Navarro's

Silent Film Guide

Navarro's
Silent Film Guide

A comprehensive look at American silent cinema

Dan Navarro

New University Press LLC

www.NewUniversityPress.com

Los Angeles   Las Vegas

iv

Cover and photo formatting by Trescela Sampson
The front cover features a publicity still for the film *7th Heaven* starring Charles Farrow and Janet Gaynor

Published by New University Press LLC

For information about bulk discounts for educational use, contact
www.NewUniversityPress.com

ISBN 978-0-9829219-0-6

Library of Congress Control Number: 2012956237

Contents

PREFACE

The guiding force behind this work was a long-felt desire to see catalogued, in convenient format, the titles of all the silent feature-length motion pictures produced in the United States. These data have been available for years, but only in widely scattered sources: studio pressbooks, trade magazines from the era, AFI catalogues, contemporary film reviews, Harrison's Reports, and so on. My hope is that this new directory will make it easier for fans and scholars of silent film to research this fascinating subject.

In compiling this book, I've included the title of each film, the director's name, the names of the principal players, and a brief plot summary. For certain outstanding films, I've also provided extended commentaries.

"What's in a name?" asked Juliet. Some silent film performers must have shared Juliet's ambivalence over nomenclature, which may be why you'll see different spellings, even different configurations, of names in this directory. Was Miss Nixon's given name Marion or Marian? Was Mr. Love Montagu or Montague? Was director Ford John or Jack? Their screen credits vary. The willowy brunette who graced many Universal films of the 1920s as Miss DuPont was sometimes called Patty DuPont. And the quintessential silent screen idol, Rudolph Valentino, appeared in films under fully a dozen different appellations before settling on the name that would mark his legend forever.

A word on definitions: A silent film is one that was conceived and produced as silent, even if it incorporates sound effects, music, and/or some talking sequences. A sound film that was also released in the silent format is not a silent film. At the end of the 1920s, when theaters were scrambling to install sound equipment to accommodate the new flood of talkies, many films were released in both formats, or as hybrids using both silent and sound sequences.

Some will question the inclusion here of very old, very minor films that are lost forever, and that no one will ever get a chance to view again. The dismal survival rate of silent movies is troubling, but recent experience tells us that yesterday's lost film is today's stunning new find; and no one can say with certainty what missing treasures will be unearthed tomorrow, next week, or next year.

D.W. Griffith's *A Romance of Happy Valley* (1919) was thought lost to the world until a print of it was found in Russia in 1971. The film has been restored and is available on videocassette. Thomas Edison's 1910 one-reel version of *Frankenstein* was found in a private collection and is also now available. Lost Laurel and Hardy shorts were found in the central film exchanges in Czechoslovakia in the 1980s. In addition to serendipitous finds like these, we know that many silent films lie unscreened for decades in various archives, in studio vaults, and in private collections. I don't know how strong the will is within the film preservation community to secure these hidden treasures, restore them, and make them available for public viewing again. But in the past two decades home video tapes, laser discs, DVDs has proved profitable enough that many rare films have, in fact, been driven out of hiding and into the marketplace. Given the base of new silent film fans created by video and public screenings, it is difficult to believe that no more "lost" films will ever be restored and made available.

Because of video and public screenings, there are probably more fans of silent film today than there have been at any time since the films themselves were new. We are on the threshold of a renaissance fueled by videotapes, DVDs, cable presentations, and screenings at film festivals throughout the world that seek out the best of silent cinema. On the Internet, dedicated and informative websites help keep the form alive, such as the sites run by The Silents Majority, Annette D'Agostino Lloyd, David B. Pearson, Tim Lussier, and many others. It's likely that silent films enjoy more popularity today than they did in the very late 1920s, when they were being sacrificed, ingloriously, on the altar of the optical sound track.

This volume is concerned only with silent features, those films with running times of at least five reels, or about 60 minutes. Of course it seems a shame not to include the short films, for there are many favorites among them. I fondly remember the wonderfully zany Keystone short comedies, with expert clowns such as Charlie Chaplin, Mabel Normand, and Roscoe Arbuckle plying their justly celebrated nonsense; the short dramas turned out by D.W. Griffith; and what is surely the gut-wrenchingly funniest 20 minutes ever recorded on film, Laurel and Hardy's *Big Business* (1929).

But the scenes most of us recall when thinking about the silent era all spring from feature films, not shorts. Whether it's Harold Lloyd dangling precariously from the hands of a giant clock several stories above the street; the sudden, horrific unmasking of the Phantom of the Opera; the furious dash of chariots as Ben Hur and Messala fight their way to the finish line; or the giant close-up of the Little Tramp as the once-blind flower girl sees him for the first time — whatever images our memories call forth when we think of silent films, they are likely to be images from full-length features.

This, then, is our tribute to American Silent Features. Let the houselights dim, let the smell of popcorn and nitrate fill the auditorium, let the ladies with the large hats be so kind as to remove them. We are about to sample the fare of a magical era.

Dan Navarro
Ventura, California, 2013

INTRODUCTION

A supernova is defined as an explosion in the sky, resulting in "an extremely bright, short-lived object that emits vast amounts of energy." The dictionary writers were defining a celestial phenomenon but they could easily have been describing the silent cinema.

For their first 30 years or so, motion pictures were mute. They were a novelty at first—imagine, a picture that moves!—but there was no sound to accompany them, no voices, no music, no sound effects. Then, as more enterprising film makers entered the field, the novelty began to develop into an art form; still, there was no audible dialogue, but the sophisticated showmen that now ran the picture business had created a tapestry of images that were complete in and of themselves, and could convey meanings without the use of words.

Today's moviegoers may think of silent film as an intermediate form, a phase of development that cinema had to pass through in order to achieve apotheosis in the wide-screen blockbusters of today. But a growing number of fans and scholars are looking back and finding that silent film was no phase, but a mature art form complete unto itself. Its passion and vitality offered much more than merely a pictorial record of the early 20th century. Silent film was an artistic expression totally unlike any other. Like a supernova, it radiated a great deal of light and energy. Like the supernova, it died much too soon.

Its beginnings were humble: magic lantern shows, Kinetoscopes, penny arcades. These crude, inchoate forms were stepping stones that would lead to the real thing, but change didn't happen overnight. Even after Auguste and Louis Lumière presented the first picture show in Paris in 1895, and pioneers such as George Méliès and Edwin S. Porter followed with their own innovative films, motion pictures were still considered cheap, inferior entertainment for the masses. All that would change with the arrival of David Wark Griffith. The early pioneers had taken still pictures and given them motion. Griffith would give them *life*.

Kentucky-born, D.W. Griffith ventured north to the Biograph studio in New York one day in 1908, and launched the career that would earn him the title "The Father of Motion Pictures." In collaboration with cinematographer G.W. "Billy" Bitzer, director Griffith developed such progressive devices as the fadeout, backlighting, the iris shot, crosscutting, and the panoramic long shot. All these techniques had been available to filmmakers before Griffith's time, but what he did was stretch their limits—push the envelope, in newspeak—creating a sparkling new lexicon of film language. Neither did he invent the closeup—*that* had been around since at least 1896's harmlessly ribald one-minute *The Kiss*—but he did develop new ways of incorporating closeups into his narratives, forever liberating the camera from its accustomed stationary position at long-shot distance in front of the actors. Griffith's camera would *move*. His motion pictures would display a sweeping fluidity not seen in films before.

Griffith, perhaps alone among filmmakers of his time, saw in the new gimmick of moving pictures an instrument of art. Certainly none of the early pioneers thought of movies as art. Even the Lumière brothers dismissed their invention as merely "a scientific curiosity."

But when Griffith's masterpiece, the three hour-long *The Birth of a Nation*, premiered in 1915 with live symphonic accompaniment, it took the world by storm. Audiences were stunned by its majesty, and perhaps a little shocked to find that film had such power to engage the intellect and touch the soul. Since that moment, the notion that a motion picture can be a work of art no longer seemed inappropriate. Griffith *legitimized* film.

Lillian Gish liked to call *The Birth of a Nation* "the first feature-length film." It wasn't quite that, though we can understand Miss Gish's affection for the motion picture that would make her one of the screen's "immortals" at the age of 21. As commonly understood, a feature is a film with a running time of at least five reels, or about 60 minutes and films of that length had been around for three years before Griffith's masterpiece hit the screen. A reel, in Hollywood usage, is a term generally taken to mean 1,000 feet of 35mm film. It could run as little as ten minutes on screen, or as long as eighteen. This is because in the days before sound, there was no strict standard speed at which film was projected. The operator would simply put his hand to the rheostat and alter the film speed from scene to scene, even from shot to shot.

This volume is concerned only with silent features, as that term is defined above, and only those produced in the United States. There were, of course, many thousands of one- and two-reel films produced in the silent era, but they are outside the scope of this work. One source recently estimated their number as in excess of 100,000. Assuming this figure is close to being correct, the reader will quickly understand that all the silent shorts cannot possibly be catalogued in a work of this size.

Of course, the short films came first. During his five-year association with Biograph Studios, D.W. Griffith turned out more than 500 films of one, two, and three reels each. In France, George Méliès produced 400 short films between 1896 and 1902. This was the era of shoot-and-run filmmaking, with quantity prized above quality by the nickelodeon operators, eager to entice repeat customers with fresh fare nearly every week.

The pace was hectic, but despite the assembly-line nature of filmmaking, some quality works managed to emerge. Edwin S. Porter's ten-minute *The Great Train Robbery*, seen through modern eyes that are used to blazing color and eye-popping computer graphics, may not seem noteworthy today but it caused a sensation in 1903. The famous closing scene shows a bewhiskered outlaw pointing a gun directly at the camera (at us!), taking aim, and firing. We hear no gunshot; we see no lifelike color; but if we imagine ourselves in the place of the nickelodeon audience who had that pistol pointed at them in 1903, we can feel some of the panic they must have felt.

Because that is what a good film *does*. It engages our emotions and makes us surrender logic to its muse, and we are drawn into a new logic, that of the photoplay unfolding before us. Today's filmmakers accomplish this seduction with the help of reality-simulating devices such as color, multichannel sound, and wide-screen formats that approximate the boundaries of human peripheral vision. Curiously, silent film accomplished the same thing because of, rather than in spite of, the absence of these devices.

Consider the limitations of early film. Although a way had been found to make pictures appear to move, they were still two-dimensional, lacking real life's third dimension of depth. They were photographed in non-lifelike black and white. And though the people in the pictures spoke, they could not be heard. These defects hardly mattered in the beginning, when moving pictures were still a crude novelty—when, in the words of the Lumière brothers, they were merely "a scientific curiosity." But once film had progressed past the novelty stage and found the excitement of storytelling, a new artistry was needed. There was a broad new canvas waiting to be filled. And the new breed of artists found a way, by making film's own limitations work in its favor.

Paul Klee, the Swiss master of abstract painting, wrote, "Art does not reproduce what we see. It *makes* us see." D.W. Griffith understood this principle, and he applied it, ingeniously, in the ways he used the camera. One example—perhaps the most famous example—is the scene in *The Birth of a Nation* where a Confederate soldier returns home from the war to a mother who has not seen her son in many months. He approaches the door; we see the door open; there is a moment of hesitation while realization sinks in; and then we see the mother's arms, joyfully outstretched through the door, and they embrace the soldier and pull him close. We don't see the mother's face, only her hands and her arms. We are denied her expression of surpassing joy, and are left to imagine it for ourselves. Yet it is one of the most poignant scenes in movie history, all the more so because the artist—Griffith—has left out details and let the viewers supply those details in their own minds.

The Impressionist painters of the 19th century—Monet, Manet, Renoir and the rest—tried to depict reality in a new way, by *not* letting us see everything we could see in real life. They tried to give a feeling or "impression" of the way something looked, rendering not the thing itself, but rather the sensation of it. Thus the viewer is drawn into the art and is engaged in its creation. By using flat, two-dimensional, mute and monochrome motion pictures to create their own kind of art, early filmmakers were, consciously or not, using the Impressionist formula and extending it in exciting new ways.

One of the tools of this new artistry was a factor sometimes regarded as a drawback: black and white images. Real life is ablaze with color, but early movies were not. It is perfectly true that some silent films were tinted, but nobody pretends that they delivered full color as it is experienced in real life. And yet, monochrome fueled the rapport between artist and viewer; the less "real life" the film delivers, the more we must supply for ourselves. Besides, black and white are the colors of the subconscious, that fantasy realm where we experience all our dreams. Small wonder that those xii

monochrome pictures found ready acceptance with movie audiences; the human psyche feels very much at home in a black-and-white world.

In his indispensible 2002 volume *The Great Movies*, Roger Ebert states the case for monochrome with the authority of a knowing, internationally celebrated observer of films: "[Y]ou cannot know the history of the movies, or love them, unless you understand why b&w can give more, not less, than color."

What about sound? Well, the absence of sound might be considered a handicap, but only by people who are now used to the talkies. As Chesterton wrote, "Art consists of limitation." Nickelodeon customers knew that the limitations of silent film drew them into the action; and worldwide, audiences thrilled to the experience. Silence permitted every audience member to interpret the action on screen in relation to his or her own sensibilities.

The interplay between the minds of the artists and the minds of the audience produced an exquisite sensation, one not easily forgotten nor casually surrendered. Silent films created a kind of reverie, blissfully undisturbed by intrusive dialogue that rivets everything in place. We were offered a deliberately incomplete canvas and invited to fill in the blanks. As one writer observed, "When we made the transition from silent films to talkies, we lost as much as we gained."

Lillian Gish wrote about the time when D.W. Griffith overheard one of his new actresses referring to films as "flickers." He told the young starlet never to use that word again. She was, he said, working in the universal language that had been predicted in the Bible, which was to make all men brothers because they would understand each other. It's clear that Griffith thought highly of this new art, even ascribing to it Messianic powers. The universal language he spoke of involved film's own silence. Through the faces, gestures, and actions of his players—and the artistry of his cinematographers—he meant to convey a world of meaning without the use of spoken language. He succeeded brilliantly, and in the process helped launch the "golden era"—twenty years of the most unique theatergoing experience ever, a supernova for the ages.

Index of Company Names

To conserve space, the names of many studios and distribution companies appearing in this directory have been abbreviated or shown as acronyms. The following are the full names of these companies.

Acme Film Corp.
Albert Capellani Productions, Inc.
All Star Feature Corp.
Allan Dwan Productions
American Commercial Film Co.
American Film Co.
American Film Mfg. Co.
America's Feature Film Co.
Anchor Film Distributors
Anita Stewart Productions, Inc.
Arrow Film Corp.
Art Cinema Corp.
Art Dramas, Inc.
Artco Productions, Inc.
Artcraft Pictures Corp.
Associated First National Pictures
Associated Producers, Inc.
Astra Film Corp.
Aywon Film Corp.
Balboa Amusement Producing Co.
B.B. Features
Betzwood Film Co.
Biograph Co.
Blaché Features, Inc.
Bluebird Photoplays, Inc.
Bosworth, Inc.
Box Office Attraction Co.
Brentwood Film Corp.
Buster Keaton Productions
Charles Ray Productions, Inc.
C.K.Y. Film Corp.
Clara Kimball Young Film Corp.
Columbia Pictures Corp.
Commonwealth Pictures Corp.
Continental Pictures Corp.
Cosmopolitan Productions
Cosmos Feature Film Corp.
David Horsley Productions
David W. Griffith Corp.
Dorothy Gish Productions
Douglas Fairbanks Pictures Corp.
D.W. Griffith, Inc.
Eclectic Film Co.

Educational Films Corp. Of America
Empire All Star Corp.
Epoch Producing Corp.
Equitable Motion Pictures Corp.
Essanay Film Mfg. Co.
Exhibitors Mutual Distributing Corp.
Falcon Features
Famous Players Film Co.
Famous Players-Lasky Corp.
FBO Pictures
Film Booking Offices of America
Fine Arts Film Co.
Fine Arts Pictures
First National Exhibitors Circuit
First National Pictures
Fox Film Corp.
Frohman Amusement Corp.
Gaumont Co.
General Film Co.
Goldwyn Distributing Corp.
Goldwyn Pictures Corp.
Harold Lloyd Corp.
Haworth Pictures Corp.
Herbert Brenon Film Corp.
High Art Productions, Inc.
International Film Service, Inc.
International Film Service Co.
Ivan Film Productions, Inc.
J. Stuart Blackton Feature Pictures, Inc.
Jack Pickford Film Co.
Jesse D. Hampton Productions
Jesse L. Lasky Feature Play Co.
Jewel Productions, Inc.
Kalem Co.
Kinemacolor Co.
King Vidor Productions
Klaw & Erlanger
Kleine-Edison Feature Service
Léonce Perret Productions
Life Photo Film Corp.
Lois Weber Productions
Louis B. Mayer Productions
Lubin Manufacturing Co.

Mabel Normand Feature Film Co.
Mack Sennett Comedies.
Majestic Motion Picture Co.
Marion Davies Film Corp.
The Mark Twain Co.
Marshall Neilan Productions
Mary Pickford Co.
Mary Pickford Film Corp.
Maurice Tourneur Productions, Inc.
Metro Pictures Corp.
Metro-Goldwyn-Mayer Pictures
Micheaux Book and Film Co.
Monrovia Feature Film Co.
Mutual Film Corp.
National Film Corp. of America
Nazimova Productions, Inc.
New York Motion Picture Corp.
Norma Talmadge Film Corp.
Oliver Morosco Photoplay Co.
Pallas Pictures
Paragon Films, Inc.
Paralta Plays, Inc.
Paramount-Artcraft Pictures
Paramount Famous Lasky Corp.
Paramount Pictures Corp.
Pathé Exchange, Inc.
Pathé Freres
Peerless Pictures Co.
Pioneer Film Corp.
Popular Plays and Players
Preferred Pictures
Quality Pictures Corp.
Realart Pictures Corp.
Realart Pictures, Inc.
Regent Feature Film Co.
Reliance Motion Picture Corp.
Republic Distributing Corp.
Republic Pictures
Rex Beach Pictures Co.
Robertson-Cole Co.
Robertson-Cole Distributing Corp.
Rolfe Photoplays, Inc.
Screen Classics, Inc.

Select Photo Play Producing Co.
Select Pictures Corp.
Selig Polyscope Co.
Selznick Pictures Corp.
Shubert Film Corp.
Solax Co.
Success Pictures Co.
Sunset Pictures Corp.
Sunset Productions
Super Art, Inc.
Sun Photoplay Co.
Technicolor Motion Picture Corp.
Thanhouser Film Corp.
The Nazimova Productions
The William S. Hart Co.
Thomas A. Edison, Inc.
Thomas H. Ince Productions
Tiffany Film Corp.
Tiffany Productions
Tiffany-Stahl Productions
Triangle Distributing Corp.
Triangle Film Corp.
Triumph Film Corp.
United Artists Corp.
United Picture Theaters of America, Inc.
Universal Film Mfg. Co.
Universal Pictures
U.S. Amusement Corp.
Virginia Pearson Photoplays, Inc.
Vitagraph Co. of America
Wark Producing Corp.
Warner Bros.
Warner's Features, Inc.
Weber Productions, Inc.
Wharton, Inc.
Willat Productions, Inc.
William A. Brady Picture Plays, Inc.
William S. Hart Productions, Inc.
World Film Corp.
W.W. Hodkinson Corp.
Yorke Film Corp.
Zane Grey Pictures, Inc.

List of Publicity Stills

NAVARRO'S SILENT FILM GUIDE

A – Z

The A.B.C. of Love (Pathé, 1919)
d: Leonce Perret. 6 reels.
Mae Murray, H.E. Herbert, Dorothy Green, Arthur Donaldson.
A playwright is attracted to an uneducated but charming young woman.

The Abandonment (Mutual, 1916)
d: Donald MacDonald. 5 reels.
E. Forrest Taylor, Harry Von Meter, Helene Rosson.
Rejected by the woman he loves, a physician moves away and becomes a derelict. But their paths will cross again.

Abie's Imported Bride (Trio Productions, 1925)
d: Roy Calnek. 7 reels.
No cast credits.
A professional matchmaker arranges a marriage between a Russian girl and the son of a prosperous American. The young man vehemently opposes the arrangement... until he sets eyes on the girl.

Abie's Irish Rose (Paramount, 1928)
d: Victor Fleming. 7 reels. (Synchronized music and sound effects.)
Charles Buddy Rogers, Nancy Carroll, J. Farrell MacDonald, Jean Hersholt, Thelma Todd, Bernard Gorcey, Rosa Rosanova.
During World War I, a wounded American soldier falls in love with an entertainer. They plan to marry, but because they are of different faiths—he's Jewish, she's Irish Catholic—they face the difficult task of smoothing things over with their families.

The Ableminded Lady (Pacific Film Co., 1922)
d: Ollie Sellers, Don Gamble. 5 reels.
Henry B. Walthall, Elinor Fair, Helen Raymond.
A bachelor cowpoke works on a ranch owned by a three-time widow, the "ableminded lady" of the title.

Abraham Lincoln (Rocket-Lincoln Film Co./Associated First National, 1924)
d: Phil Rosen. 12 reels.
Fay McKenzie, Westcott B. Clarke, George A. Billings, Ruth Clifford, Irene Hunt, Charles French, Ed Burns, Calvert Carter, Louise Fazenda.
Ambitious biographical drama about Abraham Lincoln, from birth to death. The original title of this film was *The Dramatic Life of Abraham Lincoln.*

Absent (Rosebud Film Corp., 1928)
d: Harry A. Gant. 6 reels.
Clarence Brooks, George Reed, Virgil Owens, Rosa Lee Lincoln, Floyd Shackelford, Clarence Williams.
A shell-shocked veteran gets help when he needs it, and a new lease on life.

The Absentee (Mutual, 1915)
d: William Christy Cabanne. 5 reels.
Robert Edeson, A.D. Sears, Arthur Paget, George A. Beranger, Charles Lee, Otto Lincoln, Augustus Carney, Loretta Blake, Mildred Harris, Olga Gray.
Allegorical tale about success and justice, and the social conflicts between the two.

The Abysmal Brute (Universal, 1923)
d: Hobart Henley. 8 reels.
Reginald Denny, Mabel Julienne Scott, Charles French, Hayden Stevenson, David Torrence, George Stewart, Buddy Messinger, Crauford Kent, Dorothea Wolbert.
A gentlemanly prize-fighter loves a society girl, but she doesn't approve of boxing.

The Accidental Honeymoon (High Art Productions, 1918)
d: Léonce Perret. 5 reels.
Robert Warwick, Elaine Hammerstein, Frank McGlynn, Blanche Craig, Frank Norcross, Edward Kimball.
Two lost souls meet and fall in love.

The Accomplice (Art Dramas, Inc., 1917)
d: Ralph Dean. 5 reels.
Dorothy Bernard, Jack Sherrill, W.J. Brady, Joseph Granby, Jean Stuart, Florence Hamilton, John Milton, Tom Ward.
Katherine, a spoiled daughter of wealth, dallies with a tango dancer and winds up in a jam when his sweetheart is found murdered.

According to Hoyle (David Butler Productions, 1922)
d: W.S. Van Dyke. 5 reels.
David Butler, Helen Ferguson, Phil Ford, Fred J. Butler, Harry Todd, Buddy Ross, Hal Wilson.
Simmons, a tramp, passes himself off as a millionaire and becomes the target of swindlers.

According to Law (Mutual, 1916)
d: Richard Garrick. 5 reels.
Mildred Gregory, Howard Hall, E.K. James, Madison Weeks, Alan Robinson, Albert Macklin, John Reinhard, Charles W. Travis.

A young woman is considered illegitimate because her parents never remarried after their brief divorce from each other. But there's a glitch in the law....

According to the Code (Essanay, 1916)
d: E.H. Calvert. 5 reels.
Lewis Stone, Marguerite Clayton, Florence Oberle, E.H. Calvert, Sydney Ainsworth.
A Civil War veteran is tried in court on assault charges. The old man is innocent, but the young prosecutor presses on with the case, unaware that the defendant is his real father.

Accused (Independent Pictures, 1925)
d: Dell Henderson. 5 reels.
Dorothy Drew, Eric Mayne, Charles Delaney, Charles Gerrard, Miss DuPont, Sheldon Lewis, Spottiswoode Aitken.
A young woman learns that she is adopted, and goes looking for her natural father. Complications arise, and she and a young man end up imprisoned in a lair of thieves.

Ace High (Fox, 1918)
d: Lynn Reynolds. 5 reels.
Tom Mix, Lloyd Perl, Lewis Sargent, Kathleen Connors, Virginia Lee Corbin, Lawrence Peyton, Colin Chase, Jay Morley, Pat Chrisman.
A Royal Canadian mountie rescues a girl three times—once when she is a baby, then twice later when she's a young adult.

Ace of Action (Action Pictures/Associated Exhibitors, 1926)
d: William Bertram. 5 reels.
Wally Wales, Alma Rayford, Charles Colby, Hank Bell, Charles Whitaker, Fanny Midgley, William Hayes, Frank Ellis.
Out west, a family feud is settled... but not without a lot of fussing and fighting.

Ace of Cactus Range (Aywon Film Corp., 1924)
d: Denver Dixon. 5 reels.
Art Mix, Virginia Warwick, Clifford Davidson, Harvey Stafford, Dorothy Chase, Charles Colby.
A gang of diamond thieves terrorize a family.

The Ace of Cads (Famous Players-Lasky/Paramount, 1926)
d: Luther Reed. 8 reels.
Adolphe Menjou, Alice Joyce, Norman Trevor, Philip Strange, Suzanne Fleming.
Two British officers are in love with the same girl.

The Ace of Clubs (Anchor Films, 1926)
d: J.P. McGowan. 50 minutes.
Al Hoxie, Minna Redman, Andrew Waldron, Peggy Montgomery, Jules Cowles.
A murderer leaves the Ace of Clubs pinned to each of his victims.

The Ace of Hearts (Goldwyn, 1921)
d: Wallace Worsley. 6 reels.
Leatrice Joy, John Bowers, Lon Chaney, Hardee Kirkland, Raymond Hatton, Roy Laidlaw, Edwin Wallock.
Murder is on a secret society's agenda.

Ace of the Saddle (Universal, 1919)
d: John Ford. 6 reels.
Harry Carey, Duke R. Lee, Vester Pegg, Joel Harris, Peggy Pearce, Jack Walters, William Cartwright.
A rancher learns that the local sheriff is in cahoots with cattle rustlers.

The Acquittal (Universal, 1923)

d: Clarence Brown. 7 reels.
Claire Windsor, Norman Kerry, Richard Travers, Barbara Bedford, Charles Wellesley, Frederick Vroom, Ben Deeley, Harry Mestayer, Emmett King, Dot Farley, Hayden Stevenson.
Murder mystery centered on a millionaire with two adopted sons.

Acquitted (Triangle, 1916)
d: Paul Powell. 5 reels.
Wilfred Lucas, Mary Alden, Bessie Love, Carmen DeRue, Elmer Clifton, Sam DeGrasse, Spottiswoode Aitken.
John Carter, an honest bookkeeper, is accused of murder.

Acquitted (Columbia, 1928)
d: Frank Strayer. 7 reels. (Also released in sound version.)
Margaret Livingston, Sam Hardy, Lloyd Hughes, Charles Wilson, George Rigas, Charles West, Otto Hoffman.
A gangster's moll meets a man doing time for a crime committed by her boyfriend.

Across the Atlantic (Warner Bros., 1928)
d: Howard Bretherton. 7 reels.
Monte Blue, Edna Murphy, Burr McIntosh, Irene Rich, Robert Ober.
A World War I aviator is missing in action and presumed dead... but he's really alive, suffering from amnesia.

Across the Border (Aywon Film Corp., 1922)
w, d: Charles R. Seeling. 5 reels.
Big Boy Williams, Patricia Palmer, William McCall, Chet Ryan.
Cattle rustlers thrive under the secret leadership of the town's sheriff.

Across the Continent (Famous Players-Lasky/Paramount, 1922)
d: Philip E. Rosen. 6 reels.
Wallace Reid, Mary MacLaren, Theodore Roberts, Betty Francisco, Walter Long, Lucien Littlefield, Jack Herbert, Guy Oliver, Sidney D'Albrook.
The son of an automobile manufacturer foils an attempt by his dad's competitor to "fix" a transcontinental road race.

Across the Dead-line (Universal, 1922)
d: Jack Conway. 5 reels.
Frank Mayo, Russell Simpson, Molly Malone, Wildred Lucas, Lydia Knott, Frank Thorwald, Josef Swickard, William Marion.
A lumber town is divided by two branches of the same family—one straight-laced, the other lustful.

Across the Deadline (William Steiner Productions, 1925)
d: Leo Maloney. 5 reels.
Leo Maloney, Josephine Hill, Thomas Lingham, Bud Osborne, Florence Lee, Rulon Slaughter, Pat Rooney.
A family feud of 30 years' standing flares anew when the daughter of one clan falls for the son of her family's enemies.

Across the Divide (Playgoers Pictures, 1921)
d: John Holloway. 6 reels.
Rex Ballard, Rosemary Theby, Ralph Fee McCullough, Thomas Delmar, Gilbert Clayton, Dorothy Manners, Flora Hollister.
The heir to a ranch is left by his dying mother in the care of a halfbreed. The boy is unaware of his true identity; but when his corrupt father returns and tries to steal the lad's inheritance from him, his halfbreed guardian hatches a plan to outwit the old scoundrel at his own game.

Across the Great Divide — see: Across the Divide (1921)

Across the Pacific (World Film Corp., 1914)
d: Edwin Carewe. 5 reels.
Dorothy Dalton, Sam Hines.
During the Spanish-American War, a woman disguises herself as a soldier and travels to the Phillipines to be with the man she loves.

Across the Pacific (Warner Bros., 1926)
d: Roy Del Ruth. 8 reels.
Monte Blue, Myrna Loy, Jane Winton, Walter McGrail, Charles Stevens.
An American adventurer enlists to fight in the Spanish-American War. Once in the Phillipines, he attracts the attentions of a lovely half-caste girl, who helps him locate the headquarters of the insurrectionist leader. Like the earlier *Across the Pacific* (World Film Corp., 1914), this film is based on Charles E. Blaney's 1904 novel of the same name; but the plot was reworked to focus on the adventurer rather than on his sweetheart, as was the case in the earlier film.

Across to Singapore (MGM, 1928)
d: William Nigh. 7 reels.
Ramon Novarro, Joan Crawford, Ernest Torrence, Frank Currier, Edward Connelly, Dan Wolheim, Duke Martine, James Mason, Anna May Wong.
Two brothers love the same girl. The eldest, a ship's captain, is victimized by a mutinous crew that leaves him stranded in Singapore. The younger brother sails to Singapore to rescue the captain, who then gives his blessing to the union of his brother and the woman they both love.

Action (Universal, 1921)
d: Jack Ford. 5 reels.
Hoot Gibson, Clara Horton, Francis Ford, J. Farrell MacDonald, Buck Connors, William Robert Daly, Dorothea Wolbert, Byron Munson.
Rangers discover precious ore on an orphan's ranch.

The Action Craver (Rayart Pictures, 1927)
d: Victor Potel. 5 reels.
Dick Hatton.
A rancher and his foreman vie for the love of the ranch owner's niece.

Action Galore (Artclass Pictures, 1925)
d: Robert Eddy. 5 reels.
Buddy Roosevelt, Toy Gallagher, Charles Williams, Joe Rickson, Jack O'Brien, Raye Hamilton, Ruth Royce.
A ranger on the trail of a dangerous criminal finds himself trapped in a burning cabin with a young woman.

The Actress (MGM, 1928)
d: Sidney Franklin. 8 reels.
Norma Shearer, Owen Moore, Gwen Lee, Roy D'Arcy, Lee Moran, Ralph Forbes, O.P. Heggie.
An actress leaves her theater repertory company for a rich young aristocrat, then repents.

Adam and Eva (Cosmopolitan/Paramount, 1923)
d: Robert G. Vignola. 8 reels.
Marion Davies, Tom Lewis, William Norris, Percy Ames, Luella Gear, T. Roy Barnes.
Heeding her father's advice, a young woman squirrels away her money against an uncertain future. Sure enough, when the family hits hard times, her savings are their salvation. It turns out, however, that Papa isn't really broke, he's just trying to teach his spendthrift daughter a lesson.

Adam and Evil (MGM, 1927)
d: Robert Z. Leonard. 7 reels.
Lew Cody, Aileen Pringle, Gwen Lee, Hedda Hopper, Roy D'Arcy.
A married man pretends to be his own twin brother while having an affair.

Adam's Rib (Famous Players-Lasky/Paramount, 1923)
d: Cecil B. DeMille. 10 reels.
Milton Sills, Elliot Dexter, Theodore Roberts, Anna Q. Nilsson, Pauline Garon, Julia Faye, Clarence Geldert, George Field, Robert Brower, Clarence Burton, Gino Corrado.
The wife of a successful businessman feels neglected, so she becomes romantically involved with a recently deposed European monarch. But she comes to realize the impropriety of her actions, and returns to her husband.

Adele (United Picture Theatres of America, 1919)
d: Wallace Worsley. 6 reels.
Kitty Gordon, Mahlon Hamilton, Wedgewood Nowell, Joseph J. Dowling.
A heroic Red Cross nurse aids the war effort and falls in love with a British captain.

The Adopted Son (Metro, 1917)
d: Charles Brabin. 6 reels.
Francis X. Bushman, Beverly Bayne, Leslie Stowe, J.W. Johnston, John Smiley, Gertrude Norman, Pat O'Malley.
Feuding families in the mountains lay down their arms only after an outsider intervenes.

The Adorable Cheat (Chesterfield, 1928)
d: Burton King. 6 reels.
Lila Lee, Cornelius Keefe, Burr McIntosh, Reginald Sheffield, Gladden James, Harry Allen, Alice Knowland, Virginia Lee.
A daughter of privilege falls in love with a lowly clerk. Then, when he's invited to a weekend party at the family estate, he becomes implicated in a burglary investigation.

The Adorable Deceiver (R-C Pictures/F.B.O. of America, 1926)
d: Phil Rosen. 5 reels.
Alberta Vaughn, Dan Makarenko, Harlan Tucker, Frank Leigh, Jane Thomas, Cora Williams, Rose Gore.
A deposed European king flees to the United States with his daughter, Princess Sylvia.

The Adorable Savage (Universal, 1920)
d: Norman Dawn. 5 reels.
Edith Roberts, Jack Perrin, Dick Cummings, Noble Johnson, Dr. Arthur Jervis, Lucille Moulton, Lily Phillips.
A young American woman journeys to Fiji, where she adopts native customs and agrees to marry the tribal chief.

Adoration (First National/Warner Bros., 1928)
d: Frank Lloyd. 7 reels. (Synchronized musical score.)
Billie Dove, Antonio Moreno, Lucy Doraine, Nicholas Soussanin, Nicholas Bela.
A Russian prince suspects his wife of infidelity. After the Revolution, they flee to Paris, where the princess is finally able to convince her husband that her love for him is true.

Adventure (Famous Players-Lasky/Paramount, 1925)
d: Victor Fleming. 7 reels.
Tom Moore, Pauline Starke, Wallace Beery, Raymond Hatton, Walter McGrail, Duke Kahanamoku, James Spencer, Noble Johnson.
Treachery, love, and adventure in the Solomon Islands.

The Adventurer (Art Dramas Inc., 1917)

d: Alice Blaché. 5 reels.
Marian Swayne, Pell Trenton, Ethel Stanard, Kirk Brown, Charles Halton, Martin Hayden, Yolande Doquette.
A millionaire's son poses as a slum-dweller in order to investigate a conspiracy.

The Adventurer (Fox, 1920)
d: J. Gordon Edwards. 6 reels.
William Farnum, Estelle Taylor, Paul Cazeneuve, Kenneth Casey, Dorothy Drake, Harry Southard, Pat Hartigan, James Devine, Sadie Radcliffe.
In 17th century Spain, a condemned nobleman is forced to enter into a sham marriage with a mysterious veiled bride. But he escapes execution, and his bride turns out to be — surprise! — the young woman he has loved all along.

The Adventurer (MGM, 1928)
d: Viachetslav Tourjansky. 5 reels.
Tim McCoy, Dorothy Sebastian, Charles Delaney, George Cowl, Michael Visaroff, Gayne Whitman.
An American mining engineer gets involved in a South American revolution.

The Adventures of Buffalo Bill (Essanay, 1917)
d: Theodore Wharton. 5 reels.
William Frederick Cody, Nelson Appleton Miles, Jesse M. Lee, Frank D. Baldwin, Marion P. Maus, Chief Tall Bull, Chief Sitting Bull, Charles A. King, H.G. Sickles.
The life of "Buffalo Bill" Cody, chief Indian scout for the U.S. cavalry, is reviewed.

The Adventures of Carol (World Film Corp., 1917)
d: Harley Knoles. 5 reels.
Madge Evans, George MacQuarrie, Rosina Henley, Carl Axzell, Nicholas Long, Kate Lester, Jack Drumier, Frances Miller.
A little girl is lost, has numerous adventures, and in the end is reunited with her mother.

The Adventures of Kathlyn (Selig Polyscope, 1916)
d: F.J. Grandon. 10 reels.
Kathlyn Williams, Charles Clary, Lafayette McKee, Thomas Santschi, Hurri Tsingh, William Carpenter, Goldie Colwell, Effie Sackville, Roy Watson.
This film, a re-edited version of an earlier 27-reel serial, follows a California girl on her adventures in East India..

An Adventuress (Republic Distributing Co., 1920)
d: Fred J. Balshofer. 5 reels.
Julian Eltinge, Fred Covert, William Clifford, Leo White, Virginia Rappe, Rodolph Valentino, Stanton Beck, Charles Millsfield.
Three American adventurers journey to a European kingdom and become involved in its civil strife. Originally conceived as an anti-war film in 1918, this project underwent some rewrites after the armistice. The focus was changed to the exploits of one of the adventurers, who dons female attire to outwit his enemies, thus becoming an "adventuress". A re-edited version appeared in 1922 under the title *The Isle of Love*.

The Adventurous Sex (Howard Estabrook Productions/Associated Exhibitors, 1925)
d: Charles Giblyn. 6 reels.
Clara Bow, Herbert Rawlinson, Earle Williams, Harry T. Morey, Mabel Beck, Flora Finch, Joseph Burke.
A girl dumps her sweetie when he seems to be spending too much time tinkering with his airplane. She goes on a romantic spree, then regrets it. Finally, the girl ends up floating in the river above Niagara Falls, about to plunge to her death... and that's the cue for her former sweetie and his plane to fly to her rescue.

The Adventurous Soul (Hi-Mark Productions, 1927)
d: Gene Carroll. 6 reels.
Mildred Harris, Jimmy Fulton, Tom Santschi, Arthur Rankin, Charles K. French.
A shipping clerk is shanghaied by a gang of roughnecks who mistake him for a rich man's son.

An Affair of Three Nations (Pathé, 1915)
d: Arnold Daly, Ashley Miller. 5 reels.
Arnold Daly, Sheldon Lewis, William Harrigan, Charles Laite, Charles Krauss, Geoffrey Stein, Martin Sabine, Louise Rutter, Doris Mitchell.
The truth about a secret international treaty comes to light.

The Affairs of Anatol (Famous Players-Lasky/Paramount, 1921)
d: Cecil B. DeMille. 9 reels.
Wallace Reid, Gloria Swanson, Elliott Dexter, Bebe Daniels, Monte Blue, Wanda Hawley, Theodore Roberts, Agnes Ayres, Theodore Kosloff, Polly Moran, Raymond Hatton, Charles Ogle.
Stylish comingling of drama and romantic comedy, told with the legendary DeMille flair. Anatol is a wealthy married man who loves his wife dearly, but is a pushover for damsels in distress, especially if they are young and pretty. Leaving his wife with a trusted friend, he goes to ridiculous lengths to try to reform a gold-digger; failing that, he again leaves his wife to go to the aid of a young country woman with a larcenous streak. Failing a second time, Anatol learns that his wife is tired of being neglected and has decided to sow a few wild oats of her own — never mind that Anatol has been scrupulously faithful to her all along.
In Anatol's third adventure, he ventures into the dungeon-like domain of "the wickedest woman in New York," one Satan Synne (Bebe Daniels, who makes a meal of her role). He — and we — are expecting Miss Synne to be a fire-snorting she-devil, but instead she turns out to be a devoted housewife who's just trying to make enough money to buy a needed operation for her critically ill husband.

Affinities (Ward Lascelle Productions/W.W. Hodkinson Corp., 1922)
d: Ward Lascelle. 6 reels.
John Bowers, Colleen Moore, Joe Bonner, Grace Gordon, Pietro Sosso.
Romantic comedy about two married couples who vacation together, and one of the husbands finds himself shipwrecked with the other fellow's wife.

Aflame in the Sky (R-C Pictures, 1927)
d: J.P. McGowan. 6 reels.
Sharon Lynn, Jack Luden, William Humphreys, Robert McKim, Billy Scott, Charles A. Stevenson, Bill Franey, Mark Hamilton, Walter Ackerman, Jane Keckley.
In New Mexico, two aviators intervene to foil a forced marriage.

Afraid to Fight (Universal, 1922)
d: William Worthington. 5 reels.
Frank Mayo, Lillian Rich, Lydia Knott, Peggy Cartwright, W.S. McDunnough, Tom McGuire, Harry Mann, Wade Boteler, Al Kaufman, Roscoe Karns, Guy Tiney, James Quinn.
Tom, a former Army boxing champ, has suffered gas

THE AFFAIRS OF ANATOL (1921). Gloria Swanson and Wallace Reid costar as husband and wife in this stylish commingling of drama and romantic comedy. Reid plays Anatol, a wealthy man with a loving wife, who foolishly seeks to improve the lives of less fortunate women, just as long as they are young and pretty.

* * * * *

poisoning and is under doctor's orders to refrain from exerting himself. Not an easy rule to follow, since Tom finds himself threatened by the town bully in front of his girlfriend.

Afraid to Love (Paramount, 1927)
d: E.H. Griffith. 7 reels.
Clive Brook, Florence Vidor, Norman Trevor, Jocelyn Lee, Arthur Lubin.
Romantic comedy about a young man who stands to lose a large inheritance unless he gives up his sweetheart and marries another woman—*any* other woman—within 24 hours.

After Business Hours (Columbia, 1925)
d: Mal St. Clair. 6 reels.
Elaine Hammerstein, Lou Tellegen, Phyllis Haver, John Patrick, Lillian Langdon, William Scott, Lee Moran.
A society wife runs up excessive gambling debts.

After Dark (World Film Corp., 1915)
d: Frederic Thomson. 5 reels.
Alec B. Francis, Eric Maxon, Melville Stewart, Norman Trevor, J.H. Goldworthy, Charles Dungan, Bertram Marburgh, Dorothy Green, Kathryn Adams.
A proud Army officer, stung by the discovery that his wife is unfaithful, is reduced to the life of a vagabond loner. The years pass, and the vagabond, now known as "Old Tom," saves the lives of a young married couple. It turns out that the young wife is Tom's daughter, all grown up and ready to welcome her father back into her life.

After Five (Lasky Feature Play Co./Paramount, 1915)
d: Oscar Apfel, Cecil B. DeMille. 5 reels.
Edward Abeles, Sessue Hayakawa, Betty Schade, Jane Darwell, Theodore Roberts, Monroe Salisbury, James Neil, Ernest Joy, Jode Mullally, Ernest Garcia.
Depressed and in debt, Ted Ewing arranges to have himself killed after five o'clock in the afternoon. It all sounds terribly sinister, but in fact it's a comedy. All the hero's attempts to kill himself fail miserably, and he winds up rich and in love.

After His Own Heart (Metro, 1919)
d: Harry L. Franklin. 5 reels.
Hale Hamilton, Naomi Childers, Mrs. Louis, Frank Hayes, Harry Carter, William V. Mong, Herbert Pryor, Stanley Sanford.
A man in need of money sells his heart for $250,000... then he discovers that the surgeon doesn't want to wait for him to die, he wants the heart *now!*

After Marriage (Sun Motion Pictures/Madoc Sales, 1925)
w, d: Norman Dawn. 5 reels.
Margaret Livingston, George Fisher, Helen Lynch, Herschel Mayall, Annette Perry, Mary Young, Arthur Jasmine.
David, a newlywed, quickly grows tired of his wife and becomes infatuated with Alma, an actress. Unknown to David, his own father is Alma's lover.

After Midnight (Selznick/Select, 1921)
d: Ralph Ince. 5 reels.
Conway Tearle, Zena Keefe, Warren Black.
A man falls in love with his twin brother's wife.

After Midnight (MGM, 1927)
w, d: Monta Bell. 7 reels.
Norma Shearer, Gwen Lee, Lawrence Gray, Eddie Sturgis, Philip Sleeman.

Mary struggles to save money while her husband toils as a taxi driver. But their values are rocked when Mary's sister Maizie, a fickle gold digger, brandishes a $1,000 bond she received from an admirer.

After the Ball (Photo Drama Co., 1914)
d: Pierce Kingsley. 6 reels.
Herbert Kelcey, Effie Shannon, Robert Vaughn.
Deeply in love, a lawyer is distraught to find his intended embracing another man, not realizing he's her brother.

After the Ball (Renco Film Co., 1924)
d: Dallas M. Fitzgerald. 7 reels.
Gaston Glass, Miriam Cooper, Thomas Guise, Robert Frazer, Edna Murphy, Eddie Gribbon.
Arthur, a playboy, is unjustly convicted and sent to jail.

After the Show (Famous Players-Lasky/Paramount, 1921)
d: William DeMille. 6 reels.
Jack Holt, Lila Lee, Charles Ogle, Eve Southern, Shannon Day, Carlton King, Stella Seager, Ethel Wales.
Taylor, a millionaire, desires Eileen, a showgirl... but finds that she has a protector in "Pop" O'Malley, the stagedoor watchman, who has taken a paternal interest in the girl.

After the Storm (Columbia, 1928)
d: George B. Seitz. 6 reels.
Hobart Bosworth, Maude George, Charles Delaney, Eugenia Gilbert, George Kuwa, Linda Loredo.
Dane, a ship's captain, believes his wife to be unfaithful, so he takes his young son and sails away. Twenty years pass, and the three are brought together again.

After the War (Universal, 1919)
d: Joseph de Grasse. 5 reels.
Grace Cunard, Herbert Prior, Edward Cecil, Frank Whitson, Dora Rogers, Gertrude Astor, L.M. Wells, Harry Carter, Gretchen Lederer.
A famous stage actress reveals that she has an illegitimate baby, stemming from an encounter with a German officer during World War I.

After Your Own Heart (Fox, 1921)
d: George E. Marshall. 5 reels.
Tom Mix, Ora Carew, George Hernandez, William Buckley, Sid Jordan, E. C. Robinson, Bill Ward.
Parker, a rancher, finds himself falling in love with the daughter of a neighboring rancher, although her father is contesting Parker's water rights.

Against All Odds (Fox, 1924)
d: Edmund Mortimer. 5 reels.
Buck Jones, Dolores Rousse, Ben Hendricks Jr., William Scott, Thais Valdemar, William N. Ailey, Bernard Seigel, Jack McDonald.
Out West, a cowpoke named Newton saves his friend from a lynch mob.

The Age of Desire (Arthur H. Jacobs Corp./Associated First National, 1923)
d: Frank Borzage. 6 reels.
Joseph Swickard, William Collier Jr., Frank Truesdell, Bruce Guerin, Frankie Lee, J. Farrell MacDonald, Mary Jane Irving, Myrtle Stedman, Aggie Herring, Mary Philbin, Edithe Yorke.
Reading that a wealthy woman has offered a reward for news of her long-lost son, a swindler goes after the reward by preparing a street orphan to pose as the boy. Unknown to the cheat, this young "orphan" really *is* the woman's son.

Ain't Love Funny? (R-C Pictures/Film Booking Offices of

America, 1927)
d: Del Andrews. 5 reels.
Alberta Vaughn, Thomas Wells, Syd Crossley, Babe London, Johnny Gough, Charles Hill Mailes.
World War I comedy about a girl whose home is converted into a dwelling for doughboys, and she's wooed by every one of them.

The Air Circus (Fox, 1928)
d: Howard Hawks. 8 reels. (Includes talking sequences.)
Louise Dresser, David Rollins, Arthur Lake, Sue Carol, Charles Delaney, Heinie Conklin, Earl Robinson.
Blake, a student of aviation, overcomes his fear of flying when his best friend's plane is badly in need of repairs in mid-air.

The Air Hawk (Van Pelt-Wilson Productions, 1924)
d: Bruce Mitchell. 5 reels.
Al Wilson, Webster Cullison, Frank Tomick, Emmett King, Virginia Brown Faire, Lee Shumway, Frank Rice, Leonard Clapham.
Aviators foil a gang of platinum mine thieves.

The Air Legion (FBO Pictures/RKO Productions, 1929)
d: Bert Glennon. 7 reels.
Antonio Moreno, Ben Lyon, Martha Sleeper, John Gough, Colin Chase.
Dave, an airmail pilot, turns coward but is given a chance to redeem himself.

The Air Mail (Famous Players-Lasky/Paramount, 1925)
d: Irvin Willat. 8 reels.
Warner Baxter, Billie Dove, Mary Brian, Douglas Fairbank Jr., George Irving, Richard Tucker, Guy Oliver, Jack Byron, John Webb Dillon, Lloyd Whitlock.
Kane, intent on larceny, manages to obtain work as an airmail pilot. As his training period unfolds, however, the would-be thief becomes inspired by the spirit of the service, and gets involved in a life-saving effort that wins him the love of a grateful young woman.

The Air Mail Pilot (Superlative Pictures/Hi-Mark Productions, 1928)
d: Gene Carroll. 6 reels.
James F. Fulton, Earl Metcalfe, Blanche Mehaffey, DeWitt Jennings, Max Hawley, Carl Stockdale.
A young pilot wins laurels when he foils a plot to rob the mail.

The Air Patrol (Universal, 1928)
d: Bruce Mitchell. 5 reels.
Al Wilson, Elsa Benham, Jack Mower, Frank Tomick, Monte Montague, Taylor Duncan, Art Goebel, Frank Clark.
Air Patrol pilots foil a gang of smugglers.

An Alabaster Box (Vitagraph, 1917)
d: Chester Withey. 5 reels.
Alice Joyce, Marc MacDermott, Harry Ham, Patsey DeForest, Frank Crane.
The daughter of a convicted embezzler returns to town to clear her father's name.

Aladdin and the Wonderful Lamp (Fox, 1917)
d: C.M. Franklin, S.A. Franklin. 5 reels.
Francis Carpenter, Fred Turner, Virginia Lee Corbin, Alfred Paget, Violet Radcliffe, Buddy Messinger, Lewis Sargent, Gertrude Messinger, Marie Messinger, Carmen DeRue, Raymond Lee, Lloyd Perl, Joe Singleton, Elmo Lincoln.
When Aladdin, a simple tailor, discovers the magic lamp in an underground cave, he uses its powers to gain wealth and pursue his courtship of a princess. But a sinister magician is after the lamp, too.

Aladdin From Broadway (Vitagraph, 1917)
d: William Wolbert. 5 reels.
Edith Storey, Antonio Moreno, William Duncan, Otto Lederer, Laura Winston, George Holt.
An Englishwoman is sold into slavery in a foreign country. A Broadway chap, disguised as a beggar, tries to get her out.

Aladdin's Other Lamp (Metro, 1917)
d: John H. Collins. 5 reels.
Viola Dana, Robert Walker, Augustus Phillips, Henry Hallam, Ricca Allen, Edward Elkas, Nellie Grant, Louis B. Foley.
An orphan girl dreams of owning Aladdin's magic lamp.

Alarm Clock Andy (Famous Players-Lasky/Paramount, 1920)
d: Jerome Storm. 5 reels.
Charles Ray, George Webb, Millicent Fisher, Tom Guise, Andrew Robson.
Bashful and insecure, a lowly clerk is mistaken for the firm's swaggering, confident efficiency expert.

The Alaskan (Famous Players-Lasky/Paramount, 1924)
d: Herbert Brenon. 7 reels.
Thomas Meighan, Estelle Taylor, John Sainpolis, Frank Campeau, Anna May Wong, Alphonse Ethier, Maurice Cannon, Charles Ogle.
In Alaska, a young man seeks vengeance on the gang that killed his father.

An Alaskan Romance—see: The Girl Alaska (1919)

The Albany Night Boat (Tiffany-Stahl Productions, 1928)
d: Alfred Raboch. 6 reels.
Olive Borden, Ralph Emerson, Duke Martin, Nellie Bryden, Helen Marlowe.
Ken, a searchlight operator, marries his true love and they settle down in a home overlooking the Hudson River. There, Ken will have to conduct a daring riparian adventure to rescue his wife from the clutches of a would-be seducer.

Alex the Great (FBO Pictures, 1928)
d: Dudley Murphy. 7 reels.
Richard "Skeets" Gallagher, Albert Conti, Patricia Avery, Ruth Dwyer, Charles Byer, J. Barney Sherry.
A small-town boy makes good in the Big City.

Ali Baba and the Forty Thieves (Fox, 1918)
d: S.A. Franklin, C.M. Franklin. 5 reels.
George Stone, Gertrude Messinger, Lewis Sargent, Buddy Messinger, G. Raymond Nye, Raymond Lee, Charles Hincus, Marie Messinger, Jack Hull.
A poor woodsman discovers a cave filled with stolen treasure.

Alias Jimmy Valentine (World Film Corp., 1915)
d: Maurice Tourneur. 5 reels.
Robert Warwick, Robert Cummings, Alec B. Francis, Fred Truesdell, Ruth Shepley, John Hines, David Flanagan, Walter Craven, John Boone.
By day, he's a respectable businessman; by night, he robs banks.

Alias Jimmy Valentine (Metro, 1920)
d: Edmund Mortimer, Arthur D. Ripley. 6 reels.
Bert Lytell, Vola Vale, Eugene Pallette, Wilton Taylor, Marc Robbins, Robert Dunbar, Winter Hall, James Farley, Fred

8

Kelsey.
Remake of the 1915 *Alias Jimmy Valentine*.

Alias Jimmy Valentine (MGM, 1928)
d: Jack Conway. 8 reels. (Part talkie.)
William Haines, Karl Dane, Tully Marshall, Lionel Barrymore, Leila Hyams, Howard Hickman, Billy Butts, Evelyn Mills.
Jimmy Valentine, a reformed safecracker, must risk suspicion in order to open a safe and rescue a trapped child.

Alias Julius Caesar (Charles Ray Productions, 1922)
d: Charles Ray. 5 reels.
Charles Ray, Barbara Bedford, William Scott, Robert Fernandez, Fred Miller, Eddie Gribbon, Tom Wilson, Harvey Clark, Milton Ross, S.J. Binhgam, Phillip Dunham.
Locked in the shower as a practical joke, Billy escapes wearing only the shower curtain, and is arrested as a dangerous lunatic. But he'll prove his sanity, and his usefulness, by capturing a jewel thief.

Alias Ladyfingers (Metro, 1921)
d: Bayard Veiller. 6 reels.
Bert Lytell, Ora Carew, Frank Elliott, Edythe Chapman, DeWitt Jennings, Stanley Goethals.
"Ladyfingers," a safecracker known for the dexterity of his sensitive fingers, is actually the long-lost grandson of the rich lady he is accused of robbing.

Alias Mary Brown (Triangle, 1918)
d: H. D'Elba. 5 reels.
Pauline Starke, Casson Ferguson, Arthur N. Millett, Eugene Burr, Sidney DeGray, Walter Belasco, Dick Rosson, Alberta Lee.
A young man vows revenge on the men who defrauded his father and hastened the old man's death. To help carry out his scheme, he disguises himself as a woman called Mary Brown.

Alias Mary Flynn (Film Booking Offices of America, 1925)
d: Ralph Ince. 6 reels.
Evelyn Brent, Malcolm McGregor, William V. Mong, Gladden James, Lou Payne, Wilson Benge, John Gough, Jacques D'Auray.
Mary Flynn, a notorious jewel thief, finds love and decides to go straight.

Alias Mike Moran (Famous Players-Lasky/Paramount, 1919)
d: James Cruze. 5 reels.
Wallace Reid, Ann Little, Emory Johnson, Charles Ogle, Edythe Chapman, William Elmer, Winter Hall, Jean Calhoun, Guy Oliver.
A ribbon clerk switches identities with an ex-convict.

Alias Miss Dodd (Universal, 1920)
d: Harry Franklin. 5 reels.
Edith Roberts, Johnnie Cook, Walter Richardson, Harry Van Meter, Margaret McWade, Vida Johnson, Ruth King.
Jeanne, a book binder's assistant, reads of scandalous doings in a diary she is supposed to be binding.

Alias Mrs. Jessop (Metro, 1917)
d: William S. Davis. 5 reels.
Emily Stevens, Howard Hall, William H. Tooker, Donald Hall, Lillian Paige, Eldean Steuart, Sue Balfour.
A girl impersonates her identical cousin.

Alias the Lone Wolf (Columbia, 1927)
d: Edward H. Griffith. 7 reels.
Bert Lytell, Lois Wilson, William V. Mong, Ned Sparks, James Mason, Paulette Duval, Ann Brody, Alphonz Ethier.
A sympathetic thief known as "The Lone Wolf" helps a lady smuggle diamonds into the U.S.A., but changes his mind when he finds himself falling in love with her.

Alias the Night Wind (Fox, 1923)
d: Joseph Franz. 5 reels.
William Russell, Maude Wayne, Charles K. French, Wade Boteler, Donald MacDonald, H. Milton Ross, Charles Wellesley, Mark Fenton, Otto Matieson, Bob Klein, Bert Lindley.
"Lady Kate," a female detective, takes on the case of the "Night Wind" robberies.

The Alibi (Vitagraph, 1916)
d: Paul Scardon. 5 reels.
James Morrison, Paul Scardon, Betty Howe, Edward Elkas, Robert Whitworth, Stanley Walpole, Robert Gaillard.
A bank cashier is falsely convicted of embezzlement, but his fiancée continues to believe in his innocence.

Alice Adams (Encore Pictures/Associated Exhibitors, 1923)
d: Rowland V. Lee. 6 reels.
Florence Vidor, Claude Gillingwater, Harold Goodwin, Margaret McWade, Thomas Ricketts, Margaret Landis, Gertrude Astor, Vernon Steele.
First feature film version of the famous Booth Tarkington novel *Alice Adams*, in which the title character strives to outgrow her family's modest station in life and gain a place in polite society.

Alice in Wonderland (Nonpareil Feature Film Corp., 1915)
d: W.W. Young. 5 reels.
Viola Savoy.
Fantasy based on Lewis Carroll's *Alice's Adventures in Wonderland*.

Alicia of the Orphans—see: The Ragged Princess (1916)

The Alien (New York Motion Picture Corp., 1915)
d: Thomas H. Ince. 8 reels.
George Beban, Blanche Schwed, Edward Gillespie, Jack Nelson, Hayward Ginn, Andrea Lynne, Thelma Salter, Jack Davidson, Edith MacBride, J. Frank Burke, William J. Kane, Ida Lewis, Fanny Midgley, Maude Gilbert, Claire Hillier, Nona Thomas.
An Italian immigrant, grieving over the death of his only daughter, is unjustly accused of kidnapping.

An Alien Enemy (W.W. Hodkinson Corp., 1918)
d: Wallace Worsley. 7 reels.
Louis Glaum, Mary Jane Irving, Thurston Hall, Albert Allardt, Charles Hammond, Jay Morley, Roy Laidlaw, Joseph J. Dowling, Clifford Alexander.
During World War I, an American girl is forced to spy for the Germans.

Alien Souls (Lasky Feature Play Co./Paramount, 1916)
d: Frank Reicher. 5 reels.
Sessue Hayakawa, Tsuru Aoki, Earle Foxe, Grace Benham, J. Parks Jones, Violet Malone, Dorothy Abril.
A Japanese girl living in America is courted by a fortune-hunter.

Alimony (Paralta Plays, Inc./First National, 1917)
d: Emmett J. Flynn. 6 reels.
Lois Wilson, George Fisher, Josephine Whittell, Wallace Worsley, Arthur Allardt, Joseph J. Dowling, Ida Lewis, Marguerite Livingston.

Hell hath no fury, etc. A malicious woman schemes to break up the marriage of her former lover and his refreshingly innocent young wife.

Alimony (R-C Pictures/Film Booking Offices of America, 1924)
d: James W. Horne. 7 reels.
Grace Darmond, Warner Baxter, Ruby Miller, William A. Carroll, Jackie Saunders, Clyde Fillmore, Herschel Mayall, Alton Brown.
When a married man makes a success of his business and enters elite society, his wife notices he has developed a wandering eye.

All Aboard (B&H Enterprises/First National, 1927)
d: Charles Hines. 7 reels.
Johnny Hines, Edna Murphy, Dot Farley, Henry Barrows, Frank Hagney, Babe London, Sojin, James Leonard.
There's comic chaos when Johnny, a failed former shoe clerk, becomes an international tourist guide—with disastrous results.

All Around Frying Pan (R-C Pictures/Film Booking Offices of America, 1925)
d: David Kirkland. 6 reels.
Fred Thomson, James Marcus, William Courtwright, John Lince, Clara Horton, Monte Collins, Elmo Lincoln, Newton Barbar.
Out West, a lonesome cowpoke becomes a champion rodeo rider and embarks on a series of adventures, including romance with a rancher's daughter.

All at Sea (MGM, 1928)
d: Alf Goulding. 6 reels.
Karl Dane, George K. Arthur, Josephine Dunn, Herbert Prior, Eddie Baker.
U.S. sailors and marines converge on a theater where one of their mates has been "hypnotized."

All Dolled Up (Universal, 1921)
d: Rollin Sturgeon. 5 reels.
Gladys Walton, Edward Hearn, Richard Norton, Florence Turner, Helen Bruneau, Fred Malatesta, Ruth Royce, John Goff, Frank Norcross, Muriel Godfrey Turner, Lydia Yeamans Titus.
Farcical comedy about a wealthy spinster who "adopts" a grown couple who have fallen in love.

All For a Girl (Mirograph Corp., 1915)
d: Roy Applegate. 5 reels.
Renee Kelly, Edward G. Longman, Frank DeVernon, Sue Balfour, E.T. Roseman, Roy Applegate, Margaret Willard, Georgia Harvey, Al Grady, Gerald Hevener, Sidney D'Albrook.
A charming but penniless young man courts a girl he thinks is a housemaid... but she's really a wealthy heiress.

All For a Husband (Fox, 1917)
d: Carl Harbaugh. 5 reels.
Herbert Evans, Virginia Pearson, Dorothy Quincy, Gladys Kelly, Carl Moody.
Henry, a mayoral candidate, is pursued by two women: one, a harmless but amorous lady, the other a dangerous lunatic. He has trouble telling them apart.

All For the Love of a Girl—see: All For a Girl (1915)

All Man (World Film Corp., 1916)
d: Emile Chautard. 5 reels.
Robert Warwick, Mollie King, Gerda Homes, Louis Grisel, Charles Duncan, Alec B. Francis, George MacQuarrie, Johnny Hines, Henry West.
A wealthy ne'er-do-well journeys West, where he gets the chance to prove he can be a productive citizen.

All Man (Vitagraph, 1918)
d: Paul Scardon. 5 reels.
Harry Morey, Betty Blythe, Robert Gaillard, George Majeroni, Carlton King, Bernard Siegel.
Steelworker John Olsen embarks on a criminal career, but finds it treacherous... especially when he falls in love with a female criminal and must sacrifice his own freedom so that she can escape the arm of the law.

All Night (Universal, 1918)
d: Paul Powell. 5 reels.
Carmel Myers, Rodolfo di Valentina, Charles Dorian, Mary Warren, William Dyer, Wadsworth Harris, Jack Hull.

A married couple pose as their own servants during an important dinner party. Universal remade this film in 1921 as *A Shocking Night*.

All of a Sudden Norma (Robertson-Cole, 1919)
d: Howard Hickman. 5 reels.
Bessie Barriscale, Joseph J. Dowling, Albert Cody, R. Henry Grey, Frank Leigh, Melbourne MacDowell.
Norma Brisbane, a stylish but penniless status-seeker, tries her hand at jewel theft, gambling, and blackmail. But in the end, she learns that honesty is the best policy.

All-of-a-Sudden-Peggy (Famous Players-Lasky/Paramount, 1920)
d: Walter Edwards. 5 reels.
Marguerite Clark, Jack Mulhall, Lillian Leighton, Maggie Fischer, Orral Humphrey, Sylvia Jocelyn, Eddie Sutherland, Tom Ricketts, Virginia Foltz.
Indifferent Peggy pays no heed to Jimmy's romantic overtures until she learns that her widowed mother is postponing her own marriage until after Peggy is wed. With that news, indifferent Peggy becomes "all-of-a-sudden-Peggy," and a double wedding looms.

All Souls' Eve (Realart Pictures, 1921)
d: Chester Franklin. 5 reels.
Mary Miles Minter, Jack Holt, Carmen Phillips, Clarence Geldert, Mickey Moore, Fanny Midgley, Lottie Williams.
Daft melodrama about a nursemaid who assumes the soul of her deceased mistress, and marries the widower. Miss Minter plays both the nursemaid and the deceased wife.

All the Brothers Were Valiant (Metro, 1923)
d: Irvin V. Willat. 7 reels.
Malcolm McGregor, Billie Dove, Lon Chaney, William H. Orlamond, Robert McKim, Robert Kortman, Otto Brower, Curt Rehfeld, William V. Mong, Leo Willis, Shannon Day.
After his brother Mark is presumed lost at sea, Joel assumes command of Mark's whaling ship. But it turns out that Mark is not dead after all, and returns to make trouble.

All the World to Nothing (Pathé, 1918)
d: Henry King. 6 reels.
William Russell, Winifred Westover, J. Morris Foster, Hayward Mack.
Delicious complications ensue when a young woman goes through a marriage of convenience, simply to qualify for a large inheritance. Her instant groom disappears and she forgets him. But much later, the now-wealthy heiress meets him again, fails to recognize him as her benefactor, and falls

in love with him.

All Woman (Goldwyn Pictures Corp., 1918)
d: Hobart Henley. 6 reels.
Mae Marsh, Jere Austin, Arthur Housman, John Sainpolis, Jack Dillon, Joe Henaway, Hazel Alden, Madelyn Dlare, Elsie Sothern, Lois Alexander, Dan Mason, Jules Cowles, Alvina Alstadt.
Filled with enthusiasm, a New York woman arrives at a hotel in the mountains she has just inherited... only to find it a rundown, seedy establishment frequented by derelicts. But she stays on, and with the help of a virtuous local lawyer, whips the place into shape.

All Wrong (Pathé, 1919)
d: William Worthington, Raymond B. West. 5 reels.
Bryant Washburn, Mildred Davis, Charles Bennett, Helen Dunbar, Fred Montague, Marguerite Livingston.
A salesman decides that his marriage should be an "Unending Courtship", and so he convinces his bride that they should live separately and see each other only once a week, just as they did during the courtship. Bad idea that gets worse.

All's Fair in Love (Goldwyn, 1921)
d: E. Mason Hopper. 5 reels.
May Collins, Richard Dix, Marcia Manon, Raymond Hatton, Stuart Holmes, Andrew Robson.
After she loses her husband to a temptress, Natalie tries to win him back by employing the vamp's own seductive methods.

Alma, Where Do You Live? (Newfields Producing Corp., 1917)
d: Hal Clarendon. 6 reels.
Ruth MacTammany, George Larkin, Jack Newton, John Webb Dillon, Frank McNish, Walter Mack, Mattie Keene, Marian Kinmaird, George Gaston, Joseph Phillips.
Alma is in love with a portrait painter, but there's a problem: She's been hired to make another man fall in love with her.

The Almighty Dollar (Paragon Films/World Film Corp., 1916)
d: Robert Thornby. 5 reels.
June Elvidge, Frances Nelson, George Anderson, E.K. Lincoln, Miss Humphries, Deborah Nanson, J. Jackson Meredith.
Feeling neglected by her husband, a young wife agrees to meet with an old flame.

Almost a Husband (Goldwyn, 1919)
d: Clarence G. Badger. 5 reels.
Will Rogers, Peggy Wood, Cullen Landis, Herbert Standing, Clara Horton, Ed Brady, Sidney DeGray, Gus Saville.
A law student plays a game in which he "marries" the prettiest girl in town. Then they discover that the marriage is legal.

Almost a Lady (Metropolitan Pictures/Producers Distributing Corp., 1926)
d: E. Mason Hopper. 6 reels.
Harrison Ford, George K. Arthur, Marie Prevost, John Miljan, Trixie Friganza, Barney Gilmore.
Romantic comedy about Marcia, a store model, who is persuaded to impersonate a famous writer.

Almost Human (DeMille Pictures/Pathé, 1927)
d: Frank Urson. 6 reels.
Vera Reynolds, Kenneth Thomson, Majel Coleman, Claire McDowell, Ethel Wales, Fred Walton.
John and Mary meet, fall in love, and are married; then they secure employment in a fashionable home as chauffeur and housemaid. Misunderstanding develops when John chances to meet his former girlfriend, and Mary leaves him. But the couple are brought back together through the intervention of the family dog, whose instincts are "almost human."

Almost Married (Metro, 1919)
d: Charles Swickard. 5 reels.
May Allison, Walter I. Percival, Frank Currier, Harry Rattenbury, James Wharton James, Hugh Fay.
The son of an American millionaire loves a Swiss entertainer, but his dad marries her first... or does he? Junior follows the pair on their "honeymoon" to find out.

Aloha Oe (Triangle, 1915)
d: Richard Stanton, Charles Swickard. 5 reels.
Willard Mack, Enid Markey, Margaret Thompson, Frank Borzage, J. Frank Burke, J. Barney Sherry.
A San Francisco lawyer takes a cruise, and settles on a Polynesian isle.

Aloma of the South Seas (Famous Players-Lasky/Paramount, 1926)
d: Maurice Tourneur. 9 reels.
Gilda Gray, Percy Marmont, Warner Baxter, Harry Morey, Julanne Johnston, Joseph Smiley, Frank Montgomery, Mme. Burani, Ernestine Gaines, Aurelio Coccia, William Powell.
First feature film version of the story of Aloma, an island princess who falls in love with a vacationing American.

Along Came Ruth (MGM, 1924)
d: Edward Cline. 5 reels.
Viola Dana, Walter Hiers, Tully Marshall, Raymond McKee, Victor Potel, Gale Henry, DeWitt Jennings, Adele Farrington, Brenda Lane.
Romantic comedy about a girl who rents a room above a struggling furniture store, and uses her personality and her wit to increase business and to get the owner's nephew to fall in love with her.

The Alster Case (Essanay, 1915)
d: J. Charles Haydon. 5 reels.
Bryant Washburn, John H. Cossar, Ruth Stonehouse, Anne Leigh, Louise Crolius, Betty Scott, Arthur W. Bates, Rod LaRocque, Beatrice Styler.
When a wealthy spinster is found murdered, a famous detective is called in on the case.

The Altar Stairs (Universal, 1922)
d: Lambert Hillyer. 5 reels.
Frank Mayo, Louise Lorraine, Dagmar Godowsky, Lawrence Hughes, J.J. Lanoe, Harry DeVere, Hugh Thompson, Boris Karloff, Nick DeRuiz.
Passion in the South Seas, where a seaman falls in love with another sailor's wife.

Altars of Desire (MGM, 1926)
d: Christy Cabanne. 7 reels.
Mae Murray, Conway Tearle, Robert Edeson, Andre de Beranger.
A fun-loving American girl is sent to Paris by her father to acquire some sophistication.

Always Audacious (Famous Players-Lasky/Paramount, 1920)
d: James Cruze. 6 reels.
Wallace Reid, Margaret Loomis, Clarence Geldart, J.M.

Dumont, Rhea Haines, Carmen Phillips, Guy Oliver, Fannie Midgely.

Reid plays a double role, as a rich wastrel and as a master criminal who resembles him.

Always in the Way (Metro, 1915)
d: J. Searle Dawley. 6 reels.
Mary Miles Minter, Ethelmary Oakland, Lowell Sherman, Edna M. Holland, Mabel B. Green, Harold Meltzer, James Riley, Arthur Evers, Charlotte Shelby, Hal Clarendon.
Rejected by her stepmother, a girl runs away and winds up in Africa, teaching Christianity to the natives. But she yearns to return to America and be reunited with her real father.

Always the Woman (Betty Compson Productions/Goldwyn, 1922)
w, d: Arthur Rosson. 6 reels.
Betty Compson, Emory Johnson, Doris Pawn, Gerald Pring, Richard Rosson, Arthur Delmore, Macey Harlam.
International intrigue aboard a steamship carrying a colorful assortment of weirdos.

Amarilly of Clothes-Line Alley (Pickford/Famous Players-Lasky, 1918)
d: Marshall A. Neilan. 5 reels.
Mary Pickford, William Scott, Norman Kerry, Ida Waterman, Margaret Landis, Kate Price, Tom Wilson, Fred Goodwins, Herbert Standing, Wesley Barry, Frank Butterworth.
A tenement girl is loved by both a bartender and a wealthy sculptor.

The Amateur Adventuress (Metro, 1919)
d: Henry Otto. 5 reels.
Emmy Wehlen, Allan Sears, Eugene Pallette, William V. Mong, Marion Skinner, Lucille Ward, Victor Potel, Rosemary Theby, Bonnie Hill.
Feeling unappreciated and unloved, a stenographer decides to go on a fling.

An Amateur Devil (Famous Players-Lasky/Paramount, 1920)
d: Maurice Campbell. 5 reels.
Bryant Washburn, Anny May, Charles Wyngate, Christine Mayo, Sidney Bracey, Norris Johnson, Graham Pettie, Anna Hernandez.
Rejected by his fiancée for being too dull, a young man sets out to change his image.

The Amateur Gentleman (Inspiration Pictures/First National, 1926)
d: Sidney Olcott. 8 reels.
Richard Barthelmess, Dorothy Dunbar, Gardner James, Nigel Barrie, Brandon Hurst, John Miljan, Edwards Davis, Billie Bennett, Herbert Grimwood, Gino Corrado, Sidney DeGray, John Peters.
In England, a parvenu ascends in social status and craves the love of a noblewoman.

An Amateur Orphan (Thanhouser/Pathé, 1917)
d: Van Dyke Brooke. 5 reels.
Gladys Leslie, Isabel Vernon, Thomas A. Curran, Jean Armour, Chester Morris, Ray Halor, Justus Barnes, Carey L. Hastings, Grace DeCarlton.
On a lark, a wealthy young woman trades places with an orphan... and gets herself adopted.

An Amateur Widow (World Film Corp., 1919)
d: Oscar Apfel. 5 reels.
Zena Keefe, Hugh Dillman, Jack Drumier, William Black, Pauline Dempsey, Mary B. Davis, Eugenie Woodward, Florence Ashbrooke, Charles Hartley, Charles Ascott.
When her sweetheart disappears and is thought dead, a madcap heiress decides to pass herself off as his widow.

The Amateur Wife (Famous Players-Lasky/Paramount, 1920)
d: Edward Dillon. 6 reels.
Irene Castle, William P. Carleton, Arthur Rankin, S.J. Warrington, A. Saskin, Augusta Anderson, Mrs. Charles Dewey, Ellen Olson.
A drab convent girl returns home to find her mother a flashy stage actress with loads of male admirers.

The Amazing Impostor (American Film Co./Pathé, 1919)
d: Lloyd Ingraham. 5 reels.
Mary Miles Minter, Edward Jobson, Margaret Shelby, Carl Stockdale, Allan Forrest, Henry Barrows, George Periolat, Demetrius Mitsoras, John Gough.
After switching identites with a phony Russian "countess," a chewing gum heiress finds herself pursued by Bolshevik spies, would-be jewel thieves, and one detective who turns out to be a pretty nice guy.

The Amazing Vagabond (FBO Pictures/RKO Productions, 1929)
d: Wallace W. Fox. 6 reels.
Bob Steele, Tom Lingham, Jay Morley, Perry Murdock, Lafe McKee, Thelma Daniels, Emily Gerdes.
Out West, a lumberman tries to make a man out of his son by having him kidnapped and challenging him to escape his captors. The lad does all that and more. He falls in love with the lumber foreman's daughter and foils timber rustlers as well.

The Amazing Wife (Universal, 1919)
d: Ida May Park. 5 reels.
Mary MacLaren, Frank Mayo, Stanhope Wheatcroft, Ethel Lynne, Seymour Zeiliff.
Grieving the loss of her own husband, a young woman decides to pass herself off as the widow of an Army lieutenant whose name was the same as her husband's. All goes well until the lieutenant turns up wounded instead of deceased.

The Amazing Woman (Lloyd Carleton Productions/Republic, 1920)
d: John G. Adolfi. 5 reels.
Edward Coxen, Ruth Clifford, Andrew Robson, Richard Morris, Mrs. Orlamonde.
She's a vamp, she's a scamp, she's Anitra Frane, a singer who bills herself as "The Flame." Anitra toys with her wealthy suitors, even causing one to commit suicide over her. But there's a tender side to Anitra, too. With some of her money, she builds a free clinic for children.

The Amazons (Famous Players Film Co./Paramount, 1917)
d: Joseph Kaufman. 5 reels.
Marguerite Clark, Elsie Lawson, Helen Greene, William Hinckley, Helen Robinson, Edgar Norton, Andre Bellon, Roxanne Lancing, Tammany Young.
Three sisters are raised as boys, because that's what their mother wanted.

Ambition (Fox, 1916)
d: James Vincent. 5 reels.
Bertha Kalich, Kenneth Hunter, William H. Tooker, W.W.

Black, Kittens Reichert, Gelbert Rooney, Barnett Greenwood, May Price.

An assistant district attorney proves to be too ambitious, prizing his career over his obligations to his wife.

The Ambition of Mark Truitt — see: Fruits of Desire (1916)

Ambitious Annie — see: Five and Ten Cent Annie (1928)

America   (World Film Corp., 1914)
d: Lawrence McGill.   6 reels.
Bert Shepherd, The Australian Wood Choppers, The Phyllis Equestrians, Arthur Voegtlin, William J. Wilson.
Filmed version of a stage production, including novelty acts.

America   (D.W. Griffith, Inc./United Artists, 1924)
d: D.W. Griffith.   14 reels.
Neil Hamilton, Carol Dempster, Lionel Barrymore, Arthur Donaldson, Frank Walsh, Arthur Dewey, Harry Semels, John Dunton, Frank McGlynn, Louis Wolheim.
The American Revolution, as seen through the eyes of one American family.

American Aristocracy   (Triangle, 1917)
d: Lloyd Ingraham.   5 reels.
Douglas Fairbanks, Jewel Carmen, Charles DeLima, Albert Parker, Arthur Ortego.
An entomologist finds himself in all sorts of daring escapades.

The American Beauty   (Paramount, 1916)
d: William D. Taylor.   5 reels.
Myrtle Stedman, Elliott Dexter, Howard Davies, Jack Livingston, Adelaide Woods, Edward Ayers.
A baby girl, found floating at sea, is raised by a fisherman and his wife. She grows up a charmer, and gets to model for an artist who paints her as "The American Beauty."

American Beauty   (First National, 1927)
d: Richard Wallace.   7 reels.
Lloyd Hughes, Billie Dove, Walter McGrail, Margaret Livingston, Lucien Prival, Edythe Chapman, Alice White, Yola D'Avril.
Millicent, an ambitious young woman bent on improving her status in life, wins the heart of a wealthy young man, who proposes.   But Millicent comes to her senses and decides to stick with her true love, a struggling young chemist.

American Buds   (Fox, 1918)
d: Kenean Buel.   6 reels.
Jane Lee, Katherine Lee, Albert Gran, Regina Quinn, Lucille Southerwaite, Leslie Austin, H.D. Southard, Nora Cecil, William Hays, Maggie Weston.
When their mother dies, two sisters try to find the father they've never known.

The American Consul   (Lasky Feature Play Co./Paramount, 1917)
d: Rollin Sturgeon.   5 reels.
Theodore Roberts, Ernest Joy, Maude Fealy, Charles West, Raymond Hattan, Tom Forman.
Intrigue and danger erupt south of the border when a newly-appointed diplomat and his daughter arrive in Central America.

An American Gentleman   (Liberty Motion Picture Co., 1915)
d: John Gorman.   5 reels.
William Bonelli, Grace Lowell, Charles Graham, Virginia Fairfax, Douglas Sibole, Martha Illington, Wilbur Hudson, George W. Middleton.
Gypsies find an abandoned four-year-old girl and raise her as their own. The "American Gentleman" of the title shows up when the girl is 18... and he not only restores her to her rightful parents, he falls in love with her besides.

An American Live Wire   (Vitagraph, 1918)
d: Thomas R. Mills.   5 reels.
Earle Williams, Grace Darmond, Hal Clements, Miss Toner, Orral Humphrey, Margaret Bennett, Malcolm Blevins.
Confusion reigns when a lovelorn New Yorker living in the South American country of Coralio accidentally apprehends a crook; his former sweetie arrives in Coralio and is mistaken for the president's mistress; and a detective looking for an embezzler erroneously arrests the country's president. But it's all sorted out, and the lovers are reunited.

American Maid   (Mutual, 1917)
d: Albert Capellani.   5 reels.
Edna Goodrich, George Henry, William B. Davidson, John Hopkins.
A senator's daughter working as a Red Cross nurse falls in love with one of her patients, a wounded American soldier.

American Manners   (Richard Talmadge Productions/Truart Film Corp., 1924)
d: James W. Horne.   6 reels.
Richard Talmadge, Mark Fenton, Lee Shumway, Helen Lynch, Arthur Millett, William Turner, Pat Harmon, George Warde.
After years in Paris, an American returns home just in time to foil a gang of smugglers operating from his father's ship.

American Methods   (Fox, 1917)
d: Frank Lloyd.   5 reels.
William Farnum, Jewel Carmen, Bertram Grassby, Willard Louis, Lillian West, Genevieve Blinn, Alan Forrest, Florence Vidor, Mortimer Jaffe, Marc Robbins, Josef Swickard.
Romantic entanglements ensue when an American visits France to claim an inheritance.

American Pluck   (Chadwick Pictures, 1925)
d: Richard Stanton.   6 reels.
George Walsh, Wanda Hawley, Sidney DeGrey, Frank Leigh, Tom Wilson, Leo White, Dan Mason.
A playboy is turned out of his disgusted father's house and told not to return until he has earned $5,000. The young man will more than satisfy his father's demands, as he becomes a boxing champion, saves a princess from a kidnapping, and wins her royal hand.

American — That's All   (Triangle, 1917)
d: Arthur Rosson.   5 reels.
Jack Devereaux, Winifred Allen, Walter Walker, Blanche Davenport, Jack Raymond, Charles Mussett, George Renevant, Miss Cummins.
Pickles and vinegar are the main ingredients in this frothy mix about a "pickle king."

The American Venus   (Famous Players-Lasky/Paramount, 1926)
d: Frank Tuttle.   8 reels.   (Includes some Technicolor scenes.)
Esther Ralston, Lawrence Gray, Ford Sterling, Fay Lanphier, Louise Brooks, Edna May Oliver, Kenneth MacKenna, William B. Mack, George DeCarlton, W.T. Benda, Ernest Torrence, Douglas Fairbanks Jr.
Mary Gray, daughter of a cold cream tycoon, enters a beauty contest with the intention of endorsing her father's product

if she wins.

The American Way   (World Film Corp., 1919)
d: Frank Reicher. 5 reels.
Arthur Ashley, Dorothy Green, Franklin Hamma, Lisle Leigh, Carl Sauerman, Ed Roseman, Robert Fisher, Harry Semels, Charles Wellsley, John Adrizoni, Hazel Sexton.
Class distinctions power this tale about an English aristocrat pursuing an American girl who likes her men rough and ready.

An American Widow   (Metro, 1917)
d: Frank Reicher. 5 reels.
Ethel Barrymore, Irving Cummings, Dudley Hawley, Ernest Stallard, Augustus Tucker, Charles Dickson, Alfred Kappler, Arthur Lewis, Pearl Browne.
A wealthy American widow pays a penniless playwright to marry her, then get a quickie divorce, all to satisfy some tangled provisions in her former husband's will. But what happens when her new husband's play is a success, and he is suddenly prosperous?

The Americano   (Triangle, 1917)
d: John Emerson. 6 reels.
Douglas Fairbanks, Alma Reubens, Spottiswood Aitken, Carl Stockdale, Charles Stevens, Lillian Langdon, Tote DuCrow, Lillian Langdon, Tom Wilson.
In a South American country, an American adventurer rescues the country's president and his beautiful daughter from rebels.

The Ancient Highway   (Famous Players-Lasky/Paramount, 1925)
d: Irvin Willat. 7 reels.
Jack Holt, Billie Dove, Montagu Love, Stanley Taylor, Lloyd Whitlock, William A. Carroll, Marjorie Bonner, Christian J. Frank.
Along Canada's St. Lawrence river, Brant, a man seeking vengeance against the wealthy miser who swindled his father, meets another of the miser's victims: a young woman with whom Brant falls in love.

The Ancient Mariner   (Fox, 1926)
d: Henry Otto, Chester Bennett. 6 reels.
Clara Bow, Earle Williams, Leslie Fenton, Nigel DeBrulier, Paul Panzer, Gladys Brockwell, Robert Klein.
Melodrama loosely based on the Samuel Taylor Coleridge poem, *The Rime of the Ancient Mariner*.

And a Still Small Voice   (Robertson-Cole, 1918)
w, d: Bertram Bracken. 5 reels.
Henry B. Walthall, Joseph J. Dowling, Fritzi Brunette, George Fisher.
A cashier becomes a gentleman thief.

And the Children Pay   (Veritas Photoplay Co., 1918)
d: Jacques Tyrol. 7 reels.
Gareth Hughes, Bliss Milford, Gerbert Pattee, Etta Mansfield, John P. Campbell, Judge Charles N. Goodnow, Judge John R. Newcomer, Kate Addams, Harry B. Miller.
Tragic tale of adultery, abandonment, and a crippled child.

And the Law Says   (Mutual, 1916)
d: Thomas Ricketts. 5 reels.
Richard Bennett, George Periolat, Adrienne Morrison, Alan Forrest, William Carroll.
A severe judge sentences an innocent young man to the electric chair, not realizing the man is his own son, abandoned by the judge years before.

Angel Child   (W.W. Hodkinson, 1918)
d: Henry Otto. 5 reels.
Kathleen Clifford, Leslie T. Peacocke, Rita Harlan, Fred Church, Daniel Gilfether, Neil Hardin, Gordon Sackville.
She's mischievous and a troublemaker, but she's still her dad's "Angel Child."

Angel Citizens   (William M. Smith Productions, 1922)
d: Francis Ford. 5 reels.
Franklyn Farnum, "Shorty" Hamilton, Peggy O'Day, Max Hoffman, Terris Hoffman.
In "Angel City," a shiftless loner becomes inspired by the love of a good woman, and embarks on a career as a lawman.

The Angel Factory   (Pathé, 1917)
d: Lawrence McGill. 5 reels.
Antonio Moreno, Helene Chadwick, Armand Cortez, Margaret Greene, Suzanne Willa, Francis X. Conlan.
"The Angel Factory" is a settlement house in the slums of New York.

The Angel of Broadway   (DeMille Pictures/Pathé, 1927)
d: Lois Weber. 7 reels.
Leatrice Joy, Victor Varconi, May Robson, Alice Lake, Elsie Bartlett, Ivan Lebedeff, Jane Keckley, Clarence Burton.
Babe, a cabaret dancer, begins attending Salvation Army meetings.

The Angel of Crooked Street   (Vitagraph, 1922)
d: David Smith. 5 reels.
Alice Calhoun, Ralph McCullough, Scott McKee, Rex Hammel, William McCall, Nellie Anderson, Martha Mattox, Mary Young, George Stanley, Walter Cooper.
Jennie, an honest housemaid, is unjustly accused when her employer is robbed.

Ankles Preferred   (Fox, 1927)
d: J.G. Blystone. 6 reels.
Madge Bellamy, Lawrence Gray, Barry Norton, Allan Forrest, Marjorie Beebe, J. Farrell MacDonald, Joyce Compton, William Strauss, Lillian Elliott, Mary Foy.
Nora, a free-thinking young woman, wants to be promoted on the basis of her mental abilities, not her shapely ankles.

Anna Ascends   (Famous Players-Lasky/Paramount, 1922)
d: Victor Fleming. 6 reels.
Alice Brady, Robert Ellis, David Powell, Nita Naldi, Charles Gerrard, Edward Durand, Florence Dixon, Grace Griswold, Frederick Burton.
Anna, a Syrian immigrant, gets involved with jewel smugglers.

Anna Christie   (First National, 1923)
d: John Griffith Wray. 8 reels.
Blanche Sweet, William Russell, George F. Marion, Eugenie Besserer, Ralph Yearsley, George Siegmann, Chester Conklin, Victor Potel, Fred Kohler.
Anna, the daughter of a sea captain, is raised by relatives who mistreat her. She runs away to the city, but unable to find her father, she soon becomes a prostitute. When she finally finds her father, she tells him nothing of her shameful life and he takes her in. But she falls in love with a sailor under his command, and knows she must reveal the facts of her sordid past.

Anna Karenina   (Fox, 1915)
d: J. Gordon Edwards. 5 reels.
Betty Nansen, Edward José, Richard Thornton, Stella

Hammerstein, Mabel Allen.

Anna, a Russian baroness, succumbs to the charms of a handsome cavalry officer and becomes his mistress. But he tires of their relationship and leaves her, even though her husband has already sent her packing. This film was based on the 1876 novel of the same name by Leo Tolstoy. During the silent era, another version of the novel was filmed, entitled *Love* (MGM, 1927), starring Greta Garbo and John Gilbert.

Anne of Green Gables (Realart Pictures, Inc., 1919)
d: William Desmond Taylor. 6 reels.
Mary Miles Minter, Paul Kelly, Marcia Harris, Frederick Burton, Leila Romer, Lincoln Stedman, Hazel Sexton, Russell Hewitt, Albert Hackett, Laurie Lovelle, Carolyn Lee.
Anne, a spirited young girl, is adopted and goes to live on a farm.

Annexing Bill (Astra Film Corp./Pathé, 1918)
d: Albert Parker. 5 reels.
Gladys Hulette, Creighton Hale, Mark Smith, Margaret Greene, Kate Lester.
Bill and Enid are in love, but they can't marry because she's got a million dollars, and he refuses to marry a woman with more money than himself. What to do?

Annie-For-Spite (Mutual, 1917)
d: James Kirkwood. 5 reels.
Mary Miles Minter, George Fisher, Eugenie Forde, Gertrude Le Brandt, George Periolat, Robert Klein, Charles Newton, Emma Kluge, Nellie Wilden, Lucille Ward.
Love changes a homely girl into a lovely young woman.

Annie Laurie (MGM, 1927)
d: John S. Robertson. 9 reels.
Lillian Gish, Norman Kerry, Creighton Hale, Joseph Striker, Hobart Bosworth, Patricia Avery, Russell Simpson, Brandon Hurst, David Torrence, Frank Currier.
Story of the clash between Scottish clans, the MacDonalds and the Campbells, and the girl who comes between them, Annie Laurie.

Ann's Finish (Mutual, 1918)
d: Lloyd Ingraham. 5 reels.
Margarita Fischer, Jack Mower, Adelaide Elliott, David Howard, John Gough, Robert Klein, Perry Banks.
A finishing-school girl invents a husband for herself, then announces that he was drowned at sea. Then he shows up.

Another Chance—see: *Man and Woman* (1920)

Another Man's Boots (Ivor McFadden Productions, 1922)
d: William J. Craft. 5 reels.
Francis Ford, Harry Smith, Elvira Weil, Frank Lanning, Robert Kortman.
Out West, a stranger assumes another man's identity at his request, and falls in love with the man's sister.

Another Man's Shoes (Universal, 1922)
d: Jack Conway. 5 reels.
Herbert Rawlinson, Una Trevelyn, Barbara Bedford, Nick DeRuiz, Josef Swickard, Jean DeBriac, Harry Carter, Nelson McDowell, Lillian Langdon, Jessie Deparnette.
Granger, a businessman trying to avoid underworld cutthroats, gets his cousin to impersonate him without telling him why.

Another Man's Wife (Regal Pictures/Producers Distributing Corp., 1924)
d: Bruce Mitchell. 5 reels.

James Kirkwood, Lila Lee, Wallace Beery, Matt Moore, Zena Keefe, Chester Conklin.
Newlyweds John and Helen quarrel, but reunite when they find both their lives threatened.

Another Scandal (Tifford Cinema Corp./W.W. Hodkinson Corp., 1924)
d: Edward H. Griffith. 8 reels.
Lois Wilson, Herbert Holmes, Ralph Bunker, Flora LeBreton, Ralph W. Chambers, Hedda Hopper, Zeffie Tilbury, Bigelow Cooper, Allan Simpson, Harry Grippe.
On a cruise ship, a happily-married man is pursued by a vamp.

The Answer (Triangle, 1918)
d: E. Mason Hopper. 7 reels.
Alma Rubens, Joe King, Francis McDonald, Claire Anderson, Charles Dorian, Jean Hersholt.
Social workers establish homes for the poor.

The Antics of Ann (Famous Players/Paramount, 1917)
d: Edward Dillon. 5 reels.
Ann Pennington, Harry Ham, Ormi Hawley, Crauford Kent, W.T. Carleton, Charlotte Granville.
Ann Wharton is incorrigible. She dresses in boys' clothes and gets into a football game, she scandalizes public morality by appearing in a one-piece bathing suit, she impersonates a Russian ballet dancer... but she's a scamp with a heart of gold.

Anton the Terrible (Lasky Feature Films/Paramount, 1916)
d: William C. DeMille. 5 reels.
Anita King, Horace B. Carpenter, Harrison Ford, Edythe Chapman, Theodore Roberts, Delia Trombly, Hugo B. Koch.
An embittered cossack becomes head of the Russian secret police.

Any Home—see: Daddy's Girl (1918)

Any Wife (Fox, 1922)
d: Herbert Brenon. 5 reels.
Pearl White, Holmes Herbert, Gilbert Emery, Lawrence Johnson, Augustus Balfour, Eulalie Jensen.
Happily married Myrtle dreams that she has a lover.

Any Woman (Famous Players-Lasky/Paramount, 1925)
d: Henry King. 6 reels.
Alice Terry, Ernest Gillen, Margarita Fisher, Lawson Butt, Aggie Herring, Henry Kolker, Thelma Morgan, George Periolat, Lucille Hutton, Arthur Hoyt, Malcolm Denny.
A secretary tries to get her bosses interested in backing her boyfriend's new invention, a soft drink.

Anybody Here Seen Kelly? (Universal, 1928)
d: William Wyler. 6 reels.
Bessie Love, Tom Moore, Tom O'Brien, Kate Price, Addie MacPhail, Bruce Gordon, Alfred Allen.
A fun-loving American G.I. in Europe invites a local girl to come visit him in the United States. Much to his surprise, she does. Now he's a traffic cop in New York City, and he must contend not only with the girl's amorous intentions, but also her shaky immigration status.

Anything Once (Universal, 1917)
d: Joseph DeGrasse. 5 reels.
Franklyn Farnum, Lon Chaney, Claire du Brey, Marjory Lawrence, Mary St. John, Sam DeGrasse, H.M. Thurston, Raymond Wells, William Dyer, Frank Tokunaga, Eugene Owen.
A New Yorker inherits a ranch in the Old West.

The Apache (Columbia, 1928)
d: Philip Rosen. 6 reels.
Margaret Livingston, Warner Richmond, Don Alvarado, Philo McCullough.
In Marseilles, a young dancer goes from the frying pan into the fire, when she is rescued from thieves by a policeman, who then tries to rape her.

The Apache Raider (Leo Maloney Productions/Pathé, 1928)
d: Leo D. Maloney. 6 reels.
Leo Maloney, Eugenia Gilbert, Don Coleman, Tom London, Jack Ganzhorn, Frederick Dana, Joan Renee, William Merrill McCormick, Robert C. Smith, Walter Shumway.
Out West, a rancher runs afoul of cattle rustlers and crooked politicians.

The Apaches of Paris (Kalem/General Film Co., 1915)
d: Robert Ellis. 4 reels.
Robert Ellis, Marion Whitney, Edna Hibbard, Arthur Houseman, Paula Sherman, Joseph Smith, Laura Hamilton.
Tragedy ensues when an American girl living in Paris falls for a heel.

Apartment 29 (Vitagraph, 1917)
d: Paul Scardon. 5 reels.
Earle Williams, Ethel Gray Terry, Denton Vane, Billie Billings, Bernard Siegle, Frank Mason, Tommy Brett.
A drama critic walks into a web of murder, deceit, and violence.

The Apostle of Vengeance (Triangle, 1916)
d: William S. Hart, Cliff Smith. 5 reels.
William S. Hart, Nona Thomas, Joseph J. Dowling, Fanny Midgley, Jack Gilbert, Marvel Stafford, Gertrude Claire.
Kentucky clans war against each other; a northern minister tries to restore peace.

The Appearance of Evil (World Film Corp., 1918)
d: Lawrence C. Windom. 5 reels.
June Elvidge, Frank Mayo, Douglas Redmond Jr., Clay Clement Jr., George MacQuarrie, Nora Cecil, Inez Marcel, Louis Grisel, Jack Drumier.
There's a scandal in town when a wealthy widow entertains a man in her home in an exclusive neighborhood. But the pair are actually husband and wife, though secretly because of a "no remarriage" clause in her former husband's will.

Appearances (Famous Players-Lasky/Paramount, 1921)
d: Donald Crisp. 5 reels.
David Powell, Mary Glynne, Langhorne Burton, Mary Dibley, Marjorie Hume, Percy Standing.
Desperate to keep up appearances of prosperity, an architect speculates in risky investments.

Applause (Famous Players-Lasky/Paramount, 1929)
d: Rouben Mamoulian. 9 reels. (Also released in sound version.)
Helen Morgan, Joan Peers, Fuller Mellish Jr., Jack Cameron, Henry Wadsworth, Dorothy Cumming.

Kitty, a veteran burlesque performer, wants to raise her daughter properly. But against her better judgment, she is persuaded by her lover, an unscrupulous burlesque comic, to bring her daughter into the show. Mamoulian's much-admired directorial debut, *Applause* is better remembered as an early talkie than a silent film, though it was released in both formats. Helen Morgan's touching performance as the over-the-hill burlesque queen is often regarded as her finest moment in the movies.

The Apple-Tree Girl (Edison/Perfection Pictures, 1917)
d: Alan Crosland. 5 reels.
Shirley Mason, Joyce Fair, Jessie Stevens, Raymond McKee, Edward Coleman, Mabel Guilford, Graham Double, Harry Hollingsworth, Andy Clark, Mabel Strickland, Paul Perez.
A girl who was raised in the shadow of an old apple tree goes to live with her aunt.

April (American Film Co./Mutual, 1916)
d: Donald MacDonald. 5 reels.
Helene Rosson, E. Forrest Taylor, Harry Von Meter, Louise Lester, Charles Newton, Al Fordyce, Marie Van Tassell, Harry McCabe, Nellie Widen.
Little April is kidnapped as a baby and taken to be raised by strangers. But class will tell, and as the girl grows up, she exhibits great gentleness and kindness.

April Folly (Cosmopolitan/Paramount, 1920)
d: Robert Z. Leonard. 5 reels.
Marion Davies, Conway Tearle, Madeline Marshall, Herbert Frank, Hattie de Laro, Amelia Summerville, Charles Peyton, Spencer Charters, Warren Cooke.
A young woman writer pitches a love story to her publisher so convincingly, the two of them fall for each other.

April Fool (Chadwick Pictures, 1926)
d: Nat Ross. 7 reels.
Alexander Carr, Mary Alden, Raymond Keane, Snitz Edwards, Baby Peggy Montgomery.
A successful businessman has to decide whether to give it all up to please his daughter.

April Showers (Preferred Pictures, 1923)
d: Tom Forman. 6 reels.
Colleen Moore, Kenneth Harlan, Ruth Clifford, Priscilla Bonner, Myrtle Vane, James Corrigan, Jack Byron, Ralph Faulkner, Tom McGuire, Kid McCoy, Danny Goodman.
Danny, son of an Irish-American cop, wants to join the force too.

The Arab (Lasky Feature Play Co./Paramount, 1915)
d: Cecil B. DeMille. 5 reels.
Edgar Selwyn, Horace B. Carpenter, Milton Brown, Billy Elmer, Sydney Deane, Gertrude Robinson, Park Jones, Theodore Roberts, Raymond Hatton, Irvin S. Cobb.
Bedouin treachery triggers an attack on local Christians. But the sheik's son and heir falls in love with a missionary's daughter.

The Arab (Metro-Goldwyn Pictures, 1924)
d: Rex Ingram. 7 reels.
Ramon Novarro, Alice Terry, Maxudian, Jean DeLimur, Paul Vermoyal, Justa Uribe, Gerald Robertshaw, Paul Francesci, Giuseppe DeCompo.
In Turkey, an Arab guide falls in love with a Christian missionary. Remake of the 1915 Paramount film *The Arab*, both films being based on the play of the same name by Edgar Selwyn (who also starred in the 1915 version).

Arabia (Fox, 1922)
w, d: Lynn Reynolds. 5 reels.
Tom Mix, Barbara Bedford, George Hernandez, Norman Selby, Edward Piel, Ralph Yearsley, Hector Sarno.
Comedic western takes a horseman to Arabia, where he gets involved with a treacherous sultan, fights off pretenders to the Arab throne, and rescues a kidnapped heiress.

An Arabian Knight (Haworth Pictures/Robertson-Cole,

1920)
d: Charles Swickard. 5 reels.
Sessue Hayakawa, Lillian Hall, Jean Acker, Marie Pavis, Elaine Inexcourt, Harvey Clarke, Fred Jones, Roy Coulson, Tom Bates.
An Egyptian donkey driver saves the lives of a visiting archeologist and his sister.

Arabian Love (Fox, 1922)
d: Jerome Storm. 5 reels.
John Gilbert, Barbara Bedford, Barbara LaMarr, Herschel Mayall, Robert Kortman, William H. Orlamond.
Nadine, a newlywed, is kidnapped by Arabian bandits and winds up the "property" of an American who's on the run from the law.

Are All Men Alike? (Metro, 1920)
d: Philip E. Rosen. 6 reels.
May Allison, Wallace MacDonald, John Elliott, Winifred Greenwood, Emanuel Turner, Ruth Stonehouse, Lester Cuneo, Harry Lamont.
"Teddy" is a madcap socialite, a bit of a tomboy, and a certified mischief-maker.

Are Parents People? (Famous Players-Lasky/Paramount, 1925)
d: Malcolm St. Clair. 7 reels.
Betty Bronson, Florence Vidor, Adolphe Menjou, Lawrence Gray, André Beranger, Mary Beth Milford, Emily Fitzroy, William Courtwright.
When her parents separate and file for divorce, young Lita decides to run away and cause them so much distress that the foolish pair will have no choice but to reconcile.

Are Passions Inherited? — see: Inherited Passions (1916)

Are You a Failure? (Preferred Pictures, 1923)
d: Tom Forman. 6 reels.
Lloyd Hughes, Madge Bellamy, Tom Santschi, Hardee Kirkland, Jane Keckley, Hallam Cooley, Myrtle Vane, Samuel Allen.
A pampered rich boy has everything he wants except self-esteem, so he takes a mail order course in "How to be a Success."

Are You a Mason? (Famous Players/Paramount, 1915)
d: Thomas N. Heffron. 5 reels.
John Barrymore, Helen Freeman, Charles Dixon, Harold Lockwood, W. Dickinson, Dodson Mitchell, Alfred Hickman, Jean Acker.
An inebriated gent accidentally enters the wrong house, then insists he was just performing a Masons' initiation rite.

Are You Legally Married? (Success Pictures, 1919)
d: Robert T. Thornby. 5 reels.
Lew Cody, Rosemary Theby, Nanon Welsh, Henry Woodward, H.J. Barrows, Roy Laidlaw.
Unable to obtain a New York divorce, a neglected wife goes to Reno.

Argentine Love (Famous Players-Lasky/Paramount, 1924)
d: Allan Dwan. 6 reels.
Bebe Daniels, Ricardo Cortez, James Rennie, Mario Majeroni, Russ Whital, Alice Chapin, Julia Hurley, Mark Gonzales, Aurelio Coccia.
In Argentina, Consuelo is promised in marriage to Juan. But she really loves Philip, an American engineer.

The Argonauts of California--1849 (Monrovia Feature Film Co., 1916)

d: Henry Kabierske. 10 reels.
Grant Churchill, Gertrude Kaby, Dorothy Barrett, Emma Kost, Ethel Smith, Vera Lewis, Gale Brooks, William Reiffel.
New Englanders head West during the California Gold Rush.

The Argument (Triangle, 1918)
d: Walter Edwards. 5 reels.
J. Barney Sherry, Pauline Starke, Audelle Higgins, Howard Davies, Eugene Corey, Edward Jobson, George Chase.
An attorney boasts to his friend that he could kill his wife and get off on a plea of temporary insanity. Tragically, he gets the chance to do just that... but his friend is involved, too.

The Argyle Case (Warwick Film Corp./Selznick, 1917)
d: Ralph W. Ince. 6 reels.
Robert Warwick, Charles Hines, Frank McGlynn, Arthur Albertson, Gazelle Marche, Elaine Hammerstein, John Fleming, H. Cooper Cliffe, Mary Alden, Robert Vivian, Frank Evans.
Millionaire John Argyle is found murdered, and all evidence points to Mary, his adopted daughter. But a shrewd detective uses modern science to disclose the real killer.

The Argyle Case (Warner Bros., 1929)
d: Howard Bretherton. 9 reels. (Also released in sound version.)
Thomas Meighan, H.B. Warner, Lila Lee, John Darrow, ZaSu Pitts, Bert Roach, Wilbur Mack, Douglas Gerrard, Alona Marlowe, James Quinn, Gladys Brockwell, Lew Harvey.
Remake of the Warwick Film Corp.'s 1917 film, *The Argyle Case.*

Arizona (All-Star Feature Corp., 1913)
d: Augustus Thomas. 6 reels.
Robert Broderick, Cyril Scott, Gail Kane, William Conklin, Francis Carlyle, H.D. Blakemore, Alma Bradley, Gertrude Shipman, Wong Ling, Elizabeth McCall, Charles Graham.
Western drama based on Thomas' play of the same name. Remade in 1918 by the Douglas Fairbanks company.

Arizona (Fairbanks/Famous Players-Lasky Corp., 1918)
d: Albert Parker. 5 reels.
Douglas Fairbanks, Theodore Roberts, Kate Price, Frederick Burton, Harry S. Northrup, Frank Campeau, Kathleen Kirkham, Marjorie Daw, Marguerite de la Motte, Raymond Hatton, Albert McQuarrie, Katherine Griffith, Ernest Butterworth.
A cavalry lieutenant sacrifices his career rather than speak out against the faithless wife of a superior officer.

Arizona Bound (Famous Players-Lasky/Paramount, 1927)
d: John Waters. 5 reels.
Gary Cooper, Betty Jewel, El Brendel, Jack Dougherty, Christian J. Frank, Charles Crockett, Joe Butterworth, Guy Oliver.
Out West, a playful, irresponsible cowboy finds he must "grow up" fast, when the local gold shipment is targeted by bandits.

The Arizona Cat Claw (World Film Corp., 1919)
d: William Bertram. 5 reels.
Edythe Sterling, William Quinn, Gordon Sackville, Leo Maloney, Steve Clemento, Apuline Becker, J. Montgomery Carlyle.
Tempers fly in the Old West when a fiery ranch girl flirts with the wrong man.

Arizona Cyclone (Universal, 1928)
d: Edgar Lewis. 5 reels.
Fred Humes, George K. French, Margaret Gray, Cuyler Supplee, Pee Wee Holmes, Benny Corbett, Dick L'Estrange, Scotty Mattraw.
Out West, a ranch foreman has a near-identical cousin who's on the wrong side of the law. Humes does double duty as Larry and Tom, the lookalike cousins.

Arizona Days (El Dorado Productions/Syndicate Pictures, 1928)
d: J.P. McGowan. 5 reels.
Bob Custer, Peggy Montgomery, John Lowell Russell, J.P. McGowan, Mack V. Wright, Jack Ponder.
A cattleman goes undercover to infiltrate a gang of rustlers.

The Arizona Express (Fox, 1924)
d: Thomas Buckingham. 7 reels.
Pauline Starke, Evelyn Brent, Anne Cornwall, Harold Goodwin, David Butler, Francis McDonald, Frank Beal, William Humphrey.
When an innocent man is railroaded for murder and sentenced to die, his sister launches her own investigation, and with the help of a charming mail clerk, locates the real killer.

The Arizona Kid (J. Charles Davis Productions, 1929)
w, d: Horace B. Carpenter. 5 reels.
Art Acord, Cliff Lyons, Bill Conant, Carol Lane, George Hollister, Lynn Sanderson, James Tromp, Horace B. Carpenter.
"The Arizona Kid" rides to the rescue after a gang robs a stagecoach and kidnap the guard and his daughter.

The Arizona Romeo (Fox, 1924)
d: Edmund Mortimer. 5 reels.
Buck Jones, Lucy Fox, Maine Geary, Thomas R. Mills, Hardee Kirkland, Marcella Daly, Lydia Yeamans Titus, Harvey Clark, Hank Mann.
Out West, a city girl falls in love with a local rancher, though she is engaged to marry the son of her father's business partner.

The Arizona Sweepstakes (Universal, 1926)
d: Clifford Smith. 6 reels.
Hoot Gibson, Helen Lynch, Philo McCullough, George Ovey, Emmett King, Tod Brown, Kate Price, Jackie Morgan, Billy Kent Schaeffer, Turner Savage.
A cowpoke enters a sweepstakes race to help bail out a struggling ranch owner.

The Arizona Wildcat (Fox, 1927)
d: R. William Neill. 5 reels.
Tom Mix, Dorothy Sebastian, Ben Bard, Gordon Elliott, Monte Collins Jr., Cissy Fitzgerlad, Doris Dawson, Marcella Daly.
Tom, an Arizonan, enters a polo match in Santa Barbara to help defeat swindlers targeting his girlfriend's family.

Arms and the Girl (Famous Players Film Co./Paramount, 1917)
d: Joseph Kaufman. 5 reels.
Billie Burke, Thomas Meighan, Louise bates, J. Malcolm Dunn, A. Bower, William David, George S. Trimble, Harry Lee.
An American couple are stranded in Belgium at the outset of World War I.

Arms and the Woman (Astra Film Corp./Pathé, 1916)
d: George Fitzmaurice. 5 reels.
Mary Nash, Lumsden Hare, H. Cooper Cliffe, Robert Broderick, Rosalind Ivan, Carl Harbaugh, Susanne Willa.
Happily married and with a brilliant operatic career in America, a Hungarian woman finds her loyalties wracked when World War I breaks out in Europe.

Armstrong's Wife (Lasky Feature Play Co./Paramount, 1915)
d: George H. Melford. 5 reels.
Edna Goodrich, Thomas Meighan, James Cruze, Hal Clements, Ernest Joy, Raymond Hatton, Horace B. Carpenter.
Childhood sweethearts part when the girl marries a gambler and the boy leaves, broken-hearted, for Canada. But their paths will cross again.

The Arrival of Perpetua (William A. Brady/World, 1915)
d: Emile Chautard. 5 reels.
Vivian Martin, Milton Sills, Julia Stuart, Nora Cecil, M.T. O'Donahue, Alec B. Francis, Fred C. Truesdell, Kenneth Hill, John Hines, John Troyano, Donald Devlin.
Perpetua is an heiress with a million dollars, and plenty of suitors who are after her money. But she's aware of their greed, and chases them away with the "news" that she has lost her fortune. Now the field is down to one man who loves her for herself: He's her guardian, and he's available.

Arsene Lupin (Vitagraph, 1917)
d: Paul Scardon. 5 reels.
Earle Williams, Brinsley Shaw, Henry Leone, Bernard Siegel, Gordon Gray, Logan Paul, Hugh Wynn, Ethel Gray Terry, Billie Billings, Julia Swayne Gordon, Frank Crayne.
Arsene Lupin, a master thief, sets about stealing rare works of art and jewels... but then he falls, inconveniently, in love.
Film based on the 1908 play *Arsene Lupin*, by Francis de Croisset. Other American films in the silent era based on the Lupin character are *The Teeth of the Tiger* (1919) and *813* (1920).

Artie, the Millionaire Kid (Vitagraph, 1916)
d: Harry Handworth. 5 reels.
Ernest Truex, Dorothy Kelly, Albert Roccardi, John T. Kelly, Etienne Girardot, William R. Dunn.
Expelled from college and given the boot by his wealthy father, Artie swears to make a fortune on his own.

The Aryan (Triangle, 1916)
d: William S. Hart. 5 reels.
William S. Hart, Gertrude Claire, Charles K. French, Louise Glaum, Herschel Mayall, Ernest Swallow, Bessie Love.
A wanderer sets out to visit his mother, but he's cheated of his gold by a conniving dance hall girl. He drags her into the desert, where he rallies men around him and becomes their bandit chief.

As a Man Lives (Achievement Films/American Releasing Corp., 1923)
d: J. Searle Dawley. 6 reels.
Robert Frzer, Gladys Hulette, Frank Losee, J. Thornton Baston, Alfred E. Wright, Kate Blanke, Tiny Belmont, Charles Sutton.
Mason, a shiftless playboy, is shattered when Nadia refuses his proposal of marriage. He takes a trip to Europe and becomes involved with underworld characters and with a kindly surgeon who undertakes to reshape Mason's character.

As a Man Thinks (Artco/Four Star Pictures, 1919)

d: George Irving. 5 reels.
Leah Baird, Henry Clive, Warburton Gamble, Charles C. Brandt, Betty Howe, Alexander Herbert, Elaine Amazar, Joseph Smiley, Jane Jennings, Bobby Ward.
A New York publisher has an affair with a Paris model. When his wife finds out, she decides that two can play at that game; so she renews her acquaintance with an old beau.

As a Woman Sows (Mutual, 1916)
d: William F. Haddock. 5 reels.
Gertrude Robinson, Alexander Gaden, Covington Barrett, John Reinhard, Charles W. Travis, Mathilde Baring, Yvonne Chappelle.
Feeling neglected, the young wife of a busy mayor engages in a flirtation.

As in a Looking Glass (World Film Corp., 1916)
d: Frank Crane. 5 reels.
Kitty Gordon, F. Lumsden Hare, Frank Goldsmith, Gladden James, Teddy Sampson, Charles Eldridge, Eugenie Woodward, George Majeroni, Lillian Cook, Philip W. Masi.
When a European temptress tries to vamp a U.S. Navy man to obtain information from him, they unexpectedly fall in love.

As Man Desires (First National, 1925)
d: Irving Cummings. 8 reels.
Milton Sills, Viola Dana, Ruth Clifford, Rosemary Theby, Irving Cummings, Paul Nicholson, Tom Kennedy, Hector Sarno, Lou Payne, Anna May Walthall, Frank Leigh. In the South Seas, a British army deserter finds love with a native girl.

As Man Made Her (World Film Corp., 1917)
d: George Archainbaud. 5 reels.
Gail Kane, Frank Mills, Gerda Holmes, Edward T. Langford, Miss Layton, Miss McDonald.
A finishing-school grad becomes a wealthy man's mistress—not exactly what Mom and Dad had in mind.

As Men Love (Pallas Pictures/Paramount, 1917)
d: E. Mason Hopper. 5 reels.
House Peters, Myrtle Stedman, J.W. Johnston, Helen Jerome Eddy.
A married socialite falls in love with her husband's best friend.

As the Sun Went Down (Metro, 1919)
d: E. Mason Hopper. 5 reels.
Edith Storey, Lewis J. Cody, Harry S. Northrup, William Brunton, F.A. Turner, Frances Burnham, Za Su Pitts, F.E. Spooner, Alfred Hollingsworth, Vera Lewis, George W. Berrell.
Folks in a California mining camp fear and respect "Colonel Billy," a female gunfighter.

As Ye Sow (Brady Picture Plays/World, 1914)
d: Frank Hall Crane. 5 reels.
Alice Brady, Walter Fischter, Beverly West, Douglas MacLean, Johnny Hines, Edmund Mortimer, George Moss, Charles Dungan, Lydia Knott.
New York heiress Dora Leland, looking for her long-lost husband and baby, finds room and board in the home of a Cape Cod lady and her adopted child. Little does Dora know, that's *her* child.

Ashamed of Parents (Warner Bros., 1922)
d: H. G. Plimpton. 5 reels.
Charles Eldridge, Edith Stockton, Walter McEvan, Jack

Lionel Bohn, W.J. Gross.
A hard-working shoemaker struggles to send his son to college.

Ashes (Amalgamated Producing Corp./East Coast Productions, 1922)
d: G.M. Anderson. 5 reels.
William Courtleigh, Leona Anderson, Margaret Landis, Myrtle Stedman, Wedgewood Nowell, George Howard, Carrie Clark Ward, Stanton Heck.
A young couple plot to extort money from a neighbor they believe is wealthy.

Ashes of Desire—see: The Curse of Iku (1919)

Ashes of Embers (Famous Players Film Co./Paramount, 1916)
d: Joseph Kaufman. 5 reels.
Pauline Frederick, Earle Foxe, Frank Losee, J. Herbert Frank, Maggie Halloway Fisher, Jay Wilson.
Miss Frederick has a double role in this tale of twin sisters, one good and one evil.

Ashes of Hope (Triangle, 1917)
d: Walter Edwards. 5 reels.
Belle Bennett, Jack Livingston, Jack Richardson, Percy Challenger, Josie Sedgwick.
Jim Gordon's a stranger in a Western mining town, and he doesn't drink, gamble, or play around. Naturally, the local dance hall hostess takes that as a challenge.

Ashes of Love (Graphic Film Corp., 1918)
d: Ivan Abramson. 6 reels.
James K. Hackett, Effie Shannon, Ruby DeRemer, Mabel Juliene Scott, Hugh Thompson, Paula Shay, Dora Mills Adams, William B. Davidson, William Bechtel, Thea Talbot.
To provide for her ailing mother, a young woman weds a wealthy older man. But she can't resist entering into an affair with her cousin's husband.

Ashes of Vengeance (Norma Talmadge Film Co., 1923)
d: Frank Lloyd. 10 reels.
Norma Talmadge, Conway Tearle, Wallace Beery, Jeanne Carpenter, Josephine Crowell, Betty Francisco, Claire McDowell, Courtenay Foote, Howard Truesdell, Forrest Robinson.
Political and religious intrigue in 16th century France.

At Bay (Pathé, 1915)
d: George Fitzmaurice. 5 reels.
Florence Reed, Frank Sheridan, Lyster Chambers, DeWitt C. Jennings, Charles Waldron, Richard Taber.
Gamblers try to intimidate a crusading gubernatorial candidate, even going so far as to compromise his daughter.

At First Sight (Famous Players/Paramount, 1917)
d: Robert Z. Leonard. 5 reels.
Mae Murray, Sam T. Hardy, Jules Rancourt, Julia Bruns, W.T. Carlton, Nellie Lindreth, William Butler, Edward Sturgis, Estar Banks.
A romance writer on vacation thwarts a mismatch between a local girl and a fortune-hunting cad.

At Piney Ridge (Selig Polyscope, 1916)
d: William Robert Daly. 5 reels.
Fritzi Brunette, Al W. Filson, Leo Pierson, Edward J. Piel, Frank Clark, Vivian Reed, James Bradbury, William Scott, Lillian Hayward.
When a scoundrel gets his girlfriend pregnant, he refuses to marry her, and instead blames the seduction on another

man.

At the Cross Roads (Select Photo Plays/Alliance Films, 1914)
d: Frank L. Dear. 5 reels.
Estha Williams, Rae Forde, Mrs. Stuart Robson, Arthur Morrison, Master Martin, Frank L. Dear, Madge Loomis, Jack Gordon, Elmer Peterson, Charles H. Streimer, Edward Thorne.
A former slave is raped by a clergyman's son, then abandoned when he learns she is carrying his child.

At the End of the World (Famous Players-Lasky/Paramount, 1921)
d: Penrhyn Stanlaws. 6 reels.
Milton Sills, Betty Compson, Mitchell Lewis, Cason Ferguson, Spottiswoode Aitken, Joseph Kilgour, Goro Kino.
Feeling trapped in an unhappy marriage, a young woman accepts the attentions of her husband's clerk.

At the Mercy of Men (Select Pictures Corp., 1918)
d: Charles Miller. 5 reels.
Alice Brady, Frank Morgan, Jack Johnson, Robert Walker, C. Porches, Helen Lindroth, W.C. Carleton, Yolande Buquette, Tula Bell.
Outraged when he learns that a woman has been attacked by three of his officers and raped, the Czar of Russia orders one of the three to marry her. The wedding takes place, but the reluctant groom stubbornly refuses to name the actual rapist. That changes, though, when the Bolshevik revolution breaks out and the woman saves her husband's life.

At the Sign of the Jack O'Lantern (Renco Film Co./W.W. Hodkinson, 1922)
d: Lloyd Ingraham. 6 reels.
Betty Ross Clark, Earl Schenck, Wade Boteler, Victor Potel, Clara Clark Ward, Monte Collins, William Courtwright, Mrs. Raymond Hatton, Newton Hall, Zella Ingraham.
Heir to a country home and a small sum of money, Harlan learns that his uncle's will provides for an even larger legacy if he entertains the uncle's relatives "properly." Harlan and his wife invite the relatives and warmly welcome them, but their guests turn out to be disagreeable misanthropes who make life miserable for their hosts. Finally, though he feels certain he will lose the legacy, Harlan orders his rude, obnoxious guests out of the house. Then comes the dawn: The family lawyer discloses that this is precisely what his uncle meant by treating them "properly," and Harlan receives his legacy.

At the Stage Door (R-C Pictures, 1921)
w, d: William Christy Cabanne. 6 reels.
Frances Hess, Elizabeth North, Miriam Battista, Billie Dove, Margaret Foster, William Collier Jr., C. Elliott Griffin, Myrtle Maughan, Charles Craig, Viva Ogden, Billy Quirk, Huntly Gordon, Katherine Spencer, Doris Eaton.
In New York, a Broadway showgirl confounds her peers by insisting on living a chaste life. But her insistence on decorum leads to a true and lasting love.

The Atom (Triangle, 1918)
d: William Dowlan. 5 reels.
Pauline Starke, Belle Bennett, Harry Mestayer, Ruth Handforth, Walter Perkins, Lincoln Stedman, Gene Burr, Tom Buckingham.
Disfigured in an accident, a popular actor loses the admiration of his public. But he finds love and a good future with his boarding-house maid.

Atonement (Humphrey Pictures, 1919)
d: William Humphrey. 5 reels.
Grace Davison, Conway Tearle, Huntley Gordon, Sally Crute, Anthony Merlo, Gretchen Hartman, Jean Gautier, Arthur Donaldson.
A bank president arranges a loan for his cash-poor brother, and comes to regret it.

Atta Boy (Monty Banks Enterprises/Pathé, 1926)
d: Edward H. Griffith. 6 reels.
Monty Banks, Virginia Bradford, Ernie Wood, Fred Kelsey, Virginia Pearson, Henry A. Barrows, Earl Metcalf, Mary Carr, Jimmie Phillips, Alfred Fisher, George Periolat, America Chedister, William Courtwright, Lincoln Plummer, Kewpie Morgan.
Monty, a newspaper copy boy, follows up on a story about the kidnapping of a baby. Though the child's father will not allow an interview, Monty finds a ransom note on the premises. He follows the leads and, disguised as a waiter in a gambling den, finds and captures the kidnapper.

Atta Boy's Last Race (Fine Arts/Triangle, 1916)
d: George Seigmann. 5 reels.
Dorothy Gish, Keith Armour, Carl Stockdale, Adele Clifton, Loyola O'Connor, Joe Neery, Fred A. Turner, Tom Wilson.
The daughter of a race horse owner enters his lame thoroughbred, "Atta Boy," in a race which, unbeknown to her, is fixed.

The Auction Block (Rex Beach Film Corp./Goldwyn, 1917)
d: Larry Trimble. 7 reels.
Rubye DeRemer, Florence Deshon, Dorothy Wheeler, Florence Johns, Tom Powers, Walter Hitchcok, Ned Burton, Charles Graham, George Cooper, Alec B. Francis.
A former showgirl marries a wealthy drunk, but refuses to consummate the marriage until he cures his drinking habit.

The Auction Block (MGM, 1925)
d: Hobart Henley. 7 reels.
Charles Ray, Eleanor Boardman, Sally O'Neil, David Torrence, Ned Sparks.
A rich New Yorker takes a job in a shoe store to impress a Deep South beauty contest winner he fancies.

Auction of Souls (First National, 1919)
d: Oscar Apfel. 8 reels.
Aurora Mardiganian, Irving Cummings, Anna Q. Nilsson, Henry Morgenthau, Howard Davies, Hector Dion, Frank Clark, Miles McCarthy, Eugenie Besserer, Lillian West.
A Christian Armenian girl rebuffs the advances of a Turkish governor, with grave consequences.

The Auction of Virtue (Art Dramas, Inc., 1917)
d: Herbert Blaché. 6 reels.
Naomi Childers, Mrs. Miller, Evelyn Dumo, Leslie Austen, Wyndham Standing, Kirke Brown.
To help a friend in need, a girl decides to auction herself to the highest bidder.

The Auctioneer (Fox, 1927)
d: Alfred E. Green. 6 reels.
George Sidney, Marion Nixon, Gareth Hughes, Doris Lloyd, Ward Crane, Sammy Cohen, Claire McDowell.
In New York, a pawnbroker raises a little girl whose parents perished at sea.

Audrey (Famous Players/Paramount, 1916)
d: Robert Vignola. 5 reels.
Pauline Frederick, Charles Waldron, Margarete Christians,

Helen Lindroth, Henry Hallam, Jack Clark.
Ostracized as an orphan, a girl nevertheless grows up cheerily, and finds love.

Autumn (Universal, 1916)
d: O.A.C. Lund. 5 reels.
Violet Mersereau, Percy Richards, Lester Stowe, Elizabeth Mudge, Paul Panzer, Clara Byers, Lindsay Hall, Fred Probet.
Autumn Arden, a young woman who has never known her father, asks a Royal Canadian Mountie to help her locate him.

The Avalanche (Famous Players-Lasky/Paramount, 1919)
d: George Fitzmaurice. 5 reels.
Elsie Ferguson, Lumsden Hare, Zeffie Tilbury, Fred Esmelton, William Roselle, Grace Field, Warner Oland, Harry Wise, George Dupree.
Gambling debts force a young woman to take extreme measures.

Avalanche (Paramount, 1928)
d: Otto Brower. 6 reels.
Jack Holt, Doris Hill, Baclanova, John Darrow, Guy Oliver, Dick Winslow.
Gritty western tale of a gambler whose adopted son starts an affair with the gambler's mistress. The two men fight, then the son escapes with his new girlfriend. The gambler follows them and, just in time, saves their lives during an avalanche.

The Avenging Rider (FBO Pictures, 1928)
d: Wallace Fox. 6 reels.
Tom Tyler, Florence Allen, Frankie Darro, Al Ferguson, Bob Fleming, Arthur Thalasso.
Sally, the niece of a deceased rancher, learns that she has inherited one-half of her uncle's ranch. Coming west to inspect her new property, she takes an instant dislike to the owner of the other half, an attractive foreman named Tom. He dislikes her as well. With the battle lines so clearly drawn, can love be far behind?

The Avenging Trail (Metro, 1917)
d: Francis Ford. 5 reels.
Harold Lockwood, Sally Crute, Joseph Dailey, Walter P. Lewis, Louis Wolheim, William Clifford, Warren Cook, Lettie Ford, Art Ortego, Edward Draham, Floyd Buckley.
Lumber country drama about a heroic woodsman and his bride.

The Average Woman (C.C. Burr Productions Inc., 1924)
d: W. Christy Cabanne. 6 reels.
Pauline Garon, David Powell, Burr McIntosh, William Tooker, Russell Griffin, DeSacia Mooers, Coit Albertson.
Jimmy, a reporter working on an article about "the average woman," becomes smitten with Sally, the girl he is researching.

The Awakening (World Film Corp., 1917)
d: George Archainbaud. 5 reels.
Montagu Love, Dorothy Kelly, John Davidson, Frank Beamish, Joseph Granby, Josephine Earle.
A French farmer moves to Paris to become an artist.

The Awakening (Goldwyn/United Artists, 1928)
d: Victor Fleming. 9 reels.
Vilma Banky, Walter Byron, Louis Wolheim, George Davis, William Orlamond, Carl Hartmann.
A French convent girl loves a German officer.

The Awakening of Helena Richie (Rolfe

Photoplays/Metro, 1916)
d: John W. Noble. 5 reels.
Ethel Barrymore, Robert Cummings, Frank Montgomery, J.A. Furey, Maury Steuart, Hassan Mussalli, William Williams, Robert Whittier, Charles Goodrich, Hattie Delaro, Mary Asquith, Kathleen Townsend.
An unmarried man and woman adopt a son.

The Awakening of Ruth (Edison/Perfection Pictures, 1917)
d: Edward H. Griffith. 5 reels.
Shirley Mason, George J. Forth, Joseph Burke, William Hayes, Donald Hall, Sally Crute, Jessie Stevens, Edward Elkas, David Davies, Caroline Lee.
While rummaging through a cave in the Florida Keys, a young woman finds two chests that may contain riches.

Away Goes Prudence (Famous Players-Lasky/Paramount, 1920)
d: John S. Robertson. 5 reels.
Billie Burke, Percy Marmont, Maude Turner Gordon, Charles Lane, Dorothy Walters, Bradley Barker, M.W. Rale, Albert Hackett.
Prudence, a society aviatrix, outwits a gang of kidnappers.

The Awful Truth (Peninsula Studios, 1925)
d: Paul Powell. 6 reels.
Agnes Ayres, Warner Baxter, Phillips Smalley, Raymond Lowney, Winifred Bryson, Carrie Clark Ward.
While Norman is out of town on business, a fire breaks out in his apartment building. When he gets home, he finds his wife Lucy in her pajamas on the fire escape, along with a similarly attired neighbor Norman knows to be a womanizer. Furious, the aggrieved husband demands and obtains a divorce. But he can't live without her, and Lucy knows it. So she arranges a fake "tryst" with the womanizing neighbor, and allows Norman to "rescue" her, proving their love is still alive.

Bab the Fixer (Mutual, 1917)
d: Sherwood Donald. 5 reels.
Jackie Saunders, Leslie T. Peacocke, Mollie McConnell, Ruth Lackaye, R. Henry Grey, Arthur Shirley, Clara Kahler.
Bab, a transplanted Easterner, turns into a real cowgirl out West.

Babbitt (Warner Bros., 1924)
d: Harry Beaumont. 8 reels.
Willard Louis, Mary Alden, Carmel Myers, Raymond Kee, Maxine Elliott Hicks, Cissy Fitzgerald, Clara Bow, Virginia Loomis, Robert Randall, Lucien Littlefield, Dale Fuller.
Drama based on the Sinclair Lewis novel *Babbitt*, about a prosperous middle-aged man who feels bored with life and decides to take a fling with a young charmer.

Babbling Tongues (Ivan Films, 1917)
d: William J. Humphrey. 7 reels.
Arthur Donaldson, Grace Valentine, James Morrison, Paul Capellani, Gladden James, Louise Beaudet, Carolyn Birch, Richard Tucker, Robert E. Hill.
Gossip flies when an older man and his young wife take in a struggling playwright.

Babe Comes Home (First National, 1927)
d: Ted Wilde. 6 reels.
Babe Ruth, Anna Q. Nilsson, Louise Fazenda, Ethel Shannon, Arthur Stone, Lou Archer, Tom McGuire, Mickey Bennett, James Bradbury, Big Boy Williams, James Gordon.
A star baseball player loves to chew tobacco, but it always makes his uniforms filthy. His girlfriend tries to reform him,

but soon they learn there is some relationship between his messy tobacco habit and his baseball prowess.

The Babes in the Woods (Fox, 1917)
d: Chester M. Franklin. 5 reels.
Francis Carpenter, Virginia Lee Corbin, Violet Radcliffe, Carmen de Rue, Herschell Mayall, Rosita Marstini, Robert Lawler, Scott McKee, Teddy Billings, Buddie Messinger.
Variant on the "Hansel und Gretel" fairy tale, considerably updated.

Babette (Vitagraph, 1917)
d: Charles J. Brabin. 5 reels.
Marc MacDermott, Peggy Hyland, Tamplar Saxe, William Dunn.
Raveau, a gentleman crook, loves Babette... and for her he promises to reform. But turning his life around isn't so easy.

Bab's Burglar (Famous Players/Paramount, 1917)
d: J. Searle Dawley. 5 reels.
Marguerite Clark, Leone Morgan, Richard Barthelmess, Frank Losee, Isabel O'Madigan, Helen Greene, Nigel Barrie, Guy Coombs, George Odell, Daisy Belmore.
A girl sets a trap for a "burglar," only to find he is her sister's fiancé, bent on eloping.

Babs' Candidate (Vitagraph, 1920)
d: Edward Griffith. 5 reels.
Corinne Griffith, George Fawcett, Webster Campbell, Charles Abbe, William Holden, Roy Applegate, Blanche Davenport, Harvey A. Fisher, Walter Horton, Wes Jenkins.
Babs, a woman in love, is put in the unusual position of having to support a political candidate who is running against her sweetheart.

Bab's Diary (Famous Players/Paramount, 1917)
d: J. Searle Dawley. 5 reels.
Marguerite Clark, Nigel Barrie, Leonora Morgan, Frank Losee, Isabel O'Madigan, Richard Barthelmess, Helen Greene, Guy Coombs, Jack O'Brien, George Odell.
To attract some attention, a spoiled girl invents a story that she is the sweetheart of a certain famous actor. But what can she do when the real actor shows up at her door?

Bab's Matinee Idol (Famous Players/Paramount, 1917)
d: J. Searle Dawley. 5 reels.
Marguerite Clark, Helen Greene, Isabel O'Madigan, Frank Losee, Nigel Barrie, Cyril Chadwick, Vernon Steel, George Odell, Daisy Belmore.
A girl smitten with a handsome actor schemes to promote some publicity for him. *Bab's Matinne Idol* was the third and last of the "Bab" stories produced by Famous Players in 1917 and starring Marguerite Clark in the title role. All three films were released within a period of seven weeks.

The Baby Cyclone (MGM, 1928)
d: Edward Sutherland. 7 reels.
Lew Cody, Aileen Pringle, Robert Armstrong, Gwen Lee, Nora Cecil, Fred Esmelton, Clarissa Selwynne, Wade Boteler.
Comedy based on the George M. Cohan play of the same name, about a Pekingese dog that goes by the name "the baby cyclone."

Baby Mine (Goldwyn, 1917)
d: John S. Robertson, Hugo Ballin. 6 reels.
Madge Kennedy, Kathryn Adams, John Cumberland, Frank Morgan, Sonia Marcelle, Virginia Madigan, Jack Ridgway, Nellie Fillmore.
To strengthen her marriage, a young wife announces to her husband that he's about to become a father. Trouble is, she isn't pregnant... so she sets about trying to adopt, borrow, or steal every baby she can get hold of.

Baby Mine (MGM, 1927)
d: Robert Z. Leonard. 6 reels.
Karl Dane, George K. Arthur, Charlotte Greenwood, Louise Lorraine.
A young doctor is tricked into marrying a girl he doesn't really fancy, so he leaves her. One year later, he hears that he is a father, so he returns home to meet the new addition to the family, and try to mend his broken marriage.

Bachelor Apartments (Arrow Film Corp., 1920)
d: Johnny Walker. 5 reels.
Frederick Howard, Georgia Hopkins, George Dupree, George Reynolds, Edward M. Favor, Eva Gordon, Ruby Davis, Edwin Bouldon, Joseph Donohue, Ben Nedell, Zadee Burbank.
Stumbling home drunk after his bachelor party, a would-be bridegroom mistakenly enters the wrong apartment. He's caught in the bedroom of the family's daughter, outraging her dad—who demands a shotgun wedding, first thing in the morning. Things get even more complicated when the reluctant couple are marched to the very church where the bachelor's fiancée is waiting for him, ready to get married.

Bachelor Brides (DeMille Pictures/Producers Distributing Corp., 1926)
d: William K. Howard. 6 reels.
Rod LaRocque, Eulalie Jensen, Elinor Fair, George Nichols, Julia Faye, Lucien Littlefield, Sally Rand, Eddie Gribbon, Paul Nicholson.
Mary, an American heiress, is engaged to marry Percy Ashfield in a Scottish castle. But on the eve of the wedding, a strange woman appears with a baby and announces that Percy is the child's father, causing a scandal.

The Bachelor Daddy (Famous Players-Lasky/Paramount, 1922)
d: Alfred E. Green. 7 reels.
Thomas Meighan, Leatrice Joy, Maude Wayne, Adele Farrington, J. Farrell MacDonald, Laurance Wheat, Charlotte Jackson, Barbara Maier, Bruce Guerin.
A bachelor mine owner agrees to care for the five children of his dying foreman.

The Bachelor Girl (Columbia, 1929)
d: Richard Thorpe. 7 reels. (Part talkie.)
Jacqueline Logan, William Collier Jr.
A secretary falls in love with an unenterprising stock boy. Realizing he is not good enough for her, he leaves. Still, she keeps trying to build up his self-respect.

The Bachelor's Baby (Columbia, 1927)
d: Frank Strayer. 6 reels.
Helene Chadwick, Harry Myers, Pat Harmon, Midget Gustav.
A midget is pressed into service to impersonate a couple's baby.

A Bachelor's Children (Vitagraph, 1918)
d: Paul Scardon. 5 reels.
Harry T. Morey, Florence Deshon, Alice Terry, Denton Vane, William Shea, Jessie Stevens, Aida Horton.
Three sisters pursue their father's claim after his death.

Bachelor's Paradise (Tiffany-Stahl Productions, 1928)
d: George Archainbaud. 7 reels.

THE BARKER (1928). Milton Sills (standing), a sideshow barker, hopes his son (Douglas Fairbanks Jr., right) will take up the legal profession and escape carnival life. But the father's dreams are being challenged by a charming blonde carny (Dorothy Mackaill), who does her best to vamp the young man into staying with the show. Here, the blonde seems to be momentarily winning the familial tug-of-war.

* * * * *

Sally O'Neill, Ralph Graves, Eddie Gribbon, Jimmy Finlayson, Sylvia Ashton, Jean Laverty.

Knocked to the canvas by a ferocious blow from his opponent, a boxer visualizes the girl he left at the altar... and is inspired to get up and win the fight. Then, he seeks out the girl, begs her forgiveness, and gets it.

The Bachelor's Romance (Famous Players/Paramount, 1915)
d: Daniel Frohman. 4 reels.
John Emerson, Lorraine Huling, George Le Guere, Robert Cain, Sybilla Pope, Maggie Fisher, Philip Hahn, Thomas McGrath.
A bachelor drama critic becomes the guardian of a 10-year-old girl. As she grows up, she blossoms into a dazzling beauty, and her guardian falls in love with her. But he realizes he must step aside for youth.

A Bachelor's Wife (American Film/Pathé, 1919)
d: Emmett J. Flynn. 5 reels.
Mary Miles Minter, Alan Forrest, Myrtle Reeves, Lydia Knott, Charles spere, Margaret Shelby, Harry Holden.
An Irish colleen comes to America, where she helps save her cousin's marriage.

Back Fire (Sunset Productions/Aywon Film Corp., 1922)
w, d: Alvin J. Neitz. 5 reels.
Jack Hoxie, George Sowards, Lou Meehan, William Lester, Poke Williams, Bert Rollins.
Two innocent cowpokes are accused when somebody robs the local express office.

Back Home and Broke (Famous Players-Lasky/Paramount, 1922)
d: Alfred E. Green. 8 reels.
Thomas Meighan, Lila Lee, Frederick Burton, Cyril Ring, Charles Abbe, Florence Dixon, Gertrude Quinlan, Richard Carlyle, Maude Turner Gordon, Lauance Wheat, Ned Burton, James Marlowe, Eddie Borden.
A young man whose father died and left him saddled with debt goes west to seek his fortune, and finds it... in oil.

Back to God's Country (Shipman-Curwood Prod./First National, 1919)
d: David M. Hartford. 5 reels.
Nell Shipman, Wheeler Oakman, Ronald Byram, Wellington Playter, Roy Laidlaw.
In the Canadian wilderness, a contented young woman lives with her father and bonds with wild animals. After her father is killed by a bandit, the young woman flees her nature home and takes up with a forest ranger.

Back to God's Country (Universal, 1927)
d: Irvin Willat. 6 reels.
Renee Adoree, Robert Frazer, Walter Long, Mitchell Lewis, James Mason, Walter Ackerman, Adolph Milar.
In the great Northwest, a trapper's daughter is endangered when her father is threatened by a drunken sea captain who covets the daughter.

Back to Life (Postman Pictues/Associated Exhibitors, 1925)
d: Whitman Bennett. 6 reels.
Patsy Ruth Miller, David Powell, Lawford Davidson, Mary Thurman, George Stewart, Frederick Burton, Frankie Evans.
John, an American serving in World War I, is reported killed in action. His widow, Margaret, remarries but still carries a torch for her "late" husband. But John lives, though he has suffered major facial damage and plastic surgery has given him a new face. Upon returning to the United States, he learns that his wife has remarried—and to save her from scandal, he introduces himself as a friend of her late husband. She does not recognize him, but gratefully welcomes the gentle stranger.

Back Pay (Cosmopolitan Productions/Paramount, 1922)
d: Frank Borzage. 7 reels.
Seena Owen, Matt Moore, J. Barney Sherry, Ethel Duray, Charles Craig, Jerry Sinclair.
Hester, an innocent country girl, goes to the big city and falls in with a "fast" crowd.

Back to the Woods (Goldwyn, 1918)
d: George Irving. 5 reels.
Mabel Normand, Herbert Rawlinson, T. Henderson Murray, Arthur Housman, James Laffey.
In a lumber town, a wealthy woman in disguise meets a novelist in disguise.

Back to Yellow Jacket (Ben Wilson Productions/Arrow Film Corp., 1922)
d: Ben Wilson. 6 reels.
Roy Stewart, Kathleen Kirkham, Earl Metcalfe, Jack Pratt.
Out West, a prospector's wife grows bored with her daily routine and leaves to become a dance hall girl in the city.

The Back Trail (Universal, 1924)
d: Clifford Smith. 5 reels.
Jack Hoxie, Alton Stone, Eugenia Gilbert, Claude Payton, William Lester, William McCall, Buck Connors, Pat Harmon.
A cowpoke suffers from amnesia due to war injuries.

Backbone (Distinctive Pictures/Goldwyn, 1923)
d: Edward Sloman. 7 reels.
Edith Roberts, Alfred Lunt, William B. Mack, Frankie Evans, James D. Doyle, L. Emile LaCroix, Charles Fang, Marion Abbott, Frank Hagney, Sam J. Ryan, George MacQuarrie.
In a logging town near the Canadian border, a lumberman's daughter falls in love with her father's business rival.

Backstage (Tiffany Productions, 1927)
d: Phil Stone. 6 reels.
William Collier Jr., Barbara Bedford, Alberta aughn, Eileen Percy, Shirley O'Hara, Gayne Whitman, Jocelyn Lee, Guinn Williams, Jimmy Harrison, Brooks Benedict.
In New York, a chorus girl winds up broke and evicted from her home when the show she is in folds. She finds lodging in the apartment of a kind stranger, but her irate boyfriend refuses to believe the arrangement is innocent.

The Bad Boy (Triangle, 1917)
d: Chester Withey. 5 reels.
Robert Harron, Richard Cummings, Josephine Crowell, Mildred Harris, William H. Brown, James Harrison, Colleen Moore, Elmo Lincoln, Harry Fischer.
Jimmie Bates, a juvenile delinquent, runs away from home and joins a gang of crooks. When the gang decides to rob his father's bank, Jimmie has a change of heart.

Bad Company (St. Regis Pictures/Associated Exhibitors, 1925)
d: E.H. Griffith. 6 reels.
Madge Kennedy, Bigelow Cooper, Conway Tearle, Lucille Lee Stewart, Charles Emmett Mack.
A young woman tries to prevent her brother from marrying a golddigger.

The Bad Lands (Hunt Stromberg Corp., 1925)
d: Dell Henderson. 6 reels.
Harry Carey, Wilfred Lucas, Lee Shumway, Gaston Glass,

Joe Rickson, Trilby Clark, Buck Black.
In the Bad Lands of Dakota, when his garrison is attacked by Indians, a young lieutenant finds he must fight not only the attackers, but also his own cowardice.

The Bad Man (Edwin Carewe Productions/Associated First National Pictures, 1923)
d: Edwin Carewe. 7 reels.
Holbrook Blinn, Jack Mulhall, Walter McGrail, Enid Bennett, Harry Myers, Charles A. Sellon, Stanton Heck, Teddy Sampson, Thomas Delmar, Frank Lanning, Peter Vanzuella.
On the Mexican border, a notorious bandido decides to help out an embattled American rancher who once saved his life.

Bad Man's Bluff (Action Pictures/Associated Exhibitors, 1926)
d: Alvin J. Neitz. 5 reels.
Buffalo Bill Jr., Molly Malone, Frank Whitson, Robert McKenzie, Wilbur McGaugh.
Out West, a young man stands to inherit a half interest in a prosperous ranch, but only if he marries Alice, a neighbor who is suspicious of his intentions.

Bag and Baggage (Finis Fox Corp./Selznick, 1923)
d: Finis Fox. 6 reels.
Gloria Grey, John Roche, Carmelita Geraghty, Paul Weigel, Adele Farrington, Arthur Stuart Hull, Fred Kelsey, Harry Dunkinson, R.D. MacLean, Doreen Turner, Ned Grey.
In the big city, a country girl's handbag is stolen by a crook who mistakenly believes it is filled with jewels.

The Bait (Mutual, 1916)
d: William J. Bowman. 5 reels.
Betty Hart, William Clifford, Oliver C. Allen, Frederick Montague, Edward Alexander, Marvel Spencer, Margaret Gibson.
Margot Sloan works as "bait," enticing men to enter her husband's saloon.

The Bait (Paramount, 1921)
d: Maurice Tourneur. 5 reels.
Hope Hampton, Harry Woodward, Jack McDonald, James Gordon, Rae Ebberly, Joe Singleton, Poupee Andriot.
After being saved from the ravages of a deadly lion at a Paris exposition, an American shopgirl falls in love with her rescuer.

The Ballet Girl (William A. Brady/World Film Corp., 1916)
d: William A. Brady. 5 reels.
Alice Brady, Holbrook Blinn, Robert Frazer, Julia Stuart, Harry Danes, Laura McClure, Jesse Lewis, Alec B. Francis, George Ralph, Fred Radcliffe, Robert Kegeris.
A successful stage dancer gets caught up in the lure of wealth and status.

The Bandbox (W.W. Hodkinson Corp./Pathé, 1919)
d: R. William Neill. 6 reels.
Doris Kenyon, Walter McEwen, Gretchen Hartman, Edward Keppler, Maggie Weston, Logan Paul, Lorraine Harding, Alexander Gaden, William Brotherhood, Helene Montrose.
On an ocean voyage, identical hatboxes are switched; identical, that is, except that one of them contains a priceless necklace.

The Bandit Buster (Action Pictures/Associated Exhibitors, 1926)
d: Richard Thorpe. 5 reels.
Buddy Roosevelt, Molly Malone, Lafe McKee, Winifred Landis, Robert Homans, Charles Whitaker, Al Taylor.

Well-meaning Sylvia, daughter of an overworked banker, plots with two men to have her father kidnapped and taken to a remote cabin, so he can finally get some rest.

The Bandit's Baby (R-C Pictures/Film Booking Offices of America, 1925)
d: James P. Hogan. 5 reels.
Fred Thomson, Helen Foster, Harry Woods, Mary Louise Miller, Clarence Geldert, Charles W. Mack.
On the lam from the law, a cowboy unjustly accused of robbery and murder comes into custody of a baby.

The Bandolero (MGM, 1924)
w, d: Tom Terriss. 8 reels.
Manuel Granado, Renee Adoree, Gustav von Seyffertitz, Gordon Begg, Pedro DeCordoba, Arthur Donaldson, Jose DeRueda, Dorothy Rush, Marie Valray.
A boy is kidnapped by a bandit and raised to be a matador.

The Banker's Daughter (Life Photo Film Corp., 1914)
d: Edward M. Roskam, William F. Haddock. 5 reels.
Katherine LaSalle, William H. Tooker, David Wall, Henry Spingler, William Bailey, Joseph Bailey, Ethel Phillips, Kitty Baldwin, Mab Rae, Philip Robson.
To help her father escape bankruptcy, a girl marries a wealthy man she does not love.

Bar Nothin' (Fox, 1921)
d: Edward Sedgwick. 5 reels.
Buck Jones, Ruth Renick, Arthur Carew, James Farley, William Buckley.
Out West, a ranch foreman is robbed by thieves and left in the desert. Against all odds, he returns to the ranch and not only outwits the men who robbed and deserted him, he foils the head crook's attempt to marry the ranch's pretty owner.

The Bar-C Mystery (Pathé, 1926)
d: Robert F. Hill. 5 reels.
Dorothy Phillips, Wallace MacDonald, Ethel Clayton, Philo McCullough, Johnny Fox, Violet Schram, Fred DeSilva.
Jane, a New Yorker, goes West to take possession of a gold mine she's inherited. But first she'll have to contend with claim jumpers and a malevolent cabaret owner.

The Bar Sinister (Edgar Lewis Productions, 1917)
d: Edgar Lewis. 8 reels.
Preston Rollow, Mary Doyle, William Anderson, Florence St. Leonard, Hedda Nova, Mitchell Lewis, Frank Reilly, George Dangerfield, J.R. Chamberlin, Victor Sutherland.
In the South, a black woman kidnaps a white baby girl and raises her as her own.

Barbara Frietchie (Metro, 1915)
d: Herbert Blaché. 5 reels.
Mary Miles Minter, Mrs. Thomas W. Whiffen, Guy Coombs, Fraunie Fraunholz, Louis Sealy, Frederick Heck, Wallace Scott, Anna Q. Nilsson, Myra Brooks, Charles Hartley.
During the Civil War, a southern girl loves a Yankee officer, but the romance ends in tragedy. (See following item.)

The Barbarian (Pioneer Film Corp., 1921)
d: Donald Crisp. 6 reels.
Monroe Salisbury, George Burrell, Jane Novak, Alan Hale, Barney Sherry, Lillian Leighton, Elinor Hancock, Anne Cudahy, Michael Cudahy, Milton Markwell.
Skullduggery in a mining camp, where claim jumpers try to cheat a nature-loving boy out of his inheritance.

Barbary Sheep (Artcraft Pictures Corp./Paramount, 1917)
d: Maurice Tourneur. 5 reels.

Elsie Ferguson, Lumsden Hare, Pedro DeCordoba, Macy Harlam, Alex Shannon, Maude Ford.

In Arabia, an Englishwoman falls for the charms of a handsome Arab.

Barbed Wire (Sunset Productions/Aywon Film Corp., 1922)
d: Frank Grandon. 5 reels.
Jack Hoxie, Jean Porter, Olah Norman, William Lester, Joe McDermott, Jim Welsh.
Out West, a miner fences in his claim with barbed wire, then has to fight off claim jumpers, who go as far as to try and frame him for murder.

Barbed Wire (Paramount, 1927)
d: Rowland V. Lee. 7 reels.
Clive Brook, Pola Negri, Einar Hanson, Claude Gillingwater, Charles Lane, Gustav von Seyffertitz, Clyde Cook.
In World War I, a French girl is in love with a German prisoner. The townspeople, aflame with hatred of Germans, are vehemently against their union... until the girl's brother, blinded in the war, speaks out in favor of tolerance and forgiveness.

Bardelys the Magnificent (MGM, 1926)
d: King Vidor. 9 reels.
John Gilbert, Eleanor Boardman, George K. Arthur, Roy D'Arcy, Theodore von Eltz, Emily Fitzroy, Lionel Belmore, Arthur Lubin, Karl Dane, Edward Connelly, Fred Malatesta.
In 17th century France, a courtier wagers his entire fortune that he will be able to win the heart of Roxalanne, the wealthiest woman in the kingdom.

Bare-Fisted Gallagher (Robertson-Cole, 1919)
d: J.J. Franz. 5 reels.
William Desmond, Agnes Vernon, Arthur Malette, Frank Lanning, Caroline Rankin, Bill Patton, Scotty McGregor.
Sparks fly when a two-fisted cowpoke takes a liking to a grownup tomboy.

Bare Knees (Gotham/Lumas Film Corp., 1928)
d: Erie C. Kenton. 6 reels.
Virginia Lee Corbin, Donald Keith, Jane Winton, Johnny Walker, Forrest Stanley, Maude Fulton.
A vivacious flapper upsets her sister's birthday party and the staid guests. But she hits it off big with her sister's brother-in-law, who sees in the youngster a bracing breath of fresh air.

Bare Knuckles (Fox, 1921)
w, d: James P. Hogan. 5 reels.
William Russell, Mary Thurman, Correan Kirkham, George Fisher, Edwin B. Tilton, Charles Gorman, Jack Roseleigh, John Cook, Joe Lee, Charles K. French, Jack Stevens.
In the California Sierras, a dam engineer fights off a kidnap attempt of his boss' daughter, saves the day, and wins the girl.

Baree, Son of Kazan (Vitagraph, 1918)
d: David Smith. 5 reels.
Nell Shipman, Alfred Whitman, Al Garcia, Joe Rickson.
In the Canadian Northwest, a valiant dog hunts down a trapper's killer.

Baree, Son of Kazan (Vitagraph, 1925)
d: David Smith. 7 reels.
Anita Stewart, Donald Keith, Jack Curtis, Joe Rickson.
Remake, by the same director, of the 1918 *Baree, Son of Kazan.*

The Barefoot Boy (Columbia, 1923)

d: David Kirkland. 6 reels.
John Bowers, Frankie Lee, Marjorie Daw, Sylvia Breamer, George McDaniel, Raymond Hatton, Tully Marshall, George Periolat, Virginia True Boardman, Brinsley Shaw.
An embittered young man returns to the town that once scorned him, vowing to close down the mill he has inherited and throw many people out of work. Can his childhood sweetheart persuade him to change his mind?

The Bargain (New York Motion Picture Co., 1914)
d: Reginald Barker. 5 reels.
William S. Hart, J. Frank Burke, James Dowling, Clara Williams, J. Barney Sherry.
A notorious two-gun bandit is reformed by a young woman's love. Thoroughly repentant, he is captured by a sheriff who turns out to be not so simon-pure himself. Together, the erstwhile foes enter into a bargain that may benefit both.

The Barker (Selig Polyscope, 1917)
d: J.A. Richmond. 5 reels.
Lew Fields, Amy Leah Dennis, James Harris, William Fables, Frank Hamilton, Fred Eckhart, A. Francis Lenz, Fannie Cohen, Mabel Bardine, Pat O'Malley.
A circus barker befriends a trapeze artist, unaware that she is his long-lost daughter.

The Barker (First National, 1928)
d: George Fitzmaurice. 8 reels.
Douglas Fairbanks Jr., George Cooper, Milton Sills, John Erwin, S.S. Simon, Dorothy Mackaill, Betty Compson, Sylvia Ashton.
A carnival barker raises his son to be a lawyer, then is dismayed to learn that the boy prefers carnival life.

The Barnstormer (Charles Ray Productions/Associated First National, 1922)
d: Charles Ray. 6 reels.
Charles Ray, Wilfred Lucas, Florence Oberle, Lionel Belmore, Phillip Dunham, Gus Leonard, Lincoln Plummer, Charlotte Pierce, George Nichols, Blanche Rose, Bert Offord.
Joel, a farm boy, is fascinated by a touring carnival show when it comes to town.

The Barnstormers (Kalem, 1915)
d: James W. Horne. 4 reels.
Myrtle Tannehill, William H. West, William Brunton, Marin Sais, Frank Jonasson, True Boardman, Ollie Kirby.
A theatrical troupe persuades a hotelier to finance their show, aware that he is smitten with the ingenue of the cast.

Barnum Was Right (Universal, 1930)
d: Del Lord. 5 reels. (Also released in sound version.)
Glenn Tryon, Merna Kennedy, Otis Harlan, Basil Radford, Clarence Burton, Lew Kelly, Isabelle Keith, Gertrude Sutton.
To drum up business, a hotel owner spreads a story that there's hidden treasure stashed somewhere in the building.

The Barricade (Rolfe Photoplays, Inc./Metro, 1917)
d: Edwin Carewe. 5 reels.
Mabel Taliaferro, Frank Currier, Clifford Bruce, Robert Rendel, Emile Collins, Lorna Volare, Mary Doyle.
A vengeful woman entices a securities banker into marrying her, intending to make his life miserable for causing the ruin of her father's business. Trouble is, she's got it all wrong. Papa lost his fortune through his own incompetence, and his new son-in-law actually helped him get out of debt. What does the wife do now?

26

The Barricade (R-C Pictures/Robertson-Cole, 1921)
d: William Christy Cabanne. 6 reels.
William H. Strauss, Katharine Spencer, Kenneth Harlan, Eugene Borden, Dorothy Richards, James Harrison, John O'Connor.
In New York, an East Side doctor falls in love with a socialite who persuades him to move his practice "uptown." He does so, but his heart remains with the folks in his old neighborhood.

The Barrier (Rex Beach Pictures, 1917)
d: Edgar Lewis. 10 reels.
Mabel Julienne Scott, Russell Simpson, Howard Hall, Victor Sutherland, Mitchell Lewis, Edward Roseman, W.J. Gross, Mary Kennevan Carr.
A white lieutenant loves a half-breed Alaskan girl.

The Barrier (MGM, 1926)
d: George Hill. 7 reels.
Lionel Barrymore, Marceline Day, Norman Kerry, Henry B. Walthall, George Cooper, Bert Woodruff, Princess Neola, Mario Carillo, Pat Harmon, Shannon Day.
Race prejudice flares up when a half-caste girl raised by a righteous seaman discovers her true parentage. Her fiancé, a southern aristocrat, is shocked by the news. But after he risks his life to save her from a shipwreck in the icy Alaskan sea, the aristocrat realizes the depth of his love for the girl, and they are reunited.

Barriers Burned Away (Encore Pictures/Associated Exhibitors, 1925)
d: W.S. Van Dyke. 7 reels.
Mabel Ballin, Eric Mayne, Frank Mayo, Wanda Hawley, Wally Van, Arline Pretty, Lawson Butt, Tom Santschi, Harry T. Morey, James Mason, J.P. Lockney, Mrs. Charles Craig.
Wayne loves Christine, but a quarrel over an art forgery has driven a wedge between them. They reunite only after Wayne risks his life to rescue her during the great Chicago fire of 1871.

Barriers of Society (Universal, 1916)
d: Clark Irvine. 5 reels.
Dorothy Davenport, Emory Johnson, Richard Morris, Alfred Allen, Frederick Montague.
When a wealthy socialite accepts an invitation to go sailing, little does she know the yacht owner plans an "accidental" shipwreck on an uncharted island.

Barriers of the Law (Independent Pictures, 1925)
d: J.P. McGowan. 5 reels.
J.P. McGowan, Helen Holmes, William Desmond, Albert J. Smith, Norma Wills, Marguerite Clayton.
Rita, daughter of a sea captain, joins up with a gang of bootleggers, then has a change of heart. But she finds that quitting the gang is no easy task.

Bashful Buccaneer (Harry J. Brown Productions/Rayart Pictures, 1925)
d: Harry J. Brown. 5 reels.
Reed Howes, Dorothy Dwan, Sheldon Lewis, Bull Montana, Jimm Aubrey, Sam Allen, George French, Sailor Sharkey.
Comedy about an author who writes lusty tales of seafaring men, but has never been to sea himself. That changes when he charters a schooner, sets sail in search of pirate gold, and falls in love with the young lady who owns the ship.

The Bat (United Artists, 1926)
d: Roland West. 9 reels.
Tullio Carminati, Louise Fazenda, Eddie Gribbon, Jewel Carmen, Andre Berenger, Charles Herzinger, Jack Pickford, Emily Fitzroy, Arthur Houseman, Robert McKim.
A detective searches for stolen loot that's hidden in a creaky old house that might be haunted.

The Battle Cry of Peace (Vitagraph, 1915)
d: Wilfred North. 9 reels.
Charles Richman, L. Rogers Lytton, James Morrison, Mary Maurice, Louise Beaudet, Harold Hubert, Jack Crawford, Charles Kent, Julia Swayne Gordon, Evart Overton, Belle Bruce, Norma Talmadge, Lucille Hamill, George Stevens, Thais Lawton, Lionel Braham.
In the years prior to America's entry into World War I, a peace-loving American becomes convinced that military preparedness will be his country's salvation. The young man is ridiculed as an alarmist by many, including his own brother, his fiancée's father, and the mysterious "Mr. Emanon" ("No Name" spelled backwards), leader of a peace movement in New York City. The young man is proven right when a peace rally run by Emanon erupts in violence, and many Americans are brutally killed. This film is considered a milestone in that it was commended by several American public figures who supported military preparedness—among them Theodore Roosevelt, Admiral George Dewey, and Assistant Secretary of the Navy Franklin D. Roosevelt.

The Battle of Ballots (Good Luck Film Co., 1915)
d: Frank B. Coigne. 6 reels.
William Wells, Mayre Hall, Baroness Dorothy Van Raven, Robert Web Lawrence, Laura Mackin, Mary Navarro, G. Charles Bryant, Frank Whitson, Frank B. Coigne, Wilfred Jessop.
A saloonkeeper comes to blows with an iceman he believes voted for Prohibition. Their children are cautioned not to associate with each other, but it's too late: The barkeep's daughter and the iceman's son are in love.

The Battle of Gettysburg (New York Motion Picture Co./Mutual, 1913)
d: Thomas H. Ince. 5 reels.
Burton King, Joe King, Gertrude Claire, Shorty Hamilton, Willard Mack, Ann Little.
Story of the famous Civil War battle, interwoven with a love story between a Southern girl and a Yankee soldier.

The Battle of Hearts (Fox, 1916)
d: Oscar Apfel. 5 reels.
William Farnum, Elda Furry, Wheeler Oakman, William Burress, Willard Louis.
Maida Rhodes is loved by a fishing fleet owner, and also by the son of the lighthouse keeper.

The Battle of Life (Fox, 1916)
d: James Vincent. 5 reels.
Gladys Coburn, Art Acord, Richard Neill, William Sheer, Frank Evans, Violet DeBiccari, Alex Shannon.
Crooks decide to go straight, but only after "one last heist."

The Battle of the Sexes (Reliance/Majestic/Mutual, 1914)
w, d: D.W. Griffith. 5 reels.
Lillian Gish, Donald Crisp, Mary Alden, Owen Moore, Robert Harron, Fay Tincher.
A sexy new neighbor seduces a married man. Griffith would remake this film for United Artists in 1928.

The Battle of the Sexes (United Artists, 1928)

d: D.W. Griffith. 10 reels. (Synchronized music and sound effects.)

Phyllis Haver, Jean Hersholt, Belle Bennett, Sally O'Neil, William Bakewell, Don Alvarado.

A pretty gold digger vamps a married man.

Remake of Griffith's own 1914 *The Battle of the Sexes*.

The Battler (World Film Corp., 1919)

d: Frank Reicher. 6 reels.

Earl Metcalfe, Virginia Hammond, Harry C. Brown, Edwin Dennison, Irving Brooks, Florence Malone, Frank Haganey, Al H. Stewart, Barry Whitcomb.

A prizefighter steps in to stop another boxer from beating his own wife. But the wife-beater will do it again, with more serious consequences.

Battling Buddy (Artclass Pictures, 1924)

d: Richard Thorpe. 5 reels.

Buddy Roosevelt, Violet LaPlante, William Lowery, Kewpie King, Shorty Hendrix, Charles E. Butler.

After a young man inherits his uncle's ranch, he finds that the unscrupulous foreman has a claim to it too... and will apparently stop at nothing to deny the young man his inheritance.

Battling Bunyon (Crown Productions, 1925)

d: Paul Hurst. 5 reels.

Wesley Barry, Molly Malone, Frank Campeau, Harry Mann, Chester Conklin.

A young man takes up boxing to impress his sweetheart.

Battling Butler (MGM, 1926)

d: Buster Keaton. 7 reels.

Buster Keaton, Sally O'Neil, Snitz Edwards, Francis McDonald. A fop in love must masquerade as a champion prize-fighter to win the approval of his inamorata's father and brothers. The plot thickens when the real champion shows up and decides to take revenge on the impostor.

The Battling Fool (Columbia, 1924)

d: W.S. Van Dyke. 5 reels.William Fairbanks, Eva Novak, Pat Harmon.

A minister's son becomes a champion boxer.

Battling Jane (Famous Players-Lasky/Paramount, 1918)

d: Elmer Clifton. 5 reels.

Dorothy Gish, George Nichols, Katherine MacDonald, May Hall, Ernest Marion, Adolphe Lestina, Bertram Grassby, Kate Toncray.

Jane, a loveable waitress, adopts a baby when its mother dies, then enters the tyke in a baby beauty show. All the while, Jane must ward off the child's abusive father and his thuggish friend until help arrives.

The Battling Orioles (Hal Roach Studios, 1924)

d: Ted Wilde, Fred Guiol. 6 reels.

Glenn Tryon, Blanche Mehaffey, John T. Prince, Noah Young, Sam Lufkin, Robert Page.

Formerly members of the Battling Orioles baseball team, wealthy retirees go to bat to help the son of a former fan.

Bavu (Universal, 1923)

d: Stuart Paton. 8 reels.

Wallace Beery, Forrest Stanley, Estelle Taylor, Sylvia Breamer, Josef Swickard, Nick DeRuiz, Martha Mattox.

A revolutionary tries to destroy palaces of the Russian aristocracy.

Bawbs O' Blue Ridge (New York Motion Picture Co./Triangle, 1916)

d: Charles Miller. 5 reels.

Bessie Barriscale, Arthur Shirley, Joe Dowling, J. Frank Burke.

Having inherited $5,000, a young woman is super cautious about romantic entanglements, thinking men will want to marry her only for her money. But then true love comes along.

Be a Little Sport (Fox, 1919)

d: Scott Dunlap. 5 reels.

Albert Ray, Elinor Fair, Lule Warrenton, George Hernandez, Leota Lorraine, Eugene Pallette.

Wedding bells ring, but for the wrong couple. They're just friends, going through a sham wedding to satisfy a relative. But a real minister shows up instead of a fake one.

Beach of Dreams (Haworth Studios/Robertson-Cole, 1921)

d: William Parke. 5 reels.

Edith Storey, Noah Beery, Sidney Payne, Jack Curtis, George Fisher, Joseph Swickard, Margarita Fisher, W. Templar Powell, Gertrude Norman, Cesare Gravina.

Cleo, a bored Parisienne socialite, goes on a cruise and is promptly shipwrecked on a deserted island.

Beans (Universal, 1918)

d: Jack Dillon. 5 reels.

Edith Roberts, William E. Lawrence, Lew Cody, Charles Gerrard, Harry Carter, John Cossar.

Misadventures beset a young woman on a business trip.

The Bearcat (Universal, 1922)

d: Edward Sedgwick. 5 reels.

Hoot Gibson, Lillian Rich, Charles French, Joe Harris, Alfred Hollingsworth, Harold Goodwin, William Buckley, Fontaine LaRue, James Alamo, J.J. Allen, Stanley Fitz.

A lone cowboy known as "the Bearcat" earns a job on a prosperous cattle ranch when he saves the rancher's daughter from a runaway horse. He'll win the girl, too.

The Beast (Fox, 1916)

d: Richard Stanton. 5 reels.

George Walsh, Anna Luther, Herschell Mayall, Edward Cecil, Henry DeVere, Clyde Benson.

An East coast girl is "roughed up" on a trip out West, then decides one of her tormentors isn't such a bad guy.

Beating Back (Thanhouser/Mutual, 1914)

d: Caryl S. Fleming. 5 reels.

Al J. Jennings, Frank Jennings, Frank Farrington, Albert Froome, Mignon Anderson, Fan Bourke, Madeline Fairbanks.

An Oklahoma attorney is unjustly accused of robbery.

Beating the Game (Goldwyn, 1921)

d: Victor Schertzinger. 6 reels.

Tom Moore, Hazel Daly, DeWitt Jennings, Dick Rosson, Nick Cogley, Tom Ricketts, Lydia Knott, William Orlamond, Lydia Yeamans Titus.

Charlie, a professional safecracker, gets a chance to tread the straight and narrow when one of his victims sees in him a streak of honesty. The would-be victim sets him up in business, and by year's end, Charlie's a legitimate success.

Beating the Odds (Vitagraph, 1919)

d: Paul Scardon. 5 reels.

Harry T. Morey, Betty Blythe, Jean Paige, George Majeroni, Robert Gaillard, Eulalie Jensen, Robert Mowbray, Frank Norcross.

Driven out of New York by the district attorney, a former

criminal becomes a patent medicine salesman.

Beau Broadway (MGM, 1928)
w, d: Malcolm St. Clair. 7 reels.
Lew Cody, Aileen Pringle, Sue Carol, Heinie Conklin.
A boxing promoter adopts the daughter of a dying fighter, then realizes he must amend his way of life.

Beau Brummel (Warner Bros., 1924)
d: Harry Beaumont. 10 reels.
John Barrymore, Mary Astor, Willard Louis, Irene Rich, Alec B. Francis, Carmel Myers, Richard Tucker, William Humphreys, Andre de Beranger, Clarissa Selwynne, John J. Richardson, Claire DeLorez, Michael Dark, Templar Saxe, James A. Marcus, Elizabeth Brice, Roland Rushton, Carol Holloway, Kate Lester, Rose Dione.
A British fop worms his way into the monarchy's inner circles.

Beau Geste (Famous Players-Lasky/Paramount, 1927)
d: Herbert Brenon. 10 reels.
Ronald Colman, Neil Hamilton, Ralph Forbes, Alice Joyce, Mary Brian, Noah Beery, William Powell, Victor McLaglen, Norman Trevor, Donald Stuart, George Rigas.
Three English brothers join the French Foreign Legion, where they must deal with a sadistic commander and fight wars against the Arabs.

Beau Revel (Thomas H. Ince/Paramount, 1921)
d: John Griffith Wray. 6 reels.
Lloyd Hughes, Florence Vidor, Lewis Stone, Kathleen Kirkham, Richard Ryan, Harlan Tucker, William Conklin, Lydia Yeamans Titus, William Musgrave, Joseph Campbell.
Revel, a wealthy womanizer, objects to his son's infatuation with Nellie, a cabaret singer, and forbids the young man to see her. Unwittingly, Revel falls in love with her himself.

Beau Sabreur (Paramount, 1928)
d: John Waters. 7 reels.
Gary Cooper, Evelyn Brent, Noah Beery, William Powell, Roscoe Karns, Mitchell Lewis, Arnold Kent, Raoul Paoli, Joan Standing, Frank Reicher, Oscar Smith, H.J. Uttenhore.
A young Frenchman goes to North Africa on a diplomatic mission, and there he meets and falls for a visiting American girl. Filmed as a sequel to the 1927 hit, *Beau Geste*.

The Beautiful Adventure (Empire All Star Corp./Mutual, 1917)
d: Dell Henderson. 5 reels.
Ann Murdock, Ada Boshell, Edward Fielding, David Powell, Kate Sergeantson, Edgar Norton, Carl Sauerman, Vera Fuller Mellish, Mercelta Esmond, Anton Ascher, Victor Le Roy.
In Paris, a young woman flees an arranged marriage.

The Beautiful and Damned (Warner Brothers, 1923)
d: Sidney Franklin. 7 reels.
Marie Prevost, Louis Fazenda, Kenneth Harlan, Harry Myers, Tully Marshall, Cleo Ridgely, Emmett King, Walter Long, Clarence Burton, Parker McConnell, Charles McHugh.
Film based on the F. Scott Fitzgerald novel of the same name, about the irresponsible, hard-drinking "lost generation" of the 1920s.

Beautiful but Dumb (Tiffany-Stahl Productions, 1928)
d: Elmer Clifton. 7 reels.
Patsy Ruth Miller, Charles Byer, George E. Stone, Shirley Palmer, Greta Yoltz, William Irving, Harvey Clark.
Another caterpillar-turns-butterfly romantic comedy, about a plain Jane who changes her clothes and her ways, and

becomes a real dish.

The Beautiful Cheat (Universal, 1925)
d: Edward Sloman. 7 reels.
Laura LaPlante, Harry Myers, Bertram Grassby, Alexander Carr, Youcca Troubetzkoy, Helen Carr, Robert Anderson.
A shopgirl poses as an aristocratic Russian actress.

The Beautiful City (Inspiration/First National, 1925)
d: Kenneth Webb. 7 reels.
Richard Barthelmess, Dorothy Gish, William Powell, Florence Auer, Frank Puglia.
In New York, a young Italian-American takes the blame for a robbery his brother committed.

The Beautiful Gambler (Universal, 1921)
d: William Worthington. 5 reels.
Grace Darmond, Jack Mower, Harry Van Meter, Charles Brinley, Herschel Mayall, Willis Marks.
Molly, daughter of a heavy gambler, grows up and marries the owner of a gambling parlor.

The Beautiful Liar (Preferred Pictures/Associated First National Pictures, 1921)

d: Wallace Worsley. 6 reels.
Katherine MacDonald, Charles Meredith, Joseph J. Dowling, Kate Lester, Wilfred Lucas.
At a resort hotel for the wealthy, a show is jeopardized when the actress selected for the lead declines to perform. Desperate, the show's promoter finds a secretary who resembles the actress, and gets her to perform in the star's place.
Miss MacDonald plays both parts, the star and her lookalike.

The Beautiful Lie (Metro, 1917)
d: John W. Noble. 5 reels.
Frances Nelson, Harry S. Northrup, Edward Earle, Elsie MacLeod, Sally Crute, John Davidson, Mrs. Allan Walker, Emile Collins.
A wealthy lothario plots a fake marriage ceremony for himself and his bride.

The Beautiful Mrs. Reynolds (World Film Corp., 1918)
d: Arthur Ashley. 6 reels.
June Elvidge, Carlyle Blackwell, Arthur Ashley, Carl Girard, Hubert Wilke, Evelyn Greeley, Lionel Belmore, George MacQuarrie, Betty Peterson, Alec B. Francis, Florence Beresford, John Smiley, Rose Tapley.
Story behind the famous duel between Alexander Hamilton and Aaron Burr.

The Beautiful Rebel — see: Janice Meredith

The Beautiful Sinner (Columbia, 1924)
d: W.S. Van Dyke. 5 reels.
William Fairbanks, Eva Novak, Carl Stockdale, George Nichols, Kate Lester, Carmen Phillips, Edward Borman.
Avery, an amateur detective, helps solve a baffling jewel theft mystery. In the process, he falls in love with Alice, apparently a member of the criminal gang. It turns out, however, that she's really an undercover detective herself.

Beautifully Trimmed (Universal, 1920)
d: Marcel de Sano. 5 reels.
Carmel Myers, Irving Cummings, Pell Trenton, Alred Fisher, Victory Bateman, George B. Williams, Lee Kohlmar, Herbert Bethew, Myrtle Reeves.
Swindlers sell worthless oil company stock to a wealthy veteran. Then, the oil company strikes a gusher.

THE BATTLE OF THE SEXES (1928). What's sauce for the goose isn't necessarily sauce for the gander, or so thinks Papa (Jean Hersholt, left). He's furious when he catches his daughter Ruth (Sally O'Neil) in the arms of a gigolo (Don Alvarado). But Ruth will remind Papa that he might be a tad bit hypocritical reproaching her, since he's seeing a mistress (platinum-tressed Phyllis Haver).

* * * * *

Beauty and Bullets (Universal, 1928)
d: Ray Taylor. 5 reels.
Ted Wells, Wilbur Mack, Duane Thompson, Jack Kenney.
Out West, a lawman foils a gang of payroll thieves, then recognizes one of them as his sweetheart's brother.

Beauty and the Rogue (American Film Co./Mutual, 1918)
d: Henry King. 5 reels.
Mary Miles Minter, Alan Forrest, Orral Humphrey, George Periolat, Lucille Ward, Spottiswood Aitken, Clarence Burton.
A girl with a strong social conscience persuades her father to hire an ex-crook.

Beauty in Chains (Universal, 1918)
d: Elsie Jane Wilson. 5 reels.
Emory Johnson, Ruby LaFayette, Ella Hall, Winter Hall, Maxfield Stanley, Harry M. Holden, George E. McDaniel, Gretchen Lederer, William Hakeem.
In Spain, a young woman is betrothed by arrangement to a man she's never met.

The Beauty Market (First National, 1919)
d: Colin Campbell. 6 reels.
Katherine MacDonald, Roy Stewart, Kathleen Kirkham, Wedgwood Nowell, Winter Hall, Robert Brower.
Tale of a girl who learns the hard way that some people will sell their souls for profit.

The Beauty Prize (MGM, 1924)
d: Lloyd Ingraham. 6 reels.
Viola Dana, Pat O'Malley, Eddie Phillips, Edward Connelly, Eunice Vin Moore, Edith Yorke, Joan Standing, Federick Truesdell.
A manicurist enters a beauty contest while masquerading as a society belle.

Beauty-Proof (Vitagraph, 1919)
d: Paul Scardon. 5 reels.
Harry T. Morey, Betty Blythe, George Majeroni, Denton Vane, Robert Gaillard, Tenny Wright.
A Canadian mountie is considered "beauty-proof" because he seems to hate women. But there's a story behind his distrust of the opposite sex.

The Beauty Shop (Cosmopolitan Productions/Paramount, 1922)
d: Edward Dillon. 7 reels.
Raymond Hitchcock, Billy B. Van, James J. Corbett, Louise Fazenda, Madeline Fairbanks, Marion Fairbanks, Diana Allen, Montagu Love, Laurance Wheat.
Budd, a struggling beauty shop owner, tries to boost his business by using a nobleman's crest on the labels of his products. But when he's mistaken for the real nobleman, he's expected to fight a duel with a European outlaw.

Beauty Shoppers (Tiffany Productions, 1927)
d: Louis J. Gasnier. 6 reels.
Mae Busch, Doris Hill, Ward Crane, Thomas Haines, Cissy Fitzgerald, James A. Marcus, Leo White, Dale Fuller, William A. Carroll, Luca Flamma.
A country girl comes to New York, eager to begin a career in art. Instead, she's forced to work in a "fat farm" shop window. Her beauty, however, endears her to various eligible gentlemen.

Beauty's Worth (Cosmopolitan/Paramount, 1922)
d: Robert G. Vignola. 7 reels.
Marion Davies, Forrest Stanley, June Elvidge, Truly Shattuck, Halam Cooley, Antrim Short, Aileen Manning, Thomas Jefferson, Martha Mattox.
An artist transforms a simple girl into a sophisticated beauty, and soon she is the belle of society. But then she realizes she isn't happy in her new status.

Because of a Woman (Triangle, 1917)
d: Jack Conway. 6 reels.
Jack Livingston, Belle Bennett, George Chesbro, Louella Maxam, Lillian Langdon, Josef Swickard, George Pearce.
A business executive is falsely accused of mismanagement and forced to resign. He goes West, but his love for the girl who was once his fiancée prompts him to return home and clear his name.

The Beckoning Flame (New York Motion Picture Corp./Triangle, 1916)
d: Charles Swickard. 5 reels.
Henry Woodruff, Tsuru Aoki, Rhea Mitchell, J. Frank Burke, Louis Morrison, J. Barney Sherry, Roy Laidlaw, Joseph Dowling.
In India on an official mission, an Englishman becomes enamored of a Hindu maiden.

Beckoning Roads (B.B. Features/Robertson-Cole, 1919)
d: Howard Hickman. 5 reels.
Bessie Barriscale, Niles Welch, George Periolat, Joseph J. Dowling, Emmett King, Dorcas Matthews, Thomas Holding.
Class prejudice brings about the downfall of the marriage between a financier and a boarding-school girl.

The Beckoning Trail (Universal, 1916)
d: Jack Conway. 5 reels.
J. Warren Kerrigan, Maude George, Harry Carter, Harry Griffith, Lois Wilson, Raymond Hanford.
A New York playboy goes West to work the mine he has inherited.

Becky (Cosmopolitan/MGM, 1927)
d: John P. McCarthy. 7 reels.
Owen Moore, Sally O'Neil, Tom Moore, Matt Moore, Gertrude Olmstead, Harry Crocker, Mack Swain, Claude King.
Becky, a rough-hewn girl from the tenements, gets a job acting in a comedy version of *Faust*. Determined to improve her lot, she attends theatrical parties to meet "the right people," and finds love with one of them.

The Bedrooom Window (Famous Players-Lasky/Paramount, 1924)
d: William DeMille. 7 reels.
May McAvoy, Malcolm McGregor, Ricardo Cortez, Robert Edeson, George Fawcett, Ethel Wales, Charles Ogle, Medea Radzina, Guy Oliver, Lillian Leighton.
Lovestruck Robert is shocked to find the dead body of his sweetheart's father. He's arrested on suspicion of murder, but his sweetie's aunt, an amateur criminologist, comes to his aid and finds the real killer.

A Beggar in Purple (Pathé, 1920)
d: Edgar Lewis. 6 reels.
Leonard C. Shumway, Charles Arling, Stanhope Wheatcroft, Betty Brice, Ruth King, Stanton Heck, Dorothea Wolbert, Ernest Butterworth, Louis Fitzroy, William F. Moran.
When a wealthy businessman refuses to help a poor man get needed medication for his dying mother, the grieving son swears revenge. In time, he builds a company that competes on even terms with that of the heartless businessman.

The Beggar of Cawnpore (New York Motion Picture

Corp./Triangle, 1916)
d: Charles Swickard. 6 reels.
H.B. Warner, Lola May, Wyndham Standing, A.F. Hollingsworth, H.E. Entwhistle, Wedgwood Nowell.
A British doctor practicing medicine in India becomes a morphine addict.

Beggar on Horseback (Famous Players-Lasky/Paramount, 1925)
d: James Cruze. 7 reels.
Edward Everett Horton, Esther Ralston, Erwin Connelly, Gertrude Short, Ethel Wales, Theodore Kosloff, James Mason, Frederick Sullivan.
Comedy about Neil, a struggling composer, who loves Cynthia but seriously considers proposing marriage to wealthy Gladys as a way out of poverty.

The Beggar Prince (Haworth Pictures/Robertson-Cole, 1920)
d: William Worthington. 5 reels.
Sessue Hayakawa, Beatrice LaPlante, Thelma Percy, Bert Hadley, Robert Bolder, Joseph Swickard, Buddy Post.
Hayakawa plays a double role, as a poor fisherman and the ruling prince.

Beggars of Life (Paramount, 1928)
d: William Wellman. 9 reels. (Synchronized music and sound effects.)
Richard Arlen, Louise Brooks, Wallace Beery, Edgar Washintgton Blue, H.A. Morgan, Andy Clark, Mike Donlin, Robert Perry.
A young woman is on the run from the law after killing her abusive foster father.

Behind Closed Doors (Triumph Films/Equitable/World Film Corp., 1916)
d: Joseph A. Golden. 5 reels.
Marie Empress, Marian Swayne, Wright Huntington, Regan Hughston, Paul Irving, Thomas Tracy.
When a casino owner is murdered, the evidence points to his romantic rival.

Behind Closed Doors (Columbia, 1929)
d: Roy William Neill. 6 reels.
Gaston Glass, Fanny Midgley, Virginia Valli, Otto Matiesen, Andre DeSegurola, Torben Meyer, Broderick O'Farrell.
A revolution is brewing in a foreign country, and Washington is watching.

Behind Masks (Famous Players-Lasky/Paramount, 1921)
d: Frank Reicher. 5 reels.
Dorothy Dalton, Frederick Vogeding, William P. Carleton, Julia Swayne Gordon, Gladys Valerie, Kempton Greene, Lewis Broughton, Alex Kaufman.
Jeanne, an orphan, discovers thieves at work and, pursued by them, escapes by diving into the sea and swimming for help.

Behind the Curtain (Universal, 1924)
d: Chester M. Franklin. 5 reels.
Lucille Rickson, Johnny Harron, Winifred Bryson, Charles Clary, Eric Mayne, George Cooper, Clarence Geldert, Pat Harmon.
After Belmont discovers that his son has eloped with his mistress' sister, he cries foul and, shortly thereafter, is found murdered.

Behind the Door (Thomas H. Ince/Paramount, 1919)
d: Irvin V. Willat. 7 reels.

Jane Novak, Hobart Bosworth, Wallace Beery, Gibson Gowland, Tom Ashton, James Gordon, Dick Wain, J.P. Lockney, Otto Hoffman.
An American couple are captured by a German submarine and treated savagely. When the husband breaks free, he exacts a fearsome revenge on the German captain.

Behind the Front (Famous Players-Lasky/Paramount, 1926)
d: Edward Sutherland. 6 reels.
Wallace Beery, Raymond Hatton, Mary Brian, Richard Arlen, Hayden Stevenson, Tom Kennedy, Chester Conklin, Frances Raymond, Melbourne MacDowell.
Wry comedy about a pair of dimwits who are persuaded to enlist in the Army by a young woman who tells each of them that she loves only him.

Behind the Lines (Universal, 1916)
d: Henry MacRae. 5 reels.
Harry Carey, Edith Johnson, Ruth Clifford, Marc Fenton, Miriam Shelby, Bill Human.
In Mexico, a diplomat's daughter spies for the Revolution.

Behind the Mask (Art Dramas, Inc., 1917)
d: Alice Blaché. 5 reels.
Catherine Calvert, Richard Tucker, Kirke Brown, Charles Dungan, Flora Nason, Charles Halton.
A woman marries for revenge, but finds that love is stronger than vengeance.

Behind the Scenes (Famous Players/Paramount, 1914)
d: James Kirkwood. 5 reels.
Mary Pickford, James Kirkwood, Lowell Sherman, Ida Waterman, Russell Bassett.
A successful actress moves West to become a farmer's wife.

Behind Two Guns (Sunset Productions, 1924)
d: Robert N. Bradbury. 5 reels.
J.B. Warner, Hazel Newman, Marin Sais, Jay Morley, Jim Welch, Otto Lederer, William Calles, Jack Waltemeyer, Emily Gerdes, Bartlett A. Carré, Robert North Bradbury.
Out West, a master hypnotist places a woman under his spell and orders her to steal her husband's gold for him.

Behold My Wife (Famous Players-Lasky/Paramount, 1920)
d: George Melford. 7 reels.
Milton Sills, Mabel Julienne Scott, Elliott Dexter, Winter Hall, Helen Dunbar, Ann Forrest, Maude Wayne, Fred Huntley, F.R. Butler, Mark Fenton, F. Templer-Powell, Clarence Burton, Jane Wolfe.
Lali, a half-breed Indian girl, marries the son of a British aristocrat.

Behold the Man (Pathé, 1921)
d: Spencer Gordon Bennett. 6 reels. (Includes Pathécolor sequences.)
H.O. Pettibone, Sybil Sheridan, Monsieur Moreau, Madame Moreau, Le Petit Briand, Richard Ross, Violet Axzelle, Monsieur Norman, Monsieur Jacquinet.
As a mother tells her children the story of Jesus Christ, the events of his life are depicted on the screen.

Behold This Woman (Vitagraph, 1924)
d: J. Stuart Blackton. 7 reels.
Irene Rich, Marguerite DeLaMotte, Charles A. Post, Harry Myers, Rosemary Theby, Anders Randolph.
Tale of an ill-fated romance between a cattleman and a movie star.

Being Respectable   (Warner Bros., 1924)
d: Phil Rosen.   8 reels.
Monte Blue, Irene Rich, Marie Prevost, Frank Currier, Louise Fazenda, Theodore von Eltz, Eulalie Jensen, Lila Leslie, Sidney Bracey.
Wealthy and respectable, a staid married man is tempted to stray when his old flame returns to town.

The Belgian   (Sidney Olcott Players/U.S. Exhibitors, 1918)
d: Sidney Olcott.   8 reels.
Walker Whiteside, Valentine Grant, Arda LaCroix, Sally Crute, Georgio Majeroni, Anders Randolf, Henry Leone, Blanche Davenport.
World War I romance involving a sculptor, his girlfriend, and a German spy.

Believe Me Xantippe   (Famous Players-Lasky/Paramount, 1918)
d: Donald Crisp.   5 reels.
Wallace Reid, Ann Little, Ernest Joy, Henry Woodward, Noah Beery, James Cruze, Winifred Greenwood, James Farley, Charles Ogle, Clarence Geldert.
On a bet, a wealthy young man commits petty theft and tries to elude capture for one year.

Belinda Puts Her Hair Up—see: The Girl-Woman (1919)

Bell Boy 13   (Thomas H. Ince/Associated First National, 1923)
d: William A. Seiter.   5 reels.
Douglas MacLean, Margaret Loomis, John Steppling, Jean Walsh, Eugene Burr, William Courtright, Emily Gerdes.
Disinherited by his uncle, young Harry becomes a bellboy in a hotel. When his uncle decides to buy the hotel just so he can fire his nephew, Harry persuades all the employees to go on strike.

Bella Donna   (Famous Players/Paramount, 1915)
d: Edwin S. Porter, Hugh Ford.   5 reels.
Pauline Frederick, Thomas Holding, Julian L'Estrange, Eugene Ormonde, George Majeroni, Edmund Shalet, Helen Sinnot.
While living in Egypt, a married Englishwoman begins an affair with a wealthy brute.

Bella Donna   (Famous Players-Lasky/Paramount, 1923)
d: George Fitzmaurice.   8 reels.
Conway Tearle, Pola Negri, Conrad Nagel, George K. Arthur, Adolphe Menjou, Claude King, Lois Wilson, Macey Harlam, Robert Schable.
Remake of the 1915 *Bella Donna* starring Pauline Frederick.

The Bellamy Trial   (MGM, 1928)
d: Monta Bell.   8 reels.   (Part talkie.)
Leatrice Joy, Cosmo Kyrle Bellew, Margaret Livingston, Betty Bronson, Eddie Nugent, George Barraud.
Courtroom drama, told largely in flashbacks.

Belle of Alaska   (Chester Bennett Productions, 1922)
d: Chester Bennett.   5 reels.
J. Frank Glendon, Jane Novak, Noah Beery, Florence Carpenter, Leslie Bates.
Stranded in Alaska, a young woman takes up with a gambler and becomes a dance hall girl known as "Chicago Belle."

The Belle of Broadway   (Columbia, 1926)
d: Harry O. Hoyt.   6 reels.
Edith Yorke, Betty Compson, Herbert Rawlinson, Armand Kaliz, Ervin Renard, Max Berwyn, Albert Roccardi, Edward Warren, Tom Ricketts, Edward Kipling, Wilfrid North.
A young vaudevillian impersonates a former Parisienne music hall star, and is accepted by the public as the star herself, miraculously untouched by the ravages of age.

The Belle of New York   (Marion Davies Film Corp./Select Pictures, 1919)
d: Julius Steger.   5 reels.
Marion Davies, Etienne Girardot, Rogers Lytton, Franklyn Hanna, Raymond Bloomer.
A New York actress in the Follies spurns the attentions of a wealthy young man. When he despairs and takes to drinking, she nurses him back to health and sobriety.

The Belle of the Season   (Metro, 1919)
d: S. Rankin Drew.   5 reels.
Emmy Wehlen, S. Rankin Drew, Walter Hitchcock, John Mackin, Louis Wolheim.
A society lady tries to improve conditions for the poor.

The Bells   (Pathé, 1918)
d: Ernest C. Warde.   4 reels.
Frank Keenan, Lois Wilson, Edward Coxen, Carl Stockdale, Albert Cody, Joseph J. Dowling, Ida Lewis, Bert Law.
Severely strapped for money, an innkeeper robs and murders one of his guests. Thereafter, he is haunted by the sounds of the murdered man's sleigh bells.

The Bells   (Chadwick Pictures, 1926)
d: James Young.   7 reels.
Lionel Barrymore, Fred Warren, Boris Karloff, Lola Todd, Eddie Phillips.
A murderer is haunted by the sound of bells.

The Beloved Adventuress   (World Film Corp., 1917)
d: Edmund Lawrence.   5 reels.
Kitty Gordon, Jack Drumier, Inez Shanon, Madge Evans, Lillian Cook, Robert Forsyth, Edward Elkas, R. Payton Gibbs, Frederick Truesdell, William Sherwood, Pinna Nesbit.
Popular stage star Juliette LaMonde is beloved by millions. Unfortunately, her heart belongs to the husband of another woman.

The Beloved Blackmailer   (World Film Corp., 1918)
d: Dell Henderson.   5 reels.
Carlyle Blackwell, W.T. Carleton, Isabelle Berwin, Evelyn Greeley, Charles Dungan, Jack Drumier, Rex MacDougal.
After faking his own kidnapping, a wealthy young man finds he must return home to rescue his sweetheart from the advances of a scheming lecher.

The Beloved Brute   (Vitagraph, 1924)
d: J. Stuart Blackton.   7 reels.
Marguerite DeLaMotte, Victor McLaglen, William Russell, Stuart Holmes, Frank Brownlee, Wilfrid North, Ernie Adams, D.D. McLean, William Moran, George Ingleton.
Out West, an itinerant wrestler takes on all comers, and beats all of them except his own brother. Humbled by his loss, the wrestler offers his girlfriend to the victorious brother. She declines the alienation, affirming that she loves the wrestler anyway.

The Beloved Cheater   (Astra Film Corp./Robertson-Cole, 1919)
d: William Christy Cabanne.   5 reels.
Lew Cody, Doris Pawn, Eileen Percy, Jack Mower, Alice Fleming, Frederick Vroom, Andrew Robson, Kathleen Kirkham.

It seems there's an "Anti-Kiss Cult", whose member ladies don't permit themselves to be kissed before marriage.

The Beloved Impostor (Vitagraph, 1918)
d: Joseph Gleason. 5 reels.
Gladys Leslie, Huntley Gordon, Denton Vane, Mrs. Hurley, Frances Grant, Gwen Williams, Miriam Miles.
To win the love of a confirmed mysogynist, an attractive young woman masquerades as a 12-year-old girl.

Beloved Jim (Universal, 1917)
d: Stuart Paton. 6 reels.
Harry Carter, Joseph Girard, Priscilla Dean, J. Morris Foster, Charles Hill Mailes, Frank Deshon, Sydney Deane, Edward Brown, Mrs. A.E. Witting.
Suspicions arise when a newlywed brings his bride home to meet his nephew, and learns that the two have met before. In what capacity?

The Beloved Rogue (United Artists, 1927)
d: Alan Crosland. 10 reels.
John Barrymore, Conrad Veidt, Marceline Day, Lawson Butt, Henry Victor, Mack Swain, Slim Summerville, Otto Matieson, Rose Dione, Bertram Grassby, Lucy Beaumont, Angelo Rossito, James Winton, Martha Franklin, Nigel DeBrulier, Dick Sutherland, Dickie Moore.
The French poet-swordsman François Villon and his army of vagabonds rescue a fair maiden from marriage to an unworthy scoundrel.

Beloved Rogues (American Film Co./Mutual, 1917)
d: Al Santel. 5 reels.
C. William Kolb, Max M. Dill, May Cloy, Clarence Burton, Harry von Meter.
Self-sacrificing hardware dealers sell everything, then steal additional money to pay for an operation to restore their blind niece's sight.

The Beloved Traitor (Goldwyn, 1918)
d: William Worthington. 5 reels.
Mae Marsh, E.K. Lincoln, Hedda Hopper, George Fawcett, Bradley Barker, J.A. Furey, Louis R. Grisel, Chester Morris.
An art student becomes smitten with his benefactor's daughter.

The Beloved Vagabond (Pathé, 1915)
d: Edward Jose. 6 reels.
Edwin Arden, Kathryn Browne-Decker, Bliss Milford, Harold Crane, Eric Mayne, Stephen Grattan, Boris Korlin.
Treachery and deceit undo a young architect, who then turns to the streets and becomes a roving musician.

Below the Deadline (Chesterfield Motion Picture Corp., 1929)
d: J.P. McGowan. 5 reels.
H.B. Warner, Lillian Biron, Bert Sprotte, Robert Anderson.
Donovan, a detective on the trail of a murderer, falls in love with his prey's wife.

Below the Line (Warner Bros., 1925)
d: Herman Raymaker. 7 reels.
Rin-Tin-Tin, John Harron, June Marlowe, Pat Hartigan, Victor Potel, Charles Conklin, Gilbert Clayton, Edith Yorke, Taylor Duncan.
A noble dog rescues his master from attackers, and leads detectives to clues incriminating a murderous reprobate.

Below the Surface (Thomas H. Ince/Famous Players-Lasky/Paramount, 1920)
d: Irvin V. Willat. 6 reels.
Lloyd Hughes, Hobart Bosworth, Grace Darmond, George Webb, Gladys George, Joseph P. Lockney, Edith Yorke, George Clair.
Father-and-son divers hunt for sunken treasure.

Ben Blair (Paramount, 1916)
d: William Desmond Taylor. 5 reels.
Dustin Farnum, Winifred Kingston, Herbert Standing, Lamar Johnstone, Virginia Foltz, Frank H. Bonn, Gordon Griffith.
Unsavory tale about desertion, alcoholism, and revenge.

Ben Bolt (Solax Co., 1913)
d: Howell Hansel. 4 reels.
Joseph Levering, Fraunie Fraunholz, Claire Whitney, James O'Neill, Jack Burns.
Unlucky in love, a young man changes his fortunes when he locates a lost ship belonging to the father of the girl he loves.

Ben-Hur (MGM, 1925)
d: Fred Niblo. 12 reels. (Technicolor sequences.)
Ramon Novarro, Francis X. Bushman, May McAvoy, Carmel Myers, Claire McDowell, Betty Bronson, Mitchell Lewis, Nigel de Brulier.

Big-screen spectacle based on Lew Wallace's novel about the time of Christ. Judah Ben-Hur, a Jewish slave, gains his freedom when he saves the life of a Roman tribune, who later adopts him. Judah returns to Jerusalem in time to see his mother and sister, both lepers, cured by Jesus along the Way of the Cross. Director Niblo and his crew fill the screen with spectacular scenes, including a furious chariot race, a violent sea battle (both directed by second unit helmsman Reaves Eason), and an earthquake that topples tall buildings into the path of onlookers. There are heart-rending moments, too, as in the cruelty shown to the galley slaves; the valley of the lepers; and the Crucifixion scene. With it all, a pleasing mix of Technicolor and tints along with standard black-and-white scenes make *Ben-Hur* a feast for the eyes.

Beneath the Czar (Solax Co., 1914)
d: Alice Blaché. 4 reels.
Claire Whitney, Fraunie Fraunholz.
In Czarist Russia, a woman hired to spy on a revolutionary falls in love with him instead.

Berlin Via America (Fordart Films, Inc., 1918)
d: Francis Ford. 6 reels.
Francis Ford, Edna Emerson, Jack Newton, George Henry, Ed Dorhan, George Jones, William Willis, William Canfield, Emma Warren, Lois Scott, Francis Feeney.
During World War I, a young American is thought to be disloyal to his country. But in reality he's an American spy, braving dangerous incursions behind enemy lines and into Germany.

Bertha, the Sewing Machine Girl (Fox, 1926)
d: Irving Cummings. 6 reels.
Madge Bellamy, Allan Simpson, Sally Phipps, Paul Nicholson, Anita Garvin, J. Farrell MacDonald, Ethel Wales, Arthur Housman, Harry Bailey.
Bertha, a sewing machine girl, loses her job but finds another as model for a lingerie company.

The Best Bad Man (Fox, 1925)
d: J.G. Blystone. 5 reels.
Tom Mix, Clara Bow, Buster Gardner, Cyril Chadwick, Tom Kennedy, Frank Beal, Judy King, Paul Panzer, Tom Wilson.

In Colorado, an absentee ranch owner masquerades as a traveling salesman in order to investigate the way his businesses are being run.

The Best Man (Falcon Features/General Film Co., 1917)
d: Bertram Bracken. 4 reels.
William Ehfe, Gordon Sackville, Capt. Nicholson, Margaret Landis, Mollie McConnell, Clifford B. Gray, Frank Brownlee.
The love of a good woman helps a businessman conquer his alcoholism.

The Best Man (Hampton Productions/Pathé, 1919)
d: Thomas Heffron. 5 reels.
J. Warren Kerrigan, Lois Wilson, Alfred Whitman, Frances Raymond, Clyde Benson, R.D. MacLean, Bert Appling, Ed Tilton, Mary Land, Fred Montague.
A Secret Service agent goes undercover to intercept an important document, knowing that his orders are to "stop at nothing" to complete his mission... even if it means marrying a woman he doesn't know!

The Best of Luck (Metro, 1920)
d: Ray C. Smallwood. 6 reels.
Kathryn Adams, Jack Holt, Lilie Leslie, Fred Malatesta, Frances Raymond, Emmett King, Robert Dunbar, Effie Conley, Jack Underhill, Carl Sawyer, Irish Meusel.
An American woman goes to Scotland and is wooed by two suitors.

The Best People (Famous Players-Lasky/Paramount, 1925)
d: Sidney Olcott. 6 reels.
Warner Baxter, Esther Ralston, Kathlyn Williams, Edwards Davis, William Austin, Larry Steers, Margaret Livingston, Joseph Striker, Margaret Morris, Ernie Adams.
Class-conscious comedy about a brother and sister who—against their parents' wishes—plan to marry members of the working class.

Betrayal (Paramount, 1929)
d: Lewis Milestone. 8 reels. (Music and sound effects.)
Emil Jannings, Esther Ralston, Gary Cooper, Jada Weller, Douglas Haig, Bodil Rosing.
In a Swiss town, the mayor discovers that one of his two sons was actually fathered by his late wife's former lover.

Betrayed (Thanhouser/Mutual, 1916)
d: Howard M. Mitchell. 5 reels.
Grace DeCarlton, Robert Whittier, Roy Pilcher, Gladys Leslie.
Race prejudice between an Indian and a white man leads to tragedy and death.

Betrayed (Fox, 1917)
d: R.A. Walsh. 5 reels.
Miriam Cooper, James Marcus, Hobart Bosworth, Monte Blue, Wheeler Oakman.
A Mexican girl is attracted to a bandido, but she's also keen on the *gringo* who's been sent to capture him.

Betsy Ross (World Film Corp., 1917)
d: Travers Vale, George Cowl. 5 reels.
Alice Brady, John Bowers, Lillian Cook, Victor Kennard, Eugenie Woodward, Kate Lester, Frank Mayo, George McQuarrie, Justine Cutting, Robert Forsyth, Robert Cummings.
Story of the legendary seamstress who helped fashion the first American flag.

Betsy's Burglar (Fine Arts Film Co./Triangle, 1917)
d: Paul Powell. 5 reels.

Constance Talmadge, Kenneth Harlan, Monte Blue, Joseph Singleton, Josephine Crowell, Clyde Hopkins, Hal Wilson, Kate Bruce.
A housemaid dreams of working as a detective. She gets her chance when a mysterious stranger moves into the boarding house and involves her in a stolen-jewel caper.

The Better Half (Select Pictures Corp., 1918)
d: J.S. Robertson. 5 reels.
Alice Brady, David Powell, Crauford Kent, W.T. Carleton, Isabel O'Madigan, Richard Allen.
Identical twin girls are lookalikes only, not at all similar in nature and temperament. The selfish twin marries and subsequently leaves her husband, and when he is later beaten by hoodlums, the sweet-natured sister nurses him back to health.

The Better Man (Famous Players Film Co., 1914)
d: Edwin S. Porter. 4 reels.
William Courtleigh, Arthur Hoops, Alice Claire Elliott, Robert Broderick.
Two reverend ministers are in love with the same woman.

The Better Man (Selig-Rork Productions/Aywon Film Corp., 1921)
d: Wilfred Lucas. 5 reels.
Snowy Baker, Brownie Vernon, Charles Villiers, Wilfred Lucas.

Rev. Harland, a former prizefighter, tries to win over his congregation with modern methods.

The Better Man (Richard Talmadge Productions/FBO, 1926)
d: Scott R. Dunlap. 5 reels.
Richard Talmadge, Ena Gregory, John Steppling, Margaret Campbell, Herbert Prior, Charles Hill Mailes, Percy Williams.
Sprightly comedy of errors and mistaken identity, with an English lord masquerading as a manservant to an American industrialist.

The Better 'Ole (Warner Bros., 1926)
d: Charles F. Reisner. 9 reels.
Sydney Chaplin, Theodore Lorch, Doris Hill, Harold Goodwin, Jack Ackroyd, Edgar Kennedy, Charles Gerrard.

A British sergeant in World War I discovers that his major is really a German spy. This was the second Warner Bros. film to be presented with a synchronized musical score. *Don Juan* (1926) was the first.

Better Times (Brentwood Film/Exhibitors Mutual, 1919)
d: King Vidor. 5 reels.
ZaSu Pitts, David Butler, Jack McDonald, William DeVaulle, Hugh Fay, George Hackathorne, Georgia Woodthorpe, Julianne Johnstone.
A hotelier's daughter decides to drum up some new business.

The Better Way (Columbia, 1927)
d: Ralph Ince. 6 reels.
Dorothy Revier, Ralph Ince, Eugene Strong, Armand Kaliz, Hazel Howell.

A homely secretary can't get men to notice her. One day she hears a tip on the stock market, invests, and makes a small fortune. Now she gets a beauty makeover and blossoms forth as a livin' doll... and the guys are all trying to date her. But are they interested in her, or in her money?

The Better Wife (Select Pictures Corp., 1918)
d: William P.S. Earle. 5 reels.
Clara Kimball Young, Nigel Barrie, Edward M. Kimball, Kathlyn Williams, Ben Alexander, Lillian Walker, Barbara Tennant, Irving Cummings.
To protect her little stepson from scandal, his new mother hides from her husband the fact that his first wife died while being unfaithful to him.

The Better Woman (Triumph Film Corp./World Film Corp., 1915)
d: Joseph A. Golden. 5 reels.
Lenore Ulrich, Edith Thornton, Lowell Sherman, Ben Graham, Charles Hutchinson, Will Browning.
Starved for romance, an uneducated girl flirts with a bridge engineer. At first he ignores her, but when stung by a romantic setback of his own, he angrily marries her. Now the engineer's bride must decide whether to admit she did a little "engineering" of her own in arranging for that romantic setback.

Bettina Loved a Soldier (Universal, 1916)
d: Rupert Julian. 5 reels.
Francelia Billington, Louise Lovely, Douglas Gerrard, Rupert Julian, Geroge Berrill, Zoe DuRae, Elsie Jane Wilson.
A wealthy American girl goes to France, and is courted by the local males.

Betty and the Buccaneers (American Film Co./Mutual, 1917)
d: Rollin S. Sturgeon. 5 reels.
Juliette Day, Charles Marriott, Joe King, Tote DuCrow, William Kyle, Gordon Russell, Harold Wilson.
Betty fantasizes about exciting adventures, but gets her fill when she goes to sea and gets marooned on a deserted island.

Betty Be Good (Balboa Amusement Producing Co./Mutual, 1917)
d: Sherwood MacDonald. 5 reels.
Jackie Saunders, Arthur Shirley, Leslie T. Peacocke, Mollie McConnell, Mrs. Marsh, Ben Rossier, Dad Voute, William Reed, Mignon LeBrun, Albert B. Ellis.
A spoiled rich girl goes joyriding in her wealthy dad's car, unaware that it carries critically important documents.

Betty in Search of a Thrill (Bosworth, Inc./Paramount, 1915)
d: Phillips Smalley, Lois Weber. 5 reels.
Elsie Janis, Owen Moore, Juanita Hansen, Harry Ham, Roberta Hickman, Herbert Standing, Vera Lewis.
Having just graduated from a convent school, Betty is desperate for excitement. She finds it, in spades, in several ill-advised escapades, including a fling as a cabaret dancer.

Betty of Greystone (Triangle/Fine Arts, 1916)
d: Allan Dwan. 5 reels.
Dorothy Gish, Owen Moore, Kate Bruce, George Fawcett, John Beck, Grace Rankin, Eugene Ormond, Marcey Harlan, Leonore Harris.
A caretaker's daughter falls in love with an aristocrat, but creates a scandal and is forced to leave town. She has the last laugh, though, when she returns married to the heir of Greystone and is accepted as the town's first lady.

Betty Takes a Hand (Triangle, 1918)
d: Jack Dillon. 5 reels.
Olive Thomas, Frederick Vroom, Bliss Chevalier, Mary Warren, George Hernandez, Charles Gunn, Margaret Cullington, Graham Pette, June DeLisle, Anna Dodge.
Believing that her late father was cheated by a business partner, a young woman seeks revenge. She finds love instead, with the son of her dad's former partner.

Betty to the Rescue (Lasky Feature Plays/Paramount, 1917)
d: Frank Reicher. 5 reels.
Fannie Ward, Jack Dean, Lillian Leighton, James Neill, Charles West, Ted Duncan.
An orphan girl's "worthless" mine turns out to contain a rich vein of ore.

Between Dangers (Action Pictures/Pathé, 1927)
d: Richard Thorpe. 5 reels.
Buddy Roosevelt, Alma Rayford, Rennie Young, Al Taylor, Charles Thurston, Allen Sewall, Edward W. Borman, Hank Bell.
An Eastern tenderfoot inherits a ranch in Cactus City. He's robbed on his way West, his ID papers are stolen, and he's unable to prove his claim. Still, the sheriff's pretty daughter believes in him and helps the tenderfoot regain his property.

Between Friends (Vitagraph, 1924)
d: J. Stuart Blackton. 7 reels.
Lou Tellegen, Anna Q. Nilsson, Norman Kerry, Alice Calhoun, Stuart Holmes, Henry Barrows.
After Jessica elopes with her artist husband's best friend, she suffers pangs of remorse and commits suicide.

Between Men (New York Motion Picture Co./Triangle, 1916)
d: William S. Hart. 5 reels.
William S. Hart, Enid Markey, House Peters, J. Barney Sherry, Bert Wesner, Robert McKim.
A westerner journeys east to help an old friend battle a ruthless business rival.

Beulah (Balboa Amusement/Alliance Films, 1915)
d: Bertram Bracken. 6 reels.
Henry B. Walthall, Joyce Moore, Mae Prestell, Clifford Gray, Marguerite Nichols, Elsie Allen, Gypsy Abbott, Corinne Grant, Leopold Medan, Mollie McConnell, Henry Stanley.
Adopted by a kind doctor, an orphan girl must deal with the barbs of his jealous kin.

Beverly of Graustark (Cosmopolitan/MGM, 1926)
d: Sidney Franklin. 7 reels. (Part color.)
Marion Davies, Antonio Moreno, Creighton Hale, Roy D'Arcy.
A girl tries to stand in for her male cousin, the Prince of Graustark, while he mends from a skiing accident.

Beware (Warner Bros., 1919)
d: William Nigh. 9 reels.
Maurine Powers, Regina Quinn, Leslie Ryecroft, William Nigh, Frank Norcross, Julia Hurley, Halbert W. Brown, Herbert Standing.
Following World War I, Kaiser Wilhelm is depicted as being on trial before an international tribunal.

Beware of Bachelors (Warner Bros., 1928)
d: Roy Del Ruth. 6 reels.
Audrey Ferris, William Collier Jr., Tom Ricketts, Andre Beranger, Clyde Cook, Dave Morris, Margaret Livingston.
A young couple are due for a financial windfall if they remain married for at least one year... otherwise, the money goes to a relative. The relative, naturally, is keen to break up the marriage.

Beware of Blondes (Columbia, 1928)
d: George B. Seitz. 6 reels.
Dorothy Revier, Matt Moore, Hazel Howell.
A jewelry store clerk vacations in Hawaii, and meets a blonde girl who may be a thief.

Beware of Married Men (Warner Bros., 1928)
d: Archie L. Mayo. 6 reels.
Irene Rich, Audrey Ferris, Clyde Cook, Myrna Loy, Richard Tucker, Stuart Holmes, Hugh Allan.
Myra, secretary to a famous divorce lawyer, tries to rescue her sister from the advances of a predatory married man. She succeeds, but then finds that she herself is the predator's next target.

Beware of Strangers (Selig Polyscope, 1917)
d: Colin Campbell. 8 reels.
Fritzi Brunette, Thomas Santschi, Bessie Eyton, Edward Coxen, Jack Richardson, Vivian Rich, Al W. Filson, Frank Clark, Eugenie Besserer, Harry Lonsdale.
A respected businessman is actually a master criminal.

Beware of the Bride (Fox, 1920)
d: Howard M. Mitchell. 5 reels.
Eileen Percy, Walter McGrail, Hallam Cooley, Harry Dunkinson, Jane Miller, Ethel Shannon, George W. Banta.
While a businessman's work interferes with his honeymoon, his bride whiles away her time at a masquerade ball.

Beware of the Law (Jawitz Pictures, 1922)
d: W.A.S. Douglas. 5 reels.
Marjorie Payne, William Coughey, Henry Van Bousen, Ann Deering, D.W. Reyolds, John Altieri, Willard Cooley.
In the woods, a forester discovers a wounded federal agent, and nurses him back to health. Ironically, the agent is on the trail of moonshiners, one of whom is the father of the forester's sweetheart.

Beware of Widows (Universal, 1927)
d: Wesley Ruggles. 6 reels.
Laura LaPlante, Bryant Washburn, Paulette Duval, Walter Hiers, Tully Marshall, Kathryn Carver, Heinie Conklin, Otto Hoffman.
Romantic comedy about Joyce, a girl who breaks up with her fiancé because she suspects him of fooling around with married women. But despite precipitating their separation, Joyce isn't all that ready to give up on her young man.

Beyond (Famous Players-Lasky/Paramount, 1921)
d: William D. Taylor. 5 reels.
Ethel Clayton, Charles Meredith, Earl Schenck, Fontaine LaRue, Winifred Kingston, Lillian Rich, Charles French, Spottiswoode Aitken, Herbert Fortier.
On her way home to her fiancé in England, a young woman is shipwrecked and washed up on a desert island. Her disconsolate fiancé believes her dead, finds solace in another woman's arms, and marries her. One year later, the castaway is rescued and returns to England. Upon finding her sweetheart married to another woman, she decides not to complicate his life by re-entering it.

Beyond London Lights (FBO Pictures, 1928)
d: Tom Terriss. 6 reels.
Adrienne Dore, Lee Shumway, Gordon Elliott, Herbert Evans, Jacqueline Gadsden, Florence Wix, Templar Saxe, Blanche Craig, Katherine Ward.
Kitty Carstairs, a postmaster's daughter, is engaged to be married, but her fiancé's mother disapproves of her. Made to feel unwanted, Kitty goes to the city and becomes a professional model. When her former fiancé comes to his senses and realizes he still loves Kitty, it's too late. She has already fallen in love with a new beau.

Beyond Price (Fox, 1921)
d: J. Searle Dawley. 5 reels.
Pearl White, Vernon Steel, Nora Reed, Arthur Gordini, Louis Haines, Maude Turner Gordon, Byron Douglas, Ottola Nesmith, Dorothy Walters, Dorothy Allen, J. Thornton Baston, Charles Sutton.
Sally, a restless wife, wishes her life were more exciting and glamorous. She decides to leave her husband, then discovers by a string of rapid-fire occurences that there is such a thing as too much excitement. Gratefully, she returns to her husband before he knows she has left.

Beyond the Border (Ragstrom Productions, 1925)
d: Scott R. Dunlap. 5 reels.
Harry Carey, Mildred Harris, Tom Santschi, Jack Richardson, William Scott.
Out West, a sheriff unjustly accused of corruption must fight to clear his name and his reputation.

Beyond the Crossroads (Pioneer Film Corp., 1922)
d: Lloyd Carleton. 5 reels.
Ora Carew, Lawson Butt, Melbourne MacDowell, Stuart Morris.
A businessman returns home from a trip and finds his wife has left him for another man.

Beyond the Law (Southern Feature Film Corp., 1918)
d: Theodore Marston. 6 reels.
Emmett Dalton, Harris Gordon, Ida Pardee, William Dunn, Mabel Bordine, Jack O'Loughlin, Dick Clark, Virginia Lee.
Out West, the Dalton brothers turn to a life of crime.

Beyond the Rainbow (Robertson-Cole Pictures, 1922)d: William Christy Cabanne. 6 reels.Harry Morey, Billie Dove, Virginia Lee, Diana Allen, James Harrison, Macey Harlam, Rose Coughlan, William Tooker, George Fawcett, Marguerite Courtot, Edmund Breese, Walter Miller, Charles Craig, Clara Bow, Huntley Gordon.
Marion, a secretary who needs money to care for her sick brother, agrees to a scheme that will pay her $250. She is to impersonate a famous flirt at a society ball, hoping to lure wealthy investors to her benefactor's business.

Beyond the Rockies (Independent Pictures, 1926)
d: Jack Nelson. 5 reels.
Bob Custer, Eugenie Gilbert, David Dunbar, Bruce Gordon, Milton Ross, Eddie Harris, Max Holcomb, Roy Laidlaw, Max Asher.
An agent employed by a cattlemen's association infiltrates a gang of rustlers.

Beyond the Rocks (Famous Players-Lasky, 1922)
d: Sam Wood. 7 reels.
Rudolph Valentino, Gloria Swanson, Edythe Chapman, Alec B. Francis, Robert Bolder, Mabel Van Buren, Gertrude Astor, Helen Dunbar, Raymond Blathwayt, F.R. Butler, June Elvidge.
While mountain climbing in the Alps, a married woman is rescued by a dashing young nobleman. They fall in love, but restrain themselves out of respect for the woman's marriage vows.

Beyond the Shadows (Triangel, 1918)
d: J.W. McLaughlin. 5 reels.
William Desmond, Josie Sedgwick, Ed Brady, Graham Pette,

Hugh Sutherland, Bert Apling, Ben Lewis, John Wild, John Lince, Alberta Lee.

In the Canadian Northwest, brothers become involved in a fur traders' war.

Beyond the Sierras (MGM, 1928)
d: Nick Grinde. 6 reels.
Tim McCoy, Sylvia Beecher, Polly Moran, Roy D'Arcy, Richard R. Neill.
Out West, a mysterious masked man rides to the rescue of homesteaders threatened by claim jumpers.

Beyond the Trail (Chesterfield Motion Picture Corp., 1926)
d: Al Herman. 5 reels.
Bill Patton, Eric Wayne, Janet Dawn, Sheldon Lewis, Stuart Holmes, Clara Horton, James F. Fulton.
In this light-hearted western, a bumbling hired hand must rescue a ranch lady from black-hearted villains.

Biff Bang Buddy (Approved Pictures/Artclass, 1924)
d: Frank L. Inghram. 5 reels.
Buddy Roosevelt, Jean Arthur, Buck Connors, Robert Fleming, Al Richmond.
Out West, a lone cowpoke rescues a young woman from attackers.

The Big Adventure (Universal, 1921)
d: Reaves Eason. 5 reels.
Breezy Eason Jr., Fred Herzog, Lee Shumway, Molly Shafer, Gertrude Olmstead.
Patches, a slum orphan, rescues Sally, a judge's daughter, from kidnappers.

Big Brother (Famous Players-Lasky/Paramount, 1923)
d: Allan Dwan. 7 reels.
Tom Moore, Edith Roberts, Raymond Hatton, Joe King, Mickey Bennett, Charles Henderson, Paul Panzer, Neill Kelley, William Black, Martin Faust, Milton Herman.
Donovan, a notorious gangster, becomes guardian to Midge, a 7-year-old boy, and decides to reform in order to raise the lad properly. The authorities have their doubts about Donovan, but he allays their fears by recovering a stolen payroll and becoming a hero.

The Big City (MGM, 1927)
d: Tod Browning. 7 reels.
Lon Chaney, Betty Compson, James Murray, Marceline Day.
A sinister cabaret owner secretly runs a jewelry-theft operation.

Big Dan (Fox, 1923)
d: William A. Wellman. 6 reels.
Charles Jones, Marian Nixon, Ben Hendricks, Trilby Clark, Jacqueline Gadsden, Charles Coleman, Lydia Yeamans Titus, Monte Collins, Charles Smiley, Harry Lonsdale, J.P. Lockney.
"Big Dan," a World War veteran, turns his ranch into a boys' camp and teaches them boxing.

The Big Diamond Robbery (FBO Pictures/RKO Productions, 1929)
d: Eugene Forde. 7 reels.
Tom Mix, Kathryn McGuire, Frank Beal, Martha Mattox, Ernest Hilliard, Barney Furey, Ethan Laidlaw.
Tom, a ranch foreman, fights off diamond thieves and rescues his boss' daughter in a race with a runaway stagecoach.

Big Game (Metro, 1921)
d: Dallas M. Fitzgerald. 6 reels.

May Allison, Forrest Stanley, Edward Cecil, Zeffie Tilbury, William Elmer, Sidney D'Albrook.
In the Canadian northwest, a pampered Boston fop must prove he is a real man when his wife is assaulted by a would-be seducer.

Big Happiness (Farnum Productions/Robertson-Cole, 1920)
d: Colin Campbell. 7 reels.
Dustin Farnum, Kathryn Adams, Fred Malatesta, Violet Schram, Joseph J. Dowling, William H. Brown, Aggie Herring.
Farnum has a double role as brothers: one loveable, the other his evil twin.

The Big Hop (Buck Jones Productions, 1928)
d: James W. Horne. 7 reels.
Buck Jones, Jobyna Ralston, Ernest Hilliard, Charles K. French, Charles Clary, Duke Lee, Edward Hearne, Jack Dill.
Buck, a devil-may-care aviator, falls for the daughter of his wealthy backer in a high-stakes airplane race.

Big Jim Garrity (Pathé, 1916)
d: George Fitzmaurice. 5 reels.
Robert Edeson, Eleanor Woodruff, Carl Harbaugh, Lyster Chambers, Charles Compton, Carleton Macey.
Cocaine addiction threatens a miner's business, and even his wife.

The Big Killing (Paramount, 1928)
d: F. Richard Jones. 6 reels.
Wallace Beery, Raymond Hatton, Anders Randolph, Mary Brian, Gardner James, Lane Chandler, Paul McAllister, James Mason, Ralph Yearsley, Ethan Laidlaw, Leo Willis.
Feuding mountain families bury the shotgun when the son of one clan marries the daughter of the other.

The Big Little Person (Universal, 1919)
d: Robert Z. Leonard.
Mae Murray, M. Rodolpho De Valentina, Clarissa Selwynne, Allan Sears, Mrs. Bertram Grassby.
A teacher contracts scarlet fever and loses her hearing. But she finds love in spite of her handicap.

The Big Noise (First National, 1928)
d: Allan Dwan. 8 reels.
Chester Conklin, Alice White, Bodil Rossing, Sam Hardy, Jack Egan, Ned Sparks, David Torrence.
In New York, a subway policeman wants to marry off his daughter to the son of his friend... but the young lady has other ideas.

The Big Parade (MGM, 1925)
d: King Vidor. 12 reels.
John Gilbert, Renee Adoree, Hobart Bosworth, Claire McDowell, Tom O'Brien, Claire Adams, Robert Ober, Karl Dane, Rosita Marstini.
A wealthy young man joins the army when World War I breaks out, and is assigned to France. He falls in love with a French farm girl, even though he knows he's expected to marry a girl back home.

The Big Punch (Fox, 1921)
d: Jack Ford. 5 reels.
Buck Jones, Barbara Bedford, George Siegmann, Jack Curtis, Jack McDonald, Jennie Lee, Edgar Jones, Irene Hunt, Eleanore Gilmore.
Buck, a paroled prisoner, falls for a Salvation Army girl.

The Big Sister (Famous Players/Paramount, 1916)

d: John B. O'Brien. 5 reels.
Mae Murray, Matty Roubert, Harry C. Browne, Ida Darling, Armand Cortes, Tammany Young, Florence Flinn, Joe Gleason, J. Albert Hall.
On the run from a white slaver, a girl and her younger brother find refuge in a wealthy man's home.

Big Stakes (Clifford S. Elfelt Productions, 1922)
d: Clifford S. Elfelt. 6 reels.
J.B. Warner, Elinor Fair, Wilamae Carson, Les Bates, H.S. Karr, Robert H. Gray.
Love is the prize when a cowboy and a villain square off in a contest to win a lady's hand.

Big Timber (Morosco Photoplays/Paramount, 1917)
d: William D. Taylor. 5 reels.
Kathlyn Williams, Wallace Reid, Joe King, Alfred Paget, Helen Bray.
A former concert singer loses her voice, and takes a job as cook in a lumber camp.

Big Timber (Universal, 1924)
d: William J. Craft. 5 reels.
William Desmond, Olive Hasbrouck, Betty Francisco, Ivor McFadden, Lydia Yeamans Titus, Albert J. Smith.
Northwest melodrama about a city boy traveling to timber company and doing battle with villainous lumberjacks.

Big Town Ideas (Fox, 1921)
d: Carl Harbaugh. 5 reels.
Eileen Percy, Kenneth Gibson, Jimmie Parrott, Lon Poff, Laura LaPlante, Leo Sulky, Harry DeRoy, Lefty James, Larry Bowes, Paul Kamp, Paul Cazeneuve, Wilson Hummell.
Farce about a lovestruck waitress who falls for a jail-bound prisoner, decides he's really innocent, and contrives to get him released from prison.

Big Town Round-Up (Fox, 1921)
d: Lynn Reynolds. 5 reels.
Tom Mix, Gilbert Holmes, Ora Carew, Harry Dunkinson, Laura LaPlante, William Buckley, William Elmer, William Crinley.
Larry, an Arizona rancher, is smitten with a vacationing San Francisco heiress.

Big Tremaine (Yorke Film Corp./Metro, 1916)
d: Henry Otto. 5 reels.
Harold Lockwood, May Allison, Lester Cuneo, Albert Ellis, Lillian Hayward, William Ephe, Andrew Arbuckle, Josephine Rice, William DeVaull, Virginia Southern.
A plantation owner, still smarting over a romantic setback, falls in love again.

The Bigger Man (Rolfe Photoplays/Metro, 1915)
d: John W. Noble. 5 reels.
Henry Kolker, Renee Kelly, Orlando Daly, Elsie Balfour, J.H. Goldsworthy, Mayme Kelso, Edwin Boring, Richard Lee.
Heavily symbolic tale of the eternal squabble between labor and management, beginning with scenes from the caveman days and the Biblical era, and continuing to modern times.

Bigger Than Barnum's (R-C Pictures/F.B.O. of America, 1926)
d: Ralph Ince. 6 reels.
Viola Dana, Ralph Lewis, George O'Hara, Ralph Ince, Lucille Mendez, Dan Makarenko, George Holt, William Knight, Rhody Hathaway.
After a circus tightrope walker refuses to perform without a net, he is branded a coward and leaves the circus. Much

later, the "coward" is present when a hotel catches fire, and breaking through the crowd, he walks across a telephone wire and rescues his father from the flames.

The Biggest Show on Earth (Thomas H. Ince/Paramount, 1918)
d: Jerome Storm. 5 reels.
Enid Bennett, Earl Rodney, Ethel Lynn, Bliss Chevalier, Carl Stockdale, Melbourne MacDowell, Jack Nelson.
Roxie's a lion tamer in a circus. When she falls in love with a scion of wealth, his social-climbing mother instantly disapproves.

Bill Apperson's Boy (Jack Pickford/First National, 1919)
d: James Kirkwood. 6 reels.
Jack Pickford, Russell Simpson, Gloria Hope, George Nicholls.
A young man whose mother has died just can't warm up to his dad's new wife.

Bill Henry (Thomas H. Ince/Paramount, 1919)
d: Jerome Storm. 5 reels.
Charles Ray, Edith Roberts, William Carroll, Bert Woodruff, Jennie Lee Courtright, Walter Perkins, Walter Hiers.
When he learns that the girl he loves has inherited a worthless swamp, a hotel clerk offers to buy it from her. He does, and they discover the land is an oil field.

Billions (Metro, 1920)
d: Ray C. Smallwood. 6 reels.
Nazimova, Charles Bryant, William J. Irving, Victor Potel, John Steppling, Marian Skinner, Bonnie Hill, Emmett King, Eugene H. Klum.
Money—too much of it—is an impediment to the romance between a Russian princess and an American poet. Eventually both lose their fortunes, and feel free to proclaim their love for each other.

Billy and the Big Stick (Thomas A. Edison, Inc., 1917)
d: Edward H. Griffith. 4 reels.
Raymond McKee, Yona Landowska, William Wadsworth, Jessie Stevens, Bradley Barker, Joseph Burke.
It's "Lights Out!" in Haiti, when the president refuses to pay his electric bills.

Billy Jim (Fred Stone Productions/R-C Pictures, 1922)
d: Frank Borzage. 5 reels.
Fred Stone, Millicent Fisher, George Hernandez, William Bletcher, Marian Skinner, Frank Thorne.
Billy Jim, seemingly a lonesome cowpoke, is actually an incognito millionaire.

Bing Bang Boom (Sol Lesser Productions, 1922)
d: Fred J. Butler. 5 reels.
David Butler, Doris Pawn, Edwin Wallock, Kate Toncray, Jack Carlyle, Carl Stockdale, William Walling, Bert Hadley, William Duvall.
Bertrand Boom, nicknamed "Bing Bang," is persuaded to buy a country hotel, sight unseen. He soon discovers he's been taken for a ride, but recovers by turning the place into a health resort and promoting it, successfully, to wealthy customers.

A Bird of Prey (Thanhouser Film Corp./Mutual, 1916)
d: Eugene Nowland. 5 reels.
John Lehnberg, Kathryn Adams, Robert Whittier, Tula Belle, Madeline Fairbanks.
After a disenchanted wife leaves her husband and runs away with his unscrupulous business associate, the husband

tries to track them down. Instead of finding the couple, he finds their abandoned baby daughter, and raises her as his own.

The Bird of Prey (Fox, 1918)
d: Edward J. Le Saint. 5 reels.
Gladys Brockwell, Herbert Heyes, L.C. Shumway, Willard Louis.
An American man and woman who dislike each other find themselves in Mexico, united in trying to escape murderous bandidos.

Birds of Prey (Columbia, 1927)
d: William James Craft. 6 reels.
William H. Tooker, Hugh Allen, Priscilla Dean, Ben Hendricks Jr., Gustav von Seyffertitz, Sidney Bracey, Fritz Becker.
Smith, formerly a prosperous big city banker, conspires with an underworld gang to rob his bank in an attempt to cover up the shortages in his accounts. But his son, who's unaware of the plot, outwits the bandits, locks them in the vault, and falls in love with the female member of the gang.

The Birth of a Man (Balboa Amusement Producing Co., 1916)
d: Harry Harvey. 5 reels.
Henry Walthall, Joyce Moore, Henry Stanley, Jay Herman, Dick Johnson, William Reed, William Sheer.
When a selfish and self-righteous millionaire finds himself robbed and in tatters, he gets a new perspective on life.

The Birth of a Nation (Griffith/Epoch, 1915)
w, d: D. W. Griffith. 12 reels.

Henry B. Walthall, Mae Marsh, Miriam Cooper, Lillian Gish, Wallace Reid, Donald Crisp, Raoul Walsh, Eugene Pallette, Walter Long.

Famous epic recounting events leading up to the American Civil War, the war itself, and its effects on families of the survivors. The film was originally titled *The Clansman*, based on the Thomas Dixon Jr. novel of that name, but its title was changed to *The Birth of a Nation* for its New York opening, and it has been known by that title ever since.
Scholars have called *The Birth of a Nation* "the single most important film of all time." It arrived on the scene at a time when motion pictures were still considered little better than arcade peep shows, yet with this one film Griffith established the motion picture as art. Its many contributions include the introduction of night photography, definitive use of the still shot and the closeup, extensive use of tracking shots, and heart-rendingly beautiful imagery that conveys with a frame of film what thousands of words are inadequate to say.
But *The Birth of a Nation* has also been condemned as racist in its depiction of several of the black characters as evil, lecherous, or shiftless, particularly in the film's second half. This criticism was intensified during the decades when America was becoming more liberal in its race relations; indeed, the film was condemned by the NAACP as "the meanest vilification of the Negro race."
Significantly, all the complaints about the film's racial insensitivity—some of them justified—have done nothing to diminish the stature of *The Birth of a Nation* as an important milestone of filmmaking. Its honors are many and have come from all directions, but perhaps one small example can put the matter in perspective. In the 1976 Peter Bogdanovich film *Nickelodeon*, an affectionate tribute to the earliest days of the movies, a small group of film makers take a break from their labors to attend the premiere of *The Clansman*. They, like the other audience members, are overwhelmed by the artistry they see on the screen. Afterwards, none of them feel much like making movies any more. One character puts the group's thoughts into words: "Might as well quit. The best damn picture that's ever gonna be made, has already been made."

The Birth of a Soul (Vitagraph, 1920)
d: Edwin L. Hollywood. 5 reels.
Harry T. Morey, Jean Paige, Charles Eldridge, George Cooper, Charles Kent, Walter Lewis, Robert Gaillard, Bernard Siegel.
In an updated and Americanized variant on *A Tale of Two Cities*, a rejected lover trades places with his lookalike rival for the lady's hand, and goes to his death by hanging. Double role for Harry T. Morey.

The Birth of Patriotism (Universal, 1917)
d: E. Magnus Ingleton. 5 reels.
Irene Hunt, Ann Kronan, Ernie Shields, Leo Pierson, Frank Coffray, Lydia Yeamans Titus, Edward Brown.
Feeling unsure of himself, a man leaves his wife and takes up with the innkeeper's daughter. But the start of World War I brings out the man's innate decency, and he enlists in the Army.

Birthright (Hemmer Superior Productions, 1920)
d: Edward Hemmer. 5 reels.
Maud Sylvester, Flora Finch, Sidney Mason, Pete Raymond, Margaret Beecher, Henry Sedley, Milton Berlinger, Mabel Wright, Horace Weston, Norman Wells, Opie Reed, John A. Boone, Bessie Stinson.
An orphaned girl leaves her small town and strikes out on her own, in search of her birthright.

Birthright (Micheaux Film Corp., 1924)
d: Oscar Micheaux. 10 reels.
J. Homer Tutt, Evelyn Preer, Salem Tutt Whitney, Lawrence Chenault, W.B.F. Crowell.
A noble black youth graduates from Harvard, but his college education has left him ill-prepared for the bigotry he encounters on the outside.

The Bishop of the Ozarks (Cosmopolitan/FBO of America, 1923)
d: Finis Fox. 6 reels.
Milford W. Howard, Derelys Perdue, Cecil Holland, William Kenton, R.D. MacLean, Mrs. Milo Adams, Rosa Melville, Fred Kelsey, George Reed.
An escaped convict masquerades as a minister and finds to his surprise that he is well-suited to life as a country parson.

The Bishop's Emeralds (Pathé, 1919)
d: John B. O'Brien. 6 reels.
Virginia Pearson, Robert Broderick, Frank Kingsley, Lucy Fox, Marcia Harris, Walter Newman, Sheldon Lewis.
The son of an Anglican bishop is engaged to be married, but questions are raised about the young lady's parentage.

A Bit O' Heaven (Frieder Film Corp., 1917)
d: Lule Warrenton. 5 reels.
Mary Louise, Harold Skinner, Ella Gilbert, Donald Watson, Madeline Eastin, Carl Miller, Mary Talbot, Gertrude Short, Roy Clark, Gertrude Messinger, John Starling, Marvel Spencer.
A 9-year-old crippled girl has her family invite a poor family over for Christmas dinner.

THE BIRTH OF A NATION (1915). During a lull between the calamities that beset them, Henry B. Walthall and Lillian Gish flirt shamelessly while caressing a pigeon.

* * * * *

A Bit of Heaven (Excellent Pictures, 1928)
d: Cliff Wheeler. 7 reels.
Bryant Washburn, Lila Lee, Martha Mattox, Lucy Beaumont, Richard Tucker, Otto Lederer, Jacqueline Gadsdon, Sybil Grove, Edwin Argus.
Roger marries Fola, a Broadway dancer, though his wealthy family severely disapproves of him marrying "beneath his station."

A Bit of Jade (American Film Co./Mutual Film Corp., 1918)
d: Edward S. Sloman. 5 reels.
Mary Miles Minter, Alan Forrest, David Howard, Vera Lewis, Alfred Ferguson, Clarence Burton.
An innocent mixup of overcoats touches off a frantic jewel hunt, involving a girl dressed in a man's clothing, a Hindu idol, and attempted mayhem.

A Bit of Kindling (Mutual, 1917)
d: Sherwood Macdonald. 5 reels.
Jackie Saunders, Arthur Shirley, J.P. Wade, Charles Dudley, Ethel Ritchey, Edward Jobson, H.C. Russell, Daniel Gilfether.
"Sticks," a tough little tomboy news vendor, sticks up for her favorite customer when thugs try to rob him. They both get knocked unconscious, then upon awakening they bond like old buddies. You can bet there's romance in their future.

Bits of Life (First National, 1921)
d: Marshall Neilan. 6 reels.
Wesley Barry, Rockliffe Fellowes, Lon Chaney, Noah Beery, Anna May Wong, John Bowers, Teddy Sampson, Dorothy Mackaill, Edythe Chapman, Frederick Burton, James Bradbury Jr., Tammany Young, Harriet Hammond, James Neill, Scott Welsh.
Anthology film presenting four separate short stories woven together for their irony.

Bitter Apples (Warner Bros., 1927)
w, d: Harry Hoyt. 6 reels.
Monte Blue, Myrna Loy.
A misguided young woman sets out to avenge her father's suicide against the man she considers responsible. Instead, she falls in love with him.

Bitter Sweets (Peerless Pictures, 1928)
d: Charles Hutchison. 6 reels.
Barbara Bedford, Ralph Graves, Crauford Kent, Joy McKnight, Ethan Laidlaw, Frank Crane, Richard Belfield, John Dillon, Oscar Smith.
Bitter society drama, about a blackmailer who holds incriminating love letters written by an heiress.

The Bitter Truth (Fox, 1917)
d: Kenean Buel. 6 reels.
Virginia Pearson, Jack Hopkins, William H. Tooker, Alice May, Sidney d'Albrook.
A young woman sentenced to prison plots an extraordinary revenge against the judge. Instead, she falls in love with him.

The Black Bag (Universal, 1922)
d: Stuart Paton. 5 reels.
Herbert Rawlinson, Ben Roach, Virginia Valli, Clara Beyers, Charles L. King, Herbert Fortier, Lew Short, Jack O'Brien.
Society mystery about a "stolen" diamond necklace which turns out not to be stolen after all.

Black Beauty (Vitagraph, 1921)
d: David Smith. 7 reels.
Jean Paige, James Morrison, George Webb, Bobby Mack, John Steppling, Capt. Leslie T. Peacock, Adele Farrington, Charles Morrison, Molly McConnell, Colin Kenny, Georgia French.
Heart-warming drama based on the famous Anna Sewell story of a black colt that grows to become a valuable thoroughbred, and the people who love him.

The Black Bird (MGM, 1926)
d: Tod Browning. 7 reels.
Lon Chaney, Renee Adoree, Doris Lloyd, Andy MacLennan, William Weston, Eric Mayne, Sidney Bracy, Ernie S. Adams, Owen Moore, Lionel Belmore, Billy Mack, Peggy Best.
Chaney plays a character called "the Black Bird," a master thief in the Limehouse district of London. But the Black Bird hides behind a second identity, as a cripple who runs a rescue mission.

Black Butterflies (Quality Distributing Corp., 1928)
d: James W. Horne. 7 reels.
Jobyna Ralston, Mae Busch, Robert Frazer, Lila Lee, Cosmo Kyrle Bellew, Robert Ober, Ray Hallor, George Periolat.
Wealthy Dorinda seeks her kicks with a shady group of thrill-seekers known as "The Black Butterflies."

The Black Butterfly (Metro, 1916)
d: Burton L. King. 5 reels.
Mme. Petrova, Mahlon Hamilton, Anthony Merlo, Count Lewenhaupt, Edward Brennan, Violet B. Reed, John Hopkins, Morgan Jones, Norman Kaiser, Roy Pilcher, Evelyn Dumo.
An opera star billed as "The Black Butterfly" falls in love with a man who had once loved a younger woman and left her. As their affair develops, the soprano comes to learn that her lover's former inamorata is none other than her own daughter.

The Black Circle (World Film Corp., 1919)
d: Frank Reicher. 5 reels.
Creighton Hale, Virginia Valli, Jack Drumier, Walter Horton, Clarette Clare, Edwin Denison, John Davidson, Carl Sauerman, Eva Gordon, Adolph Millar.
Crusading newshounds expose a gang of smugglers noted for giving its foes "the Black Circle"—a mark symbolizing death.

The Black Crook (Kalem, 1916)
d: Julian Alfred. 5 reels.
E.P. Sullivan, Gladys Coburn, Roland Bottomley, Henry Hallem, Charles DeForrest, Mae Thompson, Frank Leonard, Helen Lindroth.
In a Faust-like scenario, a man makes a pact with the devil.

Black Cyclone (Hal Roach, 1925)
d: Fred Jackman. 5 reels.
Guinn Williams, Kathleen Collins, Christian Frank.
A cowboy and his faithful horse save the heroine from disaster.

Black Diamond Express (Warner Bros., 1927)
d: Howard Bretherton. 6 reels.
Monte Blue, Edna Murphy, Myrtle Stedman, Claire McDowell, William Demarest, J.W. Johnston, Carroll Nye.
Dan, a railroad engineer, meets and falls for Jeanne, an heiress. She's willing to break her engagement to a society swell and marry Dan, but her snobbish mother intervenes and Jeanne is forced to go through with her wedding. Fate will bring them together again, however, when Dan is

assigned to drive the train carrying Jeanne and her new husband. Train robbers attack, and Dan is forced to risk his life to protect the newlyweds.

Black Fear (Rolfe Photoplays, Inc./Metro, 1915)
w,d: John W. Noble. 5 reels.
Grace Ellison, Grace Valentine, Edward Brennan, Paul Everton, Frank Hannah, John Tansey, Mrs. Allan Walker, Edwin Polk, Albert Hackett, Del Lewis.
Cocaine addiction leads to the death of a messenger boy, and to the disgrace of his sisters.

Black Friday (Universal, 1916)
d: Lloyd Carleton. 5 reels.
Dorothy Davenport, Richard Morris, Wilfred Roger, Mrs. Maurese, Emory Johnson, Gretchen Lederer, Virginia Southern, Marc Fenton.
During the financial panic of 1869, a businessman learns that his wife has been targeted for seduction by one of his own associates.

The Black Gate (Vitagraph, 1919)
d: Theodore Marston. 5 reels.
Earle Williams, Ruth Clifford, Harry Spingler, Park Jones, Clarissa Selwyn, Brinsley Shaw, J. Barney Sherry.
A womanizing impresario is shot and killed while trying to rape a young charmer. The police take a suspect into custody, and it appears likely he will eventually enter "the black gate," i.e., the door to the death chamber. But another man steps forward and offers to confess to the crime, if the suspect's family will pay $100,000 to his brother.

Black is White (Thomas H. Ince/Paramount, 1920)
d: Charles Giblyn. 6 reels.
Dorothy Dalton, Claire Mersereau, Lillian Lawrence, Holmes E. Herbert, Jack Crosby, Joseph Granby, Patrick Barrett, Tom Cameron.
When her husband turns her out, a woman goes to live with her twin sister. The twin dies, and the rejected wife takes her place.

Black Jack (Fox, 1927)
d: Orville O. Dull. 5 reels.
Buck Jones, Barbara Bennett, Theodore Lorch, George Berrell, Harry Cording, William Caress, Buck Moulton, Murdock MacQuarrie, Frank Lanning, Mark Hamilton, Sam Allen.
Out West, a cardsharp helps a girl locate hidden treasure.

Black Lightning (Gotham Productions/Lumas Film Corp., 1924)
d: James P. Hogan. 6 reels.
Clara Bow, Harold Austin, Eddie Philips, Joe Butterworth, Mark Fenton, John Pringle.
A World War veteran falls for a mountain girl.

Black Orchids (Universal, 1916)
d: Rex Ingram. 5 reels.
Cleo Madison, Wedgewood Nowell, Howard Crampton, Richard La Reno, Francis McDonald, William J. Dyer, John George, Joe Martin.
Marie, a convent school girl, loves to flirt when she is home on vacation.

Black Oxen (Frank Lloyd Productions/First National, 1924)
d: Frank Lloyd. 8 reels.
Corinne Griffith, Conway Tearle, Thomas Ricketts, Thomas Guise, Clara Bow, Kate Lester, Harry Mestayer, Lincoln Stedman, Claire McDowell, Alan Hale, Clarissa Selwynne,

Fred Ganbod, Percy Williams, Otto Nelson, Eric Mayne, Otto Lederer, Carmelita Geraghty.
A mysterious woman claims to be an Austrian countess who has had her youth restored by surgery.

The Black Panther's Cub (Ziegfeld Cinema Corp./Equity Pictures, 1921)
d: Emile Chautard. 6 reels.
Florence Reed, Norman Trevor, Henry Stephenson, Paul Ducet,m Don Merrifield, Henry Carvill, Louis Grisel, Eale Foxe, William Roselle, Paula Shay, Halbert Brown, Tyrone Power.
In Paris, a young woman is protected by her adoptive father from the deadly influence of her dissolute mother, mistress of a gambling establishment known as "the Black Panther."

Black Paradise (Fox, 1926)
d: R. William Neill. 5 reels.
Leslie Fenton, Madge Bellamy, Edmund Lowe, Edward Piel, Harvey Clark, Paul Panzer, Marcella Daly, Samuel Blum, Doris Lloyd, Patrick Kelly, Mary Gordon.
Graham, a detective, is shanghaied and winds up on a South Seas island. There he falls in love with the sister of his captor, and the two wind up being the only survivors of a devastating volcanic eruption.

The Black Pearl (Trem Carr Productions/Rayart, 1928)
d: Scott Pembroke. 6 reels.
Lila Lee, Ray Hallor, Carlton Stockdale, Howard Lorenz, Adele Watson, Thomas Curran, Sybil Grove, Lew Short, George French, Baldy Belmont, Art Rowlands.
A black pearl stolen from a sacred Indian statue torments those who possess it.

The Black Pirate (Fairbanks/United Artists, 1926)
d: Albert Parker. 9 reels. (Technicolor.)
Douglas Fairbanks, Billie Dove, Tempe Pigott, Sam DeGrasse, Anders Randolf, Charles Stevens, Donald Crisp.
In one of the first Technicolor films, Fairbanks stars as an athletic nobleman who swears revenge on the pirates who killed his father. He joins forces with another pirate crew, avenges his father's death, and rescues an aristocratic lady, with whom he falls in love.

Black Roses (Hayakawa Feature Play Co./Robertson-Cole, 1921)
d: Colin Campbell. 6 reels.
Sessue Hayakawa, Myrtle Stedman, Tsura Aoki, Andrew Robson, Toyo Fujita, Henry Hebert, Harold Holland, Carrie Clark Ward.
A suave Japanese nobleman is not all he pretends to be. He's really an escaped prisoner who was unjustly convicted of murder, and now he's out to find the real killers and exact his revenge.

Black Shadows (Fox, 1920)
d: Howard M. Mitchell. 5 reels.
Peggy Hyland, Albert Roscoe, Correan Kirkham, Henry J. Hebert, Edwin Booth Tilton, Estelle Evans, Cora Drew.
Hypnotic suggestion turns an innocent young woman into a jewel thief... or so it seems.

A Black Sheep (Selig Polyscope, 1915)
d: Thomas N. Heffron. 5 reels.
Otis Harlan, Rita Gould, Grace Darmond, John Charles, James Bradbury, John D. Murphy, Fred Morley, Lou Kelso, Jack Rollins, Emma Glenwood, Virginia Ainsworth.
A miner in love with a burlesque dancer learns he's in line to inherit two million dollars... but there several conditions

attached. For one thing, he has to become "cultured."

The Black Sheep of the Family   (Universal, 1916)
d: Jay Hunt. 5 reels.
Francelia Billington, Jack Holt, Gilmore Hammond, Paul Byron, Mina Jeffreys, C. Norton Hammond, Mrs. Jay Hunt, Hector V. Sarno, W.F. Musgrave.
A young wife and her former sweetheart enter into a secret arrangement.

Black Tears   (John Gorman Productions/Hollywood Pictures, 1927)
w, d: John Gorman. 6 reels.
Bryant Washburn, Vola Vale, Hedda Hopper, Jack Richardson.
Gold digger meets gold digger... she's a Broadway show girl, he's a man with a mine.

The Black Wolf   (Lasky Feature Plays/Paramount, 1917)
d: Frank Reicher. 5 reels.
Lou Tellegen, Nell Shipman, H.J. Herbert, James Neill, Paul Weigel.
Tale of a Spanish Robin Hood.

The Blackbird   (MGM, 1925)
w, d: Tod Browning. 7 reels.
Lon Chaney, Renee Adoree, Owen Moore, Doris Lloyd, Sidney Bracey, Lionel Belmore.
A Limehouse thief wears a disguise as a cripple with contorted legs. After a theft in which he kills a policeman, he finds his legs have become permanently contorted.

Blackbirds   (Lasky Feature Plays/Paramount, 1915)
d: J.P. McGowan. 5 reels.
Laura Hope Crews, Thomas Meighan, George Gebhardt, Raymond Hatton, Jane Wolf, Florence Dagmar, Evelyn Desmond, Ed Harley, Frederick Wilson.
The son of a famous detective apprehends jewel thieves, thwarts the theft of a priceless oriental rug, and brings two lovers together.

Blackbirds   (Realart Pictures Corp., 1920)
d: Jack Dillon. 5 reels.
Justine Johnstone, William Boyd, Charles Gerard, Jessie Arnold, Walter Walker, Marie Shotwell, Grace Parker, Ada Boshell, Alex Saskins, Mabel Bert.
Remake of the 1915 *Blackbirds*, with some plot alterations.

Blackie's Redemption   (Metro, 1919)
d: John Ince. 5 reels.
Bert Lytell, Alice Lake, Henry Kolker, Bernard Durning, Jack Duffy, William Musgrave, Little Squirrel, Gertrude Short, Ah Toy, Joseph Kilgour.
Boston Blackie, a reformed crook, is framed for jewel theft on the eve of his wedding.

The Blacklist   (Lasky Feature Plays/Paramount, 1916)
d: William C. DeMille. 5 reels.
Blanche Sweet, Charles Clary, Ernest Joy, Billy Elmer, Horace B. Carpenter, Lucien Littlefield, Jane Wolf.
Colorado miners go on strike and elect one of their own to shoot the mining company president.

Blackmail   (Screen Classics, Inc./Metro, 1920)
d: Dallas M. Fitzgerald. 6 reels.
Viola Dana, Alfred Allen, Wyndham Standing, Edward Cecil, Florence Turner, Jack Roi, Lydia Knott, Fred Kelsey.
A female con artist tries to trap a wealthy greenhorn with a breach-of-promise scam, but it backfires when she falls in love with her pigeon's attorney.

Blarney   (MGM, 1926)
d: Marcel de Sano. 6 reels.
Ralph Graves, Renee Adoree, Paulette Duval, Malcolm Waite, Margaret Seddon.
There's much wearin' of the green in this tale of Irish immigrants in New York City.

Blazing Arrows   (Doubleday Productions/Western Pictures Exploitation Co., 1922)
w, d: Henry McCarty. 5 reels.
Lester Cuneo, Francelia Billington, Clark Comstock, Laura Howard, Lafayette McKee, Lew Meehan, Jim O'Neill.
Sky Fire, an Indian studying at Columbia University, falls in love with Martha, a white coed. Their love is doomed because of race prejudice until it is revealed that Sky Fire is actually a white boy who was raised by Indians.

Blazing Days   (Universal, 1927)
d: William Wyler. 5 reels.
Fred Humes, Churchill Ross, Ena Gregory, Bruce Gordon, Eva Thatcher, Bernard Siegel, Dick L'Estrange.
Out West, a stagecoach robbery leads to a relentless manhunt.

Blazing Love   (Fox, 1916)
d: Keenan Buel. 5 reels.
Virginia Pearson, Frank Burbeck, Wilmuth Merkyl, Lew Stern, Frank Goldsmith, George Selby, Louise Huff, Mattie Ferguson.
Malicious gossip ruins the marriage of a woman and her elderly husband when she's accused of seeing a younger man.

The Blazing Trail   (Universal, 1921)
d: Robert Thornby. 5 reels.
Frank Mayo, Frank Holland, Mary Philbin, Verne Winter, Bert Sprotte, Madge Hunt, Lillian Rich, Ray Ripley, Joy Winthrop, Helen Gilmore.
Medical researchers try desperately to develop a serum to cure blood poisoning.

The Blind Adventure   (Vitagraph, 1918)
d: Wesley H. Ruggles. 5 reels.
Edward Earle, Betty Howe, Frank Norcross, William Bailey, Gilbert Rooney, C.A. Stevenson, George Wright, P.D. Standing, Eulalie Jensen, John Sturgeon.
Smitten with a young woman he spied in a restaurant, a man invents a torrid tale of murder and suspense to get her attention. The story is so convincing, the young woman tries to protect him from the law.

Blind Alleys   (Famous Players-Lasky/Paramount, 1927)
d: Frank Tuttle. 6 reels.
Thomas Meighan, Evelyn Brent, Greta Nissen, Hugh Miller, Thomas Chalmers, Tammany Young.
Dan, a sea captain, is injured by an automobile in New York and taken to the hospital. Because he is unconscious, he cannot get word to his young Cuban bride who comes to fear her new husband has abandoned her.

A Blind Bargain   (Goldwyn, 1922)
d: Wallace Worsley. 5 reels.
Lon Chaney, Raymond McKee, Virginia True Boardman, Fontaine LaRue, Jacqueline Logan, Aggie Herring, Virginia Madison.
To raise money for his invalid mother, a struggling author subjects himself to a monstrous experiment by a mad doctor who wants to turn him into an ape man.

The Blind Goddess (Famous Players-Lasky/Paramount, 1926)
d: Victor Fleming.   8 reels.
Jack Holt, Ernest Torrence, Esther Ralston, Louise Dresser, Ward Crane, Richard Tucker, Louis Payne, Charles Clary, Erwin Connelly, Charles Lane.
Political melodrama about a noble district attorney who resigns his post in order to defend his fiancée's mother in a murder trial.

Blind Hearts (Hobart Bosworth Productions/Associated Producers, 1921)
d: Rowland V. Lee.   6 reels.
Hobart Bosworth, Wade Boteler, Irene Blackwell, Colette Forbes, Madge Bellamy, Raymond McKee, William Conklin, Lule Warrenton, Henry Hebert.
Paul and Julia and want to get married, but Julia's father opposes the match because he suspects that the happy couple, unknown to them, are actually half-siblings.

Blind Husbands (Universal, 1919)
d: Erich von Stroheim.   8 reels.
Erich von Stroheim, Francelia Billington, Sam DeGrasse, T.H. Gibson Gowland, Fay Holderness, Ruby Kendrick, Valerie Germonprez, Jack Perrin, Richard Cummings, Louis Fitzroy, William Duvalle, Jack Mathes, Percy Challenger.
An Austrian army officer toys with an American woman's affections.

Blind Love (Aywon Film Corp., 1920)
d: Oliver D. Bailey.   6 reels.
Lucy Cotton, Thurlow Bergen, George LeGuere, Frank O'Connor, Lillian Bacon, Morgan Coman, Edouard Durand, Bert Leigh, James Cullen.
Love blossoms at a resort casino.

Blind Man's Eyes (Metro, 1919)
d: John Ince.   5 reels.
Bert Lytell, Frank Currier, Naomi Childers, Joseph Kilgour, Richard Morris, Morris Foster, Gertrude Claire, Mignon Anderson, Effie Conley.
An unjustly convicted prisoner escapes, and falls in love with the daughter of his blind lawyer. The young lady is so helpful to her father, she is known as "the blind man's eyes."

Blind Man's Holiday (Broadway Star Features/General Film Co., 1917)
d: Martin Justice.   4 reels.
Jean Paige, Carlton King, John Costello, Aida Horton.
A man with a past meets and falls for a mysterious woman.

Blind Man's Luck (Astra Film Corp./Pathé, 1917)
d: George Fitzmaurice.   5 reels.
Mollie King, Earle Foxe, William Riley Hatch, Zeffie Tilbury, Helene Chadwick, Francis Byrne.
When the train they are riding is wrecked and his bride killed, a man agrees to let another passenger pose as his new wife, so that she can avoid a detective who's trailing her.

Blind Wives (Fox, 1920)
d: Charles J. Brabin.   9 reels.
Marc MacDermott, Estelle Taylor, Harry Southern.
Angry because her husband has canceled her credit accounts, a spendthrift wife goes to bed and has nightmares that cure her of her exhorbitant habits.

Blind Youth (National Pictures/Select Pictures, 1920)
d: Edward Sloman, Al Green.   6 reels.
Walter McGrail, Leatrice Joy, Ora Carew, Claire Macdowell,
Joseph Swickard, Buddy Post, Leo White, Helen Howard, Clara Horton, Colin Kenny.
Depressed and contemplating suicide, a sculptor meets a young woman who inspires him to his greatest creation, "Blind Youth."

Blindfold (Fox, 1928)
d: Charles Klein.   6 reels.
Lois Moran, George O'Brien, Maria Alba, Earle Foxe, Don Terry, Fritz Feld, Andy Clyde, Crauford Kent, Robert E. Homans, John Kelly, Phillips Smalley.
After a policeman is discharged for arresting several V.I.P.s with little or no evidence to hold them, he pursues the case as a civilian. With the help of a young lady who was one of the crime gang's victims, he uncovers enough evidence to return the culprits to custody and get back his job on the force.

Blindfolded (Paralta Plays, Inc./W.W. Hodkinson, 1918)
d: Raymond B. West.   5 reels.
Bessie Barriscale, Joseph J. Dowling, Patrick Calhoun, David Kirby, Jay Morley, Edward Coxen, Helen Dunbar, H.M. O'Connor.
A female safecracker wants to pull off one last job, then go straight.

The Blinding Trail (Universal, 1919)
d: Paul Powell.   6 reels.
Monroe Salisbury, Claire Anderson, Helen Jerome Eddy, Arthur Maude, Johnnie Cooke, Alfred Allen, Milton Markwell.
In a logging camp, a worker is temporarily blinded during an accident, but he marries the boss' daughter anyway.

The Blindness of Devotion (Fox, 1915)
d: J. Gordon Edwards.   5 reels.
Robert B. Mantell, Genevieve Hamper, Stuart Holmes, Claire Whitney, Henry Leone, Charles Young, Jack Standing.
Downbeat, labyrinthine plot includes foster siblings in love with each other; an amoral temptress marrying a Count but secretly romancing his adopted son; another couple marrying "in name only" out of a sense of duty; poison; strangulation; and suicide.

The Blindness of Divorce (Fox, 1918)
d: Frank Lloyd.   6 reels.
Charles Clary, Rhea Mitchell, Nancy Caswell, Bertram Grassby, Marc Robbins, Willard Louis, Fred Church, Al Fremont, Bertha Mann.
Suspicion of infidelity drives a man to divorce his wife, but he's got it wrong.

The Blindness of Love (Rolfe Photoplays, Inc./Metro, 1916)
d: Charles Horan.   5 reels.
Julius Steger, George Le Guere, Grace Valentine, Edgar L. Davenport, Walter Hitchcock, Maud Hill, Charles F. Gotthold, Harry Neville.
A widowed piano maker gives all his love and support to his son, even after the boy repeatedly disappoints him.

The Blindness of Virtue (Essanay, 1915)
d: Joseph Byron Totten.   5 reels.
Bryant Washburn, Edna Mayo, Thomas MacLarnie, George Le Guere, Betty Brown, Renee Noel, John Cossar, Harry Dunkinson, Betty Scott.
A girl with no knowledge about sexual matters cozies up to a young cad.

THE BLACK PIRATE (1926). Douglas Fairbanks, as The Black Pirate, exhorts his fellow buccaneers to hold the captured princess (Billie Dove) for ransom, rather than ravage her in the accustomed manner of sea brigands. He's secretly on her side, trying to save her life. *The Black Pirate* was one of the few silent feature films photographed entirely in Technicolor.

* * * * *

Blinky (Universal, 1923)
d: Edward Sedgwick. 6 reels.
Hoot Gibson, Esther Ralston, Mathilde Brundage, DeWitt Jennings, Elinor Field, Donald Hatswell, Charles K. French, John Judd, William E. Lawrence, W.T. McCulley.
"Blinky," a cavalryman and a former scout, solves a case and rescues an officer's daughter from kidnappers... using Boy Scout techniques.

The Block Signal (Gotham Productions/Lumas Film Corp., 1926)
d: Frank O'Connor. 6 reels.
Ralph Lewis, Jean Arthur, Hugh Allan, George Cheeseboro, Sidney Franklin, Leon Holmes, "Missouri" Royer.
A railroad engineer who is color blind and can't distinguish the block signals invents an automatic signaling device.

Blockade (FBO Pictures, 1928)
d: George B. Seitz. 7 reels.
Anna Q. Nilsson, Wallace MacDonald, James Bradbury Sr., Walter McGrail.
Bess, a female pirate chieftain, blocks rumrunners on the Carribean... but it's only a front, for Bess is really a Secret Service agent.

Blonde for a Night (Pathé/DeMille, 1928)
d: E. Mason Hopper. 6 reels.
Harrison Ford, Marie Prevost, Franklin Pangborn, T. Roy Barnes, Lucien Littlefield.
To test her husband's fidelity, a newlywed bride dons a blonde wig and poses as a "femme fatale."

Blonde or Brunette (Famous Players-Lasky/Paramount, 1927)
d: Richard Rosson. 6 reels.
Adolphe Menjou, Greta Nissen, Arlette Marchal, Mary Carr, Evelyn Sherman, Emile Chautard, Paul Weigel, Henry Sedley, André Lanoy, Henri Menjou.
In Paris, a playboy marries a sweet, unspoiled girl from the countryside. After spending some time away on business, he returns to find his bride has taken to "fast" living, corrupted by his own society friends.

The Blonde Saint (Sam E. Rork Productions/First National, 1926)
d: Svend Gade. 7 reels.
Lewis Stone, Doris Kenyon, Ann Rork, Gilbert Roland, Cesare Gravina, Malcolm Denny, Albert Conti, Vadim Uraneff, Lillian Langdon, Leo White.
In New York, a Sicilian novelist falls in love with a ravishing American beauty... but she's so chaste and pure, she is known as "the blonde saint." Undeterred, the novelist tricks her into traveling back to Sicily with him, where, after several adventures, he gets her to admit her love for him.

Blondes by Choice (Gotham Productions/Lumas Film Corp., 1927)
d: Hampton Del Ruth. 6 reels.
Claire Windsor, Allan Simpson, Walter Hiers, Bodil Rosing, Bess Flowers, Leigh Willard, Jack Gardner, Louise Carver, Mai Wells, Alice Belcher, Joseph Belmont.
Bonnie, a small town girl, opens a beauty shop and, to drum up business, bleaches her own hair. This sets the local Ladies' Auxiliary against her and they try to shut her down on moralist grounds. But when Bonnie is championed by a wealthy society lady, the tide turns and soon all the spinsters in town are at her shop, seeking beauty treatments.

Blood and Sand (Famous Players-Lasky, 1922)

d: Fred Niblo. 9 reels.
Rudolph Valentino, Lila Lee, Nita Naldi, George Field, Walter Long, Rosa Rosavona, Leo White, Charles Belcher, Jack Winn, Marie Marstini, Gilbert Clayton, Harry LaMont, George Periolat, Sidney DeGray, Dorcas Matthews, Fred Becker, William Lawrence.
A great Spanish bullfighter, though happily married, is tempted by a faithless vamp who later rebuffs him. Struggling to regain his confidence through his profession, he overestimates his skill and is killed in the ring.

The Blood Barrier (Pathé, 1920)
d: J. Stuart Blackton. 6 reels.
Sylvia Breamer, Robert Gordon, William R. Dunn, Eddie Dunn, Louis Dean, Margaret Barry, Gus Alexander.
An insanely jealous man, erroneously believing his wife to be unfaithful, shoots and wounds her, then kills himself.

The Blood of His Fathers (Horsley Productions/Art Dramas, 1917)
d: Harrish Ingraham, Crane Wilbur. 5 reels.
Crane Wilbur, Jode Mullally, Gene Crosby, Don Bailey, Jake Abraham, Doc Crane, Ruth King, Richie Carpenter, Ray Thompson, Julia Jackson.
A likeable chap has friends and a fiancée... but he's fighting to control the curse of alcoholism, inherited from his grandfather.

The Blood Ship (Columbia, 1927)
d: George B. Seitz. 7 reels.
Walter James, Hobart Bosworth, Jacqueline Logan, Richard Arlen, Fred Kohler, James Bradbury Sr., Arthur Rankin, Syd Crossley, Frank Hemphill, Chappell Dossett.
Swope, a ruthless martinet of a sea captain, takes on additional crewmen in San Francisco. Once out to sea, however, the captain recognizes that one of his new crew is in fact the father of the girl Swope kidnapped when she was a child, years before.

Blood Will Tell (New York Motion Picture Corp./Triangle, 1917)
d: Charles Miller. 5 reels.
William Desmond, Enid Markey, David M. Hartford, Howard Hickman, Margaret Thompson, Charles Gunn, J. Frank Burke, J. Barney Sherry, Fannie Midgley, Robert McKim.
Disgraced and disinherited, a financier's son uses a rare talent—safecracking—to save the day when his dad's fortune is threatened by unscrupulous traders.

Blood Will Tell (Fox, 1927)
d: Ray Flynn. 5 reels.
Buck Jones, Kathryn Perry, Lawford Davidson, Robert Kortman, Harry Gripp, Austin Jewel.
Out West, a rancher rescues a damsel from a runaway horse. He soon learns that she is heading for his own ranch... and that she claims ownership!

The Bloodhound (Independent Pictures, FBO of America, 1925)
d: William James Craft. 5 reels.
Bob Custer, David Dunbar, Ralph McCullough, Mary Beth Milford, Emily Barrye.
In the Northwest, a mountie is assigned to go after a murder suspect. Upon locating him, the mountie discovers the man is his own twin brother.

The Blooming Angel (Goldwyn, 1920)
d: Victor L. Schertzinger. 5 reels.

Madge Kennedy, Pat O'Malley, Margery Wilson, Arthur Housman, Robert Chandler, Vera Lewis, B.F. Blinn, Billy Courtwright.
An innovative young wife decides to enhance the family's income by marketing her own complexion cream—and using it on an elephant!

The Blot (Lois Weber Productions, 1921)
d: Lois Weber. 7 reels.
Louis Calhern, Claire Windsor, Philip Hubbard, Margaret McWade, Marie Walacamp.
Phil, a rich boy, loves Amelia, the daughter of a struggling professor. "The blot" that separates them—her poverty—threatens to keep them apart.

Blow Your Own Horn (R-C Pictures/FBO of America, 1923)
d: James W. Horne. 6 reels.
Warner Baxter, Ralph Lewis, Derelys Perdue, Eugene Acker, William H. Turner, Ernest C. Warde, John Fox jr., Mary Jane Sanderson, Eugenie Forde, Dell Boone, Stanhope Wheatcroft.
Jack, a young inventor, perfects a wireless electronic device.

The Bludgeon (Equitable Motion Pictures/World Film Corp., 1915)
d: Webster Cullison. 5 reels.
Kathryn Osterman, John Dunn, Frank Beamish, Clara Whipple, Roy Applegate, Katherine Lee.
A chemist invents a formula that makes him rich, but finds that money can't buy marital bliss.

The Blue Bandanna (Hampton Productions/Robertson-Cole, 1919)
d: Joseph J. Franz. 5 reels.
William Desmond, Russell Simpson, Jean Acker, Frank Lanning, Richard LaReno.
A wealthy broker goes West, on doctor's orders, to relieve stress. But amid stagecoach robberies, gunfights, and an affair of the heart, he finds more excitement than he bargained for.

The Blue Bird (Famous Players-Lasky/Artcraft, 1918)
d: Maurice Tourneur. 6 reels.
Tula Belle, Robin Macdougall, Edwin E. Reed, Emma Lowry, William J. Gross, Florence Anderson, Edward Elkas, Katherine Bianchi, Lillian Cook, Gertrude McCoy, Lyn Donelson, Charles Ascot, Tom Corless, Mary Kennedy, Eleanor Masters, Charles Craig, Sam Blum.
Whimsical fantasy based on the 1890 play by Maurice Maeterlinck. The story portrays the innocence of childhood, as a boy and his sister explore a dazzling fantasy world of Light, Happiness, and Luxury, only to find that their true happiness is with them at all times.

Blue Blazes (Universal, 1926)
d: Joseph Franz. 5 reels.
Pete Morrison, Jim Welsh, Barbara Starr, Dick LaReno Jr., Les Bates, Jerome LaGrasse, James Lowe.
Out West, an honest cowpoke rescues a damsel who is looking for her late grandfather's stash of money. Soon, ornery critters are looking for it too, leaving the honest cowpoke no choice but to find it first.

Blue Blazes Rawden (Wm. S. Hart Productions/Artcraft, 1918)
d: William S. Hart. 5 reels.
William S. Hart, Maude George, Gertrude Claire, Robert McKim, Robert Gordon, Hart Hoxie.
A tough lumberjack kills another man in a duel, fair and square. But he finds it next to impossible to live down his "triumph."

Blue Blood (Selexart Pictures/Goldwyn, 1918)
d: Eliot Howe. 6 reels.
Howard Hickman, George Fisher, Mary Mersch, Nona Thomas, Ida Lewis.
Though he's wealthy and has a loving wife, an aristocrat lives in fear that the insanity that once ran in his family will be passed on to his son.

Blue Blood (Chadwick Pictures, 1925)
d: Scott Dunlap. 6 reels.
George Walsh, Cecile Evans, Philo McCullough, Joan Meredith, Robert Bolder, Harvey Clark, G. Howe Black, Eugene Borden.
Geraldine, willful daughter of a chewing gum magnate, is being pressured to marry malted milk tycoon Horton. But Horton's real fortune is in bootleg booze.

Blue Blood and Red (Fox, 1916)
d: Raoul Walsh. 5 reels.
George Walsh, Martin Kinney, Doris Pawn, James Marcus, Jack Woods, Augustus Carney.
Algernon DuPont is a blue blood and an heir, but when he's thrown out of the family mansion in disgrace, he has to make it on his own. Algie's surprised to find he isn't bad with his hands, so he builds a good life out West, even getting married and fathering twins.

The Blue Bonnet (National Film/Pathé, 1919)
d: Louis William Chaudet. 6 reels.
Billie Rhodes, Ben Wilson, Irene Rich, Stanhope Wheatcroft, William A. Carroll, Scott R. Beal, Charlotte Merriam, Lloyd Bacon.
An abandoned baby girl is found and raised by a pawnbroker. As an adult, she joins the Salvation Army to help unfortunate people such as the ones she observed in the pawn shop.

The Blue Danube (DeMille Pictures/Pathé, 1928)
d: Paul Sloane. 7 reels.
Leatrice Joy, Joseph Schildkraut, Nils Asther, Seena Owen, Albert Gran, Frank Reicher.
Tale of love, treachery, and redemption overlooking the Danube.

The Blue Eagle (Fox, 1926)
d: John Ford. 7 reels.
George O'Brien, Janet Gaynor, Robert Edeson, William Russell, David Butler, Phillip Ford, Ralph Sipperly, Margaret Livingston, Harry Tenbrook, Lew Short, Jerry Madden.
Rival gangleaders join the Navy during World War I, and continue their rivalry on board ship.

The Blue Envelope Mystery (Vitagraph, 1916)
d: Wilfrid North. 5 reels.
Lillian Walker, John D. Bennett, Bob Hay, Charles Kent, Josephine Earle, Harry Northrup, Florence Radinoff, Isabelle West, William Shea.
Entrusted with delivering an important government formula to Washington, a chemist's assistant finds she must fend off foreign spies.

Blue-Eyed Mary (Fox, 1918)
d: Harry Millarde. 5 reels.
June Caprice, Helen Tracy, Blanche Hines, Bernard Randall, Thomas Fallon, Jack McLean, Florence Ashbrooke, Henry

Hallam.

Because her son married beneath his station, a wealthy dowager disinherits him and names her nephew as her sole heir. She later regrets it.

Blue Grass (Equitable Motion Pictures/World Film Corp., 1915)
d: Charles Seay. 5 reels.
Thomas A. Wise, Clara Whipple, George Soule Spencer, Ray Tuckerman, Frank Beamish, Bess Sankey, Tommy Mead.
A Kentucky colonel owns "Blue Grass," a spirited race horse.

Blue Jeans (Metro, 1917)
d: John H. Collins. 7 reels.
Viola Dana, Robert Walker, Sally Crute, Clifford Bruce, Hanry Hallam, Russell Simpson, Margaret McWade, Augustus Phillips.
An aging couple adopt a poor orphan, not realizing she is really their lost granddaughter.

The Blue Moon (American Film Co./Pathé, 1920)
d: George L. Cox. 6 reels.
Pell Trenton, Elinor Field, Harry S. Northrup, James Gordon, Margaret McWade, Herbert Standing, Sidney Franklin, Frederick Monley.
"The Blue Moon" is a priceless pearl, coveted by heroes and villains alike.

The Blue Pearl (Weber Photo Dramas/Republic Distributing Corp., 1920)
d: George Irving. 6 reels.
Edith Hallor, Lumsden Hare, Earl Schenck, Jack Halliday, Corliss Giles, Faire Binney, Florence Billings, Jack Raymond, Charles Angelo, Adel Dumo.
When the lights go out at a fancy party, a priceless jewel is stolen from its owner.

The Blue Streak (Fox, 1917)
d: William Nigh. 5 reels.
William Nigh, Violet Palmer, Ruth Thorp, Martin Faust, Ned Finley, Edward Roseman, Tom Cameron, Danny Sullivan, Ed Kennedy, Bert Grudgeon, Marc Robbins.
Ousted from his wealthy home, a ne'er-do-well goes out West and wins a new reputation, earns new respect, and finds a new lady love.

The Blue Streak (Richard Talmadge Productions/FBO of America, 1926)
d: Noel Mason. 5 reels.
Richard Talmadge, Charles Clary, Louise Lorraine, Henry Herbert, Charles Hill Mailes, Victor Dillingham, Tote DuCrow.
Out West, a chap falls in love with a mine owner's daughter, and winds up rescuing both her and the ore shipments from a dastardly scoundrel.

Blue Streak McCoy (Universal, 1920)
d: Reaves Eason. 5 reels.
Harry Carey, Lila Leslie, Charles Arling, Breezy Eason, Ruth Golden, Ray Ripley, Charles Le Moyne, Ruth Royce.
A westerner thwarts mine-robbers.

Bluebeard's Eighth Wife (Famous Players-Lasky/Paramount, 1923)
d: Sam Wood. 6 reels.
Gloria Swanson, Huntley Gordon, Charles Green, Lianne Salvor, Paul Weigel, Frank Butler, Robert Agnew, Irene Dalton, Majel Coleman, Thais Valdemar.

A french noblewoman falls for a wealthy American, and they plan to marry. But she's reticent when she discovers that he's already married and divorced, seven times.

Bluebeard's Seven Wives (First National Pictures, 1926)
d: Alfred Santell. 8 reels.
Ben Lyon, Lois Wilson, Blanche Sweet, Dorothy Sebastian, Diana Kane, Sam Hardy, Dick Bernard, Andrew Mack, B.C. Duval, Wilfred Lytell, Dorothy Sebastian, Katherine Ray.
John, a movie extra and a bit of a naif, is promoted to leading man and gets the full star treatment. The publicity department quickly generates seven marriages and seven divorces for the bewildered newcomer. He ends up escaping his motion picture career on the dead run, and settling down on a farm, married to his childhood sweetheart.

Bluff (American Film Co./Mutual, 1916)
d: Rea Berger. 5 reels.
C. William Kolb, Max M. Dill, May Cloy, Thomas Chatterton, George Ahern, Clarence Burton, Harry Bernard, Charles Lynch.
A janitor hopes to make billions peddling a formula for making gold, but settles for millions when the formula instead creates puncture-proof rubber.

The Bluffer (World Film Corp., 1919)
d: Travers Vale. 5 reels.
June Elvidge, Irving Cummings, Frank Mayo, George MacQuarrie, Muriel Ostriche, Elizabeth Garrison, Louis Grisel, Jack Davidson, Jack Raymond.
A disillusioned young woman cynically believes it is better to bluff one's way through life than to be honest with oneself and others.

The Blushing Bride (Fox, 1921)
w, d: Jules G. Furthman. 5 reels.
Eileen Percy, Herbert Heyes, Philo McCullough, Jack LaReno, Rose Dione, Harry Dunkinson, Bertram Johns, Herschel Mayall, Sylvia Ashton, Earl Crain, Madge Orlamond, Robert Klein.
Follies girl Beth accepts wealthy Ames' proposal of marriage, insisting all along that she is the niece of a duke. When she reaches the Ames home, she is flabbergasted to recognize the butler as her own uncle! Later, the butler's cousin shows up and introduces himself as Beth's supposed uncle, the duke.

Bob Hampton of Placer (Marshall Neilan Productions/Associated First National, 1921)
d: Marshall Neilan. 7 reels.
James Kirkwood, Wesley Barry, Marjorie Daw, Pat O'Malley, Noah Beery, Frank Leigh, Dwight Crittenden, Tom Gallery, Priscilla Bonner, Charles West, Bert Sprotte, Carrie Clark Ward, Victor Potel, Buddy Post.
Bob, a U.S. Army captain, is unjustly convicted of murder and serves a minimum term. After becoming a gambler out West, he finds the real killer and gets his name cleared... just in time to join General Custer at the Battle of Little Big Horn.

Bobbed Hair (Realart Pictures/Paramount, 1922)
d: Thomas N. Heffron. 5 reels.
Wanda Hawley, William Boyd, Adele Farrington, Leigh Wyant, Jane Starr, Margaret Vilmore, William P. Carleton, Ethel Wales, Junior Coghlan, Robert Kelly.
Pretty Polly is wooed by Dick, a respectable businessman, but she wants a life of glamour and excitement. She finds excitement, in spades, when she takes up with a Bohemian

artist and poet who, unknown to Polly, is married with children.

Bobbed Hair (Warner Bros., 1925)
d: Alan Crosland. 6 reels.
Marie Prevost, Louise Fazenda, Kenneth Harlan, John Roche, Emily Fitzroy, Reed Howes, Dolores Costello, Helene Costello, Pat Hartigan.
A girl has two beaus: one who likes girls with bobbed hair, and one who doesn't.

Bobbie of the Ballet (Universal, 1916)
d: Joseph DeGrasse. 5 reels.
Louise Lovely, Jay Belasco, Lon Chaney, Jean Hathaway, Gretchen Lederer, Gilmore Hammond, Lule Warrenton.
Bobbie, a ballet dancer, pretends that her young brother and sister are her own children to keep them out of the clutches of the orphan asylum.

Body and Soul (Frohman Amusement Corp./World Film Corp., 1915)
d: George Irving. 5 reels.
Florence Rockwell, Kenneth Hunter, Robert Whitworth, Jack Sherrill, Mrs. Cecil Raleigh, Frazer Coulter, George Irving.
Amnesia strikes a wealthy woman, leading her to various colorful adventures.

Body and Soul (Metro, 1920)
d: Charles Swickard. 6 reels.
Alice Lake, William Lawrence, Stuart Holmes, Carl Gerard, Fontaine LaRue, William Orlamond, Hugh Saxon.
Remake of the 1915 *Body and Soul*. Both films are based on William Hurlbut's play of the same title.

Body and Soul (Micheaux Film Corp., 1925)
d: Oscar Micheaux. 5 reels.
Paul Robeson, Julia Theresa Russell, Mercedes Gilbert.
A reverend minister is led astray by greed, liquor, and sex.

Body and Soul (MGM, 1927)
d: Reginald Barker. 6 reels.
Lionel Barrymore, Aileen Pringle, Norman Kerry, T. Roy Barnes.
Leyden, an alcoholic surgeon, tricks a Swiss waitress into marrying him, then fights the burden of guilt when her true lover returns.

The Body Punch (Universal, 1929)
d: Leigh Jason. 5 reels.
Virginia Brown Faire, Jack Daugherty, George Kotsonaros, Wilbur Mack, Monte Montague, Arthur Millett.
When a boxer and a wrestler get together for a charity match, it's Turner, a fortune-hunting weasel and a thief, who delivers the body punch. Turner plants a stolen bracelet in the boxer's dressing room to divert suspicion from himself.

The Boer War (Kalem, 1914)
d: George Melford. 5 reels.
Edward Clisbee, Jane Wolfe, Marin Said, William Brunton, Larry Peyton, William H. West.
A British army captain falls in love with a general's daughter.

Bolshevism on Trial (Mayflower Photoplays/Select Pictures Corp., 1919)
d: Harley Knoles. 6 reels.
Robert Frazer, Leslie Stowe, Howard Truesdell, Jim Savage, Pinna Nesbit, Ethel Wright, Valda Valkyrien, May Hopkins, Chief Standing Bear, J.G. Davis.
The bolshevist notions of a utopian society are given a trial run on a private island.

The Bolted Door (Universal, 1923)
d: William Worthington. 5 reels.
Frank Mayo, Charles A. Stevenson, Phyllis Haver, Nigel Barrie.
Natalie, an heiress, marries a mechanic who loves her, though she's indifferent about him. She continues to live the high life and flirt with other men while her husband works on perfecting his invention. One night, as she meets with a lover behind bolted doors, a telegram comes telling her that her fortune has been wiped out. What now?

The Bonanza Buckaroo (Action Pictures/Associated Exhibitors, 1926)
d: Richard Thorpe. 5 reels.
Buffalo Bill Jr., Harry Todd, Judy King, Lafe McKee, Winifred Landis, Al Taylor, Charles Whitaker, Dutch Maley, Emily Barrye, Bill Ryno.
Hi-jinx out West, where a drifter rescues a wealthy lady in danger of tumbling over a steep cliff. He's introduced to her family and begins to fancy the lady's daughter, but with no real hopes of winning her hand. But fate steps in again, when the drifter gets the chance to save the wealthy family from swindlers.

The Bond Between (Pallas Pictures/Paramount, 1917)
d: Donald Crisp. 5 reels.
George Beban, John Burton, Nigel DeBrulier, Paul Weigel, Colin Chase, Eugene Pallette, W.H. Bainbridge, Vola Vale, Signor Buzzi, Mrs. Buehler.
A female secret service agent investigates a suspected art forger. Turns out he's innocent, so together they capture the real thief, then fall in love.

The Bond Boy (Inspiration Pictures/Associated First National, 1922)
d: Henry King. 7 reels.
Richard Barthelmess, Charles Hill Mailes, Ned Sparks, Lawrence D'Orsay, Robert Williamson, Leslie King, Jerry Sinclair, Thomas Maguire, Lucia Backus Seger, Virginia Magee.
Joe, a bonded servant, intervenes when his master's wife is trying to run away with her lover, and is quickly assumed to be the lover himself.

The Bond of Fear (Triangle, 1917)
d: Jack Conway. 5 reels.
Roy Stewart, Belle Bennett, Melbourne McDowell, George Webb, John Lince.
A fire-breathing law enforcement judge accidentally kills his brother.

Bondage (Universal, 1917)
d: Ida May Park. 5 reels.
Dorothy Phillips, William Stowell, Gretchen Lederer, Gertrude Astor, J.B. McLaughlin, Jean Porter, Eugene Owen.
Bohemian in her tastes and suspicious of a lawyer who tries to change her ways, a girl marries a free-thinking radical who proceeds to cheat on her.

The Bondage of Barbara (Goldwyn, 1919)
d: Emmett J. Flynn. 5 reels.
Mae Marsh, Matt Moore, Jack McLean, Arthur Housman, Henry Hallam, Edwin Sturgis.
A self-sacrificing young woman must deal with crooks who rob her cashier's box and try to pin the crime on her brother.

The Bondage of Fear (World Film Corp., 1917)

d: Travers Vale. 5 reels.
Ethel Clayton, Edward M. Kimball, John Bowers, Rockliffe Fellowes, Arthur Ashley, Frances Miller, William Nash, George Morgan, Elsa Bambrick.
Although she is innocent of any wrongdoing, a young bride is compromised when her old sweetheart is killed in her room.

The Bonded Woman (Famous Players-Lasky/Paramount, 1922)
d: Philip E. Rosen. 6 reels.
Betty Compson, John Bowers, Richard Dix, J. Farrel MacDonald, Ethel Wales.
Angela, in love with a sea captain with a weakness for drink, sets out to find him when he disappears in the South Seas.

The Bondman (Fox, 1916)
d: Edgar Lewis. 5 reels.
William Farnum, L.O. Hart, Dorothy Bernard, Charles Graham, Doris Wooldridge, Charles Brooke, Julia Hurley, Carey Lee, Harry Spingler.
Half-brothers love the same woman.

Bonds of Honor (Haworth Pictures Corp./Robertson-Cole, 1919)
d: William Worthington. 5 reels.
Sessue Hayakawa, Tsuri Aoki, Marin Sais, Dagmar Godowsky, Herschel Mayall, Toyo Fujita, M. Foshida.
Hayakawa plays a double role, as twin brothers—one virtuous, the other an evil schemer.

Bonds of Love (Goldwyn, 1919)
d: Reginald Barker. 5 reels.
Pauline Frederick, Percy Standing, Betty Schade, Leslie Stuart, Charles Clary, Kate Lester, Frankie Lee.
A young boy is saved from drowning by his valiant governess.

Bondwomen (Kleine-Edison Feature Service, 1915}
d: Edwin August. 5 reels.
Maude Fealy, John Sainpolis, Iva Shepard, Mildred Gregory, David Landau, Harry Knowles, Harmon McGregor, Shirley DeMe, Maurice Steuart Jr., Frederic Sumner.
A docile wife decides to stand up for her rights... in this case, a joint bank account.

Bonnie Annie Laurie (Fox, 1918)
d: Harry Millarde. 5 reels.
Peggy Hyland, Henry Hallam, William Bailey, Sidney Mason, Marion Singer.
When a young woman who's engaged to marry a soldier meets an injured lieutenant and takes care of him, she begins to experience doubts about her commitment to her fiancé.

Bonnie Bonnie Lassie (Universal, 1919)
d: Tod Browning. 6 reels.
Mary MacLaren, Spottiswoode Aitken, David Butler, Arthur Carewe, Fred Turner, Clarissa Selwyn, Eugenie Forde.
Two young people are "betrothed," sight unseen, in a marital arrangement. Furious, the young man refuses the arrangement and leaves home to make his own living as a billboard painter. In that job, he meets a sympathetic young woman who gladdens his life. They fall in love and marry, and the young man takes his bride home to meet his favorite uncle. There, he learns that his bride is none other than the girl his family had chosen for him in the first place.

The Bonnie Brier Bush (Famous Players-Lasky/Paramount, 1921)

d: Donald Crisp. 5 reels.
Donald Crisp, Mary Glynne, Alec Fraser, Dorothy Fane, Jack East, Langhorne Burton, Jerrold Robertshaw, H.H. Wright.
In Scotland, a young lord is persuaded into a betrothal with the lovely Kate, although his true love is Flora. Escaping for the moment from his family and the church elders, the young lord takes Flora to the brier bush and invokes an ancient Scottish rite, declaring her his wife in front of the bush with a witness present.

Bonnie May (Callaghan Productions/Federated Film Exchanges, Inc., 1920)
d: Ida May Park. 5 reels.
Bessie Love, Miss Dupont, William Bainbridge, Charles Gordon, Lon Poff.
A girl helps her friend rewrite his play, making it a great success.

The Boob (MGM, 1926)
d: William Wellman. 6 reels.
George K. Arthur, Joan Crawford, Gertrude Olmstead, Charles Murray, Antonio D'Algy, Hank Mann, Babe London.
Peter, a lovestruck farmer, adores Amy, but she goes for fast-living city boys.

The Book Agent (Fox, 1917)
d: Otis Turner. 5 reels.
George Walsh, Doris Pawn, William Burress, Reginald Everett, Willard Louis, Joseph Swickard, Velma Whitman, Phil Gastrock.
An itinerant book peddler meets a young private nurse, and they fall in love.

The Boomerang (National Film Corp./Pioneer Film Corp., 1919)
d: Bertram Bracken. 7 reels.
Henry B. Walthall, Melbourne McDowell, Nina Byron, Dick Johnson, Richard Norris, Helen Jerome Eddy, Jack MacDonald, Nigel DeBrullier, Beulah Booker, Gordon Sackville, Maryland Morne, Lloyd Whitlock, William Ryno, Bert Appling.
A crusading lawyer uncovers a racket that traffics in tainted meat.

The Boomerang (B.P. Schulberg Productions, 1925)
d: Louis Gasnier. 7 reels.
Anita Stewart, Bert Lytell, Donald Keith, Mary McAllister, Ned sparks, Arthur Edmund Carew, Philo McCullough, Winter Hall.
A physician decides to jump on the psychology bandwagon, so he opens a sanitarium with himself as the head shrink.

Boomerang Bill (Cosmopolitan Productions/Paramount, 1922)
d: Tom Terriss. 6 reels.
Lionel Barrymore, Marguerite Marsh, Margaret Seddon, Frank Shannon, Matthew Betts, Charlie Fong, Harry Lee, Miriam Battista, Helen Kim.
In New York, a young man is dissuaded from a life of crime by a kindly cop.

The Bootlegger's Daughter (Playgoers Pictures/Associated Exhibitors, 1922)
d: Victor Scherzinger. 5 reels.
Enid Bennett, Fred Niblo, Donald MacDonald, Melbourne MacDowell, Virginia Southern, Billy Elmer, J.P. Lockney, Caroline Rankin, Otto Hoffman, Harold Goodwin.
Against all odds, a bootlegger's daughter is persuaded to

turn away from her prosperous father's illicit profession. She goes so far as to marry the reverend minister who did the persuading.

Boots (Paramount, 1919)
d: Elmer Clifton. 5 reels.
Richard Barthelmess, Dorothy Gish, Ed Peil, Fontaine LaRue, Edward Peil, Kate Toncray, Raymond Cannon.
A London working girl falls in love with an American Secret Service agent.

Border Blackbirds (Leo Maloney Productions/Pathé, 1927)
d: Leo Maloney. 6 reels.
Leo Maloney, Eugenia Gilbert, Nelson McDowell, Joseph Rickson, Bud Osborne, Frank Clark, Morgan Davis, Tom London, Don Coleman, Allen Watt.
Two drifters seek shelter in a remote cabin, where they find the body of a murdered man.

Border Intrigue (Independent Pictures, 1925)
d: J.P. McGowan. 5 reels.
Franklyn Farnum, Jack Vernon, Mathilda Brundage, Dorothy Wood, Robert E. Cline, Mack V. Wright, "Slender" Whittaker, Emily Barrye, J.P. McGowan, Dot Farley.
There's a battle at the border when two brothers refuse to sell their farm rights to a Mexican speculator. To try and settle things down, one of the brothers rides south into Mexico, where he is drawn into the web of a wily señorita.

The Border Legion (Goldwyn, 1918)
d: T. Hayes Hunter. 5 reels.
Blanche Bates, Hobart Bosworth, Eugene Strong, Horace Morgan, Russell Simpson, Arthur Morrison, Bull Montana, Richard Souzade, Kate Elmore.
Accused by his fiancée of cowardice, a westerner joins an outlaw gang.

The Border Legion (Famous Players-Lasky/Paramount, 1924)
d: William K. Howard. 7 reels.
Antonio Moreno, Helene Chadwick, Rockliffe Fellowes, Gibson Gowland, Charles Ogle, James Corey, Edward Gribbon, Luke Cosgrave.
Above-average western follows a young man who joins a band of outlaws known as "the border legion" and the young woman who tries to extricate him from the gang.

The Border Patrol (Charles R. Rogers Productions/Pathé, 1928)
d: James P. Hogan. 5 reels.
Harry Carey, Kathleen Collins, Phillips Smalley, Richard Tucker, James Neill, James Marcus.
A Texas Ranger finds himself falling in love with an eastern girl, on the road to El Paso.

The Border Raiders (Diando Film Corp./Pathé, 1918)
d: Stuart Paton. 5 reels.
Betty Compson, George Larkin, Frank Deshon, H.C. Carpenter, Claire DuBrey, Howard Crampton, Fred M. Malatesta.
A western ranch is taken over by opium smugglers.

The Border Sheriff (Universal, 1926)
d: Robert North Bradbury. 5 reels.
Jack Hoxie, Olive Hasbrouck, S.E. Jennings, Gilbert Holmes, Buck Moulton, Tom Lingham, Bert DeMarc, Frank Rice, Floyd Criswell, Leonard Trainer.
On leave from his duties in Cayuse County, the sheriff anonymously saves the life of a businessman and captures a gang of dope smugglers.

Border Vengeance (Harry Webb Productions/Aywon, 1925)
d: Harry Webb. 5 reels.
Jack Perrin, Minna Redman, Vondell Darr, Jack Richardson, Josephine Hill, Leo Clapham.
Fury and fisticuffs in the Old West, as a cowpoke fights for his lady and an old mine.

The Border Wildcat (Universal, 1929)
d: Ray Talor. 5 reels.
Ted Wells, Tom London, Kathryn McGuire, William Malan.
Out West, an intrepid sheriff routs gunmen and saves the life of his future father-in-law.

The Border Wireless (Wm. S. Hart Productions/Paramount, 1918)
d: William S. Hart. 5 reels.
William S. Hart, Wanda Hawley, Charles Arling, James Mason, E. Von Ritzen, Bert Sprotte, Marcia Manon.
Unwittingly, a wireless operator in the U.S.A. transmits coded messages to Berlin.

Borderland (Famous Players-Lasky/Paramount, 1922)
d: Paul Powell. 6 reels.
Agnes Ayres, Fred Huntley, Milton Sills, Bertram Grassby, Casson Ferguson, Ruby Lafayette, Sylvia Ashton, Frankie Lee, Mary Jane Irving, Dale Fuller.
Supernatural drama about a woman's ghost looking for her lost child.

Born Rich (Garrick Pictures/First National, 1924)
d: Will Nigh. 8 reels.
Claire Windsor, Bert Lytell, Cullen Landis, Doris Kenyon, Frank Morgan, J. Barney Sherry, Maude Turner Gordon, Jackie Ott, William Burton.
A wealthy woman returns from travel in Europe to find that her husband has been fooling around with scarlet women. Instead of confronting him, she tries to arouse his jealousy by having some affairs of her own.

Born to Battle (R-C Pictures/FBO of America, 1926)
d: Robert DeLacy. 5 reels.
Tom Tyler, Jean Arthur, Ray Childs, Fred Gambold, Frankie Darro, Buck Black, LeRoy Mason, Ethan Laidlaw.
Out West, a ranch foreman discovers there is oil in the land his boss has just sold. Now it's up to the foreman to ride to the rescue and get that deed back!

Born to the West (Famous Players-Lasky/Paramount, 1926)
d: John Waters. 6 reels.
Jack Holt, Margaret Morris, Raymond Hatton, Arlette Marchal, George Siegmann, Bruce Gordon, William A. Carroll, Tom Kennedy, Richard Neill, Edith Yorke, E. Alyn Warren.
Sparks fly when cowpunchers clash over the love of the same woman.

Borrowed Clothes (Universal, 1918)
d: Lois Weber, Phillips Smalley. 6 reels.
Mildred Harris, Edward J. Peel, Helen Rosson, Lew Cody, George Nichols, Edythe Chapman, Fontaine LaRue.
When a bath-house fire destroys her clothes, a young woman has to borrow the flashy finery of a worldly woman. Her father, her fiancé, and her sister all assume The Worst.

Borrowed Finery (Tiffany Productions, 1925)
d: Oscar Apfel. 7 reels.

Louise Lorraine, Ward Crane, Lou Tellegen, Taylor Holmes, Hedda Hopper, Gertrude Astor, Trixie Friganza, Barbara Tennant, Otto Lederer.

Sheila, a shopgirl, borrows a fancy gown to wear to a party and meets Mr. Right.

Borrowed Husbands (Vitagraph, 1924)
d: David Smith. 7 reels.
Florence Vidor, Rockliffe Fellowes, Earle Williams, Robert Gordon, Kathryn Adams, Violet Palmer, Alpheus Lincoln, Claire DuBrey, Charlotte Merriam, J.W. Irving.
While her husband's away on business, vivacious Nancy engages in several flirtations.

Borrowed Plumage (Triangle, 1917)
d: Raymond B. West. 5 reels.
Bessie Barriscale, Arthur Maude, Dorcas Matthews, Barney Sherry, Wallace Worsley, Tod Burns.
Left behind in an abandoned castle, a kitchen maid dons her mistress' clothes and entertains an infantry brigade.

The Boss (Brady Picture Plays/World, 1915)
d: Emile Chautard. 5 reels.
Alice Brady, Holbrook Blinn, Douglas MacLean, Charles F. Abbe, William Marion, Fred C. Truesdell, Julia Stuart, Robert Frazer, Bert Starkey, R.B. Mantell Jr.
A saloon owner begins a freight business and becomes a major success.

The Boss of Camp 4 (Fox, 1922)
d: W.S. Van Dyke. 5 reels.
Charles Jones, Fritzi Brunette, G. Raymond Nye, Francis Ford, Sid Jordan, Milton Ross.
Chet, a road crew member, foils attempted sabotage against the project and saves the life of his boss' daughter... who promptly falls in love with him.

The Boss of the Lazy Y (Triangle, 1918)
d: Cliff Smith. 5 reels.
Roy Stewart, Jose Sedgwick, Frank MacQuarrie, Graham Pette, Walt Whitman, Aaron Edwards, Frankie Lee, William Ellingford, Bill Patton.
After years of drifting, a rancher's son returns to the old homestead and takes charge.

Boston Blackie (Fox, 1923)
d: Scott Dunlap. 5 reels.
William Russell, Eva Novak, Frank Brownlee, Otto Matieson, Spike Robinson, Frederick Esmelton.
Boston Blackie, a gentleman thief who despises violence, serves his term in jail and then gets the warden fired for using a cruel torture on his prisoners.

Boston Blackie's Little Pal (Metro, 1918)
d: E. Mason Hopper. 5 reels.
Bert Lytell, Rhea Mitchell, Rosemary Theby, Joel Jacobs, Howard Davies, John Burton, Frank Whitson.
Boston Blackie, a gentleman thief, plans to rob a mansion. But when the young son of the family enters, the two become fast friends.

The Bottle Imp (Lasky Feature Play Co./Paramount, 1917)
d: Marshall Neilan. 5 reels.
Sessue Hayakawa, Lehua Waipahu, H. Komshi, George Kuwa, Guy Oliver, James Neill.
Exotic tale about love and adventure in the Hawaiian islands, and a magic bottle containing a powerful god who grants wishes.

The Bottom of the Well (Vitagraph, 1917)
d: John S. Robertson. 5 reels.
Evart Overton, Agnes Ayres, Adele DeGarde, Ned Finley, Herbert Pryor, Robert Gaillard, Alice Terry, Bigelow Cooper.
There's trouble afoot, courtesy of a secret organization known as "The Well."

Bought (Shubert Film/World Film Corp., 1915)
d: Barry O'Neil. 5 reels.
Frederick Lewis, Ethel Grey Terry.
When the *Titanic* sinks and her pregnant daughter's fiancé goes down with it, a wealthy woman offers a struggling writer $10,000 and a job to be her daughter's husband "in name only."

Bought and Paid For (Brady Picture Plays, Inc./World Film Corp., 1916)
d: Harley Knoles. 5 reels.
Alice Brady, Josephine Drake, Frank Conlan, Montagu Love.
A wealthy alcoholic treats his wife kindly when sober, but it's a different story when he's in his cups.

Bought and Paid For (Famous Players-Lasky/Paramount, 1922)
d: William C. DeMille. 6 reels.
Agnes Ayres, Jack Holt, Walter Hiers, Leigh Wyant, George Kuwa, Bernice Frank, Ethel Wales.
Remake of the 1916 *Bought and Paid For*, originally produced by Brady Picture Plays.

Bound in Morocco (Douglas Fairbanks/Famous Players-Lasky/Paramount, 1918)
d: Allan Dwan. 5 reels.
Douglas Fairbanks, Pauline Curley, Edythe Chapman, Tully Marshall, Frank Campeau, Jay Dwiggins, Fred Burns, Albert McQuarrie.
An adventurer in Morocco fights to save an American girl from being sold into a harem.

The Bowery Bishop (Rellimeo Film Syndicate/Selznick, 1924)
d: Colin Campbell. 6 reels.
Henry B. Walthall, Leota Lorraine, George Fisher, Lee Shumway, Edith Roberts, William H. Ryno, Norval MacGregor.
Scandal rules the Bowery when a missionary is accused of fathering the illegitimate child of one of the local girls.

A Bowery Cinderella (Excellent Pictures, 1927)
d: Burton King. 7 reels.
Gladys Hulette, Pat O'Malley, Kate Bruce, Ernest Hilliard, Rosemary Theby, Pat Hartigan, Pauline Carr, Howard Mitchell, Leo White, John Webb Dillon.
Nora, a fashionable dressmaker, is innocently caught in what looks like a "compromising" position with a known womanizer.

Boy Crazy (Hunt Stromberg Productions/R-C Pictures, 1922)
d: William A. Seiter. 5 reels.
Doris May, Fred Gambold, Jean Hathaway, Frank Kingsley, Harry Myers, Otto Hoffman, Gertrude Short, Eugenia Tuttle, Ed Brady, James Farley.
Kidnappers nab the wrong woman and spirit her away to their remote cabin. They are foiled, though, when their real target, her wealthy father, and the boyfriend of the abducted girl all converge on the cabin and bring the cops with them.

The Boy Friend (MGM, 1926)
d: Monta Bell. 6 reels.

Marceline Day, George K. Arthur, Gwen Lee, John Harron, Elizabeth Patterson, Ward Crane, Gertrude Astor, Otto Hoffman, Maidel Turner, Edgar Norton, Clarence Geldart. Though she has a handsome boyfriend who loves her, small-town girl Ida May yearns to escape to the glamour of the big city. It's up to the boyfriend to dissuade her.

The Boy Girl   (Universal, 1917)
d: Edwin Stevens.   5 reels.
Violet Mersereau, Sidney Mason, Florida Kingsley, Caroline Harris, Maud Cooling, Tina Marshall, Charles Mason, James O'Neill, Dean Raymond, Byron Dean.
Her father wanted a son, so his daughter is raised as "Jack" Channing.

A Boy of Flanders   (Jackie Coogan Productions/Metro-Goldwyn Distributing Corp., 1924)
d: Victor Schertzinger.   7 reels.
Jackie Coogan, Nigel DeBrulier, Lionel Belmore, Nell Craig, Jean Carpenter, Russ Powell, Aimé Charland, Eugene Tuttle, Lydia Yeamans Titus, Larry Fisher, Josef Swickard.
After his grandfather dies, a little boy is left homeless, with no one but his pet dog to keep him company.

Boys Will be Boys   (Goldwyn, 1921)
d: Clarence G. Badger.   5 reels.
Will Rogers, Irene Rich, C.E. Mason, Sydney Ainsworth, Edward Kimball, H. Milton Ross, C.E. Thurston, May Hopkins, Cordelia Callahan, Nick Cogley, Burton Halbert.
When O'Day, a small-town "hick," unexpectedly inherits a small fortune, a crooked lawyer decides to bilk him of it. The shyster sends O'Day a slinky charmer claiming to be a long-lost relative, and demanding her share of the inheritance.

Brace Up   (Universal, 1918)
d: Elmer Clifton.   5 reels.
Herbert Rawlinson, Claire du Brey, Alfred Allen, Sam DeGrasse.
A habitual coward finds courage at the crucial moment.

The Bramble Bush   (Vitagraph, 1919)
d: Tom Terriss.   5 reels.
Corinne Griffith, Julia Swayne Gordon, Miss Bohamar, Denton Vane, Frank Mills, Robert W. Frazer.
An innocent rural girl goes to New York and finds employment.   Soon, she is being pursued by a notorious womanizer.

The Brand   (Rex Beach/Goldwyn, 1919)
d: Reginald Barker.   7 reels.
Kay Laurell, Russell Simpson, Robert McKim, Robert Kunkel, Mary Jane Irving, Gus Saville.
A vaudeville dancer ventures north to Alaska and meets and marries a lonely miner.   Though he treats her well, she grows bored and soon takes up with a former beau.

The Brand of Cowardice   (Rolfe Photoplays, Inc./Metro, 1916)
d: John W. Noble.   5 reels.
Lionel Barrymore, Grace Valentine, Robert Cummings, Kate Blancke, John Davidson, Frank Montgomery, Louis Wolheim, Tula Belle.
A national guardsman refuses a call to action and is branded a coward.   But he enlists in the army and makes amends, fighting valiantly at the Mexican border and rescuing a young woman who has been taken hostage.

Brand of Cowardice   (Phil Goldstone Productions/Truart Film Corp., 1925)
d: John P. McCarthy.   5 reels.
Bruce Gordon, Carmelita Geraghty, Cuyler Supplee, Ligio DeColconda, Harry Lonsdale, Charles McHugh, Mark Fenton, Sidney DeGrey.
Out West, a U.S. marshal goes undercover as a bandit.

The Brand of Lopez   (Haworth Pictures Corp./Robertson-Cole, 1920)
d: Joseph DeGrasse.   5 reels.
Sessue Hayakawa, Florence Turner, Sidney Payne, Evelyn Ward, Eugenie Besserer, Gertrude Norman, Kitty Bradbury.
Class differences cause the breakup of the marriage of a matador and an opera singer.

The Brand of Satan   (World Film Corp., 1917)
d: George Archainbaud.   5 reels.
Montagu Love, Gerda Holmes, Evelyn Greeley, Albert Hart, Nat C. Gross, J. Herbert Frank, Emile LeCroix, Katherine Johnston.
In Paris, an attorney lives a double life.   By day, he is a tireless prosecutor in service to the law; by night, he assumes the identity of a master criminal.

Branded Man   (Trem Carr Productions/Rayart Pictures, 1928)
d: Scott Pembroke.   6 reels.
Charles Delaney, June Marlowe, Gordon Griffith, George Riley, Andy Clyde, Erin LaBissoniere, Lucy Beaumont, Henry Roquemore.
Unhappily married to a compulsive flirt, Colgate drifts away and is eventually presumed dead.   But he's become a prize fighter south of the border, where he begins a new life.

The Branded Sombrero   (Fox, 1928)
d: Lambert Hillyer.   5 reels.
Buck Jones, Leila Hyams, Jack Baston, Stanton Heck, Francis Ford, Josephine Borio, Lee Kelly.
On his deathbed, a rancher reveals that his sombrero is etched with the number of cattle he rustled from each competitor.   After the man's death, his sons strive to make restitution.

A Branded Soul   (Fox, 1917)
d: Bertram Bracken.   5 reels.
Gladys Brockwell, Colin Chase, Vivian Rich, Willard Louis, Lewis J. Cody, Gloria Payton, Fred Whitman, Barney Furey.
Conchita, a choir singer, is lusted after by a wealthy oil man, though she loves a poor farm worker.

The Branded Woman   (Joseph M. Schenck/First National, 1920)
d: Albert Parker.   5 reels.
Norma Talmadge, Percy Marmont, Vincent Serrano, George Fawcett, Grace Studdiford, Gaston Glass, Jean Armour, Edna Murphy, H.J. Carvill, Charles Lane, Sydney Herbert, Edouard Durand, Henrietta Floyd.
In Paris, an American girl marries well and is happy with her husband and child.   But a woman who knows a scandalous secret about the girl's family shows up and threatens to expose the truth.

Branding Broadway   (Wm. S. Hart Productions/Paramount, 1918)
d: William S. Hart.   5 reels.
William S. Hart, Seena Owen, Arthur Shirley, Andrew Robeson, Lewis W. Short.
An Arizona cowboy becomes the guardian to a New York millionaire's son.

The Branding Iron (Goldwyn, 1920)
d: Reginald Barker. 7 reels.
Barbara Castleton, James Kirkwood, Russell Simpson, Richard Tucker, Sidney Ainsworth, Gertrude Astor, Albert Roscoe, Marion Colvin, Joan Standing, Louie Cheung.
An estranged couple watch a play based on their lives, and are moved to reconcile.

Brand's Daughter (Falcon Features/General Film Co., 1917)
d: E.D. Horkheimer. 4 reels.
Danile Gilfether, Julien Beaubien, Gloria Payton, R. Henry Grey, Kathleen Kirkham, Melvin Mayo, Robert Weycross.
Wealthy banker Robert Brand insists that his daughter's beau acquire a small fortune before he can marry her.

Brass (Warner Bros., 1923)
d: Sidney Franklin. 9 reels.
Monte Blue, Irene Rich, Marie Prevost, Harry Myers, Cyril Chadwick, Frank Keenan, Helen Ferguson, Vera Lewis, Margaret Seddon, Winter Hall.
A wife tries to mend her broken marriage.

The Brass Bottle (Maurice Tourneur Productions, 1923)
d: Maurice Tourneur. 6 reels.
Harry Myers, Ernest Torrence, Tully Marshall, Clarissa Selwyn, Ford Sterling, Aggie Herring, Charlotte Merriam, Edward Jobson, Barbara LaMarr, Otis Harlan, Hazel Keener, Julanne Johnston.
Takeoff on the old tale of Aladdin and his magic lamp, told in comedic fashion.

The Brass Bowl (Fox, 1924)
d: Jerome Storm. 6 reels.
Edmund Lowe, Claire Adams, Jack Duffy, J. Farrell MacDonald, Leo White, Fred Butler.
Maitland, a country gentleman, is the exact double of Anisty, a jewel thief.
Lowe plays both roles, as Maitland and Anisty.

Brass Buttons (American Film Co./Pathé, 1919)
d: Henry King. 5 reels.
William Russell, Eileen Percy, Helen Howard, Frank Brownlee, Bull Montana, Wilbur Higby, Carl Stockdale.
Double deception, when a wealthy man borrows a uniform and pretends to be a cop in order to woo a girl he thinks is a housemaid. The object of his affections is in reality a wealthy woman, but she likes the "cop," so she lets him go on thinking she's a maid.

The Brass Check (Metro, 1918)
d: William S. Davis. 5 reels.
Francis X. Bushman, Beverly Bayne, Augustus Phillips, Frank Currier, Ollie Cooper, Frank Joyner, Rudolph DeCordova, Robert Williamson, Hugh Jeffrey, John Smiley, Hugh D'Arcy, Jack Newton, Syn DeConde.
An inventor is framed by a large corporation when he refuses to turn over his new formula. But his daughter hires a detective to learn the truth, and he does, even though the "detective" is actually the corporate president's son, who's fallen in love with her.

Brass Commandments (Fox, 1923)
d: Lynn F. Reynolds. 5 reels.
William Farnum, Wanda Hawley, Tom Santschi, Claire Adams, Charles LeMoyne, Joe Rickson, Lon Poff, Al Fremont, Joseph Gordon, Cap Anderson.
Steve Lanning, a westerner who's spent some time in the east, returns home just in time to foil a gang of rustlers.

Brass Knuckles (Warner Bros., 1927)
d: Lloyd Bacon. 7 reels.
Monte Blue, Betty Bronson, William Russell, George E. Stone, Paul Panzer, Jack Curtis.
A former convict adopts the teen-age daughter of a former cellmate.

The Brat (Metro, 1919)
d: Herbert Blaché. 7 reels.
Nazimova, Charles Bryant, Amy Veness, Frank Currier, Darrell Foss, Bonnie Hill, Milla Davenport, Henry Kolker, Ethelbert Knott.
A chorus girl known as "The Brat" is asked to help in the creation of a new novel.

Brave and Bold (Fox, 1918)
d: Carl Harbaugh. 5 reels.
George Walsh, Francis X. Conlon, Dan Mason, Mabel Bunyea, Regina Quinn, A.B. Conkwright.
Industrial espionage confuses the life of a man about to marry.

Braveheart (Cinema Corp. of America/Cecil B. DeMille, 1925)
d: Alan Hale. 7 reels.
Rod LaRocque, Robert Edeson, Lillian Rich, Arthur Housman, Frank Hagney, Jean Acker, Tyrone Power, Sally Rand, Henry Victor.
A young Indian brave goes east to study the law. While in college, he becomes an All-American football player.

The Bravest Way (Famous Players-Lasky/Paramount, 1918)
d: George H. Melford. 5 reels.
Sessue Hayakawa, Florence Vidor, Tsuru Aoki, U Aoyama, Jane Wolff, Winter Hall, Tom Kurahara, Josephine Crowell, Goro Kino, Clarence Geldart, Guy Oliver, Billy Elmer.
At great personal sacrifice, a Japanese gardener marries the widow of his friend, though the gardener's own sweetheart is waiting for him.

Brawn of the North (Trimble-Murfin Productions/Associated First National, 1922)
d: Laurence Trimble. 8 reels.
Irene Rich, Lee Shumway, Joseph Barrell, Roger James Manning, Philip Hubbard, Jean Metcalf, Baby Evangeline Bryant.
In Alaska, a valiant dog saves the life of a baby threatened by a pack of wolves.

Bread (Universal, 1918)
d: Ida May Park. 6 reels.
Mary MacLaren, Edward Cecil, Gladys Fox, Kenneth Harlan, Louis Morrison.
Aggravated by what she considers patronizing by an impresario and a playwright, a young actress storms out and leaves theater life behind. But she's soon down to her last crust of bread. Now what?

Bread (MGM, 1924)
d: Victor Schertzinger. 7 reels.
Mae Busch, Pat O'Malley, Robert Frazer, Wanda Hawley, Hobart Bosworth, Eugenie Besserer. Myrtle Stedman, Ward Crane.
Fiercely independent Jeanette works as a stenographer. In time, though, she'll come to realize that true happiness lies in marriage.

Break the News to Mother (Select Pictures Corp., 1919)

d: Julius Steger. 6 reels.
Pearl Shepard, Gertrude Berkeley, Raymond Bloomer, Alice Gerard, Forrest Robinson, William Bailey, Louis Stern, Joseph Smiley, Chester Barnett.
On his return from Europe, a war hero learns that the girl who spurned him has had a change of heart.

The Breaker (Essanay, 1916)
d: Fred E. Wright. 5 reels.
Bryant Washburn, Nell Craig, Ernest Maupain.
A salesman is duped into passing counterfeit money.

Breakers Ahead (Metro, 1918)
d: Charles J. Brabin. 5 reels.
Viola Dana, Clifford Bruce, Mabel Van Buren, Russell Simpson, Eugene Pallette, Sydney Deane, T.H. Gowland, Lorena Foster, Helen Jerome Eddy.
Wagging tongues spread the word that a neighbor girl is illegitimate. She is ostracized by the community for a while, until her father, a sea captain, comes ashore and proves them wrong.

Breakfast at Sunrise (First National, 1927)
d: Malcolm St. Clair. 7 reels.
Constance Talmadge, Bryant Washburn, Paulette Duval, Marie Dressler, Burr McINtosh, Alice White, David Mir, Don Alvarado, Nelly Bly Baker.
In Paris, a wealthy madamoiselle and a boulevardier meet, and both having been rejected by their lovers, decide to marry each other for spite. But what begins in rancor develops into true love.

Breaking into Society (Hunt Stromberg Productions/FBO of America, 1923)
d: Hunt Stromberg. 5 reels.
Carrie Clark Ward, Bull Montana, Kalla Pasha, Francis Trebaol, Florence Gilbert, Leo White, Tiny Sandford, Stanhope Wheatcroft, Chuck Reisner, Gertrude Short.
Nouveau riche moderns learn that it takes more than money to become accepted in the upper echelons of polite society.

The Breaking Point (J.L. Frothingham Productions/W.W. Hodkinson, 1921)
d: Paul Scardon. 6 reels.
Bessie Barriscale, Walter McGrail, Ethel Grey Terry, Eugenie Besserer, Pat O'Malley, Winter Hall, Wilfred Lucas, Joseph J. Dowling, Lydia Knott, Irene Yeager.
A mismatch if there ever was one: Sweet young Ruth is forced to marry wealthy Richard, who cares nothing for her and even gives their child to one of his mistresses!

The Breaking Point (Famous Players-Lasky/Paramount, 1924)
d: Herbert Brenon. 7 reels.
Nita Naldi, Patsy Ruth Miller, George Fawcett, Matt Moore, John Merkyl, Theodore von Eltz, Edythe Chapman, Cyril Ring, W.B. Clarke, Edward Kipling, Milt Brown, Naida Faro.
Believing himself guilty of murder, a young doctor worries himself into a state of amnesia.

The Breath of Scandal (B.P. Schulberg Productions, 1924)
d: Louis Gasnier. 7 reels.
Betty Blythe, Patsy Ruth Miller, Jack Mulhall, Myrtle Stedman, Lou Tellegen, Forrest Stanley, Frank Leigh, Phyllis Haver, Charles Clary.
Settlement worker Marjorie is shocked to discover that her father is an adulterer.

The Breath of the Gods (Universal, 1920)
d: Rollin Sturgeon. 6 reels.
Tsuri Aoki, Pat O'Malley, Stanhope Wheatcroft, Arthur Carewe, Barney Sherry, Marion Skinner, Ethel Shannon, Missao Seki, Mai Wells, Paul Weigel.
Racial prejudice erupts from both sides when a Japanese girl studying in America falls in love with a French diplomat, and he with her.

The Breathless Moment (Universal, 1924)
d: Robert F. Hill. 6 reels.
William Desmond, Charlotte Merriam, Alfred Fisher, Robert E. Homans, Lucille Hutton, John Steppling, Margaret Cullington, Harry Van Meter, Albert Hart.
Quinn, a kindly cop, was once good friends with Carson, a crook. To avoid sending Carson to jail, Quinn "sentences" him instead to spend a year in a small town. There, Carson falls in love, goes straight, and becomes a respectable citizen.

Bred in Old Kentucky (R-C Pictures/FBO of America, 1926)
d: Eddie Dillon. 6 reels.
Viola Dana, Jerry Miley, Jed Prouty, James Mason, Roy Laidlaw, Josephine Crowell.
Katie's horse is accidentally killed by another horse during a race. Rather than resenting the horse's owner, Katie falls in love with him.

Breed of Men (Wm. S. Hart Productions/Paramount, 1919)
d: William S. Hart. 5 reels.
William S. Hart, Seena Owen, Bert Sprotte, Buster Irving.
A rootless cowpoke settles in Arizona to become the new sheriff.

The Breed of the Border (Harry Garson Productions, FBO of America, 1924)
d: Harry Garson. 5 reels.
Lefty Flynn, Dorothy Dwan, Louise Carver, Milton Ross, Frank Hagney, Fred Burns, Joe Bennett, Bill Donovan.
In a dusty border town, a drifter becomes a hero when he rescues a damsel from a masher, saves her father from a mob, and prevents a bank robbery.

Breed of the Sea (R-C Pictures/FBO of America, 1926)
d: Ralph Ince. 6 reels.
Ralph Ince, Margaret Livingston, Pat Harmon, Alphonz Ethier, Dorothy Dunbar, Shannon Day.
Twin brothers follow disparate paths. One becomes a missionary, the other a pirate.
Ince wears three hats here, playing both twins as well as directing the film.

Breed of the Sunsets (FBO Pictures, 1928)
d: Wallace W. Fox. 5 reels.
Bob Steele, Nancy Drexel, George Bunny, Dorothy Kitchen, Leo White, Larry Fisher.
Out West, a cowpoke falls for a señorita who is betrothed to another.

Breezy Bill (Big Productions Film Corp., 1930)
d: J.P. McGowan. 5 reels.
Bob Steele, Alfred Hewston, George Hewston, Edna Aslin, Perry Murdock, Bud Osborne, Cliff Lyons, J.P. McGowan.
Out West, an adopted son battles bandits eager to get their hands on his foster father's millions.

Breezy Jim (Triangle, 1919)
d: Lorimer Johnson. 5 reels.
Crane Wilbur, Juanita Hansen.
When a bored New York woman goes West to find

excitement, she finds more than she bargained for.

Brewster's Millions (Lasky Feature Plays, 1914)
d: Cecil B. DeMille. 5 reels.
Edward Abeles, Winifred Kingston, Joseph Singleton, Sydney Dean, Miss Bartholomew, Mabel Van Buren, Dick La Reno, Bernadine Zuber, Monroe Salisbury, Murine Rasmussen.
Monty Brewster has inherited a million dollars. But if he spends the first million within a year without telling why, he stands to inherit seven million more.

Brewster's Millions (Famous Players-Lasky/Paramount, 1921)
d: Joseph Henabery. 6 reels.
Roscoe "Fatty" Arbuckle, Betty Ross Clark, Fred Huntley, Marian Skinner, James Corrigan, Jean Acker, Charles Ogle, Neely Edwards, William Boyd, L.J. McCarthy, Parker J. McConnell, John MacFarland, Walter A. Coughlin.
One of Monte Brewster's grandfathers leaves him $2 million dollars, but his other grandfather promises the young man a sum of $10 million if he can spend his inheritance in one year while remaining single, and not telling anyone why he is being such a spendthrift. Perversely, every attempt of his to lose money nets him even more money.
Remake, with some plot alterations, of the 1914 Lasky *Brewster's Millions.*

The Bride of Fear (Fox, 1918)
d: S.A. Franklin. 5 reels.
Jewel Carmen, Charles Gorman, L.C. Shumway, Charles Bennett.
The bride of a thief learns that her husband was killed in an attempted prison break, so she makes plans to marry again. But she was misinformed.

The Bride of Hate (New York Motion Picture Corp./Triangle, 1917)
d: David M. Hartford. 5 reels.
Frank Keenan, Margery Wilson, Jerome Storm, David M. Hartford, Elvira Weil, Mrs. J. Hunt, J.P. Lockney, Nona Thomas, Jack Gilbert.
In the old South, a beautiful slave with only a trace of Negro blood is forced by her master to trick his enemy into falling in love with her.

The Bride's Awakening (Univesal, 1918)
d: Robert Leonard. 6 reels.
Mae Murray, Lewis Cody, Ashton Dearholt, Clarissa Selwynne, Harry Carter, Joe Girard.
A couple marry, but the husband wants to continue an affair "on the side."

The Bride's Play (Cosmopolitan/Paramount, 1921)
d: George Terwilliger. 7 reels.
Marion Davies, Wyndham Standing, Carlton Miller, Jack O'Brien, Eleanor Middleton, Richard Cummings.
Modern lovers decide to play the ancient game of "The Bride's Play" at their wedding, a custom which permits the bride to ask each of the male guests if he, and not the groom, is her true love.

The Bride's Silence (American Film Co./Mutual, 1917)
d: Henry King. 5 reels.
Gail Kane, Lewis J. Cody, Henry A. Barrows, James Lee Farley, Robert Klein, Ashton Dearholt.
When a wealthy young man is mysteriously stabbed to death, his sister lets the police arrest the family butler for the crime, though she knows he didn't do it.

The Bridge of San Luis Rey (MGM, 1929)
d: Charles Brabin. 10 reels. (Part talkie.)
Lily Damita, Ernest Torrence, Don Alvarado, Raquel Torres, Henry B. Walthall, Duncan Renaldo, Emily Fitzroy, Tully Marshall, Jane Winton, Gordon Thorpe, Mitchell Lewis.
In Peru, a bridge that was blessed by St. Louis himself collapses on his feast day, and five villagers fall to their death. Though the people interpret this occurrence as a sign of God's disfavor, a kindly priest examines the lives of the five and determines that each of them had made his peace with the Lord, and they were simply being reunited with Him.

The Bridge of Sighs (Warner Bros., 1925)
d: Phil Rosen. 7 reels.
Creighton Hale, Dorothy Mackaill, Alec B. Francis, Richard Tucker, Ralph Lewis, Clifford Saum, Fanny Midgley, Aileen Manning.
Craig, a steamship executive, has his son shanghaied on one of his ships rather than let the larcenous young man be imprisoned for theft.

Bridges Burned (Popular Plays/Metro, 1917)
d: Perry N. Vekroff. 5 reels.
Mme. Olga Petrova, Mahlon Hamilton, Arthur Hoops, Maury Steuart, Robert Broderick, Mathilde Brundage, Louis Stern, Thomas Cameron.
When his daughter becomes pregnant, an Irish gentleman insists on a shotgun wedding.

Brigadier Gerard (Universal, 1916)
d: Bert Haldane. 5 reels.
Lewis Waller, A.E. George, Madge Titheridge, Fernand Mailly, Frank Cochrane.
Adventure tale about a charismatic brigadier in the Napoleonic Wars, based on the Arthur Conan Doyle stories.

Bright Lights (MGM, 1925)
d: Robert Z. Leonard. 7 reels.
Charles Ray, Pauline Starke, Lilyan Tashman, Ned Sparks, Lawford Davidson.
A farm boy falls for a Broadway dancer, and tries to keep up with her big-city friends.

Bright Lights of Broadway (Principal Pictures, 1923)
d: Webster Campbell. 7 reels.
Harrison Ford, Doris Kenyon, Edmund Breese, Claire DeLorez, Lowell Sherman, Charles Murray, Effie Shannon, Tyrone Power.
In New York, a small-town girl is lured by the bright lights of Broadway, and marries a cad who promises to make her a star.

The Bright Shawl (Inspiration/First National, 1923)
d: John S. Robertson. 8 reels.
Richard Barthelmess, Dorothy Gish, Edward G. Robinson, Mary Astor, Andre de Beranger, Margaret Seddon, Jetta Goudal, William Powell, Luis Alberni, George Humbert, Anders Randolf.
A Cuban dancer is persuaded to spy on the Spanish army.

Bright Skies (Brentwood Film Corp./Robertson-Cole, 1920)
d: Henry Kolker. 5 reels.
ZaSu Pitts, Tom Gallery, Jack Pratt, Kate Price, Edward Delavanti, Jack Braughall.
An old organ grinder befriends a street waif and makes her his assistant.

Bring Him In (Vitagraph, 1921)

d: Earle Williams, Robert Ensminger.   5 reels.

Earle Williams, Fritzi Ridgeway, Elmer Dewey, Ernest Van Pelt, Paul Weigel, Bruce Gordon.

In the Great Northwest, a doctor who mistakenly believes he killed a gambler is pursued by a mountie who is also convinced of the doctor's guilt.

Bringin' Home the Bacon   (Action Pictures, 1924)

d: Richard Thorpe.   5 reels.

Buffalo Bill Jr., Jean Arthur, Bert Lindley, Lafe McKee, George F. Marion, Wilbur McGaugh, Victor King, Laura Miskin, Frank Ellis.

Out West, an amorous rancher puts his courtin' on hold while he foils stagecoach robbers.

Bringing Home Father   (Universal, 1917)

d: William Worthington.   5 reels.

Franklyn Farnum, Brownie Vernon, Florence Mayon, Arthur Hoyt, Richard La Reno.

A political candidate running on the Prohibition ticket winds up hosting a party which turns into a drunken brawl.

Bringing Up Betty   (World Film Corp., 1919)

d: Oscar Apfel.   5 reels.

Evelyn Greeley, Lyster Chambers, Reginald Denny, Ben Johnson, Grace Carlyle, Joseph Weber, Maude Turner Gordon, Oliver Smith, Grace Hansen, Morgan Wallace.

Fortune hunters swarm to a lawn party honoring a wealthy girl.

Bringing Up Father   (MGM, 1928)

d: Jack Conway.   7 reels.

Marie Dressler, J. Farrell McDonald, Polly Moran, Gertrude Olmstead, Grant Withers, Rose Dione.

Comedy based on the comic strip about a social climber and her prosperous but henpecked husband.

The Brink   (New York Motion Picture Corp./Mutual, 1915)

d: Charles Swickard.   4 reels.

Forrest Winant, Rhea Mitchell, Arthur Maude, Joseph Dowling, Lewis Durham.

After losing a bundle to gamblers, a young man is attracted to a life of crime.

Broad Daylight   (Universal, 1922)

d: Irving Cummings.   5 reels.

Lois Wilson, Jack Mulhall, Ralph Lewis, Kenneth Gibson, Wilton Taylor, Ben Hewlett, Robert Walker.

A crime lord known as "the Scarab" forces an honest man into a life of crime.

The Broad Road   (Associated Authors/Associated First National, 1923)

d: Edmund Mortimer.   6 reels.

Richard C. Travers, May Allison, Ben Hendricks Jr., D.J. Flanagan, Mary Foy, Charles McDonald, L. Emile LaCroix, Roy Kelly, Alicia Collins.

In a lumber camp, two men war over the love of the same girl.

Broadway After Dark   (Warner Bros., 1924)

d: Monta Bell.   7 reels.

Adolphe Menjou, Edward Burns, Anna Q. Nilsson, Carmel Myers, Vera Lewis, Willard Louis, Mervyn LeRoy, Norma Shearer, Otto Hoffman.

In New York, a wealthy playboy wearies of life in the fast lane, and turns his attention to a poor but honest working girl.

Broadway After Midnight   (Krelbar Pictures, 1927)

d: Fred Windermere.   7 reels.

Matthew Betz, Priscilla Bonner, Cullen Landis, Gareth Hughes, Ernest Hilliard, Barbara Tennant, William Turner, Hank Mann, Paul Weigel.

In New York, a nightclub singer is forced by underworld thugs to marry a gangster, and later must stand trial for a murder she did not commit.

Broadway Arizona   (Triangle, 1917)

d: Lynn F. Reynolds.   5 reels.

Olive Thomas, George Chesebro, George Hernandez, Jack Curtis, Dana Ong, Thomas S. Guise, Leola Mae, Robert N. Dunbar.

A cattle rancher falls for a Broadway star.

Broadway Bill   (Metro, 1918)

d: Fred J. Balshofer.   5 reels.

Harold Lockwood, Martha Mansfield, Cornish Beck, Stanton Heck, Raymond C. Hadley, Bert Starkey, W.W. Black, Tom Blake, William Clifford, Art Ortego.

Alcoholic playboy Bill Clayton takes a job in a lumber camp, hoping the change will do him good.

Broadway Billy   (Rayart Pictures, 1926)

d: Harry J. Brown.   5 reels.

Billy Sullivan, Virginia Brown Faire, Jack Herrick, Hazel Howell.

"Broadway Billy," a New York boxer, must win a major bout to pay his wife's hospital bills.

The Broadway Boob   (Associated Exhibitors, 1926)

d: Joseph Henabery.   6 reels.

Glenn Hunter, Mildred Ryan, Antrim Short, Beryl Halley, Margaret Irving.

Danny, a small-town boy, lands a role in a Broadway play. Although his role is small, the hometown folks fantasize that their Danny has achieved stardom.

Broadway Broke   (Selznick, 1923)

d: J. Searle Dawley.   6 reels.

Mary Carr, Percy Marmont, Gladys Leslie, Dore Davidson, Maclyn Arbuckle, Macey Harlam, Edward Earle, Pierre Gendron, Billy Quirk, Henrietta Crosman, Sally Crute.

A retired Broadway actress turns to writing plays, and finds success when her work is purchased by a Hollywood producer.

The Broadway Bubble   (Vitagraph, 1920)

d: George L. Sargent.   5 reels.

Corinne Griffith, Joseph King, Stanley Warmerton, Robert Gaillard.

When she gets her big break to appear on the Broadway stage, a married woman persuades her twin sister to "stand in" for her at home, while she pursues a musical comedy career. But what happens when her husband and her twin fall deeply in love?

A Broadway Butterfly   (Warner Bros., 1925)

d: William Beaudine.   7 reels.

Dorothy Devore, Louise Fazenda, Willard Louis, John Roche, Cullen Landis.

A girl from the sticks descends on Broadway, looking for fame and fortune.

A Broadway Cowboy   (Pathé, 1920)

d: Joseph Franz.   5 reels.

William Desmond, Betty Francisco, Thomas Delmar, J.P. Lockney, Paddy McGuire, Clark Comstock, Evelyn Selbie.

A Montana gal falls for a Broadway actor, but that doesn't

set well with her admirer back home — the sheriff!

Broadway Daddies (Columbia, 1928)
d: Fred Windemere. 6 reels.
Jacqueline Logan, Rex Lease, Alec B. Francis, Phillips Smalley, DeSacia Mooers, Clarissa Selwynne, Betty Francisco.
Eve, a nightclub performer, has plenty of wealthy suitors, but her heart belongs to a nice guy without much money.

The Broadway Drifter (Samuel Zierfler Photoplay Corp., 1927)
d: Bernard McEveety. 6 reels.
George Walsh, Dorothy Hall, Bigelow Cooper, Arthur Donaldson, Paul Doucet, Nellie Savage, Gladys Valerie, Donald Laskley, George Offerman Jr.
Bob, a disowned playboy, tries desperately to make it on his own.

Broadway Fever (Tiffany-Stahl Productions, 1929)
d: Edward Cline. 6 reels.
Sally O'Neil, Roland Drew, Corliss Palmer, Calvert Carter.
In New York, an aspiring actress can't get an audition with Broadway's leading producer, so she goes to work for him as his maid... and wins his heart.

Broadway Gold (Edward Dillon Productions/Truart Film Corp., 1923)
d: Edward Dillon, J. Gordon Cooper. 7 reels.
Elaine Hammerstein, Elliott Dexter, Kathlyn Williams, Eloise Goodale, Richard Wayne, Harold Goodwin, Henry Barrows, Marshall Neilan.
Sunny's a Broadway chorus girl who's suspected of murder.

Broadway Jones (Cohan Feature Film Co./Artcraft, 1917)
d: Joseph Kaufman. 6 reels.
George M. Cohan, Marguerite Snow, Russell Bassett, Crawford Kent, Ida Darling, Joe Smiley.
A chewing-gum heir travels to New York in search of excitement.

Broadway Lady (R-C Pictures/FBO of America, 1925)
d: Wesley Ruggles. 6 reels.
Evelyn Brent, Marjorie Bonner, Theodore von Eltz, Joyce Compton, Clarissa Selwyn, Ernest Hilliard, Johnny Gough.
Rosalie, a Broadway chorus girl, becomes implicated in a shooting when she tries to prevent her best friend's elopement with a cad.

Broadway Love (Universal, 1917)
d: Ida May Park. 5 reels.
William Stowell, Lon Chaney, Dorothy Phillips, Juanita Hansen, Harry Von Meter, Gladys Tennyson, Eve Southern.
Chorus girls have man trouble, but it all leads to wedding bells.

Broadway Madness (Excellent Pictures, 1927)
d: Burton King. 7 reels.
Marguerite DeLaMotte, Donald Keith, Betty Hilburn, Margaret Cloud, George Cowl, Louis Payne, Robert Dudley, Orral Humphreys, Thomas Ricketts, Alfred Fisher, Jack Haley.
Enchanted by her radio personality, a small-town boy is attracted to a Broadway actress. Against all odds, he'll meet and marry her.

The Broadway Madonna (Quality Film Productions/FBO of America, 1922)
d: Harry Revier. 6 reels.
Dorothy Revier, Jack Connolly, Harry Van Meter, Eugene Burr, Juanita Hansen, Lee Willard, Lydia Knott.
At a masked ball, a judge is murdered when he spots a costumed guest robbing his safe.

Broadway Nights (First National, 1927)
d: Joseph C. Boyle. 7 reels.
Lois Wilson, Sam Hardy, Louis John Bartels, Philip Strange, Barbara Stanwyck.
Fannie and Johnny, music hall performers, marry and have a child, but they are forced to separate when their careers take them in opposite directions. Finally, Fannie joins the cast of a show for which Johnny has written the music, and the couple are reunited.

Broadway or Bust (Universal, 1924)
d: Edward Sedgwick. 6 reels.
Hoot Gibson, Ruth Dwyer, Gertrude Astor, King Zany, Stanhope Wheatcroft, Fred Malatesta.
After a precious mineral lode is found beneath their ranch, two partners sell out and go to New York to try and crash into high society.

The Broadway Peacock (Fox, 1922)
d: Charles J. Brabin. 5 reels.
Pearl White, Joseph Striker, Doris Eaton, Harry Southard, Elizabeth Garrison.
May, a cabaret hostess, falls for wealthy Harold, but loses him to a country charmer.

Broadway Rose (Tiffany Productions/Metro, 1922)
d: Robert Z. Leonard. 6 reels.
Mae Murray, Monte Blue, Raymond Bloomer, Ward Crane, Alma Tell, Charles Lane, May Turner Gordon, Jane Jennings, Pauline Dempsey.
Although his wealthy parents oppose the match, a New Yorker secretly weds a Broadway dancer.

A Broadway Saint (World Film Corp., 1919)
d: Harry O. Hoyt. 5 reels.
Montagu Love, George Bunny, Helen Weer, Emile LaCroix, Mrs. Burmeister, Emily Fitzroy, Annie Laurie Spence, Mrs. Stuart Robson, Edward Arnold, Sally Crute.
A New Yorker leaves the big city to find a nice small-town girl. When he meets Mazie, she is all he dreamed of, until he discovers she's really a burlesque performer.

A Broadway Scandal (Universal, 1918)
d: Joseph de Grasse. 5 reels.
Carmel Myers, Edwin August, Lon Chaney, W.H. Bainbridge, Andrew Robson, S.K. Shilling, Frederick Gamble.
Overseas service during World War I opens a New Yorker's eyes to the courage of the French people.

The Broadway Sport (Fox, 1917)
d: Carl Harbaugh. 5 reels.
Stuart Holmes, Wanda Petit, Dan Mason, Mabel Rutter, W.B. Green, Mario Majeroni, Jay Wilson.
A day-dreaming bookkeeper fantasizes about living the high life on Broadway, and about marrying the boss' daughter.

Broken Barriers (MGM, 1924)
d: Reginald Barker. 6 reels.
Norma Shearer, Ruth Stonehouse, George Fawcett, Margaret McWade, Adolphe Menjou, James Kirkwood, Mae Busch.
A young woman reveals to her well-to-do family that she is in love with a married man.

Broken Barriers (Excellent Pictures, 1928)
d: Burton King. 6 reels.

Helene Costello, Gaston Glass, Joseph Girard, Frank Beal, Carlton Stockdale, Frank Hagney.

Hill, a crusading newspaper reporter, aims his editorial guns at an amoral political boss.

Broken Blossoms (Griffith/United Artists, 1919)
w, d: D. W. Griffith. 6 reels.
Lillian Gish, Donald Crisp, Richard Barthelmess, Arthur Howard, Edward Peil, George Beranger, Norman Selby.
A young Chinaman befriends a street waif who has been physically abused by her father.

The Broken Butterfly (Maurice Tourneur Productions/Robertson-Cole, 1919)
d: Maurice Tourneur. 5 reels.
Lew Cody, Mary Alden, Pauline Starke, Peaches Johnson, Nina Byron.
Passionate romance occurs when an American composer meets a Canadian "nature girl."

Broken Chains (Brady Picture Plays/World Film Corp., 1916)
d: Robert Thornby. 5 reels.
John Tansy, Carlyle Blackwell, Herbert Barrington, Stanhope Wheatcroft, Herbert Delmore, Henry West, Louis Grisel, William Sherwood, Madge Evans, Ethel Clayton.
Federal agents crack down on Southern moonshiners.

Broken Chains (Goldwyn, 1922)
d: Allen Holubar. 7 reels.
Malcolm McGregor, Colleen Moore, Ernest Torrence, Claire Windsor, James Marcus, Beryl Mercer, William Orlamond, Gerald Pring, Edward Peil, Leo Willis.
Disgusted with his own lack of courage, an easterner heads to the American West to "find himself." There, he summons the courage to fight for a woman he has fallen in love with, and he wins not only the girl, but his own self-esteem.

Broken Commandments (Fox, 1919)
d: Frank Beal. 5 reels.
Gladys Brockwell, William Scott, Thomas Santschi, G. Raymond Nye, Spottiswoode Aitken, Margaret McWade, Lule Warrenton.
After getting a girl pregnant, an escaped convict tries to get a minister to marry them, but instead he's recaptured and sent back to prison. The girl marries an old flame, and together they raise her child for three years. Then the convict re-enters her life.

A Broken Doll (Allan Dwan Productions/Associated Producers, 1921)
d: Allan Dwan. 5 reels.
Tommy, a ranch hand, goes to the city to buy a new doll for the foreman's young daughter. He will encounter violence, adventure, even false imprisonment; but after the storm Tommy returns triumphantly with a new doll for the little girl... and a new bride for himself!

Broken Fetters (Universal, 1916)
d: Rex Ingram. 5 reels.
Violet Mersereau, Frank Smith, William Garwood, Kittens Reichert, Charles Francis, Earl Simmons, William Dyer, Paul Panzer, Isabel Patterson, Paddy Sullivan, Guy Morville.

An orphan girl is brought from China to America by a slave trader.

The Broken Gate (J.L. Frothingham Productions/Pathé, 1920)
d: Paul Scardon. 6 reels.

Bessie Barriscale, Joseph Kilgour, Sam DeGrasse, Marguerite DeLaMotte, Arnold Gregg, Lloyd Bacon, Evelyn Selbie, Alfred Allen.
Judgmental neighbors ostracize a young man and his mother because they know he was conceived out of wedlock.

The Broken Gate (Tiffany Productions, 1927)
d: James C. McKay. 6 reels.
Dorothy Phillips, William Collier Jr., Jean Arthur, Phillips Smalley, Florence Turner, Gibson Gowland, Charles A. Post, Caroline Rankin, Vera Lewis, Jack McDonald, Adele Watson.
In a small town, a single mother is shunned by the community for having borne a child out of wedlock.

Broken Hearts of Broadway (Irving Cummings Productions, 1923)
d: Irving Cummings. 7 reels.
Colleen Moore, John Walker, Alice Lake, Tully Marshall, Kate Price, Creighton Hale, Anthony Merlo, Arthur Stuart Hull, Freeman Wood.
In the world of Broadway glitz and glamour, a simple country girl has trouble "fitting in." First, she refuses a casting director's advances, then finds herself falsely accused of murder.

Broken Hearts of Hollywood (Warner Bros., 1926)
d: Lloyd Bacon. 8 reels.
Patsy Ruth Miller, Douglas Fairbanks Jr., Louise Dresser, Jerry Miley, Stuart Holmes, Barbara Worth.
In Hollywood, an over-the-hill actress fights to keep her ingenue daughter from being seduced by an unscrupulous talent agent.

The Broken Law (Fox, 1915)
d: Oscar C. Apfel. 5 reels.
William Farnum, Dorothy Bernard, Mary Martin, Bertram Marburgh, Richard Neill, Nicholas Dunaeu, Lyster Chambers, Christine Mayo.
After he learns that he has a half-sister among the Romany Gypsies, a novelist decides to join the clan.

The Broken Mask (Morris R. Schlank Productions/Anchor Film Distributors, 1928)
d: James P. Hogan. 6 reels.
Cullen Landis, Barbara Bedford, William V. Mong, Wheeler Oakman, James Marcus, Philippe DeLacy, Ina Anson, Nanci Price, Pat Harmon.
Fiery Argentine dancers fall in love, but the man's career is jeopardized because of his scarred face.

The Broken Melody (Selznick/Select Pictures Corp., 1919)
d: William P.S. Earle. 5 reels.
Eugene O'Brien, Lucy Cotton, Corinne Barker, Donald Hall, Ivo Dawson, Gus Weinberg, Jack Johnstone, Helen Reinecke.
Two hopeful artists—he, a painter; she, a singer—love each other though an ocean apart.

The Broken Silence (Pine Tree Pictures/Arrow Film Corp., 1922)
d: Del Henderson. 6 reels.
Zena Keefe, Robert Elliott, J. Barney Sherry, Jack Hopkins, Jack Drumier, James Milady, Roy Gordon, Gypsy O'Brien, Dorothy Allen, Ted Griffen, Joseph Depew, William Fisher.
In the Canadian Northwest, a brother and sister team up to bring a murderer to justice.

The Broken Spur (Ben Wilson Productions/Arrow Film Corp., 1921)
d: Ben Wilson. 5 reels.

Jack Hoxie, Evelyn Nelson, Jim Welch, Wilbur McGaugh, Edward Berman, Harry Rattenberry, Marin Sais.

Knowing he bears a strong resemblance to Joe, a railroad engineer, a bandit poses as his lookalike to prevent a railroad line from being built.

Joe and the bandit are both played by Jack Hoxie.

Broken Ties (World Film Corp., 1918)
d: Arthur Ashley. 5 reels.
June Elvidge, Montagu Love, Arthur Ashley, Pinna Nesbit, Alec B. Francis, Kate Lester, Arthur Matthews, Frances Miller.
Racial hatred threatens a match between a white man and a West Indian girl.

The Broken Violin (Atlantic Features/Arrow Film Corp., 1923)
d: Jack Dillon. 6 reels.
Joseph Blake, Warren Cook, Henry Sedley, Sydney Deane, Reed Howes, Dorothy Mackaill, Rita Rogan, J.H. Lewis, Zena Keefe, Gladden James, Edward Roseman.
Siblings John and Beatrice are attacked by hoodlums seeking to steal their inheritance.

The Broken Wing (B.P. Schulberg Productions/Preferred Pictures, 1923)
d: Tom Forman. 6 reels.
In a town on the Mexican border, a ranchero's daughter prays for a husband. When Marvin, an American pilot, crashlands his plane on the rancho, the lovesick girl believes he's the answer to her prayers.

The Broncho Twister (Fox, 1927)
d: Orville O. Dull. 6 reels.
Tom Mix, Helene Costello, George Irving, Dorothy Kitchen, Paul Nicholson, Doris Lloyd, Malcolm Waite, Jack Pennick, Otto Fries, Tony the wonder horse.
Tom, a returning U.S. Marine, finds his family's ranch is under siege by a villainous landowner.

The Bronze Bell (Thomas H. Ince Productions/Paramount, 1921)
d: James W. Horne. 6 reels.
Courtenay Foote, Doris May, John Davidson, Claire DuBrey, Noble Johnson, Otto Hoffman, Gerald Pring, C. Norman Hammond, Howard Crampton, Fred Huntley.
David, a British officer who bears a strong resemblance to a recently deceased East Indian prince, travels to India and arrives just in time to help defeat a rebellion.
Courtenay Foote plays both the Indian prince and his British double.

The Bronze Bride (Universal, 1917)
d: Henry MacRae. 5 reels.
Claire McDowell, Frank Mayo, Frankie Lee, Edward Clark, Charles Hill Mailes, Eddie Polo, Harry Archer, Winter Hall, Betty Schade.
Caught in a powerful bear trap in the Canadian woods, a hunter is rescued by a beautiful Indian maiden.

Brooding Eyes (Banner Productions, 1926)
d: Edward J. LeSaint. 6 reels.
Lionel Barrymore, Ruth Clifford, Robert Ellis, Montagu Love, William V. Mong, Lucien Littlefield, John Miljan, Dot Farley, Alma Bennett.
Gangsters try to take over the estate of a "deceased" lord. Unknown to them, the lord is very much alive.

Brotherly Love (MGM, 1928)

d: Charles Reisner. 7 reels. (Part talkie.)
Karl Dane, George K. Arthur, Jean Arthur, Richard Carlyle, Edward Connelly, Marcia Harris.
Jerry, a convict, is the star player on his prison football team. After his term of imprisonment is up, he deliberately tries to get re-arrested so that he can participate in the Big Game against a rival prison.

Brothers Divided (Pathé, 1919)
d: Frank Keenan. 5 reels.
Frank Keenan, Wallace MacDonald, Ruth Langston, James O. Barrows, Gertrude Claire, Russ Powell, Mary Talbot, Paul Mullen, Curtiss G. Powell.
An ex-con returns home and becomes a successful mill owner, winning the respect and love of his brother and his own son, who had been raised by his uncle.

Brothers Under the Skin (Goldwyn, 1922)
d: E. Mason Hopper. 6 reels.
Norman Kerry, Claire Windsor, Pat O'Malley, Helene Chadwick, Mae Busch.
Though far apart in the corporate hierarchy, a shipping clerk and the company's vice president share a common curse: shrewish wives.

The Brown Derby (C.C. Burr Pictures/First National, 1926)
d: Charles Hines. 7 reels.
Johnny Hines, Diana Kane, Ruth Dwyer, Flora Finch, Edmund Breese, J. Barney Sherry, Bradley Barker, Herbert Standing, Harold Foshay, Bob Slater.
Comedy about a young plumber who gets mistaken for a wealthy gent named "Plummer," and winds up marrying Plummer's niece. He believes he owes his good fortune to his brown derby, left to him by an uncle who promised it would bring him luck.

Brown of Harvard (Selig Polyscope, 1918)
d: Harry Beaumont. 6 reels.
Tom Moore, Hazel Daly, Sydney Ainsworth, Warner Richmond, Walter McGrail, Nancy Winston, Alice Gordon, Kempton Greene, Frank Joyner, Robert Ellis, Lydia Dalzell, Walter Hiers, Arthur Hausman, Johnnie Walker.
Misunderstandings threaten to break up a college hero and his sweetie.

Brown of Harvard (MGM, 1926)
d: Jack Conway. 8 reels.
William Haines, Jack Pickford, Mary Brian, Francis X. Bushman Jr., David Torrence, Mary Alden, Edward Connelly, Guinn Williams.
Two college roommates love the same girl.

The Bruiser (American Film Co./Mutual, 1916)
d: Charles Bartlett. 5 reels.
William Russell, Charlotte Burton, George Ferguson, Lizette Thorne, Roy Stewart, Pete Morrison, Al Fordyce, Eric Jacobs.
Longshoremen trying to negotiate a new labor contract pin their hopes on winning the waterfront boxing contest.

The Brute (Warner Bros., 1927)
d: Irving Cummings. 7 reels.
Monte Blue, Leila Hyams, Clyde Cook, Carol Nye, Paul Nicholson.
Out West, an easygoing cowhand falls for the fair Jennifer... but finds that she is "owned" by Felton, a crooked gambler. The cowpoke bides his time, and when he comes into some money he offers to "buy" Jennifer from Felton.

The Brute Breaker (Universal, 1919)

d: Lynn Reynolds. 6 reels.
Frank Mayo, Kathryn Adams, Harry Northrup, Jack Curtis, Burwell Hamrick, Bert Sprotte, Frank Brownlee, Charles Le Moyne.
In a French Canadian lumber camp, a mysterious stranger charms the boss' daughter but rouses the ire of several roughneck loggers.

The Brute Master (J. Parker Read Jr./Pathé, 1920)
d: Roy H. Marshall. 5 reels.
Hobart Bosworth, Anna Q. Nilsson, William Conklin, Margaret Livingston.
The love of a good woman mellows a ship's captain once known as "the Brute."

Bubbles (Pioneer Film Corp., 1920)
d: Wayne Mack. 5 reels.
Mary Anderson, Jack Connolly, Bert Woodruff, Adelaide Elliott, Jack Mower, Arthur Millet, Mary Land.
"Bubbles" is a tomboy who often dresses as a male. Eventually, a man who loves her persuades her to give up the tomboy act and marry him.

Buchanan's Wife (Fox, 1918)
d: Charles J. Brabin. 5 reels.
Virginia Pearson, Marc McDermott, Victor Sutherland, Ned Finley.
After her husband disappears, a woman remarries. Then, the first husband returns.

Buck Privates (Universal, 1928)
d: Melville W. Brown. 7 reels.
Lya DePutti, ZaSu Pitts, Malcolm McGregor, James Marcus, Eddie Gribbon, Ted Duncan, Bud Jamison, Les Bates.
In occupied Germany after the Armistice, an American buck private falls for the daughter of a German officer he once captured.

The Buckaroo Kid (Universal, 1926)
d: Lynn Reynolds. 6 reels.
Hoot Gibson, Ethel Shannon, Burr McIntosh, Harry Todd, James Gordon.
Out West, a young ranch foreman is assigned the task of managing a repossessed ranch. The former owner, however, is disinclined to let the young man take over, and a gunfight ensues.

Bucking Broadway (Universal, 1917)
d: Jack Ford. 5 reels.
Harry Carey, Molly Malone, Vester Pegg, L.M. Wells, William Gettinger.
A cowpoke follows his gal when a devious slicker lures her to the big city.

Bucking the Barrier (Fox, 1923)
d: Colin Campbell. 5 reels.
Dustin Farnum, Arline Pretty, Leon Barry, Colin Chase, Hayford Hobbs, Sidney D'Albrook.
Carew, in Alaska working his mine, gets word that he has inherited a fortune, and must travel to England to claim it.

Bucking the Line (Fox, 1921)
d: Carl Harbaugh. 5 reels.
Maurice B. Flynn, Molly Malone, Norman Selby, Edwin B. Tilton, Kathryn McGuire, J. Farrell MacDonald, James Farley, Leslie Casey, George Kerby.
Monty, a railroad worker, discovers that the foreman is conspiring with the owner's business rivals to delay the project. Monty foils the treachery, sees the railroad line to completion, and wins the hand of the owner's daughter.

Bucking the Tiger (Selznick, 1921)
d: Henry Kolker. 6 reels.
Conway Tearle, Winifred Westover, Gladden James, Helene Montrose, Harry Lee, George A. Wright, Templar Saxe.
In Alaska, four failed prospectors decide on a grim solution to their financial woes: They will pool their remaining money to buy an insurance policy on the life of one of the men, whichever one loses in a game of cards. That man will commit suicide, and the remaining three would be his beneficiaries. The fatal card is drawn, and the loser returns glumly to working his mine claim before killing himself. Predictably, the prospector strikes gold, everyone prospers, the insurance plan is cancelled, and the prospector falls in love with a good woman.

Bucking the Truth (Universal, 1926)
d: Milburn Morante. 5 reels.
Pete Morrison, Brinsley Shawj, Bruce Gordon, William LaRoche, Charles Whittaker, Ione Reed, Vester Pegg.
Out West, an honest cowpoke is mistaken for a desperado.

Buckshot John (Bosworth/Paramount, 1915)
d: Hobart Bosworth. 5 reels.
Art Acord, Hobart Bosworth, Courtenay Foote, Helen Wolcott, Herbert Standing, Marshall Stedman, Frank Lanning, Oscar Linkenhelt, Rhea Haines.
After serving fifteen years for robbery, a convict decides to come clean about the location of the stolen loot. Trouble is, he contacts a phony clairvoyant to assist him, and the charlatan gets to the gold before he does. Now it's up to the ex-con to steal the gold a second time.

The Bugle Call (New York Motion Picture Corp./Triangle, 1916)
d: Reginald Barker. 5 reels.
William Collier Jr., Wyndham Standing, Anna Lehr, Thomas Guise, Joe Goodboy.
In the Wild West, a young boy saves his stepmother during an Indian raid.
This film was remade by MGM in 1927 as a vehicle for Jackie Coogan.

The Bugle Call (MGM, 1927)
d: Edward Sedgwick. 6 reels.
Jackie Coogan, Claire Windsor, Herbert Rawlinson, Johnny Mack Brown, Tom O'Brien, Harry Todd, Nelson McDowell, Sarah Padden.
Nineteenth century frontier drama about an orphan who serves as bugle boy at a U.S. cavalry post.
Remake of the 1916 New York Motion Picture Company film *The Bugle Call*, both versions being based on the story by C. Gardner Sullivan.

The Bugler of Algiers (Universal, 1916)
d: Rupert Julian. 5 reels.
Kingsley Benedict, Ella Hall, Rupert Julian.
Wartime tale of a soldier in love with his best friend's sister.

The Builder of Bridges (World Film Corp., 1915)
d: George Irving. 5 reels.
C. Aubrey Smith, Marie Edith Wells, Jack B. Sherrill, Fred Eric, Edward R. Mawson, G.W. Anson, Kate Meek, Helen Weer, Sidney Mason.
A devious girl flirts with a bridge builder, who falls for her and proposes marriage. When he learns that she tricked him, he leaves. But now the girl decides she loves him after all.

Builders of Castles (Thomas A. Edison, Inc., 1917)
d: Ben Turbett. 5 reels.
Marc MacDermott, Miriam Nesbitt, William Wadsworth, Robert Brower, Edward Longman, Jessie Stevens, Florence Stover, Nellie Grant, Simon P. Gillies, Frank Trainor.
An honest businessman is duped into joining a fly-by-night enterprise.

Bulldog Courage (Clinton Productions/Russell Productions, 1922)
d: Edward Kull. 5 reels.
George Larkin, Bessie Love, Albert MacQuarrie, Karl Silvera, Frank Whitman, Bill Patton, Barbara Tennant.
Out West, an young man starts to pick a fight with a rancher, but hesitates when he falls in love with Gloria, the rancher's daughter.

Bunty Pulls the Strings (Goldwyn, 1921)
d: Reginald Barker. 7 reels.
Leatrice Joy, Russell Simpson, Raymond Hatton, Cullen Landis, Casson Ferguson, Josephine Crowell, Edythe Chapman, Roland Rushton, Georgia Woodthorpe, Sadie Gordon, Otto Hoffman.
In Scotland, a canny lass controls her father and two brothers through her feminine wiles.

Bullet Proof (Universal, 1920)
d: Lynn Reynolds. 5 reels.
Harry Carey, Kathleen O'Connor, Fred Gamble, William Ryno, J. Farrell McDonald, Beatrice Burnham, Bob McKenzie, Joe Harris, Charles LeMoyne, Robert McKim.
Vengeance drives a westerner to hunt down a murderous bandit.

Bullets and Brown Eyes (Triangle, 1916)
d: Scott Sidney. 5 reels.

William Desmond, Bessie Barriscale, Wyndham Standing, Joseph J. Dowling, J. Barney Sherry, Roy Laidlaw, Louise Brownell, Leonard Smith, Jack Gilbert.

Love among the royals, in opposing European countries.

A Bunch of Keys (Essanay, 1915)
d: Richard Foster Baker. 5 reels.
John Slavin, William Burress, June Keith, Charlotte Mineau, Leota Chrider, William Castelet, Royal Douglas, Fred Wyatt.
Three girl cousins, all surnamed Keys, are due to inherit their late uncle's hotel. However, their lawyer, an unethical weasel, concocts a phony clause in the will saying that the hotel will pass only to the cousin deemed the homeliest. Then he romances the girl he thinks is the homeliest, hoping to snag some of her fortune for himself. But the girls smell a rat.

The Burden of Proof (Marion Davies Film Corp./Select Pictures, 1918)
d: Julius Steger, John G. Adolfi. 5 reels.
Marion Davies, Mary Richards, Eloise Clement, John Merkyl, L. Rogers Lytton, Willard Cooley, Fred Hearn, Fred Lenox, Maude Lowe.
German spies try to compromise the young bride of a U.S. government official.

The Burglar (World Film Corp., 1917)
d: Harley Knoles. 5 reels.
Carlyle Blackwell, Harry La Mont, Richard Clarke, Justine Cutting, Evelyn Greeley, Rosina Henley, Frank Mayo, Madge Evans, Victor Kennard, Jack Drumier, Henry Drehle.
A young prankster's life is ruined by a single "thrill" robbery.

The Burglar and the Lady (Sun Photoplay Co., 1914)
d: Herbert Blaché. 5 reels.
James J. Corbett, Edward Cecil, Claire Whitney, Fraunie Fraunholz, Calvin Reisland, Augusta Burmeister.
Two brothers, raised separately, follow divergent career paths. One becomes a burglar, the other a clergyman. Ironically, both fall in love with the same girl.
The brother who became a thief is played by James J. Corbett, who had been heavyweight boxing champion of the world in the 1890s.

Burglar by Proxy (Jack Pickford Productions/First National, 1919)
w, d: Jack Dillon. 5 reels.
Jack Pickford, Gloria Hope, Jack Dillon, Robert Walker.
When a young man is falsely accused of stealing some important papers from his girlfriend's father, he must become a temporary burglar to steal those papers back from the real thief, and clear his name.

A Burglar For a Night (Paralta Plays, Inc./ W.W. Hodkinson, 1918)
d: Ernest C. Warde. 5 reels.
J. Warren Kerrigan, Lois Wilson, William Elmer, Herbert Prior, Robert Brower, Charles French, Lydia Yeamans Titus, Arma Roma.
The son of a railroad owner fights a takeover plot by his dad's business rivals.

Burglar Proof (Famous Players-Lasky/Paramount, 1920)
d: Maurice Campbell. 5 reels.
Bryant Washburn, Lois Wilson, Grace Morse, Emily Chichester, Clarence H. Geldart, Clarence Burton, Tom D. Bates, Hayward Mack, Blanche Gray.
After losing his girlfriend due to his poverty, a young man resolves never to be poor again. He applies himself to a new career, and after a few years, becomes wealthy. Now he'd like to reclaim his old sweetie... but would such a gold digger be worth going after?

Buried Treasure (Cosmopolitan/Paramount, 1921)
d: George D. Baker. 7 reels.
Marion Davies, Norman Kerry, Anders Randolf, John Charles, Edith Shayne, Earl Schenck, Thomas Findlay.
A tale of buried treasure, reincarnation, and the searchers who recover the treasure centuries later.

Burlesque on Carmen — see: Charlie Chaplin's Burlesque on Carmen (1916)

Burn 'em Up Barnes (Mastodon Films/Affiliated Distributors, 1921)
d: George André Beranger, Johnny Hines. 6 reels.
Johnny Hines, Edmund Breese, George Fawcett, Betty Carpenter, J. Barney Sherry, Matthew Betts, Richard Thorpe, Julia Swayne Gordon, Dorothy Leeds, Harry Fraser.
Wealthy Whitney Barnes, disgusted with his son's cavalier ways, disowns the youngster, who's known as "Burn 'em Up Barnes" because of his fondness for fast motor cars. The young man lives as a hobo for a while, but finds a streak of responsibility within him when he comes to the aid of a young woman in trouble.

Burning Bridges (Charles R. Rogers Productions/Pathé, 1928)
d: James P. Hogan. 6 reels.
Harry Carey, Kathleen Collins, William N. Bailey, Dave

Kirby, Raymond Wells, Edward Phillips, Florence Midgely, Henry A. Barrows, Sam Allen.
Twin brothers Bob and Jim take on a crooked sheriff. Carey portrays both twins.

Burning Daylight (Metro, 1920)
d: Edward Sloman. 6 reels.
Mitchell Lewis, Helen Ferguson, William V. Mong, Alfred Allen, Edward Jobson, Robert Bolder, Gertrude Astor, Arthur E. Carew, Louis Morrison, Newton Hall, Aaron Edwards.
When Burning Daylight, a miner, strikes gold, he ignites a gold rush in his part of Alaska. Based on the Jack London novel of the same name.

Burning Daylight (First National, 1928)
d: Charles J. Brabin. 7 reels.
Doris Kenyon, Milton Sills, Arthur Stone, Guinn Williams, Lawford Davidson, Jane Winton, Stuart Holmes, Edmund Breese, Howard Truesdale, Frank Hagney, Harry Northrup.
An Alaska real estate mogul is fleeced by a group of investors. Remake of the 1920 Metro film *Burning Daylight*, both versions based on the novel by Jack London.

Burning Sands (Famous Players-Lasky/Paramount, 1922)
d: George Melford. 7 reels.
Milton Sills, Wanda Hawley, Louise Dresser, Jacqueline Logan, Robert Cain, Fenwick Oliver, Winter Hall, Harris Gordon, Albert Roscoe, Cecil Holland, Joe Ray.
Lane, a British subject who maintains a home in Arabia, falls in love with Muriel, a fellow Brit, at an embassy ball.

Burning the Candle (Essanay, 1917)
d: Harry Beaumont. 5 reels.
Henry B. Walthall, Mary Charleson, Julien Barton, Frankie Raymond, Thurlow Brewer, Patrick Calhoun.
Newly married, a Southern boy and his bride move to New York. Their dream of happiness is shattered, however, when his new big-city job drags him into a vortex of alcoholism and despair.

Burning the Wind (Universal, 1929)
d: Henry MacRae. 6 reels.
Hoot Gibson, Virginia Brown Faire, Cesare Gravina, Boris Karloff, Pee Wee Homes, Robert Homans, George Grandee.
In New Mexico, fellow ranch owners plot to have the son of one marry the daughter of the other. Because the young people would never go along with an "arranged" courtship, the two fathers have to set a trap for them... and the youngsters fall into it.

The Burning Trail (Universal, 1925)
d: Arthur Rosson. 5 reels.
William Desmond, Albert J. Smith, Mary McIvor, James Corey, Jack Dougherty, Edmund Cobb, Dolores Roussey, Harry Tenbrook.
Out West, a former prizefighter gets a job as a cook on a ranch, but finds that his physical talents are needed when a major fire breaks out.

Burning Up Broadway (Sterling Pictures, 1928)
d: Phil Rosen. 6 reels.
Helene Costello, Robert Frazer, Sam Hardy, Ernest Hilliard, Max Asher, Jack Rich.
In the Prohibition era, an undercover revenue agent falls for a bootlegger's girlfriend.

Burning Words (Universal, 1923)
d: Stuart Paton. 5 reels.

Roy Stewart, Laura LaPlante, Harold Goodwin, Edith Yorke, Alfred Fisher, William Welsh, Noble Johnson, Eve Southern, Harry Carter, George McDaniels.
In the Canadian Northwest, brother Mounties fall in love with the same dance hall girl.

Burnt Wings (Universal, 1920)
d: W. Christy Cabanne. 5 reels.
Josephine Hill, Frank Mayo, Rudolph Christians, Betty Blythe, Beatrice Burnham.
To make ends meet, a struggling artist's wife is forced into prostitution. Remake of Universal's 1915 film *The Primrose Path*.

The Bush Leaguer (Warner Bros., 1927)
d: Howard Bretherton. 7 reels.
Monte Blue, Leila Hyams, Clyde Cook, William Demarest.
A garage mechanic yearns to be a baseball player, and decides to pursue his dream.

The Busher (Paramount, 1919)
d: Jerome Storm. 5 reels.
Charles Ray, Colleen Moore, Jack Gilbert, Jay Morley, Otto Hoffman, Jack Nelson.
A young minor-league ballplayer is given his chance to make it in the big leagues.

The Bushranger (MGM, 1928)
d: Chet Withey. 7 reels.
Tim McCoy, Marian Douglas, Russell Simpson, Arthur Lubin, Ed Brady, Frank Baker, Dale Austen, Richard R. Neill, Rosemary Cooper.
To avenge a lady's honor, an Englishman fights a duel that results in the death of his rival. He is arrested and sentenced to prison, but escapes to a new life in Australia.

Business is Business (Universal, 1915)
d: Otis Turner. 6 reels.
Gretchen Lederer, Nat Goodwin, Maude George, Marc Robbins, Frank Newburg, Wellington Plater, Wyndham Standing, Hobart Bosworth.
A newly successful businessman lets wealth and privilege go to his head.

The Business of Life (Vitagraph, 1918)
d: Tom Terriss. 5 reels.
Alice Joyce, Betty Blythe, Walter McGrail, Percy Standing, Nellie Spaulding, Templer Saxe, Herbert Pattee.
While working for an antique collector, a young woman falls in love with him.

The Buster (Fox, 1923)
d: Colin Campbell. 5 reels.
Dustin Farnum, Doris Pawn, Gilbert Holmes, Francis McDonald, Lucille Hutton.
Out West, a rancher arranges a fake kidnapping of a city girl, to "teach her a lesson." He intends to "rescue" her, but complications occur when a stranger interferes and throws the plan off schedule.

Bustin' Thru (Universal, 1925)
d: Clifford Smith. 5 reels.
Jack Hoxie, Helen Lynch, William Norton Bailey, Alfred Allen, Georgie Grandee.
Out West, a rancher falls in love with a young woman, not knowing she is the daughter of the man who is out to steal his property.

The Butter and Egg Man (First National, 1928)
d: Richard Wallace. 7 reels.

Jack Mulhall, Greta Nissen, Sam Hardy, William Demarest, Gertrude Astor.

Jones, a small town boy who's always dreamed of being a Broadway producer, gets his chance when a crooked promoter sells him a "worthless" play. But Jones goes ahead with the production anyway, and after he and the leading lady fall in love, their play has an SRO Broadway run.

Butterflies in the Rain   (Universal, 1926)
d: Edward Sloman.   8 reels.

Laura LaPlante, James Kirkwood, Robert Ober, Dorothy Cumming, Oscar Beregi, Grace Ogden, Dorothy Stokes, Edwards Davis, Edward Lockhart, James Anderson, Clarence Thompson, Rose Burdick, George Periolat.

Tina, a fire-breathing feminist, agrees to marry John, but only on the condition that she enjoy absolute freedom to go about as she pleases.

The Butterfly   (Shubert Film Corp./World Film Corp., 1915)
d: O.A.C. Lund.   5 reels.

Howard Estabrook, Barbara Tennant, O.A.C. Lund, Jessie Lewis, Julia Stuart, Fred Radcliffe, Albert Edmondson.

Revenge takes center stage when a hunchback impresario plots against a woman who once spurned him.

Butterfly   (Universal, 1924)
d: Clarence Brown.   8 reels.

Laura LaPlante, Norman Kerry, Kenneth Harlan, Ruth Clifford, Cesare Gravina, Margaret Livingston, Freeman Wood.

A spiteful young woman makes a play for her sister's sweetheart.

The Butterfly Girl   (Mutual, 1917)
d: Henry Otto.   5 reels.

Margarita Fischer, Baby Marie Kiernan, Jack Mower, J. Gordon Russell, Della Pringle, John Steppling.

On the run from a lecherous agent, a young woman joins a troupe of Hawaiian dancers.

The Butterfly Girl   (Playgoers Pictures/Pathé, 1921)
d: John Gorman.   5 reels.

Marjorie Daw, Fritzi Brunette, King Baggot, Jean DeBriac, Ned Whitney Warren.

Edith, a wealthy small-town flirt, decides to go to the big city and ensnare men.

The Butterfly Man   (L.J. Gasnier Productions/Robertson-Cole, 1920)
d: Ida May Park.   6 reels.

Lew Cody, Louise Lovely, Lilie Leslie, Rosemary Theby, Martha Mattox, Mary Land, Alberta Lee, Augustus Phillips, Alec B. Francis, Andrew Robson.

A sleazy gigolo seeks to marry wealth; but in a rare about-face, he unselfishly saves a child from a burning building and is proclaimed a hero.

A Butterfly on the Wheel   (Shubert Film Corp./World Film Corp., 1915)
d: Maurice Tourneur.   5 reels.

Holbrook Blinn, Vivian Martin, George Ralph, June Elvidge, John Hines.

Suspicions of infidelity intrude on the blissful union of two socialites.

Buttons   (MGM, 1927)
w, d: George Hill.   7 reels.

Jackie Coogan, Lars Hanson, Gertrude Olmstead, Polly

Moran, Roy D'Arcy, Paul Hurst, Jack McDonald, Coy Watson Jr.

Buttons, a street waif, gets a job as page boy on a large steamship. Though his antics on board have him thrown in the brig by the exasperated captain, Buttons eventually shows his mettle by saving the captain from drowning after a shipwreck.

The Buzzard's Shadow   (American Film Co./Mutual, 1915)
d: Thomas Ricketts.   5 reels.

Harold Lockwood, May Allison, William Stowell, Harry Von Meter, Alice Ann Rooney, Dick La Reno, Betty Hart, Virginia Fordyce.

On a mission across the desert, a U.S. Army scout finds his enemy has poisoned him.

By Divine Right   (Grand-Asher Distributing Corp., 1924)
d: R. William Neill.   7 reels.

Mildred Harris, Anders Randolf, Elliott Dexter, Sidney Bracey, Jeanne Carpenter, Grace Carlyle, DeWitt Jennings.

To escape a would-be seducer, a young woman takes a job in a mission and soon falls in love with the chief missionary.

By Hook or Crook   (World Film Corp., 1918)
d: Dell Henderson.   5 reels.

Carlyle Blackwell, Evelyn Greeley, Jack Drumier, Frank Doane, Jennie Ellison, Nora Cecil, Alice Chapin, Henry Warwick.

To help his girlfriend outwit her villainous uncle, a socialite turns to cracking safes.

By Proxy   (Triangle, 1918)
d: Cliff Smith.   5 reels.

Roy Stewart, Maude Wayne, Walter Perry, Wilbur Higby, John Lince, Harry Yamamoto.

Trying to help a friend, a cowpoke fetches the girl he thinks his pal's in love with—but she's the wrong gal.

By Right of Possession   (Vitagraph, 1917)
d: William Wolbert.   5 reels.

Mary Anderson, Antonio Moreno, Otto Lederer, Leon Kent.

Out West, a liberated woman runs for the office of Sheriff.

By Right of Purchase   (Select Pictures Corp., 1918)
d: Charles Miller.   6 reels.

Norma Talmadge, Eugene O'Brien, Ida Darling, William Courtleigh Jr., Charles Wellesley, Florence B. Billings.

A girl who married for money finds herself falling in love with her husband.

By the World Forgot   (Vitagraph, 1918)
d: David Smith.   5 reels.

Hedda Nova, J. Frank Glendon, Ed Alexander, Patricia Palmer, R.S. Bradbury, George Kunkel, Otto Lederer.

Shanghaied, a young man finds love on a Pacific island.

By Whose Hand?   (World Film Corp., 1916)
d: James Durkin.   5 reels.

Edna Wallace Hopper, Charles J. Ross, Muriel Ostriche, Nicholas Dunaew, John Dillion, James Ryley.

When a wealthy investor is found murdered, suspicion points at two lovers.

By Whose Hand?   (Columbia, 1927)
d: Walter Lang.   6 reels.

Eugenia Gilbert, William Scott, Ricardo Cortez, J. Thornton Baston, Tom Dugan, Edgar Washington Blue, Lillian Leighton, John Steppling, DeSacia Mooers.

At a Long Island society party, a dowager's jewels are stolen during an electric blackout.

C.O.D. (Vitagraph, 1915)
d: Tefft Johnson. 4 reels.
Harry Davenport, Hughie Mack, Charles Brown, Eulalie Jensen, Mabel Kelly, Edwina Robbins, Jack Bulger, William Dunn, Stephen Lennon, William Shea, Minnie Storey.
Three men, all of whose initials are C.O.D., take a vacation trip together.

The Cabaret (World Film Corp., 1918)
d: Harley Knoles. 5 reels.
June Elvidge, Montagu Love, Carlyle Blackwell, Captain Charles, John Bowers, George MacQuarrie.
Helene, a cabaret dancer, becomes a portrait model for four artists, all of whom fall in love with her.

Cabaret (Famous Players-Lasky/Paramount, 1927)
d: Robert G. Vignola. 7 reels.
Gilda Gray, Tom Moore, Chester Conklin, Mona Palma, Jack Egan, William Harrigan, Charles Byer, Anna Lavsa.
Gloria, a child of the New York tenements, grows up to become a headliner in a posh night club.

The Cabaret Girl (Universal, 1918)
d: Douglas Gerrard. 5 reels.
Ruth Clifford, Ashton Dearholt, Carmel Phillips, Harry Van Meter, Jack Nelson.
Failing in her attempts to become an opera singer, a girl turns to cabaret singing instead.

Cactus Crandall (Triangle, 1918)
d: Cliff Smith. 5 reels.
Roy Stewart, Marion Marvin, Pete Morrison, William Ellingford, Joe Rickson.
In the Southwest, a cattle rancher battles Mexican bandidos.

The Cactus Cure (Ben Wilson Productions/Arrow Film Corp., 1925)
d: Ward Hayes. 5 reels.
Dick Hatton, Yakima Canutt, Wilbur McGaugh, Marilyn Mills.
Out West, a transplanted New York boy tries to mend his intemperate ways.

Cactus Trails (Unique/Aywon, 1926)
d: Harry S. Webb. 5 reels.
Jack Perrin, Alma Rayford, Nelson McDowell, Wilbur McGaugh.
A returned World War I hero rescues a girl in a runaway carriage, and later has to rescue the same girl from kidnappers.

A Cafe in Cairo (Hunt Stromberg Productions, 1924)
d: Chet Withey. 6 reels.
Priscilla Dean, Robert Ellis, Carl Stockdale, Evelyn Selbie, Harry Woods, John Steppling, Carmen Phillips, Larry Steers, Ruth King, Vincent Orona.
In the Arabian desert, the orphaned daughter of slain British parents grows up believing that she is Arab. One day, she is assigned by a renegade shiek to steal an important document from a visiting American soldier, but falls in love with him instead.

The Caillaux Case (Fox, 1918)
d: Richard Stanton. 7 reels.
Madlaine Traverse, Henry Warwick, George Majeroni, Eugene Ormonde, Philip Van Loan, Emile La Croix, Norma McCloud, George Humbert, Frank McGlynn.
Heavy drama about a social climbing woman who marries, divorces, then remarries, each time ascending the ladder of prestige. Eventually it leads to her doom.

Caleb Piper's Girl (Astra Film Corp./Pathé, 1919)
d: Ernest Traxler. 5 reels.
Helene Chadwick, Spottiswood Aitken, William A. Lawrence.
Comedy-drama about a charming girl and her dad who are threatened with foreclosure. To raise money, she turns their home into a hotel.

The Calendar Girl (American film Co./Mutual, 1917)
d: Rollin S. Sturgeon. 5 reels.
Juliette Day, Ashton Dearholt, Clarissa Selwynne, Lamar Johnstone, Kathleen Kirkham, Ruth Hanford, Sherry Hall, John Gough, Cora Drew, Fritzie Ridgway.
Romantic comedy about a dressmaker's model who tries on a new bathing suit, wears it to the beach, and is photographed by news hounds. Her picture turns up on a calendar against her wishes, so she hires a lawyer—and promptly falls in love with him.

The Calgary Stampede (Universal, 1925)
d: Herbert Blache. 6 reels.
Hoot Gibson, Virginia Brown Faire, Clark Comstock, Ynez Seabury, Jim Corey, Philo McCullough, W.T. McCulley, Ena Gregory, Charles Sellon, Tex Young, Bob Gillis.
Dan, an American rodeo champion, travels north to Canada and promptly falls in love with a Calgary girl.

California (MGM, 1927)
d: W.S. Van Dyke. 5 reels.
Tim McCoy, Dorothy Sebastian, Marc MacDermott, Frank Currier, Fred Warren, Lillian Leighton, Edwin Terry.
During the Mexican War, an American officer falls in love with a Mexican señorita.

California in '49 (Arrow Film Corp., 1924)
d: Jacques Jaccard. 6 reels.
Edmund Cobb, Neva Gerber, Charles Brinley, Ruth Royce, Wilbur McGaugh.
Coleman, a frontier guide leading the Donner party across the mountains, leaves the snowbound wagon train and rides to Sutter's fort to seek help. There, he finds not only help for the wagon trains, but also love with John Sutter's daughter, Sierra.
California in '49 originated as a serial, *Days of '49*, from which this feature-length film was crafted.

The California Mail (First National/Warner Bros., 1929)
d: Albert Rogell. 6 reels.
Ken Maynard, Dorothy Dwan, Lafe McKee, Paul Hurst, Fred Burns.
During the Civil War, a federal agent is dispatched to California to secure gold shipments for the Union cause.

California or Bust (R-C Pictures/FBO of America, 1927)
d: Phil Rosen. 5 reels.
George O'Hara, Helen Foster, John Steppling, Johnny Fox, Irving Bacon.
When an automobile executive's car break down in Arizona, the local garage mechanic sees his chance to sell the exec his invention: a powerful new engine.

A California Romance (Fox, 1922)
d: Jerome Storm. 5 reels. 5 reels.
John Gilbert, Estelle Taylor, George Siegmann, Jack McDonald, Charles Anderson.
In Old California, after a señorita surmises that her beau Fernando is a coward, she renounces him. Eventually,

Fernando storms the renegade camp where the girl is being imprisoned, routs the villains, and reclaims her love.

California Straight Ahead (Universal, 1925)
d: Harry A. Pollard. 7 reels.
Reginald Denny, Tom Wilson, Gertrude Olmstead, Charles Gerrard, Lucille Ward, John Steppling, Fred Esmelton.
A wild and zany comedy that sends a would-be bridegroom (Reginald Denny) and his friends on a cross-country car chase. At the finish is his inamorata, unkissed but still willing to be a bride if her sweetheart can get his act together.

The Call of Courage (Universal, 1925)
d: Clifford Smith. 5 reels.
Art Acord, Olive Hasbrouck, Duke R. Lee, Frank Rice, John T. Prince, Turner Savage, Floyd Shackelford, Mrs. C. Martin.
Out West, a miner is falsely accused of murder.

The Call of Her People (Columbia/Metro, 1917)
d: John W. Noble. 7 reels.
Ethel Barrymore, Robert Whittier, William B. Davidson, Frank Montgomery, William Mandeville, Mrs. Allan Walker, Helen Arnold, Hugh Jeffrey.
A Gypsy woman is taken from her camp by a wealthy man who claims to be her true father. Though he treats her well, she is irresistibly drawn to return to the Gypsies.

The Call of Home (R-C Pictures, 1922)
d: Louis J. Gasnier. 6 reels.
Leon Barry, Irene Rich, Ramsey Wallace, Margaret Mann, Jobyna Ralston, Genevieve Blinn, Wadsworth Harris, James O. Barrows, Carl Stockdale, Emmett King, Sidney Franklin.
Misunderstandings lead to a marital separation, and George heads for South America. There, he prospers in the plantation business until a great flood overflows his property and leaves him devastated. Just when things look darkest, he receives word through a friend that his wife is still loyal to him, has just given birth to his son, and awaits George's return home.

The Call of the Canyon (Famous Players-Lasky/Paramount, 1923)
d: Victor Fleming. 7 reels.
Richard Dix, Lois Wilson, Marjorie Daw, Noah Beery, Ricardo Cortez, Fred Huntley, Lillian Leighton, Helen Dunbar, Leonard Clapham, Edward Clayton, Dorothy Seastrom.
Out West, a war veteran is brought back to health by a nurse who falls in love with him, despite the fact that he is already spoken for.

The Call of the Cumberlands (Pallas Pictures/Paramount, 1916)
d: Julia Crawford Ivers. 5 reels.
Dustin Farnum, Winifred Kingston, Herbert Standing, Page Peters, Howard Davies, Dick Le Strange, Joe Ray, Myrtle Stedman, Virginia Foltz, Michael Hallvard.
A mountain man goes to New York to learn to paint, and becomes a success in cafe society. But his yearnings for home, and especially the gal he left behind, lead him to return.

The Call of the East (Lasky Feature Plays/Paramount, 1917)
d: George H. Melford. 5 reels.
Sessue Hayakawa, Tsuru Aoki, Jack Holt, Margaret Loomis, James Cruze, Ernest Joy, Guy Oliver, Jane Wolff.
East meets West when a Japanese businessman plans to seduce an American girl visiting in Japan. She flees to the image of Kwannon, a sacred spot, and there the would-be seducer bows down and begs her forgiveness. But she is irresistibly drawn to him. Upon learning that her mother had Japanese blood, the young woman realizes she is simply answering the call of the East.

Call of the Heart (Universal, 1928)
d: Francis Ford. 5 reels.
Dynamite, the dog, Joan Alden, Edmund Cobb, William A. Steele, Maurice Murphy, George Plews, Frank Baker, Owen Train.
Out West, homesteaders are terrorized by lawless gangs out to seize their property. But the homesteaders, Molly and her young brother, are befriended by a government agent, and the gangs are put to rout.

The Call of the Klondike (Paul Gerson Pictures/Rayart, 1926)
d: Oscar Apfel. 6 reels.
Gaston Glass, Dorothy Dwan, Earl Metcalfe, Sam Allen, William Lowery, Olin Francis, Harold Holland, Jimmy Aubrey.
In Alaska, a young engineer and miner intervenes to save a dancehall girl when she is threatened with the advances of a wealthy lecher.

Call of the Mate (Phil Goldstone Productions/Renown Pictures, 1924)
d: Alvin J. Neitz. 5 reels.
William Fairbanks, Dorothy Revier, Milton Ross, Billie Bennett, Earl Close, Neil Keller, Stanley Bingham, Marguerite Neitz.
Out West, a cowpoke agrees to marry a single mother who saved his life.

The Call of the North (Lasky Feature Plays, 1914)
d: Oscar Apfel, Cecil B. DeMille. 5 reels.
Robert Edeson, Theodore Roberts, Winifred Kingston, Horace B. Carpenter, Florence Dagmar, Milton Brown, Vera McGarry, Jode Mulally, Sydney Deane, Fred Montague.
In the Canadian Northwest, a tradesman seeks shelter in a storm, and falls in love.

The Call of the North (Famous Players-Lasky/Paramount, 1921)
d: Joseph Henabery. 5 reels.
Jack Holt, Madge Bellamy, Noah Beery, Francis McDonald, Edward Martindel, Helen Ferguson, Jack Herbert.
Remake of the 1914 Lasky Feature Plays film *The Call of the North*, both versions based on the novel *Conjuror's House* by Stewart Edward White.

The Call of the Soul (Fox, 1919)
d: Edward J. Le Saint. 5 reels.
Gladys Brockwell, William Scott, Lydia Yeamans Titus, Charles Clary, Nancy Caswell.
On an arctic expedition, an explorer falls for a nurse.

The Call of the Wild (Hal Roach Studios/Pathé, 1923)
d: Fred Jackman. 7 reels.
Jack Mulhall, Walter Long, Sidney D'Albrook, Laura Roessing, Frank Butler, Buck, the dog.
In the Frozen North, a prospector rescues Buck, a St. Bernard, from his cruel owner. Later, when the prospector's life is threatened, Buck returns the favor by saving his new owner's life.

Call of the Wilderness (Associated Exhibitors, 1926)

THE CAMERAMAN (1928). Buster Keaton plays a shutterbug who's asked a beautiful lady (played by Marceline Day) out on a date. Here, he's at her rooming house to pick her up, but first he must run the gauntlet laid down by several of her comely housemates. Can Buster pass muster?

* * * * *

d: Jack Nelson. 5 reels.
Sandow, the dog, Lewis Sargent, Edna Marion, Sydney D. Grey, Al Smith, Max Asher.
Tale of a man, his dog, and a land agent's daughter.

The Callahans and the Murphys (MGM, 1927)
d: George Hill. 7 reels.
Marie Dressler, Sally O'Neil, Lawrence Gray, Polly Moran, Gertrude Olmstead, Eddie Gribbon, Frank Currier, Turner Savage, Jackie Coombs, Dawn O'Day, Monty O'Grady.
Tenement neighbors Callahan and Murphy discover that their children, Dan and Ellen, are in love with each other. When her daughter delivers a baby, Mrs. Callahan tries to adopt the child and keep its existence a secret. It turns out, though, that Dan and Ellen are secretly married.

Calvert's Valley (Fox, 1922)
d: Jack Dillon. 5 reels.
Jack Gilbert, Sylvia Breamer, Philo McCullough, Herschel Mayall, Lule Warrenton.
When a wealthy landowner tumbles off a cliff to his death, the police want to know: Did he fall, or was he pushed?

The Cambric Mask (Vitagraph, 1919)
d: Tom Terriss. 5 reels.
Alice Joyce, Herbert Pattee, Maurice Costello, Roy Applegate, Bernard Siegel, Jules Cowles, Martin Faust, Florence Deshon.
Rebel outlaws try to force an entomologist to sell them his land.

Cameo Kirby (Lasky Feature Plays/Paramount, 1914)
d: Oscar Apfel. 5 reels.
Dustin Farnum, Fred Montague, James Neill, Jode Mullally, Winifred Kingston, Dick La Reno, Ernest Joy.
In this historical drama, an antebellum gambler survives bankruptcy, a deadly duel, and a trumped-up murder charge... and finds the girl he loves.

Cameo Kirby (Fox, 1923)
d: John Ford. 7 reels.
John Gilbert, Gertrude Olmstead, Alan Hale, Eric Mayne, William E. Lawrence, Richard Tucker, Phillips Smalley, Jack McDonald, Jean Arthur, Eugenie Ford.
Remake of the 1914 Lasky film *Cameo Kirby*, both versions based on the play of the same name by Booth Tarkington and Harry Leon Wilson.

The Cameraman (MGM, 1928)
d: Edward Sedgwick. 8 reels.
Buster Keaton, Marceline Day, Harry Gribbon, Harold Goodwin, Sidney Bracy.
A newsreel cameraman is kept busy covering various news events while trying to win the heart of a girl he's just met. Last of the great Buster Keaton silent comedies.

Camille (Shubert Film Corp./World Film Corp., 1915)
d: Albert Capellani. 5 reels.
Clara Kimball Young, Paul Capellani, Lillian Cook, Robert Cummings, Dan Baker, Stanhope Wheatcroft, Frederick C. Truesdell, William Jefferson, Edward M. Kimball.
In 18th century France, a courtesan loves a young lawyer but is committed to be with her sponsor, Count de Varville.

Camille (Fox, 1917)
d: J. Gordon Edwards. 5 reels.
Theda Bara, Albert Roscoe, Walter Law, Glen White, Alice Gale, Claire Whitney.
A kept woman yearns to belong to another man, Armand Duvall. She breaks away from her lover to be with Duvall, but is forced to give him up. Then she dies of consumption.
This was the second American feature film based on the famous Alexandre Dumas story and play. Over the years, the durable tale has been filmed at least twenty times, beginning with its first film version, in Denmark in 1907.

Camille (Metro, 1921)
d: Ray C. Smallwood. 6 reels.
Rudolph Valentino, Alla Nazimova, Arthur Hoyt, Zeffie Tillbury, Rex Cherryman, Edward Connelly, Patsy Ruth Miller, Consuelo Flowerton, William Orlamond.
Modern-day version of the Dumas tale, with Nazimova as an ill-fated call girl who nobly rejects the man she loves, rather than burden his life with so disreputable a woman as herself.
Ray C. Smallwood is the credited director, but a persistent legend tells us that Nazimova did most of the directing herself.

Camille (Norma Talmadge Productions, 1927)
d: Fred Niblo. 9 reels.
Norma Talmadge, Gilbert Roland, Lilyan Tashman, Rose Dione, Oscar Beregi, Harvey Clark, Helen Jerome Eddy, Alec B. Francis, Albert Conti, Michael Visaroff, Evelyn Selbie, Etta Lee, Maurice Costello.
Fourth feature length retelling of the famous Alexandre Dumas tale, *La Dame aux Camélias*.

Camille of the Barbary Coast (Associated Exhibitors, 1925)
d: Hugh Dierker. 6 reels.
Mae Busch, Owen Moore, Fritzi Brunette, Burr McIntosh, Harry Morey, Tammany Young, Dorothy King, Robert Daly, Dagmar Godowsky.
Love conquers all when an ex-convict falls for a Barbary Coast saloon girl. They marry, and in time the hard-working husband overcomes the stigma of a prison record with support from his doting wife.

A Camouflage Kiss (Fox, 1918)
d: Harry Millarde. 5 reels.
June Caprice, Bernard Thornton, Pell Trenton, George Bunny, Lola May.
A kiss in the dark convinces a girl she's engaged to the wrong guy.

The Campus Flirt (Famous Players-Lasky/Paramount, 1926)
d: Clarence Badger. 7 reels.
Bebe Daniels, James Hall, El Brendel, Charles Paddock, Joan Standing, Gilbert Roland, Irma Kornelia, Jocelyn Lee.
Patricia, a snobbish society girl, incurs the dislike of many of her classmates at college, but is befriended by the old janitor. One day, Pat spots the janitor's pet mouse and runs away screaming. So fast, in fact, that she catches the eye of the girls' track coach. After joining the varsity track team, she mends her snobbish ways and becomes a star athlete.
Charles Paddock, who plays himself in this film, was the 1920 Olympic champion in the 100-meter dash.

Campus Knights (Chesterfield Motion Picture Company, 1929)
d: Albert Kelly. 6 reels.
Raymond McKee, Shirley Palmer, Marie Quillan, Jean Laverty, J.C. Fowler.
McKee in a dual role: He's twins, one a playboy, the other a college professor.

Can a Woman Love Twice? (R-C Pictures/FBO of America,

1923)

d: James W. Horne. 7 reels.

Ethel Clayton, Muriel Dana, Kate Lester, Fred Esmelton, Victory Bateman, Wilfred Lucas, Anderson Smith, Al Hart, Malcolm McGregor, Theodore von Eltz, Clara Clark Ward.

Mary, a war widow with a young son, gratefully accepts Abner Grant's offer to live with him on his ranch. But the offer is based on mistaken identity: Abner, who lost a son in the war, thinks his son was Mary's husband because of the similarity of names. When his son turns out to be very much alive, and not Mary's husband at all, Abner feels he's been tricked. That passes, when Mary and the returned veteran fall in love and decide to marry.

The Canadian (Famous Players-Lasky/Paramount, 1926)
d: William Beaudine. 8 reels.

Thomas Meighan, Mona Palma, Wyndham Standing, Dale Fuller, Charles Winninger, Billy Butts.

Romantic drama about a struggling wheat farmer and an antagonistic woman who is angry over losing her wealth. Strange bedfellows, these; but they need each other, and so they marry. The man promises to release her from the marriage with some money, if his planned crop is successful. Then, as they work the land together, antagonism turns to love.

The Canary Murder Case (Paramount, 1929)
d: Malcolm St. Clair. 7 reels.

William Powell, Louise Brooks, Jean Arthur, James Hall, Gustav von Seyffertitz, Charles Lane, Eugene Pallette, Ned Sparks, Louis John Bartels, Lawrence Grant, E.H. Calvert, Oscar Smith, George Y. Harvey.

"The Canary," an amoral Broadway dancer, plans to marry for wealth but is killed before the nuptials can take place. Philo Vance (played by Powell), an amateur detective, sorts out the mystery and names the murderer from among the many Broadway denizens "the Canary" had wronged.

Conceived and filmed as a silent, *The Canary Murder Case* wrapped production in October 1928 but was caught in a squeeze when sound pictures began to take over the screen. Hurriedly, the producers recalled the cast members to dub their own voices over their action and turn the film into a talkie. But Louise Brooks, who plays the unscrupulous dancer, had left for Europe to star in Germany productions, so "the Canary's" voice was dubbed by actress Margaret Livingston.

The Cancelled Debt (Banner Productions/Sterling Pictures Distributing Corp., 1927)
d: Phil Rosen. 6 reels.

Rex Lease, Charlotte Stevens, Florence Turner, Billy Sullivan, James Gordon, Ethel Grey Terry.

June's a girl who loves to speed but always seems to get stopped and ticketed by Patrick, a young traffic cop. They develop a strong dislike for each other, until they learn that June's dad has proposed marriage to Patrick's widowed mom.

The Candy Girl (Thanhouser/Pathé, 1917)
d: W. Eugene Moore. 5 reels.

Gladys Hulette, Helen Badgley, William Park Jr., J.H. Gilmour, Thomas A. Curran.

His drug addiction clouds the future for a young married couple.

The Canvas Kisser (Paul Gerson Pictures, 1925)
d: Duke Worne. 5 reels.

Richard Holt, Ruth Dwyer, Garry O'Dell, Cecil Edwards.

A prizefighter has an unbeatable system for success: He bets against himself, then takes a dive in his fights.

The Canyon of Adventure (Charles R. Rogers Productions, 1928)
d: Albert Rogell. 6 reels.

Ken Maynard, Virginia Brown Faire, Eric Mayne, Theodore Lorch, Tyrone Grereton, Hal Salter, Billy Franey, Charles Whitaker.

In the new state of California, a U.S. land agent falls in love with a señorita who's engaged to a ne'er-do-well.

Capital Punishment (B.P. Schulberg Productions/Preferred Pictures, 1925)
d: James P. Hogan. 6 reels.

Elliot Dexter, George Hackathorne, Clara Bow, Margaret Livingston, Robert Ellis, Mary Carr, Fred Warren, Wade Boteler.

Hoping to discredit the practice of capital punishment, a welfare worker weaves a bizarre plot to throw suspicion of murder on an innocent man, and then, after the man has been convicted and sentenced, produce the "victim" alive and well, thus causing the prisoner to be freed. All goes as planned until the supposed victim is accidentally killed.

The Capitol (Artco Productions, Inc./Pathé, 1919)
d: George Irving. 6 reels.

Leah Baird, Robert T. Haines, Alexander Gaden, William B. Davidson, Downing Clarke, Ben Hendricks, Donald Hugh McBride, Mildred Rhoads, Ben Hendricks Jr., Brian Darley.

The wife of a young congressman tries to help his cause by fingering his chief nemesis as the man who seduced her mother and broke up their family.

Cappy Ricks (Famous Players-Lasky/Paramount, 1921)
d: Tom Forman. 6 reels.

Thomas Meighan, Charles Abbe, Agnes Ayres, Hugh Cameron, John Sainpolis, Paul Everton, Eugenie Woodward, Tom O'Malley, Ivan Linow, William Wally, Jack Dillon.

An able seaman takes command of his ship after the captain is killed, and later marries the shipowner's daughter.

Caprice of the Mountains (Fox, 1916)
d: John G. Adolfi. 5 reels.

June Caprice, Harry S. Hilliard, Joel Day, Lisle Leigh, Richard Hale, Albert Gran, Tom Burrough, Robert D. Walker, Sara Alexander, Harriet Thompson.

When a playboy from the city dallies with a country girl, the result is a shotgun wedding.

The Caprices of Kitty (Paramount, 1915)
d: Phillips Smalley. 5 reels.

Elsie Janis, Courtenay Foote, Herbert Standing, Vera Lewis, Martha Mattox, Myrtle Stedman.

Romantic comedy about a lively young heiress who plays pranks, speeds in her racing car, and adopts several disguises to win her man.

Captain Alvarez (Vitagraph, 1914)
d: Rollin S. Sturgeon. 6 reels.

Edith Storey, William D. Taylor, George S. Stanley, George Holt, Otto Lederer, Myrtle Gonzalez, George Kunkel.

On a mission to Argentina, an American businessman falls in love with a young revolutionary. He decides to aid her cause as "Captain Alvarez," fighting against the despotic establishment.

Captain Blood (Vitagraph, 1924)
d: David Smith. 11 reels.

70

J. Warren Kerrigan, Jean Paige, Charlotte Merriam, James Morrison, Allan Forrest, Bertram Grassby, Otis Harlan, Jack Curtis, Wilfrid North, Otto Matiesen, Robert Bolder, Templar Saxe, Henry Barrows, Boyd Irwin, Henry Hebert, Miles McCarthy, Tom McGuire.
In the Caribbean, an enslaved Irishman organizes other slaves and together they commandeer a Spanish galleon.

Captain Careless (FBO Pictures, 1928)
d: Jerome Storm. 6 reels.
Bob Steele, Mary Mabery, Jack Donovan, Barney Furey, Perry Murdock, Wilfred North.
Adventure in the South Seas, with a daring aviator searching for a girl who's been reported lost at sea.

Captain Courtesy (Bosworth/Paramount, 1915)
d: Lois Weber, Phillips Smalley. 5 reels.
Dustin Farnum, Herbert Standing, Winifred Kingston, Courtenay Foote, Carl Von Schiller, Jack Hoxie, Winona Brown.
In 1840, a masked highwayman known as "Captain Courtesy" terrorizes outlaw bands running riot in Mexican-controlled California.

Captain Cowboy (J. Charles Davis Productions, 1929)
d: J.P. McGowan. 5 reels.
Yakima Canutt, Ione Reed, Charles Whittaker, John Lowell, Bobby Dunn, Betty Carter, Lynn Sanderson, Scotty Mattraw, Cliff Lyons.
Out West, a cowpoke battles hoodlums who are trying to take over a peaceful ranch and its occupants.

Captain Fly-by-Night (R-C Pictures/FBO of America, 1922)
d: William K. Howard. 5 reels.
Johnnie Walker, Francis McDonald, Shannon Day, Edward Gribbon, Victory Bateman, James McElhern, Charles Stevens, Bert Wheeler, Fred Kelsey.
A notorious bandit known as "Captain Fly-by-Night" terrorizes a small western outpost.

Captain January (Principal Pictures, 1923)
d: Edward F. Cline. 6 reels.
Baby Peggy, Irene Rich, Hobart Bosworth, Lincoln Stedman, Harry T. Morey, Barbara Tennant, Emmett King.
A lighthouse keeper finds a baby girl washed up on shore, and takes her in as his own daughter. Trouble arises when, years later, the girl's real relatives try to take her away.

Captain Kidd Jr. (Pickford/Famous Players-Lasky/Paramount, 1919)
d: William Desmond Taylor 5 reels.
Mary Pickford, Robert Gordon, Douglas MacLean, Spottiswoode Aitken, Marcia Manon, Winter Hall, Victor Potel, Clarence Geldert, Vin Moore, William Hutcheson.
Fortune hunters dig up an old farm, looking for treasure.

Captain Kiddo (Pathé, 1917)
d: W. Eugene Moore. 5 reels.
Baby Marie Osborne, Marion Warner, Philo McCullough, Harry Von Meter, Ray Clark.
"Captain Kiddo" is little Marie, who finds a strange cross while playing pirates with her friends.

Captain Lash (Fox, 1929)
d: John Blystone. 6 reels. (Music and sound effects.)
Victor McLaglen, Claire Windsor, Jane Winton, Clyde Cook, Arthur Stone, Albert Conti, Jean Laverty, Frank Hagney, Boris Charsky.
On board ship, a stoker falls for a stylish young woman.

Unknown to him, she's a jewel thief.

Captain of His Soul (Triangle, 1918)
d: Gilbert P. Hamilton. 5 reels.
William Desmond, Claire McDowell, Charles Gunn, Jack Richardson, Walt Whitman, Jules Friquet, Mitzi Gould, Eugene Burr, Percy Challenger, Lucretia Harris.
When the manager of a gunworks is found dead, the former owner's sons are the prime suspects.

The Captain of the Gray Horse Troop (Vitagraph, 1917)
d: William Wolbert. 5 reels.
Antonio Moreno, Edith Storey, Mrs. Bradbury, Otto Lederer, Al Jennings, Neola May, Robert Burns, H.A. Barrows.
A cavalry captain rides herd on cattlemen and Indians alike, to keep the peace.

Captain Salvation (MGM, 1927)
d: John S. Robertson. 8 reels.
Lars Hanson, Pauline Starke, George Fawcett, Ernest Torrence, Marceline Day.
A theology student takes over a convict ship from a corrupt captain, saves the crew, and reforms the convicts.

Captain Swagger (Pathé, 1928)
d: Edward H. Griffith. 7 reels.
Rod LaRocque, Sue Carol, Richard Tucker, Victor Potel, Ulrich Haupt.
A big spender goes broke, and then turns to crime to pay his bills.

Captain Swift (Life Photo Film Corp., 1914)
d: Edgar Lewis. 5 reels.
David Wall, George DeCarlton, William H. Tooker, Frank B. Andrews, Harry Spingler, Thomas O'Keefe, Iva Shepherd, Maxine Brown, Ethel Wayne, Philip Robson, Emily Loraine.
The bastard son of an aristocratic Englishwoman is raised in a foster home, escapes, and becomes a notorious Australian outlaw known as Captain Swift. Eventually, he dies in battle. However, see the next entry.

Captain Swift (Vitagraph, 1920)
d: Tom Terriss. 5 reels.
Earle Williams, Florence Dixon, Edward Martindale, Adelaide Prince, Downing Clarke, Barry Baxter, Alice Calhoun, James O'Neill, Herbert Pattee.
Second film adaptation of the C. Haddon Chambers play *Captain Swift*. Here, the title character does not die; instead, he falls in love and marries.

The Captain's Captain (Vitagraph, 1919)
d: Tom Terriss. 5 reels.
Alice Joyce, Arthur Donaldson, Percy Standing, Julia Swayne Gordon, Eulalie Jensen, Maurice Costello.
A grizzled old storekeeper spins yarns about a fictitious and flamboyant sea captain.

Captivating Mary Carstairs (National Film Corp., 1915)
d: Bruce Mitchell. 5 reels.
Norma Talmadge, Alan Forrest, Bruce Mitchell, Jack Livingston, Frank Brown.
Mary Carstairs is a young woman who has not seen her father in years, since he and her mother split up. Finally, her father hires a young man to kidnap Mary and bring her to him. Predictably, Mary "captivates" the young fellow just as he is trying to captivate *her*, and they are married on their way back to Dad.

The Captive (Lasky Feature Plays/Paramount, 1915)
d: Cecil B. DeMille. 5 reels.

THE CAMPUS FLIRT (1926). Bebe Daniels was a spirited comedienne who could be tomboyish and charming at the same time. As a nine-year-old, she was the screen's first Dorothy in an early version of *The Wizard of Oz*, and later partnered Harold Lloyd in 44 short comedies. Here, she teams with real-life Olympic sprint champion Charles Paddock in a lightweight collegiate frolic.

* * * * *

Blanche Sweet, House Peters, Gerald Ward, Page Peters, Jeanie MacPherson, Theodore Roberts, Billy Elmer.
Heavy drama chronicling the woes of a Balkan family during the War of 1912.

The Captive God (Triangle, 1916)
d: Charles Swickard. 5 reels.
William S. Hart, Enid Markey, Dorothy Dalton, Robert McKim, P.D. Tabler, Dorcas Matthews, Herbert Farjean, Robert Kortman.
In the 16th century, a white boy known as Chiapa is raised by Mexican Indians. Because the tribe enjoys great prosperity since Chiapa's arrival, he is proclaimed a god.

The Car of Chance (Universal, 1917)
d: William Worthington. 5 reels.
Franklyn Farnum, Agnes Vernon, Molly Malone, Helen Wright, Mark Fenton, H.J. Bennett, Walter Belasco, Harry DeMore.
Cut loose by his fiancée's family after being disinherited, an enterprising young man gets into the jitney business and challenges his former intended in-laws' trolley company. In no time, his business is cutting into the trolley company's profits. Can a merger be far behind?

The Cardboard Lover (MGM, 1928)
d: Robert Z. Leonard. 8 reels.
Marion Davies, Nils Asther, Jetta Goudal, Andres de Segurola, Pepi Lederer.
To avoid a predatory female, a tennis star hires a girl to pose as his fiancée.

Cardinal Richelieu's Ward (Thanhouser Film Corp., 1914)
d: Frank L. Gereghty. 5 reels.
James Cruze, Florence La Badie, J. Morris Foster, Lila Chester, Justus D. Barnes, Arthur Bower, Nolan Gane.
Intrigue and treachery intrude in a simple love match in 17th century France, when the Cardinal's ward is betrothed to the man she loves. It seems she is desired by both a king and a count, and they are committed to derailing the marriage.

The Career of Katherine Bush (Famous Players-Lasky/Paramount, 1919)
d: Roy W. Neill. 5 reels.
Catherine Calvert, John Goldsworthy, Crauford Kent, Mathilda Brundage, Helen Montrose, Ann Dearing, Augusta Anderson, Norah Reed, Claire Whitney, Albert Hackett.
Katherine, a middle-class Brit, strives to reach the upper echelons of society.

Carmen (Lasky Feature Plays/Paramount, 1915)
d: Cecil B. DeMille. 5 reels.
Geraldine Farrar, Wallace Reid, Pedro de Cordoba, Horace B. Carpenter, William Elmer, Jeanie Macpherson, Anita King, Milton Brown.
At feature length, perhaps the most filmed story in the silent era was Prosper Mérimée's novel *Carmen*. In the United States alone, four full-length versions of the classic were brought to the silent screen. The first was this one, starring Geraldine Farrar, then at the height of her Metropolitan Opera career. A competing version starring Theda Bara opened less than a month later.
Miss Farrar brings a full range of operatic gestures and mannerisms to her role as the gypsy girl whose coquettish charms cause the ruination of a proud Spanish army officer. She flashes her eyes, teases her prey with pouts and smiles, and thoroughly destroys the doomed lieutenant, Don José, with her charms. Miss Farrar's acting style might seem

overly flamboyant, even hammy, in a sound film; but on the silent screen, with its strong emphasis on visual flair, extravagant gestures win the day.
The four American silent features based on Mérimée's novel are: *Carmen* (Lasky/Paramount, 1915); *Carmen* (Fox, 1915); *Charlie Chaplin's Burlesque on Carmen* (Essanay, 1916); and *Loves of Carmen* (Fox, 1927). In addition, there were two 3-reel versions of *Carmen* produced in 1913, and a German feature, known in the U.S. as *Gypsy Blood*, starring Pola Negri and directed by Ernst Lubitsch, in 1918.

Carmen (Fox, 1915)
d: Raoul Walsh. 5 reels.
Theda Bara, Einar Linden, Carl Harbaugh, James A. Marcus, Elsie MacLeod, Fay Tunis, Emil de Varney, Joseph P. Green,
Bara stars as the feisty gypsy girl in the second feature to be based on the novel *Carmen*. This version was filmed virtually simultaneously with the Geraldine Farrar version. They opened within weeks of each other, on competing screens.

Carmen of the Klondike (Selexart Pictures, Inc., 1918)
d: Reginald Barker. 7 reels.
Clara Williams, Herschel Mayall, Edward Cosen, Joseph J. Dowling.
Dorothy, a lively vaudeville dancer, heads for the Klondike to cash in on the gold rush.

The Carnation Kid (Christie Film Co./Paramount, 1929)
d: E. Mason Hopper. 7 reels. (Talking sequences, music score.)
Douglas MacLean, Frances Lee, William B. Davidson, Lorraine Eddy, Charles Hill Mailes, Francis McDonald, Maurice Black, Ben Swor Jr., Carl Stockdale.
Comedy about mistaken identity when a simple typewriter salesman is mistaken for a notorious gangster known as The Carnation Kid.

The Carnival Girl (Associated Exhibitors, 1926)
d: Cullen Tate. 5 reels.
Marion Mack, Gladys Brockwell, Frankie Darro, George Siegmann, Allan Forrest, Jack Cooper, Victor Potel, Max Asher.
Circus drama about orphaned siblings whose guardian is a brutal weightlifter. The strong man is a bootlegger on the side.

Carolyn of the Corners (Pathé, 1919)
d: Robert Thornby. 5 reels.
Bessie Love, Charles Edler, Charlotte Mineau, Eunice Moore, Prince the dog.
A girl whose parents are believed lost at sea goes to live with her uncle, and finds a way to reunite him with his old flame.

The Carpet From Bagdad (Selig Polyscope, 1915)
d: Colin Campbell. 5 reels.
Kathlyn Williams, Wheeler Oakman, Guy Oliver, Eugenie Besserer, Frank Clark, Charles Clary, Harry Lonsdale, Fred Huntley.
Would-be bank robbers plan to tunnel into the bank's vault, aided by a magic carpet stolen from an eastern Pasha.

A Case at Law (Triangle, 1917)
d: Arthur Rosson. 5 reels.
Dick Rosson, Pauline Curley, Riley Hatch, Jack Dillon, Ed Sturgis.
A reformed alcoholic becomes a fiery spokesman for prohibition.

The Case of Becky (Lasky Feature Plays/Paramount, 1915)
d: Frank Reicher. 5 reels.
Blanche Sweet, Theodore Roberts, James Neill, Carlyle Blackwell, Jane Wolff, Gertrude Kellar.
Dual personality afflicts a girl who's sweet as Dorothy, devilish as Becky.

The Case of Becky (Realart Pictures/Paramount, 1921)
d: Chester M. Franklin. 6 reels.
Constance Binney, Glenn Hunter, Frank McCormack, Montague Love, Margaret Seddon, Jane Jennings.
Remake of the 1915 Lasky drama *The Case of Becky*. Both versions were based on the play of the same name by Edward Locke.

The Case of Lena Smith (Paramount, 1929)
d: Josef von Sternberg. 8 reels.
Esther Ralston, James Hall, Gustav von Seyffertitz, Emily Fitzroy, Fred Kohler, Betty Aho, Lawrence Grant, Leone Lane, Kay Deslys, Alex Woloshin, Anny Brody, Wally Albright Jr., Warner Klinger.
In a village in Hungary, a naive peasant girl is seduced by a cavalry officer and bears his child. When the soldier's father finds out, he tries to take the baby away from her, but she has her last name officially changed to Smith, and escapes with her child.

Casey at the Bat (Fine Arts Film Co./Triangle, 1916)
d: Lloyd Ingraham. 5 reels.
DeWolf Hopper, Kate Toncray, May Garcia, Carl Stockdale, William H. Brown, Marguerite Marsh, Frank Bennett, Robert Lawler, Bert Hadley, Hal Wilson, Frank Hughes.

Mighty Casey still strikes out, but in this version there's a good reason: He's worried about his niece, who is seriously ill.

Casey at the Bat (Famous Players-Lasky/Paramount, 1927)
d: Monte Brice. 6 reels.
Wallace Beery, Sally Blane, ZaSu Pitts, Sterling Holloway, Spec O'Donnell, Iris Stuart, Sidney Jarvis, Lotus Thompson, Rosalind Byrne, Anne Sheridan, Doris Hill.
Another film "inspired" by the Ernest Thayer poem of the same name. In this version, Casey is a small-town junk dealer who wins a tryout with the New York Giants.

Casey Jones (Trem Carr Productions/Rayart Pictures, 1927)
d: Charles J. Hunt. 7 reels.
Ralph Lewis, Kate Price, Al St. John, Jason Robards, Anne Sheridan, Brooks Benedict, Violet Kane, Jimmy Kane, Charlie Kane.
Railroad engineer Casey Jones turns hero when he and his son foil bandits who try to steal a train. In the bargain, Casey Jr. wins the love of Peggy, a charming young passenger.

Cassidy (Triangle, 1917)
d: Arthur Rosson. 5 reels.
Dick Rosson, Frank Currier, Pauline Curley, Mac Alexander, Eddie Sturgis, John O'Connor, Jack Snyder.
Though suffering from a terminal illness, a young man is able to repay a kindness to a friend by rescuing the man's daughter from kidnappers.

The Cast-Off (Triangle, 1918)
d: Raymond B. West. 6 reels.
Bessie Barriscale, Howard Hickman, Jack Livingston, Dorcas Matthews, Thomas Guise, Aggie Herring, Margaret Thompson.

After years of suffering ridicule and rejection, a young woman achieves theatrical stardom.

Castles For Two (Lasky Feature Plays/Paramount, 1917)
d: Frank Reicher. 5 reels.
Marie Doro, Elliott Dexter, Mayme Kelson, Jane Wolff, Harret Sorenson, Lillian Leighton, Julia Jackson, Horace B. Carpenter, Billy Elmer, Marie Mills.
An American heiress journeys to Ireland in search of leprechauns, and finds love instead.

Castles in the Air (Metro, 1919)
d: George D. Baker. 5 reels.
May Allison, Ben Wilson, Clarence Burton, Walter I. Percival, Irene Rich, Mother Anderson, Viola Dolan, Ruth Maurice.
Lecher? Or lonely guy? An Englishman who behaves like the former insists he's the latter.

The Cat and the Canary (Universal, 1927)
d: Paul Leni. 8 reels.
Creighton Hale, Laura LaPlante, Forrest Stanley, Tully Marshall, Flora Finch, Gertrude Astor, Arthur Edmund Carewe, Lucien Littlefield, Martha Mattox, George Siegmann.
Eerily atmospheric haunted-house comedy centered on the reading of a will. Close relatives of the deceased are shocked to learn that the entire estate goes to a distant cousin (Miss LaPlante), but there's a catch: First she must be proved sane!

Catch My Smoke (Fox, 1922)
d: William Beaudine. 5 reels.
Tom Mix, Lillian Rich, Claude Peyton, Gordon Griffith, Harry Griffith, Robert Milash, Pat Chrisman, Cap Anderson, Ruby Lafayette.
A returning war veteran finds that a pretty girl has taken over his family's ranch. It seems his dad died, and had named the girl's father the executor of his will. Believing the son to be killed in action, the executor, now deceased, had assumed control of the ranch. Now that the son is back, he's entitled to the ranch... but he fancies the girl and proposes marriage.

The Cat's Pajamas (Famous Players-Lasky/Paramount, 1926)
d: William Wellman. 6 reels.
Betty Bronson, Ricardo Cortez, Arlette Marchal, Theodore Roberts, Gordon Griffith, Tom Ricketts.
Don Cesare, an opera singer, sees a cat wandering around backstage and impulsively declares that he will marry the first woman the cat leads him to. Not a good idea at all, for that feline heads straight for Riza, a dancer with glorious talent and a temper to match.

The Catspaw (Thomas A. Edison, Inc., 1916)
d: George A. Wright. 5 reels.
Miriam Nesbitt, Marc MacDermott, William Wadsworth, Yale Benner, Mabel Dwight, Harry Eytinge, Grace Morrissey, James Harris, Brad Sutton.
An innovative crook assigns his spittin' image lookalike to take his place in public, while he pulls off a heist.

Caught Bluffing (Universal, 1922)
d: Lambert Hillyer. 5 reels.
Frank Mayo, Wallace MacDonald, Edna Murphy, Jack Curtis, Andrew Arbuckle, Ruth Royce, Bull Durham, Jack Walters, Scott Turner, Martin Best, Tote DuCrow.

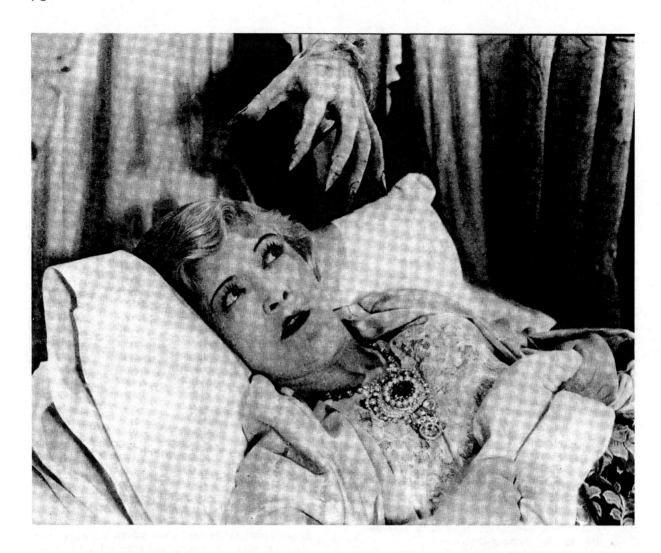

THE CAT AND THE CANARY (1927). Laura LaPlante tries to get some sleep—fat chance!
—while a hideous claw tries to attack her. Wearing such an expensive-looking necklace to
bed, what did she expect?

* * * * *

In Alaska, an honest gambler falls for a girl who loves an inveterate loser.

Caught in the Act   (Fox, 1918)
d: Harry Millarde.   5 reels.
Peggy Hyland, Leslie Austen, George Bunny, Carlotta Coer, Jack Raymond, Wally McKeown, Elizabeth Garrison, Ellen Cassidy, Henry Hallam.
What happens when a shady businessman tries to frame the crusading journalist who's out to expose him and winds up with an incriminating candid photo of the journalist with the businessman's own daughter?

Caught in the Fog   (Warner Bros., 1928)
d: Howard Bretherton. 7 reels.   (Part talkie.)
May McAvoy, Conrad Nagel, Mack Swain, Charles Gerrard, Ruth Cherrington, Emil Chautard, Hugh Herbert.
Too many crooks spoil the farce in this one-joke comedy about waves of jewel thieves competing for the same diamonds.

Cause for Divorce   (Hugh Dierker Productions/Selznick, 1923)
d: Hugh Dierker. 7 reels.
Fritzi Brunette, David Butler, Charles Clary, Helen Lynch, Pat O'Malley, Peter Burke, Cleve Moore, James O. Barrows, Harmon MacGregor, Junior Coughlan.
Two wives feel neglected by their husbands, and together search for a solution.

The Cavalier   (Tiffany-Stahl Productions, 1928)
d: Irvin Willat. 7 reels.
Richard Talmadge, Barbara Bedford, Nora Cecil, David Torrence, David Mir, Stuart Holmes, Christian Frank, Oliver Eckhardt.
In Old California, a Spanish nobleman disguised as a highwayman saves a girl from a disastrous planned marriage, and elopes with her himself.

Cavanaugh of the Forest Rangers   (Vitagraph, 1918)
d: William Wolbert. 5 reels.
Nell Shipman, Alfred Whitman, Otto Lederer, Laura Winston, Rex Downs, Joe Rickson, Hal Wilson, Hattie Buskirk.
Love blossoms amid a cattlemen-sheepherders war.

The Cave Girl   (Inspiration Pictures, 1921)
d: Joseph J. Franz. 5 reels.
Teddie Gerard, Charles Meredith, Wilton Taylor, Eleanor Hancock, Lillian Tucker, Frank Coleman, Boris Karloff, Jake Abrahams, John Beck.
In the American wilderness, a professor experiments with primitive methods of living.   All very well, but in the meantime Margot, his young ward, gets hungry and begins to steal from a nearby camp. After numerous adventures including a near-death experience with a waterfall, Margot falls in love with Bates, whose father owns the camp she's been robbing.

The Cave Man   (Vitagraph, 1915)
d: Theodore Marston. 5 reels.
Robert Edeson, Fay Wallace, Lillian Burns, George DeBeck, Frances Connelly, John T. Kelly, Charles Eldridge, William Sellery, Charles Morrison.
Anticipating *Pygmalion, Trading Places,* and several other scenarios, this tale deals with a cynical socialite who turns a tramp into a respectable gentleman.

The Caveman   (Warner Bros., 1926)

d: Lewis Milestone.   7 reels.
Marie Prevost, Matt Moore, Myrna Loy, Phyllis Haver, John Patrick, Hedda Hopper.
An idle society girl comes up with an innovative way to stir up some fun: She tears a $100 bill in two and lets half of it fly, together with a note to the finder to look her up.

Cecilia of the Pink Roses   (Marion Davies Film Corp./Select Pictures, 1918)
d: Julius Steger. 6 reels.
Marion Davies, Harry Benham, Edward O'Connor, Willette Kershaw, Charles Jackson, George Le Guere, Daniel J. Sullivan, John Charles, Eva Campbell, Joseph Burke.
Cecilia is daughter to a bricklayer/inventor who comes up with a revolutionary type of brick and makes a fortune. But wealth doesn't guarantee happiness.

The Celebrated Scandal   (Fox, 1915)
d: J. Gordon Edwards. 5 reels.
Betty Nansen, Edward José, Walter Hitchcock, Stuart Holmes, Wilmuth Merkyl, Helen Robertson.
When a Spanish nobleman invites a needy friend of the family to live with him and his young wife, wagging tongues are quick to concoct a fictional affair between the new tenant and the mistress of the house. Scandal ensues, followed by a duel to the death between the tenant and his chief accuser.

Celebrity   (Pathé, 1928)
d: Tay Garnett. 7 reels.
Robert Armstrong, Clyde Cook, Lina Basquette, Dot Farley, Jack Perry, Otto Lederer, David Tearle.
Comedy about a fight manager who drums up a preposterous scheme to publicize his boxer: He hires a poet to write flowery poems and sign the boxer's name to them, then has them printed in the society columns.

A Certain Rich Man   (Great Authors Pictures, 1921)
d: Howard Hickman. 6 reels.
Carl Gantvoort, Claire Adams, Robert McKim, Jean Hersholt, Joseph J. Dowling, Lydia Knott, Frankie Lee, Mary Jane Irving, Harry Lorraine, J. Gunnis Davis, Charles Colby.
Weepy melodrama about two young lovers, the man's banker father, and the financier who has led the banker to embezzle funds.

A Certain Young Man   (MGM, 1928)
d: Hobart Henley. 6 reels.
Ramon Novarro, Carmel Myers, Renee Adoree, Marceline Day, Huntley Gordon, Willard Louis, Bert Roach.
A lecher who specializes in conquering married women is startled to find himself falling in love for the very first time.

The Chain Invisible   (Equitable Motion Pictures Corp., 1916)
d: Frank E. Powell. 5 reels.
Bruce McRae, Gerda Holmes, Alfred Hickman, Tom McGrath, Lillian Page, Victor Benoit, Margaret Livingston.
A lumberjack falls in love with a society girl.

Chain Lightning   (Ben Wilson Productions/Arrow Film Corp., 1922)
d: Ben Wilson. 5 reels.
Norval MacGregor, Joseph W. Girard, William Carroll, Jack Dougherty, Ann Little.
Chain Lightning is Peggy's favorite horse, but her debt-ridden father is forced to sell it to a southern colonel. Peggy's dad wagers the last of his money on Chain Lightning to win the big race, but all seems lost when the

jockey suffers a traffic accident and is unable to ride. No problem, says Peggy: She dons the jockey's silks and rides Chain Lightning to victory.

Chains of Evidence (Hallmark Pictures Corp., 1920)
d: Dallas M. Fitzgerald. 5 reels.
Edmund Breese, Marie Shotwell, Anna Lehr, Wallace Ray, Joseph Granby, Peggy Worth, James F. Cullen, George Cooper, Edward Elkas, Glenn Kunkel, Eva Gordon, Joseph P. Mack.
Unjustly jailed by a tough judge, a reporter learns that his mother has married the judge.

The Chalice of Courage (Vitagraph, 1915)
d: Rollin S. Sturgeon. 5 reels.
William Duncan, Myrtle Gonzalez, Natalie DeLontan, George Holt, George Kunkel, William V. Ranous, Otto Lederer, Anne Schaefer.
A wealthy prospector becomes snowbound in his cabin with the young woman he loves, though his affection for her remains unspoken during their long winter of isolation. With the spring thaw comes a rescue party, and the prospector is finally free to declare his love.

The Chalice of Sorrow (Bluebird Photoplays, Inc., 1916)
d: Rex Ingram. 5 reels.
Cleo Madison, Blanche White, Charles Cummings, John McDermott, Wedgewood Nowell, Howard Crampton, Albert McQuarrie, Rhea Haines.
Tragedy ensues when an American opera singer charms a Mexican governor.

Chalk Marks (Peninsula Studios, 1924)
d: John G. Adolfi. 7 reels.
Marguerite Snow, Ramsey Wallace, June Elvidge, Lydia Knott, Rex Lease, Helen Ferguson, Priscilla Bonner, Harold Holland, Verna Mercereau, Fred Church, Lee Willard.
Drama about young lovers who drift apart, pursue separate careers, but stay in touch and come together later in life.

The Challenge (Star Productions/American Releasing Corp., 1922)
d: Tom Terriss. 5 reels.
Rod LaRocque, Dolores Cassinelli, Warner Richmond, DeSacia Mooers, Jane Jennings, Frank Norcross.
When Barbara chooses between her two suitors, Stanley and Ralph, the loser remains bitter, and anonymously tries to create a rift between the newlyweds.

The Challenge Accepted (Pathé, 1918)
d: Edwin L. Hollywood. 5 reels.
Zena Keefe, Charles Eldridge, Russell Simpson, Chester Barnett, Joel Day, Sidney D'Albrook, John Hopkins, Warren Cook.
In the Blue Ridge mountains, a reluctant recruit hesitates before going off to war, but is finally convinced by his sweetie and his friends that it's the right thing to do.

The Challenge of Chance (Continental Pictures Corp., 1919)
d: Harry Revier. 7 reels.
Jess Willard, Arline Pretty, Albert Hart, Lee Hill, Harry Van Meter.
A gruff but conscientious horse buyer must deal with animal cruelty, unscrupulous dealers, and a young couple in love. Jess Willard, who plays the lead, was heavyweight boxing champion of the world when this film was released.

The Challenge of the Law (Fox, 1920)
d: Scott Dunlap. 5 reels.
William Russell, Helen Ferguson, Arthur Morrison, James Farley, Robert Klein, D.J. Mitsoras, Fred Malatesta.
Ordered to put a stop to the fur smuggling trade, a Canadian mountie is torn between love and duty when he falls for a smuggler's daughter.

The Chamber Mystery (Schomer-Ross Productions, Inc./Arrow Film Corp., 1920)
d: Abraham Schomer. 5 reels.
Claire Whitney, Earl Metcalfe, Sam Edwards, Robert Lee Allen, Camilla Dalberg, Dorothy Walker, Howard Morgan, Ricca Allen, Fred Stanton.
Lovers take the devious road to matrimony when they trick a detective into arresting both her dad and the loser fiancé Dad had picked out for her.

Champion of Lost Causes (Fox, 1925)
d: Chester Bennett. 5 reels.
Edmund Lowe, Barbara Bedford, Walter McGrail, Jack McDonald, Alec Francis.
Murder mystery set in a gambling casino.

Changing Husbands (Famous Players-Lasky/Paramount, 1924)
d: Frank Urson. 7 reels.
Leatrice Joy, Victor Varconi, Raymond Griffith, Julia Faye, ZaSu Pitts, Helen Dunbar, William Boyd.
Miss Joy plays a double role, as actresses who greatly resemble each other.

The Changing Woman (Vitagraph, 1918)
d: David Smith. 5 reels.
Hedda Nova, J. Frank Glendon, Otto Lederer, George Kunkel.
Comedy-drama about a temperamental soprano on tour in South America who is captured by a tribe of mountain Indians. She is rescued by an intrepid young man who has no use for her artistic temper, but finds that in captivity she is tender, even demure. Now smitten, he returns her to civilization and restores her to the spotlight, only to see her once again become a vainglorious, fire-breathing prima donna. Disgusted by the change, her new lover kidnaps her again and takes her back to the mountains.

Channing of the Northwest (Selznick/Select, 1922)
d: Ralph Ince. 5 reels.
Eugene O'Brien, Gladden James, Norma Shearer, James Seeley, Pat Hartigan, Nita Naldi, Harry Lee, J.W. Johnston.
Channing, a disinherited London chap, travels to Canada and joins the Northwest Mounted Police.

The Chaperon (Essanay, 1916)
d: Arthur Berthelet. 5 reels.
Edna Mayo, Eugene O'Brien, Sydney Ainsworth, Frankie Raymond, John Cossar, Marion Skinner, Leona Ball, Gertrude Glover, Renee Clements, Teddy Virgo.
An American heiress is forced to marry a titled fortune hunter.

A Chapter in her Life (Universal, 1923)
d: Lois Weber. 6 reels.
Claude Gillingwater, Jane Mercer, Jacqueline Gadsden, Frances Raymond, Robert Frazer, Eva Thatcher, Ralph Yearsley, Fred Thomson, Beth Rayon.
After her husband dies, a young woman continues to live in her in-laws' home, but they steadily begin to resent her presence.

Charge It (Equity Pictures/Jans Film Service, 1921)
d: Harry Garson. 7 reels.
Clara Kimball Young, Herbert Rawlinson, Edward M. Kimball, Betty Blythe, Nigel Barrie, Hal Wilson, Dulcie Cooper.
Julia, a spenthrift newlywed, gets her husband to agree to giving her a charge account. *Big* mistake!

Charge It to Me (American Film Co./Pathé, 1919)
d: Roy William Neill. 5 reels.
Margarita Fisher, Emory Johnson, Augustus Phillips, L.S. McKee, Budd Post, Bull Montana, George Swann, J. Farrell MacDonald, Sophie Todd.
An enterprising young wife starts her own taxi service to earn enough money to buy her husband a birthday present.

The Charge of the Gauchos (Ajuria Productions, 1928)
d: Albert Kelly. 6 reels.
Francis X. Bushman, Jacqueline Logan, Guido Trento, Paul Ellis, Henry Kolker, Charles Hill Mailes, John Hopkins, Charles K. French, Olive Hasbrouck, Mathilde Comont, Jack Ponder, Ligo Conley, Gino Corrado, Frank Hagney.
In old Argentina, a fearless gaucho leads his people against the Spanish loyalists.

Charity (Frank Powell Productions, Inc., 1916)
d: Frank Powell. 6 reels.
Linda A. Griffith, Creighton Hale, Sheldon Lewis, John Dunn, Elizabeth Burbridge, Veta Searl, Sam J. Ryan.
On trial for killing her own child, an innocent woman is heartened to learn that her younger brother, whom she hasn't seen in years, is now a lawyer and a member of her defense team.

Charity Castle (American Film Co./Mutual, 1917)
d: Lloyd Ingraham. 5 reels.
Mary Miles Minter, Clifford Callis, Alan Forrest, Eugenie Ford, Henry A. Barrows, Ashton Dearholt, Robert Klein, Spottiswoode Aitken, George Ahearn, Gordon Russell.
A young orphan girl and her little brother are taken in by the son of a millionaire.

The Charlatan (Universal, 1929)
d: George Melford. 7 reels. (Part talkie.)
Holmes Herbert, Margaret Livingston, Philo McCullogh, Anita Garvin, Crauford Kent, Rose Tapley, Dorothy Gould.
A murder mystery, with suspicions being leveled at a master of disguise in the demise of his ex-wife.

Charley's Aunt (Christie Film Co./Producers Distributing Corp., 1925)
d: Scott Sidney. 8 reels.
Sydney Chaplin, Ethel Shannon, James E. Page, Lucien Littlefield, Alec B. Francis, Phillips Smalley, Eulalie Jensen, David James, Jimmy Harrison, Mary Akin, Priscilla Bonner.
Well-worn comedy about two young swains who press a friend into impersonating "Charley's Aunt" in order to provide a chaperone for a meeting with their sweethearts. Complications multiply when the real aunt shows up.

The Charm School (Famous Players-Lasky/Paramount, 1921)
d: James Cruze. 5 reels.
Wallace Reid, Lila Lee, Adele Farrington, Beulah Bains, Edwin Stevens, Grace Morse, Patricia Magee, Lincoln Stedman, Kate Toncray, Minna Redman, Snitz Edwards, Tina Marshall.
Comedy about a chap who inherits a school for girls.

The Charmer (Universal, 1917)
d: Jack Conway. 5 reels.
Ella Hall, Martha Mattox, Belle Bennett, James McCandlas, Gelorge Webb, Frank McQuarrie, A.E. Witting, Lincoln Stedman.
Prefiguring Mary Pickford's *Pollyanna* by three years, this tale has Ella Hall as an irrepressibly cheerful orphan who goes about cheering the lives of those around her.

The Charmer (Paramount, 1925)
d: Sidney Olcott. 6 reels.
Pola Negri, Wallace MacDonald, Robert Frazer, Trixie Friganza, Cesare Gravina, Gertrude Astor, Edwards Davis, Mathilda Brundage.
Comedy, with serious overtones, about a Spanish dancer imported to New York by a pair of her love-struck beaus.

The Chaser (Harry Langdon Corp./First National, 1928)
d: Harry Langdon. 5 reels.
Harry Langdon, Gladys McConnell, Helen Hayward, William Jamison, Charles Thurston.
Harry, the little fellow accused of being a "chaser"—as in skirt chaser—is nothing of the sort. He's a befuddled, and *very* henpecked, husband whose bullying wife is determined to put him in his place. Her mother, a hateful shrew, comes along to heap even more abuse on poor Harry. At a divorce hearing, even the judge decides the little fellow "needs to be taught a lesson," and instead of granting a divorce, he sentences Harry to spend 30 days as the "wife" of the family. Not exactly the first of Langdon's films to hint that his career was going south, this inglorious exhibition hastened his decline as a star. *The Chaser* has no narrative flow to speak of, just one humiliation after another piled onto its lead character.

Chasing Rainbows (Fox, 1919)
d: Frank Beal. 5 reels.
Gladys Brockwell, William Scott, Richard Rosson, Harry Dunkinson, Irene Aldwyn, Walter Long, Claire McDowell.
Love blossoms in the desert, between a waitress and the restaurant manager.

Chasing the Moon (Fox, 1922)
d: Edward Sedgwick. 5 reels.
Tom Mix, Eva Novak, William Buckley, Sid Jordan, Elsie Danbric, Wynn Mace.
Mix tries chase comedy in this film, playing a millionaire who accidentally breaks a vial containing a deadly poison. He learns that the only known antidote is in the hands of a professor who has disappeared somewhere in Russia, and decides to launch a sea-and-air search to locate him. Meanwhile, we learn that the vial didn't contain poison after all, but if the Mix character finds the antidote and takes it, it will kill him.

Chasing Through Europe (Fox, 1929)
d: David Butler. 6 reels. (Talking sequences and sound effects.)
Sue Carol, Nick Stuart, Gustav von Seyffertitz, Gavin Gordon, E. Alyn Warren.
A newsreel photographer escorts an American heiress through various European landmarks.

Chasing Trouble (Universal, 1926)
d: Milburn Morante. 5 reels.
Pete Morrison, Ione Reed, Tom London, Franklin Pangborn, Roy Watson, Frances Friel, Milton Fahrney, Jew Bennett, J.A. Wiley, Al Richmond, Skeeter Bill Robbins, Lilly Harris.

Out West, a good-natured gunman is hired to foil a gang of cattle rustlers.

Chastity (Preferred Pictures/Associated First National, 1923)
d: Victor Schertzinger. 6 reels.
Katherine MacDonald, J. Gunnis Davis, J. Gordon Russell, Huntley Gordon, Frederick Truesdell, Edythe Chapman.
Norma, a virtuous young actress, becomes the target of mudslinging publicists who hint that her backer is also her lover.

The Chattel (Vitagraph, 1916)
d: Fred Thomson, 5 reels.
E.H. Sothern, Peggy Hyland, Rose Tapley, Charles Kent, John Lark Taylor, Florence Radinoff.
A businessman loves his possessions, and even includes his wife as one of them.

Cheap Kisses (C. Gardner Sullivan Productions/FBO of America, 1924)
d: John Ince. 7 reels.
Lillian Rich, Cullen Landis, Vera Reynolds, Phillips Smalley, Louise Dresser, Jean hersholt, Bessie Eyton, Lincoln Stedman, Kathleen Myers, Sidney DeGrey, Michael Dark.
Donald, a scion of wealth, incurs his family's disapproval when he marries a chorus girl.

Cheaper to Marry (MGM, 1924)
d: Robert Z. Leonard. 7 reels.
Conrad Nagel, Marguerite De La Motte, Lewis Stone, Paulette Duval, Louise Fazenda, Claude Gillingwater.

While a lawyer romances an artist, his partner is squandering partnership funds on a faithless golddigger.

The Cheat (Lasky Feature Plays/Paramount, 1915)
d: Cecil B. DeMille. 5 reels.
Fannie Ward, Jack Dean, Sessue Hayakawa, James Neill, Utake Abe, Hazel Childers.
A socialite misappropriates charity funds to invest in the stock market. When her investments go sour, she must borrow from a human snake named Tori.

The Cheat (Paramount, 1923)
d: George Fitzmaurice. 8 reels.
Jack Holt, Charles de Roche, Dorothy Cummings, Pola Negri, Robert Schable, Charles Stevenson, Helen Dunbar, Richard Wayne, Guy Oliver, Edward Kimball, Frank Campeau, Noah Beery.
Remake of 1914's *The Cheat*.

Cheated Hearts (Universal, 1921)
d: Hobart Henley. 5 reels.
Herbert Rawlinson, Warner Baxter, Marjorie Daw, Doris Pawn, Winter Hall.
Love of a good woman cures a southern colonel's lust for alcohol.

Cheated Love (Universal, 1921)
d: King Baggot. 5 reels.
Carmel Myers, Allen Forrest, John Davidson, George B. Williams, Ed Brady, Snitz Edwards, Smoke Turner, Virginia Harris, Inez Gomez, Clara Greenwood, Meyer Ouhayou.
Sonya, an immigrant, is loved by one man while she desires another.

The Cheater (Screen Classics, Inc./Metro, 1920)
d: Henry Otto. 6 reels.
May Allison, King Baggot, Rudolph Valentino, Frank Currier, Harry Ven Meter, May Geraci, Percy Challenger,

Lucille Ward, Alberta Lee, P. Dempsey Tabler.
What's a phony faith healer to do when she actually heals someone?

The Cheater Reformed (Fox, 1921)
d: Scott Dunlap. 5 reels.
William Russell, Seena Owen, John Brammall, Sam DeGrasse, Ruth King.
His congregation doesn't know it, but the Reverend McCall has a twin brother who's an embezzler. After the good reverend is killed in a train accident, the larcenous twin takes his place in the pulpit. But virtue wins out, as the fake minister is reformed by his new calling.
Russell plays a double role here, as both the minister and his duplicitous twin.

Cheating Cheaters (C.K.Y. Film Corp./Select Pictures, 1919)
d: Allan Dwan. 5 reels.
Clara Kimball Young, Anna Q. Nilsson, Jack Holt, Frederick Burton, Frank Campeau, Mayme Kelso, Tully Marshall, Ira Lazarre, Edwin Stevens, Jess Singleton, Eleanor Hancock.
A gang of thieves poses as a respectable family, in order to rob the respectable family next door. Trouble is, the "family" next door is a gang of thieves as well.

Cheating Herself (Fox, 1919)
d: Edmund Lawrence. 5 reels.
Peggy Hyland, Harry Hilliard, Molly McConnell, Mrs. Jack Mulhall, William Elmer, Edwin Booth Tilton, Edward Jobson.
Convinced that her millionaire parents would be happier without constantly worrying over their money, an heiress decides to rob their safe.

Cheating the Public (Fox, 1918)
d: Richard Stanton. 7 reels.
Enid Markey, Ralph Lewis, Bertram Grassby, Tom Wilson, Edward Peil, Charles Edler, Wanda Petit, Carrie Clark Ward, Fanny Midgley, Baby Cohen, James Titus, Henry Peal.
A greedy industrialist is shot during a struggle with a young woman who represents his striking workers. She's tried for murder and is found guilty... but we know better.

The Checkered Flag (Banner Productions, 1926)
d: John G. Adolfi. 6 reels.
Elaine Hammerstein, Wallace MacDonald, Lionel Belmore, Robert Ober, Peggy O'Neil, Lee Shumway, Flora Maynard.
Fired unjustly from his job, a mechanic takes his new invention—a revolutionary carburetor—to the race track and seeks to win the big race with it.

Checkers (All Star Feature Corp., 1913)
d: Augustus Thomas. 6 reels.
Thomas W. Ross, Jack Regan, Gertrude Shipman, Katherine La Salle, Alfred Sidwell, Charles Graham, William A. Williams, Harriet Worthington, Marie Taylor, Carl Hartberg.
An amiable loser finally has his day, when he bets his last dime on a horse named "Remorse." It wins him five thousand dollars.

The Checkmate (Mutual, 1917)
d: Sherwood McDonald. 5 reels.
Jackie Saunders, Frank Mayo, Daniel Gilfether, Mollie McConnell, R. Henry Grey, Margaret Landis, Cullen Landis, Edward Jobson.
It's "checkmate" in a game of hearts, when a girl in love replaces her twin sister at the nuptial altar.

The Cheer Leader (Gotham Productions/Lumas Film Corp., 1928)
d: Alvin J. Neitz. 6 reels.
Ralph Graves, Gertrude Olmstead, Shirley Palmer, Ralph Emerson, Harold Goodwin, Donald Stuart, Duke Martin, Harry Northrup, Ruth Cherrington, James Leonard.
College hi-jinx have a pair of freshmen falling for two coeds, being rebuffed, then going out on the field to win the Big Game.

The Cheerful Fraud (Universal, 1927)
d: William A. Seiter.   7 reels.
Reginald Denny, Gertrude Olmstead, Otis Harlan, Emily Fitzroy, Charles Gerrard, Gertrude Astor.
Farcical comedy set in London about Michael, a gent who pretends to be a social secretary to be near Ann Kent, his beloved, and a crook who then impersonates Michael to be near the Kent jewels.

Cheerful Givers (Fine Arts Film Co./Triangle, 1917)
d: Paul Powell. 5 reels.
Bessie Love, Kenneth Harlan, Josephine Crowell, Spottiswoode Aitken, Bessie Buskirk, Pauline Starke, Winifred Westover, Loyola O'Connor, William H. Brown.
Strapped for cash, a young woman dresses as a man to apply for a job, and gets it.

The Cherokee Kid (FBO Pictures, 1927)
d: Robert DeLacy. 5 reels.
Tom Tyler, Sharon Lynn, Jerry Pembroke, Robert Burns, Robert Reeves, Ray Childs, James Van Horn, Carol Holloway.
Out West, a cowboy returning home learns he is suspected of murder.

Cheyenne (First National/Warner Bros., 1929)
d: Albert Rogell. 6 reels.
Ken Maynard, Gladys McDonnell, James Bradbury Jr., William Franey, Charles Whitaker.
Cal, an expert rodeo rider, helps a girl get her father out of debt.

Chicago (DeMille Pictures/Pathé, 1927)
d: Frank Urson. 9 reels.
Phyllis Haver, Victor Varconi, Eugene Palette, Virginia Bradford, Clarence Burton, Warner Richmond, T. Roy Barnes, Sidney D'Albrook, Otto Lederer, May Robson, Julia Faye, Robert Edeson.
Roxie Hart is at the center of a scandalous trial, accused of murdering a car salesman. She's innocent of that crime, but guilty of adultery because, though Roxie is married, the murdered man was her lover.

Chicago After Midnight (FBO Pictures, 1928)
d: Ralph Ince. 7 reels.
Ralph Ince, Jola Mendez, Lorraine Rivero, James Mason, Carl Axzelle, Helen Jerome Eddy, Ole M. Ness, Robert Seiter, Frank Mills, Christian J. Frank.
Boyd, an ex-con, leaves jail after 15 years, and goes after the man whose treachery put him behind bars. He finds him and kills him during a fight, then pins the crime on an innocent man who's engaged to marry Mona, a night club dancer. What Boyd doesn't know—yet—is that Mona is his own daughter, all grown up now, and in love.

Chicken A La King (Fox, 1928)
d: Henry Lehrman. 7 reels.
Nancy Carroll, George Meeker, Arthur Stone, Ford Sterling, Frances Lee, Carol Holloway.
Romantic comedy about a millionaire who, though married, consorts with lovely chorus girls. When his wife learns of his dalliances, she has two choices: One, confront the scoundrel; two, put some effort into making herself look young and attractive again to try and win him back. She chooses the latter, wiser choice.

Chicken Casey (New York Motion Picture Corp./Triangle, 1917)
d: Raymond B. West. 5 reels.
Dorothy Dalton, Charles Gunn, Howard Hickman, Thomas Guise.
To win a stage role as a street waif, an actress adopts a ragged disguise.

The Chicken in the Case (Selznick/Select, 1921)
w, d: Victor Heerman. 5 reels.
Owen Moore, Vivian Ogden, Teddy Sampson, Edgar Nelson, Katherine Perry, Walter Walker.
Threatened with loss of his inheritance unless he gets married, young Steve "borrows" his friend's wife and presents her to his family as his fiancée. But the plot thickens when Steve falls in love for real with a girl who knows nothing of the hoax.

Chickens (Thomas H. Ince/Paramount, 1921)
d: Jack Nelson. 5 reels.
Douglas MacLean, Gladys George, Claire McDowell, Charles H. Mailes, Edith Yorke, Raymond Cannon, Willie Marks, Al W. Filson.
Deems, a chicken farmer, loves Julia, the girl from the neighboring farm. But his mortgage holder is about to foreclose and drive Deems off his land. What to do?

Chickie (First National, 1925)
d: John Francis Dillon. 8 reels.
Dorothy Mackaill, John Bowers, Hobart Bosworth, Gladys Brockwell, Paul Nicholson, Myrtle Stedman, Olive Tell, Lora Sonderson, Louise Mackintosh.
Chickie, a stenographer, is seduced by a law clerk and finds herself with child.

The Child of Destiny (Columbia/Metro, 1916)
d: William Nigh. 5 reels.
Irene Fenwick, Madama Ganna Walska, Robert Elliott, Roy Applegate, Roy Clair, William Yearance, Martin J. Faust, William Davidson, R.A. Bresee, Elizabeth Le Roy.
A confirmed bachelor finally marries... but it's a mismatch.

Child of M'Sieu (Triangle, 1919)
d: Harrish Ingraham. 5 reels.
Baby Marie Osborne, Philo McCullough, Harrish Ingraham, Claire Alexander, Katherine MacLaren.
A little orphan girl brings happiness to all those around her.

A Child of Mystery (Universal, 1916)
d: Hobart Henley. 5 reels.
Gertrude Selby, Thomas Jefferson, Paul Byron, Alfred Allen, Mark Fenton, Nanine Wright, Hobart Henley.
Denizens of New York's Little Italy live in fear of an evil secret society.

A Child of the Paris Streets (Fine Arts/Triangle, 1916)
d: Lloyd Ingraham. 5 reels.
Mae Marsh, Robert Harron, Jennie Lee, Carl Stockdale, Tully Marshall, Loyola O'Connor, Bert Hadley, Josephine Crowell, Paul LeBlanc.
Snatched from her Parisian home, a girl is raised as an apache.

A Child of the Wild (Fox, 1917)
d: John G. Adolfi. 5 reels.
June Caprice, Frank Morgan, Tom Brooke, Richard Neill, Jane Lee, John W. Kellette, John G. Adolfi, Tom Cameron.
A tomboy falls for her handsome teacher.

Children in the House (Fine Arts/Triangle, 1916)
d: C.M. Franklin. 5 reels.
Norma Talmadge, Alice Rae, Jewel Carmen, William Hinckley, W.E. Lawrence, George Pearce, Eugene Pallette, Walter Long, Alva D. Blake, George Stone, Violet Radcliffe.
Dallying with a callous wench from the local cabaret, a married man finds himself under financial pressure, and so engineers a robbery.

Children Not Wanted (Crest Pictures/Republic, 1920)
d: Paul Scardon. 6 reels.
Edith Day, Ruth Sullivan, Joe King, Lumsden Hare, Jean Robertson, Mario Majeroni, K.C. Beaton, Dorothy Walters.
A young woman and her foster daughter learn it's difficult to find an apartment that will accept children.

Children of Banishment (Select Pictures Corp., 1919)
d: Norval MacGregor. 5 reels.
Mitchell Lewis, Bessie Eyton, Herbert Heyes, Arthur Morrison, Tom Bates, George Nichols, Jane Keckley.
In the Pacific northwest, a lumberman finds that he is falling in love with his partner's wife.

Children of Divorce (Famous Players-Lasky/Paramount, 1927)
d: Frank Lloyd, Josef von Sternberg. 7 reels.
Clara Bow, Esther Ralston, Gary Cooper, Einar Hanson, Norman Trevor, Hedda Hopper, Edward Martindel, Julia Swayne Gordon, Tom Ricketts, Albert Gran, Iris Stuart, Margaret Campbell, Percy Williams, Joyce Coad, Yvonne Pelletier, Don Marion.
Weepy melodrama about a boy and a girl, childhood friends who grow up in love with each other, but find the road to romance is littered with broken hearts.

Children of Dust (Associated First National, 1923)
d: Frank Borzage. 7 reels.
Lloyd Hughes, Bert Woodruff, Johnnie Walker, Frankie Lee, Pauline Garon, Josephine Adair, Hewton Hall, George Nichols.
Neighbor boys love the same girl. When World War I beckons, they enlist in the service, but on their return the girl must choose between them.

Children of Destiny (Weber Productions, Inc./Republic, 1920)
d: George Irving. 6 reels.
Edith Hallor, William Courtleigh, Arthur E. Carew, Emory Johnson, Frederick Garvin.
A fleeting indiscretion in Italy comes to haunt an American wife, years later.

Children of Eve (Thomas A. Edison, Inc., 1915)
d: John H. Collins. 5 reels.
Viola Dana, Robert Conness, Thomas F. Blake, Nellie Grant, Robert Walker, William Wadsworth, James Harris, Hubert Dawley, Warren Cook, Brad Sutton.
Heavy drama aimed at reforming the child labor laws.

Children of Jazz (Famous Players-Lasky/Paramount, 1923)
d: Jerome Storm. 6 reels.
Theodore Kosloff, Ricardo Cortez, Robert Cain, Eileen Percy, Irene Dalton, Alec B. Francis, Frank Currier, snitz Edwards, Lillian Drew.
Babs, a frivolous "Jazz baby," is engaged to be married. Before her swain can take her to the altar, however, he must reform her from her madcap ways.

Children of the Feud (Fine Arts Film Co./Triangle, 1916)
d: Joseph Henabery. 5 reels.
Charles Gorman, Dorothy Gish, Violet Radcliffe, Beulah Burns, Thelma Burns, Tina Rossi, Georgie Stone, A.D. Sears, F.A. Turner, Sam De Grasse, Alberta lee, Elmo Lincoln.
Feuding mountain clans are finally stopped by the love of one of their own women.

Children of the Ghetto (Box Office Attraction Co./Fox, 1915)
d: Frank Powell. 5 reels.
Wilton Lackaye, Ruby Hoffman, Ethel Kaufman, Frank Andrews, Louis Alberni, Irene Boyle, Victor Benoit, David Bruce, William R. Hatch, J. Albert Hall.
Drama focuses on the problems of a poor Jewish family.

Children of the Ritz (First National, 1929)
d: John Francis Dillon. 7 reels. (Music and sound effects.)
Dorothy Mackaill, Jack Mulhall, James Ford, Richard Carlyle, Evelyn Hall, Kathryn McGuire, Frank Crayne, Ed Burns, Doris Dawson, Aggie Herring, Lee Moran.
A spoiled, pampered heiress seduces the family chauffeur and gets him to marry her.

Children of the Whirlwind (Whitman Bennett Productions/Arrow Pictures, 1925)
d: Whitman Bennett. 7 reels.
Lionel Barrymore, Johnny Walker, Marguerite De La Motte, J.R. Roser, Marie Haynes, Bert Tuey, Frank Montgomery, Ruby Blaine.
Larry, an ex-con, tries to get his old friends to go straight.

The Chimes (U.S. Amusement Corp./World Film Corp., 1914)
d: Herbert Blaché. 5 reels.
Tom Terriss, Faye Cusick, Alfred Hemming, Clarence Harvey, Harry Hitchcock, Robert Vivian, Milly Terriss, Vinnie Burns, William Terriss, Eliza Mason.
Is it a sin for the poor to marry? This film seriously poses that question.

China Bound (MGM, 1929)
d: Charles Reisner. 7 reels.
Karl Dane, George K. Arthur, Polly Moran, Josephine Dunn, Carl Stockdale, Harry Woods.
When his girlfriend's father puts her on an ocean liner bound for China, Eustis follows along, hoping to pursue their courtship.

Chinatown Charlie (First National, 1928)
d: Charles Hines. 7 reels.
Johnny Hines, Louise Lorraine, Harry Gribbon, Fred Kohler, Scooter Lowry, Sojin, Anna May Wong, George Kuwa, John Bradette.
Hines plays Chinatown Charlie, a tour guide who is forced to defend one of his female passengers from a gang of jewel thieves.

Chinatown Nights (Paramount, 1929)
d: William A. Wellman. 8 reels. (Part talkie.)
Wallace Beery, Florence Vidor, Warner Oland, Jack McHugh, Jack Oakie, Tetsu Komai, Frank Chew, Mrs. Wong Wing, Pete Morrison, Freeman Wood.
A socialite falls in love with one of the leaders in a

Chinatown tong war.

The Chinese Parrot (Universal, 1927)
d: Paul Leni. 7 reels.
Marian Nixon, Florence Turner, Hobart Bosworth, Edward Burns, Alber Conti, Sojin, Fred Esmelton, Edgar Kennedy, George Kuwa, Slim Summerville, Dan Mason, Anna May Wong, Etta Lee, Jack Trent.
The mystery of stolen jewels may be unraveled by a Chinese parrot who witnessed the robbery.

Chip of the Flying U (Universal, 1926)
d: Lynn Reynolds. 7 reels.
Hoot Gibson, Virginia Brown Faire, Philo McCullough, Nora Cecil, DeWitt Jennings, Harry Todd, Pee Wee Holmes, Mark Hamilton, Willie Sung, Steve Clements.
Chip, a confirmed misogynist, nevertheless falls head over heels in love with his rancher boss' sister.

Chivalrous Charley (Selznick/Select, 1921)
d: Robert Ellis. 5 reels.
Eugene O'Brien, George Fawcett, Nancy Deaver, D.J. Flanagan, Huntley Gordon.
Charley, a bachelor who is chivalrous to a fault, takes in a supposed lady in distress for the night only to find, the following morning, that her father insists they get married.

The Chocolate Soldier (Daisy Feature Film Co./Alliance, 1915)
d: Walter Morton, Stanislaus Stange. 5 reels.
Alice Yorke, Tom Richards, Lucille Saunders, Francis J. Boyle, George Tallman, William H. White.
Flirtations among the nobility in the Balkans. Story is based on the operetta *The Chocolate Soldier*, which in turn was based on George Bernard Shaw's *Arms and the Man*.

The Chorus Girl's Romance (Metro, 1920)
d: William C. Dowlan. 5 reels.
Viola Dana, Gareth Hughes, Phil Ainsworth, William Quinn, Jere Sundin, Sidney DeGrey, Lawrence Grant, Tom Gallery, Edward Jobson, Martyn Best, Anne Schaefer.
Falling madly in love with a shimmy dancer, a wealthy bookworm renounces his inheritance for the right to marry her.

The Chorus Kid (Gotham Productions/Lumas Film Corp., 1928)
d: Howard Bretherton. 6 reels.
Virginia Brown Faire, Bryant Washburn, Thelma Hill, Hedda Hopper, John Batten, Tom O'Brien, Sheldon Lewis.
Beatrice, a chorus girl, has set her sights on marrying a rich man... and she's got one in the cross hairs.

The Chorus Lady (Lasky Feature Plays/Paramount, 1915)
d: Frank Reicher. 5 reels.
Cleo Ridgely, Marjorie Daw, Wallace Reid, Richard Grey, Mrs. Lewis McCord.
When a respectable chorus dancer is found in dishabille in a man's apartment, her fiancé is livid and wants to call off the engagement. But the lady has a perfectly good excuse: She was trying to save her stagestruck kid sister from making a fool of herself.

The Chorus Lady (Regal Pictures, 1924)
d: Ralph Ince. 7 reels.
Margaret Livingston, Alan Roscoe, Virginia Lee Corbin, Lillian Elliott, Lloyd Ingraham, Philo McCullough, Eve Southern, Mervyn LeRoy.
Remake of the 1915 Lasky film *The Chorus Lady*, both

versions based on the 1906 play of the same name by James Forbes.

The Christian (Vitagraph, 1914)
d: Frederick A. Thomson. 8 reels.
Earle Williams, Edith Storey, Harry S. Northrup, James Morrison, Jane Fearnley, Donald Hall, Edward Kimball, Charles Kent, J.W. Sambrook, James Lackaye, Carlotta de Felice.

Hopelessly in love with a successful stage actress, a social worker tries to forget her by establishing a settlement house in a London slum.

The Christian (Goldwyn, 1923)
d: Maurice Tourneur. 8 reels.
Richard Dix, Mae Busch, Gareth Hughes, Phyllis Haver, Cyril Chadwick, Mahlon Hamilton, Joseph Dowling, Claude Gillingwater, John Herdman, Beryl Mercer, Robert Bolder, Milla Davenport, Alice Hesse, Aileen Pringle, Harry Northrup, Eric Mayne, William Moran.
Remake of the 1914 Vitagraph film *The Christian*, both versions based on the play of the same name by Hall Caine.

Christina (Fox, 1929)
d: William K. Howard. 7 reels. (Also released in sound version.)
Janet Gaynor, Charles Morton, Rudolph Schildkraut, Harry Cording, Lucy Dorraine.
In Holland, a girl falls for a "knight" in shining armor. Actually, he's an actor playing that role in a traveling carnival show.

Christine of the Big Tops (Banner Productions/Sterling Pictures, 1926)
d: Archie Mayo. 6 reels.
Pauline Garon, Cullen Landis, Otto Matiesen, Robert Graves, John Elliott, Martha Mattox, Betty Noon.
A disillusioned physician joins the circus as a veterinarian. There, he falls for Christine, a trapeze artist, and through her love wins back his confidence to practice medicine.

Christine of the Hungry Heart (Thomas H. Ince Corp./First National, 1924)
d: George Archainbaud. 8 reels.
Florence Vidor, Clive Brook, Ian Keith, Warner Baxter, Walter Hiers, Lillian Lawrence, Dorothy Brock.
Christine, twice-married and still dissatisfied, tries love a third time.

The Cigarette Girl (Astra Film Corp./Pathé, 1917)
d: William Parke. 5 reels.
Gladys Hulette, Warner Oland, William Parke Jr., Florence Hamilton, Arthur Sullivan.
To foil a blackmail scheme against him, a sympathetic cigarette girl enters into a platonic marriage to a wealthy young man, who then transfers all his assets to his wife. The blackmailers are thus put to rout, and the newlyweds now discover that they do, in fact, love each other.

The Cinderella Man (Goldwyn, 1917)
d: George Loane Tucker. 5 reels.
Mae Marsh, Tom Moore, Alec B. Francis, George Fawcett, Louis R. Grisel, George Farren, Elizabeth Arians, Dean Raymond, Harry Scarborough, Royce Coombs.
By pretending to be a secretary, a wealthy young woman hopes to appeal to the impoverished young poet she fancies.

Cinderella of the Hills (Fox, 1921)
d: Howard M. Mitchell. 5 reels.

Barbara Bedford, Carl Miller, Cecil Van Auker, Wilson Hummel, Tom McGuire, Barbara LaMarr Deely.

In the Ozark mountains, a girl disguises herself as a boy and earns money by playing the violin. But what she's really trying to do is reunite her separated parents.

Cinderella's Twin (Metro, 1920)
d: Dallas M. Fitzgerald. 6 reels.
Viola Dana, Wallace MacDonald, Ruth Stonehouse, Cecil Foster, Edward Connelly, Victory Bateman, Gertrude Short, Irene Hunt, Edward Cecil, Calvert Carter.
A 20th century scullery maid is put through a series of adventures that remarkably parallel the famous story of Cinderella—up to, and including, a Prince Charming.

The Cinema Murder (Cosmopolitan/Paramount, 1919)
d: George D. Baker. 6 reels.
Marion Davies, Peggy Parr, Nigel Barrie, Eulalie Jensen, Anders Randolph, W. Scott Moore, Reginald Barlow.
A young woman falls in love with a suspected murderer.

Circe the Enchantress (Tiffany Productions/MGM, 1924)
d: Robert Z. Leonard. 7 reels.
Mae Murray, James Kirkwood, William Haines.
A vengeful young woman, having been abused by a man as a convent girl, turns against men and treats them like dirt.

The Circle (MGM, 1925)
d: Frank Borzage. 6 reels.
Eleanor Boardman, Eulalie Jensen, Malcolm McGregor, Alec B. Francis, Creighton Hale, Eugenie Besserer, George Fawcett, Lucille LeSueur.
Film version of Somerset Maugham's stage play about marital infidelity.

The Circular Staircase (Selig Polyscope, 1915)
d: Edward J. Le Saint. 5 reels.
Guy Oliver, Eugenie Besserer, Stella Razeto, Edith Johnson, William Howard, Anna Dodge, Jane Watson, F.J. Tyler, Fred Huntly, Clyde Benson, George Hernandez, Bert Grasby.
Summer vacation turns deadly for a family leasing a large home with a circular staircase.

Circumstantial Evidence (William Steiner Productions, 1920)
w, d: Tom Collins. 5 reels.
Glenn White, Leo Delaney, Jane McAlpin, Alfred Warman, David Wall, Robert Taber, Marie Treador.
Having been wrongly convicted of murder on circumstantial evidence, an innocent man wins a pardon, finds the real murderer, and devotes his life to solving crimes.

Circumstantial Evidence (Chesterfiled Motion Picture Corp., 1929)
w, d: Wilfred Noy. 7 reels.
Cornelius Keefe, Helen Foster, Alice Lake, Charles Gerrard, Ray Hallor, Fred Walton, Jack Tanner.
Ladies' man Henry Lord is found murdered, and circumstantial evidence points to an innocent stenographer.

The Circus (Chaplin/United Artists, 1928)
w, d: Charles Chaplin. 7 reels.
Charles Chaplin, Merna Kennedy, Betty Morrissey, Harry Crocker, Allan Garcia, Henry Bergman, Stanley J. Sanford, George Davis, John Rand, Steve Murphy, Doc Stone, Albert Austin, Heinie Conklin.
A little tramp joins the cast of a traveling circus and becomes the comic hit of the show. He falls in love with the show's equestrienne, but gives her up so she can marry the tightrope walker she fancies.

When the first Academy Awards were given out in 1929, Chaplin received a "special" award for his work in *The Circus*. But he deserved more acclaim than an honorary trophy bestows. By 1929, Chaplin was already the greatest talent in films and had a spectacular string of hits behind him, beginning with his memorable two-reelers at Keystone, Essanay, and Mutual, and continuing through the 1920s with *The Kid* (1921), *The Pilgrim* (1923), and his masterpiece, *The Gold Rush* (1925).

In *The Circus*, he gives a moving performance as the drifter who is hired as a property man for a carnival show, and soon becomes its star. His antics are hilarious and his warmth is genuine. But his love for Merna, the bareback rider, is unrequited, for she loves another. Realizing this, the humble tramp encourages the two to marry, helps them to elope, even throws rice at the happy couple after the wedding. Here, Chaplin gives us an eloquent lesson in selfless love. The tramp is happy because the woman he loves is happy; and for the moment, that is all that matters to him.

Chaplin finally received his deserved praise—and a standing ovation—from the Hollywood community in 1972, when he was presented with a second special Academy Award, for a lifetime of achievement in films.

The Circus Ace (Fox, 1927)
d: Ben Stoloff. 5 reels.
Tom Mix, Natalie Joyce, Jack Baston, Duke Lee, James Bradbury, Stanley Blystone, Dudley Smith, Buster Gardner, Tony the wonder horse.
Out West, a cowboy falls in love with a circus aerialist.

The Circus Cyclone (Universal, 1925)
d: Albert S. Rogell. 5 reels.
Art Acord, Nancy Deaver, Moe McRae, Cesare Gravina, Albert J. Smith, Hilliard Karr, George Austin, Gertrude Howard, Jim Corey, Ben Corbett.
Pepe, a circus clown, is accused of bank robbery. Fortunately Jack, who fancies Pepe's equestrienne daughter, is sure that the clown was framed for the holdup, and goes after the real robbers.

Circus Days (Sol Lesser/Associated First National Pictures, 1923)
d: Edward F. Cline. 6 reels.
Jackie Coogan, Barbara Tennant, Russell Simpson, Claire McDowell, Cesare Gravina, Peaches Jackson, Sam DeGrasse, DeWitt Jennings, Nellie Lane, William Barlow.
Feeling abused by his guardian, Toby Tyler runs away from home and joins the circus.

The Circus Man (Lasky Feature Plays/Paramount, 1914)
d: Oscar C. Apfel. 5 reels.
Theodore Roberts, Mabel Van Buren, Florence Dagmar, Hubert Whitehead, Jode Mullally, Raymond Hatton, Frank Hickman, Fred Montague, Billy Elmer, James Neill.
Evidence in a murder case points to a clown in a traveling circus.

The Circus of Life (Universal, 1917)
d: Rupert Julian. 5 reels.
Pomeroy Cannon, Elsie Jane Wilson, Harry Carter, Emory Johnson, Zoe Rae.
A new father loves his daughter, although he suspects she isn't really his.

A Circus Romance (Equitable Motion Pictures Corp., 1916)

CHILDREN OF THE RITZ (1929). Jack Mulhall (right, in chauffeur's uniform) prepares to fight a rival (Ed Burns) for the woman he loves (Dorothy MacKaill, center) in spite of his "inferior" status in life. Soon, the chauffeur will win a large sum at the race track and thus gain new stature to woo the lady. In silent era films, true love was never enough; the couple also had to share equal economic status for the romance to succeed, even if—as here—one's fortune came as a surprise.

* * * * *

84

d: Charles M. Seay. 5 reels.
Muriel Ostriche, Edward Davis, Jack Hopkins, Catherine Calhoun, George Larkin.
Fear of public disapproval leads a respected businessman to disavow his illegitimate daughter, a circus dancer. Later, when he confesses his past to his wife and she forgives him, the businessman opens his arms and his home to his daughter.

Circus Rookies (MGM, 1928)
d: Edward Sedgwick. 6 reels.
Karl Dane, George K. Arthur, Louise Lorraine, Sidney Jarvis, Fred Humes.
Oscar, an animal trainer for the circus, vies with newcomer Francis for the hand of the fair La Belle, the circus owner's daughter.

The City (World Film Corp., 1916)
d: Theodore Wharton. 5 reels.
Thurlow Bergen, William Riley Hatch, Elsie Esmond, Bessie E. Wharton, Richard Stewart, Allan Murnane.
A candidate for governor must face not only his political rivals, but also the treacherous young man he believes to be his half-brother.

The City (Fox, 1926)
d: R. William Neill. 6 reels.
Nancy Nash, Robert Frazer, George Irving, Lillian Elliott, Walter McGrail, Richard Walling, May Allison, Melbourne MacDowell, Bodil Rosing.
When the son of a reformed criminal runs for mayor of his city, his father's past is used to smear his political image.

City Girl (Fox, 1930)
d: F.W. Murnau. 7 reels. (Also released in sound version.)
Charles Farrell, Mary Duncan, Guinn Williams, David Torrence, Edith Yorke, Dawn O'Day, Dick Alexander, Tom Maguire, Jack Pennick, Ed Brady, Ed Clay, Helen Lynch.
When a country boy brings home a bride from the big city, she is met with scorn by his father, a wheat farmer who suspects his new daughter-in-law is a fortune hunter. She tries repeatedly to win the farmer's approval, but to no avail... until the ranch foreman tries to seduce her, and the struggle is witnessed by her father-in-law.

The City Gone Wild (Paramount, 1927)
d: James Cruze. 6 reels.
Thomas Meighan, Marietta Millner, Louise Brooks, Fred Kohler, Duke Martin, Nancy Phillips, Wyndham Standing, Charles Hill Mailes, King Zany.
While a crime wave erupts in the big city, a young woman is caught in the crossfire between a criminal lawyer and a district attorney who loves her.

City Lights (United Artists, 1931)
w, d: Charles Chaplin. 9 reels.
Charles Chaplin, Virginia Cherrill, Harry Myers, Hank Mann, Florence Lee, Allan Garcia, Eddie Baker, Henry Bergman, Albert Austin, James Donnelly, Robert Parrish, John Rand, Stanhope Wheatcroft.

Released three years after the birth of the talkies, this silent film has a lush musical score (composed by Chaplin) and synchronized sound effects, but no dialogue. Chaplin's story of a tramp who befriends a blind flower girl contains some of the most inventive comedy turns ever filmed, and some of the finest pathos. The famous closing scene, where the now-cured flower girl sees her benefactor—the tramp—for the first time, is a heart-rending mixture of joy and sadness. James Agee wrote: "It is enough to shrivel the heart to see, and it is the greatest piece of acting and the highest moment in movies." Of that scene, Al Capp wrote: "...because he is the most understanding and exquisite of artists, Chaplin's final tragedy became somehow our tragedy. He entered into us."

The City of Comrades (Goldwyn, 1919)
d: Harry Beaumont. 5 reels.
Tom Moore, Seena Owen, Otto Hoffman, Albert Roscoe, Alec B. Francis, Ralph Walker, Mary Warren, Kate Lester.
A settlement house known as "The City of Comrades" shelters derelicts and gives them a second chance at life.

The City of Dim Faces (Famous Players-Lasky/Paramount, 1918)
d: George Melford. 5 reels.
Sessue Hayakawa, Doris Pawn, Marin Sais, James Cruze, Winter Hall, Togo Yama, James Wang, George King, Larry Steers.
Jang Lung, the product of a marriage between a Chinese man and a white woman, meets a white girl and brings her home to San Francisco's Chinatown.

The City of Illusion (Ivan Film Productions, 1916)
w, d: Ivan Abramson. 6 reels.
Mignon Anderson, Joseph Burke, Blanche Craig, Carleton Macy, Mathilde Brundage, Bradley Barker, Paula Shay, Maxine Brown, Willard Case, Guido Colucci, D.H. Gould.
A scheming Southern woman claims she is having an affair with a New York lawyer.

The City of Masks (Famous Players-Lasky/Paramount, 1920)
d: Thomas N. Heffron. 5 reels.
Robert Warwick, Lois Wilson, Theodore Kosloff, Edward Jobson, J.M. Dumont, Robert Dunbar, Helen Dunbar, Anne Schaefer, Frances Raymond, William Boyd, Snitz Edwards.
Penniless European nobles find consolation among their own kind, in New York City.

The City of Purple Dreams (Selig Polyscope, 1918)
d: Colin Campbell. 7 reels.
Thomas Santschi, Bessie Eyton, Fritzi Brunette, Harry Lonsdale, Frank Clark, A.D. Sears, Lafayette Mckee, Fred Huntley, William Scott, Eugenie Besserer, Cecil Holland.
When a derelict involved in a blackmail scheme realizes his victim is the father of a woman who once showed him some kindness, he rejects the criminal life.

City of Silent Men (Famous Players-Lasky/Paramount, 1921)
d: Tom Forman. 6 reels.
Thomas Meighan, Lois Wilson, Kate Bruce, Paul Everton, George MacQuarrie, Guy Oliver.
After being framed for a murder he didn't commit, a young man escapes from prison and begins a new life in another state. There, he becomes a model citizen and a loving husband.

The City of Tears (Universal, 1918)
d: Elsie Jane Wilson. 5 reels.
Carmel Myers, Edwin August, Earl Rodney, Leatrice Joy, Lettie Kruse.

A young singer finds herself out of a job and penniless, but is befriended by the owner of an Italian delicatessen.

A City Sparrow (Famous Players-Lasky/Paramount, 1920)
d: Sam Wood. 5 reels.

Ethel Clayton, Walter Hiers, Clyde Fillmore, Lillian Leighton, William Boyd, Rose Cade, Robert Brower, Helen Jerome Eddy, Sylvia Ashton.

After an injury leaves her unable to bear children, a vaudeville dancer turns bitter and rejects all suitors. But the love of a good man restores her good spirits.

The City That Never Sleeps (Famous Players-Lasky/Paramount, 1924)
d: James Cruze. 6 reels.
Louise Dresser, Ricardo Cortez, Kathlyn Williams, Virginia Lee Corbin, Pierre Gendron, James Farley, Ben Hendricks, Vondell Darr.

Heavy weeper about a widowed mother who runs a Bowery saloon, but unselfishly decides to give up her young daughter to a refined family. Years later, the daughter returns to the saloon as a callous, self-centered flapper. She remembers nothing about her real mother and cares less.

Civilian Clothes (Famous Players-Lasky/Paramount, 1920)
d: Hugh Ford. 6 reels.
Thomas Meighan, Martha Mansfield, Maude Turner Gordon, Alfred Hickman, Frank Losee, Marie Shotwell, Warren Cook, Albert Gran, Isabelle Garrison, Halbert Brown.

What's a young "widow" to do when her impending marriage is interrupted by the return of her former Army husband, in civilian clothes?

Civilization (Triangle, 1916)
d: Thomas H. Ince, Reginald Barker. 10 reels.
Howard Hickman, Enid Markey, Lola May, Kate Bruce, Charles K. French, Fanny Midgley, George Fisher, Ethel Ullman, Claire DeBrey, J. Frank Burke, Herschel Mayall.

Strongly symbolic tale about a submarine commander who's really a pacifist. He perishes at sea and goes to his eternal reward, then the Lord God Himself intervenes in earthly matters to bring the war to an end.

Civilization's Child (New York Motion Picture Corp./Triangle, 1916)
d: Charles Giblyn. 5 reels.
William H. Thompson, Anna Lehr, Jack Standing, Dorothy Dalton, Clyde Benson, J.P. Lockney, J. Barney Sherry.

Tragedy results when a Russian immigrant in New York is cheated out of her husband, her job, and her baby.

The Claim (Metro, 1918)
d: Frank Reicher. 5 reels.
Edith Storey, Wheeler Oakman, Mignon Anderson, Marian Skinner, Paul Weigel, Fred Malatesta.

A brother and sister adopt an abandoned baby girl. But the child's mother returns and demands that they give her back her child or pay blackmail.

Clancy's Kosher Wedding (R-C Pictures/FBO of America, 1927)
d: Arvid E. Gillstrom. 6 reels.
George Sidney, Will Armstrong, Ann Brody, Mary Gordon, Sharon Lynn, Rex Lease, Ed Brady.

Rival haberdashers Cohen and Clancy have a problem that's bigger than business: Cohen's daughter and Clancy's son are in love with each other, to their parents' chagrin.

The Clansman — see: The Birth of a Nation

Clarence (Famous Players-Lasky/Paramount, 1922)
d: William DeMille. 7 reels.
Wallace Reid, Agnes Ayres, May McAvoy, Kathlyn Williams, Edward Martindel, Robert Agnew, Adolphe Menjou, Bertram Johns, Dorothy Gordon, Mayme Kelso.

Comedy about Clarence, a war veteran, who is hired as a handyman to a high-strung, neurotic family. He falls in love with the family's governess, and together they prevent the family's daughter from eloping with a fortune hunter, while at the same time fending off the wife's amorous advances to Clarence.

The Clarion (Equitable Motion Pictures Corp./World Film Corp., 1916)
d: James Durkin. 5 reels.
Carlyle Blackwell, Howard Hall, Marion Dentler, Charles Mason, George Soule Spencer, Rosemary Dean, Philip Hahn.

An idealistic young man buys a newspaper, The Clarion, and wages a crusade against slumlords, quack doctors, and other miscreants.

Clash of the Wolves (Warner Bros., 1925)
d: Noel Smith. 7 reels.
Rin-Tin-Tin, Charles Farrell, June Marlowe, Charlie Conklin, Pat Hartigan.

A wild dog is leader of a pack of wolves, until he is befriended by a kindly human.

Classified (Corinne Griffith Productions/First National Pictures, 1925)
d: Alfred Santell. 7 reels.
Corinne Griffith, Jack Mulhall, Ward Crane, Carroll Nye, Charles Murray, Edythe Chapman, Jacqueline Wells, George Sidney, Bernard Randall.

Edna Ferber tale about Babs, a girl who works in the newspaper's classified ads section. She's a looker who openly flirts with wealthy men, hoping to attract a rich husband. But she comes to love a garage mechanic and, in time, becomes convinced that he's her best "catch."

Classmates (Inspiration Pictures/First National, 1924)
d: John S. Robertson. 7 reels.
Richard Barthelmess, Madge Evans, Claude Brooke, Charlotte Walker, Reginald Sheffield, Beach Cooke, James Bradbury Jr., Henry B. Lewis, Richard Harlan, Antrim Short.

Remake of the 1914 film *Classmates*, both versions based on the play of the same name by Margaret Turnbull and William C. DeMille.

The Claw (Select Pictures, 1918)
d: Robert G. Vignola. 5 reels.
Clara Kimball Young, Milton Sills, Henry Woodward, Mary Mersch, Jack Holt, Edward M. Kimball, Marcia Manon.

In South Africa, a girl is engaged to marry a British major, until he is reported killed in a native revolution. Sorrowfully, his fiancée marries someone else. Then comes word that the Major is still alive.

The Claw (Universal, 1927)
d: Sidney Olcott. 6 reels.
Norman Kerry, Claire Windsor, Arthur Edmund Carewe, Tom Guise, Helene Sullivan, Nelson McDowell, Larry Steers, J. Gordon Russell, Myrta Bonillas, Dick Sutherland, Jacques D'Auray, Pauline Neff, Bertram Johns, Billie Bennett, Annie Ryan.

Dierdre, a young Englishwoman, becomes infatuated with a dashing British major and follows him when he returns to his post in East Africa.

The Claws of the Hun (Thomas H. Ince/Paramount, 1918)
d: Victor L. Schertzinger. 5 reels.
Charles Ray, Jane Novak, Robert McKim, Dorcas Matthews,

Melbourne MacDowell, Mollie McConnell, Henry A. Barrows.
A young American foils a German spy intent on stealing an important formula.

Clay Dollars (Selznick/Select, 1921)
d: George Archainbaud. 5 reels.
Eugene O'Brien, Ruth Dwyer, Frank Currier, Arthur Houseman, Jim Tenbrooke, Florida Kingsley, Tom Burke, Jerry Devine, Bruce Reynolds.
A local squire informs a man's heir, Bruce, that his father traded away all his property for worthless swampland before he died. But Bruce suspects that the squire is trying to pull a fast one, so with the help of a lovely young woman, eventually cons the con man into restoring his rightful inheritance.

The Clean Heart (Vitagraph, 1924)
d: J. Stuart Blackton. 8 reels.
Percy Marmont, Otis Harlan, Marguerite De La Motte, Andrew Arbuckle, Martha Petelle, Violet LaPlante, George Inleton, Anna Lockhardt.
Philip, a successful writer, suffers a nervous breakdown and goes to the country to recuperate. There, he finds not only a restoration of his health, but love with a good woman as well.

The Clean-Up (Universal, 1917)
d: William Worthington. 5 reels.
Franklyn Farnum, Brownie Vernon, Mark Fenton, Mary Talbot, Martha Mattox, Claire McDowell, Clyde Benson, Albert MacQuarrie.
Members of a small-town "Purity League" try to keep a burlesque show from opening.

The Clean Up (Universal, 1923)
d: William Parke. 5 reels.
Herbert Rawlinson, Claire Adams, Claire Anderson, Herbert Fortier, Margaret Campbell, Frank Farrington.
Monte's grandfather dies and leaves thousands of dollars to the town's citizens, but only one dollar to his grandson. Monte is disappointed and depressed... until he finds true love with a young secretary, and then discovers that the old man's will was double-tiered, and he really has a fortune coming to him!

The Clean-up Man (Universal, 1928)
d: Ray Taylor. 5 reels.
Ted Wells, Peggy O'Day, Henry Hebert, George Reed, Tom Carter.
Out West, a rancher battles a phony minister who's really the leader of a gang of road agents.

Clear the Decks (Universal, 1929)
d: Joseph E. Henabery. 6 reels. (Part talkie.)
Reginald Denny, Olive Hasbrouck, Otis Harlan, Lucien Littlefield, Collette Marten, Robert Anderson, Elinor Leslie, Brooks Benedict.
Love-struck Armitage pursues the object of his affection on an ocean voyage.

Clearing the Trail (Universal, 1928)
d: Reaves Eason. 6 reels.
Hoot Gibson, Dorothy Gulliver, Fred Gilman, Cap Anderson, Philo McCullough, Andy Waldron, Duke Lee, Monte Montague.
Out West, two brothers infiltrate the gang that's taken over their late father's ranch.

The Clemenceau Case (Fox, 1915)
d: Herbert Brenon. 5 reels.
William E. Shay, Theda Bara, Mrs. Allan Walker, Stuart Holmes, Jane Lee, Mrs. Cecil Raleigh, Frank Goldsmith, Sidney Shields.
Tragic romance, with a self-centered model manipulating her suitors and their families. She marries for spite, then turns to adultery with one wealthy admirer, and then another.

Cleopatra (Helen Gardner Picture Players, 1912)
d: Charles L. Gaskill. 6 reels.
Helen Gardner, Mr. Sindelar, Harley Knoles, Mr. Waite, Mr. Howard, Miss Winter, Mr. Osborne, Miss Sindelar, Robert Gaillard.
Cleopatra, queen of Egypt under the Roman Empire, dallies with the married Marc Antony. When his vengeful brother-in-law Octavius threatens to overrun Egypt with his armed forces, Antony rouses his own army to aid Cleopatra's cause.

Cleopatra (Fox, 1917)
d: J. Gordon Edwards. 11 reels.
Theda Bara, Fritz Leiber, Thurston Hall, Albert Roscoe, Genevieve Blinn, Henry de Vries, Dorothy Drake, Dell Duncan, Hector V. Sarno, Herschel Mayall, Dorothy Blake, Helen Tracy, Alfred W. Fremont, Art Acord.
Massive spectacle based on three plays about the life and loves of Cleopatra, Queen of the Nile. Studio publicity claimed that 10,000 extras and 3,000 horses were used in the production, which tells Cleopatra's story from her defeat at Alexandria at the hands of Julius Caesar, to her return to power with Marc Antony at her side. In the end, grieving over Antony's death, she puts a poisonous asp to her breast and takes her own life.

The Clever Mrs. Carfax (Lasky Feature Plays/Paramount, 1917)
d: Donald Crisp. 5 reels.
Julian Eltinge, Daisy Robinson, Noah Beery, Rosita Marstini, Jennie Lee, Fred Church, Fred DeShon.
A male newspaper publisher writes a "letters to the lovelorn" column under the name "Mrs. Carfax."

The Climbers (Lubin Mfg. Co., 1915)
d: Barry O'Neil. 5 reels.
Gladys Hanson, Walter Hitchcock, Dorothy DeWolff, Charles Brandt, George Soule Spencer, Eleanor Barry, Ruth Bryan, Frankie Mann, Edith Ritchie, Clarence Jay Elmer.
Speculative stock investments bring ruin to a family striving to maintain its social position. Based on the Clyde Fitch play of the same name.

The Climbers (Vitagraph, 1919)
d: Tom Terriss. 5 reels.
Corinne Griffith, Hugh Huntley, Percy Marmont, Henry Hallam, Josephine Whittell, Jane Jennings, James C. Spottswood, Corinne Barker, Emily Fitzroy, Charles Halton, James A. Furey.
Second film version of Clyde Fitch's play *The Climbers*.

The Climbers (Warner Bros., 1927)
d: Paul Stein. 7 reels.
Irene Rich, Clyde Cook, Forrest Stanley, Flobelle Fairbanks, Myrna Loy, Dot Farley, Anders Randolf, Rosemary Cooper, Nigel Barrie, Joseph Striker, Hector Sarno, Max Barwyn, Martha Franklin.
Romantic intrigue among the Spanish nobility ends with a duchess and her lover being exiled to a distant island.

CLEOPATRA (1917). Theda Bara, who personified the modern "vamp" in her 1915 starring debut, *A Fool There Was*, is seen here as Queen of the Nile. Only three of Miss Bara's 42 films exist today, but *Cleopatra*, alas, is not one of them. Contemporary reviews gave rave notices to not only the film—a massive production budgeted at $500,000—but to Miss Bara's performance as well. True to her vampish credentials, she played Cleopatra as a wily seductress who ensnares and exploits men.

* * * * *

The Clinging Vine   (DeMille Pictures/Producers Distributing Corp., 1926)
d: Paul Sloane.   7 reels.
Leatrice Joy, Tom Moore, Toby Claude, Robert Edeson, Dell Henderson, Snitz Edwards.
The real brains behind the success of a large paint company is Ann, a secretary. She makes most of the big business decisions and keeps the profits rolling in. But Ann's love life is going nowhere, until her boss' grandmother gives her tips on how to soften her hard-boiled exterior and blossom forth as a raving beauty.

The Clock   (Universal, 1917)
d: William Worthington.   5 reels.
Franklyn Farnum, Agnes Vernon, Frank Whitson, Mark Fenton, Frederick Montague, Willis Marks.
Always late, and with little regard for the time of day, a man is tricked by his fiancée into developing punctual habits.

The Clodhopper   (New York Motion Picture Corp./Triangle, 1917)
d: Victor Schertzinger.   5 reels.
Charles Ray, Charles K. French, Margery Wilson, Lydia Knott, Thomas Guise.
A prodigal son comes home in time to save his father's business.

Closed Doors   (Vitagraph, 1921)
d: G.V. Seyffertitz.   5 reels.
Alice Calhoun, Harry C. Browne, Bernard Randall, A.J. Herbert, Betty Burwell, Charles Brook.
When an ambitious businessman starts spending all his time on his work, his young wife feels neglected and seeks amusement outside the home.

Closed Gates   (Sterling Pictures, 1927)
d: Phil Rosen.   6 reels.
Johnny Harron, Jane Novak, Lucy Beaumont, Sidney DeGrey, LeRoy Mason, Rosemary Cooper, Ruth Handforth, Bud Jamison.
Shell shocked in World War I, a scion of wealth loses his memory. He eventually marries his nurse but still doesn't remember who he is, until the sight of his invalid mother's old wheelchair brings it all back.

The Closed Road   (Paragon Films, Inc./World Film Corp., 1916)
d: Maurice Tourneur.   5 reels.
House Peters, Barbara Tennant, Lionel Adams, Leslie Stowe, George Cowl.
When a terminally ill man confesses to a murder he didn't commit, he is sentenced to die in the electric chair. But on death row he learns he's not sick after all, and a furious scramble begins to find the real criminal.

Closin' In   (Triangle, 1918)
d: J.W. McLaughlin.   5 reels.
William Desmond, Maud Wayne, George Pearce, Darrell Foss, Alberta Lee, Louis Durham, Bob Thompson, Graham Pette, Claire McDowell.
In the Canadian Northwest, a fugitive from justice discovers gold on his land.

The Closing Net   (Pathé, 1915)
d: Edward José.   5 reels.
Howard Estabrook, Madeline Traverse, Arthur Albro, Kathryn Browne-Decker, Bliss Milford, Frederick Macklyn, Eric Wayne.
Aiming to go straight, a jewel thief renounces his life of

crime, but his former partners are hard to convince.

Clothes   (Metro, 1920)
d: Fred Sittenham.   5 reels.
Olive Tell, Crauford Kent, Cyril Chadwick, Zeffie Tilbury, Rae Allen, Frank Currier, Mary Beaton.
Believing she has inherited a fortune, a woman spends lavishly, and then finds she is penniless.
Remake, with some alterations, of the 1914 film four-reel *Clothes.*

Clothes Make the Pirate   (First National, 1925)
d: Maurice Tourneur.   9 reels.
Dorothy Gish, Leon Errol, Nita Naldi, James Rennie, George Marion, Tully Marshall, Frank Lawler, Edna Murphy, Reginald Barlow, Walter Law.
In 18th century Boston, a timid tailor dreams of being a feared pirate on the Spanish Main.

Clothes Make the Woman   (Tiffany-Stahl Productions, 1928)
w, d: Tom Terriss.   6 reels.
Eve Southern, Walter Pidgeon, Charles Byer, George E. Stone, Adolph Millar, Duncan Renaldo, Gordon Begg, Catherine Wallace, Corliss Palmer, Margaret Selby, H.D. Pennell.
In Hollywood, the exiled Princess Anastasia of Russia turns up incognito as a movie extra. She works her way to stardom and is assigned to a movie about the Bolshevik Revolution, in which she will play—herself!

The Cloud   (Van Dyke Film Corp./Art Dramas, Inc., 1917)
d: Will S. Davis.   5 reels.
Jean Sothern, Mae Melvin, Franklin Hanna, Arthur Housman, Richard Tucker, Walter Miller, Ogden Crane, Mrs. Charles Willard.
Under the cloud of scandal, a young woman is forced to give up an inheritance.

The Cloud Dodger   (Universal, 1928)
d: Bruce Mitchell.   5 reels.
Al Wilson, Gloria Grey, Joe O'Brien.
A jilted aviator goes after his ex-love and her new intended.

The Cloud Rider   (Van Pelt-Wilson/F.B.O., 1925)
d: Bruce Mitchell.   5 reels.
Al Wilson, Virginia Lee Crobin, Harry von Meter, Helen Ferguson, Frank Rice, Melbourne MacDowell, Brinsley Shaw, Frank Tomick, Boyd Monteith, Frank Clark.
Torrence, a daredevil aviator, is also a Secret Service agent.

The Clouded Name   (World Film Corp., 1919)
d: Caryl S. Fleming.   5 reels.
John Lowell, Corene Uzzell, Charles Edwards, Charles A. Robins, Jules Cowles, Edgar Keller.
In a lumber camp, one of the workers is wrongly suspected of scandalous doings.

A Clouded Name   (Logan Productions/Playgoers Pictures, 1923)
d: Austin O. Huhn.   5 reels.
Norma Shearer, Gladden James, Yvonne Logan, Richard Neill, Charles Miller, Frederick Eckhart.
Ben, a strange old codger who lives in the woods with his little girl, is really a wealthy man whose memory has been erased.

Clover's Rebellion   (Vitagraph, 1917)
d: Wilfrid North.   5 reels.
Anita Stewart, Rudolph Cameron, Brinsley Shaw, Eulalie

Jensen, Charles Stevenson, Julia Swayne Gordon, William Dunn.

Clover Dean is a wealthy heiress with three suitors, but only one worthy of her.

The Clown (Lasky Feature Plays/Paramount, 1916)
d: William C. DeMille. 5 reels.
Victor Moore, Thomas Meighan, Ernest Joy, Florence Dagmar, Jerold Ward, Tom Forman, Horace B. Carpenter, Wallace Pike, Billie Jacobs.
A big-hearted circus clown marries a girl in need, then must give her up.

The Clown (Columbia, 1927)
d: William James Craft. 6 reels.
John Miljan, Barbara Tennant, William V. Mong, Dorothy Revier, Johnny Walker.

An embittered man, jailed for his part in an accidental death, escapes from prison dressed as a clown, goes to the circus tent, and turns a lion on his tamer.

The Clue (Lasky Feature Plays/Paramount, 1915)
d: James Neill, Frank Reichert. 5 reels.
Blanche Sweet, Gertrude Keller, Edward Mackay, Sessue Hayakawa, Page Peters, Ernest Joy, Billy Elmer.
International intrigue is the focus, as Russian brothers plot to sell Japanese secrets to the Germans. Two American women also get involved.

The Clutch of Circumstance (Vitagraph, 1918)
d: Henry Houry. 5 reels.
Corinne Griffith, Robert Gaillard, David Herblin, Florence Deshon, Denton Vane, Esta Banks.
A faithful wife goes onstage and becomes a Broadway star... but her husband is deeply suspicious about her relationship with the show's producer.

Coals of Fire (Famous Players-Lasky/Paramount, 1918)
d: Victor L. Schertzinger. 5 reels.
Enid Bennett, Fred Niblo, Melbourne MacDowell, Billy Elmer, Virginia Southern, John P. Lockney, Donald MacDonald.
In a temperance showdown, a reverend minister is attracted to a barkeep's daughter.

The Coast of Folly (Famous Players-Lasky/Paramount, 1925)
d: Allan Dwan. 7 reels.
Gloria Swanson, Anthony Jowitt, Alec Francis, Dorothy Cumming, Jed Prouty, Eugenie Besserer, Arthur Housman, Lawrence Gray.
In Paris, an expatriate American woman, Nadine, learns that the daughter she abandoned 20 years earlier is in trouble. Now Nadine, who has become a countess, travels home to try and help her daughter out of her difficulties.

The Coast of Opportunity (Robert Brunton Productions/W.W. Hodkinson, 1920)
d: Ernest C. Warde. 5 reels.
J. Warren Kerrigan, Herschel Mayall, Fritzi Brunette, Eddy Hearn, Flo Hollister, Carl Stockdale, William V. Mong.
An American engineer hopes to mine a rich copper field in Mexico.

The Coast Patrol (Bud Barsky Corp., 1925)
d: Bud Barsky. 5 reels.
Kenneth McDonald, Claire DeLorez, Fay Wray, Spottiswoode Aitken, Geno Corrado.
Off the coast of Maine, smugglers set a trap for the lighthouse keeper's daughter, but they are foiled by agents of the Coast Patrol.

Coax Me (World Film Corp., 1919)
d: Gilbert Hamilton. 5 reels.
June Elvidge, Earl Metcalfe, Arthur Donaldson, Lola Humphrey, A.J. Herbert, Lillian Hall, Austin Webb, Ivan Christy, Varnum Mills.
What's a widower to do, when his daughter disapproves of his impending remarriage?

Cobra (Ritz-Carlton Pictures/Paramount, 1925)
d: Joseph Henabery. 6 reels.
Rudolph Valentino, Nita Naldi, Casson Ferguson, Gertrude Olmstead, Claire DeLorez, Hector V. Sarno, Eileen Percy, Lillian Langdon, Rosa Rosanova, Henry Barrows.
A playboy count incurs great debts with his extravagant lifestyle, and must go to work. Since this count is played by Rudolph Valentino, he soon finds himself enmeshed in affairs of the heart, including the presence of a vamp (Nita Naldi) who winds herself around him like a cobra.

The Code of Marcia Gray (Oliver Morosco Photoplay Co./Paramount, 1916)
d: Frank Lloyd. 5 reels.
Constance Collier, Harry DeVere, Forrest Stanley, Herbert Standing, Howard Davies, Helen Jerome Eddy, Frank Bonn.
When Marcia's husband is sent to jail for bank fraud, she turns to an old lover for bail money. He agrees, and the husband is released. When hubby learns where the money came from, his basest suspicions are aroused.

Code of the Air (Bischoff Productions, 1928)
d: James P. Hogan. 6 reels.
Kenneth Harlan, June Marlowe, Arthur Rankin, William V. Mong, Paul Weigel, James Bradbury Jr., Edna Mae Cooper.
Air pirates conspire to capture commercial planes carrying valuable cargo.

Code of the Range (Morris R. Schlank Productions/Rayart, 1927)
d: Bennett Cohn. 5 reels.
Jack Perrin, Nelson McDowell, Pauline Curley, Lew Meehan, Chic Olsen.
Out West, a cowboy seeks revenge against the human snake who wronged his sister.

Code of the Scarlet (Charles R. Rogers Productions/First National, 1928)
d: Harry J. Brown. 6 reels.
Ken Maynard, Gladys McConnell, Ed Brady, J.P. McGowan, Dot Farley, Sheldon Lewis, Hal Salter, Joe Rickson, Robert Walker.
In the Canadian Northwest, two mounties capture a gang of murderous thieves.

Code of the Sea (Famous Players-Lasky/Paramount, 1924)
d: Victor Fleming. 6 reels.
Rod LaRocque, Jacqueline Logan, George Fawcett, Maurice B. Flynn, Luke Cosgrave, Lillian Leighton, Sam Appel.
In a stormy sea, a young man whose father was believed to be a coward proves his own mettle by commandeering a storm-tossed ship and saving all the passengers, including the young lady who loves him.

Code of the West (Famous Players-Lasky/Paramount, 1925)
d: William K. Howard. 7 reels.
Owen Moore, Mabel Balin, Charles Ogle, David Butler,

George Bancroft, Gertrude Short, Constance Bennett, Lillian Leighton, Pat Hartigan, Frankie Lee.

Out West, a rancher and a pretty New Yorker can hardly stand each other, until fate places them together in a cabin that's threatened by a raging forest fire.

Code of the West (Syndicate Pictures, 1929)
d: J.P. McGowan. 5 reels.
Bob Custer, Vivian Bay, Bobby Dunn, Martin Cichy, Bud Osborne, Cliff Lyons, Tom Bay, Buck Bucko.
Mail thieves terrorize the railroads out West, until a special agent tracks them down.

Code of the Wilderness (Vitagraph, 1924)
d: David Smith. 7 reels.
John Bowers, Alice Calhoun, Alan Hale, Charlotte Merriam, Otis Harlan, Kitty Bradbury, Joseph Rickson, Cliff Davidson.
Ruth, an eastern girl, goes west to take possession of her inherited ranch.

Code of the Yukon (Select Pictures Corp., 1918)
d: Bertram Bracken. 6 reels.
Mitchell Lewis, Tom Santschi, Arthur Morrison, William Effee, Jack McDonald, Franklyn Hall, Vivian Rich, Margaret Landis, Goldie Caldwell.
In the Canadian Northwest, a miner is betrayed by his wife and seeks revenge.

The Cohens and the Kellys (Universal, 1926)
d: Harry Pollard. 8 reels.
Charlie Murray, George Sidney, Jason Robards, Bobby Gordon, Kate Price, Vera Gordon.
A Jewish merchant and an Irish cop lock horns, but reconcile in time for the merchant's daughter and the cop's son to marry.

The Cohens and the Kellys in Atlantic City (Universal, 1929)
d: William James Craft. 8 reels. (Part talkie.)
George Sidney, Vera Gordon, Mack Swain, Kate Price, Cornelius Keefe.
Cohen's daughter and Kelly's son stage a beauty contest.

The Cohens and the Kellys in Paris (Universal, 1928)
d: William Beaudine. 8 reels.
George Sidney, J. Farrell MacDonald, Vera Gordon, Kate Price, Gertrude Astor, Charles Delaney, Sue Carol, Gino Corrado, Charlie Murray.
The Cohens and the Kellys travel to Paris, get into a vigorous quarrel with an apache, and nearly destroy a restaurant.

Coincidence (Metro, 1921)
d: Chet Withey. 5 reels.
Robert Harron, June Walker, Bradley Barker, William Frederic, Frank Belcher, June Ellen Terry.
Comedy about a young clerk who falls in love with a stenographer, then loses his job. But just when things look bleakest, word comes that his wealthy aunt has died and left him a small fortune.

The Cold Deck (Triangle, 1917)
d: William S. Hart. 5 reels.
William S. Hart, Alma Rubens, Mildred Harris, Sylvia Breamer, Charles O. Rush, Edwin N. Wallock, Joe Knight.
A reformed gambler meets a fiery dance hall girl.

Cold Steel (L.J. Meyberg/Robertson-Cole, 1921)
d: Sherwood MacDonald. 6 reels.
J.P. McGowan, Kathleen Clifford, Stanhope Wheatcroft,

Arthur Millett, Charles E. Insley, Milt Brown, Nigel DeBrulier, George Clair, Andy Waldron, Elinor Fair, V.L. Barnes.
The son of a framed man takes on the gang that plotted his father's downfall.

Colleen (Fox, 1927)
d: Frank O'Connor. 6 reels.
Madge Bellamy, Charles Morton, J. Farrell MacDonald, Tom Maguire, Sammy Cohen, Marjorie Beebe, Ted McNamara, Tom McGuire, Sarah Padden, Sidney Franklin, Carl Stockdale.
Titled but penniless, an Irish lord loves the daughter of his wealthy neighbors.

Colleen of the Pines (Chester Bennett Productions/FBO of America, 1922)
d: Chester Bennett. 5 reels.
Jane Novak, Edward Hearn, Alfred Allen, J. Gordon Russell, Charlotte Pierce, Ernest Shields.
In the Canadian Northwest, love blossoms between a mountie and the daughter of a fur trader.

College (Joseph M. Schenck Productions/United Artists, 1927)
d: James Horne. 6 reels.
Buster Keaton, Anne Cornwall, Flora Bramley, Harold Goodwin, Buddy Mason, Grant Withers, Snitz Edwards, Carl Harbaugh, Sam Crawford, Florence Turner.
"Brains vs. brawn" is the mantra of an erudite college freshman who demeans all athletic endeavors. But when he falls for a girl who insists she can love only an athlete, Our Hero goes all out to make the track team. So far so good, but now his girl has been kidnapped, and it's up to him to save her—even if the task requires he perform a dazzling variety of athletic stunts in the process.

The College Boob (Harry Garson Productions, 1926)
d: Harry Garson. 6 reels.
Lefty Flynn, Jean Arthur, Jimmy Anderson, Bob Bradbury Jr., Cecil Ogden, Dorothea Wolbert, William Malan, Raymond Turner.
Appleby, newly installed in college, promises his family he will not participate in sports. But after some of the upper classmen razz the youngster and try to make him the college boob, Appleby responds by knocking out one of them. The football coach is impressed, and urges him to try out for the team.

The College Coquette (Columbia, 1929)
d: George Archainbaud. 6 reels. (Also released in sound version.)
William Collier Jr., Jobyna Ralston, Ruth Taylor, John Holland, Adda Gleason.
A college girl makes a play for her roommate's boyfriend.

College Days (Tiffany Productions, 1926)
d: Richard Thorpe. 8 reels.
Marceline Day, Charles Delaney, James Harrison, Duane Thompson, Brooks Benedict, Kathleen Key, Edna Murphy, Robert Homans, Charles Wellesley, Gibson Gowland.
Gordon, a newcomer to the university, falls for a coed but soon has to explain why he was seen with a pair of campus vamps.

The College Hero (Columbia, 1927)
d: Walter Lang. 6 reels.
Bobby Agnew, Rex Lease, Pauline Garon, Ben Turpin, Churchill Ross, Joan Standing, Charles Paddock.

At college, roommates vie for the love of the same girl.

The College Orphan (Universal, 1915)
d: William Dowlan. 6 reels.
Carter de Haven, Flora Parker de Haven, Miss Edwards, Louis Morrison, Gloria Fonda, Val Paul, Lule Warrenton, William Canfield, Doc Crane.
Comedy-drama about a restless college boy who gets into all manner of scrapes, including wild parties, adventures at a burlesque house, fights, and frame-ups.

The College Widow (Lubin Mfg. Co., 1915)
d: Barry O'Neil. 5 reels.
Charles Brandt, Ethel Clayton, Edith Ritchie, Ferdinand Tidmarsh, Howard Missimer, Clarence Jay Elmer, Peter Lang, George Soule Spencer, George Clarke, Joseph Kaufman.
"The College Widow" is the nickname of a college president's daughter who keeps losing fiancés to graduation. In this comedy, based on the play of the same name by humorist George Ade, she tries to charm a talented football player into playing for her dad's college.

The College Widow (Warner Bros., 1927)
d: Archie Mayo. 7 reels.
Dolores Costello, William Collier Jr., Douglas Gerrard, Guinn Williams, Anders Randolph.
To inspire a college football team to perform its best, a young lady flirts with every member of the team and makes each one think he is her one and only. Remake of Lubin's 1915 *The College Widow*.

Collegiate (R-C Pictures/FBO of America, 1926)
d: Del Andrews. 5 reels.
Alberta Vaughn, Donald Keith, John Steppling, Alys Murrell, William Austin, Frankie Adams, Charles Cruz.
Patricia, a madcap heiress, loves a working stiff she meets in college.

Colorado (Universal, 1915)
d: Norval MacGregor. 5 reels.
Hobart Bosworth, Anna Lehr, Louise Baxter, Carl von Schiller, Albert MacQuarrie, Edward Brown, Ronald Bradbury.
In Colorado, a newcomer is persuaded to buy ranchland that's basically worthless, because it has no water. But his luck changes when his neighbor strikes gold, exposing an underground river they both can share.

Colorado Pluck (Fox, 1921)
d: Jules G. Furthman. 5 reels.
William Russell, Margaret Livingston, William Buckley, George Fisher, Helen Ware, Bertram Johns, Ray Berger.
A newly rich American rancher travels to London and falls in love with Angela, daughter of a penniless but proud family. He proposes marriage, and her family urges her to accept for their sake. Angela finally agrees, but stubbornly declares she will be his wife in name only. She'll change her mind.

The Combat (Vitagraph, 1916)
d: Ralph W. Ince. 6 reels.
Anita Stewart, John Robertson, Richard Turner, Virginia Norden, Winthrop Mandell.
When a young woman's husband is reported killed in another part of the country, she mourns him for a time and then remarries. Her new husband, a successful lawyer, rises to the rank of district attorney... and then husband number one shows up alive and well.

The Combat (Universal, 1926)
d: Lynn Reynolds. 7 reels.
House Peters, Wanda Hawley, Walter McGrail, C.E. Anderson, Charles Mailes, Steve Clemento, Howard Truesdale.
In a lumber camp, two men vie for the love of the same girl. Her choice is made easy when a forest fire engulfs her and one of the men rushes through the flames to save her.

Combat (Burton King Productions/Pathé, 1927)
d: Albert Hiatt. 6 reels.
George Walsh, Bradley Barker, Claire Adams, Gladys Hulette, Dex Reynolds.

When Jack, an inventor, perfects a new formula and his rights to it are challenged, he decides to fight it out in court. But his adversary hires a dangerous criminal to intimidate Jack, and the young inventor escapes to the Florida Keys to await his court date.

Come Across (Universal, 1929)
d: Ray Taylor. 6 reels. (Part talkie.)
Lina Basquette, Reed Howes, Flora Finch, Crauford Kent, Gustav von Seyffertitz, Clarissa Selwynne.
Mary, a night club entertainer, is recruited by gangsters to assist in swindling a millionaire. At first she agrees, but then thinks better of it and turns the tables on the crooks.

Come Again Smith (Jesse D. Hampton Productions/W.W. Hodkinson, 1919)
d: E. Mason Hopper. 5 reels.
J. Warren Kerrigan, H.A. Barrows, William Conklin, Winifred Greenwood, Lois Wilson, Charles French, Walter Perry.
When a wealthy businessman invites a park bench idler to his home as a gesture to all humanity, he learns that the "idler" is really a millionaire's son.

The Come-Back (Quality Pictures Corp./Metro, 1916)
d: Fred J. Balshofer. 5 reels.
Harold Lockwood, May Allison, George Henry, Howard Truesdell, Lester Cuneo, Bert Starkey, Mitchell Lewis, Clara Selwynne.
A wealthy mill owner disowns his layabout son. Unbeknown to Dad, the youngster gets a job in his father's mill and, after months of hard work and exercise, he develops character and falls in love with a worthy young woman... and gets back in Dad's good graces.

Come On Cowboys! (Ben Wilson Productions/Arrow Film Corp., 1924)
d: Ward Hayes. 5 reels.
Dick Hatton, Marilyn Mills, Harry Fenwick, Philip Sleeman.
Jim, a cowpoke in love with a New York girl, and two of his pals ride to the rescue when he hears that she's being forced into a loveless marriage.

Come On In (Famous Players-Lasky/Paramount, 1918)
d: John Emerson. 5 reels.
Shirley Mason, Ernest Truex, Charles DePlanta, Joseph Burke, Renault Tourneur, Bernard Randall, Blanche Craig, Meyer Berenson, Richie Ling, Louis Hendricks.
World War I farce about a stenographer who's courted by two suitors, and vows to marry the more patriotic of the two. When she makes her choice, her new hubby turns out to be—a German spy!

Come Out of the Kitchen (Famous Players-Lasky/Paramount, 1919) d: John S. Robertson. 5 reels.

Marguerite Clark, Frances Kaye, Bradley Barker, Albert M. Hackett, George Stevens, May Kitson, Eugene O'Brien, Frederick Esmelton, Crauford Kent, Augusta Anderson.

Penniless aristocrats earn some money by leasing out their Virginia mansion and posing as its servants.

Come Through (Universal, 1917)
d: Jack Conway. 7 reels.

Herbert Rawlinson, Alice Lake, George Webb, Jean Hathaway, Roy Stewart, Charles Hill Mailes, Margaret Whistler, William Dyer.

Mistaken identity leads to a shotgun wedding between two total strangers.

This film was remade by Conway in 1922 under the title *Don't Shoot.*

The Coming of Amos (Cinema Corp. of America, 1925)
d: Paul Sloane. 6 reels.

Rod LaRocque, Jetta Goudal, Noah Beery, Richard Carle, Arthur Hoyt, Trixie Friganza, Clarence Burton, Ruby Lafayette, Amos Burden.

A sheep rancher travels to the French Riviera, where he meets and falls for an exiled Russian princess.

The Coming of the Law (Fox, 1919)
d: Arthur Rosson. 5 reels.

Tom Mix, Brownie Vernon, Jane Novak, George Nicholls, Jack Curtis, Sid Jordan, B.M. Turner, Charles LeMoyne, Pat Chrisman, Lewis Sargent, Jack Dill, Harry Dunkinson.

Out West, a transplanted easterner decides to run for sheriff.

Coming Through (Famous Players-Lasky/Paramount, 1925)
d: Edward Sutherland. 7 reels.

Thomas Meighan, Lila Lee, John Miltern, Wallace Beery, Laurance Wheat, Frank Campeau, Gus Weinberg, Alice Knowland.

Rand, a mine president, dislikes Tom, his employee and new son-in-law, because his daughter married him against her father's wishes.

The Common Cause (Blackton Productions, Inc./Vitagraph, 1919)
d: J. Stuart Blackton. 7 reels.

Effie Shannon, Irene Castle, Herbert Rawlinson, Sylvia Breamer, Huntley Gordon, Lawrence Grossmith, Violet Heming, Julia Arthur, Marjorie Rambeau, Philip Van Loan.

Filmed in support of the war effort, this comedy-drama relates the story of a Red Cross nurse, her husband, and her lover. The latter, fatally wounded in World War I, finds the moral strength to reunite husband and wife and bless their marriage, just before he dies.

Common Clay (Astra Film Corp./Pathé, 1919)
d: George Fitzmaurice. 7 reels.

Fannie Ward, Easter Walters, Fred Goodwins, John Cossar, Helen Dunbar, W.E. Lawrence, John Barrows, Mary Alden, Andrew Arbuckle, Henry A. Barrows.

When a housemaid becomes pregnant by the son of her employer, his scandalized family refers the case to a judge. Ironically, it turns out that the housemaid is the illegitimate daughter of the judge himself.

Common Ground (Lasky Feature Plays/Paramount, 1916)
d: William C. DeMille. 5 reels.

Marie Doro, Thomas Meighan, Theodore Roberts, Mary Mersch, Horace B. Carpenter, Florence Smythe, Mrs. Lewis McCord.

A crusading judge is framed by a vengeful rival.

The Common Law (Clara Kimball Young Film Corp./Selznick, 1916)
d: Albert Capellani. 7 reels.

Clara Kimball Young, Conway Tearle, Paul Capellani, Edna Hunter, Lillian Cook, Julia Stuart, Edward M. Kimball, Lydia Knott, D.J. Flanagan.

Romanced by two painters, an artist's model decides to accept neither. But the strength of love inevitably brings her together with the more persistent of the two.

The Common Law (Selznick Pictures, 1923)
d: George Archainbaud. 8 reels.

Corinne Griffith, Conway Tearle, Elliott Dexter, Hobart Bosworth, Lillian Lawrence, Bryant Washburn, Doris May, Harry Myers, Miss DuPont, Phyllis Haver, Wally Van, Dagmar Godowsky.

Remake of the 1916 Clara Kimball Young film, both versions based on the 1911 play of the same name by Robert William Chambers.

Common Property (Universal, 1919)
d: Paul Powell. 6 reels.

Robert Anderson, Nell Craig, Colleen Moore, Johnnie Cooke, Frank Leigh, Arthur Jasmine, Richard Cummings, Robert Lawler, Arthur Maude.

For a short time, a modern form of slavery arises in Russia, decreeing that all women are considered common property of the state.

The Common Sin (Burton King Productions/Hallmark Pictures, 1920)
d: Burton King. 6 reels.

Grace Darling, Rod LaRocque, Anders Randolf, Nita Naldi, James Cooley, Stephen Gratton, Alice Gordon, Virginia Valli.

Greed and vindictiveness cause the downfall of a marriage, as a woman is forced to marry a man she does not love, and the man's mistress falsely accuses the wife of infidelity.

The Companionate Marriage (First National/Warner Bros., 1928)
d: Erle C. Kenton. 7 reels.

Betty Bronson, Richard Walling, Alec B. Francis, June Nash, Edward Martindel, Arthur Rankin, Hedda Hopper, William Welsh, Sarah Padden, Ruth Moore.

Sally and Donald, two innocents disillusioned by marriage because of the sad experiences of others, decide to marry, but only conditionally. A legal contract is drawn up that specifies that either party can nullify the marriage at will after a certain period of time. Perhaps because each of them knows the contract is in place, the two are on their best behavior... and their marriage lasts a lifetime.

Compromise (Warner Bros., 1925)
d: Alan Crosland. 7 reels.

Clive Brook, Irene Rich, Louise Fazenda, Pauline Garon, Raymond McKee, Helen Dunbar, Winter Hall, Frank Butler, Lynn Cowan.

While on his honeymoon, a newlywed is vamped by his bride's younger sister.

Comrade John (Pathé, 1915)
d: Bertram Bracken. 5 reels.

William Elliott, Ruth Roland, Madeline Pardee, Lewis J. Cody, William Lampe.

An idealistic architect builds a "Dream City" for a cult leader, but the dream turns into a nightmare.

The Concealed Truth (Ivan Film Productions, Inc., 1915)
w, d: Ivan Abramson. 5 reels.
Gertrude Robinson, James Cooley, Carrey Lee, Frank Whitson, Frank de Vernon, Sue Balfour, James McDuff.
Grieving because the woman he loves has married his brother, a once-promising composer lapses into despair and poverty. But a twist of fate will reunite the broken man with his beloved.

Conceit (Selznick/Select Pictures, 1921)
d: Burton George. 5 reels.
Maurice Costello, William B. Davidson, Betty Hilburn, Hedda Hopper, Pat Hartigan, Charles Gerard, Warren Cook, Red Eagle.
Crombie, though wealthy and comfortable, is plagued by cowardice. On a hunting trip he becomes enamored of a young woman who lives in the woods, but is afraid to challenge another hunter for her. Even Crombie's own wife disdains him and takes a lover. But the worm will turn, and eventually Crombie is emboldened to fight for what is his.

The Concert (Goldwyn, 1921)
d: Victor Schertzinger. 6 reels.
Lewis S. Stone, Myrtle Stedman, Raymond Hatton, Mabel Julienne Scott, Gertrude Astor, Russ Powell, Lydia Yeamans Titus, Frances Hall, Louie Cheung.
Sophisticated comedy about a concert pianist with an eye for the ladies.

Conductor 1492 (Warner Bros., 1923)
d: Charles Hines, Frank Griffin. 7 reels.
Johnny Hines, Doris May, Dan Mason, Dorothy Burns, Byron Sage, Ruth Renick, Robert Cain, Fred Esmelton, Michael Dark.
An Irishman transplanted to America gets a job running a streetcar.

Coney Island (FBO Pictures, 1928)
d: Ralph Ince. 7 reels.
Lois Wilson, Lucilla Mendez, Eugene Strong, Rudolph Cameron, William Irving, Gus Leonard, Orlo Sheldon, Carl Axzelle.
Burke, owner of a seaside roller coaster, fights the syndicate that wants to take over.

A Coney Island Princess (Famous Players/Paramount, 1916)
d: Del Henderson. 5 reels.
Irene Fenwick, Owen Moore, Eva Francis, Clifford B. Gray, William Bailey, Kate Lester, Dora Mills Adams, Russell Bassett.
Slumming at Coney Island, a wealthy playboy falls for a shimmy dancer.

Confession (Fox, 1918)
d: S.A. Franklin. 5 reels.
Jewel Carmen, L.C. Shumway, Fred Warren, Jack Brammall, Charles Gorman, Andrew Arbuckle.
Newlyweds are robbed while on their honeymoon, then are forced to sleep in a hotel parlor because they cannot prove they are married to each other.

The Confession (National Film Corp. of America, 1920)
d: Bertram Bracken. 7 reels.
Henry B. Walthall, Francis McDonald, William Clifford, Margaret McWade, Margaret Landis, Barney Furey.
A priest learns in the confessional who committed a murder, and is bound by secrecy even when his own brother is accused of the crime.

Confessions of a Queen (MGM, 1925)
d: Victor Seastrom. 7 reels.
Lewis Stone, Alice Terry, John Bowers, Eugenie Besserer, Andre de Beranger, Helena D'Algy, Frankie Darro, Joseph Dowling, Bert Sprotte, Wilbur Higby, Otto Hoffman.
In a tiny European kingdom, the king prepares to marry a chaste young princess, but has eyes only for his mistresses.

Confessions of a Wife (Excellent Pictures, 1928)
d: Albert Kelly. 6 reels.
Helene Chadwick, Arthur Clayton, Ethel Grey Terry, Walter McGrail, Carl Gerard, Clarissa Selwynne, Sam Lufkin, DeSacia Mooers, Suzanne Rhoades.
Gangsters plot to infiltrate a party of swells to steal their jewels, aided and abetted by Marion, a socialite and compulsive gambler who owes the gang a large debt.

Confidence (Universal, 1922)
d: Harry Pollard. 5 reels.
Herbert Rawlinson, Harriet Hammond, Lincoln Plummer, William A. Carroll, Otto Hoffman, William Robert Daly, Hallam Cooley, John Steppling, Melbourne MacDowell.
Mortimer, a timid traveling salesman, is emboldened when he finds a satchel full of money.

The Confidence Man (Famous Players-Lasky/Paramount, 1924)
d: Victor Heerman. 8 reels.
Thomas Meighan, Virginia Valli, Laurence Wheat, Charles Dow Clark, Helen Lindroth, Jimmie Lapsley, Margaret Seddon, George Nash, Dorothy Walters, David Higgins.
Two con men try to fleece the locals in a small Florida town.

The Conflict (Vitagraph, 1916)
d: Ralph W. Ince. 5 reels.
Lucille Lee Stewart, Jessie Miller, Huntley Gordon, William Lytell Jr., Frank Currier, John Robertson, Richard Turner.
A wealthy woman callously steals another woman's lover, then discards him.

The Conflict (Universal, 1921)
d: Stuart Paton. 7 reels.
Priscilla Dean, Herbert Rawlinson, Martha Mattox, Hector Sarno, Edward Connelly, Olah Norman, L.C. Shumway, Sam Allen, C.E. Anderson, Knute Erickson, Bill Gillis.
After her father dies, a socialite moves into the home of her uncle, a sullen lumber baron. There, she finds herself in a fight over land rights, and successfully leads the lumbermen in a fight against the would-be usurpers.

A Connecticut Yankee in King Arthur's Court (Fox, 1920)
d: Emmett J. Flynn. 8 reels.
Harry Myers, Pauline Starke, Rosemary Theby, Charles Clary, William V. Mong, George Siegmann, Charles Gordon, Karl Formes, Herbert Fortier, Adele Farrington, Wilfred McDonald.
Dreams transport a 20th-century wastrel into the Age of Chivalry, where he meets King Arthur and Morgan le Fay, and wins a tilting contest with Sir Sagamore.

Conquered Hearts (Ivan Film Productions, Inc., 1918)
d: Francis J. Grandon. 7 reels.
Marguerite Marsh, Corinne Uzzelle, Emma Lowry, Eileen Walker, Richard Turner, Harry Myers, R. Paton Gibbs, Dean Raymond, Barney Gilmore, Frank Evans, Sheridan Tansey.
A young wife "on leave" from her marriage becomes an artist's model, and then a movie star. But in her heart she knows she belongs with her husband.

The Conquering Christ — see: Restitution (1918).

The Conquering Power (Metro, 1921)
d: Rex Ingram. 6 reels.
Rudolph Valentino, Alice Terry, Eric Mayne, Ralph Lewis, Edna Demaurey, Edward Connelly, Willard Lee Hall, Mark Fenton, George Atkinson, Bridgetta Clark, Ward Wing, Mary Hearn, Eugene Poouyet, Andrée Tourneur.
Financially ruined and thinking he has nothing to live for, an investor commits suicide. His son is sent to live with his rich uncle, who is just as much a miser as his late brother had been. The boy falls in love with his beautiful cousin, and together they escape the suffocating atmosphere of the uncle's tight-fisted world.

Conquering the Woman (King Vidor Productions/Associated Exhibitors, 1922)
d: King Vidor. 6 reels.
Florence Vidor, Bert Sprotte, Mathilde Brundage, David Butler, Roscoe Karns, Peter Burke, Harry Todd.
When a spoiled socialite starts putting on airs to snare a wealthy foreign husband, her father decides she needs a lesson in humility. He arranges to have her marooned on a deserted island with only a lonesome cowpoke for company. But Papa's gambit pays off in an unexpected way, when she and the cowboy fall in love.

The Conqueror (New York Motion Picture Corp./Triangle, 1916)
d: Reginald Barker. 5 reels.
Willard Mack, Enid Markey, J. Barney Sherry, Margaret Thompson, Louise Brownell.
Though he rose from poverty through the free enterprise system, a new millionaire still hates the rich. He uses his new wealth to power into society, and even tries to "buy" himself a fashionable wife. Finally he realizes he's being a jerk, and tries to mend his ways.

The Conqueror (Fox, 1917)
d: Raoul A. Walsh. 8 reels.
William Farnum, Jewel Carmen, Charles Clary, James A. Marcus, Carrie Clarke Ward, William Chisolm, Robert Dunbar, Owen Jones, William Eagle Shirt, Chief Birdhead, Little Bear.

Sam Houston rises from illiterate mountaineer to become governor of Texas. He romances and wins the hand of Eliza Allen, the aristocratic beauty he has loved for years.

The Conquest of Canaan (Famous Players-Lasky/Paramount, 1921)
d: R. William Neill. 7 reels.
Thomas Meighan, Doris Kenyon, Diana Allen, Ann Egleston, Alice Fleming, Charles Abbe, Malcolm Bradley, Paul Everton, Macey Harlam, Henry Hallam, Louis Hendricks.
Louden, a small town lawyer, defends a man accused of murdering a romantic rival.

Conrad in Quest of His Youth (Famous Players-Lasky/Paramount, 1920)
d: William C. DeMille. 6 reels.
Thomas Meighan, Mabel Van Buren, Mayme Kelso, Bertram Johns, Margaret Loomis, Sylvia Ashton, Kathlyn Williams, Charles Ogle, Ruth Renick, Eddie Sutherland.
Newly returned to London from the Indian wars, a Brit attempts to regain his youth.

Conscience (Fox, 1917)
d: Bertram Bracken. 5 reels.

Gladys Brockwell, Marjorie Daw, Eugenie Forde, Eve Southern, Genevieve Blinn, Douglas Gerrard, Edward Cecil, Harry G. Lonsdale, Colin Chase, Bertram Grassby.
Highly allegorical tale, with Conscience, Lust, Avarice, Vanity and other emotions interacting with modern folks who love not wisely, but too well.

The Conscience of John David (Mutual, 1916)
d: Crane Wilbur. 5 reels.
Crane Wilbur, Alice Rinaldo, Frederick Montague, John Oaker, Mae Gaston, Louis Durham, Francis Raymond.
Misguided feelings of guilt almost doom a young man's happiness, but in the end he realizes he has done nothing wrong.

A Continental Girl (Continental Photoplay Corp., 1915)
d: Joseph Adelman. 5 reels.
May Ward, George Harcourt, William Sorell, Olaf Skavian, William H. Cone, Jack Murray, George Brugger, Elys Lotus, Mabel Scott, E.B. Tilton.
During the American Revolution, a young woman is loved by two soldiers: one American, one British.

Contraband (Famous Players-Lasky/Paramount, 1925)
d: Alan Crosland. 7 reels.
Lois Wilson, Noah Beery, Raymond Hatton, Raymond McKee, Charles Ogle, Luke Cosgrave, Edwards Davis, Johnny Fox, Victor Potel, Alphonse Ethier, Cesare Gravina.
Carmel, a young woman, inherits a newspaper and soon finds herself leading a press crusade against bootleggers and murderers.

Convict 993 (Astra Film Corp./Pathé, 1918)
d: William Parke. 5 reels.
Irene Castle, Warner Oland, Helen Chadwick, Harry Benham, J.H. Gilmore, Paul Everton, Bert Starkey, Ethyle Cook.
A women's prison inmate, "Convict 993," breaks out of jail and begins a new life. When her former cellmate is released, she and her gang of thieves try to blackmail the fugitive, and in so doing, they play right into her hands. It seems 993 was really a Secret Service agent all along.

Convoy (Robert Kane Productions/First National, 1927)
d: Joseph C. Boyle. 8 reels.
Lowell Sherman, Dorothy Mackaill, William Collier Jr., Lawrence Gray, Ian Keith, Gail Kane, Vincent Serrano, Donald Reed, Eddie Gribbon, Jack Ackroyd, Ione Holmes.
Sylvia, whose fiancé and brother have both enlisted to serve in World War I, discovers that one of her male friends is a German spy.

The Cook of Canyon Camp (Oliver Morosco Photoplay Co./Paramount, 1917)
d: Donald Crisp. 5 reels.
George Beban, Monroe Salisbury, Florence Vidor, Helen Jerome Eddy, John Burton.
A cook in a Quebec lumber camp doubles as a romance counselor.

The Cop (DeMille Pictures/Pathé, 1928)
d: Donald Crisp. 8 reels.
William Boyd, Alan Hale, Jacqueline Logan, Robert Armstrong, Tom Kennedy, Louis Natheaux, Phil Sleeman.
Smith, a new cop on the beat, must arrest a gangster who was once his friend.

The Copperhead (Famous Players-Lasky/Paramount, 1920)

d: Charles Maigne. 7 reels.
Lionel Barrymore, William P. Carlton, Frank Joyner, Richard Carlyle, Arthur Rankin, Leslie Stowe, Nicholas Schroell, William David, Harry Bartlett, Jack Ridgway, Doris Rankin, Carolyn Lee, Anne Cornwall.
During the Civil War, a Northerner is considered a traitor by his family and friends because he has joined the Copperheads, an organization sympathetic to the South. What they don't know is that he is working undercover, for President Lincoln.

Cora (Rolfe Photoplays, Inc./Metro, 1915)
d: Edwin Carewe. 5 reels.
Emily Stevens, Edwin Carewe, Ethel Stewart, Frank Elliot.
Cora, an opera star, attracts the wrong sort of men as her suitors.

Cordelia the Magnificent (Metro, 1923)
d: George Archainbaud. 7 reels.
Clara Kimball Young, Huntley Gordon, Carol Halloway, Lloyd Whitlock, Jacqueline Gadsden, Lewis Dayton, Mary Jane Irving, Catherine Murphy, Elinor Hancock.
Cordelia, a socialite whose family has fallen on hard financial times, is recruited as an accomplice to a crooked lawyer.

The Co-respondent (Universal, 1917)
d: Ralph W. Ince. 5 reels.
Elaine Hammerstein, Wilfred Lucas, George Anderson, Winifred Harris, Richard Neill, Charles Smith, Josephine Morse, Hattie Horne, Robert Cain, Edna Hunter.
A female reporter learns that she's been named co-respondent in a divorce case.

The Corner (New York Motion Picture Corp./Triangle, 1916)
d: Walter Edwards. 5 reels.
George Fawcett, Willard Mack, Clara Williams, Louise Brownell, Charles Miller.
Melodrama about a ruthless millionaire who corners the food market and drives thousands of people into hunger and abject poverty.

The Corner Grocer (World Film Corp., 1917)
d: George Cowl. 5 reels.
Lew Fields, Madge Evans, Lillian Cook, Nick Long Jr., William Sherwood, Justine Cutting, George Cowl, Pinna Nesbit, Viva Ogden, Stanhope Wheatcroft.
A kindly grocer adopts a little orphan girl.

A Corner in Colleens (New York Motion Picture Corp./Triangle, 1916)
d: Charles Miller. 5 reels.
Bessie Barriscale, Charles Ray, Margery Wilson, Roy Neill, Aggie Herring, Walter Perry, Alice Taafe, Alice Lawrence, Charles French.
In Ireland, four orphan sisters live on land that's been inherited by an American. Their fears that he will throw them out when he comes to claim his inheritance are allayed when he falls in love with one of them.

A Corner in Cotton (Metro, 1916)
d: Fred J. Balshofer. 5 reels.
Marguerite Snow, Frank Bacon, Zella Call, Howard Truesdell, Lester Cuneo, J.H. Goldsworthy, William Clifford, Wilfred Roger, Helen Dunbar.
It's father versus daughter, as Dad tries to corner the cotton market while Peggy sells off her shares to keep a failing cotton mill in business.

Cornered (Warner Bros., 1924)
d: William Beaudine. 7 reels.
Marie Prevost, Rockliffe Fellowes, Vera Lewis, John Roche, Raymond Hatton, Cissy Fitzgerald, George Pearce, Bartine Burkett, Billy Fletcher, Ruth Dwyer, Bertram Johns.
In a dual role, Miss Prevost plays a wealthy young woman and her conniving lookalike from the wrong side of the tracks.

Corporal Kate (DeMille Pictures/Producers Distributing Corp., 1926)
d: Paul Sloane. 8 reels.
Vera Reynolds, Julia Faye, Majel Coleman, Kenneth Thompson, Fred Allen.
A pair of manicurists from Brooklyn put together a dance routine to entertain the troops during the war.

Corruption (Super Art Film Corp., 1917)
d: Jack Gorman. 6 reels.
Helen Martin, Henry J. Sedley, John J. Dunn, Florence Hackett, Arthur J. Pickens, Lucile Dorrington, Marian Stephenson.
Heavy drama that features adultery, abortion, forced marriage, wife-beating, and attempted suicide.

The Corsican Brothers (United Picture Theatres of America, Inc., 1920)
d: Colin Campbell. 6 reels.
Dustin Farnum, Winifred Kingston, Wedgewood Nowell, Will Machin, Ogden Crane, Fanny Midgley, Andrew Robson, Sidney Payne, Evert Mitchell, Tote Du Crow, Pearl Levier.
Conjoined twins are physically separated at birth, but they remain attached emotionally.

The Cossack Whip (Thomas A. Edison, Inc., 1916)
d: John H. Collins. 5 reels.
Viola Dana, Grace Williams, Bob Walker, Frank Farrington, Richard Tucker, Sally Crute, William Wadsworth, Robert Brower, Saul Harrison.
When Cossacks raid a village and whip a young woman to death, her sister swears revenge and gets it, after becoming a prima ballerina and seducing the Cossacks' leader.

The Cossacks (MGM, 1928)
d: George Hill, Clarence Brown. 10 reels.
John Gilbert, Renee Adoree, Ernest Torrence, Nils Asther, Paul Hurst, Dale Fuller, Mary Alden, Josephine Borio, Yorke Sherwood, Joseph Mari.
In Russia, a cossack is unjustly branded a coward; even Maryana, his sweetheart, believes the charge and turns against him. In time, though, he will lead his troops valiantly into battle, incur war wounds, and prove his heroism. Now he's home again to great acclaim, and Maryana wants him again... but he's changed his mind about her.

The Cost (Famous Players-Lasky/Paramount, 1920)
d: Harley Knoles. 6 reels.
Violet Heming, Edwin Mordant, Jane Jennings, Ralph Kellard, Ed Arnold, Clifford Gray, Carlotta Monterey, Aileen Savage, Warburton Gamble, Florence McGuire, Julia Hurley.
When she catches her husband philandering, a young woman calls it quits and moves back to Mom and Dad's house.

The Cost of Hatred (Lasky Feature Plays/Paramount, 1917)
d: George H. Melford. 5 reels.

Kathlyn Williams, Theodore Roberts, Tom Forman, J.W. Johnston, Jack Holt, Charles Ogle, Walter Long, Horace B. Carpenter, Mayme Kelso, Louise Mineugh, Lucien Littlefield.

A callous brute abuses his wife, shoots his neighbor, and then conspires to get his neighbor's son Ned convicted on false charges and sentenced to hard labor. He is stung by remorse, however, when he finds that his own daughter has married Ned and refuses to see her father ever again.

The Cotton King (Brady Picture Plays/World Film Corp., 1915)
d: Oscar Eagle. 5 reels.
George Nash, Julia Hay, Eric Mayne, Fred Truesdell, Julia Stuart, Mario Majeroni.
A wheeler-dealer becomes known as "The Cotton King" because of his control of the cotton exchange on the stock market.

Counsel for the Defense (Burton King/Associated Exhibitors, 1925)
d: Burton King. 7 reels.
Jay Hunt, Betty Compson, House Peters, Rockliffe Fellowes, Emmett King, Bernard Randall, George MacDonald, George MacDowell, William Conklin, Joan Standing.
Katherine, the ink on her law school diploma barely dry, takes on her scientist father as her first client.

The Count of Luxembourg (Chadwick Pictures, 1926)
d: Arthur Gregor. 7 reels.
George Walsh, Helen Lee Worthing, Michael Dark, Charles Requa, James Morrison, Lola Todd, Joan Meredith.
What a tangled web these foolish royals weave. A duke loves Angela, an actress, but she is a commoner and therefore prevented from marrying him. To get around the technicality, the duke arranges for Angela to marry the Count of Luxembourg, sight unseen, then divorce him and return to the duke as a countess. Good plan, until Angela meets her new husband, and Cupid's arrow strikes.

The Count of Monte Cristo (Famous Players Film Co., 1912)
d: Edwin S. Porter. 5 reels.
James O'Neill, Eugenie Besserer, Hobart Bosworth.
Historical drama based on the famous novel by Alexandre Dumas. Edmond Dantes, a young Frenchman, is falsely accused of treason and sentenced to the notorious island prison, the Chateau D'If. There he languishes for years, until he finally sees a chance to escape and, miraculously, succeeds. He sails for the remote island of Monte Cristo and recovers a hidden treasure he learned about while in jail. Now wealthy, and calling himself the Count of Monte Cristo, Dantes returns to France to avenge himself against the men who had him imprisoned.
This was the first feature-length version of the Dumas story, and would be followed by many other versions, in both the silent and sound eras. *The Count of Monte Cristo* was filmed once previously, in 1907 by the Selig Polyscope Company, in a three-reel version. That film has the distinction of being the first commercial movie ever made entirely in what would come to be known as Hollywood, and is credited with touching off a mass migration of the New York-based movie business to California

The Count of Ten (Universal, 1928)
d: James Flood. 6 reels.
Charles Ray, Jobyna Ralston, Arthur Lake, James Gleason, Charles Sellon, Edythe Chapman, George Magrill, Jackie Coombs.
A prize-fighter gets married against his manager's wishes, and comes to regret it.

Counterfeit (Famous Players-Lasky/Paramount, 1919)
d: George Fitzmaurice. 5 reels.
Elsie Ferguson, David Powell, Helene Montrose, Charles Kent, Charles Gerard, Ida Waterman, Robert Lee Keeling, Fred Jenkins, Elizabeth Breen.
Secret Service agents are on the trail of a counterfeiting ring.

Counterfeit Love (Murray W. Garsson/Playgoers Pictures, 1923)
d: Roy Sheldon. 6 reels.
Joe King, Marian Swayne, Norma Lee, Jack Richardson, Irene Boyle, Isabel Fisher, Alexander Giglio, Danny Hayes, Frances Grant, William Jenkins.
Mary, an impoverished young woman who's the sole support of her sickly brother and sister, needs money for the mortgage. Now desperate, Mary accepts money she knows to be counterfeit and bets it on a horse race, losing it all. Now she'll be forced to marry a bounder for his money... unless that nice Secret Service agent who's been following the trail of the funny money can be induced to marry her instead.

The Countess Charming (Lasky Feature Plays/Paramount, 1917)
d: Donald Crisp. 5 reels.
Julian Eltinge, Florence Vidor, Tully Marshall, George Kuwa, Edythe Chapman, Mabel Van Buren, Gustav Von Seyffertitz, Billy Elmer.
She's Russian... she's royal... she's a countess! Nope, "she's" really a male in drag, preying on the pettiness and fragile egos of a country club set.

The Country Beyond (Fox, 1926)
d: Irving Cummings. 6 reels.
Olive Borden, Ralph Graves, Gertrude Astor, J. Farrell MacDonald, Evelyn Selbie, Fred Kohler, Lawford Davidson, Alfred Fisher, Lottie Williams.
In the Canadian Northwest, a valiant mountie takes the blame for a crime supposedly committed by the young woman he loves.

The Country Boy (Lasky Feature Plays/Paramount, 1915)
d: Frederick Thomson. 5 reels.
Marshal Neilan, Florence Dagmar, Dorothy Green, Loyola O'Connor, Mrs. Lewis McCord, Horace B. Carpenter, Edward Lewis, Ernest Joy, Tex Driscoll, Al Ernest Garcia.
Challenged by his girlfriend's father to prove he can support a wife, a young rustic goes to New York to make his fortune.

The Country Cousin (Selznick Pictures/Select Pictures Corp., 1919)
d: Alan Crosland. 5 reels.
Elaine Hammerstein, Marguerite Sidden, Lumsden Hare, Genevieve Tobin, Reginald Sheffield, Walter McGrail, Bigelow Cooper, Helene Montrose, Gilbert Rooney.
A country girl goes to New York to visit her cousin, a *nouveau riche* heiress.

The Country Doctor (DeMille Pictures, 1927)
d: Rupert Julian. 8 reels.
Rudolph Schildkraut, Junior Coghlan, Sam DeGrasse, Virginia Bradford, Gladys Brockwell, Frank Marion, Jane Keckley, Louis Natheaux, Ethel Wales.
Amos, a heroic country doctor, accepts an orphaned brother and sister into his home.

The Country Flapper (Paramount, 1922)
d: F. Richard Jones. 5 reels.
Dorothy Gish, Glenn Hunter, Harlan Knight, Mildred Marsh, Tom Douglas, Albert Hackett, Raymond Hackett, Catherine Collins.
A bucolic tease connives to get her bashful beau to the altar.

The Country Kid (Warner Bros., 1923)
d: William Beaudine. 6 reels.
Wesley Barry, Spec O'Donnell, Kate Toncray, Helen Jerome Eddy, Bruce Guerin.
Three orphaned brothers learn they are in danger of losing the farm they inherited..

The Country That God Forgot (Selig Polyscope, 1916)
w, d: Marshall Neilan. 5 reels.
Thomas Santschi, George Fawcett, Mary Charleson, Will Machin, Charles Gerrard, Victoria Forde, Charles LeMoyne.
Bitter drama about a miner whose wife deserts him for another man.

Courage (Sidney A. Franklin Productions, 1921)
d: Sidney A. Franklin. 6 reels.
Naomi Childers, Sam DeGrasse, Lionel Belmore, Adolphe Menjou, Lloyd Whitlock, Alec B. Francis, Ray Howard, Gloria Hope, Charles Hill Mailes.
Stephan, a young inventor, is unjustly accused and convicted of murdering his former employer. But his wife, Jean, continues to work on perfecting his invention and praying for her husband's release. Just as the invention is ready to market, the true murderer confesses and Stephan is freed and reunited with his wife.

Courage for Two (World Film Corp., 1919)
d: Dell Henderson. 5 reels.
Carlyle Blackwell, Evelyn Greeley, Rosina Henley, George MacQuarrie, Arda Lacroix, Henry West, Albert Gaston, Jack Drumier, Isabel O'Madigan, Lettie Ford.
Cal and Tony are cousins who bear a striking physical resemblance to each other, but have very different personalities.
Blackwell does double duty as the cousins.

The Courage of Marge O'Doone (Vitagraph, 1920)
d: David Smith. 7 reels.
Pauline Starke, Niles Welch, George Stanley, Jack Curtis, William Dyer, Boris Karloff, Billie Bennett, James O'Neill, Vincent Howard.
During a harsh winter in the icy Northwest, a man and his wife are lost and leave behind their young daughter. Years later, through a series of near-incredible coincidences, the family is reunited.

The Courage of Silence (Vitagraph, 1917)
d: William P.S. Earle. 5 reels.
Alice Joyce, Harry T. Morey, Willie Johnson, Mildred May, Cleo Ayres, Robert Gaillard, Walter McGrail, Anders Randolf, Dorothy Conroy.
An American businessman in London falls for a lady of Spain, though they are both happily married.

The Courage of the Common Place (Thomas A. Edison, Inc., 1917)
d: Ben Turbett. 5 reels.
Leslie Austin, Wililam Calhoun, Mildred Havens, Jessie Stevens, William Wadsworth, Lucia Moore, Stanley Wheatcroft, Ben La Mar, Charlotte Lambert, Lima Kaya.
Though he fails in his try for a high academic honor, a young man remains cheerful. Years later, his heroism during a raging fire earns him acclaim at his former college.

The Courageous Coward (Haworth Pictures/Robertson-Cole, 1919)
d: William Worthington. 5 reels.
Sessue Hayakawa, Tsuru Aoki, Toyo Fujita, Geroge Hernandez, Francis J. McDonald, Buddy Post.
A Japanese-American is appointed assistant district attorney, and proves his mettle in a difficult prosecution.

The Courageous Coward (Sable Productions/Usla Co., 1924)
d: Paul Hurst. 5 reels.
Jack Meehan, Jackie Saunders, Mary MacLaren, Earl Metcalf, Bruce Gordon, James Gordon.
A timid young engineer finds the courage to stand up to his larcenous employer, and to propose to the young lady he fancies.

The Courtesan (American Film Co./Mutual, 1916)
d: Arthur Maude. 5 reels.
Eugenie Forde, Hal Cooley, Al Fordyce, Charles Wheelock, William Carroll, Nell Franzen.
A newly-elected district attorney's reputation is almost ruined when his foes turn up proof that his mother is a paid mistress.

Court-Martial (Columbia, 1928)
d: George B. Seitz. 7 reels.
Jack Holt, Frank Austin, Betty Compson, Pat Harmon, Doris Hill, Frank Lackteen, George Cowl, Zack Williams.
During the Civil War, a Union officer tries to infiltrate a guerilla band, and falls for the notorious Belle Starr.

The Courtship of Miles Standish (Charles Ray Productions, 1923)
d: Frederick Sullivan. 9 reels.
Charles Ray, Enid Bennett, E. Alyn Warren, Joseph Dowling, Sam DeGrasse, Norval MacGregor, Thomas Holding, Frank Farrington, William Sullivan.
Historical drama based on the poem of the same name by Henry Wadsworth Longfellow.

Cousin Kate (Vitagraph, 1921)
d: Mrs. Sidney Drew. 5 reels.
Alice Joyce, Gilbert Emery, Beth Martin, Inez Shannon, Leslie Austin, Freddie Verdi, Frances Miller Grant, Henry Hallam.
Kate, a romance novelist, meets Heath on the rebound, and they fall in love even as Heath's former love is getting married.

The Covered Wagon (Famous Players-Lasky/Paramount, 1923)
d: James Cruze. 10 reels.
J. Warren Kerrigan, Lois Wilson, Alan Hale, Ernest Torrence, Tully Marshall, Charles Ogle, Ethel Wales, Guy Oliver, John Fox.
Historical drama about romance and treachery aboard two wagon trains heading west.

The Coward (Triangle, 1915)
d: Reginald Barker. 5 reels.
Charles Ray, Frank Keenan, Gertrude Claire, Margaret Gibson, Nick Cogley, Charles K. French.
During the Civil War, a young man thought to be a coward makes good.

The Coward (R-C Pictures/FBO of America, 1927)
d: Alfred Raboch. 6 reels.

Warner Baxter, Sharon Lynn, Freeman Wood, Raoul Paoli, Byron Douglas, Charlotte Stevens, Hugh Thomas.

After losing a fistfight to a romantic rival, wealthy young Philbrook is made a laughing stock and forced to leave town. He travels to Canada and becomes a trapper and a logger, learning the outdoorsman's way of life. Upon returning to the city, he finds his socialite girlfriend still available and proposes to her. .

Cowardice Court (Fox, 1919)
d: William C. Dowlan. 5 reels.
Peggy Hyland, Jack Livingston, Arthur Hoyt, Kathryn Adams, Burton Law, Bull Montana, Harry Lonsdale, Bertram Grassby, Gung Wong, Al McKinnon, Bonnie Hill.
Feuding develops between neighbors when a mountain dweller refuses to give up his shack and land to the wealthy family next door.

The Cowboy and the Countess (Fox, 1926)
d: R. William Neill. 6 reels.
Buck Jones, Helen D'Algy, Diana Miller, Harvey Clark, Monte Collins Jr., Fletcher Norton, Chappell Dossett, Jere Austin.
While his Wild West show is on tour in Europe, a cowboy learns that a countess is about to marry a duke who's really a jewel thief. The intrepid cowpoke abducts the countess to save her from the misalliance, then trounces the larcenous duke.

The Cowboy and the Lady (Rolfe Photoplays, Inc./Metro, 1915)
d: Edwin Carewe. 5 reels.
S. Miller Kent, Helen Case, Gertrude Short, Fred W. Hornby, Bert Hadley, William Ryno, Eith Stevens.
Refused permission to court the girl he loves, a young man goes West and becomes a cowboy. Years later, the now-experienced cowpoke rescues a girl from a runaway horse, and discovers that she's the girl he left behind.

The Cowboy Cavalier (Action Pictures/Pathé, 1928)
d: Richard Thorpe. 5 reels.
Buddy Roosevelt, Olive Hasbrouck, Charles K. French, Fannie Midgley, Robert Walker, Bob Clark, William Ryno.
A cowpoke rides to the rescue when a young woman is kidnapped and forced to sign a confession to a crime she didn't commit.

The Cowboy Cop (R-C Pictures/Film Booking Offices of America, 1926)
d: Robert DeLacey. 5 reels.
Tom Tyler, Jean Arthur, Irvin Renard, Frankie Darro, Pat Harmon, Earl Haley.
McGill, an Arizona cowboy, joins the police force in Los Angeles and finds himself involved in a jewel theft case.

The Cowboy Kid (Charles R. Seeling Productions/Aywon, 1922)
d: Charles R. Seeling. 5 reels.
Big Boy Williams, Patricia Palmer, Elizabeth DeWitt, William Austin, Chet Ryan, Bill Dyer, Mae Summers.
Smiley, a ranch foreman, fights crooks involved in a land grab.

The Cowboy Musketeer (R-C Pictures/ Film Booking Offices of America, 1925)
d: Robert DeLacy. 5 reels.
Tom Tyler, Jim London, Frances Dare, David Dunbar, Frankie Darro.
Out West, a cowboy helps a young lady recover the map to her late father's gold mine.

The Crab (New York Motion Picture Corp./Triangle, 1917)
d: Walter Edwards. 5 reels.
Thelma Salter, Frank Keenan, Ernest Butterworth, Gertrude Claire, J.P. Lockney, Thomas Guise.
An embittered man—the "crab" of the title—adopts an orphan girl. Though he treats her well, there is no laughter and no fun in his home. But all that changes one day, when the man is falsely accused of cruelty... and on the witness stand, his adopted daughter tells the court what a wonderful man her "dad" is, and how much she loves him. Exonerated, and deeply touched by the girl's testimony, he takes her home, and will be a crab no longer.

Crack O' Dawn (Harry J. Brown Productions/Rayart, 1925)
d: Albert Rogell. 5 reels.
Reed Howes, J.P. McGowan, Ruth Dwyer, Henry A. Barrows, Eddie Barry, Tom O'Brien, Ethan Laidlaw.
Feuding automobile company partners are reunited when they learn their children, Earl and Etta, are in love and have successfully created a champion race car.

The Crackerjack (East Coast Films, 1925)
d: Charles Hines. 7 reels.
Johnny Hines, Sigrid Holmquist, Henry West, Bradley Barker, J. Barney Sherry.
Perkins, a flapjack flipper, learns of a plot to smuggle bullets inside pickles to be shipped to headquarters of a revolution.

The Cradle (Famous Players-Lasky/Paramount, 1922)
d: Paul Powell. 5 reels.
Ethel Clayton, Charles Meredith, Mary Jane Irving, anna Lehr, Walter McGrail, Adele Farrington.
Doris, daughter of a divorced couple, spends half a year with each parent. In time, she'll see to it that Ma and Pa are reunited.

The Cradle Buster (Film Guild, 1922)
w, d: Frank Tuttle. 5 reels.
Glenn Hunter, Marguerite Courtot, Mary Foy, William H. Tooker, Lois Blaine, Osgood Perkins, Townsend Martin, Beatrice Morgan.
Benjamin, a boy who's been pampered all his life, decides on his 21st birthday to assert his manhood. He starts by smoking a cigar, drinking alcohol, and romancing a cabaret dancer... who, as it turns out, takes a fancy to him and agrees to become his bride. Now Benjamin's about to discover another side of being a man: Responsibility.

The Cradle of Courage (Famous Players-Lasky/Paramount, 1920)
w, d: Lambert Hillyer. 5 reels.
William S. Hart, Ann Little, Tom Santschi, Gertrude Claire, Francis Thorwald, George Williams.
Upon his return from duty in World War I, a former safecracker decides to amend his life, and becomes a San Francisco policeman... much to the consternation of his former gang.

The Cradle Snatchers (Fox, 1927)
d: Howard Hawks. 7 reels.
Louise Fazenda, J. Farrell MacDonald, Ethel Wales, Franklin Pangborn, Dorothy Phillips, William Davidson, Joseph Striker, Nick Stuart, Arthur Lake, Dione Ellis, Sammy Cohen, Tyler Brook.
Three wives who feel neglected plot to make their husbands jealous.

Craig's Wife   (Pathé, 1928)
d: William C. DeMille.   7 reels.
Irene Rich, Warner Baxter, Virginia Bradford, Carroll Nye, Lilyan Tashman, George Irving, Jane Keckley, Mabel Van Buren, Ethel Wales, Rada Rae.
The eponymous Mrs. Craig is fastidious and tyrannical, and soon alienates her husband and her own sister.

The Crash   (First National/Warner Bros., 1928)
d: Eddie Cline.   8 reels.
Milton Sills, Thelma Todd, Wade Boteler, William Demarest, Fred Warren, Sylvia Ashton, DeWitt Jennings.
Though it seems like a prophetic warning of the infamous Wall Street panic of the following year, the "crash" of this title refers instead to a train wreck that occurs in the final reel.

Crashin' Thru   (R-C Pictures/FBO of America, 1923)
d: Val Paul.   6 reels.
Harry Carey, Cullen Landis, Myrtle Stedman, Vola Vale, Charles LeMoyne, Winifred Bryson, Joseph Harris, Donald MacDonald, Charles Hill Mailes.
Out West, a rancher with an eye for the ladies finds he should have been keeping at least one eye on his stock. Before the rancher knows it, cattle rustlers have cleaned him out.

Crashing Through   (Liberty Pictures/Pathé, 1928)
d: Thomas Buckingham.   5 reels.
Jack Padjan, Sally Rand, William Eugene, Buster Gardner, Tom Santschi, Duke Lee, Jack Livingston.
Out West, a noble cowpoke is given a job on a cattle ranch by Rita, a girl he once saved from a horse stampede. He'll have his work cut out for him, for one of the ranch partners is a thief by night and a cattle rustler by day.

The Craving   (American Film Co./Mutual, 1916)
d: Charles Bartlett.   5 reels.
William Russell, Helene Rosson, Rea Berger, Roy Stewart, Charlotte Burton, Robert Miller.
Expelled from college because of his addiction to alcohol, a formerly respected football player and school hero determines to start over.

The Craving   (Universal, 1918)
d: Jack Ford.   5 reels.
Francis Ford, Mae Gaston, Peter Gerald, Duke Worne, Jean Hathaway.
Determined to obtain a secret formula, an East Indian has his lovely ward try to seduce its inventor.

Crazy to Marry   (Famous Players-Lasky/Paramount, 1921)
d: James Cruze.   5 reels.
Roscoe "Fatty" Arbuckle, Lila Lee, Laura Anson, Edwin Stevens, Lillian Leighton, Bull Montana, Allen Durnell, Sidney Bracey, Genevieve Blinn, Clarence Burton, Henry Johnson, Charles Ogle, Jackie Young, Lucien Littlefield.
Comedy of the absurd, with Arbuckle as a wacky surgeon who decides to elope with one girl while he has another one waiting at the altar.

Creaking Stairs   (Universal, 1919)
d: Rupert Julian.   6 reels.
Mary MacLaren, Herbert Prior, Jack Mulhall, Clarissa Selwyn, Lucretia Harris.
Newlyweds start life together in a modest home which, unbeknownst to them, is owned by her former lover.

The Cricket   (Universal, 1917)
d: Elsie Jane Wilson.   5 reels.
Zoe Rae, Harry Holden, Rena Rogers, Fred Warren, Winter Hall, George Hupp, Hal Cooley, Gretchen Lederer.
Cricket, an orphan girl, is raised by three foster fathers.

The Cricket on the Hearth   (Paul Gerson Pictures/Selznick, 1923)
d: Lorimer Johnston.   7 reels.
Josef Swickard, Fritzi Ridgeway, Paul Gerson, Virginia Brown Faire, Paul Moore, Lorimer Johnston, Margaret Landis, Joan Standing.
In 19th century England, a young couple marry and move into a village home with a large hearth. The bride sees a cricket on the hearth, and considers it a sign of good luck.

Crime and Punishment   (Arrow Film Corp./Pathé, 1917)
d: Lawrence B. McGill.   5 reels.
Derwent Hall Caine, Cherrie Coleman, Lydia Kott, Carl Gerard, Sidney Bracey, Marguerite Courtot, Robert Cummings.
Raskolnikoff, an immigrant from Russia, settles in New York. He is touched by the misery endured by poor people on the East Side, and to help them he robs a pawnshop, killing the pawn broker in the process. But when an innocent man is accused of the crime, Raskolnikoff is torn between his sense of altruism and his conscience.

The Criminal   (New York Motion Picture Co./Triangle, 1916)
d: Reginald Barker.   5 reels.
Clara Williams, William Desmond, Enid Willis, Joseph J. Dowling, Gertrude Claire, Charles K. French, Walt Whitman.
Naneta, an Italian immigrant in New York, finds an abandoned baby and decides to raise it. Because Naneta is not proficient in English, however, her intentions are misconstrued and she is arrested for kidnapping. But she's bailed out by a friend, and all ends happily.

The Crimson Canyon   (Universal, 1928)
d: Ray Taylor.   5 reels.
Ted Wells, Wilbur Mack, Lotus Thompson, Buck Connors, George Atkinson, Henri DeVelois.
Out West, a cowpoke "rescues" a damsel from a runaway stagecoach... then learns that it was only a motion picture scene, and he's ruined the take!

The Crimson Challenge   (Famous Players-Lasky/Paramount, 1922)
d: Paul Powell.   5 reels.
Dorothy Dalton, Jack Mower, Frank Campeau, Irene Hunt, Will R. Walling, Howard Ralston, Clarence Burton, George Field, Fred Huntly.
Feminist western, with the daughter of a murdered rancher taking up arms against her enemies.

The Crimson City   (Warner Bros., 1928)
d: Archie Mayo.   6 reels.
Myrna Loy, John Miljan, Matthew Betz, Leila Hyams, Anna May Wong, Richard Tucker, Anders Randolph, Sojin.
Kent, a young Englishman, takes refuge in China when he is accused of embezzlement. There, he finds himself coveted by a Chinese maiden, and forced to make a deal with her to clear himself of the false charges.

The Crimson Dove   (World Film Corp., 1917)
d: Romaine Fielding.   5 reels.
Carlyle Blackwell, June Elvidge, Marie La Varre, Henry West, Edward N. Hoyt, Dion Titheradge, Maxine Hicks,

Louis R. Grisel, Norman Hackett, George Cowl, Mildred Beckwith.

Sparks fly when a minister falls for a stage star, thinking she is a simple country girl.

The Crimson Gardenia (Rex Beach Pictures/Goldwyn, 1919)
d: Reginald Barker. 6 reels.
Owen Moore, Hedda Nova, Hector V. Sarno, Sydney Deane, Tully Marshall, Sydney Ainsworth, Edwin Stevens, Gertrude Claire, Betty Schade, Alec B. Francis, Kate Lester.
Mardi Gras in New Orleans serves up adventure and romance when a New Yorker is mistaken for an escaped counterfeiter, by gangsters and by the criminal's lovely cousin.

The Crimson Runner (Hunt Stromberg Corp./Producers Distributing Corp., 1925)
d: Tom Forman. 6 reels.
Priscilla Dean, Bernard Siegel, Alan Hale, Ward Crane, James Neill, Charles Hill Mailes, Ilsa DeLindt, Mitchell Lewis, Taylor Holmes, Arthur Millett.
In Vienna, a young rape victim dedicates her life to stealing from the "upper classes" she blames for her misfortune. As the leader of a gang of expert thieves, she becomes known as "The Crimson Runner."

The Crimson Wing (Essanay, 1915)
d: E.H. Calvert. 6 reels.
E.H. Calvert, John Cossar, Ruth Stonehouse, Beverly Bayne, Bryant Washburn, Betty Scott, Harry Dunkinson, Grant Foreman.
World War I intrudes, tragically, on the love affair between a German army officer and his lovely French sweetheart.

Crinoline and Romance (Metro, 1923)
d: Harry Beaumont. 6 reels.
Viola Dana, Claude Gillingwater, John Bowers, Allan Forrest, Betty Francisco, Mildred June, Lillian Lawrence, Gertrude Short, Lillian Leighton, Nick Cogley.
Emmy Lou is a southern belle who's been raised by her grandfather in near-seclusion, in a sheltered area of North Carolina. She has no idea about the "outside world" until she visits one of the larger cities and learns about jazz and flappers. Emmy Lou catches on to these decadent icons quickly.

The Crippled Hand (Universal, 1916)
d: Robert Leonard, David Kirkland. 5 reels.
Ella Hall, Robert Leonard, Marc Robbins, Gladys Rockwell, Kingsley Benedict.

During a quarrel, a stage actress cuts her boyfriend's hand, ending his career as a musician. Naturally, he swears revenge.

The Crisis (Selig Polyscope, 1916)
d: Colin Campbell. 7 reels.
George Fawcett, Matt B. Snyder, Bessie Eyton, Thomas Santschi, Eugenie Besserer, Marshall Neilan, Frank Weed, Will Machin, Sam D. Drane, Cecil Holland, Leo Pierson.
Ambitious tale of the War Between the States, dealing with divided loyalties among Americans, North and South alike.

The Crook of Dreams (World Film Corp., 1919)
d: Oscar Apfel. 5 reels.
Louise Huff, Virginia Hammond, Florence Billings, Kempton Greene, Josephine Williams, Edward Elkas, Kate Lester, Frank Mayo.

Constance, a petty crook, poses as the long-lost daughter of a wealthy widow. The widow accepts her, and showers her new-found "daughter" with gifts and clothes and gives her a good home. Over time, Constance acquires grace and sophistication, and concludes that her scam has worked perfectly. But what she doesn't know—and neither do we, until the final reel—is that this child of the streets really *is* the widow's daughter, stolen from her mother in infancy.

Crooked Alley (Universal, 1923)
d: Robert F. Hill. 5 reels.
Thomas Carrigan, Laura LaPlante, Tom Guise, Owen Gorine, Albert Hart.
A reformed thief tries to arrange a pardon for a dying friend.

Crooked Straight (Thomas H. Ince/Famous Players-Lasky, 1919)
d: Jerome Storm. 5 reels.
Charles Ray, Wade Butler, Margery Wilson, Gordon Mullen, Otto Hoffman.
Swindled out of his life's savings by a city slicker, country boy Ben Trimble reluctantly turns to safecracking to get some money.

Crooked Streets (Famous Players-Lasky/Paramount, 1920)
d: Paul Powell. 5 reels.
Ethel Clayton, Jack Holt, Clyde Fillmore, Clarence H. Geldart, Josephine Crowell, Frederick Starr.
An American girl in China barely escapes abduction.

Crooks Can't Win (FBO Pictures, 1928)
d: George M. Arthur. 7 reels.
Ralph Lewis, Thelma Hill, Sam Nelson, Joe Brown, Eugene Strong, James Eagle, Charles Hall.
Malone, a police officer, leaves his post guarding a warehouse in order to help his brother. When the warehouse is looted, Malone is blamed and is thrown off the force. But through his connections, he gets advance information on where the thieves will strike next and foils them, regaining his good name.

The Cross Bearer (World Film Corp., 1918)
d: William A. Brady. 5 reels.
Montagu Love, Jeanne Eagels, Anthony Merlo, George Morgan, Edward Elkas, Charles Brandt, Eloise Clement, Albert Hart, Alexander Francis, Kate Lester, Fanny Cogan.
A courageous Cardinal defends his church, his townspeople, and his ward when German forces invade their Belgian town during World War I.

Cross Breed (Bischoff Productions, 1927)
d: Noel Mason Smith. 6 reels.
Johnnie Walker, Gloria heller, Charles K. French, Frank Glendon, Henry Hebert, Joseph Mack, Olin Francis.
A war veteran and his valiant dog fight off timber thieves.

Cross Currents (Fine Arts Film Co./Triangle, 1916)
d: Francis Grandon. 5 reels.
Helen Ware, Courtenay Foote, Teddy Sampson, Sam DeGrasse, Vera Lewis.
When the yacht they are on catches fire, a couple are forced to swim to a desert island.

Cross Roads (William M. Smith Productions/Merit Film Corp., 1922)
d: Francis Ford. 5 reels.
Franklyn Farnum, Shorty Hamilton, Genevieve Bert, Al Hart.
Out West, a homeless girl thought to be an omen of bad luck

helps a cowpoke clear himself of false murder charges.

Crossed Signals (Rayart, 1926)
d: J.P. McGowan. 5 reels.
Helen Holmes, Henry Victor, Georgie Chapman, William Lowery, Milla Davenport, Nelson McDowell, Clyde McAtee.
Counterfeiters scheme to swap their phony money for the real thing, using a female train station agent as their dupe.

Crossed Trails (Independent Pictures, 1924)
d: J.P. McGowan. 5 reels.
Franklyn Farnum, William Buehler, V.L. Barnes, Mack V. Wright, Alyce Mills, Buck Black, Billie Bennett, J.P. McGowan.
Out West, a lawman tries to protect the father of the girl he loves... even though ol' Dad is an outlaw.

Crossed Wires (Universal, 1923)
d: King Baggot. 5 reels.
Gladys Walton, George Stewart, Tom Guise, Lillian Langdon, William Robert Daly, Kate Price, Eddie Gribbon, Marie Crisp, Eloise Nesbit, Helen Broneau, Lewis Mason.
Marcel, a telephone operator and socialite wannabe, wangles an invitation to a party of swells—and winds up engaged to marry the heir to the estate.

Crossing Trails (Cliff Smith Productions/Associated Photoplays, 1921)
d: Cliff Smith. 5 reels.
Pete Morrison, Esther Ralston, John Hatton, Lew Meehan, Floyd Taliaferro, J.B. Warner, Billie Bennett.
When Helen, an heiress, is falsely accused of murder, she flees from the law. Her accuser chases after her, but his intentions are dishonorable... because *he's* the real killer.

The Crossroads of New York (Mack Sennett Productions/Associated First National, 1922)
d: F. Richard Jones. 6 reels.
George O'Hara, Noah Beery, Ethel Grey Terry, Ben Deely, Billy Bevan, Herbert Standing, Dot Farley, Eddie Gribbon, Kathryn McGuire, Robert Cain, Mildred June.
Michael, a country boy, takes a job in the big city as a street sweeper. In spite of his lowly position, he's soon pursued by numerous women. The reason: It's rumored that Michael is an heir to his wealthy uncle's estate.

The Crowd (MGM, 1928)
w, d: King Vidor. 9 reels.
James Murray, Eleanor Boardman, Bert Roach, Del Henderson, Lucy Beaumont, Estelle Clark, Daniel G. Tomlinson, Freddie Burke, Alice Mildred Puter.

Episodes in the lives of two ordinary people, their hopes, their marriage, their triumphs, and their tragedies. This film attracted high critical praise for its realism, partly due to hidden cameras which recorded daily life in bustling New York City.

The Crowded Hour (Famous Players-Lasky/Paramount, 1925)
d: E. Mason Hopper. 7 reels.
Bebe Daniels, Kenneth Harlan, T. Roy Barnes, Frank Morgan, Helen Lee Worthing, Armand Cortez, Alice Chapin, Warner Richmond.
In World War I, Peggy, a Red Cross nurse, loves a doughboy named Billy. He's married, though, so Peggy keeps her love locked in her heart... until Billy is assigned to a dangerous mission and Peggy learns that he will be facing certain death by ambush. Will she follow him into danger to alert him?

The Crown of Lies (Famous Players-Lasky/Paramount, 1926)
d: Dimitri Buchowetski. 5 reels.
Pola Negri, Noah Beery, Robert Ames, Charles a. Post, Arthur Hoyt, Mikhael Vavitch, Cissy Fitzgerald, May Foster, Frankie Bailey, Edward Cecil, Erwin Connelly.
In the Balkan kingdom of Sylvania, a New York girl is mistaken for the country's "lost queen" and is forced to ascend the throne.

The Crown Prince's Double (Vitagraph, 1916)
d: Van Dyke Brooke. 5 reels.
Maurice Costello, Norma Talmadge, Howard Hall, Anders Randolf, Thomas R. Mills, Thomas Brooke, Daniel Leighton, Anna Laughlin, Leila Blau.
An uprising in a small European country cancels a crown prince's wedding plans. Instead, he sails to the U.S.A., where he meets and marries an American girl. But he is still pursued by his enemies, so the prince enlists the aid of an American who looks just like him.

The Crow's Nest (Sunset Productions/Aywon, 1922)
d: Paul Hurst. 5 reels.
Jack Hoxie, Ruddel Weatherwax, Evelyn Nelson, Tom Lingham, William Lester, William Dyer, Mary Bruce, Bert Lindley, Augustina Lopez.
Esteban, a young Indian brave, falls in love with a white girl, but fears she will reject him because of his race. What he doesn't know—yet—is that he is really a white orphan boy who was raised by an Indian squaw.

The Cruel Truth (Sterling Pictures, 1927)
d: Phil Rosen. 6 reels.
Hedda Hopper, Constance Howard, Hugh Allan, Frances Raymond, Ruth Handforth.
Reggie, a scion of wealth, meets a lovely "girl" at the beach, and is smitten. The lady is, in fact, a youthful-looking matron old enough to be Reggie's mother, and with a daughter Reggie's age.

The Cruise of the Jasper B (DeMille Pictures/Producers distributing Corp., 1926)
d: James W. Horne. 6 reels.
Rod LaRocque, Mildred Harris, Jack Ackroyd, Snitz Edwards, Otto Lederer, James Mack.
In order to claim his inheritance, a landlubber must get married at sea on the deck of the family's ancient ship. But she isn't seaworthy.

The Cruise of the Make-Believes (Famous Players-Lasky/Paramount, 1918)
d: George Melford. 5 reels. 5 reels.
Raymond Hatton, Harrison Ford, Lila Lee, Parks Jones, Spottiswoode Aitkens, Bud Duncan, Eunice Moore, Mayme Kelso, Jane Wolff, Nina Byron, William Brulton, John McKinnon, William McLaughlin.
A slum girl gets a chance to spend a month in a luxurious estate.

The Crusader (Fox, 1922)
d: Howard M. Mitchell. 5 reels.
William Russell, Gertrude Claire, Helen Ferguson, Fritzi Brunette, George Webb, Carl Grantvoort.
Out West, a miner is trapped in a cave-in. He'll be fished out by friends, but then must face angry citizens who have been fleeced in the sale of worthless mining stock.

The Cry of the Weak (Astra Film Corp./Pathé, 1919)
d: George Fitzmaurice. 5 reels.

102

Fannie Ward, Frank Elliott, Walt Whitman, Paul Willis.
Socially conscious tale about whether or not criminals can be rehabilitated.

The Crystal Cup (Henry Hobart Productions/First National, 1927)
d: John Francis Dillon. 7 reels.
Dorothy Mackaill, Rockliffe Fellowes, Jack Mulhall, Clarissa Selwynne, Jane Winton, Edythe Chapman.
A man-hating woman finds herself suddenly being ardently wooed by not one but two admirers.

The Crystal Gazer (Paramount, 1917)
d: George Melford. 5 reels.
Raymond Hatton, Harrison Ford, Fannie Ward, Jack Dean, Winifred Greenwood, Edythe Chapman, Jane Wolff.
Orphan sisters are adopted, one by a wealthy family, the other by poor folks.

The Cub (William A. Brady Picture Plays, Inc./World Film Corp., 1915)
d: Maurice Tourneur. 5 reels.
John Hines, Martha Hedman, Robert Cummings, Dorothy Farnum, Jessie Lewis, Bert Starkey.
A cub reporter sent to cover a rural feud gets into all manner of scrapes, including an innocent flirtation with one of the mountain girls that turns deadly when her family takes exception to his attentions.

A Cumberland Romance (Realart Pictures Corp., 1920)
d: Charles Maigne. 6 reels.
Mary Miles Minter, Monte Blue, John Bowers, Martha Mattox, Robert Brower.
A civil engineer from the city woos a mountain girl.

The Cup of Fury (Rupert Hughes/Goldwyn, 1920)
d: Claude Camp. 6 reels.
Helene Chadwick, Rockcliffe Fellowes, Frank Leigh, Clarissa Selwyn, Kate Lester, Herbert Standing, Florence Deshon, Dwight Crittenden, Sydney Ainsworth, H.A. Morgan, Marion Colvin, Wade Boteler, Elinor Hancock.
Marie, a German expatriate working in the U.S., is approached by a German spy and urged to betray her adopted country.

The Cup of Life (New York Motion Picture Corp./Mutual, 1915)
d: Raymond B. West, Thomas H. Ince. 5 reels.
Bessie Barriscale, Enid Markey, Charles Ray, Frank Borzage, Arthur Maude, J. Barney Sherry, Louise Glaum, Harry Keenan, Howard Hickman, Jerome Storm.
Sisters grow up with very different priorities: One yearns for wealth, luxury, and exotic romances; the other wants only to marry her sweetheart and make him happy.

The Cup of Life (Thomas H. Ince Productions/Associated Producers, 1921)
d: Rowland V. Lee. 6 reels.
Hobart Bosworth, Madge Bellamy, Niles Welch, Tully Marshall, Monte Collins, May Wallace.
In Singapore, a pearl smuggler plies a priceless jewel to win a bride for his son.

Cupid by Proxy (Diando Film Co./Pathé, 1918)
d: William Bertram. 5 reels.
Baby Marie Osborne, Minnie Danvers, J.N. McDowell, Mary Talbot, John Steppling, Mildred Harris, Antrim Short, Kenneth Nordyke.
When the daughter of an upscale family wishes to marry the "ordinary fella" she loves, her parents panic and try to find her an "acceptable" mate among the wealthy, but to no avail.

Cupid Forecloses (Viatagraph, 1919)
d: David Smith. 5 reels.
Bessie Love, Dorothea Wolbert, Wallace McDonald, Frank Hayes, Jim Donnelly, Aggie Herring, Jake Abrams, Anne Schaefer, Gordon Griffith, Otto Lederer, Ruth Fuller Golden.
An impoverished family subsists on the salary of their schoolteacher daughter Geraldine, but they are deeply in debt and facing foreclosure. Fortunately, the mortgage holder falls in love with Geraldine and the debt is forgiven.

Cupid, the Cowpuncher (Goldwyn, 1920)
d: Clarence G. Badger. 5 reels.
Will Rogers, Helene Chadwick, Andrew Robson, Lloyd Whitlock, Guinn Williams, Tex Parker, Roy Laidlaw, Katherine Wallace, Nelson McDowell, Cordelia Callahan.
A ranch foreman has eyes for a girl who's training for an opera career.

Cupid's Brand (Unity Photoplays/Arrow Film Corp., 1921)
d: Rowland V. Lee. 6 reels.
Jack Hoxie, Wilbur McGaugh, Charles Force, Mignon Anderson, William Dyer, A.T. Van Sicklen.
In a desert town, counterfeiters try to ply their trade, but find that the sheriff is on to them. To their great surprise, the lawman merely wants a cut of the take.

Cupid's Fireman (Fox, 1923)
d: William A. Wellman. 5 reels.
Charles Jones, Marian Nixon, Brooks Benedict, Eileen O'Malley, Lucy Beaumont, Al Fremont, Charles McHugh, Mary Warren, L.H. King.
McGee, a fireman, rescues a lovely lady from a burning building and then marries her.

Cupid's Roundup (Fox, 1918)
d: Edward J. LeSaint. 5 reels.
Tom Mix, Wanda Petit, E.B. Tilton, Roy Watson, Verne Mesereau, Al Padgett, Fred Clark, Eugenie Forde.
Engaged to be married, a young Westerner takes a job on a ranch, hoping to have a fling with the maid at the ranch next door. What he doesn't know is that the "maid" is his fiancée.

Cupid's Rustler (Dearholt Productions/Arrow Film Corp., 1924)
d: Francis Ford. 5 reels.
Edmund Cobb, Florence Gilbert, Clark Coffey, Ashton Dearholt, Wilbur McGaugh.
Out West, an unlucky gambler tries to help a dance hall girl start her own ranch.

The Curious Conduct of Judge Legarde (Life Photo Film Corp., 1915)
d: Will Davis. 5 reels.
Lionel Barrymore, Edna Pendleton, William H. Tooker, Roy Applegate, W.W.M. Draper, August Balfour, Charles Graham, Arthur Morrison, Ed Roseman, Thomas O'Keefe.
After suffering a blow to the head, a judge develops a dual personality.

Curlytop (Fox, 1924)
d: Maurice Elvey. 6 reels.
Shirley Mason, Wallace MacDonald, Warner Oland, Diana Miller, George Kuwa, Ernest Adams, Nora Hayden, LaVerne Lindsay.
In London, a curly-haired blonde shopgirl falls for a

charming but irresponsible young man. Her love changes him into a vital, energetic optimist. Good thing, too, because soon the girl will need her man to rescue her from a sinking ship.

The Curse of Drink (Weber & North, 1922)
w, d: Harry O. Hoyt. 6 reels.
Harry T. Morey, Edmund Breese, Marguerite Clayton, George Fawcett, Miriam Battista, Brinsley Shaw, Alice May, Albert L. Barrett, June Fuller.
Bootleg hooch leads to the near-ruination of a respected railroad engineer.

Curtain (First National, 1920)
d: James Young. 5 reels.
Katherine MacDonald, E.B. Tilton, Earl Whitlock, Charles Richman, Florence Deshon.
Bitter drama about a couple who can't agree on her theatrical career, leading them to get a divorce.

The Custard Cup (Fox, 1922)
d: Herbert Brenon. 7 reels.
Mary Carr, Myrta Bonillas, Miriam Battista, Jerry Devine, Ernest McKay, Peggy Shaw, Leslie Leigh, Frederick Esmelton, Henry Sedley, Louis Hendricks, Edward Boring.
"The Custard Cup" is a close-knit neighborhood housing, among others, an elderly widow and her three children, and husband-and-wife counterfeiters.

Cy Whittaker's Ward (Thomas A. Edison, Inc., 1917)
d: Ben Turbett. 5 reels.
William Wadsworth, Shirley Mason, William Burton, Carter Harkness, Mary Elizabeth Forbes, Emily Lorraine, Leslie Hunt, Wally Clark, Ed Bunnell, George O'Donnell, Hugh Gillen.
A retired sea captain takes in a homeless young girl.

The Cycle of Fate (Selig Polyscope, 1916)
d: Marshall Neilan. 5 reels.
William Machin, Edith Johnson, Bessie Eyton, Wheeler Oakman, Al W. Filson, Lewis Cody, Marion Warner, Marshall Neilan, Fred Hearn, Frank Clark.
Brother and sister twins are separated as infants. They follow different paths in life—he becomes a gangster, she a schoolteacher—but when a twist of fate brings them together again, they are reconciled and the brother leaves his criminal past behind.

The Cyclone (Fox, 1920)
d: Cliff Smith. 5 reels.
Tom Mix, Colleen Moore, Henry Hebert, William Ellingford.
In the rugged Northwest, a Canadian mountie rounds up a gang of smugglers.

The Cyclone Cowboy (Action Pictures/Pathé, 1927)
d: Richard Thorpe. 5 reels.
Wally Wales, Violet Bird, Raye Hampton, Richard Lee, Ann Warrington, George Magrill.
Out West, a rancher's daughter is sought by two men: the ranch foreman and a city slicker. She's torn between the love of both men, but makes her mind up when the foreman shows courage during a storm and the city boy turns tail.

Cyclone Higgins, M.D. (Metro, 1918)
d: William Christy Cabanne. 5 reels.
Francis X. Bushman, Beverly Bayne, Baby Ivy Ward, Charles Fang, John Prescott, Helen Dunbar, Eugene Borden, Sue Balfour, Pop Kennard, Robert Carson.
"Cyclone" Higgins is a preacher whose mission is to tame a rough Southern town.

Cyclone of the Range (FBO Pictures, 1927)
d: Robert DeLacy. 5 reels.
Tom Tyler, Elsie Tarron, Harry O'Connor, Richard Howard, Frankie Darro, Harry Woods.
Out West, a cowpoke searches for the outlaw who killed his brother.

The Cyclone Rider (Fox, 1924)
d: Thomas Buckingham. 7 reels.
Reed Howes, Alma Bennett, William Bailey, Margaret McWade, Frank Beal, Evelyn Brent, Eugene Pallette, Ben Deeley, Charles Conklin, Bud Jamison, Ben Hendricks Jr.
Armstrong, an automobile racer, falls in love with a tycoon's daughter. Though Papa doesn't approve of the match, he agrees to it if Armstrong wins the big race.

Cynthia-of-the-Minute (Gibraltar Pictures/W.W. Hodkinson, 1920)
d: Perry Vekroff. 6 reels.
Leah Baird, Burr McIntosh, Hugh Thompson, Alexander Gaden, Mathilde Brundage, Ruby Hoffman, John Webb Dillion, William Welsh, Wallace Widdecombe, Ashton Newton.
A girl who knows Morse code intercepts a criminal message, and saves the day.

Cytherea (Madison Productions/Associated First National, 1924)
d: George Fitzmaurice. 8 reels. (Technicolor sequence.)
Irene Rich, Lewis Stone, Norman Kerry, Betty Bouton, Charles Wellesley, Peaches Jackson, Mickey Moore, Constance Bennett, Hugh Saxon, Lee Hill, Lydia Yeamans Titus, Brandon Hurst.
Romance-minded businessman Lee Randon meets a woman who appears to resemble Cytherea, Goddess of Love. He pursues her passionately and they begin an affair, but the woman dies tragically. Heartbroken but repentant, Randon returns home to his wife and children and is welcomed with open arms.

Daddies (Warner Bros., 1924)
d: William A. Seiter. 7 reels.
Harry Myers, Mae Marsh, Willard Lewis, Crauford Kent, Claude Gillingwater, Claire Adams, Boyce Combe, Otto Hoffman, King Evers, the DeBriac twins, Georgia Woodthorpe.
The solace of an exclusive men's club is shattered by the arrival of six children.

Daddy (Jackie Coogan Productions/Associated First National, 1923)
d: E. Mason Hopper. 6 reels.
Jackie Coogan, Arthur Carewe, Josie Sedgwick, Cesare Gravina, Bert Woodruff, Anna Townsend, Willard Louis, George Kuwa.
Jackie, an orphan, lives on a farm but is forced to move on when his foster parents lose their property. By chance, he meets a violin virtuoso who recognizes with joy that Jackie is his own long lost son. The musician takes the boy into his own home and shows his gratitude to the foster parents who sheltered him by buying their farm back for them.

Daddy Long Legs (Pickford/First National, 1918)
d: Marshall Neilan. 7 reels.
Mary Pickford, Milla Davenport, Miss Percy Haswell, Fay Lemport, Mahlon Hamilton, Lillian Langdon, Betty Bouton, Audrey Chapman, Marshall A. Neilan, Carrie Clarke Ward.

A good-natured orphan girl is "adopted" by an unknown benefactor who pays her expenses on condition that she never try to see him.

Daddy's Girl (Diando Film Corp./Pathé, 1918)
d: William Bertram. 5 reels.
Baby Marie Osborne, Marion Warner, Lew Cody, Katherine McLaren, Herbert Standing.
Life is good for little Marie, until she learns that Papa is being untrue to Mama.

Daddy's Gone A'Hunting (MGM, 1925)
d: Frank Borzage. 6 reels.
Alice Joyce, Percy Marmont, Virginia Marshall, Ford Sterling, Holmes Herbert, Helena D'Algy, Edythe Chapman.
Julian, an artist, grows weary of his domestic life and asks his wife to take a job so he can study in Europe. She does so, but when Julian returns from abroad, he is full of bohemian ideas and cannot stand her bourgeois ways. He'll come to his senses, though, when he realizes that he is in danger of losing his wife to another man.

Damaged Goods (American Film Manufacturing Co., 1914; Mutual, 1915)
d: Thomas Ricketts. 7 reels.
Richard Bennett, Adrienne Morrison, Maud Milton, Olive Templeton, Josephine Ditt, Jacqueline Moore, Florence Short, Louis Bennison, John Steppling, William Bertram, George Ferguson, Charlotte Burton.
Tragic tale of a successful young lawyer who, in a moment's weakness, contracts syphilis and later passes the disease to his wife and their baby.
Richard Bennett was a famous stage actor and director and the father of actresses Joan and Constance Bennett. Their mother was Adrienne Morrison, the leading lady in *Damaged Goods*.

Damaged Hearts (Pilgrim Pictures, 1924)
d: T. Hayes Hunter. 6 reels.
Mary Carr, Jerry Devine, Helen Rowland, Tyrone Power, Jean Armour, Thomas Gillen, Edmund Breese, Effie Shannon, Rolinda Bainbridge, Eugene Strong, Florence Billings.
David, a young man whose sister was abused as a child and died, swears revenge on the parties responsible. As part of his plan, he kidnaps the wife of one of the abusers. What happens next is something David didn't count on: He falls in love with his captive.

Dame Chance (David Hartford Productions, 1926)
d: Bertram Bracken. 7 reels.
Julanne Johnston, Gertrude Astor, Robert Frazer, David Hartford, Lincoln Stedman, Mary Carr, John T. Prince.
Stafford, a prosperous businessman, offers to support Gail, a struggling actress... but there are strings attached.

Dames Ahoy! (Universal, 1930)
d: William James Craft.   6 reels.   (Also released in sound version.)
Glenn Tryon, Eddie Gribbon, Otis Harlan, Helen Wright, Gertrude Astor.
Three sailors on shore leave track the scheming blonde who bilked one of the trio out of half his pay.

Damon and Pythias (Universal, 1914)
d: Otis Turner. 6 reels. 6 reels.
William Worthington, Herbert Rawlinson, Frank Lloyd, Anna Little, Cleo Madison.
In ancient Greece, two men are good and loyal friends to each other, even at the risk of their own lives.

A Damsel in Distress (Albert Capellani Productions, Inc./Pathé, 1919)
d: George Archainbaud. 5 reels.
June Caprice, Creighton Hale, William H. Thompson, Charlotte Granville, Arthur Albro, George Trimble, Katherine Johnson, Mark Smith.
On the run from her pushy relatives, a girl ducks into a taxi occupied by a musical comedy composer, and finds love.

Dance Madness (MGM, 1925)
d: Robert Z. Leonard. 7 reels.
Claire Windsor, Conrad Nagel, Hedda Hopper, Douglas Gilmore, Mario Carillo.
A fun-loving wife decides to test her husband's fidelity by trying to seduce him while disguised as a notorious, sensual dancer.

Dance Magic (Robert Kane Productions/First National, 1927)
d: Victor Halperin. 7 reels.
Pauline Starke, Ben Lyon, Louis John Bartels, Isabel Elson, Harlan Knight, Judith Vosselli.
Melodrama about a girl who leaves her strict religious community to become a dancer on Broadway.

The Dancer of Paris (First National Pictures, 1926)
d: Alfred Santell. 7 reels.
Conway Tearle, Dorothy Mackaill, Robert Cain, Henry Vibart, Paul Ellis, Frances Miller Grant.
In Paris, a dancer breaks off her engagement to a wealthy roué. Aching to avenge himself, the rejected fiancé follows her and tries to get her dancing partner to injure her during one of their routines.

The Dancer of the Nile (William P.S. Earle Productions, 1923)
d: William P.S. Earle. 6 reels.
Carmel Myers, Malcolm McGregor, Sam DeGrasse, Bertram Grassby, June Eldridge.
In ancient Egypt, a princess desires the prince of a nearby country although he's spoken for. Not used to having her desires go unfulfilled, the princess orders her rival killed; but eventually the girl's life is spared.

The Dancers (Fox, 1925)
d: Emmett J. Flynn. 7 reels.
George O'Brien, Alma Rubens, Madge Bellamy, Templar Saxe, Joan Standing, Alice Hollister, Freeman Wood, Walter McGrail, Noble Johnson, Tippy Grey.
In a South American country, a dancehall is owned and run by Tony, an expatriate Briton.

The Dancer's Peril (World Film Corp., 1917)
d: Travers Vale. 5 reels.
Alice Brady, Philip Hahn, Harry Benham, Montagu Love, Alexis Kosloff, Auguste Burmeister, Louis Grisel, Jack Drumier, Johnny Hines, Sydeny Dalbrook.
When the star pupil in a Russian dancing academy is refused permission to dance in a Paris ballet, she disguises herself as a boy and runs away to France on her own.

The Dancin' Fool (Famous Players-Lasky/Paramount, 1920)
d: Sam Wood. 5 reels.
Wallace Reid, Bebe Daniels, Raymond Hatton, Willis Marks, George B. Williams, Lillian Leighton, Carlos San Martin, William H. Brown, Tully Marshall, Ruth Ashby, Ernest Joy.

A country boy in the big city meets a cabaret dancer, they work up a duo act, and soon the two are a hit on Broadway.

The Dancing Cheat (Universal, 1924)
d: Irving Cummings. 5 reels.
Herbert Rawlinson, Alice Lake, Robert Walker, Edwin J. Brady, Jim Blackwell, Harmon MacGregor.
Infuriated over being refused entrance to a large casino, a gambler persuades his wife to help him blackmail the owner.

Dancing Days (Preferred Pictures, 1926)
d: Albert Kelley. 6 reels.
Helene Chadwick, Forrest Stanley, Gloria Gordon, Lillian Rich, Robert Agnew, Thomas Ricketts, Sylvia Ashton.
Ralph and Alice, a comfortably married young couple, are faced with a crisis when he develops a wandering eye.

The Dancing Girl (Famous Players/Paramount, 1915)
d: Daniel Frohman. 5 reels.
Florence Reed, Fuller Mellish, Lorraine Huling, Malcolm Williams, William Russell, Eugene Ormonde, William Lloyd, Minna Gale.
Success on the stage doesn't spoil a girl who yearns to return to her Quaker community.

Dancing Mothers (Famous Players-Lasky/Paramount, 1926)
d: Herbert Brenon. 8 reels.
Alice Joyce, Conway Tearle, Clara Bow, Donald Keith, Dorothy Cumming, Elsie Lawson, Norman Trevor.
After discovering that her husband is cheating on her, a socialite determines to travel to Paris and start a new life.

Danger Ahead (Universal, 1921)
d: Rollin Sturgeon. 5 reels.
Mary Philbin, James Morrison, Jack Mower, Minna Redman, George Bunny, George B. Williams, Jane Starr, Emily Rait, Helene Caverly.
When a proud family is forced to take in boarders, their daughter Tressie falls in love with one of them.

The Danger Game (Goldwyn, 1918)
d: Harry Pollard. 5 reels.
Madge Kennedy, Tom Moore, Paul Doucet, Ned Burton, Mabel Ballin, Kate Blancke.
When a society girl sets out to prove that her novel about a socialite-thief is plausible, she runs into unexpected complications.

The Danger Girl (Metropolitan/Producers Distributing Corp., 1926)
d: Edward Dillon. 6 reels.
Priscilla Dean, John Bowers, Gustav von Seyffertitz, Cissy Fitzgerald, Arthur Hoyt, William Humphreys, Clarence Burton, Erwin Connelly.
Two reclusive brothers live together in relative isolation from the rest of the community, until one night when a young woman dressed in a bridal gown comes to their home and pleads for them to take her in.

Danger Go Slow (Universal, 1918)
d: Robert Leonard. 6 reels.
Mae Murray, Jack Mulhall, Lon Chaney, Lydia Knott, Joseph Girard.
A tomboy living on the shady fringes of society decides to "go straight."

The Danger Line (R-C Pictures/FBO of America, 1924)
d: E.E. Violet. 6 reels.
Sessue Hayakawa, Tsuru Aoki, Gina Palerme, Cady Winter, Felix Ward.
The happy marriage of two Japanese nobles is threatened when a westerner professes his love for the wife.

The Danger Mark (Famous Players-Lasky/Paramount, 1918)
d: Hugh Ford. 5 reels.
Elsie Ferguson, Mahlon Hamilton, Crauford Kent, Gertrude McCoy, Edward Burns, Maud Turner Gordon, W.T. Carlton.
At her coming-out party, a deb gets drunk, and learns that she has inherited a tendency to alcoholism.

Danger Patrol (Duke Worne Productions/Rayart, 1928)
d: Duke Worne. 6 reels.
William Russell, Virginia Browne Faire, Wheeler Oakman, Rhea Mitchell, Ethan Laidlaw, S.D. Wilcox.
In the Canadian Northwest, a young woman falls in love with the mountie who has captured her father, an accused murderer.

The Danger Point (Halperin Productions/American Releasing Corp., 1922)
d: Lloyd Ingraham. 6 reels.
Carmel Myers, William P. Carleton, Vernon Steel, Joseph J. Dowling, Harry Todd, Margaret Joslin.
Alice, a city girl, marries an older man whose main interest is his oil wells. She leaves him, but returns after she survives a train wreck, convinced that the accident is a sign for her to continue loving her husband.

The Danger Rider (Universal, 1928)
d: Henry MacRae. 6 reels.
Hoot Gibson, Eugenia Gilbert, Reaves Eason, Monty Montague, King Zany, Frank Beal, Milla Davenport, Bud Osborne.
The son of a prison warden falls for a girl who directs a kind of reform school for ex-convicts. To be near her, he masquerades as one of the toughest ex-cons.

The Danger Signal (George Kleine/Kleine-Edison Feature Service, 1915)
d: Walter Edwin. 5 reels.
Arthur Hoops, Ruby Hoffman, John Davidson, Frank Belcher, Tom Walsh, Billy Wherwood, Della Connor, Florence Coventry.
A large but timid Irish-American boy rises from the ash heap of society to wealth and power by training himself to be courageous.

The Danger Signal (Columbia, 1925)
d: Erle C. Kenton. 6 reels.
Gaston Glass, Robert Gordon, Dorothy Revier, Jane Novak, Robert Edeson, Mayme Kelso, Lee Shumway, Lincoln Stedman.
Twins take disparate paths in life: One becomes a shiftless idler, the other a bright young man with a strong work ethic.

Danger Street (FBO Pictures, 1928)
d: Ralph Ince. 6 reels.
Warner Baxter, Martha Sleeper, Duke Martin, Frank Mills, Harry Tenbrook, Harry Allen Grant, Ole M. Ness, Spec O'Donnell.
Weary of his decadent life, a society man turns to a street gang, hoping he will be caught in the crossfire and killed. Instead, he meets a working girl and falls in love with her.

The Danger Trail (Selig Polyscope, 1917)
d: Frederick A. Thompson. 5 reels.

H.B. Warner, Violet Heming, W. Lawson Butt, Arthur Donaldson, Richard Thornton, Harold Howard, William Cooper, S.M. Unander, Arthur Cozine.

In the frozen North, a railroad agent meets and falls in love with a local girl, but her three brothers are unhappy with the arrangement.

Danger Within (Universal, 1918)
d: Rae Berger. 5 reels.
Zoe Rae, Charles H. Mailes, William Carroll, Winifred Greenwood, Harry Dunkinson, True Boardman.
A wealthy man's housemaid learns that her employer is the target of a plot.

The Danger Zone (Fox, 1918)
d: Frank Beal. 5 reels.
Madlaine Traverse, Thomas Holding, Fritzie Ridgeway, Edward Cecil.
After her unsavory lover rejects her, a soprano rises to operatic fame and marries a wealthy Senator. All is well until her sleazy ex-flame wants her back.

The Dangerous Age (Louis B. Mayer Productions/Associated First National, 1922)
d: John M. Stahl. 7 reels.
Lewis Stone, Cleo Madison, Edith Roberts, Ruth Clifford, Myrtle Stedman, James Morrison, Helen Lynch, Lincoln Stedman, Edward Burns, Richard Tucker.
Unhappy because his wife takes him for granted, a businessman meets a young charmer on a trip, and succumbs to her charms. He plans to go away with her and, accordingly, sends a letter to his wife telling her he will not return to her. *Big* mistake! The businessman finds that his Circe already has a fiancé whom she loves. Now it's up to the businessman to race the mail train and hope to retrieve the letter to his wife.

The Dangerous Blonde (Universal, 1924)
d: Robert F. Hill. 5 reels.
Laura LaPlante, Philo McCullough, Edward Hearn, Arthur Hoyt, Rolfe Sedan, Eve Southern, Margaret Campbell, Dick Sutherland, Frederick Cole.
A southern colonel asks his daughter to retrieve some ill-advised letters he wrote to a vamp who is now trying to blackmail him with them.

Dangerous Business (Associated First National, 1920)
d: R. William Neill. 6 reels.
Constance Talmadge, Kenneth Harlan, George Fawcett, Matilda Brundage, Jack Raymond, Florida Kingsley, Nina Cassavant.
A spoiled socialite makes a sport of falling in and out of love, while ignoring the attentions of the one man truly devoted to her.

The Dangerous Coward (Monogram Pictures/FBO of America, 1924)
d: Albert Rogell. 5 reels.
Fred Thomson, Hazel Keener, Frank Hagney, Andrew Arbuckle, David Kirby, Al Kaufman, Lillian Adrian, Jim Corey.
Out West, a boxer believes he has caused permanent injury to his ring opponent, and swears off boxing. But his opponent was only playing possum.

Dangerous Curves Ahead (Goldwyn, 1921)
d: E. Mason Hopper. 6 reels.
Helene Chadwick, Richard Dix, Maurice B. Flynn, James Neill, Edythe Chapman, Kate Lester.

At a summer resort while her husband is away on business, a young mother with two children meets her old lover, and the flame is rekindled.

Dangerous Days (Eminent Authors Pictures, Inc./Goldwyn, 1920)
d: Reginald Barker. 7 reels.
Lawson Butt, Clarissa Selwynne, Rowland Lee, Ann Forrest, Stanton Heck, H. Milton Ross, Pauline Starke, Bertram Grassby, Frank Leigh, Eddie McWade, Barbara Castleton.
A German spy plots to blow up an American munitions factory.

The Dangerous Dub (Action Pictures/Associated Exhibitors, 1926)
d: Richard Thorpe. 5 reels.
Buddy Roosevelt, Peggy Montgomery, Joseph Girard, Fanny Midgley, Al Taylor, Curley Riviere.
Out West, a cowpoke falls for a pretty girl whose stepdad is up to no good.

The Dangerous Dude (Harry J. Brown Productions/Rayart, 1926)
d: Harry J. Brown. 5 reels.
Reed Howes, Bruce Gordon, Dorothy Dwan, Billy Franey, Dave Kirby, Richard Travers.
A young man foils saboteurs out to destroy a dam, and wins the love of the dam builder's daughter.

The Dangerous Flirt (Gothic Pictures, 1924)
d: Tod Browning. 6 reels.
Evelyn Brent, Edward Earle, Sheldon Lewis, Clarissa Selwynne, Pierre Gendron.
Sheila, an innocent girl raised by a prudish maiden aunt, is fearful of her own husband's advances on their wedding night. Thinking she doesn't love him, the frustrated bridegroom goes off on a business trip to South America. But Sheila comes to her senses and follows him.

A Dangerous Game (Universal, 1922)
d: King Baggot. 5 reels.
Gladys Walton, Otto Hoffman, Spottiswoode Aitken, Rosa Gore, William Robert Daly, Kate Price, Robert Agnew, Edward Jobson, Anne Schaefer, Christine Mayo, Harry Carter.
Young Gretchen runs away from home and finds shelter with a wealthy oilman.

Dangerous Hours (Thoms H. Ince/Famous Players-Lasky, 1919)
d: Fred Niblo. 7 reels.
Lloyd Hughes, Barbara Castleton, Claire DuBrey, Jack Richardson, Walt Whitman, Lew Morrison, Gordon Mullen.
An idealistic young American falls under the influence of the Russian revolution.

Dangerous Innocence (Universal, 1925)
d: William A. Seiter. 7 reels.
Laura LaPlante, Eugene O'Brien, Jean Hersholt, Alfred Allen, Milla Davenport, Hedda Hopper, William Humphrey, Martha Mattox.
On a ship bound for India, a British girl falls for a handsome military officer who, unknown to her, was once in love with her mother.

The Dangerous Little Demon (Universal, 1922)
d: Clarence G. Badger. 5 reels.
Marie Prevost, Jack Perrin, Robert Ellis, Anderson Smith, Fontaine LaRue, Edward Martindel, Lydia Knott, Herbert

Prior.

Teddy, a flirtatious young socialite, has man trouble and winds up being arrested during a raid on a gambling den. But the man who truly loves her will bail her out.

The Dangerous Maid (Joseph M. Schenck Productions/Associated First National, 1923)
d: Victor Heerman. 8 reels.
Constance Talmadge, Conway Tearle, Morgan Wallace, Charles Gerrard, Marjorie Daw, Kate Price, Tully Marshall, Lou Morrison, Phillip dunham, Otto Matiesen, Wilson Hummel.
In 17th century England, a young woman, though engaged to be married, falls in love with a military captain.

The Dangerous Moment (Universal, 1921)
d: Marcel De Sano. 5 reels.
Carmel Myers, George Rigas, Lule Warrenton, W.T. Fellows, Billy Fay, Bonnie Hill, Herbert Heyes, Fred G. Becker, Marian Skinner, Smoke Turner.
Sylvia, a Greenwich Village waitress, is unjustly accused of murder, but she's saved from the false charges by the actions of an artist she has grown to love.

Dangerous Money (Paramount, 1924)
d: Frank Tuttle. 7 reels.
Bebe Daniels, Tom Moore, Dolores Cassinelli, Mary Foy, William Powell, Edward O'Connor, Peter Lang, Charles Slattery, Diana Kane.
Adele, a humble tenement dweller, unexpectedly inherits a valuable property and is thrust into the whirl of money and adventure. Now filled with hifalutin airs, she travels to Europe and becomes involved with an Italian gigolo. Meanwhile, back home the young man who truly loves Adele discovers that he is the rightful heir to the property Adele thinks she inherited. What now?

The Dangerous Paradise (Selznick/Select Pictures Corp., 1920)
d: William P.S. Earle. 5 reels.
Louis Huff, Harry Benham, Ida Darling, Jack Raymond, Nora Reed, Templar Saxe, William Brille, Maude Hill.
A capricious socialite hires a man to pose as her husband, then proceeds to flirt with someone else, hoping to ignite some passion.

Dangerous Pastime (Louis J. Gasnier Productions, 1922)
d: James W. Horne. 5 reels.
Lew Cody, Cleo Ridgely, Elinor Fair, Mrs. Irving Cummings.
Barry loves Celia, but she won't accept his marriage proposal because she thinks he prefers wandering to settling down. Reasoning that if he's going to have the name he may as well have the game, Barry goes off in search of adventure. Eventually he and Celia meet again.

Dangerous Paths (Berwilla Film Corp./Arrow Film Corp., 1921)
d: Duke Worne. 5 reels.
Neva Gerber, Ben Wilson, Edith Stayart, Joseph W. Girard, Henry Van Sickle, Helen Gilmore.
When a girl's stepmother tries to marry her off to a wealthy old geezer, the girl leaves town and seeks her fortune in the city.

The Dangerous Talent (American Film Co./Pathé, 1920)
d: George L. Cox. 6 reels.
Margarita Fisher, Harry Hilliard, Beatrice Van, Harvey Clark, Neil Hardin, George Periolat, Mary Talbot.
A stenographer with a talent for forging handwriting finds

that it can be both a blessing and a curse.

Dangerous to Men (Screen Classics, Inc./Metro, 1920)
d: W.C. Dowlan. 6 reels.
Viola Dana, Milton Sills, Edward Connelly, Josephine Crowell, Marian Skinner, John P. Morse, James Barrows, Mollie McConnell, Helen Raymond, Mary Beaton.
When an 18-year-old girl dresses and behaves like a child to fool her new guardian, she finds herself secretly falling in love with him.

Dangerous Toys (Bradley Feature Film Corp., 1921)
d: Samuel Bradley. 7 reels.
Frank Losee, Marion Elmore, Marguerite Clayton, William Desmond, Frances Devereaux, Lillian Greene.
After his wife walks out on him, Hugo loses all faith in womankind. He goes so far as to try to destroy the marriage of one of his own clerks. But when the husband and wife in question see that they truly belong together, Hugo is forced to rethink his own circumstances.

Dangerous Traffic (Goodwill Pictures, 1926)
w, d: Bennett Cohn. 5 reels.
Francis X. Bushman Jr., Jack Perrin, Mildred Harris, Tom London, Ethan Laidlaw, Hal Walters.
A reporter in search of a scoop infiltrates a gang of smugglers.

Dangerous Trails (Rocky Mountain Productions/Anchor Productions, 1923)
d: Alvin J. Neitz. 6 reels.
Irene Rich, Tully Marshall, Noah Beery, Allan Penrose, William Lowery, Jack Curtis, Jane Talent.
While on the trail of opium smugglers, a mountie falls for a dancehall girl who's engaged to one of the smugglers.

Dangerous Waters (Jesse D. Hampton Productions/Robertson-Cole, 1919)
d: Parke Frame, J.J. Franz. 5 reels.
William Desmond, Marguerite DeLaMotte, Arthur Carew, Beatrice LaPlante, Ida Lewis, Walter Perry, William P. DeVaull.
Several of New York's social elite participate in a "Feast of the Gods", in which everyone comes dressed as a character from Greek mythology.

Dante's Inferno (Fox, 1924)
d: Henry Otto. 6 reels.
Ralph Lewis, William Scott, Josef Swickard, Lawson Butt.
A stone-hearted businessman refuses to feel sympathy for the less fortunate. Then someone sends him a copy of Gustave Dore's classic, "Dante's Inferno", and after reading it the businessman falls asleep and has a disturbing dream which has Dante escorting him on a tour of hell.

Daphne and the Pirate (Fine Arts/Triangle, 1916)
d: William Christy Cabanne. 5 reels.
Lillian Gish, Elliott Dexter, Howard Gaye, Walter Long, Lucille Young, Richard Cummings, Jack Cosgrove, Joseph Singleton, George Pearce, W.E. Lawrence, Pearl Elmore.

A young Frenchwoman is brought to 1718 Louisiana to be married.

The Daredevil (Gail Kane Productions/Mutual, 1918)
d: Francis Grandon. 5 reels.
Gail Kane, Norman Trevor, W.W. Crimans, Roy Applegate, Duncan McRae, Henry Sedley, Corinne Uzzell, Walter Dowling, Walter Hiers, Mildred Marsh.
After her father dies in the War, a 16-year-old girl goes to

live with her uncle, who's expecting a nephew, not a niece. So she don's boy's clothes and passes herself off as "Bob." Fluent in the French language, "Bob" goes to work as a translator. While at work, she falls for her boss, reintroduces herself as a girl, and wins his love.

The Daredevil (Fox, 1920)
d: Tom Mix. 5 reels.
Tom Mix, Eva Novak, Charles K. French, L.C. Shumway, Sid Jordan, Lucille Younge, L.S. McKee, Pat Chrisman, George Hernandez, Harry Dunkinson.
An eastern ne'er-do-well is sent out West where he falls in love, catches train robbers, and foils a kidnapping.

Daredevil Kate (Fox, 1916)
d: Keenan J. Buel. 6 reels.
Virginia Pearson, Victor Sutherland, Mary Martin, Kenneth Hunter, Alex Shannon, Leighton Stark, Fred R. Stanton, Jane Lee, Katherine Lee, Minna Philips.
Two orphan sisters, separated as children, find each other years later in a western boom town.

Daredevil's Reward (Fox, 1928)
d: Eugene Forde. 5 reels.
Tom Mix, Natalie Joyce, Lawford Davidson, Billy Bletcher, harry Cording, William Welch.
Tom, a Texas Ranger, is on the trail of a gang of highwaymen. Then he falls in love with the head gangster's niece.

Daring Chances (Universal, 1924)
d: Clifford Smith. 5 reels.
Jack Hoxie, Alta Allen, Claude Payton, Jack Pratt, Catherine Wallace, Doreen Turner, Genevieve Danninger, newton Campbell, William McCall.
Out West, a rodeo rider adopts his orphaned niece.

Daring Danger (Cliff Smith Productions/Associated Photoplays, 1922)
d: Cliff Smith. 5 reels.
Pete Morrison, Esther Ralston, Billy Ryno, Lew Meehan, Bob Fleming.
Horton, a rancher, is enlisted by the federal government to crack a sinister gang of cattle rustlers.

Daring Days (Universal, 1925)
d: John B. O'Brien. 5 reels.
Josie Sedgwick, Edward Hearn, Frederick Cole, Zama Zamoria, Harry Rattenberry, Ted Oliver, Harry Todd, T.C. Jack, Ben Corbett.
Out West, a town with no women advertises for a lady mayor.

Daring Hearts (Vitagraph, 1919)
d: Henry Houry. 6 reels.
Francis X. Bushman, Beverly Bayne, L. Rogers Lytton, Karl Dane, Jean Paige, Arthur Donaldson, George Des Lyon, Charles Kent.
Just prior to World War I, an Alsatian girl is attacked by German soldiers but rescued by a visiting American. After war is declared, the American joins the French forces and comes back to the Alsatian girl, a hero.

Daring Love (Hoffman Productions/Truart film Corp., 1924)
d: Roland G. Edwards. 6 reels.
Elaine Hammerstein, Huntly Gordon, Walter Long, Gertrude Astor, Johnny Arthur, Cissy Fitzgerald, Morgan Wallace.

Stedman, an alcoholic, finds true love with a woman who helps him overcome his addiction. Later he serves honorably in World War I, marries the woman who helped him, and is elected governor. All this, while successfully repelling his first wife's efforts to win him back.

The Daring of Diana (Vitagraph, 1916)
d: S. Rankin Drew. 5 reels.
Anita Stewart, Charles Wellesley, Anders Randolf, Julia Swayne Gordon, Francis Morgan, Donald MacBride, Doc Donohue, Lou Johnson.
The publisher of a New York tabloid hires a young woman as investigative reporter, and she uncovers a sordid tale of corruption in high places.

The Daring Years (Daniel Carson Goodman Corp./Equity Pictures, 1923)
d: Kenneth Webb. 7 reels.
Mildred Harris, Charles Emmett Mack, Mary Carr, Joe King, Tyrone Power, Skeets Gallagher, Clara Bow, Jack Richardson, Joseph Depew, Helen Rowland, Sam Sidman.
Susie, a spiteful nightclub dancer, accuses an innocent man of murder.

Daring Youth (B.F. Zeidman/Principal Pictures, 1924)
d: William Beaudine. 6 reels.
Bebe Daniels, Norman Kerry, Lee Moran, Arthur Hoyt, Lillian Langdon, George Pearce.
Alita and John love each other, but she's inherited her mother's feminist ideas. She insists that she and her new husband have two breakfasts a week together, no more,and that she have complete freedom the rest of the time. This'll never work....

The Dark Angel (Goldwyn, 1925)
d: George Fitzmaurce. 8 reels.
Vilma Banky, Ronald Colman, Wyndham Standing, Frank Elliott, Charles Lane, Helen Jerome Eddy, Florence Turner.
Multiple-hanky weeper about Trent, a British military officer who is ordered into battle on the eve of his scheduled wedding. He is blinded in battle and captured by the Germans. After the war, Trent makes a quiet living writing short stories, but cannot bear to be reunited with his fiancée because of his blindness. When she comes to him, he tells her he no longer loves her. She knows better, however, and through her loving kindness they are reconciled.

A Dark Lantern (Realart Pictures Corp., 1920)
d: John S. Robertson. 6 reels.
Alice Brady, James L. Crane, Reginald Denny, Brandon Hurst, Marie Burke, David Montero, Carolyn Irwin, Roni Pursell, Russel McDermot, Virginia Huppert, Dorothy Betts.
When an Englishwoman visits the country of Argovinia, she falls in love with the Crown Prince and dares expect the best. But the Prince asks her to be his mistress, not his wife.

The Dark Mirror (Famous Players-Lasky/Paramount, 1920)
d: Charles Giblyn. 5 reels.
Dorothy Dalton, Huntley Gordon, Walter Neeland, Jessie Arnold, Lucille Carney, Pedro de Cordoba, Donald MacPherson, Bert Starkey.
A young woman has terrifying dreams, and tells her physician about them. He listens intently, then slowly realizes that the people and events she has been dreaming about really exist: They're in the news! Upon investigation, the doctor learns that his patient has an evil twin who's been committing the crimes her sister has been dreaming about.

The Dark Road (Triangle, 1917)
d: Charles Miller. 5 reels.
Dorothy Dalton, Robert McKim, Jack Livingston, Jack Gilbert, Walt Whitman, Lydia Knott.
Dark melodrama about a married woman of extraordinary beauty who, once her husband goes off to the War, entices one lover after another. One of the men turns out to be a German sympathizer who makes her his slave.

Dark Secrets (Famous Players-Lasky/Paramount, 1923)
d: Victor Fleming. 6 reels.
Dorothy Dalton, Robert Ellis, José Ruben, Ellen Cassidy, Pat Hartigan, Warren Cook, Julia Swayne Gordon.

Ruth, a New York socialite, goes to Egypt to be cured of her lameness, but finds that the doctor expects her hand in marriage as his fee.

The Dark Silence (World Film Corp., 1916)
d: Albert Capellani. 5 reels.
Clara Kimball Young, Edward T. Langford, Paul Capellani, Barbara Gilroy, Jessie Lewis.
During World War I, two men love the same Red Cross nurse.

Dark Stairways (Universal, 1924)
d: Robert F. Hill. 5 reels.
Herbert Rawlinson, Ruth Dwyer, Hayden Stevenson, Robert E. Homans, Walter Perry, Bonnie Hill, Kathleen O'Connor, Dolores Rousse, Emmett King, Lola Todd, Tom McGuire.
A man unjustly jailed for theft breaks out of prison to find and capture the real thieves.

The Dark Star (Cosmopolitan/Paramount, 1919)
d: Allan Dwan. 6 reels.
Marion Davies, Norman Kerry, Dorothy Green, Matt Moore, Ward Crane, Arthur Earle, Emil Hoch, George Cooper, Fred Hearn.
A pastor's daughter is drawn into a spy plot revolving around the theft of a priceless artifact said to have fallen from a dark star.

The Dark Swan (Warner Bros., 1924)
d: Millard Webb. 7 reels.
Marie Prevost, Helene Chadwick, Monte Blue, John Patrick, Lilyan Tashman, Vera Lewis, Carlton Miller, Mary MacLaren, Arthur Rankin.
Cornelia loves Lewis, but neither of them has a chance against the wiles of Cornelia's sister Eve, a maneating vamp who gets Lewis to marry her and almost immediately commences a series of affairs.

The Darkest Hour (Vitagraph, 1919)
d: Paul Scardon. 5 reels.
Harry T. Morey, Anna Lehr, Jean Paige, George Howard, George Majeroni, Robert Gaillard, Louis Wolheim, Herbert Pattee, Harry Hallem, Jane Jennings.
Suffering from amnesia, a wealthy New Yorker doesn't know who he is, and gets a job as a lumberjack, calling himself "John Doe."

Darkest Russia (World Film Corp., 1917)
d: Travers Vale. 5 reels.
Alice Brady, John Bowers, J. Herbert Frank, Norbert Wicki, Jack Drumier, Kate Lester, Lillian Cook, Frank De Vernon, Boris Korlin, Herbert Barrington.
In Czarist Russia, two lovers are sentenced to ten years in Siberia, but escape.

Darling Mine (Selznick, 1920)

d: Laurence Trimble. 5 reels.
Olive Thomas, Walter McGrail, Walt Whitman, Barney Sherry, Margaret McWade, Betty Schade, Richard Tucker, Colin Kenny, Andrew Arbuckle.
An Irish lass in New York finds love and a career in the theater.

The Darling of New York (Universal, 1923)
d: King Baggot. 6 reels.
Baby Peggy Montgomery, Sheldon Lewis, Frank Currier, Gladys Brockwell, Pat Hartigan, Junior Coghlan, Max Davidson, Emma Steel and Walter O'Donnell.
A five-year-old orphan, separated from her family, is cared for by gangsters.

The Darling of Paris (Fox, 1917)
d: J. Gordon Edwards. 5 reels.
Theda Bara, Glen White, Walter Law, Herbert Heyes, Carey Lee, Alice Gale, John Webb Dillon, Louis Dean.
In 19th-century Paris, a hunchback saves the life of a condemned gypsy girl.
This was the first feature-length version of the 1831 Victor Hugo novel *Notre-Dame de Paris*. In the silent era, the tale would be filmed once again, by Universal in 1923, as *The Hunchback of Notre Dame*.

D'Artagnan (New York Motion Picture Corp./Triangle, 1916)
d: Charles Swickard. 5 reels.
Orrin Johnson, Dorothy Dalton, Louise Glaum, Harvey Clark, Walt Whitman, Arthur Maude, George Fisher, Rhea Mitchell, Edward Kenny, C.N. Mortensen, J.P. Lockney, Alfred Hollingsworth.
In 17th century France, D'Artagnan, the young Gascon who has joined with the Three Musketeers, assists Queen Anne, though it almost costs him his life.

Daughter of Destiny (Petrova Picture Co./First National, 1917)
d: George Irving. 5 reels.
Olga Petrova, Thomas Holding, Anders Randolf, Robert Broderick, Henri Leone, Richard Garrick, Carl Dietz, Anita Allen, Beatrix Sherman.
During World War I, an ambassador's daughter accepts the proposal of the Crown Prince of a neutral nation... not knowing that her first husband, a German spy, is still alive.

A Daughter of France (Fox, 1918)
d: Edmund Lawrence. 5 reels.
Virginia Pearson, Hugh Thompson, Herbert Evans, George Moss, Ethel Kaufman, Anthony Merlo, Maude Hill, Nadia Gary.
A French girl must fend off amorous advances by invading German troops.

The Daughter of MacGregor (Famous Players/Paramount, 1916)
d: Sidney Olcott. 5 reels.
Valentine Grant, Sidney Mason, Arda La Croix, Helen Lindreth, Daniel Pennell, Edward Davis.
Ugly gossip drives an innocent young woman away from home.

Daughter of Mine (Goldwyn, 1919)
d: Clarence G. Badger. 5 reels.
Madge Kennedy, John Bowers, Tully Marshall, Arthur Carew, Abraham Schwartz.
A Jewish tailor in New York objects to his daughter's romance with a gentile.

A Daughter of the City (Essanay, 1915)
d: E.H. Calvert. 5 reels.
Marguerite Clayton, E.H. Calvert, John Junior, Camille D'Arcy, Florence Oberle, Betty Scott, Ernest Maupain.
A wealthy roué covets a dressmaker's daughter, though he is already married.

A Daughter of the Gods (Fox, 1916)
d: Herbert Brenon. 10 reels.
Annette Kellerman, William E. Shay, Hal De Forest, Mlle. Marcelle Hontabat, Edward Boring, Violet Horner, Jane Lee, Katharine Lee, Stuart Holmes, Ricca Allen, Henrietta Gilbert, Walter James, Milly Liston, Walter McCullough, Mark Price, Louise Rial, Barbara Castleton.
Grand-scale epic with Miss Kellerman as Anitia, a free-spirited girl who loves a prince but is captured and forced to join the sultan's harem.

A Daughter of the Law (Universal, 1921)
d: Jack Conway. 5 reels.
Carmel Myers, Jack O'Brien, Fred Kohler, Jack Walters, Dick LaReno, Charles Arling, Joe Bennett.
Nora, a police inspector's daughter, tries to dissuade her brother from his ties to the underworld.

A Daughter of the Old South (Famous Players-Lasky/Paramount, 1918)
d: Emile Chautard. 5 reels.
Pauline Frederick, Pedro De Cordoba, Vera Beresford, Rex MacDougall, Mrs. T. Randolph, Myra Brooks, J.P. Laffey.
A Creole girl is infatuated with a suave novelist, but she has a rival for his attentions.

A Daughter of the Poor (Fine Arts Film Co./Triangle, 1917)
d: Edward Dillon. 5 reels.
Bessie Love, Carmel Myers, Max Davidson, George Beranger, Carl Stockdale, Roy Stewart, Tina Rossi.
Subtly hilarious comedy that begins with all the principals leaning toward socialism and thinking the rich are evil scum. The story ends with a socialist earning a bundle on royalties from a book he has published, and his girlfriend flirting with a wealthy young man who doesn't seem so bad after all.

The Daughter of the Sea (Equitable Motion Picture Corp./World Film Corp., 1915)
d: Charles Seay. 5 reels.
Muriel Ostriche, W.H. Tooker, Catherine Calhoun, Clara Whipple, Clifford Gray, Roy Applegate, Ethel Langtry, Myrtis Coney, Eloise Clement.
 Margot, a fisherman's daughter, falls in love with a wealthy young man living across the bay. After she rescues the young man's mother from her burning boat, the lovestruck Margot is introduced into high society.

Daughter of the War—see: A Continental Girl (1915)

A Daughter of the Wolf (Famous Players-Lasky/Paramount, 1919)
d: Irvin Willat. 5 reels.
Lila Lee, Elliott Dexter, Clarence Geldart, Raymond Hatton, Richard Wayne, Minnie Provost, James Mason, Jack Herbert, Marcia Manon, James Neill, Clyde Benson, Roy Diem.
Love blossoms in the frozen land of the Northwest.

A Daughter of Two Worlds (Norma Talmadge Film Corp./First National, 1920)
d: James L. Young. 6 reels.
Norma Talmadge, Jack Crosby, Virginia Lee, Silliam Shea, Frank Sheridan, Joe Smiley, Gilbert Rooney, Charles Slattery,

E.J. Radcliffe, Winifred Harris, Millicent Martin, Ned Burton.
A girl with a shady past tries to hide by enrolling in an exclusive school under an assumed name. But to derail an outrageous miscarriage of justice, she decides to reveal what she knows, even though it means exposing her errant past.

The Daughter Pays (Selznick, 1920)
d: Robert Ellis. 5 reels.
Elaine Hammerstein, Norman Trevor, Robert Ellis, Theresa Maxwell, Bryson Russell, Dore Davidson, Evelyn Times, Augustus Fleming, Nora Cecil.
Revenge triggers a marriage when a wealthy cynic proposes to the daughter of the woman who had rejected him years earlier. Though he intends to humiliate his bride and her family, the new bridegroom instead is touched by her sincerity and openness. In time, he comes to realize that he really loves her, too.

The Daughters of Men (Lubin/General Film Co., 1914)
d: George Terwilliger. 5 reels.
Percy Winter, W.H. Turner, Gaston Bell, George Soule, Arthur Matthews, Earl Metcalfe, Ethel Clayton, Robert Dunbar, Kempton Greene, Bernard Siegel, James Daly, Lilie Leslie.
Two brothers and their cousin run a conglomerate. When labor troubles arise, love steps in and helps everyone resolve their differences.

Daughters of Pleasure (B.F. Zeidman Productions Ltd./Principal Pictures, 1924)
d: Louis Gasnier. 7 reels.
Monte Blue, Marie Prevost, Clara Bow, Edythe Champman, Wilfred Lucas.
A philanderer discovers that his young mistress and his daughter are good friends.

David Garrick (Pallas Pictures/Paramount, 1916)
d: Frank Lloyd. 5 reels.
Dustin Farnum, Winifred Kingston, Herbert Standing, Frank Bonn, Lydia Yeamans Titus, Olive White, Mary Mersch.
David Garrick, a thespian in 18th century London, falls madly in love with a young woman in the audience during his performance as Romeo.

David Harum (Famous Players/Paramount, 1915)
d: Allan Dwan. 5 reels.
William H. Crane, Kate Meeks, May Allison, Harold Lockwood, Hal Clarendon, Guy Nichols.
A country banker is a bit of a philanthropist, and a Dan Cupid as well.

Davy Crockett (Pakkas Pictures/Paramount, 1916)
d: William Desmond Taylor. 5 reels.
Dustin Farnum, Winifred Kingston, Harry De Vere, Herbert Standing, Howard Davies, Page Peters, Lydia Yeamans Titus, Ida Darling.
The famous Indian fighter loves Eleanor and she loves him, but he is so timid about declaring his love, she gives up and arranges to marry someone else. Then, on the day of the wedding, Davy kidnaps Eleanor and marries her himself.

Dawn (Pathé, 1919)
d: J. Stuart Blackton. 6 reels.
Robert Gordon, Sylvia Breamer, Harry Davenport, James Furey, Fanny Rice, Flora Finch, Gladys Valerie, Margaret Barry, Eddie Dunn, Gus Alexander, George Bunny, George Pauncefort.
Blinded in an accident, a young man finds love and marriage anyway.

The Dawn Maker (New York Motion Picture
Corp./Triangle, 1916)
d: William S. Hart. 5 reels.
William S. Hart, Blanche White, William Desmond, J. Frank
Burke, Joe Goodboy.
A noble half-breed suffers starvation during a snowstorm,
that others may live.

The Dawn of a Tomorrow (Famous Players/Paramount,
1915)
d: James Kirkwood. 5 reels.
Mary Pickford, David Powell, Forrest Robinson, Robert
Cain, Margaret Seddon, Blanche Craig, Ogden Childe.
In the London slums, a cheerful girl persuades her crooked
sweetheart to go straight.

The Dawn of a Tomorrow (Famous Players-
Lasky/Paramount, 1924)
d: George Melford. 6 reels.
Jacqueline Logan, David Torrence, Raymond Griffith,
Roland Bottomley, Harris Gordon, Guy Oliver, Tempe
Piggot, Mabel Van Buren, Marguerite Clayton, Alma
Bennett, Warren Rodgers.
Remake of the 1915 Mary Pickford vehicle about a cheerful
slum girl who brightens the lives of those around her.

The Dawn of Freedom (Vitagraph, 1916)
d: Paul Scardon, Theodore Marston. 5 reels.
Charles Richman, Arline Pretty, Billie Billings, James
Morrison, Thomas R. Mills, Edward Elkas, Joseph Kilgour,
Templar Saxe.
A wounded Revolutionary War veteran is frozen in a state of
suspended animation, then awakens in 1916 to find his
landowner descendants have been unfairly exploiting
workers since his "demise."

The Dawn of Love (Rolfe Photoplays, Inc./Metro, 1916)
d: Edwin Carewe. 5 reels.
Mabel Taliaferro, Robert W. Frazer, Leslie M. Stowe, Peter
Lang, Martin J. Faust, D.H. Turner, Frank Bates, Jack La
Mond.
A fisherman's daughter falls for the G-man who's
investigating charges that her dad is secretly a smuggler.

Dawn of Revenge (Charles E. Bartlett
Productions/Aywon, 1922)
d: Bernard Siegel. 5 reels.
Richard C. Travers, Muriel Kingston, Charles Graham,
Florence Foster, Louis Dean, May Daggert.
Bitter over losing his lady love to a rival, Ace Hall kidnaps
their infant son and raises the boy as his own. Years later,
the still-resentful Hall plots to make his revenge shockingly
complete by engineering a romance between the boy and his
own sister (they don't recognize each other, having been
apart for years) and maneuvering them into marriage. At
the wedding, however, it is revealed that the girl was
adopted... and you can just imagine Hall muttering, "Curses!
Foiled again!"

Dawn of the East (Realart Pictures/Paramount, 1921)
d: E.H. Griffith. 5 reels.
Alice Brady, Kenneth Harlan, Michio Ito, America Chedister,
Betty Carpenter, Harriet Ross, Sam Kim, Frank Honda, H.
Takemi, Patricio Reyes.
In Shanghai, a Russian countess is forced to support herself
by dancing and singing in a cabaret.

The Dawn of Understanding (Vitagraph, 1918)
d: David Smith. 5 reels.

Bessie Love, G.A. Williams, Jack Gilbert, J. Frank Glendon,
George Kunkel, Jack Abrams.
When the circus comes to town, an unhappy wife meets a
volatile acrobat who's only too happy to show her a good
time under the Big Top.

Day Dreams (Goldwyn, 1919)
d: Clarence G. Badger. 5 reels.
Madge Kennedy, John Bowers, Jere Austin, Alec B. Francis,
Grace Henderson, Marcia Harris.
A sheltered girl dreams of a white knight on a charger who
will sweep her away. When it really happens, it seems to
good to be true... and it *is*. The knight is a paid impostor, but
paid or unpaid, he falls in love with her anyway.

The Day of Faith (Goldwyn, 1923)
d: Tod Browning. 7 reels.
Eleanor Boardman, Tyrone Power, Raymond Griffith,
Wallace MacDonald, Ford Sterling, Charles conklin, Ruby
Lafayette, Jane Mercer, Edward Martindel, winter Hall,
Emmett King, Jack Curtis, Frederick Vroom, John Curry,
Henry Herbert, Myles McCarthy.
When a scion of wealth falls in love with the young woman
who runs the local mission, his father tries to sabotage their
alliance by bribing a reporter to attack the mission in print.
But even the reporter is won over to the young woman's
side, when he sees that her commitment to missionary work
is sincere.

The Day She Paid (Universal, 1919)
d: Rex Ingram. 5 reels.
Francelia Billington, Charles Clary, Harry Van Meter, Lillian
Rich, Nancy Caswell.
"Sowing one's wild oats is okay for a man, but not for a
woman!" With that thunderous edict, Warren Rogers
throws out his loving wife, who he has just learned had a
brief affair before their marriage. Rogers will regret his
attitude, however, and try to win back his wife's love.

Daybreak (Metro, 1917)
d: Albert Capellani. 5 reels.
Emily Stevens, Julian L'Estrange, Herman Lieb, Augustus
Phillips, Frank Joyner, Evelyn Brent, Joe Daley, Evelyn
Axzell.
An alcoholic businessman loses his wife, and almost his son,
because of his addiction.

Daytime Wives (R-C Pictures/Film Booking Offices of
America, 1923)
d: Emile Chautard. 7 reels.
Derelys Perdue, Wyndham Standing, Grace Darmond,
William Conklin, Edward Hearn, Katherine Lewis, Kenneth
Gibson, Christina Mott, Jack Carlyle, Craig Biddle Jr.
Adams, an architect, is married to both a jealous wife and his
job.

The Dazzling Miss Davison (Frank Powell Producing
Corp./Mutual, 1917)
d: Frank Powell. 5 reels.
Marjorie Rambeau, Fred Williams, Aubrey Beattie, Agnes
Eyre, Robert Elliott, Winifred Harris, Frank Ford, Lillian
Page, Ruth Byron, Dore Flowden, Bert Starkey, George
Paige.
Rachel Davison is an accomplished pickpocket, but on the
side of law and order.

The Dead Alive (Mutual, 1916)
d: Henry J. Vernot. 5 reels.
Marguerite Courtot, Sydney Mason, Henry W. Pemberton,

James Levering.

Miss Courtot has a double role... as Jessie, who dies in a car crash, and as her twin sister Mary, who falls in love with her newly widowed brother-in-law.

Dead Game (Universal, 1923)
d: Edward Sedgwick. 5 reels.
Hoot Gibson, Laura LaPlante, Robert McKim, Harry Carter, William Welsh, Tony West, William A. Steele.
Out West, a determined cowpoke breaks up a misalliance by abducting his girlfriend from the church where she's scheduled to marry someone else.

The Dead Line (Fox, 1920)
d: Dell Henderson. 5 reels.
George Walsh, Irene Boyle, Baby Anita Lopez, Joseph Hanaway, Al Hart, Henry Pemberton, James Milady, Gus Weinberg, G.A. Stryker, Virginia Valli, James Birdsong.
A pacifist member of a mountain clan is thought a coward by his kin.

The Dead Line (Independent Pictures/FBO of America, 1926)
d: Jack Nelson. 5 reels.
Bob Custer, Nita Cavalier, Robert McKim, Tom Bay, Marianna Moya, Billy Franey, Gino Corrado.
Out West, a cowpoke named Sonora Slim gets involved in tracking down killers and a secret mine.

Dead Man's Curve (FBO Pictures, 1928)
d: Richard Rosson. 6 reels.
Douglas Fairbanks Jr., Sally Blane, Charles Byer, Arthur Metcalfe, Kit Guard, Byron Douglas, James Mason.
Keith, a racing driver, redesigns his car and makes it a winner.

Dead Men Tell No Tales (Vitagraph, 1920)
d: Tom Terriss. 7 reels.
Catherine Calvert, Percy Marmont, Holmes E. Herbert, George von Seyffertitz, Walter James, Roy Applegate, India Wakara, Bernard Siegel.
Pirates plunder and destroy a ship carrying gold, but there's a twist: The sole surviving passenger is a man in love with the pirate's daughter.

Dead or Alive (Unity Photoplays/Arrow Film Corp., 1921)
d: Dell Henderson. 5 reels.
Jack Hoxie, Joseph Girard, Marin Sais, C. Ray Florhe, Wilbur McGaugh, Evelyn Nelson.
Out West, a sheriff is on the trail of two wanted men, each traveling under assumed names.

Dead Shot Baker (Vitagraph, 1917)
d: William Duncan. 5 reels.
William Duncan, Carol Holloway, J.W. Ryan, S.E. Jennings, R.L. Rogers, Otto Lederer, Charles Wheelock.
A dedicated sheriff heads a posse in search of outlaws who've kidnapped two girls.

The Deadlier Sex (Pathé, 1920)
d: Robert Thornby. 6 reels.
Blanche Sweet, Winter Hall, Roy Laidlaw, Mahlon Hamilton, Russell Simpson, Boris Karloff.
When a young woman inherits her father's railroad business, she decides how to deal with her principal competitor: She has him kidnapped!

Deadline at Eleven (Vitagraph, 1920)
d: George Fawcett. 5 reels.
Corinne Griffith, Frank Thomas, Webster Campbell, Alice

Calhoun, Maurice Costello, Dodson Mitchell, James Bradbury, Emily Fitzroy, Ernest Lambert.
A socialite takes a job as a newspaper's advice to the lovelorn columnist.

The Deadwood Coach (Fox, 1924)
d: Lynn Reynolds. 7 reels.
Tom Mix, George Bancroft, DeWitt Jennings, Buster Gardner, Lucien Littlefield, Jane Keckley, Doris May, Norma Wills, Frank Coffyn, Sid Jordan, Ernest Butterworth, Nora Cecil.
Out West, a gunslinger searches for the notorious bandit who killed his parents.

Dearie (Warner Bros., 1927)
d: Archie Mayo. 6 reels.
Irene Rich, William Collier Jr., Edna Murphy, Anders Randolph, Richard Tucker, Arthur Rankin, Douglas Gerrard.
A mother supports her son by appearing in night clubs under the name "Dearie."

The Death Dance (Select Pictures Corp., 1918)
d: J. Searle Dawley. 5 reels.
Alice Brady, H.E. Herbert, Mahlon Hamilton, Helene Montrose, Robert Cain, Rita Spear, Charles Slattery, Nadia Gray.
Cabaret dancers turn deadly.

The Debt (Frank Powell Producing Corp./Mutual, 1917)
d: Frank Powell. 5 reels.
Marjorie Rambeau, Henry Warwick, T. Jerome Lawlor, Paul Everton, Nadia Gary, Anne Sutherland, Agnes Eyre, Robert Elliott.
Melodramatic tale of almost unrelieved misery. A count's daughter has a father who commits suicide, an abductor who rapes her, a husband who is killed in a fight, and a mother-in-law who can't stand the sight of her.

The Debt of Honor (Fox, 1918)
d: O.A.C. Lund. 5 reels.
Peggy Hyland, Eric Mayne, Irving Cummings, Frank Goldsmith, Hazel Adams.
During World War I, a senator catches his wife having an affair with a German agent.

The Deciding Kiss (Universal, 1918)
d: Tod Browning. 5 reels.
Edith Roberts, Hal Cooley, Winifred Greenwood, Thornton Church, Lottie Kruze, Edwin Cobb.
When a wealthy New York woman adopts an orphan girl, she unknowingly creates an opponent for herself in the game of love.

Declasse (Corinne Griffith Productions/First National, 1925)
d: Robert G. Vignola. 8 reels.
Corinne Griffith, Clive Brook, Lloyd Hughes, Rockliffe Fellowes, Lilyan Tashman, Hedda Hopper, Bertram Johns, Gale Henry, Louise Fazenda, Eddie Lyons, Marc Carillo, Paul Weigel.
Lady Helen, an unhappily married British subject, falls for Ned, a visiting American, but cannot bring herself to ask for a divorce and the disgrace that comes with it. Eventually her husband initiates the divorce himself and Helen, now free to remarry, goes to America only to learn that Ned has left for Africa. Soon penniless, the expatriate lady agrees to become an art collector's mistress.

The Decoy (Mutual, 1916)

d: George W. Lederer. 5 reels.
Frances Nelson, Gladden James, Leonore Harris, Robert W. Frazer, Frank Beamish.
An orphan girl is unwittingly used as a decoy by a gang of crooks.

The Deemster (Arrow Film Corp., 1917)
d: Howell Hansel. 7 reels.
Derwent Hall Caine, Marian Swayne, Sidney Bracy, Albert Froom, K. Barnes Clarendon, Alexander Hall, James Levering, Ben Lodge, Thomas O'Malley, Lee Post, William V. Miller.
Ostracized by his community, an outcast nevertheless comes back to rescue his accusers from the plague by virtue of an antidote he alone possesses.

The Deep Purple (World Film Corp., 1915)
d: James Young. 5 reels.
Milton Sills, Clara Kimball Young, E.M. Kimball, Mary Hopkins, Crauford Kent, Walter Craven, Grace Aylesworth, Fred C. Truesdell, W.J. Ferguson.
An innocent young woman is duped into becoming a con man's accomplice.

The Deep Purple (Mayflower Photoplays/Realart, 1920)
d: R. A. Walsh. 6 reels.
Miriam Cooper, Helen Ware, Vincent Serrano, W.J. Ferguson, Stuart Sage, William B. Mack, Lincoln Plumer, Ethel Hallor, Harold Horne, Lorraine Frost, Louis Mackintosh.
Remake of 1915's *The Deep Purple*, both films based on the play of the same name by Paul Armstrong.

Deep Waters (Paramount, 1920)
d: Maurice Tourneur. 5 reels.
Broerken Christians, Barbara Bedford, Jack Gilbert, Florence Deshon, Jack McDonald, Henry Woodward, George Nichols, Lydia Yeamans Titus, Marie Van Tassell, James E. Gibson, Ruth Wing, B. Edgar Stockwell, Charles Millsfield, Siggrid McDonald.
Lust and lighthouses highlight this sea tale about divers and their wives.

Defend Yourself (W.T. Lackey Productions/Ellbee Pictures, 1925)
d: Dell Henderson. 5 reels.
Dorothy Drew, Miss DuPont, Robert Ellis, Sheldon Lewis.
To support herself and her younger brother, an orphan gets work as a masked dancer in a cabaret.

Defying Destiny (Rellimeo Film Syndicate/Selznick, 1923)
d: Louis Chaudet. 6 reels.
Monte Blue, Irene Rich, Tully Marshall, Jackie Saunders, Z. Wall Covington, Russell Simpson, James Gordon, Frona Hale, Laura Ames, George Reehm.
A man who's rescued his girlfriend from a burning bank building suffers facial scars in the fire. He goes to another city where a plastic surgeon gives him a new face and a new life.

Defying the Law (William B. Brush Productions/Gothan Productions, 1924)
d: Bertram Bracken. 5 reels.
Lew Cody, Renee Adoree, Josef Swickard, Charles "Buddy" Post, Naldo Morelli, Dick Sutherland, James B. Leon, Evelyn Adamson, Kathleen Chambers, Marguerite Kosik.
Michelo, disconsolate and bent on suicide, throws his daughter into the ocean. The girl is picked up in a fisherman's net, however, and is taken to a village to start a new life.

The Delicious Little Devil (Universal, 1919)
d: Robert Z. Leonard. 6 reels.
Mae Murray, Rudolpho De Valentina, Harry Rattenbury, Richard Cummings, Ivor McFadden, Bertram Grassby, Edward Jobson.
A tenement girl gets a job as a roadhouse dancer and falls for a wealthy customer.

Delirium — see: The Craving (1918)

Deliverance (Helen Keller Film Corp., 1919)
d: George Foster Platt. 9 reels.
Helen Keller, Anne Sullivan Macy, Etna Ross, Edythe Lyle, Roy Stewart, Betty Schade, Ann Mason, Josef de Serino, Ivan Tchkowski, Herbert Hayes, Thomas Jefferson, Jenny Lind, Joy Montana, John Cosgrove, Tula Belle, James Howarth, Henry Russell, Ardita Mellinino.
Inspirational telling of the story of Helen Keller, who lost her sight and hearing in infancy. Little Helen's education is entrusted to Anne Sullivan, who herself had been handicapped as a child. In time, and with a great deal of patience, Anne manages to instill in Helen a keen understanding of life around her. It helps that Helen is blessed with great intelligence and a receptive nature.

DeLuxe Annie (Norma Talmadge/Select Pictures, 1918)
d: Roland West. 7 reels.
Norma Talmadge, Eugene O'Brien, Frank Mills, Edna Hunter, Fred R. Stanton, Joseph Burke, Edwards Davis, Harriet Jenkins, David Burns.
Knocked unconscious by a blow to the head, a law-abiding woman awakens to become "DeLuxe Annie," a gangster's moll.

The Demi-Bride (MGM, 1926)
d: Robert Z. Leonard. 7 reels.
Carmel Myers, Lew Cody, Norma Shearer, Dorothy Sebastian, Lionel Belmore, Tenen Holtz, Nora Cecil.
In Paris, a fun-loving girl named Criquette tricks a young man into falling in love and marrying her.

The Demon (Metro, 1918)
d: George D. Baker. 5 reels.
Edith Storey, Lewis Cody, Charles Gerard, Virginia Chester, Molly McConnell, Laura Winston, Fred Malatesta, Frank Deshon, Alice Knowland, Anne Schaefer.
Sold as a slave and purchased by a kind-hearted Englishman, a young Persian princess comes to love her benefactor.

The Demon (Universal, 1926)
d: Clifford Smith. 5 reels.
Jack Hoxie, Lola Todd, William Welsh, Jere Austin, Al Jennings, Georgie Grandee, Harry Semels.
Out West, a rancher poses as an ex-convict to infiltrate a gang of smugglers.

The Demon Rider (Davis, 1926)
d: Paul Hurst. 5 reels.
Ken Maynard, Alma Rayford, Fred Burns, Tom London, James Lowe.
A rugged ranch foreman captures a mysterious outlaw and his gang. As matters play out, the foreman himself gets accused of the gang's crimes.

The Denial (MGM, 1925)
d: Hobart Henley. 5 reels.
Claire Windsor, Lucille Rickson, Robert Agnew, Emily

Fitzroy, William Haines.
A stern mother must deal with her daughter's wish to marry a young officer.

Denny From Ireland (W.H. Clifford Photoplay Co., 1918)
d: W.H. Clifford. 5 reels.
Shorty Hamilton, Ellen Terry, Florence Drew, Andrew Arbuckle, Pomeroy Cannon, Ralph Bell, Louis Morrison, U.G. Calvin.
A newlywed Irishman ships out to America to make his fortune, intending to send for his bride later. She does join him in America, after the young man has experienced numerous adventures on an Arizona ranch.

The Denver Dude (Universal, 1927)
d: Reaves Eason. 6 reels.
Hoot Gibson, Blanche Mehaffey, Glenn Tryon, Robert McKim, George Summerville, Howard Truesdell, Mathilde Brundage, Rolfe Sedan, Grace Cunard, Buck Carey, Pee Wee Holmes.
Out West, when a stagecoach is held up by robbers, all the passengers flee except for Randall, who fights it out with the bandits and drives them off. He then assumes the identity of another passenger, "The Denver Dude," because Randall has fallen in love with the picture of the pretty lady the Dude was on his way to see.

The Derelict (Fox, 1917)
d: Carl Harbaugh. 5 reels.
Stuart Holmes, Mary Martin, June Daye, Carl Eckstrom, Dan Mason, Wanda Petit, Olive Trevor.
After faking his own death to free his wife from her marriage vows, an irresponsible loner hits bottom and becomes an alcoholic drifter.

Desert Blossoms (Fox, 1921)
d: Arthur Rosson. 5 reels.
William Russell, Helen Ferguson, Wilbur Higbny, Willis Robards, Margaret Mann, Dulcie Cooper, Charles Spere, Gerald Pring.
Brent, a construction engineer, is accused of deliberately using defective materials in the building of a bridge. He's innocent, but unselfishly quits his job rather than expose the man really responsible.   It turns out to be a good move, because on his next job Brent meets the woman he wants to marry.

The Desert Bride (Columbia, 1928)
d: Walter Lang. 6 reels.
Allan Forrest, Betty Compson, Otto Matiesen, Roscoe Karns, Frank Austin.
Cloak and scimitar melodrama on the sand, with a French intelligence officer and his lady love being taken captive by Arab nationalists.

The Desert Demon (Action Pictures/Artclass Pictures, 1925)
d: Richard Thorpe. 5 reels.
Buffalo Bill Jr., Betty Morrissey, Frank Ellis, Harry Todd, Jack O'Brien, Frank Austin, Margaret Martin.
Out West, a gallant cowpoke helps a girl and her dad from losing their mine to bandits.

Desert Driven (R-C Pictures/FBO of America, 1923)
d: Val Paul. 6 reels.
Harry Carey, Marguerite Clayton, George Waggner, Charles J. LeMoyne, Alfred Allen, Camille Johnson, Dan Crimmins, Catherine Kay, Tom Lingham, Jack Carlyle, Jim Wang.
York, a rancher, shelters a fugitive wrongly accused of murder.

Desert Dust (Universal, 1927)
d: William Wyler. 5 reels.
Ted Wells, Lotus Thompson, Bruce Gordon, Jimmy Phillips, Charles "Slim" Cole, George Ovey, Dick L'Estrange.
Helen, a senator's daughter, has three prisoners paroled in her care to work on her ranch. One of the three, Frank, is actually innocent, and proves his gallantry when Helen is kidnapped, her money is stolen, and he stops the culprits. Ultimately Frank wins Helen's hand in marriage.

The Desert Flower (First National, 1925)
d: Irving Cummings. 7 reels.
Colleen Moore, Lloyd Hughes, Kate Price, Geno Corrado, Fred Warren, Frank Brownlee, Isabelle Keith, Anna May Walthall, William Norton Bailey, Monte Collins, Edna Gregory.
Out West, lovebirds Maggie and Rance each confess to a murder to clear the other. Turns out the death is ruled a suicide, and the lovers are free to marry.

Desert Gold (Zane Grey Pictures/W.W. Hodkinson, 1919)
d: T. Hayes Hunter. 5 reels.
E.K. Lincoln, Margery Wilson, Eileen Percy, W. Lawson Butt, Russell Simpson, Walter Long, Arthur Morrison, Edward Cosen, Frank Lanning, Frank Brownlee, William H. Bainbridge, Laura Winston, Mrs. Dark Cloud, Mary Jane Irving.
When an adventurer gets involved with Mexican bandits near the border, he takes refuge in a local ranch. There, he finds that the rancher's adopted daughter Nell is an American girl abandoned by her parents years before. The adventurer knows that Nell is the heir to a fabulous desert gold mine, and once the pesky bandidos are disposed of, he takes her to her claim. Can love be far behind?
First film version of the Zane Grey novel of the same name. In the silent era, it would be filmed once more, by Famous Players-Lasky in 1926.

Desert Gold (Famous Players-Lasky/Paramount, 1926)
d: George B. Seitz. 7 reels.
Robert Frazer, Neil Hamilton, Shirley Mason, Joseph Swickard, George Irving, Eddie Gribbon, William Powell, Frank Lackteen, Richard Howard, Aline Goodwin, George Rigas.
Remake of the 1919 *Desert Gold*, based on the Zane Grey novel of the same name.

Desert Greed (Goodwill Pictures, 1926)
d: Jacques Jaccard. 5 reels.
Yakima Canutt, Rose Blossom, Henry Hebert, Lucille Young.
A border deputy rescues a desperate girl who's lost her job and is being forced by her stepfather to marry for money.

Desert Love (Fox, 1920)
d: Jacques Jaccard. 5 reels.
Tom Mix, Francelia Billington, Eva Novak, Lester Cuneo, Charles K. French, Jack Curtis.
Out West, the son of a murdered lawman swears revenge on his killers.

The Desert Man (Triangle, 1917)
d: William S. Hart. 5 reels.
William S. Hart, Margery Wilson, Buster Irving, Henry Belmar, Milton Ross, Walter Whitman, Josephine Headley, Jack Livingston.
In the desert, a prospector comes upon a dying woman who begs him to care for her child.

Desert Nights (MGM, 1929)

d: William Nigh. 7 reels. (Also released in sound version.)
John Gilbert, Mary Nolan, Ernest Torrence.
Thieves kidnap the manager of an African diamond mine, but find that they must rely on their captive to help them survive the desert.

Desert of the Lost (Action Pictures/Pathé, 1927)
d: Richard Thorpe. 5 reels.
Wally Wales, Peggy Montgomery, William J. Dyer, Edward Cecil, Richard Neill, Kelly Cafford, Ray Murro, George Magrill, Charles Whitaker.
Drake, an American fugitive sought for murder but who actually killed in self defense, escapes into Mexico, with a detective in hot pursuit.

The Desert Outlaw (Fox, 1924)
d: Edmund Mortimer. 6 reels.
Buck Jones, Evelyn Brent, DeWitt Jennings, William Haynes, Claude Payton, William Gould, Bob Klein.
Halloway, a reluctant thief who steals because of need, flees to the desert to outpace the posse on his trail.

The Desert Pirate (FBO Pictures, 1927)
d: James Dugan. 5 reels.
Tom Tyler, Frankie Darro, Duane Thompson, Edward Hearne, Tom Lingham.
Out West, an ex-sheriff adopts an orphan boy, then falls in love with a girl who might just make a good mother for the lad.

The Desert Rider (MGM, 1929)
d: Nick Grinde. 6 reels.
Tim McCoy, Raquel Torres, Bert Roach, Edward Connelly, Harry Woods, Jess Cavin.
Pony express bandits seize a valuable land deed, but are foiled by a Galahad of the range.

The Desert Secret (H & B Film Co./Madoc Sales, 1924)
d: Fred Reel Jr. 5 reels.
Bill Patton, Pauline Curley.
Mining partners strike a rich vein, but would-be claim jumpers force them into a race to the land office to file their claim.

The Desert Sheik (Truart Film Corp./FBO of America, 1924)
d: Tom Terriss. 6 reels.
Wanda Hawley, Nigel Barrie, Pedro DeCordoba, Edith Craig, Arthur Cullen, Stewart Rome, Douglas Munro, Percy Standing, Cyril Smith, Hamed El Gabrey.
In Egypt, a British touring party is attacked by desert bandits.

Desert Valley (Fox, 1926)
d: Scott R. Dunlap. 5 reels.
Buck Jones, Virginia Brown Faire, Malcolm Waite, J.W. Johnston, Eugene Pallette, Charles Brinley.
Monty, an adventuresome cowboy, intervenes in the desert saga of ranchers vs. water profiteers.

A Desert Wooing (Thomas H. Ince Corp./Paramount, 1918)
d: Jerome Storm. 5 reels.
Enid Bennett, Jack Holt, Donald MacDonald, John P. Lockney, Charles Spere, Elinor Hancock.
A girl whose family needs money marries a wealthy rancher, but confides to her friends that the marriage is for convenience only, and means nothing more. To her

surprise, her new husband decides to make a real marriage out of it.

Deserted at the Altar (Phil Goldstone Productions, 1922)
d: William K. Howard, Al Kelley. 7 reels.
Tully Marshall, Bessie Love, William Scott, Barbara Tennant, Eulalie Jensen, Fred Kelsey, Frankie Lee, Wade Boteler, Les Bates, Edward McQuade, Helen Howard.
An unscrupulous householder tries to derail the marriage of his beautiful ward.

The Deserter (New York Motion Picture Corp./Triangle, 1916)
d: Scott Sidney. 5 reels.
Charles Ray, Rita Stanwood, Wedgwood Nowell, Hazel Belford, Joseph J. Dowling.
Devastated because the girl of his dreams loves another man, a soldier goes on a drunken spree and winds up being listed as a deserter. But he remains loyal to his country, and gets the chance to prove it.

The Desert's Crucible (Ben Wilson, Productions/Arrow Film Corp., 1922)
d: Roy Clements. 5 reels.
Jack Hoxie, Claude Payton, Andrée Tourneur.
Hardy, an eastern tenderfoot, tries to win a ranch girl by proving himself equal to the challenges of the West.

The Desert's Price (Fox, 1925)
d: W.S. Van Dyke. 6 reels.
Buck Jones, Florence Gilbert, Edna Marion, Ernest Butterworth, Arthur Houseman, Montague Love, Carl Stockdale, Harry Dunkinson, Henry Armetta.
Out West, a noble cattle rancher intervenes to prevent the lynching of an innocent young woman.

The Desert's Toll (MGM, 1926)
d: Clifford Smith. 6 reels.
Francis McDonald, Kathleen Key, Tom Santschi, Anna May Wong, Chief Big Tree, Lew Meehan, Guinn Williams.
Cooper, a dying miner, confides in a friend the location of his gold strike.

Desire (Metro, 1923)
d: Rowland V. Lee. 7 reels.
Marguerite De La Motte, John Bowers, Estelle Taylor, David Butler, Walter Long, Edward Connelly, Ralph Lewis, Chester conklin, Vera Lewis, Nick Cogley, Sylvia Ashton.
Melodrama that follows two former lovers as they separate and marry others not suited to them.

Desire of the Moth (Universal, 1917)
d: Rupert Julian. 5 reels.
Ruth Clifford, Monroe Salisbury, W.H. Bainbridge, Rupert Julian, Milton Brown, Al Sears.
An innocent man accused of cattle theft takes refuge in a remote mountain cabin.

The Desired Woman (Vitagraph, 1918)
d: Paul Scardon. 5 reels.
Harry Morey, Florence Deshon, Jean Paige, Charles Hutchinson, William Cameron, Eulalie Jensen, Harold Foshay, Aida Horton, Julia Swayne Gordon, Herbert Potter.
Fickleness is the downfall of a stockbroker who finds Miss Right, but vacillates and marries Miss Wrong.

The Desired Woman (Warner Bros., 1927)
d: Michael Curtiz. 7 reels.
Irene Rich, William Russell, William Collier Jr., Douglas Gerrard, Jack Ackroyd, John Miljan, Richard Tucker.

Lady Diana is desired by three British soldiers.

Desperate Courage (Action Pictures/Pathé, 1928)
d: Richard Thorpe. 5 reels.
Wally Wales, Olive Hasbrouck, Tom Bay, Lafe McKee, Fanchon Frankel, Bill Dyer, Charles Whitaker, Al Taylor, S.S. Simon.
Out West, a cowpoke rides to the rescue when villains try to steal the Halliday ranch through the use of fraudulent land deeds.

The Desperate Game (Universal, 1926)
d: Joseph Franz. 5 reels.
Pete Morrison, James Welsh, Dolores Garner, Jere Austin, J.P. Lockney, Al Richmond, Virginia Warwick, Lew Meehan, Milburn Morante, William Merrill McCormick.
Wesley, an eastern tenderfoot, gets involved in a western donnybrook over water rights.

The Desperate Hero (Selznick Pictures Corp., 1920)
d: Wesley Ruggles. 6 reels.
Owen Moore, Gloria Hope, Emmett King, Henry Miller Jr., Arthur Hoyt, Charles Arling, Nell Craig, Virginia Caldwell, Tom Ricketts.
A debt-ridden man raffles off his car to earn money to satisfy his creditors.

A Desperate Moment (Banner Productions, 1926)
d: Jack Dawn. 6 reels.
Wanda Hawley, Theodore von Eltz, Sheldon Lewis, Leo White, Dan Mason, James Neill, Bill Franey.

On the high seas, a young woman and her father are taken captive by a mutinous crew.

Desperate Trails (Universal, 1921)
d: Jack Ford. 5 reels.
Harry Carey, Irene Rich, Georgie Stone, Helen Field, Edward Coxen, Barbara LaMarr, George Siegmann, Charles E. Insley.
A lady named Lou uses her feminine wiles to trick a cowpoke into confessing to a crime her "brother" committed. What the cowpoke doesn't know is that the "brother" is really Lou's lover.

Desperate Youth (Universal, 1921)
d: Harry B. Harris. 5 reels.
Gladys Walton, J. Farrell MacDonald, Lewis Willoughby, Muriel Godfrey Turner, Hazel Howell, Harold Miller, Lucretia Harris, Jim Blackwell.
Rosemary, daughter of a murdered miner, is sent to live with a southern family, and finds love.

The Despoiler (New York Motion Picture Corp./Triangle, 1915)
d: Reginald Barker. 6 reels.
Frank Keenan, Enid Markey, Charles K. French, Roy Laidlaw, Fanny Midgley, Agnes Herring, J. Frank Burke.
In World War I, a victorious colonel takes a Balkan town, then allows his allies to unleash their men on the town's women.

Destiny (Universal, 1919)
d: Rollin Sturgeon. 6 reels.
Dorothy Phillips, William Stowell, Tom Ashton, Antrim Short, Stanhope Wheatcroft, Walt Whitman, Nanine Wright, Harry Hilliard, Allan Sears, Gertrude Astor, Edgar Sherrod.
A young man with a burning ambition to succeed leaves the farm and moves to New York, where he becomes a titan of finance. In his ruthlessness, however, he makes many enemies and even alienates his own brother and sister.

Finally, his family in ruins, the "titan of finance" is destroyed by one of his own business rivals.
At this point, the movie winks, "Just kidding." In an alternate ending, the young man stays home on the farm, becomes an engineer, and he and his family lead happy, productive lives.

Destiny; Or, the Soul of a Woman (Rolfe Photoplays, Inc./Metro, 1915)
d: Edwin Carewe. 5 reels.
Emily Stevens, George Le Guere, Walter Hitchcock, Theodore Babcock, Fred Stone, Howard Truesdell, Henry Bergman, Effingham Pinto, Del DeLois, Florence Short, Vivian Oakland, Ralph Austin, Edwin Martin.
Allegorical tale pitting the souls of a woman and her son against the Seven Deadly Sins.

Destiny's Isle (Willaim P.S. Earle Pictures/American Releasing Corp., 1922)
d: William P.S. Earle. 6 reels.
Virginia Lee, Ward Crane, Florence Billings, Arthur Housman, George Fawcett, William B. Davidson, Mario Majeroni, Ida Darling, Albert Roccardi, Pauline Dempsey.
Jilted by his sweetheart, a young man takes to sea and is shipwrecked. He is nursed back to health by Lola, an island girl with whom he falls in love.

Destiny's Toy (Famous Players/Paramount, 1916)
d: John B. O'Brien. 5 reels.
Louise Huff, John Bowers, J.W. Johnston, Harry Lee, Mary Gray, John Dillon, Hattie Forsythe, Tammany Young, Ed Sturgis, Kat Lester, Florence Johns.
After a gang of thieves bungles a job, the conscientious youngest member, Nan, cooperates with the police and the gang chieftain is sent to jail. In gratitude, the family that was targeted by the thieves takes in the "orphaned" Nan... and the paterfamilias soon recognizes a scar on her arm that proves she is his long-lost daughter.

The Destroyers (Vitagraph, 1916)
d: Ralph W. Ince. 5 reels.
Lucille Lee Stewart, Huntley Gordon, John Robertson, Richard Turner, Virginia Norden, Florence Natol, Harry Mayo.
A hermit nurses a wounded Mountie back to health.

The Destroying Angel (Thomas A. Edison, Inc., 1915)
d: Richard Ridgely. 5 reels.
Mabel Trunnelle, Marc McDermott, Walter Craven, George Wright, Fred Jones, John Sturgeon, William West.
Because all her lovers seem to die prematurely, an actress is known as "The Destroying Angel."

The Destroying Angel (Arthur F. Beck/Associated Exhibitors, 1923)
d: W.S. Van Dyke. 6 reels.
Leah Baird, John Bowers, Noah Beery, Ford Sterling, Mitchell Lewis.
Whittaker, a New Yorker, believes he has only a few months to live. As a gesture of compassion, he agrees to marry a young woman to prevent her from falling into scandal, then takes a voyage to Europe. But in Europe, Whittaker recovers his health. When he returns to New York to start a new life, he falls in love with Sara, an actress, not realizing she is the girl he unselfishly married... and she's still his wife!

Destruction (Fox, 1915)
d: Will S. Davis. 5 reels.
Theda Bara, J.A. Furey, Carleton Macy, Esther H. Hoier,

Warner Oland, J. Herbert Frank, Frank Evans, Arthur Morrison, Gaston Bell, Master Tansey, Arthur Morrison.
After a wealthy industrialist marries a scheming temptress against his son's advice, the misalliance results in spending sprees, labor strife, rape, disgrace, and attempted murder.

Detectives (MGM, 1928)
d: Chester Franklin. 7 reels.
Karl Dane, George K. Arthur, Polly Moran, Marceline Day, Tenen Holtz, Felicia Drenova, Tetsu Komai, Clinton Lyle.
Comedic tale about a hotel bellhop who outwits both a jewel thief and the house detective, to win the love of the hotel's stenographer.

Deuce Duncan (Triangle, 1918)
d: Thomas N. Heffron. 5 reels.
William Desmond, Luella Maxim, Ed Brady, George Field, William Ellingford, Joe Singleton.
A noble cowpoke rescues a barmaid from attack by a man she thought was her brother.

Deuce High (Action Pictures/Artclass Pictures, 1926)
d: Richard Thorpe. 5 reels.
Buffalo Bill Jr., Alma Rayford, Robert Walker, J.P. Lockney, Harry Lord.
Thinking he has killed a man in a fight, a cowpoke risks his life to save the ranch. After the danger has passed, he learns that his opponent was merely knocked unconscious.

The Deuce of Spades (Charles Ray Productions/Frist National Exhibitors, 1922)
d: Charles Ray. 5 reels.
Charles Ray, Marjorie Maurice, Lincoln Plumer, Phillip Dunham, Andrew Arbuckle, Dick Sutherland, Jack Richardson, J.P. Lockney, Gus Leonard, Bert Offord, William Courtwright.
A mild easterner goes West, is forced to buy a decrepit old restaurant, and against all odds turns it into a model of cleanliness and haute cuisine.

The Devil (New York Motion Picture Corp./Mutual, 1915)
d: Reginald Barker. 4 reels.
Bessie Barriscale, Arthur Maude, Rhea Mitchell, Edward Connelly, J. Barney Sherry, Clara Williams.
Melodrama shows Satan himself, escorting two adulterers to Hell.

The Devil (Associated Exhibitors/Pathé, 1921)
d: James Young. 6 reels.
George Arliss, Sylvia Breamer, Lucy cotton, Mrs. George Arliss, Edmund Lowe, Roland Bottomley.
Fantasy about an evil degenerate who tries to manipulate people's lives so as to ruin them, and about the fearsome price he pays.

The Devil at His Elbow (Popular Plays/Metro, 1916)
d: Burton L. King. 5 reels.
Clifford Bruce, Dorothy Green, J.K. Roberts, Frank McDonald, Mary Sandway, Adolphe Menjou, Edward Martindel.
An engineer turns to drink when faced with a production deadline.

The Devil Dancer (Goldwyn/United Artists, 1927)
d: Fred Niblo. 8 reels.
Gilda Gray, Clive Brook, Anna May Wong, Serge Temoff, Michael Vavitch, Sojin, Uta Mita, Ann Schaeffer, Albert Conti, Clarissa Selwynne, James Leong, Martha Mattox, William H. Tooker, Claire DuBrey, Nora Cecil, Barbara Tennant, Kalla Pasha.
In the Himalayas, a white girl is raised in the Tibetan faith.

The Devil Dodger (Triangle, 1917)
d: Cliff Smith. 5 reels.
Roy Stewart, Jack Gilbert, Carolyn Wagner, John Lince, Anna Dodge, George Willis.
Out West, a new minister tries to reform a town controlled by a saloon owner.

The Devil Horse (Hal Roach, 1926)
d: Fred Jackman. 65 minutes.
Yakima Canutt, Gladys Morrow, Roy Clements, Fred Jackson, Robert Kortman.
In the Old West, a young boy sees his family massacred by Indians, but he and his black colt escape. Years later, a new terror sweeps the tribe, centered on the fear of a black "devil horse" with an intense hatred of Indians.

The Devil-Stone (Artcraft, 1917)
d: Cecil B. DeMille. 5 reels.
Geraldine Farrar, Wallace Reid, Hobart Bosworth, Tully Marshall James Neill, Gustav Von Seyffertitz, Ernest Joy, Mabel Van Buren, Lillian Leighton, Burwell Hamrick, Horace B. Carpenter, Theodore Roberts, Raymond Hatton.
A priceless emerald brings only grief to those who possess it: a fishery owner and his unfaithful wife.

The Devil to Pay (Robert Brunton Productions/Pathé, 1920)
d: Ernest C. Warde. 6 reels.
Roy Stewart, Robert McKim, Fritzi Brunette, George Fisher, Evelyn Selbie, Joseph J. Dowling, Richard Lapan, Mark Fenton, William Marion.
Though pre-eminent in the power circles of politics and high finance, a murderer is brought to justice through the efforts of a tenacious district attorney.

The Devil Within (Fox, 1921)
d: Bernard J. Durning. 6 reels.
Dustin Farnum, Virginia Valli, Nigel DeBrulier, Bernard Durning, Jim Farley, Tom O'Brien, Bob Perry, Charles Gorman, Otto Hoffman, Kirk Incas, Evelyn Selbie.
In the South Seas, a native witch casts a curse on a rampaging sea captain.

The Devil's Apple Tree (Tiffany-Stahl Productions, 1929)
d: Elmer Clifton. 7 reels.
Dorothy Sebastian, Larry Kent, Edward Martindel, Ruth Clifford, George Cooper, Cosmo Kyrle Bellew.
Dorothy, a young woman who has become engaged by proxy to a man she has never met, travels to the tropics to meet her intended. But Dorothy falls for a colonel's dashing son instead.

The Devil's Bondswoman (Universal, 1916)
d: Lloyd Carleton. 5 reels.
Emory Johnson, Dorothy Davenport, Richard Morris, Adele Farrington, William Canfield, Miriam Shelby.
Though married, a faithless vamp works her seductive magic on other men.

The Devil's Cage (Chadwick Pictures, 1928)
d: Wilfred Noy. 6 reels.
Pauline Garon, Ruth Stonehouse, Donald Keith, Armand Kaliz, Lincoln Stedman.
In Paris, a French apache dancer falls for a visiting American artist.

The Devil's Cargo (Famous Players-Lasky/Paramount,

118

1925)
d: Victor Fleming. 8 reels.
Wallace Beery, Pauline Starke, Claire Adams, William Collier Jr., Raymond Hatton, George Cooper, Dale Fuller, Spec O'Donnell, Emmett C. King, John Webb Dillon.
John, a crusading newspaper publisher, is shanghaied onto a ship bound for the Far East, along with a gambler's daughter and several other "undesirables."

Devil's Chaplain (Trem Carr Productions/Rayart, 1929)
d: Duke Worne. 6 reels.
Cornelius Keefe, Virginia Brown Faire, Josef Swichard, Boris Karloff, Wheeler Oakman, Leland Carr, George McIntosh.
When a Balkan prince is forced to flee to the United States after a revolution in his country, a U.S. Secret Service agent is assigned to protect the prince and his betrothed, Princess Therese. Eventually the Balkan strife ends and the prince is restored to his kingdom... but without the princess, who has fallen in love with the Secret Service agent.

The Devil's Circus (MGM, 1925)
w, d: Benjamin Christensen. 7 reels.
Norma Shearer, Charles Emmett Mack, John Miljan, Carmel Myers, Claire McDowell, Yoce Coad.
Mary, a circus trapeze artist, finds that the lion tamer has fallen in love with her. His mistress resents the young aerialist, however, and weakens her trapeze equipment, causing her to fall and become seriously injured.

The Devil's Claim (Haworth Pictures/Robertson-Cole, 1920)
d: Charles Swickard. 5 reels.
Sessue Hayakawa, Rhea Mitchell, Colleen Moore, William Buckley, Sidney Payne, Joe Wray.
Devil worship drives a wedge between a novelist and Indora, the Persian girl he loves.

The Devil's Daughter (Fox, 1915)
d: Frank Powell. 5 reels.
Theda Bara, Paul Doucet. Victor Benoit, Robert Wayne, Jane Lee, Doris Haywood, Jane Miller, Elaine Evans, Edouard Durad, Clifford Bruce.
Deserted by her lover, a scorned woman vows to avenge herself by destroying other men.

Devil's Dice (Banner Productions/Sterling Pictures, 1926)
d: Tom Forman. 6 reels.
Barbara Bedford, Robet Ellis, Josef Swickard, Tom Forman, James Gordon, Jack Richardson.
In San Francisco, a gambler comes up winner in a dice game; but his adversaries are so resentful that they make his life a living hell.

The Devil's Dooryard (Ben Wilson Productions/Arrow Film Corp., 1923)
d: Lewis King. 5 reels.
William Fairbanks, Ena Gregory, Joseph Girard, Bob McKenzie, Claude Payton, Wilbur McGaugh, William White.
Out West, a loner finds a cache of stolen money and sets out to find its rightful owner. When the owner arrives, she turns out to be a beautiful young woman; and she and the loner are pursued by the thieves, who aim to retake their loot.

The Devil's Double (Triangle, 1916)
d: William S. Hart. 5 reels.
William S. Hart, Enid Markey, Robert McKim, Thomas Kurihara.
After agreeing to pose for an artist's depiction of Lucifer, a westerner finds himself attracted to the artist's wife.

The Devil's Garden (Whitman Bennett Productions/First National, 1920)
d: Kenneth Webb. 6 reels.
Lionel Barrymore, Doris Rankin, H. Cooper Cliffe, May McAvoy.
A postmaster catches his wife with her lover and kills the man, then must live with the guilt.

Devil's Island (Chadwick Pictures, 1926)
d: Frank O'Connor. 7 reels.
Pauline Frederick, Marion Nixon, George Lewis, Richard Tucker, William Dunn, Leo White, John Miljan, Harry Northrup.
Valyon, a once-respected Paris surgeon, is sentenced to seven years imprisonment on Devil's Island, the infamous penal colony.

The Devil's Masterpiece (Sanford F. Arnold, 1927)
d: John P. McCarthy. 6 reels.
Virginia Brown Faire, Gordon Brinkley, Fred Kohler.
In the Canadian Northwest, a mountie searches for his father's killers.

The Devil's Needle (Fine Arts Film Co./Triangle, 1923)
d: Chester Withey. 5 reels.
Tully Marshall, Norma Talmadge, Marguerite Marsh, F.A. Turner, Howard Gaye, John Brennan, Paul LeBlanc.
Drug addiction almost ruins the lives of an artist and his wife.

The Devil's Partner (Iroquois Productions/Independent Pictures, 1923)
d: Caryl S. Fleming. 5 reels.
Norma Shearer, Charles Delaney, Henry Sedley, Edward Roseman, Stanley Walpole.
In a Canadian village, a notorious smuggler is known as "the Devil's Partner."

The Devil's Pass Key (Universal, 1920)
w, d: Erich von Stroheim. 7 reels.
Sam DeGrasse, Una Trevelyan, Clyde Fillmore, Maude George, Mae Busch.
A Parisian wife runs up large bills, expecting her writer husband's new play to be a big success. But things don't turn out quite that way.

The Devil's Pay Day (Universal, 1917)
d: William Worthington. 5 reels.
Franklyn Farnum, Gertrude Astor, Leah Baird, Charles Perley, Countess DuCello, Seymour Hastings.
When a naïve girl marries a worthless cad, she sets off a string of tragic consequences.

The Devil's Playground (Monmouth Film Corp./State Rights, 1918)
d: Harry McRae Webster. 7 reels.
Vera Michelena, Harry Springler, Lillian Cook, George S. Trimble, William H. Tooker, Robert Cummings.
Father-and-son cabaret patrons fall for dissolute women, and come to regret it.

The Devil's Prayer-Book (George Kleine/Kleine-Edison Features, 1916)
d: Fraser Tarbutt. 5 reels.
Arthur Hoops, Alma Hanlon, Frank Belcher, Ruby Hoffman, Carlyle Fleming, Tom Coventry.
A girl who's been raised as a thief is caught during the bungled robbery of a businessman's home. When the

businessman hears her story, he comes to realize the girl is his own daughter, deserted by him when she was an infant.

The Devil's Prize (Vitagraph, 1916)
d: Marguerite Bertsch. 5 reels.
Antonio Moreno, Naomi Childers, Albert S. Howson, Clio Ayres, Mildred Platz, Templar Saxe, Lark Taylor.
When a husband and father learns that the daughter he raised is not his own, he reacts violently... but finally he mellows and realizes he loves his wife and daughter, regardless.

The Devil's Riddle (Fox, 1920)
d: Frank Beal. 5 reels.
Gladys Brockwell, William Scott, Richard Cummings, Claire McDowell, Easter Walters, Nicholas Dunaew, Kate Price, Louis Fitzroy, Chance Ward, Vera Lewis, Louis Natho.
Misunderstandings drive a wedge between an actress and a doctor who love each other.

The Devil's Saddle (Charles R. Rogers Productions/First National, 1927)
d: Albert Rogell. 6 reels.
Ken Maynard, Kathleen Collins, Francis Ford, Will Walling, Earl Metcalfe, Paul Hurst.
In the old West, a white man takes the side of the Indians when they try to fight off the white invaders of their lands.

The Devil's Skipper (Tiffany-Stahl Productions, 1928)
d: John G. Adolfi. 6 reels.
Belle Bennett, Montagu Love, Gino Corrado, Mary McAllister, Cullen Landis, G. Raymond Nye, Pat Hartigan, Adolph Millar, Caroline Snowden, Stepin Fetchit.
Off the coast of Louisiana, a slave ship trades in human cargo.
Film version of the Jack London story "Demetrios Contos."

Devil's Tower (Trem Carr Productions/Rayart, 1928)
d: J.P. McGowan. 5 reels.
Buddy Roosevelt, Frank Earle, J.P. McGowan, Thelma Parr, Art Rowlands, Tommy Bay.
Out West, an outlaw gang tries to blackmail the contractor of a new dam, claiming damage to their grazing land.

The Devil's Toy (Equitable Motion Pictures/World Film Corp., 1916)
d: Harley Knoles. 5 reels.
Adele Blood, Edwin Stevens, Montagu Love, Jack Halliday, Madge Evans, Arnold Lucy.
When an untalented painter sells his soul to the Devil, he immediately becomes talented and prosperous. But in the end, he sadly finds that Lucifer got the better of the bargain.

The Devil's Trademark (FBO Pictures, 1928)
d: Leo Meehan. 6 reels.
Belle Bennett, William V. Mong, Marian Douglas, William Blakewell, Patrick Cunning, William Desmond, Olin Francis.
Husband-and-wife thieves decide to reform their ways for the sake of their children. The husband, however, believes that thievery is an inherited trait, and that it's only a matter of time before the kids launch a criminal career. He's wrong.

The Devil's Trail (World Film Corp., 1919)
d: Stuart Paton. 5 reels.
Betty Compson, George Larkin, William Quinn, Fred M. Malatesta, Claire Du Brey, H.C. Carpenter, J.J. France, Howard Crampton, Robert Magowan.
A Canadian mountie rescues a girl from the smuggler who kidnapped her years before.

The Devil's Twin (Leo Maloney Productions/Pathé, 1927)
d: Leo Maloney. 6 reels.
Leo Maloney, Josephine Hill, Don Coleman, Albert Hart, Joseph Rickson, Tom London, Bud Osborne, Bert Apling, William Rhine.
Out West, an ex-judge runs afoul of con artists who try to swindle him with forged documents purportedly signed by his son.

The Devil's Wheel (Fox, 1918)
d: Edward Le Saint. 5 reels.
Gladys Brockwell, William Scott, Lucille Young, Bertram Grassby, T.D. Crittendon, Pietro Buzzi, Andrew Robson.
The "devil's wheel" of the title is the roulette wheel, where fortunes are made and lost, and volcanic passions aroused.

Devotion (Associated Producers, 1921)
d: Burton George. 6 reels.
Hazel Dawn, E.K. Lincoln, Violet Palmer, Renita Randolph, Bradley Barker, Henry G. Sell, Wedgewood Nowell.
Marsh, an escaped convict, turns to his now remarried ex-wife to hide him from the law.

The Diamond Bandit (Ben Wilson Productions/Arrow Film Corp., 1924)
w, d: Francis Ford. 5 reels.
Arthur George, Florence Gilbert, Frank Baker, Robert McGowan, Ashton Dearholt, Harry Dunkinson, Francis Ford.
In a South American village, the local Indians look to a masked man, Pinto Pete, to rescue them from the oppression of their cruel masters.

Diamond Handcuffs (Cosmopolitan/MGM, 1928)
d: John P. McCarthy. 7 reels.
Conrad Nagel, Gwen Lee, Eleanor Boardman, Lawrence Gray, Lena Malena.
Tale of a stolen diamond and the disasters it brings, told in three separate stories.

The Diamond Runners (Signal Film Corp./Mutual, 1916)
w, d: J.P. McGowan. 5 reels.
Helen Holmes, Paul Hurst, Thomas Lingham, Katherine Goodrich, William G. Brunton, Charles G. Wells.
A girl working with a gang of South African diamond smugglers turns against her cronies when she falls in love with the G-man investigating her crimes.

Diamonds Adrift (Vitagraph, 1921)
d: Chester Bennett. 5 reels.
Earle Williams, Beatrice Burnham, Otis Harlan, George Field, Jack Carlisle, Hector Sarno, Melbourne MacDowell.
In Mexico, an American playboy wins a Persian cat in a card game and then cavalierly gives the animal to Consuelo, a Mexican girl. Not until he returns home does he learn that the cat was wearing a priceless diamond necklace. Now it's a race against time to get back to Consuelo and the cat before anyone else finds out.

Diamonds and Pearls (World Film Corp., 1917)
d: George Archainbaud. 5 reels.
Milton Sills, Kitty Gordon, Curtis Cooksey, George MacQuarrie, Henrietta Simpson, Katherine Johnson, Ed Burns, C.W. Dungan, Francis Miller.
The social-climbing Violetta marries wealth, but finds that even her husband's fortune cannot insulate her from her gambling addiction.

Diane of the Follies   (Fine Arts Film Co./Triangle, 1916)
d: William Christy Cabanne.   5 reels.
Lillian Gish, Sam DeGrasse, Howard Gaye, Lillian Langdon, A.D. Sears, Wilbur Higby, William de Vaull, Wilhelmina Siegmann, Adele Clifton, Clara Morris, Helen Walcott.

Because he believes that people's natures can be changed by a change of environment, a wealthy sociologist marries a girl from the follies and tries to introduce her to the high-society life.

Diane of the Green Van   (Winsome Stars Corp./Robertson-Cole, 1919)
d: Wallace Worsley.   5 reels.
Alma Rubens, Nigel Barrie, Lamar Johnstone, Josephine Crowell, Harry von Meter, Wedgwood Nowell, Ed Brady, Alfred Hollingsworth, Irene Rich, Sydney Hayes.
A bored heiress tries to escape her humdrum life in a green van, not knowing that her new life will soon be anything but boring, since four men are chasing her for various reasons.

Dice of Destiny   (Pathé, 1920)
d: Henry King.   5 reels.
H.B. Warner, Lillian Rich, Howard Davis, Harvey Clark, J.P. Lockney, Claude Payton, Frederick Huntley, Rosemary Theby.
Imprisoned for a crime he did not commit, an ex-con decides to tread the straight and narrow.   He winds up as a medical assistant and, as fate would have it, is called upon to perform an appendectomy on the very detective who framed him in the first place.

The Dice Woman   (Metropolitan Pictures Corp., 1927)
d: Edward Dillon.   6 reels.
Priscilla Dean, John Bowers, Gustav von Seyffertitz, Lionel Belmore, Phillips smalley, Malcolm Denny, William Humphrey, George Kuwa.
Anita, a spoiled socialite who's lucky with dice, impulsively hops aboard a steamship bound for China.   Once there, Anita attracts the amorous attentions of a hotel owner, a potentate and a government agent.

Dick Turpin   (Fox, 1925)
d: John G. Blystone.   7 reels.
Tom Mix, Kathleen Myers, Philo McCullough, James Marcus, Lucille Hutton, Alan Hale, Bull Montana, Fay Holderness, Fred Kohler.
An English highwayman robs from the rich to give to the poor.

The Dictator   (Famous Players/Paramount, 1915)
d: Oscar Eagle.   5 reels.
John Barrymore, Ivan F. Simpson, Charlotte Ives, Robert Broderick, Thomas McGrath, Walter Craven, Harry West, Esther Lyon, Ruby Hoffman, Mario Majerino.
Through various misunderstandings and misadventures, a New York playboy ends up impersonating a Central American dictator and fighting revolutionaries in his new country.

The Dictator   (Famous Players-Lasky/Paramount, 1922)
d: James Cruze.   6 reels.
Wallace Reid, Theodore Kosloff, Lila Lee, Kalla Pasha, Sidney Bracey, Fred J. Butler, Walter Long, Alan Hale.
Remake of the 1915 *The Dictator*, based on the 1904 play of the same name by Richard Harding Davis.

Dimples   (Columbia/Metro, 1916)
d: Edgar Jones.   5 reels.

Mary Miles Minter, William Cowper, John J. Donough, Thomas J. Carrigan, Schuyler Ladd, Fred Tidmarsh, Peggy Hopkins, Charlotte Shelby, Harry Ford, William Rausher.
Money hidden in a girl's doll saves a friend on the brink of financial disaster.

Dinty   (First National, 1920)
d: Marshall Neilan, John McDermott.   6 reels.
Wesley Barry, Colleen Moore, Tom Gallery, J. Barney Sherry, Marjorie Daw, Noah Beery, Walter Chung, Pat O'Malley, Kate Price, Tom Wilson, Aaron Mitchell, Newton Hall, Yung Hipp, Hal Wilson, Anna May Wong.
Dinty's a poor Irish lad who sells newspapers in San Francisco.

Diplomacy   (Famous Players/Paramount, 1916)
d: Sidney Olcott.   5 reels.
Marie Doro, Elliott Dexter, Edith Campbell Walker, George Majeroni, Frank Losee, Russell Bassett, Ruth Rose.
Mother-and-daughter husband hunters strike it rich in Europe.

Diplomacy   (Famous Players-Lasky/Paramount, 1926)
d: Marshall Neilan.   7 reels.
Blanche Sweet, Neil Hamilton, Arlette Marchal, Matt Moore, Gustav von Seyffertitz, Earle Williams, Arthur Edmund Carew, Julia Swayne Gordon, David Mir, Charles "Buddy" Post, Mario Carillo, Sojin, Edgar Norton, Linda Landi.
Remake of the Famous Players film *Diplomacy*, first filmed in 1916.

A Diplomatic Mission   (Vitagraph, 1918)
d: Jack Conway.   5 reels.
Earle Williams, Grace Darmond, Leslie Stuart, Kathleen Kirkham, Gordon Russell.
An American soldier of fortune finds love and adventure in the South Seas.

The Discard   (Essanay, 1916)
d: Lawrence Windom.   5 reels.
Virginia Hammond, Ernest Maupain, Harry Beaumont, Betty Brown, Charles J. Stine, Patrick Calhoun, Gertrude Glover.
A girl grows up well cared for, but never knowing her own mother.   Then, after the young lady is happily married, Mama shows up... and she's a con artist.

The Discarded Woman   (Hallmark Pictures Corp., 1920)
d: Burton L. King.   6 reels.
Grace Darling, James Cooley, Madeline Clare, E.J. Radcliffe, John Nicholson, W.D. Corbett, Rod LaRocque.
Destiny brings together a cad and the woman he abused while he was drunk.

The Disciple   (New York Motion Picture Co./Triangle, 1915)
d: William S. Hart.   5 reels.
William S. Hart, Dorothy Dalton, Thelma Salter, Robert McKim, Charles K. French, Jean Hersholt, Wegewood Nowell.
A frontier preacher, his wife and daughter arrive in a new town to provide spiritual leadership.   However, the local saloon owner develops a liking for the preacher's wife, and soon the lady has a heavy decision to make.

Discontented Husbands   (Columbia, 1924)
d: Edward J. LeSaint.   6 reels.
James Kirkwood, Cleo Madison, Grace Darmond, Arthur Rankin, Vernon Steele, Carmelita Geraghty, Baby Muriel

McCormack.

Although he is married and his wife is faithful, Frazer, an inventor, starts an affair of the heart with his architect's wife. Her husband retaliates by running away with Frazer's daughter.

Discontented Wives (Herald Productions/Playgoers Pictures, 1921)
d: J.P. McGowan. 5 reels.
J.P. McGowan, Fritzi Brunette, Jean Perry, Andy Waldron.
Ruth, a New Yorker, gives up city life to marry and move with her new husband to the great outdoors in the West. But she'll have second thoughts about that.

Disraeli (United Artists, 1921)
d: Henry Kolker. 7 reels.
George Arliss, E.J. Ratcliffe, Louise Huff, Reginald Denny, Florence Arliss, Margaret Dale, Frank Losee, Henry Carvill, Grace Griswold.
Tale of the British prime minister's role in acquiring the Suez Canal for his country and his queen. Arliss would reprise his title role in the 1929 sound film *Disraeli*, for which he won an Oscar.

The District Attorney (Lubin, 1915)
d: Barry O'Neil. 5 reels.
Dorothy Bernard, George Soule Spencer, Charles Brandt, A.H. Van Buren, Walter Law, Peter Lang, Florence Williams, Rosetta Brice, Ruth Bryan, Ferdinand Tidmarsh.
A crooked contractor is able to get his son-in-law elected district attorney, but cannot persuade the honest lad to call off a grand jury investigation of the contractor's crimes.

The Dividend (New York Motion Picture Corp./Triangle, 1916)
d: Walter Edwards. 5 reels.
William H. Thompson, Charles Ray, Ethel Ullman, Margaret Thompson.
A slumlord forsakes his tenants, his employees, even his own son, to make profits.

The Divine Lady (First National/Warner Bros., 1929)
d: Frank Lloyd.   12 reels.   (Music, singing, and sound effects.)
Corinne Griffith, Victor Varconi, Marie Dressler, H.B. Warner, Ian Keith, William Conklin, Michael Vavitch, Montagu Love, Evelyn Hall.
Picturesque drama based on the story of Lord Nelson and Emma, the cook's daughter who rose to a position of great prestige as Lady Hamilton.

The Divine Sacrifice (World Film Corp., 1918)
d: George Archainbaud. 5 reels.
Kitty Gordon, Celene Johnson, Jean Angelo, Frank Goldsmith, Charles Dungan, Mildred Beckwith, Vera Beresford, Ethel Burner, Harry Fraser.
Thinking his first wife dead, a man remarries and he and his bride have a daughter. Years later, the first wife shows up alive, and must decide whether to intervene, or to sacrifice her own happiness for her husband's new family.

Divine Sinner (Trem Carr Productions/Rayart, 1928)
d: Scott Pembroke. 6 reels.
Vera Reynolds, Nigel DeBrulier, Bernard Seigel, Ernest Hilliard, John Peters, Carol Lombard, Harry Northrup, James Ford, Alphonse Martel.
In Europe, a comely forger is arrested but given a chance to escape jail by vamping the crown prince.

The Divine Woman (MGM, 1928)
d: Victor Seastrom. 8 reels.
Greta Garbo, Lars Hanson, Lowell Sherman, John Mack Brown, Polly Moran, Dorothy Cumming, Paulette Duval, Jean de Briac.
It's the rags to riches to rags story of a peasant girl who rises to wealth and fame as a stage actress, then breaks down on stage after learning her lover has walked out on her. She is disgraced and must leave her acting career. But there's a happy ending of sorts.

Divorce (Film Booking Offices of America, 1923)
d: Chester Bennett. 6 reels.
Jane Novak, John Bowers, James Corrigan, Edythe Chapman, Margaret Livingston, Freeman Wood, George McGuire, George Fisher, Philippe DeLacy.
When a young, married businessman achieves success and develops an interest in the office vamp, his wife employs a novel technique to put an end to his nonsense: She asks his boss to fire him.

Divorce and the Daughter (Thanhouser Film Corp./Pathé, 1916)
d: Frederick Sullivan. 5 reels.
Florence La Badie, Edwin Stanley, Sam Niblack, Kathryn Adams, J.H. Gilmour, Zenaide Williams, Ethelmary Oakland, Arthur Le Vien.
A happily-married man has a midlife crisis and takes up with another woman. His daughter, taking her cue from Dad, breaks off her engagement and begins an affair with a "free love" zealot. In time, both father and daughter realize their mistakes, and scramble to return to their uncomplicated lives with people who truly love them.

Divorce Coupons (Vitagraph, 1922)
d: Webster Campbell. 6 reels.
Corinne Griffith, Holmes E. Herbert, Mona Lisa, Diana Allen, Cyril Ring, Vincent Coleman.

Small town girl Linda accepts the proposal of a wealthy man she doesn't love, expecting that eventually she will divorce him and live on generous alimony payments. But after the wedding, the unthinkable happens: Linda falls in love with her husband.

The Divorce Game (World Film Corp., 1917)
d: Travers Vale. 5 reels.
Alice Brady, John Bowers, Arthur Ashley, Kate Lester, Joseph Herbert, John Drumier, Marie Lavarre.
Married, penniless aristocrats decide to divorce so that the wife can claim the large inheritance that is hers only if she is single. They plan to remarry later, but when the newly-divorced husband appears to begin an affair with an attractive mademoiselle "just to make it look good," his ex-wife decides that maybe this wasn't such a great plan after all.

A Divorce of Convenience (Selznick/Select, 1921)
d: Robert Ellis. 5 reels.
Owen Moore, Katherine Perry, George Lessey, Nita Naldi, Frank Wunderley, Dan Duffy, Charles Craig.
What's a girl to do when she finds herself saddled with two husbands, and loves neither?

The Divorce Trap (Fox, 1919)
d: Frank Beal. 5 reels.
Gladys Brockwell, Francis MacDonald, William Sheer, John Steppling, Betty Schade, William Scott, Herschel Mayall.
Bored with his marriage, an amoral banker decides to frame

his wife as an adultress, and then divorce her.

The Divorcee (Vitagraph, 1917)
d: William Wolbert. 5 reels.
Mary Anderson, Alfred Vosburgh, Pliny Goodfriend, Jean Hathaway.
Curious about Reno's lively "divorce colony," an eastern woman who's never been in love decides to visit Reno and pose as a divorcee.

The Divorcee (Metro, 1919)
d: Herbert Blaché. 5 reels.
Ethel Barrymore, E.J. Ratcliffe, H.E. Herbert, Naomi Childers, John Goldsworthy, Joseph Kilgour, Maud Turner Gordon, Harold Entwhistle, Eugene Strong, Ricca Allen.
An unhappily married woman sacrifices her own reputation to help out her foolish sister, and pays for her kind gesture when her titled husband divorces her.

The Dixie Flyer (Trem Carr Productions/Rayart, 1926)
d: Charles J. Hunt. 6 reels.
Cullen Landis, Eva Novak, Pat Harmon.
A railroad foreman falls for the company president's daughter, then together they foil a plot to oust her dad from the top job.

The Dixie Handicap (MGM, 1925)
d: Reginald Barker. 7 reels.
Lloyd Hughes, Otis Harlan, Claire Windsor, Joseph Morrison, Frank Keenan, John Sainpolis, Otto Hoffman, Edward Martindel, Ruth King, Loyal Underwood, William Quirk, James Quinn, Bert Lindley, William Orlamond, Milton Ross, J.P. Lockney.
Financially on the rocks, a former judge is rescued from a life of despair when his filly wins the big race and a purse of $50,000.

The Dixie Merchant (Fox, 1926)
d: Frank Borzage. 6 reels.
J. Farrell Macdonald, Madge Bellamy, Jack Mulhall, Claire McDowell, Harvey Clark, Edward Martindel, Evelyn Arden, Onest Conly, Paul Panzer.
A once-prosperous horse owner loses his home, his car, and his wife. Finally left with nothing but his horse, he enters her in a high-stakes race and wins the big prize.

Do and Dare (Fox, 1922)
d: Edward Sedgwick. 5 reels.
Tom Mix, Dulcie Cooper, Claire Adams, Claude Peyton, Jack Rollins, Hector Sarno, Wilbur Higby, Bob Klein, Gretchen Hartman.
An American in a South American country gets involved in a revolution, and rescues the president's daughter from rebels.

Do Your Duty (First National/Warner Bros., 1928)
d: William Beaudine. 7 reels.
Charlie Murray, Charles Delaney, Lucien Littlefield, Ed Brady, Washington Blue, Doris Dawson, Aggie Herring, George Pierce.
An honest police sergeant is framed and suffers an unjust demotion in rank, but clears his name by the final reel.

The Docks of New York (Paramount, 1928)
d: Josef von Sternberg. 8 reels.
Betty Compson, George Bancroft, Baclanova, Clyde Cook, Mitchell Lewis, Gustav von Seyffertitz, Guy Oliver, May Foster, Lillian Worth.
Roberts, an itinerant seaman, gets shore leave in New York

and meets and marries Sadie, a waterfront vamp. Next morning he will leave her, but once out to sea Roberts realizes he really loves his bride and jumps ship to return to her.

The Doctor and the Woman (Universal, 1918)
d: Lois Weber, Phillips Smalley. 6 reels.
Mildred Harris, True Boardman, Albert Roscoe, Zella Caull, Carl Miller.
When a mysterious stranger is faced with a life-or-death situation, he must acknowledge his identity as a famous, though discredited, surgeon. He comes out of seclusion and performs an operation that saves a man's life.

Doctor Jack—see: Dr. Jack (1922)

Doctor Jim—see: Dr. Jim (1921)

Doctor Neighbor (Universal, 1916)
d: Lloyd Carleton. 5 reels.
Gretchen Lederer, Hobart Bosworth, Dorothy Davenport, Emory Johnson, Charles Hickman, Adele Farrington, Margaret Whistler.
An unselfish doctor sacrifices everything, including his own life, to help others.

Dodging a Million (Goldwyn, 1918)
d: George L. Tucker. 6 reels.
Tom Moore, Armand Cortez, Mabel Normand, Rita Dane, J. Herbert Frank, John Sutherland, Shirley Aubert, Norah Sprague, Bruce Biddle.
Mabel Normand plays Arabella, a flighty heiress who quickly spends her entire inheritance on clothes, then has to scramble to avoid creditors.

Does it Pay? (Fox, 1923)
d: Charles Horan. 7 reels.
Hope Hampton, Robert T. Haines, Florence Short, Walter Petri, Peggy Shaw, Charles Wellesley, Mary Thurman, Claude Brooke, Pierre Gendron, Roland Bottomley, Bunny Grauer.
John, a successful family man, is seduced by a vamp and divorces his loving wife. He'll marry the vamp, but he'll also live to regret it.

A Dog of the Regiment (Warner Bros., 1927)
d: D. Ross Lederman. 5 reels.
Rin-Tin-Tin, Tom Gallery, John Peters, Dorothy Gulliver.
In World War I, a valiant dog rescues a pilot from an airplane wreck.

Doing Our Bit—see: Doing Their Bit (1917)

Doing Their Bit (Fox, 1917)
d: Kenean Buel. 5 reels.
Jane Lee, Katherine Lee, Franklyn Hanna, Gertrude Le Brandt, Alex Hall, Beth Ivins, Kate Lester, William Pollard, Jay Strong, Aimee Abbott, Edwin Sturgis, R.R. Neill, Jack Gilbert.
Two Irish sisters living with their American uncle foil a German spy plot.

The Dollar and the Law (Vitagraph, 1916)
d: Wilfred North. 5 reels.
Lillian Walker, Edward Elkas, Walter McGrail, Thomas R. Mills, Arnold Storrer, Josephine Earle, Victor Norman, Vera Norman, Hugh Wynn, Harry Fisher, Frank A. Vanderlip.
Newlyweds are unaware that her stingy father is actually a millionaire.

The Dollar-a-Year Man (Famous Players-

Lasky/Paramount, 1921)
d: James Cruze. 5 reels.
Roscoe "Fatty" Arbuckle, Lila Lee, Winifred Greenwood, J.M. Dumont, Edward Sutherland, Edwin Stevens, Henry Johnson.
High-society comedy about Franklin, the laundry man for a yacht club, who manages to rescue a visiting monarch from kidnappers.

Dollar Devils (Victor Schertzinger/W.W. Hodkinson, 1923)
d: Victor Schertzinger. 6 reels.
Joseph Dowling, Miles McCarthy, Cullen Landis, Lydia Knott, Neyneen Farrell.
In New England, a con man tries to get an entire town to invest in his phony scheme.

Dollar Down (Co-Artists Productions/Truart Film Corp., 1925)
d: Tod Browning. 6 reels.
Ruth Roland, Henry B. Walthall, Maym Kelso, Earl Schenck, Claire McDowell, Roscoe Karns, Jane Mercer, Lloyd Whitlock, Otis Harlan, Edward Borman.
To forestall creditors, a girl pawns a ring she hasn't yet paid for. She'll be sorry.

Dollar for Dollar (Pathé, 1920)
d: Frank Keenan. 5 reels.
Frank Keenan, Kathleen Kirkham, Kate Van Buren, Harry Van Meter, Jay Belasco, Gertrude Claire, Larry Steers, Harry Kendall.
After an unsuccessful businessman commits suicide, his widow reacts violently against his business partners.

The Dollar Mark (World Film Corp., 1914)
d: O.A.C. Lund. 5 reels.
Robert Warwick, Barbara Tennant, Eric Mayne, Edward F. Roseman, J.S. Hale, Lindsey J. Hall, Stanley Walpole, Bert Starkey, Charles B. Morgan, Sofia Blair, Nini Goodstadt.
A mine owner and his rival's sister find love while on a raft during a flood.

Dollars and Sense (Goldwyn, 1920)
d: Harry Beaumont. 5 reels.
Madge Kennedy, Kenneth Harlan, Willard Louis, Florence Deshon, Richard Tucker.
Unlucky in love and just about everything else, a girl finds the milk of human kindness runs deep, when it comes to her friends.

Dollars and the Woman (Lubin, 1916)
d: Joseph Kaufman. 6 reels.
Tom Moore, Ethel Clayton, Crauford Kent, Bartley McCullum, Herbert Fortier.
An impoverished inventor suspects his wife of infidelity.

Dollars and the Woman (Vitagraph, 1920)
d: George Terwilliger. 6 reels.
Alice Joyce, Robert Gordon, Crauford Kent, Jessie Stevens.
Second film version of Albert Payson Terhune's novel of the same name. Here, Crauford Kent plays the same supporting role he had in Lubin's 1916 version.

A Doll's House (Universal, 1917)
d: Joseph DeGrasse. 5 reels.
Dorothy Phillips, Lon Chaney, William Stowell, Sidney Dean, Miriam Shelby, Helen Wright.
In Denmark, a subservient young wife is kept in blissful ignorance by her husband.

A Doll's House (Famous Players-Lasky/Artcraft, 1918)
d: Maurice Tourneur. 5 reels.
Elsie Ferguson, H.E. Herbert, Alex K. Shannon, Ethel Grey Terry, Warren Cook, Zelda Crosby, Mrs. R.S. Anderson, Ivy Ward, Tula Belle, Douglas Redmond, Charles Crompton.
Second feature version of the Ibsen play about a young wife who discovers that her husband is selfish and domineering.

A Doll's House (United Artists, 1922)
d: Charles Bryant. 7 reels.
Alla Nazimova, Alan Hale, Wedgewood Nowell, Florence Fisher, Nigel de Brulier.
Third feature film version of Henrik Ibsen's classic novel, with the fiery Nazimova in the central role of Nora.

Domestic Meddlers (Tiffany-Stahl Productions, 1928)
d: James Flood. 6 reels.
Claire Windsor, Lawrence Gray, Roy D'Arcy.
A suave ladies' man tries to romance his partner's wife.

Domestic Relations (Preferred Pictures/Associated First National, 1922)
d: Chet Withey. 6 reels.
Katherine MacDonald, William P. Carleton, Frank Leigh, Brbara LaMarr, Gordon Mullen, George Fisher, Lloyd Whitlock.
A domestic dilemma: Should a judge mete out a harsh sentence for a convicted wife-beater and still treat his own wife with neglect?

Domestic Troubles (Warner Bros., 1928)
d: Ray Enright. 6 reels.
Clyde Cook, Arthur Rankin, Betty Blythe, Jean Lafferty, Louise Fazenda.
Twin brothers swap places—and wives.

Don Dare Devil (Universal, 1925)
d: Clifford Smith. 5 reels.
Jack Hoxie, Duke R. Lee, Cathleen Calhoun, William Welch, Thomas G. Lingham, Evelyn Sherman, William A. Steele, Cesare Gravina, Tommy Grime, Demetrius Alexis.
Jack, a rootin' tootin' cowpoke, goes south of the border and catches a killer, frees an innocent man from jail, and rescues a maiden threatened with a Fate Worse than Death. All in a day's work.

Don Desperado (Leo Maloney Productions/Pathé, 1927)
d: Leo Maloney. 6 reels.
Leo Maloney, Eugenia Gilbert, Frederick Dana, Charles Bartlett, Bud Osborne, allen Watt, Morgan Davis, Harry W. Ramsey.
Out West, a deputy sheriff has to deal with stagecoach robbers on the one side, and an angry lynch mob on the other.

Don Juan (Warner Brothers, 1926)
d: Alan Crosland. 10 reels.
John Barrymore, Mary Astor, Warner Oland, Estelle Taylor, Myrna Loy, Phyllis Haver, Willard Louis, Montague Love, Helene Costello, Myrna Loy, Jane Winton, John Roche, June Marlowe, Yvonne Day, Phillip De Lacy, John George, Helene D'Algy, Josef Swickard, Lionel Braham, Phyllis Haver, Nigel De Brulier, Hedda Hopper, Helen Lee Worthing, Emily Fitzroy, Gustav von Seyffertitz, Sheldon Lewis, Gibson Gowland, Dick Sutherland.
The first silent film to be produced with a fully synchronized Vitaphone musical score and sound effects. Energetic swashbuckler with Barrymore in full swash, and Mary Astor ravishing as his damsel in distress.

Don Juan's Three Nights   (Henry Hobart Productions/First National, 1926)
d: John Francis Dillon.   7 reels.
Lewis Stone, Shirley Mason, Malcolm McGregor, Myrtle Stedman, Betty Francisco, Kalla Pasha, Alma Bennett, Natalie Kingston, Mario Carillo, Jed Prouty, Gertrude Astor, Madeline Hurlock.
Johann, a concert pianist, has an ardent admirer in Ninette, but she's only 16. To try to discourage the girl's amorous attentions, Johann throws a boisterous party and invites Ninette, then lets her see him get drunk and disgusting. That does the trick.

Don Q, Son of Zorro   (Fairbanks/United Artists, 1925)
d: Donald Crisp.   11 reels.
Douglas Fairbanks, Mary Astor, Donald Crisp, Jack MacDonald, Warner Oland, Jean Hersholt, Lottie Pickford Forrest.
Not exactly a sequel to Fairbanks' *The Mark of Zorro* (1920), this story takes place in old Madrid rather than California. But Fairbanks' derring-do, acrobatics and sword-fighting skills are as valiant and entertaining as in the earlier movie.

Don Quickshot of the Rio Grande   (Universal, 1923)
d: George Marshall.   5 reels.
Jack Hoxie, Emmett King, Elinor Field, Fred C. Jones, William A. Steele, Bob McKenzie, Harry Woods, Hank Bell, Ben Corbett, Skeeter Bill Robbins.
Out West, an imaginative cowboy tries to emulate Don Quixote.

Don Quixote   (Fine Arts Film Co./Triangle, 1916)
d: Edward Dillon.   5 reels.
DeWolf Hopper, Fay Tincher, Max Davidson, Rhea Mitchell, Chester Mithey, Julia Faye, George Walsh, Edward Dillon, Carl Stockdale, William Brown.
A slightly unbalanced Spaniard believes himself to be a chivalrous knight, and sallies forth to battle windmills and other "villains," accompanied by his squire Sancho Panza.
Action adventure based on the famous novel by Miguel de Cervantes Saavedra.

Don't   (MGM, 1925)
d: Alf Goulding.   6 reels.
Sally O'Neil, John Patrick, Bert Roach, Ethel Wales, James Morrison, Estelle Clark, DeWitt Jennings, Johnny Fox, Dorothy Seay, Evelyn Pierce, Helen Hoge, Brinsley Shaw.
Tracey, a strong-willed flapper, rejects the arranged marriage her parents have planned for her and goes after her own choice, a pleasure-seeking lad.

Don't Call it Love   (Famous Players-Lasky/Paramount, 1924)
d: William C. DeMille.   7 reels.
Agnes Ayres, Jack Holt, Nita Naldi, Theodore Kosloff, Rod LaRocque, Robert Edeson, Julia Faye.
Rita, a tempestuous opera star, vamps a man away from his fiancée.

Don't Call Me Little Girl   (Realart Pictures, 1921)
d: Joseph Henabery.   5 reels.
Mary Miles Minter, Winifred Greenwood, Ruth Stonehouse, Jerome Patrick, Edward Flanagan, Fannie Midgley.
A maiden lady who's had the same fiancé for 12 years discovers, on her wedding day, that she isn't going to marry him, but rather another man who has adored her from afar.

Don't Change Your Husband (Famous Players-Lasky/Artcraft, 1919)
d: Cecil B. DeMille.   5 reels.
Gloria Swanson, Lew Cody, Elliott Dexter, Sylvia Ashton, Theodore Roberts, Julia Faye, James Neill.
Feeling unappreciated and underloved, Leila divorces her husband and marries a second time. She finds she's jumped out of the frying pan and into the fire.

Don't Doubt Your Husband   (Metro, 1924)
d: Harry Beaumont.   6 reels.
Viola Dana, Allan Forrest, Winifred Bryson, John Patrick, Willard Louis, Adele Watson, Robert Dunbar.
A newlywed husband is accused of infidelity, but it turns out to be a case of mistaken identity.

Don't Doubt Your Wife   (Leah Baird Productions/Associated Exhibitors, 1922)
d: James W. Horne.   5 reels.
Leah Baird, Edward Peil, Emory Johnson, Mathilde Brundage, Katherine Lewis.
After a rainstorm, Rose arrives home wearing the overcoat of Herbert, a friend who had offered it to protect her from the showers. John, her impulsive husband, immediately suspects Rose of infidelity and files for divorce. After the divorce, Herbert offers to marry her and the despairing Rose accepts; but when he learns that Rose is carrying John's child, Herbert informs the hard-headed ex, and on the wedding day John appears and begs Rose to take him back.

Don't Ever Marry   (Marshall Neilan Productions/First National, 1920)
d: Marshall Neilan, Victor Heerman.   6 reels.
Matt Moore, Marjorie Daw, Tom Guise, Adele Farrington, Thomas Jefferson Jr., Mayme Kelso, Betty Bouton, Christine Mayo, Herbert Standing, David Butler, Wesley Barry.
Lovers must marry in secret because the girl's eccentric father has threatened to kill any man who touches his daughter. But after several escapades, the couple finds bliss when her Dad meets a dazzling female and falls head over heels, himself.

Don't Get Personal   (Universal, 1922)
d: Clarence G. Badger.   5 reels.
Marie Prevost, George Nichols, Daisy Robinson, Roy Atwell, T. Roy Barnes, G. Del Lorice, Sadie Gordon, Alida B. Jones, Ralph McCullouch.
Comedy about Pat, an ex-chorus girl who intervenes when the son of a friend is being vamped away from his fiancée. Her involvement raises all sorts of suspicions, but in the end Pat is not only exonerated, but wins a husband for herself.

Don't Marry   (Fox, 1928)
d: James Tinling.   6 reels.
Lois Moran, Neil Hamilton, Henry Kolker, Claire McDowell, Lydia Dickson.
Priscilla, a jazz-age flapper, masquerades as her own sedate cousin to win the heart of an old-fashioned guy she fancies.

Don't Marry for Money   (Weber & North Productions, 1923)
d: Clarence L. Brown.   6 reels.
House Peters, Rubye DeRemer, Aileen Pringle, Cyril Chadwick, Christine Mayo, Wedgewood Nowell, George Nichols, Hank Mann, Charles Wellesley.
Marion, married to a millionaire, finds him boring and begins flirting with a gigolo.

Don't Neglect Your Wife   (Goldwyn, 1921)
d: Wallace Worsley.   6 reels.

Mabel Julienne Scott, Lewis S. Stone, Charles Clary, Kate Lester, Arthur Hoyt, Josephine Crowell, Darrel Foss, Norma Gordon, Richard Tucker, R.D. MacLean.

Nineteenth century drama about a society wife who feels neglected by her husband. She is courted by a young writer, but as their love cannot be, they part and he drifts into alcoholism. Finally the wife obtains a divorce and goes to the writer to save him from despair.

Don't Shoot (Universal, 1922)
d: Jack Conway. 6 reels.
Herbert Rawlinson, Edna Murphy, William Dyer, Harvey Clarke, Wade Boteler, Margaret Campbell, George Fisher, Tiny Sanford, Duke Lee, Mrs. Bertram Grassby, Fred Kelsey, L.J. O'Connor.
Velma, forced to marry a man she does not love, tries to reform him from his criminal ways.
Remake, by director Jack Conway, of his 1917 film *Come Through*.

Don't Tell Everything (Famous Players-Lasky/Paramount, 1921)
d: Sam Wood. 5 reels.
Wallace Reid, Gloria Swanson, Elliott Dexter, Dorothy Cumming, Genevieve Blinn, Baby Gloria Wood, DeBriac Twins.
Romantic comedy-drama about a girl who's loved by both a polo player and his best friend.

Don't Tell the Wife (Warner Bros., 1927)
d: Paul Stein. 7 reels.
Irene Rich, Huntly Gordon, Lilyan Tashman, Otis Harlan, William Demarest.
In Paris, a young wife rightly suspects her husband of dallying with an adventuress.

Don't Write Letters (S-L Pictures/Metro, 1922)
d: George D. Baker. 5 reels.
Gareth Hughes, Bartine Burkett, Herbert Hayes, Harry Lorraine, Margaret Mann, Lois Lee, Victor Potel.
During World War I, an undersized doughboy writes love letters to a lady who likes her men big and strong.

Doomsday (Famous Players-Lasky/Paramount, 1928)
d: Rowland Lee. 6 reels.
Gary Cooper, Florence Vidor, Lawrence Grant, Charles Stevenson.
Mary, who has lived in near poverty, accepts the marriage proposal of wealthy Percival although she really loves a poor farmer.

The Door Between (Universal, 1917)
d: Rupert Julian. 5 reels.
Monroe Salisbury, Ruth Clifford, George McDaniels, W.H. Bainbridge.
Tragedy intrudes on the uneasy marriage between a singer and an unprincipled drunk.

Dorian's Divorce (Rolfe Photoplays, Inc./Metro, 1916)
d: O.A.C. Lund. 5 reels.
Lionel Barrymore, Grace Valentine, Edgar L. Davenport, William Davidson, L. Robert Wolheim, Lindsay J. Hall, Buckley Starkey, John Leach, Jerome Wilson.
Carefree newlyweds decide to divorce, then face a real hardship that proves to them that they really love each other.

The Dormant Power (World Film Corp., 1917)
d: Travers Vale. 5 reels.
Ethel Clayton, Joseph Herbert, Edward T. Langford, Montagu Love, Muriel Ostriche, George Morgan.
Left alone after her father's death, a distraught girl unwisely marries a cad.

Dorothy Vernon of Haddon Hall (Pickford/United Artists, 1924)
d: Marshall Neilan. 10 reels.
Mary Pickford, Allan Forrest, Estelle Taylor, Clare Eames, Marc MacDermott, Wilfred Lucas, Courtenay Foote, Lottie Pickford Forrest.
In 16th century England, a young aristocratic woman is torn between her love for her man and her loyalty to the Queen.

Double Action Daniels (Action Pictures/Artclass Pictures, 1925)
d: Richard Thorpe. 5 reels.
Buffalo Bill Jr., Lorna Palmer, Edna Hall, J.P. Lockney, Edward Piel, D'Arcy Corrigan, N.E. Hendrix, Lafe McKee, Harry Belmore, Clyde McClary, William Ryno, Cy Belmore.
Rapid-fire western action with young Bill Daniels falling for Ruth, the leading lady in a traveling show. When the show closes, Bill gets her a job on his father's ranch, but the old man fires her when he learns she's an actress. Then a con man talks Old Bill into signing over his ranch and, before you know it, everyone is homeless. Young Bill beats up the con man and is thrown in jail. Meanwhile, back at the ranch... Ruth learns that there is a hidden deed which transfers the land rights to her. Retrieving it, she is assaulted by the con man. But Young Bill, who's just broken out of jail, rides to the rescue and everything ends happily.

Double Crossed (Famous Players/Paramount, 1917)
d: Robert G. Vignola. 5 reels.
Pauline Frederick, Crauford Kent, Riley Hatch, Clarence Handyside, Harris Gordon, Joseph Smiley.
A double crosser is double crossed when his "pigeon's" wife overhears his plans.

Double Daring (Action Pictures/Artclass Pictures, 1926)
d: Richard Thorpe. 5 reels.
Wally Wales, J.P. Lockney, Jean Arthur, Hank Bell, Charles Whittaker, Toby Wing, N.E. Hendrix.
Out West, a cowpoke named Meeker intervenes when highwaymen threaten to loot the local bank and all its depositors. He wins the banker's daughter, too.

Double Dealing (Universal, 1923)
d: Henry Lehrman. 5 reels.
Hoot Gibson, Helen Ferguson, Eddie Gribbon, Betty Francisco, Gertrude Claire, Otto Hoffman, Frank Hayes, Jack Dillon.
Western comedy about Ben, a man who is duped into buying "worthless" land and sees it increase in value, much to the chagrin of the con man who sold it to him.

A Double Dyed Deceiver (Goldwyn, 1920)
d: Al Green. 5 reels.
Jack Pickford, Marie Dunn, James Neill, Edythe Chapman, Sydney ainsworth, Manuel R. Ojeda.
South of the border, an outlaw impersonates the missing heir of a wealthy family with the intention of stealing their jewels. But he falls in love with the family's niece, and has a change of heart.

The Double O (Ben Wilson Productions/Arrow Film Corp., 1921)
w, d: Roy Clements. 5 reels.
Jack Hoxie, Steve Clemento, William Lester, Ed La Niece,

Evelyn Nelson.
In a ranch near the Mexican border, love blossoms between the foreman and the ranch's lady owner.

The Double Room Mystery (Universal, 1917)
d: Hobart Henley. 5 reels.
Edwin H. Brady, Hayward Mack, Gertrude Selby, Edward Hearn, Ernest Shields.
A shyster lawyer appropriates stolen gems and frames a housemaid for the theft.

Double Speed (Famous Players-Lasky/Paramount, 1920)
d: Sam Wood. 5 reels.
Wallace Reid, Wanda Hawley, Theodore Roberts, Tully Marshall, Lucien Littlefield, Guy Oliver, Maxine Elliott Hicks.

Robbed of all his possessions during a New York-to-L.A. auto trip, a millionaire arrives in Los Angeles looking like a bum.

The Double Standard (Universal, 1917)
d: Phillips Smalley. 5 reels.
Roy Stewart, Hazel Page, Frank Brownlee, Clarissa Selwyn, Joseph Girard, Frank Elliott, Irene Aldwyn, Maxfield Stanley.
A newly-elected judge swears to uphold the law, as usual, but some of his friends think His Honor is being too strict when it comes to laws concerning saloons and cabarets.

Double Trouble (Fine Arts film Co./Triangle, 1915)
d: William Christy Cabanne. 5 reels.
Douglas Fairbanks, Richard cummings, Olga Grey, Margery Wilson, Gladys Brockwell, Monroe Salisbury, W.E. Lowery, Tom Kennedy, Kate Toncray, Lillian Langdon.
After five years in a coma, a young banker awakens with an entirely different personality.

Doubling for Romeo (Goldwyn, 1922)
d: Clarence Badger. 6 reels.
Will Rogers, Sylvia Breamer, Raymond Hatton, Sydney Ainsworth, Al Hart, John Cossar, C.E. Thurston, Cordelia Callahan, Roland Rushton, Jimmy Rogers, William Orlamond.
Western comedy about Sam, an Arizona cowpoke who's in love with Lulu, a lady with many admirers. Haughty Lulu tells Sam that she'll have nothing to do with him until he can love her as Romeo loved Juliet. So he acquires a copy of the Shakespeare classic, reads it, and readdresses the task at hand. He comes on like Romeo, Arizona style, and wins the lady.

Doubling With Danger (Richard Talmadge Productions/FBO of America, 1926)
d: Scott R. Dunlap. 5 reels.
Richard Talmadge, Ena Gregory, Joseph Girared, Fred Kelsey, Harry Dunkinson, Douglas Gerrard, Paul Dennis, Herbert Prior, Joseph Harrington.
Mystery surrounding the whereabouts of plans for a secret airplane after its inventor is murdered.

The Dove (United Artists, 1928)
d: Roland West. 9 reels.
Gilbert Roland, Norma Talmadge, Noah Beery, Eddie Borden, Harry Myers, Michael Vavitch, Brinsley Shaw, Kalla Pasha, Charles Darvas, Michael Dark, Walter Daniels.
A dance-hall girl is coveted by a ruthless aristocrat, but she loves another.

The Down Grade (Gotham Productions/Lumas Film Corp., 1927)
d: Charles Hutchison. 5 reels.
William Fairbanks, Alice Calhoun, Charles K. French, Big Boy Williams, Jimmy Aubrey.
Aided by his girlfriend, a young man foils a gang of train robbers.

Down Home (Willat Productions, Inc./W.W. Hodkinson, 1920)
d: Irvin V. Willat. 7 reels.
Leatrice Joy, James Barrows, Edward Hearn, Aggie Herring, Edward Nolan, Robert Daly, Sidney a. Franklin, Bert Hadley, Frank Braidwood, Robert Chandler, Nelson McDowell, Florence Gilbert, J.P. Lockney, William Sloane, Helen Gilmore, Willis Robards.
A girl who plays the piano in a roadhouse comes into a surprise inheritance.

Down on the Farm (Mack Sennett/United Artists, 1920)
d: Mack Sennett. 5 reels.
Louise Fazenda, Bert Roach, James Finlayson, Harry Gibbon, Ben Turpin, Marie Prevost, Billy Armstrong, Teddy the dog.
A madcap girl is urged by her father to settle down and marry his solid, dependable banker friend. But she prefers her local sweetheart.

Down the Stretch (Universal, 1927)
d: King Baggot. 7 reels.
Robert Agnew, Marian Nixon, Virginia True Boardman, Otis Harlan, Lincoln Plummer, Jack Daugherty, Ward Crane, Ben Hall, Ena Gregory.
Though weakened through malnutrition to "make the weight," a jockey rides his mount to victory.

Down to Earth (Fairbanks/Artcraft, 1917)
d: John Emerson. 5 reels.
Douglas Fairbanks, Eileen Percy, Gustave von Seyffertitz, Charles McHugh, Charles Gerrard, William Keith, Ruth Allen, Fred Goodwins, Florence Mayon, Herbert Standing.
A game hunter is in love with a socialite, but she wants nothing to do with him. When the two are shipwrecked on a desert island, she does learn to love him. Then she discovers that the "island" is merely an uninhabited area in Florida, not far from where she lives. Indignant, she returns to her socialite friends, but finds that the love she knew with the hunter is real.

Down to the Sea in Ships (Whaling Film Corporation/W.W. Hodkinson, 1922)
d: Elmer Clifton. 12 reels.
Raymond McKee, William Walcott, William Cavanaugh, Leigh R. Smith, Elizabeth Foley, Thomas White, Juliette Courtot, Clarice Vance, Curtis Pierce, Ada Laycock, Marguerite Courtot, Clara Bow, James Turfler, Pat Hartigan, Raymond McKee.
Adventures aboard a whaling ship, but with a romantic twist. Patience, a Quaker girl, loves Allan; but her father has decreed that Patience must marry only a man who is both Quaker and whaleman, and Allan is neither. Allan's response is to convert to the Quaker faith and sign aboard a whaling ship, where he earns distinction as a capable seaman. *Down to the Sea in Ships* is generally remembered today as Clara Bow's first film. Only sixteen, she plays the role of an effervescent, life-affirming young girl. Though her role was small, her ebullient performance resonated strongly with an audience on the threshhold of the Flapper Age.

Down Upon the Suwanee River (Royal Palm Productions,

1925)
d: Lem F. Kennedy. 6 reels.
Charles Emmett Mack, Mary Thurman, Arthur Donaldson, Wally Merrill, Walter Lewis, Blanch Davenport, Charles Shannon.
Bill, an atheist, signs on as deckhand on a ship about to take a world tour. After many adventures, he returns home a reformed man and a true believer.

Dr. Jack (Pathé, 1922)
d: Fred Newmeyer. 6 reels.
Harold Lloyd, Mildred Davis, John T. Prince, Eric Mayne, C. Norman Hammond, Mickey Daniels.
A small-town doctor dispenses common sense as readily as he does pills.

Dr. Jekyll and Mr. Hyde (Famous Players-Lasky/Paramount, 1920)
d: John S. Robertson. 7 reels.
John Barrymore, Nita Naldi, Brandon Hurst, Martha Mansfield, Louis Wolheim, Charles Lane, J. Malcolm Dunn, Cecil Clovelly, George Stevens, Louis Wolheim.
Feature-length version of the famous Robert Louis Stevenson story in which a scientist accidentally invents a formula that releases the dark sides of the human personality. There were at least five versions of the story filmed in the silent era, beginning with Selig Polyscope's in 1908 and Thanhouser's in 1912, but those were one-reelers. The Paramount version with Barrymore was the first feature-length *Dr. Jekyll and Mr. Hyde*. In the sound era, the story has been filmed several times, including a number of spoofs.

Dr. Jekyll and Mr. Hyde (Pioneer, 1920)
d: Charles J. Hayden. 5 reels.
Sheldon Lewis, Alexander Shannon, Dora Mills Adams, Gladys Field, Harold Forshay, Leslie Austin.
Second feature-length film based on the Robert Louis Stevenson classic, released only one month after the Famous Players-Lasky version.

Dr. Jim (Universal, 1921)
d: William Worthington. 5 reels.
Frank Mayo, Claire Windsor, Oliver Cross, Stanhope Wheatcroft, Robert Anderson, Herbert Heyes, Gordon Sackville.
Helen, the wife of a dedicated surgeon, begins to resent his devotion to his work.

Dr. Rameau (Fox, 1915)
d: Will S. Davis. 5 reels.
Frederick Perry, Stuart Holmes, George Alison, Dorothy Bernard, Jean Sothern, Edith Hallor, Bertha Brundage, Mayme Kelso, Graham Velsey, Thomas Carnahan Jr.
Buffeted by outrageous fortune, an atheist finally prays that his beloved daughter survives a serious illness.

Draft 258 (Metro, 1917)
d: William Christy Cabanne. 7 reels.
Mabel Taliafero, Walter Miller, Earl Brunswick, Eugene Borden, Sue Balfour, William H. Tooker, Camilla Dalberg, Baby Ivy Ward, Sidney D'Albrook, Robert Anderson.
During World War I, when draft number 258 is called and the young man refuses to report to his draftboard, his patriotic sister offers to go in his place.

Drag Harlan (Fox, 1920)
d: J. Gordon Edwards. 6 reels.
William Farnum, Jackie Saunders, Arthur Millett, G.

Raymond Nye, Herschel Mayall, Frank Thurwald, Kewpie Morgan, Al Fremont, Erle Crane.
A western avenger searches for the killer of a mine owner.

The Dragnet (Paramount, 1928)
d: Josef von Sternberg. 8 reels.
George Bancroft, Evelyn Brent, William Powell, Fred Kohler, Leslie Fenton, Francis McDonald.
Nolan, a tough police detective, resigns in despair after he accidentally shoots and kills his partner in a gang shoot-out. But Nolan will learn that the deadly bullet was fired not by him, but by the gang's leader.

The Dragon (Equitable Motion Pictures Corp./World Film Corp., 1916)
d: Harry Pollard. 5 reels.
Margarita Fischer, Katherine Calhoun, Bennett Southard, Joseph Harris, Harry Leighton, Thomas J. McGrane, Sheridan Block.
Whimsical drama about a convent girl who comes home to find her family home in a state of chaos. With innocence and love, she goes about setting everything right.

The Dragon Horse—see: The Silk Bouquet (1926)

The Dragon Painter (Haworth Pictures Corp./Robertson-Cole, 1919)
d: William Worthington. 5 reels.
Sessue Hayakawa, Toyo Fujita, Edward Peil, Tsuru Aoki.
An eccentric Japanese painter searches for a fantastic dragon princess.

The Dramatic Life of Abraham Lincoln—see: Abraham Lincoln (1924)

The Dream Cheater (Robert Brunton Productions/W.W. Hodkinson, 1920)
d: Ernest C. Warde. 5 reels.
J. Warren Kerrigan, Wedgewood Nowell, Alice Wilson, Joseph J. Dowling, Thomas H. Guise, Fritzi Brunette, Aggie Herring, Sam Sothern.
Like Aladdin finding a lamp, a penniless writer finds a magic skin that grants its owners wishes. But those wishes come with a price attached.

The Dream Doll (Essanay, 1917)
d: Howard S. Moss. 5 reels.
Marguerite Clayton, John Cossar, Rod LaRocque, Bobby Bolder, Ernest Maupin.
In this fantasy, a chemist discovers a formula that brings dolls to life.

The Dream Girl (Lasky Feature Plays/Paramount, 1916)
d: Cecil B. DeMille. 5 reels.
Mae Murray, Theodore Roberts, Charles West, James Neill, Earle Foxe, Mary Mersch.
A girl imagines she has met her Sir Galahad in the boy next door.

The Dream Lady (Universal, 1918)
d: Elsie Jane Wilson. 5 reels.
Carmel Myers, Thomas Holding, Kathleen Emerson, Harry Von Meter, Philo McCullough, Elizabeth Janes.
Dreams come true, as a young fortune teller spins her magic.

The Dream Melody (Excellent Pictures, 1929)
d: Burton King. 6 reels.
John Roche, Mabel Julienne Scott, Rosemary Theby, Robert Walker, Adabelle Driver, Adolph Faylor, Elinor Leslie.
Richard, a struggling composer, writes a love song that

DR. JEKYLL AND MR. HYDE (1920). John Barrymore, as the depraved Mr. Hyde, paws a comely wench (actress uncredited, alas) in Hyde's favorite hangout, the local opium den.

* * * * *

makes him famous—but not rich, since he's under contract to a cabaret that reaps the earnings and pays him a salary. But with the help of his sweetheart, Mary Talbot, Richard launches his own career and looks forward to a bountiful future.

Dream of Love (MGM, 1928)
d: Fred Niblo. 6 reels.
Joan Crawford, Aileen Pringle, Nils Asther, Warner Oland, Carmel Myers, Harry Reinhardt, Alphonse Martell, Harry Myers, Fletcher Norton.
Adrienne, a gypsy girl, falls in love with a prince and helps him secure his throne from a usurper.

A Dream or Two Ago (American Film Co./Mutual, 1916)
d: James Kirkwood. 5 reels.
Mary Miles Minter, Dodo Newton, Lizette Thorne, Clarence Burton, John Gough, Orral Humphrey, Gertrude Le Brandt, William Carroll.
Millicent lives as a pickpocket by day, and cabaret dancer by night—but there's a lot more to this girl than meets the eye.

Dream Street (Griffith/United Artists, 1921)
d: D.W. Griffith. 9 reels.
Carol Dempster, Ralph Graves, Charles Emmet Mack, Tyrone Power, Morgan Wallace, Edward Peil.
Allegory pitting Good versus Evil, centered in the story of a London dance-hall girl who bewitches three men.

Dreams of Monte Carlo—see: Monte Carlo

Dress Parade (DeMille Pictures/Pathé, 1927)
d: Donald Crisp. 7 reels.
William Boyd, Bessie Love, Hugh Allan, Walter Tennyson, Maurice Ryan, Louis Natheaux, Clarence Geldert.
Vic, an amateur boxing champion, falls for Janet, the daughter of the West Point commandant. Pulling a few strings, he wangles an appointment to the academy, intent on wooing Janet. But life in the academy proves to be tougher than a mere game of skirt-chasing.

Dressed to Kill (Fox, 1928)
d: Irving Cummings. 7 reels.
Edmund Lowe, Mary Astor, Ben Bard, Robert Perry, Joe Brown, Tom Dugan, John Kelly, Robert E. O'Connor, R.O. Pennell, Ed Brady, Charles Morton.
Barry, a gang leader, seeks to help a girl get her sweetheart released from prison.

The Dressmaker from Paris (Famous Players-Lasky/Paramount, 1925)
d: Paul Bern. 8 reels.
Leatrice Joy, Sally Rand, Ernest Torrence, Allan Forrest, Mildred Harris, Lawrence Gray, Charles Crockett, Rosemary Cooper, Spec O'Donnell.
In a midwestern city, Brent, manager of a clothing store, hires a Parisienne dressmaker to put on a fashon show. When she arrives, Brent is surprised and delighted to learn that she is Fifi, the girl he had fallen in love with as a doughboy in France during World War I.

The Drifter (Gaumont Co./Mutual, 1916)
d: Richard Garrick. 5 reels.
Alexander Gaden, Lucille Taft, Albert Macklin, Iva Shepard, Stockton Quincy.
After a reverend minister is killed in a train wreck, a gambler takes his place.

The Drifter (FBO Pictures/RKO, 1929)
d: Robert DeLacy. 6 reels.

Tom Mix, Dorothy Dwan, Barney Furey, Al Smith, Ernest Wilson, Frank Austin, Joe Rickson, Wynn Mace.
Tom, a deputy marshal, goes undercover as a ranch hand to locate a hidden gold mine.

The Drifters (Jesse D. Hampton Productions/W.W. Hodkinson, 1919)
d: Jesse D. Hampton. 5 reels.
J. Warren Kerrigan, William Conklin, Casson Ferguson, Lois Wilson, Walter Perry.
Three men living in a remote cabin in Alaska have their lives changed by the arrival of a young woman in need of their help.

Driftin' Thru (Charles R. Rogers Productions/Pathé, 1926)
d: Scott R. Dunlap. 5 reels.
Harry Carey, Stanton Heck, Ruth King, G. Raymond Nye, Joseph Girard, Harriet Hammond, Bert Woodruff.
Out West, a drifter helps a girl ranch owner locate gold deposits on her land.

Drifting (Universal, 1923)
d: Tod Browning. 7 reels.
Priscilla Dean, Wallace Beery, Matt Moore, J. Farrell MacDonald, Rose Dione, Edna Tichenor, William V. Mong, Anna May Wong, Bruce Guerin, Marie DeAlbert, William Moran.
An American girl smuggling opium in China is thwarted by a U.S. agent. After she reforms, romance blossoms between them.

Driftwood (Ocean Film Corp., 1916)
d: Marshall Farnum. 5 reels.
Vera Michelena, Clarissa Selwynne, Dora Heritage, Harry Spingler, Leslie Stowe, Charles Graham, Joseph Daly, Vida Johnson, David McCauley, Etta Mansfield.
A secretary has an affair with her married boss, unaware that he is her brother-in-law.

Driftwood (Columbia, 1928)
d: Christy Cabanne. 7 reels.
Don Alvarado, Marceline Day, Alan Roscoe, J.W. Johnston, Fred Holmes, Fritzi Brunette, Nora Cecil, Joe Mack.
When her yachtsman companion tries to force his attentions on her, Daisy jumps overboard and swims to the nearest island. There, she meets an American beachcomber and they form an uneasy alliance.

Driven (Universal, 1923)
d: Charles J. Brabin. 6 reels.
Charles Emmett Mack, Emily Fitzroy, Elinor Fair, George Bancroft, Burr McIntosh, Fred Kohler, Ernest Chandler, Leslie Stowe.
Brothers in a Southern moonshiner family are rivals for the love of the same girl.

Driven From Home (Chadwick, 1927)
d: James Young. 7 reels.
Ray Hallor, Virginia Lee Corbin, Pauline Garon, Anna May Wong, Sojin, Melbourne MacDowell, Margaret Seddon, Sheldon Lewis, Virginia Pearson, Eric Mayne, Alfred Fisher.
A girl elopes with her dad's male secretary, infuriating Pa.

The Drivin' Fool (Regent Pictures/W.W. Hodkinson, 1923)
d: Robet T. Thornby. 6 reels.
Alec B. Francis, Patsy Ruth Miller, Wilton Taylor, Wally Van, Ramsey Wallace, Wilfred North, Jessie J. Aldriche, Kenneth R. Bush.
Hal, a fast-car fancier, faces a time limit as he races from the

west coast to New York City, to deliver an important document before the deadline.

The Drop Kick   (First National, 1927)
d: Millard Webb.   7 reels.
Richard Barthelmess, Barbara Kent, Dorothy Revier, Eugene Stong, Alberta Vaughn, Hedda Hopper.
Jock Hamill, a college football star, is between a rock and a hard place: He's suspected of killing his coach (the old guy actually committed suicide), and now the coach's widow is aggressively romancing Jock. With problems like these, can a guy be expected to concentrate on delivering the drop kick that wins the big game? You betcha.

Drug Store Cowboy   (Independent Pictures, 1925)
d: Park Frame.   5 reels.
Franklyn Farnum, Robert Walker, Jean Arthur, Malcolm Denny, Ronald Goetz, Dick LaReno.
A drug store clerk gets his chance to act in movies when an actor dies suddenly and he's the only man available to take his place.

The Drug Traffic   (Irving Cummings, 1923)
d: Irving Cummings. 5 reels.
Bob Walker, Gladys Brockwell, Barbara Tennant.
A respected physician succumbs to drugs and alcohol, losing everything.

Drugged Waters   (Universal, 1916)
d: William Dowlan. 5 reels.
Gloria Fonda, E.P. Evers, George Berrell, William Dowlan, Lule Warrenton, H.F. Crane, Mary Ruby, William Quinn.
The "natural" waters at a health spa are actually drugged.

Drums of Fate   (Famous Players-Lasky/Paramount, 1923)
d: Charles Maigne.   6 reels.
Mary Miles Minter, Maurice B. Flynn, George Fawcett, Robert Cain, Casson Ferguson, Bertram Grassby, Noble Johnson.
Believing herself a widow, Carol remarries. But her first husband isn't dead, he's been lost in the jungle and now he's ready to come home.

The Drums of Jeopardy   (Hoffman Productions/Truart Film Corp., 1923)
d: Edward Dillon. 7 reels.
Elaine Hammerstein, Jack Mulhall, Wallace Beery, David Torrence, Maude George, Eric Mayne, Forrest Seabury.
Priceless emeralds are sealed in the heads of drums, and exert a sinister power over those who come near them.

Drums of Love   (United Artists, 1928)
d: D.W. Griffith. 9 reels.
Mary Philbin, Don Alvarado, Lionel Barrymore, Tully Marshall, Eugenie Besserer, William Austin, Charles Hill Mailes, Rosemary Cooper.
Emanuella, a noblewoman, loves Leonardo, but marries his brother, the hunchbacked Duke Cathos. After the wedding, Emanuella and Leonardo continue their affair, but are caught by the Duke and put to death. Director Griffith now supplies an alternate ending: The Duke dies, and with his last breath he blesses the union of the two lovers.

Drums of the Desert   (Paramount, 1927)
d: John Waters. 6 reels.
Warner Baxter, Marietta Millner, Ford Sterling, Wallace MacDonald, Heinie Conklin, George Irving, Bernard Siegel, Guy Oliver.
In old Arizona, a band of white men try to force Indians off

their land, but they are foiled by Curry, a white man who's a friend of the Indians.

Drusilla With a Million   (Associated Arts Corp./FBO of America, 1925)
d: F. Harmon Weight. 7 reels.
Mary Carr, Priscilla Bonner, Kenneth Harlan, Henry Barrows, William Humphreys, Claire DuBrey.
Upon inheriting a million dollars from a distant relative, Drusilla turns her home into an orphanage. That move gets the neighbors steamed.

Dry Martini   (Fox, 1928)
d: H. D'Abbadie D'Arrast. 7 reels.
Mary Astor, Matt Moore, Jocelyn Lee, Sally Eilers, Albert Gran, Albert Conti, Tom Ricketts, Hugh Trevor, John Webb Dillon, Marcelle Corday.
In Paris, a divorced American learns that he will receive a visit from his daughter, Elisabeth, whom he has not seen for years. Since Dad has mistresses and is a heavy drinker, he decides to clean up his act before his daughter arrives.

Du Barry   (George Kleine, 1914)
d: Edoardo Bencivenga. 6 reels.
Mrs. Leslie Carter, Richard Thornton, Hamilton Revelle, Campbell Gollan, Louis Payne.
In 18th century Paris, a millinery model becomes the King's mistress.

Du Barry   (Fox, 1917)
d: J. Gordon Edwards. 7 reels.
Theda Bara, Charles Clary, Fred Church, Herschel Mayall, Genevieve Blinn, Willard Louis, Hector Sarno, Dorothy Dranke, Rosita Marstini, Joe King, James Conley.
Louis XV of France takes Jeanette Du Barry as his mistress, though their union enrages several members of his court.

The Dub   (Famous Players-Lasky/Paramount, 1919)
d: James Cruze. 5 reels.
Wallace Reid, Charles Ogle, Ralph Lewis, Raymond Hatton, Winter Hall, Nina Byron, Guy Oliver, H.M. O'Connor, Billy Elmer, Clarence H. Geldart.
Former brokerage-firm partners fight over the option on a valuable mine.

The Duchess of Buffalo   (Constance Talmadge Productions/First National, 1926)
d: Sidney Franklin. 7 reels.
Constance Talmadge, Tullio Carminati, Rose Dione, Chester Conklin, Lawrence Grant, Jean De Briac, Edward Martindel, Martha Franklin.
An American entertainer and a Russian officer fall in love, but the Grand Duke wants her too, so the couple are compelled to flee. When they get to a new region, the locals accept the American as their grand duchess.

The Duchess of Doubt   (Metro, 1917)
d: George D. Baker. 5 reels.
Emmy Wehlen, Ricca Allen, Frank Currier, George Stuart Christie, Peggy Parr, Kate Blancke, Walter Horton, Ilean Hume, Charles Eldridge, Fred C. Truesdell.
After she receives a $7,000 inheritance, a housemaid travels while posing as a duchess.

Ducks and Drakes   (Realart Pictures, 1921)
d: Maurice Campbell. 5 reels.
Bebe Daniels, Jack Holt, Mayme Kelso, Edward Martindel, William E. Lawrence, Wade Botelier, Maurie Newell, Elsie Andrean.

Teddy, a spoiled and flirtatious young lady, likes to trifle with many men, although she is engaged to be married. But her fiancé is on to her, and with the aid of friends schemes to teach Teddy a lesson.

Duds (Goldwyn, 1920)
d: Thomas R. Mills. 5 reels.
Tom Moore, Naomi Childers, Christine Mayo, Edwin Stevens, Lionel Belmore, Edwin Wallock, Wilson Hummell, H. Milton Ross, Betty Lindley, Florence Deshon, Jack Richardson.
A war hero becomes a special agent, and apprehends jewel smugglers.

The Duke Steps Out (MGM, 1928)
d: James Cruze. 8 reels.
William Haines, Joan Crawford, Delmer Daves, Eddie Nugent, Karl Dane, Tenen Holtz, Jack Roper, Luke Cosgrave, Herbert Prior.
A profligate playboy decides to take up prizefighting.

Dulcie's Adventure (American Film Co./Mutual, 1916)
d: James Kirkwood. 5 reels.
Mary Miles Minter, Bessie Banks, Marie Van Tassell, Harry Von Meter, Alan Forrest, Mellie Schafer, Perry Banks, John Gough, Gertrude Le Brandt, William Carroll, Robert Klein.
Dulcie is a Southern girl, off to California in search of a rich husband.

Dulcy (Constance Talmadge Film Co./Associated First National, 1923)
d: Sidney A. Franklin. 7 reels.
Constance Talmadge, Claude Gillingwater, Jack Mulhall, May Wilson, Johnny Harron, Anne Cornwall, Andre Beranger, Gilbert Douglas, Frederick Esmelton, Milla Davenport.
Dulcy, a feather-headed but earnest bride, charms her husband's business clients.

The Dumb Girl of Portici (Universal, 1916)
d: Lois Weber, Phillips Smalley. 7 reels.
Anna Pavlova, Rupert Julian, Douglas Gerrard, John Holt, Betty Schade, Edna Maison, Hart Hoxie.
A poor Italian girl loves a Spanish Duke.

The Dummy (Famous Players/Paramount, 1917)
d: Francis J. Grandon. 5 reels.
Jack Pickford, Frank Losee, Edwin Stanley, Helen Greene, Ethelmary Oakland, Ruby Hoffman, Hal Wilson.
While her parents bicker and consider separation, a little girl is kidnapped.

The Dungeon (Micheaux Film Corp., 1922)
d: Oscar Micheaux. 7 reels.
William E. Fountaine, Shingzie Howard, J. Kenneth Goodman, W.B.F. Crowell, Earle Browne Cook, Blanche Thompson.
Lassiter, a deranged scoundrel, compels a young woman to marry him by having her hypnotized.

The Dupe (Lasky Feature Plays/Paramount, 1916)
d: Frank Reicher. 5 reels.
Blanche Sweet, Ernest Joy, Veda McEvers, Thomas Meighan.
A secretary is blackmailed by her employer, a woman who needs a "dupe" to help her win a divorce from her wealthy husband.

Durand of the Badlands (Fox, 1917)
d: Richard Stanton. 5 reels.
Dustin Farnum, Winifred Kingston, Tom Mix, Babe Cressman, Lee Morris, Amy Jerome, Frankie Lee.
In this comedy western, a young outlaw stops to help a group of settlers fight off some Indians, and becomes an unlikely hero.

Durand of the Badlands (Fox, 1925)
d: Lynn Reynolds. 6 reels.
Buck Jones, Marion Nixon, Malcolm Waite, Fred DeSilva, Luke Cosgrave, George Lessey, Buck Black, Seesel Ann Johnson, James Corrigan, Carol Lombard.
Remake of Fox's 1917 film of the same name, starring Dustin Farnum.

Dusk to Dawn (Florence Vidor Productions/Associated Exhibitors, 1922)
d: King Vidor. 6 reels.
Florence Vidor, Jack Mulhall, Truman Van Dyke, James Neill, Lydia Knott, Herbert Fortier, Norris Johnson, Nellie Anderson, Sidney Franklin.
A young woman is troubled by nightly dreams of a Doppelganger, a dancer in India.

Dust (American Film Co./Mutual, 1916)
d: Edward Sloman. 5 reels.
Franklin Ritchie, Winifred Greenwood, Harry Von Meter, William Marshall, Margaret Nichols, Louis Lester.
Factory employees are forced to work under deplorable conditions until a crusading author arouses public outrage against the firm.

The Dust Flower (Goldwyn, 1922)
d: Rowland V. Lee. 6 reels.
Helene Chadwick, James Rennie, Claude Gillingwater, Mona Kingsley, Edward Peil, George Periolat.
In a modern variant of the Cinderella story, a slavey is rescued by a millionaire who falls in love with her.

Dust of Desire (World Film Corp., 1919)
d: Perry Vekroff. 5 reels.
Rubye de Remer, Thomas J. Carrigan, Stuart Holmes, Betty Blythe, Marion Barney, Betty Hutchinson.
Newlyweds go to South America on the husband's business trip, and there they encounter the bride's former lover.

The Dust of Egypt (Vitagraph, 1915)
d: George D. Baker. 6 reels.
Antonio Moreno, Edith Storey, Hughie Mack, Charles Brown, Jay Dwiggins, William Shea, Edward Elkas, J. Herbert Frank, Nicholas Dunaew, George Stevens, Jack Brawn.
An amateur archeologist entrusts his friend Geoffrey with the care of an Egyptian mummy. In his dreams Geoffrey sees the mummy come to life as a beautiful but demanding princess.

The Dwelling Place of Light (Pathé, 1920)
d: Jack Conway. 7 reels.
Claire Adams, King Baggot, Robert McKim, Ogden Crane, Lassie Young, Lydia Knott, George Berrell, Beulah Booker, William Mong, Aggie Herring, Nigel de Brulier, C.B. Murphy.
Disgruntled mill workers threaten to strike, and their actions imperil a secretary and a stockholder who are trying to improve conditions for the workers.

Dynamite Allen (Fox, 1921)
d: Del Henderson. 5 reels.
George Walsh, Edna Murphy, Dorothy Allen, Carola Parsons, J. Thornton Baston, Byron Douglas, Nellie Parker

Spaulding, Lottie Ford, Brigham Royce, Frank Nelson, Billy Gilbert.

Allen, a mine owner, is mistakenly convicted of murder. Years later, and before the man is to be executed, his son "Dynamite" Allen re-opens the case and uncovers the real killer.

Dynamite Dan (Sunset Productions/Aywon, 1924)
d: Bruce Mitchell. 5 reels.
Kenneth McDonald, Frank Rice, Boris Karloff, Eddie Harris, Diana Alden, Harry Woods, Jack Richardson, Emily Gerdes, Jack Waltemeyer, Max Ascher, Frank Rice.
A hod carrier with an explosive punch becomes a prize fighter and wins the championship.

Dynamite Smith (Thomas H. Ince Corp./Pathé, 1924)
d: Ralph Ince. 7 reels.
Charles Ray, Jacqueline Logan, Bessie Love, Wallace Beery, Lydia Knott, S.D. Wilcox, Russell Powell, Adelbert Knott.
Smith, a meek newspaper reporter, is assigned to cover a murder case, and falls for the culprit's wife.

Each Pearl a Tear (Lasky Feature Plays/Paramount, 1916)
d: George Melford. 5 reels.
Fannie Ward, Charles Clary, Jack Dean, Paul Weigel, Jane Wolff.
A string of pearls is cause for disaster and disillusionment.

Each to His Kind (Lasky Feature Plays/Paramount, 1917)
d: Edward J. LeSaint. 5 reels.
Sessue Hayakawa, Tsuru Aoki, Vola Vale, Ernest Joy, Eugene Pallette, Guy Oliver, Walter Long, Paul Weigel, Cecil Holland.
East meets West, with unhappy results.

Eager Lips (Chadwick Pictures, 1927)
d: Wilfred Noy. 7 reels.
Pauline Garon, Betty Blythe, Gardner James, Jack Richardson, Evelyn Selbie, Fred Warren, Erin La Bissoniere.
Paula, owner of a traveling carnival show, takes an orphan girl under her wing.

The Eagle (Universal, 1918)
d: Elmer Clifton. 5 reels.
Monroe Salisbury, Edna Earle, Ward King, Alfred Allen.
Cheated of his inheritance by a massive mining corporation, a young man becomes "The Eagle," a thief determined to overthrow the company.

The Eagle (United Artists, 1925)
d: Clarence Brown. 7 reels.
Rudolph Valentino, Vilma Banky, Louise Dresser, Albert Conti, James Marcus, George Nichols, Spottiswoode Aitken, Michael Pleschkoff, Gustav von Seyffertitz, Otto Hoffman, Mario Carillo, Eric Mayne, Jean De Briac, Carrie Clark Ward.
To avenge his father's death, a Russian officer terrorizes the wealthy and decadent while disguised as a bandit named The Black Eagle.

Eagle of the Sea (Paramount, 1926)
d: Frank Lloyd. 8 reels.
Ricardo Cortez, Florence Vidor, Sam DeGrasse, Andre de Beranger, Mitchell Lewis, Guy Oliver, George Irving, James Marcus, Ervin Renard, Charles Anderson.
The notorious pirate Jean Lafitte champions a young American woman in early 19th century New Orleans.

The Eagle's Feather (Metro, 1923)
d: Edward Sloman. 7 reels.
James Kirkwood, Elinor Fair, Mary Alden, Lester Cuneo, George Siegmann, Crauford Kent, John Elliott, Charles McHugh, William Orlamond, Jim Wang.
Delia, a ranch owner, hires a foreman who loves her niece. Delia, however, comes to mistake his intentions, thinking the new foreman's affections are for her alone.

The Eagle's Mate (Famous Players/Paramount, 1914)
d: James Kirkwood. 5 reels.
Mary Pickford, James Kirkwood, Ida Waterman, Robert Broderick, Harry C. Browne, Helen Gillmore, Jack Pickford, R.J. Henry, J. Albert Hall.
In the Virginia mountains, rival clan members clash over a feisty young woman.

The Eagle's Nest (Lubin, 1915)
d: Romaine Fielding. 6 reels.
Edwin Arden, Romaine Fielding, Harry Kenneth, Clark Comstock, Eileen Sedgwick.
Western drama about a man raised in the shadow of an eagle's nest.

The Eagle's Wings (Universal, 1916)
d: Rufus Steele. 5 reels.
Rodney Ronous, Herbert Rawlinson, Grace Carlyle, Vola Smith, Charles Hill Mailes, Charles Gunn, Albert McQuarrie, Malcolm Blevins, Walter Belasco.
Propaganda film boosting war preparedness.

The Earl of Pawtucket (Universal, 1915)
d: Harry C. Myers. 5 reels.
Lawrence D'Orsay, Rosemary Theby, Harry C. Myers, Flora Mason, Emile Hoch, Helen Gilmore, Bradley Barker, Thomas Curran, Louis Leon Hall, Charles Dungan, Leonard Gray.
While helping an American tourist douse a fire in her London apartment, an earl falls in love with her.

The Early Bird (East Coast Films, 1925)
d: Charles Hines. 7 reels.
Johnny Hines, Sigrid Holmquist, Wyndham Standing, Edmund Breese, Maude Turner, Bradley Barker, Flora Finch, Jack DeLacey.
Seriocomedy about an independent milkman who tries to combat the price-fixing milk trust. Along the way, he falls in love with a pretty girl dressed in a maid's outfit. But she's dolled up for a costume party, and is really the powerful president of the milk trust.

Early to Wed (Fox, 1926)
d: Frank Borzage. 6 reels.
Matt Moore, Kathryn Perry, Albert Gran, Julia Swayne Gordon, Arthur Housman, Rodney Hildebrand, ZaSu Pitts, Belva McKay, Ross McCutcheon, Harry Bailey.
Newlyweds Tommy and Daphne try to impress their friends by appearing prosperous.

The Earth Woman (Mrs. Wallace Reid Productions, 1926)
d: Walter Lang. 6 reels.
Mary Alden, Priscilla Bonner, Russell Simpson, Carroll Nye, Joe Butterworth, John Carr, Johnny Walker, William Scott.
Martha, a strong-willed wife and mother, follows her daughter's would-be seducer and, in a scuffle, he falls and is killed.

Earthbound (Goldwyn, 1920)
d: T. Hayes Hunter. 8 reels.
Wyndham Standing, Naomi Childers, Billie Cotton, Mahlon Hamilton, Flora Revalles, Alec B. Francis, Lawson Butt, Kate Lester.

After an unfaithful husband is killed by his rival, his spirit remains earthbound until he can expiate his sins against his wife and the couple he tried to split up.

The Easiest Way (C.K.Y. Film Corp./Selznick, 1917)
d: Albert Capellani. 7 reels.
Clara Kimball Young, Louise Bates, Joseph Kilgour, Rockcliffe Fellowes, Cleo Desmond, George Stevens, Frank Kingdon, May Hopkins, Walter McEwen.
What's a girl to do, when her wealthy lover won't marry her, and the young man she really fancies hasn't a cent to his name?

East is West (Constance Talmadge Productions/Associated First National, 1922)
d: Sidney Franklin. 8 reels.
Constance Talmadge, Edward Burns, E.A. Warren, Warner Oland, Frank Lanning, Nick DeRuiz, Nigel Barrie, Lillian Lawrence, Winter Hall, Jim Wang.
Benson, an American visiting China, buys Ming Toy, a girl being auctioned off. He sends her to America to liberate her. But in San Francisco's Chinatown, Ming Toy is terrorized by local predators, and Benson must step in again, this time to declare his love for the girl.

East Lynne (Fox, 1916)
d: Bertram Bracken. 5 reels.
Theda Bara, Claire Whitney, Stuard Holmes, William H. Tooker, Ben Deely, Stanhope Wheatcroft, Eugenie Woodward, H.F. Hoffman, James O'Connor, Emily Fitzroy, Loel Stewart, Elden Stewart, Frank Norcross, Ethel Fleming.
Melodrama based on the 19th-century novel of the same name, about a woman who abandons her husband and children, then returns in disguise as her children's governess.

East Lynne (Hugo Ballin Productions/W.W. Hodkinson, 1921)
d: Hugo Ballin. 7 reels.
Edward Earle, Mabel Ballin, Gladys Coburn, Gilbert Rooney, Henry G. Sell, Nellie Parker Spaulding, Doris Sheerin.
Remake of the 1916 Fox picture *East Lynne*, both versions based on the 19th-century novel by Ellen Wood.

East Lynne (Fox, 1925)
d: Emmett Flynn. 9 reels.
Alma Rubens, Edmund Lowe, Lou Tellegen, Frank Keenan, Marjorie Daw, Leslie Fenton, Belle Bennett, Paul Panzer, Lydia Knott, Harry Seymour, Richard Headrick, Virginia Marshall, Martha Mattox, Eric Mayne.
Third feature-film version of the multiple-hanky weeper based on Ellen Wood's story.

East of Broadway (Encore Pictures/Associated Exhibitors, 1924)
d: William K. Howard. 6 reels.
Owen Moore, Marguerite De La Motte, Mary Carr, Eddie Gribbon, Francis McDonald, Betty Francisco, George Nichols, Ralph Lewis.
Peter, a young Irishman, yearns to be one of New York's Finest, but he's too short and flunks the written exam besides. Still, out of sympathy the commissioner allows Peter to wear the uniform for one night only, and to accompany an officer on his beat. Peter and his companion find a robbery in progress, the companion is shot and wounded, and Peter captures the crooks and winds up a hero.

East of Suez (Paramount, 1925)

d: Raoul Walsh. 7 reels.
Edmund Lowe, Pola Negri, Rockliffe Fellowes, Noah Beery, Sojin Kamiyama, Mrs. Wong Wing, Florence Regnart, Charles Reque, E.H. Calvert.
Daisy, a London-educated young lady, returns to her birthplace in China. There, she makes a startling discovery: Her real mother was an Oriental. Daisy's new half-caste status makes her a pariah in China, and creates problems for her and her English fiancé.

East Side, West Side (Principal Pictures, 1923)
d: Irving Cummings. 6 reels.
Kenneth Harlan, Eileen Percy, Maxine Elliott Hicks, Lucille Hutton, Lucille Ward, John Price, Betty May, Charles Hill Mailes, Wally Van.
When a successful author falls in love with his secretary, his social-climbing mother rejects the idea because of the girl's working-class status.

East Side, West Side (Fox, 1927)
d: Allan Dwan. 9 reels.
George O'Brien, Virginia Valli, J. Farrell MacDonald, Dore Davidson, Sonia Nodalsky, June Collyer, John Miltern, Dan Wolheim, Johnny Dooley, John Kearney, Edward Garvey.
In New York, an orphan boy drifts into prizefighting and becomes the protegé of a millionaire. Unknown to both men, the millionaire is the "orphan's" real father.

Eastward Ho! (Fox, 1919)
d: Emmett J. Flynn. 5 reels.
William Russell, Lucille Lee Stewart, Johnnie Hines, Charles A. Stevenson, Mary Hay, Robert Cain, Thomas Delmar, Colin Chase, Dorothy Dickson, Carl Hyson.
When an Arizonan goes East to straighten out a business matter concerning some cattle stock, he falls for the daughter of an east coast kingpin.

Easy Come, Easy Go (Paramount, 1928)
d: Frank Tuttle. 6 reels.
Richard Dix, Nancy Carroll, Charles Sellon, Frank Currier, Arnold Kent, Christian J. Frank, Joseph J. Franz, Guy Oliver.
Comedy about an honest chap who finds he has unknowingly become an accomplice in a bank robbery.

Easy Going Gordon (Paul Gerson Pictures, 1925)
d: Duke Worne. 5 reels.
Richard Holt, Kathryn McGuire, Gordon Russell, Fernando Galvez, Harris Gordon, Roy Cushing.
Gordon, a scion of wealth, foils a pair of thieves who have robbed him and his fiancée. Then, faced with a major business problem, Gordon uses the same two thieves to help him steal proxies to save his father from financial ruin.

Easy Money (World Film Corp., 1917)
d: Travers Vale. 5 reels.
Ethel Clayton, John Bowers, Frank Mayo, Louise Vale, Jack Drumier, Charles Morgan, Eugenie Woodward.
After he enters into a marriage in name only, in order to please his grandfather, a young man slowly begins to fall in love with his wife, and she with him.

Easy Money (Harry J. Brown Productions/Rayart, 1925)
d: Albert Rogell. 6 reels.
Cullen Landis, Mildred Harris, Mary Carr, Crauford Kent, Gertrude Astor, Gladys Walton, Rex Lease, David Kirby, Joseph Swickard, Wilfred Lucas.
A young man is persuaded to impersonate a missing heir.

Easy Pickings (First National, 1927)

d: George Archainbaud. 6 reels.

Anna Q. Nilsson, Kenneth Harlan, Philo McCullough, Billy Bevan, Jerry Miley, Charles Sellon, Zack Williams, Gertrude Howard.

Stewart, a larcenous lawyer, schemes to secure a portion of the Van Horne estate, intended to be divided between cousins Peter and Dolores. The cunning counselor knows that Dolores is dead, so he persuades Mary, a petty thief, to impersonate her. As the plot plays out, Stewart is foiled when it is revealed that Mary herself is entitled to a portion of the estate.

The Easy Road (Famous Players-Lasky/Paramount, 1921)
d: Tom Forman. 5 reels.

Thomas Meighan, Gladys George, Grace Goodall, Arthur Carew, Lila Lee, Laura Anson, Viora Daniels.

Leonard, a seafaring novelist, marries wealthy Isabel, but their marriage stalls when he senses that she and her frivolous society friends have dried up his creative juices. Isabel takes a trip to Europe to give Leonard time to sort things out, but instead of regaining inspiration, Leonard drifts into depression and becomes suicidal. Isabel's return home heals all psychic wounds, and they resume their married life with new optimism.

Easy to Get (Famous Players-Lasky/Paramount, 1920)
d: Walter Edwards. 5 reels.

Harrison Ford, Marguerite Clark, Rod La Rocque, Helen Greene, Herbert Barrington, Kid Broad, H. Van Bausch, Julia Hurley, Walter Jones.

To test her husband's love, a newlywed pretends she has been kidnapped.

Easy to Make Money (Metro, 1919)
d: Edwin Carewe. 5 reels.

Bert Lytell, Gertrude Selby, Frank Currier, Stanton Heck, Ethel Shannon, Edward Connelly, Bull Montana, Hal Wilson.

A carefree ne'er-do-well bets $25,000 that he can go one year without being arrested more than once... and wins, by sassing a judge into giving him a twelve-month sentence.

Ebb Tide (Famous Players-Lasky/Paramount, 1922)
d: George Melford. 8 reels.

Lila Lee, James Kirkwood, Raymond Hatton, George Fawcett, Noah Beery, Jacqueline Logan.

Three burned-out losers sail to a tropical island where there are only two white inhabitants, a pearl merchant and his daughter. While two of the newcomers scheme to steal the pearls, the third falls in love with the girl. Together they foil the thieves and start a life together.

Eden and Return (Hunt Stromberg Productions/R-C Pictures, 1921)
d: William A. Seiter. 5 reels.

Doris May, Emmett King, Margaret Livingston, Earl Metcalfe, Margaret Campbell, Buddy Post, Frank Kingsley.

Love-struck Betty buys a wishing ring and hopes for a handsome, blue-eyed man to come sweep her off her feet. Something like that will actually happen to her, but not in the ways she expected.

The Edge of the Abyss (New York Motion Picture Corp./Triangle, 1915)
d: Walter Edwards. 5 reels.

Mary Boland, Robert McKim, Frank Mills, Willard Mack.

Sparks fly when a social butterfly marries a lawyer who is more interested in his career than in his marriage.

The Edge of the Law (Universal, 1917)
d: Louis Chaudet. 5 reels.

Ruth Stonehouse, Betty Schade, Lloyd Whitlock, Lydia Yeamans Titus, Henry Dunkinson, M.W. Testa, J. Webster Dill.

A girl who's been trained as a pickpocket falls in love with one of her intended victims.

The Education of Elizabeth (Famous Players-Lasky/Paramount, 1921)
d: Edward Dillon. 5 reels.

Billie Burke, Lumsden Hare, Edith Sharpe, Donald Cameron, Frederick Burton.

A scion of wealth courts a chorus girl who's a lot sharper than she seems.

The Education of Mr. Pipp (All Star Features/Alco, 1914)
d: Augustus Thomas. 5 reels.

Digby Bell, Kate Jopson, Belle Daube, George Irving, Stanley Dark, H.D. Blakemore, Mona Ryan, Frank Patton, William A. Evans.

A nouveau riche family tries to climb the social ladder.

Efficiency Edgar's Courtship (Essanay, 1917)
d: L.C. Windom. 5 reels.

Taylor Holmes, Virginia Valli, Ernest Maupin.

An efficiency expert applies business methods to his courtship.

The Egg Crate Wallop (Thomas H. Ince/Paramount, 1919)
d: Jerome Storm. 6 reels.

Charles Ray, Colleen Moore, Jack Connolly, J.P. Lockney, George Williams, Fred Moore, Otto Hoffman, Ed Jobson, Dewitt Van Court, Arthur Millett, Al Kauffman, Cliff Jordan.

Big biceps and a winning smile are a country bumpkin's main assets.

813 (Christie Films/Robertson-Cole, 1920)
d: Scott Sidney, Charles Christie. 6 reels.

Wedgwood Nowell, Ralph Lewis, Wallace Beery, J.P. Lockney, William V. Mong, Colin Kenny, H. Milton Ross, Thornton Edwards, Frederick Vroom, Mark Fenton, Kathryn Adams, Laura LaPlante, Vera Steadman.

Gentleman crook Arsene Lupin finds himself framed for murder.

The Eleventh Commandment (Advanced Motion Picture Corp., 1918)
d: Ralph W. Ince. 5 reels.

Lucille Lee Stewart, Grace Beal, Carleton Macy, Walter Miller, Huntley Gordon.

Foolishly, a young woman rejects her sweetheart in favor of marriage to a wealthy man. Turns out he isn't really wealthy; he's merely a charming fraud.

The Eleventh Hour (Fox, 1923)
d: Bernard J. Durning. 7 reels.

Shirley Mason, Charles Jones, Richard Tucker, Alan Hale, Walter McGrail, June Elvidge, Fred Kelsey, Nigel DeBrulier, Fred Kohler.

A demented foreign monarch intends to take over the world with a doomsday weapon.

Ella Cinders (First National, 1926)
d: Alfred E. Green. 7 reels.

Colleen Moore, Lloyd Hughes, Vera Lewis, Doris Baker, Emily Gerdes, Jed Prouty, Jack Duffy, Alfred E. Green, Mike Donlin, Jack Duffy, Harry Allen, D'Arcy Corrigan, Al E. Green, Harry Langdon (cameo).

Spoof of the famous Cinderella story, with Miss Moore as Ella, a put-upon slavey who makes good in Hollywood.

Elope if You Must (Fox, 1922)
d: C.R. Wallace. 5 reels.
Eileen Percy, Edward Sutherland, Joseph Bennett, Mildred Davenport, Mary Huntress, Harvey Clarke, Larry Steers.
Comedy about Nancy and Hennessy, out-of-work actors stranded in a hick town. Luck comes their way when a wealthy man offers them $10,000 if they can keep his daughter from eloping with a suitor Dad deems undesireable.

Elusive Isabel (Universal, 1916)
d: Stuart Paton. 6 reels.
Florence Lawrence, Sydney Bracey, Harry Millarde, Wallace Clarke, William Welsh, Paul Panzer, Jack Newton, Sonia Marcel.
The U.S. Secret Service thwarts an international plot to take over the world.

The Embarrassment of Riches (Lillian Walker Pictures/General Film, 1918)
d: Edward Dillon. 5 reels.
Lillian Walker, Carl Brickert, John Costello, Edward Keenan, Henry Sedley, Edward Roseman, Harriet Ross, Reeva Greenwood, Peggy Lundeen, Howard Truesdale, John Dillon.
While incognito, a newly rich heiress meets and falls for a social reformer who despises the wealthy.

Embers (American Film Co./Mutual, 1916)
d: Arthur Maude. 5 reels.
Constance Crawley, Arthur Maude, Nell Franzen, William Carroll.
After learning that she cannot have children, a self-sacrificing woman offers her husband a divorce so that he can find a wife who can give him a "normal" marriage. But he isn't so eager to dispose of his wife, fertile or otherwise.

Emmy of Stork's Nest (Columbia/Metro, 1915)
d: William Nigh. 5 reels.
Mary Miles Minter, Niles Welch, Charles Prince, William Cowper, Mathilde Brundage, Martin Faust.
Two men vie for the love of a mountain girl.

The Empire of Diamonds (Pathé, 1920)
d: Léonce Perret. 6 reels.
Robert Elliott, Lucy Fox, Henry G. Sell, Leon Mathot, Jacques Volnys, Ruth Hunter.
The head of an American diamond exchange and his sister sail to Paris on the trail of a special formula for creating near-perfect imitation diamonds.

The Empress (United States Amusement Corp./Pathé, 1917)
d: Alice Guy Blaché. 5 reels.
Doris Kenyon, Holbrook Blinn, William Morse, Lyn Donaldson.
An artist takes his beautiful model on a trip to the country... but his intentions aren't as honorable as she thinks.

Empty Arms (Park-Whiteside Productions, 1920)
d: Frank Reicher. 6 reels.
Gail Kane, Thurston Hall, J. Herbert Frank, Irene Blackwell, Warren Chandler, Howard Truesdell, Beverly Bruce.
Pathologically fearful of motherhood, a young woman agrees to marry her sweetheart, but only if he agrees that the marriage never be consummated.

The Empty Cab (Universal, 1918)
d: Douglas Gerrard. 5 reels.
Franklyn Farnum, Eileen Percy, Fred Kelsey, Harry De More, Frank Brownlee, Harry Lindsey.
An intrepid cub reporter takes on mobsters, counterfeiters, and kidnappers to get a story.

The Empty Cradle (State Pictures/Truart Film Corp., 1923)
d: Burton King. 7 reels.
Mary Alden, Harry T. Morey, Mickey Bennett, Edward Quinn, Helen Rowland, Coit Albertson, Madeline LaVarre, Rica Allen.
Alice, a poverty-stricken young mother, dreams she has been offered a large sum of money to part with one of her children.

Empty Hands (Famous Players-Lasky/Paramount, 1924)
d: Victor Fleming. 7 reels.
Jack Holt, Norma Shearer, Charles Clary, Hazel Keener, Gertrude Olmstead, Ramsey Wallace, Ward Crane, Charles Stevens, Hank Mann, Charles Green.
Claire, a society vamp, finally exasperates her decorous father so much that he takes her out of the social whirl and on a trip to the Canadian Northwest.

Empty Hearts (Banner Productions, 1924)
d: Al Santell. 6 reels.
John Bowers, Charles Murray, John Miljan, Clara Bow, Buck Black, Lillian Rich, Joan Standing.
Kimberlin, who still grieves for his late wife, tries matrimony a second time.

Empty Pockets (Herbert Brenon Film Corp./First National, 1918)
d: Herbert Brenon. 6 reels.
Barbara Castleton, Bert Lytell, Peggy Betts, Malcolm Williams, Ketty Galanta, Susanne Willa, Ben Graham, J. Thornton Baston.
When a millionaire is found murdered, evidence implicates four women in the crime.

The Enchanted Barn (Vitagraph, 1919)
d: David Smith. 5 reels.
Bessie Love, J. Frank Glendon, Joe Singleton, William Horne, Frank Butterworth, Ella Wolbert, Darbey A. Walker, Jane Hathaway, Otto Lederer.
A stenographer falls in love with a young man who's fixing up a barn for her family.

The Enchanted Cottage (First National, 1924)
d: John S. Robertson. 7 reels.
Richard Barthelmess, May McAvoy, Ida Waterman, Alfred Hickman, Florence Short, Marion Coakley, Holmes E. Herbert, Ethel Wright, Harry Allen.
Oliver, a battle-weary veteran of World War I, moves into an isolated cottage in search of peace and quiet. One day he meets Laura, a lonely, introverted woman who shares Oliver's longing for solitude. They marry but find they have little in common besides their negative attitudes. Finally, Oliver and Laura decide to try and make their marriage work by sharing love and laughter. Through their efforts, the two lonely souls emerge from their self-imposed isolation, fully and freely in love with each other.

Enchantment (Cosmopolita/Paramount, 1921)
d: Robert G. Vignola. 7 reels.
Marion Davies, Edith Shayne, Forrest Stanley, Tom Lewis, Corinne Barker, Maude Turner Gordon, Edith Lyle, Arthur Rankin, Huntley Gordon.

A flighty jazz baby needs to be put in her place, and her father thinks he knows how.

The End of the Game (Jesse D. Hampton Productions/Pathé, 1919)
d: Jesse D. Hampton. 5 reels.
J. Warren Kerrigan, Lois Wilson, Alfred Whitman, Jack Richardson, George Field, Milton Ross, Walter Perry, Elinor Fair, Bert Appling, J.J. Franz.
Out West, a Virginia gambler saves a girl from the clutches of a bloodthirsty gang.

The End of the Rainbow (Universal, 1916)
d: Lynn Reynolds. 5 reels.
Myrtle Gonzalez, Val Paul, George Hernandez, Jack Curtis, Fred Church, Joe Ryan.
A lumberman's wily daughter disguises herself and gets a job as secretary to her dad's unscrupulous business rival.

The End of the Road (American Film Co./Mutual, 1915)
d: Thomas Ricketts. 5 reels.
Harold Lockwood, May Allison, William Carroll, Helene Rosson, William Stowell, William Ehfe, Lizette Thorne, Harry von Meter, Hal Clements, Beatrice Van, Nan Christie.
Counterfeiters and moonshiners endanger the love of a wealthy Northerner and his new Southern sweetheart.

The End of the Road (Famous Players-Lasky, 1919)
d: Edward H. Griffith. 7 reels.
Richard Bennett, Helen Ferguson, Claire Adams, Joyce Fair, Raymond McKee, Maude Hill, Robert Cain, Arthur Housman, Alice Brady.
Instructional drama dealing with the evils of syphillis and other sexual diseases.

The End of the Tour (Columbia/Metro, 1917)
d: George D. Baker. 5 reels.
Lionel barrymore, Ethel Dayton, Frank Currier, Walter Hiers, J. Herbert Frank, Richard Thornton, Maud Hill, Kate Blancke, Hugh Jeffrey, Mary Taylor, Charles Eldridge.
When a traveling theatrical company stages a performance in Mayville, it unexpectedly reunites a brother and sister who haven't seen each other since childhood.

The End of the Trail (Fox, 1916)
d: Oscar C. Apfel. 5 reels.
William Farnum, Gladys Brockwell, Willard Louis, Eleanor Crowe, H.A. Barrows, William Burress, Harry De Vere, Hermina Louis, Henry J. Hebert, Ogden Crane, Charles Whittaker.
After a Canadian trapper takes a young widow for his bride, they discover that her first husband isn't dead after all.

Enemies of Children (Fisher Productions/Mammoth Pictures, 1923)
d: Lillian Ducey, John M. Voshell. 6 reels.
Anna Q. Nilsson, George Siegmann, Claire McDowell, Lucy Beaumont, Joseph Dowling, Raymond Hatton, Ward Crane, Charles Wellesley, Virginia Lee Corbin, Kate Price, Boyd Irwin, Eugenie Besserer, William Boyd, Mary Anderon.
A child of the streets, presumed to be an orphan, is adopted by a wealthy family.

Enemies of Women (Cosmopolitan Pictures/Goldwyn, 1923)
d: Alan Crosland. 11 reels.
Lionel Barrymore, Alma Rubens, Pedro De Cordoba, Gareth Hughes, Gladys Hulette, William Thompson, William Collier Jr., Mario Majeroni, Betty Bouton, Madame Jean Brindeau, Ivan Linow, Paul Panzer, Clara Bow.
In Paris, an exiled Russian price who's been unlucky in love forms a society called "Enemies of Women."

Enemies of Youth (Atlas Educational Film Co., 1925)
d: Arthur Berthelet. 6 reels.
Mahlon Hamilton, Gladys Leslie, J. Barney Sherry, Jack Drumier, Jane Jennings, Burr McIntosh, Charles Delaney, Gladys Walton.
A young attorney runs for mayor on a platform of "fun."

The Enemy (Vitagraph, 1916)
d: Paul Scardon. 7 reels.
Charles Kent, Julia Swayne Gordon, Peggy Hyland, Evart Overton, Billie billings, James Morrison, Edward Elkas, Charles Wellesley.
"The enemy" of the title is demon rum.

The Enemy (MGM, 1928)
d: Fred Niblo. 9 reels.
Lillian Gish, Ralph Forbes, Ralph Emerson, Frank Currier, George Fawcett, Fritzi Ridgeway, John S. Peters, Karl Dane, Polly Moran, Billy Kent Shaeffer.
In World War I Vienna, a newlywed couple are separated by the war, with tragic consequences.

An Enemy of Men (Columbia, 1926)
d: Frank Strayer. 6 reels.
Dorothy Revier, Cullen Landis, Barbara Luddy, Charles Clary.
What's a man-hating woman to do when she meets Mr. Right?

The Enemy Sex (Famous Players-Lasky/Paramount, 1924)
d: James Cruze. 8 reels.
Betty Compson, Percy Marmont, Sheldon Lewis, Huntley Gordon, DeWitt Jennings, William H. Turner, Dot Farley, Ed Faust, Pauline Bush, Kathlyn Williams.
Sinister tale of a chorus girl who's invited to a party, and there finds that all the men are wealthy, insensitive boors.

An Enemy to Society (Columbia/Metro, 1915)
d: Edgar Jones. 5 reels.
Hamilton Revelle, William C. Cowper, L.M. Horne, f.G. Bell, Henry Bergman, Lois Meredith, H. Cooper Cliffe, John O'Hara.
After falling in love with a girl of curious ethics, a reformed thief promises her he will commit one final crime... because it is for "a good cause."

An Enemy to the King (Vitagraph, 1916)
d: Frederick A. Thomson. 6 reels.
E.H. Sothern, Edith Storey, John Robertson, Fred Lewis, Brinsley Shaw, Roland Buckstone, Mildred Manning, Pierre Colone, Charles Muzitt, Denton Vane.
Sixteenth-century costume drama centers on a girl who agrees to help the French authorities trap a famous fugitive in return for the release of her father from prison.

Enter Madame (Metro, 1922)
d: Wallace Worsley. 7 reels.
Clara Kimball Young, Elliott Dexter, Louise Dresser, Lionel Belmore, Wedgewood Nowell, Rosita Marstini, Ora Devereaux, Arthur Rankin, Mary Jane Sanderson, George Kuwa.
Lisa, a fiery prima donna, receives her husband's request for a divorce. But the lady lacks docility and instead of giving up, decides to fight for her man, and wins him back.

Enticement (Thomas H. Ince Corp./First National, 1925)

d: George Archainbaud. 7 reels.
Mary Astor, Clive Brook, Ian Keith, Louise Dresser, Edgar Norton, Vera Lewis, Lillian Langdon, Lorimer Johnston, Maxine Elliott Hicks, Fenwick Oliver, Florence Wix, George Bunny, Roland Bottomley, Aileen Manning.
Leonore and Henry's happy marriage is given a jolt when they receive word that she's been named corespondent in another woman's divorce case.

Environment (American Film Co./Mutual, 1917)
d: James Kirkwood. 5 reels.
Mary Miles Minter, George fisher, Harvey Clark, George Periolat, Emma Kluge, Margaret Shelby, Arthur Howard, Al Vosburgh, Lucille Ward, Jack Vosburgh.
Miss Minter plays Liz, a small-town girl of high principles. When she learns that her best friend's brother has threatened to kill a local artist if he finds his sister with him, Liz sacrifices her honor and takes the girl's place in the artist's arms. Though Liz is disgraced in her community, the local minister learns the truth and clears her name.

Environment (Principal Pictures, 1922)
d: Irving Cummings. 6 reels.
Milton Sills, Alice Lake, Ben Hewlett, Gertrude Claire, Richard Headrick, Ralph Lewis.
"Chicago Sal," a young female thief, is placed on probation. Although she falls in love with her probation officer, Sal finds that old habits die hard, and soon she's back in the rackets. Now her new lover has to try and reform her, permanently.

Envy (McClure Pictures/Triangle, 1917)
d: Richard Ridgeley. 5 reels.
Anna Murdock, Shirley Mason, George Le Guere, Lumsden Hare, Jessie Stevens, William Wadsworth, Robert Cain.
Eve, a simple country girl, envies Betty, a celebrated stage actress. But not all that glitters is golden, as Eve finds out when she meets the tragic, tortured celebrity.

Ermine and Rhinestones (Jans Productions, 1925)
d: Burton King. 6 reels.
Edna Murphy, Niles Welch, Ruth Stonehouse, Coit Albertson, Sally Crute, Bradley Barker, Marguerite McNulty.
At a fashion show in New York, a girl persuades her fiancé to buy her an ermine wrap trimmed in rhinestones. The girl modeling the wrap, however, recognizes the fiancé as the man who sent her boyfriend to jail, and soon there's hell to pay.

Erstwhile Susan (Realart Pictures, 1919)
d: John S. Robertson. 6 reels.
Constance Binney, Jere Austin, Alfred Hickman, Mary Alden, Anders Randolph, Georges Renavent, Bradley Barker, Leslie Hunt.
The aptly-surnamed Dreary family live a pretty grim existence until the widowed father of the clan meets and marries a vibrant, upbeat woman who changes their lives.

The Escape (Majestic Motion Picture Co./Mutual, 1914)
d: David W. Griffith. 7 reels.
Donald Crisp, F.A. Turner, Robert Harron, Blanche Sweet, Mae Marsh, Owen Moore, Ralph Lewis, Tammany Young, Fay Tincher, Walter Long.
A brutal, ignorant father turns his children into sadists, prostitutes, and scoundrels. One daughter, blessed with a virtuous nature, survives and sets her family straight.

The Escape (Universal, 1926)
d: Milburn Morante. 5 reels.

Pete Morrison, Frank Norcross, Barbara Starr, Bruce Gordon, Elmer Dewey, Jane Arden, Tex Young.
Out West, an intrepid cowpoke foils a gnag of bank robbers.

The Eternal City (Famous Players/Select Film, 1915)
d: Edwin S. Porter, Hugh Ford. 8 reels.
Pauline Frederick, Thomas Holding, Kittens Reickert, Arthur Oppenheim, George Stillwell, Della Bella, Frank Losee, Fuller Mellish, Jiquel Lanoe, George Majeroni.
In Italy, a guardsman loses his wife in a drowning accident. He enters a monastery and, years later, becomes Pope Pius XI.

The Eternal City (Madison Productions/Associated First National, 1923)
d: George Fitzmaurice. 8 reels.
Barbara LaMarr, Lionel Barrymore, Richard Bennett, Bert Lytell, Montagu Love.
In Rome, a young orphan is adopted by a doctor. Raised along with the doctor's daughter, he and the daughter grow to love each other. However, the onset of World War I separates them and they go widely disparate ways: He joins the Fascists, she the Communists.

The Eternal Flame (Norma Talmadge Film Co./Associated First National, 1922)
d: Frank Lloyd. 8 reels.
Norma Talmadge, Adolphe Menjou, Wedgewood Nowell, Conway Tearle, Rosemary Theby, Kate Lester, Thomas Ricketts, Otis Harlan, Irving Cummings.
In 19th century Paris, a flirtatious duchess vamps a general, then falls genuinely in love with him. She pursues him vainly, and after a year passes, resigns herself and enters a convent.

The Eternal Grind (Famous Players/Paramount, 1916)
d: John B. O'Brien. 5 reels.
Mary Pickford, Loretta Blake, Dorothy West, John Bowers, Robert Cain, J. Albert Hall.
Sons of a sweatshop manager fall in love with two of the working girls. One of them, our little Mary, will eventually force management to improve the workers' conditions.

Eternal Love (Universal, 1917)
d: Douglas Gerrard. 5 reels.
Ruth Clifford, Myrtle Reeves, Douglas Gerrard, George Gebhart, Edward Clark, Dan Duffy.
In Brittany, a charming but fickle artist falls in love with Mignon, a lovely orphan girl. They swear eternal love, but when he returns to Paris and the high life there, he forgets Mignon and resumes his womanizing. It takes a while, but eventually Mignon will gain wealth of her own and the artist will beg to see her again.

Eternal Love (United Artists, 1929)
d: Ernst Lubitsch. 9 reels. (Synchronized music and sound effects.)
John Barrymore, Camilla Horn, Victor Varconi, Hobart Bosworth, Bodil Rosing, Mona Rico, Evelyn Selbie.
Star-crossed lovers flee to the mountains, but there's an avalanche acomin'....

The Eternal Magdalene (Goldwyn, 1919)
d: Arthur Hopkins. 5 reels.
Charles Dalton, Margaret Marsh, Charles Trowbridge, Donald Gallaher, Maud Cooling, Vernon Steele, Maxine Elliott.
A morally upright citizen launches a campaign to drive out his town's prostitutes.

The Eternal Mother   (Metro, 1917)
d: Frank Reicher. 5 reels.
Ethel Barrymore, Frank Mills, Jack W. Johnston, Charles W. Sutton, Kaj Gynt, Louis R. Wolheim, Maxine Elliott Hicks, J. Van Cortlandt.
When a mill owner's wife discovers that her husband employs child labor, she and her minister try to convince the husband that the practice is morally wrong. Imagine her reaction when she discovers that one of the underage drudges is, in fact, her own daughter from her first marriage.

The Eternal Mother   (Tribune Productions/Pioneer Film Corp., 1920)
d: William Davis. 5 reels.
Florence Reed, Lionel Atwill, Jere Austin, Gareth Hughes, Robert Broderick.
A socialite becomes fascinated by tales of an East Indian goddess.

The Eternal Question   (Popular Plays and Players/Metro, 1916)
d: Burton L. King. 5 reels.
Olga Petrova, Mahlon Hamilton, Arthur Hoops, Warner Oland, Edward Martindel, Henry Leone, Howard Messimer, Evelyn Dumo.
Yet another variant on the "Pygmalion" theme, this one has two bored playboys wagering whether a peasant woman can be turned into a socialite in only three months.

The Eternal Sapho   (Fox, 1916)
d: Bertram Bracken. 5 reels.
Theda Bara, James Cooley, Walter Lewis, Harriet Delaro, Einar Linden, Mary Martin, Kittens Reichert, George MacQuarrie, Warner Oland, Frank Norcross, Caroline Harris.
After a young woman poses for an artist's sculpture of Sapho, the poetic muse of the Aegean, the resulting publicity makes her an overnight sensation.   But far from guaranteeing her happiness, the notoriety leads to tragedy, and even insanity.
In modern usage, the name of the muse is usually spelled Sappho, but in all contemporary references to this film, the spelling is Sapho.

The Eternal Sin   (Herbert Brenon Film Corp./Selznick, 1917)
d: Herbert Brenon. 6 reels.
Florence Reed, William E. Shay, Stephen Grattan, Richard Barthelmess, Alexander Shannon, A.G. Parker, M.J. Briggs, Edward Thorne, Elmer Patterson, Anthony Merlo, Henry Armetta, William Welsh, Juliet Brenon, Jane Fearnley, Henrietta Gilbert.
Historical melodrama about Gennaro, who is unaware that he is the son of the infamous Lucretia Borgia. A lot of blood is shed during the Borgia family's reign of terror before Gennaro learns his true heritage.

The Eternal Struggle   (Metro, 1923)
d: Reginald Barker. 8 reels.
Renee Adoree, Earle Williams, Barbara LaMarr, Pat O'Malley, Wallace Beery, Josef Swickard, Pat Harmon, Anders Randolf, Edward J. Brady, Robert Anderson, George Kuwa.
In the Canadian Northwest, two mounties are attracted to a cafe owner's daughter.

The Eternal Temptress   (Famous Players/Paramount, 1917)
d: Emile Chautard. 5 reels.

Lina Cavalieri, Elliott Dexter, Mildred Conselman, Alan Hale, Edward Fielding, Hallen Mostyn, James Laffey, Pierre De Matteis, Peter Barbier.
During World War I, an American emissary to Venice falls in love with a princess.

The Eternal Three   (Goldwyn, 1923)
d: Marshall Neilan. 7 reels.
Hobart Bosworth, Claire Windsor, Raymond Griffith, Bessie Love, George Cooper, Tom Gallery, Helen Lynch, Alec Francis, William Orlamond, Charles West, Maryon Aye, William Norris, James F. Fulton, Irene Hunt, Peaches Jackson, Victory Batement, Lillian Leighton.
The "eternal three" of the title are these: a surgeon, his neglected wife, and the surgeon's son, who's attracted to his stepmom.

The Eternal Woman   (Columbia, 1929)
d: John P. McCarthy. 6 reels.
Olive Borden, Nina Quartaro, Josef Swickard, Ralph Graves, Ruth Clifford, John Miljan, Julia Swayne Gordon.
During a storm at sea, an Argentine girl saves the life of an American named Hartley, then falls in love with him. Love turns to fury when the girl finds a picture that suggests Hartley is the man who murdered her father. So now the life-saver becomes the huntress, as she tries to take the life she saved. She is unsuccessful in her attempt at murder, and it's a good thing, too—for Hartley is not her father's killer.

Eternal Youth—see: West Point (1927)

Evangeline   (Fox, 1919)

d: R.A. Walsh. 6 reels.
Miriam Cooper, Albert Roscoe, Spottiswoode Aitken, James Marcus, Paul Weigel.
Historical drama based on Henry Wadsworth Longfellow's poem "Evangeline."

Evangeline   (United Artists, 1929)
d: Edwin Carewe. (Synchronized music.) 8 reels.
Dolores Del Rio, Roland Drew, Alec B. Francis, Donald Reed, Paul McAllister, James Marcus, George Marion, Bobby Mack.
The wedding plans of a young Acadian couple are disrupted when the region is invaded by British troops.

Eve in Exile   (American Film Co./Pathé, 1919)
d: Burton George. 7 reels.
Charlotte Walker, Thomas Santschi, Wheeler Oakman, Melbourne MacDowell, Violet Palmer, Martha Mattox, L.C. Shumway, Perry Banks.
A socialite spends some time in a seaside village, and falls in love.

Even as Eve   (A.H. Fischer Features/First National, 1920)
d: B.A. Rolfe. 6 reels.
Grace Darling, Ramsaye Wallace, E.J. Ratcliffe, Sally Crute, Marc MacDermott, Gustav von Seyffertitz, John Goldsworthy, John L. Shine, Robert Paton Gibbs.
Cult leaders scheme to steal valuable land from an innocent young woman.

Even as You and I   (Universal, 1917)
d: Lois Weber. 5 reels,
Maude George, Priscilla Dean, Ben Wilson, Mignon Anderson, Bertram Grassby, Harry Carter, Hayward Mack, Earle Page, E.N. Wallock, Seymour Hastings.
Allegorical morality tale, using actors as the Deadly Sins and also as virtues such as Wisdom, Loyalty, and Repentance.

An Even Break   (Triangle, 1917)
d: Lambert Hillyer.   5 reels.
Olive Thomas, Charles Gunn, Margaret Thompson, Darrel Foss, Charles K. French, J. Frank Burke, Louis Durnham.
Childhood small-town friends Claire and Jimmy meet again, years later, in the big city... and their friendship develops into love.

Evening Clothes   (Famous Players-Lasky/Paramount, 1927)
d: Luther Reed.   7 reels.
Adolphe Menjou, Virginia Valli, Noah Beery, Louise Brooks, Lido Manetti, André Cheron.

In France, a wealthy farmer tries to acquire urban polish to please his wife.

Ever Since Eve   (Fox, 1921)
d: Howard M. Mitchell.   5 reels.
Shirley Mason, Herbert Heyes, Eva Gordon, Mrs. Vin Moore, Charles Spere, Frances Hancock, Ethel Lynn, Louis King.
Celestine, a French orphan, is adopted by a successful artist who promptly falls in love with the girl.

The Everlasting Whisper   (Fox, 1925)
d: J.G. Blystone.   6 reels.
Tom Mix, Alice Calhoun, Robert Cain, Geroge Berrell, Walter James, Virginia Madison, Karl Dane.
Mark, a prospector, performs several feats of derring-do in the service of folks in distress. His wife yearns to move to the city, but Mark prefers "the everlasting whisper" of the forest pines.

Every Girl's Dream   (Fox, 1917)
d: Harry Millarde.   6 reels.
June Caprice, Kittens Reichert, Harry Hilliard, Margaret Fielding, Marcia Harris, Dan Mason.
In a Dutch village, a boy and a girl are raised in poverty, until it is discovered that the boy had been stolen from his royal parents as a baby and is really the heir to the throne.

Every Man's Wife   (Fox, 1925)
d: Maurice Elvery.   5 reels.
Elaine Hammerstein, Hebert Rawlinson, Robert Cain, Diana Miller, Dorothy Phillips.
Newlyweds grapple with the green-eyed monster as the wife suspects her husband of infidelity.   He's innocent, though, and by the final reel he proves it.

Every Mother's Son   (Fox, 1918)
d: Raoul Walsh.   5 reels.
Charlotte Walker, Percy Standing, Edwin Stanley, Ray Howard, Gareth Hughes, Corone Paynter, Bernard Thornton.
Pro-war effort drama tells the story of three brothers who enlist in World War I.

Every Woman's Husband   (Triangle, 1918)
d: Gilbert P. Hamilton.   5 reels.
Gloria Swanson, Joe King, Lillian Langdon, George Pearce, Lillian West, Jack Livingston, Walt Whitman, Ed Brady.
A newlywed follows her mother's advice and treats her new husband sternly, laying down strict rules of behavior. Soon, the embattled husband seeks and finds the loving attention of another woman.

Every Woman's Problem   (Plymouth Pictures, 1921)
d: Willis Robards.   5 reels.
Dorothy Davenport, Willis Robards, Maclyn King, Wilson DuBois.
Every woman's problem?   Surely not.   This particular woman is a judge who is later elected to governor, and her "problem" is that her own husband has been unjustly convicted of murder.   Should she give him an official pardon or not?

Everybody's Acting   (Famous Players-Lasky/Paramount, 1926)
d: Marshall Neilan.   7 reels.
Betty Bronson, Ford Sterling, Louise Dresser, Lawrence Gray, Henry Walthall, Raymond Hitchcock, Stuart Holmes, Edward Martindel, Philo McCullough, Jed Prouty, Jocelyn Lee.
Doris, a member of an acting troupe, falls for a taxi driver who's really a wealthy man doing research for a novel.

Everybody's Girl   (Vitagraph, 1918)
d: Tom Terriss.   5 reels.
Alice Joyce, May Hopkins, Walter McGrail, Percy Standing, W.T. Carleton, Victor Stewart, Bernard Siegel.
Florence lives in a working-class tenement building, and is forced to meet her men friends in the park.   After she and a wealthy gent fall in love, he is shocked to learn that she "meets men in the park," assuming The Worst.   Soon, however, he becomes convinced of Florence's virtuous character and discovers that he owns the tenement she lives in, and is moved to improve conditions there.

Everything But the Truth   (Universal, 1920)
d: Eddie Lyons, Lee Moran.   5 reels.
Kathleen Lewis, Eddie Lyons, Lee Moran, Anne Cornwall, Nelson McDowell, Willis Marks, Elizabeth Witt.
After a newlywed man and his newlywed neighbor lady are forced by a deranged lunatic to spend a night together in a remote farmhouse, they are hard-pressed to explain the truth to their respective spouses.

Everything for Sale   (Realart Pictures/Paramount, 1921)
d: Frank O'Connor.   5 reels.
May McAvoy, Eddie Sutherland, Kathlyn Williams, Edwin Stevens, Richard Tucker, Betty Schade, Dana Todd, Jane Keckley.
Helen's engaged to marry rich boy Lee Morton, but he's got a mistress on the side.

Everywoman   (Famous Players-Lasky/Paramount, 1919)
d: George H. Melford.   7 reels.
Theodore Roberts, Violet Heming, Clara Horton, Wanda Hawley, Margaret Loomis, Mildred Reardon, Edythe Chapman, Bebe Daniels, Monte Blue, Irving Cummings, James Neill, Raymond Hatton, Lucien Littlefield, Noah Beery, Jay Dwiggins, Tully Marshall, Robert Brower, Charles Ogle, Fred Huntley, Clarence Geldart.
In one of many allegorical morality tales that were so popular in the early silent era, a girl is confronted by incarnate versions of Modesty, Conscience, Truth, Vice, and Love.

Eve's Daughter   (Famous Players-Lasky/Paramount, 1918)
d: James Kirkwood.   5 reels.
Billie Burke, Thomas Meighan, Lionel Atwill, William Riley Hatch, Florence Flynn, Harriet Ross, Lucille Carney, Mary Navaro, Henry Lee.
A naïve heiress decides to have a fling with a big-city chap who's really just a fortune-hunting phony.   He tricks her into "eloping" with him, though he has no intention of really marrying her.   Not to worry, though.   The heiress and her virtue are saved in the last reel by the arrival of her former small-town beau.

140

Eve's Leaves (DeMille Pictures, 1926)
d: Paul Sloane. 7 reels.
Leatrice Joy, William Boyd, Robert Edeson, Walter Long, Arthur Hoyt, Richard Carle, Sojin, Nambu.
In China, westerners meet and fall in love.

Eve's Lover (Warner Bros., 1925)
d: Roy Del Ruth. 7 reels.
Irene Rich, Bert Lytell, Clara Bow, Willard Louis, John Steppling, Arthur Hoyt.
An industrialist schemes to acquire ownership of a certain lady's steel mill.

Eve's Secret (Famous Players-Lasky/Paramount, 1925)
d: Clarence Badger. 6 reels.
Betty Compson, Jack Holt, William Collier Jr., Vera Lewis, Lionel Belmore, Mario Carillo.

In Europe, a duke falls in love with a peasant girl. He sends her to Paris to be educated, but he isn't prepared for the "education" she receives—in sexuality, sophistication, and poise.

Evidence (World Film Corp., 1915)
d: Edwin August. 5 reels.
Lillian Tucker, Edwin August, Haidee Wright, Florence Hackett, Richard Buhler, Richard Temple, Lionel Pape, Maurice Stewart.
Though innocent of any wrongdoing, a young wife is accused by her husband of infidelity after she's caught with an unscrupulous cad—*twice!*

Evidence (Selznick, 1922)
d: George Archainbaud. 5 reels.
Elaine Hammerstein, Niles Welch, Holmes Herbert, Ernest Hilliard, Constance Bennett, Marie Burke, Mathilda Metevien.
Florette, an actress, marries an aristocrat in spite of their different social status. She is ostracized by her husband's family, but by a clever ruse she makes them finally accept her.

The Evil Eye (Lasky Feature Plays/Paramount, 1917)
d: George Melford. 5 reels.
Blanche Sweet, Tom Forman, Webster Campbell, J. Parks Jones, Walter Long, Ruth King, William Dale.
A female physician answers the call to minister to mine workers during an outbreak of diphtheria. But some of the workers are suspicious of the doctor's tiny flashlight, calling it an "evil eye."

The Evil Men Do—see: The Weakness of Strength (1916)

The Evil Thereof (Famous Players/Paramount, 1916)
d: Robert G. Vignola. 5 reels.
Frank Losee, Crauford Kent, Grace Valentine, Henry Hallam, George Le Guere.
After a wealthy cad seduces a manicurist, humiliation and murder follow.

The Evil Women Do (Universal, 1916)
d: Rupert Julian. 5 reels.
Elsie Jane Wilson, Francelia Billington, Douglas Gerrard, Hobart Henley, Rupert Julian, C.N. Hammond, Tom Lockhart, Sydney Dean.
An amoral vamp preys on wealthy but gullible men.

The Exalted Flapper (Fox, 1929)
d: James Tinling. 6 reels. (Music score.)
Sue Carol, Barry Norton, Irene Rich, Albert Conti, Sylvia Field, Stuart Erwin, Lawrence Grant, Charles Clary, Michael Visaroff.
Farce about a "flapper princess" who refuses to go through with an arranged marriage to the prince of a neighboring country. She falls in love with him, though, when she meets him incognito.

Excess Baggage (MGM, 1928)
d: James Cruze. 8 reels.
William Haines, Josephine Dunn, Ricardo Cortez, Kathleen Clifford, Greta Granstedt.
A married couple are a hit in vaudeville, but their marriage is strained when she makes it big on her own, in the movies.

An Exchange of Wives (MGM, 1925)
d: Hobart Henley. 7 reels.
Eleanor Boardman, Lew Cody, Renee Adoree, Creighton Hale.
Lew and Eleanor and Creighton and Renee anticipate *Bob and Carol and Ted and Alice* by 44 years.

Excitement (Universal, 1924)
d: Robert F. Hill. 5 reels.
Laura LaPlante, Edward Hearn, William Welsh, Frances Raymond, Fred DeSilva, Margaret Cullington, Albert Hart, Rolfe Sedan, Bert Roach, Stanley Blystone, Lon Poff.
Nila, a newlywed with a penchant for thrills and excitement, gets more than she bargained for when she is kidnapped, stuffed into a sarcophagus, and shipped to an Egyptian prince.

The Exciters (Famous Players-Lasky/Paramount, 1923)
d: Maurice Campbell. 6 reels.
Bebe Daniels, Antonio Moreno, Burr McIntosh, Diana Allen, Cyril Ring, Bigelow Cooper, Ida Darling, Jane Thomas, Allan Simpson, George Backus, Henry Sedley, Erville Alderson, Tom Blake.
Ronny, a girl who must marry before her 21st birthday to collect her inheritance, picks a gangster named Pierre for her husband. His gang tries to blackmail the heiress, and when Pierre resists, they try to kill him. In the end, Pierre is revealed to be a U.S. Secret Service agent and Madcap Ronny is a bit disappointed that her husband isn't a real desperado. But she stays with him anyway.

Exclusive Rights (Preferred Pictures, 1926)
d: Frank O'Connor. 6 reels.
Gayne Whitman, Lillian Rich, Gloria Gordon, Raymond McKee, Gaston Glass, Grace Cunard, Sheldon Lewis, Charles Mailes, Shirley Palmer, James Bradbury Jr., Fletcher Norton.
Wharton, a war hero and newly elected governor, clashes with organized crime in his state.

Excuse Me (Henry W. Savage, Inc./Pathé, 1915)
d: Henry W. Savage. 5 reels.
George F. Marion, Geraldine O'Brien, Harrison Ford, Robert Fischer, J.B. Hollis, Vivian Blackburn.
Aboard a train, an engaged couple, a divorcing couple, a disillusioned minister, and several other colorful characters meet.

Excuse Me (MGM, 1924)
d: Alf Goulding. 6 reels.
Conrad Nagel, Norma Shearer, Renee Adoree, John Boles, Walter Hiers, Bert Roach.
A naval officer and his fiancée search for a clergyman to marry them.
Remake of Pathé's 1915 *Excuse Me*. Both films were based on the 1911 play of the same name by Rupert Hughes.

Excuse My Dust (Famous Players-Lasky/Paramount, 1920)
d: Sam Wood. 5 reels.
Wallace Reid, Ann Little, Tully Marshall, Guy Oliver, Otto Brower, Theodore Roberts, James Gordon, Walter Long, Jack Herbert, Fred Huntley, Byron Morgan, Will M. Ritchey.
Sequel to 1919's *The Roaring Road* finds the same cheerful young man entering another auto race, and this time, sabotage is afoot.

Exile (Lasky Feature Plays/Paramount, 1917)
d: Maurice Tourneur. 5 reels.
Olga Petrova, Wyndham Standing, Mahlon Hamilton, Warren Cook, Charles Martin, Violet Reed.
An amoral colonial governor sends his wife to offer sexual favors to his rival, in return for an incriminating letter.

The Exiles (Fox, 1923)
d: Edmund Mortimer. 5 reels.
John Gilbert, Betty Bouton, John Webb Dillon, Margaret Fielding, Fred Warren.
Alice, an American who's a suspect in a murder mystery, flees to North Africa. The district attorney, who is secretly very fond of Alice, discovers she is innocent and personally follows her to Tangiers and brings her home.

Exit Smiling (MGM, 1926)
d: Sam Taylor. 7 reels.
Beatrice Lillie, Jack Pickford, Harry Myers, Doris Lloyd, DeWitt Jennings, Louise Lorraine, Franklin Pangborn.
Comedy about actors in a repertory theater company and its worst actress.

Exit the Vamp (Famous Players-Lasky/Paramount, 1921)
d: Frank Urson. 5 reels.
Ethel Clayton, Theodore Roberts, T. Roy Barnes, Fontaine laRue, William Boyd, Mickey Moore, Mattie Peters.
Romantic comedy about a devoted wife who schemes to get her husband out of the clutches of a vamp.

Experience (Famous Players-Lasky/Paramount, 1921)
d: George Fitzmaurice. 7 reels.
Richard Barthelmess, John Miltern, Marjorie Daw, E.J. Radcliffe, Betty Carpenter, Kate Bruce, Lilyan Tashman, Joseph Smiley, Helen Ray, Jed Prouty, Barney Furey, Edna Wheaton.
Allegory about a young man who is enticed to follow Temptation and Pleasure in the city, and lives to regret it.

Experimental Marriage (Select Pictures, 1919)
d: Robert G. Vignola. 5 reels.
Harrison Ford, Constance Talmadge, Walter Hiers, Vera Sisson, Edythe Chapman, Raymond Hatton, Mayme Kelso, James Gordon.
A headstrong feminist agrees to marry her beau, but on the condition that they live together only from Saturday to Monday of each week.
Marital comedy whose plot suspiciously resembles that of another 1919 film, Pathé's *All Wrong*, in which the newlywed husband decided to spend only one evening a week with his bride. In both films, the idea of "part-time" marriage is soundly discredited.

The Explorer (Lasky Feature Plays/Paramount, 1915)
d: George Melford. 5 reels.
Lou-Tellegen, Tom Forman, Dorothy Davenport, James Neill, Horace B. Carpenter.
A shiftless ne'er-do-well signs on for a mission to Africa, and finds courage.

The Exquisite Sinner (MGM, 1926)
d: Josef von Sternberg, Phil Rosen. 6 reels.
Conrad Nagel, Renee Adoree, Paulette Duval, Frank Currier, George K. Arthur, Myrna Loy, Matthew Betz, Helena D'Algy, Claire DuBrey.
In France, a soldier decides to join a band of gypsies.

The Exquisite Thief (Universal, 1919)
d: Tod Browning. 6 reels.
Priscilla Dean, Sam De Grasse, J. Milton Ross, Thurston Hall, Jean Calhoun.
A lady jewel thief meets a gentleman thief during a heist.

Extra! Extra! (Fox, 1922)
d: William K. Howard. 5 reels.
Edna Murphy, Johnnie Walker, Herschel Mayall, Wilson Hummell, John Steppling, Gloria Woodthorpe, Theodore von Eltz, Edward Jobson.
Barry, a cub reporter, is assigned to a story but runs into complications. Disguising himself as a butler, he gains admission to the house of an industrialist and there finds the information he needs to write his story.

The Extra Girl (Mack Sennett Productions/Associated Exhibitors, 1923)
d: F. Richard Jones. 6 reels.
Mabel Normand, George Nichols, Anna Hernandez, Ralph Graves, Vernon Dent, Ramsey Wallace, Charlotte Mineau, Elsie Tarron, Charles K. French, Mary Mason, Max Davidson, Louise Carver, William Desmond, Carl Stockdale, Harry Gribbon, Billy Bevan, Andre Beranger, Teddy the Dog, Duke the Lion.
Sue, a small town girl, wins a trip to Hollywood and gets a job in a studio wardrobe department.

Extravagance (Popular Plays and Players/Metro, 1916)
d: Burton L. King. 5 reels.
Olga Petrova, H. Cooper cliffe, Mahlon Hamilton, Arthur Hoops, J.W. Hartman, Edward Martindel, Tom Cameron.
When a desirable damsel chooses to marry one beau instead of the other, the rejected suitor plots revenge against both of them.

Extravagance (Thomas H. Ince/Paramount, 1919)
d: Victor Schertzinger. 5 reels.
Dorothy Dalton, Charles Clary, J. Barney Sherry, Donald Macdonald, Philo McCullough.
A high-living stockbroker and his equally extravagant wife live on the verge of bankruptcy.

Extravagance (Metro, 1921)
d: Philip E. Rosen. 6 reels.
May Allison, Robert Edeson, Theodore von Eltz, William Courtwright, Grace Pike, Lawrence Grant.
Vane, a young lawyer and newlywed, can't keep up with his wife's spendthrift ways.

Eye for Eye (Nazimova Productions Inc./Metro, 1918)
d: Albert Capellani. 7 reels.
Alla Nazimova, Charles Bryant, Donald Gallaher, Sally Crute, E.L. Fernandez, John Reinhard, Louis Stern, Charles Eldridge, Hardee Kirkland, Miriam Battista, William Cohill.
The exotic Nazimova plays a sheik's daughter in love with a French officer.

The Eye of God (Universal, 1916)
d: Lois Weber, Phillips Smalley. 5 reels.
Lois Weber, Ether Weber, Tyrone Power, Charles Gunn.
A murderer sees an innocent man convicted for his crime,

then feels "the eye of God" trained on him.

The Eye of the Night (New York Motion Picture Corp./Triangle, 1916)
d: Walter Edwards. 5 reels.
William H. Thompson, Margery Wilson, Thornton Edwards, J.P. Lockney, Agnes Herring, Jack Gilbert.
After her fiancé goes to war, a young woman asks a lighthouse keeper to take her and her baby in, despite the disapproval of the community.

Eyes of Julia Deep (American Film Co./Pathé, 1918)
d: Lloyd Ingraham. 5 reels.
Mary Miles Minter, Alan Forrest, Alice Wilson, George Periolat, Ida Easthope, Eugenie Besserer, Carl Stockdale.
A dissolute playboy bent on suicide is dissuaded by Julia, his young neighbor.

The Eyes of Mystery (Metro, 1918)
d: Tod Browning. 5 reels.
Edith Storey, Bradley Barker, Harry S. Northrup, Frank Andrews, Kempton Greene, Grank Fisher Bennett, Louis R. Wolheim, Anthony Byrd, Pauline Dempsey.
A girl who lives with her uncle is abducted by her father, whom she hasn't seen in years. It turns out he isn't her father at all.

Eyes of the Forest (Fox, 1923)
d: Lambert Hillyer. 5 reels.
Tom Mix, Pauline Starke, Sid Jordan, Buster Gardner, J.P. Lockney, Tom Lingham, Edwin Wallock.
Bruce, a flying forest ranger, nabs a girl accused of murdering her stepfather. She's proved innocent, though, so Bruce and his fellow rangers go after the real killer.

Eyes of the Heart (Realart Pictures, 1920)
d: Paul Powell. 5 reels.
Mary Miles Minter, Edward Burns, Lucien Littlefield, Florence Midgely, Burton Law, John Cook, Fred Turner, William E. Parsons, Loyola O'Connor.
When a blind girl has an operation that restores her sight, she comes to realize the sordidness of her situation. She's been living with thieves, but now she prevails upon them to amend their lives and follow the straight and narrow.

Eyes of the Soul (Famous Players-Lasky/Paramount, 1919)
d: Emile Chautard. 5 reels.
Elsie Ferguson, Wyndham Standing, George Backus, Cora Williams.
A cabaret dancer, deeply sympathetic to a blinded former soldier, renounces the chance to marry a wealthy man and marries the blind man instead.

Eyes of the Totem (H.C. Weaver Productions/Pathé, 1927)
d: W.S. Van Dyke. 7 reels.
Wanda Hawley, Tom Santschi, Anne Cornwall, Gareth Hughes, Bert Woodruff, Monte Wax, Violet Palmer, Mary Louise Jones, Dorothy Llewellyn, Nell Barry Taylor.
Miriam, a widow whose husband was stabbed and robbed by a stranger, lives with her young daughter in poverty on the streets of Tacoma. She meets a beggar who makes a living pretending he is blind, and is convinced to do the same. For her daughter's sake, Miriam becomes a "blind" beggar and takes her position under a large totem pole. In time, she and her daughter escape poverty, and Miriam finally finds her husband's killer and brings him to justice.

Eyes of the Underworld (Universal, 1929)
d: Leigh Jason. 5 reels.

Bill Cody, Sally Blane, Arthur Lubin, Harry Tenbrook, Charles Clary, Monty Montague.
Vicious mobsters turn on a newspaper publisher who holds incriminating evidence against them.

The Eyes of the World (Clune Film Producing Co., 1917)
d: Donald Crisp. 7 reels.
Monroe Salisbury, Jack Livingstone, Jane Novak, Jack McDonald, Kathleen Kirkham, Edward Peil, Lurline Lyons, Arthur Tavares, Beatrice Burnham, Fred Burns, Ah Wing.
An artist paints a flattering portrait of a wealthy and worldly socialite, then meets an innocent girl that inspires him to even greater heights of artistry. The socialite is not amused.

The Eyes of Youth (Garson Productions/Equity, 1919)
d: Albert Parker. 7 reels.
Clara Kimball Young, Edmund Lowe, Pauline Starke, Ralph Lewis, Milton Sills, Rudolfo Valentino, Gareth Hughes, Sam Sothern, Vincent Serrano, William Courtleigh, Norman Selby, Edward Kimball.
Confused about her future, a young woman consults a fortune teller.

Eyes Right! (Otto K. Schreier Productions/Goodwill Pictures, 1926)
d: Louis Chaudet. 5 reels.
Francis X. Bushman Jr., Flobelle Fairbanks, Dora Dean, Larry Kent, Frederick Vroom, Robert Hale.
At a military academy, Ted, a young cadet, proves his athleticism on the football field, but is barred from the big game on trumped-up scandal charges. During the game, the academy team is being soundly beaten, so the commandant's niece, who loves Ted, tells her uncle that Ted was "set up" and is innocent. The commandant buys it, Ted gets sent into the game, and leads the team to a come-from-behind victory.

The Face at Your Window (Fox, 1920)
d: Richard Stanton. 7 reels.
Gina Reilly, Earl Metcalfe, Edward Roseman, Boris Rosenthal, Walter McEwen, Diana Allen, Alice Reeves, Fraser Coulter, William Corbett, Robert Cummings, Henry Armetta.
Class-conscious drama about two factory owners and the very different ways they treat their employees.

The Face Between (Metro, 1922)
d: Bayard Veiller. 5 reels.
Bert Lytell, Andrée Tourneur, Sylvia Breamer, Hardee Kirkland, Gerard Alexander, Frank Brownlee, Burwell Hamrick, Joel Day, DeWitt Jennings.
Tommy, confused and in love, agrees to marry Marianna, but really loves Sybil.

The Face in the Dark (Goldwyn, 1918)
d: Hobart Henley. 6 reels.
Mae Marsh, Niles Welch, Alec B. Francis, Harry C. Myers, Donald Hall, Joseph Smiley, Isabelle Lamon, Alice Wilson, Willard Dashiell.
A retired Secret Service agent is called back to take part in one last investigation.

The Face in the Fog (Cosmopolitan/Paramount, 1922)
d: Alan Crosland. 7 reels.
Lionel Barrymore, Seena Owen, Lowell Sherman, Louis Wolheim, Mary MacLaren, Macey Harlam, Gustav von Seyffertitz, Joe King, Tom Blake, Marie Burke, Joseph Smiley.
Boston Blackie, a reformed society thief, must safeguard the

Romanov crown jewels.

The Face in the Moonlight (World Film Corp., 1915)
d: Albert Capellani. 5 reels.
Robert Warwick, Stella Archer, H. Cooper Cliffe, Montague Love, Dorothy Fairchild, George D. MacIntyre.
In 19th century France, an aristocrat loves a peasant girl, but is pressured to marry a woman of noble rank.

Face of the World (Willat Productions/W.W. Hodkinson, 1921)
d: Irvin V. Willat. 6 reels.
Edward Hearn, Barbara Bedford, Harry Duffield, lloyd Whitlock, Gordon Mullen, J.P. Lockney, Fred Huntley.
Harold, a dedicated young surgeon, unselfishly agrees to operate and save the life of the man who stole his wife.

The Face on the Barroom Floor (Fox, 1923)
d: Jack Ford. 6 reels.
Henry B. Walthall, Ruth Clifford, Walter Emerson, Frederick Sullivan, Alma Bennett, Norval MacGregor, Michael Dark, Gus Saville.
Stevens, a burnt-out drunk, paints a girl's face on a barroom floor, then tells his story. He was once a successful artist, and the girl behind the face was his fiancée.

Face Value (Universal, 1917)
d: Robert Z. Leonard. 5 reels.
Mae Murray, Wheeler Oakman, Clarissa Selwynne, Casson Ferguson. Florence Carpenter.
Though she tries hard to go straight, a street waif keeps getting into trouble.

Face Value (Sterling Pictures, 1927)
d: Robert Florey. 5 reels.
Fritzi Ridgeway, Gene Gowing, Betty Baker, Paddy O'Flynn, Jack Mower, Edwards Davis, Joe Bonner.
Howard, a scar-faced veteran, remains in France after the war, although he has a sweetheart waiting for him at home. He's afraid she will be revolted by his appearance, and when he finally does return to her, his worst fears are confirmed.

The Faded Flower (Ivan Film Productions, Inc., 1916)
d: Ivan Abramson. 6 reels.
Marguerite Snow, Rose Coghlan, Arthur Donaldson, Alma Hanlon, Edward Mackay.
Lillian loves Henry, but marries her wealthy boss instead. Then there's the devil to pay, when Henry comes over to woo Lillian's new stepdaughter.

Faint Perfume (B.P. Schulberg Productions, 1925)
d: Louis Gasnier. 6 reels.
Seena Owen, William Powell, Alyce Mills, Mary Alden, Russell Simpson, Betty Francisco, Jacqueline Saunders, Philo McCullough, Ned Sparks, Dicky Brandon, Joan Standing.
Powers, a divorced father, visits his wife to see his son... and falls in love with his ex-wife's cousin.

Fair and Warmer (Screen Classics, Inc./Metro, 1919)
d: Henry Otto. 6 reels.
May Allison, Pell Trenton, Eugene Pallette, Christine Mayo, William Buckley, Effie Conley.
A married man and a married woman, left alone for the evening by their inconsiderate spouses, plot an elaborate revenge.

The Fair Barbarian (Paramount, 1917)
d: Robert W. Thornby. 5 reels.
Vivian Martin, Clarence H. Geldert, Jane Wolff, Josephine Crowell, William Hutchinson, Mae Busch, Douglas

MacLean, Alfred Paget, Elinor Hancock, Charles Gerrard, Helen Jerome Eddy, John Burton, Ruth Hancock, Charles Ogle.
Octavia, an American cowgirl, shakes up the populace in a staid English village.

The Fair Cheat (R-C Pictures, 1923)
d: Burton King. 6 reels.
Edmund Breese, Wilfred Lytell, Dorothy Mackaill, Marie White, William Robyns, Harold Foshay, Bradley Barker, Jack Newton, Tom Blake.
Camilla loves John, but her wealthy father is against their alliance. Papa makes a deal with his daughter: While he's in Europe on business, she is not to marry John or even let him know where she is. Camilla agrees, but she's got a way to let John find her without telling him her whereabouts. First, she becomes a chorus girl....

The Fair Co-Ed (MGM, 1927)
d: Sam Wood. 7 reels.
Marion Davies, Johnny Mack Brown, Jane Winton, Thelma Hill, Lillian Leighton.
A bubbly flapper goes to college, where she meets the man of her dreams. Trouble is, he's taken... that is, until our jazz baby joins the girls' basketball team and helps win the big game.

Fair Enough (American Film Co./Pathé, 1918)
d: Edward Sloman. 5 reels.
Margarita Fisher, Eugenie Forde, Alfred Hollingsworth, Alice Knowland, Harry McCoy, Jack Mower, Bull Montana, J. Farrel McDonald.
When her nouveau riche parents try to break into high society, a down-to-earth girl remains refreshingly frank— and antagonizes nearly all her parents' new friends.

Fair Lady (Whitman Bennett/United Artists, 1922)
d: Kenneth Webb. 7 reels.
Betty Blythe, Macey Harlam, Thurston Hall, Robert Elliott, Gladys Hulette, Florence Auer, Walter James.
A young woman gets involved with a Mafia gang, a secret agent, and a crooked banker.

Fair Play (William Steiner Productions, 1925)
d: Frank Crane. 5 reels.
Edith Thornton, Lou Tellegen, Gaston Glass, Betty Francisco, David Dunbar, Simon Greer.
It's an age-old story. Secretary loves boss, she can't do enough for him, but he pays no attention to her and instead marries an unworthy dame. When the frivolous bride is accidentally killed, her hubby is convicted of murder on circumstantial evidence. So once again, the secretary rides to the rescue. Will he notice her this time?

The Fair Pretender (Goldwyn, 1918)
d: Charles Miller. 5 reels.
Madge Kennedy, Tom Moore, Robert Walker, Paul Doucet, Wilmer Walter, Emmett King, John Terry, Charles Slattery, Florence Billings, Grace Stevens.
Two working-class misfits masquerade as members of high society at a grand party, meet, and fall in love.

A Fair Rebel (Biograph, 1914)
d: D.W. Griffith. 5 reels.
Dorothy Gish, Linda Arvidson, Clara T. Bracey, Charles West, Charles Perley, Walter Lewis, Jack Brammall, Robert Drouet, Florence Ashbrook.
Civil War romance in three parts, with Dorothy Gish as a Southern belle in love.

LOUISE BROOKS (1928). Curiously, the exquisite Louise Brooks didn't become a star until *after* she left Hollywood. She appeared in 14 American silent films including *The Canary Murder Case* (for which she posed in this publicity still), then left for Europe. *Canary* was filmed in 1928, the year that sound would take over the screen, so the studio decided to turn it into a talkie by having the actors dub their voices into their scenes. But not our Miss Brooks. She was, by then, busy becoming an international star in German films.

* * * * *

Fair Week   (Famous Players-Lasky/Paramount, 1924)
d: Rob Wagner.   5 reels.
Walter Hiers, Constance Wilson, Carmen Phillips, J. Farrell MacDonald, Bobby Mack, Mary Jane Irving, Earl Metcalf, Knute Erickson, Jane Keckley.
A trio of con artists descend on a small Missouri town, looking to rob the bank during county fair week.

The Fairy and the Waif   (World Film Corp., 1915)
d: George Irving.   5 reels.
Mary Miles Minter, Percy Helton, Will Archie, William T. Carleton, Hubert Wilke, Ina Brooks, Ralph Dean, Yolanda Bianca, Maud Brooks, Richard Dupont, Edwin Dupont.
An orphan girl plays a fairy on stage, and meets a young waif who believes she is a real fairy.

Faith   (American Film Co./Mutual, 1916)
d: James Kirkwood.   6 reels.
Mary Miles Minter, Clarence Burton, Lizette Thorne, Margaret Shelby, Josephine Taylor, Perry Banks, Gertrude Le Brandt, John Gough, King Clark.
Faith, an orphan girl, becomes a servant in a wealthy man's house with neither of them realizing they are grandfather and granddaughter.

Faith   (Metro, 1919)
d: Charles Swickard.   5 reels.
Bert Lytell, Rosemary Theby, Edythe Chapman, Edwin Stevens, Nancy Chase.
A bank employee in charge of the safe-deposit boxes has his honesty sorely tested.

Faith   (Fox, 1920)
d: Howard M. Mitchell.   5 reels.
Peggy Hyland, J. Parks Jones, Edward Hearn, Winter Hall, Edwin B. Tilton, Milla Davenport, Frederick Herzog.
In Scotland, a local schoolteacher is also a faith healer.

Faith Endurin'   (Triangle, 1918)
d: Cliff Smith.   5 reels.
Roy Stewart, W.A. Jeffries, Fritzie Ridgeway, Joe Bennett, Edward Brady, Walter Perkins, Graham Pette, Walter Perry.
Cattle ranch partners split up, then meet again when one is accused of murder, and the other is in a position to help him.

The Faith Healer   (Famous Players-Lasky/Paramount, 1921)
d: George Melford.   7 reels.
Ann Forrest, Milton Sills, Fontaine LaRue, Frederick Vroom, Adolphe Menjou, Loyola O'Connor, May Giraci, John Curry, Edward Vroom, Robert Brower, Winifred Greenwood.
Michaelis, a young shepherd, has the divine power to heal sickness. However, once he falls in love with a woman, he finds his gift for healing has disappeared.

The Faith of the Strong   (Selznick, 1919)
d: Robert North Bradbury.   6 reels.
Mitchell Lewis, Gloria Payton, Patricia Palmer, Frank Whitson.
In a French Canadian lumber camp, rivals battle for the love of the same woman.

Faithful Wives   (Platinum Pictures, 1926)
d: Norbert Myles.   6 reels.
Wallace MacDonald, Edythe Chapman, Doris May, Niles Welch, Philippe DeLacy, Myrda Dagmarna, Dell Boone, William Lowery, William Conklin, Alec B. Francis.
Intervention by his wife saves an innocent man from execution.

The Faithless Sex   (Signet Films, 1922)
d: Henry J. Napier.   5 reels.
Frances Nelson, Leonore Harris, Gladden James, Robert Frazer, Frank Beamish.
In New York, a gambler known as "the Black Duke" runs crooked card games in his establishment.   One of his customers, a young man named Latimer, loses a lot of money and tires of the games—until the Black Duke finds a girl to attract Latimer's attention.   She does so, but falls in love with him and exposes the crooked scheme.

The Faker   (Columbia, 1929)
d: Phil Rosen.   6 reels.
Jacqueline Logan, Gaston Glass, Charles Hill Mailes, Warner Oland, Charles Delaney, Flora Finch, David Mir, Lon Poff, Fred Kelsey.
Frank, a recently disinherited young scoundrel, arranges for a fake seance to try to win back his wealthy father's good graces—and his checkbook.

The Fall of a Nation   (National Drama Corp., 1916)
d: Thomas Dixon.   7 reels.
Lorraine Huling, Percy Standing, Arthur Shirley, Flora MacDonald, Paul Willis, Philip Gastrock, C.H. Geldart, Leila Frost, Edna May Wilson, Mildred Bracken, May Geraci, Beulah Burns, A.E. Witting, Ernest Butterworth.
A wealthy American leads a conspiracy to overthrow the government.

The Fall of Babylon   (D.W. Griffith, 1919)
w, d: D.W. Griffith.   7 reels.
Tully Marshall, Constance Talmadge, Elmer Clifton, Alfred Paget, Carl Stockdale, Seena Owen, Elmo Lincoln, James Curley, Kate Bruce, Howard Scott, Alma Rubens, Ruth Darling, Margaret Mooney, George Fawcett, Mildred Harris, Pauline Stark, Winnifred Westover.
Spectacle drama about the Persian siege of Babylon in 539 B.C.

The Fall of the Romanoffs   (Iliodor Pictures Corp./First National, 1918)
d: Herbert Brenon.   8 reels.
Edward Connelly, Iliodor, Alfred Hickman, Conway Tearle, Charles Craig, George Deneuburg, R. Paton Gibbs, William E. Shay, Lawrence Johnson, W. Francis Chapin, Peter Barbierre, Ketty Galanta, Sonia Marcelle, Nance O'Neil, Charles Edward Russell.
Ambitious historical drama chronicles the rise of Rasputin, a false prophet who is installed in the Czar's court and plays an important role in the Russian revolution.

The Fallen Angel   (Fox, 1918)
d: Robert Thornby.   5 reels.
Jewel Carmen, Charles Clary, L.C. Shumway, Herbert Heyes, Daisy Robinson, Lavine Monsch.
A kept woman inherits her lover's millions when he dies, then later falls in love and makes plans to marry.   But when her groom's intended best man turns out to be her former lover's son, the ex-paramour faces exposure and disgrace.

A Fallen Idol   (Fox, 1919)
d: Kenean Buel.   5 reels.
Evelyn Nesbit, Lillian Lawrence, Sidney Mason, Lyster Chambers, Pat J. Hartigan, Harry Semels, Thelma Parker, Marie Newton, Fred C. Williams.
Race prejudice rears its ugly head when a Hawaiian girl falls in love with a white American, and his influential aunt schemes to keep them apart.

The False Alarm (Columbia, 1926)
d: Frank O'Connor. 6 reels.
John Harron, Dorothy Revier, Ralph Lewis, George O'Hara.
Brothers scrap over the love of the same girl.

False Ambition (Triangle, 1918)
d: Gilbert P. Hamilton. 5 reels.
Alma Rubens, Peggy Pearce, Alberta Lee, Edward Peil, Walt Whitman, Iris Ashton, Myrtle Rishell, Lillian Langdon, Lee Phelps, Ward Caulfield, Lee Hill, Alice Crawford.
Driven by social ambition, a young woman masquerades as a fortune-teller to the rich.

False Brands (World Film Corp./Pacific Film Co., 1922)
d: William J. Craft. 5 reels.
Joe Moore, Eileen Sedgwick, C.W. Williams, Robert Kentman.
A college prankster is sent home to his father's ranch, where he renews an old romance with his former sweetheart.

The False Code (Pathé, 1919)
d: Ernest C. Warde. 5 reels.
Frank Keenan, Myles McCarthy, Joseph J. Dowling, Clyde Benson, Edward J. Brady, T.D. Crittenden, Helene Sullivan, Irene Yaeger, Jean Calhoun, Pell Trenton.
A ship builder is betrayed by his partners, and winds up in prison.

False Colours (Paramount, 1914)
d: Phillips Smalley. 5 reels.
Phillips Smalley, Lois Weber, Dixie Carr, Adele Farrington, Charles Marriott, Courtenay Foote, Herbert Standing.
When his wife dies in childbirth, an actor is crushed and, irrationally, blames his new daughter.

False Evidence (Metro, 1919)
d: Edwin Carewe. 5 reels.
Viola Dana, Wheeler Oakman, Joe King, Edward J. Connelly, Patrick O'Malley, Peggy Pearce, Virginia Ross.
While still in her infancy, a girl is betrothed to a wealthy man. As she matures, she falls for his cousin instead.

The False Faces (Thomas H. Ince/Paramount, 1919)
d: Irvin V. Willat. 7 reels.
Henry B. Walthall, Mary Anderson, Lon Chaney, Milton Ross, Thornton Edwards, William Bowman, Garry McGarry, Ernest Pasque.
A professional thief known as "The Lone Wolf" aids the Allies in World War I.

False Fathers (El Dorado Productions/J. Charles Davis Productions, 1929)
d: Horace B. Carpenter. 5 reels.
Noah Beery, Horace B. Carpenter, Francis Pomerantz, E.A. Martin.
Out West, two prospectors find an abandoned baby and take it in and care for it.

The False Friend (World Film Corp., 1917)
d: Harry Davenport. 5 reels.
Robert Warwick, Gail Kane, Jack Drumier, Earl Schenck, E.J. Rollow, Louis Edgard, Pinna Nesbit.
He's in love with a judge's daughter and wants to marry her, but first there's a little matter about his mistress....

False Fronts (Herold Brothers/American Releasing Corp., 1922)
d: Samuel R. Bradley. 5 reels.
Edward Earle, Madelyn Clare, Frank Losee, Barbara Castleton, Bottles O'Reilly.

A working-class youth decides to make his fortune in the world by pretending to be rich.

False Kisses (Universal, 1921)
d: Paul Scardon. 5 reels.
Miss DuPont, Pat O'Malley, Lloyd Whitlock, Camilla Clark, Percy Challenger, Madge Hunt, Fay Winthrop, Joseph Hazelton, Mary Philbin.
Paul, a blind lighthouse keeper, regains his sight and finds his wife kissing his former best friend.

The False Road (Thomas H. Ince/Paramount, 1920)
d: Fred Niblo. 6 reels.
Lloyd Hughes, Enid Bennett, Wade Boteler, Lucille Young, Charles Smiley, Edith Yorke, Gordon Mullen.
After paying his debt to society, a professional thief tries to go straight. But his sweetie, who's also a crook, wants to continue along "the false road."

False Women (Pandora Productions/Aycie Pictures, 1921)
w, d: R. Dale Armstrong. 5 reels.
Sheldon Smith, Audrey Chapman, Catherine Bradley, Antonio Corsi, Wheeler Dryden.
Upon meeting a lovely young woman, a seminarian finds himself being distracted from his studies for the priesthood.

Fame and Fortune (Fox, 1918)
d: Lynn F. Reynolds. 5 reels.
Tom Mix, Kathleen Connors, George Nicholls, Charles McHugh, Annette DeFoe, Val Paul, Jack Dill, E.N. Wallock, Clarence Burton.
A cowboy returns home to find his family ranch has been confiscated by crooks.

The Family Closet (Ore-Col Film Corp./Playgoers Pictures, 1921)
d: John B. O'Brien. 6 reels.
Holmes Herbert, Alice Mann, Kempton Greene, Byron Russell, Josephine Frost, Walter Ware, John Dillon, Verne Layton, Walter Lewis, May Kitson.
Purcell, a newspaper publisher, is being sued for libel by Dinsmore. A sticky situation, since their children happen to be in love with each other.

The Family Cupboard (World Film Corp., 1915)
d: Frank Crane. 5 reels.
Holbrook Blinn, Clinton Preston, Frances Nelson, John Hines.
A newly wealthy family has trouble adjusting to success.

The Family Honor (World Film Corp., 1917)
d: Emile Chautard. 5 reels.
Robert Warwick, June Elvidge, Alec B. Francis, Henry Hull, Gerda Holmes, Frank Beamish.
When a young man forsakes his fiancée to pursue a charming actress, his brother tries to talk the actress into giving him up. He then falls for the actress himself.

The Family Honor (First National, 1920)
d: King Vidor. 5 reels.
Florence Vidor, Roscoe Karns, Ben Alexander, Charles Meredith, George Nichols, J.P. Lockney, Willis Marks, Harold Goodwin.
A young woman scrimps and saves to send her younger brother through college. But the kid's a rascal, spending most of his time drinking and gambling.

The Family Secret (Universal, 1924)
d: William A. Seiter. 6 reels.
Gladys Hulette, Baby Peggy Montgomery, Edward Earle,

Frank Currier, Cesare Gravina, Martin Turner, Elizabeth Mackey, Martha Mattox, Lucy Beaumont.
A couple are secretly married, leading to ticklish problems when the husband comes home to see their baby and finds his father-in-law in the house.

The Family Skeleton (Thomas H. Ince/Paramount, 1918)
d: Victor L. Schertzinger. 5 reels.
Charles Ray, Sylvia Bremer, Andrew Arbuckle, Billy Elmer, Otto Hoffman, Jack Dyer.
Though he craves the bottle, a young man fights off his alcohol problem to protect his girlfriend from an abductor.

The Family Stain (Fox, 1915)
d: Will S. Davis. 5 reels.
Frederick Perry, Einar Linden, Walter Miller, Stephen Grattan, Carey Lee, Dixie Compton, Helen Tiffany, Frank Evans, Edith Hallor, Mayme Kelso, Louis Hendricks.
In a small French town, a detective investigates a homicide in which the murdered woman had been paid to switch two babies at birth.

The Family Upstairs (Fox, 1926)
d: J.G. Blystone. 6 reels.
Virginia Valli, Allan Simpson, J.Farrell MacDonald, Lillian Elliott, Edward Piel Jr., Dot Farley, Cecille Evans, Jacqueline Wells.
Louise falls in love with Charles, a bank teller, but her uppity family nearly runs him off. They'll meet again at Coney Island, and plan a future together.

The Famous Mrs. Fair (Metro, 1923)
d: Fred Niblo. 8 reels.
Myrtle Stedman, Huntly Gordon, Marguerite De La Motte, Cullen Landis, Ward Crane, Carmel Myers, Helen Ferguson, Lydia Yeamans Titus, Dorcas Matthews, Frankie Bailey.
Mrs. Fair, a nurse who served meritoriously in the war, returns home to find her family in shambles.

Fan Fan (Fox, 1918)
d: Sidney A. Franklin, Chester M. Franklin. 5 reels.
Virginia Lee Corbin, Francis Carpenter, Carmen De Rue, Violet Radcliffe, Bud Messinger, Joe Singleton, Gertie Messinger, Louis Sargent.
The Japanese emperor's son elopes with Fan Fan, a lovely girl who is decidedly not the emperor's choice for his son.

Fanatics (Triangle, 1917)
d: Raymond B. Wells. 5 reels.
Ada Gleason, J. Barney Sherry, William V. Mong, Donald Fullen, Olga Grey, Eugene Burr, Edward Hayden, W.A. Jeffries.
Revenge is the motive when a young widow schemes to undo the factory owner she believes is responsible for her husband's death.

Fanchon the Cricket (Famous Players/Paramount, 1915)
d: James Kirkwood. 5 reels.
Mary Pickford, Jack Standing, Lottie Pickford, Gertrude Norman, Russell Bassett, Richard Lee, Jack Pickford.
Miss Pickford plays a "nature girl" who lives in the forest.

Fangs of Destiny (Universal, 1927)
d: Stuart Paton. 5 reels.
Dynamite, the dog, Edmund Cobb, Betty Caldwell, George Periolat, Carl Sepulveda, Al Ferguson, Joan Hathaway, Brick Cannon.
Out West, a treacherous rancher tries to run his neighbor out of business by arranging for rustlers to deplete his herd. But

the villains hadn't counted on dealing with the foreman and his wonder dog Dynamite.

Fangs of the Wild (FBO Pictures, 1928)
d: Jerome Storm. 5 reels.
Ranger, the dog, Dorothy Kitchen, Sam Nelson, Tom Lingham, Syd Crossley.
A valiant dog protects Blossom, a Kentucky girl, from the attentions of a drunken masher.

Fantasma (Thomas A. Edison, Inc./General Film, 1914)
d: Charles M. Seay. 5 reels.
Edwin Clark, Marie La Manna, William T. Carlton, William Ruge, George Schrode, Grace Goodall, George Hanlon Jr., William Fables, Richard Neill, Matholda Baring.
Whimsical fantasy about a mythical ruler who loves a princess.

The Far Call (Fox, 1929)
d: Allan Dwan. 6 reels.
Charles Morton, Leila Hyams, Arthur Stone, Warren Hymer, Dan Wolheim, Stanley J. Sandford, Ullrich Haupt, Charles Middleton, Pat Hartigan, Charles Gorman, Ivan Linow.
In the desolate North, a poacher goes to St. Paul Island to rob the seal hatchery. But he'll change his plans—and turn his life around—when he discovers that he's the long-lost son of a respected member of the island community.

The Far Cry (First National, 1926)
d: Silvano Balboni. 8 reels.
Blanche Sweet, Jack Mulhall, Myrtle Stedman, Hobart Bosworth, Leo White, Julia Swayne Gordon, William Austin, John Sainpolis, Dorothy Revier, Mathilde Comont.
Two Americans in Paris fall in love and plan to marry, but meet with massive opposition from their respective parents.

The Farmer's Daughter (Fox, 1928)
d: Norman Taurog. 6 reels.
Marjorie Beebe, Frank Albertson, Arthur Stone, Lincoln Stedman, Jimmie Adams, Charles Middleton.
Small-town girl Marjorie falls for a slick talker from the city.

Fascinating Youth (Famous Players-Lasky/Paramount, 1926)
d: Sam Wood. 7 reels.
Charles (Buddy) Rogers, Ivy Harris, Jack Luden, Claude Buchanan, Mona Palma, Walter Goss, Thelma Todd, Josephine Dunn, Irving Hartley, Gregory Blackton, Charles Brokaw, Iris Gray, Joseph Burke, Harry Sweet, Lois Wilson.
The son of a resort owner hatches a plot to drum up business, involving his pals, an ice boat race, and several visiting movie stars.

Fascination (Tiffany Productions/Metro, 1922)
d: Robert Z. Leonard. 8 reels.
Mae Murray, Creighton Hale, Charles Lane, Emily Fitzroy, Robert Frazer, Vincent Coleman, Courtenay Foote, Helen Ware, Frank Puglia.
In Spain, an American girl disguises herself as a señorita in order to meet a famous bullfighter.

Fashion Madness (Columbia, 1928)
d: Louis J. Gasnier. 7 reels.
Claire Windsor, Reed Howes, Laska Winters, Donald McNamee, Boris Snegoff.
Gloria, a flighty socialite, reluctantly goes to a remote cabin in the Canadian wilderness with Victor, her fiancé. When Victor contracts an infection, Gloria overcomes her self-centeredness and drags him on a sled through the snow to

the nearest town, several miles away.

Fashion Row   (Tiffany Productions/Metro, 1923)
d: Robert Z. Leonard.   7 reels.
Mae Murray, Earle Foxe, Freeman Wood, Mathilde Brundage, Elmo Lincoln, Sidney Franklin, Rosa Rosanova.
Olga and Zita, two Russian sisters fleeing from the Bolshevik revolution, make their way to America.

Fashionable Fakers   (R-C Pictures, 1923)
d: William Worthington.   5 reels.
Johnnie Walker, Mildred June, George Cowl, J. Farrell MacDonald, Lillian Lawrence, Robert Balder, George Rigas.
Plummer, a furniture store worker, buys an oriental rug that seems to have magical powers.

Fashions for Women   (Famous Players-Lasky/Paramount, 1927)
d: Dorothy Arzner.   7 reels.
Esther Ralston, Raymond Hatton, Einar Hanson, Edward Martindel, William Orlamond, Agostino Borgato, Edward Faust, Yvonne Howell, Maude Wayne, Charles Darvas.
When a socialite is counseled by her press agent to take some time off to get a face lift, a cigarette girl who resembles her is persuaded to take her place in a fashion show... and wins!
Esther Ralston portrays both women, the cigarette girl and her lookalike society friend.

Fast and Fearless   (Action Pictures/Arclass Pictures, 1924)
d: Richard Thorpe.   5 reels.
Buffalo Bill Jr., Jean Arthur, William Turner, George Magrill, Julian Rivero, Emily Barrye, Kewpie King, Steve Clemento, Victor Allen.
Wild and wooly action out West, as a sharpshooter sets out after a border bandit.

Fast and Furious   (Universal, 1927)
d: Melville W. Brown.   6 reels.
Reginald Denny, Barbara Worth, Claude Gillingwater, Armand Kaliz, Lee Moran, Charles K. French, Wilson Benge, Robert E. Homans, Kingsley Benedict, Edgar Norton.
Comedy about a young man who loves fast cars, and has wrecked a few.

Fast Company   (Universal, 1918)
d: Lynn Reynolds.   5 reels.
Franklyn Farnum, Juanita Hansen, Lon Chaney, Fred Montague, Katherine Griffith, Edward Cecil.
A pampered playboy gets his act together in time to rescue his fiancée from the clutches of an amoral scoundrel.

Fast Fightin'   (Approved Pictures/Artclass Pictures, 1925)
d: Richard Thorpe.   5 reels.
Buddy Roosevelt, Nell Brantley, Joe Rickson, Emily Barrye, Sherry Tansey, Emma Tansey, Leonard Trainor.
Out West, a cowboy is falsely accused of theft. He not only proves himself innocent, but also learns of the culprits' other nefarious plans, and foils them.

The Fast Mail   (Fox, 1922)
d: Bernard J. Durning.   6 reels.
Charles Jones, Eileen Percy, James Mason, William Steele, Adolphe Menjou, Harry Dunkinson.
Carson, a rugged cowpoke, learns that a gal he fancies has been kidnapped. Chasing the culprits by land, water, and rail, he finds the captive and sets her free. Along the way, he also rescues a family from a fire.

The Fast Set   (Famous Players-Lasky/Paramount, 1924)
d: William DeMille.   8 reels.
Betty Compson, Adolphe Menjou, Elliott Dexter, ZaSu Pitts, Dawn O'Day, Grace Carlyle, Claire Adams, Rosalind Byrne, Edgar Norton, Louis Natheaux, Fred Walton.
Romantic comedy about a novelist and his "neglected" wife, and the scoundrel who tries to take advantage of her.

The Fast Worker   (Universal, 1924)
d: William A. Seiter.   7 reels.
Reginald Denny, Laura LaPlante, Ethel Grey Terry, Muriel Frances Dana, Lee Moran, Richard Tucker, Margaret Campbell, Betty Morrisey, Mildred Vincent, John Steppling, T.D. Crittenden, Clarissa Selwynne.
Comic chaos ensues when the friend of an architect substitutes for him on a Catalina cruise.

The Fatal Card   (Famous Players/Paramount, 1915)
d: James Kirkwood.   5 reels.
John Mason, Hazel Dawn, Russell Bassett, Helen Weir, David Powell, William J. Ferguson.
A thief is saved from the hands of a violent mob by a visiting stranger. The thief offers the stranger his card, together with a promise of assistance should the need ever arise. Little does the thief know that keeping that promise could cost him his life.

The Fatal Hour   (Metro, 1920)
d: George W. Terwilliger.   6 reels.
Thomas W. Ross, Wilfred Lytell, Francis X. Conlan, Lionel Pape, Jack Crosby, Henry Hallam, Louis Sealey, Frank Currier, Gladys Coburn, Thea Talbot, Jennie Dickerson, Florence Court, Marie Shaffer, Effie Conley.
When a nobleman has his ancestry—and his title—questioned, he must journey to a monastery in Switzerland where the royal papers are stored, to prove his nobility.

The Fatal Mistake   (Columbia, 1924)
d: Scott Dunlap.   5 reels.
William Fairbanks, Eva Novak, Wilfred Lucas, Dot Farley, Bruce Gordon, Harry McCoy, Paul Weigel, Frank Clark.
A cub reporter is instrumental in preventing a jewel heist.

The Fate of a Flirt   (Columbia, 1925)
d: Frank Strayer.   6 reels.
Forrest Stanley, Dorothy Revier, Tom Ricketts, Clarissa Selwynne, Phillips Smalley, William Austin, Charles West, Louis Payne.
An English lord poses as a chauffer to be near the girl he loves.

Fate's Boomerang   (Paragon Films, Inc./World Film Corp., 1916)
d: Frank H. Crane.   5 reels.
Mollie King, Charles Gotthold, June Elvidge, Frank Goldsmith, Harry Redding.
A vengeful woman schemes to place her innocent husband with a female friend, hoping to obtain grounds for divorce.

Father and Son   (Mutual, 1916)
d: T. Hayes Hunter.   5 reels.
Henry E. Dixey, Millicent Evans, Gladden James, Mabel Montgomery.
When a widower and his business rival, a widow, find that their son and daughter have fallen in love and eloped, the rivals decide to merge their business interests as well.

Father and Son   (Columbia, 1929)
d: Erle C. Kenton.   7 reels.   (Part talkie.)
Jack Holt, Mickey McBan, Dorothy Revier, Wheeler

Oakman, Helene Chadwick.
A father gives his son a recording machine for his birthday, and it eventually is used to clear Dad of unjust criminal charges.

Father and the Boys (Universal, 1915)
d: Joseph de Grasse. 5 reels.
Digby Bell, Harry Ham, Louise Carbasse, Colin Chase, Yona Landowska, Mae Gaston, Lon Chaney, Hayward Mack, Thomas Chatterton, Jean Hathaway.
A stockbroker plans to marry off his two sons, but first he has a few adventures of his own, involving a young singer-dancer from out of town.

Father Tom (O'Brien Productions/Playgoers Pictures, 1921)
d: John B. O'Brien. 5 reels.
Tom Wise, James Hill, May Kitson, Myra Brooks, Ray Allen, Harry Boler, Alexander Clark, James Wallace, Nancy Deaver.
A small-town preacher called Father Tom is beloved for his understanding and his charity towards all.

Fathers of Men (Vitagraph, 1916)
d: William Humphrey. 6 reels.
Robert Edeson, William Humphrey, Naomi Childers, Harry S. Northup, Stanley Dunn, Kalman Matus, Logan Paul, Robert Gaillard, Carolyn Birch, Bobby Connelly, Betty Howe.
A young man must face three brothers who blame his father for the death of their own dad. While preparing to fight, they are interrupted by two women in distress. In assisting the women, the four young men find they have bonded, and agree to end their quarrel.

A Favor to a Friend (Metro, 1919)
d: John Ince. 5 reels.
Emmy Wehlen, Jack Mulhall, Hugh Fay, Joseph Kilgour, Effie Conley, Jack Miller Jr., Harry Todd, Fred H. Warren.
Comedy hi-jinks ensue when a young woman on the run is seized by inept kidnappers who mistake her for her friend, a musical comedy star.

Fazil (Fox, 1928)
d: Howard Hawks. 7 reels. (Musical score and sound effects.)
Charles Farrell, Greta Nissen, Mae Busch, Vadim Uraneff, Tyler Brooke, Eddie Sturgis, Josephine Borio, John Boles, John T. Murray, Erville Alderson, Dale Fuller, Hank Mann.
When a Parisienne marries an Arab prince, she doesn't figure on living amid the sand dunes. Once she tires of desert life, she leaves her husband... who promptly establishes a harem for himself.

Fear-Bound (Vitagraph, 1925)
w, d: Will Nigh. 6 reels.
Marjorie Daw, Will Nigh, Niles Welch, Louise Mackintosh, Edward Roseman, James Bradbury Jr., Warner Richmond, Dexter McReynolds, Jean Jarvis, Frank Conlon.
Heavy drama of the frontier days, involving an abandoned wife who must turn her son against his father.

The Fear Fighter (Rayart, 1925)
d: Albert Rogell. 5 reels.
Billy Sullivan, Ruth Dwyer, J.P. McGowan, "Gunboat" Smith, Phil Salvadore, Spike Robinson, Jack Herrick, Billy Franey.
After recovering from amnesia, a boxer is booked to fight the champ. He takes a fearful pounding for several rounds, until a blow to the head restores memories of fighting lessons he learned while an amnesiac. His memory thus refreshed, he proceeds to trounce the champion.

The Fear Market (Realart Pictures Corp., 1920)
d: Kenneth Webb. 5 reels.
Alice Brady, Frank Losee, Harry Mortimer, Richard Hatteras, Edith Stockton, Bradley Barker, Nora Reed, Fred Burton, Alfred Hickman, Sara Biala.
Unaware that her own dad is the publisher of a scandal sheet, a young woman takes steps to shut it down.

Fear Not (Universal, 1917)
d: Allen Holubar. 5 reels.
Myles McCarthy, Brownie Vernon, Murdock MacQuarrie, Joseph Girard, Frank Borzage.
Two brothers who are cocaine addicts believe their craving is hereditary.

The Fear Woman (Goldwyn, 1919)
d: John A. Barry. 5 reels.
Milton Sills, Pauline Frederick, Walter Hiers, Emmett King, Harry Northrup, Ernest Pasque, Beverly Travers, Lydia Yeamans Titus.
An heiress sacrifices her own reputation to save that of an adulterous friend.

The Fearless Lover (Columbia, 1925)
d: Henry MacRae. 5 reels.
William Fairbanks, Eva Novak, Arthur Rankin, Tom Kennedy.
A cop in love arrests his sweetheart's brother, then learns the boy was under the spell of a criminal mastermind.

The Fearless Rider (Universal, 1928)
d: Edgar Lewis. 5 reels.
Fred Humes, Barbara Worth, Ben Corbett, Pee Wee Holmes, Buck Connors, William Steele.

A rodeo star tries to help a girl and her father protect their gold claim from thieves.

The Feast of Life (Paragon Films, Inc./World Film Corp., 1916)
d: Albert Capellani. 5 reels.
Clara Kimball Young, E.M. Kimball, Paul Capellani, Doris Kenyon, Robert Frazer.
Family debts force a young woman to marry a man she does not love.

Feathertop (Gaumont Co./Mutual, 1916)
d: Henry Vernot. 5 reels.
Marguerite Courtot, James Levering, Gerald Griffin, Mathilde Baring, Charles Graham, Sidney Mason, John Reinhard.
A sweet and simple country girl goes to visit the big city, and is seduced by the glitz and glamour of it all.

Fedora (Famous Players-Lasky/Paramount, 1918)
d: Edward José. 5 reels.
Pauline Frederick, Alfred Hickman, Jere Austin, W.L. Abingdon, Wilmuth Merkyll.
Fedora, a princess in Czarist Russia, is involved in lethal affairs of the heart.

Feel My Pulse (Paramount, 1928)
d: Gregory La Cava. 6 reels.
Bebe Daniels, Richard Arlen, Melbourne MacDowell, George Irving, Charles Sellon, William Powell, Heinie Conklin.
Barbara, a hypochondriac, visits a sanitarium to improve her health... and finds the place run over with hijackers and bootleggers.

150

Feet of Clay (Famous Players-Lasky/Paramount, 1924)
d: Cecil B. DeMille. 10 reels.
Rod LaRocque, Julia Faye, Ricardo Cortez, Robert Edeson, William Boyd, Vera Reynolds, Theodore Kosloff, Victor Varconi.
Drama with a touch of the supernatural, as a married couple try to commit suicide but are rejected by Death. They live on, and are inspired to resolve their problems.

Felix O'Day (Jesse D. Hampton Productions/Pathé, 1920)
d: Robert Thornby. 5 reels.
H.B. Warner, Marguerite Snow, Lillian Rich, Ray Ripley, Karl Formes, George Williams.
Felix wants revenge against the man who stole his wife, and goes after him. Along the way he falls in love with another woman—this time for keeps.

The Female (Famous Players-Lasky/Paramount, 1924)
d: Sam Wood. 7 reels.
Betty Compson, Warner Baxter, Noah Beery, Dorothy Cumming, Freeman Wood, Helen Butler, Pauline French, Edgar Norton, Florence Wix.
A lady from South Africa fancies a big game hunter, but marries her wealthy patron instead.

The Female of the Species (New York Motion Picture Corp./Triangle, 1916)
d: Raymond B. West. 5 reels.
Dorothy Dalton, Enid Markey, Howard Hickman, Gertrude Claire, Roy Laidlaw, Aggie Herring.
When a predatory female loses her man to a more demure woman, the vamp schemes to recapture her prey.

The Fettered Woman (Vitagraph, 1917)
d: Tom Terriss. 5 reels.
Alice Joyce, Webster Campbell, Donald McBride, Lionel Grey, Templer Saxe.
An unjustly imprisoned young woman lives in fear that her prison record will jeopardize her future happiness.

The Feud (Fox, 1919)
d: Edward Le Saint. 5 reels.
Tom Mix, Eva Novak, Claire McDowell, J. Arthur Mackley, John Cossar, Mollie McConnell, Lloyd Bacon, Joseph Bennett, Jean Calhoun, Frank Thorne, Guy Eakins, Sid Jordan.
Children of feuding families secretly nurture a romance.

The Feud Girl (Famous Players/Paramount, 1916)
d: Frederic Thompson. 5 reels.
Hazel Dawn, Irving Cummings, Arthur Morrison, Hardee Kirkland, Russell Simpson, Gertrude Norman, George Majeroni, Edna Holland.
In the mountains, a Haddon girl and a Bassett boy fall in love and get married, bringing to an end the generations-long feud between their clans.

The Field of Honor (Universal, 1917)
d: Allen Holubar. 5 reels.
Louise Lovely, M.K. Wilson, Allen Holubar, Sidney Dean, Helen Wright, Frank MacQuarrie, Frankie Lee.
Civil War melodrama about two men in love with the same woman.

Fields of Honor (Goldwyn, 1918)
d: Ralph W. Ince. 5 reels.
Mae Marsh, Marguerite Marsh, George Cooper, John Wessel, Vernon Steele, Neil Moran, Maud Cooling, Ned Hay, Edward Lynch.

European immigrants to America have their lives entangled by World War I.

Fifth Avenue (Belasco Productions/Producers Distributing Corp., 1926)
d: Robert G. Vignola. 6 reels.
Marguerite De La Motte, Allan Forrest, Louise Dresser, William V. Mong, Crauford Kent, Lucille Lee Stewart, Anna May Wong, Lillian Langdon, Josephine Norman, Sally Long, Flora Finch.
Misunderstandings ensue when a proper southern girl goes north and stays in the home of a lady she met on the train. As it turns out, the "home" is a house of ill repute.

Fifth Avenue Models (Universal, 1925)
d: Sven Gade. 7 reels.
Mary Philbin, Josef Swickard, Norman Kerry, William Conklin, Rosemary Theby, Rose Dione, Jean Hersholt, Cesare Gravina.
A mannequin is forced to pay for a damaged gown. Her artist father tries to help her out, but breaks the law and is arrested. However, one of his paintings is identified as a masterpiece and all ends happily.

Fifty-Fifty (Fine Arts Film Co./Triangle, 1916)
d: Allan Dwan. 5 reels.
Norma Talmadge, J.W. Johnston, Marie Chambers, Ruth Darling, H.S. Northrup, Frank Currier, Dodson Mitchell, W.P. Richmond.
A "perfect couple" find their serenity undone by a scheming vamp.

Fifty-Fifty (Encore Pictures, 1925)
d: Henri Diamant. 5 reels.
Louise Glaum, Hope Hampton, Lionel Barrymore, J. Moy Bennett, Arthur Donaldson, Jean Del Val.
Harmon, an American in Paris, meets and falls in love with Ginette, an apache dancer. However, after he takes her home to the U.S., his eye wanders and he starts a fling with a divorcee. Ginette learns of the affair and decides that what's good for the gander is good for the goose.

The Fifty-Fifty Girl (Paramount, 1928)
d: Clarence Badger. 7 reels.
Bebe Daniels, James Hall, William Austin, George Kotsonaros, Johnnie Morris, Alfred Allen, John O'Hara.
Kathleen and her sweetheart Jim become owners of a gold mine in California.

$50,000 Reward (Clifford S. Elfelt Productions, 1924)
d: Clifford S. Elfelt. 5 reels.
Ken Maynard, Esther Ralston, Bert Lindley, Edward Peil, Lillian Leighton, Charles Newton, Frank Whitson.
Tex, a cowhand whose inherited land is indispensable to a new dam project, rides to the county seat to register his title. But a gang of hoodlums is out to stop him, spurred by greedy speculators who hope to steal the land for themselves.

Fig Leaves (Fox, 1926)
w, d: Howard Hawks. 7 reels. (Part Technicolor.)
George O'Brien, Olive Borden, Heinie Conklin, Phyllis Haver.
"Battle of the sexes" comedy with Adam (O'Brien) and Eve (Miss Borden) battling it out in the Garden of Eden and also in Roaring '20s America.

A Fight for Honor (Columbia, 1924)
d: Henry MacRae. 5 reels.

Wilfred Lucas, Eva Novak, William Fairbanks, Claire McDowell, Jack Byron, Marion Harlan, Derry Welford.
Railroad thieves are thwarted at every turn by two sisters, a young man, and their dog.

A Fight for Love (Universal, 1919)
d: Jack Ford. 6 reels.
Harry Carey, Neva Gerber, Joe Harris, Mark Fenton, J. Farrell McDonald.
An outlaw escapes a sheriff's posse by crossing the border into Canada. He thinks he's home free, but his troubles have just begun.

A Fight to the Finish (Columbia, 1925)
d: Reeves Eason. 5 reels.
William Fairbanks, Phyllis Haver, Tom Ricketts, Pat Harmon, William Bolder, Leon Beauman.
A millionaire pretends he has lost his fortune in order to shock his playboy son into showing some initiative.

The Fighter (Selznick/Select, 1921)
d: Henry Kolker. 5 reels.
Conway Tearle, Winifred Westover, Arthur Housman, Ernest Lawford, George Stewart, Warren Cook, Helen Lindroth.
Caleb, a railroad president, is in love with his ward. Before he can declare his love, however, he must fight scoundrels who try to take over his organization.

Fighter's Paradise (Phil Goldstone Productions, 1924)
d: Alvin J. Neitz. 5 reels.
Rex Baker, Andrew Waldron, dick Sutherland, Jack Curtis, Harry Burns, Kenneth Benedict, Margaret Landis.
A small-town soda jerk is mistaken for a famous boxer and forced to fight.

The Fightin' Comeback (Action Pictures/Pathé, 1927)
d: Tenny Wright. 5 reels.
Buddy Roosevelt, Clara Horton, Sidney M. Goldin, Richard Neill, Robert Homans, Charles Thurston, Richard Alexander.
In Arizona, a cowpoke who was cheated out of a large sum of money by a crooked gambler decides to avenge himself by stealing the cash back and escaping.

Fightin' Mad (William Desmond Productions/Metro, 1921)
d: Joseph J. Franz. 6 reels.
William Desmond, Virginia Brown Faire, Doris Pawn, Rosemary Theby, Joseph J. Dowling, William lawrence, Emmett C. King, Jack Richardson, William J. Dyer, Bert Lindley.
McGraw, a combat veteran, returns to his Pa's cattle ranch, but finds peace and tranquility boring. Itching to get back into some kind of action, McGraw finds all he can handle with the Texas Border Police.

Fightin' Odds (Anchor Film Distributors, 1925)
d: Bennett Cohn. 5 reels.
Bill Patton, Doris Dare, Jack House, Jack Ganzhorn, Hugh Saxon, Alfred Hewston, Edmund Burns.
Out West, a crooked judge and sheriff conspire to cheat an heir out of his land. But against all odds, the heir fights back and, after several adventures, manages to redeem his land and get the culprits arrested.

The Fightin' Redhead (FBO Pictures, 1928)
d: Louis King. 5 reels.
Buzz Barton, Duane Thompson, Milburn Morante, Bob Fleming, Edmund Cobb, Edward Hearn.
Two drifters, "Red" Hepner and his pal Steve, ride into town

and help the local authorities capture a notorious bandit.

The Fighting American (Universal, 1924)
d: Tom Forman. 6 reels.
Pat O'Malley, Mary Astor, Raymond Hatton, Warner Oland, Edwin J. Brady, Taylor Carroll, Clarence Geldert, Alfred Fisher.
A college boy proposes to a girl purely as a gag, but falls in love with her anyway. When she learns about the deception, the disillusioned girl runs off to join her missionary father in China, but her new "fiancé" follows her there.

Fighting Back (Triangle, 1917)
d: Raymond Wells. 5 reels.
William Desmond, Claire McDowell, Jack Richardson, Curley Baldwin, Pete Morrison, William Ellingford, Thomas S. Guise, Thornton Edwards, Josie Sedgwick.
A court-martialed soldier labeled "the weakling" fights back, proves his bravery, and has his record cleared of all charges.

The Fighting Blade (Inspiration Pictures, 1923)
d: John S. Robertson. 9 reels.
Richard Barthelmess, Lee Baker, Morgan Wallace, Bradley Barker, Frederick Burton, Stuart Sage, Philip Tead, Walter Horton, Dorothy Mackaill, Allyn King, Marcia Harris.
Swordplay and derring-do highlight this tale of a Flemish soldier and his exploits during the English Civil War in the 17th century.

Fighting Blood (Fox, 1916)
d: Oscar C. Apfel. 5 reels.
William Farnum, Dorothy Bernard, Fred Huntley, Henry J. Herbert, H.A. Barrows, Dick Le Strange, Willard Louis.
When a lumberjack is framed of embezzling funds and sent to prison, instead of turning bitter he turns to religion and becomes a reverend minister.

Fighting Bob (Rolfe Photoplays, Inc./Metro, 1915)
d: John W. Noble. 5 reels.
Orrin Johnson, Olive Wyndham, Edward Brenon, Frederick Vroom, John Sheehan.
An American college student goes south of the border and foils a rebel attempt to overthrow the government of a Central American republic.

The Fighting Boob (R-C Pictures/FBO of America, 1926)
d: Jack Nelson. 5 reels.
Bob Custer, Frank Whitson, Sherry Tansey, Hugh Saxon, Violet Palmer, Andrew Arbuckle, Sam Lufkin, Tom Bay, Joan Meredith, Bobby Nelson, Artie Ortega.
A mysterious bandit known as "The Tiger" stands in for a former war pal in a face-off against kidnappers who are out to blackmail the buddy's uncle and steal his ranch.

The Fighting Buckaroo (Fox, 1926)
d: R. William Neill. 5 reels.
Buck Jones, Sally Long, Lloyd Whitlock, Frank Butler, E.J. Ratcliffe, Ben Hendricks Jr., Ray Thompson, Frank Rice.

Rapid-fire western comedy about Crawford, a rancher who falls for a girl he meets in the city. He tries to win her favor but alienates her father with his antics. Meanwhile, a gang of larcenous toughs is after Crawford to steal his ranch.

The Fighting Chance (Famous Players-Lasky/Paramount, 1920)
d: Charles Maigne. 6 reels.
Conrad Nagel, Anna Q. Nilsson, Clarence Burton, Dorothy Davenport, Herbert Pryor, Ruth Helms, Bertram Grassby, Maude Wayne, Frederick Stanton, William H. Brown.

A woman engaged to a wealthy scoundrel falls in love with another man.

The Fighting Cheat (Action Pictures/Artclass Pictures, 1926)
d: Richard Thorpe. 5 reels.
Wally Wales, Jean Arthur, Ted Rackerby, Fanny Midgley, Charles whitaker, V.L. Barnes, Al Taylor.
Out West, a bandit who thinks he's dying entrusts a stranger with some money to take to the bandit's mother. The patient recovers, however, and when he goes to his mother's home he finds that his sister has met and fallen in love with the kind stranger.

A Fighting Colleen (Vitagraph, 1919)
d: David Smith. 5 reels.
Bessie Love, Ann Schaefer, Charles Spere, Jay Marley, George Kunkel, Beulah Clark.
"Shrimpy" Malone, a wee lass from Ireland, helps the district attorney crack a case involving illegal payoffs.

Fighting Courage (Clifford S. Elfelt Productions, 1925)
d: Clifford S. Elfelt. 5 reels.
Ken Maynard, Peggy Montgomery, Melbourne MacDowell, Frank Whitson, Henry Ward, Gus Saville, James Barry Jr.
Kingsley, a wealthy New Yorker, is sent by his father to Colorado to search for a lost mine. Along the way he has several adventures and misadventures, and falls in love with a chorus girl.

The Fighting Coward (Famous Players-Lasky, 1924)
d: James Cruze. 7 reels.
Cullen Landis, Ernest Torrence, Mary Astor, Noah Beery, Phyllis Haver, Richard R. Neill, Bruce Covington, Helen Dunbar, Carmen Phillips, Frank Jonasson.
Tom, a young man raised by Quakers, refuses to accept a duel when he is challenged. Thought of as a coward by most in the community, Tom secretly learns to use swords and firearms, and in time proves he is no coward after all.

Fighting Cressy (Pathé, 1920)
d: Robert T. Thornby. 6 reels.
Blanche Sweet, Russell Simpson, Edward Peil, Pell Trenton, Antrim Short, Frank Lanning, Billie Bennett, Georgie Stone, Walter Perry, Eunice Moore.
Feuding Kentucky clans settle in California, but continue their discord.

The Fighting Cub (Crown Productions/Truart Film Corp., 1925)
d: Paul Hurst. 6 reels.
Wesley Barry, Mildred Harris, Pat O'Malley, Mary Carr, George Fawcett, Stuart Holmes.
O'Toole, a copy boy for a city newspaper, tries for a promotion to cub reporter by getting an interview with a famous philanthropist. He does arrange for a meeting, but then O'Toole discovers much more than he expected: The "philanthropist" is secretly a gang leader.

The Fighting Demon (Richard Talmadge Productions/FBO of America, 1925)
d: Arthur Rosson. 6 reels.
Richard Talmadge, Lorraine Eason, Dick Sutherland, Peggy Shaw, Herbert Prior, Charles Hill Mailes, Stanton Heck, Jack Hill, Dave Morris, Andre Cheron, Frank Elliott.
Drake, an outstanding college athlete, gets innocently involved in a bank conspiracy in South America, and ends up having to enter the prize ring to win enough money to exonerate himself.

Fighting Destiny (Vitagraph, 1919)
d: Paul Scardon. 5 reels.
Harry T. Morey, Betty Blythe, Arthur Donaldson, George Majeroni, Templar Saxe.
When a girl breaks her engagement on the eve of her wedding, the puzzled fiancé takes steps to find out why... and stumbles into an opium den.

The Fighting Eagle (DeMille Pictures, 1927)
d: Donald Crisp. 8 reels.
Rod LaRocque, Phyllis Haver, Sam DeGrasse, Max Barwyn, Julia Faye, Sally Rand, Clarence Burton, Alphonse Ethier.
In Napoleon's army, a brigadier helps to expose a traitorous foreign minister.

The Fighting Edge (Warner Bros., 1926)
d: Henry Lehrman. 7 reels.
Patsy Ruth Miller, Kenneth Harlan, Charlie Conklin, David Kirby, Pat Hartigan, Lew Harvey, Eugene Pallette, Pat Harmon, W.A. Carroll.
Drama, with some slapstick elements, about government agents fighting a gang that smuggles aliens into the U.S. across the Mexican border.

The Fighting Failure (Alpine Productions/Hollywood Pictures, 1926)
d: E.G. Boyle. 6 reels.
Cullen Landis, Peggy Montgomery, Lucy Beaumont, Sidney Franklin, Ernest Hilliard.
Out West, a prize fighter falls in love with a lovely ranch owner and uncovers a takeover plot.

Fighting Fate (Harry J. Brown Productions/Rayart, 1925)
d: Albert Rogell. 5 reels.
Billy Sullivan, Johnny Sinclair, Nancy Deaver, Tom McGuire.
When a prizefighter is unjustly accused of throwing a match, he fights back to salvage his reputation... and the hand of the girl he loves.

Fighting for Gold (Fox, 1919)
d: Edward J. LeSaint. 5 reels.
Tom Mix, Teddy Sampson, Sid Jordan, Jack Nelson, Robert Dunbar, Hattie Buskirk, Frank Clark, Lucille Young.
A British heir in the American West is forced to fight to defend his mining claim.

Fighting for Love (Universal, 1916)
d: Raymond Wells. 5 reels.
Ruth Stonehouse, Jack Mulhall, Noble Johnson, Jean Hersholt, J.F. Briscoe, Ruby Marshall.
American cowboys journey to a foreign kingdom and join in its war with its neighbor.

Fighting Fury (Universal, 1924)
d: Clifford Smith. 5 reels.
Jack Hoxie, Helen Holmes, Fred Kohler, Duke R. Lee, Bert DeMare, Al Jennings, George Connors, Art Manning.
Out West, an orphan swears revenge on the three desperadoes who murdered his parents.

The Fighting Grin (Universal, 1918)
d: Joseph de Grasse. 5 reels.
Franklyn Farnum, Edith Johnson, J. Morris Foster, Charles H. Mailes, Fred Montague.
A plucky young man bets $10,000 that he will marry his sweetheart within a week, even though both his father and hers are opposed to their union.

The Fighting Gringo (Universal, 1917)

d: Fred A. Kelsey. 5 reels.
Harry Carey, Claire du Brey, George Webb, Rex DeRosselli, T.D. Crittendon, Tote DuCrow, Bill Gettinger, Vester Pegg.
While trying to reconcile a couple who have separated, a western Dan Cupid also finds time to help the government crush a local uprising.

The Fighting Guide (Vitagraph, 1922)
d: William Duncan, Don Clark. 5 reels.
William duncan, Edith Johnson, Harry Lonsdale, William McCall, Sidney D'Albrook, Charles Dudley, Fred DeSilva, Mrs. Harry Burns.
Ned, a guide for a Northwest trading post, foils a plot to frame an innocent man for murder.

A Fighting Heart (Hercules Film Productions, 1924)
w, d: Jack Nelson. 6 reels.
Frank Merrill, Margaret Landis, Milburn Morante, May Sherman, Otto Lederer, Alphonse Martell, Kathleen Calhoun.
Jack, a collegiate track champion, returns home and finds that his father has died and his entire estate has been left to the doctor who treated him in his last days. Upon investigating, Jack learns that the "doctor" is a crook who's trying to steal another fortune by hypnotizing his new patient, the aunt of Jack's sweetheart.

The Fighting Heart (Fox, 1925)
d: John Ford. 7 reels.
George O'Brien, Billie Dove, J. Farrell MacDonald, Victor McLaglen, Diana Miller, Bert Woodruff, Francis Ford, Hazel Howell, Edward Piel, James Marcus.
In New York, a boxer who gets a shot at the champion is vamped by the champ's sweetie.

The Fighting Hombre (Bob Custer Productions/FBO of America, 1927)
d: Jack Nelson. 5 reels.
Bob Custer, Mary O'Day, Bert Sprotte, David Dunbar, Carlo Schipa, Zita Makar, Walter Maly, Jack Anthony.
Western drama about a girl who accidentally kills a gambler, but gets away with it because another girl, Marie, confesses to the crime. Since Marie had once been seduced by the murdered man, she is freed by the sympathetic authorities.

The Fighting Hope (Lasky Feature Plays/Paramount, 1915)
d: George Melford. 5 reels.
George Gebhardt, Laura Hope Crews, Gerald Ward, Thomas Meighan, Richard Morris, Florence Smythe, Theodore Roberts, Cleo Ridgely, Tom Forman, Billy Elmer.
When a fraudulent transaction causes a bank to fail, the bank's treasurer is sentenced to ten years in jail. His wife goes undercover to prove his innocence, but her research uncovers evidence that tends to incriminate him even more.

The Fighting Kentuckians (Sterling Features/State Rights, 1920)
d: J. Harrison Edwards. 5 reels.
Thornton Baston, Irma Harrison, Tom Burroughs, Adele Kelly, Colin Chase, Peter Raymond, Thomas Swinton, May Wick, Myra Brooks, Clifford Williams.
Rivals for a Kentucky girl go to France during World War I.

Fighting Love (DeMille Pictures/Producers Distributing Corp., 1927)
d: Nils Olaf Chrisander. 7 reels.
Jetta Goudal, Victor Varconi, Henry B. Walthall, Louis Natheaux, Josephine Crowell.
In Africa, the wife of an Italian officer is seduced by a charming young soldier.

The Fighting Lover (Universal, 1921)
d: Fred Leroy Granville. 5 reels.
Frank Mayo, Elinor Hancock, Gertrude Olmstead, Jackson Read, Colin Kelly, Jacqueline Logan, Joe Singleton, Gordon Sackville, Jean Calhoun, Ruth Ashby, Fred G. Becker.
 Andrew bets his friend Ned a large sum of money that he (Ned) will fall in love with one of three girls within a month. Ned can't dodge Cupid's darts, though, and after several adventures, he is glad to hand over the money to be united with Anna, his new love.

Fighting Mad (Universal, 1917)
d: Edward J. Le Saint. 5 reels.
William Stowell, Helen Gibson, Betty Schade, Hector Dion, Alfred Allen, Mildred Davis, M.K. Wilson.
Abandoned by his wife, a preacher loses his faith in humanity. He deposits his baby daughter on a doorstep, leaves town, and becomes a drunkard. Several years later, he staggers back into town and meets his grown daughter, who has blossomed into a radiant beauty, both in body and soul.

The Fighting Marine (Pathé, 1926)
d: Spencer Gordon Bennett. 7 reels.
Gene Tunney, Marjorie Gay, Walter Miller, Virginia Vance, Sherman Ross, Mike Donlin, Jack Anthony, Anna May Walthall, Frank Hagney.
An ex-Marine becomes guardian to a young woman who's trying to fulfill the requirements of an eccentric relative's will.

Fighting Odds (Goldwyn, 1917)
d: Allan Dwan. 6 reels.
Maxine Elliott, Henry Clive, Charles Dalton, George Odell, Regan Hughston, William T. Carleton, Eric Hudson.
When an honest industrialist is betrayed by his partners and winds up being sentenced to prison on trumped-up evidence, his wife disguises herself to gain the partners' trust and find proof of her husband's innocence.

The Fighting Peacemaker (Universal, 1926)
d: Clifford Smith. 5 reels.
Jack Hoxie, Lola Todd, Ted Oliver, William A. Steele, Robert McKenzie, Clark Comstock, Frank Rice.
Parker, a ranch foreman who fancies the owner's daughter, is convicted of a crime on perjured testimony. He's be released from prison early for good behavior, then gets to work solving the crime himself.

The Fighting Romeo (J.J. Fleming Productions, 1925)
d: Al Ferguson. 5 reels.
Al Ferguson, Elaine Eastman, Paul Emery, George Routh, William Dills.
Out West, a ranch foreman takes Jim, an old friend, under his wing as an apprentice. The apprentice learns well. Soon, when the ranch owner's daughter is kidnapped, it's Jim who rides to the rescue.

The Fighting Roosevelts (McClure Productions, Inc./First National, 1919)
d: William Nigh. 6 reels.
Francis J. Noonan, Herbert Bradshaw, E.J. Ratcliffe.
Biodrama based on the life of Theodore Roosevelt.

The Fighting Sap (Monogram, 1924)
d: Albert Rogell. 6 reels.
Fred Thomson, Hazel Keener, Wilfred Lucas, George

Williams, Frank Hagney, Ralph Yearsley, Bob Williamson, Robert Fleming.

Disowned by his disgusted father, a young man changes his indolent ways and becomes a geological engineer. Now involved in research at his father's gold mine, the youngster learns of a plot among the workers to steal from the mine. He foils the crooks, is welcomed back by his father, and wins the hand of the mine superintendent's daughter.

The Fighting Shepherdess (First National, 1920)
d: Edward José. 5 reels.
Anita Stewart, Wallace MacDonald, Noah Beery, Walter Long, Eugenie Besserer, John Hall, Gibson Gowland, Calvert Carter, Billie Devall, Maud Wayne, Ben Lewis, Will Jeffries.
When her best friend, a man who was like a father to her, is murdered, a docile girl becomes like a "fighting shepherdess" in her zeal to find his killer.

The Fighting Sheriff (Independent Pictures, 1925)
d: J.P. McGowan. 5 reels.
Bill Cody, Frank Ellis, Walter Shumway, Hazel Holt.
Out West, a battling sheriff takes on platinum thieves.

The Fighting Smile (Independent Pictures, 1925)
d: Jay Marchant. 5 reels.
Bill Cody, Jean Arthur, Charles Brinley, George Magrill, Billie Bennett.
A rancher's son discovers that Dad's assistant is rustling his cattle.

The Fighting Stranger (William N. Selig/Canyon Pictures, 1921)
d: Webster Cullison. 5 reels.
Franklyn Farnum, Flora Hollister, W.A. Alleman, Vester Pegg, W.A. Bartlett, Churchill Scott, Emma Burns.

Joe, an ex-con, attempts a bank robbery but apparently bungles it. Meanwhile, his gang gets the goods on a prominent citizen who's secretly a bandit, and Joe then springs the trap: He's not a real criminal, but a Secret Service man in disguise.

The Fighting Streak (Fox, 1922)
d: Arthur Rosson. 5 reels.
Tom Mix, Patsy Ruth Miller, Gerald Pring, Al Fremont, Sidney Jordan, Bert Sprotte, Robert Fleming.
Engaging western melodrama about Andy, a law-abiding blacksmith who is forced by circumstances to become a fugitive.

Fighting the Flames (Columbia, 1925)
d: Reeves Eason. 6 reels.
William Haines, David Torrence, Dorothy Devore, Frankie Darro, Sheldon Lewis, William Welsh, Charles Murray.
A judge's son is blamed for obstructing firemen, then later rescues two people from another burning building.

The Fighting Three (Universal, 1927)
d: Albert S. Rogell. 5 reels.
Jack Hoxie, Olive Hasbrouck, Marin Sais, Fanny Warren, William Malan, Buck Connors, William Dyer, Henry Roquemore, William Norton Bailey.
Out West, a traveling Follies company plays in Conway's town, and he becomes enamored of one of the stars. Soon, he finds himself accused of murdering the girl's father, and takes to the hills with the girl in tow. But you can bet that he'll be exonerated—*and* win the girl—by the final reel.

Fighting Through (W.W. Hodkinson/Pathé, 1919)
d: William Christy Cabanne. 6 reels.

E.K. Lincoln, Spottiswoode Aitken, Millicent Fisher, Frederick Vroom, Helen Dunbar, Hayward Mack.
A son of the Old South finally buries his resentment against the American flag.

Fighting Youth (Columbia, 1925)
d: Reeves Eason. 5 reels.
William Fairbanks, Pauline Garon, Frank Hagney, George Periolat, William Norton Bailey, Pat Harmon, Tom Carr, Jack Britton.
Dick, a young hothead, promises his girlfriend that he will stop fighting. It's a promise he'll find difficult to keep.

The Figurehead (Selznick, 1920)
d: Robert Ellis. 5 reels.
Eugene O'Brien, Alla W. Nilsson, Ora Carew, Edwin Stevens, Joseph Girard, Frances Parks, Kate Price.
Two political bosses decide to run a figurehead for mayor, but much to their dismay, the candidate takes politics seriously and refuses to play their game.

Figures Don't Lie (Paramount, 1927)
d: Edward Sutherland. 6 reels.
Esther Ralston, Richard Arlen, Ford Sterling, Doris Hill, Blanche Payson, Natalie Kingston.
Janet is beautiful, and a very efficient secretary... thus putting her boss at odds with his extraordinarily jealous wife.

Filling His Own Shoes (Essanay, 1917)
d: Harry Beaumont. 1917. 5 reels.
Bryant Washburn, Hazel Daly, Roderick LaRock, Lydia Dalzell, Virginia Valli, Helen Ferguson, Louis Long, Julien Barton, Alice Hawley, Arthur Metcalfe.
When an American shoe clerk saves the life of a wealthy Turk, the grateful man bequeaths to his benefactor his entire estate. Later, when the Turk dies, the shoe clerk learns that in addition to a large sum of money, he has inherited guardianship of three lovely young women.

The Final Close-up (Famous Players-Lasky/Paramount, 1919)
d: Walter Edwards. 5 reels.
Shirley Mason, Francis McDonald, James Gordon, Betty Bouton, Eugene Burr, Mary Warren.
A shopgirl receives an anonymous check for $200 and goes to a seaside resort on vacation. Her money is stolen and she must resort to washing dishes at the resort; but soon she discovers a plot to loot the hotel safe, and captures the thief. She is cleared of all debt by the grateful hotel management, then finds that her anonymous benefactor is a young fellow she's had eyes for, and winds up in his arms in the final close-up.

The Final Extra (Gotham Productions/Lumas Film Corp., 1927)
d: James P. Hogan. 6 reels.
Marguerite De la Motte, Grant Withers, John Miljan, Frank Beal, Joseph W. Girard, Billy "Red" Jones, Leon Holmes.
Riley, a newspaper reporter, works on the entertainment news but yearns to be assigned to cover a juicy crime story. He soon gets his wish when a chorus girl is abducted by an unscrupulous promoter, and Riley becomes involved in rescuing the girl, foiling the promoter, and getting his scoop.

The Final Judgment (Rolfe Photoplays, Inc./Metro, 1915)
d: Edwin Carewe. 5 reels.
Ethel Barrymore, Beatrice Maude, Mahlon Hamilton, H. Cooper Cliffe, Percy G. Standing, Paul Lawrence, M.W. Rale.

An actress must prove her husband innocent of murder.

The Final Payment (Fox, 1917)
d: Frank Powell. 5 reels.
Nance O'Neil, Jane Miller, Clifford Bruce, Leslie Austin, Alfred Hickman, Dorothy Bernard.
Two fishermen love the same girl. When she gives her heart to one of them, his rival becomes insanely jealous and wages an all-out war against them both.

Find the Woman (Vitagraph, 1918)
d: Tom Terriss. 5 reels.
Alice Joyce, Walter McGrail, Henry Houry, Jessie Stevens, Jean Paige, Arthur Donaldson, Martin Faust, Victor A. Stewart.
In New Orleans, a French opera star is falsely accused of stealing $20,000.

Find the Woman (Cosmopolitan/Paramount, 1922)
d: Tom Terriss. 6 reels.
Alma Rubens, Harrison Ford, George MacQuarrie, Norman Kerry, Arthur Donaldson, Henry Sedley, Eileen Hoban, Sydney Deane.
A midwest girl opts for a Broadway career, and finds more excitement than she dreamed she would when a theatrical agent is murdered in a baffling mystery.

Find Your Man (Warner Bros., 1924)
d: Mal St. Clair. 7 reels.
Rin-Tin-Tin, Eric St. Clair, Pat Hartigan, June Marlowe, Raymond Mckee, Lew Harvey.
A clever dog solves a murder his master is accused of, and tracks down the real culprit.

Finders Keepers (Art-O-Graph Productions/Pioneer Pictures, 1921)
d: Otis B. Thayer. 6 reels.
Violet Mersereau, Edmund Cobb, Dorothy Simpson, Verne Layton, May Stone.
Small-town girl Amy, who sang in the church choir, goes to New York to try making it on Broadway. But it's tough going in the big city, and Amy winds up as a cabaret singer.

Finders Keepers (Universal, 1928)
d: Wesley Ruggles. 6 reels.
Laura LaPlante, John Harron, Edmond Breese, William Gorman, Eddie Phillips, Arthur Rankin, Joe Mack.
When her soldier sweetie is ordered to go overseas, Barbara can't bear to see him leave. So she dresses up as a soldier and tries to join him.

Fine Feathers (Cosmos Features/World Film Corp., 1915)
d: Joseph A. Golden. 5 reels.
Janet Beecher, David Powell, Lyster Chambers, Alberta Gallatin, Geraldine McCann.
When a chemist's wife develops a liking for fine clothes, she soon drags her husband along in a greedy search for luxuries.

Fine Feathers (Metro, 1921)
d: Fred Sittenham. 6 reels.
Eugene Pallette, Blaire Whitney, Thomas W. Ross, Warburton Gamble, June Elvidge.
Morbid melodrama about a construction engineer who is induced to use inferior concrete in the construction of a dam. The dam bursts, there is much loss of life, and the guilt-tormented engineer kills the man who persuaded him to do shoddy work, then takes his own life.

Fine Manners (Famous Players-Lasky/Paramount, 1926)
d: Richard Rosson. 7 reels.
Gloria Swanson, Eugene O'Brien, Helen Dunbar, Walter Goss, John Miltern.
A society swell tries to transform a chorus girl into a lady of fine manners.

Finger Prints (Warner Bros., 1927)
d: Lloyd Bacon. 7 reels.
Louise Fazenda, Edgar Kennedy, Myrna Loy, Helene Costello, Warner Richmond, William Demarest, John T. Murray, Franklin Pangborn.
A gang of thieves searches for hidden loot, but they are thwarted by secret panels, trap doors, and some cheerfully inept lawmen.

Finnegan's Ball (Graf Brothers Studio/First Division Pictures, 1927)
d: James P. Hogan. 7 reels.
Blanche Mehaffey, Mack Swain, Cullen Landis, Aggie Herring, Charles McHugh, Westcott B. Larke, Kewpie Morgan, Mimi Finnegan.
Two Irish clans—the Finnegans and the Flanagans—migrate to the U.S., and continue their feuding ways.

The Fire Brigade (MGM, 1926)
d: William Nigh. 9 reels.
Charles Ray, Tom O'Brien, May McAvoy, Eugenie Besserer, Holmes Herbert, Warner P. Richmond, Bert Woodruff, Vivia Ogden, DeWitt Jennings, Dan Mason, Erwin Connelly.
Three generations of fire fighters are involved in dousing a huge conflagration of suspicious origin.

The Fire Cat (Universal, 1921)
d: Norman Dawn. 5 reels.
Edith Roberts, Walter Long, William Eagle Eye, Olga D. Mojean, Beatrice Dominguez, Arthur Jasmine, Wallace MacDonald.
In the Andes, a cabaret dancer vows revenge on an American drifter who killed her mother. While she seeks her revenge, the volcano Cotopaxi erupts and engulfs the drifter, as the dancer flees the advancing lava with another Americano.

The Fire Eater (Universal, 1921)
d: Reaves Eason. 5 reels.
Hoot Gibson, Louis Lorraine, Walter Perry, Tom Lingham, Fred Lancaster, Carmen Phillips, George Berrell, W. Bradley Ward, George A. Williams.
U.S. forest rangers try to win acceptance among the inhabitants of a valley which is to be incorporated into a national park. It won't be easy.

The Fire Flingers (Universal, 1919)
d: Rupert Julian. 6 reels.
Clyde Fillmore, Fred Kelsey, Jane Novak, Rupert Julian, E.A. Warren, Fay Tincher, Fritzie Ridgeway, William Lloyd, Will Jeffries.
Two print shop workers are about to be fired by their unfeeling boss because he's learned they are ex-convicts. Before you know it, one of the ex-cons is impersonating the boss, and the boss' wife doesn't seem to mind.

The Fire Patrol (Hunt Stromberg Productions/Chadwick Pictures, 1924)
d: Hunt Stromberg. 7 reels.
Anna Q. Nilsson, William Jeffries, Spottiswoode Aitken, Jack Richardson, Madge Bellamy, Helen Jerome Eddy, Dicky Brandon, Johnny Harron, Gale Henry, Frances Ross.
Ferguson, a sea captain who was blinded in a pirate attack

on his ship years before, finally catches up to the former pirate when both are rescued from a burning ship by the fire patrol.

The Firebrand (Fox, 1918)
d: Edmund Lawrence. 5 reels.
Virginia Pearson, Victor Sutherland, Carleton Macy, Herbert Evans, Jane Courtney, Willard Cooley, Nicholas Dunaew.
In Russia during the revolution, a princess falls in love with an American ex-patriot.

The Firebrand (Phil Goldstone Productions, 1922)
d: Alvin J. Neitz. 5 reels.
Franklyn Farnum, Ruth Langdon, Fred Gamble, Pat Harmon, William Lester, Tex Keith.
Out West, a homesteader helps the sheriff capture a gang of cattle rustlers.

Firebrand Trevision (Fox, 1920)
d: Thomas N. Heffron. 5 reels.
Buck Jones, Winifred Westover, Martha Mattox, Stanton Heck, Katherine Van Buren, Frank Clark, Joe Ray, Pat Harnman, Fong Hong.
Eager to obtain certain ranchland, a railroad executive tries to undermine the ranch owner's title and grab the land for next to nothing.

The Firefly of France (Famous Players Lasky/Paramount, 1918)
d: Donald Crisp. 5 reels.
Wallace Reid, Ann Little, Charles Ogle, Raymond Hatton, Winter Hall, Ernest Joy, Clarence Geldert, William Elmer, Henry Woodward, Jane Wolff.
In World War I, an American joins forces with French patriots.

The Firefly of Tough Luck (Triangle, 1917)
d: E. Mason Hopper. 5 reels.
Alma Rueben, Charles Gunn, Walt Whitman, Darrel Foss, Jack Curtis, Aaron Edwards, Laura Sears.
Fresh from New York city, a music hall dancer lands in a western town with a miner called "Tough Luck" Baxter.

Fireman, Save My Child (Paramount, 1927)
d: Edward Sutherland. 6 reels.
Wallace Beery, Raymond Hatton, Josephine Dunn, Tom Kennedy, Walter Goss, Joseph Girard.
Farcical comedy about childhood pals who later become members of the town's fire department.

The Fires of Conscience (Fox, 1916)
d: Oscar Apfel. 5 reels.
William Farnum, Gladys Brockwell, Nell Shipman, H.A. Barrows, H.J. Herbert, William Burress, Eleanor Crowe, Willard Louis, Brooklyn Keller, Fred Huntley.
Finding his wife has been unfaithful, a cuckold husband kills his rival. He escapes, but finds that he cannot live with his guilt, and so returns to face trial.

Fires of Faith (Famous Players-Lasky/Paramount, 1919)
d: Edward José. 6 reels.
Catherine Calvert, Eugene O'Brien, Ruby de Remer, Helen Dunbar, Theodore Roberts, Charles Ogle, Clarence Geldart, James Neill, Edythe Chapman, Pat Moore, Fred Huntley, Lucille Ward, Mowbray Berkeley, Robert Anderson.
Tangled drama about a young farm woman who gets raped, and a man who is a friend of her family. They don't know each other, but meet when he saves her from a second attack, this time in New York city.

Fires of Rebellion (Universal, 1917)
d: Ida May Park. 5 reels.
Dorothy Phillips, Lon Chaney, William Stowell, Belle Bennett, Golda Madden, Alice May Youst, Edward Brady, Richard LaReno.
After a girl spurns her plain beau's proposal for fear of a drab existence, she moves to the big city to find some excitement—and finds more than she had hoped for.

Fires of Youth (Universal, 1918)
d: Rupert Julian. 5 reels.
Ralph Lewis, Ruth Clifford, George Fisher.
A lovely young woman marries an older man for his money, then finds herself attracted to his young friend.

The Fires of Youth (Thanhouser Film Corp./Pathé, 1917)
d: Emile Chautard. 5 reels.
Frederick Warde, Helen Badgley, Ernest Howard, Jeanne Eagels, Robert Vaughn, James Ewens, Carey Hastings.
A steel magnate who has spent his life amassing millions but has wasted his youth, now seeks to recapture the boyhood he once knew.

The Firing Line (Famous Players-Lasky/Paramount, 1919)
d: Charles Maigne. 6 reels.
Irene Castle, Isabelle West, May Kitson, Anne Cornwall, Gladys Coburn, R. Vernon Steele, David Powell, J.H. Gilmore, Frank Losee, Rudolph de Cordova, Charles Craig.
Ill-advised scenario appears to condone suicide as the "noble" way out when a man discovers his wife loves another man.

The First Auto (Warner Bros., 1927)
d: Roy Del Ruth. 7 reels.
Charles Emmett Mack, Russell Simpson, Barney Oldfield, Patsy Ruth Miller, Frank Campeau, William Demarest, Paul Kruger.
Comedic tale about Hank, an old-fashioned man who resents that new-fangled contraption, the "horseless carriage." Unfortunately for Hank, his own son takes to the new machines like a duck to water.

The First Born (Robertson-Cole, 1921)
d: Colin Campbell. 5 reels.
Sessue Hayakawa, Helen Jerome Eddy, Sonny Boy Warde, Goro Kino, Marie Pavis, Clarence Wilson, Frank M. Seki, Anna May Wong.
Bitter drama about a man who seeks revenge on a neighbor because his son was killed in a fall from the neighbor's window.

The First Degree (Universal, 1923)
d: Edward Sedgwick. 5 reels.
Frank Mayo, Sylvia Breamer, George A. Williams, Harry Carter.
Sam, a man who thinks he's killed his brother Will, discovers that Will is very much alive... and a blackmailer!

The First Kiss (Paramount, 1928)
d: Rowland V. Lee. 6 reels.
Fay Wray, Gary Cooper, Lane Chandler, Leslie Fenton, Paul Fix, Malcolm Williams, Monroe Owsley.
After the Talbot family falls from glittering prominence to pitiful decay in only two generations, one of the four sons finally decides he will pull the family up by the bootstraps. Along the way to redemption, he kisses a girl he's fallen for, but she rejects him. Six years later, however, the Talbots are back on the high road, and that girl is back in his life again, this time for good.

The First Law (Astra Film Corp./Pathé, 1918)
d: Lawrence McGill. 5 reels.
Irene Castle, Antonio Moreno, J.H. Gilmour, Marguerite Snow, Edward J. Connelly.
A boarding-house owner loves one of her tenants and he loves her, but they cannot marry because she is already in a loveless marriage entered into in haste.

First Love (Realart Pictures/Paramount, 1921)
d: Maurice Campbell. 5 reels.
Constance Binney, Warner Baxter, George Webb, Betty Schade, George Hernandez, Fannie Midgley, Edward Jobson, Agnes Adams, Maxine Elliott Hicks, Dorothy Gordon.
Kathleen loves Harry, an ambulance driver. Trouble is, he's Mr. Wrong. Eventually she sees the light when she spots him in a restaurant with another girl. Fortunately, Mr. Right is there to cushion the blow.

The First Night (Tiffany Productions, 1927)
d: Richard Thorpe. 6 reels.
Bert Lytell, Dorothy Devore, Harry Myers, Frederic Kovert, Walter Hiers, Lila Leslie, James Mack, Hazel Keener, Joan Standing.
A doctor and his new fiancée have a rough engagement, since her former boyfriend has sworn to prevent their marriage from ever taking place.

The First Year (Fox, 1926)
d: Frank Borzage. 6 reels.
Matt Moore, Kathryn Perry, John Patrick, Frank Currier, Frank Cooley, Virginia Madison, Carolynne Snowden, J. Farrell MacDonald.
Marital comedy about newlyweds surviving a rocky first year together.

Five and Ten Cent Annie (Warner Bros., 1928)
d: Roy Del Ruth. 5 reels.
Louise Fazenda, Clyde Cook, William Demarest, Gertrude Astor, Tom Ricketts, Douglas Gerrard, Andre Beranger.
A street sweeper inherits a million dollars, but there are strings attached. So the heir and his sweetheart scramble furiously to untie them.

Five Days to Live (R-C Pictures, 1922)
d: Norman Dawn. 6 reels.
Sessue Hayakawa, Tsuru Aoki, Goro Kino, Misao Seki, Toyo Fujita, George Kuwa.
A Chinese woodcarver falls for a girl whose foster father, Chong, will not release her. Finally the woodcarver secures her freedom by offering Chong a large sum of money — but he almost dies trying to raise the funds.

The Five Dollar Baby (Metro, 1922)
d: Harry Beaumont. 6 reels.
Viola Dana, Ralph Lewis, Otto Hoffman, John Harron, Tom McGuire, Arthur Rankin, Marjorie Maurice, Ernst Pasque.
After a tramp finds a needy young orphan girl, he takes her and hocks her with a pawnbroker for five dollars, promising a large reward when the girl turns 18.

The Five Faults of Flo (Thanhouser Film Corp./Mutual, 1916)
d: George Foster Platt. 5 reels.
Florence La Badie, Harris Gordon, Samuel Niblack, Ernest Howard, Grace DeCarlton, Bertha Smith, Helen Eldridge.
Flo has five faults she must lose: pride, envy, fickleness, extravagance, and jealousy.

The $5,000,000 Counterfeiting Plot (Dramascope Co., 1914)
d: Bertram Harrison. 6 reels.
William J. Burns, Glen White, Joseph Sullivan, Clifford P. Saum, Hector Dion, Jack Sharkey, William Cavanaugh, Charles E. Graham, Harry Lillford, James Ayling, John Ransom, Jean Acker, Eileen Hume, Sir Arthur Conan Doyle.
The daughter of a counterfeiter touches off an investigation when she innocently passes off one of her dad's "products." Eventually, the counterfeiter and all his cronies are jailed. Sir Arthur Conan Doyle, the author of the Sherlock Holmes stories, appears in the film as himself.

Five Thousand an Hour (Metro, 1918)
d: Ralph W. Ince. 5 reels.
Hale Hamilton, Lucille Lee Stewart, Gilbert Douglas, Florence Short, Robert Whittier, Robert Middlemass, Isabel O'Madigan, William Frederic, Warren Cook, Charles Edwards.
Comedy about a loveable loser whose partner absconds with the company funds and leaves him nearly penniless. When he learns that the girl he loves will inherit one million dollars if she marries the felonious partner within six weeks, our hero decides to earn an equal amount — $5,000 an hour — and beat his rival to the altar.

$5,000 Reward (Universal, 1918)
d: Douglas Gerrard. 5 reels.
Franklyn Farnum, Gloria Hope, William Lloyd, J. Farrell MacDonald, Wharton Jones, Marc Fenton, Frank Brownlee, Lule Warrenton, Grace McLean.
When a wealthy man threatens to disinherit his nephew and is later found dead, all evidence points to the nephew. But he's innocent, so he and his wife scramble to find the real killer.

Fixed by George (Universal, 1920)
d: Eddie Lyons, Lee Moran. 5 reels.
Eddie Lyons, Lee Moran, Hazel Howell, Beatrice LaPlante, Fred Gamble, Daisy Robinson, Earl Martin, Jack Byron, Maude Wayne.
A spoiled, neurotic woman pays her therapist $1,000 a week, and eventually falls in love with him. But he's already married, a fact he tries to hide from his wealthy patient.

Flame of the Argentine (R-C Pictures/FBO of America, 1926)
d: Edward Dillon. 5 reels.
Evelyn Brent, Orville Caldwell, Frank Leigh, Dan Makarenko, Rosita Marstini, Evelyn Selbie, Florence Turner.
In Argentina, a con man hires a cabaret singer to impersonate a wealthy woman's long-lost daughter.

The Flame of Life (Universal, 1923)
d: Hobart Henley. 7 reels.
Priscilla Dean, Wallace Beery, Robert Ellis, Fred Kohler, Beatrice Burnham, Emmett King, Kathryn McGuire, Frankie Lee.
A coal mine foreman's life is endangered by a surly workman, whose own daughter is secretly in love with the foreman.

Flame of the Desert (Diva Pictures, Inc./Goldwyn, 1919)
d: Reginald Barker. 5 reels.
Geraldine Farrar, Lou Tellegen, Alec B. Francis, Edythe Chapman, Casson Ferguson, Macey Harlam, Syn DeConde, Milton Ross, Miles Dobson, Jim Mason, Louis Durham, Ely Stanton, J. Montgomery Carlyle.
Differences of race and class are addressed in this tale of a

British lady who loves an Egyptian Sheik.

The Flame of the Yukon (Triangle, 1917)
d: Charles Miller. 5 reels.
Dorothy Dalton, Melbourne MacDowell, Kenneth Harlan, Margaret Thompson, Carl Ullman, May Palmer.
"The Flame" is a dance hall girl who performs in a Yukon territory cabaret.

The Flame of the Yukon (Metropolitan Pictures Corp. of California, 1926)
d: George Melford. 6 reels.
Seena Owen, Arnold Gray, Matthew Betz, Jack McDonald, Vadim Uraneff, Winifred Greenwood.
Remake of the 1917 Triangle film of the same name, both versions based on a story by Monte Katterjohn.

The Flame of Youth (Universal, 1917)
d: Elmer Clifton. 5 reels.
Jack Mulhall, Ann Kronan, Donna Moon, Hayward Mack, Alfred Allen, Ed Brady, Fred Montague, Burton Law, Percy Challenger, Harry Mann, Harry Morris.
Dispatched to an island off the coast of California on a business mission, a young man becomes infatuated with one of the local girls.

Flame of Youth (Fox, 1920)
d: Howard M. Mitchell. 5 reels.
Shirley Mason, Raymond McKee, Philo McCullough, Cecil Van Auker, Adelbert Knott, Betty Schade, Karl Formes.
When a worldly cad meets an innocent peasant girl and makes her fall in love with him, she spurns the farm boy who loves her dearly.

Flames (Associated Exhibitors, 1926)
d: Lewis H. Moomaw. 6 reels.
Eugene O'Brien, Virginia Valli, Jean Hersholt, Bryant Washburn, Cissy Fitzgerald, George Nichols, Boris Karloff.
Landis, a construction engineer, is secretly in love with his boss' daughter. She doesn't realize it, though, until a raging fire breaks out and she's trapped in it... and Landis risks his own life to save her.

The Flames of Chance (Triangle, 1918)
d: Raymond Wells. 5 reels.
Margery Wilson, Jack Mulhall, Anna Dodge, Wilbur Higbee, Percy Challenger, Ben Lewis, Eugene Corey, Lee Phelps.
During World War I, a young woman in New York sends letters and gifts to soldiers in the field, always describing herself as an elderly woman. She nearly panics when she learns that one of the soldiers has been released and is coming to New York to visit her. But panic turns to love, when she meets him and realizes she has found her soulmate.

Flames of Desire (Fox, 1924)
d: Denison Clift. 6 reels.
Wyndham Standing, Diana Miller, Richard Thorpe, Frank Leigh, George K. Arthur, Jackie Saunders, Frances Beaumont, Hayford Hobbs, Charles Clary, Eugenia Gilbert.
After a fight between erstwhile friends results in the accidental death of one of the men, the survivor promises to raise the dead man's daughter. Years pass, and both guardian and ward realize they have fallen in love with each other. But what's a girl to do when she knows her sweetheart was responsible for the death of her dad?

The Flames of Johannis (Lubin, 1916)
d: Edgar Lewis. 5 reels.

Nance O'Neil, George Clarke, Eleanor Barry, Ethel Tully, Victor Sutherland, Irving Dillon, Violet Axzell, Rosemary Carr.
Foster siblings love each other, but their union is forbidden by tradition.

Flames of the Flesh (Fox, 1920)
d: Edward J. LeSaint. 5 reels.
Gladys Brockwell, William Scott, Harry Spingler, Ben Deely, Charles K. French, Louis Fitzroy, Rosita Marstini, Josephine Crowell, Nigel DeBrullier.
Betrayed by her lover, a woman contemplates suicide but instead decides to exact revenge on all men. After a crash course in vamping, she blossoms forth as an exotic seductress.

Flaming Barriers (Famous Players-Lasky/Paramount, 1924)
d: George Melford. 6 reels.
Jacqueline Logan, Antonio Moreno, Walter Hiers, Charles Ogle, Robert McKim, Luke Cosgrave, Warren Rogers, Claribel Campbell.
Malone, inventor of a revolutionary fire-fighting machine, meets resistance when he tries to bring his device to market. When a large fire breaks out in town and the local firemen have trouble dousing a burning bridge, Malone puts his gizmo to work, it quenches the fire, and Malone ends up a wealthy hero.

The Flaming Clue (Vitagraph, 1920)
d: Edwin L. Hollywood. 5 reels.
Harry T. Morey, Lucy Fox, Sidney Dalbrook, Jack McLean, Eleanor Barry, R.E. Milasch, Robert Gaillard, Bernard Siegel, Frank Evans.
A Secret Service agent tracks counterfeiters to the basement of an old country residence.

The Flaming Forest (MGM, 1926)
d: Reginald Barker. 7 reels. (Part color.)
Antonio Moreno, Renee Adoree, William Austin, Tom O'Brien, Gardner James, Bert Roach, Emile Chautard, Oscar Beregi, Clarence Geldart, Frank Leigh, Charles Ogle, Claire McDowell.
In the Canadian northwest, an orphan girl falls in love with a mountie who rescues her from a forest fire.

The Flaming Frontier (Universal, 1926)
d: Edward Sedgwick. 9 reels.
Hoot Gibson, Anne Cornwall, Dustin Farnum, Ward Crane, Kathleen Key, Eddie Gribbon, Harry Todd, Harold Goodwin, George Fawcett, Noble Johnson, Charles K. French, William Steele, Walter Rodgers, Ed Wilson, Joe Bonomo.
Retelling of the story of the Battle of Little Big Horn. After the slaughter of General Custer and his command of 400 troopers by the Sioux, an Indian fighter (Gibson) leads the angry settlers in an attack on the traitors who conspired with Sitting Bull in the massacre.

Flaming Hearts (Metropolitan Pictures, 1922)
d: Clifford S. Elfelt. 5 reels.
J.B. Warner, Kathleen Myers, Alma Bennett, George Hernandez, Frankie Lee.
Hartman, an effete easterner, goes West to "toughen up."

The Flaming Hour (Universal, 1922)
d: Edward Sedgwick. 5 reels.
Frank Mayo, Helen Ferguson, Melbourne MacDowell, Charles Clary, Albert MacQuarrie, Tom Kennedy.

Lucille and Bruce marry against her father's wishes, but after a misunderstanding she leaves him. Bruce hangs around, though, long enough to run to the rescue when Lucille and her dad are trapped in a burning factory.

The Flaming Omen (Vitagraph, 1917)
d: William Wolbert. 5 reels.
Alfred Whitman, Mary Anderson, Luella Smith, Otto Lederer, S.E. Jennings, Clara King.
An English lord finds a deserted Peruvian orphan and takes the boy home to raise as his own son. As he grows to maturity, however, the young man is haunted by visions of an Incan goddess.

Flaming Passion — see: Lucretia Lombard

The Flaming Sword (Rolfe Photoplays, Inc./Metro, 1915)
d: Edwin Middleton. 5 reels.
Lionel Barrymore, Jane Grey, M.E. Middleton, Glenn White.
Deciding to end his life, a well-educated man leaves home and puts out to sea on a small boat. He drifts for days, then is washed onto a sparsely-populated island where he will learn, from the natives, life-affirming truths that put thoughts of suicide out of his mind.

Flaming Waters (Associated Arts Corp./FBO of America, 1925)
d: F. Harmon Weight. 7 reels.
Malcolm McGregor, Pauline Garon, Mary Carr, John Miljan, Johnny Gough, Mayme Kelso.
Thorne, a crooked dealer in oil stock, cheats a widow out of her life savings. When her son Danny returns from a sea voyage, he goes after Thorne and gets some of the money back, then impulsively invests it in some oil stock of his own. When the investment pays off, Thorne vengefully starts a fire near the well and puts Danny's girlfriend in danger for her life. Not to worry — Danny will come through yet again.

Flaming Youth (First National, 1923)
d: John Francis Dillon. 9 reels.
Colleen Moore, Milton Sills, Elliott Dexter, Sylvia Breamer, Myrtle Stedman, Betty Francisco, Walter McGrail, Phillips Smalley, Ben Lyon, George Barraud, Sidney Rathbone, John Patrick, Gino Corrado.
Jazz-age romantic drama about a girl who feels discouraged about marriage, having seen too many failed uunions in her own family. Later, when she goes yachting and finds herself overboard, she is rescued by a dashing young man who, now that she thinks about it, might make a pretty good husband after all.

The Flapper (Selznick, 1920)
d: Alan Crosland. 6 reels.
Olive Thomas, Warren Cook, Theodore Westman Jr., Katherine Johnston, Arthur Houseman, Louise Lindroth, Charles Craig, William P. Carlton, Marcia Harris, Bobby Connelly, Norma Shearer, Athole Shearer, Dorothy Kent, Russell Hewitt, Aleene Bergman.
Ginger's a small-town girl who dreams of glamour and adventure. She sets out to conquer new worlds, and after dallying with a pair of jewel thieves, returns home dressed as a lady of affairs. However, soon her bubble bursts.

Flapper Wives (Selznick, 1924)
d: Jane Murfin, Justin H. McCloskey. 7 reels.
May Allison, Rockliffe Fellowes, Vera Reynolds, Edward Horton, Harry Mestayer, William V. Mong, Edward Phillips, Tom O'Brien, Evelyn Selbie, Robert Dudley.

A defrocked clergyman is reinstated to the church due to the efforts of a charming young divorcee.

"Flare-Up" Sal (Thomas H. Ince Corp./Paramount, 1918)
d: Roy William Neill. 5 reels.
Dorothy Dalton, Thurston Hall, William Conklin, J.P. Lockney, Milton Ross.
A fiery dance hall girl connects with a fugitive bandit, and they fall in love.

Flash O' Lightning (William Steiner Productions, 1925)
d: Leo Maloney. 5 reels.
Leo Maloney, Josephine Hill, Evelyn Thatcher, Whitehorse, Bud Osborne.
Out West, con men persuade Flash, a good-nature cowpoke, to impersonate the heir to a late rancher's large estate, hoping to cash in on the deception. Flash goes along with their scheme and meets the rancher's family, taking a special interest in the pretty young woman who was the rancher's ward.

The Flash of an Emerald (World Film Corp., 1915)
d: Albert Capellani. 5 reels.
Robert Warwick, Dorothy Fairchild, Jean Stuart, Julia Stuart, Georgia May Fursman, Clarissa Selwynne, June Elvidge, Paul Gordon.
A society thief engineers the heist of a priceless emerald.

The Flash of Fate (Universal, 1918)
d: Elmer Clifton. 5 reels.
Herbert Rawlinson, Mary MacGregor, Sally Star, Jack Nelson, Dana Ong, Madge Kirby, Willis Marks, Charles West, George Brooks.
After suffering personal and financial disaster, an embittered man determines to rebuild his fortune by any means necessary. He becomes an underworld gang chief, enriching himself by robbing banks and wealthy homes, but is won back to honesty by the love of a good woman.

Flashing Spurs (Independent Pictures/FBO of Amrica, 1924)
d: Reeves Eason. 5 reels.
Bob Custer, Edward Coxen, Marguerite Clayton, Joe Bennett, William Hayes, William Malan, Andy Waldron, Park Frame.
Stuart, a Texas ranger, finds evidence implicating a pretty girl in a gangland conspiracy to rob her own father's safe.

The Flashlight (Universal, 1917)
d: Ida May Park. 5 reels.
Dorothy Phillips, Lon Chaney, William Stowell, Alfred Allen, George Berrill, Evelyn Selbie, Clyde Benson, O.C. Jackson, Mark Fenton.
A nature photographer invents a new flashlight photo process, but before he can bring it to market it causes him to be unjustly accused of a crime.

Flattery (Mission Film Corp./Chadwick Pictures, 1925)
d: Tom Forman. 6 reels.
John Bowers, Marguerite De La Motte, Alan Hale, Grace Darmond, Edwards Davis, Louis Morrison, Larry Steers.
Mallory, a dandified child of privilege who has embarked on a career as a civil engineer, is swayed by the flattery of crooked politicians and gets involved in their corrupt scheme. Before major damage is done, Mallory pulls out of his self-involvement, denounces the schemers, and dynamites the half-finished firetrap they have started to build.

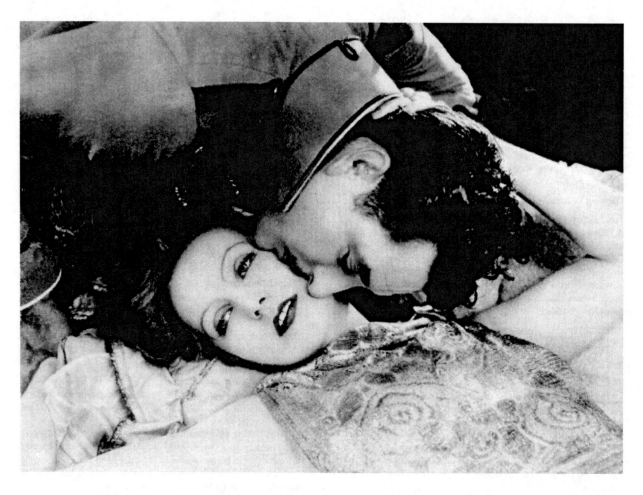

FLESH AND THE DEVIL (1926). John Gilbert and Greta Garbo exchange sweet nothings during one of their steamy love scenes in this, the first of their five screen pairings. As the amoral Felicitas, the sultry Garbo plays both title roles.

* * * * *

The Fleet's In (Paramount, 1928)
d: Malcolm St. Clair. 8 reels.
Clara Bow, James Hall, Jack Oakie, Bodil Rosing, Eddie Dunn, Jean Laberty, Dan Wolheim, Richard Carle, Joseph Girard.
The fleet's in town and the girls from the Roseland dancehall are there to greet the guys.

Fleetwing (Fox, 1928)
d: Lambert Hillyer. 5 reels.
Barry Norton, Dorothy Janis, Ben Bard, Robert Kortman, Erville Alderson, James Anderson, Blanche Frederici.
In Arabia, young Jaafor rides off with a slave girl and a thoroughbred horse named Fleetwing—but both properties belong to the sheik, who recaptures them. Now it's up to Jaafor to rescue the slave girl and take her for his wife.

Flesh and Blood (Western Pictures Exploitation Co., 1922)
d: Irving Cummings. 6 reels.
Lon Chaney, Edith Roberts, DeWitt Jennings, Noah Beery, Ralph Lewis, Jack Mulhall, Togo Yamamoto, Kate Price, Wilfred Lucas.
Webster, unjustly imprisoned for 15 years, breaks out of jail. To escape detection, he disguises himself as a crippled beggar and goes looking for his daughter. When he finds her, he is shocked to learn that she is in love with the son of the man whose perjured testimony sent Webster to jail in the first place.

Flesh and the Devil (MGM, 1926)
d: Clarence Brown. 9 reels.
Greta Garbo, John Gilbert, Lars Hanson, Marc McDermott, Barbara Kent, Lars Hanson, George Fawcett, William Orlamond, Eugenie Besserer, Marcelle Corday.

A married temptress toys with men, including two Austrian soldiers who have sworn eternal friendship to each other.

The Flight of the Duchess (Thanhouser/Mutual, 1916)
d: Eugene Nowland. 5 reels.
Gladys Hulette, Robert Gray, Burnett Parker, Nellie Parker Spaulding, Wayne Arey, Caroline Lee.
Class-conscious comedy in which a modern duke decides to live as in medieval days, including ordering servants about and demanding marriage with a local girl. Needless to say, the duke's medieval days are numbered.

The Flirt (Universal, 1916)
d: Lois Weber, Phillips Smalley. 5 reels.
Marie Walcamp, Grace Benham, Antrim Short, Ogden Crane, Nannine Wright, Juan de la Cruz, Paul Byron, Fred Church, Robert Lawlor, Robert M. Dunbar.
She's a flirt, he's a swindler, and they deserve each other.

The Flirt (Universal, 1922)
d: Hobart Henley. 8 reels.
George Nichols, Lydia Knott, Eileen Percy, Helen Jerome Eddy, Buddy Messenger, Harold Goodwin, Nell Craig, Tom Kennedy, Lloyd Whitlock, Edward Hearn, Bert Roach.
Remake of the 1916 Universal film *The Flirt*, both versions based on the Booth Tarkington story of the same name.

Flirting With Death (Universal, 1917)
d: Elmer Clifton. 5 reels.
Herbert Rawlinson, Brownie Vernon, Frank MacQuarrie, Marc Fenton, H.F. Crane, Red Unger.
Carnival con men go into the "aero-chute" business.

Flirting With Fate (Fine Arts Film Co./Triangle, 1916)
d: Christy Cabanne. 5 reels.

Douglas Fairbanks, Howard Gaye, Jewel Carmen, W.E. Lawrence, George Beranger, Dorothy Haydel, Lillian Langdon, J.P. McCarty, Wilbur Higby.
Black comedy about a rejected lover who hires a hit man to murder him, then finds true love and changes his mind about dying. Can he stop the hit man before the hit man stops him?

Flirting With Love (First National, 1924)
d: John Francis Dillon. 7 reels.
Colleen Moore, Conway Tearle, Winifred Bryson, Frances Raymond, John Patrick, Alan Roscoe, William Gould, Marga LaRubia.
When the chairman of a morality group stops the production of her play, star Gilda Lamont goes undercover as an unknown actress and tries to get him to back her in another production. Instead of destroying each other, the actress and the reformer fall in love.

The Floating College (Tiffany-Stahl Productions, 1928)
d: George J. Crone. 6 reels.
Sally O'Neil, William Collier Jr., Georgia Hale, Harvey Clark, Georgie Harris, E.J. Ratcliffe, Virginia Sale.
Two sisters love the same swimming instructor, and enroll in his floating college—a ship that travels around the world.

The Floor Below (Goldwyn, 1918)
d: Clarence G. Badger. 6 reels.
Mabel Normand, Tom Moore, Wallace McCutcheon, Willard Dashiell, Helen Dahl, Herbert Rawlinson, Louis R. Grisel, A. Romaine Calender, Lincoln Plummer, Charlotte Granville, Texas Charwaite.
Patricia's a high-spirited imp who works as a copy girl for a local newspaper. When she gets an assignment to investigate a series of local robberies, she winds up in love with the chief suspect!

A Florida Enchantment (Vitagraph, 1914)
d: Sidney Drew. 5 reels.
Sidney Drew, Edith Storey, Charles Kent, Jane Morrow, Ada Gifford, Ethel Lloyd, Lillian Burns, Grace Stevens, Allan Campbell, Cortland Van Deusen, Frank O'Neil.
Disconsolate when she finds her lover in the arms of another woman, an heiress swallows a pill that changes her into a man. Now unable to locate the heiress, the confused fiancé thinks the new "man" has killed "her." But the heiress (now an heir?) gives him one of the pills, and instantly he turns into a woman. Not to worry, it's only a dream. Could this be the screen's first gender-bender comedy?

The Flower of Doom (Universal, 1917)
d: Rex Ingram. 5 reels.
Yvette Mitchell, Gypsy Hart, Wedgwood Nowell, Nicholas Dunaew, M.K. Wilson, Tommy Morrissey, Frank Tokunaga, Gordo Keeno, Evelyn Selbie.
Because she innocently wears a flower that has symbolic meaning, a cabaret dancer is kidnapped by Chinatown gangsters.

Flower of Night (Paramount, 1925)
d: Paul Bern. 7 reels.
Pola Negri, Joseph Dowling, Youcca Troubetskoy, Warner Oland, Edwin J. Brady, Eulalie Jensen, Cesare Gravina, Gustav von Seyffertitz, Helen Lee Worthing, Manuel Acosta.
In Old California, a Mexican girl whose father had his gold mine stolen from him by American scoundrels goes to San Francisco and becomes a cabaret dancer. There, she joins forces with an American hoodlum who promises to help her

recover her family mine.

The Flower of No Man's Land   (Columbia/Metro, 1916)
d: John H. Collins.   5 reels.
Viola Dana, Duncan McRae, Harry C. Brown, Mitchell Lewis, Fred Jones, Nellie G. Mitchell, Eldine Steuart, Marcus Moriarity.
When an unspoiled orphan girl falls for a big-city entertainer, she is duped into marrying him, although he already has a wife.

Flower of the Dusk   (Metro, 1918)
d: John H. Collins.   5 reels.
Viola Dana, Howard Hall, Guy Coombs, Alice Martin, Jack McGowan, Margaret McWade, Bliss Milford, Charles Sutton, Maggie Breyer.
Heavy melodrama about a blind man, his crippled daughter, and his suicidal wife.

Flower of the North   (Vitagraph, 1921)
d: David Smith.   7 reels.
Henry B. Walthall, Pauline Starke, Harry Northrup, Joe Rickson, Jack Curtis, Emmett King, Walter Rodgers, William McCall, Vincent Howard.
Jeanne, known as "the flower of the North," lives with her woodsman father in the Canadian wilds.

Flowing Gold   (First National, 1924)
d: Joseph De Grasse.   8 reels.
Anna Q. Nilsson, Milton Sills, Alice Calhoun, Crauford Kent, John Roche, Cissy Fitzgerald, Josephine Crowell, Bert Woodruff, Charles Sellon.
Gray, an adventurer, goes to work for a Texas family who have struck it rich in the oil business. He has his work cut out for him, as plenty of scoundrels are after that oil money.

The Fly God   (Triangle, 1918)
d: Cliff Smith.   5 reels.
Roy Stewart, Edward Peil, Claire Anderson, Aaron Edwards, Percy Challenger, Walter Perry.
Unjustly accused of murder, a man winds up being tried by a corrupt jury that bases its final decision on whether a crawling fly makes it to the top of a window pane.

Flyin' Thru   (Al Wilson Pictures/Davis Distribution, 1925)
d: Bruce Mitchell.   6 reels.
Al Wilson, Elinor Fair, George French, James McElhern, Clarence Burton, Fontaine LaRue, Garry O'Dell.
Willis, a World War I aviator, returns home and solves a baffling murder mystery. He then marries his sweetheart as they soar through the clouds on his plane.

Flying Colors   (Triangle, 1917)
d: Frank Borzage.   5 reels.
William Desmond, Golda Madden, Jack Livingston, Laura Sears, J. Barney Sherry, George W. Chase, John P. Lockney, Bert Offerd, Mary McIvor, Ray Jackson.
Once a pole vaulter in college, an amateur sleuth finds his athletic skill comes in handy to help solve a mysterious jewel theft.

The Flying Buckaroo   (Action Pictures/Pathé, 1928)
d: Richard Thorpe.   5 reels.
Wally Wales, Jack D'Oise, J.P. Lockney, Fanny Midgley, Duane Thompson, Mabel Van Buren, Charles K. French, Charles Whitaker, Helen Marlowe, Bud McLure.
When his sweetheart is abducted, Matthews valiantly follows the kidnappers in his airplane and parachutes into their mountain lair, routing the scoundrels and rescuing his

lady.

The Flying Cowboy   (Universal, 1928)
d: Reaves Eason.   6 reels.
Hoot Gibson, Olive Hasbrouck, Harry Todd, William Bailey, Buddy Phillips, Ann Carter.
Hammond, a Wild West stunt man, makes a splash when he parachutes into a swimming pool, then rousts two gunmen who are trying to rob the ranch.

The Flying Dutchman   (R-C Pictures/FBO of America, 1923)
d: Lloyd B. Carleton.   6 reels.
Lawson Butt, Nola Luxford, Ella Hall, Edward Cosen, Walter Law.
Fantasy retelling of the story of Peter Van Dorn, condemned to sail the seas in a phantom ship forever, reaching port only once every seven years.

The Flying Fleet   (MGM, 1928)
d: George Hill.   11 reels.   (Synchronized musical score.)
Ramon Novarro, Anita Page, Ralph Graves, Eddie Nugent, Carroll Nye, Sumner Getchell, Gardner James, Alfred Allen.
Naval academy grads fly to Honolulu for romance.

Flying Fool   (Sunset Productions/Aywon, 1925)
d: Frank S. Mattison.   5 reels.
Gaston Glass, Dick Grace, Wanda Hawley, Mary Land, Dorothy Vernon, Dick Sutherland, Eddie Harris, Milburn Morante.
When the groom is late getting to his own wedding, his outraged bride-to-be storms off with the best man instead. But the tenacious groom follows them on a flying trip to a distant city, and tries to win his bride back.

The Flying Fool   (Pathé, 1929)
d: Tay Garnett.   7 reels.
William Boyd, Marie Prevost, Russell Gleason, Tom O'Brien.
A World War I pilot returns home and falls for his brother's girlfriend.

Flying Hoofs   (Universal, 1925)
d: Clifford Smith.   5 reels.
Jack Hoxie, Bartlett A. Carre, William Welsh, Gordon Russell, Charlotte Stevens, Alys Murrell, Duke R. Lee.
Out West, a sheriff searches for a mysterious bandit known only as The Raven.

The Flying Horseman   (Fox, 1926)
d: Orville O. Dull.   5 reels.
Buck Jones, Gladys McConnell, Bruce Covington, Walter Percival, Silver Buck, Hank Mann, Harvey Clark, Vester Pegg, Joseph Rickson.
When an itinerant cowpoke intervenes in a plot against a rancher and his daughter, the villain has the cowpoke framed for murder.

Flying Luck   (Monty Banks Enterprises/Pathé, 1927)
d: Herman C. Raymaker.   7 reels.
Monty Banks, Jean Arthur, J.W. Johnston, Kewpie Morgan, Eddie Chandler, Silver Harr.
Farcical comedy about a young flying enthusiast who enlists in the army but—through multiple bureacratic errors— winds up an emissary to a foreign country.

The Flying Mail   (Al Wilson Productions/Associated Exhibitors, 1926)
d: Noel Mason.   5 reels.
Al Wilson, Joseph W. Girard, Kahtleen Myers, Carmelita Geraghty, Harry Van Meter, Eddie Gribbon, Frank Tomick.

Gillespie, a pilot who flies the U.S. mail, gets involved with airplane thieves and a scheming gold digger.

Flying Pat (Paramount, 1920)
d: F. Richard Jones. 5 reels.
Dorothy Gish, James Rennie, Harold Vizard, Morgan Wallace, William Black, Tom Blake, Kate Bruce, Porter Strong.
The wife of an airplane manufacturer becomes a flying enthusiast herself.

Flying Romeos (First National, 1928)
d: Mervin LeRoy. 7 reels.
Charlie Murray, George Sidney, Fritzi Ridgeway, Lester Bernard, Duke Martin, James Bradbury Jr., Belle Mitchell.
Two barbers have their eyes on the same girl: their manicurist. She has a thing for aviators, though, so the tonsorial twosome sign up for flying lessons.

The Flying Torpedo (Fine Arts Film Co./Triangle, 1916)
d: John B. O'Brien. 5 reels.
John Emerson, Spottiswoode Aitken, William E. Lawrence, Fred J. Butler, Raymond Wells, Lucille Younge, Erich von Stroheim, Viola Barry, Bessie Love, Ralph Lewis.
In this drama set in the future, American officials offer a reward to anyone inventing a weapon capable of repelling an invading foreign power. Result: a flying torpedo!

The Flying U Ranch (R-C Pictures/FBO of America, 1927)
d: Robert DeLacy. 5 reels.
Tom Tyler, Nora Lane, Bert Hadley, Grace Woods, Frankie Darro, Olin Francis.
Bennett, owner of the Flying U Ranch, is threatened with foreclosure. His niece Sally agrees to marry their slimy neighbor in order to save the ranch, but she is spared that fate when a U.S. Secret Agent discovers the neighbor has been rustling Bennett's cattle.

The Fog (Max Graf Productions/Metro, 1923)
d: Paul Powell. 7 reels.
Mildred Harris, Louise Fazenda, Louise Dresser, Marjorie Prevost, Ann May, Ethel Wales, Cullen Landis, Ralph Lewis, David Butler, Frank Currier, Edward Phillips.
Nathan, a war veteran, goes to work for the Red Cross. Ironically, he meets and falls in love with a girl from his own home town, while working in far-off Siberia.

Fog Bound (Famous Players-Lasky/Paramount, 1923)
d: Irvin Willat. 6 reels.
Dorothy Dalton, David Powell, Martha Mansfield, Maurice Costello, Jack Richardson, Ella Miller, Willard Cooley, William David, Warren Cook.
Roger, a wealthy New Yorker vacationing in Florida, meets and falls in love with the daughter of a federal agent. She rejects him when she learns he is suspected of being her father's murderer, but Roger eventually proves he's no killer. After the real murderer is brought to justice, the girl accepts Roger's proposal of marriage.

The Follies Girl (Triangle, 1919)
d: Jack Dillon. 5 reels.
Olive Thomas, Wallace MacDonald, William V. Mong, Claire McDowell, J.P. Wild, Lee Phelps, Ray Griffith.
Scheming relatives hire a girl from the Follies to impersonate a dying man's granddaughter, hoping the old man will leave his estate to her and she will then distribute it to them. These plans start to go awry, however, when the girl endears herself to the old man and, in his joy, he recovers from his illness.

The Folly of Vanity (Fox, 1924)
d: Maurice Elvey. 6 reels.
Billie Dove, Jack Mulhall, Betty Blythe, John Sainpolis, Fred Becker, Otto Matiesen, Byron Munson, Consuelo, Jean LaMotte, Bob Klein, Ena Gregory, Edna Mae Cooper.
At a lavish party, a newlywed wife impulsively accepts an expensive gift from the host, causing her husband to suspect the worst.

Follow the Girl (Universal, 1917)
d: Louis Chaudet. 5 reels.
Ruth Stonehouse, Jack Dill, Roy Stewart, Claire Du Brey, Alfred Allen, Harry Dunkinson.
A Swedish orphan sails to America and finds true love. Unbeknown to her, a gang of criminals have hidden secret documents in her baggage, and she is pursued all over the U.S.A. by both the law and the criminals.

Food for Scandal (Realart Pictures Corp., 1920)
d: James Cruze. 5 reels.
Wanda Hawley, Harrison Ford, Ethel Gray Terry, Margaret McWade, Minnie Provost, Juan de la Cruz, Sidney Bracey, Lester Cuneo.
When a struggling young attorney leaves his sweetheart to go seek his fortune, she looks around for a job. Failing to find anything else, she settles for a job in a "Vanities" chorus line... and becomes a huge success.

The Food Gamblers (Triangle, 1917)
d: Albert Parker. 5 reels.
Wilfred Lucas, Elda Millar, Mac Barnes, Russell simpson, Jack Snyder, Eduardo Cianelli.
A female reporter takes on a ring of food speculators that drive up prices.

The Fool (Fox, 1925)
d: Harry Millarde. 10 reels.
Edmund Lowe, Raymond Bloomer, Henry Sedley, Paul Panzer, A.J. Herbert, Downing Clarke, George Lessey, Blanche Craig, Fred C. Jones, Rose Blossom, Anne Dale, Helena D'Algy, Mary Thurman, Lucille Lee Stewart, Brenda Bond, Marie Shaffer, Joseph Burke.
After being dismissed from his church for his supposedly radical views, a former minister begins a mission where he helps the poor and the unfortunate.

A Fool and His Money (Selznick, 1920)
d: Robert Ellis. 5 reels.
Eugene O'Brien, Rubye De Remer, Emile La Croix, Anne Brody, Finnstron Erics, George Dowling, Frank Goldsmith, Wray Page, Ned Hay, Louise Prussing, Arthur Housman, Charles Craig, Jules Cowles, Elizabeth Garrison.
When an American author purchases an old castle in Switzerland, he finds a young woman and her baby hiding in it.

A Fool and His Money (Columbia, 1925)
d: Erle C. Kenton. 6 reels.
William Haines, Madge Bellamy, Stuart Holmes, Alma Bennett, Charles Conklin, Lon Poff, Carrie Clark Ward, Eugenie Besserer, Edwards Davis, Baby Billie Jean Phyllis.
Remake of the 1920 Selznick film *A Fool and His Money*, both versions based on the novel of the same name by George Barr McCutcheon.

A Fool There Was (Fox, 1915)
d: Frank Powell. 6 reels.
Theda Bara, Edward Jose, May Allison, Clifford Bruce, Mabel Fremyear, Victor Benoit, Runa Hodges, Mina Gale,

Frank Powell.

Schuyler, a happily-married, respectable diplomat, is sent to Europe on a brief mission. He reluctantly leaves his charming wife and their little daughter, then sets sail on the U.S.S. "Gigantic." Unfortunately for him, one of the other passengers is an alluring, exotic seductress who lives only for attracting men and then destroying them. She targets Schuyler as her prey and soon makes him her sex slave. He ends up dishonored, addicted to drugs and alcohol, and a mere shell of his former manly self.

Theda Bara costars as the seductress, identified only as "the vamp."

A Fool There Was (Fox, 1922)
d: Emmett J. Flynn. 7 reels.
Estelle Taylor, Lewis Stone, Irene Rich, Muriel Dana, Marjorie Daw, Mahlon Hamilton, Wallace MacDonald, William V. Mong, Harry Lonsdale.
Remake, with some plot variations, of the 1915 Fox film *A Fool There Was*. In this version, the vamp has a name: Gilda.

The Foolish Age (Hunt Stromberg Productions/Robertson-Cole, 1921)
d: William A. Seiter. 5 reels.
Doris May, Hallam Cooley, Otis Harlan, Arthur Hoyt, Lillian Worth, Bull Montana, Billy Elmer, Spike Robinson.
Comedy about Margie, who mistakenly believes her sweetheart Homer is suicidal, and decides to go to his aid whether he wants it or not. Imagine her surprise when she finds the very life-affirming Homer in the arms of a chorus girl!

The Foolish Matrons (Maurice Tourneur Productions/Associated Producers, 1921)
d: Maurice Tourneur. 6 reels.
Hobart Bosworth, Doris May, Mildred Manning, Kathleen Kirkham, Betty Schade, Margaret McWade, Charles Meredith, Wallace MacDonald, Michael Dark, Frankie Lee.
Melodrama about three women and their lives, their loves, and their mistakes.

The Foolish Virgin (C.K.Y. Film Corp./Selznick, 1916)
d: Albert Capellani. 5 reels.
Clara Kimball Young, Conway Tearle, Paul Capellani, Catherine Proctor, Sheridan Tansey, William Welsh, Marie Lines, Agnes Mapes, Edward Elkas, Jaqueline Morhange.
A dreamy-eyed schoolteacher thinks she's found her Sir Galahad, but secretly he's a jewel thief.

The Foolish Virgin (Columbia, 1924)
d: George W. Hill. 6 reels.
Robert Frazer, Elaine Hammerstein, Gladys Brockwell, Phyllis Haver, Lloyd Whitlock, Irene Hunt, Howard Truesdell, Jack Henderson, Roscoe Karns, Oliver Cross, Edward Borman.
A reformed crook meets a classy lady and they fall in love. When she learns about his past, she wants to call the whole thing off. But then he rescues her from a fire, and she comes to respect him and believe in his love.
Remake, with some plot revisions, of the 1916 *The Foolish Virgin*.

Foolish Wives (Universal, 1922)
w, d: Erich von Stroheim. 10 reels.
Erich Von Stroheim, Maude George, Mae Busch, Miss Du Pont, Rudolph Christians, Robert Edeson, Cesare Gravina, Dale Fuller, Al Edmundsen, Louis K. Webb, C.J. Allen, Edward Reinach.

A phony but charming Russian count preys on gullible women.

Fools and Riches (Universal, 1923)
d: Herbert Blache. 5 reels.
Herbert Rawlinson, Katherine Perry, Tully Marshall, Doris Pawn, Arthur S. Hull, Nicholas DeRuiz, Roy Laidlaw, John Cossar.
Extravagant in his spending habits, Jimmy finds that when his father dies, he's inherited little more than a treasure map. To find the bulk of his inheritance, Jimmy has to get an honest job, foil a gang of thieves, and stick with a good woman. With her help, the young heir finds the hidden trove at last.

Fools and Their Money (Metro, 1919)
d: Herbert Blaché. 5 reels.
Emmy Wehlen, Jack Mulhall, Emmett King, Mollie McConnell, Betty K. Peterson, William V. Mong, Gerard Grassby, John Stepping, Bertram Grassby, Gordon Marr, Charles Hill Mailes.
Though they've inherited a fortune, the Tompkins family doesn't care to join in the social swim... until Mrs. Tompkins talks her husband and children into it.

The Fool's Awakening (Metro, 1924)
d: Harold Shaw. 6 reels.
Harry Northrup, Evelyn Sherman, Harrison Ford, John Sainpolis, Pauline French, Edward connelly, Mark Fenton, Arline Pretty, Lorimer Johnston.
An Englishman working in Russia at the time of the Revolution escapes and finds his true calling: writing of the exploits of a charismatic Russian noble, whom he also impersonates.

Fools First (Marshall Neilan Productions, 1922)
d: Marshall Neilan. 6 reels.
Richard Dix, Claire Windsor, Claude Gillingwater, Raymond Griffith, Baby Peggy, George Siegmann, Helen Lynch, Shannon Day, George Dromgold, Leo White, Robert Brower.
Tommy, an ex-con, and his girlfriend Ann decide to rob the bank where she works. The heist goes according to plan and Tommy escapes with a large sum of money, ready to meet Ann at the railroad station to complete their getaway. But Tommy has pangs of conscience and decides to return the money, with Ann's consent. But they are restrained by his former gang members, who want their share of the loot.

Fools For Luck (Essanay, 1917)
d: Lawrence C. Windom. 5 reels.
Taylor Holmes, Helen Ferguson, Bobbie Bolder, Frankie Raymond, John Cossar, James C. Carroll, Ed Cooke.
An accountant who's superstitious to a fault finds he has excellent luck at gambling—until the day he accidentally walks under a ladder. It all goes south from there, but in time he learns that the love of a good woman is the best luck he can have.

Fools For Luck (Paramount, 1928)
d: Charles Reisner. 6 reels.
W.C. Fields, Sally Blane, Chester Conklin, Jack Luden, Mary Alden, Arthur Houseman, Robert Dudley, Martha Mattox.
An itinerant con man engineers a scheme to promote some worthless oil fields, then frantically tries to buy back the stock when a real gusher erupts.

Fool's Gold (Washington Motion Picture Corp./Arrow, 1919)
d: Laurence Trimble. 6 reels.

Mitchell Lewis, Wellington Playter, Florence Turner, Sarah Truex, Francis Joyner, Kempton Greene, Evelyn Brent, Marguerite Serruys, Harry Hyde, Loan Star Dietz.
Two partners in a gold-mine operation love the same schoolteacher.

Fool's Highway (Universal, 1924)
d: Irving Cummings. 7 reels.
Pat O'Malley, Mary Philbin, Kate Price, William Collier Jr., Lincoln Plummer, Edwin J. Brady, Max Davidson, Charles Murray.
A Bowery fighter's crude behavior interferes with his romance, until his lady love inspires him to mend his ways.

Fools in the Dark (R-C Pictures/FBO of America, 1924)
d: Al Santell. 8 reels.
Patsy Ruth Miller, Matt Moore, Bertram Grassby, Charles Belcher, Tom Wilson, John Steppling.
Chaotic comedy about a young man who just wants to get married, but gets sidetracked in the laboratory of a crazy scientist, eventually escaping in an airplane with the aid of the U.S. Marines.

Fools of Fashion (Tiffany Productions, 1926)
d: James C. McKay. 7 reels.
Mae Busch, Marceline Day, Theodore von Eltz, Robert Ober, Hedda Hopper, Rose Dione, James Mack, Albert Roccardi.
Society drama about wives who love not wisely, but too well.

Fools of Fortune (Golden State Films, 1922)
d: Louis Chaudet. 6 reels.
Frank Dill, Russell Simpson, Tully Marshall, Frank Brownlee, Thomas Ricketts, Lillian Langdon, Marguerite De La Motte.
Four westerners go east, to claim inheritance from a wealthy relative.

A Fool's Paradise (Ivan Film Productions, Inc., 1916)
d: Ivan Abramson. 6 reels.
Joseph Burke, Paula Shay, Jack J. Clarke, Violet Axzell, Chrystine Mayo, James Cooley.
When a wealthy widower consults a crystal ball gazer about his future, she recommends that they marry.

Fool's Paradise (Famous Players-Lasky/Paramount, 1921)
d: Cecil B. DeMille. 9 reels.
Dorothy Dalton, Mildred Harris, Conrad Nagel, Theodore Kosloff, John Davidson, Julia Faye, Clarence Burton, Guy Oliver, Kamuela C. Searle, Jacqueline Logan.
Phelps, a war veteran, falls in love with two dancers and can't decide between them. When he is temporarily blinded by an exploding cigar, one of the dancers impersonates the other's voice and makes him choose her for his wife. He has his sight restored by an operation, and then his troubles *really* begin. Phelps embarks on a world-wide trip to find the girl he left behind... but eventually realizes he unwittingly picked the right girl, after all.

The Fool's Revenge (Fox, 1916)
d: Will S. Davis. 5 reels.
William H. Tooker, Maude Gilbert, Ruth Findlay, Richard Neal.
Revenge takes a grisly turn when a cuckold kills his wife and then tries to avenge himself against her lover.

Footfalls (Fox, 1921)
d: Charles J. Brabin. 8 reels.
Tyrone Power, Tom Douglas, Estelle Taylor, Gladden James.

Atmospheric melodrama about a blind cobbler who must decide whether a man burned beyond recognition—even by the sighted—is his son or not.

The Footlight Ranger (Fox, 1923)
d: Scott Dunlap. 5 reels.
Charles Jones, Fritzi Brunette, James Mason, Lillian Langdon, Lydia Yeamans Titus, Henry Barrows.
Out West, a cowpoke falls for a pretty actress from New York.

Footlights (Famous Players-Lasky/Paramount, 1921)
d: John S. Robertson. 7 reels.
Elsie Ferguson, Reginald Denny, Marc MacDermott, Octavia Handworth.
Lizzie, an American girl with a gift for impersonations, achieves success on the stage when she magically "becomes" Lisa, a Russian actress fleeing the Revolution.

Footlights and Shadows (Selznick Pictures Corp., 1920)
d: John W. Noble. 5 reels.
Olive Thomas, Alex Onslow, Ivo Dawson, May Hicks, E. Van Beusen, Robert Keeling.
When a golddigging Follies dancer sets her cap for a wealthy man, little does she know that the amnesiac stranger she's been nursing back to health is, in fact, just what she wants.

The Footlights of Fate (Vitagraph, 1916)
d: William Humphrey. 5 reels.
Naomi Childers, Marc MacDermott, Templar Saxe, William Shea, Katherine Lewis.
A secretary is encouraged to become a stage actress.

The Footloose Widows (Warner Bros., 1926)
d: Roy Del Ruth. 7 reels.
Louise Fazenda, Jacqueline Logan, Jason Robards, Arthur Hoyt, Neely Edwards, Douglas Gerrard, John Miljan, Jane Winton.
Two wealthy widows turn out to be neither wealthy nor widowed, but merely golddiggers on the prowl.

For a Woman's Fair Name (Vitagraph, 1916)
d: Harry Davenport. 5 reels.
Robert Edeson, Eulalie Jensen, Belle Bruce, Harry Morey, William Dunn, Jack Brawn.
Because of tangled circumstances involving the protection of a good woman's name, a man is forced to allow a rival to romance his sweetheart.

For a Woman's Honor (Robertson-Cole, 1919)
d: Park Frame. 5 reels.
H.B. Warner, Marguerite De La Motte, John Gilbert, Carmen Phillips, Hector V. Sarno, Olive Acorn, Roy Coulson, Carl Stockdale.
Though innocent of any wrongdoing, a medical corps captain steps aside when his fidelity is questioned on the eve of his wedding.

For Alimony Only (DeMille Pictures/Producers Distributing Corp., 1926)
d: William DeMille. 7 reels.
Leatrice Joy, Clive Brook, Lilyan Tashman, Casson Ferguson, Toby Claude.
Married life is trying for a newlywed couple who are trying to cope while he pays exhorbitant alimony to his vindictive first wife.

For Another Woman (Rayart, 1924)
d: David Kirkland. 6 reels.
Kenneth Harlan, Florence Billings, Henry Sedley, Mary

Thurman, Kathryn Riddell, Arnold Daly, Alan Hale, Tyrone Power.

After inheriting a large estate in Canada, a New York playboy feels he can neglect his new responsibilities... until a fetching Canadian lass comes to Gotham to persuade him otherwise.

For Better, For Worse (Famous Players-Lasky/Paramount, 1919)
d: Cecil B. DeMille. 7 reels.
Elliott Dexter, Tom Forman, Gloria Swanson, Sylvia Ashton, Raymond Hatton, Theodore Roberts, Wanda Hawley, Winter Hall, Jack Holt, Fred Huntley.

During World War I, a young woman is loved by both Edward, a doctor, and Richard, an architect. She spurns Edward as a coward and accepts Richard because the latter enlists in the service and goes off to the battlefields of Europe. But in time she discovers that she rejected Edward for all the wrong reasons.

For Big Stakes (Fox, 1922)
w, d: Lynn Reynolds. 5 reels.
Tom Mix, Patsy Ruth Miller, Sid Jordan, Bert Sprotte, Joe Harris, Al Fremont, Earl Simpson.
Out West, a villain ties the rancher's daughter to a tree and sets fire to the ranch. Not to worry, though: A handsome stranger arrives just in time to rescue the girl and reveal that he is the ranch's rightful owner.

For France (Vitagraph, 1917)
d: Wesley H. Ruggles. 5 reels.
Edward Earle, Betty Howe, Arthur Donaldson, Mary Maurice, Frank Anderson, Eric Von Stroheim.
At the outset of World War I, an American in Paris enlists in the French army.

For Freedom (Fox, 1918)
d: Frank Lloyd. 6 reels.
William Farnum, Ruby De Remer, Anna Lehr, Herbert Frank, G. Raymond Nye, John Slaven, Marc Robbins.
Battlefield heroics in World War I earn a convict a new hearing and, eventually, exoneration.

For Heaven's Sake (Harold Lloyd Corp./Paramount, 1926)
d: Sam Taylor. 6 reels.
Harold Lloyd, Jobyna Ralston, Noah Young, James Mason, Paul Weigel.
A wealthy ne'er-do-well falls for the daughter of a mission preacher.

For Husbands Only (Universal, 1918)
d: Lois Weber, Phillips Smalley. 6 reels.
Mildred Harris, Lewis J. Cody, Fred Goodwins, Kathleen Kirkham, Henry A. Barrows.
A rich girl marries for spite, then flirts with another man.

For Ladies Only (Columbia, 1927)
d: Scott Pembroke, Henry Lehrman. 6 reels.
John Bowers, Jacqueline Logan, Edna Marion, Ben Hall, William H. Strauss, Templar Saxe, Kathleen Chambers, Henry Roquemore.
A businessman fires all his female employees because he believes they are all vain creatures, more concerned with cosmetics and perfume than with work. Not surprisingly, this policy runs afoul of public opinion.

For Liberty (Fox, 1917)
d: Bertram Bracken. 5 reels.
Gladys Brockwell, Charles Clary, Bertram Grassby, Willard

Louis, Colin Chase, Clara Graham, Norbig Miles, Ryno William, George Routh.
When World War I breaks out, a young American woman living in Berlin begins spying for the Allies.

For Love or Money (Hallmark Pictures/State Rights, 1920)
d: Burton King. 6 reels.
Virginia Lee, Harry Benham, Roger Lytton, Stephen Gratton, Julia Swayne Gordon, Mildred Wayne, Hugh Huntley.
Social-climbing Helen Gerard arranges for her daughter to marry for wealth rather than love. The daughter does so, but the marriage is doomed from the start.
This film is also known as *The Road to Arcady*.

For Love or Money — see: The Crossroads of New York (1922)

For Sale (Astra Film Corp./Pathé, 1918)
d: Fred Wright. 5 reels.
Gladys Hulette, Creighton Hale, Helene Chadwick.
Treachery by the former boyfriend threatens a new marriage.

For Sale (Associated First National, 1924)
d: George Archainbaud. 8 reels.
Claire Windsor, Adolphe Menjou, Robert Ellis, Mary Carr, Tully Marshall, Joh Patrick, Vera Reynolds, Jule Power, Lou Payne, Phillips Smalley, Christine Mayo, Jean Vachon.
A young socialite is persuaded by her cash-strapped father to marry a wealthy man, but she isn't happy about it.

For the Defense (Lasky Feature Plays/Paramount, 1916)
d: Frank Reicher. 5 reels.
Fannie Ward, Jack Dean, Paul Byron, Horace B. Carpenter, Camille Astor, James Neill, Gertrude Kellar.
When a convent novice witnesses a murder, she takes leave from her vocation to pose as a maid so that she can trick the murderer into confessing.

For the Defense (Famous Players-Lasky/Paramount, 1922)
d: Paul Powell. 5 reels.
Ethel Clayton, Vernon Steele, ZaSu Pitts, Bertram Grassby, Mayme Kelso, Sylvia Ashton, Mabel Van Buren.
When a famous hypnotherapist is found murdered, suspicion falls on Anne, a popular singer who was one of his patients; and on his assistant Jennie, who is found to have money taken from the doctor's safe. Whodunit?

For the Freedom of the World (Goldwyn, 1917)
d: Romaine Fielding. 8 reels.
E.K. Lincoln, Barbara Castleton, Romaine Fielding, Neil Moran, Jane Adler, Walter Weems.
World War I drama about a gung-ho American who joins the Canadian army before his own country has entered the war.

For the Love of Mike (Robert Kane Productions/First National, 1927)
d: Frank Capra. 7 reels.
Claudette Colbert, Ben Lyon, George Sidney, Ford Steling, Hugh Cameron, Richard "Skeets" Gallagher, Rudolph Cameron, Mabel Swor.
In New York, three old bachelors raise a foundling child — Mike — as their own.

For the Soul of Rafael (Garson/Equity, 1920)
d: Harry Garson. 7 reels.
Clara Kimball Young, Bertram Grassby, Eugenie Besserer, Juan De La Cruz, J. Frank Glendon, Ruth King, Helene Sullivan Paula Merritt, Maude Emery, Edward M. Kimball.

A FOOL THERE WAS (1915). Theda Bara burst onto the screen in her star-making role as the cruel and sensual "vamp" whose only purpose in life is to charm wealthy, gullible men and drag them down the path of moral degradation.

* * * * *

In old California, a convent-bred girl is coerced into an arranged marriage... but the man she truly loves doesn't give up that easily.

For Those We Love (Betty Compson Productions/Goldwyn, 1921)
d: Arthur Rosson. 6 reels.
Betty Compson, Richard Rosson, Camille Astor, Bert Woodruff, Harry Duffield, Walter Morosco, George Cooper, Frank Campeau, Lon Chaney.
Bernice, fiercely loyal to her brother, tries to persuade their father that the young man did not steal money from him... although she knows that he did, and lost it in a gambling scandal.

For Valour (Triangle, 1917)
d: Albert Parker. 5 reels.
Winifred Allen, Richard Barthelmess, Henry Weaver, Mabel Ballin.
Melia Nobbs helps her brother enlist in World War I, through great personal sacrifice of her own. When he returns with multiple decorations for valour, she realizes her sacrifice was not in vain.

For Wives Only (Metropolitan Pictures Corp. Of California, 1926)
d: Victor Heerman. 6 reels.
Marie Prevost, Victor Varconi, Charles Gerrard, Arthur Hoyt, Claude Gillingwater, Josephine Crowell, Dorothy Cumming, William Courtright.
In Vienna, it's open courting season. A young society doctor tries to solicit funds for a new sanitarium, but instead finds himself being vamped by the countess whose donation he sought.

Forbidden (Universal, 1919)
d: Lois Weber, Phillips Smalley. 6 reels.
Mildred Harris, Henry Woodward, Fred Goodwins, Priscilla Dean.
A country girl marries a big-city chap, and expects she will be treated to the high life, New York style. Her anticipation sours, though, when her new husband decides to settle down in the country.

The Forbidden Box—see: Forbidden (1919)

Forbidden Cargo (Gothic Productions/FBO of America, 1925)
d: Thomas Buckingham. 5 reels.
Evelyn Brent, Robert Ellis, Boris Karloff.
Burke, a Secret Service agent, assigned to halt illegal rum trafficking between the Bahamas and the United States, falls in love with the female captain of the rumrunning ship.

The Forbidden City (Select Pictures, 1918)
d: Sidney A. Franklin. 5 reels.
Norma Talmadge, Thomas Meighan, A.E. Warren, Michael Rayle, L. Rogers Lytton, Reid Hamilton.
Miss Talmadge plays two roles, as mother and daughter, in this "East-meets-West" romantic drama.

Forbidden Fruit (Ivan Film Productions, 1915)
w, d: Ivan Abramson. 5 reels.
Paula Shay, Everett Butterfield, Minna Phillips, James Cooley, Kittens Reichert, Walter Gould, June Janin, Daddy Lewis.
Indiscretion with a former lover brings down a woman's happy marriage.

Forbidden Fruit (Famous Players-Lasky/Paramount, 1921)

d: Cecil B. DeMille. 8 reels.
Agnes Ayres, Clarence Burton, Theodore Roberts, Kathlyn Williams, Forrest Stanley, Theodore Kosloff, Shannon Day, Bertram Johns, Julia Faye.
Mary, a seamstress with an indolent husband, agrees to impersonate a debutante to "fill in" at a society party—and winds up staying in the society whirl, courtesy of a wealthy oil executive.

Forbidden Grass (Oscar Price/General Pictures, 1928)
d: E.M. Eldridge. 5 reels.
William Anderson, Evelyn Nicholas, Jack Padjan, Otto Meek, Walter Long, Elsie Duane, Billy Nichols.
Ranchers must round up the wild horses roaming the plains of Utah, to save the grazing fields for their sheep.

Forbidden Hours (MGM, 1928)
d: Harry Beaumont. 6 reels.
Ramon Novarro, Renee Adoree, Dorothy Cumming, Roy D'Arcy, Edward Connelly, Mitzi Cummings, Alberta Vaughn.
A Ruritanian monarch loves a commoner.

Forbidden Love (Wistaria Productions/Playgoers Pictures, 1921)
d: Philip Van Loan. 6 reels.
Creighton Hale, George MacQuarrie, Marguerite Clayton, Thomas Cameron, Peggy Shaw, Harold Thomas, Baby Ivy Ward.
Two brothers love the same girl. The shadier of the two schemes to get his brother out of the way.

Forbidden Paradise (Famous Players-Lasky/Paramount, 1924)
d: Ernst Lubitsch. 8 reels.
Rod LaRocque, Pola Negri, Adolphe Menjou, Pauline Starke, Nick DeRuiz, Mme. D'Aumery, Fred Malatesta, Madame Daumery.
In a small European kingdom, the Czarina's lover discovers she has been unfaithful to him. Defiantly, he joins a band of revolutionaries sworn to overthrow the monarchy.

The Forbidden Path (Fox, 1918)
d: J. Gordon Edwards. 6 reels.
Theda Bara, Hugh Thompson, Sidney Mason, Walter Law, Florence Martin, Wynne Hope Allen, Alphonse Ethier, Lisle Leigh, Reba Porter.
While posing for a painting of the madonna, a young woman is seduced by the artist's wealthy friend.

Forbidden Paths (Lasky Feature Plays/Paramount, 1917)
d: Robert T. Thornby. 5 reels.
Sessue Hayakawa, Vivian Martin, Tom Forman, Carmen Phillips, James Neill, Ernest Joy, Paul Weigel.
An American girl living with her Japanese guardian feels great friendship for him, but not the deep love he feels for her.

The Forbidden Room (Fox, 1919)
d: Lynn F. Reynolds. 5 reels.
Gladys Brockwell, William Scott, J. Barney Sherry, Harry Dunkjinson, Al Fremont, William Burress, T.S. Guise, Louis King, Robert Dunbar, Lillian West, Virginia Lee Corbin, Francis Carpenter.
Turnabout is foul play, as a corrupt chief of police finds out. After framing a district attorney and his innocent secretary, the framer becomes the framed, when the secretary uses her feminine wiles to lure the chief into a trap.

The Forbidden Thing (Allan Dwan/Associated Producers, Inc., 1920)
d: Allan Dwan. 6 reels.
James Kirkwood, Helen Jerome Eddy, Marcia Manon, King Baggot, Gertrude Claire, Jack Roseleigh, Arthur Thalasso, Newton Hall, Harry Griffith, Katherine Norton, J. Montgomery Carlyle.
A straight-laced fellow who's engaged to be married goes to a dance hall with friends and falls under the influence of a notorious seductress.

The Forbidden Trail (Sunset Productions, 1923)
d: Robert North Bradbury. 5 reels.
Jack Hoxie, Evelyn Nelson, Frank Rice, William Lester, Joe McDermott, Tom Lingham.
Out West, a cowboy falls in love with the daughter of his enemy.

Forbidden Trails (Fox, 1920)
d: Scott Dunlap. 5 reels.
Buck Jones, Winifred Westover, Stanton Heck, William Elmer, George Kunkel, Harry Dunkinson, Fred Herzog, Edwin Booth Tilton.
On his deathbed, an old rancher asks his partner to find and protect his missing daughter.

Forbidden Valley (Pathé, 1920)
d: J. Stuart Blackton. 5 reels.
May McAvoy, Bruce Gordon, William R. Dunn, Charles Kent, Warren Chandler, Nellie Anderson, Gene Layman, Emil Mink, Harry Kiefer.
Feuding and fighting in the Kentucky hills.

Forbidden Waters (Metropolitan Pictures, 1926)
d: Alan Hale. 6 reels.
Priscilla Dean, Walter McGrail, Dan Mason, Casson Ferguson, DeSacia Mooers.
Nancy goes to Reno seeking a divorce. Trouble is, she still loves her husband.

The Forbidden Woman (Garson/Equity, 1920)
d: Harry Garson. 6 reels.
Clara Kimball Young, Conway Tearle, Jiquet Lanoe, Kathryn Adams, Winter Hall, Milla Davenport, Stanton Williams, John MacKinnon.
After one of her suitors commits suicide over her, a famous French actress relocates to America. But even in New York, the tragedy haunts her.

The Forbidden Woman (DeMille Pictures/Pathé, 1927)
d: Paul L. Stein. 7 reels.
Jetta Goudal, Ivan Lebedeff, Leonid snegoff, Josephine Norman, Victor Varconi, Joseph Schildkraut.
Pierre, a French colonel, falls in love with a beautiful Moroccan woman and they marry. What Pierre doesn't know is that his wife is a spy and that she's transmitting military secrets to hostile troops. The tragic triangle is complete when Pierre is called back to Paris, and there his wife meets her brother-in-law and falls desperately in love with him.

Foreign Devils (MGM, 1927)
d: W.S. Van Dyke. 5 reels.
Tim McCoy, Claire Windsor, Cyril Chadwick, Emily Fitzroy, Sojin, Frank Currier.
Kelly, an American diplomat in China, falls for an imprisoned British lady and will eventually undergo several hardships to free her from her captors.

The Foreign Legion (Universal, 1928)
d: Edward Sloman. 8 reels.
Norman Kerry, Lewis Stone, Mary Nolan, June Marlowe, Walter Perry, Crauford Kent.
Foreign intrigue with a twist: An American joins the Foreign Legion, then learns that the commanding officer is his own father, whom he hasn't seen in decades.

Forest Rivals (World Film Corp., 1919)
d: Harry O. Hoyt. 5 reels.
Dorothy Green, Arthur Ashley, Jack Drumier, Kempton Greene, Clay Clement, John Davidson, Frank Montgomery, Evelyn Axzel, Madge Lee.
In the French Canadian woods, a young woman is chased by three men, only one of them with honorable intentions.

Forever (Famous Players-Lasky/Paramount, 1922)
d: George Fitzmaurice. 7 reels.
Wallace Reid, Elsie Ferguson, Montagu Love, George Fawcett, Dolores Cassinelli, Paul McAllister, Elliott Dexter, Barbara Dean, Nell Roy Buck, Charles Eaton, Jerome Patrick.
Tragic drama about two lovers, one of them Peter Ibbetson, adopted son of a wealthy Englishman, and the other his life-long sweetheart, Mimsi.

Forever After (First National, 1926)
d: F. Harmon Weight. 7 reels.
Lloyd Hughes, Mary Astor, Hallam Cooley, David Torrence, Eulalie Jensen, Alec B. Francis, Lila Leslie.
Overseas, an American infantry officer is wounded in action. He is taken to the field hospital, and there is reunited with the girl he left behind, now a Red Cross nurse.

The Forfeit (Sunset Pictures Corp./Pathé, 1919)
d: Frank Powell. 5 reels.
House Peters, Jane Miller, William Human, Hector V. Sarno, L.H. Welles, Blanche Abbott, George Murdock.
Grim western drama about two brothers, one of whom leads a gang of rustlers.

The Forged Bride (Universal, 1920)
d: Douglas Gerrard. 5 reels.
Mary MacLaren, Thomas Jefferson, Harold A. Miller, Dorothy Hagan, J. Barney Sherry, Dagmar Godowsky, Frances Raymond.
A convicted forger breaks out of jail to do one last job.

Forget-Me-Not (World Film Corp., 1917)
d: Emile Chautard. 5 reels.
Kitty Gordon, Montagu Love, Alec B. Francis, George MacQuarrie, James Furey, Norma Phillips, Lillian Herbert, Henrietta Simpson.
A reckless adventuress ruins the lives of two men, and very nearly a third.

Forget-Me-Not (Louis Burston Productions/Metro, 1922)
d: W.S. Van Dyke. 6 reels.
Irene Hunt, William Machin, Bessie Love, Gareth Hughes, Otto Lederer, Myrtle Lind, Hal Wilson, Gertrude Claire, Sam Allen, William Lawrence.
Melodrama about a poverty-stricken single mother who must leave her infant daughter on the steps of an orphanage. The girl is eventually adopted by a musician and becomes a violin virtuoso.

Forgotten Faces (Paramount, 1928)
d: Victor Schertzinger. 8 reels.
Clive Brook, Baclanova, Jack Luden, Fred Kohler, Mary Brian, William Powell.

Bitter melodrama about a father who loves his daughter so much, he is willing to go to jail for life so that she will be happy and free of the influence of her vicious mother.

The Forgotten Law (Metro, 1922)
d: James W. Horne. 7 reels.
Jack Mulhall, Cleo Ridgeley, Alec B. Francis, Milton Sills, Muriel Dana, Alice Hollister, Lucretia Harris, Walter Law.
Victor, an unfaithful husband, is so irate when his wife confronts him with the truth, he has his will changed to deny her custody of their daughter in the event of his death.

Forlorn River (Paramount, 1926)
d: John Waters. 6 reels.
Jack Holt, Raymond Hatton, Arlette Marchal, Edmund Burns, Tom Santschi, Joseph Girard, Christian J. Frank, Albert Hart, Nola Luxford, Chief Yowlache, Jack Moore.
Out West, an accused rustler on the run falls in love with a rancher's daughter and is encouraged to return to society and clear his name.

Forsaking All Others (Universal, 1922)
d: Emile Chautard. 5 reels.
Colleen Moore, Cullen Landis, Sam DeGrasse, Mrs. Wallace, June Elvidge, David Torrence, Melbourne MacDowell, Elinor Hancock, Lucille Rickson.
To dissuade her son from courting a girl she disapproves of, a dowager points him in the direction of another young lady. Big mistake! The lady is married, and to a very jealous husband.

The Fortunate Youth (Ocean Film Corp./State Rights, 1916)
d: Joseph Smiley. 5 reels.
Wilmuth Merkyl, William Cohill, John A. Smiley, G. Davison Clark, Charles Graham, Lilie Leslie, Rita Fitzgerald, Sue Balfour, Marguerite Forrest, Betty Holton.
In England, an unknown runs for parliament... and is astounded to learn that his opponent is his father, whom he hadn't seen in years.

The Fortune Hunter (Lubin/General Film, 1914)
d: Barry O'Neil. 6 reels.
William Elliott, George Soule Spencer, Charles Brandt, Ethel Clayton, Rosetta Brice, Joseph Kaufman, Florence Williams, James Daly, Gaston Bell, Ruth Bryan, Frank Backus.
After squandering his fortune, Nat Duncan is at the end of his rope. So he's rescued by an old friend, who proposes a novel solution: Nat should move to a small town, give up his vices, and marry a rich woman. He makes good on the first two suggestions, then marries a non-affluent girl he really loves, and all ends happily.

The Fortune Hunter (Vitagraph, 1920)
d: Tom Terriss. 7 reels.
Earle Williams, Jean Paige, Van Dyke Brooke, Nancy Lee, William Holden, Charles Trowbridge, Frank Norcross, Billy Hoover, Louise Lee, Earl Metcalfe.
Remake of the 1914 Lubin film *The Fortune Hunter*. Both films were based on the play of the same name by Winchell Smith.

The Fortune Hunter (Warner Bros., 1927)
d: Charles F. Reisner. 7 reels.
Sydney Chaplin, Helene Costello, Clara Horton, Duke Martin, Thomas Jefferson, Erville Alderson, Paul Kruger, Nora Cecil, Louise Carver, Bob Perry, Babe London.
Nat, who's looking for a wealthy woman to marry, settles in a new town and hones in on the banker's daughter. She's interested, but before Nat can make his move he notices Betty, a working-class girl, and it's love at first sight.
Second feature-length remake of *The Fortune Hunter*, from Winchell Smith's play.

The Fortune Teller (Robertson-Cole, 1920)
d: Albert Capellani. 7 reels.
Marjorie Rambeau, Frederick Burton, Raymond McKee, Franklin Hanna, Virginia Lee, T.M. Koupal, Cyprian Giles.
When a discouraged young man goes to a circus fortune teller, she inspires him with predictions of great future success... and it all comes true for him. What the young man doesn't know is that the fortune teller is his own mother, from whom he was separated as a little boy.

Fortune's Child (Vitagraph, 1919)
d: Joseph Gleason. 5 reels.
Gladys Leslie, Kempton Greene, Stanley Walpole, Frances Mann, Fred Smith, Jessie Stevens, Denton Vane, Frank Norcross, Miriam Miles, Shirley Brule.
When she's falsely accused of stealing at her cheap boarding house, a young drudge runs away and comes to rest on the doorstep of an artist who's also a prizefighter.

Fortune's Mask (Vitagraph, 1922)
d: Robert Ensminger. 5 reels.
Earle Williams, Patsy Ruth Miller, Henry Hebert, Milton Ross, Eugenie Ford, Arthur Tavares, Frank Whitson, Oliver Hardy, William McCall.
Maloney, an Irishman, lands in a Central American country and charms the residents.

The Fortunes of Fifi (Famous Players/Paramount, 1917)
d: Robert G. Vignola. 5 reels.
Marguerite Clark, William Sorelle, John Sainpolis, Yvonne Chevalier, Kate Lester, Jean Gauthier, J.K. Murray.
An old soldier is kind to an out-of-work actress, but when she realizes she's in love with him, he refuses to marry her, thinking himself too old.

Forty-Five Minutes From Broadway (First National, 1920)
d: Joseph De Grasse. 5 reels.
Charles Ray, Dorothy Devore, Hazel Howell, Eugenie Besserer, May Foster, Donald McDonald, Harry Myers, William Courtright.
Love among the idle rich and the not-so-rich in New Rochelle.
Based on the George M. Cohan musical comedy *Forty-Five Minutes From Broadway*.

40-Horse Hawkins (Universal, 1924)
d: Edward Sedgwick. 6 reels.
Hoot Gibson, Anne Cornwall, Richard Tucker, Helen Holmes, Jack Gordon Edwards, Ed Burns, Edward Sedgwick, John Judd.
Hawkins, an all-around handyman, falls for the leading lady in a traveling carnival show.

'49-'17 (Universal, 1917)
w, d: Ruth Ann Baldwin. 5 reels.
Joseph Girard, Jean Hersholt, Donna Drew, Leo Pierson, William J. Dyer, Martha Witting, George Pearce.
A retired judge goes West to restore Nugget Notch, a formerly prosperous Gold Rush town.

Forty Winks (Famous Players-Lasky/Paramount, 1925)
d: Frank Urson. 7 reels.
Viola Dana, Raymond Griffith, Theodore Roberts, Cyril Chadwick, Anna May Wong, William Boyd.

Foreign intrigue in California, as a double agent steals important military papers from an American officer. When Lord Chumley, a British agent, is accused of the theft, he goes all out to clear his name and restore the stolen documents, avert a suicide, and win the love of the girl in the case.

The Foundling (Famous Players/Paramount, 1916)
d: John D. O'Brien. 5 reels.
Mary Pickford, Edward Martindale, Maggie Weston, Mildred Morris, Marcia Harris.
Spurned by her father because his beloved wife died in childbirth, young Molly grows up in an orphanage. But as the years go by, Molly's dad comes to regret his mistake, and returns to claim his daughter. He's tricked into taking a different girl... but, after several misadventures handled with the usual Mary Pickford charm, young Molly is reunited with her dad at last.

4 Devils (Fox, 1928)
d: F.W. Murnau. 12 reels. (Music, sound effects, part talkie.)
J. Farrell MacDonald, Janet Gaynor, Charles Morton, Nancy Drexel, Barry Norton, Anders Randolf, Claire McDowell, Jack Parker, Philippe DeLacy, Dawn O'Day, Anita Fremault, Mary Duncan, Michael Visaroff, George Davis, Andre Cheron, Wesley Lake.
Two couples—circus trapeze performers all—fall in love, but one of the men is distracted by the enticements of an aristocratic woman.

Four Feathers (Dyreda Art Film Corp./Metro, 1915)
d: J. Searle Dawley. 5 reels.
Edgar L. Davenport, Fuller Mellish, Ogden Child Jr., Howard Estabrook, Arthur Evers, George Moss, Irene Warfield, David Wall.
Classic tale of courage under fire, based on the British novel *The Four Feathers*, by Alfred E.W. Mason. In the silent era, it would be remade in a 1921 British version and in a 1929 Paramount film that incorporated music and sound effects.

The Four Feathers (Paramount, 1929)
d: Merian C. Cooper. 8 reels. (Synchronized music and effects.)
Richard Arlen, Fay Wray, Clive Brook, William Powell, Theodore von Eltz, Noah Beery, Zack Williams, Noble Johnson, Harold Hightower, Philippe DeLacy, E.J. Radcliffe.
Ambitious retelling of the famous A.E.W. Mason story, with location shooting in Africa.
A British officer is accused of cowardice after he resigns his commission to be married just as his unit is to be sent to the Sudan. His supposed cowardice is symbolized by four white feathers sent to him by his disillusioned comrades. Although he is out of the service, the disgraced former officer clears his name by going to Africa and joining in the fight.

The Four-Flusher (Metro, 1919)
d: Harry L. Franklin. 5 reels.
Hale Hamilton, Ruth Stonehouse, Harry Holden, Ralph Bell, Robert Badger, Louis Fitzroy, Frederic Malatesta, Effie Conley.
Comedy about an unqualified fraud who passes himself off as a businessman, spending lavishly to impress a visiting importer.

The Four-Footed Ranger (Universal, 1928)
d: Stuart Paton. 5 reels.

Dynamite, the dog, Edmund Cobb, Marjorie Bonner, Pearl Sindelar, Francis Ford, Pat Rooney, Frank M. Clark, Carl Sepulveda, Lee Lin.
A Texas Ranger and his wonder dog, Dynamite, foil a gang of cattle rustlers.

The Four Horseman of the Apocalypse (Metro, 1921)
d: Rex Ingram. 11 reels.
Pomeroy Cannon, Josef Swickard, Bridgetta Clark, Rudolph Valentino, Virginia Warwick, Alan Hale, Mabel Van Buren, Stuart Holmes, John Sainpolis, Alice Terry, Mark Fenton, Derek Ghent, Nigel De Brulier, Broadwitch Turner, Edward Connelly, Wallace Beery, Harry Northrup, Arthur Hoyt.
Sprawling epic that covers three generations, and moves from turn-of-the-century Argentina to Europe during the first World War.
Star-making vehicle for Valentino, who is magnetic as the young scoundrel, Julio.

Four Sons (Fox, 1928)
d: John Ford. 9 reels. (Synchronized music and sound effects.)
George Meeker, Margaret Mann, Francis X. Bushman Jr., James Hall, Charles Morton, Earle Foxe, June Collyer, Albert Gran, Frank Reicher, Hughie Mack, Michael Mark, June Collyer.
Heavy melodrama about a widow with four sons, all of whom die in the war except the youngest, Joseph.

Four Walls (MGM, 1928)
d: William Nigh. 8 reels.
John Gilbert, Joan Crawford, Carmel Myers, Vera Gordon, Robert Emmet O'Connor, Louis Natheaux, Jack Byron.
A convicted criminal reforms while in jail, and faces a showdown with his old gang when he is released.

The Fourflusher (Universal, 1928)
d: Wesley Ruggles. 6 reels.
George Lewis, Marion Nixon, Eddie Phillips, Churchill Ross, Jimmie Ayre, Burr McIntosh, Otto Hoffman, Wilfred North, Knute Erickson, Patricia Caron, Marian Fauche.
Comedy about Andy, a shoe salesman who's invented a revolutionary new arch support.

The Fourteenth Lover (Metro, 1922)
d: Harry Beaumont. 5 reels.
Viola Dana, Jack Mulhall, Theodore von Eltz, Kate Lester, Alberta Lee, Frederick Vroom, Fronzie Gunn.
Daffy comedy about a girl with a dozen eligible suitors, who nevertheless sets her cap for a penniless gardener.

The Fourteenth Man (Famous Players-Lasky/Paramount, 1920)
d: Joseph Henabery. 5 reels.
Robert Warwick, Bebe Daniels, Walter Hiers, Robert Milash, Norman Selby, Sylvia Ashton, James Farley, C.H. Geldart, Viora Daniel, Robert Dudley, Lucien Littlefield, John McKinnon.
A Scotsman flees his country after an altercation, and is followed by sinister detectives. Once in New York and established with the love of an American girl, he learns that the detectives pursuing him merely want to notify him of an inheritance.

The Fourth Commandment (Universal, 1927)
d: Emory Johnson. 7 reels.
Henry Victor, June Marlowe, Belle Bennett, Leigh Willard, Mary Carr, Brady Cline, Catherine Wallace, Frank Elliott, Knute Erickson, Kathleen Myers, Robert Agnew.

Melodrama that traces the lives of childhood sweethearts through the years. They are split apart as young adults, live calamitous lives with other spouses, then are reunited in later years.

The Fourth Estate (Fox, 1916)
d: Frank Powell. 5 reels.
Clifford Bruce, Ruth Blair, Victor Benoit, Alfred Hickman, Samuel J. Ryan, Aline Bartlett, Stacey Van Patten Jr.
Newspaper reporters launch a crusade against a corrupt judge.

The Fourth Musketeer (R-C Pictures/FBO of America, 1923)
d: William K. Howard. 6 reels.
Johnnie Walker, Eileen Percy, Eddie Gribbon, William Scott, Edith Yorke, Georgie Stone, James McElhern, Philo McCullough, Kate Lester.
O'Brien, a prizefighter turned mechanic, loses his wife to another, but regains her love in the end.

The Fox (Universal, 1921)
d: Robert Thornby. 7 reels.
Harry Carey, George Nichols, Gertrude Olmstead, Betty Ross, Johnny Harron, Gertrude Claire, Alan Hale, George Cooper, Breezy Eason, Charles LeMoyne, C.E. Anderson.
Tale of western derring-do by a Secret Agent who poses as a tramp, then proceeds to clean up a corrupt town.

The Frame-up (Universal, 1915)
d: Otis Turner. 5 reels.
George Fawcett, Maude George, Harry Carter, Albert McQuarrie, Olive Fuller Golden, Lule Warrenton.
Handed the mayorship by a corrupt political boss, Luke Simms is expected to "play ball" with the controlling powers — but Luke has a mind of his own.

The Frame Up (American Film Co./Mutual, 1917)
d: Edward Sloman. 5 reels.
William Russell, Harvey Clark, Lucille Ward, Francelia Billington, Alfred Ferguson, Charles Newton, Clarence Burton, Manuel Sampson, John Goff.
Rejecting his father's offer of a soft job, a scion of wealth instead chooses the life of an adventurer.

Framed (First National, 1927)
d: Charles J. Brabin. 6 reels.
Milton Sills, Natalie Kingston, E.J. Ratcliffe, Charles Gerrard, Burr McIntosh, Natli Barr, John Miljan.
During World War I, a French army officer is courtmartialed for crimes he did not commit. He emigrates to Brazil and becomes a foreman in a diamond mine, but even there trouble pursues him.

Framing Framers (Triangle, 1917)
d: Ferris Hartman, Henri D'Elba. 5 reels.
Charles Gunn, Edward Jobson, George Pearce, Laura Sears, Edward Martin, Lee Phelps, Mildred Delfino, Eugene Burr, Anna Dodge, Verne Peterson, Leo Willis, Arthur Millet.
Comedy about a gung-ho young reporter who inadvertently gets mixed up in a war between political rivals. When one politico has the reporter beaten senseless and left looking like a bum, he is singled out by the other rival as a tramp who needs redeeming. Playing along, the reporter allows his handlers to make a "respectable gentleman" of him, then turns on the charm and wins the hand of the daughter of one of the dueling political rivals.

Freckles (Lasky Feature Plays/Paramount, 1917)
d: Marshall Neilan. 5 reels.
Jack Pickford, Louis Huff, Hobart Bosworth, Lillian Leighton, Billy elmer, Guy Oliver.
Freckles is a one-armed waif who is often the butt of the other children's jokes. Fortunately, he is redeemed by the love of a good girl.

Freckles (FBO Pictures, 1928)
d: Leo Meehan. 7 reels.
John Fox Jr., Gene Stratton Porter, Hobart Bosworth, Eulalie Jensen, Billy Scott, Lafe McKee.
Freckles, an orphan, works in a loggers' camp and succeeds in foiling timber thieves. He finds the girl of his dreams, too.

Free and Equal (Thomas H. Ince, 1918)
d: R. William Neill. 5 reels.
Charles K. French, Gloria Hope, Jack Curtis, Lydia Knott, Jack Richardson, Thoms J. Guise, J.J. Dowling.
When a sympathetic judge creates an organization that encourages integration of the white and Negro races, he opens a Pandora's box. In the end, the brilliant mulatto at the center of the drama is revealed to be a lustful, vengeful bigamist.
During the brief exhibition of the film *Free and Equal*, city authorities in Los Angeles and other cities denounced the film as racist and began litigation to have it shut down.

Free Lips (James Ormont Productions, 1928)
d: Wallace MacDonald. 6 reels.
June Marlowe, Frank Hagney, Jane Novak, Ernie Shields, Olin Francis, Edna Hearn.
When an innocent farm girl goes to the city and gets work in a night club, her eyes are opened to a world of sin and corruption — but also true love.

Free to Love (B.P. Schulberg Productions/Preferred Pictures, 1925)
d: Frank O'Connor. 5 reels.
Clara Bow, Donald Keith, Raymond McKee, Hallam Cooley, Winter Hall.
Miss Bow plays a young and charming defendant in a criminal trial who is found guilty and imprisoned. We never doubt her innocence, however, and after she is cleared of all wrongdoing and released, she is adopted by the very judge who sentenced her.

Freedom of the Press (Universal, 1928)
d: George Melford. 7 reels.
Lewis Stone, Malcolm McGregor, Marceline Day, Henry B. Walthall, Robert E. O'Connor, Thomas Ricketts, Hayden Stevenson, Robert Ellis, Boris Baronoff, Morgan Thorpe.
After a newspaper publisher is brutally murdered, his son takes over and leads a successful crusade against the corrupt politicians who are trying to take over the city.
This film is also known by the title *Graft*.

The Freeze Out (Universal, 1921)
d: John Ford. 5 reels.
Harry Carey, Joe Harris, Helen Ferguson, Charles LeMoyne, J. Farrell MacDonald, Lydia Yeamans Titus.
There's a new hombre in town, and he'll clean up the saloons and drives the varmints out into the desert.

The French Doll (Tiffany Productions/Metro, 1923)
d: Robert Z. Leonard. 7 reels.
Mae Murray, Orville Caldwell, Rod LaRocque, Rose Dione, Paul Cazeneuve, Willrd Louis, Bernard Randall, Lucien Littlefield.
Comedy with a Gallic air, about a French antiques dealer

(female) who emigrates to America and falls in love with a Palm Beach zillionaire.

French Dressing (First National Pictures, 1927)
d: Allan Dwan. 7 reels.
H.B. Warner, Clive Brook, Lois Wilson, Lilyan Tashman.
Cynthia, a tightly-wound socialite, suspects her husband of having an affair with her friend Peggy. In a huff, the wife demands a divorce and storms off for Paris. There, she flirts with a boulevardier, and come to realize that coquettishness doesn't necessarily lead to adultery. Her husband, who has followed her to France, arrives just in time to take her back into his arms.

French Heels (Holtre Productions/W.W. Hodkinson, 1922)
d: Edwin L. Hollywood. 7 reels.
Irene Castle, Ward Crane, Charles Gerard, Howard Truesdale, Tom Murray.
The manager of a lumber camp marries a cabaret dancer, despite his wealthy father's disapproval.

The Freshie (Frederick Herbst Productions, 1922)
d: W. Hughes Curran. 5 reels.
Guinn "Big Boy" Williams, Molly Malone, Lincoln Stedman, James McElhern, Edward Burns, Lee Phelps, Sam Armstrong, J. Buckley Russell, Jules Hauft.
Subjected to a hazing ritual at his new college, a former cowboy fights back against his tormentors.

The Freshman (Pathé, 1925)
d: Fred Newmeyer, Sam Taylor. 7 reels.
Harold Lloyd, Jobyna Ralston, Brooks Benedict, James Anderson, Pat Harmon, Joe Harrington, Hazel Keener.
A college freshman longs to be accepted by his peers, but he gets no respect. Even when he tries out for the football squad, he is assigned to be a live tackling dummy. After many misadventures, this square peg finally fits in—when he scores the winning touchdown in the school's Big Game.

Friday the Thirteenth (World Film Corp., 1916)
d: Emile Chautard. 5 reels.
Robert Warwick, Clarence Harvey, Charles Brandt, Gerda Holmes, Montagu Love, Lenore Harris.
Revenge on her mind, a ruined Southerner's daughter takes a job in the New York investment firm she believes devastated her family fortune. While looking for ways to sabotage the company, she falls for the son of her boss, and in the end there's a North-South reconciliation.

Friend Husband (Goldwyn, 1918)
d: Clarence G. Badger. 5 reels.
Madge Kennedy, Rockliffe Fellowes, George Bunny, Paul Everton, William Davidson, Jean Armour.
When a young woman with modern ideas learns she must be married to claim an inheritance, she pays a man $10,000 to go through a wedding with her and then leave her in peace. He agrees, but after they are married he saves her from thieves and cutthroats, and her gratitude for the young man matures into love.

Friendly Enemies (Belasco Productions, 1925)
d: George Melford. 7 reels.
Lew Fields, Joe Weber, Virginia Brown Faire, Jack Mulhall, Stuart Holmes, Lucille Lee Stewart, Eugenie Besserer, Nora Hayden, Jules Hanft, Fred Kelsey, Johnny Fox, Edward Porter.
American immigrants from Germany find their loyalties divided when World War I breaks out.

A Friendly Husband (Fox, 1923)
d: John Blystone. 5 reels.
Lupino Lane, Alberta Vaughn, Eva Thatcher.
Newlyweds buy a trailer and embark on a camping trip, but are joined at the last moment by the wife's family.

The Fringe of Society (Backer-Foursquare, 1917)
d: Robert Ellis. 7 reels.
Milton Sills, Ruth Roland, J. Herbert Frank, Leah Baird, George Larkin, Ollie Kirby, Tammany Young, Jules Cowles.
A publisher who supports Prohibition clashes with a politician who doesn't.

Frisco Sally Levy (MGM, 1927)
d: William Beaudine. 7 reels.
Sally O'Neil, Mickey Daniels, Tenen Holtz, Kate Price, Charles Delaney, Leon Holmes, Turner Savage, Helen Levine, Roy D'Arcy.
Sally, whose father is Jewish and whose mother is Irish, finds herself juggling similarly contrasting boyfriends.

The Frisky Mrs. Johnson (Famous Players-Lasky/Paramount, 1920)
d: Edward Dillon. 5 reels.
Billie Burke, War Crane, Jane Warrington, Lumsden Hare, Huntley Gordon, Jean de Briac, Robert Agnew, Leonora Ottinger, Emily Fitzroy.
Belle Johnson, a flirtatious widow living in Paris, finds that her sister's marriage is headed for trouble unless she (Belle) acts fast. At the risk of her own future happiness, Belle steps in and allows herself to be caught with her sister's lover. Fortunately, the complications are all sorted out by the final reel.

Frivolous Sal (J.K. McDonald Productions/First National, 1925)
d: Victor Scherzinger. 8 reels.
Eugene O'Brien, Mae Busch, Ben Alexander, Tom Santschi, Mitchell Lewis, Mildred Harris.
Keene, a widower, falls in love with Sal, a young saloon owner, and they marry. Sal devotes herself to taking care of her husband's young son Benny and leaves the running of the saloon to her husband. *Big* mistake! Unknown to Sal, her husband is a recovered alcoholic and with temptation so close at hand now, he reverts to his drinking habits. It will take all the love she and Benny can muster to pull Keene out of the bottle this time.

Frivolous Wives—see: The Married Virgin (1918)

From Broadway to a Throne (Universal, 1916)

d: William Bowman. 5 reels.
Carter de Haven, Yona Landowska, Malcolm Blevins, Duke Worne, Walter Belasco, Marvel Spencer, Frank MacQuarrie, Albert MacQuarrie, William Canfield, T.D. Crittenden.
Just before a bout, a New York prizefighter receives a medallion that may—or may not—bring him good luck.

From Headquarters (Vitagraph, 1919)
d: Ralph Ince. 5 reels.
Anita Stewart, Earle Williams, Anders Randolf, Templar Saxe, Ruth Edwards.
A tough police detective loves his innocent daughter, but he unreasonably forbids her to be around men.

From Headquarters (Warner Bros., 1929)
d: Howard Bretherton. 7 reels. (Talking sequences.)
Monte Blue, Guinn Williams, Gladys Brockwell, Lionel Belmore, Henry B. Walthall, Ethlyne Claire, Pat Hartigan.

A squad of U.S. Marines goes searching in the Central American jungle for a lost party of sightseers.

From Now On (Fox, 1920)
d: Raoul Walsh. 5 reels.
George Walsh, Regina Quinn, Mario Majeroni, Paul Everton, J.A. Marcus, Tom Walsh, Cesare Gravina, Robert Byrd.
When a young man is bilked of his money by race track crooks and he later steals the money back, he is arrested for theft and jailed. But his sentence ends five years later, and he heads straight for his stash... followed closely by both the crooks and the police.

From the Ground Up (Goldwyn, 1921)
d: E. Mason Hopper. 5 reels.
Tom Moore, Helene Chadwick, DeWitt Jennings, Grace Pike, Hardee Kirkland, Darrel Foss.
Terence, a construction worker, falls for a gal from the upper crust of society.

From the Manger to the Cross (Kalem, 1912)
d: Sidney Olcott. 5 reels.
R. Henderson Bland, Alice Hollister, James D. Ainsley, Percy Dyer, Gene Gauntier, George Kellog, Sidney Olcott, Robert G. Vignola, Sidney Baber, Jack Clark, J.P. MacGowan.
An ambitious retelling of the story of Christ, this was the first major film to be shot "on location", as that term is now used. Kalem sent its entire company to the Holy Land for photography in the areas where the original New Testament story took place.

From the Valley of the Missing (Fox, 1915)
d: Frank Powell. 5 reels.

Jane Miller, Vivian Tobin, Harry Spingler, W.N. "Bill" Bailey, William Riley Hatch, Robert Cummings, Kate Cummings, Arline Hackett, Clifford Bruce, Catherine Calhoun.
Lost children turn up in their parents' lives, years later.

From Two to Six (Triangle, 1918)
d: Albert Parker. 5 reels.
Winifred Allen, Earle Foxe, Forrest Robinson, Robert Fischer, Margaret Greene, Clarence Handyside, Charles B. Wells, Madeline Marshall, Amy Somers, Riley Hatch.
Comedic romp about espionage and stolen plans.

The Frontier of the Stars (Famous Players-Lasky/Paramount, 1921)
d: Charles Maigne. 6 reels.
Thomas Meighan, Faire Binney, Alphonz Ethier, Edward Ellis, Gus Weinberg, Florence Johns.
On a tenement roof in New York, a gangster on the run from the police meets a young crippled girl and they fall in love. Through her continuing love, the crook's attitude softens and he renounces his life of crime.

The Frontier Trail (Charles R. Rogers Productions/Pathé, 1926)
d: Scott R. Dunlap. 6 reels.
Harry Carey, Mabel Julienne Scott, Ernest Hilliard, Frank Campeau, Nelson McDowell, Charles Mailes, Harvey Clark, Aggie Herring, Chief Big Tree.
Out West, a major's daughter must travel through dangerous Indian territory to reach her father.

The Frontiersman (MGM, 1927)
d: Reginald Barker. 5 reels.
Tim McCoy, Claire Windsor, Tom O'Brien, Louise Lorraine, Russell Simpson, Lillian Leighton, May Foster, Chief Big

Tree, Frank Hagney, John Peters.
Members of Andrew Jackson's Tennessee Militia try to make peace with the Sioux, but are finally forced to fight.

Frozen River (Warner Bros., 1929)
d: F. Harmon Weight. (Part talkie.) 6 reels.
Rin-Tin-Tin, Davey Lee, Nina Quartero, Josef Swickard, Raymond McKee, Duane Thompson, Frank Campeau.
Rinty saves an old man's small fortune from being stolen.

The Frozen Warning (Commonwealth Pictures, 1917)
d: Oscar Eagle. 6 reels.
Charlotte Hayward, Jack Meredith, Seymour Rose, Ralph Johnson, Charles Gardner, Esther Lynn, Gerald Kaehm, Courtland J. Van Deusen.
An ice-skater in love with an inventor tries to warn him of danger by carving a message on the ice during an exhibition.

The Fruit of Divorce — see: San Francisco Nights (1928)

Fruits of Desire (World Film Corp., 1916)
d: Oscar Eagle. 5 reels.
Robert Warwick, Madeline Traverse, Dorothy Fairchild, Robert Cummings, Alec B. Francis, Ralph Delmore, D.J. Flannigan, James Mack, James Ewens, Adolphe Lestina.
Love blossoms when a country boy comes to Pittsburgh to learn the steel business, and the boss' daughter falls for him.

The Fuel of Life (Triangle, 1917)
d: Walter Edwards. 5 reels.
Belle Bennett, F.H. Newburg, J. Barney Sherry, Texas Guinan, Lee Hill, Margaret Shillingford, Alberta Lee, Lee Phelps, Eugene Burr, Edward Hayden, Thomas S. Guise.
A woman whose husband has been unfaithful to her declares a war of vengeance on all men.

The Fugitive (Thanhouser, 1916)
d: Frederick Sullivan. 5 reels.
Florence La Badie, Ethyle Cook, George Marlo, Hector Dion, J.H. Gilmour, Samuel N. Niblack, Robert Vaughn, Dorothy Benham.
When her sister accidentally kills a man bent on seduction, Margery Carew takes the blame to protect her sister's family.

The Fugitive (Arrow Pictures, 1925)
d: Ben Wilson. 5 reels.
Ruth Stonehouse, Wilbur McGaugh, Ben Wilson, Natalie LaSupervia, Joseph Girard, Helene Rosson.
Out West, an embittered man hunts for the desperadoes who killed his sister in a rape attempt.

A Fugitive From Matrimony (Robertson-Cole, 1919)
d: Henry King. 5 reels.
H.B. Warner, Seena Owen, Adele Farrington, Walter Perry, Christine Mayo, Matthew Biddulph, John Gough, Lule Warrenton.
A confirmed bachelor impersonates an escaped convict and gets into a jam from which only matrimony can extricate him.

Fugitives (Fox, 1929)
d: William Beaudine. 6 reels.
Madge Bellamy, Don Terry, Arthur Stone, Earle Foxe, Matthew Betz, Lumsden Hare, Edith Yorke, Jean Laverty, Hap Ward.
Alice, a nightclub singer, is convicted of murder on circumstantial evidence. After her boyfriend helps her escape prison, they take to the road, but are forced to halt their getaway to rescue a man under attack by thieves. It turns out the man is the same D.A. who prosecuted the

singer and got her convicted.

A Full House   (Famous Players-Lasky/Paramount, 1920)
d: James Cruze. 5 reels.
Bryant Washburn, Lois Wilson, Guy Milham, Hazel Howell, Vera Lewis, Beverly Travers, Lottie Williams, John Wild, Z. Wall Covington, Frank Jonasson, Lillian Leighton.
A comedy of errors ensues when newlyweds, a thief, a chorus girl, and a friend of the groom all gather at the same house, and the police forbid anyone to leave.

Full of Pep   (Metro, 1919)
d: Harry L. Franklin. 5 reels.
Hale Hamilton, Alice Lake, Alice Knowland, Fred Malatesta, Charles Hill Mailes, Victor Potel, R.D. MacLean.
"Pep," a very popular patent medicine, is in reality straight whiskey. A super salesman not only peddles the stuff, he parlays his Pep into a peppy romance with a south-of-the-border señorita.

The Furnace   (Realart, 1920)
d: William Desmond Taylor. 7 reels.
Agnes Ayres, Milton Sills, Jerome Patrick, Edward Martindel, Betty Francisco, Theodore Roberts, Lucien Littlefield, Helen Dunbar, Fred Turner, Robert Bolder, Mayme Kelso.
When a millionaire learns that his wife has married him only for his money, he retaliates by insisting on a marriage in name only.

Fury   (Inspiration/Associated First National, 1923)
d: Henry King. 9 reels.
Richard Barthelmess, Dorothy Gish, Pat Hartigan, Tyrone Power, Barry Macallum, Jessie Arnold, Harry Blakemore, Adolph Milar, Ivan Linow, Emily Fitzroy, Lucia Backus.
Bitter melodrama about a young man who is bent on avenging his father's death by seeking out the man who caused his mother to desert his father.

Fuss and Feathers   (T.H. Ince/Famous Players-Lasky/Paramount, 1918)
d: Fred Niblo. 5 reels.
Enid Bennett, John P. Lockney, Douglas MacLean, Charles K. French, Sylvia Ashton, Robert McKim, Lucile Young.
A nouveau riche father and daughter find that their money won't help them in the social whirl unless they cultivate some manners. So, the daughter hires an etiquette instructor.

The Gaiety Girl   (Universal, 1924)
d: King Baggot. 8 reels.
Mary Philbin, Joseph Dowling, William Haines, James O. Barrows, DeWitt Jennings, Freeman Wood, Otto Hoffman, Grace Darmond, Thomas Ricketts, William Turner, Duke R. Lee.
In England, a penniless aristocrat and his granddaughter move to London, where she joins the Gaiety Theater acting troupe.

The Gallant Fool   (Duke Worne Productions/Rayart, 1926)
d: Duke Worne. 5 reels.
Billy Sullivan, Hazel Deane, Ruth Boyd, Ruth Royce, Frank Baker, Jimmy Aubrey, Ferdinand Schumann-Heink, Robert Walker.
Billy, a brash young American, travels to the kingdom of Valdonia on business. While there, he impersonates a prince and wins the heart of the queen.

The Galley Slave   (Fox, 1915)
d: J. Gordon Edwards. 5 reels.
Theda Bara, Stuart Holmes, Claire Whitney, Lillian Lawrence, Jane Lee, Ben Hendricks, Hardee Kirkland, Henry Leone, A.H. Van Buren.
Deserted by her uncaring husband when he inherits wealth and a title, a woman tries to support herself and her daughter by working as an artist's model.

The Galloping Ace   (Universal, 1924)
d: Robert North Bradbury. 5 reels.
Jack Hoxie, Margaret Morris, Robert McKim, Frank Rice, Julia Brown, Dorothea Wolbert, Fred Humes.
A war veteran gets a job working at a ranch owned by a pretty boss lady.

The Galloping Cowboy   (Western Star Productions/Associated Exhibitors, 1926)
d: William J. Craft. 5 reels.
Bill Cody, Alex Hart, Edmund Cobb, Barney Gilmore, Florence Ulrich, Richard Cummings, David Dunbar.
Out West, fun-loving Bill discovers that his cousin Jack is a notorious fugitive.

The Galloping Devil   (Canyon Pictures Corp./State Rights, 1920)
d: Nate Watt. 6 reels.
Franklyn Farnum, Genevieve Berte, Bud Osborne, Joseph Chatterton, Vester Pegg.
In the old West, a ranch foreman falls for his predecessor's young ward.

Galloping Fish   (Thomas H. Ince Corp./Associated First National, 1924)
d: Thomas H. Ince. 6 reels.
Louise Fazenda, Sydney Chaplin, Ford Sterling, Chester Conklin, Lucille Ricksen, John Steppling.
Newlyweds quarrel, and the husband is sent packing by his bride. Innocently, he wanders into a theater where an exotic lady is performing with a trained seal... and somehow, he gets involved with the actress, her seal, lawyers, bill collectors, and finally with his bride, who wants to take him back and give love another chance.

Galloping Fury   (Universal, 1927)
d: Reaves Eason. 6 reels.
Hoot Gibson, Otis Harlan, Sally Rand, Frank Beal, Gilbert "Pee Wee" Holmes, Max Asher, Edward Coxen, Duke R. Lee.
Western comedy about the characters at a ranch with miraculous mud. That's right, mud. It cures disease and even makes you look better.

The Galloping Gobs   (Action Pictures/Pathé, 1927)
d: Richard Thorpe. 5 reels.
Buffalo Bill Jr., Morgan Brown, Betty Baker, Raye Hampton, Walter Maly, Robert Homans, Jack Barnell, Fred Burns.
Sailors on leave settle into a dilapidated ranch they won in a poker game.

The Galloping Kid   (Universal, 1922)
d: Nat Ross. 5 reels.
Hoot Gibson, Edna Murphy, Lionel Belmore, Leon Barry, Jack Walters, Percy Challenger.
Out West, a cowboy is hired to chaperone a rancher's daughter.

Galloping Thunder   (Bob Custer Productions/FBO of America, 1927)
d: Scott Pembroke. 5 reels.

Bob Custer, Anne Sheridan, J.P. Lockney, Richard R. Neill, Fernando Galvez.

Judith, a ranch owner's daughter, is desired by both the foreman and a train robber.

Gambier's Advocate (Famous Players/Paramount, 1915)
d: James Kirkwood. 5 reels.

Hazel Dawn, James Kirkwood, Fuller Mellish, Dorothy Bernard, Robert Broderick, Maude Odell.

A young woman catches her stepmother in an embrace with Steve Gambier, a man not her husband, and suspects The Worst. To save her father grief, the young woman introduces Gambier as her fiancé. What she doesn't know is that the embrace was a completely innocent token of gratitude. But she finds out, after Gambier falls in love with her and becomes her fiancé for real.

A Gamble in Souls (New York Motion Picture Corp./Triangle, 1916)
d: Walter Edwards. 5 reels.

William Desmond, Dorothy Dalton, P.D. Tabler, Charles K. French, Jack Vosburgh.

Passion mingles with preaching when a minister and a chorus girl are shipwrecked together on a desert isle.

The Gamblers (Lubin, 1914)
d: George W. Terwilliger. 5 reels.

George Soule Spencer, William H. Turner, Gaston Bell, Lilie Leslie, Earle Metcalfe, Ethel Clayton, Kempton Greene, Gilbert Ely, Jack Ridgeway.

Tempers flare when a woman marries a man she does not love, while her true soul mate, a weak-willed banker, is sentenced to prison for speculating with bank funds.

The Gamblers (Vitagraph, 1919)
d: Paul Scardon. 6 reels.

Harry T. Morey, Charles Kent, Agnes Ayres, Helen Ferguson, Eric Mayne, George Majeroni, George Backus.

Remake of Lubin's 1914 *The Gamblers*, both films based on the play of the same name by Charles Klein.

The Gambling Fool (Independent Pictures, 1925)
d: J.P. McGowan. 5 reels.

Franklyn Farnum, Otto Myers, Fred Holmes, Harry Northrup, Jack Pearce, Ralph Yearsley, Mary Louise Montague, Joseph W. Girard, Ruth Dwyer.

Out West, a gambler wins a ranch in a poker game, and finds it comes with an orphan boy attached.

Gambling in Souls (Fox, 1919)
d: Harry Millarde. 6 reels.

Madlaine Traverse, Herbert Heyes, Murdock MacQuarie, Lew Zehring, Mary McIvor, Henry Barrows, Marion Skinner, William Clifford.

Because her husband committed suicide after being ruined financially by an unscrupulous trader, his widow vows revenge on the culprit.

The Game Chicken (Realart Pictures/Paramount, 1922)
d: Chester M. Franklin. 5 reels.

Bebe Daniels, Pat O'Malley, James Gordon, Martha Mattox, Gertrude Norman, Hugh Thompson, Max Weatherwax, Mattie Peters, Charles Force, Edwin Stevens.

Inez, an American girl living in Cuba, is desired by two men — a U.S. revenue agent and a bootlegger.

A Game of Wits (American Film Co./Mutual, 1917)
d: Henry King. 5 reels.

Gail Kane, George Periolat, Spottiswoode Aitken, Lewis J. Cody.

An aging roué is outwitted by the girl he planned to seduce.

A Game With Fate (Vitagraph, 1918)
d: Paul Scardon. 5 reels.

Harry T. Morey, Betty Blythe, Denton Vane, Percy Standing, Robert Gaillard, Stanley Walpole.

Friends concoct a deadly gamble, with one pretending to murder the other.

The Game's Up (Universal, 1919)
d: Elsie Jane Wilson. 5 reels.

Ruth Clifford, Al Ray, Harry Holden, Mildred Lee, Margaret Cullington, Clifford Gray, John Hay Cossar.

When a young woman in the West pretends to her east coast friend that she is successful and wealthy, she weaves a tangled web of deceit. Her friend arrives with a chaperone, and they expect to be treated luxuriously.

The Gangsters of New York — see: The Gangsters (1914)

The Garden of Allah (Selig Polyscope, 1916)
d: Colin Campbell. 10 reels.

Helen Ware, Thomas Santschi, Will Machin, Matt B. Snyder, Harry Lonsdale, Eugenie Besserer, James Bradbury, Al W. Filson, Cecil Holland, Frank Clark, Billy Jacobs.

At a remote oasis in the Sahara desert, a young woman meets and falls in love with a man of mystery... who turns out to be a defrocked priest.

The Garden of Allah (MGM, 1927)
d: Rex Ingram. 9 reels.

Alice Terry, Ivan Petrovich, Marcel Vibert, H.H. Wright, Madame Paquerette, Armand Dutertre, Ben Sadour, Gerald Fielding, Michael Powell, Rehba Ben Salah, Claude Fielding.

Ambitious retelling of the Robert Smythe Hichens tale about a defrocked priest who resumes his birth name, Boris Androvsky, and falls in love with a young woman.

Reworking of the 1916 Selig Polyscope movie of the same name.

The Garden of Eden (United Artists, 1928)
d: Lewis Milestone. 8 reels.

Corinne Griffith, Louise Dresser, Lowell Sherman, Charles Ray, Maude George, Edward Martindel, Freeman Wood, Hank Mann.

A young singer rises to the rank of baroness.

Garden of Lies (Universal, 1915)
d: John H. Pratt. 5 reels.

Jane Cowl, William Russell, Philip Hahn, Violet Horner, Ethelbert Hale, David Wall, Claude Cooper, Adele Carson.

An American woman weds a European prince, but suffers aphasia when involved in a vehicle accident on her wedding day. To calm her fears, a stranger offers to pose as her absent husband temporarily, and they fall in love.

The Garden of Weeds (Famous Players-Lasky/Paramount, 1924)
d: James Cruze. 6 reels.

Betty Compson, Rockliffe Fellowes, Warner Baxter, Charles Ogle, King Zany, William Austin, Lucille Thorndike, William Turner, Toyo Fujita, Lilyan Tashman, Al St. John.

Dorothy, a showgirl, refuses a wealthy promoter's advances at his estate, "The Garden of Weeds." However, to save her job, she does eventually give in to him. Later, when Mr. Right enters the picture, Dorothy is afraid to tell him of her "checkered" past. She marries him anyway, and when the pressure of her guilt gets too intense, she breaks down and tells him everything. Her husband gently replies that he knew about her indiscretion all along, but loves her anyway.

Garments of Truth (S-L Pictures/Metro, 1921)
d: George D. Baker. 5 reels.
Gareth Hughes, Ethel Grandin, John Steppling, Frances Raymond, Margaret McWade, Graham Pettie, Frank Norcross, Harry Lorraine, Walter Perry, Gerbert Fortier, Eileen Hume.
Comedy about Lester, a compulsive liar who makes himself such a nuisance that the townfolk send him to a specialist to be cured. After treatment, Lester not only stops telling lies, he speaks nothing but the truth, about everything. After Lester's unflagging honesty ruins a couple of real estate deals and other business transactions, the townspeople yearn for the old, loveable liar they transformed. In the end, only love can solve his problem... and he finds it, with a beauty to whom telling the truth will be an endless joy.

Garrison's Finish (United Artists, 1923)
d: Arthur Rosson. 8 reels.
Jack Pickford, Madge Bellamy, Clarence Burton, Charles Ogle, Charles A. Stevenson, Ethel Grey Terry.
A jockey suffering from amnesia enters the Kentucky Derby, and wins it.

The Garter Girl (Vitagraph, 1920)
d: Edward H. Griffith. 5 reels.
Corinne Griffith, Sallie Crute, Earl Metcalfe, Rod LaRocque, James Tarbell.
When a former vaudeville dancer meets and falls for a young minister, she tries to unearth information about his past... and learns too much. It seems the reverend has dark secrets.

Gas, Oil and Water (Charles Ray Productions/Associated First National, 1922)
d: Charles Ray. 5 reels.
Charles Ray, Otto Hoffman, Charlotte Pierce, Robert Grey, William Carroll, Dick Sutherland, Bert Offord, Whiskers Ray.
Susie, a girl whose Dad owns a hotel on the Mexican border, falls for the new gent who's just opened a gas station nearby. What she doesn't know is that he's a Secret Service agent on the trail of smugglers.

Gasoline Gus (Famous Players-Lasky/Paramount, 1921)
d: James Cruze. 5 reels.
Roscoe "Fatty" Arbuckle, Lila Lee, Charles Ogle, Theodore Lorch, Wilton Taylor, Knute Erickson, Fred Huntley.
Comedy about Gus, a jolly fat man who finds a way to make a dry oil well pay off.
This is the film that was playing in the nation's theaters when the Virginia Rappe scandal broke in September 1921. Because of the public outrage over Arbuckle's role in the incident, the studios withdrew his films from distribution. For the rest of his life, Arbuckle would be held publicly accountable for Miss Rappe's tragic death, despite the fact that he faced three trials for her murder, and was never convicted.

The Gate Crasher (Universal, 1928)
d: William James Craft. 6 reels.
Glenn Tryon, Patsy Ruth Miller, T. Roy Barnes, Beth Laemmle, Fred Malatesta, Claude Payton, Russell Powell, Tiny Sandford, Al Smith, Monte Montague.
Henshaw, a would-be detective who's studying via a correspondence course, goes to New York and solves the mystery of a Broadway actress' stolen jewels.

Gates of Brass (Pathé, 1919)
d: Ernest C. Warde. 5 reels.
Frank Keenan, Lois Wilson, George Fisher, Clyde Benson, Edwin Tilton, Lillian Langdon, Frank DeLoan, Tula Belle, Bobbie Mack.
A professional swindler gains wealth but loses family and friends.

The Gates of Doom (Universal, 1917)
d: Charles Swickard. 5 reels.
Claire McDowell, L.C. Shumway, Jack Connolly, Mark Fenton, Tommie Dale, Alfred Allen, Francis MacDonald, Lena Baskette.
After marrying an English captain and bearing his child, an Indian woman is captured by a Bengali prince and imprisoned in his harem.

The Gates of Eden (Columbia/Metro, 1916)
d: John H. Collins. 5 reels.
Viola Dana, Augustus Phillips, Robert Walker, Edward Earle, Grace E. Stevens, Fred Jones, Harry Linson, George Melville.
Sweethearts in a Shaker community are ostracized and the young man is driven out of town, but not before his girlfriend bears their child.

Gates of Gladness (World Film Corp., 1918)
d: Harley Knoles. 5 reels.
Madge Evans, George MacQuarrie, Niles Welch, Rosina Henley, Gerda Holmes.
Disowned by his father, a young man brings his wife and little girl back to the family estate years later, when his brother is the new lord of the manor.

The Gateway of the Moon (Fox, 1928)
d: John Griffith Wray. 6 reels.
Dolores Del Rio, Walter Pidgeon, Anders Randolf, Ted McNamara, Adolph Millar, Leslie Fenton, Noble Johnson, Virginia LaFonde.
In South America, a ruthless contractor tries to kill the inspector who's investigating his work methods. The inspector is shot and left for dead, but is rescued by the contractor's own niece.

The Gaucho (Fairbanks/United Artists, 1928)
d: F. Richard Jones. 10 reels.
Douglas Fairbanks, Lupe Velez, Michael Vavitch, Gustave von Seyffertitz, Charles Stevens, Nigel de Brulier, Albert MacQuarrie, Mary Pickford (cameo).
The leader of an outlaw band tries to oust a corrupt head of state.

The Gauntlet (Vitagraph, 1920)
d: Edwin L. Hollywood. 5 reels.
Harry T. Morey, Louiszita Valentine, Frank Hagney, Walter Horton, Charles Eldridge, Arden Page, Eleanor Barry, Robert Gaillard.
In Tennessee, a young man falls for the daughter of moonshiners, then has to fight off a whole clan of them.

Gay and Devilish (R-C Pictures, 1922)
d: William A. Seiter. 5 reels.
Doris May, Cullen Landis, Otis Harlan, Jacqueline Logan, Bull Montana, Lila Leslie, Ashley Cooper, Arthur Millett, Kingsley Benedict, Milton Ross, George Periolat.
Fanchon, a young charmer, agrees to marry a wealthy elderly man to help her cash-strapped guardian. Instead,

she falls in love with the elderly man's nephew.

The Gay Deceiver (MGM, 1926)
d: John M. Stahl. 7 reels.
Lew Cody, Carmel Myers, Marceline Day, Malcolm McGregor, Roy D'Arcy, Dorothy Phillips, Edward Connelly, Antonio D'Algy.
In Paris, a young woman tries to reunite her estranged parents.

The Gary Defender (Paramount, 1927)
d: Gregory LaCava. 7 reels.
Richard Dix, Thelma Todd, Fred Kohler, Jerry Mandy, Robert Brower, Harry Holden, Fred Esmelton, Frances Raymond, Ernie S. Adams.
In Old California, the son of a land baron loves Ruth, daughter of a U.S. commissioner.

The Gay Lord Quex (Goldwyn, 1919)
d: Harry Beaumont. 5 reels.
Tom Moore, Gloria Hope, Naomi Childers, Hazel Daly, Sydney Ainsworth, P.H. McCullough, Arthur Housman, Kate Lester, Henry Miller Jr., Kathleen Kirkham.
Society drama about two womanizers who hone in on the same lady.

The Gay Lord Waring (Universal, 1916)
d: Otis Turner. 5 reels.
J. Warren Kerrigan, Lois Wilson, Maude George, Bertram Grassby, Duke Worne.
Desperate for money, a penniless nobleman borrows from a relative who insists on harsh terms: If the nobleman cannot pay the money back in six months, he must commit suicide!

The Gay Old Bird (Warner Bros., 1927)
d: Herman Raymaker. 7 reels.
Louise Fazenda, Edgar Kennedy, John Steppling, John T. Murray, Frances Raymond, William Demarest, Jane Winton.
A housemaid is compelled to temporarily replace the lady of the house.

The Gay Old Dog (Pathé, 1919)
d: Hobart Henley. 6 reels.
John Cumberland, Mary Chambers, Emily Lorraine, Inez Marcel, Frances Neilson, Gertrude Robinson, Nell Tracy.
Despite the title, this drama's a downer: A romantically-inclined young man promises his dying mother not to marry before his three sisters do. Two of the sisters eventually do marry, but in the meantime their brother has grown old and is condemned to a life of loneliness.

The Gay Retreat (Fox, 1927)
d: Ben Stoloff. 6 reels.
Gene Cameron, Betty Francisco, Judy King, Sammy Cohen, Jerry the Giant, Holmes Herbert, Ted McNamara, Charles Gorman.
Wright, a somnambulist, joins an ambulance unit to aid in the war effort. By beaurocratic blunder, however, he gets sent to France as part of the U.S. Army—and helps to win the war!

The General (Keaton/United Artists, 1927)
d: Buster Keaton, Clyde Bruckman. 8 reels.
Buster Keaton, Marion Mack, Glen Cavender, Jim Farley, Frederick Vroom, Joseph Keaton.
Action comedy usually voted among the best silent films ever made. Keaton plays a railroad engineer in the South whose train is stolen—and his girlfriend abducted—by Yankee spies during the Civil War. Keaton gives chase,

eventually freeing both train and girl, and winning the respect of those who had written him off as a coward.

The Gentle Cyclone (Fox, 1926)
d: William S. Van Dyke. 5 reels.
Buck Jones, Rose Blossom, Will Walling, Reed Howes, Stanton Heck, Grant Withers, Kathleen Myers, Jay Hunt, Oliver Hardy, Marion Harlan.
When June, an orphan girl, inherits a strip of valuable land lying between the farms of her two uncles, the occasion sets off a feud between the two men.

The Gentle Intruder (American Film Co./Mutual, 1917)
d: James Kirkwood. 5 reels.
Mary Miles Minter, George Fisher, Eugenie Forde, Harvey Clarke, Franklin Ritchie.
Cheated of her inheritance by an unscrupulous attorney, a young woman goes to work for the lawyer's family as a maid. In time, her cheerful, understanding nature lets the attorney see the error of his ways, and he humbly returns to the heiress what is rightfully hers. Meanwhile, the genial maid has captured the heart of her employer's son.

Gentle Julia (Fox, 1923)
d: Rowland V. Lee. 6 reels.
Bessie Love, Harold Goodwin, Frank Elliott, Charles K. French, Clyde Benson, Harry Dunkinson, Jack Rollins, Frances Grant, William Irving, Agnes Aker, William Lester, Gypsy Norman, Mary Arthur, Richard Billings.
Julia's got plenty of beaus back home, but she falls instead for a gent from the city. Trouble is, he's already married!

The Gentleman From America (Universal, 1923)
d: Edward Sedgwick. 5 reels.
Hoot Gibson, Tom O'Brien, Louise Lorraine, Carmen Phillips, Frank Leigh, Jack Crane, Bob McKenzie, Albert Prisco, Rosa Rosanova.
Comedy about a pair of doughboys who go to Spain on leave and fall in love with señoritas.

The Gentleman From Indiana (Pallas Pictures/Paramount, 1915)
d: Frank Lloyd. 5 reels.
Dustin Farnum, Winifred Kingston, Herbert Standing, Page Peters, Howard Davies, Juan de la Cruz, Joe Ray, Elsie Cort, C. Norman Hammond, Helen Eddy.
A former college football star becomes a crusading newspaper publisher.

A Gentleman of Leisure (Lasky Feature Plays/Paramount, 1915)
d: George Melford. 5 reels.
Wallace Eddinger, Sydney Deane, Gertrude Kellar, Tom Forman, Carol Hollaway, Frederick Vroom, Francis Tyler, Monroe Salisbury, Florence Dagmar, Lucien Littlefield.
A gentleman crook robs from the rich... until he falls in love with the daughter of one of his victims.

A Gentleman of Paris (Paramount, 1927)
d: Harry D. D'Arrast. 6 reels.
Adolphe Menjou, Shirley O'Hara, Arlette Marchael, Ivy Harris, Nicholas Soussanin, Lawrence Grant, William Davidson, Lorraine Eddy.
A Parisian roué announces he is ready to settle down and marry, and sends notice to all his mistresses.

A Gentleman of Quality (Vitagraph, 1919)
d: James Young. 5 reels.
Earle Williams, Katherine Adams, Joyce Moore, James

THE GARDEN OF EDEN (1928). Charles Ray and Corinne Griffith portray lovebirds in old Budapest, in this lively romantic comedy with a wacky sense of fun.

* * * * *

Carpenter, Robert Bolder, George Pierce, Ronald Byram.
Double role for Williams, as twin brothers separated at birth.
One of them grows up to fall in love with a beautiful lady,
but when he disappears on his wedding day, the other
brother shows up and fills in for him at the altar.

A Gentleman's Agreement (Vitagraph, 1918)
d: David Smith. 5 reels.
Alfred Whitman, Nell Shipman, Juan de la Cruz, Jake
Abraham, Hattie Buskirk, Jack Wetherby, Al Garcia, Patricia
Palmer.
When a mining engineer engaged to an east coast beauty is
seriously injured and thought dead, his grieving fiancée
agrees to marry another man.

Gentlemen Prefer Blondes (Paramount, 1928)
d: Malcolm St. Clair. 7 reels.
Ruth Taylor, Alice White, Ford Sterling, Holmes Herbert,
Mack Swain, Emily Fitzroy, Trixie Friganza, Blanche
Frederici, Ed Faust, Eugene Borden, Margaret Seddon, Luke
Cosgrave, Chester Conklin, Yorke Sherwood, Mildred Boyd.
The first screen appearance of Lorelei Lee, the beguiling
blonde gold-digger from Little Rock. Curiously, the elfin
Alice White, who made a career of playing bubbly blonde
flappers, is here given the role of brunette Dorothy, Lorelei's
level-headed girlfriend.

George Washington Cohen (Tiffany-Stahl Productions,
1928)
d: George Archainbaud. 6 reels.
George Jessel, Robert Edeson, Corliss Palmer, Lawford
Davidson, Florence Allen, Jane LaVerne, Paul Panzer, Edna
Mae Cooper.
In New York, a chap gets a job as private secretary to a
banker. When the secretary learns that his boss' wife is
having an extra-marital affair, he'll have to be careful of his
next move: tell the boss or keep it himself?

George Washington Jr. (Warner Bros., 1924)
d: Malcom St. Clair. 6 reels.
Wesley Barry, Leon Barry, Gertrude Olmstead, Charles
Conklin, Otis Harlan, William Courtwright, Edward
Phillips.
A young man with principles cannot tell a lie, and that's the
problem.

Gerald Cranston's Lady (Fox, 1924)
d: Emmett J. Flynn. 7 reels.
James Kirkwood, Alma Rubens, Walter McGrail, J. Farrell
MacDonald, Lucien Littlefield, Spottiswoode Aitken,
Templar Saxe, Richard Headrick, Marguerite De La Motte.
In England, a genteel noblewoman accepts marriage to a
businessman who has worked his way up from the bottom.
Neither has any romantic illusions about their union; they
are marrying each other for convenience only. However, as
time goes by and each of them has their commitment tested
through conflict, the husband and wife learn to love each
other, and convenience has nothing to do with it.

Geraldine (Pathé, 1929)
d: Melville Brown. 7 reels.
Marian Nixon, Eddie Quillan, Albert Gran, Gaston Glass.
Wygate, a businessman, hires Eddie to instruct his daughter
Geraldine in the fine art of being a lady.

Get-Rich-Quick Wallingford (Cosmopolitan/Paramount,
1921)
d: Frank Borzage. 7 reels.
Sam Hardy, Norman Kerry, Doris Kenyon, Diana Allen,

William T. Hayes, Billie Dove, Edgar Nelson, Mac Barnes,
Horace James, Mrs. Charles Willard, John Woodford.
A couple of scam artists drum up interest in a phony
manufacturing scheme, and sell hundreds of shares of stock
in their enterprise. But crime never pays—or does it? When
a large company places a huge order for their product, the
scam artists bewilderedly find themselves awash in honest
profits.

Get Your Man (Fox, 1921)
d: George W. Hill. 5 reels.
Buck Jones, William Lawrence, Beatrice Burnham, Helen
Rosson, Paul Kamp.
In Canada, a girl falls for the mountie who had suspected
her father of embezzlement.

Get Your Man (Paramount, 1927)
d: Dorothy Arzner. 6 reels.
Clara Bow, Charles (Buddy) Rogers, Josef Swickard,
Josephine Dunn, Harvey Clarke, Frances Raymond.
In Paris, a visiting American girl (played by Miss Bow) falls
for a French nobleman. He's already engaged, though, so
our intrepid Yankee gal must engineer a fake auto wreck,
snoop into the family's private affairs, and wangle a
marriage proposal from the fiancée's dad, all in the name of
getting her prey to drop the other girl and marry *her*. It
works.

Getting Gertie's Garter (Metropolitan Pictures Corp. Of
Calif., 1927)
d: E. Mason Hopper. 7 reels.
Marie Prevost, Charles Ray, Harry Myers, Sally Rand,
William Orlamond, Fritzi Ridgeway, Franklin Pangborn, Del
Henderson, Lila Leslie.
Massive misunderstandings liven the comedy in this
production of the famous Avery Hopwood/Wilson Collison
play. Gertie owns a diamond-studded garter given to her by
an old flame, but now that she's engaged to another man,
she tries to return the garter to her former beau... who's
trying to reclaim it before *his* new fiancée learns of it.

Getting Mary Married (Cosmopolitan/Select Pictures,
1919)
d: Allan Dwan. 5 reels.
Marion Davies, Norman Kerry, Frederick Burton, Matt
Moore, Amelia Summerville, Constance Beaumar, Elmer
Grandin.
A young woman with a large inheritance stands to lose it if
she marries.

The Ghost Breaker (Lasky Feature Plays/Paramount, 1914)
d: Cecil B. DeMille. 5 reels.
H.B. Warner, Rita Stanwood, Theodore Roberts, Betty
Johnson, Jode Mullally, Horace B. Carpenter, Jeanne
McPherson, Mabel Van Buren, Billy Elmer, Dick La Strange,
Fred Montague.
The secret to the whereabouts of a long-lost treasure is
contained in a tiny locket.

The Ghost Breaker (Famous Players-Lasky/Paramount,
1922)
d: Alfred E. Green. 5 reels.
Wallace Reid, Lila Lee, Walter Hiers, Arthur Carewe, J.
Farrell MacDonald, Frances Raymond, Snitz Edwards.
In the hills of Kentucky, a girl and her beau try to find a
treasure that's thought to be hidden in or near her ancestral
home.

Ghost City (Helen Holmes Productions/Associated

Photoplays, 1921)
d: William Bertram. 5 reels.
Helen Holmes, Ann Schaeffer, Leo Maloney, Leonard Clapham, Jack Connolly.
Using an ancient map, a girl and her dad are out to find a hidden cache of silver. A pair of bootleggers pursue them, looking to cut themselves in on any uncovered treasure.

The Ghost Flower (Triangle, 1918)
d: Frank Borzage. 5 reels.
Alma Rubens, Charles West, Francis McDonald, Dick Rosson, Emory Johnson, Naida Lessing, Tote Ducrow.
In Italy, a wine merchant's daughter is menaced by a secret society.

The Ghost House (Lasky Feature Plays/Paramount, 1917)
d: William C. DeMille. 5 reels.
Jack Pickford, Louise Huff, Olga Grey, James Neill, Eugene Pallette, Mrs. Lewis McCord, Horace B. Carpenter, Edythe Chapman, Lillian Leighton.
Love blossoms in a "haunted" house, between a poor girl and a college boy.

The Ghost in the Garret (Paramount, 1921)
d: F. Richard Jones. 5 reels.
Dorothy Gish, William E. Park, Mrs. David Landau, Downey Clark, Tom Blake, Ray Gray, Porter Strong.
Banished from her aunt and uncle's home when they think they've caught her stealing, a young woman hides out in a "haunted house" and, with the help of a friend, catches the real crooks.

The Ghost of Old Morro (Thomas A. Edison, Inc., 1917)
d: Richard Ridgely. 5 reels.
Helen Strickland, Herbert Prior, Robert Conness, Mabel Trunnelle, Marie LaCorio, Dorothy Graham, Bigelow Cooper, Francisco Castillo.
The ghost of a murdered innkeeper haunts Morro castle by the sea.

The Ghost of Rosy Taylor (American Film Company, 1918)
d: Edward S. Sloman. 5 reels.
Mary Miles Minter, Alan Forrest, George Periolat, Helen Howard, Emma Kluge, Kate Price, Ann Schaefer.
A former housekeeper, supposedly dead, continues to clean the family mansion.

The Ghost Patrol (Universal, 1923)
d: Nat Ross. 5 reels.
Ralph Graves, Bessie Love, George Nichols, George B. Williams, Max Davidson, Wade Boteler, Melbourne MacDowell.
In New York, a dedicated cop is forced to retire because of age, but continues to walk his daily rounds and help keep the peace.

Ghosts (Majestic/Mutual, 1915)
d: George Nicholls. 5 reels.
Henry Walthall, Mary Alden, Loretta Blake. Erich von Stroheim, Nigel de Brulier.
Venereal disease afflicts the children of a playboy.

The Ghosts of Yesterday (Norma Talmadge Film Corp./Select Pictures, 1918)
d: Joseph M. Schenck. 6 reels.
Norma Talmadge, Eugene O'Brien, Stuart Holmes, John Daly Murphy, Henry J. Hebert, Ida Darling, Blanche Douglas.
After an artist's true love dies, he becomes disconsolate and

moves to Paris. There he meets a cabaret singer who closely resembles his lady love.
Double role for Miss Talmadge, who plays both women.

The Gift Girl (Universal, 1917)
d: Rupert Julian. 5 reels.
Louise Lovely, Emory Johnson, Wadsworth Harris, Rupert Julian, Frederick Montague, Winter Hall, Rex Roselli.
When his son begins to neglect his studies in favor of the life of a playboy, a French marquis sends his ward, a young English woman, to reform him.

Gift O' Gab (Essanay, 1917)
d: W.S. Van Dyke. 5 reels.
Jack Gardner, Helen Ferguson, Frank Morris, John Cossar, Margaret A. Wiggin.
A college boy with a talent for persuasion finds success as a salesman, and marries a railroad tycoon's daughter.

The Gift Supreme (C.R. Macauley Photoplays/Republic, 1920)
d: Ollie L. Sellers. 6 reels.
Bernard Durning, Seena Owen, Melbourne McDowell, Tully Marshall, Eugenie Besserer, Lon Chaney, Jack Curtis, Dick Morris, Anna Dodge, Claire McDowell.
A nurse in love with her patient gives her blood to save his life.

Gigolo (DeMille Pictures/Producers Distributing Corp., 1926)
d: William K. Howard. 7 reels.
Rod LaRocque, Jobyna Ralston, Louise Dresser, Cyril Chadwick, George Nichols, Ina Anson, Sally Rand.
Gideon, a scion of wealth, joins the Lafayette Escadrille and is wounded in action. He is taken to a field hospital, where he undergoes such extensive plastic surgery that his girlfriend Mary, who has joined the war effort as a nurse, meets Gideon in the hospital but does not recognize him.

The Gilded Butterfly (Fox, 1926)
d: John Griffith Wray. 6 reels.
Alma Rubens, Bert Lytell, Huntly Gordon, Frank Keenan, Herbert Rawlinson, Vera Lewis, Arthur Hoyt, Carolynne Snowden.
Morally suspect melodrama about a young woman who, finding herself short of funds, burns her own wardrobe in order to collect on the insurance. She is caught and arrested, but on the way to the police station the patrol car is involved in an accident and she makes her escape to another country.

The Gilded Cage (World Film Corp., 1916)
d: Harley Knoles. 5 reels.
Alice Brady, Alec B. Francis, Gerda Holmes, Montagu Love, Arthur Ashley, Sidney Dalbrook, Clara Whipple, Irving Cummings.
When the young queen of a mythical kingdom goes incognito among her discontented people, she meets and falls in love with their leader.

The Gilded Dream (Universal, 1920)
d: Rollin Sturgeon. 5 reels.
Carmel Myers, Elsa Lorimer, Thomas Chatterton, Zola Claire, May McCulley, Boyd Irwin, Eddie Dennis, Maxine Elliott Hicks.
When a small-town girl travels to New York and meets the man of her dreams, she is crushed to hear reports that he is already in an illicit love affair. Disconsolate, she returns home. But the young man, who's innocent and really loves her, gets there first and meets her as her train arrives.

A Gilded Fool (Fox, 1915)
d: Edgar Lewis. 5 reels.
William Farnum, Maude Gilbert, Margaret Vale, Charles Guthrie, Harry Spingler, George De Carlton.
Embittered by the loss of his dear mother, a wealthy young man becomes "a gilded fool," spending money on debauchery... until he meets his true love. There will be other complications, but at the end he mends his dissolute ways and gets his sweetheart to agree to marriage.

The Gilded Highway (Warner Bros., 1926)
d: J. Stuart Blackton. 7 reels.
Dorothy Devore, Macklyn Arbuckle, Florence Turner, John Harron, Myrna Loy, Andre Tourneur.
A family of pleasure seekers live the high life, then learn their fortune is severely limited.

Gilded Lies (Selznick, 1921)
d: William P.S. Earle. 5 reels.
Eugene O'Brien, Martha Mansfield, Frank Whitson,m George Stewart, Arthur Donaldson.
After her Arctic explorer fiancé is reported lost, Hester marries another man not for love but for money. Now, the fiancé has returned and wants back into Hester's life.

The Gilded Lily (Famous Players-Lasky/Paramount, 1921)
d: Robert Z. Leonard. 7 reels.
Mae Murray, Lowell Sherman, Jason Robards, Charles Gerard, Leonora Ottinger.
Lillian, a cafe hostess with an alcoholic husband, is desired by another man.

The Gilded Spider (Universal, 1916)

 d: Joseph De Grasse. 5 reels.
Louise Lovely, Lon Chaney, Lule Warrenton, Gilmore Hammond, Marjorie Ellison, Hayward Mack, Jay Belasco.
Morbid melodrama about a dissolute American who causes an Italian woman's suicide; her husband and daughter's subsequent trip to America, which causes the seducer's death; and the eventual suicide of the young girl's father.

The Gilded Youth (American Film Co./Mutual, 1917)
d: George L. Sargent. 5 reels.
Richard Bennett, Rhea Mitchell, Adrienne Morrison, George Periolat, Alfred Hollingsworth, Charles Newton.John and Mary, a poor boardinghouse tenant and a housemaid, plan to marry. But first, John plans to strike it rich in the stock market.

Gimme (Goldwyn, 1923)
d: Rupert Hughes. 6 reels.
Helene Chadwick, Gaston Glass, Kate Lester, Eleanor Boardman, David Imboden, May Wallace, Georgia Woodthorpe, H.B. Walthall, Jean Hope.
Fanny loves Ferris, but his tightfisted ways threaten their happiness.

Ginger (World Film Corp., 1919)
d: Burton George. 5 reels.
Violet Palmer, Raymond Hackett, Paul Everton, Garreth Hughes.
Raised lovingly by her adoptive father, young Ginger grows up to become a Red Cross nurse and serves in World War I. While in France, she ministers to her childhood sweetheart, who dies in her arms. But there's a happy ending, as Ginger marries another soldier: the son of her adoptive father.

Ginger, the Bride of Chateau Thierry—see: Ginger (1919)

The Gingham Girl (R-C Pictures/FBO of America, 1927)

d: David Kirkland. 7 reels.
Lois Wilson, George K. Arthur, Charles Crockett, Hazel Keener, Myrta Bonillas, Jerry Miley, Betty Francisco, Derelys Perdue, Jed Prouty, Maude Fulton.
A small town girl specializes in making home-baked cookies. Upon moving to New York, she'll join with a biscuit manufacturer and create a large cookie empire.

Ginsberg the Great (Warner Bros., 1927)
d: Byron Haskins. 6 reels.
George Jessel, Audrey Ferris, Theodore Lorch, Gertrude Astor, Douglas Gerrard, Jack Santoro, Jimmie Quinn, Stanley J. Sanford.
Ginsberg, a stage-struck tailor, joins a traveling carnival show.

The Girl Alaska (World Film Corp., 1919)
d: Al Ira Smith, Henry Bolton. 5 reels.
Lottie Kruse, Henry Bolton, C. Edward Cone.
An orphan girl disguises herself as a boy nicknamed "Alaska" and heads for the Yukon.

The Girl and the Crisis (Universal, 1917)
d: William V. Mong. 5 reels.
Dorothy Davenport, Charles Perley, Harry Holden, William V. Mong, Alfred Hollingsworth, Forrest Seaberry.
Encouraged by his kindhearted fiancée, a state governor mulls over whether to commute an assassin's death sentence.

The Girl and the Judge (Mutual, 1918)
d: John B. O'Brien. 5 reels.
Olive Tell, David Powell, Charlotte Granville, Eric Mayne, Marie Reichert, Paul Stanton, Marie Burke, Thomas Curran.
Kleptomania brings a girl and a young judge together.

The Girl Angle (Mutual, 1917)
d: Edgar Jones. 5 reels.
Anita King, Robert Ensminger, Ruth Lackaye, Joseph Ryan, Frank Erlanger, Daniel Gilfether, William Reed, Gordon Sackville, Mollie McConnell.
A confirmed man-hater settles in the Southwest, but she can't avoid the attentions of the local sheriff and a charming bandit.

A Girl at Bay (Vitagraph, 1919)
d: Tom Mills. 5 reels.
Corinne Griffith, Walter Miller, Harry Davenport, Denton Vane, Walter Horton.
After a young judge marries his secretary, detectives uncover evidence that seem to point to the bride as the culprit who murdered the judge's brother.

The Girl at Home (Lasky Feature Plays/Paramount, 1917)
d: Marshall Neilan. 5 reels.
Vivian Martin, Jack Pickford, James Neill, Olga Grey, Edythe Chapman, Billy Elmer.
At college, a young man falls for a shallow co-ed, ignoring the loving attentions of his girl back home.

The Girl by the Roadside (Universal, 1917)
d: Theodore Marston. 5 reels.
Violet Mersereau, Allen Edwards, Cecil Owen, Ann Andrews, Robert F. Hill, Royal Byron, Kenneth Hall, Sam B. Minter.
Husband-and-wife counterfeiters are hunted by a Secret Service agent.

The Girl Dodger (Thomas H. Ince Corp./Paramount, 1919)
d: Jerome Storm. 5 reels.

Charles Ray, Doris Lee, Hal Cooley, Jack Nelson, Leota Lorraine.

Comedic tale of mistaken identity, with an amiable but absent-minded collegian pretending to be his own roommate and falling in love with the roommate's girl.

The Girl From Beyond (Vitagraph, 1918)
d: William Wolbert. 5 reels.
Nell Shipman, Alfred Whitman, Bob Burns, Hattie Buskirk, Ed Alexander, Patricia Palmer, A.W. Wing.

A marriage of convenience is imperiled when the wife falls in love with another man and decides to ask her husband for a divorce. But upon meeting his rival, the husband recognizes him as the scoundrel who caused his sister to commit suicide, years before. What now?

The Girl From Chicago (Warner Bros., 1927)
d: Ray Enright. 6 reels.
Conrad Nagel, Myrna Loy, Carol Nye, Paul Panzer, Erville Anderson, William Russell.

Mary, a Southern girl, must pose as a tough-as-nails Chicago doll to infiltrate an underworld gang.

The Girl From Coney Island—see: Just Another Blonde (1926)

The Girl From Gay Paree (Tiffany Productions, 1927)
d: Phil Stone. 6 reels.
Lowell Sherman, Barbara Bedford, Malcolm McGregor, Betty Blythe, Walter Hiers, Margaret Livingston, Templar Saxe, Leo White.

Mary, a big city girl, is down on her luck and hungry. She steals food from a restaurant but is observed and followed by the police. Frantic to escape, she ducks into a French cafe where she finds refuge in a group of girls waiting to be interviewed for a part in the Folies Bergère. Do you suppose Mary will be the chosen one?

The Girl From God's Country (Nell Shipman Productions/F.B. Warren Corp., 1921)
d: Nell Shipman. 7 reels.
Nell Shipman, Edward Burns, Al Filson, George Berrell, Walt Whitman, C.K. VanAuker, Lillian Leighton, L.M. Wells, Milla Davenport.

After finding a lost halfbreed girl while on a hunting expedition, a millionaire adopts her and takes her home, never realizing that she is his own daughter by an indiscretion of years before.

The Girl From Mexico—see: Mexicali Rose

The Girl From Montmartre (First National, 1926)
d: Alfred E. Green. 6 reels.
Barbara LaMarr, Robert Ellis, Lewis Stone, William Eugene, E.H. Calvert, Mario Carillo, Mathilde Comont, Edward Piel, Nicholas DeRuiz, Bobby Mack.

Emilia, a Spanish girl, works as a dancer in Paris during World War I. There she attracts the attentions of Jerome, an English officer, and Ewing, an unprincipled fellow performer.

The Girl From Nowhere (National Film Corp./Pioneer, 1919)
d: Wilfred Lucas. 5 reels.
Cleo Madison, Wilfred Lucas, Frank Brownlee, Val Paul, Mary Talbot, John Cook.

In the rugged Northwest, a dance hall girl suffers from amnesia, but has many admirers.

The Girl From Nowhere (Selznick/Select, 1921)

d: George Archainbaud. 5 reels.
Elaine Hammerstein, William B. Davidson, Huntley Gordon, Louise Prussing, Colin Campbell, Al H. Stewart, Warren Cook, Vera Conroy.

After eluding an attempt to frame her for robbery, Mavis runs away with Jimmy. The two runaways find themselves drawn to each other, and become husband and wife.

The Girl From Outside (Rex Beach/Goldwyn, 1919)
d: Reginald Barker. 7 reels.
Clara Horton, Cullen Landis, Sydney Ainsworth, Hallam Cooley, Colin Kenny, Walter McNamara, Ernest Spencer, Wilton Taylor, Louie Cheung, Bert Sprotte.

A girl alone in 1900 Alaska is befriended by gamblers, traders, saloon keepers, and assorted colorful characters.

The Girl From Rio (Gotham Productions/Lumas Film Corp., 1927)
d: Tom Terriss. 6 reels. (Includes Technicolor sequences.)
Carmel Myers, Walter Pidgeon, Richard Tucker, Henry Herbert, Mildred Harris, Edouard Raquello.

Sinclair, an American coffee distributor in Rio de Janeiro on business, becomes smitten with Lola, a cabaret dancer with an insanely jealous boyfriend and a likewise infatuated dancing partner.

The Girl From Rocky Point (Pacific Film Co., 1922)
d: Fred G. Becker. 5 reels.
Milton Ross, Ora Carew, Gloria Joy, Charles Spere, E.G. Davidson, Theodore von eltz, Verna Brooks, Walt Whitman.

Betty falls in love with a shipwreck survivor, but must deal with the displeasure of the town cynic.

The Girl From State Street —see: State Street Sadie (1928)

The Girl Glory (New York Motion Picture Corp./Triangle, 1917)
d: R. William Neill.
Enid Bennett, Walt Whitman, William Warters, Margery Bennett, Darrell Foss, J.P. Lockney.

Glory is a girl with a grandpa who's a Civil War veteran, and also the town drunk. She sets out to cure his drinking habit by ridding their town of its only saloon, but it won't be easy.

The Girl He Didn't Buy (Dallas M. Fitzgerald Productions, 1928)
d: Dallas M. Fitzgerald. 6 reels.
Pauline Garon, Allan Simpson, William Eugene, Gladden James, Rosemary Cooper, May Prestelle, James Aubrey.

Ruth, who aspires to a showbiz career on the stage, agrees to marry a prospective backer at the end of one year. However, during that year she sails to Havana, meets another man, and they are married by the ship's captain.

The Girl I Left Behind Me (Box Office Attraction Co./Fox, 1915)
d: Lloyd B. Carleton. 5 reels.
Robert Edeson, Stuart Holmes, Irene Warfield, Claire Whitney, Walter Hitchcock.

Out West, two Army lieutenants vie for the love of the general's daughter.

The Girl I Loved (United Artists, 1923)
d: Joseph DeGrasse. 8 reels.
Charles Ray, Patsy Ruth Miller, Ramsey Wallace, Edyth Chapman, William Courtwright.

A country bumpkin is in love with his adopted sister.

A Girl in Bohemia (Fox, 1919)

d: Howard M. Mitchell. 5 reels.
Peggy Hyland, Josef Swickard, L.C. Shumway, Betty Schade, Edward Cecil, Melbourne MacDowell, Winter Hall, J. Montgomery Carlyle.
Rejected by her publisher after writing a novel about Bohemian life, a girl moves to Greenwich Village to study Bohemia first-hand.

A Girl in Every Port   (Fox, 1928)
d: Howard Hawks. 6 reels.
Victor McLaglen, Louise Brooks, Maria Casajuana, Natalie Joyce, Dorothy Mathews, Elena Jurado, Francis McDonald, Phalba Morgan, Felix Valle, Greta Yoltz, Leila Hyams, Robert Armstrong, Sally Rand, Natalie Kingston, Caryl Lincoln.
Spike, a career Navy man, loves the ladies... and he's got one in every port of call!

The Girl in His House   (Vitagraph, 1918)
d: Thomas R. Mills. 5 reels.
Earle Williams, Grace Darmond, James Abrahams, Irene Rich, Margaret Allen, Harry Lonsdale.
After six years overseas, a wealthy man returns home and finds that a strange but lovely girl has been living in his house.

The Girl in His Room   (Vitagraph, 1922)
d: Edward José. 5 reels.
Alice Calhoun, Warner Baxter, Robert Anderson, Faye O'Neill, Eve Southern.
Remake of the 1918 Vitagraph film *The Girl in His House*.

The Girl in Number 29   (Universal, 1920)
d: Jack Ford. 5 reels.
Frank Mayo, Elinor Fair, Claire Anderson, Robert Bolder, Ruth Royce, Ray Ripley, Bull Montana, Arthur Hoyt, Harry Hilliard.
Bored after turning out one successful play, a writer idles away the time at home until he sees a beautiful girl in a nearby apartment, attempting to commit suicide. Bored no longer, the playwright springs into action to rescue the girl from her demons.

The Girl in the Checkered Coat   (Universal, 1917)
d: Joseph de Grasse. 5 reels.
Dorothy Phillips, Lon Chaney, William Stowell, Mrs A.E. Witting, David Kirby.
Miss Phillips plays a double role as two sisters—one larcenous, the other virtuous.

The Girl in the Dark   (Universal, 1918)
d: Stuart Paton. 5 reels.
Carmel Myers, Ashton Dearholt, Betty Schade, Frank Tokanaga, Frank Deshon, Harry Carter, Alfred Allen.
A girl wearing a mysterious ring is abducted by a secret Chinese society.

The Girl in the Glass Cage   (First National/Warner Bros., 1929)
d: Ralph Dawson. 6 reels.
Loretta Young, Carroll Nye, Ralph Lewis, Matthew Betz, George E. Stone, Lucien Littlefield, Julia Swayne Gordon, Majel Coleman, Charles Sellon, Robert T. Haines.
Gladys, a box-office cashier at a movie house must try to fend off the attentions of a shady underworld character.

The Girl in the Limousine   (Chadwick Pictures/Associated First National, 1924)
d: Larry Semon. 6 reels.

Larry Semon, Claire Adams, Charles Murray, Lucille Ward, Larry Steers, Oliver Hardy.
Tony, a rejected suitor, is kidnapped by two scoundrels in a limousine and taken to the home of his ex-girlfriend. He hides by dressing in her pajamas and appearing to be a female. When the crooks try to steal the girl's diamonds, Tony asserts his manhood and chases down the thieves, capturing them and becoming a hero.

The Girl in the Pullman   (Pathé/De Mille, 1927)
d: Erle C. Kenton. 6 reels.
Harrison Ford, Marie Prevost, Franklin Pangborn, Kathryn McGuire, Ethel Wales, Harry Myers.
Comedy about a doctor who's divorcing his wife, but who remains in love with her and she with him. Can these crazy kids ever get together again?

The Girl in the Rain   (Universal, 1920)
d: Rollin Sturgeon. 5 reels.
Lloyd Bacon, Anne Cornwall, Jessalyn Van Trump, James Farley, George Kunkel, James Liddy, Neal Hardin.
Love blossoms between a man and a young woman marooned together during a storm.

The Girl in the Taxi   (Carter DeHaven Productions/Associated First National, 1921)
d: Lloyd Ingraham. 6 reels.
Mrs. Carter DeHaven, Carter DeHaven, King Baggot, Grace Cunard, Otis Harlan, Tom McGuire, Margaret Campbell, Lincoln Plumer, Freya Sterling, John Gough.
Considered a wimp and a loser, Stewart nevertheless winds up at a society party with a ravishing beauty he met when they shared a taxicab ride.

The Girl in the Web   (Pathé, 1920)
d: Robert Thornby. 6 reels.
Blanche Sweet, Nigel Barrie, Thomas Jefferson, Adele Farrington, Hayward Mack, Christine Mayo, Peaches Jackson.
The private secretary of a socialite is blamed when the socialite's safe is robbed.

A Girl Like That   (Famous Players/Paramount, 1917)
d: Del Henderson. 5 reels.
Irene Fenwick, Owen Moore, Tom O'Keefe, Edwin Sturgis, Harry Lee, Jack Dillon, Olive Thomas, William Butler.
A gang of crooks try to persuade a bank stenographer to rob the bank's safe.

A Girl Named Mary   (Famous Players-Lasky/Paramount, 1919)
d: Walter Edwards. 5 reels.
Marguerite Clark, Kathlyn Williams, Wallace MacDonald, Aggie Herring, Charles Clary, Lillian Leighton, Pauline Pulliam, Eddie Sutherland, Helene Sullivan.
Mary, separated from her wealthy parents in childhood, is finally reunited with her widowed mother, years later. But the mother's society friends officially disapprove of Mary's blue-collar companions.

The Girl O' Dreams   (American Film Co., 1918)
d: Thomas Ricketts. 5 reels.
Audrey Munson, Nigel de Brulier, Eugenie Forde, William Stowell, Josephine Phillips, William Carroll, Margaret Nichols, Roy Stewart.
When an unconscious girl is washed ashore on a private island, its sole occupant, a sculptor, nurses her back to health, shelters her, and makes her his new model.

The Girl of Gold (Regal Pictures/Producers Distributing Corp., 1925)
d: John Ince. 6 reels.
Florence Vidor, Malcolm McGregor, Alan Roscoe, Bessie Eyton, Claire DuBrey, Charles French.
Helen's the "girl of gold," heiress to a mine fortune but snubbed by high society. Schuyler is her opposite, the scion of a socially prominent family, but one that's fallen on hard financial times. The plan is for them to marry each other, with Helen thus buying social acceptability with her family's hard-earned money. While they are in her father's mine and the cave collapses, nearly burying them alive, their mutual struggle to survive ignites the spark of love. By the time they are rescued, Helen and Schuyler are fervently in love with each other.

The Girl of My Dreams (National Film Corp./Robertson-Cole, 1918)
d: Martin L. Doner. 6 reels.
Billie Rhodes, Jack MacDonald, Lamar Johnston, Golda Mawden, Jane Keckley, Frank MacQuarrie, Benjamin Suslow, Leo Pierson.
A charming young mountain girl saves the life of a car crash victim, and while she is nursing his wounds, they fall in love.

The Girl of My Heart (Fox, 1920)
d: Edward J. LeSaint. 5 reels.
Shirley Mason, Raymond McKee, Martha Mattox, Al Fremont, Cecil Van Auker, Calvin Weller, Hooper Toler, Alfred Weller.
A runaway orphan girl is given shelter by a wealthy landowner.

The Girl of the Golden West (Lasky Feature Plays/Paramount, 1915)
d: Cecil B. DeMille. 5 reels.
Mabel Van Buren, Theodore Roberts, House Peters, Anita King, Sydney Deane, Billy Elmer, Jeane McPherson, Raymond Hatton, Dick Le Strange, Tex Driscol, James Griswold.
During the Gold Rush of 1849, a young woman runs a saloon in the town of Cloudy, California. She is courted by two suitors: a former gambler turned sheriff, and a bandit who agrees never to rob her saloon.

The Girl of the Golden West (First National, 1923)
d: Edwin Carewe. 7 reels.
Sylvia Breamer, J. Warren Kerrigan, Russell Simpson.
Remake of the 1915 *The Girl of the Golden West*. Both films were based on the 1905 stage play by David Belasco.

The Girl of Lost Lake (Universal, 1916)
d: Lynn Reynolds. 5 reels.
Myrtle Gonzales, Val Paul, Mary Du Cello, Ruby Cox, Fred Church, George Hernandez, Jack Curtis, Bertram Grassby, Jack Connelly, Bobby Mack.
When a country girl falls for a city boy on a visit to Lost Lake, she breaks off with her former sweetheart. But the rejected fellow isn't amused, and determines to start trouble.

A Girl of the Limberlost (Gene Stratton Porter Productions, 1924)
d: James Leo Meehan. 6 reels.
Gloria Grey, Emily Fitzroy, Arthur Currier, Raymond McKee, Arthur Millett, Cullen Landis, Gertrude Olmstead, Alfred allen, Virginia Boardman, Myrtle Vane, Jack Daugherty.
Elnora loves Philip, but there's a problem: He's already engaged to be married.

Girl of the Sea (Submarine Film Corp./Republic, 1920)
d: J. Winthrop Kelley. 6 reels.
Betty Hilburn, Chester Barnett, Kathryn Lean, Alex Shannon.
After a shipwreck, a baby girl is washed ashore on a South Seas island, with the deed to her father's valuable gold mine tied around her neck. Years later, the girl, beautifully grown to adulthood, teams with a seaman to find the mine and establish her claim—but not without several complications setting in first.

The Girl of the Timber Claims (Fine Arts Film Co./Triangle, 1917)
d: Paul Powell. 5 reels.
Constance Talmadge, A.D. Sears, Clyde Hopkins, Beau Byrd, Wilbur Higby, Bennie Schuman, Joseph Singleton, F.A. Turner, Charles Lee.
In the Pacific Northwest, a girl who holds a valuable homestead claim is menaced by claim jumpers.

The Girl of Today (Vitagraph, 1918)
d: John Robertson. 5 reels.
Corinne Griffith, Marc MacDermott, Charles A. Stevenson, Ida Darling, Webster Campbell.
During World War I, a charming young woman is wooed by two suitors—one of them a German secret agent!

A Girl of Yesterday (Famous Players/Paramount, 1915)
d: Allan Dwan. 5 reels.
Mary Pickford, Jack Pickford, Gertrude Norman, Donald Crisp, Marshall Neilan, Frances Marion, Lillian Langdon, Claire Alexander, Glenn Martin.
A young woman and her brother are raised to appreciate old-fashioned values.

The Girl on the Barge (Universal, 1929)
d: Edward Sloman. 7 reels. (Part talkie.)
Sally O'Neil, Jean Hersholt, Malcolm McGregor, Morris McIntosh, Nancy Kelly, George Offerman Jr., Henry West, J. Francis Robertson.
Barge captain's daughter falls for tugboat pilot, much to her father's chagrin.

The Girl on the Stairs (Peninsula Studios/Producers Distributing Corp., 1924)
d: William Worthington. 7 reels.
Patsy Ruth Miller, Frances Raymond, Arline Pretty, Shannon Day, Niles Welch, Freeman Wood, Bertram Grassby, Michael Dark, George Periolat.
When Dora's former boyfriend is found murdered and she is accused of the crime, her present fiancé, a hotshot new attorney, undertakes her defense. The truth about the murder comes out in dramatic fashion, after Dora is hypnotized on the witness stand by a professional mesmerist.

Girl Overboard (Universal, 1929)
d: Wesley Ruggles. 8 reels. (Part talkie.)
Mary Philbin, Fred Mackaye, Edmund Breese, Otis Harlan, Francis McDonald, Wilfred North, Mary Alden.
A parolee saves a young woman from drowning, and they fall in love.

The Girl Philippa (Vitagraph, 1917)
d: S. Rankin Drew. 8 reels.
Anita Stewart, S. Rankin Drew, Frank Morgan, Billie

Billings, Captain Eyerman, Ned Hay, Mis Curley, Stanley Dunn, Alfred Rabock, Jules Cowles, Betty Young, Anders Randolf.

In Europe, a cabaret dancer is courted by two suitors, an American and an Englishman.

The Girl Problem (Vitagraph, 1919)
d: Kenneth Webb. 5 reels.
Corinne Griffith, Agnes Ayres, Walter McGrail, William David, Julia Swayne Gordon, Eulalie Jensen, Frank Kingsley, Harold Foshay.
She's a model by day, an author by night—but a handsome novelist mistakes her for a "flapper."

Girl Shy (Harold Lloyd Corp./Pathé, 1924)
d: Fred Newmeyer, Sam Taylor. 8 reels.
Harold Lloyd, Jobyna Ralston, Richard Daniels, Carlton Griffin, Dorothy Dorr, Joe Cobb, Priscilla King, Nola Luxford.
Harold, a bashful tailor with a speech impediment, is clueless about women, but that doesn't keep him from writing a how-to book on handling the opposite sex. When this loveable loser finally does find the girl of his dreams, she's about to be married to someone else. The tailor returns sadly to his work, hoping to forget her... until he discovers that the girl's fiancé is really a fortune-hunting bigamist. That sets off one of the grandest, dizziest, most hilarious chases in movie history, as Harold commandeers every sort of conveyance in sight—automobiles, motorcycles, a streetcar, a team of horses—in a furious race to the altar, to halt the nuptials before the final "I do."
Girl Shy was Lloyd's first independent film, and it is his finest, freshest, most memorable achievement. Not a bad rating, in an *oeuvre* that includes the gems *Safety Last* (1923), *The Freshman* (1925), and *The Kid Brother* (1927).

The Girl-Shy Cowboy (Fox, 1928)
d: R.L. Hough. 5 reels.
Rex Bell, George Meeker, Patsy O'Leary, Donald Stuart, Margaret Coburn, Betty Caldwell, Joan Lyons, Ottola Nesmith.
Out West, two friends compete for the love of the same girl.

The Girl Who Came Back (Famous Players-Lasky/Paramount, 1918)
d: Robert G. Vignola. 5 reels.
Ethel Clayton, Elliott Dexter, Theodore Roberts, James Neill, Charles West, Jane Wolff, John McKinnon, Pansy Perry.
Like father, like daughter. Michael's a crook; his daughter Lois is a trained burglar—until she meets a man who inspires her to reform.

The Girl Who Came Back (B.P. Schulberg Productions/Preferred Pictures, 1923)
d: Tom Forman. 6 reels.
Miriam Cooper, Gaston Glass, Kenneth Harlan, Fred Malatesta, Joseph Dowling, Ethel Shannon, Mary Culver, ZaSu Pitts.
Sheila, a country girl who gets talked into marrying a fellow she barely knows, soon regrets it. Her hubby's a car thief, and when he is apprehended by the law, both he and Sheila wind up in the slammer. But after her release from prison, Sheila falls in love again, and this time there's a happy ending: It turns out her "marriage" to the car thief was invalid.

The Girl Who Couldn't Grow Up (Pollard Picture Plays/Mutual, 1917)

d: Harry Pollard. 5 reels.
Margarita Fischer, John Stepling, Jean Hathaway, Jack Mower, Joseph Harris, Lule Warrenton, Leota Lorraine, Marjorie Blinn.
Peggy doesn't get along with her new stepmother and her snobbish daughters, so she runs away and sneaks aboard a yacht. Much to her surprise, the yacht owner is a nobleman who catches the little stowaway. Peggy runs away again, but the nobleman, smitten with love for the girl, follows her and persuades her to become his wife. Could this be the first movie version of *Cinderella*?

The Girl Who Dared (Republic, 1920)
d: Cliff Smith. 5 reels.
Edythe Sterling, Jack Carlyle, Steve Clemento, Yakima Canutt, Gordon Sackville.
There's a new sheriff in town, and he's a she. Not only that, but in one of her first official duties, she has to jail her own Pa, who's suspected of cattle rustling.

The Girl Who Ran Wild (Universal, 1922)
d: Rupert Julian. 5 reels.
Gladys Walton, Marc Robbins, Vernon Steele, Joseph Dowling, William Burress, Al Hart, Nelson McDowell, Lloyd Whitlock, Lucille Ricksen.
A mountain girl is orphaned at an early age and becomes a hard-bitten tomboy.

The Girl Who Stayed at Home (Paramount, 1919)
d: D.W. Griffith. 6 reels.
Adolphe Lestina, Carol Dempster, Richard Barthelemess, George Fawcett, Syn De Conde Kate Bruce, Robert Harron, Edward Peil, Clarine Seymour, Tully Marshall, David Butler.
A Southerner who defected from the United States rather than surrender to the Union forces after the Civil War finds himself in France at the time of World War I. His granddaughter urges him to join the cause against Germany. So he does, bringing along a friend's young brother, who enlists in the war and leaves his sweetheart, "the girl who stayed at home."

The Girl Who Wanted to Live—see: Her Life and His (1917)

The Girl Who Won Out (Universal, 1917)
d: Eugene Moore. 5 reels.
Violet MacMillan, P.L. Pembroke, Barbara Conley, Mrs. A.E. Witting, Charles Hill Mailes, Gertrude Astor, L.M. Wells, Sherman Bainbridge.
Orphan sisters are placed in separate foster homes, but the older girl misses her sister and goes all out to be with her again—even if it means cutting her hair short and dressing as a boy!

The Girl Who Wouldn't Quit (Universal, 1918)
d: Edgar Jones. 5 reels.
Louise Lovely, Mark Fenton, Charles H. Mailes, Henry A. Barrows, Gertrude Astor, William Chester, Philo McCullough, Clyde Benson.
A mining camp foreman is unjustly convicted of murder, but his daughter never stops believing in his innocence.

The Girl Who Wouldn't Work (B.P. Schulberg Productions, 1925)
d: Marcel DeSano. 6 reels.
Lionel Barrymore, Marguerite De La Motte, Henry B. Walthall, Lilyan Tashman, Forrest Stanley, Winter Hall, Thomas Ricketts.
Thinking (erroneously) that his daughter has lost her chastity to a philanderer and therefore must be punished, a

distraught father goes to the womanizer's apartment, shoots, and accidentally kills the wrong person.

The Girl With No Regrets (Fox, 1919)
d: Harry Millarde. 5 reels.
Peggy Hyland, Charles Clary, Gene Burr, Betty Shade, Jack Nelson, Al Fremont, Harry Von Meter, Beverly Travers, William Ellingford.
When she learns that her sister and brother-in-law are trained burglars, a girl moves out of their home in disgust, and takes a position with a dealer in rare gems. Sure enough, who should show up to rob the place but Sis and her husband.

The Girl With the Champagne Eyes (Fox, 1918)
d: C.M. Franklin. 5 reels.
Jewel Carmen, L.C. Shumway, Charles Edler, G. Raymond Nye, Alfred Padget, Charles Gorman, Eleanor Washinton, Francis Carpenter, Gertrude Messinger, Carmen De Rue.
On board ship, a felonious young woman steals a wallet and slips it into a stranger's pocket to avoid capture. When the stranger is accused and jailed, the girl has pangs of guilt, and plots to help him escape.

The Girl With the Jazz Heart (Goldwyn, 1920)
d: Lawrence C. Windom. 5 reels.
Madge Kennedy, Joe King, Leon Pierre Glendron, William Walcott, Helen Du Bois, Robert Vaughn, Emile Hoch, Lillian Worth, Robert Tansey, Dorothy Haight.
Trying to avoid an arranged marriage, a young woman runs away to the big city, and finds love.

The Girl Without a Soul (Metro, 1917)
d: John H. Collins. 5 reels.
Viola Dana, Robert Walker, Fred Jones, Henry Hallam, Margaret Seddon, Margaret Vaughan.
A country violin maker has two daughters, one of whom has inherited her mother's musical talent. The other girl, who apparently lacks talent, is known derisively as "the girl without a soul." But in time, this girl will prove to her father and everyone else, that she has talents none of them dreamed of.

The Girl-Woman (Vitagraph, 1919)
d: Thomas R. Mills. 5 reels.
Gladys Leslie, Maurice Costello, Priestley Morrison, William E. Lawrence, Joe Burke, Frank Norcross, Julia Swayne Gordon, Walter Horton.
Tired of being treated like a child, a 17-year-old girl throws a party and shows up wearing a long dress and with her hair in an upsweep.

Girls (Famous Players-Lasky/Paramount, 1919)
d: Walter Edwards. 5 reels.
Harrison Ford, Marguerite Clark, Helene Chadwick, Mary Warren, Lee Hill, Clarissa Selwynne, Arthur Carewe, Thomas D. Perse, Tom Ricketts, Virginia Fultz, Myrtle Richelle.
Unlucky in love, three girls firmly resolve never to marry. But one by one, each girl's resolve is broken as the right man comes along.

A Girl's Desire (Vitagraph, 1922)
d: David Divad. 5 reels.
Alice Calhoun, Warner Baxter, Frank Crane, Lillian Lawrence, Victory Bateman, James Donnelly, Sadie Gordon, Charles Dudley, Lydia Yeamans Titus, Harry Pringle.
A nouveaux riche American tries to "buy" a British title for her daughter.

Girls Don't Gamble (D.N. Schwab Productions, 1920)
d: Fred J. Butler, Hugh C. McClung. 5 reels.
David Butler, Wilbur Higby, Elsie Bishop, Harry Todd, Eleanor Field, Rhea Haines, Alice Knowland, William De Vaull, Rex Zane, Elmer Dewey, R.J. Davenport.
When a city girl starts dating a truck driver, her sisters and their beaus disapprove, and try to frame the trucker for robbery.

A Girl's Folly (Paragon Films/World Film Corp., 1917)
d: Maurice Tourneur. 5 reels.
Doris Kenyon, Robert Warwick, Johnny Hines, Chester Barnett, Jane Adair, June Elvidge, Leatrice Joy, Maurice Tourneur.
A naive young woman breaks into the movie business, but there are perils along the way.

Girls Gone Wild (Fox, 1929)
d: Lewis Seiler. 6 reels. (Music and sound effects.)
Sue Carol, Nick Stuart, William Russell, Roy D'Arcy, Leslie Fenton, Hedda Hopper, John Darrow, Matthew Betz, Edmund Breese, Minna Ferry, Louis Natheaux, Lumsden Hare.
Babs, rich and spoiled, tries to get a speeding ticket "fixed," but the transaction is prevented by an honest cop. Later, she'll unknowingly fall in love with that same cop's son.

Girls Men Forget (Principal Pictures, 1924)
d: Maurice Campbell. 6 reels.
Johnnie Walker, Patsy Ruth Miller, Alan Hale, Mayme Kelso, Carrie Clark Ward, Wilfred Lucas, Frances Raymond, Shannon Day.
Kitty, a jazz baby who's the life of every party, learns to hold her impulses in check and becomes a modest, retiring maiden in order to snare a husband.

Girls Who Dare (Trinity Pictures, 1929)
d: Frank S. Mattison. 6 reels.
Rex Lease, Priscilla Bonner, Rosemary Theby, Ben Wilson, Steve Hall, Eddie Brownell, Sarah Roberts, May Hotely, Hall Cline.
Sally, a chorus girl, loves Chet, but his snobbish father refuses to give their union his blessing—in spite of the fact that the old goat is romancing a nightclub hostess himself.

Give and Take (Universal, 1928)
d: William Beaudine. 7 reels. (Part talkie.)
Jean Hersholt, George Sidney, Sam Hardy, George Lewis, Sharon Lynn.
A cannery owner must contend with an employees' strike—organized by his own son!

Giving Becky a Chance (Oliver Morosco Photoplays/Paramount, 1917)
d: Howard Estabrook. 5 reels.
Vivian Martin, Jack Holt, Jack Richardson, Pietro Sosso, Alice Knowland.
Ashamed that her parents are simple shopkeepers, Becky pretends to be as wealthy as her stuffy classmates. But soon Becky's bluff is called and she takes a job as a cabaret dancer to save the family store.

Glass Houses (Metro, 1922)
d: Harry Beaumont. 5 reels.
Viola Dana, Gaston Glass, Maym Kelso, Helen Lynch, Claire DuBrey, Ellsworth Gage, John Steppling.
Joy, an heiress with nothing to inherit, must find work. She applies for a job as an old lady's companion—and falls in love with the matron's nephew.

Gleam o' Dawn (Fox, 1922)
d: Jack Dillon. 5 reels.
John Gilbert, Barbara Bedford, James Farley, John Gough, Wilson Hummel, Edwin Booth Tilton.
In Canada, an artist living in the wilds befriends an elderly man and his daughter. In time, the artist will come to learn that his elderly friend is actually his adoptive father, who got lost while panning for gold years before.

The Glimpses of the Moon (Famous Players-Lasky/Paramount, 1923)
d: Allan Dwan. 7 reels.
Bebe Daniels, Nita Naldi, David Powell, Maurice Costello, Rubye DeRemier, Charles Gerard, William Quirk, Pearl Sindelar, Beth Allen, Mrs. George Peggram, Dolores Costello.
Penniless newlyweds Susan and Nick struggle to live on love.

Gloriana (Universal, 1916)
d: E. Mason Hopper. 5 reels.

Zoe Rae, Virginia Foltz, William Canfield, Clarissa Selwynne, Gordon Griffith, Irene Hunt, Mary Talbot, John J. Cook, Buddie Messinger.
Young, innocent Gloriana teaches her adoptive mother a lesson about charity beginning at home.

The Glorious Adventure (Goldwyn, 1918)
d: Hobart Henley. 5 reels.
Mae Marsh, Wyndham Standing, Sara Alexander, Paul Ballin, A. Voorhees Nood, Ivan Christy, Mammy Lou, Gladys Wilson, Irene Blackwell.
Not to be confused with the 1922 all-color British film of the same name, this Southern drama tells of a family that clings to the old-fashioned costumes and quaint manners of the ante-bellum South.

Glorious Betsy (Warner Bros., 1928)
d: Alan Crosland. 7 reels.
Dolores Costello, Conrad Nagel, John Miljan, Marc McDermott, Betty Blythe, Paul Panzer, Michael Vavitch, Pasquale Amato.
Napoleon's younger brother loves an American girl, but the Emperor turns thumbs down on their union, wishing his brother to marry royalty instead.

The Glorious Fool (Goldwyn, 1922)
d: E. Mason Hopper. 6 reels.
Helene Chadwick, Richard Dix, Vera Lewis, Kate Lester, Otto Hoffman, John Lince, Theodore von Eltz, Frederick Vroom, Lillian Langdon, George Cooper.
Injured in an automobile accident, Grant winds up in the hospital. But he's afraid to die because he doesn't want his greedy relatives to inherit his property, so he proposes to his nurse—and she accepts.

The Glorious Lady (Selznick/Select, 1919)
d: George Irving. 5 reels.
Olive Thomas, Matt Moore, Evelyn Brent, Robert Taber, Huntley Gordon, Marie Burke, Mona Kingsley.
Class prejudice informs this tale about a Duke who falls in love with a commoner.

The Glorious Trail (First National/Warner Bros., 1928)
d: Albert Rogell. 6 reels.
Ken Maynard, Gladys McConnell, Frank Hagney, James Bradbury, Chief Yowlache.
Out West, workmen stringing telegraph wire across the

Great Plains are attacked by Indians. The superintendent investigates and discovers that a white renegade is inciting the red men to riot.

Glory (M.L.B., 1917)
d: Maud Lillian Berri. 7 reels.
Juanita Hansen, William Kolb, Max Dell, May Cloy, Wellington Playter, Alan Forest, William Lampe, Doris Baker, Frank Mayo.
Glory is both a girl and the town she's named after.

The Glory of Clementina (R-C Pictures, 1922)
d: Emile Chautard. 6 reels.
Pauline Frederick, Edward Martindel, George Cowl, Lincoln Plummer, Edward Hearn, Jean Calhoun, Wilson Hummel, Louise Dresser, Helen Stone, Lydia Yeamans Titus.
Clementina, a renowned artist, is commissioned to paint the portrait of a wealthy but unhappy man, Quixtus. She begins work on the painting, but her observant eye tells her that her wealthy subject is being cheated by Lena, an amoral temptress. Clementina will have none of that. Showing up one day transformed from her usual drab self into a glorious beauty, she wins Quixtus' love and rescues him from the conniving Lena.

The Glory of Love—see: While Paris Sleeps (1923)

The Glory of Yolanda (Vitagraph, 1917)
d: Marguerite Bertsch. 5 reels.
Anita Stewart, John Ardizoni, Denton Vane, Evart Overton, Bernard Seigel.
In Czarist Russia, a peasant girl longs to become a ballet dancer, and a kindly duke offers her the chance. But there are strings attached.

Go and Get It (Marshall Neilan Productions/First National, 1920)
d: Marshall Neilan. 7 reels.
Pat O'Malley, Wesley Barry, Agnes Ayres, J. Barney Sherry, Charles Mailes, Noah Beery, Bull Montana, Walter Long, Lydia Yeamans Titus, George C. Dromgold, Ashley Cooper.
A lurid story involving a gorilla with the transplanted brain of a murderer is uncovered by a star reporter who scoops the competition, wins fame, and marries the publisher's daughter.

Go Get 'Em Garringer (Astra Film Corp/Pathé, 1919)
d: Ernest Traxler. 5 reels.
Helene Chadwick, Franklyn Farnum, Joseph Rickson, Dick Loreno.
A cowpoke is hired to infiltrate a dangerous gang and bring them to justice.

Go Straight (Universal, 1921)
d: William Worthington. 5 reels.
Frank Mayo, Cora Drew, Harry Carter, Lillian Rich, George F. Marion, Lassie Young, Charles Brinley.
In backwoods Kentucky, there's a new preacher in town—but not all the community's residents are happy about that. The town pols are in league with outlaws, and they train their cross-hairs on the sermonizer.

Go Straight (B.P. Schulberg Productions 1925)
d: Frank O'Connor. 6 reels.
Owen Moore, Mary Carr, George Fawcett, Ethel Wales, Gladys Hulette, Lillian Leighton, Robert Edeson, DeWitt Jennings, Francis McDonald, Anita Stewart, Larry Semon.
Gilda, a former thief, decides to go straight and finds work in a bank. Her old gang tries to persuade her to help them

rob the bank, but Gilda refuses and finds a novel way of preventing the theft: She takes all the bank's money home with her, so that when the gang strikes, the bank is empty.

Go West (MGM, 1925)
w, d: Buster Keaton. 7 reels.
Buster Keaton, Howard Truesdale, Kathleen Myers, Ray Thompson, Joe Keaton, Roscoe Arbuckle (cameo).
A homeless man decides to take Horace Greeley's advice. Once out west, he befriends a cow with big brown eyes, then fights to free her when she's scheduled for a one-way trip to the slaughterhouse.

Go West, Young Man (Goldwyn, 1918)
d: Harry Beaumont. 5 reels.
Tom Moore, Ora Carew, Melbourne MacDowell, Jack Richardson, Mollie Mc Connell, Edward Coxen, Robert Chandler, Hector V. Sarno.
A tenderfoot from back East goes West, and is appointed sheriff in a lawless town.

The Goat (Paramount, 1918)
d: Donald Crisp. 5 reels.
Fred Stone, Fannie Midgely, Charles McHugh, Rhea Mitchell, Sylvia Ashton, Philo McCullough, Winifred Greenwood, Noah Beery, Raymond Hatton, Charles Ogle, Ernest Joy, Clarence Geldart.
Chuck wants to be an actor, but instead he winds up as a stuntman, performing daredevil feats that are credited to the leading men.

God Gave Me Twenty Cents (Famous Players-Lasky/Paramount, 1926)
d: Herbert Brenon. 7 reels.
Lois Moran, Lya DePutti, Jack Mulhall, William Collier Jr., Adrienne D'Ambricourt, Leo Feodoroff, Rosa Rosanova, Claude Brooke, Tommy Madden, Phil Bloom, Eddie Kelly, Jack Sharkey, Harry Lewis.
During the boisterous Mardi Gras season in New Orleans, visiting sailor Steve falls hard for Mary, a cafe waitress.

The Goddess of Lost Lake (Louise Glaum Organization/W.W. Hodkinson, 1918)
d: Wallace Worsley. 5 reels.
Louise Glaum, W. Lawson Butt, Hayward Mack, Joseph J. Dowling, Frank Lanning.
Race prejudice is the key here, as a half-breed girl must choose between two suitors: one who loves her for herself, and another who wants her to suppress her Indian roots.

The Godless Girl (C.B. DeMille Productions/Pathé, 1929)
d: Cecil B. DeMille. 12 reels. (Part talkie.)
Lina Basquette, Marie Prevost, George Duryea, Noah Beery, Eddie Quillan, Mary Jane Irving, Clarence Burton, Dick Alexander, Kate Price, Hedwig Reicher, Julia Faye, Viola Louie.
Judith, a staunch atheist, joins forces with Bob, a devout Christian, when both are in the state reformatory.

Godless Men (Goldwyn, 1920)
d: Reginald Barker. 7 reels.
Russell Simpson, James Mason, Helene Chadwick, John Bowers, Alec B. Francis, Robert Kortman, Irene Rich, Lionel Belmore.
Lusty seamen sail the South Seas looking for women and adventure.

God's Country and the Woman (Vitagraph, 1916)
d: Rollin S. Sturgeon. 8 reels.

William Duncan, Nell Shipman, George Holt, William Brainbridge, Nell Clark Keller, Edgar Keller, George Kunkel.
In the Far North, a marriage of convenience slowly turns into the real thing.

God's Crucible (Universal, 1916)
d: Lynn Reynolds. 5 reels.
George Hernandez, Val Paul, Myrtle Gonzalez, Frederick Montague, Jack Curtis, Edward J. Brady, Francis Lee, Harvey Griffith.
Father disowns son, but later when the chips are down, the family comes together again.

God's Gold (Pinnacle Productions, 1921)
d: Webster Cullison. 5 reels.
Neal Hart, Audrey Chapman, James McLaughlin, Al Kaufman, C.D. Rehfeld, Jacob Abrams, Charles Holly, Dick Sutherland.
On a voyage to the South Seas to hunt for buried treasure, seaman Cameron takes charge of the ship when a mutiny is threatened.

God's Great Wilderness (David M. Hartford Productions, 1927)
d: David M. Hartford. 6 reels.
Lillian Rich, Joseph Bennett, Russell Simpson, Mary Carr, John Steppling, Rose Tapley, Edward Coxen, Tom Bates, Wilbur Higby, Roy Laidlaw.
In the North country, a merchant named Goodheart battles a hard-hearted competitor named Stoner for the soul of the community.

God's Half Acre (Rolfe Photoplays/Metro, 1916)
d: Edwin Carewe. 5 reels.
Mabel Taliaferro, J.W. Johnston, Helen Dahl, Lorraine Frost, Richard Neill, John Smiley, Daniel Jarrett, Miriam Hutchins.
God's Half Acre is an orphanage, where a novelist and a nurse meet and fall in love.

God's Law and Man's (Columbia/Metro, 1917)
d: John H. Collins. 5 reels.
Viola Dana, Robert Walker, Augustus Phillips, Henry Hallam, Frank Currier, Marie Adell, George A. Wright, Floyd Buckley.
Incredible coincidence arises when a young doctor in India takes Ameia, a local girl, for his wife, then returns to England and is dismayed to learn that his father has arranged for him to marry Olive, the daughter of a certain British general. It seems the doctor has *already* married the general's daughter, though not the one his family expected: Ameia turns out to be the general's illegitimate daughter, abandoned by her father years before.

The Gods of Fate (Lubin, 1916)
d: Jack Pratt. 5 reels.
Richard Buhler, Rosetta Brice, Arthur Housman, William H. Turner, Francis Joyner, Inez Buck.
After stealing his friend's plans for an important invention, the thief is stricken by conscience and adopts the inventor's orphaned daughter.

God's Outlaw (Metro, 1919)
d: William Christy Cabanne. 5 reels.
Francis X. Bushman, Beverly Bayne, Helen Dunbar, Samuel Framer, Charles A. Fang, Belle Bruce, Valentine Mott, Emily Chichester.
Out West, a sheriff and a blacksmith both love the same girl.

Going Crooked (Fox, 1926)

d: George Melford. 6 reels.

Bessie Love, Oscar Shaw, Gustav von Seyffertitz, Ed Kennedy, Leslie Fenton, Lydia Knott, Bernard Siegel.

Marie, a thief, disguises herself as an old woman to help a gang pull off a jewel heist. When the theft results in murder, she has a change of heart and assists the D.A. in prosecuting the case.

Going Some (Rex Beach/Goldwyn, 1920)
d: Harry Beaumont. 6 reels.
Cullen Landis, Helen Ferguson, Lillian Hall, Lillian Langdon, Kenneth Harlan, Ethel Grey Terry, Willard Louis, Walter Hiers, Frank Braidwood, Nelson McDowell, Snitz Edwards.
Comedic tale of a young fellow who pretends to be a talented sprinter, then is forced to run a race on which his friends have bet everything.

Going Straight (Fine Arts Film Co., 1916)
d: C.M. Franklin, S.A. Franklin. 5 reels.
Norma Talmadge, Ralph Lewis, Nino Fovieri, Francis Carpenter, Fern Collier, Ruth Handforth, Eugene Pallette, George Stone, Kate Toncray, Carmen De Rue, Violet Radcliffe.
A married couple, formerly criminals, go straight and become respected members of the community. But an old gang member threatens to expose them unless they help him pull one more robbery.

Going Up (Associated Exhibitors, 1923)
d: Lloyd Ingraham. 6 reels.
Douglas MacLean, Mervy Le Roy, Hallam Cooley, Arthur Stuart Hall, Francis McDonald Hughie Mack, Wade Boteler, John Streppling, Marjorie Daw, Edna Murphy, Lillian Langdon.
Robert, a best-selling author of aviation thrillers, has a dark secret: He's scared to death of airplanes.

Gold and Grit (Approved Pictures, 1925)
d: Richard Thorpe. 5 reels.
Buddy Roosevelt, Ann McKay, William H. Turner, L.J. O'Connor, Wilbur Mack, Nelson McDowell, Hank Bell.
Out West, a stagecoach driver crosses swords with a crooked miner.

Gold and the Girl (Fox, 1925)
d: Edmund Mortimer. 5 reels.
Buck Jones, Elinor Fair, Bruce Gordon, Claude Peyton, Lucien Littlefield, Alphonz Ethier.
Prentiss, a special agent for a mining company, is sent west to investigate a string of robberies. He'll catch the crooks and, in the bargain, win the love of a good woman.

Gold and the Woman (Fox, 1916)
d: James Vincent. 6 reels.
Theda Bara, H. Cooper Cliffe, Alma Hanlon, Harry Hilliard, Chief Black Eagle, Jude Hurley, Caroline Harris, Ted Griffin, Louis Stern, James Sheehan.
Heavy melodrama about thousands of acres of land stolen from an Indian tribe, and the white woman who tries to restore the Indians' title to them.

The Gold Cure (Metro, 1919)
d: John H. Collins. 5 reels.
Viola Dana, John McGowan, Elsie MacLeod, Howard Hall, Fred Jones, William B. Davidson, Franklyn Hanna, Ed Mack, Julia Hurley, George Dowling.
Two lonely girls conceive of a novel plan to snare men friends: Strew tacks on the main street, then reel 'em in when the boys get flat tires.

The Gold Diggers (Warner Bros., 1923)
d: Harry Beaumont. 8 reels.
Wyndham Standing, Louise Fazenda, Hope Hampton, Alec B. Francis, Jed Prouty, Louise Beaudet, Gertrude Short, Arita Gillman, Peggy Browne, Margaret Seddon, Johnny Harron.
Broadway showgirls live the high life in the Roaring Twenties, but one of them sacrifices everything to ensure her sister's happiness.

Gold From Weepah (Bill Cody Productions/Pathé, 1927)
d: William Bertram. 5 reels.
Bill Cody, Doris Dawson, Dick LaReno, Joe Harrington, Fontaine LaRue, David Dunbar.
Elsie, a violin-playing dance hall girl, is desired by her employer and his henchmen.

Gold Grabbers (W.M. Smith Productions/Merit Film Corp., 1922)
d: Francis Ford. 5 reels.
Franklyn Farnum, Shorty Hamilton, Al Hart, Genevieve Berte.
Out West, greed nearly overcomes two partners in a gold mine business.

The Gold Rush (Chaplin/United Artists, 1925)
w, d: Charles Chaplin. 9 reels.
Charles Chaplin, Georgia Hale, Mack Swain, Henry Bergman, Tom Murray.

Enormously successful comedy by Chaplin at the peak of his powers. A lone prospector in the Yukon meets and bonds with another prospector, finds true love with a dance hall girl and, after several adventures, strikes it rich. Two scenes stand out: The Thanksgiving dinner at which snowbound Charlie and his friend are forced to eat a boiled shoe; and the riotous, and justly famous, scene where the two men are stranded in a cabin that is dangling on the edge of a precipice.

The Golden Bed (Famous Players-Lasky/Paramount, 1925)
d: Cecil B. DeMille. 9 reels.
Lillian Rich, Henry B. Walthall, Vera Reynolds, Theodore Kosloff, Rod LaRocque, Warner Baxter, Robert Cain, Robert Edeson, Julia Faye, Charles Clary, Jacqueline Wells.
Flora Lee, an unprincipled sybarite, marries wealthy men and destroys them financially.

The Golden Chance (Lasky Featue Plays/Paramount, 1916)
d: Cecil B. DeMille. 5 reels.
Leo Ridgely, Wallace Reid, Horace B. Carpenter, Edythe Chapman, Ernest Joy, Raymond Hatton.
An unhappily-married seamstress falls for a millionaire, and he with her.

The Golden Claw (New York Motion Picture Corp./Triangle, 1915)
d: Reginald Barker. 5 reels.
Bessie Barriscale, Frank Mills, Wedgewood Nowell, Truly Shattuck, Robert N. Dunbar, J. Barney Sherry.
After a young woman marries for money, she learns to love her husband—even after he loses his fortune.

The Golden Cocoon (Warner Bros., 1925)
d: Millard Webb. 7 reels.
Helene Chadwick, Huntly Gordon, Richard Tucker, Frank Campeau, Margaret Seddon, Carrie Clark.
A political science professor is in love with two different

women.

Golden Dreams (Benjamin B. Hampton/Goldwyn, 1922)
d: Benjamin B. Hampton. 5 reels.
Rose Dione, Claire Adams, Norris McKay, Carl Gantwoort, Audrey Dhapman, Ida Ward, Bertram Grassby, Frank Leigh, Gordon Mullen, Pomeroy Cannon, Frank Hayes, Babe London.
In a mythical Latin American country, a countess urges her niece to wed a duke instead of the young engineer she fancies.

The Golden Fetter (Lasky Feature Plays/Paramount, 1917)
d: Edward J. LeSaint. 5 reels.
Wallace Reid, Anita King, Tully Marshall, Guy Oliver, Walter Long, Mrs. Lewis McCord, C.H. Geldert, Larry Peyton, Lucien Littlefield.
Out West, an east coast schoolteacher finds that the gold mine she bought is worthless. But she also finds true love.

The Golden Fleece (Triangle, 1918)
d: Gilbert P. Hamilton. 5 reels.
Joe Bennett, Peggy Pearce, Jack Curtis, Harvey Clark, Graham Pette.
An enterprising country boy goes to the big city to sell his inventions.

The Golden Gallows (Universal, 1922)
d: Paul Scardon. 5 reels.
Miss DuPont, Edwin Stevens, Eve Southern, Jack Mower, George B. Williams, Douglas Gerrard, Elinor Hancock, Barbara Tennant.
A chorus girl named Willow discovers that she's inherited the entire estate of a former admirer. Peter, her current boyfriend, irately denounces the girl and storms off, thinking her relationship with the admirer had been improper. But Willow is innocent—literally so—and in time Peter will come to his senses.

The Golden Gift (Metro, 1922)
d: Maxwell Karger. 5 reels.
Alice Lake, John Bowers, Harriet Hammond, Joseph Swickard, Bridgetta Clark, Louis Dumar, Geoffrey Webb, Camilla Clark.
Nita, a singer and dancer, must face life alone after her husband deserts her and their little daughter Joy. The husband remarries, then dies... and his widow adopts a young girl from a missionary orphanage. Yes, the child is Joy, though the widow does not realize her new adoptive daughter is her late husband's child.

The Golden Goal (Vitagraph, 1918)
d: Paul Scardon. 5 reels.
Harry T. Morey, Florence Deshon, Jean Paige, Arthur Donaldson, Denton Vane, Robert Gaillard, Bernard Siegel.
When a longshoreman determines to get "class" and an education, he persuades a young stenographer to help him. Once he has acquired some polish, he courts the daughter of a wealthy shipbuilder. But in the end, after fighting off the shipbuilder's ruthless attempt to ruin a business rival, the former longshoreman realizes he is better off with the steno who helped him when he was in need.

The Golden Idiot (Essanay, 1917)
d: Arthur Berthelet. 5 reels.
Bryant Washburn, Virginia Valli, Arthur Metcalfe.
Under the peculiar terms of their uncle's will, nephews are due to inherit his millions in proportion to their own personal savings. Not too promising for the nephew who

happens to be penniless. But his fortunes do change.

The Golden Princess (Famous Players-Lasky/Paramount 1925)
d: Clarence Badger. 9 reels.
Betty Bronson, Neil Hamilton, Rockliffe Fellowes, Phyllis Haver, Joseph Dowling, Edgar Kennedy, George Irving, Norma Wills, Mary Schoene, Don Marion.
Betty, a child of the California Gold Rush, is raised by a priest after her mother runs off with her dad's killer. Years later Betty returns to California and looks up an old friend of her father's, and is rewarded with a share in his gold mine.

Golden Rule Kate (Triangle, 1917)
d: Reginald Barker. 5 reels.
Louise Glaum, William Conklin, Jack Richardson, Mildred Harris, John Gilbert, Gertrude Claire, J.P. Lockney, H. Milton Ross, Josephine Headley.
Kate, a saloon owner in a gold-rush mining town, has problems with the local preacher.

Golden Shackles (Dallas M. Fitzgerald Productions/Peerless Pictures, 1928)
d: Dallas M. Fitzgerald. 6 reels.
Grant Withers, Priscilla Bonner, LeRoy Mason, Ruth Stewart.
Vengeful Lucy marries the man she believes responsible for her father's death, bent on making her husband suffer. Soon, however, she learns that her husband is innocent of any wrongdoing. Now what?

The Golden Shower (Vitagraph, 1919)
d: John W. Noble. 5 reels.
Gladys Leslie, Robert Cummings, Frank Morgan, Estelle Taylor, Corinne Barker, Karl Lowenhaupt.
After a wealthy roué dies of a heart attack while chasing a resistant female, it is learned that he has willed most of his estate to her.

The Golden Snare (David Hartford Productions/Associated First National, 1921)
d: David M. Hartford. 6 reels.
Lewis Stone, Wallace Beery, Melbourne MacDowell, Ruth Renick, Wellington Playter, DeWitt Jennings, Francis McDonald, Little Esther Scott.
In the Canadian Northwest, a mountie trails an escaped killer.

The Golden Strain (Fox, 1925)
d: Victor Scherzinger. 6 reels.
Hobart Bosworth, Kenneth Harlan, Madge Bellamy, Lawford Davidson, Ann Pennington, Frank Beal, Frankie Lee, Coy Watson, Robert Frazer, Oscar Smith, George Reed, Grace Morse.
Out West, a disgraced West Point graduate regains respect when he leads a battalion in a successful Indian raid.

The Golden Trail (American Lifeograph Co., 1920)
d: L.H. Moomaw, Jean Hersholt. 6 reels.
Jane Novak, Jack Livingston, Jean Hersholt, Bert Sprotte, Otto Matiesen, Al Garcia, Broderick O'Farrell, William Dills, Allen Hersholt.
In Alaska, a prospector yearns for the girl he left back home.

The Golden Wall (World Film Corp., 1918)
d: Dell Henderson. 5 reels.
Carlyle Blackwell, Evelyn Greeley, John Hines, Winifred Leighton, Madge Evans, Jack Drumier, Kate Lester, George MacQuarrie, Florence Coventry, A.G. Corbell, Louise de Rigny.

THE GOLDEN PRINCESS (1925). Neil Hamilton comforts Betty Bronson in this adaptation of a story by Bret Harte. Hamilton will carry Betty to his Golden Princess Mine, where they will fall in love and marry.

* * * * *

Penniless though of noble birth, a Marquis falls in love with the daughter of a wealthy American. However, he vows never to marry her until the two of them are equally prosperous. In time, the Marquis' financial venture pays off, and the "golden wall" of wealth between him and his beloved falls away.

The Golden Web (Gotham Productions/Lumas Film Corp., 1926)
d: Walter Lang. 6 reels.
Lillian Rich, Huntly Gordon, Jay Hunt, Lawford Davidson, Boris Karloff, Nora Hayden, Syd Crossley, Joe Moore.
Tale of intrigue and murder, centered on questions of ownership of a valuable gold mine in South Africa.

The Goldfish (Constance Talmadge Productions, 1924)
d: Jerome Storm. 7 reels.
Constance Talmadge, ZaSu Pitts, Jack Mulhall, Frank Elliott, Jean Hersholt, Edward Connelly, William Conklin, Leo White, Nellie Bly Baker, Kate Lester, Eric Mayne, William Wellesley, Jacqueline Gadsden, Percy Williams, John Patrick.
Romantic comedy about Jennie, a social-climbing wife who goes from husband to husband, always seeking higher status.

Golf Widows (Columbia, 1928)
d: Erle C. Kenton. 6 reels.
Will Stanton, Vera Reynolds, Kathleen Key, Vernon Dent, Sally Rand, John Patrick, Harrison Ford.
Ethel and Mary, two fed-up golf widows, take off for Tijuana while their husbands are on the back nine.

Good and Naughty (Paramount, 1926)
d: Malcolm St. Clair. 6 reels.
Pola Negri, Tom Moore, Ford Sterling, Miss Dupont, Stuart Homes, Marie Mosquini, Warner Richmond.
Germaine loves her employer, Gerald, but he scarcely notices her. So the smitten secretary dresses as a vamp and goes on the same yachting trip as her boss. She wins attention, breaks some hearts, and Gerald is finally forced to take a good look at her — and likes what he sees.

Good as Gold (Fox, 1927)
d: Scott Dunlap. 5 reels.
Buck Jones, Frances Lee, Carl Miller, Charles French, Adele Watson, Arthur Ludwig, Mickey Moore.
Out West, a young boy sees his father's mine stolen from him, and plans revenge for when he gets older. Years later, he confronts the new "owner" of the mine and finds that she's a pretty girl.

The Good Bad Man (Fine Arts Film Co./Triangle, 1916)
d: Allan Dwan. 5 reels.
Douglas Fairbanks, Sam De Grasse, Doc Cannon, Joseph Singleton, Bessie Love, Mary Alden, George Beranger, Fred Burns.
Out West, a cowboy Robin Hood steals from the rich and gives to children born out of wedlock, out of belief that he is illegitimate himself.

The Good-Bad Wife (Vera McCord Productions, 1921)
d: Vera McCord. 5 reels.
Sidney Mason, Dorothy Green, Leslie Stowe, Mathilde, Brundage, Albert Hackett, Beatrice Jordan, Pauline Dempsey, Wesley Jenkins, J. Thornton Baston, Erville Alderson, John Ardizoni.
Fanchon, a Parisian dancer, marries into an aristocratic American family, and instantly antagonizes them with her unconventional ways.

Good-By Girls! (Fox, 1923)
d: Jerome Storm. 5 reels.
William Russell, Carmel Myers, Tom Wilson, Kate Price, Robert Klein.
McPhee, a successful author, finds a mystery woman hiding in his home.

Good-Bye, Bill (Famous Players-Lasky/Paramount, 1918)
d: John Emerson. 5 reels.
Shirley Mason, Ernest Truex, Joseph Allen, Joseph Burke, Carl de Planta, H.E. Koser, Herbert Frank.
During World War I, a German-American creates a new invention and is called to Germany to mass-produce it.

The Good-Bye Kiss (First National/Warner Bros., 1928)
d: Mack Sennett. 8 reels.
Johnny Burke, Sally Eilers, Wheeler Oakman, Irving Bacon, Lionel Belmore, Eugene Pallette, Andy Clyde.
In World War I, an American doughboy is thought to be a coward, but he proves otherwise.

The Good For Nothing (World Film Corp., 1917)
d: Carlyle Blackwell. 5 reels.
Carlyle Blackwell, Evelyn Greeley, Kat Lester, Charles Duncan, William Sherwood, Muriel Ostriche, Eugenie Woodward, Katherine Johnston, Pinna Nesbit.
After his widowed mother remarries, a ne'er-do-well son decides to go to work for his new stepfather, and cleans up his act enough to win the gratitude of his new family.

Good Gracious, Annabelle (Famous Players-Lasky/Paramount, 1919)
d: George Melford. 5 reels.
Billie Burke, Herbert Rawlinson, Gilbert Douglas, Crauford Kent, Frank Losee, Leslie Casey, Gordon Dana, Delle Duncan, Olga Downs, Thomas A. Braidon, Billie Wilson.
Forced into marriage with a bearded hermit and then sent away to live in New York, a young woman gets herself into all sorts of trouble. With the help of a new friend, she resolves her legal problems and then determines to return to her husband. Then she learns that the handsome, clean-shaven man who helped her out is, in fact, her husband, the former recluse.

A Good Little Devil (Famous Players Film Co., 1914)
d: Edwin S. Porter. 5 reels.
Mary Pickford, Ernest Truex, William Norris, Iva Merlin, Wilda Bennett, Arthur Hill, Edward Connelly, David Belasco.
A mischievious little boy is befriended by a blind girl, who spins tales of fairies and enchants the boy's soul.

A Good Loser (Triangle, 1918)
d: Dick Donaldson. 5 reels.
Lee Hill, Arthur Millett, Peggy Pearce, Dick Rosson, Graham Pette, Pete Morrison.
Two men, Harry and Jim, are close friends, until Jim goes East, falls in love, and marries. By incredible coincidence, the bride is Harry's former fiancée.

Good Men and Bad (F.W. Kraemer/American Releasing Corp., 1923)
d: Merrill McCormick. 5 reels.
Marin Sais, Steve Carrie, Merrill McCormick, George Guyton, Faith Hope.
In Argentina, a rancher tries to give his daughter as collateral for a loan.

Good Men and True (R-C Pictures/FBO of America, 1922)

d: Val Paul. 6 reels.
Harry Carey, Vola Vale, Thomas Jefferson, Noah Beery, Charles J. LeMoyne, Tully Marshall, Helen Gilmore.
Out West, an unprincipled candidate for sheriff pushes his opponent over the edge of a cliff. The opponent survives, though, and not only wins the election but the heart of a lovely girl.

Good Morning, Judge (Universal, 1928)
d: William A. Seiter. 6 reels.
Reginald Denny, Mary Nolan, Otis Harlan, Dorothy Gulliver, William Davidson, Bull Montana, William Worthington, Sailor Sharkey, Charles Coleman, William H. Tooker.
Freddie, a wealthy playboy, meets Julia, an attractive social worker, and falls for her. But to get her attention Freddie must claim he is a criminal seeking repentance.

Good Night, Paul (Select Pictures Corp., 1918)
d: Walter Edwards. 5 reels.
Constance Talmadge, Norman Kerry, Harrison Ford, John Steppling, Beatrice Van, Rosita Marstini.
When a business gets into dire financial straits, the wife of one of the partners agrees to pose as the bride of the other partner, knowing that his wealthy uncle will give him a large sum of money when he marries. The plan goes well, until the uncle decides to move in.

The Good Provider (Cosmopolitan Productions/Paramount, 1922)
d: Frank Borzage. 8 reels.
Vera Gordon, Dore Davidson, Miriam Battista, Vivienne Osborne, William "Buster" Collier Jr., John Roche, Ora Jones, Edward Phillips, Muriel Martin, James Devine.
In a small American town, a Jewish immigrant begins as a peddler, then gradually becomes prosperous enough to move his family to New York. Once in the big city, however, the former peddler finds himself and his business subjected to pressures unheard of in small towns.

Good References (First National, 1920)
d: R. William Neill. 5 reels.
Constance Talmadge, Vincent Coleman, Ned Sparks, Nellie P. Spaulding, Mona Liza, Matthew L. Betts, Arnold Lucy, Dorothy Walters.
A private secretary falls in love with her employer's trouble-prone nephew.

Good Time Charley (Warner Bros., 1927)
d: Michael Curtiz. 7 reels.
Warner Oland, Helene Costello, Clyde Cook, Montague Love, Hugh Allan, Julanne Johnston.
A veteran character actor suffers various misfortunes bravely.

Good Women (Robertson-Cole Pictures, 1921)
d: Louis J. Gasnier. 6 reels.
Rosemary Theby, Hamilton Revelle, Irene Blackwell, Earl Schenck, William P. Carleton, Arthur Stuart Hull, Rhea Mitchell, Eugenie Besserer.
Katherine's wealthy, but unlucky in love. She elopes with a married man, but he soon leaves her. Then she goes to Italy, finds another married man, and tries again to form a relationship. In the end, though, she'll realize that she has no rightful claim on him, and sends him back to his wife.

The Goose Girl (Lasky Feature Plays/Paramount, 1915)
d: Frederick Thomson. 5 reels.
Marguerite Clark, Monroe Salisbury, Lawrence Peyton,

Sidney Deane, E.N. Dunbar, James Neill, P.E. Peters, H.B. Carpenter, Ernest Joy, J.M. Cassidy, Jane Darwell.
Abducted as an infant and raised by peasants, she's known as "The Goose Girl." But in reality, she is the princess of the realm.

The Goose Hangs High (Famous Players-Lasky/Paramount, 1925)
d: James Cruze. 6 reels.
Constance Bennett, Myrtle Stedman, George Irving, Esther Ralston, William R. Otis Jr., Edward Peil Jr., Gertrude Claire, James A. Marcus, Anne Schaefer, Z. Wall Covington.
Although their parents struggle to put their three children through college, the kids are a bunch of ingrates.

The Goose Woman (Universal, 1925)
d: Clarence Brown.
Louise Dresser, Jack Pickford, Constance Bennett, Spottiswoode Aitken, George Cooper, Gustav von Seyffertitz, George Nichols, Marc MacDermott.
A retired opera singer seeks some sensational publicity, but her efforts backfire.

The Gorilla (First National, 1927)
d: Alfred Santell. 8 reels.
Charlie Murray, Fred Kelsey, Alice Day, Tully Marshall, Claude Gillingwater, Walter Pidgeon, Gaston Glass, Brooks Benedict, Aggie Herring, Syd Crossley, John Gough.
Mystery about a murder believed to have been committed by a gorilla. But is it a real ape, or a man in a gorilla costume?

Gossip (Universal, 1923)
d: King Baggot. 5 reels.
Gladys Walton, Ramsey Wallace, Albert Prisco, Freeman Wood, Carol Halloway.
Caroline, a southern charmer, brings sunshine to the dreary life of a weary businessman.

The Governor's Lady (Lasky Feature Plays/Paramount, 1915)
d: George Melford. 5 reels.
James Neill, Edith Wynne Mathison, Tom Forman, Theodore Roberts, May Allison.
After a miner strikes it rich, he moves into high society and is eventually elected governor. But through it all, his loving wife prefers the quiet life of their earlier years together.

The Governor's Lady (Fox, 1923)
d: Harry Millarde. 8 reels.
Robert T. Haines, Jane Grey, Ann Luther, Frazer Coulter, Leslie Austen.
Remake of the 1915 Paramount film *The Governor's Lady*, both versions based on the play of the same name by Alice Brady.

The Gown of Destiny (Triangle, 1917)
d: Lynn F. Reynolds. 5 reels.
Alma Rubens, Herrera Tejedde, Allan Sears, Lillian West, J. Barney Sherry, Pietro Buzzi, Frederick Vroom, Bliss Chevalier, Kathleen Emerson, Dorothy Marshall.
Magically, a special gown designed by a French dressmaker helps win World War I.

Graft—see: Freedom of the Press (1928)

Grafters (Triangle, 1917)
d: Arthur Rosson. 5 reels.
Jack Devereaux, Anna Lehr, Frank Currier, Irene Leonard, George Siegmann, Robert Crimmins.

Newly rich, a young man becomes ensnared with a mysterious woman and a gang of grafters.

The Grail (Fox, 1923)
d: Colin Campbell. 5 reels.
Dustin Farnum, James Gordon, Carl Stockdale, Alma Bennett, Peggy Shaw, Leon Barry, Frances Raymond, Jack Rollins, Frances Hatton.
Out West, a Texas Ranger impersonates a preacher to flush two outlaws out of hiding.

The Grain of Dust (Ogden Pictures Corp., 1918)
d: Harry Revier. 6 reels.
Lillian Walker, Ramsey Wallace, Ralph Delmore, James O'Neill, Corinne Uzzell, Edith Day, Richard Wangerman, Jacques Tyrol, Cecil Fletcher, Elizabeth Ferris, George Henry.
A Wall Street stenographer is courted by the firm's junior partner, but the attraction isn't mutual—at least, not at first.

The Grain of Dust (Tiffany-Stahl Productions, 1928)
d: George Archainbaud. 7 reels.
Ricardo Cortez, Claire Windsor, Alma Bennett, Richard Tucker, John St. Polis, Otto Hoffman.
Remake of the 1918 Ogden Pictures film *The Grain of Dust*, both versions based on the novel by David Graham Phillips.

The Grand Duchess and the Waiter (Paramount, 1926)
d: Malcolm St. Clair. 7 reels.
Florence Vidor, Adolphe Menjou, Lawrence Grant, Andre Beranger, Dot Farley, Barbara Pierce, Brandon Hurst, William Courtright.
In Paris, a wealthy sportsman falls for an exiled Russian countess.

Grand Larceny (Goldwyn, 1922)
d: Wallace Worsley. 6 reels.
Claire Windsor, Elliott Dexter, Richard Tucker, Tom Gallery, Roy Atwell, John Cossar, Lowell Sherman.
Kathleen, a southern coquette, goes through two northern husbands, and discards them both.

The Grand Passion (Universal, 1918)
d: Ida May Park. 7 reels.
Dorothy Phillips, William Stowell, Jack Mulhall, Lon Chaney, Bert Appling, Evelyn Selbie, Alfred Allen.
Two friends love the same woman, but the town they're living in is a powder keg, rife with corruption. When the woman is kidnapped and held captive in the local brothel, her two suitors rush to the rescue as the town burns to the ground.

Grandma's Boy (Hal Roach/Associated Exhibitors, 1922)
d: Fred Newmeyer. 5 reels.
Harold Lloyd, Anna Townsend, Mildred Davis, Charles Stevenson, Dick Sutherland, Noah Young.
A timorous young man must face a bully who's terrorizing the neighborhood. At first he shrinks from the obligation, but he summons up courage when his grandmother tells the young man about his grandfather's valiant exploits in the Civil War.

The Grasp of Greed (Universal, 1916)
d: Joseph de Grasse. 5 reels.
Louise Lovely, C.M. Hammond, Jay Belasco, Lon Chaney.
A greedy publisher seeks to disinherit his nephew, but repents and decides to alter his will by having a new will tattooed on a girl's back.

Graustark (Essanay, 1915)
d: Fred E. Wright. 6 reels.

Francis X. Bushman, Beverly Bayne, Edna Mayo, Thomas Commerford, Helen Dunbar, Albert Roscoe, Lester Cuneo, Bryant Washburn, Ernest Maupain.
Two strangers, a wealthy American male and a foreign girl, meet on a train traveling through the American West. They spend some quality time together, then part. But later, on a trip to the Balkan kingdom known as Graustark, the American meets the girl again, and learns she is Graustark's princess and heiress to the throne.

Graustark (Joseph M. Schenck Productions/First National, 1925)
d: Dimitri Buchowetzki. 7 reels.
Norma Talmadge, Eugene O'Brien, Marc MacDermott, Roy D'Arcy, Albert Gran, Lillian Lawrence, Michael Vavitch, Frank Currier, Winter Hall, Wanda Hawley.
Remake of the 1915 Essanay film *Graustark*, both films based on the novel of the same name by George Barr McCutcheon.

The Gray Horizon (Haworth Pictures Corp./Robertson-Cole, 1919)
d: William Worthington. 5 reels.
Sessue Hayakawa, Bertram Grassby, Eileen Percy, Mary Jane Irving, Tsuru Aoki, Andrew Robson.
Though struggling to make a living, a Japanese artist living in America nobly refuses to help an unscrupulous businessman reproduce counterfeit bonds.

The Gray Mask (Shubert Film Corp./World Film Corp., 1915)
d: Frank Crane. 5 reels.
Edwin Arden, Barbara Tennant, Frank Monroe, Georgio Majeroni, Buckley Starkey, Hugh Jeffrey, John Hines.
A dedicated police inspector dons a gray mask to infiltrate a gang and bring them to justice.

The Gray Towers Mystery (Vitagraph, 1919)
d: John W. Noble. 5 reels.
Gladys Leslie, Frank Morgan, Warner Richmond, Warren Chandler, Charles Craig, George Henry, Marie Burke, Cecil Kern.
Out West, a woman rancher has two suitors: her half-breed foreman and the local sheriff.

Greased Lightning (Thomas H. Ince/Paramount, 1919)
d: Jerome Storm. 5 reels.
Charles Ray, Wanda Hawley, Robert McKim, Willis Marks, Bert Woodruff, John P. Lockney, Otto Hoffman.
An inventive country chap takes a jalopy and converts it into a snazzy racing car.

Greased Lightning (Universal, 1928)
d: Ray Taylor. 5 reels.
Ted Wells, Betty Caldwell, Walter Shumway, Lon Poff, George Dunning, Myrtis Crinley, Victor Allen.
Out West, a ranch foreman and his pards race to the rescue, when the pretty ranch owner is kidnapped.

The Great Accident (Goldwyn, 1920)
d: Harry Beaumont. 6 reels.
Tom Moore, Jane Novak, Andrew Robson, Willard Louis, Lillian Langdon, Ann Forrest, Philo McCullough, Otto Hoffman, Roy Laidlaw, Edward McWade, Don Bailey, Lefty Flynn.
The boozing son of a Prohibition party candidate is mistakenly elected mayor.

The Great Adventure (Pathé, 1918)
d: Alice Blaché. 5 reels.

Bessie Love, Flora Finch, Donald Hall, Chester Barnett, Florence Short, John W. Dunn, Walter Craven.
Small-town girl makes good in a Broadway show.

The Great Adventure (Whitman Bennett Productions/Associated First National, 1921)
d: Kenneth Webb. 6 reels.
Lionel Barrymore, Doris Rankin, Octavia Broske, Thomas Braidon, Arthur Rankin, Paul Kelly, Maybeth Carr, Dharles Land, Jed Prouty, E.J. Ratcliffe, Ivo Dawson, Katherine Stewart.
Romantic comedy about a portrait painter who seeks to escape from the "curse" of stardom. He switches identities with his recently deceased valet and retreats from the world of his fans. He meets a girl, falls in love, and marries. But he can't escape his own talent, and soon he is painting again and being recognized for the artist he is.

The Great Air Robbery (Universal, 1919)
d: Jacques Jaccard. 6 reels.
Alan Forrest, Francelia Billington, Ormer Locklear, Ray Ripley, Carmen Phillips.
Aerial pirates menace the U.S. Mail Service.

The Great Alone (West Coast Films/American Releasing Corp., 1922)
d: Isadore Bernstein. 6 reels.
Monroe Salisbury, Laura Anson, Walter Law, Maria Law, George Waggoner, Richard Cummings.
Duval, half Indian and half white, is discriminated against on racial grounds and forced to give up college. But when a girl who befriended him there is reported lost in a blinding snowstorm, he braves the icy drifts and rescues her.

The Great Deception (Robert Kane Productions/First National, 1926)
d: Howard Higgin. 6 reels.
Ben Lyon, Aileen Pringle, Basil Rathbone, Sam Hardy, Charlotte Walker, Amelia Summerville, Hubert Wilke, Lucien Prival, Lucius Henderson, Mark Gonzales.
During World War I, a young Englishman is a double agent for Germany and England.

The Great Diamond Mystery (Fox, 1924)
d: Denison Clift. 5 reels.
Shirley Mason, Jackie Saunders, Harry von Meter, John Cossar, Philo McCullough, Hector V. Sarno, William Collier Jr., Eugenia Gilbert, Mary Mayo, Hardee Kirkland.
Murder mystery with a last-second reprieve that saves the life of an innocent man.

The Great Divide (Lubin, 1915)
d: Edgar Lewis. 5 reels.
Ethel Clayton, House Peters, Marie Sterling, Hayden Stevenson, Mary Moore, Warner P. Richmond, Ferdinand O'Beck, Ray Chamberlain.
Alone in her new Arizona home, a young woman is threatened with rape by three drunks. Incredibly, she marries one of them.

The Great Divide (MGM, 1924)
d: Reginald Barker. 8 reels.
Wallace Beery, Alice Terry, Conway Tearle, Huntly Gordon, Allan Forrest, George Cooper, ZaSu Pitts, William Orlamond.
Ghent, a tough gold miner, falls in love with Ruth, a genteel girl. Having rescued her from two roughnecks, he forces her to marry him, then loses her when her brother turns up and takes her back home. But Ghent will show great valor in

getting medical help through the wilderness for Ruth, and in the end she realizes she really loves her husband.

The Great Divide (First National, 1929)
d: Reginald Barker. 8 reels.
Dorothy Mackaill, Ian Keith, Myrna Loy, Lucien Littlefield, Creighton Hale, George Fawcett, Claude Gillingwater, Roy Stewart, Ben Hendricks Jr., Jean Laverty.
Remake of the MGM film *The Great Divide*, with some plot alterations. Both versions are based on the play of the same name by William V. Moody.

Great Expectations (Famous Players/Paramount, 1917)
d: Robert G. Vignola. 5 reels.
Louise Huff, Jack Pickford, Frank Losee, W.W. Black, Marcia Harris, Grace Barton, Herbert Prior.
In the first feature film version of the Charles Dickens novel, Jack Pickford plays Pip, the boy who aids an escaped convict and later falls in love with Estella, his foster mother's ward.

The Great Gatsby (Famous Players-Lasky/Paramount, 1926)
d: Herbert Brenon. 8 reels.
Warner Baxter, Lois Wilson, Neil Hamilton, Georgia Hale, George Nash, Eric Blore, Carmelita Geraghty, William Powell, Gunboat Smith, Claire Whitney, Hale Hamilton.
Gatsby, an Army officer in World War I, loves Daisy, a high society girl. When he returns from the war, he finds Daisy married to an irresponsible patrician. Gatsby himself rises to a high caste in Long Island society, and cautiously he and Daisy resume their affair.

The Great Impersonation (Famous Players-Lasky/Paramount, 1921)
d: George Melford. 7 reels.
James Kirkwood, Ann Forrest, Winter Hall, Truly Shattuck, Fontaine LaRue, Alan Hale, Bertram Johns, William Burress, Cecil Holland, Tempe Pigott, Lawrence Grant, Louis Dumar.
College roommates—an aristocratic Englishman and a German baron—look so much alike their friends can barely tell them apart. Not a problem in school, but when World War I breaks out and the two roommates must take opposite sides in the great conflict, their resemblance to each other lends an air of intrigue to the roles each must take.
Kirkwood plays both roles, the English peer and his German counterpart.

The Great K&A Train Robbery (Fox, 1926)
d: Lewis Seiler. 6 reels.
Tom Mix, Dorothy Dwan, William Walling, Harry Grippe, Carl Miller, Edward Peil, Curtis McHenry.
When a railroad company becomes the target of several robberies, a detective goes undercover to solve the crimes and bring the criminals to justice.
Generally considered the best of the Tom Mix silent westerns, *The Great K&A Train Robbery* is non-stop action, with Mix and his wonder horse Tony performing some of their most spectacular stunts. Among other things, Mix slides down a rope from the top of a mountain, scrambles underneath a train, and rides his horse into a swimming pool and out again.

The Great Love (Famous Players-Lasky/Paramount, 1918)
d: D.W. Griffith. 7 reels.
Lillian Gish, Robert Harron, Henry B. Walthall, Gloria Hope, Maxfield Stanley, George Fawcett, Rosemary Theby, George Siegmann.
During World War I, an Australian heiress marries an

American soldier in London.

The Great Love (MGM, 1925)
d: Marshall Neilan. 6 reels.
Viola Dana, Robert Agnew, ZaSu Pitts, Frank Currier, Chester Conklin, Junior Coughlan, Malcolm Waite.
After a circus stops in a country town and the local doctor cures Norma, the elephant, of a burn, Norma keeps returning to the doc, no matter where the circus travels.

The Great Lover (Goldwyn, 1920)
d: Frank Lloyd. 6 reels.
John Sainpolis, Claire Adams, John Davidson, Alice Hollister, Lionel Belmore, Rose dion, Richard Tucker, Tom Ricketts, Frederick Vroom, Jean Corey.
When a famous opera baritone is accidentally injured between acts of an opera, his son goes on in his place and wins public acclaim.

The Great Moment (Famous Players-Lasky/Paramount, 1921)
d: Sam Wood. 7 reels. 7 reels.
Gloria Swanson, Alec B. Francis, Milton Sills, F.R. Butler, Helen Dunbar, Julia Faye, Clarence Geldart, Raymond Brathwayt, Ann Grigg.
In Nevada, an English girl is bitten by a snake and is attended to by a local engineer. But when Papa finds them together in the engineer's cabin, he suspects the worst and forces the two to marry. To her great surprise, the girl isn't at all displeased.

The Great Night (Fox, 1922)
d: Howard M. Mitchell. 5 reels.
William Russell, Eva Novak, Winifred Bryson, Henry Barrows, Wade Boteler, Harry Lonsdale, Earl Metcalfe.
An heir must marry by midnight or lose a fortune.

The Great Problem (Universal, 1916)
d: Rex Ingram. 5 reels.
Violet Mersereau, Lionel Adams, Dan Hanlon, Kittens Reicherts, William J. Dyer, Mrs. J.J. Brundage, Howard Crampton.
A convict's daughter is befriended by a kindly district attorney.

The Great Redeemer (Metro, 1920)
d: Clarence Brown. 5 reels.
House Peters, Marjorie Daw, Jack McDonald, Joseph Singleton.
Unrepentant crook Dan Malloy, who has artistic talent, is sentenced to ten years in jail. On his cell wall he draws a picture of Jesus Christ. Incredibly, the sight of the picture ennobles the hardened inmates, and leads to Dan's own conversion.

The Great Romance (Yorke Film Corp./Metro, 1919)
d: Henry Otto. 6 reels.
Harold Lockwood, Ruby de Remer, Joseph Granby, Frank Currier, Helen Lindroth, Franklyn Hanna, Clare Grenville, Louis Stern, Morgan Thorpe, J.P. Laffey.
Raised by adoptive parents, an American college student travels to the kingdom of Rugaria, where it is discovered that he is actually the heir to the throne.

The Great Ruby (Lubin, 1915)
d: Barry O'Neil. 5 reels.
Beatrice Morgan, George Soule Spencer, Octavia Handworth, Eleanor Barry, Frankie Mann, Jeanette Hackett, Peter Lang, Chauncey Keim, Walter Hitchcock, Ferdinand Tidmarsh.
Ambitious tale tracking the path of a priceless ruby through the ages.

The Great Sensation (Columbia, 1925)
d: Jay Marchant. 5 reels.
William Fairbanks, Pauline Garon, Adelaide Hallock, Lloyd Whitlock,
A scion of wealth masquerades as chauffeur to a lovely flapper.

The Great Shadow (Adanac Producing Co./Republic, 1920)
d: Harley Knoles. 6 reels.
Tyrone Power, Donald Hall, Dorothy Bernard, John Rutherford, Louis Stern.
Bolsheviks try to infiltrate an American labor union.

The Great Victory, Wilson or the Kaiser? (Screen Classics/Metro, 1919)
d: Charles Miller. 6 reels.
Creighton Hale, Florence Billings, E.J. Connelly, Helen Ferguson, Frank Currier, Fred C. Truesdell, Margaret McWade, Earl Schenck, Florence Short, Andrew Clarke, J.A. Furey.
World War I drama (with an unwieldy title) that follows an Alsace-Lorraine patriot from duty in the German army, to his disgust with the Kaiser's policies, and eventually his conversion to the Allied side as a doughboy.

The Great White Way (Cosmopolitan, 1924)
d: E. Mason Hopper. 10 reels.
Anita Stewart, Tom Lewis, T. Roy Barnes, Oscar Shaw, Dore Davidson, Ned Wayburn, G.L. (Tex) Rickard, Harry Watson, Hal Forde, Olin Howland, Pete Hartley, Fay King.
As a publicity stunt, a showgirl is romantically paired with a prizefighter.

The Greater Claim (Metro, 1921)
d: Wesley Ruggles. 6 reels.
Alice Lake, Jack Dougherty, Edward Cecil, DeWitt Jennings, Florence Gilbert, Lenore Lynard.
When a chorus girl elopes with a scion of wealth, his angry father has the young man kidnapped and tenders his new daughter-in-law an offer to annul the marriage. Fortunately she rejects the offer, and after the birth of their child, the couple is reunited.

The Greater Glory (First National, 1926)
d: Curt Rehfeld. 11 reels.
Conway Tearle, Anna Q. Nilsson, May Allison, Ian Keith, Lucy Beaumont, Jean Hersholt, Nigel DeBrulier, Bridgetta Clark, John Sainpolis, Marcia Manon, Edward Earle, Virginia Southern, Isabelle Keith, Kathleen Chambers.
Fanny, an aristocratic Austrian lady, loves a count, but he calls off the engagement when she courts disgrace by helping a needy young woman. The outbreak of the World War throws their lives into tumult, and eventually Fanny prospers as the partner of an arms dealer. At War's end, the count seeks her hand again—but this time, it's no dice.

The Greater Law (Universal, 1917)
d: Lynn Reynolds. 5 reels.
Myrtle Gonzalez, George Hernandez, Gretchen Lederer, Maud Emory, G.M. Ricketts.
In the frozen North, a young woman searches for her brother's killer.

Greater Love Hath No Man (Popular Plays and

Players/Metro, 1915)
d: Herbert Blaché. 5 reels.
Emmett Corrigan, Crauford Kent, Thomas Curran, Mabel Wright, William Morse, Mary Martin, Lawrence Grattan, Albert Lang, Edward Hoyt.
To protect his foster mother, a young man confesses to a murder that her son committed.

The Greater Profit (Haworth Studios/R-C Pictures, 1921)
d: William Worthington. 5 reels.
Edith Storey, Pell Trenton, Willis Marks, Lloyd Bacon, Bobbie Roberts, Ogden Crane, Lillian Rambeau, Dorothy Wood.
In New York, a young woman skilled at safecracking gets a crack at an honest job.

Greater Than a Crown (Fox, 1925)
d: R. William Neill. 5 reels.
Edmund Lowe, Dolores Costello, Margaret Livingston, Ben Hendricks, Paul Panzer, Anthony Merlo, Robert Klein.
Improbable but tantalizing comedy about an American who rescues a strange girl from attackers in London. He then finds her accomodations for the night with Molly, an actress friend. Next morning, the strange girl has disappeared and so have Molly's jewels. Molly and the American give chase, only to discover that the missing girl is actually the crown princess of a European kingdom, and she's on the lam to avoid an arranged marriage. The princess didn't take Molly's jewels, her kidnappers did... and in the ensuing scramble, it turns out that Molly is also royalty incognito.

Greater Than Fame (Selznick/Select, 1920)
d: Alan Crosland. 5 reels.
Elaine Hammerstein, Walter McGrail, W.H. Tooker, Julia Swayne Gordon, Albert Roccardi, Cora Williams, John Walker, Arthur Donaldson, Flora Kingsley, Eugenie Woodward.
A naïve young singer goes to the city in search of a career, but gets more propositions than theater roles.

Greater Than Love (J. Parker Read Jr. Productions/Associated Producers, 1921)
d: Fred Niblo. 6 reels.
Louise Glaum, Patricia Palmer, Rose Cade, Eve Southern, Willie May Carson, Betty Francisco, Mahlon Hamilton, Donald MacDonald, Edward Martindel, Gertrude Claire, Stanhope Wheatcroft.
Tragedy strikes a group of young women living in a New York apartment when one of them takes her own life.

Greater Than Marriage (Romance Pictures/Vitagraph, 1924)
d: Victor Hugo Halperin. 7 reels.
Marjorie Daw, Lou Tellegen, Peggy Kelly, Tyrone Power, Mary Thurman, Dagmar Godowsky, Raymond Bloomer, Effie Shannon, Florence Billings, William Ricciardi, Ed Roseman.
Masters, a playwright, disapproves of his wife's ambitions to become a stage actress. Nevertheless, while he's out of town she tries out for a part, nails it, and becomes the star. Now she's a big success, but meantime her husband's play is a failure. What now?

The Greater Will (Premo Film Co./Pathé, 1915)
d: Harley Knoles. 5 reels.
Cyril Maude, Lois Meredith, Montague Love, H.J. Carvill, William T. Carleton, Charles Francis, Margot Williams, Lionel Belmore, Walter Craven.

Grieving the death of his daughter, a man vows revenge against the man responsible, a master hypnotist who drove the girl to her death.

The Greater Woman (Frank Powell Producing Corp./Mutual, 1917)
d: Frank Powell. 5 reels.
Marjorie Rambeau, Aubrey Beattie, Hassan Mussalli, Sara Haidez, Frank Ford, Josephine Park, Margaret Grey, H.H. Pattee, Louis Stern.
After marrying an artist in Paris, an American woman returns home and finds that a former suitor is insanely jealous of her husband.

The Greatest Love (Select Pictures Corp., 1920)
d: Henry Kolker. 6 reels.
Vera Gordon, Bertram Marburgh, Yvonne Shelton, Hugh Huntley, William H. Tooker, Ray Dean, Donald Hall, Sally Crute, Jessie Simpson.
Lorenzo, an Italian immigrant, learns that his sister has been seduced by a theatrical impresario, and goes to the man's office to confront him. But Lorenzo finds the man dead, just as the police arrive, and they arrest him on suspicion of murder. His family never doubts Lorenzo's innocence, and in time they find the true culprit.

The Greatest Power (Rolfe Photoplays, Inc./Metro, 1917)
d: Edwin Carewe. 5 reels.
Ethel Barrymore, William B. Davidson, Harry S. Northrup, Frank Currier, William Black, Cecil Owen, Fred C. Truesdell, Redfield Clark, Rudolph de Cordova, W.M. Armstrong.
When two young scientists—a man and a woman—come up with a formula for a powerful explosive, pacifist John refuses to allow it to be used for war, while patriotic Miriam urges that they turn it over to the government. The matter is settled once the pair find a German spy trying to get his hands on their invention. That swings the tide in favor of wartime use.

The Greatest Question (Griffith/First National, 1919)
d: D.W. Griffith. 6 reels.
Lillian Gish, Robert Harron, Ralph Graves, Eugenie Besserer, George Fawcett, Tom Wilson, Josephine Crowell, George Nichols.
An orphan girl is given shelter by a farm family and becomes their servant. But the family has a dark secret: They are murderers.

The Greatest Thing in Life (D.W. Griffith/Paramount, 1918)
d: D.W. Griffith. 7 reels.
Lillian Gish, Robert Harron, Adolphe Lestina, David Butler, Elmo Lincoln, Edward Peil, Kate Bruce, Peaches Jackson.
A French girl living in America journeys to France in hopes of finding love. Ironically, an American boy she knew in the States turns up and realizes he loves her.

Greed (McClure Pictures/Triangle, 1917)
d: Theodore Marston. 5 reels.
Nance O'Neil, Shirley Mason, Alfred Hickman, Harry Northrup, Robert Elliott, George Le Guere.
Not to be confused with the 1924 Erich von Stroheim classic, this picture deals with a couple who get involved with stock market trading, and their greedy obsessions.

Greed (MGM, 1924)
d: Erich von Stroheim. 10 reels.

Gibson Gowland, ZaSu Pitts, Jean Hersholt, Chester

Conklin, Dale Fuller, Sylvia Ashton, Joan Standing, Austin Jewel, Oscar Gottell, Otto Gottell, Frank Hayes, FannyMidgley, Hughie Mack, Jack Curtis, Tempe Pigott.

A dentist marries a grasping, avaricious woman whose greed eventually drives him to desperation and murder. Von Stroheim's adaptation of Frank Norris' powerful novel *McTeague* was filmed with meticulous fidelity to the original story, and ran nine hours (forty-two reels) when von Stroheim was finished. Studio moguls Louis B.Mayer and Irving Thalberg then had the film edited down to ten reels (about two hours running time), over von Stroheim's cries of "butchery." But the resulting film is still considered a classic.

McTeague had been filmed in 1916 by American Film Corp. as *Life's Whirlpool*.

The Green Cloak (George Kleine/Kleine-Edison Feature Service, 1915)
d: Walter Edwin. 5 reels.
Irene Fenwick, Blanche Aimee, Della Connor, Kathryn Brook, Anna Reader, Roland Bottomley, John Davidson, Frank Belcher, Richie Ling, William Anker.
A young woman is arrested for the murder of a stranger because the police find a green tassle clutched in his hand, and it has come from the woman's cloak.

The Green-Eyed Monster (Fox, 1916)
d: J. Gordon Edwards. 5 reels.
Robert Mantell, Genevieve Hamper, Stuart Holmes, Henry Leone, Charles Davidson.
Jealousy leads Raymond de Mornay to poison his brother, who had married the woman Raymond loved.

Green Eyes (Thomas H. Ince/Paramount, 1918)
d: R. William Neill. 5 reels.
Dorothy Dalton, Jack Holt, Emory Johnson, Doris Lee, Robert McKim, Clyde Benson, Charles French.
Bitterness and jealousy attend a wealthy Southern family when a plantation owner finds his new bride in conversation with another man. The owner's future sister-in-law is likewise stricken by the green-eyed monster when her fiancé is found conversing with another woman.

The Green Flame (Robert Brunton Productions/Pathé, 1920)
d: Ernest C. Warde. 5 reels.
J. Warren Kerrigan, Fritzi Brunette, Jay Morley, Claire duBrey, Myles McCarthy, Edwin Wallock, William Moran.
"The Green Flame" is a priceless emerald, and it seems everyone is after it.

The Green God (Vitagraph, 1918)
d: Paul Scardon. 5 reels.
Harry T. Morey, Betty Blythe, Arthur Donaldson, George Majeroni, Bernard Siegel, Robert Gaillard, Joseph Burke.
Antique hunters have their sights set on a green Buddha idol.

The Green Goddess (Distinctive Productions/Goldwyn, 1923)
d: Sidney Olcott. 8 reels.
George Arliss, Alice Joyce, David Powell, Harry T. Morey, Jetta Goudal, Ivan Simpson, William Worthington.
Three British citizens in India are imperiled by a Hindu uprising.

Green Grass Widows (Tiffany-Stahl Productions, 1928)
d: Alfred Raboch. 6 reels.
Walter Hagen, Gertrude Olmstead, John Harron, Hedda Hopper, Lincoln Stedman, Ray Hallor.
Golf pro Walter Hagen plays himself in this dramedy about a college boy trying to earn some needed money by winning in a golf tournament against Hagen.

Green Stockings (Vitagraph, 1916)
d: Wilfrid North. 5 reels.
Lillian Walker, Frank Currier, Louise Beaudet, Adele De Garde, Lillian Burns, Stanley Dark, Charles Brown, John T. Kelly, Denton Vane, Robert Vivian, Charles Wellesley.
In England, a young woman invents for herself a fictional fiancé named "Colonel Smith" for herself. She is pleasantly startled when Colonel Smith turns out to be both real and eligible.

The Green Temptation (Famous Players-Lasky/Paramount, 1922)
d: William D. Taylor. 6 reels.
Betty Compson, Mahlon Hamilton, Theodore Kosloff, Neely Edwards, Edward Burns, Lenore Lynard, Mary Thurman, William von Hardenburg, Betty Brice, Arthur Hull.
In Paris, larcenous apache dancers operate in league with a sinister clown to steal from customers. But when World War I breaks out, the female dancer becomes a Red Cross nurse and, in her new profession, discovers values that turn her away from her life of crime.

The Grell Mystery (Vitagraph, 1917)
d: Paul Scardon. 5 reels.
Earle Williams, Miriam Miles, Jean Dunbar, Denton Vane, Mabel Trunnelle, Frank Crayne, Bernard Siegel, Robert Gaillard.

Mistaken identity fuels this tale of a man who believes his fiancée has committed murder, and tries to throw suspicion on himself.

The Grey Chiffon Veil —see: The Veiled Adventure (1919)

The Grey Devil (George Blaisdell Productions/Rayart, 1926)
d: Bennett Cohn. 5 reels.
Jack Perrin, Tom London, Lorraine Eason, Andy Waldron, Jerome LaGrasse, Milburn Morante.
Out West, a ranch hand is suspected of cattle rustling.

The Grey Mask —see: The Gray Mask (1915)

The Grey Parasol (Triangle, 1918)
d: Lawrence Windom. 5 reels.
Claire Anderson, Wellington Cross, Joe Bennett, Ed Brady, Frank Thorne, William Quinn.
The handle of a grey parasol contains an important formula, and thugs are out to steal it.

The Greyhound Limited (Warner Bros., 1929)
d: Howard Bretherton. 7 reels. (Music, sound effects, part talkie.)
Monte Blue, Grant Withers, Edna Murphy, Lew Harvey, Ernie Shields.
An engineer comes to the rescue when his pal is arrested for a crime he did not commit.

The Grim Comedian (Goldwyn, 1921)
d: Frank Lloyd. 6 reels.
Phoebe Hunt, Jack Holt, Gloria Hope, Bert Woodruff, Laura LaVarnie, May Hopkins, John Harron, Joseph J. Dowling.
Marie, a successful stage actress, finds that her lover has asked her daughter to elope with him.

The Grim Game (Famous Players-Lasky/Paramount, 1919)

d: Irvin Willat. 5 reels.
Harry Houdini, Thomas Jefferson, Ann Forrest, Augustus Phillips, Tully Marshall, Arthur Hoyt, Mae Busch, Ed Martin, Jane Wolfe.
Real-life escape artist Harry Houdini plays a reporter who's unjustly arrested for murder. He then displays remarkable escapes from chains, handcuffs, and a straitjacket.

Grinning Guns (Universal, 1927)
d: Albert S. Rogell. 5 reels.
Jack Hoxie, Robert Milasch, Ena Gregory, Arthur Morrison, George French, Dudley Hendricks, Alphonse Martell.
Out West, a crooked town boss tries to get "Grinner" Martin, an honest cowboy, lynched.

The Grip of Jealousy (Universal, 1916)
d: Joseph De Grasse. 5 reels.
Louise Lovely, Lon Chaney, Jay Belasco, Walter Belasco, Harry Hamm, Marcia Morse, Grace Thompson.
Melodrama about two feuding Southern families.

Grip of the Yukon (Universal, 1928)
d: Ernst Laemmle. 7 reels.
Francis X. Bushman, Neil Hamilton, June Marlowe, Otis Harlan, Burr McIntosh, James Farley.
Prospector buddies fall for a dance hall girl.

Grit (Film Guild/W.W. Hodkinson Corporation, 1924)
d: Frank Tuttle. 6 reels.
Glenn Hunter, Helenka Adamowska, Roland Young, Osgood Perkins, Townsend Martin, Clara Bow, Dore Davidson, Martin Broder, Joseph Depew.
F. Scott Fitzgerald tale about two gang members, a man and a young woman, who attempt to go straight but meet resistance from their gang.

Grit Wins (Universal, 1929)
d: Joseph Levigard. 5 reels.
Ted Wells, Kathleen Collins, Al Ferguson, Buck Connors, Nelson McDowell, Edwin Moulton.
After a ranch owner is framed for murder and imprisoned, the victim's own son helps exonerate him.

Grumpy (Famous Players-Lasky/Paramount, 1923)
d: William DeMille. 6 reels.
Theodore Roberts, May McAvoy, Conrad Nagel, Casson Ferguson, Bertram Johns, Charles Ogle, Robert Bolder, Charles French, Bernice Frank, Bertram Frank.
An irascible lawyer solves a baffling mystery, using a gardenia as his main clue.

The Guardian (World Film Corp., 1917)
d: Arthur Ashley. 5 reels.
Montagu Love, June Elvidge, Arthur Ashley, William Black, Robert Broderick.
When a young woman learns that her romantic choice is a scheming blackmailer, she turns to her guardian for advice.

Guardians of the Wild (Universal, 1928)
d: Henry MacRae. 5 reels.
Jack Perrin, Ethlyne Clair, Al Ferguson, Bernard Siegel, Robert Homans.
A gritty forest ranger rescues his fiancée and her father from a rampaging gang intent on forcing them off their land. Later, the girl is trapped in a forest fire, and the ranger rides to the rescue once again.

Guile of Women (Goldwyn, 1921)
d: Clarence Badger. 5 reels.
Will Rogers, Mary Warren, Bert Sprotte, Lionel Belmore,
Charles A. Smiley, Nick Cogley, Doris Pawn, John Lince, Jane Starr.
In San Francisco, a Swedish sailor laments the loss of his girlfriend from the old country, but finds consolation with a new love. He is shocked, however, when he finds his new love in the arms of his best friend. Downhearted, the sailor returns to the docks and finds his old girlfriend, who has made it all the way to America looking for him.

The Guilt of Silence (Universal, 1918)
d: Elmer Clifton. 5 reels.
Monroe Salisbury, Ruth Clifford, Alfred Allen, Betty Schade, Sam De Grasse.
During the Alaska gold rush, a prospector loses his voice in a violent snowstorm.

A Guilty Conscience (Vitagraph, 1921)
d: David Smith. 5 reels.
Antonio Moreno, Betty Francisco, Harry Van Meter, Lila Leslie, John MacFarlane.
In a story with echoes of the Biblical story of David and Bathsheba, a military commander sends an officer to a distant and dangerous post because the commander covets the officer's wife.

The Guilty Man (Thomas H. Ince/Paramount, 1918)
d: Irvin V. Willat. 5 reels.
Vivian Reed, Gloria Hope, William Garwood, J.P. Lockney, Charles French, Hal Cooley, John Steppling, Hayward Mack.
In Paris, a young woman is accused of murdering a lecher she shot in self-defense. At her trial, the prosecutor learns that the defendant is his own daughter, abandoned by him years before. He shamefacedly names himself as "the guilty man."

Guilty of Love (Famous Players-Lasky/Paramount, 1920)
d: Harley Knoles. 5 reels.
Dorothy Dalton, Julia Hurley, Henry J. Carvil, Augusta Anderson, Edward Langford, Charles Lane, Douglas Redmond, Ivy Ward, Lawrence Johnson.
A brief affair leads to pregnancy and a shotgun wedding.

The Guilty One (Famous Players-Lasky/Paramount, 1924)
d: Joseph Henabery. 6 reels.
Agnes Ayres, Edward Burns, Stanley Taylor, Crauford Kent, Cyril Ring, Thomas R. Mills, Catherine Wallace, George Siegmann, Clarence Burton, Dorothea Wolbert.
An innocent "affair" between a married woman and her husband's rakish client is really only a friendship.

The Gulf Between (Technicolor Motion Picture Corp., 1917)
d: Wray Physioc. 7 reels. (Technicolor.)
Grace Darmond, Niles Welch, Herbert Fortier, Charles C. Brandt, George DeCarlton, Joseph Dailey, Caroline Harris, Virginia Lee, Violet Axzell, Louis Montjoy.
A lost little girl is adopted by a kindly sea captain and raised as his own daughter. Years later, when the grown girl falls in love with a scion of wealth, his parents forbid their marriage because of "the gulf between" them in social class. But love wins out, when it is discovered that the girl is really the daughter of a wealthy family, who lost her all those years ago.
The Gulf Between was the first feature film released in two-color Technicolor. In 1914, England had produced a 5-reel feature, *The World, the Flesh and the Devil*, in a process called Kinemacolor. Except for a few short films, these two were the first color motion pictures. The next American feature to

be produced in Technicolor was Metro's *The Toll of the Sea* (1922), which used a color system far superior to the primitive additive process used for *The Gulf Between*.

The Gun Fighter (Triangle, 1917)
d: William S. Hart. 5 reels.
William S. Hart, Margery Wilson, Roy Laidlaw, Joseph J. Dowling, Milton Ross, George Stone, J.P. Lockney.
In old Arizona, a gun fighter finds he cannot escape his reputation.

A Gun-Fighting Gentleman (Universal, 1919)
d: Jack Ford. 5 reels.
Harry Carey, Kathleen O'Connor, Barney Sherry, Harry Meter, Lydia Titus, Duke Lee, Joe Harris, Johnnie Cooke, Ted Brooks.
Interesting western drama about Cheyenne Harry, an honest rancher who's being blackmailed by an unscrupulous cattle baron. Harry starts robbing the baron's payroll; but each time he does, he sends his adversary a receipt for the amount. Eventually, the cattle baron's own daughter falls in love with Harry.
Harry Carey played the role of Cheyenne Harry in several films directed by Jack Ford, who later used the name John Ford in his spectacular film career.

Gun Gospel (Charles R. Rogers Productions/First National, 1927)
d: Harry J. Brown. 7 reels.
Ken Maynard, Bob Fleming, Romaine Fielding, Virginia Brown Faire, J.P. McGowan, Jerry Madden, Noah Young, Bill Dyer, Slim Whittaker.
Out West, a dying ranch owner tells his friend that the "gospel of the gun" is wrong, and elicits his promise not to avenge his death. The friend agrees, lays the dead man to rest, and goes after his killer.

Gun Law (FBO Pictures/RKO, 1929)
d: Robert DeLacey, John Burch. 6 reels.
Tom Tyler, Barney Furey, Ethlyne Clair, Frankie Darro, Lew Meehan, Tom Brooker, Harry Woods.
Out West, a cowboy courts the rancher's daughter.

The Gun Runner (Tiffany-Stahl Productions, 1928)
d: Edgar Lewis. 6 reels.
Ricardo Cortez, Nora Lane, Gino Corrado, John St. Polis.
Action and intrigue in a Central American country.

Gun Shy (Phil Goldstone Productions, 1922)
d: Alvin J. Neitz. 5 reels.
Franklyn Farnum, Florence Gilbert, Andrew Waldron, Robert Kortman, George F. Marion, William Dyer.
A U.S. marshal is sent to a western town to restore law and order.

The Gun Woman (Triangle, 1918)
d: Frank Borzage. 5 reels.
Texas Guinan, Edward Brady, Francis McDonald, Walter Perkins, Thornton Edwards, George Chase.
In the old West, a tough lady named "the Tigress" runs the local dance hall.

The Gunfighter (Fox, 1923)
d: Lynn F. Reynolds. 5 reels.
William Farnum, Doris May, L.C. Shumway, J. Morris Foster, Virginia True Boardman, Irene Hunt, Arthur Morrison, Cecil Van Auker, Jerry Campbell.
Feuding mountain families spar over a girl who was taken from one of the families as a child.

A Gutter Magdalene (Lasky Feature Plays/Paramount, 1916)
d: George H. Melford. 5 reels.
Fannie Ward, Jack Dean, Charles West, Billy Elmer, Gertrude Kellar, Robert Bradbury, James Neill.
When a gambler turns thief, his sweetheart leaves him. After several adventures, she winds up engaged to the man her ex-boyfriend robbed.

The Guttersnipe (Universal, 1922)
d: Dallas M. Fitzgerald. 5 reels.
Gladys Walton, Walter Perry, Kate Price, Jack Perrin, Sidney Franklin, Carmen Phillips, Edward Cecil, Hugh Saxon, Seymour Zeliff, Eugene Corey, Lorraine Weiler, Christian J. Frank.
Mazie, a New York girl who loves to read pulp magazine stories, recognizes in a new acquaintance the attributes of one of her pulp heroes.

Gypsy of the North (Trem Carr Productions/Rayart, 1928)
d: Scott Pembroke. 6 reels.
Georgia Hale, Huntley Gordon, Jack Dougherty, William Quinn, Hugh Saxon, Henry Roquemore, Erin LaBissoniere.
In the frozen North, a dance hall girl searches for her brother's killer.

The Gypsy Trail (Famous Players-Lasky/Paramount, 1918)
d: Walter Edwards. 5 reels.
Bryant Washburn, Wanda Hawley, Casson Ferguson, C.H. Geldart, Georgie Stone, Edythe Chapman.
Incurable romantic Frances loves Edward, and would like to be swept off her feet and carried away; but because Edward is too bashful to try anything so intrepid, he hires a friend to do it for him.

The Habit of Happiness (Fine Arts/Triangle, 1916)
d: Allan Dwan. 5 reels.
Douglas Fairbanks, George Fawcett, Macey Harlam, Dorothy West, George Backus, Grace Rankin, William Jefferson.
A relentlessly cheerful young man brightens the spirits of everyone around him.

Hail the Woman (Thomas H. Ince/Associated Producers, 1921)
d: John Griffith Wray. 8 reels.
Lloyd Hughes, Florence Vidor, Theodore Roberts, Gertrude Claire, Madge Bellamy, Vernon Dent, Edward Martindel, Charles Meredith, Mathilde Brundage, Eugene Hoffman, Frances Dana.
A conservative preacher tries to run his children's lives for them, but his daughter rebels.

Hair Trigger Casey (American Film Co., 1922)
d: Frank Borzage. 5 reels.
Frank Borzage, Ann Little, Chick Morrison, Jack Richardson.
Re-edited and revised version of the 1916 American Film Company's *Immediate Lee*.

Hairpins (Thomas H. Ince/Paramount, 1920)
d: Fred Niblo. 5 reels.
Enid Bennett, Matt Moore, William Conklin, Margaret Livingston, Grace Morse, Al Filson, Aggie Herring.
When a frump notices her husband is beginning a flirtation with his pretty secretary, she takes a look in the mirror and decides she could use some sprucing up. After getting a complete makeover, the ugly duckling emerges as a beautiful swan, attracts the attention of playboys and businessmen... and more importantly, wins back the love of

her husband.

Haldane of the Secret Service   (Houdini Picture Corp./FBO of America, 1923)
d: Harry Houdini.   6 reels.
Harry Houdini, Gladys Leslie, William Humphrey,. Richard Carlyle, Jane Jennings, Charles Fang, Myrtle Morse, Irving Brooks, Edward Bouldin.
Standard Houdini escape-artist stunts liven this tale of the son of a murdered detective hunting for his father's killers.

Half a Bride   (Paramount, 1928)
d: Gregory LaCava.   7 reels.
Esther Ralston, Gary Cooper, William Worthington, Freeman Wood, Mary Doran, Guy Oliver, Ray Gallagher.
The ill-named Patience rushes into a quickie marriage, then regrets it.

Half a Chance   (Pathé, 1920)
d: Robert Thornby.   6 reels.
Mahlon Hamilton, Mary McAllister, Lillian Rich, Sydney Ainsworth, Tom Maguire, Wilton Taylor, John Gough, William Lion West, Josephine Crowell.
A prisoner convicted of a crime he did not commit gets a second chance when he escapes the prison ship during a violent storm.

Half-a-Dollar Bill   (Graf Productions/Metro, 1924)
d: William S. Van Dyke.   6 reels.
Anna Q. Nilsson, William P. Carleton, Raymond Hatton, Mitchell Lewis, Alec B. Francis, George MacQuarrie, Frankie Darro, Rosa Gore.
A sea captain finds an abandoned baby boy with a half-dollar pinned to his clothing, together with a note from the baby's desperate mother.

Half a Rogue   (Universal, 1916)
d: Henry Otto.   5 reels.
King Baggot, Clara Beyers, Joseph Castellanos, Howard Crampton, Lettie Ford, Mathilde Brundage, Edna Hunter, Henry Otto.
Political foes try to smear a candidate's name, but the plot backfires.

Half an Hour   (Famous Players-Lasky/Paramount, 1920)
d: Harley Knoles.   5 reels.
Dorothy Dalton, Charles Richman, Albert Barrett, Frank Losee, H. Cooper Cliffe.
A woman whose husband's love for her is unrequited decides to elope with her former beau, and leaves behind a letter of explanation. But when she arrives to join her lover, she learns that he's been killed in a traffic accident. Now she's got to hurry home and get back that letter!

The Half-Breed   (Fine Arts/Triangle, 1916)
d: Allan Dwan.   5 reels.
Douglas Fairbanks, Alma Reubens, Sam DeGrasse, Tom Wilson, Frank Brownlee, Jewel Carmen, George Beranger.
Race prejudice informs this tale about a half-breed who is forced to live on the outskirts of town, in spite of the fact that his father is the town's sheriff.

The Half Breed   (Oliver Morosco Productions, 1922)
d: Charles A. Taylor.   6 reels.
Wheeler Oakman, Ann May, King Evers, Joseph Dowling, Lew Harvey, Herbert Pryor, Sidney DeGray, Nick DeRuiz, Leela Lane, Eugenia Gilbert, Carl Stockdale, Evelyn Selbie.
Spavinaw, a civilized half-breed, covets the daughter of a

judge.

The Half Million Bribe   (Columbia/Metro, 1916)
d: Edgar Jones.   5 reels.
Hamilton Revelle, Marguerite Snow, Carl Brickert, Fred C. Williams, Fred Heck, John Smiley, Ferdinand Tidmarsh, Carol Seymour, Diane D'Aubrey.
Though her husband Lawrence is unfaithful to her, Miriam gives up her entire fortune to bribe the prosecutor when her husband is accused of murder. The D.A. takes the money, but prosecutes forcefully and wins a conviction. Treachery? Not quite. There's method in the D.A.'s madness. After the real murderer confesses and Lawrence is set free, he and Miriam, now penniless, move to the slums. There they rekindle their love and Lawrence gives up his tomcat habits for good.   That's just what the D.A. predicted would happen—so he returns the money.

The Half-Way Girl   (First National, 1925)
d: John Francis Dillon.   8 reels.
Lloyd Hughes, Doris Kenyon, Hobart Bosworth, Tully Marshall, Sam Hardy, Charles Wellesley, Martha Madison, Sally Crute.
In Singapore, love blossoms between a police chief's son and Poppy, an actress stranded by her theatrical troupe.

Ham and Eggs at the Front   (Warner Bros., 1927)
d: Roy Del Ruth.   6 reels.
Tom Wilson, Charlie Conklin, Myrna Loy, William J. Irving, Noah Young.
A pair of doughboys in an all-Negro army regiment fall for a waitress while stationed in France.

The Hand at the Window   (Triangle, 1918)
d: Raymond Wells.   5 reels.
Joe King, Margery Wilson, Francis McDonald, Irene Hunt, Aaron Edwards, Arthur Millett.
Arrested by the police on the day of his wedding, a counterfeiter swears he will get his revenge on the arresting officer on *his* wedding day.

The Hand Invisible   (World Film Corp., 1919)
d: Harry O. Hoyt.   5 reels.
Montagu Love, Virginia Hammond, William Sorrelle, Marguerite Gale, Martha Mansfield, Kate Lester, George Le Guere, Muriel Ostriche.
When a businessman callously divorces his wife because she is unable to bear children, he triggers a chain of events that lead to his eventual heartbreak and demise.

The Hand of Peril   (Paragon Films, Inc./World Film Corp., 1916)
d: Maurice Tourneur.   5 reels.
House Peters, June Elvidge, Ralph Delmore, Doris Sawyer, Ray Pilcer.
Crime drama about Secret Service agents and counterfeiters.

The Hand That Rocks the Cradle   (Universal, 1917)
d: Lois Weber, Phillips Smalley.   6 reels.
Lois Weber, Phillips Smalley, Priscilla Dean, Evelyn Selbie, Wedgewood Nowell, Harry De More.
Pro-birth control film, this drama was banned in New York state.

Handcuffs or Kisses   (Selznick/Select, 1921)
d: George Archainbaud.   6 reels.
Elaine Hammerstein, Julia Swayne Gordon, Dorothy Chappell, Robert Ellis, Alison Skipworth, Florence Billings, Ronald Schabel, George Lessey, Ronald Colman.

Lois, an orphan, is shunted from orphanage to reform school to foster home. Still she grows in beauty and grace, and wins the love of a good man.

Handle With Care (Rockett Film Corp./Associated Exhibitors, 1921)
d: Philip E. Rosen. 5 reels.
Grace Darmond, Harry Myers, James Morrison, Landers Stevens, William Austin, William Courtleigh, Patsy Ruth Miller.
Romantic comedy about a girl with numerous beaus, all of whom swear they would die for her. She finally marries one of them, but after the honeymoon they have a silly spat. Now the pouting bride threatens to return to her former beaus and let them fight over her... but none of them will give her a tumble.

Hands Across the Border (R-C Pictures/FBO of America, 1926)
d: David Kirkland. 6 reels.
Fred Thomson, Tyrone Power, Bess Flowers, William Courtwright, Clarence Geldert, Tom Santschi.
Lots of border action in this tale of a horse breeder who rescues a captive señorita.

Hands Down (Universal, 1918)
d: Rupert Julian. 5 reels.
Monroe Salisbury, Ruth Clifford, W.H. Bainbridge, Rupert Julian, Rita Pickering, Al Filson.
Claim jumpers try to gun down a dead miner's surviving daughter.

The Hands of Nara (Samuel Zierler Photoplay Corp./Metro, 1922)
d: Harry Garson. 6 reels.
Clara Kimball Young, Count John Orloff, Elliott Dexter, Edwin Stevens, Vernon Steele, John Miltern, Margaret Loomis, Martha Mattox, Dulcie cooper, Ashley Cooper, Myrtle Stedman, Eugenie Besserer.
Nara, a Russian emigrée, is convinced that her hands have healing powers.

Hands Off (Fox, 1921)
d: George E. Marshall. 5 reels.
Tom Mix, Pauline Curley, Charles K. French, Lloyd Bacon, Frank Clark, Sid Jordan, William McCormick, Virginia Warwick, J. Webster Dill, Marvin Loback.
Tex, a ranch hand, rescues two sisters from being mauled by beasts, one of them the two-legged variety.

Hands Off (Universal, 1927)
d: Ernst Laemmle. 5 reels.
Fred Humes, Helen Foster, George Connors, Nelson McDowell, Bruce Gordon, William Dyer, William Ellingford, Bert Apling.
Out West, a drifter promises a dying prospector he'll take care of his young daughter.

Hands Up! (Fine Arts/Triangle, 1917)
d: Tod Browning, Wilfred Lucas. 5 reels.
Wilfred Lucas, Colleen Moore, Monte Blue, Beatrice Van, Rhea Haynes, Bert Woodruff, Kate Toncray.
Western drama about a train robbery and the romance that springs up between one of the outlaws and the daughter of the railroad company's president.

Hands Up! (Famous Players-Lasky/Paramount, 1926)
d: Clarence Badger. 6 reels.
Raymond Griffith, Marion Nixon, Virginia Lee Corbin,
Montagu Love, Mack Swain, George Billings.
Hilarious Civil War comedy, probably Griffith's best film. Two secret agents—one from the South, one from the North—race to a Nevada gold mine whose riches could shift the balance of power in the war. Along the way, the Southern spy falls in love with two sisters, and they with him. He wants to marry both girls, an insoluble dilemma—until a stranger from Utah provides him with a workable, if unconventional, solution.

The Handsome Brute (Columbia, 1925)
d: Robert Eddy. 5 reels.
William Fairbanks, Lee Shumway, Virginia Lee Corbin, Robert Bolder, J.J. Bryson, Daniel Belmont.
A cop facing suspension redeems himself by unmasking a clever crook.

Hangman's House (Fox, 1928)
d: John Ford. 7 reels.
June Collyer, Larry Kent, Hobart Bosworth, Baron O'Brien, Earle Fox, Victor McLaglen.
In Ireland, a retired judge who sent many people to the gallows is now near death himself. To please her dying father, the judge's daughter agrees to marry a man she does not love.

Happiness (Triangle, 1917)
d: Reginald Barker. 5 reels.
Enid Bennett, Charles Gunn, Thelma Salter, Andrew Arbuckle, Gertrude Claire, Adele Belgrade, Jack Gilbert.
Doris, a college girl, is thought to be a snob, but she's merely shy. Though ostracized by other coeds, she develops a romance with a nice guy who's working his way through school.

Happiness (Metro, 1924)
d: King Vidor. 8 reels.
Laurette Taylor, Pat O'Malley, Hedda Hopper, Cyril Chadwick, Edith Yorke, Patterson Dial, Joan Standing, Lawrence Grant, Charlotte Mineau.
Though she is penniless and works as a shopgirl, Jenny forges an amiable relationship with two members of elite society.

Happiness a la Mode (Select, 1919)
d: Walter Edwards. 5 reels.
Harrison Ford, Constance Talmadge, Betty Schade, Myrtle Richelle, Paul Weigel, Thomas D. Persse, A. Fremont.
Newlyweds love each other deeply, but a misunderstanding drives a wedge between them. They agree to divorce, but when the wife learns there's another woman in the picture, she redoubles her efforts to keep her man—and succeeds.

Happiness Ahead (First National, 1928)
d: William A. Seiter. 8 reels.
Colleen Moore, Edmund Lowe, Charles Sellon, Edythe Chapman, Carlos Durand, Lilyan Tashman, Robert Elliott, Diane Ellis.
Stewart, a crooked gambler, is on the lam when he meets and falls in love with Mary, daughter of a local shopkeeper.

Happy Though Married (T.H. Ince/Famous Players-Lasky/Paramount, 1919)
d: Fred Niblo. 5 reels.
Enid Bennett, Philo McCullough, Douglas MacLean, Vola Vale, Hallam Cooley, Lydia Yeamans Titus, Charles K. French, Norine Johnson.
Misunderstandings and mistaken identity trigger the green-eyed monster, as a newlywed begins to doubt her new

husband's fidelity.

The Happy Warrior (Vitagraph, 1925)
d: J. Stuart Blackton. 8 reels.
Malcolm McGregor, Alice Calhoun, Anders Randolf, Olive Borden, Gardner James, Otto Matieson, Wilfred North, Eulalie Jensen, Andrée Tourneur, Jack Herrick, Philippe DeLacy, Bobby Gordon.
Ralph and Rollo are good friends despite the fact that Rollo is a member of the British nobility and Ralph is a commoner. On the day Rollo is to marry his true love, Ralph learns from a relative that he, and not Rollo, is the true heir to the title.

Hard Boiled (Thomas H. Ince/Paramount, 1919)
d: Victor L. Schertzinger. 5 reels.
Dorothy Dalton, C.W. Mason, Billy Courtwright, Gertrude Claire, Walter Hiers, Nona Thomas.
Stranded in a tiny Arizona town, a Broadway diva finds she likes small-town living.

Hard Boiled (Fox, 1926)
d: J.G. Blystone. 6 reels.
Tom Mix, Helene Chadwick, William Lawrence, Charles Conklin, Emily fitzroy, Phyllis Haver, Dan Mason, Walter "Spec" O'Donnell, Ethel Grey Terry, Edward Sturgis, Eddie Boland.
Comedy western for Mix, who plays Tom, a scion of wealth sent west to help operate a health resort. When Tom surmises that the out-of-town guests crave some "real western action," he supplies it—fake Indian raids, stagecoach chases, even a daring robbery of the hotel safe. But some of his "actors" get carried away and hit the safe for real, and Tom is duty-bound to round them up and bring them to justice, bringing even more cheers from his clueless guests.

Hard Boiled Haggerty (First National, 1927)
d: Charles J. Brabin. 8 reels.
Milton Sills, Molly O'Day, Mitchell Lewis, Arthur Stone, George Fawcett, Yola D'Avril.
High-flying aviator Haggerty is a hero in World War I, but he hasn't a clue when it comes to down-to-earth dealings with the opposite sex.
Miss O'Day plays twin sisters who confuse and delight Haggerty (Sills).

Hard Fists (Universal, 1927)
d: William Wyler. 5 reels.
Art Acord, Louise Lorraine, Lee Holmes, Albert J. Smith.
Out West, a sinister colonel enlists a ranch hand in illegal schemes.

The Hard Rock Breed (Triangle, 1918)
d: Raymond Wells. 5 reels.
Jack Livingston, Margery Wilson, Jack Curtis, J. Barney Sherry, Marion Skinner, Lee Phelps, George Chase, Louis Durham, Thornton Edwards, Aaron Edwards.
A ne'er-do-well rich boy is sent to his dad's rock quarries, where he must fight to earn respect.

Hardboiled (FBO Pictures, 1929)
d: George Arthur. 7 reels.
Sally O'Neil, Donald Reed, Lilyan Tashman, Bob Sinclair, Ole M. Ness, Tom O'Grady.
Kyle, playboy son of a wealthy family, meets and marries Teena, a Broadway showgirl. Soon after the honeymoon, however, Kyle's disgusted father cuts off his income and the newlyweds learn they must live by honest toil. After the son has made good, however, Papa relents.

Hardboiled Rose (Warner Bros., 1929)
d: F. Harmon Weight. 6 reels. (Music, sound effects, part talkie.)
Myrna Loy, William Collier Jr., John Miljan, Gladys Brockwell, Lucy Beaumont, Ralph Emerson, Edward Martindel, Otto Hoffman, Floyd Shackelford.
Rose, daughter of a banker who has committed suicide rather than admit to purloining bank securities, decides to clear the family name by retrieving those securities by vamping the gambler who swindled her Pa in the first place.

Harold Teen (First National, 1928)
d: Mervyn LeRoy. 8 reels.
Arthur Lake, Alice White, Hedda Hopper, Mary Brian, Lucien Littlefield, Jack Duffy, Jack Egan, Ben Hall, William Bakewell, Lincoln Stedman, Fred A. Kelsey, Jane Keckley, Edward Brady, Virginia Sale.
Comedy based on the popular comic strip *Harold Teen*, about a farm boy who moves to the city and becomes a high school football star.

A Harp in Hock (DeMille Pictures/Pathé, 1927)
d: Renaud Hoffman. 6 reels.
Rudolph Schildkraut, Junior Coghlan, May Robson, Bessie Love, Louis Natheaux, Elsie Bartlett, Mrs. Charles Mack, Joseph Striker, Adele Watson, Lillian Harmen, Clarence Burton.
In New York, a Jewish pawnbroker adopts the Irish son of a dying scrubwoman.

The Harvest of Hate (Universal, 1929)
d: Henry MacRae. 5 reels.
Jack Perrin, Helen Foster, Tom London.
Out West, a cowboy and his valiant horse rescue a damsel from a crooked carnival owner.

The Harvester (R-C Pictures/FBO of America, 1927)
d: Leo Meehan. 8 reels.
Orville Caldwell, Natalie Kingston, Will R. Walling, Jay Hunt, Lola Todd, Edward Hern, Fanny Midgley.
Langston, a harvester of medicinal plants, comes across a young woman who accuses him of "stealing" the herbs from the forest. They will meet again, and their initial animosity is transformed into love and marriage.

Has the World Gone Mad! (Daniel Carson Goodman Corp./Equity, 1923)
d: J. Searle Dawley. 7 reels.
Robert Edeson, Hedda Hopper, Vincent Coleman, Mary Alden, Charles Richman, Elinor Fair, Lyda Lola.
Propriety seems to collapse when an attractive widow decides to have an affair with her son's future father-in-law.

Hashimura Togo (Lasky Feature Plays/Paramount, 1917)
d: William C. DeMille. 5 reels.
Sessue Hayakawa, Florence Vidor, Mabel Van Buren, Walter Long, Tom Forman, Raymond Hatton, Ernest Joy, Margaret Loomis, Horin Konishi.
A Japanese butler saves his employer's family from financial ruin.

Hate (Metro, 1922)
d: J. Searle Dawley. 7 reels.
Alice Lake, Conrad Nagel, Harry Northrup, Charles Clary, John Ince.
Two gamblers are crazy in love with a chorus girl—so much so, that one of them plans his own suicide and sees that his rival is blamed for his murder.

The Hater of Men (Triangle, 1917)
d: Charles Miller. 5 reels.
Bessie Barriscale, Charles K. French, Jack Gilbert.
Deeply affected by the sordid details of a divorce case she is covering, a female reporter decides to break off her own engagement.

The Haunted Bedroom (Thomas H. Ince/Paramount, 1919)
d: Fred Niblo. 5 reels.
Enid Bennett, Dorcas Matthews, Jack Nelson, William Conklin, Harry Archer, Otto Hoffman, Joseph Anthony.
A New York reporter is sent to the South to investigate a reportedly haunted house.

The Haunted House (First National/Warner Bros., 1928)
d: Benjamin Christensen. 7 reels. (Music, sound effects, part talkie.)
Chester Conklin, Thelma Todd, Larry Kent, Edmund Breese, Barbara Bedford, Flora Finch, Montagu Love, Sidney Bracy, Barbara Bedford, Flora Finch, William V. Mong.
An aging millionaire gives each of his four presumed heirs a sealed envelope, not to be opened until after his death. All of them disobey the old man's instructions and open their envelopes right away. What they read sets all four off on a treasure hunt in an old haunted house "occupied" by ghosts, goblins, and ghouls. That is,until the millionaire reappears, informs the unlucky quartet that the otherworldly creatures were only actors, and he was merely putting the heirs to the test: a test which, of course, they all flunk.

The Haunted Manor (Gaumont Co./Mutual, 1916)
d: Edwin Middleton. 5 reels.
Earl Schenck, Iva Sheppard, Mathilde Baring, Gertrude Robinson, Olive Trevor, Henry W. Pemberton, William H. Hopkins, Robert Klugston, Joseph Levering, Mary G. Davis.
Convinced that her scarlet past will make her husband despise her if he knew of it, a former kept woman decides to disappear, as if in an accident.

The Haunted Pajamas (Yorke Film Corp./Metro, 1917)
d: Fred J. Balshofer. 5 reels.
Harold Lockwood, Carmel Myers, Edward Sedgwick, Lester Cuneo, Paul Willis, Harry de Roy, Helen Ware, William DeVaull, Gordo Kino.
Comedic farce about a pair of enchanted pajamas that transform the wearer into someone else entirely.

The Haunted Range (Davis Distributing Division, 1926)
d: Paul Hurst. 5 reels.
Ken Maynard, Alma Rayford, Harry Moody, Al Hallett, Fred Burns, Bob Williamson.
Out West, a cowpoke uncovers a phony "haunted ranch" ploy that's only a coverup for cattle rustling.

The Haunted Ship (Tiffany-Stahl Productions, 1927)
d: Forrest K. Sheldon. 5 reels.
Dorothy Sebastian, Montagu Love, Tom Santschi, Ray Hallor, Pat Harmon, Alice Lake, Bud Duncan, Blue Washington, Sojin, Andrée Tourneur, William Lowery.
Gant, a sea captain, sets his wife and son adrift on a small boat because he believes she has been unfaithful and that the boy is the son of his first mate. This cruelty comes back to haunt Gant and his ship.

Haunting Shadows (Jesse D. Hampton Productions/Robertson-Cole, 1920)
d: Henry King. 5 reels.
H.B. Warner, Edward Peil, Charles Hill, Frank Lanning, Florence Oberle, Marguerite Livingston, Harry Kendall, Patricia Fox, Charles French.
In order to gain an inheritance, a young man is forced to live in his grandfather's supposedly haunted mansion for one year.

The Havoc (Essanay, 1916)
d: Arthur Berthelet. 5 reels.
Gladys Hanson, Lewis Stone, Bryant Washburn.
After a businessman marries his stenographer, he invites an associate to live with them, although the arrangement could lead to the "eternal triangle." Sure enough, it does.

Havoc (Fox, 1925)
d: Rowland V. Lee. 9 reels.
Madge Bellamy, George O'Brien, Walter McGrail, Eulalie Jensen, Margaret Livingston, Leslie Fenton, David Butler, Harvey Clark, Wade Boteler, Edythe Chapman, Bertram Grassby.
During World War I, fellow officers are rivals for the love of a girl who's no good for either of them.

The Hawk (Vitagraph, 1917)
d: Paul Scardon. 5 reels.
Earle Williams, Ethel Grey Terry, Denton Vane, Julia Swayne Gordon, Mario Majerone, Katherine Lewis.
A master gambler known as "the Hawk" wins regularly at the roulette tables, but he's less lucky in love.

The Hawk's Nest (First National, 1928)
d: Benjamin Christensen. 8 reels.
Milton Sills, Montagu Love, Mitchell Lewis, Doris Kenyon, Stuart Holmes, Sojin Kamamura.
In San Francisco's Chinatown, a cafe owner known as "the Hawk" undergoes plastic surgery to transform his appearance into that of a gangster.

Hawthorne of the U.S.A. (Famous Players-Lasky/Paramount, 1919)
d: James Cruze. 5 reels.
Wallace Reid, Harrison Ford, Lila Lee, Tully Marshall, Charles Ogle, Edwin Stevens, Clarence Burton, Theodore Roberts, Ruth Rennick, Robert Brower, Frank Bonner.
Vacationing Americans win big in Monte Carlo, then take part in a revolution in a small European kingdom.

Hay Foot, Straw Foot (Thomas H. Ince/Paramount, 1919)
d: Jerome Storm. 5 reels.
Charles Ray, Doris Lee, William Conklin, Spottiswoode Aitken, J.P. Lockney.
During World War I, a young recruit falls in love with a dancer performing in a show to boost the troops' morale.

Hazardous Valley (Ellbee Pictures, 1927)
d: Alvin J. Neitz. 6 reels.
Vincent Brownell, Virginia Brown Faire, Sheldon Lewis, Pat Harmon, David Torrence, Andrew Arbuckle, Burr McIntosh.
A timber baron's son must brave the odds to see that an important shipment of logs is delivered on time.

He Comes Up Smiling (Fairbanks/Paramount, 1918)
d: Allan Dwan. 5 reels.
Douglas Fairbanks, Herbert Standing, Marjorie Daw, Frank Campeau, Bull Montana, Albert McQuarrie, Kathleen Kirkham, Jay Dwiggins, Billy Elmer.
A cheerful bank clerk decides he prefers life as a hobo. His indigence doesn't last long, though. When his clothes are stolen during a swim, he steps easily into the fine threads of a New York swell, and eventually charms his way to the top.

He Fell in Love With His Wife (Bosworth,

Inc./Paramount, 1916)
d: William D. Taylor. 5 reels.
Florence Rockwell, Forrest Stanley, Page Peters, Lydia Yeamans Titus, Howard Davis.
A marriage of convenience slowly turns into the real thing.

He Who Gets Slapped (MGM, 1924)
d: Victor Seastrom. 7 reels.
Norma Shearer, Lon Chaney, John Gilbert, Tully Marshall, Marc MacDermott, Ford Sterling, Paulette Duval, Harvey Clark, Ruth King, Clyde Cook.
After losing his wife to another man, a scientist begins a new career as a circus clown in an effort to forget his sorrow. Alas, even in the circus the former scientist is rejected once again, this time by Consuelo, a bareback rider he has grown to love.

He Who Laughs Last (Bud Barsky Corp., 1925)
d: Jack Nelson. 5 reels.
Kenneth McDonald, Margaret Cloud, David Torrence, Gino Corrado, Harry Northrup.
Jim Taylor is accused of robbery and murder—but he's innocent, and he'll prove it.

The Head Man (First National/Warner Bros., 1928)
d: Eddie Cline. 7 reels.
Charlie Murray, Lucien Littlefield, Loretta Young, Larry Kent, E.J. Ratcliffe, Irving Bacon, Harvey Clark, Sylvia Ashton, Dot Farley, Martha Mattox, Rosa Gore.
Rejected by the voters after being defamed by a political mob he refused to cozy up to, an ex-senator finds a new career as mayor of his town.

The Head of the Family (Gotham Productions/Lumas Film Corp., 1928)
d: Joseph C. Boyle. 7 reels.

William Russell, Mickey Bennett, Virginia Lee Corbin, Richard Walling, Alma Bennett, William Welsh, Aggie Herring
When a faithful but henpecked husband is told to go away for his health, he leaves his friend Eddie in charge of his family.   Eddie deals with the man's shrewish wife, coquettish daughter, and wastrel son and straightens them all out.

Head Over Heels (Goldwyn, 1922)
d: Victor L. Schertzinger, Paul Bern. 5 reels.
Mabel Normand, Hugh Thompson, Russ Powell, Raymond Hatton, Adolphe Menjou, Lilyan Tashman, Lionel Belmore.
Tina, an Italian acrobat, is talented but plain and unstylish. When she is signed to perform in the United States, a press agent arranges for this ugly duckling to turn into a glamorous swan.

Head Winds (Universal, 1925)
d: Herbert Blache. 6 reels.
House Peters, Patsy Ruth Miller, Richard Travers, Arthur Hoyt, William Austin.
When Peter, a yachtsman, learns that the girl he loves is planning to marry another man, he lures her aboard his yacht and then shanghais her.   Not the most romantic approach, perhaps, but in this case it works: The captain and his lady love are married aboard ship.

Headin' Home (Kessel & Baumann/Yankee Photo Corp., 1920)
d: Lawrence Windom. 5 reels.
George Herman "Babe" Ruth, Ruth Taylor, William Sheer,

Margaret Sedden, Frances Victory, James A. Marcus, George Halman, Ralph Harolds, Charles Hurt, George Halpin.
Somewhat fictional story about Babe Ruth's climb to fame as a New York Yankee.

Headin' North (Arrow Film Corp., 1921)
d: Charles Bartlett. 5 reels.
Pete Morrison, Jack Walters, Gladys Cooper, Dorothy Dickson, William Dills, Barney Furey, Will Franks.
Out West, a broken-hearted swain plots revenge against the careless stagecoach driver who accidentally killed his sweetheart.

Headin' South (Fairbanks/Paramount, 1918)
d: Arthur Rosson. 5 reels.
Douglas Fairbanks, Frank Campeau, Katherine MacDonald, James Mason, Johnny Judd, Tommy Grimes, Art Acord, Hoot Gibson, Ed Burns.
In a small town on the Mexican border, two outlaws fall in love with a rancher's daughter.

Headin' Through (Maloford Productions/Photo Drama Co. 1924)
d: Leo D. Maloney. 5 reels.
Leo D. Maloney, Josephine Hill, Horace Carpenter, Robert Williamson, Jim Corey, Chet Ryan, Leonard Clapham.
Baxter, a man who is wanted by the law, lives quietly but manages to fall in love with Rhoda, the rancher's daughter. When one of his rivals for her hand threatens to expose Baxter's past, Rhoda investigates and learns that he is covering for his brother-in-law, the real culprit.

Headin' West (Universal, 1922)
d: William J. Craft. 5 reels.
Hoot Gibson, Gertrude Short, Charles LeMoyne, Jim Corey, Leo White, Louise Lorraine, George A. Williams, Frank Whitson, Mark Fenton.
Perkins, a war veteran, heads west. In his new surroundings, he learns that a crooked foreman is plotting to steal the ranch from its absentee owner, who has never been seen. After Perkins mobilizes the good people in town, he routs the foreman and his gang, claims a pretty neighbor gal for his wife, and reveals that he himself is the ranch's true owner, an absentee no longer.

Heading' Westward (El Dorado Productions/Syndicate Pictures, 1928)
d: J.P. McGowan. 5 reels.
Bob Custer, Mary Mayberry, John Lowell, J.P. McGowan, Charles Whittaker, Mack V. Wright, Cliff Lyons, Dorothy Vernon.
Out West, Mary, a rancher's daughter, leads a team of cowpokes against cattle rustlers.

The Headless Horseman (Sleepy Hollow Corp./W.W. Hodkinson Corp., 1922)
d: Edward Venturini. 7 reels.
Will Rogers, Lois Meredith, Ben Hendricks Jr., Mary Foy, Charles Graham.
Dramedy re-working of Washington Irving's *The Legend of Sleepy Hollow*, with Will Rogers as Ichabod Crane.

Headlines (St. Regis Productions/Associated Exhibitors, 1925)
d: E.H. Griffith. 6 reels.
Alice Joyce, Malcolm McGregor, Virginia Lee Corbin, Harry T. Morey, Ruby Blaine, Elliott Nugent.
Phyllis, a newspaper reporter with a steady fella, reveals that she's the mother of a teenage girl.

Heads Up (Harry Garson Productions/FBO of America, 1925)
d: Harry Garson. 6 reels.
Maurice B. Flynn, Kathleen Myers, Kalla Pasha, Jean Perry, Milton Ross, Harry McCoy, Hazel Rogers, Ray Ripley, Robert Cautier, Raymond Turner.
Action comedy about a usually dull chap who yearns for adventure, and gets it in spades. He's assigned to deliver a message to a South American president, but when he arrives he finds that the country is in the midst of a revolution and the president and his daughter have been taken prisoners. It's Our Hero's job to stop the revolution, restore the presidency, and marry El Presidente's daughter... though not necessarily in that order.

Heart and Soul (Fox, 1917)
d: J. Gordon Edwards. 5 reels.
Theda Bara, Harry Hilliard, Glen White, Claire Whitney, Walter Law, Edwin Holt, John Webb Dillon, Alice Gale, Kittens Reichert, Margaret Laird.
On a plantation in Puerto Rico, two sisters fall in love with the same man.

The Heart Bandit (Metro, 1924)
d: Oscar Apfel. 5 reels.
Viola Dana, Milton Sills, Gertrude Claire, Wallace MacDonald, Bertram Grassby, DeWitt Jennings, Nelson McDowell, Mathew Betz, Edward Wade.
"Angel Face Molly," a small-time crook, is rehabilitated by a woman whose own son is involved with miscreants.

The Heart Buster (Fox, 1924)
d: Jack Conway. 5 reels.
Tom Mix, Esther Ralston, Cyril Chadwick, William Courtwright, Frank Currier, Tom Wilson.
Tod, a love-struck young fellow, loses his girlfriend to another man, and wedding plans are made. Tod knows his rival is already married... but can he prove it in time?

The Heart Line (Leah Baird Productions/Pathé, 1921)
d: Frederick A. Thompson. 6 reels.
Leah Baird, Jerome Patrick, Frederick Vroom, Ruth Sinclair, Ivor McFadden, Philip Sleeman, Mrs. Charles Craig, Martin Best, Ben Alexander.
In San Francisco, a businessman consults a phony medium, looking for his former foster child.

Heart o' the Hills (First National, 1919)
d: Sidney Franklin. 6 reels.
Mary Pickford, Harold Goodwin, Sam De Grasse, Claire McDowell, Fred W. Huntley, Jack Gilbert, William Bainbridge, Betty Bouton, Allan Sears, Henry J. Herbert, Fred Warren.
Miss Pickford plays a feisty 13-year-old who has a way with guns.

The Heart of a Child (Metro, 1920)
d: Ray C. Smallwood. 6 reels.
Nazimova, Charles Bryant, Ray Thompson, Nell Newman, Victor Potel, Eugene Klum, Claire Du Brey, Jane Sterling, John Steppling, William J. Irving, Myrtle Rishell, Joseph Kilgour.
In London, a girl rises from poverty to become a graceful model, then a star on the stage.

The Heart of a Follies Girl (First National, 1928)
d: Richard A. Rowland. 7 reels.
Billie Dove, Larry Kent, Lowell Sherman, Clarissa Selwynne, Mildred Harris.
Derek falls head over heels in love with a Follies dancer. Trouble is, she's his boss' girlfriend.

The Heart of a Girl (World Film Corp., 1918)
d: John G. Adolfi. 5 reels.
Barbara Castleton, Irving Cummings, Charles Wellesley, Kate Lester, Ricca Allen, W.T. Carleton, Gladys Valerie, Florence Coventry, Clay Clement Jr., Anthony Byrd, Inez Shannon.
Betty Lansing loves a congressman, and in this light-hearted drama she helps her love win his party's nomination for governor.

The Heart of a Hero (World Film Corp., 1916)
d: Emile Chautard. 6 reels.
Robert Warwick, Gail Kane, Alec B. Francis, George McQuarrie, Clifford Gray, Henry West, Charles Jackson, Clara Whipple, Mildred Havens.
Historical drama centering on Revolutionary War hero Nathan Hale.

The Heart of a Lion (Fox, 1917)
d: Frank Lloyd. 5 reels.
William Farnum, Mary Martin, William Courtleigh Jr., Wanda Petit, Walter Law, Marc Robbins, Rita Bori.
Two brothers love the same girl, but it turns out she isn't worthy of either of them.

Heart of a Siren (Associated Pictures/First National, 1925)
d: Phil Rosen. 7 reels.
Barbara LaMarr, Conway Tearle, Harry Morey, Paul Doucet, Ben Finney, Florence Auer, Ida Darling, William Ricciardi, Clifton Webb, Florence Billings, Mike Rayle, Katherine Sullivan.
In France, a beautiful vamp sets out to seduce an Englishman who has previously proved impervious to her charms.

The Heart of a Woman (Peerless Pictures Co., 1920)
d: Jack Pratt. 5 reels.
Mignon Anderson, Jack Richardson, George Fisher, Clara Horton, Pat O'Malley, Francis Brainard.
Tear-jerker that asks: Should a wife stay with her husband although he is abusive and a bad father to their daughter?

The Heart of Broadway (Duke Worne Productions/Rayart, 1928)
d: Duke Worne. 6 reels.
Pauline Garon, Bobby Agnew, Wheeler Oakman, Oscar Apfel, Duke Lee.
Roberta, a country girl, hits the big town and becomes a cabaret dancer.

The Heart of Ezra Greer (Thanhouser/Pathé, 1917)
d: Emile Chautard. 5 reels.
Frederick Warde, Leila Frost, George Forth, Lillian Mueller, Gerald Badgley, Carey Hastings, Thomas A. Curran, Helen Badgley.
Mary, a college girl and the daughter of Ezra, a faithful old butler, meets a wealthy student and falls in love with him. But he forsakes her and leaves her pregnant. After the baby is born, Mary deposits the child on the doorstep of its father's mansion, and leaves. What she does not know is that her father is that mansion's new butler, and it falls to Ezra to try and locate the infant's mother, not knowing she is his own daughter.

Heart of Gold (World Film Corp., 1919)
d: Travers Vale. 5 reels.

Louise Huff, Grace Barton, Johnny Hines, Marion Barney, Robert Fischer, Anthony Merlo, William Williams, Peggy Vaughan, Louis Rheinhardt.

"Heart of Gold" is the name of a dress design created by a poor seamstress in support of the war effort in WWI.

The Heart of Humanity (Universal, 1919)
d: Allen Holubar. 9 reels.
Dorothy Phillips, Erich von Stroheim, William Stowell, Margaret Mann, Robert Anderson, Frank Braidwood, George Hackathorne, Walt Whitman.
A World War I pilot saves his bride from an insufferable cad.

The Heart of Jennifer (Famous Players/Paramount, 1915)
d: James Kirkwood. 5 reels.
Hazel Dawn, James Kirkwood, Irene Howley, Russell Bassett, Harry Brown.
Amid numerous complications, a lumber camp foreman weds Jennifer, a girl from the city.

The Heart of Lincoln (New Era Productions/Anchor Film Distributors, 1922)
d: Francis Ford. 5 reels.
Francis Ford, Grace Cunard, Ella Hall, William Quinn, Elmer Morrow, Lew Short.
During the Civil War, Abraham Lincoln shows clemency toward a young Union soldier accused of treason for letting a Confederate prisoner (his sweetheart's brother) escape.

The Heart of Maryland (Tiffany Film Corp./Metro, 1915)
d: Herbert Brenon. 6 reels.
Mrs. Leslie Carter, William E. Shay, J. Farrell MacDonald, Matt Snyder, Raymond Russell, Marcia Moore, Vivian Reed, Doris Baker, Herbert Brenon, Joe Hazelton, Bert Hadley.
Civil War drama, with families torn by divided loyalties.

The Heart of Maryland (Vitagraph, 1921)
d: Tom Terriss. 6 reels.
Catherine Calvert, Crane Wilbur, William Collier Jr., Warner Richmond, Bernard Siegel, Henry Hallam, Victoria White, Marguerite Sanchez, Jane Jennings.
Remake of the Tiffany Film Corp.'s *The Heart of Maryland*, released in 1915. Warner Bros. Remade the film again in 1927. (See below.)

The Heart of Maryland (Warner Bros., 1927)
d: Lloyd Bacon. 6 reels.
Dolores Costello, Jason Robards, Myrna Loy, Warner Richmond, Charles Bull, Helene Costello.
During the American Civil War, a Northern man loves a Southern girl.
Second remake of the 1915 Tiffany Film Corp. film *The Heart of Maryland*.

The Heart of Nora Flynn (Lasky Feature Plays/Paramount, 1916)
d: Cecil B. DeMille. 5 reels.
Marie Doro, Elliott Dexter, Ernest Joy, Lola May, Charles West, Billy Jacobs, Peggy George.
To save the marriage of her employers, Nora, the Stones' family maid, pretends that the man Mrs. Stone is seeing is really her own lover.

The Heart of Paula (Pallas Pictures/Paramount, 1916)
d: William Taylor, Julia Crawford Ivers. 5 reels.
Lenore Ulrich, Velma Lefler, Jack Livingstone, Forrest Stanley, Howard Davies, Herbert Standing.
In Mexico, a bandit leader kidnaps an American mining engineer who has captured the heart of Paula, the woman the bandit leader loves.

The Heart of Rachael (Paralta Plays, Inc./General Film, 1918)
d: Howard Hickman. 5 reels.
Bessie Barriscale, Herschel Mayall, Ella Hall, Herbert Heyes, Gloria Hope, Ben Alexander, Edward Coxen, Mary Jane Irving.
Rachael falls in love twice, marries twice, and is neglected twice.

The Heart of Romance (Fox, 1918)
d: Harry Millarde. 5 reels.
June Caprice, Bernard Thornton, George Bunny, Joseph Kilgour, Lilian Page, Jack Martin, Jack Raymond.
A judge is convinced that his ward's boyfriend is interested only in her money, so he announces (falsely) that he is bankrupt. Imagine his delighted surprise when the boyfriend is his ward's only friend who sticks by her in this "crisis!"

The Heart of Salome (Fox, 1927)
d: Victor Schertzinger. 6 reels.
Alma Rubens, Walter Pidgeon, Holmes Herbert, Robert Agnew, Erin LaBissoniere, Walter Dugan, Barry Norton, Virginia Madison.
Tale of a modern Salome, swearing revenge on the man who scorned her.

The Heart of Texas Ryan (Selig, 1916)
d: E.A. Martin. 5 reels.
Tom Mix, George Fawcett, Bessie Eyton, Frank Campeau, William Rhino, Charles Gerrard, Goldie Colwell.
Texas Ryan is the Eastern-educated daughter of a Western rancher, and she's an eyeful who captures the heart of a cowpoke (played by Mix).

The Heart of the Blue Ridge (World Film Corp., 1915)
d: James Young. 5 reels.
Clara Kimball Young, Chester Barnett, Robert Cummings, Edwin L. Hollywood.
In Tennessee's Blue Ridge mountains, a farmer and a moonshiner scrap over the heart of a pretty mountain girl.

The Heart of the Hills (Thomas A. Edison, Inc., 1916)
d: Richard Ridgely. 5 reels.
Mabel Trunnelle, Conway Tearle, Bigelow Cooper, Ray McKee, Marie LaCorio, Herbert Prior, George Wright, Robert Conness, Edith Strickland, Crawford Kent, Charles Sutton.
Kidnapped in India by a group of revolutionaries, an English girl is brainwashed by her captors and sent home to recover a precious ruby from her own father.

Heart of the Sunset (Rex Beach/Goldwyn, 1918)
d: Frank Powell. 7 reels.
Anna Q. Nilsson, Herbert Heyes, Robert Taber, E.L. Fernandez, Jane Miller, William Frederic, Irene Boyle.
A Texas ranger falls for a cattle rancher's widow.

Heart of the Wilds (Famous Players-Lasky/Paramount, 1918)
d: Marshall Neilan. 5 reels.
Thomas Meighan, Elsie Ferguson, Joseph Smiley, Matt Moore, Escamilo Fernandez, Sidney D'Albrook.
In the Canadian Northwest, a tavern keeper and his daughter get involved with a Mountie sergeant who's trying to crack a baffling case.

The Heart of the Yukon (H.C. Weaver Productions/Pathé,

1927)
d: W.S. Van Dyke. 7 reels.
John Bowers, Anne Cornwall, Edward Hearn, Frank Campeau, Russell Simpson, George Jeske.
Anita, an heiress, travels to Alaska to find her long-lost father.

The Heart of Twenty (Brentwood Film Corp., 1920)
d: Henry Kolker. 5 reels.
ZaSu Pitts, Jack Pratt, Percy Challenger, Hugh Saxon, Tom Gallery, Aileen Manning, Billie Lind, Verne Winter.
When a suspected car thief announces he is running for mayor, Katie Abbott urges her honest friend, Mr. Higginbotham, to oppose him.

The Heart of Wetona (Norma Talmadge Film Corp./Select Pictures, 1919)
d: Sidney A. Franklin. 6 reels.
Norma Talmadge, Fred Huntley, Thomas Meighan, Gladden James, Fred Turner, Princess Uwane Yea, Charles Edler, White Eagle, Black Wolf, Black Lizard.
A beautiful half-breed is betrayed by her white lover and rebounds into the arms of a handsome Government agent. He loves her and forgives her her sins, and her Indian chief father bestows his blessing on their union.

The Heart of Youth (Famous Players-Lasky/Paramount, 1919)
d: Robert G. Vignola. 5 reels.
Lila Lee, Tom Forman, Buster Irving, Charles Ogle, Fanny Midgley, Guy Oliver, Lydia Knott, Fay Lemport, Gertrude Short, Cameron Coffey, Vera Sisson, Lewis Sargent.
Country lovers have to deal with a fued between their families.

The Heart Raider (Famous Players-Lasky/Paramount, 1923)
d: Wesley Ruggles. 6 reels.
Agnes Ayres, Mahlon Hamilton, Charles Ruggles, Frazer Coulter, Marie Burke, Charles Riegal.
Muriel's a jazz baby, and she drives too fast. Her father finally takes out an insurance policy to cover any damages she may cause, leading the insurance company to intervene in Muriel's life and get her married off.

The Heart Specialist (Realart Pictures/Paramount, 1922)
d: Frank Urson. 5 reels.
Mary Miles Minter, Allan Forrest, Roy Atwell, Jack Matheis, Noah Beery, James Neill, Carmen Phillips.
Rosalie, a newspaper reporter, falls in love with Bob, the subject of one of her investigations.

Heart Strings (Universal, 1917)
d: Allan Holubar. 5 reels.
Allan Holubar, Francelia Billington, Paul Byron, Maude George, Irene Hunt, Charles Cummings, Virginia Cobin, Zoe Rae.
An adoptive daughter discovers she is love with the doctor who adopted her and has looked over her since childhood.

Heart Strings (Fox, 1920)
d: J. Gordon Edwards. 6 reels.
William Farnum, Gladys Coburn, Betty Hilburn, Paul Cazeneuve, Robert Cain, Rowland G. Edwards, Kate Blancke.
When a girl is seduced by a scoundrel, her violinist brother puts his career on hold so that he can take of her.

The Heart Thief (Metropolitan Pictures Corp. of California, 1927)
d: Nils Olaf Chrisander. 6 reels.
Joseph Schildkraut, Lya DePutti, Robert Edeson, Charles Gerrard, Eulalie Jensen, George Reehm, William Bakewell.
In Budapest, a war veteran loves a girl but considers himself unworthy of her. Later he is hired by two conspirators to compromise a young woman they consider an obstacle to their greedy ambitions, and the war veteran is delighted to discover that his "mark" is none other than the girl he loves.

Heart to Heart (First National, 1928)
d: William Beaudine. 7 reels.
Lloyd Hughes, Mary Astor, Louise Fazenda, Lucien Littlefield, Thelma Todd, Ray McKee, Eileen Manning, Virginia Gray.
Romantic comedy about an American-born princess of Italy who, newly widowed, returns to her home town and finds that her old sweetheart still loves her.

A Heart to Let (Realart Pictures Co., 1921)
d: Edward Dillon. 5 reels.
Harrison Ford, Justine Johnstone, Marcia Harris, Thomas Carr, Elizabeth Garrison, Winifred Bryson, Claude Cooper, James Harrison.
After putting up her newly-inherited mansion for rent, young Agatha finds love with one of her prospective tenants.

Heart Trouble (First National/Warner Bros., 1928)
d: Harry Langdon. 6 reels.
Harry Langdon, Doris Dawson, Madge Hunt, Lionel Belmore, Bud Jamieson, Mark Hamilton, Nelson McDowell.
During World War I, an American of German ancestry tries to enlist in the U.S. Army to prove to his girlfriend that he is 100 per cent American. He is rejected, however, for a variety of medical reasons, none of them serious. In due course, this eager-beaver American chap becomes a hero by foiling German spies operating off the U.S. coast.

Hearts Aflame (Louis B. Mayer Productions/Metro, 1923)
d: Reginald Barker. 9 reels.
Frank Keenan, Anna Q. Nilsson, Craig Ward, Richard Headrick, Russell Simpson, Richard Tucker, Stanton Heck, Martha Mattox, Walt Whitman, Joan Standing, Lee Shumway.
Early conservation piece set in Michigan's timber country, where a lumberman tries to get a young woman to sell her land to his company. She refuses to do so until he promises to replant a new tree for every one he cuts down.

Hearts and Fists (H.C. Weaver Productions/Associated Exhibitors, 1926)
d: Lloyd Ingraham. 6 reels.
John Bowers, Marguerite De La Motte, Alan Hale, Dan Mason, Lois Ingraham, Howard Russell, Jack Curtis, Kent Mead, Charles Mailes.
Two rival lumbermen tangle, each trying to beat the other in getting his logs to the mill.

Hearts and Masks (Federated Productions/FBO of America, 1921)
d: William A. Seiter. 5 reels.
Elinor Field, Francis McDonald, Lloyd Bacon, John Cossar, Molly McConnell.
Alice, a coquette, charms Richard at the society ball. When jewelry is discovered missing, Alice fears that Richard is guilty, and tries to hide him. In so doing, she generates accusations that she is an accomplice. But in the end, the

real culprit is captured, and Alice and Richard are free to consider their future together.

Hearts and Spangles (Gotham Productions/Lumas Film Corp., 1926)
d: Frank O'Connor. 6 reels.
Wanda Hawley, Robert Gordon, Barbara Tennant, Eric Mayne, Frankie Darrow, Larry Steers, J.P. Lockney, George Cheeseboro, Charles Force.
A failed medical student takes a job with the circus.

Hearts and Spurs (Fox, 1925)
d: William S. Van Dyke. 5 reels.
Buck Jones, Carol Lombard, William Davidson, Freeman Wood, Jean LaMotte, J. Gordon Russell, Walt Robbins, Charles Eldridge.
Out West, an eastern tenderfoot loses large sums to crooked gamblers, and is forced to hold up a stagecoach to settle his gambling debts. He receives support from his sister and an honest cowpoke, who, acting together, foil the larcenous gamblers and exonerate the tenderfoot.

Hearts and the Highway (Vitagraph, 1915)
d: Wilfred North. 5 reels.
Lillian Walker, Darwin Karr, Donald Hall, L. Rogers Lytton, Charles Kent, Charles Eldridge, Charles Wellesley, Anders Randolf, Ned Finley, Harry Northrup, William Gilson, Rose Tapley.
A noblewoman dons male clothing in a ploy to get her father released from prison.

Hearts Are Trumps (Metro, 1920)
d: Rex Ingram. 6 reels.
Winter Hall, Frank Brownlee, Alice Terry, Francelia Billington, Joseph Kilgour, Brinsley Shaw, Thomas Jefferson, Norman Kennedy, Edward Connelly, Bull Montana.
When a lady of nobility secretly marries a common gamekeeper, her father has the gamekeeper beaten and banished from his estate. But years later, he *does* return, and this time he has the upper hand—and it's holding the mortgage on the old man's manor.

Hearts Asleep (B.B. Features, Inc./Robertson-Cole, 1919)
d: Howard Hickman. 5 reels.
Bessie Barriscale, Vola Vale, Frank Whitson, George Fisher, Henry Woodward, Tom Guise, Anna Dodge.
Though raised by a criminal, a scrub girl for a wealthy estate remains honest and pure. Her wholesome nature shines through when a gentleman puts her through five years of training, and then passes her off as a lady born to wealth.

Heart's Desire (Famous Players/Paramount, 1917)
d: Francis J. Grandon. 5 reels.
Marie Doro, Albert Roscoe, Mario Majeroni, Jean Gauthier, Helen Dahl, Harry Lee, Gertrude Norman, Ida Darling, Edwin Sturgis.
Fleurette, an island girl, brings happiness to a visiting landowner.

Heart's Haven (Benjamin B. Hampton Productions/W.W. Hodkinson, 1922)
d: Benjamin B. Hampton. 6 reels.
Robert McKim, Claire Adams, Carl Gantvoort, Claire McDowell, Betty Brice, Frankie Lee, Mary Jane Irving, Jean Hersholt, Frank Hayes.
Joe, secretary to a railroad executive, antagonizes his sensitive wife when he allows his mother to move in with them. Joe's mother is merely there to help with the couple's two children, but the wife curiously continues to regard her

presence with suspicion.

Hearts in Dixie (Fox, 1929)
d: Paul Sloane. 8 reels.
Clarence Muse, Eugene Jackson, Stepin Fetchit, Bernice Pilot, Clifford Ingram, Mildred Washington, Zack Williams, Gertrude Howard, Dorothy Morrison, Vivian Smith, Robert Brooks.
Down South, an old Negro works his farm while his son-in-law loafs.

Hearts of Men (Hiram Abrams, 1919)
d: George Beban. 6 reels.
George Beban, Sarah Kernan, George Beban Jr., Mabel Van Buren, Harry Rattenbury, George Pierson, Clarence Burton, Hop Sing.
An Italian immigrant buys arid land in Arizona, but strikes oil.

Hearts of Oak (Fox, 1924)
d: John Ford. 6 reels.
Hobart Bosworth, Pauline Starke, Theodore von Eltz, James Gordon, Francis Powers, Jennie Lee, Francis Ford.
Dunnivan, a sea captain, loves the girl he adopted as a child, and proposes marriage. Although she accepts, Dunnivan learns she has a younger beau who would be more suitable for her, and he gives way so that the youngsters can be together.

Hearts of the World (D.W. Griffith, 1918)
d: D.W. Griffith. 12 reels.
Lillian Gish, Dorothy Gish, Adolphe Lestina, Josephine Crowell, Robert Harron, Jack Cosgrave, Kate Bruce, Ben Alexander, Robert Anderson, George Fawcett, George A. Seigmann, Fay Holderness, Eugene Pouyet, Anna Mae Walthall, Herbert Sutch, Alphonse Dufort, Jean Dumercier, George Nichols, Noel Coward.
World War I drama about a grief-stricken French girl who believes her lover has been killed in action when the Germans capture her village.

Hearts or Diamonds? (William Russell Productions/Mutual, 1918)
d: Henry King. 5 reels.
William Russell, Charlotte Burton, Howard Davies, Carl Stockdale, John Gough, Robert Klein.
Jewel thieves prey upon a trusting diamond collector who's infatuated with the young woman traveling with the gang.

A Heart's Revenge (Fox, 1918)
d: O.A.C. Lund. 5 reels.
Sonia Markova, David Herblin, Frank Goldsmith, Eric Mayne, Bradley Barker, Helen Long, Stanley Heck, Fred Ratcliffe.
Jealous because the Russian countess he loves has fallen for an American army lieutenant, a baron has the American abducted. But his sweetheart follows the baron, finds her sweetheart, and helps him to escape.

Hearts Up! (Universal, 1920)
d: Val Paul. 5 reels.
Harry Carey, Arthur Millett, Charles LeMoyne, Frank Braidwood, Mignonne Golden.
Out West, a rancher named David learns that an old friend has died just before he was to meet his daughter Lorelei, returning home after an absence of many years. David meets her ship, intending to break the bad news to her; but when Lorelei mistakes him for her dad, David cannot bring himself to break her heart, and lets her believe he *is* her dad.

Heartsease (Goldwyn, 1919)
d: Harry Beaumont. 5 reels.
Tom Moore, Helene Chadwick, Larry Steers, Alec B. Francis, Sydney Ainsworth, Herbert Pryor, William Burress, Rosemary Theby, Mary Warren.
Though penniless, a composer dedicates a song, "Heartsease," to a wealthy young lady.

Heartstrings (Universal, 1917)
d: Allan Holubar. 5 reels.
Maude George, Irene Hunt, Francelia Billington, Paul Byron, Irene Hunt, Charles Cummings, Virginia Corbin, Zoe Rae.
A heartless vamp enjoys destroying men. When she trains her charms on a young doctor who's engaged to be married, however, the vamp gets a shock upon realizing that his fiancée is the daughter she deserted as a child.

Heaven on Earth (MGM, 1927)
d: Phil Rosen. 7 reels.
Conrad Nagel, Renee Adoree, Gwen Lee, Julia Swayne Gordon, Marcia Manon, Pat Hartigan.
In France, a young silk miller finds love with a Gypsy girl.

Hedda Gabler (Frank Powell Producing Corp./Mutual, 1917)
d: Frank Powell. 5 reels.
Nance O'Neil, Aubrey Beattie, Lillian Paige, Einar Linden, Ruth Byron, Alfred Hickman, Edith Campbell Walker, Frank Ford.
Hedda, though recently married, still imagines herself in the arms of her former lover.
First feature film version of the play of the same name by Henrik Ibsen.

Heedless Moths (Perry Plays/Equity Pictures, 1921)
d: Robert Z. Leonard. 6 reels.
Holmes E. Herbert, Hedda Hopper, Ward Crane, Tom Burroughs, Audrey Munson, Jane Thomas, Henry Duggan.
Miss Munson, who was in real life an artist's model, plays herself in this melodrama about a model who innocently poses for a sculptor but incites jealousy in the sculptor's wife.

The Heights of Hazard (Vitagraph, 1915)
d: Harry Lambart. 5 reels.
Eleanor Woodruff, Charles Richman, Charles Kent, Hattie de Lara, Frank Holland.
A young woman declares that romance is dead, and says she wishes she could be courted as in days of old, when a man would climb "the heights of hazard" for love. Soon after, she is abducted by a handsome masked man who takes her to his apartment and wins her heart.

The Heir of the Ages (Pallas Pictures/Paramount, 1917)
d: Edward J. LeSaint. 5 reels.
House Peters, Eugene Pallette, Nina Byron, John Burton, Henry A. Barrows, Adele Farrington.
Two brothers, one weak, one strong, love the same girl.

The Heir to the Hoorah (Lasky Feature Plays/Paramount, 1916)
d: William C. DeMille. 5 reels.
Thomas Meighan, Anita King, Edythe Chapman, Horace B. Carpenter, Charles Ogle, Ernest Joy, Joane Woodbury.
"The Hoorah" is a gold mine in California, and its owners are three single men. Lamenting that they have no one to inherit their good fortune, the three decide that one of them should get married and produce an heir.

The Heiress at Coffee Dan's (Fine Arts Film Co./Triangle, 1916)
d: Edward Dillon. 5 reels.
Bessie Love, Frank Bennett, Max Davidson, Lucille Younge, Alfred Paget, Alva Blake.
Waffles, a friendly coffee shop waitress, is duped into believing she's heiress to a fortune. She isn't, but when she puts in an appearance at the manor, her charming ways captivate a wealthy neighbor, and Waffles wins his love.

Heiress for a Day (Triangle, 1918)
d: Jack Dillon. 5 reels.
Olive Thomas, Joe King, Eugene Burr, Graham Pette, Lillian Langdon, Mary Warren, Anna Dodge.
When a manicurist learns she is to inherit her grandfather's estate, she runs up a lot of bills on clothing and jewelry. Then comes the dawn: her inheritance is limited to $1,000.

Held by the Enemy (Famous Players-Lasky/Paramount, 1920)
d: Donald Crisp. 6 reels.
Agnes Ayres, Wanda Hawley, Josephine Crowell, Lillian Leighton, Lewis Stone, Jack Holt, Robert Cain, Walter Hiers, Robert Brower, Clarence H. Geldart.
During the Civil War, a young widow is "held by the enemy" when her Southern estate is within the area occupied by Yankee troops.

Held by the Law (Universal, 1927)
d: Edward Laemmle. 7 reels.
Ralph Lewis, Johnnie Walker, Marguerite De La Motte, Robert Ober, Fred Kelsey, Maude Wayne, E.J. Ratcliffe.
Mary and Tom are engaged to be married, but tragically, during their engagement party, Tom's father is murdered. Wedding plans are put on hold until the lovebirds solve the mystery and bring the guilty party to justice.

Held in Trust (Metro, 1920)
d: John E. Ince. 6 reels.
May Allison, Darrell Foss, Walter Long, John H. Elliott, Lawrence Grant.
Mary Manchester is the spittin' image of Adelaide, a wealthy woman who is dying. Fearful that upon her death her entire estate will revert to her brother, Adelaide's husband and his cohorts hire Mary to impersonate her and keep the estate in their hands. But the plan backfires when Mary meets Adelaide's brother and they fall in love.

Held to Answer (Metro, 1923)
d: Harold Shaw. 6 reels.
House Peters, Grace Carlyle, John Sainpolis, Evelyn Brent, James Morrison, Lydia Knott, Bull Montana, Gale Henry, Thomas Guise, Robert Daly, charles West, Charles Mailes.
Hell hath no fury, etc.... When a stage actor gives up his actress girlfriend and his career and moves to a small town to become a minister, the scorned actress follows him and tries to destroy his reputation.

Heléne of the North (Famous Players/Paramount, 1915)
d: J. Searle Dawley. 5 reels.
Marguerite Clark, Conway Tearle, Elliott Dexter, Robert Rogers, Katherine Adams, Frank Losee, David Wall, Ida Darling, Theodore Guise, James Kearney, Brigham Royce, Eleanor Flowers.
The daughter of a whisky runner near the Canadian border falls in love with a Mountie.

Helen's Babies (Principal Pictures, 1924)
d: William A. Seiter. 6 reels.

Baby Peggy, Clara Bow, Jean Carpenter, Edward Everett Horton, Claire Adams, George Reed, Mattie Peters, Richard Tucker.

Uncle Harry finds himself saddled with a precocious infant while her parents travel.

Heliotrope (Cosmopolitan/Paramount, 1920)
d: George D. Baker. 7 reels.
Wilfred Lytell, Ben Hendricks, Julia Swayne Gordon, Betty Hilburn, Diana Allen, Fred Burton, Clayton White, William B. Mack, William H. Tooker, Thomas J. Findlay.
"Heliotrope Harry," so-called because of his fondness for the scent of heliotrope perfume, is serving a life sentence in the penitentiary. But he obtains a leave from the governor when he learns that his daughter is in a jam, and runs to her aid.

Hell Bent (Universal, 1918)
d: Jack Ford. 6 reels.
Harry Carey, Neva Gerber, Duke Lee, Vester Pegg, Joseph Harris.
Carey again plays "Cheyenne Harry," this time in the town of Rawhide, where he befriends a dance hall girl in trouble.

Hell-Bent for Heaven (Warner Bros., 1926)
d: J. Stuart Blackton. 7 reels.
Patsy Ruth Miller, John Harron, Gayne Whitman, Gardner James, James Marcus, Wilfred North, Evelyn Selbie.
A villain bent on seduction is rebuffed by the object of his lust; in revenge, he decides to dynamite a dam.

The Hell Cat (Goldwyn, 1918)
d: Reginald Barker. 6 reels.
Geraldine Farrar, Milton Sills, Tom Santschi, Evelyn Axzell, William W. Black, Harry Lee, Clarence Williams, George Hopkins, Raymond Wallace, Dudley Smith, Clarence Snyder.
High-spirited Pancha O'Brien, feisty daughter of a ranch owner, is desired by two men: the local sheriff, and his sworn enemy Outlaw Jim.

The Hell Diggers (Famous Players-Lasky/Paramount, 1921)
d: Frank Urson. 5 reels.
Wallace Reid, Lois Wilson, Alexander Broun, Frank Gelbert, Lucien Littlefield, Clarence Geldert, Buddy Post.
Tale of pro-constructions forces vs. pro-conservationists.

The Hell-Hound of Alaska — see: The Darkening Trail (1915)

Hell Morgan's Girl (Universal, 1917)
d: Joseph DeGrasse. 5 reels.
Dorothy Phillips, William Stowell, Alfred Allen, Lon Chaney, Lilyan Rosine, Joseph Girard.
The daughter of a Barbary Coast saloon owner falls in love with the saloon's piano player. Neither of them know it, but he's about to inherit millions.

Hell Roarin' Reform (Fox, 1919)
d: Edward J. LeSaint. 5 reels.
Tom Mix, Kathleen Connors, George Berrell, B.M. Turner, Jack Curtis, Cupid Morgan.
When outlaws demolish his church, a cowboy turned minister pursues them and finds that the outlaw gang is headed by the local sheriff.

Hell-To-Pay Austin (Triangle, 1916)
d: Paul Powell. 5 reels.
Bessie Love, Wilfred Lucas, Ralph Lewis, Mary Alden, Eugene Pallette, James O'Shea, Clyde Hopkins, Marie Wilkinson, A.D. Sears, William H. Brown, Tom Wilson.

Miss Love plays Briar, an orphan girl who's adopted by lumberjacks.

The Hellion (American Film Co./Pathé, 1919)
d: George L. Cox. 5 reels.
Margarita Fisher, Emory Johnson, Charles Spere, Henry Barrows, Lillian Langdon, George Periolat, Frank Clark, Bull Montana.
A cabaret dancer is persuaded to impersonate an heiress.

Hello Cheyenne (Fox, 1928)
d: Eugene Forde. 5 reels.
Tom Mix, Caryl Lincoln, Jack Baston, Martin Faust, Joseph Girard, Al St. John, William Caress.
In Wyoming, rival telephone companies race to be the first to bring service to Cheyenne.

Hell's Crater (Universal, 1918)
w, d: W.B. Pearson. 5 reels.
Grace Cunard, George McDaniel, Ray Hanford, Eileen Sedgwick.
After being robbed by a dance hall owner and his gal, a prospector retaliates by abducting the woman and forcing her to work in his gold mine, known as "Hell's Crater." The relationship begun in enmity gradually softens, and the two fall in love.

Hell's End (Triangle, 1918)
d: J.W. McLaughlin. 5 reels.
William Desmond, Josie Sedgwick, Bull Durham, Dorothy Hagar, Charles Dorian.
"Hell's End" is a slum neighborhood in New York. Two who escape it come back in later years, and work to improve conditions.

Hell's 400 (Fox, 1926)
d: John Griffith Wray. 6 reels.
Harrison Ford, Margaret Livingston, Henry Kolker, Wallace MacDonald, Marceline Day, Rodney Hildebrand, Amber Norman.
Evelyn, a gold digger, marries wealth but then faces an ethical dilemma: Should she come forward with evidence to exonerate a man accused of murder, knowing that her own husband is the true culprit?

Hell's Highroad (Cinema Corp. Of America, 1925)
d: Rupert Julian. 6 reels.
Leatrice Joy, Edmund Burns, Robert Edeson, Julia Faye, Helene Sullivan.
Bitter drama about Judy, a young woman who loves Ronald, a working-class engineer. She meets with a wealthy playboy and persuades him to clear the way for Ronald to become successful. He does so, and they are married; but soon after, the newly-prosperous Ronald neglects his wife to court a wealthy widow. Stung by this rejection, Judy returns to the playboy who helped Ronald and, offering herself as the prize, challenges him to ruin Ronald's career.

Hell's Hinges (Triangle, 1916)
d: William S. Hart, Charles Swickard. 5 reels.
William S. Hart, Alfred Hollingsworth, Clara Williams, Jack Standing, Louise Glaum, Robert McKim, J. Frank Burke, Jean Hersholt, Robert Kortman, Leo Willis.
Powerful and spectacular western drama about sin and redemption. A minister comes West to assume the spiritual guidance of a frontier community. The town's saloon owner (and *de facto* mayor) senses a threat to his way of life, and hires a gunfighter (played by Hart) to run the minister and his sister out of town. But rather than degenerate into a

routine shootout between good and evil, *Hell's Hinges* takes the dramatic high road. As it turns out, the minister is weak and unworthy of his calling. He permits himself to be seduced by a local harlot, and then, consumed with self-hatred, he launches into a wild orgy of drinking that culminates in his leading a pack of ruffians to burn down his own church. The gunfighter, meanwhile, has seen the truth and finds that only the reverend's sister is worthy of his protection.

Hell's Hole (Fox, 1923)
d: Emmett J. Flynn. 6 reels.
Charles Jones, Maurice B. Flynn, Eugene Pallette, George Siegmann, Ruth Clifford, Kathleen Key, Hardee Kirkland, Charles K. French, Henry Miller Jr., Fred Kohler, Dick Sutherland.
Two cowpoke stowaways on a train bound west get thrown off, then dream of overtaking the train and robbing it.

Hell's Oasis (Pinnacle Productions/Independent Films Association, 1920)
d: Neal Hart. 5 reels.
Neal Hart, William Quinn, Hal Wilson, Betty Brown, John Tyke, Inez Gomez, Allen Smith.
Father-and-daughter missionaries arrive in the town of Little Hell, ready to save the heathens. The heathens put up a struggle, but in the end they are won over by the missionaries and a noble cowboy who falls in love with the female missionary.

Hellship Bronson (Gotham Productions/Lumas Film Corp., 1928)
d: Joseph E. Henabery. 7 reels.
Noah Beery, Mrs. Wallace Reid, Reed Howes, Helen Foster, James Bradbury Jr., Jack Anthony.
Bronson, a sea captain, believes his wife to be unfaithful, so he takes their young son and goes to sea. Twenty years later, the youngster falls in love with the daughter of a woman his father once loved.

Help! Help! Police! (Fox, 1919)
d: Edward Dillon. 5 reels.
George Walsh, Eric Mayne, Henry Hallam, Marie Burke, Alice Mann, Alan Edwards, Evelyn Brent, Joseph Burke.
A young man becomes infatuated with the daughter of his dad's business rival. But there's another fellow after her too, and after a series of escapades—including an auto race, robberies, abductions, and a huge fire—our hero and his sweetie finally get together.

Help Wanted (Oliver Morosco Photoplays/Paramount, 1915)
d: Hobart Bosworth. 5 reels.
Lois Meredith, Lillian Elliott, Hobart Bosworth, Owen Moore, Adele Farrington, Helen Wolcott, Carl Von Schiller, Myrtle Stedman, Herbert Standing.
When his stepdad hires a stenographer for her looks and not her ability, Jack smells trouble. Sure enough, stepdad puts some moves on the girl. But Jack intervenes in time to save everyone's honor, and ends up marrying the inept stenographer.

Help Wanted—Male (Pathé, 1920)
d: Henry King. 6 reels.
Blanche Sweet, Henry King, Frank Leigh, Mayme Kelso, Thomas Jefferson, Jay Belasco, Jean Acker.
After receiving a small inheritance, a girl spends it on a wardrobe and a resort vacation, hoping to snag a rich husband.

Help Yourself (Goldwyn, 1920)
d: Hugo Ballin. 5 reels.
Madge Kennedy, Joseph Striker, Mrs. David Landau, Helen Greene, E.J. Ratcliffe, Sidney Vautier, Nellie Beaumont, Roy Applegate, Edward Bernard, Renault Tourneur.
Emily's wealthy aunt Carmen dismisses Emily's choice of beaus, favoring instead a visiting Bolshevik. But it doesn't take long for the ladies to see through him.

Her Accidental Husband (Columbia, 1923)
d: Dallas M. Fitzgerald. 6 reels.
Forrest Stanley, Miriam Cooper, Mitchell Lewis, Richard Tucker, Kate Lester, Maude Wayne.
Swept away in a raging storm, wealthy Gordon is about to drown when he is rescued by Rena and her father. However, the father drowns and Gordon feels obliged to marry Rena and carry on the family fishing business. This uneasy arrangement lasts only six months, after which time Gordon persuades Rena to return to the city with him and meet his family. There's a different kind of storm raging there, for Gordon's wealthy relatives don't approve of the fishy new addition to the family.

Her American Husband (Triangle, 1918)
d: E. Mason Hopper. 5 reels.
Tedy Sampson, Darrell Foss, Leota Lorraine, Thomas Kurihara, Misao Seki, Jack Abbe, W.A. Jeffries, Arthur Millet, Ludwig Lowry, Kathleen Emerson.
Wry variant on "Madame Butterfly," with an American taking a Japanese bride and bringing her home to America with him.

Her Beloved Enemy (Thanhouser, 1917)
d: Ernest Warde. 5 reels.
Doris Grey, Wayne Arey, J.H. Gilmour, Gladys Leslie.
A young woman swears to avenge her father's death by targeting the man she holds responsible. But as matters play out, her father was a traitorous spy, and the man she sought to kill is in reality a Secret Service agent.

Her Beloved Villain (Realart Pictures Co., 1920)
d: Sam Wood. 5 reels.
Harrison Ford, Ramsey Wallace, F. Templar Powell, Tully Marshall, Lillian Leighton, Gertrude Claire, Robert Bolder, Margaret McWade, Wanda Hawley, Irma Coonly, Jay Peters.
When a young bride discovers that her new husband lied about her to his rival in order to deflect his attention, she determines to get even with "her beloved villain."

Her Better Self (Famous Players/Paramount, 1917)
d: Robert G. Vignola. 5 reels.
Pauline Frederick, Thomas Meighan, Alice Hollister, Maude Turner Gordon, Charles Wellesley, Frank De Rheim, Armand Cortez.
Debutante Vivian Tyler offers to help the poor by working in a sanitarium. But once there, Vivian finds some unsettling indications that the doctor in charge is leading women into prostitution.

Her Big Adventure (Kerman Films/A.G. Steen, 1926)
d: John Ince. 5 reels.
Herbert Rawlinson, Grace Darmond, Vola Vale, Carlton Griffin, William Turner, Edward Gordon.
Ralph, whose father is wealthy, decides to make it on his own, and gets a job as bellhop in a fashionable hotel. His father's secretary, who is unknown to Ralph, checks into the hotel posing as a countess, and she and Ralph fall in love.

Then the real countess shows up. Then Ralph's dad shows up. Now what?

Her Big Night (Universal, 1926)
d: Melville W. Brown. 8 reels.

Laura LaPlante, Einar Hansen, ZaSu Pitts, Tully Marshall, Lee Moran, Mack Swain, John Roche, William Austin, Nat Carr, Cissy Fitzgerald.

An unalloyed comedy delight. Miss LaPlante kicks up her heels in two roles: as Frances, a shopgirl who closely resembles big movie star Daphne Dix, and as the impetuous movie star herself. One night when Daphne is frolicking aboard a millionaire's yacht when she should be attending the big premiere of her latest film, her studio's press agent spots Frances and offers her $1,000 to pose as Miss Dix at the premiere and throw a few kisses to her loyal fans. The deception works, but it also leads to several humorous complications that keep this frothy comedy bubbling at a merry pace.

Among the comedy highlights is Mack Swain --who had played the giant prospector, "Big Jim," in the previous year's *The Gold Rush*—as the studio head who gives Frances lessons on how to prance and curtsy daintily before Daphne's fans. The sight of this lumbering hulk of a man trying to display feminine grace and charm is screamingly funny, and after you see it you won't soon forget it.

Miss LaPlante, who cut her acting teeth on Christie comedies, is perfect in her roles as the shopgirl and the movie star she resembles. In the film's final scene—after all the plot complications have been resolved—the two women say farewell with a kiss, in a triumph of film technology. For it is Laura LaPlante, kissing *herself*, and seamlessly. The two mirror images are juxtaposed with no technical flaws. Before we can ask ourselves, How the hell did they do *that*? the film fades to black and we are left with a happy glow, like the sensation of having just finished a tasty dessert.

This film is also known as *Local Girl Makes Good*.

Her Bitter Cup (Universal, 1916)
d: Cleo Madison. 5 reels.

Edward Hearn, William V. Mong, Cleo Madison, Adele Farrington, Ray Hanford, Lule Warrenton, Willis Marks.

While crusading for better working conditions, a young woman falls in love with her boss' son.

Her Bleeding Heart (Lubin, 1916)
d: Jack Pratt. 5 reels.

Rosetta Brice, Richard Buhler, Crauford Kent, Inez Buck, Karva Poloskova, William Turner.

Pregnant and abandoned, a young woman pretends she is a widow and marries a sympathetic doctor.

Her Body in Bond (Universal, 1918)
d: Robert Leonard. 5 reels.

Mae Murray, Kenneth Harlan, Al Roscoe, Joseph Girard, Paul Weigel, Mabelle Harvey.

Husband-and-wife cabaret performers separate when he goes West for his health. But they remain very much in love, although a slimy millionaire is interested in the wife.

Her Boy (Metro, 1918)
d: George Irving. 5 reels.

Effie Shannon, Niles Welch, Pauline Curley, James T. Galloway, Pat O'Malley, William A. Bechtel, Charles W. Sutton, Charles Riegel, Violet Axzell, Robert Chandler, Anthony Byrd.

During World War I, a widow worries that her only son will be taken into combat.

Her Code of Honor (Tribune Productions., Inc., 1919)
d: John M Stahl. 6 reels.

Florence Reed, William Desmond, Robert Frazer, Irving Cummings, Alec B. Francis, Marcelle Roussillon, George Stevens.

A horrified bride-to-be learns that her intended husband may be her half-brother.

Her Condoned Sin (Biograph, 1917)
d: D.W. Griffith. 6 reels.

Blanche Sweet, Mae Marsh, Henry B. Walthall, Lillian Gish, Dorothy Gish, Robert Harron, Kate Bruce.

Re-issued version of the 1914 *Judith of Bethulia*. After D.W. Griffith left Biograph, the company collected two reels worth of outtakes, worked them into the original film, and re-released it as *Her Condoned Sin*.

Her Country First (Famous Players-Lasky/Paramount, 1918)
d: James Young. 5 reels.

Vivian Martin, John Cossar, Florence Oberle, J. Parks-Jones, Larry Steers, Brydine Zuber, Louis Willoughby, James Farley, Lillian Leighton, Jack McDonald, Audrey Chapman.

Thunderingly patriotic tale about a finishing-school grad who rallies her neighbors into supporting America's war effort.

Her Country's Call (American Film Co./Mutual, 1917)
d: Lloyd Ingraham. 5 reels.

Mary Miles Minter, George Periolat, Alan Forrest, Harry A. Barrows, Margaret Shelby, Ashton Dearholt, Nellie Widen, Spottiswoode Aitken.

The daughter of a moonshiner overhears spies planning to seize a military ammo depot, and saves the day.

Her Debt of Honor (Columbia/Metro, 1916)
d: William Nigh. 5 reels.

Valli Valli, William Davidson, William Nigh, J.H. Goldsworthy, Frank Bacon, Ilean Hume, Frank Montgomery, David H. Thompson, R.A. Bresee, Jack Murray.

After her father's death, a young woman continues to receive a monthly stipend from a friend of her dad's until his own death. Then, feeling indebted, she nurses the man's dying son.

Her Decision (Triangle, 1918)
d: Jack Conway. 5 reels.

Gloria Swanson, J. Barney Sherry, Darrell Foss, Ann Kroman.

To help pay for her sister's hospital bills, a young woman agrees to marry a wealthy man she does not love.

Her Double Life (Fox, 1916)
d: Gordon Edwards. 6 reels.

Theda Bara, Stuart Holmes, A.H. Van Buren, Walter Law, Madeleine Le Nard, Carey Lee, Katherine Lee, Lucia Moore, Franklin Hanna, Jane Lee.

In World War I, a front line nurse poses as an aristocratic lady, in order to evade the unwanted advances of a crude war correspondent.

Her Elephant Man (Fox, 1920)
d: Scott Dunlap. 5 reels.

Shirley Mason, Albert Roscoe, Henry J. Hebert, Ardito Mellonino, Harry Todd, Dorothy Lee.

On an elephant hunt in Africa, a colonel and his party

HER BIG NIGHT (1926). The horizontal lady is blonde, beautiful Laura LaPlante, being spanked by John Roche, as an irate husband who thinks he's caught his wife cheating on him. But Laura plays Frances, a dead ringer for the gentleman's wife, and she's innocent of any wrongdoing. At right, Nat Carr tries to explain away the error, but gets there a little too late to save Frances' hide.

* * * * *

encounter an orphaned white girl, and take her back to America with them. The girl grows older and becomes a graceful beauty, and soon love blossoms between her and the colonel.

Her Excellency, the Governor (Triangle, 1917)
d: Albert Parker. 5 reels.
Wilfred Lucas, Elda Millar, Joseph Kilgour, Regan Hughston, Walter Walker, Edith Speare, Albert Perry.
After her beau is elected governor, a young lawyer decides to run for lieutenant governor, and she's elected.

Her Face Value (Realart Pictures/Paramount, 1921)
d: Thomas N. Heffron. 5 reels.
Wanda Hawley, Lincoln Plummer, Dick Rosson, T. Roy Barnes, Winifred Bryson, Donald MacDonald, Harvey Clark, George Periolat, Eugene Burr, Ah Wing.
Peggy, a chorus girl, goes to Hollywood and makes good in the movies.

Her Fatal Millions (Metro, 1923)
d: William Beaudine. 6 reels.
Viola Dana, Huntly Gordon, Allan Forrest, Peggy Browne, Edward Connelly, Kate Price, Joy Winthrop.
Small town girl Mary hears that Fred, her former boyfriend, has made good in the big city and is coming home for a visit. Wishing to appear prosperous herself, Mary borrows jewels and costly clothes and tells Fred that she's married wealth. Eventually, Fred sees through her deception and offers to marry her himself.

Her Father Said No (R-C Pictures/FBO of America, 1927)
d: Jack McKeown. 7 reels.
Mary Brian, Canny O'Shea, Al Cooke, Kit Guard, John Steppling, Frankie Darro, Gene Stone, Betty Caldwell.
Danny, a prizefighter, and Charlotte fall in love. But her dad hates prizefighting and so disapproves of the courtship. Danny is turned away and quits the ring to open a health resort, and Charlotte's father becomes one of his first customers. Soon, Danny and Charlotte elope and Papa grudgingly accepts his new son-in-law.

Her Father's Gold (Thanhouser, 1916)
d: W. Eugene Moore. 5 reels.
Harris Gordon, Barbara Gilroy, William Burt, Louise Emerald Bates.
A reporter goes to Florida to find gold, and finds love besides.

Her Father's Keeper (Fine Arts Film Co./Triangle, 1917)
d: Arthur Rosson, Dick Rosson. 5 reels.
Irene Howley, Jack Devereux, Frank Currier, Jack Raymond, John Hanneford, Walter Bussell.
A financier's daughter enters the business world and is startled to learn that her father is involved in shady dealings.

Her Father's Son (Oliver Morosco Photoplays/Paramount, 1916)
d: William D. Taylor. 5 reels.
Vivian Martin, Alfred Vosburgh, Herbert Standing, Helen Jerome Eddy, Joe Massey, Jack Lawton, Lucille Ward, Tom Bates.
To satisfy an eccentric uncle, young Frances disguises herself as a boy and presents herself to him as his nephew. The masquerade works up to a point, but when the disguised female meets and falls in love with a dashing lieutenant, the boys' clothes go into mothballs, and out come the crinolines and lace.

Her Final Reckoning (Famous Players-Lasky/Paramount, 1918)
d: Emile Chautard. 5 reels.
Pauline Frederick, John Miltern, Robert Cain, Warren Cooke, Joseph Smiley, James Laffey, Karl Dane, Florence Beresford, Louis Reinhart, Edith Ellwood.
In Hungary, a beautiful gypsy woman dallies with a married count, but she really fancies the Hungarian prince.

Her First Elopement (Realart Pictures, 1920)
d: Sam Wood. 5 reels.
Wanda Hawley, Jerome Patrick, Nell Craig, Lucien Littlefield, Jay Eaton, Helen Dunbar, Herbert Standing, Edwin Stevens, Margaret Morris, Ann Hastings, John MacKinnon.
When Christina tries to end her cousin's flirtation with a disreputable snake dancer, she is herself mistaken for the dancer. Going along with the charade for the fun of it, Christina finds herself falling in love with a handsome stranger.

Her Five-Foot Highness (Universal, 1920)
d: Harry Franklin. 5 reels.
Edith Roberts, Ogden Crane, Stanhope Wheatcroft, Virginia Ware, Harold Miller, Kathleen Kirkham, Rudolph Christians, Hugh Saxon, Leota Lorraine, Leonard Clapham.
Ellen, a Texas ranch owner, inherits an English estate.

Her Game (Tribune, 1919)
d: Frank H. Crane. 5 reels.
Florence Reed, Conway Tearle, Jed Prouty, Florence Billings, Mathilda Brundage.
An heiress discovers that her new husband has an evil twin.

Her Gilded Cage (Famous Players-Lasky/Paramount, 1922)
d: Sam Wood. 6 reels.
Gloria Swanson, Harrison Ford, David Powell, Anne Cornwall, Walter Hiers, Charles A. Stevenson.
In Paris, a cabaret performer who met the king only briefly, agrees to be billed as "the favorite of King Fernando."

Her Good Name (Van Dyke Film Production Co., 1917)
d: George Terwilliger. 5 reels.
Jean Sothern, William H. Turner, Earl Metcalfe, Etherl Tully, Arthur Housman, Barbara Castleton, Nellie Parker Spaulding.
After her drunken father shoots and kills her beau, an innocent young woman is torn with indecision: Should she testify that the young man had violated her and thus save her father, or should she tell the truth and send her dad to prison?

Her Great Chance (Select Pictures Corp., 1918)
d: Charles Maigne. 5 reels.
Alice Brady, David Powell, Nellie Parker-Spaulding, Gloria Goodwin, Gertrude Barry, Hardy Kirkland, Ormi Hawley, C.A. de Lima, Jefferson de Angelis, Louis Sherwin.
Lola's in love with a rich guy, but she rejects him because he's too reckless and irresponsible to settle down. All that changes, though, when his dad disowns him. Now sober and trustworthy, he's just what she wants, and Lola marries him for better or worse.

Her Great Hour (Equitable Motion Pictures Corp./World Film Corp., 1916)
d: S.E.V. Taylor. 5 reels.
Molly McIntyre, Gerda Holmes, Richard Lynn, Martin Alsop, P.J. LeMae.

Convinced of a young woman's innocence, a district attorney drops theft charges against her, and brings her home as a companion for his wife.

Her Great Match (Popular Plays and Players/Metro, 1915)
d: Rene Plaisetty. 5 reels.
Gail Kane, Vernon Steel, Ned Burton, Clarissa Selwynne, Lawrence Grattan, Julia Hurley.
Visiting in America, the prince of Syravia meets and falls for an American girl.

Her Great Price (Rolfe Photoplays, Inc./Metro, 1916)
d: Edwin Carewe. 6 reels.
Mabel Taliaferro, Henry Mortimer, Richard Barbee, George Pauncefort, William Cahill, Jeanette Horton, Ruth Chester.
A mystery writer invites guests to a party at which her own body will be found, apparently dead.

Her Greatest Love (Fox, 1917)
d: J. Gordon Edwards. 5 reels.
Theda Bara, Glenn White, Harry Hilliard, Walter Law, Marie Curtis, Alice Gale.
After being forced by her mother to marry a prince she does not love, Vera discovers her husband has a mistress. When she objects, the prince banishes her to a convent. But Vera's prayers are answered when, after the prince is killed in a duel, she is at last free to marry the man she loves.

Her Honor the Governor (R-C Pictures/FBO of America, 1926)
d: Chet Withey. 7 reels.
Pauline Frederick, Carroll Nye, Greta von Rue, Tom Santschi, Stanton Heck, Boris Karloff, Jack Richardson, Charles McHugh, Kathleen Kirkham, William Worthington.
Bob, the son of the state's lady governor, tangles with a political boss out to have his mother impeached.

Her Honor the Mayor (Fox, 1920)
d: Paul Cazeneuve. 5 reels.
Eileen Percy, Ramsey Wallace, Charles Force, Edwin Booth Tilton, William Fletcher.
A young woman is elected mayor on the suffrage ticket.

Her Hour (World Film Corp., 1917)
d: George Cowl. 6 reels.
Kitty Gordon, George Morgan, George MacQuarrie, Edward Burns, Lillian Cook, Eric Mayne, Yolande Brown, Jean Wilson, Frank Beamish, Justine Cutting.
Weepy melodrama about a betrayed woman who puts her daughter in a convent rather than expose her to disgrace.

Her Husband's Friend (Thomas H. Ince/Paramount, 1920)
d: Fred Niblo. 5 reels.
Enid Bennett, Roland Lee, Tom Chatterton, Mae Busch, Aileen Manning,
George Pierce, Robert Dunbar.
A divorced wife learns that her husband's friend has been paying her alimony.

Her Husband's Honor (Mutual, 1918)
d: Burton King. 5 reels.
Edna Goodrich, David Powell, Thomas Tommamato, Barbara Allen, Clarence Heritage.
Usually frivolous Nancy learns that her husband's firm is in dire financial straits, and arranges for a foreign businessman to sign a lucrative contract that will save the firm. But first, she's got to fight off the foreigner's advances, which are amorous rather than financial.

Her Husband's Secret (Frank Lloyd Productions/First National, 1925)
d: Frank Lloyd. 7 reels.
Antonio Moreno, Patsy Ruth Miller, Ruth Clifford, David Torrence, Walter McGrail, Phyllis Haver, Pauline Neff, Margaret Fielding, Edwards Davis, Frank Coffyn, Fred warren, Frankie Darro, Frances Teague.
When Kent, a neglectful husband, discovers that his wife spent the night in the home of Brewster, a neighbor, he becomes furious and divorces her, taking their young son with him. But the wife's actions were perfectly innocent, a claim Kent refuses to accept. Twenty-five years later, all the chickens come home to roost when Kent's son shows up with his new fiancée—and she's Brewster's daughter.

Her Husband's Trademark (Famous Players-Lasky/Paramount, 1922)
d: Sam Wood. 5 reels.
Gloria Swanson, Richard Wayne, Stuart Holmes, Lucien Littlefield, Charles Ogle, Edythe Chapman, Clarence Burton, James Neill.
Berkeley, whose ambitions of great wealth have never been realized, nevertheless displays his trophy wife, his "trademark."

Her Husband's Wife (Ivan Film Productions, Inc., 1916)
d: Ivan Abramson. 5 reels.
Sally Crute, Mignon Anderson, Augustus Phillips, Edward Mackey, Kittens Reichart, William Bechtel, Bradley Barker, Arthur Law, Brinsley Shaw, J.H. Lewis, Guido Colucci.
Fickleness, thy name is Belle. A woman of that name marries and divorces three times, seemingly never satisfied with any one man. But she is stunned when she learns that one of her former husbands is remarried—to her own daughter by an earlier marriage.

Her Inspiration (Metro, 1918)
d: Robert Thornby. 5 reels.
May Allison, Herbert Heyes, Charles Edler, Allan D. Sears, Jack Brammall.
A young playwright visits the Kentucky mountains to absorb local color.

Her Life and His (Thanhouser/Pathé, 1917)
d: Frederick Sullivan. 5 reels.
Florence La Badie, H.E. Herbert, Ethyle Cooke, Sam Niblack, Justus D. Barnes.
After serving time for petty theft, a young woman turns her attention to the cause of prison reform.

Her Lord and Master (Vitagraph, 1921)
d: Edward José. 6 reels.
Alice Joyce, Holmes Herbert, Walter McEwen, Frank Sheridan, Marie Shotwell, Louise Beaudet, Eugene Acker, John Sutherland, Ida Waterman.
A spoiled American girl has trouble adjusting to the ways of her new husband's aristocratic family.

Her Love Story (Famous Players-Lasky/Paramount, 1924)
d: Allan Dwan. 7 reels.
Gloria Swanson, Ian Keith, George Fawcett, Echlin Gayer, Mario Majeroni, Sidney Herbert, Donald Hall, Baroness de Hedemann, Jane Auburn, Bert Wales.
In a Balkan kingdom, a princess falls in love with a commoner.

Her Mad Bargain (Anita Stewart Productions/Associated First National, 1921)
d: Edwin Carewe. 6 reels.
Anita Stewart, Arthur Edmund Carew, Helen Raymond,

Adele Farrington, Margaret McWade, Percy Challenger, Walter McGrail, Gertrude Astor, George B. Williams.

The penniless Alice, an artist's model, makes a bargain to insure her life for $35,000, receive a portion of the money from her employer, a sculptor... and then take her own life six months later. But before the fateful day arrives, the sculptor falls in love with his model, and calls off the "bargain."

Her Majesty (Playgoers Pictures/Associated Exhibitors, 1922)
d: George Irving. 5 reels.
Mollie King, Creighton Hale, Rose Tapley, Neville Percy, Jerome Lawler.
Identical twin orphan girls are adopted separately, and they develop very different personalities.
Mollie King plays both twins, Susan and Rosalie.

Her Man (Advanced Motion Picture Corp./Pathé, 1918)
d: Ralph W. Ince, John E. Ince. 6 reels.
Elaine Hammerstein, W. Lawson Butt, George Anderson, Carleton Macy, Erville Alderson, Cecil Chichester, George Cooper, Violet Palmer, Josephine Morse.
A Northern woman of privilege goes South to help educate illiterate mountain folk.

Her Man o' War (DeMille Pictures/Producers Distributing Corp., 1926)
d: Frank Urson. 6 reels.
Jetta Goudal, William Boyd, Jimmie Adams, Grace Darmond, Kay Deslys, Frank Reicher, Michael Vavitch, Robert Edeson, Junior Coghlan.
During World War I, two U.S. Army deserters escape into a German village. They settle down on a farm operated by a German girl, who becomes quite fond of one of them. Slowly, the two men return to their pro-American sympathies, and begin sending wireless messages to help the Allied forces, aided by the German girl.

Her Market Value (Paul Powell Productions/Producers Distributing Corp., 1925)
d: Paul Powell. 6 reels.
Agnes Ayres, George Irving, Anders Randolf, Hedda Hopper, Edward Earle, Taylor Holmes, Gertrude Short, Sidney Bracy.
In a peculiar bequest, a dying man leaves his beautiful wife to his three friends, "in trust."

Her Marriage Vow (Warner Bros., 1924)
w, d: Millard Webb. 7 reels.
Monte Blue, Beverly Bayne, John Roache, Willard Louis, Margaret Livingston, Priscilla Moran, Mary Grabhorn, Martha Petelle, Arthur Hoyt.
Marital misunderstandings arise when a wife is seen apparently flirting with her former boyfriend.

Her Maternal Right (Paragon Films, Inc./World Film Corp., 1916)
d: Robert Thornby. 5 reels.
Kitty Gordon, Zena Keefe, George Ralph, Frank Evans, Warner Richmond.
Even after a bank cashier embezzles money to help satisfy his money-mad sweetheart, she dumps him. When he later marries, his pregnant wife goes to the golddigger and forces her to reimburse her husband the full amount.

Her Moment (Author's Photo-Plays, Inc./General Film Co., 1918)
d: Frank Beal. 7 reels.

Anna Luther, William Garwood, Alida Jones, Ann Schaeffer, Frank Brownlee.
After her sweetheart goes to America to study, a Rumanian girl is sold into slavery. Her cruel owner beats her and abuses her; but when he finally takes her to America, she again meets her old sweetheart, now a successful engineer.

Her Mother's Secret (Fox, 1915)
d: Frederick A. Thomson. 5 reels.
Ralph Kellard, Dorothy Green, Julie Power, Jane Meredith, Edward Davies.
Heartbreak results when a young man and his sweetheart plan to marry, only to discover that they are half-siblings.

Her New York (Thanhouser/Pathé, 1917)
d: Oscar Lund, Eugene Moore. 5 reels.
Gladys Hulette, Riley Chamberlain, Carey Hastings, William Parke Jr., Robert Vaughn, Ethyle Cooke.
When a poet from the city falls for a simple country girl, wedding bells get set to chime. But first, he's got to explain: Where did his baby come from, and who's the mother?

Her Night of Nights (Universal, 1922)
d: Hobart Henley. 5 reels.
Marie Prevost, Edward Hearn, Hal Cooley, Betty Francisco, Charles Arling, Jane Starr, George B. Williams, William Robert Daly, Richard Daniels.
In New York, a fashion model yearns for a life of wealth and luxury. But when Mr. Right shows up, he's a working-class clod.

Her Night of Romance (Constance Talmadge Productions/First National, 1924)
d: Sidney A. Franklin. 8 reels.
Constance Talmadge, Ronald Colman, Jean Hersholt, Albert Gran, Robert Rendel, Sidney Bracey, Joseph Dowling, Templar Saxe, Eric Mayne, Emily Fitzroy, Clara Bracey.
In England, an American heiress meets a penniless nobleman, and they fall in love.

Her Official Fathers (Triangle/Fine Arts, 1917)
d: Elmer Clifton, Joseph Henabery. 5 reels.
Dorothy Gish, Frank Bennett, Sam De Grasse, Fred A. Turner, Charles Lee, Milton Schumann, Jennie Lee, Hal Wilson, Fred Warren, Bessie Buskirk.
A wealthy young woman controls a bank's board of directors.

Her One Mistake (Fox, 1918)
d: Edward J. Le Saint. 5 reels.
Gladys Brockwell, William Scott, Willard Louis, Charles Perley, Mark Fenton, Helen Wright.
When a wealthy young woman falls for a gentleman thief and he later abandons her, she decides to avoid men forever.But then she meets John, and her misgivings are forgotten.

Her Only Way (Norma Talmadge Film Corp./Select Pictures, 1918)
d: Sidney A. Franklin. 6 reels.
Norma Talmadge, Eugene O'Brien, Ramsey Wallace, E.A. Warren, Jobyna Howland.
A young woman plans to marry for money, but finally true love wins the day.

Her Own Free Will (Eastern Productions/W.W. Hodkinson, 1924)
d: Paul Scardon. 6 reels.
Helene Chadwick, Holmes Herbert, Allan Simpson, George

Backus, Violet Mersereau.
Ever the faithful daughter, Nan marries a wealthy man primarily to save her father from bankruptcy.

Her Own Money (Famous Players-Lasky/Paramount, 1922)
d: Joseph Henabery. 5 reels.
Ethel Clayton, Warner Baxter, Charles French, Clarence Burton, Mae Busch, Jean Acker, Roscoe Karns.
Mildred, a thrifty wife, manages to save $2,000 without her husband's knowledge. Then, when he is desperately in need of funds, she plots with their neighbor Harry to loan her husband the money. But this arrangement triggers a suspicion that Mildred and Harry are having an affair.

Her Own People (Pallas Pictures/Paramount, 1917)
d: Scott Sidney. 5 reels.
Lenore Ulrich, Colin Chase, Howard Davies, Adelaide Woods, Jack Stark, Gail Brooks, Joy Lewis, William Winter Jefferson, Ada Lewis, Mary Mersch, William Gettinger.
A girl of white and American Indian parentage finds race prejudice among her boarding school classmates.

Her Own Way (Popular Plays and Players, Inc./Metro, 1915)
d: Herbert Blaché. 5 reels.
Florence Reed, Blanche Davenport, Clarissa Selwynne, Robdert H. Barrat, Fraunie Fraunholz, William A. Morse, John Karney, James O'Neill.
Childhood sweethearts grow up unaware of how much they love each other. Their love is put to the test when the boy goes off to fight in the Phillipines.

Her Price (Fox, 1918)
d: Edmund Lawrence. 5 reels.
Virginia Pearson, Edward F. Rosen, Victor Sutherland, Henri Leone, Charles H. Martin, Paul Stanton, Mrs. Allan Walker.
Deserted by her wealthy lover, an opera singer vows revenge on him and his family. But she is deterred when his brother offers her true love.

Her Private Affair (Pathé, 1919)
d: Paul Stein. 7 reels. (Sound effects, part talkie.)
Ann Harding, Harry Bannister, John Loder, Kay Hammond, Arthur Hoyt, William Orlamond, Lawford Davidson, Elmer Ballard, Frank Reicher.
While separated from her husband, Vera writes compromising letters to a man who turns out to be a cad. Later, when Vera and her husband are reunited, the cad tries to use those letters to blackmail her.

Her Purchase Price (B.B. Features/Robertson-Cole, 1919)
d: Howard Hickman. 5 reels.
Bessie Barriscale, Albert Roscoe, Joseph Dowling, Kathlyn Williams, Stanhope Wheatcroft, Irene Rich, Henry Kolker, Wedgewood Nowell, Una Trevelyn.
A British baby girl is kidnapped by an Arab chieftain and placed in his harem. When she grows up, she is purchased by an Englishman, who takes her home and tries to instruct her in western ways.

Her Reckoning (Rolfe Photoplays, Inc./Metro, 1915)
d: Charles Horan. 5 reels.
Emmy Wehlen, J. Frank Glendon, Leslie Austin, Walter Hitchcok, Jeannette Horton, Edgar L. Davenport, H. Cooper Cliffe.
To humor his girlfriend, a wealthy college boy agrees to go through a wedding ceremony, but secretly plans to have a fake minister. His roommate, however, delivers a real minister instead.

Her Reputation (Thomas H. Ince/Associated First National, 1923)
d: John Griffith Wray. 7 reels.
May McAvoy, George Larkin, Lloyd Hughes, James Corrigan, Eric Mayne, Winter Hall, Jane Wray, Gus Leonard.
Though innocent, Jacqueline finds her reputation in danger because of a news story that paints her as responsible for the death of her guardian.

Her Right to Live (Vitagraph, 1917)
d: Paul Scardon. 5 reels.
Peggy Hyland, Antonio Moreno, Bobby Connelly, Helen Connelly, Mildred Platz, John Robertson, Jack Ellis, Julia Swayne Gordon.
When an innocent man is accused of murder and refuses to give an alibi for fear of compromising the girl he was with, the girl bravely comes forward and testifies on his behalf.

Her Sacrifice (Sanford Productions, 1926)
d: Wilfred Lucas. 6 reels.
Gaston Glass, Bryant Washburn, Herbert Rawlinson, Gladys Brockwell, Wilfred Lucas, Ligia Golconda, Gene Crosby, Hector Sarno, Charles "Buddy" Post, Barbara Tennant.
Margarita refuses a proposal of marriage from the man she loves because she fears exposure of her past, during which she was seduced by a scoundrel.

Her Second Chance (First National/Vitagraph, 1926)
d: Lambert Hillyer. 7 reels.
Anna Q. Nilsson, Huntly Gordon, charlie Murray, Sam DeGrasse, William J. Kelly, Mike Donlin, Dale Fuller, Jed Prouty, Corliss Palmer.
Bitter over having been sent to a reformatory, Caroline emerges and swears to take revenge on the judge who sent her there.

Her Second Husband (Mutual, 1917)
d: Dell Henderson. 5 reels.
Edna Goodrich, William B. Davidson, Richard R. Neill, Miriam Folger.
After a businessman neglects his wife she divorces him and goes to work for one of his friends. Later, she is invited to attend a masquerade ball with a blind date. At the dance, she and her masked date hit it off so famously that they decide to marry. You guessed it, her second husband is her ex, who's had time to regret his mistakes, and is a reformed man.

Her Secret (Vitagraph, 1917)
d: Perry N. Vekroff. 5 reels.
Alice Joyce, Harry Morey, Robert Kelley, Mary Maurice, George Cooper, Patsey De Forest, Kittens Reichert, Nellie Anderson.
Raped by a bearded stranger and then abandoned, a young woman learns she is pregnant. She has the baby, then goes to work as a stenographer. She and her boss fall in love and marry, and he adopts her child. All seems rosy, until the truth slowly sets in: The clean-shaven man she's married is the stranger who raped her.

Her Silent Sacrifice (Select Pictures, 1917)
d: Edward José. 5 reels.
Alice Brady, Henry Clive, R. Payton Gibbs, Edmund Pardo, Blanche Craig, Arda LaCroix.
So that the penniless artist she loves can receive money to live on and help further his career, Arlette reluctantly agrees to sell her body to a lecherous art connoisseur.

Her Sister From Paris (Joseph M. Schenck
Productions/First National, 1925)
d: Sidney Franklin. 7 reels.
Constance Talmadge, Ronald Colman, George K. Arthur,
Margaret Mann, Gertrude Claire.
After Helen, a neglected wife, is cast away by her husband,
she turns to her twin sister Lola, a cabaret entertainer, for
comfort. Lola devises a plan that will send Helen back to her
husband, but dressed in Lola's glamorous clothes and
makeup and pretending to be Lola herself. Will that make a
difference to the husband? Yes it will.
Miss Talmadge plays both twins, mousy Helen and
glamorous Lola.

Her Social Value (Katherine MacDonald
Pictures/Associated First National, 1921)
d: Jerome Storm. 6 reels.
Katherine MacDonald, Roy Stewart, Bertram Grassby, Betty
Ross Clarke, Winter Hall, Joseph Girard, Lillian Rich,
Vincent Hamilton, Helen Raymond, Violet Phillips, Arthur
Gibson.
Marion, a shopgirl, falls for James, a young architect, and
soon they are married. But their happiness comes with a
price tag: James' career was being financed by a plutocrat
who fancied the young man as a husband for his daughter.
With his protegé now married to someone else, the sponsor
drops him and James is ostracized. Now it's up to James to
climb the career ladder on his own.

Her Soul's Inspiration (Universal, 1917)
d: Jack Conway. 5 reels.
Ella Hall, Marc Robbins, Edward Hearn, Marcia Moore,
Richar Ryan, Margaret Whistler, Alice May Youse, Ray
Whittaker.
A young woman who loves to dance gets her chance when
her grandpa buys a traveling show.

Her Strange Wedding (Lasky Feature Plays/Paramount,
1917)
d: George H. Melford. 5 reels.
Fannie Ward, Jack Dean, Tom Forman, Billy Elmer.
Unknowingly, a young woman marries an embezzler.

Her Sturdy Oak (Realart Pictures, 1921)
d: Thomas N. Heffron. 5 reels.
Wanda Hawley, Walter Hiers, Sylvia Ashton, Mayme Kelso,
Leo White, Frederick Stanton.
Belle, the ranch boss, is a sturdy young woman with
mannish clothes and manners. She's engaged to marry
Samuel, but on a trip he meets the attractive and feminine
Violet, and has a change of heart.

Her Summer Hero (FBO Pictures, 1928)
d: James Dugan. 6 reels.
Hugh Trevor, Harold Goodwin, Duane Thompson, James
Pierce, Cleve Moore, Sally Blane.
Lifeguard Ken saves the lovely Joan from drowning, and
they become sweethearts.

Her Surrender (Ivan Film Productions, Inc., 1916)
w, d: Ivan Abramson. 5 reels.
Anna Nilsson, William H. Tooker, Wilmuth Merkyl, Rose
Coghlan, Harry Spingler, Frankie Mann.
In critical condition, a young woman needs a massive blood
transfusion. Her donor turns out to be a man whose love for
her has always been unrequited. Now that he's saved her
life, she begins to see him in a different light.

Her Temporary Husband (Associated First National, 1923)

d: John McDermott. 7 reels.
Owen Moore, Sydney Chaplin, Sylvia Breamer, Tully
Marshall, Charles Gerrard, George Cooper, Chuck Reisner,
John Patrick.
Pressured to marry quickly in order to inherit a fortune,
Blanche selects an old man for her groom. She's tricked,
however, for after the ceremony the happy couple go home
and the groom sheds his disguise and is revealed to be a
handsome young man.

Her Temptation (Fox, 1917)
d: Richard Stanton. 5 reels.
Gladys Brockwell, Bertram Grassby, Ralph Lewis, Beatrice
Burnham, James Cruze.
Through the power of hypnotism, a young woman is made
to poison her aged husband.

Her Unwilling Husband (Jesse D. Hampton
Productions/Pathé, 1920)
d: Paul Scardon. 5 reels.
Blanche Sweet, Albert Roscoe, Edwin Stevens.
When a young actress' former fiancé comes to call, she
falsely introduces another man as her husband. Her ex-
flame sees through the deception, though, and decides to try
once more to win her love.

Her Wild Oat (First National, 1927)
d: Marshall Neilan. 7 reels.
Colleen Moore, Larry Kent, Hallam Cooley, Gwen Lee,
Martha Mattox, Charles Giblyn, Julanne Johnston.
Mary Brown, a working-class girl, disguises herself as a
duchess in an effort to enter high society.

Her Winning Way (Realart Pictres/Paramount, 1921)
d: Joseph Henabery. 5 reels.
Mary Miles Minter, Gaston Glass, Carrie Clark Ward, Fred
Goodwins, Helen Dunbar, Grace Morse, John Elliott, Omar
Whitehead.
When Ann, a newspaper reporter, is assigned to interview a
reclusive author, she devises a clever plan to gain access to
his apartment: She hires on as his maid.

Here Comes the Bride (Famous Players-Lasky/Paramount,
1919)
d: John S. Robertson. 5 reels.
John Barrymore, Frank Losee, Faire Binney, Frances Kaye,
Alfred Hickman, William David, Leslie King, Harry
Semmels.
Light-hearted comedy about a young lawyer whose fiancée's
father won't give his consent to their marriage.
Downhearted but back at work, the lawyer takes on a client
who wants him to marry her "in name only," to satisfy some
provision in a will. He does so, then his fiancée decides to
elope with him, giving him one wife too many.

Heredity (World Film Corp., 1918)
d: William P.S. Earle. 5 reels.
Madge Evans, Barbara Castleton, Jennie Ellison, Anne
Warrington, Jack Drumier, John Bowers, Joseph Smiley,
George MacQuarrie.
A young girl develops a crush on a handsome man who was
kind to her after a traffic accident. Years later, circumstances
bring them together again, and now the age difference
doesn't seem so daunting.

The Heritage of Hate (Universal, 1916)

d: Burton George. 5 reels.
William Quinn, Betty Schade, Roberta Wilson, Lillian

Concord, Eileen Sedgwick, Alfred Wertz, Paul Byron, Betty Hart.

Born illegitimate because her father deserted her mother, a young woman schemes to ruin him financially.

The Heritage of the Desert (Paramount, 1924)
d: Irvin Willat. 6 reels. (Includes Technicolor sequences.)
Bebe Daniels, Ernest Torrence, Lloyd Hughes, Noah Beery, Anne Schaefer, James Mason, Richard R. Neill, Leonard Clapham.

Out West, a rancher finds a tenderfoot in the desert and takes him home. There, the easterner falls in love with the halfbreed girl tending to his care.

The Hero (Preferred Pictures, 1923)
d: Louis J. Gasnier. 7 reels.
Gaston Glass, Barbara LaMarr, John Sainpolis, Martha Mattox, Frankie Lee, David Butler, Doris Pawn, Ethel Shannon.

Oswald, a war hero, returns home and is given a warm reception. He has an eye for the ladies, however, and it gets him into more trouble than he ever encountered overseas.

A Hero for a Night (Universal, 1927)
d: William James Craft. 6 reels.
Glenn Tryon, Patsy Ruth Miller, Lloyd Whitlock, Burr McINtosh, Robert Milash, Ruth Dwyer.

Comedy about Hiram, a taxi driver who decides to build his own airplane and fly it across the Atlantic.

The Hero of Submarine D-2 (Vitagraph, 1916)
d: Paul Scardon. 5 reels.
Charles Richman, James Morrison, Anders Randolph, Charles Wellesley, Thomas Mills, L. Rogers Lytton, Eleanor Woodruff, Zena Keefe.

Though he flunked out of Annapolis, a young man enlists as a sailor, and during an attack on the American fleet, he saves the life of the officer who flunked him.

Hero of the Big Snows (Warner Bros., 1926)
d: Herman Raymaker. 5 reels.
Rin-Tin-Tin, Alice Calhoun, Don Alvarado, Leo Willis, Mary Jane Milliken.

A courageous dog braves a violent snowstorm to deliver an urgent message.

Hero of the Hour (Universal, 1917)
d: Raymond Wells. 5 reels.
Jack Mulhall, Fritzi Ridgeway, Wadsworth Harris, Eugene Owen, Fred Burns, M.K. Wilson, Grace MacLean, Noble Johnson.

Perfume salesman Billy Brooks doesn't fit his dad's idea of what a man should be, so Dad arranges to have Billy kidnapped and roughed up a bit, to "make a man of him."

A Hero on Horseback (Universal, 1927)
d: Del Andrews. 6 reels.
Hoot Gibson, Ethlyne Clair, Edward Hearn, Edwards Davis, Dan Mason.

Fast-moving western drama about a cowpoke who loses big at the gaming table, then joins an oldtimer in prospecting. Along the way, he falls for the boss' daughter and is fired because of their courtship. But the girl somehow gets locked in the bank vault, and it's up to the cowpoke to rescue her.

Heroes and Husbands (Preferred Pictures, 1922)
d: Chet Withey. 6 reels.
Katherine MacDonald, Nigel Barrie, Charles Clary, Charles Gerrard, Mona Kingsley, Ethel Kay.

Susanne, a novelist, enacts a play in which she shoots her publisher with what she thought was a prop gun. Surprise... it's real, and it's loaded.

Heroes in Blue (Duke Worne Productions/Rayart, 1927)
d: Duke Worne. 5 reels.
John Bowers, Sally Rand, Gareth Hughes, Ann Brody, Lydia Yeamans Titus, George Bunny, Barney Gilmore.

Two Irish clans, the Dugans and the Kellys, clash when the Dugan boy, a pyromaniac and thief, is tracked by the Kellys, who are on the police force.

Heroes of the Night (Gotham Productions/Lumas Film Corp., 1927)
d: Frank O'Connor. 7 reels.
Cullen Landis, Marion Nixon, Rex Lease, Wheeler Oakman, Sarah Padden, J.P. Lockney, Robert E. Homans, Lois Ingraham.

Two brothers—a policeman and a fireman—love the same girl, but neither of them realizes it at first.

Heroes of the Street (Warner Brothers, 1923)
d: William Beaudine. 6 reels.
Wesley Barry, Marie Prevost, Jack Mulhall, Wilfred Lucas, Aggie Herring, Joe Butterworth, Phil Ford.

A street kid tries to solve his policeman father's murder.

Hesper of the Mountains (Vitagraph, 1916)
d: Wilfred North. 5 reels.
Lillian Walker, Donald Hall, Evart Overton, Donald MacBride, Denton Vane, Rose E. Tapley, Templar Saxe, Josephine Earle.

New York born and bred, Ann still yearns for the rustic West.

Hey Rube! (FBO Pictures, 1928)
d: George B. Seitz. 7 reels.
Hugh Trevor, Gertrude Olmstead, Ethlyne Clair, Bert Moorehouse, Walter McGrail, James Eagle.

Carnival performers clash in the eternal triangle.

Hickville to Broadway (Fox, 1921)
w, d: Carl Harbaugh. 5 reels.
Eileen Percy, William Scott, Rosemary Theby, John P. Lockney, Margaret Morris, Ray Howard, Paul Kamp, Ed Burns.

Small-town girl Anna Mae goes to the big city and, with the help of a benefactor, meets high-living jazz babies and is introduced to the fast life.

Hidden Aces (Louis T. Rogers Productions/Pathé, 1927)
d: Howard Mitchell. 5 reels.
Charles Hutchinson, Alice Calhoun, Barbara Tennant, Paul Weigel, Harry Norcross, James Bradbury Jr., Frank Whitson.

When two thieves make a daring daylight theft of a visiting princess' jewels, the police soon catch up with them, and discover that the "thieves" are really Secret Service agents, recovering stolen loot.

Hidden Charms (Argus Motion Picture Co., 1920)
d: Samuel Brodsky. 5 reels.
Daniel Kelly, Mrs. Charles Willard, Florence Dixon, William Mortimer, Robert Adams, Cecil Owens, George Fox.

To avoid a shallow suitor's unwelcome advances, young Mary disguises her face to appear that she was disfigured in an accident. Right on cue, the suitor forsakes her, and beautiful Mary is free to marry her true love.

The Hidden Children (Yorke Film Corp./Metro, 1917)
d: Oscar C. Apfel. 5 reels.

Harold Lockwood, May Allison, Lillian West, Henry Herbert, George MacDaniel, Lester Cuneo, A.B. Ellis, Lillian Hayward, Howard Davies, Daniel Davies, Clara Lucas.

Two white children, a boy and a girl, are hidden away from rampaging Indian tribes, in separate incidents. As they grow older, circumstances bring the two together.

The Hidden Code (Pioneer Film Corp., 1920)
d: Richard Lestrange. 5 reels.
Grace Davison, Ralph Osborne, Richard Lestrange, Clayton Davis.
A girl's tattoo contains an important formula for a new explosive.

Hidden Fires (Goldwyn, 1918)
d: George Irving. 5 reels.
Mae Marsh, Rod La Rocque, Florida Kingsley, Alec B. Francis, Jere Austin.
Louise is on her way home to America, but the ship she's booked on is torpedoed. With her mother emotionally distraught, the mother's doctor hires Peggy, a clerk who bears a resemblance to Louise, to pose as the lost girl.
Double duty for Miss Marsh, who plays both Louise and her lookalike, Peggy.

Hidden Loot (Universal, 1925)
d: Robert North Bradbury. 5 reels.
Jack Hoxie, Olive Hasbrouck, Edward Cecil, Jack Kenney, Buck Connors, Bert DeMarc, Charles Brinley.
Out West, a ranch lady becomes furious with a stranger she considers rash and stupid. Later, however, he breaks up a gang that have stolen the ranch payroll... and earns the lady's everlasting respect.

Hidden Pearls (Lasky Feature Plays/Paramount, 1918)
d: George H. Melford. 5 reels.
Sessue Hayakawa, Margaret Loomis, Florence Vidor, Theodore Roberts, James Cruze, Noah Beery, Clarence Geldart, Jack Holt, Gustav von Seyffertitz, Henry F. Woodward.
The son of a white man and a Hawaiian princess learns of a cache of pearls, hidden on his mother's island.

The Hidden Scar (World Film Corp., 1916)
d: Barry O'Neil. 5 reels.
Ethel Clayton, Holbrook Blinn, Irving Cummings, Montagu Love, Madge Evans, Edward M. Kimball.
When a minister preaches tolerance and understanding, his wife is emboldened to tell him about her own checkered past.

The Hidden Spring (Yorke Film Corp./Metro, 1917)
d: E. Mason Hopper. 5 reels.
Harold Lockwood, Herbert Standing, Lester Cuneo, H.F. Crane, Arthur Millette, Vera Sisson, Billie West.
In Copper City, a young lawyer fights for the rights of the working class.

Hidden Valley (Thanhouser, 1916)
d: Ernest Warde. 5 reels.
Vakyrien, Boyd Marshall, Ernest Warde, Arthur Bower.
In Africa, a young seminarian helps the natives bring water to their land by building an irrigation system.

The Hidden Way (Joseph DeGrasse/Associated Exhibitors, 1926)
d: Joseph DeGrasse. 6 reels.
Mary Carr, Gloria Grey, Tom Santschi, Arthur Rankin, Ned Sparks, Jane Thomas, Billie Jeane Phelps, Wilbur Mack, William Ryno.
Three ex-convicts find a natural spring and decide to bottle its water and market it as a miraculous medicine.

High and Handsome (R-C Pictures/FBO of America, 1925)
d: Harry Garson. 6 reels.
Maurice B. Flynn, Ethel Shannon, Tom Kennedy, Ralph McCulough, Jean Perry, Marjorie Bonner, John Gough, Lydia Knott.
Joe, a conscientious policeman, tries to get a fight promoter to repair the flimsy stands in his boxing arena. Instead, Joe gets suspended from the force. The promoter then matches Joe and a club fighter in his main event and, after Joe knocks out his opponent and the gallery stands collapse, Joe is vindicated and welcomed back to the force.

High Finance (Fox, 1917)
d: Otis Turner. 5 reels.
George Walsh, Doris Pawn, Willard Louis, Charles Clary, Herschel Mayall, Rosita Marstini, William Marr.
When a millionaire disowns his son, the lad decides to show Dad that making money is not all that difficult. He does so, but the underhanded mine swindle that Junior engineers doesn't make either of them happy.

The High Hand (Favorite Players Film Co./Alliance Films, 1915)
d: William D. Taylor. 6 reels.
Carlyle Blackwell, Neva Gerber, William Brunton, Douglas Gerrard, Richard Willis, John Sheehan, Henry Kernan.
A steel mill superintendent decides to run for governor.

The High Hand (Leo Maloney Productions/Pathé, 1926)
d: Leo Maloney. 6 reels.
Leo Maloney, Josephine Hill, Paul Hurst, Murdock MacQuarrie, Whitehorse, Gus Saville, Dick LaReno, Florence Lee.
Out West, a cowpoke assists a rancher and his pretty daughter in their battle against rustlers.

High Hat (Robert Kane Productions/First National, 1927)
d: James Ashmore Creelman. 7 reels.
Ben Lyon, Mary Brian, Sam Hardy, Lucien Prival, Osgood Perkins, Jack Ackroyd, Iris Gray, Ione Holmes.

Comedy about an extra in a movie studio who's taken a fancy to the wardrobe mistress.

High Heels (Universal, 1921)
d: Lee Kohlmar. 5 reels.
Gladys Walton, William Worthington, Frederick Vogeding, Freeman Wood, George Hackathorne, Charles DeBriac, Raymond DeBriac, Milton Markwell, Dwight Crittenden, Robert Dunbar, Ola Norman, Leigh Wyant, Jean DeBriac, Hugh Saxon.
Christine, a self-centered socialite, thinks of no one but herself and routinely ignores her wealthy father and her siblings. But the old man dies and, to everyone's surprise, leaves nothing but debts.

High Pockets (Betzwood Film Co./Goldwyn, 1919)
d: Ira M. Lowry. 5 reels.
Louis Bennison, Katherine MacDonald, William Black, Frank Evans, Edward Roseman, Francis Joyner, Sam Ryan, Neil Moran.
U.S. Marshal "High Pockets" Henderson is one tough customer. Almost single-handedly, he solves a murder, rounds up cattle thieves, and brings peace to the American West.

The High Road (Rolfe Photoplays, Inc./Metro, 1915)
d: John W. Noble. 5 reels.
Valli Valli, Frank Elliott, C.H. Brenon, Fred L. Wilson.
Sweatshop workers in a shirt factory are locked in and forced to work overtime. When a fire breaks out, several of the workers die in the flames. But one (Miss Valli) escapes, takes "the high road," and agrees to help prosecute the owner.

High School Hero (Fox, 1927)
d: David Butler. 6 reels.
Nick Stuart, Sally Phipps, William N. Bailey, John Darrow, Wade Boteler, Brandon Hurst, David Rollins, Charles Paddock.
High schoolers Pete and Bill, friends since childhood, clash over their mutual admiration of Eleanor, a new girl in school.

The High Sign (Universal, 1917)
d: Elmer Clifton. 5 reels.
Herbert Rawlinson, Brownie Vernon, Nellie Allen, Hayward Mack, Ed Brady, Marc Fenton, Frank McQuarrie, Al McQuarrie.
As a fraternity initiation prank, a collegian is made to impersonate a Balkan prince. Trouble arises when violent anarchists mistake him for the real prince.

High Speed (Universal, 1917)
d: George L. Sargent. 5 reels.
Jack Mulhall, Fritzi Ridgeway, Harry Rattenbury, Lydia Yeamans Titus, Albert MacQuarrie, J. Morris Foster.
Her social-climbing mother wants Susan to marry a count, but Susan prefers a down-to-earth young businessman.

High Speed (Hallmark Pictures Corp., 1920)
d: Charles Miller. 5 reels.
Edward Earle, Gladys Hulette, Roger Lytton, Charles Husted, Fay Evelyn, Aida Horton.
A race-car driver takes a job as chauffeur to a socialite.

High Speed (Universal, 1924)
d: Herbert Blache. 5 reels.
Herbert Rawlinson, Carmelita Geraghty, Bert Roach, Otto Hoffman, Percy Challenger, Jules Cowles, Cleo Bartlett, J. Buckley Russell.
Moreland, a high school athlete, woos the bank president's daughter, but Papa has picked out a more "suitable" match for her.

High Stakes (Triangle, 1918)
d: Arthur Hoyt. 5 reels.
J. Barney Sherry, Jane Miller, Harvey Clark, Ed Washington, Myrtle Rishell, Ben Lewis, J.P. Wild, Dick Rosson.
When a gentleman thief settles down to become a husband and father, he thinks the police will finally leave him alone. But soon, there's another jewel theft, and who do you think is the chief suspect?

High Steppers (Edwin Carewe Productions/First National, 1926)
d: Edwin Carewe. 7 reels.
Dolores Del Rio, Lloyd Hughes, Mary Astor, Emily Fitzroy, Rita Carewe, John T. Murray, Edwards Davis, Alec B. Francis, Clarissa Selwynne, Charles Sellon, John Steppling.
Two former Oxford students, Julian and Audrey, become reporters for a scandal magazine and actually uncover a serious criminal plot.

High Tide (Triangle, 1918)
d: Gilbert P. Hamilton. 5 reels.
Harry Mestayer, Yvonne Pavis, Jean Calhoun, Frederick Vroom, Graham Pettie, Julia Jackson, Leo Pierson, Jack Rollens.
In Greenwich Village, a writer falls in love, but because of his hereditary illness, he hesitates to propose matrimony.

The Highbinders (Worthy Pictures/Associated Exhibitors, 1926)
d: George W. Terwilliger. 6 reels.
William T. Tilden, Marjorie Daw, Ben Alexander, George Hackathorne, Edmund Breese, Walter Long, George F. Marion, Effie Shannon, Hugh Thompson.
After an attack by burglars, an author develops amnesia. He manages to fall in love, however, and when a later knock on the head restores his memory, he still remembers his new beloved.

The Highest Bid (American Film Co./Mutual, 1916)
d: Jack Prescott, William Russell. 5 reels.
Charlotte Burton, Marie Van Tassell, William Russell, Harry Keenan, William S. Hooser.
After his fiancée breaks off their engagement, a disconsolate young man goes west to mine for gold—and finds it.

The Highest Bidder (Goldwyn, 1921)
d: Wallace Worsley. 6 reels.
Madge Kennedy, Lionel Atwill, Vernon Steele, Ellen Cassity, Zelda Sears, Joseph Brennan, Reginald Mason, Brian Darley, William Black.
Once bitten, a millionaire is chary of falling in love again. Still, he falls in love with Sally, until he learns that she wants to marry him only for his money. For revenge, he finds a sewer rat, cleans him up and trains him, then introduces him to Sally as one even richer than he.

The Highway of Hope (Oliver Morosco Photoplays/Paramount, 1917)
d: Howard Estabrook. 5 reels.
House Peters, Kathlyn Williams, James Farley, Harry Devere.

Trying to forget his troubles, a former playboy marries a saloon girl while drunk. Comes the dawn, he faces his new married life with grit—and he and his bride discover gold.

The Hill Billy (United Artists, 1924)
d: George W. Hill. 6 reels.
Jack Pickford, Lucille Ricksen, Ralph Yearsley, Frank Leigh, Jane Keckley, Snitz Edwards.
A country bumpkin is unjustly accused of murder.

The Hillcrest Mystery (Astra Film Corp./Pathé, 1918)
d: George Fitzmaurice. 5 reels.
Irene Castle, J.H. Gilmour, Ralph Kellard, Wyndham Standing.
Marion wants to marry Gordon, but her dad, a wealthy shipbuilder, has other plans for her. What Dad doesn't know is that the man he's picked out for his little girl is a foreign spy.

Hills of Kentucky (Warner Bros., 1927)
d: Howard Bretherton. 7 reels.
Rin-Tin-Tin, Jason Robards, Dorothy Dwan, Tom Santschi, Billy Kent Shaeffer.
A wild dog is injured by violent mountain people, then is nursed back to health in secret by a crippled boy.

Hinton's Double (Thanhouser, 1917)

d: Ernest Warde. 5 reels.
Frederick Ware, Kathryn Adams, Eldean Steuart, Wayne Arey.
Sentenced to prison, a con man gets his lookalike to serve the sentence for him, in return for certain favors. Ware does double duty as the crook and his double.

The Hired Man (Thomas H. Ince/Paramount, 1918)
d: Victor L. Schertzinger. 5 reels.
Charles Ray, Charles K. French, Gilbert Gordon, Doris Lee, Lydia Knott, Carl Ullman.
Love blossoms on a New England farm, as a rancher's daughter falls for the hired hand.

His Birthright (Haworth Pictures Corp./Mutual, 1918)
d: William Worthington. 5 reels.
Sessue Hayakawa, Marin Sais, Howard Davies, Mary Anderson, Tsuru Aoki, Sydney De Grey, Harry Von Meter, Mayme Kelso.
The son of an American father and a Japanese mother becomes involved with German spies, but sees the light and joins the American war effort.

His Bonded Wife (Metro, 1918)
d: Charles J. Brabin. 5 reels.
Emmy Wehlen, Frank Currier, Creighton Hale,
John Terry, Warda Howard, William Frederick.
When a vacationing heiress falls in love with a working man, she tries to hide the difference in their status by posing as a department store clerk.

His Bridal Night (Select Pictures Corp., 1919)
d: Kenneth Webb. 5 reels.
Alice Brady, James L. Crane, Edward Earle, Daniel Pennell, Daisy Belmore.
On his wedding night, a bridegroom mistakenly takes his bride's twin sister on the honeymoon.

His Brother's Wife (World Film Corp., 1916)
d: Harley Knoles. 5 reels.
Carlyle Blackwell, Ethel Clayton, Paul McAllister.
To help pay her husband's medical bills, a wife agrees to a one-night stand with a wealthy man. What she doesn't know is that the man is her husband's brother.

His Captive Woman (First National/Warner Bros., 1929)
d: George Fitzmaurice. 8 reels. (Part talkie.)
Dorothy Mackaill, Milton Sills, Gladden James, Jed Prouty, Sidney Bracey, George Fawcett, William Holden, Gertrude Howard, Marion Byron, Frank Riecher, Doris Dawson.
A young woman goes on trial for murder, but she says there were extenuating circumstances.

His Debt (Haworth Pictures Corp./Robertson-Cole, 1919)
d: William Worthington. 5 reels.
Sessue Hayakawa, Jane Novak, Francis MacDonald, Fred Montague.
When a Japanese-American gambling house owner is shot and wounded by a sore loser, the loser's own fiancée, a nurse, helps to save his life.

His Divorced Wife (Universal, 1919)
d: Douglas Gerrard. 5 reels.
Monroe Salisbury, Charles West, Charles le Moyne, Alfred Allen, Alice Elliott, Raymond Gallagher, Pat Moore.
In the Kentucky mountains, a blacksmith fights for the honor of his wife.

His Enemy, the Law (Triangle, 1918)
d: Raymond Wells. 5 reels.

Jack Richardson, Irene Hunt, Jack Livingston, Graham Pette, Dorothy Hagar, Walt Whitman, May Giraci.
Because his father was shot while committing a robbery, a young man grows up with an intense hatred of legal authority.

His Father's Son (Rolfe Photoplays, Inc./Metro, 1917)
d: George D. Baker. 5 reels.
Lionel Barrymore, Irene Howley, Frank Currier, Charles Eldridge, George A. Wright, Phil Sanford, Walter Horton, Hugh Jeffrey, Florence Natol, Ilean Hume.
When a young man flunks out of college, his exasperated father cuts off his allowance and bets him that he cannot hold a job for a month. The lad gets a job as a detective, foils a jewel robbery, and wins the bet and the love of the jewelry owner's daughter.

His Father's Wife (World Film Corp., 1919)
d: Frank Crane. 5 reels.
June Elvidge, Sam B. Hardy, Malcolm Fassatt, W.T. Carleton, Marion Barney, Virginia Valli, William Parke, Lou Gorey, David Davies, Clio St. Bau, Ann Eggleston, J.W. Jenkins.
When an elderly millionaire seems to be getting too friendly with his private secretary, his greedy relatives try to discredit her. The old man's son investigates their slanderous accusations, and not only finds them untrue, but falls in love with the secretary himself.

His First Flame (Mack Sennett/Pathé, 1927)
d: Harry Edwards. 6 reels.
Harry Langdon, Ruth Hiatt, Natalie Kingston, Vernon Dent, Bud Jamison, Dot Farley.
A lovestruck young man is dismayed to learn that his sweetheart is really just a faithless gold-digger. He spends the night in his uncle's fire station, trying to forget his troubles—until the clamor of a fire alarm presents him with the chance to be a hero.
His First Flame, filmed mostly in 1925, was apparently Harry Langdon's first feature film; however, Mack Sennett Productions delayed its release until May of 1927, after the comedian had starred in two successful features for First National Pictures: *Tramp, Tramp, Tramp* and *The Strong Man*, both released in 1926.

His Great Triumph (Columbia/Metro, 1916)
w, d: William Nigh. 5 reels.
William Nigh, Julius D. Cowles, Roy Applegate, R.A. Bresee, Robert Elliott, Martin J. Faust, David Thompson, Victor De Linsky, Frank Montgomery, Marguerite Snow.
When tenement dweller Buttsy Gallagher is falsely convicted of murder, he gains a sort of celebrity status among his peers. But then the real killer is uncovered, and Gallagher's false reputation disappears—until he gets a chance to be a hero for real, by saving an honest judge from a gang of cutthroats.

His Hour (MGM, 1924)
d: King Vidor. 7 reels.
John Gilbert, Aileen Pringle, Emily Fitzroy, Lawrence Grant, Jacqueline Gadsden, George Waggoner, Carrie Clark Ward, Bertram Grassby, Jill Reties, Wilfred Gough.
Elinor Glyn tale about Tamara, an English beauty who becomes infatuated with a Russian womanizer.

His House in Order (Famous Players-Lasky
Corp./Paramount, 1920)
d: Hugh Ford. 5 reels.
Elsie Ferguson, Holmes E. Herbert, Vernon Steele, Margaret

Linden, Marie Burke, Lawrence Johnson, William P. Carlton, Forrest Robinson, Jane Jennings, Lewis Sealy.

After his unfaithful wife is killed in an accident, a young father looks to his son's governess, and finds in her a good prospect for a wife, and an excellent stepmother for the boy.

His Jazz Bride (Warner Bros., 1926)
d: Herman Raymaker. 7 reels.
Marie Prevost, Helen Dunbar, George Irving, Matt Moore, John Patrick, Gayne Whitman.
Dick's married to a jazz baby, and that's the problem. How to keep up with her extravagant ways?

His Last Haul (FBO Pictures, 1928)
d: Marshall Neilan. 6 reels.
Tom Moore, Seena Owen, Charles Mason, Al Roscoe, Henry Sedley.
Joe, a notorious thief, confesses his sins to a Salvation Army girl.

His Lucky Day (Universal, 1929)
d: Edward Cline. 6 reels. (Part talkie.)
Reginald Denny, Lorayne DuVal, Otis Harlan, Eddie Phillips, Cissy Fitzgerald.
Charles, a real estate broker, falls for one of his tenants.

His Majesty, Bunker Bean (Oliver Morosco Photoplays/Paramount, 1918)
d: William D. Taylor. 5 reels.
Jack Pickford, Louise Huff, Jack McDonald, Frances Clanton, Peggy O'Connell, Edythe Chapman, Hart Hoxie, Gustav von Seyffertitz, Edith M. Lessing.
A timid male stenographer is duped into thinking he is the reincarnation of Napoleon and also of an ancient Egyptian king.

His Majesty, Bunker Bean (Warner Bros., 1925)
d: Harry Beaumont. 8 reels.
Matt Moore, Dorothy Devore, David Butler, George Nichols, Helen Dunbar.
A timid male stenographer finds himself emboldened by the "discovery" that he is a reincarnation of Napoleon... but it's all a fake.
Remake of the 1918 Paramount film *His Majesty, Bunker Bean*. Both films were based on the novel *Bunker Bean*, by Harry Leon Wilson.

——**His Majesty, the American** (Fairbanks/United Artists, 1919)
d: Joseph Henabery. 8 reels.
Douglas Fairbanks, Marjorie Daw, Frank Campeau, Lillian Langdon, Jay Dwiggins, Sam Sothern.

A New Yorker is heir to the throne of a small kingdom.
This was the first film to be released by the newly-formed United Artists company.

His Master's Voice (Gotham Productions, 1925)
d: Renaud Hoffman. 6 reels.
Thunder the dog, George Hackathorne, Marjorie Daw, Mary Carr, Will Walling, Brooks Benedict.
Bob, a World War I doughboy, tries to desert the army, but his dog Thunder, who was taken overseas as part of a Red Cross unit, won't let him. Eventually Bob and Thunder become heroes, and Bob marries a Red Cross nurse.

His Majesty, the Scarecrow of Oz (Oz Film Manufacturing Co., 1914)
w, d: L. Frank Baum. 5 reels.
Violet Macmillan, Frank Moore, Pierre Couderc, Raymond

Russell, Tod Wright, Mildred Harris, Vivian Reed, May Wells, Fred Woodward.
Dorothy has many adventures in Oz, with Button Bright, the Tin Woodman, and the Cowardly Lion.

His Mother's Boy (Thomas H. Ince/Paramount, 1917)
d: Victor L. Schertzinger. 5 reels.
Charles Ray, Doris Lee, William Elmer, Joseph Swickard, Jerome Storm, Gertrude Claire, Lydia Knott.
A lad thought to be a "mama's boy" solves a mysterious oil shortage and wins the heart of a lovely lady, besides.

His Mystery Girl (Universal, 1923)
d: Robert F. Hill. 5 reels.
Herbert Rawlinson, Ruth Dwyer, Margaret Campbell, Jere Austin, Ralph Fee McCullough, William Quinn.
Kerry thinks he's found a damsel in distress, but it's all just a practical joke.

His New York Wife (Preferred Pictures, 1926)
d: Albert Kelley. 6 reels.
Alice Day, Theodore von Eltz, Ethel Clayton, Fontaine LaRue, Charles Cruz, Edith Yorke.
In New York, the secretary to a socially prominent young widow is forced to impersonate her.

His Nibs (Exceptional Pictures, 1921)
d: Gregory LaCava. 5 reels.
Charles (Chic) Sale, Colleen Moore, Joseph Dowling, J.P. Lockney, Walt Whitman, Lydia Yeamans Titus, Harry Edwards.
At a rural movie theater, the proprietor announces to the audience that he's snipped all the titles out of the film they are about to see, but that he will explain the plot as it goes along.

His Official Fiancée (Famous Players-Lasky/Paramount, 1919)
d: Robert G. Vignola. 5 reels.
Vivian Martin, Forrest Stanley, Vera Sisson, Hugh Huntley, Mollie McConnell, Kathryn Sohn, Tom Ricketts, Bobbie Bolder, James Neill, Katherine Van Buren, Virginia Foltz.
When a businessman asks his secretary to act as his fiancée for appearance's sake, she agrees to do so. But in her heart, she yearns to be his fiancée for real.

His Own Home Town (Famous Players-Lasky/Paramount, 1918)
d: Victor L. Schertzinger. 5 reels.
Charles Ray, Katherine MacDonald, Charles K. French, Otto Hoffman, Andrew Arbuckle, Carl Formes, Milton Ross.
It's old home week when a playwright from a small town writes a hit play, and a girl from the same small town stars in that play on Broadway.

His Own People (Vitagraph, 1917)
d: William P.S. Earle. 5 reels.
Harry Morey, Gladys Leslie, Arthur Donaldson, William Dunn, Betty Blythe, Stanley Dunn.
The village smithy rivals a British nobleman, as both love a spirited lass.

His Pajama Girl (Southern California Production Co., 1920)
d: Donald Edwards. 5 reels.
Billie Rhodes, Harry Ham, Nigel de Brulier, Harry Edwards, Harry Rattenbury, Eddie Barry, George French.
Newlyweds have a hectic bridal night when she's "abducted" by her mischievous girl friends, and he captures a crook who has escaped from jail.

His Parisian Wife (Famous Players-Lasky/Paramount, 1919)
d: Emile Chautard. 5 reels.
Elsie Ferguson, David Powell, Courtney Foote, Frank Losee, Cora Williams.
When an American lawyer in Paris marries a piquant French girl and brings her home to his icy-hearted parents, the marriage gets off to a rocky start.

His People (Universal, 1925)
d: Edward Sloman. 9 reels.
George Lewis, Blanche Mehaffey, Rudolph Schildkraut, Arthur Lubin, Rosa Rosanova, Bobby Gordon, Albert Bushaland, Jean Johnson, Kate Price, Virginia Brown Faire, Edgar Kennedy, Nat Carr, Charles Sullivan, Sidney Franklin.
A pushcart peddler has two sons: an ambitious law student and a humble newsie who also works as a prizefighter.

His Picture in the Papers (Triangle, 1916)
d: John Emerson. 5 reels.
Douglas Fairbanks, Clarence Handyside, Rene Boucicault, Jean Temple, Charles Butler, Loretta Blake, Homer Hunt.
Through a curious set of circumstances, a young man is required to get his picture in the papers in order to marry his sweetheart.

His Private Life (Paramount, 1928)
d: Frank Tuttle. 5 reels.
Adolphe Menjou, Kathryn Carver, Margaret Livingston, Eugene Pallette, André Cheron, Sybil Grove, Paul Guertzman, Alex Melesh, Alex Woloshin.
In Paris, a playboy who's attracted to a visiting American girl moves into the hotel where she's staying. Trouble is, the hotel is owned by his former fiancée and her husband—and when his ex sees the playboy, she leaps to the conclusion that he wants to resume *their* affair!

His Rise to Fame (Excellent Pictures, 1927)
d: Bernard McEveety. 6 reels.
George Walsh, Peggy Shaw, Bradley Barker, Mildred Reardon, Martha Petelle, William Nally, Ivan Linow.
A loser named Jerry finds good reason to amend his ways: the love of a good woman.

His Robe of Honor (Paralta Plays, Inc./W.W. Hodkinson, 1918)
d: Rex Ingram. 7 reels.
Henry B. Walthall, Mary Charleson, Lois Wilson, Noah Beery, J.J. Dowling, Roy Laidlaw, Fred Montague, Eugene Pallette, Guy Newhard.
After a shady lawyer becomes a judge through the intervention of machine politicians, he has a change of heart and decides to be an upstanding jurist. The love of a true-hearted woman makes his decision even easier.

His Royal Highness (World Film Corp., 1918)
d: Carlyle Blackwell. 5 reels.
Carlyle Blackwell, Evelyn Greeley, Kate Lester, Bert Honey, Lionel Belmore, Kitty Johnson, Herbert Barrington, George Morgan.
American college boys journey to France and get involved with a gangster's daughter.

His Secretary (MGM, 1925)
d: Hobart Henley. 7 reels.
Norma Shearer, Lew Cody, Willard Louis, Karl Dane, Gwen Lee, Ernest Gillen.
Romantic comedy about an ugly duckling secretary who overhears her handsome boss say he wouldn't kiss her for a

thousand dollars. She goes to a beauty parlor and... well, we all know what happens to ugly ducklings in the movies.

His Supreme Moment (Goldwyn/First National, 1925)
d: George Fitzmaurice. 8 reels.
Blanche Sweet, Ronald Colman, Kathleen Myers, Belle Bennett, Cyril Chadwick, Ned Sparks, Nick DeRuiz.
John, a mining engineer, proposes to Carla, an actress. She agrees to marry, but only on the condition that they live together the first year as brother and sister. The "supreme moment" of the title occurs after John and Carla have become convinced that their platonic experiment has failed. They separate and both find other loves, until the realization hits that they are passionately in love with each other, and they resume their marriage, this time for real.

His Temporary Wife (Joseph Levering Productions/Gaumont, 1920)
d: Joseph Levering. 6 reels.
Rubye de Remer, Edmund Breese, Eugene Strong, Mary Boland, W.T. Carleton, Armand Cortes.
When an eccentric millionaire dies, he leaves a will saying that his son will inherit only on the express condition that he marry someone other than his current golddigging girlfriend. So the heir decides to contract with the old man's nurse to become his "temporary wife."

His Tiger Lady (Paramount, 1928)
d: Hobart Henley. 5 reels.
Adolphe Menjou, Evelyn Brent, Rose Dione, Emil Chautard, Mario Carillo, Leonardo DeVesa, Jules Rancourt.
In Paris, a stage extra who dresses in a rajah's costume falls for an imperious duchess, the "Tiger Lady" of the title.

His Wife (Thanhouser/Mutual, 1915)
d: George Foster Platt. 5 reels.
Geraldine O'Brien, H.E. Herbert, Lorraine Huling, Inda Palmer, Theodore Von Eltz.
In England, two brothers love the same girl. One marries her.

His Wife's Friend (Thomas H. Ince/Paramount, 1919)
d: Joseph DeGrasse. 6 reels.
Dorothy Dalton, Warren Cook, Henry Mortimer, Richard Niel, Paul Cazeneuve, Tom Cameron, William Williams.
Love among the nobles: Lady Marion is married to Sir Robert, but secretly desires his friend John.

His Wife's Good Name (Vitagraph, 1916)
d: Ralph Ince. 5 reels.
Lucille Lee Stewart, Jessie Miller, Huntley Gordon, Frank Currier, John Robertson, William Lytell Jr.
When a millionaire's son marries a simple country girl, Dad tries to break them up.

His Wife's Husband (Pyramid Pictures/American Releasing Corp., 1922)
d: Kenneth Webb. 6 reels.
Betty Blythe, Huntley Gordon, Arthur Carewe, George Fawcett, Grace Goodall, Blanche Davenport, Rita Maurice.
She marries him for his money, he marries her for her looks. Can this marriage be saved?

His Wife's Money (Selznick/Select Pictures, 1920)
d: Ralph Ince. 5 reels.
Eugene O'Brien, Zena Keefe, Ned Hay, Louise Prussing, Cyril Chadwick, Dorothy Kent.
When a simple miner marries a wealthy heiress, they are happy at first, but eventually her money comes between

them.

Hit and Run (Universal, 1924)
d: Edward Sedgwick. 6 reels.
Hoot Gibson, Marion Harlan, Cyril Ring.
A lanky westerner has an amazing talent for sandlot baseball. He is signed to play in the major leagues, but finds that at that level, racketeers are involved in the game.

Hit of the Show (FBO Pictures, 1928)
d: Ralph Ince. 7 reels.
Joe E. Brown, Gertrude Olmstead, William Norton Bailey, Gertrude Astor, Ole M. Ness, Lee Shumway, William Francis Dugan, Ione Holmes, LeRoy Mason, Frank Mills, Daphne Pollard.
Show-biz comedy with a tear in its eye. A vaudeville comic gets to star in his own show, and also gets a spot for a charming but penniless girl. But the comic has a weak heart, and after fighting off a villain and then performing two roles on opening night, he collapses and dies right after the final curtain.

Hit or Miss (World Film Corp., 1919)
d: Dell Henderson. 5 reels.
Carlyle Blackwell, Evelyn Greeley, Charles Sutton, Jack Drumier, Richard Neal, Escamillo Fernandez, Joel Day.
Comedy about a chap whose wealthy father dies, leaving him only a tiny fraction of his estate until he can prove himself worthy in some capacity. The fellow scrambles about, trying to make himself useful somehow, and after several escapades, finally proves himself a hero by saving an inventor from his burning laboratory. That satisfies his father's will, and he inherits.

Hit-the-Trail Holliday (Famous Players-Lasky/Paramount, 1918)
d: Marshall A. Neilan. 5 reels.
George M. Cohan, Marguerite Clayton, Robert Broderick, Pat O'Malley, Russell Bassett, Richard Barthelmess, William Walcott, Estar Banks.
When a bartender loses his job for refusing to serve liquor to minors, he embarks on a grand crusade for prohibition.

Hitchin' Posts (Universal, 1920)
d: Jack Ford. 5 reels.
Frank Mayo, J. Farrell McDonald, Beatrice Burnham, Joseph Harris, Dagmar Godowsky, Mark Fenton, C.E. Anderson, Duke Lee.
After a riverboat gambler wins four race horses, the last possessions of a proud Kentucky colonel, the old man kills himself. Filled with remorse, the gambler tries to square accounts with the proud colonel's daughter, and together they go West, where they stake a claim to government land and start a new life together.

Hitting the High Spots (Metro, 1918)
d: Charles Swickard. 5 reels.
Bert Lytell, Eileen Percy, Winter Hall, Helen Dunbar, Gordon Griffith, Fred Goodwins, Ilean Hume, Stanton Heck, Al Edmundson, William Eagle Eye, William Courtright.
South of the border during the Mexican Revolution, two Americans vie for a girl's love.

Hitting the Trail (World Film Corp., 1918)
d: Dell Henderson. 5 reels.
Carlyle Blackwell, Evelyn Greeley, Joseph Smiley, George MacQuarrie, Mabel Bunyea, Muriel Ostriche, Walter Green, Edward Elkas.
In New York's lower East Side, a gangster reforms for the love of a flower girl.

Hoarded Assets (Vitagraph, 1918)
d: Paul Scardon. 5 reels.
Harry T. Morey, Betty Blythe, George Majeroni, Robert Gaillard, Jean Paige, Bernard Siegel.
It's larceny on the river, when a crook substitutes sand for gold dust in kegs.

Hogan's Alley (Warner Bros., 1925)
d: Roy Del Ruth. 7 reels.
Monte Blue, Willard Louis, Patsy Ruth Miller, Louise Fazenda, Ben Turpin, Max Davidson, Herbert Spencer Griswold, Mary Carr, Nigel Barrie.
Lefty, a prizefighter, is engaged to Patsy Ryan, but her father doesn't approve.

Hold 'em Yale! (DeMille Pictures/Pathé, 1928)
d: Edward H. Griffith. 8 reels.
Rod LaRocque, Jeanette Loff, Hugh Allan, Joseph Cawthorn, Tom Kennedy, Jerry Mandy.
Farcical doings, as an Argentine goes to Yale, bringing his pet monkey with him.

Hold That Lion (Paramount, 1926)
d: William Beaudine. 6 reels.
Douglas MacLean, Walter Hiers, Constance Howard, Cyril Chadwick, Wade Boteler, George C. Pearce.
Comedy about Jimmy, a romantic youth who's so infatuated with Marjorie that he follows her and her father all over the world. The title "Hold That Lion" relates to their stopover in darkest Africa.

Hold Your Horses (Goldwyn, 1921)
d: E. Mason Hopper. 5 reels.
Tom Moore, Sylvia Ashton, Naomi Childers, Bertram Grassby, Mortimer E. Stinson, Sydney Ainsworth.
Humorous tale about an Irish immigrant streetcleaner who goes from pushing brooms to becoming the city's mayor.

The Hole in the Wall (Metro, 1921)
d: Maxwell Karger. 6 reels.
Alice Lake, Allan Forrest, Frank Brownlee, Charles clary, William DeVaull, Kate Lester, Carl Gerrard, John Ince, Claire DuBrey.
Three crooks persuade a girl to impersonate a fashionable medium who has died.

Hollywood (Famous Players-Lasky/Paramount, 1923)
d: James Cruze. 8 reels.
Hope Drown, Luke Cosgrave, George K. Arthur, Harris Gordon, Bess Flowers, Eleanor Lawson, King Zany, Cecil B. DeMille, William S. Hart, Walter Hiers, May McAvoy, Owen Moore, Baby Peggy, Viola Dana, Anna Q. Nilsson, Bull Montana, Laurence Wheat, Jack Holt, Jacqueline Logan, Nita Naldi, Mary Astor, William de Mille, Jack Pickford, Lloyd Hamilton, Will Rogers, T. Roy Barnes, Thomas Meighan, Betty Compson, Leatrice Joy, Theodore Kosloff, George Fawcett, Bryant Washburn, Hope Hampton, Eileen Percy, Stuart Holmes, Ricardo Cortez, Lila Lee, Lois Wilson, Noah Beery, Alfred E. Green, Anita Stewart, Ben Turpin, J. Warren Kerrigan, Ford Sterling, Sigrid Holmquist, Roscoe Arbuckle.
Angela, an Ohio girl, decides to go to Hollywood and get into the movies. She trudges about from studio to studio, but gets no work. Ironically, all her family members and her boyfriend find movie roles without even trying. Standard wish-fulfillment entertainment, but with a stellar cast of real Hollywood stars appearing in cameos as themselves.

The Hollywood Reporter (Hercules Film Productions, 1926)
d: Bruce Mitchell. 5 reels.
Frank Merrill, Charles K. French, Peggy Montgomery, William Hayes, Jack Richardson, Violet Schram.
Billy, a reporter, loves the daughter of his publisher. Papa won't consent, though, until Billy gets a scoop that will put the publisher's chief rival behind bars.

Home (New York Motion Picture Corp./Triangle, 1916)
d: Raymond B. West, C. Gardner Sullivan. 5 reels.
Bessie Barriscale, Charles Ray, Clara Williams, George Fisher, Agnes Herring, Thomas S. Guise, Louis Glaum, Joseph J. Dowling.
When her newly wealthy relatives begin acting like snobs, young Bessie searches for a way to snap some sense into them.

Home (Universal, 1919)
w, d: Lois Weber. 6 reels.
Frank Elliott, Mildred Harris, Clarissa Selwynne, John Cossar, Dwight Crittenden, Lydia Knott, Helen Yoder, Al Ray.
After putting on airs to impress her wealthy classmates, a plumber's daughter learns the virtues of being herself.

Home James (Universal, 1928)
d: William Beaudine. 7 reels.
Laura LaPlante, Charles Delaney, Aileen Manning, Joan Standing, George Pearce, Arthur Hoyt, Sidney Bracy.
Laura, a shopgirl, hires a "chauffeur" to impress some visiting relatives. The chap isn't really a chauffeur, but her boss' son. He goes along with the gag because it amuses him, and in the end he and Laura fall in love.

Home Made (B & H Enterprises/First National, 1927)
d: Charles Hines. 7 reels.
Johnny Hines, Margaret Seddon, DeWitt Jennings, Maude Turner Gordon, Edmund Breese, Marjorie Daw, Charles Gerrard.
Small-town boy Johnny goes to the big city to promote his mom's home-made jam.

The Home-Maker (Universal, 1925)
d: King Baggot. 8 reels.

Clive Brook, Alice Joyce, George Fawcett, Billy Kent Schaeffer, Jacqueline Wells, Maurice Murphy, Martha Mattox, Virginia Boardman, Rank Newburg.
A husband and father suffers an injury and is confined to a wheelchair. Now he must swap roles with his wife, who turns out to be a better provider than he was. The husband discovers that he is a better home-maker and parent than his wife was, so they find this unorthodox arrangement to their liking. But what happens when the husband is healed of his injury, and regains the use of his legs?

The Home Stretch (T.H. Ince/Famous Players-Lasky/Paramount, 1921)
d: Jack Nelson. 5 reels.
Douglas MacLean, Beatrice Burnham, Walt Whitman, Margaret Livingston, Wade Boteler, Mary Jane Irving, Charles H. Mailes, Joe Bennett, George Homes, Jack Singleton.
Johnny, a young man, inherits a prize thoroughbred. His primary interest, though, is Margaret, the girl who's captured his heart. When his horse wins the big race, Johnny gets up the nerve to romance Margaret and finds, to his delight, that the lady wonders what took him so long!

Home Struck (R-C Pictures/FBO of America, 1927)
d: Ralph Ince. 6 reels.
Viola Dana, Alan Brooks, Tom Gallery, Nigel Barrie, George Irving, Charles Howard.
Barbara's a chorine who longs to be married. Dick, a bank clerk, proposes to her and they are soon married, but he likes to attend wild parties, which isn't exactly the home life Barbara had envisioned.

Home Stuff (Metro, 1921)
d: Albert Kelley. 6 reels.
Viola Dana, Tom Gallery, Josephine Crowell, Nelson McDowell, Priscilla Bonner, Robert Chandler, Aileen Manning, Philip Sleeman.
Madge, a stage actress, is replaced in the cast by a star-struck newcomer. Fuming privately, Madge goes out and falls asleep on a haystack. Next morning, she's discovered by the farmer, Robert, who falls in love with her and marries her. By the sheerest coincidence, he's the brother of the girl who replaced Madge in the show.

Home Sweet Home (Mutual, 1914)
d: D.W. Griffith. 6 reels.
Henry B. Walthall, Josephine Crowell, Fay Tincher, Lillian Gish, Dorothy Gish, Mae Marsh, Spottiswood Aitken, Robert Harron, Miriam Cooper, Mary Alden, James Kirkwood, Jack Pickford, Fred Burns, Courtenay Foote, Blanche Sweet, Owen Moore, Edward Dillon.
Four stories, all based on the song "Home Sweet Home" and the life of its composer, John Howard Payne.

Home Talent (Mack Sennett Productions/Associated Producers, 1921)
d: Mack Sennett. 5 reels.
Charlie Murray, Ben Turpin, James Finlayson, Eddie Gribbon, Kalla Pasha, Phyllis Haver, Dot Farley, Kathryn McGuire, Harriet Hammond.
Stranded vaudeville performers decide to put on a show to pay their rent.

The Home Town Girl (Famous Players-Lasky/Paramount, 1919)
d: Robert G. Vignola. 5 reels.
Vivian Martin, Ralph Graves, Lee Phelps, Carmen Phillips, Stanhope Wheatcroft, Herbert Standing, Pietro Sosso, Edythe Chapman, William Courtwright, Tom D. Bates.
Small-town girl Nell urges her soda jerk boyfriend to go to New York and prosper.

The Home Trail (Vitagraph, 1918)
d: William Wolbert. 5 reels.
Nell Shipman, Alfred Whitman, Joe Rickson, Patricia Palmer, Hal Wilson, S.E. Jennings.
Out West, a ranch foreman and a schoolteacher marry. But she becomes restless and is soon persuaded to leave him.

Home Wanted (World Film Corp., 1919)
d: Tefft Johnson. 5 reels.
Madge Evans, W.T. Carleton, Anna Lehr, Jack Drumier, Hugh Thompson, Charles Sutton, Maude Turner Gordon, Winifred Leighton, Michael J. Hanlon.
An orphan girl finds a home at last, with a kindly old Major and his family.

The Homebreaker (Thoms H. Ince/Paramount, 1919)
d: Victor Schertzinger. 5 reels.
Dorothy Dalton, Douglas Maclean, Edwin Stevens, Frank Leigh, Beverly Travis, Nora Johnson, Mollie McConnell.
Mary loves Raymond, but he's too busy living the high life

to notice her. So she and his father hatch a plan to make Raymond jealous.

Homer Comes Home (Thomas H. Ince/Paramount, 1920)
d: Jerome Storm. 5 reels.
Charles Ray, Otto Hoffman, Priscilla Bonner, Ralph McCullough, Walter Higby, John H. Elliot, Harry Hyde, Gus Leonard, Joe Hazelton, Bert Woodruff, Lew Morrison.
When Homer, a small town lad, returns home from the big city, the old crowd assumes he's become prosperous.

Homespun Folks (Thomas H. Ince/Famous Players-Lasky, 1920)
d: John Griffith Wray. 6 reels.
Lloyd Hughes, Gladys George, George Webb, A.W. Filson, Charles H. Mailes, Lydia Knott, Gordon Sackville, Willis Marks, James Gordon, Edith Yorks, Jeff Osborne, Jess Herring.
Love blossoms between a young lawyer and the daughter of a newspaper publisher.

A Homespun Vamp (Realart Pictures/Paramount, 1922)
d: Frank O'Connor. 5 reels.
May McAvoy, Darrel Foss, Lincoln Stedman, Josephine Crowell, Charles Ogle, Guy Oliver, Helen Dunbar, Kathleen Kirkham.
Stephen, an author from out of town, settles in a small village. The natives are inhospitable, though, and after being accused of theft, he is attacked and injured. Hometown girl Meg nurses his wounds, but when her guardians see them together, they consider her compromised and demand a shotgun wedding. Stephen goes along with it, thinking to have the marriage annulled some day. But his new bride makes herself so desirable to him, all thoughts of annulment are ended.

The Homesteader (Micheaux Book and Film Co., 1919)
w, d: Oscar Micheaux. 7 reels.
Charles D. Lucas, Evelyn Preer, Iris Hall, Inez Smith, Vernon S. Duncan, Charles S. Moore, Trevy Woods, William George.
After marrying a preacher's daughter, a man discovers that his new father-in-law is mentally unbalanced and uses his pulpit for evil purposes.

Homeward Bound (Famous Players-Lasky/Paramount, 1923)
d: Ralph Ince. 7 reels.
Thomas Meighan, Lila Lee, Charles Abbe, William P. Carleton, Hugh Cameron, Gus Weinberg, Maude Turner Gordon, Cyril Ring, Katherine Spencer.
A first mate takes over command of a yacht, in place of its alcoholic captain and against the wishes of the ship's owner. All ends well, however, when the first mate rescues the yacht from destruction in a stormy sea. He even winds up marrying the shipowner's daughter.

Honest Hutch (Goldwyn, 1920)
d: Clarence G. Badger. 5 reels.
Will Rogers, Mary Alden, Priscilla Bonner, Tully Marshall, Nick Cogley, Byron Munson, Eddie Trebaol, Jeanette Trebaol, Yves Trebaol.
When an idler discovers a stash of hidden money, he's forced to take a job to cover up his new-found wealth.

An Honest Man (Triangle, 1918)
d: Frank Borzage. 5 reels.
William Desmond, Mary Warren, Ann Kroman, Graham Pette.
A wealthy farmer asks a friend to deliver $50,000 to his daughter in the city.

Honesty—The Best Policy (Fox, 1926)
d: Chester Bennett. 5 reels.
Rockliffe Fellowes, Pauline Starke, Johnnie Walker, Grace Darmond, Mickey Bennett, Mack Swain, Albert Gran, Johnnie Walker, Dot Farley, Heinie Conklin.
An author who is having trouble getting published invents a shady criminal past for himself and his wife. Now his publisher is anxious to buy the author's memoirs.—but the lies threaten to get out of hand.

The Honey Bee (American Film Co./Pathé, 1920)
d: Rupert Julian. 6 reels.
Marguerita Sylva, Thomas Holding, Nigel Barrie, Albert Ray, George Hernandez, Harvey Clark, Dell Boone, Ethel Ullman, Charlotte Merriam, Ruth Maurice, Harry Tenbrook.
Flitting about, from New York to Paris to London, Hilda Wilson tries to find love, and eventually does— back home where she started.

The Honeymoon (Select Pictures, 1917)
d: Charles Giblyn. 5 reels.
Constance Talmadge, Earle Foxe, Maude Turner Gordon, Russell Bassett, Harris Gordon, Lillian Cook, Julia Bruns, Sam Coit.
To cure a new bride of her senseless jealousy, her lawyer uncle pretends to accede to her wish for a divorce, but without actually filing the papers.

Honeymoon (MGM, 1928)
d: Robert A. Golden. 6 reels.
Harry Gribbon, Polly Moran, Bert Roach, Flash, the dog.
Newlyweds receive a dog as a wedding gift from the bride's rejected lover. Trouble is, the dog has been carefully trained to allow nobody to touch the bride—including her new spouse.

The Honeymoon Express (Warner Bros., 1926)
d: James Flood. 7 reels.
Irene Rich, Willard Louis, Helene Costello, Jason Robards, Virginia Lee Corbin, Holmes Herbert, John Patrick, Jane Winton, Harold Goodwin, Robert Brower.
A wife and mother decides to walk out on her philandering husband, and becomes a successful interior decorator.

Honeymoon Flats (Universal, 1928)
d: Millard Webb. 6 reels.
George Lewis, Dorothy Gulliver, Phillips Smalley, Kathlyn Williams, Ward Crane, Bryant Washburn, Jane Winton, Patricia Caron, Eddie Phillips.
A snobbish woman resents the fact that her daughter did not marry for money, and tries to break up the daughter's marriage to a working man.

Honeymoon Hate (Paramount, 1927)
d: Luther Reed. 6 reels.
Florence Vidor, Tullio Carminati, Wiliam Austin, Corliss Palmer, Shirley Dorman, Effie Ellsler, Genaro Spagnoli, Marcel Guillaume.
In Venice, an imperious American heiress meets an Italian nobleman, and they fall in love and marry. The honeymoon is short-lived, though. When business calls him away, the bride is furious and locks herself in the bedroom. The Italian, seeing that this "honeymoon hate" is just an old-fashioned tantrum, sits calmly until the heiress returns to him and they resume their idyllic life together.

Honor Among Men (Fox, 1924)

d: Denison Clift. 5 reels.
Edmund Lowe, Claire Adams, Sheldon Lewis, Diana Miller, Frank Leigh, Fred Becker, Paul Weigel, Hector Sarno, Fred Malatesta, Walter Wilkinson.
In the kingdom of Messina, a visiting American heiress falls in love with the crown prince, and he with her.

Honor Bound (Universal, 1920)
d: Jacques Jaccard. 5 reels.
Frank Mayo, J. Farrell McDonald, Beatrice Burnham, Dagmar Godowsky, Nick de Ruiz, Irene Blackwell, Helen Lynch, Gordon Sackville, Max Willink, C.W. Herzinger.
While working on a South American rubber plantation, an American learns that the foreman is having an affair with a local girl. When the foreman's wife comes to visit, the American allows her to think the local girl is with him — but the deception doesn't work.

Honor Bound (Fox, 1928)
d: Alfred E. Green. 7 reels.
George O'Brien, Estelle Taylor, Leila Hyams, Tom Santschi, Frank Cooley, Sam DeGrasse, Al Hart, Harry Gripp, George Irving.
After a woman accidentally kills her husband, a devoted admirer of hers accepts the blame and is sent to prison. In gratitude, the woman has the prisoner released to her charge as her chauffeur.

Honor First (Fox, 1922)
d: Jerome Storm. 5 reels.
John Gilbert, Renee Adoree, Hardee Kirkland, Shannon Day, Wilson Hummel.
During World War I, twin brothers serve in the French army. One is a coward and runs away, the other presses on and wins a glorious victory.
Gilbert plays both twins, cowardly Honoré and brave Jacques.

The Honor of His House (Famous Players-Lasky/Paramount, 1918)
d: William C. DeMille. 5 reels.
Sessue Hayakawa, Florence Vidor, Jack Holt, Mayme Kelso, Tom Kurahara, Forrest Seabury.
Two men love a Nisei girl they met on a desert island.

The Honor of Mary Blake (Universal, 1916)
d: Edwin Stevens. 5 reels.
Violet Mersereau, Sidney Mason, Tina Marshall, Caroline Harris, James O'Neill.
An actress is duped into marrying a theatrical producer who already has a wife.

The Honor System (Fox, 1917)
d: Raoul A. Walsh. 5 reels.
Milton Sills, Cora Drew, James A. Marcus, Charles Clarey, Gladys Brockwell, Roy Rice, Arthur Mackley, Miriam Cooper, Geroge Walsh, P.J. Cannon, Johnny Reese, Carrie Clark Ward.
Unjustly convicted of murder and sentenced to life in prison, Joe Stanton becomes a model prisoner and works to bring about an "honor system." But a crooked politician schemes to abolish the honor system, using Joe as his patsy.

Honor Thy Name (New York Motion Picture Corp./Triangle, 1916)
d: Charles Giblyn. 5 reels.
Frank Keenan, Louise Glaum, Charles Ray, Blanche White, Gertrude Claire, George Fisher, Dorcas Matthews, Agnes Herring, Harvey Clarke, Jack Vosburgh.

A Southern colonel devises a novel though tragic way to save his son from a loveless marriage to an unfaithful vamp.

The Honorable Algy (New York Motion Picture Corp./Triangle, 1916)
d: Raymond B. West. 5 reels.
Charles Ray, Margaret Thompson, Howard Hickman, Margery Wilson, Albert Cody, Jerome Storm, Charles French, Louise Brownell, Thomas S. Guise, Walt Whitman.
To honor his parents' request that he marry an American heiress, Algy leaves England and heads for New York — but his heart is still with his English sweetheart.

The Honorable Friend (Lasky Feature Plays/Paramount, 1916)
d: Edward J. Le Saint. 5 reels.
Sessue Hayakawa, Tsuri Aoki, Raymond Hatton, Billy Elmer.
A wealthy Nisei sends away to Japan for a girl to be his bride, but when she arrives in America, his employee sees her, falls in love with her, and marries her himself.

Honor's Altar (New York Motion Picture Corp./Triangle, 1916)
d: Walter Edwards. 5 reels.
Walter Edwards, Bessie Barriscale, Lewis s. Stone, Lola May, Robert McKim.
Having reached the pinnacle of his profession, a financier wants to dump the wife who stood by him all through the lean years.

The Hoodlum (First National, 1919)
d: Sidney A. Franklin. 7 reels.
Mary Pickford, Ralph Lewis, Kenneth Harlan, Melvin Messenger, Dwight Crittenden, Aggie Herring, Andrew Arbuckle, Max Davidson, Paul Mullen, Buddy Messinger.
When a wealthy girl moves into a New York slum with her sociologist father to do research for a book, she quickly gets the hang of having fun, the poor folks' way.

Hoodman Blind (Fox, 1923)
d: John Ford. 6 reels.
David Butler, Gladys Hulette, Regina Connelly, Frank Campeau, Marc MacDermott, Trilby Clark, Jack Walters, Eddie Gribbon.
A confused young man marries twice and deserts his wife both times. But there are two daughters born of these unions, and when they grow up they will be reunited with their father. Miss Hulette plays a double role as the two daughters.

Hoodoo Ann (Fine Arts/Triangle, 1916)
d: Lloyd Ingraham. 5 reels.
Mae Marsh, Robert Harron, William H. Brown, Wilbur Higby, Loyola O'Connor, Mildred Harris, Pearl Elmore, Anna Hernandez, Charles Lee, Elmo Lincoln, Robert Lawler.
In an orphanage, a young girl is greatly impressed by the "hoodoo" practiced by the resident cook. As a consequence, she believes herself bewitched later in life.

Hoofbeats of Vengeance (Universal, 1929)
d: Henry MacRae. 5 reels.
Jack Perrin, Helen Foster, Al Ferguson, Rex the Wonder Horse.
Rex the Wonder Horse assists the mounties in their hunt for a dangerous criminal.

Hook and Ladder (Universal, 1924)
d: Edward Sedgwick. 6 reels.

Hoot Gibson, Frank Beal, Mildred June, Edwards Davis, Philo McCullough.
A cowboy turned fireman wins the girl of his dreams when he rescues her from a conflagration.

A Hoosier Romance (Selig Polyscope/Mutual, 1918)
d: Colin Campbell. 5 reels.
Colleen Moore, Thomas Jefferson, Harry McCoy, Edward Jobson, Eugenie Besserer, Frank Hayes.
A tender-hearted farm girl wants to marry her sweetie, the hired hand. But Pa forbids it, insisting instead that she marry an ancient but wealthy family acquaintance.

The Hoosier Schoolmaster (Whitman Bennett Productions/W.W. Hodkinson, 1924)
d: Oliver L. Sellers. 6 reels.
Henry Hull, Jane Thomas, Frank Dane, Mary Foy, Walter Palm, Nat Pendleton, Dorothy Allen, G.W. Hall, George Pelzer, Arthur Ludwig, Frank Andrews, Harold McArthur.
Ralph, an Indiana schoolmaster, is falsely accused of theft. He not only defends himself and wins acquittal, he helps expose the real thieves.

Hop, the Devil's Brew (Universal, 1916)
d: Lois Weber, Phillips Smalley. 5 reels.
Charles Hammond, Marie Walcamp, Phillips Smalley, Lois Weber, Juan De La Cruz, Ethel Weber.
Tragedy ensues when a customs official investigating the opium trafficking problem discovers that his own wife is addicted to the drug.

The Hope (Metro, 1920)
d: Herbert Blaché. 6 reels.
Jack Mulhall, Marguerite de la Motte, Ruth Stonehouse, Frank Elliott, Lillian Langdon, Mayme Kelso, Arthur Clayton, J.P. Morse, Bobby Mack, Herbert Grimwood.
A heartless cad courts a girl for her money, gets her pregnant, then abandons her. In her desperation the girl flees to Italy, where her family finally catches up with her and forgives her.

The Hope Chest (Paramount, 1919)
d: Elmer Clifton. 5 reels.
Richard Barthelmess, Dorothy Gish, Sam De Grasse, George Fawcett, Kate Toncray, Bertram Grassby, Carol Dempster.
The daughter of a vaudeville performer falls in love with a young man of standing. His mother is violently opposed to their union, but the young people's fathers favor it.

The Hopper (Triangle, 1918)
d: Thomas N. Heffron. 5 reels.
Walt Whitman, George Hernandez, Irene Hunt, William V. Mong, Eugene Corey, Thomas Kurahara, Peaches Jackson, Lillian West, Louis Durham.
Rival antique collectors despise each other so much that when their children marry each other, the kids are promptly disinherited.

The Hornet's Nest (Vitagraph, 1919)
d: James Young. 5 reels.
Earle Williams, Brinsley Shaw, Vola Vale, Ogden Crane, Kathleen Kirkman, Edward McWade.
Suspecting her guardians of trying to rob her of her estate, a teenage girl seeks help from her cousin, a burglar known as "The Hornet."

Horse Shoes (Monty Banks Enterprises/Pathé, 1927)
d: Clyde Bruckman. 6 reels.
Monty Banks, Ernie Wood, Henry Barrows, John Elliott, Jean Arthur, Arthur Thalasso, George French, Agostino Borgato, Bert Apling.
Monty, fresh from law school, gets a case involving a possibly forged will. He wins the case by proving that the horseshoe-shaped watermark on the "will" is dated later than the document itself!

The Hostage (Lasky Feature Plays/Paramount, 1917)
d: Robert Thornby. 5 reels.
Wallace Reid, Dorothea Abril, Gertrude Short, C.H. Geldert, Guy Oliver, Camille Ankewich, Noah Beery, Georgie D. Spaulding, Lillian Leighton, Lucien Littlefield.
In a mythical kingdom, rival clans unite to fight a common enemy.

Hot Heels (Universal, 1928)
d: William James Craft. 6 reels.
Glenn Tryon, Patsy Ruth Miller, Greta Yoltz, James Bradbury Sr., Tod Sloan, Lloyd Whitlock.
In a gesture more romantic than cerebral, a small hotel owner buys a stranded theatrical troupe.

Hot News (Paramount, 1928)
d: Clarence Badger. 7 reels.
Bebe Daniels, Neil Hamilton, Paul Lukas, Alfred Allen, Spec O'Donnell, Ben Hall, Mario Carillo, Maude Turner Gordon.
When his publisher hires a young woman as a cameraman—oops, camera *person*—the paper's male cameraman resigns in protest. This couple is off to such a rocky start, you can't help but know that by the final reel, they'll be in romantic embrace.

Hot Stuff (First National/Warner Bros., 1929)
d: Mervyn LeRoy. (Part talkie.) 7 reels.
Alice White, Louise Fazenda, William Bakewell, Doris Dawson, Ben Hall, Charles Sellon, Buddy Messinger, Andy Devine.
A lady has a financial windfall, decides to send her niece to college, and goes along with her.

Hot Water (Pathé, 1924)
d: Fred Newmeyer, Sam Taylor. 5 reels.
Harold Lloyd, Jobyna Ralston, Josephine Crowell.

A flustered husband spends his day trying to transport groceries—and a live turkey—home on a streetcar. Later, he suggests that he and his wife take their new automobile for a trial spin, only to find that the whole family has invited themselves along, too.

Hotel Imperial (Paramount, 1927)
d: Mauritz Stiller. 8 reels.
Pola Negri, James Hall, George Seigmann, Max Davidson, Mikhail Vavitch, Otto Fries, Nicholas Soussanim, Golden W. Adams.
During World War I, a weary Hungarian officer falls asleep outside the Hotel Imperial in a Russian-occupied border town. Come morning, the hotel servants find the officer and persuade him to masquerade as the hotel waiter to avoid detection. In that capacity, he learns of Russian plans to devastate Hungarian forces. He acts fast, alerts his troops, and foils the Russians' plans.

The Hottentot (First National, 1923)
d: James W. Horne. 5 reels.
Douglas MacLean, Madge Bellamy, Lila Leslie, Martin Best, Stanhope Wheatcroft, Raymond Hatton, Dwight Crittenden, Harry Booker, Bert Lindley.
Comedy about a fellow who's deathly afraid of horses, but is

THE KID (1921). Charlie Chaplin and the six-year-old phenom, Jackie Coogan, are warily looking out for the law—unaware that "the law"—in the person of 6-foot-two-inch Tom Wilson—stands right behind them, eager for an arrest.   Since Chaplin stood only 5 feet five, he usually chose very tall actors to play his nemeses.

* * * * *

mistaken for a champion steeplechase rider.

The Hound of Silver Creek (Universal, 1928)
d: Stuart Paton.   5 reels.
Dynamite, the dog, Gloria Grey, Edmund Cobb, Gladden James, Billy "Red" Jones, Frank Rice, Frank Clark.
Tale of a man, a woman, and his faithful dog.

The Hour of Reckoning (John E. Ince/George H. Davis, 1927)
d: John E. Ince.   6 reels.
John E. Ince, Herbert Rawlinson, Grace Darmond, Harry von Meter, Virginia Castleman, John J. Darby, Edwin Middleton.
A clerk in a safe-manufacturing firm saves the boss' son from suffocation, by managing to unlock a safe that has trapped the lad.

The House Built Upon Sand (Triangle/Fine Arts, 1917)
d: Edward Morrisey.   5 reels.
Lillian Gish, Roy Stuart, Kate Bruce, Josephine Crowell, Jack Brammall, William H. Brown, Bessie Buskirk.
A pampered debutante learns to love her husband.

A House Divided (J. Stuart Blackton Productions, Inc., 1919)
d: J. Stuart Blackton.   5 reels.
Sylvia Breamer, Herbert Rawlinson, Lawrence Grossmith, Shirley Huxley, Sally Crute, William Humphrey, Eric Mayne, Marie Burke, Charles Stuart Blackton, Violet Blackton.
Weepy melodrama about a young woman who finally marries a man she's loved for years, only to find that he already has a wife and child.

The House Next Door (Lubin/General Film Co., 1914)
d: Barry O'Neil.   5 reels.
Edwin Barbour, Gaston Bell, Ethel Clayton, George Soule Spencer, Florence Williams, Joseph Kaufman, Frankie Mann, Ferdinand Tidmarsh, Peter Lang, Edwin Booth Tilton.
Anti-Semitism plagues the romances of two couples.

The House of a Thousand Candles (Selig Polyscope, 1915)
d: Thomas N. Heffron.   5 reels.
Harry Mestayer, Grace Darmond, John Charles, George Backus, Forrest Robinson.
A young man is forced to live in a mysterious house for one year, in order to qualify for an inheritance.
This Selig film, based on the play of the same name by George Middleton, was remade in 1920 by Jesse D. Hampton Productions as *Haunting Shadows*.

The House of a Thousand Scandals—see: The House of Scandals (1915)

The House of Bondage (Photo Drama Motion Picture Co., 1914)
d: Pierce Kingsley.   6 reels.
Lottie Pickford, Armand F. Cortes, Sue Willis, Robert Lawrence, Herbert Barrington, Vivian De Wolfe, Brian Darley, Amelia Badarracco, Anna Jordan, Julia Walcott, Fred Nicholls.
A young woman finds that, after having worked in a bordello, she can now find no respectable work anywhere.

The House of Glass (C.K.Y. Film Corp./Select Pictures, 1918)
d: Emile Chautard.   5 reels.
Clara Kimball Young, Pell Trenton, Corliss Giles, Edward Kimball, James T. Laffey, Jose Sadler, Norman Selby, William Waltman, Peggy Burke, Doris Field.

After serving time for a robbery she did not commit, a young woman goes West to make a new life for herself. But in so doing, she's violating her parole.

The House of Gold (Metro, 1918)
d: Edwin Carewe.   5 reels.
Emmy Wehlen, Joseph Kilgour, Hugh Thompson, Helen Lindroth, Maud Hill.
Riotous parties are a regular occurrence at the home of a dissolute wastrel, who's tricked an honest girl into marriage.

The House of Horror (First National/Warner Bros., 1929)
d: Benjamin Christensen.   7 reels.
Louise Fazenda, Chester Conklin, Thelma Todd, James Ford, William V. Mong, Dale Fuller.
Not a horror movie *per se*, this one's about an antique shop with trap doors, sliding panels, and all manner of strange characters popping in and out.

The House of Intrigue (Haworth Pictures/Robertson-Cole, 1919)
d: Lloyd Ingraham.   5 reels.
Mignon Anderson, Helene Sullivan, Peggy May, Bert Hadley, Lloyd Bacon, Donald McDonald, Josephine Crowell, Alfred Fisher, Virginia Boardman.
An out-of-work actress agrees to impersonate an heiress.

The House of Lies (Oliver Morosco Photoplays/Paramount, 1916)
d: William D. Taylor.   5 reels.
Edna Goodrich, Juan de la Cruz, Kathleen Kirkham, Lucille Ward, Harold Holland, Herbert Standing.
To avoid a forced marriage, a young woman deliberately burns her face with acid, to make herself look homely. When she finally finds a man who loves her and will marry her in spite of her scars, she accepts... and reveals that the acid was not real, and her scars are no more than greasepaint.

The House of Mirth (Metro, 1918)
d: Albert Capellani.   6 reels.
Katherine Harris Barrymore, Henry Kolker, Christine Mayo, Joseph Kilgour, Lottie Briscoe, Edward Abeles, Maggie Western, Pauline Welch, Nellie Parker-Spaulding.
What's a young woman to do when she's loved by two wealthy men, but her own true love is a fellow of modest means?

The House of Scandal (Tiffany-Stahl Productions, 1928)
d: King Baggot.   6 reels.
Pat O'Malley, Dorothy Sebastian, Harry Murray, Gino Corrado, Lee Shumway, Jack Singleton, Ida Darling, Lydia Knott.
Danny, an Irish immigrant, is mistaken for a police officer during a jewel theft. He tries to aid a comely young woman at the scene, but it turns out that she is one of the thieves, and Danny is shot. He comes out of it okay, and the girl goes to jail, but when she is released Danny and a marriage proposal are waiting for her.

The House of Shame (Chesterfield Motion Picture Corp., 1928)
d: Burton King.   6 reels.
Creighton Hale, Virginia Browne Faire, Lloyd Whitlock, Florence Dudley, Fred Walton, Carlton King.
Convoluted tale about a romantic triangle that turns out not to be a triangle at all, but a set-up.

The House of Silence (Famous Players-Lasky/Paramount,

1918)
d: Donald Crisp. 5 reels.
Wallace Reid, Ann Little, Adele Farrington, Winter Hall, Ernest Joy, H.A. Barrows.
There's a violent death in the local bordello... but was it murder or self-defense?

The House of Tears (Rolfe Photoplays/Metro, 1915)
d: Edwin Crane. 5 reels.
Emily Stevens, Henry Bergman, Walter Hitchcock, George Brennan, Madge Tyrone, Bernard Randall.
Frivolous and self-absorbed, a bored woman callously deserts her husband and daughter and moves to another town, where she remarries. Years later, she returns to New York only to find that her new husband is cheating on her with her own daughter.

The House of the Lost Court (Thomas A. Edison, Inc./Paramount, 1915)
d: Charles J. Brabin. 5 reels.
Robert Conness, Duncan McRae, Helen Strickland, Sally Crute, Viola Dana, Mrs. Wallace Erskine, Gertrude McCoy, William West.
In England, a young nobleman is sentenced to hang for a murder he did not commit. The following morning, the jailer finds him dead, apparently from self-inflicted poison. But that's not the end of the story. The nobleman's "death" was a hoax to lure the real culprit into coming forward... and it works.

The House of the Tolling Bell (J. Stuart Blackton Features/Pathé, 1920)
d: J. Stuart Blackton. 6 reels.
May McAvoy, Bruce Gordon, Morgan Thorpe, Edward Elkas, Eulalie Jensen, William R. Dunn, Edna Young, William Jenkins.
The only two heirs to an old man's estate are forced to live in his creaky—and possibly haunted—residence for one year before claiming their inheritance.

The House of Toys (American Film Co./Pathé, 1920)
d: George L. Cox. 6 reels.
Seena Owen, Pell Trenton, Helen Jerome Eddy, Lillian Leighton, George Hernandez, Stanhope Wheatcroft, Henry Barrows, Marian Skinner, William Buckley, Perry Banks.
A young woman ignores her wealthy aunt's advice and marries for love instead of for money. Initially she'll regret her decision, but the passing years invest both husband and wife with a new realization of the true value of marriage.

The House of Youth (Regal Pictures/Producers Distributing Corp., 1924)
d: Ralph Ince. 7 reels.
Jacqueline Logan, Malcolm McGregor, Vernon Steele, Gloria Grey, Richard Travers, Lucilla Mendez, Edwin Booth Tilton, Aileen Manning, Hugh Metcalf, Barbara Tennant.
Melodrama about Corinna, a socialite who loves not wisely but too well, and ends up forsaking all her lovers in favor of opening a youth farm.

The House That Jazz Built (Realart Pictures, 1921)
d: Penrhyn Stanlaws. 6 reels.
Wanda Hawley, Forrest Stanley, Gladys George, Helen Lynch, Clarence Geldert, Helen Dunbar, Robert Bolder.
Frank and Cora are an ideal couple until he gets a high-salaried position in a big New York company. The new lifestyle agrees with Frank, but Cora just overeats and grows fat and lazy. When Frank gets close to a young, trim girl in his firm, Cora hears the wake-up call and gets her act together, regains her figure and her vitality, and keeps her man.

The House With the Golden Windows (Lasky Feature Plays/Paramount, 1916)
d: George Melford. 5 reels.
Wallace Reid, Cleo Ridgely, Billy Jacobs, James Neill, Mabel Van Buren, Marjorie Daw.
The wife of a shepherd grows weary of always being poor, and aspires to own the mansion down the lane.

How Baxter Butted In (Warner Bros., 1925)
d: William Beaudine. 7 reels.
Matt Moore, Dorothy Devore, Ward Crane, Wilfred Lucas, Adda Gleason, Turner Savage, Otis Harlan.
An amiable day-dreamer yearns to be a success.

How Could You, Caroline? (Pathé, 1918)
d: Frederick Thompson. 5 reels.
Bessie Love, James Morrison, Dudley Hawley, Henry Hallam, Edna Earl, Amelia Summerville.
Comedic hi-jinks ensue when a bride-to-be attends her fiancé's bachelor party disguised as a cooch dancer.

How Could You, Jean? (Famous Players-Lasky/Paramount, 1918)
d: William D. Taylor. 5 reels.
Mary Pickford, Casson Ferguson, Spottiswoode Aitken, Herbert Standing, Fanny Midgley, Larry Peyton, ZaSu Pitts, Mabell Harvey, Lucille Ward, Emma Gerdes, Wesley Barry.
Jean is a high-spirited girl who's working as a cook in a fancy residence, and attracting all the eligible young men in the neighborhood.

How to Educate a Wife (Warner Bros., 1924)
d: Monta Bell. 7 reels.
Monte Blue, Creighton Hale, Marie Prevost, Claude Gillingwater, Vera Lewis, Betty Francisco, Edward Earle, Nellie Bly Baker.
There's friction and misunderstanding when an attractive young woman goes to work in her husband's business.

How to Handle Women (Universal, 1928)
d: William J. Craft. 6 reels.
Glenn Tryon, Raymond Keane, Marian Nixon, Mario Carillo, Bull Montana, Cesare Gravina, Robert T. Haines.
A commercial artist saves a European kingdom from bankruptcy and wins the love of a beautiful journalist in the bargain.

Huck and Tom: Or the Further Adventures of Tom Sawyer (Paramount, 1918)
d: William D. Taylor. 5 reels.
Jack Pickford, Robert Gordon, George Hackathorne, Alice Marvin, Edythe Chapman, Frank Lanning, Clara Horton, Tom Bates, Helen Gilmore, Antrim Short, Jane Keckley.
Second part of William D. Taylor's two-part series based on Mark Twain's novels *The Adventures of Tom Sawyer* and *Huckleberry Finn*. Part one, also starring Jack Pickford as Tom and Robert Gordon as Huck, was titled *Tom Sawyer*.

Huckleberry Finn (Famous Players-Lasky/Paramount, 1920)
d: William D. Taylor. 7 reels.
Lewis Sargent, Katherine Griffith, Martha Mattox, Frank Lanning, Orral Humphrey, Tom D. Bates, Gordon Griffith, Edythe Chapman, Thelma Salter, George Reed, L.M. Wells.
This version of Mark Twain's tale of a fugitive boy and his

friend Jim, the slave, stars Lewis Sargent as the runaway Huck.

Hugon, the Mighty (Universal, 1918)
d: Rollin Sturgeon. 5 reels.
Monroe Salisbury, Margery Bennett, Antrim Short, Thomas H. Pearse, George Holt, Tote Du Crow, Roy Watkins.
Hugon, a Canadian woodsman, loves Marie but fears she doesn't love him back. He's wrong.

Hula (Paramount, 1927)
d: Victor Fleming. 6 reels.
Clara Bow, Clive Brook, Arlette Marchal, Arnold Kent, Maude Truax, Albert Gran, Agostino Borgato.
A free-spirited girl who has grown up in Hawaii reaches the age where she begins to notice men, and they her.

Hulda From Holland (Famous Players/Paramount, 1916)
d: John B. O'Brien. 5 reels.
Mary Pickford, Frank Losee, John Bowers, Russell Bassett, Harold Hollacher, Charles E. Vernon.
Young Hulda arrives in the U.S. from Holland, and instantly sets hearts spinning.

Human Collateral (Vitagraph, 1920)
d: Lawrence C. Windom. 5 reels.
Corinne Griffith, Webster Campbell, Maurice Costello, W.T. Carleton, Charles Kent, Alice Calhoun.
When a young woman's father asks her wealthy fiancé for a loan, she is resentful, feeling she is mere human collateral. She's wrong, of course.

Human Desire (Associated First National, 1919)
d: Wilfrid North. 6 reels.
Anita Stewart, Conway Tearle, Robert Steele, Naomi Childers, Templar Saxe, Eulalie Jensen, Hattie Delaro.
Filled with altruistic desire, a convent-bred Italian girl journeys to America to help care for impoverished infants.

Human Driftwood (Shubert Film Corp./World Film Corp., 1916)
d: Emile Chautard. 5 reels.
Robert Warwick, Frances Nelson, Leonore Harris, Alec B. Francis, Albert S. Hart.
In Alaska, a lawman falls in love with Velma, the niece of Myra, a dance hall owner. Though he doesn't recognize Myra at first, the lawman learns that she is the woman he once loved, years before. Then, she hits him with this news: Velma isn't her niece, she's her daughter—and she's the lawman's daughter, too.

Human Hearts (Universal, 1922)
d: King Baggot. 7 reels.
House Peters, Russell Simpson, Gertrude Claire, George Hackathorne, George West, Lucretia Harris, Edith Hallor, Ramsey Wallace, Mary Philbin, H.S. Karr, Snitz Edwards.
A big-city con artist tries to maneuver a yokel into marrying her so she can get her hands on some of his family's fortune.

Human Stuff (Universal, 1920)
d: Reaves Eason. 5 reels.
Harry Carey, Rudolph Christians, Charles Le Moyne, Joe Harris, Fontaine La Rue, Ruth Fuller, Mary Charleson, Bobby Mack.
Out West, a lonely rancher wires his dad to find him a suitable bride. When an attractive and high-spirited young lady blows in from the East, the rancher assumes she's his bride-to-be, and starts courting. But—surprise!—she's there for another reason entirely, and rebuffs his advances. With

such an unpromising beginning, can love be far behind?

The Human Tornado (R-C Pictures/FBO of America, 1925)
d: Ben Wilson. 5 reels.
Yakima Canutt, Bert Sprotte, Nancy Leeds, Lafe McKee, Joe Rickson, Slim Allen.
Out West, a thief robs the safe in a mining office run by two brothers.

Human Wreckage (Thomas H. Ince, 1923)
d: John Griffith Wray. 8 reels.
Bessie Love, Mrs. Wallace Reid, James Kirkwood, George Hackathorne, Claire McDowell, Robert McKim, Harry Northrup, Victory Bateman, Eric Mayne, Philip Sleeman.
Sordid tale about a family who become addicted to morphine.

Humdrum Brown (Paralta Play, Inc./W.W. Hodkinson, 1918)
d: Rex Ingram. 6 reels.
Henry B. Walthall, Mary Charleson, Dorothy Love, Howard Crampton, Kate Price, Joseph J. Dowling, Joe Harris, Ida Lewis.
A shy and retiring bank clerk leads such an uneventful life, his nickname is "Humdrum Brown." But there's nothing boring about the way Humdrum leaps into action to capture a fleeing bank robber, or the way he finally sweeps his lady love off her feet.

The Humming Bird (Famous Players-Lasky/Paramount, 1924)
d: Sidney Olcott. 8 reels.
Gloria Swanson, Edward Burns, William Ricciardi, Cesare Gravina, Mario Majeroni, Adrienne D'Ambricourt, Helen Lindroth, Rafael Bongini, Regina Quinn, Aurelio Coccia.
In Paris, a female leader of an apache gang is known as "The Humming Bird."

Humoresque (Cosmopolitan/Paramount, 1920)
d: Frank Borzage. 6 reels.
Vera Gordon, Gaston Glass, Alma Rubens, Dore Davidson, Bobby Connelly, Helen Connelly, Ann Wallick, Sidney Carlyle, Joseph Cooper, Maurice Levigne, Ruth Sabin.
When a promising young violinist goes off to war, his right arm is severely injured and he fears he will never be able to play the violin again.

The Hun Within (Famous Players-Lasky/Paramount, 1918)
d: Chet Withey. 5 reels.
Douglas MacLean, George Fawcett, Dorothy Gish, Charles Herrard, Kate Bruce, Herbert Sutch, Erich von Stroheim, Max Davidson, Robert Anderson, Lillian Clark, Adolphe Lestina.
During World War I, a girl is loved by two men, one pro-German and the other pro-Allies.

The Hunch (S-L Productions/Metro, 1921)
d: George D. Baker. 6 reels.
Gareth Hughes, Ethel Grandin, John Steppling, Edward Flanagan, Harry Lorraine, Gale Henry, William H. Brown.
Comedy about a jolly soul who receives a hunch on the stock market, borrows money to buy the shares, then has to effect a mysterious disappearance to cover his losses. In the end, just as all seems lost, the stock stages a miraculous comeback, and our hero makes good on all his debts.

The Hunchback of Notre Dame (Universal, 1923)
d: Wallace Worsley. 12 reels.

Lon Chaney, Patsy Ruth Miller, Ernest Torrence, Norman Kerry, Raymond Hatton, Tully Marshall, Nigel de Brulier, Kate Lester, Gladys Brockwell, Brandon Hurst, Raymond Hatton.

Spectacular version of the Victor Hugo novel *Notre-Dame de Paris*, with Chaney at his grotesque best as the misshapen, suffering Quasimodo. The hunchbacked bellringer of Notre Dame cathedral rescues Esmeralda, a gypsy girl unjustly convicted of a capital crime.

The classic Hugo tale was filmed in feature length earlier, by Fox in 1917, under the title *The Darling of Paris*.

Hungry Eyes (Universal, 1918)
d: Rupert Julian. 5 reels.
Monroe Salisbury, Ruth Clifford, Rupert Julian, W.H. Bainbridge, H.A. Barrows, Arthur Tavares, Gretchen Lederer, George McDaniel, Rita Pickering.
A rancher's daughter falls for a hard-working new ranch hand—who happens to be an ex-con.

A Hungry Heart (World Film Corp., 1917)
d: Emile Chautard. 5 reels.
Alice Brady, Edward Langford, George McQuarrie, Gerda Holmes, Alec B. Francis, John Dudley, Edna Whistler, Charles Hartley, Josephine Earle, Horace Haine, Ray Carrara.
In France, two sisters—one frivolous, one sensible—love the same Marquis.

The Hungry Heart (Famous Players/Paramount, 1917)
d: Robert G. Vignola. 5 reels.
Pauline Frederick, Howard Hall, Robert Cain, Helen Lindroth, Eldean Steuart.
Neglected by her chemist husband, Courtney begins to eye his friend Basil.

Hungry Hearts (Goldwyn, 1922)
d: E. Mason Hopper. 7 reels.
Bryant Washburn, Helen Ferguson, E.A. Warren, Rosa Rosanova, George Siegmann, Otto Lederer, Millie Schottland, Bert Sprotte, Edwin B. Tilton.
Drama about Jewish immigrants from Russia who have a difficult time making ends meet, even though everyone in the family is working.

The Hunted Woman (Vitagraph, 1916)
d: S. Rankin Drew. 5 reels.
Virginia Pearson, S. Rankin Drew, Frank Currier, George Cooper, Charles Wellesley, Ned Finley, Denton Vane, Harold Foshay, Mae Greene, Billie Billings.
Joanne's unfaithful husband turns up dead... or does he?

The Hunted Woman (Fox, 1925)
d: Jack Conway. 5 reels.
Seena Owen, Earl Schenck, Diana Miller, Cyril Chadwick, Francis McDonald, Edward Piel, Victor McLaglen.
In the lawless Northwest, gold fever infects two miners who have struck it rich. Into the drama comes a sophisticated woman from the American east, and the miners cannot hold their tongues about their claim. Soon all the thugs in Alaska are scrambling to locate the claim for themselves.

The Hunting of the Hawk (Astra Film Corp./Pathé, 1917)
d: George Fitzmaurice. 5 reels.
William Courtenay, Marguerite Snow, Robert Clugston.
Diana is unhappily married to a notorious criminal known as The Hawk. Will the new playboy in her life bring her happiness, or is he really an undercover officer trying to capture her husband?

The Huntress (Associated First National, 1923)
d: Lynn F. Reynolds. 6 reels.
Colleen Moore, Lloyd Hughes, Lila Leslie, Snitz Edwards, Russell Simpson, Walter Long, Charles Anderson, Wilfred North, Helen Raymond, William Marion, Lawrence Steers, Helen Walron, John Lance, Lalo Encinas, Chief Big Tree.
Bela, a girl raised in an Indian family, learns that she is a white woman.

A Huntress of Men (Universal, 1916)
d: Lucius Henderson. 5 reels.
Mary Fuller, Lon Chaney, Joseph Girard, Sydney Bracey.
A fiery socialite has a reputation as a voracious man-eater. One fellow decides to try and tame the beast.

The Hurricane Kid (Universal, 1925)
d: Edward Sedgwick. 6 reels.
Hoot Gibson, Marion Nixon, William A. Steele, Arthur Machley, Violet LaPlante, Harry Todd, Fred Humes.
Out West, a cowpoke known as the Hurricane Kid tames a wild horse and enters it in a race, with himself as the rider.

Hurricane's Gal (Allen Holubar Pictures/Associated First National, 1922)
d: Allen Holubar. 8 reels.
Dorothy Phillips, Robert Ellis, Wallace Beery, James O. Barrows, Gertrude Astor, William Fong, Jack Donovan, Frances Raymond.
Lola's a smuggler, and a dangerous lady—as the government agent assigned to her case will soon find out.

Husband and Wife (World Film Corp., 1916)
d: Barry O'Neil. 5 reels.
Ethel Clayton, Holbrook Blinn, Madge Evans, Montagu Love, Emmett Corrigan, Dion Titheradge, Gerda Holmes, Alec B. Francis, Frank Beamish.
After a spendthrift wife drives her husband to bankruptcy and attempted suicide, she sees the light and promises to be more frugal and more understanding.

The Husband Hunter (Fox, 1920)
d: Howard M. Mitchell. 5 reels.
Eileen Percy, Emory Johnson, Jane Miller, Evans Kirk, Edward McWade, John Stepling, Harry Dunkinson.
Warned that his fiancée is a flirt, a bridegroom-to-be decides to teach her a lesson.

Husband Hunters (Tiffany Productions, 1927)
d: John G. Adolfi. 6 reels.
Mae Busch, Charles Delaney, Jean Arthur, Walter Hiers, Duane Thompson, Mildred Harris, Robert Cain, Jimmy Harrison, Nigel Barrie, James Mack, Marcin Asher, Fred Fisher.
In New York, chorus girls size up the eligible bachelors.

Husbands and Lovers (Louis B. Mayer Productions/First National, 1924)
d: John M. Stahl. 8 reels.
Lewis S. Stone, Florence Vidor, Dale Fuller, Winter Hall, Edithe Yorke.
When Grace changes her dowdy appearance and emerges as a flapper type, her husband is decidedly annoyed by the transformation. His friend Rex, however, finds Grace's new look refreshing. So much so, that she contemplates eloping with him.

Husbands for Rent (Warner Bros., 1927)
d: Henry Lehrman. 6 reels.
Owen Moore, Helene Costello, Claude Gillingwater, John

Miljan, Kathryn Perry, Arthur Hoyt.
A husband and wife ponder divorce plans after only six months together, but her dad plots to keep them together.

Hush (Equity Pictures/Jans Film Service, 1921)
d: Harry Garson. 6 reels.
Clara Kimball Young, J. Frank Glendon, Kathlyn Williams, Jack Pratt, Bertram Grassby, Gerard Alexander, Beatrice LaPlante, John Underhill.
A happily married woman still suffers from the memory of an early affair.

Hush Money (Realart Pictures/Paramount, 1921)
d: Charles Maigne. 5 reels.
Alice Brady, George Fawcett, Laurence Wheat, Harry Benham, Jerry Devine.
When Evelyn, a daughter of wealth, runs down and injures a newsboy with her car, she is persuaded by a friend to flee the scene. But the accident was witnessed, and Evelyn's dad must pay hush money to keep the witness quiet.

The Hushed Hour (Harry Garson Productions/State Rights, 1919)
d: Edmund Mortimer. 5 reels.
Winter Hall, Lydia Knott, Wilfred Lucas, Blanche Sweet, Milton Sills, Rosemary Theby, Gloria Hope, Harry Northrup, Mary Anderson, Wyndham Standing, Ben Alexander.
The four offspring of a recently-deceased judge pay their respects at his coffin, one at a time... and all four come to realize they have not lived up to their father's high standards.

Hutch of the U.S.A. (William Steiner Productions, 1924)
d: James Chapin. 5 reels.
Charles Hutchison, Edith Thornton, Frank Leigh, Ernest Adams, Jack Mathis, Natalie Warfield, Alphonse Martell, Frederick Vroom.
Hutch, an American reporter, investigates a brewing revolution in a Latin American country, and finds love with the rebel leader's daughter.

Hypocrisy (Fox, 1916)
d: Keenan Buel. 6 reels.
Virginia Pearson, Alfred Swenson, John Webb Dillon, Ida Darling.
When his bride accepts a check from her former beau, a new husband suspects the worst, and confronts her with his accusations.

I Accuse (Gaumont/Mutual, 1916)
d: William F. Haddock. 5 reels.
Alexander Gaden, Charles W. Travis, Helen Marten, Albert Macklin, Henry W. Pemberton, John Reinhard, John Macklin, W.J. Butler, Iva Shepard, James Levering.
When a girl chooses a young judge for her husband, his rival for her hand swears revenge, and begins by accusing her preacher father of murder.

I Am Guilty (J. Parker Read Jr. Productions/Associated Producers, 1921)
d: Jack Nelson. 7 reels.
Louise Glaum, Mahlon Hamilton, Claire duBrey, Joseph Kilgour, Ruth Stonehouse, May Hopkins, George Cooper, Mickey Moore, Frederic DeKovert.
A neglected wife attends a wild party while her husband is on a business trip.

I Am the Law (Edwin Carewe Productions/Affiliated Distributors, 1922)

d: Edwin Carewe. 7 reels.
Alice Lake, Kenneth Harlan, Rosemary Theby, Gaston Glass, Noah Beery, Wallace Beery.
In the Canadian Northwest, a mountie is forced to arrest his own brother on suspicion of murder.

I Am the Man (Chadwick Pictures, 1924)
d: Ivan Abramson. 7 reels.
Lionel Barrymore, Seena Owen, Gaston Glass, Martin Faust, Flora LeBreton, James Keane, Joseph Striker.
Convoluted melodrama about McQuade, a political boss, who desires an aristocratic beauty named Julia, who loves another. McQuade blackmails Julia into marrying him by framing her father for embezzlement. Later, when McQuade kills his own brother and tries to lay the blame on an actress named Corrine, he discovers to his dismay that Corrine is his own daughter.

I Can Explain (S-L Pictures/Metro, 1922)
d: George D. Baker. 5 reels.
Gareth Hughes, Bartine Burkett, Grace Darmond, Herbert Hayes, Victor Potel, Nelson McDowell, Edwin Wallock, Albert Breig, Harry Lorraine, Tina Modotti, Sidney D'Albrook, Stanton Heck.
Business partners find their relationship strained when one of the partners is suspected of dalliances with the other's wife.

I Love You (Triangle, 1918)
d: Walter Edwards. 7 reels.
Alma Rubens, John Lince, Francis McDonald, Wheeler Oakman, Frederick Vroom, Lillian Langdon, Peaches Jackson.
In Italy, a free-spirited beauty has her portrait painted by a traveling artist, who then falls in love with her.

I Want My Man (First National, 1925)
d: Lambert Hillyer. 7 reels.
Doris Kenyon, Milton Sills, Phyllis Haver, May Allison, Kate Bruce, Paul Nicholson, Louis Stern, Theresa Maxwell Conover, Charles Lane, George Howard.
Julian, an American soldier who was blinded in the war, is operated on successfully in France and recovers his sight. However, he finds that his wife, a former army nurse, has left him and returned to the U.S., where she obtains a divorce. Years later, their paths cross again; but Julian, who has never seen his wife, does not recognize her. Though he is now engaged to marry another girl, Julian falls in love with his former wife all over again. When she reveals her identity and her change of heart, the couple are ready to start a new life together.

I Want to Forget (Fox, 1918)
d: James Kirkwood. 5 reels.
Evelyn Nesbit, Russell Thaw, Henry Clive, Alphonse Ethier, William R. Dunn, Jane Jennings.
During World War I, an Austrian-American girl is suspected by her lieutenant sweetheart of consorting with the enemy. What the officer doesn't know is that she is working on an undercover mission with the American Secret Service.

I Will Repay (Vitagraph, 1917)
d: William P.S. Earle. 5 reels.
Corinne Griffith, William Dunn, George J. Forth, Mary Maurice, Arthur Donaldson, Eulalie Jensen.
A literary agent tries to help a woman writer leave her abusive husband.

The Ice Flood (Universal, 1926)

d: George B. Seitz. 6 reels.
Kenneth Harlan, Viola Dana, Frank Hagney, Fred Kohler, De Witt Jennings, Kitty Barlow, James Gordon.
An Oxford graduate travels to an Oregon lumber camp, where he encounters love, conflict, and a spectacular ice avalanche.

Icebound (Famous Players-Lasky/Paramount, 1924)
d: William DeMille. 7 reels.
Richard Dix, Lois Wilson, Helen DuBois, Edna May Oliver, Vera Reynolds, Mary Foy, Joseph Depew, Ethel Wales, Alice Chapin, John Daly Murphy, Frank Shannon.
In New England, a chastened ne'er-do-well returns home, having left after he had accidentally caused a large fire.

Idle Hands (Park-Whiteside Productions/Pioneer Pictures, 1921)
d: Frank Reicher. 6 reels.
Gail Kane, Thurston Hall, J. Herbert Frank, William Bechtel, Nellie Burt, Paul Lane, Norbert Wicki.
Small-town sisters move to the big city, and tragedy ensues.

The Idle Rich (Metro, 1921)
d: Maxwell Karger. 5 reels.
Bert Lytell, Virginia Valli, John Davidson, Joseph Harrington, Thomas Jefferson, Victory Bateman, Leigh Wyant, Max Davidson.
Sam, whose wealth has vanished as the result of irresponsible speculation, becomes a junk dealer... and becomes prosperous all over again.

Idle Tongues (Thomas H. Ince/First National, 1924)
d: Lambert Hillyer. 6 reels.
Percy Marmont, Doris Kenyon, Claude Gillingwater, Lucille Ricksen, David Torrence, Malcolm McGregor, Vivia Ogden, Marguerite Clayton, Ruby Lafayette, Dan Mason, Mark Hamilton.
A self-sacrificing doctor serves 5 years in prison for a crime his wife committed.

Idle Wives (Universal, 1916)
d: Lois Weber, Phillips Smalley. 7 reels.
Lois Weber, Phillips Smalley, Neva Gerber, Mary McLaren, Edwin Hearn, Seymour Hastings, Pauline Aster, Cecilia Matthews, Ben Wilson, Maude George.
Several moviegoers attend a screening of a film called *Life's Mirror*, which has the effect of letting each audience member see his or her own life, and its consequences.

The Idol Dancer (D.W. Griffith/First National, 1920)
d: D.W. Griffith. 7 reels.
Richard Barthelemess, Clarine Seymour, Creighton Hale, George MacQuarrie, Anders Randolf, Kate Bruce, Thomas Carr, Florence Short.

Drama of moral regeneration and spiritual rebirth in the South Pacific. An alcoholic beachcomber is rescued from one of his stupors by the stepdaughter of the local missionary minister, and is brought home to become "part of the family."

The Idol of the North (Famous Players-Lasky/Paramount, 1921)
d: R. William Neill. 6 reels.
Dorothy Dalton, Edwin August, E.J. Ratcliffe, Riley Hatch, Jules Cowles, Florence St. Leonard, Jessie Arnold, Marguerite Marsh, Joe King.
In the Canadian Northwest, a drifter is coerced into marrying Colette, a dance hall girl.

The Idol of the Stage (Gaumont/Mutual, 1916)
d: Richard Garrick. 5 reels.
Malcolm Williams, Charles W. Travis, John Mackin, Lucille Taft, Richard Garrick, James Levering, Helen Marten, Charles Winston, Harry Chira, James Arbuckle Jr.
Years after abandoning his wife, a traveling actor returns to town and meets a newsboy who, he later learns, is his own son.

Idolators (Triangle, 1917)
d: Walter Edwards. 5 reels.
Louise Glaum, George Webb, Dorcas Matthews, Lee Hill, T.S. Guise, Hugo Koch, Milton Ross.
Sordid melodrama about a hack playwright who, though married, falls in love with his self-absorbed leading lady, and the degeneration that follows for both of them.

Idols of Clay (Famous Players-Lasky/Paramount, 1920)
d: George Fitzmaurice. 7 reels.
Mae Murray, David Powell, Dorothy Cummings, George Fawcett, Leslie King, Richard Wangermann, Claude King.
Raised in a South Seas paradise, a young woman falls in love with a traveling British sculptor. She follows him home to England, but is corrupted by the manners and morals of his conceited society friends.

If I Marry Again (First National, 1925)
d: John Francis Dillon. 8 reels.
Lloyd Hughes, Doris Kenyon, Frank Mayo, Hobart Bosworth, Anna Q. Nilsson, Myrtle Stedman, Dorothy Brock.
When the son of a proud businessman decides to marry a well-known prostitute, his father threatens to disown the young man. However, the bride turns out to be an exceptionally good wife and, later, mother.

If I Were King (Fox, 1920)
d: J. Gordon Edwards. 8 reels.
William Farnum, Betty Ross, Fritz Lieber, Walter Law, Harry Carvill, Claude Payton, V.V. Clogg, Harold Clairmont, Renita Johnston, Kathryn Chase.
François Villon rides again in this Fox version of the novel by Justin Huntly McCarthy. In the silent era, the story would be told again in feature length, as *The Beloved Rogue* (1927), starring John Barrymore.

If I Were Single (Warner Bros., 1927)
d: Roy Del Ruth. 7 reels.
May McAvoy, Conrad Nagel, Myrna Loy, Andre Beranger.
Ted and May, married to each other and very much in love, nevertheless engage in occasional flirtations.

If Marriage Fails (C. Garner Sullivan Productions/FBO of America, 1925)
d: John Ince. 7 reels.
Jacqueline Logan, Belle Bennett, Clive Brook, Jean Hersholt, Donald MacDonald, Mathilde Comont, Cissy Fitzgerald.
In an effort to save their imperfect marriage, Joe and Eleanor go to see a fortune teller. She turns out to be a lovely young woman, and Joe is instantly smitten. So much for crystal ball therapy.

If My Country Should Call (Universal, 1916)
d: Joseph De Grasse. 5 reels.
Dorothy Phillips, Jack Nelson, Lon Chaney, Adele Farrington, Frank Whitson, Albert MacQuarrie, Carl Von Schiller, Gretchen Lederer, Gordon Griffith, Clyde Benson.
Pro-war drama that tells of a pacifist woman who dreams of dire consequences, should she prevent her husband and son

from fighting in the war.

'If Only' Jim (Universal, 1921)
d: Jacques Jaccard. 5 reels.
Harry Carey, Carol Holloway, Ruth Royce, Duke Lee, Roy Coulson, Charles Brinley, George Bunny, Joseph Hazelton, Minnie Prevost, Thomas Smith.
Out West, a gold miner fights off claim jumpers while adopting a baby and romancing the postmistress, all at the same time.

If Winter Comes (Fox, 1923)
d: Harry Millarde. 14 reels.
Percy Marmont, Arthur Metcalfe, Sidney Herbert, Wallace Kolb, William Riley Hatch, Raymond Bloomer, Russell Sedgwick, Leslie King, George Pelzer, James Ten Brook.
Unhappy tale of an emotionless marriage, which is further exacerbated when the husband agrees to take in a homeless young woman with a baby.

If You Believe It, It's So (Paramount, 1922)
d: Tom Forman. 7 reels.
Thomas Meighan, Pauline Starke, Joseph Dowling, Theodore Roberts, Charles Ogle, Laura Anson, Charles French, Tom Kennedy, Ed Brady.
Preparing to relieve an old man of his wallet, professional thief Chick Harris finds himself helping the old geezer instead—and decideing to embark on a life of honesty.

I'll Get Him Yet (Paramount, 1919)
d: Elmer Clifton. 5 reels.
Richard Barthelmess, Dorothy Gish, Ralph Graves, George Fawcett, Porter Strong.
A rich girl sets her cap for a young reporter.

I'll Say So (Fox, 1918)
d: Raoul A. Walsh. 5 reels.
George Walsh, Regina Quinn, William Bailey, James Black, Ed Keeley.
Rejected by Army recruiters because of flat feet, a patriot finds other ways to serve his country, such as foiling German agents at the Mexican border, and saving his girl from marrying a German secret agent just before the final "I do."

I'll Show You the Town (Universal, 1925)
d: Harry Pollard. 8 reels.
Reginald Denny, Marion Nixon, Edward Kimball, Lilyan Tashman, Hayden Stevenson, Cissy Fitzgerald, Neely Edwards, William A. Carroll, Martha Mattox, Helen Greene.
Comedy about a young college professor who must talk fast to extricate himself from a three-way mess: He has agreed to take out three women, all on the same night, all separately.

The Illustrious Prince (Haworth Pictures Corp./Robertson-Cole, 1919)
d: William Worthington. 5 reels.
Sessue Hayakawa, Mabel Ballin, Harry Lonsdale, Beverly Traverse, Robert Lawler, Bertram Grassby, Toyo Fujita, Edward Peil.
Swearing vengeance on the English con man who caused his father to commit *hara-kiri*, a Japanese prince follows the scoundrel to London's financial district.

The Image Maker (Thanhouser/Pathé, 1917)
d: Eugene Moore. 5 reels.
Valda Valkyrien, Harris Gordon, Arthur Bauer, Inda Palmer, Morgan Jones.
Strongly attracted to each other but not understanding why,

a young actress and her sweetheart discover that they may be reincarnated lovers from ancient Egypt.

Immediate Lee (American Film Co./Mutual, 1916)
d: Frank Borzage. 5 reels.
Frank Borzage, Anna Little, Jack Richardson, Chick Morrison, William Stowell, Harry McCabe, George Clark, John Smith, Charles Newton.
Out West, a quick-draw artist gets the nickname "Immediate Lee."
Also see *Hair Trigger Casey*, a 1922 re-issue of this film with revised titles and role names.

The Immigrant (Lasky Feature Plays/Paramount, 1915)
d: George Melford. 5 reels.
Valeska Suratt, Thomas Meighan, Theodore Roberts, Jane Wolf, Hal Clements, Ernest Joy, Raymond Hatton, Gertrude Kellar.
Masha, an immigrant from Russia, is forced to become the mistress of a wealthy contractor... but her heart is with the young American engineer she met on the boat.

The Immortal Flame (Ivan Film Productions, Inc., 1916)
w, d: Ivan Abramson. 5 reels.
Maude Fealy, Charles Edwards, Joseph Burke, Louise Guischard, James Cooley, Paula Shay, Edna Luby, Kittens Reichart, Willard Case.
Sudsy mix of infidelity, self-sacrifice, insanity, and drowning.

The Imp (Selznick/Select, 1919)
d: Robert Ellis. 6 reels.
Elsie Janis, Joseph King, Ethel Stewart, E.J. Ratcliffe, Duncan Penwarden, Arthur Marion, John Sutherland, William Fredericks, Edith Forrest, Joseph Granby, Jack Ridgeway.
Conked on the head by an errant golf ball, a young woman is knocked unconscious, and wakes up with a rare type of amnesia: She thinks she's a notorious pickpocket who plies her trade while dressed as a man.

Impossible Catherine (Pathé, 1919)
d: John B. O'Brien. 5 reels.
Virginia Pearson, William B. Davidson, J.H. Gilmour, Ed Roseman, James Hill, Mabel McQuade, John Walker, Sheldon Lewis.
Timberland version of *The Taming of the Shrew*, with an impossibly unruly Catherine being tamed by her new husband at a North Woods lumber camp.

The Impossible Mrs. Bellew (Famous Players-Lasky/Paramount, 1922)
d: Sam Wood. 8 reels.
Gloria Swanson, Conrad Nagel, Robert Cain, Richard Wayne, Frank Elliott, Gertrude Astor, June Elvidge, Herbert Standing, Mickey Moore, Pat Moore, Helen Dunbar, Arthur Hull, Clarence Burton.
A husband is outraged when he finds his wife with a male acquaintance, and shoots him—even though the husband has a mistress on the side.

Impossible Susan (American Film Co./Mutual, 1918)
d: Lloyd Ingraham. 5 reels.
Margarita Fisher, Jack Mower, Hayward Mack, Beverly Travers, L.M. Wells, Anne Schaefer, Lloyd Hughes.
Susan, a high-spirited orphan girl, is being cared for by a family that decides to educate her in proper dress and manners. Their lessons are so successful, Susan blossoms forth as a thoroughly desireable female, as in: All the male members of the family now desire *her*.

The Impostor (Brady Picture Plays/World Film Corp., 1915)
d: Albert Capellani. 5 reels.
Jose Collins, Alec B. Francis, Leslie Stowe, Sumner Gard, E.M. Kimball, Dorothy Fairchild.
When a hard-hearted mine owner dies overseas, his near-identical brother impersonates him and returns to England, where he institutes social reforms in the mines and agrees to improve working conditions.

The Impostor (Empire All Star Corp./Mutual, 1918)
d: Dell Henderson. 5 reels.
Ann Murdock, David Powell, Lionel Adams, Richie Ling, Charlotte Granville, Eleanor Seybolt, Edyth Latimer, Charles Mussett, Charles MacDonald, Anita Rothe, George Abbott.
Out of work and broke, a girl is befriended by a family that introduces her as their wealthy sister-in-law.

The Impostor (Gothic Productions/FBO of America, 1926)
d: Chet Withey. 6 reels.
Evelyn Brent, Carroll Nye, James Morrison, Frank Leigh, Jimmy Quinn, Carlton Griffin, Edna Griffin.
Gilbert, an irresponsible playboy, purloins his family's jewels in order to pay off gambling debts.

Impulse (Berwilla Film Corp./Arrow Film Corp., 1922)
d: Norval MacGregor. 5 reels.
Neva Gerber, Jack Dougherty, Goldie Madden, Douglas Gerrard, Ashton Dearholt, Helen Gilmore.
Deserted by her husband, Julia decides to treat herself to a vacation at a luxury hotel—and there, she falls in love.

In a Moment of Temptation (R-C Pictures/FBO of America, 1927)
d: Philip Carle. 6 reels.
Charlotte Stevens, Grant Withers, Cornelius Keefe, Marie Walcamp, Kit Guard, Tom Ricketts, John MacKinnon.
A shopgirl is unjustly accused of theft and imprisoned. When she is released, she seeks to avenge herself against the family who framed her, by helping to rob their residence.

In Again—Out Again (Fairbanks/Paramount, 1917)
d: John Emerson. 5 reels.
Douglas Fairbanks, Arline Pretty, Walter Walker, Arnold Lucy, Helen Greene, Homer Hunt, Albert Parker, Bull Montana, Ada Gilman, Frank Lalor, Betty Tyrel, Spike Robinson.
While in prison on a minor charge, a playboy falls in love with the jailer's daughter. After his release, he keeps trying to get re-arrested and sent back to prison, but with little success.

In Bad (American Film Co./Mutual, 1918)
d: Edward Sloman. 5 reels.
William Russell, Francelia Billington, Harvey Clark, Bull Montana, Fred Smith, Lucille Ward, Carl Stockdale.
A rowdy street fighter gets won over by a pretty girl, and follows her on a treasure hunt to the Yucatan peninsula.

In Borrowed Plumes (Welcome Pictures/Arrow Pictures, 1926)
d: Victor Hugo Halperin. 6 reels.
Marjorie Daw, Niles Welch, Arnold Daly, Louise Carter, Peggy Kelly, Wheeler Oakman, Dagmar Godowsky.
Posing as a countess, a destitute socialite meets and falls in love with Philip, a scion of wealth.

In Every Woman's Life (Associated First National, 1924)
d: Irving Cummings. 7 reels.
Lloyd Hughes, Virginia Valli, Marc MacDermott, George Fawcett, Vara Lewis, Ralph Lewis, Stuart Holmes, John Sainpolis.
In Paris, an American girl finds herself desired by three men—one of whom is her soulmate.

In Fast Company (Carlos Productions/Truart Film Corp., 1924)
d: James W. Horne. 6 reels.
Richard Talmadge, Midlred Harris, Sheldon Lewis, Douglas Gerrard, Jack Herrick, Charles Clary, Snitz Edwards, Lydia Yeamans Titus.
Perry, an irresponsible playboy, pulls one wild stunt too many and is disinherited by his father. But he'll become resourceful, and win back his father's respect as well as the heart of a good woman.

In Folly's Trail (Universal, 1920)
d: Rollin Sturgeon. 5 reels.
Carmel Myers, Thomas Holding, Arthur Clayton, George B. Williams, Viola Lind, W.H. Bainbridge, Beth Ivans.
When an aristocrat marries a chorus girl, they find they blend like oil and water.

In For Thirty Days (Metro, 1919)
d: Webster Cullison. 5 reels.
May Allison, Robert Ellis, Mayme Kelso, Rex Cherryman, Jay Dwiggins, George Berrell, Bull Montana.
Rollicking comedy about a madcap heiress who gets thrown into a Southern jail for driving recklessly. Seems there's an ancient law on the books that allows anyone to hire prisoners for 20 cents a day, so the heiress soon finds herself cooking and cleaning in the home of one of the fellows whose cars she hit. But when the reluctant domestic starts falling for her "employer," she resists her family's attempts to get her released from custody.

In His Brother's Place (Metro, 1919)
d: Harry L. Franklin. 5 reels.
Hale Hamilton, Emmett C. King, Ruby La Fayette, Mary McIvor, Marguerite Snow, Jessie De Jarnette, Howard Crampton, Ward Wing.
When a poor country preacher finds his congregation dwindling, he appeals for help to his twin brother, a successful business executive.

In Hollywood With Potash and Perlmutter (Goldwyn, 1924)
d: Alfred Green. 7 reels.
George Sidney, Alexander Carr, Betty Blythe, Belle Bennett, Anders Randolph, Peggy Shaw, Charles Meredith, Lillian Hackett, David Butler, Sidney Franklin, Joseph W. Girard, Norma Talmadge, Constance Talmadge.
Textile producers Potash and Perlmutter decide to turn their efforts to producing motion pictures.

In Honor's Web (Vitagraph, 1919)
d: Paul Scardon. 5 reels.
Harry T. Morey, Gladden James, George Backus, Agnes Ayres, Myrtle Stedman, George Majeroni, Bernard Siegel, Robert Gaillard.
Accused of a murder he did not commit, an honorable businessman refuses to offer an alibi, believing that by doing so he is saving a lady from disgrace.

In Judgment Of (Metro, 1918)
d: Will S. Davis. 5 reels.
Anna Q. Nilsson, Franklyn Farnum, Herbert Standing, Edward Alexander, Lydia Knott, Harry S. Northrup,

Spottiswoode Aitken, Katherine Griffith, Robert Dunbar.
Here's a scenario you don't see every day: Presiding over a murder trial, a judge is forced to admit that he, not the defendant, killed the victim—in self-defense. Not only that, but the judge is also the defendant's long-lost father!

In Love with Love   (Fox, 1924)
d: Rowland V. Lee.   6 reels.
Marguerite De La Motte, Allan Forrest, Harold Goodwin, William Austin, Mary Warren, Will Walling, Allan Sears, Mabel Forrest.
Romantic comedy about Ann, a spoiled coquette who gets engaged to three different men at the same time.

In Old Kentucky   (First National, 1919)
d: Marshall Neilan.   7 reels.
Anita Stewart, Mahlon Hamilton, Edward Coxen, Charles Arling, Edward Connolly, Adele Farrington, Marcia Manon, Frank Duffy, John Currie.
In the Blue Ridge Mountains, a visiting city dweller falls in love with an illiterate country girl, and teaches her to read and write.

In Old Kentucky   (MGM, 1927)
d: John M. Stahl.   7 reels.
James Murray, Helene Costello, Wesley Barry, Stepin Fetchit, DorothyCumming, Edward Martindel, Harvey Clark, Carolynne Snowden, Nick Cogley.
Jimmy, a war veteran, returns to his Kentucky home and finds the old homestead verging on bankruptcy. But he'll be reunited with the horse he rode in the war, and together they'll win a rich Derby race.

In Pursuit of Polly   (Famous Players-Lasky/Paramount, 1918)
d: Chet Withey.   5 reels.
Billie Burke, Thomas Meighan, Frank Losee, A.J. Herbert, William Davidson, Alfred Hickman, Ben Deely.
Polly, a frivolous heiress, gets herself engaged to three men at once. When all three pursue her racing car, the flighty Polly somehow gets entangled in an international conspiracy, and winds up marrying the Secret Service man who rides to her rescue.

In Search of a Sinner   (Constance Talmadge Film Co./First National, 1920)
d: David Kirkland.   5 reels.
Constance Talmadge, Rockliffe Fellowes, Corliss Giles, William Roselle, Marjorie Milton, Evelyn C. Carrington, Lillian Worth, Arnold Lucy, Charles Whittaker, Ned Sparks.
Flirtatious Georgiana, a new widow whose husband was a saintly bore, completes a suitable period of mourning, then begins her "search for a sinner"—i.e., a beau who can bring out the devil in her.

In Search of a Thrill   (Metro, 1923)
d: Oscar Apfel.   5 reels.
Viola Dana, Warner Baxter, Mabel Van Buren, Templar Saxe, Robert Schable, Walter Wills, Rosemary Theby, Billy Elmer, Leo White.
A shallow American socialite learns respect for other people's problems during a trip to the impoverished, war-torn areas of Europe.

In Slumberland   (Fine Arts Film Co./Triangle, 1917)
d: Irvin Willat.   5 reels.
Thelma Salter, Laura Sears, Jack Livingston, J.P. Lockney, Walter Perry, Georgie Stone.
A salacious landlord covets his tenant's wife.

In the Balance   (Vitagraph, 1917)
d: Paul Scardon.   5 reels.
Earle Williams, Grace Darmond, Miriam Miles, Denton Vane, Robert Gaillard, Templar Saxe, Julia Swayne Gordon.
Though he's fearful of a family curse that warns against going to the big city, a country boy follows the actress he loves into the heart of Gotham.

In the Days of the Thundering Herd   (Selig Polyscope, 1914)
d: Colin Campbell.   5 reels.
Tom Mix, Bessie Eyton, Wheeler Oakman, Red Wing.
Lots of action in this early Tom Mix western, as Tom saves his girlfriend from a buffalo stampede, then heads up a wagon train heading west. The wagon train is attacked by savage Indians, and only Tom and his sweetie survive.

In the Diplomatic Service   (Quality Pictures Corp./Metro, 1916)
d: Francis X. Bushman.   5 reels.
Francis X. Bushman, Beverly Bayne, Helen Dunbar, Henri Bergman, Belle Bruce, Edmond Elton, William Davidson, Charles Fang, Harry D. Blakemore, Liza Miller.
Foreign spies seek out the inventor of a powerful new weapon that will revolutionize warfare. But fear not, the "inventor" is Our Hero in disguise, setting a trap for the spies.

In the First Degree   (Sterling Pictures, 1927)
d: Phil Rosen.   6 reels.
Alice Calhoun, Bryant Washburn, Gayne Whitman, Trilby Clark, Gareth Hughes, Joseph Girard, Milton Fahrney, William DeVaull.
Pendleton, an assistant to a wealthy stock broker, admires his boss' daughter and wishes to marry her. But first, there's this murder rap he's got to beat.

In the Headlines   (Warner Bros., 1929)
d: John Adolfi.   8 reels.
Grant Withers, Marion Nixon, Clyde Cook, Edmund Breese, Pauline Garon, Frank Campeau, Vivian Oakland, Hallam Cooley, Spec O'Donnell.
A reporter and his girlfriend investigate a double murder.

In the Heart of a Fool   (Mayflower Photoplay Corp./Associated First National, 1920)
d: Allan Dwan.   6 reels.
James Kirkwood, Anna Q. Nilsson, Mary Thurman, Philo McCullough, Ward Crane, John Burton, Margaret Campbell, Percy Challenger, Arthur Hoyt, Harold A. Miller.
Four lives are nearly ruined by a thoughtless flirtation.

In the Hollow of Her Hand   (Select Pictures Corp., 1918)
d: Charles Maigne.   5 reels.
Alice Brady, Myrtle Stedman, A.J. Herbert, Louise Clark, Harold Entwistle, Percy Marmont, Henry Miller Jr.
The widow of a murdered playboy suspects her new employee of the crime.

In the Name of Love   (Famous Players-Lasky/Paramount, 1925)
d: Howard Higgin.   6 reels.
Ricardo Cortez, Greta Nissen, Wallace Beery, Raymond Hatton, Lillian Leighton, Edythe Chapman, Richard Arlen.
Romantic comedy about Raoul, a naturalized American who revisits France in search of the girl he left behind.

In the Name of the Law   (Emory Johnson Productions/FBO of America, 1922)

d: Emory Johnson. 7 reels.
Ralph Lewis, Claire McDowell, Ella Hall, Emory Johnson, Johnnie Walker, Ben Alexander, Josephine Adair, Johnny Thompson, Richard Morris, Jean Adair.
In San Francisco, a law student from a respectable family is accused of theft.

In the Palace of the King (Essanay, 1915)
d: Fred Wright. 6 reels.
E.J. Ratcliffe, Richard C. Travers, Arline Hackett, Lewis Edgard, Lillian Drew, Nell Craig, Ernest Maupain, Thomas Commerford, Sydney Ainsworth, Charles J. Stine.
Spain has defeated the Moors, but instead of feeling euphoric, King Philip feels suspicion that his half-brother, Don Juan of Austria, seeks to capture his throne.

In the Palace of the King (Goldwyn, 1923)
d: Emmett Flynn. 9 reels.
Blanche Sweet, Edmund Lowe, Hobart Bosworth, Pauline Starke, Sam DeGrasse, William V. Mong, Aileen Pringle, Lucien Littlefield, Charles Clary, Harvey Clarke, Tom Bates, D.N. Clugston, Charles Gorham, Jack Pitcairn, David Kirby, Ena Gregory, Bruce Sterling.
Historical drama about King Philip of Spain, who is jealous of his brother's popularity and sends him to a mission from which he will almost certainly not return. But he does.

In the Shadow (Excelsior Feature Film Co./Alliance Films, 1915)
d: Harry Handworth. 5 reels.
Gordon De Maine, William A. Williams, Harry Handworth, Octavia Handworth, Marie Boyd, Henry Blossom, Victor Herbert.
Tom, a college boxer, thinks he's killed his opponent, his sweetheart's brother.

In the Web of the Grafters (Signal Film Corp./Mutual, 1916)
d: Murdock MacQuarrie, Al V. Jefferson. 5 reels.
Edythe Sterling, Norbert A. Myles, Millard K. Wilson, Francis J. MacDonald, Louise Hutchinson.
When a policeman is framed for murdering the mayor, his sweetheart clears him by posing as a fortuneteller and getting the truth out of the real killers.

In the West (Wild West Productions/Arrow Film Corp., 1923)
w, d: George Holt. 5 reels.
Neva Gerber, Richard Hatton, Arthur Morrison, Elias Bullock, Robert McKenzie.
An eastern tenderfoot goes west, tries to make good, and wins the heart of a pretty gal. But in the end, discouraged by the rough western lifestyle, the easterner heads back to his city roots and leaves the gal to her cowboy sweetheart.

In Wrong (First National, 1919)
d: James Kirkwood. 5 reels.
Jack Pickford, Marguerite de la Motte, Clara Horton, George Dromgold, Hardee Kirkland, Rubin Williamson, Lydia Knott, Jake Abrams.
A small-town grocery delivery boy loves a local girl, but she couldn't care less.

The Indestructible Wife (Select Pictures Corp., 1919)
w, d: Charles Maigne. 5 reels.
Alice Brady, Saxon Kling, Sue Balfour, George Backus, Roy Adams, W.A. Williams, Anne Cornwall, Percy Marmont, Leonore Hughes, Thomas Donnelly.
Newlyweds fill their honeymoon with sports activities and late-night dancing. The husband is baffled that his bride can keep up the pace, so he sets out to test her limits.

Indiscreet Corinne (Triangle, 1917)
d: Jack Dillon. 5 reels.
Olive Thomas, George Chesebro, Joseph Bennett, Josie Sedgwick, Annette DeFoe, Lillian Langdon, Thomas H. Guise, Lou Conley, Thornton Edwards, Edwin J. Brady.
Corinne's a nice girl who wants to live a little. So, she poses as a shady lady and vamps a fellow who's only too happy to get the attention.

Indiscretion (Vitagraph, 1917)
d: Wilfrid North. 5 reels.
Lillian Walker, Walter McGrail, Richard Wangemann, Katharine Lewis, Thomas R. Mills, Josephine Earle, Thomas Brooke, Robert Gaillard.
Feeling restrained by society's standards, a young woman decides to carry on a flirtation with a married man.

Indiscretion (A.J. Bimberg/Pioneer Film Corp., 1921)
d: William Davis. 6 reels.
Florence Reed, Lionel Atwill, Gareth Hughes.
Though engaged to marry Howard, Laura becomes fascinated by his friend Stephen, a recent convert to an eastern cult.

The Inevitable (Erbograph Co./Art Dramas, Inc., 1917)
d: Ben Goetz. 5 reels.
Anna Q. Nilsson, Albert Tavernier, Wilson Reynolds, Chester Barnett, William Bailey, Lucile Dorrington.
When a man dies after a violent argument with his business partner, the dead man's daughter resolves to avenge his death by vamping the partner's son and destroying him.

Inez From Hollywood (Sam E. Rork Productions/First National, 1924)
d: Alfred E. Green. 7 reels.
Anna Q. Nilsson, Lewis Stone, Mary Astor, Laurence Wheat, Rose Dione, Snitz Edwards, Harry Depp, Ray Hallor, E.H. Calvert.
Inez, a screen actress who has built her reputation on her roles as a "vamp," is actually a man-hater.

The Infamous Miss Revell (Metro, 1921)
d: Dallas M. Fitzgerald. 6 reels.
Alice Lake, Cullen Landis, Jackie Saunders, Lydia Knott, Herbert Standing, Alfred Hollingsworth, Stanley Goethals, Francis Carpenter, May Giraci, Geraldine Condon.
Twin sisters have a musical act, but away from the footlights their lives border on the sinister.
Miss Lake has a double role here, as the twins.

Infatuation (Corinne Griffith Productions/First National, 1925)
d: Irving Cummings. 7 reels.
Corinne Griffith, Percy Marmont, Malcolm McGregor, Warner Oland, Clarissa Selwyn, Leota Lorraine, Claire DuBrey, Martha Mattox, Howard Davies.
In Cairo, a British nobleman devotes himself to his work, his wife at his side. However, he devotes rather too much time to work, allowing his wife to become infatuated with his male secretary.

The Inferior Sex (First National, 1920)
d: Joseph Henabery. 5 reels.
Milton Sills, Mildred Harris Chaplin, Mary Alden, John Steppling, Bertram Grassby, James O. Barrows, Yvette Mitchell.

When a man spends time tending to business matters, his new bride feels neglected.

Infidel (Preferred Pictures/Associated First National, 1922)
w, d: James Young. 6 reels.
Katherine MacDonald, Robert Ellis, Joseph Dowling, Boris Karloff, Melbourne MacDowell, Oleta Otis, Charles Smiley, Loyola O'Connor, Barbara Tennant, Charles Force.
Lola, a lovely young actress, is transported to a South Seas island, ostensibly for a film role. Once there, however, she finds herself in the midst of a native uprising.

Infidelity (Erbograph Co./Art Dramas, Inc., 1917)
w, d: Ashley Miller. 5 reels.
Anna Q. Nilsson, Eugene Strong, Miriam Nesbitt, Warren Cook, Fred Jones, Elizabeth Spencer, Arthur Morrison.
Under hypnotism, an art school student is induced to go to her classmate's private studio.

The Inn of the Blue Moon (De Luxe Pictures, Inc., 1918)
d: John B. O'Brien. 6 reels.
Doris Kenyon, Harry C. Browne, Crauford Kent, William Walcott, Harriet Ross, Lyn Donaldson, John Hopkins.
Twin sisters separated in childhood are reunited years later, at the Inn of the Blue Moon.

The Inner Chamber (Vitagraph, 1921)
d: Edward José. 6 reels.
Alice Yoce, Jane Jennings, Pedro DeCordoba, Holmes E. Herbert, John Webb Dillon, Grace Barton, Ida Waterman, Josephine Whittell, Mrs. DeWolf Hopper.
Claire, grateful for the kindnesses of Ned Wellman to her mother and herself, falls in love with him. She soon learns, however, that the kindly Wellman is already married, and his wife is insane.

The Inner Man (Syracuse Motion Picture Co./Playgoers Pictures, 1922)
d: Hamilton Smith. 5 reels.
Wyndham Standing, J. Barney Sherry, Louis Pierce, Leslie Hunt, Dorothy Mackaill, Gustav von Seyffertitz, Arthur Dewey, Martin Kinney, Kathryn Kingsley, Nellie Parker Spaulding, Arthur Caldwell Jr.
When confronted by villainy at his father's mine in Kentucky, a mild-mannered professor of mathematics finds he is not so mild-mannered after all.

The Inner Shrine (Lasky Feature Plays/Paramount, 1917)
d: Frank Reicher. 5 reels.
Margaret Illington, Hobart Bosworth, Jack Holt, Elliott Dexter, Adele Farrington, Paul Weigel, Ernest Joy, Jack Stark.
In France, a viscount and a marquis vie for the love of a woman.

The Inner Struggle (American Film Co./Mutual, 1916)
d: Edward Sloman. 5 reels.
Franklin Ritchie, Winnifred Greenwood, Roy Stewart.
Melodrama about a doctor who loves a married woman. To forget about her, he takes a position at a leper colony.

Innocence (Columbia, 1923)
d: Edward J. Le Saint. 6 reels.
Anna Q. Nilsson, Earle Foxe, Freeman Wood, Marion Harlan, Wilfred Lucas, William Scott.
A Broadway dancer marries a scion of privilege, then finds that her new husband's family disapproves of her.

The Innocence of Lizette (American Film Co./Mutual, 1916)
d: James Kirkwood. 5 reels.
Mary Miles Minter, Eugene Ford, Harvey Clark, Eugenie Forde, Ashton Dearholt, Blanche Hanson.
Naively innocent, a girl finds a baby and claims it is her own—but since she doesn't really know where babies come from, she's mystified at people's response to her news.

The Innocence of Ruth (Thomas A. Edison, Inc., 1916)
d: John H. Collins. 5 reels.
Edward Earle, Viola Dana, Augustus Phillips, Lena Davril, Brad Sutton, Nellie Grant.
An orphan girl is treated with fatherly attention by her wealthy guardian, although they are close enough in age to be romantically involved.

Innocent (Astra Film Corp./Pathé, 1918)
d: George Fitzmaurice. 5 reels.
Fannie Ward, John Miltern, Armand Kaliz, Frederick Perry, Nathaniel Sack.
In Paris, an orphan girl becomes smitten with an unscrupulous gambler.

An Innocent Adventuress (Famous Players-Lasky, 1919)
d: Robert G. Vignola. 5 reels.
Vivian Martin, Edythe Chapman, Gertrude Norman, Jane Wolff, Thomas D. Bates, Hal Clements, James Farley, Spottiswoode Aitken, Lloyd Hughes.
Misunderstandings lead an innocent girl to fear she has committed a felony.

The Innocent Cheat (Ben Wilson Productions/Arrow Film Corp., 1921)
d: Ben Wilson. 6 reels.
Roy Stewart, Sidney DeGray, George Hernandez, Rhea Mitchell, Kathleen Kirkham.
Murdock, a railroad engineer, accidentally causes a train wreck and loses his job. He wanders the streets aimlessly, becomes a hobo, and at long last finds the woman who was the cause of his distractions at work. It's a bittersweet ending of sorts, for although Murdock is jobless, he discovers that he now has a child.

The Innocent Lie (Famous Players/Paramount, 1916)
d: Sidney Olcott. 5 reels.
Valentine Grant, Jack J. Clark, Morris foster, Hunter Arden, Robert Cain, Frank Losee, William Courtleigh Jr., Helen Lindroth, Charles Ferguson.
Nora's a colleen from Ireland, visiting America. When she suffers a bump on the head and temporarily loses her memory, she is mistaken for another Nora, and is placed with that woman's family. Eventually our heroine recovers her memory and realizes there's been a mistake—but by now she's in love with her new "cousin," and decides to make her ties to the family permanent.

An Innocent Magdalene (Triangle/Fine Arts, 1916)
d: Allan Dwan. 5 reels.
Lillian Gish, Sam DeGrasse, Mary Alden, Spottiswoode Aitken, Jennie Lee, Seymour Hastings.
A Southern belle marries a reformed gambler.

The Innocent Sinner (Fox, 1917)
d: Raoul Walsh. 5 reels.
Miriam Cooper, Charles Clary, Jack Standing, Jane Novak, Rosita Marstini, William E. Parsons, Johnny Reese, Jennie Lee.
Widowed when her husband is killed in a fight, a young woman lives in a state of fear. But she is rescued when a kindly doctor takes a romantic interest in her, and it turns

244

out that he's her husband's cousin.

Innocent's Progress (Triangle, 1918)
d: Frank Borzage. 5 reels.
Pauline Starke, Lillian West, Alice Knowland, Jack Livingston, Charles Dorian, Graham Pette.
Tessa's a country girl who yearns for love and a career in the big city.

The Inside of the Cup (Cosmopolitan/Paramount, 1921)
d: Albert Capellani. 7 reels.
William P. Carleton, David Torrence, Edith Hallor, John Bohn, Marguerite Clayton, Richard Carlyle, Margaret Seddon, Albert Roccardi, Frank A. Lyon, Henry Morey, Irene Delroy, George Storey.
A new minister preaches against infamy and intolerance, and becomes a hero.

Inside the Lines (Delcah Photoplays, Inc./World Film Corp., 1918)
d: David M. Hartford. 6 reels.
Lewis Stone, Marguerite Clayton, George Field, Arthur Allardt, David M. Hartford, Joseph Singleton, Helen Dunbar, Willard Wayne, William Durall, Fritz von Hardenburg.
World War I espionage drama, with Lewis Stone in the role as a double agent.

Inspiration (Thanhouser, 1915)
d: George Foster Platt. 5 reels.
Audrey Munson, Thomas A. Curran, George Marlo, Bert Delaney, Carey L. Hastings, Ethyle Cooke, Louise Emerald Bates.
While preparing to create a statue for a new fountain, a sculptor almost despairs of finding the right model for his work. Then he does meet her, and she inspires his artistry to magnificent heights.
Audrey Munson was an artist's model in real life. Her beauty was so luminous that her nude posing scenes in this film were considered beyond censorship, and were allowed to remain in the finished print. She would play an artist's model again, in the American Film Co.'s *Purity* (1916). After the success of *Purity*, Thanhouser re-released *Inspiration* in 1918 under the title *The Perfect Model*.

Inspiration (Excellent Pictures, 1928)
d: Bernard McEveety. 7 reels.
George Walsh, Gladys Frazin, Marguerite Clayton, Earle Larrimore, Bradley Barker, Ali Yousoff, John Costello, Buddy Harris, Bernice Vert.
When Gerald Erskine is accused of fathering an illegitimate child, his chaste sweetheart decides she'll have nothing more to do with him. But Gerald is innocent.

The Interferin' Gent (Action Pictures/Pathé, 1927)
d: Richard Thorpe. 5 reels.
Buffalo Bill Jr., Olive Hasbrouck, Al Taylor, Harry Todd, Jack McDonald.
Out West, a beautiful young ranch owner is under siege from thugs who are trying to steal her property. She is protected by her long-lost brother, who happens along at just the right time. Once the danger is over, however, she learns to her delight that her protector is not her brother at all—and, with the real brother's blessing, they face a happy future together.

The Interloper (World Film Corp., 1918)
d: Oscar C. Apfel. 5 reels.
Kitty Gordon, Irving Cummings, Warren Cook, Isabelle

Berwin, June Blackman, Frank Mayo, George MacQuarrie, Anthony Byrd, Tom Cameron.
When a Southern girl marries a Northern gent and moves into his home, his family and friends who strongly admired his deceased first wife make her feel like an interloper.

An International Marriage (Oliver Morosco/Paramount, 1916)
d: Frank Lloyd. 5 reels.
Rita Jolivet, Marc Robbins, Elliott Dexter, Grace Carlisle, Olive White, Courtenay Foote, Page Peters, Herbert Standing, Adelaide Woods, Jean Woodbury.
Marital mixups drive this comedy about an American girl who must obtain a title before she can marry a duke. Her route to the altar takes her through a "temporary" marriage with a count, but she finds that detour fraught with complications.

Into Her Kingdom (Corinne Griffith Productions/First National, 1926)
d: Svend Gade. 7 reels.
Corinne Griffith, Einar Hanson, Claude Gillingwater, Charles Crockett, Evelyn Selbie, Larry Fisher, H.C. Simmons, Elinor Vanderveer, Byron Sage, Tom Murray, Marcelle Corday.
When a Russian peasant is sent to Siberia for an alleged crime against the Grand Duchess, he swears revenge. He gets his chance a few years later when the Bolsheviks topple the Czarist regime and take over Russia. But the duchess is beautiful, and the peasant shirks from causing her any more pain. Together they escape to America, where they settle down in New Jersey as husband and wife.

Into No Man's Land (Excellent Pictures, 1928)
d: Cliff Wheeler. 7 reels.
Tom Santschi, Josephine Norman, Jack Daugherty, Betty Blythe, Crawford Kent, Mary McAllister, Syd Crossley.
Multiple-hanky weeper about a crook who conceals his criminal activities from the daugher he cherishes.

Into the Night (Raleigh Pictures, 1928)
d: Duke Worne. 6 reels.
Agnes Ayres, Forrest Stanley, Robert Russell, Rom Lingham, Rhody Hathaway, Allan Sears, Corliss Palmer, Arthur Thalasso.
Unfairly convicted of crime, a man faces jail unless his devoted daughter can find evidence to exonerate him.

Into the Primitive (Selig Polyscope, 1916)
d: T.N. Heffron. 5 reels.
Kathlyn Williams, Guy Oliver, Harry Lonsdale.
Three castaways—two men and a woman—are washed ashore on a desert island.

Intolerance (Griffith, 1916)
w, d: D.W. Griffith. 13 reels.
Mae Marsh, Lillian Gish, Constance Talmadge, Robert Harron, Elmo Lincoln, Eugene Pallette, Fred Turner, Sam DeGrasse, Vera Lewis, Mary Alden, Lucille Brown, Miriam Cooper, Walter Long, Tom Wilson, Ralph Lewis, A.W. McClure, Max Davidson, Monte Blue, Marguerite Marsh, Tod Browning, Edward Dillon, Clyde Hopkins, William Brown, Albert Lee, Howard Gaye, Lillian Langdon, Olga Grey, Erich von Stroheim, Bessie Love, George Walsh, Eugene Pallette, Spottiswoode Aitken, Ruth Handforth, A.D. Sears, Josephine Crowell, Constance Talmadge, W.E. Lawrence, Joseph Henabery, Elmer Clifton, Alfred Paget, Seena Owen, Carl Stockdale, Tully Marshall, George

Siegmann, George Fawcett, Kate Bruce, Ruth St. Denis, Loyola O'Connor, James Curley, Howard Scott, Alma Rubens, Mildred Harris, Margaret Mooney, Pauline Starke, Winifred Westover.

Massively ambitious spectacle film, divided into four separate but interwoven stories—set in Belshazzar's Babylon, in Judea at the time of the Crucifixion, in Renaissance France, and in early 20th century America. The unifying theme is intolerance, i.e., man's inhumanity to man.

Intrigue (Vitagraph, 1917)
d: John Robertson. 5 reels.
Peggy Hyland, Marc MacDermott, Bobby Connelly, Templar Saxe, Brinsley Shaw, Harry Southwell, Nellie Spitzer.
In a mythical European kingdom, an American girl finds that the Grand Duke is being held hostage. The ransom: her romantic affections.

The Intrigue (Pallas Pictures/Paramount, 1916)
d: Frank Lloyd. 5 reels.
Lenore Ulrich, Cecil Van Auker, Howard Davies, Florence Vidor, Paul Weigel, Herbert Standing.
When an American inventor develops a revolutionary new weapon, the bidding is opened to several European powers.

Introduce Me (Associated Exhibitors, 1925)
d: George J. Crone. 7 reels.
Douglas MacLean, Robert Ober, E.J. Ratcliffe, Lee Shumway, Wade Boteler, Anne Cornwell.
Madcap comedy about a timid American who's mistaken for a champion mountain climber and is forced to keep up appearances by scaling an alp.

The Intrusion of Isabel (American Film Co./Pathé, 1919)
d: Lloyd Ingraham. 5 reels.
Mary Miles Minter, J. Parks Jones, Lucretia Harris, Alan Forrest, Margaret Shelby, George Periolat, Mary Land, Carl Stockdale.
Sibling southerners Isabel and Bert land in New York and start new lives.

The Invisible Bond (Famous Players-Lasky/Paramount, 1919)
d: Charles Maigne. 5 reels.
Irene Castle, Huntley Gordon, Claire Adams, Fleming Ward, George Majeroni, Helen Green, Ida Waterman, Warburton Gamble.
After an evil flirt causes a rift between husband and wife, the pair divorce. But even years later, an "invisible bond" exists between them.

The Invisible Divorce (National Picture Theaters/Select Pictures, 1920)
d: Thomas R. Mills, Nat C. Deverich. 6 reels.
Walter McGrail, Leatrice Joy, Walter Miller, Grace Darmond, Tom Bates.
Jimmy, a newlywed, runs his oil drilling business with money borrowed from the husband of an old flame. The business is successful, but Jimmy finds the pressure of dealing with his former sweetheart is putting a strain on his marriage.

The Invisible Fear (Anita Stewart Productions/Associated First National, 1921)
d: Edwin Carewe. 6 reels.
Anita Stewart, Walter McGrail, Allan Forrest, Hamilton Morse, Estelle Evans, George Kuwa, Edward Hunt, Ogden Crane.
Believing she has murdered a man, Sylvia is tormented by

fear of discovery.

The Invisible Power (Goldwyn, 1921)
d: Frank Lloyd. 7 reels.
House Peters, Irene Rich, DeWitt Jennings, Sydney Ainsworth, Jessie DeJainette, William Friend, Gertrude Claire, Lydia Yeamans Titus.
Chambers, an ex-con, gets married to a lady who knows his past but cares for him anyway.

Irene (First National, 1926)
d: Al E. Green. 9 reels. (Technicolor sequences.)
Lloyd Hughes, Colleen Moore, George K. Arthur, Charles Murray, Kate Price, Ida Darling, Eva Novak, Edward Earle, Lawrence Wheat, Maryon Aye, Bess Flowers, Lydia Yeamans Titus, Cora Macey.
Fresh and winsome Irene, an Irish lass, comes to New York City and finds a job as a fashion model. She falls in love with Donald, a son of wealth, but his uptight mother is not amused by the young lady's Irish ancestry.

Irish Eyes (Triangle, 1918)
d: William Dowlan. 5 reels.
Pauline Starke, Ward Caulfield, Virginia Ware, Gus Saville, Joe King, Eugene Burr, Rae Godfrey.
After her alcoholic father is killed in a brawl, an Irish colleen runs away to the seaside and is taken in by a kindly nobleman.

Irish Hearts (Warner Bros., 1927)
d: Byron Haskins. 6 reels.
May McAvoy, Jason Robards, C. Graham Baker, Bess Meredyth, Walter Perry.
An Irish girl journeys to America to be with her beau, but he dumps her. Soon after, she meets Mr. Right.

Irish Luck (Famous Players-Lasky/Paramount, 1925)
d: Victor Heerman. 7 reels.
Thomas Meighan, Lois Wilson, Cecil Humphreys, Claude King, Ernest Lawford, Charles Hammond, Louise Grafton, S.B. Carrickson, Charles McDonald, Mary Foy.
Donahue, a New Yorker, wins a trip to Ireland, where he goes and looks up his relatives. He finds that he's a lookalike for Lord Fitzhugh, a young nobleman, and the two men become good friends. In time, Donahue will be needed to impersonate the young lord and put to rout a foul scheme against the family.
Meighan does double duty here, playing both the American and his aristocratic relative.

The Iron Hand (Universal, 1916)
d: Ulysses Davis. 5 reels.
Hobart Bosworth, Maud George, William V. Mong, Jack Curtis, Frank Newberg, Winifred Harris, Jane Novak.
Political corruption lies at the heart of this tale about a politician whose foster son sides against him.

The Iron Heart (Astra Film Corp./Pathé, 1917)
d: George Fitzmaurice. 5 reels.
Edwin Arden, Forrest Winant, Helene Chadwick, Leonore Harris, Gertrude Berkeley.
A ruthless industrialist runs his steel works with an iron hand and, it's said, an iron heart.

The Iron Heart (Fox, 1920)
d: Denison Clift, Paul Caseneuve. 5 reels.
Madlaine Traverse, George McDaniel, Edwin Booth Tilton, Melbourne McDowell, Ben Deely.
When an industrialist dies, his daughter takes over his steel

mills.

The Iron Horse (Fox, 1924)
d: John Ford. 10 reels.
George O'Brien, Madge Bellamy, Cyril Chadwick, Fred Kohler, J. Farrel MacDonald, Charles Edward Bull, Gladys Hulette, Francis Powers, James Welch, Jack O'Brien, Peggy Cartwright, Will Walling.
Epic western documenting the building of a railroad into Nevada. Climaxes with a mammoth Indian attack on trapped locomotives, while the U.S. Cavalry races to the rescue.

The Iron Man (Whitman Bennett Productions/Chadwick Pictures, 1925)
d: Whitman Bennett. 5 reels.
Lionel Barrymore, Mildred Harris, Winifred Barry, Dorothy Kingdon, Alfred Mack, J. Moy Bennett, Isobel DeLeon, Jean Del Val.
A jilted bride finds happiness of sorts with a wealthy steel executive—but it's a marriage in name only.

The Iron Mask (Fairbanks/United Artists, 1929)
d: Allan Dwan. 11 reels. (Music, sound effects, part talkie.)
Douglas Fairbanks, Marguerite de la Motte, Ulrich Haupt, Nigel de Brulier, Leon Barry, Dorothy Revier, Stanley Sandford, Gino Corrado, Rolfe Sedan, Belle Bennett, William Bakewell, George Thorpe.
D'Artagnan and the Three Musketeers fight to restore the rightful king to his throne after his evil twin has taken his place.

The Iron Rider (Fox, 1920)
d: Scott Dunlap. 5 reels.
William Russell, Vola Vale, Arthur Morrison, Wadsworth Harris, George Nicholls.
Out West, folks in a lawless town yearn for the days of the Iron Riders, a masked band who took the law into their own hands and kept the town crime-free and peaceful. Soon a new masked man rides, emulating the Iron Riders of old.

The Iron Ring (World Film Corp., 1917)
d: George Archainbaud. 5 reels.
Edward Langford, Gerda Holmes, Arthur Ashley, Herbert Frank, George MacQuarrie, George Cowl, Alexandria Carewe, Gladys Thompson, Victor Kennard, Richard Clarke.
Feeling neglected by her husband, Bess is tempted to encourage her new suitor. But when she arrives at his flat for a party and finds that she is the only guest, Bess sees the light and hightails it back to her husband.

The Iron Strain (New York Motion Picture Corp./Triangle, 1915)
d: Reginald Barker. 6 reels.
Dustin Farnum, Enid Markay, Charles K. French, Louise Glaum, Truly Shattuck, Joseph Dowling, Nigura Eagle Feather, Joe Goodboy, Louis Morrison.
In Alaska, a wealthy girl is kidnapped and forced to marry her abductor.

Iron to Gold (Fox, 1922)
d: Bernard J. Durning. 5 reels.
Dustin Farnum, Marguerite Marsh, William Conklin, William Elmer, Lionel Belmore, Glen Cavender, Robert Perry, Dan Mason.
Western melodrama about an outlaw who rescues a young woman from thieves and then learns she's the wife of the man who stole his mining claim.

The Iron Trail (Whitman Bennett/United Artists, 1921)
d: Roy William Neill. 7 reels.
Wyndham Standing, Thurston Hall, Alma Tell, Reginald Denny, Harlan Knight, Betty Carpenter, Lee Beggs, Bert Starkey, Danny Hayes, Eulalie Jensen.
Two railroad men fight to complete an Alaskan rail line.

The Iron Woman (Popular Plays and Players, Inc./Metro, 1916)
d: Carl Harbaugh. 6 reels.
Nance O'Neil, Einar Linden, Alfred Hickman, Evelyn Brent, Vera Sisson, William Postance, Christine Mayo.
A steel mill is owned and operated by a widow with two children.

The Irresistible Lover (Universal, 1927)
d: William Beaudine. 7 reels.
Norman Kerry, Lois Moran, Gertrude Astor, Lee Moran, Myrtle Stedman, Phillips Smalley, Arthur Lake, Walter James, George Pearce.
Romantic comedy about Gray, a wealthy womanizer who finds himself engaged to two different women.

Is Life Worth Living? (Selznick, 1921)
d: Alan Crosland. 5 reels.
Eugene O'Brien, Winifred Westover, Arthur Housman, George Lessey, Warren Cook, Arthur Donaldson, Florida Kingsley.
A troubled man, despondent and bent on suicide, meets a young woman with worse problems than his own.

Is Love Everything? (Garson Enterprises/Associated Exhibitors, 1924)
d: William Christy Cabanne. 6 reels.
Alma Rubens, Frank Mayo, H.B. Warner, Walter McGrail, Lilyan Tashman, Marie Schaefer, Irene Howley.
When a yachting expedition turns into a shipwreck, the only apparent survivors are Virginia, a married woman, and Robert, her former sweetheart. The flame of their love is rekindled now that her husband is apparently lost at sea. But then he shows up. What now?

Is Matrimony Available? (Famous Players-Lasky/Paramount, 1922)
d: James Cruze. 6 reels.
T. Roy Barnes, Lila Lee, Lois Wilson, Walter Hiers, ZaSu Pitts, Tully Marshall, Arthur Hoyt, Lillian Leighton, Adolphe Menjou, Otis Harlan, Sylvia Ashton, Charles Ogle.
Young lovers Margaret and Arthur elope and head for their honeymoon hotel, only to be informed that their marriage is not valid because the license clerk had not been sworn in. When the frustrated Arthur returns to the clerk's office to complain, he learns that because of the beaureaucratic blunder, all marriages for the past 30 years are null and void.

Is Money Everything? (D.M. Film Corp./Lee-Bradford Corp., 1923)
w, d: Glen Lyons. 6 reels.
Norman Kerry, Miriam Cooper, Andrew Hicks, John Sylvester, Martha Mansfield, William Bailey, Lawrence Brooke.
The inordinate love of money nearly ruins a happy marriage.

Is That Nice? (R-C Pictures/FBO of America, 1926)
d: Del Andrews. 5 reels.
George O'Hara, Doris Hill, Stanton Heck, Charles Thrston, Roy Laidlaw, Babe London, "Red" Kirby, Ethan Laidlaw.
Daffy comedy about Ralph, a cub reporter who writes a

damaging story about a political boss. When his editor balks at printing it because of the potential for libel, the reporter must retrieve the one copy of his article that is making its way into the hands of the political boss himself—even if it means disguising himself as a window washer outside the man's office.

Is Zat So? (Fox, 1927)
d: Alfred E. Green. 7 reels.
George O'Brien, Edmund Lowe, Kathryn Perry, Cyril Chadwick, Doris Lloyd, Dione Ellis, Richard Maitland, Douglas Fairbanks Jr., Philippe DeLacy, Jack Herrick.
After losing the big fight, a boxer and his manager must take jobs as servants in a millionaire's mansion. But the boxer will live to fight another day.

The Island of Desire (Fox, 1916)
d: Otis Turner. 5 reels.
George Walsh, Margaret Gibson, Anna Luther, Herschel Mayall, William Burress, William Clifford, Sam Searles, Hector Sarno, Marie McKeen, Willard Louis.
Treasure seekers find a fortune in pearls on a South Sea island.

The Island of Intrigue (Metro, 1919)
d: Henry Otto. 5 reels.
May Allison, Jack Mower, Frederick Vroom, Lucille Ward, Gordon Marr, Lillian West, Hector V. Sarno, Tom Kennedy, Chance Ward, Edward Alexander.
An oil tycoon's daughter is kidnapped and held hostage on a sheltered island.

The Island of Regeneration (Vitagraph, 1915)
d: Harry Davenport. 6 reels.
Edith Storey, Bobby Connelly, Antonio Moreno, S. Rankin Drew, Leo Delaney, Naomi Childers, Jack Brawn, Lillian Herbert, Logan Paul.
A young woman who thinks platonic friendship between a man and a woman is purely a case of mind over matter finds her theory sorely tested.

The Island of Surprise (Vitagraph, 1916)
d: Paul Scardon. 5 reels.
William Courtenay, Charles Kent, Anders Randolf, Charles Wellesley, Denton Vane, Eleanor Woodruff, Zena Keefe, Julia Swayne Gordon, Caroline Cook, Logan Paul.
What's a chap to do when he gets shipwrecked on a desert island with two women, both of whom claim to be his wife?

Island Wives (Vitagraph, 1922)
d: Webster Campbell. 5 reels.
Corinne Griffith, Charles Trowbridge, Rockliffe Fellowes, Ivan Christy, Edna Hibbard, Norman Rankow, Peggy Parr, Barney Sherry, John Galsworthy.
A mainland girl becomes disenchanted with living on a South Seas island, and seeks adventure. She ends up finding more adventure than she bargained for.

The Isle of Conquest (Norma Talmadge Film Co./Select, 1919)
d: Edward José. 5 reels.
Norma Talmadge, Wyndham Standing, Charles Gerard, Hedda Hopper, Natalie Talmadge, Claire Whitney, Gareth Hughes, Joe Smiley.
When their pleasure boat sinks, a deck hand rescues an heiress and manages to swim with her to a deserted island.

Isle of Doubt (Syracuse Motion Picture Co./Playgoers Pictures, 1922)
d: Hamilton Smith. 6 reels.
Wyndham Standing, Dorothy Mackaill, George Fawcett, Marie Burke, Warner Richmond, Arthur Dewey.
Penniless and bitter, Eleanor marries wealthy Dean with the intention of making him miserable and getting a large divorce settlement. It doesn't quite work out that way.

Isle of Forgotten Women (Columbia, 1927)
d: George B. Seitz. 6 reels.
Conway Tearle, Alice Calhoun, Dorothy Sebastian.
An innocent man confesses to his father's crimes, then flees to a South Seas island.

The Isle of Hope (Richard Talmadge Productions/FBO of America, 1925)
d: Jack Nelson. 6 reels.
Richard Talmadge, Helen Ferguson, James Marcus, Bert Strong, Howard Bell, Edward Gordon, George Reed.
While at sea, a yachtsman suffers a mutiny and winds up stranded on a deserted island—with the captain's daughter for company.

The Isle of Life (Universal, 1916)
d: Burton George. 5 reels.
Frank Whitson, Roberta Wilson, Hayward Mack, T.D. Crittendon, Lillian Concord, Hector V. Sarno, Dick Ryan, Babe Sedgwick.
A scruffy but dynamic ne'er-do-well kidnaps an heiress and takes her to an uncharted island.

The Isle of Lost Men (Trem Carr Productions/Rayart Pictures, 1928)
d: Duke Worne. 6 reels.
Tom Santschi, James Marcus, Allen Connor, Patsy O'Leary, Paul Weigel, Jules Cowles, Maude George, Sailor Sharkey.
A millionaire's daughter is kidnapped by pirates and winds up on an island with only men.

The Isle of Lost Ships (First National, 1923)

d: Maurice Tourneur. 8 reels.
Milton Sills, Anna Q. Nilsson, Frank Campeau, Walter Long, Bert Woodruff, Aggie Herring, Herschel Mayall.
Survivors of a shipwreck are washed up on an island in the Sargasso Sea.

The Isle of Love (Gaumont Co./Mutual, 1916)
d: Edwin Middleton. 5 reels.
Gertrude McCoy, Earl O. Schenck, Robert Clugston, Iva Shepard, Charles W. Travis.
An actress is marooned on a desert island with a man who thinks he's in love with her.

The Isle of Love (1922)—see: An Adventuress (1920)

The Isle of Retribution (R-C Pictures/FBO of America, 1926)
d: James P. Hogan. 7 reels.
Lillian Rich, Robert Frazer, Victor McLaglen, Mildred Harris, Kathleen Kirkham, David Torrence, Inez Gomez.

In the Alaskan seas, a shipwreck strands a group of wealthy voyagers on an island owned by a brute with an ugly temper.

Isn't Life Wonderful? (Griffith/United Artists, 1924)
d: D.W. Griffith. 9 reels.
Carol Dempster, Neil Hamilton, Helen Lowell, Erville Alderson, Frank Puglia, Marcia Harris, Lupino Lane, Hans von Schlettow, Paul Rehkopf, Robert Scholz, Walter Plimmer Jr.

A tale of trial and hardship in post-WW I Germany, and the family love that conquers all.

Isobel; Or, the Trail's End   (George H. Davis, 1920)
d: Edwin Carewe.   6 reels.
House Peters, Jane Novak, Edward Pell, Tom Wilson, Bob Walker, Pearlie Norton, Dick La Reno, Horin Konishi.
A Northwest mountie falls in love with a woman whose husband he must arrest.

It   (Paramount, 1927)
d: Clarence G. Badger.   7 reels.
Clara Bow, Antonio Moreno, William Austin, Priscilla Bonner, Jacqueline Gadsdon, Julia Swayne Gordon, Elinor Glyn (as herself), Gary Cooper.
A shopgirl fancies her handsome boss, and charms her way into his heart.   The romance stalls, however, when a newspaper mistakenly reports that the girl is an unwed mother.   The misunderstanding is cleared up, but not before several complications set in.

It Can Be Done   (Earle Williams Productions/Vitagraph, 1921)
d: David Smith.   5 reels.
Earle Williams, Elinor Fair, Henry Barrows, Jack Mathies, Jack Carlisle, Alfred Aldridge, William McCall, Florence Hart, Mary Huntress.
An author of seemingly implausible detective stories replicates one of them, proving that his plots do make sense in real life.

It Can Be Done   (Universal, 1929)
d: Fred Newmeyer.   7 reels.   (Music, sound effects, part talkie.)
Sue Carol, Richard Carlyle, Richard Carle, Jack Egan, Tom O'Brien.
A mild-mannered clerk is mistaken for an important publisher.

It Happened in Honolulu   (Universal, 1916)

d: Lynn Reynolds.   5 reels.
Myrtle Gonzales, Val Paul, George Hernandez, Lule Warrenton, C. Norman Hammond, Fred church, Bertram Grassby, Jack Curtis.
Though she's headed for an arranged marriage with a wealthy dolt, a girl manages to marry her true love instead.

It Happened to Adele   (Thanhouser, 1917)
d: Van Dyke Brooke.   5 reels.
Gladys Leslie, Carey Hastings, Peggy Burke, Charlie Emerson, Clarine Seymour, Wayne Arey, Justus Barnes.
When an important broker offers to help an aspiring dancer, and she takes him up on it, the arrangement sparks an affair of the heart.

It is the Law   (Fox, 1924)
d: J. Gordon Edwards.   7 reels.
Arthur Hohl, Herbert Heyes, Mimi Palmeri, George Lessey, Robert Young, Florence Dixon, Byron Douglas, Olaf Hytten, DeSacia Mooers, Guido Trento, Byron Russell.
Rejected by his lady love in favor of another man, Woodruff schemes to make it seem that he has been killed by his rival. The man is sentenced to prison and serves a long sentence. Years later, he really does kill Woodruff, but is immune from prosecution because he cannot be convicted of the same crime twice.

It Isn't Being Done This Season   (Vitagraph, 1921)
d: George L. Sargent.   5 reels.

Corinne Griffith, Sally Crute, Webster Campbell, Charles Wellesley, John Charles.
Marcia loves Oliver, but George is the suitor with money.

It Might Happen to You   (Artclass Pictures Corp., 1920)
d: Al Santell.   5 reels.
Billy Mason, Doris Dare, William Harcourt, Walter Beckwith, Violet Mack, Edward Scanlon, Helen Adams.
Comedic tale about a wealthy playboy and skirt chaser whose father orchestrates a lavish hoax to convince his son he's got the d.t.'s and get him to give up alcohol.

It Must be Love   (John McCormick Productions/First National, 1926)
d: Alfred E. Green.   7 reels.
Colleen Moore, Jean Hersholt, Malcolm McGregor, Arthur Stone, Bodil Rosing, Dorothy Seastrom, Cleve Moore, Mary O'Brien, Ray Hallor.
Comedy about a delicatessen owner's daughter who can't stand the smell of her dad's shop, and yearns to break free of it.   She meets Jack and they fall in love, and soon they are engaged.   Then Jack buys a deli of his own.   What now?

It Pays to Advertise   (Famous Players-Lasky/Paramount, 1919)
d: Donald Crisp.   5 reels.
Bryant Washburn, Lois Wilson, Frank Currier, Walter Hiers, Clarence Geldart, Julia Faye, Guy Oliver.
After a soap tycoon angrily disinherits his son, the lad uses his inherited business sense to build a soap empire of his own.

The Italian   (New York Motion Picture Corp., 1915)
d: Reginald Barker.   5 reels.
George Beban, Clara Williams, J. Frank Burke.
Tragic tale of an immigrant in New York City whose baby falls ill and dies during a heat wave.

Itching Palms   (R-C Pictures/FBO of America, 1923)
d: James W. Horne.   6 reels.
Tom Gallery, Herschel Mayall, Virginia Fox, Tom Wilson, Joseph Harrington, Victor Potel, Gertrude Claire, Robert Walker, Tom Lingham, Richard Cummings.
Two crooks conspire to steal a large sum of money that turns out to be counterfeit.

It's a Bear   (Triangle, 1919)
d: Lawrence Windom.   5 reels.
Taylor Holmes, Vivian Reed, Howard Davies, Edna Phillips Holmes.
Out West, a transplanted Bostonian outsmarts the local wise guys and falls in love with the pretty schoolmarm.

It's a Great Life   (Eminent Authors/Goldwyn, 1920)
d: E. Mason Hopper.   6 reels.
Cullen Landis, Molly Malone, Clara Horton, Howard Halston, Otto Hoffman, Tom Pearse, Ralph Bushman, E.J. Mack, John Lynch.

When a couple of prep school buddies find a pearl in a dish of oysters, they envision a life filled with riches. But all they get are tummy aches from eating their fill of oysters, trying to find more pearls.

It's the Old Army Game   (Paramount, 1926)
d: Edward Sutherland.   7 reels.
W.C. Fields, Louise Brooks, Blanche Ring, William Gaxton, Mary Foy, Mickey Bennett, Josephine Dunn, Jack Luden, George Currie.
Wild farce involving a village druggist (played by Fields)

who is awakened in the middle of the night by a female customer who wants to buy a 2-cent stamp. He gets no sleep the rest of the night, as one calamity after another visits the tormented storekeeper. Finally he gets some sleep by having himself locked up in jail.

The Ivory Snuff Box (World Film Corp., 1915)
d: Maurice Tourneur. 5 reels.
Holbrook Blinn, Alma Belwin, Norman Trevor, Robert Cummings.
In Europe, an American detective and his bride pursue the theft of a snuff box that turns out to contain a top secret code.

Jack and Jill (Oliver Morosco Photoplays/Paramount, 1917)
d: William Desmond Taylor. 5 reels.
Jack Pickford, Louise Huff, Leo Houck, Don Bailey, J.H. Holland, Hart Hoxie, Beatrice Burnham.
A young boxer quits the ring after killing an opponent, and goes West to forget.

Jack and the Beanstalk (Fox, 1917)
d: C.M. Franklin, S.A. Franklin. 10 reels.
Francis Carpenter, Virginia Lee Corbin, Violet Radcliffe, Carmen Fay DeRue, J. G. Traver, Vera Lewis, Ralph Lewis, Eleanor Washington, Ione Glennon, Buddy Messinger.
Fantasy based on the famous children's story about a boy who sells the family cow for a handful of beans instead of money. The beans are magical, and when planted, they sprout into a giant vine that reaches beyond the clouds. Jack then climbs the beanstalk, and finds trouble and treasure, in about equal measure.

Jack o' Clubs (Universal, 1924)
d: Robert F. Hill. 5 reels.
Herbert Rawlinson, Ruth Dwyer, Eddie Gribbon, Esther Ralston, Joseph Girard, Florence D. Lee, John Fox Jr., Noel Stewart.
Jack's a cop in the city's toughest neighborhood—and he straightens it out.

Jack o' Hearts (David Hartford/American Cinema Association, 1926)
d: David Hartford. 6 reels.
Cullen Landis, Gladys Hulette, Bert Cummings, Antrim Short, John T. Dwyer, John Price, Vester Pegg.
Jack, a young minister, is framed for robbery and spends time in prison. Instead of making him bitter, the experience emboldens him to preach of love, forgiveness and repentance.

Jack Spurlock, Prodigal (Fox, 1918)
d: Carl Harbaugh. 6 reels.
George Walsh, Dan Mason, Ruth Taylor, Robert Vivian, Mike Donlin, Jack Goodman.
After a young college cut-up gets expelled, he goes to work and makes a fortune buying and selling onions for use in a health tonic.

Jack Straw (Famous Players-Lasky/Paramount, 1920)
d: William C. DeMille. 5 reels.
Robert Warwick, Carol McComas, Charles Ogle, Irene Sullivan, Monte du Mont, Frances Parks, Lucien Littlefield, Robert Brower, Sylvia Ashton.
When a waiter impersonates a nobleman, the deception works almost too well. The young waiter falls in love with a wealthy young American woman, and she with him.

The Jack-Knife Man (First National, 1920)
d: King Vidor. 6 reels.
Fred Turner, Harry Todd, Bobby Kelso, Willis Marks, Lillian Leighton, James Corrigan, Claire MacDowell, Florence Vidor.
A lonely riverboat man adopts a baby boy, and raises him lovingly. But the law tries to take the child away from him.

Jackie (Fox, 1921)
d: Jack Ford. 5 reels.
Shirley Mason, William Scott, Harry Carter, George Stone, John Cook, Elsie Bambrick.
On the streets of London, a crippled boy plays the accordion while Jackie, an orphan girl from Russia, dances for the customers. Though the two fall prey to an opportunistic lecher who wants to include Jackie in his acting troupe and there take advantage of her, they are spotted by Carter, a wealthy American who takes up their cause. Carter sends the boy for an operation that will restore his health, and falls in love with Jackie.

Jacqueline, or Blazing Barriers (Pine Tree Pictures/Arrow Film Corp., 1923)
d: Dell Henderson. 7 reels.
Marguerite Courtot, Helen Rowland, Gus Weinberg, Effie Shannon, Lew Cody, Joseph Depew, Russell Griffin, J. Barney Sherry, Edmund Breese, Edria Fisk, Sheldon Lewis, Charles Fang, Paul Panzer.
In a lumber camp, passions—and a forest fire—are ignited when the camp boss and his enemy fight over the love of Jacqueline. But Jacqueline isn't having either of them, for she loves Raoul instead.

The Jade Cup (Gothic Productions/FBO of America, 1926)
d: Frank Hall. 5 reels.
Evelyn Brent, Jack Luden, Eugene Borden, George Cowl, Charles Delaney, Violet Palmer.
A chorus girl agrees to pose for a famous artist. While waiting for him in his studio, however, she is abducted by crooks who are there to steal the artist's paintings.

Jaffery (International Film Service, Inc., 1916)
d: George Irving. 6 reels.
C. Aubrey Smith, Eleanor Woodruff, Florence Deshon, Eric Blind, Paul Doucet, Ben Hendricks, Doris Sawyer, George Irving.
To help out a widow he admires, a budding writer presents her with a manuscript he has written, and tells her it was left by her late husband.

The Jaguar's Claws (Lasky Feature Plays/Paramount, 1917)
d: Marshall Neilan. 5 reels.
Sessue Hayakawa, Fritzi Brunette, Tom Moore, Marjorie Daw, Tom Forman, Mabel Van Buren, Horace B. Carpenter, Lucien Littlefield.
El Jaguar is a bandido who terrorizes folks on both sides of the U.S.-Mexico border.

The Jailbird (T.H. Ince/Famous Players-Lasky/Paramount, 1920)
d: Lloyd Ingraham. 5 reels.
Lew Morrison, Douglas MacLean, William Courtright, Wilbur Higby, Otto Hoffman, Bert Woodruff, Monty Collins, Doris May, Edith Yorke, Joe Hazelton.
After escaping from prison, a jailbird tries to settle in a small town and fleece the local yokels by selling them shares in a phony oil scheme. But destiny deals him a double whammy:

First, he falls in love with a local girl; second, the oil well he's been touting really does strike oil, and all his investors stand to get rich.

Jake the Plumber (R-C Pictures/FBO of America, 1927)
d: Edward I. Luddy. 6 reels.
Jess Devorska, Sharon Lynn, Rosa Rosanova, Ann Brody, Bud Jamison, Carol Halloway, William H. Tooker, Dolores Brinkman, Eddie Harris, Fanchon Frankel.
Comedy about Jake, an apprentice plumber who's barely making ends meet, but hopes to marry Sarah, who supports her entire family. Through a series of chance events, Jake winds up jockeying the winning horse in a rich stakes race—and can finally afford to marry Sarah.

Jane (Oliver Morosco Photoplays/Paramount, 1915)
d: Frank Lloyd. 5 reels.
Charlotte Greenwood, Sydney Grant, Myrtle Stedman, Forrest Stanley, Howard Davies, Herbert Standing, Lydia Yeamans Titus, Syd de Grey.
Jane's the maid in a wealthy household. When her unmarried boss receives word that his wealthy uncle is coming to visit, and wants to meet the "wife" his nephew has married, Jane's boss pleads with her to pose as his wife for the duration of the uncle's stay. She agrees, but it's no piece of cake, since Jane is secretly married to the butler, who now must wait on them and keep his mouth shut.

Jane Eyre (Whitman Features Co., 1914)
d: John William Kellette. 5 reels.
Lisbeth Blackstone, Dallas Tyler, Harrish Ingraham, John Charles.
Jane Eyre is hired as governess for the daughter of a supposed widower, Edward Rochester. Jane doesn't understand the reason for her employer's persistent moodiness until one day she learns that Rochester's wife is not deceased but insane, and is being kept prisoner in a separate wing of the mansion.
This was the first feature film version of *Jane Eyre*, the 19th century novel by Charlotte Bronte. In the silent era it would be remade twice—as *Woman and Wife* (1918) and as *Jane Eyre* (1921).

Jane Eyre (Hugo Ballin Productions/W.W. Hodkinson, 1921)
d: Hugo Ballin. 7 reels.
Norman Trevor, Mabel Ballin, Crauford Kent, Emily Fitzroy, John Webb Dillon, Louis Grisel, Stephen Carr, Vernie Atherton, Elizabeth Aeriens, Harlan Knight, Helen Miles.
Jane, an orphan, takes a position as companion to the ward of Mr. Rochester. The guardian soon takes an interest in Jane and offers a marriage proposal, which she accepts. But then she learns that the first Mrs. Rochester is not deceased but insane.
This was the second feature film based on the Charlotte Bronte novel. In the silent era, it first appeared as *Jane Eyre* in 1914 and subsequently as *Woman and Wife* (1918).

Jane Goes A-Wooing (Famous Players-Lasky/Paramount, 1919)
d: George H. Melford. 5 reels.
Vivian Martin, Niles Welch, Casson Ferguson, Spottiswoode Aitken, Helen Dunbar, Byrdine Zuber, Clyde Benson, the McKenzie twins, Herbert Standing, Frank Hays.
Jane, a temporary "mother" to her twin sisters, is surprised to learn that her recently deceased employer has willed his estate to her.

Janice Meredith (Cosmopolitan/MGM, 1924)
d: E. Mason Hopper. 11 reels.
Marion Davies, Ken Maynard, W.C. Fields, Harrison Ford, Maclyn Arbuckle, Joseph Kilgour, Olin Howland, Tyrone Power, Helen Lee Worthing, Spencer Charters, Holbrook Blinn, Hattie Delaro, George Nash, Robert Thorne, George Siegmann, W.C. Fields, Helen Lee Worthing.
The stories of Paul Revere's ride, the Boston Tea Party, and Washington crossing the Delaware are recounted in this American Revolution romantic drama.

A Japanese Nightingale (Astra Film Corp./Pathé, 1918)
d: George Fitzmaurice. 5 reels.
Fannie Ward, W.E. Lawrence.
Madame Butterfly with a twist: This time, the Japanese girl's Western husband remains faithful to her.

Java Head (Famous Players-Lasky/Paramount, 1923)
d: George Melford. 8 reels.
Leatrice Joy, Jacqueline Logan, Frederick Strong, Albert Roscoe, Arthur Stuart Hull, Rose Tapley, Violet Axzelle, Audrey Berry, Polly Archer, Betty Bronson, George Fawcett, Raymond Hatton, Helen Lindroth, Dan Pennell, George Stevens, Mimi Sherwood.
Sorrowful tale about Gerrit, a New England seaman who sails to China and marries Taou Yuen, a Manchu dynasty princess. He brings her home to Massachusetts, where he meets again with his former sweetheart. Because Taou Yuen surmises that love still exists between Gerrit and his ex-girlfriend, the self-sacrificing princess takes her own life to give her husband his freedom.
Leatrice Joy portrays the exotic Chinese princess, Taou Yuen.

Jaws of Steel (Warner Bros., 1927)
d: Ray Enright. 6 reels.
Rin-Tin-Tin, Jason Robards, Helen Ferguson, Mary Louise Miller, Jack Curtis, Robert Perry, George Connors.
It's Rinty to the rescue once again, as a young married couple and their baby try to put down roots in a desert town. A shady local merchant puts the moves on the bride, then kills the husband's mining partner; but the valiant dog foils him at every turn.

The Jazz Age (FBO Pictures, 1929)
d: Lynn Shores. 7 reels.
Douglas Fairbanks Jr., Marceline Day, H.B. Walthall, Myrtle Stedman, Gertrude Messinger, Joel McCrea, William Bechtel, E.J. Ratcliffe, Ione Holmes, Edgar Dearing.
Rival promoters clash over city politics. Meanwhile the daughter of one and the son of another are falling in love.

The Jazz Bride—see: The Companionate Marriage (1928)

The Jazz Girl (Motion Picture Guild, 1926)
d: Howard Mitchell. 6 reels.
Gaston Glass, Edith Roberts, Howard Truesdale, Murdock MacQuarrie, Coit Albertson, Ernie Adams, Sabel Johnson, Dick Sutherland, Lea Delworth.
A weary Jazz-age flapper, looking for some real excitement, turns amateur sleuth.

Jazz Mad (Universal, 1928)
d: F. Harmon Weight. 7 reels.
Jean Hersholt, George Lewis, Marion Nixon, Roscoe Karns, Torben Meyer, Andrew Arbuckle, Charles Clary, Clarissa Selwynne, Patricia Caron, Alfred Hertz.
A composer suffers a nervous breakdown, and is cured when a major symphony orchestra decides to play his latest composition.

The Jazz Singer (Warner Bros., 1927)
d: Alan Crosland.   9 reels.   (Music, sound effects, part talkie.)
Al Jolson, May McAvoy, Warner Oland, Eugenie Besserer, Joseph Rosenblatt, Otto Lederer, William Demarest, Anders Randolf, Will Walling, Roscoe Karns, Myrna Loy.
Watershed film that revolutionized the motion picture industry. This was the first feature-length "talkie," although only a few hundred words are spoken, and most of the film is silent and dependent on the customary dialogue titles. Not only the first part-talkie but also the first "singie," as Jolson gets to display his Broadway charm, warbling four songs in his inimitable style. Jolson's mesmerizing vocal display outshines the basic plot, about a rabbi's son who wants to be in show business rather than follow in his father's footsteps.

Jazzland (A. Carlos/Quality Distributing Corp., 1928)
d: Dallas M. Fitzgerald.   6 reels.
Bryant Washburn, Vera Reynolds, Carroll Nye, Forrest Stanley, Virginia Lee Corbin, Violet Bird, Carl Stockdale, Edward Cecil, George Raph, Nicholas Caruso, Florence Turner.
Citizens of a small New England town fight the intrusion in their lives of a big city nightclub, the Jazzland.

Jazzmania (Tiffany Productions/Metro, 1923)
d: Robert Z. Leonard.   8 reels.
Mae Murray, Rod LaRocque, Robert Frazer, Edward Burns, Jean Hersholt, Lionel Belmore, Herbert Standing, Mrs. J. Farrell MacDonald, Wilfred Lucas, J. Herbert Frank.
Ninon, the queen of Jazzmania, meets a charming American in Monte Carlo, and they fall in love.

Jealous Husbands (Maurice Tourneur Productions, 1923)
d: Maurice Tourneur.   7 reels.
Earle Williams, Jane Novak, Ben Alexander, Don Marion, George Siegmann, Emily Fitzroy, Bull Montana, J. Gunnis Davis, Carl Miller, Wedgewood Nowell, Carmelita Geraghty.
A jealous husband suspects his wife of infidelity. He condemns her and, in a parting gesture, gives away their baby boy to a band of gypsies.

Jealousy (Fox, 1916)
d: Will S. Davis.   5 reels.
Valeska Suratt, Lew Walter, Charline Mayfield, Curtis Benton, Joseph Granby, George M. Adams.
With selfishness as her primary motivation, a troubled woman enters into two marriages, and destroys them both.

Jenny Be Good (Realart, 1920)
d: William Desmond Taylor.   6 reels.
Mary Miles Minter, Jay Belasco, Margaret Shelby, Frederick Stanton, Sylvia Ashton, Edwin Brown, Lillian Rambeau, Catherine Wallace, Fanny Cossar, Maggie Halloway Fisher, Grace Pike.
Jenny supports herself by weaving and selling rugs, but her dream is to become a concert violinist.

Jes' Call Me Jim (Goldwyn, 1920)
d: Clarence G. Badger.   6 reels.
Will Rogers, Irene Rich, Lionel Belmore, Raymond Hatton, Jimmy Rogers, Bert Sprotte, Nick Cogley, Sydney De Grey.
Congenial Jim is a do-gooder who'll do most anything for his sweetie, the local milliner.

Jesse James (Paramount, 1927)
d: Lloyd Ingraham.   8 reels.

Fred Thomson, Nora Lane, Montagu Love, Mary Carr, James Pierce, Harry Woods, William Courtright.
Jesse James, a Civil War veteran, becomes an outlaw when he tries to avenge his mother, who was maimed by Union sympathizers.

Jesus of Nazareth (Ideal Pictures, 1928)
d: Jean Conover.   6 reels.
Philip Van Loan, Anna Lehr, Charles McCaffrey.
The story of Jesus is told, from birth to death to Ascension.

Jewel (Universal, 1915)
d: Phillips Smalley.   5 reels.
Ella Hall, Rupert Julian, Hilda Hollis Sloman, Frank Elliot, T.D. Crittenden, Dixie Carr, T.W. Gowland, Abe Mundon, Jack Holt, Lule Warrenton.
A Pollyanna-like girl radiates sunshine and brightens up a gloomy family.

A Jewel in Pawn (Universal, 1917)
d: Jack Conway.   5 reels.
Ella Hall, Antrim Short, Walter Belasco, Maie Hall, Jack Connolly, George Pearce, Marshall Mackaye.
When her mother dies after leaving her with a kindly pawnbroker, a girl named Jewel becomes known as "a Jewel in pawn."

The Jilt (Universal, 1922)
d: Irving Cummings.   5 reels.
Marguerite De La Motte, Ralph Graves, Matt Moore, Ben Hewlett, Harry DeVere, Eleanor Hancock.
A man who was blinded during the war is cured by a specialist, but keeps the cure a secret from friends and family.

Jilted Janet (American Film Co./Mutual, 1918)
d: Lloyd Ingraham.   5 reels.
Margarita Fischer, Jack Mower, Edward Peil, Golda Madden, David Howard, Jean Robbins, Fred Smith.
After being jilted by her lover, Janet tries to get even by telling him she is now living in a mansion. The cad and his new wife come to visit while Janet is "housesitting" the mansion, and she seems to be pulling off the ruse until the mansion's real owner comes home during their visit. The owner is so taken by Janet's winning personality, he proposes marriage—and soon, the mansion really *is* Janet's home.

Jim Bludso (Fine Arts Film Co./Triangle, 1917)
d: Tod Browning, Wilfred Lucas.   5 reels.
Wilfred Lucas, Olga Grey, George Stone, Charles Lee, Winifred Westover, Sam DeGrasse, James O'Shea, Monte Blue.
A Civil War veteran returns home to find his wife has deserted him.

Jim Grimsby's Boy (New York Motion Picture Corp./Triangle, 1916)
d: Reginald Barker.   5 reels.
Frank Keenan, Enid Markey, Robert McKim, Fanny Midgley, J.P. Lockney.
Jim Grimsby's "boy" is really a girl, raised by her father to be tough and resourceful.

Jim the Conqueror (Metropolitan Pictures Corp. of California, 1927)
d: George B. Seitz.   6 reels.
William Boyd, Elinor Fair, Walter Long, Tully Marshall, Tom Santschi, Marcell Corday.

Out West, love blossoms between Jim and Polly, neighboring ranch owners.

Jim the Penman (Famous Players/Paramount, 1915)
d: Edwin S. Porter. 5 reels.
John Mason, Harold Lockwood, Russell Bassett, Frederick Perry, William Roselle, Marguerite Leslie.
Rejected by his sweetheart, James Ralston becomes a forger known as "Jim the Penman."

Jim the Penman (Whitman Bennett Productions/Associated First National, 1921)
d: Kenneth Webb. 6 reels.
Lionel Barrymore, Doris Rankin, Anders Randolf, Douglas MacPherson, Gladys Leslie, Charles Coghlan, James Laffey, Ned Burton, Arthur Rankin.
Remake of the 1915 Famous Players film *Jim the Penman*, both versions based on the play of the same name by Charles Lawrence Young.

Jimmie's Millions (Carlos Productions/FBO of America, 1925)
d: James P. Hogan. 6 reels.
Richard Talmadge, Betty Francisco, Charles Clary, Brinsley Shaw, Dick Sutherland, Ina Anson, Lee Moran, Wade Boteler.
Jimmie, a world-class procrastinator, is always late for everything. To cure him of his tardiness, his wealthy uncle puts a clause in his will providing that Jimmie will inherit his fortune only if he demonstrates punctuality for a specified period of time. After the old fellow dies, Jimmie tries to comply with the terms of the will—but another nephew, who stands to collect if Jimmie fails, is dead set on keeping him from complying.

Jinx (Goldwyn, 1919)
d: Victor L. Schertzinger. 5 reels.
Mabel Normand, Cullen Landis, Frances Carpenter, Gertrude Claire, Ogden Crane, Clarence Arper.
"Jinx" is the nickname of a girl who does menial jobs for a traveling circus. In time, she gets to perform under the Big Top, and even falls in love with the circus "Wild Man," who isn't really wild at all.

Joan of Plattsburg (Goldwyn, 1918)
d: George L. Tucker. 6 reels.
Robert Elliot, Mabel Normand, Edward Elkas, John Webb Dillon, William Fredericks, Joseph Smiley, Willard Dashiell, Edith McAlpin, Isabel Vernon.
When an orphan girl who is enchanted with the story of Joan of Arc hears sinister and threatening voices, she believes them to be products of her own imagination. But the voices are real; they belong to German spies plotting against the U.S. Like her namesake, little Joan will soon help to foil the enemies of her country.

Joan the Woman (Cardinal Film Corp./Paramount, 1916)
d: Cecil B. DeMille. 10 reels.
Geraldine Farrar, Wallace Reid, Raymond Hatton, Walter Long, Hobart Bosworth, Theodore Roberts, Charles Clary, James Neill, Tully Marshall, Larry Peyton, Lillian Leighton.
The story of Joan of Arc is told in a flashback from World War I.

Joanna (Edwin Carewe Productions/First National, 1925)
d: Edwin Carewe. 8 reels.
Dorothy Mackaill, Jack Mulhall, Paul Nicholson, George Fawcett, John T. Murray, Rita Carewe, Dolores Del Rio, Lillian Langdon, Edwards Davis, Bob Hart.

Intriguing drama about Joanna, a young woman who mysteriously inherits $1 million from an unknown benefactor. Naturally she becomes a magnet for numerous greedy suitors, and finally has to travel to Europe to get away from the confusion. Upon her return, she'll discover that the bequest was the result of a sporting proposition between two millionaires, who bet on her chastity!

Johanna Enlists (Pickford/Famous Players-Lasky/Paramount, 1918)
d: William Desmond Taylor. 5 reels.
Mary Pickford, Wallace Beery, Monte Blue, Douglas MacLean, Anne Schaefer, Fred Huntley, Emory Johnson, John Steppling, Wesley Barry, June Prentis, Jean Prentis.
The daydreams of a Pennsylvania farm girl come true when a regiment of doughboys move onto her family farm for maneuvers—and she becomes the focus of their attention.

John Barleycorn (Bosworth, Inc./W.W. Hodkinson, 1914)
d: Hobart Bosworth. 6 reels.
Elmer Clifton, Antrim Short, Matty Roubert, Viola Barry, Hobart Bosworth, Joe Ray.
Author-adventurer Jack London spins tales about his bout with alcoholism.

John Ermine of Yellowstone (Universal, 1917)
d: Francis Ford. 5 reels.
Mae Gaston, Burwell Hamrick, William Carroll, Mark Fenton, Duke Worne, Burwell Hamrick, William Carroll, Joe Flores, Elsie Ford, John Darkcloud.
When a white man who was raised by Indians falls in love with a colonel's daughter and offers her his heart, she haughtily rejects him, thinking him to be a half-breed.

John Needham's Double (Universal, 1916)
d: Lois Weber, Phillips Smalley. 5 reels.
Tyrone Power, Marie Walcamp, Agnes Emerson, Frank Elliott, Walter Belasco, Frank Lanning, Buster Emmons.
The unscrupulous guardian of a young man's fortune plans to spend the money himself.

John Petticoats (Paramount, 1919)
d: Lambert Hillyer. 5 reels.
William S. Hart, Walter Whitman, Winifred Westover, George Webb, Ethel Shannon, Andrew Arbuckle.
Rare comedy from William S. Hart, with the star playing a tough lumberjack who inherits a big-city dress shop.

John Smith (Selznick/Select, 1922)
d: Victor Heerman. 6 reels.
Eugene O'Brien, Viva Ogden, W.J. Ferguson, Tammany Youn, Estar Banks, Frankie Mann, Mary Astor, George Fawcett, J. Barney Sherry, John Butler, Walter Greene, Warren Cook, Henry Sedley, Daniel Haynes.
Dramedy about John Smith, a chap who's unjustly imprisoned and upon his release becomes a charity worker.

Johnny Get Your Gun (Famous Players-Lasky/Paramount, 1919)
d: Donald Crisp. 5 reels.
Fred Stone, Mary Anderson, Casson Ferguson, James Cruze, Sylvia Ashton, Nina Byron, Mayme Kelso, Raymond Hatton, Hart Hoxie, Dan Crimmins, Fred Huntley, Noah Beery.
Out West, a tough guy who left his Palm Beach home as a boy gets into trouble and is sentenced to jail. Then, he receives word that he is desperately needed back home, since his father has died, his sister is engaged to a cad, and the family stands to lose its fortune. Imprisoned and unable to leave, he sends his best friend to impersonate him with

the folks at home — but his rough-hewn pard rubs a lot of the Palm Beach folks the wrong way.

Johnny Get Your Hair Cut (MGM, 1926)
d: B. Reeves Eason, Archie Mayo. 7 reels.
Jackie Coogan, Harry Carey, Maurice Costello, Mattie Witting, Pat Hartigan, James Corrigan, Knute Erickson.
An orphan boy is befriended by a racehorse owner, gets to ride the horse in the big race, and wins.

Johnny-on-the-Spot (Metro, 1919)
d: Harry L. Franklin. 5 reels.
Hale Hamilton, Louise Lovely, Philo McCullough, Ruth Orlamond, Edward J. Connelly, Hardee Kirkland, Lilie Leslie, E.N. Wallack, Fred H. Warren, Neal Hardin, Oral Humphreys.
Comedic tale of a penniless would-be author whose motto is "take it easy." He finds that life isn't that simple.

The Johnstown Flood (Fox, 1926)
d: Irving Cummings. 6 reels.
George O'Brien, Florence Gilbert, Janet Gaynor, Anders Randolf, Paul Nicholson, Paul Panzer, George Harris, Max Davidson, Walter Perry, Sid Jordan.
In Pennsylvania, a lumber camp owner fails to heed the flood warnings until it is too late and the dam bursts, destroying the town and taking numerous lives.

The Jolt (Fox, 1921)
d: George E. Marshall. 5 reels.
Edna Murphy, Johnnie Walker, Raymond McKee, Albert Prisco, Anderson Smith, Wilson Hummell, Lule Warrenton.
Johnny, a veteran, brings home Georgette, his French war bride. He's unable to find a job, however, and under the pressure of mounting bills, Johnny agrees to pull a con job for a former gangland friend.

Josselyn's Wife (Tiffany Productions, 1926)
d: Richard Thorpe. 6 reels.
Pauline Frederick, Holmes Herbert, Josephine Kaliz, Josephine Hill, Carmelita Geraghty, Freeman Wood, Pat Harmon, Ivy Livingston, W.A. Carroll.
A newlywed bride is faced with a dilemma when her former lover returns from Europe and tries to romance her.

Jordan is a Hard Road (Triangle/Fine Arts, 1915)
d: Allan Dwan. 5 reels.
Owen Moore, Dorothy Gish, Sarah Truax, Frank Campeau, Ralph Lewis, Mabel Wiles, Lester Perry, Fred Burns, Jim Ked, Joseph Singleton, Walter Long, Elmo Lincoln.
An incorrigible thief leaves his baby girl to be raised by a friend, then goes off to prison. Years later, he attends a revival meeting at which his grown daughter is one of the featured speakers, and as a result he reforms. But before all the loose ends can be tied up, he must perform one last, daring robbery.

Josselyn's Wife (B.B. Features, Inc./Robertson-Cole, 1919)
d: Howard Hickman. 5 reels.
Bessie Barriscale, Nigel Barrie, Kathleen Kirkham, Joseph Dowling, Ben Alexander, Leslie Stewart, Marguerite De La Motte, Josephine Crowell, George Hackathorn, Helen Dunbar.
A married artist is vamped by his flirtatious young stepmother.

Journey's End (World Film Corp., 1918)
d: Travers Vale. 5 reels.
Ethel Clayton, John Bowers, Muriel Ostriche, Jack Frumier, Louise Vale, Frank Mayo, Victor Kennard, Jean Loew.
When a husband with a wandering eye flirts openly with a stage actress, his wife gets him to sign an agreement that gives each of them three months of "freedom from marriage." Then the wife decides to sow some wild oats of her own.

The Journey's End (Hugo Ballin Productions/W.W. Hodkinson, 1921)
d: Hugo Ballin. 7 reels.
Mabel Ballin, George Bancroft, Wyndham Standing, Georgette Bancroft, Jack Dillon.
Maudlin melodrama about a convent-bred girl who marries a steelworker to escape a distasteful life in her uncle's home.

The Joy Girl (Fox, 1927)
d: Allan Dwan. 7 reels.
Olive Borden, Neil Hamilton, Marie Dressler, Mary Alden, William Norris, Helen Chandler, Frank Walsh, Jerry Miley, Clarence J. Elmer, Peggy Kelly, Jimmy Grainger Jr.
Mistaken identity comedy about a girl who loves a chauffeur but rejects him because she intends to marry for money. She meets a millionaire and marries him, unaware that he's merely a proxy groom, a working-class chap who's subbing for the real millionaire, who is — guess who? That's right, the "chauffeur."

Joy Street (Fox, 1929)
d: Raymond Cannon. 7 reels. (Music, sound effects, part talkie.)
Lois Moran, Nick Stuart, Rex Bell, José Crespo, Dorothy Ward, Ada Williams, Maria Alba, Sally Phipps, Florence Allen, Mabel Vail, Carol Wines, John Breeden, Marshall Ruth, James Barnes, Allen Dale.
Mimi is suddenly rich and thoroughly irresponsible.

The Joyous Troublemaker (Fox, 1920)
d: J. Gordon Edwards. 6 reels.
William Farnum, Louise Lovely, Henry J. Hebert, Harry Devere, G. Raymond Nye, Clarence Morgan, George Nichols, Sedley Brown, John Underhill, Harry Archer, Molly Bishop.
Out West, sparks fly when a businessman buys a stretch of land that his high-spirited neighbor Beatrice insists encroaches on her own property.

Jubilo (Goldwyn, 1919)
d: Clarence G. Badger. 5 reels.
Will Rogers, Josie Sedgwick, Charles French, Willard Louis, James Mason.
Jubilo's a jolly but shiftless drifter. Shiftless, that is, until he falls in love with a rancher's daughter and then helps her dad foil a gang of blackmailers.

The Jucklins (Famous Players-Lasky/Paramount, 1920)
d: George Melford. 6 reels.
Winter Hall, Mabel Julienne, Monte Blue, Ruth Renick, Fannie Midgely, Zell Covington, J.M. Dumont, Clarence Burton, Guy Oliver, Robert Brower, Jack Herbert, Jack Hull, Charles Ogle, Walter Scott, Frank Weatherwax, William Boyd, Jack Byron.
While teaching school in a North Carolina town, a former rancher falls in love with the daughter of a prominent local family, the Jucklins.

Judge Not, or The Woman of Mona Diggings (Universal, 1915)
d: Robert Z. Leonard. 6 reels.
Harry Carey, Julia Dean, Harry Carter, Marc Robbins,

Kingsley Benedict, Joe Singleton, Paul Machette, Lydia Yeamans Titus, Walter Belasco.
A woman shoots her husband in self-defense, and must stand trial.

The Judgement House (J. Stuart Blackton Productions/Paramount, 1917)
d: J. Stuart Blackton. 6 reels.
Violet Heming, Wilfred Lucas, Conway Tearle, Paul Doucet, Crazy Thunder, Florence Deshon, Lucille Hamill.
When her marriage begins to turn sour, a young woman looks to a former suitor for a way to escape her bitter bonds of matrimony.

Judgment of the Hills (R-C Pictures/FBO of America, 1927)
d: James Leo Meehan. 6 reels.
Virginia Valli, Frankie Darro, Orville Caldwell, Frank McGlynn Jr., Johnny Gough.
Brant, a denizen of the Kentucky hills, is drafted into World War I. But he's an alcoholic, and it will take more than an army stint to cure him of his addiction.

Judgment of the Storm (Palmer Photoplays/FBO of America, 1924)
d: Del Andrews. 7 reels.
Lloyd Hughes, Lucille Ricksen, George Hackathorne, Claire McDowell, Myrtle Stedman, Philo McCullough, Bruce Gordon, Frankie Darro, Fay McKenzie.
After a man is accidentally killed in a gambling parlor, the noble son of the establishment's owner offers to support the man's family.

Judith of the Cumberlands (Signal Film Corp./Mutual, 1916)
d: J.P. McGowan. 5 reels.
Helen Holmes, Leo D. Maloney, Paul C. Hurst, Thomas G. Lingham, William Brunton, Clara Mosher, Harry Lloyd, Sam Morje, G.H. Wischussen.
Mountaineers seek to lynch a judge they think killed one of their own.

Judy Forgot (Universal, 1915)
d: T. Hayes Hunter. 5 reels.
Marie Cahill, Samuel B. Hardy.
Misunderstandings and mistaken identity result when a young woman cannot help winking every time she smiles.

Judy of Rogue's Harbor (Realart Pictures Corp., 1920)
d: William D. Taylor. 6 reels.
Mary Miles Minter, Charles Meredith, Herbert Standing, Theodore Roberts, Clo King, Fritzie Ridgeway, Allan Sears, Frankie Lee, George Periolat.
Judy's an orphan girl who discovers a plot on the governor's life in time to save him.

The Juggernaut (Vitagraph, 1915)
d: Ralph W. Ince. 5 reels.
Anita Stewart, Earle Williams, Julia Swayne Gordon, William Dunn, Frank Currier, Eulalie Jensen, Paul Scardon, Jack Brawn.
Two friends take up different careers: One becomes a district attorney, the other a railroad president. But the railroad is unsafe, and they both know it.

Jules of the Strong Heart (Lasky Feature Plays/Paramount, 1918)
d: Donald Crisp. 5 reels.
George Beban, Helen Jerome Eddy, Charles Ogle, Raymond Hatton, Guy Oliver, Ernest Joy, Horace B. Carpenter, Edward Martin, James Neill.
In the Northwest woods, two lumberjacks vie for the love of the same woman.

June Madness (Metro, 1922)
d: Harry Beaumont. 6 reels.
Viola Dana, Bryant Washburn, Gerald Pring, Leon Barry, Eugenie Besserer, Snitz Edwards, Anita Fraser.
An uncertain bride-to-be jilts her fiancé on the day of the wedding, then runs off with a jazz musician.

The Jungle Child (New York Motion Picture Corp./Triangle, 1916)
d: Walter Edwards. 5 reels.
Dorothy Dalton, Howard Hickman, Gertrude Claire, Dorcas Matthews, Frederick Vroom, Elsa Lorrimer, Leo Willis.
An orphan girl is raised in the jungle by South American Indians.

The Jungle Princess (Selig Polyscope, 1920)
d: E.A. Martin. 7 reels.
Juanita Hansen, George Chesebro, Frank Clark, Hector Dion, Alfred Ferguson.
Jungle adventures, assembled into a feature film from various episodes of a 15-part serial, *The Lost City*.

The Jungle Trail (Fox, 1919)
d: Richard Stanton. 5 reels.
William Farnum, Anna Luther, Lyster Chambers, Sara Alexander, Anna Schaeffer, Edward Roseman, Henry Armetta, G. Raymond Nye, Ann Lehr, George Stone.
A New Yorker goes to Africa to hunt tigers, and finds love and adventure besides.

Jungle Trail of the Son of Tarzan (National Film Corp./Howells Sales Co., 1923)
d: Harry Revier. 6 reels.
Dempsey Tabler, Karla Schramm, Gordon Griffith, Kamuela C. Searle, Manilla Martans, Lucille Rubey, DeSacia Saville, Kathleen May, Frank Morrell, Ray Thompson, Eugene Burr.
Back in England and living as Lord and Lady Greystoke, Tarzan and Jane find that their son Jack has inherited his parents' love of the jungle.
Re-edited and greatly shortened version of a 15-episode serial, *Son of Tarzan*.

The Jury of Fate (Metro, 1917)
d: Tod Browning. 5 reels.
William Sherwood, Frank Fisher Bennett, Charles Fang, Albert Tavernier, Bradley Barker, H.F. Webber, Dee Dorsey.
When boy and girl twins capsize while rafting, the boy drowns but the girl survives. To save her blind father from a heart attack over the loss of his beloved son, the girl selflessly cuts her hair and pretends to be her own brother, letting her father think it was his daughter who died.

Just a Song at Twilight (Dixie Film Co./State Rights, 1916)
d: Carlton S. King. 5 reels.
Evelyn Greeley, Pedro de Cordoba, Richard Barthelmess, Charles Wellesley, Nellie Grant, Frank Lyons.
When a gardener falls in love with his employer's daughter, her dad objects to their union. But then he has a change of heart, when he remembers his own youthful days.

Just a Wife (National Picture Theaters, Inc./Select, 1920)
d: Howard Hickman. 5 reels.
Roy Stewart, Leatrice Joy, Albert Van, Kathlyn Williams, William Lion West.

After a socialite and a wealthy industrialist enter into a marriage of convenience, they then attempt to live separate lives. But in time, they both decide they are truly in love.

Just a Woman (S & S Photoplays, Inc./State Rights, 1918)
d: Julius Steger. 6 reels.
Charlotte Walker, Lee Baker, Forrest Robinson, Henry Carvill, Edwin Stanley, Anna Williams, Paul Perez, Charles Kraus, Lorna Volare, Cornish Beck, Florence Deshon.
After investing in a new invention and making good, a steel worker rises to become president of the company. But he knows he would not have succeeded without his wife to encourage him.

Just a Woman (First National, 1925)
d: Irving Cummings. 7 reels.
Claire Windsor, Conway Tearle, Dorothy Brock, Percy Marmont, Dorothy Revier, George Cooper, Edward Gribbon.
Remake of the 1918 S & S Photoplays film *Just a Woman*, both versions based on the play of the same name by Eugene Walter.

Just Another Blonde (Al Rockett Productions/First National, 1926)
d: Alfred Santell. 6 reels.
Dorothy Mackaill, Jack Mulhall, Louise Brooks, William Collier Jr.
Jimmy and Scotty are good pals until Scotty falls for Diana, who operates a Coney Island shooting gallery. But Diana has a friend, Jeanne, who's just right for Jimmy.
This film is also known as *The Girl From Coney Island*.

Just Around the Corner (Cosmopolitan Productions/Paramount, 1921)
d: Frances Marion. 7 reels.
Margaret Seddon, Lewis Sargent, Sigrid Holmquist, Edward Phillips, Fred Thomson, Peggy Parr, Rosa Rosanova, William Nally.
Essie's engaged to Joe, but he's a thoughtless layabout who prefers to shoot pool than meet his fiancée's family. Finally, when Essie's mother is dying of heart disease, the girl pleads with Joe to come home and meet her mother. Still he refuses. In desperation, Essie turns to a stranger with a kind smile and asks him to pose as her fiancé to meet her mother. He does so, and—Essie and the stranger get married!

Just For Tonight (Goldwyn, 1918)
d: Charles Giblyn. 5 reels.
Tom Moore, Lucy Fox, Henry Sedley, Henry Hallam, Robert Broderick, Ethel Grey Terry, Edwin Sturgis, Phil Ryley, Maude Turner Gordon.
Larceny powers this tale of stolen stock certificates and the pair of lovers who crack the case together.

Just Like a Woman (Grace S. Haskins/W.W. Hodkinson, 1923)
d: Scott R. Beal. 5 reels.
Marguerite De La Motte, George Fawcett, Ralph Graves, Jane Keckley, J. Frank Glendon, Julia Calhoun.
Romantic comedy about a girl who behaves like a prim and proper lady at home, but cavorts like a jazz baby when prowling for men.

Just Married (Paramount, 1928)
d: Frank Strayer. 6 reels.
James Hall, Ruth Taylor, William Austin, Harrison Ford, Ivy Harris, Tom Ricketts, Maude Turner Gordon, Lila Lee, Arthur Hoyt, Wade Boteler.

In Paris, a scorned woman strikes back when her ex-lover connects with a new woman.

Just Off Broadway (Fox, 1924)
d: Edmund Mortimer. 6 reels.
John Gilbert, Marion Nixon, Trilby Clark, Pierre Gendron, Ben Hendricks Jr.
A musical comedy actress falls in with gangsters.

Just Off Broadway (Chesterfield Motion Picture Corp., 1929)
d: Frank O'Connor. 7 reels.
Donald Keith, Ann Christy, Larry Steers, DeSacia Mooers, Jack Tanner, Sid Saylor, Beryl Roberts, Albert Dresden.
In New York, a fugitive falls in love with a Broadway dancer.

Just Out of College (Goldwyn, 1920)
d: Alfred Green. 5 reels.
Jack Pickford, Molly Malone, George Hernandez, Edythe Chapman, Otto Hoffman, Irene Rich, Maxfield Stanley, Maurice B. Flynn, Loretta Blake.
To discourage Ed, his daughter's beau, a businessman offers him $20,000 and a challenge to double the money within two months, or forget about marrying his daughter. Ed not only meets his goal, but he winds up selling his new company to his prospective father-in-law!

Just Pals (Fox, 1920)
d: Jack Ford. 5 reels.
Buck Jones, Johnny Cooke, Helen Ferguson, William Buckley, George Stone, Edwin B. Tilton, Duke R. Lee, Eunice Murdock Moore, Bert Apling, Slim Padgett, Pedro Leone.
A lazy but honest tramp befriends a runaway boy, then comes to realize he must mend his ways and show some responsibility. Then, through a series of complications, the hobo is falsely accused of stealing a large sum of money from the local school.

Just Suppose (Inspiration Pictures/First National, 1926)
d: Kenneth Webb. 7 reels.
Richard Barthelmess, Lois Moran, Geoffrey Kerr, Henry Vibart, George Spelvin, Harry Short, Bijou Fernandez, Prince Rokneddine.
Romantic fantasy about Rupert, a European prince who comes to the U.S. and falls for an American girl. There's an anxious moment when he learns that his monarch, the crown prince, has died and left Rupert the heir apparent to the throne... meaning he will be forced into a royal marriage. But then, the widow of the late monarch gives birth to an heir, freeing Rupert to marry his American sweetheart.

Just Sylvia (World Film Corp., 1918)
d: Travers Vale. 5 reels.
Barbara Castleton, Johnny Hines, Jack Drumier, Gertrude Berkeley, Franklyn Hanna, Henry Warwick, Anthony Merlo, Eloise Clement, Theresa Maxwell Conover.
Sylvia's a fashion model with a lot of class—because secretly she's also a royal princess.

Just Tony (Fox, 1922)
d: Lynn Reynolds. 5 reels.
Tom Mix, Claire Adams, Duke Lee, J.P. Lockney, Frank Campeau, Walt Robbins.
A roving cowboy seeks revenge against an enemy. During his search, the cowpoke finds a magnificent wild stallion, and also finds love—with the daughter of his enemy.

Justice of the Far North (Columbia, 1925)

d: Norman Dawn. 6 reels.
Arthur Jasmine, Marcia Manon, Laska Winter, Chuck Reisner, Max Davidson, George Fisher, Katherine Dawn, Steve Murphy.
In the frozen North, a trader covets the half-breed wife of an Eskimo.

K - The Unknown (Universal, 1924)
d: Harry Pollard. 9 reels.
Virginia Valli, Percy Marmont, Margarita Fisher, Francis Feeney, John Roche, Maurice Ryan, Myrtle Vane, William A. Carroll.
A rooming house boarder known only as "K" is revealed to be a gifted surgeon.

The Kaiser, Beast of Berlin (Universal, 1918)
d: Rupert Julian. 7 reels.
Ruth Clifford, Robert Gordon, Rupert Julian, Elmo Lincoln, Nigel De Brulier, Lon Chaney, Harry Von Meter, Harry Carter, Joseph Girard, Harry Holden, Gretchen Lederer.
Patriotic tale about Kaiser Wilhelm II and his lust for conquest.

The Kaiser's Finish (First National, 1918)
d: John Joseph Harvey, Clifford P. Saum. 6 reels.
Earl Schenck, Claire Whitney, Percy Standing, John Sunderland, Louise Keene, Philip Van Loan.
World War I fiction about an illegitimate son of the German Kaiser who enters Germany with a mission to kill both the Kaiser and his son.

The Kaiser's Shadow, or the Triple Cross (Thomas H. Ince/Paramount, 1918)
d: R. William Neill. 5 reels.
Dorothy Dalton, Thurston Hall, Edward Cecil, Leota Lorraine, Otto Hoffman, Charles French.
World War I espionage drama about an inventor being captured by German spies. Paula, one of the spies, is actually a French double agent, and Hugo, another German spy, is really an American Secret Service agent. After all the complications are played out, Paula and Hugo fall in love.

Kathleen Mavourneen (Fox, 1919)
d: Charles J. Brabin. 5 reels.
Theda Bara, Edward O'Connor, Jennie Dickenson, Raymond McKee, Marc McDermott, Marcia Harris, Henry Hallam, Harry Gripp, Morgan Thorpe.
Kathleen, a poor Irish girl, attracts the unwanted attentions of a Squire who owns the land her family lives on.

Kazan (William N. Selig/Export & Import Film Co., 1921)
d: Bertram Bracken. 6 reels.
Jane Novak, Ben Deeley, William Ryno, Benjamin Haggerty, Edwin Wallock.
In the Canadian Northwest, Kazan, a valiant dog, comes to the rescue of a girl threatened by her father's murderer.

Keep Moving (George Kleine, 1915)
d: Louis Myll. 5 reels.
Harry Watson Jr., George Bickel, Cissie Fitzgerlad, Rose Gore, Dan Crimmins, Snitz Edwards, Ruby Hoffman, Alma Hanlon, Tom Nawn, Frank Belcher, Maxfield Moree.
Whimsical fantasy about the prince of Blunderland, who yearns to visit the outside world. After several misadventures on the outside, the prince is happy to return to his cozy palace in Blunderland.

Keep Smiling (Monty Banks Pictures/Associated Exhibitors, 1925)

d: Gilbert W. Pratt. 6 reels.
Monty Banks, Robert Edeson, Anne Cornwall, Stanhope Wheatcroft, Glen Cavender, Donald Morelli, Syd Crossley, Ruth Holly, Martha Franklin, Jack Huff.
Farcical comedy about a young man who invents a revolutionary life preserver, then has to drive a speedboat through dangerous waters in order to prove his invention's worth.

Keeper of the Bees (Gene Stratton Porter Productions/FBO of America, 1925)
d: James Leo Meehan. 7 reels.
Robert Frazer, Josef Swickard, Martha Maddox, Clara Bow, Alyce Mills, Gene Stratton, Anise Charland, Billy Osborne, Joe Coppa.
Convoluted melodrama about a man who must marry twice—first to provide a wedding certificate for an unwed mother, then again to marry his true love.

Keeping Up With Lizzie (Rockett Film Corp./W.W. Hodkinson, 1921)
d: Lloyd Ingraham. 6 reels.
Enid Bennett, Otis harlan, Leo White, Victory Bateman, Landers Stevens, Edward Hearn, Harry Todd, Lila Leslie.
Comedy of blunders about small-town Lizzie, who gets herself engaged to a "wealthy" count. However, Lizzie's bankrupt dad has to borrow money from a loan shark to finance the large dowry demanded by the fiancé. Meanwhile, Lizzie's true love, Dan, discovers that the "count" is a phony, halts the wedding, and chases down the villain as he tries to abscond with the funds.

Keith of the Border (Triangle, 1918)
d: Clifford Smith. 5 reels.
Roy Stewart, Josie Sedgwick, Norbert Gills, Pete Morrison, William Ellingford, Wilbur Higbee, Alberta Lee.
A fightin' Texas Ranger locks horns with a gang called the Border Wolves.

Kennedy Square (Vitagraph, 1916)
d: S. Rankin Drew. 5 reels.
Charles Kent, Antonio Moreno, Muriel Ostriche, Tom Brooke, Raymond Bloomer, Dan Jarrett, Hattie Delaro, Harold Foshay, Herbert Barry, Logan Paul.
After the owner of Kennedy Square mortgages his home to pay off a friend's debts, the friend leaves for South America. Years later, the young man returns wealthy with plantation money, and pays off his friend's mortgage.

The Kentuckians (Famous Players-Lasky/Paramount, 1921)
d: Charles Maigne. 6 reels.
Monte Blue, Wilfred Lytell, Diana Allen, Frank Joyner, J.H. Gilmour, John Miltern, Thomas S. Brown, J.W. Johnston, Russell Parker, John Carr, Albert Hewitt, Eugenie Woodward, Wesley Jenkins, Grace Reals.
In Kentucky, a mountain dweller is elected to the state legislature, and immediately is at odds with the establishment.

A Kentucky Cinderella (Universal, 1917)
d: Rupert Julian. 5 reels.
Ruth Clifford, Rupert Julian, Harry Carter, Zoe Rae, Lucretia Harris, Myrtle Reeves, Aurora Pratt, Eddie Polo, Emory Johnson, Frank Lanning.
An orphan girl moves in with her uncle and his wife, but gets a rude reception.

The Kentucky Colonel (National Film Corp./W.W.

Hodkinson, 1920)
d: William A. Seiter. 6 reels.
Joseph J. Dowling, Frederick Vroom, Elinor Field, Francis McDonald, Cora Drew, Lloyd Bacon, Jill Woodward, Fred Kohler, Gordon Griffith, Mary Talbot, Thelma Salter, Ed Brady.
Old friends tangle over a misunderstanding.

Kentucky Days (Fox, 1923)
d: David Soloman. 5 reels.
Dustin Farnum, Margaret Fielding, Miss Woodthrop, Bruce Gordon, William DeVaull.
In antebellum days, a young southerner leaves his wife and home to seek his fortune. He strikes gold and returns home years later, eager to tell his wife the good news—and finds her kissing another man.

The Kentucky Derby (Universal, 1922)
d: King Baggot. 6 reels.
Reginald Denny, Lillian Rich, Emmett King, Walter McGrail, Gertrude Astor, Lionel Belmore, Kingsley Benedict, Bert Woodruff, Bert Tracy, Harry Carter, Wilfred Lucas.
Donald, son of a Kentucky colonel, reveals his secret marriage and raises his father's ire.   The colonel ousts Donald and his bride from his mansion, but three years later Donald returns in time to save the colonel's racehorse from elimination from the Kentucky Derby.

Kentucky Pride (Fox, 1925)
d: John Ford. 7 reels.
Henry B. Walthall, J. Farrell MacDonald, Gertrude Astor, Malcolm Waite, Belle Stoddard, Winston Miller, Peaches Jackson.
The owner of a stable of racehorses loses most of them at the gambling table, but keeps one, Virginia's Future, which he hopes will win the Futurity and put him back in business.

The Key to Power (Educational Film Corp. of America, 1920)
d: William Parke. 5 reels.
Hugh Thompson, Claire Adams, J.H. Gilmour, Frazier Nounnan, Tom Burrough, J.J. Dunn, Fred Radcliffe, George Pauncefort, Stephen Grattan, L.F. Kennedy, Stephen Carr.
The owner of a West Virginia coal mine stays home rather than enlist during World War I and is thought a coward, even by his fiancée. But he proves his mettle when German agents try to take over his mine, and he fights them off.

Keys of the Righteous (Thomas H. Ince/Paramount, 1918)
d: Jerome Storm. 5 reels.
Enid Bennett, Earl Rodney, George Nichols, Josef Swickard, Carl Formes, Gertrude Claire, Lydia Knott, Melbourne MacDowell.
Rejected by his wife and even his own father, a former alcoholic returns home and finds that his daughter Mary accepts him with an understanding heart.

The Kick Back (R-C Pictures/FBO of America, 1922)
d: Val Paul. 6 reels.
Harry Carey, Henry B. Walthall, Charles J. LeMoyne, Vester Pegg, Mingenne, Ethel Grey Terry.

Out West, White Horse Harry is threatened by a lynch mob, but a Mexican girl he once befriended brings the Texas Rangers to the rescue.

Kick In (Astra Film Corp./Pathé, 1917)
d: George Fitzmaurice. 5 reels.
William Courtenay, Robert Clugston, Mollie King, Richard Tabor, Suzanne Willa, John Boyle.
Partners in crime come to a parting of the ways when one of them heeds his wife's advice to go straight.

Kick In (Famous Players-Lasky/Paramount, 1922)
d: George Fitzmaurice. 7 reels.
Betty Compson, Bert Lytell, May McAvoy, Gareth Hughes, kathleen Clifford, Maym Kelso, Mohn Miltern, Walter Long, Robert Agnew, Jed Prouty, Carlton King, Charles Ogle.
Hewes, an ex-con, resolves to go straight after his release. But he finds the behavior of "respectable people" so disgusting that he decides to pull one last burglary.

The Kick-Off (Excellent Pictures, 1926)
d: Wesley Ruggles. 6 reels.
George Walsh, Leila Hyams, Bee Amann, Earle Larrimore, W.L. Thorne, Joseph Burke, Jane Jennings.
Tom, a college newcomer, rescues a girl from the unwanted attentions of Frank, a football player. The vengeful Frank resolves that Tom will never make the varsity team, and even engineers several "accidents" to prevent Tom from reporting to the squad. But in the end, Tom does get to play quarterback for his beleaguered team, and leads them from behind to victory.

The Kid (Vitagraph, 1916)
d: Wilfrid North. 6 reels.
Lillian Walker, Ned Finley, Eulalie Jensen, Robert Gaillard.
This "kid" is a 19-year-old girl who was raised by an adoptive father. Now that she's a big city reporter, she crusades against political corruption, and in the process, discovers her true parents' identities.

The Kid (First National, 1921)
w, d: Charles Chaplin. 6 reels.
Charles Chaplin, Jackie Coogan, Carl Miller, Edna Purviance, Chuck Riesner, Tom Wilson, Albert Austin, Nellie Bly Baker, Monta Bell, Henry Bergman, Lita Grey, Raymond Lee.
Chaplin's first feature-length comedy since *Tillie's Punctured Romance*, and the first made entirely under his control. Chaplin plays a slum dweller who finds an abandoned baby boy and raises the child himself. Five years later, the tramp and the kid, having attained a father-son relationship, find their little world rocked by various outside forces, including the medical establishment, the law, and the kid's real mother.
The critics were virtually unanimous in finding Chaplin's first independent feature a success. Variety said it was "one of the best things he has ever done." Theatre Magazine was less restrained, calling *The Kid* "a screen masterpiece."

Kid Boots (Famous Players-Lasky/Paramount, 1926)
d: Frank Tuttle. 6 reels.
Eddie Cantor, Clara Bow, Billie Dove, Lawrence Gray, Natalie Kingston, Malcolm Waite, William Worthington, Harry von Meter, Fred Esmelton.
Feature film debut for Cantor, the renowned vaudeville entertainer, has him working as an apprentice tailor and helping his handsome friend get out of a jam.

The Kid Brother (Paramount, 1927)
d: Ted Wilde. 8 reels.
Harold Lloyd, Jobyna Ralston, Walter James, Leo Wills, Olin Francis, Eddie Boland, Constantine Romanoff.
In a tale that suggests a male Cinderella story, the youngest son of a county Sheriff is considered less worthy than his robust brothers. But the lad has guts, and proves it when a

gang of itinerant crooks try to make off with county funds entrusted to his dad.

Kid Gloves (Warner Bros., 1929)
d: Ray Enright. 7 reels. (Music, sound effects, part talkie.)
Conrad Nagel, John Davidson, Lois Wilson, Tommy Dugan, Maude Turner Gordon, Richard Cramer.
When a bootlegger finds his socialite girlfriend with another man, he forces the two strangers to marry.

The Kid is Clever (Fox, 1918)
d: Paul Powell. 5 reels.
George Walsh, Doris Pawn, Ralph Lewis, A. Burt Wesner, Don Likes, Clyde Hopkins, James Marcus.
Comedy of the absurd, as a little-known French director named Hoe Beaux is assigned to write and direct a motion picture, and he creates an aimless adventure with no rhyme or reason.

The Kid Sister (Columbia, 1927)
d: Ralph Graves. 6 sisters.
Ann Christy, Marguerite De La Motte, Malcolm McGregor, Brooks Benedict, Tom Dugan, Sally Long, Barrett Greenwood.
Small-town girl Mary travels to New York to join her chorus girl sister.

Kidder and Ko (Diando Film Corp./Pathé, 1918)
d: Richard Foster Baker. 5 reels.
Bryant Washburn, Harry Dunkinson, Gertrude Selby, Wadsworth Harris, Carl Stockdale.
A young pool hustler gets involved with a tin can tycoon and his daughter Julie. Next thing you know, he's invented a revolutionary new can, made a fortune, and is asking for Julie's hand in marriage.

The Kid's Clever (Universal, 1929)
d: William James Craft. 6 reels.
Glenn Tryon, Kathryn Crawford, Russell Simpson, Lloyd Whitlock, George Chandler, Joan Standing, Max Asher, Virginia Sale, Stepin Fetchit.
An inventor turns out a new kind of automobile, and tries to market it. But first, he must contend with a rival inventor's sabotage.

Kiki (Norma Talmadge Productions/First National, 1926
d: Clarence Brown. 9 reels.
Norma Talmadge, Ronald Colman, Gertrude Astor, Marc MacDermott, George K. Arthur, William Orlamond, Erwin Connelly, rankie Darro, Mack Swain.
In Paris, Kiki, a street girl who sells newspapers, decides to try out for the chorus line in a stage show, and is accepted. But it will be tough going, because one of Kiki's first accomplishments is to anger Paulette, the show's tempestuous star.

Kildare of Storm (Metro, 1918)
d: Harry L. Franklin. 5 reels.
Emily Stevens, King Baggot, Crauford Kent, Florence Short, Edwards Davis, Helen Lindroth, Maggie Breyer, Fred H. Warren.

To please her mother, young Kate marries Kildare, lord of the Southern plantation Storm.

The Killer (Benjamin B. Hampton Productions/Pathé, 1921)
d: Howard Hickman. 6 reels.
Claire Adams, Jack Conway, Frankie Lee, Frank Campeau, Tod Sloan, Edward Peil, Frank Hayes, Will Walling, Milton

Ross, Tom Ricketts, Zack Williams.
On the Mexican border, a killer double-crosses an old friend and ensnares his two children in a heinous scheme.

Kilmeny (Oliver Morosco Photoplays/Paramount, 1915)
d: Oscar Apfel. 5 reels.
Lenore Ulrich, William Desmond, Baby Doris Baker, Herbert Standing, Howard Davies, Gordon Griffith, Marshall Mackaye, Frederick Wilson, Myrtle Stedman, Victory Bateman.
Kilmeny's a girl who was kidnapped by gypsies as a child. Now an attractive young woman, she charms several men, both in the gypsy band and outside it.

Kindled Courage (Universal, 1923)
d: William Worthington. 5 reels.
Hoot Gibson, Beatrice Burnham, Harold Goodwin, Harry Tenbrook, James Gordon Russell, J. Russell Powell, Albert Hart.
Out West, a perceived "coward" becomes a hero, and wins the job of sheriff.

Kindred of the Dust (R.A. Walsh Co./Associated First National, 1922)
d: R.A. Walsh. 8 reels.
Miriam Cooper, Ralph Graves, Lionel Belmore, Eugenie Besserer, Maryland Morne, Elizabeth Waters, W.J. Ferguson, Caroline Rankin, Pat Rooney, John Herdman.
Nan, who has discovered that her husband is a bigamist and she is not legally married to him, takes her baby with her and returns to her family home in the Pacific Northwest. But the narrow-minded townfolk ostracize her.

King Cowboy (FBO Pictures, 1928)
d: Robert DeLacy. 7 reels.
Tom Mix, Sally Blane, Lew Meehan, Barney Furey, Frank Leigh, Wynn Mace, Robert Fleming.
Tex, a ranch foreman from out West, leads a daring rescue attempt in North Africa.

King Lear (Thanhouser, 1916)
d: Ernest Warde. 5 reels.
Frederick Warde, Ernest Warde, Ina Hammer, Wayne Arey, Edith Diestal, Charles Brooks, Lorraine Huling, J.H. Gilmour, Boyd Marshall, Hector Dion, Edwin Stanley, Robert Whittier.
Lear suspects that his daughter Cordelia does not love him, and so gives his kingdom to his other daughters, Regan and Goneril. Only much later, after Cordelia has died, does the grieving Lear realize that she was the one daughter who truly loved him.
First feature film version of the famous Shakespeare drama. Vitagraph had made a two-reel version in 1909. Wisely, perhaps, there would be no other silent film versions of *King Lear*; but after the birth of the talkies, filmmakers took full advantage of the Bard's resonant prose to mount several versions of this and other Shakespearean plays.

The King of Diamonds (Vitagraph, 1918)
d: Paul Scardon. 6 reels.
Harry T. Morey, Betty Blythe, Jean Paige, Geroge Majeroni, William Dennison.
A cuckold is convinced by his rival that he is dying, so he rows out into deep waters to drown himself. His will to live is too strong, though, so instead he boards a steamer to Cape Town, South Africa, where he strikes it rich in the diamond business.

The King of Kings (Pathé, 1927)

d: Cecil B. DeMille.   14 reels.   (Includes Technicolor sequence.)

H.B. Warner, Lionel Belmore, Joe Bonomo, Dorothy G. Cummings, William Boyd, Sam De Grasse, Ernest Torrence, Joseph Schildkraut, James Neill, Robert Edeson, Jacqueline Logan, Rudolph Schildkraut, James Farley, Frances Dale, Kathleen Chambers, George Siegmann, May Robson, Dot Farley, Tom London, Monte Collins, Sojin, Sally Rand, Noble Johnson, Brandon Hurst, Victor Marconi.

Spectacular epic based on the adult life of Jesus of Nazareth. Many actors have tackled the role, but Warner's is the definitive Jesus, played with gentleness and a quiet dignity. The movie tells the story of the New Testament miracles, the Last Supper, the Crucifixion, and the Resurrection. Typically, DeMille tantalized audiences with glimpses of decadence within the Bible story, including a lovely and seductive pre-conversion Mary Magdalene (Jacqueline Logan). The Resurrection sequence at the end is presented in two-strip Technicolor.

King of the Rodeo (Universal, 1929)
d: Henry MacRae. 6 reels.
Hoot Gibson, Kathryn Crawford, Slim Summerville, Charles K. French, Monty Montague, Joseph W. Girard, Jack Knapp, Harry Todd, Bodil Rosing.
The Montana Kid, a champion rider, goes to Chicago for a rodeo and promptly falls in love with the daughter of one of the officials.

King of the Turf (Film Booking Offices of America, 1926)
d: James P. Hogan. 7 reels.
George Irving, Patsy Ruth Miller, Kenneth Harlan, Al Roscoe, Kathleen Kirkham, Mary Carr, David Torrence, Dave Kirby, William Franey, Eddie Phillips.
Fairfax, a southern colonel, is unjustly imprisoned for embezzlement, the victim of a frame-up. While the colonel quietly serves his time, the real culprit dies and leaves a deathbed confession exonerating Fairfax. In the final reel, the colonel's prize stallion wins the big race.

The King of Wild Horses (Hal Roach/Pathé, 1924)
d: Fred Jackman. 5 reels.
Leon Barry, Edna Murphy, Charles Parrott, Sidney DeGray, Pat Hartigan, Frank Butler.
Out West, a cowboy tries to capture and tame a wild black stallion.

The King on Main Street (Famous Players-Lasky/Paramount, 1925)
d: Monta Bell. 6 reels. (Technicolor sequences.)
Adolphe Menjou, Bessie Love, Greta Nissen, Oscar Shaw, Joseph Kilgour, Edgar Norton, Mario Majeroni, Carlotta Monterey, Marcia Harris, Edouard Durand.
The king of a European country travels to America and, tiring of diplomatic routine, sneaks off to Coney Island, makes new friends, and falls in love with an American girl.

King, Queen, Joker (Famous Players-Lasky/Paramount, 1921)
w, d: Sydney Chaplin. 5 reels.
Sydney Chaplin, Lottie MacPherson.
A European king ponders whether to grant his people the freedoms they crave, or to deny them and risk a revolution.

The Kingdom of Youth (Goldwyn, 1918)
d: Clarence G. Badger. 5 reels.
Madge Kennedy, Tom Moore, Marie DeWolfe, Lee Baker, Jennie Dickerson.

Charming in an ageless way, a fifty-something widow tries to win a young husband away from his wife.

The Kingdom Within (Producers Security Corp./W.W. Hodkinson, 1922)
d: Victor Schertzinger. 7 reels.
Russell Simpson, Z. Wall Covington, Gaston Glass, Pauline Starke, Hallam Cooley, Ernest Torrence, Gordon Russell, Marion Feducha.
Amos and Emily, next-door neighbors who are shunned by the community for a variety of reasons, form a close attachment.

The Kingfisher's Roost (Pinnacle Productions, 1922)
d: Louis Chaudet, Paul Hurst. 5 reels.
Neal Hart, Yvette Mitchell, William Quinn, Ben Corbett, Chet Ryan, Jane Fosher, Floyd Anderson, W.S. Weatherwax, John Judd, Earl Simpson, Earl Dwyer.
Out West, a suspected cattle thief escapes across the Mexican border and locates the Kingfisher gang, the outlaws who framed him.

King's Creek Law (William Steiner Productions/Photo Drama Co., 1923)
d: Leo Maloney, Bob Williamson. 5 reels.
Leo Maloney, Horace Carpenter, Frank Ellis, Milton Brown, Chet Ryan, Josephine Hill.
Hardy, a Texas Ranger, rides into the isolated town of King's Creek, where a local strongman has made himself the law.

The King's Game (Pathé, 1916)
d: Ashley Miller. 5 reels.
George Probert, Pearl White, Sheldon Lewis, Nora Moore, George Parks.
Philip, a Russian grand duke, falls in love with a New York girl.

Kinkaid, Gambler (Universal, 1916)
d: Raymond Wells. 5 reels.
Ruth Stonehouse, R.A. Cavin, Raymond Whittaker, Noble Johnson, Harry Mann, Harry Griffith, J.H. Knowles, Cleo Loring.
Kinkaid's a thief who robs from the rich to give to the poor.

Kismet (Waldorf Film Corp./Robertson-Cole, 1920)
d: Louis J. Gasnier. 5 reels.
Otis Skinner, Rosemary Theby, Elinor Fair, Mathilda Comont, Nicholas Dunaev, Herschel Mayall, Fred Lancaster, Leon Bary, Sidney Smith, Hamilton Revelle, Thomas Kennedy, Sam Kaufman, Emmett C. King, Fanny Ferrari, Emily Seville, Georgia Woodthorpe.
Hajj, an Arabian beggar, is also a thief, a gambler, and an attempted murderer. But his greatest adventure comes when he saves his daughter from being forced into a sultan's harem.

The Kiss (Famous Players/Paramount, 1916)
d: Dell Henderson. 5 reels.
Owen Moore, Marguerite Courtot, Kate Lester, Virginia Hammond, Adolph Menjou, Gus Weinberg, Thomas O'Keefe, Viola Trent, Frances Kaye, Elsie Lewis, Florence Hamilton.
Though he can have almost any girl he wants, a French flying corps hero falls head over heels for a mystery woman who kisses him at a masked ball. Who can she be?

The Kiss (Universal, 1921)
d: Jack Conway. 5 reels.
George Periolat, Carmel Myers, William E. Lawrence, J.P.

260

Lockney, Harvey Clarke, J.J. Lanoe, Jean Acker, Ed Brady.
In old California, a ranchero expects his son to marry the girl he has selected for him. But Junior's got other plans.

The Kiss (MGM, 1929)
d: Jacques Feyder. 7 reels. (Music score.)
Greta Garbo, Conrad Nagel, Lew Ayres, Holmes Herbert, Anders Randolf, Holmes Herbert, George Davis.
A married woman who is already having an affair is attracted to the 18-year-old lad who walks her dogs.

The Kiss Barrier (Fox, 1925)
d: R. William Neill. 6 reels.
Edmund Lowe, Claire Adams, Diana Miller, Marion Harlan, Thomas Mills, Charles Clary, Grace Cunard.
In France during World War I, an injured American aviator steals a kiss from his Red Cross nurse. He'll meet her again, back home....

A Kiss for Cinderella (Famous Players-Lasky/Paramount, 1925)
d: Herbert Brenon. 10 reels.
Betty Bronson, Tom Moore, Esther Ralston, Henry Vibart, Dorothy Cumming, Ivan Simpson, Dorothy Walters, Flora Finch, Juliet Brenon, Marilyn McLain, Pattie Coakley.
Reworking of the famous Cinderella story. This time, the heroine is a charwoman for a struggling artist, and also runs a small shop that cares for hungry war orphans.

A Kiss for Susie (Pallas Pictures/Paramount, 1917)
d: Robert Thornby. 5 reels.
Vivian Martin, Tom Forman, John Burton, Jack Nelson, Pauline Perry, Chris Lynton, Elinor Hancock.
To learn the business from the ground up, a contractor's son takes a beginner's job. That's when he meets and falls for Susie, the daughter of one of his coworkers.

A Kiss in a Taxi (Paramount, 1927)
d: Clarence Badger. 7 reels.
Bebe Daniels, Chester Conklin, Douglas Gilmore, Henry Kolker, Richard Tucker, Agostino Borgato, Eulalie Jensen, Rose Burdick, Jocelyn Lee.
Romantic farce about Ginette, a Parisian waitress in love with a struggling artist.

A Kiss in the Dark (Famous Players-Lasky/Paramount, 1925)
d: Frank Tuttle. 6 reels.
Adolphe Menjou, Aileen Pringle, Lillian Rich, Kenneth MacKenna, Ann Pennington, Kitty Kelly.
Romantic misadventures arise when two married couples tour Havana together, then for the boat trip back home, the husband of one couple is accidentally left behind with the wife of the other.

Kiss Me Again (Warner Bros., 1925)
d: Ernst Lubitsch. 7 reels.
Marie Prevost, Monte Blue, John Roche, Clara Bow, Willard Louis.
In Paris, Gaston finds that his lovely wife is infatuated with Maurice, a shallow musician. The husband pretends to go along with her flirtations, even offering to grant his wife a divorce so she can be with Maurice forever. But Gaston has a secret agenda: to make her want to return to him exclusively, and finally she does.
Much-admired effort which exemplified what came to be known as "The Lubitsch Touch", this simple tale of a romantic triangle is delivered with wit and charm.

The Kiss of Hate (Columbia/Metro, 1916)
d: William Nigh. 5 reels.
Ethel Barrymore, H. Cooper Cliffe, Robert Elliott, Roy Applegate, Niles Welch, William L. Abingdon, Victor De Linsky, Martin J. Faust, William Boyd, Frank Montgomery, Ilean Hume.
Anti-Semitism leads to many tragic deaths in a Russian province.

Kiss or Kill (Universal, 1918)
d: Elmer Clifton. 5 reels.
Herbert Rawlinson, Priscilla Dean, Alfred Allen, Harry Carter.
Out of a job and desperate, an Army veteran turns to petty theft. That's when he meets and falls in love with Ruth, an impoverished girl who stands to gain an inheritance through the document the veteran has just stolen.

Kissed (Universal, 1922)
d: King Baggot. 5 reels.
Marie Prevost, Lillian Langdon, Lloyd Whitlock, J. Frank Glendon, Arthur Hoyt, Percy Challenger, Harold Miller, Marie Crisp, Harold Goodwin.
Connie, comfortably engaged to marry a millionaire, nevertheless mopes about not having enough romance and excitement in her life. She'll get more of both than she bargained for.

Kisses (Metro, 1922)
d: Maxwell Karger. 5 reels.
Alice Lake, Harry Myers, Edward Connelly, Edward Jobson, Dana Todd, Mignon Anderson, John MacKinnon, Eugene Pouyet.
Candy kisses, that is. Entrepreneurial Betty manufactures them, and she and they are a big success.

Kit Carson (Paramount, 1928)
d: Alfred L. Werker. 8 reels.
Fred Thompson, Dorothy Janis, Nora Lane, Raoul Paoli, William Courtright, Nelson McDowell, Raymond Turner.
In New Mexico, government agent Kit Carson finds he must protect an Indian chief's daughter from attack by one of his fellow agents.

Kitty Kelly, M.D. (B.B. Features, Inc./Robertson-Cole, 1919)
d: Howard Hickman. 5 reels.
Bessie Barriscale, Jack Holt, Joseph J. Dowling, Wedgewood Nowell, Mildred Manning, Tom Guise.
The new doctor in town is a pretty lady, and all the gents start coming to her with imaginary ailments.

Kitty MacKay (Vitagraph, 1917)
d: Wilfrid North. 5 reels.
Lillian Walker, Jewell Hunt, Charles Kent, Don Cameron, Isabelle West, Thomas Mills, William Shea, William Ferguson, Nellie Anderson, Beatrice Anderson.
Kitty's a Scottish lass who learns, to her dismay, that the young man she fancies may be her half-brother. But the smiles return when a deathbed confession by an aged relative discloses Kitty was adopted, and therefore no blood relation to her young man.

The Knickerbocker Buckaroo (Artcraft/Famous Players-Lasky, 1919)
d: Albert Parker. 6 reels.
Douglas Fairbanks, Marjorie Daw, William Wellman, Frank Campeau, Edythe Chapman, Albert MacQuarrie, Theodore "Ted" Reed, James Mason, Ernest Butterworth.

KING OF KINGS (1927). Jesus of Nazareth (H.B. Warner) ministers to some of his followers in Cecil B. DeMille's spectacular version of the New Testament story. Kneeling at Jesus' feet is the reformed Mary Magdalene (Jacqueline Logan). In the background we can see Matthew (Robert Edeson), John (Joseph Striker), and the giant apostle Peter (Ernest Torrance). Judas (Joseph Schildkraut) can be seen at the right, behind the pillar.

* * * * *

A happy-go-lucky New York playboy is expelled from his private club for his inconsiderate ways. Seeking to amend his life, he heads west and winds up in a dusty border town complete with a crooked sheriff, hostile bandidos, and a damsel in distress.

The Knife (Select Pictures Corp., 1918)
d: Robert G. Vignola. 5 reels.
Alice Brady, Frank Morgan, Crauford Kent, Helen Lackaye, Paul Doucet, Alice Hollister, Johnnie Walker, Frank Evans, Anne Cornwall, Myra Brook.
Drugged and kidnapped into a den of vice, a young woman slowly goes insane.

A Knight of the Range (Universal, 1916)
d: Jacques Jaccard. 5 reels.

Harry Carey, Olive Golden, Hoot Gibson, William Canfield, Bud Osborne, A.D. Blake, Bill Gettinger, Peggy Coudray.
Selflessly, a cowpoke takes the blame for a crime committed by the man his beloved plans to marry.

A Knight of the West (W.B.M. Photoplays, 1921)
d: Robert McKenzie. 5 reels.
Olin Francis, Estelle Harrison, Billy Franey, Otto Nelson, May Foster, Claude Peyton, Fay McKenzie.
Out West, a crooked ranch foreman tries to transfer suspicion to his rival for the hand of the ranch owner's daughter.

The Knockout (First National, 1925)
d: Lambert Hillyer. 8 reels.
Milton Sills, Lorna Duveen, John Philip Kolb, Ed Lawrence, Harry Cording, Frankie Evans, Harlan Knight, Jed Prouty, Claude King.
Donlin, a former prizefighter, takes a job as foreman in a lumber camp. He meets Jean, the daughter of his boss' biggest rival, and in spite of the animosities between the two camps, Donlin and Jean grow to love each other.

The Knockout Kid (Harry Webb Productions/Rayart, 1925)
d: Albert Rogell. 5 reels.
Jack Perrin, Molly Malone, Eva Thatcher, Bud Osborne, Martin Turner, Ed Burns, Jack Richardson.
Out West, a former prizefighter finds himself suspected of rustling cattle.

Know Your Men (Fox, 1921)
d: Charles Giblyn. 6 reels.
Pearl White, Wilfred Lytell, Downing Clarke, Harry C. Browne, Estar Banks, Byron Douglas, William Eville.
After Ellen, a small-town girl, is discarded by her fiancé, she is comforted by Barrett, a neighbor. Their friendship grows into love and eventually marriage. Ellen's married life is no picnic, since she has a nagging mother-in-law; and in a weak moment, she considers leaving her husband and child and accepting her former fiancé's proposal to join him.

Kosher Kitty Kelly (R-C Pictures/FBO of America, 1926)
d: James W. Horne. 7 reels.
Viola Dana, Tom Forman, Vera Gordon, Kathleen Myers, Nat Carr, Stanley Taylor, Carroll Nye, Aggie Herring.
Comedy, with some serious overtones, about the uneasy relationship between an Irish and a Jewish family in New York.

The Kreutzer Sonata (Fox, 1915)
d: Herbert Brenon. 5 reels.
Nance O'Neil, Theda Bara, William E. Shay, Mimi Yvonne.

Five-hanky weeper about a pregnant Russian girl whose parents will not let her marry her lover. The lover then kills himself, and his sweetie is forced into a loveless marriage with a gigolo, who flirts with his bride's sister and gets *her* pregnant. When the bride finds out, she shoots them both, then turns the gun on herself.

Kultur (Fox, 1918)
d: Edward J. Le Sainte. 6 reels.
Gladys Brockwell, Georgia Woodthorpe, William Scott, Willard Louis, Charles Clary, Nigel de Brulier, William Burress, Alfred Fremont.
Fictionalized version of the assassination of the Archduke Ferdinand of Austria, which led to the start of World War I.

La Belle Russe (Regent Feature Film Co., 1914)
d: William J. Hanley. 5 reels.
Evelyn Russell, Lawrence Gordon, Frank Sidney Wood, Harry Knowles, Irene Warren, Mary Stewart, Bertha Kirkstein.
Sprawling chronicle that takes twin sisters from England to France to India and back again. Miss Russell plays a double role.

La Boheme (MGM, 1925)
d: King Vidor. 9 reels.
Lillian Gish, John Gilbert, Renee Adoree, George Hassell, Roy D'Arcy, Edward Everett Horton, Karl Dane, Frank Currier, Matilde Comont, Gino Corrado, Gene Pouyet, David Mir, Catherine Vidor, Valentina Zimina.
In 1830 Paris, a poor playwright named Rodolphe meets a waif named Mimi, and they fall in love. Mimi inspires Rodolphe, and he launches with a newfound passion into writing his new play. But there are complications, for example a Count Paul, who lusts after Mimi and has the power to help Rodolphe professionally.
This was the first film Lillian Gish would make for MGM under her new long-term contract, a coup for the studio. Her preparation techniques startled her coworkers; for example, for three days before shooting Mimi's death scene, the dedicated Miss Gish refused to allow liquid to touch her lips, to achieve the parched look of a woman wasting away. She also trained herself to breathe without any visible movement.

La La Lucille (Universal, 1920)
d: Eddie Lyons, Lee Moran. 5 reels.
Eddie Lyons, Lee Moran, Gladys Walton, Anne Cornwall, Fred Gamble, Henry Meyer, Frank Earle, Charles McHugh, Rosa Gore, Arthur Thalasso, Dorothea Wolbert, Sam Appel, Burton Halbert, Marion Skinner.
Zany comedy about a young couple, John and Lucille, who are forced to divorce so that he can receive a large inheritance from his eccentric aunt's estate. They set up a fake "tryst" with a friend's wife, to create the appearance of impropriety so that Lucille will have grounds to seek a divorce. They plan to re-marry later. Good plan, but it starts to unravel quickly when Lucille arrives to find John with an entirely different woman in his apartment.

La Tosca (Famous Players-Lasky/Paramount, 1918)
d: Edward José. 5 reels.
Pauline Frederick, Frank Losee, Jules Raucourt, Henry Hebert, W.H. Forestelle.
Floria Tosca, an operatic diva, loves Mario but finds that to save him from torture by the police, she must consent to the villainous Baron Scarpia's romantic demands.

La Vie de Boheme (Paragon Films, Inc./World Film Corp., 1916)
d: Albert Capellani. 5 reels.
Alice Brady, Paul Capellani, June Elvidge, Leslie Stowe, Chester Barnett, Zena Keefe, Fred Truesdell, D.J. Flanagan.
Mimi, a Parisian waif, is found by well-to-do Rudolphe, and they fall in love. But his family disapproves, and eventually Rudolphe is persuaded to leave Mimi. With her true love gone, Mimi's health deteriorates and she tries to commit suicide. She is rescued, but finally dies in her own bed, with Rudolphe at her side.

The Labyrinth (Equitable Motion Pictures Corp./World Film Corp., 1915)
d: E. Mason Hopper. 5 reels.
Gail Kane, Dolly Larkin, Richard Neal, Edward Roseman, Polly Champlain, Walter Hiers.
To squirm out of her loveless marriage and an obnoxious theatrical contract, an actress creates a labyrinth of lies.

The Lad and the Lion (Selig Polyscope, 1917)
d: Alfred Green. 5 reels.
Vivian Reed, Will Machin, Charles Le Moyne, Al W. Filson, Lafayette McKee, Captain Ricardo, Cecil Holland, Gertrude Oakman, Frank Clark.
Shipwrecked and stricken with amnesia, an American drifts to North Africa, accompanied by a lion he has befriended. Whimsical adventure tale, based on a short story by Edgar Rice Burroughs.

The Ladder Jinx (Vitagraph, 1922)
d: Jess Robbins. 6 reels.
Edward Horton, Margaret Landis, Tully Marshall, Otis Harlan, Colin Kenny, Tom McGuire, Will R. Walling, Tom Murray, Ernest Shields, Max Asher.
Comedy about Helen, a highly superstitious girl, who makes her boyfriend Arthur walk back under a ladder he walked under earlier in the day. This simple maneuver makes Arthur a suspect in a robbery and he is pursued by the police. Never fear, though, after numerous pratfalls and other misadventures, Arthur proves his innocence, captures the real crook, and marries Helen.

The Ladder of Lies (Famous Players-Lasky/Paramount, 1920)
d: Tom Forman. 5 reels.
Ethel Clayton, Clyde Fillmore, Jean Acker, Irving Cummings, Charles Meredith, Ruth Ashby.
Trying to save a friend from marrying a golddigger, a woman gets trapped in a ladder of lies.

Laddie (Gene Stratton Porter Productions/FBO of America, 1926)
d: James Leo Meehan. 7 reels.
John Bowers, Bess Flowers, Theodore von Eltz, Eugenia Gilbert, David Torrence, Eulalie Jensen, Arthur Clayton, Fanny Midgley, Aggie Herring, Gene Stratton, John Fox Jr.
Laddie, son of an Ohio family, falls in love with Pamela, a neighbor girl from England, though her parents exhibit a supercilious distaste for Laddie's family.   Through a remarkable coincidence, Laddie's sister becomes enamored of an attorney who turns out to be Pamela's long-lost brother.

Ladies at Ease (Chadwick Pictures/First Division Distributors, 1927)
d: Jerome Storm. 6 reels.
Pauline Garon, Gertrude Short, Gardner James, Raymond

Glenn, Lillian Hackett, Jean Van Vliet, William H. Strauss, Charles Meakin, Henry Roquemore.
Comedy of blunders, about two lingerie models who steal the beaus of a pair of sisters who perform on stage. Furious, the sisters have the models fired from their jobs.   No problem for the former models: they replace the sisters on stage, and their inexperience is translated into fun for the audience, who greet the new act enthusiastically.

Ladies at Play (First National, 1926)
d: Alfred E. Green. 7 reels.
Lloyd Hughes, Louise Fazenda, Doris Kenyon, Virginia Lee Corgin, Phil McCullough, Hallam Colley, John Patrick, Ethel Wales, Thomas Ricketts.
Naughty farce about Ann, a girl who can inherit a small fortune if she is married within three days. But her spinster aunts dislike all of Ann's boyfriends and refuse to give their consent. So Ann decides to vamp a young man and place herself in a compromising situation, to force her aunts' consent to her marriage.

Ladies Beware (R-C Pictures/FBO of America, 1927)
d: Charles Giblyn. 5 reels.
George O'Hara, Nola Luxford, Florence Wix, Kathleen Myers, Mario Carillo, Alan Brooks, Byron Douglas, Bud Jamieson, Jimmy Aubrey.
A jewel thief infiltrates a house party with the intention of stealing a precious ruby. Instead, he falls in love with Jeannie, an employee of the ruby's owner, and ends up thwarting the robbery attempt of another crook.

Ladies Must Live (Mayflower Photoplay Corp./Paramount, 1921)
d: George Loane Tucker. 8 reels.
Robert Ellis, Maylon Hamilton, Betty Compson, Leatrice Joy, Hardee Kirkland, Gibson Gowland, John Gilbert, Cleo Madison, Snitz Edwards, Lucille Hutton, Lule Warrenton, William V. Mong, Jack McDonald, Marcia Manon, Arnold Gregg.
Four women, all from different social classes, have romance on their minds.

Ladies' Night in a Turkish Bath (Asher-Small-Rogers/First National, 1928)
d: Edward Cline. 7 reels.
Dorothy Mackaill, Jack Mulhall, Sylvia Ashton, James Finlayson, Guinn Williams, Harvey Clarke, Reed Howes, Ethel Wales, Fred Kelsey.
Dawson, a steelworker, is dismayed when the sweet, simple girl he fancies begins dressing "modern style," with bare legs and short skirts. The girl and her mother go to a Turkish Bath, followed closely by Dawson and his friend, but the two men are routed when they discover that it's ladies' night.

Ladies of Leisure (Columbia, 1926)
d: Thomas Buckingham. 6 reels.
T. Roy Barnes, Elaine Hammerstein, Robert Ellis, Gertrude Short, Thomas Ricketts, James Mason, Joseph W.Girard.
Marian is smitten with Eric, but he's a bachelor and wants to stay that way. Then, in rapid succession, Eric stops a girl from committing suicide and takes her to his home; Marian's brother follows them, thinking to accuse Eric of the unthinkable; and just as he gets there, the would-be suicide exits out a side door and Marian walks in. Now Eric has got Marian compromised and must marry her... right?

Ladies of the Mob (Paramount, 1928)

d: William Wellman. 7 reels.

Clara Bow, Richard Arlen, Helen Lynch, Mary Alden, Carl Gerrald, Bodil Rosing, Lorraine Rivero, James Pierce.

A trio of bank robbers, two men and a young woman, live in a seedy underworld of violence and despair. After several desperate confrontations with the law, the young woman begs her man to abandon this life of crime so they can live in peace... but he isn't convinced.

Ladies of the Night Club (Tiffany-Stahl Productions, 1928)
d: George Archainbaud. 7 reels.

Ricardo Cortez, Barbara Leonard, Lee Moran, Douglas Gerrard, Cissy Fitzgerald, Charles Gerrard.

The male half of a night club act is in love with his partner— but she's already spoken for.

Ladies to Board (Fox, 1924)
d: J.G. Blystone. 6 reels.

Tom Mix, Gertrude Olmstead, Philo McCullough, Pee Wee Holmes, Gertrude Claire, Dolores Rousse.

A young man inherits an old ladies' home.

The Lady (Norma Talmadge Productions/First National, 1925)
d: Frank Borzage. 8 reels.

Norma Talmadge, Wallace MacDonald, Brandon Hurst, Alf Goulding, Doris Lloyd, Walter Long, George Hackathorne, Marc MacDermott, Paulette Duval, John Fox Jr., Emily Fitzroy, John Herdman, Margaret Seddon.

After an irresponsible playboy takes Polly, a music hall singer, for his wife, the playboy's father disinherits him. Not long after, the husband dies and Polly finds herself reduced to singing in waterfront dives to support herself and her son.

Lady Audley's Secret (Fox, 1915)
d: Marshall Farnum. 5 reels.

Theda Bara, Clifford Bruce, William Riley Hatch, Stephen Gratten, Warner Richmond.

After her husband disappears and she thinks him dead, Helen marries again and becomes Lady Audley. But then her lost husband returns.

Lady Barnacle (Metro, 1917)
d: John H. Collins. 5 reels.

Viola Dana, Robert Walker, Augustus Phillips, William B. Davidson, Henry Hallam, Marie Adell, Fred Jones, Henry Leone, Ricca Allen, Harry Linson, Gerald Griffin, Nellie Grant.

In India, two lovers named Krishna and Lakshima are denied permission to marry by their Maharajah fathers. The young man is then sent to America to get an education, and the grief-stricken girl tries to drown herself in the ocean. But she's fished out of the water by an American skipper, who hides her on board his ship and takes her to America and a reconciliation with her lover, Krishna.

Lady Be Good (First National, 1928)
d: Richard Wallace. 7 reels.

Jack Mulhall, Dorothy Mackaill, John Miljan, Nita Martan, Dot Farley, James Finlayson, Aggie Herring, Jay Eaton, Eddie Clayton, Yola D'Arvil.

Vaudeville partners Jack and Mary are in love. They quarrel and separate, then discover that neither is a success without the other.

The Lady From Hell (Stuart Paton Productions/Associated Exhibitors, 1926)
d: Stuart Paton. 6 reels.

Roy Stewart, Blanche Sweet, Ralph Lewis, Frank Elliott,

Edgar Norton, margaret Campbell, Ruth King, Mickey Moore.

A Scottish nobleman lives a double life, doubling as a ranch foreman in the American West.

The Lady From Longacre (Fox, 1921)
d: George E.Marshall. 5 reels.

William Russell, Mary Thurman, Mathilde Brundage, Robert Klein, Jean DeBriac, Francis Ford, William Brunton, Douglas Gerard, Lillian Worth, Arthur Van Sickle.

Isabel, a princess of a European kingdom, has a lookalike in Molly, a stage actress. Together they concoct a plot to get Isabel out of an odious arranged marriage.

Miss Thurman plays both the princess and her double.

The Lady in Ermine (Corinne Griffith Productions/First National, 1927)
d: James Flood. 7 reels.

Corinne Griffith, Francis X. Bushman, Einar Hansen, Ward Crane, Jane Keckley.

During the Napoleonic Wars, an Austrian countess is coveted by a French general.

A Lady in Love (Famous Players-Lasky/Paramount, 1920)
d: Walter Edwards. 5 reels.

Harrison Ford, Ethel Clayton, Boyd Irwin, Ernest Joy, Elsa Lorimer, Clarence Geldert, Ernest Goodleigh, Frances Raymond.

Barbara's in love with John, but she's still married to a man who deserted her. So she files for a quiet divorce, fearing that John may discover she's been married before. Luck is with her, as she discovers that her ex was already married, hence their marriage was invalid.

A Lady of Chance (MGM, 1928)
d: Robert Z. Leonard. 8 reels. (Part talkie.)

Norma Shearer, Lowell Sherman, Gwen Lee, Johnny Mack Brown, Eugenie Besserer, Buddy Messinger.

"Angel Face" is her monicker, and swindling gullible men is her trade.

A Lady of Quality (Famous Players Film Co., 1914)
d: Daniel Frohman. 5 reels.

Cecilia Loftus, Geraldine O'Brien, House Peters, peter Lang, Hal Clarendon, Edna Weick, Roy Pilser, Dave Wall, Alexander Gaden, Henrietta Goodman.

A girl who was raised as a boy by her widowed father finally blossoms forth as a beautiful woman.

A Lady of Quality (Universal, 1924)
d: Hobart Henley. 8 reels.

Virginia Valli, Earle Foxe, Milton Sills, Lionel Belmore, Margaret Seddon, Peggy Cartwright, Florence Gibson, Dorothea Wolbert, Bert Roach, Leo White, Willard Louis, Bobby Mack, Yvonne Armstrong, Patterson Dial.

In 18th century London, a young woman falls for a cad, who later threatens her with blackmail.

The Lady of Red Butte (Thomas H. Ince/Paramount, 1919)
d: Victor L. Schertzinger. 5 reels.

Dorothy Dalton, Thomas Holding, Tully Marshall, William Courtright, Joseph Swickard, May Garcia.

In a small mining town, a theology student falls in love with a lady saloon-keeper.

Lady of the Harem (Paramount, 1926)
d: Raoul Walsh. 6 reels.

Ernest Torrence, William Collier Jr., Greta Nissen, Louise Fazenda, André de Beranger, Sojin, Frank Leigh, Noble

Johnson, Daniel Makarenko, Christian Frank, Snitz Edwards, Chester Conklin, Brandon Hurst, Leo White.

Arabian Nights-style entertainment about a young man who arrives in town to rescue his beloved from the slave market, where she has been imprisoned by a cruel sultan.

Lady of the Night (MGM, 1924)
d: Monta Bell. 6 reels.
Norma Shearer, Malcolm McGregor, George K. Arthur.
A villainess and a debutante closely resemble each other. Miss Shearer plays both roles.

Lady of the Pavements (Art Cinema Corp./United Artists, 1929)
d: D.W. Griffith. 8 reels. (Music, part talkie, three songs.)
Lupe Velez, William Boyd, Jetta Goudal, Albert Conti, George Fawcett, Henry Armetta,William Bakewell, Franklin Pangborn.
In Paris, a Prussian officer breaks off his engagement to a French countess, declaring that he would sooner marry "a woman of the streets." The enraged countess then arranges for him to do just that.

The Lady of the Photograph (Thomas A. Edison, Inc./Perfection Pictures, 1917)
d: Ben Turbett. 5 reels.
Shirley Mason, Raymond McKee, Royal Byron, Dudley Hill, William Calhoun, Gerald Pring, Jane Harvey.
Left penniless when his father dies, a young English nobleman sails to America, confident of making a success in the New World. The titular "lady of the photograph" is the American girl he falls in love with.

Lady Raffles (Columbia, 1928)
d: Roy William Neill. 6 reels.
Estelle Taylor, Ronald Drew, Lilyan Tashman, Ernest Hilliard.
A lady jewel thief is mistaken for a temporary maid, and put to work.

Lady Robinhood (R-C Pictures/FBO of America, 1925)
d: Ralph Ince. 6 reels.
Evelyn Brent, Robert Ellis, Boris Karloff, William Humphrey, D'Arcy Corrigan, Robert Cauterio.
Catalina, a noble Spanish lady, dons a mask and turns into an avenger of injustice.

Lady Rose's Daughter (Famous Players-Lasky/Paramount, 1920)
d: Hugh Ford. 5 reels.
Elsie Ferguson, Frank Losee, David Powell, Holmes E. Herbert, Ida Waterman, Warren Cook.
The "daughter" of the title is Julie, a girl born out of wedlock to a noblewoman. Her disdainful relatives never let Julie forget her bastard status, but finally she meets and falls in love with a decent man who loves her for herself.

The Lady Who Lied (First National, 1925)
d: Edwin Carewe. 8 reels.
Lewis Stone, Virginia Valli, Louis Payne, Nita Naldi, Edward Earle, Leo White, Purnell Pratt, Sam Appel, Zalla Zarana, George Lewis.

On an African safari, an Englishwoman and her alcoholic husband are joined by her former lover.

Lady Windermere's Fan (Warner Bros., 1925)
d: Ernst Lubitsch. 8 reels.
Irene Rich, May McAvoy, Bert Lytell, Ronald Colman, Edward Martindale, Helen Dunbar, Carrie Daumery, Billie Bennett.
The Lubitsch touch spices a visual rendition of the famous Oscar Wilde play about amorous misunderstandings among the very rich.

The Ladybird (Chadwick Pictures/First Division Pictures, 1927)
d: Walter Lang. 7 reels.
Betty Compson, Malcolm McGregor, Sheldon Lewis, Hank Mann, Leo White, John Miljan, Ruth Stonehouse, Joseph Girard, Jean DeBriac, Mathew Matron.
Diana, a bored socialite, decides to earn her own living by dancing in a New Orleans cabaret.

Ladyfingers (Metro, 1921)
d: Bayard Veiller. 6 reels.
Bert Lytell, Ora Carew, Frank Elliott, Edythe Chapman, DeWitt Jennings, Stanley Goethals.
Rachel, a fiercely proud woman of wealth, rejects her daughter when she marries against Rachel's wishes. Years later, with the daughter dead, Rachel's grandson enters her life as a safecracker.

A Lady's Name (Select Pictures, 1919)
d: Walter Edwards. 5 reels.
Harrison Ford, Constance Talmadge, Emory Johnson, Vera Doria, James Farley, Fohn Steppling, Truman Van Dyke, Lillian Leighton, Emma Gerdes, ZaSu Pitts.
Talented, but engaged to a jerk, a lady writer advertises for a husband just to gather material for a new novel. But when one of the applicants turns out to be charming and sincere, she accepts his proposal, and the jerk is history!

Lafayette, We Come! (Perret Productions/Exhibitor's Mutual, 1918)
d: Leonce Perret. 6 reels.
E.K. Lincoln, Dolores Cassinelli, Emmett C. King, Ethel Winthrop, Ernest Maupain, Valentine Petit Perret.
In France, an American pianist falls in love with a mysterious woman, who soon departs and leaves him heartbroken. World War I breaks out and, at the front, the young American finds the enigmatic woman again, working as an Army nurse. But that's only one of her many disguises.

The Lair of the Wolf (Universal, 1917)
d: Charles Swickard. 5 reels.
Gretchen Lederer, Donna Drew, Joseph Girard, Chester Bennett, Val Paul, Charles Mailes, Peggy Custer, George Berrell, Martha Mattox.
Unknowingly, a kind-hearted widow marries a vicious, unrepentant scoundrel.

The Lamb (Triangle, 1915)
d: W. Christy Cabanne. 5 reels.
Douglas Fairbanks, Seena Owen, William E. Lowery, Lillian Langdon, Monroe Salisbury, Kate Toncray, Alfred Paget.
A scion of wealth woos a fair lady, but he's considered a weakling. He proves his bravery when, on vacation out West, he rescues the lady from bloodthirsty savages.
Fairbanks made his film debut in *The Lamb*, playing the lead. He was a star from the beginning.

The Lamb and the Lion (National Film Corp. of America, 1919)
d: Francis J. Grandon. 5 reels.
Billie Rhodes, Melbourne MacDowell, Al Garcia, William Griffin, Walter Hiers, Maud George, Vera Lewis, Hal Clements, Harry Devere, Charles Spere.

"Boots," a tomboy who's also a petty thief, is caught by a wealthy widow who resolves to make a lady of her, then marry her off to a rich young man.

The Lamplighter (Fox, 1921)
d: Howard M. Mitchell. 6 reels.
Shirley Mason, Raymond McKee, Albert Knott, Edwin Booth Tilton, Iris Ashton, Philo McCullough, Madge Hunt.
Gertie, a mistreated orphan, runs away from her foster home and is taken in by an old lamplighter. In later years, the grown Gertie will find a job as companion to a blind woman who turns out to be her own mother.

Land o' Lizards (American Film Co./Mutual, 1916)
d: Frank Borzage. 5 reels.
Frank Borzage, Harvey Clark, Laura Sears, Perry Banks, Anna Little, Jack Richardson.
When gold is discovered on a western ranch, rivals battle it out for rightful ownership.

The Land of Jazz (Fox, 1920)
d: Jules Furthman. 5 reels.
Eileen Percy, Ruth Stonehouse, Herbert Heyes, George Fisher, Franklyn Farnum, Hayward Mack, Rose Dione, Carry Ward, Blanch Payson, Wilson Hummel, Harry Dunkinson.
Friends Nina and Nancy are both are engaged to be married. But in this comedy of errors involving mistaken identity, insane asylums, and island dancers, Nina and Nancy wind up with each other's beaus.

The Land of Long Shadows (Essanay, 1917)
d: W.S. Van Dyke. 5 reels.
Jack Gardner, Ruth King, C.J. Lionel, Carl Stockdale.
In the Canadian northwest, a trapper and a saloon keeper's daughter fall in love.

The Land of Promise (Famous Players-Lasky/Paramount, 1917)
d: Joseph Kaufman. 5 reels.
Billie Burke, Thomas Meighan, Helen T. Tracy, J.W. Johnson, Mary Alden, Margaret Seddon, Walter McEwen, Grace Studeford, John Raymond.
Nora, penniless after her long servitude to a wealthy woman who died suddenly, marries a farmer with the stipulation that their marriage be in name only. But it won't be that way for long.

Land of the Lawless (Liberty/Pathé, 1927)
d: Thomas Buckingham. 5 reels.

Jack Padjan, Vivian Winston, Tom Santschi, Joe Rickson, Duke Lee, Charles Clary.
A Texas Ranger is assigned to break up a gang of desperadoes.

The Landloper (Yorke Film Corp./Metro, 1918)
d: George Irving. 5 reels.
Harold Lockwood, Pauline Curley, Stanton Heck, William Clifford, Bert Starkey, Gertrude Maloney.
A wealthy man makes a bet that he can live a hobo's life in perfect happiness.

The Lane That Had No Turning (Famous Players-Lasky/Paramount, 1922)
d: Victor Fleming. 5 reels.
Agnes Ayres, Theodore Kosloff, Mahlon Hamilton, Wilton Taylor, Frank Campeau, Lillian Leighton, Charles West, Robert Bolder, Fred Vroom.
Madelinette, who aspires to an operatic career, receives a welcome bequest from a deceased relative of her husband's. As she follows her dream, the relative's family busily tries to revoke her inheritance.

Langdon's Legacy (Universal, 1915)
d: Otis Turner. 5 reels.
J. Warren Kerrigan, Lois Wilson, Maude George, Bertram Grassby, Harry Carter, G.A. Williams, Mary Talbot.
Jack Langdon gets appointed head of a woman's school in Massachussetts. By coincidence, one of the students is the daughter of his old enemy from South America.

L'Apache (Famous Players-Lasky/Paramount, 1919)
d: Joseph De Grasse. 6 reels.
Dorothy Dalton, Robert Elliott, Macey Harlam, Austin Webber, George Furry, Frank Cluxon, Alice Gale, Louis Darclay, Clara Beyers.
Miss Dalton plays a double role: as a French apache dancer, and the American woman she resembles.

The Lariat Kid (Universal, 1929)
d: Reaves Eason. 6 reels.
Hoot Gibson, Francis Ford, Ann Christy, Cap Anderson, Mary Foy, Walter Brennan, Andy Waldron, Bud Osborne, Joe Bennett, Jim Corey, Joe Rickson.
Out West, a deputy sheriff cleans up a wild town and captures the killers of his father, the former sheriff.

Lasca (Universal, 1919)
d: Norman Dawn. 5 reels.
Edith Roberts, Frank Mayo, Veola Harty, Lloyd Whitlock, Arthur Jasmine.
Lasca's a Rio Grande maiden in love with an American rancher.

The Lash (Lasky Feature Plays/Paramount, 1916)
d: James Young. 5 reels.
Marie Doro, Elliott Dexter, James Neill, Thomas Delmar, Jane Wolff, Veda McEvers, Raymond Hatton, Josephine Rice.
On the island of St. Ba'tiste, there's a custom that any woman found in a pre-marital affair will be lashed at the stake. Sidonie, one of the local girls, apparently runs afoul of that custom; but just as she is being prepared for the whipping, her lover comes forward and reveals that they are really married.

The Lash of Destiny (Van Dyke Film Corp./Art Dramas, Inc., 1916)
d: George Terwilliger. 5 reels.
Gertrude McCoy, Duncan McRae, Helen Greene, Arthur Housman, Mabel Juline Scott, Margaret Milne.
A small-town girl goes to the big city and immediately falls under the spell of a two-timing cheat.

The Lash of Power (Universal, 1917)
d: Harry Solter. 5 reels.
Carmel Myers, Kenneth Harlan, Helen Wright, Charles Hill Mailes, T.D. Crittenden, Jack Nelson, Gertrude Astor.
Fixated on Napoleonic ambition, a young man dreams of obtaining wealth and power.

The Last Act (New York Motion Picture Corp./Triangle, 1916)
d: Walter Edwards. 5 reels.
Bessie Barriscale, Clara Williams, Harry Keenan, Robert McKim.
Ethel's an actress in a play where her character is having an affair with a married man. By eerie coincidence, the real life Ethel begins an affair with a married man herself.

The Last Alarm (Paul Gerson Pictures/Rayart, 1926)
d: Oscar Apfel. 6 reels.
Rex Lease, Wanda Hawley, Maurice Costello, Florence Turner, Theodore von Eltz, Hazel Howell, Jimmy Aubrey.
Firemen buddies Tom and Joe each love the other's sister.

The Last Card (Metro, 1921)
d: Bayard Veiller. 6 reels.
May Allison, Albert Roscoe, Stanley Goethals, Frank Elliott, Irene Hunt, Dana Todd, Wilton Taylor.
Gannell, an insanely jealous husband, suspects his wife of infidelity with their neighbor.

The Last Command (Paramount, 1927)
d: Josef Von Sternberg. 9 reels.
Emil Jannings, Evelyn Brent, Jack Raymond, Nicholas Soussanin, William Powell, Michael Visaroff, Vlacheslav Savitsky, Fritz Feld, Harry Semels, Alex Ikonnikov.
Alexander, a former general in the Russian army, has fled to the United States and now finds himself working as a movie extra in Hollywood. In a devastating irony, Alexander is cast in a film as a Russian general, and must take orders from a director who was once one of the revolutionaries the true-life general was sworn to kill.

The Last Door (Selznick, 1921)
d: William P.S. Earle. 5 reels.
Eugene O'Brien, Charles Craig, Nita Naldi, Helen Pillsbury, Martha Mansfield, Katherine Perry, Warren Cook.
A famous libertarian declares that he would be willing to shield any female convict who is on the run from the law. Soon after that, a young woman comes to him and asks for assistance, saying she's on the lam. He takes her into his home, where she advises him that she was merely playing a joke on him, and is not really a criminal. That's okay, he says... he's not who she thinks he is either.

The Last Edition (Emory Johnson Productions/FBO of America, 1925)
d: Emory Johnson. 7 reels.
Ralph Lewis, Lila Leslie, Ray Hallor, Frances Teague, Rex Lease, Lou Payne, David Kirby, Wade Boteler, Cuyler Supplee, Leigh Willard, Will Frank, Ada Mae Vaughn.
The foreman at a big-city newspaper becomes involved with intrigue when he and his son, an assistant D.A., are framed for bootlegging.

The Last Egyptian (Oz Film Manufacturing Co./Alliance Films, 1914)
w, d: L. Frank Baum. 5 reels.
J. Farrell Macdonald, Vivian Reed, Jefferson Osborne, Mai Wells, Jane Urban, J. Charles Haydon, Howard Davies, Frank Moore, Ora Buckley.
In Cairo, a descendant of the pharaohs proposes marriage to an English girl.

The Last Frontier (Metropolitan Pictures Corp. of California, 1926)
d: George B. Seitz. 8 reels.
William Boyd, Marguerite De La Motte, Jack Hoxie, Junior Coghlan, Mitchell Lewis, Gladys Brockwell, Frank Lacksteen.
Following the Civil War, a southern family heads west to replenish its lost fortune.

The Last Hour (Mastodon Films, 1923)
d: Edward Sloman. 7 reels.
Carmel Myers, Pat O'Malley, Milton Sills, Jack Mower, Alec B. Francis, Charles Clary, Walter Long, Eric Mayne, Wilson Hummell.
Reever, an outraged father, kills his daughter's blackmailer. Their friend Steve, however, takes the blame and is convicted of murder and sentenced to hang. At the execution, the gallows fail to function properly, and after Reever's confession, Steve is set free.

The Last Man (Vitagraph, 1916)
d: William Wolbert. 5 reels.
William Duncan, Corinne Griffith, Mary Anderson, Jack Mower, Otto Lederer.
In the Phillipines, two American married couples find themselves under attack by rebels.

The Last Man on Earth (Fox, 1924)
d: J.G. Blystone. 7 reels.
Earle Foxe, Grace Cunard, Maurice Murphy, William Steele, Jean Dumas, Harry Dunkinson, Gladys Tennyson, Derelys Perdue, Maryon Aye, Clarissa Selwynne, Pauline French.
Fantasy about Elmer, a swain whose proposal of marriage is rejected by his sweetheart, and whose response is to retreat into the forest and live as a hermit. Subsequently, a deadly virus envelops the earth and kills all males except Elmer. Now he returns to civilization and finds himself, to put it mildly, in demand.

The Last Moment (J. Parker Read Jr./Goldwyn, 1923)
d: J. Parker Read Jr. 6 reels.
Henry Hull, Doris Kenyon, Louis Wolheim, Louis Calhern, William Nally, Mickey Bennett, Harry Allen, Donald Hall, Danny Hayes, Jerry Peterson, Robert Hazelton.
Sweethearts Nap and Alice are shanghaied and forced aboard an unwanted sea cruise by a brutal sea captain. The captain keeps a caged ape on board to intimidate his passengers. During a fierce storm, the captain and crew perish, and leave Nap and Alice alone with the ape. Now what?

The Last Moment (Freedman-Spitz/Zakoro, 1928)
w, d: Paul Fejos. 6 reels.
Otto Matiesen, Julius Molnar Jr., Lucille La Verne, Anielka Elter, Georgia Hale, Isabelle Lamore, Vivian Winston.
A drowning man sees his life flash before him.

The Last of His People (Select Pictures Corp., 1919)
d: Robert North Bradbury. 5 reels.
Mitchell Lewis, Harry Lonsdale, Yvette Mitchell, Catherine Van Buren, J.J. Bryson, Eddie Hearn, Joseph Swickard.
Stranded in the Canadian northwest, an Indian youth and his sister are adopted by a lone woodsman.

The Last of the Carnabys (Astra Film Corp./Pathé, 1917)
d: William Parke. 5 reels.
Gladys Hulette, William Parke Jr., Eugenie Woodward, Paul Everton, Harry Benham, J.H. Gilmour, Helene Chadwick.
After her mother dies, a young woman is left with numerous unpaid bills and an irresponsible brother on her hands.

The Last of the Duanes (Fox, 1919)
d: J. Gordon Edwards. 7 reels.
William Farnum, Frankie Raymond, Harry DeVere, Charles Clary, G. Raymond Nye, Clarence Burton, Lamar Johnstone, Henry J. Hebert, C. Edward Hatton, Louise Lovely, Genevieve Blinn, Orra Gardner, Frederic Herzog.
Out West, the son of an outlaw yearns to live honestly and in peace, but is continually being tempted by lawless gangs to join them.

The Last of the Duanes (Fox, 1924)

d: Lynn Reynolds. 7 reels.

Tom Mix, Marian Nixon, Brinsley Shaw, Frank Nelson, Lucy Beaumont, Harry Lonsdale.

Buck, a reformed outlaw, is forced to fight to retain his new respectability.

Remake of the 1919 Fox film *The Last of the Duanes*, both versions based on the Zane Grey novel of the same name.

The Last of the Ingrams (New York Motion Picture Corp./Triangle, 1917)

d: Walter Edwards. 5 reels.

William Desmond, Margery Wilson, Robert McKim, Walt Whitman, Mary Armlyn, Thelma Salter.

In a Puritan community, the sight of an unmarried man keeping company with an unmarried woman is considered unseemly—and the citizens start boiling tar and plucking feathers.

The Last of the Mohicans (Associated Producers, Inc., 1920)

d: Maurice Tourneur, Clarence Brown. 6 reels.

Albert Roscoe, Barbara Bedford, Wallace Beery, Lillian Hall, Henry Woodward, James Gordon, George Hackathorne, Nelson McDowell, Harry Lorraine, Theodore Lerch, Jack F. McDonald, Sydney Deane, Joseph Singleton.

During colonial days, a British fort is attacked by the Huron tribe.

The Last Outlaw (Paramount, 1927)

d: Arthur Rosson. 6 reels.

Gary Cooper, Jack Luden, Betty Jewel, Herbet Prior, Jim Corey, Billy Butts.

Out West, a drifter rescues a girl from a runaway horse and is rewarded with being named sheriff by the local judge. But he'll find that the judge is actually behind a conspiracy to rustle cattle from the ranchers.

The Last Performance (Universal, 1929)

d: Paul Fejos. 7 reels. (Music, sound effects, part talkie.)

Conrad Veidt, Mary Philbin, Leslie Fenton, Fred Mackaye, Gustav Partos, William H. Turner, Anders Randolf, Sam DeGrasse, George Irving.

Erik, a professional mesmerist, loves his young assistant Julie, but so does Mark, another assistant.

The Last Rebel (Triangle, 1918)

d: Gilbert P. Hamilton. 5 reels.

Belle Bennett, Walt Whitman, Lillian Langdon, Joe Bennett, Joe King, Jack Curtis, Lucretia Harris, Anna Dodge.

Fifty years after the Civil War, descendants of two old wartime foes happen to meet and fall in love.

The Last Sentence (Thomas A. Edison, Inc., 1916)

d: Ben Turbett. 5 reels.

Marc MacDermott, Miriam Nesbitt, Grace Williams, Herbert Prior, Florence Stover, Gladys Gane, Elaine Ivans, Raymond McKee, Mrs. Wallace Erskine, Jessie Stevens, Fred Jones.

Sitting in judgment over a young woman charged with murder, a judge comes to realize that the defendant is the daughter he deserted years before.

The Last Straw (Fox, 1920)

d: Denison Clift. 5 reels.

Buck Jones, Vivian Rich, Jane Tallent, Colin Kenny, Charles LeMoyne, Bob Chandler, William Gillis, H.W. Padgett, Hank Bell, Zeib Morris, Lon Poff.

Jones plays Tom Beck, a ranch hand who almost single-handedly foils a gang of cattle rustlers and wins the love of Jane, the ranch's owner.

The Last Trail (Fox, 1921)

d: Emmett J. Flynn. 7 reels.

Maurice B. Flynn, Eva Novak, Wallace Beery, Rosemary Theby,Charles K. French, Harry Springler, Harry Dunkinson.

When a masked bandit known as "The Night Hawk" terrorizes a small western town, the citizens become wary of all strangers.

The Last Trail (Fox, 1927)

d: Lewis Seiler. 6 reels.

Tom Mix, Carmelita Geraghty, William Davidson, Frank Hagney, Lee Shumway.

A newcomer to a western town may actually be an infamous bandit.

Remake of Fox's 1921 film *The Last Trail*, both versions based on the Zane Grey story of the same name.

The Last Volunteer (Pathé Freres/Eclectic Film Co., 1914)

d: Oscar C. Apfel. 5 reels.

Eleanor Woodruff, Paul Panzer, Robert Broderick, Irving Cummings, Edward N. Hoyt, Mary Gray, Harold Crane, A.H. Barstar.

While traveling incognito, a European prince falls in love with an innkeeper's daughter.

The Last Warning (Universal, 1928)

d: Paul Leni. 8 reels. (Music, sound effects, part talkie.)

D'Arcy Corrigan, Laura LaPlante, John Boles, Roy D'Arcy, Margaret Livingston, Montague Love, Burr McIntosh, Bert Roach, Carrie Daumery, Slim Summerville, Torben Meyer.

A leading actor is murdered during a stage performance, and the remaining players are all under suspicion, but no arrests are made. When the same play is scheduled to be performed five years later on the same stage, the ghost of the dead actor returns to warn the company not to perform that play, and old suspicions are rekindled.

The Latest From Paris (MGM, 1927)

d: Sam Wood. 8 reels.

Norma Shearer, Ralph Forbes, George Sidney, Tenen Holtz, William Bakewell, Margaret Landis, Bert Roach.

Traveling salespersons for competing clothing firms fall in love.

Laugh, Clown, Laugh (MGM, 1928)

 d: Herbert Brenon. 8 reels.

Lon Chaney, Nils Asther, Loretta Young, Bernard Siegel, Cissy Fitzgerald, Gwen Lee.

Tito, a circus clown, grows to love his young ward as she matures into a beautiful woman. By now, however, she is desired by someone else.

Laughing at Danger (Carlos Productions/FBO of America, 1924)

d: James W. Horne. 6 reels.

Richard Talmadge, Joe Girard, Eva Novak, Joe Harrington, Stanhope Wheatcroft.

Comedy of terrors, as Alan, a scion of wealth, continually scoffs at attempts on his life, thinking they are all part of a game. But they're real.

Laughing at Death (FBO Pictures, 1929)

d: Wallace W. Fox. 6 reels.

Bob Steele, Natalie Joyce, Captain Vic, Kai Schmidt, Ethan Laidlaw, Armand Trillor, Hector V. Sarno, Golden Wadhams.

Bob, an American college student, swaps identities with a

foreign dignitary, then has to dodge plotters out to assassinate him.

Laughing Bill Hyde (Rex Beach Pictures/Goldwyn, 1918)
d: Hobart Henley. 6 reels.
Will Rogers, Anna Lehr, John M. Sainpolis, Mabel Ballin, Clarence Oliver, Joseph Herbert, Robert Conville, Dan Mason.
In Alaska, an ex-con discovers that a mine superintendent is stealing gold from his employer. So the ex-con steals it back.

Lavender and Old Lace (Renco Film Co./W.W. Hodkinson, 1921)
d: Lloyd Ingraham. 6 reels.
Marguerite Snow, Seena Owen, Louis Bennison, Victor Potel, Zella Ingraham, Lillian Elliott, James Corrigan.
Sentimental tale about Mary, a spinster who has waited 30 years for her seafaring lover to return and marry her. When a young stranger comes to town and meets Mary, she is startled by his resemblance to her old beau. He turns out to be the son of her beau, now dead.

The Lavender Bath Lady (Universal, 1922)
d: King Baggot. 5 reels.
Gladys Walton, Edward Burns, Charlotte Pierce, Tom Ricketts, Lydia Yeamans Titus, Mary Winston, Al MacQuarrie, Harry Lorraine, Earl Crain.
A shopgirl foils a kidnapping attempt and gains a sweetheart in the detective investigating the case.

The Law and the Lady (Marlborough Productions/Aywon, 1924)
d: John L. McCutcheon. 6 reels.
Len Leo, Alice Lake, Mary Thurman, Tyrone Power, Maurice Costello, Henry Sedley, Cornelius Keefe, Joseph Depew, Tom Blake, Joseph Burke, Jack McLean, Raphaella Ottiano.
A young attorney investigates the case of a possible robbery-abduction.

Law and the Man (Trem Carr Productions/Rayart, 1928)
d: Scott Pembroke. 6 reels.
Tom Santschi, Gladys Brockwell, Robert Ellis, Tom Ricketts, Florence Turner, James Cain, Henry Roquemore.
A formerly shady politician cleans up his act for the love of a lady.

The Law and the Woman (Famous Players-Lasky/Paramount, 1922)
d: Penrhyn Stanlaws. 7 reels.
Betty Compson, William P. Carleton, Cleo Ridgley, Casson Ferguson, Henry Barrows, Helen Dunbar, Clarence Burton, J.S. Stembridge.
Framed for murder, a man is tried and convicted on the day his first child is born. His wife, however, learns that the real killer is her husband's former mistress, and gets her to confess.

The Law Decides (Vitagraph, 1916)
d: Marguerite Bertsch, William P.S. Earle. 7 reels.
Donald Hall, Dorothy Kelly, Harry Morey, Bobby Connelly, Louise Beaudet. Adele Kelly, Bonnie Taylor.
A greedy woman tries to break up her wealthy stepson's marriage and get him to marry her own daughter.

The Law Forbids (Universal, 1924)
d: Jesse Robbins. 6 reels.
Robert Ellis, Baby Peggy Montgomery, Elinor Fair, Joseph Dowling, Winifred Bryson, James Corrigan, Anna Hernandez, Joseph Dowling, Eva Thatcher, Victor Potel, Bobby Bowes.
The parents of little Peggy separate, and each is awarded custody of the child 6 months out of each year. But Peggy knows that her parents still love each other, and schemes to get them back together.

The Law of Compensation (Norma Talmadge Film Corp./Selznick Pictures, 1917)
d: Julius Steger, Joseph A. Golden. 6 reels.
Norma Talmadge, Frederick Esmelton, Chester Barnett, John Charles, Sally Crute, Fred G. Hearn, Mary Hall, Edwin Stanley, Robert Cummings, Marie Reichardt, Harry Burkhardt.
Ruth, a young wife, wants to leave her husband and marry a songwriter. But then her dad tells her the story of his own sad experiences with infidelity and divorce, and Ruth comes to learn that there is a "law of compensation" at work.

The Law of Men (Thomas H. Ince/Paramount, 1919)
d: Fred Niblo. 5 reels.
Enid Bennett, Niles Welch, Andrew Robson, Dorcas Matthews, Donald MacDonald, Frankie Lee.
Talented but naive, a sculptress believes the man who takes her to another town with the promise of a commission for one of her sculptures.

The Law of the Great Northwest (Triangle, 1918)
d: Raymond Wells. 5 reels.
Will Jeffries, Eugene Corey, William Dyer, Louis Durham, William V. Mong, Margery Wilson, J.P. Wild, Leo Willis, Arthur Willet.
Fur traders in the Canadian northwest run afoul of a brutal gang of thieves.

The Law of the Land (Lasky Feature Plays/Paramount, 1917)
d: Maurice Tourneur. 5 reels.
Olga Petrova, Wyndham Standing, Mahlon Hamilton, J.D. Haragan, William Riley Hatch.
To save her young son from being beaten by his brutal father, the mother shoots and kills her husband. At her trial for murder, the woman's former beau testifies that he saw the man beat his son on many occasions, and the mother is acquitted.

The Law of the Lawless (Famous Players-Lasky/Paramount, 1923)
d: Victor Fleming. 7 reels.
Dorothy Dalton, Theodore Kosloff, Charles DeRoche, Tully Marshall, Fred Huntley, Margaret Loomis.
In Eastern Europe, a Tartar girl is sold at slave auction to a gypsy chief. At first the girl is furious, but in time she comes to realize she has fallen in love with her new master.

The Law of the North (Thomas A. Edison, Inc., 1917)
d: Burton George. 5 reels.
Shirley Mason, Pat O'Malley, Richard Tucker, Charles Sutton, Sally Crute, Fred Jones, Robert Keggerris.
In the Canadian northwest, a young woman has two suitors. She revels in the attention until she discovers that one of the two men is an adulterer and murderer.

The Law of the North (Thomas H. Ince/Paramount, 1918)
d: Irvin V. Willat. 5 reels.
Charles Ray, Doris Lee, Robert McKim, Gloria Hope, Charles K. French, Manuel Ojeda.
At a French Canadian trading post, Alain falls in love with Therese. But the discovery that her father is a murderer casts a dark shadow over their relationship.

The Law of the Range   (MGM, 1927)
d: William Nigh.   6 reels.
Tim McCoy, Joan Crawford, Rex Lease, Bodil Rosing, Tenen Holtz.
Out West, a Texas Ranger hunting a desperate criminal captures him, and discovers they are long-lost brothers.

The Law of the Yukon   (Mayflower Photoplay Corp./Realart Pictures, 1920)
d: Charles Miller.   6 reels.
Edward Earle, Joseph Smiley, Nancy Deaver, June Elvidge, Bigelow Cooper, Tom Velmar, Warburton Gamble, Sara Biala, Nadine Nash, Thomas O'Malley, Jack Dillon.
When a newspaperman is unjustly charged with safe-cracking and robbery, he refuses to give an alibi. That's because at the time of the robbery, he was with a certain young woman whose reputation he wants to protect.

The Law Rustlers   (Ben Wilson Productions/Arrow Film Corp., 1923)
d: Lewis King.   5 reels.
William Fairbanks, Edmund Cobb, Joseph Girard, Ena Gregory, Ashton Dearholt, Wilbur McGaugh, Claude Payton.
Two cowpokes wander into an Alaskan town with a corrupt leadership, and champion the cause of a girl trying to avenge her brother's recent murder.

The Law That Divides   (Plaza Pictures/W.W. Hodkinson Corp., 1918)
d: Howard M. Mitchell.   5 reels.
Kathleen Clifford, Kenneth Harlan, Gordon Sackville, Corinne Grant, Patrick Calhoun, Stanley Pembroke, Ruth Lackaye, Mabel Hyde.
Weepy melodrama about a couple who divorce, with each of them taking one of the children. Years later, the boy is a grown man, and he is attracted to a new girl he's just met. Yep, she's his sister.

A Law Unto Herself   (Paralta Plays, Inc./W.W. Hodkinson Corp., 1918)
d: Wallace Worsley.   5 reels.
Louise Glaum, Samuel DeGrasse, Joseph J. Dowling, Edward Coxen, Irene Rich, Elvira Weil, Roy Laidlaw, Burwell Hamerick, George Hackathorne, Peggy Schaffer, Jess Herring.
Alouette, a young French widow, is forced into marriage with a cruel but wealthy German. The years go by, Alouette's young son by her first marriage grows to maturity, and when World War I breaks out, he enlists in the French army against his stepfather's wishes.

A Law Unto Himself   (Centaur Film Co./Mutual, 1916)
d: Robert Broadwell.   5 reels.
Crane Wilbur, Louis Durham, E.W. Harris, Carl von Schiller, Francis Raymond, Steve Murphy, George Clare, Virginia Kirtley.
Out West, an outlaw that's terrorizing a small town bears a striking resemblance to the town's sheriff. Crane Wilbur does double duty as the sheriff and his lookalike.

Lawful Cheaters   (B.P. Schulberg Productions, 1925)
d: Frank O'Connor.   5 reels.
Clara Bow, David Kirby, Edward Hearn, Raymond McKee.
This one requires a real stretch. The Clara Bow character dresses in a boy's clothes and somehow makes an outlaw gang believe she's the real thing.

Lawful Larceny   (Famous Players-Lasky/Paramount, 1923)
d: Allan Dwan.   6 reels.
Hope Hampton, Conrad Nagel, Nita Naldi, Lew Cody, Russell Griffin, Yvonne Hughes, Dolores Costello, Gilda Gray, Florence O'Denishawn, Alice Maison.
A very gutsy lady disguises herself and vamps a gambler in order to retrieve from his vault a check her loser husband gave him.

The Lawless Legion   (Warner Bros., 1929)
d: Harry J. Brown.   6 reels.
Ken Maynard, Nora Lane, Richard Talmadge, Paul Hurst, J.P. McGowan, Frank Rice, Howard Truesdell.
In Texas, a cattle drover is drugged by rustlers and loses his herd. But the drover recovers, disguises himself as a cattle buyer, recovers the herd, and captures the criminals.

Lawless Love   (Fox, 1918)
d: Robert Thornby.   5 reels.
Jewel Carmen, Henry Woodward, Edward Hearn.
In old Arizona, two vaudeville dancers are abducted by a notorious bandit. Incredibly, the female half of the act falls in love with the bandit, and together they escape to a new life.

The Law's Lash   (Fred J. McConnell Productions/Pathé, 1928)
d: Noel Mason Smith.   5 reels.
Klondike the dog, Robert Ellis, Mary Mayberry, Jack Marsh, Richard r. Neill, LeRoy Mason, William Walters.
In the Canadian Northwest, a valiant dog helps a mountie bring to justice a gang of killers.

The Law's Outlaw   (Triangle, 1918)
d: Cliff Smith.   5 reels.
Roy Stewart, Fritzi Ridgeway, Harry Rattenberry, Norbert Gills, Pete Morrison, Bob Thompson, Lou Durham, William Ellingford, Alfred Hollingsworth, Percy Challenger.
Two men who opposed each other in the election for sheriff join forces to bring an outlaw gang to justice.

Lazy Lightning   (Universal, 1926)
d: William Wyler.   5 reels.
Art Acord, Fay Wray, Bobby Gordon, Vin Moore, Arthur Morrison, George K. French, Rex DeRoselli.
Out West, Lighton, a shiftless drifter known as "Lazy Lightning," springs into action to save a crippled boy from a fatal accident.

Lazybones   (Fox, 1925)
d: Frank Borzage.   8 reels.
Charles "Buck" Jones, Madge Bellamy, Virginia Mrshall, Edythe Chapman, Leslie Fenton, Jane Novak, Emily Fitzroy, ZaSu Pitts, William Norton Bailey.
In the early 1900s, a chap known as "Lazybones" adopts Kit, a little girl. World War I comes along, Lazybones enlists and serves in France, then upon his return he decides he wants to marry Kit, who has grown into a lovely young woman.

Leap to Fame   (World Film Corp., 1918)
d: Carlyle Blackwell.   5 reels.
Carlyle Blackwell, Evelyn Greeley, Muriel Ostriche, Alec B. Francis, Frank Beamish, Philip Van Loan, Lionel Belmore, William Bailey, Benny Nedell.
A judge's son makes a name for himself when he foils two German spies and recovers the formula for an important invention. Along the way, he falls in love with the inventor's daughter.

Leap Year   (Famous Players-Lasky/Paramount, 1921)

d: James Cruze. 5 reels.

Roscoe "Fatty"Arbuckle, Mary Thurman, Lucien Littlefield, Clarence Colbert, Harriet Hammond, Allen Durnell, Gertrude Short, John McKinnon, Maude Wayne, Winifred Greenwood.

Historically significant picture, only because this was the last feature film comedy starring the disgraced Arbuckle. Though an American production, *Leap Year* was never released in the United States. It is also known as *Skirt Shy*.

The Learnin' of Jim Benton (Triangle, 1917)
d: Cliff Smith. 5 reels.

Roy Stewart, Fritzie Ridgeway, Walter Perry, Edward Brady, Thornton Edwards, William Ellingford, John P. Wild, Harry Rattenberry.

Out West, a rancher hires a schoolteacher to teach him readin' and writin'.

Learning to Love (First National, 1925)
d: Sidney A. Franklin. 7 reels.

Constance Talmadge, Antonio Moreno, Emily Fitzroy, Edythe Chapman, Johnny Harron, Ray Hallor, Wallace MacDonald, Alf Goulding, Byron Munson, Edgar Norton.

Miss Talmadge kicks up her heels as Patricia, a flirt who gets engaged to four men at the same time, then leaves them all. Her stern guardian, Warner, warns the little coquette that he will force her to marry the next man she gets romantically involved with... unaware that it will be *him!*

The Leatherneck (Ralph Block Productions/Pathé, 1929)
d: Howard Higgin. 8 reels. (Part talkie.)

Alan Hale, William Boyd, Robert Armstrong, Fred Kohler, Diane Ellis, James Aldine, Paul Weigel, Jules Cowles, Wade Boteler, Jack Richardson, Joseph Girard, Lee Shumway.

A U.S. Marine stationed in China goes AWOL to rescue his Russian bride, Tanya, from whom he was separated during the revolution in her country.

Leave it to Gerry (Ben Wilson Productions/Grand-Asher Distributing Corp., 1924)
d: Arvid E. Gillstrom. 6 reels.

Billie Rhodes, William Collier Jr., Claire McDowell, kate Lester, Kathleen Kirkham, Joseph W. Girard, Alla Cavan.

Geraldine, a young hoyden, comes to the rescue when her mother is driven off her property by the mortgage holder. It seems the gentleman has discovered the lady's land is rich in oil, and he wants all of it.

Leave It to Me (Fox, 1920)
d: Emmett J. Flynn. 5 reels.

William Russell, Eileen Percy, Marcella Daley, Hal Cooley, Lucille Cavanaugh, William Elmer, Harvey Clark, Milla Davenport.

When an idle playboy angers his fiancée by refusing to work, he decides to buy a detective agency to prove to her his usefulness.

Leave It to Susan (Goldwyn, 1919)
d: Clarence G. Badger. 5 reels.

Madge Kennedy, Wallace MacDonald, Alfred Hollingsworth, Anna Hernandez, Walter Hiers, George Kunkel, Bill Patton, William McPherson, Tuck Reynolds, Walter Cameron.

Comedy western about a rich girl who meets a young man she thinks is a crook. He's actually an engineer, but to play along with her fantasies, he starts acting like a crook.

The Leavenworth Case (Whitman Bennett Productions/Vitagraph, 1923)

d: Charles Giblyn. 6 reels.

Seena Owen, Martha Mansfield, Wilfred Lytell, Bradley Barker, Paul Doucet, William Walcott, Frances Miller Grant, Fred Miller.

An heiress is suspected of murdering her wealthy uncle.

Legally Dead (Universal, 1923)
d: William Parke. 6 reels.

Milton Sills, Claire Adams, Margaret Campbell, Edwin Sturges, Fay O'Neill, Charles A. Stevenson, Joseph W. Girard, Albert Prisco, Herbert Fortier, Brandon Hurst, Charles Wellesley.

Will, a crusading news reporter, tries to get evidence that most prisoners condemned to death are actually innocent. He gets himself arrested, is wrongly found guilty of murder, and is sentenced to be hanged. After the execution, Will is declared legally dead just as evidence of his innocence is brought to light. A sad ending? Not really. The hangman was too hasty in his judgment, and Will is revived by smelling salts... alive and free to write his news article from an insider's point of view.

The Legend of Hollywood (Charles R. Rogers Productions, 1924)
d: Renaud Hoffman. 6 reels.

Percy Marmont, ZaSu Pitts, Alice Davenport, Dorothy Dorr.

Smith, a struggling screenwriter eager to sell his scenario but lacking confidence in himself, goes to absurd lengths to insulate himself against failure.

The Legion of Death (Metro, 1918)
d: Tod Browning. 7 reels.

Edith Storey, Philo McCullough, Fred Malatesta, Charles Gerard, Pomeroy Cannon, Norma Nichols, R.O. Pennell, Grace Aide, H.L. Swisher, Francis Marion, Harry Moody.

Princess Marya of Russia organizes the peasant women into a fighting unit, "the Legion of Death."

Legion of the Condemned (Paramount, 1928)
d: William A. Wellman. 8 reels.

Fay Wray, Gary Cooper, Barry Norton, Lane Chandler, Francis MacDonald, Albert Conti, Charlotte Bird, Voya George, Freeman Wood, E.H. Calvert, Toto Guette.

A daredevil squadron of World War I pilots, patterned after the storied Lafayette Escadrille, serves as background for the love story of an American warrior and a female spy.

Lena Rivers (Chord Pictures/Arrow Pictures, 1925)
d: Whitman Bennett. 9 reels.

Earle Williams, Johnny Walker, Gladys Hulette, Edna Murphy, Marcia harris, Doris Rankin, Irma Harrison, Frank Sheridan, Herman Lieb, Harlan Knight, William T. Hayes, Frank Andrews.

Lena falls in love with Henry Rivers and they marry. But his wealthy father, disapproving of the match, has his son kidnapped and shanghaied on a steamship. Lena, now alone, dies in childbirth; but her little daughter, also called Lena, is taken in by her mother's uncle John.

Lend Me Your Husband (C.C. Burr Pictures, 1924)
d: William Christy Cabanne. 6 reels.

Doris Kenyon, David Powell, Dolores Cassinelli, J. Barney sherry, Violet Mersereau, Burr McIntosh, Connie Keefe, Coit Albertson, Helen D'Algy.

Henry, a bounder, has an affair with the gardener's daughter and nearly drives her to suicide.

Lend Me Your Name (Yorke Film Corp./Metro, 1918)
d: Fred J. Balshofer. 5 reels.

Harold Lockwood, Pauline Curley, Bessie Eyton, Bert Starkey, Stanton Heck, Peggy Prevost, Harry DeRoy.
Lookalike brothers trade identities to confound the shrewish wife of one of them.

The Leopard Lady (DeMille Pictures/Pathé, 1928)
d: Rupert Julian. 7 reels.
Jacqueline Logan, Alan Hale, Robert Armstrong, Hedwig Reicher, James Bradbury Sr., Dick Alexander, William Burt, Sylvia Ashton, Kay Deslys, Willie May Carson.
Paula, a circus performer, tames wild cats and is known as "The Leopard Lady."

The Leopard Woman (J. Parker Read Jr. Productions, 1920)
d: Wesley Ruggles. 7 reels.
Louise Glaum, House Peters, Noble Johnson.
"The Leopard Woman" is a foreign secret agent, out to derail British efforts in Africa.

The Leopardess (Famous Players-Lasky/Paramount, 1923)
d: Henry Kolker. 6 reels.
Alice Brady, Edward Langford, Montau Love, Charles Kent, George André Beranger, Marguerite Forrest, Glorie Eller.
An acrimonious soldier of fortune finds a half-breed girl on a South Sea island, and they marry. He takes her aboard his ship bound for New York, but he mistreats her and subjects her to the same physical whippings he regularly gives his pet leopard. Eventually the leopard will break out of its cage and devour its master, leaving the native girl free to love the ship's captain.

Les Miserables (Fox, 1918)
d: Frank Lloyd. 9 reels.
William Farnum, George Moss, Hardee Kirkland, Sonia Markova, Kittens Reichert, Jewel Carmen, Harry Spingler, Dorothy Bernard, anthony Phillips, Edward Elkas, Mina Ross.
The first feature film version of the Victor Hugo classic novel, with Farnum as Jean Valjean and Hardee Kirkland as the obsessed Javert.

Less Than Kin (Famous Players-Lasky/Paramount, 1918)
d: Donald Crisp. 5 reels.
Wallace Reid, Ann Little, Raymond Hatton, Noah Beery, James Neill, Charles Ogle, Jane Wolff, James Cruze, Guy Oliver, Calvert Carter, Gustav Seyffertitz.
A fugitive from justice decides to trade identities with a wealthy man who's just died.

Less Than the Dust (Mary Pickford Film Corp./Artcraft, 1916)
d: John Emerson. 7 reels.
Mary Pickford, David Powell, Frank Losee, Mary Alden, Mario Majeroni, Cesare Gravina, Francis Joyner, Russell Bassett, Walter Morgan, Mercita Esmonde, Nathaniel Sack.
Our Mary plays a half-caste Hindu woman whose father was British.

The Lesson (Select Pictures Corp., 1918)
d: Charles Giblyn. 5 reels.
Constance Talmadge, Tom Moore, Walter Hiers, Herbert Heyes, Joseph Smiley, Lillian Rambeau, Dorothy Green, Christy Walker.
When a small-town girl grows tired of the languid pace of her home town, she falls for a New York architect and goes with him to the big city. After several unpleasant adventures, she forsakes Gotham and returns to her roots, and to her small-town boyfriend.

Lessons in Love (Constance Talmadge Productions/Associated First National, 1921)
d: Chet Withey. 6 reels.
Constance Talmadge, Flora Finch, James Harrison, George Fawcett, Frank Webster, Kenneth Harlan, Florence Short.
Older relatives plan to marry off nephew Henry to Leila, a young heiress. The young man refuses, choosing instead to select his own wife. Leila is stung by the rejection and resolves to get even. She disguises herself as a maid, goes to work in Henry's home, and makes him fall in love with her.

Let 'er Buck (Universal, 1925)
d: Edward Sedgwick. 6 reels.
Hoot Gibson, Marion Nixon, Charles K. French, G. Raymond Nye, William A. Steele, Jose Sedgwick, Fred Humes.
Bob, a rodeo rider, falls for Jacqueline, the ranch owner's daughter. But their romance is opposed by several individuals, both male and female.

Let 'er Go Gallagher (Pathé/De Mille, 1928)
d: Elmer Clifton. 6 reels.
Harrison Ford, Frank "Junior" Coghlan, Elinor Fair, Wade Boteler, E.H. Calvert, Ivan Lebedeff.
Callahan, a news reporter, gets tips from a youngster, Gallagher.

Let it Rain (Paramount, 1927)
d: Eddie Cline. 7 reels.
Douglas MacLean, Boris Karloff, Wade Boteler, Shirley Masion, Frank Campeau, James Bradbury Jr., Lincoln Stedman, Lee Shumway, James Mason, Edwin Sturgis, Ernest Hilliard.
A marine sergeant teams up with sailors to foil a mail robbery.

Let Katie Do It (Fine Arts Film Co./Triangle, 1916)
d: C.M. Franklin, S.A. Franklin. 5 reels.
Jane Grey, Tully Marshall, Charles West, Ralph Lewis, Walter Long, Charles Gorman, George Pearce, Violet Radcliffe, George Stone, Carmen de Rue, Francis Carpenter, Lloyd Pearl.
Katie becomes a surrogate mother to her seven nieces and nephews, when their parents die in a train accident.

Let Women Alone (Peninsula Studios/Producers Distributing Corp., 1925)
d: Paul Powell. 6 reels.
Pat O'Malley, Wanda Hawley, Wallace Beery, Ethel Wales, J. Farrell MacDonald, Harris Gordon, Betty Jane Snowdon, Lee Willard, Marjorie Morton.
Her husband reported lost at sea, a young woman supports herself and her daughter by working as an interior decorator. She falls in love again, but then her husband shows up alive.

Let's Be Fashionable (T.H. Ince/Famous Players-Lasky/Paramount, 1920)
d: Lloyd Ingraham. 5 reels.
Douglas MacLean, Doris May, Wade Boteler, Grace Morse, George Webb, Wilbur Higby, Molly McConnell, Norris Johnson.
Innocent flirtations—the "fashionable" kind—imperil the marriage on a newlywed couple.

Let's Elope (Famous Players-Lasky/Paramount, 1919)
d: John S. Robertson. 5 reels.
Marguerite Clark, Frank Mills, Gaston Glass, Helen Green, Blanche Standing, George Stevens, Albert Busby.
A newlywed feeling neglected by her husband turns to a

friend, who asks her to elope with him.

Let's Get a Divorce (Famous Players-Lasky/Paramount, 1918)
d: Charles Giblyn. 5 reels.
Billie Burke, John Miltern, Pinna Nesbit, Armand Kaliz, Rod La Rocque, Helen Tracy, Wilmuth Merkyl, Cesare Gravina.
A bored convent girl dreams romantic fantasies, so she's all for it when her sweetheart suggests they elope. But after the honeymoon, the bride gets bored again and turns her attention to her new husband's cousin, who is out to do some serious flirting.

Let's Get Married (Paramount, 1926)
d: Gregory LaCava. 7 reels.
Richard Dix, Lois Wilson, Nat Pendleton, Douglas MacPherson, Gunboat Smith, Joseph Kilgour, Tom Findley, Edna May Oliver.
Comedy about college boy Dexter, who is arrested for disturbing the peace after a football game. He promises he will reform his raucous ways; but to make certain, his father sends him to a missionary who sells hymnals by mail order. The "missionary" turns out to be an alcoholic female, who persuades Dexter to accompany her to a cabaret. There, Dexter is arrested again. In the end, the chastened college boy returns to his girlfriend and vows to stay away from cabarets and missionaries.

Let's Go (Richard Talmadge Productions/Truart Film Corp., 1923)
d: William K. Howard. 6 reels.
Richard Talmadge, Eileen Percy, George Nichols, Tully Marshall, Bruce Gordon, Al Fremont, Matthew Betz, Louis King, Aggie Herring, John Steppling.
Barry, son of a cement manufacturer, foils a plot to steal funds set aside for a new paving contract.

Let's Go Gallagher (R-C Pictures/FBO of America, 1925)
d: Robert DeLacey, James Gruen. 5 reels.
Tom Tyler, Barbara Starr, Olin Francis, Sam Peterson, Alfred Heuston, Frankie Darro.
Out West, a cowpoke foils mail thieves.

Lew Tyler's Wives (Preferred Pictures, 1926)
d: Harley Knoles. 7 reels.
Frank Mayo, Ruth Clifford, Hedda Hopper, Helen Lee Worthing, Lew Brice, Robert T. Haines, Warren Cook.
Lew, having failed at marriage, tries to drown his sorrows in drink. He is rescued by the father of his former sweetheart, who brings Lew together with his daughter and gives them a chance to start life anew.

Li Ting Lang (Haworth Pictures/Robertson-Cole, 1920)
d: Charles Swickard. 5 reels.
Sessue Hayakawa, Allan Forrest, Charles E. Mason, Doris Pawn, Frances Raymond, Marc Robbins.
Racial prejudice strikes when a white American girl is ostracized because of her relationship with a Chinese college student.

The Liar (Fox, 1918)
d: Edmund Lawrence. 5 reels.
Virginia Pearson, Alexander Frank, Edward F. Roseman, Victor Sutherland, Eugene Borden, Albert Roccardi, Liane Held Carrera, Myra Brooke, Matilda Brundage.
When the woman he loves marries another man, an ardent swain decides to make trouble for her.

The Libertine (Triumph Film Corp./State Rights, 1916)
d: Julius Steger, Joseph A. Golden. 6 reels.
John Mason, Alma Hanlon, Marie Alexander, Walter Hitchcock, Edward Langford, Jean Stuart, Doris Sawyer.
Just before she is to be married, Elsie meets a man who embodies lust and lasciviousness, and falls for him. She breaks her engagement and follows her new Svengali into the depths of profligacy until—well, until she wakes up and realizes she's been having a bad dream.

The Lie (Famous Players-Lasky/Artcraft, 1918)
d: J. Searle Dawley. 5 reels.
Elsie Ferguson, David Powell, John L. Shine, Percy Marmont, Charles Sutton, Bertha Kent, Maude Turner Gordon, Betty Howe.
After Elinor helps her sister Lucy through her pregnancy with an illegitimate child, the faithless Lucy then tells her sister's fiancé that it was Elinor, not she, who had the baby.

Lieutenant Danny, U.S.A. (New York Motion Picture Corp./Triangle, 1916)
d: Walter Edwards. 5 reels.
William Desmond, Enid Markey, Gertrude Claire, Thornton Edwards, Robert Kortman.
A new West Point graduate sees action on the U.S.-Mexico border, and falls in love with a Mexican maiden.

Life (William A. Brady/Famous Players-Lasky, 1920)
d: Travers Vale. 5 reels.
Nita Naldi, Herbert Druce, Jack Mower, J.H. Gilmour, Arline Pretty, Leeward Meeker, Rod La Rocque, Edwin Stanley, Curtis Cooksey, Geoffrey Stein, Effingham Pinto.
When a banker is murdered, the culprits contrive to cast the blame on an innocent clerk.

The Life and Death of Lieutenant Petrosino —see: The Adventures of Lieutenant Petrosino

The Life Line (Maurice Tourneur Productions, Inc./Paramount, 1919)
d: Maurice Tourneur. 6 reels.
Jack Holt, Seena Owen, Wallace Beery, Pauline Stark, Tully Marshall, Lewis J. Cody.
A devil-may-care adventurer lives with the gypsies rather than among the social set his family belongs to. But all that changes when he meets Ruth, and falls in love.

The Life Mask (Petrova Picture Co./First National, 1918)
d: Frank Crane. 6 reels.
Olga Petrova, Thomas Holding, Wyndham Standing, Christine Mayo, Lucille LaVerne, Matilda Brundage, Edward J. Burns, Edith Hinckle, Gene Burnell.
To save her mother from scandal, a girl marries a millionaire she doesn't love.

The Life of an Actress (Chadwick Pictures, 1927)
d: Jack Nelson. 7 reels.
Barbara Bedford, Bert Sprotte, Lydia Knott, John Patrick, Sheldon Lewis, James Marcus, John Hyams, Bobby Nelson, Mary Foy.
Make that a would-be actress. Nora tries hard, but she never makes it as a principal player, and winds up marrying her former boyfriend and settling down.

The Life of Moses (Vitagraph, 1910)
d: J. Stuart Blackton. 5 reels.
Ambitious depiction of the Old Testament story of Moses, including the parting of the Red Sea and the delivery of the Ten Commandments.
The Life of Moses was released in 1909 as a five-part serial,

with the reels being shown in theaters in successive weeks. By 1910, however, exhibitors were screening it as a feature-length film comprising all five parts. In effect, this coalescing of the chapters made *The Life of Moses* the first American feature film.

It was also one of the first films to alternate closeups with distance shots within the same scene. It may surprise modern moviegoers to learn that this technique, so essential to the integrity of today's photoplays, was protested vigorously by some movie critics, who apparently found it distracting. The reviewer in Motion Picture World in July 1909 wrote:

"Now, here there is a total lack of uniformity, due entirely to a want of intelligence on the part of the producer and the photographer, and the effect on the minds of the people who saw this picture was extreme dissatisfaction."

The Life of Riley   (First National, 1927)
d: William Beaudine.   7 reels.
Charlie Murray, George Sidney, Stephen Carr, June Marlowe, Myrtle Stedman, Sam Hardy, Bert Woodruff, Edwards Davis.
Riley's a fireman, and he and his friend Meyer, the chief of police, are both enamored of Penelope, a charming widow.

The Life of the Party   (Famous Players-Lasky/Paramount, 1920)
d: Joseph Henabery.   5 reels.
Roscoe "Fatty" Arbuckle, Viola Daniel, Winifred Greenwood, Roscoe Karns, Julia Faye, Frank Campeau, Allen Connor, Frederick Starr, Ben Lewis, Viora Daniel.
Deeply infatuated with a pretty secretary, a heavy-set attorney (Arbuckle) argues her case in court *pro bono*, although he hasn't a penny to his name.

Life or Honor?   (Ivan Film Productions, Inc./State Rights, 1918)
d: Edmund Lawrence.   7 reels.
Leah Baird, James Morrison, Violet Palmer, Harry Burkhardt, Edward MacKay, Ben Hendricks, Mathilda Brundage, Joseph Burke, Florence Sottong.
Although an innocent man has been convicted of murder, a witness who saw the killing refuses to come forward for fear of compromising the woman in whose room he was staying.

Life's a Funny Proposition   (Jesse D. Hampton Productions/Robertson-Cole, 1919)
d: Thomas N. Heffron.   5 reels.
William Desmond, Jay Belasco, Vera Doria, Louise Lovely, John Steppling, Lillie Sylvester, Joseph Franz, John McGregor, Ernest Marion.
Humor abounds when, after a penniless young lawyer falls for his friend's sister, his rich uncle offers him a small fortune if he will marry his fat cousin. Then somebody leaves a baby on the lawyer's doorstep, and he tries desperately to hide its cries from both his sweetie and her mother, for fear they'll think it's his.

Life's Blind Alley   (American Film Co./Mutual, 1916)
d: Thomas Ricketts.   5 reels.
Harold Lockwood, May Allison, Nell Franzen, Robert Klein, Perry Banks, Warren Ellsworth, William Tedmarsh, Carl Morrison, Pete Morrison.
Walt and Helen are in love with each other, but each is in a loveless marriage to someone else. When their spouses fall into quicksand, Walt and Helen see their chance to let them die and be free to marry. But would it be right?

Life's Darn Funny   (Metro, 1921)
d: Dallas M. Fitzgerald.   6 reels.
Viola Dana, Gareth Hughes, Eva Gordon, Kathleen O'Connor, Mark Fenton.
Zoe, by profession a violinist, and Clay, an artist, enter into a dress-designing business.

Life's Greatest Game   (Emory Johnson Productions/FBO of America, 1924)
d: Emory Johnson.   7 reels.
Tom Santschi, Jane Thomas, Dicky Brandon, Johnnie Walker, David Kirby, Gertrude Olmstead.
Donovan, manager of the New York Giants, hires a young player, not realizing it's his own son, lost to him since childhood.

Life's Mockery   (Chadwick Pictures, 1928)
d: Robert F. Hill   7 reels.
Betty Compson, Alec B. Francis, Russell Simpson, Theodore von Eltz, Dorothy Cumming.
Fullerton, a former prison warden, believes that changes in environment can reform criminals, and he obtains permission to experiment on one of them.
Life's Mockery is also known as *Reform*.

Life's Shadows   (Columbia/Metro, 1916)
d: William Nigh.   5 reels.
William Nigh, Irene Howley, Will Stevens, Robert Elliott, Roy Clair, Kathleen Allaire, Ruth Thorp, Grace E. Stevens, William Yerance, Frank Montgomery, David Thompson.
The town of Purity has a devoted servant in Martin. Trouble is, he's a drunk.

Life's Shop Window   (Box Office Attraction Co./Fox, 1914)
d: J. Gordon Edwards.   5 reels.
Claire Whitney, Stuart Holmes.
In Arizona, new immigrants cope with their ranch, their new baby, and the wife's new attraction to a would-be seducer.

Life's Twist   (B.B. Features/Robertson-Cole, 1920)
d: William Christy Cabanne.   6 reels.
Bessie Barriscale, Walter McGrail, King Baggot, Claire Dubrey, George Periolat, Truly Shattuck, William V. Mong, Marcia Manon.
When a man marries a beautiful woman only for her money, she discovers this on their wedding night and moves out on her own. Now alone, the new husband sees a slum girl who bears a striking resemblance to his wife, and decides to remake her in his wife's image.
Miss Barriscale, who seemed to relish doing double duty in her films, plays the roles of both the wife and her slum lookalike. She previously had played twins in Triangle's *The Snarl* (1917), and another double role in *A Trick of Fate* (B.B. Features, 1919).

Life's Whirlpool   (World Film Corp., 1916)
d: Barry O'Neil.   5 reels.
Holbrook Blinn, Walter Green, Phil Robson, Fania Marinoff, Julia Stuart, Rosemary Dean, Eleanore Blanchard.
After his wife wins $5,000 in a lottery, a dentist learns that she is consumed by greed.
This film and the 1925 Erich von Stroheim drama *Greed* are based on the novel *McTeague* by Frank Norris.

Life's Whirlpool   (Metro, 1917)
d: Lionel Barrymore.   5 reels.
Ethel Barrymore, Paul Everton, Alan Hale, Reginald Carrington, Ricca Allen, Frank Leigh, Walter Hiers, Harvey Bogart.

A long-suffering woman spends her youth caring for her father, and after his death marries a cold-hearted man who offers her shelter but not much else.

The Lifted Veil (Metro, 1917)
d: George D. Baker. 5 reels.
Ethel Barrymore, Frank Gilmore, William B. Davidson, Robert Ellis, Ilean Hume, Maude Hill, Ricca Allen, Myra Brooke, George Stevenson.
Guilt over an affair with a married man drives a woman to hiding behind veils and doing charity work.

Lifting Shadows (Pathé, 1920)
d: Leonce Perret. 6 reels.
Emmy Wehlen, Stuart Holmes, Wyndham Standing, Julia Swayne Gordon.
The daughter of a Russian revolutionary escapes to America.

The Light (Fox, 1919)
d: J. Gordon Edwards. 5 reels.
Theda Bara, Eugene Ormonde, Robert Walker, George Revenant, Florence Martin.
After a sculptor is blinded in the war, the woman he loved agrees to pose for him while he sculpts her figure by touch.

Light in Darkness (Thomas A. Edison, Inc., 1917)
d: Alan Crosland. 5 reels.
Shirley Mason, Frank Morgan, William H. Tooker, J. Frank Glendon, George Trimble, Bigelow Cooper, William Wadsworth, Sam Niblack, Charles Martin.
Two prison parolees, a man and a woman, fall in love and get married.

The Light in the Clearing (Dial Film Co./W.W. Hodkinson, 1921)
d: T. Hayes Hunter. 7 reels.
Eugenie Besserer, Clara Horton, Edward Sutherland, George Hackathorne, Frank Leigh, Andrew Arbuckle, Arthur Morrison, Alberta Lee, Jack Roseleigh, Virginia Madison, J. Edwin Brown.
An orphan boy encounters a seeress who foretells a successful future for him.

The Light in the Dark — see: The Light of Faith (1922)

A Light in the Window (Trem Carr Productions/Rayart, 1927)
d: Scott Pembroke. 6 reels.
Henry B. Walthall, Patricia Avery, Erin LaBissoniere, Henry Sedley, Tom O'Grady, Cornelius Keefe.
Dorothy, sheltered daughter of a loving but stern father, yearns to break free and live life to the fullest. She gets her chance, but it doesn't bring the happiness she expected.

The Light of Faith (Hope Hampton Productions/Associated First National, 1922)
d: Clarence L. Brown. 7 reels.
Lon Chaney, Hope Hampton, E.K. Lincoln, Theresa Maxwell Conover, Dorothy Walters, Charles Mussett, Edgar Norton, Dore Davidson.
A goblet purportedly has the properties of the Holy Grail.
Also known as *The Light in the Dark*.

The Light of Happiness (Columbia/Metro, 1916)
d: John H. Collins. 5 reels.
Viola Dana, George Melville, Lorraine Frost, Harry Linsen, Edward Earle, Jack Busby, Mona Kingsley, Robert Walker, Charles Boone.
The daughter of the town drunk is persuaded to impersonate a wealthy young man's fiancée.

Light of Victory (Universal, 1919)
d: William Wolbert. 5 reels.
Monroe Salisbury, Betty Compson, Fred Kelsey, Bob Edmond, Andrew Robson, Fred Wilson, Norval MacGregor, Beatrice Dominguez, George Nichols.
Disgraced by his uncontrolled alcoholism, a U.S. Navy lieutenant is court-martialed and put ashore on a desert island. But he'll recover in time to aid the war effort.

The Light of Western Stars (United Pictures, 1918)
d: Charles Swickard. 7 reels.
Dustin Farnum, Winifred Kingston, Bert Appling, Joseph Swickard, Virginia Eames, Charles Rogers, Jeanne Maddock, George Fields, Frank Clark, Eddie Hearne, Ogden Crane.
Out West, a drunken cowpoke meets a girl for the first time, and forces the local padre to marry them. As it turns out, the girl is the sister of the cowboy's boss! But that isn't the worst of his problems, for soon he'll be facing a firing squad in Mexico.
Re-made by Famous Players-Lasky in 1925.

The Light of Western Stars (Famous Players-Lasky/Paramount, 1925)
d: William K. Howard. 7 reels.
Jack Holt, Billie Dove, Noah Beery, Alma Bennett, William Scott, George Nichols, Mark Hamilton, Robert Perry, Eugene Pallette.
Remake, with some plot variances, of the 1918 United Pictures film *The Light of Western Stars*, both versions based on the Zane Grey novel of the same name.

The Light That Failed (Famous Players-Lasky/Paramount, 1923)
d: George Melford. 7 reels.
Jacqueline Logan, Percy Marmont, David Torrence, Sigrid Holmquist, Mabel Van Buren, Luke Cosgrave, Peggy Schaffer, Winston Miller, Mary Jane Irving.
Heldar, a famous painter, persuades a young woman of the streets to pose for his greatest—and last --masterpiece, since he is going blind.

The Light Within (Petrova Picture Co./First National, 1918)
d: Larry Trimble. 6 reels.
Olga Petrova, Lumsden Hare, Thomas Holding, Clarence Heritage, Freddie Verdi, Evelyn Dumo, Fred C. Jones, Frank McDonald, Matilda Brundage.
Though she loves another, a lab researcher marries a wealthy man in order to finance her experiments.

A Light Woman (American Film Co./Pathé, 1920)
d: George L. Cox. 6 reels.
Helen Jerome Eddy, Hallam Cooley, Claire DuBrey, Charles Clary, Guy Milham, Frances Raymond, Nancy Chase.
Enamored of a gold digger, a young man soon discovers her shallowness.

The Lighthouse by the Sea (Warner Bros., 1925)
d: Mal St. Clair. 7 reels.
Rin-Tin-Tin, Louise Fazenda, William Collier Jr., Charles Hill Mailes, Douglas Gerrard, Matthew Betz.
A seafarer and his dog are shipwrecked near a lighthouse and find, respectively, romance and shelter with the lighthouse-keeper's daughter.

Lightnin' (Fox, 1925)
d: John Ford. 8 reels.
Jay Hunt, Madge Bellamy, Wallace MacDonald, J. Farrell MacDonald, Ethel Clayton, James Marcus, Edythe Chapman,

276

Otis harlan, Brandon Hurst, Richard Travers, Peter Mazutis.
Comedy about "Lightnin' Bill," an amiable drunk, who strangely is the only obstacle to a group of real estate swindlers trying to obtain the soon-to-be valuable land of a local lady and her stepdaughter.

Lightnin' Shot (Trem Carr Productions/Rayart, 1928)
d: J.P. McGowan. 5 reels.
Buddy Roosevelt, J.P. McGowan, Frank Earle, Carol Lane, Jimmy Kane, Tommy Bay.
Out West, a pair of ranchers are feudin' over ownership of a strip of land, while the son of one rancher and the daughter of the other are falling in love.

Lightning (Tiffany Productions, 1927)
d: James C. McKay. 7 reels.
Jobyna Ralston, Margaret Livingston, Robert Frazier, Guinn Williams, Pat Harmon.
"Lightning" is a wild stallion who consistently evades capture... until he's lured by the pet mare of one of the wranglers chasing him.

Lightning Bill (Goodwill Pictures, 1926)
d: Louis Chaudet. 5 reels.
Bill Bailey, Jean Arthur, Edward Heim, Jack Henderson, Charles Meakin, Tom Shirley.
Out West, an intrepid rancher loses his nerve after a near-fatal fall from a cliff. But when land swindlers try to steal his oil-rich property, the rancher recovers his nerve quickly, and routs the chiselers from his land.

Lightning Lariats (R-C Pictures/FBO of America, 1927)
d: Robert DeLacey. 5 reels.
Tom Tyler, Dorothy Dunbar, Frankie Darro, Ruby Blaine, Fred Holmes, Ervin Renard, Carl Silvera, Leroy Scott.
Exiled Europeans find refuge in America's wild west.

The Lightning Rider (Stellar Productions/W.W. Hodkinson, 1924)
d: Lloyd Ingraham. 6 reels.
Harry Carey, Virginia Brown Faire, Thomas G. Lingham, Frances Ross, Leon Barry, Bert Hadley, Madame Sul-Te-Wan.
A western town is menaced by a masked bandit.

The Lights of New York (Vitagraph, 1916)
d: Van Dyke Brooke. 5 reels.
Leah Baird, Walter McGrail, Arthur Cozine, Adele DeGarde, Leila Blow, Agnes Wadleigh, Don Cameron, Edwina Robbins, John Costello.
There's a new gent in the social swirl, but look out—he's a murderer.

The Lights of New York (Fox, 1922)
d: Charles J. Brabin. 6 reels.
Marc MacDermott, Margaret Seddon, Estelle Taylor, Frank Currier, Florence Short, Charles Gerard.
In New York, a financier is stunned when he learns that his fiancée has left him for another man. Near despair, he is rescued when friends invite him to a bachelor party and he discovers that the host is the son of his former lady love. The financier and his lady are reunited.

Lights of Old Broadway (MGM, 1925)
d: Monta Bell. 7 reels.
Marion Davies, Conrad Nagel, Frank Currier, George K. Arthur, Julia Swayne Gordon, Matthew Betz, Charles McHugh, Eleanor Lawson, Wilbur Higbee, George Bunny.
Twin orphan girls are adopted; one by a wealthy family, one by a poor one. By coincidence, the scion of the wealthy family meets and falls for the poor sister.
Miss Davies does double duty here, as both orphan twins.

Lights of the Desert (Fox, 1922)
d: Harry Beaumont. 5 reels.
Shirley Mason, Allan Forrest, Edward Burns, James Mason, Andrée Tourneur, Josephine Crowell, Lillian Langdon.
Yvonne, stranded with her theatrical troupe in a remote Nevada city, elects to stay after her coworkers have moved on.

Lights Out (R-C Pictures/FBO of America, 1923)
d: Al Santell. 7 reels.
Ruth Stonehouse, Walter McGrail, Marie Astaire, Theodore von Eltz, Ben Deely, Hank Mann, Ben Hewlett, Mabel Van Buren, Fred Kelsey, Harry Fenwick, Chester Bishop.

When a mobster sees a movie and recognizes his own character on the screen, he decides to go to the movie studio and confront the scenarist.

Like Wildfire (Universal, 1917)
d: Stuart Paton. 5 reels.
Herbert Rawlinson, Neva Gerber, Johnnie Cook, Howard Crampton, L.M. Wells, Burton Law, Willard Wayne.
Disowned by his disgusted father, a dime store heir finds a way to set up shop on his own—and provide competition for Dad's business.

Lilac Time (First National, 1928)
d: George Fitzmaurice. 11 reels. (Synchronized music and sound effects.)
Colleen Moore, Gary Cooper, Burr McIntosh, George Cooper, Cleve Moore, Kathryn McGuire, Eugenie Besserer, Emile Chautard, Jack Stone, Edward Dillon, Dick Grace, Stuart Knox, Harlan Hilton, Richard Jarvis, Jack Ponder, Dan Dowling.
Romance blossoms between a British Air Force captain and a French girl during the first World War.

Lilies of the Field (Corinne Griffith Productions/First National, 1924)
d: John Francis Dillon. 8 reels.
Corinne Griffith, Conway Tearle, Alma Bennett, Myrtle Stedman, Crauford Kent, Sylvia Breamer, Charlie Murray, Phyllis Haver, Cissy Fitzgerald, Edith Ransom, Charles Gerrard, Dorothy Brock, Mattie Peters, Anna May Wong.
Mildred, who has been divorced by her husband and deprived of her child, must work as a model to make ends meet. She then meets Louis, a wealthy roué, and rejects his advances but accepts his help in regaining custody of her child.

Lilies of the Streets (Belban Productions/FBO of America, 1925)
d: Joseph Levering. 7 reels.
Virginia Lee Corbin, Wheeler Oakman, Peggy Kelly, Johnnie Walker, Irma harrison, Mary E. Hamilton, Elizabeth J. Monroe.
Judith, a fun-loving flapper, is mistakenly arrested and charged as a prostitute.

The Lily (Fox, 1926)
d: Victor Schertzinger. 7 reels.
Belle Bennett, Ian Keith, Reata Hoyt, Barry Norton, John St. Polis, Richard Tucker, Gertrude Short, James Marcus, Lydia Yeamans Titus, Thomas Ricketts, Vera Lewis, Carmelita Geraghty, Rosa Rudami.

In France, a nobleman nearly ruins the future happiness of his two daughters by his selfish behavior.

The Lily and the Rose (Triangle, 1915)
d: Paul Powell. 5 reels.
Lillian Gish, Rozsika Dolly, Wilfred Lucas, Mary Alden, Elmer Clifton, Loyola O'Connor, William Hinckley, Cora Drew.
After a young woman loses her husband to a vamp, she turns to her former sweetheart.

Lily of the Desert (Famous Players-Lasky/Paramount, 1924)
d: Dimitri Buchowetzki. 7 reels.
Ben Lyon, Pola Negri, Noah Beery, Raymond Griffith, William J. Kelly, Jeanette Daudet.
Lily, a bookseller, falls for an army officer but is swept off her feet by his superior and marries him. The loveless marriage does not last long, however, and Lily is soon in the arms of another.

The Limited Mail (Warner Bros., 1925)
d: George Hill. 7 reels.
Monte Blue, Tom Gallery, Vera Reynolds, Willard Louis, Jack Huff.
In the Old West, a railroad engineer becomes a hobo after his best friend dies in a train accident. But he regains his self-esteem when called on to prevent another train wreck.

Limousine Life (Triangle, 1918)
d: Jack Dillon. 5 reels.
Olive Thomas, Lee Phelps, Joe Bennett, Lillian West, Virginia Foltz, Alberta Lee, Lottie Du Vaulle, Lillian Langdon, Harry Rattenberry, Jules Friquet.
While in Chicago, a small town girl charms and captures the heart of a wealthy playboy.

The Lincoln Highwayman (Fox, 1919)
d: Emmett J. Flynn. 5 reels.
William Russell, Lois Lee, Frank Brownlee, Jack Connolly, Edward Piel, Harry Springler, Edwin Booth Tilton.
He isn't Robin Hood or the Cisco Kid, but the modern automobile bandit still charms the ladies, even as he steals their jewels.

Linda (Mrs. Wallace Reid Productions, 1929)
d: Mrs. Wallace Reid. 7 reels. (Music, sound effects.)
Helen Foster, Warner Baxter, Noah Beery, Mitchell Lewis, Kate Price, Alan Connor, Bess Flowers.
A young woman is forced to marry a much older man. He tries hard to make his bride happy, but she has eyes only for a young doctor.

Lingerie (Tiffany-Stahl, 1928)
d: George Melford. 6 reels.
Malcolm McGregor, Mildred Harris, Armand Kaliz, Alice White, Cornelia Kellogg, Kit Guard, Victor Potel, Richard Carlyle, Marcella Corday.
Boyd, a war veteran, replaces his unfaithful wife with "Lingerie," a French girl he meets while overseas.

The Lion and the Mouse (Lubin/General Film Co., 1914)
d: Barry O'Neil. 6 reels.
Ethel Clayton, Gaston Bell, George Soule Spencer, Bartley McCullom, Robert Dunbar, Eleanor Barry, Lilie Leslie, Richard Morris, Carlotta Doti, Ruth Bryan, Walter C. Prichard.
While a business tycoon wages a crusade against a Supreme Court Justice, the judge's daughter and the businessman's

son secretly fall in love.
This film, based on a popular play of the same title by Charles Klein, was remade in 1919 and again in 1928.

The Lion and the Mouse (Vitagraph, 1919)
d: Tom Terriss. 6 reels.
Alice Joyce, Conrad Nagel, Anders Randolf, Henry Hallam, W.T. Carlton, Mona Kingsley, Jane Jennings, W.H. Burton, Templar Saxe, Mary Carr.
Romance gets in the way of impeachment proceedings against a federal judge.
Remake of Lubin's 1914 *The Lion and the Mouse*. The film would be remade again, by Warner Bros., in 1928.

The Lion and the Mouse (Warner Bros., 1928)
d: Lloyd Bacon. 7 reels. (Part talkie.)
Lionel Barrymore, May McAvoy, William Collier Jr., Alec B. Francis, Emmett Corrigan, Jack Ackroyd.
Part talkie based on Charles Klein's play *The Lion and the Mouse*. There were two prior feature film versions of the play, in 1914 and in 1919.

The Lion's Den (Metro, 1919)
d: George D. Baker. 5 reels.
Bert Lytell, Alice Lake, Joseph Kilgour, Edward Connelly, Augustus Phillips, Howard Crampton, Seymour Rose, Alice Nowland.
A minister and a businessman lock horns over the financing of a local boys' club.

Listen Lester (Sacramento Pictures/Principal Pictures, 1924)
d: William A. Seiter. 6 reels.
Louise Fazenda, Harry Myers, Eva Novak, George O'Hara, Lee Moran, Alec Francis, Dot Farley.
Colonel Dodge, a womanizing widower, hires a detective to retrieve some incriminating letters from one of his old flames.

The Little Adventuress (DeMille Pictures/Producers Distributing Corp., 1927)
d: William DeMille. 7 reels.
Vera Reynolds, Phyllis Haver, Robert Ober, Theodore Kosloff, Victor Varconi, Fred Walton.
After five years of marriage, Leonard and Victoria decide to call it quits... but that's easier said than done.

The Little American (Artcraft, 1917)
d: Cecil B. DeMille. 6 reels.
Mary Pickford, Jack Holt, Raymond Hatton, Hobart Bosworth, Guy Oliver, Ben Alexander, Lillian Leighton, Walter Long.
Angela, an American girl, takes a trip to France during World War I, only to be captured when the Germans move in. But she is saved when recognized by a German officer who loved her when he lived in the United States.

Little Annie Rooney (Pickford/United Artists, 1925)
d: William Beaudine. 5 reels.
Mary Pickford, William Haines, Spec O'Donnell, Hugh Fay, Walter James, Gordon Griffith, Carlo Schipa, Vola Vale, Joe Butterworth, Oscar Rudolph.
The young daughter of a widowed New York City policeman manages the house for her dad, and runs a local kids' gang as well.

The Little Boss (Vitagraph, 1919)
d: David Smith. 5 reels.
Bessie Love, Wallace McDonald, Harry Russell, Otto

Lederer, Joe Rickson, Clara Knight, Karl Formes.
In a Northwest lumber camp, the timber boss is a lady.

The Little Boy Scout (Famous Players/Paramount, 1917)
d: Francis J. Grandon. 5 reels.
Ann Pennington, Owen Moore, Fraunie Fraunholtz, Marcia Harris, George Burton, Harry Lee.
The "little boy scout" of the title is Justina, a Mexican-American girl.

The Little Brother (New York Motion Picture Corp./Triangle, 1917)
d: Charles Miller. 5 reels.
Enid Bennett, William Garwood, Josephine Headley, Dorcas Matthews, Carl Ullman.
When a man who's interested in the Big Brother movement sponsors one of the young lads, he is surprised that his "little brother" is really a girl!

A Little Brother of the Rich (Universal, 1915)
d: Otis Turner. 5 reels.
Hobart Bosworth, Jane Novak, Hobart Henley, Maud George, Albert MacQuarrie, Carl Von Schiller, William Clark, Edmond Brown, Walter Belasco, Jane Bernoudy, Bob Vernon.
Paul breaks up with Sylvia when he meets big-city temptress Muriel. But Muriel's no good for him, as Paul discovers too late.
This film is based on the novel of the same name by Joseph M. Patterson, and would be remade by Universal in 1919.

A Little Brother of the Rich (Universal, 1919)
d: Lynn Reynolds. 6 reels.
J. Barney Sherry, Frank Mayo, Kathryn Adams, Lily Leslie, Jack Gilbert.
Remake of the 1915 film *A Little Brother of the Rich*. Both films are based on the Joseph M. Patterson novel of the same name.

The Little Chevalier (Thomas A. Edison, Inc., 1917)
d: Alan Crosland. 4 reels.
Shirley Mason, Ray McKee, Richard Tucker, Joseph Burke, William Wadsworth.
Feuding French families continue their animosity into the New World, when their descendants confront each other in New Orleans.

The Little Church Around the Corner (Warner Brothers, 1923)
d: William A. Seiter. 6 reels.
Kenneth Harlan, Claire Windsor, Alec B. Francis, George Cooper, Wallis Long, Hobart Bosworth, H.B. Warner, Pauline Starke, Walter Long.
A priest quells a riot, falls in love, and miraculously restores a dumb girl's gift of speech.

The Little Clown (Realart Pictures, 1921)
d: Thomas N. Heffron. 5 reels.
Mary Miles Minter, Jack Mulhall, Winter Hall, Helen Dunbar, Cameron Coffey, Neely Edwards, Wilton Taylor, Lucien Littlefield, Zelma Maja, Laura Anson.
Down South, a young girl clown falls in love with the son of an aristocratic family.

Little Comrade (Famous Players-Lasky/Paramount, 1919)
d: Chester Withey. 5 reels.
Vivian Martin, Niles Welch, Gertrude Claire, Richard Cummings, L.W. Steers, Eleanor Hancock, Nancy Chase, Pearl Lovci.

During World War I, a soldier goes AWOL for one night. He returns home to the family ranch, falls in love with the new girl working there, and returns to duty engaged to be married.

The Little Diplomat (Diando Film Corp./Pathé, 1919)
d: Stuart Paton. 5 reels.
Baby Marie Osborne, Lydia Knott, William Welsh, Jack Connolly, Murdock MacQuarrie, Velma Clay, Al MacQuarrie, Betty Compson.
Marie, a war orphan, is adopted by an American antique collector.

The Little Duchess (World Film Corp., 1917)
d: Harley Knoles. 5 reels.
Madge Evans, Pinna Nesbit, Jack Drumier, James Davis, Patrick Foy, Maxine Elliott Hicks, Sheridan Tansey, Mrs. Nellie Anderson, Charles Hartley, Richard clarke, Harry Bartlett.
Lord Carmichael, a crusty old misogynist, is forced to take in an orphan girl. Though he resents her presence at first, the girl's charming ways win him over.

The Little Dutch Girl (Shubert Film Co./World Film Corp., 1915)
d: Emile Chautard. 5 reels.
Vivian Martin, W.J. Gross, Chester Barnett, Dorothy Fairchild, John Bowers, Julia Stuart.
A foundling child is raised by an old gardener.

Little Eva Ascends (S-L Pictures/Metro, 1922)
d: George D. Baker. 5 reels.
Gareth Hughes, May Collins, Unice Vin Moore, Benjamin Haggerty, Edward Martindel, Harry Lorraine, Mark Fenton, Eleanor Fields, John Prince, Fred Warren, W.H. Brown.
A touring company of "Uncle Tom's Cabin" runs into problems when the leading lady discovers that the hotel they are registered in is owned by her ex-husband.

Little Eve Edgarton (Universal, 1916)
d: Robert Leonard. 5 reels.
Ella Hall, Thomas Jefferson, Doris Pawn, Gretchen Lederer, Herbert Rawlinson, Marc Fenton.
Eve, a quiet student of botany, agrees to marry an older man who can help her further her studies. Complications arise when Eve meets a fellow her own age who arouses passions in her that the little scientist has never had to deal with.

The Little Firebrand (Hurricane Film Corp./Pathé, 1927)
d: Charles Hutchison. 5 reels.
Edith Thornton, George Fawcett, Lou Tellegen, Eddie Phillips, Joan Standing, Lincoln Stedman, Gino Corrado, Helen Crawford, Ben Walker.
Dorothy, daughter of a wealthy widower, is wild, unruly and irresponsible. When he goes on a business trip, Papa leaves Dorothy in the care of Harley, one of his junior partners, and Harley makes a game try at roping in the girl's enthusiasm.

The Little Fool (Metro, 1921)
d: Philip E. Rosen. 6 reels.
Ora Carew, Milton Sills, Nigel Barrie, Byron Munson, Marjorie Prevost, Helen Howard, Iva Forrester.
Bucolic drama based on the Jack London novel "The Little Lady in the Big House."

The Little 'Fraid Lady (Robertson-Cole, 1920)
d: John G. Adolfi. 6 reels.
Mae Marsh, Tully Marshall, Kathleen Kirkham, Charles

Meredith, Herbert Prior, Gretchen Hartman, George Bertholon Jr.

Shy and wary of strangers, a young painter is dubbed "the little 'fraid lady."

The Little French Girl (Famous Players-Lasky/Paramount, 1925)
d: Herbert Brenon. 6 reels.
Alice Joyce, Mary Brian, Neil Hamilton, Esther Ralston, Anthony Jowitt, Jane Jennings, Mildred Ryan, Eleanor Shelton, Maurice Cannon, Maude Turner Gordon, Paul Doucet, Julia Hurley, Mario Majeroni.
After his brother is killed in the war, Giles tries to effect a reconciliation between the brother's sweetheart, his mistress, and the mistress' daughter.

The Little Giant (Universal, 1926)
d: William Nigh. 7 reels.
Glenn Hunter, Edna Murphy, David Higgins, James Bradbury Jr., Leonard Meeker, Louise Mackintosh, Thomas McGuire, Dodson Mitchell, Peter Raymond.
Elmer, a whiz-bang salesman of washing machines, finds his efforts being undermined by the company president's son, who has an agenda all his own.

A Little Girl in a Big City (Lumas Film Corp., 1925)
d: Burton King. 6 reels.
Gladys Walton, Niles Welch, Mary Thurman, J. Barney Sherry, Coit Albertson, Helen Shipman, Sally Crute, Nellie Savage.
Mary, a small-town girl, wins a beauty contest and heads for the big city to meet the contest's sponsor—a human skunk.

The Little Girl Next Door (Blair Coan Productions, 1923)
d: W.S. Van Dyke. 6 reels.
Pauline Starke, James Morrison, Carmel Myers, Mitchell Lewis, Edward Kennedy.
James, a young man from a small town, heads for Chicago to seek his fortune. But he'll learn the truth of the saying that the bluebird of happiness is in one's own backyard, back home.

The Little Grey Mouse (Fox, 1920)
d: James P. Hogan. 5 reels.
Louise Lovely, Sam DeGrasse, Rosemary Theby, Philo McCullough, Wilson Hummel, Miss Gerard Alexander, Willis Marks, Thomas Jefferson.
When his wife Beverly helps him to write a best-selling novel, Stephen lets success go to his head before finding out, too late, that Beverly is his source of inspiration.

The Little Gypsy (Fox, 1915)
d: Oscar C. Apfel. 5 reels.
Dorothy Bernard, Thurlow Bergen, Raymond Murray, W.J. Herbert, William Riley Hatch.
The daughter of a Scottish lord cavorts like a wild gypsy; maybe because she really is the daughter of gypsies, abandoned by them as an infant and raised by the nobleman.

The Little Intruder (World Film Corp., 1919)
d: Oscar Apfel. 5 reels.
Louise Huff, George MacQuarrie, Christine Mayo, John Hines, Stuart Holmes, Albert Hart.
George, suspicious of his wife Virginia's flirtations with a neighbor, hires a shady lady to spy on them.

The Little Irish Girl (Warner Bros., 1926)
d: Roy Del Ruth. 7 reels.
Dolores Costello, John Harron, Dot Farley, Matthew Betz, Lee Moran, Gertrude Claire.
Dot, a shill for racketeers, falls in love with one of her "marks."

Little Italy (Realart Pictures, 1921)
d: George Terwilliger. 5 reels.
Alice Brady, Norman Kerry, George Fawcett, Jack Ridgway, Gertrude Norman, Luis Alberni, Marguerite Forrest.
An Italian-American girl vows to marry the next man she meets. As fate would have it, he's a trucker whose family is feuding with her own.

Little Johnny Jones (Warner Brothers, 1923)
d: Arthur Rosson. 7 reels.
Johnny Hines, Wyndham Standing, Margaret Seddon, Herbert Prior, Molly Malone, George Webb, Mervyn LeRoy.
An English earl decides to enter an American horse in the Epsom Derby.

A Little Journey (MGM, 1926)
d: Robert Z. Leonard. 7 reels.
William Haines, Claire Windsor, Harry Carey.

A young woman takes a trip to join her fiancé, then falls in love with a fellow she meets on the train.

Little Lady Eileen (Famous Players/Paramount, 1916)
d: J. Searle Dawley. 5 reels.
Marguerite Clark, Vernon Steele, John L. Shine, J.K. Murray, Harry Lee, Maggie Halloway Fisher, Russell Bassett.
Fairy tale about Eileen, an Irish girl, who falls in love but accidentally marries her fiancé's twin brother.

The Little Liar (Fine Arts Film Co., 1916)
d: Lloyd Ingraham. 5 reels.
Mae Marsh, Robert Harron, Olga Gray, Carl Stockdale, Jenny Lee, Ruth Handforth, Tom Wilson, Loyola O'Connor.
When a girl who has a reputation for lying is accused of shoplifting and pleads innocent, nobody believes her.

Little Lord Fauntleroy (Pickford/United Artists, 1921)
d: Alfred E. Green, Jack Pickford. 10 reels.
Mary Pickford, Claude Gillingwater, Joseph Dowling, Rose Dione, Frances Marion.
Miss Pickford plays both Cedric, the little lord of the title, and his mother in this adaptation of the Frances Hodgson Burnett novel.

Little Lost Sister (Selig Polyscope, 1917)
d: Alfred Green. 5 reels.
Vivian Reed, Bessie Eyton, George Fawcett, Marion Warner, Tom Bates, Eugenie Besserer, T.C. Jack, Joseph Singleton, Will Machin, Al W. Filson, Harry Lonsdale.
Innocent little Elsie is lured to the big city and forced into a life of prostitution.

The Little Mademoiselle (World Film Corp., 1915)
d: Oscar Eagle. 6 reels.
Vivian Martin, Mario Majeroni. E.M. Kimball, Arthur Ashley, Lila Chester.
Lili, a French girl traveling in America, is stranded in a small town. Fortunately, a race car driver understands some French and comes to her aid—and Lili wins his heart.

Little Mary Sunshine (Balboa Feature Film Co./Pathé, 1916)
d: Henry King. 5 reels.
Baby Marie Osborne, Henry King, Marguerite Nichols, Andrew Arbuckle, Mollie McConnell.
When Bob, an irresponsible drunk, finds a little orphan girl

who's been abandoned, he takes her into his home and raises her. Bob's new responsibilities have a positive effect on him, and because of the girl he becomes sober and trustworthy.

Little Meena's Romance (Triangle/Fine Arts, 1916)
d: Paul Powell. 5 reels.
Owen Moore, Dorothy Gish, Marguerite Marsh, Robert Lawler, Fred J. Butler, Alberta Lee, George Pierce, Mazie Radford, Fred A. Turner, James O'Shea, Kate Toncray, William Brown.
A romance blossoms between little Meena and a German nobleman.

Little Mickey Grogan (FBO Pictures, 1927)
d: Leo Meehan. 6 reels.
Frankie Darrow, Lassie Lou Ahern, Jobyna Ralston, Carroll Nye, Billy Scott, Vadim Uraneff, Don Bailey, Crauford Kent.
After Susan, a factory worker, takes in a street orphan, the kid shows his appreciation by introducing her to the man who will become her husband.

The Little Minister (Famous Players-Lasky/Paramount, 1922)
d: Penrhyn Stanlaws. 6 reels.
Betty Compson, George Hackathorne, Edwin Stevens, Nigel Barrie, Will R. Walling, Guy Oliver, Fred Huntly, Robert Brower, Joseph Hzelton, Mary Wilkinson.
In Scotland, a young gypsy girl intervenes in a strike between weavers and manufacturers. She wins the heart of Gavin, the "little minister" of the title, and in the end the girl discloses that she is really a member of the nobility.

The Little Minister (Vitagraph, 1922)
d: David Smith. 6 reels.
Alice Calhoun, James Morrison, Henry Hebert, Alberta Lee, William McCall, Dorothea Wolbert, Maud Emery, George Stanley, Richard Daniels, Charles Wheelock.
Apparently simultaneous remake of the Famous Players film of the same title, also released in 1922.
Both versions are based on the story of the same name by James Matthew Barrie.

Little Miss Happiness (Fox, 1916)
d: John G. Adolfi. 5 reels.
June Caprice, Harry Hilliard, Zena Keefe, Sara Alexander, Sidney Bracy, Leo Kennedy, Robert Vivian, Lucia Moore, Genevieve Raynold, Grace Beaumont, Edward N. Hoyt.
An unmarried young woman braves the condemnation of the local gossips, who think she has had a child out of wedlock. But she's merely baby-sitting for a married friend who has reason to keep her maternity a secret.

Little Miss Hawkshaw (Fox, 1921)
d: Carl Harbaugh. 5 reels.
Eileen Percy, Francis Feeney, Eric Mayne, Leslie Casey, Frank Clark, Vivian Ransome, Fred L. Wilson, J. Farrell MacDonald, Glen Cavender.

Patsy, a poor Bowery girl, works at selling newspapers. One day an emissary comes to New York, searching for the long-lost granddaughter of a wealthy Irishman. An unscrupulous police official decides to pass Patsy off as the heiress and cut himself in for a portion of the Irishman's fortune—until, upon further investigation, it is learned that Patsy really *is* the heiress, orphaned as a baby and taken in by an American family.

Little Miss Hoover (Famous Players-Lasky/Paramount, 1918)
d: John S. Robertson. 5 reels.
Marguerite Clark, Eugene O'Brien, Alfred Hickman, Forrest Robinson, Hal Reid, Frances Kaye, John Tansey, J.M. Mason, J.J. Williams.
During World War I, an Army officer working on an undercover assignment is unjustly thought to be a "slacker."

Little Miss No-Account (Vitagraph, 1918)
d: William P.S. Earle. 5 reels.
Gladys Leslie, Frank O'Connor, William Calhoun, Eulalie Jensen, Wet Jenkins, Richard Wangeman, Carlton King, Stephen Carr.
After being lured into a den of iniquity by a scheming gambler, a young heiress is rescued by the lawyer who's admired her from afar.

Little Miss Nobody (Universal, 1917)
d: Harry F. Millarde. 5 reels.
Violet Mersereau, Clara Beyers, Helen Lindroth, Sidney Mason, Dean Raymond, John Mackin, James O'Neil, Robert Clugston, Sidney Mason, Willis Baker.
Bullied by her foster father, an orphan girl is taken in by a playwright and his sister.

Little Miss Optimist (Pallas Pictures/Paramount, 1917)
d: Robert Thornby. 5 reels.
Vivian Martin, Tom Moore, Charles West, Ernest Joy, Charles Gerard, Helen Bray.
In a sensational moment, a murderer is unmasked, in church, before the whole congregation.

Little Miss Rebellion (Famous Players-Lasky/Paramount, 1920)
d: George Fawcett. 5 reels.
Dorothy Gish, Ralph Graves, Riley Hatch, George Seigmann, Marie Burke.
An exiled duchess comes to the United States, works in a restaurant, and falls in love.

Little Old New York (Cosmopolitan/Goldwyn, 1923)
d: Sidney Olcott. 11 reels.
Marion Davies, Harrison Ford, Courtenay Foote, Mahlon Hamilton, Andrew Dillon, Charles Kennedy, Sam Hardy, Andrew Dillon, Harry Watson, George Barraud, Riley Hatch, Louis Wolheim, J.M. Kerrigan, Stephen Carr, Marie R. Burke.
A young Irish woman must impersonate her dead brother in order to collect an inheritance in America. Complications arise when the *faux* male develops a liking for a boy she's met.

The Little Orphan (Universal, 1917)
d: Jack Conway. 5 reels.
Ella Hall, Gretchen Lederer, Gertrude Astor, Jack Conway, Richard La Reno, George Webb, George Hupp, Chandler House, Ernie Shields, Margaret Whistler.
After adopting a Belgian war orphan, a bachelor tries to find a suitable wife to be a mother to his little girl. In the end, he realizes that he and his ward love each other, and that they should not be guardian and ward, but husband and wife.

Little Orphan Annie (Selig Polyscope/Pioneer, 1918)
d: Colin Campbell. 6 reels.
Colleen Moore, Thomas Santschi, Harry Lonsdale, Eugenie Besserer, Doris Baker, Lillian Wade, Ben Alexander, Billy Jacobs, James Whitcomb Riley, Mae Gaston, Lillian Hayward, Lafayette McKee.
A young girl loses her mother and is sent to an orphanage,

where she delights the other orphans with her stories.

Little Pal (Famous Players/Paramount, 1915)
d: James Kirkwood. 5 reels.
Mary Pickford, Russell Bassett, George Anderson, William Lloyd, Constance Johnson, Joseph Manning, Bert Hadley.
During the Alaskan Gold Rush, a saloon keeper loses his daughter, "Little Pal," in a crap game.

The Little Pirate (Universal, 1917)
d: Elsie Jane Wilson. 5 reels.
Zoe Rae, Burwell Hamrick, Charles West, Frank Brownlee, Gretchen Lederer, M.F. Titus, Lillian Peacock.
Hidden treasure awaits two youngsters, a boy and a girl, who play at being pirates.

The Little Princess (Pickford Film Corp./Artcraft, 1917)
d: Marshall Neilan. 5 reels.
Mary Pickford, Norman Kerry, Katherine Griffith, Ann Schaefer, ZaSu Pitts, William E. Lawrence, Theodore Roberts, Gertrude Short, Gustav Von Seyffertitz, Loretta Blake.
Sara, the daughter of a British officer and heiress to his fortune, nevertheless is made to work as a scullery maid in a girls' school in London.

The Little Red Schoolhouse (Martin J. Heyl/Arrow Film Corp., 1923)
d: John G. Adolfi. 6 reels.
Martha Mansfield, Harlan Knight, Sheldon Lewis, E.K. Lincoln, Edmund Breese, Florida Kingsley, Paul Everton.
Bootleggers ply their trade in a school basement.

Little Robinson Crusoe (MGM, 1924)
d: Edward Cline. 7 reels.
Jackie Coogan, Tom Santschi, Noble Johnson, Gloria Grey, Daniel J. O'Brien, Will Walling, C.H. Wilson, Eddie Boland, Tote DuCrow, Bert Sprotte.
An orphan boy shipwrecked on a desert island is captured by natives.

The Little Rowdy (Triangle, 1919)
d: Harry Beaumont. 5 reels.
Hazel Daly, Harry Hilliard, Sydney Ainsworth.
Boarding school is turned into a funhouse when irrepressible Betty arrives and starts playing pranks on everyone, including the headmistress.

The Little Runaway (Vitagraph, 1918)
d: William P.S. Earle. 5 reels.
Gladys Leslie, Edward Earle, Jessie Stevens, Mary Maurice, William Dunn, Betty Blythe, William Calhoun.
When Eileen, a wealthy man's fiancée, walks out on him, he comes to realize that his true love is not Eileen, but Ann, the little lacemaker who has followed him from Ireland to the United States.

The Little School Ma'am (Triangle/Fine Arts, 1916)
d: Charles M. Franklin, Sidney A. Franklin. 5 reels.
Dorothy Gish, Elmer Clifton, Jack Brammall, George Pierce, Howard Gaye, Luray Huntley, Josephine Crowell, Millard Webb, George E. Stone, Hal Wilson.
A schoolteacher in a small Western town is lonely until she meets a vacationing Virginian. Their romance sparks rumors and then a scandal, but her devoted students come to the rescue.

The Little Shepherd of Kingdom Come (Goldwyn, 1920)
d: Wallace Worsley. 6 reels.
Jack Pickford, Clara Horton, Pauline Starke, J. Park Jones,

Clark Marshall, Edythe Chapman, James Neill, R.D. McLean, Dwight Crittenden, Aileen Manning, Dudley Hendricks.
In Civil War days, a mountain boy is indoctrinated into Southern society.

The Little Shepherd of Kingdom Come (First National, 1928)
d: Alred Santell. 8 reels.
Richard Barthelmess, Molly O'Day, Nelson McDowell, Martha Mattox, Victor Potel, Mark Hamilton, William Bertram, Walter Lewis, Gardner James, Ralph Yearsley, Gustav von Seyffertitz, Robert Milasch, Claude Gillingwater, David Torrence, Eulalie Jensen.
Remake of the 1920 Goldwyn film *The Little Shepherd of Kingdom Come*, both versions based on the story of the same name by John William Fox.

Little Shoes (Essanay, 1917)
d: Arthur Berthelet. 5 reels.
Henry B. Walthall, Mary Charleson, Mary McAlister, U.K. Haupt, Patrick Calhoun, Victor Benoit, Bowd M. Turner, Jack Paul.
When a rich girl gives him her own shoes to cover his bare feet during a cold winter, poor David is inspired to get his life together and achieve success. Fifteen years later, David comes back to town a wealthy man, and looks for the girl who inspired him to greatness. In a bittersweet moment, he finds her and her father poverty-stricken, and himself in a position to help them.

A Little Sister of Everybody (Pathé, 1918)
d: Robert T. Thornby. 5 reels.
Bessie Love, George Fisher, Joseph J. Dowling, Hector Sarno.
Celeste, a tenement girl, is friendly to everyone, and becomes known as "the little sister of everybody."

The Little Snob (Warner Bros., 1928)
d: John Adolfi. 6 reels. (Music, sound effects.)
May McAvoy, Robert Frazier, Alec Francis, John Miljan, Virginia Lee Corbin, Frances Lee, John Miljan.
May, a girl from a Coney Island neighborhood, is sent to finishing school by her hard-working father. At the school, May develops a snobbish attitude and comes to consider her childhood friends beneath her dignity. But she'll straighten out.

The Little Terror (Universal, 1917)
d: Rex Ingram. 5 reels.
Violet Mersereau, Sidney Mason, Ed Porter, Ned Finlay, Robert Clugston, Jack Raymond, Mathilde Brundage.
Miss Mersereau plays two roles, as a circus performer and as her daughter—the "little terror" of the title.

The Little Wanderer (Fox, 1920)
d: Howard M. Mitchell. 5 reels.
Shirley Mason, Raymond McKee, Cecil Vanauker, Alice Wilson, Jack Pratt.
The son of a crusading newspaper editor takes on a crusade of his own: reforming the condition of slum dwellers. That's when he meets Jenny, a poor girl who dresses as a boy, and the two fall in love.

The Little White Savage (Universal, 1919)
d: Paul Powell. 5 reels.
Carmel Myers, Harry Hilliard, William Dyer, Richard Cummings, John Cook.
Two circus people concoct a wild tale about their main attraction, "The Savage."

The Little Wild Girl (Hercules Film Production/Trinity Pictures, 1928)
d: Frank S. Mattison. 6 reels.
Lila Lee, Cullen Landis, Frank Merrill, Sheldon Lewis, Boris Karloff, Jimmy Aubrey, Bud Shaw, Arthur Hotaling.
Marie, a girl from the Candian Northwest, goes to New York and becomes a Broadway star.

Little Wildcat (Vitagraph, 1922)
d: David Divad. 5 reels.
Alice Calhoun, Ramsey Wallace, Herbert Fortier, Oliver Hardy, Adele Farrington, Arthur Hoyt, Frank Crane, James Farley, Henry Hebert, Maud Emery.
In a variation on "Pygmalion," a wealthy man takes into his custody a rough-hewn girl of the streets, determined to turn her into a fine lady.

The Little Wildcat (Warner Bros., 1929)
d: Ray Enright. 6 reels. (Music, sound effects, part talkie.)
George Fawcett, Audrey Ferris, James Murray, Doris Dawson, Robert Edeson, Hallam Cooley.
Grandpa, a Civil War vet, objects to his granddaughter's new beau, an aviator.

Little Women (Paramount, 1919)
d: Harley Knoles. 6 reels.
Isabel Lamon, Dorothy Barnard, Lillian Hall, Florence Flynn, Henry Hull, Conrad Nagel, Kate Lester, George Kelson, Julia Hurley, Lynn Hammond, Frank de Vernon.
This first feature film version of the Louisa May Alcott novel depicts the life of the March family and their four daughters, in the days before the Civil War.

The Little Yank (Triangle/Fine Arts, 1917)
d: George Seigmann. 5 reels.
Dorothy Gish, Frank Bennett, Hal Wilson, A.D. Sears, Robert Burns, Kate Toncray, Fred A. Turner, Alberta Lee.
A Yankee girl falls in love with a captured Confederate officer, and saves his life.

The Littlest Rebel (Photoplay Productions Co., 1914)
d: Edgar Lewis. 6 reels.
E.K. Lincoln, William J. Sorelle, Estelle Coffin, Mimi Yvonne, Elaine Ivans, Martin Reagan, Fred Fleck, Bert S. Frank, Paul Pilkerton.
Virgie is "the littlest rebel" on her family's Southern plantation during the Civil War.

Live and Let Live (Robertson-Cole/R-C Pictures, 1921)
d: William Christy Cabanne. 6 reels.
Harriet Hammond, George Nichols, Dulcie Cooper, Harris Gordon, Gerald Pring, Dave Winter, Helen Lynch, Josephine Crowell, Cora Drew, Helen Muir.
Mary, a former thief, meets a woman on a train and learns that she is about to elope instead of continuing on to her grandparents' home. So Mary detrains at that station and presents herself to the family as the long-lost granddaughter.

Live Sparks (Robert Brunton Productions/Pathé, 1920)
d: Ernest C. Warde. 5 reels.
J. Warren Kerrigan, Mary Talbot, Roy Laidlaw, Fritzi Brunette, Clyde Benson, Beth Ivins, Zelma Maja, John Steppling, Arthur Millette, Joseph Dowling, Mary Jane Irving.
In Texas, two scoundrels tap into an oil company's pipeline.

The Live Wire (First National, 1925)
d: Charles Hines. 8 reels.
Johnny Hines, Edmund Breese, Mildred Ryan, J. Barney Sherry, Bradley Barker, Flora Finch.
A former circus stunt performer gets a job at the power company, and finds that his old circus talents will come in handy there.

Live Wires (Fox, 1921)
d: Edward Sedgwick. 5 reels.
Johnnie Walker, Edna Murphy, Alberta Lee, Frank Clark, Bob Klein, Hayward Mack, Wilbur Higby, Lefty James.
A much-beset college boy has problems at home, but he is airlifted from the roof of a speeding train and flown to the football field, arriving in time to win the Big Game.

Living Lies (Mayflower Photoplay Corp., 1922)
d: Emile Chautard. 5 reels.
Edmund Lowe, Mona Kingsley, Kenneth Hill.
A young newspaper reporter comes into possession of documents that prove crooked operations by a group of financiers.

Loaded Dice (Pathé, 1918)
d: Herbert Blaché. 5 reels.
Frank Keenan, Florence Billings, Guy Coombs, Madeline Marshall.
In an attempt to corner the market for food supplies, a speculator stoops to blackmail and even murder.

The Loaded Door (Universal, 1922)
d: Harry A. Pollard. 5 reels.
Hoot Gibson, Bill Ryno, Gertrude Olmstead, Eddie Sutherland, Noble Johnson, Joseph Harris, Charles Newton, Charles A. Smiley, Victor Potel, C.L. Sherwood.
Out West, a ranch hand rousts drug smugglers and cattle rustlers.

Local Girl Makes Good — see: Her Big Night (1926).

Locked Doors (Famous Players-Lasky/Paramount, 1924)
d: William C. DeMille. 7 reels.
Betty Compson, Theodore Roberts, Kathlyn Williams, Theodore von Eltz, Robert Edeson, Elmo Billings.
Mary, a young woman, marries an older man for security's sake. Later, while on a vacation with friends, she meets and falls in love with John. He feels the same way about her, but suppresses his feelings because of her married status. Later still, John is invited to spend a week in the home of a business associate, and sure enough, it turns out to be the home of Mary and her husband. What now?

The Locked Heart (Oakdale Productions/General Film, 1918)
d: Henry King. 5 reels.
Gloria Joy, Henry King, Vola Vale, Daniel Gilfether, Leon Perdue.
When his wife dies in childbirth, Harry is crushed and cannot bear to look at his new daughter. He leaves her with relatives and goes on a long European trip to try and forget. When Harry finally returns home, still despondent, he is befriended by a spunky little girl who tries to cheer him up, and actually succeeds. Imagine Harry's joy when he discovers that his new friend is his own daughter!

Locked Lips (Universal, 1920)
d: William Dowlan. 5 reels.
Tsuru Aoki, Magda Lane, Stanhope Wheatcroft.
East meets West in this tragic tale of a mixed marriage gone sour.

Loco Luck (Universal, 1927)
d: Clifford Smith. 5 reels.

Art Acord, Fay Wray, Aggie Herring, William A. Steele, Al Jennings, George F. Marion, M.E. Stimson, George Grandee, George Kesterson.

Out West, a cowpoke enters a horse race to win enough money to pay off the mortgage.

The Lodge in the Wilderness (Tiffany Productions, 1926)
d: Henry McCarthy. 6 reels.
Anita Stewart, Edmund burns, Duane Thompson, Lawrence Steers, Victor Potel, Eddie Lyons, James Farley.

Melodrama about love and murder in a logging camp in the Great Northwest.

Lombardi, Ltd. (Metro, 1919)
d: Jack Conway. 6 reels.
Bert Lytell, Alice Lake, Vera Lewis, Juanita Hansen, George McDaniel, Joseph Kilgour, Thomas Jefferson, Thea Talbot, Ann May, John Steppling, Jean Acker, Virginia Caldwell.
Lombardi is a couturier with fabulous designs, but not much business sense.

London After Midnight (MGM, 1927)
d: Tod Browning. 7 reels.
Lon Chaney, Polly Moran, Conrad Nagel, Marceline Day, Henry B. Walthall, Percy Williams, Edna Tichenor, Claude King.
In London, a police inspector solves a murder mystery using hypnotism on his primary suspects.

The Lone Chance (Fox, 1924)
d: Harold Mitchell. 5 reels.
John Gilbert, Evelyn Brent, John Miljan, Edwin Booth Tilton, Harry Todd, Frank Beal.
Saunders, an inventor with a cash flow problem, agrees to plead guilty to a murder he didn't commit, in return for $20,000 and the promise of his freedom after one year behind bars.

The Lone Eagle (Universal, 1927)
d: Emory Johnson. 6 reels.
Raymond Keane, Nigel Barrie, Barbara Kent, Jack Pennick, Donald Stuart, Cuyler Supplee, Frank Camphill, Marcella Daly, Eugene Pouyet, Wilson Benge, Brent Overstreet.
Holmes, an American aviator in World War I, is accused of cowardice for failing to confront the enemy. We know he's no coward, though, and after gaining inspiration from Mimi, his French sweetheart, he takes to the skies again and shoots down the German ace who's been tailing him.

The Lone Hand (Universal, 1922)
d: Reaves Eason. 5 reels.
Hoot Gibson, Marjorie Daw, Helen Holmes, Hayden Stevenson, Jack Pratt, William Welch, Robert Kortman.
A cowpoke from Laramie helps a pretty gal and her dad protect their mine from swindlers.

Lone Hand Saunders (R-C Pictures/FBO of America, 1926)
d: B. Reeves Eason. 6 reels.
Fred Thomson, Bess Flowers, Billy Butts, Frank Hagney, Albert Priscoe, Bill Dyer, William Courtwright.
Out West, a rancher is known as "Lone Hand" Saunders because he uses only his left hand, never his right. But there's a reason: Saunders is a surgeon who mourns the death of his sister, who died before he could operate on her. He has sworn never again to use the hand that might have saved her life.

The Lone Horseman (J.P. McGowan Productions/Syndicate Pictures, 1929)

d: J.P. McGowan. 5 reels.
Tom Tyler, J.P. McGowan, Charlotte Winn, Tom Bay, Mack V. Wright.
Gardner, a rancher, has his property sold out from under him by swindlers.

The Lone Rider (D.M. Productions/Rollo Sales Corp., 1922)
d: Denver Dixon. 5 reels.
Denver Dixon, Alma Rayford, Edward Heim, Charles Force, Clyde McClary, Tommy Hines.
Out West, an innocent hobo is framed for cattle rustling by a crooked sheriff and his partner. Ruth, the local rancher's daughter, believes the young man is innocent, however. And apparently so does the mystery man known as "The Lone Rider," who appears sporadically to thwart the sheriff's evil deeds. In the last reel, we learn that the mystery man and the innocent hobo are one and the same.

Lone Star (American Film Co./Mutual, 1916)
d: Edward Sloman. 5 reels.
William Russell, Charlotte Burton, Harry Von Meter, Alfred Ferguson, Ashton Dearholt.
Lone Star is an Indian who decides to study medicine as it is practiced by white doctors.

The Lone Star Ranger (Fox, 1919)
d: J. Gordon Edwards. 5 reels.
William Farnum, Louise Lovely, G. Raymond Nye, Charles Clary, Lamar Johnstone, Frederic Herzog, Irene Rich.
Captain Neil of the Texas Rangers wages war against cattle rustlers.

The Lone Star Ranger (Fox, 1923)
d: Lambert Hillyer. 6 reels.
Tom Mix, Billie Dove, L.C. Shumway, Stanton Heck, Edward Peil, Frank Clark, Minna Redman, Francis Carpenter, William Conklin, Tom Lingham.
Remake of the Fox film *The Lone Star Ranger*, both versions based on the novel of the same name by Zane Grey.

The Lone Wolf (Herbert Brenon Film Corp./Selznick, 1917)
d: Herbert Brenon. 8 reels.
Hazel Dawn, Bert Lytell, Cornish Beck, Stephen Grattan, Alfred Hickman, Ben Graham, Robert Fisher, William Riley Hatch, Joseph Chailles, William E. Shay, Edward Abeles.
In Paris, a master crook baffles the police.

The Lone Wolf (John McKeown/Associated Exhibitors, 1924)
d: S.E.V. Taylor. 6 reels.
Dorothy Dalton, Jack Holt, Wilton Lackaye, Tyrone Power, Charlotte Walker, Lucy Fox, Edouard Durand, Robert T. Haines, Gustav von Seyffertitz, Alphonse Ethier, William Tooker.
Lanyard, an internationally famous thief known as "the Lone Wolf," is retained by the United States government to recover stolen plans for a strategic weapon.

The Lone Wolf Returns (Columbia, 1926)
d: Ralph Ince. 6 reels.
Bert Lytell, Billie Dove, Freeman Wood, Gustav von Seyffertitz, Gwen Lee, Alphonse Ethier.
Lanyard, "the Lone Wolf," returns to his crooked ways, but in the middle of a jewel theft he is interrupted by detectives. In eluding them, he stumbles into an ongoing masked ball. There, he meets and falls in love with the young woman whose jewels he was trying to steal.

The Lone Wolf's Daughter (Pathé, 1919)
d: William P.S. Earle. 7 reels.
Bertram Grassby, Louise Glaum, Edwin Stevens, Thomas Holding, Fred L. Wilson.
In a London estate, young Sonia thinks she is the maid's daughter. Actually, she is the daughter of a princess and the mysterious master thief, "the Lone Wolf."

The Lone Wolf's Daughter (Columbia, 1929)
d: Albert Rogell. 7 reels. (Part talkie.)
Bert Lytell, Gertrude Olmstead, Charles Gerard, Lilyan Tashman, Donald Keith, Florence Allen, Robert Elliott, Ruth Cherrington.
Lanyard, a former master thief, adopts the daughter of an old friend and watches her grow to young adulthood. When she announces her engagement to a wealthy young man, Lanyard throws her a party and recognizes among the guests a "count" and "countess" who are, in fact, international jewel thieves.

The Lonely Road (Preferred Pictures/Associated First National, 1923)
d: Victor Schertzinger. 6 reels.
Katherine MacDonald, Orville Caldwell, Kathleen Kirkham, Eugenie Besserer, William Conklin, James Neill, Frank Leigh, Charles French, Stanley Goethals.
Betty's married to a suspicious fellow who insists on her sticking close to him. That will be difficult, when their son is injured and Betty must take the boy to see a doctor.

The Lonely Woman (Triangle, 1918)
d: Thomas N. Heffron. 5 reels.
Belle Bennett, Lee Hill, Percy Challenger, Anna Dodge, Blanche Gray, Alberta Lee, Walter Perkins.
There's a new woman in town, and the local gossips don't know what to make of her—especially when she hires the town drunk to be her handyman.

Lonesome (Universal, 1928)
d: Paul Fejos. 7 reels. (Sound effects, part talkie.)
Barbara Kent, Glenn Tryon, Gustav Partos, Eddie Phillips, Fay Holderness.
Two lonely souls live in the same apartment building but don't know each other. Then one day they meet at the beach, fall in love, and are forcibly separated. After they return, mournfully, to their dwellings, they learn the joyful truth that they are neighbors.

The Lonesome Chap (Pallas Pictures/Paramount, 1917)
d: Edward J. LeSaint. 5 reels.
Louise Huff, House Peters, John Burton, Eugene Pallette, J. Parks Jones, Betty Johnson.
Renée, a girl whose dad was killed in a mining accident, is raised by Stuart, a kind friend of her father's. Stuart sends the girl to boarding school, but after she graduates at age 18, she comes home to him. When he sees her as a grownup, Stuart is moved to propose marriage.

Lonesome Corners (Playgoers Pictures/Pathé, 1922)
w, d: Edgar Jones. 5 reels.
Edgar Jones, Henry Van Bousen, Edna May Sperl, Walter Lewis, Lillian Lorraine.
Another "Pygmalion" clone, in which an unsophisticated backwoods girl is tutored to become a refined young lady.

Lonesome Ladies (First National, 1927)
d: Joseph Henabery. 6 reels.
Lewis Stone, Anna Q. Nilsson, Jane Winton, Doris Lloyd,
Edward Martindel, Fritzi Ridgeway, DeSacia Mooers, E.H. Calvert, Grace Carlisle, Fred Warren.
Fosdick, a complacent husband, learns that wives can stray if they are not cared for.

The Long Arm of Mannister (National Film Corp./Pioneer, 1919)
d: Bertram Bracken. 6 reels.
Henry B. Walthall, Helene Chadwick, William Clifford, Olive Ann Alcorn, Charles Wheelock, John Cossar, Matthew Biddolph, Barney Furey, Hallam Cooley.
Two fugitives, a man and a woman, are pursued across the globe by the woman's jealous husband.

The Long Chance (Universal, 1915)
d: Edward J. LeSaint. 6 reels.
Frank Keenan, Stella Razeto, Beryle Boughton, Fred Church, Jack Nelson, Clyde Benson, Harry Blaising, Walter Newman, Jack Curtis.
Out West, a gambler keeps his love for a married woman a secret. Then, after both the woman and her husband die, the gambler raises their daughter as a proper father would.

The Long Chance (Universal, 1922)
d: Jack Conway. 5 reels.
Henry B. Walthall, Marjorie Daw, Ralph Graves, Jack Curtis, Leonard Clapham, Boyd Irwin, William Bertram, Grace Marvin, George A. Williams.
Out West, a gambler promises a dying woman to care for her young daughter.

The Long Lane's Turning (National Film Corp. of America, 1919)
d: Louis William Chaudet. 5 reels.
Henry B. Walthall, Harry M. O'Connor, Jack Richardson, Joe Dowling, Ralph Lewis, Mary Charleson, Vera Lewis, Melbourne MacDowell, William DeVaul.
Though brilliant at his job, a lawyer drinks to excess and loses his fiancée. But he wins her back after he gives up alcohol, recovers her father's stolen property, and is nominated to run for governor.

Long Live the King (Metro, 1923)
d: Victor Schertzinger. 10 reels.
Jackie Coogan, Rosemary Theby, Ruth Renick, Vera Lewis, Alan Hale, Allan Forrest, Walt Whitman, Robert Brower, Raymond Lee, Monte Collins, Sam Appel, Ruth Handforth.
In the kingdom of Livonia, the young crown prince just wants to live like a normal little boy. He gets his chance, for a while at least.

The Long Loop on the Pecos (Leo Maloney Productions/Pathé, 1927)
d: Leo Maloney. 6 reels.
Leo Maloney, Eugenia Gilbert, Frederick Dana, Albert Hart, Tom London, Bud Osborne, Chet Ryan, William Merrill McCormick Robert Burns, Dick LaReno, Murdock MacQuarrie.
In the Pecos country, a newcomer takes on the infamous Long Loop Gang, a deadly bunch of cattle rustlers.

Long Pants (Harry Langdon Corp./First National, 1927)
d: Frank Capra. 6 reels.
Harry Langdon, Priscilla Bonner, Alma Bennett, Frankie Darro, Gladys Brockwell, Al Roscoe.

A young man is expected to marry his childhood sweetheart, but instead he falls for a hard-boiled, big-city temptress who's in trouble with the law.

In some ways, this is the most peculiar comedy ever made. William K. Everson called it "the closest that silent comedy ever came to a Luis Buñuel type of *noir* comedy...." Langdon's character is a "youngster" who's kept in knee-pants by his overprotective parents until they think he's old enough to wear long pants. But Langdon was 43 years old at the time, and he doesn't look much younger than that in the film. Also, there's a strange scene where this awkward man-child actually tries to *murder* his fiancée in order to be free to marry a vamp he's met! He wants to shoot his fiancée in cold blood, but quickly puts away his gun when he sees a posted sign that says: "No shooting on these premises." Musn't disobey the law, you know. It's all very odd, but to Langdon's credit he pulls it off and still retains our sympathy for his character. In the end, of course, he sees the light, forsakes the vamp and returns to his stainless small-town sweetheart.

The Long Trail (Famous Players/Paramount, 1917)
d: Howell Hansell. 5 reels.
Lou-Tellegen, Mary Fuller, Winifred Allen, Sydney Bracy, Franklin Woodruff, Ferdinand Tidmarsh, Frank Farrington.
In the frozen Northwest, a trapper shelters a young woman from the storm.

Look Your Best (Goldwyn, 1923)
d: Rupert Hughes. 6 reels.
Colleen Moore, Antonio Moreno, William Orlamond, Orpha Alba, Earl Metcalfe, Martha Mattox, Francis McDonald.
In New York's "Little Italy," a willowy young woman is given a job as a tight rope walker, in place of a girl who has put on too much weight.

Looking for Trouble (Universal, 1926)
d: Robert North Bradbury. 5 reels.
Jack Hoxie, Marceline Day, J. Gordon Russell, Clark Comstock, Edmund Cobb, Bud Osborne, Peggy Montgomery, William Dyer, Harry Russell.
In Texas, a young man learns that a local newspaper is really a "front" for jewel smugglers.

The Lookout Girl (Quality Pictures, 1928)
d: Dallas M. Fitzgerald. 7 reels.
Jacqueline Logan, Ian Keith, William H. Tooker, Lee Moran, Gladden James, Henry Herbert, Jimmy Aubrey, Broderick O'Farrell, Jean Huntley, Geraldine Leslie.
When he rescues a girl whose canoe has tipped over in the lake, Richardson falls in love with her. He proposes marriage, but she agrees only on the condition that he ask no questions about her past. What can she be hiding?

Looped for Life (J. Joseph Sameth Productions, 1924)
d: Park Frame. 5 reels.
Art Acord, Jack Richardson, Marcella Pershing, Charles Adler.
Out West, jealousy makes fast friends into fast enemies.

Loose Ankles—see: Ladies at Play (1926)

Loot (Universal, 1919)
d: William Dowlan. 6 reels.
Joseph Girard, Ora Carew, Frank Thompson, Darrell Foss, Alfred Allen, Wadsworth Harris, Arthur Mackley, Gertrude Astor, Frank MacQuarrie, Helen Gibson.
An emissary travels from London to New York to secure a priceless diamond necklace. Along the way, he is shadowed by thieves and also by a young actress, all eager to get their hands on the "loot."

Lord and Lady Algy (Goldwyn, 1919)
d: Harry Beaumont. 6 reels.
Tom Moore, Naomi Childers, Leslie Stuart, Frank Leigh, William Burress, Alec B. Francis, Philo McCullough, Mabel Ballin, Kate Lester, Hal Taintor, Herbert Standing.
Society comedy features Lord and Lady Algy, who bet on horse races... sometimes against each other.

Lord Jim (Famous Players-Lasky/Paramount, 1925)
d: Victor Fleming. 7 reels.
Percy Marmont, Shirley Mason, Noah Beery, Raymond Hatton, Joseph Dowling, George Magrill, Nick DeRuiz, J. Gunnis Davis, Jules Cowles, Duke Kahanamoku.
Jim, a disgraced former seaman, drifts into a Moslem kingdom and befriends the natives.

Lord Loveland Discovers America (American Film Co./Mutual, 1916)
d: Arthur Maude. 5 reels.
Arthur Maude, Constance Crawley, William Carroll, Charles Newton, William Frawley, George Clancy, Nell Franzen.
When a penniless British nobleman comes to America in search of a rich wife, he gets sidetracked instead into a variety of jobs: waiter, actor, chauffeur.

The Lord Loves the Irish (Pathé, 1919)
d: Ernest C. Warde. 5 reels.
J. Warren Kerrigan, Aggie Herring, James O. Barrows, Fritzi Brunette, William Ellingford, Wedgwood Nowell, Joseph J. Dowling.
Miles, an Irish lad, is smitten with an American girl and follows her home to New York.

The Lords of High Decision (Universal, 1916)
d: Jack Harvey. 5 reels.
Cyril Scott, Joseph Girard, Mildred Gregory, Willilam Welsh, Margaret Scervin, Mathilde Brundage.
Heavy drama about strained relations between a mine owner and his overworked men.

Lorelei of the Sea (Marine Film Co./State Rights, 1917)
d: Henry Otto. 6 reels.
Tyrone Power, Frances Burnham, Henry Otto, John Oaker, Jay Belasco, Agnes Blanchard, Winifred Greenwood, Gypsy Abbott.
When a South Seas girl named Lorelei decides to act out her fantasies and sing the siren's song, she attracts a young yachtsman to her shore. Can love be far behind?

Lorna Doone (Thomas H. Ince/Associated First National, 1922)
d: Maurice Tourneur. 7 reels.
Madge Bellamy, John Bowers, Frank Keenan, Jack McDonald, Donald MacDonald, Norris Johnson, May Giraci, Charles Hatton.
A noblewoman is kidnapped as a child and raised by a band of outlaws.

Lorraine of the Lions (Universal, 1925)
d: Edward Sedgwick. 7 reels.
Norman Kerry, Patsy Ruth Miller, Fred Humes, Doreen Turner, Harry Todd, Philo McCullough, Joseph J. Dowling, Frank Newburg, Rosemary Cooper.
Lorraine, young daughter of a circus performer, is shipwrecked alone on a desert island. She has a natural way with wild animals, thus she is cared for by the lions and a gorilla as she grows to maturity.

Lost and Found on a South Sea Island (Goldwyn, 1923)

286

d: R.A. Walsh. 7 reels.
House Peters, Pauline Starke, Antonio Moreno, Mary Jane Irving, Rosemary Theby, George Siegmann, William V. Mong, Carl Harbaugh, David Wing.
In the South Seas, a captain's wife and daughter are stolen from him by a white slaver.

Lost and Won (Lasky Feature Plays/Paramount, 1917)
d: James Young. 5 reels.
Marie Doro, Elliott Dexter, Carl Stockdale, Mayme Kelso, Robert Gray, C.H. Geldert.
Another variant of the "Pygmalion" story, this one's about a bank director who spruces up a little newsgirl and turns her into a ravishing beauty.

Lost at Sea (Tiffany Productions, 1926)
d: Louis J. Gasnier. 7 reels.
Huntly Gordon, Lowell Sherman, Jane Novak, Natalie Kingston, Billy Kent Schaefer, Joan Standing, William Walling, Neal Dodd.
Richard, a rejected lover, finds years later that his former sweetheart has been abandoned by her husband on a desert island. He goes to her and tries to rekindle their romance, but the dog-in-the-manger husband refuses to give her a divorce.

Lost at the Front (John McCormick Productions/First National, 1927)
d: Del Lord. 6 reels.
George Sidney, Charlie Murray, Natalie Kingston, John Kolb, Max Asher, Brooks Benedict, Ed Brady, Harry Lipman, Nita Martan, Nina Romano.
Two pals, an Irish-American and a German, find themselves on opposite sides when World War I breaks out.

The Lost Bridegroom (Famous Players/Paramount, 1916)
d: Jakes Kirkwood. 5 reels.
John Barrymore, Catherine Harris, Ida Darling, June Dale, Hardie Kirkland, Edward Sturgis, Jack Dillon.
Comedy about a bridegroom-to-be who gets knocked cold after his bachelor party and develops amnesia. Remembering nothing, he wanders around until a gang of crooks finds him and trains him to be a thief. Sure enough, the first place he is assigned to rob is his fiancée's house.

The Lost Chord (Chord Pictures/Arrow Film Corp., 1925)
d: Wilfred Noy. 7 reels.
David Powell, Alice Lake, Dagmar Godowsky, Henry Sedley, Faire Binney, Louise Carter, Charles Mack, Dorothy Kingdon, Samuel Hines, Signor N. Salerno, Rita Maurice.
Arnold, a concert organist, loves but one woman; and he loses her—*twice*.

Lost in a Big City (Blazed Trail Productions/Arrow Film Corp., 1923)
d: George Irving. 8 reels.
John Lowell, Baby Ivy Ward, Jane Thomas, Charles Beyer, Evangeline Russell, James Watkins, Edgar Keller, Whitney Haley, Edward Phillips, Ann Brody, Charles A. Robins.
Upon his return from Alaska, a gold prospector learns that his sister's husband has abandoned her and their daughter. The prospector sets out after him, seeking to bring him to justice.

A Lost Lady (Warner Bros., 1925)
d: Harry Beaumont. 7 reels.
Irene Rich, George Fawcett, Matt Moore, John Roche, June Marlowe, Victor Potel, Eva Gordon, Nanette Valone.
Bored with her marriage and her lifestyle, a young woman looks for options.

Lost in Transit (Pallas Pictures/Paramount, 1917)
d: Donald Crisp. 5 reels.
George Beban, Helen Jerome Eddy, Pietro Sosso, Vera Lewis, Henry Barrows, Frank Bennett, Bob White.
On his way home to see the father he has never known, a young boy is kidnapped.

Lost Money (Fox, 1919)
d: Edmund Lawrence. 5 reels.
Madlaine Traverse, George McDaniel, Henry Hebert, Edwin B. Tilton.
Desperate and near bankruptcy, a South African diamond miner appropriates his absent neighbor's wealth.

The Lost Paradise (Famous Players/Paramount, 1914)
d: J. Searle Dawley. 5 reels.
H.B. Warner, Catherine Carter, Mark Price, Arthur Hoops, Rita Stan, Amy Sumers, Phillips Tead, Trixie Jennery, Wellington A. Playter, August Balfour, Marcus Moriarity.
The foreman of an iron mill discovers that his invention was stolen by his employer and is being used to amass a fortune.

The Lost Princess (Fox, 1919)
d: Scott Dunlap. 5 reels.
Albert Ray, Elinor Fair, George Hernandez, Maggie Halloway Fisher, Edward Cecil, Burt Wesner, H.C. Simmons, Fred Bond.
Farm boy Sam leaves the country and heads for the city, where he gets work as a feature writer for a newspaper. There, he dreams up the story of a lost European princess who is hiding in the United States.

The Lost Romance (Famous Players-Lasky/Paramount, 1921)
d: William C. DeMille. 7 reels.
Jack Holt, Lois Wilson, Fontaine LaRue, conrad Nagel, Mickey Moore, Mayme Kelso, Robert Brower, Barbara Gurney, Clarence Geldert, Clarence Burton, Lillian Leighton.
After six years of marriage, a couple find their romance has grown cold.

The Lost World (First National, 1925)
d: Harry Hoyt. 10 reels.
Lewis Stone, Bessie Love, Lloyd Hughes, Wallace Beery, Bull Montana, Marguerite McWade, Arthur Hoyt, Jules Cowles, George Bunny, Alma Bennett, Virginia Brown Faire.
Fascinating tale of a team of explorers who happen upon a strange land where prehistoric monsters are very much alive. Technical wizard Willis O'Brien and cameraman Arthur Edeson were the creators of the much-admired special effects.

Lost—a Wife (Famous Players-Lasky/Paramount, 1925)
d: William C. DeMille. 7 reels.
Adolphe Menjou, Greta Nissen, Robert Agnew, Edgar Norton, Mario Carillo, Genaro Spagnoli, Eugenio DiLiguro, Henrietta Floyd, Toby Claude, Marcelle Corday.
In France, a gambler loses his wife to divorce, then goes all out to get her back.

The Lottery Man (Famous Players-Lasky/Paramount, 1919)
d: James Cruze. 5 reels.
Wallace Reid, Harrison Ford, Wanda Hawley, Fannie Midgley, Sylvia Shton, Carolyn Rankin, Wilton Taylor, Clarence Geldert, Marcia Manon, Winifred Greenwood, Fred Huntley.

To increase his paper's circulation, a news reporter dreams up the idea of a lottery—with his hand in marriage as the winner's prize!

Lotus Blossom (Wah Ming Motion Picture Co./First National, 1921)
d: Frank Grandon. 7 reels.
Lady Tsen Mei, Tully Marshall, Noah Beery, Jack Abbe, Goro Kino, James Wang, Chow Young.
In China, the sacred clock of a village cracks and the emperor commissions a clockmaker to mend it. Failing to do so, the clockmaker is threatened with execution. To save her father's honor, his daughter Moy Tai sacrifices her life to appease the gods, and the clock mends itself.

The Lotus Eater (Marshall Neilan Productions/First National, 1921)
d: Marshall Neilan. 7 reels.
John Barrymore, Colleen Moore, Anna Q. Nilsson, Ida Waterman, Frank Currier, J. Barney Sherry, Wesley Barry.
Jacques, a young man who has grown up sheltered and in complete ignorance of the opposite sex, falls in love when he finally does see a woman.

The Lotus Woman (Kalem/General Film Co., 1916)
d: Harry Millarde. 5 reels.
Alice Hollister, Harry Millarde, Arthur Albertson, John E. Mackin, James B. Ross.
In a Latin American country, a convent-bred girl undergoes a transformation from innocent señorita to seductive vamp.

Louisiana (Famous Players-Lasky/Paramount, 1919)
d: Robert G. Vignola. 5 reels.
Vivian Martin, Robert Ellis, Noah Beery, Arthur Allardt, Lillian West, Lillian Leighton.
Louisiana isn't a state, she's a girl living in the Blue Ridge mountains of Tennessee.

Love (J. Parker Read Jr. Productions, 1920)
d: Wesley Ruggles. 6 reels.
Louise Glaum, Peggy Cartwright, James Kirkwood, Joseph Kilgour, Edith Yorke.
Natalie, a proper but poverty-stricken girl, becomes a rich man's mistress in order to pay her sister's doctor bills.

Love (MGM, 1927)
d: Edmund Goulding. 8 reels.
John Gilbert, Greta Garbo, Brandon Hurst, Philippe de Lacy, George Fawcett, Emily Fitzroy, Philippe de Lacy.
Gilbert-Garbo vehicle based on Leo Tolstoy's "Anna Karenina." In Czarist Russia, Anna falls in love with a handsome Count, although she is already married. The match leads to tragedy.
The story was filmed earlier, as *Anna Karenina* (Fox, 1915).

Love Aflame (Universal, 1917)
d: Raymond Wells. 5 reels.
Ruth Stonehouse, Jack Mulhall, Noble Johnson, Jean Hersholt, Raymond Whitaker, Fronzie Gunn, Nita White.
When a young adventurer bets that he can travel from New York to Constantinople without spending a dime, he starts his journey in the company of a tramp who also wants to get away. Little does he know, that "tramp" is really a lovely woman, in disguise.

Love and Glory (Universal, 1924)
d: Rupert Julian. 7 reels.
Charles DeRoche, Ford Sterling, Wallace MacDonald, Madge Bellamy, Gibson Gowland, Priscilla Moran, Charles DeRavenne, André Lancy, Madame DeBodamere.
Gabrielle, a French girl, has a brother and a lover serving in the same regiment in Algeria—and loses them both.

Love and Hate (Fox, 1916)
d: James Vincent. 6 reels.
Bertha Kalich, Stuart Holmes, Kenneth Hunter, Madeleine Le Nard, Jane Lee, Katherine Lee.
Bitter drama about a would-be seducer who drives a happily married couple to divorce, and the murder that follows when he tries to force his attentions on the ex-wife.

Love and Learn (Paramount, 1928)
d: Frank Tuttle. 6 reels.
Esther Ralston, Lane Chandler, Hedda Hopper, Claude King, Jack J. Clark, Jack Trent, Hal Craig, Helen Lynch, Catherine Parrish, Martha Franklin, Jerry Mandy, Dorothea Wolbert.
To keep her parents from obtaining a divorce, young Nancy gets herself into all sorts of trouble, knowing that they'll stay together as long as they think she needs them.

Love and Sacrifice—see: America (1924)

Love and the Devil (First National/Warner Bros., 1929)
d: Alexander Korda. 7 reels. (Synchronized music, sound effects.)
Milton Sills, Maria Korda, Ben Bard, Nellie Bly Baker, Amber Norman.
When a British lord falls in love with a tempestuous Italian opera diva, they marry and he takes her to live with him in England. But the diva longs for the Italian sunshine and the limelight she once enjoyed.

Love and the Law (Edgar Lewis Productions, 1919)
d: Edgar Lewis. 6 reels.
Glen White, Josephine Hill, Arnold Storrer, Paul Ker, W.T. Clark, Tom Williams.
Curly, a hired hand, loves his boss' niece, but still suspects the boss is up to no good. Sure enough, it turns out the old man is a German agent, and Curly must prevent him from sabotaging a troop train.

Love and the Woman (World Film Corp., 1919)
d: Tefft Johnson. 5 reels.
June Elvidge, Donald Hall, Marion Barney, Ed Roseman, Lillian Lawrence, Rod LaRocque, George MacQuarrie, Laura Burt.
Switched at birth with a baby girl who dies, a young woman grows up in the home of a widower not related to her. Troubles develop years later, when the man attains wealth, and his "daughter's" true identity is discovered by two scoundrels bent on blackmail. But when it's all sorted out, the widower assures her that she will always be his little girl.

The Love Auction (Fox, 1919)
d: Edmund Lawrence. 5 reels.
Virginia Pearson, Elizabeth Garrison, Gladys MacClure, Hugh Thompson, Edwin Stanley, Thurlow Bergen, Charles Mason.
When a young woman marries for money rather than for love, she discovers she would have been better off to have followed her heart.

The Love Bandit (Charles E. Blaney Productions/Vitagraph, 1924)
d: Dell Henderson. 6 reels.
Doris Kenyon, Victor Sutherland, Jules Cowles, Christian Frank, Mary Walters, Miss Valentine, Cecil Spooner,

Gardner James, Walter Jones, Edward Bouldin.
Out West, a lumberman falls in love with a vacationing New York girl.

The Love Brand   (Universal, 1923)
d: Stuart Paton.   5 reels.
Roy Stewart, Wilfred North, Margaret Landis, Arthur Hull, Sidney DeGrey, Marie Wells.
For financial purposes, a young woman tries to get a rancher to fall in love with her. He does so, then learns she had an ulterior motive.   But now the young lady has fallen genuinely in love with her "mark," and to prove it she offers to submit to being branded by him.

The Love Brokers   (Triangle, 1918)
d: E. Mason Hopper.   5 reels.
Alma Rubens, Texas Guinan, Joseph Bennett, Lee Hill, Betty Pearce, George Pearce.
Charlotte's a struggling songwriter, eager for a big break. A pair of schemers convince her to marry Gerard, a rich man, since he is near death anyway. Charlotte agrees, and goes through with the marriage... but to everyone's surprise, Gerard recovers his health.

The Love Burglar   (Famous Players-Lasky/Paramount, 1919)
d: James Cruze.   5 reels.
Wallace Reid, Anna Q. Nilsson, Raymond Hatton, Wallace Beery, Wilton Taylor, Edward Burns, Alice Taffe, Dick Wayne, Henry Woodward, Loyola O'Connor.
To avoid the unwelcome attentions of an ex-con, cabaret singer Joan Grey claims to be engaged to someone else. A friendly stranger agrees to help Joan by going through a phony marriage ceremony with her. In due course, Joan and the stranger fall in love with each other and decide on a real marriage.

The Love Call   (National Film Corp. of America, 1919)
d: Louis William Chaudet.   5 reels.
Billie Rhodes, T. Lloyd Whitlock, Art Hoxan, William Dyer, Frank Whitson, Harry Devere, John Pettie.
Out West, a young woman yearns to get an education, though she hasn't the foggiest notion how to go about it.

The Love Charm   (Realart Pictures/Paramount, 1921)
d: Thomas N. Heffron.   5 reels.
Wanda Hawley, Mae Busch, Sylvia Ashton, Warner Baxter, Carrie Clark Ward, Molly McGowan.
Romantic comedy about Ruth, an orphan who lives in her aunt's household. Ruth and her cousin Hattie both set their caps for the same young banker; and Ruth, in an effort at one-upmanship, plays the scandalous vamp for his benefit.

The Love Cheat   (Albert Capellani Productions, Inc./Pathé, 1919)
d: George Archainbaud.   5 reels.
June Caprice, Creighton Hale, Edwards Davis, Alfred Hickman, Charles Coleman, Jessica Brown, Katherine Johnson.
A struggling artist falls for a debutante and, without considering the consequences, impersonates a wealthy man in order to win her heart.

The Love Defender   (World Film Corp., 1919)
d: Tefft Johnson.   5 reels.
June Elvidge, Frank Mayo, Madge Evans, Tefft Johnson, Eloise Clement, Isabel O'Madigan, Marie Burke.
After his sweetheart jilts him, a broken-hearted young doctor settles down and marries his mentor's daughter. The marriage is comfortable but unexciting—until his old sweetheart returns and decides to reclaim her old flame.

Love 'Em and Leave 'Em   (Paramount, 1926)
d: Frank Tuttle.   7 reels.
Louise Brooks, Evelyn Brent, Lawrence Gray, Osgood Perkins, Jack Egan, Marcia Harris, Edward Garvey, Vera Sisson, Joseph McClunn, Arthur Donaldson, Elise Cabanna, Dorothy Mathews.
Mame and Janie are sisters who share the same philosophy about men: Love 'em and leave 'em.

The Love Expert   (Constance Talmadge Film Co./First National, 1920)
d: David Kirkland.   6 reels.
Constance Talmadge, John Halliday, Arnold Lucy, Natalie Talmadge, Fanny Bourke, Nellie P. Spaulding, Marion Sitgreave, James Spottswood, David Kirkland, Edward Kepler.
Though they've been engaged for six years, a couple cannot marry until he finds husbands for his two sisters and his maiden aunt.

The Love Flower (United Artists, 1920)
w, d: D.W. Griffith. 7 reels.
Carol Dempster, Richard Barthelmess, George MacQuarrie, Anders Randolf, Florence Short, Crauford Kent, Adolphe Lestina, William James, Jack Manning.
A detective pursues a murder suspect to the South Pacific.

The Love Gamble   (Banner Productions, 1925)
d: Edward LeSaint.   6 reels.
Lillian Rich, Robert Frazer, Pauline Garon, Kathleen Clifford, Larry Steers, Bonnie hill, Arthur Rankin, Brooks Benedict, James Marcus.
Peggy Mason, owner of a Boston tearoom, is in the enviable position of juggling proposals of marriage from two ardent suitors.

The Love Gambler   (Fox, 1922)
d: Joseph Franz.   5 reels.
John Gilbert, Carmel Myers, Bruce Gordon, Cap Anderson, William Lawrence, James Gordon, Barbara Tennant, Edward Cecil, Doreen Turner.
Out West, a ranch hand bets that he can tame a wild horse and also tame a wild lady he's got his eyes on.

The Love Girl   (Universal, 1916)
d: Robert Leonard.   5 reels.
Ella Hall, Harry Depp, Adele Farrington, Grace Marvin, Betty Schade, Wadsworth Harris.
When an eastern mystic kidnaps a young woman and holds her for ransom, his captive's cousin comes to her aid.

Love, Hate and a Woman   (J.G. Pictures/Arrow Film Corp., 1921)
d: Charles Horan.   6 reels.
Grace Davison, Ralph Kellard, Robert Frazer, Lila Peck, Charles McDonald, Julia Swayne Gordon.
Daryl, a working girl, masquerades as a socialite at an exclusive resort, and meets Lockwood, a handsome young artist.

The Love Hermit   (American Film Co./Mutual, 1916)
d: Jack Prescott.   5 reels.
William Russell, Charlotte Burton, William Stowell, Harry Von Meter, Queenie Rosson, Ashton Dearholt.
Confounded by a failed love affair, a young man throws himself into his work and rises in the business world to a

position of wealth and prominence. Then she comes back into his life.

Love, Honor and --? (Charles Miller Productions/Hallmark Pictures, 1919)
d: Charles Miller. 5 reels.
Ellen Cassidy, Stuart Holmes, Corliss Giles, Florence Short, Edouard Durand.
Returning from his tour of duty in World War I, an aviator learns that his wife has behaved shamefully.

Love, Honor and Behave (Mack Sennett/Associated First National, 1920)
d: Richard Jones, Erle Kenton. 5 reels.
Charles Murray, Ford Sterling, Phyllis Haver, Marie Prevost, George O'Hara, Charlotte Mineau, Billy Bevan, Kalla Pasha, Eddie Gribbon, Fanny Kelly, Billy Armstrong.

Recalling how he himself was once blackmailed on the basis of circumstantial evidence, a judge ponders uneasily the case before him: Should he declare a husband unfaithful because his wife has discovered another woman's picture in his pocket? Yep, it's a comedy.

Love, Honor and Obey (Metro, 1920)
d: Leander de Cordova. 6 reels.
Wilda Bennett, Claire Whitney, Henry Harmon, Kenneth Harlan, George Cowl, E.J. Ratcliffe.
Falsely accused of scandalous activities, a young writer finds that his fiancée has left him and married another man. But the writer will get a second chance.

The Love Hour (Vitagraph, 1925)
d: Herman Raymaker. 7 reels.
Huntley Gordon, Louise Fazenda, Willard Louis, Ruth Clifford, John Roche, Charles Farrell, Gayne Whitman.
An unspeakable cad drugs a husband in order to pursue the man's wife.

Love Hungry (Fox, 1928)
d: Victor Heerman. 6 reels.
Lois Moran, Lawrence Gray, Marjorie Beebe, Edythe Chapman, James Neill, John Patrick.
Tom, a struggling writer, loves a chorus girl—and wins her on the rebound.

Love in a Hurry (World Film Corp., 1919)
d: Dell Henderson. 5 reels.
Carlyle Blackwell, Evelyn Greeley, Isabel O'Madigan, George MacQuarrie, William Bechtel, Kid Broad, Dick Collens, Louis Grisel.
Charles, a mysterious American, travels to England, where he falls in love with Lady Joan Templar. But before making wedding plans, Charles must tend to his official duties: He's a secret agent, on the trail of German spies.

Love in the Dark (Metro, 1922)
d: Harry Beaumont. 6 reels.
Viola Dana, Cullen Landis, Arline Pretty, Bruce Guerin, Edward Connelly, Margaret Mann, John Harron, Charles West.
Tim, a man with a wife and child, has a mysterious malady that allows him to see only at night.

Love in the Desert (FBO Pictures, 1929)
d: George Melford. 7 reels.
Olive Borden, Hugh Trevor, Noah Beery, Frank Leigh, Pearl Varvell, William H. Tooker, Ida Darling, Alan Roscoe, Fatty Carr.
Bob, an irrigation engineer, is sent on a construction project to North Africa. There, he is kidnapped by outlaws, then assisted in his escape by a beautiful Arabian girl, with whom he falls in love.

Love Insurance (Famous Players-Lasky/Paramount, 1919)
d: Donald Crisp. 5 reels.
Bryant Washburn, Lois Wilson, Theodore Roberts, Frances Raymond, Frank Elliott, Edwin Stevens, Clarence Geldart, Eddie Sutherland, P. Dempsey Tabler, Fred Wright.
What happens when an insurance man, assigned to see that a wedding goes smoothly, falls in love with the bride-to-be?

Love is an Awful Thing (Owen Moore Film Corp./Selznick, 1922)
w, d: Victor Heerman. 7 reels.
Owen Moore, Thomas Guise, Marjorie Daw, Kathryn Perry, Arthur Hoyt, Douglas Carter, Charlotte Mineau, Snitz Edwards, Alice Howell.
Anthony loves Helen, and they are about to be married. Then an old girlfriend shows up and swears he has promised to marry *her*, instead.

Love is Love (Fox, 1919)
d: Scott Dunlap. 5 reels.
Albert Ray, Elinor Fair, William Ryno, Hayward Mack, Harry Dunkinson, John Cossar.
An ex-safe cracker decides to go straight, and love is the reason.

The Love Letter (Universal, 1923)
d: King Baggot. 5 reels.
Gladys Walton, Fontaine LaRue, George Cooper, Edward Hearne, Walt Whitman, Alberta Lee, Lucy Donohue.
Mary Ann, who works in an overalls factory, puts love letters into the pockets of the overalls being shipped. One of them eventually wins her a husband.

Love Letters (Thomas H. Ince/Paramount, 1917)
d: R. William Neill. 5 reels.
Dorothy Dalton, William Conklin, Dorcas Matthews, Thurston Hall, Hayward Mack, William Hoffman.
When a free-love advocate spins his web, young Eileen writes him several letters. But less than a year later, the scoundrel will try to blackmail her with those letters.

Love Letters (Fox, 1924)
d: David Soloman. 5 reels.
Shirley Mason, Gordon Edwards, Alma Francis, John Miljan, William Irving.
Evelyn and Julia, starry-eyed sisters, write love letters to the same guy.

The Love Light (Pickford/United Artists, 1921)
w, d: Frances Marion. 8 reels.
Mary Pickford, Fred Thomson, Edward Philips, Evelyn Duynn, Albert Frisco, Raymond Bloomer, Georges Rigas.
During World War I, an Italian girl marries a man she believes to be American, but who is actually a German spy.

Love Madness (J. Parker Read Jr. Productions, 1920)
d: Joseph Henabery. 6 reels.
Louise Glaum, Matt Moore, William Conklin, Noah Beery, Jack Nelson, Arthur Millet, Peggy Pearce.
Mary's husband Lloyd is in jail, suspected of killing a gang member. But Mary knows he's innocent, so she goes undercover as a woman of the streets and infiltrates the gang to find the real killer.

Love Makes 'em Wild (Fox, 1927)
d: Albert Ray. 6 reels.

Johnny Harron, Sally Phipps, Ben Bard, Arthur Housman, J. Farrell MacDonald, Natalie Kingston, Albert Gran, Florence Gilbert, Earle Mohan, Coy Watson Jr., Noah Young, William B. Davidson.

When a mild-mannered clerk is erroneously diagnosed by his doctors as having a fatal disease, he finds the courage to face up to those who have pushed him around in the past. Now that he's pushed back, he learns that he's going to live after all.

The Love Mart (First National, 1927)
d: George Fitzmaurice. 8 reels.
Billie Dove, Gilbert Roland, Raymond Turner, Noah Beery, Armand Kaliz, Emil Chautard, Boris Karloff, Mattie Peters.
When a popular southern belle is rumored to have Negro blood, she is sold at auction as a slave. But the rumor proves false, and the lady wins not only her freedom, but love with her new "owner."

The Love Mask (Lasky Feature Plays/Paramount, 1916)
d: Frank Reicher. 5 reels.
Cleo Ridgley, Wallace Reid, Earle Foxe, Robert Fleming, Dorothy Abril.
After her mining claim is stolen from her, a woman prospector decides to take the law into her own hands and reclaim her gold.

Love Me (Thomas H. Ince/Paramount, 1918)
d: R. William Neill. 5 reels.
Dorothy Dalton, Jack Holt, William Conklin, Dorcas Matthews, Melbourne MacDowell, Elinor Hancock, Robert McKim.
When a wealthy easterner marries a mining town girl and takes her home to Philadelphia, she gets the cold shoulder from his snobbish family members. But the new bride knows a thing or two about winning people over, and she works her charm on them.

Love Me and the World is Mine (Universal, 1928)
d: E.A. DuPont. 6 reels.
Mary Philbin, Norman Kerry, Betty Compson, Henry B. Walthall, Mathilde Brundage, Charles Sellon, Martha Mattox, George Siegmann, Robert Anderson, Albert Conti, Emily Fitzroy.
In World War I Vienna, a girl consents to marry a wealthy older man when she hears that the man she loves is involved with another girl. But she's wrong about him, and on her wedding day the presumptive bride dashes away from the altar and pursues her true love, who is now in the service and is about to be sent to war.

The Love Net (World Film Corp., 1918)
d: Tefft Johnson. 5 reels.
Madge Evans, Jack Drumier, Charles Sutton, W.T. Carleton, Charles Ascott, Blanche Craig, Kate Lester, Sam Ryan, Charles Jackson, Nora Cecil, Estar Banks, Kathleen Blackburn.
Patty Barnes, a youngster, lives with her grandpa on a modest income... but though there are not many material comforts, the love of family permeates their lives.

Love Never Dies (Universal, 1916)
d: William Worthington. 5 reels.
Ruth Stonehouse, Franklyn Farnum, Dorothy Clark, Maurice Kusell, Kingsley Benedict, Arthur Hoyt, William Canfield, Wadsworth Harris, T.D. Crittenden.
In Paris, love blossoms between a prima ballerina and a struggling composer.

Love Never Dies (First National, 1921)
d: King Vidor. 7 reels.
Lloyd Hughes, Madge Bellamy, Joe Bennett, Lillian Leighton, Fred Gambold, Julia Brown, Frank Brownlee, Winifred Greenwood, Claire McDowell.
A happy marriage is broken up by the wife's possessive father. Dad insists she marry the fellow he's picked out for her, but his daughter still pines for her first love.

The Love of Sunya (United Artists, 1927)
d: Albert Parker. 8 reels.
Gloria Swanson, John Boles, Andres De Segurola, Anders Randolph, Raymond Hackett, Ivan Lebedeff, Ian Keith, Florabelle Fairbanks.
A woman in love has her future disclosed to her by a crystal ball.

Love of Women (Selznick, 1924)
d: Whitman Bennett. 6 reels.
Helene Chadwick, Montague Love, Maurice Costello, Mary Thurman, Lawford Davidson, Marie Shotwell, Frankie Evans.
A persistent suitor continues to court a young woman even after she marries another.

Love or Justice (New York Motion Picture Corp./Triangle, 1917)
d: Walter Edwards. 5 reels.
Louise Glaum, Charles Gunn, Jack Richardson, J. Barney Sherry, Dorcas Matthews, Charles K. French, Louis Durham, Jack Gilbert.
Once a successful lawyer but now a drugged-out loser, Jack Dunn begins a comeback with the help of a woman's love.

Love Over Night (Pathé, 1928)
d: Edward H. Griffith. 6 reels.
Rod LaRocque, Jeanette Loff, Richard Tucker, Tom Kennedy, Mary Carr.
Comedy of errors about a subway employee who pursues a young woman he thinks guilty of theft. He, in turn, is being pursued by a detective who suspects *him*.

The Love Pirate (Richard Thomas Productions/FBO of America, 1923)
d: Richard Thomas. 5 reels.
Melbourne MacDowell, Carmel Myers, Charles Force, Kathryn McGuire, Clyde Fillmore, John Tonkey, Carol Halloway, Edward W. Borman, Spottiswoode Aitken.
Melodrama about a love triangle that turns deadly.

The Love Song—see: Valencia (1926)

The Love Special (Famous Players-Lasky/Paramount, 1921)
d: Frank Urson. 5 reels.
Wallace Reid, Agnes Ayres, Theodore Roberts, Lloyd Whitlock, Sylvia Ashton, William Gaden, Clarence Burton, Snitz Edwards, Ernest Butterworth, Zelma Maja.
Harrison, one of the directors of a western railroad line, tries to win the hand of the daughter of the company's president by bribing him with a needed parcel of land.

A Love Sublime (Fine Arts film Co./Triangle, 1917)
d: Wilfred Lucas, Tod Browning. 5 reels.
Wilfred Lucas, Carmel Myers, Fred A. Turner, Alice Rae, George Beranger, Jack Brammall, James O'Shea, Bert Woodruff, Mildred Harris.
Philip loves Toinette, and when she is injured in an car accident, he keeps watch at her hospital room window night

THE LOVE MART (1927). Gilbert Roland (seated) plays a disconsolate southern gentleman who feels conflicted because he has heard a rumor that the woman he loves (Billie Dove, standing) is of mixed race. Apparently that information was shocking to 1927 audiences.

* * * * *

292

after night.

The Love Swindle (Univesal, 1918)
d: Jack Dillon. 5 reels.
Edith Roberts, Leo White, Clarissa Selwynne, Emmanuel Turner, Reggie Morris.
Wealthy Diana loves Dick, but his dislike of the idle rich keeps him from loving her back. So, Diana tells him she has a twin sister who is a working girl. Dick meets her, falls head over heels, and proposes. After the wedding, the bride tells Dick the truth: the two girls are one and the same.

The Love That Dares (Fox, 1919)
d: Harry Millarde. 5 reels.
Madlaine Traverse, Thomas Santschi, Frank Elliott, Mae Gaston, Thomas Guise, George B. Williams.
Marital mishaps erupt when a wife's extravagance forces her husband to devote more hours to his work.

The Love That Lives (Famous Players/Paramount, 1917)
d: Robert G. Vignola. 5 reels.
Pauline Frederick, John Sainpolis, Pat O'Malley, Joseph Carroll, Violet Palmer, Frank Evans, Eldean Stewart.
Molly's a scrubwoman who sacrifices everything, even her life, so that her son can escape the slums.

The Love Thief (Fox, 1916)
d: Richard Stanton. 5 reels.
Gretchen Hartman, Alan Hale, Frances Burnham, Edward Cecil, Willard Louis, Jack McDonald, Charles Ehler.
Juanita, a Mexican rebel leader, has unrequited love for an American captain.

The Love Thief (Universal, 1926)
d: John McDermott. 7 reels.
Norman Kerry, Greta Nissen, Marc MacDermott, Cissy Fitzgerald, Agostino Borgato, Carrie Daumery, Oscar Beregi, Nigel Barrie, Vladimir Glutz, Charles Puffy, Alphonse Martel.
A princess is used as a pawn in the battle between her own country and its belligerent neighbor.

The Love Thrill (Universal, 1927)
d: Millard Webb. 6 reels.
Laura LaPlante, Tom Moore, Bryant Washburn, Jocelyn Lee, Arthur Hoyt, Nat Carr.
Comedy about an insurance saleswoman who poses as the widow of an explorer who died in Africa. Her imposture begins to unravel about the time the explorer shows up very much alive.

The Love Toy (Warner Bros., 1926)
d: Erle C. Kenton. 6 reels.
Lowell Sherman, Willard Louis, Gayne Whitman, Helene Costello, Ethel Gray Terry.
A young man jilted on the eve of his wedding departs for Europe.

The Love Trap (Ben Wilson Productions, 1923)
d: John Ince. 6 reels.
Bryant Washburn, Mabel Forrest, Wheeler Oakman, Kate Lester, Mabel Trunnelle, William J.Irving, Wilbur Higby, Laura LaVarnie, Sidney Franklin, Edith Stayart, Betty Small.
Joyce, a socialite, is engaged to Garrison, not knowing he's already got a wife, and he's abandoned her.

The Love Trap (Universal, 1929)
d: William Wyler. 8 reels. (Part talkie.)
Laura LaPlante, Neil Hamilton, Norman Trevor, Robert Ellis, Clarissa Selwynne, Rita Le Roy, Jocelyn Lee.
A chorus girl marries a young taxi driver, but his family doesn't approve—especially not his uncle, a judge who met the chorus girl briefly once, at a wild party.

Love Watches (Vitagraph, 1918)
d: Henri Houry. 5 reels.
Corinne Griffith, Denton Vane, Florence Deshon, Edward Burns, Julia Swayne Gordon, Alice Terry, Nellie Parker, Charles A. Stevenson, Carola Carson, Alice Nash, Edna Nash.
In France, a count's wife suspects her husband is being unfaithful, so she seeks solace with an old friend, a man who is secretly in love with her.

Lovebound (Fox, 1923)
d: Henry Otto. 5 reels.
Shirley Mason, Albert Roscoe, Richard Tucker, Joseph Girard, Edward Martindel, Fred Kelsey.
A girl who's engaged to the local district attorney has a secret criminal past.

The Lovelorn (Cosmopolitan/MGM, 1927)
d: John P. McCarthy. 7 reels.
Sally O'Neil, James Murray, Molly O'Day, Larry Kent, Charles Delaney, George Cooper, Allan Forrest, Dorothy Cumming.
Two sisters in love with the same man seek advice from Beatrice Fairfax, a columnist for the lovelorn.

Lovely Mary (Columbia/Metro, 1916)
d: Edgar Jones. 5 reels.
Mary Miles Minter, Frank De Vernon, Russell Simpson, Schuyler Ladd, Fred Tidmarsh, Myra Brooks, Harry Blakemore, Thomas Carrigan.
When a young woman and her cousin try to sell the land they've inherited, they run afoul of greedy speculators.

The Lover of Camille (Warner Bros., 1924)
d: Harry Beaumont. 8 reels.
Monte Blue, Marie Prevost, Willard Louis, Pierre Gendron, Pat Moore, Carlton Miller, Rosa Rosanova, Winifred Bryson, Brandon Hurst, Rose Dione, Trilby Clark.
In Paris, a young actor follows in his father's footsteps as a prince of players.

Lovers? (MGM, 1927)
d: John Stahl. 6 reels.
Ramon Novarro, Alice Terry, Edward Connelly, John Miljan, George K. Arthur, Edward Martindel, Lillian Leighton, Holmes Herbert, Roy D'Arcy.
A young man falls in love with his guardian's wife.

Lovers in Quarantine (Famous Players-Lasky/Paramount, 1925)
d: Frank Tuttle. 7 reels.
Harrison Ford, Bebe Daniels, Alfred Lunt, Eden Gray, Edna May Oliver, Diana Kane, Ivan Simpson, Marie Shotwell.
Diana, thought to be unattractive and a tomboy, secretly desires her sister's fiancé.

Lover's Island (Encore Pictures/Associated Exhibitors, 1925)
d: Henri Diamant-Berger. 5 reels.
Hope Hampton, James Kirkwood, Louis Wolheim, Ivan Linow, Flora Finch, Flora LeBreton, Jack Raymond.
In a small fishing village, a young woman is attacked and raped. When pressed to name the man, she deliberately names a different fellow, one she's had her eyes on.

Lovers' Lane (Warner Bros., 1924)

d: Phil Rosen. 7 reels.

Robert Ellis, Gertrude Olmstead, Maxine Elliott Hicks, Kate Toncray, Norval McGregor, Crauford Kent, Charles Sellon, George Periolat, Frances Dale, Bruce Guerin, Ethel Wales.

Mary, a country girl, is engaged to the local doctor; but bored with the rural life, she instead goes after a fellow who promises to take her to the big city.

A Lover's Oath   (Astor Pictures, 1925)
d: Ferdinand P. Earle. 6 reels.

Ramon Novarro, Kathleen Key, Edwin Stevens, Frederick Warde, Hedwig Reicher, Snitz Edwards, Charles A. Post, Arthur Edmund carew, Paul Weigel, Philippe DeLacy, Warren Rodgers.

Romantic drama inspired by a passage from *The Rubaiyat of Omar Khayyam*, about the love of one Ben Ali for the most beautiful women in the tribe.

Love's Blindness   (MGM, 1926)
d: John Francis Dillon. 7 reels.

Antonio Moreno, Pauline Starke, Lilyan Tashman, Sam de Grasse, Tom Ricketts, Kate Price, Ned Sparks, Douglas Gilmore.

A penniless nobleman marries for money, then discovers he loves his wife.

Love's Boomerang   (Famous Players-Lasky/Paramount, 1922)
d: John S. Robertson. 6 reels.

Ann Forrest, Bunty Fosse, David Powell, John Miltern, Roy Byford, Florence Wood, Geoffrey Kerr, Lillian Walker, Lionel D'Aragon, Ollie Emery, Amy Williard.

An artist falls in love with his ward, and she with him.

Love's Conquest   (Famous Players-Lasky/Paramount, 1918)
d: Edward José. 5 reels.

Lina Cavalieri, Courtenay Foote, Fred Radcliffe, Frank Lee, J.H. Gilmore, Isabelle Berwin, Fredi Verdi.

When a duchess learns her young son has fallen into a lion pit, she swears to marry the man who saves him. But it turns out that the boy's savior is a commoner, something the status-conscious duchess hadn't counted on.

Love's Crucible   (Wm. A. Brady/World, 1916)
d: Emile Chautard. 5 reels.

Douglas MacLean, Frances Nelson, June Elvidge, Lumsden Hare, John Hyland, Edythe Thornton, Mildred Havens, Jessie Lewis, E.M. Kimball, Fred C. Truesdell.

While in New York city, a small town girl with a flair for painting becomes an international success. She is courted by many suitors, but unwisely picks a pretentious fop who grows tired of her and breaks off the affair. Having been tested by love's crucible, the young artist decides to devote her life to her art.

Love's Greatest Mistake   (Famous Players-Lasky/Paramount, 1927)
d: Edward Sutherland. 6 reels.

Evelyn Brent, James Hall, Josephine Dunn, Frank Morgan, Iris Gray, William Powell, Betty Byrne.

Honey, a small-town girl, travels to New York and finds numerous romantic adventures.

Love's Harvest   (Fox, 1920)
d: Howard M. Mitchell. 5 reels.

Shirley Mason, Raymond McKee, Edwin Booth Tilton, Lilie Leslie.

In Paris, an American girl studying music is visited by an old friend from home, and falls in love with him.

Love's Lariat   (Universal, 1916)
d: George Marshall, Harry Carey. 5 reels.

Harry Carey, Olive Golden, Neal Hart, William Quinn, Pedro Leon, Joe Rickson.

A cowboy receives a large inheritance from his uncle, but there's a catch: to collect, he must live in the big city for a year.

Love's Law   (Fox, 1917)
d: Tefft Johnson. 5 reels.

Joan Sawyer, Stuart Holmes, Olga Grey, Leo Delaney, Richard Neill, Frank Goldsmith.

Whimsical fantasy about a young girl who roams the forest and becomes involved with a band of gypsies.

Love's Law   (Mutual, 1918)
d: Francis J. Grandon. 5 reels.

Gail Kane, Courtenay Foote, Reed Hamilton, Frederick Jones, Augusta Perry, Walter Deming, Mathilde Baring, Emile La Croix, Frank Lenox.

Sonia's a young Polish American with a great musical gift but not much money. To finance her studies and her eventual debut, she accepts a loan from a millionaire without thinking what he might demand in return.

Love's Masquerade   (Selznick/Select, 1922)
d: William P.S. Earle. 5 reels.

Conway Tearle, Winifred Westover, Danny Hayes, Arthur Houseman, Robert Schable.

Carrington, hopelessly in love with a married woman, takes the blame when her husband is murdered, believing the wife is the actual murderer.

Loves of an Actress   (Paramount, 1928)
d: Rowland V. Lee. 8 reels.

Pola Negri, Paul Lukas, Nils Asther, Mary McAllister, Richard Tucker, Phil Strange, Nigel De Brulier, Robert Fischer, Helene Giere.

In France, Rachel, a peasant girl, is sponsored by three wealthy men and becomes the toast of the Comédie Française. All three men pursue her love, but Rachel's heart belongs to Raoul, a young diplomat.

Loves of Carmen   (Fox, 1927)
d: Raoul Walsh. 9 reels.

Dolores Del Rio, Don Alvarado, Victor McLaglen, Nancy Nash, Rafael Valverda, Mathilde Comont, Jack Baston, Carmen Costello, Fred Kohler.

A feisty gypsy girl flirts with many men, and succeeds in destroying the career of a Spanish cavalry lieutenant. Energetic, physical performance by the vivacious Dolores Del Rio as the fiery coquette, Carmen.

The Loves of Letty   (Goldwyn, 1919)
d: Frank Lloyd. 5 reels.

Pauline Frederick, John Bowers, Lawson Butt, Willard Louis, Florence Deshon, Leila Bliss, Leota Lorraine, Sydney Ainsworth, Harland Tucker, Joan Standing.

Letty's a clerk who dreams of fine clothes and social standing, and seeks to attain them through affairs with wealthy men. She comes to her senses, though, and forsakes her chance at riches, settling down with a photographer who loves her.

Love's Old Sweet Song   (Norca Pictures/Hopp Hadley, 1923)
d: Oscar Lund. 5 reels.

Louis Wolheim, Helen Weir, Donald Gallagher, Helen Lowell, Baby Margaret Brown, Ernest Hilliard.

A tramp wanders into a town where a crooked bank cashier is determined to ruin the owner of a marble quarry. But the "tramp" is really a Secret Service agent, and soon the villain is behind bars.

Love's Pay Day (Triangle, 1918)
d: E. Mason Hopper. 5 reels.
Rosemary Theby, Pete Morrison, Billy Dale, Lillian West, Alberta Lee, Harvey Clark, John Lince.
In Newfoundland, a young bride gets talked into selling her new husband's packing plant to a big city combine.

Love's Penalty (Hope Hampton Productions/Associated First National, 1921)
w, d: John Gilbert. 5 reels.
Hope Hampton, Irma Harrison, Mrs. Phillip Landau, Percy Marmont, Jack O'Briend, Virginia Valli, Douglas Redmond, Charles Lane, Mrs. L. Faure.
A villainous ship owner sends his wife to Europe aboard an ill-fated liner.

Love's Pilgrimage to America (Universal, 1915)
d: Harry C. Myers. 5 reels.
Lulu Glaser, Jack Richards, Adila Comer, Thomas Keeswald, Sarah Brundage, Henry Norman, Joe Girard, William Sloan, A.C. Marston, Hudson Liston, E. Cooper Willis.
In England, Lulu and Tom are in love and want to be married, but their families oppose the match. So they elope to America, where they have numerous adventures before finally settling down to wedded bliss.

Love's Prisoner (Triangle, 1919)
d: Jack Dillon. 6 reels.
Olive Thomas, Joe King, William V. Mong.
An embittered young woman turns to a life of crime.

Love's Redemption (Norma Talmadge Film Co./Associated First National, 1921)
d: Albert Parker. 6 reels.
Norma Talmadge, Harrison Ford, Montagu Love, Ida Waterman, H. Cooper Cliffe, Michael M. Barnes, Frazer Coulter, E.L. Fernandez.
Ginger, an orphan who grew up in Jamaica, falls in love with a plantation owner.

Love's Toll (Lubin, 1916)
d: Jack Pratt. 5 reels.
Rosetta Brice, Richard Buhler, Crauford Kent, Inez Buck, Karva Poloskova, William H. Turner.
Upon learning that his new bride once had a lover, a doctor is determined to throw her out of his house forever.

Love's Whirlpool (Regal Pictures/W.W. Hodkinson, 1924)
d: Bruce Mitchell. 6 reels.
James Kirkwood, Lila Lee, Robert Agnew, Mathew Betz, Edward Martindel, Margaret Livingston, Madge Bellamy, Clarence Geldert, Joseph Mills.
Jim, a former criminal, tries to wreak vengeance on a heartless banker by abducting his daughter.

Love's Wilderness (Corinne Griffith Productions/First National, 1924)
d: Robert Z. Leonard. 7 reels.
Corinne Griffith, Holmes E. Herbert, Ian Keith, Maurice Cannon, Emily Fitzroy, Anne Schaefer, Bruce Covington, David Torrance, Frank Elliott, Adolph Millar, Jim Blackwell.
Linda, an orphan raised by maiden aunts, falls in love with David, a medical missionary. He leaves for Africa, however, and Linda accepts marriage with Paul, a drifter. Paul deserts her, and Linda returns to David, thinking her husband dead. They marry and she accompanies him to Devil's Island, where the prisoners have just broken free. Linda is shocked to find that one of the escapees is her first husband Paul.

Lovetime (Fox, 1921)
d: Howard M. Mitchell. 5 reels.
Shirley Mason, Raymond McKee, Frances Hatton, Edwin B. Tilton, Mathilde Brundage, Wilson Hummell, Harold Goodwin, Charles A. Smiley, Correan Kirkham.
In the French countryside, a painter finds his muse in the person of Marie, a peasant girl.

Lovey Mary (MGM, 1926)
d: King Baggot. 7 reels.
Bessie Love, William Haines, Jackie Coombs, Mary Alden, Eileen Percy, Martha Mattox.
Lovey Mary, an orphan, falls in love with Tommy, a fellow orphan. When his mother comes to the orphanage to take Tommy away, Mary and Tommy flee together.

Loving Lies (United Artists, 1924)
d: W.S. Van Dyke. 7 reels.
Monte Blue, Evelyn Brent, Charles Gerrard, Joan Lowell, Ralph Faulkner, Ethel Wales, Andrew Waldron, Tom Kennedy.
When a sea captain's wife suffers a miscarriage while he is away, her jealous former sweetheart takes advantage of her fragile condition and lies to her, saying that the captain has been unfaithful.

Loyal Lives (Postman Pictures/Vitagraph, 1923)
d: Charles Giblyn. 6 reels.
BrandonTynan, Mary Carr, Faire Binney, William Collier Jr., Charles McDonald, Blanche Craig, Chester Morris, Tom Blake, Blanche Davenport, John Hopkins, Mickey Bennett.
O'Brien, a postal employee, raises a son and a daughter both dedicated to hard work and integrity.

Luck (C.C. Burr/Mastodon Films, 1923)
d: C.C. Burr. 7 reels.
Johnny Hines, Robert Edeson, Edmund Breese, Violet Mersereau, Charles Murray, Flora Finch, Warner Richmond, Polly Moran, Harry Fraser, Matthew Betts.
Carter, a gambler, wagers that he can start with nothing and end the year with $10,000.

Luck and Pluck (Fox, 1919)
d: Edward Dillon. 5 reels.
George Walsh, Virginia Lee, Joe Smiley, George Fisher, Corinne Uzzell, George Halpin.
It's farewell to the criminal life when a master thief spots a beautiful girl in Central Park.

Luck and Sand (Maloford Productions/Weiss Brothers Clarion Photoplays, 1925)
d: Leo Maloney. 5 reels.
Leo Maloney, Josephine Hill, Homer Watson, Florence Lee, Leonard Clapham, Roy Watson, Hal Gilbert.
Con men resort to murder when they can't get a railroad engineer to divulge the company's secret plans for a new right of way.

Luck in Pawn (Famous Players-Lasky/Paramount, 1919)
d: Walter Edwards. 5 reels.
Marguerite Clark, Charles Meredith, Leota Lorraine, Richard

Wayne, John Steppling, Lillian Langdon, Myrtle Richelle, Lydia Knott, Paul Weigel, Thomas D. Persse, Pat Moore.
Annabel's a struggling artist who has sold only one painting. On the verge of calling it quits, she is persuaded to stay on for a while by a millionaire who's fallen for her.

The Luck of Geraldine Laird (B.B. Features, 1920)
d: Edward Sloman. 5 reels.
Bessie Barriscale, Niles Welch, Boyd Irwin, Dorcas Matthews, William Mong, Rosita Marstini, Ashton Dearholt, George Hall, Nannine Wright, Mary Jane Irving.
Geraldine's husband is a playwright who never seems to sell any plays. She follows him to the big city, and there she lucks into a job that makes her a theatrical star.

The Luck of the Irish (Mayflower Photoplay Corp., 1920)
d: Allan Dwan. 7 reels.
James Kirkwood, Anna Q. Nilsson, Harry Northrup, Ward Crane, Ernest Butterworth, Gertrude Messenger, Madame Deione, Louise Lester.
When a plumber who works in a basement falls in love with a pretty pair of feet he spies through the window, he follows and finds their owner, a lovely schoolteacher.

Lucky Boy (Tiffany-Stahl Productions, 1929)
d: Norman Taurog. 10 reels. (Part talkie.)
George Jessel, Gwen Lee, Richard Tucker, Gayne Whitman, Margaret Quimby, Rosa Rosanova, William Strauss, Mary Doran.
After several false starts, a jeweler's apprentice finally makes it big in show business.

Lucky Carson (Vitagraph, 1921)
d: Wilfrid North. 5 reels.
Earle Williams, Earl Schenck, Betty Ross Clarke, Gertrude Astor, Colette Forbes, James Butler, Loyal Underwood.
In England, a gambler blows all his money betting on the horses. Not to be dissuaded, he makes his way to America and adopts the name "Lucky" Carson.

Lucky Devil (Famous Players-Lasky/Paramount, 1925)
d: Frank Tuttle. 6 reels.
Richard Dix, Esther Ralston, Edna May Oliver, Tom Findlay, Anthony Jowitt, Joseph Burke, Mary Foy, Gunboat Smith, Charles Sellon, Charles Hammond, Charles McDonald.
Zany comedy about a fellow who wins a racing car in a raffle and must drive it in a race with the sheriff continually at his side.

Lucky Horseshoe (Fox, 1925)
d: J.G. Blystone. 5 reels.
Tom Mix, Billie Dove, Malcolm Waite, J. Farrell MacDonald, Clarissa Selwynne, Ann Pennington, J. Gunnis Davis.
Knocked on the head, a ranch foreman dreams he is the fabled Don Juan.

The Lucky Lady (Paramount, 1926)
d: Raoul Walsh. 6 reels.
Greta Nissen, Lionel barrymore, William Collier Jr., Marc MacDermott, Madame Daumery, Sojin.
In a European kingdom, the prime minister decrees that the princess must marry the rakish Count Ferranzo. The princess, however, has her eyes on a handsome American.

Lucky Star (Fox, 1929)
d: Frank Borzage. 9 reels. (Music, sound effects, part talkie.)
Janet Gaynor, Charles Farrell, Guinn Williams, Paul Fix, Hedwig Reicher, Gloria Grey, Hector Sarno.

A poor farm girl meets her dream man just as word comes that war has been declared. He enlists in the army and goes to the battlefields of Europe, where he is wounded and loses the use of his legs. Home again, and in a wheelchair, the young man finds himself powerfully attracted to the farm girl, but his physical handicap prevents him from declaring his love for her. (But there's a happy ending.)

Lucretia Lombard (Warner Brothers, 1923)
d: Jack Conway. 7 reels.
Irene Rich, Marc McDermott, Monte Blue, Norma Shearer, Alec B. Francis, John Roche, Lucy Beaumont, Otto Hoffman.
A young woman is in a loveless marriage with an older man. When he dies, she looks forward to a happier future, but various disasters intervene, including a forest fire, an explosion, and a mighty flood.

The Lullaby (R-C Pictures/FBO of America, 1924)
d: Chester Bennett. 7 reels.
Jane Novak, Robert Anderson, Fred Malatesta, Dorothy Brock, Cleo Madison, Otis Harlan, Peter Burke, Lydia Yeamans Titus.
Weepy melodrama about pregnant Felipa, who is sentenced to prison as accessory to murder. Her baby is born in prison, but the child is taken from her and adopted by the judge who sentenced her.

The Lunatic at Large (First National Pictures, 1927)
d: Fred Newmeyer. 6 reels.
Leon Errol, Dorothy Mackaill, Jack Raymond, Warren Cook, Kenneth MacKenna, Tom Blake, Charles Slattery, Theresa Maxwell Conover.
Comedy about a pair of sane chaps who get tricked into checking into a sanitarium, then have to finagle their way out.

The Lure of Ambition (Fox, 1919)
d: Edmund Lawrence. 5 reels.
Theda Bara, Thurlow Bergen, William B. Davidson, Dan Mason, Ida Waterman, Amelia Gardner, Robert Paton Gibbs, Dorothy Drake, Tammany Young.
Olga, a poor tenement girl, has major ambitions. She persuades an admirer to take her to Europe, and once there she wangles an introduction to the Duke of Rutledge, whom she fancies.

Lure of Gold (William Steiner Productions, 1922)
d: Neal Hart. 5 reels.
Neal Hart, William Quinn, Ben Corbett.
Out West, a concert diva falls for a rodeo champion.

The Lure of Heart's Desire (Popular Plays and Players/Metro, 1916)
d: Francis J. Grandon. 5 reels.
Edmund Breese, Arthur Hoops, John Mahon, Jeannette Horton, Evelyn Brent.
Rejected by his socialite sweetie because of his low-income status, Jim goes on a prospecting trip to Alaska and strikes it rich.

The Lure of Jade (Robertson-Cole/R-C Pictures, 1921)
d: Colin Campbell. 6 reels.
Pauline Frederick, Thomas Holding, Arthur Rankin, Leon Bary, Hardee Kirkland, L.C. Shumway, Clarissa Selwynne, Togo Yamamoto, Goro Kino.
An admiral with an impressive collection of jade lures a beautiful woman into his chamber to view it. Because his servant locks the door behind them, the lady is forced to protect her reputation by fleeing through a window.

The Lure of Luxury   (Universal, 1918)
d: Elsie Jane Wilson.   5 reels.
Ruth Clifford, Edward Hearn, Harry Von Meter, Elizabeth Janes, George Hopp, Janet Sally.
Childhood sweethearts meet again as adults and realize they are still in love.

The Lure of the Night Club   (R-C Pictures/FBO of America, 1927)
d: Thomas Buckingham.   6 reels.
Viola Dana, Robert Ellis, Jack Daugherty, Bert Woodruff, Lydia Yeamans Titus, Robert Dudley.
A romantic tug-of-war develops between an entertainer's manager and her home-town boyfriend.

The Lure of the Wild   (Columbia, 1925)
d: Frank Strayer.   6 reels.
Alan Roscoe, Jane Novak, Billie Jean, Richard Tucker, Mario Carillo, Pat Harmon.
In the Canadian Northwest, the father of a little girl is ruthlessly murdered, but his faithful dog valiantly protects the daughter.

Lure of the Yukon   (Norman Dawn Alaska Co./Lee-Bradford Corp., 1924)
w, d: Norman Dawn.   6 reels.
Eva Novak, Spottiswoode Aitken, Kent sanderson, Arthur Jasmine, Howard Webster, Katherine Dawn.
In the frozen Klondike, a gold prospector and his daughter are pursued by would-be claim jumpers.

The Lure of Youth   (Metro, 1921)
d: Philip E. Rosen.   6 reels.
Cleo Madison, William Conklin, Gareth Hughes, Lydia Knott, William Courtwright, Helen Weir.
On Broadway, a famous actress sponsors a young playwright.

Luring Lips   (Universal, 1921)
d: King Baggot.   5 reels.
Darrel Foss, Ramsey Wallace, Edith Roberts, William Welsh, Carlton King, M.E. Stimson.
Dave, a bank teller, is accused of embezzling $50,000, but the real culprit is the office manager, who's also out to snag Dave's girlfriend.

The Lust of the Ages   (Ogden Pictures Corp., 1917)
d: Harry Revier.   7 reels.
Lillian Walker, Jack Mower, Harry Revier, Nellie Parker Spaulding, W.J. Everett, Frances Sanson, Betty Mack.
After reading a book titled "The Lust of the Ages," a young man abandons his pursuit of money and settles instead for a home and family.

Lydia Gilmore   (Famous Players/Paramount, 1915)
d: Edwin S. Porter, Hugh Ford.   5 reels.
Pauline Frederick, Vincent Serrano, Thomas Holding, Robert Cain, Helen Luttrell, Jack Curtis, Michael Rale.
Though enamored of a humble workman, Lydia marries a wealthy doctor—and lives to regret it.

Lying Lips   (American Film Co./Mutual, 1916)
d: Edward Sloman.   5 reels.
Winnifred Greenwood, Franklin Ritchie, Eugenie Forde, Clarence Burton, Roy Stewart, George Webb.
Nobly, a stage actress agrees to let her husband's sister live with them.   When the sister's actions unjustly cause her brother to believe his wife is having an affair, he confronts his wife.   She soon sets his mind to rest, and Sis is sent packing.

Lying Lips   (Thomas H. Ince/Associated Producers, 1921)
d: John Griffith Wray.   7 reels.
House Peters, Florence Vidor, Joseph Kilgour, Margaret Livingston, Margaret Campbell, Edith Yorke, Calvert Carter, Emmett C. King.
Nancy, an English aristocrat, is engaged to one man but enamored of another.

The Lying Truth   (Eagle Producing Co./American Releasing Corp., 1922)
d: Marion Fairfax.   5 reels.
Noah Beery, Marjorie Daw, Tully Marshall, Pat O'Malley, Charles Mailes, Claire McDowell, Adele Watson, George Dromgold, Robert Brauer, Wade Boteler.
Bill is accused of murdering his adoptive father—but the old man actually took his own life.

Lying Wives   (Ivan Players, 1925)
w, d: Ivan Abramson.   7 reels.
Clara Kimball Young, Richard Bennett, Madge Kennedty, Edna Murphy, Niles Welch, J. Barney Sherry, Buddy Harris, Bee Jackson.
Though married herself, a spiteful woman tries to break up the marriage of a stenographer and a millionaire through innuendo.

The Mad Dancer   (Jans Productions, 1925)
d: Burton King.   7 reels.
Ann Pennington, Johnny Walker, Coit Albertson, John Woodford, Frank Montgomery, Rica Allen, William F. Haddock, John Costello, Nellie Savage, Echlin Gayer.
After posing in the nude for a statue of "The Mad Dancer," Mimi gets the cold shoulder from her high-society friends.

Mad Hour   (First National, 1928)
d: James C. Boyle.   7 reels.
Sally O'Neil, Donald Reed, Lowell Sherman, Norman Trevor, Alice White, Tully Marshall, James Farley, Roe Dione, Margaret Livingston, Kate Price, Mary Foy, Ione Holmes.
Heavy weeper about a taxi driver's daughter who marries unwisely, becomes implicated in a robbery scheme, and bears a child while in prison for a crime she didn't commit.

The Mad Lover   (Robert Warwick Film Corp./Pathé, 1917)
w, d: Leonce Perret.   5 reels.
Robert Warwick, Elaine Hammerstein, Valentine Petit, Edward Kimball, George Flateau, Frank McGlynn.
When a comfortably married man sees his wife playing Desdemona in a charity performance of *Othello*, he becomes upset watching her in the love scenes.

The Mad Marriage   (Universal, 1921)
d: Rollin Sturgeon.   5 reels.
Carmel Myers, Truman Van Dyke, William Brunton, Virginia Ware, Margaret Cullington, Jane Starr, Arthur Carewe, Nola Luxford, Lydia Yeamans Titus.
Melodrama about Jane, a playwright who marries Jerry, a struggling artist.

The Mad Marriage   (Rosemary Films, 1925)
d: Frank F. Donovan.   5 reels.
Maurice Costello, Harrison Ford, Rosemary Davis, Richard Carle, Paul Panzer, Florence Turner, Gaston Glass, Montagu Love, Walter McGrail, Mary Thurman.
After leaving his teenage wife and child, an author goes on to build a name for himself in literary circles. Years pass, he

falls in love with a young woman, and they plan to be married. But hold on, Mr. Write: She's the daughter you left behind.

The Mad Whirl (Universal, 1925)
d: William A. Seiter. 7 reels.
May MacAvoy, Jack Mulhall, Myrtle Stedman, Alex B. Francis, Barbara Bedford, George Nichols, Ward Crane, George Fawcett, Marie Astaire, Joe Singleton.
Jazz-age parents try to keep up with their son's party-loving friends.

Madam Who (Paralta Plays Inc./General Film Co., 1918)
d: Reginald Barker. 7 reels.
Bessie Barriscale, Edward Coxen, Howard Hickman, Joseph J. Dowling, David M. Hartford, Fanny Midgley, Nicholas Cogley, Eugene Pallette, Wallace Worsley, Clarence Barr.
During the Civil War, a southern girl falls for a northerner.

Madame Behave (Christie Film Co., 1925)
d: Scott Sidney. 6 reels.
Julian Eltinge, Ann Pennington, Lionel Belmore, David James, Tom Wilson, Jack Duffy, Stanhope Wheatcroft, Evelyn Francisco.
Zany farce about two roommates in danger of becoming homeless, who resort to female impersonation to solve their dilemma.

Madame Bo-Peep (Fine Arts Film Co./Triangle, 1917)
d: Chester Withey. 5 reels.
Seena Owen, A.D. Sears, F.A. Turner, James Harrison, Sam De Grasse, Pauline Starke, Kate Bruce, Jennie Lee.
After a socialite rejects her fiancé to marry for money, her decision will come back to haunt her.

Madame Butterfly (Famous Players/Paramount, 1915)
d: Sidney Olcott. 5 reels.
Mary Pickford, Olive West, Jane Hall, Lawrence Wood, Caroline Harris, M.W. Rale, W.T. Carleton, David Burton, Frank Dekum, Marshall Neilan, Caesere Gravina.
In Japan, a girl named Cho-Cho-San marries a white American officer, Lieutenant Pinkerton. It is a tragic mismatch, as Pinkerton leaves his bride to return to the United States, and she has their baby alone.

Madame Du Barry — see: Du Barry (1917)

Madame Jealousy (Famous Players/Paramount, 1918)
d: Robert G. Vignola. 5 reels.
Pauline Frederick, Thomas Meighan, Frank Losee, Charles Wellesley, Isabel O'Madigan, Elsie MacLeod, Ina Rorke, Frances Cappelano, Grace Barton, Edwin Sturgis, Marcia Harris.
Allegorical tale about a happily married couple named Charm and Valor, and the troubles they have when targeted by the green-eyed monster, Jealousy.

Madame La Presidente (Oliver Morosco Photoplays/Paramount, 1916)
d: Frank Lloyd. 5 reels.
Anna Held, Forrest Stanley, Herbert Standing, Page Peters, Lydia Yeamans Titus, Helen Eddy, Howard Davies, Dick La Strange, Robert Newcomb, Frank Bonn.
In France, a charming actress masquerades as the wife of a presiding judge.

Madame Peacock (Metro, 1920)
d: Ray C. Smallwood. 6 reels.
Nazimova, George Probert, John Steppling, William Orlamond, Rex Cherryman, Albert Cody, Gertrude Claire, Georgie Woodthorpe.
Ambitious and self-centered, a successful stage actress banishes her tubercular husband and their daughter to a sanitarium and continues to climb the ladder of success alone. Some years later, she finds herself being outperformed and upstaged by a young actress. Sure enough, it is none other than the daughter she abandoned.

Madame Sans-Gêne (Paramount, 1925)
d: Léonce Perret. 10 reels.
Gloria Swanson, Emile Drain, Charles DeRoche, Madelaine Guitty, Warwick Ward, Henry Favieres, Renée Heribelle, Suzanne Bianchetti, Denise Lorys, Jacques Marney.
In 18th century Paris, a laundress known as Madame Sans-Gêne serves a young lieutenant named Napoleon. Little do they know that in the future, they will be brought together again after the French Revolution ends and Napoleon is proclaimed Emperor.

Madame Sphinx (Triangle, 1918)
d: Thomas N. Heffron. 5 reels.
Alma Rubens, Wallace McDonald, Gene Burr, Frank MacQuarrie, William Dyer, Dick Rosson, Betty Pearce, Wilbur Higby, Arthur Millett, John Lince.
The only clue to a baffling murder mystery is a cuff link bearing a picture of a sphinx.

Madame Spy (Universal, 1918)
d: Douglas Gerrard. 5 reels.
Jack Mulhall, Donna Drew, Wadsworth Harris, George Gebhart, Jean Hersholt, Claire Du Brey, Maude Emory.
Rejected by the Annapolis naval academy, an admiral's son determines to do something to aid the war effort. He gets his chance when he impersonates a German woman, gains the trust of some spies, and turns them over to the authorities.

Madame X (Henry W. Savage, Inc./Pathé, 1916)
d: George F. Marion. 6 reels.
Dorothy Donnelly, John Bowers, Edwin Fosberg, Ralph Morgan, Robert Fischer, Charles Bunnell, Gladys Coburn.
In Paris, a young lawyer is assigned to defend a suspected murderess known only as Madame X. He wins her acquittal, and is then overjoyed to learn that Madame X is really his long-lost mother.

Madame X (Goldwyn, 1920)
d: Frank Lloyd. 7 reels.
Pauline Frederick, William Courtleigh, Casson Ferguson, Maud Louis, Hardee Kirkland, Albert Roscoe, John Hohenvest, Correan Kirkham, Sidney Ainsworth, Lionel Belmore.
Remake of the 1916 *Madame X*. Both films were based on the play *La Femme X...* by Alexandre Bisson.

The Madcap (Universal, 1916)
d: William Dowlan. 5 reels.
Flora Parker de Haven, Richard Sterling, Vera Doria.
In France, a young woman falls in love with an artist, but their relationship is threatened when a self-centered actress, consumed by jealousy, tries to drive them apart.

Madcap Madge (New York Motion Picture Corp./Triangle, 1917)
d: Raymond B. West. 5 reels.
Olive Thomas, Charles Gunn, Dorcas Matthews, Aggie Herring, Jack Livingston, J. Barney Sherry, J. Frank Burke, Gertrude Claire.
Madge is the youngest sister in a social-climbing family.

She's also the liveliest, and the first to snare a rich husband.

Made For Love (Cinema Corp. of America, 1926)
d: Paul Sloane. 7 reels.
Leatrice Joy, Edmund Burns, Ethel Wales, Brandon Hurst, Frank Butler.
American tourists, husband and wife, are trapped in a tomb in Egypt.

Made in Heaven (Goldwyn, 1921)
d: Victor Schertzinger. 5 reels.
Tom Moore, Helene Chadwick, Molly Malone, Kate Lester, Al Filson, Freeman Wood, Charles Eldridge, Renee Adoree, Herbert Prior, Fronzie Gunn, John Cossar.
Romantic comedy about a couple who enter into a marriage of convenience, then find they truly love each other.

A Made-To-Order Hero (Universal, 1928)
d: Edgar Lewis. 5 reels.
Ted Wells, Marjorie Bonner, Pee Wee Holmes, Pearl Sindelar, Jack Pratt, Ben Corbett, Scotty Mattraw, Dick L'Estrange.
Out West, a rancher must prove to his sweetheart that he's worthy of her.

Mademoiselle Midnight (MGM, 1924)
d: Robert Z. Leonard. 7 reels.
Mae Murray, Monte Blue, Johnny Arthur, Robert McKim, Paul Weigel, John Sainpolis, Clarissa Selwynne, Earl Schenck, Nick DeRuiz, Nigel DeBrulier, Johnny Arthur, Otis Harlan.
A Frenchwoman inherits a Mexican ranch, then falls in love with an American.

Mademoiselle Modiste (Corinne Griffith Productions/First National, 1926)
d: Robert Z. Leonard. 7 reels.
Corinne Griffith, Norman Kerry, Willard Louis, Dorothy Cumming, Rose Dione.
In Paris, a visiting American becomes interested in buying a dressmaker's shop... providing Fifi, a charming saleslady, is part of the package.

The Madness of Helen (World Film Corp., 1916)
d: Travers Vale. 5 reels.
Ethel Clayton, Carlyle Blackwell, Earl Schenck, Jack Drumier, Charles Duncan, Stanhope Wheatcroft, Mildred Cheshire, Frank Evans, Maude Forde, Julia Stuart.
After Helen elopes with a Navy man, he is recalled to his ship, and she goes to a village where she suffers an automobile accident that leaves her partially deranged. While in a semi-lucid state, Helen is tended to by a young man who falls in love with her, not realizing she is married.

The Madness of Youth (Fox, 1923)
d: Jerome Storm. 5 reels.
John Gilbert, Billie Dove, Donald Hatswell, George K. Arthur, Ruth Boyd, Luke Lucas, Julanne Johnston.
A young thief goes about preaching of forgiveness and redemption, but his preachments are only a cover for his larceny. That is, until he meets Nanette and learns that his sermons about love and virtuous living make sense after all.

Madonna of the Streets (First National, 1924)
d: Edwin Carewe. 8 reels.
Nazimova, Milton Sills, Claude Gillingwater, Courtenay Foote, Wallace Beery, Anders Randolf, Tom Kennedy, Vivian Oakland, Harold Goodwin, Rose Gore, Herbert Prior.
A reverend minister inherits a large sum from his uncle and proceeds to use it for charity. But his uncle's former mistress, who considers some of that money her own, is outraged at the reverend's munificence and plots to marry him in order to recover some of the fortune for herself.

Madonnas and Men (Jans Pictures, Inc., 1920)
d: B.A. Rolfe. 7 reels.
Anders Randolf, Edmund Lowe, Gustav Von Seyffertitz, Raye Dean, Evan-Burrows Fontaine, Blanche Davenport, Faire Binney.
In the old Roman Empire, the son of the emperor falls for a Christian girl about to be fed to the lions.

The Maelstorm (Vitagraph, 1917)
d: Paul Scardon. 5 reels.
Earle Williams, Dorothy Kelly, Julia Swayne Gordon, Gordon Gray, Bernard Seigel, Denton Vane, John Robertson, Robert Gaillard, Frank Crayne.
Confusing mystery yarn about an innocent young man drawn into a maelstorm of intrigue, extortion, and murder—and of course, romance too.

Magda (C.K.Y. Film Corp./Select Pictures, 1917)
d: Emile Chautard. 5 reels.
Clara Kimball Young, Alice Gale, Kitty Baldwin, Maude Ford, Thomas Holding, Edmund Fielding, George Merlo.
Melodrama about Magda, a proud, independent girl who leaves her family home and goes to the city to build a singing career. One failed love affair and one baby later, Magda realizes her mistakes—mistakes she gets a chance to make again.

A Magdalene of the Hills (Rolfe Photoplays, Inc./Metro, 1917)
d: John W. Noble. 5 reels.
Mabel Taliaferro, William Garwood, Frank Montgomery, William B. Davidson, William Black, Charles Brown.
In the high timber country, the daughter of a landowner secretly marries his rival's son.

Maggie Pepper (Famous Players-Lasky Corp./Paramount, 1919)
d: Chester Withey. 5 reels.
Ethel Clayton, Elliott Dexter, Winifred Greenwood, Tully Marshall, Edna Mae Wilson, Raymond Hatton, Marcia Manon, Clyde Benson, Billy Elmer, Bud Duncan, C.H. Geldart.
Maggie's a high-spirited saleswoman for a dry goods merchant. When the boss hears her plans to improve business, he fires her from her sales job and hires her as his assistant.

The Magic Cup (Realart Pictures, 1921)
d: John S. Robertson. 5 reels.
Constance Binney, Vincent Coleman, Blanche Craig, William H. Strauss, Charles Mussett, J.H. Gilmour, Malcolm Bradley, Cecil Owen.
Mary, a scullery maid, tries to help a recently evicted neighbor by pawning a silver chalice owned by her employer.

The Magic Eye (Universal, 1918)
d: Rea Berger. 5 reels.
Zoe Rae, H.A. Burrows, Claire DuBrey, Charles H. Mailes, William Carroll, Elwood Burdell.
During World War I, a ship's captain sets sail in spite of warnings that his ship may be torpedoed. The omen comes true, but the captain's daughter, who is a clairvoyant, sees that her father will be rescued. And so it comes to pass.

The Magic Flame (Goldwyn/United Artists, 1927)
d: Henry King. 9 reels.
Ronald Colman, Vilma Banky, Augustino Borgato, Gustave von Seyffertitz, Harvey Clarke, Shirley Palmer, Cosmo Kyrle Bellew, George Davis, André Cheron, Vadim Uraneff.
A clown in a traveling circus bears an uncanny resemblance to a certain unsavory monarch.

The Magic Garden (Gene Stratton Porter Productions/FBO of America, 1927)
d: J. Leo Meehan. 7 reels.
Joyce Coad, Margaret Morris, Philippe DeLacy, Raymond Keane, Charles Clary, William V. Mong, Cesare Gravina, Paulette Duval, Walter Wilkinson, Earl McCarthy, Alfred Allen.
Amaryllis, a love-struck young woman, falls for a young violinist who takes her for a visit in his "magic garden."

The Magic Skin (Thomas A. Edison, 1915)
d: Richard Ridgely. 5 reels.
Everett Butterfield, Mabel Trunnelle, Bigelow Cooper, Frank A. Lyon, William West, George A. Wright, Nellie Grant, Harry Linson, Sally Crute, Herbert Prior.
In Paris, a musician loves his landlady's daughter, but in turn is desired by Flora, an exotic vamp.

The Magician (MGM, 1926)
d: Rex Ingram. 7 reels.
Ivan Petrovich, Alice Terry, Paul Wegener, Firmin Gemier, Gladys Hamer.
Fantasy about a worshiper of the occult who puts a young woman in a hypnotic spell and schemes to extract her virgin blood for one of his experiments.

The Magnificent Brute (Universal, 1921)
d: Robert Thornby. 5 reels.
Frank Mayo, Dorothy Devore, Percy Challenger, Alberta Lee, J.J. Lance, William Eagle Eye, Charles Edler, Dick Sutherland, Eli Stanton, Buck Moulton, Lillian Ortez.
In the Canadian Northwest, a trapper and a marquis vie for the love of the lovely Yvonne.

The Magnificent Flirt (Paramount, 1928)
d: Harry D'Aarrast. 7 reels.
Florence Vidor, Albert Conti, Loretta Young, Matty Kemp, Marietta Millner, Ned Sparks.
In Paris, a count tries to dissuade his nephew from the temptations of a girl he considers an incorrigible flirt, just like her mother.

The Magnificent Meddler (Vitagraph, 1917)
d: William Wolbert. 5 reels.
Antonio Moreno, Mary Anderson, Otto Lederer, Leon D. Kent, George Kunkel.
Out West, the crusading young owner of a town newspaper leads a drive for annexation to a larger town, thus enraging the local boss. That's more than just inconvenient, because the young publisher has fallen in love with the town boss' daughter, and she with him.

Maid o' the Storm (Peralta Plays, Inc./General Film Co., 1918)
d: Raymond B. West. 6 reels.
Bessie Barriscale, George Fisher, Herschel Mayall, Joseph J. Dowling, Myra Davis, Nick Cogley, Howard Hickman, Jack Abrams, Ida Lewis, Helen Dunbar, Lois Wilson, Pietro Buzzi, Clifford Alexander, Nona Thomas.
During a storm at sea, a baby girl is washed ashore. The fisherman who finds her names her Ariel, and she grows to be a magnificent beauty and a renowned dancer.

The Maid of Belgium (World Film Corp., 1917)
d: George Archainbaud. 5 reels.
Alice Brady, Louise de Rigney, George MacQuarrie, Richard Clarke, Lotta Burnell, Anthoney Merlo.
Adoree, a Belgian girl, is so horrified by the war violence, she blots out the memories and develops amnesia. She is adopted by an American couple, who take her home. Only then does it become clear that Adoree is pregnant. Now... how to find the father?

Maid of the West (Fox, 1921)
d: Philo McCullough. 5 reels.
Eileen Percy, William Scott, Hattie Buskirk, Charles Meakin, June LaVere, Jack Brammall, Frank Clark.
Betty loves Bert, an aviator from Texas, but her guardians don't approve.

The Mailman (Emory Johnson/FBO of America, 1923)
d: Emory Johnson. 7 reels.
Ralph Lewis, Johnnie Walker, Martha Sleeper, Virginia True Boardman, Dave Kirby, Josephine Adair, Taylor Graves, Hardee Kirkland, Richard Morris, Rosemary Cooper.
Johnnie, a veteran mailman, is accused of mail theft aboard ship, but he's innocent.

The Main Event (DeMille Pictures/Pathé, 1927)
d: William K. Howard. 7 reels.
Vera Reynolds, Rudolph Schildkraut, Julia Faye, Charles Delaney, Robert Armstrong, Ernie Adams.
Glory, a cabaret dancer, vamps the upcoming opponent of her boxer boyfriend in an attempt to keep the opponent from getting into proper shape. But Glory does her vamping too well, and falls in love with her victim.

Main Street (Warner Bros., 1923)
d: Harry Beaumont. 9 reels.
Florence Vidor, Monte Blue, Harry Myers, Robert Gordon, Noah Beery, Alan Hale, Louis Fazenda, Anne Schaefer, Josephine Crowell, Otis Harlan, Gordon Griffith, Lon Poff, J.P. Lockney, Gilbert Clayton, Jack McDonald, Michael Dark, Estelle Short, Glen Cavender, Kathryn Perry, Aileen Manning, Josephine Kirkwood.
Carol, a sensitive and intelligent city girl, marries Dr. Kennicott and moves with him to his small-town home. Soon she becomes annoyed with the small town's stodgy and unprogressive ways, and determines to change them.

The Mainspring (Universal, 1916)
d: Jack Conway. 5 reels.
Francelia Billington, Wilbur Higby, Ben Wilson, Henry Holland, Clyde Benson, Raymond Whittaker, Marc Robbins, Thomas Jefferson, E.J. Brady.
When a reporter is assigned to cover a Wall Street story, he is mistaken for Larry, the son of a financial mogul. Surprisingly, the family urges him to continue the masquerade, for the real son has been kidnapped, and the reporter's presence as "Larry" will help in the family's fight against a hostile takeover bid. When it's all sorted out, the real Larry returns—and the reporter, his job done, wins the hand of Larry's sister in marriage.

The Majesty of the Law (Bosworth, Inc./Paramount, 1915)
d: Julia Crawford Ivers. 5 reels.
George Fawcett, Jane Wolfe, William Desmond, Myrtle Stedman, John Oaker, Charles Ruggles, Herbert Standing.
When a judge's son refuses to explain how a stolen necklace got into his possession, his father turns him out of his home.

The lad is merely being silent to protect a friend, and in time he will get the chance to present his case.

The Make-Believe Wife (Famous Players-Lasky/Paramount, 1918)
d: John Stuart Robertson. 5 reels.
Billie Burke, Afred Hickman, Ida Darling, David Powell, Wray Page, Isabel O'Madigan, Frances Kaye, Bigelow Cooper, Howard Johnson, F. Gatenbery Bell.
Romantic entanglements ensue, when two engaged couples go rock climbing and a storm isolates one of the ladies with her girlfriend's fiancé.

Makers of Men (Bud Barsky Corp., 1925)
d: Forrest Sheldon. 6 reels.
Kenneth McDonald, Clara Horton, J.P. McGowan, William Burton, William Lowery, Ethan Laidlaw.
During World War I, a weakling comes under the influence of a tough-as-nails sergeant and, as a result, becomes tough himself.

Making a Man (Famous Players-Lasky/Paramount, 1922)
d: Joseph Henabery. 6 reels.
Jack Holt, J.P. Lockney, Eva Novak, Bert woodruff, Frank Nelson, Robert Dudley.
A wealthy snob finds himself forced into a menial life of servitude.

The Making of Maddalena (Oliver Morosco Photoplays/Paramount, 1916)
d: Frank Lloyd. 5 reels.
Edna Goodrich, Forrest Stanley, Howard Davies, John Burton, Mary Mersch, Colin Chase, Juan delaCruz, Laura LaVernie, Katherine Griffith, Mary Bunting, Violet White.
In Rome, an American painter marries his model, Maddalena.

The Making of O'Malley (First National, 1925)
d: Lambert Hillyer. 8 reels.
Milton Sills, Dorothy Mackail, Helen Rowland, Warner Richmond, Julia Hurley, Thomas Carrigan, Claude King, Charles Craig, Blanche Ring, Allen Brander.
Jim O'Malley, a loyal police officer, learns that the leader of a gang of bootleggers is the fiancé of the girl Jim loves.

Making the Grade (Fox, 1929)
d: Alfred E. Green. 6 reels.
Edmund Lowe, Lois Moran, Lucien Littlefield, Albert Hart, James Ford, Rolfe Sedan, John Alden, Sherman Ross, Gino Conti, Mary Ashley, Lia Tora.
Comedy based on the George Ade tale about a loveable klutz.

Making the Varsity (Excellent Pictures, 1928)
d: Cliff Wheeler. 7 reels.
Rex Lease, Arthur Rankin, Gladys Hulette, Edith Yorke, Florence Dudley, Carl Miller, James Latta.

Ed and Wally, brothers as different as night and day, attend the same college and make the football team.

Male and Female (Famous Players-Lasky/Paramount, 1919)
d: Cecil B. DeMille. 115 minutes.
Gloria Swanson, Thomas Meighan, Theodore Roberts, Raymond Hatton, Bebe Daniels, Lila Lee, Wesley Barry.
Glamorous retelling of James Barrie's *The Admirable Crichton*, with Swanson as the spoiled daughter of privilege and Meighan as her family's super-efficient butler Crichton. The family yacht is shipwrecked at sea, and all survivors are forced to cope on a desert island, where class distinctions are meaningless.
This was the first of many cinema versions of Barrie's tale, and despite the 1919 date, it remains the most cinematic, thanks to DeMille's talent for spectacle. The film's most famous scene is vintage DeMille: In a dream sequence, we see Meighan as the King of Babylon in ancient days, and Miss Swanson as a Christian slave. Given her choice, the slave opts to be thrown to the lions rather than submit to the pagan monarch. She enters the pit and lies awaiting her fate, while a real lion approaches her and places his paw on her prostrate form. The lion was tame, but Miss Swanson was terrified... and, legend tells us, she insisted there be no retakes!

Mama's Affair (Constance Talmadge Film Co./Associated First National, 1921)
d: Victor Fleming. 6 reels.
Constance Talmadge, Effie Shannon, Katherine Kaelred, George LeGuere, Kenneth Harlan, Gertrude LeBrandt.
Eve, a faithful daughter to her widowed mother, balks at her mother's choice of a bridegroom for her.

The Man Above the Law (Triangle, 1918)
d: Raymond Wells. 5 reels.
Jack Richardson, Josie Sedgwick, Claire McDowell, May Giraci.
In New Mexico, a white man marries an Indian maid and together they raise a daughter.

Man and Beast (Universal, 1917)
d: Henry MacRae. 5 reels.
Eileen Sedgewick, Park Jones, Harry Clifton, Kingsley Benedict, L.M. Wells, Parks Jones, Joe Martin.
In South Africa, a Hatfield-McCoy-style feud erupts between two families.

A Man and His Mate (Reliance/Mutual, 1915)
d: John G. Adolfi. 4 reels.
Henry Woodruff, Sam DeGrasse, Gladys Brockwell, F.A. Turner, Walter Long, Josephine Crowell, Fred Hamer.
Out West, a transplanted easterner is accused of murdering a ranch owner. But he's innocent and in love with the rancher's daughter.

A Man and His Money (Goldwyn Pictures, 1919)
d: Harry Beaumont. 5 reels.
Tom Moore, Seena Owen, Sydney Ainsworth, Kate Lester, Claire DuBrey, Sydney Deane, Edwin Sturgis.
After losing his fiancée because of his drunkenness, a reformed alcoholic takes a job as a handyman. In his new position, he cares for an estate, keeps an eye on his employer's niece, and wins her love when he rescues her from a would-be seducer.

Man and His Soul (Metro, 1916)
d: John W. Noble. 5 reels.
Francis X. Bushman, Beverly Bayne, Edward Brennan, Charles H. Prince, John Davidson, Helen Dunbar, Grace Valentine, Etta Mansfield, Fred Sittenham.
A thoroughly altruistic man finds it impossible to do anything dishonest.

Man and His Woman (Pathé, 1920)
d: J. Stuart Blackton. 6 reels.
Herbert Rawlinson, Eulalie Jensen, May McAvoy, Warren Chandler, Louis Dean, Charles Kent.
Upon discovering that his fiancée loves another, a young doctor turns to opium and becomes addicted. He is nursed

MALE AND FEMALE (1919). Gloria Swanson, at left, plays a lady of wealth and privilege reduced to coping on a desert island along with her family and two servants, played by Lila Lee (center) and Thomas Meighan (seated, as the admirable Crichton).

* * * * *

302

back to health by the tender care of Eva, a nurse with whom he falls in love.

Man and Maid (MGM, 1925)
d: Victor Schertzinger. 6 reels.
Lew Cody, Renee Adoree, Harriet Hammond, Paulette Duval, Alec B. Francis, Crauford Kent, Jacqueline Gadsden.
A playboy must choose between a saucy wench and his chaste secretary.

Man and Wife (Effanem Productions/Arrow Film Corp., 1923)
d: John L. McCutcheon. 5 reels.
Maurice Costello, Gladys Leslie, Norma Shearer, Edna May Spooner, Robert Elliott, Ernest Hilliard.
After his wife perishes in a fire, a young doctor goes to the country to try and forget. There, he will meet and fall in love with a charming young woman who, it turns out, is his wife's sister.

Man Bait (Metropolitan Pictures/Producers Distributing Corp., 1926)
d: Donald Crisp. 6 reels.
Marie Prevost, Kenneth Thomson, Douglas Fairbanks Jr., Louis Natheaux, Eddie Gribbon, Betty Francisco, Adda Leason, Sally Rand, Fritzi Ridgeway.
Madge, a taxi dancer, catches the eye—and the heart—of Jeff, a scion of wealth.

The Man Behind the Curtain (Vitagraph, 1916)
d: Courtlandt J. Van Deusen. 5 reels.
Lillian Walker, Evart Overton, Templar Saxe, William Dunn, John Costello, Bobby Connelly.
Edna, a young secretary, finds her employer dead. A man steps out from behind a curtain and accuses Edna of the crime, but she's innocent and in time will prove it.

The Man Beneath (Haworth Pictures/Robertson-Cole, 1919)
d: William Worthington. 5 reels.
Sessue Hayakawa, Helen Jerome Eddy, Pauline Curley, Jack Gilbert, Fountain LaRue, Wedgewood Nowell.
Racial prejudice derails a romance between a Scottish girl and a Hindu doctor.

The Man Between (Finis Fox Productions, 1923)
d: Finis Fox. 6 reels.
Allan Forrest, Edna Murphy, Fred Malatesta, Vola Vale, Kitty Bradbury, Philo McCullough, Dorren Turner.
Jules, a convict, meets a fellow con who closely resembles him, and persuades him to take Jules' place when he is released.

Man Crazy (Charles R. Rogers Productions/First National, 1927)
d: John Francis Dillon. 6 reels.
Dorothy Mackaill, Jack Mulhall, Edythe Chapman, Phillips Smalley, Walter McGrail, Ray Hallor.
Clarissa, a devil-may-care society girl, annoys her staid family with her modern ways.

A Man Four-Square (Fox, 1926)
d: R. William Neill. 5 reels.
Buck Jones, Marion Harlan, Harry Woods, William Lawrence, Jay Hunt, Sidney Bracey, Florence Gilbert, Frank Beal.
Out West, an honest rancher is accused of rustling cattle.

The Man From Beyond (Houdini Picture Corp., 1922)
d: Burton King. 7 reels.

Harry Houdini, Arthur Maude, Frank Montgomery, Nita Naldi, Albert Tavernier, Erwin Connelly, Frank Montgomery, Luis Alberni, Yale Benner, Jane Connelly, Nita Naldi.
Houdini portrays a man frozen in a block of ice in suspended animation for 100 years.

The Man From Bitter Roots (Fox, 1916)
d: Oscar C. Apfel. 5 reels.
William Farnum, Charles Whitaker, H.A. Barrows, Willard Louis, William Burress, Henry De Vere, Betty Schade, Betty Harte, Ogden Crane.
After two partners hit a gold strike and one of them dies, the survivor tries to find the dead partner's family, to share the profits from the mine.

The Man From Brodney's (Vitagraph, 1923)
d: David Smith. 8 reels.
J. Warren Kerrigan, Alice Calhoun, Wanda Hawley, Miss DuPont, Pat O'Malley, Kathleen Key, Bertram Grassby.
Chase, an American attorney, goes to an East African island to help two heirs confirm their title to the island.

The Man From Downing Street (Vitagraph, 1922)d: Edward José. 5 reels.
Earle Williams, Charles Hill Mailes, Boris Karloff, Betty Ross Clarke, Kathryn Adams, Herbert Prior, Eugenia Gilbert James Butler, George Stanley.
A British secret agent disguises himself as a rajah to infiltrate Indian society.

The Man From Funeral Range (Famous Players-Lasky/Paramount, 1918)
d: Walter Edwards. 5 reels.
Wallace Reid, Ann Little, Lottie Pickford, Willis Marks, Tully Marshall, George McDaniel, Phil Ainsworth, Tom Guise.
Out West, a prospector is framed for murder.

The Man From Glengarry (Ernest Shipman/W.W. Hodkinson, 1923)
d: Henry MacRae. 6 reels.
Anders Randolph, Warner P. Richmond, Harlan Knight, Marian Swayne, E.L. Fernandez, Jack Newton, Pauline Garon, Frank Badgley, William Colvin, Marion Lloyd.
In a Northwest lumber camp, a feud arises between a Scotsman and the French-Canadian who killed the Scot's father in a fight.

The Man From God's Country (Phil Goldstone Productions, 1924)
d: Alvin J. Neitz. 5 reels.
William Fairbanks, Dorothy Revier, Lew Meehan, Milton Ross, Carl Silvera, Andrew Waldron.
In a border town, an American and a Mexican vie for the hand of a Mexican girl.

The Man From Hardpan (Leo Maloney Productions/Pathé, 1927)
d: Leo D. Maloney. 6 reels.
Leo Maloney, Eugenia Gilbert, Rosa Gore, Murdock MacQuarrie, Paul Hurst, Ben Corbett, Albert Hart.
Out West, an escaped convict poses as the heir to a ranch.

The Man From Hell's River (Irving Cummings Productions, 1922)
d: Irving Cummings. 5 reels.
Irving Cummings, Eva Novak, Wallace Beery, Frank Whitson, Robert Klein, William Heford, Rin-Tin-Tin.
A valiant dog rescues a reluctant bride from her brutal new

husband.

The Man From Home (Lasky Feature Plays/Paramount, 1914)
d: Cecil B. DeMille. 5 reels.
Charles Richman, Theodore Roberts, Fred Montague, Monroe Salisbury, Horace B. Carpenter, Jode Mullally, Dick La Reno, Dorothy Quincy, Anita King.
When a girl from Indiana becomes smitten with a fortune-hunting Italian nobleman in his country, she calls for her guardian to come to Italy and bless their union. He does make the trip, but withholds his blessing because he's in love with his ward himself!

The Man From Home (Famous Players-Lasky/Paramount, 1922)
d: George Fitzmaurice. 7 reels.
James Kirkwood, Anna Q. Nilsson, Geoffrey Kerr, Norman Kerry, Dorothy Cumming, José Ruben, Annette Benson, John Miltern, Clifford Grey.
Remake of the Lasky film of 1914 of the same name.

The Man From Lost River (Goldwyn, 1921)
d: Frank Lloyd. 6 reels.
House Peters, Fritzi Brunette, Allan Forrest, James Gordon, Monte Collins, Milla Davenport.
The plague strikes while a New Yorker and a local are sparring over the love of the same woman in a remote North Woods community.

The Man From Manhattan (American Film Co./Mutual, 1916)
d: Jack Halloway. 5 reels.
William Stowell, Charles Wheelock, Rhea Mitchell, Jo Taylor, Jack Prescott, Warren Ellsworth, Otto Nelson, Perry Banks, George Bally, Harry Edmonson, William Tedmarsh.
After a Manhattan businessman disowns his son for his literary fantasies, the lad journeys to a small town and buys the local newspaper.

The Man From Mexico (Famous Players/Paramount, 1914)
d: Thomas N. Heffron. 5 reels.
John Barrymore, Wellington A. Playter, Harold Lockwood, Pauline Neff, Anton Ascher, Fred Annerly, Winona Winters, Nathaniel Sack.
When a married playboy is arrested during a fight in a night club and sentenced to thirty days in jail, he tries to keep the whole thing from his wife, by telling her he is going on a thirty-day business trip to Mexico.

The Man From Montana (Universal, 1917)
d: George Marshall. 5 reels.
Neal Hart, Vivian Rich, George Berrell, E.J. Piel, Betty Lamb, Willard Wayne, Edward Steele.
On the trail of claim jumpers, Duke Farley runs afoul of a frameup: he's accused under the Mann Act of leading a minor girl astray. To outwit the scoundrels, and also because he's in love with her, Duke trumps the charge by marrying the girl.

The Man From Nowhere (Universal, 1916)
d: Henry Otto. 5 reels.
King Baggot, Irene Hunt, Joseph Granby, Frank Smith, Joseph W. Gerard, Helen Marten, Johnny Walker.
Imprisoned for a crime he did not commit, a convict becomes a model prisoner and is made a trustee. In time, he is able to prove his innocence and to woo the warden's daughter, with whom he has fallen in love.

The Man From Nowhere (Ben Wilson Productions/Arrow Film Corp., 1920)
d: Francis Ford. 5 reels.
Jack Hoxie, Fred Moore, Pansy Porter, Francis Ford, Sam Polo.
Out West, a miner seeks revenge against his former partner Duke, who turned his sweetheart against him so that Duke could marry her himself.

The Man From Oklahoma (Rayart Pictures, 1926)
d: Harry Webb, Forrest Sheldon. 5 reels.
Jack Perrin, Josephine Hill, Lou Meehan, Lafe McKee, Edmund Cobb.
A man and his wonder dog clear up a murder mystery.

The Man From Oregon (New York Motion Picture Corp./Mutual, 1915)
d: Reginald Barker. 5 reels.
Howard Hickman, Fanny Midgley, Herschel Mayall, Clara Williams, Joseph J. Dowling.
Oregon senator Jim Martin fights against a fraudulent railroad bill, and runs afoul of lobbyists who try to frame him with "incriminating" photos of the senator and a young woman.

The Man from Painted Post (Fairbanks/Artcraft Pictures, 1917)
d: Joseph Henabery. 5 reels.
Douglas Fairbanks, Eileen Percy, Frank Campeau, Frank Clark, Herbert Standing, William Lowery, Rhea Haines, Charles Stevens, Monte Blue.
A range detective is hired by ranchers to drive away rustlers.

The Man From Red Gulch (Hunty Stromberg Productions, 1925)
d: Edmund Mortimer. 6 reels.
Harry Carey, Harriet Hammond, Frank Campeau,k Mark Hamilton, Lee Shumway, Doris Lloyd, Frank Norcross, Vrginia Davis, Mickey Moore.
Gold Rush drama about Sandy, a prospector out to avenge the death of his partner.

The Man From the West (Universal, 1926)
d: Albert S. Rogell. 5 reels.
Art Acord, Eugenia Gilbert, Irvin Renard, William Welsh, Vin Moore, Dick Gilbert, Georgie Grandee, Eunice Vin Moore.
Louden, a ranch foreman who's disenchanted with modern women and their pushy, aggressive ways, sees a newspaper photo of Iris, who appears to possess all the feminine qualities he admires. When he meets her, however, Louden finds Iris as pushy and snobbish as all the others. But Iris is nothing if not adaptable. Once she recognizes Louden for the "catch" he is, she turns her attentions to satisfying his image of a respectable female.

The Man From Wyoming (Universal, 1924)
d: Robert North Bradbury. 5 reels.
Jack Hoxie, Lillian Rich, William Welsh, Claude Payton, Ben Corbett, Lon Poff, George Kuwa, James Corrigan.
Out West, a sheep rancher is accused of murdering a cattleman.

The Man Hater (Triangle, 1917)
d: Albert Parker. 5 reels.
Winifred Allen, Jack Meredith, Harry Neville, Jessie Shirley, Marguerite Gale, Robert Vivian, Anna Lehr.
A young woman develops a hatred of men. She agrees to marry her suitor only on the condition that they be married

304

in name only... and his love for her is so great that he agrees. After the wedding, the bride continually avoids her husband, but is roused to action when a home-wrecking female enters the picture. Okay, so *now* she's interested in being his wife!

The Man Hunt (World Film Corp., 1918)
d: Travers Vale. 5 reels.
Ethel Clayton, Rockliffe Fellowes, Henry Warwick, John Adrizonia, Herbert Barrington, Jack Drumier, Al Hart, John Dungan.
Newly wealthy from an inheritance, a young woman is besieged by golddigging suitors, but resolves to find True Love.

The Man Hunter (Fox, 1919)
d: Frank Lloyd. 6 reels.
William Farnum, Louise Lovely, Charles Clary, Marc Robbins, Leatrice Joy.
Melodrama follows a London bachelor from the heights of riches to the depths of poverty, and back again.

The Man in Blue (Universal, 1925)
d: Edward Laemmle. 6 reels.
Herbert Rawlinson, Madge Bellamy, Nick DeRuiz, André de Beranger, Cesare Gravina, Jackie Morgan, Dorothy Brock, D.J. Mitsoras, Carrie Clark Ward, C.F. Roark, Martha Mattox.
In New York's Little Italy, an Irish cop falls for Tina, the florist's daughter.

The Man in Hobbles (Tiffany-Stahl Productions, 1928)
d: George Archainbaud. 6 reels.
John Harron, Lila Lee, Lucien Littlefield, Sunshine Hart, Betty Egan, Eddie Nugent, William Anderson, Vivian Oakland.
A love-struck young man marries the girl of his dreams, but it's a nightmare when she brings her whole family along.

The Man in the Moonlight (Universal, 1919)
d: Paul Powell. 6 reels.
Monroe Salisbury, Colleen Moore, William Stowell, Alfred Allen, Harry DuRoy, Sydney Franklin, Virginia Foltz, Arthur Jasmine.
In Canada, a mountie postpones his wedding to search for escaped convicts, one of whom is his future brother-in-law.

Man in the Open (United Picture Theatres of America, 1919)
d: Ernest C. Warde. 6 reels.
Dustin Farnum, Joseph Dowling, Irene Rich, Lamar Johnstone, Claire DuBrey, Herschall Mayall.
Out West, a cowpoke meets an opera singer and they fall in love.

Man in the Rough (FBO Pictures, 1928)
d: Wallace Fox. 5 reels.
Bob Steele, Marjorie King, Tom Lingham, William Norton Bailey, Jay Morley.
A cowboy tries to warn a prospector and his daughter of an impending attack on them, but succeeds primarily on heaping suspicion on himself.

The Man in the Saddle (Universal, 1926)
d: Lynn Reynolds. 6 reels.
Hoot Gibson, Charles H. Mailes, Fay Wray, Clark Comstock, Sally Long, Emmett King, Lloyd Whitlock, Duke R. Lee, Yorke Sherwood, William Dyer.
Out West, a cowpoke who's a crack shot but is otherwise

awkward is scammed in a plot to rob the camping party under his care. But he fights back, chasse the robbers to their lair, and forces a confession from their chieftain.

The Man Inside (Universal, 1916)
d: J.G. Adolfi. 5 reels.
Edwin Stevens, Harry Benham, Tina Marshall, Charles Burbridge, Justina Huff, William Armstrong, Sid Bracy, Louis Leon Hall, Gustave Thomas, Florence Crawford.
After being accused of sabotage, an American disappears and is thought dead. But his daughter continues to harbor hope of seeing her father alive again—and she will, in a flurry of events that unravel that mystery and several others.

The Man Life Passed By (Metro, 1923)
w, d: Victor Shertzinger. 7 reels.
Jane Novak, Percy Marmont, Eva Novak, Cullen Landis, Lydia Knott, Hobart Bosworth, Gertrude Short, Ralph Bushman, Lincoln Stedman, George Siegmann, André de Beranger, Larry Fisher, William Humphrey.
An inventor swears vengeance on the wealthy steel mogul who stole his new formula.

A Man Must Live (Famous Players-Lasky/Paramount, 1924)
d: Paul Sloane. 7 reels.
Richard Dix, Jacqueline Logan, George Nash, Edna Murphy, Charles Beyer, Dorothy Walters, William Ricciardi, Arthur Houseman, Lucius Henderson, Jane Jennings.
A reporter for a scandal magazine finds he has too much compassion to do a good hatchet job on the subjects of his interviews.

The Man Next Door (Vitagraph, 1923)
d: Victor Schertzinger, David Smith. 7 reels.
David Torrence, Frank Sheridan, James Morrison, Alice Calhoun, John Steppling, Adele Farrington, Mary Culver, Bruce Boteler.
Bonnie, a cultured young lady, inexplicably falls in love with the gardener for the family next door. Her father vehemently opposes her union with a common working man, until it is revealed that he's no gardener, but actually the son of a prominent society family.

A Man of Action (Thomas H. Ince Corp., 1923)
d: James W. Horne. 6 reels.
Douglas MacLean, Raymond Hatton, Arthur Millett, Marguerite DeLaMotte, Wade Boteler, Kingsley Benedict, Arthur Steward Hull, William Courtright, Katherine Lewis.
Zany farce about a chap who's been urged by his fiancée to prove he's a man of action. He'll prove it when, after being mistaken for a famous Chicago gangster, he leads the gang on a supposed heist—right into the hands of the police.

The Man of Bronze (Pyramid Photo Plays, Inc./World Film Corp., 1918)
d: David M. Hartford. 5 reels.
Lewis S. Stone, Marguerite Clayton, Richard Cummings, Harry Von Meter, May Gaston.
While studying art in New York, a wholesome Arizona girl gets used to the Bohemian life, and finds her values being put to the test.

A Man of Iron (Chadwick Pictures, 1925)
d: Whitman Bennett. 6 reels.
Lionel Barrymore, Mildred Harris, Winifred Barry, Dorothy Kingdon, Alfred Mack, J. Moy Bennett, Isobel DeLeon, Jean Del Val.
A marriage of convenience turns into the real thing, when

the husband is forced to fight a duel to defend his wife's honor.

The Man of Mystery (Vitagraph, 1917)
d: Frederick a. Thompson. 5 reels.
E.H. Sothern, Charlotte Ives, Vilda Varesi, Brinsley Shaw, Bernard Siegel.
In Italy, a deformed oldster is transformed into a young and healthy man when his body is covered with burning lava from Mt. Vesuvius.

A Man of Quality (Excellent Pictures, 1926)
d: Wesley Ruggles. 6 reels.
George Walsh, Ruth Dwyer, Brian Donlevy, Lucien Prival, Laura DeCardi.
Banning, a secret service agent, goes undercover as "Strongarm Samson," a crook.

The Man of Shame (Universal, 1915)
d: Harry C. Myers. 5 reels.
Wilton Lackaye, Rosemary Theby, Evelyn Dubois, Harry C. Myers, Victor Lewis, Franklin Paul, Katherine Mendel, Louis Leon Hall, Joel Day.
During the Franco-Prussian War, an injured duelist swears revenge on his nemesis.

A Man of Sorrow (Fox, 1916)
d: Oscar C. Apfel. 5 reels.
William Farnum, Dorothy Bernard, Willard Louis, Mary Ruby, Fred Huntley, Harry DuRoy, Henry J. Herbert, William Burress, H.A. Barrows, Thelma Burns, William Scott.
Thinking his wife unfaithful, a man decides to commit suicide. But before he can throw himself into the ocean, he sees a woman attempt suicide by the same means, and jumps in to save her.

The Man of Stone (Selznick/Select, 1921)
d: George Archainbaud. 5 reels.
Conway Tearle, Betty Howe, Martha Mansfield, Colin Campbell, Warren Cook, Charles D. Brown.
A British officer known as "The Man of Stone" falls in love with a girl he met while on duty in Arabia.

Man of the Forest (Famous Players-Lasky/Paramount, 1926)
d: John Waters. 6 reels.
Jack Holt, Georgia Hale, El Brendel, Warner Oland, Tom Kennedy, George Fawcett, Ivan Christie, Bruce Gordon, Vester Pegg, Willard Cooley, Guy Oliver, Walter Ackerman, Duke R. Lee.
In order to save a young heiress from being kidnapped, an intrepid cowboy kidnaps her himself.

The Man of the Hour (World Film Corp., 1914)
d: Maurice Tourneur. 5 reels.
Robert Warwick, Alec B. Francis, Ned Burton, Eric Mayne, John Hines, Belle Adair, Chester Barnett, Thomas Jackson, Bert Starkey, Charles Dungan.
After his father is ruined financially by a swindler, a prospector swears revenge on the culprit. He changes his name and becomes the swindler's protegé, then runs for mayor of New York, and wins.

The Man on the Box (Lasky Feature Plays, 1914)
d: Oscar C. Apfel. 5 reels.
Max Figman, C.F. Le None, Fred Montague, Fred L. Wilson, Betty Jonson, Mabel Van Buren, Harry Fisher, James Neill, Lolita Robertson, Horace B. Carpenter, Jane Darwell.

While on a leave of absence from the military, a cavalry lieutenant travels to Monte Carlo, falls in love, and foils the plans of a Russian secret agent.

The Man on the Box (Warner Bros., 1925)
d: Charles Reisner. 8 reels.
Sydney Chaplin, David Butler, Alice Calhoun, Kathleen Calhoun, Theodore Lorch, Helene Costello, E.J. Ratcliffe, Charles F. Reisner, Charles Gerrard, Henry Barrows.
A headstrong bachelor takes a job as a gardener to be near his lady love.

Man Power (Paramount, 1927)
d: Clarence Badger. 6 reels.
Richard Dix, Mary Brian, Philip Strange, Charles Hill Mailes, Oscar Smith, George Irving, Charles Clary, Charles Schaeffer.
Tom, an ex-Army officer, gets a job with a company that makes tractors. His knowledge of army tanks helps Tom to perfect the tractors, and wins him the love of the owner's daughter.

Man Rustlin' (Independent Pictures/FBO of America, 1926)
d: Del Andrews. 5 reels.
Bob Custer, Florence Lee, Jules Cowles, Sam Allen, James Kelly, Pat Beggs, Howard Fay, Skeeter Bill Robbins.
Comedy western about a hick reporter who has a natural nose for news—and a talent for trouble.

The Man Tamer (Universal, 1921)
d: Harry B. Harris. 5 reels.
Gladys Walton, Roscoe Karns, Norman Hammond, William Welsh, Rex DeRosselli, C.G. Murphy, Parker J. McConnell.
A female lion-tamer finds she must fight off two-legged beasts as well.

Man to Man (Universal, 1922)
d: Stuart Paton. 6 reels.
Harry Carey, Lillian Rich, Charles Le Moyne, Harold Goodwin, Willis Robards.
Out West, a new rancher discovers his foreman is guilty of sabotage.

The Man Trackers (Universal, 1921)
d: Edward Kull. 5 reels.
George Larkin, Barney Furey, Josephine Hill, Al Smith, Ruth Royce, Harold Holland, Ralph Fee McCullough.
In the Canadian northwest, a mountie meets with treachery at the hands of a gang of outlaws who frame him on an assault charge.

The Man Trail (Essanay, 1915)
d: E.H. Calvert. 6 reels.
Richard C. Travers, June Keith, Ernest Maupain, Thomas McLarnie, Arthur W. Bates, John Lorenz, Betty Scott, Jack Meredith, Hugh Thompson, John Cossar, Sam Cramer.
In a Northwest timber camp, a young man from Philadelphia falls in love with his uncle's adopted daughter.

The Man Trap (Universal, 1917)
d: Elmer Clifton. 5 reels.
Herbert Rawlinson, Sally Starr, Ruby La Fayette, Jack Nelson, Mark Fenton, Franck MacQuarrie, Hal Wilson.
Convicted and sentenced to jail for a crime he did not commit, a reporter escapes and seeks evidence that will implicate the real criminals.

The Man Unconquerable (Famous Players-Lasky/Paramount, 1922)

306

d: Joseph Henabery. 6 reels.
Jack Holt, Sylvia Breamer, Clarence Burton, Ann Schaeffer, Jean DeBriac, Edwin Stevens, Willard Louis.
Kendall, a New Yorker, inherits a pearl fishery in the South Seas.

The Man Under Cover (Universal, 1922)
d: Tod Browning. 5 reels.
Herbert Rawlinson, George Hernandez, William Courtwright, George Webb, Edwin Booth Tilton, Gerald Pring, Barbara Bedford, Willis Marks, Betty Eliason, Betty Stone.
Porter, a con artist, decides to reform for the love of a good woman. And reform he does, but his old tricks come in handy later on, when to save the townspeople's money he has to swindle a pair of swindlers.

The Man Upstairs (Warner Bros., 1926)
d: Roy Del Ruth. 7 reels.
Monte Blue, Dorothy Devore, John Roche, Charlie Conklin, Helen Dunbar, Stanley Taylor, Carl Stockdale.
A hotel guest tries to impress a young lady by inventing a murder case he is involved in, then finds to his dismay that such a murder did in fact take place.

Man Wanted (Herbert L. Steiner/Clark-Cornelius Corp., 1922)
d: John Francis Dillon. 5 reels.
Arthur Housman, Frank Losee, Flora Finch, Huntley Gordon, Diana Allen.
Edgar, a wealthy layabout, fancies Helen, but there's a problem: Helen's dad has decreed that her future husband must be a working man. This sets Edgar on a wild search for a steady job... and he goes from being a soda jerk to being a handyman to being a hypnotist's assistant. In the end, he rescues Helen from the clutches of her abductor, and wins her dad's approval.

The Man Who (Metro, 1921)
d: Maxwell Karger. 6 reels.
Bert Lytell, Lucy Cotton, Virginia Valli, Frank Currier, Tammany Young, Fred Warren, Clarence Elmer, William Roselle, Mary Louise Beaton, Frank Strayer.
Comedy about a chap who, to protest the high price of shoes, takes to walking the streets of New York barefoot.

The Man Who Came Back (Fox, 1924)
d: Emmett Flynn. 9 reels.
George O'Brien, Dorothy Mackaill, Cyril Chadwick, Ralph Lewis, Emily Fitzroy, Harvey Clark, Edward Piel, David Kirby, James Gordon, Walter Wilkinson, Brother Miller.
Henry and Marcelle, a pair of misfits at home, travel to other lands, and meet again in Shanghai.

The Man Who Could Not Lose (Favorite Players Film Co., 1914)
d: Carlyle Blackwell. 5 reels.
Carlyle Blackwell, Hal Clements, William Branton, James J. Sheehan, J.M. Strong, Thomas Delmar, Henry Kernan, Gypsie Abbott, Ruth Hartman.
Whimsical drama about a writer who writes a novel based on sheer fantasy and then meets his heroine, in the flesh, in the publisher's daughter.

The Man Who Couldn't Beat God (Vitagraph, 1915)
d: Maurice Costello, Robert Gaillard. 5 reels.
Maurice Costello, Robert Gaillard, Denton Vane, Estelle Mardo, Edwina Robbins, Thomas Mills, Marion Henry, Naomi Childers, Mary Maurice, Charles Eldridge, Harry Morey.
In England, a groundskeeper fights with and kills his employer. He escapes to America, becomes a success in business, and is eventually elected to high political office. But he cannot escape the nightmarish vision of his crime.

The Man Who Dared (Fox, 1920)
d: Emmett J. Flynn. 6 reels.
William Russell, Eileen Percy, Frank Brownlee, Fred Warren, Lon Poff, Joe Ray.
While in jail, a condemned murderer spends the night before his execution sculpting a figure of Jesus Christ.

The Man Who Fights Alone (Famous Players-Lasky/Paramount, 1924)
d: Wallace Worsley. 7 reels.
William Farnum, Lois Wilson, Edward Horton, Lionel Belmore, Barlowe Borland, George Irving, Dawn O'Day, Rose Tapley, Frank Farrington.
An engineer, stricken with paralysis, fantasizes that his wife is being unfaithful to him.

The Man Who Forgot (World Film Corp., 1917)
d: Emile Chautard. 5 reels.
Robert Warwick, Doris Kenyon, Gerda Holmes, Alex K. Shannon, Ralph Delmore, John Reinhard, Frederick C. Truesdell.
In Washington, an amnesiac fights for passage of a Prohibition bill.

The Man Who Found Himself (World Film Corp., 1915)
d: Frank H. Crane. 5 reels.
Johnny Hines, Robert Warwick, Paul McAllister, Arline Pretty, E.M. Kimball, Charles Dungan, Madge Evans, Ruth Finley, Leone Morgan, Phyllis Hazelton, Douglas MacLean, Martin Faust, Richard Neill.
A convicted embezzler escapes from prison, falls in love, then willingly returns to jail to finish out his term so that he can get married with a clear conscience.

The Man Who Found Himself (Famous Players-Lasky/Paramount, 1925)
d: Alfred E. Green. 7 reels.
Thomas Meighan, Virginia Valli, Frank Morgan, Ralph Morgan, Charles Stevenson, Julia Hoyt, Lynne Fontanne, Mildred Ryan, Hugh Cameron, Victor Moore, Russell Griffin.
Tom, a former bank director who was railroaded by another banker in an embezzlement scheme, plans his vengeance while serving his sentence.

The Man Who Had Everything (Goldwyn, 1920)
d: Alfred E. Green. 5 reels.
Jack Pickford, Lionel Belmore, Priscilla Bonner, Shannon Day, Alec B. Francis, William Machin.
Harry's a wealthy young man who has everything he wants, but he finds that it doesn't bring him happiness.

The Man Who Laughs (Universal, 1928)
d: Paul Leni. 10 reels. (Synchronized music and sound effects.)
Conrad Veidt, Mary Philbin, Olga Baclanova, Josephine Crowell, George Siegmann, Brandon Hurst, Sam De Grasse, Stuart Holmes, Cesare Gravina, Nick De Ruiz.
A man whose features are permanently distorted into a smile becomes a circus performer and finds love with a blind girl. Then word comes that he is heir to the nobility, and he must make a decision whether to assume his title, or stay with the circus and his lady love.

A minor controversy exists regarding the true release date of *The Man Who Laughs*. Some sources report that the film was completed in April of 1927 but withheld from release until a year later, after a musical score and sound effects had been added. Other sources report that the film actually premiered in late April of 1927, then was pulled from distribution while the sound track was added. Whichever version is true, the film certainly bears a copyright date of 1928.

The Man Who Lost Himself (Selznick, 1920)
d: George D. Baker. 5 reels.
William Faversham, Hedda Hopper, Violet Reed, Radcliffe Stelle, Claude Payton, Mathilde Brundage, Emily Fitzroy, Downing Clarke.
In London, an Earl meets a young American who bears an uncanny resemblance to him. Double role for Faversham, as the nobleman and the visiting Yank.

The Man Who Married His Own Wife (Universal, 1922)
d: Stuart Paton. 5 reels.
Frank Mayo, Sylvia Breamer, Marie Crisp, Howard Crampton, Francis McDonald, Joe Girard.
Morton, a sea captain, rescues Elsie, a shipwreck victim, but suffers disfiguring injuries to his face in the incident. Once they reach port, the two are married; but Morton comes to fear that his wife secretly hates him because of his ugly scars. So he arranges to disappear from her life and be presumed dead. After receiving cosmetic surgery to restore his face to its natural look, Morton re-enters his wife's life and learns that she loved him all along, scars or no scars.

The Man Who Paid (Producers Security Corp., 1922)
d: Oscar Apfel. 5 reels.
Wilfred Lytell, Norma Shearer, Florence Rogan, Fred C. Jones, Bernard Siegel, David Hennessy, Charles Beyer, Erminie Gagnon, Frank Montgomery.
Thornton, convicted of a crime he did not commit, finds refuge—and the love of a good woman—in the woods of the Great Northwest.

The Man Who Played God (United Artists, 1922)
d: Harmon Wright. 6 reels.
George Arliss, Effie Shannon, Edward Earle, Margaret Seddon, J.B. Walsh, Pierre Gendron, Mary Astor.
A deafened ex-pianist learns to lip-read, and through this newly developed talent he eavesdrops on strangers' conversations and learns of their troubles. Arliss would play this role again, in a sound version with the same title, in 1932.

The Man Who Played Square (Fox, 1924)
d: Al Santell. 7 reels.
Buck Jones, Ben Hendricks Jr., David Kirby, Hank Mann, Howard Foster, William Scott, Wanda Hawley.
Matt inherits one-half of a successful gold mine, the other half going to Bertie, daughter of one of the original owners. There will be mistrust between the two new owners, and they will have to face down the treachery of a dishonest foreman. But in the end, Matt and Bertie fall in love and decide to merge their mine shares into one.

The Man Who Saw Tomorrow (Famous Players-Lasky/Paramount, 1922)
d: Alfred E. Green. 7 reels.
Thomas Meighan, Theodore Roberts, Leatrice Joy, Albert Roscoe, Alec Francis, June Elvidge, Eva Novak, Laurance Wheat, John Miltern, Robert Brower, Edward Patrick, Jacqueline Dyris.

Burke, a man who must decide which of two women he will marry, consults a hypnotist who lets him see what his future will be like with each of them.

The Man Who Stayed at Home (Metro, 1919)
d: Herbert Blaché. 6 reels.
King Baggot, Claire Whitney, Robert Whittier, Alexandre Herbert, Lilie Leslie, Frank Fisher Bennett, Ricca Allen, Robert Paton Gibbs, Julia Calhoun, Ida Darling, Betty Hutchinson.
During World War I, a young man is thought a slacker because he refuses to enlist in the service. But he's really working for the Secret Service.

The Man Who Stood Still (World Film Corp., 1916)
d: Frank Crane. 5 reels.
Lew Fields, Doris Kenyon, George Trimble, Viola Trent, Harry Fraser, Edward O'Connor, John Powers, Dave Ferguson, Auguste Burmester.
Dad's got his daughter's future all mapped out. But then she elopes.

The Man Who Took a Chance (Universal, 1917)
d: William Worthington. 5 reels.
Franklyn Farnum, Agnes Vernon, Lloyd Whitlock, Marc Fenton, Charles Perley, Arthur Hoyt.
Constance is surrounded by suitors, but can't decide on any of them. So, she stages her own kidnapping to see which one of them tries to "rescue" her.

The Man Who Woke Up (Triangle, 1918)
d: J.W. McLaughlin. 5 reels.
William V. Mong, Pauline Starke, George Hernandez, Estelle Evans, Darrell Foss, Harry Depp, George Pearce, Jean Calhoun, Alberta Lee.
In the Deep South, a newspaper publisher is still deeply resentful of the Yankees. That is, until his own daughter, a true magnolia blossom, falls in love with a visiting New Yorker.

The Man Who Won (Vitagraph, 1919)
d: Paul Scardon. 5 reels.
Harry T. Morey, Maurice Costello, Betty Blythe, Bernard Siegel, Robert Gaillard, Denton Vane.
After recovering a load of platinum and hiding it for the United States government, a U.S. agent develops amnesia.

The Man Who Won (Fox, 1923)
d: William Wellman. 5 reels.
Dustin Farnum, Jacqueline Gadsden, Lloyd Whitlock, Ralph Cloninger, Mary Warren, Pee Wee Holmes, Harvey Clark, Lon Poff, Andy Waldron, Ken Maynard, Muriel McCormac, Mickey McBan, Bob Marks.
Out West, a miner named Zip leaves his three children in the care of his friend Wild Bill and sets out to find the man who stole his wife.

The Man Who Would Not Die (American Film Co./Mutual, 1916)
d: William Russell, John Prescott. 5 reels.
William Russell, Charlotte Burton, Harry Keenan, Leona Hutton.
Agnes has a double dilemma: she's loved by twin brothers.

The Man Who Wouldn't Tell (Vitagraph, 1918)
d: James Young. 5 reels.
Earle Williams, Grace Darmond, Charles Spere, Edward Cecil.
During World War I, a charming, polo-playing Englishman

is suspected of being a slacker—but he's really an incognito Secret Service agent.

The Man With Two Mothers (Goldwyn, 1922)
d: Paul Bern. 5 reels.
Cullen Landis, Sylvia Breamer, Mary Alden, Hallam Cooley, Fred Huntly, Laura LaVarnie, Monte Collins, William Elmer.
Dennis, an Irish lad, comes to the United States with his mother to take over his aunt's junkyard business.

The Man Without a Conscience (Warner Bros., 1925)
d: James Flood. 7 reels.
Willard Louis, Irene Rich, June Marlowe, John Patrick, Robert Agnew, Helen Dunbar, Kate Price.
Amos, an unscrupulous young man with a driving ambition to get rich, swindles his own fiancée on his way to wealth. In the end, though, Amos' unethical schemes land him in prison, and the fiancée falls in love with another.

The Man Without a Country (Universal, 1917)
d: Ernest C. Warde. 6 reels.
H.H. Herbert, Florence LaBadie, J.H. Gilmour, Carey Hastings, Ernest Howard, Charles Dundan.
Reworking of the patriotic tale by Edward Everett Hale.

The Man Without a Country (Fox, 1925)
d: Rowland W. Lee. 10 reels.
Edward Hearn, Pauline Starke, Lucy Beaumont, Richard Tucker, Earl Metcalf, Edward Coxen, Wilfred Lucas, Francis Powers, Harvey Clark, William Walling, William Conklin, Edward Peil, Albert Hart, Emmett King, George Billings.
Classic tale of an army officer who is tried for treason and angrily renounces his allegiance to the United States.

The Man Without a Heart (Banner Productions, 1924)
d: Burton King. 6 reels.
Kenneth Harlan, Jane Novak, David Powell, Faire Binney, Bradley Barker, Tommy Tremaine, Mary McCall, Muriel Ruddell, Tom Blake.
To save his sister's marriage, Rufus abducts the woman he thinks guilty of infidelity with his brother-in-law.

Man, Woman and Sin (MGM, 1927)
d: Monta Bell. 7 reels.
Jeanne Eagels, John Gilbert, Marc MacDermott, Gladys Brockwell, Philip Anderson, Hayden Stevenson, Charles K. French, Aileen Manning.
A timid man with a strong attachment to his mother decides to visit a brothel.
Change-of-pace role for John Gilbert, who was often asked to portray a nonchalant womanizer. Here, his character is as meek as a little white mouse, until he meets a worldly woman named Vera (Miss Eagels).

Man, Woman, and Wife (Universal, 1929)
d: Edward Laemmle. 7 reels.
Marian Nixon, Norman Kerry, Pauline Starke, Byron Douglas, Kenneth Harlan, Crauford Kent.
A widow remarries, then learns her first husband isn't dead after all.

Man-Made Women (DeMille Pictures/Pathé, 1928)
d: Paul L. Stein. 6 reels.
Leatrice Joy, H.B. Warner, John Boles, Seena Owen, Jay Eaton, Jeanette Loff, Sidney Bracy.
John and Nan are happily married, but there's a problem: She thinks his friends are boring, he thinks her friends are scandalous. Can this marriage survive?

Man-Woman-Marriage (Allen Holubar/Associated First National, 1921)
d: Allen Holubar. 9 reels.
Dorothy Phillips, Ralph Lewis, Margaret Mann, James Kirkwood, Robert Cain, J. Barney Sherry, Shannon Day, Frances Parks, Emily Chichester.
Victoria, wife of a successful attorney, feels neglected by him when he is nominated as a candidate for U.S. Senator and becomes busy with campaign matters.

The Man Worth While (Romaine Fielding Productions, 1921)
d: Romaine Fielding. 5 reels.
Joan Arliss, Lawrence Johnson, Eugene Acker, Margaret Seddon, Frederick Eckhart, Peggy Parr, Herbert Standing, Vanda Tierendelli, Barney Gilmore, Natalie O'Brien.
Mary, engaged to marry Ward, is tricked into marriage with the wealthy son of a lumber magnate instead.

Mandarin's Gold (World Film Corp., 1919)
d: Oscar Apfel. 5 reels.
Kitty Gordon, Irving Cummings, George MacQuarrie, Marguerite Gale, Veronica Lee, Warner Oland, Joseph Lee, Marion Barney, Tony Merlo, Charles Fang, Alice Lee.
When a New York socialite insists on running up debts by playing bridge, she finds herself in a quandary: either pay with cash, or pay with her body, to the cad who holds her IOUs.

Manhandled (Famous Players-Lasky/Paramount, 1924)
d: Allan Dwan. 7 reels.
Gloria Swanson, Tom Moore, Lilyan Tashman, Ian Keith, Arthur Housman, Paul McAllister, Frank Morgan, Marie Shelton, Ann Pennington, Carrie Scott.
A shopgirl who's good at imitations is hired by a businessman to bring class to his shop by impersonating a Russian countess.

Manhattan (Famous Players-Lasky/Paramount, 1924)
d: R.H. Burnside. 7 reels.
Richard Dix, Jacqueline Logan, Gregory Kelly, George Siegmann, Gunboat Smith, Oscar Brimberton Figman, Edna May Oliver, Alice Chapin, James Bradbury.
A wealthy New Yorker tires of the easy life and decides to go incognito to Hell's Kitchen, looking for some excitement. He finds plenty of it.

Manhattan Cocktail (Paramount, 1928)
d: Dorothy Arzner. 8 reels.
Nancy Carroll, Richard Arlen, Danny O'Shea, Paul Lukas, Lilyan Tashman.
Two small-town youths go to the big city to make their fortune.

Manhattan Cowboy (El Dorado Productions, 1928)
d: J.P. McGowan. 5 reels.
Bob Custer, Lafe McKee, Mary Mayberry, Charles Whittaker, John Lowell Russell, Lynn Sanderson, Mack V. Wright, Cliff Lyons, Dorothy Vernon.
An east coast playboy is sent out west to learn about hard work.

A Manhattan Knight (Fox, 1920)
d: George A. Beranger. 5 reels.
George Walsh, Virginia Hammond, William H. Budd, Warren Cook, John Hopkins, William T. Hayes, Cedric Ellis, Charles Slattery, Louis R. Wolheim, Jack Raymond, Walter Mann, Pauline Garon, W.A. Sullivan.
In New York, a young man helps a girl whose half-brother has just attempted suicide.

Manhattan Knights   (Excellent Pictures, 1928)
d: Burton King.   7 reels.
Barbara Bedford, Walter Miller, Betty Worth, Ray Hallor, Crauford Kent, Eddie boland, Noble Johnson, Joseph Burke, Leo white, Maude Truax.
Siblings Jimmy and Margaret, and Margaret's sweetheart Bob, go after crooked card sharps. It turns out the sharps are also into arson, kidnapping, and murder.

Manhattan Madness   (Fine Arts Film Co./Triangle, 1916)
d: Allan Dwan.   5 reels.
Douglas Fairbanks, Jewel Carmen, George Beranger, Ruth Darling, Eugene Ormonde, Macey Harlan, W.P. Richmond.
In Manhattan, a former cowboy fights off citified villains and captures a pretty gal for himself.

Manhattan Madness   (Fine Arts Pictures, 1925)
d: John McDermott.   6 reels.
Jack Dempsey, Estelle Taylor, George Siegmann, Frank Campeau, Bull Montana, Nelson McDowell, Bill Franey, Theodore Lorch, Jane Starr, Robert Graves, Tom Wilson.
Remake of the 1916 Fine Arts/Triangle film of the same name.

The Manicure Girl   (Famous Players-Lasky/Paramount, 1925)
d: Frank Tuttle.   6 reels.
Bebe Daniels, Edmund Burns, Dorothy Cumming, Hale Hamilton, Charlotte Walker, Ann Brody, Marie Shotwell, Mary Foy.
Maria, a hotel manicurist, is romanced by Morgan, a wealthy guest. She's engaged to be married, but Morgan presses his pursuit of her anyway.

Mannequin   (Paramount, 1926)
d: James Cruze.   7 reels.
Alice Joyce, Warner Baxter, Dolores Costello, ZaSu Pitts, Walter Pidgeon, Freeman Wood, Charlot Bird.
Annie, a newly-orphaned girl of the tenements, finds work as a clothing model.

Manon Lescaut   (Playgoers Film Co., 1914)
d: Herbert Hall Winslow.   6 reels.
Lina Cavalieri, Lucien Muratore, Dorothy Arthur, W.L. Abingdon, Charles Hammond, Frank H. Westerton, Henry Weaver, Frank Hardy, H.L. Winslow, Cecil Walter.
Classic tale about Manon, a French convent girl who marries a count and then is seduced by his rival. Reunited again with her husband, the pair flee to New Orleans, where more tragedy awaits them.
This film is based on the famous 18th-century novel by Abbé Prévost, which also inspired an opera by Giacomo Puccini and several later films, including *When a Man Loves* (1927), starring John Barrymore and Dolores Costello.

Man's Desire   (Lewis S. Stone Productions/Exhibitors Mutual, 1919)
d: Lloyd Ingraham.   5 reels.
Lewis S. Stone, Jane Novak, Jack Curtis, Bill Dyer, Charlotte Burton, George Pearce, Joe Bennett.
Violent, action-packed saga of the Northwest lumber camps. A mill owner enrages his lumberjacks by insisting they abstain from liquor, and is subsequently targeted by dynamiters.

A Man's Fight   (United Picture Theaters of America, Inc., 1919)
d: Thomas N. Heffron.   5 reels.
Dustin Farnum, Dorothy Wallace, J. Barney Sherry,
Wedgwood Nowell, Harry Von Meter, Lois Wilson, Miles McCarthy, Betty Bouton, Dick La Reno, Aggie Herring.In Arizona, a former New York playboy buys a copper mine and becomes embroiled in a management-labor beef.

A Man's Home   (Selznick/Select, 1921)
d: Ralph Ince.   6 reels.
Harry T. Morey, Kathlyn Williams, Faire Binney, Margaret Seddon, Grace Valentine, Roland Bottomley, Matt Moore.
Osborn, a self-made millionaire, finds himself too occupied with business to concern himself with family matters.

A Man's Making   (Lubin, 1915)
d: Jack Pratt.   5 reels.
Herbert Fortier, Richard Buhler, George Clarke, Rosetta Brice, Nelson Hall, William H. Turner.
Disowned by his wealthy father, a university student finds himself penniless and stranded in a small village. But he recovers his dignity and fights his way back to success, aided by the love of a good woman.

A Man's Man   (Peralta Plays, Inc./W.W. Hodkinson, 1918)
d: Oscar Apfel.   7 reels.
J. Warren Kerrigan, Lois Wilson, Kenneth Harlan, Ed Coxen, Ida Lewis, Harry Von Meter, Eugene Pallette, Ernst Pasque, Arthur Allardt, Joseph J. Dowling, John Steppling.
A soldier of fortune prospects for gold in the West, rescues a girl from a would-be seducer, then goes to Central America to fight for a deposed president who, thanks to the American's help, regains the presidency. In the glow of success that follows, the American marries the president's sister, who turns out to be the girl he rescued from the masher.

A Man's Man   (MGM, 1929)
d: James Cruze.   8 reels.
William Haines, Josephine Dunn, Mae Busch, Sam Hardy, Gloria Davenport, John Gilbert, Greta Garbo.
Small-town girl Peggy goes to Hollywood to try to break into the movies.   John Gilbert and Greta Garbo play themselves, in small roles.

A Man's Mate   (Fox, 1924)
d: Edmund Mortimer.   6 reels.
John Gilbert, Renee Adoree, Noble Johnson, Wilfrid North, Thomas Mills, James Neill, Jack Giddings, Patterson Dial.
In Paris, an artist develops amnesia from a blow on the head, but it doesn't keep him from falling in love with an apache dancer and producing a masterful portrait of her.

A Man's Past   (Universal, 1927)
d: George Melford.   6 reels.
Conrad Veidt, Ian Keith, Barbara Bedford, Arthur Edmund Carew, Charles Puffy, Corliss Palmer, Edward Reinach.
A surgeon serving a prison sentence for performing euthanasia on a dying patient breaks out and starts a new life under a new name.

Man's Plaything   (Republic, 1920)
d: Charles T Horan.   6 reels.
Montague Love, Grace Davison, Stuart Holmes, J.W. Johnston, Eric Mayne.
In a downtown nightery, a young woman working as a flower girl falls for a wealthy patron, and he with her. It's love at first sight, but there's a catch: her boss wants her too.

Man's Size   (Fox, 1921)
d: Howard M. Mitchell.   5 reels.
William Russell, Alma Bennett, Stanton Heck, Charles K.

French, James Gordon, Carl Stockdale.
In Canada, a brutal father "sells" his daughter to a bootlegger.

Man's Woman (World Film Corp., 1917)
d: Travers Vale. 5 reels.
Ethel Clayton, Rockcliffe Fellowes, Frank Goldsmith, Justine Cutting, Eugenie Woodward, John Hines, Ned Burton, Edward Kimball.
The embattled wife of an assistant district attorney must contend with the constant interference of her husband's maiden aunts.

A Man's World (Metro, 1918)
d: Herbert Blaché. 5 reels.
Emily Stevens, John Merkyl, Frederick Truesdell, Florence Short, Baby Ivy Ward, Walter Hiers, Sidney Bracy, Vera Roger, Lucile Dorrington, Vinney Binns.
In Paris, a visiting American woman comforts a dying girl, and decides to adopt the girl's illegitimate baby and bring it home to New York. Once she's home, she writes a bitter book denouncing the "system" that makes this "a man's world." Imagine her surprise when her own publisher, who had visited Paris, turns out to be the father of her adopted baby!

A Man's World (1925)—see: Daddy's Gone A'Hunting

The Mansion of Aching Hearts (B.P. Schulberg Productions, 1925)
d: James P. Hogan. 6 reels.
Ethel Clayton, Brbara Bedford, Priscilla Bonner, Philo McCullough, Edward Delaney, Cullen Landis, Sam DeGrasse, Eddie Phillips, Edward Gribbon, Helen Hogo.
Weepy melodrama about a banker who unjustly believes his wife unfaithful, and drives her and her infant son from their home. Years later, mother and son become separated, and the banker finds the boy and takes him under his wing, not knowing the lad is his own son.

Manslaughter (Famous Players-Lasky/Paramount, 1922)
d: Cecil B. DeMille. 10 reels.
Thomas Meighan, Leatrice Joy, Lois Wilson, John Miltern, George Fawcett, Julia Faye, Edythe Chapman, Jack Mower, Dorothy Cumming, Casson Ferguson, Mickey Moore, James Neill, Sylvia Ashton, Raymond Hatton, Mabel Van Buren, Dale Fuller, Charles Ogle.
Typically ornate DeMille near-epic about Lydia, a young socialite who likes to drive fast cars. When her driving causes a person's death, the district attorney prosecutes Lydia vigorously and has her sent to prison. But in the meantime, the D.A. has fallen in love with her. What now?

The Mantle of Charity (American Film Co./Pathé, 1918)
d: Edward Sloman. 5 reels.
Margarita Fisher, Jack Mower, Daniel Gilfether, Louella Maxam, Gordon Russell, Kate Price.
Light comedy has a young woman dressing her Pekinese pooch in baby clothes to get him into her Pullman coach, and consequently being thought an unwed mother.

Mantrap (Famous Players-Lasky/Paramount, 1926)
d: Victor Fleming. 6 reels.
Ernest Torrence, Clara Bow, Percy Marmont, Eugene Pallette, Tom Kennedy, William Orlamond, Charles Stevens, Josephine Crowell, Miss DuPont, Charlot Bird.
An attractive young manicurist is swept off her feet by a backwoodsman, who marries her and takes her back to his remote home on a Canadian lakefront. Now she's got

security, but she still likes to flirt... and she gets to do plenty of that, with several men, including a mountie.

The Marble Heart (Fox, 1916)
d: Keenan Buel. 5 reels.
Violet Horner, Louise Rial, Walter Miller, Rhy Alexander, Henry Armetta, Walter McCullough, Harry Burkhardt, Hal De Forrest, Mark Price, Arthur Leslie.
Tragedy based on Emile Zola's novel *Thérése Raquin*. In France, young Thérése marries a boring lad, and soon tires of him. She and her new lover drown her husband and then, after a suitable mourning period, they marry. But their guilt constantly torments them and leads them to mutual destruction.

The March Hare (Realart Pictures, 1921)
d: Maurice Campbell. 5 reels.
Bebe Daniels, Grace Morse, Herbert Sherwood, Mayme Kelso, Helen Jerome Eddy, Sidney Bracey, Frances Raymond, Melbourne MacDowell, Harry Myers.
A young socialite makes a bet that she can survive on only 75 cents for a week.

Mare Nostrum (MGM, 1925)
d: Rex Ingram. 10 reels.
Antonio Moreno, Alice Terry, Uni Apollon, Alex Nova, Hughie Mack, Mademoiselle Kithnou, Michael Brantford, Rosita Ramirez, Kada-Abdel-Kader, Frederick Mariotti.
World War I drama about a Spanish sea captain who falls in love with a beautiful German spy. When he learns that his son has been killed by a German torpedo, he turns against his lovely foil and prosecutes her ruthlessly, leading to her death in front of a French firing squad.

Maria Rosa (Lasky Feature Plays/Paramount, 1916)
d: Cecil B. DeMille. 5 reels.
Geraldine Farrar, Wallace Reid, Pedro de Cordoba, Ernest Joy, Anita King, Horace B. Carpenter, James Neill.
In Spain, two men court the same woman. When she chooses one to marry, his resentful rival frames the would-be bridegroom for murder and has him thrown in jail.

Marianne (MGM, 1929)
d: Robert Z. Leonard. 7 reels. (Also released in sound, with different supporting cast.)
Marion Davies, Oscar Shaw, Robert Castle, Robert Ames, Scott Kolk, Mack Swain, Emil Chautard.
A French girl falls for an American G.I., then impersonates an officer to help get her man out of the stockade.

Marie, Ltd. (Select Pictures Corp., 1919)
d: Kenneth Webb. 5 reels.
"Marie, Ltd." is a New York milliner's shop where customers are regularly overcharged for their purchases.

The Mark of Cain (Universal, 1916)
d: Joseph DeGrasse. 5 reels.
Lon Chaney, Frank Whitson, Dorothy Phillips, Gilmore Hammond, T.D. Crittenden, Gretchen Lederer, Lydia Yeamans Titus, Mark Fenton, Georgia French.
Dick, an ex-con, and Doris, a despondent girl, are both bent on suicide. But then they meet and fall in love.

The Mark of Cain (Astra Film Corp./Pathé, 1917)
d: George Fitzmaurice. 5 reels.
Irene Castle, Antonio Moreno, J.H. Gilmour, Elinor Black, John Sainpolis.
Alice, whose adoptive father has been murdered, works hard to prove his nephew innocent of the crime.

The Mark of Zorro (Fairbanks/United Artists, 1920)
d: Fred Niblo. 8 reels.
Douglas Fairbanks, Marguerite de la Motte, Robert McKim, Noah Beery, Charles Hill Mailes, Claire McDowell, Walt Whitman.
A Spanish nobleman in early California is thought a pretentious fop, but in his other identity he is Zorro, masked crusader for the rights of the poor.

A Marked Man (Universal, 1917)
d: Jack Ford. 5 reels.
Harry Carey, Molly Malone, Harry Rattenbury, Vester Pegg, William Gettinger.
Carey again plays Cheyenne Harry, this time falsely accused of murder in connection with a stagecoach robbery.

Marked Men (Universal, 1920)
d: Jack Ford. 5 reels.
Harry Carey, Joe Harris, Ted Brooks, Winifred Westover, J. Farrell MacDonald, Charles Lemoyne.
A remake of *The Three Godfathers* (Universal, 1916). Three bank robbers on the lam run across a dying woman and her child, and find themselves obliged to care for the child after the mother's death.

Marked Money (Pathé, 1928)
d: Spencer Gordon Bennett. 6 reels.
Junior Coghlan, George Duryea, Virginia Bradford, Tom Kennedy, Bert Woodruff, Jack Richardson.
Grace, a sea captain's daughter, is kidnapped and held for ransom.

The Marked Woman (World Film Corp., 1914)
d: O.A.C. Lund. 5 reels.
Dorothy Tennant, O.A.C. Lund, Joseph Baker, Walter Connolly, Jane Stuart.
In China, a Russian woman becomes the wife of the Chinese prime minister, although her heart is with an American Navy officer.

The Market of Souls (Thomas H. Ince/Paramount, 1919)
d: Joseph DeGrasse. 6 reels.
Dorothy Dalton, Holmes E. Herbert, Philo McCullough, Dorcas Matthews, Donald McDonald, George Williams.
Helen spends New Year's Eve with her married cousin Evelyn and her husband. When both Evelyn and her spouse are unfaithful, Helen finds herself involved in trying to straighten them out.

The Market of Vain Desire (New York Motion Picture Co./Triangle, 1916)
d: Reginald Barker. 5 reels.
H.B. Warner, Clara Williams, Charles Miller, Gertrude Claire, Leona Hutton.
When a status-seeking socialite secures a title for her daughter by arranging to marry her off to a nobleman, the local minister suggests that such a move is little better than outright prostitution.

Marlie the Killer (Fred J. McConnell Productions/Pathé, 1928)
d: Noel Mason Smith. 5 reels.
Klondike, a dog, Francis X. Bushman Jr., Joseph Girard, Blanche Mehaffey, Richard Alexander, Sheldon Lewis.
Crooked officials try to delay completion of a dam project. The hero is waylaid by the villains, but his dog Marlie chases the chief crook to the edge of a cliff and sends him off.

Marooned Hearts (National Picture Theatres, Inc./Select, 1920)
d: George Archainbaud. 5 reels.
Conway Tearle, Zena Keefe, Ida Darling, Tom Blake, Eric Mayne, George Backus, Joseph Flanagan, Lavilla Seibert.
Resentful of her doctor fiancé's dedication to his work, a spoiled socialite intercepts an emergency call intended for him. The missed call means the end of the young doctor's career, and an end to his engagement. But he and the socialite will meet again a year later, when by coincidence both are washed ashore on the same desert island.

Marriage (Fox, 1927)
d: R. William Neill. 6 reels.
Virginia Valli, Allan Durant, Gladys McConnell, Lawford Davidson, Donald Stuart, Frank Dunn, Edwards Davis, James Marcus, Billie Bennett.
Marjorie doesn't fancy the fellow she's engaged to, so instead she elopes with a young inventor.

Marriage á la Carte — see: Marrying Money (1915)

The Marriage Bond (Mirror Films, Inc., 1916)
d: Lawrence Marston. 5 reels.
Nat C. Goodwin, Margaret Green, Anne Jeffson, Raymond Bloomer, P.J. Rollow.
When a young woman breaks her engagement to the man she loves and instead marries for money, she sets in motion a chain of tragic events.

Marriage By Contract (Tiffany-Stahl Productions, 1928)
d: James Flood. 8 reels.
Patsy Ruth Miller, Lawrence Gray, Robert Edeson, Ralph Emerson, Shirley Palmer, John St. Polis, Claire McDowell, Ruby Lafayette, Duke Martin, Raymond Keane.
Margaret and her fiancé Don marry, but she soon leaves him. Entering into marriage again, with Dirk, she gets a taste of her own medicine when *he* leaves *her*. Then she marries a wealthy old man, and soon divorces him. Now she's up to her fourth husband, a ne'er-do-well named Drury, whom she murders. As she is dragged off to jail by the police, Margaret wakes up. Yep, it's all been a bad dream; soon she must get ready to meet Don at church to get married.

The Marriage Chance (American Releasing Corp., 1922)
w, d: Hampton Del Ruth. 6 reels.
Milton Sills, Alta Allen, Henry B. Walthall, Tully Marshall, Irene Rich, Mitchell Lewis, Laura LaVarnie, Nick Cogley.
Eleanor, about to marry a young district attorney, has second thoughts.

The Marriage Cheat (Thomas H. Ince/Associated First National, 1924)
d: John Griffith Wray. 7 reels.
Leatrice Joy, Percy Marmont, Adolphe Menjou, Laska Winter, Henry Barrows, J.P. Lockney.
Helen, shipwrecked on a South Seas island, falls in love with a missionary.

The Marriage Circle (Warner Bros., 1924)
d: Ernst Lubitsch. 8 reels.
Florence Vidor, Monte Blue, Marie Prevost, Creighton Hale, Adolphe Menjou, Harry Myers, Dale Fuller, Esther Ralston.
Comedy of marriage manners and morals, set in pre-World War I Vienna.

The Marriage Clause (Universal, 1926)
d: Lois Weber. 8 reels.
Billie Dove, Francis X. Bushman, Warner Oland, Henri La

Garde, Grace Darmond,
Caroline Snowden, Andre Cheron.
A Broadway star and her director fall in love, but they are prevented from marrying because of a clause in her contract.

Marriage For Convenience (Frank A. Keeney Pictures Corp., 1919)
d: Sidney Olcott. 5 reels.
Catherine Calvert, Ann May, George Majeroni, Henry Sedley, Blanche Davenport, Edward Burns, Sadie Leonard, George Pauncefort, Caesar Gravina, Edward Slow.
When Barbara is accosted by a would-be seducer, she tries to escape and in the attempt loses her eyesight. Her sister, determined to fund an operation to restore Barbara's sight, marries a wealthy suitor instead of the young man she truly loves. Little does she realize, her new husband is the cad who attacked her sister.

Marriage in Transit (Fox, 1925)
d: R. William Neill. 5 reels.
Edmund Lowe, Carol Lombnard, Adolph Milar, Frank Beal, Harvey Clark, Fred Walton, Wade Boteler, Fred Butler, Byron Douglas, Fred Becker, Edward Chandler.
Gordon, a Secret Service agent, looks so much like a certain gang leader that he has no trouble impersonating him and infiltrating the gang. But he didn't count on this: The gang leader is engaged to marry the beautiful Celia... and to make the masquerade work, Gordon must go through with the wedding.
Lowe portrays both the U.S. agent and the lookalike mobster.

The Marriage Lie (Universal, 1918)
d: Harvey Gates. 5 reels.
Carmel Myers, Kenneth Harlan, Harry Carter, William Quinn, Joe Girard.
Douglas offers to support penniless Eileen if she will pose as his wife so he can obtain a management position with a construction firm. The arrangement works just fine, until Douglas catches his boss trying to force his attentions on Eileen. After Douglas tosses the boss out on his ear, he and Eileen realize they are truly in love, and decide to get married for real.

The Marriage Market (World Film Corp., 1917)
d: Arthur Ashley. 5 reels.
June Elvidge, Arthur Ashley, Carlyle Blackwell, Frederick Truesdell, Jack Drumier, Charles Duncan, Eugenie Woodward, Lewis Edgard.
In an effort to gain financial independence from her boorish husband, Helen tries to sell her thoroughbred horse. She sees a prospective buyer, but discovers that all he really wants is to force his attentions on her.

The Marriage Market (Columbia, 1923)
d: Edward J. Le Saint. 6 reels.
Pauline Garon, Jack Mulhall.
Theodora, a daughter of privilege, is expelled from boarding school.

Marriage Morals (Weber & North Productions, 1923)
w, d: William Nigh. 7 reels.
Tom Moore, Ann Forrest, Russell Griffin, John Goldsworthy, Harry T. Morey, Edmund Breese, Florence Billings, Ben Hendricks Jr., Shannon Day, Mickey Bennett, Charles Craig.
Love-struck Mary reads about marital bliss, and dreams of her own future wedding.

The Marriage of Kitty (Lasky Feature Plays/Paramount, 1915)
d: George Melford. 5 reels.
Fannie Ward, Richard Morris, Jack Dean, Cleo Ridgeley, Tom Forman.
Breezy romantic comedy about an Englishman who's engaged to one girl but must marry a different girl, Kitty, in order to gain his inheritance. The plan is for he and Kitty to marry for six months, then divorce, and for her trouble Kitty will pocket $50,000. But secretly, Kitty plans to hang on to her man.

The Marriage of Molly-O (Fine Arts Film Co./Triangle, 1916)
d: Paul Powell. 5 reels.
Mae Marsh, Kate Bruce, Robert Harron, James O'Shea, Walter Long, Alice Knowland.
In Ireland, Molly-O loves Larry but agrees to marry Denny for financial security.

The Marriage of William Ashe (Metro, 1921)
d: Edward Sloman. 6 reels.
May Allison, Wyndham Standing, Zeffie Tillbury, Frank Elliott, Robert Bolder, Lydia Yeamans Titus, Clarissa Selwynne.
Kitty, a convent-bred girl, marries William Ashe, a British government official. She is skilled at drawing cartoons, and produces several sketches of cabinet memers, which are then published in the newspaper. This leads to a scandal that ruptures the marriage, but in the end they realize they still love each other, and are reconciled.

The Marriage Pit (Universal, 1920)
d: Fred Thomson. 5 reels.
Frank Mayo, Lillian Tucker, Ray Ripley, Frederick Vroom, Hal Wilson, Dagmar Godowsky, Belle Stoddard Johnstone, Boyd Irwin, Robert Dunbar, Judson Vernon, Will Herford.
Elinor marries a financier out of gratitude, but after several bumps along the road of matrimony, learns to her joy that she really loves her husband.

The Marriage Price (Famous Players-Lasky/Paramount, 1919)
d: Emile Chautard. 5 reels.
Elsie Ferguson, Wyndham Standing, Lionel Atwill, Robert Schable, Maud Hosford, Marie Temper, Clairette Anthony, Zelda Crosby.
A sybaritic young woman is surrounded by suitors, but only one of them is Mr. Right.

The Marriage Ring (Thomas H. Ince/Paramount, 1918)
d: Fred Niblo. 5 reels.
Enid Bennett, Jack Holt, Robert McKim, Maude George, Charles K. French, Lydia Knott, John Cossar.
Fleeing from her dishonest and violent husband, a San Francisco girl makes her way to Honolulu, where she finds true love. But look out, hubby's following close behind.

The Marriage Speculation (Vitagraph, 1917)
d: Ashley Miller. 5 reels.
Charles Kent, Mildred Manning, Wallace MacDonald, Augustus Phillips.
Clara loves Billy, but she can't resist an old man's offer to send her to the best finishing schools that money can buy, so that she can then attract a wealthy suitor. Clara completes her courses and blossoms forth as a polished and confident beauty. Now it's up to Billy to see if he can compete with the noble young gentlemen competing for Clara's hand.

The Marriage Whirl (First National, 1925)

d: Al Santell. 8 reels.
Corinne Griffith, Kenneth Harlan, Harrison Ford, E.J. Ratcliffe, Charles Lane, Edgar Norton, Nita Naldi.
Marian, a shy and decorous girl, marries wild jazz-age partygoer Arthur. It won't last.

Marriages Are Made (Fox, 1918)
d: Carl Harbaugh. 5 reels.
Peggy Hyland, Edwin Stanley, George Clarke, Al Lee, Dan Mason, Ellen Cassidy, William H. Boyd, Ed Begley, George Halpin.
Susan loves James, but because he's related to an enemy of the family, Susan's dad discourages their marriage plans.

Married? (Herman Janus Films, 1925)
d: George Terwilliger. 6 reels.
Owen Moore, Evangeline Russell, Julia Hurley, Constance Bennett, Nick Thomas, Antrim Short.
Marcia, a frivolous flapper, agrees to marry a lumberman she doesn't know, by telephone. After the "ceremony," her new husband arrives and takes her to the North Woods, where they will learn to love each other.

Married Alive (Fox, 1927)
d: Emmett Flynn. 5 reels.
Lou Tellegen, Margaret Livingston, Matt Moore, Claire Adams, Gertrude Claire, Marcella Daly, Henry Sedley, Eric Mayne, Charles Lane, Emily Fitzroy.
At the seashore, a vacationing college professor meets a man who claims to be married simultaneously to four different women.

The Married Flapper (Universal, 1922)
d: Stuart Paton. 5 reels.
Marie Prevost, Kenneth Harlan, Philo McCullough, Frank Kingsley, Lucille Rickson, Kathleen O'Connor, Hazel Keener, Tom McGuire, Burton Wilson, William Quinn, Lydia Titus.
When her race driver husband is injured, Pam takes his place and wins the big race.

Married Flirts (MGM, 1924)
d: Robert Vignola. 7 reels.
Pauline Frederick, Conrad Nagel, Mae Busch, Huntley Gordon, Paul Nicholson, Patterson Dial, Alice Hollister. A married man is lured to the arms of another woman, who later rejects him.

Married in Haste (Fox, 1919)
d: Arthur Rosson. 5 reels.
Albert Ray, Elinor Fair, Robert Klein, Don Bailey, B.M. Turner, Thomas Jefferson, William Carroll, William Elmer.
Comedic tale about a rich wastrel whose bride tries to break him of his spendthrift ways.

Married in Name Only (Ivan Productions, 1917)
d: Edmund Lawrence. 6 reels.
Milton Sills, Gretchen Hartman, Marie Shotwell, Dora Mills Adams, William Desmond.
On his wedding day, a bridegroom learns that his grandparents were insane. Now fearful of passing on the insanity genes to his children, he resolves to keep his wife at arm's length. It's a dreary marriage until, one day, the young man learns another family secret: He was adopted!

Married Life (Mack Sennett/Associated First National, 1920)
d: Mack Sennett. 5 reels.
Ben Turpin, Charles Conklin, James Finlayson, Phyllis Haver, Charlotte Mineau, Kalla Pasha, Charlie Murray, Ford Sterling, Louise Fazenda, Eddie Gribbon.
Typically frenetic comedy from the Sennett studio, involving an actor who is injured by falling scenery, a mad dash to the hospital, and a not-quite-right doctor who decides to operate.

Married People (Hugo Ballin Productions/W.W. Hodkinson, 1922)
d: Hugo Ballin. 6 reels.
Mabel Ballin, Percy Marmont, Ernest Hilliard, Bobby Clarke, Dick Lee, Bertha Kent, John Webb Dillon, Louis Dean, Charles Fang, Baby Peggy Rice.
A couple whose marriage is on the rocks find bliss when they adopt two children, a boy and a girl.

The Married Virgin (Maxwell Productions/Fidelity Pictures, 1920)
d: Joseph Maxwell. 6 reels.
Vera Sisson, Frank Newberg, Kathleen Kirkham, Rodolfo Di Valentina, Edward Jobson.
To help her father discharge a large debt, a young woman agrees to a marriage in name only.

Marry in Haste (Phil Goldstone Productions, 1924)
d: Duke Worne. 5 reels.
William Fairbanks, Dorothy Revier, Alfred Hollingsworth, Gladden James, William Dyer, Al Kaufman.
Out West, a wealthy rancher disowns his son for marrying in haste. But the father will eventually forgive him and welcome his daughter-in-law home.

Marry Me (Famous Players-Lasky/Paramount, 1925)
d: James Cruze. 6 reels.
Florence Vidor, Edward Everett Horton, John Roche, Helen Jerome Eddy, Fanny Midgley, Ed Brady, Z. Wall Covington, Anne Schaefer, Erwin Connelly.
Comedy about a schoolmarm who wins a marriage proposal from one John Smith, and sets the date for the wedding. But years go by, and her groom never shows up. Finally she receives a message that John Smith is coming to town to see her, and the lady gets herself ready for the big ceremony. But this fellow is not the same John Smith she consented to marry. No matter; they get married anyway.

Marry the Girl (Sterling Pictures, 1928)
d: Philip Rosen. 6 reels.
Barbara Bedford, Robert Ellis, DeWitt Jennings, Freddie Frederick, Florence Turner, Paul Weigel, Allan Roscoe.
A conniving brother and sister convince a wealthy old man that his son, who has disappeared, is dead. They then produce Elinor and her little boy, claiming that Elinor is the heir's widow and her little boy is the old man's grandson. The schemers hope to lay their hands on the old man's fortune, but they are foiled when the real heir returns and drives them out. But he rather fancies Elinor, and soon the old man's dreams come true when his boy marries Elinor for real.

Marrying Money (World Film Corp., 1915)
d: James Young. 5 reels.
Clara Kimball Young, Ina Brooks, Chester Barnett, William W. Jefferson, Winthrop Chamberlain, Cyril Chadwick, Alice Gordon, E.M. Kimball.
Two fortune hunters marry, neither one knowing that the other is really impoverished.

Marse Covington (Rolfe Photoplays, Inc./Metro, 1915)
d: Edwin Carewe. 5 reels.

Edward Connelly, Louise Huff, John J. Williams, Lyster Chambers, Howard Truesdell, Paul Dallzell.
After the Civil War, a proud Confederate captain refuses to allow his daughter to marry her sweetheart, a Yankee.

Martha's Vindication (Fine Arts Film Co./Triangle, 1916)
d: C.M. Franklin, S.A. Franklin. 5 reels.
Norma Talmadge, Seena Owen, Ralph Lewis, Tully Marshall, Charles West, William Hinckley, Francis Carpenter, George Stone, Alice Knowland, Alberta Lee, Edwin Harley.
Newly-engaged Martha is accused before the church congregation of being an unwed mother. But the baby she is protecting isn't hers, and Martha is vindicated when the real mother comes forward.

The Martin Mystery—see: The Master Cracksman (1914)

The Martyr Sex (Phil Goldstone Productions, 1924)
d: Duke Worne. 5 reels.
William Dyer, William Fairbanks, Les Bates, Billie Bennett, Dorothy Revier, Pat Harmon, Frank Hagney.
In a mountain community, feuding relatives scheme to ambush a kindly doctor. But the doctor outwits them and saves a life by tricking the schemers into "donating" blood for a transfusion for their cousin.

The Martyrdom of Philip Strong (Thomas A. Edison, Inc./Paramount, 1916)
d: Richard Ridgely. 5 reels.
Robert Conness, Mabel Trunnelle, Janet Dawley, Bigelow Cooper, Helen Strickland, Frank Lyons, William Wadsworth, Herbert Prior, Olive Wright, Edith Wright, Brad Sutton.
Philip, a conscience-stricken minister, decides to give up all his material wealth and dedicate himself to live among the poor.

The Martyrs of the Alamo (Fine Arts Film Co./Triangle, 1915)
d: W. Christy Cabanne. 5 reels.
Sam DeGrasse, Walter Long, A.D. Sears, Alfred Paget, Fred Burns, John Dillon, Juanita Hansen, Ora Carew, Tom Wilson, Augustus Carney, Douglas Fairbanks, Jack Prescott.
Retelling of the 1836 storming of the Alamo by Mexican general Santa Anna, and the tragic battle that took the lives of Davy Crockett and James Bowie.
Douglas Fairbanks had a supporting role in this, his first motion picture.

Mary Ellen Comes to Town (Paramount, 1920)
d: Elmer Clifton. 5 reels.
Dorothy Gish, Ralph Graves, Adolphe Lestina, Kate Bruce, Charles Gerrard, Bert Apling, Raymond Cannon, Rhea Haines.
A stage-struck girl comes to the big city in search of a career.

Mary Janes's Pa (Vitagraph, 1917)
d: William P.S. Earle. 5 reels.
Marc MacDermott, Mildred Manning, Eulalie Jensen, Emmett King, Clio Ayres, William Dunn, Templar Saxe, Edward Elkas, Mary Maurice.
Hiram Perkins returns home to his wife and two daughters after an absence of 15 years.

Mary Lawson's Secret (Thanhouser, 1917)
d: John B. O'Brien. 5 reels.
Charlotte Walker, William Davidson, J.H. Gilmour, N.S. Wood, Inda Palmer, Robert Vaughn, Gene LaMotte.

When the local doctor makes a pass at her, Mary Lawson grows furious with him. Later, when the medic is found murdered, Mary is accused of the crime. But she's really innocent, and in time will prove it.

Mary of the Movies (Columbia, 1923)
d: John McDermott. 7 reels.
Marion Mack, Harry Cornelli, Florence Lee, Douglas MacLean, Bryant Washburn, Mary Kane, John Gough, Raymond Cannon, Rosemary Cooper, Creighton Hale, Frances McDonald, Barbara La Marr, Johnnie Walker, J. Warren Kerrigan, Herbert Rawlinson, Alec B. Francis, Richard C. Travers, David Butler, Louise Fazenda, Anita Stewart, Estelle Taylor, Rosemary Theby, Bessie Love, Marjorie Daw, Tom Moore, Elliott Dexter, ZaSu Pitts, Carmel Myers, Rex Ingram, Maurice Tourneur, Edward J. Le Saint, Wanda Hawley.
A girl goes to Hollywood to break into the movies, but the closest she gets is as waitress in a studio restaurant. Her luck changes, though, when somebody notices that she closely resembles one of the studio's stars—a star that has taken ill.

Mary Regan (Anita Stewart Productions/First National, 1919)
d: Lois Weber. 7 reels.
Anita Stewart, Frank Mayo, Carl Miller, Barney Sherry, Brinsley Shaw, George Hernandez, L.W. Steers, Hedda Nova, Syn DeCona.
Mary's the daughter of a convicted thief, and because of her family's past she refuses to marry her beau, a district attorney, for fear of hurting his career.

Mary's Ankle (T.H. Ince/Famous Players-Lasky/Paramount, 1920)
d: Lloyd Ingraham. 5 reels.
Douglas MacLean, Doris May, Victor Potel, Neal Burns, James Gordon, Lisette Thorne, Ida Lewis.
Knowing that his wealthy uncle has promised a sizeable sum as a wedding present, a young doctor's friends spread the rumor that he is engaged to be married. When the presumed bride-to-be learns of the deception, she confronts the doctor and, in her haste, sprains her ankle. The doctor treats her injury and, in the process, they fall in love.

Mary's Lamb (Pathé, 1915)
d: Donald MacKenzie. 5 reels.
Richard Carle, Jessie Ralph, Marie Wayne, Lillian Thatcher.
An unhappily married scientist secretly loves the widow next door.

The Mask—see: The Mask of Riches (1918)

The Mask of Lopez (Monogram Pictures, 1924)
d: Albert Rogell. 5 reels.
Fred Thomson, Wilfred Lucas, David Kirby, Hazel Keener, Frank Hagney, George Magrill, Pee Wee Holmes, Bob Reeves, Dick Sutherland.
Out West, a cowpoke foils a ranch foreman who's been rustling cattle from his employer.

The Mask of Riches (Triangle, 1918)
d: Thomas N. Heffron. 5 reels.
Claire Anderson, Rae Godfrey, Grace Marvin, Bliss Chevalier, John Gilbert, Edward Hearn, Harry Holden, Marie Van Tassel, Lillian West.
Disinherited by his wealthy uncle, a thoughtless playboy changes his ways and falls in love with a sweet and simple girl.

Masked Angel   (Chadwick Pictures, 1928)
d: Frank O'Connor. 6 reels.
Betty Compson, Erick Arnold, Wheeler Oakman, Jocelyn Lee, Grace Cunard, Lincoln Plummer, Robert Homans, Jane Keckley.
A cabaret singer falls in love with a crippled soldier.

The Masked Bride   (MGM, 1925)
d: Josef von Sternberg, Christy Cabanne. 6 reels.

Mae Murray, Roy D'Arcy, Francis X. Bushman, Basil Rathbone.
An apache dancer has a sideline: robbing rich men.

The Masked Heart   (American Film Co./Mutual, 1917)
d: Edward Sloman. 5 reels.
William Russell, Francelia Billington, William Conklin, Kathleen Kirkham, Ashton Dearholt.
Society drama about a young man who meets a mystery woman at a masked ball, and yearns to be with her again... but who is she?

The Masked Rider   (Quality Pictures Corp./Metro, 1916)
d: Fred J. Balshofer. 5 reels.
Harold Lockwood, May Allison, Lester Cuneo, H.W. Willis, John MacDonald, Harry Burkhardt, Clarissa Selwynnn, Harry Linkey, Howard Truesdell.
North Carolina moonshiners are pursued by the Secret Service, including a mysterious masked man.

The Masked Woman   (First National, 1927)
d: Silvano Balboni. 6 reels.
Anna Q. Nilsson, Holbrook Blinn, Einar Hansen, Charlie Murray, Gertrude Short, Ruth Roland, Richard Pennell, Cora Macey, Paulette Day.
Tolento, an unscrupulous baron, invites his physician's beautiful wife to a party at his house while the doctor is out of town.

Masks of the Devil   (MGM, 1928)
d: Victor Seastrom. 8 reels.
John Gilbert, Eva von Berne, Polly Ann Young, Alma Rubens, Ralph Forbes, Theodore Roberts, Frank Reicher, Ethel Wales.
In Vienna, an aristocrat becomes attracted to a charming schoolgirl who's engaged to his best friend.

The Masquerade Bandit   (R-C Pictures/FBO of America, 1926)
d: Robert DeLacey. 5 reels.
Tom Tyler, Dorothy Dunbar, Ethan Laidlaw, Alfred Heuston, Ray Childs, Raye Hamilton, Earl Haley, Frankie Darro.
Western derring-do about a chase after a concealed cache of stolen goods.

The Masquerader   (Richard Walton Tully Productions/Associated First National, 1922)
d: Wilfred Buckland. 8 reels.
Guy Bates Post, Ruth Sinclair, Edward M. Kimball, Herbert Standing, Lawson Butt, Marcia Manon, Barbara Tennant.
Chilcote, a member of the British parliament, has dissipated all his life and is on the verge of losing his political career. Ailing, he persuades his cousin, John Loder, who is the spitting image of Chilcote, to replace him in parliament and in life. Loder agrees, and not only revives the M.P.'s career but reawakens the love of his wife. This latter dilemma is resolved when Chilcote passes away quietly.
Guy Bates Post plays a double role, as Chilcote and his lookalike cousin Loder.

The Masqueraders   (Famous Players/Paramount, 1915)
d: James Kirkwood. 5 reels.
Hazel Dawn, Elliot Dexter, Frank Losee, Norman Tharp, Ida Darling, Evelyn Farris, Nina Lindsey, Charles Bryant, Russell Bassett.
When a barmaid marries a volatile nobleman to escape her poverty, she soon learns that she would have been better off marrying for love.

The Master Cracksman   (Progressive Motion Picture Co., 1914)
d: Harry Carey. 6 reels.
Harry Carey, E.A. Locke, Rexford Burnett, Fern Foster, Herbert Russell, Marjorie Bonner, Juliette Day, Louis Morrell, William H. Power, Gregory Allen, Roland DeCastro.
When a diamond merchant is mysteriously murdered, an innocent man is accused of the crime. Ironically, the miscarriage of justice is derailed by a gentleman jewel thief who witnessed the murder while he was planning a robbery.

The Master Hand   (Premo Feature Film Corp./World Film Corp., 1915)
d: Harley Knoles. 5 reels.
Nat C. Goodwin, Theodore Babcock, Julia Stuart, Florence Malone, Carroll Fleming, Alex Calvert, Clarissa Selwynne, Katherine Lee, Madge Evans.
When a scheming husband contrives to take control of his stepdaughter's assets, he finds that a volatile stock market is the least of his worries.

The Master Man   (Pathé, 1919)
d: Ernest C. Warde. 5 reels.
Frank Keenan, Kathleen Kirkham, Joseph J. Dowling, Joseph McManus, Jack Brammall, William V. Mong, Hardee Kirkland, J. Barney Sherry, Joseph Rae.
Corruption in high places finds a state governor being killed, and his murder blamed on an innocent young senator.

The Master Mind   (Jesse L. Lasky Feature Play Co., 1914)
d: Cecil B. DeMille, Oscar C. Apfel. 5 reels.
Edmund Breese, Fred Montague, Jane Darwell, Dick LaReno, Harry Fisher, Mabel Van Buren, Richard La Strage, Monroe Salisbury, Billy Elmer.
When a crook, known as the Master Mind, tries to avenge his brother's death by execution, he persuades a female crook to seduce the district attorney responsible... but she falls in love with the D.A. instead.

The Master Mind   (Whitman Bennet Productions/Associated First National, 1920)
d: Kenneth Webb. 6 reels.
Lionel Barrymore, Gypsy O'Brien, Ralph Kellard, Bradley Barker, Charles Brandt, Marie Shotwell, Bernard Randall, Charles Edwards.
Remake of the 1914 *The Master Mind*, with minor plot variations.

Master of His Home   (Triangle, 1917)
d: Walter Edwards. 5 reels.
William Desmond, Alma Ruben, Joseph J. Dowling, Eleanor Hancock, Robert McKim, Susie Light Moon, Will H. Bray.
A socialite wishes her daughter to marry someone of equal station, but the girl instead falls for a scruffy gold miner.

The Master of His House   (Triumph Film Corp./World Film Corp., 1915) d: Joseph A. Golden. 5 reels.

Julius Steger, Grace Reals, Margot Williams, Austin Webb, Ralph Morgan, Gertrude Shelby, Charles Hutchinson.

The title's a wry joke, for the "master of his house" is a man who is seduced by his children's governess, a saucy flirt who soon fritters away the man's life savings and forces him to return, hat in hand, to his wife and family.

The Master Passion (Thomas A. Edison, Inc., 1917)

d: Richard Ridgely. 5 reels.

Mabel Trunnelle, Robert Conness, Helen Strickland, Richard Tucker, William Wadsworth, Ann Leonard, Raymond McKee, Olive Wright, Bigelow Cooper, Grace Williams.

In Paris, an opera singer attains fame and renown. Secretly, though, she's a woman who has deserted her husband and daughter.

A Master Stroke (Vitagraph, 1920)

d: Chester Bennett. 5 reels.

Earle Williams, Vola Vale, Lee Hill, H.A. Barrows, John Elliot, Rhea Haines, Frank Crayne, Paul Wiegle, Ethel Shannon.

About to commit suicide because he has squandered all his money, a young man is dissuaded long enough to help his fiancée's father out of his own financial troubles by using a few tricks he learned in the stock market.

Masters of Men (Vitagraph, 1923)

d: David Smith. 7 reels.

Earle Williams, Alice Calhoun, Cullen Landis, Wanda Hawley, Dick Sutherland, Charles Mason, Jack Curtis, Martin Turner.

During the Spanish-American War, a U.S. sailor and his lieutenant are shanghaied by a rebel sea captain. They fight valiantly and escape, and are rejoined with their crew in time to sink a Spanish warship.

The Match Breaker (Metro, 1921)

d: Dallas M. Fitzgerald. 5 reels.

Viola Dana, Jack Perrin, Edward Jobson, Julia Calhoun, Wedgewood Nowell, Kate Toncray, Lenore Lynard, Fred Kelsey, Arthur Millett.

A young woman hires herself out as a "match breaker"— meaning that she'll break up romantic misalliances before they reach the critical stage.

The Mate of the Sally Ann (American Film Co./Mutual, 1917)

d: Henry King. 5 reels.

Mary Miles Minter, Alan Forrest, George Periolat, Jack Connolly, Adele Farrington.

Resentful of high society, a salty sea captain lives on his ship with his granddaughter Sally. One day, Sally wanders onto shore and falls in love with a young man who works for a judge, the dean of a great manor. It turns out that the judge is Sally's long-lost father, and soon there's a reconciliation of all parties involved.

Maternity (World Film Corp., 1917)

d: John B. O'Brien. 5 reels.

Alice Brady, Marie Chambers, John Bowers, David Powell, Herbert Barrington, Florence Crane, Stanhope Wheatcroft, Charles Duncan, Louis Grisel, Julia Stuart, Madge Evans, John Dugley.

Ellen and John get married, but because she is fearful of childbirth, she refuses to bear him children. She'll get over it.

The Matinee Idol (Columbia, 1928)

d: Frank Capra. 6 reels.

Bessie Love, Johnny Walker, Lionel Belmore, Ernest Hilliard, Sidney D'Albrook.

A rural theater group is given a chance to perform before a New York audience. But their earnest dramatic efforts are so corny, the performance is greeted with derisive howls by the big city sophisticates. Disillusioned, the small troupe returns home... closely followed by a genuine Broadway star, who has fallen in love with the company's lead actress.

Matinee Ladies (Warner Bros., 1927)

d: Byron Haskins. 7 reels.

May McAvoy, Malcolm McGregor, Hedda Hopper, Margaret Seddon, Richard Tucker, Jean Lefferty, Cissy Fitzgerald, William Demarest.

A group of bored housewives decide to party with paid escorts at an afternoon club.

The Mating (New York Motion Picture Corp./Mutual, 1915)

d: Raymond B. West. 5 reels.

Bessie Barriscale, Lewis J. Cody, Enid Markey, Walter Whitman, Margaret Thompson, Ida Lewis.

When a lovelorn college girl "invents" a beau by writing herself a love letter, who do you think shows up? That's right, the beau... and they fall in love.

The Mating (Vitagraph, 1918)

d: Frederic Thomson. 5 reels.

Gladys Leslie, Herbert Rawlinson, Forest Robertson, John Thomson, Aida Horton, Stephen Carr, Frances Miller Grant.

In a small town, an eccentric perfects his latest invention while his family almost starves. Not to worry, though — the boy next door will market the man's invention, bring him fame and fortune, and marry the inventor's daughter.

The Mating Call (Caddo Co./Paramount, 1928)

d: James Cruze. 7 reels.

Thomas Meighan, Evelyn Brent, Renee Adoree, Alan Roscoe, Gardner James, Helen Foster, Luke Cosgrave, Cyril Chadwick, Will R. Walling.

Hatton, a war veteran, returns home and finds that his wife has had their marriage annulled and taken up with another man. Disappointed but not despairing, Hatton persuades Catherine, a Russian immigrant, to marry him in return for a permanent home in America. In time, their union blossoms into true love.

The Mating of Marcella (Thomas H. Ince/Paramount, 1918)

d: R. William Neill. 5 reels.

Dorothy Dalton, Thurston Hall, Juanita Hansen, William Conklin, Donald MacDonald, Milton Ross, Spottiswoode Aitken, Buster Irving.

Marcella's a poor girl who gets hired by a bored socialite to impersonate her in Reno while the socialite dallies with a lover. When the socialite's cuckold husband finally visits Reno and discovers the truth, he falls in love with Marcella and she with him.

The Matrimaniac (Triangle, 1916)

d: Paul Powell. 5 reels.

Douglas Fairbanks, Constance Talmadge, Wilbur Higby, Clyde Hopkins, Fred Warren, Winfred Westover.

Comedic farce which has Jimmie (played by Fairbanks) trying to elope with his sweetie and running into all sorts of complications. They finally end up getting married over the telephone!

The Matrimonial Web   (Vitagraph, 1921)
d: Edward José.   5 reels.
Alice Calhoun, Joseph Striker, William Riley Hatch, Armand Cortez, Charles Mackay, Elsie Fuller, Ernest Hilliard, Marion Barney, Edith Stockton, G.C. Frye, Richard Lee.
The daughter of a government agent helps her dad track down an opium smuggler who was trying to force another young woman into a compromising situation.

Matrimony   (New York Motion Picture Corp./Triangle, 1915)
d: Scott Sidney.   5 reels.
Julia Dean, Howard Hickman, Thelma Salter, Louise Glaum, Elizabeth Burbridge, Lou Salter.
Feeling neglected by her husband, a young woman decides to act the vamp and flirt with other men in an effort to attract her husband's attention.

May Blossom   (Famous Players/Paramount, 1915)
d: Allan Dwan.   4 reels.
Gertrude Robinson, Donald Crisp, Marshall Neilan, Russell Bassett, Gertrude Norman.
Civil War drama about a Southern girl in love with two different beaux.

Mayblossom   (Astra Film Corp./Pathé, 1917)
d: Edward José.   5 reels.
Pearl White, Hal Ford, Fuller Mellish.
Anabel Lee finds herself deserted when her husband takes up with an opera singer.

The Mayor of Filbert   (Triangle, 1919)
d: William Christy Cabanne.   7 reels.
Jack Richardson, Belle Bennett, J. Barney Sherry, Bennie Alexander, George Pearce, Wilbur Higby, William Dyer, Joseph Singleton, Millicent Fisher, Louise Lester, Grace Parker.
His honor the mayor is a tad corrupt, so when he's knocked unconscious and develops amnesia, some citizens prevail upon the mayor's straight-arrow twin brother to replace him.

Maytime   (B.P. Schulberg Productions/Preferred Pictures, 1923)
d: Louis Gasnier.   8 reels.
Ethel Shannon, Harrison Ford, William Norris, Clara Bow, Wallace MacDonald, Josef Swickard, Martha Mattox, Betty Francisco, Robert McKim.
Romantic tale about Richard and Ottilie, who fall in love with each other and marry, three generations after their grandparents had loved each other but were prevented from marrying.

McFadden's Flats   (Asher-Small-Rogers/First National, 1927)
d: Richard Wallace.   8 reels.
Charlie Murray, Chester Conklin, Edna Murphy, Larry Kent, Aggie Herring, DeWitt Jennings, Cissy Fitzgerald, Dorothy Dwan, Freeman Wood, Dot Farley, Leo White.
McFadden, an Irishman, and McTavish, a Scotsman, are frequently and hilariously at odds; but their children are in love with each other.

McGuire of the Mounted   (Universal, 1923)
d: Richard Stanton.   5 reels.
William Desmond, Louise Lorraine, Willard Louis, Vera James, J.P. Lockney, William A. Lowery, Peggy Browne, Frank Johnson, Jack Walters.
In the Canadian Northwest, a mountie named McGuire trails opium smugglers.

McVeagh of the South Seas   (Progressive Motion Picture Co., 1914)
d: Harry Carey, Cyril Bruce.   5 reels.
Harry Carey, Fern Foster, Herbert Russell, Kathleen Butler, Jack Terry.
In the South Seas, a former ship's captain is reduced to dissipation by his unrequited love for a woman who chooses another man.

Me and Captain Kidd   (World Film Corp., 1919)
d: Oscar Apfel.   5 reels.
Evelyn Greeley, Raymond McKee, W.T. Carleton, Arthur Donaldson, Charles Mackay, Raymond Van Sickle, Robert Broderick, Betty Hutchinson, Pauline Dempsey, William Brooks.
Contrived romantic plot about a girl who spins tales about Captain Kidd, and the young man who falls in love with her.

Me, Gangster   (Fox, 1928)
d: Raoul Walsh.   7 reels.
June Collyer, Don Terry, Anders Randolf, Stella Adams, Burr McIntosh, Walter James, Gustav von Seyffertitz, Al Hill, Herbert Ashton, Bob Perry, Nigel DeBrulier, Carol Lombard.
Jimmy, a product of the slums, steals $50,000 but is quickly arrested and sentenced to two years in jail. During that time, a social worker named Mary helps Jimmy to see the light and forget his rude upbringing. Upon his release, he attempts to give the $50,000 back to its rightful owners, but has to battle members of his old gang to accomplish the feat. Having won back his self-respect, Jimmy settles down with Mary in a new life.

The Meanest Man in the World   (Principal Pictures/Associated First National, 1923)
d: Edward F. Cline.   6 reels.
Bert Lytell, Blanche Sweet, Bryan Washburn, Maryon Aye, Lincoln Stedman, Helen Lynch, Ward Crane, Frances Raymond, Carl Stockdale, Tom Murray, Forrest Robinson.
When Clarke, an attorney, decides to clamp down on his debtors and collect all that is owed him, he finds that one of them, "J. Hudson," is actually Jane Hudson, a lovely young woman. Instead of forcing her to pay off her debt, he helps her to finance her business, and they wind up falling in love.

The Measure of a Man   (Universal, 1916)
d: Jack Conway.   5 reels.
J. Warren Kerrigan, Louise Lovely, Katherine Campbell, Ivor MacFadden, Marion Emmons, Harry Carter, Marc Robbins.
An ex-semanarian converts the rowdy, hard-drinking workers in a lumber camp.

The Measure of a Man   (Universal, 1924)
d: Arthur Rosson.   5 reels.
William Desmond, Albert J. Smith, Francis Ford, Marin Sais, William J. Dyer, Bobby Gordon, Harry Tenbrook, Zala Davis, William Turner, Mary McAllister.
Remake of the 1916 Universal film of the same name.

The Meddler   (Universal, 1925)
d: Arthur Rosson.   5 reels.
William Desmond, Dolores Rousse, Claire Anderson, Albert J. Smith, Jack Daugherty, C.L. Sherwood, Kate Lester, Georgie Grandee, Donald Hatswell.

Gilmore, a stuffy New York businessman, decides to change

318

his lifestyle by going west and becoming a highway thief.
But it's all for sport, as Gilmore returns all the loot he steals.
Eventually, he robs a girl he finds irresistible, and they fall in
love.

Meddling Women (Chadwick Pictures, 1924)
w, d: Ivan Abramson. 7 reels.
Lionel Barrymore, Sigrid Holmquist, Ida Darling, Dagmar
Godowsky, Hugh Thompson, Alice Hegeman, Antonio
D'Algy, William Bechtel.
Edwin marries Grace, but his disapproving mother does all
in her power to make their married life miserable.

The Mediator (Fox, 1916)
d: Otis Turner. 5 reels.
George Walsh, Juanita Hansen, James Marcus, Lee Willard,
Pearl Elmore, Sedley Brown.
Out West, a newcomer to town proves his toughness in
action and his skills of persuasion in mediations between
opposing gangs.

The Medicine Man (Triangle, 1917)
d: Cliff Smith. 5 reels.
Roy Stewart, Ann Kronan, Percy Challenger, Aaron
Edwards, Carl Ulman, Wilbur Higbee.
In the small town of El Dorado, performers in a traveling
medicine show are stunned to learn that their dancing girl is
the rightful owner of a local mine.

Meet the Prince (Metropolitan Pictures Corp. of California,
1926)
d: Joseph Henabery. 6 reels.
Joseph Schildkraut, Marguerite De La Motte, Vera
Steadman, Julia Faye, David Butler, Helen Dunbar, Bryant
Washburn, Bessie Love.
Prince Nicholas, an ex-patriot from Russia after the
revolution, finds love with a New York girl named
Annabelle.

Melissa of the Hills (American Film Co./Mutual, 1917)
d: James Kirkwood. 5 reels.
Mary Miles Minter, Spottiswoode Aitken, Allan Forrest,
George Periolat, Perry Banks, Harvey Clark, Frank
Thompson, John Gough, Gertrude LeBrandt, Emma Kluge,
Ann Schaefer.
Tennessee hill folk feud among themselves, but little Melissa
is there to offer pleas for harmony.

Melting Millions (Fox, 1917)
d: Otis Turner. 5 reels.
Sidney Dean, Cecil Holland, Velma Whitman, George
Walsh, Frank Alexander, Anna Luther, Charles Gerrard.
Jack is heir to his uncle's millions, but the will stipulates that
Jack must first prove that he's a success. Not an easy task,
since Jack is a good-natured bumbler. But after he goes out
West and rescues a pretty lady from an attempted
kidnapping, the stipulation is satisfied and Jack gets both his
inheritance and the girl.

Memory Lane (John M. Stahl Productions/First National,
1926)
d: John M. Stahl. 8 reels.
Eleanor Boardman, Conrad Nagel, William Haines, John
Seppling, Eugenie Ford, Frankie Darrow, Dot Farley, Joan
Standing, Kate Price, Florence Midgley, Dale Fuller, Billie
Bennett.
Mary's engaged to Jimmy, but just before their scheduled
wedding she's abducted by a former sweetheart.

Men (Famous Players-Lasky/Paramount, 1924)
d: Dimitri Buchowetzki. 7 reels.
Pola Negri, Robert Frazer, Robert Edeson, Joseph Swickard,
Monti Collins, Gino Corrado, Edgar Norton.
Cleo, a Parisienne stage star, uses men as tools to gain
luxury and privilege.

Men and Women (Famous Players-Lasky/Paramount,
1925)
d: William DeMille. 6 reels.
Richard Dix, Claire Adams, Neil Hamilton, Henry
Stephenson, Robert Edeson, Flora Finch.
The eternal triangle nearly dooms a bank cashier who covets
his friend's wife.

Men of Daring (Universal, 1927)
d: Albert s. Rogell. 7 reels.
Jack Hoxie, Francis Ford, Ena Gregory, Marin Sais, James
Kelly, Ernie Adams, Robert Milash, Bert Lindley, Bert
Apling, William Malan, John Hall, Joseph Bennett.
Out West, three pals agree to take over the wagon train of a
religious sect after the sect's leader is killed in an Indian
attack.

Men of Steel (First National, 1926)
d: George Archainbaud. 10 reels.
Doris Kenyon, Milton Sills, May Allison, Victor McLaglen,
Frank Currier, George Fawcett, John Kolb, Harry Lee, Henry
West, Taylor Graves.
A steel mill worker fights violent strikers and saves the life
of the mill owner's daughter.

Men of the Desert (Essanay, 1917)
d: W.S. Van Dyke. 5 reels.
Jack Gardner, Ruth King, Carl Stockdale.
When a wandering cowpoke enters a Western town beset
with violent feuding, he accepts the chance to become a
lawman and end the strife.

Men of the Night (Sterling Pictures, 1926)
d: Albert Rogell. 6 reels.
Herbert Rawlinson, Gareth Hughes, Wanda Hawley,l Lucy
Beaumont, Jay Hunt, Mathilda Brundage.
Mrs. Abbott, an elderly news vendor, is in league with two
art thieves, though she doesn't know it. The men are simply
using her as their "cover."

The Men of Zanzibar (Fox, 1922)
d: Rowland V. Lee. 7 reels.
William Russell, Ruth Renick, Claude Peyton, Harvey
Clarke, Arthur Morrison, Michael Dark, Lila Leslie.
American detectives trail a fugitive to the African coast.

The Men She Married (World Film Corp., 1916)
d: Travers Vale. 5 reels.
Gail Kane, Arthur Ashley, Montagu Love, Louise M. Bates,
Muriel Ostriche.
Wealthy Beatrice loves not wisely but too well... and too
often. She's a bigamist.

Men, Women and Money (Famous Players-
Lasky/Paramount, 1919)
d: George Melford. 5 reels.
Ethel Clayton, James Neill, Jane Wolfe, Lew Cody, Sylvia
Ashton, Irving Cummings, Winifred Greenwood, Edna Mae
Cooper, Leslie Stewart Jr., Mayme Kelso, Lillian Leighton.
Though she's down on her luck, a young woman refuses a
millionaire's cynical offer of support in return for sexual
favors.

The Menace (Vitagraph, 1918)
d: John Stuart Robertson. 5 reels.
Corinne Griffith, Evart Overton, Herbert Prior, Ned Finley, Leila Blow, Frank A. Ford.
What matters most in determining character: Environment or heredity? The son of a convicted thief is put to the test.

The Merry Cavalier (Richard Talmadge Productions/FBO of America, 1926)
d: Noel Mason. 5 reels.
Richard Talmadge, Charlotte Stevens, William H. Tooker, Joseph Harrington, Jack Richardson.
In the timber country, a lumberman rescues a girl and her father from the schemes of a land-grabbing cheat.

Merely Mary Ann (Fox, 1916)
d: John G. Adolfi. 5 reels.
Vivian Martin, Edward N. Hoyt, Harry Hilliard, Laura Lyman, Isabel O'Madigan, Sidney Bracy, Niles Welch.
In London, young orphan Mary Ann works as a drudge until word comes that she is heiress to a fortune.

Merely Mary Ann (Fox, 1920)
d: Edward J. LeSaint. 5 reels.
Shirley Mason, Casson Ferguson, Harry Spingler, Georgia Woodthorpe, Babe London, H.A. Morgan, Jean Hersholt, Paul Weigel.
Remake of Fox's own 1916 film, *Merely Mary Ann*, about a poor young woman who is startled to learn she is an heiress.

Merely Players (World Film Corp., 1918)
d: Oscar Apfel. 5 reels.
Kitty Gordon, Irving Cummings, George MacQuarrie, John Hines, Pinna Nesbit, Muriel Ostriche, Florence Coventry, Dore Davidson.
A wealthy widow who loves the theater builds a private one—stage and all—in her own home.

The Merry-Go-Round (Fox, 1919)
d: Edmund Lawrence. 5 reels.
Peggy Hyland, Jack Mulhall, Edward Jobson, Edwin B. Tilton, Vera Lewis, Robert Walker, Willard Louis, Lule Warrenton, Joe Martin.
A down-on-his-luck businessman buys a broken-down carnival show, and makes it a success.

The Merry-Go-Round (Universal, 1923)
d: Rupert Julian. (Work commenced by Erich von Stroheim.) 10 reels.
Norman Kerry, Mary Philbin, Cesare Gravina, Dorothy Wallace, Spottiswoode Aitken, George Hackathorne, Edith Yorke. George Siegmann, Dale Fuller, Lillian Sylvester, Ed Edmundsen, Maude George.
Sumptuous romantic drama set in Vienna before, during, and just after World War I. An Austrian count falls for a puppeteer's daughter, but cannot express his love because he is irreversibly engaged to a woman of high standing.

The Merry Widow (MGM, 1925)
d: Erich von Stroheim. 10 reels.
Mae Murray, John Gilbert, Roy D'Arcy, Tully Marshall, Edward Connelly, Josephine Crowell, George Fawcett, Albert Conti, Sidney Bracey, Don Ryan, Hughie Mack Ida Moore, Lucille von Lent, Dale Fuller, Charles Magelis, Harvey Karels, Edna Tichenor, Zala Zorana.
A former showgirl, once rejected by a prince, returns to society as a wealthy young widow. When she meets the prince again, she finds the old fire still burning.

Merry Wives of Gotham —see: Lights of Old Broadway (1925)

Merton of the Movies (Famous Players-Lasky/Paramount, 1924)
d: James Cruze. 8 reels.
Viola Dana, Glenn Hunter, Charles Sellon, DeWitt Jennings, Elliott Roth, Charles Ogle, Ethel Wales, Sadie Gordon, Gale Henry, Luke Cosgrave, Frank Jonasson, Eleanor Lawson.
Merton, a country boy, comes to Hollywood with a vague idea about getting into the movies. After several misadventures, he finds a part in a comedy satire which he mistakes for a serious drama—and he's legitimately surprised to learn that he's a hit.

A Message From Mars (Metro, 1921)
d: Maxwell Karger. 6 reels.
Bert Lytell, Raye Dean, Maude Milton, Alphonz Ethier, Gordon Ash, Leonard Mudie, Mary Louise Beaton, Frank Currier, George Spink.
Parker, a brilliant but selfish young inventor, works on a device for communicating with distant planets. In his sleep, he pictures himself being visited by a messenger from Mars, who then shows him true poverty and suffering among people in his (Parker's) own home town. Upon awaking, the inventor vows to be selfish no more.

The Message of the Mouse (Vitagraph, 1917)
d: J. Stuart Blackton. 5 reels.
Anita Stewart, Julia Swayne Gordon, Rudolph Cameron, L. Rogers Lytton, Franklin Hanna, Robert Gaillard, Bernard Seigel.
In preparation for the War, foreign agents try to inveigle an American businessman into investing in their international steamship lines.

A Message to Garcia (Thomas A. Edison, Inc., 1916)
d: Richard Ridgely. 5 reels.
Mabel Trunnelle, Robert Conness, Herbert Prior, Robert Kegerreis, Bradley Sutton, Charles Sutton, Paul Everton, Helen Strickland, Ray Fairchild, Bigelow Cooper.
During the War of 1898, an American lieutenant is dispatched to Cuba to offer U.S. support to the revolutionaries.

Mexicali Rose (Columbia, 1929)
d: Erle C. Kenton. 7 reels. (Music, sound effects, part talkie.)
Barbara Stanwyck, Sam Hardy, William Janney, Arthur Rankin, Louis Natheaux, Harry Vejar, Louis King, Julia Beharano.
A saucy flirt chases men, then discards them. Finally, one of her rejects has her thrown out of town. To get even with him, she marries his younger brother, then continues giving the eye to every man she meets.

Miami (Tilford Cinema Corp./W.W. Hodkinson, 1924)
d: Alan Crosland. 7 reels.
Betty Compson, Lawford Davidson, Hedda Hopper, J. Barney Sherry, Lucy Fox, Benjamin F. Finney Jr.
In Miami, a popular socialite is pursued by two men, only one of them worthy of her.

Mice and Men (Famous Players/Paramount, 1916)
d: J. Searle Dawley. 5 reels.
Marguerite Clark, Marshall Neilan, Charles Waldron, Clarence Handyside, Maggie Halloway Fisher, Helen Dahl, Robert Conville, William McKey, Ada Deaves, Francesca Warde.

In the antebellum South, a young man tries to raise an orphan girl to be the ideal wife.

Michael O'Halloran (Gene Stratton Porter Productions/W.W. Hodkinson, 1923)
d: James Leo Meehan. 7 reels.
Virginia True Boardman, Ethelyn Irving, Irene Rich, Charles Clary, Claire McDowell, Charles Hill Mailes, Josie Sedgwick, William Boyd.
Though an orphan himself, young news vendor Michael O'Halloran takes in a little crippled girl after her grandmother's death leaves her alone in the world.

The Michigan Kid (Universal, 1928)
d: Irvin Willat. 6 reels.
Renee Adoree, Conrad Nagel, Fred Esmelton, Virginia Grey, Conrad Nagel, Maurice Murphy, Adolph Milar, Lloyd Whitlock, Donald House.
Jimmy, a youngster from Michigan, goes to Alaska to strike it rich so that he can marry his childhood sweetheart.

Mickey (Mabel Normand Feature Film Co., 1918)
d: F. Richard Jones, James Young. 7 reels.
Mabel Normand, Wheeler Oakman, Lew Cody, George Nichols, Minta Durfee, Laura LaVarnie, Tom Kennedy, Minnie HaHa.
A young woman is forced to be a servant in her rich aunt's house.

The Microbe (Metro, 1919)
d: Henry Otto. 5 reels.
Viola Dana, Kenneth Harlan, Arthur Maude, Bonnie Hill, Ned Norworth, Lucy Donahue.
Charming tale about a street urchin knicknamed "The Microbe" who dresses like a boy, fights like a boy, but is nonetheless one hundred per cent female.

The Microscope Mystery (Fine Arts Film Co./Triangle, 1916)
d: Paul Powell. 5 reels.
Wilfred Lucas, F.A. Turner, Constance Talmadge, Pomeroy Cannon, Winnifred Westover, Monte Blue, Fred Warren, James O'Shea, Jack Sealock, Kate Bruce.
When a rich hypochondriac can't get his doctor to find anything wrong with him, he goes to a quack who gleefully diagnoses multiple diseases.

Mid-Channel (Garson Studios, 1920)
d: Harry Garson. 6 reels.
Clara Kimball Young, J. Frank Glendon, Edward M. Kimball, Bertram Grassby, Eileen Robinson, Helen Sullivan, Katherine Griffith, Jack Livingston.
A married couple tire of each other's company and seek diversion elsewhere.

The Midlanders (Andrew J. Callaghan Productions, Inc., 1920)
d: Ida May Park, Joseph DeGrasse. 6 reels.
Bessie Love, Truman Van Dyke, Sydney Deane, Frances Raymond, Curt Rehfeld, C. Norman Hammond, Lloyd Bacon, Jack Donovan.
An orphan girl is adopted by a Mississippi boat captain, and grows up to be a beauty contest winner.

Midnight (Realart Pictures/Paramount, 1922)
d: Maurice Campbell. 5 reels.
Constance Binney, William Courtleigh, Sidney Bracey, Arthur S. Hull, Herbert Fortier, Helen Lynch, Edward Martindel, Jack Mulhall.

Edna loves Jack, and they plan to marry at midnight. But before they can, Edna's first husband, whom she thought dead, shows up alive. Now what?

A Midnight Adventure (Duke Worne Productions/Rayart Pictures, 1928)
d: Duke Worne. 6 reels.
Cullen Landis, Edna Murphy, Ernest Hilliard, Jack Richardson, Allan Sears, Virginia Kirkley, Maude Truax, Ben Hall, Betty Caldwell, Tom O'Grady, Fred Kelsey, Edward Cecil, Amber Norman.
When one of the guests is murdered during a large gathering at a country estate, the evidence points to the women who knew him intimately and were all being blackmailed by him.

The Midnight Alarm (Vitagraph, 1923)
d: David Smith. 7 reels.
Alice Calhoun, Percy Marmont, Cullen Landis, Joseph Kilgour, Maxine Elliott Hicks, George Pearce, Kitty Bradbury, J. Gunnis Davis, Jean Carpenter, May Foster, Fred Behrle.
Having killed his former business partner and caused the death of the man's widow, a villain sets his sights on doing away with their daughter.

A Midnight Bell (Charles Ray Productions/Associated First National, 1921)
d: Charles Ray. 6 reels.
Charles Ray, Donald MacDonald, Van Dyke Brooke, Doris Pawn, Clyde McCoy, Jess Herring, S.J. Bingham, Bert Offord.
Martin, a traveling salesman, stops in a country village and takes a bet he cannot spend all night in a certain house that's said to be haunted. It's haunted all right, but by crooks, not by supernatural beings.

The Midnight Bride (Vitagraph, 1920)
d: William J. Humphrey. 5 reels.
Gladys Leslie, James Morrison, Gladden James, Nellie Spaulding, Roy Applegate, Virginia Valli, Denton Vane.
An innocent girl meets a wealthy playboy in Central Park.

The Midnight Express (Columbia, 1924)
d: George W. Hill. 6 reels.
William Haines, Elaine Hammerstein, George Nichols.
A dishonored young man is given a second chance at life when he prevents a potentially disastrous railroad collision.

The Midnight Flyer (R-C Pictures/FBO of America, 1925)
d: Tom Forman. 7 reels.
Cullen Landis, Dorothy Devore, Buddy Post, Charles Mailes, Frankie Darro, Claire McDowell, Barbara Tennant, Elmo Billings, Alphonz Ethier.
In the West Virginia hills, an ages-old feud imperils the success of the new railroad.

The Midnight Girl (Chadwick Pictures, 1925)
d: Wilfred Noy. 7 reels.
Lila Lee, Gareth Hughes, Dolores Cassinelli, Bela Lugosi, Charlotte Walker, Ruby Blaine, John D. Walsh, William Harvey, Sidney Paxton, Signor N. Salerno.
Anna, a Russian emigree with a beautiful singing voice, gets a job dancing in a floor show as "The Midnight Girl."

The Midnight Guest (Universal, 1923)
d: George Archainbaud. 5 reels.
Grace Darmond, Mahlon Hamilton, Clyde Fillmore, Pat Harmon, Mathilde Brundage.
Caught in the act of burglarizing a wealthy man's home,

young Gabrielle finds him more than forgiving: He offers her a home and his protection.

The Midnight Kiss (Fox, 1926)
d: Irving Cummings. 5 reels.
Richard Walling, Janet Gaynor, George Irving, Doris Lloyd, Gene Cameron, Arthur Houseman, Tempe Pigott, Gladys McConnell, Herbert Prior, Bodil Rosing.
Thomas, an enterprising youngster, raises money by threatening to expose an inappropriate love affair.

Midnight Life (Gotham Productions/Lumas Film Corp., 1928)
d: Scott R. Dunlap. 5 reels.
Francis X. Bushman, Gertrude Olmstead, Eddie Buzzell, Monte Carter, Cosmo Kyrie Bellew, Carlton King.
Logan, a New York police detective, trails the murderer of Logan's close friend.

Midnight Limited (Paul Gerson Pictures/Rayart, 1926)
d: Oscar Apfel. 6 reels.
Gaston Glass, Wanda Hawley, Sam Allen, William Humphrey, Mathilda Brundage, Richard Holt, L.J. O'Connor, Eric Mayne, Fred Holmes, Hayford Hobbs.
A petty crook with a soft heart goes to the aid of a man he was attempting to rob, when the old fellow suffers a stroke.

Midnight Lovers (John McCormick Productions/First National, 1926)
d: John Francis Dillon. 7 reels.
Lewis Stone, Anna Q. Nilsson, John Roche, Chester Conklin, Dale Fuller, Purnell Pratt, Harvey Clark.
Ridgewell, a World War I flying ace, takes his bride on an airborne honeymoon.

Midnight Madness (Universal, 1918)
d: Rupert Julian. 5 reels.
Ruth Clifford, Kenneth Harlan, Harry M. Holden, Harry Van Meter, Claire DuBrey, Louis Willoughby.
International intrigue ensues when a jewel thief tails a lovely but felonious young woman to Paris.

Midnight Madness (DeMille Pictures/Pathé, 1928)
d: F. Harmon Weight. 6 reels.
Jacqueline Logan, Clive Brook, Walter McGrail, James Bradbury, Oscar Smith, Vadim Uraneff, Louis Natheaux, Clarence Burton, Virginia Sale, Frank Hagney, Emmett King.
A gold digger marries for wealth, then learns to her dismay that her explorer husband has planned a honeymoon for them in the jungles of Africa.

The Midnight Man (Universal, 1917)
d: Elmer Clifton. 5 reels.
Jack Mulhall, Ann Kronan, Al McQuarrie, Warda Lamont, Hal Wilson, Wilbur Higby, J. Montgomery Carlyle.
Bob's a young inventor in love, and to win his lady fair, he must open a "burglar proof" safe containing precious gems.

The Midnight Message (Goodwill Pictures, 1926)
d: Paul Hurst. 5 reels.
Wanda Hawley, Mary Carr, John Fox Jr., Stuart Holmes, Creighton Hale, Mathilda Brundage, Otis Harlan, Earl Metcalf, Karl Silvera, Wilson Benge.
It's Western Union calling... and this time, the messenger interrupts a robbery in progress.

Midnight Molly (Gothic Pictures/FBO of America, 1925)
d: Lloyd Ingraham. 6 reels.
Evelyn Brent, John Dillon, Bruce Gordon, Leon Bary, John Gough.

Molly, a sneak thief, masquerades as the wife of a prominent politician.

The Midnight Patrol (Thomas H. Ince/Select, 1918)
d: Irvin V. Willat. 5 reels.
Thurston Hall, Rosemary Theby, Kino, Charles French, Marjorie Bennett, Harold Holland, William Musgrave, Yamamoto, Harold Johnstone.
Drama about drug smugglers in Chinatown.

A Midnight Romance (Anita Stewart Productions/First National, 1919)
d: Lois Weber. 6 reels.
Anita Stewart, Jack Holt, Edward Tilton, Elinor Hancock, Helen Yoder, Juanita Hansen, Montague Dumont.
On a seaside vacation, wealthy Roger Sloan falls in love with a girl who turns out to be a Russian princess.

Midnight Rose (Universal, 1928)
d: James Young. 6 reels.
Lya De Putti, Kenneth Harlan, Henry Kolker, Lorimer Johnston, George Larkin, Gunboat Smith, Wendell Phillips Franklin, Frank Brownlee.
Formula weeper about Midnight Rose, a cabaret dancer who, against her better judgment, falls in love with a mobster.

The Midnight Sun (Universal, 1926)
d: Dimitri Buchowetski. 9 reels.
Laura LaPlante, Pat O'Malley, Raymond Keane, George Siegmann, Arthur Hoyt, Earl Metcalf, Mikhael Vavitch, Nicholas Soussanin, Cesare Gravina,l Nina Romano.
Olga, an American girl, rises to the rank of prima ballerina in the Imperial Russian Ballet.

The Midnight Trail (American Film Co./Mutual, 1918)
d: Edward Sloman. 5 reels.
William Russell, Francelia Billington, Sydney Deane, Jermoe Sheler, Carl Stockdale, Edward Jobson, Harvey Clark, Clarence Burton, Helen Howard, Alfred Ferguson.
An amateur detective gets the chance to prove his skill when he's involved in the case of a beautiful sleepwalker who carries her jewels with her on her midnight walks.

The Midshipman (MGM, 1925)
d: Christy Cabanne. 8 reels.
Ramon Novarro, Harriet Hammond, Wesley Barry, Crauford Kent, Margaret Seddon, Pauline Key, Maurice Ryan, Harold Goodwin, William Boyd.
At the Naval Academy, a midshipman falls for the sister of a plebe. She's engaged, however, and her fiancé is not amused by the middie's attentions to his girl.

Midstream (Tiffany-Stahl Productions, 1929)
d: James Flood. 8 reels. (Music, part talkie.)
Ricardo Cortez, Claire Windsor, Montagu Love, Larry Kent, Helen Jerome Eddy, Leslie Brigham, Louis Alvarez, Genevieve Schrader, Florence Foyer.
An aging stockbroker tries to restore his former youthful appearance through surgery.

Midsummer Madness (Famous Players-Lasky/Paramount, 1921)
d: William C. DeMille. 6 reels.
Jack Holt, Conrad Nagel, Lois Wilson, Lila Lee, Betty Francisco, Claire McDowell, Charlotte Jackson, Ethel Wales, Charles Ogle, Lillian Leighton, George Kuwa.
Left alone on a midsummer weekend when his wife visits relatives, a young man falls prey to the romantic advances of

his friend's wife.

Might and the Man   (Fine Arts film Co./Triangle, 1917)
d: Edward Dillon.   5 reels.
Elmo Lincoln, Carmel Myers, Wilbur Higby, Lillian Langdon, Clyde Hopkins, Carl Stockdale, Luray Huntley, Mazie Radford.
Lincoln, the screen's first "Tarzan," has a field day here, performing several athletic stunts in his role as a physical trainer involved with dispelling enemy agents.

Mighty Lak'a Rose   (Edwin Carewe
Productions/Associated First National, 1923)
d: Edwin Carewe.   8 reels.
James Rennie, Sam Hardy, Anders Randolf, Harry Short, Dorothy Mackaill, Helene Montrose, Paul Panzer, Dora Mills Adams.
Rose, a blind violinist, so enchants the local gang that they all decide to go straight. But first, they plan to pull one last heist, to gain enough money to buy Rose a sight-restoring operation.

Mignon   (California Motion Picture Co./World Film Corp., 1915)
d: William Nigh.   5 reels.
Beatriz Michelena, Clara Beyers, William Pike, House Peters, Belle Bennett, Ernest Joy, Andrew Robson, Emil Krushe, Harold B. Meade, Frank Hollins.
After his baby daughter, Mignon, is stolen from him by a band of gypsies, a nobleman drifts into amnesia and becomes a wanderer. But they'll be reunited years later, when Mignon is sixteen.

Mike   (MGM, 1926)
w, d: Marshall Neilan.   7 reels.
Sally O'Neil, Charles Murray, William Haines, Ned Sparks, Ford Sterling, Frankie Darro, Junior Coghlan.
A railroad girl lives in a converted freight car and loves a telegraphist.

Milady of the Beanstalk   (Diando Film Corp./Pathé, 1918)
d: William Bertram.   5 reels.
Baby Marie Osborne, Ellen Cassity, Jack Connolly.
Little Marie, who is enchanted by the story of Jack and the Beanstalk, decides to climb her make-believe "beanstalk" — the fire escape outside her tenement building.

Mile-a-Minute Kendall   (Famous Players-
Lasky/Paramount, 1918)
d: William D. Taylor.   5 reels.
Jack Pickford, Louise Huff, Charles Arling, Jane Wolff, Casson Ferguson, Lottie Pickford, Jack McDonald, W.E. Lawrence, John Burton.
Jack Kendall's a high-living playboy and skirt chaser... but his real love is tinkering with motor engines.

The Mile-a-Minute Man   (Camera Pictures/Lumas Film
Corp., 1926)
d: Jack Nelson.   5 reels.
William Fairbanks, Virginia Brown Faire, George Periolat, Jane Keckley, George Cheeseboro, Barney Furey, Paul Dennis, Hazel Howell.
"Old Ironsides" Rockett, a race car manufacturer, finds that his competition, the Greydon Corporation, has installed a jazzy new motor in their racing machine. Now it's up to Rockett's son to perfect his own new carburetor, to beat the Greydons in the big race.

Mile-a-Minute Romeo   (Fox, 1923)

d: Lambert Hillyer.   6 reels.
Tom Mix, Betty Jewel, J. Gordon Russell, James Mason, Duke Lee, James Quinn.
Out West, three cowpokes vie for the love of the same girl.

The Mill on the Floss   (Thanhouser/Mutual, 1915)
d: W. Eugene Moore.   5 reels.
Mignon Anderson, Harris Gordon, George Marlo, W. Eugene Moore, Fanny Hoyt, Arthur Bauer, Leo Wirth, Boyd Marshall.
Tom and his sister Maggie, heirs to a water mill on the Floss River, quarrel over her fascination with her cousin's fiancé.
First feature film version of the famous novel by Mary Ann Evans, who wrote under the pseudonym George Eliot.

A Million a Minute   (Quality Pictures/Metro, 1916)
d: John W. Noble.   5 reels.
Francis X. Bushman, Beverly Bayne, Robert Cummings, William Bailey, Helen Dunbar, John Davidson, Charles Prince, Carl Brickert, Mary Moore, Jerome Wilson.
A wealthy old bachelor bequeaths his fortune to a friend's son provided he marries the bachelor's ward by a certain date. But the bequest touches off a frenzy of impostures, because the prospective bride and groom have never met!

A Million Bid   (Warner Bros., 1927)
d: Michael Curtiz.   7 reels.
Betty Blythe, Warner Oland, Dolores Costello, Malcolm McGregor, William Demarest, Douglas Gerrard, Grace Gordon.
Remake of the 1914 Vitagraph melodrama *A Million Bid*.

The Million Dollar Collar   (Warner Bros., 1929)
d: D. Ross Lederman.   6 reels.
Rin-Tin-Tin, Evelyn Pierce, Matty Kemp, Tommy Dugan, Allan Cavin, Philo McCullough, Grover Liggon.
Thieves are looking for a valuable necklace, but it's hidden in Rinty's collar.

The Million Dollar Dollies   (Emerald Pictures/Metro, 1918)
w, d: Leonce Perret.   5 reels.
Yancsi Dolly, Roszika Dolly, Bradley Barker, Huntley Gordon, Paul Doucet, Dolores Cassinelli, Ernest Maupain, Marshall Phillip.
The Dolly sisters try to help a psychologist solve a puzzling case involving an affair of the heart.

The Million Dollar Handicap   (Metropolitan Pictures, 1925)
d: Scott Sidney.   6 reels.
Vera Reynolds, Edmund Burns, Ralph Lewis, Ward Crane, Tom Wilson, Clarence Burton, Danny Hoy, Rosa Gore, Walter Emerson, Lon Poff.
When her horsebreeder father falls critically ill, a young woman disguises herself as a boy and rides his thoroughbred to victory in the big race.

The Million Dollar Mystery   (Thanhouser Film Corp., 1918)
d: Howell Hansell.   6 reels.
Sidney Bracey, Marguerite Snow, Florence La Badie, James Cruze, Mitchell Lewis, Frank Farrington, Lila Chester, Irving Cummings.
Re-edited version of a 1914 serial about the efforts of an immigrant and his daughter to make a living in the United States while hiding from Russian agents.

Million Dollar Mystery   (Trem Carr Productions/Rayart, 1927)
d: Charles J. Hunt.   6 reels.

James Kirkwood, Lila Lee, Henry Sedley, Erin LaBissoniere, Elmer Dewey, Edward Gordon, John Elliott, Ralph Whiting. Norton, a former gangster, goes straight and becomes legitimately wealthy. Now his old gang is pestering him and his daughter, apparently looking for "their cut."

A Million For Love (Sterling Pictures, 1928)
d: Robert F. Hill. 6 reels.
Reed Howes, Josephine Dunn, Lee Shumway, Mary Carr, Lewis Sargent, Jack Rich, Frank Baker, Alfred Fisher.
The principal suspect in a mob killing refuses to tell the police his whereabouts on the night of the murder, because he's trying to protect the reputation of the girl he was with. The lady in question is the district attorney's own daughter, and she comes forward with the truth that sets her man free.

A Million for Mary (American Film Co./Mutual, 1916)
d: Rea Berger. 5 reels.
C. William Kolb, Max Dill, Dodo Newton, May Cloy, King Clark.
Two druggists, wards of a teenage girl, invent a pill that's said to be a cure-all.

A Million to Burn (Universal, 1923)
d: William Parke. 5 reels.
Herbert Rawlinson, Kalla Pasha, Beatrice Burnham, Tom McGuire, Melbourne MacDowell, Margaret Landis, George F. Marion, Frederick Stanton, Frederick Bertrand.
Comedy about Tom, a young man who inherits a million dollars and uses it to buy a hotel. His idea of good management is to let all his employees do whatever they wish... and, not surprisingly, the hotel is soon headed for bankruptcy.

The Millionaire (Universal, 1921)
d: Jack Conway. 5 reels.
Herbert Rawlinson, Bert Roach, William Courtwright, Verne Winter, Lillian Rich, Margaret Mann, Fred Vroom, Mary Huntress, Doris Pawn, E.A. Warren.
Norman, the heir to an $80 million dollar estate, learns that the criminals who murdered his benefactor are now after *him*.

The Millionaire (Micheaux Film Corp., 1927)
w, d: Oscar Micheaux. 7 reels.
Grace Smith, J. Lawrence Criner, Cleo Desmond, Lionel Monagas, William Edmonson, Vera Bracker, S.T. Jacks, E.G. Tatum.
Pelham, a black American, travels to South America and, after much hard work, becomes wealthy. Upon his return to New York, Pelham meets a girl he could learn to love—but first she must sever her ties to the underground.

The Millionaire Baby (Selig Polyscope, 1915)
d: Lawrence Marston. 6 reels.
Grace Darmond, Harry Mestayer, John Charles, Frederick Hand, Charlotte Stevens, Mrs.A.C. Marston, Charles Siddon, Robert Sherwood.
Because her husband has left her, an actress decides to give up her baby for adoption by a wealthy couple. What she doesn't know is that her estranged husband is now employed by the girl's new foster father, and will inevitably meet his own daughter.

A Millionaire For a Day (Guy Empey Productions/Pioneer Film Corp., 1921)
d: Wilfred North. 6 reels.
Arthur Guy Empey, Harry Burkhardt, Florence Martin, Templar Saxe, Williams Eville.

Bobby, a somewhat naive investor, proves the old adage that a fool and his money are soon parted. He makes a million, then loses it all to sharp speculators. Battered but not beaten, Bobby climbs back onto the fast track and earns another million, being careful not to be fooled again. In the process, he gains the love of a good woman.

The Millionaire Pirate (Universal, 1919)
d: Rupert Julian. 5 reels.
Monroe Salisbury, Ruth Clifford, Lillian Langdon, Harry Holden, Jack Mower, Clyde Fillmore.
A pearl diver discovers buried treasure... and a beautiful girl.

The Millionaire Policeman (Banner Productions, 1926)
d: Edward J. LeSaint. 5 reels.
Herbert Rawlinson, Eva Novak, Eugenie Besserer, Arthur Rankin, Lillian Langdon.
Wallace, the son of a millionaire, joins the police force to prove he is no coward.

The Millionaire Vagrant (Triangle, 1917)
d: Victor L. Schertzinger. 5 reels.
Charles Ray, Sylvia Breamer, J. Barney Sherry, Jack Gilbert, Elvira Weil, Dorcas Matthews, Aggie Herring, Josephine Headley, Carolyn Wagner, Walt Whitman.
To win a bet, a millionaire dons rags and moves to the slums—for a while.

Millionaires (Warner Bros., 1926)
d: Herman Raymaker. 7 reels.
George Sidney, Vera Gordon, Nat Carr, Helene Costello, Arthur Lubin, Jane Winton, Otto Hoffman, William Strauss.
Rags-to-riches tale of a humble tailor and his wife. They're now ready for high society, but is high society ready for them?

The Millionaire's Double (Rolfe Photoplays, Inc./Metro, 1917)
d: Harry Davenport. 5 reels.
Lionel Barrymore, Evelyn Brent, Harry S. Northrup, H.H. Pattee, John Smiley, Jack Raymond, Louis Wolheim.
When a millionaire on vacation reads in the paper that he has "committed suicide," naturally he realizes there's a scheme afoot, and he returns home to investigate.

Mind Over Motor (Ward Lascelle Productions/Principal Pictures, 1923)
d: Ward Lascelle. 5 reels.
Trixie Friganza, Ralph Graves, Clara Horton, Lucy Handforth, Grace Gordon, Pietro Sosso, George Guyton, Larry Steers, Edward Hearne.
Tish, a wealthy young woman who's mad about automobiles, gets the opportunity to drive one to victory in a major road race.

Mind the Paint Girl (Vitagraph, 1919)
d: Wilfrid North. 6 reels.
Anita Stewart, Conway Tearle, Victor Steele, Templar Saxe, Arthur Donaldson, Robert Lee Keeling, Virginia Norden, Hattie Delaro, George Stewart, Gladys Valerie.
"Mind the Paint Girl" is a song warning men about actresses wearing too much makeup.

The Mine With the Iron Door (Sol Lesser Productions/Principal Pictures, 1924)
d: Sam Wood. 8 reels.
Pat O'Malley, Dorothy Mackaill, Raymond Hatton, Charlie Murray, Bert Woodruff, Mitchell Lewis, Creighton Hale,

Mary Carr, William Collier Jr., Robert Frazer, Clarence Burton.

Marta, an orphan girl who was raised by two prospectors, grows to maturity and falls in love with a young fugitive with a price on his head.

Minnie (Marshall Neilan Productions/Associated First National, 1922)
d: Marshall Neilan. 7 reels.

Leatrice Joy, Matt Moore, George Barnum, Josephine Crowell, Helen Lynch, Raymond Griffith, Richard Wayne, Tom Wilson, George Dromgold.

Minnie's known as "the ugliest girl in town." To deflect taunts and ridicule, she pretends to have a lover who sends her candy and love letters. Eventually, Minnie finds a young man who sees through her facial defects to her beautiful soul, and he falls in love with her.

The Miracle Baby (R-C Pictures/FBO of America, 1923)
d: Val Paul. 6 reels.

Harry Carey, Margaret Landis, Charles J.L. Mayne, Edward Hearn, Hedda Nova, Edmund Cobb, Alfred Allen, Bert Sprotte.

Out West, a young fugitive from justice becomes partners with his victim's father, and together they adopt a baby.

The Miracle Man (Mayflower/Famous Players-Lasky, 1919)
d: George Loane Tucker. 8 reels.

Thomas Meighan, Betty Compson, Lon Chaney, J.M. Dumont, W. Lawson Butt, Elinor Fair, F.A. Turner, Lucille Hutton, Joseph J. Dowling, Frankie Lee.

Four crooks, three men and a woman, scheme to exploit an aged man as a "worker of miracles" for their own profit.

The Miracle of Life (S.E.V. Taylor/Associated Exhibitors, 1926)
d: S.E.V. Taylor. 5 reels.

Percy Marmont, Mae Busch, Nita Naldi.

Remake of the 1915 Mutual film *The Miracle of Life.*

The Miracle of Love (Cosmopolitan/Paramount, 1919)
d: Robert Z. Leonard. 7 reels.

Lucy Cotton, Blanche Davenport, Lila Blow, Jackie Saunders, Wyndham Standing, Ivo Watson, Percy Standing, Edward Earle, Ida Darling.

In England, love develops between a married noblewoman and the brother of a duke.

The Miracle of Manhattan (Selznick/Select, 1921)
d: George Archainbaud. 5 reels.

Elaine Hammerstein, Matt Moore, Ellen Cassity, Nora Reed, Walter Greene, Leonora Ottinger, Jack Raymond.

In New York, a socialite decides to launch a career as a singer. She soon becomes a popular cabaret songstress and attracts several suitors, not all of them with her best interests at heart.

The Miracle of Money (Hobart Henley Productions/Pathé, 1920)
d: Hobart Henley. 5 reels.

Bess Gearhart Morrison, Margaret Seddon, David Briggs, Walter Soders, Grace Klebold.

Small-town milliners inherit a fortune, and move to the big city.

The Mirage (Regal Pictures, 1924)
d: George Archainbaud. 6 reels.

Florence Vidor, Clive Brook, Alan Roscoe, Vola Vale, Myrtle Vane, Charlotte Stevens.

Romantic comedy about small-town girl Irene, who goes to the big city and finds a part in a stage show. There she meets and charms Henry, a wealthy businessman, who sees in Irene his dream girl.

Mirandy Smiles (Famous Players-Lasky/Paramount, 1918)
d: William C. De Mille. 5 reels.

Vivian Martin, Lewis Willoughby, Gean Gennung, William Freeman, Maym Kelso, Douglas MacLean, Elinor Hancock, Frances Beech.

Mirandy's a scrub lady who befriends a Sunday school teacher and helps her in her romance with the local minister.

The Mirror (Mutual, 1917)
d: Frank Powell. 5 reels.

Robert Elliott, Marjorie Rambeau, Irene Warfield, Paul Everton, Aubrey Beattie, Frank Ford, T. Jerome Lawlor.

When an artist paints a portrait of his beautiful wife, the picture draws much acclaim... and also the unwelcome attention of an unscrupulous playboy.

The Mischief Maker (Fox, 1916)
d: John G. Adolfi. 5 reels.

June Caprice, Harry Benham, John Reinhard, Margaret Fielding, Inez Marcel, Minnie Milne, Tom Brooke, Nellie Slattery.

A boarding school girl whose mother has already picked for her a husband, rejects him because she's never met the man. Soon fate will bring them together anyway.

A Misfit Earl (Betzwood Film Co./Goldwyn, 1919)
d: Ira M. Lowry. 5 reels.

Louis Bennison, Samuel Ross, Charles Brandt, Neil Moran, Ida Waterman, Claire Adams, Herbert Standing, Barbara Allen.

Out West, a cowpoke learns he has inherited an estate in England.

The Misfit Wife (Metro, 1920)
d: Edwin Mortimer. 6 reels.

Alice Lake, Forrest Stanley, Billy Gettinger, Frederic Vroom, Graham Pettie, Edward Martindel, Leota Lorraine, Helen Pillsbury, Jack Livingston, Jim Blackwell.

After a wealthy playboy falls in love with a manicurist and marries her, his status-conscious family tries to get the marriage annulled.

The Misleading Lady (Essanay, 1916)
d: Arthur Berthelet. 5 reels.

Henry B. Walthall, Edna Mayo, Sydney Ainsworth, Edward Arnold, Harry Dunkinson, John Junior, John H. Cossar, Charles J. Stine, Grant Mitchell, Renee Clemmons.

A high-society flirt charms an explorer into proposing to her, then laughs that it was all just a practical joke. But it's no joke to the explorer, who kidnaps his "fiancée" and carries her off to his home in the wilderness.

The Misleading Lady (Metro, 1920)
d: George Irving, George W. Terwilliger. 6 reels.

Bert Lytell, Lucy Cotton, Frank Currier, Stephen Grattan, Rae Allen, Cyril Chadwick, Barnet Parker, Arthur Hausman.

Remake of Essanay's 1916 romantic comedy *The Misleading Lady.* Both films were based on the stage play of the same name by Charles Goddard and Paul Dickey.

The Misleading Widow (Famous Players-Lasky/Paramount, 1919)
d: John S. Robertson. 5 reels.

Billie Burke, James L. Crane, Frank Mills, Madeline Clare, Fred Hearn, Frederick Esmelton, Dorothy Waters.
Comedic tale about a woman whose husband has left her, and her seemingly improper hospitality toward a visiting military officer.

Mismates (First National, 1926)
d: Charles Brabin. 7 reels.
Doris Kenyon, Warner Baxter, May Allison, Philo McCullough, Chalres Murray, Maude Turner Gordon, John Kolb, Cyril Ring, Nancy Kelly.
When a scion of wealth marries Judy, a manicurist, he is promptly disinherited by his family. Even after the couple have a child, Judy's in-laws refuse to re-open lines of communication.

Miss Adventure (Fox, 1919)
d: Lynn F. Reynolds. 5 reels.
Peggy Hyland, Gertie Messinger, Edward Burns, Lewis Sargent, Frank Brownlee, George Hernandez, George Webb, Alice Mason.
When a cabin boy on a schooner is entrusted with the care of an orphan girl, he little realizes that, in years to come, he and the girl will fall in love and marry.

Miss Ambition (Vitagraph, 1918)
d: Henry Houry. 5 reels.
Corinne Griffith, Walter McGrail, Betty Blythe, Fred Smith, Denton Vane, Templar Saxe, Harry Kendall.
Marta, lady's maid to a wealthy socialite, poses for a statue entitled "Miss Ambition." As matters turn out, that label will suit Marta quite well.

Miss Bluebeard (Paramount, 1925)
d: Frank Tuttle. 7 reels.
Bebe Daniels, Robert Frazer, Kenneth MacKenna, Raymond Griffith, Martha Madison, Diana Kane, Lawrence D'Orsay, Florence Billings, Ivan Simpson.
Comedy farce about Colette, a Parisienne actress who finds love with Larry, a wealthy American, and marries him. The only problem is, this chap isn't Larry, he's a friend filling in for the real Larry. Can this proxy marriage be saved?

Miss Brewster's Millions (Famous Players-Lasky/Paramount, 1926)
d: Clarence Badger. 7 reels.
Bebe Daniels, Warner Baxter, Ford Sterling, André de Beranger.
Feminist riff on the basic "Brewster's Millions" plot, this time with a young lady as the heir(ess) of millions that she must spend within a stated period of time.

Miss Crusoe (World Film Corp., 1919)
d: Frank Crane. 5 reels.
Virginia Hammond, Rod LaRocque, Nora Cecil, Irving Brooks, Albert Hart, Edwin Sturgis, W.R. Randall.
Adventure-seeking Dorothy finds plenty of action—involving crooks, detectives, and a deadly bottle of nitroglycerin—when she vacations at an island in Chesapeake Bay.

Miss Deception (Van Dyke Films/Art Dramas, Inc., 1917)
d: Eugene Knowland. 5 reels.
Jean Sothern, Robert Kegeris, Jack Newton, Mary Moore, Edwin Stanley, Jack Ellis, Hal Peel.
Though cultured and well-educated, a country girl pretends to her big-city relatives that she's an illiterate hick with crude manners.

Miss Dulcie From Dixie (Vitagraph, 1919)
d: Joseph Gleason. 5 reels.
Gladys Leslie, Charles Kent, Arthur Donaldson, Julia Swayne Gordon, James Morrison.
Southern girl Dulcie must live with her New York uncle for a year in order to claim an inheritance.

Miss George Washington (Famous Players/Paramount, 1916)
d: J. Searle Dawley. 5 reels.
Marguerite Clark, Frank Losee, Niles Welch, Florence Marten, Joseph Gleason, Maude Turner Gordon, Billy Watson, Herbert Prior.
When a girl claims to be the bride of a young diplomat in order to explain her presence in his hotel room, a judge and his wife insist that the "newlyweds" stay with them.

Miss Hobbs (Realart Pictures Corp., 1920)
d: Donald Crisp. 5 reels.
Harrison Ford, Wanda Hawley, Helen Jerome Eddy, Jack Mulhall, Walter Hiers, Julianne Johnston, Emily Chichester, Frances Raymond.
When a fire-breathing feminist talks two girlfriends into leaving their men, the rejected chaps ask a resourceful friend to tame the feminist and restore order.

Miss Innocence (Fox, 1918)
d: Harry Millarde. 5 reels.
June Caprice, Marie Shotwell, Robert Walker, Frank Beamish, Carleton Macy.
Dolores, a convent-bred girl, yearns for travel and adventure.

Miss Jackie of the Army (American Film Co./Mutual, 1917)
d: Lloyd Ingraham. 5 reels.
Margarita Fischer, Jack Mower, L.C. Shumway, Hal Clements.
Jackie, an Army brat, alerts her colonel father and his command that saboteurs are about to blow up a troop train.

Miss Jackie of the Navy (Pollard Picture Plays/Mutual, 1916)
d: Harry Pollard. 5 reels.
Margarita Fischer, Jack Mower, J. Gordon Russell.
Jackie, looking for love, disguises herself as a sailor and stows away on a ship bound for an exotic island.

Miss Lulu Bett (Famous Players-Lasky/Paramount, 1921)
d: William C. DeMille. 7 reels.
Lois Wilson, Milton Sills, Theodore Roberts, Helen Ferguson, Mabel Van Buren, Clarence Burton, Ethel Wales, Taylor Graves, Charles Ogle, May Garici.
Lulu, a lonely spinster, meets Deacon, the brother of her dentist brother-in-law. Deacon takes pity on the charming Lulu and arranges a party in her honor. As part of the hijinks, he and Lulu go through a phony marriage ceremony, with her brother-in-law presiding. Not until after the party does anyone realize that the her brother-in-law the dentist is also the local justice of the peace. Does that make the marriage binding?

Miss Nobody (Astra Film Corp./Pathé, 1917)
d: William Parke. 5 reels.
Gladys Hulette, Cesare Gravina, H.G. Andrews, William Parke Jr., Sidney Mather.
Two pawnbrokers raise a girl left in their care. As she grows up, she hears taunts from classmates that she's a "nobody"—but the locket she's always worn will establish that she's a

326

member of the British nobility.

Miss Nobody (First National, 1926)
d: Lambert Hillyer. 7 reels.
Anna Q. Nilsson, Walter Pidgeon, Louise Fazenda, Mitchell Lewis, Clyde Cook, Arthur Stone, Anders Randolf, Claire DuBrey, Jed Prouty, Caroline Rankin, George Nichols, Oleta Otis, James Gordon, Fred Warren.
Barbara, a girl disguised as a boy, is "adopted" by a street gang.

Miss Petticoats (World Film Corp., 1916)
d: Harley Knoles. 5 reels.
Alice Brady, Arthur Ashley, Isabel Berwin, Robert Elliott, Johnny Hines, Lila Chester, Edward M. Kimball, Alec B. Francis, Charles K. Gerard, Louis Grisel.
"Miss Petticoats" is the the pet name of a girl raised in America by her sea captain grandfather. One day, the girl will learn that she is descended from the French nobility.

Miss Robinson Crusoe (Rolfe Photoplays, Inc./Metro, 1917)
d: William Christy Cabanne. 5 reels.
Emmy Wehlen, Walter C. Miller, Harold Entwhistle, Sue Balfour, Margaret Seddon, Augustus Phillips, Daniel Jarrett, Ethel Hallor.
Flirtatious Pamela yearns to meet a daring young man, but despairs of finding one among the idlers of New York society. But when Pamela finds herself on a remote island, under attack from foreign agents, it is one of the society lads who rescues her and wins her hand.

Miss U.S.A. (Fox, 1917)
d: Harry Millarde. 5 reels.
June Caprice, William Courtleigh Jr., Frank Evans, Tom Burroush, Al Hall.
An heiress narrowly escapes death, not once but several times.

Missing (Famous Players-Lasky/Paramount, 1918)
d: James Young. 5 reels.
Thomas Meighan, Sylvia Breamer, Robert Gordon, Winter Hall, Ola Humphrey, Mollie McConnell, Kathleen O'Connor.
In World War I, newlyweds are separated when the husband goes to the battlefields of Europe.

Missing Daughters (Choice Productions/Selznick, 1924)
d: William H. Clifford. 7 reels.
Eileen Percy, Pauline Starke, Claire Adams, Eva Novak, Walter Long, Robert Edeson, Rockliffe Fellowes, Sheldon Lewis, Walt Whitman, Frank Ridge, Chester Bishop.
Fast-moving drama about three girls who are abducted and flown to a distant getaway, only to be rescued by closely-following Secret Service agents.

The Missing Link (Warner Bros., 1927)
d: Charles F. Reisner. 7 reels.
Sydney Chaplin, Ruth Hall, Tom McGuire, Crauford Kent, Sam Baker, Otto Fries, Kewpie Morgan.
Farcical doings on safari, where a phony explorer falls in love with the daughter of the real explorer's friend, Colonel Braden.

The Missing Links (Fine Arts Film Co./Triangle, 1916)
d: Lloyd Ingraham. 5 reels.
Thomas Jefferson, Elmer Clifton, Robert Harron, Loyola O'Connor, William Higby, Elinor Stone, Norma Talmadge, Jack Brammall, Hal Wilson, Constance Talmadge.

When a bank president is found murdered, the husband of his stepdaughter is suspected of the crime. But a pair of cufflinks found at the scene point detectives to the real culprit.

Missing Millions (Famous Players-Lasky/Paramount, 1922)
d: Joseph Henabery. 6 reels.
Alice Brady, David Powell, Frank Losee, Riley Hatch, John B. Cooke, William B. Mack, George LeGuere, Alice May, H. Cooper Cliffe, Sydney Deane, Beverly Travers, Sidney Herbert.
Mary, a lady crook, and Boston Blackie steal millions in gold to aid her father, who's in prison, having been railroaded by a treacherous financier.

Mister 44 (Yorke Film Corp./Metro, 1916)
d: Henry Otto. 5 reels.
Harold Lockwood, May Allison, Lester Cuneo, Yona Landowska, Henry Otto, Aileen Allen, Belle Hutchinson, Lee Arms.
Sadie, a shirt factory worker, yearns for a man with a size 44 chest. So, she slips a note into the pocket of a size 44 shirt and awaits an answer from her dream man.

Mistress Nell (Famous Players/Paramount, 1915)
d: James Kirkwood. 5 reels.
Mary Pickford, Owen Moore, Arthur Hoops, Ruby Hoffman, Amelia Rose, J. Albert Hall, Nathaniel Sack.
Actress Nell Gwynn, who is in love with King Charles II of England, learns of a treasonous plot against the king, and takes action to upset the traitors' plans.
Not precisely the same story as in the 1926 British film *Nell Gwynn*, which starred Dorothy Gish, though some of the characters are the same.

The Mistress of Shenstone (Robertson-Cole Pictures, 1921)
d: Henry King. 6 reels.
Pauline Frederick, Roy Stewart, Emmett C. King, Arthur Clayton, John Willink, Helen Wright, Rosa Gore, Helen Muir, Lydia Yeamans Titus.
In England, a World War I widow grieves for her dead husband at the seashore. There, she meets and falls in love with a war veteran who saves her from drowning... not realizing he is the man who gave the military order that resulted in her husband's death.

Mixed Blood (Universal, 1916)
d: Charles Swickard. 5 reels.
Claire McDowell, George Beranger, Roy Stewart, Wilbur Higby, Jessie Arnold, Harry Archer, Doc Crane.
Nita, a half-Irish and half-Spanish girl, is attracted to two men: violent, adventurous Carlos and Jim, a big-hearted American sheriff.

Mixed Faces (Fox, 1922)
d: Rowland V. Lee. 5 reels.
William Russell, Renee Adoree, DeWitt Jennings, Elizabeth Garrison, Charles French, Aileen Manning, Harvey Clarke.
A famous politician's lookalike is persuaded to impersonate him during the campaign.

M'Liss (World Film Corp., 1915)
d: O.A.C. Lund. 5 reels.
Barbara Tennant, Howard Estabrook, O.A.C. Lund.
The wild and carefree M'Liss is heiress to a valuable oil fortune, but she doesn't know it. There are men, however, who would try to do her out of her inheritance.

M'Liss (Pickford/Famous Players-Lasky/Artcraft, 1918)
d: Marshall Neilan. 5 reels.
Mary Pickford, Theodore Roberts, Thomas Meighan, Tully Marshall, Charles Ogle, Monte Blue, Winifred Greenwood, Helen Kelly, Val Paul, W.H. Brown, John Burton, Bud Post.
During the 1849 Gold Rush, a crusty prospector earns a fortune, and then dies. His enemies then conspire to cheat his flighty but loveable daughter, "M'Liss," out of her inheritance.

Moana of the South Seas (Paramount, 1926)
d: Robert Flaherty. 7 reels.
Ta'avale, Fa'amgase, Tu'ugaita, Moana, Pe'a.
A virtually plotless documentary-style picture about life in the South Pacific.

Mockery (MGM, 1927)
w, d: Benjamin Christensen. 7 reels.
Lon Chaney, Barbara Bedford, Ricardo Cortez, Emily Fitzroy, Kai Schmidt.
In Siberia during the Bolshevik Revolution, a peasant risks his life to save a countess he loves.

The Model (World Film Corp., 1915)
d: Frederick Thomson. 5 reels.
William Elliott, Cynthia Day, Alec B. Francis, Dorothy Green, Henry Leone.
After Dick Seymour inherits a large estate, a fortune hunter persuades his girlfriend to pose as an artist's model and seduce the young heir.

A Model's Confession (Universal, 1918)
d: Ida May Park. 5 reels.
Mary MacLaren, Kenneth Harlan, Edna Earle, Herbert Prior, Louis Willoughby, Gretchen Lederer.
When a fashion model is forced to call upon a customer to retrieve some unpaid-for gowns, she meets the father she hasn't seen in many years.

A Modern Cinderella (Fox, 1917)
d: John G. Adolfi. 5 reels.
June Caprice, Frank Morgan, Betty Prendergast, Stanhope Wheatcroft, Grace Stevens, Tom Brooke.
She's sweet, she's winsome, but she's also a flirt. She's Joyce, the modern Cinderella.

Modern Daughters (Trem Carr Productions/Rayart, 1927)
d: Charles J. Hunt. 6 reels.
Edna Murphy, Bryant Washburn, Ernest Hilliard, Virginia Lyons, Jack Fowler, Hazel Flint.
Jazz-age youngsters stir up a troubling brew.

Modern Husbands (National Film Corp./Mutual, 1919)
d: Francis J. Grandon. 5 reels.
Henry B. Walthall, Ethel Fleming, Neil Hardin, Melbourne McDowell, Clare DuBrey, Olga Gray.
When she feels her wealthy husband is neglecting her, Julia takes a lover.

Modern Love (Universal, 1918)
d: Robert Leonard. 6 reels.
Mae Murray, George Cheesboro, Philo McCullough, Arthur Shirley, Claire DuBrey.
A young actress' honor is compromised by her lecherous costar.

Modern Love (Universal, 1929)
d: Arch Heath. 6 reels. (Part talkie.)
Kathryn Crawford, Charley Chase, Jean Hersholt, Edward Martindel.
A career woman must decide between business and a domestic married life.

A Modern Magdalen (Life Photo Film Corp., 1915)
d: Will S. Davis. 5 reels.
Catherine Countiss, Lionel Barrymore, William H. Tooker, Charles Graham, Marjorie Nelson.
Katinka, a factory worker, becomes the mistress of the mill owner in order to provide her sister with living expenses.

Modern Marriage (F.X.B. Pictures/American Releasing Corp., 1923)
d: Lawrence C. Windom. 7 reels.
Francis X. Bushman, Beverly Bayne, Roland Bottomley, Ernest Hilliard, Zita Moulton, Frankie Evans, Arnold Lucy, Pauline Dempsey, Blanche Craig.
Varley, a neglectful husband, finds that his wife has strayed into the arms of another.

Modern Matrimony (Selznick, 1923)
w, d: Victor Heerman. 5 reels.
Owen Moore, Alice Lake, Mayme Kelso, Frank Campeau, Kate Lester, Victor Potel, Snitz Edwards, Douglas Carter.
Chester, a working class chap, surreptitiously marries a socialite, then announces their marriage at a party thrown by her family to announce her engagement to someone else.

A Modern Monte Cristo (Thanhouser, 1917)
d: W. Eugene Moore. 5 reels.
Vincent Serrano, Thomas Curran, Helen Badgley, Gladys Dore, Boyd Marshall.
After a patient dies on the operating table, the surgeon is accused of accepting a bribe in return for allowing the patient to die.

Modern Mothers (Columbia, 1928)
d: Philip Rosen. 6 reels.
Helene Chadwick, Barbara Kent, Douglas Fairbanks Jr.
A Broadway actress visits her daughter, and falls for the girl's boyfriend.

A Modern Musketeer (Fairbanks/Artcraft, 1917)
d: Allan Dwan. 5 reels.
Douglas Fairbanks, Marjorie Daw, Eugene Ormonde, Tully Marshalkl, Edythe Chapman.
Ned, a Kansas boy, has the spirit of D'Artagnan running in his veins, and he gets the chance to show his bravery when he must rescue a young woman from Indians near the Grand Canyon.

A Modern Salome (Metro, 1920)
w, d: Leonce Perret. 6 reels.
Hope Hampton, Sidney L. Mason, Percy Standing, Arthur Donaldson, Wyndham Standing, Agnes Ayres.
Virginia's a devil-may-care rich girl and a flirt, but she exceeds decorum when she cavalierly accuses her husband's employee of attacking her and gets him fired. In a nightmare, Virginia sees herself as a modern Salome, guilty of causing the ruination of St. John the Baptist. Upon awakening, she quickly makes amends and sees that the employee's good name and career are restored.

A Modern Thelma (Fox, 1916)
d: John G. Adolfi. 5 reels.
Vivian Martin, Harry Hilliard, William H. Tooker, Albert Roccardi, Maud Sinclair, Elizabeth Kennedy, Allen Walker, Stuart Russell, Albert Tovell, Richard Neill, Pauline Barry.
Sir Philip, an English nobleman, journeys abroad and falls in love with Thelma, a Norwegian girl.

Modern Times (United Artists, 1936)
w, d: Charles Chaplin. 9 reels. (Part talkie)
Charles Chaplin, Paulette Goddard, Henry Bergman, Chester Conklin, Stanley Sanford, Hank Mann, Louis Natheaux, Allan Garcia, Richard Alexander, Heinie Conklin, Lloyd Ingraham, Edward Kimball, Wildred Lucas, Mira McKinney, John Rand, Walter James.
A factory worker runs afoul of modern machinery and modern conventions. After several adventures, he and an orphan girl escape the city to find a better world together.
Modern Times signaled the end of the silent era. Chaplin had clung stubbornly to the silent genre, years after Hollywood embraced the talkies, but with this parting shot he ended the career of the most recognizable figure the screen had ever created: the Little Tramp. *Modern Times* has a synchronized musical score (composed by Chaplin), there are some audible words barked by the plant manager, and Chaplin's voice is heard on film for the first time, singing a nonsense ditty to a café audience. Otherwise, the film is mute... and it would be the final grace note in the glorious symphony of silence.

The Mohican's Daughter (P.T.B., Inc./American Releasing Corp., 1922)
d: S.E.V. Taylor. 5 reels.
Nancy Deaver, Hazel Washburn, Szon Kling, William Thompson, Jack Newton, Paul Panzer, Nick Thompson, Mortimer Snow, John Webb Dillon, Myrtle Morse, Rita Abrams.
Out West, a half-breed girl falls for the local trading post manager.

Molly and I (Fox, 1920)
d: Howard M. Mitchell. 5 reels.
Shirley Mason, Albert Roscoe, Harry Dunkinson, Lilie Leslie.
To help out an author who is losing his eyesight, Molly persuades him that she is an old maid with a large dowry, in need of a husband. In fact, she has a small inheritance, and she gladly gives it to her new husband so that he can get an operation to have his eyesight restored.

Molly and Me (Tiffany-Stahl Productions, 1929)
d: Albert Ray. 8 reels.
Belle Bennett, Joe E. Brown, Alberta Vaughn, Charles Byer.
After hitting the big time on Broadway, a vaudeville performer falls in love with his new co-star despite the fact that he is already married.

Molly Entangled (Paramount, 1917)
d: Robert Thornby. 5 reels.
Harrison Ford, Vivian Martin, Noah Beery, G.S. Spaulding, Helen Dunbar, Gibson Gowland, Jane Keckley, William A. Carroll.
Out of respect for the family's wishes, Molly marries a dying man so he can receive his inheritance. Trouble is, the "dying" bridegroom recovers!

Molly, Go Get 'Em (American Film Co./Mutual, 1918)
d: Lloyd Ingraham. 5 reels.
Margarita Fischer, Jack Mower, Hal Clements, Margaret Allen, David Howard, Emma Kluge, True Boardman.
Mischievous and feisty, young Molly awaits her debut into society.

Molly Make-Believe (Famous Players/Paramount, 1916)
d: J. Searle Dawley. 5 reels.
Marguerite Clark, Mahlon Hamilton, Master Dick Gray, Helen Dahl, Gertrude Norman, J.W. Johnston, Edwin Mordant.
Molly, whose pastime is writing letters to shut-ins and the lonely, falls in love with an unseen penpal, and he with her.

Molly O' (Mack Sennett Productions/First National, 1921)
d: F. Richard Jones. 8 reels.
George Nichols, Mabel Normand, Eugenie Besserer, Anna Hernandez, Jack Mulhall, Albert Hackett, Jacqueline Logan, Ben Deeley, Eddie Gribbon, Carol Stockdale, Lowell Sherman, Gloria Davenport.
Frenetic high-jinks about Molly, a young washerwoman, who falls in love with Bryant, a young millionaire, and sets out to nab him. At a masked ball at the country club, Bryant mistakes Molly for his fiancée, and what follows is a breathtaking chase involving Molly, Bryant, his fiancée, Molly's working-class beau, her own dad, and a high-society crook with a flying blimp.

Molly of the Follies (American Film Co./Pathé, 1919)
d: Edward Sloman. 5 reels.
Margarita Fischer, Jack Mower, Lule Warrenton, Millard L. Webb, J. Farrell MacDonald, Mary Lee Wise.
In a carnival at Coney Island, dancer Molly loves diver Joe. But she's attracted to wealthy customer Chauncy and elopes with him, with Joe in hot pursuit.

The Mollycoddle (Fairbanks/United Artists, 1920)
d: Victor Fleming. 6 reels.
Douglas Fairbanks, Wallace Beery, Ruth Renick, Paul Burns, Lewis Hippe, Albert MacQuarrie, Betty Bouton, Morris Hughes.
A wealthy playboy who's suspected of being a "cream puff" proves his detractors wrong.

The Moment Before (Famous Players/Paramount, 1916)
d: Robert G. Vignola. 5 reels.
Pauline Frederick, Thomas Holding, Frank Losee, J.W. Johnston, Edward Sturgis, Henry Hallam.
An elderly duchess sees her entire life, in an instant, just before she dies.

The Money Changers (Federal Photoplays Inc./Pathé, 1920)
d: Jack Conway. 6 reels.
Robert McKim, Claire Adams, Roy Stewart, Audrey Chapman, George Webb, Betty Brice, Edward Peil, Harvey Clark, Harry Tennebrook, Stanton Heck, George Hernandez.
Underworld crime lords deal in narcotics and white slavery.

The Money Corral (Paramount, 1919)
d: William S. Hart. 5 reels.
William S. Hart, Jane Novak, Herschel Mayall, Winter Hall, Rhea Mitchell, Patricia Palmer, Ira McFadden.
In Chicago, a rodeo performer is offered a job guarding the railroad's large vault, which has just been robbed. He declines the job, but after falling for the niece of the railroad boss, the cowpoke goes searching for the robbers in their lair, "the Money Corral."

Money Isn't Everything (American Film Co./Pathé, 1918)
d: Edward Sloman. 5 reels.
Margarita Fisher, Jack Mower, J. Morris Foster, Wedgwood Nowell, Kate Price.
Comedic tale of a lawyer who hires a pretty girl for her looks, believing her to be empty-headed. As it turns out, the girl is plenty smart, and soon foils a fraudulent real estate scheme and wins the lawyer's heart.

Money Mad (Goldwyn, 1918)

d: Hobart Henley. 5 reels.

Mae Marsh, Rod LaRocque, John Sainpolis, Macey Harlam, Alec B. Francis, Corinne Barker, Florida Kingsley.

After murdering his wealthy client, the executor of her estate squanders all her fortune except for some precious jewels. The client's daughter learns of his treachery and, with the aid of her fiancé, sets out to trap the culprit and his seductive girlfriend and regain the jewels.

Money Madness (Universal, 1917)
d: Henry MacRae. 5 reels.

Don Bailey, Charles H. Mailes, Mary MacLaren, Alfred Vosburg, Rex de Roselli, Eddie Polo.

When his bank is on the verge of collapse, a banker calls in a famous detective, "Whispering Smith," to investigate. Smith discovers that the bank's vice president is guilty of willful mismanagement.

Money Magic (Vitagraph, 1917)
d: William Wolbert. 5 reels.

Antonio Moreno, Laura Winston, Edith Storey, William Duncan, Florence Dye.

Poor but lovely Bertha marries Marshall, a wealthy cripple, and has every intention of remaining true to him. But when she meets Ben, her attraction to him is almost more than she can bear.

The Money Maniac (Leonce Perret/Pathé, 1921)
w, d: Leonce Perret. 5 reels.

Robet Elliott, Henry G. Sell, Marcya Capri, Lucy Fox, Ivo Dawson, Eugene Breon.

En route to the United States, a con artist sells phony stock to his fellow immigrants.

The Money Master (Kleine-Edison Feature Service, 1915)
d: George Fitzmaurice. 5 reels.

Frank Sheridan, Paul McAllister, Calvin Thomas, Sam Reid, Anne Meredith, Fania Marinoff, Bert Gudgeon, Malcolm Duncan.

Ruthless and hard-driving, an industrialist rises to the pinnacle of success by crushing his competition. However, his obsession with making money costs him the love of his wife, who leaves him and takes their young son.

The Money Mill (Vitagraph, 1917)
d: John Robertson. 5 reels.

Dorothy Kelly, Evart Overton, Gordon Gray, Edward elkas, Charles Kent, Logan Paul.

After her father's death, the daughter of a wealthy miner decides to move to New York and climb the social ladder.

Money! Money! Money! (Preferred Pictures/Associated First National Pictures, 1923)
d: Tom Forman. 6 reels.

Katherine MacDonald, Carl Stockdale, Frances Raymond, Paul Willis, Hershcel Mayall, Brenda Fowler, Margaret Loomis, Charles Clary, Jack Dougherty.

Priscilla, a social climber, persuades her factory owner father to borrow money from a loan shark.

Money Talks (MGM, 1926)
d: Archie Mayo. 6 reels.

Owen Moore, Claire Windsor, Ned Sparks, Bert Roach, Kathleen Key, Phillips Smalley, Dot Farley.

Sam, whose wife has left him over his spendthrift ways, tries to win her back by promoting an island hotel as a health spa—with his wife as one of the customers. Things go well until the lady doctor Sam has hired turns up missing, and he is forced to impersonate her to proceed with the charade.

Money to Burn (Fox, 1922)
d: Rowland V. Lee. 5 reels.

William Russell, Sylvia Breamer, Hallam Cooley, Harvey Clark, Otto Matieson.

A Wall Street speculator is known as "Lucky" because of his success in the market.

Money to Burn (Gotham Productions/Lumas Film corp., 1926)
d: Walter Lang. 6 reels.

Malcolm McGregor, Dorothy Devore, Eric Mayne, Nina Romano, George Chesebro, Orfa Casanova, Jules Cowles, John Price, Arnold Melvin.

Dolores, a South American beauty, and Dan, the American doctor she loves, travel to her country and uncover a counterfeiting operation.

The Monkey Talks (Fox, 1927)
d: Raoul Walsh. 6 reels.

Olive Borden, Jacques Lerner, Don Alvarado, Malcolm Waite, Raymond Hitchcock, Ted McNamara, Jane Winton, August Tollaire.

To raise money, three stranded members of a French circus troupe decide that the smallest of them will pose as a talking monkey.

Monsieur Beucaire (Famous Players-Lasky, 1924)
d: Sidney Olcott. 10 reels.

Rudolph Valentino, Bebe Daniels, Lois Wilson, Doris Kenton, Lowell Sherman, John Davidson, Paulette Duval, Oswald Yorke, Flora Finch, Templar Powell, Downing Clarke, Yvonne Hughes, John Davidson, Louis Waller, Ian MacLaren, Frank Shannon.

A male hairdresser wins the heart of a French princess.

The Monster (MGM, 1925)
d: Roland West. 7 reels.

Lon Chaney, Walter James, Gertrude Olmstead, Hallam Cooley, Johnny Arthur, Charles A. Sellon, Knute Erickson, George Austin, Edward McWade, Ethel Wales.

Ziska, a mad scientist, believes he can bring the dead back to life.

Montana Bill (Western Star Productions/Pioneer Film Corp., 1921)
d: Phil Goldstone. 5 reels.

William Fairbanks, Maryon Aye, Robert Kortman, Jack Waltemeyer, Ernest Van Pelt, Hazel Hart.

Out West, a new ranch hand runs afoul of the jealous foreman when he takes an interest in the ranch owner's pretty daughter.

Monte Carlo (MGM, 1926)
d: Christy Cabanne. 7 reels.

Lew Cody, Gertrude Olmstead, Roy D'Arcy, ZaSu Pitts, Harry Myers, Karl Dane, Trixie Friganza, Margaret Campbell, André Lanoy, Max Barwyn, Barbara Shears, Harry Myers.

Sally, a small-town schoolteacher, wins a trip to Monte Carlo, where she meets and mingles with princes, millionaires... and Tony, a penniless but charming American.

Monte Cristo (Fox, 1922)
d: Emmett J. Flynn. 10 reels.

John Gilbert, Estelle Taylor, Robert McKim, William V. Mong, Virginia Brown Faire, Renee Adoree, George Siegmann, Spottiswoode Aitken, Ralph Cloninger, Albert Prisco, Gaston Glass, Al Filson, Hary Lonsdale, Francis

McDonald, Jack Cosgrove, Maude George.
Retelling of the Alexandre Dumas tale *Le Comte de Monte Cristo*, in which Dantes, an innocent French sailor, is framed for treason and imprisoned in an impenetrable dungeon. Dumas' story was first filmed as a three-reeler in 1907 by the Selig Polyscope Company, and again in 1912 by Edwin S. Porter for the Famous Players Film Co.

Montmartre Rose (Excellent Pictures, 1929)
d: Bernard F. McEveety, Frederick Hiatt. 6 reels.
Marguerite De La Motte, Rosemary Theby, Harry Myers, Paul Ralli, Frank Leigh, Martha Mattox.
In Paris, a jeweler named Henri becomes engaged to Rose, a cabaret entertainer.

Moon Madness (Haworth Studios/Robertson-Cole, 1920)
d: Colin Campbell. 6 reels.
Edith Storey, Sam DeGrasse, Josef Swickard, Wallace MacDonald, Irene Hunt, William Courtleigh, Frankie Lee, Frederic Starr.
In Paris, a girl who's desperately in love with an artist offers herself to him, but he isn't interested. Not to worry, though. The young man who has stood behind the girl throughout her "moon madness" is still very much in love with her.

Moonlight and Honeysuckle (Realart Pictures, 1921)
d: Joseph Henabery. 5 reels.
Mary Miles Minter, Monte Blue, Willard Louis, Grace Goodall, Guy Oliver, William Boyd, Mabel Van Buren.
Romantic comedy about a U.S. senator in love with a widow who refuses to marry him while his daughter, Judith, is still single. Judith has several beaus but is playing the waiting game—until a political-style "leak" declares that she has eloped. The rumor isn't true, but it brings her several suitors together to wage an all-out effort to win her hand.

Moonlight Follies (Universal, 1921)
d: King Baggot. 5 reels.
Marie Prevost, Lionel Belmore, Marie Crisp, George Fisher, George Fillmore.
Romantic comedy about Nan, a high-spirited girl who flirts with nearly every man she meets. Finally Anthony, previously thought to be a misogynist, proposes marriage to Nan, and she accepts. But it's in her nature to tease, so after their betrothal she cheerfully denounces him in front of guests and says she's changed her mind about marriage. Not one to be so easily dismissed, Anthony carries Nan off, kicking and screaming, and takes her to his mountain cabin, there to await the minister.

The Moonshine Trail (J. Stuart Blackton Features/Pathé, 1919)
d: J. Stuart Blackton. 6 reels.
Sylvia Breamer, Robert Gordon, Julia Swayne Gordon, Van Dyke Brooke, Margaret Barry, Robert Milasch, Slim Rube, Jay Strong, Louis Dean, Leo Delaney, Eddie Dunn.
The daughter of Kentucky moonshiners goes to New York and, ironically, falls in love with a man with a drinking problem.

Moonshine Valley (Fox, 1922)
d: Herbert Brenon. 6 reels.
William Farnum, Sadie Mullen, Holmes Herbert, Dawn O'Day.
After his wife leaves him to marry a doctor, Connors lapses into drunkenness. After finding a lost little girl and bringing her into his home, Connors reforms his ways.

The Moonstone (World Film Corp., 1915)

d: Frank Crane. 5 reels.
Eugene O'Brien, Elaine Hammerstein, William Rosell, Ruth Findlay, Edmund Mortimer.
After an Englishman steals a diamond from the Temple of the Moon in India, he and his family are cursed with misfortune and disaster.

The Moral Code (Erbograph, 1917)
d: Ashley Miller. 5 reels.
Anna Q. Nilsson, Walter Hitchcock, Florence Hamilton, Richard Barthelmess.
There's melodrama afoot, when a young man with high morals marries a girl with none.

Moral Courage (World Film Corp., 1917)
d: Romaine Fielding. 5 reels.
Muriel Ostriche, Arthur Ashley, Edward Elkas, Clarence Elmer, Robert Forsyth, Julia Stuart, Richard Turner, Edmund Cobb.
Joshua, a captain of industry, expects his college-educated son to marry well, but the lad has his eyes on one of the girls who work in his dad's factory.

The Moral Deadline (World Film Corp., 1919)
d: Travers Vale. 5 reels.
June Elvidge, Frank Mayo, Ned Burton, Grace Stevens, Alice Weeks, Jane Sterling, Muriel Ostriche, Gertrude Webber, Louis Grizel, Louise DuPre, Joseph Smiley.
Hal loves Evelyn, and so they marry. But his financier father thinks the girl is beneath him, and tries every trick to get Hal and Evelyn to divorce.

The Moral Fabric (New York Motion Picture Corp./Triangle, 1916)
d: Charles Miller. 5 reels.
Frank Mills, Edith Reeves, Howard Hickman, Louise Brownell.
Bitter drama about a man whose wife cheats on him, and his subsequent revenge.

Moral Fibre (Vitagraph, 1921)
d: Webster Campbell. 6 reels.
Corinne Griffith, Catherine Calvert, William Parke Jr., Harry C. Browne, Joe King, Alice Concord.
Marion, a successful illustrator, swears vengeance on the woman she considers responsible for her brother's suicide.

The Moral Law (Fox, 1918)
d: Bertram Bracken. 5 reels.
Gladys Brockwell, Rosita Marstini, Joseph singleton, Colin Chase, Bertram Grassby, Cora Rankin Drew.
Half-sisters resemble each other in appearance, but they're poles apart in moral quality.
Double role for Miss Brockwell, as half-sisters Isobel and Anita.

The Moral Sinner (Famous Players-Lasky/Paramount, 1924)
d: Ralph Ince. 6 reels.
Dorothy Dalton, James Rennie, Alphonse Ethier, Frederick Lewis, Walter Percival, Paul McAllister, Florence Fair.
In Paris, the daughter of a thief follows in Papa's footsteps, but she doesn't feel right doing it.

Morals (Realart Pictures/Paramount, 1921)
d: William D. Taylor. 5 reels.
May McAvoy, William P. Carleton, Starke Patterson, William Lawrence, Kathlyn Williams, Bridgetta Clark, Sidney Bracey.

Carlotta, a young woman raised in a Turkish harem, escapes to London in search of true love.

Morals For Men (Tiffany Productions, 1925)
d: Bernard Hyman. 8 reels.
Conway Tearle, Agnes Ayres, Alyce Mills, Otto Matieson, Robert Ober, John Miljan, Mary Beth Milford, Eve Southern, Marjery O'Neill.
Bitter melodrama that visits the age-old question: Does society have one standard of conduct for men, and another for women?

The Morals of Hilda (Universal, 1916)
d: Lloyd Carleton. 5 reels.
Gretchen Lederer, Lois Wilson, Frank Whitson, Richard Morris, Adele Farrington, Emory Johnson.
Heavy drama about a politician, himself illegitimate, who fights for the rights of illegitimate children.

The Morals of Marcus (Famous Players/Paramount, 1915)
d: Edwin S. Porter, Hugh Ford. 5 reels.
Marie Doro, Eugene Ormonde, Ida Darling, Julian L'Estrange, Russell Bassett, Frank Andrews, Wellington A. Playter, Phyllis Carrington, Helen Freeman, J.W. Austin.
Marcus, a wealthy philosopher, falls in love with a girl brought up in a Turkish harem.

Moran of the Lady Letty (Famous Players-Lasky, 1922)
d: George Melford. 7 reels.
Rudolph Valentino, Dorothy Dalton, Charles Brinley, Walter Long, Emil Jorgenson, Maude Wayne, Cecil Holland, George Kuwa, Charles K. French.
Shanghaied aboard a smugglers' ship, playboy Ramon regains his self-respect and leads a mutiny against the villainous captain.

Moran of the Marines (Paramount, 1928)
d: Frank Strayer. 7 reels.
Richard Dix, Ruth Elder, Roscoe Karns, Brooks Benedict, Capt. E.H. Calvert, Duke Martin, Tetsu Komai.
Moran, a high-spirited Marine, kisses the general's daughter and is quickly court-martialed. But his boldness will come in handy after the girl is abducted by bandits, and Moran leads a Marine detachment to her rescue.

More Deadly Than the Male (Famous Players-Lasky/Paramount, 1919)
d: Robert G. Vignola. 5 reels.
Ethel Clayton, Edward Hoxen, Herbert Heyes, Hallam Cooley, Peggy Pearce.
When a wealthy soldier of fortune declares that pursuing hot-blooded women in underdeveloped countries is more of a challenge than wooing civilized American women, one of the latter decides to prove him wrong.

The More Excellent Way (Vitagraph, 1917)
d: Perry Vekroff. 5 reels.
Anita Stewart, Charles Richman, Rudolph Cameron, Charles A. Stevenson, Katherine Lewis, Josephine Earle, Gordon Gray.
Chrissey, a naive young woman, marries her guardian but continues to be fascinated by her husband's roguish business rival.

More Pay, Less Work (Fox, 1926)
d: Albert Ray. 6 reels.
Albert Gran, Mary Brian, E.J. Ratcliffe, Charles Rogers, Otto Hoffman, Charles Conklin.
Rival shipowners have to contend not only with each other's

business shenanigans, but also with the unsettling truth that their children are in love with each other.

More to be Pitied than Scorned (Columbia, 1922)
d: Edward J. Le Saint. 6 reels.
J. Frank Glendon, Alice Lake, Rosemary Theby, Philo McCullough, Gordon Griffith, Josephine Adair.
Domestic dramedy, with hubby mistakenly thinking his wife is cheating on him.

More Trouble (Pathé, 1918)
d: Ernest C. Warde. 5 reels.
Frank Keenan, John Gilbert, Ida Lewis, Roberta Wilson, Jospeh J. Dowling, Jack Rollins, Helen Dunbar, Al Ray, Clyde Benson, Aggie Herring, Lule Warrenton.
After an exemplary young man graduates college with honors and enters business, he learns that one of his fraternity brothers is forging his name to large debts.

More Truth Than Poetry (Metro, 1917)
d: Burton L. King. 5 reels.
Mme. Olga Petrova, Mahlon Hamilton, Charles Martin, Violet Reed, Harry Burkhardt, Mary Sands, William B. Davidson, Anthony Merlo.
Is there one law for a woman and another for a man? That's the question raised at the trial of a young wife who shot her husband when she found him in the arms of another woman.

Morgan's Last Raid (MGM, 1929)
d: Nick Grinde. 6 reels.
Tim McCoy, Dorothy Sebastian, Wheeler Oakman, Allan Garcia, Hank Mann, Montague Shaw.
During the Civil War, a Tennesseean named Claibourne leads Morgan's raiders to rescue an abducted confederate lady.

Morgan's Raiders (Universal, 1918)
d: Bess Meredyth, Wilfred Lucas. 5 reels.
Violet Mersereau, Barbara Gilroy, Edward Burns, Frank Holland, William Cavanaugh.
Civil War tale of a courageous Confederate battalion known as "Morgan's Men."

Morganson's Finish (Tiffany Productions, 1926)
d: Fred Windemere. 7 reels.
Anita Stewart, Johnnie Walker, Mahlon Hamilton, Victor Potel, Crauford Kent, Rose Tapley.
In the frozen North, a prospector in love makes a rich strike but is harassed by a jealous romantic rival.

A Mormon Maid (Lasky Feature Plays/Friedman Enterprises, Inc., 1917)
d: Robert Leonard. 5 reels.
Mae Murray, Frank Borzage, Hobart Bosworth, Edythe Chapman, Noah Beery, Richard Cummings.
Anti-Mormon sentiment permeates this picture, which tells the story of a married man who is forced to marry a second wife, and his first wife's consequent suicide.

The Mortal Sin (Columbia/Metro, 1917)
d: John H. Collins. 5 reels.
Viola Dana, Robert Walker, Augustus Phillips, Lady Thompson, Henry Leone, Louis B. Foley, Ricca Allen.
When a struggling author completes a novel titled *The Mortal Sin*, about a woman who sacrifices her honor for the sake of her husband, little does he realize that the scenario will be played out in his own married life.

The Mortgaged Wife (Universal, 1918)

d: Allen Holubar. 6 reels.
Dorothy Phillips, William Stowell, Albert Roscoe, Sam DeGrasse, Edwin August.
Gloria loves her husband Ralph so much, she "mortgages" her honor to the bank president from whom Ralph has embezzled $50,000.

Mortmain (Vitagraph, 1915)
d: Theodore Marston. 5 reels.
Robert Edeson, Donald Hall, Edward Elkas, Joseph Weber, Muriel Ostriche, Karin Norman, James Morrison, J. Herbert Frank, Gladden James, Roland Osborne, Helen Pillsbury.
Mortmain's an art collector who gets talked into being used in an exotic experiment—the amputation of his hand in return for having another man's hand grafted in its place.

The Moth (Norma Talmadge Film Corp./Select, 1917)
d: Edward José. 6 reels.
Norma Talmadge, Hassard Short, Eugene O'Brien, Virginia Dare, Adolph Menjou, donald Hall, Maude Allen, Frank Kingdon, Robert Vivian, Kenneth Worms, Aida Armand.
Lucy's an heiress whose fortune-seeking husband is unfaithful to her.

Mother (R-C Pictures/FBO of America, 1927)
d: J. Leo Meehan. 7 reels.
Belle Bennett, Crauford Kent, William Bakewell, Joyce Coad, Mabel Julienne Scott, Sam Allen, Charlotte Stevens.
Melodrama about a middle-class American family, their struggles, their dreams, and the fruits of their success.

The Mother and the Law—see: Corruption (1917)

The Mother and the Law (D.W. Griffith, 1919)
w, d: D.W. Griffith. 7 reels.
Mae Marsh, Robert Harron, Miriam Cooper, Vera Lewis, Sam DeGrasse, Clyde Hopkins, Fred Turner, Walter Long, Tom Wilson, Ralph Lewis, Edward Dillon, A.W. McClure, Lloyd Ingraham, William Brown, Max Davidson, Alberta Lee, Margaret Marsh, Tod Browning.
The sister of a wealthy mill owner is persuaded to joining a reformers' group, where she is systematically abused and betrayed.
The Mother and the Law is a re-edited version of one of the episodes from Griffith's 1916 box office failure (but critical success), *Intolerance*.

The Mother Heart (Fox, 1921)
w, d: Howard M. Mitchell. 5 reels.
Shirley Mason, Raymond McKee, Edwin Booth Tilton, Cecil Van Auker, William Buckley, Peggy Eleanor, Mrs. Raymond Hatton, Lillian Langdon.
May, a girl whose mother is dead and whose father is in jail for stealing food for his family, is befriended by a grocer.

The Mother Instinct (Triangle, 1917)
d: Roy William Neil. 5 reels.
Enid Bennett, Rowland V. Lee, Margery Wilson, Tod Burns, Jack Gilbert, Gertrude Claire, Carl Ullman.
In Paris, an fashion model pretends to be the mother of her sister's illegitimate son.

Mother Knows Best (Fox, 1928)
d: John Blystone. 9 reels. (Music, sound effects.)
Madge Bellamy, Louise Dresser, Barry Norton, Albert Gran, Joy Auburn, Annette DeKirby, Stuart Erwin, Ivor DeKirby, Lucien Littlefield, Dawn O'Day.
A star-struck, ambitious mother drives her talented daughter through a career in show business, leading to Broadway stardom.

Mother Machree (Fox, 1928)
d: John Ford. 7 reels. (Music, sound effects.)
Belle Bennett, Neil Hamilton, Philippe DeLacy, Pat Somerset, Victor McLaglen, Ted McNamara, John MacSweeney, Eulalie Jensen, Constance Howard, Ethel Clayton, William Platt, Jacques Rollens, Rodney Hildebrand, Joyce Wirard, Robert Parrish.
In America, an Irish widow sacrifices everything for her son's happiness.

Mother o' Mine (Universal, 1917)
d: Rupert Julian. 5 reels.
Ruby La Fayette, Rupert Julian, Elsie Jane Wilson, Ruth Clifford, W.E. Warner.
A successful son rejects his elderly mother, but later repents.

Mother o' Mine (Thomas H. Ince/Associated Producers, 1921)
d: Fred Niblo. 7 reels.
Lloyd Hughes, Betty Ross Clark, Betty Blythe, Joseph Kilgour, Claire McDowell, Andrew Robson, Andrew Arbuckle.
In New York, a young man gets a position as a bank clerk, not knowing the boss is his own father, who deserted his family years before.

The Mother of His Children (Fox, 1920)
d: Edward J. LeSaint. 5 reels.
Gladys Brockwell, William Scott, Frank Leigh, Nigel deBrullier, Golda Madden, Nancy Caswell, Jean Eaton.
It's love at first sight when a foreign princess journeys to Paris and falls for a talented sculptor. Trouble is, he has a wife and children.

Motherhood (Mutual, 1917)
d: Frank Powell. 5 reels.
Marjorie Rambeau, Frank Ford, Robert Elliott, Paul Everton, Aubrey Beattie, Agnes Eyre, Ruth Byron, Lillian Page, Anne Sutherland, Frank Frayne, Robert Eaton, Lorna Volare.
When Albert, a World War I soldier, returns home, he is overjoyed that his wife has borne a son... until he learns that she was raped by an enemy soldier, and the child isn't Albert's.

A Mother's Confession (Ivan Film Productions, Inc., 1915)
w, d: Ivan Abramson. 5 reels.
Chrystine Mayo, Otto Kruger, Margaret Adair, Austin Webb, Carrie Reynolds, Sidney L. Mason, Ned Nye.
Louise, a widow, is forced to confess details of her past in order to stop her son's wedding. It seems the lad is unknowingly engaged to his half-sister.

Mothers-in-Law (B.P. Schulberg Productions/Preferred Pictures, 1923)
d: Louis Gasnier. 7 reels.
Ruth Clifford, Gaston Glass, Vola Vale, Crauford Kent, Josef Swickard, Edith Yorke, Doris Stone.
After a farm boy marries a city girl and they have a baby, his widowed mother comes to live with them.

Mothers of Men (Reid-Robards Pictures Co., 1917)
d: Willis Robards. 5 reels.
Willis Robards, Dorothy Davenport, Hal Reid, Katherine Griffith, Arthur Tavares, Billie Bennett, Marcella Russell, Harry Griffith, Grace Blake, George Utell.
Clara, a suffragette and a successful politician, is elected governor of her state, but it isn't entirely a happy situation.

Now she must decide whether to pardon her husband, on death row for a crime he didn't commit, or uphold her principles and let him die.

Mothers of Men (Edward José/Film Specials, Inc., 1920)
d: Edward José. 6 reels.
Claire Whitney, Lumsden Hare, Martha Mansfield, Miss E. Roma, Cesare Gravina, Arthur Donaldson, William Gaton, Zeffie Tilbury, Gaston Glass, Pierre Collosse, Julia Hurley.
During World War I, Marie, an Austrian girl, is raped by a Prussian officer and escapes to France. There, she falls in love with a Frenchman and they plan to be married. But before the wedding she discovers that one of the household's new servants is none other than the Prussian who abused her, in disguise.

A Mother's Ordeal (Van Dyke Film Production Co., 1917)
w, d: Will S. Davis. 5 reels.
Jean Sothern, Walter Miller, Alice May, Arthur Housman, Charles A. Boyd.
Deserted by her husband, a young woman drifts into life as a prostitute.

A Mother's Secret (Universal, 1918)
d: Douglas Gerrard. 5 reels.
Ella Hall, Mary Hirsch, Emory Johnson, T.D. Crittenden, Mrs. L.C. Harris, Grace McLean.
When a widowed English noblewoman moves to the United States and decides to remarry, she forces her 18-year-old daughter to dress as a child, to conceal the noblewoman's true age.

A Mother's Sin (Vitagraph, 1918)
d: Thomas R. Mills. 5 reels.
Earle Williams, Miriam Miles, Ernest Maupain, Denton Vane, Fred Peters, Louise DePre, Eleanor Lawson, Betty Blythe.
After a woman leaves her husband for another man, her son is disinherited by his father's family. In time, the lad will prove himself worthy of the family's trust.

Moulders of Men (R-C Pictures/FBO of America, 1927)
d: Ralph Ince. 7 reels.
Conway Tearle, Margaret Morris, Frankie Darro, Rex Lease, Eugene Pallette, Jola Mendez, William Knight.
A young man joins a gang running drugs in order to pay for an operation for his crippled brother.

Mountain Dew (Triangle, 1917)
d: Thomas N. Heffron. 5 reels.
Margery Wilson, Charles Gunn, Thomas Washington, Al W. Filson, Jack Richardson, Aaron Edwards, Mary Boland.
A city boy travels to the mountains to romance the daughter of a man who distills "mountain dew," also known as moonshine whiskey.

Mountain Madness (Lloyd Carleton Productions/Republic, 1920)
d: Lloyd Carleton. 5 reels.
Mignon Anderson, Harold Miller, Ora Carew, Edward Coxen, Stuart Morris, Jack Lott, Grace Pike, Alfred Allen, Edna Pennington.
Vacationing in mountain country, a young couple have a spat and separate... for a while.

The Mountain Woman (Fox, 1921)
d: Charles Giblyn. 6 reels.
Pearl White, Corliss Giles, Richard C. Travers, George Barnum, Warner Richmond, John Webb Dillon, Thornton Baston, Charles Graham.
Alexander, a girl with a boy's name, is raised by her father to be tough, to be prepared, and to assist in his   logging operation.

Mountains of Manhattan (Gotham Productions/Lumas Film Corp., 1927)
d: James P. Hogan. 6 reels.
Dorothy Devore, Charles Delaney, Kate Price, Bobby Gordon, George Chesebro, James P. Hogan, Clarence H. Wilson, Robert E. Homans.
Jerry, a former boxing champ, gets a job building skyscrapers and eventually takes over as foreman.

Mr. Barnes of New York (Vitagraph, 1914)
d: Maurice Costello, Robert Gaillord. 6 reels.
Maurice Costello, Mary Charleson, Darwin Karr, Naomi Childers, Adele De Garde, Robert Gaillord, William Humphrey, Charles Kent, S. Rankin Drew, Donald Hall.
Mr. Barnes of New York visits Corsica and Egypt, and is drawn into a murder mystery.

Mr. Barnes of New York (Goldwyn, 1922)
d: Victor Schertzinger. 5 reels.
Tom Moore, Anna Lehr, Naomi Childers, Lewis Willoughby, Ramon Samaniegos, Otto Hoffman, Sydney Ainsworth.
Remake of Vitagraph's 1914 *Mr. Barnes of New York*, both versions based on the novel of the same name by Archibald Clavering Gunter.

Mr. Billings Spends His Dime (Famous Players-Lasky/Paramount, 1923)
d: Wesley Ruggles. 6 reels.
Walter Hiers, Jacqueline Logan, George Fawcett, Robert McKim, Patricia Palmer, Joseph Swickard, Guy Oliver, Edward Patrick, Clarence Burton, George Field, Lucien Littlefield.
Comedy about a chap who falls madly in love with the face of a girl whose picture he sees on a cigar band. He travels to her country, just in time to aid her father, el presidente, fight off an imminent revolution.

Mr. Dolan of New York (Universal, 1917)
d: Raymond Wells. 5 reels.
Noble Johnson, Jack Mulhall, Julia Ray, Al MacQuarrie, Harry Mann, Ernest Shields, Francis MacDonald, Grace MacLean.
While in Europe, an American boxer accepts an offer to impersonate a prince.

Mr. Fix-It (Famous Players-Lasky/Artcraft Pictures, 1918)
d: Allan Dwan. 5 reels.
Douglas Fairbanks, Wanda Hawley, Marjorie Daw, Leslie Stuart, Ida Waterman, Alice Smith, Mrs. H.R. Hancock, Frank Campeau, Fred Goodwins, Margaret Landis.
"Mr. Fix-It," so named because he mends broken hearts, intervenes in an ill-begotten romance and sets the participants on correct paths. Then he finds a true love of his own.

Mr. Goode, the Samaritan (Fine Arts Film Co./Triangle, 1916)
d: Edward Dillon. 5 reels.
DeWolf Hopper, Fay Tincher, Edward Dillon, Chester Withey, Margaret Marsh, Lillian Langdon, Max Davidson.
Kindness begets kindness, after a goodhearted soul helps out a pair of ex-cons.

Mr. Grex of Monte Carlo (Lasky Feature Play

Co./Paramount, 1915)
d: Frank Reicher. 5 reels.
Theodore Roberts, Dorothy Davenport, Carlyle Blackwell, James Neill, Horace B. Carpenter, Frank Elliot, Jack McDermott, Bob Gray, Gertrude Kellar, Lucien Littlefield.
Foreign intrigue drama centering on the attempts of a Russian duke to involve France and Germany in a treaty alliance opposing England.

Mr. Logan, U.S.A. (Fox, 1918)
d: Lynn F. Reynolds. 5 reels.
Tom Mix, Kathleen Connors, Dick LaReno, Charles LeMoyne, Jack W. Dill, Val Paul.
In New Mexico, a tungsten mine operator tries to increase production to aid the U.S. war effort.

Mr. Opp (Universal, 1917)
d: Lynn Reynolds. 5 reels.
Arthur Hoyt, George Cheesboro, Neva Gerber, George Hernandez, Jack Curtis, Elsie Maison, Anne Lockhart, Jane Bernoudy.
Perpetually optimistic, Mr. Opp stares misfortune in the face and ends up a winner.

Mr. Wu (MGM, 1927)
d: William Nigh. 8 reels.
Lon Chaney, Louise Dresser, Ralph Forbes, Renee Adoree, Anna May Wong, Holmes Herbert, Gertrude Olmstead, Mrs. Wong Wing, Sonny Loy, Claude King.
A young Englishman loves a Chinese girl and wants to marry her, but her father is adamantly opposed to the union.

Mrs. Balfame (Mutual, 1917)
w, d: Frank Powell. 6 reels.
Nance O'Neil, Frank Belcher, Robert Elliott, Agnes Eyre, Anna Raines, Alfred Hickman, Grace Gordon, Aubrey Beattie, Elsie Earle.
Deeply impressed by a raging feminist's tirade against men, Mrs. Balfame plots to murder her husband.

Mrs. Dane's Defense (Famous Players/Paramount, 1918)
d: Hugh Ford. 5 reels.
Pauline Frederick, Frank Losee, Leslie Austen, Maude Turner Gordon, Ormi Hawley, John L. Shine, Ida Darling, Cyril Chadwick, Amelia Summerville, Frank Kingdon, Howard Hall.
Left an inheritance by her Canadian cousin Mrs. Dane, an Englishwoman decides to take her cousin's name and break into British society.

Mrs. Leffingwell's Boots (Select, 1918)
d: Walter Edwards. 5 reels.
Constance Talmadge, Harrison Ford, George Fisher, Fred Goodwin, Mercedes Temple, Vera Doria, Herbert Prior, Julia Faye.
There's a merry marital mixup when a jealous husband believes his wife is being unfaithful to him with his friend. The reason: Her fancy new shoes are identical to a pair worn by his friend's maid.

Mrs. Plum's Pudding (Universal, 1915)
d: Al E. Christie. 5 reels.
Marie Tempest, W. Graham Brown, Eddie Lyons, Violet MacMillan.
A widow becomes a millionaire overnight when oil is discovered on her ranch.

Mrs. Slacker (Astra Film Corp./Pathé, 1918)
d: Hobart Henley. 5 reels.
Gladys Hulette, Creighton Hale, Paul Clerget, Walter Hiers.
During World War I, a coward marries Susie, a washer woman, in order to escape the draft. When she learns of his reasons, Susie declares that she will not be a "Mrs. Slacker," and decides to aid the war effort herself.

Mrs. Temple's Telegram (Famous Players-Lasky/Paramount, 1920)
d: James Cruze. 5 reels.
Bryant Washburn, Wanda Hawley, Carmen Phillips, Walter Hiers, Sylvia Ashton, Leo White, Anne Schaefer, Edward Jobson.
There are comedic mixups galore, when a jealous wife suspects her husband of flirting with a glamorous vamp.

Mrs. Wiggs of the Cabbage Patch (California Motion Picture Corp./World Film Corp., 1914)
d: Harold Entwhistle. 5 reels.
Beatriz Michelena, Blanche Chapman, Andrew Robson, House Peters, LaBelle Carmen, Belle Bennett, William Pike.
Lovey Mary, an adorable orphan girl, is mistreated by her carnival owner foster father. When Mary sees her chance, she flees with Tommy, the son of the circus' bareback rider, and they seek refuge in Mrs. Wiggs' cabbage patch.

Mrs. Wiggs of the Cabbage Patch (Famous Players-Lasky/Paramount, 1919)
d: Hugh Ford. 5 reels.
Marguerite Clark, Mary Carr, Gareth Hughes, Gladys Valerie, Vivia Ogden, May McAvoy, Robert Milash.
Lovey Mary, a teenage orphan, lovingly looks after the younger children in the orphanage. Trouble develops when a surly young woman—a "graduate" of the orphanage—drops off her baby son Tommy at the institution. Lovey Mary and the boy form a close friendship and life is good—until word comes that the wayward mother is coming back to claim her boy. In an impulsive burst of courage, Lovey Mary and Tommy bolt to freedom, finding refuge at the Wiggs' cabbage farm.
Remake of the 1914 *Mrs. Wiggs of the Cabbage Patch*, both films based on the novel by Alice Hegan Rice.

The Mummy and the Humming Bird (Famous Players/Paramount, 1915)
d: James Durkin. 5 reels.
Charles Cherry, Lillian Tucker, Arthur Hoops, William Sorelle, Claire Zobelle, Charles Coleman, Nina Lindsey.
Obsessed with his laboratory projects, a scientist unwittingly drives his neglected wife into the arms of another man.

The Music Master (Fox, 1927)
d: Allan Dwan. 8 reels.
Alec B. Francis, Lois Moran, Neil Hamilton, Norman Trevor, Charles Lane, William T. Tilden, Helen Chandler, Marcia Harris, Kathleen Kerrigan, Howard Cull, Armand Cortez.
Anton, a formerly renowned orchestra conductor, leaves his post to search for his long-lost daughter. Working as a music teacher, he finally finds his daughter when she comes to his studio seeking music lessons.

Must We Marry? (Trinity Pictures, 1928)
d: Frank S. Mattison. 6 reels.
Pauline Garon, Lorraine Eason, Bud Shaw, Vivian Rich, Edward Brownell, Louise Carver, Charles Hall, Thomas A. Curran.
Thelma, a gold digging vamp, tries to win the heart of Kenneth, a wealthy but attached young man.

A Mute Appeal (Van Dyke Films/Art Dramas, Inc., 1917)

d: Walter Edwin. 5 reels.
Jean Sothern, Donald Cameron, Tom Magrane, Elsie Mason.
Faith's a country girl raised by deaf-mute parents. When she travels to New York, she meets a sympathetic soul who will introduce Faith to a world she's never known.

Mutiny (Universal, 1917)
d: Lynn Reynolds. 5 reels.
Myrtle Gonzales, Val Paul, George Hernandez, Jack Curtis, Fred Harrington, E.J. Brady.
Esther, a ship owner's daughter, becomes pregnant and is thought to be a dishonored lady. But she's secretly married.

The Mutiny of the Elsinore (C.E. Shurtleff, Inc./Metro, 1920)
d: Edward Sloman. 6 reels.
Mitchell Lewis, Helen Ferguson, Noah Beery Jr., Casson Ferguson, William V. Mong, Norval MacGregor, Sidney D'Albrook, J.P. Lockney.
Mutineers try to commandeer a ship during a storm.

My American Wife (Famous Players-Lasky/Paramount, 1922)
d: Sam Wood. 6 reels.
Gloria Swanson, Antonio Moreno, Josef Swickard, Eric Mayne, Gino Corrado, Edythe Chapman, Aileen Pringle, Walter Long, F.R. Butler, Jacques D'Auray, Loyal Underwood.
Love blossoms between a Kentucky girl and an Argentinean.

My Best Girl (Pickford/United Artists, 1927)
d: Sam Taylor. 9 reels.
Mary Pickford, Charles "Buddy" Rogers, Lucien Littlefield, Sunshine Hart, Carmelita Geraghty, Hobart Bosworth, Evelyn Hall, Mack Swain.
A scion of wealth decides to work incognito in his father's store, and falls for a charming clerk. She loves him too, but there's a problem: Her family is overly dependent on her, and she's reluctant to leave them.

My Boy (Jackie Coogan Productions/Associated First National, 1921)
d: Victor Herman, Albert Austin. 5 reels.
Jackie Coogan, Claude Gillingwater, Methilde Brundage.
A runaway orphan joins an old sea captain.

My Country First (Terriss Film Corp., 1916)
d: Tom Terriss. 6 reels.
Tom Terriss, Helene Ziegfield, John Hopkins, Alfred Heming, Joseph Baker, Joseph Sterling, Jill Woodward, Harold Vosburgh, A.B. Thaw.
Foreign agents try to steal an inventor's new formula for a powerful explosive device.

My Cousin (Famous Players-Lasky/Artcraft, 1918)
d: Edward José. 5 reels.
Enrico Caruso, Henry Leone, Carolina White, Joseph Ricciardi, A.G. Corbelle, Bruno Zirato, William Bray.
In New York, a poor but honorable sculptor claims to be related to a famous opera tenor.

My Fighting Gentleman (American Film Co./Mutual, 1917)
d: Edward Sloman. 5 reels.
William Russell, Francelia Billington, Charles Newton, Jack Vosburgh, Clarence Burton, Harry Von Meter, William Carroll, Sid Algier, Lucille Ward.
Though ostracized by his own people, a southerner who sided with the North in the Civil War decides to run for

senator from Virginia.

My Four Years in Germany (First National, 1918)
d: William Nigh. 9 reels.
Halbert Brown, William Daschiell, Earl Schenck, George Kiddell, Frank Stone, Karl Dane, Fred Herd, Percy Standing, William Bittner, James Gerard (as himself).
Documentary-style patriotic film, based on U.S. Ambassador James Gerard's dealings with the German Kaiser. Much real-life footage made it into the film, including scenes of uncommon brutality and violence.

My Friend From India (DeMille Pictures/Pathé, 1927)
d: E. Mason Hopper. 6 reels.
Franklin Pangborn, Elinor Fair, Ben Hendricks Jr., Ethel Wales, Jeanette Loff, Tom Ricketts, Louis Natheaux, Tom Dugan, George Ovey, Edgar Norton.
William, a wealthy playboy, falls for a girl he met overseas.

My Friend, the Devil (Fox, 1922)
d: Harry Millarde. 8 reels.
Charles Richman, Ben Grauer, William Tooker, Adolph Milar, John Tavernier, Myrtle Stewart, Barbara Castleton, Alice May, Peggy Shaw, Robert Frazer, Mabel Wright.
Dryden, a surgeon who's also an atheist, cherishes his daughter. When the girl becomes critically ill, he tries everything in his power to heal her. Failing, he finally appeals to God to save her life.

My Home Town (Trem Carr Productions/Rayart, 1928)
d: Scott Pembroke. 6 reels.
Gladys Brockwell, Gaston Glass, Violet LaPlante, Carl Stockdale, Henry Sedley, William Quinn, Ruth Cherrington, Frank Clark.
A fugitive from justice falls in love with the honest sister of a gangster.

My Husband's Other Wife (J. Stuart Blackton Features/Pathé, 1920)
d: J. Stuart Blackton. 6 reels.
Sylvia Breamer, Robert Gordon, Warren Chandler, May McAvoy, Fanny Rice.
Adelaide's an actress whose fierce pursuit of a career alienates her husband. He divorces her, then remarries. Now Adelaide wants him back.

My Husband's Wives (Fox, 1924)
d: Maurice Elvey. 5 reels.
Shirley Mason, Bryant Washburn, Evelyn Brent, Paulette Duval.
Young Mrs. Harvey invites an old friend for a visit, not realizing that the friend was Mr. Harvey's first wife.

My Lady Friends (Carter DeHaven Productions/Associated First National, 1921)
d: Lloyd Ingraham. 6 reels.
Carter DeHaven, Mrs. Carter DeHaven, Thomas G. Lingham, Helen Raymond, Helen Lynch, Lincoln Stedman, May Wallace, Hazel Howell, Clara Morris, Ruth Ashby.
Marital comedy about a nouveau riche publisher with a super-thrifty wife.

My Lady Incog. (Famous Players/Paramount, 1916)
d: Sidney Olcott. 5 reels.
Hazel Dawn, George Majeroni, Robert Cain, Dora Mills Adams, Franklyn Hanna, Frank Wunderlee.
Posing as a baroness, a lady detective tries to outwit some society thieves.

My Lady of Whims (Dallas M. Fitzgerald

Productions/Arrow, 1926)
d: Dallas M. Fitzgerald. 7 reels.
Clara Bow, Donald Keith, Carmelita Geraghty, Francis McDonald, Lee Moran.
A girl's father hires a detective to follow her and keep her out of trouble.

My Lady's Garter (Famous Players-Lasky/Paramount, 1920)
d: Maurice Tourneur. 5 reels.
Wyndham Standing, Sylvia Breamer, Holmes E. Herbert, Warner Richmond, Paul Clerget, Warren Cook, Louise Derigney, Charles Craig.
After a fabled jeweled garter is stolen from a museum, Secret Service agents and international crooks collide in a frantic search for the culprit.

My Lady's Latchkey (Katherine MacDonald Pictures/Associated First National, 1921)
d: Edwin Carewe. 6 reels.
Katherine MacDonald, Edmund Lowe, Claire DuBrey, Howard Gaye, Lenore Lynard, Thomas Jefferson, Helena Phillips.
Anne, a newlywed, discovers that her husband is a jewel thief.

My Lady's Lips (B.P. Schulberg Productions, 1925)
d: James P. Hogan. 7 reels.
Clara Bow, Alyce Mills, William Powell, Frank Keenan, Ford Sterling, John Sainpolis, Gertrude Short, Matthew Betz, Sojin Kamamura.
Scott, a newspaper reporter, poses as a crook to infiltrate a gang and get a scoop. But he didn't count on falling in love with Dora, the beautiful gang leader.

My Lady's Past (Tiffany-Stahl Productions, 1929)
d: Albert Ray. 9 reels. (Music, sound effects, part talkie.)
Belle Bennett, Joe E. Brown, Alma Bennett, Russell Simpson, Joan Standing, Billie Bennett, Raymond Keane.
Long-engaged sweethearts Sam and Mamie finally decide to marry. First, though, they suffer a number of mishaps until, in the final reel, Sam storms a wedding party to save Mamie from marrying somebody else.

My Lady's Slipper (Vitagraph, 1916)
d: Ralph W. Ince. 5 reels.
Anita Stewart, Earle Williams, Joseph Kilgour, Julia Swayne Gordon, Harry Northrup, George O'Donnell, Albert Roccardi, Charles Chapman, George Stevens.
In the 18th century, a cad tries to compromise a countess by obtaining her slipper and displaying it.

My Little Boy (Universal, 1917)
d: Elsie Jane Wilson. 5 reels.
Ella Hall, Zoe Rae, Emory Johnson, Winter Hall, Harry Holden, Gretchen Lederer.
In a variant on Dickens' A Christmas Carol, a spiteful old man comes to his senses just in time to wish everyone a Merry Christmas.

My Little Sister (Fox, 1919)
d: Kenean Buel. 5 reels.
Evelyn Nesbit, Leslie Austen, Lillian Hall, Kempton Greene, Lyster Chambers, Herbert Standing, Caroline Lee, Amelia Summerville, Ben Hendricks, Louise Rial, Martha Mayo.
Two sisters on their way to London are intercepted and taken to a brothel instead.

My Madonna (Metro, 1915)

d: Alice Blaché. 5 reels.
Mme. Olga Petrova, Guy Coombs, Evelyn Dumo, Albert Howson, James O'Neill, Albert Derbil, Yahne Fleury.
Inspired to paint a portrait of the Madonna, an artist chooses a wealthy prostitute for a model because he believes she radiates the ideal countenance. The finished painting is a huge success, and it changes the lives of both artist and model.

My Man (Vitagraph, 1924)
d: David Smith. 7 reels.
Patsy Ruth Miller, Dustin Farnum, Niles Welch, Margaret Landis, George Webb, William Norris, Edith Yorke, Violet Palmer, Sidney DeGrey.
Sledge, an alderman, loves Molly, but she's engaged to marry a ne'er-do-well who's only after her money. So Sledge kidnaps Molly on her wedding day and arranges for her father's investments to turn sour. Feeling betrayed, the unworthy fiancé cancels the wedding, while Molly plans to marry Sledge, who restores her father's bank account.

My Man (Warner Bros., 1928)
d: Archie Mayo. 7 reels. (Music, sound effects, part talkie.)
Fanny Brice, Guinn Williams, Edna Murphy, André DeSegurola, Richard Tucker, Billy Seay, Arthur Hoyt, Ann Brody, Clarissa Selwynne.
Fanny, a girl who works in theatrical costuming, loves Joe, and they plan to be married. But what's this? Fanny finds Joe kissing her coquettish sister, and angrily calls off the wedding. But they'll be together again by the final reel.

My Neighbor's Wife (Clifford S. Elfelt Productions, 1925)
d: Clarence Geldert. 6 reels.
E.K. Lincoln, Helen Ferguson, Edwards Davis, Herbert Rawlinson, William Russell, William Bailey, Chester Conklin, Tom Santschi, Mildred Harris, Douglas Gerard, Philippe DeLacy.
Jack, a struggling film director, borrows $40,000 from his girlfriend's dad to finance his picture.

My Official Wife (Vitagraph, 1914)
d: James Young. 5 reels.
Clara Kimball Young, Harry T. Morey, Earle Williams, L. Roger Lytton, Rose E. Tapley, Mary Anderson, Arthur Cozine, Eulalie Jensen, Charles Wellesley, Louise Beaudet.
In Russia, a traveling American allows a mysterious woman to pose as his wife, not knowing that she intends to assassinate the Czar.

My Official Wife (Warner Bros., 1926)
d: Paul Stein. 8 reels.
Irene Rich, Conway Tearle, Gustav von Seyffertitz, Jane Winton, Stuart Holmes, John Miljan, Emile Chautard, Sidney Bracey.

An aristocratic lady dresses as a peasant girl for a masquerade party, but is kidnapped on her way to the affair. Her abductors treat her shabbily, but incredibly, she falls in love with one of them.

My Old Dutch (Universal, 1915)
d: Larry Trimble. 5 reels.
Albert Chevalier, Florence Turner, Henry Edwards.
An elderly couple are rescued from the poorhouse by their successful son.

My Old Dutch (Universal, 1926)
d: Lawrence Trimble. 8 reels.
May McAvoy, Pat O'Malley, Jean Hersholt, Cullen Landis,

Patsy O'Byrne, Edgar Kennedy, Frank Crane, Rolfe Sedan, Violet Kane, Kathleen O'Malley, Sheila O'Malley, Jane Winton, George Siegmann.
Remake of Universal's own 1915 film *My Old Dutch*.

My Old Kentucky Home (Pyramid Pictures/American Releasing Corp., 1922)
d: Ray C. Smallwood. 7 reels.
Monte Blue, Julia Swayne Gordon, Frank Currier, Sigrid Holmquist, Arthur Carew, Lucy Fox, Matthew Betz, Billy Quirk, Pat Hartigan, Tom Blake.
Richard, unjustly convicted of another's crime, serves his time and is released. He returns to his mother's home and helps groom her prize filly to win the Kentucky Derby.

My Own Pal (Fox, 1926)
d: J.G. Blystone. 5 reels.
Tom Mix, Olive Borden, Tom Santschi, Virginia Marshall, Bardson Bard, William Colvin, Virginia Warwick, Jay Hunt, Hedda Nova, Tom McGuire, Helen Lynch.
Tom, a cowboy in the big city, gets a job on the police force and rescues a kidnapped young lady.

My Own United States (Frohman Amusement Corp./Metro, 1918)
d: John W. Noble. 8 reels.
Arnold Daly, Charles E. Graham, Duncan McRae, Sidney Bracey, P.R. Scammon, Thomas Donnelly, James Levering, Edward Dunn, Claude Cooper, William V. Miller, Frederick Truesdell, Anna Lehr, Helen Mulholland, J.A. Furey, Mary Kennevan Carr.
Thunderingly patriotic version of Edward Everett Hale's "The Man Without a Country," updated to include 20th-century scenes involving Philip Nolan IV, descendant of the novel's eponymous hero.

My Son (First National, 1925)
d: Edwin Carewe. 7 reels.
Alla Nazimova, Jack Pickford, Hobart Bosworth, Ian Keith, Mary Akin, Constance Bennett, Charles A. Murray, Dot Farley.
In New England, the quiet atmosphere of a fishing village is disrupted when a wealthy woman and her vampish flapper daughter come to town, angling for men.

My Unmarried Wife (Universal, 1917)
d: George Siegmann. 5 reels.
Carmel Myers, Kenneth Harlan, Beatrice Van, Patrick Calhoun, Mark Fenton, Jack Hutchinson.
Blinded in an explosion, a young writer learns that only a very delicate and expensive operation can restore his sight. His doctor's nurse has fallen in love with him, and offers to finance the operation if he agrees to marry her immediately. He agrees, they marry, and the operation is a success. But now that the writer has his sight back, his wife has disappeared—and he doesn't even know what she looks like. Will they find each other again?

My Wife (Empire All-Star Corp./Mutual, 1918)
d: Dell Henderson. 5 reels.
Ann Murdock, Rex MacDougal, Hubert Druce, Amy Veness, Ferdinand Gottschalk, Grace Carlyle, Carl Sautermann, Harriet Thompson, Romaine Callender, Dudley Hill.
Beatrice stands to inherit a million dollars, but alas: The will stipulates that she must be married in order to claim the inheritance, and Bea's beau is off in France, fighting the Germans. So she arranges to marry a friend instead, collect the inheritance, and he agrees to divorce her as soon as

Sweetie returns. Trouble is, once they're married, Bea's new husband starts to grow on her.

My Wife and I (Warner Bros., 1925)
d: Millard Webb. 7 reels.
John Harron, Constance Bennett, Irene Rich, Huntly Gordon, John Roche, Tom Ricketts, Claire de Lorez.
A father and his son are rivals for the same girl.

My Wild Irish Rose (Vitagraph, 1922)
d: David Smith. 7 reels.
Pat O'Malley, Helen Howard, Maud Emery, Pauline Starke, Edward Cecil, Henry Hebert, James Farley, Bobby Mack, Frank Clark, Richard Daniels.
Robert, an Irish villager, is framed on trumped-up evidence and imprisoned. His friend helps him to escape, and Robert returns to his village in time to rescue his sweetheart Rose from the attack of the man who framed him.

The Mysterious Client (Astra/Pathé, 1918)
d: Fred Wright. 5 reels.
Irene Castle, Milton Sills, Warner Oland, Caesar Gravina, Helene Chadwick.
Dramedy serves up a ladleful of hi-jinks when a beautiful woman hires a lawyer and leads him into a maze of twists and complications.

The Mysterious Island (MGM, 1929)
w, d: Lucien Hubbard. 10 reels. (Part talkie, part Technicolor.)
Lionel Barrymore, Jane Daly, Lloyd Hughes, Montagu Love, Gibson Gowland, Dolores Brinkman.
A 19th century nobleman creates a submarine that takes him and his party of adventurers to a hidden, underwater city.
Part talkie, part color version of the famous Jules Verne tale.

The Mysterious Lady (MGM, 1928)
d: Fred Niblo. 9 reels.
Greta Garbo, Conrad Nagel, Gustav von Seyffertitz, Albert Pollet, Edward Connelly, Richard Alexander.
Karl, an Austrian officer, falls in love with Tania, the Russian spy who betrayed him.

The Mysterious Miss Terry (Famous Players/Paramount, 1917)
d: J. Searle Dawley. 5 reels.
Billie Burke, Thomas Meighan, Walter Hiers, Gerald O. Smith, George A. Wright, Bessie Hearn.
Mavis Terry is a real mystery: A wealthy heiress who pretends she is a tenement dweller, too poor to pay her rent.

The Mysterious Mr. Tiller (Universal, 1917)
d: Rupert Julian. 5 reels.
Ruth Clifford, Frank Brownlee, Wedgewood Nowell, Rupert Julian, Harry Rattenberry, E.A. Warren, Lloyd Whitlock, William Higby.
Police detectives track a jewel thief known as "the Face."

The Mysterious Mrs. M (Universal, 1917)
d: Lois Weber. 5 reels.
Harrison Ford, Evelyn Selbie, Mary MacLaren, Willis Marks, Frank Brownlee, Bertram Grassby, Charles H. Mailes.
Mrs. M is a fortune teller, or so she says. Actually, she's an actress hired by an unhappy man's friends to cheer him up.

The Mysterious Rider (Paramount, 1927)
d: John Waters. 6 reels.
Jack Holt, Betty Jewel, Charles Sellon, David Torrence, Tom Kennedy, Guy Oliver, Albert Hart, Ivan Christie, Arthur Hoyt.

THE MYSTERIOUS LADY (1928). Greta Garbo, perhaps the most carnally erotic of all silent film actresses, is cast as Tania, a bewitching Russian spy who ensnares an Austrian captain (Conrad Nagel) in her web of deceit. The film opts for a happy ending, though, and by the fadeout Tania and her captain are playing for the same team—*his*.

* * * * *

In Old California, a mysterious rider helps homesteaders withstand the treachery of land pirates.

The Mysterious Stranger (Carlos Productions/FBO of America, 1925)
d: Jack Nelson. 6 reels.
Richard Talmadge, Joseph Swickard, Carmelita Geraghty, Sheldon Lewis, Duane Thompson, Bert Bradley, Robert Carleton.
A young man who has led a sheltered life all his 21 years walks in his sleep one night and discovers the world and the love of a young woman.

The Mystery Club (Universal, 1926)
d: Herbert Blache. 7 reels.
Matt Moore, Edith Roberts, Mildred Harris, Charles Lane, Warner Oland, Henry Herbert, Charles Puffy, Alphonse Martell, Finch Smiles, Earl Metcalf, Nat Carr, Jed Prouty, Alfred Allen.
A secret organization made up of millionaires makes a bet among its members that the perfect crime can be committed by one of them.

The Mystery Girl (Famous Players-Lasky/Paramount, 1918)
d: William C. DeMille. 5 reels.
Ethel Clayton, Henry Woodward, Clarence Burton, Charles West, Winter Hall, Mayme Kelso, Parks Jones.
In World War I, a small European country is overrun by the Germans, who install a puppet ruler. The new ruler covets Countess Therese, niece of the deposed monarch—but Therese escapes and lends her services as an ambulance driver in France, where she falls in love.

The Mystery of Number 47 (Selig Polyscope, 1917)
d: Otis B. Thayer. 5 reels.
Ralph Herz, Nellie Hartley, Louiszita Valentine, Edgar Murray Jr., James Fulton, Fred Eckhart, Casson Ferguson, Lloyd Sedgwick, Tony West, May White, Mrs. Wiggin.
Scotland Yard is called in to investigate the disappearance of a model citizen's wife and cook, both of whom appear to be victims of foul play. But the whole thing's a hoax.

The Mystery of the Yellow Room (Mayflower Photoplay Corp./Realart, 1919)
w, d: Emile Chautard. 6 reels.
William S. Walcott, Edmund Elton, George Cowl, Ethel Grey Terry, Lorin Raker, Jean Gauthier, W.H. Burton, Henry S. Koser, Jean Ewing, William Morrison, Louis Grisel.
Police detectives seem baffled by a case in which a young woman is attacked in her yellow room, and her scientist father's formulas stolen. The doors and windows were all locked and protected by iron bars... so how did the intruder escape?

Mystery Valley (Trem Carr Productions, 1928)
d: J.P. McGowan. 5 reels.
Buddy Roosevelt, Carol Lane, Tommy Bay, Jimmy Kane, Art Rowlands.
Out West, the son of a murdered rancher finds that his dad was killed by a greedy gambler after gold was discovered on the property.

The Mystic (MGM, 1925)
d: Tod Browning. 7 reels.
Aileen Pringle, Mitchell Lewis, Conway Tearle, Gladys Hulette, Robert Ober, Stanton Heck, David Torrence, DeWitt Jennings.
An heiress' guardian schemes to get control of her fortune by means of fake seances.

Mystic Faces (Triangle, 1918)
d: E. Mason Hopper. 5 reels.
Jack Abbe, Martha Taka, Larry Steers, Clara Morris, Liu Chung, W.H. Bainbridge.
In Chinatown, a charming delivery boy rescues an American woman from German spies.

The Mystic Hour (Apollo Pictures, Inc./Art Dramas, Inc., 1917)
d: Richard Ridgely. 5 reels.
Alma Hanlon, Charles Hutchinson, John Sainpolis, Florence Short, Helen Strickland.
Freud's influence is felt in this film, in which a young man who dreams he murdered the husband of the woman he loves is forced to interpret his dream.

Naked Hearts (Universal, 1916)
d: Rupert Julian. 5 reels.
Francelia Billington, Zoe Bech, Jack Holt, Douglas Gerrard, Gordon Griffith, Rupert Julian, George Hipp, Ben Horning, Paul Weigle, Nanine Wright.
Childhood sweethearts grow up and are separated by war.

Name the Man (Goldwyn, 1924)
d: Victor Seastrom. 8 reels.
Mae Busch, Conrad Nagel, Hobart Bosworth, Creighton Hale, Patsy Ruth Miller, Winter Hall, Aileen Pringle, DeWitt Jennings, Evelyn Selbie, Mark Fenton, Anna Hernandez, Mrs. Charles Craig, Cecil Holland, Lucien Littlefield, William Orlamond, Charles Mailes.
On the Isle of Man, a judge is forced to try a young unmarried woman for infanticide.

Name the Woman (Columbia, 1928)
d: Erle C. Kenton. 6 reels.
Gaston Glass, Anita Stewart, Huntly Gordon, Chappell Dossett, Julanne Johnston, Jed Prouty.
A man on trial for murder is acquitted at court when the woman he was with on the night of the killing testifies on his behalf. Because the woman in question is the wife of the prosecuting attorney, she will have a lot to answer for; but even her husband admits she did the right thing by stepping forward to free an innocent man.

Nameless Men (Tiffany-Stahl Productions, 1928)
d: Christy Cabanne. 6 reels.
Claire Windsor, Antonio Moreno, Eddie Gribbons, Ray Hallor, Charles Clary, Carolynne Snowden, Sally Rand, Stepin Fetchit.
After a man is convicted of robbery and goes to prison, a detective poses as a fellow convict in order to learn from the thief the whereabouts of the loot.

Nan of Music Mountain (Lasky Feature Plays/Paramount, 1917)
d: George H. Melford. 5 reels.
Wallace Reid, Anna Little, Theodore Roberts, James Cruze, Charles Ogle, Raymond Hatton, Hart Hoxie, Guy Oliver, James P. Mason, Henry Woodward, Ernest Joy, Alice Marc.
Out West, the war between a stagecoach line and a band of armed robbers heats up when the stage line's general manager falls in love with Nan, daughter of the outlaw chief.

Nancy Comes Home (Triangle, 1918)
d: Jack Dillon. 5 reels.
Myrtle Lind, George Pierce, Myrtle Rishell, Eugene Burr, Anna Dodge, Percy Challenger, Jack Gilbert, J.P. Wild.

Nancy wants to enter society, so she pawns her mother's jewels to buy the necessary clothes.

Nancy From Nowhere (Realart Pictures/Paramount, 1922)
d: Chester M. Franklin. 5 reels.
Bebe Daniels, Edward Sutherland, Vera Lewis, James Gordon, Myrtle Stedman, Alberta Lee, Helen Holly, Dorothy Hagan.
Halliday, a scion of wealth, finds a slavey named Nancy and feels compelled to save her from her drudgery.

Nancy's Birthright (Signal Film Corp./Mutual, 1916)
d: Murdock MacQuarrie. 5 reels.
Murdock MacQuarrie, Edythe Sterling, Norbert A. Myles, Millard K. Wilson, V.T. Henderson, Belle Hutchinson, Antrim Short, F.M. Van Norman, Walter Rogers.
Multiple handkerchief weeper about a girl who elopes against her father's wishes, only to learn that her new husband is a brute.

Nanette of the Wilds (Famous Players/Paramount, 1916)
d: Joseph Kaufman. 5 reels.
Pauline Frederick, Willard Mack, Macey Harlan, Charles Brandt, Frank Joyner, Daniel Pennell, Wallace MacDonald, Jean Stewart, Robert Conville.
Nanette, daughter of the leader of a gang of smugglers, falls in love with the Canadian Mountie who's investigating the gang's illegal activities.

Nanook of the North (Revillion Fréres/United Artists, 1922)
w, d: Robert J. Flaherty. 6 reels.
Nanook, Nyla, Allee, Cunayou, Comock.
Documentary about Eskimo life in the Far North.

The Narrow Path (Universal, 1916)
d: Francis J. Grandon. 5 reels.
Violet Mersereau, Lenora Von Ottinger, Niles Welch, William J. Welsh, Nellie Slattery, Anthony Merlo, Clara Beyers, Joseph Girard, George Gardner.
Tenement dweller Bessie has brains, talent, and beauty... and they lead her to a career on Broadway.

The Narrow Path (Astra/Pathé, 1918)
d: George Fitzmaurice. 5 reels.
Fannie Ward, W.E. Lawrence, Irene Aldwyn, Sam DeGrasse, Mary Alden, Antrim Short.
Marion the manicurist is named co-respondent in a divorce suit. But it's all a mistake, as she's only covering for a friend. Cleared of all suspicion, Marion wins her one true love.

The Narrow Street (Warner Bros., 1925)
d: William Beaudine. 7 reels.
Matt Moore, Dorothy Devore, David Butler, Russell Simpson, Gertrude Short, Kate Toncray, Mademoiselle Sultewan.
A milquetoast bachelor is dismayed to find that a pretty lady has taken up residence in his home.

The Narrow Trail (William S. Hart/Artcraft Pictures Corp., 1917)
d: Lambert Hillyer. 5 reels.
William S. Hart, Sylvia Breamer, Milton Ross, Robert Kortman.
"Ice" Harding, a charming jewel thief, falls in love with Betty, who he believes is a society girl. But Betty's not what she appears to be. When "Ice" finds her performing as a dancer in a waterfront saloon, the barriers between them are removed, and they begin a new life together.

The Nation's Peril (Lubin, 1915)
d: George Terwilliger. 5 reels.
Ormi Hawley, William H. Turner, Earl Metcalfe, Eleanor Barry, Arthur Matthews, Herbert Fortier.
Defiantly anti-war, Ruth angrily rejects her U.S. Navy lieutenant fiancé when he uncovers his new invention, an aerial torpedo. Soon, she is being courted by a smooth-talking stranger who asks questions about the lieutenant's invention and wants to locate the plans for the new weapon. Her new beau, it turns out, is a foreign spy.

The Natural Law (France Films, Inc., 1917)
d: Charles H. France. 7 reels.
Marguerite Courtot, Howard Hall, George Larkin, Jack Ellis, Charles H. France, Lila Blow, Gordon Gray, Leah Peck.
Though engaged to an older man, young Ruth falls for an athlete and they conceive a child. Now the question is, should she get an abortion?

The Nature Girl (Universal, 1918)
d: O.A.C. Lund. 5 reels.
Violet Mersereau, Donald Stewart, Señorita de Cordoba, Frank Wonderly.
Under a cloud of mystery, an American girl lives with her guardian on a South American island.

Naughty Baby (First National, 1929)
d: Mervyn LeRoy. 7 reels. (Music, sound effects.)
Jack Mulhall, Alice White, Benny Rubin, Andy Devine, Georgie Stone, Thelma Todd, Doris Dawson, Natalie Joyce, Frances Hamilton, Fred A. Kelsey, Rose Dione, Raymond Turner, Jay Eaton.
Comedy about a hatcheck girl who pursues a wealthy playboy.

Naughty But Nice (John McCormick Productions/First National, 1927)
d: Millard Webb. 7 reels.
Colleen Moore, Donald Reed, Claude Gillingwater, Kathryn McGuire, Hallam Cooley, Edythe Chapman, Clarissa Selwynne, Burr McIntosh.
After oil is discovered on the family's property, a plain Jane decides to upgrade her appearance, and blossoms forth as a ravishing beauty.

The Naughty Duchess (Tiffany-Stahl Productions, 1928)
d: Tom Terriss. 6 reels.
Eve Southern, H.B. Warner, Duncan Renaldo, Maude Turner Gordon, Gertrude Astor, Martha Mattox, Herbert Evans.
Hortense, a beauty on the lam from the law, takes refuge in the train compartment of a duke and pleads with him to protect her.

Naughty Nanette (R-C Pictures/FBO of America, 1927)
d: James Leo Meehan. 5 reels.
Viola Dana, Patricia Palmer, Edward Brownell, Helen Foster, Joe Young, Sidney DeGray, Alphonse Martel, Mary Gordon, Florence Wix, Barbara Clayton.
Nanette, a Hollywood extra, takes in a poor girl who's been thrown out of her home by her heartless grandfather. To help her new friend, Nanette decides to vamp Grandpa.

Naughty, Naughty! (Thomas H. Ince Corp./Paramount, 1918)
d: Jerome Storm. 5 reels.
Enid Bennett, Earl Rodney, Marjorie Bennett, Cloria Hope, Andrew Arbuckle.
Roberta's a small-town girl who returns from a visit to the big city with a fresh, modern attitude that scandalizes the

folks back home.

The Naulahka   (Astra/Pathé, 1918)
d: George Fitzmaurice. 6 reels.
Antonio Moreno, Doraldina, Helene Chadwick, J.H. Gilmour, Warner Oland, Mary Alden, Edna Hunter.
Exotic tale of an adventurer who travels to India to obtain a precious jewel known as the Naulahka.

The Navigator   (MGM, 1924)
d: Buster Keaton, Donald Crisp. 6 reels.
Buster Keaton, Kathryn McGuire, Frederick Vroom, Noble Johnson, Clarence Burton, H.M. Clugston.
Keaton plays a dim-bulb millionaire who finds himself adrift on a ship. He thinks he's the only one on board, but there's also a girl... and she thinks she's alone, too.

The Near Lady   (Universal, 1923)
d: Herbert Blache. 5 reels.
Gladys Walton, Jerry Gendron, Hank Mann, Kate Price, Otis Harlan, Florence Drew, Emmett King, Henrietta Floyd.
Wealthy young Basil and the butcher's daughter Nora pretend to be in love to please their parents. What the youngsters don't realize is that they really are falling in love.

Nearly a King   (Famous Players/Paramount, 1915)
d: Frederick Thomson. 5 reels.
John Barrymore, Catherine Harris, Russell Bassett, Beatrice Prentice, Martin Alsop, Fred McGuirk, Adolphe Menjou.
Whimsical tale about a prince who's in love with a dancer, but is facing an arranged marriage to a princess he doesn't love.

Nearly a Lady   (Bosworth, Inc./Paramount, 1915)
d: Hobart Bosworth. 5 reels.
Elsie Janis, Frank Elliott, Owen Moore, Myrtle Stedman, Harry Ham, Roberta Hickman.
Frederica is fascinated by an elegant swell named Lord Cecil, but her heart is with a cowboy named Jack.

Nearly Married   (Goldwyn, 1917)
d: Chester Withey. 5 reels.
Madge Kennedy, Frank Thomas, Mark Smith, Alma Tell, Richard Barthelmess, Hedda Hopper.
Betty and Harry are in love and they marry, but before the honeymoon can begin, a misunderstanding causes her to file for divorce.

'Neath Western Skies   (J.P. McGowan Productions/Syndicate Pictures, 1929)
d: J.P. McGowan. 5 reels.
Tom Tyler, Hank Bell, Harry Woods, J.P. McGowan, Bobby Dunn, Lotus Thompson, Alfred Huston, Barney Furey.
Out West, the owner of oil property finds his drilling has been sabotaged, and he sets out to get the bad guys and win the girl.

The Necessary Evil   (First National, 1925)
d: George Archainbaud. 7 reels.
Ben Lyon, Viola Dana, Frank Mayo,1 Thomas Holding, Gladys Brockwell, Mary Thurman, Betty Jewel, Martha Madison, Arthur Housman, Beach Cooke.
Seeking what is best for the young man, a guardian sends his ward to a remote island to temper his recklessness.

Nedra   (Pathé, 1915)
d: Edward José. 5 reels.
George Probert, Fania Marinoff, Margaret Greene, Crawford Kent.
Engaged to be married, Hugh and Grace board a yacht to take a cruise. After a sudden storm tosses the ship about, Hugh is washed up on a desert island with a young woman who isn't his intended.

The Ne'er-Do-Well   (Selig Polyscope, 1916)
d: Colin Campbell. 10 reels.
Wheeler Oakman, Kathlyn Williams, Harry Lonsdale, Frank Clark, Norma Nichols, Will Machin, Jack McDonald, Sidney Smith, Fred Huntley, Lamar Johnstone, Harry DeVere.
Kirk, a former football hero, is shanghaied aboard a steamer bound for Panama.

The Ne'er-Do-Well   (Famous Players-Lasky/Paramount, 1923)
d: Alfred E. Green. 8 reels.
Thomas Meighan, Lila Lee, Gertrude Astor, John Miltern, Gus Weinberg, Sid Smith, George O'Brien, Jules Cowles, Laurance Wheat, Cyril Ring.
Remake of the 1916 Selig film *The Ne'er-Do-Well*, both films based on the novel of the same name by Rex Beach.

Neighbors   (World Film Corp., 1918)
d: Frank Crane. 5 reels.
Madge Evans, Johnny Hines, Violet Palmer, J.A. Furey, Maxine Elliott Hicks, Mathilde Brundage, Herbert Pattee, Kitty Johnson, Frank Beamish, Charles Hartley, Anthony Merlo.
Ruth's in love with the boy next door, but his status-conscious mother wants him to marry a socialite.

Nellie, the Beautiful Cloak Model   (Goldwn, 1924)
d: Emmett Flynn. 7 reels.
Claire Windsor, Betsy Ann Hisle, Edmund Lowe, Mae Busch, Raymond Griffith, Lew Cody, Hobart Bosworth, Lilyan Tashman, Dorothy Cumming, Will Walling, Mayme Kelso, William Orlamond, Arthur Housman, David Kirby.
Nellie, an orphan, is taken in by a kind man and grows up to become a beautiful fashion model.

Neptune's Daughter   (Universal, 1914)
d: Herbert Brenon. 7 reels.
Annette Kellerman, William Welsh, William E. Shay, Edmund Mortimer, Lewis Hooper, Francis Smith, Leah Baird, Herbert Brenon, Katherine Lee, Millie Liston.
A daughter of King Neptune falls in love with a mortal.

Nero   (Fox, 1922)
d: J. Gordon Edwards. 12 reels.
Jacques Gretillat, Alexander Salvini, Guido Trento, Enzo DeFelice, Nero Bernardi, Adolfo Trouche, Nello Carolenuto, Americo DeGiorgio, Paulette Duval, Edy Darclea, Violet Mersereau, Lina Talba.
Spectacular historical drama chronicles the rise to power of Nero, his infatuation with a young Christian girl, and her love for a Roman tribune.

The Nervous Wreck   (Christie Film Co./Producers Distributing Corp., 1926)
d: Scott Sidney. 7 reels.
Harrison Ford, Phyllis Haver, Chester Conklin, Mack Swain, Hobart Bosworth, Paul Nicholson, Vera Steadman, Charles Gerrard, Clarence Burton.
Farcical comedy about a chap who believes he's dying, and goes West for his health.

The Nest   (Excellent Pictures, 1927)
d: William Nigh. 8 reels.
Holmes Herbert, Thomas Holding, Pauline Frederick, Ruth Dwyer, Reginald Sheffield, Rolland Flander, Jean Acker,

Wilfred Lucas.

A widow tries to manage her boisterous children—a "jazz age" son and daughter—but it's a losing proposition, until her late husband's best friend enters the picture.

The Net (Thanhouser, 1916)
d: George Foster Platt. 5 reels.
Bert Delaney, Marion Swayne, Inda Palmer, Ethel Jewett, Arthur Bauer, Morgan Jones.
A fisherman falls in love with a woman who has washed ashore.

The Net (Fox, 1923)
d: J. Gordon Edwards. 7 reels.
Barbara Castleton, Raymond Bloomer, Albert Roscoe, Peggy Davis, William H. Tooker, Helen Tracy, Eliah Nadel, Claire DeLorez, Arthur Gordini, Alexander Gaden, Byron Douglas.
Fleeing the scene of his crime, a murderer runs into an amnesiac stranger and switches identities with him.

Nevada (Famous Players-Lasky/Paramount, 1927)
d: John Waters. 7 reels.
Gary Cooper, Thelma Todd, Philip Strange, William Powell, Ernie S. Adams, Christine J. Frank, Ivan Christy, Guy Oliver.
A cowpoke and his pal go after cattle rustlers.

Never Say Die (Douglas MacLean Productions/Associated Exhibitors, 1924)
d: George J. Crone. 6 reels.
Douglas MacLean, Lillian Rich, Helen Ferguson, Hallam Cooley, Lucien Littlefield, Tom O'Brien, Wade Boteler, Eric Mayne, William Conklin, George Cooper.
Comedy about a chap whose doctors mistake the sound of buzzing bees for heart murmurs, and give him only three months to live.

Never Say Quit (Fox, 1919)
d: Edward Dillon. 5 reels.
George Walsh, Florence Dixon, Henry Holland, William Frederic, Frank Jacobs, Joe Smiley, Jean Acker.
Adventure mixes with comedy in this tale of an unlucky loser with a life history of failure and disappointment. But he hangs in there, and finally gets lucky when he saves a millionaire from would-be kidnappers, and wins the heart of the millionaire's daughter.

Never the Twain Shall Meet (Cosmopolitan/MGM, 1925)
d: Maurice Tourneur. 8 reels.
Anita Stewart, Huntley Gordon, Bert Lytell, Justine Johnstone, Georghe Siegmann, Lionel Belmore, William Norris, Emily Fitzroy, Marie de Bourbon, Florence Turner.
A South Seas girl travels to San Francisco and falls for an American.

New Brooms (Famous Players-Lasky/Paramount, 1925)
d: William DeMille. 6 reels.
Neil Hamilton, Bessie Love, Phyllis Haver, Robert McWade, Fred Walton, Josephine Crowell, Larry Steers, James Neill.
When a broom manufacturer's son criticizes the old man's business methods, Papa lets the youngster take over the business for a year.

The New Champion (Columbia, 1925)
d: Reeves Eason. 5 reels.
Frank Hagney, William Fairbanks, Edith Roberts, Lotus Thompson, Lloyd Whitlock, Al Kaufman, Marion Court, Bert Apling.
A substitute fighter enters a championship fight, and wins.

The New Commandment (First National Pictures, 1925)

d: Howard Higgin. 7 reels.
Blanche Sweet, Ben Lyon, Holbrook Blinn, Clare Eames, Effie Shannon, Dorothy Cumming, Pedro DeCordoba, George Cooper, Diana Kane, Lucius Henderson, Betty Jewel.
Billy, an American in Paris, falls in love with Renée, an artist's model.

The New Disciple (Federation Film Corp., 1921)
d: Ollie Sellers. 6 reels.
Pell Trenton, Alfred Allen, Norris Johnson, Margaret Mann, Walt Whitman, Alice H. Smith, Arthur Stuart Hull, Walter Perkins, Charles Prindley.
Fanning, a businessman, is nearly ruined by a workers' strike, but is saved when the workers agree to buy him out.

The New Klondike (Famous Players-Lasky/Paramount, 1926)
d: Lewis Milestone. 8 reels.
Thomas Meighan, Lila Lee, Paul Kelly, Hallie Manning, Robert Craig, George DeCarlton, J.W. Johnston, Brenda Lane, Tefft Johnson, Danny Hayes.
Animosity between a ballplayer and his manager force them both to make sacrifices.

New Lives For Old (Famous Players-Lasky/Paramount, 1925)
d: Clarence Badger. 7 reels.
Betty Compson, Wallace MacDonald, Theodore Kosloff, Sheldon Lewis, Jack Joyce, Margaret Seddon, Joseph Dowling, Helen Dunbar, Gale Henry, Marvel Quivey, Ed Faust.
In the aftermath of World War I, an American captain marries a girl he believes to be a French peasant, but she turns out to have been a secret agent in the service of France.

New Love For Old (Universal, 1918)
d: Elsie Jane Wilson. 5 reels.
Ella Hall, Emory Johnson, Gretchen Lederer, Winter Hall, E.A. Warren, Harry Holden.
Disheartened when the woman he loves deserts him, Scott wanders to a small village and falls in love again... not realizing this girl is the sister of the woman he lost.

The New Moon (Norma Talmadge Film Corp./Select, 1919)
d: Chester Withey. 6 reels.
Stuart Holmes, Norma Talmadge, Pedro de Cordoba, Charles Gerard, Stuart Holmes, Marc McDermott, Ethel Kaye, Harry Sothern, Marguerite Clayton.
In a Balkan country, the new dictator decrees that all unmarried young women must be registered with the state. In reality, he's trying to locate the princess of the deposed regime, who has gone undercover as a shopkeeper.

The New School Teacher (C.C. Burr Pictures, 1924)
d: Gregory LaCava. 6 reels.
Doris Kenyon, Charles "Chic" Sale, Mickey Bennett, Russell Griffin, Freddy Strange, Kent Raymond, Henry O'Connor, Edward Weisman, Edward Quinn.
When a schoolteacher rescues a child from a burning building and becomes a hero, his students change their attitudes toward him.

The New Teacher (Fox, 1922)
d: Joseph Franz. 5 reels.
Shirley Mason, Allan Forrest, Earl Metcalf, Otto Hoffman, Ola Norman, Pat Moore, Kate Price.
Constance, a socialite, takes a job as a schoolteacher in a poor section of New York.

New Toys (Inspiration Pictures/First National, 1925)
d: John S. Robertson. 8 reels.
Richard Barthelmess, Mary Hay, Katherine Wilson, Clifton Webb, Francis Conlon, Bijou Fernandez, Tammany Young, Pat O'Connor, Jules Jordon, Jacob Kingsbury.
Newlyweds find their life together disrupted by the arrival of the husband's ex-sweetheart.

New Year's Eve (Fox, 1929)
d: Henry Lehrman. 7 reels. (Music, sound effects.)
Mary Astor, Charles Morton, Earle Foxe, Florence Lake, Arthur Stone, Helen Ware, Freddie Frederick, Jane LaVerne, Sumner Getchell, Stuart Erwin, Virginia Vance.
Marjorie, an innocent, goes to work for a gambler, sees him murdered, then finds herself accused of the crime.

New York (Pathé, 1916)
d: George Fitzmaurice. 5 reels.
Florence Reed, Fania Marinoff, Jessie Ralph, John Miltern, Forrest Winant.
In New York, a businessman takes in a boy who has lost his mother, because the man believes the lad to be his own son.

New York (Famous Players-Lasky/Paramount, 1927)
d: Luther Reed. 7 reels.
Ricardo Cortez, Lois Wilson, Estelle Taylor, Norman Trevor, Richard Skeets Gallagher, William Powell, Margaret Quimby, Lester Scharff, Charles Byers.
Old friends find their loyalties tested when one of them accidentally kills a girl and her "murder" is attributed to someone else.

The New York Idea (Realart Pictures Corp., 1920)
d: Herbert Blaché. 6 reels.
Alice Brady, Lowell Sherman, Hedda Hopper, George Howell, Lionel Pape, Margaret Linden, Edwards Davis, Harry Hocky, Nina Herbert, Emily Fitzroy, Julia Hurley, Marie Burke.
Socialites John and Cynthia quarrel constantly, and when Cynthia catches her husband in an innocent flirtation, she is quick to file divorce papers. But can this divorce last?

New York Luck (American Film Co./Mutual, 1917)
d: Edward Sloman. 5 reels.
William Russell, Francelia Billington, Harvey Clark, Clarence Burton, Edward Peil, Alfred Ferguson, Frederick Vroom, Carl Stockdale.
Nick, an ambitious writer, concocts a wild story in which he tells of meeting a mysterious beauty, impersonating a British nobleman, then getting involved with jewel thieves. Against all odds, the story impresses a movie director, who buys the script and hires Nick as his new scriptwriter.

The New York Peacock (Fox, 1917)
d: Kenean Buel. 5 reels.
Valeska Suratt, Harry Hilliard, Eric Mayne, Alice Gale, Claire Whitney, W.W. Black, John Mackin, Frank Goldsmith.
Cautionary tale about a young man who is lured into the world of gambling and loses all his money.

The News Parade (Fox, 1928)
d: David Butler. 7 reels.
Nick Stuart, Sally Phipps, Brandon Hurst, Cyril Ring, Earle Foxe, Franklin Underwood, Truman Talley.
Nick, a newsreel photographer, averts a kidnapping and gets the footage besides.

The Next Corner (Famous Players-Lasky/Paramount, 1924)

d: Sam Wood. 7 reels.
Conway Tearle, Lon Chaney, Dorothy Mackaill, Ricardo Cortez, Louise Dresser, Remea Radzina, Dorothy Cumming, Bertha Feducha, Bernard Seigel.
In Paris, a neglected wife turns to a nobleman for love.

Nice People (Famous Players-Lasky/Paramount, 1922)
d: William DeMille. 7 reels.
Wallace Reid, Bebe Daniels, Conrad Nagel, Julia Faye, Claire McDowell, Edward Martindel, Eve Southern, Bertram Jones, William Boyd, Ethel Wales.
Known as "Teddy" to her friends, Theodora is one of a group of jazz-age "nice people"—meaning she flirts, but doesn't let a fellow get past first base. One night Teddy meets a chap who wants to hit a home run.

The Night Bird (Universal, 1928)
d: Fred Newmeyer. 7 reels.
Reginald Denny, Betsy Lee, Sam Parker, Harvey Clark, Corliss Palmer, Jocelyn Lee, Alphonse Martel, George Bookasta, Michael Visaroff.
Davis, a light heavyweight boxer, meets a young woman in Central Park and they fall in love. Later, when Davis is in the ring taking a beating from a superior opponent, the young woman's brother shows up at ringside and tells the boxer that she is being forced to marry another man. That turns the tide. Davis quickly kayos his opponent, then rushes to the girl's side, stops the wedding, and steps in for the groom.

The Night Bride (Metropolitan Pictures/Producers Distributing Corp., 1927)
d: E. Mason Hopper. 6 reels.
Harrison Ford, Franklin Pangborn, Marie Prevost, Robert Edeson, Richard Crawford, George Kuwa.
When a flapper's roadster gets into a fender bender with the auto driven by a handsome woman hater, the sparks fly. But as things turn out, the sparks ignite their love.

The Night Club (Famous Players-Lasky/Paramount, 1925)
d: Frank Urson, Paul Iribe. 6 reels.
Raymond Griffith, Vera Reynolds, Wallace Beery, Louise Fazenda.
A professed woman-hater is stung by Cupid's arrow, but is rejected by the object of his affection. He considers suicide, but in the end the lady consents to marry him after all.

The Night Cry (Warner Bros., 1926)
d: Herman Raymaker. 7 reels.
Rin-Tin-Tin, June Marlowe, Don Alvarado, John Harron, Gayne Whitman, Heinie Conklin, Mary Louise Miller.
A dog is accused of killing sheep and, under the law of the range, must be destroyed. But the clever animal discovers the real killer, a giant condor, and rescues a child it has stolen.

The Night Flyer (James Cruze, Inc./Pathé, 1928)
d: Walter Lang. 7 reels.
William Boyd, Jobyna Ralston, Philo McCullough, Ann Schaeffer, DeWitt Jennings, John Milerta, Robert Dudley.
A locomotive fireman gets the chance to engineer the mail train through rugged territory.

The Night Hawk (Stellar Productions/W.W. Hodkinson, 1924)
d: Stuart Paton. 6 reels.
Harry Carey, Claire Adams, Joseph Girard, Fred Malatesta, Nicholas DeRuiz.
Out West, a mysterious thief known as "the Night Hawk"

falls in love with the sheriff's daughter and decides to mend his ways.

The Night Horsemen   (Fox, 1921)
w, d: Lynn F. Reynolds.   5 reels.
Tom Mix, May Hopkins, Harry Lonsdale, Joseph Bennett, Sid Jordan, Bert Sprotte, Cap Anderson, Lon Poff, Charles K. French.
Out West, a man known as Whistling Dan gets into a saloon fight and wounds his opponent. He stays to tend to the man's wounds, though Dan is warned that his opponent's brother is trailing him with vengeance in mind.

Night Life   (Tiffany Productions, 1927)
d: George Archainbaud.   7 reels.
Alice Day, Johnny Harron, Eddie Gribbon, Walter Hiers, Lionel Braham, Kitty Barlow, Dawn O'Day, Mary Jane Irving, Audrey Sewell, Earl Metcalf, Lydia Yeamans Titus.
In postwar Vienna, a gentleman thief meets a young woman who has been reduced by poverty to picking pockets, and they fall in love.

Night Life of New York   (Paramount, 1925)
d: Allan Dwan.   8 reels.
Rod LaRocque, Dorothy Gish, Helen Lee Worthling, Ernest Torrence, George Hackathorne, Riley Hatch, Arthur Housman.
A big-city telephone operator yearns for the wide open spaces, then meets a young man from the plains of Iowa.

The Night Message   (Universal, 1924)
d: Perley Poore Sheehan.   5 reels.
Howard Truesdale, Gladys Hulette, Charles Cruz, Margaret Seddon, Norman Rankow, Robert Gordon, Edgar Kennedy, Joseph W. Girard.
During a country feud, a telephone operator accidentally shoots a member of the Lefferts clan.

The Night of Love   (Goldwyn/United Artists, 1927)
d: George Fitzmaurice.   8 reels.
Ronald Colman, Vilma Banky, Montague Love, Natalie Kingston, Sally Rand, John George, Laska Winter.
A gypsy bandit out for revenge against a villainous duke steals the duke's bride from him on his wedding night.

A Night of Mystery   (Paramount, 1928)
d: Lothar Mendes.   6 reels.
Adolphe Menjou, Evelyn Brent, Nora Lane, William Collier Jr., Raoul Paoli, Claude King, Frank Leigh, Margaret Burt.
In France, an army captain pays a surreptitious visit to his former sweetheart, who has married another. As he leaves, he chances upon a murder in progress but is prevented from reporting it, for fear that the killer may have seen him exiting his ex-sweetheart's apartment. The captain then learns that an innocent man has been accused of the murder.

The Night Patrol   (Richard Talmadge Productions/FBO of America, 1926)
d: Noel Mason Smith.   6 reels.
Richard Talmadge, Rose Blossom, Mary Carr, Art Conrad, Gardner James, Josef Swickard, Grace Darmond, Victor Dillingham.
A police officer goes undercover to infiltrate a gang he suspects of murdering another officer.

The Night Riders   (Samuelson Film Mfg. Co./Second National Pictures, 1920)
d: Alexander Butler.   5 reels.
Maudie Dunham, Albert Ray, Andrea Beaulieu, Russell Gordon, Jose delaCruz.
In the Canadian northwest, a gang called "the Night Riders" is led by Red Mask, a man who is blind by day but sees clearly at night.

The Night Rose   (Goldwyn, 1921)
d: Wallace Worsley.   6 reels.
Leatrice Joy, Lon Chaney, John Bowers, Cullen Landis, Richard Tucker, Mary Warren, Edythe Chapman, Betty Schade, Maurice B. Flynn, H. Milton Ross, John Cossar.
In a fashionable San Francisco night spot, a young woman is horrified to see a policeman gunned down. She and her escort is later implicated in the D.A.'s investigation because of the young man's underworld connections.

The Night Ship   (Gotham Productions/Lumas Film Corp., 1925)
w, d: Henry McCarthy.   6 reels.
Mary Carr, Tom Santschi, Robert Gordon, Margaret Fielding, Charles A. Sellon, Willis Marks, Charles W. Mack, Mary McLane, L.J. O'Connor, Julian Rivero.
A seaman returns from the South Seas and finds that his sweetheart has married a drug smuggling sea captain.

The Night Watch   (Warner Bros., 1928)
d: Alexander Korda.   7 reels.   (Music, sound effects.)
Paul Lukas, Billie Dove, Donald Reed, Nicholas Soussanin, Anita Garvin, Gustav Partos, Nicholas Bela.
A ship's captain faces court-martial after shooting one of his own crew.

The Night Workers   (Essanay, 1917)
d: J. Charles Haydon.   5 reels.
Marguerite Clayton, Jack Gardner, Julien Barton, Mabel Bardine, Arthur W. Bates.
Clyde's a youngster who works long hours as an office boy, and to relieve the pressure, he turns to drinking. He soon meets Ethel, a young woman who persuades him to give up the bottle and join her as co-editor on the newspaper she has inherited.

The Nightingale   (All Star Feature Corp./Alco Film Corp., 1914)
d: Augustus Thomas.   5 reels.
Ethel Barrymore, William Courtleigh Jr., Frank Andrews, Conway Tearle, Charles A. Stevenson, Irving Brooks, Mario Majeroni, Philip Hahn, Ida Darling, Bobby Stewart.
In Ethel Barrymore's film debut, she plays Isola, a street singer who rises to the rank of star at the Metropolitan opera.

Nina, the Flower Girl   (Fine Arts Film Co./Triangle, 1917)
d: Lloyd Ingraham.   5 reels.
Bessie Love, Elmer Clifton, Bert Hadley, Loyola O'Connor, Alfred Paget, Fred Warren, Adele Clifton, Rhea Haines, Jennie Lee.
Nina's a blind girl who sells artificial flowers on street corners. She's poor, but she has a "protector" — Jimmy, the crippled newsboy who's in love with her.

Nine and Three-fifths Seconds   (A.G. Steen, 1925)
d: Lloyd B. Carleton.   6 reels.
Charles Paddock, Helen Ferguson, George Fawcett, Jack Giddings, Peggy Schaffer, G. Raymond Nye, Otis Harlan.
Disowned by his father, a former college athlete becomes a hobo and starts riding the rails. He is saved by the love of a good woman who encourages him to develop his running skills—so much so, in fact, that he runs in the Olympics and sets a new world record.

Charles Paddock was, in real life, the 100-meter champion at the 1920 Olympic Games.

A Nine O'Clock Town (Thomas H. Ince/Paramount, 1918)
d: Victor L. Schertzinger. 5 reels.
Charles Ray, Jane Novak, Otto Hoffman, Gertrude Claire, Catherine Young, Dorcas Matthews, Milton Ross, Melbourne MacDowell, Caroline "Spike" Rankin.
A small-town boy goes to New York to seek his fortune. He runs afoul of con artists in the big city, and returns home to manage his dad's store—but the con artists will follow him there, too.

Nine Points of the Law (Rainbow Film Co., 1922)
d: Wayne Mack. 6 reels.
Helen Gibson, Edward Coxen, Leo Maloney, Aggie Herring.
In a western town, an orphan child is adopted by a dance hall girl.

Nine-Tenths of the Law (North Woods Producing Co./Balboa Amusement, 1918)
w, d: Reaves Eason. 6 reels.
Mitchell Lewis, Jimsy Maye, Reaves Eason, Breezy Reeves, Julius Frankenburg, Molly Shafer.
Kidnappers abduct a small boy, but he escapes and is found by a childless married couple who want to keep him.

Nineteen and Phyllis (Charles Ray Pictures/Associated First National, 1920)
d: Joseph DeGrasse. 6 reels.
Charles Ray, George Nichols, Cora Drew, Clara Horton, Frank Norcross, Lincoln Stedman.
Andrew, a poor but honest clerk, loves Phyllis.

The Ninety and Nine (Vitagraph, 1916)
d: Ralph W. Ince. 5 reels.
Lucille Lee Stewart, William Courtenay, Josephine Lovett, Frank Currier, William Lytell, William Dangman.
Abner, a respected farmer, mistakenly believes his daughter is having an affair with a local workman, and turns her out of his house. But Abner will have a lot to apologize for, when his daughter and the workman return and save his life when his farmhouse catches fire.

The Ninety and Nine (Vitagraph, 1922)
d: David Smith. 7 reels.
Warner Baxter, Colleen Moore, Lloyd Whitlock, Gertrude Astor, Robert Dudley, Mary Young, Arthur Jasmine, Ernest Butterworth, Aggie Herring, Dorothea Wolbert, Rex Hammel.
Remake of Vitagraph's own 1916 production *The Ninety and Nine*, both versions based on the play of the same name by Ramsay Morris.

Niobe (Famous Players/Paramount, 1915)
d: Hugh Ford, Edwin S. Porter.
Hazel Dawn, Charles Abbe, Maude Odell, Marie Leonard, Leigh Denny, Irene Haisman, Wilmuth Merkyl.
When a businessman obtains a valuable statue of Niobe, of Greek mythology fame, he is so fascinated by it that the statue comes to life for him. Or is it only a dream?

No Children Wanted (Oakdale Productions/General Film Co., 1918)
d: Sherwood MacDonald. 5 reels.
Gloria Joy, Ethel Ritchie, R. Henry Grey, Edward Jobson, Neil Hardin, Daniel Gilfether, H.E. Archer, Ruth Lackaye, Edward Saunders.
Uncaring parents pack off their young daughter to boarding school, so they can move into a fashionable apartment complex that doesn't permit children.

No Control (Metropolitan Pictures, 1927)
d: Scott Sidney, E.J. Babille. 6 reels.
Harrison Ford, Phyllis Haver, Jack Duffy, Tom Wilson, Tony Claude, E.J. Ratcliffe, Larry Steers.
A young businessman falls for a circus owner's daughter and together—with the help of a dancing horse—they revive the show's flagging appeal and make it a success.

No Defense (Vitagraph, 1921)
d: William Duncan. 6 reels.
William Duncan, Edith Johnson, Jack Richardson, Henry Hebert, Mathilde Brundage, Charles Dudley.
Melodrama about a young woman who marries an up-and-coming lawyer although she still loves her first husband, who is missing and may be alive.

No Defense (Warner Bros., 1929)
d: Lloyd Bacon. 7 reels. (Music, sound effects, part talkie.)
Monte Blue, May McAvoy, Kathryn Carver, William Desmond, Lee Moran, William Tooker.
To shield the miscreant's aged father from shock, a construction foreman takes the blame for a bridge collapsing, even though his partner was responsible.

The No-Good Guy (New York Motion Picture Corp./Triangle, 1916)
d: Walter Edwards. 5 reels.
William Collier, Enid Markey, Charles K. French, Robert Kortman, J. Frank Burke, Walter Edwards.
A carefree bachelor opens a detective agency, but his heart isn't in it—until one day, while working on a case, he falls in love with Lucia, one of the gang members he's investigating.

No Man's Gold (Fox, 1926)
d: Lewis Seiler. 6 reels.
Tom Mix, Eva Novak, Frank Campeau, Forrest Taylor, Harry Grippe, Malcolm Waite, Mickey Moore, Tom Santschi.
Out West, Tom and his sidekick find a dying miner, who gives them a map to his lost gold mine.

No Man's Land (Metro, 1918)
d: William S. Davis. 5 reels.
Bert Lytell, Anna Q. Nilsson, Charles Arling, Mollie McConnell, Eugene Pallette, Edward Alexander, Sydney Deane.
When his girlfriend is kidnapped by a German spy and taken to a remote island, intrepid Garrett follows them, determined to rescue her.

No Man's Law (Hal Roach/Pathé, 1928)
d: Fred Jackman. 7 reels.
Theodore von Eltz, Barbara Kent, Oliver Hardy, James Finlayson.
Desert hoodlums plot to murder an aging miner and his stepdaughter.

No More Women (United Artists, 1924)
d: Lloyd Ingraham. 6 reels.
Matt Moore, Madge Bellamy, Kathleen Clifford, Stanhope Wheatcroft, George Cooper, Clarence Burton, George Cooper, H. Reeves-Smith.
Following a heartbreaking experience, a bachelor swears off women forever. But he hasn't counted on the tenacity of a certain waitress who fancies him.

No Mother to Guide Her (Fox, 1923)
d: Charles Horan. 7 reels.

Genevieve Tobin, John Webb Dillon, Lolita Robertson, Katherine Downer, Dolores Rousse, Frank Wunderlee, Maude Hill, Ruth Sullivan, J.D. Walsh, Jack Richardson.

Kathleen and Donald marry in secret, then she has a baby. But Kathleen is shocked to discover that the clergyman who officiated at their wedding was a phony, and the marriage is null and void.

No Other Woman (Fox, 1928)
d: Lou Tellegen. 6 reels.
Dolores Del Rio, Don Alvarado, Ben Bard, Paulette Duval, Rosita Marstini, André Lanoy.

Carmelita, a South American heiress, marries in haste, then discovers that her new husband is a fortune hunter.

No Place to Go (First National, 1927)
d: Mervyn LeRoy. 7 reels.
Lloyd Hughes, Mary Astor, Hallam Cooley, Virginia Lee Corbin, Myrtle Stedman, Jed Prouty, Russell Powell.

Minor comedy about newlyweds who unknowingly visit an island that's inhabited by cannibals.

No Trespassing (Holtre Productions/W.W. Hodkinson, 1922)
d: Edwin L. Hollywood. 7 reels.
Irene Castle, Howard Truesdale, Emily Fitzroy, Ward Crane, Eleanor Barry, Blanche Frederici, Charles Eldridge, Leslie Stowe, Betty Bouton, Al Roscoe, Harry Fisher.

In a Cape Cod fishing village, a local landowner permits the townspeople to use a lane across his property. But when he becomes desperate for funds, he considers selling the land to a developer who may shut off the public's right of way.

No Woman Knows (Universal, 1921)
d: Tod Browning. 7 reels.
Bernice Radom, Raymond Lee, Earl Schenck, Max Davidson, Snitz Edwards, Grace Marvin, Danny Hoy, E.A. Warren, Joseph Swickard, Richard Cummings, Joseph Sterns.

Small-town girl Fanny sacrifices so that her young brother can study the violin.

Noah's Ark (Warner Bros., 1928)
d: Michael Curtiz. 11 reels. (Music, part talkie.)
Dolores Costello, George O'Brien, Noah Beery, Louise Fazenda, Paul McAllister, Guinn Williams, Myrna Loy, Malcolm Waite, Nigel DeBrulier, Anders Randolf, Armand Kaliz.

The Biblical story is retold paralleling a World War I romance.

Ambitious spectacle film told in epic style, with massive sets and special effects to depict the great flood.

Nobody (Roland West Productions/Associated First National, 1921)
w, d: Roland West. 7 reels.
Jewel Carmen, William Davidson, Kenneth Harlan, Florence Billings, J. Herbert Frank, Gracer Studiford, George Fawcett, Lionel Pape, Henry Sedley, Ida Darling, Charles Wellesley.

Intriguing mystery drama about a wealthy man found murdered in his study. His butler is accused of the crime and brought to trial. But one of the jurors knows for a fact that the butler is innocent.

Nobody Home (Famous Players-Lasky/Paramount, 1919)
d: Elmer Clifton. 5 reels.
Dorothy Gish, Ralph Graves, Raymond Cannon, Vera McGinnis, George Fawcett, Emily Chichester, Rodoph Valentine, Norman McNeil, Kate V. Toncray, Porter Strong.

In this romantic comedy, Miss Gish plays Frances, a

superstitious woman who lives her life by following signs, omens, and astrological predictions. Even when she gets married, she postpones the wedding night because the stars aren't right!

Nobody's Bride (Universal, 1923)
d: Herbert Blache. 5 reels.
Herbert Rawlinson, Edna Murphy, Alice Lake, harry Van Meter, Frank Brownlee, Sidney Bracey, Phillips Smalley, Robert Dudley, Lillian Langdon.

Doris is engaged to marry Jimmy, but jilts him. Then she becomes engaged to another man and jilts him also.

Nobody's Fool (Universal, 1921)
d: King Baggot. 5 reels.
Marie Prevost, Helen Harris, R. Henry Guy, Vernon Snively, Percy Challenger, Harry Myers, George Kuwa, Lucretia Harris, Lydia Yeamans Titus.

College girl Polly is considered unattractive until the day she inherits a half million dollars. Now she's got suitors springing out of the woodwork.

Nobody's Kid (Robertson-Cole, 1921)
d: Howard Hickman. 5 reels.
Mae Marsh, Kathleen Kirkham, Anne Schaefer, Maxine Elliott Hicks, John Steppling, Paul Willis.

Mary, a parentless girl mistreated by the orphanage matron, learns the identity of her father and contacts his brother. Her uncle, rejoicing that he has a niece he didn't know about, rescues her from the orphanage and brings her home to live with him.

Nobody's Money (Famous Players-Lasky/Paramount, 1923)
d: Wallace Worsley. 6 reels.
Jack Holt, Wanda Hawley, Harry Depp, Robert Schable, Walter McGrail, Josephine Crowell, Julia Faye, Charles Clary, Will R. Walling, Clarence Burton, Aileen Manning.

When Webster, the manager of the governor's reelection campaign, discovers that bribe money has been planted in the governor's safe, he steals it. Now nobody will claim the money.

Nobody's Widow (DeMille Pictures/Producers Distributing Company, 1927)
d: Donald Crisp. 7 reels.
Leatrice Joy, Charles Ray, Phyllis Haver, David Butler, Dot Farley, Fritzi Ridgeway, Charles West.

Roxanne, an American girl, marries a European duke, unaware of his reputation as a ladies' man. But on their wedding night she catches him kissing another woman and, furious, returns to the United States, claiming her husband died suddenly. But they'll meet again.

Nobody's Wife (Universal, 1918)
d: Edward le Saint. 5 reels.
Hart Hoxie, Louise Lovely, Betty Schade, Alfred Allen, A.G. Kenyon, Grace McLean.

In Canada, a Mountie falls in love with a girl who's minding her sister's baby. Because he is working undercover on a case, she takes him for an outlaw, and he takes her for the baby's mother. Does this romance stand a chance?

A Noise in Newboro (Metro, 1923)
d: Harry Beaumont. 6 reels.
Viola Dana, David Butler, Eva Novak, Allan Forrest, Betty Francisco, Alfred Allen, Malcolm McGregor, Joan Standing, Bert Woodruff, Hank Mann.

Small-town girl Martha goes to New York, develops her

talent as an artist, and becomes wealthy. Now she's returned home to her old sweetheart, but finds him involved with another girl. When he learns she has come into money, he transfers his attentions back to Martha... but it's too late.

Noisy Neighbors (Paul Bern/Pathé, 1929)
d: Charles Reisner. 6 reels.
Eddie Quillan, Alberta Vaughn, Theodore Roberts, Ray Hallor, Russell Simpson, Robert Perry, Mike Donlin, Billy Gilbert.
Vaudevillians find themselves heirs to a southern mansion... and to the feud that goes with it.

Nomads of the North (First National, 1920)
d: David M. Hartford. 6 reels.
Lon Chaney, Lewis Stone, Betty Blythe, Melborne MacDowell, Francis McDonald, Spottiswood Aitken.
In the Pacific northwest, a man tries to elude the law after an accidental killing.

None But the Brave (Fox, 1928)
d: Albert Ray. 6 reels. (Technicolor sequence.)
Charles Morton, Sally Phipps, Sharon Lynn, J. Farrell MacDonald, Tom Kennedy, Billy Butts, Alice Adair, Tyler Brooke, Earle Foxe, Gertrude Short, Dorothy Knapp.
Charles, a lifeguard, helps an injured fellow win an obstacle race, and wins the love of a girl in the beach beauty pageant.

None So Blind (State Pictures/Arrow Film Corp., 1923)
d: Burton King. 6 reels.
Dore Davidson, Zena Keefe, Anders Randolf, Edward Earle, Sonia Nodell, Bernard Siegel, Robert Bentley, Maurice Costello, Gene Burnell.
Rachel, daughter of a Jewish pawnbroker, and Russell, son of a wealthy gentile, fall in love and marry, but their fathers are dead set against the match and resolve to terminate it.

The Noose (First National, 1928)
d: John Francis Dillon. 8 reels.
Richard Barthelmess, Montagu Love, Robert E. O'Connor, Lina Basquette, Thelma Todd, Ed Brady, Fred Warren, Charles Giblyn, Alice Joyce, William Walling, Robert T. Haines.
When a young man kills a gangster, he is arrested and tried for murder. After being sentenced to die, he learns that the governor's wife has prevailed upon her husband to grant him a pardon. Small wonder. The governor's wife is the prisoner's mother.

North of Hudson Bay (Fox, 1923)
d: Jack Ford. 5 reels.
Tom Mix, Kathleen Key, Jennie Lee, Frank Campeau, Eugene Pallette, Will Wailing, Frank Leigh, Fred Kohler.
Action thriller, with Mix playing a rancher whose brother has been murdered.

North of Nevada (Monogram/FBO of America, 1924)
d: Albert Rogell. 5 reels.
Fred Thomson, Hazel Keener, Josef Swickard, Joe Butterworth, Chester Conklin, Taylor Graves, George Magrill, Wilfred Lucas.
Out West, a ranch foreman rides to the rescue when Marion, an eastern girl who's just inherited the ranch, is kidnapped.

North of Nome (Arrow Pictures, 1925)
d: Raymond K. Johnston. 6 reels.
Robert McKim, Gladys Johnston, Robert N. Bradbury, Howard Webster, William Dills.
In an Alaskan trading post, a stranger appears just in time to rescue a girl who's being attacked by a crazed miner.

North of the Rio Grande (Famous Players-Lasky/Paramount, 1922)
d: Rollin Sturgeon. 5 reels.
Jack Holt, Bebe Daniels, Charles Ogle, Alec B. Francis, Will R. Walling, Jack Carlyle, Fred Huntley, Shannon Day, Edythe Chapman, George Field, W.B. Clarke.
Out West, a rancher becomes leader of an outlaw gang.

North of 36 (Famous Players-Lasky/Paramount, 1924)
d: Irvin Willat. 8 reels.
Ernest Torrence, Jack Holt, Lois Wilson, Noah Beery, David Dunbar, Stephen Carr, Guy Oliver, William Carroll, Clarence Geldert, George Irving, Ella Miller.
Taisie, the female owner of a large ranch, is determined to drive her cattle through a thousand miles of Indian territory.

North of '53 (Fox, 1917)
d: Richard Stanton. 5 reels.
Dustin Farnum, Winifred Kingston, William Conklin, Edward Alexander, Frank Lanning, Rex Downs.
Bill loves Hazel, but because she has been touched by scandal, she thinks he wouldn't be interested in her if he knew the truth. She's wrong.

North Star (Howard Estabrook Productions/Associated Exhibitors, 1925)
d: Paul Powell. 5 reels.
Virginia Lee Corbin, Stuart Holmes, Ken Maynard, Harold Austin, Clark Gable, William Riley, Syd Crossley, Jerry Mandy, Marte Faust, Jack Fowler.
A fugitive from justice takes for the North Woods.

The North Wind's Malice (Rex Beach/Goldwyn, 1920)
d: Carl Harbaugh, Paul Bern. 7 reels.
Tom Santschi, Jane Thomas, Joe King, Henry West, William H. Strauss, Walter Abel, Vera Gordon, Edna Murphy, Dorothy Wheeler, Julia Stewart.
A constantly quarreling husband and wife finally separate, and the husband goes on a gold mining expedition to get away from the marital acrimony. What he doesn't know is that his wife is pregnant with their first child.

Northern Code (Gotham Productions/Lumas, 1925)
d: Leon De La Mothe. 6 reels.
Robert Ellis, Eva Novak, Francis McDonald, Josef Swickard, Jack Kenney, Claire DeLorez, Raye Hampton.
In the Canadian Northwest, a woman shoots her drunken husband and, thinking she's killed him, runs away. She falls in love again and remarries, but then her first husband shows up alive and angry.

Northern Lights (Life Photo Film Corp., 1914)
d: Edgar Lewis. 5 reels.
William H. Tooker, Harry Knowles, Harry Springler, George DeCarlton, William F. Sorrell, Iva Shepard, Anna Laughlin, Katherine LaSalle, David Wall.
In college, a young man thought to be a coward makes friends with an Indian boy who's studying to be a doctor. Later, they join the Army, and with the help of his Indian friend, the formerly timorous lad redeems himself by a selfless act of bravery.

Not a Drum Was Heard (Fox, 1924)
d: William A. Wellman. 5 reels.
Charles Jones, Betty Bouton, Frank Campeau, Rhody Hathaway, Al Fremont, William Scott, Mickey McBan.
Melodrama about a single man who takes the blame for his

friend's larceny so that the friend can go back to his wife and child without disgrace.

Not Built for Runnin' (William Steiner Productions/Ambassador Pictures, 1924)
d: Leo Maloney. 5 reels.
Leo Maloney, Josephine Hill, Whitehorse, Milton Fahrney, Bud Osborne, Leonard Clapham, Evelyn Thatcher, Won Lefong.
Confusing western comedy about a rancher who kidnaps Louise, his neighbor, only to discover that she is his long lost daughter.

Not for Publication (Ralph Ince Productions/FBO of America, 1927)
d: Ralph Ince. 7 reels.
Ralph Ince, Roy Laidlaw, Rex Lease, Jola Mendez, Eugene Strong, Thomas Brower.
A newspaper publisher attacks the awarding of a dam contract to a local construction firm as political cronyism.

Not Guilty (Triumph Film Corp./World Film Corp., 1915)
d: Joseph Golden. 5 reels.
Cyril Scott, Catherine Proctor, Ada Boshell, Mark Ellison, Charles Hutchison.
Because of maliciously false testimony from the dead man's brother, Ed Andrews is found guilty of accidental homicide and sentenced to jail. Twenty years go by and Ed is released, only to find that his daughter is now engaged to the perjurer's son.

Not Guilty (Whitman Bennett Productions/Associated First National, 1921)
d: Sidney A. Franklin. 7 reels.
Sylvia Breamer, Richard Dix, Molly Malone, Elinor Hancock, Herbert Prior, Lloyd Whitlock, Alberta Lee, Charles West, Alice Forbes.
When Arthur is accused of murder, his twin brother Paul sacrifices his own freedom by switching places with Arthur. But it turns out that neither of them is guilty.

Not My Sister (New York Motion Picture Corp./Triangle, 1916)
d: Charles Giblyn. 5 reels.
Bessie Barriscale, William Desmond, Franklin Ritchie, Alice Taafe, Louise Brownell.
"Not my sister too!" That's the cry from Grace, a happily married woman who learns that her younger sister is now involved with the same artist who seduced Grace, years before.

Not Quite Decent (Fox, 1929)
d: Irving Cummings. 5 reels. (Music, sound effects, part talkie.)
Louise Dresser, June Collyer, Allan Lane, Oscar Apfel, Paul Nicholson, Marjorie Beebe, Ben Hewlett, Jack Kenney.
Small-town girl Linda travels to the big city, hoping for a career on the stage. There, she will meet Mame, a saloon singer, never realizing that Mame is her own mother, who gave Linda up as a baby.

Not So Long Ago (Famous Players-Lasky/Paramount, 1925)
d: Sidney Olcott. 7 reels.
Betty Bronson, Ricardo Cortez, Edwards Davis, Julia Swayne Gordon, Laurence Wheat, Jacquelin Gadsdon, Dan Crimmins.
Betty, the daughter of a struggling inventor, goes to work as a domestic for the wealthy Ballard family. She quickly falls

for Billy Ballard and invents a fictitious romance between them, telling her friends about it as if it were true. When Billy finds out about the fabrication, he takes his first good look at Betty—and soon, a real romance blossoms between them.

Nothing But Lies (Taylor Holmes Productions, Inc./Metro, 1920)
d: Lawrence C. Windom. 6 reels.
Taylor Holmes, Justine Johnstone, Jack McGowan, Rapley Holmes, John Junior, Ann Wallack, Gypsy O'Brien, Dodson Mitchell.
Ad agency mischief is exposed as a pack of lies... or is it really a clever new advertising gimmick?
This comedy is a sequel of sorts to Holmes' previous film, *Nothing But the Truth*, also released in 1920.

Nothing But the Truth (Taylor Holmes Productions, Ince./Metro, 1920)
d: David Kirkland. 6 reels.
Taylor Holmes, Elsie Mackaye, Ned Sparks, Marcelle Carroll, Ben Hendricks, Radcliffe Steele, Elizabeth Garrison, Charles Craig, Colin Campbell, Beth Franklyn, Edna Phillips.
Chaos results when a playboy bets $30,000 that he can go for one week telling nothing but the truth. His friends' wives ask him personal questions about their husbands' private activities, and the playboy is forced to answer truthfully, though it lands his friends in hot water. In retaliation, his friends have him committed to an insane asylum... but that still isn't the end of the playboy's troubles.
Following his appearance in this film Taylor Holmes appeared in *Nothing But Lies*, also released in 1920. Though the two comedies have no characters in common, they are sometimes regarded as prequel and sequel because of the similarity in titles, plus the fact that in each film Holmes' character is a befuddled everyman trapped in comic predicaments partly of his own making.

Nothing to Wear (Columbia, 1928)
d: Erle C. Kenton. 6 reels.

Jacqueline Logan, Theodore von Eltz, Bryant Washburn.
When her husband won't buy her a fur coat, a woman asks her ex-boyfriend to get it for her. Numerous complications ensue, with the fur coat changing hands rapidly.

Notoriety (L. Lawrence Weber/Apollo Trading Corp., 1922)
w, d: William Nigh. 8 reels.
Maurine Powers, Mary Alden, Rod LaRocque, George Hackathorne, Richard Travers, J. Barney Sherry, Mona Lisa, Anders Randolf, John Goldsworthy, Ida Waterman.
A girl who seeks notoriety confesses to a murder she didn't commit.

The Notorious Lady (First National, 1927)
d: King Baggot. 7 reels.
Lewis Stone, Barbara Bedford, Ann Rork, Earl Metcalfe, Francis McDonald, Grace Carlyle, E.J. Ratcliffe, J. Gunnis Davis.
An Army officer kills a man when he finds his own wife in the man's room. Although the wife is innocent of any wrongdoing, she swears to the authorities that she and the dead man were having an affair, in order to spare her husband from a murder conviction.

The Notorious Miss Lisle (Associated First National, 1920)
d: James Young. 5 reels.

Katherine MacDonald, Nigel Barrie, Margaret Campbell, Ernest Joy, William Clifford, Dorothy Cummings.

Disgraced by her apparent involvement in a sensational divorce, Miss Lisle leaves England and meets Peter, falls in love, and marries him. When Peter learns of the scandal in Paris, he determines to return to England and clear his wife's name.

The Notorious Mrs. Sands (B.B. Features/Robertson-Cole, 1920)
d: William Christy Cabanne. 5 reels.
Bessie Barriscale, Forrest Stanley, Dorothy Cumming, Harry Meyers, Ben Alexander.
Mary loves Ronald, but since Ronald doesn't have a dime, her mother talks her into marrying Mr. Sands for his money.

Now We're in the Air (Paramount, 1927)
d: Frank Strayer. 6 reels.
Wallace Beery, Raymond Hatton, Russell Simpson, Louise Brooks, Emile Chautard, Malcolm Waite, Duke Martin.
Comedy about Wally and Ray, daft cousins who get innocently involved with foreign spies during the first World War.

The Nth Commandment (Cosmopolitan/Paramount, 1923)
d: Frank Borzage. 8 reels.
Colleen Moore, James Morrison, Eddie Phillips, Charlotte Merriam, George Cooper.
To help move herself and her consumptive husband to a milder climate, a young wife accepts money from a chap who fancies her.

Nugget Nell (Paramount, 1919)
d: Elmer Clifton. 5 reels.
Dorothy Gish, Raymond Cannon, Regina Sarle, David Butler, James Farley, Wilbur Higeby, Bob Fleming, Emily Chichester, Regina Sarle.
Western burlesque, with Dorothy Gish as a two-gun tomboy in mining country.

Number 99 (Robert Brunton Productions/Pathé, 1920)
d: Ernest C. Warde. 5 reels.
J. Warren Kerrigan, Fritzi Brunette, Emmett King, Charles Arling, Kathleen Kirkham, John Steppling, Lila Leslie, R.D. MacLean, W.V. Mong, Thomas S. Guise.
Unjustly sentenced to jail for a crime he didn't commit, a convict escapes and persuades a young socialite to help him clear his name by finding the true criminal.

Nurse Marjorie (Realart Pictures Corp., 1920)
d: William Desmond Taylor. 6 reels.
Mary Miles Minter, Clyde Fillmore, George Periolat, Mollie McConnell, Frankie Lee, Vera Lewis, Arthur Hoyt, Frankie Lee, Lydia Yeamans Titus, Joe Murphy.
Marjorie, a young aristocrat with a compassionate heart, volunteers as a nurse in a local rest home. Into the home comes a new patient, a political reformer who will win Nurse Marjorie's love.

The Nut (Fairbanks/United Artists, 1921)
d: Ted Reed. 7 reels.
Douglas Fairbanks, Marguerite De La Motte, Gerald Pring, Morris Hughes, William Lowery, Barbara LaMarr, Sidney de Grey.
An eccentric inventor falls in love with a charity worker and tries to get "big money" interests to assist in her work.

The Nut-Cracker (Associated Exhibitors, 1926)
d: Lloyd Ingraham. 6 reels.

Edward Everett Horton, Mae Busch, Harry Myers, Thomas Ricketts, Martha Mattox, George Kuwa, Katherine Lewis, Albert Priscoe, George Periolat.
Farce about a chap who feigns amnesia after a traffic accident in order to get a large settlement from the insurance company.

A Nymph of the Foothills (Vitagraph, 1918)
d: Frederick A. Thomson. 5 reels.
Gladys Leslie, Alfred Kappeler, Walter Hiers, Charles A. Stevenson, Arnold Lucy, Charles Hope, John Pierson, Bradley Barker, Jane Jennings, Greta Ardin.
City boy meets mountain girl, sparks fly, and they marry. But there's a problem, because her lovin' pa has sworn to kill his city-bred son-in-law.

The Oakdale Affair (World Film Corp., 1919)
d: Oscar Apfel. 5 reels.
Evely Greeley, Eric Mayne, Maude Turner Gordon, Charles Mackay, Eric Dalton, Mona Kingsley, Reginald Denny, Frank Joyner, Albert Hart, Eddie Sturgis, George E. Murphy.
Rebelling against an arranged marriage, Gail leaves her family's luxurious home and takes to the road dressed as a boy. There, she meets Arthur, a friendly hobo. They travel together and share several adventures, and in the end, it turns out that neither the *faux* boy nor the hobo are really what they pretend to be.

The Oath (Mayflower Photoplay Corp., 1921)
d: R.A. Walsh. 8 reels.
Miriam Cooper, Robert Fischer, Conway Tearle, Henry Clive, Ricca Allen, Anna Q. Nilsson.
Coleman loves Minna and they get married, although her Jewish banker father will never accept a gentile as his son-in-law.

Obey the Law (Columbia, 1926)
d: Alfred Raboch. 6 reels.
Bert Lytell, Edna Murphy, Hedda Hopper, Larry Kent, Eugenia Gilbert, Sarah Paden, William Welsh.
Norma, an American girl, gets her education in Paris, then returns home with a wealthy family who have taken a liking to her. What none of them know is that Norma's father is now in jail for grand larceny.

Obey Your Husband (Morris R. Schlank Productions/Anchor Film Distributors, 1928)
d: Charles J. Hunt. 6 reels.
Gaston Glass, Dorothy Dwan, Alice Lake, Henry Sedley, Robert Homans, Robert Elliott, Jack Johnston, Joseph Burke.
A married couple with a weakness for card games are suspected in the murder of a gambler.

Object - Alimony (Columbia, 1928)
d: Scott R. Dunlap. 7 reels.
Hugh Allan, Douglas Gilmore, Lois Wilson, Roscoe Karns, Ethel Grey Terry, Carmelita Geraghty, Dickey Moore, Jane Keckley, Thomas Curran.
A department store heir finds his wife in the arms of another man, and suspects the worst. But she's really innocent of any wrongdoing.

The Obligin' Buckaroo (Action Pictures/Pathé, 1927)
d: Richard Thorpe. 5 reels.
Buffalo Bill Jr., Olive Hasbrouck, Sherry Tansey, Harry Todd, Raye Hampton, Charles Whitaker.
Out West, a miner inherits a broken-down hotel. Then, when a theatrical troupe is stranded in town, the miner offers them free lodging in return for their help in fixing up

the place.

Occasionally Yours   (Lew Cody Films Corp./Robertson-Cole, 1920)
d: James W. Horne.   5 reels.
Lew Cody, Betty Blythe, J. Barney Sherry, Elinor Fair, Yvonne Gardelle, Cleo Ridgely, Lillian Rambeau, Lloyd Hamilton, Gertrude Astor, William Quinn.
Bruce, a playboy and occasional artist, loves women but is frightened by thoughts of spending a lifetime with just one.

The Ocean Waif   (International Film Service, Inc./Golden Eagle Features, 1916)
d: Alice Blaché.   5 reels.
Carlyle Blackwell, Doris Kenyon, William Morse, Fraunie Fraunholz, Lyn Donaldson, August Burmester, Edgar Norton.
When a novelist takes a house in a quiet coastal town, thinking to concentrate on writing his next book, he's surprised to find that a young woman has already broken in and is living there.

An Odyssey of the North   (Bosworth, Inc./Paramount, 1914)
d: Hobart Bosworth.   6 reels.
Hobart Bosworth, Rhea Haines, Gordon Sackville, Joe Ray.
Bitter adventure tale about an Alaskan who exacts a terrible revenge on the woman who deserted him and the man she married in his place.

Off the Highway   (Hunt Stromberg Corp./Producers Distributing Corp., 1925)
d: Tom Forman.   8 reels.
William V. Mong, Marguerite De La Motte, John Bowers, Charles Gerard, Geno Corrado, Buddy Post, Joseph Swickard, Smoke Turner.
When a wealthy skinflint's butler dies, the skinflint takes the butler's place and lets the world believe that he himself has died. In this way, the old miser can keep an eye on just how his "heir" deals with his inheritance... and he doesn't like what he sees.

The Off-Shore Pirate   (Metro, 1921)
d: Bayard Veiller.   6 reels.
Viola Dana, Jack Mulhall, Edward Jobson, Edward Cecil.
When Ardita, a socialite, is romanced by a gold digging Russian, her disapproving uncle makes plans to get him out of the way.

The Office Scandal   (Pathé, 1929)
d: Paul L. Stein.   7 reels.   (Part talkie.)
Phyllis Haver, Leslie Fenton, Raymond Hatton, Margaret Livingston, Jimmie Adams, Jimmy Aldine, Dan Wolheim.
A cub reporter cracks a murder case after the detectives on the case are stumped.

Officer 666   (George Kleine Attractions, 1914)
d: Frank Powell.   5 reels.
Howard Estabrook, Sydney Seaward, Lois Burnett, Della Connor, Ada Nevil, Dan Moyles, Harold Howard, Makoto Inokuchi.
After spending some time abroad, a millionaire art collector returns to his U.S. mansion, only to find a strange young lady there, waiting to marry him. Realizing the girl has been duped, the art collector borrows the police uniform of "Officer 666" and sets a trap for the impostor.

Officer 666   (Goldwyn, 1920)
d: Harry Beaumont.   5 reels.

Tom Moore, Jean Calhoun, Jerome Patrick, Harry Dunkinson, Raymond Hatton, Priscilla Bonner, Kate Lester, Hardee Kirkland, M.B. Flynn, George Kuwa, Al Edmundson.
Remake of the 1914 George Kleine production *Officer 666*.

Oh, Baby!   (Universal, 1926)
d: Harley Knoles.   7 reels.
Little Billy, David Butler, Madge Kennedy, Creighton Hale, Ethel Shannon, Flora Finch, Joe Humphreys, Bugs Baer, Graham McNamee, Fred Veats, Damon Runyon, S. Jay Kaufman.
A midget who manages a contender for the heavyweight boxing champion must help a pal by shuttling between Madison Square Garden and his pal's home on the night of the big match. It seems his friend is pretending to his maiden aunt that he has a wife and young daughter; and Billy, to help him out, is playing the role of the daughter, complete with blonde wig and crinoline drag.

Oh, Boy!   (Albert Capellani Productions, Inc./Pathé, 1919)
w, d: Albert Capellani.   6 reels.
June Caprice, Creighton Hale, Zena Keefe, Flora Finch, W.H. Thompson, Grace Reals, Joseph Conyers, J.K. Murray, Maurice Bennett Flynn, Albert Capellani, Ben Taggart.
Anti-prohibition comedy about college students George and Lou Ellen, sweethearts who want to get married. No dice, says Lou Ellen's dad, a judge who's a leader of the prohibition movement, because George admits he sometimes takes a drink. But things get out of hand when the judge, a lovely actress, and George's aunt all get roaring drunk due to circumstances very much under their control.

Oh, Doctor!   (Universal, 1925)
d: Harry A. Pollard.   7 reels.
Reginald Denny, Mary Astor, Otis Harlan, William V. Mong, Tom Ricketts, Lucille Ward, Mike Donlin, Clarence Geldert, Blanche Payton, George Kuwa, Martha Mattox, Helen Lynch.
Farce about Rufus, a hypochondriac who promises to repay a loan with money he is due to inherit in three years. To keep him alive that long, his creditors hire a pretty nurse to look after him. One look at his nurse, though, and the frail Rufus is madly in love, and pulling all sorts of dangerous stunts to impress her, much to his creditors' dismay.

Oh, Johnny!   (Betzwood Film Co./Goldwyn, 1918)
d: Ira M. Lowry.   5 reels.
Louis Bennison, Alphonse Ethier, Edward Roseman, John Daly Murphy, Frank Goldsmith, Virginia Lee, Anita Cortez, Louise Brownell, Russell Simpson.
Out West, a cowboy joins forces with a prospector's daughter to develop a potentially valuable gold strike.

Oh, Kay!   (First National, 1928)
d: Mervyn LeRoy.   6 reels.
Colleen Moore, Lawrence Gray, Alan Hale, Ford Sterling, Claude Gillingwater, Julanne Johnston, Claude King, Edgar Norton, Percy Williams, Fred O'Beck.
Although scheduled to be married to others the following day, Kay and Jimmy fall in love, scrap old wedding plans, and draw up new ones.

Oh, Lady! Lady!   (Realart Pictures Corp., 1919)
d: Maurice Campbell.   5 reels.
Harrison Ford, Bebe Daniels, Walter Hiers, Charlotte Woods, Lillian Langdon, Jack Doud.
Finch is engaged to Molly, but he fears that May, his former

girlfriend, will try to upset their wedding plans. His worst suspicions are confirmed when May shows up at the wedding rehearsal, but her presence there is purely coincidental... or is it?

Oh, Mabel Behave (Triangle Film Corporation/Photocraft Productions, 1922)
d: Mack Sennett, Ford Sterling. 5 reels.
Mabel Normand, Mack Sennett, Ford Sterling, Owen Moore.
An innkeeper has his daughter Mabel betrothed to the wealthy local squire, but her heart belongs to young Randolph.

Oh Mary be Careful (Goldwyn/Pioneer Film Corp., 1921)
d: Arthur Ashley. 5 reels.
Madge Kennedy, George Forth, George Stevens, Bernard Thornton, Marguerite Marsh, Harry Fraser, Dixie Thompson, Mae Rogers, Kathleen McEchran, Harry Myers, Marcia Harris.
Mary, a popular college girl, finds that living with her maiden aunt tends to curtail her own social life.   So she hatches a plot to get around Auntie.

Oh, What a Night! (Sterling Pictures, 1926)
d: Lloyd Ingraham. 5 reels.
Raymond McKee, Edna Murphy, Charles K. French, Ned Sparks, Jackie Coombs, Hilliard Karr, Frank Alexander.
Comedy about a playwright who is asked by his producer to rewrite the last act the night before his play is to be produced.   On his way to the producer's home, the playwright gets into numerous entanglements with thieves, butlers, babies, and a pretty girl named June who, against all odds, believes all his sad stories and wins his heart.

Oh, What a Nurse! (Warner Bros., 1926)
d: Charles F. Reisner. 7 reels.
Sydney Chaplin, Patsy Ruth Miller, Gayne Whitman, Matthew Betz, Pat Hartigan, Edgar Kennedy, Edith Yorke, David Torrence.
A jealous man disguises himself as a woman and showers attentions on the rival for his sweetheart's affections.

Oh, You Women (Famous Players-Lasky/Paramount, 1919)
d: John Emerson. 5 reels.
Ernest Truex, Joseph Burke, Bernard Randall, Gaston Glass, Louise Huff, Betty Wales, Mercita Esmonde, Ida Fitzhugh, Josephine Stevens.
Comedy about militant feminists in a small town, where the women don men's clothes and do "men's" work.

The Oklahoma Kid (J.P. McGowan Productions, 1929)
d: J.P. McGowan. 5 reels.
Bob Custer, Henry Roguemore, Vivian Ray, Tommy Bay, J.P. McGowan, Walter Patterson.
Out West, a cattle drover is held up and robbed, but battles his way out of trouble and into the heart of a pretty girl.

Old Age Handicap (Trinity Pictures, 1928)
d: Frank S. Mattison. 6 reels.
Alberta Vaughn, Gareth Hughes, Vivian Rich, Olaf Hytten, Mavis Villiers, Bud Shaw, Jimmy Humes, Carolyn Wethall, Robert Rodman, Frank Mattison Jr., Ford Jessen, Hall Cline.
A cabaret dancer substitutes for the jockey and rides a horse to victory in the big race.

Old Clothes (MGM, 1925)
d: Edward Cline. 6 reels.
Jackie Coogan, Max Davidson, Joan Crawford, Allan Forrest,
Lillian Elliott, James Mason, Stanton Heck.
In this sequel to 1924's *The Rag Man*, the junk man and the young boy are still partners in the salvage business. Now they take in a homeless but lovely waif, and she winds up with a rich sweetheart.

The Old Code (Morris R. Schlank Productions/Anchor Film Distributors, 1928)
d: Benjamin Franklin Wilson. 6 reels.
Walter McGrail, Lillian Rich, Cliff Lyons, Melbourne MacDowell, J.P. McGowan, Neva Gerber, Ervin Renard, Mary Gordon, Rhody Hathaway, John Rainbow.
In the Canadian Northwest, a French trapper is loved by a beautiful Indian girl.

Old Dad (Chaplin-Mayer Pictures Co./Associated First National, 1920)
d: Lloyd Ingraham. 5 reels.
Mildred Harris Chaplin, George Stewart, John Sainpolis, Myrtle Stedman, Irving Cummings, Hazel Howell, Edwin Brown, Loyola O'Connor, Bess Mitchell, Tula Belle.
Dad has his hands full with Daphne, his daughter with an eye for dashing young men.

Old Dutch (Shubert Film Corp./World Film Corp., 1915)
d: Frank Crane. 5 reels.
Lew Fields, Vivian Martin, George Hassell, Marie Embpress, Charles Judels, W.J. Ferguson, Chester Barnett.
"Old Dutch," an inventor with a hot new device that transmits images over the telephone, gets backing from a wealthy investor. But inventor and investor alike will find that the new gadget causes as many problems as it solves.

An Old Fashioned Boy (Thomas H. Ince/Paramount, 1920)
d: Jerome Storm. 5 reels.
Charles Ray, Wade Boteler, Ethel Shannon, Alfred Allen, Grace Morse, Gloria Joy, Frankie Lee, Hal Cooley, Virginia Brown.
After a young couple impulsively break their engagement, the girl's father, a doctor, sees a way to get the youngsters to reconcile: He orders the house they are in to be quarantined!

An Old Fashioned Young Man (Fine Arts Film Co./Triangle, 1917)
d: Lloyd Ingraham. 5 reels.
Robert Harron, Thomas Jefferson, Loyola O'Connor, Colleen Moore, Adele Clifton, Charles Lee, Wilbur Higby, Winifred Westover, Alberta Lee, Sam DeGrasse, Bert Hadley.
Raised with a deep respect for women, a young man springs into action when he learns a political candidate is planning a smear campaign against his female opponent.

The Old Folks at Home (Fine Arts Film Co./Triangle, 1916)
d: Chester Withey. 5 reels.
Herbert Beerbohm Tree, Josephine Crowell, Elmer Clifton, Mildred Harris, Lucille Younge, W.E. Lawrence, Spottiswoode Aitken, Alfred Paget, Wilbur Higby.
When a senator's son is implicated in a "love triangle" murder case, the senator tries to pull strings to have him acquitted.

The Old Fool (W.W. Hodkinson Corp., 1923)
d: Edward Venturini. 6 reels.
Lloyd Hughes, James Barrows, Henry Hunt, Barbara Tenant, Betty Francisco, Bernard Hendricks, O.V. Harrison, Louise Fazenda, Monte Collins, Tom Mead.
When a crooked sheriff is accused of smuggling contraband across the Mexican border, he is unexpectedly thwarted by

an old timer—a Civil War veteran who still knows how to use his sword.

Old Hartwell's Cub (Triangle, 1918)
d: Thomas N. Heffron. 5 reels.
William Desmond, Mary Warren, Eugene Burr, Walt Whitman, Percy Challenger, Dorothy Hagar, Graham Pette, Edwin J. Brady, William Ellingford.
Although his late father was the town drunk, Bill Hartwell is respected by the local minister and his daughter.

Old Heidelberg (Triangle, 1915)
d: John Emerson. 5 reels.
Wallace Reid, Dorothy Gish, Karl Forman, Erich von Stroheim, Madge Hunt, Raymond Wells, Erik von Ritzau, Harold Goodwin, Kate Toncray, Francis Carpenter.
A tavern waitress falls in love with a prince who's in disguise.

Old Heidelberg—see: The Student Prince in Old Heidelberg (1927).

Old Home Week (Famous Players-Lasky/Paramount, 1925)
d: Victor Heerman. 7 reels.
Thomas Meighan, Lila Lee, Charles Dow Clark, Max Figman, Charles Sellon, Zelma Tiden, Sidney Paxton, Joseph Smiley, Jack Terry, Leslie Hunt, Isabel West, Clayton Frye.
Clark, a New York gasoline jockey, returns to his home town in time to outsmart a pair of swindlers who deal in phony oil wells.

The Old Homestead (Famous Players/Paramount, 1915)
d: James Kirkwood. 5 reels.
Frank Losee, Creighton Hale, Denman Maley, Louise Huff, Horace Newman, Thomas Wood, Margaret Seddon, Russell Simpson.
After several misadventures, a prodigal son returns to the old homestead.

The Old Homestead (Famous Players-Lasky/Paramount, 1922)
d: James Cruze. 8 reels.
Harrison Ford, Theodore Roberts, George Fawcett, T. Roy Barnes, Fritzi Ridgeway, James Mason, Kathleen O'Connor, Ethel Wales, Edwin J. Brady, Frank Hayes, C. Wall Covington, Charles Williams.
Remake of the 1915 Famous Players film *The Old Homestead*, both versions based on the play of the same name by Denman Thompson.

Old Ironsides (Paramount, 1926)
d: James Cruze. 8 reels.
Esther Ralston, Wallace Beery, George Bancroft, Charles Farrell, Johnny Walker, George Godfrey, Guy Oliver, Eddie Fetherston, Effie Ellsler, William Conklin, Fred Kohler, Charles Hill Mailes, Nick De Ruiz, Mitchell Lewis, Frank Jonasson, Frank Bonner, Duke Kahanamoku, Arthur Lugwig, Spec O'Donnell, Boris Karloff, Tetsu Komai.
"Millions for defense, but not one cent for tribute!" These are the historic words that launch the U.S.S. Constitution into battle against the pirates of the Barbary States in 1815. *Old Ironsides* tells the story of that battle, and the resultant attack on Tripoli harbor, which signalled America's first victory on foreign soil.

Old Lady 31 (Screen Classics, Inc./Metro, 1920)
d: John E. Ince. 6 reels.
Emma Dunn, Henry Harmon, Clara Knott, Carrie Clark Ward, Sadie Gordon, Winifred Westover, Antrim Short, Lawrence Underwood, Graham Pettie, Martha Mattox, May Wells.
When a destitute aged couple find they have no choice but to move the wife to the Old Ladies Home and leave the husband to fend for himself, the residents of the home decide to accept the husband also—as "Old Lady 31."

Old Love For New (Triangle, 1918)
d: Raymond Wells. 5 reels.
Margery Wilson, Lee Hill, Blanche Gray, George Pearce, Irene Hunt, Leo Willis, Pete Morrison, Lee Phelps.
Gwen and Harvey, a wealthy young couple, find their extravagant lifestyle threatened when Harvey's dad decides his son must earn his own living or be disinherited.

Old Loves and New (Sam E. Rork Productions/First National, 1926)
d: Ben Silvey. 8 reels.
Lewis Stone, Barbara Bedford, Walter Pidgeon, Katherine MacDonald, Tully Marshall, Ann Rork, Arthur Rankin, Albert Conti.
A British doctor whose wife has left him decides to move to Algeria and tend to the needs of the desert people. There he becomes revered and is given the name El Hakim.

The Old Maid's Baby (Diando Film Corp./Pathé, 1919)
d: William Bertram. 5 reels.
Baby Marie Osborne, Jack Richardson, Marion Werner, Jack Connelly, Claire DuBrey, William Quinn, Georgia Woodthorpe, Little Sambo.
When a young girl's parents are killed in a circus parachute accident, she is taken in by her aunt Sylvia, who's considered an "old maid." But Sylvia has a beau... and now that she has a child to be responsible for, marriage lies just ahead.

The Old Nest (Goldwyn, 1921)
d: Reginald Barker. 8 reels.
Dwight Crittenden, Mary Alden, Nick Cogley, Fanny Stockbridge, Laura LaVarnie, Johnny Jones, Richard Tucker, Marshall Ricksen, Buddy Messenger, Cullen Landis, Lucille Ricksen, Louis Lovely, Robert DeVilbiss, J. Parks Jones, Helene Chadwick, Theodore von Eltz.
A country doctor and his wife raise a large family, but one by one they all move away to other cities, and become forgetful of their parents.

The Old Oregon Trail (Aywon Film Corp., 1928)
d: Denver Dixon. 5 reels.
Art Mix, Delores Booth, F.C. Rose, Art Seales, Grace Underwood, Sid Seales.
A small band of settlers break off from a wagon train to make a new life near the Old Oregon Trail.

Old San Francisco (Warner Bros., 1927)
d: Alan Crosland. 8 reels.
Dolores Costello, Warner Oland, Joseph Swickart, Charles Emmett Mack, John Miljan, Anna May Wong, Anders Randolf, Sojin, Angelo Rossitto.
In 1906 San Francisco, a self-styled warlord presides over corruption in the Chinese community. Vicious and consumed with hatred, he tries to seize one of the last remaining Spanish estates, even going so far as to try selling the heiress into white slavery. Excellent special effects include a realistic depiction of the 1906 San Francisco earthquake.

Old Shoes (Peerless Productions/Hollywood Pictures,

1925)
w, d: Frederick Stowers. 7 reels.
Noah Beery, Johnny Harron, Viora Daniels, Ethel Grey Terry, ZaSu Pitts, Russell Simpson, Snitz Edwards.
Weepy melodrama about a widow with a young son who, against her better judgment, marries her late husband's heartless brother.

The Old Soak (Universal, 1926)
d: Edward Sloman. 8 reels.
Jean Hersholt, George Lewis, Louise Fazenda, June Marlowe, William V. Mong, Gertrude Astor, Lucy Beaumont, Adda Gleason, Tom Ricketts, George Siegmann.
Clem, a young banker, takes an interest in Ina, a New York showgirl.

An Old Sweetheart of Mine (Harry Garson Productions/Metro, 1923)
d: Harry Garson. 6 reels.
Pat Moore, Elliott Dexter, Mary Jane Irving, Helen Jerome Eddy, Turner Savage, Lloyd Whitlock, Barbara Worth, Arthur Hoyt, Gene Cameron.
A married couple reminisce about the day they met, and their early life together.

The Old Swimmin' Hole (Charles Ray Productions/Associated First National, 1921)
d: Joseph DeGrasse. 5 reels.
Charles Ray, James Gordon, Laura LaPlante, Blanche Rose, Marjorie Prevost, Lincoln Stedman, Lon Poff.
Young love blossoms between Ezra and Esther at the local swimming hole.

Old Wives For New (Famous Players-Lasky/Artcraft Pictures, 1918)
d: Cecil B. DeMille. 6 reels.
Elliott Dexter, Sylvia Ashton, Wanda Hawley, Florence Vidor, Theodore Roberts, Helen Jerome Eddy, Marcia Manon, Julia Faye, Edna Mae Cooper, Gustav von Seyffertitz.
After twenty years of marriage, a couple drift apart.

The Oldest Law (World Film Corp., 1918)
d: Harley Knoles. 5 reels.
June Elvidge, Captain Charles, John Bowers, Eloise Clement, Frank Norcross, Frank Andrews.
Down to her last three dollars, a poverty-stricken young woman decides to spend it all on a good meal in a fashionable restaurant. While there, she meets a wealthy man who is looking for a good housekeeper. She ends up with not only a job, but later a proposal of marriage from her boss.

Oliver Twist (General Film Co., 1912)
d: H.A. Spanuth. 5 reels.
Nat C. Goodwin, Vinnie Burns, Charles Rogers, Mortimer Martine, Beatrice Moreland, Edwin McKim, Daniel Read, Hudson Liston, Frank Kendrick, Stuart Holmes, Will Scherer.
In a London slum, young Oliver is sent to the workhouse with other poor orphans. Later he is rescued from his drab life by a benefactor.

Oliver Twist (Famous Players-Lasky/Paramount, 1916)
d: James Young. 5 reels.
Marie Doro, Tully Marshall, Hobart Bosworth, Raymond Hatton, Edythe Chapman, James Neill, Harry L. Rattenbury, Carl Stockdale, Elsie Jane Wilson, W.S. Van Dyke.
Oliver, a young orphan boy, escapes from a cruel London workhouse and joins up with a gang of thieves. He will have several dangerous adventures before his benefactor, Mr. Brownlow, finds him and takes him in.
Marie Doro, a popular actress with the Lasky company, plays the role of the orphan boy, Oliver Twist, in this remake of the 1912 film based on the Charles Dickens novel of the same name.

Oliver Twist (First National, 1922)
d: Frank Lloyd. 8 reels.
Lon Chaney, Jackie Coogan, Gladys Brockwell, George Siegmann, Edouard Trebaol, Lionel Belmore, Carl Stockdale, Eddie Boland, Taylor Graves, Lewis Sargent, James Marcus, Aggie Herring, Joan Standing, Esther Ralston, Florence Hale, Nelson McDowell, Joseph Hazelton, Gertrude Claire.
A child of the streets is lured into a life of crime. After several brushes with the law and with other criminals, the young boy finally gets a break and becomes "respectable."
Second remake of *Oliver Twist*, which was filmed in 1912 and 1916, all versions based on the novel of the same name by Charles Dickens.

Oliver Twist Jr. (Fox, 1921)
d: Millard Webb. 5 reels.
Harold Goodwin, Lillian Hall, George Nichols, Harold Esboldt, Scott McKee, Wilson Hummell, G. Raymond Nye, Hayward Mack, Pearl Lowe, George Clair, Fred Kirby, Irene Hunt.
Modern twist on the familiar *Oliver Twist* tale. In this version, Oliver is 17 years old when he falls in with Fagin and his gang.

O'Malley of the Mounted (William S. Hart Co./Paramount, 1921)
w, d: Lambert Hillyer. 6 reels.
William S. Hart, Eva Novak, Antrim Short, Leo Willis, Bert Sprotte, Alfred Allen.
O'Malley, a Canadian mountie, is sent into the U.S. to search for a wanted killer.

Omar the Tentmaker (Richard Walton Tully Productions, 1922)
d: James Young. 8 reels.
Guy Bates Post, Virginia Brown Faire, Nigel DeBrulier, Noah Beery, Rose Dione, Patsy Ruth Miller, Douglas Gerrard, Will Jim Hatton, Boris Karloff, Evenly Selbie, Maurice B. Flynn.
In Ancient Persia, a young bride is taken from Omar, her new husband; forced into the harem of a Shah; and finally, sold into slavery. But as the years pass, Omar comes into power under a new government, and frees his wife and reunites her with their daughter.

On Dangerous Ground (World Film Corp., 1917)
d: Robert Thornby. 5 reels.
Carlyle Blackwell, Gail Kane, William Bailey, Stanhope Wheatcroft, Frank Leigh, Florence Ashbrook, John Burkell.
Bradford, an American, and his best friend Ritter, a German, are separated when World War I breaks out. Later, when a French girl who has become Bradford's sweetheart is sentenced to be executed by the Germans, the German commander—Ritter—pardons her, remembering his old friend.

On Probation (William Steiner Productions, 1924)
d: Charles Hutchinson. 5 reels.
Edith Thornton, Robert Ellis, Joseph Kilgour, Wilfred Lucas, Helen Lynch, Eddie Phillips, Betty Francisco, Lincoln Stedman.

Mary, a socialite who loves fast cars, is constantly being arrested for speeding.

On Record (Lasky Feature Plays/Paramount, 1917)
d: Robert Leonard. 5 reels.
Mae Murray, Tom Forman, Henry A. Barrows, Charles Ogle, Louis Morrison, Bliss Chevalier, Gertrude Maitland.
Small-town girl Helen moves to the big city and finds work as a secretary... but that's not all she finds there. She crosses paths with men both predatory and considerate, and it's up to Helen to figure out which is which.

On the Banks of the Wabash (Vitagraph, 1923)
d: J. Stuart Blackton. 7 reels.
Mary Carr, Burr McIntosh, James Morrison, Lumsden Hare, Mary MacLaren, Madge Evans, George Neville, Marcia Harris, Ed Roseman.
Laid-back melodrama partially inspired by the lyrics of "On the Banks of the Wabash Far Away."

On the Go (Action Pictures/Weiss Brothers Artclass Pictures, 1925)
d: Richard Thorpe. 5 reels.
Buffalo Bill Jr., Helen Foster, Lafe McKee, Nelson McDowell, Raye Hampton, Charles Whitaker, Louis Fitzroy, George F. Marion, Alfred Hewston, Morgan Davis, Pietro Sosso.
Out West, a ranch hand rescues a young woman who has fainted, and gives her shelter. Can romance be far behind?

On the High Seas (Famous Players-Lasky/Paramount, 1922)
d: Irvin Willat. 6 reels.
Dorothy Dalton, Jack Holt, Mitchell Lewis, Winter Hall, Michael Dark, Otto Brower, William Boyd, James Gordon, Alice Knowland, Vernon Tremaine.
Tragedy on the high seas casts three survivors adrift—a young woman, and two men. One man will abuse the lady, the other will rescue her from his advances and win her love. But will they ever get off this raft?

On the Jump (Fox, 1918)
d: Raoul A. Walsh. 6 reels.
George Walsh, Frances Burnham, James Marcus, Henry Clive, Ralph Faulkner.
During World War I, a reporter interviews President Wilson and then submits the finished interview, a thunderingly patriotic article on war preparedness, to his newspaper. But the article is scrapped by the publisher, who is secretly a German agent.

On the Level (Paramount, 1917)
d: George Melford. 5 reels.
James Cruze, Fannie Ward, Harrison Ford, Jack Dean, Edythe Chapman, Jane Wolff, Lottie Pickford, James Mason, Henry Woodward.
Out West, a drug addict falls in love with Mae, a saloon dancer. Despite his addiction, he's basically a decent sort, and with the help of Mae's love he is able to cure his habit.

On the Night Stage (New York Motion Picture Co./Mutual, 1914)
d: Reginald Barker. 5 reels.
Robert Edeson, Rhea Mitchell, William S. Hart, Herschel Mayall, Gladys Brockwell, Shorty Hamilton.
In a small Texas town, a dance hall queen is loved by two men: a bandit and the local minister.

On the Quiet (Famous Players-Lasky, 1918)
d: Chet Withey. 5 reels.

John Barrymore, Lois Meredith, Frank Losee, J.W. Johnston, Alfred Hickman, Helen Greene, Cyril Chadwick, Frank H. Belcher.
Comedy of manners about a girl whose inheritance depends on her brother's approval of the man she will marry, and who then marries a ne'er-do-well "on the quiet."

The On-the-Square Girl (Astra Film Corp./Pathé, 1917)
d: George Fitzmaurice. 5 reels.
Mollie King, L. Rogers Lytton, Aimee Dalmores, Donald Hall, Ernest Lawford, Richard Tucker.
Upon her mother's death, Anne finds letters that prove that the old lecher who tried to seduce Anne was—unknown to both of them—her father.

On the Stroke of Three (Associated Arts Corp., 1924)
d: F. Harmon Weight. 7 reels.
Kenneth Harlan, Madge Bellamy, Mary Carr, John Miljan, Robert Dudley, Leonore Mater, Edwards Davis, Edward Phillips, Dorothy Dahm.
An engineer plans to build a massive power development, but needs one more parcel of land to begin. Unfortunately for the developer, the owner is a young inventor who refuses to sell.

On the Threshold (Renaud Hoffman Productions/Producers Distributing Corp., 1925)
d: Renaud Hoffman. 6 reels.
Gladys Hulette, Henry B. Walthall, Robert Gordon, Willis Marks, Sam DeGrasse, Charles Sellon, Margaret Seddon.
After suffering the loss of his wife in childbirth, a man vows never to let his baby—a girl—get married. Eighteen years later, he'll have trouble keeping that vow.

On Thin Ice (Warner Bros., 1925)
d: Mal St. Clair. 7 reels.
Edith Roberts, Tom Moore, William Russell, Theodore von Eltz, Wilfred North, Gertrude Robinson.
Sweet and simple Rose finds a bag that's supposedly loaded with stolen loot.

On Time (Carlos Productions/Truart Film Corp., 1924)
d: Henry Lehrman. 6 reels.
Richard Talmadge, Billie Dove, Stuart Holmes, George Siegmann, Tom Wilson, Charles Clary, Douglas Gerard, Fred Kirby, Frankie Mann.
To impress his girlfriend, Harry promises to make $10,000 in just six months. But can he deliver?

On to Reno (James Cruze, Inc./Pathé, 1928)
d: James Cruze. 6 reels.
Marie Prevost, Cullen Landis, Ethel Wales, Ned Sparks, Jane Keckley.
Marital comedy about a young married woman who goes to Reno to get a divorce. But it isn't for her, it's for the woman she's impersonating. Both husbands get wise and join the ladies in Reno to try and smooth things over.

On Trial (Essanay, 1917)
d: James Young. 6 reels.
Barbara Castleton, Sydney Ainsworth, Mary McAlister, James Young, Corene Uzzell, Patrick Calhoun, John Cossar.
On trial for murder, a man admits the killing but refuses to testify on his own behalf. When the defense attorney questions his wife and daughter, however, it comes out that the motive for the killing was that the victim had seduced the defendant's wife.

On With the Dance (Famous Players-Lasky/Paramount,

1920)
d: George Fitzmaurice. 7 reels.
Mae Murray, David Powell, Alma Tell, John Miltern, Robert Schable, Ida Waterman, Zola Talma, James A. Furey.
Two mismatched couples clash when the wife of one man becomes a dancer in the other man's cabaret.

On Your Toes (Universal, 1927)
d: Fred Newmeyer. 6 reels.
Reginald Denny, Barbara Worth, Hayden Stevenson, Frank Hagney, Mary Carr, Gertrude Howard, George West.
A dance instructor turns to prize-fighting.

On Ze Boulevard (MGM, 1927)
d: Harry Millarde. 6 reels.
Lew Cody, Renee Adoree, Dorothy Sebastian, Anton Vaverka, Roy D'Arcy.
In France, a waiter wins the lottery and starts spending wildly, while his sweetheart tries to rein in his sudden extravagance.

Once a Plumber (Universal, 1920)
d: Eddie Lyons, Lee Moran. 5 reels.
Eddie Lyons, Lee Moran, Sidney Deane, George B. Williams, Jeff Osborne, Lillian Hackett, Edna Mae Wilson, Jane Elliott, Ethel Ritchie, Lew Short, Harry Archer, Doc Bytell.
Bill and Joe, partners in a plumbing business, run afoul of high-society swindlers.

Once and Forever (Tiffany Productions, 1927)
d: Phil Stone. 6 reels.
Patsy Ruth Miller, John Harron, Burr McIntosh, Emily Fitzroy, Adele Watson, Vadim Uraneff.
On an isolated French island, a tomboy falls in love with the governor's son.

Once in a Lifetime (Paul Gerson Pictures, 1925)
d: Duke Worne. 5 reels.
Richard Holt, Mary Beth Milford, Wilbur Higgins, Theodore Lorch, Les Bates, Jack O'Brien.
Glenn, a young golfer, finds himself in the right place at the right time, and gets to rescue the mayor's daughter from a would-be kidnapper.

Once to Every Man (Frohman Amusement Corp., 1918)
d: T. Hayes Hunter. 6 reels.
Jack Sherrill, Mabel Withee, Roy Applegate, Charles DeForrest, George Kline, Eddie Kelly, William Powers, Kid Broad.
After his wife leaves him over a misunderstanding, Denny is so angry at the world that he decides to take out his agressiveness in the gymnasium. He enters the world of boxing, and defeats the world's lightweight champion after hearing from his wife that all is forgiven.

Once to Every Woman (Universal, 1920)
d: Allen Holubar. 7 reels.
Dorothy Phillips, William Ellingford, Rudolph Valentino, Mrs. Margaret Mann, Emily Chichester, Elinor Field, Mary Wise, Rosa Gore, Robert Anderson, Frank Elliott, Dan Crimmins.
Small-town girl Aurora has a glorious singing voice, and uses it to become a major international star. However, heartbreak comes with her success, and after losing a lover, several friends, and then her own mother, Aurora returns to her small town roots and marries her childhood sweetheart.

One a Minute (Thomas H. Ince/Paramount, 1921)
d: Jack Nelson. 5 reels.

Douglas MacLean, Marian DeBeck, Victor Potel, Frances Raymond, Andrew Robson, Graham Pettie.
Comedy about a chap who inherits a drugstore and proceeds to make a success by perfecting a cure-all medicine.

One Clear Call (First National, 1922)
d: John M. Stahl. 8 reels.
Claire Windsor, Hanry B. Walthall, Irene Rich, Milton Sills, Stanley Goethals, William Marion Jr., Joseph J. Dowling, Edith Yorke, Doris Pawn, Donald MacDonald, Shannon Day, Annette De Foe, Fred A. Kelsey, Albert MacQuarrie.
Weepy melodrama about Garnett, an outcast who operates a seedy gambling hall, and the fiercely loyal mother who believes in her boy despite his notorious reputation.

One Day (B.S. Moss Motion Picture Corp., 1916)
d: Hal Clarendon. 5 reels.
Jeanne Iver, Victor Sutherland, Barclay Barker, Robert Broderick, John Webb Dillon, Arthur Evers, Hal Clarendon, Walter D. Nealand, Frank Whitson, William Bechtel.
In a Balkan country, a princess is betrothed in an arranged marriage to a prince she does not love. She agrees to the union, but before the nuptials she goes on a vacation trip to England—and there, she falls in love with an exiled prince from her own country.

One Dollar Bid (Paralta Plays, Inc./W.W. Hodkinson, 1918)
d: Ernest C. Warde. 5 reels.
J. Warren Kerrigan, Lois Wilson, Joseph J. Dowling, Leatrice Joy, Arthur Allardt, Jess Herring, Elvira Weil, Clifford Alexander, Jack Gilbert.
In the hills of Kentucky, a moonshiner falls under the influence of the local politicians and is sold into servitude—for one dollar!

One Exciting Night (Griffith/United Artists, 1922)
w,d: D.W. Griffith. 11 reels.
Carol Dempster, Henry Hull, Morgan Wallace, C.H. Croker-King, Margaret Dale, Charles Emmett Mack, Porter Strong.
A woman discovers the key to a murder mystery and learns the truth about her own past.

One Glorious Day (Famous Players-Lasky/Paramount, 1922)
d: James Cruze. 5 reels.
Will Rogers, Lila Lee, Alan Hale, John Fox, George Nichols, Emily Rait, Clarence Burton.
Will Rogers plays a mild-mannered professor who tells his friends he plans to "leave his body" and escape spiritually, then return in an altered form. Sure enough, something like that does happen, though not exactly as the professor and his friends imagined. He mysteriously becomes an aggressor, swaggering about and trouncing some crooked politicians and a cad who has designs on the professor's sweetie. As quickly as it came, the trance leaves him and the prof reverts to his meek state. Now, he at least has the courage to ask his girlfriend to marry him.

One Glorious Night (Columbia, 1924)
d: Scott Dunlap. 6 reels.
Al Roscoe, Elaine Hammerstein, Freeman Wood, Phyllis Haver, Lillian Elliott, Clarissa Selwynne.
Girl loves noble poor boy, but marries wealthy fop instead. The marriage flops and the couple's newborn baby is put up for adoption. But *One Glorious Night* earns its title when, five years later, the girl is reunited with her former sweetheart

and her child.

One Glorious Scrap (Universal, 1927)
d: Edgar Lewis. 5 reels.
Fred Humes, Dorothy Gulliver, Robert McKenzie, Francis Ford, George French, Cuyler Supplee, Benny Corbett, Gilbert Holmes, Dick L'Estrange, Scotty Mattraw.
Out West, drought-plagued ranchers try to hire a rainmaker.

One Hour (B.S. Moss Motion Picture Corp., 1917)
d: Paul McAllister, Edwin L. Hollywood. 6 reels.
Zena Keefe, Alan Hale, D.J. Flanagan, Ina Brooks, Warren Cook, Henry W. Pemberton, William Marion, Franklyn Hanna, Herbert Dansey.
In the Canadian wilderness, young Opal falls in love with Stanley, a neighboring youth. Neither of them know it, but they are both of royal blood—and in time, they will be summoned to their native countries to assume their rightful roles.

One Hour Before Dawn (Jesse D. Hampton Productions/Pathé, 1920)
d: Henry King. 5 reels.
H.B. Warner, Anna Q. Nilsson, Augustus Phillips, Frank Leigh, Howard Davies, Adele Farrington, Lillian Rich, Dorothy Hagan, Thomas Guise, Ralph McCullough, Edward Burns.
At a social gathering, a hypnotist plants in a guest's mind the suggestion that he kill his neighbor "one hour before dawn." Next morning, when the neighbor is found murdered, all suspicions point to the hypnotist and his subject.

One Hour of Love (Tiffany Productions, 1927)
d: Robert Florey. 7 reels.
Jacqueline Logan, Robert Frazer, Montagu Love, Taylor Holmes, Duane Thompson, Mildred Harris, Hazel Keener, William Austin, Henry Sedley, Billy Bletcher.
A spoiled socialite bets her friends she can coax a marriage proposal from a certain tough engineer within one week.

One Increasing Purpose (Fox, 1927)
d: Harry Beaumont. 8 reels.
Edmund Lowe, Lila Lee, Holmes Herbert, May Allison, Lawford Davidson, Emily Fitzroy, George Irving, Huntley Gordon, Josef Swickard, Jane Novak, Nicholas Soussanin, Tom Maguire, Gwynneth Bristowe.
A war veteran and his wife go on a crusade to spread the message of brotherly love.

One Law For Both (Ivan Film Productions, Inc., 1917)
d: Ivan Abramson. 8 reels.
Rita Jolivet, James Morrison, Leah Baird, Vincent Serrano, Paul Capellani, Helen Arnold, Pedro de Cordoba, Margaret Greene, Anders Randolf, Hassan Mussalli, Walter Gould.
When an American lawyer learns that his foreign-born wife had slept with another man in her native country, he turns her out of his house. But the lawyer's sister then reminds him that he had argued a case in court in which he defended a man who had had an illegitimate child. Should there be a different law for each sex, or one law for both?

A One Man Game (Universal, 1927)
d: Ernst Laemmle. 5 reels.
Fred Humes, Fay Wray, Harry Todd, Clarence Geldert, Norbert Myles, Lotus Thompson, William Malan, Julia Griffith, Bud Osborne.
Out West, a rancher fancies a frilly eastern society girl, but ultimately falls in love with a tomboy he's known for years.

One Man in a Million (Sol Lesser/Robertson-Cole, 1921)
d: George Beban. 6 reels.
George Beban, Helen Jerome Eddy, Irene Rich, Lloyd Whitlock, George B. Williams, Jennie Lee, Wade Boteler, George Beban Jr.
A young woman is attracted to a pound worker because of his love for animals.

The One-Man Trail (Fox, 1921)
d: Bernard J. Durning. 5 reels.
Buck Jones, Beatrice Burnham, Helene Rosson, James Farley.
Tom, an itinerant cowpoke, returns home to learn that his Pa's been murdered by a gambler who desires Tom's sister.

One Million Dollars (Rolfe Photoplays, Inc./Metro, 1915)
d: John W. Noble. 5 reels.
William Faversham, Henry Bergman, George LeGuere, Mayme Kelso, Carlotta DeFelice, Arthur Morrison, Charles Graham, Camilla Dalberg.
In England, a detective solves a murder by using a crystal ball given him in India.

One Million in Jewels (William B. Brush/American Releasing Corp., 1923)
w, d: J.P. McGowan. 5 reels.
Helen Holmes, J.P. McGowan, Elinor Fair, Nellie Parker spaulding, Charles Craig, Leslie Casey, Herbert Pattee.
Burke, a Secret Service agent, is on the case when a gang tries to smuggle a million dollars worth of jewels from Cuba to the United States. Complicating the mission is the fact that Helen, the gang's leader, is secretly in love with Burke.

One Minute to Play (R-C Pictures/FBO of America, 1926)
d: Sam Wood. 8 reels.
Red Grange, Mary McAllister, Charles Ogle, George Wilson, Ben Hendricks Jr., Lee Shumway, Al Cooke, Kit Guard, Lincoln Stedman, Jay Hunt, Edythe Chapman.
Red, a high school football phenom, goes to college but is forbidden to play football there because his wealthy donor father fears injuries to his son. But Dad will change his mind.

One More American (Lasky Feature Plays/Paramount, 1918)
d: William C. DeMille. 5 reels.
George Beban, Camille Ankewich, May Giraci, Helen Jerome Eddy, Raymond Hatton, Jack Holt, Horace B. Carpenter, Hector Dion, May Palmer, Ernest Joy.
An Italian puppeteer in New York wants to become an American citizen, but a crooked local official won't release his naturalization papers without a bribe.

One Night in Rome (MGM, 1924)
d: Clarence Badger. 7 reels.
Laurette Taylor, Warner Oland, Tom Moore, Alan Hale, Miss Dupont, Warner Oland, Brandon Hurst, Edna Tichenor, Ralph Yearsley.
A fortune-teller's client recognizes her as a woman with a scandalous past.

One of Many (Columbia/Metro, 1917)
d: William Christy Cabanne. 5 reels.
Frances Nelson, Niles Welch, Mary Mersch, Harold Entwhistle, Richard Dix, Walter Worden, Adella Barker, Caroline Harris.
In desperate straits, a young woman becomes a wealthy man's mistress.

One of the Bravest (Gotham Productions/Lumas Film

Corp., 1925)
d: Frank O'Connor. 6 reels.
Ralph Lewis, Edward Hearn, Sidney Franklin, Pat Somerset, Claire McDowell, Marion Mack.
Kelly, a fireman, is deathly afraid of fires. But when a blaze breaks out and it's up to Kelly to save his father's life, he overcomes his fear and becomes a hero.

One of the Finest (Goldwyn, 1919)
d: Harry Beaumont. 5 reels.
Tom Moore, Seena Owen, Peaches Jackson, Mollie McConnell, Mary Warren, Hallam Cooley, Edwin Sturgis, Frederick Vroom, Adelaide Elliott.
When a New York cop sends a criminal to prison and leaves the man's little daughter homeless, the kindly cop takes her into his own home. Complications arise when the cop's girlfriend wants to know what's the deal with the little girl, but it's all straightened out by the final reel.

One-Round Hogan (Warner Bros., 1927)
d: Howard Bretherton. 7 reels.
Monte Blue, Leila Hyams, James J. Jeffries, Tom Gallery, Frank Hagney.
A prizefighter responds to a friend's death in the ring by holding back in his own fights.

One Shot Ross (Triangle, 1917)
d: Clifford Smith. 5 reels.
Roy Stewart, Josie Sedgwick, Jack Richardson, Louis Durham, William Ellingford, Leo Willis.
Out West, a lawman known as "One Shot" Ross decides to give up his firearms when he sees the daughter of one of his victims sobbing uncontrollably over her father's body. Ross' conversion lasts until he sees another girl, distraught and inconsolable, grieving over her dead father who was shot by outlaws. Now seeing both sides of the moral dilemma, Ross decides to get back to work, rounds up a posse, and leads the men to the outlaws' hideaway, where he shoots it out with the outlaw chief and rescues his lovely hostage.

One Splendid Hour (Excellent Pictures, 1929)
d: Burton King. 6 reels.
Viola Dana, George Periolat, Allan Simpson, Lewis Sargent, Jack Richardson, Lucy Beaumont, Florice Cooper, Ernie S. Adams, Hugh Saxon, Charles Hickman.
Bobbie, a callous socialite, decides to "go slumming" on skid row, to laugh at the dregs of society. Instead, she meets a charismatic social worker who inspires her to amend her life.

One Stolen Night (Vitagraph, 1923)
d: Robert Ensminger. 5 reels.
Alice Calhoun, Herbert Heyes, Otto Hoffman, Adele Farrington, Russ Powell.
Wealthy Diana and her family travel to the Sahara to visit her fiancé. Once there, she is kidnapped by a sheik and threatened with imprisonment in his harem, but she is rescued by a strange Arab. After the danger is over, Diana discovers that the "Arab" who saved her is her fiancé in disguise.

One Stolen Night (Warner Bros., 1929)
d: Scott R. Dunlap. 6 reels. (Part talkie.)
William Collier Jr., Betty Bronson, Harry Schultz, Mitchell Lewes, Harry Todd, Charles Hill Mailes, Nina Quartero, Otto Lederer.
A British soldier joins a vaudeville troupe and wins the heart of a showgirl.

One-Thing-at-a-Time O'Day (Metro, 1919)

d: John Ince. 5 reels.
Bert Lytell, Joseph Kilgour, Eileen Percy, Stanton Heck, William A. Carroll, Jules Hanft, John Hack, Bull Montana.
Circus comedy has a good-natured chap falling in love with a bareback rider, then fighting off a felonious circus strongman.

One Thousand Dollars (Vitagraph, 1918)
d: Kenneth Webb. 5 reels.
Edward Earle, Agnes Ayres, Florence Deshon, Templar Saxe, Anne Brody.
Eddie loves Margaret, but spends most of his time with Lotta, a burlesque dancer. When his wealthy uncle dies and leaves Eddie only $1,000, Lotta dumps him, clearing the way for Margaret to claim Eddie for herself.

One Touch of Nature (Thomas A. Edison, Inc., 1917)
d: Edward H. Griffith. 5 reels.
John Drew Bennett, Viola Cain, Edward O'Connor, George Henry, Helen Strickland, John J. McGraw, Edward Lawrence.
William, a scion of wealth, is disinherited by his dad when the lad marries a vaudeville dancer. Left to his own devices, William parlays his college baseball experience into a job with the New York Giants... and wins the big game with a home run.
John J. McGraw, manager of the New York Giants, plays himself in this film.

One Touch of Sin (Fox, 1917)
d: Richard Stanton. 5 reels.
Gladys Brockwell, Jack Standing, Willard Louis, Sedley Brown, Carrie Clark Ward, Frankie Lee, Charles Edhler, Jack MacDonald.
Hard-luck Mary is deserted by her lover, loses her father, and turns to stealing in order to eat. But her luck changes when she meets Tabor, a good man who truly loves her.

One Way Street (First National, 1925)
d: John Francis Dillon. 6 reels.
Ben Lyon, Anna Q. Nilsson, Marjorie Daw, Dorothy Cumming, Lumsden Hare, Mona Kingsley, Thomas Holding.
A famous opera singer loses her voice and fears the loss of her social status.

The One Way Trail (Republic, 1920)
d: Fred Kelsey. 5 reels.
Edythe Sterling, Gordon Sackville, Jack Connolly, J. Webster Dill, Alfred Hollingsworth.
In the Canadian northwest, a Mountie on the trail of a dangerous outlaw appoints his sweetheart's father as his deputy—not knowing that the dad is an escaped convict.

One Week of Life (Goldwyn, 1919)
d: Hobart Henley. 5 reels.
Pauline Frederick, Thomas Holding, Sydney Ainsworth, Corinne Barker, Percy Challenger.
An unhappily married woman is dying to spend a week alone with her lover. She gets her chance when she meets a lookalike who can take her place at home with her husband for the seven days of freedom she needs. Alas, the illicit lovers are drowned during a storm and the husband is left with the impostor... who, as it turns out, is perfectly suited to him.
Pauline Frederick does double duty here, playing both the unhappy wife and her lookalike.

One Week of Love (Selznick, 1922)

d: George Archainbaud. 7 reels.
Elaine Hammerstein, Conway Tearle, Kate Lester, Hallam Cooley.
A frivolous society girl flies her own airplane and crashlands in Mexico. She's unhurt in the crash, but is found by a rough-hewn American expatriate, and they become lovers.

One Wild Week (Realart Pictures, 1921)
d: Maurice Campbell. 5 reels.
Bebe Daniels, Frank Kingsley, Mayme Kelso, Frances Raymond, Herbert Standing, Edwin Stevens, Edythe Chapman, Carrie Clark Ward, Bull Montana.
Pauline is due to inherit a fortune, but only if the family lawyer considers her spotless and well-behaved. Wouldn't you know it, the day before the inheritance is to kick in, Pauline is framed for picking pockets and gets thrown into jail. But she's innocent, and with the friendly help of an amorous young lawyer who's got more on his mind than simple justice, the comely heiress wins her freedom, her inheritance, and a new love.

The One Woman (National Drama Corp./Select, 1918)
d: Reginald Barker. 6 reels.
Lawson Butt, Clara Williams, Herschel Mayall, Thurston Hall, Ben Alexander, Adda Gleason, Mary Jane Irving.
Gordon, an idealistic preacher who dreams of founding a "Temple of Man" and who opposes war, comes to feel that idealism has its limits. So, he divorces his wife and enters into a common law relationship with another woman. But that doesn't bring him happiness either.

The One Woman Idea (Fox, 1929)
d: Berthold Viertel. 7 reels.
Rod LaRocque, Marceline Day, Shirley Dorman, Sharon Lynn, Sally Phipps, Ivan Lebedeff, Douglas Gilmore, Gino Corrado, Joseph W. Girard, Arnold Lucy, Coy Watson.
Ahmed, a Persian prince, falls in love with the wife of a British nobleman.

One Woman to Another (Paramount, 1927)
d: Frank Tuttle. 5 reels.
Florence Vidor, Theodore von Eltz, Marie Shotwell, Hedda Hopper, Roy Stewart, Joyce Coad, Jimsy Boudwin.
Comedy about John and Rita, desperately in love and eager to marry, but finding the bridal trail strewn with obstacles.

One Wonderful Night (Universal, 1922)
d: Stuart Paton. 5 reels.
Herbert Rawlinson, Lillian Rich, Sidney Bracey, Dale Fuller, Sidney DeGrey, Joseph W. Girard, Jean DeBriac, Amelio Mendez, Spottiswoode Aitken.
Curtis, a gentleman and a sport, marries a young woman so that she will not have to marry the obnoxious—and *phony*—count her dad has picked out for her.

One Year to Live (First National, 1925)
d: Irving Cummings. 7 reels.
Aileen Pringle, Dorothy Mackaill, Sam DeGrasse, Rosemary Theby, Leo White, Joseph Kilgour, Antonio Moreno, Rose Dione, Chester Conklin.
A love-struck doctor tells his pretty patient that she has only one year to live, but it's just a ploy to weaken her resistance to his amorous attentions. The ploy doesn't work.

Only a Shop Girl (Columbia, 1922)
d: Edward J. Le Saint. 7 reels.
William Scott, Estelle Taylor, Wallace Beery, Josephine Adair, Mae Busch.
Murder mystery, with an ex-con the primary suspect. But he didn't do it.

The Only Road (Metro, 1918)
d: Frank Reicher. 5 reels.
Viola Dana, Casson Ferguson, Edythe Chapman, Fred Huntley, Monte Blue, Paul Weigel, Marie Van Tassell, Gertrude Short.
Nita is the tomboy daughter of poor California ranch workers, or so she thinks. In fact, she was stolen from her parents at birth and raised by the ranch workers. But Nita will soon be reunited with her mother, and will find a handsome new husband.

The Only Thing (MGM, 1925)
d: Jack Conway. 6 reels.
Conrad Nagel, Eleanor Boardman, Edward Connelly, Arthur Edmund Carewe, Vera Lewis, Dale Fuller, Ned Sparks, Louis Payne, Carrie Clark Ward, Mario Carillo, Joan Crawford.
In a small European kingdom, a revolution breaks out just as the king is about to marry the princess of a neighboring country.

Only 38 (Famous Players-Lasky/Paramount, 1923)
d: William C. DeMille. 7 reels.
May McAvoy, Lois Wilson, Elliott Dexter, George Fawcett, Robert Agnew, Jane Keckley, Lillian Leighton, Taylor Graves, Anne Cornwall.
Lucy, a young widow with teenage twins, decides to change her looks and lead a glamorous life style—much to her children's dismay.

The Only Woman (Norma Talmadge Productions/First National, 1924)
d: Sidney Olcott. 7 reels.
Norma Talmadge, Eugene O'Brien, Edwards Davis, Winter Hall, Matthew Betz, E.H. Calvert, Stella DiLanti, Murdock MacQuarrie, Neal Dodd, Brooks Benedict, Charles O'Malley.
Helen is forced into marriage with Rex, a weakling with a drinking problem. Desperately unhappy, she takes her husband on a cruise, hoping a change of scenery will help the situation. It does, but not in the way she imagined. They are shipwrecked on an island far away from liquor and other comforts, and Rex is forced to develop character. By the time the couple are rescued, they are in new, everlasting love.

Open All Night (Famous Players-Lasky/Paramount, 1924)
d: Paul Bern. 6 reels.
Viola Dana, Jetta Goudal, Adolphe Menjou, Raymond Griffith, Maurice B. Flynn, Gale Henry, Jack Giddings, Charles Puffy.
Comedy about Therese, who's married to a mild-mannered gent and longs for a dash of adventure.

The Open Door (Artclass Pictures Corp./Robertson-Cole, 1919)
d: Dallas M. Fitzgerald. 5 reels.
John P. Wade, Sam J. Ryan, Robert Broderick, Frank Evans, Anna Lehr, Edith Stockton, Walter Miller, Diana Allen, William Cavanaugh, Johnnie Walker.
Joe Moore, a former bookkeeper, serves fifteen years in prison for embezzlement, a crime he did not commit. When he's released from prison, the truth comes out: He agreed to take the rap in return for assurances that his motherless little girl would be taken care of.

Open Places (Essanay, 1917)
d: W.S. Van Dyke. 5 reels.

Jack Gardner, Carl Stockdale, Ruth King.
In Montana, a schoolteacher marries a dapper outdoorsman, unaware that he's a thoroughly bad egg.

Open Range (Paramount, 1927)
d: Clifford S. Smith. 6 reels.
Betty Bronson, Lane Chandler, Fred Kohler, Bernard Siegel, Guy Oliver, Jim Corey, George Connors.
Out West, a cowpoke is unjustly charged with cattle rustling.

Open Your Eyes (Warner Bros., 1919)
d: Gilbert P. Hamilton. 7 reels.
Ben Lyon, Gaston Glass, Faire Binney, Emilie Marceau, Jack Warner.
An educational film cautioning against indiscriminate sex and its medical consequences, presented in narrative format.

Opened Shutters (Universal, 1921)
d: William Worthington. 5 reels.
Joseph Swickard, Edith Roberts, Joe Singleton, Mai Wells, Clark Comstock, Edward Burns, Charles Clary, Floye Brown, Nola Luxford, Andrew Waldron, Lorraine Wieler.
A newly orphaned girl living with her aunt and uncle feels unwanted,. But her charm and grace slowly win over her new guardians, as well as most of the townfolk—especially a young lawyer who has captured her heart.

The Opening Night (Columbia, 1927)
d: Edward H. Griffith. 6 reels.
Claire Windsor, John Bowers, E. Alyn Warren, Grace Goodall, Bobby Mack, William Welsh.
Bowers, a theater producer, is lost at sea and presumed drowned. Three months later he returns home and finds his wife remarried. Now what?

Opportunity (Metro, 1918)
d: John H. Collins. 5 reels.
Viola Dana, Hale Hamilton, Frank Currier, Edward Abeles, Sally Crute, Joseph Burke, Frank Lyon, Elsie MacLeod.
Tomboy Mary dresses in boys' clothes to attend prizefights.

Orchids and Ermine (First National, 1927)
d: Alfred Santell. 7 reels.
Colleen Moore, Jack Mulhall, Sam Hardy, Gwen Lee, Alma Bennett, Hedda Hopper, Kate Price, Jed Prouty, Emily Fitzroy, Caroline Snowden, Yola D'Avril, Brooks Benedict.
Dreams come true for a telephone operator who dreams of orchids and ermine... and love.

The Ordeal (Famous Players-Lasky/Paramount, 1922)
d: Paul Powell. 5 reels.
Clarence Burton, Agnes Ayres, Conrad Nagel, Edna Murphy, Anne Schaefer, Eugene Corey, Adele Farrington, Edward Martindel, Shannon Day, Claire DuBrey.
Heavy drama about a wife who, tired of her marriage to an older man, allows him to die of a heart attack. She inherits his fortune on condition that she never remarry, then has to rethink her decision when she falls in love with a young doctor.

The Ordeal of Elizabeth (Vitagraph, 1916)
d: Wilfrid North. 6 reels.
Lillian Walker, Evart Overton, Denton Vane, Ollie Walker, Kate Price, L. Rogers Lytton, Templar Saxe, R.M.S. Putnam, Karin Norman, Walter McGrail.
While her husband is away in Europe, impulsive Elizabeth starts up a romance with a new lover.

The Ordeal of Rosetta (Select Pictures Corp., 1918)
d: Emile Chautard. 5 reels.

Alice Brady, Crauford Kent, Ormi Hawley, Henri Leone, Maude Turner Gordon, Hazel Washburn, Ed Burns, George Henry.
In New York, a Sicilian girl is haunted by the specter of her twin sister, who was killed in an earthquake.

The Orphan (Fox, 1920)
d: J. Gordon Edwards. 6 reels.
William Farnum, Louise Lovely, Henry J. Hebert, Earl Crain, G. Raymond Nye, George Nichols, Harry DeVere, Olive White, Al Fremont, Carrie Clark Ward.
Out West, a bandit known as "the Orphan" joins forces with lawmen to repel an Indian attack.

Orphans of the Storm (Griffith/United Artists, 1921)
w, d: D.W. Griffith. 14 reels.
Lillian Gish, Dorothy Gish, Joseph Schildkraut, Lucille LaVerne, Morgan Wallace, Frank Puglia, Creighton Hale, Monte Blue, Sidney Herbert, Sheldon Lewis, Frank Losee, Katherine Emmett, Leslie King, Monte Blue, Lee Kohlmar, Adolphe Lestina, Kate Bruce, Flora Finch, Louis Wolheim, Kenny Delmar, Herbert Sutch, James Smith, Rose Smith.
Two adoptive sisters, one of them blind, are caught up in the French Revolution.
Spectacular costume drama which includes a furious race to the rescue after one of the sisters is sentenced to the guillotine.

The Other Girl (Raver Film Corp., 1916)
d: Percy Winter. 5 reels.
James J. Corbett, Paul Gilmore, Horace Vinton, Mortimer Martini, Louis Thiel, Rawland Ratcliffe, Henry Redding, Ten Eyck Clay, Mona Ryan, Becky Bruce, Edith Luckett.
Though engaged to be married, socialite Catherine Fulton agrees to a romantic rendezvous with a prizefighter. Her sister overhears them, however, and schemes to take Catherine's place.

The Other Half (Brentwood Film Corp., 1919)
d: King Vidor. 5 reels.
Florence Vidor, Charles Meredith, ZaSu Pitts, David Butler, Alfred Allen, Frances Raymond, Hugh Saxon, Thomas Jefferson, Arthur Redden.
The high-minded son of an industrialist decides he wants to start at the bottom and work his way up, with no special favoritism.

The Other Man (Vitagraph, 1918)
d: Paul Scardon. 5 reels.
Harry T. Morey, Grace Darmond, Florence Deshon, Frank Norcross, Jessie Stevens, Stanley Walpole.
Disillusioned after finding his wife in the arms of another man, a young doctor becomes a derelict and lives in a slum. There, he meets and falls in love with Dorothy, not knowing that she is wealthy and is living an austere life for only a short time, to win a bet.

Other Men's Daughters (Fox, 1918)
d: Carl Harbaugh. 5 reels.
Peggy Hyland, Eric Mayne, Elizabeth Garrison, Regina Quinn, Riley Hatch, Frank Goldsmith, Robert Middlemas.
When her father is suspected of philandering, Shirley pays him a secret visit and learns that the suspicions are true.

Other Men's Shoes (Edgar Lewis Productions, Inc./Pathé, 1920)
d: Edgar Lewis. 7 reels.
Crauford Kent, Irene Boyle, Stephen Gratton, Jean Armour, Harold Foshay, John P. Wade, Phil Sanford, Bobby Connelly,

Edna May Sperl, Jack Sharkey.
After a minister suffers a nervous breakdown, his brother steps in and takes over his flock. What the brother hasn't told anyone is that he's just recently been released from prison.

Other Men's Wives (Thomas H. Ince/Paramount, 1919)
d: Victor L. Schertzinger. 5 reels.
Dorothy Dalton, Forrest Stanley, H.E. Herbert, Dell Boone, Elsie Larimer, Hal Clements.
Destitute after the death of her father, a socialite accepts an offer of money from a wealthy cad to blackmail one of his rivals for another woman's hand.

Other People's Money (Thanhouser/Mutual, 1916)
d: William Parke. 5 reels.
Gladys Hulette, Fraunie Fraunholz, J.H. Gilmour, Yale Benner, Kathryn Adams.
A millionaire and a banker's daughter use a "sting" operation to outwit a husband-and-wife team of swindlers.

The Other Side of the Door (American Film Co./Mutual, 1916)
d: Thomas Ricketts. 5 reels.
Harold Lockwood, May Allison, William Stowell, Harry Von Meter, Dick LaReno, Josephine Humphreys, Roy Stewart.
Out West, a newcomer falls in love with a casino owner's mistress.

The Other Woman (Astra Film Corp./Pathé, 1918)
d: Albert Parker. 5 reels.
Milton Sills, Ethel Clayton, John Davidson, Frank de Vernon, Walter James, Peggy Hyland, Anna Lehr.
Small-town girl Eleanor moves to New York, where she becomes friends with a stock broker. The friendship is strictly platonic at first, but when the broker and his wife have a rift, he turns to his young friend from the country.

The Other Woman (J.L. Fothingham Productions/W.W. Hodkinson, 1921)
d: Edward Sloman. 5 reels.
Jerome Patrick, Jane Novak, Helen Jerome Eddy, William Conklin, Joseph J. Dowling, Frankie Lee, Lincoln Palmer, Kate Price.
Langdon, an amnesiac, has no memory of his wife and children, and thus feels perfectly free to marry.

Other Women's Clothes (Hugo Ballin Productions/W.W. Hodkinson, 1922)
d: Hugo Ballin. 6 reels.
Mabel Ballin, Raymond Bloomer, Crauford Kent, May Kitson, William H. Strauss, Aggie LaField, Rose Burdick.
Tale about a wealthy bachelor who comes up with a novel way of making his girlfriend's dreams come true: He invents an unknown benefactor, who then "dies" and leaves a fortune to the girlfriend.

Other Women's Husbands (Warner Bros., 1926)
d: Erle C. Kenton. 7 reels.
Marie Prevost, Monte Blue, Huntley Gordon, Phyllis Haver, Marjorie Gay, John Patrick.
At a masked ball, a betrayed wife wears a costume identical to that of her husband's mistress and tries to win him away from her.

Our Better Selves (Astra Film Corp./Pathé, 1919)
d: George Fitzmaurice. 5 reels.
Fannie Ward, Lewis J. Cody, Charles Hill Mailes, Mary Lee Wise.

Two wealthy idlers marry, and seem destined to continue their selfish ways. But the start of World War I galvanizes their better selves, and they join the war effort and help defeat the enemy.

Our Dancing Daughters (MGM, 1928)
d: Harry Beaumont. 9 reels.
Joan Crawford, Johnny Mack Brown, Dorothy Sebastian, Anita Page, Nils Asther, Eddie Nugent, Dorothy Cumming.
Jazz-age seriocomedy finds a wild deb breaking up a marriage.

Our Hospitality (Metro, 1923)
d: Buster Keaton, Jack Blystone. 7 reels.
Buster Keaton, Natalie Talmadge, Joseph Keaton, Buster Keaton Jr., Kitty Bradbury, Joe Roberts, Leonard Clapham, Craig Ward, Ralph Bushman, Edward Coxen, Jean Dumas.
In 1830, New York city's Willie McKay (Keaton) discovers he is heir to property in the South. He journeys to Kentucky to claim his inheritance, only to learn that his family was involved in a feud of several generations' standing. As the youngest of the McKays, he finds himself in the cross-hairs of the enemy clan wherever he goes. To complicate matters, he and the daughter of his enemy have fallen in love.
Most Keatonphiles praise the comedian's trio of "major" works—*The Navigator* (1924), *Sherlock Jr.* (1924), and *The General* (1926)—as his most stunning accomplishments. But *Our Hospitality* should be added to make it a quartet. No Keaton film boasts more rapid-fire gags, and the plot elements flow more smoothly here than in most feature-length comedies. There's also a gasp-inducing stunt in the final third of the movie, where McKay rescues his lady love from certain death, nanoseconds before she is to plunge over a deadly waterfall. There was surely a double for Miss Talmadge, but Keaton, as usual, did his own stunt work. And, as in the best silent comedies, there's a visual gag at the fadeout that tops another one just moments earlier.

Our Leading Citizen (Famous Players-Lasky/Paramount, 1922)
d: Alfred E. Green. 7 reels.
Thomas Meighan, Lois Wilson, William P. Carleton, Theodore Roberts, Guy Oliver, Laurence Wheat, James Neill, Lucien Littlefield, Charles Ogle, Tom Kennedy, Sylvia Ashton.
Bentley, a decorated war hero, is persuaded by his sweetheart to run for Congress against the nominee of the political machine.

Our Little Wife (Goldwyn, 1918)
d: Edward Dillon. 6 reels.
Madge Kennedy, George Forth, Walter Hiers, William Davidson, Kempton Greene, Marguerite Marsh, Wray Page.
Marital comedy with an incredible premise: An impulsive bride insists that she and her new husband take her three former beaus on the honeymoon with them!

Our Modern Maidens (MGM, 1929)
d: Jack Conway. 8 reels. (Music, sound effects, part talkie.)
Joan Crawford, Douglas Fairbanks Jr., Rod LaRocque, Anita Page, Eddie Nugent, Josephine Dunn.
Jazz-age lovers Billie and Gil get married, travel to Paris, and find their union threatened by Gil's extra-marital affair.

Our Mrs. McChesney (Metro, 1918)
d: Ralph W. Ince. 5 reels.
Ethel Barrymore, Huntley Gordon, Wilfred Lytell, Lucille Lee Stewart, John Daly Murphy, Walter Percival, William H.

St. James, Ricca Allen, George Trimble, Sammy Cooper, Fred Walters.

Emma McChesney is not only a successful petticoat saleswoman, she's also a terrific designer. To save her company from bankruptcy, she creates a new skirt that takes the fashion world by storm.

Our Teddy — see: The Fighting Roosevelts (1919)

Out All Night (Universal, 1927)
d: William A. Seiter. 6 reels.
Reginald Denny, Marian Nixon, Wheeler Oakman, Dorothy Earle, Dan Mason, Alred Allen, Robert Seiter, Ben Hendricks Jr., Billy Franey, Harry Tracey, Lionel Braham.
Molly, a star of musical comedies, falls in love with Graham and they are married. But her contract stipulates a salary cut in case she should marry, so the newlyweds try desperately to stay close together, yet far enough apart to deflect any suspicion that they are husband and wife.

Out of a Clear Sky (Famous Players-Lasky/Paramount, 1918)
d: Marshall Neilan. 5 reels.
Marguerite Clark, Thomas Meighan, E.J. Radcliffe, Bobby Connelly, Raymond Bloomer, Robert Dudley, Walter P. Lewis, Maggie H. Fisher, Helene Montrose, Robert Vivian, Nell Clark Keller.
Fleeing from an enemy, a Belgian countess in the United States gets off her train at the first station, a small town in Tennessee. There, she meets and falls in love with an American who promises to protect her from her pursuer.

Out of Luck — see: Nobody Home (1919)

Out of Luck (Universal, 1923)
d: Edward Sedgwick. 6 reels.
Hoot Gibson, Laura LaPlante, Howard Truesdale, Elinor Hancock, DeWitt Jennings, Freeman Wood, Jay Morley, Kansas Moehring, John Judd.
Sam, a westerner, enlists in the Navy by mistake and then can't get out of it. But he'll become a hero when he saves his captain from an attacker, and earns a promotion.

Out of the Chorus (Realart Pictures, 1921)
d: Herbert Blache. 5 reels.
Alice Brady, Vernon Steel, Charles Gerard, Emily Fitzroy, Constance Berry, Edith Stockton, Ben Probst, Richard Carlyle.
A square peg in a round hole... that's what her mother-in-law thinks of Flo, a chorine who's married into high society.

Out of the Darkness (Lasky Feature Plays/Paramount, 1915)
d: George Melford. 5 reels.
Charlotte Walker, Thomas Meighan, Marjorie Daw, Hal Clements, Tom Forman, Loyola O'Connor.
When her yacht is involved in an accident at sea, an heiress receives a blow to the head that brings on amnesia.

Out of the Drifts (Famous Players/Paramount, 1916)
d: J. Searle Dawley. 5 reels.
Marguerite Clark, J.W. Johnston, Albert Gran, William Courtleigh Jr., Ivan Simpson, DeWitt Lillibridge, Kitty Brown, Florence Johns, Robert Conville.
In Switzerland, a world-weary Londoner meets and woos a shepherd girl.

Out of the Dust (McCarthy Picture Productions, 1920)
d: John P. McCarthy. 6 reels.
Russell Simpson, Dorcas Matthews, Robert McKim, Francis Powers, Master Pat Moore, Bert Sprotte, Master Mickey Moore.
In the Old West, a cavalry captain fights Indians, but can't keep his wife from getting bored with Army life.

Out of the Fog (Metro, 1919)
d: Albert Capellani. 7 reels.
Nazimova, Charles Bryant, Henry Harman, Nancy Palmer, T. Morse Koupal, George W. Davis, Charles Smiley, Tom Blake, Hugh Jeffrey, Dorothy Smoller, Marie Grant, Ada Scovill.
After being sheltered by her obsessive uncle all her life, a 20-year-old woman is impulsively kissed by a sailor, and her romantic impulses are awakened.

Out of the Night (Frank A. Keeney Pictures Corp., 1918)
d: James Kirkwood. 6 reels.
Catherine Calvert, Herbert Rawlinson, Frederick Esmelton, Emmett King, Harry C. Myers, Ida Darling, Bessie Stinson, Eldean Stuart, Harry Lee, Dan Malloy, Barney Gilmore.
Denied a loan and desperate for funds, a young woman becomes a prostitute. But circumstances bring her together with the company officer who turned down her loan and with his son, who falls in love with the fallen woman.

Out of the Past (Dallas M. Fitzgerald Pictures/Peerless Pictures, 1927)
d: Dallas M. Fitzgerald. 6 reels.
Robert Frazer, Mildred Harris, Ernest Wood, Rose Tapley, Mario Marano, Joyzelle Joyner, Harold Miller, Byron Sage, William Clifford.
Formula weeper about Dora, a girl whose lover is reported killed in the war. While she mourns him, she's persuaded to marry a wealthy man she doesn't love and barely knows. Sure enough, the "dead" soldier returns, alive and well.

Out of the Ruins (First National Pictures, 1928)
d: John Francis Dillon. 7 reels.
Richard Barthelmess, Robert Frazer, Marian Nixon, Emile Chautard, Bodil Rosing, Eugene Pallette, Rose Dione.
During World War I, a soldier leaves the front lines during a lull and returns to his sweetheart in Paris, where they are married. Upon returning to duty, he is court-martialed for desertion and sentenced to a firing squad. However, his comrades-in-arms don't have the heart to kill him, and he escapes. After the war, the ex-soldier returns to his wife, upsetting her father's plans for her to marry a wealthy suitor.

Out of the Shadows (Famous Players-Lasky/Paramount, 1919)
d: Emile Chautard. 5 reels.
Pauline Frederick, Wyndham Standing, Ronald Byram, William Gross, Emma Campbell, Nancy Hathaway, Agnes Wakefield, Jack W. Johnson, Synd DeConde, Henry Heaton.
Newly widowed Ruth, whose husband was murdered, is taken in by a kindly philanthropist. But in the murder investigation that follows, Ruth's benefactor is considered one of the prime suspects.

Out of the Silent North (Universal, 1922)
d: William Worthington. 5 reels.
Frank Mayo, Barbara Bedford, Frank Leigh, Harris Gordon, Christian J. Frank, Frank Lanning, Louis Rivera, Dick LaReno.
In the Canadian Northwest, rival gold miners race to the recorder's office with competing claims on a gold strike.

Out of the Snows (National Picture Theaters, Inc./Select,

1920)
d: Ralph Ince. 6 reels.
Ralph Ince, Zena Keefe, Patrick Hartigan, Gladys Coburn, Huntley Gordon, Red Eagle, Jacques Suzanne, H.L. Atkins.
In the Canadian northwest, a Mountie is engaged to marry Ruth Hardy. That is, until she hears from a mutual friend that her fiancé is the man who killed her father.

Out of the Storm (Eminent Authors Pictures, Inc./Goldwyn, 1920)
d: William Parke. 5 reels.
Barbara Castleton, John Bowers, Sydney Ainsworth, Doris Pawn, Elinor Hancock, Lawson Butt, Edythe Chapman, Ashton Dearholt, Carrie Clark Ward, Lincoln Stedman, Clarissa Selwynne.
A poor girl with a glorious singing voice is guided to an operatic career by a benefactor, whom she promises to marry. But meantime, she's fallen in love with a nobleman. What's a diva to do?

Out of the Storm (Tiffany Productions, 1926)
d: Louis J. Gasnier. 6 reels.
Jacqueline Logan, Tyrone Power, Edmund Burns, Montagu Love, Eddie Phillips, George Fawcett, Crawford Kent, Jay Hunt, Joseph W. Girard, Leon Holmes, Frona Hale.
Three-hankie weeper about Mary, a girl with two suitors who sees one of them kill the other over her, then has to live with the guilt.

Out of the West (R-C Pictures/FBO of America, 1926)
d: Robert DeLacy. 5 reels.
Tom Tyler, Bernice Welch, L.J. O'Connor, Ethan Laidlaw, Alfred Hewston, Frankie Darro, Gertrude Claire, Barney Furey.
Rival ranchers, each with his own a baseball team, find their competition escalating beyond the merely friendly.

Out of the Wreck (Oliver Morosco Photoplay Co./Paramount, 1917)
d: William Desmond Taylor. 5 reels.
Kathlyn Williams, William Clifford, William Conklin, Stella Razeto, William Winter Jefferson, Don Bailey.
Sensation-seeking reporters find a scandal in the past of a senatorial candidate.

Out With the Tide (Peerless Pictures, 1928)
d: Charles Hutchison. 6 reels.
Dorothy Dwan, Cullen Landis, Crauford Kent, Mitchell Lewis, Ernest Hilliard, Sojin, James Aubrey, Arthur Thalasso, Etta Lee, Harry Semels, Charles Alexandra.
Templeton, a news reporter, is unjustly accused of murder.

Out Yonder (Selznick/Select, 1919)
d: Ralph Ince. 5 reels.
Olive Thomas, Huntley Gordon, Mary coverdale, Louise Prussing, John Smiley, Cyril Chadwick, Edward Ellis.
The daughter of a lighthouse keeper guides a yacht to shore with lanterns when the lighthouse beam goes out.

Outcast (Empire All-Star Corp./Mutual, 1917)
d: Dell Henderson. 6 reels.
Ann Murdock, David Powell, Catherine Calvert, Richard Hatteras, Jules Raucourt, Herbert Ayling, Reginald Carrington, Kate Sargeantson, H. Ashton Tonge, V.L. Granville.
Seduced and abandoned, young Miriam turns to prostitution to provide for her new baby. But there's a happy ending to Miriam's story when, after several setbacks, she finds true love with a London barrister.

Outcast (Paramount, 1922)
d: Chet Withey. 7 reels.
Elsie Ferguson, David Powell, William David, Mary MacLaren, William Powell, Charles Wellesley, Teddy Sampson.
Poor Miriam. She's alone, out of work, and hungry. Then she meets Geoffrey and they fall in love. Now enjoying real happiness at last, Miriam learns that Geoffrey's former sweetheart wants him back. So Miriam, figuring her good luck has run out, runs away. But Geoffrey wants Miriam—not his ex—and he pursues her to South America to prove it and declare his love.

Outcast (First National/Warner Bros., 1928)
d: William A. Seiter. 8 reels. (Music, sound effects.)
Corinne Griffith, Edmund Lowe, James Ford, Huntly Gordon, Kathryn Carver, Louise Fazenda, Patsy O'Byrne.
Remake of Paramount's 1922 film *Outcast*, both versions based on the play of the same name by Hubert Henry Davies.

Outcast Souls (Sterling Pictures, 1928)
d: Louis Chaudet. 6 reels.
Priscilla Bonner, Charles Delaney, Ralph Lewis, Lucy Beaumont, Tom O'Brien.
Alice and Charles meet cute, get arrested for petting in public, then decide to marry.

The Outcasts of Poker Flat (Universal, 1919)
d: Jack Ford. 6 reels.
Harry Carey, Gloria Hope, Cullen Landis, Joseph Harris.
An Arizona gambling-hall owner falls in love with his pretty ward.

The Outlaw Breaker (Goodwill, 1926)
d: Jacques Jaccard. 5 reels.
Yakima Canutt, Nelson McDowell, Harry Northrup, Alma Rayford, Dick La Reno.
A cattleman finds himself accused of murdering his sweetheart's father.

The Outlaw Express (Leo Maloney Productions/Pathé, 1926)
d: Leo D. Maloney. 6 reels.
Leo Maloney, Joan Renee, Melbourne MacDowell, Albert Hart, Henry Otto, Paul Hurst, Bud Osborne, Evelyn Thatcher, Nelson McDowell, Fred Burns, Frank Ellis.
Out West, a Wells Fargo agent searches for stagecoach robbers.

Outlawed (FBO Pictures, 1929)
d: Eugene Forde. 7 reels.
Sally Blane, Tom Mix, Frank M. Clark, al Smith, Ethan Laidlaw, Barney Furey, Al Ferguson.
In a spectacular rescue, Tom (Tom Mix) saves Anne and her father from a wild horse stampede. Later, he and Anne fall in love.

Outlaws of Red River (Fox, 1927)
d: Lewis Seiler. 6 reels.
Tom Mix, Marjorie Daw, Lee Shumway, Ellen Woonston, Arthur Clayton, Virginia Marshall, Duke Lee, Francis McDonald.
A Texas Ranger searching for his parents' killer meets a young woman who was also orphaned by the same culprit. They team up to bring the killer to justice.

Outside the Law (Universal, 1921)
d: Tod Browning. 8 reels.

Priscilla Dean, Wheeler Oakman, Lon Chaney, Stanley Goethals, Ralph Lewis, E.A. Warren, Melbourne McDowell, Wilton Taylor.

A society crook and her cohort ponder whether to continue their wicked ways or go straight. They finally turn to a disciple of Confucius for advice.

Lon Chaney received high critical praise for his dual role as an arch-criminal and the Confucian who counsels the troubled pair.

The Outside Woman (Realart Pictures, 1921)
d: Thomas N. Heffron. 5 reels.
Wanda Hawley, Clyde Fillmore, Sidney Bracey, Rosita Marstini, Misao Seki, Thena Jasper, Mary Winston, Jacob Abrams.

Marital comedy about Dorothy, a newlywed who swaps one of her husband's old statuettes for a shawl, then learns that the "statuette" is actually an invaluable Aztec idol. She scrambles frantically to find the idol's new owner, and upon finding him she pleads for its return. The fellow is a gentleman, and returns the idol to Dorothy for no more compensation than a kiss. Dorothy agrees, and pays the "ransom." That's when her husband and the gentleman's wife walk in.

The Outsider (Metro, 1917)
d: William C. Dowlan. 6 reels.
Emmy Wehlen, Herbert Heyes, Florence Short, Virginia Palmer, Jules Raucourt, Harry Benham, Ilean Hume, Gladys Fairbanks.

In New York, a shopgirl accidentally uncovers a plot to steal valuable gems.

The Outsider (Fox, 1926)
d: Rowland V. Lee. 6 reels.
Jacqueline Logan, Lou Tellegen, Walter Pidgeon, Roy Atwell, Charles Lane, Joan Standing, Gibson Gowland, Bertram Marburgh, Crauford Kent, Louis Payne.

In England, an injured dancer is cured by a Gypsy mystic.

Outwitted (Metro, 1917)
d: George D. Baker. 5 reels.
Emily Stevens, Earle Foxe, Frank Currier, Ricca Allen, Paul Everton, Frank Joyner, Fred Truesdell, Joseph Burke.

At the reception, a wedding guest announces that the bride is a thief.

Outwitted (Independent Pictures, 1925)
w, d: J.P. McGowan. 5 reels.
Helen Holmes, William Desmond, J.P. McGowan, Grace Cunard, Alec Francis, Emily Fitzroy.

Jack, a Treasury agent, captures a counterfeiter but the culprit escapes on his way to jail. Now Jack's got to bring him in again within 48 hours or be suspended from the department.

The Oval Diamond (Thanhouser, 1916)
d: W. Eugene Moore. 5 reels.
Harris Gordon, Barbara Gilroy, Arthur Bauer.

When Sylvia and her father discover a large diamond in South Africa, they find their lives in peril from greedy miners who want to steal the diamond from them.

Over Night (World Film Corp., 1915)
d: James Young. 5 reels.
Vivian Martin, Sam B. Hardy, Herbert Yost, Florence Morrison, William Jefferson, Jessie Lewis, Kitty Baldwin, Jere Austin, Ada Stirling, Lucile LaVerne, Dorothy Farnum.

Wife swapping? Not exactly. In this romantic comedy, two married couples plan to take a boat trip together. But Richard and Elsie are on board when the ship sails, while their spouses are still ashore. To prevent a scandal, the uncomfortable pair must pose as husband and wife throughout the trip, with amusing consequences.

Over the Border (Famous Players-Lasky/Paramount, 1922)
d: Penrhyn Stanlaws. 7 reels.
Betty Compson, Tom Moore, J. Farrell MacDonald, Casson Ferguson, Sidney D'Albrook, L.C. Shumway, Jean DeBriac, Edward J. Brady, Joe Ray.

In the Canadian Northwest, a mountie is loved by the daughter of the moonshiner he's sworn to capture.

Over the Garden Wall (Vitagraph, 1919)
d: David Smith. 5 reels.
Bessie Love, Myrtle Reeves, Willis Marks, James Blackwell, Edward Hearn, Otto Lederer, Allen Forrest, Anne Schaefer, Jay Morley, Truman Van Dyke, Ruth Fuller Golden.

When an important contract is misplaced and his funds are tied up, an investor is forced to rent out his home and move his family "over the garden wall" to the gardener's house.

Over the Hill (Astra Film Corp./Pathé, 1917)
d: William Parke. 5 reels.
Gladys Hulette, J.H. Gilmour, Dan Mason, William Parke Jr., Chester Barnett, Richard Thornton, Joyce Fair, Paul Clerget, Tula Belle, Inda Palmer, Johnny Carr, William Sullivan.

Esther, a minister's daughter, takes a job on the local newspaper staff and targets the paper's policy of yellow journalism.

Over the Hill — see: Over the Hill to the Poorhouse (1920)

Over the Hill to the Poorhouse (Fox, 1920)
d: Harry Millarde. 11 reels.
Johnny Walker, Mary Carr, William Welch, Sheridan Tansey, Noel Tearle, Stephen Carr, John Dwyer, Jerry Devine, James Sheldon, Wallace Ray, Rosemary Carr, Edna Murphy.

A large, struggling family ekes out a living — though the father is shiftless and a thief — and most of the children drift away as soon as they are old enough to escape. But the mother and her youngest son, John, keep the family going and earn a share of dignity for themselves.

Over the Top (Vitagraph, 1918)
d: Wilfred North. 9 reels.
Arthur Guy, Lois Meredith, James Morrison, Arthur Donaldson, Julia Swayne Gordon, Mary Maurice, Betty Blythe, Nellie Anderson, William Calhoun, William H. Stucky.

Ambitious World War I drama that deals with an American's adventures in the British army, his love affair with a girl whose brother serves under the American's command, and various villains who capture the American and his sweetheart and try to force the girl to marry a German officer.

Over the Wire (Metro, 1921)
d: Wesley Ruggles. 6 reels.
Alice Lake, Al Roscoe, George Stewart, Alan Hale.

Kathleen, a vengeful young woman, secures a job with the man who drove her brother to suicide, and makes him fall in love with her.

Over There (Charles Richman Pictures Corp./Select, 1917)
d: James Kirkwood. 6 reels.
Charles Richman, Anna Q. Nilsson, Walter McGrail,

Gertrude Berkeley, Walter Hiers, Veta Searl, James A. Furey. During World War I, Monty Jackson is thought a coward because he refuses to enlist. He finally does enlist, proves his courage under fire, and wins the love of a good woman.

Overalls (American Film Co./Mutual, 1916)
d: Jack Halloway. 5 reels.
William Stowell, Perry Banks, Warren Ellsworth, Rhea Mitchell, Sylvia Ashton, Estelle Allen, George Ahern, Jack Prescott, George Bailey.
"Overalls" Drew is a camp foreman who's in love with the boss' daughter.

The Overcoat (American Film Co./Mutual, 1916)
d: Rea Berger. 5 reels.
Rhea Mitchell, William Stowell, Perry Banks, Clarence Burton, Warren Ellsworth.
Ex-con Maurice loves prostitute Belle, and together they resolve to amend their lives.

Overland Red (Universal, 1920)
d: Lynn Reynolds. 6 reels.
Harry Carey, Charles LeMoyne, Harold Goodwin, Vola Vale, David B. Gally, Joe Harris.
Out West, an old prospector and his young friend find a dying miner who holds a bag of gold dust and the map to a secret mine.

The Overland Limited (Gotham Productions/Lumas Film Corp., 1925)
d: Frank O'Neill. 6 reels.
Malcolm McGregor, Olive Borden, Alice Lake, Ethel Wales, Ralph Lewis, John Miljan, Roscoe Karns, Emmett King, Charles Hill Mailes, Charles West, Evelyn Jennings.
An insanely jealous man sabotages his romantic rival's new railroad bridge and causes a train to derail.

The Overland Stage (Charles R. Rogers Productions/First National, 1927)
d: Albert Rogell. 7 reels.
Ken Maynard, Kathleen Collins, Tom Santschi, Sheldon Lewis, Dot Farley, Florence Turner, Jay Hunt, William Malan, Paul Hurst, Fred Burns.
At a trading post in Dakota territory, a scout for the Overland Stage must deal with crooked traders and Sioux attacks.

The Overland Telegraph (MGM, 1929)
d: John Waters. 6 reels.
Tim McCoy, Lawford Davidson, Dorothy Janis, Frank Rice.
During the Civil War, an army captain must keep the peace in the West, against Indian attackers.

The Pace That Kills (Willis Kent Productions, 1928)
d: Norton S. Parker. 7 reels.
Owen Gorin, Thelma Daniels, Florence Turner, Florence Dudley, Harry Todd, Arnold Dallas, Virginia Roye.
Unsavory tale with an anti-drug message, about a country girl and her brother who go to the big city and become addicted to narcotics.

The Pace That Thrills (First National, 1925)
d: Webster Campbell. 7 reels.
Ben Lyon, Mary Astor, Charles Beyer, Tully Marshall, Wheeler Oakman, Thomas Holding, Evelyn Walsh Hall, Warner Richmond, Fritzi Brunette, Paul Ellis.
Melodrama about a mother who risks everything to protect her child from the abuses of her alcoholic husband, and winds up killing him and going to jail.

Paddy O'Hara (New York Motion Picture Corp./Triangle, 1917)
d: Walter Edwards. 5 reels.
William Desmond, Mary McIvor, Robert McKim, J.J. Dowling, Walt Whitman.
Paddy's an intrepid newspaper reporter who not only reports the news, but gets involved in it. At least that's what happens when he meets a beautiful countess in a jam.

Padlocked (Paramount, 1926)
d: Allan Dwan. 7 reels.
Lois Moran, Noah Beery, Louise Dresser, Helen Jerome Eddy, Allan Simpson, Florence Turner, Richard Arlen, Charles Lane, Douglas Fairbanks Jr., Charlot Bird, Josephine Crowell.
Discovering that his young daughter has taken a job as a cabaret dancer, a proud millionaire has the girl sent to reform school.

The Pagan (MGM, 1929)
d: W.S. Van Dyke. 7 reels. (Includes singing and talking sequences.)
Ramon Novarro, Renee Adoree, Dorothy Janis, Donald Crisp.
A half-caste South Sea Islander is healthy, wealthy, and charming. Several women are attracted to him, but his heart belongs to a local girl who is, like himself, half islander and half European. Trouble is, her guardian is a pious hypocrite who wants the girl for himself, and aims to destroy his competition.

The Pagan God (Jesse D. Hampton Productions/Robertson-Cole, 1919)
d: Park Frame. 5 reels.
H.B. Warner, Carmen Phillips, Ed Peil, Jack Abbe, Carl Stockdale, Marguerite DeLaMotte, Walter Perry.
To fulfill his mission in Mongolia, a U.S. secret agent must romance a female Chinese agent. He does his job almost too well, losing his American fiancée in the process.

Pagan Passions (Rellimeo Film Syndicate/Selznick, 1924)
d: Colin Campbell. 6 reels.
Wyndham Standing, June Elvidge, Barbara Bedford, Raymond McKee, Sam DeGrasse, Rosemary Theby, Tully Marshall.
Two westerners fall in love in China. However, it isn't long before they are both swallowed up into the Chinese drug underworld.

The Page Mystery (World Film Corp., 1917)
d: Harley Knoles. 5 reels.
Carlyle Blackwell, June Elvidge, Frank Goldsmith, Alec B. Francis, Arthur Ashley, Charles Duncan, Pinna Nesbit, Albert Hart, Charles Charles, Lilah Chester.
Alan, a young Englishman, comes to America and takes a job as caretaker at a country lodge—and soon finds himself involved in a murder mystery.

Paid Back (Universal, 1922)
d: Irving Cummings. 5 reels.
Gladys Brockwell, Mahlon Hamilton, Stuart Holmes, Lillian West, Kate Price, Edna Murphy, Arthur Stuart Hull, Wilfred Lucas.
Carol, an heiress who's in an unhappy marriage, tries to forget by helping a friend.

Paid in Advance (Universal, 1919)
w, d: Allen Holubar. 6 reels.
Dorothy Phillips, Frank Brownlee, William Stowell, Lon

Chaney, Joseph Gerard, Priscilla Dean, Bill Buress, Harry De More.

Joan, the orphan daughter of a fur trader, reaches Dawson City and soon finds herself pursued by every lecher and lothario in town. Besieged on all sides by amorous brutes, she comes up with a novel solution: She auctions herself off—in marriage—to the highest bidder!

Paid in Full (All Star Feature Corp., 1914)
d: Augustus Thomas. 5 reels.
Tully Marshall, Caroline French, William Riley Hatch, George H. Irving, Winifred Kingston, Hattie Russell, Irving Southard, Alfred Sidwell.

When a payroll clerk is blackmailed by his employer and threatened with prison, the clerk tries to avoid prosecution by asking his wife to give in to the employer's romantic demands.

Another version of this film was made by Famous Players-Lasky in 1919.

Paid in Full (Famous Players-Lasky/Paramount, 1919)
d: Emile Chautard. 5 reels.
Pauline Frederick, Robert Cain, Wyndham Standing, Frank Losee, Jane Farrell.

Remake, with some plot alterations, of the 1914 film *Paid in Full*. Both versions were based on the play of the same title by Eugene Walter.

Paid To Love (Fox, 1927)
d: Howard Hawks. 7 reels.
Virginia Valli, George O'Brien, J. Farrell MacDonald, William Powell, Thomas Jefferson, Merta Sterling, Hank Mann.

In Europe, a crown prince falls in love with an apache dancer.

Paint and Powder (Chadwick Pictures, 1925)
d: Hunt Stromberg. 7 reels.
Elaine Hammerstein, Theodore von Eltz, Mrs. Charles Craig, John Sainpolis, Stuart Holmes, Derelys Perdue, Pat Hartigan, Russell Simpson, Charles Murray.

In a New York cabaret, a singing waiter loves a dancer so much that he steals money for her to buy proper clothes to audition for a Broadway show. He's caught and jailed, but she becomes a hit in the show.

The Painted Flapper (Chadwick Pictures, 1924)
d: John Gorman. 6 reels.
James Kirkwood, Pauline Garon, Crauford Kent, Kathlyn Williams, Claire Adams, Hal Cooley, John Harron, Maine Geary, Anita Simons, Al Roscoe, Carlton Griffin, Pauline French.

Arline, a Roaring Twenties jazz baby, stops doing the Charleston long enough to get serious and rescue her sister from marriage to an insufferable bore.

The Painted Lady (Fox, 1924)
d: Chester Bennett. 7 reels.
George O'Brien, Dorothy Mackaill, Harry T. Morey, Lucille Hutton, Lucille Ricksen, Margaret McWade, John Miljan, Frank Elliott, Lucien Littlefield.

Violet accepts the blame for her sister's crime and is sent to prison. Upon her release, she discovers she has become a pariah, and so turns to the Oldest Profession. But Violet is basically a good girl, and she'll meet a sailor who can appreciate her on those terms.

The Painted Lie (David Horsley Productions/Mutual, 1917)
d: Harrish Ingraham. 5 reels.
Crane Wilbur, Harrish Ingraham, Mae Gaston, Ida Lewis, Marie Corteaux.

After Diana, a socialite, finishes sitting for her portrait, the artist tries to force his romantic attentions on her. She refuses him, and leaves in a huff. For revenge, the artist paints a nude body on her portrait, creating a major scandal.

The Painted Lily (Triangle, 1918)
d: Thomas N. Heffron. 5 reels.
Alma Rubens, William V. Mong, Jack Richardson, Dorothy Hagar, Francis McDonald, Alberta Lee, Gene Burr.

A gambling hall owner uses his naive wife to attract customers.

Painted Lips (Universal, 1918)
d: Edward LeSaint. 5 reels.
Louise Lovely, Lewis Cody, Alfred Allen, Betty Schade, Hector Dion, Beatrice Van.

Though she's had a strict and proper upbringing, a young woman is induced to paint her lips and strut like a woman abandoned.

The Painted Madonna (Fox, 1917)
d: Oscar A.C. Lund. 5 reels.
Sonia Markova, Sidney Mason, William Lampe, David Herblin, Albert Tavernier, Anita Navarro, Edith Reeves, Julia Stuart.

"The Black Nightingale," a wealthy courtesan, is really Stella, a simple country girl.

Painted People (Associated First National, 1924)
d: Clarence Badger. 7 reels.
Colleen Moore, Ben Lyon, Charlotte Merriam, Joseph Striker, Charles Murray, Russell Simpson, Mary Alden, Mary Carr, Sam DeGrasse, June Elvidge, Anna Q. Nilsson, Bull Montana.

Childhood sweethearts grow up, go their separate ways, then meet again as playwrights working on the same show.

Painted Ponies (Universal, 1927)
d: Reaves Eason. 6 reels.
Hoot Gibson, William Dunn, Ethlyne Clair, Charles Sellon, Otto Hoffman, Slim Summerville, Chief White Spear, Mary Lopez.

Buck, a rodeo champion, gets the chance to ride a jerry-rigged carousel, to the delight of his friends—but not the delight of his sweetheart.

The Painted Soul (New York Motion Picture Corp./Mutual, 1915)
d: Scott Sidney. 5 reels.
Bessie Barriscale, Charles Ray, Truly Shattuck.

When a convicted prostitute is recruited by an artist to pose for his new painting, "A Fallen Woman," she agrees. But instead she is so impressed by "The Resurrection," his magnificent earlier work, that she reforms instantly, and is no longer right for the second painting.

The Painted Trail (Trem Carr Productions/Rayart, 1928)
d: J.P. McGowan. 5 reels.
Buddy Roosevelt, Betty Baker, Leon De La Mothe, Lafe McKee, Tommy Bay.

Out West, a federal agent takes on a gang of border smugglers.

The Painted World (Vitagraph, 1919)
d: Ralph Ince. 5 reels.
Anita Stewart, E.K. Lincoln. Julia Swayne Gordon, Harry

Northrup, Janice Cummings, R.A. Roberts.
When a burlesque queen gives birth to a baby girl, she decides her daughter will not grow up in the seamy backstage world of strippers and con men.

Painting the Town (Universal, 1927)
d: William James Craft. 6 reels.
Glenn Tryon, Patsy Ruth Miller, Charles Gerrard, George Fawcett, Sidney Bracey, Max Ascher, Monte Collins.
Comedy about Hector, a small town boy with big city ideas.

A Pair of Cupids (Metro, 1918)
d: Charles J. Brabin. 5 reels.
Francis X. Bushman, Beverly Bayne, Charles Sutton, Gerald Griffin, Jessie Stevens, Edgar Norton, Lou Gorey, Thomas Blake, Louis R. Wolheim, John Judge, Elwell Judge.
The "pair of cupids" that brings two young people together are twin babies, "borrowed" by the young man's uncle to give the couple a craving for marriage and family.

A Pair of Silk Stockings (Select, 1918)
d: Walter Edwards. 5 reels.
Harrison Ford, Constance Talmadge, Wanda Hawley, Sylvia Ashton, Vera Doria, Florence Carpenter, Thomas Persse, Lewis Willoughby, Helen Haskell, L.W. Steers.
Sam and Molly are happy together until a silly argument drives a wedge between them, and they get a divorce. But they're reunited during an amateur play when a stranger wanders into the wrong dressing room, and thinking him a burglar, Sam and Molly overcome the man and tie him up with a pair of Molly's silk stockings.

A Pair of Sixes (Essanay, 1918)
d: Lawrence C. Windom. 6 reels.
Taylor Holmes, Robert Conness, Alice Mann, Edna Phillips Holmes, Cecil Owen, Maude Eburne, C.E. Ashley, John Cossar, Byron Aldenn, Virginia Bowker, Tommy Carey.
Partners in business quarrel so much, they decide to settle matters with a hand of poker.

Pajamas (Fox, 1927)
d: J.G. Blystone. 6 reels.
Olive Borden, John J. Clark, Lawrence Gray, Jerry Miley.
A vivacious, headstrong girl steps in as pilot in her dad's private plane, which is carrying a young businessman she's keen for.

Pal o' Mine (Columbia, 1924)
d: Edward J. Le Saint. 6 reels.
Irene Rich, Josef Swickard, Pauline Garon, Willard Louis.
An opera star's husband loses his job and faces shame, until his wife secretly sees to it that he is given work, so that he can regain his confidence. Then an uppity underling spills the beans.

The Palace of Darkened Windows (National Picture Theatres, Inc./Select, 1920)
d: Henry Kolker. 6 reels.
Claire Anderson, Arthur Edmund Carew, Jay Belasco, Christine Mayo, Gerald Pring, Adele Farrington, Virginia Caldwell, Nicholas Dunaev.
Traveling through India, a young woman is courted by both an American and a British officer.

The Palace of Pleasure (Fox, 1926)
d: Emmett Flynn. 6 reels.
Edmund Lowe, Betty Compson, Henry Kolker, Harvey Clark, Nina Romano, Francis McDonald, George Siegmann.
In old Portugal, a young man is madly in love with actress and singer Lola Montez.

The Paliser Case (Goldwyn, 1919)
d: William Parke. 5 reels.
Pauline Frederick, Albert Roscoe, James Neil, Hazel Brennan, Kate Lester, Carrie Lee Ward, Warburton Gamble, Alec Francis, Eddie Sutherland, Tom Ricketts, Virginia Foltz.
When a society scoundrel is found murdered, the evidence appears to incriminate the girl he had tried, unsuccessfully, to win for his wife.

The Palm Beach Girl (Famous Players-Lasky/Paramount, 1926)
d: Erle Kenton. 7 reels.
Bebe Daniels, Lawrence Gray, Josephine Drake, Marguerite Clayton, John G. Patrick, Armand Cortez, Roy Byron, Maude Turner Gordon.
A farm girl travels to Palm Beach for a visit with her high-society aunts.

Pals (Truart Film Corp., 1925)
d: John P. McCarthy. 5 reels.
Louise Lorraine, Art Acord, Leon Kent, Andrew Waldron.
When his dog discovers an abandoned baby, a bachelor is forced to raise the child himself.

Pals First (Yorke Film Corp./Metro, 1918)
d: Edwin Carewe. 6 reels.
Harold Lockwood, James Lackaye, Ruby DeRemer, Frank DeVernon, Richard R. Neill, Anthony Byrd, Pauline Dempsey, Walter P. Lewis, Rollo Llloyd.
When a tramp is mistaken for Richard, a wealthy gent thought lost at sea, he steps easily into the role... perhaps because he really *is* Richard, with a private agenda.
Carewe would make another film based on the same material, *Pals First*, in 1926.

Pals First (First National, 1926)
d: Edwin Carewe. 7 reels.
Dolores Del Rio, Lloyd Hughes, Alec B. Francis, George Cooper, Edward Earle, Hamilton Morse, George Reed, Alice Nichols, Alice Belcher.
There's double deception afoot, when a wealthy landowner is reported missing at sea and his scheming cousin grabs the chance to make a move on the landowner's fiancée. But the landowner returns in disguise, ousts his conniving cousin, and reclaims his lady love.
Remake of Metro's 1918 film *Pals First*, also directed by Carewe. Both films were based on the novel of the same name by Francis Perry Elliott.

Pals in Paradise (Metropolitan Pictures Corp. of California, 1926)
d: George B. Seitz. 7 reels.
Marguerite De La Motte, John Bowers, Rudolph Schildkraut, May Robson, Alan Brooks, Ernie Adams, Bruce Gordon.
During the California Gold Rush, a young prospector battles a young woman who claims ownership of his mine.

Pals in Peril (Action Pictures/Pathé, 1927)
d: Richard Thorpe. 5 reels.
Buffalo Bill Jr., George Ovey, Edward Hearn, Robert Homans, Bert Lindley, Olive Hasbrouck, Harry Belmore, Raye Hampton.
Out West, a pair of cowpokes search for stolen cattle.

Pampered Youth (Vitagraph, 1925)
d: David Smith. 7 reels.
Cullen Landis, Ben Alexander, Allan Forrest, Alice Calhoun,

Emmett King, Wallace MacDonald, Charlotte Merriam, Kathryn Adams, Aggie Herring, William J. Irving.

Turn of the century drama about the Ambersons, a leading family in a small town in Indiana. After young Isabel Amberson makes a poor choice in selecting a husband, her rejected lover leaves town and goes on to great success in the automobile business. Later he returns to his home town, re-acquaints himself with the Ambersons, and rescues Isabel from a fire in her mansion.

First feature film version of Booth Tarkington's *The Magnificent Ambersons*, which would be famously remade by Orson Welles in 1942.

Panthea (Norma Talmadge Film Corp./Selznick, 1917)
d: Allan Dwan. 5 reels.
Norma Talmadge, Earle Foxe, Roger Lytton, George Fawcett, Murdock McQuarrie, Erich von Stroheim, Norbert Wicki, William Abington, Winifred Harris, Eileen Percy, J.S. Furey.
Panthea's a beautiful, talented pianist who's married to a composer. When her husband despairs of ever getting his opera produced, Panthea offers herself to a wealthy baron on the condition that her husband's opera be produced and given a chance to be heard by the public.

Pants (Essanay, 1917)
d: Arthur Berthelet. 5 reels.
Little Mary McAlister, John Cossar, Marion Skinner, Charles Koeppe, Russell McDermott, Arthur Metcalfe, Caroline Irwin.
Betty, a wealthy and charming young girl who wants to live life to the fullest, decides to go to the beach and make new friends.

Paradise (First National, 1926)
d: Irvin Willat. 8 reels.
Betty Bronson, Milton Sills, Noah Beery, Lloyd Whitlock, Kate Price, Charlie Murray, Claude King, Charles Brook, Ashley Cooper.
Tony, a World War I aviator, returns home and is given the deed to a South Seas island called Paradise.

Paradise For Two (Paramount, 1927)
d: Gregory LaCava. 7 reels.
Richard Dix, Edmund Breese, Betty Bronson, André Beranger, Peggy Shaw.
Steve, a bachelor playboy, learns that his allowance will be cut off unless he marries.

Paradise Garden (Yorke Film Corp./Metro, 1917)
d: Fred J. Balshofer. 6 reels.
Harold Lockwood, Vera Sisson, Virginia Rappe, William Clifford, Lester Cuneo, Catherine Henry, Little George Hupp.
Jerry, young heir to a large estate, must remain on the grounds until he turns 21.

The Parasite (B.P. Schulberg Productions, 1925)
d: Louis Gasnier. 6 reels.
Owen Moore, Madge Bellamy, Bryant Washburn, Mary Carr, Lilyan Tashman, Bruce Guerin.
After a wife sheds her husband and he becomes wealthy, she tries to win him back.

Pardners (Thomas A. Edison, Inc./Mutual, 1917)
d: Alan Crosland. 5 reels.
Charlotte Walker, Richard Tucker, Leo Gordon, Charles Sutton, Redfield Clarke.
When a railroad engineer's marriage is threatened because of some doctored photographs, his partner obtains proof of the deception and saves the marriage.

Pardon My French (Goldwyn, 1921)
d: Sidney Olcott. 6 reels.
Vivian Martin, George Spink, Thomas Meighan, Nadine Beresford, Ralph Yearsley, Grace Studiford, Walter McEwen, Wallace Ray.
When their stage troupe gets stranded in a small town, the show's ingenue and leading man take jobs with a wealthy family... as French maid and butler.

Pardon My Nerve (Fox, 1922)
d: Reaves Eason. 5 reels.
Charles Jones, Eileen Percy, Mae Busch, G. Raymond Nye, Joe Harris, Otto Hoffman, William Steele, Robert Daly.
Out West, a gunfighter helps derail a miscarriage of justice, and saves the ranch its owner had been coerced into signing away.

Paris (MGM, 1926)
d: Edmund Goulding. 6 reels.
Charles Ray, Joan Crawford, Douglas Gilmore, Rose Dione, Michael Visaroff, Jean Galeron.
In Paris, a wealthy American falls in love with an apache dancer and tries to help her escape her life of abuse at the hands of her dance partner. In the end, though, the American comes to realize that even though the man beats and mistreats her, she loves him still.

Paris at Midnight (Metropolitan Pictures, 1926)
d: E. Mason Hopper. 7 reels.
Jetta Goudal, Lionel Barrymore, Mary Brian, Edmund Burns, Emile Chautard, Brandon Hurst, Jocelyn Lee, Mathilde Comont, Carrie Daumery, Fannie Yantis, Jean DeBriac.
In Paris, an ex-con moves into a rooming house where almost all the tenants have domestic problems. Patiently, he solves their problems, one by one; then he moves on.

Paris Green (Thomas H. Ince/Paramount, 1920)
d: Jerome Storm. 5 reels.
Charles Ray, Ann May, Bert Woodruff, Gertrude Claire, Donald McDonald, Gordon Douglas Mullen, Norris Johnson, William Courtright, Ida Lewis, Otto Hoffman.
After the war ends, a doughboy known by his friends as "Paris Green" meets a French girl and, though neither can speak the other's language, they fall in love.

The Parish Priest (Jesse D. Hampton Productions, 1920)
d: Joseph J. Franz. 6 reels.
William Desmond, Thomas Ricketts, Carl Miller, J. Morris Foster, Walter Perry, Margaret Livingston, Ruth Renick, Billie Bennett, L.M. Wells, Lydia Kott.
Pastor John devotes himself to granting his mother's dying wish: that a certain young doctor and his sweetheart get married.

The Parish Priest (Herman J. Garfield, 1921)
d: Joseph Franz. 6 reels.
William Desmond, Thomas Ricketts, Carl Miller, J. Morris Foster, Walter Perry, Margaret Livingston, Ruth Renick, Billie Bennett.
Remake of the Jesse D. Hampton 1920 film *The Parish Priest*, both versions based on the play of the same name by Daniel L. Hart.

Parisian Love (B.P. Schulberg Productions/Preferred Pictures, 1925)
d: Louis Gasnier. 7 reels.
Clara Bow, Donald Keith, Lillian Leighton, James Gordon

Russell, Hazel Keener, Lou Tellegen, Jean De Briac, Otto Matiesen, Alyce Mills.

In Paris, two dancers—one male, one female—try to rob a rich man's home, but they're caught. Nevertheless, the wealthy homeowner falls in love with the female, Marie, and they are married.

Parisian Nights (Gothic Pictures/FBO of America, 1925)
d: Al Santell. 7 reels.
Elaine Hammerstein, Gaston Glass, Lou Tellegen, William J. Kelly, Boris Karloff, Renee Adoree.
In Paris, an American sculptress induces a French thief to pose for her.

A Parisian Romance (Fox, 1916)
d: Frederick A. Thompson. 5 reels.
H. Cooper Cliffe, Dorothy Green, Dion Titheradge, Margaret Skirvin, Angelica Spier, Isabel O'Madigan, Clarence Heritage, Harold Hartzelle.
In Paris, a misalliance takes place when an old playboy forces marriage on young Therese, who is in love with Henri. On the rebound, Henri marries a thoughtless flirt.

A Parisian Scandal (Universal, 1921)
d: George L. Cox. 5 reels.
George Periolat, Marie Prevost, Lillian Lawrence, Bertram Grassby, George Fisher, Lillian Rambeau, Tom Gallery, Mae Busch, Rose Dione.
Basil, a dry, humorless young scientist, visits Paris and meets a girl who instantly tries to vamp him. Not quite what the young intellectual had in mind at first... but he gets to liking it.

The Parisian Tigress (Metro, 1919)
d: Herbert Blaché. 5 reels.
Viola Dana, Darrell Foss, Henry Kolker, Edward Connelly, Clarissa Selwynne, Louis Darclay, Paul Weigel, Mitzi Goodstadt, Maree Beaudet.
Jeanne, an apache dancer, is being pressured to marry an aging roué.

Parlor, Bedroom and Bath (Metro, 1920)
d: Edward Dillon. 6 reels.
Eugene Pallette, Ruth Stonehouse, Kathleen Kirkham, Charles H. West, Dorothy Wallace, Helen Sullivan, Henry Miller Jr., George Periolat, Josephine Hill, Graham Pettie.
A flaky housewife can't truly love her husband unless she thinks other women are after him. In desperation, the husband tries several ploys to convince his wife that he is attractive to other women.

The Parson of Panamint (Paramount, 1916)
d: William Desmond Taylor. 5 reels.
Dustin Farnum, Winifred Kingston, Pomeroy "Doc" Cannon, Howard Davies, Colin Chase, Ogden Crane, Jane Keckley, Tom Bates.
In the western town of Panamint, a new preacher turns a casino into a church.
This film would be remade in 1922 by Paramount as *While Satan Sleeps.*

The Part Time Wife (Gotham Productions/Lumas Film Corp., 1925)
d: Glenn Belt. 6 reels.
Alice Calhoun, Robert Ellis, Freeman Wood, Edwards Davis, Janice Peters, Patricia Palmer, Charles West.
Kenneth, a journalist, marries movie star Doris Fuller. At first they are happy, but before long he perceives that society considers him "Mr. Doris Fuller," and his pride is devastated.

Parted Curtains (Warner Bros., 1922)
d: James C. Bradford, Bertram Bracken. 6 reels.
Henry B. Walthall, Edward Cecil, Mary Alden, Margaret Landis, Edward Cecil.
An ex-con tries to go straight, but can't find acceptance in society until a kind-hearted painter takes the time to show him some compassion.

Partners Again (Goldwyn/United Artists, 1926)
d: Henry King. 6 reels.
George Sidney, Alexander Carr, Betty Jewel, Allan Forrest, Robert Schable, Lillian Elliott, Lew Brice, Earl Metcalf, Gilbert Clayton, Anna Gilbert.
Potash and Perlmutter, former partners in the auto business, are reunited after a brief fling in other ventures.

Partners in Crime (Paramount, 1928)
d: Frank B. Strayer. 7 reels.
Wallace Beery, Raymond Hatton, Mary Brian, Arthur Housman, William Powell, Jack Luden, Albert Roccardi, Joseph W. Girard, George Irving, Bruce Gordon, Jack Richardson.
Deming, an assistant district attorney, is imprisoned by a gang of thieves, then rescued when a pair of wannabe detectives accidentally ignite a box full of tear bombs and flush the crooks out of their lair.

Partners of Fate (Fox, 1921)
d: Bernard Durning. 5 reels.
Louise Lovely, William Scott, Rosemary Theby, Philo McCulloughm, George Siegmann, Richard Cummings, Eileen O'Malley.
Two pairs of newlyweds sail for their honeymoons on the same ship.

Partners of the Night (Goldwyn, 1920)
d: Paul Scardon. 6 reels.
Pinna Nesbit, William B. Davidson, William Ingerson, Emmett Corrigan, Mario Majeroni, Vincent Coleman, Frank Kingdon, Tenny Wright, Lew O'Connor.
There's a bad apple on the police force, and he's the chief of detectives.

Partners of the Sunset (Western Pictures, 1922)
d: Robert H. Townley. 5 reels.
Allene Ray, Robert Frazer, Mildred Bright, J.W. Johnston.
Out West, two sisters are torn between a swindler's offer to buy their ranch and the urging of a young geologist not to sell.

Partners of the Tide (Irvin V. Willat Productions/W.W. Hodkinson, 1921)
d: L.V. Jefferson. 7 reels.
Jack Perrin, Marion Faducha, Gordon Mullen, Daisy Robinson, Gertrude Norman, J.P. Lockney, Joe Miller, Bert Hadley, Fred Kohler, Florence Midgley, Ashley Cooper.
Melodrama on the high seas, as a first mate struggles to overcome sabotage of his ship.

Partners Three (Thomas H. Ince/Paramount, 1919)
d: Fred Niblo. 5 reels.
Enid Bennett, Casson Ferguson, John P. Lockney, Robert McKim, Lydia Yeamans Titus.
Abandoned by her husband, a New York songstress out West forms a partnership with two desert rats and together they strike gold.

Pasquale (Oliver Morosco Photoplay Co./Paramount,

1916)
d: William D. Taylor. 5 reels.
George Beban, Helen Jerome Eddy, Page Peters, Jack Nelson, Myrtle Stedman, Nigel de Brulier.
Pasquale, an Italian immigrant living in America, is drafted into the Italian army.

Passers By (Equitable Motion Pictures Corp./World Film Corp., 1916)
d: Stanner E.V. Taylor. 5 reels.
Charles Cherry, Marguerite Skirvin, Mary Charleson, Kate Sarjeanston, Donald Kite.
Class distinctions break up a romance between an Englishman and his sister's housemaid, but years later the maid returns to introduce her former lover to his 8-year-old son.

Passers By (Pathé, 1920)
d: J. Stuart Blackton. 6 reels.
Herbert Rawlinson, Leila Valentine, Ellen Cassity, Pauline Coffyn, William J. Ferguson, Tom Lewis, Dick Lee, Charles Blackton.
Remake of the 1916 World Film Corp. movie *Passers By*. Both versions were based on the play of the same name by C. Haddon Chambers.

Passing Thru (Thomas H. Ince/Paramount, 1921)
d: William A. Seiter. 5 reels.
Douglas MacLean, Madge Bellamy, Otto Hoffman, Cameron Coffey, Willard Robards, Edith Yorke, Fred Gambold, Margaret Livingston, Louis Natheaux, Bert Hadley.
Billy, a bank teller, takes the blame for a cash shortage although he isn't responsible. Then he spots the banker's daughter, and it's love at first sight.

Passion (McClure Pictures, Inc./Triangle, 1917)
d: Richard Ridgeley. 5 reels.
Shirley Mason, George LeGuere, Clifford Bruce, Bigelow Cooper, Ruby Hoffman, Mabel Strickland, Edith Wright, Edmund Dalby, Harry Gripp.
Adam and Eve—not the originals, but the 1917 couple—have a spat when Eve wants to flirt with a strongman who runs a diving show.

The Passion Flower (First National, 1921)
d: Herbert Brenon. 7 reels.
Norma Talmadge, Courtenay Foote, Harrison Ford, Eulalie Jenson, Charles Stevenson, Alice May, Herbert Vance, H.D. McClellan, Austin Harrison, Robert Agnew, Harold Stern, Natalie Talmadge, Walter Wilson, Mildred Adams, Augustus Balfour, Elsa Fredericks.
Tragic melodrama about a young woman who's engaged to her cousin, but is betrayed by a jealous lover's lie.

Passion Fruit (Metro, 1921)
d: John E. Ince. 6 reels.
Doraldina, Edward Earle, Stuart Holmes, Sidney Bracey, Florence Turner, W.H. Bainbridge.
On a South Sea island, an unscrupulous foreman plots to separate a landowner from both his estate and his daughter.

The Passion Song (Excellent Pictures/Interstate Pictures, 1928)
d: Harry O. Hoyt. 6 reels.
Gertrude Olmsted, Noah Beery, Gordon Elliott, Edgar Washington Blue.
Van Ryn, retired in England after years of working in South Africa, receives an old friend from that country and finds that the friend is in love with Van Ryn's wife.

The Passionate Pilgrim (Cosmopolitan/Paramount, 1921)
d: Robert G. Vignola. 7 reels.
Matt Moore, Mary Newcomb, Julia Swayne Gordon, Tom Guise, Frankie Mann, Rubye DeRemer, Claire Whitney, Van Dyke Brooke, Charles Gerard, Sam J. Ryan, Arthur Donaldson.
A reporter writes an exposé about the crooked mayor, who then gets the reporter fired. But the newspaper owner's invalid daughter hears about the miscarriage of justice, grants an interview to the reporter, and together they work to have the corrupt politician put behind bars.

The Passionate Quest (Warner Bros., 1926)
d: J. Stuart Blackton. 7 reels.
Willard Louis, May McAvoy, Louise Fazenda, Holmes Herbert, Vera Lewis, Frank Butler, Jane Winton.
Three friends in workaday situations decide to take a stab at the high life.

Passionate Youth (Truart Film Corp., 1925)
d: Dallas M. Fitzgerald. 6 reels.
Beverly Bayne, Frank Mayo, Pauline Garon, Bryant Washburn, Carmelita Geraghty, Ralph McCullough, Ernest Wood, Lawrence Underwood, Jack Fowler, Walter Deming, James McElhern.
Henrietta is accused of murdering her lover, who was courting both her and her mother.

Passion's Pathway (Jean Perry & Edward Small Co., 1924)
d: Bertram Bracken. 6 reels.
Estelle Taylor, Jean Perry, Wilfred Lucas, Tully Marshall, Snitz Edwards, Margaret Landis, Kate Price, Edward Kimball, Fred DeSilva, Kenneth Gibson, Ben Deely.
Kenyon, an honest and hard-working man, is fired by his boss because of false charges invented by the boss' associate, a rejected suitor of Kenyon's wife. But truth and justice shall prevail.

Passion's Playground (First National, 1920)
d: J.A. Barry. 5 reels.
Katherine MacDonald, Norman Kerry, Nell Craig, Rudolph Valentino, Edwin Stevens, Virginia Ainsworth, Alice Wilson, Fanny Ferrari, Howard Gaye, Walt Whitman.
Convent-bred Mary Grant travels to Monte Carlo, and right into a scandal.

The Patchwork Girl of Oz (Oz Film Mfg. Co./Paramount, 1914)
d: J. Farrell MacDonald. 5 reels.
Mildred Harris, Frank Moore, Pierre Couderc, Raymond Russell, Violet Macmillan, Bobby Gould, Vivian Reed, Juanita Hansen, Al Roach, Fred Woodward, Vivian Reed.
Colorful characters on their way to Oz search for magic ingredients to undo a curse that has turned their friends to stone.

The Patent Leather Kid (First National, 1927)
d: Alfred Santell. 12 reels.
Richard Barthelmess, Molly O'Day, Lawford Davidson, Matthew Betz, Arthur Stone, Raymond Turner, Hank Mann, Walter James, Lucien Prival, Nigel DeBrulier, Fred O'Beck.
A New York boxer is drafted into World War I, but has no passion for his country. That will change.

The Path Forbidden (Excelsior Feature Films/Alliance Films, 1914)
d: Harry Handworth. 5 reels.
Octavia Handworth, Gordon DeMaine, William A. Williams, Hamilton Crane, Francis Pierlot, Tom Tempest, John B.

Hymer, James Allbaugh.

Adult twin girls are unaware of each other's existence until they run into each other in a hotel. Though they are identical in appearance, one girl is a shameless vamp, the other is a solid, respectable family person.

Miss Handworth has a triple role, portraying not only both twins, but also their mother.

The Path of Happiness (Universal, 1916)
d: Elaine Sterne. 5 reels.
Violet Mersereau, Harry Benham, Joseph Phillips, Sidney Bracey, Dorothy Benham, Florence Crawford, Leland Benham.
Joan, a "nature girl," lives in the woods with her father.

The Path She Chose (Universal, 1920)
d: Philip Rosen. 5 reels.
Anne Cornwall, Claire Anderson, J. Farrell McDonald, Genevieve Blinn, Dagmar Godowsky, Kathleen O'Connor, Edward Coxen, William Moran, Harry Schumm.
Virginia, a girl with a dysfunctional family, leaves home and tries to get honest work. She succeeds, but after being promoted to plant manager, her unsavory family finds her and they threaten to muck up her new life.

Paths to Paradise (Famous Players-Lasky/Paramount, 1925)
d: Clarence Badger. 7 reels.
Raymond Griffith, Betty Compson, Tom Santschi, Bert Woodruff, Fred Kelsey.
Two thieves, male and female, are both after a priceless diamond.

The Patriot (Triangle, 1916)
d: William S. Hart. 5 reels.
William S. Hart, Georgie Stone, Francis Carpenter, Joe Goodboy, Roy Laidlaw, Milton Ross, P.D. Tabler, Charles K. French.
Furious with unfair treatment by a U.S. government agent, an American prospector rebels and joins a gang of Mexican guerillas.

The Patriot (Paramount, 1928)
d: Ernst Lubitsch. 10 reels. (Music, sound effects, part talkie.)
Emil Jannings, Florence Vidor, Lewis Stone, Vera Voronina, Neil Hamilton, Harry Cording, Carmenetti.
Story of treachery and intrigue in Czarist Russia.

Patriotism (Paralta Plays, Inc./General Film Co., 1918)
d: Raymond B. West. 6 reels.
Bessie Barriscale, Charles Gunn, Herschel Mayall, Arthur Allardt, Joseph J. Dowling, Mary Jane Irving, Ida Lewis, Clifford Alexander.
In Scotland, a young woman aids the war effort by turning her home into a convalescent hospital for soldiers.

Patsy (Fox, 1917)
d: John G. Adolfi. 5 reels.
June Captice, Harry Hilliard, John Smiley, Edna Munsey, Ethyle Cooke, Alma Muller, Fred Hearn, Jane Lee.
Patsy's a tomboy who is sent East to learn femininity and refinement. While there, she falls in love with a young man named Dick, and he with her. But he cannot propose marriage to Patsy because he's already been trapped into marriage with a maneater named Helene.

Patsy (Truart Film Corp., 1921)
d: John McDermott. 5 reels.

ZaSu Pitts, John MacFarlane, Tom Gallery, Marjorie Daw, Fannie Midgley, Wallace Beery, Harry Todd, Milla Davenport, Henry Fortson.
In California, a runaway tomboy joins a neighborhood gang and must fight the boys to earn their respect.

The Patsy (MGM, 1928)
d: King Vidor. 8 reels.
Marion Davies, Marie Dressler, Jane Winton, Del Henderson, Lawrence Gray.
An underappreciated daughter cons her parents—and her sister's boyfriend—into paying some attention to her. This is the celebrated comedy in which Marion Davies does hilarious impressions of screen stars Lillian Gish, Mae Murray, Pola Negri... and even Charlie Chaplin! Arguably Miss Davies' best comedy performance, in a close decision over her follow-up film, *Show People*, also directed by Vidor. Nineteen twenty-eight was a big year for Marion.

The Pawn of Fate (Shubert Film Corp./World Film Corp., 1916)
d: Maurice Tourneur. 5 reels.
George Beban, Doris Kenyon, Charles W. Charles, John Davidson, John Hines, Alec B. Francis, Mary Booth.
In Normandy, a painter of still life lives happily with his charming young wife, Marcine. But their idyllic existence is disrupted when a Parisian playboy comes to woo Marcine, and to gain the husband's acceptance he offers to arrange a Paris showing of his art.

Pawn Ticket 210 (Fox, 1922)
d: Scott Dunlap. 5 reels.
Shirley Mason, Robert Agnew, Irene Hunt, Jacob Abrams, Dorothy Manners, Fred Warren.
A young girl is left in a pawnshop and is cared for by the pawnbroker. Years later, the girl's mother returns to "claim" her.

Pawned (Select Pictures/Selznick, 1922)
d: Irvin V. Willat. 5 reels.
Tom Moore, Edith Roberts, Charles Gerard, Josef Swickard, Mabel Van Buren, James Barrows, Eric Mayne, Billy Elmer.
Claire, who operates a mobile pawnshop, becomes romantically involved with a night club manager and also with a drug-addicted doctor.

Paws of the Bear (New York Motion Picture Corp./Triangle, 1917)
d: Reginald Barker. 5 reels.
William Desmond, Clara Williams, Robert McKim, Wallace Worsley, Charles K. French.
During World War I, a Russian girl marries an American traveler, and they head for the United States. On board ship, the American meets an old friend who is now a German agent, and gets involved in international espionage.

Pay As You Enter (Warner Bros., 1928)
d: Lloyd Bacon. 5 reels.
Clyde Cook, William Demarest, Louise Fazenda, Myrna Loy.
Mary, a lunch wagon waitress, loves Bill the conductor, but he's too infatuated with a gold digger to notice.

Pay Day (Metro, 1918)
d: Sidney Drew, Mrs. Sidney Drew. 5 reels.
Sidney Drew, Mrs. Sidney Drew, Florence Short, Emily Lorraine, Charles Reigel, Linda Farley, Dan Baker, Richard A. Rowland, Joseph Engel, Mrs. Samuel Zucker.
On the Metro lot, husband-and-wife comedians pitch a script about the life and loves of an unscrupulous lothario.

Pay Dirt (Knickerbocker Star Features/General Film, 1916)
d: Henry King. 5 reels.
Henry King, Marguerite Nichols, Gordon Sackville, Mollie McConnell, Daniel Gilfether, Charles Dudley, Philo McCullough, Ruth White, Bruce Smith.
Each evening a gold miner gambles away whatever gold he finds during the day.

Pay Me (Universal, 1917)
d: Joseph DeGrasse. 5 reels.
Dorothy Phillips, Lon Chaney, Evelyn Selbie, Ed Brown, William Clifford, Evelyn Selbie, Tom Wilson, Claire DuBrey, William Stowell.
Out West, a saloon owner named Lawson has a guilty secret: As a young man, he strangled his mining partner and shot the man's wife. But Lawson has raised the couple's baby, now a beautiful young woman who's in love with a handsome lumberjack.

Paying His Debt (Triangle, 1918)
d: Cliff Smith. 5 reels.
Roy Stewart, Josie Sedgwick, Walter Perkins, William Ellingford, Dixie Doll, Harry Yamamoto, William Dyer, Arthur Millett.
To repay a debt of gratitude, Frank offers to provide alibis for Pete, a crook whom he closely resembles, by posing as Pete whenever the crook is away pulling another theft.
Double role for Roy Stewart, who plays both the thief and his "honest" lookalike.

Paying the Piper (Famous Players-Lasky/Paramount, 1921)
d: George Fitzmaurice. 6 reels.
Dorothy Dickson, Alma Tell, George Fawcett, Rod LaRocque, Robert Schable, Katherine Emmett, Reginald Denny.
Spoiled society brats Larry and Barbara embark on a marriage of convenience, while both continue to pursue other loves.

Paying the Price (Paragon Films, Inc./World Film Corp., 1916)
d: Frank H. Crane. 5 reels.
Gail Kane, Robert Cummings, Lydia Knott, George Ralph, Gladden James, George Majeroni, June Elvidge.
When a U.S. naval officer introduces his sweetheart to a friend of his, he isn't prepared for what comes next: Sweetie and the friend get married! But that isn't the end of the story. The marriage goes sour when hubby runs up large gambling debts, and to pay them off he turns to treason, leaving an opening for the navy man to win Sweetie back.

Paying the Price (Columbia, 1927)
d: David Selman. 6 reels.
Marjorie Bonner, Priscilla Bonner, John Miljan, George Hackathorne, Mary Carr, Eddie Phillips, William Welsh, William Eugene.
When an innocent man is accused of murder on circumstantial evidence and stands trial, he seems certain to be convicted. But one juror dissents, and we know why: The juror is the guilty party.

The Payment (New York Motion Picture Corp./Triangle, 1916)
d: Raymond B. West. 5 reels.
Bessie Barriscale, Charles Miller, Katherine Kirkwood, William Desmond, Thomas S. Guise, Gertrude Claire.
Phyllis, a struggling artist, compromises her honor in order to pay for her studies in Europe. Years later, when she's attained fame and fortune, she falls in love with her former lover's brother-in-law and must consider his marriage proposal in light of her earlier indiscretions.

Payment Guaranteed (American Film Co./Pathé, 1921)
d: George L. Cox. 5 reels.
Margarita Fisher, Cecil Van Auker, Hayward Mack, Harry Lonsdale, Harvey Clark, Marjorie Manners, Alice Wilson.
Fenton, a stock trader, faces bankruptcy unless his girlfriend can wangle a loan from a businessman who's got eyes for her. Sweetie goes to bat for her lover, then finds she has more fondness for the businessman than she ever could for Fenton.

The Peace of Roaring River (Goldwyn, 1919)
d: Hobart Henley. 5 reels.
Pauline Frederick, Hardee Kirkland, Corinne Barker, Lydia Yeamans Titus, Edwin Sturgis, Thomas Holding.
Mail order bride Madge, a young woman from the midwest, arrives in the town of Roaring River seeking a husband. She is spurned at first, and denounced by citizens who consider her an opportunist; but she wins the heart of her intended.

Peaceful Peters (Ben Wilson Productions/Arrow Film Corp., 1922)
d: Lewis King. 5 reels.
William Fairbanks, Harry LaMont, W.L. Lynch, Evelyn Nelson, Wilbur McGaugh, Monte Montague.
Out West, Peters hears a dying miner's last wish: That his newly discovered mine go to his niece, "Buddy's Gal." With nothing but that to go on, Peters has his work cut out for him. But his investigation does turn up the missing niece, a girl he's fallen in love with and must rescue from the clutches of an unscrupulous dancehall owner.

Peaceful Valley (Charles Ray Productions, Inc./Associated First National, 1920)
d: Jerome Storm. 5 reels.
Charles Ray, Harry Myers, Lincoln Stedman, Walter Perkins, William Courtright, Vincent C. Hamilton, Jesse Herring, Ann May, Lydia Knott, Charlotte Pierce, Ida Lewis.
When Hosiah's farmland is found to contain highly desirable waters, unscrupulous speculators scheme to cash in on it.

Peacock Alley (Tiffany Productions/Metro, 1922)
d: Robert Z. Leonard. 8 reels.
Mae Murray, Monte Blue, Edmund Lowe, W.J. Ferguson, Anders Randolph, William Tooker, Howard Lang, William Frederic, Jeffrys Lewis.
Elmer, an American diplomat, falls in love with Cleo, a French dancer.

Peacock Feathers (Universal, 1925)
d: Sven Gade. 7 reels.
Jacqueline Logan, Cullen Landis, Ward Crane, George Fawcett, Emmett King, Youcca Troubetzkoy, Aggie Herring, Dunbar Raymond.
Mimi's a gold digger eager to marry wealth. When she meets Jerry, who's just inherited a ranch, Mimi marries him, anticipating that they will be rich together. But she's dismayed to discover that the ranch is unprofitable and a nuisance. Mimi is almost lured away by a wealthy former beau, but at the last minute decides to honor her commitment and stay with her husband, whom she has come to love.

The Pearl of Paradise (Pollard Picture Plays/Mutual, 1916)

w, d: Harry Pollard. 5 reels.
Margarita Fischer, Joseph Harris, Harry Pollard, Beatrice Van, J. Gordon Russell.
Gomez, a Spanish matador, and his baby daughter are stranded on a deserted island. The girl grows to adulthood on the island, with little or no knowledge of the outside world until, one day, a young engaged couple are shipwrecked there, and their presence awakens desires the young girl had never felt.

The Pearl of the Antilles (Terriss Feature Film Co./Picture Playhouse Film Co., 1915)
d: Tom Terriss. 5 reels.
Tessie DeCordova, Rodney Hickok, Ethel Mitchell, Lionel Pape, Rienzi DeCordova, Tom Terriss.
Pearl, the daughter of a Southern colonel, is sent to live in Jamaica, far from corrupting mainland civilization. But she'll find plenty of corruption on the island also.

Peck o' Pickles (American Film Co./Mutual, 1916)
d: T.N. Heffron. 5 reels.
C. William Kolb, May Cloy, Max M. Dill, Frank Thompson, Marie Van Tassell, Josephine Clark, Burdell Jacobs, Alan Forrest.
Humorous tale of a cobbler and his friend who spike the punch at a temperance picnic.

Peck's Bad Boy (First National, 1921)
d: Sam Wood. 5 reels.
Jackie Coogan, Wheeler Oakman, Doris May, Raymond Hatton, James Corrigan, Lillian Leighton, Charles Hatton, Gloria Wood.
A youngster has a talent for trouble. He and his best pal visit the circus, and can't resist helping a lion escape his cage. Later, they rescue every stray dog from the dogcatcher. More a series of skits than a cohesive plot, this film nevertheless was a hit, in part because the public was eager to see Jackie Coogan in this, his first movie since his star-making appearance in Chaplin's *The Kid* (1921).

Peck's Bad Girl (Goldwyn, 1918)
d: Charles Giblyn. 5 reels.
Mabel Normand, Earle Foxe, Corinne Barker, Blanche Davenport, William Riley Hatch, Leslie Hunt, E.M. Favor, Edwin Sturgis, Joseph Granby, F.G. Patton, Auge Becker.
Minnie's a scamp who always gets into trouble. Angry with a bank because she thinks it owes her dad money, Minnie gets out the word that the bank is insolvent, causing a run. Later, she accidentally douses all the depositors with a fire hose. On the verge of being sent to reform school, Minnie saves herself by uncovering a plot to rob the bank, and emerges a heroine.

The Peddler (U.S. Amusement Corp./Art Dramas, Inc., 1917)
d: Herbert Blaché. 5 reels.
Joe Welch, Sidney Mason, Catherine Calvert, Kittens Reichert, Sally Crute.
Wistful tale of an old peddler who loses a son but gains an adopted daughter.

The Peddler of Lies (Universal, 1920)
d: William Dowlan. 5 reels.
Frank Mayo, Ora Carew, Ora Devereaux, Harold A. Miller, Dagmar Godowsky, Bonnie Hill, Flora Hollister, Truman Van Dyke, James Barrow, William Brown, Ray Ripley.
During a power failure at a ritzy party, a priceless diamond disappears. William, the idler son of a wealthy family, is

suspected, but his sister and a mysterious peddler come to his defense. It turns out that the peddler is really a Secret Service agent, on the trail of the real jewel thieves.

Peer Gynt (Oliver Morosco Photoplays/Paramount, 1915)
d: Oscar Apfel. 5 reels.
Cyril Maude, Myrtle Stedman, Fanny Y. Stockbridge, Mary Reubens, Mary Ruby, Winifred Bryson, Evelyn Duncan, Kitty Stevens, Herbert Standing, Charles Ruggles.
Peer Gynt, a high-spirited Norwegian, travels the world in search of beautiful women.

Peg o' My Heart (Metro, 1922)
d: King Vidor. 8 reels.
Laurette Taylor, Mahlon Hamilton, Russell Simpson, Ethel Grey Terry, Nigel Barrie, Lionel Belmore, Vera Lewis, Sidna Beth Ivins, D.R.O. Hatswell, Aileen O'Malley.
In England, Peg, an Irish lass, lives uncomfortably in a house full of snobs. She'll be taken away from all this by Jerry, a neighbor boy who loves her and is, in fact, a nobleman.

Peg o' the Sea (Van Dyke Film Production Co., 1918)
d: Eugene Nowland. 5 reels.
Jean Sothern, Charles Sutton, Jere Austin, Stanley Walpole, Mae Megin.
Young Peg lives with her grandfather in a fishing village, where she is romanced by a young inventor.

Peg of the Pirates (Fox, 1918)
d: O.A.C. Lund. 5 reels.
Peggy Hyland, Carleton Macy, Sidney Mason, Frank Evans, James Davis, Ajax Carrol, Eric Mayne, Louis Walheim.
Margaret, known as "Peg," is abducted by pirates at her own engagement party.

Pegeen (Vitagraph, 1920)
d: David Smith. 5 reels.
Bessie Love, Edward Burns, Ruth Fuller Golden, Charles Spere, Juan DeLACruz, Major McGuire, George Stanley, Anne Schaefer, Jay Morley.
Tragic tale about a man who loses his beloved wife and becomes mentally unbalanced, and his daughter, Pegeen, who sees him through the torment he suffers.

Peggy (New York Motion Picture Corp./Triangle, 1916)
d: Thomas H. Ince. 7 reels.
Billie Burke, William H. Thompson, William Desmond, Charles Ray, Nona Thomas, Gertrude Claire, Truly Shattuck.
Billie Burke's movie debut has her playing Peggy, a young New York socialite who is forced to move to Scotland. Though out of her element on the moors, Peggy tries to maintain her madcap big city lifestyle, and wins the grudging respect of the townspeople and the love of the bachelor minister.

Peggy Does Her Darndest (Metro, 1919)
d: George D. Baker. 5 reels.
May Allison, Rosemary Theby, Frank Currier, Augustus Phillips, Robert Ellis, Wilton Taylor, Dick Rosson, Sylvia Ashton, Ernest Morrison.
Peggy, a charming hoyden, plays at being a detective, and actually captures a crook.

Peggy Leads the Way (American Film Co./Mutual, 1917)
d: Lloyd Ingraham. 5 reels.
Mary Miles Minter, Andrew Arbuckle, Carl Stockdale, Alan Forrest, Emma Kluge, Margaret Shelby, George Ahern, Frank C. Thompson, William Spencer.
When Peggy, a finishing school grad, comes home to

California, she finds that her dad's grocery store is steadily losing money. So she rolls up her sleeves and goes to work, and with her school smarts and her naturally peppy personality, Peggy has the store turning a profit in no time.

Peggy of the Secret Service (Davis Pictures, 1925)
d: J.P. McGowan. 5 reels.
Peggy O'Day, Eddie Phillips, William H. Ryno, Clarence L. Sherwood, Dan Peterson, Richard Neill, V.L. Barnes, Ethel Childers.
Comedy about an Arabian chap who flees his country for the United States and takes the sultan's harem with him. Naturally, this becomes an affair of State—and Peggy, a crack Secret Service agent, is put on the case and winds up in the harem.

Peggy Puts it Over (Vitagraph, 1921)
d: Gustav von Seyffertitz. 5 reels.
Alice Calhoun, Edward Langford, Leslie Stowe, Charles Mackay, Helen Lindroth, Cornelius MacSunday, Dick Lee.
Peggy, a recent graduate in civil engineering, takes on the task of remaking a town.

The Penalty (Goldwyn, 1920)
d: Wallace Worsley. 7 reels.
Lon Chaney, Ethel Grey Terry, Charles Clary, Claire Adams, Kenneth Harlan, James Mason, Edouard Trebaol, Milton Ross, Wilson Humel, J. Montgomery Carlyle.
A double-amputee crime boss schemes to loot the city of San Francisco.

The Penitentes (Fine Arts Film Co./Triangle, 1915)
d: John Conway. 5 reels.
Orrin Johnson, Seena Owen, Paul Gilmore, Irene Hunt, Josephine Crowell, F.A. Turner, Charles Clary, A.D. Sears, Dark Cloud.
In 17th century New Mexico, a fanatical cult seizes all the property belonging to a family that's been nearly wiped out in an Indian attack. A baby named Manuel, one of the survivors, grows up to be the man who finally defeats the cult and reclaims his family's property.

Pennington's Choice (Quality Pictures/Metro, 1915)
d: O.A.C. Lund. 5 reels.
Francis X. Bushman, Wellington Playter, William Farris, Beverly Bayne, Helen Dunbar, Lester Cuneo, Morris Cytron, J.J. Jeffries.
Pennington, a New Yorker, falls for Eugenia, a Canadian visitor, but must travel to her northwest wilderness area to meet her family and ask for her hand in marriage. Pennington survives the trip but is intimidated by Eugenia's rough and ready brothers. So he takes boxing lessons from a former champion (J.J. Jeffries, playing himself in his film debut) and then whips two bullies who are scheming to take over the family's property.

Penny of Top Hill Trail (Andrew J. Callaghan, 1921)
d: Arthur Berthelet. 5 reels.
Sam Lauder, Bessie Love, Wheeler Oakman, Raymond Cannon, Harry DeVere, Lizette Thorne, Gloria Hunt, George Stone, Herbert Hertier.
When Penny, a stranger in town, arouses suspicion, a deputy sheriff takes her in tow. It turns out that Penny is no criminal, but a movie celebrity seeking anonymity.

The Penny Philanthropist (Wholesome Films Corp., 1917)
d: Guy McConnell. 5 reels.
Ralph Morgan, Peggy O'Neil, Frank Wood, James C. Carroll, D.E. Ehrich, William Burt, Rex Adams, Grace Arnold, Thomas Carey, Merribelle Laflin, Mrs. Margaret A. Wiggin.
Peggy's a tomboy who sells newspapers on a Chicago street corner. From her meager earnings, she gives away a penny each day to those less fortunate than herself.

Penrod (Marshall Neilan Productions, 1922)
d: Marshall Neilan. 8 reels.
Baby Peggy, Wesley Barry, Tully Marshall, Claire McDowell, John Harron, Sunshine Morrison, Gordon Griffith, Newton Hall, Harry Griffith, Cecil Holland, Marjorie Daw.
Penrod, a lively youth, presides over a "gang" called the American Boys' Protective Association. Their objective: Reporting the evils inflicted on kids by adults.

Penrod and Sam (J.K. McDonald/Associated First National, 1923)
d: William Beaudine. 7 reels.
Ben Alexander, Joe Butterworth, Buddy Messinger, Newton Hall, Gertrude Messinger, Rockliffe Fellowes, Gladys Brockwell, Mary Philbin, Gareth Hughes, William V. Mong.
Sequel to *Penrod*, exploring the friendship between boyhood pals.

The People vs. John Doe (Universal, 1916)
d: Lois Weber. 6 reels.
Harry DeMore, Evelyn Selby, Willis Marks, Leah Baird, George Berrell, Maud George, Charles Mailes, Robert Smith.
When a farmer and his family are found murdered, the hired hand, John Doe, is suspected of the crime.

The People vs. Nancy Preston (Hunt Stromberg Productions, 1925)
d: Tom Forman. 7 reels.
Marguerite De La Motte, John Bowers, Frankie Darro, David Butler, William V. Mong, Alphonz Ethier, Ed Kennedy, Gertrude Short, Ray Gallagher, Jackie Saunders, Mary Gordon.
Mike and Nancy, fugitives from injustice, go to a small town to live, but are followed by a Jauvert-like detective.

Peppy Polly (Paramount, 1919)
d: Elmer Clifton. 5 reels.
Richard Barthelmess, Dorothy Gish, Emily Chichester, Ed Peil, Kate Toncray, Josephine Crowell.
A tomboy in trouble with the law falls for a young doctor.

Perch of the Devil (Universal, 1927)
d: King Baggot. 7 reels.
Mae Busch, Pat O'Malley, Jane Winton, Mario Carillo, Theodore von Eltz, Lincoln Stedman, George Kuwa, Gertrude Oakman, Martha Franklin.
Ida, a young wife helping her husband prospect for gold in Montana, yearns for a more citified life. When she gets it, she learns that there is a lot to be said for the peace and tranquility of a country existence.

Percy (Thomas H. Ince/Pathé, 1925)
d: R. William Neill. 6 reels.
Charles Ray, Louise Dresser, Joseph Kilgour, Clyde McAtee, Dave Winter, Charles Murray, Victor McLaglen, Betty Blythe, Barbara Bedford, Don Marion.
Rogeen, a senatorial candidate, feels ashamed of his son Percy, who plays the violin and is thought to be a sissy. But his campaign manager takes the youngster in hand and introduces him to a world of cabarets, liquor, and women. Percy will never be the same again, and neither will dear old Dad.

The Perfect Clown (Chadwick Pictures, 1925)

d: Fred Newmeyer. 6 reels.
Larry Semon, Oliver Hardy, Kate Price, Dorothy Dwan, Joan Meredith, Otis Harlan.
There's a hectic, hilarious night awaiting a clerk who's trying to deliver a bag containing $10,000 to the bank. He finds the bank closed and, not wishing to be burdened with the money overnight, tries to get to the bank president's home, with many adventures along the way, including a rendezvous with a pretty girl.

A Perfect Crime (Allan Dwan Productions/Associated Producers, 1921)
d: Allan Dwan. 5 reels.
Monte Blue, Jacqueline Logan, Stanton Heck, Hardee Kirkland.
Griggs, a meek bank clerk, lives a second life as a romantic adventurer.

The Perfect Crime (FBO Pictures, 1928)
d: Bert Glennon. 7 reels.
Clive Brook, Irene Rich, Ethel Wales, Carroll Nye, Gladys McConnell, Edmund Breese, James Farley, Phil Gastrock, Tully Marshall, Jane LaVerne.
Benson, a famous criminologist, becomes obsessed with the notion of committing the perfect crime.

The Perfect Flapper (Associated First National, 1924)
d: John Francis Dillon. 7 reels.
Colleen Moore, Sydney Chaplin, Phyllis Haver, Lydia Knott, Frank Mayo, Charles Wellesley.
A young and modest debutante finds herself rejected by her fun-loving jazz-age friends.

A Perfect Gentleman (Monty Banks Enterprises/Pathé, 1928)
d: Clyde Bruckman. 6 reels.
Monty Banks, Ernest Wood, Henry Barrows, Ruth Dwyer, Arthur Thalasso, Hazel Howell, Agostino Borgato, Mary Foy, Syd Crossley, Jackie Coombs.
Comedy of the absurd has Monty, a bank clerk, engaged to marry the bank president's daughter. He gets accidentally drunk, however, and his behavior has him thrown out of the bride's house. But Monty will get back in the family's good graces when he foils a crook trying to embezzle bank funds.

A Perfect Lady (Goldwyn, 1918)
d: Clarence G. Badger. 5 reels.
Madge Kennedy, Jere Austin, Walter Law, Rod LaRocque, Ben Hendricks Sr., Harry Spingler, Agnes Marc, Mae McAvoy.
Lucille, a dancer in a burlesque revue, runs afoul of a moralizing preacher who aims to run her out of town.

The Perfect Lover (Selznick, 1919)
d: Ralph Ince. 5 reels.
Eugene O'Brien, Lucille Lee Stewart, Marguerite Courtot, Mary Boland, Martha Mansfield, Tom McRayne.
Brian, a struggling artist, becomes a society favorite after he exhibits his portrait of a wealthy socialite.

The Perfect Model—see: Inspiration (1915)

The Perfect Sap (Ray Rockett Productions/First National, 1927)
d: Howard Higgin. 6 reels.
Ben Lyon, Virginia Lee Corbin, Lloyd Whitlock, Diana Kane, Byron Douglas, Christine Compton, Charles Craig, Sam Hardy, Tammany Young, Helen Rowland.
While studying to be a detective, Herbert runs into thieves George and Polly, who assume Herbert is one of them.

A Perfect 36 (Goldwyn, 1918)
d: Charles Giblyn. 5 reels.
Rod LaRocque, Mabel Normand, Flora Zabelle, Leila Romer, Louis R. Grisel.
Star comedy turn for Miss Normand, who plays Mabel, a traveling corset saleswoman.

The Perfect Woman (Joseph M. Schenck Productions/First National, 1920)
d: David Kirkland. 6 reels.
Constance Talmadge, Charles Meredith, Elizabeth Garrison, Joseph Burke, Ned Sparks.
Comedic romp in which Mary (Miss Talmadge) seeks a job but is turned down by the woman-hating employer because she is too attractive. After going home and mussing her hair, changing into dowdy clothes and misapplying her makeup, she applies for the job again and is hired. But with her handsome boss won't remain a woman-hater for long.

The Perils of Divorce (World Film Corp., 1916)
d: Edwin August. 5 reels.
Edna Wallace Hopper, Frank Sheridan, Macey Harlan, Ruby Hoffman, Alec Francis, John Morgan, Zoe Gregory.
Happily married John and Constance are split apart by the conniving of a jealous former lover.

Periwinkle (American Film Co./Mutual, 1917)
d: James Kirkwood. 5 reels.
Mary Miles Minter, George Fisher, Arthur Howard, Clarence Burton, Alan Forrest, Harvey Clark, George Periolat, Ann Schaefer, George Ahern.
Lifeguards rescue a baby girl from a shipwreck, and name her Periwinkle.

Perjury (Fox, 1921)
d: Harry Millarde. 9 reels.
William Farnum, Sally Crute, Wallace Erskine, Alice Mann, Gilbert Rooney, Grace LaVell, Jack Crane, Frank Joyner, Frank Shannon, John Webb Dillon.
Weeper about a man who is unjustly convicted of murder. He goes to prison for 20 years and loses his wife; but just as he is released, the real culprit confesses.

Persuasive Peggy (Mayfair Film Corp., 1917)
d: Charles J. Brabin. 6 reels.
Peggy Hyland, William Davidson, Mary Cecil, Gertrude Norman, Charles Sutton, Jules Cowles, Arthur Houseman.
Newlywed Peggy is an independent imp, as her befuddled new husband is soon to learn.

The Pest (Goldwyn, 1919)
d: William Christy Cabanne. 5 reels.
John Bowers, Mabel Normand, Charles Girard, Alec B. Francis, Leota Lorraine, Asher Blodgett, Amy Blodgett, Jack Curtis, Pearl Elmore, James Bradbury.
A country girl with backwoods ways finds happiness with a judge's nephew, but not before she gets involved in an elaborate scheme involving stolen jewelry, frame-ups and attempted murder.

The Petal on the Current (Universal, 1919)
d: Tod Browning. 6 reels.
Mary MacLaren, Robert Anderson, Gertrude Claire, Fritzie Ridgeway, Beatrice Burnham, Victor Potel, David Butler.
Meandering story about a poor but honest shopgirl who is invited to a party to meet a man she might want to get interested in. He never shows up, and the shopgirl drinks

too much and winds up getting arrested and thrown into jail. Later she loses her job and her mother dies suddenly; but just when all seems darkest, she meets the man of her dreams. Yep, he's the fellow she was supposed to meet at the party.

Peter Pan (Famous Players-Lasky/Paramount, 1924)

d: Herbert Brenon. 10 reels.

Betty Bronson, Mary Brian, Esther Ralston, Cyril Chadwick, George Ali, Anna May Wong, Ernest Torrence, Virginia Brown Faire, Philippe DeLacey, Jack Murphy.

Whimsical fairy-tale magic at its best. Eighteen-year-old Betty Bronson plays the irrepressible Peter Pan in this first—and still best—film version of the James M. Barrie classic. Peter, "the boy who refused to grow up," flies into the lives of the Darling children one evening and, charming them, gets them to fly away with him to Never-Never Land.

Unlike most treasures of the Silent Era, *Peter Pan* happily exists in a near-pristine 35mm print. In 1999 the film was lovingly restored by film historian David Pierce for Kino International and made available to the public in videotape and DVD editions, with a new orchestral score.

When *Peter Pan* was first performed on stage at Christmastime in 1903, Peter was played by actress Maude Adams, and it became a tradition that the role would always be portrayed by a female—partly because petite actresses were easier for invisible wires to lift on stage during the flying scenes.

Of course, Peter's costume varies slightly with each production. For the 1924 film version, Miss Bronson played the entire film barefoot and bare-legged.

Upon reviewing the DVD release in 1999, one writer observed: "Betty Bronson displays the best pair of legs ever, for a Peter Pan." An indelicate comment, perhaps, but absolutely true.

A Petticoat Pilot (Paramount, 1918)

d: Rollin S. Sturgeon. 5 reels.

Harrison Ford, Vivian Martin, Theodore Roberts, James Neill, Helen Gilmore, Richard Cummings, Jane Wolff, Bert Hadley, John Burton, Cecil Lione, Jane Keckley, Antrim Short.

Cape Cod business partners adopt the orphaned daughter of a former ally. In later years, she goes off to school in Boston, where she meets and falls for a schoolmate; alas, he's the son of a scoundrel who swindled her adoptive fathers years before. Sadly convinced that their alliance can never take place, the girl returns to Cape Cod to help run the family business. But she'll meet her young man again.

Petticoats and Politics (Plaza Pictures/W.W. Hodkinson, 1918)

d: Howard M. Mitchell. 5 reels.

Anita King, R. Henry Grey, Gordon Sackville, Charles Dudley, Ruth Lackaye.

Ambitious women aim to reform a wide-open Nevada town by getting elected to office.

Pettigrew's Girl (Famous Players-Lasky/Paramount, 1919)

d: George H. Melford. 5 reels.

Ethel Clayton, Monte Blue, James Mason, Charles Gerard, Clara Whipple.

At his army base, Private Pettigrew feels lonely because the other soldiers in his unit regularly receive mail from their loved ones, but Pettigrew is alone in the world. So he buys a picture of a chorus girl and pretends she is his sweetheart.

Sure enough, that very same chorus girl will find her way into Pettigrew's life.

The Phantom (Triangle, 1916)

d: Charles Giblyn. 5 reels.

Frank Keenan, Enid Markey, Robert McKim, P.D. Tabler, Charles K. French, J. Barney Sherry, Jack Gilbert.

Known as "the Phantom" for his seeming ability to disappear at will, a jewel thief plans to steal a valuable necklace. But he changes his mind when he meets its owner, Avis, and falls in love with her.

The Phantom Buccaneer (Essanay, 1916)

d: J. Charles Haydon. 5 reels.

Richard C. Travers, Gertrude Glover, Thurlow Brewer, R.P. Thompson, Carrol C. James, Arthur W. Bates, Ethel Davis.

After killing a high-ranking government official in South America, an adventurous Englishman escapes to London, but is pursued by the official's revenge-minded cohorts.

The Phantom Bullet (Universal, 1926)

d: Clifford Smith. 6 reels.

Hoot Gibson, Eileen Percy, Pat Harmon, Allan Forrest, Nelson McDowell, Pee Wee Holmes, Rosemary Cooper, John T. Prince, William H. Turner.

A cowpoke hunts for his father's killer.

The Phantom City (First National/Warner Bros., 1929)

d: Albert Rogell. 6 reels.

Ken Maynard, Eugenia Gilbert, James Mason, Charles Mailes, Jack McDonald.

Out West, a gang of crooks try to wrest a goldmine from its true owner.

The Phantom Express (Banner Productions, 1925)

d: John Adolfi. 5 reels.

Ethel Shannon, George Periolat, David Butler, Frankie Darro, George Siegmann, William Tooker, John Webb Dillon.

Jack, a substitute engineer, takes over and saves the Phantom Express from saboteurs.

Phantom Fortunes (Vitagraph, 1916)

d: Paul Scardon. 5 reels.

Barney Bernard, James Morrison, Lester Bernard, Edward Elkas, Adele DeGarde, Mary Maurice, L. Roger Lytton, Robert Gaillard.

Deceived by foreign criminals, a tailor makes enough army coats to outfit a battalion, but he's left with the coats when the crooks are carted off to jail.

The Phantom Honeymoon (J. Searle Dawley Productions/Hallmark Pictures, 1919)

d: J. Searle Dawley. 6 reels.

Marguerite Marsh, Vernon Steele, Hal Clarendon, Leon Dadmun, Henry Guy Carlton, Charles P. Patterson, Grace Bryant, Harriet Cox, Katherine Perkins, Edwin Poffley.

In Ireland, a professor and his two daughters search for answers to a mystery: It seems a castle is said to be haunted by lovers who died on their honeymoon.

The Phantom Horseman (Universal, 1924)

d: Robert North Bradbury. 5 reels.

Jack Hoxie, Lillian Rich, Neil McKinnon, Wade Boteler, William McCall, Ben Corbett, George A. Williams, Ruby Lafayette.

Out West, a phantom horseman rides at night, robbing the rich to help the poor.

A Phantom Husband (Triangle, 1917)

PETER PAN (1924). Betty Bronson was a teenager from New Jersey, toiling away at bit parts when J.M. Barrie spotted her and insisted that she play his hero, Peter Pan, in the Paramount film of his story. The ballet-trained youngster proved to be a perfect choice.

* * * * *

d: Ferris Hartman. 5 reels.
Ruth Stonehouse, J.P. Wild, Charles Gunn, Evelyn Driskell, Don Likes, Mary McIvor, Estelle Lacheur.
Humorous happenings, when a wallflower decides to invent a fictitious "fiancé" for herself.

Phantom Justice (Richard Thomas Productions/FBO of America, 1924)
d: Richard Thomas. 7 reels.
Rod LaRocque, Garry O'Dell, Kathryn McGuire, Frederick Vroom, Lillian Leighton, Frederick Moore, Gordon Dumont, Estelle Taylor, Rex Ballard, Norval MacGregor.
A lawyer falls asleep in the dentist's chair and dreams of a sensational murder case, with himself as the star attorney.

The Phantom Melody (Universal, 1920)
d: Douglas Gerrard. 6 reels.
Monroe Salisbury, Henry Barrows, Jean Calhoun, J. Barney Sherry, Ray Gallagher, Charles West, Lois Lee, Joe Ray, Milton Markwell.
In Italy, a count loves an English girl whose family owns a neighboring estate. His love is unrequited, however, because his worthless cousin also fancies the girl, and the count keeps his distance out of respect for his cousin. But that will change.

The Phantom of the Forest (Gotham Productions/Lumas Film Corp., 1926)
d: Henry McCarthy. 6 reels.
Thunder the dog, Betty Francisco, Eddie Phillips, James Mason, Frank Foster Davis, Irene Hunt, Rhody Hathaway.
In the forest, a smart, valiant dog protects a young woman from land thieves.

The Phantom of the Opera (Universal, 1925)
d: Rupert Julian. 10 reels. (Part Technicolor.)
Lon Chaney, Mary Philbin, Norman Kerry, Gibson Gowland, Arthur Edmund Carewe, Snitz Edwards, Mary Fabian, John Sainpolis, Virginia Pearson, Edith Yorke, Cesare Gravina, John Miljan, Chester Conklin.
A disfigured misfit lures a beautiful opera singer into his cavernous lair beneath the Paris Opera House.
Considered one of the most brilliant and effective horror movies ever, certainly the best in the silent era. Lon Chaney's makeup was as extensive as his getup for *The Hunchback of Notre Dame* (1923) had been, and the resulting face was so hideous, several theater patrons were reported to have fainted at first sight of it. Universal took care that no pictures of the phantom's face were published in any of the advertising or promotional literature prior to the film's premiere, to ensure maximum shock appeal... and it worked!

Phantom of the Range (FBO Pictures, 1928)
d: James Dugan. 5 reels.
Tom Tyler, Charles McHugh, Duane Thompson, Frankie Darro, James Pierce, Marjorie Zier.
Out West, a stranded actor fights off land thieves who are trying to swindle a local rancher and make off with his daughter.

Phantom of the Turf (Duke Worne Productions/Rayart, 1928)
d: Duke Worne. 6 reels.
Helene Costello, Rex Lease, Forrest Stanley, Danny Hoy, Clarence H. Wilson.
John, the son of a racing horse owner, returns home after hearing of his father's death, and sees that Phantom, his dad's thoroughbred, is entered in the big race. Despite

attempted sabotage by a rival horse owner, Phantom wins by a nose.

The Phantom Riders (Universal, 1918)
d: Jack Ford. 5 reels.
Harry Carey, Buck Connor, Molly Malone, Vester Pegg, Billy Gettinger.
Out West, a range war erupts when squatters claim ownership of Paradise Creek.

The Phantom's Secret (Universal, 1917)
d: Charles Swickard. 5 reels.
Mignon Anderson, Hayward Mack, Mark Fenton, Daniel Leighton, Molly Malone, L.C. Shumway, Fred Church, Nellie Allen, Nanine Wright.
Upon the death of a French count, his daughter is shocked to learn that he was a mysterious criminal known only as "the Phantom."

Phil-For-Short (World film Corp., 1919)
d: Oscar Apfel. 6 reels.
Evelyn Greeley, Charles Walcott, James Furey, Jack Drumier, Ann Egelston, Hugh Thompson, Henrietta Simpson, Charles Duncan, Ethel Grey Terry, Edward Arnold, John Adrizani, Tony Merlo, Florence Short, Henry Hallam.
Her Greek professor father named her Damophilia, but the young lady prefers to be called "Phil" for short. The nickname comes in handy, when Phil is forced to wear overalls and masquerade as a boy while trying to nurture a friendship with woman-hater John Alden, whom Phil (as a girl) adores.

Philip Holden—Waster (American film Co./Mutual, 1916)
d: George Sargent. 5 reels.
Richard Bennett, George Periolat, Adrienne Morrison, Rhea Mitchell, Clarence Burton, Orral Humphrey.
Philip, a poet smitten with love for Louise, determines to land a paying job so that he can afford to propose to her. Though his shady employer pays him in worthless shares in a dried-up gold mine, the day comes when the mine begins producing gold again... and Philip becomes wealthy enough to court Louise *and* write poetry.

Phyllis of the Follies (Universal, 1928)
d: Ernst Laemmle. 6 reels.
Alice Day, Matt Moore, Edmund Burns, Lilyan Tashman, Duane Thompson.
To teach an old roué a lesson, a lawyer's wife asks Phyllis, a Follies girl, to impersonate her at a meeting with the womanizer.

Picadilly Jim (Selznick/Select, 1920)
d: Wesley Ruggles. 5 reels.
Owen Moore, Zena keefe, George Bunny, William T. Hays, Dora Mills Adams, Alfred Hickman, Reginald Sheffield, Harlem Tommy Murphy, George Howard.
In London, a madcap American's wild adventures win him the nickname "Picadilly Jim."

Pidgin Island (Yorke Film Corp./Metro, 1916)
d: Fred J. Balshofer. 5 reels.
Harold Lockwood, May Allison, Doc Pomeroy Cannon, Lester Cuneo, Fred Wilson, Lillian Hayward, Elizah Zerr, Yukio Avyoma.
On Pidgin Island in the St. Lawrence River, a vacationing Secret Service agent begins a romance with the daughter of a smuggler he brought to justice.

Pied Piper Malone (Famous Players-Lasky/Paramount,

THE PHANTOM OF THE OPERA (1925). Lon Chaney stars as Erik, the grotesque "phantom" who lives in the catacombs beneath the Paris Opera House. He kidnaps an ingénue (Mary Philbin) and forces her to live with him in his bizarre underworld. The famous unmasking scene, when she rips off Erik's mask and reveals his hideous face, still packs a wallop. That face—Chaney's own creation—was so gruesome, the studio wisely kept it from appearing in publicity stills until after the film's premiere.

* * * * *

1924)

d: Alfred E. Green. 8 reels.

Thomas Meighan, Lois Wilson, Emma Dunn, Charles Stevenson, George Fawcett, Cyril Ring, Claude Brook, Joseph Burke, Peaches Jackson, Charles Winninger, Hugh Cameron, Dorothy Walters, Pearl Sindelar, Marie Schaefer, Elizabeth Henry, Jean Armour, Blanch Standing, Mollie Ring, Charles Mussett, Walter Downing, Henry Mayo, Lawrence Barnes, David Wall, Ed Williams, Helen Mack, Marilyn McLain, Florence Rogan, Rita Rogan, Louise Jones, Marie Louise Bobb, Louise Sirkin, Billy Lauder, Charles Walters, Edwin Mills, Leonard Connelly, Bobby Jackson, Dorothy McCann, Billy Baker, Marshall Green, Douglas Green.

A loveable seaman is hero to the children in his New England home town, but his rival schemes to dishonor the seaman's name.

Pilgrims of the Night (J.L. Frothingham/Associated Producers, 1921)

d: Edward Sloman. 6 reels.

Lewis S. Stone, Rubye DeRemer, William V. Mong, Kathleen Kirkham, Raymond Hatton, Walter McGrail, Frank Leigh.

In Paris, a vengeful daughter tries to kill the man she believes had her father imprisoned. What she doesn't know is that the prisoner is neither innocent nor her father at all. Her real dad, in fact, is the very man she wants to kill.

Pillars of Society (Fine Arts Film Co./Triangle, 1916)

d: Raoul Walsh. 5 reels.

Henry Walthall, Mary Alden, Juanita Archer, George Beranger, Josephine B. Crowell, Olga Gray.

Though he prides himself on being a pillar of society, a shipping tycoon knows in his heart that he rose to the top using trickery and deceit, and even fathered an illegitimate daughter.

The Pillory (Thanhouser, 1916)

d: Frederic Sullivan. 5 reels.

Florence LaBadie, George Marlo, Marie Shotwell, Marie Haynes, Nellie Parker Spaulding, Ethyle Cooke, Yale Benner, James Seeley.

Earnest commentary on society's shameful treatment of children unlucky enough to be born out of wedlock.

The Pinch Hitter (New York Motion Picture Corp./Triangle, 1917)

d: Victor L. Schertzinger. 5 reels.

Charles Ray, Sylvia Bremer, Joseph J. Dowling, Jerome Storm, Darrel Foss, Louis Durham.

Joel, a college boy and a blunderer, has been disparaged all his life. Lacking confidence, he has only one friend: Abbie, a shopgirl, who is the only person who ever tries to lift his spirits. Joel is on the college baseball team, but strictly as a bench-warmer who never gets to play. That is, not until one day when his team needs a pinch hitter, and Joel is the only player left.

The Pinch Hitter (Associated Exhibitors, 1926)

d: Joseph Henabery. 7 reels.

Glenn Hunter, Jack Drumier, Reginald Sheffield, Constance Bennett, Antrim Short, George Cline, Mary foy, James E. Sullivan, Joseph Burke.

Remake of the 1917 Triangle film of the same name.

Pink Gods (Famous Players-Lasky/Paramount, 1922)

d: Penrhyn Stanlaws. 8 reels.

Bebe Daniels, James Kirkwood, Anna Q. Nilsson, Raymond Hatton, Adolphe Menjou, Guy Oliver, George Cowl, Arthur Trimble.

Quelch, a fabulously wealthy owner of diamond mines, is also fabulously neurotic about his wealth, and questions the intentions of everyone he comes in contact with.

Pink Tights (Universal, 1920)

d: B. Reeves Eason. 5 reels.

Gladys Walton, Jack Perrin, Reeves Eason Jr., Dave Dyas, Stanton Hack, Rosa Gore, Dan Crimmins, Dorothea Wolbert.

Mazie, a circus performer in pink tights, accidentally ignites a scandal involving the local minister.

Pinto (Goldwyn, 1920)

d: Victor L. Schertzinger. 5 reels.

Cullen Landis, Edward Jobson, Mabel Normand, George Nichols, Edythe Chapman, William Elmer, Hallam Cooley, Dwight Crittenden, Andrew Arbuckle, Richard Cummings.

Miss Normand plays Pinto, an orphan girl who's been raised on an Arizona ranch by five wealthy adoptive fathers. Now that she's 18 years old, they send her to New York to acquire breeding... but find that you can take a girl out of the West, but you can't take the West out of a girl. At least not this one!

The Pioneer Scout (Paramount, 1928)

d: Lloyd Ingraham. 7 reels.

Fred Thomson, Nora Lane, William Courtwright, Tom Wilson.

In frontier days, a scout falls in love with the daughter of a wagonmaster.

Pioneer Trails (Vitagraph, 1923)

d: David Smith. 7 reels.

Cullen Landis, Alice Calhoun, Bertram Grassby, Otis Harlan, Dwight Crittenden, Virginia True Boardman, Aggie Herring, Nelson McDowell, Joe Rickson.

After an Indian raiding party attacks a wagon train, the only survivor is Jack, a 4-year-old boy. In years to come, Jack will become a hero, saving a wagon train from sure disaster.

Pioneer's Gold (Sanford Productions, 1924)

d: Denver Dixon. 5 reels.

Pete Morrison, Kathryn McGuire, Virginia Warwick, Spottiswood Aitken, Louis Emmons, Madge Lorese Bates, Merrill McCormick, Les Bates, George King, William McCormick.

A dying rancher plans to leave his estate to his brother's children, whom he's never met.

Pioneers of the West (J.P. McGowan Productions, 1929)

w, d: J.P. McGowan. 5 reels.

Tom Tyler, J.P. McGowan, George Brownhill, Mack V. Wright, Tommy Bay, Charlotte Winn.

After a train holdup the culprit's father takes the blame in order to save his son from a life in prison.

The Piper's Price (Universal, 1916)

d: Joseph DeGrasse. 5 reels.

Dorothy Phillips, William Stowell, Lon Chaney, Claire du Brey, Maud George.

Though he's now married to Amy, Ralph can't stop pining for his ex-wife, Jessica.

Pirates of the Sky (Hurricane Film Co./Pathé, 1927)

d: Charles Andrews. 5 reels.

Charles Hutchison, Wanda Hawley, Crauford Kent, Jimmy Aubrey, Ben Walker.

After a U.S. mail plane is lost, the Secret Service turns to

Manning, a criminologist with considerable flying experience.

The Pit (William A. Brady/World, 1914)
d: Maurice Tourneur. 5 reels.
Milton Sills, Wilton Lackaye, Alec B. Francis, Chester Barnett, E.P. Roseman, Bert Starkey, Slim Wiltsie, Gunnis Davis, William A. Orlamond, George Ingleton, Gail Kane, Jessie Lewis, Julia Stewart, Hattie Delaro, Betty Riggs.
In Chicago, a stock broker falls for another man's sweetheart and decides to pursue her.

Pitfalls of a Big City (Fox, 1919)
d: Frank Lloyd. 5 reels.
Gladys Brockwell, William Scott, William Sheer, Neva Gerber, Al Fremont, Ashton Dearholt, Janis Wilson.
Molly, a city dweller with a shady past, tries to operate a restaurant and take care of her younger sister. But two ex-cons Molly once knew catch up with her and threaten to expose her past crimes.

The Place Beyond the Winds (Universal, 1916)
d: Joseph DeGrasse. 5 reels.
Dorothy Phillips, Jack Mulhall, Lon Chaney, Joseph DeGrasse, C. Norman Hammond, Alice May Youse, Grace Carlyle.
In the Canadian wilderness, a young woman is sent packing by her straight-laced father after she stays out all night.

The Place of Honeymoons (Atlas Film Corp./Pioneer Film Corp., 1920)
d: Keenan Buel. 5 reels.
Emily Stevens, Frankie Mann, Joseph Selman, Mabel Bardine, Herbert Evans, Montagu Love, Charles Coleman, Edward Cullen, Harry Guy Carleton, Nila Devi, Antonia Petrucelli.
Mysterious happenings, when an opera singer is apparently kidnapped and later names a man named Edward as her abductor. But Edward is not charged with the crime; to the contrary, he becomes good friends with the singer's father.

Plain Jane (New York Motion Picture Corp./Triangle, 1916)
d: Charles Miller. 5 reels.
Bessie Barriscale, Charles Ray, Mabel Johnson, Fanny Midgley.
Jane, who works in a rooming house, loves John, one of the tenants, but he's too busy to notice her. When "plain Jane" is given a new hairdo and nice clothes in order to pose for a fashion photographer, she blossoms forth as an enchanting beauty... and John can no longer look away.

The Planter (Nevada Motion Picture Corp./Mutual, 1917)
d: T.N. Heffron. 7 reels.
Tyrone Power, Lamar Johnstone, Helen Bateman, Lucille King, Mabel Wiles, Pearl Elmore, George R. Odell, Alice Winchester, James Donald, Louis Fitzroy, Grace Whitehead.
When a spoiled New Englander travels to Mexico to safeguard his mother's plantation investment, he finds cruelty against Yaqui slaves, a housemaid who swims in the nude, and an epidemic of yellow fever. But he also finds love with the daughter of a slave trader.

Plastered in Paris (Fox, 1928)
d: Benjamin Stoloff. 6 reels.
Sammy Cohen, Jack Pennick, Lola Salvi, Ivan Linow, Hugh Allan, Marion Byron, Michael Visaroff, Albert Conti, August Tollaire.
Comedy about a pair of ex-doughboys, veterans of the Great War, who return to Paris for a tenth anniversary celebration of the Armistice. Among several other complications, our heroes get accidentally drafted into the French Foreign Legion. Once at their new post in North Africa, they get the chance to rescue the commandant's daughter from a sheik's harem.

The Plastic Age (B.P. Schulberg Productions/Preferred Pictures, 1925)
d: Wesley Ruggles. 7 reels.
Donald Keith, Clara Bow, Henry B. Walthall, Gilbert Roland, Mary Alden, Felix Balle, David Butler, J. Gordon Edwards Jr.
Hugh, a world-class athlete, enrolls in Prescott College and meets his waterloo in Cynthia, a world-class flirt. Through their infatuation, Hugh begins dissipating and falls out of shape. Eventually, by his senior year, both Hugh and Cynthia have come to their senses, and he recovers his athletic prowess in time to win the big football game.
Stylistically, *The Plastic Age* is a pedestrian exercise, with static staging and little if any innovation in camera technique. Still, the film is rewarding because it showcases the Clara Bow persona of legend. Here she is, all flashing eyes and winsome smiles, the promise of sex percolating just beneath her powder-and-paint exterior. Those kewpie doll lips, that *faux* demureness, the winks and the suggestive (though never lewd) body language... she unleashes the full arsenal here. It isn't a great movie, but Miss Bow puts on a great show.

The Play Girl (Fox, 1928)
d: Arthur Rosson. 6 reels.
Madge Bellamy, John Mack Brown, Walter McGrail, Lionel Belmore, Anita Garvin, Thelma Hill, Harry Tenbrook.
It's love in bloom, between a flower shop girl and her new customer.

Play Safe (Monty Banks Enterprises/Pathé, 1927)
d: Joseph Henabery. 5 reels.
Monty Banks, Virginia Lee Corbin, Charles Mailes, Charles Gerard, Bud Jamieson, Rosa Gore, Syd Crossley, Max Ascher, Fatty Alexander.
Monty springs to the rescue when Virginia, a new heiress, is menaced by the estate's untrustworthy trustee.

Play Square (Fox, 1921)
d: William K. Howard. 5 reels.
Johnnie Walker, Edna Murphy, Hayward Mack, Laura LaPlante, Jack Brammall, Wilbur Higby, Nanine Wright, Harry Todd, Al Fremont.
Johnny, a boy who was once induced to commit petty theft, gets a second chance at life from a sympathetic judge.

Playing Dead (Vitagraph Company of America, 1915)
d: Sidney Drew..
Sidney Drew, Mrs. Sidney Drew, Donald Hall, Harry English, Isadore Marcil, Alice Lake.
When a loving husband discovers his wife is interested in another man, he gallantly decides to fake his own death, so she will be free of him. But the will he signed, leaving her his entire estate, is lost. So the husband sneaks back into his own house disguised as a burglar, to find that will, and gets "caught" by his wife, who decides she prefers the man she married, after all.

Playing it Wild (Vitagraph, 1923)
d: William Duncan. 6 reels.
William Duncan, Edith Johnson, Francis Powers, Dick LaReno, Edmund Cobb, Frank Beal, Frank Weed.

Out West, an itinerant cowpoke wins the local newspaper in a poker game.

Playing the Game (Thomas H. Ince/Paramount, 1918)
d: Victor L. Schertzinger. 5 reels.
Charles Ray, Doris Lee, Harry Rattenberry, Robert McKim, Billy Elmer, Leota Lorraine, Charles Perley, Melbourne MacDowell.
When a wealthy easterner and his valet go west to inspect the Bar X Ranch—one of the easterner's investments—they are robbed by thieves. So they arrive at the ranch looking like a pair of bums and with no identification, giving the foreman no alternative but to put them to work.

Playing With Fire (Popular Plays and Players/Metro, 1916)
d: Francis J. Grandon. 5 reels.
Olga Petrova, Arthur Hoops, Evelyn Brent, Pierre LeMay, Catherine Calhoun, Philip Hahn, Claire Lillian Barry.
When a cash-strapped girl marries a wealthy man but is honest enough to warn him that she intends to play the faithful wife overtly but not in privacy, he loves her enough to go through with the marriage anyway. She'll change her mind.

Playing With Fire—see: Let's be Fashionable (1920)

Playing With Fire (Universal, 1921)
d: Dallas M. Fitzgerald. 5 reels.
Gladys Walton, Kathryn McGuire, Hayward Mack, Hallam Cooley, Eddie Gribbon, Harold Miller, Sidney Franklin, Lydia Knott, Harriet Laurel, Elinor Hancock, Danny Hoy.
Janet, a young socialite, helps a shopgirl cultivate good manners. In return, the shopgirl and her friends go after a signed affidavit that would clear Janet's father of financial wrongdoing.

Playing With Souls (Thomas H. Ince Corp./First National, 1925)
d: Ralph Ince. 7 reels.
Jacqueline Logan, Mary Astor, Belle Bennett, Clive Brook, William Collier Jr., Jessie Arnold, Don Marion, Helen Hoge, Josef Swickard.
Young newlyweds Matt and Amy decide to separate and put their son Matthew into a school where he will be well taken care of, but remain ignorant of his parents.

The Plaything of Broadway (Realart Pictures, 1921)
d: Jack Dillon. 5 reels.
Justine Johnstone, Crauford Kent, Macey Harlam, Edwards Davis, George Cowl, Lucy Parker, Claude Cooper, Garry McGarry, Gertrude Hillman, Mrs. Charles Willard.
Lola, a Broadway dancer, vamps a good doctor who's trying to help slum children.

Playthings (Universal, 1918)
d: Douglas Gerrard. 5 reels.
Myrtle Reeves, Lewis Cody, Fritzi Brunette, Charles Gerrard, Phil Dunham, Mary Anderson, Fred A. Turner.
Marjorie, a shopgirl, has a baby by the store owner, but is dismayed to learn that he has no intention of honoring his obligations as a father, nor to marry her.

Playthings of Desire (Jans Productions, 1924)
d: Burton King. 7 reels.
Estelle Taylor, Mahlon Hamilton, Dagmar Godowsky, Mary Thurman, Lawrence Davidson, Walter Miller, Edmund Breese, Bradley Barker, Ida Pardee.
Gloria, a stage actress honeymooning in Canada, is rescued from a steep waterfall by Pierre, a forest guide. When Gloria learns that her new husband is being unfaithful to her, she is drawn to Pierre and they fall in love.

Playthings of Destiny (Anita Stewart Productions/Associated First National, 1921)
d: Edwin Carewe. 7 reels.
Anita Stewart, Herbert Rawlinson, Walter McGrail, Grace Morse, William V. Mong, Richard Headrick.
Fleeing from what she believes is a bigamous marriage, Julie takes her child and moves to Jamaica, where she will find new love. She remarries, then discovers that her former husband was true to her all along. Now what?

Playthings of Fate—see: Playthings of Passion (1919)

Playthings of Passion (United Picture Theaters of America, Inc., 1919)
d: Walace Worsley. 5 reels.
Kitty Gordon, Mahlon Hamilton, W. Lawson Butt, Dick Rosson.
When wealthy Henry Rowland agrees to make charitable donations to a young minister doing social work in the slums, nobody is prepared for what comes next: Henry's wife Helen falls head over heels in love with the minister!

Please Get Married (Screen Classics, Inc./Metro, 1919)
d: John E. Ince. 5 reels.
Viola Dana, Antrim Short, Margaret Campbell, Harry Todd, Emmett King, Ralph Bell, Thoms Ricketts, Hugh Fay, Joseph Hazelton, W.K. Mesick, William F. Moran, Daisy Robinson.
Comedic tale about Ferdie and Muriel, lovers who are determined to get married. They take their vows before a strange preacher, then leave on their honeymoon. But panic strikes when the groom's father learns the "preacher" was a phony, and now Papa frantically phones ahead to the hotel, ordering the management not to let the happy couple into the bridal suite.

Please Help Emily (Empire All Star Corp./Mutual, 1917)
d: Dell Henderson. 5 reels.
Ann Murdock, Herbert Druce, Amy Veness, Grace Carlisle, Katherine Stewart, Rex McDougall, Ferdinand Gottschalk, John Harwood, Jules Raucourt, Hal Brown.
Emily, a madcap heiress, meets a boy at a club dance and, upon realizing that she left her house key at home, decides to spend the night at his place.

Pleasure Before Business (Columbia, 1927)
d: Frank Strayer. 6 reels.
Max Davidson, Virginia Brown Faire, Pat O'Malley.
A daughter dips into her dowry to help support her father after he becomes ill.

The Pleasure Buyers (Warner Bros., 1925)
d: Chester Withey. 7 reels.
Irene Rich, Clive Brook, Gayne Whitman, June Marlowe, Chester Conklin, Don Alvarado, Edward Peil, Frank Campeau, Winter Hall, Frank Leigh.
Workman, a retired detective, is called back to solve a perplexing murder case.

Pleasure Mad (Louis B. Mayer Productions/Metro, 1923)
d: Reginald Barker. 8 reels.
Huntley Gordon, Mary Alden, Norma Shearer, William Collier Jr., Winifred Bryson, Ward Crane, Frederick Truesdell, Joan Standing.
Carried away by sudden financial success, a husband and father goes on a spree with a younger woman.

Pleasure Seekers (Selznick, 1920)

d: George Archainbaud. 5 reels.

Elaine Hammerstein, James A. Furey, Webster Campbell, Marguerite Clayton, Frank Currier.

When a wealthy playboy meets a girl in the quaint village of South Paradise and they get married, it appears she is the only one who takes the marriage seriously.

Pleasures of the Rich (Tiffany Productions/Renown Pictures, 1926)

d: Louis Gasnier. 7 reels.

Helene Chadwick, Mary Carr, Marcin Asher, Jack Mulhall, Lillian Langdon, Dorothea Wolbert, Hedda Hopper, Julanne Johnston, Katherine Scott.

Wilson, a self-made man, becomes enamored of a divorcee who, on the other hand, is trying to win the affections of Clayton, who's in love with Wilson's daughter. Clear?

The Plow Girl (Lasky Feature Plays/Paramount, 1916)

d: Robert Leonard. 5 reels.

Mae Murray, Elliott Dexter, Theodore Roberts, Charles Gerard, Edythe Chapman, Horace B. Carpenter, William Elmer, Lillian Leighton.

When a London attorney is sent to South Africa to try and locate a long-lost heiress, he is unsuccessful, but he does find a girl who is being abused by her brutal guardian. The attorney rescues the girl and takes her back to London, introducing her as the missing heiress. The ruse works perfectly, but then the girl's former guardian shows up, and produces evidence that she really *is* the heiress everyone's been looking for.

The Plow Woman (Universal, 1917)

d: Charles Swickard. 5 reels.

Mary MacLaren, H.C. DeMore, Marie Hazelton, L.C. Shumway, Kingsley Benedict, Hector V. Sarno, Clara Horton, Eddie Polo, George Hupp, Tommy Burns.

Mary, the overworked daughter of a brutish father, keeps house for him and also looks after her little sister Ruth.

The Plunderer (Fox, 1915)

d: Edgar Lewis. 5 reels.

William Farnum, Harry Spingler, William Riley Hatch, Claire Whitney, Elizabeth Eyre, William J. Gross, George DeCarlton, Henry Armetta.

Out West, two partners in a gold mine discover that their neighbor has been plundering a vein from beneath their land.

The Plunderer (Fox, 1924)

d: George Archainbaud. 6 reels.

Frank Mayo, Evelyn Brent, Tom Santschi, James Mason, Peggy Shaw, Edward Phillips, Dan Mason.

Remake of the 1915 Fox film *The Plunderer*, both versions based on the novel of the same name by Roy Norton.

The Plunger (Fox, 1920)

d: Dell Henderson. 5 reels.

George Walsh, Virginia Valli, Byron Douglas, Richard R. Neill, Edward Bouldon, Inez Shannon, Irving Brooks, Robert Vivian, W.S. Harkins.

Schuyler, an office boy for a brokerage firm, rises to the position of Wall Street broker.

The Point of View (Selznick/Select, 1920)

d: Alan Crosland. 6 reels.

Elaine Hammerstein, Rockcliffe Fellowes, Arthur Houseman, Hugh Huntley, Helen Lindroth, Cornish Beck, Warren Cook.

Marjory, managing her fashionable family's affairs since they lost their fortune, rents out an apartment on the family estate to a westerner who's a millionaire. They fall in love and marry, but even in hard times, her family still is so proud that they look down on the westerner.

The Pointing Finger (Universal, 1919)

d: Tod Browning. 5 reels.

Mary MacLaren, Robert Anderson, Gertrude Claire, David Butler, Johnnie Cook, Carl Stockdale, Charlotte Woods.

Mary, a runaway orphan, goes to the city and gets a job. But first she has to disguise her good looks, because the prospective employer doesn't believe attractive girls can be good workers.

Points West (Universal, 1929)

d: Arthur Rosson. 6 reels.

Hoot Gibson, Alberta Vaughn, Frank Campeau, Jack Raymond, Martha Franklin, Milt Brown, Jim Corey.

It's home, home on derange, when a psychotic outlaw goes gunning for the man who had him sent to jail.

The Poison Pen (World Film Corp., 1919)

d: Edwin August. 5 reels.

June Elvidge, Earl Metcalfe, Joseph Smiley, Marion Barney, Jeanne Loew, George Bunny, Irving Brooks, John M. Sainpolis, J. Arthur Young, Henry West, Charles Mackay.

In an English village, the townsfolk are startled by a series of anonymous letters that disparage several of their most outstanding citizens.

Poisoned Paradise (Preferred Pictures, 1924)

d: Louis Gasnier. 7 reels.

Kenneth Harlan, Clara Bow, Barbara Tennant, Andre de Beranger, Raymond Griffith, Carmel Myers, Josef Swickard, Evelyn Selby, Michael Varconi, Frankie Lee, Peaches Jackson.

In Monte Carlo, a girl loses all her money at the gaming tables, but meets a dashing artist who covers all her losses and marries her besides.

Poker Faces (Universal, 1926)

d: Harry A. Pollard. 8 reels.

Edward Everett Horton, Laura LaPlante, Dorothy Revier, George Siegmann, Harry Curlew, Tom O'Brien.

A businessman borrows a prizefighter's wife to pose as his own for an important dinner engagement.

The Police Patrol (Gotahm Productions/Lumas Film Corp., 1925)

d: Burton King. 6 reels.

James Kirkwood, Edna Murphy, Edmund Breese, Bradley Barker, Frankie Evans, Joseph Smiley, Robert McKim, Blanche Craig, Edward Roseman, Tammany Young, Charles Craig.

Ryan, a police officer, loves Alice, but there's a problem: She's a dead ringer for Dorothy, a notorious jewel thief.

Edna Murphy portrays both roles: the cop's inamorata and his nemesis.

The Politic Flapper — see: The Patsy (1928)

Polly Ann (Triangle, 1917)

d: Charles F. Miller. 5 reels.

Bessie Love, J.P. Lockney, Rowland Lee, William Ellingford, Darrell Foss, Alfred Hollingsworth, Josephine Headley, Walt Whitman.

Polly Ann, an orphan girl, runs away with an itinerant theater company and befriends Howard, a carefree soul who's been disowned by his wealthy father.

Polly of the Circus (Goldwyn, 1917)
d: Charles T. Horan, Edwin L. Hollywood.   8 reels.
Mae Marsh, Vernon Steele, Charles Eldridge, Wellington Playter, George Trimble, Lucille Laverne, Dick Lee, Charles Riegel, Lucille Satterthwaite, J.B. Hollis, Helen Salinger.
Little Polly is raised by a circus clown and learns to be a bareback rider. When she's injured in a fall from her horse, Polly is taken to the local minister's house to recover and ends up finding true love, with the reverend himself.

Polly of the Follies (Constance Talmadge Film Co./Associated First National, 1922)
d: John Emerson.   7 reels.
Constance Talmadge, Horace Knight, Thomas Carr, Harry Fisher, Frank Lalor, George Fawcett, Ina Rorke, Mildred Arden, Kenneth Harlan, Paul Doucet, Theresa Maxwell.
Bob and Alysia are in love and want to be married, but their parents urge them to wait six months first. While the lovebirds are waiting, Alysia's younger sister Polly lands a role in the Ziegfeld Follies, but suffers stage fright and is unable to go on. Quickly, Alysia takes her place on stage and is an instant success. Alysia gets the part, and Polly gets Bob.

Polly of the Movies (James Ormont Productions, 1927)
d: Scott Pembroke.   7 reels.
Jason Robards, Gertrude Short, Mary Foy, Corliss Palmer, Stuart Holmes, Jack Richardson, Rose Dione.
Small-town girl Polly goes to Hollywood to break into the movies. Her boyfriend takes his $25,000 inheritance and sinks it all into Polly's initial opus, a heavy drama. But the "drama" turns out to be unintentionally hilarious, so the studio quickly promotes it as a comedy—and Polly and her sweetie have their first hit.

Polly of the Storm Country (Chaplin-Mayer Pictures Co./First National, 1920)
d: Arthur H. Rosson.   5 reels.
Mildred Harris Chaplin, Emory Johnson, Charlotte Burton, Harry Northrup, Maurice Valentine, Ruby Lafayette, Charles West, Mickey Moore.
The romance appears doomed when Polly, the daughter of squatters, falls in love with a wealthy landowner. But Polly's charm and ingenuity win over the doubters.

Polly Put the Kettle On (Universal, 1916)

d: Douglas Gerrard.   5 reels.
Douglas Gerrard, Thomas Jefferson, Ruth Clifford, Miss Maddox, Marvel Spencer, Lena Baskette, Zoe Rae, Anna Dodge, George Gebhardt, Lawrence Noskowski, Armin Von Harder.
When a young man enters a burning building to save Polly and her sisters, he saves the girls, but loses his eyesight in the process.

Polly Redhead (Universal, 1917)
d: Jack Conway.   5 reels.
Gertrude Astor, Charles H. Mailes, Gretchen Lederer, Ella Hall, George Webb, Dick LaReno, Raymond Whittaker, William Worthington Jr., Helen Wright.
Twelve-year-old Polly toils as a domestic in the home of a wealthy attorney. Before long, Polly's employer notices that she bears a strong resemblance to a girl involved in a custody dispute with the family of the attorney's fiancée. So he decides to have her impersonate that girl, to give the dispute time to resolve itself.

Polly With a Past (Metro, 1920)

d: Leander de Cordova.   6 reels.
Ina Claire, Ralph Graves, Marie Wainwright, Harry Benham, Clifton Webb, Louiszita Valentine, Myra Brooks, Frank Currier.
Rex loves Myrtle, but she's so wrapped up in her charity work she can't find time for him. To make the lady jealous and attract her attention, Rex hires Polly, his friends' maid, to impersonate a wicked woman and appear to vamp him. The charade works, but too well: Rex shifts his affection to Polly.

Pollyanna (Pickford/United Artists, 1920)
d: Paul Powell.   6 reels.
Mary Pickford, J. Wharton James, Katherine Griffith, Howard Ralston, William Courtleigh, Herbert Prior, Helen Jerome Eddy, George Berrell, Howard Ralston.
An eternally happy 14-year-old gladdens the hearts of those around her, then is injured while trying to save a child's life. This was Miss Pickford's first production to be released by United Artists, the company she helped found. She was 28 years old when she played the 14-year-old Pollyanna, but the customers didn't seem to mind—or even notice—the age difference.

Ponjola (Sam E. Rork Productions/Associated First National, 1923)
d: Donald Crisp.   7 reels.
Anna Q. Nilsson, James Kirkwood, Tully Marshall, Joseph Kilgour, Bernard Randall, Ruth Clifford, Claire DuBrey, Claire McDowell, Charles Ray, Edwin Sturgis.
Disguised as a man, Countess Flavia follows the man she loves to Africa.

The Pony Express (Famous Players-Lasky/Paramount, 1925)
d: James Cruze.   10 reels.
Betty Compson, Ricardo Cortez, Ernest Torrence, Wallace Beery, George Bancroft, Frank Lackteen, John Fox Jr., William Turner, Al Hart.
In antibellum days, a Pony Express rider valiantly fights political conspirators, Indian raids, and natural disasters to carry the message to California that Abraham Lincoln has been elected president.

The Pool of Flame (Universal, 1916)
d: F. McGraw Willis.   5 reels.
Lois Wilson, Maud George, J. Warren Kerrigan, Harry Carter, Bertram Grassby, H.L. Holland, Frank MacQuarrie, Earl Rogers.
"The Pool of Flame" is a priceless ruby that's been stolen from a statue of Buddha, in Burma. Now an American adventurer, Terence O'Rourke, is commissioned to find the jewel and return it to the authorities.

The Poor Boob (Famous Players-Lasky/Paramount, 1919)
d: Donald Crisp.   5 reels.
Bryant Washburn, Wanda Hawley, Dick Rosson, Theodore Roberts, Raymond Hatton, Jay Dwiggins, Charles Ogle, Jane Wolff, Mary Thurman, Guy Oliver, Clarence Geldart.
When Simpson, a loveable loser, goes to the big city after losing his factory and his girlfriend, he meets Hope, a secretary, and Jimmy, an office boy, and they become fast friends. The trio return to Simpson's home town and pull off a scam that wins back his factory. Simpson doesn't return to his old girlfriend, though; he's fallen in love with Hope, and he now sheds his loser image once and for all.

Poor, Dear Margaret Kirby (Selznick Pictures, 1921)

d: William P.S. Earle. 5 reels.

Elaine Hammerstein, William B. Donaldson, Ellen Cassidy, Helen Lindroth, Warburton Gamble.

A financially burdened man attempts suicide, but fails. His patient, understanding wife nurses him back to health and, through the efforts of a sympathetic admirer, obtains enough funds to see them through this hardship.

Poor Girls (Columbia, 1927)

d: William James Craft. 6 reels.

Dorothy Revier, Edmund Burns, Ruth Stonehouse, Lloyd Whitlock, Marjorie Bonner.

Peggy, a young socialite, is stunned to learn that her mother is secretly Texas Kate, a saloon owner.

A Poor Girl's Romance (R-C Pictures/FBO of America, 1926)

d: F. Harmon Weight. 6 reels.

Creighton Hale, Gertrude Short, Rosa Rudami, Clarissa Selwyn, Charles Requa, Johnny Gough, Forrest Taylor.

At a New York party, a tenement girl is introduced by her wealthy escort as a royal princess.

Poor Little Peppina (Famous Players/Paramount, 1916)

d: Sidney Olcott. 7 reels.

Mary Pickford, Eugene O'Brien, Antonio Maiori, Ernesto Torti, Edwin Mordant, Jack Pickford, Edith Shayne, Cesare Gravina, W.T. Carleton, Mrs. A. Maiori, Francesca Guerra.

Peppina, an Italian girl fleeing the Mafia, dresses as a boy and stows away on a boat bound for America.

The Poor Little Rich Girl (Artcraft Pictures Corp., 1917)

d: Maurice Tourneur. 6 reels.

Mary Pickford, Madeline Traverse, Charles Wellesley, Gladys Fairbanks, Frank McGlynn, Emile LaCroix, Marcia Harris.

A daughter of wealth and privilege is neglected by her parents and mistreated by the servants.

Poor Men's Wives (Preferred Pictures/Al Lichtman Corp., 1923)

d: Louis J. Gasnier. 7 reels.

Barbara LaMarr, David Butler, Betty Francisco, Richard Tucker, ZaSu Pitts, Muriel McCormac, Mickey McBan.

Laura, the wife of a taxicab driver, is induced by a well-off girlfriend to attend a fancy dress ball with her.

The Poor Nut (Jess Smith Productions/First National, 1927)

d: Richard Wallace. 7 reels.

Jack Mulhall, Charlie Murray, Jean Arthur, Jane Winton, Glenn Tryon, Cornelius Keefe, Maurice Ryan, Henry Vibart, Bruce Gordon, William Courtwright.

Comedy about John, a collegian with a huge inferiority complex who must be forced to go out for sports. Once on the team, he discovers unexpected athletic prowess.

A Poor Relation (Goldwyn, 1921)

d: Clarence Badger. 5 reels.

Will Rogers, Sylvia Breamer, Wallace MacDonald, Sydney Ainsworth, George B. Williams, Molly Malone, Robert DeVilbiss, Jeanette Trebaol, Walter Perry.

A struggling book peddler ekes out a living for himself and his two adopted children while he works on perfecting an invention.

Poor Relations (Brentwood Film Corp./Robertson-Cole, 1919)

d: King Vidor. 5 reels.

Florence Vidor, Lillian Leighton, William DuVaull, Roscoe

Karns, ZaSu Pitts, Charles Meredith.

Dorothy, daughter of poor country folk, goes to the city to study architecture, and becomes a success. She marries Monty, a scion of wealth, but even her business success doesn't placate her in-laws, who still regard Dorothy as "poor relations."

The Poor Rich Man (Metro, 1918)

d: Charles J. Brabin. 5 reels.

Francis X. Bushman, Beverly Bayne, Stuart Holmes, Sally Crute, William Frederic, C.J. Williams, Jules Cowles, Louis R. Wolheim.

When a wealthy man's son fails to show any initiative whatsoever, his disgusted father decides to put the boy to a test. Papa has his attorney proclaim that the old man has died, and has left a will directing that his son must make a success of himself within six months, or lose his inheritance.

The Poor Simp (Selznick/Select, 1920)

d: Victor Heerman. 5 reels.

Owen Moore, Nell Craig, Harry Rattenbury, Vera Lewis, Herbert Prior, Lassie Young, Tom Kennedy, Douglas S. Carter, Max Stanley.

Humorous doings, when a bashful young man can't bring himself to propose marriage to his girlfriend and instead winds up getting knocked out in a bar fight. Next morning, his sweetie and her mother visit the poor simp, and find him being attended to by a barmaid. The outraged sweetie and her mama want answers!

Poppy (Norma Talmadge Film Corp./Selznick, 1917)

d: Edward José. 8 reels.

Norma Talmadge, Eugene O'Brien, Frederick Perry, Jack Meredith, Dorothy Rogers, Edna Whistler, Marie Haines.

Tangled story of a young woman's loves and misadventures, beginning in Africa where she was a young orphan and culminating in her career as a successful novelist in London.

The Poppy Girl's Husband (Paramount, 1919)

d: William S. Hart. 5 reels.

William S. Hart, Juanita Hansen, Walter Long, Fred Starr, David Kirby, Georgie Stone.

Bittersweet drama about the love of a convict for his unfaithful wife.

The Port of Missing Girls (Brenda Pictures, 1928)

d: Irving Cummings. 8 reels.

Barbara Bedford, Malcolm McGregor, Natalie Kingston, Hedda Hopper, George Irving, Wyndham Standing, Charles Gerard, Paul Nicholson, Edith Yorke, Bodil Rosing, Rosemary Theby, Lotus Thompson, Amber Norman.

Ruth, an aspiring singer, gets trapped into a phony "stage school" that is run by its owner solely for immoral purposes.

The Port of Missing Men (Famous Players Film Co., 1914)

d: Francis Powers. 5 reels.

Arnold Daly, Marguerite Skirvin, Edward Mackay, Frederick Bock, Augustus Balfour, Minna Haines, Mortimer Martini, Dave Wall.

In a European monarchy, an evil archduchess plots to engineer a coup d'etat.

Ports of Call (Fox, 1925)

d: Denison Clift. 6 reels.

Edmund Lowe, Hazel Keener, william Davidson, William Conklin, bobby Mack, Lilyan Tashman, Alice Ward, Mary McLean.

Seen as a coward by the girl he loves, Kirk becomes a drifter, eventually ending up in Manila. There he gets a chance to show bravery when he rescues Lillie, another American, from a masher in a bar.

Potash and Perlmutter (Goldwyn, 1923)
d: Clarence Badger. 8 reels.
George Sidney, Alexander Carr, Barney Bernard, Vera Gordon, Martha Mansfield, Ben Lyon, Edward Durand, Hope sutherland, DeSacia Mooers, Jerry Devine, Lee Kohlmar.
Comedy about Abe Potash and Morris Perlmutter, partners in a tailor shop in New York.

Pots-and-Pans Peggy (Thanhouser/Pathé, 1917)
d: Eugene Moore. 5 reels.
Gladys Hulette, Wayne Arey, George Marlo, Kathryn Adams, Arthur Bauer, Grace Henderson, Helen Badgley, Gerald Badgley.

Peggy's only a housemaid, but she gets involved in the private affairs of her employer's family; fortunately so, because in time she will derail a planned misalliance at the altar, sober up the employer's drunken son, and prevent a traitorous scheme to sell War Department secrets.

The Potters (Famous Players-Lasky/Paramount, 1927)
d: Fred Newmeyer. 7 reels.
W.C. Fields, Mary Alden, Ivy Harris, Jack Egan, Richard "Skeets" Gallagher, Joseph Smiley, Bradley Barker.
Comedy about Pa Potter, a lowly dreamer who sinks the family's meager "fortune" —$4,000— into highly speculative oil stock.

The Poverty of Riches (Goldwyn, 1921)
d: Reginald Barker. 6 reels.
Richard Dix, Leatrice Joy, John Bowers, Louise Lovely, Irene Rich, DeWitt Jennings, Dave Winter, Roy Laidlaw, John Cossar, Frankie Lee, Dorothy Hughes.
Bitter drama about a woman who wants to have children, but accedes to her husband's wish to wait until their financial situation improves. When it does, she again proposes starting a family, but the husband wants to improve their social status, and so they continue to wait. Eventually the wife is involved in an automobile accident and suffers injuries that make it impossible for her to bear children.

Powder (American Film Co./Mutual, 1916)
d: Arthur Maude. 5 reels.
Arthur Maude, Constance Crawley, Jack Prescott, Jack Farrell, William Carroll, Lizette Thorne, George Ahearn.
A munitions manufacturer believes in selling firepower to the highest bidder, even if it be a warlike nation. But he changes forever when his own son is killed by an explosive made by the father's own company.

Powder My Back (Warner Bros., 1928)
d: Roy Del Ruth. 7 reels.
Irene Rich, Anders Randolph, Carol Nye, Andre Beranger, Audrey Ferris.
A crusading politician wants to close down a stage show he considers immoral, but the lead actress persuades him otherwise... and marries him, too.

Power (Pathé, 1928)
d: Howard Higgin. 7 reels.
William Boyd, Alan Hale, Jacqueline Logan, Jerry Drew, Joan Bennett, Carol Lombard, Pauline Curley.
Two pals in the dam construction business get scammed by a predatory female who exacts a proposal of marriage from

each of them—separately, of course—after first obtaining from each man his life's savings.

The Power and the Glory (World Film Corp., 1918)
d: Lawrence C. Windom. 5 reels.
June Elvidge, Frank Mayo, Madge Evans, Johnny Hines, Albert Hart, Clay Clement, Jack Drumier, Ricca Allen, Ned Burton, Sheridan Tansey, Charley Jackson, Inez Marcel, Violet Reed.
When an old man locates a lost silver mine, he is beaten by claim-jumpers who steal his find. One of the thieves covets Jonnie, the miner's niece, but she clings to Gray, the owner of a nearby mill, and together they work to reclaim the mine.

The Power of a Lie (Universal, 1922)
d: George Archainbaud. 5 reels.
Mabel Julienne Scott, David Torrence, Maude George, Phillips Smalley, Ruby Lafayette, Earl Metcalfe, June Elvidge, Stanton Heck, Winston Heck.
Richard, an architect, is accused of forging a promissory note and is put on trial. But he's innocent, and he'll prove it.

The Power of Decision (Rolfe Photoplays, Inc./Metro, 1917)
d: John W. Noble. 5 reels.
Frances Nelson, Richard Tucker, John Davidson, Sally Crute, Mary Asquith, Fuller Mellish, Hugh Jeffrey.
It's a ticklish situation when a novelist asks his wife to pose for the illustrations in his new book, and the artist turns out to be the wife's former husband.

The Power of Evil (Balboa Amusement Producing Co., 1916)
d: H.M. Horkheimer, E.D. Horkheimer. 5 reels.
Henry King, Marguerite Nichols, Lillian West, Frank Erlanger, Victory Bateman, Edward Peters, Gordon Sackville, Philo McCollough.
When a wealthy playboy marries and amends his carousing ways, he finds that his wife, unlike himself, has no real interest in settling down.

The Power of Love (Perfect Pictures, 1922)
d: Nat Deverich. 5 reels.
Elliott Sparling, Barbara Bedford, Noah Beery, Aileen Manning, Albert Prisco, John Herdman.
In Old California, a visiting American falls in love with a señorita, and she with him.

The Power of Silence (Tiffany-Stahl Productions, 1928)
d: Wallace Worsley. 6 reels.
Belle Bennett, John Westwood, Marian Douglas, Anders Randolf, John St. Polis, Virginia Pearson, Raymond Keane, Jack Singleton.
It's puzzling when a woman on trial for murder declines to offer an alibi. But she is simply sacrificing her own self-interest to save the woman she knows committed justifiable homicide.

The Power of the Press (Columbia, 1925)
d: Frank Capra. 7 reels.
Douglas Fairbanks Jr., Jobyna Ralston, Edwards Davis, Mildred Harris, Philo McCullough, Wheeler Oakman.
A crusading reporter fights to clear a young woman of murder charges.

The Power of the Weak (Chadwick Pictures/Independent Pictures, 1926)
d: William J. Craft. 7 reels.
Arnold Gregg, Alice Calhoun, Carl Miller, Spottiswoode

386

Aitken, Marguerite Clayton.
In the north woods, a lady owner of a lumber camp enlists the help of a newcomer to overthrow her rival.

Powers That Prey (American Film Co./Mutual, 1918)
d: Henry King. 5 reels.
Mary Miles Minter, Alan Forrest, Harvey Clark, Clarence Burton, Lucille Ward, Emma Kluge, Perry Banks, Robert Miller.
After taking over a newspaper her father left her, young Sylvia cuts a wide swath with sensational scoops, including an exposé of a crooked politician that recommends he be "tarred and feathered."

The Prairie King (Universal, 1927)
d: Reaves Eason. 6 reels.
Hoot Gibson, Barbara Worth, Albert Prisco, Charles Sellon, Rosa Gore, Sidney Jarvis, George Periolat.
Out West, a dying prospector bequeaths his mine to three beneficiaries, but on certain conditions that only one of the three can meet.

The Prairie Pirate (Producers Distributing Corp., 1926)
d: Edmund Mortimer. 5 reels.
Harry Carey, Jean Dumas, Lloyd Whitlock, Trilby Clark, Fred Kohler, Robert Edeson.
A westerner searches for the man responsible for the death of his sister.

Prairie Trails (Fox, 1920)
d: George Marshall. 5 reels.
Tom Mix, Charles K. French, Kathleen O'Connor, Robert Walker, Gloria Hope, Sid Jordan, Harry Dunkinson, William Elmer.
Mix performs several daredevil feats in this Western comedy about a cowboy in love with a sheep rancher's daughter.

The Prairie Wife (MGM, 1924)
w, d: Hugo Ballin. 7 reels.
Gibson Gowland, Dorothy Devore, Herbert Rawlinson, Boris Karloff.
In the Old West, a brutal homesteader menaces his new bride.

The Praise Agent (World Film Corp., 1919)
d: Frank Crane. 5 reels.
Arthur Ashley, Dorothy Green, Jack Drumier, Lucille LaVerne, J.W. Johnston, Lola Frink, Mrs. Priestly Morrison.
Political comedy about a publicity agent who drums up support for the suffragette cause.

The Precious Packet (Pathé, 1916)
d: Donald MacKenzie. 5 reels.
Ralph Kellard, Lois Meredith, W. Tabor Wetmore, Clara Heath, Charles Angelo, George Pauncefort, Walter Shindler.
In Canada, a British Secret Service agent is assigned to marry a female revolutionary leader to take some of the steam out of her cause.

Prep and Pep (Fox, 1928)
d: David Butler. 6 reels.
David Rollins, Nancy Drexel, John Darrow, E.H. Calvert, Frank Albertson, Robert Peck.
Comedy about Cyril, son of a famous athlete, who doesn't seem to have inherited his father's talent for sports. Eventually Cyril will find that his talent isn't in football or track, but in taming and riding horses, and he goes on to glory in his school's equestrian program.

The Pretender (Triangle, 1918)
d: Cliff Smith. 5 reels.
William Desmond, Ethel Fleming, Eugene Burr, Joseph J. Franz, C.E. Thurston, Graham Pettie, Percy Challenger, Walter Perkins, Joe Singleton.
Raucous comedy western that takes place in a town called Freloe Beanos and features a thespian named Otheloe Actwell. "The Pretender" refers to Desmond's character, a well-meaning stranger who fills in for the ailing schoolmaster in town, though his students probably know more about the subjects than he does.

The Pretenders (Rolfe Photoplays, Inc./Metro, 1916)
d: George D. Baker, Charels J. Hundt. 5 reels.
Emmy Wehlen, Paul Gordon, Charles Eldridge, Kate Blancke, Edwin Holt, William Davidson, Howard Truesdell, Jerome Wilson, Ilean Hume, Hugh Jeffrey, Harry Neville, George Stevens.
Country bumpkins strike oil, and with their new millions, they move to New York to join the social set. But the uppity social set won't have them... until one of the bumpkins makes friends with an English nobleman.

Pretty Clothes (Sterling Pictures, 1927)
d: Phil Rosen. 6 reels.
Jobyna Ralston, Gertrude Astor, Johnny Walker, Lloyd Whitlock, Charles Clary, Jack Mower, Lydia Knott.
To discourage his son from pursuing a certain poor girl, a millionaire persuades the son's friend to try and "compromise" the girl.

Pretty Ladies (MGM, 1925)
d: Monta Bell. 6 reels.
ZaSu Pitts, Tom Moore, Norma Shearer, Conrad Nagel, Ann Pennington, George K. Arthur, Lilyan Tashman, Roy D'Arcy, Gwen Lee, Myrna Loy, Lucille LeSueur.
A Broadway star loses her husband to one of the show's chorines.

Pretty Mrs. Smith (Oliver Morosco Photoplays/Paramount, 1915)
d: Hobart Bosworth. 5 reels.
Fritzi Scheff, Louis Bennison, Forrest Stanley, Owen Moore, Leila Bliss.
A young woman marries three times, always to a man named Smith.

The Pretty Sister of Jose (Famous Players/Paramount, 1915)
d: Allan Dwan. 5 reels.
Marguerite Clark, Jack Pickford, Edythe Chapman, Gertrude Norman, William Lloyd, Rupert Julian, Teddy Sampson, Dick Rosson.
Pepita, who saw her mother kill herself over a man, swears eternal hatred of men.   That's before Spanish torero Sebastiano enters her life....

Pretty Smooth (Universal, 1919)
d: Rollin Sturgeon. 6 reels.
Priscilla Dean, Francis McDonald, George McDaniels, Gertrude Astor, Walt Whitman, Claire Greenwood, Joseph Swickard, H. Milton Ross.
Gertie and Jimmy, both notorious thieves, fall in love at first sight.

The Prey (Vitagraph, 1920)
d: George L. Sargent. 6 reels.
Alice Joyce, Henry Hallam, Jack McLean, Harry Benham, L. Rogers Lytton, Herbert Pattee, William Turner, Cecil Kern, Roy Applegate.

A crooked investment banker tries to frame the district attorney, who was once in love with the banker's wife.

The Price (Equitable Motion Pictures/World Film Corp., 1915)
d: Joseph A. Golden. 5 reels.
Helen Ware, Wilmuth Merkyl, James Cooley, Blanche Douglas.
Infidelity and revenge power this tale about a girl who has an affair with a married artist, and repents.

The Price — see: The Dark Road (1917)

A Price for Folly (Vitagraph, 1915)
d: George D. Baker. 5 reels.
Edith Storey, Antonio Moreno, Louise Beaudet, Charles Kent, Harry T. Morey, Ethel Corcoran, Helen Pillsbury, John Hines, Arthur Cozine, Hughie Mack.
The wild, ne'er-do-well son of a duke loves a ballet dancer — not wisely, but too well.

The Price Mark (Thomas H. Ince/Paramount, 1917)
d: Roy W. Neill. 5 reels.
Dorothy Dalton, William Conklin, Thurston Hall, Adele Farrington, Edwin Wallock, Dorcas Matthews, Clio Ayres.
While serving as his model, Paula falls victim to an artist's charm and is dishonored.

The Price of a Good Time (Universal, 1917)
d: Lois Weber, Phillips Smalley. 5 reels.
Mildred Harris, Kenneth Harlan, Gertrude Astor, Alfred Allen, Helene Rosson, Adele Farrington, Ann Schaeffer.
A poor but honorable shopgirl accepts a rich man's offer of "a good time," but finds there is a price she must pay.

The Price of a Party (Pathé, 1924)
d: Charles Giblyn. 6 reels.
Hope Hampton, Harrison Ford, Arthur Edmund Carew, Mary Astor, Dagmar Godowsky, Fred Hadley, Florence Richardson, Edna Richmond, Daniel Pennell, Joy Bennett, Edward Lawrence, Claire Luce, Ward Fox, Esther Muir.
An unscrupulous stockbroker schemes with a cabaret dancer to distract his business rival.

The Price of Applause (Triangle, 1918)
d: Thomas N. Heffron. 5 reels.
Jack Livingston, Claire Anderson, Joe King, Walt Whitman.
During World War I, an attention-craving poet proclaims loudly that he is an American patriot willing to die for his country. He'll soon get his chance.

The Price of Fame (Vitagraph, 1916)
d: Charles J. Brabin. 5 reels.
Marc MacDermott, Naomi Childers, L. Rogers Lytton, Logan Paul, Mary Maurice.
When a senatorial candidate dies during his campaign, his twin brother steps in to take his place — not only in the campaign, but also in the life of the candidate's sweetheart.

The Price of Fear (Universal, 1928)
d: Leigh Jason. 5 reels.
Bill Cody, Duane Thompson, Grace Cunard, Tom London, Monty Montague, Ole M. Ness, Jack Raymond.
Rival detectives — a man and a woman — wind up working together undercover.

The Price of Happiness (Triumph Film Corp./World Film Corp., 1916)
d: Edmond Lawrence. 5 reels.
Mary Boland, Marion Singer, Enid Francis, Carlotta DeFelico, Albert Bechtel, Dave Wall, Adolphe Menjou.

Morality play about a young woman, married to a master cobbler, who envies her three single girlfriends their glamorous lifestyles and their ways of juggling lovers with ease. When the cobbler's wife sets about delivering three pairs of new shoes to her friends as gifts, she gets to see the ugly sides of their licentious ways.

The Price of Her Soul (Variety Films Corp., 1917)
d: Oscar Apfel. 6 reels.
Gladys Brockwell, Jack Standing, Monroe Salisbury, Brooklyn Keller, Eleanor Crowe, Jack Abbott, Willard Louis.
Powerful anti-drug drama, with a man named Connor trying to find the fiend who caused his brother's addiction. Upon learning that the perpetrator is none other than his own sweetheart's father, Connor makes the unusual move of getting his sweetheart hooked on drugs, to teach her father a lesson.

The Price of Honor (Columbia, 1927)
d: E.H. Griffith. 6 reels.
Dorothy Revier, Malcolm McGregor, William V. Mong, Gustav von Seyffertitz, Erville Alderson, Dan Mason.
Hoyt, a man unjustly convicted and sent to prison, is released after 15 years and goes to visit his niece without telling her of his identity.

The Price of Innocence (Buffalo Motion Picture Corp./First National, 1919)
d: Frank Gordon Kirby. 5 reels.
Stella K. Talbot, Howard Hall, Anders Randolf, Margaret Campbell, John Smiley, Stanely Walpole, Jack Johnson, George Trimble.
When a wealthy heir tries to evict squatters from his father's land, they resist. But the heir finds himself attracted to Mary, the lovely ward of the squatters' minister. Callously, he hatches a plan to trade her physical favors for the land.

The Price of Malice (Rolfe Photoplays/Metro, 1916)
d: O.A.C. Lund. 5 reels.
Hamilton Revelle, Barbara Tennant, William Davidson, Helen Dunbar, William Calhoun, Frank Glendon, Hugh Jeffrey, William Heck.

A British secret agent turns the tables on a jealous army officer who was trying to blackmail him.

The Price of Pleasure (Universal, 1925)
d: Edward Sloman. 7 reels.
Virginia Valli, Norman Kerry, Louise Fazenda, Kate Lester, George Fawcett, T. Roy Barnes, James O. Barrows, Marie Astaire.
Linnie, a shopgirl, and Garry, son of a wealthy family, fall in love and are married. But his family members strongly disapprove of Linnie and they let her know it in no uncertain terms.

The Price of Possession (Famous Players-Lasky/Paramount, 1921)
d: Hugh Ford. 5 reels.
Ethel Clayton, Rockliffe Fellowes, Maude Turner Gordon, Reginald Denny, Clarence Heritage, George Backus, Isabel West, Pearl Shepard.
Competing claimants to an estate decide to merge their interests: They get married.

The Price of Pride (World Film Corp., 1917)
d: Harley Knoles. 5 reels.
Carlyle Blackwell, June Elvidge, Frank Mills, Evelyn Greeley, George MacQuarrie, Charles Charles, Pinna Nesbit.

Out West, a shiftless idler named William fritters away his time in the gambling hall run by his mother and stepfather. Into William's life comes an eastern visitor—David—who, though neither of them knows it, is William's half-brother. Blackwell plays both brothers, William and David.

The Price of Redemption (Metro, 1920)
d: Dallas M. Fitzgerald. 7 reels.
Bert Lytell, Seena Owen, Cleo Madison, Landers Stevens, Edward Cecil, Arthur Morrison, Wilbur Higby, Mickey Moore, Rose Marie de Courelle.
Leigh, a British officer with commendations for honorable service in India, falls in love with Jean, and they marry. But when Leigh takes to drinking and Jean repulses him, he disappears and fakes his own death in a railroad crash. Years later, when Jean and her new husband visit India, they are threatened in a native uprising, and Leigh is the instrument of their salvation.

The Price of Silence (Universal, 1916)
d: Joseph DeGrasse. 5 reels.
Dorothy Phillips, Vola Smith, Lon Chaney, Frank Whitson, Evelyn Selbie, Jay Belasco, Jack Mulhall, Eddie Brown.
Helen, who had an illegitimate son by another man years before she married her present husband—and kept quiet about it—is shocked to learn that her grown daughter is engaged to marry the son she abandoned, years before.

The Price of Silence (Fox, 1917)
d: Frank Lloyd. 5 reels.
William Farnum, Frank Clark, Vivian Rich, Brooklyn Keller, Charles Clary, Ray Hanford, Gordon Griffith.
A self-sacrificing senator faces prison for accepting a bribe, although he did so only to protect the daughter of an unscrupulous, now-deceased judge.

The Price of Success (Columbia, 1925)
d: Tony Gaudio. 6 reels.
Lee Shumway, Alice Lake, Alma Bennett, Gaston Glass, Florence Turner, Spec O'Donnell, Edward Kipling.
Learning that her husband is having an affair, Ellen begins flirting with other men, thinking to win back her husband by making him jealous.

The Price of Youth (Berwilla Film Corp./Arrow Film Corp., 1922)
d: Ben wilson. 5 reels.
Neva Gerber, Spottiswoode Aitken, Ashton Dearholt, Charles L. King, Joseph Girard, Jack Pratt, Pietro Sosso.
Country girl Adele, whose father has died, moves to the big city to try to launch a singing career. There, she meets Spencer, a wealthy broker, who gains her confidence. In time, Adele will learn that Spencer is the man her mother ran off with years before, causing a great rift in her family.

The Price She Paid (Clara Kimball Young Film Corp./Selznick, 1917)
d: Charles Giblyn. 7 reels.
Clara Kimball Young, Louise Beaudet, Cecil Fletcher, Charles Bowser, Snitz Edwards, Alan Hale, David Powell, Cesare Gravina.
Mildred, forced to marry a rich scoundrel, soon leaves him and Paris and goes to America to study voice.

The Price She Paid (Columbia, 1924)
d: Henry MacRae. 6 reels.
Alma Rubens, Eugenie Besserer, William Welsh, Frank Mayo, Lloyd Whitlock, Otto Hoffman, Edwards Davis, Wilfred Lucas, Ed Brady, Freeman Wood.

A society girl marries for money, to help save her extravagant mother from bankruptcy.

The Price Woman Pays (California Motion Picture Corp., 1919)
d: George Terwilliger. 6 reels.
Lois Wilson, Frances Burnham, Beatriz Michelena, Albert Morrison, William Scott, Harvey Miller, Mina Gleason.
After a single indiscretion, a young woman reads the story of *Faust*, about a man who sells his soul to the devil for some instant gratification. The story makes such an impression on the girl, she resolves never to tempt fate again.

Pride (McClure Pictures, Inc./Triangle, 1917)
d: Richard Ridgely. 5 reels.
Holbrook Blinn, Shirley Mason, George LeGurer, Helen Strickland, Guido Colucci.
Eve, a newly rich young woman, eludes her sweetheart and sails to Europe with a phony count. Fortunately for her, the sweetheart has stowed away and is able to denounce Eve's "count" as a fortune-hunting phony.

Pride and the Devil (Apollo Pictures, Inc./Art Dramas, Inc., 1917)
d: Richard Ridgley. 5 reels.
Alma Hanlon, Leo Delaney, Bigelow Cooper, Pamela Vale, Charles Hutchinson, Harold Vermilye.
In a sensational murder case, an attorney wins acquittal for his client by blaming the crime on his client's wife.

Pride and the Man (American Film Co./Mutual, 1917)
d: Edward Sloman. 5 reels.
William Russell, Francelia Billington, Clarence Burton, George Fisher, Antrim Short, Al Kaufman, Tom Moran, Paul Weigel.
A prizefighter gives up the ring to marry the woman he loves.

The Pride of New York (Fox, 1917)
d: R.A. Walsh. 5 reels.
George Walsh, James A. Marcus, William Bailey, Regina Quinn.
Derring-do in World War I, as an intrepid aviation captain pursues a German officer who's abducted a Red Cross nurse. After several adventures, he rescues her and they escape together.

The Pride of Palomar (Cosmopolitan/Paramount, 1922)
d: Frank Borzage. 8 reels.
Forrest Stanley, Marjorie Daw, Tote DuCrow, James Barrows, Joseph Dowling, Alred Allen, George Nichols, Warner Oland, Mrs. Jessie Hebbard, Percy Williams.
In Old California, a returned war veteran fights to keep land pirates from taking over the family ranch.

The Pride of Pawnee (FBO Pictures, 1929)
d: Robert DeLacy. 6 reels.
Tom Tyler, Ethlyne Clair, Barney Furey, Frankie Darrow, Jack Hilliard, Lew Meehan, Jimmy Casey.
Out West, a gang of white marauders pose as Indians to stage raids on stagecoaches.

The Pride of the Clan (Pickford/Artcraft, 1916)
d: Maurice Tourneur. 7 reels.
Mary Pickford, Matt Moore, Warren Cook, Kathryn Browne Decker, Ed Roseman.
On a small Scottish island where life is harsh, a young woman falls in love with a local fisherman, and they plan to marry. But their love is complicated by revelations that the

fisherman is of noble blood.

The Pride of the Force (Rayart, 1925)
d: Duke Worne. 5 reels.
Tom Santschi, Edythe Chapman, Gladys Hulette, James Morrison, Francis X. Bushman Jr., Crauford Kent, Joseph Girard.
Moore, a scrupulously honest police officer, sets a trap and captures a criminal gang, even though it means he must also run in his own daughter, who appears to be a gang accomplice. Later, when proof of the girl's innocence is uncovered, Moore happily accepts his promotion to sergeant.

The Prima Donna's Husband (Triumph Film Corp./A.&W. Film Corp., 1916)
d: Julius Steger, Joseph A. Golden. 5 reels.
Holbrook Blinn, Kathryn Browne-Decker, Clara Whipple, Walter Hitchcock, Marie Reichardt, Fred Esmelton.
A selfish opera singer rejects both her husband and her daughter in her climb to stardom.

The Primal Law (Fox, 1921)
d: Bernard J. Durning. 6 reels.
Dustin Farnum, Mary Thurman, Harry Dunkinson, Philo McCullough, William Lowery, Charles Gorman, Glen Cavender, Frankie Lee, Rosita Marstini, Allan Cavan, Edwin Booth Tilton.
Out West, a rancher is tricked into selling his land to a scoundrel who has secretly discovered oil on the property. Upon learning of the duplicity, the rancher tries to destroy the deed and nullify the transfer of ownership, but finds this difficult, because the villain is prepared to use even the forces of law and order to validate his claim.

The Primal Lure (New York Motion Picture Corp./Triangle, 1916)
d: William S. Hart. 5 reels.
William S. Hart, Margery Wilson, Robert McKim, Jerome Storm, Joe Goodboy.
In the Pacific northwest, a trading post officer falls in love with a girl he believes is a thief.

The Primitive Call (Fox, 1917)
d: Bertram Bracken. 5 reels.
Gladys Coburn, Fritz Leiber, John Webb Dillion, George Alan Larkin, Lewis Sealy, Velma Whitman, Kittens Reichert.
Betty, an unscrupulous socialite, schemes to defraud an educated Indian brave out of his tribe's land.

The Primitive Lover (First National, 1922)
d: Sidney Franklin. 7 reels.
Constance Talmadge, Harrison Ford, Kenneth Harlan, Joe Roberts, Charles Pina, Chief Big Tree, Matilda Brudage, Clyde Benson.
An embattled husband is determined to stop his wife's divorce proceedings and prove that he still loves her. So, he kidnaps her.

The Primitive Woman (American Film Co./Mutual, 1918)
d: Lloyd Ingraham. 5 reels.
Margarita Fisher, Jack Mower, Millard Wilson, Emma Kluge, Helen Howard, Molly McConnell, Edward Peil.
Stephen, a misogynist professor, takes refuge in his mountain cabin. There, he meets Nan, a mountain girl in ragged clothes, and falls in love with her. But Nan's really a sophisticated city girl, out to disprove the professor's theories on modern women.

The Primrose Path (Universal, 1915)
d: Lawrence Martson. 5 reels.
Hal Forde, Gladys Hanson, William J. Welsh, E. Cooper Willis, Nina Blake.
In Paris, an artist's wife sells her body to provide money to cure her husband's illness.
This film was remade by Universal in 1920 as *Burnt Wings*.

The Primrose Path (Arrow Pictures, 1925)
d: Harry O. Hoyt. 6 reels.
Wallace MacDonald, Clara Bow, Arline Pretty, Stuart Holmes, Pat Moore, Lydia Knott, Tom Santschi, Templar Saxe.
Bruce, a disgraced son of a wealthy family, joins a smuggling ring in order to repay his gambling debts.

The Primrose Ring (Lasky Feature Plays/Paramount, 1917)
d: Robert Leonard. 5 reels.
Mae Murray, Tom Moore, Winter Hall, Little Billy Jacobs, Mayme Kelso.
Margaret is a kindly nurse who's devoted to her charges in the crippled children's ward. When the chief physician dies, however, his son takes over and decides to close the hospital and send the children away. Margaret will change his mind.

The Prince and Betty (Jesse D. Hampton Productions/Pathé, 1919)
d: Robert Thornby. 5 reels.
William Desmond, Mary Thurman, Anita Kay, George Swann, Walter Perry, Wilton Taylor, William Devaull, Frank Lanning, Boris Karloff.
On the small island country of Mervo, an American poses as a prince to drum up attendance at the island's casino.

The Prince and the Pauper (Famous Players/Paramount, 1915)
d: Edwin S. Porter, Hugh Ford. 5 reels.
Marguerite Clark, Robert Broderick, William Barrows, William Sorelle, William Frederick, Alfred Fisher, Nathaniel Sack.
In 16th century England, young Edward, the Prince of Wales, longs for a respite from his royal duties. He happens to meet Tom, a street beggar who strongly resembles Edward, and suggests that they exchange identities for a while. After the boys swap clothes, each finds himself swept up in the other's life, with all the pains and pleasures that go with it. But when Edward's father the king dies and his successor must assume the monarchy, Tom knows that he must somehow find Edward and return him to his rightful position to be crowned the new king.
This was the first feature film version of the enormously popular Mark Twain novel, *The Prince and the Pauper*, first published in 1882.

The Prince Chap (Selig Polyscope, 1916)
d: Marshall Neilan. 5 reels.
Marshall Neilan, Mary Charleson, Bessie Eyton, Camille D'Arcy, George Fawcett, Margaret Fawcett, Cecil Holland, Charles Gerard, Fannie Cohen.
William, an American painter studying in London, takes on a responsibility he hadn't counted on: a foster daughter, Claudia. Somehow the arrangement doesn't sit well with Alice, William's fiancée, so she gives him an ultimatum: Either the girl goes, or Alice does.

The Prince Chap (Famous Players-Lasky/Paramount, 1920)
d: William DeMille. 6 reels.

Thomas Meighan, Charles Ogle, Kathlyn Williams, Casson Ferguson, Ann Forrest, Peaches Jackson, May Giraci, Lila Lee, Lillian Leighton, Bertie Johns, Florence Hart, Theodore Kosloff, Clarence Geldart, Yvonne Gardelle.
Remake of Selig's 1916 film *The Prince Chap*. Both films are based on the play of the same name by Edward Peple.

Prince Dimitri — see: Resurrection (1927)

A Prince in a Pawnshop (Vitagraph, 1916)
d: Paul Scardon. 5 reels.
Barney Bernard, Garry McGarry, Bobby Connelly, Charlotte Ives, Edna Hunter, Brinsley Shaw, Lester Bernard.
David, a warm-hearted banker, charges high interest rates from wealthy clients so that he can carry on charity work in the slums.

A Prince of a King (Z.A. Stegmuller/Selznick, 1923)
d: Albert Austin. 6 reels.
Dinky Dean, Virginia Pearson, Eric Mayne, John Sainpolis, Joseph Swickard, Mitchell Lewis, Sam DeGrasse.
In a fictional European kingdom, a usurper poisons the king and tries to kill Price Gigi, the rightful heir. But the prince escapes to safety with a troupe of Gypsies, who will help him secure the throne and drive away the usurper's forces.

The Prince of Avenue A (Universal, 1920)
d: Jack Ford. 5 reels.
James Corbett, Richard Cummings, Cora Drew, Frederick Vroom, Mary Warren, George Fisher, Harry Northrup, Mark Fenton, Johnnie Cooke, Lydia Yeamans Titus.
Because Barry dresses elegantly, he's thought to be a sissy. But he'll prove otherwise.

The Prince of Broadway (Chadwick Pictures, 1925)
d: John Gorman. 6 reels.
George Walsh, Alyce Mills, Freeman Wood, Robert Roper, Tommy Ryan, Charles McHugh, G. Howe Black, Frankie Genaro, Ad Wolgast, Billy Papke, Leach Cross.
Gorman, a boxing champion, spends his evenings drinking and dancing; not surprisingly, he gets knocked out in his next bout and loses the championship. But his childhood sweetheart will help him get back in training and, eventually, Gorman wins back his title.

The Prince of Graustark (Essanay, 1916)
d: Fred E. Wright. 5 reels.
Bryant Washburn, Marguerite Clayton, Sydney Ainsworth, Ernest Maupain, Florence Oberle, John Cossar.
When the prince of a small Balkan nation refuses to marry a neighboring princess because he has never met her, he inadvertently places his country on the fast track to bankruptcy.

The Prince of Headwaiters (Sam E. Rork Productions/First National, 1927)
d: John Francis Dillon. 7 reels.
Lewis Stone, Priscilla Bonner, E.J. Ratcliffe, Lilyan Tashman, John Patrick, Robert Agnew, Ann Rork, Cleve Moore, Dick Folkens, Lincoln Stedman, Cecille Evans.
In Paris, a headwaiter learns that one of the three college boys he is serving is his own son, born after the waiter's wife had left him.

A Prince of His Race (Colored Players Film Corp., 1926)
d: Roy Calnek. 8 reels.
Harry Henderson, William A. Clayton Jr., Lawrence Chenault, Arline Mickey, Ethel Smith, Shingzie Howard.
Tom, an innocent man, is railroaded into a prison term by false friends.

The Prince of Pep (Carlos Productions/FBO of America, 1925)
d: Jack Nelson. 5 reels.
Richard Talmadge, Nola Luxford, Carol Wines, Marcella Daly, Brinsley Shaw, Arthur Conrad, Victor Dillingham.
Leland, a philanthropist, is knocked unconscious by an assailant and left for dead. When he comes to, he has lost his memory and soon develops two personalities: one, as a clinic worker, and the other as a bandit who robs from the rich to benefit the clinic.

The Prince of Pilsen (Belasco Productions/Producers Distributing Corp., 1926)
d: Paul Powell. 7 reels.
George Sidney, Anita Stewart, Allan Forrest, Myrtle Stedman, Otis Harlan, Rose Tapley, William von Brincken, William von Hardenburg.
In Europe, a visiting American chef is mistaken for a prince.

The Prince of Tempters (Robert Kane Productions/First National, 1926)
d: Lothar Mendes. 8 reels.
Lois Moran, Ben Lyon, Lya DePutti, Ian Keith, Mary Brian, Olive Tell, Sam Hardy, Henry Vibart, Judith Vosselli, Frazer Coulter, J. Barney Sherry.
In Italy, a boy grows up in a monastery, never realizing he is the heir to a British estate and a title.

A Prince There Was (Famous Players-Lasky/Paramount, 1922)
d: Tom Forman. 6 reels.
Thomas Meighan, Mildred Harris, Guy Oliver, Arthur Hull, Sylvia Ashton, Fred Huntley.
Martin, a wealthy playboy, buys out a magazine publisher so he can begin publishing the stories of a girl he's fallen in love with.

The Princess From Hoboken (Tiffany Productions, 1927)
d: Allan Dale. 6 reels.
Edmund Burns, Blanche Mehaffey, Ethel Clayton, Lou Tellegen, Babe London, Will R. Walling, Charles McHugh, Aggie Herring, Charles Crockett, Robert Homans, Harry Bailey.
In Hoboken, New Jersey, a restaurant owner transforms his place of business into a Russian Tea Room and has his daughter impersonate a certain famous Russian princess. On opening night, the real princess shows up. Now what?

Princess Jones (Vitagraph, 1921)
d: Gustav von Seyffertitz. 5 reels.
Alice Calhoun, Vincent Coleman, Helen DuBois, Robert Lee Keeling, Robert Gaillard, Joseph Burke, Sadie Mullen.
A small-town girl passes herself off as a Balkan princess.

The Princess on Broadway (Dallas M. Fitzgerlad Productions/Pathé, 1927)
d: Dallas M. Fitzgerald. 6 reels.
Pauline Garon, Dorothy Dwan, Johnny Walker, Harold Miller, Ethel Clayton, Neely Edwards, Ernest Wood, George Walsh.
A waitress turned chorus girl is introduced to an admirer as a real-life Russian princess.

The Princess of Park Row (Vitagraph, 1917)
d: Ashley Miller. 5 reels.
Mildred Manning, Wallace MacDonald, William Dunn, John Costello, Anne Brody.

In New York, a reporter meets and romances a girl he thinks is a maid—but she's really the crown princess of a European kingdom.

The Princess of Patches (Selig Polyscope, 1917)
d: Al Green. 5 reels.
Violet DeBiccari, Vivian Reed, Burke Wilbur, Hildor Hoberg, Roy Southerland, Cora Lambert, Frank Weed, Charles LeMoyne, Maude Baker, R.H. Kelly.
A kindly Southern colonel takes in an orphan girl in ragged clothes and raises her as his own. Years later, the girl is identified as the heiress to a large plantation.

Princess of the Dark (Triangle, 1917)
d: Charles Miller. 5 reels.
Enid Bennett, Jack Gilbert, Alfred Vosburgh, Walt Whitman, J. Frank Burke.
In a small mining town, a girl who has been blind since birth spins elaborate fantasies.

Princess Romanoff (Fox, 1915)
d: Frank Powell. 5 reels.
Nance O'Neil, Clifford Bruce, Dorothy Bernard, Stuart Holmes.
Fedora, the Princess Romanoff, follows the trail of her fiancé's killer all the way to New York, and then falls in love with him.

Princess Virtue (Universal, 1917)
d: Robert Z. Leonard. 5 reels.
Mae Murray, Wheeler Oakman, Jean Hersholt, Lule Warrenton, Clarissa Selwynne, Gretchen Lederer, Harry Van Meter, Paul Nicholson.
A sweet and simple American girl has her innocence tested by Parisian life.

The Printer's Devil (Warner Brothers, 1923)
d: William Beaudine. 6 reels.
Wesley Barry, Harry Myers, Kathryn McGuire, Louis King, George Pearce, Raymond Cannon.
The crusading publisher of a small local newspaper is arrested for a robbery he did not commit.

The Prison Without Walls (Lasky Feature Plays/Paramount, 1917)
d: E. Mason Hopper. 5 reels.
Wallace Reid, Myrtle Stedman, William Conklin, Billy Elmer, Camille Ankewich, James Neill, Lillian Leighton, Clarence H. Geldert.
Prison reformers run afoul of a graft-seeking prison administrator.

The Prisoner (Universal, 1923)
d: Jack Conway. 5 reels.
Herbert Rawlinson, Boris Karloff, Eileen Percy, George Cowl, June Elvidge, Lincoln Stedman, Gertrude Short, Bertram Grassby, Mario Carillo, Hayford Hobbs, Lillian Langdon, Bert Sprotte, Esther Ralston, J.P. Lockney.
Dorothy, an American girl in Europe, is engaged to marry a prince. Unknown to her, though, the "prince" is an imposter who is wanted for murder.

The Prisoner of Zenda (Metro, 1922)
d: Rex Ingram. 10 reels.
Ramon Novarro, Lewis Stone, Stuart Holmes, Barbara La Marr, Alice Terry, Robert Edeson, Malcolm McGregor, Edward Connelly, Lois Lee, John George, Snitz Edwards.
Rudolf of Ruritania is preparing to be crowned king, but his brother the duke is determined to thwart the coronation.

The duke's henchman Rupert drugs the king-designate's wine and Rudolf is spirited off to a remote hunting lodge. But there's a twist: Rudolf's cousin, an exact lookalike, is persuaded to impersonate him and go through with the coronation, until the real king can be returned.

Prisoners (First National/Warner Bros., 1929)
d: William A. Seiter. 8 reels. (Part talkie.)
Corinne Griffith, Ian Keith, Otto Matiesen, Juanne Johnston, Baron von Hesse, Bela Lugosi.
A lawyer falls in love with his client, a petty—and pretty—crook.

Prisoners of Love (Betty Compson Productions/Goldwyn, 1921)
d: Arthur Rosson. 6 reels.
Betty Compson, Ralph Lewis, Claire McDowell, Clara Horton, Emory Johnson, Kate Toncray, Roy Stewart.
Blanche, a small-town girl, goes to San Francisco and gets work in a law firm. Before long, she becomes the mistress of one of the partners. When her father and younger sister come to the city to visit her, Blanche's common-law husband falls rapturously in love with the sister.

Prisoners of the Pines (Jesse D. Hampton Productions, 1918)
d: Ernest C. Warde. 5 reels.
J. Warren Kerrigan, Lois Wilson, Walter Perry, Claire DuBrey.
In the Canadian northwest, lumbermen earn good wages, but each time they try to go home, they stop in a saloon and are seduced out of their money by a beautiful woman.

Prisoners of the Storm (Universal, 1926)
d: Lynn Reynolds. 6 reels.
House Peters, Peggy Montgomery, Walter McGrail, Harry Todd, Fred DeSilva, Clark Conmstock, Evelyn Selbie.
Murder mystery set in the frozen North pits a wounded mountie against a homicidal physician.

Private Affairs (Renaud Hoffman Productions, 1925)
d: Renaud Hoffman. 6 reels.
Gladys Hulette, Robert Agnew, Mildred Harris, David Butler, Arthur Hoyt, Betty Francisco, Willis Marks, Charles Sellon, Hardee Kirkland, J. Frank Glendon, Frank Coffyn.
Four small-town residents finally receive mail sent to them five years previously, and their lives are affected dramatically by the letters' contents.

Private Izzy Murphy (Warner Bros., 1926)
d: Lloyd Bacon. 8 reels.
Gorge Jessel, Patsy Ruth Miller, Vera Gordon, Gustav von Seyffertitz, Nat Carr, William Strauss, Spec O'Donnell.
In Jessel's debut film, he plays a Jewish boy in love with a Catholic girl.

The Private Life of Helen of Troy (First National, 1927)
d: Alexander Korda. 8 reels.
Maria Corda, Lewis Stone, Ricardo Cortez, George Fawcett, Gordon Elliott, Tom O'Brien, Bert Sprotte, Mario Carillo, Alice White, Charles Puffy, George Kotsonaros, Constantine Romanoff, Emilio Borgato, Alice Adair, Helen Fairweather, Virginia Thomas.
Paris steals Helen of Troy away from her husband and precipitates the Trojan War.

A Private Scandal (Realart Pictures, 1921)
d: Chester Franklin. 5 reels.
May McAvoy, Bruce Gordon, Ralph Lewis, Kathlyn

Williams, Lloyd Whitlock, Gladys Fox.
To save her adoptive mother from gossip, a French orphan declares that the mother's lover is really her own.

The Probation Wife (Norma Talmadge Film Corp./Select, 1919)
d: Sydney A. Franklin. 5 reels.
Norma Talmadge, Thomas Meighan, Florence Billings, Alec B. Francis, Walter McEwen, Amelia Summerville.
Josephine, a child of the slums, grows up frequenting sordid bars and cafes, earning her money by cheating customers. Finally, after escaping from reform school, she offers her body to a man of substance, hoping that in return he will get her a place to stay and some good clothes. But he's a true gentleman, and Josephine will get far more than that in the long run.

Prodigal Daughters (Famous Players-Lasky/Paramount, 1923)
d: Sam Wood. 6 reels.
Gloria Swanson, Ralph Graves, Vera Reynolds, Theodore Roberts, Louise Dresser, Charles Clary, Robert Agnew, Maude Wayne, Jiquel Lanoe, Eric Mayne, Antonio Corsi.
Two daughters of wealth leave home and take up the jazz life in Greenwich Village, but come to regret it.

The Prodigal Judge (Vitagraph, 1922)
d: Edward José. 8 reels.
Jean Paige, Maclyn Arbuckle, Ernest Torrence, Earle Foxe, Arthur Carew, Horace Braham, Charles Kent, Charles Eaton, Robert Milasch, George Bancroft, Peggy Shanor.
In the antebellum South, a respected judge becomes a drifter after his wife leaves him.

The Prodigal Liar (Jesse D. Hampton Features Corp./Robertson-Cole, 1919)
d: Thomas N. Heffron. 5 reels.
William Desmond, Betty Compson, Louis Morrison, Walter Perry, Frank Lanning.
It starts as a practical joke, when an innocent man poses as a wanted criminal to impress a girl. But things get serious when the real criminal comes after both of them, fire in his eyes.

The Prodigal Wife (Screencraft Pictures/Pioneer Film Corp., 1918)
d: Frank Reicher. 6 reels.
Mary Boland, Lucy Cotton, Raymond Bloomer, Alfred Keppler, Harris Gordon, Vincent Coleman, Mrs. Stuart Robson.
Bored with her husband, Marion leaves him for another man and severs ties with not only her husband, but their daughter as well. Years later, sadder but wiser, Marion returns incognito to take a position as nanny to her own grandchild.

The Profiteer (Arrow Film Corp., 1919)
d: John K. Holbrook. 6 reels.
Jack Sherrill, Alma Hanlon, Robin H. Townley, Charles Bowell, F.W. Stewart, Dorothy Kingdon, E.L. Howard, Louise Hotelling.
When one of his employees comes up with an invention for bringing sunken ships to the surface, his boss, a war profiteer, tries to claim the rights to it.

The Profiteers (Astra Film Corp./Pathé, 1919)
d: George Fitzmaurice. 5 reels.
Fannie Ward, John Miltern, Leslie Stuart, Edwin Stevens.
Food profiteers attempt to blackmail the wife of a crusading attorney.

Prohibition (Photo Drama Co./Prohibition Film Corp., 1915)
w, d: Hal Reid. 6 reels.
Thurlow Bergen, David Wall, Charles Trowbridge, Charles Dow Clark, Virginia Westbrook, Mary Moore, Roberta Paine, Lila Barclay, Mario Maroney, Edward Nannery.
Pro-temperance drama about two brothers who fight for the love of the same woman. One brother abstains from liquor, the other does not.

The Promise (Yorke Film Corp./Metro, 1917)
d: Fred J. Balshofer. 5 reels.
Harold Lockwood, May Allison, Lester Cuneo, Paul Willis, Lillian Hayward, W.H. Bainbridge, George Fisher, Leota Lorraine, John Steppling, T.H. Gibson Gowland.
In a lumber camp out West, an eastern playboy matures into a rugged outdoorsman.

The Prophet's Paradise (Selznick/Select, 1922)
d: Alan Crosland. 5 reels.
Eugene O'Brien, Sigrid Holmquist, Bigelow Cooper, Arthur Housman, Nora Booth, Joseph Burke, John Hopkins.
In old Constantinople, a visiting American buys a lovely young woman at a slave auction. She turns out to be an American girl who was kidnapped by renegade Turks.

Protection (Fox, 1929)
d: Benjamin Stoloff. 7 reels.
Robert Elliott, Paul Page, Dorothy Burgess, Ben Hewlett, Dorothy Ward, Joe Brown, Roy Stewart, William H. Tooker, Arthur Hoyt.
A crusading news reporter brings down a bootlegging operation and the duplicitous city officials who have been covering it up.

Proud Flesh (MGM, 1925)
d: King Vidor. 7 reels.
Eleanor Boardman, Harrison Ford, Pat O'Malley, Trixie Friganza, Margaret Seddon.
Orphaned by the San Francisco earthquake, a girl is adopted by relatives in Spain.

Prowlers of the Night (Universal, 1926)
d: Ernst Laemmle. 5 reels.
Fred Humes, Barbara Kent, Slim Cole, John T. Prince, Joseph Belmont, Walter Maly.
Out West, a sheriff falls in love with the daughter of the outlaw he is sworn to bring to justice.

Prowlers of the Sea (Tiffany-Stahl Productions, 1928)
d: John G. Adolfi. 6 reels.
Carmel Myers, Ricardo Cortez, George Fawcett, Gino Corrado, Frank Lackteen, Frank Leigh, Shirley Palmer.
In Cuba, an incorruptible officer is placed in charge of the Coast Guard. Gun smugglers try to bribe the new captain, but he remains true to his duty until the smugglers come up with a trump card: Mercedes, a seductive siren who will command el capitan's attention.

Proxies (Cosmopolitan/Paramount, 1921)
d: George D. Baker. 7 reels.
Norman Kerry, Zena Keefe, Raye Dean, Jack Crosby, Paul Everton, William H. Tooker, Robert Broderick.
The new butler and maid in a fashionable home are more than servants, they are former crooks.

Prudence on Broadway (Triangle, 1919)
d: Frank Borzage. 5 reels.

Olive Thomas, Francis McDonald, Harvey Clark, John P. Wild, Alberta Lee, Lillian West, Edward Peil, Mary Warren, Lillian Langdon, Claire McDowell.

Prudence, daughter of strict Quaker parents, goes to New York to learn first hand about the ways of the devil.

Prudence the Pirate (Thanhouser, 1916)
d: William Parke. 5 reels.
Gladys Hulette, Flora Finch, Riley Chamberlain, William Parke Jr., Barnett Parker.
Rebelling against pressure to marry a man she doesn't love, young Prudence rents a ship and plans on becoming a pirate.

Prunella (Famous Players-Lasky/Paramount, 1918)
d: Maurice Tourneur. 5 reels.
Marguerite Clark, Jules Raucourt, Harry Cecil, William J. Gross, A. Voorhees Wood, Charles Hartley, Arthur Kennedy.
Sheltered all her young life by three maiden aunts, Prunella finally makes a break for it, eloping with an itinerant actor.

The Prussian Cur (Fox, 1918)
d: R.A. Walsh. 8 reels.
Miriam Cooper, Sidney Mason, Horst von der Goltz, Leonora Stewart, James Marcus, Patrick O'Malley, Walter McEwen, William W. Black, Ralph Faulkner, Walter M. Lawrence.
During World War I, German spies in America cause unrest by organizing labor strikes, train derailings, and various other domestic crises.

The Public be Damned (Public Rights Film Corp., 1917)
w, d: S.E.V. Taylor. 5 reels.
Mary Fuller, Charles Richman, Chester Barnett, Joe Smiley, Russell Bassett.
Socially conscious drama about farmers who are unable to make a profit because of artificially depressed food prices. Herbert Hoover, U.S. Food Administrator (and later president), is seen in the film.

The Public Defender (Harry Raver, Inc./Apollo Pictures, Inc., 1917)
d: Burton King. 6 reels.
Frank Keenan, Alma Hanlon, Robert Edeson, John Sainpolis, Florence Short, Louis Sterns, C.H. Martin, William B. Green, Tex LaGrove, Harry Kingsley, Helen Conwell.
David, a young bank clerk, is accused of murdering a bank president who in fact died accidentally when he fell into an open elevator shaft.

Public Opinion (Lasky Feature Plays/Paramount, 1916)
d: Frank Reicher. 5 reels.
Blanche Sweet, Earle Foxe, Edythe Chapman, Tom Forman, Elliott Dexter, Raymond Hatton, Robert Henry Gray.
When a debilitated woman dies while under a nurse's care, public opinion turns against the innocent caregiver and she is accused of poisoning her patient.

Publicity Madness (Fox, 1927)
d: Albert Ray. 6 reels.
Lois Moran, Edmund Lowe, E.J. Ratcliffe, James Gordon, Arthur Housman, Byron Munson, Norman Peck.
Comedy about Pete, a publicity man who wagers $10,000 that a non-stop flight to Hawaii is impossible. Then word comes that Lindbergh has crossed the Atlantic, suddenly making the Hawaii flight seem possible. So it's up to Pete to enter the contest himself, fly an airplane to Hawaii, and try to win his own money.

Pudd'nhead Wilson (Lasky Feature Plays/Paramount, 1916)
d: Frank Reicher. 5 reels.
Theodore Roberts, Alan Hale, Thomas Meighan, Florence Dagmar, Jane Wolff, Ernest Joy, Gertrude Kellar.
In the antebellum South, a lawyer known as "Pudd'nhead Wilson" argues a case that turns on the reliability of fingerprints as evidence.

The Pulse of Life (Universal, 1917)
d: Rex Ingram. 5 reels.
Wedgewood Nowell, Gypsy Hart, William Dwyer, Dorothy Barrett, Molly Malone, Nicholas Dunaew, Millard K. Wilson, Albert MacQuarrie, Edward Brown, Seymour Hastings.
On the isle of Capri, love blossoms between a New Yorker and a fisherman's daughter.

The Puppet Crown (Lasky Feature Plays/Paramount, 1915)
d: George Melford. 5 reels.
Ina Claire, Carlyle Blackwell, Christian Lynton, Cleo Ridgely, Horace Carpenter, John Abraham, George Gebhardt, Tom Forman, Marjorie Daw.
Alexia, a European princess studying in the U.S. incognito, falls in love with an American millionaire.

Puppets (First National, 1926)
d: George Archainbaud. 8 reels.
Milton Sills, Gertrude Olmstead, Francis McDonald, Mathilde Comont, Lucien Prival, William Ricciardi, Nick Thompson.
In New York, a puppet master falls in love with a winsome runaway girl.

Puppy Love (Famous Players-Lasky/Paramount, 1919)
d: R. William Neill. 5 reels.
Lila Lee, Charles Murray, Harold Goodwin, Helen Dunbar, Lincoln Stedman, Josephine Crowell, Emma Gerdes, Alice Knowland.
When teenage Gloria falls in love with James, she is restrained from seeing him by her three old maid aunts. Undaunted, James becomes a newspaper writer and prints a scathing editorial on "the large spinster population" of their town.

Pure Grit (Universal, 1923)
d: Nat Ross. 5 reels.
Roy Stewart, Jack Mower, Esther Ralston, Jere Austin, Verne Winter.
Evans, a Texas Ranger, battles rustlers, kidnappers, and a raging cabin fire.

Puritan Passions (Film Guild/W.W. Hodkinson, 1923)
d: Frank Tuttle. 7 reels.
Glenn Hunter, Mary Astor, Osgood Perkins, Maude Hill, Frank Tweed, Dwight, Wiman, Thomas Chalmers.
Fantasy about a Salem, Massachusetts, community in which a wronged woman makes a pact with Satan himself.

Purity (American Film Co./Mutual, 1916)
d: Rea Berger. 7 reels.
Audrey Munson, Nigel de Brulier, Alfred Hollingsworth, William A. Carroll, Eugenie Forde, Clarence Burton, Nela Drinkwitz, Molly Shafer, Marie Van Tassell, Ellen Howard, Mary Dunham, Alice Anaroni, Hazel West, Nell Franzen, Wallace MacDonald, Ashton Dearholt.

An idealistic poet becomes enraptured with a young woman who seems to him to represent the ideal of purity. The girl appeals the same way to a painter, who persuades her to pose for his new canvas, "Virtue".

An interesting scenario in many ways, not least because the movie features Miss Munson in various non-erotic nude poses. It's said that the artistic merits of the film are so strong that the censors could not bring themselves to object to the nudity. Unfortunately, *Purity* is, at this writing, a "lost" film.

Purple Dawn (Charles R. Seeling/Aywon, 1923)
d: Charles R. Seeling. 5 reels.
Bert Sprotee, William E. Aldrich, James B. Leong, Edward Piel, Bessie Love, William Horne, Priscilla Bonner.
In San Francisco, Chinese Tong leaders entangle a young American sailor in their opium smuggling operations.

The Purple Highway (Kenma Corp./Paramount, 1923)
d: Henry Kolker. 7 reels.
Madge Kennedy, Monte Blue, Vincent Coleman, Pedro DeCordoba, Dore Davidson, Emily Fitzroy, William H. Tooker, Winifred Harris, John W. Jenkins, Charles Kent.
Say, kids... why don't we put on a show? Three unknowns do just that, and produce a musical that captivates Broadway.

The Purple Lady (Rolfe Photoplays/Metro, 1916)
d: George A. Lessey. 5 reels.
Ralph Herz, Irene Howley, Alan Hale, Howard Truesdell, George Pauncefote, Guido Colucci, Gretchen Hartman, Mrs. William Bechtel, Cora Williams.
Social reformers go to a shady nightclub to study its corrupting influence... just as the police arrive to raid the place, and reformers and corrupters alike are rounded up.

The Purple Lily (World Film Corp., 1918)
d: George Kelson. 5 reels.
Kitty Gordon, Frank Mayo, Muriel Ostriche, Charles Wellesley, Clay Clement, Henry West, Howard Kyle, John Dudley, Carl Axzell.
In Canada on business, an Englishman hires the beautiful wife of a gambler to steal some important papers for him.

Pursued (W.T. Lackey Productions/Ellbee Pictures, 1925)
d: Dell Henderson. 5 reels.
Gaston Glass, Dorothy Drew, George Siegmann, Arthur Rankin, Gertrude Astor, Stuart Holmes, Lafe McKee.
A kidnapped district attorney's girlfriend tracks down his abductors by posing as "Chicago Ann," a notorious female criminal.

The Pursuit of the Phantom (Bosworth, Inc./Paramount, 1914)
w, d: Hobart Bosworth. 5 reels.
Hobart Bosworth, Rhea Haines, Helen Wolcott, Courtney Foote, Myrtle Stedman, E.J. Flynn, Nigel DeBrullier.
Years after he stole an artist's sweetheart and married her himself, a millionaire learns that his son is courting the artist's daughter.

Put 'em Up (Universal, 1928)
d: Edgar Lewis. 5 reels.
Fred Humes, Gloria Grey, Pee Wee Holmes, Tom London, Harry Semels, Ben Corbett, Charles Colby, Bert Starkey.
Out West, a fearless cowboy fights off stagecoach robbers.

Put Up Your Hands (American Film Co./Pathé, 1919)
d: Edward Sloman. 5 reels.
Margarita Fisher, George Periolat, Emory Johnson, Hayward Mack, William Mong, Gordon Russell, Kate Price, Marion Lee.

Olive, a mischievous young woman, scandalizes society with her antics, such as staging a prizefight during one of her aunt's genteel parties.

Putting It Over (Famous Players-Lasky/Paramount, 1919)
d: Donald Crisp. 5 reels.
Bryant Washburn, Shirley Mason, Adele Farrington, Winifred Greenwood, Edna Mae Cooper, Casson Ferguson, C.H. Geldart, Edward Alexander, Robert Dunbar, Guy Oliver.
Buddy Marsh is only a soda jerk, but he's got ambitious plans. With the help of his new sweetheart Mary, Buddy convinces his boss to open a new lunchroom that makes them all rich.

Putting It Over (Phil Goldstone Productions, 1922)
d: Grover Jones. 5 reels.
Richard Talmadge, Doris Pawn, Thomas Ricketts, Harry Ven Meter, Henry Barrows, Victor Metzetti, William Horne, Earl Schaeffer, Andrew Waldron.
Political comedy about a young fellow who decides to run for mayor, then falls for his opponent's daughter and switches to the other side.

Putting One Over (Fox, 1919)
d: Edward Dillon. 5 reels.
George Walsh, Edith Stockton, Ralph J. Locke, Frank Beamish, Robert L. Keeling, Matthew L. Betts, Jack Dillon, Mrs.
Elizabeth Garrison, Marcia Harris, Henry Hallam.
When Horace, the heir to a fortune, is killed in a train accident, his unscrupulous advisors force a lookalike to impersonate the heir for their financial advantage. The deception goes smoothly until the *faux* heir falls in love with Horace's cousin.
George Walsh does double duty here, portraying both Horace and the impostor.

The Quality of Faith (Gaumont Co./Mutual, 1916)
d: Richard Garrick. 5 reels.
Alexander Gaden, Gertrude Robinson, Lucille Taft, Charles W. Travis, John Reinhard, Henry W. Pemberton, Alan Robinson, John Mackin.
When a minister tries to reform a prostitute, he finds himself falling in love with her.

Quality Street (Cosmopolitan/MGM, 1927)
d: Sidney Franklin. 8 reels.
Marion Davies, Conrad Nagel, Helen Jerome Eddy, Flora Finch, Margaret Seddon, Kate Price, Marcelle Corday.
A woman scorned transforms her appearance to win back her man.

Quarantined Rivals (Gotham Productions/Lumas Film Corp., 1927)
d: Archie Mayo. 7 reels.
Robert Agnew, Kathleen Collins, John Miljan, Ray Hallor, Viora Daniels, Big Boy Williams, Clarissa Selwynne, George Pierce, William A. O'Connor, Josephine Borio.
Comedy of errors leads to Bob and Bruce, rivals for the hand of Elsie, having to spend two weeks together in a quarantined house.

The Quarterback (Paramount, 1926)
d: Fred Newmeyer. 8 reels.
Richard Dix, Esther Ralston, Harry Beresford, David Butler, Robert Craig, Mona Palma.
Preposterous comedy about a college quarterback who led his team to defeat in 1899, and vows to remain a student

until his school beats its arch-rival. It's 1926, and he's still waiting.

Queen Kelly (United Artists, 1928)
d: Erich von Stroheim. 8 reels.
Gloria Swanson, Walter Byron, Seena Owen, Tully Marshall, Sidney Bracey, William von Brincken.
An American girl is courted by a European prince.
Legendary star turn by Miss Swanson, who as producer was forced to fire the lavishly extravagant von Stroheim when, after four hours worth of film were in the can, only one-third of the picture had been shot. The film was edited down and fitted with an ending of sorts, but was never released in the United States. *Queen Kelly* exists today in a 96-minute video version that is sometimes shown on cable television.

Queen o' Diamonds (R-C Pictures/FBO of America, 1926)
d: Chet Withey. 6 reels.
Evelyn Brent, Elsa Lorimer, Phillips Smalley, William N. Bailey, Theodore von Eltz.
A chorus girl is mistakenly accused of theft and, later, murder.

The Queen of Hearts (Fox, 1918)
d: Edmund Lawrence. 5 reels.
Virginia Pearson, Joseph Smiley, Victor Sutherland, Edward J. Burns, Peggy Shanor, John Webb Dillon, James A. Furey, Adelaide Lawrence.
When a casino owner is found murdered, his daughter Pauline vows to bring the culprit to justice. There are three suspects, all of them in love with Pauline.

The Queen of Sheba (Fox, 1921)
d: J. Gordon Edwards. 9 reels.
Betty Blythe, Fritz Leiber, Claire DeLorez, George Siegmann, Herbert Heyes, Herschel Mayall, G. Raymond Nye, George Nichols, Genevieve Blinn, Pat Moore, Joan Gordon, William Hardy, Paul Cazeneuve, John Cosgrove, Nell Craig, Al Fremont, Earl Crain.
Epic drama covering the romance of King Solomon and the Queen of Sheba.

Queen of the Chorus (Morris R. Schlank Productions/Anchor Film Distributors, 1928)
d: Charles J. Hunt. 6 reels.
Virginia Browne Faire, Rex Lease, Lloyd Whitlock, Betty Francisco, Harriet Hammond, Charles Hill Mailes, Crauford Kent.
Queenie, a chorus cutie, falls for a young fan who's impersonating a millionaire.

Queen of the Moulin Rouge (Pyramid Pictures/American Releasing Corp., 1922)
d: Ray C. Smallwood. 7 reels.
Martha Mansfield, Joseph Striker, Henry Harmon, Fred T. Jones, Jane Thomas, Tom Blake, Mario Carillo.
To teach his violin student the value of suffering, a music teacher conspires to get the student's beloved a job as a dancer at the notorious Moulin Rouge. The girl carries out her part of the bargain, and perhaps more; she becomes so popular that she is voted the Queen of the Moulin Rouge.

Queen of the Sea (Fox, 1918)
d: John G. Adolfi. 6 reels.
Annette Kellerman, Hugh Thompson, Mildred Keats, Walter Law, Beth Irvins, Philip Van Loan, Fred Parker, Louis Dean, Carrie Lee, Minnie Methol.
Fantasy about Merilla, queen of the sea, who must save four human lives in order to be transformed into a human

herself.

Queen X (Mutual, 1917)
d: John B. O'Brien. 5 reels.
Edna Goodrich, Hugh Thompson, Lucille Taft, Dora Adams, William Wolcott, Jack Hopkins.
In an unsavory New York neighborhood filled with opium dens and sleazy bars, U.S. agents capture one of the leading drug dealers, a woman known as Queen X.

Queenie (Fox, 1921)
d: Howard M. Mitchell. 6 reels.
Shirley Mason, George O'Hara, Wilson Hummell, Aggie Herring, Lydia Titus, Adophe Menjou, Clarissa Selwynne.
Comedy about an old recluse and the odd folks he has working as servants: his housekeeper Pansy, his valet Abner, and Pansy's niece Queenie. The latter is engaged to a noodle king with poetic aspirations.
Wilson Hummell plays a double role, as both the recluse and his valet.

The Quest (American Film Mfg. Co./Mutual, 1915)
d: Harry Pollard. 5 reels.
Harry Pollard, Margarita Fischer, Lucille Ward, Joseph E. Singleton, Nan Christy, Robyn Adair, William Carroll.
Bored with society life, a wealthy bachelor travels to the South Seas in search of his "dream girl."

The Quest of Life (Famous Players/Paramount, 1916)
d: Ashley Miller. 5 reels.
Florence Walton, Maurice (no last name), Julian L'Estrange, Royal Byron, Daniel Burke, Russell Bassett, Mrs. William Bechtel, Kathleen Townsend.
When a famous dancer falls seriously ill and is ordered by her doctor to move to a dry and sunny climate, she decides she would rather live a short, glamorous life on the stage than a long, boring life in the desert.

The Question (Equitable Motion Pictures Corp./World Film Corp., 1916)
d: Harry Handworth. 5 reels.
Marguerite Leslie, George Anderson, Marie Benton, Lorell Gibson, Louise Evans, Clara Whipple, Bernard Randall.
Ralph wants children, but his wife Grace does not. Crushed, Ralph turns to his secretary for solace, and they have an affair. When the secretary dies in childbirth, her baby is put up for adoption—just in time for Grace, who has had a change of heart, to adopt the child.

The Question (Vitagraph, 1917)
d: Perry N. Vekroff. 5 reels.
Harry Morey, Alice Joyce, Charles Kent, Gladden James, Amy Remley, Edward Davis.
The question is: Which is more important—to gain one's heart's desire, or to forgo marriage and remain in the laboratory, working on a formula which may revolutionize medicine?

A Question of Honor (Anita Stewart Productions/Associated First National, 1922)
d: Edwin Carewe. 7 reels.
Anita Stewart, Edward Hearn, Arthur Stuart Hull, Walt Whitman, Bert Sprotte, Frank Beal, Adele Farrington, Mary Land, Ed Brady, Doc Bytell.
Shannon, a construction engineer, falls for the fiancée of his chief rival.

Quick Triggers (Universal, 1928)
d: Ray Taylor. 5 reels.

QUEEN KELLY (1928). Hell having no fury like a woman scorned, the queen of Ruritania (Seena Owen) whips convent girl Patricia Kelly, who the queen suspects of stealing the heart of her fiancé, Prince Wolfram. She's right. In director Erich von Stroheim's lavish 11-reel version (later cut to 8 reels by producer Swanson), Patricia undergoes several adventures and finally does marry the prince and ascends the throne.

* * * * *

Fred Humes, Derelys Perdue, Wilbur Mack, Robert Chandler, Gilbert "Pee Wee" Holmes, Scotty Mattraw, Dick L.Estrange, Ben Corbett.
Out West, a ranch foreman falls in love with the daughter of a cattle rustler.

The Quickening Flame (World Film Corp., 1919)
d: Travers Vale. 5 reels.
Montagu Love, June Elvidge, Mabel Ballin, Albert Hart, Jack Drumier, Frank Quong, Rodney McKeever, Bert Leigh.
Dazzled by her beauty, an attorney impulsively marries a burlesque queen... but he'll live to regret it.

Quicksand (Thomas H. Ince Corp./Paramount, 1918)
d: Victor L. Schertzinger. 5 reels.
Dorothy Dalton, Ed Coxen, Philo McCullough, Henry A. Barrows, Frankie Lee.
When her husband Jim is framed for forgery and sent to prison, Mary goes to work in the cabaret where the bogus check was cashed, hoping to find the real culprit.

Quicksands (Agfar Corp./American Releasing Corp., 1923)
d: Jack Conway. 6 reels.
Helene Chadwick, Richard Dix, Alan Hale, Noah Beery, J. Farrell MacDonald, George Cooper, Tom Wilson, Dick Sutherland, Hardee Kirkland, Louis King, Jean Hersholt.
At the Mexican border, an American lieutenant battles narcotic smugglers who have kidnapped his sweetheart.

Quincy Adams Sawyer (Sawyer-Lubin Productions/Metro, 1922)
d: Clarence Badger. 8 reels.
John Bowers, Blanche Sweet, Lon Chaney, Barbara LaMarr, Elmo Lincoln, Louise Fazenda, Joseph Dowling, Claire McDowell, Edward Connelly, June Elvidge, Victor Potel.
A Boston lawyer travels to small-town America to aid a widow in settling her late husband's estate.

The Quitter (Rolfe Photoplays, Inc./Metro, 1916)
d: Charles Horan. 5 reels.
Lionel Barrymore, Marguerite Skirvin, Paul Everton, Charles Prince, Julius D. Cowles, Edward Brennan.
Out West, a miner signs over his claim to his "mail order bride" in lieu of fulfilling his promise to marry her. But when she arrives in town, the miner gets his first look at the woman, and falls head over heels in love.

The Quitter (Columbia, 1929)
d: Joseph Henabery. 6 reels.
Ben Lyon, Fred Kohler, Dorothy Revier, Charles McHugh, Sherry Hall, Jane Daly, Henry Otto, Claire McDowell.
A discouraged surgeon decides to give up, then gets the opportunity to save the life of a stranger.

R.S.V.P. (Charles Ray Productions/Associated First National, 1921)
d: Charles Ray. 6 reels.
Charles Ray, Florence Oberle, Harry Myers, Tom McGuire, Jean Calhoun, Robert Grey, William Courtright, Ida Schumaker.
Richard, a struggling artist, paints the portrait of Betty, a girl who has long loved him from afar.

The Race (Lasky Feature Plays/Paramount, 1916)
d: George H. Melford. 5 reels.
Victor Moore, Anita King, Robert Bradbury, William Dale, Mrs. Louis McCord, Ernest Joy, Horace B. Carpenter.
When he's disinherited for his spendthrift ways, Jimmy rolls up his sleeves, goes to work, and invents a revolutionary car engine that will make him wealthy in his own right.

A Race for Life (Warner Bros., 1928)
d: D. Ross Lederman. 5 reels.
Rin-Tin-Tin, Bobby Gordon, Virginia Brown Faire, Carol Nye, Pat Hartigan.
A boy and his faithful dog head for a race track, where the lad seeks employment as a jockey.

Race Suicide (Lubin, 1916)
d: George W. Terwilliger. 6 reels.
Ormi Hawley, Earl Metcalfe, Kempton Greene, Octavia Handworth, Herbert Fortier, Hazel Hubbard.
Cautionary tale that studies "race suicide" through the ages—child murder in prehistoric times, child neglect during the Roman Empire, and, in contemporary times, the refusal to have children.

Racing Blood (Gotham Productions/Lumas Film Corp., 1926)
d: Frank Richardson. 6 reels.
Robert Agnew, John Elliott, Clarence Geldert, Charles A. Sellon, Robert Hale.
In California, a young news reporter buys a horse at auction and decides to enter it in a steeplechase. He is rejected as the rider, however, because he is over the weight limit; whereupon Muriel, his girlfriend, dons the jockey's silks and rides the horse herself... to victory.

Racing For Life (Columbia, 1924)
d: Henry MacRae. 5 reels.
Eva Novak, William Fairbanks, Philo McCullough, Wilfred Lucas, Ralph DePalma, Lydia Knott, Frankie Darro, Edwin Booth Tilton, Frank Whitson, Harley Moore, Harry LaVerne.
Jack, a novice driver, enters an automobile race to win the money for his girlfriend's debt-ridden father.

Racing Hearts (Famous Players-Lasky/Paramount, 1923)
d: Paul Powell. 6 reels.
Agnes Ayres, Richard Dix, Theodore, Roberts, Robert Cain, Warren Rogers, J. Farrell MacDonald, Edwin J. Brady, Fred J. Butler, Robert Brower, Kalla Pasha, James A. Murphy.
Virginia, daughter of an automobile manufacturer, enters Dad's car in the big race and drives it to victory herself.

Racing Luck (Grand-Asher Distributing Corp./Associated Exhibitors, 1924)
d: Herman C. Raymaker. 6 reels.
Monty Banks, Helen Ferguson, Martha Franklin, D.J. Mitsoras, Lionel Belmore, Francis McDonald, William Blaisdell, Al Martin, Al Thompson.
Mario, an Italian immigrant, is mistaken for a well-known race driver. Seeing his chance, Mario signs with an auto manufacturer to drive his car in the big race... and wins it.

Racing Romance (Harry J. Brown Productions/Rayart, 1926)
d: Harry J. Brown. 5 reels.
Reed Howes, Virginia Brown Faire, Harry S. Northrup, Mathilda Brundage, Victor Potel, Ethan Laidlaw.
Although the villains try to force him out of the race, a young Kentuckian rides his girlfriend's horse in the big race, wins it, and with the prize money the girl's family can retire their mortgage.

A Racing Romeo (R-C Pictures/FBO of America, 1927)
d: Sam Wood. 7 reels.
Harold "Red" Grange, Jobyna Ralston, Trixie Friganza, Walter Hiers, Ben Hendricks Jr., Warren Rogers, Ashton

Dearholt, Jerry Zier.

Zany comedy about a chap who enters a motor sweepstakes to ingratiate himself with his fiancée, who's furious because she caught him flirting with a movie star.

The Racing Strain (Goldwyn, 1918)
d: Emmett J. Flynn. 5 reels.
Mae Marsh, Clarence Oliver, Clifford Bruce, W.T. Carleton, Edwin Sturgis, Tammany Young.
When the family estate is threatened with foreclosure, a Kentucky colonel's daughter saves the day by entering her filly in a high stakes horse race, which it wins.

The Rack (William A. Brady/World Film Corp., 1916)
d: Emile Chautard. 5 reels.
Milton Sills, Alice Brady, Chester Barnett, George Cowl, June Elvidge, Doris Kenyon.
When a womanizing playboy is murdered, the evidence seems to implicate Tom, whose wife is the best friend of the playboy's widow. When the police move against Tom, his wife confesses in order to save her husband. But neither of them did it.

The Racket (Paramount, 1928)
d: Lewis Milestone. 8 reels.
Thomas Meighan, Marie Prevost, Louis Wolheim, George Stone, John Darrow, Skeets Gallagher, Lee Moran, Lucien Prival, Tony Marlo, Henry Sedley, Sam DeGrasse, Burr McIntosh.
Scarsi, the leader of a gang of liquor bootleggers, is freed through the efforts of a corrupt politician. But soon Scarsi murders a policeman, is arrested, then shot dead trying to escape.

Radio Mania (Teleview Corp./W.W. Hodkinson, 1923)
d: R. William Neill. 6 reels.
Grant Mitchell, Margaret Irving, Gertrude Hillman, W.H. Burton, Isabelle Vernon, J.D. Walsh, Peggy Smith, Betty Borders, Alice Effinger, Peggy Williams.
Wyman, an inventor, tries to develop a radio with which he can communicate with Mars.

Raffles, the Amateur Cracksman (Lawrence Weber Photo Dramas, Inc., 1917)
d: George Irving. 7 reels.
John Barrymore, Frank Morgan, Betty Riggs, Christine Mayo, Nita Allen, Mathilda Brundage, Frederick Perry, H. Cooper Cliffe, Mike Donlin.
A modern-day Robin Hood robs from the rich to give to the poor.

Raffles, the Amateur Cracksman (Universal, 1925)
d: King Baggot. 6 reels.
House Peters, Miss DuPont, Hedda Hopper, Frederick Esmelton, Walter Long, Winter Hall, Kate Lester, Freeman Wood.
A gentleman thief robs from the rich to help the poor.

The Rag Man (MGM, 1924)
d: Edward Cline. 6 reels.
Jackie Coogan, Max Davidson, Lydia Yeamans Titus, Robert Edeson, William Conklin.
An orphanage runaway finds a home with a junk man. Successful vehicle for young Coogan, this film spawned a sequel, *Old Clothes*, in 1925.

The Ragamuffin (Lasky Feature Plays/Paramount, 1916)
w, d: William C. DeMille. 5 reels.
Blanche Sweet, Tom Forman, Minnette Barrett, Mrs. Lewis McCord, Park Jones, James Neill, William Elmer, Agnes de Mille.
Jenny, in tattered clothes, breaks into a wealthy man's house to rob him. He catches her, but instead of turning her over to the police he exacts her promise not to take anything, and lets her go. Jenny is touched by this act of kindness and decides to walk the straight and narrow. She even comes to the man's aid later on, when he finds himself in a jam.

The Rage of Paris (Universal, 1921)
d: Jack Conway. 5 reels.
Miss DuPont, Elinor Hancock, Jack Perrin, Leo White, Ramsey Wallace, Freeman Wood, Eve Southern, Mathilde Brundage, J.J. Lanoe.
Joan runs away from a loveless marriage and goes to France, where she becomes a dancer known as The Rage of Paris.

The Ragged Edge (Distinctive Pictures/Goldwyn-Cosmopolitan Distributing Corp., 1923)
d: Harmon Weight. 7 reels.
Alfred Lunt, Mimi Palmeri, Charles Fang, Wallace Erskine, George MacQuarrie, Charles Slattery, Christian Frank, Grace Griswold, Alice May, Percy Carr, Marie Day, Charles Kent.
Though innocent, a fugitive from the law travels to China to evade capture.

The Ragged Earl (Popular Plays and Players, Inc./Alco Film Corp., 1914)
d: Lloyd B. Carleton. 5 reels.
Andrew Mack, William Conklin, Ormi Hawley, Eleanor Dunn, Edward J. Peil.
When a debt-ridden earl meets a young man on the run, he takes the lad into his castle—and discovers that "he" is really a beautiful young woman!

The Ragged Girl of Oz—see: The Patchwork Girl of Oz (1914)

The Ragged Heiress (Fox, 1922)
d: Harry Beaumont. 5 reels.
Shirley Mason, John Harron, Edwin Stevens, Cecil Van Auker, Claire McDowell, Aggie Herring, Eileen O'Malley.
Melodrama with a double twist on the old mistaken identity scenario. As a child, Lucia runs away from her tyrannical uncle's home, in the custody of her nurse. Years later, after the nurse has died, Lucia obtains work as a domestic in the home of her uncle, neither of them realizing who the other is. Finally Lucia's father returns home from his long prison term and asks to see his daughter. His brother, ashamed to admit the girl ran away from his home, persuades Lucia to pose as the long-lost daughter... never suspecting she is exactly who she pretends to be!

The Ragged Princess (Fox, 1916)
d: John G. Adolfi. 5 reels.
June Caprice, Harry Hilliard, Richard Neill, Tom Burrough, Florence Ashbrook, Sid Bracy, Caroline Harris, Little Jane Lee, Little Katherine Lee.
An orphan girl is adopted by a wealthy mine owner, but he's not to be trusted. His half-brother intervenes when he learns that the mine owner is trying to seduce his new daughter.

The Raggedy Queen (Universal, 1917)
d: Theodore Marston. 5 reels.
Grace Barton, Frank Otto, Violet Mersereau, Donald Hall, Robert F. Hill, Charles Slattery, James O'Neill.
"Tatters" is a girl who lives in and around a mining camp, and she's convinced she has royal blood. When the mines are threatened by labor strife and the owner's representative

David comes to mediate a settlement, he is roughed up by agitators and left for dead. "Tatters" finds David and nurses him back to health, winning the gratitude and admiration of both him and the mine owner, who recognizes her as his long-lost daughter.

Raggedy Rose (Hal Roach Studios/Pathé, 1926)
d: Richard Wallace. 5 reels.
Mabel Normand, James Finlayson, Carl Miller, Anita Garvin, Laura LaVarnie.
Miss Normand plays Raggedy Rose, poor but plucky assistant to a junk dealer. While sorting out various salvage items in the junkyard, Rose dreams of a handsome prince who will carry her away from her sordid life... and, against all odds, she does find her dream man.

Raggedy Rose is a clever and funny variant on the Cinderella story. The cruel stepmother and stepsisters of the fairy tale are replaced by Anita Garvin and her scheming harridan of a mother, played by Laura LaVarnie, both of whom pull every trick they can think of to keep Rose from uniting with her "prince." But unite with him she does, exhilaratingly.

Rags (Famous Players/Paramount, 1915)
d: James Kirkwood. 5 reels.
Mary Pickford, Marshall Neilan, Joseph Manning, Joseph Farrell MacDonald.
Rags, the daughter of a boisterous drunk, is all sweetness and light despite her father's vulgar ways. When a young engineer comes to town and Rags' father makes plans to rob him, she calls the police who stop the theft, but in the process mortally wounding the would-be thief. Before he dies, Rags' father performs one decent act: He asks the engineer to look after his daughter. In time, love blossoms between the engineer and the little ragamuffin.

Rags to Riches (Warner Brothers, 1921)
d: Wallace Worsley. 7 reels.
Niles Welch, Wesley Barry, Russell Simpson, Minna Redman, Ruth Renick, Richard Tucker, Eulalie Jensen, Jane Keckley, Sam Kaufman, Dick Sutherland, Jimmy Quinn, Snitz Edwards, Aileen Manning.
Marmaduke, a scion of wealth who yearns for adventure, leaves home and joins up with a gang of thieves.

Ragtime (James Ormont Productions/First Division Distributors, 1927)
d: Scott Pembroke. 7 reels.
John Bowers, Marguerite De La Motte, Robert Ellis, Rose Dione, William H. Strauss, Kate Bruce, Bernard Siegel.
In New York's Tin Pan Alley, love blossoms between a songwriter and a socialite.

The Raiders (New York Motion Picture Co./Triangle, 1916)
d: Charles Swickard. 5 reels.
H.B. Warner, Dorothy Dalton, Henry Belmar, Robert McKim, George Elwell, J. Barney Sherry.
Drama about a Wall Street clerk's frantic attempt to halt the hostile takeover of the railroad company run by his sweetheart's father.

The Raiders (William N. Selig Productions, 1921)
d: Nate Watt. 5 reels.
Franklyn Farnum, Bud Osborne, Vester Pegg, Claire Windsor, Frederick Soult.
In the Canadian Northwest, two mounties and their Indian guide track a gang of rumrunners.

The Rail Rider (Paragon Films, Inc./World Film Corp., 1916)
d: Maurice Tourneur. 5 reels.
House Peters, Bertram Marburgh, Harry West, Zena Keefe.
When the best engineer on the railroad is fired, he demands to know why. To find out, he has to make a trip back east to confront the boss—but when he does, the engineer discovers that the company is being run by a shadow management that is up to no good.

Railroaded (Universal, 1923)
d: Edmund Mortimer. 5 reels.
Herbert Rawlinson, Esther Ralston, Alfred Fisher, David Torrence, Lionel Belmore, Mike Donlin, Herbert Fortier.
In England, a judge's son is framed for murder.

The Railroader (Triangle, 1919)
d: Colin Campbell. 5 reels.
George Fawcett, Virginia Eames, Frank Elliott, Velma Whitman, Thomas Santschi, Fritzi Brunette, Goldie Colwell.
Conover, a railroad section manager, drives his way to the top and, through tenacity and harassment, becomes a feared political boss.

Rainbow (Vitagraph, 1921)
d: Edward José. 5 reels.
Alice Calhoun, Jack Roach, William Gross, Charles Kent, Tom O'Malley, George Lessey, Cecil Kern, Tammany Young, Ivan Christie.
Rainbow, an orphan girl, is willed a copper mine by her father. One day, however, a young man from Chicago arrives to take ownership of the mine, claiming it is rightfully his.

The Rainbow (Tiffany-Stahl Productions, 1929)
d: Reginald Barker. 7 reels. (Sound effects.)
Dorothy Sebastian, Lawrence Gray, Sam Hardy, Harvey clarke, Paul Hurst, Gino Corrado, King Zany.
Out West, a gang of crooks start a human stampede by declaring that gold has been found in a ghost town.

The Rainbow Girl (American Film Co./Mutual, 1917)
d: Rollin S. Sturgeon. 5 reels.
Juliette Day, George Fisher, Charles Bennett, Lillian Hayward, Louis Morrison, Emma Kluge, Marie Robertson.
Sweet-natured Mary Beth rents a room to Richard, a penniless composer who is trying to sell his songs but is having no luck... until Mary Beth inspires him to write his greatest composition yet.

The Rainbow Princess (Famous Players/Paramount, 1916)
d: J. Searle Dawley. 5 reels.
Ann Pennington, William Courtleigh Jr., Augusta Anderson, Grant Stewart, Charles Sutton, Harry Lee, Edwin Sturgis, Clifford Gray, Herbert Rice, Queen Pearl, Amy Manning.
Hope, the star dancer for a circus company, is billed as "The Rainbow Princess."

Rainbow Rangers (William Steiner Productions, 1924)
w, d: Forrest Sheldon. 5 reels.
Pete Morrison, Peggy Montgomery, Lew Meehan, Eddie Dennis, Nelson McDowell, Milburn Morante, Martin Turner, Lafe McKee, Victor Allen, Raye Hampton.
Out West, a girl and her father are attacked by brigands but rescued by an itinerant band of law-enforcement rangers.

Rainbow Riley (Burr and Hines Enterprises/First National, 1926)
d: Charles Hines. 7 reels.
Johnny Hines, Brenda Bond, Bradley Barker, Dan Mason,

John Hamilton, Harlan Knight, Gerbert Standing, Ben Wilson, Lillian Ardell.

In the Kentucky hills, feuding clans stop long enough to gang up on a hapless reporter who's been sent to cover their colorful quarrels.

The Rainbow Trail (Fox, 1918)

d: Frank Lloyd. 6 reels.

William Farnum, Ann Forrest, Mary Mersch, William Burress, William Nye, Genevieve Blinn, George Ross, Buck Jones.

Out West, a cowboy named Shefford rides to the rescue of a young woman who's been abducted by a Mormon elder seeking to make her one of his wives.

Film version of the Zane Grey novel, a sequel to his *Riders of the Purple Sage*. This film would be remade once in the silent era, by Fox in 1925.

The Rainbow Trail (Fox, 1925)

d: Lynn Reynolds. 6 reels.

Tom Mix, Anne Cornwall, Diana Miller, Thomas Delmar, Vivien Oakland, George Bancroft, Lucien Littlefield, Fred De Silva, Mark Hamilton, Steve Clements.

Remake of Fox' 1918 *The Rainbow Trail*, both films based on the Zane Grey novel of the same name.

The Rainmaker (Paramount, 1926)

d: Clarence Badger. 7 reels.

William Collier Jr., Georgia Hale, Ernest Torrence, Brandon Hurst, Joseph Dowling, Tom Wilson, Martha Mattox, Charles K. French, Jack Richardson, Melbourne MacDowell.

Robertson has a reputation as a rainmaker—but it's only because a war wound lets him know what kind of weather to expect.

The Ramblin' Kid (Universal, 1923)

d: Edward Sedgwick. 6 reels.

Hoot Gibson, Laura LaPlante, Harold Goodwin, William Welsh, W.T. McCulley, Charles K. French, G. Raymond Nye, Carol Holloway, Goober Glenn, George King.

Out West, a cowpuncher wins a rodeo competition in spite of the treachery of his rival for Carolyn, a lovely eastern girl.

The Rambling Ranger (Universal, 1927)

d: Del Henderson. 5 reels.

Jack Hoxie, Dorothy Gulliver, C.E. Anderson, Monte Montague Jr., Charles Avery.

Kinney, a Texas Ranger, finds an abandoned infant and seeks to adopt the child himself.

Ramona (Clune Film Producing Co., 1916)

d: Donald Crisp. 10 reels.

Adda Gleason, Mabel Van Buren, Anna Lehr, Monroe Salisbury, Nigel de Brulier, Richard Sterling, Princess Red Wing, Lurline Lyons, Alice Morton Otten, James Needham.

In 19th century California, racial bias threatens the union of a full-blooded Indian and his bride Ramona, who is half European and half Indian.

First feature film version of the novel by Helen Hunt Jackson. It would be remade once in the silent era, by Inspiration Pictures in 1928.

Ramona (United Artists, 1928)

d: Edwin Carewe. 8 reels.

Dolores Del Rio, Warner Baxter, Vera Lewis, Roland Drew, John J. Prince, Michael Visaroff, Mathilde Comont, Carlos Amor, Jess Cavin, Rita Carewe.

A beautiful half-caste elopes with an Indian against her guardian's wishes.

Remake of Clune Film's *Ramona* (1916), both versions based on the novel by Helen Hunt Jackson.

Ramshackle House (Tilford Cinema Corp./Producers Distributing Corp., 1924)

d. Harmon Weight. 6 reels.

Betty Compson, Robert Lowing, John Davidson, Henry James, William Black, Duke Pelzer, Josephine Norman.

In Southern Florida, a girl helps a fugitive from injustice hide from his pursuers.

The Range Boss (Essanay, 1917)

d: W.S. Van Dyke. 5 reels.

Jack Gardner, Ruth King, Carl Stockdale.

"The Range Boss" is a lovely young woman who inherits a ranch, then goes West to claim her inheritance.

Range Courage (Universal, 1927)

d: Ernst Laemmle. 5 reels.

Fred Humes, Gloria Grey, Dick Winslow, William A. Steele, Robert Homans, Arthur Millett, Monte Montague, Charles L. King, Morgan Brown.

Out West, a young man considered a wimp proves that he's anything but.

The Range Riders (Ben Wilson Productions/Rayart, 1927)

d: Ben Wilson. 5 reels.

Ben Wilson, Neva Gerber, Al Ferguson, Ed LaNiece, Earl C. Turner.

Out West, a ranger tracks a gang of thieves, even though he's fallen in love with the sister of one of the crooks.

The Range Terror (Independent Pictures/FBO of America, 1925)

d: William James Craft. 5 reels.

Bob Custer, Thais Valdemar, Claire DeLorez, Boris Bullock, H.J. Herbert, Bobby Mack, Tom Sharkey, Milburn Morante.

Speed, a Texas Ranger, enlists the aid of a dance hall girl to track down a killer.

The Ranger (W.H. Clifford Photoplay Co., 1918)

d: Bob Gray. 5 reels.

Shorty Hamilton, Charles Arling, William Colvin, Mattie Connolly, Kenneth Nordyke.

During World War I, a Texas Ranger learns that pro-German activities are being conducted along the Mexican border, and he rides to stop them.

The Ranger and the Law (Capital Film Co., 1921)

d: Robert Kelly. 5 reels.

Lester Cuneo, Walter I. McCloud, Francelia Billington, Clark Comstock, Roy Watson, Phil Gastrock, Maxwell Morgan, Fernando Galvez, David Kirby, Lester Howley.

Out West, a tough Texas Ranger tracks down a gang of whisky runners, brings them to justice, and saves the daughter of one of them, proposing marriage to her as he does so.

Ranger of the Big Pines (Vitagraph, 1925)

d: William S. Van Dyke. 7 reels.

Kenneth Harlan, Helene Costello, Eulalie Jensen, Will Walling, Lew Harvey, Robert Graves.

Cavanagh, a forest ranger, must enforce a new tax on grazing land, but finds cattle baron Sam Gregg a formidable foe of the tax.

Ranger of the North (FBO Pictures, 1927)

d: Jerome Storm. 5 reels.

Ranger, the dog, Hugh Trevor, Lina Basquette, Bernard Siegel, Jules Rancourt, William Van Vleck.

In the northern woods, a city boy and his dog fight malevolent trappers and loggers.

The Ransom   (Triumph Film Corp./World Film Corp., 1916)
d: Edmund Lawrence.   5 reels.
Julia Dean, Louise Huff, James Hall, Ethel Lloyd, Willard Case, Kenneth Hunter, William Mackey, Lorna Volare, Evelyn Dumo, Adelaide Lawrence.
Formula weeper about a woman who abandons her husband and daughter to take up with a lover. Years later, alone in the world, she learns that her daughter has become a famous actress, and takes a job as her maid without ever telling the actress she is her mother.

Ransom   (Columbia, 1928)
w, d: George B. Seitz.   6 reels.
Edmund Burns, William V. Mong, Lois Wilson, Blue Washinton, James B. Leong, Jackie Coombs.
Wu Fang, a Chinese underworld leader, plots to steal a new poison gas formula developed by the U.S. government. To help him obtain the formula, Wu Fang kidnaps the young son of Lois, fiancée to the inventor who developed it.

Ranson's Folly   (Inspiration Pictures, Inc./First National, 1926)
d: Sidney Olcott.   8 reels.
Richard Barthelmess, Dorothy Mackaill, Anders Randolf, Pat Hartigan, William Norton Bailey, Brooks Benedict, Pauline Neff.
A soldier is suspected in a stagecoach theft and murder.
Remake of the 1915 Edison film *Ranson's Folly*. Both versions were based on the novel of the same name, by Richard Harding Davis.

Rasputin, the Black Monk   (World Film Corp., 1917)
d: Arthur Ashley.   7 reels.
Montagu Love, June Elvidge, Arthur Ashley, Violet Axzell, Lillian Cook, Irving Cummings, Julia Dean, Pinna Nesbit, Hubert Wilke, Florence Beresford, Charles Crompton.
In pre-revolution Russia, a peasant named Gregory disguises himself as a monk and becomes known as Rasputin. With his immense charisma, Rasputin gains converts to his ideas about living free of inhibitions—ideas that both the Czarists and the Communists consider dangerous.

The Rattler   (Ermine Productions, 1925)
d: Paul Hurst.   5 reels.
Jack Mower, George Williams, Alma Rayford, William Buckley, Vester Pegg.
Rivals for the hand of a rancher's daughter clash, with the better man finally winning by distracting his foe with the imitated sound of a snake's rattle.

The Raven   (Essanay, 1915)
d: Charles J. Brabin.   6 reels.
Henry B. Walthall, Wanda Howard, Ernest Maupain, Eleanor Thompson, Marion Skinnet, Harry Dunkinson, Grant Foreman, Hugh E. Thompson, Peggy Meredith.
Walthall plays Edgar Allan Poe in this biopic.

Rawhide   (Action Pictures/Associated Exhibitors, 1926)
d: Richard Thorpe.   5 reels.
Buffalo Bill Jr., Al Taylor, Molly Malone, Joe Rickson, Charles Whitaker, Harry Todd, Ruth Royce, Lafe McKee.
Out West, "Rawhide" Rawlins tries to exonerate himself from false charges of murder.

The Re-Creation of Brian Kent   (Principal Pictures, 1925)
d: Sam Wood.   7 reels.
Kenneth Harlan, Helene Chadwick, Mary Carr, ZaSu Pitts, Rosemary Theby, T. Roy Barnes, Ralph Lewis, Russell Simpson, DeWitt Jennings, Russell Powell.
Kent, a henpecked husband, feels pressure from his demanding wife and so embezzles money from his bank.

Reaching for the Moon   (Fairbanks/Artcraft, 1917)
d: John Emerson.   5 reels.
Douglas Fairbanks, Richard Cummings, Millard Webb, Eileeen Percy, Eugene Ormonde, Frank Campeau.
Comedy about a button clerk who fantasizes about becoming royalty.

Ready Money   (Lasky Feature Plays/Paramount, 1914)
d: Oscar C. Apfel.   5 reels.
Edward Abeles, Monroe Salisbury, Jode Mullally, Jane Darwell, Bessie Barriscale, Florence Dagmar, James Neill, Theodore Roberts, Billy Elmer, Sydney Deane, Dick LaReno.
Western comedy has a tenderfoot going West, buying a worthless mine, gullibly accepting $50,000 in counterfeit money... and *still* coming out a winner!

The Real Adventure   (Florence Vidor Productions/Associated Exhibitors, 1922)
d: King Vidor.   5 reels.
Florence Vidor, Clyde Fillmore, Nellie Peck Saunders, Lilyan McCarthy, Philip Ryder.
Rose, married to a good, solid, dependable man, is nevertheless dissatisfied because she has never succeeded in anything on her own. So, in quick succession, she takes up the study of law, becomes a chorus girl, learns costume design, and opens her own boutique, which becomes a great success.

Real Folks   (Triangle, 1918)
d: Walter Edwards.   5 reels.
Francis McDonald, Alberta Lee, J. Barney Sherry, Fritzi Ridgeway, Marion Skinner, Betty Pearce, George Pearce, T.D. Crittenden.
When Irish immigrant Pat Dugan strikes oil on his California land, he is suddenly rich, and insists that his family move upscale in society. But Jimmy, Pat's son, is perfectly happy living modestly and wooing Joyce, who is poor but charming.

The Reapers   (Triumph Film Corp./World Film Corp., 1916)
d: Burton King.   5 reels.
John Mason, Clara Whipple, Joan Morgan, Rene Dentling, Warner Oland, Pierre LeMay.
When her husband Albert becomes paralyzed from the waist down, his fair-weather wife Rita leaves him and their daughter and takes up with a gambler.

The Reason Why   (C.K.Y. Film Corp./Select, 1918)
d: Robert G. Vignola.   5 reels.
Clara Kimball Young, Milton Sills, Florence Billings, Frank Losee, John Sunderland, Kate Lester, J.W. Johnson, Eldean Stewart.
In London, a young woman lives with her wealthy uncle, who is unaware that she was once married and has a son. When the uncle compels her to marry a certain nobleman, she does so grudgingly, and soon has to explain about her little boy.

Rebecca of Sunnybrook Farm   (Artcraft, 1917)
d: Marshall Neilan.   6 reels.

Mary Pickford, Eugene O'Brien, Helen Jerome Eddy, Charles Ogle, Marjorie Daw, Josephine Crowell, Jack McDonald, Mayme Kelso, Janae Wolff, Violet Wilkey, Frank Turner, Kate Toncray, Emma Gerdes.

A frisky young girl is adopted by her stern maiden aunts.

The Rebellious Bride (Fox, 1919)
d: Lynn F. Reynolds. 5 reels.
Peggy Hyland, George Nicholls, George Hernandez, Pell Trenton, Charles LeMoyne, Kathleen Emerson, Lillian Langdon, Harry Dunkinson.
Cynthy, a high-spirited girl from the Ozarks, rebels against her family's decision on whom she should marry. When Cynthy does make her choice, it's to marry Arthur, an aviator she's never met before, and who consents to the marriage only at gunpoint.

Received Payment (Vitagraph, 1922)
d: Charles Maigne. 5 reels.
Corinne Griffith, Kenneth Harlan, David Torrence, William David, Charles Hammond, Henry Sedley, Regina Quinn, Dorothy Walters, Dan Duffy.
Years after Milton, a millionaire, has disowned his only daughter, a strange young woman comes to him and declares that she is his granddaughter.

The Reckless Age (Universal, 1924)
d: Harry Pollard. 7 reels.
Reginald Denny, Ruth Dwyer, John Steppling, May Wallace, William Austin, Tom McGuire, Fred Malatesta, Henry A. Barrows, Frederick Vroom, William E. Lawrence, Hayden Stevenson, Frank Leigh.
Comedy about an insurance agent who's sent to a wedding to insure the life of the bride, and ends up falling in love with her.

Reckless Courage (Action Pictures/Artclass Pictures, 1925)
d: Tom Gibson. 5 reels.
Buddy Roosevelt, J.C. Fowler, Helen Foster, William McIllwain, Jay Morley, Jack O'Brien, N.E. Hendrix, Merrill McCormick, Eddie Barry, Robert Burns.
Out West, a ranch foreman and a wealthy girl embark on a series of adventures in search of a stolen diamond necklace.

The Reckless Lady (First National, 1926)
d: Howard Higgin. 8 reels.
Belle Bennett, James Kirkwood, Lois Moran, Lowell Sherman, Ben Lyon, Marcia Harris, Charlie Murray.
In Monte Carlo, a young American woman shows a romantic interest in a dashing Russian, who turns out to be the same man who, years before, seduced her mother, the "reckless lady" of the title.

Reckless Romance (Christie Film Co./Producers Distributing Corp., 1924)
d: Scott Sidney. 6 reels.
T. Roy Barnes, Harry Myers, Wanda Hawley, Sylvia Breamer, Tully Marshall, Jack Duffy, Lincoln Plumer, Morgan Wallace, George French.
Comedy about a young fellow who can't marry his sweetie because her dad won't give his consent. He gets a $10,000 gift from his uncle, however, and bets his girl's dad that he can hang on to the money for a month, with the girl's hand in marriage as the prize if he wins. Her dad gladly consents, knowing that this loser is sure to blow the money recklessly. But he's got a surprise coming.

The Reckless Sex (Phil Goldstone Productions/Truart Film Corp., 1925)

d: Alvin J. Neitz. 6 reels.
Madge Bellamy, William Collier Jr., Wyndham Standing, Claire McDowell, Johnnie Walker, Gertrude Astor, Alec B. Francis, Gladys Brockwell, David Torrence, Helen Dunbar.
In a border town, a Bostonian on business befriends a stranded actress from a touring production of *Uncle Tom's Cabin*. Since she played the role of Little Eva in the show, she is still in costume, so the Boston chap mistakes her for a little girl. But she's a fully-developed young woman, as her benefactor will soon discover.

Reckless Youth (Selznick, 1922)
d: Ralph Ince. 6 reels.
Elaine Hammerstein, Miles Welch, Myrtle Stedman, Robert Lee Keeling, Huntley Gordon, Louise Prussing, Frank Currier, Kate Cherry, Constance Bennett.
Convent-bred Alice yearns to escape the discipline and regimentation of her situation, so she elopes with a lodge keeper.

The Reckoning Day (Triangle, 1918)
d: Harry Clements. 5 reels.
Belle Bennett, Jack Richardson, J. Barney Sherry, Tom Buckingham, Lenore Fair, Louise Lester, Lee Phelps, Lucille Desmond, Sidney DeGrey, Joe Bennett.
In this World War I drama, a lady lawyer helps to break up a phony charity organization that's really a front for international spies.

Reclamation (American Film Co./Mutual, 1916)
d: Edward Sloman. 5 reels.
Winnifred Greenwood, Franklyn Ritchie, Dick LaReno, Clarence Burton, Margaret Nichols, Harry McCabe, Roy Stewart.
Ranchers and businessmen square off in a battle to control water rights out West.

The Recoil (Astra Film Corp./Pathé, 1917)
d: George Fitzmaurice. 5 reels.
William Courtenay, Lillian Greuze, Frank Belcher, Dora Mills Adams, William Raymond.
When a Secret Service agent is kidnapped by a spy ring, his wife thinks he has been killed, and marries again.

The Recoil (Goldwyn/Metro-Goldwyn, 1924)
d: T. Hayes Hunter. 7 reels.
Mahlon Hamilton, Betty Blythe, Clive Brook, Fred Paul, Ernest Hilliard.
In Paris, wealthy Gordon Kent marries a poor girl with a checkered past.

Recompense (Warner Bros., 1925)
d: Harry Beaumont. 7 reels.
Monte Blue, Marie Prevost, John Roche, George Siegmann, Charles Stevens, Virginia Brown Faire, William B. Davidson, Etta Lee.
Graham, a British minister with an eye for the ladies, tries to put his romantic urges behind him by becoming an Army chaplain. He ends up marrying the winsome nurse he meets while on duty in South Africa.

Red Clay (Universal, 1927)
d: Ernst Laemmle. 5 reels.
William Desmond, Marceline Day, Albert J. Smith, Byron Douglas, Billy Sullivan, Lola Todd, Noble Johnson, Felix Whitefeather, Ynez Seabury.
Racial bigotry rears its ugly head in this tale about an Indian who earns military decorations in World War I, yet is scorned at home by the man whose life he saved during the

war.

Red Courage (Universal, 1921)
d: Reaves Eason. 5 reels.
Hoot Gibson, Joel Day, Molly Malone, Joe Girard, William Merrill McCormick, Charles Newton, Arthur Hoyt, Joe Harris, Dick Cummings, Mary Philbin, Jim Corey, Mac V. Wright.
Out West, a colorful pair of characters become crusading newspapermen and drive the corrupt mayor and local crime boss out of town.

The Red Dance (Fox, 1928)
d: Raoul Walsh. 10 reels. (Synchronized music.)
Charles Farrell, Dolores Del Rio, Ivan Linow, Boris Charsky, Dorothy Revier, Andres De Segurola, Demetrius Alexis.
In Russia, a peasant girl is ordered by revolutionaries to shoot a grand duke, but misses on purpose, because she fancies him. After the Bolsheviks take over, the same girl surfaces as the Red Dancer of Moscow, not without influence in the new order. But she is again drawn to the grand duke whose life she saved.

Red Dice (DeMille Pictures/Producers Distributing Corp., 1926)
d: William K. Howard. 7 reels.
Rod LaRocque, Marguerite De La Motte, Ray Hallor, Gustav von Seyffertitz, George Cooper, Walter Long, Edithe Yorke, Clarence Burton, Charles Clary, Alan Brooks.
Beckwith, desperately in need of funds, strikes a macabre bargain with an underworld leader: For $300 in cash, Beckwith will insure his life in favor of the gangster, and on the 24th of the month—a date determined by the "red dice" of the title—he will be killed by one of the gangster's henchmen. But once the deal is underway, Beckwith meets his true love, and he tries desperately to renegotiate the "bargain."

Red Foam (Selznick/Select, 1920)
d: Ralph Ince. 6 reels.
Zena Keefe, Harry Tighe, Huntley Gordon, Daniel Hays, Peggy Worth, Johnny Butler.
After an unbalanced traveling salesman discovers that his bride and their neighbor were once romantically involved, he repeatedly forces them to see each other, hoping to stir up feelings of envy.

Red Hair (Paramount, 1928)
d: Clarence Badger. 7 reels. (Technicolor sequence.)
Clara Bow, Lane Chandler, William Austin, Jacqueline Gadsdon, Lawrence Grant, Claude King, William Irving.
Bubbles McCoy, a jazz-age gold digger, decides to marry a young man who's under the joint guardianship of three of her beaus.

The Red-Haired Cupid (Triangle, 1918)
d: Cliff Smith. 5 reels.
Roy Stewart, Charles Dorian, Peggy Pearce, Ray Griffith, Aaron Edwards, Walter Perry.
Oklahoma ranch hands prepare for the worst when they learn the owner's niece will be visiting them from back east. The cowpokes expect an old prune, but instead they find a young beauty. Foreman "Red" Saunders smooths the way for one of the hands to woo the newcomer.

Red Hot Dollars (Thomas H. Ince/Paramount, 1919)
d: Jerome Storm. 5 reels.
Charles Ray, Gladys George, Charles Mailes, William Conklin, Mollie McConnell.
In an iron foundry, a worker saves the millionaire owner from being crushed to death, and is rewarded with an executive position. The young man then hires his sweetie as his secretary, not realizing that her father and the foundry owner were once business rivals, and remain bitter enemies.

Red Hot Leather (Universal, 1926)
d: Albert S. Rogell. 5 reels.
Jack Hoxie, William Malan, Ena Gregory, Tom Shirley, William H. Turner, George K. French, Billy Engle, Jim Corey, Leo Sailor.
Out West, a rancher's son enters a rodeo to try and win money to pay off the mortgage.

Red Hot Romance (John Emerson and Anita Loos Productions, 1922)
d: Victor Fleming. 6 reels.
Basil Sydney, Henry Warwick, Frank Lalor, Carl Stockdale, Olive Valerie, Edward Connelly, May Collins, Roy Atwell, Tom Wilson, Lillian Leighton, Snitz Edwards.
Stone, an American chap whose dad is a dim-bulb diplomat, goes to the kingdom of Bunkonia to protect the family's insurance business by defending the marked-for-assassination, alcoholic king.

Red Hot Speed (Universal, 1929)
d: Joseph E. Henabery. 7 reels. (Part talkie.)
Alice Day, Reginald Denny, Thomas Ricketts, Charles Byer, De Witt Jennings, Fritzi Ridgeway, Hector V. Sarno.
A newspaper publisher's daughter is arrested for speeding while her father is energetically waging an anti-speeding campaign through his newspaper. The daughter is paroled into the custody of a charming assistant D.A., and they fall in love.

Red Hot Tires (Warner Bros., 1925)
d: Erle C. Kenton. 7 reels.
Monte Blue, Patsy Ruth Miller, Lincoln Stedman, Charles Conklin, Fred Esmelton.
Comedy about a fellow who rides a buggy because he has a fear of motor vehicles. Not good news for his fast-car-loving girlfriend.

Red Kimono (Mrs. Wallace Reid Productions, 1925)
d: Walter Lang. 7 reels.
Priscilla Bonner, Theodore von Eltz, Tyrone Power, Mary Carr, Virginia Pearson, Mrs. Wallace Reid.
In New Orleans, a prostitute falls in love with a doughboy.

The Red Lane (Universal, 1920)
d: Lynn Reynolds. 5 reels.
Frank Mayo, Lillian Rich, James L. Mason, Jean Hersholt, James O'Neill, Karl Formes, Paul Weigel, Frank Thorne, Harry Lamont, Fred Herzog.
The convent-bred daughter of a smuggler is alarmed to learn that her father expects her to marry a member of his gang.

The Red Lantern (Metro, 1919)
d: Albert Capellani. 7 reels.
Alla Nazimova, Margaret McWade, Virginia Ross, Frank Currier, Winter Hall, Amy Veness, Darrell Foss, Noah Beery, Harry Mann, Yukio Aoyamo, Edward J. Connelly.
Tragic melodrama about a Eurasian girl in China during the Boxer Rebellion.

Red Lights (Goldwyn, 1923)
d: Clarence Badger. 7 reels.
Marie Prevost, Raymond Griffith, Johnnie Walker, Alice Lake, Dagmar Godowsky, William Worthington, Frank

RED DICE (1926). Rod LaRocque and Marguerite DeLaMotte strike a romantic pose in this drama involving a forced marriage where the two initially reluctant partners actually do fall in love with each other.

* * * * *

Elliott, Lionel Belmore, Jean Hersholt, George Reed, Charles West.

In Los Angeles, a railroad heiress is menaced by mysterious figures appearing at night and sporting flashing red lights.

The Red Lily (MGM, 1924)
w, d: Fred Niblo. 7 reels.
Ramon Novarro, Enid Bennett, Wallace Beery, Frank Currier, Rosemary Theby, Mitchell Lewis, Emily Fitzroy.
In France, destitute lovers turn to crime to support themselves.

Red Lips (Universal, 1928)
d: Melville W. Brown. 7 reels.
Marion Nixon, Charles Buddy Rogers, Stanley Taylor, Hayden Stevenson, Andy Devine, Robert Seiter, Hugh Trevor, Earl McCarthy.
Carver, a top athlete, is thrown off the college track team because of his indiscretions with a flirt, Cynthia Day. But these kids will get their act together and Carver will return to the team and set a world record.
Remake of the 1925 film *The Plastic Age*, which starred Donald Keith and Clara Bow.

Red Love (Lowell Film Productions, 1925)
d: Edgar Lewis. 6 reels.
John Lowell, Evangeline Russell, F. Serrano Keating, William Calhoun, Ann Brody, William Cavanaugh, Wallace Jones, Charles W. Kinney, Frank Montgomery, Dexter McReynolds, Chick Chandler.
Out West, a college-educated Sioux falls in love with Starlight, a halfbreed girl. But then he learns that his son is in love with her as well.

The Red Mark (James Cruze, Inc./Pathé, 1928)
d: James Cruze. 8 reels.
Nina Quartaro, Gaston Glass, Gustav von Seyffertitz, Rose Dione, Luke Cosgrave, Eugene Pallette, Jack Roper, Charles Dervis.
On a South Seas island, an executioner is about to behead a young prisoner when he notices the boy has a red birthmark on his neck—an indication that he is the executioner's long-lost son.

The Red Mill (Cosmopolitan/MGM, 1926)
d: Roscoe Arbuckle (as William Goodrich). 7 reels.
Marion Davies, Owen Moore, Louise Fazenda, Karl Dane, George Seigmann, Snitz Edwards, J. Russell Powell, William Orlamond, Fred Gambold, Louis Fazenda.
A Dutch workmaid and her man collaborate to help a girl escape a forced marriage.

The Red Raiders (First National, 1927)
d: Albert Rogell. 7 reels..
Ken Maynard, Ann Drew, Paul Hurst, J.P. McGowan, Chief Yowlache, Harry Shutan, Tom Day, Hal Salter.
With Indians on the warpath, a young cavalry officer is assigned to a fort in Sioux territory.

The Red, Red Heart (Universal, 1918)
d: Wilfred Lucas. 5 reels.
Monroe Salisbury, Ruth Clifford, Val Paul, Gretchen Lederer, Allan Sears, Monte Blue, Princess Neola.
When a sickly girl is taken to Arizona to try to regain her health, she is befriended by an Indian who teaches her the curative ways of the desert.

The Red Rider (Universal, 1925)
d: Clifford Smith. 5 reels.

Jack Hoxie, Mary McAllister, Jack Pratt, Natalie Warfield, Marin Sais, William McCall, Francis Ford, George Connors, Frank Lanning, Clark Comstock, Duke R. Lee, Chief Big Tree.
Out West, an Indian chief falls in love with a white girl and rescues her when she is captured by a renegade tribe and set adrift in a canoe headed for a deadly waterfall.

Red Signals (Sterling Pictures, 1927)
d: J.P. McGowan. 5 reels.
Wallace MacDonald, Earle Williams, Eva Novak, J.P. McGowan, Sylvia Ashton, William Moran, Robert McKenzie, Billy Franey, Frank Rice.
Out West, a railroad agent does battle with a gang of train robbers.

The Red Sword (FBO Pictures/RKO, 1929)
d: Robert G. Vignola. 7 reels.
William Collier Jr., Carmel Myers, Demetrius Alexis, Allan Roscoe, Charles Darvas, Barbara Bozoky.
In Russia, a drunken Cossack assaults an innkeeper's wife. In her efforts to escape him, the victim falls over the balcony to her death. In years to come, the woman's death will be avenged by her daughter.

The Red Viper (Tyrad Pictures, 1919)
d: Jacques Tyrol. 6 reels.
Gareth Hughes, Ruth Stonehouse, Jack Gilbert, Irma Harrison, R.H. Fitzsimmons, Alberta Lee, Alfred Hollingsworth.
On New York's east side, a foreign-born newsboy joins a gang of anarchists, but comes to regret it.

The Red Warning (Universal, 1923)
d: Robert North Bradbury. 5 reels.
Jack Hoxie, Elinor Field, Fred Kohler, Frank Rice, Jim Welsh, William Welsh, Ben Corbett, Ralph Fee McCullough.
Thrilling western melodrama in which two strangers help a girl find a lost gold mine.

Red, White and Blue Blood (Metro, 1917)
d: Charles J. Brabin. 5 reels.
Francis X. Bushman, Beverly Bayne, Adelia Barker, William H. Tooker, Duncan McRae, Cecil Fletcher, Jack Raymond, C.R. McKinney, Arthur Houseman.
John, an intrepid adventurer, saves Helen from a train robbery, from drowning, and from marrying the wrong man.

The Red Widow (Famous Players/Paramount, 1916)
d: James Durkin. 5 reels.
John Barrymore, Flora Zabelle, John Hendricks, Eugene Redding, Millard Benson, George E. Mack, Lillian Tucker.
In this farcical comedy, Barrymore plays Cicero Hannibal Butts, an American corset salesman who plans to take his new bride to Russia on their honeymoon.

Red Wine (Fox, 1928)
w, d: Raymond Cannon. 7 reels.
June Collyer, Conrad Nagel, Arthur Stone, Sharon Lynn, E. Alyn Warren, Ernest Hilliard, Ernest wood, Marshall Ruth, Dixie Gay, Margaret LaMarr, Bo Ling, Dolores Johnson.
A faithful young husband is persuaded by friends to join them at a wild party, where he drinks too much wine, makes a fool of himself, and passes out. Just for laughs, his "friends" make it appear that, when the chap wakes up the next morning, he has been unfaithful to his wife. The following evening is his wedding anniversary, and he's ill at ease—to say the least—when his wife insists he take her to

the same restaurant where the party was held.

The Red Woman (World Film Corp., 1917)
d: Emile Chautard. 5 reels.
Gail Kane, Mahlon Hamilton, Ed F. Roseman, June Elvidge, Charlotte Granville, Gladys Earlcott.
After his father's death, a playboy discovers that his disgusted dad cut him out of the will, except for leaving him some mining properties in Mexico. Sobered by the revelation, the young man goes to Mexico, and there falls in love with an American-educated Indian maiden.

Redeeming Love (Oliver Morosco Photoplays/Paramount, 1916)
d: William D. Taylor. 5 reels.
Kathlyn Williams, Thomas Holding, Wyndham Standing, Herbert Standing, Jane Keckley, Helen Jerome Eddy, Don Bailey.
Naomi, a tough-minded woman, rises to the top as chief of gambling operations in her city. Now she has to face John, the minister she once loved, who heads an organization dedicated to fighting the corrupting influence of gambling.

The Redeeming Sin (Vitagraph, 1925)
d: J. Stuart Blackton. 7 reels.
Nazimova, Lou Tellegen, Carl Miller, Otis Harlan, Rosita Marstini, William Dunn.
In Paris, a fiery apache dancer falls for a sculptor and enlists his aid in teaching her to become a lady of manners.

The Redeeming Sin (Warner Bros., 1929)
d: Howard Bretherton. 8 reels. (Music, sound effects, part talkie.)
Dolores Costello, Conrad Nagel, Warner Richmond, Philippe de Lacey, Lionel Belmore.
A vengeful young woman tries to take out her wrath on an innocent doctor.

Redemption (Triumph Film Corp., 1917)
d: Julius Steger, Joseph A. Golden. 6 reels.
Evelyn Nesbit-Thaw, Russell Thaw, Charles Wellsley, Mary Hall, William Clarke, Joyce Fair, Edward Lynch, George Clarke, Marie Reichard.
Harry loves Grace, but her father Stephen will not permit their marriage because he still bears ill will against Harry's mother, Stephen's former lover.

The Redemption of Dave Darcey (Vitagraph, 1916)
d: Paul Scardon. 5 reels.
James Morrison, Belle Bruce, Billie Billings, Emanuel A. Turner, Mary Maurice, Robert Gaillard, Gerald Gordon, John Costello, Logan Paul, Dan Hayes, Charles J. Giegerich Jr.
After a shootout with other hoodlums, Dave, a gangster, takes refuge in a private home. The couple who own the house allow Dave to stay if he promises to give up his life of crime, and they even get him a job in a munitions factory. Once on the job, Dave justifies his benefactors' faith in him by identifying, and helping to bring to justice, a foreign spy bent on sabotage.

Redhead (Select Pictures Corp., 1919)
d: Charles Maigne. 5 reels.
Alice Brady, Conrad Nagel, Robert Schable, Charles A. Stevenson, Charles Eldridge, May Brettone.
A cabaret dancer known as "Redhead" agrees to marry an immature playboy, hoping she'll be able to change him.

Redheads Preferred (Tiffany Productions, 1926)
d: Allan Dale. 6 reels.
Raymond Hitchcock, Marjorie Daw, Theodore von Eltz, Cissy Fitzgerald, Vivian Oakland, Charles A. Post, Leon Holmes, Geraldine Leslie.
Hearing that her businessman husband plans to take a redheaded woman to a fancy party to win a lucrative contract, Angela decides to buy a red wig and take the lady's place.

Redskin (Paramount, 1929)
d: Victor Schertzinger. 9 reels. (Technicolor sequences, music score, sound effects.)
Richard Dix, Jack Duane, Gladys Belmont, Jane Novak, Larry Steers, Tully Marshall, Bernard Siegel, George Rigas, Augustina Lopez, Noble Johnson, Joseph W. Girard.
Wing Foot, a college-educated Navajo, becomes an outcast among his own people. Fleeing into the desert, he strikes oil and must then wage a furious race to the recorder's office to file his claim ahead of rival prospectors. Wing Foot gets there first, files his claim, then announces to his tribe that these riches will be for the good of all the Indian nations.

The Reed Case (Universal, 1917)
d: Allen Holubar. 5 reels.
Alfred Allen, Louise Lovely, Fred Montague, Allen Holubar, George Pearce, Sydney Dean, Nanine Wright, Ernest Shields, Edward Brady.
When a detective stays in a mountain cabin that's said to be haunted, he discovers who the "ghost" is: A lovely girl who's been kidnapped and is being held there.

The Referee (Selznick/Select, 1922)
d: Ralph Ince. 5 reels.
Conway Tearle, Anders Randolf, Gladys Hulette, Gus Platz, Frank Ryan, Joe Humphries, Patsy Haley.
McArdle, a former boxer, loves Janie, but her father objects to their union because he disapproves of the fighting profession and its "questionable" scruples.

Reform — see: Life's Mockery (1928)

The Reform Candidate (Pallas Pictures/Paramount, 1915)
d: Frank Lloyd. 5 reels.
Maclyn Arbuckle, Forrest Stanley, Myrtle Stedman, Malcolm Blevins, Charles Ruggles, Mary Ruby, Howard Davies, Jane Darwell, Fanny Stockbridge, Mary Higby.
When Frank, the reform candidate for mayor, decides to dig up some dirt on Art, his opponent, he learns that Art's young daughter is not really his child, but a foundling he has raised. Upon further digging, Frank finds another nugget: The girl is Frank's own long-lost daughter.

The Refuge (Preferred Pictures/Associated First National, 1923)
d: Victor Schertzinger. 6 reels.
Katherine MacDonald, Hugh Thompson, J. Gunnis Davis, J. Gordon Russell, Eric Mayne, Arthur Edmund Carew, Mathilde Brundage, Fred Malatesta, Grace Morse, Victor Potel, Olita Otis.
In a mythical kingdom, a prince hopes to marry a countess and thus cement his claim to the throne. The rightful heir, however, is a soldier who arrives home just in time to prevent the bogus marriage and claim the throne for himself.

The Regenerates (Triangle, 1917)
d: E. Mason Hopper. 5 reels.
Alma Rubens, Walt Whitman, Darrel Foss, John Lince, Allan Sears, Louis Durnham, William Brady, Pauline Stark.
Catherine loves Paul, and together they adopt the orphan

baby of Catherine's cousin.

Regeneration (Fox, 1915)
d: R.A. Walsh. 5 reels.
Rockcliffe Fellowes, Anna Q. Nilsson, William Sheer, Carl Harbaugh, James Marcus, Maggie Weston, John McCann, Peggy Barn.
Mistreated by his foster parents, a 10-year-old orphan runs away and makes his way through life on his own. By age 25, he has become a hardened veteran of the streets, but retains a sense of decency and falls in love with Marie, a kind settlement worker.

Reggie Mixes In (Triangle, 1916)
d: W. Christy Cabanne. 5 reels.
Douglas Fairbanks, Bessie Love, Joseph Singleton, W.A. Lowery, Wilbur Higby, Frank Bennett, Lillian Langdon, Alma Reubens, Alberta Lee, Tom Wilson.
Reggie, a scion of wealth, falls for a girl who dances in a saloon.

A Regular Fellow (Triangle, 1919)
d: Christy Cabanne. 5 reels.
Taylor Holmes, Millicent Fisher, Edna Phillips Holmes, Frank Leigh, Aileen Manning, Bert Apling, Lillian Langdon, Bill Durham, Leo Willis.
In order to claim his inheritance, a misogynist must marry a girl he's never met.

A Regular Fellow (Famous Players-Lasky/Paramount, 1925)
d: Edward Sutherland. 5 reels.
Raymond Griffith, Mary Brian, Tyrone Power, Edgar Norton, Nigel DeBrulier, Gustav von Seyffertitz, Kathleen Kirkham, Carl Stockdale, Michael Dark, Lincoln Plumer, Jacqueline Gadsden, Jerry Austin.
Comedy about a Balkan prince who loves a commoner but is unable to marry her because his family insists his wife be of royal status. No problem for this prince. He arranges with an anarchist to stage a revolution; the revolution is bloodless and a success; and the monarchy is ousted. Now the prince is free to marry the woman he loves, and is elected the first president of the new republic.

A Regular Girl (Selznick/Select, 1919)
d: James Young. 5 reels.
Elsie Janis, Robert Lyton, Matt Moore, Robert Ayerton, Tammany Young, Ernie Adams, Jerry Delaney, Frank Murdock, Mrs. Jeffrey Lewis.
During World War I, a patriotic-minded society girl becomes an Army nurse.

A Regular Scout (R-C Pictures/FBO of America, 1926)
w, d: David Kirkland. 6 reels.
Fred Thomson, Olive Hasbrouck, William Courtright, T. Roy Barnes, Margaret Seddon, Buck Black, Robert McKim, Harry Woods.
Out West, Blake learns that a dying bandit is the long-lost son of a prominent local family. Blake impersonates the son and arrives at the family estate just in time to prevent crooked lawyers from swindling the family.

The Rejected Woman (Distinctive Pictures/Goldwyn, 1924)
d: Albert Parker. 8 reels.
Alma Rubens, Bela Lugosi, George MacQuarrie, Conrad Nagel, Frederick Burton, Antonio D'Algy, Aubrey Smith, Wyndham Standing, Juliette LaViolette, Leonora Hughes.
John, an American aviator, runs into rough flying weather over Canada, and while seeking shelter he meets Diane, with whom he falls in love. Diane gets permission from her family to visit John in New York; and though the two are happy together, she is "rejected" by his society friends because of her rough-hewn manners.

The Rejuvenation of Aunt Mary (Metropolitan Pictures, 1927)
d: Erle C. Kenton. 6 reels.
Harrison Ford, May Robson, Phyllis Haver, Arthur Hoyt, Franklin Pangborn, Robert Edeson, Betty Brown.
When his wealthy Aunt Mary decides to visit him, a racing car designer hastily converts his garage into a sanitarium, with friends of his pretending to be patients. You see, Aunt Mary thinks her favorite nephew is studying to be a doctor, not a speed demon.

Remember (Columbia, 1927)
d: David Selman. 6 reels.
Dorothy Phillips, Earle Metcalfe, Lola Todd, Lincoln Stedman, Eddie Featherstone.
A war hero returns home blinded, to rejoin the girl he loves... but she's doesn't want him any more. Her sister, though, loves the ex-soldier and lets him think she is his girl. When his sight is restored after an operation, he finds he was blind in more ways than one, and lovingly clings to the sister who stuck with him through it all.

Remembrance (Goldwyn, 1922)
w, d: Rupert Hughes. 6 reels.
Claude Gillingwater, Kate Lester, Patsy Ruth Miller, Cullen Landis, Max Davidson, Richard Tucker, Dana Todd, Nell Craig, Esther Ralston, Helen Hayward, Lucille Ricksen.
Drama about a businessman who works himself into a heart attack, and the daughter who sticks by him.

The Remittance Woman (R-C Pictures/FBO of America, 1923)
d: Wesley Ruggles. 6 reels.
Ethel Clayton, Rockliffe Fellowes, Mario Carillo, Frank Lanning, Tom Wilson, Etta Lee, James B. Leong, Edward Kimball, Toyo Fujita.
Marie, a blushing bride-to-be, is so extravagant that her exasperated father weighs sending her to China as punishment.

Remodeling Her Husband (New Art Film Co./Paramount, 1920)
d: Lillian Gish. 5 reels.
Dorothy Gish, James Rennie, Downing Clarke, Marie Burke, Frank Kingdon.
A man considers his wife dowdy, until he notices how other men react to her.

Remorseless Love (Selznick/Select, 1921)
d: Ralph Ince. 5 reels.
Elaine Hammerstein, Niles Welch, Jerry Devine, Ray Allen, James Seeley, Effingham Pinto.
To save his fiancée from disgrace, an accused murderer refuses to offer an alibi for his whereabouts.

The Rendezvous (Goldwyn, 1923)
d: Marshall Neilan. 8 reels.
Conrad Nagel, Lucille Ricksen, Richard Travers, Kathleen Key, Emmett Corrigan, Elmo Lincoln, Sydney Chaplin, Kate Lester, Cecil Holland, Lucien Littlefield, Max Davidson, Eugenie Besserer, R.O. Pennell.
In Russia, an American soldier saves a girl from attack by a lustful Cossack.

Reno (Goldwyn, 1923)
w, d: Rupert Hughes. 7 reels.
Helene Chadwick, Lew Cody, George Walsh, Carmel Myers, Dale Fuller, Hedda Hopper, Kathleen Key, Rush Hughes, Marjorie Bonner, Robert DeVilbiss, Virginia Loomis, Richard Wayne, Hughie Mack.
Dora, a recently divorced mother of two, falls in love with Walter and they marry. Soon, however, they discover that her Reno divorce is not legal in their home state. To make matters worse, her ex-husband is trying to take her children from her.

A Reno Divorce (Warner Bros., 1927)
w, d: Ralph Graves. 6 reels.
May McAvoy, Ralph Graves, Robert Ober, Hedda Hopper, Anders Randolf, Edwards Davis, William Demarest.
Carla, a high society deb, falls for a struggling artist.

Rent Free (Famous Players-Lasky/Paramount, 1922)
d: Howard Higgin. 5 reels.
Wallace Reid, Lila Lee, Henry Barrows, Gertrude Short, Lillian Leighton, Clarence Geldert, Claire McDowell, Lucien Littlefield.
A penniless artist tries to help a socialite who's been cheated out of her inheritance.

Reported Missing (Owen Moore Pictures/Selznick/Select, 1922)
d: Henry Lehrman. 7 reels.
Owen Moore, Pauline Garon, Tom Wilson, Frank Wunderlee, Robert Cain, Nita Naldi, Mickey Bennett.
Boyd, a shipping magnate, and his fiancée, Pauline, are shanghaied by a rival shipping tycoon.

Reputation (Mutual, 1917)
d: John B. O'Brien. 5 reels.
Edna Goodrich, William Hinckley, Frank Goldsmith, Carey Lee, Esther Evans, Nellie Parker Spaulding, Mrs. Mathilde Brundage.
In New York, a dress model is propositioned by her employer. She resists him, resigns and returns to her home town, but still the man pursues her.

Reputation (Universal, 1921)
d: Stuart Paton. 7 reels.
Priscilla Dean, Mae Giraci, Harry Van Meter, Harry Carter, Niles Welch, Spottiswoode Aitken, William Welsh.
A famous theatrical actress hits the skids after being fired from a production.

The Rescue (Universal, 1917)
d: Ida May Park. 5 reels.
Dorothy Phillips, Lon Chaney, William Stowell, Gretchen Lederer, Molly Malone, Claire DuBray, Gertrude Astor.
Romantic tale with a twist: An actress is asked by a friend to intervene in the marriage of the friend's daughter and the actress' ex-husband. She does so, and in the process discovers she is still in love with him.

The Rescue (Goldwyn/United Artists, 1929)
d: Herbert Brenon. 9 reels. (Music, sound effects.)
Ronald Colman, Lily Damita, Alfred Hickman, Theodore von Eltz, John Davidson, Philip Strange, Bernard Siegel, Sojin, Harry Cording, Laska Winters, Duke Kahanamoku, George Rigas.
Lingard, a British ship owner, is drawn into a local revolution in the South Seas.

The Rescuing Angel (Famous Players-Lasky/Paramount, 1919)
d: Walter Edwards. 5 reels.
Shirley Mason, Forrest Stanley, Arthur Carew, John Steppling, Carol Edwards, James Neill, Edythe Chapman, T.D. Crittenden, J. Park Jones.
After marrying Angela, a millionaire hears gossip implying that she married him for his money. He confronts her angrily and, feeling insulted, she leaves him to begin divorce proceedings. When the lovesick millionaire learns that the gossip is untrue, he sets out in a fast car to find Angela and get her to drop the divorce.

Respectable by Proxy (J. Stuart Blackton Features/Pathé, 1920)
d: J. Stuart Blackton. 6 reels.
Sylvia Breamer, Robert Gordon, William R. Dunn, Bessie Stinson, Eulalie Jensen, Margaret Barry, Morgan Thorpe.
John, a wealthy Southerner, marries a temperamental actress, but they quarrel so severely that after a few days he leaves for Europe. When his ship sinks and all are reported dead, the actress lets her sickly friend Betty pose as John's widow, so that Betty might inherit his stately mansion. Betty proves to be a big comfort to John's grieving mother... so much so, that when John returns home unharmed, he falls in love with his "proxy wife."

Restitution (Mena Film Co., 1918)
d: Howard Gaye. 9 reels.
Lois Gardner, Eugene Corey, Alfred Garcia, Frank Whitson, Amy Jerome, Pomeroy Cannon, Frederick Vroom, Mabel Harvey, Harold Quintin, Howard Gaye, F.A. Turner, John Steppling, Mary Wise, C. Norman Hammond, Venita Fitzhugh, Edward Cecil, Virginia Chester.
Allegorical drama that begins with the fall of Adam and Eve, and takes us through the centuries to the modern era. Satan is depicted as the causal agent of the Crucifixion, the torture of Christians in Nero's empire, the Inquisition, and the establishment of Kaiser Wilhelm in Germany. But in the end Christ conquers Satan and raises the dead to life eternal.
This film was also known as *The Conquering Christ*.

The Restless Sex (Cosmopolitan/Paramount, 1921)
d: Robert Z. Leonard. 6 reels.
Marion Davies, Ralph Kellard, Charles Lane, Robert Vivian, Stephen Carr, Carlyle Blackwell, Corinne Barker, Vivian Osborne.
Stephanie loves her foster brother Jim, but he doesn't seem interested in her.

Restless Souls (Triangle, 1919)
d: William C. Dowlan. 6 reels.
Alma Rubens, Katherine Adams, Jack Conway, Harvey Clark, J. Barney Sherry, Eugene Burr.
Friends Judith and Marion are both unhappy in their marriages, but for very different reasons. Judith is wealthy but restless, and both she and her husband take lovers. Marion, on the other hand, is constant and loving, but yearns for the day her husband will sell the invention he's working on, and bring some money into the home.

Restless Souls (Vitagraph, 1922)
d: Albert E. Smith. 5 reels.
Earle Williams, Francelia Billington, Arthur Hoyt, Martha Mattox, Nick Cogley.
Suspecting that his wife is unfaithful to him, a millionaire feigns suicide and goes into seclusion. He returns after learning of the battle royal raging over ownership of his estate. And when he does, he discovers that his wife has

been faithful all along.

Restless Wives (C.C. Burr Pictures, 1924)
d: Gregory LaCava. 7 reels.
Doris Kenyon, James Rennie, Montague Love, Edmund Breese, Burr McIntosh, Coit Albertson, Naomi Childers, Maud Sinclair, Edna May Oliver, Richard Thorpe, Fren Oakley.
Still in love with the wife who divorced him, Benson kidnaps her to try and win her hand all over again.

Restless Youth (Columbia, 1928)
d: Christy Cabanne. 7 reels.
Ralph Forbes, Marceline Day, Norman Trevor, Robert Ellis, Mary Mabery, Gordon Elliott, Roy Watson.
After accidentally killing a man who tried to assault her, a young woman is placed on trial for murder.

Resurrection (Famous Players-Lasky/Paramount, 1918)
d: Edward José. 5 reels.
Pauline Frederick, Robert Elliott, John Sainpolis, Jere Austin.
In Russia, a peasant woman becomes pregnant by a prince, who deserts her. Later the woman becomes a prostitute and eventually is sent to be exiled in Siberia. But even in adversity, she finds happiness in the love of a fellow prisoner.

Resurrection (United Artists, 1927)
d: Edwin Carewe. 10 reels.
Rod LaRocque, Dolores Del Rio, Lucy Beaumont, Vera Lewis, Marc MacDermott, Count Ilyha Tolstoy, Clarissa Selwynne, Eve Southern.
A Russian nobleman is overcome with remorse when he recognizes a woman as a girl he had once seduced.

The Return of Boston Blackie (Chadwick Pictures, 1927)
d: Harry O. Hoyt. 6 reels.
Corliss Palmer, Raymond Glenn, Rosemary Cooper, Coit Albertson, William Worthington, Florence Wix, J.P. Lockney, Strongheart the dog.
Boston Blackie, the quintessential gentleman crook, performs one last "heist" — to return a stolen necklace to its rightful owner.

The Return of Draw Egan (Triangle, 1916)
d: William S. Hart. 5 reels.
William S. Hart, Louise Glaum, Margery Wilson, Robert McKim, J.P. Lockney.
Now installed as marshal of Yellow Dog, Draw Egan is on his way to making the town a model community... until a bandit comes to town and threatens to expose Egan's criminal past.

The Return of Eve (Essanay, 1916)
d: Arthur Berthelet. 5 reels.
Edna Mayo, Eugene O'Brien, Edward Mawson, Edward Arnold, Emily Fitzroy, Leona Ball, John Cossar, Renee Clemons.
Orphans known only as Adam and Eve grow up in a wilderness known as Eden, put there by a kindly millionaire who hates civilization.

Return of Grey Wolf (Ambassador Pictures, 1926)
d: Jacques Rollens. 6 reels.
Leader, the dog, James Pierce, Helen Lynch, Walter Shumway.
A dog rescues his master and mistress.
Entertaining and unusual tale, told in flashbacks from the point of view of the dog.

The Return of Mary (Metro, 1918)
d: Wilfred Lucas. 5 reels.
May Allison, Clarence Burton, Claire McDowell, Darrell Foss, Frank Brownlee, Joseph Belmont.
Fourteen years after they lost their little daughter Mary in a kidnapping, the Denbys get her back... or do they? After three years of bonding, they learn that the new "Mary" is not their daughter, but an impostor. But there's one member of the Denby family who isn't alarmed by the news: Jack, who has learned to love his new "sister," and now will propose marriage.

The Return of Peter Grimm (Fox, 1926)
d: Victor Schertzinger. 8 reels.
Alec B. Francis, John Roche, Janet Gaynor, Richard Walling, Elizabeth Patterson, Lionel Belmore, Bodil Rosing, Mickey McBan, Florence Colbert, Sammy Cohn, John Sainpolis.
The spirit of a dead man returns to set matters right with those he left behind.

The Return of Tarzan (Numa Pictures Corp./Goldwyn, 1920)
d: Harry Revier. 7 reels.
Gene Pollar, George Romain, Waler Miller, Armand Cortez, Louis Stearns, Karla Schramm, Estelle Taylor, Franklin B. Coates, Betty Turner, Peggy Hannon, Estelle Evans, Fred A. Turner, Evelyn Fariss, Phil Gastrock, Arthur Morrison, Jack Leonard, Harry Lonsdale.
Back in western civilization, Tarzan encounters several adventures among card cheats, decadent European noblemen, and blackmailers. Eventually the ape-man is happy to return to Africa, where he resumes his primitive life and also hooks up again with Jane.

Revelation (Metro, 1918)
d: George D. Baker. 7 reels.
Nazimova, Charles Bryant, Frank Currier, Syn de Conde, Bigelow Cooper, John Martin, Eugene Borden, Philip Sanford, True James, Dave Turner, Fred Radcliffe, A.C. Hadley.
Using a flirtatious cabaret dancer, Joline, as his model, a struggling painter makes a breakthrough and attains fame and success. Finally he receives his greatest commission, to paint "the Madonna of the Rosebush," and that experience so moves Joline that she leaves the worldly life and becomes a Red Cross nurse in World War I.
This film was remade by MGM in 1924, with Viola Dana as the dancer/model.

Revelation (MGM, 1924)
w, d: George D. Baker. 9 reels.
Viola Dana, Monte Blue, Lew Cody, Marjorie Daw, Frank Currier, Edward Connelly, Kathleen Key, Ethel Wales, George Siegmann, Otto Matiesen, Bruce Guerin.
A Montmarte apache dancer poses for an American artist, who paints her as the Madonna. The girl is so overwhelmed by the picture, she reforms her wicked ways.
Remake of Metro's 1918 *Revelation*.

Revelations (American Film Co./Mutual, 1916)
d: Arthur Maude. 5 reels.
Constance Crawley, Arthur Maude, William Carroll, Nell Franzen, Madeline Fordyce, Sylvia Ashton, Robert Klein, Jack Farrell.
The daughter of a German army officer goes to Paris, falls in love, and gets pregnant. Though her lover deserts her, the girl has her baby, then studies voice and becomes an operatic star.

Revenge (Metro, 1918)
d: Tod Browning. 5 reels.
Edith Storey, Wheeler Oakman, Ralph Lewis, Alberta Ballard, Charles West.
The fiancée of a murdered man swears revenge on his killer.

Revenge (United Artists, 1928)
d: Edwin Carewe. 7 reels.
Dolores Del Rio, Leroy Mason, James Marcus, Sophia Ortiga, Sam Appel, Rita Carewe, Jess Cavin, José Crespo, Marta Golden.
The fiery daughter of a bear tamer meets her match in a handsome gypsy.

The Revenge of Tarzan—see: The Return of Tarzan (1920).

The Revolt (World Film Corp., 1916)
d: Barry O'Neill. 5 reels.
Frances Nelson, Arthur Ashley, Madge Evans, Clara Whipple, Frank Beamish, Augusta Burmeister, George McQuarrie, Ada Price, Justine Cutting.
Anna, the wife of a philanderer, decides to sow some wild oats of her own.

The Reward of Patience (Famous Players/Paramount, 1916)
d: Robert G. Vignola. 5 reels.
Louise Huff, John Bowers, Lottie Pickford, Kate Lester, Adolphe Menjou, Gertrude Norman.
Patience, a Quaker girl, becomes enamored of a city man. However, he marries a frivolous girl who is more interested in his money than in him, and Patience becomes their nanny when they have a baby. While she nurses the baby, she also nurtures her love for the baby's father... until the inevitable moment when the frivolous wife goes off with another lover, and Daddy sees the light.

The Reward of the Faithless (Universal, 1917)
d: Rex Ingram. 5 reels.
Wedgewood Nowell, Betty Schade, Claire DuBray, Nicholas Dunaew, Richard LeReno, William J. Dyer, Yvette Mitchell, Jim Brown, Bill Rathbone.
To exact revenge from her unfaithful husband, a princess feigns her own death, then comes back to him as another woman and forces him to fall in love with her all over again.

Rich But Honest (Fox, 1927)
d: Albert Ray. 6 reels.
Nancy Nash, Clifford Holland, Charles Morton, J. Farrell MacDonald, Tyler Brooke, Ted McNamara, Marjorie Beebe, Ernie Shields, Doris Lloyd.
At the height of the jazz age, a flapper wins a Charleston contest, gets a role in the theater, and poses as Lady Godiva.

Rich Girl, Poor Girl (Universal, 1921)
d: Harry B. Harris. 5 reels.
Gladys Walton, Gordon McGregor, Harold Austin, Antrim Short, Joe Neary, Wadsworth Harris, Charles W. Herzinger.
Miss Walton has a double role here, as a tenement girl and her lookalike heiress.

Rich Man, Poor Man (Famous Players-Lasky/Paramount, 1918)
d: J. Searle Dawley. 5 reels.
Marguerite Clark, Richard Barthelmess, George Backus, Frederick Warde, J.W. Herbert, Augusta Anderson, Donald Clayton, William Wadsworth, Ottola Nesmith, Mary Davis.
Betty, a hard-working housemaid with a sunny disposition, goes to live with an old millionaire who suspects she may be his long-lost granddaughter.

A Rich Man's Darling (Universal, 1918)
d: Edgar Jones. 5 reels.
Louise Lovely, Philo McCullough, Harry Holden, Edna Maison, Harry Mann.
Infatuated with a picture of a young millionaire, Julie tries to meet him by posing as his father's mistress.

A Rich Man's Plaything (Fox, 1917)
d: Carl Harbaugh. 5 reels.
Valeska Suratt, Edward Martindel, John Dillon, Charles Craig, Robert Cummings, Gladys Kelly.
Lloyd, a millionaire tenement owner, falls for a New England girl who inspires him to improve living conditions for his tenants.

Rich Men's Sons (Columbia, 1927)
d: Ralph Graves. 6 reels.
Ralph Graves, Shirley Mason.
The son of a business tycoon falls for Carla, the daughter of a factory owner.

Rich Men's Wives (Preferred Pictures/Al Lichtman Corp., 1922)
d: Louis J. Gasnier. 7 reels.
House Peters, Claire windsor, Rosemary Theby, Gaston Glass, Myrtle Stedman, Richard Headrick, Mildred June, Charles Clary, Carol Holloway, Martha Mattox, William Austin.
Catching his wife in an innocent flirtation with a guest, the wealthy husband orders her out of his house and forbids her to see their son. But he'll repent.

The Rich Slave (Jaxon Film Corp., 1920)
d: Romaine Fielding. 6 reels.
Mabel Taliaferro, Romaine Fielding, Joseph Smiley, June Day, Arthur Elton, Martha Forrest, Edgar Viller, Ira M. Hards, Herbert Standing Jr., A.H. Busby, Barney Gilmore.
Gladys, who lives in a squalid orphanage, is actually heiress to millions.

Richard the Brazen (Vitagraph, 1917)
d: Perry N. Vekroff. 5 reels.
Harry T. Morey, Alice Joyce, William Frederic, Franklyn Hanna, Robert Kelly, Agnes Eyre, Charles Wellesley, William Bailey.
Richard, a Texan filling in for his British friend, delivers some important contracts to a munitions manufacturer, and falls in love with the industrialist's daughter.

Richard the Lion-Hearted (United Artists, 1923)
d: Chet Withey. 8 reels.
Wallace Beery, Marguerite De La Motte, Kathleen Clifford, Charles Gerrard, John Bowers, Clarence Geldert, Wilbur Highby.
Epic treatment of the story of King Richard and the Crusades.

Richard III (Sterling Camera and Film Co./State Rights, 1912)
d: James Keene. 5 reels.
Frederick Warde, Mr. Gomp, James Keane, Violet Stuart.
Political intrigue, kidnapping, and murder elevate Richard of Gloucester to the British throne. After Richard tries (unsuccessfully) to marry his niece Elizabeth, his strongest supporters desert him, and he is eventually killed in battle.

Originally copyrighted under the wordy title *Mr. Frederick Warde in Shakespeare's Masterpiece "The Life and Death of King*

Richard III", this picture is said to be America's oldest surviving feature film. It was discovered and restored by the American Film Institute in 1996.

The Richest Girl (Empire All Star Corp./Mutual, 1918)
d: Albert Capellani. 5 reels.
Ann Murdock, David Powell, Charles Wellesley, Herbert Ayling, Gladys Wilson, Paul Capellani, Cyril Chadwick.
When an heiress motoring through the country has a flat tire near Paul's cottage, she nonchalantly asks Paul for assistance and shelter for the night. It's all very innocent, but the following morning Paul's fiancée arrives, sees the heiress having breakfast with her sweetie, and storms out. Paul loses a sweetheart, but gains a new love with the heiress.

Riddle Gawne (Famous Players-Lasky/Paramount, 1918)
d: William S. Hart. 5 reels.
William S. Hart, Katherine MacDonald, Lon Chaney, Gretchen Lederer, Gertrude Short, E.B. Tilton, Milton Ross, George Field, Leon Kent.
Out West, a cowpoke searches for the man who killed his brother.

The Riddle: Woman (Associated Exhibitors, Inc./Pathé, 1920)
d: Edward José. 6 reels.
Geraldine Farrar, Montague Love, Adele Blood, William P. Carleton, Frank Losee, Madge Bellamy, Louis Stern.
In New York, two natives of Denmark are happily married... until an old lover of the wife comes to town and threatens to expose their affair to her husband.

Ride 'em High (Action Pictures/Pathé, 1927)
d: Richard Thorpe. 5 reels.
Buddy Roosevelt, Charles K. French, Olive Hasbrouck, Robert Homans, George Magrill.
Out West, a rodeo rider must fight off his own villainous cousin.

Ride for Your Life (Universal, 1924)
d: Edward Sedgwick. 6 reels.
Hoot Gibson, Laura LaPlante, Harry Todd, Robert McKim, Howard Truesdell, Fred Humes, Clark Comstock, Mrs. George Hernandez, William Robert Daly.
Watkins, a ranch owner, loses everything to a crooked gambler... then gets it back by impersonating a notorious criminal.

The Rider of the Law (Universal, 1919)
d: Jack Ford. 6 reels.
Harry Carey, Claire Anderson, Jennie Lee, Vesta Pegg, Ted Brooks, Joe Harris, Jack Woods, Duke Lee, Gloria Hope.
Jim, a former outlaw, becomes a Texas Ranger and rides with the law.

Riders of Mystery (Independent Pictures, 1925)
d: Robert North Bradbury. 5 reels.
Bill Cody, Frank Rice, Tom Lingham, Peggy O'Dare, Mack V. Wright.
Out West, a stagecoach driver is secretly the leader of an outlaw gang.

Riders of the Dark (MGM, 1928)
d: Nick Grinde. 6 reels.
Tim McCoy, Bert Roach, Roy D'Arcy, Rex Lease, Dorothy Dwan, Frank Currier.
The cavalry really *does* come riding to the rescue, when a newspaper editor's daughter is menaced by the bandits who killed her father.

Riders of the Dawn (Zane Grey Pictures, Inc./Pathé, 1920)
d: Hugh Ryan Conway. 6 reels.
Roy Stewart, Claire Adams, Marc Robbins, Joseph J. Dowling, Robert McKim, Frederick Starr, Violet Schram, Frank Brownlee, Marie Messenger, Arthur Morrison.
Kurt, an ex-doughboy, is asked to join "the riders of the dawn," a law enforcement group intent on cracking down on labor agitators.

Riders of the Law (Sunset Productions, 1922)
w, d: Robert North Bradbury. 5 reels.
Jack Hoxie, Frank Rice, Marin Sais.
In the Great Northwest, two adventurers rescue a sheriff and his daughter from imprisonment by smugglers.

Riders of the Night (Metro, 1918)
d: John H. Collins. 5 reels.
Viola Dana, George Cheseboro, Clifford Bruce, Russell Simpson, Mabel Van Buren, Monte Blue.
In the Kentucky hills, settlers are subjected to a series of raids by murdering hoodlums.

Riders of the Purple Sage (Fox, 1918)
d: Frank Lloyd. 7 reels.
William Farnum, William Scott, Marc Robbins, Murdock MacQuarrie, Mary Mersch, Katherine Adams, Nancy Caswell, Charles Clary, Jack Nelson, Buck Jones.
Lassiter, a Texas Ranger, seeks vengeance against the man who kidnapped his sister and forced her to join a sect.
First film version of the famous Zane Grey novel. It would be remade once in the silent era, by Fox in 1925, with Tom Mix as the Texas Ranger.

Riders of the Purple Sage (Fox, 1925)
d: Lynn Reynolds. 6 reels.
Tom Mix, Beatrice Burnham, Arthur Morrison, Seesel Ann Johnson, Warner Oland, Fred Kohler, Charles Newton, Harold Goodwin, Mabel Ballin.
Second film version of the Zane Grey classic, dealing with a cowboy's search for his abducted sister.

Riders of the Rio Grande (J.P. McGowan Productions, 1929)
d: J.P. McGowan. 5 reels.
Bob Custer, Edna Aslin, H.B. Carpenter, Kip Cooper, Bob Erickson, Martin Cichy, Merrill McCormick.
Out West, a professional engraver is forced by a gang to turn out counterfeit money.

Riders of Vengeance (Universal, 1919)
d: Jack Ford. 6 reels.
Harry Carey, Seena Owen, Joseph Harris, Jennie Lee, J. Farrell McDonald, Alfred Allen.
Cheyenne Harry vows to avenge the deaths of his bride and his parents.

Riders Up (Universal, 1924)
d: Irving Cummings. 5 reels.
Creighton Hale, George Cooper, Kate Price, Robert Brower, Ethel Shannon, Edith Yorke, Charlotte Stevens, Harry Tracey, Hank Mann.
In Tijuana, a race track tout charitably gives up his own winnings to help an elderly blind man.

Ridgeway of Montana (Universal, 1924)
d: Clifford Smith. 5 reels.
Jack Hoxie, Olive Hasbrouck, Herbert Fortier, Lew Meehan, Charles Thurston, Pat Harmon, Lyndon Hobart.
In Montana, a cattle man is pursued aggressively by his

neighbor's daughter.

Ridin' Comet (Ben Wilson Productions/FBO of America, 1925)
d: Ben Wilson. 5 reels.
Yakima Canutt, Dorothy Woods, Bob Walker, Bill Donovan, Archie Ricks, William Hackett.
A rancher must fight off land developers while trying to win a gal's affection.

The Ridin' Demon (Universal, 1929)
d: Ray Taylor. 5 reels.
Ted Wells, Kathleen Collins, Lucy Beaumont, Otto Bibber.
Out West, twin brothers Pat and Dan develop wildly different personalities.

The Ridin' Kid from Powder River (Universal, 1924)
d: Edward Sedgwick. 6 reels.
Hoot Gibson, Gladys Hulette, Tully Marshall, Gertrude Astor, Walter Long, Sidney Jordan, William A. Steele, Howard Truesdell, Frank Rice, Nelson McDowell, Fred Humes.
Watkins, a homesteader, falls in love with the daughter of the man who shot his foster father.

Ridin' Luck (Trem Carr Productions/Rayart, 1927)
d: Edward R. Gordon. 5 reels.
Tex Maynard, Ruby Blaine, Jack Anthony, Charles O'Malley, Charles Schaeffer, Art Wilting, Marshall Ruth.
Out West, a rancher's son rescues a girl from assault by a scoundrel, and then saves her brother from a "necktie party."

Ridin' Pretty (Universal, 1925)
d: Arthur Rosson. 5 reels.
William Desmond, Ann Forrest, Stanhope Wheatcroft, Billy Sullivan, Slim Cole, Tex Young, Bill Gillis, Frank Rice.
Parker, an Arizonan, inherits his uncle's estate, but it comes with strings attached. To claim his bequest, he must live in the uncle's San Francisco mansion for one year. Doesn't sound too tough... but Parker's evil cousin tries to scuttle the inheritance with the aid of a vamp. She falls in love with the Arizonan, however, and in the end he asks her to marry him.

The Ridin' Rascal (Universal, 1926)
d: Clifford Smith. 5 reels.
Art Acord, Olive Hasbrouck, Al Jennings.
A homesteader is suspected of cattle rustling.

A Ridin' Romeo (Fox, 1921)
d: George E. Marshall. 5 reels.
Tom Mix, Rhea Mitchell, Pat Chrisman, Sid Jordan, Harry Dunkinson, Eugenie Ford.
Western with comedy overtones, as a cowboy tries to rescue a widow from stagecoach thieves, only to discover that they're all hired actors.

Ridin' Thunder (Universal, 1925)
d: Clifford Smith. 5 reels.
Jack Hoxie, Jack Pratt, Catherine Grant, Francis Ford, George Connors, Bert DeMarc, William McCall, Broderick O'Farrell.
Douglas, an honest rancher, is accused of murder, convicted on circumstantial evidence, and sentenced to hang. In a thrill-a-minute sequence, Douglas' son rides cross-country to obtain the governor's pardon and save his dad's life.

Ridin' Wild (Universal, 1922)
d: Nat Ross. 5 reels.
Hoot Gibson, Edna Murphy, Wade Boteler, Jack Walker, Otto Hoffman, Wilton Taylor, Bert Wilson, Gertrude Claire,

William Welsh.
A Quaker lad is made an object of scorn by the townsfolk when he refuses to fight a bully. But eventually the bully will push the young man too far, and the lamb will show his fangs.

Riding for Fame (Universal, 1928)
d: Reaves Eason. 6 reels.
Hoot Gibson, Ethlyne Clair, Charles K. French, George Summerville, Allan Forrest, Ruth Cherrington, Chet Ryan, Robert Burns.
Out West, a bronco bustin' cowboy is unjustly suspected of theft.

Riding With Death (Fox, 1921)
d: Jacques Jaccard. 5 reels.
Charles Jones, Betty Francisco, Jack Mower, J. Farrell MacDonald, H. Von Sickle, William Steele, William Gettinger, Bill Gillis, Artie Ortega, Tina Medotti.
Dorsey, a Texas Ranger, must solve the murder of his pal.

The Right Direction (Pallas Pictures/Paramount, 1916)
d: E. Mason Hopper. 5 reels.
Vivian Martin, Colin Chase, Herbert Standing, Alfred Hollingsworth, Billy Mason, Baby Jack White, William W. Jefferson.
Angered that his son is romancing Polly, a woman from "the lower class," a mine owner gets her fired from her job. But when his own miners stage a revolt and threaten their employer with violence, Polly is the plucky lady who rescues him.

The Right of the Strongest (Zenith Pictures/Selznick, 1924)
d: Edgar Lewis. 7 reels.
E.K. Lincoln, Helen Ferguson, George Siegmann, Tom Santschi, Robert Milasch, F.B. Phillips, Tully Marshall, James Gibson, Coy Watson, Gertrude Norman, Milla Davenport, Niles Welch, June Elvidge, Beth Kosick, Leonard Clapham.
In a small country town, the residents regard their new neighbor with suspicion. It turns out he's an agent from a utility company, looking to buy land for a dam project.

The Right of Way (Rolfe Photoplays, Inc./Metro, 1915)
d: John W. Noble. 5 reels.
William Faversham, Jane Grey, Edward Brennan, Henry Bergman, Harold DeBecker.
Steele, a brilliant criminal lawyer who is lapsing slowly into alcoholism, hits the skids and is near death when a former client rescues him and takes him to a Canadian village to recuperate.
This film would be remade once in the silent era, by Screen Classics in 1920.

The Right of Way (Screen Classics, Inc./Metro, 1920)
d: Jack Dillon. 7 reels.
Bert Lytell, Gibson Gowland, Leatrice Joy, Virginia Caldwell, Antrim Short, Carmen Phillips, Frank Currier, Henry Harmon, Larry Steers.
After a brilliant but alcoholic attorney is injured in a barroom brawl, he is taken to a small village and meets Rosalie, who will restore his faith in God.
Remake of the Rolfe/Metro 1915 film of the same name.

Right Off the Bat (Arrow Film Corp., 1915)
d: Hugh Reticker. 5 reels.
Roy Hauck, Henry Grady, Fan Bourke, Doris Farrington, George Henry, Mabel Wright, Harry Six, Peter Conroy, Mike Donlin, John J. McGraw, Claire Mersereau, Rita Ross Donlin.
Young Mike Donlin works his way up from poor boy to

mechanic to, eventually, minor league baseball player. His heroics help his team win a tight pennant race, after which he is signed up by a major league scout... and he's finally able to propose to his childhood sweetheart.

The Right That Failed (Metro, 1922)
d: Bayard Veiller. 5 reels.
Bert Lytell, Virginia Valli, DeWitt Jennings, Philo McCullough, Otis Harlan, Max Davidson.
A boxing champion tries to woo a socialite at a summer resort.

The Right to be Happy (Universal, 1916)

d: Rupert Julian. 5 reels.
John Cook, Claire McDowell, Emory Johnson, Rupert Julian, Francis Lee, Harry Carter, Roberta Wilson, Francelia Billington, Wadsworth Harris, Dick LeStrange, Tom Figee.
On Christmas Eve, miserly businessman Ebenezer Scrooge is haunted by the ghost of his old business partner, and by other spectral visitors. They take him back to the days of his childhood and early adulthood, and try to rekindle in Scrooge the fires of human compassion. He responds by changing his grouchy outlook and resolving to help the poor and less fortunate for the rest of his life.
First feature film to be based on Charles Dickens' famous novel *A Christmas Carol*.

The Right to Happiness (Universal, 1919)
d: Allen Holubar. 8 reels.
Dorothy Phillips, William Stowell, Robert Anderson, Henry Barrows, Winter Hall, Margaret Mann, Stanhope Wheatcroft, Alma Bennett, Hector Sarno, Maxine Elliott.
An American businessman living with his twin daughters in Russia finds life increasingly hazardous because of social unrest. During a particularly violent riot, the American escapes with one daughter, Vivian, believing the other twin, Sonia, has been killed. But Sonia survives, and years later she will come to America as a Communist revolutionary and find her father and sister living in capitalistic luxury.
Miss Phillips plays both twins, Vivian and Sonia.

The Right to Lie (Pathé, 1919)
d: Edwin Carewe. 7 reels.
Dolores Cassinelli, Frank Mills, Joseph King, Warren Cook, Grace Reals, George Deneubourg, Claire Grenville, Violet Reed, John A. Boone.
When her husband shoots and kills a blackmailer, Carlotta saves him from a murder conviction by lying on the witness stand that she and the blackmailer were lovers.

The Right to Love (Famous Players-Lasky/Paramount, 1920)
d: George Fitzmaurice. 7 reels.
Mae Murray, Holmes E. Herbert, David Powell, Frank Losee, Alma Tell, Macey Harlam, Marcia Harris, Lawrence Johnson.
In Constantinople, the American wife of an English noblewoman faces disgrace when her husband makes plans to frame her for adultery.

The Right Way (Thomas Mott Osborne/Standard Productions, 1921)
d: Sidney Olcott. 7 reels.
Edwards Davis, Helen Lindroth, Joseph Marquis, Vivienne Osborne, Sidney D'Albrook, Annie Ecleston, Helen Ferguson, Elsie McLeod, Tammany Young, Thomas Brooks.
Stark prison-reform drama, about the harsh methods used in dealing with some prisoners.

The Rights of Man: A Story of War's Red Blotch (Lubin, 1915)
d: John H. Pratt. 5 reels.
George Clark, Richard Buhler, Rosetta Brice, Francis Joyner, Charles Brandt, Walter Law, Florence Williams, Margaret Moore, Marie Sterling, Clara Lambert, Richard Wangemann.
War drama about a self-sacrificing princess who marries an American doctor, but continues to carry out her father's agenda in war-torn Europe.

Riley of the Rainbow Division (Anchor Film Distributors, 1928)
d: Robert Ray. 6 reels.
Creighton Hale, Al Alt, Pauline Garon, Joan Standing, Jack Carlyle, Lafayette McKee, Rolfe Sedan, Jack Raymond.
Comedy about a couple of doughboys in training camp, who get tossed into the brig on the day they were planning to marry their girlfriends. Not to be dissuaded, the girls gain admission to the camp by disguising themselves as soldiers.

Riley the Cop (Fox, 1928)
d: John Ford. 6 reels.
Farrell MacDonald, Louise Fazenda, Nancy Drexel, David Rollins, Harry Schultz, Mildred Boyd, Ferdinand Schumann-Heink, Del Henderson, Mike Donlin, Russell Powell, Tom Wilson, Billy Bevan, Otto Fries.
Riley, a likeable street cop, is sent on a special mission to Europe to bring back an escaped fugitive from justice.

Rimrock Jones (Lasky Feature Plays/Paramount, 1918)
d: Donald Crisp. 5 reels.
Wallace Reid, Anna Little, Charles Ogle, Paul Hurst, Guy Oliver, Fred Huntley, Edna Mae Cooper, Tote DuCrow, Gustav Von Seyffertitz, Ernest Joy, George Kuwa, Mary Mersch.
Out West, Rimrock Jones discovers copper in his mine, then must fight off poachers with designs both on his mine and his girlfriend.

Rinty of the Desert (Warner Bros., 1928)
d: D. Ross Lederman. 5 reels.
Rin-Tin-Tin, Audrey Ferris, Paul Panzer, Otto Hoffman, Carol Nye.
The irrepressible Rinty comes through again, leading a police detective to an underworld lair where scoundrels are holding a museum owner captive.

Rio Grande (Edwin Carewe Productions, Inc./Pathé, 1920)
d: Edwin Carewe. 7 reels.
Rosemary Theby, George Stone, Allan Sears, Peaches Jackson, Hector V. Sarno, Adele Farrington, Arthur Carew, Harry S. Duffield.
Separated in childhood, a Mexican girl and her American foster brother find themselves on opposite sides in a border war.

Rip Roarin' Roberts (Approved Pictures/Artclass Pictures, 1924)
d: Richard Thorpe. 5 reels.
Buddy Roosevelt, Brenda Lane, Joe Rickson, Al Richmond, John Webb Dillon, Bert Lindley, Lew Bennett.
Out West, a deputy sheriff searches for an elusive criminal known only as "The Hawk."

The Rip Snorter (Ben Wilson Productions/Arrow Pictures, 1925)
d: Ward Hayes. 5 reels.
Dick Hatton, Archie Ricks, William Rhine, Robert Walker, Milburn Morante, Robert McGowan, Marilyn Mills, Emma

Gertes.

Meadows, a bronco buster, rides to his girlfriend's aid when he learns she is being held against her will to become the bride of a dishonest ranch foreman.

Rip Van Winkle (B.A. Rolfe Photoplays, Inc., 1914)
d: John W. Noble. 5 reels.
Thomas Jefferson, Clairet Claire, H.D. Blackmore, Daisy Robinson, Wallace Scott, William Cavanaugh, William Chamberlain, Loel Stewart, Maurice Stewart.
Dramatization of the famous short story by Washington Irving, about a layabout who meets strange little mountain people who give him a drink that puts him to sleep for 20 years.

The Rip Tide (A.B. Maescher/Arrow Film Corp., 1923)
d: Jack Pratt. 6 reels.
Dick Sutherland, George Rigas, J. Frank Glendon, Stuart Holmes, Russell Simpson, Rosemary Theby, Diana Alden.
A prince of India goes to England, learns British ways, and becomes a minister in the Church of England.

The Rise of Jennie Cushing (Famous Players-Lasky/Artcraft, 1917)
d: Maurice Tourneur. 5 reels.
Elsie Ferguson, Elliott Dexter, Fania Marinoff, Frank Goldsmith, Sallie Delatore, Mae Bates, Edith McAlpin, Isabel Vernon.

Jennie, a street urchin, is a scrapper who winds up in reform school. Upon her release she decides to "go straight," studies at a beauty academy, and becomes a lady's maid. But upon receiving a proposal of marriage, Jennie decides that her sordid past would be too big a burden for the young man to bear, and rejects him. She'll change her mind.

The Rise of Susan (World Film Corp., 1916)
d: S.E.V. Taylor. 5 reels.
Clara Kimball Young, Jenny Dickerson, Warner Oland, Marguerite Skirwin, Eugene O'Brien.
Susan, a shopgirl, agrees to impersonate a countess at a socialite's dinner party... never knowing that at the gathering, she'll meet and fall in love with Mr. Right.

Risky Business (Universal, 1920)
d: Harry B. Harris. 5 reels.
Gladys Walton, Fred Malatesta, Lillian Lawrence, Maude Wayne, Nanine Wright, Grant McKay, John Gough, Louis Willoughby, Fred Andrews.
Mrs. Renwick, a wealthy socialite, holds a masquerade party at her lavish estate. But one of the invited guests, a Captain Chantry, is really a society thief with designs on the Renwick jewels.

Risky Business (DeMille Pictures/Producers Distributing Corp., 1926)
d: Alan Hale. 7 reels.
Vera Reynolds, ZaSu Pitts, Ethel Clayton, Kenneth Thomson, Ward Crane, Lous Natheaux, George Irving, Louise Cabo.
The course of true love runs, but not smoothly, through the lives of a country doctor and his pampered inamorata.

The Risky Road (Universal, 1918)
d: Ida May Park. 5 reels.
Dorothy Phillips, William Stowell, Juanita Hansen, Claire DuBrey, George Cheseboro, Edward Cecil, Joseph Girard, Sally Starr.
Marjorie, a steno of solid moral character, meets a millionaire whose intentions may not be honorable.

Ritzy (Paramount, 1927)
d: Richard Rosson. 6 reels.
Betty Bronson, James Hall, William Austin, Joan Standing, George Nichols, Roscoe Karns.
Ritzy is an American girl who yearns to become a duchess. Fat chance, in her country, right? But soon she meets a real British duke, who's young, single, and looking for love.

The River (Fox, 1929)
d: Frank Borzage. 7 reels. (Music score, part talkie.)
Charles Farrell, Mary Duncan, Ivan Linow, Margaret Mann, Alfred Sabato, Bert Woodruff.
Allen, a young man with a barge, floats it down the river and meets his dream girl... but she's the former mistress of a condemned murderer.

The River of Romance (Yorke Film Corp./Metro, 1916)
d: Henry Otto. 5 reels.
Harold Lockwood, May Allison, Lester Cuneo, Bert Busby, Lee Walker, Mathilde Brundage, Lillian Halpern, Phil Masi, Dan Hanlon.
Rosalind goes on a river cruise and falls for the boat captain.

The River Pirate (Fox, 1928)
d: William K. Howard. 7 reels.
Victor McLaglen, Lois Moran, Nick Stuart, Earle Foxe, Donald Crisp, Robert Perry.
In reform school, young Sandy learns from a former convict the "art" of robbing warehouses. He'll ply that trade until love steps in, in the form of a detective's daughter who urges Sandy to go straight.

The River Woman (Gotham Productions, 1928)
d: Joseph Henabery. 7 reels.
Lionel Barrymore, Charles Delaney, Mary Doran, Sheldon Lewis, Jacqueline Logan, Harry Todd.
Melodrama about Lefty, a tough saloon owner who loves a cabaret hostess but discovers she is devoted to the piano player he has just hired.

The River's End (Marshall Neilan Productions/First National, 1920)
d: Marshall Neilan, Victor Heerman. 6 reels.
Lewis Stone, Marjorie Daw, Jane Novak, J. Barney Sherry, George Nichols, Charles West, Togo Yamamoto.
In the Canadian northwest, a mountie and his captive exchange places.
Lewis Stone plays both roles, that of the mountie and his lookalike prisoner.

The Road Between (Erbograph Co./Art Dramas, Inc., 1917)
d: Joseph Levering. 5 reels.
Marian Swayne, Bradley Barker, Armand Cortes, Gladys Fairbanks, Frank Andrews, Kirke Brown, Sallie Tyscher.
Martin, a chemist who has fought poverty for years, finally develops a formula that makes him and his family wealthy. But now that they've moved up the economic ladder, they face new predators: society cheats.

The Road Called Straight (Betzwood Film Co./Goldwyn, 1919)
d: Ira M. Lowry. 5 reels.
Louis Bennison, Ormi Hawley, Henry Mortimer, Burton Churchill, Jane Adler, John Daly Murphy.
Betty, a girl from an upscale Chicago family, marries a wealthy cattle rancher, but considers her new husband her social inferior, and keeps her distance from him. Impetuously, she reaches out to her old beau... but when he tries to force his attentions on her and her husband stops

him, Betty gains new respect for her man.

The Road Demon (Fox, 1921)
d: Lynn Reynolds. 5 reels.
Tom Mix, Claire Anderson, Charles K. French, George Hernandez, Lloyd Bacon, Sid Jordan, Charles Arling, Harold Goodwin, Billy Elmer, Frank Tokawaja, Lee Phelps.
Higgins, an automobile enthusiast, acquires a jalopy and turns it into one of the finest racing machines in the West.

Road House (Fox, 1928)
d: Richard Rosson, James Kevin McGuinness. 5 reels.
Maria Alba, Warren Burke, Lionel Barrymore, Julia Swayne Gordon, Tempe Piggott, Florence Allen, Eddie Clayton, Jack Oakie, Jane Keckley, Joe Brown, Kay Bryant.
At a road house that caters to a jazz-age crowd, young Grayson falls head over heels for Marla, a vamp.

The Road of Ambition (Selznick/National Picture Theatres, Inc., 1920)
d: William P.S. Earle. 6 reels.
Conway Tearle, Florence Dixon, Gladden James, Florence Billings, Arthur Housman, Tom Brooks, Tom McGuire, Adolph Milar.
Bill, a steel mill foreman, perfects a new labor-saving device and becomes wealthy. Now that he has money, he'd like to break into high society, but finds that road narrow and treacherous.

The Road Through the Dark (Clara Kimball Young Film Corp./Select, 1918)
d: Edmund Mortimer. 5 reels.
Clara Kimball Young, Jack Holt, Henry Woodward, Elinor Fair, Bobby Connelly, John Steppling, Lillian Leighton, Edward M. Kimball, Elmo Lincoln, Eugenie Besserer.
During World War I, a French girl is forced to become a German officer's mistress, but she remains loyal to the Allied cause.

The Road to Arcady—see: For Love or Money (1920)

The Road to Arcady (J.W. Film Corp., 1922)
d: Burton King. 5 reels.
Virginia Lee, Harry Benham, Roger Lytton, Stephen Gratton, Julia Swayne Gordon, Mildred Wayne, Hugh Huntley.
Helen, a social climber, forces her daughter to marry a millionaire although the girl is in love with a working-class chap.
Remake of the 1920 Hallmark Pictures film *For Love or Money*.

The Road to Divorce (Universal, 1920)
d: Philip Rosen. 5 reels.
Mary MacLaren, Edward Pell, Bonnie Hill, William Ellingford, Alberta Lee, Eugenie Forde, Gloria Holt, Arthur Redden, Ray Stecker, Helen Davidge.
The marriage of newlyweds Mary and Myron is threatened when her stylish girlfriend arrives for a visit.

The Road to France (World Film Corp., 1918)
d: Dell Henderson. 7 reels.
Carlyle Blackwell, Evelyn Greeley, Jack Drumier, Muriel Ostriche, George DeCarlton, Jane Sterling, Richard R. Neill, Inez Shannon, Henry West, Alex K. Shannon, Joseph Smiley.
A wastrel is disinherited by his father and rejected by the draft board. Nevertheless he pulls himself together and gets a job in a defense plant, where he discovers that three of his coworkers are actually German spies.

The Road to Glory (Fox, 1926)

d: Howard Hawks. 6 reels.
May McAvoy, Leslie Fenton, Ford Sterling, Rockliffe Fellowes, Milla Davenport, John MacSweeney.
Judith, depressed over having lost both her father and her eyesight, denounces God and moves to a remote mountain village. But her fiancé David, still in love with Judith despite her blindness, goes looking for her and is badly injured during a storm. In working to nurse his wounds, Judith realizes how much she loves this young man, and prays for his recovery. Through the power of prayer—and of love— David's wounds are healed and Judith's eyesight is restored.

The Road to Love (Oliver Morosco Photoplay Co./Paramount, 1916)
d: Scott Sidney. 5 reels.
Lenore Ulrich, Colin Chase, Lucille Ward, Estelle Allen, Alfred Vosburgh, Herschell Mayall, Joe Massey, Alfred Hollingsworth.
Gordon, an American adventurer in Algiers, falls for a local girl, Hafsa.

The Road to Mandalay (MGM, 1926)
d: Tod Browning. 7 reels.
Lon Chaney, Owen Moore, Lois Moran, Sojin, Henry B. Walthall.
Partners in crime have a falling out over a girl.

The Road to Romance (MGM, 1927)
d: John S. Robertson. 7 reels.
Ramon Novarro, Marceline Day, Marc McDermott, Roy D'Arcy, Cesare Gravina, Bobby Mack, Otto Matiesen, Jules Cowles.
Romance and adventure mingle in this tale of a Spanish soldier of fortune who arrives at a Cuban isle and falls in love with Serafina, a girl being held captive by the island's governor.

The Road to Ruin (Cliff Broughton Productions, 1928)
d: Norton S. Parker. 6 reels.
Helen Foster, Grant Withers, Florence Turner, Charles Miller, Virginia Roye, Tom Carr, Don Rader.
Seamy saga about a girl who goes down the primrose path, big time. She becomes addicted to alcohol and tobacco, has numerous affairs, is arrested during a strip poker game, and finally turns to prostitution.

The Road to Yesterday (DeMille Pictures/Producers Distributing Corp., 1925)
d: Cecil B. DeMille. 10 reels.
William Boyd, Joseph Schildkraut, Jetta Goudal, Junior Coghlan, Vera Reynolds.
A train wreck magically transports the passengers back through time to medieval days.

Roads of Destiny (Goldwyn, 1921)
d: Frank Lloyd. 5 reels.
Pauline Frederick, John Bowers, Richard Tucker, Jane Novak, Hardee Kirkland, Willard Louis, Maude George, Maurice B. Flynn.
Two brothers vie for the love of the same woman.

A Roadside Impresario (Pallas Pictures/Paramount, 1917)
d: Donald Crisp. 5 reels.
George Beban, Harrison Ford, Joseph E. Melville, Julia Faye, Fred Huntley, W.A. Carrol, Adele Farrington, Bruno the bear.
In Italy, a strolling musician with a daughter and a dancing bear tries to rescue a shipwrecked stranger. He not only fails in the rescue attempt but loses his daughter as well. Years

later, the musician journeys to America and joyfully discovers that his daughter is alive and well... and engaged to marry the "stranger" he tried to rescue.

A Roaring Adventure   (Universal, 1925)
d: Clifford Smith.   5 reels.
Jack Hoxie, Mary McAllister, Marin Sais, J. Gordon Russell, Jack Pratt, Francis Ford, Margaret Smith.
Duffy, an eastern tenderfoot, returns to his western home and learns that cattle rustlers are on the verge of ruining his rancher father.

Roaring Fires   (Ellbee Pictures, 1927)
d: W.T. Lackey.   6 reels.
Roy Stewart, Alice Lake, Lionel Belmore, Bert Berkeley, Raymond Turner, Spottiswoode Aitken, Robert Walker.
Sylvia, a wealthy young woman with a strong social conscience, tries to pressure slumlords into making their firetrap tenements safe.

Roaring Rails   (Stellar Productions/Producers Distributing Corp., 1924)
d: Tom Forman.   6 reels.
Harry Carey, Frankie Darro, Edith Roberts, Wallace MacDonald, Frank Hagney.
Bill, a railroad engineer, has adopted a war orphan. When the child is injured during an explosion and loses his sight, Bill decides the boy needs a mother, and sets out to woo the foreman's daughter. In the end, Bill saves the railroad by driving his engine through a raging forest fire, he marries the girl, and his adoptive son's sight is restored by an operation paid for by the grateful railroad president.

The Roaring Road   (Famous Players-Lasky/Paramount, 1919)
d: James Cruze.   5 reels.
Wallace Reid, Ann Little, Theodore Roberts, Guy Oliver, Clarence Geldart, Jack Duffy.
A young racing-car enthusiast uses ingenuity and a bit of luck to win a major road race, but gets no respect from the president of the company that manufactured the car. The exec's daughter loves the young man and they want to get married, but Papa refuses to bestow his blessing. Things get a bit sticky, however, when Papa sees the opportunity to set a new land speed record, and he needs his daughter's suitor as the driver. Will the young man swallow his pride? Will Papa swallow his? Stay tuned....

Robes of Sin   (William Russell Productions/Jans Productions, 1924)
d: Russell Allen.   6 reels.
Sylvia Breamer, Jack Mower, Lassie Lou Ahern, Bruce Gordon, Gertrude Astor, Helene Sullivan, William Buckley.
Rogens, a federal agent trying to break up a gang of bootleggers, is neglectful of his wife and doesn't even realize it, until he finds her dallying with one of the gang.

Robin Hood   (Fairbanks/United Artists, 1922)
d: Allan Dwan.   11 reels.
Douglas Fairbanks, Wallace Beery, Enid Bennett, Sam DeGrasse, Paul Dickey.
Robin, the outlaw of Sherwood Forest, battles to unseat the pretender Prince John and prepare for King Richard's return from the crusades.

Rocking Moon   (Metropolitan Pictures/Producers distributing Corp., 1926)
d: George Melford.   7 reels.
Lilyan Tashman, John Bowers, Rockliffe Fellowes, Laska Winters, Luke Cosgrave, Eugene Pallette.
On an island off the coast of Alaska, a young female owner of a fox ranch hires an adventurer to protect her property from pelt poachers.

Rogues and Romance   (George B. Setiz Productions/Pathé, 1920)
d: George B. Seitz.   6 reels.
June Caprice, George B. Seitz, Harry Semels, Marguerite Courtot, William P. Burt, Frank Redman.
Hot gypsy blood intrudes on the romance between a Spaniard and an American girl, when the fiery Carmelita warns Pedro she will knife him if she sees them together.

A Rogue's Romance   (Vitagraph, 1919)
d: James Young.   5 reels.
Earle Williams, Brinsley Shaw, Harry Van Meter, Maude George, Herbert Standing, Sidney Franklin, Katherine Adams, Karl Formes, Rudolpho de Valentina, Marion Skinner, Harry Dunkinson, Peaches Jackson, Jenette Trebol, Gladys McMurray.
Picard, a master criminal, gives up his life of crime for the love of a good woman.

Rolled Stockings   (Paramount, 1927)
d: Richard Rosson.   7 reels.
James Hall, Louise Brooks, Richard Arlen, Nancy Phillips, El Brendel, David Torrence, Chance Ward.
At college, two brothers are in love with the same vampish coed.

Rolling Home   (Universal, 1926)
d: William A. Seiter.   7 reels.
Reginald Denny, Marian Nixon, E.J. Ratcliffe, Ben Hendricks Jr., Margaret Seddon, George Nichols, Alfred Allen, C.E. Thurston, George F. Marion, Alfred Knott, Anton Vaverka, Howard Enstedt, Adele Watson.
Comedy about Nat, an exuberant promoter who can't seem to promote success for himself. He fails in a business deal and gets thrown out of his office by his millionaire boss. Playing a hunch, Nat buys the local power franchise with a rubber check, then accepts a higher offer from a plutocrat eager to get in on the deal... thus covering his own bad check.   Oh yes, and there's a girl too, who loves Nat regardless of his yo-yoing economic situation.

Rolling Stones   (Famous Players/Paramount, 1916)
d: Del Henderson.   5 reels.
Owen Moore, Marguerite Courtot, Denham Maley, Alan Hale, Gretchen Hartman, W.J. Butler, Ida Fitzhugh.
Comedic tale about a strange inheritance: Jerry and Norma must marry each other in order to inherit, and if either of them marries someone else, the unmarried heir will get the entire estate. But Jerry gets married before he learns about the provisions of the will. What now?

Roman Candles   (Master Pictures, 1920)
d: Jack Pratt.   5 reels.
J. Frank Glendon, Phalba Morgan, Edward M. Kimball, Hector Sarno, Sidney D'Albrook, Jack Pratt, Mechtilde Price, Lola Smith, William Connant, Jack Waldermeyer.
John, a struggling fireworks manufacturer, needs to move merchandise, fast. So he journeys to the republic of Santa Maria, where a successful revolution has just taken place, and the populace needs fireworks for the celebration. It's a sale! But once there, John falls in love with Zorra, the daughter of the ousted president, and determines to engineer a second revolution to restore Zorra's dad... and

sell more fireworks.

Romance (United Artists, 1920)
d: Chet Withey. 7 reels.
Basil Sydney, Doris Keane, June Ellen Terry, Arthur Rankin, Betty Ross Clarke, Amelia Summerville, Vangie Valentine, A.J. Herbert, Gilda Varesi, John Davidson.
When Harry falls in love with an actress and decides to propose, his uncle the bishop tries to discourage the romance, citing his own failed love affair with an opera singer, years before.

Romance and Arabella (Select, 1919)
d: Walter Edwards. 5 reels.
Harrison Ford, Constance Talmadge, Gertrude Claire, Monte Blue, Antrim Short, James Neill, Arthur Carew.
Young widow Arabella is determined that her second marriage will provide her with the romantic flair that was lacking in her first.

Romance Land (Fox, 1923)
d: Edward Sedgwick. 5 reels.
Tom Mix, Barbara Bedford, Frank Brownlee, George Webb, Pat Chrisman, Wynn Mace.
Hawkins, a romance-minded westerner, falls for a rancher's daughter and must win her hand by competing against his rival in an athletic tournament.

The Romance of a Million Dollars (J.G. Bachmann/Preferred Pictures, 1926)
d: Tom Terriss. 6 reels.
Glenn Hunter, Alyce Mills, Gaston Glass, Jane Jennings, Bobby Watson, Lea Penman, Thomas Brooks.
Breck, a former doughboy, returns from the war to find that his uncle has died and left him a considerable sum of money. But his inheritance is under a cloud because Breck is suspected of robbing a guest. To clear his name and win the hand of the army nurse he's fallen in love with, Breck must solve the robbery and bring the true culprit to justice.

Romance of a Rogue (A. Carlos/Quality Distributing Corp., 1928)
d: King Baggot. 6 reels.
H.B. Warner, Anita Stewart, Alfred Fisher, Charles Gerrard, Fred Esmelton, Billy Franey.
Bitter melodrama about a man who is unjustly imprisoned on the eve of his wedding, and his revenge against the false friend who betrayed him.

A Romance of Billy Goat Hill (Universal, 1916)
d: Lynn Reynolds. 5 reels.
Myrtle Gonzales, Val Paul, Joseph Jefferson, George Hernandez, Fred Church, Frankie Lee, Jack Connelly, Jack Curtis.
When the only apparent witness to a gunfight leaves town, he is immediately made the primary suspect. But he didn't do it, and will be acquitted when exonerated by a surprise witness.

A Romance of Happy Valley (Famous Players-Lasky/Paramount,1919)
d: D.W. Griffith. 6 reels.
Lillian Gish, Robert Harron, Lydia Yeamans Titus, Kate Bruce, George Fawcett, George Nicholls, Adolphe Lestina, Bertram Grassby, Porter Strong, Frances Sparks.

A country boy makes good in the big city, then returns home after several years to find his loved ones suffering. His embittered father, not recognizing his own son, plans to murder the new arrival and steal his money.

The Romance of Tarzan (National Film Corp. Of America, 1918)
d: Wilfred Lucas. 7 reels.
Elmo Lincoln, Enid Markey, Cleo Madison, Thomas Jefferson, Colin Kenny, Nigel de Brulier, Monte Blue, Clyde Benson, Phil Dunham, Gordon Griffith, John Cook.
Lord Greystoke, reared in the African jungle by apes and now known as Tarzan, falls in love with Jane Porter after he saves her from being mauled by a lion.

A Romance of the Redwoods (Artcraft, 1917)
d: Cecil B. DeMille. 7 reels.
Mary Pickford, Elliott Dexter, Charles Ogle, Tully Marshall, Raymond Hatton, Walter Lang, Winter Hall.
Jenny goes West and falls in love with an outlaw. The outlaw is kind to her, however, and affection grows between them. When he is arrested and sentenced to hang, Jenny devises a clever way to save him: She displays some doll's clothes and declares that she and the outlaw are having a baby.

Romance of the Underworld (Fox, 1928)
d: Irving Cummings. 7 reels.
Mary Astor, Ben Bard, Robert Elliott, John Boles, Oscar Apfel, Helen Lynch, William H. Tooker.
Melodrama about Judith, a simple country girl who goes to the big city and is lured into a life of prostitution.

The Romance Promoters (Vitagraph, 1920)
d: Chester Bennett. 5 reels.
Earle Williams, Helen Ferguson, Charles Wyngate, Tom McGuire, Jack Matheis, Ernest Pasque, Parker McConnell, Mary Huntress, Otis Harlan.
When Betty, a charming lass, appears likely to inherit a fortune, she is besieged by opportunists, frauds, and other greedy suitors... but her dad devises a plan to find the worthiest man for his daughter, and he's none of the above.

Romance Ranch (Fox, 1924)
d: Howard M. Mitchell. 5 reels.
John Gilbert, Virginia Brown Faire, John Miljan, Bernard Siegel, Evelyn Selbie.
Squatters occupy a ranch, but the rightful owner plans to evict them. That is, until he sets eyes on Carmen, the family's lovely daughter.

Romance Road (Granada Productions/Truart Film Corp., 1925)
d: Fred Windemere. 5 reels.
Raymond McKee, Billy Bletcher, Marjorie Meadows, Dick Gordon, Gertrude Claire, Billy Fletcher.
Patrick, a war veteran, comes home and invents a revolutionary new carburetor. When his invention makes him wealthy, Patrick gets up the nerve to propose to Mary, a lovely girl from a prominent family.

A Romantic Adventuress (Famous Players-Lasky/Paramount, 1920)
d: Harley Knoles. 5 reels.
Dorothy Dalton, Charles Meredith, Howard Lang, Augusta Anderson, Ivo Dawson, John Ardizoni, Robert Schable, Lewis Broughton.
Alice is a successful stage dancer, but she'll have to do extra fancy footwork to avoid the forced marriage her mother and stepfather have planned for her.

The Romantic Age (Columbia, 1927)

d: Robert Florey. 6 reels.

Eugene O'Brien, Alberta Vaughn, Bert Woodruff, Stanley Taylor.

A girl's guardian makes plans to marry her, but finds the bridal path obstructed by his ne'er-do-well younger brother.

The Romantic Journey (Astra Film Corp./Pathé, 1916)
d: George Fitzmaurice. 5 reels.

William Courtenay, Macey Harlan, Alice Dovey, Norman Thorpe.

By hypnotizing a young widow, an East Indian mystery man plans to secure her late husband's vast fortune... but the young man who's in love with her steps in to foil the mystic's plans.

Romeo and Juliet (Quality Pictures Corp./Metro, 1916)
d: John W. Noble. 8 reels.

Francis X. Bushman, Beverly Bayne, Horace Vinton, John Davidson, Eric Hudson, Edmund Elton, Leonard Grover, Fritz Leiber, Olaf Skavlan, W. Lawson Butt, Robert Cummings.

First feature film version of Shakespeare's tragic tale of star-crossed lovers.

This film was apparently produced simultaneously with the Fox version of the same play. The Metro version debuted in theaters October 23, 1916, beating Fox to the screen by less than one week.

Romeo and Juliet (Fox, 1916)
d: J. Gordon Edwards. 7 reels.

Theda Bara, Harry Hilliard, Glen White, Walter Law, John Webb Dillon, Einar Linden, Edwin Eaton, Edwin Holt, Alice Gale, Victory Bateman, Jane Lee, Helen Tracy.

Silent feature film version of the Shakespeare play about feuding families and the tragedy that befalls two young people who dare to love across the battle lines.

Romola (Inspiration/MGM, 1924)
d: Henry King. 12 reels.

Lillian Gish, Dorothy Gish, Ronald Colman, William H. Powell, Charles Lane, Herbert Grimwood, Bonaventura Ibanez, Frank Puglia, Amelia Summerville, Tina Ceccacci Renaldi, Eduilio Mucci, Angelo Scatigna, Alfredo Bertone, Ugo Uccellini, Alfredo Martinelli, Gino Borsi, Pietro Nistri, Isabella Romanoff.

Tragic drama about a Florentine peasant girl tricked into a mock marriage.

The Roof Tree (Fox, 1921)
d: John Francis Dillon. 5 reels.

William Russell, Florence Deshon, Sylvia Breamer, Robert Daly, Arthur Morrison, Al Fremont.

In the Kentucky hills, love blossoms between Dorothy and Ken, the latter being accused of killing his brother-in-law. The charge is false, however, and in the end the mystery is solved.

Rookies (MGM, 1927)
d: Sam Wood. 7 reels.

Karl Dane, George K. Arthur, Marceline Day, Louise Lorraine, Tom O'Brien, Frank Currier, E.H. Calvert, Charles Sullivan, Lincoln Stedman, Gene Stone.

Comedy about two soldiers: one, a professional dancer who is thought to be effeminate; the other, his rough-hewn sergeant. In a spectacular action scene, the ex-dancer parachutes to the rescue of the sergeant and his girlfriend when they are trapped in a runaway balloon.

The Rookie's Return (T.H. Ince/Famous Players-Lasky/Paramount, 1921)
d: Jack Nelson. 5 reels.

Douglas MacLean, Doris May, Frank Currier, Leo White, Kathleen Kay, Aggie Herring, Elinor Hancock, Frank Clark, Wallace Beery, Aggie Herring.

James, a youngster who served in the War, inherits a large estate from his aunt.

Room and Board (Realart Pictures/Paramount, 1921)
d: Alan Crosland. 5 reels.

Constance Binney, Tom Carrigan, Malcolm Bradley, Arthur Housman, Jed Prouty, Blanche Craig, Ben Hendricks Jr., Ellen Cassidy, Arthur Barry.

Lady Noreen, the penniless owner of an old castle in Ireland, finds she must rent it out in order to meet her bills. She stays with the castle when tenants move in, pretending to be the housemaid... and falls in love with her new tenant.

Roped (Universal, 1919)
d: Jack Ford. 6 reels.

Harry Carey, Neva Gerber, Molly McConnell, Arthur Shirley, J. Farrell McDonald.

A wealthy rancher is tricked into marriage with a New York socialite, but he learns to love her and they have a child. Then, treachery enters the picture through the rancher's greedy mother-in-law and an embittered rival for his wife's affections.

The Rosary (Selig Polyscope, 1915)
d: Colin Campbell. 7 reels.

Kathlyn Williams, Charles Clary, Wheeler Oakman, Gertrude Ryan, Eugenie Besserer, Harry Lonsdale, Roland Sharp, Frank Clark, Sidney Smith, Fred Huntly, Utahna LaReno.

Father Kelly, an Irish priest, settles in New York and helps to send a young man to college. Out of gratitude, the now prosperous young man builds a cathedral.

The Rosary (Selig-Rork Productions/Associated First National, 1922)
d: Jerome Storm. 7 reels.

Lewis S. Stone, Jane Novak, Wallace Beery, Robert Gordon, Eugenie Besserer, Dore Davidson, Pomeroy Cannon, Bert woodruff, Mildred June, Harold Goodwin.

Remake of the 1915 Selig Polyscope film *The Rosary*, both versions based on the play of the same name by Edward E. Rose.

Rose Marie (MGM, 1927)
d: Lucien Hubbard. 8 reels.

Joan Crawford, James Murray, House Peters, Creighton Hale, Gibson Gowland.

In the Canadian northwest, the daughter of a trading post owner loves a trapper who's on the wrong side of the law.

Rose o' Paradise (Paralta Plays, Inc./General Film, 1918)
d: James Young. 6 reels.

Bessie Barriscale, Howard Hickman, David M. Hartford, Norman Kerry, Edythe Chapman, William Delmar, Lucille Young, Arthur Allardt.

Virginia, a young girl who is due to come into her inheritance on her 18th birthday, is shunted about by her scheming guardian, who wants to get his hands on her fortune.

Rose o' the River (Famous Players-Lasky/Paramount, 1919)
d: Robert Thornby. 5 reels.

Lila Lee, Darrell Foss, George Fisher, Robert Brower,

Josephine Crowell, Sylvia Ashton, Jack Brammall.
Rose, a naive country girl, falls in love with a lumberjack, but is dissuaded from seeing him by a duplicitous scoundrel.

The Rose of Blood (Fox, 1917)
d: J. Gordon Edwards.
Theda Bara, Richard Ordynski, Charles Clary, Herschel Mayall, Marie Keirnan, Bert Turner, Genevieve Blinn, Joe King, Hector V. Sarno.
In Russia, a princess secretly dedicated to the revolution quietly assassinates those who stand in its way, and leaves a red rose on each victim.

The Rose of Kildare (Gotham Productions/Lumas Film Corp., 1927)
d: Dallas M. Fitzgerald. 7 reels.
Helene Chadwick, Pat O'Malley, Henry B. Walthall, Lee Moran, Edwin J. Brady, Ena Gregory, Carroll Nye.

Eileen, an Irish singer whose fiancé left for South Africa and never returned, mourns his passing until one day she is booked to appear at a dance hall in that country. There, she runs into her former beloved and learns that he is married.

The Rose of Nome (Fox, 1920)
d: Edward J. LeSaint. 5 reels.
Gladys Brockwell, William Scott, Herbert Prior, Gertrude Ryan, Edward Peel, Stanton Heck, Frank Thorne, Lule Warrenton, Georgie Woodthorpe.
In the frozen northwest, Rose and Jack, a couple fleeing from her husband, settle in Nome and open a dance hall.

The Rose of Paris (Universal, 1923)
d: Irving Cummings. 7 reels.
Mary Philbin, Robert Cain, John Sainpolis, Rose Dione, Dorothy Revier, D.J. Mitsoras, Gino Corrado, Charles Puffy, Frank Currier, Cesare Gravina.
A convent-bred girl is rightful heir to a fortune, but finds that claiming the estate is easier said than done.

Rose of the Alley (Rolfe Photoplays, Inc./Metro, 1916)
d: Charles Horan. 5 reels.
Mary Miles Minter, Daniel B. Hogan, Frederick Heck, Geraldine Berg, Allen Edwards, Thomas J. Carrigan.
Nell, a girl who's loyal to a fault, defends her drunken criminal of a brother.

Rose of the Bowery (David M. Hartford Productions/American Cinema Corp., 1927)
d: Bertram Bracken. 6 reels.
Johnny Walker, Edna Murphy, Mildred Harris.
When a young woman leaves her husband and hides her baby girl in a black bag, that bag is taken by crooks who think it's filled with money.

Rose of the Golden West (First National, 1927)
d: George Fitzmaurice. 7 reels.
Mary Astor, Gilbert Roland, Gustav von Seyffertitz, Montagu Love, Flora Finch, Harvey Clark, Roel Muriel, André Cheron, Romaine Fielding, Thur Fairfax, William Conklin.
In Old California, a patriot loves a convent-bred rich girl.

Rose of the Rancho (Lasky Feature Plays/Paramount, 1914)
d: Cecil B. DeMille. 5 reels.
Bessie Barriscale, Jane Darwell, Dick LaReno, J.W. Johnston, Monroe Salisbury, James Neill, Sydney Deane, William Elmer, Jeanie McPherson, Padre Francisca de la Vinna.
In old California, a U.S. Secret Service agent falls in love with a Spanish señorita.

Rose of the South (Vitagraph, 1916)
d: Paul Scardon. 5 reels.
Peggy Hyland, Antonio Moreno, Mary Maurice, Arthur Cozine, Charles Kent, Rose E. Tapley, Gordon Gray.
Fifty years after the War Between the States, a woman who loved two soldiers—one from the North, one from the South—recalls memories of the war that killed them both.

Rose of the Tenements (R-C Pictures/FBO of America, 1926)
d: Phil Rosen. 7 reels.
Shirley Mason, Johnny Harron, Evelyn Selbie, Sidney Franklin, James Gordon, Frank McGlynn Jr., Scott McKee, Jess Devorska, Mathilde Comont, Valentina Zimina, Kalla Pasha.
In New York's East Side, two orphans—a boy and a girl—are raised by an elderly couple who run a flower shop. As the orphans grow to adulthood, love blossoms between them.

Rose of the West (Fox, 1919)
d: Harry Millarde. 5 reels.
Madlaine Traverse, Frank Leigh, Beatrice LaPlante, Thomas Santschi, Henry J. Hebert, Minna Prevost, Jack Nelson.
Tragedy stalks Rose, whose Canadian trapper husband was reported dead in an avalanche, but who returns on her wedding day and threatens to sell their daughter Angela to a wealthy landowner.

The Rose of the World (Famous Players-Lasky/Artcraft, 1918)
d: Maurice Tourneur. 5 reels.
Elsie Ferguson, Wyndham Standing, Percy Marmont, Ethel Martin, Clarence Handysides, June Sloane, Marie Benedetta, Gertrude LeBrant, Sloane DeMasber.
When an English soldier is reported killed in battle in India, his grief-stricken wife begins to have delusions. Even after she remarries, she is still unable to forget her noble first husband.

Rose of the World (Warner Bros., 1925)
d: Harry Beaumont. 7 reels.
Rockliffe Fellowes, Patsy Ruth Miller, Alan Forrest, Pauline Garon, Barbara Luddy, Alec B. Francis, Helen Dunbar, Lydia Knott.
A disillusioned girl marries a man on the rebound, then finds he only wants her money.

Rosemary (Quality Pictures Corp./Metro, 1915)
d: William Bowman, Fred J. Balshofer. 5 reels.
Marguerite Snow, Virginia Craft, William Clifford, Paul Gilmore, George F. Hernandez, Frank Bacon, Maurice Cytron.
Young lovers elope, then must take refuge in a nobleman's house in a storm. What they don't know is that the nobleman is deeply in love with the bride.

Rosemary Climbs the Heights (American Film Co./Pathé, 1918)
d: Lloyd Ingraham. 5 reels.
Mary Miles Minter, Allan Forrest, Margaret Shelby, Charlotte Mineau, George Periolat, Nanine Wright, Jack Farrell, Carl Stockdale, Lewis King, Rosita Marstini.
Rosemary, a country girl, has a knack for carving wooden dolls, and goes to New York to sell her work. There, she finds friendship, jealousy, murder, and finally love.

Rosie O'Grady (Apollo Pictures/Art Dramas, Inc., 1917)
d: John H. Collins. 5 reels.
Viola Dana, Thomas F. Blake, James Harris.
Rosie, a tomboy who sells newspapers on the East Side, meets a gent who might be right for her... or is he just a phony, setting her up for a fall?

Rosita (Pickford/United Artists, 1923)
d: Ernst Lubitsch. 9 reels.
Mary Pickford, George Walsh, Holbrook Blinn, Irene Rich, Charles Belcher, Snitz Edwards.
In old Toledo, a winsome dancing girl is courted by the King of Spain to be his mistress, but she's in love with a dashing nobleman.

Rouge and Riches (Universal, 1920)
d: Harry Franklin. 6 reels.
Mary MacLaren, Robert Walker, Alberta Lee, Wallace McDonald, Marguerite Snow, Syn de Conde, Lloyd Whitlock, Dorothy Abril, Harry Dunkinson, Helen Sullivan.
Becky, a poor but ambitious girl, gets a job in a Broadway chorus, hoping to snag a millionaire.

Rouged Lips (Metro, 1923)
d: Harold Shaw. 6 reels.
Viola Dana, Tom Moore, Nola Luxford, Sidney DeGray, Arline Pretty, Francis Powers, Georgia Woodthorpe, Burwell Hamrick.
James, a young millionaire, falls for Nora, a chorus girl, but wonders if she might have a sugar daddy when he sees her new clothes and pearls. Nope, it turns out Nora is simply a thrifty shopper. Her frocks are from the bargain bin, and the pearls are fake.

Rough and Ready (Fox, 1918)
d: Richard Stanton. 6 reels.
William Farnum, Violet Palmer, Alphonse Ethier, Jessie Arnold, David Higgins, Frank Newton, Mabel Bardine, Frank McGlynn.
In an Alaskan mining town, Bill laments losing his girl, who broke their engagement over a misunderstanding. But Bill gets a chance to win her again, when he saves her from being attacked by a masher.

Rough and Ready (Universal, 1927)
d: Albert S. Rogell. 5 reels.
Jack Hoxie, William A. Steele, Ena Gregory, Jack Pratt, William A. Steele, Monte Montague, Clark Comstock, Marin Sais, Bert DeMarc.
Out West, a cowhand rescues the rancher's daughter from marrying a man she does not love, saves her daddy's herd from rustlers, and wins the lady's hand for himself.

The Rough Diamond (Fox, 1921)
d: Edward Sedgwick. 5 reels.
Tom Mix, Eva Novak, Hector Sarno, Edwin J. Brady, Sid Jordan.
Hank, a circus performer, falls for the daughter of the ex-president of a European kingdom.

Rough House Rosie (Paramount, 1927)
d: Frank Strayer. 6 reels.
Clara Bow, Reed Howes, Arthur Housman, Doris Hill, Douglas Gilmore, John Miljan, Henry Kolker.
Rosie, a cabaret dancer, helps her boxer boyfriend win his big fight by distracting his opponent with her feminine charms.

The Rough Lover (Universal, 1918)
d: Joseph de Grasse. 5 reels.
Franklyn Farnum, Juanita Hansen, Catherine Henry, Martha Mattox, Fred Montague.
Romantic comedy in which Farnum plays two roles—a shy bookworm and a tough boxer—and both are in love with the same girl.
Farnum had previously played a double role in Universal's 1916 film *A Stranger From Somewhere*.

The Rough Neck (World Film Corp., 1919)
d: Oscar Apfel. 5 reels.
Montagu Love, Robert Broderick, George DeCarlton, Barbara Castleton, Frank Mayo, Albert Hart, James Davis, Robert Milash, H.E. Herbert.
John, a lumberjack, comes into possession of documents that incriminate several big-city political crooks. Unfortunately, one of the scoundrels is the father of the girl he loves.

The Rough Riders (Famous Players-Lasky/Paramount, 1927)
d: Victor Fleming. 13 reels.
Noah Beery, Charles Farrell, George Bancroft, Charles Emmett Mack, Mary Astor, Frank Hopper, Col. Fred Lindsay, Fred Kohler, Ed Jones.
Romantic drama centered around Teddy Roosevelt's band of Rough Riders and their famous charge up San Juan Hill during the Spanish-American war.

Rough Riding Romance (Fox, 1919)
d: Arthur Rosson. 5 reels.
Tom Mix, Juanita Hansen, Pat Chrisman, Spottiswoode Aitken, Jack Nelson, Sid Jordan, Frankie Lee.
Out West, an incognito princess in distress comes to town. She'll be rescued and romanced by a daring, hard-riding cowpoke.

The Roughneck (Fox, 1924)
d: Jack Conway. 8 reels.
George O'Brien, Billie Dove, Harry T. Morey, Cleo Madison, charles A. Sellon, Anne Cornwall, Harvey Clark, Maryon Aye, Edna Eichor, Buddy Smith.
After Jerry, a professional boxer, gets into a warehouse fight and knocks his opponent unconscious, he thinks he's killed him. Fearing a murder charge, Jerry stows away on a ship bound for the South Seas... but he'll return one day and learn that the chap he knocked cold has recovered.

Roulette (Aetna Pictures/Selznick, 1924)
d: S.E.V. Taylor. 5 reels.
Edith Roberts, Norman Trevor, Maurice Costello, Mary Carr, Walter Booth, Effie Shannon, Montagu Love, Henry Hull, Flora Finch, Jack Raymond, Diana Allen, Dagmar Godowsky.
Lois, the ward of a professional gambler, offers herself as the prize in a game of roulette.

The Roundup (Famous Players-Lasky/Paramount, 1920)
d: George Melford. 7 reels.
Roscoe "Fatty" Arbuckle, Jean Acker, Tom Forman, Mabel Julienne Scott, Guy Oliver, Wallace Beery, Irving Cummings, Fred Huntley, Jane Wolfe, Lucien Littlefield, George Kuwa, Edward Sutherland, Buster Keaton (bit).
When a long-lost engineer returns home, he finds his sweetheart marrying another man.

The Rowdy (Universal, 1921)
d: David Kirkland. 5 reels.
Rex DeRoselli, Anna Hernandez, Gladys Walton, C.B. Murphy, Jack Mower, Frances Hatton, Bert Roach, Alida B.

Jones.

The "rowdy" of the title is a young woman—Kit—who was found as a baby and adopted by a crusty sea captain. As she grows to teenage, Kit becomes an energetic presence around the docks, and she's as tough and as brave as any male her age.

A Royal Family (Columbia/Metro, 1915)
d: William Nigh. 5 reels.
Fuller Mellish, Montague Love, Ann Murdock, William Nigh, Lila Barclay, Mathilde Brundage, W.J. Draper, Edwin Mordant, Niles Welch, Albert Lewis, J.D. Cowles.
To ease international tensions, a marriage is proposed between the prince of one nation and the princess of another. Neither of them is thrilled with the idea, since they don't know each other. But the prince will go incognito into the neighboring kingdom, woo the princess, and then declare his love.

The Royal Pauper (Thomas A. Edison, Inc., 1917)
d: Ben Turbett. 5 reels.
Francine Larrimore, Walter Bauer, Richard Tucker, William Wadsworth, Herbert Pattee, Nellie Grant, Leo Gordon, Helen Strickland, Charles Sutton.
Irene, a poor girl, weaves fantasies about a fairy godmother who will come and rescue her from her poverty.

The Royal Rider (First National/Warner Bros., 1929)
d: Harry J. Brown. 7 reels.
Ken Maynard, Philippe de Lacey, Olive Hasbrouck, Theodore Lorch, Joseph Burke.
A cowpoke rides to the rescue when an innocent boy monarch faces a revolution.

Royal Romance (Fox, 1917)
d: James Vincent. 5 reels.
Virginia Pearson, Royce Coombs, Irving Cummings, Charles Craig, Nora Cecil, Grace Henderson, Nellie Slattery, Alex K. Shannon, Emil DeVarney.
When an emperor proposes marriage to Sylvia, the princess of a nearby principality, she irately refuses because the proposal is diplomantic, not romantic. Sylvia is curious, though, so she disguises herself as a commoner and shows up at the emperor's hunting lodge. Can true love be far behind?

Rubber Heels (Paramount, 1927)
d: Victor Heerman. 7 reels.
Ed Wynn, Chester Conklin, Thelma Todd, Bradley Barker, Armand Cortez, Ruth Donnelly, Mario Majeroni, Truly Shattuck.
Comedy about Homer, a private detective, who is thought a fool but shows real cunning in retrieving jewels stolen from visiting foreign dignitaries.

Rubber Tires (DeMille Pictures/Producers Distributing Corp., 1927)
d: Alan Hale. 7 reels.
Harrison Ford, Bessie Love, Irwin Connelly, Frank "Junior" Coghlan, May Robson, John Patrick, Clarence Burton.
It's "California or Bust" for a family of New Yorkers as they travel west in their dilapidated auto. Unbeknownst to them, their car has been declared a priceless antique, and soon they are being chased across the country by fortune hunters.

The Rug Maker's Daughter (Bosworth, Inc./Paramount, 1915)
d: Oscar Apfel. 5 reels.
Maud Allan, Forrest Stanley, Jane Darwell, Howard Davies, Herbert Standing, Laura Woods Cushing, Harrington Gibbs, Mary Ruby.
Demetra, daughter of a Turkish rug maker, is promised in marriage to a rug dealer, but instead she falls for a visiting American.

Rugged Water (Famous Players-Lasky/Paramount, 1925)
d: Irvin Willat. 6 reels.
Lois Wilson, Wallace Beery, Warner Baxter, Phyllis Haver, Dot Farley, J.P. Lockney, James Mason, Willard Cooley, Walter Ackerman, Knute Erickson, Thomas Delmar.
During a violent storm, a valiant sea rescue captain puts out into the rugged waters and saves an endangered vessel and its occupants.

Ruggles of Red Gap (Essanay, 1918)
d: Lawrence C. Windom. 7 reels.
Taylor Holmes, Frederick Burton, Lawrence D'Orsay, Virginia Valli, Edna Phillips, Lillian Drew, Rose Mayo, Charles Lane, Rod LaRocque, Frances Conrad, James F. Fulton, Ferdinand Munier.
In a gentlemanly card game, a British peer loses his valet, Ruggles, to a U.S. Senator. The senator then takes the impeccably polite and well-groomed Ruggles home with him to Red Gap, Arizona, where the valet will cut quite a swath with the down-home Americans.

Ruggles of Red Gap (Famous Players-Lasky/Paramount, 1923)
d: James Cruze. 8 reels.
Edward Horton, Ernest Torrence, Lois wilson, Fritzi Ridgeway, Charles Ogle, Louise Dresser, anna Lehr, William Austin, Lillian Leighton, Thomas Holding, Frank Elliott, Kalla Pasha, Sidney Bracey, Milt Brown, Guy Oliver.Remake of the 1918 Essanay comedy *Ruggles of Red Gap*, both versions based on the novel of the same name by Harry Leon Wilson.

Rule G (Blazon Film Producing Co./Paramount, 1915)
d: George W. Lawrence, G.M. Noble. 5 reels.
Harry L. Stevenson, Lawrence Katzenberg, A.C. Posey, Paul Gillette, Jack O'Connor, Kathleen Emerson.
"Rule G" prohibits drinking during working hours at a railroad machinists' shop. Several workers will run afoul of that rule, and some will be fired, only to try to avenge themselves by sabotaging the railroad.

Ruler of the Road (Pathé, 1918)
d: Ernest C. Warde. 5 reels.
Frank Keenan, Kathryn Lean, Thomas Jackson, Frank Sheridan, Ned Burton, John Charles.
In a variant on Dickens' *A Christmas Carol*, a railroad owner works his employees relentlessly. Hugh, one of his overworked engineers, finally falls asleep at the switch and is fired. But the railroad owner secretly provides Hugh and his family with free lodging, and even gives them presents on Christmas Eve.

The Ruling Passion (United Artists, 1922)
d: Harmon Wright. 7 reels.
George Arliss, Edward J. Burns, J.W. Johnston, Doris Kenyon, Ida Darling.
A millionaire feels that retirement is hazardous to his health, so he assumes a new identity and moves back into the workplace.

The Rummy (Fine Arts Film Co./Triangle, 1916)
d: Paul Powell. 5 reels.
Wilfred Lucas, Pauline Starke, William H. Brown, James

422

O'Shea, Harry Fisher, A.D. Sears, Clyde Hopkins.
A reporter takes to drink after losing his wife and his job.

The Runaway (Empire All Star Corp./Mutual, 1917)
d: Dell Henderson. 5 reels.
Julia Sanderson, Ada St. Claire, Dore Plowden, Jennie Ellison, Norman Trevor, Rex McDougall, Edward Fielding, W.H. St. James, Josephine Morse, Stanhope Wheatcroft.
Alice, a small town girl, runs away to the big city to be with an artist she fancies.

The Runaway (Famous Players-Lasky/Paramount, 1926)
d: William C. De Mille. 7 reels.
Clara Bow, Warner Baxter, William Powell, George Bancroft, Edythe Chapman.
Cynthia, a movie actress on location in the South, falls for a Kentucky mountaineer.

The Runaway Express (Universal, 1926)
d: Edward Sedgwick. 6 reels.
Jack Daugherty, Blanche Mehaffey, Tom O'Brien, Charles K. French, William A. Steele, Harry Todd, Madge Hunt, Sid Taylor.
Foley, a valiant railroad engineer, saves his train and all its passengers from doom by halting the "runaway express" just before it reaches a dynamited bridge.

Runaway Girls (Columbia, 1928)
d: Mark Sandrich. 6 reels.
Shirley Mason, Edward Earle, Arthur Rankin.
A girl leaves home and becomes a salon model, attracting lecherous suitors.

Runaway Romany (Ardsley Art Film Corp./Pathé, 1917)
d: George W. Lederer. 5 reels.
Marion Davies, Joseph Kilgour, Matt Moore, Ormi Hawley, Gladden James, Boyce Combe, W.W. Bittner, Pedro de Cordoba.
Romany, a beautiful "gypsy," is in reality the daughter of a millionaire, stolen in infancy.

The Running Fight (Pre-Eminent Films, Ltd./Paramount, 1915)
d: James Durkin. 5 reels.
Robert Cummings, Violet Heming, Thurlow Bergen, Robert Cain, William T. Carleton, Clarissa Selwynne, George Pauncefort, Alfred Kappeler, Philip Robson.
Wilkinson, a scheming bank president, diverts his bank's funds into a personal account, causing the firm to go bankrupt.

Running Wild (Paramount, 1927)
d: Gregory LaCava. 7 reels.
W.C. Fields, Mary Brian, Claud Buchanan, Marie Shotwell, Barney Raskle, Frederick Burton, J. Moy Bennett, Frankie Evans, Ed Roseman, Tom Madden.
Finch, henpecked by his wife and browbeaten by his employer, happens onto stage during a hypnotist's act and is mesmerized into becoming an aggressive, courageous lion of a man.

Rupert of Hentzau (Selznick, 1923)
d: Victor Heerman. 9 reels.
Elaine Hammerstein, Bert Lytell, Lew Cody, Claire Windsor, Hobart Bosworth, Bryant Washburn, Marjorie Daw, Mitchell Lewis, Adolphe Menjou, Elmo Lincoln, Irving Cummings, Josephine Crowell, Nigel DeBrulier, Gertrude Astor.
The exiled Rupert, who had conspired in the plot against the king of Ruritania, returns and gets involved in more intrigue.
This adaptation of Anthony Hope's 1898 novel is a sequel to his *The Prisoner of Zenda*.

The Ruse of the Rattler (Herald Productions/Playgoers Pictures, 1921)
d: J.P. McGowan. 5 reels.
J.P. McGowan, Lillian Rich, Jean Perry, Gordon McGregor, Stanley Fritz, Dorothea Wolbert.
Out West, an adventurer is hired to drive ranchers from their land.

Rush Hour (DeMille Pictures/Pathé, 1928)
d: E. Mason Hopper. 5 reels.
David Butler, Marie Prevost, Harrison Ford, Seena Owen, Ward Crane, Arthur Hoyt, Franklin Pangborn.
Margie dreams of travel and adventure, while her sweetie Dan is a stay-at-home kind of guy. Finally desperate to have some exotic fun before marrying, Margie stows away on an ocean liner bound for France.

The Rustle of Silk (Famous Players-Lasky/Paramount, 1923)
d: Herbert Brenon. 7 reels.
Betty Compson, Conway Tearle, Cyril Chadwick, Anna Q. Nilsson, Leo White, Charles Stevenson, Tempe Piggot, Frederick Esmelton.
Lola, a loyal housemaid in the home of a British M.P., secretly loves her employer.

Rustlers' Ranch (Universal, 1926)
d: Clifford Smith. 5 reels.
Art Acord, Olive Hasbrouck, Duke R. Lee, George Chesebro, Edith Yorke, Matty Kemp, Stanton Heck, Lillian Worth, Ned Bassett.
Out West, an itinerant cowpoke signs on as a ranch hand and gets to rescue his new employer from a swindlin' coyote.

Rustling a Bride (Famous Players-Lasky/Paramount, 1919)
d: Irvin Willat. 5 reels.
Lila Lee, Monte Blue, L.C. Shumway, Manuel Ojeda, Ruby LaFayette, Guy Oliver, Alice Knowland, Jim Farley, Dick LaReno, Tom Walsh, Roy Marshall.
Comedy western about a shy cowboy who proposes to an eastern gal by mail, but sends his handsome friend's picture instead of his own. When the gal accepts his proposal and goes West, the down-hearted cowpoke, not wanting to let her down, leads her to his friend. But the friend, good looks and all, is a horse rustler and a blackmailer, leading the eastern gal to turn to the cowpoke who wooed her in the first place.

Rustling for Cupid (Fox, 1926)
d: Irving Cummings. 5 reels.
George O'Brien, Anita Stewart, Russell Simpson, Edith Yorke, Herbert Prior, Frank McGlynn Jr., Sid Jordan.
The son of a cattle rancher falls for the new school marm in town.

S.O.S. (Sunshine Film Corp., 1917)
d: William Buckley. 5 reels.
Richard C. Travers, William Buckley, Eleanor Shannon, Mary Evelynne, Jane Thomas, Marjory LaFern, Suzanne Feday, William Burns, George Offerman, Grant Forman.
Dark melodrama about venereal disease and its consequences.

S.O.S. Perils of the Sea (Columbia, 1925)

d: James P. Hogan. 6 reels.
Elaine Hammerstein, Robert Ellis, William Franey, Pat Harmon, Jean O'Rourke, Frank Alexander, J.C. Fowler.
Fisherman brothers Ralph and Jim vie for the love of a girl they rescued from a shipwreck at sea.

The Sable Blessing (American Film Co./Mutual, 1916)
d: George L. Sargent. 5 reels.
Richard Bennett, Rhea Mitchell, Adrienne Morrison, Charles Newton, George Periolat, Alfred Hollingsworth.
John loves Mary, but he's too poor to propose marriage. Meanwhile, his uncle is trying to arrange a match between John and Bess, a movie star of his acquaintance who loves luxury.

Sackcloth and Scarlet (Kagor Productions/Paramount, 1925)
d: Henry King. 7 reels.
Alice Terry, Orville Caldwell, Dorothy Sebastian, Otto Matiesen, Kathleen Kirkham, John Miljan, Clarissa Selwynne, Jack Huff.
Melodrama about two sisters, one of them an unmarried mother, the other a caring person who chucks her own chance at happiness to care for her sister and niece.

Sacred and Profane Love (Famous Players-Lasky/Paramount, 1921)
d: William Desmond Taylor. 5 reels.
Elsie Ferguson, Maxine Elliott Hicks, Conrad Nagel, Thomas Holding, Helen Dunbar,
Winifred Greenwood, Raymond Brathwayt, Clarissa Selwyn, Howard Gaye, Forrest Stanley.
In Paris, a woman dedicates her life to helping her former lover recover from addiction to absinthe.

The Sacred Flame (Schomer-Ross Productions, Inc., 1920)
d: Abraham S. Schomer. 6 reels.
Emily Stevens, Muriel Ostriche, Maud Hill, Violet Axzelle, Earl Schenck, Lionel Adams, Frederic Clayton, James P. Laffey.
Rosalie, a schoolteacher, carries a torch for Lionel, but it's Paul who's really worthy of her.

The Sacred Ruby (William Steiner Productions, 1920)
d: Glenn White. 5 reels.
Glenn White, Arthur E. Sprague, David Wall, Jack Newton, Jane Drake, Willard Cooley, Ethel Russell, Marie Treador, Walter Dowling.
The theft of a priceless ruby sparks a manhunt that ranges from India to New York.

Sacred Silence (Fox, 1919)
d: Harry Millarde. 6 reels.
William E. Russell, Agnes Ayres, George MacQuarrie, James Morrison, Tom Brooke.
Capt. Craig, an officer and a gentleman, keeps his silence about an illicit affair between his friend and a married woman; but the captain is unwittingly drawn into the scandal anyway.

Sacrifice (Lasky Feature Plays/Paramount, 1917)
d: Frank Reicher. 5 reels.
Margaret Illington, Jack Holt, Winter Hall, Noah Beery.
During wartime, a self-sacrificing young woman exchanges places with her half-sister before a firing squad.

The Saddle Hawk (Universal, 1925)
d: Edward Sedgwick. 6 reels.
Hoot Gibson, Marion Nixon, G. Raymond Nye, Josie Sedgwick, Charles French, Tote DuCrow, Fred Humes, William Steele, Frank Campeau.
Ben, a westerner, infiltrates an outlaw gang to rescue their captive, the daughter of a sheep rancher.

Saddle Mates (Action Pictures/Pathé, 1928)
d: Richard Thorpe. 5 reels.
Wally Wales, Hank Bell, J. Gordon Russell, Peggy Montgomery, Charles Whitaker, Lafe McKee, Edward Cecil, Lillian Allen.
Saddle pals Benson and Mannick ride into town on the trail of the villainous Shelby.

Sadie Goes to Heaven (Essanay, 1917)
d: W.S. Van Dyke. 5 reels.
Little Mary McAlister, Jenny St. George, Russell McDermott, Frankie Raymond, Rod LaRocque, Kathryn Kennedy, Bobby Bolder.
Sadie, a child of the slums, fantasizes about Heaven, and wonders what it would be like to go there. One day she hops into a rich woman's limousine and is delivered to the mansion door, and spends a memorable day in her "Heaven on earth."

Sadie Love (Famous Players-Lasky/Paramount, 1919)
d: John S. Robertson. 5 reels.
Billie Burke, James L. Crane, Helen Montrose, Hedda Hopper, Jed Prouty, Shaw Lovett, Margaret Wiggins, May Rogers, Charles Craig, Ida Waterman.
Romantic comedy of errors has Sadie paired with Jim, who's already married; Luigi, who's on the rebound; and Mumford, the ex-husband of Jim's wife.

Sadie Thompson (United Artists, 1928)
d: Raoul Walsh. 9 reels.
Gloria Swanson, Lionel Barrymore, Blanche Frederici, James Marcus, Charles Lane, Raoul Walsh, Florence Midgley, Sophia Artega, Will Stanton.
Somerset Maugham's famous strumpet heats up the sands of Pago Pago, undeterred by a reformer who's trying to save her soul.

The Safety Curtain (Norma Talmadge Film Corp./Select, 1918)
d: Sidney A. Franklin. 6 reels.
Norma Talmadge, Eugene O'Brien, Anders Randolph, Gladden James, Lillian Hall.
When a London music hall catches fire, a dancer is rescued by an army captain, and falls in love with him. But there's a problem: The dancer is already married—to an actor who may or may not have survived the fire.

Safety Last (Hal Roach/Pathé, 1923)
d: Sam Taylor, Tim Whelan. 7 reels.
Harold Lloyd, Mildred Davis, Bill Strothers, Noah Young, Westcott Clarke, Mickey Daniels, Anna Townsend.
Harold, a shy store clerk, tries to impress his girlfriend by climbing the outside of a tall building. Hilarious comedy which mixes thrills and laughs in about equal measure.

A Sage Brush Hamlet (Jesse D. Hampton Productions, 1919)
d: Joseph J. Franz. 5 reels.
William Desmond, Florence Gibson, Edward Piel, Frank Lanning, Walter Perry, Harrish Ingraham, Marguerite de la Motte, George Fields, Bill Patton, Rosalie Sershon.
Out West, a rancher sets out to avenge his father's death.

The Sage Hen (Edgar Lewis/Pathé, 1921)

d: Edgar Lewis.   6 reels.
Gladys Brockwell, Wallace MacDonald, Richard Headrick, Lillian Rich, Alfred Allen, James Mason, Arthur Morrison, Edgar Lewis.
In the late 19th century, the era of this story, "sage hen" was a customary term for a woman of questionable morals. The film tells of such a woman, driven from town with her young son by the local Purity League. But she'll be back, and so will her son, by then a handsome lieutenant in the U.S. cavalry.

The Sagebrush Trail (Hugh B. Evans Jr./Western Pictures Exploitation Co., 1922)
d: Robert T. Thornby.   5 reels.
Roy Stewart, Marjorie Daw, Johnny Walker, Wallace Beery.
Out West, a sheriff forbids firearms within his town... a rule that's sure to get broken, and frequently is.

Sahara (J. Parker Rade Jr. Productions/Pathé, 1919)
d: Arthur Rosson.   6 reels.
Louise Glaum, Matt Moore, Edwin Stevens, Pat Moore, Nigel de Brulier.
Mignon, a music hall singer, marries an engineer and accompanies him on a mission to the Sahara desert. But she's used to gaiety and laughter, not sand and solitude, so she leaves her husband and son in the desert and takes up with a baron in Cairo.

Sailor Izzy Murphy (Warner Bros., 1927)
d: Henry Lehrman.   7 reels.
George Jessel, Audrey Ferris, Warner Oland, John Miljan.
A perfume salesman seeks the lady whose picture is on the perfume labels, and stumbles into a mad plot to murder the lady's father.

A Sailor's Sweetheart (Warner Bros., 1927)
d: Lloyd Bacon.   6 reels.
Louise Fazenda, Clyde Cook, John Miljan, Tom Rickett, Myrna Loy.
A headmistress is bequeathed a fortune, but there's a catch. To collect, she must prove that no scandal will ever besmirch her name. Needless to say, scandals galore lurk just around the corner.

Sailor's Wives (First National, 1927)
d: Joseph Henabery.   6 reels.
Lloyd Hughes, Mary Astor, Ruth Dwyer, Earle Foxe, Robert Schable, Gayne Whitman, Bess True, Burr McIntosh, Jack Mollen, Olive Tell.
Drama about Carol, a woman who knows she is going blind, trying to have one last fling before the darkness sets in.

Saint, Devil and Woman (Thanhouser, 1916)
d: Frederic Sullivan.   5 reels.
Florence LaBadie, Wayne Arey, Hector Dion, Claus Bogel, Ethyle Cooke, Ernest Howard.
Florence, a convent-bred girl, inherits her uncle's factory. The executor of the will, however, has a private agenda, and he uses hypnosis to persuade Florence to institute radical changes in the employees' salaries and working conditions.

A Sainted Devil (Famous Players-Lasky, 1924)
d: Joseph Henabery.   9 reels.
Rudolph Valentino, Nita Naldi, Helen D'Algy, Dagmar Godowsky, Jean Del Val, Antonio D'Algy, George Siegmann, Isabel West, Louis Lagrange, Rafael Bongini, Frank Montgomery, William Betts, Edward Elkas, Rogers Lytton, Ann Brody, Marie Diller.
In Argentina, an outlaw known as "El Tigre" abducts a bride on her wedding day.

The Saintly Sinner (Universal, 1916)
d: Raymond Wells.   5 reels.
Ruth Stonehouse, Jack Mulhall, Alida Hayman, Dorothy Drake, Henry Devries, Raymond Whittaker, Frederick Montague, T.D. Crittenden.
Jane, a simple and honest stenographer, is framed for robbery and sent to prison. After her release she dedicates her life to social reform. But she still has one item on her vengeance agenda: the ruination of the man who framed her.

The Saint's Adventure (Essanay, 1917)
d: Arthur Berthelet.   5 reels.
Henry B. Walthall, Mary Charleson, Frankie Raymond, Bert Weston, Patrick Calhoun, Ellis Paul.
Socially-conscious drama in which a minister gets the chance to clean up the slums by assuming the identity of another man.

Saints and Sinners (Famous Players/Paramount, 1916)
d: James Kirkwood.   5 reels.
Peggy Hyland, William C. Lampe, Albert Tavernier, Clarence Handysides, Hal Forde, Estar Banks, Horace Newman.
Thundering with righteous indignation, a banker forces a preacher to resign his mission because of a rumored scandal involving Letty, the preacher's daughter. Later, after the innocent Letty has become a volunteer nurse during an epidemic, the banker and the townspeople rethink their actions, and the two pariahs are allowed to return—with honors.

Sal of Singapore (Pathé, 1929)
d: Howard Higgin.   7 reels.   (Music score, sound effects, part talkie.)
Phyllis Haver, Alan Hale, Fred Kohler, Noble Johnson, Dan Wolheim, Jules Cowles, Pat Harmon, Harold William Hill.
A sea captain adopts an abandoned baby and persuades a prostitute, Singapore Sal, to help him care for it.

The Salamander (B.S. Moss Motion Picture Corp., 1916)
d: Arthur Donaldson.   5 reels.
Ruth Findlay, Iva Shepard, John Sainpolis, J. Frank Glendon, Edgar L. Davenport, Dan Baker, J. Albert Hall, H.H. Pattee, Mabel Trinnear, Beatrice James, Rita Allen, Violet Davis.
Dore, a simple country girl, travels to the big city to face the swindler who caused the bankruptcy of her parents.

The Saleslady (Famous Players/Paramount, 1916)
d: Frederick A. Thomson.   5 reels.
Hazel Dawn, Irving Cummings, Dorothy Rogers, Clarence Handysides, Arhur Morrison.
When Bruce, a wealthy man's son, falls in love with Helen, a struggling actress, his status-conscious father disowns him. But the youngsters get married anyway, and after a lot of hard work, Helen becomes a star. In this identity, she attracts Bruce's father, who is only too happy to shower the beautiful actress with gifts and attention. Then comes the dawn.

Sally (First National, 1925)
d: Alfred E. Green.   12 reels.
Colleen Moore, Lloyd Hughes, Leon Errol, Dan Mason, John T. Murray, Eva Novak, Ray Hallor, Carlo Schipa, Myrtle Stedman, E.H. Calvert, Louise Beaudet.
Sally, an orphan, is raised by a lady who teaches dancing. The dance training will come in handy later in life when

Sally, now working as a dishwasher, gets the chance to impersonate a famous Russian dancer at a gala, and charms the audience. Among the spectators is Florenz Ziegfeld, who asks Sally to dance in his Follies.

Sally in a Hurry (Vitagraph, 1917)
d: Wilfrid North. 5 reels.
Lillian Walker, Don Cameron, Thomas R. Mills, William Shea, Eulalie Jensen.
Sally's a lowly waitress, but she's got a nobleman in love with her.

Sally in Our Alley (Peerless Features/World Film Corp., 1916)
d: Travers Vale. 5 reels.
Muriel Ostriche, Carlyle Blackwell, Pat Foy, Walter D. Greene, Jean Shelby, Betty K. Peterson.
Tenement dweller Sally attracts the attentions of a wealthy young man, much to his sweetheart's chagrin.

Sally in Our Alley (Columbia, 1927)
d: Walter Lang. 6 reels.
Shirley Mason, Alec B. Francis, William H. Strauss, Paul Panzer, Kathlyn Williams, Richard Arlen, Florence Turner, Harry Crocker.
In New York, an orphan girl is cared for by three foster fathers—an Irishman, a Jew, and an Italian. Eventually she grows into a teenage charmer, and attracts the romantic attentions of Jimmy, a young plumber.

Sally, Irene and Mary (MGM, 1925)
w, d: Edmund Goulding. 6 reels.
Constance Bennett, Henry Kolker, Sally O'Neil, William Haines, Joan Crawford, Ray Howard, Douglas Gilmore.
Three Broadway chorines enjoy varying degrees of success in their love lives.

Sally of the Sawdust (D.W. Griffith, Inc./United Artists, 1925)
d: D.W. Griffith. 10 reels.
Carol Dempster, W.C. Fields, Alfred Lunt, Erville Alderson, Effie Shannon, Charles Hammond, Roy Applegate, Florence Fair, Marie Shotwell.
A carnival performer raises Sally, an orphan girl, as his own. When Sally comes of age, she falls for a handsome local chap... but his wealthy father disapproves, and collaborates with a local judge to find a way to thwart the union. What the judge doesn't know is that he is actually Sally's grandfather. Nobody knows except the carny who raised her, and he's just been arrested.

Sally of the Scandals (FBO Pictures, 1928)
d: Lynn Shores. 7 reels.
Bessie Love, Irene Lambert, Allan Forrest, Margaret Quimby, Jimmy Phillips, Jack Raymond, Jerry Miley.
Broadway showgirl Sally is wooed by two attractive gentlemen: Steve, a legitimate impresario, and Bill, a gangster who masquerades as an honest businessman.

Sally's Shoulders (FBO Pictures, 1928)
d: Lynn Shores. 7 reels.
Lois Wilson, George Hackathorne, Huntley Gordon, Ione Holmes, Lucille Williams, Edythe Chapman, Charles O'Malley, William Marion.
Sally, a girl who's the sole support of her ne'er-do-well brother and her frivolous sister, takes a job in a gambling establishment, hoping it's a legitimate operation. It isn't.

Salome (Fox, 1918)

d: J. Gordon Edwards. 8 reels.
Theda Bara, G. Raymond Nye, Albert Roscoe, Bertram Grassby, Herbert Heyes, Genevieve Blinn, Vera Doria, Alfred W. Fremont.
Ambitious spectacle tracing the Biblical story of Herod, tyrant of Judea, and his beautiful cousin Salome. The treacherous Salome attempts to seduce John the Baptist, who has publicly denounced Herod's rule, and when that attempt is unsuccessful, she vows to have him killed.
One of the first films able to boast: "A cast of thousands!" Publicity for the picture states that some two thousand extras were hired for the crowd scenes.

Salome (Nazimova Productions/United Artists, 1923)
d: Charles Bryant. 6 reels.
Alla Nazimova, Mitchell Lewis, Rose Dione, Nigel de Brulier, Earl Schenck, Arthur Jasmina, Rose Diane, Frederick Peters, Luis Dumer.
Nazimova brings a flamboyant interpretation to the dance of the seven veils.

Salome of the Tenements (Famous Players-Lasky/Paramount, 1925)
d: Sidney Olcott. 7 reels.
Jetta Goudal, Godfrey Tearle, José Ruben, Lazar Freed, Irma Lerna, Sonia Nodell, Elihu Tenenholtz, Nettie Tobias.
Sonya, a tenement girl, gets a big break when a rich gent invites her to dinner. She needs a new dress, though, so to finance it she obtains a $1,500 loan from a loan shark. *Big mistake.*

Salomy Jane (California Motion Picture Corp./Alco Film Corp., 1914)
d: Lucius Henderson, William Nigh. 5 reels.
Beatriz Michelena, House Peters, William Pike, Clara Byers, Lorraine Levy, Loretta Ephran, Walter Williams, Andrew Robson, Matt Snyder, Harold Meade, Clarence Arper.
Forty-niners head west, looking for gold, and bring the seductive Salomy Jane with them.

Salomy Jane (Famous Players-Lasky/Paramount, 1923)
d: George Melford. 7 reels.
Jacqueline Logan, George Fawcett, Maurice B. Flynn, William Davidson, Charles Ogle, William Quirk, G. Raymond Nye, Louise Dresser, James Neill, Tom Carrigan, Barbara Brower.
Out West, Salomy Jane kisses a desperado about to be hanged, and helps him escape.

Salt of the Earth (Thomas A. Edison, Inc., 1917)
d: Saul Harrison. 5 reels.
Peggy Adams, Chester Barnett, Russell Simpson, William Wadsworth, William Chatterton, Ivan Christie.
A crooked prospector salts his mine with gold dust and then sells it to a miner named Kincaid. His perfidy causes Kincaid's death and makes a lifelong enemy of the miner's daughter.

Salvage (Robertson-Cole, 1921)
d: Henry King. 6 reels.
Milton Sills, Pauline Frederick, Ralph Lewis, Helen Stone, Rose Cade, Raymond Hatton, Hobart Kelly.
Bernice, who has lost her own child and thinks she has nothing to live for, becomes friends with her tenement neighbor and her baby. Then the neighbor dies, leaving no one to care for her baby but Bernice. So Bernice takes care of the child and assumes the dead woman's identity. Then the dead woman's husband completes his prison term and

comes home. Now what?

The Salvation Hunters (United Artists, 1925)
w, d: Joseph von Sternberg. 6 reels.
George K. Arthur, Georgia Hale, Bruce Guerin, Otto Matiesen, Nellie Bly Baker, Olaf Hytten, Stuart Holmes.
Three waterfront denizens try a move to the city, but find it too big and impersonal.

Salvation Joan (Vitagraph, 1916)
d: Wilfred North. 7 reels.
Edna May, Harry T. Morey, Dorothy Kelly, Donald Hall, Bobby Connelly, L. Rogers Lytton, Eulalie Jensen, Belle Bruce.
Against all odds, a high-society gadabout develops a social conscience and joins the Salvation Army, dedicating herself to improving slum conditions.

Salvation Jane (R-C Pictures/FBO of America, 1927)
d: Phil Rosen. 6 reels.
Viola Dana, J. Parks Jones, Fay Holderness, Erville Alderson.
Jane, a tenement girl and reluctant thief, uses the Salvation Army as cover for her escapades.

Salvation Nell (California Motion Picture Corp./World Film Corp., 1915)
d: George E. Middleton. 6 reels.
Beatriz Michelena, William Pike, Nina Herbert, Clarence Arper, James Leslie, Irene Outtrim, Myrtle Neuman, Frank Hollins, Minnette Barrett, Andrew Robson, Katherine Angus.
Nell in Hell. That's what it seems like, for this young woman of the tenements who loses her parents in alcohol-related violence. Then she falls in love with a thief and is forced to work to support *his* drinking habit.

Salvation Nell (Whitman Bennett Productions/Associated First National, 1921)
d: Kenneth Webb. 5 reels.
Pauline Starke, Joseph King, Gypsy O'Brien, Edward Langford, Evelyn C. Carrington, Charles McDonald, Matthew Betz, Marie Haynes, William Nally, Lawrence Johnson.
In New York, a slum girl who scrubs saloon floors for a living becomes a charismatic speaker on behalf of the Salvation Army.

Samson (Universal, 1914)
d: J. Farrell MacDonald. 6 reels.
George Periolat, J. Warren Kerrigan, Lule Warrenton, Kathleen Kerrigan, Edith Bostwick, Rose Gibbons, Cleo Madison, William Worthington, Marion Emmons.
Retelling of the Old Testament story (with considerable dramatic license) about Samson, the Israelite whose enormous strength comes from his hair, and Delilah, the Philistine maiden who discovers his secret and brings about the ruination of them both.

Samson (Box Office Attraction Co., 1915)
d: Edgar Lewis. 5 reels.
William Farnum, Maud Gilbert, Edgar L. Davenport, Agnes Everett, Harry Spingler, Charles Guthrie, Carey Lee, George DeCarlton, Elmer Peterson, Edward Kyle.
Maurice, a young tough, becomes a dockhand and then, inspired by the Biblical story of Samson, goes on to become a titan of industry. Like the Samson of old, he meets his doom at the hands of a beautiful woman.

San Francisco Nights (Gotham Productions/Lumas Film Corp., 1928)
d: R. William Neill. 7 reels.
Percy Marmont, Mae Busch, Tom O'Brien, George Stone, Alma Tell, Hobart Cavanaugh.
Vickery, a promising young lawyer, believes his wife to be in love with another, and so divorces her. Desperately alone, he drifts into the underworld milieu, and becomes a lawyer for the criminals. Flo, a dance hall girl with an understanding heart, sees that something is out of joint here, and contrives to bring Vickery and his wife back together again.
This film is also known as *The Fruit of Divorce*.

Sand (Paramount, 1920)
d: Lambert Hillyer. 5 reels.
William S. Hart, Mary Thurman, G. Raymond Nye, Patricia Palmer, William Patton, Lon Poff, Hugh Jackson.
Out West, a cowpoke takes a job on a ranch and is suspected of having designs on the rancher's daughter. But his true love is Margaret, his former sweetheart who is now engaged to marry a train thief.

Sandra (Associated Pictures/First National, 1924)
d: Arthur H. Sawyer. 8 reels.
Barbara LaMarr, Bert Lytell, Leila Hyams, Augustin Sweeney, Maude Hill, Edgar Nelson, Leon Gordon, Leslie Austin, Lillian Ten Eyck, Morgan Wallace, Arthur Edmund Carewe, Helen Gardner, Alice Weaver.
Sandra, happily married but craving adventure, leaves her husband and goes on to enjoy escapades in the gay places of Europe. At last, after many affairs and many disillusionments, she returns home, thinking to end her life. But she finds her forgiving husband waiting for her.

Sands of Sacrifice (American Film Co./Mutual, 1917)
d: Edward S. Sloman. 5 reels.
William Russell, Francelia Billington, George Periolat, John Gough, Joe King.
Bill Darcey, a wealthy lodge owner, protects a young woman who is bent on revenge against the man who swindled her family out of their fortune.

Sandy (Famous Players-Lasky/Paramount, 1918)
d: George H. Melford. 5 reels.
Jack Pickford, Louise Huff, James Neill, Edythe Chapman, Julia Faye, George A. Beranger, Raymond Hatton, Clarence Geldart, Louise Hutchinson, Jennie Lee, J. Parks Jones.
In New York, a Scottish immigrant teams up with a jockey who plans to ride in the Kentucky Derby.

Sandy (Fox, 1926)
d: Harry Beaumont. 8 reels.
Harrison Ford, Madge Bellamy, Leslie Fenton, Gloria Hope, Bardson Bard, David Torrence, Lillian Leighton, Charles Farrell, Joan Standing.
Tragic tale of Sandy, a jazz baby who loves not wisely but too well.

Sandy Burke of the U-Bar-U (Betzwood Film Co./Goldwyn, 1919)
d: Ira M. Lowry. 5 reels.
Louis Bennison, Virginia Lee, Alphonse Ethier, Herbert Horton Pattee, Echlin P. Gayer, Lucy Beaumont, Wilson Bayley, Nadia Gary, Philip Sanford.
Sandy, a ranch hand, is mistaken for a stagecoach thief. Sandy proves his innocence, and all seems well... until he is forced to impersonate that same thief, in a stagecoach robbery.

The Sap (Warner Bros., 1926)
d: Erle Kenton. 6 reels.
Kenneth Harlan, David Butler, Mary McAllister, Eulalie Jensen.
A soldier returns from war a "hero", credited for an act of bravery he did not commit. Once he's back home, the deception gnaws at him until he is forced to confront his fears and admit the truth.

The Saphead (Metro, 1920)
d: Herbert Blaché. 7 reels.
Buster Keaton, William H. Crane, Irving Cummings, Carol Holloway, Beulah Booker, Edward Alexander, Jeffrey Williams, Helen Holte, Odette Taylor, Edward Connelly, Alfred Hollingsworth, Edward Jobson, Jack Livingston.
The witless son of a wealthy stockbroker must come to the rescue when the family business is threatened with bankruptcy.

Sapho (Famous Players/Paramount, 1917)
d: Hugh Ford. 5 reels.
Pauline Frederick, Frank Losee, John Sainpolis, Pedro de Cordoba, Thomas Meighan.
Struggling to escape her life of poverty, a flower vendor becomes mistress to one man after another, and soon gets used to a life of luxury. But when she falls truly in love with a young man, she fears he will leave her if he learns of her past.

Satan and the Woman (Excellent Pictures, 1928)
d: Burton King. 7 reels.
Claire Windsor, Cornelius Keefe, Vera Lewis, Thomas Holding, James Mack, Edithe Yorke, Madge Johnston, Sybil Grove, Lucy Donahue, Blanche Rose.
A misanthropic old woman tries to disinherit her granddaughter, who she believes was born out of wedlock.

Satan in Sables (Warner Bros., 1925)
d: James Flood. 8 reels.
Lowell Sherman, Pauline Garon, Gertrude Astor, Frank Butler, John Harron, Francis J. MacDonald, Otto Hoffman.
In France, a Russian prince's pre-divorce romance leads to complications.

Satan Jr. (Metro, 1919)
d: Herbert Blaché. 5 reels.
Milton Sills, Viola Dana, Lloyd Hughes, Alice Knowland, Frank Currier, Lille Leslie, George King.
When a playwright attracts the attentions of a spoiled rich girl, she determines that he will be hers, no matter what schemes she has to concoct.

Satan Town (Charles R. Rogers Productions/Pathé, 1926)
d: Edmund Mortimer. 6 reels.
Harry Carey, Kathleen Collins, Charles Clary, Trilby Clark, Richard Neill, Ben Hall, Charles Delaney, Ben Hendricks.
Scott, a prospector headed for the Alaskan gold rush, saves an orphan girl from wild horses while in Seattle. He pays a waterfront lawyer to put the girl through boarding school, then leaves her in his care. When Scott returns years later, having become wealthy, he finds that the shady lawyer has misused his funds and created a Sin City, with gambling, prostitution, and dance halls. Aligned against this wave of debauchery is Salvation Sue, a lovely girl working with the Salvation Army—the orphan girl Scott saved years before, now grown up and just waiting to be swept off her feet.

Satan's Private Door (Essanay, 1917)
d: J. Charles Haydon. 5 reels.

Mary Charleson, Webster Campbell, John Cossar, Hazel Daly, U.K. Houpt, Alice McChesney, Virginia Valli.
Orphaned when her father dies, Edith goes to live in the mansion of his old friend, a wealthy man with two very spoiled adult children.

The Satin Girl (Ben Wilson/Grand-Asher Distributing Corp., 1923)
d: Arthur Rosson. 6 reels.
Mabel Forrest, Norman Kerry, Marc MacDermott, Clarence Burton, Florence Lawrence, Kate Lester, Reed House, William H. Turner, Walter Stevens.
Lenore, a girl who has lost her memory, becomes persuaded to commit burglaries—until a patient young doctor works to restore her memory and her lawful ways.

The Satin Woman (Lumas Films, 1927)
d: Walter Lang. 7 reels.
John Miljan, Gladys Brockwell, Mrs. Wallace Reid, Rockliffe Fellowes, Laska Winters, Chares Buddy Post, Ruth Stonehouse, Alice White, Ethel Wales.
A social climbing woman neglects her husband and children.

Saturday Night (Famous Players-Lasky/Paramount, 1922)
d: Cecil B. DeMille. 9 reels.
Leatrice Joy, Conrad Nagel, Edith Roberts, Jack Mower, Julia Faye, Edythe Chapman, Theodore Roberts, John Davidson, James Neill, Winter Hall, Lillian Leighton, Sylvia Ashton.
Richard and Iris, wealthy society folk, each marry someone from the working class... and come to regret their choices.

Saturday's Children (First National/Warner Bros., 1929)
d: Gregory LaCava. 8 reels. (Music, sound effects, part talkie.)
Corinne Griffith, Grant Withers, Albert Conti, Alma Tell, Lucien Littlefield, Charles Lane, Ann Schaeffer.
Young lovers court, get engaged, get married, then split up.

Sauce for the Goose (Select, 1918)
d: Walter Edwards. 5 reels.
Harrison Ford, Constance Talmadge, Harland Tucker, Vera Doria, Edna Mae Cooper, Lewis Willoughby, Jane Keckley.
When John, a published author, is targeted for conquest by a flirtatious widow and he doesn't discourage her, his young wife Kitty feels neglected. So, she resolves to win her husband back by inventing a number of fictitious romances with other men.

The Savage (Universal, 1917)
d: Rupert Julian. 5 reels.
Ruth Clifford, Collen Moore, Monroe Salisbury, Allan Sears, W.H. Bainbridge, Arthur Tavares, George Franklin, Duke Lee.
In the Canadian northwest, a crazed half-breed kidnaps the winsome Marie Louise and carries her off to his remote mountain cabin. The exertion gives the kidnapper an attack of fever, but instead of running away when her abductor is disabled, Marie nurses him back to health. Her selfless act of charity will pay dividends in the long run.

The Savage (First National, 1926)
d: Fred Newmeyer. 5 reels.
Ben Lyon, May McAvoy, Tom Maguire, Philo McCullough, Sam Hardy, Charlotte Walker.
Comedy about a pulp writer who, as a gag, poses as a "white savage" and allows himself to be captured and caged. Just as he's about to deliver the punch line, though, he meets the daughter of the professor he's allowed to

428

"capture" him, and falls in love with her.

The Savage Woman (Clara Kimball Young Pictures/Select, 1918)
d: Edmund Mortimer, Robert G. Vignola. 5 reels.
Milton Sills, Clara Kimball Young, Edward M. Kimball, Marcia Manon, Clyde Benson.
Lost in the African wilderness, innocent young Renee is mistaken for the Queen of Sheba.

Saving the Family Name (Universal, 1916)
d: Lois Weber, Phillips Smalley. 5 reels.
Mary MacLaren, Gerrard Alexander, Phillips Smalley, Carl von Schiller Jack Holt, Harry Depp.
Estelle, a chorus girl thought to be a vamp, is kidnapped by a well-meaning young man who, during her period of captivity, falls in love with her.

Sawdust (Universal, 1923)
d: Jack Conway. 5 reels.
Gladys Walton, Edith Yorke, Niles Welch, Herbert Standing, Matthew Betz, Frank Brownlee, William Robert Daly, Mattie Peters.
A circus performer convinces a wealthy couple that she is their long-lost daughter. Her duplicity is finally discovered and she apologizes, but not before meeting her dream man and falling in love.

The Sawdust Doll (Diando Film Corp./Pathé, 1919)
d: William Bertram. 5 reels.
Baby Marie Osborne, Jack Connolly, Claire DuBrey, William Quinn.
The village blacksmith's daughter yearns for a real mother, and clings to her sawdust doll for company.

The Sawdust Paradise (Paramount, 1928)
d: Luther Reed. 7 reels.
Esther Ralston, Reed Howes, Hobart Bosworth, Tom Maguire, George French, Alan Roscoe, Mary Alden, J.W. Johnston, Frank Brownlee, Helen Hunt.
Hallie and Butch, con artists working a carnival, fall for each other.

The Sawdust Ring (New York Motion Picture Corp./Triangle, 1917)
d: Charles Miller, Paul Powell. 5 reels.
Bessie Love, Harold Goodwin, Jack Richardson, Josephine Headley, Daisy Dean, Alfred Hollingsworth.
Young Janet and her best friend Peter run away to locate Janet's father, a circus ringmaster.

The Sawdust Trail (Universal, 1924)
d: Edward Sedgwick. 6 reels.
Hoot Gibson, Josie Sedgwick, David Torrence, Charles K. French, Pat Harmon, Taylor Carroll, W.T. McCulley.
Comedy about a mild-mannered college boy who turns brave when faced with danger.

Say it Again (Paramount, 1926)
d: Gregory LaCava. 8 reels.
Richard Dix, Alyce Mills, Chester Conklin, Gunboat Smith, Bernard Randall, Paul Porcasi, Ida Waterman, William Ricciardi.

Daffy comedy about a doughboy in love with a European princess.

Say it with Sables (Columbia, 1928)
d: Frank Capra. 6 reels.
Francis X. Bushman, Helene Chadwick, Margaret Livingston, Arthur Rankin.

A wealthy widower remarries, then finds that his son's new fiancée is none other than the father's former mistress.

Say, Young Fellow! (Famous Players-Lasky/Paramount, 1918)
d: Joseph Henabery. 5 reels.
Douglas Fairbanks, Marjorie Daw, Frank Campeau, Edythe Chapman, James Neill, Ernest Butterworth.
A determined cub reporter scoops the competition with the aid of his alter ego, "The Hunch," a miniature image of himself that perches on the reporter's shoulder.

The Scales of Justice (Famous Players Film Co., 1914)
d: Thomas N. Heffron. 5 reels.
Paul McAllister, Jane Fearnley, Harold Lockwood, Hal Clarendon, Mark Price, Catherine Lee, Mary Blackburn, Beatrice Moreland, Daniel Jarrett.
When an elderly judge is murdered, his granddaughter is the chief suspect. But the district attorney who's in love with her investigates and finds the real killer.

Scandal (Universal, 1915)
d: Lois Weber and Phillips Smalley. 5 reels.
Lois Weber, Phillips Smalley, Rupert Julian, Adele Farrington, Abe Mundon, Alice Thomson, Grace Johnson, Jim Mason, Sis Matthews.
The lives of a banker, his secretary, and several others are ruined by vicious gossip.

Scandal (Selznick. 1917)
d: Charles Giblyn. 5 reels.
Constance Talmadge, Harry C. Browne, J. Herbert Frank, Aimee Dalmores, Gladden James, W.P. Carleton, Ida Darling, Mattie Ferguson.
Beatrix, a young socialite on the verge of scandal, saves her reputation by declaring that she is secretly married. But the lie just grows and grows, and she has to produce her "husband" and even go on trips with him... a development the phony spouse doesn't mind at all.

Scandal (Universal, 1929)
d: Wesley Ruggles. (Music, sound effects, part talkie.) 7 reels.
Laura LaPlante, John Boles, Huntley Gordon, Jane Winton, Julia Swayne Gordon, Eddie Phillips, Nancy Dover.
The former sweetheart of a married socialite visits her while her husband is away, on the very evening his own wife is being murdered. The widower is then arrested for the crime and, not wishing to compromise his old flame, refuses to produce an alibi.

Scandal Mongers — see: Scandal (1915)

Scandal Proof (Fox, 1925)
d: Edmund Mortimer. 5 reels.
Shirley Mason, John Roche, Freeman Wood, Hazel Howell, Frances Raymond, Ruth King, Edward Martindel, Joseph Striker, Billy Fay, Clarissa Selwynne.
To keep her employer from learning that his wife is having an affair, a housemaid quickly takes the wife's place in the arms of her lover.

The Scar (World Film Corp., 1919)
d: Frank Crane. 5 reels.
Kitty Gordon, Irving Cummings, Jennie Ellison, Eric Mayne, Charles Dungan, Frank Farrington, Ruth Findlay, Paul Doucet, David Herblin, Herbert Bradshaw, Amelia Barleon.
George, an American adventurer, brings Cora, a Spanish spitfire, to live in the United States. But Cora proves

ungrateful and even treacherous to her benefactor.

The Scar of Shame (Colored Players Film Corp., 1927)
d: Frank Peregini. 8 reels.
Harry Henderson, Lucia Lynn Moses, Ann Kennedy, Norman Johnstone, William E. Pettus, Pearl MacCormick, Lawrence Chenault.
Louise, a cabaret singer, yearns to return to her former lover—who's still trying to forget that she walked out on him, years before.

Scaramouche (Metro, 1923)
d: Rex Ingram. 10 reels.
Ramon Novarro, Lewis Stone, Alice Terry, Lloyd Ingraham, Julia Swayne Gordon, William Humphrey, otto Matiesen, George Siegmann, Lydia Yeamans Titus, Edith Allen, Nelson McDowell, Carrie Clark Ward, Edward Coxen, Tom Kennedy, Kalla Pasha.
During the French Revolution, a law student dedicates himself to the overthrow of the entrenched regime because his friend was killed in a duel with an aristocrat.

Scarlet and Gold (J.J. Fleming Productions/Davis Distributing Division, 1925)
d: Frank Grandon. 5 reels.
Al Ferguson, Lucille DuBois, Frank Granville, Yvonne Pavis.
In the Canadian northwest, a mountie gallantly marries an Indian girl in order to give her unborn child a name.

The Scarlet Car (Universal, 1917)
d: Joseph De Grasse. 5 reels.
Franklyn Farnum, Lon Chaney, Edith Johnson, Sam DeGrasse, Al Filson, Howard Crampton, William Lloyd.
Billy rescues Beatrice from a forced marriage and they escape into a storm... but their troubles aren't over with, yet.

The Scarlet Car (Universal, 1923)
d: Stuart Paton. 5 reels.
Herbert Rawlinson, Claire Adams, Edward Cecil, Norris Johnson, Tom McGuire, Marc Robbins, Tom O'Brien.
Beatrice loves Ernest, who's running for mayor as a reform candidate. But her admirer Billy learns that Ernest is really a treacherous scoundrel, and denounces him.

The Scarlet Crystal (Universal, 1917)
d: Charles Swickard. 5 reels.
Herbert Rawlinson, Betty Schade, Dorothy Davenport, Raymond Whitaker, Marie Hazelton, Gertrude Astor, Dick Ryan.
Priscilla, a spotless country girl, charms a wealthy playboy and they are soon married. But the bridegroom isn't quite ready to give up his tomcat ways.

Scarlet Days (D.W. Griffith/Paramount, 1919)
d: D.W. Griffith. 7 reels.
Richard Barthelemess, Clarine Seymour, Eugenie Besserer, Carol Dempster, Ralph Graves, Walter Long, George Fawcett, Kate Bruce, Rhea Haines, Adolph Lestina.
During Gold Rush days, a dance girl saves enough gold dust to send for her daughter to join her.

The Scarlet Dove (Tiffany-Stahl Productions, 1928)
w, d: Arthur Gregor. 6 reels.
Lowell Sherman, Robert Frazer, Josephine Borio, Margaret Livingston, Shirley Palmer, Carlos Durand, Julia Swayne Gordon.
Mara, a convent-bred Russian girl, flees an arranged marriage to be with her true love, a cavalry officer.

The Scarlet Dragon (Park-Whiteside Productions, 1920)
d: Frank Reicher. 6 reels.
Gail Kane, Thurston Hall, J. Herbert Frank, William Bechtel, Nellie Burt, Norbert Wicki, Paul Lane, Ted Lewis and his band, May Kitson, Rene Gerard.
Small-town sisters go to New York, eager for a stage career. But they'll run into several misadventures after the younger sister disappears during a visit to Chinatown.

The Scarlet Drop (Universal, 1918)
d: Jack Ford. 5 reels.
Harry Carey, Molly Malone, Vester Pegg, Betty Schade, M.K. Wilson, Martha Mattox, Steve Clemento.
During the Civil War, a Kentucky moonshiner helps the Southern cause and proves himself a gentleman when he rescues a daughter of the Confederacy from attempted rape.

The Scarlet Honeymoon (Fox, 1925)
d: Alan Hale. 5 reels.
Shirley Mason, Pierre Gendron, Allan Sears, J. Farrell MacDonald, Rose Tapley, Maine Geary, Eugenie Gilbert, Eric Mayne, Eulalie Jensen.
Pedro, son of a wealthy South American businessman, falls in love with an American stenographer while working in New York.

The Scarlet Lady (Columbia, 1928)
d: Alan Crosland. 7 reels.
Don Alvarado, Lya De Putti, Warner Oland, Otto Matiesen, John Peters, Valentina Zimina.
Rejected by the prince she loves, a Russian girl joins the Revolutionary forces and is involved in the storming of the Czar's palace.

The Scarlet Letter (Fox, 1917)
d: Carl Harbaugh. 5 reels.
Mary Martin, Stuart Holmes, Dan Mason, Kittens Reichert, Edward N. Hoyt, Robert Vivian, Florence Ashbrooke.
Hester, a Massachussetts woman of Puritan days, bears a child out of wedlock and is forced by the community to wear the scarlet letter "A" for "adultress."

The Scarlet Letter (MGM, 1926)
d: Victor Seastrom. 9 reels.
Lillian Gish, Lars Hanson, Henry B. Walthall, Karl Dane, William H. Tooker, Joyce Coad, Marceline Corday, Fred Herzog, Jules Cowles, Mary Hawkes, James A. Marcus.
Superior version of the Nathaniel Hawthorne tale, with Lillian Gish exquisite as the adulterous Hester Prynne, forced by Puritan society to wear the scarlet letter "A."

Lillian Gish could not speak Swedish and her costar, Lars Hanson, could not speak English. So they played all their scenes together in their own native tongues... and they understood each other beautifully. Miss Gish wrote of that experience: "It is always a thrill to play with a fine and true professional—in any language."

The Scarlet Lily (Preferred Pictures/Associated First National, 1923)
d: Victor Schertzinger. 6 reels.
Katherine MacDonald, Orville Caldwell, Stuart Holmes, Edith Lyle, Adele Farrington, Gordon Russell, Grace Morse, Jane Miskimin, Lincoln Stedman, Gertrude Quality.
Dora, an innocent girl, accepts a kind man's hospitable offer to stay in his house while he is out of town—and finds herself named as corespondent in his wife's divorce suit.

The Scarlet Oath (World Film Corp., 1916)
d: Frank Powell, Travers Vale. 5 reels.

Gail Kane, Philip Hahn, Carleton Macey, Lillian Paige, Alan Hale, Montagu Love, Boris Korlin.

Russian twin sisters, separated in infancy, meet again years later, during an uprising that kills their father and one of the girls. Happily, the other twin survives and is reunited with her American sweetheart.

Double duty for Miss Kane, who plays twins Olga and Nina.

The Scarlet Pimpernel (Fox, 1917)
d: Richard Stanton. 5 reels.
Dustin Farnum, Winifred Kingston, William Burgess, Bertram Grassby, Bert Hadley, Howard Gaye, Willard Louis, Jack Nelson.

During the French revolution, an English fop is regarded as a spineless idler, incapable of a serious thought. Actually, he is the outlaw known as "The Scarlet Pimpernel," who rides by night to save French aristocrats from the guillotine.

The Scarlet Road (George Kleine, 1916)
d: Walter Edwin. 5 reels.
Malcolm Duncan, Anna Q. Nilsson, Della Connor, Iva Shepard, John Jarrott.

Harry inherits a small fortune and immediately forgets about his family, his sweetheart, even the new airplane engine he is struggling to bring to market. But he falls in with false friends who dissipate the gullible heir's fortune, leaving him penniless and alone. Harry is smart enough, however, to learn from his lesson. So he works to perfect his invention and bring it to market, and stays away from chorus girls and fair-weather friends.

The Scarlet Road (Fox, 1918)
d: Edward J. LeSaint. 5 reels.
Gladys Brockwell, Betty Schade, L.C. Shumway, Charles Clary, William Scott.

Mabel, a proper girl raised by strict parents, is a fish out of water in New York's Bohemian district. But her strong moral code serves her well, when she is courted by two men—one a hard-working magazine editor, the other a wealthy lecher.

The Scarlet Saint (First National, 1925)
d: George Archainbaud. 7 reels.
Lloyd Hughes, Mary Astor, Frank Morgan, Jed Prouty, Jack Raymond, George Neville, Frances Grant, J.W. Jenkins.

Although she loves someone else, an aristocratic young lady is promised in marriage to an older man.

Scarlet Seas (First National/Warner Bros., 1929)
d: John Francis Dillon. 7 reels. (Music, sound effects.)
Richard Barthelmess, Betty Compson, Loretta Young, Knute Erickson.

A sea captain falls in love with a cabaret singer.

The Scarlet Shadow (Universal, 1919)
d: Robert Z. Leonard. 6 reels.
Mae Murray, Frank Elliot, Martha Mattox, Ralph Graves, Clarissa Selwnne, Willard Louis, J. Edwin Brown.

Elena, a girl being raised by her stiff-necked aunt, is said to possess "the scarlet strain," simply because her mother has divorced and remarried. But there isn't much Auntie can do about it, when Elena is wooed and won by the uncle of her young boyfriend.

The Scarlet West (Frank J. Carroll Productions/First National, 1925)
d: John G. Adolfi. 9 reels.
Robert Frazer, Robert Edeson, Johnnie Walker, Clara Bow, Walter McGrail, Gaston Glass, Ruth Stonehouse, Helen Ferguson, Martha Francis, Florence Crawford.

A noble red man is made a U.S. army captain, but must endure the hostility of his own people, who think he has turned against them.

The Scarlet Woman (Popular Plays and Players, Inc./Metro, 1916)
d: Edmund Lawrence. 5 reels.
Madame Petrova, Edward Martindel, Arthur Hoops, Eugene O'Brien, Frances Gordon, Frank Hanna.

When Blake, a popular candidate, wins election as district attorney, his embittered rival reveals to him that Blake's sweetheart was a trollop with a long string of conquests.

School Days (Warner Brothers, 1922)
d: William Nigh. 7 reels.
Wesley Barry, George Lessey, Nella P. Spaulding, Margaret Seddon, J.H. Gilmore, Arnold Lucy, Arlene Blackburn.

A small-town square peg moves to New York and finds he doesn't fit in.

A School For Husbands (Lasky Feature Plays/Paramount, 1917)
d: George H. Melford. 5 reels.
Fannie Ward, Jack Dean, Edythe Chapman, Frank Elliott, Mabel Van Buren, James Neill, Frank Borzage, Irene Aldwyn.When an upwardly mobile stockbroker starts neglecting his dowdy wife, she begins to dress more lavishly and learns genteel manners. She becomes so desirable that her husband eventually is willing to kill to keep her... though, in the end, he's glad it didn't come to that.

The Scoffer (Mayflower Photoplay Corp./First National, 1920)
d: Allan Dwan. 7 reels.
Mary Thurman, James Kirkwood, Philo McCullough, Rhea Mitchell, John Burton, Noah Beery, Eugenie Besserer, Georgie Stone, Bernard During, Ward Crane.

Disillusioned after an unjust stay in prison, a doctor becomes a cynic who scoffs at acts of kindness. Eventually he is persuaded to help a desperately sick boy, and returns to a life of helping others.

Scrambled Wives (Marguerite Clark Productions/Associated First National, 1921)
d: Edward H. Griffith. 7 reels.
Marguerite Clark, Leon P. Gendron, Ralph Bunker, Florence Martin, Virginia Lee, Alice Mann, Frank Badgley, America Chedister, John Mayer, John Washburn, Thomas Braidon.

Marital comedy about a divorced couple who contrive to keep their former marriage a secret from their new partners.

Scrap Iron (Charles Ray Productions/Associated First National, 1921)
d: Charles Ray. 7 reels.
Charles Ray, Lydia Knott, Vera Steadman, Tom Wilson, Tom O'Brien, Stanton Heck, Charles Wheelock, Claude Berkeley.

Steel, an amateur boxer, gives up fighting at his mother's request... but his fair-weather friends don't understand, and think he's turned yellow. He has to convince them he hasn't.

The Scrap of Paper (William Steiner Productions, 1920)
d: Tom Collins. 5 reels.
Glenn White, William Fredericks, Jane McAlpine, Joseph Striker, Leo Delaney, David Wall, Robert Taber, Joseph Sullivan, Alexander Frank.

"The scrap of paper" of the title is part of an illegal agreement for price-fixing among milk producers.

The Scrapper (Universal, 1922)
d: Hobart Henley. 5 reels.
Herbert Rawlinson, Gertrude Olmstead, William Welsh, Frankie Lee, Fred Kohler, Hal Craig, George McDaniels, Edward Jobson, Al MacQuarrie, Walter Perry.
During a construction project, a young engineer falls in love with the contractor's daughter, and she with him. But he has to fight off an attempt to sabotage the project before declaring his love.

The Scrappin' Kid (Universal, 1926)
d: Clifford Smith. 5 reels.
Art Acord, Velma Connor, Jimsy Boudwin, C.E. Anderson, Jess Deffenbach, Hank Bell, Edmund Cobb, Dudley Hendricks.
Out West, a young man fights off outlaws to get to the girl he loves.

Scratch My Back (Eminent Authors/Goldwyn, 1920)
d: Sidney Olcott. 6 reels.
T. Roy Barnes, Lloyd T. Whitlock, Helene Chadwick, Andrew Robson, Cesare Gravina.
Convent-bred Madeline yearns for a stage career but can only get jobs dancing in cheap vaudeville acts.

A Scream in the Night (A.H. Fischer Features, Inc./Select, 1919)
d: Burton King, Leander DeCordova. 6 reels.
Ruth Budd, Ralph Kellard, Edna Britton, John Webb Dillon, Ed Roseman, Stephen Grattan, Adelbert Hugo, Louis Stern.
Darwa, a senator's daughter, is kidnapped in infancy and raised in the jungle.

The Scuttlers (Fox, 1920)
d: J. Gordon Edwards. 6 reels.
William Farnum, Jackie Saunders, Herschel Mayall, G. Raymond Nye, Arthur Millett, Harry Spingler, Manuel Ojeda, Erle Crane, Kewpie Morgan, Claire Delorez, Al Fremont.
Landers, an insurance investigator, stows away to learn whether or not a captain is scuttling his ships for the insurance money.

The Sea Beast (Warner Bros., 1926)
d: Millard Webb. 10 reels.
John Barrymore, Dolores Costello, George O'Hara, Mike Donlin, Sam Baker, George Burrell, Sam Allen, Frank Nelson, Mathilde Comont, James Barrows, Frank Hagney.
Mini-epic based loosely on Melville's "Moby Dick." Barrymore plays Ahab, the sea captain obsessed with capturing a great white whale. But here, a love interest (Miss Costello) and a happy ending are provided.

The Sea Flower (Universal, 1918)
d: Colin Campbell. 5 reels.
Juanita Hansen, Al Whitman, Fred Huntley, Eugenie Besserer, Frederick Starr, George Pearce, Alfred Allen.
During World War I, a Secret Service agent falls in love with a beachcomber's daughter, but must leave for San Francisco on a mission to stop saboteurs.

The Sea Hawk (First National, 1924)
d: Frank Lloyd. 12 reels.
Milton Sills, Enid Bennett, Lloyd Hughes, Wallace MacDonald, Marc MacDermott, Wallace Beery, Frank Currier, Medea Radzina, William Collier Jr., Lionel Belmore, Kate Price, Al Jennings, Hector V. Sarno, Kathleen Key, Robert Bolder, Bert Woodruff, Claire Du Brey, Theodore Lorch, Henry O. Barrows, Fred de Silva, Albert Prisco,

George E. Romain, Christina Montt, Nancy Zann, Louis Morrison, Walter Wilkinson, Andrew Johnston.
A British aristocrat is falsely imprisoned, thrown into a ship's galley and chained to an oar. Once the ship is at sea, however, it is captured by Moorish pirates... and its slaves, including the innocent prisoner, are set free. Now adopted by a Moorish prince, the former aristocrat becomes Sakr-el-Bahr, scourge of all Christendom. But he cannot forget his past.

Sea Horses (Famous Players-Lasky/Paramount, 1926)
d: Allan Dwan. 7 reels.
Jack Holt, Florence Vidor, George Bancroft, Mack Swain, Frank Campeau, Allan Simpson, George Nichols, Mary E. Dow, William Powell, Dick La Reno, Frank Austin.
Helen, an Englishwoman with a 4-year-old daughter, sails to East Africa to join her estranged husband. To her dismay, Helen discovers that her husband has degenerated into an abusive drunkard.

The Sea Lion (Hobart Bosworth Productions/Associated Producers, 1921)
d: Rowland V. Lee. 5 reels.
Hobart Bosworth, Emory Johnson, Bessie Love, Carol Holloway, Florence Carpenter, Charles Clary, Jack Curtis, Richard Morris, J. Gordon Russell.
Nelson, an ill-humored sea captain whose wife left him 20 years earlier, sets sail and finds a young woman castaway. Though he takes her on his ship, the captain resents the girl's presence, as she reminds him of his wife. Small wonder: It turns out this girl is the daughter he's never met.

The Sea Master (American Film Co./Mutual, 1917)
d: Edward S. Sloman. 5 reels.
William Russell, Francelia Billington, George Fisher, Joe King, George Ahern, Clarence Burton, Rena Carlton, Helen Howard, Perry Banks.
Dorgan, a ship's captain, fights mutineers but still finds time to rescue and marry a Barbary Coast dancing girl.

The Sea Panther (Triangle, 1918)
d: Thomas N. Heffron. 5 reels.
William Desmond, Mary Warren, Jack Richardson, Arthur Millett, Lillian Langdon, Lee Hill.
In the 17th century Carribean, a pirate captain heads a band of bloodthirsty buccaneers... but he's tender with the ladies, especially beautiful Molly, whom he's captured from a seized British ship.

The Sea Rider (Vitagraph, 1920)
d: Edwin L. Hollywood. 5 reels.
Harry Morey, Webster Campbell, Van Dyke Brooke, Alice Calhoun, Louiszita Valentine, Frank Norcross.
Fishermen brothers quarrel over a woman... and when one of them gets her pregnant, the other brother forces him to marry her.

The Sea Tiger (First National, 1927)
d: John Francis Dillon. 6 reels.
Larry Kent. Mary Astor, Milton Sills, Emily Fitzroy, Kate Price, Milton Sills, Alice White, Arthur Stone, Joe Bonomo.
In the Canary Islands, a young fisherman falls for a girl of noble birth.

The Sea Waif (World Film Corp., 1918)
d: Frank Reicher. 5 reels.
Louise Huff, John Bowers, Anthony Merlo, Henry Warwick, Robert Broderick, Clay Clement Jr., Florence Malone, Louis Reinhart, T. Tamamato, Charles Dewey, Helen Russell.

When a stage performer takes a vacation in the country, he finds love with a young woman who has never known her real parents, and together they will find her rightful family.

The Sea Wolf   (Bosworth, Inc./W.W. Hodkinson, 1913)
d: Hobart Bosworth.   7 reels.
Hobart Bosworth, Herbert Rawlinson, Viola Barry, J. Charles Haydon, Jack London.
Ship's captain Wolf Larsen rules his domain with an iron hand. When his first mate falls in love with a young woman rescued from a shipwreck, Larsen decides he wants her too, leading to a fateful conflict between the two men.
First feature film version of the Jack London novel of the same name. It was remade twice in the silent era, by Famous Players-Lasky in 1920 and by Ralph W. Ince in 1926.

The Sea Wolf   (Famous Players-Lasky/Paramount, 1920)
d: George Melford.   7 reels.
Noah Beery, James Gordon, Raymond Hatton, Eddie Sutherland, Walter Long, Fred Huntley, Mabel Julienne Scott, Tom Forman.
Second feature film version of Jack London's novel *The Sea Wolf*, about a brutal sea captain named Wolf Larsen.

The Sea Wolf   (Ralph W. Ince Corp./Producers Distributing Corp., 1926)
d: Harold Grieve.   7 reels.
Ralph Ince, Claire Adams, Theodore von Eltz, Snitz Edwards, Mitchell Lewis.
Third feature film based on Jack London's novel *The Sea Wolf*. The durable story of Wolf Larsen was filmed in 1913 and again in 1920.

The Seal of Silence   (Vitagraph, 1918)
d: Thomas R. Mills.   5 reels.
Earle Williams, Grace Darmond, Kathleen Kirkham, Martin Best, Kate Price, Colin Kenny, Pat Moore.
A doctor wants to have a child, but his shallow, heartless wife will not hear of it. She finally leaves him, only to discover that she is pregnant. Not wanting to give her husband the satisfaction of knowing he will be blessed with an heir, the unfeeling wife swears her nurse to secrecy... but the truth has a way of coming out.

The Sealed Envelope   (Universal, 1919)
d: Douglas Gerrard.   5 reels.
William A. Sheer, Fritzi Brunette, Joseph Girard, Charles Dorian, Katherine Wallace, Ogden Crane, Martha Mattox, Francis Murphy.
Peter, an ex-con, is given a secret mission involving a sealed envelope.

Sealed Hearts   (Selznick/Select, 1919)
d: Ralph Ince.   5 reels.
Eugene O'Brien, Robert Edeson, Lucille Lee Stewart, John Dean, Ethel Kingsley, Frank Murdock, Helen Reinecke, William T. Hays.
When a millionaire marries a younger woman, he begins to suspect she is carrying on an affair with his son.

Sealed Lips   (Equitable Motion Pictures/World Film Corp., 1915)
d: John Ince.   5 reels.
William Courtenay, Arthur Ashley, Mary Charleson, Adele Ray, Marie E. Wells, Edward N. Hoyt.
Cyril, a divinity student, gets a girl pregnant, then lets a friend go to prison for a crime he did not commit. When Cyril becomes a famous preacher, he carries a heavy load of guilt.

Sealed Lips   (Columbia, 1925)
d: Tony Gaudio.   6 reels.
Cullen Landis, Dorothy Revier, Scott Turner, Lincoln Stedman, John Miljan, Barbara Luddy, Tom Ricketts.
Alan, a scion of wealth, falls for Margaret, who unwisely keeps from him the information that her father is a professional gambler.

Sealed Valley   (Metro, 1915)
d: Lawrence B. McGill.   5 reels.
Dorothy Donnelly, J.W. Johnson, Rene Ditline.
When an Indian maiden leaves her settlement in the Sealed Valley to find a doctor for her ailing mother, she inadvertently opens up the valley to gold poachers.

The Seats of the Mighty   (Colonial Motion Picture Corp./World Film Corp., 1914)
d: T. Hays Hunter.   7 reels.
Lionel Barrymore, A.P. Jackson, Clinton Preston, Millicent Evans, Glen White, Lois Meredith, Jack Hopkins, Harold Hartsell, William Cavanaugh, Charles Graham, Grace Leigh.
During the French and Indian War, a colonial captain falls in love with a Canadian girl.

Second Fiddle   (Film Guild/W.W. Hodkinson, 1923)
d: Frank Tuttle.   6 reels.
Glenn Hunter, Mary Astor, Townsend Martin, William Nally, Leslie Stowe, Mary Foy, Helenka Adamowska, Otto Lang, Osgood Perkins.
A young man who has always played second fiddle to his older brother finally gets a chance to show his courage, when he rescues his girlfriend from an attacker.

Second Hand Rose   (Universal, 1922)
d: Lloyd Ingraham.   5 reels.
Gladys Walton, Wade Boteler, George B. Williams, Eddie Sutherland, Max Davidson, Virginia Adair, Alice Belcher, Jack Dougherty, Walter Perry, Bennett Southard, Camilla Clark, Marion Faducha.
On New York's East Side, Rose, the adopted Irish daughter of a Jewish pawnbroker, juggles marriage proposals.

The Second in Command   (Quality Pictures Corp./Metro, 1915)
d: William J. Bowman.   5 reels.
Francis X. Bushman, Marguerite Snow, William Clifford, Lester Cuneo, Helen Dunbar, Paul Byron, Marcia Moore, Evelyn Greeley.
During the Boer War, two officers—one young, one older—vie for the love of the same woman.
Along with *The Birth of a Nation*, which was released earlier the same year, *The Second in Command* is one of the first silent features to make extensive and sophisticated use of tracking shots.

Second Youth   (Distinctive Pictures/Goldwyn, 1924)
d: Albert Parker.   6 reels.
Alfred Lunt, Dorothy Allen, Jobyna Howland, Lynne Fontanne, Walter Catlett, Herbert Corthell, Margaret Dale, Mimi Palmeri, Winifred Allen, Charles Lane, Lumsden Hare.
Comedy about Roland, a girl-shy clerk who is pursued relentlessly by ladies with marriage on their minds.

Secret Code   (Triangle, 1918)
d: Albert Parker.   5 reels.
Gloria Swanson, J. Barney Sherry, Rhy Alexander, Leslie Stewart, Joe King, Dorothy Wallace, Lee Phelps.
During World War I, a senator's young wife is suspected of transmitting messages to the enemy via secret code.

The Secret Game (Lasky Feature Plays/Paramount, 1917)
d: William C. DeMille. 5 reels.
Sessue Hayakawa, Jack Holt, Florence Vidor, Mayme Kelso, Raymond Hatton, Charles Ogle.
Nara-Nara, a Japanese detective, is assigned to an espionage case involving American transport ships during World War I.

The Secret Garden (Famous Players-Lasky/Paramount, 1919)
d: G. Butler Clonebough. 5 reels.
Lila Lee, Spottiswoode Aitken, Clarence H. Geldart, Dick Rosson, Fay Holderness, Ann Malone, Paul Willis, Lucille Ward, Mae Wilson, James Neill, Seymour Hastings, Larry Steers.
When the embittered father of a crippled boy is appointed guardian of a young orphan girl, his depression deepens. But the cheerful girl will brighten her guardian's life and restore his faith in humanity.

The Secret Gift (Universal, 1920)
d: Harry L. Franklyn. 5 reels.
Lee Kohlmar, Rudolph Christians, Doris Baker, Gladys Walton, Carl Gerrard, Fred Gamble, Carl Ullman, Jennie Lee, Verne Winters.
Winnie, a businessman's daughter, falls in love with Larry, but her father disapproves of their union.

The Secret Hour (Paramount, 1928)
d: Rowland V. Lee. 8 reels.
Pola Negri, Jean Hersholt, Kenneth Thompson, George Kuwa, Christian J. Frank, George Periolat.
While courting a pretty waitress by mail, a middle-aged farmer impulsively sends her a photograph of his young, attractive foreman instead of his own. *Big* mistake!

Secret Love (Universal, 1916)
d: Robert Leonard. 6 reels.
Helen Ware, Harry Carey, Jack Curtis, Dixey Carr, Harry Carter, Marc Robbins, Harry Southard, Warren Ellsworth, Ella Hall, Willis Marks, Lule Warrenton.
In 19th century England, a mine owner drives his workers hard, and resents the reform efforts of Fergus, his chief engineer... this in spite of the fact the owner's daughter is in love with Fergus.

The Secret Man (Universal, 1917)
d: Jack Ford. 5 reels.
Harry Carey, Edith Sterling, Hoot Gibson, Morris Foster, Vester Pegg, Bill Gettinger, Steve Clements, Elizabeth Janes.
Cheyenne Harry, a recent prison escapee, finds a little girl in the desert, the sole survivor of a wagon accident.

Secret Marriage (Triangle, 1919)
d: Thomas Ricketts. 5 reels.
Mary MacLaren, Fred Vroom, Edward Alexander, Harold Johnson, Vera Mersereau, B.W. Hopkins.
Mary, the daughter of a policeman, is accused of drunkenness and attempted suicide. But there are extenuating circumstances, and they all come out on the witness stand.

The Secret of Eve (Popular Plays and Players, Inc./Metro, 1917)
d: Perry Vekroff. 5 reels.
Olga Petrova, Arthur Hoops, William L. Hinckley, Edward Roseman, Laurie Mackin, Florence Moore, George Morrell.
Eve marries Brandon, a factory owner, but learns too late that he is an alcoholic and a ruthless exploiter of his employees. After a little girl is blinded while working in Brandon's factory, Eve defies her husband by joining the crusade to reform working conditions there.

The Secret of the Hills (Vitagraph, 1921)
d: Chester Bennett. 5 reels.
Antonio Moreno, Lillian Hall, Kingsley Benedict, George Clair, Walter Rodgers, Oleta Otis, J. Gunnis Davis, Frank Thorne, Arthur Sharpe.
Murder mystery set in London involving an American reporter, a kidnapping, and a lost treasure.

The Secret of the Storm Country (Norma Talmadge Film Corp./Select, 1917)
d: Charles Miller. 5 reels.
Norma Talmadge, Edwin D. Denison, J. Herbert Frank, Niles Welch, Ethel G. Terry, Mrs. J.H. Brundage, Charles Gotthold, Julia Hurley, W.W. Black, Lorna Volare, James Mack.
Tess marries a wealthy young man in secret, since they know his mother would never approve. Later, when his mother insists the young man marry a family friend, he lacks the gumption to confess he is already married, and goes ahead with the nuptials, committing bigamy. Then, Tess discovers she is pregnant. What now?

The Secret of the Swamp (Universal, 1916)
d: Lynn Reynolds. 5 reels.
Myrtle Gonzales, George Hernandez, Fred Church, Frank McQuarrie, Val Paul, Mary DuCello, Lule Warrenton, Jack Curtis.
Feuding landowners escalate their dispute into armed warfare.

The Secret Orchard (Lasky Feature Plays/Paramount, 1915)
d: Frank Reicher. 5 reels.
Cleo Ridgley, Blanche Sweet, Edward Mackey, Gertrude Kellar, Carlyle Blackwell, Theodore Roberts, Cynthia Williams, Marjorie Daw, Loyola O'Connor, Sydney Deane.
In Paris, a wealthy woman of the world has a daughter, Diane, who inherits her mother's fiery nature and eventually becomes mistress of a duke.

Secret Orders (R-C Pictures/FBO of America, 1926)
d: Chet Withey. 6 reels.
Harold Goodwin, Robert Frazer, Evelyn Brent, John Gough, Marjorie Bonner, Brandon Hurst, Frank Leigh.
During World War I, a female Secret Service agent is duped into marrying a German sympathizer.

Secret Service (Famous Players-Lasky/Paramount, 1919)
d: Hugh Ford. 6 reels.
Robert Warwick, Wanda Hawley, Theodore Roberts, Edythe Chapman, Raymond Hatton, Casson Ferguson, Robert Cain, Irving Cummings, Guy Oliver, Lillian Leighton, Shirley Mason.
During the Civil War, a Northern spy goes South... and falls in love with a southern belle.

The Secret Sin (Lasky Feature Plays/Paramount, 1915)
d: Frank Reicher. 5 reels.
Blanche Sweet, Hal Clements, Alice Knowland, Sessue Hayakawa, Thomas Meighan.
Twin sisters, one of them a morphine addict, fall in love with the same man.
Miss Sweet does double duty here, in the roles of twins Edith and Grace.

Secret Strings (Metro, 1918)

d: John Ince. 5 reels.
Olive Tell, William J. Kelly, Hugh Thompson, John Daly Murphy, Marie Wainwright, Hugh Jeffrey, Barbara Winthrop, Bert Tuey, John A. Smiley, Edward Lawrence.
Janet, shocked to learn her new husband is a gangster, leaves him and takes a job as companion to a wealthy old couple. Soon, her husband and his gang are making plans to rob Janet's employers. They arrange to have the couple's coffee drugged and then crack their safe. But just as the gang is about to make their escape with the loot, the "elderly" couple—who are actually detectives—spring into action and arrest the criminals.

The Secret Studio (Fox, 1927)
d: Victor Schertzinger. 6 reels.
Olive Borden, Clifford Holland, Noreen Phillips, Ben Bard, Kate Bruce, Joseph Cawthorn, Margaret Livingston, Walter McGrail, Lila Leslie, Ned Sparks.
Kane, a portrait painter, has a good girl pose for him, but though she is decorously attired during the sitting, his painting depicts her in the nude. Troubles ensue.

Secrets (Joseph M. Schenck/Associated First National, 1924)
d: Frank Borzage. 8 reels.
Norma Talmadge, Eugene O'Brien, Francis Feeney, Alice Day, Patterson Dial, Emily Fitzroy, Claire McDowell, Charles Ogle, George Nichols, Gertrude Astor.
An elderly lady falls asleep and dreams of her youth in England, her elopement to America, and the family's tribulations while working a western ranch.

The Secrets of Paris (Whitman Bennett Productions, 1922)
d: Kenneth Webb. 7 reels.
Lew Cody, Gladys Hulette, Effie Shannon, Montagu Love, Harry Sothern, Rose Coghlan, William Collier Jr., J. Barney Sherry, Dolores Cassinelli, Bradley Barker, Walter James.
A monarch goes incognito to search for the daughter of his former sweetheart.

Secrets of the Night (Universal, 1925)
d: Herbert Blache. 6 reels.
James Kirkwood, Madge Bellamy, Tom Ricketts, Tom Guise, ZaSu Pitts, Arthur Stuart Hull, Rosemary Theby, Tom Wilson, Joe Singleton, Bull Montana, Tyrone Brereton, Otto Hoffman.
A banker hosts a large party and stages his own murder to avoid the bank examiner.

See My Lawyer (Christie Film Co./Robertson-Cole Distributing Corp., 1921)
d: Al Christie. 6 reels.
T. Roy Barnes, Grace Darmond, Lloyd Whitlock, Jean Acker, Ogden Crane, Tom McGuire, J.P. Lockney, Lincoln Plumer, Bert Woodruff, Eugenie Ford.
A pair of sports invest in an invention said to create artifical rubber, then discover it's a fraud. But they win back their investment, and a lot more, when the formula is found to serve a very different—and very special—purpose: Instant concrete.

See You in Jail (Ray Rockett Productions/First National, 1927)
d: Joseph Henabery. 6 reels.
Jack Mulhall, Alice Day, Mack Swain, George Fawcett, Crauford Kent, John Kolb, William Orlamond, Leo White, Carl Stockdale, Burr McIntosh, Charles Clary.
Farcical doings in jail, as a disowned heir impersonates a friend and gets locked up for speeding. Once behind prison walls, he organizes the other prisoners to form their own company to mass-produce a new invention, which turns out to be a great success.

Seeds of Vengeance (C.R. Macauley Photoplays, Inc./Select, 1920)
d: Ollie L. Sellers. 5 reels.
Bernard Durning, Charles Edler, Eugenie Besserer, Jack Curtis, Evelyn Selbie, Pauline Starke, Gloria Hope, George Hernandez, Jack Levering, Burwell Hamrick George Stone.
David, a young man whose father was killed in a brutal ambush, swears to avenge his murder.

Seeing it Through (Brentwood Film Corp./Robertson-Cole, 1920)
d: Claude H. Mitchell. 5 reels.
ZaSu Pitts, Henry Woodward, Edwin Stevens, W.H. Bainbridge, Fannie Midgley, Frank Hayes, Julanne Johnson, Hughie Mack, Anna Hernandez, Fred Mack, Frankie Raymond.
Betty and her mother fall into a trap set by an unscrupulous moneylender, and end up losing their land. But Betty finds an ally to help her investigate the lender's wicked ways, and all ends happily.

Seeing's Believing (Metro, 1922)
d: Harry Beaumont. 5 reels.
Viola Dana, Allan Forrest, Gertrude Astor, Philo McCullough, Harold Goodwin, Edward Connelly, Josephine Crowell, Colin Kenny, Grace Morse, J.P. Lockney.
A young woman and a male friend are forced by a storm to take refuge for the night in a country hotel. But although the two remain innocent, they are spotted by a mutual acquaintance who, naturally, suspects the worst.

The Seekers (Universal, 1916)
d: Otis Turner. 5 reels.
Flora Parker de Haven, Edward Hearn, Paul Byron, Charles Mailes, Edwin Booth, Florence Noar, Mary DuCello.
Ruth and her brother Lem belong to a peace-loving sect called The Seekers. When Lem is falsely imprisoned, Ruth decides to enlist the town sheriff in her plan to get Lem released.

Seeking Happiness—see: Happiness (1917)

A Self-Made Failure (J.K. McDonald Productions/Associated First National, 1924)
d: William Beaudine. 8 reels.
Ben Alexander, Lloyd Hamilton, Matt Moore, Patsy Ruth Miller, Mary Carr, Sam DeGrasse, Chuck Reisner, Victor Potel, Dan Mason, Harry Todd, Alta Allen, Joel McCrea.
Comedy about Breezy, a kindly hobo who gets mistaken for a masseur in a health spa.

A Self-Made Man (Fox, 1922)
d: Rowland V. Lee. 5 reels.
William Russell, Renee Adoree, Mathilde Brundage, James Gordon, Richard Tucker, Togo Yamamoto, Harry Gribbon.
Jack, a ne'er-do-well, gets disinherited by his wealthy dad and rejected by Anita, his fiancée. These twin trauma work their magic on Jack, who becomes a dynamo of energy and a success in business, eventually winning back both Pa and Anita.

A Self-Made Widow (World Film Corp., 1917)
d: Travers Vale. 5 reels.
Alice Brady, John Bowers, Curtis Cooksey, Justine Cutting,

Richard Clarke, Henrietta Simpson, Herbert Barrington, Lila Chester.

Comedic tale about a country girl who goes to the big city to find a husband. She does even better: Passing herself off as the widow of a recent suicide, she succeeds to his estate and his fortune. The only problem is, the "suicide" has had second thoughts about ending his life, and decides to return home. What now?

The Self-Made Wife (Universal, 1923)
d: Jack Dillon. 5 reels.
Ethel Grey Terry, Crauford Kent, Phillips Smalley, Virginia Ainsworth, Dorothy Cumming, Maurice Murphy, Turner Savage, Honora Beatrice, Tom McGuire, Laura LaVarnie.
A country lawyer moves his practice to the big city, but his wife doesn't take to city life well, and the couple faces a marital crisis.

The Selfish Woman (Lasky Feature Plays/Paramount, 1916)
d: E. Mason Hopper, George Melford. 5 reels.
Wallace Reid, Cleo Ridgley, Mrs. James Neill, Charles Arling, Joseph King, Jane Wolff, William Elmer, Horace B. Carpenter, Bob Fleming, Milton Brown, Edythe Chapman.
The self-centered wife of a railroad engineer accepts a bribe to foment unrest among her husband's employees. When they decide to go on strike and begin threatening the engineer, the wife realizes she really does love her husband after all, and must do some rapid backtracking.

Selfish Yates (Wm S. Hart Productions/Paramount, 1918)
d: William S. Hart. 5 reels.
William S. Hart, Jane Novak, Ernest Butterworth, Bert Sprotte, Harry Dunkinson, Thelma Salter.
In old Arizona, a self-centered dance hall proprietor hires two orphan girls to scrub the floors, then falls in love with one of them.

The Senator (Triumph Film Corp./World Film Corp., 1915)
d: Joseph A. Golden. 5 reels.
Charles J. Ross, Joseph Burke, Ben Graham, Thomas Tracy, Philip Hahn, Dixie Compton, Constance Molineux, Gene Luneska, William Corbett.
Shortly after the Revolutionary War ends, Rivers, a newly elected senator, falls for a young woman whose father claims the government owes him compensation for property used in that war.

Señor Daredevil (Charles R. Rogers Productions/First National, 1926)
d: Albert Rogell. 7 reels.
Ken Maynard, Dorothy Devore, George Nichols, Josef Swickard, J.P. McGowan, Sheldon Lewis, Buck Black, Billy Franey.
Out West, a wagon train carrying essential supplies for a mining camp is repeatedly menaced by bandits.

Señorita (Famous Players-Lasky/Paramount, 1927)
d: Clarence G. Badger. 7 reels.
Bebe Daniels, James Hall, William Powell, Josef Swickard.
In old California, a young woman learns to excel in sports including riding, fencing, and shooting. When her grandfather in South America is plagued by treacherous neighbors, he sends for his grandchild for help, thinking it is a boy, not a girl. Not to be dissuaded, the valiant girl dons male clothes and makes the trip to her grandfather's estate... and there, she plays the female Zorro, righting injustice and bringing peace to the community.

Sensation Seekers (Universal, 1927)
d: Lois Weber. 7 reels.
Billie Dove, Huntley Gordon, Peggy Montgomery, Phillips Smalley, Raymond Bloomer, Will Gregory, Helen Gilmore, Edith Yorke, Cora Williams, Sidney Arundel, Frances Dale.
An up-to-date jazz baby frolics at road houses and cabarets, but secretly her true love is the local minister.

The Sentimental Lady (George Kleine, 1915)
d: Walter Edwin. 5 reels.
Irene Fenwick, Frank Belcher, John Davidson, Thomas McGrath, Jack Devereaux, Richie Ling, Anna Reader, Lila Barclay, Della Connor, Ben L. Taggart.
At a summer camp, a damsel in distress is rescued from swindlers by a man she has assumed is untrustworthy.

Sentimental Tommy (Famous Players-Lasky/Paramount, 1921)
d: John S. Robertson. 8 reels.
Gareth Hughes, May McAvoy, Mabel Taliaferro, George Fawcett, Harry L. Coleman, Leila Frost, Kempton Greene, Virginia Valli, Malcolm Bradley, Alfred Kappeler, Kate Davenport.
Tommy, a young author, proposes to a childhood friend once he has achieved success, but she rejects him. After he moves to Switzerland and begins a new romance, his younger girlfriend decides she'd like another chance to accept Tommy's proposal.

Serenade (R.A. Walsh Productions/Associated First National, 1921)
d: R.A. Walsh. 7 reels.
Miriam Cooper, George Walsh, Rosita Marstini, James A. Marcus, Josef Swickard, Bertram Grassby, Noble Johnson, Adelbert Knott, William Eagle Eye, Ardita Milano.
In Spain during a revolution, a girl is loved by men from both factions.

Serenade (Paramount, 1927)
d: Harry D'Abbadie D'Arrast. 6 reels.
Adolphe Menjou, Kathryn Carver, Lawrence Grant, Lina Basquette, Martha Franklin.
In Vienna, a composer neglects his wife and has a fling with the leading lady in his new operetta.

The Serpent (Fox, 1916)
d: Raoul Walsh. 5 reels.
Theda Bara, George Walsh, James Marcus, Lillian Hathaway, Charles Craig, Carl Harbaugh, Nan Carter, Marcel Morhange, Ben Nedell.
Vania, an actress from Moscow, achieves fame and fortune on the London stage. She is courted by several admirers, but Vania is interested in only one: the man who, years before in Russia, raped her and killed her fiancé. When she finds the scoundrel, she exacts a most ingenious revenge: She makes his son fall in love with her, then at the crucial moment she destroys them both.
Perhaps to pacify those who might find the scenario too shocking, a sort of epilogue was added to the film, suggesting that Vania's escapades were only a dream.

The Serpent's Tooth (American Film Co./Mutual, 1917)
d: Rollin S. Sturgeon. 5 reels.
Gail Kane, William Conklin, Edward Peil, Jane Pascal, Frederick Vroom, Mary Lee Wise, Charles P. Kellogg, Al Vosburgh.
Because he fears he can never support a wife on his tiny income, a struggling doctor gives up his fiancée and she

marries another man. But the doctor and his ex-sweetheart will meet again.

The Servant in the House (Triangle, 1920)
d: Jack Conway. 8 reels.
Jean Hersholt, Jack Curtis, Edward Peil, Harvey Clark, Clara Horton, Zenaide Williams, Claire Anderson, John Gilbert, Mrs. George Hernandez.
When a bishop comes to call, he finds a family torn with strife. He disguises himself as a servant and, in that identity, is able to effect a reconciliation among all the family members.

The Servant Question (Selznick/Select, 1920)
w, d: Dell Henderson. 5 reels.
William Collier, Virginia Lee, Buster Collier, Armand Cortez, Rapley Holmes.
High-society thieves try to steal a diamond necklace from their host, but are thwarted by the host's friend, who's posing as the butler.

Service For Ladies (Paramount, 1927)
d: Harry D'Arrast. 7 reels.
Adolphe Menjou, Kathryn Carver, Charles Lane, Lawrence Grant.
A Paris headwaiter falls hopelessly in love with an American heiress.

The Service Star (Goldwyn, 1918)
d: Charles Miller. 5 reels.
Madge Kennedy, Clarence Oliver, Maude Turner Gordon, Mabel Ballin, Victory Bateman, Tammany Young, William Bechtel, Jules Cowles, Zula Ellsworth, John A. Hemmingway, Phineas Billings, Isaace Wentworth, David Schuyler.
During World War I, a country girl pretends to be secretly married to a war hero.

Set Free (Universal, 1918)
d: Tod Browning. 5 reels.
Edith Roberts, Harry Hilliard, Harold Goodwin, Molly McConnell, Blanche Gray.
Whimsical comedy about a girl who's bored with her staid life and decides to become a gypsy. She thinks gypsies have an exciting, romantic life... but after several brushes with the law and a band of real gypsy thieves, she decides that sort of life is a tad too exciting for her.

Set Free (Universal, 1927)
d: Arthur Rosson. 5 reels.
Art Acord, Olive Hasbrouck, Claude Payton, Robert McKenzie.
Out West, a side show performer reveals himself to be an undercover detective on the trail of a claim-jumping thief.

The Set-Up (Universal, 1926)
d: Clifford Smith. 5 reels.
Art Acord, Alta Allen, Albert Schaeffer, Thomas G. Lingham, Montague Shaw, Jack Quinn, William Welsh.
Tolliver, a crooked banker, arranges for the murder of a rancher whose property he covets.

Seven Chances (MGM, 1925)
d: Buster Keaton. 6 reels. (Technicolor sequence.)
Buster Keaton, T. Roy Barnes, Snitz Edwards, Ruth Dwyer, Jean Arthur, Frankie Raymond, Jules Cowles, Erwin Connelly, Loro Bara, Hazel Deane, Marion Harlan, Pauline Toler, Judy King, Eugenie Burkette, Edna Hammon, Barbara Pierce, Connie Evans, Rosalind Mooney.

On the morning of his 27th birthday, a stock broker with massive debts learns he is to inherit $7 million, provided he gets married by 7 p.m. that day. With that big a payoff, you'd think he would have no problem getting a girl to marry him. Think again. This is a surreal comedy, one of Keaton's best, and in keeping with the theme of unreality, every girl he proposes to that morning rejects him. Time for Plan B. Now his best friend and partner decides to run a classified ad, soliciting a bride for this would-be millionaire—and the response is overwhelming.
The film's second half is a classic reversal of the first half. Earlier, he couldn't get a girl to marry him for love or money; but now Keaton's character finds himself in danger of being trampled by hundreds, maybe thousands, of eager wannabe brides. He takes to the streets, then to the open road, then to mountainous countryside, and still the hordes of predatory females pursue him like rabid pitbulls. Finally even the rocks on the hillside take on a malign life of their own, chasing Keaton's character down hill and across valley—until he ends up at the home of his true lady love, where she's waiting with a minister and a marriage license.

Seven Days (Christie Film Co./Producers distributing Corp., 1925)
d: Scott Sidney. 7 reels.
Lillian Rich, Creighton Hale, Lilyan Tashman, Mabel Julienne Scott, William Austin, Hal Cooley, Rosa Gore, Tom Wilson, Eddie Gribbon, Charles Clary.
Comedy of the absurd which puts eight wildly different people together in a house quarantined because of a smallpox scare.

Seven Footsteps to Satan (First National/Warner Bros., 1929)
d: Benjamin Christensen. 6 reels. (Synchronized music, sound effects.)
Thelma Todd, Creighton Hale, Ivan Christie, Sheldon Lewis, William V. Mong, Sojin, Laska Winters, De Witt Jennings.
A couple are kidnapped and taken to Satan's mansion. But it's all in fun.

Seven Keys to Baldpate (Cohan Feature Film Corp./Artcraft, 1917)
d: Hugh Ford. 5 reels.
George M. Cohan, Anna Q. Nilsson, Elda Furry, Corene Uzzell, Joseph Smiley, Armand Cortes, C. Warren Cook, Purnell Pratt.
A writer bets he can finish a novel in 24 hours while staying in a deserted hotel which, it turns out, is anything but deserted.

Seven Keys to Baldpate (Famous Players-Lasky/Paramount, 1925)
d: Fred Newmeyer. 7 reels.
Douglas MacLean, Edith Roberts, Anders Randolf, Crauford Kent, Ned Sparks, William Orlamond, Wade Boteler, Edwin Sturgis, Petty Francisco, Mayme Kelso, Fred Kelsey, John P. Lockney, Edith Yorke.
Remake of the 1917 Cohan Features film, both versions being based on the play of the same name by George M. Cohan.

Seven Sinners (Warner Bros., 1925)
d: Lewis Milestone. 7 reels.
Marie Prevost, Clive Brook, Charlie Conklin, Claude Gillingwater, Mathilde Brundage, Fred Kelsey.
Seven burglars all try to rob the same house on the same night.

Seven Sisters (Famous Players/Paramount, 1915)
d: Sidney Olcott. 5 reels.
Madge Evans, Dorothea Camden, Georgia Fursman, Marguerite Clark, Jean Stewart, Lola Barclay, Conway Tearle, George Renevant, Mayne Lunton, Sydney Mason, Charles Kraus.
In Hungary, a convent school girl sneaks out one evening and attends a costume ball, where she meets a handsome lieutenant who will change her life and the lives of her six sisters.

The Seven Swans (Famous Players/Paramount, 1917)
d: J. Searle Dawley. 5 reels.
Marguerite Clark, William Danforth, Augusta Anderson, Edwin Dennison, Daisy Belmore, Richard Barthelmess, Richard Allen, Jere Austin, Joseph Sterling, Frederick Merrick.
Fairy tale fantasy about a queen with magical powers who turns seven princes into swans.

Seven Years Bad Luck (Robertson-Cole, 1921)
d: Max Linder. 5 reels.
Max Linder, Thelma Percy, Alta Allen, Betty Peterson, Lola Gonzales, Harry Mann, Chance Ward, Ralph McCullogh, Hugh Saxon.
Comedy written, produced, and directed by star Max Linder. He plays an inebriated bachelor who's convinced his sweetheart wants to leave him.

Seventeen (Famous Players/Paramount, 1916)
d: Robert G. Vignola. 5 reels.
Louise Huff, Jack Pickford, Winifred Allen, Madge Evans, Walter Hiers, Dick Lee, Richard Rosson, Julian Dillon, Helen Lindroth, Anthony Merlo.
Upon turning seventeen, a youth falls in, then out of, love.

The Seventh Day (Inspiration Pictures/Associated First National, 1922)
d: Henry King. 6 reels.
Richard Barthelmess, Frank Losee, Leslie Stowe, Tammany Young, George Stewart, Alfred Schmid, Grace Barton, Anne Cornwall, Patterson Dial, Teddie Gerard, Louise Huff.
Society vacationers stop in a small town in New England and find new loves.

7th Heaven (Fox, 1927)
d: Frank Borzage. 9 reels. (Synchronized musical score.)
Janet Gaynor, Charles Farrell, Gladys Brockwell, David Butler, Albert Gran, David Butler, Marie Mosquini, Gladys Brockwell, Emile Chautard, Ben Bard, George Stone, Jessie Haslett, Brandon Hurst, Lillian West.
A Parisian street waif, battered and abused by her guardian, is rescued by a street worker. They fall in love, but before they can marry he is called to serve in the war.

The Seventh Sin (McClure Pictures, Inc./Triangle, 1917)
d: Richard Ridgeley. 7 reels.
Shirley Mason, George LeGuere, Ann Murdock, Holbrook Blinn, Nance O'Neil, Charlotte Walker, H.B. Warner.
Another McClure picture featuring a couple named Adam and Eve, following *Passion*, released earlier in 1917. *Passion* had also starred Shirley Mason and George LeGuere.

Sex (J. Parker Read Jr. Productions/Pathé, 1920)
d: Fred Niblo. 7 reels.
Louise Glaum, Irving Cummings, William Conklin, Myrtle Steadman, Peggy Pearcy.
Adrienne is a compulsive vamp who delights in stealing other women's husbands.

The Sex Lure (Ivan Film Productions, 1916)
d: Ivan Abramson. 6 reels.
James Morrison, Louise Vale, Frankie Mann, Donald Hall, Marie Reichardt, W.W. Black, George Henry, T.B. Carnahan Jr.
Rose, an orphan girl adopted and cared for by Reynolds, her late father's employer, harbors hatred against him because she believes Reynolds responsible for her father's death. As she grows older, she still feels malice against her adoptive father, and seduces him to destroy his marriage.

Shackled (Paralta Plays, Inc./W.W. Hodkinson, 1918)
d: Reginald Barker. 6 reels.
Louise Glaum, Charles West, Jack Gilbert, Roberta Wilson, Herschel Mayall.
After a wealthy man leaves his mistress to marry another, the mistress vows revenge.

Shackles of Gold (Fox, 1922)
d: Herbert Brenon. 6 reels.
William Farnum, Al Loring, Marie Shotwell, Myrtle Bonillas, Wallace Ray, C. Elliott Griffin, Ellen Cassity, Henry Carvill.
At the urging of her social-climbing mother, a young woman marries a wealthy self-made man, though she does not love him.

Shackles of Truth (American Film Co./Mutual, 1917)
d: Edward Sloman. 5 reels.
William Russell, Francelia Billington, Alfred Vosburgh, Adda Gleason, George Ahern, Lucille Ward, Frederick Vroom.
Law partners vie for the love of the same woman.

The Shadow of a Doubt (Equitable Motion Picture Corp./World Film Corp., 1916)
d: Wray Physioc. 5 reels.
Carlyle Blackwell, Jean Shelby, George Anderson, Lillian Allen, Frank Beamish.
After a distressed woman borrows $1,000 to help her husband, the lender insists that she repay the loan immediately or submit to his physical demands.

The Shadow of Rosalie Byrnes (Selznick/Select, 1920)
d: George Archinbaud. 5 reels.
Elaine Hammerstein, Edward Langford, Anita Booth, Alfred Hickman, Fanny Cogan, George Cowle, Lillian Wiggins, Juliette Benson.
Rosalie marries Gerald, a military lieutenant. Because his wealthy family objects to the match, they try to buy off his wife... but they mistakenly contact Rosalie's twin sister instead. Delighted by the family's offer, the crooked twin accepts.

The Shadow of the Law (Associated Exhibitors, 1926)
d: Walace Worsley. 5 reels.
Clara Bow, Forrest Stanley, Stuart Holmes, Ralph Lewis, William V. Mong, Adele Farrington, J. Emmett Beck, Eddie Lyons, George Cooper.
Mary, an ex-con, falls in love with a millionaire who is ignorant of her jail record. In time, a scoundrel whose knows of her background will try blackmail.

The Shadow on the Wall (Gotham Productions/Lumas Film Corp., 1925)
d: Reeves Eason. 6 reels.
Eileen Percy, Creighton Hale, William V. Mong, Dale Fuller, Jack Curtis, Hardee Kirkland, Willis Marks.
Crooks persuade a young man to pose as the long-missing

7th HEAVEN (1927). Charles Farrell and Janet Gaynor were one of the silent screen's most popular romantic couples, although only the first three of their twelve films together were made in the silent era. Here, they strike a blissful pose in their debut pairing, as Chico the street worker and Diane, the girl he rescues from an abusive relationship.

* * * * *

heir of a millionaire. Little do they know, he's the real heir.

Shadows (Goldwyn, 1919)
d: Reginald Barker. 6 reels.
Milton Sills, Geraldine Farrar, Tom Santschi, Fred C. Truesdell, George Smith, Charles Slattery, Robert Harvey, Jean Armour.
Happily married to a businessman, Muriel is startled when her husband brings home an associate who recognizes her as Cora, the former companion of his partner.

Shadows (Preferred Pictures Inc., 1922)
d: Tom Forman. 7 reels.
Lon Chaney, Marguerite de la Motte, Harrison Ford, John Sainpolis, Walter Long, Buddy Messinger, Priscilla Bonner, Frances Raymond.
A minister's wife is stunned to receive the news that her first husband, lost at sea, has survived.

Shadows and Sunshine (Balboa Amusement Co./Pathé, 1916)
d: Henry King. 5 reels.
Baby Marie Osborne, Lucy Payton, Daniel Gilfether, Mollie McConnell, R. Henry Grey.
Treacly drama about a status-climbing couple, the Jacksons, who break off relations with their son when he marries "beneath him." Meanwhile, the Jacksons grow fond of their new next-door neighbors, a mother and her precocious child... not realizing the pair are their son's wife and daughter.

Shadows of Paris (Paramount, 1924)
d: Herbert Brenon. 7 reels.
Charles DeRoche, Pola Negri, Adolphe Menjou, Gareth Hughes, Vera Reynolds, Rose Dione, Rosita Marstini, Edward Kipling, Maurice Cannon, Frank Nelson, George O'Brien.
In Paris following the end of World War I, an underground apache dancer emerges as the reigning queen of high society.

Shadows of Suspicion (Yorke Film Corp./Metro, 1919)
d: Edwin Carewe. 5 reels.
Harold Lockwood, Naomi Childers, Helen Lindroth, Kenneth Kealing, William Bailey, Bigelow Cooper, Leslie Peacock.
Espionage drama centers on a British playboy who's thought to be a coward because he is a pacifist during World War I. Actually, he's very much involved in the war—as an undercover Secret Service agent.

Shadows of the North (Universal, 1923)
d: Robert F. Hill. 5 reels.
William Desmond, Virginia Brown Faire, Fred Kohler, William Welsh, Albert Hart, James O. Barrows, Rin-Tin-Tin.
A returning war veteran finds that his father has been murdered and their mining claim confiscated by three hardened criminals—one of them the father of the veteran's own sweetheart.

Shadows of the Past (Vitagraph, 1919)
d: Ralph Ince. 5 reels.
Anita Stewart, Harry T. Morey, Rose Tapley, L. Rogers Lytton, Julia Swayne Gordon, E.K. Lincoln.
A shady politician tries to derail a rival's gubernatorial campaign by getting him involved in a sex scandal.

Shadows of the Sea (Selznick/Select, 1922)
d: Alan Crosland. 5 reels.
Conway Tearle, Jack Drumier, Crauford Kent, Arthur Houseman, J. Barney Sherry, Doris Kenyon, Frankie Mann, Harry J. Lane, William Nally.
Carson, a sea captain, rescues a doctor's widow from the grasp of a lecherous scoundrel.

Shadows of the West (Cinema Craft/Motion Picture Producing Co. Of America, 1921)
d: Paul Hurst. 8 reels.
Pat O'Brien, Hedda Nova, Virginia Dale, Seymour Zeliff, Pat Corbett.
During World War I, a pair of doughboys discover a Japanese plot to take over the United States while Americans are distracted by the war against Germany.

The Shady Lady (Pathé, 1929)
d: Edward H. Griffith. 7 reels. (Part talkie.)
Phyllis Haver, Robert Armstrong, Louis Wolheim, Russell Gleason.
In Cuba, an expatriate American woman gets involved with a gang of smugglers.

The Shakedown (Universal, 1929)
d: William Wyler. 7 reels. (Part talkie.)
James Murray, Barbara Kent, Jack Hanlon, Wheeler Oakman, George Kotsonaros, Harry Gibbon.
An itinerant boxer takes part in fixed fights.

Shall We Forgive Her? (World Film Corp., 1917)
d: Arthur Ashley. 5 reels.
June Elvidge, Arthur Ashley, John Bowers, Captain Charles, Richard Collins, George MacQuarrie, Katherine Johnston, Alexandria Carewe.
In New York, a happily-married woman has to own up to her scarlet past.

Shame (Fox, 1921)
d: Emmett J. Flynn. 8 reels.
John Gilbert, Mickey Moore, Frankie Lee, George Siegmann, William V. Mong, George Nichols, Anna May Wong, Rosemary Theby, Doris Pawn, Red Kirby.
In San Francisco, a young man is led to believe he is part Chinese.

Shameful Behavior? (Preferred Pictures, 1926)
d: Albert Kelley. 6 reels.
Edith Roberts, Richard Tucker, Martha Mattox, Harland Tucker, Grace Carlyle, Louise Carver, Hayes Robertson.
Comedy of errors in which Daphne, honest but a flirt, tries to bag her prey by telling him that she is a certain escaped lunatic, and that he had best abide by her wishes. He cautiously goes along with her whims, then engages the services of a nurse to care for her. The nurse, however, turns out to be the *real* escaped lunatic, leading to a manic mixup of identities, relationships, and romance.

The Shamrock and the Rose (Chadwick Pictures, 1927)
d: Jack Nelson. 6 reels.
Mack Swain, Olive Hasbrouck, Edmund Burns, Maurice Costello, William Strauss, Dot Farley, Rosa Rosanova, Leon Holmes, Otto Lederer, Coy Watson Jr.
Feuding food peddlers stop their warfare when Rosie, daughter of one faction, marries Tommy, son of the other.

The Shamrock Handicap (Fox, 1926)
d: John Ford. 6 reels.
Janet Gaynor, Leslie Fenton, J. Farrell MacDonald, Louis Payne, Claire McDowell, Willard Louis, Andy Clark, Georgie Harris, Ely Reynolds, Thomas Delmar, Brandon

Hurst.
Sheila, fair colleen from Ireland, falls for Neil, a young American jockey.

Shanghai Bound (Paramount, 1927)
d: Luther Reed. 6 reels.
Richard Dix, Mary Brian, Charles Byer, George Irving, Jocelyn Lee, Tom Maguire, Frank Chew, Tom Gubbins, Arthur Hoyt, Tetsu Komai.
Jim, an American naval officer, finds himself and his crew in peril when they sail into Shanghai harbor during a local uprising.

Shanghai Rose (Trem Carr Productions/Rayart, 1929)
d: Scott Pembroke. 7 reels.
Irene Rich, William Conklin, Richard Walling, Ruth Hiatt, Anthony Merlo, Sid Saylor, Robert Dudley, DeSacia Mooers.
In San Francisco, a notorious woman known as "Shanghai Rose" runs a seedy ale house that attracts the criminal element. When a young deputy district attorney comes to investigate, Rose is fearful that he will discover the truth—that he is her own son, taken from her when he was a baby and she was still a respectable woman.

Shanghaied (Ralph Ince Productions/FBO of America, 1927)
d: Ralph Ince. 7 reels.
Ralph Ince, Patsy Ruth Miller, Alan Brooks, Gertrude Astor, Walt Robbins, H.J. Jacobson.
Haley, a sea captain, has a falling out with his first mate over a woman.

Shannon of the Sixth (Kalem, 1914)
d: George Melford. 5 reels.
Edward Clisbee, Paul C. Hurst, Douglas Gerrard, William Herman West, Jack Dillon, Thomas Lingham, Marin Sais, Jane Wolfe.
In 19th century India, British officers fight to quell an insurrection, and also vie for the love of the same woman.

The Shark (Fox, 1920)
d: Dell Henderson. 5 reels.
George Walsh, Robert Broderick, William G. Nally, James Mack, Henry Pemberton, Marie Pagano, Mary Hall.
"The Shark" is a seafaring man who falls in love with a society girl.

The Shark Master (Universal, 1921)
d: Fred LeRoy Granville. 5 reels.
Frank Mayo, May Collins, Dorris Deane, Herbert Fortier, Oliver A. Cross, "Smoke" Turner, Nick De Ruiz.
An adventurer is shipwrecked in the South Seas and, despite being engaged to a girl back home, falls in love with a native girl.

Shark Monroe (Paramount, 1918)
d: William S. Hart. 5 reels.
William S. Hart, Katherine MacDonald, Joe Singleton, George McDaniel, Bert Sprotte.
In the Northwest, a girl and her drunken brother board a ship bound for Alaska. The ship's captain, "Shark" Monroe, falls for the girl, and eventually saves her from a phony wedding to a slave trader.

Sharp Shooters (Fox, 1928)
d: J.G. Blystone. 6 reels.
George O'Brien, Lois Moran, Noah Young, Tom Dugan, William Demarest, Gwen Lee, Josef Swickard.
Comedy about George, a Navy man who's got a girl in every port, and the young woman who decides to win him away from all of them.

Shattered Dreams (Universal, 1922)
d: Paul Scardon. 5 reels.
Miss Du Pont, Bertram Grassby, Herbert Heyes, Eric Mayne.
Marie, a Parisian sculptress, selects a manly apache as a model.

Shattered Idols (J.L. Frothingham Productions/Associated First National, 1922)
d: Edward Sloman. 6 reels.
Marguerite De La Motte, William V. Mong, James Morrison, Frankie Lee, Ethel Grey, Alfred Allen, Louise Lovely, Harvey Clark, Josephine Crowell, Robert Littlefield, Mary Wynn, George Periolat, Thomas Ricketts.
David, a young Englishman whose father was killed in an uprising in India, grows up and falls in love with Sarasvati, a devout Hindu.

She (Fox, 1917)
d: Kenean Buel. 5 reels.
Valeska Suratt, Ben L. Taggart, Miriam Fouche, Wigney Percyval, Tom Burrough, Martin Reagan.
Leo, descendant of an Egyptian priest who was slain by Queen Ayesha thousands of years before, seeks to avenge his ancestor's death. He encounters the ageless queen guarded by cannibals, and finds she is still ruthless... and still capable of driving men mad.

She Couldn't Help It (Realart Pictures Corp., 1920)
d: Maurice Campbell. 5 reels.
Bebe Daniels, Emory Johnson, Wade Boteler, Vera Lewis, Herbert Standing, Helen Raymond, Ruth Renick, Gertrude Short, Milla Davenport.
Fresh from the orphanage, a girl pairs up with a jewel thief.

The She-Devil (Fox, 1918)
d: J. Gordon Edwards. 6 reels.
Theda Bara, Albert Roscoe, Frederick Bond, George McDaniel.
Lolette, a Spanish spitfire, follows an artist to France and becomes his model and his lover.

She Goes to War (United Artists, 1929)
d: Henry King. 10 reels. (Music, sound effects, part talkie.)
Al St. John, Alma Rubens, Glen Walters, Eleanor Boardman, Edmund Burns, John Holland, Margaret Seddon, Yola D'Avril, Evelyn Hall, Augustino Borgato, Dina Smirnova.
Joan, a society snob, sees the coming of war as an opportunity for an overseas assignment and adventure. In France, she toys with the affections of various men, ignoring the very real sacrifices that other women in her unit are making. But when she finds her soldier lover drunk while on duty, she dons his uniform and goes to war in his place, eventually realizing the deadly seriousness of her commitment.

She Hired a Husband (Universal, 1918)
d: Jack Dillon. 5 reels.
Priscilla Dean, Pat O'Malley, Marian Skinner, Frederick Vroom, F.A. Turner, Charles Gerrard, Sam Appel, Harry Todd.
Daphne, an impetuous romantic, falls in love twice but rejects her lover each time. Finally, she vows to marry the next man she meets. The "next man" turns out to be a bearded lumberjack who does agree to marry her, but after the nuptials, he finds the impulsive Daphne a tigress who must be tamed.

The She Tiger — see: The Love Thief (1916)

The She Wolf (Frohman Amusement Corp., 1919)
d: Cliff Smith. 5 reels.
Texas Guinan, George Chesboro, Ah Wing, Charles Robertson, Anna Wild, Jack Richardson, Josie Sedgwick.
A man-hating female nevertheless is grateful to a stranger who once befriended her.

She Wolves (Fox, 1925)
d: Maurice Elvey. 6 reels.
Alma Rubens, Jack Mulhall, Bertram Grassby, Harry Myers, Judy King, Fred Walton, Diana Miller, Josef Swickard, Helen Dunbar, Charles Clary.
In France, a young woman is forced to marry for wealth instead of love. She goes through with the wedding but makes her husband's life so miserable he leaves for Paris on an extended vacation. In this case, absence does make the heart grow fonder; the young wife eventually follows her husband to Paris, where they try to make up for lost time.

The Sheik (Famous Players-Lasky/Paramount, 1921)
d: George Melford. 7 reels.
Rudolph Valentino, Agnes Ayres, Adolphe Menjou, Walter Long, Lucien Littlefield, Patsy Ruth Miller, F.R. Butler.
Diana, a vivacious young Englishwoman, meets an Arabian sheik in his country. He tries to force his attentions on her, but she resists. After Diana is captured by renegade Arabs, the sheik and his men attack the bandits and rescue her. Now the tables are turned, for Diana finds herself more than grateful to him and declares she is in love with the sheik after all.

Shell Forty-Three (New York Motion Picture Corp./Triangle, 1916)
d: Reginald Barker. 5 reels.
H.B. Warner, Enid Markey, Jack Gilbert, George Fisher, Margaret Thompson, Louise Brownell, J.P. Lockney, Charles K. French.
In World War I, a British spy enters Germany as part of the Allied strategy.

The Shell Game (Metro, 1918)
d: George D. Baker. 5 reels.
Emmy Wehlen, Henry Kolker, Joseph Kilgour, Ganny Cogan, Ricca Allen, Hugh Jeffrey, Richard Thornton, Clarence Heritage, Donald McBride.
A New York millionaire is reunited with his long-lost daughter... or so he thinks. The "daughter" is really a phony, taking part in a confidence game.

Sheltered Daughters (Realart Pictures, 1921)
d: Edward Dillon. 5 reels.
Justine Johnstone, Riley Hatch, Warner Baxter, Charles Gerard, Helen Ray, Edna Holland, James Laffey, Jimmie Lapsley, Dan E. Charles.
Jeanne and Adele, schoolgirl chums, live in a dream world supplied by their overprotective parents.

The Shepherd King (Fox, 1923)
d: J. Gordon Edwards. 9 reels.
Violet Mersereau, Edy Darclea, Virginia Lucchetti, Nero Bernardi, Guido Trento, Ferrucio Biancini, Alessandro Salvini, Mariano Bottino, Samuel Balestra, Adriano Bocanera.
Biblical drama based on the story of David and Goliath.

The Shepherd of the Hills (First National, 1928)
d: Albert Rogell. 9 reels.
Alec B. Francis, Molly O'Day, John Boles, Matthew Betz, Romaine Fielding, Otis Harlan, Joseph Bennett, Maurice Murphy, Edythe Chapman, Carl Stockdale, Marian Douglas.
In the Ozark Mountains, a stranger comes to be known as "the Shepherd of the hills."

The Sheriff of Hope Eternal (Ben Wilson Productions/Arrow Film Corp., 1921)
d: Ben Wilson. 5 reels.
Jack Hoxie, Marin Sais, Joseph Girard, William Dyer, Bee Monson, Theodore Brown, Wilbur McGaugh.
Out West, a newly elected sheriff must fight off a murdering gambler.

The Sheriff's Son (Thomas H. Ince/Paramount, 1919)
d: Victor L. Schertzinger. 5 reels.
Charles Ray, Seena Owen, John P. Lockney, Clyde Benson, Charles K. French, Otto Hoffman, Lamar Johnstone, Buck Jones.
In New Mexico, a young man seeks to avenge the death of his father, the former sheriff.

Sherlock Brown (Metro, 1922)
d: Bayard Veiller. 5 reels.
Bert Lytell, Ora Carew, Sylvia Breamer, DeWitt Jennings, Theodore von Eltz, Wilton Taylor, Hardee Kirkland, George Barnum, George Kuwa.
Comedy about "Sherlock" Brown, a correspondence-school detective, who against all odds thwarts a plot to steal a secret formula.

Sherlock Holmes (Essanay, 1916)
d: Arthur Berthelet. 7 reels.
William Gillette, Marjorie Kay, Ernest Maupain, Edward Fielding, Stewart Robbins, Hugh Thompson, Ludwig Kreiss, Mario Majeroni, William Postance, Chester Beery.
Holmes, the famous British detective, is hired by an aristocratic family to retrieve some embarrassing documents from Alice, a working class girl.

Sherlock Holmes (Goldwyn, 1922)
d: Albert Parker. 9 reels.
John Barrymore, Roland Young, Carol Dempster, Gustav von Seyffertitz, Louis Wolheim, Percy Knight, William H. Powell, Hedda Hopper, Peggy Bayfield, Margaret Kemp, Ander Randolf, Robert Schable, Reginald Denny, David Torrence, Robert Fischer, Lumsden Hare, Jerry Devine, John Willard.
Holmes is called to help a friend of Dr. Watson's who's been unjustly charged with theft.

Sherlock Jr. (Buster Keaton Productions/MGM, 1924)
d: Buster Keaton. 5 reels.
Buster Keaton, Kathryn McGuire, Ward Crane, Joseph Keaton, Horace Morgan, Jane Connelly, Erwin Connelly, Ford West, George Davis, John Patrick, Ruth Holly.
A young man dreams of being a famous detective, but he's stuck in a thankless job as projectionist for a local movie house. In a dream, he enters the world of screen make-believe, becomes the famous detective, and wins the girl.
Probably Keaton's best film, with prodigious camera effects, spectacular stunts and a hilarious climactic chase.

Sherry (Edgar Lewis Productions, Inc./Pathé, 1920)
d: Edgar Lewis. 7 reels.
Pat O'Malley, Lillian Hall, Harry Spingler, Maggie Halloway, Richard Cummings, Alred Fisher, Will Jeffries, Scott McKee.
Sheridan — known as "Sherry" — gets a job as bodyguard to a

THE SHEIK (1921). Sheik Ahmed (Rudolph Valentino) orders the English adventuress Diana (Agnes Ayres) out of his tent when she refuses to bend to his will. Filmed the year after The Four Horsemen of the Apocalypse made Valentino a superstar, The Sheik advanced his legend and set millions of female hearts to fluttering. Its popularity created a demand for a sequel, The Son of the Sheik (1926). That would be the last film for the enigmatic screen idol, for Valentino died tragically in 1926, at the age of 31.

* * * * *

wealthy family, and apprehends two burglars.

She's A Sheik (Famous Players-Lasky/Paramount, 1927)
d: Clarence Badger. 6 reels.
Bebe Daniels, Richard Arlen, Josephine Dunn, James Bradbury Jr., William Powell, Billy Franey, Paul McAllister, Al Fremont.
Zaida, granddaughter of an Arabian sheik, goes all-out to win a handsome captain at a desert carnival.

She's My Baby (Sterling Pictures, 1927)
d: Fred Windemere. 6 reels.
Robert Agnew, Kathleen Myers, Earle Williams, Grace Carlyle, Mildred Harris, Alphonse Martel, Max Asher, William Irving.
When ennui settles into their 21-year marriage, John and Mary continue to profess affection for each other, for the sake of their daughter Bernice. Both parents latch on to new lovers, but these flings are no substitute for the real thing, as they discover when their basic love for each other breaks through the frivolous facades. Bernice finds her true love, as well.

The Shield of Honor (Universal, 1927)
d: Emory Johnson. 6 reels.
Neil Hamilton, Dorothy Gulliver, Ralph Lewis, Nigel Barrie, Claire McDowell, Fred Esmelton, Harry Northrup, Thelma Todd, David Kirby, Joseph Girard, William Bakewell.
Jack, a policeman's aviator son, apprehends jewel thieves in a daring air battle.

Shifting Sands (Triangle, 1918)
d: Albert Parker. 5 reels.
Gloria Swanson, Joe King, Harvey Clark, Leone Carton, Lillian Langdon, Arthur Millett.
A young woman is unjustly sent to jail, but fights bitterness and upon her release she devotes her life to charity work. She meets and falls in love with a philanthropist and they marry. But the man who had framed her for robbery now re-enters her life and threatens to expose her shameful past.

Shifting Sands (Luxor Pictures/W.W. Hodkinson, 1923)
d: Fred Leroy Granville. 6 reels.
Peggy Hyland, Lewis Willoughby, Richard Atwood, Mademoiselle Valia, Gibson Gowland, Tony Melford, Douglas Webster.
Weepy melodrama about a wife who becomes infatuated with a Frenchman and, taking her son with her, follows him to North Africa. She'll regret doing so.

The Shine Girl (Thanhouser/Pathé, 1916)
d: William S. Parke. 5 reels.
Gladys Hulette, Wayne Arey, Kathryn Adams, Ethelmary Oakland, John Cook.
When a shoeshine girl is arrested for stealing a loaf of bread to help feed a hungry family, she's hauled into court. But the judge recognizes the girl's basic kindness.

A Ship Comes In (De Mille Pictures/Pathé, 1928)
d: William K. Howard. 7 reels.
Rudolph Schildkraut, Louise Dresser, Lucien Littlefield, Robert Edeson, Louis Natheaux.
A Hungarian immigrant in the United States has his patriotism for his new country severely tested when he is unjustly convicted of a crime.

The Ship of Doom (Triangle, 1917)
d: Wyndham Gittens. 5 reels.
Claire McDowell, Monte Blue, Arthur Millet, Aaron Edwards, Frank Brownlee.
Two lovers on a sinking ship are picked up by a slave trader.

Ship of Souls (Encore Pictures/Associated Exhibitors, 1925)
d: Charles Miller. 6 reels.
Bert Lytell, Lillian Rich, Gertrude Astor, Earl Metcalf, Russell Simpson, Ynez Seabury, Cyril Chadwick, Jean Perry, Pete Mauer, W.J. Miller, Jack Irwin.
In the great Northwest, Christine, daughter of a local proctor, falls for Barnes, a married man whose wife has deserted him.

Shipwrecked (Metropolitan Pictures Corp. of California, 1926)
d: Joseph Henabery. 7 reels.
Seena Owen, Joseph Schildkraut, Matthew Betz, Clarence Burton, Laska Winter, Lionel Belmore, Erwin Connelly.
An artist's model disguises herself as a boy and stows away on a ship.

Shirley Kaye (C.K.Y. Film Corp./Select, 1917)
d: Joseph Kaufman. 5 reels.
Clara Kimball Young, Corliss Giles, George Fawcett, George Backus, Claire Whitney, Nellie Lindrich, John Sunderland, Mrs. F.O. Winthrop, Frank Otto.
Shirley, daughter of a railroad magnate, helps save her father's business.

Shirley of the Circus (Fox, 1922)
d: Rowland V. Lee. 5 reels.
Shirley Mason, George O'Hara, Crauford Kent, Alan Hale, Lule Warrenton, Maude Wayne, Mathilde Brundage.
Nita, a circus girl, accepts an artist's kind offer of paying her way through school, but her circus blood gets the better of her and she finds her way back to the sawdust trail.

The Shock (Universal, 1923)
d: Lambert Hillyer. 7 reels.
Lon Chaney, Virginia Valli, Christina Mayo, Jack Mower, William Welsh, Henry Barrows, Harry Devere, John Beck, Walter Long.
A banker is blackmailed by a San Francisco gang leader.

The Shock Punch (Famous Players-Lasky/Paramount, 1925)
d: Paul Sloane. 6 reels.
Richard Dix, Frances Howard, Theodore Babcock, Percy Moore, Charles Beyer, Gunboat Smith, Jack Scannell, Walter Long, Paul Panzer.
Randall, a boxer with an impressive knockout record, gets a construction job just to be near his beloved, the daughter of a contractor. Once on the job, he learns that the foreman is deliberately trying to sabotage the project to ruin the contractor financially. Randall foils the foreman's plans and wins the girl's hand in marriage.

A Shocking Night (Universal, 1921)
d: Eddie Lyons. 5 reels.
Eddie Lyons, Lee Moran, Alta Allen, Lillian Hall, Lionel Belmore, Clark Comstock, Florence Mayon, Charles McHugh.
Remake of the 1918 Universal film *All Night*, in which a formerly wealthy couple run into hard times and must masquerade as their own servants during an important business dinner.

Shod With Fire (Fox, 1920)
d: Emmett J. Flynn. 5 reels.

444

SHORE LEAVE (1925). Sailor on leave "Bilge" Smith (Richard Barthelmess) courts Connie, a local dressmaker, never thinking she will take the flirtation seriously. But she does, and their lives are forever changed. First feature film version of the durable Hubert Osborne play Shore Leave. It would be remade as Hit the Deck (1930), Follow the Fleet (1936), and Hit the Deck (1955).

* * * * *

445

William Russell, Helen Ferguson, Betty Schade, Robert Cain, George Stewart, Nelson McDowell, Jack Connolly.
Out West, a young woman married to a drunk falls in love with a noble cowhand.

Shoes (Universal, 1916)
d: Lois Weber. 5 reels.
Mary MacLaren, Harry Griffith, Jessie Arnold, William V. Mong.
Drama about a family struggling to survive in poverty.

The Shoes That Danced (Triangle, 1918)
d: Frank Borzage. 5 reels.
Pauline Starke, Wallace MacDonald, Dick Rosson, Anna Dodge, Lydia Yeamans Titus, Anne Kroman, Edward Brady, William Dyer.
East Side street gangs get involved in a vaudeville show.

Shootin' for Love (Universal, 1923)
d: Edward Sedgwick. 5 reels.
Hoot Gibson, Laura LaPlante, Alfred Allen, William Welsh, William Steele, Arthur Mackley, W.T. McCulley, Kansas Moehring.
Duke, a ranchowner's son, returns from the war suffering from battle fatigue and a deadly fear of guns. But he gets over that fear fast, when a neighboring rancher tries to move in on their property.

Shootin' Irons (Paramount, 1927)
d: Richard Rosson. 6 reels.
Sally Blane, Jack Luden, Fred Kohler, Richard Carlyle, Loyal Underwood, Scott McGee, Guy Oliver, Arthur Millett.
Out West, a rancher harbors a fugitive from justice and his daughter, knowing that the fugitive is actually innocent of the crime with which he is charged.

The Shooting of Dan McGrew (Popular Plays and Players, Inc./Metro, 1915)
d: Herbert Blaché. 5 reels.
Edmund Breese, William A. Morse, Kathryn Adams, Audrine Stark, Betty Riggs, Evelyn Brent, Wallace Stopp.
In the frozen northwest, a prospector plays piano and sings a telling tale about his wife, his daughter, and dangerous Dan McGrew.

The Shooting of Dan McGrew (S-L Pictures/Metro, 1924)
d: Clarence Badger. 7 reels.
Barbara LaMarr, Lew Cody, Mae Busch, Percy Marmont, Max Ascher, Fred Warren, George Siegmann, Nelson McDowell, Bert Sprotte, Ina Anson, Philippe DeLacy, Harry Lorraine.
That lady that's known as Lou leaves her husband and runs away with Dan McGrew to Alaska, where she becomes a dance hall girl. But her husband's arrival in the Klondike forces a showdown with McGrew.

The Shop Girl (Vitagraph, 1916)
d: George D. Baker. 5 reels.
Edith Storey, Antonio Moreno, Lillian Burns, John Costello, Harold Foshay, Marion Henry, Josephine Earle, Claire McCormack, Emily Leaske, Thomas Mills, Templar Saxe.
Aboard an ocean liner, a shopgirl falls in love with a scion of wealth. She thinks he's only flirting, but after the ship docks in New York he looks her up and finds her... just in time to save her from her boss' unwelcome advances.

The Shopworn Angel (Paramount, 1928)
d: Richard Wallace. 8 reels. (Part talkie.)
Nancy Carroll, Gary Cooper, Paul Lukas, Roscoe Karns.
During World War I, an army private goes AWOL to be with his chorus girl sweetheart.

Shore Acres (All Star Feature Corp., 1914)
d: John H. Pratt. 5 reels.
Charles A. Stevenson, William Riley Hatch, Conway Tearle, E.J. Connelly, Violet Horner, Gladys Fairbanks, Harry Knowles, Philip Traub, Madge Evans.
Blake, an unscrupulous land developer, convinces a young man to mortgage his farm—against the advice of his wife and brother.
This film was remade by Screen Classics in 1920.

Shore Acres (Screen Classic, Inc./Metro, 1920)
d: Rex Ingram. 6 reels.
Alice Lake, Robert Walker, Edward Connelly, Frank Brownlee, Joseph Kilgour, Margaret McWade, Nancy Caswell, Franklyn Garland, Burwell Hamrick, Richard Headrick, Carol Jackson, John P. Morse, Mary Beaton.
Martin, a lighthouse operator, is duped into a land speculation scheme and loses his money. But Blake, the duplicitous real estate agent who now owns Martin's mortgage, offers to cancel the debt in return for amorous favors from Martin's daughter.
Remake, with some plot alterations, of the All Star's 1914 film *Shore Acres*. Both versions were based on the play of the same name by James A. Herne.

Shore Leave (Inspiration Pictures/First National, 1925)
d: John S. Robertson. 7 reels.
Richard Barthelmess, Dorothy Mackaill, Ted McNamara, Nick Long, Marie Shotwell, Arthur Metcalfe, Warren Cook, Samuel Hines.
A sailor on leave woos the village dressmaker, not realizing she is taking him seriously.

Short Skirts (Universal, 1921)
d: Harry B. Harris. 5 reels.
Gladys Walton, Ena Gregory, Jack Mower, Jean Hathaway, Scotty MacGregor, Edward Martindel, Harold Miller, William Welsh, Howard Ralston.
Seventeen-year-old Natalie resents being treated as if she were a little girl.

Shorty Escapes Marriage (New York Motion Picture Corp./Mutual, 1914)
d: Richard Stanton. 4 reels.
Shorty Hamilton, Charles Swickard, Thomas Chatterton, Rhea Mitchell.
A ranch hand falls into the hands of Mexican bandidos, who hold him captive and prevent him from marrying an eastern woman he's never met—who, it turns out, would have been wrong for him.

Should a Girl Marry? (Trem Carr Productions/Rayart, 1928)
d: Scott Pembroke. 8 reels. (Part talkie.)
Helen Foster, Donald Keith, William V. Mong, Andy Clyde, Dot Farley, George Chesebro, Dorothy Vernon.
Alice, a new girl in town, meets and falls in love with Jerry, a banker's son. But she's got a past, and after Jerry proposes marriage she'll have to decide whether to keep it bottled up or tell all and face the music.

Should a Husband Forgive? (Fox, 1919)
d: R.A. Walsh. 6 reels.
Miriam Cooper, Mrs. James K. Hackett, Eric Mayne, Vincent Coleman, Lyster Chambers, Percy Standing, Charles Craig, Martha Mansfield, James Marcus, Johnny Ries.

Mary and her son John are separated for years, until one day his sweetheart coincidentally becomes Mary's secretary.

Should a Mother Tell? (Fox, 1915)
d: J. Gordon Edwards. 5 reels.
Betty Nansen, Stuart Holmes, Runa Hodges, Jean Sothern, Stephen Grattan, Grace Everett, Ralph Johnston, Kate Blancke, Arthur Hoops, Claire Whitney, Henri Leone.
Pamela is raised by her mother's friends and, as she grows up, falls in love with their son. They are engaged to be married, but her mother wonders: Should she tell her future in-laws that Pamela's father was a murderer?

Should a Wife Forgive? (Equitable Motion Pictures Corp./World Film Corp., 1915)
d: H.M. Horkheimer. 5 reels.
Lillian Lorraine, Mabel Van Buren, Henry King, Lewis Cody, William Lampe, Mollie McConnell, Fred Whitman, Daniel Gilfether, Baby Osborne.
A happily married man begins an affair with a dance hall girl.

Should a Wife Work? (Plimpton Pictures/J.W. Film Corp., 1920)
d: Horace G. Plimpton. 5 reels.
Edith Stockton, Alice Lowe, Stuart Robson, Louis Kimball, Elinor Curtis, Walter McEwen, Harry Mowbray.
Betty marries, but is desired by a wealthy cad named Paget who controls her husband's income.

Should a Woman Divorce? (Ivan Film Productions, Inc., 1914)
d: Edward McKim. 5 reels.
Leonid Samoloff, Lea Leland, Anna Lehr, Mabel Wright, Ordean Stark, Robert Taber, Frederic Roberts, Milton S. Gould.
Grace, the farmer's daughter, marries a rancher but later regrets it. When her former beau shows up and Grace is attracted to him again, they run away together... but she'll regret that too.

Should a Woman Tell? (Screen Classics, Inc./Metro, 1919)
d: John E. Ince. 6 reels.
Alice Lake, Frank Currier, Jack Mulhall, Relyea Anderson, Lydia Knott, Don Baily, Jack Gilbert, Richard Headrick, Carol Jackson.

A small-town girl visits the big city and suffers abuse at the hands of a strange man. When she returns home, her boyfriend proposes marriage to her, but she feels ashamed of her big-city experience.

Should She Obey? (Arizona Film Co., 1917)
d: George A. Siegmann. 7 reels.
George A. Siegmann, Norbert Myles, Gene Genung, Billie West, andrew Arbuckle, Alice Wilson, James Harrison, Robert Lawlor, Herbert Sutch, Laura Winston, Margaret MacQuarrie.
Blake, an unsavory opportunist, blackmails his former friend and uses the extortion money to open a dance hall with his own daughter installed as the main attraction.

The Show (MGM, 1926)
d: Tod Browning. 7 reels.
Renee Adoree, John Gilbert, Lionel Barrymore, Edward Connelly, Gertrude Short.
Performers in a carnival side show play at love, but the man's enormous ego blocks any real affection. Finally his erstwhile lady love saves him from death by decapitation,

and the movie hints at a reconciliation. But even at the fadeout, we doubt that this charming scoundrel will ever really change.

Show Boat (Universal, 1929)
d: Harry Pollard. 12 reels. (Music, sound effects, part talkie.)
Laura LaPlante, Joseph Schildkraut, Otis Harlan, Helen Morgan, Emily Fitzroy, Alma Rubens, Elsie Bartlett, Jack McDonald, Stepin Fetchit, Neely Edwards, Theodore Lorch, Jane LaVerne, Gertrude Howard, Carl Laemmle, Florenz Ziegfeld.
The Kern-Hammerstein classic musical is given its first screen incarnation in this partially silent version.
Laemmle, Ziegfeld, and Miss Morgan appear only in the sound prologue.

The Show Down (Universal, 1917)
d: Lynn Reynolds. 5 reels.
Myrtle Gonzales, George Hernandez, Arthur Hoyt, George Chesbro, Edward Cecil, Jean Hersholt.
When an ocean liner sinks and the survivors scramble to safety on a deserted island, the experience brings out their true natures.

Show Folks (Pathé, 1928)
d: Paul L. Stein. 8 reels.
Eddie Quillan, Lina Basquette, Carol Lombard, Robert Armstrong, Bessie Barriscale.
Dance partners Eddie and Rita make a big hit on stage, but quarrel and break up. Eddie gets a new partner—a strumpet named Cleo—but she walks out in a huff on opening night. What to do? Fortunately, Rita's in the audience. When she takes Cleo's place on stage, the old magic clicks and Eddie and Rita are again a hit.

The Show Girl (Trem Carr Productions/Rayart, 1927)
d: Charles J. Hunt. 6 reels.
Mildred Harris, Gaston Glass, Mary Carr, Robert McKim, Eddie Borden, William Strauss, Sam Sidman, Aryel Darma.
Maizie, formerly a honky-tonk club owner, clicks as the star of a big theatrical production.

Show Girl (First National, 1928)
d: Alfred Santell. 7 reels.
Donald Reed, Lee Moran, Alice White, Charles Delaney, Richard Tucker, Gwen Lee, James Finlayson, Kate Price, Hugh Roman, Bernard Randall.
Miss White plays Dixie Dugan, a night club cutie, who gets involved (innocently) with sugar daddies, killers, and tabloid reporters. But she emerges with her reputation intact and gets her big chance on Broadway.
Alice White reprised her role as Dixie in a 1930 sound sequel, *Show Girl in Hollywood.*

The Show Off (Paramount, 1926)
d: Malcolm St. Clair. 7 reels.
Ford Sterling, Lois Wilson, Louise Brooks, Claire McDowell, E.W. Goodrich.
Sterling, formerly chief of the Keystone Kops, has the role of his career as the "show off" of the title. He's a raucous, annoying, insensitive boor who nevertheless is lucky in love, and marries the girl of his dreams. Unfortunately, they can't live on his meager salary, so the happy couple move in with her not-so-happy family. In time, though—and against all odds— this sorry carbuncle of a man will surprise everyone, and come through in a big way that makes him the family's savior.

Show People (MGM, 1928)
d: King Vidor. 9 reels.
Marion Davies, William Haines, Del Henderson, Paul Ralli, Tenen Holtz, Harry Gribbon, Sidney Bracey, Polly Moran, Albert Conti.
A southern belle arrives in Hollywood, eager to work in motion pictures. With help from a nice guy on the inside, she catches on as an actress with a studio making slapstick comedies, but is soon lured away by a major studio that specializes in Artistic films, with a capital "A." Now a dramatic star, the girl makes plans to marry her new costar—mainly for publicity purposes. But the nice guy at her former studio, who really loves her, breaks up the wedding and brings the southern belle back down to earth.
Major star vehicle for Miss Davies, and her second hit comedy of 1928 directed by Vidor. (*The Patsy* was the first.) Several movie stars were persuaded to appear as themselves, primarily in a commissary scene. They include: Renee Adoree, Lew Cody, Karl Dane, Douglas Fairbanks, John Gilbert, William S. Hart, Rod La Rocque, and Norma Talmadge. Charlie Chaplin also appears as himself, and Miss Davies briefly appears as Marion Davies herself.

The Showdown (Paramount, 1928)
d: Victor Schertzinger. 8 reels.
Geroge Bancroft, Evelyn Brent, Neil Hamilton, Fred Kohler, Helen Lynch, Arnold Kent, Leslie Fenton, George Kuwa.
Sibyl, the comely wife of an oil man, finds herself trapped in the Mexican jungle with three of her husband's business cronies.

The Shriek of Araby (Mack Sennett/United Artists, 1923)
d: F. Richard Jones. 5 reels.
Ben Turpin, Kathryn McGuire, Dick Sutherland, George Cooper, Ray Grey, Louis Fronde, Charles Stevenson.
A parody of *The Sheik* (Paramount, 1921), this Sennett-concocted farce features the perpetually cross-eyed comic Ben Turpin as a movie bill-poster who, in a dream, fancies himself the Lion of the Sahara.

The Shrine of Happiness (Balboa Feature Film Co./Pathé, 1916)
d: Bertram Bracken. 5 reels.
Jackie Saunders, William Conklin, Paul Gilmore, Gordon Sackville, Charles Dudley, Bruce Smith.
Marie, an orphan, is taken in by Dick, her father's mining partner, and grows to love him.

The Shuttle (Select, 1918)
d: Rollin S. Sturgeon. 5 reels.
Constance Talmadge, Albert Roscoe, Edith Johnson, E.B. Tilton, Helen Dunbar, George McDaniel, Thomas Persse, Edward Peil, Casson Ferguson.
The daughter of an American millionaire visits her married sister in England, and finds that the sister's fortune is spent and her husband is shiftless and abusive.

Siberia (Fox, 1926)
d: Victor Schertzinger. 7 reels.
Alma Rubens, Edmund Lowe, Lou Tellegen, Tom Santschi, Paul Panzer, Vadim Uraneff, Lilyan Tashman, Helen D'Algy, James Marcus, Daniel Makarenko, Harry Gripp, Samuel Blum.
It's a perilous romance when a Russian royalist falls in love with Sonia, a schoolteacher in league with the revolutionaries.

Sick Abed (Famous Players-Lasky/Paramount, 1920)
d: Sam Wood. 5 reels.
Wallace Reid, Bebe Daniels, John Steppling, Winifred Greenwood, Tully Marshall, C.H. Geldart, Lucien Littlefield, Robert Bolder, Lorenza Lazzarini, George Kuwa.
To avoid a subpoena, a man pretends to be seriously ill... and falls in love with his nurse.

The Side Show of Life (Famous Players-Lasky/Paramount, 1924)
d: Herbert Brenon. 8 reels.
Ernest Torrence, Anna Q. Nilsson, Louise Lagrange, Maurice Cannon, Neil Hamilton, William Ricciardi, Lawrence D'Orsay, Effie Shannon, Katherine Lee.
In France during World War I, a juggler joins the army and rises through the ranks to become a brigadier general.

The Sideshow (Columbia, 1928)
d: Erle C. Kenton. 7 reels.
Ralph Graves, Marie Prevost, Little Billy, Alan Roscoe, Pat Harmon, Texas Madesen, Martha McGruger, Steve Clemento, Janet Ford, Paul Dismute, Bert Price, Chester Morton.
While working in the sideshow, Queenie discovers a plot to sabotage the circus.

The Siege (Universal, 1925)
d: Sven Gade. 7 reels.
Mary Alden, Eugene O'Brien, Virginia Valli, Marc MacDermott, Harry Lorraine, Beatrice Burnham, Helen Dunbar.
A hard-headed businesswoman plans to turn over her business to her nephew, but his ultra-modern wife presents an obstacle.

The Sign Invisible (Edgar Lewis Productions, Inc./First National, 1918)
d: Edgar Lewis. 5 reels.
Mitchell Lewis, Victor Sutherland, William A. Williams, Edward F. Roseman, Mabel Julienne Scott, Hedda Nova, Phil Sanford, Ray Chamberlain, William H. Cavanaugh.
A doctor, who has lost faith in himself because his own mother died on his operating table, moves to the Northwest to forget. But when he's forced to do emergency surgery on a wounded Indian brave, the operation is successful and the doctor's confidence returns.

The Sign of the Cactus (Universal, 1925)
d: Clifford Smith. 5 reels.
Jack Hoxie, Helen Holmes, Gordon Russell, Francis Ford, Josef Swickard, Frank Newberg, Jack Pratt, Bobby Gordon, Muriel Frances Dana.
Out West, a mysterious midnight rider helps ranchers who have been cheated out of their water rights.

The Sign of the Poppy (Universal, 1916)
d: Charles Swickard. 5 reels.
Hobart Henley, Mina Cunard, Gertrude Selby, Wilbur Higby, Robert Clark, Garland Briden.
In New York's Chinatown, a drug addict kidnaps his twin brother and tries to take over his life... and his wife.
Hobart Henley has a double role, playing both twins.

The Sign of the Spade (American Film Co./Mutual, 1916)
d: Murdock MacQuarrie. 5 reels.
Alan Forest, Helene Rosson, Warren Ellsworth, Harvey Clarke, Clarence Burton, Robert Miller, George Gerhardt.
A gang of murderous thieves kill, and then pin an ace of spades on the body.

SHOW PEOPLE (1928). William Haines, at left, happily receives an autograph from Charlie Chaplin (right), but his companion Marion Davies is wary, thinking the actor is a fraud, since Chaplin is not wearing his usual tramp makeup.

* * * * *

The Sign on the Door (Norma Talmadge Productions/Associated First National, 1921)
d: Herbert Brenon. 7 reels.
Norma Talmadge, Charles Richman, Lew Cody, David Proctor, Augustus Balfour, Mac Barnes, Helen Weir, Robert Agnew, Martinie Burnlay, Paul McAllister, Louis Hendricks.
When Ann, a proper young woman, marries into society, her past comes back to haunt her in the form of an official picture of her taken during a police raid, years before.

The Signal Tower (Universal, 1924)
d: Clarence Brown. 7 reels.
Virginia Valli, Wallace Beery, Rockliffe Fellowes, J. Farrell MacDonald, Frankie Darro, Dot Farley, James O. Barrows, Clarence Brown.
A shady character accepts the hospitality of a railroad signalman, then makes a move on the signalman's wife.

Silas Marner (Thanhouser/Mutual, 1916)
d: Ernest Warde. 7 reels.
Frederick Warde, Louise Emerald Bates, Morgan Jones, Thomas Curran, Ethel Jewett, Frank L. McNish, Hector Dion, Arthur L. Rankin, Elsie Jordan.
In 19th century England, a lonely weaver gains a "daughter" when a young orphan girl finds her way into his house.

Silence (DeMille Pictures/Producers Distributing Corp., 1926)
d: Rupert Julian. 8 reels.
Vera Reynolds, H.B. Warner, Raymond Hatton, Rockliffe Fellowes, Jack Mulhall, Virginia Pearson.
Warren, a condemned man awaiting execution for murder, remains silent about the real killer in order to protect his former wife.

The Silence Sellers (Metro, 1917)
d: Burton L. King. 5 reels.
Olga Petrova, Mahlon Hamilton, Wyndham Standing, Violet Reed, Charles Dungan, Myles McCarthy, Henry Leone, Edward James.
Society drama about a rich girl whose car breaks down during a storm and who's forced to spend the night with a stranger.

The Silent Accuser (MGM, 1924)
w, d: Chester Franklin. 6 reels.
Eleanor Boardman, Raymond McKee, Edna Tichenor, Peter the Great (the dog).
A young woman dresses as a man to search for the murderer of her stepfather.

The Silent Avenger (Gotham Productions/Lumas Film Corp., 1927)
d: James P. Hogan. 6 reels.
Charles Delaney, Duane Thompson, David Kirby, George Chesebro, Robert E. Homans, Clarence H. Wilson, Buck Black, Thunder, the dog.
The son of a railroad president, in Tennessee to acquire an important right of way, is twice saved from villains by his faithful dog Thunder.

The Silent Barrier (Louis Tracy Productions, Inc./Pathé, 1920)
d: William Worthington. 6 reels.
Sheldon Lewis, Corinne Barker, Florence Dixon, Donald Cameron, Gladys Hulette, Adolf Milar, Ernest Des Baillets, Fuller Mellish, Joseph Burke, Mathilde Brundage.
Helen, a society reporter, tries to convince a Swiss mountain guide to forgive the daughter he has disowned. Meanwhile,

Helen is herself being stalked by a disagreeable millionaire.

The Silent Battle (Universal, 1916)
d: Jack Conway. 5 reels.
J. Warren Kerrigan, Lois Wilson, Maud George, Harry Carter, Ray Hanford, J.F. Connolly.
Jane falls in love with Tom, a reformed alcoholic who once tried to rape her while he was under the influence.

The Silent Command (Fox, 1923)
d: J. Gordon Edwards. 8 reels.
Edmund Lowe, Bela Lugosi, Carl Harbaugh, Martin Faust, Gordon McEdward, Byron Douglas, Theodore Babcock, George Lessey, Warren Cook, Henry Armetta, Alma Tell.
Saboteurs use a vamp to try and distract a Naval Captain from his duty at the Panama Canal, but he's on to them... and to her.

The Silent Guardian (Truart Film Corp., 1926)
d: William Bletcher. 5 reels.
Louise Lorraine, Harry Tenbrook, L.J. O'Connor, Art Acord, Grace Woods, Rex, the dog.
Out West, a valiant dog saves his master from certain death.

The Silent Hero (Duke Worne Productions/Rayart, 1927)
d: Duke Worne. 6 reels.
Robert Frazer, Edna Murphy, Ernest Hilliard, Joseph Girard, Harry Allen, Napoleon Bonaparte, the dog.
In the Frozen North, a german shepherd aids his master in routing a claim jumper.

The Silent Lady (Universal, 1917)
d: Elsie Jane Wilson. 5 reels.
Gretchen Lederer, Zoe Rae, Winter Hall, Harry Holden, Edwin Brown, Lule Warrenton, E.A. Warren.
When a nurse is hired to care for the foster daughter of a lighthouse keeper, it develops that she was once the lover of the lighthouse inspector.

The Silent Lie (Fox 1917)
d: R.A. Walsh. 5 reels.
Miriam Cooper, Ralph Lewis, Charles Clary, Monroe Salisbury, Henry A. Barrows, Howard Davies, William Eagle Shirt.
In the Northwest, a lumberjack falls in love and marries... but his bride has a crimson past that she hasn't revealed to her new husband.

The Silent Lover (First National, 1926)
d: George Archainbaud. 7 reels.
Viola Dana, Charlie Murray, Milton Sills, Natalie Kingston, William Humphrey, Arthur E. Carewe, William V. Mong, Claude King, Arthur Stone, Alma Bennett, Montagu Love.
At a Foreign Legion outpost, a French nobleman falls for a Bedouin girl.

The Silent Man (Thomas H. Ince/Artcraft, 1917)
d: William S. Hart. 5 reels.
William S. Hart, Vola Vale, Robert McKim, Harold Goodwin, J.P. Lockney, George P. Nichols, Gertrude Claire, Milton Ross, Dorcas Matthews.
Out West, a silent prospector strikes gold.

The Silent Master (Robert Warwick Film Corp./Selznick, 1917)
d: Leonce Perret. 6 reels.
Robert Warwick, Olive Tell, Donald Galaher, Anna Little, Juliette Moore, Henri Valbel, Valentin Petit, George Clark.
In Paris, a secret Apache gang has its own system of meting out justice.

Silent Movie (Twentieth Century-Fox, 1976)
d: Mel Brooks. 87 min. (About 8 reels.)
Mel Brooks, Marty Feldman, Dom DeLuise, Bernadette Peters, Sid Caesar, Paul Newman, James Caan, Liza Minnelli, Anne Bancroft, Burt Reynolds.
With this film, director/writer/star Mel Brooks created a loving homage to silent comedies. It's not a spoof, but an affectionate tribute to the silent cinema, observing silent era conventions and pacing.
There is no dialogue, only music and sound effects. The setting is 1976 modern, with color and widescreen; but where you would expect to hear dialogue, instead you see title cards, most of them infused with Brooks' manic sense of humor.
Brooks plays a once-successful film director who's hit the skids by way of the bottle. Now sober and seeking a comeback, he teams with two buddies (Feldman and DeLuise) to sell a major studio on making the first silent movie in 40 years.

The Silent Partner (Lasky Feature Plays/Paramount, 1917)
d: Marshall A. Neilan. 5 reels.
Blanche Sweet, Thomas Meighan, Henry Hebert, Ernest Joy, Mabel Van Buren, Florence Smythe, Mayme Kelso.
Jane, a super-efficient secretary for a securities firm, is so essential to the firm's success that she is, in effect, "the silent partner."

The Silent Partner (Famous Players-Lasky/Paramount, 1923)
d: Charles Maigne. 6 reels.
Leatrice Joy, Owen Moore, Robert Edeson, Robert Schable, Patterson Dial, E.H. Calvert, Maude Wayne, Bess Flowers, Laura Anson, Bert Woodruff, Robert Grey.
Lisa, wife of a big investor in the stock market, squirrels away the money he gives her instead of buying fancy clothes and jewelry. A good thing too, since the husband's investments turn sour and he loses everything. But Lisa is there with the good news: they've still got money.

The Silent Power (Gotham Productions/Lumas Film Corp., 1926)
d: Frank O'Connor. 6 reels.
Ralph Lewis, Ethel Shannon, Charles Delaney, Vadim Uraneff, Robert E. Homans.
When Rob, a young engineer, is found guilty of a murder he didn't commit and is about to take the electric chair, his own father is on duty as the man who must pull the fatal switch. But at the last minute the real killer, consumed with guilt, cuts the power line and Rob is saved.

The Silent Rider (Triangle, 1918)
d: Cliff Smith. 5 reels.
Roy Stewart, L.D. McKee, Ethel Fleming, Leo Willis.
Out West, a Texas Ranger works incognito to defeat cattle rustlers.

The Silent Rider (Universal, 1927)
d: Lynn Reynolds. 6 reels.
Hoot Gibson, Blanche Mehaffey, Otis Harlan, Ethan Laidlaw, Wendell Phillips Franklin, Arthur Morrison, Nora Cecil, Dick LaReno, Lon Poff, Dick L'Estrange.
Out West, cowpoke Jerry Alton becomes smitten with Marian, the ranch cook. The trouble is, she's looking for a husband with red hair, and Jerry's hair is black.

Silent Sanderson (Hunt Stromberg Corp./Producers Distributing Corp., 1925)

d: Scott R. Dunlap. 5 reels.
Harry Carey, Trilby Clark, John Miljan, Gardner James, Edith Yorke, Stanton Heck, Sheldon Lewis.
In the Yukon, a westerner who left home to forget the girl he lost to another man runs into her again: She's now a dance hall girl.

The Silent Stranger (Monogram Pictures/FBO of America, 1924)
d: Albert Rogell. 5 reels.
Fred Thomson, Hazel Keener, George Williams, Richard Headrick, Frank Hagney, Horace Carpenter, Bud Osborne, Bob Reeves, George Nichols.
Out West, a Secret Service agent disguised as a deaf mute arrives in town and solves the mystery of a recent string of mail thefts.

Silent Strength (Vitagraph, 1919)
d: Paul Scardon. 5 reels.
Harry T. Morey, Betty Blythe, Robert Gaillard, Bernard Siegel, Herbert pattee, James Costello.
Dan, a loner who lives in a mountain cabin, receives word from his cousin that they have inherited an estate. When Dan travels to the city to meet his cousin and claim his inheritance, he is startled to notice that his cousin closely resembles him.
Morey portrays both roles, the loner and his city cousin.

Silent Trail (El Dorado Productions, 1928)
d: J.P. McGowan. 5 reels.
Bob Custer, Peggy Montgomery, John Lowell, J.P. McGowan, Mack V. Wright, Nancy Lee, Jack Ponder.
Chased out of town following a barroom brawl, a pair of cowboys join a gang of rustlers.

The Silent Voice (Quality Pictures Corp./Metro, 1915)
d: William J. Bowman. 6 reels.
Francis X. Bushman, Marguerite Snow, Lester Cuneo, Ann Drew, Frank Bacon, Catherine Henry, William Clifford, Helen Dunbar.
Franklyn, a renowned musician, becomes deaf and learns to read lips.

The Silent Voice — see: The Man Who Played God (1922)

The Silent Vow (Vitagraph, 1922)
d: William Duncan. 5 reels.
William Duncan, Edith Johnson, Dorothy Dwan, Maud Emery, J. Morris Foster, Henry Hebert, Fred Burley, Jack Curtis, Charles Dudley.
In the great Northwest, a mountie searches for his father's killers.

The Silent Watcher (Frank Lloyd Productions/First National, 1924)
d: Frank Lloyd. 8 reels.
Glenn Hunter, Bessie Love, Hobart Bosworth, Gertrude Astor, George Nichols, Aggie Herring, Lionel Belmore, DeWitt Jennings, Alma Bennett, Brandon Hurst, David Murray.
Roberts, working for the election of a senatorial candidate, is arrested and charged with murder when a young actress dies under suspicious circumstances. Roberts' wife and the police all believe the actress was Roberts' mistress; but Roberts remains silent throughout his interrogation, knowing that the girl's lover was really the candidate he is trying to get elected.

The Silent Woman (Metro, 1918)

d: Herbert Blaché. 5 reels.

Edith Storey, Frank Mills, Joseph Kilgour, Lilie Leslie, Mathilde Brundage, Baby Ivy Ward, George Stevens, T. Tamamoto, Augusta Perry, Harry Linson, Ben Walker, John Cohill.

When Nan, governess to a married couple's little boy, becomes aware of the wife's infidelity, she remains silent about it for the family's sake. But she is torn, because secretly Nan has fallen in love with the husband.

Silent Years (R-C Pictures, 1921)
d: Louis J. Gasnier. 6 reels.

Rose Dione, Tully Marshall, George McDaniel, George Siegmann, Will Jim Hatton, Jack Mower, James O. Barrows, Jack Livingston, Ruth King, Kate Toncray, Lillian Rambeau.

Jo, a French Canadian girl, works her late father's farm and cares for her younger sister, thinking nothing of her own happiness. When a baby girl is left at her farm, Jo cares for it lovingly and the girl blossoms into a beauty. But all those years later, Jo must face the fear that her "daughter" may be taken away from her by the girl's real family.

Silk Hosiery (Thomas H. Ince/Paramount, 1920)
d: Fred Niblo. 5 reels.

Enid Bennett, Joan Standing, Geoffrey Webb, Donald MacDonald, Marie Pavis, Derrick Ghent, Vern Winters, Harold Holland, Bonnie Hill, Otto Hoffman, Sylvia Brooks, Rose Dione.

When a dashing European prince plans a visit to New York, the society world prepares to attend his gala reception. But one of the guests, Marjorie, holds incriminating evidence about the prince, and hides it in her silk stocking to keep it from falling into the wrong hands.

Silk Husbands and Calico Wives (Garson Studios, Inc./Equity, 1920)
d: Alfred E. Green. 5 reels.

House Peters, Mary Alden, Mildred Reardon, Edward Kimball, Sam Sothern, Eva Novak, Vincent Serrano.

A society temptress falls for a married attorney and tries to destroy his marriage.

Silk Legs (Fox, 1927)
d: Arthur Rosson. 6 reels.

Madge Bellamy, James Hall, Joseph Cawthorn, Maude Fulton, Margaret Seddon.

Comedy about a pair of hosiery salespersons, a young man and young woman, who try to outwit each other in business, then realize they are falling in love.

The Silk Lined Burglar (Universal, 1919)
d: Jack Dillon. 6 reels.

Priscilla Dean, Sam DeGrasse, Ashton Dearholt, Sam Appel, Lillian West, Fred Kelsey.

Boston Blackie, a high-society thief, is hired to crack the safe of an important official.

Silk Stocking Sal (Gothic Pictures/FBO of America, 1924)
d: Tod Browning. 5 reels.

Evelyn Brent, Robert Ellis, Earl Metcalfe, Alice Browning, Virginia Madison, Marylinn Warner, John Gough, Louis Fitzroy.

Silk Stocking Sal, a petty thief, is captured by the man whose townhouse she is ransacking. Rather than turn her over to the police, however, he gives her a job with his exporting firm. She'll repay his kindness, big time, when she solves a crime of which her new (and innocent) employer is accused.

Silk Stockings (Universal, 1927)

d: Wesley Ruggles. 6 reels.

Laura LaPlante, John Harron, Otis Harlan, William Austin, Marcella Daly, Heinie Conklin, Burr McIntosh.

A newlywed couple decide to separate after the suspicious wife finds a pair of silk stockings in her husband's coat pocket. Eventually, she learns that Hubby is innocent... but not before several comic complications have been played out.

Silken Shackles (Warner Bros., 1926)
d: Walter Morosco. 6 reels.

Irene Rich, Huntley Gordon, Victor Varconi, Bert Harburgh, Evelyn Selbie, Robert Schabble, Kalla Pascha.

A husband decides to teach his flirtatious wife a lesson, but it backfires.

Silks and Saddles (Universal, 1929)
d: Robert F. Hill. 6 reels.

Richard Walling, Sam DeGrasse, Marion Nixon, Montagu Love, Mary Nolan, Otis Harlan, David Torrence, Claire McDowell, John Fox Jr., Hayden Stevenson.

Spencer, a disgraced jockey, climbs back into the stable owner's favor when he rides her best horse to victory.

Silks and Satins (Famous Players/Paramount, 1916)
d: J. Searle Dawley. 5 reels.

Marguerite Clark, Vernon Steel, Clarence Handysides, W.A. Williams, Thomas Holding, Fayette Perry.

Facing a forced marriage to a man she does not love, a young woman gets up the nerve to run away from home and into the arms of her true sweetheart.

The Silver Car (Vitagraph, 1921)
d: David Smith. 6 reels.

Earle Williams, Kathryn Adams, Geoffrey Webb, Eric Mayne, Emmett King, Mona Lisa, John Steppling, Max Asher, Walter Rodgers.

International intrigue, when a gentleman crook intervenes in forging a peace treaty between two formerly hostile countries.

The Silver Girl (Robert Brunton Co./Pathé, 1919)
d: Frank Keenan. 5 reels.

Frank Keenan, Catherine Adams, George Hernandez, Donald McDonald, Herschel Mayall, Irene Rich, Cliff Alexander.

Husband and wife are partners in a mine named "The Silver Girl."

The Silver Horde (Eminent Authors Pictures, Inc./Goldwyn, 1920)
d: Frank Lloyd. 6 reels.

Myrtle Stedman, Curtis Cooksey, Betty Blythe, R.D. MacLean, Robert McKim, Hector Sarno, Bull Durham, M.B. Flynn, Neola Mae, E.J. Denecke, Frederick Stanton, Carl Gerard.

Boyd, a New Yorker, goes to Alaska to join a commercial fishing venture. With two partners—one of them an attractive woman—he fights for their share of the salmon catch known as "the silver horde," against a business trust that wants it all.

The Silver King (Famous Players-Lasky/Paramount, 1919)
d: George Irving. 5 reels.

William Faversham, Barbara Castleton, Nadia Gray, Lawrence Johnson, John Sutherland, Warburton Gamble, Helen Meyers, John Sunderland, Daniel Pennell, Cecil Yapp, William O'Day.

When an English squire believes he has killed a rival for his wife's affections, he flees to America. There, he works in silver mines, eventually amassing a fortune that earns him the title "The Silver King." But though he is a success, the squire yearns for the comforts of the home and family he left behind.

The Silver Lining (Iroquois Film Corp./Metro, 1921)
d: Roland West. 6 reels.
Jewel Carmen, Leslie Austen, Coit Albertson, Virginia Valli, Julia Swayne Gordon, J. Herbert Frank, Edwards Davis, Marie Coverdale, Gladden James, Henry Sedley, Jule Powers.
Strong, a Secret Service agent, tells the true stories of two orphan sisters, separated at birth and adopted by different families. One girl grows up in a upwardly mobile family, and makes her debut as a society belle. The other is raised by pickpockets, and learns the family "trade." But at a critical juncture in her life, the larcenous sister falls in love with a decent man and renounces her criminal career. Strong's point in telling the story is that heredity has a great influence on one's life choices.

The Silver Slave (Warner Bros., 1927)
d: Howard Bretherton. 7 reels.
Irene Rich, Audrey Ferris, Holmes Herbert, John Miljan, Carroll Nye.
Bernice, a rich widow who came from a working-class family, tries to steer her daughter in the right direction, i.e., away from poor-but-honest types and toward scions of wealth.

Silver Threads Among the Gold (K. & R. Film Co., 1915)
d: Pierce Kingsley. 6 reels.
Richard J. José, Mrs. R.E. French, Guy D'Ennery, Dora Dean, Jack Ridgway, Dick Lee, Catherine Lee, Jane Lee, Jim McCabe.
When Tom is framed for the theft of a young woman's purse, his father believes him guilty and sends him away. Tom will have many bitter adventures in New York, including a stay in prison... but his mother never gives up hope, and prays that her son and his father will become reconciled.

The Silver Treasure (Fox, 1926)
d: Rowland V. Lee. 6 reels.
George O'Brien, Jack Rollins, Helena D'Algy, Joan Renee, Evelyn Selbie, Lou Tellegen, Otto Matieson, Stewart Rome, Hedda Hopper, Daniel Makarenko, Fred Becker, Harvey Clark.
In an island country, a local strong man, Nostromo, is betrothed to Linda, though he secretly loves her cousin Giselle.

Silver Wings (Fox, 1922)
d: Edwin Carewe. 9 reels.
Mary Carr, Lynn Hammond, Claude Brook, Percy Helton, Joseph Striker, Jane Thomas, Maybeth Carr, Robert Hazelton, Roy Gordon, Jane Thomas, Florence Haas, Roger Lytton.
Weepy melodrama about a widow who is deserted by her three thoughtless children.

Simon, the Jester (Pathé, 1915)
d: Edward José. 5 reels.
Edwin Arden, Irene Warfield, Alma Tell, Crawford Kent, Edgar L. Davenport, Gerald Hevener.
Simon, a wealthy gent, learns that he has only six months to live, and decides to tell no one. He begins to live recklessly and finds himself innocently involved in a plot to kill the unfaithful husband of lovely Lola, an animal trainer. Though the plot is carried out, Simon remains innocent. Then, after his health is restored by a radical new operation, Simon sets out to find and woo Lola, the not-so-grieving new widow.

Simon the Jester (Metropolitan Pictures of California, 1925)
d: George Melford. 7 reels.
Eugene O'Brien, Lillian Rich, Edmund Burns, Henry B. Walthall, William Platt.
Remake of the 1915 Pathé melodrama *Simon, the Jester*.

Simple Sis (Warner Bros., 1927)
d: Herman Raymaker. 7 reels.
Louise Fazenda, Clyde Cook, Billy Kent Schaeffer, William Demarest, Myrna Loy, Betty Kent, Cathleeen Calhoun.
Sis, a plain girl with romantic longings, finds love with Jerry, a shy truckdriver.

Simple Souls (Jesse D. Hampton Productions/Pathé, 1920)
d: Robert Thornby. 6 reels.
Blanche Sweet, Charles Meredith, Kate Lester, Herbert Standing, Mayme Kelso, Herbert Grimwood.
In England, a charming duke takes an interest in a shopgirl's love of literature and sends her money to help her buy the books she loves. But the duke's innocent donations are misinterpreted by the girl's mother, who demands he make an "honest woman" out of her.

Sin (Fox, 1915)
d: Herbert Brenon. 5 reels.
Theda Bara, William E. Shay, Warner Oland, Louise Rial, Henry Leone.
Bitter drama about a love triangle that ends in death and dishonor.

Sin Cargo (Tiffany Productions, 1926)
d: Louis J. Gasnier. 7 reels.
Shirley Mason, Robert Frazer, Earl Metcalfe, Lawford Davidson, Gertrude Astor, Pat Harmon, William Walling, Billy Cinders, James Mack.
Gibson, an overstrapped businessman, tries to recoup his losses by dealing in pearl smuggling.

The Sin Flood (Goldwyn, 1922)
d: Frank Lloyd. 7 reels.
Richard Dix, Helene Chadwick, James Kirkwood, John Steppling, Ralph Lewis, Howard Davies, Will Walling, William Orlamond, Darwin Karr, Otto Hoffman, L.H. King.
On the banks of the mighty Mississippi, a group of dissimilar companions take refuge in a café when the river overflows and threatens to flood them out.

The Sin Sister (Fox, 1929)
d: Charles Klein. 7 reels.
Nancy Carroll, Lawrence Gray, Josephine Dunn, Myrtle Stedman, Anders Randolf, Richard Alexander.
In the great Northwest, a vaudeville dancer falls for a wealthy young man who's stranded at a trading post.

The Sin That Was His (Seznick/Select, 1920)
d: Hobart Henley. 6 reels.
William Faversham, Lucy Cotton, Pedro de Cordoba, Miss Sherman, Lulu Warrenton, Robert Conville, John Barton.
In Canada, a defrocked priest gets involved in a murder and, to escape, impersonates a priest.

Sin Town (DeMille Pictures/Pathé, 1929)

d: J. Gordon Cooper. 5 reels.
Elinor Fair, Ivan Lebedeff, Hugh Allan, Jack Oakie, Robert Perry.
Out West, a pair of itinerant handymen run afoul of the crime lords in Sin Town.

The Sin Woman (George Backer Film Corp., 1917)
d: George W. Lederer. 7 reels.
Irene Fenwick, Clifford Bruce, Reine Davies, George Morgan, Sara McVickar, Wellington Playter, Little Joan.
Grace, a seductress, makes a game of destroying men. On one occasion, the wretched victim announces he is leaving his wife; but the townspeople, roused by the pleas of the mother of one of the vamp's previous victims, go after Grace with tar and feathers.

The Sin Ye Do (New York Motion Picture Co./Triangle, 1916)
d: Walter Edwards. 5 reels.
Frank Keenan, Margery Wilson, David M. Hartford, Margaret Thompson, Louise Brownell, J.P. Lockney, Charles K. French, Howard Hickman, Jack Gilbert, Walt Whitman.
Steele, a successful lawyer who is also a notorious womanizer, must defend a woman who killed a man when he tried to rape her.

Sinews of Steel (Gotham Productions/Lumas Film Corp., 1927)
d: Frank O'Connor. 6 reels.
Alberta Vaughn, Gaston Glass, Anders Randolf, Paul Weigel, Greta von Rue, Nora Hayden, Charles Wellesley, John H. Gardener, Bobby Gordon.
Robert, the son of a powerful steel mogul, falls for Helen, owner of a competing mill.

The Singapore Mutiny (FBO Pictures, 1928)
d: Ralph Ince. 7 reels.
Ralph Ince, Estelle Taylor, James Mason, Gardner James, William Irving, Harry Allen, Carl Axzelle, Martha Mattox, Robert Gaillard, Frank Newberg.
After a shipwreck, only three survivors are cast ashore—a shipmate, a stowaway, and a New York hooker who was trying to sail away to peace and quiet.

Singed (Fox, 1927)
d: John Griffith Wray. 6 reels.
Blanche Sweet, Warner Baxter, James Wang, Alfred Allen, Clark Comstock, Howard Truesdale, Claude King, Ida Darling, Mary McAllister, Edwards Davis, Edgar Norton.
Dolly, a cabaret dancer, loves Royce and puts her own money into his oil well investment. When it pays off, he callously decides to dump her and direct his affections elsewhere... but he's reckoned without the fury of a woman scorned.

Singed Wings (Famous Players-Lasky/Paramount, 1922)
d: Penrhyn Stanlaws. 8 reels.
Bebe Daniels, Conrad Nagel, Adolphe Menjou, Robert Brower, Ernest Torrence, Mabel Trunnelle.
A Spanish dancer has a nightmare about love and violence, and fears it will come true.

Singer Jim Mckee (Famous Players-Lasky/Paramount, 1924)
d: Clifford S. Smith. 7 reels.
William S. Hart, Phyllis Haver, Gordon Russell, Edward Coxen, William Dyer, Bert Sprotte, Patsy Ruth Miller, George Siegmann, Baby Turner.
When his partner in crime is killed, McKee, a holdup man, is left with the partner's young daughter. McKee raises her as his own, but when she reaches maturity the two realize their love for each other has progressed beyond the parent-child stage.

Singing River (Fox, 1921)
d: Charles Giblyn. 5 reels.
William Russell, Vola Vale, Clark Comstock, Jack Roseleigh, Arthur Morrison, Jack McDonald, Jack Hull, Louis King, Charles L. King.
Out West, a homesteader desperate to hold on to his claim robs a bank to pay his mortgage, then escapes during a gunfight. On the banks of Singing River, he finds a lode of silver and files a claim that makes him wealthy. He not only pays off his mortgage, but proposes to Alice, his sweetheart-in-waiting.

The Single Code (David Horsley Productions/Mutual, 1917)
d: Thomas Ricketts. 5 reels.
Crane Wilbur, Florence Printy, F.A. Johnston, Harrish Ingraham, Nan Christy, John Oaker, Olive Stokes, Ernesto Garcia, Marie Corteaux, Ida Lewis.
In affairs of the heart, is there one rule for men and another for women, or one single code for both? This none-too-original question is explored yet again.

Single Handed (Universal, 1923)
d: Edward Sedgwick. 5 reels.
Hoot Gibson, Percy Challenger, Elinor Field, William Steele, Philip Sleeman, Dick LaReno, Mack V. Wright, Tom McGuire, Gordon McGregor, W.T. McCulley, C.B. Murphy, Bob McKenzie, Sidney DeGrey.
Rare comedy for Gibson, as he plays a town nuisance who plays the fiddle... terribly.

A Single Man (MGM, 1928)
d: Harry Beaumont. 7 reels.
Lew Cody, Aileen Pringle, Eddie Nugent, Marceline Day, Kathlyn Williams, Aileen Manning.
A middle-aged bachelor lights up when he sees his dowdy secretary all dolled up in glamorous attire.

The Single Standard (MGM, 1929)
d: John S. Robertson. 8 reels. (Music score, sound effects.)
Greta Garbo, Nils Asther, John Mack Brown, Lane Chandler, Dorothy Sebastian, Robert Castle, Mahlon Hamilton, Kathlyn Williams, Zeffie Tilbury.
Garbo plays a feminist who decries the so-called "double standard," the public mores as applied to the two sexes. She demands a single standard, and defiantly turns down the marriage proposal of a man of her own social set—running off instead to the South Seas, in a yacht with a prizefighter who wants to be an artist.

The Single Track (Vitagraph, 1921)
d: Webster Campbell. 5 reels.
Corinne Griffith, Richard Travers, Charles Kent, Sidney Herbert, Jessie Stevens, Edward Norton, Matthew Bettz, Fuller Mellish.
Janetta, an heiress, is shocked to learn that her inheritance is worthless unless a single-track railroad line can be constructed leading to her family's copper mine.

Single Wives (First National, 1924)
d: George Archainbaud. 8 reels.
Corinne Griffith, Milton Sills, Kathlyn Williams, Phyllis Haver, Phillips Smalley, Jere Austin, Lou Tellegen, Henry B. Walthall, John Patrick.

Domestic drama about a marriage that becomes a chore after only one year.

Sink or Swim (Fox, 1920)
d: Richard Stanton. 5 reels.
George Walsh, Enid Markey, Joe Dowling, Charles Elder, James O'Shea, Edward Sedgwick, Count Von Hardenberg, Edward Cecil, Tom Wilson.
In Texas, a rowdy young man tries to defend a pretty girl and lands in jail. Disgusted by his son's lack of restraint, the young man's dad sends him to the European nation of Lithonia to attend to some of Dad's business matters. Once there, the young man discovers that the girl he fought to defend in Texas is actually Lithonia's crown princess... and she's in trouble again, with pretenders to her country's throne.

Sinner or Saint (B.B. Productions/Selznick, 1923)
d: Lawrence Windom. 6 reels.
Betty Blythe, William P. Carleton, Gypsy O'Brien, William H. Tooker, Fuller Mellish, Richard Neill, William Collier Jr., Frances Miller Grant, Horace Braham.
Mademoiselle Iris, a comely fortune teller, is denounced as a fraud by a crusading reformer. Then, when she comes under the protection of a U.S. senator, the reformer suspects she has become the senator's mistress. Actually, she's his daughter.

Sinners (Realart Pictures Corp., 1920)
d: Kenneth Webb. 5 reels.
Alice Brady, Agnes Everett, Augusta Anderson, Lorraine Frost, Nora Reed, James L. Crane, W.P. Carleton, Frank Losee, Crauford Kent, Robert Schable.
Mary, a spotless country girl, moves to New York and encounters the cyncal ways of big-city living.

Sinners in Heaven (Famous Players-Lasky/Paramount, 1924)
d: Alan Crosland. 7 reels.
Bebe Daniels, Richard Dix, Holmes Herbert, Florence Billings, Betty Hilburn, Montagu Love, Effie Shannon, Marcia Harris.
Alan, an aviator, and his young passenger Barbara crashland on a primitive island where the natives come to worship them as gods.

Sinners in Love (FBO Pictures, 1928)
d: George Melford. 6 reels.
Olive Borden, Huntley Gordon, Seena Owen, Ernest Hilliard, Daphne Pollard, Phillips Smalley.
Ann, a simple small-town girl, falls for a big-city gambler.

Sinners in Silk (MGM, 1924)
d: Hobart Henley. 6 reels.
Conrad Nagel, Eleanor Boardman, Adolphe Menjou, Hedda Hopper, Bradley Ward, Jean Hersholt, Miss Dupont.
High society hi-jinks involve a young man, his sweetheart, and his profligate father.

Sinner's Parade (Columbia, 1928)
d: John G. Adolfi. 6 reels.
Dorothy Revier, Victor Varconi, John Patrick, Marjorie Bonner, Edna Marion, Clarissa Selwynne, Jack Mower.
Mary, a schoolteacher by day, dances in a cabaret by night.

Sins of Ambition (Ivan Film Productions, Inc., 1917)
d: Ivan Abramson. 6 reels.
James Morrison, Wilfred Lucas, Anders Randolf, Leah Baird, Barbara Castleton, Edward Lawrence, Madeline Traverse.

When a wife who feels neglected decides to pursue an acting career, she files for divorce and claims that her husband is not the father of their daughter.

Sins of Her Parent (Fox, 1916)
d: Frank Lloyd. 5 reels.
Gladys Brockwell, William Clifford, Carl Von Schiller, George Webb, Herschel Mayall, Jim Farley.
Unhappy in her marriage, a southern woman leaves her young daughter with a Virginia family and becomes a saloon dancer in Alaska.

Sins of Men (Fox, 1916)
d: James Vincent. 5 reels.
Stuart Holmes, Dorothy Bernard, Tom Burrough, Alice Gale, Stanhope Wheatcroft, Hattie Burks, Louis Hendricks, Stephen Gratten, Pauline Barry, Kittens Reichert.
When a philosopher writes a book that preaches self-centeredness and surrender to one's base impulses, he triggers ominous events that threaten to destroy him and his family.

The Sins of Rosanne (Famous Players-Lasky/Paramount, 1920)
d: Tom Forman. 5 reels.
Ethel Clayton, Jack Holt, Fontaine LaRue, Mabel Van Buren, Fred Malatesta, Grace Morse, C.H. Geldart, Dorothy Messenger, James Smith, Guy Oliver.
While under an Eastern mystic's hypnotic spell, a South African woman becomes a jewel thief.

The Sins of Society (World Film Corp., 1915)
d: Oscar Eagle. 5 reels.
Robert Warwick, Alec B. Francis, Ralph Delmore, Royal Byron, George Ingleton, Robert B. Mantell Jr., Harry Weir, Dorothy Fairchild, Frances Nelson, Lila Hayward Chester.
After swindling a pawnbroker out of a large sum of money, a schemer tries to frame an innocent woman for the crime, hoping to force her sister to marry him.

The Sins of St. Anthony (Famous Players-Lasky/Paramount, 1920)
d: James Cruze. 5 reels.
Bryant Washburn, Margaret Loomis, Lorenza Lazzarini, Viora Daniel, Frank Jonasson, May Baxter, L.J. McCarthy, Lucien Littlefield, Guy Oliver.
Humorous tale of Anthony, a scientist who isn't married to his fiancée yet, but is plenty hen-pecked already. When she postpones their marriage in order to play footsie with a foreign stranger, Anthony decides to remake his own image. He consults a dancer who instructs him on how to let down his hair, kick up his heels and have fun, and eventually becomes the life of every party. Too late, the fiancée realizes what a gem her Anthony is... and loses him to the dancer who changed his life.

Sins of the Children (Harry Rapf Productions/Pioneer Film Corp., 1918)
d: John S. Lopez. 5 reels.
Mahlon Hamilton, Alma Hanlon, Stuart Holmes, Robert Walker, Warren Cook, Lenore Cooper, Estar Banks, Madeline Marshall.
When a widower neglects to guide his children properly, they grow up to be disagreeable, unscrupulous adults.

Sins of the Fathers (Paramount, 1928)
d: Ludwig Berger. 10 reels.
Emil Jannings, Barry Norton, ZaSu Pitts, Jean Arthur, Matthew Betz, Harry Cording, Ruth Chatterton, Arthur

Housman, Frank Reicher, Douglas Hall, Dawn O'Day.
Spengler, a restaurateur, is persuaded by his mistress to break the Prohibition laws and import bootleg hooch. He does so, and eventually his own son is blinded from drinking rotgut.

Sins of the Mothers (Vitagraph, 1915)
d: Ralph W. Ince. 5 reels.
Anita Stewart, Julia Swayne Gordon, Ralph W. Ince, Earle Williams, Lucille Lee, Mary Maurice, Paul Scardon.
Convent-bred, young Trixie wishes to become a nun, but her mother persuades her instead to try society life for one year. She does, but with disastrous results.

Sins of the Parents (Ivan Film Productions, Inc., 1914)
w, d: Ivan Abramson. 5 reels.
Sarah Adler, Paul Doucet, John W. Dillon, Ralf Henderson, Mabel Wright, Louise Corbin.
Ruth, a girl who grew up believing that the woman who raised her is her mother, learns that the woman is actually her aunt. Disillusioned but not disheartened, she heads for New York to find her real mother.

Sioux Blood (MGM, 1929)
d: John Waters. 6 reels.
Tim McCoy, Marion Douglas, Chief Standing Bear, Robert Frazer, Clarence Geldert, Sidney Bracey.
An "Indian" known as Lone Eagle is really a white man who was raised by a Sioux family.

The Siren (Fox, 1917)
d: Roland West. 5 reels.
Valeska Suratt, Clifford Bruce, Robert Clugston, Isabel Rea, Cesare Gravina, Armand Kalisz, Rica Scott, Curtis Benton.
Western melodrama about a dance hall queen who lures men to their destruction.

The Siren (Columbia, 1928)
d: Byron Haskin. 6 reels.
Dorothy Revier, Norman Trevor, Tom Moore, Jed Prouty, Otto Hoffman.
Glenna, a flirtatious society girl, uses her charms to attract wealthy men to her lover's crooked poker games.

The Siren Call (Famous Players-Lasky/Paramount, 1922)
d: Irvin Willat. 6 reels.
Dorothy Dalton, David Powell, Mitchell Lewis, Edward J. Brady, will Walling, Leigh Wyant, Lucien Littlefield, George B. Williams.
In the great Northwest, a dance hall girl vamps a fur trapper.

The Siren of Seville (Hunt Stromberg Corp./Producers Distributing Corp., 1924)
d: Jerome Storm, Hunt Stromberg. 7 reels.
Priscilla Dean, Allan Forrest, Stuart Holmes, Claire DeLorez, Bert Woodruff, Matthew Betz.
In Seville, a dancer intervenes in a bullfight to save her lover, a neophite matador, from being gored.

Sirens of the Sea (Universal, 1917)
d: Allan Holubar. 5 reels.
Louise Lovely, Jack Mulhall, William Quinn, Carmel Myers, Sydney Dean, Evelyn Selbie, Helen Wright.
A yachtsman dreams about sea sirens and mermaids, then meets Lorelei, a girl who may be one of them.

The Siren's Song (Shubert Film Corp./World Film Corp, 1915)
d: Harry Revier. 5 reels.
Mademoiselle Diane, Charles Trowbridge, Albert Hart, Helen Weer, Mae Phelps, Charles Dickson, Maisie Gay, Adolph Link, Roy Hogan.
John, a divinity student who once was unjustly convicted of a white-collar crime, runs across the two crooks who framed him.

The Siren's Song (Fox, 1919)
d: J. Gordon Edwards. 5 reels.
Theda Bara, Alfred W. Fremont, Ruth Handworth, L.C. Shumway, Albert Roscoe, Paul Weigel, Carrie Clark Ward.
In a small fishing village, a girl sings beautifully. But her prudish father suspects her talent is diabolical, given to her only to drive men mad.

Sis Hopkins (Goldwyn, 1919)
d: Clarence G. Badger. 5 reels.
Mabel Normand, John Bowers, Sam DeGrasse, Thomas Jefferson, Nick Cogley, Eugenie Forde, Harry McCoy.
When a country girl and her beau accidentally tip over a large can of oil on her Pa's farm, it creates a pool that fools a greedy neighbor. He thinks the farm is brimming with black gold, and determines to buy it at any price.

Sister Against Sister (Fox, 1917)
d: James R. Vincent. 5 reels.
Virginia Pearson, Maud Hall, Walter Law, Irving Cummings, Calla Dillatore, William Battista, Archie Battista, Jane Lee.
Twin sisters separated in childhood grow up very differently. Anne becomes a sedate, virtuous young woman, while Katherine grows callous and undisciplined. As adults, their paths will cross again.

A Sister of Six (Fine Arts Film Co./Triangle, 1916)
d: C.M. Franklin, S.A. Franklin. 5 reels.
Ben Lewis, Bessie Lovie, George Stone, Violet Radcliffe, Carmen DeRue, Francis Carpenter, Beulah Burns, Lloyd Pearl, Ralph Lewis, Frank Bennett, A.D. Sears, Charles Groman.
Eastern siblings strike it rich in California's minefields.

A Sister to Salome (Fox, 1920)
d: Edward J. LeSaint. 5 reels.
Gladys Brockwell, William Scott, Edwin B. Tilton, Ben Deely.
Elinor, an operatic diva undergoing an operation, has a hallucination while under the ether, and imagines herself in ancient Rome.

Sisters (International Film Service/American Releasing Corp., 1922)
d: Albert Capellani. 7 reels.
Seena Owen, Gladys Leslie, Mildred Arden, Matt Moore, Joe King, Tom Guise, Robert Schable, Frances Grant, Fred Miller.
Interesting love quadrangle, as one girl marries Martin, and her sister marries Peter... but Peter actually is in love with his sister-in-law.

The Six Best Cellars (Famous Players-Lasky/Paramount, 1920)
d: Donald Crisp. 5 reels.
Bryant Washburn, Wanda Hawley, Clarence Burton, Elsa Lorimer, Josephine Crowell, Fred Vroom, Jane Wolfe, Richard Wayne, Julia Faye, Howard Gaye, Zelma Maja.
Down to only a few bottles of wine in his cellar during Prohibition, a party host tries to save face by proclaiming a patriotic distaste for alcohol. He's so convincing, in fact, that he is drafted to run for Congress by the Prohibition party.

Six Days (Goldwyn, 1923)
d: Charles Brabin. 9 reels.
Corinne Griffith, Frank Mayo, Myrtle Stedman, Claude King, Maude George, Spottiswoode Aitken, Charles Clary, Evelyn Walsh Hall, Paul Cazeneuve, Jack Herbert, Robert DeVilbiss.
A young woman is urged by her mother to marry a man of wealth, but the girl goes for his son instead.

Six Feet Four (American, 1919)
d: Henry King. 6 reels.
William Russell, Vola Vale, Charles French, Harvey Clark, Al Garcia, Jack Collins, Jack Brammall, Calvert Carter, Perry Banks, John Gough, Anne Schaffer.
A cowpoke does battle with a gang of thieves headed by a crooked sheriff.

The Six-Fifty (Universal, 1923)
d: Nat Ross. 5 reels.
Renee Adoree, Orville Caldwell, Bert Woodruff, Gertrude Astor, Niles Welch.
Hester, a farmer's wife, is lured to the big city and its excitements by a man who arrives in town on the "Six-Fifty" train.

Six Shooter Andy (Fox, 1918)
d: Sidney A. Franklin, Chester M. Franklin. 5 reels.
Tom Mix, Bert Woodruff, Sam DeGrasse, Charles Stevens, Pat Crisman, Bob Fleming, Enid Markey, Jack Plank, Ben Hammer, Georgie Stone, Lewis Sargent, Buddy Messenger, Virginia Lee Corbin, Violet Radcliffe, Ray Lee.
Andy, a young prospector, is forced to become his town's lawman after a crooked sheriff and his cronies kill Andy's father.

The Sixteenth Wife (Vitagraph, 1917)
d: Charles Brabin. 5 reels.
Peggy Hyland, Marc MacDermott, George J. Forth, Templar Saxe.
Mary Ann, a ballet dancer known professionally as Olette, performs for a caliph in Turkey. He is so enchanted by her grace and beauty that he offers her the honor of becoming his sixteenth wife. Olette refuses, so the caliph has her imprisoned in his harem with his fifteen other wives.

The Sixth Commandment (Encore Pictures/Associated Exhibitors, 1924)
d: William Christy Cabanne. 6 reels.
William Faversham, Charlotte Walker, John Bohn, Kathleen Martyn, Neil Hamilton, Coit Albertson, Sara Wood, Consuelo Flowerton, Charles Emmett Mack, Edmund Breese.
Brant, a reverend minister, loves one of his parishoners but keeps quiet because she is engaged to another man. Patience being a virtue, however, the good reverend is rewarded in the long run when the girl breaks her engagement.

Sixty Cents an Hour (Famous Players-Lasky/Paramount, 1923)
d: Joseph Henabery. 6 reels.
Walter Hiers, Jacqueline Logan, Ricardo Cortez, Charles Ogle, Lucille Ward, Robert dudley, Clarence Burton, Guy Oliver, Cullen Tate.
Jimmy, a soda jerk, has dreams of winning the hand of the bank president's daughter. His dreams come true when a survey reveals that the bank building encroaches on 4 feet of Jimmy's property, and he receives a settlement... and the girl of his dreams.

Skid Proof (Fox, 1923)
d: Scott Dunlap. 6 reels.
Charles Jones, Laura Anson, Fred Eric, Jacqueline Gadsden, Peggy Shaw, Earl Metcalf, Claude Peyton, Harry Tracey.
Darwin, a champion race driver, wins the hand of a movie actress.

Skin Deep (T.H. Ince/First National, 1922)
d: Lambert Hillyer. 6 reels.
Florence Vidor, Milton Sills, Marcia Manon, Charles Clary, Winter Hall, Joe Singleton, Frank Campeau, Gertrude Astor, Muriel Dana, B.H. DeLay.
Doyle, a former crook, wants to go straight but finds it almost impossible because his facial features have hardened into a criminal visage. But Doyle's desire to be an honest man is strong, so he undergoes plastic surgery and emerges with a new, "law-friendly" face.

Skinner's Baby (Essanay, 1917)
d: Harry Beaumont. 5 reels.
Bryant Washburn, Hazel Daly, James Carroll, U.K. Houpt.
William Skinner goes into ecstasy when his wife informs him she is pregnant. The proud papa-to-be makes elaborate preparations for "Junior's" arrival... then is stunned when the new heir turns out to be an heiress, instead.

Skinner's Big Idea (FBO Pictures, 1928)
d: Lynn Shores. 7 reels.
Bryant Washburn, William Orlamond, James Bradbury Sr., Robert Dudley, Ole M. Ness, Charles Wellesley, Martha Sleeper, Hugh Trevor, Ethel Grey Terry.
Workplace comedy about Skinner, a junior partner in a hardware company, who's been given the onerous task of firing three long-time employees for no reason other than their advanced age. Instead of firing them, Skinner gets this big idea: Hire a pretty girl to come in and rejuvenate the staid old firm, and pump some life into those old codgers. It works, and soon the trio are turning out more work than ever before, and they even win a big contract for the company.

Skinner's Bubble (Essanay, 1917)
d: Harry Beaumont. 5 reels.
Bryant Washburn, Hazel Daly, James C. Carroll, U.K. Houpt, Marion Skinner.
When Skinner, a junior partner in his firm, decides to branch out for himself, he learns the harsh realities of being one's own boss and paying one's own bills. Through bluff and bluster, he gets his old firm to take him back.

Skinner's Dress Suit (Essanay, 1917)
d: Harry Beaumont. 5 reels.
Bryant Washburn, Hazel Daly, Harry Dunkinson, James C. Carroll, U.K. Houpt, Florence Oberle, Frances Raymond, Marion Skinner.
Too embarrassed to admit to his wife that he lacked the gumption to ask his boss for a raise in salary, Skinner lies and tell her he got the raise. Now she embarks on a spending spree, and even makes her husband by a dress suit.

Skinner's Dress Suit (Universal, 1926)
d: William A. Seiter. 7 reels.
Reginald Denny, Laura LaPlante, Ben Hendricks Jr., E.J. Ratcliffe, Arthur Lake, Hedda Hopper, Lionel Braham, Frona Hale, William Strauss, Lucille De Nevers, Lucille Ward, Lila Leslie, Broderick O'Farrell.
A hen-pecked husband lies to his wife that he has been given

a salary increase, then is horrified when she embarks on a spending spree.

Remake of the 1917 Essanay comedy *Skinner's Dress Suit*, both versions based on the short story of the same name by Henry Irving Dodge.

Skirt Shy — see: Leap Year (1921)

Skirts (Fox, 1921)
w, d: Hampton Del Ruth. 5 reels.
Clyde Cook, Chester Conklin, Polly Moran, Jack Cooper, Billy Armstrong, Ethel Teare, Glen Cavender, Slim Summerville, Harry McCoy, Bobby Dunn, Tom Kennedy, Ed Kennedy, William Trancy, Laura LaVarnie, Alice Davenport.
Farcical comedy about a circus worker whose mother is the bearded lady in the sideshow.

Sky High (Fox, 1922)
d: Lynn Reynolds. 5 reels.
Tom Mix, Eva Novak, J. Farrell MacDonald, Sid Jordan, William Buckley, Adele Warner.
A cowboy who's really a secret agent cracks a gang of smugglers running Chinese laborers across the Mexican border.

Sky High Corral (Universal, 1926)
d: Clifford Smith. 5 reels.
Art Acord, Marguerite Clayton, Duke R. Lee, Jack Mower, Tom Lingham, Blackie Thompson, Missouri Royer, Floyd Shackelford.
Out West, a forest ranger tries to evict a rancher and his daughter, but falls in love with the daughter instead.

Sky-High Saunders (Universal, 1927)
d: Bruce Mitchell. 5 reels.
Al Wilson, Elsie Tarron, Frank Rice, Bud Osborne.
Out West, an aviator duels with a gang of smugglers.

The Sky Pilot (First National, 1921)
d: King Vidor. 7 reels.
John Bowers, Colleen Moore, David Butler, Harry Todd, James Corrigan, Donald MacDonald, Kathleen Kirkham.
In the Canadian north, a young minister helps a handicapped girl walk again.

The Sky Rider (Chesterfield Motion Picture Corp., 1928)
w, d: Alvin J. Neitz. 5 reels.
Alfred Heuston, Gareth Hughes, Josephine Hill, J.P. Lockney, John Tansey, Edward Cecil, Lew Meehan, Sheldon Lewis.
When an airline executive decides to cut his ne'er-do-well nephew out of his will, the nephew reacts violently, with explosives and an attempted kidnapping.

The Sky Skidder (Universal, 1929)
d: Bruce Mitchell. 5 reels.
Al Wilson, Helen Foster, Wilbur McGaugh, Pee Wee Holmes.
Daredevil stunts are featured in this tale of an inventor who develops a revolutionary new fuel for airplanes.

Skyfire (Pinnacle Productions, 1920)
d: Neal Hart. 5 reels.
Neal Hart, William Quinn, Rita Pickering, Hugh Saxon, Al Garcia, Artie Ortego, Les Bates, Ruth Tamison.
In the great Northwest, a Canadian mountie searches for his partner's killers.

The Skylight Room (Broadway Star Features Co./General Film, 1917)
d: Martin Justice. 4 reels.
Jean Paige, Grace Ashley, Carlton King, Nell Spencer, William Lampe, Bruno Karnum, Rex Burnett, Frank Crayne, Herbert Pattee, Ada Kingsley.
Whimsical drama about a young woman who's a self-employed typist, barely eking out a living. She occupies "the skylight room" in her apartment building, and from that vantage point she frequently scans the night skies looking for her favorite star, which she has nicknamed "Billy Jackson."

The Skyrocket (Celebrity Pictures/Associated Exhibitors, 1926)
d: Marshall Neilan. 8 reels.
Peggy Hopkins Joyce, Owen Moore, Gladys Brockwell, Gladys Hulette, Paulette Duval, Lilyan Tashman, Charles West, Junior Coughlan, Earle Williams, Bernard Randall, Muriel McCormac, Sammy Cohen, Bull Montana, Arnold Gregg, Ben Hall.
Childhood friends from a poor neighborhood wind up in Hollywood — one as a motion picture star, the other as her screenwriter.

Skyscraper (DeMille Pictures, 1928)
d: Howard Higgin. 8 reels.
William Boyd, Alan Hale, Sue Carol, Alberta Vaughn.
Construction workers vie for the love of the same girl.

The Skywayman (Fox, 1920)
d: James P. Hogan. 5 reels.
Ormer Locklear, Louise Lovely, Sam DeGrasse, Ted McCann, Jack Brammall.
Craig, a returning war hero, has lost his memory in a war-related incident.

The Slacker (Metro, 1917)
d: William Christy Cabanne. 6 reels.
Emily Stevens, Walter Miller, Leo Delaney, Daniel Jarrett, Eugene Borden, Millicent Fisher, Sue Balfour, Mathilde Brundage, Baby Ivy Ward, Charles Fang, Belle Bruce.
During World War I, a young man is suspected of rushing into marriage in order to escape military service.

The Slacker's Heart (Emerald Motion Picture Co., 1917)
d: Frederick J. Ireland. 7 reels.
Edward Arnold, Byrdine Zuber, Rhea Catto Laughlin, Lillian DeTurck, Tony West.
Frank's a pacifist who doesn't believe in war... until he meets a scoundrel who insults the American flag.

Slam-bang Jim — see: Snap Judgement (1917)

Slander (Fox, 1916)
d: Will S. Davis. 5 reels.
Bertha Kalich, Eugene Ormonde, Mayme Kelson, Edward Van Sloane, Robert Rendel, Warren Cook, T.J. Lawler.
Richard loves Helen, but there's a problem: Both of them are already married to others.

Slander the Woman (Allen Holubar Pictures/Associated First National, 1923)
d: Allen Holubar. 7 reels.
Dorothy Phillips, Lewis Dayton, Robert Anderson, Mayme Kelso, George Siegmann, Ynez Seabury, Herbert Fortier, Geno Corrado, William Orlamond, Robert Schable, Rosemary Theby, Irene Haisman, Cyril Chadwick.
In an emotional murder case, the judge denounces an innocent young woman as a probable accomplice to the crime. Later, he realizes his remarks were unethical, and tries to reach the woman to apologize to her.

The Slanderers (Universal, 1924)
d: Nat Ross. 5 reels.
Johnnie Walker, Gladys Hulette, Billy Sullivan, George Nichols, Edith Yorke, Philo McCullough, Margaret Landis, Jackie Morgan, Turner Savage.
Small-town gossips slander a widow and her two sons, one of them a war hero.

The Slave (Fox, 1917)
d: William Nigh. 5 reels.
Valeska Suratt, Violet Palmer, Eric Mayne, Herbert Heyes, Edward Burns, Edwin Roseman, Dan Mason, Tom Brooke, Martin Faust, Martin Hunt.
A shopgirl dreams that she is the pampered wife of a wealthy man.

The Slave Market (Famous Players/Paramount, 1917)
d: Hugh Ford. 5 reels.
Pauline Frederick, Thomas Meighan, Albert Hart, Ruby Hoffman, Wellington Playter.
When the ship she is sailing on is raided by pirates, a convent-bred young woman is taken prisoner and carried off to the pirates' island hideout.

Slave of Desire (Goldwyn, 1923)
d: George D. Baker. 7 reels.
George Walsh, Bessie Love, Carmel Myers, Wally Van, Edward Connelly, Eulalie Jensen, Herbert Prior, William Orlamond, Nicholas DeRuiz, William von Hardenburg.
In France, a poet falls prey to the snares of a vampish countess.

A Slave of Fashion (MGM, 1925)
d: Hobart Henley. 6 reels.
Norma Shearer, William Haines, Lew Cody, Mary Carr, James Corrigan, Vivia Ogden.
A small-town girl appropriates a crash victim's lease on a New York apartment in order to get a taste of the good life. When her family comes to visit, she pretends to be the wife of the absent owner. Then the owner shows up.

The Slaver (Morris R. Schlank Productions/Anchor Film Distributors, 1927)
d: Harry Revier. 6 reels.
Pat O'Malley, Carmelita Geraghty, John Miljan, J.P. McGowan, Billie Bennett, William Earle, Leo White, Phil Sleeman.
On the high seas off the coast of Africa, a sea captain tries to sell a young woman to a white slavery gang.

Slaves of Pride (Vitagraph, 1920)
d: George W. Terwilliger. 5 reels.
Alice Joyce, Percy Marmont, Templar Saxe, Louise Beaudet, G.V. Seyffertitz, Charles A. Stevenson.
When her greedy mother forces her to marry a wealthy man, Patricia develops an intense dislike for her new husband. Out of spite, she runs away with one of his employees... but when her husband follows her and risks his life to get her back, Patricia's attitude towards him softens.

Sleeping Fires (Famous Players/Paramount, 1917)
d: Hugh Ford. 5 reels.
Pauline Frederick, John Sainpolis, Maury Stewart, Thomas Meighan, Helen Dahl, Joseph Smiley.
After being treated scornfully by her brutish husband, Zelma leaves him. But she still wants custody of their little boy—something the husband refuses to give up without a fight.

The Sleeping Lion (Universal, 1919)
d: Rupert Julian. 6 reels.
Monroe Salisbury, Alice Elliot, Sydney Franklyn, Pat Moore, Rhea Mitchell, Herschel Mayall, Alfred Allen, Marion Skinner, Frank Leigh.
Out West, a transplanted New York Italian and his young son settle down to ranch living. But the Italian finds he must duel with the town's biggest gambler over the woman they both fancy.

A Sleeping Memory (Metro, 1917)
d: George D. Baker. 7 reels.
Emily Stevens, Frank Mills, Mario Majeroni, Walter Horton, Richard Thornton, Frank Joyner, Kate Blancke.
In New York, a shopgirl makes a pact which will bring her a life of luxury. All she has to do is give up her memory, which a wealthy surgeon intends to remove during an operation.

The Sleepwalker (Realart Pictures/Paramount, 1922)
d: Edward LeSaint. 5 reels.
Constance Binney, Jack Mulhall, Edythe Chapman, Florence Roberts, Bertram Grassby, Cleo Ridgely, Winifred Edwards.
Doris, a sleepwalker, is suspected of immorality when found in a single man's room at night.

Slide, Kelly, Slide (MGM, 1927)
d: Edward Sedgwick. 8 reels.
William Haines, Guinn Williams, Harry Carey, Karl Dane, Junior Coghlan, Sally O'Neil, Warner Richmond, Paul Kelly, Mike Donlin, Irish Meusel, Bob Meusel, Tony Lazzeri.
Kelly, a rookie pitcher for the New York Yankees, develops an ego problem.

Slightly Used (Warner Bros., 1927)
d: Archie Mayo. 7 reels.
May McAvoy, Conrad Nagel, Bobby Agnew, Audrey Ferris, Anders Randolph.
To satisfy a parental requirement, a young woman invents a husband for herself... and whaddaya know, the "fictitious" hubby turns up.

Slim Fingers (Universal, 1929)
d: Joseph Levigard. 5 reels.
Bill Cody, Duane Thompson, Wilbur Mack, Monte Montague, Arthur Morrison, Charles L. King.
Two art thieves—a man and a woman—make off with a valuable painting and are chased by police and an art connoisseur who's taken a shine to the slick-fingered lady thief.

The Slim Princess (Goldwyn, 1920)
d: Victor L. Schertzinger. 5 reels.
Mabel Normand, Hugh Thompson, Tully Marshall, Russ Powell, Lillian Sylvester, Harry Lorraine, Pomeroy Cannon.
Remake of the 1915 4-reel Essanay comedy of the same name.
Both films are based on the short story *The Slim Princess* by George Ade.

Slim Shoulders (Tilford Cinema Studios/W.W. Hodkinson Corp., 1922)
d: Alan Crosland. 6 reels.
Irene Castle, Rod LaRocque, Anders Randolph, Warren Cook, Mario Carillo, Marie Burke.
Naomi, a young socialite, tries to steal some incriminating documents from a private safe. The owner catches her in the act, but instead of turning her over to the police, he falls in love with her.

Slippy McGee (Oliver Morosco Productions/Associated First National, 1923)
d: Wesley Ruggles. 7 reels.
Wheeler Oakman, Colleen Moore, Sam DeGrasse, Edmund Stevens, Edith Yorke, Lloyd Whitlock, Pat O'Malley.
McGee, a reformed safecracker, uses his light-fingered skills once more—this time for a noble purpose.

Sloth (McClure Pictures, Inc./Triangle, 1917)
d: Theodore Marston. 5 reels.
Charlotte Walker, Jack Meredith, D.J. Flannigan, Jack Crosby, Grace Williams, Charles DeMussett, Curtis Cooksey, Emil Hach, Peter Pann, Hattie Delaro, Harry McFayden.
During World War I, a young woman rebels when her fiancé is called to the front. After she reads stories about patriotic American women of the past, however, she changes her attitude and becomes a Red Cross nurse to help wounded American soldiers.

The Small Bachelor (Universal, 1927)
d: William A. Seiter. 7 reels.
Barbara Kent, André Beranger, William Austin, Lucien Littlefield, Carmelita Geraghty, Gertrude Astor, George Davis, Tom Dugan, Vera Lewis, Ned Sparks.
Comedy about a painfully shy suitor who must somehow summon the courage to ask his beloved for her hand in marriage.

The Small Town Girl (Fox, 1917)
d: John G. Adolfi. 5 reels.
June Caprice, Jane Lee, Bernard Delaney, Ethyle Cook, Tom Brooke, Lucia Moore, Inez Marcel, Howard D. Southard, John Burkell.
In New York, a country girl and her old beau are reunited.

The Small Town Guy (Essanay, 1917)
d: L.C. Windom. 5 reels.
Taylor Holmes, Helen Ferguson, Fred Tiden, Mark Elliston, James F. Fulton.
Ernest, a small town hotel clerk, goes to Chicago to make his fortune.

A Small Town Idol (Mack Sennett Productions/Associated Producers, 1921)
d: Erle Kenton. 7 reels.
Ben Turpin, James Finlayson, Phyllis Haver, Bert Roach, Al Cooke, Charles Murray, Marie Prevost, Dot Farley, Eddie Gribbon, Kalla Pasha, Billy Bevan, George O'Hara.
Wacky comedy about a wannabe bridegroom who is chased out of his small town on suspicion of theft, of which he is innocent. Finally landing in Hollywood, the hicksville pariah makes it big as a stunt man, becoming rich and successful. Still, when he tries to return home, he finds the locals angry as ever, and must escape a lynch mob before proving himself innocent.

The Smart Set (MGM, 1928)
d: Jack Conway. 7 reels.
William Haines, Alice Day, Jack Holt, Hobart Bosworth, Coy Watson Jr., Constance Howard, Paul Nicholson, Julia Swayne Gordon.
Tommy, a self-centered chap, gets thrown off his polo team for "hot-dogging," and finds his wealthy father has disowned him besides. But in the big match, when the team loses its last player to injuries, Tommy is sent in and carries the team to victory.

The Smart Sex (Universal, 1921)
d: Fred Leroy Granville. 5 reels.

Eva Novak, Frank Braidwood, Geoffrey Webb, Mayre Hall, C. Norman Hammond, Dorothy Hagan, Calvert Carter, Margaret Mann, Jim O'Neill, Evelyn McCoy.
In a small town, big-city girl Rose wins an amateur talent show, gets a job on a ranch, and captures the heart of the local "catch."

Smashing Through (Universal, 1918)
d: Elmer Clifton. 5 reels.
Herbert Rawlinson, Sally Starr, Neal Hart, Sam DeGrasse, Millard K. Wilson, Clarissa Selwynne, Paul Hurst.
Crooked stockbrokers induce a chemist's mother to invest all her money in a worthless mining claim.

Smile, Brother, Smile (Charles R. Rogers Productions/First National, 1927)
d: John Francis Dillon. 7 reels.
Jack Mulhall, Dorothy Mackaill, Philo McCullough, E.J. Ratcliffe, Harry Dunkinson, Ernest Hilliard, Charles Clary, Jack Dillon, Yola D'Avril, Hank Mann, T. Roy Barnes.
Comedy about hi-jinx in a cosmetics firm.

Smiles (Fox, 1919)
d: Arvid E. Gillstrom. 5 reels.
Jane Lee, Katherine Lee, Etherl Fleming, Val Paul, Carmen Phillips, Charles Arling, Katherine Griffith.
Comedy of the absurd, which begins with two sisters being stuffed into a mailbag and sent via U.S. Mail across the country. The girls also manage to fit their dog into the bag.

Smiles are Trumps (Fox, 1922)
d: George E. Marshall. 5 reels.
Maurice B. Flynn, Ora Carew, Myles McCarthy, Herschel Mayall, Kirke Lucas, C. Norman Hammond.
Carson, a paymaster for a railroad company, learns that his supervisor is cheating the firm and resolves to stop him.

Smilin' Guns (Universal, 1929)
d: Henry MacRae. 6 reels.
Hoot Gibson, Blanche Mehaffey, Virginia Pearson, Robert Graves, Leo White, Walter Brennan, Jack Wise, James Bradbury Jr., Dad Gibson.
Out West, a rough-hewn cowpoke determines to remake himself into a gentleman, to vie for the hand of the visiting socialite he fancies.

Smilin' Through (First National, 1922)
d: Sidney A. Franklin. 8 reels.
Norma Talmadge, Harrison Ford, Wyndham Standing, Glenn Hunter, Alec B. Francis, Miriam Battista, Gene Lockhart, Grace Griswold.
Melodrama about John, a man who is shocked to learn that his niece is engaged to the son of the man who killed John's fiancée years before.

Smiling All the Way (D.N. Schwab Productions, Inc., 1920)
d: Fred J. Butler. 5 reels.
David Butler, Leatrice Joy, Frances Raymond, Parker McConnell, Rhea Haines, Helen Scott, Charles Smiley, Arthur Redden, P.D. Tabler, Harry Duffield, Charles McHugh.
Hannibal, a lumberjack chef, leaves his kitchen long enough to rescue a damsel from kidnappers.

Smiling Jim (Phil Goldstone Productions, 1922)
d: Joseph Franz. 5 reels.
Franklyn Farnum, Alma Bennett, Percy Challenger, Al Ferguson.
Out West, a newcomer nicknamed Smiling Jim is run out of

town by the sheriff, who believes he is a notorious bandit.

The Smiling Terror (Universal, 1929)
d: Joseph Levigard. 5 reels.
Ted Wells, Derelys Perdue, Al Ferguson, Bud Osborne.
Wayne, a smiling cowpoke, rescues the same girl three times—from a team of stampeding horses, a fall down a mine shaft, and the hands of kidnappers.

Smoke Bellew (Big 4 Productions/First Division Distributors, 1929)
d: Scott Dunlap. 7 reels.
Conway Tearle, Barbara Bedford, Mark Hamilton, Alphonse Ethier, William Scott, Alaska Jack, J.P. Lockney.
Tale of romance and rivalry among visitors to the Klondike during the 1897 gold rush, based on the novel of the same name by Jack London.

The Smoke Eaters (Trem Carr Productions/Rayart, 1926)
d: Charles Hunt, Charles Hutchinson. 6 reels.
Cullen Landis, Wanda Hawley, Edward Cecil, Aryel Darma, Broderick O'Farrell, Mae Prestelle, Harold Austin, Baby Moncur.
A girl in love with a rich wastrel becomes trapped in a raging fire and is rescued by a courageous firefighter, whom she later marries.

Smoldering Embers (Frank Keenan Productions, Inc./Pathé, 1920)
d: Frank Keenan. 5 reels.
Frank Keenan, Jay Belasco, Kate Van Buren, Russ Powell, Graham Pettie, Hardie Kirkland, Lucille Ward, Frances Raymond, Thomas Guise, Burwell Hamrick.
Conroy, a lonesome tramp, makes friends with a young man who's being pressured into marriage to a congressman's daughter to further his stepfather's political ambitions. What the young man doesn't know is that Conroy is really his long-lost father, returned home to make things right with his family.

Smooth as Satin (R-C Pictures/FBO of America, 1925)
d: Ralph Ince. 6 reels.
Evelyn Brent, Bruce Gordon, Fred Kelsey, Fred esmelton, Mabel Van Buren, John Gough.
Professional safecrackers Gertie and Jim meet while both are trying to rob the same safe, and they fall in love.

Smouldering Fires (Universal, 1925)
d: Clarence Brown. 8 reels.
Pauline Frederick, Laura LaPlante, Malcolm McGregor, Tully Marshall, Wanda Hawley, Helen Lynch, George Cooper, Bert Roach, Billy Gould.
A businesswoman marries a younger man, then learns she may have to give him up.

Smudge (Charles Ray Productions/First National, 1922)
d: Charles Ray. 5 reels.
Charles Ray, Charles K. French, Florence Oberle, Ora Carew, J.P. Lockney, Blanche Rose, Lloyd Bacon, Ralph McCullough.
Stephen, a neophite newspaper man, crusades vigorously against the use of smudge pots and drives all the local orange growers bananas.

The Smugglers (Famous Players/Paramount, 1916)
d: Sidney Olcott. 5 reels.
Donald Brian, Olive Tell, Cyril Chadwick, Margaret Greene, Harold Vosburgh, Rita Bori.
In London, a touring American buys an expensive necklace for his wife at her insistence; but in a comedy of errors, it gets mixed up with a worthless imitation necklace. Now he'll have to contend with customs officials who will judge the bauble's worth. Which one does the wife have—the real necklace or the fake?

Snap Judgement (American Film Co./Mutual, 1917)
d: Edward Sloman. 5 reels.
William Russell, Francelia Billington, Harvey Clark, Charles Newton, Perry Banks, Ada Gleason, Ashton Dearholt, Bull Montana, Ruth Everdale, Clarence Burton.
Believing she's been jilted, a bride-to-be denounces her fiancé, not knowing he's been thrown in jail by lawmen who think he's Rawley, a wanted outlaw. Then the real Rawley kidnaps the would-be-bride and her mother. Soon, Rawley's girlfriend helps the bridegroom escape from prison, believing him to be the outlaw.
William Russell plays a double role here, as both the bridegroom and the outlaw.

Snares of Paris (Fox, 1919)
d: Howard M. Mitchell. 5 reels.
Madlaine Traverse, Charles Arling, Frank Leigh, Jack Rollens, Joseph Swickard.
In Paris, an international trade agreement is jeopardized when a diplomat discovers that one of his associates had seduced the diplomat's wife, years before.

The Snarl (New York Motion Picture Corp./Triangle, 1917)
d: Raymond B. West. 5 reels.
Bessie Barriscale, Charles Gunn, Howard Hickman, Aggie Herring, J. Barney Sherry, Thomas Guise.
Twin sisters have mismatched personalities, one kind, the other evil.
Miss Barriscale, as the twins, plays a double role here. She would again play a double role in the 1919 film from B.B. Features, *A Trick of Fate*; and in the 1920 film from B.B. Features, *Life's Twist*.

The Snarl of Hate (Bischoff Productions, 1927)
d: Noel Mason Smith. 6 reels.
Johnnie Walker, Mildred June, Jack Richardson, Wheeler Oakman.
Walker plays twins, one of them murdered early in the film, the other hunting down his killer.

The Sneak (Fox, 1919)
d: Edward J. LeSaint. 5 reels.
Gladys Brockwell, William Scott, Alfred Hollingsworth, John Oaker, Harry Hilliard, Irene Rich, Gerrard Grassby.
While visiting a gypsy camp, an artist is enchanted by a gypsy maiden's beauty, and asks her to pose for him.

The Snitching Hour (Houseman Comedies/Clark-Cornelius Corp., 1922)
d: Alan Crosland. 5 reels.
Arthur Houseman, Gladys Leslie, Frank Currier, Nita Naldi, George Lessey, Mario Carillo.
Comedy about a pair of high society crooks, a man and a woman, who try to "lift" a valuable gem from their host during a weekend party. They'll get nowhere.

The Snob (Realart Pictures, 1921)
d: Sam Wood. 5 reels.
Wanda Hawley, Edwin Stevens, Walter Hiers, Sylvia Ashton, William E. Lawrence, Julia Faye, Richard Wayne.
Kathryn, a nouveau riche snob, scorns a young suitor when she learns that he works as a waiter and busboy. But she'll have a change of heart.

The Snob (MGM, 1924)
w, d: Monta Bell. 7 reels.
John Gilbert, Norma Shearer, Phyllis Haver, Conrad Nagel, Hedda Hopper, Margaret Seddon, Aileen Manning, Hazel Kennedy, Gordon Sackville, Roy Laidlaw, Nellie Bly Baker.
A married couple, both schoolteachers, face marital problems when the husband is attracted to a glamorous society woman.

Snobs (Lasky Feature Plays/Paramount, 1915)
d: Oscar Apfel. 5 reels.
Victor Moore, Anita King, Constance Johnson, Ernest Joy, Florence Dagmar, Jode Mullally.
Victor Moore's film debut has him playing a milkman who comes into an inheritance... *and* a title.

The Snow Bride (Famous Players-Lasky/Paramount, 1923)
d: Henry Kolker. 6 reels.
Alice Brady, Maurice B. Flynn, MarioMajeroni, Nick Thompson, Jack Baston, Stephen Gratton, William Cavanaugh, Margaret Morgan.
In a remote Canadian outpost, a young woman rejects a suitor and he promptly takes poison. She's convicted of his "murder," but as she's being led to the gallows an avalanche buries half the town. The superstitious townfolk take this as a sign that she's innocent, as indeed she is.

Snow White (Famous Players/Paramount, 1916)
d: J. Searle Dawley. 6 reels.
Marguerite Clark, Dorothy G. Cumming, Creighton Hale, Lionel Brtaham, Alice Washburn.
The insanely jealous Queen Brangomar hates the beautiful princess Snow White, and conspires to have her murdered. But Snow White escapes into the forest, and into the lives of seven dwarfs who have their cottage there.

The Snowbird (Rolfe Photoplays, Inc./Metro, 1916)
d: Edwin Carewe. 6 reels.
Mabel Taliaferro, Edwin Carewe, James Cruze, Warren Cook, Arthur Evers, Walter Hitchcock, Kitty Stevens, John Melody.
In the Canadian woods, a young woman impersonates a man in order to gain the confidence of a reclusive misogynist.

Snowblind (Goldwyn, 1921)
d: Reginald Barker. 6 reels.
Russell Simpson, Mary Alden, Cullen Landis, Pauline Starke.
In the Canadian northwest, a girl from a theatrical troupe goes temporarily blind from the snow drifts, and is nursed back to health by a charming trapper.

Snowdrift (Fox, 1923)
d: Scott Dunlap. 5 reels.
Bert Sprotte, Charles Jones, Irene Rich, Gertrude Ryan, G. Raymond Nye, Colin Chase, Evelyn Selbie, Dorothy Manners, Lalo Encinas, Lee Shumway, Charles Anderson, Annette Jean.
Snowdrift, an orphan white girl who's been raised by Indians, is attacked by a dance hall proprietor but rescued by a sympathetic mining engineer.

The Snowshoe Trail (Chester Bennett Productions/FBO of America, 1922)
d: Chester Bennett. 6 reels.
Jane Novak, Roy Stewart, Lloyd Whitlock, Herbert Prior, Kate Toncray, Spottiswoode Aitken, Chai Hung.
Virginia, an heiress, sets out for the great Northwest in search of her fiancé but then falls in love with the guide who gets her there.

So Big (First National, 1924)
d: Charles Brabin. 9 reels.
Colleen Moore, Sam De Grasse, John Bowers, Ben Lyon, Wallace Beery, Gladys Brockwell, Jean Hersholt, Charlotte Merriam, Dot Farley, Ford Sterling, Frankie Darrow, Henry Gerbert, Dorothy Brock, Rosemary Theby, Phyllis Haver.
Selina, formerly a young woman of high standing, is reduced to poverty after the death of her father. She marries a poor farmer and leads a hard life, but is brightened by her little son, whom she calls So Big.

So Long Letty (Christie Film Co., 1920)
d: Al Christie. 6 reels.
T. Roy Barnes, Colleen Moore, Walter Hiers, Grace Darmond.
Grace and Letty overhear their husbands planning to "swap wives," and decide not to let them get away with it.

So This is Arizona (William M. Smith Productions/Merit Film Corp., 1922)
d: Francis Ford. 6 reels.
Franklyn Farnum, Francis Ford, Shorty Hamilton, Al Hart, Genevieve Bert, Art Phillips.
Out West, a cowpoke follows a young woman all the way to her home in Arizona to return her lost purse. Along the way, however, he's hindered by policemen, crooks, and a sheriff's posse.

So This is Love (Columbia, 1928)
d: Frank Capra. 6 reels.
William Collier Jr., Shirley Mason, Johnnie Walker, Ernie Adams, Carl Gerard, William H. Strauss, Jean Laverty.
A young man is in love with a shopgirl, and she fancies him too. Trouble is, a brawny prizefighter is also in love with the girl, and he won't give her up without a fight.

So This is Marriage (MGM, 1924)
d: Hobart Henley.   7 reels. (Part color.)
Conrad Nagel, Eleanor Boardman, Lew Cody, Warner Oland, John Boles, Clyde Cook, Edward Connelly, Miss Dupont, Francis McDonald, Tom O'Brien.
A frivolous wife ponders divorcing her husband and marrying another man.

So This is Paris (Warner Bros., 1926)
d: Ernst Lubitsch. 7 reels.
Monte Blue, Patsy Ruth Miller, Lilyan Tashman, Andre de Beranger, Myrna Loy, Sidney D'Albrook.
Merry marital mixups liven this tale of a husband-and-wife dance team and their admirers.

The Soap Girl (Vitagraph, 1918)
d: Martin Justice. 5 reels.
Gladys Leslie, Frank Norcross, Harold Foshay, Ed Burns, Julia Swayne Gordon, Ed Favor.
When a young woman is pictured in magazine ads using the sponsor's soap in her bathtub, society is shocked, and promptly dubs her "The Soap Girl."

The Soapsuds Trust — see: Happiness (1917)

Social Ambition (Selexart Pictures, Inc./Goldwyn, 1918)
d: Wallace Worsley. 6 reels.
Howard Hickman, Rhea Mitchell, Katherine Kirkham, Noah Beery, Joseph J. Dowling.
When a playwright invests all his money in stock and loses it, his avaricious wife divorces him. He moves to Alaska and

marries a dance hall girl who loves him for himself, then strikes it rich in the gold fields.

Social Briars (American Film Co./Mutual, 1918)
d: Henry King. 5 reels.
Mary Miles Minter, Alan Forrest, Anne Schaefer, Edmund Cobb, George Periolat, Claire DuBrey, Milla Davenport, Jacob Abrams, Frank Whitson.
Iris, a small town charmer, moves to the big city and is promptly courted by a wealthy young alcoholic.

The Social Buccaneer (Universal, 1916)
d: Jack Conway. 5 reels.
J. Warren Kerrigan, Lois Wilson, Maud George, Louise Lovely, Harry Carter, Marc Robbins, Hayward Mack, W.T. Horne.
Determined to become a modern Robin Hood, an importer plans to steal a wealthy woman's necklace and redistribute the wealth to the poor.

The Social Celebrity (Paramount, 1926)
d: Malcolm St. Clair. 6 reels.
Adolphe Menjou, Louise Brooks, Elsie Lawson, Roger Davis, Hugh Huntley, Chester Conklin, Freeman Wood, Josephine Drake, Ida Waterman.

Max, a small-town barber, goes to New York as the guest of a society matron and tries to pass himself off as a French count.

The Social Highwayman (Shubert Film Corp./World Film Corp., 1916)
d: Edwin August. 5 reels.
Edwin August, John Sainpolis, Ormi Hawley, Alice Clair Elliott, Noah Beery.
Curtis, a self-made millionaire, feels the need to steal from his friends and distribute the money to the poor.

The Social Highwayman (Warner Bros., 1926)
d: William Beaudine. 7 reels.
John Patrick, Montague Love, Dorothy Devore, George Pearce, Lynn Cowan, James Gordon, Fred Kelsey, Charles Hill Mailes.
Walker, a cub reporter, trails a notorious bandit into the countryside.

The Social Leper (World Film Corp., 1917)
d: Harley Knoles. 5 reels.
Carlyle Blackwell, Arthur Ashley, June Elvidge, George MacQuarrie, Isabelle Berwin, Evelyn Greeley, Eugenie Woodward, Edna Whistler.
A heartless woman causes the death of her only child and, after divorcing her husband, sabotages his romance with another woman.

The Social Pirate (World Film Corp., 1919)
d: Dell Henderson. 5 reels.
June Elvidge, Laura Burt, Allan Edwards, George McQuarrie, Ned Sparks, May Hopkins, Philip Van Loan, Alex Shannon, Bertram Marburg.
Dolores, an immigrant from South America, becomes a famous violinist... but not before spending four months behind bars for a crime she didn't commit.

Social Quicksands (Metro, 1918)
d: Charles J. Brabin. 5 reels.
Francis X. Bushman, Beverly Bayne, Mabel Fremyear, Leslie Stowe, William Dunn, Lila Blow, Rolinda Bainbridge, Elsie MacLeod, Jack B. Hollis, Armorel McDowell, William Stone.
Dexter, an eligible bachelor, passes up the chance to meet a

debutante. Stung by the rejection, she makes a bet that she'll get him to propose marriage within a month... and does.

The Social Secretary (Fine Arts Film Co./Triangle, 1916)
d: John Emerson. 5 reels.
Norma Talmadge, Kate Lester, Helen Weir, Gladden James, Herbert French, Eric von Stroheim, Nathaniel Sack.
Too lovely to hold onto a secretarial job without attracting her bosses' unwanted flirtations, a young woman decides to make herself look as homely as possible. She succeeds, but then in her new job she meets a young man whose attentions she would not mind receiving. Now what?

A Society Exile (Famous Players-Lasky/Paramount, 1919)
d: George Fitzmaurice. 6 reels.
Elsie Ferguson, William P. Carleton, Warburton Gamble, Julia Dean, Henry Stephenson, Zeffie Tilbury, Bijou Fernandez, Alexander Kyle.
Nora, an American heiress, gets innocently involved in a murder-suicide case in England.

Society For Sale (Triangle, 1918)
d: Frank Borzage. 5 reels.
William Desmond, Gloria Swanson, Herbert Prior, Charles Dorian, Lillian West, Lillian Langdon.
Phyllis, a fashion model eager to break into society, pays a penniless nobleman to introduce her as his fiancée.

A Society Scandal (Famous Players-Lasky/Paramount, 1924)
d: Allan Dwan. 7 reels.
Gloria Swanson, Rod LaRocque, Ricardo Cortez, Allan Simpson, Ida Waterman, Thelma Converse, Fraser Coalter, Catherine Proctor, Wilfred Donovan, Yvonne Hughes, Marie Shelton.
Marjorie, a flirtatious wife, is sued by her husband for divorce... and sets her cap for the husband's attorney.

Society Secrets (Universal, 1921)
d: Leo McCarey. 5 reels.
Eva Novak, Gertrude Claire, George Verrell, Clarissa Selwynne, William Buckley, Ethel Ritchie, L.C. Shumway, Carl Stockdale, Lucy Donohue.
A farmer and his wife get introduced to New York society.

A Society Sensation (Universal, 1918)
d: Paul Powell. 5 reels.
Rodolpho DeValentina, Carmel Myers, Alfred Allen, Lydia Yeamans Titus, Fred Kelsey, ZaSu Pitts, Harold Goodwin.
An heir to wealth falls in love with a fisherman's daughter.

Society Snobs (Selznick/Select, 1921)
d: Hobart Henley. 5 reels.
Conway Tearle, Vivian Forrester, Ida Darling, Jack McLean, Huntley Gordon.
A spoiled socialite is introduced to a duke and falls in love with him. Trouble is, he's no duke, just a penniless waiter in disguise.

Society's Driftwood (Universal, 1917)
d: Louis Chaudet. 5 reels.
Grace Cunard, Joseph Girard, Charles West, William Musgrave.
Bitter drama about a young woman whose brother is unjustly sentenced to jail, and who determines to make the judge fall in love with her so she can destroy him.

Soft Boiled (Fox, 1923)
d: J.G. Blystone. 8 reels.
Tom Mix, Joseph Girard, Billie Dove, L.C. Shumway, Tom

Wilson, Frank Beal, Jack Curtis, Charles Hill Mailes, Harry Dunkinson, Wilson Hummell.

Out West, a cowboy must come to grips with a family flaw: He has a hair-trigger temper.

Soft Cushions (Paramount, 1927)
d: Eddie Cline. 7 reels.

Douglas MacLean, Sue Carol, Richard Carle, Russell Powell, Frank Leigh, Wade Boteler, Nigel DeBrulier, Albert Prisco, Boris Karloff, Albert Gran, Fred Kelsey, Harry Jones, Noble Johnson.

Comedy about a thief who falls for a beautiful harem girl and decides to "buy" her.

Soft Living (Fox, 1928)
d: James Tinling. 6 reels.

Madge Bellamy, John Mack Brown, Mary Duncan, Joyce Compton, Thomas Jefferson, Henry Kolker, Olive Tell, Maine Geary, Tom Dugan, David Wengren.

Nancy, secretary to a divorce lawyer, decides to jump on the gravy train herself. She gets a wealthy man to marry her, with the idea of taking him for all he's worth in a large divorce settlement. But she finds that her new husband has ideas of his own—and they *don't* include divorce.

Soiled (Phil Goldstone Productions/Truart Film Corp., 1924)
d: Fred Windemere. 7 reels.

Kenneth Harlan, Vivian Martin, Mildred Harris, Johnny Walker, Mary Alden, Robert Cain, Wyndham Standing, Maude George, Alec B. Francis, John T. Mack.

When a chorus girl named Mary borrows $2,500 and cannot pay her debt in time, the lender decides she can retire the debt by retiring to his bedroom. However, her boyfriend comes up with the money and saves Mary's honor with the lecher in mid-pounce.

Sold (Famous Players/Paramount, 1915)
d: Edwin S. Porter, Hugh Ford. 5 reels.

Pauline Frederick, Thomas Holding, Julian L'Estrange, Lowell Sherman, Lucille Fursman, Russell Bassett.

Fellow artists clash when one of them paints semi-nude poses of the other's wife.

Sold at Auction (Balboa Amusement Producing Co./Pathé, 1917)
d: Sherwood MacDonald. 5 reels.

Lois Meredith, William Conklin, Marguerite Nichols, Frank Mayo, Charles Dudley, Lucy Blake.

Nan, a girl separated from her father since childhood, winds up on the auction block at a phony matrimonial agency, and attracts lively bidding. When a millionaire outbids the others and winds up with Nan, a reporter who knows her story reveals to the millionaire that he has just purchased his own daughter.

Sold for Marriage (Fine Arts Film Co./Triangle, 1916)
d: Christy Cabanne. 5 reels.

Lillian Gish, Frank Bennett, A.D. Sears, Walter Long, Mike Siebert, Olga Grey.

A Russian girl is brought to the American South to help ease the female shortage.

A Soldier's Oath (Fox, 1915)
d: Oscar C. Apfel. 5 reels.

William Farnum, Dorothy Bernard, Kittens Reichert, Alma Frederic, Ruth Findlay, H.J. Herbert, Walter Connolly, Louise Thatcher, Benjamin Marburgh, Henry A. Barrows, Will Lois.

Pierre, a French soldier, makes a battlefield oath to deliver a dying count's jewels to the count's family.

Soldiers of Chance (Vitagraph, 1917)
d: Paul Scardon. 5 reels.

Evart Overton, Miriam Fouche, Julia Swayne Gordon, Charles Kent, Charles Henderson, Denton Vane, Ned Finley.

Two soldiers of fortune sail to a South American country torn by civil war... one to aid the government, the other to aid the rebels.

Soldiers of Fortune (All Star Feature Corp., 1914)
d: William F. Haddock. 6 reels.

Dustin Farnum, John Sainpolis, John Pratt, Leighton Stark, George A. Stillwell, William Conklin, Sam Coit, Ernest Laseby, Winthrop Chamberlain, Helen Luttrelle, Winifred Kingston.

In a South American country, an American engineer gets involved in a revolution.

Soldiers of Fortune (Mayflower Photoplay Corp./Realart Pictures, 1919)
d: Allan Dwan. 7 reels.

Norman Kerry, Pauline Starke, Anna Q. Nilsson, Melbourne MacDowell, Wallace Beery, Wilfred Lucas, Herald Lindsay, Ward Crane, Frank Wally, Fred Kohler, Philo McCullough.

Remake of the 1914 All Star Feature Corp. film *Soldiers of Fortune*.

The Solitary Sin (New Art Film Co., 1919)
d: Frederick Sullivan. 6 reels.

Jack Mulhall, Helene Chadwick, Gordon Griffith, Pauline Curley, Anne Schaefer, Irene Aldwyn, Leo Pierson, Charles Spere, Edward Jobson, Kate Lester, Berry Mills, Edward Cecil.

Cautionary tale about three teenage boys: One boy heeds his father's warnings about illicit sex and ends up marrying happily; the other two reject the warnings and live to regret it.

Some Boy! (Fox, 1917)
d: Otis Turner. 5 reels.

George Walsh, Doris Pawn, Herschel Mayall, Caroline Rankin, Hector Sarno, Velma Whitman, N.A. Myles.

A hotel's publicity agent breaks into a guest's room and steals her jewels, just to generate publicity for the hotel.

Some Bride (Metro, 1919)
d: Henry Otto. 5 reels.

Viola Dana, Irving Cummings, Ruth Sinclair, Billy Mason, Florence Carpenter.

Patricia, a young bride, really loves her new husband but can't cure her flirtatious ways.

Some Liar (American Film Co./Pathé, 1919)
d: Henry King. 5 reels.

William Russell, Eileen Percy, Haywood Mack, Gordon Russell, John Gough.

Out West, a traveling salesman gains a reputation for tall tales.

Some Pun'kins (Chadwick Pictures, 1925)
d: Jerome Storm. 6 reels.

Charles Ray, George Fawcett, Fanny Midgley, Duane Thompson, Bert Woodruff, Hallam Cooley, William Courtright, Ida Lewis.

When fire breaks out and Mary and her father are trapped in their home, a country pumpkin farmer who's had his eye on Mary saves them both with a folding ladder he invented.

464

Somebody's Mother (Gerson Pictures/Rayart, 1926)
w, d: Oscar Apfel. 5 reels.
Mary Carr, Rex Lease, Mickey McBan, Kathryn McGuire, Sidney Franklin, Edward Martindel, Robert Graves.
A street peddler known as Matches Mary wanders the streets looking for the boy who was taken from her in childhood.

Someone in the House (Metro, 1920)
d: John E. Ince. 6 reels.
Edmund Lowe, Vola Vale, Howard Crampton, William J. Irving, Clara Lee, Lawrence Grant, Edward Connelly, Henry Miller Jr., Edward Jobson, Thomas McGuire, Jack Levering.
Jewel theft with a twist: When he learns that the lead actress plans to use her own real diamonds during a play, a society crook auditions for, and lands, the costarring role opposite her.

Someone to Love (Paramount, 1928)
d: F. Richard Jones. 7 reels.
Charles Buddy Rogers, Mary Brian, William Austin, Jack Oakie, James Kirkwood, Mary Alden, Frank Reicher.
William loves Joan, but because her family is wealthy, he refuses to marry her until he has become a success himself.

Something Always Happens (Paramount, 1928)
w, d: Frank Tuttle. 5 reels.
Esther Ralston, Neil Hamilton, Sojin, Charles Sellon, Roscoe Karns, Lawrence Grant, Mischa Auer, Noble Johnson.
Roderick takes Diana, his high-spirited fiancée, to a supposedly haunted house for some laughs. The house is haunted all right, but not by ghosts: It harbors a bloodthirsty outlaw bent on gem theft and, when the couple arrives, on murder.

Something Different (Realart Pictures Corp., 1920)
d: W. William Neill. 5 reels.
Constance Binney, Lucy Fox, Ward Crane, Crane Wilbur, Gertrude Hillman, Mark Smith, Grace Scudiford, William Riley Hatch, Adolph Millar.
Alicia, an American heiress, travels to Cuba to visit friends and falls in love with a dashing army commander.

Something New (Fred H. Croghan, 1920)
d: Bert Van Tuyle. 5 reels.
Nell Shipman, Bert Van Tuyle, L.M. Wells, William McCormack.
In Mexico, a girl from the United States is kidnapped by bandidos, but a brave American rides to her rescue in an amazing car that can traverse seemingly impassable terrain.

Something to Do (Famous Players-Lasky/Paramount, 1919)
d: Donald Crisp. 5 reels.
Bryant Washburn, Ann Little, Robert Brower, Charles Gerrard, Adele Farrington, Charles Ogle, James Mason.
When a playboy decides to crash a ritzy party in the guise of a British nobleman, he discovers that most of the other guests are phonies, too.

Something to Think About (Famous Players-Lasky/Paramouont, 1920)
d: Cecil B. DeMille. 7 reels.
Elliot Dexter, Gloria Swanson, Theodore Roberts, Julia Faye, Monte Blue, Micky Moore, James Mason, Togo Yamamoto, Theodore Kosloff.
Crippled but wealthy, David pays to have local girl Ruth educated, and then falls in love with her. Unfortunately, she loves another, and soon elopes and leaves David broken-hearted. But their paths cross again... and this time, the power of positive thinking heals not only David's bitterness but also his infirmity.

Somewhere in America (Rolfe Photoplays, Inc./Metro, 1917)
d: William C. Dowlan. 5 reels.
Thomas J. Carrigan, Francine Larrimore, Herbert Hayes, Daniel Hogan, Mary Miles Minter, Jules Raucourt, Sidney D'Albrook, Harold Hilton.
Gray, a U.S. secret agent, takes a job as a draftsman with a government contractor who's suspected of having divided loyalties.

Somewhere in France (New York Motion Picture Corp./Triangle, 1916)
d: Charles Giblyn. 5 reels.
Louise Glaum, Howard Hickman, Joseph J. Dowling, Fanny Midgley, Jerome Storm, George Fisher, Carl Ullman.
During World War I, a Frenchwoman in the employ of the German government seduces several high officials and collects state secrets.

Somewhere in Georgia (Sunbeam Motion Picture Corp., 1916)
d: George Ridgwell. 6 reels.
Ty Cobb, Elsie MacLeod, Will Corbett, Harry Fisher, Eddie Boulden, Ned Burton.
A bank clerk gets a chance to play major league baseball.

Somewhere in Sonora (Charles R. Rogers Productions/First National, 1927)
d: Albert Rogell. 6 reels.
Ken Maynard, Kathleen collins, Frank Leigh, Joe Bennett, Charles Hill Mailes, Carl Stockdale, Yvonne Howell, Richard Neill, Ben Corbett, Monte Montague.
In the Southwest, a cowboy searches for a rancher's lost son. He finds the lad and plenty of excitement besides, including the love of a new woman and a narrow escape from a quicksand pit.

The Son-of-a-Gun (Golden West, 1919)
d: Jesse J. Robbins. 5 reels.
G.M. "Broncho Billy" Anderson, Joy Lewis, Fred Church, Frank Whitson, A.E. Whitting, Paul Willis.
A raucous, gun-toting drunk starts a fight in a saloon, but simmers down when a beautiful girl takes a liking to him.

A Son of Erin (Pallas Pictures/Paramount, 1916)
w, d: Julia Crawford Ivers. 5 reels.
Dennis, an impoverished Irish lad, comes to America to become a New York policeman.

The Son of His Father (Thomas H. Ince/Parmamount, 1917)
d: Victor L. Scherzinger. 5 reels.
Charles Ray, Vola Vale, Robert McKim, George Nichols, John P. Lockney, Charles K. French, George Hoffman, Harry Yamamoto.
Gordon, son of a railroad tycoon, is challenged by his father to make good on his own.

A Son of His Father (Famous Players-Lasky/Paramount, 1925)
d: Victor fleming. 7 reels.
Bessie Love, Warner Baxter, Raymond Hatton, Walter McGrail, Carl Stockdale, Billy Eugene, James Farley, Charles Stevens, Valentina Zimina, George Kuwa.
Out West, a rancher helps a girl who's come to town looking

for her wayward brother.

A Son of the Desert (F.W. Kraemer/American Releasing Corp., 1928)
w, d: William Merrill McCormick. 5 reels.
William Merrill McCormick, Marin Sais, Robert Burns, Faith Hope, James Welsh.
Helen, an American art student visiting Arabia, wishes to paint a portrait of a handsome sheik. The sheik invites her into his camp, but posing is the last thing on his mind.

Son of the Golden West (FBO Pictures, 1928)
d: Eugene Forde. 6 reels.
Tom Mix, Sharon Lynn, Tom Lingham, Duke R. Lee, Lee Shumway, Fritzi Ridgeway, Joie Ray, Mark Hamilton, Wynn Mace.
Out West, a cowboy and his wonder horse rescue a young woman from a runaway team.

A Son of the Hills (Vitagraph, 1917)
d: Harry Davenport. 5 reels.
Antonio Moreno, Belle Bruce, Robert Gaillard, Julia Swayne Gordon, Florence Radinoff, William Balfour.
A runaway country boy makes good in the big city.

A Son of the Immortals (Universal, 1916)
d: Otis Turner. 5 reels.
J. Warren Kerrigan, Lois Wilson, Bertram Grassby, Harry Carter, Maud George, H.L. Holland, George Hernandez, Girrard Alexander.
The ruler of a European principality discovers his mother was American-born, thus disqualifying him from holding his throne. Instead of being upset, though, the prince is happy to relinquish his title, because he's fallen in love with an American girl.

A Son of the Sahara (Edwin Carewe Productions/Associated First National, 1924)
d: Edwin Carewe. 8 reels.
Claire Windsor, Bert Lytell, Walter McGrail, Rosemary Theby, Marise Dorval, Montagu Love, Paul Panzer, Georges Chebat.
Raoul, a dignified Frenchman, was raised by Arabs and knows their ways. When he falls in love with Barbara and she plays hard to get, Raoul arranges for her to be stolen by renegades and to be offered for sale at a slave auction. Raoul has his bid ready.

Son of the Sheik (United Artists, 1926)
d: George Fitzmaurice. 7 reels.
Rudolph Valentino, Vilma Banky, Agnes Ayres, Bull Montana, Charles Requa, Karl Dane, William Donovan, George Fawcett, Montagu Love, Erwin Connelly.
Valentino's last film, released after his death, finds him an Arab leader prowling the sands and falling in love with Yasmin, a desert wench.

The Song and Dance Man (Paramount, 1926)
d: Herbert Brenon. 7 reels.
Tom Moore, Bessie Love, Harrison Ford, Norman Trevor, Bobby Watson, Josephine Drake, George Nash, William B. Mack, Helen Lindroth, Jane Jennings.
Happy, an entertainer, turns to petty theft when his luck goes sour. But his tutelage brings success to Leola, whose dancing lights up the Broadway stage.

The Song of Hate (Fox, 1915)
d: J. Gordon Edwards. 5 reels.
Betty Nansen, Arthur Hoops, Dorothy Bernard, Claire Whitney.
Operatic diva Floria Tosca offers herself to a Roman official in order to save the life of her lover... but there's treachery all around, and all three die violent deaths.
The first of several feature films based on the Victorien Sardou play *La Tosca*, which also spawned the Puccini opera of that title.

The Song of Life (Louis B. Mayer Productions/Associated First National, 1922)
d: John M. Stahl. 7 reels.
Gaston Glass, Grace Darmond, Georgia Woodthorpe, Richard Headrick, Arthur Stuart Hull, Wedgewood Nowell, Edward Peil, Fred Kelsey, Claude Payton.
Mary, a middle-aged woman who washes dishes for a living and seemingly has no future, becomes depressed and attempts suicide. She is stopped by a young writer, David, who takes her into his home as a companion to his wife. In time, Mary learns that David is the son she abandoned when he was a child.

The Song of Love (Norma Talmadge Productions/Associated First National, 1923)
d: Chester Franklin. 8 reels.
Norma Talmadge, Joseph Schildkraut, Arthur Edmund Carew, Laurence Wheat, Maude Wayne, Earl Schenck, Hector V. Sarno, Albert Prisco, Mario Carillo, James Cooley.
Exotic melodrama about an Arabian girl in love with an officer in the French garrison.

A Song of Sixpence (Van Dyke Film Production Co./Art Dramas, Inc., 1917)
d: Ralph Dean. 5 reels.
Marie Wayne, Robert Conness, Rowdon Hall, Alfred Hemming, Margaret Townsend, Nell Pemberton, Jean LaMotte.
Emmy, a girl from the country who yearns for a life of luxury, attains that when she marries an elderly millionaire. But she comes to realize that money isn't everything.

The Song of Songs (Famous Players-Lasky/Paramount, 1918)
d: Joseph Kaufman. 5 reels.
Elsie Ferguson, Frank Losee, Crauford Kent, Cecil Fletcher, Gertrude Berkeley, Corinne Uzzell, Charles Wellesley, Henry Leone, Robert Cummings, Ned Burton.
Lily, a beautiful girl with an artistic temperament, has many suitors... but inspires as much jealousy as affection.

The Song of the Soul (Vitagraph, 1918)
d: Tom Terriss. 5 reels.
Alice Joyce, Percy Standing, Walter McGrail, Bernard Randall, Bernard Siegel, Edith Reeves, Stephen Carr.
Upon learning that her husband is a bigamist, Ann leaves him but is also forced to leave her young son behind. Years later, after several misadventures, she wins the love of a kindly doctor who agrees to marry her and adopt her son.

The Song of the Wage Slave (Popular Plays and Players, Inc./Metro, 1915)
d: Herbert Blaché, Alice Blaché. 5 reels.
Edmund Breese, Helen Martin, J. Byrnes,Fraunie Fraunholz, Albert Froom, George MacIntyre, Wallace Scott, Mabel Wright, Claire Hillier, Kitty Reichert, William Moore.
In the Northwest, a paper mill worker marries a girl he knows still pines for her former lover.

Sonny (Inspiration Pictures/Associated First National, 1922)

d: Henry King.   7 reels.
Richard Barthelmess, Margaret Seddon, Pauline Garon, Lucy Fox, Herbert Grimwood, Patterson Dial, Fred Nicholls, James Terbell, Margaret Elizabeth Falconer, Virginia Magee.
During the War, Joe and Sonny meet in the trenches and realize they are dead ringers for each other. When Sonny is fatally wounded, he makes Joe promise he will return home in his place in order to save his mother the grief of having lost a son. Joe keeps his promise, but finds it difficult to maintain the deception when he falls in love with Sonny's sister.Barthelmess does double duty here, playing both Sonny and Joe.

Sooner or Later   (Selznick/Select, 1920)
d: Wesley Ruggles.   5 reels.
Owen Moore, Seena Owen, Clifford Gray, Amy Dennis, Jane Carleton, Marie Burke, Katherine Perry.
Mistaken-identity comedy, with a newlywed husband suspecting his bride is having an affair. He gets his friend to investigate, and the friend kidnaps the woman he thinks is the bride, only to discover she's a stranger with the same name.

Sophy of Kravonia; or, the Virgin of Paris   (Allied Artists/Harry Raver, Inc., 1920)
d: Gerard Fontaine.   6 reels.
Diana Kareni, Walter Gordon, PhilipAshley, Marjorie Strickland, Marie Paton, Lewis J. Mortimer, J.R. Phelps, Florence Temple, William Creswick, Clara Denvil.
In the kingdom of Kravonia, a housemaid meets a crown prince and saves his life.

Sorrell and Son   (United Artists, 1927)
d: Herbert Brenon.   10 reels.
H.B. Warner, Anna Q. Nilsson, Nils Asther, Mickey McBan, Carmel Myers, Lionel Belmore, Norman Trevor, Louis Wolheim, Alice Joyce, Mary Nolan.
A World War I veteran returns home to find his wife has left him and their young son.

The Sorrows of Love   (New York Motion Picture Corp./Triangle, 1916)
d: Charles Giblyn.   5 reels.
Bessie Barriscale, William Desmond, Ora Carew, Herschel Mayall, Wedgwood Nowell.
During a time of civil strife in Italy, a nun leaves the convent to join the revolution.

Sorrows of Satan   (Paramount, 1926)
d: D.W. Griffith.   9 reels.
Adolphe Menjou, Ricardo Cortez, Carol Dempster, Lya De Putti.
Menjou portrays the Devil as an all too debonair society rascal.

So's Your Old Man   (Paramount, 1926)
d: Gregory LaCava.   7 reels.
W.C. Fields, Alice Joyce, Charles Rogers, Kittens Reichert, Marcia Harris, Julia Ralph, Frank Montgomery, Jerry Sinclair.
Prototypical Fields farce, this time about a clueless but loveable inventor who somehow manages to develop a truly useful invention and bring fortune and renown to himself and his family.

A Soul Enslaved   (Universal, 1916)
d: Cleo Madison.   5 reels.
Irma Sorter, Thomas Chatterton, Cleo Madison, Douglas Gerrard, Lule Warrenton, Marguerite Gibson, Alfred Allen.

Richard, a happily married husband and father, discovers that his wife was once another man's mistress, and throws her out. On second thought, Richard muses on his own checkered past and realizes he may be judging her too harshly.

Soul-Fire   (Inspiration Pictures/First National, 1925)
d: John S. Robertson.   9 reels.
Richard Barthelmess, Bessie Love, Percy Ames, Charles Esdale, Lee Baker, Carlotta Monterey, Helen Ware, Walter Long, Harriet Sterling, Richard Harlan, Arthur Metcalfe.
Eric, a musical prodigy, travels the world over searching for inspiration for his symphonies.

A Soul for Sale   (Universal, 1918)
d: Allen Holubar.   6 reels.
Dorothy Phillips, Albert Roscoe, Catherine Kirkwood, William Burress, Harry Dunkinson, Joseph Girard.
Left penniless by the death of her husband, a woman decides to earn money by auctioning off her daughter in marriage to the highest bidder.

A Soul in Trust   (Triangle, 1918)
d: G.P. Hamilton.   7 reels.
Belle Bennett, Darrell Foss, J. Barney Sherry, Lillian West, Grover Franke, Lee Hill, Lizzie Davis, William Dyer.
On his deathbed, a leading citizen confesses to his wife that he has a baby son by another woman. The widow good-heartedly adopts the child and raises him as her own. Twenty years go by, and the young man, now a senator's aide, clashes with a group of lawbreakers—and their number includes his natural mother.

The Soul Market   (Popular Plays and Players/Metro, 1916)
d: Francis J. Grandon.   5 reels.
Olga Petrova, Arthur Hoops, Wilmuth Merkyl, Fritz DeLint, Fraunie Fraunholz, Charles Brandt, Charles Mack, Bert Tuey, Grace Florence, Cora Milholland, Evelyn Brent, Al Thomas.
A millionaire poses as a chauffeur to be near the woman he loves.

The Soul Master   (Vitagraph, 1917)
d: Marguerite Bertsch.   5 reels.
Earle Williams, Billie Billings, Katherine Lewis, Julia Swayne Gordon, Albert Howson, Annie Brody, Mildred May, Donald Cameron, Denton Vane.
Travers, embittered because his wife left him years before, owns a large department store. He finds himself irresistibly drawn to Ruth, a young ribbon clerk in his employ, and offers her a position as his secretary. Eventually Travers will learn that Ruth is his own daughter, whom he hasn't seen in eighteen years.

Soul Mates   (American Film Co./Mutual, 1916)
d: William Russell, Jack Prescott.   5 reels.
William Russell, Charlotte Burton, Leona Hutton, Harry Keenan, Dodo Newton, Robert Klein, John Gough, Lou Davis.
When Sherman, a wealthy businessman, learns that his wife is having an affair, he vengefully sends her packing and drives her lover into bankruptcy. After the lover, who is also married, commits suicide, Sherman feels guilty about the man's widow and child, and begins supporting them. What began as an act of philanthropy deepens into love.

Soul Mates   (MGM, 1925)
d: Jack Conway.   6 reels.
Aileen Pringle, Edmund Lowe, Phillips Smalley, Antonio

D'Algy, Edythe Chapman, Mary Hawes, Catherine Bennett, Lucien Littlefield, Ned Sparks.
A young woman resists being driven into a marriage arranged by her wealthy uncle.

The Soul of a Child (Pioneer Feature Film Corp., 1916)
d: Jack Gorman. 5 reels.
Em Gorman, Wellington Playter, John Dunn, Nancy Baring, Grace Lovell.
Jim, a transplanted country boy, lives the fast life in the big city. But his lifestyle undergoes some alterations when his brother and sister-in-law die in an accident, and Jim inherits Goldenlocks, his little niece.

The Soul of a Magdalen (Popular Plays and Players, Inc./Metro, 1917)
d: Burton L. King. 5 reels.
Olga Petrova, Wyndham Standing, Mahlon Hamilton, Mathilde Brundage, Violet Reed, Gene Burnell, Frances Walton, Richard Barthelmess, Boris Korlin, Frank Moore.
To support her needy family, a young woman becomes a rich man's mistress.

The Soul of Broadway (Fox, 1915)
d: Herbert Brenon. 5 reels.
Valeska Suratt, William E. Shay, Sheridan Block, Mabel Allen, Jane Lee, George W. Middleton, Gertrude Berkeley.
Grace, a self-centered Broadway star, pursues an old admirer although he now loves another.

The Soul of Buddha (Fox, 1918)
d: J. Gordon Edwards. 5 reels.
Theda Bara, Hugh Thompson, Victor Kennard, Anthony Merlow, Florence Martin, Jack Ridgway, Henry Warwick.
Bava, an incorrigible flirt, is dedicated as a sacred dancer to Buddha... but that doesn't stop her wandering eyes.

The Soul of Kura-San (Lasky Feature Plays/Paramount, 1916)
d: E.J. LeSaint. 5 reels.
Sessue Hayakawa, Myrtle Stedman, Tsuru Aoki, George Webb, Thomas Kurihara, George Kuwa.
In Japan, a girl models for an American artist and they have an affair, after which the girl dutifully commits suicide.

The Soul of Satan (Fox, 1917)
d: Otis Turner. 5 reels.
Gladys Brockwell, Bertram Grassby, Charles Clary, William Burress, Josef Swickard, Gerard Alexander, Norbert Myles, Lucille Young, Frankie Lee, Marie Kiernan.
In New York, a girl falls for a handsome gambler and lets him lure her into a fake wedding ceremony.

The Soul of the Beast (Thomas H. Ince/Metro, 1923)
d: John Griffith Wray. 5 reels.
Madge Bellamy, Oscar the elephant, Cullen Landis, Noah Beery, Vola Vale, Bert Sprotte, Harry Rattenberry, Carrie Clark Ward, Lincoln Stedman, Larry Steers, Vernon Dent.
Oscar, a prodigiously gifted circus elephant, helps a young woman escape her cruel stepfather and brings her together with a young man she will grow to love.

The Soul of Youth (Realart Pictures Corp., 1920)
d: William D. Taylor. 6 reels.
Lewis Sargent, Ernest Butterworth, Clyde Fillmore, Grace Morse, Lila Lee, Elizabeth Janes, William Collier Jr., Claude Peyton, Betty Schade, Fred Huntley, Sylvia Ashton.
When a young thief is arrested and his custody awarded to a kindly politician, the boy shows his gratitude by stealing

incriminating documents that eliminate his foster father's opponent from the election.

A Soul Without Windows (World Film Corp., 1918)
d: Travers Vale. 5 reels.
Ethel Clayton, Frank Mayo, Pinna Nesbit, Richard Clarke, Eugenie Woodward, Victor Kennard, David Davies, Gus Pixley, Zadee Burbank, Jack Drumier, Jack Roberts, Violet Axzell.
In Pennsylvania, a Shaker girl falls in love with a young man who's temporarily paralyzed.

Souls Adrift (World Film Corp., 1917)
d: Harley Knowles. 5 reels.
Milton Sills, Ethel Clayton, John Davidson, Frank DeVernon, Walter James.
Two castaways fall in love on a desert island.

The Soul's Cycle (Centaur Film Co./Mutual, 1916)
d: Ulysses Davis. 5 reels.
Margaret Gibson, John Oaker, George Claire Jr., George Stanley, Roy Watson.
In Ancient Greece, the gods punish a murderous senator by turning him into a lion. Fast forward to modern times, and the lion finally makes amends by guaranteeing the happiness of two lovers, and reverts back to being human.

Souls for Sables (Tiffany Productions, 1925)
d: James C. McKay. 7 reels.
Claire Windsor, Eugene O'Brien, Claire Adams, Edith Yorke, George Fawcett, Eileen Percy, Anders Randolf, Robert Ober.
Esther, married but neglectful of her husband, allows a scoundrel to woo her with fancy furs.

Souls for Sale (Goldwyn, 1924)
d: Rupert Hughes. 8 reels.
Eleanor Boardman, Mae Busch, Richard Dix, Lew Cody, Arthur Hoyt, Barbara LaMarr, David Imboden, Roy Atwell, William Orlamond, Forrest Robinson, Edith Yorke, Dale Fuller.
A minister's daughter leaves her new husband on their wedding night and winds up working in the movies.
Several film stars are seen playing themselves, including Charles Chaplin, Barbara Bedford, Raymond Griffith, Bessie Love, Johnny Walker, Florence Vidor, Anna Q. Nilsson, ZaSu Pitts, Blanch Sweet, Claire Windsor, Erich von Stroheim, and Alice Lake.

Souls in Bondage (Lubin, 1916)
d: Edgar Lewis. 5 reels.
Nance O'Neil, Ida Stanhope, William Corbett, Bernard Seigel.
Rosa, a humanitarian to a fault, becomes a Red Cross nurse and serves at the front.

Souls in Bondage (Sanford Productions, 1923)
d: William H. Clifford. 7 reels.
Pat O'Malley, Cleo Madison, Otto Lederer, Eugenia Gilbert, Frank Hayes, Gene Crosby, Peter Howard, Leon Artigue.
When a jewel thief loses his memory from a blow on the head, his gang sends him to a faith healer.

Souls in Pawn (American Film Co./Mutual, 1917)
d: Henry King. 5 reels.
Gail Kane, Robert Klein, Frank Rickert, Edward Peil, Ashton Dearholt, Ruth Everdale, Douglas MacLean.
In World War I, a German prince enlists the aid of Liane, a beautiful widow, as a spy. Unknown to Liane, the prince himself caused the death of her husband... but, it will turn

out, he had good cause.

Souls Triumphant (Fine Arts Film Co./Triangle, 1917)
d: John O'Brien. 5 reels.
Lillian Gish, Wilfred Lucas, Spottiswoode Aitken, Louise Hamilton.
Horrified to learn that his son has perished in a fire, an unfaithful husband goes to his wife to beg her forgiveness. But she has rescued their son, and when the wife sees her husband's concern, she forgives him his infidelity.

The Source (Famous Players-Lasky/Paramount, 1918)
d: George H. Melford. 5 reels.
Wallace Reid, Ann Little, Theodore Roberts, Raymond Hatton, James Cruze, Noah Beery, Nina Byron, Charles West, G. Butler Clonblough, Charles Ogle.
An alcoholic playboy becomes a lumberjack, kicks his habit, and wins the love of a good woman.

South of Panama (Chesterfield Motion Picture Corp., 1928)
d: Charles J. Hunt, Bernard F. McEveety. 7 reels.
Carmelita Geraghty, Edouard Raquello, Lewis Sargent, Philo McCullough, Marie Messinger, Henry Arras, Carlton King, Joseph Burke, Fred Walton.
A munitions smuggler tries to drum up business by fomenting a revolution in a South American country; but when he sets eyes on the lovely daughter of the country's president he suddenly wants to make love, not war.

South of Suva (Realart Pictures/Paramount, 1922)
d: Frank Urson. 5 reels.
Mary Miles Minter, Winifred Bryson, Walter Long, John Bowers, Roy Atwell, Fred Kelsey, Lawrence Steers.
Phyllis, who has traveled to the South Seas to search for her husband, finds him on an island in an advanced case of alcoholism.

South Sea Love (Fox, 1923)
d: David Soloman. 5 reels.
Shirley Mason, J. Frank Glendon, Francis McDonald, Lillian Nicholson, Charles A. Sellon, Fred Lancaster, Robert Conville.

On a tropical island, a young woman falls in love with her married guardian.

South Sea Love (R-C Pictures/FBO of America, 1927)
d: Ralph Ince. 7 reels.
Patsy Ruth Miller, Lee Shumway, Alan Brooks, Harry Crocker, Barney Gilmore, Gertrude Howard, Albert Conti, Everett Brown, Harry Wallace.
Stewart, an American working in the South Seas, sends money home to Charlotte, a chorus girl. But he'll have to fight off a jealous rival to win her everlasting love.

Southern Justice (Universal, 1917)
d: Lynn Reynolds. 5 reels.
Myrtle Gonzales, George Hernandez, Jack Curtis, Jean Hersholt, Charles H. Mailes, Fred Church, Elwood Bredell, Maxfield Stanley, George Marsh.
Down South, a shifty Yankee tries to swindle the locals in a land scheme.

Southern Pride (American Film Co./Mutual, 1917)
d: Henry King. 5 reels.
Gail Kane, Cora Drew, Jack Vosburgh, Robert Klein, Spottiswoode Aitken, George Periolat, Lewis J. Cody.
In New Orleans, the remnants of a poor but proud Creole clan struggle to keep their family together.

The Sowers (Lasky Feature Plays/Paramount, 1916)

d: William C. DeMille. 5 reels.
Blanche Sweet, Thomas Meighan, Mabel Van Buren, Ernest Joy, Theodore Roberts, Horace B. Carpenter, Raymond Hatton, Harold Howard.
In Russia, Prince Paul Alexis sacrifices his own happiness to marry a princess he does not love, thinking their union will encourage the Czar to improve conditions among the poor.

Sowers and Reapers (Rolfe Photoplays, Inc./Metro, 1917)
d: George D. Baker. 5 reels.
Emmy Wehlen, George Stuart Christie, Frank Currier, Peggy Parr, Harry Davenport, Claire McCormack, Emmanuel Turner, Walter Horton, Kate Blancke, David Thompson.
Earle and Annie are in love and get married, but his wealthy father disapproves and tries to have the marriage annulled.

Sowing the Wind (Anita Stewart Productions/Associated First National, 1921)
d: John M. Stahl. 9 reels.
Anita Stewart, James Morrison, Myrtle Stedman, Ralph Lewis, William V. Mong, Josef Swickard, Ben Deely, Harry Northrup, Margaret Landis, William Clifford.
Rosamond, a convent-bred girl, learns that her mother is a notorious woman earning her living in a gambling den. Her illusions shattered, Rosamond leaves home and takes to the stage, where she becomes a successful actress. Her new sweetheart is Ned, foster son of a wealthy gent, and Rosamond learns that the gent is the father she's never known.

Spangles (Universal, 1926)
d: Frank O'Connor. 6 reels.
Marian Nixon, Hobart Bosworth, Pat O'Malley, Gladys Brockwell, Jay Emmett, James Conly, Grace Gordon, Paul Howard, Tiny Ward, Charles Becker, Nelle B. Lane, Clarence Wertz.
"Spangles" Delancy, bareback riding star of a traveling circus, is sweet on a new chariot driver—but unknown to her, he's a fugitive from justice.

The Spaniard (Famous Players-Lasky/Paramount, 1925)
d: Raoul Walsh. 7 reels.
Ricardo Cortez, Jetta Goudal, Noah Beery, Mathilda Brundage, Renzo DeGardi, Emily Fitzroy, Bernard Seigel, Florence Renart.
Barrego, a Spanish matador, loves an English lady whose disdain for him wounds him more than any bull ever could. Not to worry, though; the lady will come around.

The Spanish Dancer (Paramount, 1923)
d: Herbert Brenon. 9 reels.
Wallace Beery, Antonio Moreno, Pola Negri, Gareth Hughes, Adolphe Menjou, Kathlyn Williams, Robert Agnew, Edward Kipling, Dawn O'Day, Charles A. Stevenson.
In old Spain, a gypsy dancer falls in love with an impecunious nobleman. But there's a problem: the king wants her too.

The Spanish Jade (Famous Players-Lasky/Paramount, 1922)
d: John S. Robertson. 5 reels.
David Powell, Marc MacDermott, Charles de Rochefort, Evelyn Brent, Lionel D'Aragon, Frank Stanmore, Roy Byford, Harry Ham.
In Spain, an American intervenes in a struggle to rescue a young woman from a band of hoodlums, and falls in love with her.

The Spark Divine (Vitagraph, 1919)

SPARROWS (1926). Mary Pickford (center) appears as the oldest of several "unwanted" children held captive by the evil Grimes (Gustav von Seyferrtitz, left) in the southern swamplands.

* * * * *

d: Tom Terriss. 5 reels.

Alice Joyce, William Carlton Jr., Eulalie Jensen, Frank Norcross, Mary Carr.

Raised by glum parents who show her no human warmth, Marcia grows up without love in her heart. She agrees to marry, but lets her new husband know that she can never truly love him. Even after their baby is born, Marcia goes about her maternal duties coldly... until one day the child is kidnapped, and the spark of motherhood is ignited.

Sparrows (Pickford/United Artists, 1926)
d: William Beaudine. 9 reels.

Mary Pickford, Gustav von Seyffertitz, Charlotte Mineau, Spec O'Donnell, Mary Louise Miller, Roy Stewart, Lloyd Whitlock, A.L. Schaeffer, Mark Hamilton, Monty O'Grady.

A group of orphans are held in bondage on a baby farm surrounded by the alligator-infested swamps of Louisiana.

Spawn of the Desert (Berwilla Film Corp./Arrow Film Corp., 1923)
d: Ben Wilson, Lewis King. 5 reels.

William Fairbanks, Florence Gilbert, Dempsey Tabler, Al Hart.

Out West, a desert guide learns that a visiting lady is really the long-lost daughter of the local hermit.

Special Delivery (Famous Players-Lasky/Paramount, 1927)
d: William Goodrich (Roscoe Arbuckle). 6 reels.

Eddie Cantor, Jobyna Ralston, Donald Keith, Jack Dougherty, William Powell, Victor Potel, Paul Kelly, Mary Carr.

Comedy about Eddie, an honest but blundering mailman who loves a waitress.

Speed (Banner Productions, 1925)
d: Edward J. LeSaint. 6 reels.

Betty Blythe, Pauline Garon, William V. Mong, Arthur Rankin, Alred Allen, Robert Ellis, Eddie Phillips, Fred Becker, Stella DeLanti.

Wiletta, a pleasure-loving jazz baby, gets involved with foreign crooks and finds herself kidnapped. In a wild ride, her dad and her beau catch the kidnappers' car and rescue the wayward girl just before the car goes over a cliff.

Speed Cop (Duke Worne Productions/Rayart, 1926)
d: Duke Worne. 5 reels.

Billy Sullivan, Rose Blossom, Francis Ford.

Billy, a handsome traffic cop, stops pretty Rose to give her a speeding ticket... and it's love at first citation.

The Speed Girl (Realart Pictures/Paramount, 1921)
d: Maurice Campbell. 5 reels.

Bebe Daniels, Theodore von Eltz, Frank Elliott, Walter Hiers, Norris Johnson, Truly Shattuck, William Courtright, Barbara Maier.

Movie stunt girl Betty Lee rides horses, drives sports cars and flies airplanes. But when a handsome stranger wanders into her life, she allows him to think he has rescued her from a runaway horse.

Speed Mad (Columbia, 1925)
d: Jay Marchant. 5 reels.

William Fairbanks, Edith Roberts, Charles K. French.

A speed-car driver is kidnapped the night before an important race.

The Speed Maniac (Fox, 1919)
d: Edward J. LeSaint. 5 reels.

Tom Mix, Eva Novak, Charles K. French, Hayward Mack, L.C. Shumway, Helen Wright, Jack Curtis, Georgie Stone, George H. Hackathorn, Charles Hill Mailes, Ernest Shields, Buck Jones.

In San Francisco, a visiting rancher tries to perfect a car engine he's invented, and winds up winning the big race.

The Speed Spook (East Coast Films, 1924)
d: Charles Hines. 7 reels.

Johnny Hines, Faire Binney, Edmund Breese, Warner Richmond, Frank Losee.

A race car appears to have an invisible driver.

Speed Wild (Harry Garson Productions/FBO of America, 1925)
d: Harry Garson. 5 reels.

Lefty Flynn, Ethel Shannon, Frank Elliott, Ralph McCullough, Raymond Turner, Fred Burns, Charles Clary.

Jack, a traffic cop, falls for a girl who's been smuggled aboard a smugglers' ship.

The Speeding Venus (Metropolitan Pictures Corp. of California, 1926)
d: Robert Thornby. 6 reels.

Priscilla Dean, Robert Frazer, Dale Fuller, Johnny Fox, Ray Ripley, Charles Sellon.

Emily, a young woman in love with an inventor, hops into his new car and enters a road race that will run from Detroit to California.

Speedway (MGM, 1929)
d: Harry Beaumont. 8 reels. (Music, sound effects.)

William Haines, Anita Page, John Miljan, Ernest Torrence, Polly Moran, Karl Dane, Eugenie Besserer.

Jim and his foster son Bill, both race car drivers, combine forces to drive their car to victory in the Indianapolis 500.

Speedy (Paramount, 1928)
d: Ted Wilde. 8 reels.

Harold Lloyd, Bert Woodruff, Babe Ruth, Ann Christy, Brooks Benedict, Babe Ruth, Dan Wolheim, Hank Knight.

Harold Swift—nicknamed "Speedy"—is a cab driver who can't seem to hold a job. But he rides to the rescue—literally—when his girlfriend's dad is in danger of losing his horse-drawn trolleycar franchise.

Speedy Meade (Betzwood Film Co./Goldwyn, 1919)
d: Ira M. Lowry. 5 reels.

Louis Bennison, Katherine MacDonald, Neil Moran, Claire Adams, Norman Jefferies, J.W. Johnston, Ed Roseman, Ricca Allen, William Bailey.

Speedy Meade, a Texas Ranger, battles cattle rustlers.

Speedy Spurs (Action Pictures/Artclass Pictures, 1926)
d: Richard Thorpe. 5 reels.

Buffalo Bill Jr., Charles Whittaker Jr., James Welch, Alma Rayford, Frank Ellis, Clyde McClary, William Ryno, Charles Colby, Charles Whittaker, Harry Belmour, Emily Barrye.

Out West, a cowboy is knocked unconscious by his rival, then dreams he is on a tour of Heaven and Hell. After coming to, he wins the rematch.

The Spell of the Yukon (Popular Plays and Players, Inc./Metro, 1916)
d: Burton King. 5 reels.

Edmund Breese, Arthur Hoops, Christine Mayo, Billy Sherwood, Evelyn Brent, Frank McArthur, Joseph S. Chailee, Jacques Suzanne, Mary Reed, Harry Moreville.

After striking it rich after several years in Alaska, Jim Carson returns home with the son he's adopted, and runs across his old girlfriend Helen, now happily married. Jim's adopted son soon falls in love with Helen's daughter and wishes to marry her, but Jim, still nursing his heartbreak from years before, refuses to consent to the marriage. All that changes, however, when Helen reveals a stunning secret: Her daughter is not her husband's child, but Jim's!

Spellbound (Balboa Amusement Producing Co./General Film Co., 1916)
d: Harry Harvey. 5 reels.
Lois Meredith, William Conklin, Bruce Smith, Edward J. Brady, Frank Erlanger, Edward Peters, R. Henry Grey.
In England, an engaged couple run into problems when her Hindu statuette becomes the focal point of a murder investigation.

The Spender (Pathé, 1915)
d: Donald McKenzie. 5 reels.
George Probert, James McCabe, Sam Ryan, Alma Martin, Paul Panzer.
Peter, a fortune-hunter, woos and wins the daughter of a wealthy industrialist. But her father's on to his new son-in-law, and cuts the couple off without a cent. He does, however, give Peter a job in his factory, and there the formerly mercenary young man earns his father-in-law's respect when he bravely halts a violent labor dispute.

The Spenders (Great Authros Pictures/W.W. Hodkinson, 1921)
d: Jack Conway. 5 reels.
Claire Adams, Robert McKim, Joseph J. Dowling, Niles Welch, Betty Brice, Adele Farrington, Virginia Harris, Tom Ricketts, Otto Lederer, Harold Holland.
Two young investors, a brother and sister, go to Wall Street with dreams of striking it rich. Their investments go sour, however, and they must be bailed out by their businessman uncle.

The Spendthrift (George Kleine, 1915)
d: Walter Edwin. 6 reels.
Irene Fenwick, Cyril Keightley, Malcolm Duncan, John Nicholson, Mattie Ferguson, Viola Savoy, Grace Leigh, J.C. Hackett, Roy Pilcher.
Frances, a spendthrift newlywed, squanders her husband's money on trifles, then has to arrange a loan from a sinister admirer.

The Sphinx (Universal, 1916)
d: Jack Adolphi. 5 reels.
Herbert Kelcey, Effie Shannon, Louise Luff, Beatrice Noyes, Charles Compton, William Bechtel.
"The Sphinx," an exotic dancer, is dating both a playboy and his widowed father, though neither of the two men know about the other's involvement.

The Spider (Famous Players/Paramount, 1916)
d: Robert G. Vignola. 5 reels.
Pauline Frederick, Thomas Holding, Frank Losee.
In France, a young wife gives up her husband and daughter to find excitement with a Parisian nobleman. Years later, the mature beauty takes up with a new lover, only to discover that she has a rival for his attentions: her own daughter.

The Spider and the Fly (Fox, 1916)
d: J. Gordon Edwards. 5 reels.
Robert B. Mantell, Genevieve Hamper, Stuart Holmes, Genevieve Blinn, Franklin B. Coates, Claire Whitney, Walter Miller, Ethel Mantell, Henri Leone, Stephen Grattan

In Paris, a malicious vamp weaves a spidery web that ensnares the gullible—men and women alike.

The Spider and the Rose (B.F. Zeidman Productions/Principal Pictures, 1923)
d: John McDermott. 7 reels.
Alice Lake, Richard Headrick, Gaston Glass, Joseph J. Dowling, Robert McKim, Noah Beery, Otis Harlan, Frank Campeau, Andrew Arbuckle, Alec Francis, Edwin Stevens, Louise Fazenda.
In Old California, a young don joins a band of revolutionaries in an attempt to overthrow the territory's governor.

Spider Webs (Artlee Pictures, 1927)
d: Wilfred Noy. 6 reels.
Niles Welch, Alice Lake, J. Barney Sherry, Martin Faust, Bert Harvey, Maurice Costello, Edna Richmond.
Gangsters make an innocent girl their pawn in a blackmailing scheme.

The Spider's Web (Micheaux Film Corp., 1927)
d: Oscar Micheaux. 7 reels.
Lorenzo McLane, Evelyn Preer, Edward Thompson, Grace Smythe, Marshall Rodgers, Henrietta Loveless, Billy Gulfport.
In New York's Harlem, an elderly woman loses all her savings playing the numbers game. Then, when she finally does pick a winner, she goes to the paymaster's office and finds him dead. The woman carefully takes only the amount she has coming from the paymaster's safe, but is later arrested for his murder.

The Spieler (Ralph Block Productions/Pathé, 1928)
d: Tay Garnett. 7 reels. (Music, sound effects, part talkie.)
Alan Hale, Clyde Cook, Renee Adoree, Fred Kohler, Fred Warren, Jimmy Quinn, Kewpie Morgan, Billie Latimer.
A pair of pickpockets invade a carnival owned by an honest young woman, hoping to make a big score. But one of them falls in love with the carnival owner and, when her office manager tries to make off with the day's take, captures him and retrieves the money for her.

The Spindle of Life (Universal, 1917)
d: George Cochrane. 5 reels.
Ben Wilson, Neva Gerber, Jessie Pratt, Ed Brady, Richard LaReno, Winter Hall, Hayward Mack.
The society-conscious Mrs. Harrison makes plans for her daughter to marry the son of her financial advisor, but the young lady has other plans.

The Spirit of Good (Fox, 1920)
d: Paul Cazeneuve. 5 reels.
Madlaine Traverse, Frederick Stanton, Dick LaReno, Charles Smiley, Clo King.
Out West, a dance hall girl and her boss plot to sabotage the sermons of the new minister in town.

The Spirit of Lafayette (James Vincent Film Corp./Pilgrim Film Corp., 1919)
d: James Vincent. 10 reels.
Earl Schenck, Violet de Biccary, Marion Barney, Robert Elliott, Paula Shay, Kittens Reichert, W.W. Black.
In the aftermath of the armistice following World War I, a veteran's daughter learns about France's Marquis de Lafayette and his sacrifice to help out in the American Revolution.

The Spirit of Romance (Pallas Pictures/Paramount, 1917)

d: E. Mason Hopper. 5 reels.

Vivian Martin, Percy Challenger, Colin Chase, Herbert Standing, Elinor Hancock, George Fisher, Daisy Robinson, H.F. Crane, John Burton.

To frustrate his greedy relatives, a wealthy curmudgeon pretends to die and "leaves" his entire estate to Abby, a shopgirl.

The Spirit of '17 (Lasky Feature Plays/Paramount, 1918)
d: William Desmond Taylor. 5 reels.

Jack Pickford, C.H. Geldert, Edythe Chapman, L.N. Wells, Charles Arling, Virginia Ware, Katherine McDonald, James Farley, Seymour Hasting, William Chester, Helen Jerome Eddy, John Burton.

German spies intent on dynamiting an American copper mine are foiled by the heroics of an Army brat and a group of veteran soldiers.

The Spirit of '76 (Continental Producing Co., 1916)
d: Frank Montgomery. 9 reels.

Adda Gleason, Howard Gaye, George Chesborough, Chief Dark Cloud, Doris Pawn, Jack Cosgrove, Norval McGregor, Jane Novak, William Colby, Lottie Cruez, Chief Big Tree.

Catherine, an American girl, goes to London and becomes a king's mistress.

The Spirit of the Poppy (Kinetophote Corp., 1914)
d: Frederick Thomson. 6 reels.

Edward Mackay, Edith Luckett, Anna Rose, William Dunne, Nicholas Dunaew, Dorothy Green.

Helene and her artist husband, Stephen, are introduced to heroin by Stephen's model, and become hopelessly addicted.

The Spirit of the U.S.A. (Emory Johnson Productions/FBO of America, 1924)
d: Emory Johnson. 9 reels.

Johnnie Walker, Mary Carr, Carl Stockdale, Dave Kirby, Mark Fenton, Rosemary Cooper, William S. Hooser, Gloria Grey, Cuyler Supplee, Dicky Brandon, Newton House.

Thunderingly patriotic drama of a young man who is rejected by the army for medical reasons, but finds a way to contribute to the war effort anyway.

The Spirit of Youth (Tiffany-Stahl Productions, 1929)
d: Walter Lang. 7 reels.

Dorothy Sebastian, Larry Kent, Betty Francisco, Maurice Murphy, Anita Fremault, Donald Hall, Douglas Gilmore, Charles Sullivan, Sidney D'Albrook.

Kenney, a U.S. Navy boxing champion, falls for a wealthy siren although he has a girl back home.

The Spite Bride (Selznick/Select, 1919)
d: Charles Giblyn. 5 reels.

Olive Thomas, Robert Ellis, Jack Mulhall, Claire DuBrey, Irene Rich, Dorothy Wallace, Lamar Johnston, Katherine Griffith, Molly Malone.

In New York, a vaudeville dancer marries a dissolute millionaire, then tries to get a divorce from him. But when he sobers up, she finds him charming.

Spite Marriage (MGM, 1929)
d: Edward Sedgwick. 9 reels. (Sound effects, music score.)

Buster Keaton, Dorothy Sebastian, Edward Earle, Leila Hyams, William Bechtel, John Byron, Hank Mann.

Buster plays Elmer, a pants presser who's smitten with Trilby, a stage actress, and attends her every performance. Trilby is infatuated with her leading man, but he spurns her, so she marries Elmer out of spite. Realizing the deception when she passes out drunk on their wedding night, Elmer

leaves and gets a job on a ship. But Trilby and her new husband get together again, on the high seas.

In Miss Sebastian, Keaton found his gamest leading lady yet. Her rough-and-tumble physicality seemed, incredibly, a match for the great Keaton, tumble for tumble and pratfall for pratfall. Two scenes that stand out: Buster's fumbling attempts to put his passed-out-cold bride to bed without waking her; and the two stars' furious scramble with the villains aboard a stolen yacht.

The Spitfire (Murray W. Garson Productions/Associated Exhibitors, 1924)
d: William Christy Cabanne. 7 reels.

Betty Blythe, Lowell Sherman, Elliott Dexter, Robert Warwick, Pauline Garon, Burr McIntosh, Jack Donovan, Ray Allen.

When a young banker "wins" a showgirl in a poker game, he finds that his prize is more trouble than she's worth.

The Spitfire of Seville (Universal, 1919)
d: George Siegmann. 6 reels.

Hedda Nova, Thurston Hall, Claire Anderson, Marion Skinner, Leo Maloney, Robert Gray, Edgar Allen.

In Spain, the fiery daughter of an outlaw chieftan falls in love with an American artist who asks her to pose for a portrait.

The Splendid Crime (Paramount, 1926)
w, d: William C. DeMille. 6 reels.

Bebe Daniels, Neil Hamilton, Anne Cornwall, Anthony Jowitt, Fred Walton, Lloyd Corrigan, Mickey McBan, Josephine Crowell, Marcelle Corday.

When a wealthy young man catches Jenny, a petty thief, in the act of burglary, he lectures her about honesty and lets her go free. Inspired by his thoughtfulness, Jenny decides to go straight and gets a job. Kindness begets kindness, and later, when the same young man faces bankruptcy and is tempted to commit robbery himself, Jenny stops him.

A Splendid Hazard (Allan Dwan Productions/Mayflower, 1921)
d: Allan Dwan. 5 reels.

Henry B. Walthall, Rosemary Theby, Norman Kerry, Ann Forrest, Hardee Kirkland, Thomas Jefferson, Philo McCullough, Jiquel Lanoe, Joseph Dowling.

Believing himself to be a descendant of Napoleon, a Corsican plots to restore the French monarchy.

The Splendid Road (Frank Lloyd Productions/First National, 1925)
d: Frank Lloyd. 8 reels.

Anna Q. Nilsson, Robert Frazer, Lionel Barrymore, Edwards Davis, Roy Laidlaw, DeWitt Jennings, Russell Simpson, George Bancroft, Gladys Brockwell, Pauline Garon, Marceline Day.

During the California Gold Rush, a real estate agent is sent to evict Sandra, a squatter in Reading Flat, but falls in love with her instead.

The Splendid Sin (Fox, 1919)
d: Howard M. Mitchell. 5 reels.

Madlaine Traverse, Charles Clary, Jeanne Calhoun, Wheeler Oakman, Elinor Hancock, George Hackathorn, Edwin Booth Tilton.

Though happily married, Sir Charles and Lady Marion are unable to have children. After Charles is called to Egypt on business, his sister and her lover have an affair, and she dies in childbirth. To honor the mother's dying request, Lady

Marion takes the child and cables Charles that the child is theirs.

The Splendid Sinner   (Goldwyn, 1918)
d: Edwin Carewe.   6 reels.
Mary Garden, Hamilton Revelle, Anders Randolph, Hassan Mussalli, Henry Pettibone, Roberta Bellinger.
Dolores, an American Red Cross nurse caught in the war and condemned to die, is offered her freedom in exchange for her amorous affections to the commanding General officer.

Splitting the Breeze   (R-C Pictures/FBO of America, 1927)
d: Robert DeLacey.   5 reels.
Tom Tyler, Harry Woods, Barney Furey, Tom Lingham, Peggy Montgomery, Red Lennox, Alfred Heuston, Barbara Starr.
Out West, a cowboy battles a corrupt saloon owner for the love of the sheriff's daughter.

The Spoilers   (Selig Polyscope, 1914)
d: Colin Campbell.   8 reels.
William Farnum, Tom Santschi, Kathlyn Williams, Wheeler Oakman, Bessie Eyton, Jack F. McDonald, Frank Clark, Marshall Farnum, W.H. Ryno.
Two prospectors find a rich gold strike in Alaska. A greedy business rival aims to cheat the partners out of their claim, so he sends a corrupt judge to the Yukon with fraudulent papers that will discredit them. But the judge falls ill, and in his place he sends his niece to deliver the papers. On the steamer trip north, she meets one of the prospectors and is attracted to him, not realizing she is the intended instrument of his undoing.

The Spoilers   (Jesse D. Hampton Productions/Goldwyn, 1923)
d: Lambert Hillyer.   8 reels.
Milton Sills, Anna Q. Nilsson, Barbara Bedford, Robert Edeson, Ford Sterling, Wallace MacDonald, Noah Beery, Mitchell Lewis, John Elliott, Robert McKim, Tom McGuire, Kate Price, Rockliffe Fellowes, Gordon Russell, Louise Fazenda, Sam De Grasse, Albert Roscoe, Jack Curtis.
Remake of the 1914 Selig film *The Spoilers*, both versions based on the novel (and play) of the same name by Rex Beach.

Spoilers of the West   (MGM, 1927)
d: W.S. Van Dyke.   6 reels.
Tim McCoy, William Fairbanks, Marjorie Daw, Chief Big Tree, Charles Thurston.
Out West, an army lieutenant is assigned to rescue a white girl left alone in Indian country.

Spook Ranch   (Universal, 1925)
d: Edward Laemmle.   6 reels.
Hoot Gibson, Helen Ferguson, Ed Cowles, Tote DuCrow, Robert McKim, Frank Rice.
In a western mining town, two strangers are enlisted by the sheriff to help solve the mystery of a house that's said to be haunted.

The Sporting Age   (Columbia, 1928)
d: Erle C. Kenton.   6 reels.
Holmes Herbert, Belle Bennett, Carroll Nye, Josephine Borio, Edwards Davis.
A man who has been temporarily blinded in an accident comes to realize that his wife is having an affair. He recovers his sight but conceals that fact from his wife and her lover, who continue their affair. Then the husband sets up a meeting between his niece and his wife's lover, hoping they will be attracted to each other.

Sporting Blood   (Fox, 1916)
d: Bertram Bracken.   5 reels.
Dorothy Bernard, Glen White, DeWitt C. Jennings, George Morgan, Madeleine LeNard, Claire Whitney.
Mary, a girl whose brother was swindled out of thousands of dollars by a professional gambler, decides to win back her brother's money. She coaxes the gambler into a bet on a horse race, with her payoff to be $10,000 if he loses—and her own sexual favors for him, if he wins.

A Sporting Chance   (American Film Co./Pathé, 1919)
d: Henry King.   5 reels.
William Russell, Fritzi Brunette, George Periolat, J. Farrell MacDonald, Lee Hill, Harvey Clark, Perry Banks.
Stonehouse, a suicidal millionaire, stumbles upon an attempted murder involving a stolen emerald. But it's all a frame-up by actors, to prove to a theater critic that such a convoluted plot could really take place.

A Sporting Chance   (Famous Players-Lasky/Paramount, 1919)
d: George Melford.   5 reels.
Ethel Clayton, Jack Holt, Herbert Standing, Margaret Green, Howard Davies.
An impulsive rich girl hires an escaped convict as her chauffeur.

The Sporting Chance   (Tiffany Productions/Truart Film Corp., 1925)
d: Oscar Apfel.   7 reels.
Lou Tellegen, Dorothy Phillips, George Fawcett, Theodore von Eltz, Sheldon Lewis, Andrew Clark.
When a horse owner's creditor tries to attach his prize thoroughbred the day before a big handicap race, the owner braves the creditor's thugs, steals back his horse, and his jockey rides it to victory.

The Sporting Duchess   (Lubin, 1915)
d: Barry O'Neil.   6 reels.
Rose Doghlan, Ethel Clayton, Rosetta Brice, Frankie Mann, Florence Williams, Chalres Brandt, Ruth Bryan, James Daly, George Soule Spender, Ferdinand Tidmarsh, Joseph Kaufman.
Melodrama dealing with infidelity among the British aristocracy.

The Sporting Duchess   (Vitagraph, 1920)
d: George Terwilliger.   7 reels.
Alice Joyce, Percy Marmont, G.V. Seyffertitz, Edith Campbell Walker, Lionel Pape, John Goldsworthy, Dan Comfort, May McAvoy, Robert Agnew, William Turner, Edward Keenan.
Remake of the 1915 Lubin melodrama *The Sporting Duchess*. Both versions are based on the play of the same name by Cecil Raleigh, Henry Hamilton, and Augustus Harris.

Sporting Goods   (Paramount, 1928)
d: Malcolm St. Clair.   6 reels.
Richard Dix, Ford Sterling, Gertrude Olmstead, Philip Strange, Myrtle Stedman, Wade Boteler, Claude King, Maude Turner Gordon.
Society comedy about a chap who's invented a new type of golf suit and tries to sell a lot of them to a big department store.

Sporting Life   (Maurice Tourneur Productions, Inc., 1918)

d: Maurice Tourneur. 7 reels.
Ralph Graves, Warner Richmond, Charles Eldridge, Charles Craig, Henry West, Constance Binney, Faire Binney, Willette Kershaw, Harry Harris, Eddie Kelly, Clara Beyers.
Saddled with debts, an English nobleman stakes his remaining fortune on two sporting events—a prize fight and the London Derby horse race.

Sporting Life (Universal, 1925)
d: Maurice Tournier. 7 rels.
Bert Lytell, Marian Nixon, Paulette Duval, Cyril Chadwick, Charles Delaney, George Siegmann, Oliver Eckhardt, Ena Gregory, Kathleen Clifford, Frank Finch Smiles, Ted Lewis.
A horse owner who has invested heavily in stage revues and prizefighters stands to lose everything unless his horse can win the big handicap.

The Sporting Lover (Faultless Pictures/First National, 1926)
d: Alan Hale. 7 reels.
Conway Tearle, Barbara Bedford, Ward Crane, Arthur Rankin, Charles McHugh, John Fox Jr., Bodil Rosing, George Ovey.
During World War I, a British officer falls in love with his nurse—and then discovers she's the sister of his enemy.

The Sporting Venus (MGM, 1925)
d: Marshall Neilan. 7 reels.
Blanche Sweet, Ronald Colman, Lew Cody, George Fawcett, Kate Price, Arthur Hoyt, Hank Mann.
A Scottish heiress loves a medical student, but she's spoken for by a prince.

Sporting Youth (Universal, 1924)
d: Harry A. Pollard. 7 reels.
Reginald Denny, Laura LaPlante, Hallam Cooley, Frederick Vroom, Lucille Ward, Malcolm Denny, Henry Barrows, Leo White.
A chauffeur is mistaken for a champion race car driver.

The Spotlight (Paramount, 1927)
d: Frank Tuttle. 5 reels.
Esther Ralston, Neil Hamilton, Nicholas Soussanin, Arlette Marchal, Arthur Housman.
A plain, talentless girl is transformed into a theatrical star through shrewd publicity.

Spotlight Sadie (Goldwyn, 1919)
d: Laurence Trimble. 5 reels.
Mae Marsh, Wallace MacDonald, Mary Thurman, Betty Schade, Alec B. Francis, Walter Hiers, P.M. McCullough, Wellington Playter, Lou Salter, Richard Carlyle, Alice Davenport.
Sadie, a bible-reading chorus girl, shuns the loose life of her fellow chorines.

The Spotted Lily (Universal, 1917)
d: Harry Solter. 5 reels.
Ella Hall, Gretchen Lederer, Victor Rottman, Jack Nelson, George Beranger, Charles Hill Mailes, Wilton Taylor, Leon D. Kent.
Poor but proud, a young violinist pawns his instrument rather than beg for money. He attracts the attention of Sofia, a wealthy woman, and she draws him into her web... but his sweetheart Yvonne redeems his violin and, at the same time, the young man's soul.

The Spreading Dawn (Goldwyn, 1917)
d: Lawrence Trimble. 5 reels.

Jane Cowl, Orme Caldara, Harry Springer, Florence Billings, Harry Stephenson, Alice Chapin, Helen Blair, Cecil Owen, Mabel Ballin, Edmund Lowe, Edith McAlpin.
Georgina's elderly aunt cautions her against marrying a military man, relating the story of her own marriage to a soldier, and how he was unfaithful to her. But Georgina opens the yellowed envelope containing her aunt's husband's last letter to his wife... and it proves that he was never unfaithful. Her faith restored, the aunt blesses Georgina's union with her soldier boyfriend.

The Spreading Evil (James Keane Feature Photoplay Productions, 1918)
w, d: James Keane. 7 reels.
Leo Pierson, Irene Wylie, Howard Davies, Carlyn Wagner, Joseph Clancy, William A. Hackett, G.B. Williams, Quex Bellamy, Josephus Daniels, James Keane.
Hartsell, a greedy scientist, perfects a cure for syphilis, but dispenses it only to the wealthy and disregards the poor. In a twist of fate, the scientist's own son contracts the disease and, because he is overseas, is unable to use his father's formula.

Spring Fever (MGM, 1927)
d: Edward Sedgwick. 7 reels.
William Haines, Joan Crawford, George K. Arthur, Eileen Percy, George Fawcett, Edward Earle, Bert Woodruff, Lee Moran.
A lowly clerk gains admission to an exclusive club and romances an heiress.

Springtime (Life Photo Film Corp./Alco Film Corp., 1914)
d: William S. Davis. 5 reels.
Florence Nash, Adele Ray, William H. Tooker, Edward F. Roseman, Bert Gardner, Sue Balfour, Frank Holland, E.F. Flannigan, Charles Travis, Warner P. Richmond, Armin Tooker.
During the War of 1812, wealthy Raoul loves a lovely Creole maiden and they wish to marry, but first he has to get out of a marriage arranged for him by his older cousin.

Spuds (Larry Semon Productions/Pathé, 1927)
w, d: Larry Semon. 5 reels.
Larry Semon, Dorothy Dwan, Edward Hearn, Kewpie Morgan, Robert Graves, Hazel Howell, Hugh Fay.
Comedy about Spuds, a doughboy in World War I, who braves enemy fire to retrieve a stolen vehicle and romance a French girl at the same time.

Spurs and Saddles (Universal, 1927)
d: Clifford Smith. 5 reels.
Art Acord, Fay Wray, Bill Dyer, J. Gordon Russell, C.E. Anderson, Monte Montague.
Marley, an adventurous cowpoke, takes over a Pony Express route when the driver is injured.

The Spurs of Sybil (World Film Corp., 1918)
d: Travers Vale. 5 reels.
Alice Brady, John Bowers, John Davidson, Iseth Munro, Justine Cutting, Eugenie Woodward, Herbert Barrington, Richard Clarke.
Sybil, a society gadabout, is informed that she will lose her inheritance unless she proves she can earn her own living for a year.

The Spy (Fox, 1917)
d: Richard Stanton. 6 reels.
Dustin Farnum, Winifred Kingston, William Burress, Charles Clary, William E. Lowry, Howard Gaye.

During World War I, an American spy falls in love with Greta, his German counterpart.

Square Crooks (Fox, 1928)
d: Lewis Seiler. 6 reels.
Robert Armstrong, John Mack Brown, Dorothy Dwan, Dorothy Appleby, Eddie Sturgis, Clarence Burton, Jackie Coombs, Lydia Dickson.
Eddie and Larry, former crooks, decide to tread the straight and narrow... but it's a zigzag journey at the start.

A Square Deal (World Film Corp., 1917)
d: Harley Knoles. 5 reels.
Carlyle Blackwell, June Elvidge, Henry Hull, Muriel Ostriche, Charlotte Granville.
Greater love has no man.... Hugh loves Doris, but she loves Mark, who is miserable in his life married to a golddigger. So, in an act of great friendship, Hugh poses as a millionaire to attract the golddigger's attention, and when they are caught in a compromising situation, Mark is able to obtain a divorce.

The Square Deal (American Film Co./Mutual, 1918)
d: Lloyd Ingraham. 5 reels.
Margarita Fisher, Jack Mower, Val Paul, Constance Johnson, Louis M. Wells, Nanine Wright.
Alys, a modern-thinking girl, leaves her family home to join a free love cult.

The Square Deal Man (Triangle, 1917)
d: William S. Hart. 5 reels.
William S. Hart, Mary McIvor, Joseph J. Dowling, Mary Jane Irving, J. Frank Burke, Darrel Foss, Thomas Kurihara, Milton Ross, Charles O. Rush.
Jack, an inveterate card sharp, resolves to give up gambling after one last hand. But it turns out to be a fateful hand, for it's followed by murder, a manhunt, and finally true love.

Square Deal Sanderson (Paramount, 1919)
d: William S. Hart, Lambert Hillyer. 5 reels.
William S. Hart, Ann Little, Lloyd Bacon, Frank Whitson, Andrew Robson, Edwin Wallach.
Out West, a letter found on a dead man leads "Square Deal" Sanderson to investigate a miscarriage of justice.

The Square Deceiver (Yorke Film Corp./Metro, 1917)
d: Fred J. Balshofer. 5 reels.
Harold Lockwood, Pauline Curley, William Clifford, Dora Mills Adams, Kathryn Hutchison, Betty Marvin, Dick L'Estrange.
Beset by fortune hunters, an eligible millionaire resolves to find a girl who will love him for himself alone. So he finds work as a chauffeur... and falls in love with Beatrice, his new employer.

The Square Shooter — see: The Master Cracksman (1914)

The Square Shooter (Fox, 1920)
d: Paul Cazeneuve. 5 reels.
Buck Jones, Patsey DeForest, Charles K. French, Al Fremont, Frederick Starr, Edwin Booth Tilton, Ernest Shields, Charles Force, Lon Poff, Orpha Alba.
Out West, a ranch owner who's been away returns home, and immediately goes undercover to nab his foreman, whom he suspects of illegal activities. Yep, he's rustling cattle.

Square Shoulders (Pathé, 1929)
d: E. Mason Hopper. 7 reels. (Music, sound effects, part talkie.)
Junior Coughlan, Louis Wolheim, Anita Louise, Montague Shaw, Phillipe De Lacy, Johnny Morris, Kewpie Morgan, Clarence Geldert, Erich von Stroheim Jr., Chuck Reisner Jr.
An underprivileged orphan realizes his dream of attending military school when he receives a mysterious letter notifying him that an unidentified benefactor has paid his tuition. Once at the academy, the lad gets along just fine, and he befriends a man who works in the horse stables. What we know, but the "orphan" doesn't, is that the stable worker is not only his mysterious benefactor, but also his long-lost father.

The Squaw Man (Lasky Feature Play Co., 1914)
d: Cecil B. DeMille. 6 reels.
Dustin Farnum, Winifred Kingston, Princess Red Wing, Katherine MacDonald, Monroe Salisbury, Billy Elmer, Mrs. A.W. Filson, Haidee Fuller, Dick LeReno, Foster Knox, Joseph Singleton, Fred Montague, Baby DeRue, Dick LeStrange, Art Acord.
A British sailor travels to the American Wild West and marries an Indian maid.
This movie is sometimes considered the first feature-length film to be made in the United States, because of its 6-reel length. *The Squaw Man* was released in February 1914, reaching the screen before another 6-reeler, *Tillie's Punctured Romance*, which premiered in December of that year. But there were a number of 4-reel and 5-reel films made earlier, beginning with the 5-reel *The Life of Moses* in 1910.

The Squaw Man (Famous Players-Lasky/Paramount, 1918)
d: Cecil B. DeMille. 6 reels.
Elliott Dexter, Ann Little, Katherine MacDonald, Theodore Roberts, Thurston Hall, Jack Holt, Tully Marshall, Pat Moore, Edwin Stevens, Herbert Standing, Helen Dunbar, Winter Hall, Julia Faye, Noah Beery, Jim Mason, Monte Blue, Charles Ogle, Clarence Geldart.
DeMille remakes his hit of the same title from 1914.

The Squaw Man's Son (Lasky Feature Plays/Paramount, 1917)
d: E.J. LeSaint. 5 reels.
Wallace Reid, Anita King, Dorothy Davenport, Donald Bowles, C.H. Geldart, Frank Lanning, Ernest Joy, Lucien Littlefield, Mabel Van Buren, Raymond Hatton.
Hal, son of the lovers in the original *The Squaw Man*, grows up in England and becomes Lord Effington. When he returns to America, he falls in love with an educated Indian maiden, Wah-na-gi.

St. Elmo (Fox, 1923)
d: Jerome Storm. 6 reels.
John Gilbert, Barbara La Marr, Bessie Love, Warner Baxter, Nigel DeBrulier, Lydia Knott.
A chap who's been unlucky in love becomes a confirmed misogynist.

Stage Kisses (Columbia, 1927)
d: Albert Kelly. 6 reels.
Helene Chadwick, Kenneth Harlan, Frances Raymond, John Patrick, Phillips Smalley, Ethel Wales.
Newlyweds face a crisis when the bride is found with another man. Though it looks bad, the lady is innocent of any wrongdoing.

Stage Madness (Fox, 1927)
d: Victor Schertzinger. 6 reels.
Virginia Valli, Tullio Carminati, Virginia Bradford, Lou

Tellegen, Richard Walling, Tyler Brooke, Lillian Knight, Bodil Rosing.

A prima ballerina feels threatened when a young dancer joins the company, and after murdering the stage manager, tries to frame the girl for the crime. Only then does the prima donna learn that the young dancer is the daughter she herself abandoned, years before.

A Stage Romance (Fox, 1922)
d: Herbert Brenon. 7 reels.
William Farnum, Peggy Shaw, Holmes Herbert, Mario Carillo, Paul McAllister, Etienne Gerardot, Bernard Seigel, Hal DeForrest, Edward Kipling, Harry Grippe, Augustus Balfour.
Biographical drama about an incident in the life of Edmund Kean, the noted Shakespearean actor in 19th century London.

Stage Struck (Famous Players-Lasky/Paramount, 1925)
d: Allan Dwan. 7 reels.
Gloria Swanson, Lawrence Gray, Gertrude Astor, Marguerite Evans, Ford Sterling, Carrie Scott, Emil Hoch, Margery Whittington.
When Wilson, the chef in a diner, falls for the leading lady of a visiting showboat troupe, his waitress girlfriend tries to win him back by taking a correspondence course in acting.

Stagestruck (Triangle/Fine Arts, 1917)
d: Edward Morrissey. 5 reels.
Dorothy Gish, Frank Bennett, Kate Toncray, Spottiswoode Aitken, Jennie Lee, Mazie Radford, Fred A. Warren.
A country girl takes a correspondence course in acting, then comes to the big city and learns that the correspondence school is a fake.

The Stain in the Blood (Signal Film Corp./Mutual, 1916)
d: Murdock MacQuarrie. 5 reels.
Edythe Sterling, Norbert A. Myles, Murdock J. MacQuarrie, Dorothy Nash, Millard K. Wilson.
Orphaned siblings Joe and Mary grow apart and he takes up a life of crime.

The Stainless Barrier (Triangle, 1917)
d: Thomas N. Heffron. 5 reels.
Irene Hunt, Jack Livingston, H.A. Barrows, Rowland Lee, Thomas S. Guise, J. Barney Sherry, John Lince, Kate Bruce, Lena Harris, James G. Farley.
When he kills a swindler in self-defense, Betsy's brother is tried for murder. His alibi: that he killed the victim to avenge Betsy's honor, irretrievably stained by the con man.

Stairs of Sand (Paramount, 1929)
d: Otto Brower. 6 reels.
Wallace Beery, Jean Arthur, Phillips R. Holmes, Fred Kohler, Chester Conklin, Guy Oliver, Lillian Worth, Frank Rice, Clarence L. Sherwood.
Out West, a stagecoach robber begins to regret his latest heist when he learns that some of the money he stole belonged to Ruth, a cabaret dancer he fancies.

Staking His Life (New York Motion Picture Corp., 1918)
d: William S. Hart. 5 reels.
William S. Hart, Louise Glaum, Charles Ray.
Out West, a powerful casino owner refuses to permit religious services in his town... until one day, the local minister takes a bullet meant for the casino owner.

Stand and Deliver (DeMille Pictures/Pathé, 1928)
d: Donald Crisp. 6 reels.

Rod LaRocque, Lupe Velez, Warner Oland, Louis Natheaux, James Dime, A. Palasthy, Frank Lanning, Bernard Siegel, Clarence Burton, Charles Stevens.
Norman, a British citizen, decides to join the Greek forces during the Greco-Turkish War.

The Star Dust Trail (Fox, 1924)
d: Edmund Mortimer. 5 reels.
Shirley Mason, Bryant Washburn, Thomas R. Mills, Richard Tucker, Merta Sterling, Shannon Day.
A cabaret dancer loves an actor, and they marry... but unfounded rumors of infidelity on the part of both partners threaten to tear their marriage apart.

The Star Prince (Little Players Film Company of Chicago, 1918)
d: Madeline Brandeis. 5 reels.
Zoe Rae, Dorphia Brown, John Dorland, Edith Rothschild, Marjorie Claire Bowden.
Whimsical tale about a boy who is found in the woods just after a falling star was seen, and comes to believe that he is a Star Prince.

The Star Rover (C.E. Shurtleff, Inc./Metro, 1920)
d: Edward Sloman. 6 reels.
Courtenay Foote, Thelma Percy, Doc Cannon, Dwight Crittenden, Jack Carlysle, Chance Ward, Marcella Daley.
When a doctor is unjustly accused of murder and the chief inspector begins to torture him to exact a confession, the doctor's soul goes wandering through the ages in search of the real killer.
Based on the novel of the same name by Jack London, published in 1915.

Stardust (Hobart Henley Productions/Associated First National, 1921)
d: Hobart Henley. 6 reels.
Hope Hampton, Edna Ross, Thomas Maguire, Mary Foy, Charles Mussett, Vivia Ogden, Ashley Buck, Noel Tearle, George Humbert, Gladys Wilson, Charles Wellesley, James Rennie.
Soapy melodrama about a lady fleeing an unhappy marriage.

Stark Love (Paramount, 1927)
d: Karl Brown. 7 reels.
Helen Munday, Forrest James, Silas Miracle, Reb Grogan.
In Smoky Mountain country, a young man yearns to escape his trappings and find "culture."

State Street Sadie (Warner Bros., 1928)
d: Archie Mayo. 7 reels. (Music score, part talkie.)
Conrad Nagel, Myrna Loy, George E. Stone, William Russell, Pat Hartigan.
Sadie, daughter of a murdered police officer, joins forces with a reformed gang member to find and capture the killer.

Station Content (Triangle, 1918)
d: Arthur Hoyt. 5 reels.
Gloria Swanson, Lee Hill, Arthur Millett, Nellie Allen, Ward Caulfield, May Walters, Diana Carrillo.
The young wife of a railroad telegraph agent finds life in the lonely station boring, so she joins a theatrical troupe.

The Stealers (Robertson-Cole Studios, Inc., 1920)
d: William Christy Cabanne. 7 reels.
William H. Tooker, Robert Kenyon, Myrtle Morse, Norma Shearer, Ruth Dwyer, Eugene Borden, Jack Crosby, Matthew L. Betz, Jack O'Brien, Downing Clarke, Walter Miller.

The Reverend Martin wears two hats: One, as the local minister; the other, as the leader of a gang of pickpockets.

Steamboat Bill Jr. (Keaton/United Artists, 1928)
d: Charles F. Reisner. 7 reels.
Buster Keaton, Ernest Torrence, Marion Byron, Tom McGuire, Tom Lewis.
The son of a crusty old steamboat captain returns home from college, but the lad is so dandified that he's an embarrassment to his dad. What's worse, Junior falls in love with the daughter of his dad's business rival. In due time, though, the young man proves his mettle and wins the respect of his father and the hand of his lady love.

The Steel King (World Film Corp., 1919)
d: Oscar Apfel. 5 reels.
Montagu Love, June Elvidge, Charles Mackay, Mrs. Priestly Morrison, Marion Barney, Charles Sutton, Alex Shannon, Clay Clement.
Blake, a self-made millionaire, tries to humiliate the proud family he thinks once wronged him. But in the course of his vengeance, Blake discovers that the head of that family paid for his education, and helped him make a success of his life.

Steel Preferred (Metropolitan Pictures/Producers Distributing Corp., 1926)
d: Charles Cadwallader. 7 reels.
Vera Reynolds, William Boyd, Hobart Bosworth, Charlie Murray, Walter Long, William V. Mong, Nigel Barrie, Helene Sullivan, Ben Turpin.
In a steel mill, a young engineer must fight off a jealous supervisor when both men are romantically interested in the mill owner's daughter.

Steele of the Royal Mounted (Vitagraph, 1925)
d: David Smith. 6 reels.
Bert Lytell, Stuart Holmes, Charlotte Merriam, Sidney DeGrey, John Toughey.
In the great northwest, a young woman's wry joke so incenses her suitor, he joins the Royal Canadian Mounted Police to forget her.

Steelheart (Vitagraph, 1921)
d: William Duncan. 6 reels.
William Duncan, Edith Johnson, Jack Curtis, Walter Rodgers, Euna Luckey, Ardeta Malino, Earl Crain, Charles Dudley.
Out West, a gentlemanly woman-hater meets his waterloo—named Ethel.

Stella Dallas (Goldwyn/United Artists, 1926)
d: Henry King. 11 reels.
Belle Bennett, Ronald Colman, Lois Moran, Jean Hersholt, Douglas Fairbanks Jr., Alice Joyce, Beatrix Pryor, Vera Lewis, Maurice Murphy, Jack Murphy, Newton Hall, Charles Hatten.
A status-conscious girl finds her uneducated mother an embarrassment.

Stella Maris (Famous Players-Lasky, 1918)
d: Marshall A. Neilan. 6 reels.
Mary Pickford, Conway Tearle, Marcia Manon, Ida Waterman, Herbert Standing, Josephine Crowell, Teddy the dog.
Miss Pickford plays two roles: an invalid and a young street orphan.

Stella Maris (Universal, 1925)
d: Charles J. Brabin. 7 reels.
Mary Philbin, Elliot Dexter, Gladys Brockwell, Jason Robards, Phillips Smalley, Lillian Lawrence, Robert Bolder, Aileen Manning.
A well-to-do crippled woman is loved by two men, one of whom has a wife in jail.
As Mary Pickford had done in the first version of *Stella Maris* 1918, Miss Philbin plays a dual role, as the invalid and as a street waif.

Step On It! (Universal, 1922)
d: Jack Conway. 5 reels.
Hoot Gibson, Edith Yorke, Frank Lanning, Barbara Bedford, Vic Potel, Gloria Davenport, Joe Girard, L.C. Shumway.
Out West, a cowpoke and a lady team up to fight cattle rustlers.

Stephen Steps Out (Famous Players-Lasky/Paramount, 1923)
d: Joseph Henabery. 6 reels.
Harry Myers, Douglas Fairbanks Jr., Theodore Roberts, Noah Beery, Frank Currier, James O. Barrows, Fannie Midgley, Bertram Johns, George Field, Maurice Freeman.
When Stephen, a scion of wealth, fails a course in Turkish history, his exasperated father sends the young man to Turkey to study the course "first hand."

Steppin' Out (Columbia, 1925)
d: Frank Strayer. 6 reels.
Robert Agnew, Dorothy Revier, Ford Sterling, Ethel Wales, Cissy Fitzgerald, Tom Ricketts, Harry Lorraine.
Complications arise when a businessman asks his secretary to pose as his wife.

Stepping Along (B&H Enterprises/First National, 1926)
d: Charles Hines. 7 reels.
Johnny Hines, Mary Brian, William Gaxton, Ruth Dwyer, Edmund Breese, Dan Mason, Lee Beggs.
Comedy about a newsboy who dreams of a career in politics, and the girl who helps him achieve his dream.

Stepping Lively (Carlos Productions/FBO of America, 1924)
d: James W. Horne. 6 reels.
Richard Talmadge, Mildred Harris, Norval MacGregor, Brinsley Shaw, Fred Kelsey, Mario Carillo, William Clifford, John Dillon, Victor Metzetti.
Dave, a bank employee who's in love with the banker's daughter, is accused of stealing some bonds. Innocent, he disguises himself as a crook to infiltrate the gang and find the real thief.

Stepping Out (Thomas H. Ince/Paramount, 1919)
d: Fred Niblo. 5 reels.
Enid Bennett, Niles Welch, Julia Faye, Gertrude Claire, William S. Conklin, Bota Miller.
When Robert, a bank clerk, starts "stepping out" on his wife and showing his secretary a good time, the wife decides that two can play at that game.

The Stepping Stone (New York Motion Picture Corp./Triangle, 1916)
d: Reginald Barker. 5 reels.
Frank Keenan, Mary Boland, Robert McKim, Margaret Thompson, Joseph Dowling, J. Barney Sherry.
When a Wall Street broker becomes smitten with Mary and gives her stock tips, she passes them on to her shiftless husband, who follows the tips and makes a fortune. But now he thinks he's too good for his wife, and asks for a divorce.

The Still Alarm (Selig Polyscope/Pioneer Film Corp., 1918)
d: Colin Campbell. 6 reels.
Thomas Santschi, Bessie Eyton, Eugenie Besserer, William Scott, Fritzi Brunette.
When his former employee threatens to frame a druggist for a crime he didn't commit, the druggist's family comes up with ways to thwart the blackmailer.

The Still Alarm (Universal, 1926)
d: Edward Laemmle. 7 reels.
Helene Chadwick, William Russell, Richard C. Travers, Edna Marion, Andy Todd, Edward Hearn, Erin LaBissoniere, Dot Farley, Jacques D'Auray.
Remake of the 1918 Selig film *The Still Alarm*. Both versions were based on the play of the same name by Joseph Arthur.

Still Waters (Famous Players/Paramount, 1915)
d: J. Searle Dawley. 5 reels.
Marguerite Clark, Robert Broderick, Philip Tonge, Robert Vaughn, Arthur Evers, Ottola Nesmith, Robert Conville, Harry LaPearl.
Nesta is raised by her grandfather, a fisherman who disapproved of his daughter's elopement with a circus performer. But the circus is in Nesta's blood, and when she hears the sound of calliope music she rides off on her horse, headed for the Big Top.

The Sting of Victory (Essanay, 1916)
d: J. Charles Haydon. 5 reels.
Henry B. Walthall, Antoinette Walker, Anne Leigh, John Lorenz, Thomas Commerford, Richardson Cotton, Jack Dale.
Historical drama tells the bitter story of a southerner who sides with the North in the Civil War, and his resulting ostracism among his own people.

A Stitch in Time (Vitagraph, 1919)
d: Ralph Ince. 5 reels.
Gladys Leslie, Eugene Strong, Charles Walton, Cecil Chichester, Earl Schenck, Charles Stevenson, Julia Swayne Gordon, Agnes Ayres, George O'Donnell.
In New York, an artist's assistant is in love with her boss... but he's got eyes only for a manipulative, scheming fortune-hunter.

The Stolen Bride (First National, 1927)
d: Alexander Korda. 8 reels.
Lloyd Hughes, Billie Dove, Armand Kaliz, Frank Beal, Lilyan Tashman, Cleve Moore, Otto Hoffman, Charles Wellesley, Bert Sprotte.
A Hungarian soldier falls for a countess and they decide to marry. Her father, however, disapproves.

Stolen Goods (Lasky Feature Plays/Paramount, 1915)
d: George Melford. 5 reels.
Blanche Sweet, Cleo Ridgely, House Peters, H.B. Carpenter, Sydney Deane, Theodore Roberts.

Margery, an American Red Cross nurse in Belgium, runs across Helen, who once framed Margery and had her sent to prison.

Stolen Honor (Fox, 1918)
d: Richard S. Stanton. 5 reels.
Virginia Pearson, Clay Clement, Ethel Hallor, Walter Law, Dorothy Rogers, Edward Roseman, George Majeroni, John Ardizoni.
Virginia, a promising artist, is accused of stealing a valuable painting. But it's a frame-up, engineered by a countess who is Virginia's rival for the hand of a dashing young captain.

Stolen Hours (World Film Corp., 1918)
d: Travers Vale. 5 reels.
Ethel Clayton, John Bowers, Louise DeRigney, Frank Mayo, Jack Drumier, Victor Kennard, Richard Clarke, Lila Chester, Joseph Herbert.
Diana loves Hugh, but there's a problem: He's married.

The Stolen Kiss (Realart Pictures Corp., 1920)
d: Kenneth Webb. 5 reels.
Constance Binney, Rodney LaRocque, George Backus, Bradley Barker, Robert Schable, Frank Losee, Richard Carlyle, Edyna Davies, Ada Nevil, Agnes Everett, Edward A. Fetherston.
Young Felicia has a crush on the choirboy who lives just over the garden wall. One day, the boy climbs the wall and steals a kiss from the startled but delighted girl. Their infatuation matures into love, and years later, after he rescues her from a lecher's torrid advances, Felicia and the boy of her dreams are reunited.

Stolen Kisses (Warner Bros., 1929)
d: Ray Enright. 7 reels. (Music, sound effects, part talkie.)
May McAvoy, Hallam Cooley, Reed Howes, Claude Gillingwater, Edna Murphy, Arthur Hoyt, Agnes Franey, Phyllis Crane.
Hal and May, a bickering young married couple, go on a voyage to try and smooth things over. But they can't stop nagging each other until a kind fate sends lovers into both their lives—and then, in their mutual jealousy, Hal and May discover how much they still love each other.

Stolen Love (FBO Pictures, 1928)
d: Lynn Shores. 7 reels.
Marceline Day, Rex Lease, Owen Moore, Helen Lynch, Blanche Frederici, Joy Winthrop, Betty Blythe.
Bill loves Joan, and they plan to elope. But on his way to fetch his beloved, Bill gets arrested and thrown in jail, and Joan imagines she's been jilted.

Stolen Moments (American Cinema Corp./Pioneer, 1920)
d: George Archainbaud. 6 reels.
Marguerite Namara, Albert L. Barrett, Rudolph Valentine, Henrietta Simpson, Arthur Earl, Walter Chapin, Aileen Savage, Alex K. Shannon, Gene Gauthier.
When an American girl pledges her love to a dapper South American, he accepts her affections, but scoffs at the idea of marriage.

Stolen Orders (William A. Brady, 1918)
d: Harley Knoles, George Kelson. 8 reels.
Montagu Love, Kitty Gordon, June Elvidge, Carlyle Blackwell, Madge Evans, George MacQuarrie, Frank Leigh, Edward Elkas, Robert Barring, Dore Davidson, Philip Masse.
During World War I, an American admiral's wife agrees to steal certain classified documents and turn them over to German spies, to cover her huge gambling losses.

The Stolen Paradise (World Film Corp., 1917)
d: Harley Knoles. 5 reels.
Ethel Clayton, Edward Langford, Pinna Nesbit, George MacQuarrie, Robert Forsyth, George Cowl, Lew Hart, Edward Reed, Edwin Roe, Ivan Dobble, Frank Norcross.
Joan loves David, a blind man who idolizes Katharine. When David gets married, he believes his bride is Katharine, but instead Joan takes her place. With his faithful wife at his side, David becomes a successful author, and eventually an operation restores his sight.

Stolen Pleasures (Columbia, 1927)

d: Philip E. Rosen. 6 reels.
Gayne Whitman, Helene Chadwick, Dorothy Revier, Ray Ripley, Harlan Tucker.
When two married couples bicker so furiously that they separate from their respective spouses, each of them goes looking for romance elsewhere.

The Stolen Ranch (Universal, 1926)
d: William Wyler. 5 reels.
Fred Humes, Louise Lorraine, William Norton Bailey, Ralph McCullough, Nita Cavalier, Edward Cecil, Howard Truesdell, Slim Whittaker, Jack Kirk.
Two war veterans—one of them still suffering from shell shock—return home and find that ownership of their ranch is now claimed by a squatter.

Stolen Secrets (Universal, 1924)
d: Irving Cummings. 5 reels.
Herbert Rawlinson, Kathleen Myers, Edwards Davis, Arthur Stuart Hull, Henry Herbert, William Conklin, George Siegmann, Joseph North, Alfred Allen, William A. Carroll.
A mysterious crime wave grips the city, and the help of a super crime-fighter is enlisted to find the culprits and bring them to justice.

The Stolen Treaty (Vitagraph, 1917)
d: Paul Scardon. 5 reels.
Earle Williams, Denton Vane, Bernard Seigel, Robert Gaillard, Corinne Griffith, Billie Billings, John Ellis.
Geoffrey, thought to be merely a fashion dandy, is actually a Secret Service agent. He needs all his skills here, to recover a stolen international treaty that's being held ransom for millions of dollars.

The Stolen Triumph (Rolfe Photoplays, Inc./Metro, 1916)
d: David Thompson. 5 reels.
Julius Steger, Harry Burkhardt, Clara Whipple, Clara Blandick, Marie Reichardt, Raye Dean, Helen Badgley, Edward Kenney, Maury Steuart, Kathleen Townsend.
When a theatrical agent reads a new play and realizes it is a masterpiece, he impulsively claims authorship and is soon acclaimed a genius.

Stool Pigeon (Columbia, 1928)
d: Renaud Hoffman. 6 reels.
Charles Delaney, Olive Borden, Louis Natheaux, Lucy Beaumont, Ernie Adams, Al Hill, Robert Wilber, Clarence Burton.
Jimmy, a poor young man with a sick mother, joins a criminal gang to earn enough money to care for her.

Stop Flirting (Christie Film Co./Producers Distributing Corp., 1925)
d: Scott Sidney. 6 reels.
John T. Murray, Wanda Hawley, Hallam Cooley, Ethel Shannon, Vera Steadman, Jimmie Adams, Jack Duffy, Jimmy Harrison, David James.
Comedy about newlyweds Perry and Vivian, who suffer a storm of misunderstandings when each is found (though innocently) in the arms of someone else.

Stop, Look, and Listen (Larry Semon Productions/Pathé, 1926)
d: Larry Semon. 6 reels.
Larry Semon, Dorothy Dwan, Mary Carr, William Gillespie, Lionel Belmore, Bull Montana, Babe Hardy, Curtis McHenry, Joseph Swickard.
Luther loves Dorothy, and he proposes marriage. But Dorothy decides she'd like to try a stage career instead... and

even gets Luther to finance the production.

Stop That Man (Universal, 1928)
d: Nat Ross. 6 reels.
Arthur Lake, Barbara Kent, Eddie Gribbon, Warner Richmond, Walter McGrail, George Siegmann, Joseph W. Girard.
Despondent over the loss of his girlfriend's love, Tommy decides to commit suicide. But he's not brave enough to do it himself, so he hires a gunman to knock him off without warning.   Tommy's girlfriend returns to him and reinvigorates his life... but now he's got to find that hired killer and unhire him.

Stop Thief! (George Kleine, 1915)
d: George Fitzmaurice. 5 reels.
Mary Ryan, Harry Mestayer, Harold Howard, Albert Tavernier, William Boyd, Auguste Burmester, Della Connor, Marguerite Boyd, Dan Moyles, Soldine Powell.
In this comedy of errors, a thief and his girlfriend invade a home where a double wedding is to be celebrated, and begin stealing the wedding gifts and nearly everything else. But the pre-nuptial joy radiated by the household is infectious, and soon the thieving pair return all their loot. Then, with the family's blessing, they turn the planned double ceremony into a triple wedding.

Stop Thief (Goldwyn, 1920)
d: Harry Beaumont. 5 reels.
Tom Moore, Hazel Daly, Irene Rich, Kate Lester, Molly Malone, Edward McWade, Raymond Hatton, Harris Gordon, Henry Ralston, John Lince, M.B. Flynn.
Remake of the 1915 George Kleine comedy *Stop Thief!*

The Storm (Lasky Feature Plays/Paramount, 1916)
d: Frank Reicher. 5 reels.
Blanche Sweet, Theodore Roberts, Thomas Meighan, Richard Sterling, Chandler House.
In the forest, a theology student meets a "nature girl" and teaches her to love.

The Storm (Universal, 1922)
d: Reginald Barker. 8 reels.
House Peters, Matt Moore, Virginia Valli, Josef Swickard, Frank Lanning, Gordon McGee.

Three cabin dwellers—two men and a young woman—are trapped together during the unforgiving Canadian winter.

The Storm Breaker (Universal, 1925)
d: Edward Sloman. 7 reels.
House Peters, Ruth Clifford, Nina Romano, Ray Hallor, Jere Austin, Lionel Belmore, Gertrude Claire, Mark Fenton.
Three's a crowd when a sea captain learns his young wife is in love with his own brother.

The Storm Daughter (Universal, 1924)
d: George Archainbaud. 6 reels.

Priscilla Dean, Tom Santschi, William B. Davidson, J. Farrell MacDonald, Cyril Chadwick, Bert Roach, Alfred Fisher.
A storm at sea and a mutiny imperil a ship's passengers.

Stormswept (Robert Thornby Productions/FBO of America, 1923)
d: Robert Thornby. 5 reels.
Wallace Beery, Noah Beery, Virginia Browne Faire, Arline Pretty, Jack Carlyle.
Waterfront drama about a pair of seamen who become close friends and shipmates, never dreaming that one of them would try to seduce the wife of the other.

480

A Stormy Knight (Universal, 1917)
d: Elmer Clifton. 5 reels.
Franklyn Farnum, Brownie Vernon, Jean Hersholt, Hayward Mack, Frank McQuarrie.
During a stormy night, a businessman finds a pretty girl at his door, pleading for help.

Stormy Seas (Continental Pictures/Associated Exhibitors, 1923)
d: J.P. McGowan. 5 reels.
J.P. McGowan, Helen Holmes, Leslie Casey, Harry Dalroy, Francis Seymour, Gordon Knapp.
Morgan, a sea captain, is addicted to drink; but he swears not to touch a drop while out at sea. Tragically, his cravings get the better of him, and the drunken captain wrecks his ship.

Stormy Waters (Tiffany-Stahl Productions, 1928)
d: Edgar Lewis. 6 reels.
Eve Southern, Malcolm McGregor, Roy Stewart, Shirley Palmer, Olin Francis, Norbert Myles, Bert Apling.
A sea captain sets sail for Argentina with his brother David along as shipmate. Once in Buenos Aires, David fires up a romance with a local lovely—to the great dissatisfaction of the captain, who knows that his brother is engaged to a girl back home.

The Story Without a Name (Famous Players-Lasky/Paramount, 1924)
d: Irvin Willat. 6 reels.
Agnes Ayres, Antonio Moreno, Tyrone Power, Louis Wolheim, Dagmar Godowsky, Jack Lionel Bohn, Maurice Costello, Frank Currier, Ivan Linow.
Action drama about a new weapon developed for the U.S. Government. Foreign spies want the device too, and they kidnap the inventor and his girlfriend, then try to force the man to build the same weapon for them. But he fools them by instead building a short-wave radio and broadcasting an SOS which leads to their rescue.

Straight From Paris (Equity Pictures, 1921)
d: Harry Garson. 6 reels.
Clara Kimball Young, Bertram Grassby, William P. Carleton, Betty Francisco, Thomas Jefferson, Gerard Alexander, Clarissa Selwynne.
Lucette, owner of a millinery shop, falls in love with a charming boulevardier, but she marries his even more charming uncle.

Straight is the Way (Cosmopolitan Productions/Paramount, 1921)
d: Robert G. Vignola. 5 reels.
Matt Moore, Mabel Bert, Gladys Leslie, George Parsons, Henry Sedley, Van Dyke Brooks, Emily Fitzroy, Peggy Parr.
Carter and Follett, two unsuccessful crooks, take up residence in an empty section of a dowager's large home. When they overhear a loan shark threatening the elderly homeowner with foreclosure, the crooks decide to help her out, and end up retiring her mortgage with buried treasure they have found.

Straight Shootin' (Universal, 1927)
d: William Wyler. 5 reels.
Ted Wells, Garry O'Dell, Lillian Gilmore, Joe Bennett, Wilbur Mack, George Connors, Al Ferguson.
Out West, two itinerant cowboys help a mining family that's being threatened by claim jumpers.

Straight Shooting (Universal, 1917)

d: Jack Ford. 5 reels.
Harry Carey, George Berrill, Molly Malone, Duke Lee, Vester Pegg, Ted Brooks, Milt Brown, Hoot Gibson.
Western depicting a bitter clash between ranchers and homesteaders.
Historically important in that this was John ("Jack") Ford's first feature film as director.

Straight Through (Universal, 1925)
d: Arthur Rosson. 5 reels.
William Desmond, Marguerite Clayton, Albert J. Smith, Ruth Stonehouse, Frank Brownlee, Bill Gillis, George F. Marion.
Out West, a gambler falls for the sister of his rancher friend.

The Straight Way (Fox, 1916)
d: Will S. Davis. 5 reels.
Valeska Suratt, Herbert Heyes, Glen White, Claire Whitney, Elsie Balfour, Richard Turner, Richard Rendell, Fred Jones, T. Tamamoto.
After having her baby, a woman suffers amnesia in a train accident. Not knowing who she is, she cannot return to her loved ones, and her husband assumes her dead. Years later, the amnesiac regains her memory and becomes convinced that her husband has disgraced her. So she plots to avenge herself by hiring an ex-con to seduce the woman her husband is living with... not realizing the woman is her own daughter, now grown.

Stranded (Fine Arts Film Co./Triangle, 1916)
d: Lloyd Ingraham. 5 reels.
DeWolf Hopper, Carl Stockdale, Frank Bennett, Loyola O'Connor, Bessie Love.
When a vaudeville troupe is stranded in a strange town after the manager absconds with the funds, an old Shakespearean actor in the troupe takes the young ingenue under his wing in a father-daughter relationship.

Stranded (Sterling Pictures, 1927)
d: Phil Rosen. 6 reels.
Shirley Mason, William Collier Jr., John Miljan, Florence Turner, Gale Henry, Shannon Day, Lucy Beaumont, Rosa Gore.
Small-town girl Sally goes to Hollywood dreaming of fame, but all she gets are promises, propositions, and small parts as an extra. Discouraged, she is just about to "upgrade" her career by giving in to a lecherous producer... when her small-town sweetheart arrives to take Sally home, wiser and with her virtue intact.

Stranded in Arcady (Astra Film Corp./Pathé, 1917)
d: Frank Crane. 5 reels.
Irene Castle, Elliott Dexter, Pell Trenton, Georgio Majeroni.
What happens when a man-hating woman and a misogynist are stranded together in a remote, mountainous region? Why, they fall in love, of course.

Stranded in Paris (Paramount, 1926)
d: Arthur Rosson. 7 reels.
Bebe Daniels, James Hall, Ford Sterling, Iris Stuart, Mabel Julienne Scott, Tom Ricketts, Helen Dunbar, Ida Darling, George Grandee, André Lanoy.
Comedy about Julie, an American girl who wins a free trip to Paris.

The Strange Boarder (Goldwyn, 1920)
d: Clarence G. Badger. 5 reels.
Will Rogers, Irene Rich, Jimmy Rogers, James Mason, Doris Pawn, Lionel Belmore, Jack Richardson, Sydney Deane,

Louis J. Durham.
When a rancher in the city falls victim to a gang of crooks who rob him of $10,000, he decides that the only way to get back his money is by gambling.

Strange Idols (Fox, 1922)
d: Bernard J. Durning. 5 reels.
Dustin Farnum, Doris Pawn, Philo McCullough, Richard Tucker.
Angus, a lumberjack from the great Northwest, visits New York and falls in love with Ruth, a cabaret dancer. They marry, and Angus takes her back to his remote home in the woods. Soon, though, the peppy Ruth tires of the bucolic setting and starts yearning for the fast life of the city.

A Strange Transgressor (Triangle, 1917)
d: Reginald Barker. 5 reels.
Louise Glaum, J. Barney Sherry, Colin Chase, Dorcas Matthews, May Giraci, J. Frank Burke, William H. Bray.
When a wealthy doctor decides to dump his mistress, she avenges herself by seducing his son.

The Strange Woman (Fox, 1918)
d: Edward J. LeSaint. 6 reels.
Gladys Brockwell, Charles Clary, William Scott, Harry Depp, Ruby LaFayette, G. Raymond Nye, Ada Beecher, Eunice Moore, Grace Wood, Margaret Cullington, Lucy Donahue.
John, a corn-fed Iowa boy, goes to Paris and falls for a woman who espouses the notion of Free Love.

The Stranger (B.S. Moss Motion Picture Corp./First National, 1920)
d: James Youngdeer. 5 reels.
Millard K. Wilson, Beatrice LaPlante, Billy Gettinger, Phil Gastrock, Catharine Penny.
Out West, a stranger rides into town searching for his brother's killer.

The Stranger (Famous Players-Lasky/Paramount, 1924)
d: Joseph Henabery. 7 reels.
Betty Compson, Richard Dix, Lewis Stone, Tully Marshall, Robert Schable, Mary Jane Irving, Frank Nelson, Marian Skinner.
In London, a poor but gallant janitor takes the blame for a killing he knows was justifiable, in order to save an engaged couple from disgrace.

A Stranger From Somewhere (Universal, 1916)
d: William Worthington. 5 reels.
Franklyn Farnum, Agnes Vernon, Helen Wright, Claire McDowell, Arthur Hoyt, Barney Furey.
Comedic tale about Sam, a rancher from out West, who moves to the city and falls for an heiress. It turns out that the rancher is a dead ringer for "Dippy," a con man who tries to impersonate him on one of Sam's dates with the heiress. Meanwhile, Sam is mistaken for the con man by some of "Dippy's" underworld chums.
Farnum plays both the rancher and the con man. He would again play a double role, in the 1918 Universal film *The Rough Lover.*

Stranger Than Fiction (Katherine MacDonald Pictures/Associated First National, 1921)
d: J.A. Barry. 6 reels.
Katherine MacDonald, Dave Winter, Wesley Barry, Wade Boteler, Jean Dumont, Harry O'Connor, Evelyn Burns, Tom McGuire.

After her party guests have been robbed by the notorious "Black Heart gang," a socialite demands that—before she will marry him—her fiancé locate the gang and bring them to justice.

The Stranger's Banquet (Marshall Neilan Productions/Goldwyn, 1922)
d: Marshall Neilan. 7 reels.
Hobart Bosworth, Claire Windsor, Rockliffe Fellowes, Ford Sterling, Eleanor Boardman, Thomas Holding, Eugenie Besserer, Nigel Barrie, Stuart Holmes, Claude Gillingwater, Margaret Loomis, Tom Guise, Lillian Langdon, William Humphrey, Arthur Hoyt, Aileen Pringle, Cyril Chadwick.
A shipyard owner must deal with labor unrest and the demands of a nihilist agitator.

Strangers of the Night (Louis B. Mayer Productions/Metro, 1923)
d: Fred Niblo. 8 reels.
Matt Moore, Enid Bennett, Barbara LaMarr, Robert McKim, Mathilde Brundage, Emily Fitzroy, Otto Hoffman, Thomas Ricketts.
In England, a country gentleman faces thieves who are after a legendary treasure that's hidden on his property.

The Stream of Life (Plimpton Epic Pictures/Plymouth Film Corp., 1919)
d: Horace G. Plimpton. 7 reels.
Douglas Redmond Jr., Allen Willey, Edward Keenan, Leonard Willey, Nettie Davenport, Frank Wilson, William J. Gross, Anna Cleveland, Mildred Carrie Travers, Henry Mowbray, Charles Sutton.
Philip, a financier who lives the good life with his wife and child, neglects the religious principles his parents tried to instill in him.

Street Angel (Fox, 1928)
d: Frank Borzage. 10 reels. (Music, sound effects, part talkie.)
Janet Gaynor, Charles Farrell, Alberto Rabagliati, Gino Conti, Guido Trento, Henry Armetta, Louis Liggett, Milton Dickinson, Helena Herman, Natalie Kingston, David Kashner, Jennie Bruno.
In Italy, a circus girl meets a painter who sees in her the inspiration for his painting of the Madonna.

The Street Called Straight (Goldwyn, 1920)
d: Wallace Worsley. 5 reels.
Milton Sills, Naomi Childers, Charles Clary, Irene Rich, Jane Sterling, W. Lawson Butt, Lydia Yeamans Titus, Alec B. Francis.
When the man who once loved her offers to pay the funds desperately needed by her family, Olivia feels insulted, for she does not want to be beholden to a former suitor.

The Street of Forgotten Men (Famous Players-Lasky/Paramount, 1925)
d: Herbert Brenon. 7 reels.
Percy Marmont, Mary Brian, Neil Hamilton, John Harrington, Juliet Brenon, Josephine Deffry, Riley Hatch, Agostino Borgato, Albert Roccardi, Dorothy Walters.
Charlie, a professional beggar, takes care of the little daughter of another beggar who has died. The girl is raised in the country without knowing her roots, and years later falls in love with a prominent business lawyer. Charlie's dilemma: Should he divulge the girl's parentage and risk her future happiness, or keep her in the dark forever?

The Street of Illusion (Columbia, 1928)

HARRY LANGDON. Along with Chaplin, Keaton, and Lloyd, Harry Langdon was considered by many to be one of the four great clowns of the silent era. He mined his screen persona-that of a small child inside a grown man's body-so skillfully, sometimes audiences would forget they were watching an adult. Langdon's best films were his two first features, *Tramp, Tramp, Tramp,* and *The Strong Man,* both released in 1926.

* * * * *

d: Erle C. Kenton.   7 reels.

Ian Keith, Virginia Valli, Kenneth Thomson, Harry Myers.

An unbalanced actor, outraged because the girl he helped get a job decides to fall for another man in the play, substitutes real bullets for blanks in the prop gun to be used against his rival.

The Street of Seven Stars   (DeLuxe Pictures, Inc., 1918)
d: John B. O'Brien.   6 reels.

Doris Kenyon, Hugh Thompson, Carey Hastings, Stephen Carr, Iva Shepard, Frank Crayne, John Hopkins, Harriet McConnell, Marie McConnell, George Moss, Eliza Helen Criswell, Raphael DeMise, Cesare Gravina.

In Paris, a lovely violinist falls in love with an American surgeon, but rejects his proposal as she believes marriage would interfere with her career.

The Streets of Illusion   (Astra Film Corp./Pathé, 1917)
d: William Parke.   5 reels.

Gladys Hulette, J.H. Gilmour, William Parke Jr., Richard Barthelmess, William Dudley, Warren Cook, Doris Grey, Kathryn Adams, Gerald Badgley, William P. Burt, Logan Paul.

When a U.S. soldier deserts from the war, his sister tries to keep the truth from their blind father, instead telling him tall tales of his son's bravery at the front. In time, her own courage will be rewarded, when her brother returns and rescues her from attack by a deranged neighbor. Then the young man returns to his post, determined to justify his sister's faith in him.

Streets of Shanghai   (Tiffany-Stahl Productions, 1927)
d: Louis Gasnier.   6 reels.

Pauline Starke, Kenneth Harlan, Eddie Gribbon, Margaret Livingston, Jason Robards, Mathilde Comont, Anna May Wong, Sojin, Tetsu Komai, Toshyie Ichioka, Media Ichioka.

In Shanghai, an American missionary falls in love with a Marine.

The Strength of Donald McKenzie   (American Film Co./Mutual, 1916)
d: William Russell, Jack Prescott.   5 reels.

William Russell, Charlotte Burton, Harry Keenan, George Ahern, John Prescott, Nell Franzen, Margaret Nichols.

Mabel, a publisher's daughter, meets a handsome poetry-writing lumberjack.

Strength of the Pines   (Fox, 1922)
d: Edgar Lewis.   5 reels.

William Russell, Irene Rich, Lule Warrenton, Arthur Morrison, Les Bates.

Bruce and Linda, siblings raised in an orphanage, grow to maturity and try to take possession of their parents' estate, only to find that it's been seized by a crook who forged its title documents. They launch an investigation into the transaction and discover the truth and then some: Not only does the property rightfully belong to Linda, but she isn't Bruce's sister at all. Now the pair have a double reason to celebrate, for they've loved each other for years.

The Strength of the Weak   (Universal, 1916)
d: Lucius Henderson.   5 reels.

Mary Fuller, Harry Hilliard, Edward Davis, Curtis Benton, Clara Byers.

Pauline has an affair with a middle-aged man, then falls in love with his son.

Strictly Confidential   (Goldwyn, 1919)
d: Clarence G. Badger.   5 reels.

Madge Kennedy, John Bowers, Robert Bolder, Herbert Standing, Roger McKinnon, Eugenie Forde, Gertrude Norman, Helen Muir, Lydia Yeamans Titus.

Society comedy about a vivacious girl who marries an artist, then learns that he's been keeping a secret: He's a member of the British nobility. Now she's the Lady of the manor where her relatives are all employed as servants.

String Beans   (Thomas H. Ince/Paramount, 1918)
d: Victor L. Scherzinger.   5 reels.

Charles Ray, Jane Novak, John P. Lockney, Donald MacDonald, Al Filson, Otto Hoffman.

A farm boy goes to work for a newspaper, and gets to investigate graft in the opening of a new string bean factory.

Strong Boy   (Fox, 1929)
d: John Ford.   6 reels.   (Music score, sound effects.)

Victor McLaglen, Leatrice Joy, Farrell MacDonald, Clyde Cook, Kent Sanderson, Douglas Scott, Slim Summerville, Tom Wilson, Eulalie Jensen, David Torrence, Dolores Johnson.

Strong Boy, a railroad employee, loves Mary McGregor, but the feeling isn't mutual. Then one day he prevents a holdup on her father's train, and Mary starts seeing that Strong Boy has romantic potential.

The Strong Man   (Harry Langdon Corp./First National, 1926)
w, d: Frank Capra.   7 reels.

Harry Langdon, Priscilla Bonner, Gertrude Astor, Robert McKim, Arthur Thalasso, William V. Mong.

A meek Belgian soldier fighting in World War I strikes up a penpal relationship with a blind American girl he has never met. After the war, he journeys to America as assistant to a theatrical strong man, Zandow the Great. While in America, he searches for the girl and finds her, just as word comes that Zandow is incapacitated and the little nebbish must go on stage in his place.

Considered by many critics to be Langdon's best film, *The Strong Man* has been called "structurally a perfect motion picture." The "Walls of Jericho" scene, where the walls of the villain's hangout come crashing down, is so beautifully set up that we, the audience, are no longer sophisticated adult observers, but innocents rejoicing that virtue has triumphed, and the world will be a happy place again.

Sadly, this would be Langdon's last great film. After his next effort, the better-than-average *Long Pants*, he parted company with director Frank Capra, and the later Langdon films would never equal the sparkle of his early work.

The Strong Way   (World Film Corp., 1917)
d: George Kelson.   5 reels.

June Elvidge, John Bowers, Isabel Berwin, Joseph Herbert, Rosina Henley, Grace Williams, Hubert Wilke.

Thinking him guilty of murder, a married woman protects her former lover by swearing they were together at the time of the murder.

The Stronger Love   (Oliver Morosco Photoplay Co./Paramount, 1916)
d: Frank Lloyd.   5 reels.

Vivian Martin, Edward Peil, Frank Lloyd, Jack Livingston, Alice Knowland, Herbert Standing, John McKinnon, Louise A. Emmons.

Nell, a lovely mountain girl, falls in love with a visiting stranger who is searching the mountains for precious metals.

Stronger Than Death (Nazimova Productions/Metro, 1920)
d: Herbert Blaché. 7 reels.
Nazimova, Charles Bryant, Charles W. French, Margaret McWade, Herbert Prior, William H. Orlamond, Milla Davenport, Henry Harmon.
When a famous dancer is warned that she may have a heart attack if she dances again, she moves to India and falls in love with a British Major. Eventually she learns the natives are planning an uprising, and must delay them by performing a mesmerizing dance, thus saving the lives of her lover and all the men in his British command post... but endangering her own.

The Stronger Vow (Goldwyn, 1919)
d: Reginald Barker. 6 reels.
Milton Sills, Geraldine Farrar, Kate Lester, Tom Santschi, John Davidson, Hassard Short.
Dolores, a newlywed bride, is grief-stricken to hear that her new husband killed her brother, and she resolves to avenge his death. But the charge against her husband is false, having been planted by one of Dolores' jealous former suitors.

The Stronger Will (Excellent Pictures, 1928)
d: Bernard McEveety. 7 reels.
Percy Marmont, Rita Carewe, Howard Truesdell, Merle Ferris, William Norton Bailey, Erin LaBissioniere.
The eternal triangle arises yet again when Estelle, who's engaged to marry Morton, jilts him and marries his rival Ralph instead. She'll be sorry.

The Strongest (Fox, 1920)
d: R.A. Walsh. 5 reels.
Renee Adoree, Carlo Liten, Harrison Hunter, Florence Malone, Madame Tressida, Jean Gauthier DeTrigny, Georgette Gauthier DeTrigny, Hal Horne, James Marcus, C.A. de Lima.
Claire, who feels neglected by her businessman husband, falls in love with his old friend when he comes for a short visit.

The Struggle (Equitable Motion Pictures Corp./World Film Corp., 1916)
d: John Ince. 5 reels.
Frank Sheridan, Arthur Ashley, Ethel Grey Terry, Eileen Evans, Alfred Loring, Isabelle Vernon.
A May-December romance gives way to marriage between the young woman and a doctor closer to her own age. But her new husband is a scoundrel and a philanderer, and as time goes by the wife realizes she should have married her older, but more loyal, suitor.

The Struggle (William N. Selig Productions/Canyon Pictures, 1921)
d: Otto Lederer. 5 reels.
Franklyn Farnum, Genevieve Bert, Edwin Wallock, Karl Formes, Vester Pegg, Bud Osborne, George Washinton Jones.
Storm, a weary war veteran, goes out West for some peace and quiet... but finds that goal elusive.

The Struggle Everlasting (High Art/Arrow, 1918)
d: James Kirkwood. 5 reels.
Milton Sills, Florence Reedl, Henry Rapp, Wellington Playter, Irving Cummings, Edwin N. Hoyt, Albert Hall, George Cooper, Mildred Cheshire, E.J. Ratcliffe, Fred C. Jones, Richard Hatteras, Margaret Pitt.

Allegory pitting Mind against Soul in the pursuit of Body. In the film, two brothers love the same girl.

The Student Prince in Old Heidelberg (MGM, 1927)
d: Ernst Lubitsch. 10 reels.
Ramon Novarro, Norma Shearer, Jean Hersholt, Gustav von Seyffertitz, Philippe de Lacy, Edgar Norton, Bobby Mack, Edward Connelly, Otis Harlan, John S. Peters, George K. Arthur, Edythe Chapman, Lionel Belmore, Lincoln Steadman.
Silent version of the operetta *The Student Prince*, about a Ruritanian prince in love with an innkeeper's niece.
Also known as *Old Heidelberg*.

The Studio Girl (Select Pictures Corp., 1918)
d: Lewis J. Selznick. 5 reels.
Constance Talmadge, Earle Foxe, Edna Earle, John Hines, Gertrude Norman, Isabel O'Madigan, Grace Burton, Fred Tidmarsh.
Romantic comedy about irrepressible Celia, who pursues her dream man in spite of numerous obstacles thrown in her path, by her own family and his.

Submarine (Columbia, 1928)
d: Frank Capra. 9 reels.
Jack Holt, Ralph Graves, Dorothy Revier, Clarence Burton, Arthur Rankin.
Stirring tale of a deep-sea diver on a mission to rescue a submarine and its crew, trapped 400 feet under the sea.

The Substitute Wife (Arrow Pictures, 1925)
d: Wilfred May. 6 reels.
Jane Novak, Niles Welch, Coit Albertson, Louise Carter, Gordon Standing, Mario Majeroni.
Far-fetched melodrama about a groom who's accidentally blinded on his wedding night, and whose faithless bride takes advantage of his blindness by substituting another woman in her place.

Subway Sadie (Al Rockett Productions/First National, 1926)
d: Alfred Santell. 7 reels.
Dorothy Mackaill, Jack Mulhall, Charles Murray, Peggy Shaw, Gaston Glass, Bernard Randall.
Sadie, a New York shopgirl, yearns to see Paris. She gets her chance when the firm promotes her to buyer and she is assigned to a European business trip.

Success (Murray W. Garsson/Metro, 1923)
d: Ralph Ince. 7 reels.
Brandon Tynan, Naomi Childers, Mary Astor, Dore Davidson, Lionel Adams, Stanley Ridges, Robert Lee Keeling, Billy Quirk, Helen Macks, Gaylord Pendleton, John Woodford.
Barry, a formerly renowned Shakespearean actor, falls on hard times and finds himself assigned as dresser for the leading man in a production of "King Lear." On opening night, the star gets drunk and Barry goes on in his place, wins the audience's heart, and launches a new career for himself.

A Successful Adventure (Metro, 1918)
d: Harry L. Franklin. 5 reels.
May Allison, Harry Hilliard, Frank Currier, Edward Connelly, Christine Mayo, Fred C. Jones, Kate Blancke, Pauline Dempsey, Anthony Byrd, Phoebe Starr, Maury Steuart.
Virginia, a Southern beauty, tries to reconcile her father and his long-estranged brother.

Such a Little Pirate (Famous Players-Lasky/Paramount, 1918)
d: George Melford. 5 reels.
Harrison Ford, Lila Lee, Theodore Roberts, Guy Oliver, Forest Seabury, J. Parke Jones, Adele Farrington, Sinbad the orangutan.
Rory and his girlfriend Patricia sail a schooner to a South Seas island and uncover her grandfather's hidden treasure.

Such a Little Queen (Famous Players/Paramount, 1914)
d: Edwin S. Porter, Hugh Ford. 5 reels.
Mary Pickford, Carlyle Blackwell, Russell Bassett, Arthur Hoops, Harold Lockwood.
Anna, the queen of Herzegovina, loves Stephen, the king of Bosnia... but both are overthrown and exiled to America. Can this romance flourish in the New World?

Such a Little Queen (Realart Pictures, 1921)
d: George Fawcett. 5 reels.
Constance Binney, Vincent Coleman, J.H. Gilmour, Roy Fernandez, Frank Losee, Betty Carpenter, Jessie Ralph, Henry Leone.
 Remake of the 1914 Famous Players film *Such a Little Queen*, with minor alterations. Both versions are based on the play of the same name by Channing Pollock.

The Sudden Gentleman (Triangle, 1917)
d: Thomas N. Heffron. 5 reels.
William Desmond, Mary McIvor, Jack Richardson, Margaret Shillingford, Alfred Hollingsworth, Donald Fuller, Alberta Lee, Walter Perry, Percy Challenger.
Garry, a rough-hewn Irish blacksmith, inherits a large estate in America.

Sudden Jim (Triangle, 1917)
d: Victor L. Schertzinger. 5 reels.
Charles Ray, Joseph J. Dowling, Sylvia Bremer, Lydia Knott, William Bellingford, Frank Whitson, Georgie Stone.
A plucky young man takes over his dad's manufacturing plant, but is opposed by a ruthless railroad man who considers the youngster a pushover, and decides to ruin his business. But Junior's no creampuff, as his foes soon learn.

Sudden Riches (World Film Corp., 1916)
d: Emile Chautard. 6 reels.
Robert Warwick, Gerda Holmes, Clara Whipple, Madge Evans, Lillian Cook, Jeannette Horton.
When Robert, an architect and family man, suddenly inherits his uncles's fortune, he thinks it will be the end of all his troubles. But they've just started.

Suds (Pickford/United Artists, 1920)
d: John Francis Dillon. 5 reels.
Mary Pickford, Harold Goodwin, Albert Austin, Rose Dione, Nadyne Montgomery, Darwin Karr, Hal Wilson.
A laundress fantasizes about love and fame and romance with a wealthy suitor.

Sue of the South (Universal, 1919)
d: Eugene Moore. 5 reels.
Edith Roberts, Ruby LaFayette, James Farley, P.S. Pembroke, Marie Van Tassell, Countess DuCello, George Hackathorne, L.M. Wells.
Tennessee mountain girl Sue travels to Chicago to live with Peyton, a foundry owner and an old friend of the family.

The Sultana (Balboa Amusement Co./Pathé,1916)
d: Sherwood MacDonald. 5 reels.
Ruth Roland, William Conklin, Charles Dudley, Frank

Erlanger, Daniel Gilfether, E.T. Peters, Edwin J. Brady, Gordon Sackville, R. Henry Grey, Richard Johnson.
"The Sultana" is a priceless diamond tiara that becomes the focus of an extensive manhunt after it is stolen.

Summer Bachelors (Fox, 1926)
d: Allan Dwan. 6 reels.
Madge Bellamy, Allan Forrest, Matt Moore, Hale Hamilton, Leila Hyams, Charles Winninger, Clifford Holland, Olive Tell, Walter Catlett, James F. Cullen, Cosmo Kyrle Bellew.
A cynical young woman decides if you can't beat 'em, organize 'em... so she starts a club for "summer bachelors" — married men who like to flirt with other women when their wives go away for the summer. Then the organizer falls madly in love with one of her clients.

The Summer Girl (World Film Corp., 1916)
d: Edwin August. 5 reels.
Mollie King, Arthur Ashley, Dave Ferguson, Ruby Hoffman, Harold Entwistle, Dora Mills Adams.
Mary, an heiress, loves Bruce, a struggling artist. To test Bruce's love for his daughter, Mary's dad tells him he has lost his fortune. But because Bruce remains anxious to win Mary's hand, Papa's convinced that the young man is seriously in love.

Sun-Up (MGM, 1925)
d: Edmund Goulding. 6 reels.
Pauline Starke, Lucille LaVerne, Edward Connelly, Conrad Nagel, Sam DeGrasse, George K. Arthur, Arthur Rankin, Bainard Beckwith.
A family takes in an army deserter, then learns he is the son of their enemy.

The Sunbeam (Rolfe Photoplays, Inc./Metro, 1916)
d: Edwin Carewe. 5 reels.
Mabel Taliaferro, Helen Alexandria, Raymond McKee, Gerald Griffin, Warner Anderson, Lillian Shaffner, Al Lee, Louis Wolheim, Eddie Reddway, Daniel Bertona, David Thompson.
In the New York slums, a warm-hearted girl and a reformed thief form an unlikely team to see that their elderly neighbor is well taken care of.

Sunday (World Film Corp., 1915)
d: George W. Lederer. 5 reels.
Reine Davies, Montagu Love, Barney McPhee, Charles Trowbridge, William H. Tooker, Albert Hart, Adolph Link, Jeanette Bageard, Charles Dickson.
Four lumberjacks raise an orphan girl named Sunday.

Sundown (First National, 1924)
d: Laurence Trimble, Harry O. Hoyt. 8 reels.
Bessie Love, Roy Stewart, Hobart Bosworth, Arthur Hoyt, Charles Murray, Jere Austin, Charles Crockett, E.J. Radcliffe, Margaret McWade, Bernard Randall, Charles Sellon.
The age-old struggle between ranchers and homesteaders is explored once again. This time, the son of one of the ranchers falls in love with a homesteader's daughter.

Sundown Slim (Universal, 1920)
d: Val Paul. 5 reels.
Harry Carey, Otto Meyers, Ed Jones, Mignonne, J.M. Foster, Ted Brooks, Charles LeMoyne, Frances Conrad, Duke Lee, Joseph Harris, Genevieve Blinn, Ed Price.
Out West, a genial hobo named Sundown Slim goes to work at his friend's cattle ranch, where a long-simmering feud with neighboring ranchers is about to come to a boil.

486

The Sundown Trail (Universal, 1919)
d: Rollin Sturgeon. 6 reels.
Monroe Salisbury, Alice Elliott, Clyde Fillmore, Beatrice Dominguez, Carl Stockdale.
During the California Gold Rush, the men in a mining town on the Sundown Trail send for women from the East to come and marry them.

Sunlight's Last Raid (Vitagraph, 1917)
d: William Wolbert. 5 reels.
Mary Anderson, Alfred Whitman, Fred Burns.
Out West, a rancher and a notorious outlaw vie for the love of the same girl.

Sunny Side Up (DeMille Pictures/Producers Distributing Corp., 1926)
d: Donald Crisp. 6 reels.
Vera Reynolds, Edmund Burns, George K. Arthur, ZaSu Pitts, Ethel Clayton, Sally Rand, Louis Natheaux, Jocelyn Lee, Majel Coleman.
Sunny, a vivacious young lady who sings joyfully for her neighbors, attracts the attention of a theatrical producer.

Sunrise (Fox, 1927)
d: F.W. Murnau. 10 reels.   (Released with music score and sound effects.)
George O'Brien, Janet Gaynor, Margaret Livingston, Bodil Rosing, J. Farrel MacDonald, Ralph Sipperly, Jane Winton, Arthur Housman, Eddie Boland, Sally Eilers, Gino Corrado.
A sparkling, luminous masterpiece, winner of three Academy Awards including Best Actress for Janet Gaynor. A married farmer falls for a temptress from the big city, and together they plot to kill his wife. But the man repents and confesses his intentions to his horrified wife, then must win her back by proving his love for her all over again.
It's a simple story, but the telling of it is anything but simple. German director F.W. Murnau was given a free hand to make the film his way, and the result is so stunningly cinematic that all thoughts of early cinema's "photographed stage plays" are forgotten. *Sunrise*, I think, comes closest of any film to achieving visual poetry. From opening shot to final fadeout, it has poetry's rhythms, discipline, and integrity. There's a justly celebrated shot early in the film where the farmer leaves his home, crosses his property, walks into the marsh and across it, snaking through trees, bushes, and fences, to his secret rendezvous with the city woman. They meet and kiss under a full moon, and it's a wildly erotic moment. But look at the scene again. From the moment the farmer leaves his cottage to the moment of that illicit embrace is one shot, continuous, with no cutting. Murnau has perfected the tracking shot, in one breathtaking sequence that covers a full 90 seconds of mounting tension.
Later, as the farmer and his wife are re-igniting the flame of their love, they walk together, arm in arm, and the scenery melts around them—first they are in the country, then they find themselves in the crowded, busy city. But they are oblivious to the change in their surroundings, concentrating solely on each other. It's a scene that could happen in only two places: a lover's imagination, and on film.
The closing scene, with the sunrise of the title dawning behind the joyfully reunited couple, is jaw-droppingly spectacular. But by that time, we have been treated to 98 minutes of dazzling visuals, enough for a dozen movies.
Under Murnau's masterful direction, *Sunrise* confidently seizes control of our emotions, then takes them for a wild ride. In Joe Franklin's 1959 book "Classics of the Silent Screen," written in collaboration with William K. Everson, we read: "I can recall no other film in which the honest emotion of love has been conveyed so beautifully, and no other film that is such a beautiful entity in itself."

The Sunset Derby (First National, 1927)
d: Albert Rogell. 6 reels.
Mary Astor, William Collier Jr., Ralph Lewis, David Kirby, Lionel Belmore, Burt Ross, Henry Barrows, Bobby Doyle, Michael Visaroff.
When a famous jockey suffers a spill during a race and winds up in the hospital, the owners are forced to sell the horse to pay his medical expenses. But this jockey is one scrappy kid. Later, when the same horse is entered in another race, he secretly mounts her and rides the filly to victory.

Sunset Jones (American Film Co./Pathé, 1921)
d: George L. Cox. 5 reels.
Charles Clary, James Gordon, Irene Rich, Kathleen O'Connor.
Sunset Jones, an adventurer, is hired to stop a gang of railroad thieves.

The Sunset Legion (Paramount, 1928)
d: Lloyd Ingraham. 7 reels.
Fred Thomson, William Courtright, Edna Murphy, Harry Woods.
A Texas Ranger goes undercover to infiltrate a gang of outlaws.

Sunset Pass (Paramount, 1929)
d: Otto Brower. 6 reels.
Jack Holt, Nora Lane, John Loder, Christian J. Frank, Pee Wee Holmes, Chester Conklin, Pat Harmon, Alfred Allen, Guy Oliver.
A cowpuncher falls in love with the sister of his employer, a British rancher.

The Sunset Princess (Great West Film Co., 1918)
d: Charles Webster Hitchcock, William Cooper. 5 reels.
Marjorie Daw, Wallace G. Coburn, C.M. Giffen.
Out West, a young woman raised on a ranch is smitten with a wandering stranger, and unwisely agrees to follow him to the nearest town.

Sunset Sprague (Fox, 1920)
d: Thomas N. Heffron, Paul Cazeneuve. 5 reels.
Buck Jones, Patsey DeForest, Henry J. Hebert, Gloria Payton, Edwin Booth Tilton, Noble Johnson, Jack Rollins, Gus Saville.
A cowpoke comes to the aid of a young woman and her uncle, who are threatened by an outlaw gang bent on stealing their mine. The cowboy investigates, and learns that the gang's chieftain is, secretly, none other than the girl's boyfriend.

The Sunset Trail (Paramount, 1917)
d: George Melford. 5 reels.
Harrison Ford, Vivian Martin, Henry A. Barrows, Charles Ogle, Carmen Phillips, Billy Elmer.
Bess, a tomboy raised by her father, takes up smoking and drinking, much to the dismay of Kirk, the lad who's grown fond of her.

The Sunset Trail (Universal, 1924)
d: Whyndham Gittens. 5 reels.
William Desmond, Gareth Hughes, Lucille Hutton, S.E. Jennings, Clark Comstock, Albert J. Smith, William A. Steele.

SUNRISE (1927). The night is charged with lust, as the married farmer (George O'Brien) and his "city woman" mistress (Margaret Livingston) meet under a full moon.

* * * * *

Out West, a friendly hobo finds the map to a gold mine and a photo of a beautiful girl. As he continues in his travels he'll find both the mine and the young lady.

Sunshine Alley (Goldwyn, 1917)
d: John W. Noble. 6 reels.
Mae Marsh, Robert Harron, Dion Titheradge, J.A. Furey, Ed See, John Charles, W.T. Carleton, Isabel Berwin, Mack Grey.
Nell, a slum girl who lives with her grandfather and her shiftless brother, attracts the affections of Ned, a millionaire's son.

Sunshine and Gold (Balboa Amusement Co./Pathé, 1917)
d: Henry King. 5 reels.
Baby Marie Osborne, Henry King, Daniel Gilfether, Neil Hardin.
Kidnapped by a band of gypsies, little Mary escapes into the woods, and meets an old hermit who has turned his back on the world. After an evening together, the old man comes to realize that Mary is the granddaughter he left behind.

Sunshine Dad (Fine Arts Film Co./Triangle, 1916)
d: Edward Dillon. 5 reels.
DeWolf Hopper, Fay Tincher, Chester Withey, Max Davidson, Raymond Wells, Eugene Pallette, Jewel Carmen, William DeWolf Hopper Jr.
Comedy about stolen jewels making their way from hand to hand, often unintentionally. All the while, priests from a Hindu temple follow the trail of the jewels, stolen from one of their shrines.

Sunshine of Paradise Alley (Chadwick Pictures, 1926)
d: Jack Nelson. 7 reels.
Barbara Bedford, Kenneth McDonald, Max Davidson, Nigel Barrie, Tui Lorraine, J. Parks Jones, Bobby Nelson, Frank Weed, Max Ascher, Lydia Yeamans Titus, Evelyn Sherman.
In New York's East Side, a tenement girl called "Sunshine" and her iceman boyfriend team up to thwart the bulldozers intent on leveling their building.

Sunshine Molly (Bosworth, Inc./Paramount, 1915)
d: Lois Weber, Phillips Smalley. 5 reels.
Lois Weber, Phillips Smalley, Adele Farrington, Margaret Edwards, Herbert Standing, Vera Lewis, Roberta Hickman, Frank Elliott, Charles Marriott.
"Sunshine" Molly brightens the lives of oil town workers.

Sunshine Nan (Famous Players-Lasky/Paramount, 1918)
d: Charles Giblyn. 5 reels.
Ann Pennington, Richard Barthelmess, John Hines, Helen Tracy, Charles Eldridge, J.A. Furey, Alice Joy, Frank Losee.
Nan's a reform school grad who is nevertheless always cheerful. Dan, one of her former schoolmates, becomes a chemist and invents a formula that will make him rich... if he and Nan can keep another of their old mates from stealing it.

The Sunshine Trail (Thomas H. Ince/Associated First National, 1923)
d: James W. Horne. 5 reels.
Douglas MacLean, William Courtright, Josephine Sedgwick, Barney Furey, Muriel Frances Dana, Rex Cherryman, Albert Hart, Edith Roberts.
A war veteran returns to his home town to renew acquaintances, but because he was mistakenly reported killed in action, the folks there have him arrested as an impostor.

The Super Sex (Frank R. Adams Productions/American Releasing Corp., 1922)

d: Lambert Hillyer. 6 reels.
Robert Gordon, Charlotte Pierce, Tully Marshall, Lydia Knott, Gertrude Claire, Albert MacQuarrie, Louis Natheaux, George Bunny, Evelyn Burns.
Small-town boy Miles has his constancy tested when a sharpster from the big city puts the moves on his sweetheart, and she seems to respond positively.

Super Speed (Harry J. Brown Productions/Rayart, 1925)
d: Albert Rogell. 5 reels.
Reed Howes, Mildred Harris, Charles Clary, Sheldon Lewis, Martin Turner, George Williams.
Pat, who's wealthy but prefers to work as a milkman, discovers that his girlfriend's inventor dad has developed a new supercharger for automobiles. Pat enters a big race using a car equipped with the new invention and, despite dirty work by villainous rivals, drives to victory.

The Supreme Passion (Robert W. Priest/Playgoers Pictures, 1921)
d: Samuel Bradley. 6 reels.
Robert Adams, William Mortimer, Daniel Kelly, Mrs. Charles Willard, George Fox, Cecil Owen, Florence Dixon, Madelyn Clare, Selmer Jackson, Edward Keane.
A misalliance is prevented when a bride's veil catches fire and her doctor reports that she has suffered disfiguring burns to her face, thus scaring off her cad of an intended groom. But the bride's long-suffering ex-fiancé still wants her, scars and all, and is delighted when on their wedding day she reveals that her burns were not as bad as reported.

The Supreme Sacrifice (Premo Film Corp./World Film Corp., 1916)
d: Harley Knoles, Lionel Belmore. 5 reels.
Robert Warwick, Vernon Steele, Anna Q. Nilsson, Christine Mayo, Jessie Lewis, Robert Forsyth, Dion Titherage.
Weepy melodrama about David, a struggling writer, who is stunned to learn that his friend and minister, Reverend Philip, has been embezzling church funds. When Philip dies, David valiantly takes the blame for the missing money in order to save Philip's reputation. He is convicted and sentenced to several years in jail, years that mold his outlook on life and make him a better writer.
This film is based on Leroy Scott's play *To Him That Hath*, and is also known under that title. Another film version of Scott's play was produced in 1918 by World Film Corp. under the title *To Him That Hath*.

The Supreme Temptation (Vitagraph, 1916)
d: Harry Davenport. 5 reels.
Antonio Moreno, Charles Kent, Mary Maurice, Dorothy Kelly, Kate Davenport, Evart Overton, Jack Brawn, Templar Saxe, Daniel Leighton, Marguerite Blake, John Robertson, Frank Brule.
In Paris, an American medical student goes on a spree and winds up married to a street girl. He returns home, hoping that his memory of the incident was only a bad dream. But no, his young bride is very real, and she follows him to America.

The Supreme Test (Universal, 1915)
d: Edward J. LeSaint. 5 reels.
Henrietta Crosman, Wyndham Standing, Stella Razeto, Adele Farrington, Jack Wilson, Sylvia Ashton.
A wealthy widow tries to help the poor and needy. Little does she realize, she will soon be one of them.

Sure Fire (Universal, 1921)

d: Jack Ford. 5 reels.
Hoot Gibson, Molly Malone, Fritzi Brunette, B. Reeves Eason Jr., Murdock McQuarrie, George Fisher, Charles Newton.
A vagabond cowboy rescues his sweetheart from outlaws.

Sure Fire Flint (Mastodon Films, 1922)
d: Dell Henderson. 7 reels.
Johnny Hines, Edmund Breese, Robert Edeson, Effie Shannon, Barney Sherry, Doris Kenyon, Charles Gerard.
Flint, an effervescent young man, loves the boss' daughter but nearly despairs of winning her heart. One day, though, the firm is robbed and the girl gets locked in the safe... and it's up to Flint to rescue her.

Surrender (Universal, 1927)
d: Edward Sloman. 8 reels.
Mary Philbin, Ivan Mosjukine, Otto Matieson, Nigel DeBrulier, Otto Fries, Daniel Makarenko.
During World War I, a Jewish girl falls in love with a Russian prince.

Susan Rocks the Boat (Triangle/Fine Arts, 1916)
d: Paul Powell. 5 reels.
Owen Moore, Dorothy Gish, Kate Bruce, Fred A. Turner, Fred J. Butler, Clyde E. Hopkins, Edwin Harley, James O'Shea.
A wealthy woman is inspired by her idol, Joan of Arc, to open a mission in the slums.

Susan's Gentleman (Universal, 1917)
d: Edwin Stevens. 5 reels.
Violet Mersereau, Maud Cooling, Sidney Mason, James O'Neill, William O'Neill, Bradley Barker.
Though raised in a New York slum, Susan is an heiress to the English nobility.

Susie Snowflake (Paramount, 1916)
d: James Kirkwood. 5 reels.
Ann Pennington, Leo Delaney, William Courtleigh Jr., William J. Butler, Marcia Harris, Billie Wilson.
Susie, a vivacious country girl, yearns for a dancing career on the stage.
First feature film appearance for former Ziegfeld showgirl Ann Pennington.

The Suspect (Vitagraph, 1916)
d: S. Rankin Drew. 5 reels.
Anita Stewart, S. Rankin Drew, Anders Randolf, George Cooper, Frank Wupperman, Edward Elkas, Julia Swayne Gordon, Bobby Connelly, Al Rabock, Anna Brody.
Prince Paul of Russia falls in love with a girl who's actually a revolutionary sworn to overthrow the monarchy.

Suspense (Screencraft Pictures, Inc./Picture Finance Corp., 1919)
d: Frank Reicher. 6 reels.
Mollie King, Howard Truesdell, Izeth Munro, Harris Gordon, Isabel O'Madigan, Frank Stefansky.
Ruth, daughter of a disgraced admiral, plans to exonerate her father from charges of treason by following leads that take her into the den of the real traitors.

Suspicion (M.H. Hoffman Co., 1918)
d: M.H. Hoffman. 6 reels.
Grace Davison, Warren Cook, Wilmuth Merkyl, Mathilde Brundage, Ama Dore, John O'Keefe.
During World War I, an aircraft executive invites his nephew to share his home. But soon gossips are spreading rumors about the nephew and the executive's lovely wife.

Suspicious Wives (Trojan Pictures/World Film Corp., 1921)
d: John M. Stahl. 6 reels.
H.J. Herbert, Mollie King, Ethel Grey Terry, Rod LaRocque, Gertrude Berkeley, Frank DeCamp, Warren Cook.
Molly, a new bride, leaves her husband abruptly when she finds him alone with another woman. But the other woman is really her husband's sister-in-law, and their meeting was completely innocent.

Suzanna (Mack Sennett/United Artists, 1923)
d: F. Richard Jones. 8 reels.
Mabel Norman, George Nichols, Walter McGrail, Carolyn Sherman, Leon Barry, Eric Mayne, Winifred Bryson, Carl Stockdale, Lon Poff, George Cooper, Minnie Ha Ha, Black Hawk.
In Old California, a peasant girl loves a wealthy rancher and he loves her... much to his father's chagrin.

The Swamp (Hayakawa Feature Play Co./R-C Pictures, 1921)
d: Colin Campbell. 6 reels.
Sessue Hayakawa, Bessie Love, Janice Wilson, Frankie Lee, Lillian Langdon, Harland Tucker, Ralph McCullough.
In a big-city slum, a deserted wife and her young son face hardship and cruelty. As they are about to be evicted from their humble home, Wang, a Chinese peddler, takes a liking to the pair and helps them through several trying circumstances.

The Swan (Paramount, 1925)
d: Dimitri Buchowetzki. 6 reels.
Frances Howard, Adolphe Menjou, Ricardo Cortez, Ida Waterman, Helen Lindroth, Helen Lee Worthing, Joseph Depew, George Walcott, Michael Visaroff.
A prince and a princess are being forced into an arranged marriage that neither of them wants. Surreptitiously, each of them initiates a flirtation with someone else.

Swat the Spy (Fox, 1918)
d: Arvid E. Gillstrom. 5 reels.
Jane Lee, Katherine Lee, Charles Slattery, P.C. Hartigan, Florence Ashbrooke.
Comedy of errors centering on World War I days, in which a busy inventor inadvertently hires servants who are German spies. The spies mean to steal a priceless potion their boss is working on, but after several misadventures his two lively daughters liberate the formula from the spies and save the day.

Sweet Adeline (Chadwick Pictures, 1926)
d: Jerome Storm. 7 reels.
Charles Ray, Gertrude Olmstead, Jack Clifford, John P. Lockney, Sibyl Johnston, Gertrude Short, Ida Lewis.

Two small-town brothers are rivals for the affections of Adeline, a neighbor girl.

Sweet Alyssum (Selig Polyscope, 1915)
d: Colin Campbell. 5 reels.
Tyrone Power, Kathlyn Williams, Edith Johnson, Wheeler Oakman, Frank Clark, Harry Lonsdale, Gene Frazer.
Wynne, a bank clerk whose meager salary cannot satisfy his extravagant wife's cravings, finds that she has left him for another man. The irony is that Wynne's own father had the same fate befall him, years earlier.

Sweet Daddies (First National, 1926)
d: Alfred Santell. 7 reels.

George Sidney, Charlie Murray, Vera Gordon, Jobyna Ralston, Jack Mulhall, Gaston Glass, Aggie Herring.

After being arrested on suspicion of bootlegging liquor, O'Brien and Finklebaum are released when they reveal that their "contraband" is really molasses.

Sweet Kitty Bellairs (Lasky Feature Plays/Paramount, 1916)
d: James Young. 5 reels.
Mae Murray, Tom Forman, Belle Bennett, Lucille Young, Joseph King, James Neill, Lucille Lavarney, Horace B. Carpenter, Robert Gray.
Kitty's an Irish flirt who is loved by two regiments in World War I.

Sweet Lavender (Realart, 1920)
d: Paul Powell. 5 reels.
Mary Miles Minter, Milton Sills, Harold Goodwin, Jame Watson, Theodore Roberts, Sylvia Ashton, J.M. Dumont, Stark Patterson, Jane Keckley, Flora Hollister.
Clem, a college freshman, falls in love with Lavender, his landlady's niece. Clem's status-conscious guardian tries to break up the romance on grounds of class differences, but changes his tune when it is discovered that he is, in fact, Lavender's long-lost father.

Sweet Rosie O'Grady (Columbia, 1926)
d: Frank Strayer. 7 reels.
Shirley Mason, E. Alyn Warren, William Conklin, Cullen Landis, Lester Bernard, Otto Lederer.
Rosie, an orphan girl with working-class guardians, is wooed by a young man of the upper crust.

Sweet Sixteen (Trem Carr Productions/Rayart, 1928)
d: Scott Pembroke. 6 reels.
Helen Foster, Gertrude Olmstead, Gladden James, Lydia Yeamans Titus, Reginald Sheffield, William H. Tooker, Harry Allen, Carolynne Snowden.
To save her younger sister from the cad who's been romancing her, Patricia risks scandal by going to the man's apartment and asking him to give her up.

Sweetheart of the Doomed (New York Motion Picture Corp./Triangle, 1917)
d: Reginald Barker. 5 reels.
Louise Glaum, Charles Gunn, Thomas Guise, Roy Laidlaw.
During World War I, an embittered young woman has her faith restored by the love of Paul, a young soldier. She follows him to the front as a Red Cross nurse and is privileged to attend to his wounds when he is injured in battle.

The Swell-Head (Columbia, 1927)
d: Ralph Graves. 6 reels.
Ralph Graves, Mildred Harris, Johnnie Walker, Mary Carr, Eugenia Gilbert, Tom Dugan.
Lefty Malone, part owner of a moving business, is mistaken for a prizefighter and sent into the ring.

Swim, Girl, Swim (Paramount, 1927)
d: Clarence Badger. 7 reels.
Bebe Daniels, James Hall, Gertrude Ederle, Josephine Dunn, William Austin, James Mack.
Alice, a college wallflower who craves the excitements of an athletic career, enters a channel swimming race.

Sylvia on a Spree (Metro, 1918)
d: Harry L. Franklin. 5 reels.
Emmy Wehlen, W.I. Percival, Frank Currier, Eugene Acker,

Peggy Parr, Isabel O'Madigan, Rose Wood, Bliss Milford, Francesca Ward, Alice Turner, Stephie Anderson.
Society comedy about Sylvia, a naive girl who wishes to visit the infamous Beaulieu Inn, source of many scandals.

The Symbol of the Unconquered (Micheaux Film Corp., 1920)
w, d: Oscar Micheaux. 8 reels.
Iris Hall, Walker Thompson, Lawrence Chenault, Jim Burris, Mattie Wilkes, E.G. Tatum, Leigh Whipper, James Burroush, George Catlin.
Hugh, a black fortune hunter, becomes involved with a young light-skinned Alabama woman he thinks is white.

Syncopating Sue (Corinne Griffith Productions/First National, 1926)
d: Richard Wallace. 7 reels.
Corinne Griffith, Tom Moore, Rockliffe Fellowes, Lee Moran, Joyce Compton, Sunshine Hart, Marjorie Rambeau.
Susan, a promising pianist, yearns for a role in a stage show.

Synthetic Sin (First National, 1929)
d: William A. Seiter. 7 reels.
Colleen Moore, Antonio Moreno, Edythe Chapman, Kathryn McGuire, Gertrude Howard, Gertrude Astor, Raymond Turner, Montague Love, Ben Hendricks Jr., Phil Sleeman.
A famous playwright tells his leading lady she is too unsophisticated to be a success on the stage. Her response? To move into a neighborhood crawling with lowlifes and try to learn their wicked ways.

Tabu (Paramount, 1931)
w,d: F. W. Murnau, Robert Flaherty. 8 reels.
A quasi-documentary with no stars, *Tabu* tells about South Sea life and customs.

A Tailor Made Man (United Artists, 1922)
d: Joseph DeGrasse. 9 reels.
Charles Ray, Ethel Grandin, Irene Lentz, Jacqueline Logan, Thomas Ricketts, Victor Potel, Frank Butler, Stanton Heck, Edythe Chapman, Frederick Thompson, Kate Lester.
A humble tailor's assistant tries to pass himself off as a society swell.

Tainted Money (Columbia, 1924)
d: Henry MacRae. 5 reels.
William Fairbanks, Eva Novak, Bruce Gordon, Edwards Davis, Carl Stockdale, Paul Weigel, Frank Clark.
Feuding lumber tycoons find that their children have fallen in love.

Take It From Me (Universal, 1926)
d: William A. Seiter. 7 reels.
Reginald Denny, Blanche Mehaffey, Ben Hendricks Jr., Lee Moran, Lucien Littlefield, Ethel Wales, Bertram Johns, Jean Tolley, Tom O'Brien, Vera Lewis.
A young man stands to inherit a department store on the condition that he operate it for three months at a profit. The store's manager has his own designs on the business, however, and schemes to sabotage the potential heir's efforts.

Take Me Home (Paramount, 1928)
d: Marshall Neilan. 6 reels.
Bebe Daniels, Neil Hamilton, Lilyan Tashman, Doris Hill, Joe E. Brown, Ernie Wood, Marcia Harris, Yvonne Howell, Janet MacLeod, J.W. Johnston.
Peggy, a chorus girl, brawls with the show's leading lady and renders her *hors de combat*. Now Peggy must carry the

show by herself... and she's an instant hit.

Taking Chances (Phil Goldstone Productions, 1922)
d: Grover Jones. 5 reels.
Richard Talmadge, Zella Gray, Elmer Dewey, Percy Challenger.
Richard, a book salesman, foils a plot to take over the business empire of his sweetheart's father.

Taking the Count — see: The Servant Question (1920)

A Tale of Two Cities (Fox, 1917)
d: Frank Lloyd. 7 reels.
William Farnum, Florence Vidor, Herschell Mayall, Rosita Marstini, Joseph Swickard, Mark Robbins, Jewel Carmen, Charles Clary, Ralph Lewis, William Clifford, Olive White, Willard Louis, Harry DeVere.

Epic film based on Charles Dickens' 1859 novel about love and self-sacrifice during the French Revolution. Farnum does double duty here, in the roles of Charles Darnay and Sydney Carton. When Darnay is condemned to the guillotine by the rebel court, his lookalike friend Carton switches places with him so that Darnay and his lady love, Lucie, can escape together.
 A three-reel version of *A Tale of Two Cities* featuring Maurice Costello was filmed by Vitagraph in 1911.

A Tale of Two Worlds (Goldwyn, 1921)
d: Frank Lloyd. 6 reels.
J. Frank Glendon, Leatrice Joy, Wallace Beery, E.A. Warren, Margaret McWade, Togo Yamamoto, Jack Abbe, Louie Cheune, Chow Young, Etta Lee.
A young white girl is raised as Chinese after the death of her parents in China.

The Talk of the Town (Universal, 1918)
d: Allen Holubar. 6 reels.
Dorothy Phillips, William Stowell, Lon Chaney, George Fawcett, Clarissa Selwynne, Gloria Joy, Una Fleming, Charles Hill Mailes, ZaSu Pitts, William Burgess, George Lewis.
To cure his new bride of her flirtatious habits, Lawrence hires a notorious playboy to romance the young woman and then break her heart.

The Talker (First National, 1925)
d: Alfred E. Green. 8 reels.
Anna Q. Nilsson, Lewis S. Stone, Shirley Mason, Ian Keith, Tully Marshall, Barbara Bedford, Harold Goodwin, Gertrude Short, Lydia Yeamans Titus, Cecille Evans, E.H. Calvert.
Early feminist tale about a wife who beats the drum for women's rights.

The Taming of the West (Universal, 1925)
d: Arthur Rosson. 6 reels.
Hoot Gibson, Morgan Brown, Marceline Day, Edwin Booth Tilton, Herbert Prior, Louise Hippe, Albert J. Smith, Francis Ford, Frona Hale.
Carleton, an eastern tenderfoot, goes West and wins the respect of the cowpokes by taming a bucking bronco.

Tangled Fates (World Film Corp., 1916)
d: Travers Vale. 5 reels.
Alice Brady, Arthur Ashley, Helen Weer, George Morgan, Ed Kimball, Alec Francis, Doris Sawyer, Albert Hart.
Jane, a department store mannequin, marries the boss' son but lives to regret it.

Tangled Hearts (Universal, 1916)
d: Joseph DeGrasse. 5 reels.
Louise Lovely, Agnes Vernon, Lon Chaney, Marjorie Ellison, Haywood Mack, Jay Belasco, Georgia French, Bud Chase.
When Hammond, a businessman, discovers evidence that seems to indicate his wife has been having an affair with his friend Monty, there's the devil to pay. But Monty isn't guilty of adultery, just imprudence... and now he'll have to explain to his own wife, as well.

Tangled Lives (Fox, 1917)
d: J. Gordon Edwards. 5 reels.
Genevieve Hamper, Stuart Holmes, Robert B. Mantell, Walter Miller, Henry Leone, Claire Whitney, Genevieve Blinn, Louise Rial, Millicent Liston, William Gerald.
Laura and Anne are half-sisters who are almost identical in appearance. Alas, their lives are not ideal. Anne is confined to an asylum, while Laura is confined to an unhappy marriage.
Miss Hamper does double duty here, portraying both sisters.

Tangled Lives (Vitagraph, 1918)
d: Paul Scardon. 5 reels.
Harry T. Morey, Betty Blythe, Jean Paige, Albert Roccardi, George Majeroni, Eulalie Jensen, Charles Kent.
When a jealous husband is informed — erroneously — that his wife is having an affair, he confronts his supposed rival and winds up in jail on a charge of assault.

Tangled Threads (B.B. Features/Robertson-Cole, 1919)
d: Howard C. Hickman. 5 reels.
Bessie Barriscale, Rosemary Theby, Nigel Barrie, Henry Kolker, Thomas Holding, Ben Alexander, Mary Jane Irving.
Convoluted melodrama about John, who leaves his wife and child to marry a frivolous adventuress, and their good friend Philip, who tries to help mend the rift but unintentionally complicates their lives even further.

The Tar Heel Warrior (Triangle, 1917)
d: E. Mason Hopper. 5 reels.
Walt Whitman, Ann Kroman, William Shaw, James W. McLaughlin, Dorcas Matthews, George West, Clara Knight, John P. Lockney, Wilbur Higby, Thomas S. Guise.
A proud Southern colonel tries to save his heavily mortgaged plantation from foreclosure.

The Tarantula (Vitagraph, 1916)
d: George D. Baker. 5 reels.
 Edith Storey, Antonio Moreno, Charles Kent, Eulalie Jensen, L. Rogers Lytton, Harry Hollingsworth, Emmanuel A. Turner, Raymond Walburn, Harold Foshay, Gordon Gray, Templar Saxe.
Steele, a New Yorker and a married man, goes to Cuba and has an affair with one of the local girls. When the girl is discovered pregnant, her family throws her out and she is forced to work in a seedy Havana night club, a job that eventually leads to a New York engagement and a reunion with her betrayer.

The Target (Universal, 1916)
d: Norval MacGregor. 5 reels.
Hobart Bosworth, Anna Lehr, Maud George, Ronald Bradbury, Dick LeReno, Jane Novak, Albert MacQuarrie.
Convicted for a murder he did not commit, Brent escapes from jail with his cellmate and makes a new life in Canada.

Tarnish (Goldwyn/Associated First National, 1924)
d: George Fitzmaurice. 7 reels.
May McAvoy, Ronald Colman, Marie Prevost, Albert Gran, Mrs. Russ Whytall, Priscilla Bonner, Harry Myers, Kay Deslys, Lydia Yeamans Titus, William Boyd, Snitz Edwards.

When a vampish manicurist takes a married man's money, his daughter storms the woman's apartment and demands she return it.

Tarnished Reputations (Perret Productions, Inc./Pathé, 1920)
d: Alice Blaché. 5 reels.
Dolores Cassinelli, Albert Roscoe, George Deneubourg, Ned Burton.
When an artist from the big city visits a small town and induces one of the local girls to pose for him, she takes their relationship to be one of affection. He, unfortunately, does not.

Tarzan and the Golden Lion (R-C Pictures/FBO of America, 1927)
d: J.P. McGowan. 6 reels.
James Pierce, Frederic Peters, Edna Murphy, Harold Goodwin, Liu Yu-Ching, Dorothy Dunbar, D'Arcy Corrigan, Boris Karloff, Robert Bolder.
In Africa, Lord Greystoke, aka Tarzan, greets a traveling party including his wife's niece Ruth Porter. When a renegade band of adventurers kidnap Ruth, Tarzan and his pet lion spring into action, and rescue her just before she is to be offered up in sacrifice to a false god.

Tarzan of the Apes (National Film Corp. of America, 1918)
d: Scott Sidney. 10 reels.
Elmo Lincoln, Enid Markey, Gordon Griffith, True Boardman, Kathleen Kirkham, George French, Thomas Jefferson, Bessie Toner, Jack Wilson, Colin Kenny, Fred L. Wilson.
First screen version of the famous Tarzan story, with the orphaned son of a British lord being raised in the African jungle by apes.

A Taste of Life (Universal, 1919)
d: Jack Dillon. 5 reels.
Edith Roberts, Billy Mason, George Hernandez, May Emory, Harry Todd.
Comedy about capricious Kitty, a girl who goes to work for her lawyer husband and gets involved in a divorce case he's working on.

The Tattlers (Fox, 1920)
d: Howard M. Mitchell. 5 reels.
Madlaine Traverse, Howard Scott, Jack Rollins, Ben Deely, Genevieve Blinn, Eleanor Hancock, Correan Kirkham, Frank Whitson, Edwin Booth Tilton.
Infuriated by the antics of her alcoholic husband, Bess leaves him for another man... but finds that her new lover has no intention of marrying her.

Taxi (Triangle, 1919)
d: Lawrence Windom. 5 reels.
Taylor Holmes, Irene Tams, Lillian Hall, Maude Eburne, Henry Sedley, Jane Jennings, Olive Trevor, Fred Tiden.
Robert, a taxi driver, rescues an heiress from being assaulted by her suitor and subsequently becomes vice-president of the taxi company.

The Taxi Dancer (MGM, 1926)
d: Harry Millarde. 7 reels.
Joan Crawford, Owen Moore, Marc MacDermott, Douglas Gilmore, Gertrude Astor, Rockcliffe Fellowes, William Orlamond, Claire McDowell, Bert Roach.
A taxi dancer loves a gigolo not wisely, but too well.

Taxi! Taxi! (Universal, 1927)

d: Melville W. Brown. 7 reels.
Edward Everett Horton, Marian Nixon, Burr McIntosh, Edward Martindel, William V. Mong, Lucien Littlefield, Freeman Wood.
Peter, a draftsman, falls in love with his boss' niece and they try to elope. He can't hire a taxi, though, so Peter impulsively *buys* one, not realizing it's a vehicle in which robbery and murder have been committed, and the police are still looking for it.

Taxi 13 (FBO Pictures, 1928)
d: Marshall Neilan. 7 reels. (Music, sound effects, part talkie.)
Chester Conklin, Ethel Wales, Martha Sleeper, Hugh Trevor, Lee Moran, Jerry Miley, Charles Byer.
Angus, an impecunious taxi driver with ten children, unwittingly aids a pair of safecrackers. When they are pursued by police, the crooks hide a priceless string of pearls in the lining of Angus' taxi. Fortunately for Angus, he later finds it, returns it to the police, and scores a nice reward of $5,000.

Tea for Three (MGM, 1927)
d: Robert Z. Leonard. 7 reels.
Lew Cody, Aileen Pringle, Owen Moore, Dorothy Sebastian, Phillips Smalley, Edward Thomas.
Comedy about the eternal triangle—in this case, Doris, her husband, and their friend Philip.

Tearing Through (Richard Talmadge Productions/FBO of America, 1925)
d: Arthur Rosson. 5 reels.
Richard Talmadge, Kathryn McGuire, Herbert Prior, Frank Elliott, Arthur Rankin, Marcella Daly, Dave Morris.
An assistant district attorney discovers that his girlfriend's brother is a drug addict, hooked on opium by the very gang the D.A. is trying to bring to justice.

Tears and Smiles (Lasalida Film Corp./Pathé, 1917)
d: William Bertram. 5 reels.
Baby Marie Osborne, Melvin Mayo, Marian Warner, Philo McCullough, Katherine MacLaren.
Marie, a runaway from a broken home, is adopted by a kindly millionaire. The plot thickens, however, when Marie's mother procures the job of governess in the millionaire's home, in order to be close to her own daughter.

The Teaser (Universal, 1925)
d: William A. Seiter. 7 reels.
Laura LaPlante, Pat O'Malley, Hedda Hopper, Walter McGrail, Byron Munson, Vivian Oakland, Wyndham Standing, Margaret Quimby, Frank Finch Smiles.
Ann, a shopgirl, finds herself in the unusual situation of having to reform *two* irksome acquaintances: her uptight aunt, and the frivolous young man that Ann is keen on.

Teeth (Fox, 1924)
d: John Blystone. 7 reels.
Tom Mix, Lucy Fox, George Bancroft, Edward Piel, Lucien Littlefield.
Out West, a prospector finds an injured dog—"Teeth"—that's been tossed from a moving train, and nurses it back to health.

The Teeth of the Tiger (Famous Players-Lasky/Paramount, 1919)
d: Chet Withey. 6 reels.
David Powell, Marguerite Courtot, Templar Saxe, Myrtle

Stedman, Joseph Herbert, Charles L. MacDonald, William Riley Hatch, Charles Gerard, Frederick Burton.
Reformed criminal Arsene Lupin assists in solving the murder of a wealthy friend.

The Telephone Girl (Paramount, 1927)
d: Herbert Brenon. 6 reels.
Madge Bellamy, Holbrook Blinn, Warner Baxter, May Allison, Lawrence Gray, Hale Hamilton, Hamilton Revelle, W.E. Shay, Karen Hansen.
Kitty, a telephone operator, foils a shady political scheme.

Tell it to Sweeney (Paramount, 1927)
d: Gregory LaCava. 6 reels.
Chester Conklin, George Bancroft, Jack Luden, Doris Hill, Franklin Bond, William H. Tooker.
Comedy about rival railroad engineers whose children are in love with each other.

Tell it to the Marines (Fox, 1918)
d: Arvid E. Gillstrom. 5 reels.
Jane Lee, Katherine Lee, Charles Slattery, Edward Bagley.
Trik and Trak are the fictional leaders of two great powers in a major war... but only in the imaginations of two impressionable young girls.

Tell it to the Marines (MGM, 1926)
d: George Hill. 9 reels.
Lon Chaney, William Haines, Eleanor Boardman, Carmel Myers, Warner Oland, Eddie Gribbon, Mitchell Lewis, Frank Currier, Maurice E. Kains.
A raw recruit is assigned to duty under a tough Marine sergeant.

The Tell-Tale Step (Thomas A. Edison, Inc., 1917)
d: Burton George. 5 reels.
Pat O'Malley, Shirley Mason, Guido Collucci, Charles Sutton, Bob Huggins, Nellie Grant, Bigelow Cooper, Sally Crute, Jessie Stevens, Leonora Von Ottinger, Grace Morrissey.
When a blind girl's father is murdered one fateful evening, she listens carefully to the cadence of the killer's walk. Her sight is later restored through an operation, but it is by the sound of his footsteps that she is able to identify her father's killer.

Telling the World (MGM, 1928)
d: Sam Wood. 8 reels.
William Haines, Anita Page, Eileen Percy, Polly Moran, Frank Currier, Bert Roach, William V. Mong, Matthew Betz.
Comedy about a struggling reporter who manages to wow the world with two sensational stories.

A Temperamental Wife (Constance Talmadge Film Co./First National, 1919)
d: David Kirkland. 6 reels.
Constance Talmadge, Wyndham Standing, Ben Hendricks, Eulalie Jensen, Armand Kaliz, Ned Sparks.
Temperamental is the word for Billie. She marries a senator, then when she learns that his secretary is an attractive female, Billie wants her fired.

Tempered Steel (Petrova Pictures Co./First National, 1918)
d: Ralph Ince. 5 reels.
Olga Petrova, J. Herbert Frank, Thomas Holding, William Carleton, Edith Hinckle, E.J. Radcliffe, Matilda Brundage, Lucille LaVerne.
Lucille, a Southern girl, goes to New York to make a name for herself on the dramatic stage. She becomes a star, but finds it's a mixed blessing when a fiercely jealous actor threatens to throw acid in her face before a performance.

Tempest (United Artists, 1928)
d: Sam Taylor.   10 reels.   (Synchronized music and sound effects.)
John Barrymore, Camilla Horn, Louis Wolheim, Boris De Fas, George Fawcett, Ulrich Haupt.
A Russian army officer loves his princess, but she scorns him and has him demoted. Come the Revolution, the tables are turned.

The Temple of Dusk (Haworth Pictures Corp./Mutual, 1918)
d: James Young. 5 reels.
Sessue Hayakawa, Jane Novak, Lewis Willoughby, Mary Jane Irving, Sylvia Bremer, Henry Barrows.
Akira, a Japanese poet, dedicates his life to caring for the little American girl born to the now-deceased woman Akira loved.

The Temple of Venus (Fox, 1923)
d: Henry Otto. 7 reels.
William Walling, Mary Philbin, Mickey McBan, Alice Day, David Butler, William Boyd, Phyllis Haver, Leon Barry, Celeste Lee, Robert Klein, Marilyn Boyd, Frank Keller, Helen Vigil.
Fantasy about the goddess Venus and her emissary, Cupid, who visits earth to see if true love still exists.

Temporary Marriage (Sacramento Pictures/Principal Pictures, 1923)
d: Lambert Hillyer. 7 reels.
Kenneth Harlan, Mildred Davis, Myrtle Stedman, Tully Marshall, Maude George, Stuart Holmes, Edward Coxen.
A callous woman becomes bored with her husband, a lawyer, and decides to divorce him. But she'll need his professional services—and soon.

Temptation (Lasky Feature Plays/Paramount, 1915)
d: Cecil B. DeMille. 5 reels.
Geraldine Farrar, Pedro DeCordoba, Theodore Roberts, Elsie Jane Wilson, Raymond Hatton, Anita King, Ernest Joy, Sessue Hayakawa.
Renée, a beautiful opera singer, is fired by her impresario after she refuses to yield to his sexual advances. But later, when the man she loves falls ill and needs medical attention, Renée returns to the lecherous producer to reconsider his offer.

Temptation (Columbia, 1923)
d: Edward J. LeSaint. 7 reels.
Eva Novak, Phillips Smalley, Bryant Washburn, June Elvidge, Vernon Steele.
A stockbroker concocts a theory that most women are corrupted by wealth... but proving his theory is tricky.

Temptation and the Man (Universal, 1916)
d: Robert F. Hill. 5 reels.
Hobart Henley, Sydell Dowling, Sidney Bracy, Bert Busby, Joseph Granby, Clara Beyers.
Determined to go straight after doing a stretch in prison, a reformed pickpocket finds himself involved in a crooked poker game. This time he finds that his light-fingered talents will come in handy—for a good cause.

Temptations of a Shop Girl (Chadwick Pictures/First Division Pictures, 1927)
d: Tom Terriss. 6 reels.

Betty Compson, Pauline Garon, Armand Kaliz, Raymond Glenn, William Humphreys, Cora Williams, Gladden James, John Francis Dillon.

Ruth, a self-sacrificing sort, takes the rap when her younger sister commits a crime.

The Temptress (MGM, 1926)
d: Fred Niblo. (Work commenced by Mauritz Stiller.) 9 reels.

Antonio Moreno, Greta Garbo, H.B. Warner, Lionel Barrymore, Roy D'Arcy, Marc McDermott, Virginia Brown Faire, Armand Kaliz, Alys Murrell, Robert Anderson, Hector V. Sarno, Roy Coulson.

A corrupt woman preys on men and drives them to disgrace and suicide.

The Ten Commandments (FamousPlayers-Lasky/Paramount, 1923)
d: Cecil B. DeMille. 10 reels. (Technicolor sequence.)

Theodore Roberts, Richard Dix, Rod La Rocque, Edythe Chapman, Leatrice Joy, Nita Naldi, Charles de Roche, Estelle Taylor, Julia Faye, Richard Dix, Agnes Ayres.

The famous story of Moses is retold, but with a DeMille twist: a modern sequence with many of the 1920s' references paralleling the Old Testament story.

The Ten Dollar Raise (J.L. Frothingham/Associated Producers, 1921)
d: Edward Sloman. 6 reels.

William V. Mong, Marguerite De La Motte, Pat O'Malley, Helen Jerome Eddy, Hal Cooley, Lincoln Plumer, Charles Hill Mailes.

A lowly bookkeeper is often promised a raise in salary, but it never happens. Finally the boss' conniving son unloads some swamp land on the gullible bookkeeper—but he strikes oil under all that mud, and becomes wealthy enough to buy the company he's been working for.

Ten Modern Commandments (Paramount, 1927)
d: Dorothy Arzner. 7 reels.

Esther Ralston, Neil Hamilton, Maude Truax, Romaine Fielding, El Brendel, Rose Burdick, Jocelyn Lee, Arthur Hoyt, Roscoe Karns.

Comedy about Kitten, a housemaid who falls for a struggling songwriter, and winds up singing his latest song in a new Broadway show.

Ten Nights in a Bar Room (Blazed Trail Productions/Arrow Film Corp., 1921)
d: Oscar Apfel. 8 reels.

Baby Ivy Ward, John Lowell, Neil Clarke Keller, Charles Mackay, James Phillips, Ethel Dwyer, Charles Beyer, John Woodford, Kempton Greene, Mrs. Thomas Ward, Harry Fisher, Lillian Kemble, J. Norman Wells.

When a new saloon opens near a logging camp, Morgan, a lumberman, starts drinking to excess. Eventually his new addiction will cost him not only his job but also the life of his daughter, Little Mary. When she comes to the saloon to implore her dad to come home, a thrown beer bottle hits and kills her.

Ten of Diamonds (Triangle, 1917)
d: Raymond B. West. 5 reels.

Dorothy Dalton, Jack Livingston, J. Barney Sherry, Dorcas Matthews, Billy Shaw.

Neva, a hardened cabaret performer, is hired by Warren to entice his rival and make him fall in love with her. The plan is for her to marry her victim and then humiliate him, but instead Neva, now schooled in the social graces, falls for Warren.

The Tender Hour (John McCormick Productions/First National, 1927)
d: George Fitzmaurice. 8 reels.

Billie Dove, Ben Lyon, Montagu Love, Alec B. Francis, Constantine Romanoff, Laska Winter, T. Roy Barnes, George Kotsonaros, Charles A. Post, Anders Randolph, Lionel Belmore.

In Paris, a wealthy American girl is forced to marry an expatriate Russian duke, though she loves another man.

The Tenderfoot (Vitagraph, 1917)
d: William Duncan. 5 reels.

William Duncan, Carol Halloway, Joe Ryan, Florence Dye, Walter L. Rodgers, Charles Wheelock, Hattie Buskirk, Fred Forrester.

Jim, an eastern tenderfoot, goes West and falls for Cynthia, a local girl.

Tenderloin (Warner Bros., 1928)
d: Michael Curtiz. 8 reels. (Part talkie.)

Dolores Costello, Conrad Nagel, Georgie Stone, Mitchell Lewis, Dan Wolheim, Pat Hartigan, Fred Kelsey, G. Raymond Nye, Evelyn Pierce, Dorothy Vernon, John Miljan.

Rose, a cabaret dancer, falls in love with a "reformed" bank robber—but there's still one more job for his gang to pull.

Tennessee's Partner (Lasky Feature Plays/Paramount, 1916)
d: George Melford. 5 reels.

Fannie Ward, Jack Dean, Charles Clary, Jesse Arnold, Raymond Hatton, James Neill.

Tennessee, a convent-bred girl, heads West by stagecoach to be with her guardian. En route, however, the stagecoach is held up by the same outlaw who killed Tennessee's father, years before. Now that the girl is grown, the outlaw lusts after her... but he must deal with her faithful guardian, who arrives on the scene just in time.

Tenth Avenue (DeMille Studio Productions/Pathé, 1928)
d: William C. DeMille. 7 reels.

Phyllis Haver, Victor Varconi, Joseph Schildkraut, Louis Natheaux, Robert Edeson, Ethel Wales, Casson Ferguson, Ernie S. Adams.

Lyla, manager of a Tenth Avenue rooming house, is desired by two of her tenants.

The Tenth Woman (Warner Bros., 1924)
d: James Flood. 7 reels.

John Roche, Beverly Bayne, June Marlowe, Raymond McKee, Alec B. Francis, Charles "Buddy" Post, Gilbert Holmes, Edith Yorke.

A rancher's marriage is threatened by the arrival of his former sweetheart.

The Terror (Universal, 1917)
d: Raymond Wells. 5 reels.

Jack Mulhall, Grace MacLean, Virginia Lee, Malcolm Blevins, Hugh Hoffman, Noble Johnson, Jean Hersholt, Evelyn Selbie.

Prodded by an adorable little girl, a gunman decides to end his life of crime.

The Terror (Fox, 1920)
d: Jacques Jaccard. 5 reels.

Tom Mix, Francelia Billington, Lester Cuneo, Charles K. French, Lucille Younge, Joseph Bennett, Wilbur Higby.

Carson, a deputy U.S. marshal, battles thieves intent on hijacking gold shipments.

The Terror   (Universal, 1926)
d: Clifford Smith.   5 reels.
Art Acord, Velma Connor, Dudley Hendricks, C.E. Anderson, Edmund Cobb, Jess Deffenbach, Hank Bell.
Working undercover, a Texas Ranger foils a gang headed by an Arizona bandit known as "the Terror."

Terror Island   (Famous Players-Lasky/Paramount, 1920)
d: James Cruze.   5 reels.
Houdini, Jack Brammall, Lila Lee, Wilton Taylor, Eugene Pallette, Edward Brady, Frank Bonner, Ted E. Duncan, Fred Turner, Rosemary Theby.
Adventure-mystery involving a girl, her kidnapped father, and an underwater engineer named Harper who rescues them both from South Sea natives.

Tess of the D'Urbervilles   (Famous Players, 1913)
d: J. Searle Dawley.   5 reels.
Minnie Maddern Fiske, Raymond Bond, David Torrence, John Steppling, Mary Barker, James Gordon, Maggie Weston, Irma LaPierre, Katherine Griffith, Franklin Hall, Camille Dalberg, Boots Wall, Caroline Darling, Justina Huff, John Troughton.
Tess, a dairy worker who's been abandoned by her husband, seeks the protection of Alec, her distant relative. But the brutal Alec seduces the girl as part of the "bargain."

Tess of the d'Urbervilles   (MGM, 1924)
d: Marshall Neilan.   8 reels.
Blanche Sweet, Conrad Nagel, Stuart Holmes, George Fawcett, Victory Bateman, Courtenay Foote, Joseph J. Dowling.
A servant girl is seduced by the master of the house.
Remake of the 1913 Famous Players film *Tess of the d'Urbervilles*, both versions based on the Thomas Hardy novel of the same name.

Tess of the Storm Country   (Pickford/United Artists, 1922)
d: John S. Robertson. 10 reels.
Mary Pickford, Lloyd Hughes, David Torrence, Forrest Robinson, Jean Hersholt, Gloria Hope, Danny Hoy, Robert Russell, Gus Saville.
A fisherman's daughter falls in love with the son of a wealthy landowner, but he rejects her when he believes she has had a child out of wedlock.
Miss Pickford reprises her role from the 1914 production of the same name.

Tessie   (Arrow Pictures, 1925)
d: Dallas M. Fitzgerald.   7 reels.
May McAvoy, Bobby Agnew, Lee Moran, Myrtle Stedman, Gertrude Short, Mary Gordon, Frank Perry.
Tessie, a tobacconist, falls for a scion of wealth. But his mother disapproves, and even offers to pay Tessie to back off.

The Test   (Astra Film Corp./Pathé, 1916)
d: George Fitzmaurice.   5 reels.
Jane Grey, Lumsden Hare, Claude Fleming, Carl Harbaugh, Inez Buck, Ida Darling.
To avoid his prosecuting her husband for suspected fraud, happily married Emma is forced to accept a lecherous banker's sexual advances.

The Test of Donald Norton   (Chadwick Pictures, 1926)
d: B. Reeves Eason.   7 reels.

George Walsh, Tyrone Power, Robert Graves, Eugenie Gilbert, Evelyn Selbie, Mickey Moore, True Boardman, Virginia Marshall, Jack Dillon.
Donald Norton, a halfbreed, grows up in the home of a kindly white couple and becomes manager of a fur trading post. When he receives a promotion and is reassigned, the new district manager takes an instant, unexplained disliking for Donald. Though neither man realizes it at the time, the district manager is Donald's real father.

The Test of Honor   (Famous Players-Lasky/Paramount, 1919)
d: John S. Robertson.   5 reels.
John Barrymore, Constance Binney, Marcia Manon, Robert Schable, J.W. Johnson, Bigelow Cooper, Ned Hay, Alma Aiken, Fred Miller.
When Martin, a wealthy Southerner, falls in love with a married woman, her husband finds them together, and the two men fight, resulting in the death of the husband. Martin is convicted of manslaughter, and has seven long years in prison to decide whether he wants to pursue his relationship with his former lover or return to Juliet, his worshipful neighbor.

The Testing Block   (Paramount, 1920)
w, d: Lambert Hillyer.   6 reels.
William S. Hart, Eva Novak, Gordon Russell, Florence Carpenter, Richard Headrick, Ira McFadden.
"Sierra" Bill, leader of an outlaw gang, falls for a violinist in a touring stage show.

The Testing of Mildred Vane   (Metro, 1918)
d: Wilfred Lucas.   5 reels.
May Allison, Darrell Foss, George Field, Nigel DeBrulier, Fred Goodwins.
A lovelorn schemer tries to avenge himself against the family of a woman who once rejected him.

The Texan   (Fox, 1920)
d: Lynn F. Reynolds.   5 reels.
Tom Mix, Gloria Hope, Robert Walker, Charles K. French, Sid Jordan, Pat Chrisman.
A cowpoke falls for a charming young woman from back east.

A Texas Steer   (Selig Polyscope, 1915)
d: Giles R. Warren.   5 reels.
Tyrone Power, Grace Darmond, Francis Bayless, John Charles, Mrs. Tyrone Power, Walter Roberts, Frank Weed.
Comedic tale about a Texas cattle baron who gets elected to Congress without really wanting to.
Another version of this story was filmed in 1927 by Sam E. Rork Productions, with Will Rogers in the lead.

A Texas Steer   (Sam E. Rork Productions/First National, 1927)
d: Richard Wallace.   8 reels.
Will Rogers, Louise Fazenda, Sam Hardy, ann Rork, Douglas Fairbanks Jr., Lilyan Tashman, George Marion Sr., Bud Jamieson, Arthur Hoyt, Mack Swain, William Orlamond, Lucien Littlefield.
Maverick Brander, an easygoing Texas rancher, would like to see a dam built to facilitate his cattle drives. When his hard-driving wife, daughter, and friends get on the case, Brander winds up elected to Congress before he knows what's hit him.
Remake of the 1915 Selig film *A Texas Steer*, both versions based on the play of the same name by Charles Hale Hoyt.

496

The Texas Streak (Universal, 1926)
d: Lynn Reynolds. 7 reels.
Hoot Gibson, Blanche Mehaffey, Alan Roscoe, James Marcus, Jack Curtis, George "Slim" Summerville, Les Bates, Jack Murphy, William H. Turner.
In Arizona, a trio of cowpokes gets work as movie extras on a location shoot. But there's a real life drama going on too, and the part-time extras have to choose up sides when violence erupts in a dispute over water rights.

The Texas Trail (Hunt Stromberg Corp./Producers Distributing Corp., 1925)
d: Scott R. Dunlap. 5 reels.
Harry Carey, Ethel Shannon, Charles K. French, Claude Payton, Sidney Franklin.
Betty, an eastern girl, comes West to see her rancher uncle, and winds up helping his foreman bring to justice a gang of crooks.

Thais (Goldwyn, 1917)
d: Frank H. Crane, Hugo Ballin. 5 reels.
Mary Garden, Hamilton Revelle, Crauford Kent, Lionel Adams, Alice Chapin, Margaret Townsend, Charles Trowbridge.
In ancient Alexandria, a young Roman falls in love with the beautiful Thais, a notorious femme fatale. He converts to Christianity, then imagines that it is his duty to reform Thais from her wicked ways.

Thank You (Fox, 1925)
d: John Ford. 7 reels.
Alec B. Francis, Jacqueline Logan, George O'Brien, J. Farrell MacDonald, George Fawcett, Cyril Chadwick, Edith Bostwick, Marion Harlan, Vivian Ogden, James Neill.
Diane, the ostentatious niece of the local minister, arrives in town after a Paris trip that has left her with highfalutin ways.

Thanks for the Buggy Ride (Universal, 1928)
d: William A. Seiter. 6 reels.
Laura LaPlante, Glenn Tryon, Richard Tucker, Lee Moran, David Rollins, Kate Price, Jack Raymond, Trixie Friganza.
A song writer and a dancing instructor fall in love, but complications occur when the dance teacher is also courted by a song publisher.

That Certain Thing (Columbia, 1928)
d: Frank Capra. 7 reels.
Ralph Graves, Viola Dana, Burr McIntosh, Aggie Herring.

A restaurant-chain executive disinherits his son when the boy declines to take over the family business and marries against Dad's wishes. But the newlyweds have a knack for business, too: The wife begins by making her husband box lunches, and soon they are preparing them for customers and turning a nice profit—which cuts into Dad's business.

That Devil, Bateese (Universal, 1918)
d: William Wolbert. 5 reels.
Monroe Salisbury, Ada Gleason, Lamar Johnstone, Lon Chaney, Andrew Robson.
In the woods near a Canadian village, Bateese the lumberjack rescues a schoolteacher from an attacker, then marries her. But when the teacher's former lover comes to town and she welcomes him warmly, the lumberjack begins to question his wife's love for him.

That French Lady (Fox, 1924)
d: Edmund Mortimer. 6 reels.

Shirley Mason, Theodore von Eltz, Harold Goodwin, Charles Coleman.
John, an Iowa man studying in Paris, falls in love with a free-thinking lady who disdains marriage laws.

That Girl Montana (Jesse D. Hampton/Pathé, 1921)
d: Robert Thornby. 5 reels.
Blanche Sweet, Mahlon Hamilton, Frank Lanning, Edward Peil, Charles Edler, Claire DeBrey, Kate Price, Jack Roseleigh.
Out West, a girl named Monte is raised as a boy.

That Man Jack! (Independent Pictures/FBO of America, 1925)
d: William J. Craft. 6 reels.
Bob Custer, Mary Beth Milford, Monte Collins, Hayford Hobbs, Buck Moulton.
When a cowpoke rescues a girl from being trampled by a runaway horse, he rouses the enmity of a man who fancies her.

That Model From Paris (Tiffany Productions, 1926)
d: Louis J. Gasnier. 7 reels.
Marceline Day, Bert Lytell, Eileen Percy, Ward Crane, Miss DuPont, Crauford Kent, Otto Lederer, Nellie Bly Baker, Leon Holmes, Sabel Johnson, George Kuwa.
A plain-jane cashier gets the chance to dress up and show off when she substitutes for a French model at a fashion show.

That Royle Girl (Famous Players-Lasky/Paramount, 1925)
d: D.W. Griffith. 10 reels.
Carol Dempster, W.C. Fields, James Kirkwood, Harrison Ford, Marie Chambers, Paul Everton, George Rigas, Florence Auer, Ida Waterman, Alice Laidley, Dorothea Love, Dore Davidson, Frank Allworth, Bobby Watson.
Daisy Royle, a plain and simple girl, gets involved in a sensational murder trial. After her friend is unjustly convicted of the crime, Daisy sets out to find evidence that will overturn the verdict.

That Something (Hermann Film Corp., 1920)
d: Margery Wilson, Lawrence Underwood. 5 reels.
Charles Meredith, Margery Wilson, Nigel DeBrulier, Eugenia Drake, John Hooper, Helen Wright, Carl Ulman, Gordon Griffith, James Farley, John Cossar.
Sarah, a young woman who has been taught to think positively, meets a wealthy couple who take a liking to her and begin treating her like kin. Before long, she does in fact become part of the family, by marrying the couple's successful son.

That Sort (Essanay, 1916)
w, d: Charles J. Brabin. 5 reels.
Warda Howard, Duncan McRae, Ernest Maupain, John Lorenz, Betty Brown, Peggy Sweeney, Marion Skinner.
Diana, married but feeling neglected, decides to stray and soon becomes a notorious woman. When she finally wakes up to the harm she has inflicted on her husband and daughter, it's almost too late to make amends. But Diana does re-enter her daughter's life in later years, and cautions her against making the same mistakes she did.

That Woman (F.C. Mims Productions/American Releasing Corp., 1922)
d: Harry O. Hoyt. 6 reels.
Catherine Calvert, Joseph Bruelle, William Black, George Pauncefort, William Ricciardi, Jack Newton, Norbert Wicki, Grace Field, Guy Coombs, Ralph Bunker.
When a scion of wealth marries a stage actress, his uptight

father strongly objects to their union. The old man goes so far as to offer his new daughter-in-law a large sum of money in return for a divorce, but she refuses. Papa then arranges for her to be lured to the yacht of a playboy and yield to his affections, but she still won't take the bait.

That's Good (Metro, 1919)
d: Harry L. Franklin. 5 reels.
Hale Hamilton, Stella Gray, Herbert Prior, James Duffy, Lewis Morrison, Marjorie Yeager, James McAndless.
Humorous tale about a small-town "boob" who is targeted by two con artists, one of them a beautiful young woman.

That's My Baby (Paramount, 1926)
d: William Beaudine. 7 reels.
Douglas MacLean, Margaret Morris, Claude Gillingwater, Eugenie Ford, Wade Boteler, Richard Tucker, Fred Kelsey, Harry Earles, William Orlamond.
Wacky farce about Alan, a chap who's been jilted once too often, and swears off women forever. Minutes later, however, he's wooing Helen, much to the dismay of a rival suitor. The rival then tries to torpedo the romance by presenting Alan with a baby and claiming that Alan is its father.

That's My Daddy (Universal, 1928)
d: Fred Newmeyer. 6 reels.
Reginald Denny, Jane La Verne, Lillian Rich, Barbara Kent, Tom O'Brien, Armand Kaliz, Mathilde Brundage.
A four-year-old orphan girl is adopted by a man who's about to be married.

Their Compact (Metro, 1917)
d: Edwin Carewe. 7 reels.
Francis X. Bushman, Beverly Bayne, Henry Mortimer, Harry S. Northrup, Mildred Adams, Robert Chandler, John Smiley, Thomas Delmar.
Out West, a transplanted easterner falls in love with a local girl, then has to fend off the advances of his capricious former girlfriend, who's just arrived in town.

Their Hour (Tiffany-Stahl Productions, 1928)
d: Alfred Raboch. 6 reels.
John Harron, Dorothy Sebastian, June Marlowe, John Roche, Huntley Gordon, Myrtle Stedman, John Steppling, Holmes Herbert.
Cora, a spoiled socialite, pounces on her prey—Jerry—and spirits him away in her private plane, as his frantic sweetheart gives chase.

Their Mutual Child (American Film Co./Pathé, 1920)
d: George L. Cox. 6 reels.
Margarita Fisher, Joseph Bennett, Margaret Campbell, Nigel Barrie, Harvey Clark, Andrew Robson, Beverly Travers, Pat Moore, Thomas O'Brien, William Lloyd, William Marion, Stanhope Wheatcroft.
When Ruth, overly cautious about health concerns, refuses to let her husband Kirk kiss their baby, he angrily leaves them both. But the family is reunited later, after a brief "kidnapping" of the child—actually a clever move engineered by one of Kirk's good friends.

Then I'll Come Back to You (Frohman Amusement Corp./World Film Corp., 1916)
d: George Irving. 5 reels.
Alice Brady, Jack Sherrill, Eric Blind, Leo Gordon, George Kline, Marie Edith.
Steve, a railroad engineer, is trying to complete a rail line through the Adirondack Mountains. But he's opposed by an unscrupulous businessman, who also happens to be Steve's rival for the hand of his true love.

There Are No Villains (Metro, 1921)
d: Bayard Veiller. 5 reels.
Viola Dana, Gaston Glass, Edward Cecil, DeWitt Jennings, Fred Kelsey, Jack Cosgrave.
Rosa, a Secret Service agent, falls in love with the man she is trailing in an opium smuggling case.

There You Are! (MGM, 1926)
d: No director credits. 6 reels.
Conrad Nagel, Edith Roberts, George Fawcett, Gwen Lee, Eddie Gribbon, Phillips Smalley, Gertrude Bennett.
Purely by dumb luck, an office worker captures a bandit and is proclaimed a hero, winning the hand of his boss' daughter.

They Like 'em Rough (Metro, 1922)
d: Harry Beaumont. 5 reels.
Viola Dana, William E. Lawrence, Hardee Kirkland, Myrtle Richell, Coilin Kenny, Steve Murphy, Walter Rodgers, Burton Law, W. Bradley Ward, Knute Erickson, Elsa Lorimer.
Katherine, a high-spirited young woman, flees an arranged marriage and heads for timber country, where she meets a bearded lumberjack and impulsively offers herself in marriage to him. He accepts, because underneath that beard is the face of a man who has loved Katherine for a long time.

They Shall Pay (Playgoers Pictures/Associated Exhibitors, 1921)
w, d: Martin Justine. 6 reels.
Lottie Pickford, Allan Forrest, Paul Weigel, Lloyd Whitlock, George Periolat, Katherine Griffith.
There's vengeance in the lady's eyes, as Margaret targets three men who framed her father and had him sent to prison.

They're Off (Triangle, 1917)
d: R. William Neill. 5 reels.
Enid Bennett, Rowland Lee, Melbourne MacDowell, Walter Whitman, Samuel Lincoln.
Manners, a Kentucky plantation owner, is forced to sell the old homestead to his rival. But the rival's daughter, who secretly loves Manners, helps him get the property back by manipulating the outcome of a high-stakes horse race.

The Thief (Box Office Attraction Co., 1914)
d: Edgar Lewis. 5 reels.
Dorothy Donnelly, Richard Buhler, Harry Springler, George DeCarlton, E.L. Davenport, Ivy Shepherd.
When an expected inheritance does not materialize, Marie is forced to rein in her extravagant spending habits... and to steal from a wealthy neighbor.

The Thief (Fox, 1920)
d: Charles Giblyn. 6 reels.
Pearl White, Charles Waldron, Wallace McCutcheon, George Howard, Dorothy Cummings, Eddie Featherstone, Sidney Herbert, Anthony Merlo.
Remake of the 1914 Box Office Attraction Co. film, *The Thief*.

A Thief in Paradise (George Fitzmaurice Productions/First National, 1925)
d: George Fitzmaurice. 8 reels.
Doris Kenyon, Ronald Colman, Aileen Pringle, Claude Gillingwater, Alec Francis, John Patrick, Charles Youree,

498

Etta Lee, Lon Poff.
When a beachcomber is killed by a shark in the South Seas, the widow tells his partner that her husband was the disinherited son of a San Francisco millionaire. So the partner decides to journey to the States and pass himself off as the millionaire's son, to see if maybe Papa hasn't had a change of heart.

The Thief of Bagdad (Fairbanks/United Artists, 1924)
d: Raoul Walsh. 12 reels.
Douglas Fairbanks, Julanne Johnston, Snitz Edwards, Charles Belcher, Anna May Wong, Winter Blossom, Etta Lee, Brandon Hurst, Tote Du Crow, Sojin, Noble Johnson, Sadakichi Hartmann, Mathilde Comont, Charles Stevens, Sam Baker, Jess Weldon, Scott Mattraw.

Ahmed, a lowly but acrobatic thief, falls in love with a beautiful princess.
This costume spectacular was the most ambitious Fairbanks vehicle and, at a cost of $2 million, the most expensive production to that time.

Thieves (Fox, 1919)
d: Frank Beal. 5 reels.
Gladys Brockwell, William Scott, Hayward Mack, Jeanne Calhoun, Spike Robinson, Bobby Starr, John Cossar, Yukio Aoyama, Marie James.
When a gang member decides to give up his life of crime and take a respectable job, his skeptical girlfriend challenges him to make as much money honestly as he did as a thief.

Thieves' Gold (Universal, 1918)
d: Jack Ford. 5 reels.
Harry Carey, Molly Malone, Vester Pegg, John Cook, L.M. Wells, Helen Ware, Harry Tenbrook, Martha Mattox.
Cheyenne Harry gets involved with highwaymen who operate near the Mexican border.

Thin Ice (Vitagraph, 1919)
d: Thomas R. Mills. 5 reels.
Corinne Griffith, Charles Kent, Jack McLean, L. Rogers Lytton, Walter Horton, Eulalie Jensen, Henry Gesell, Walter Miller, Alice Terry.
Alice and her brother Ned find themselves trapped in a web of deceit woven by Ned's unscrupulous employer, who accuses him of embezzlement and then tries to seduce Alice.

The Thing We Love (Famous Players-Lasky/Paramount, 1918)
d: Lou Tellegen. 5 reels.
Wallace Reid, Kathlyn Williams, Tully Marshall, Mayme Kelso, Charles Ogle, Billy Elmer.
During World War I, a factory vice president and his sweetheart discover that the company's president is secretly in league with the German government.

Think it Over (U.S. Amusement Corp./Art Dramas, Inc., 1917)
d: Herbert Blaché. 5 reels.
Catherine Calvert, Richard Tucker, A. Lloyd Lack, Eugene Borden, Auguste Burmester.
Alice, an heiress whose guardian is conspiring to seize control of her fortune, joins forces with a family friend to foil the guardian's scheme.

The Third Alarm (Emory Johnson Productions/FBO of America, 1922)
d: Emory Johnson. 7 reels.
Ralph Lewis, Johnnie Walker, Ella Hall, Virginia True Boardman, Richard Morris, Josephine Adair, Frankie Lee.
McDowell, a veteran fireman, is forcibly retired with a small pension when it turns out he can't operate modern equipment. But when fire engulfs a house, McDowell comes to the rescue using the old-fashioned methods, and is declared a hero.

The Third Degree (Lubin/General Film Co., 1913)
d: Barry O'Neil. 5 reels.
Gaston Bell, Robert Dunbar, Carlotta Doti, Robert Whittier, George Soule Spencer, Lilie Leslie, Bartley McCullum, Bernard Siegel, Robert Graham Jr.
When a struggling artist commits suicide, his friend Howard is arrested for murdering him, then has a confession beaten out of him by a sadistic police inspector.
Drama based on a popular play of the same name by Charles Klein. The film was remade twice in the silent era; by Vitagraph in 1919, and by Warner Bros. In 1926.

The Third Degree (Vitagraph, 1919)
d: Tom Terriss. 6 reels.
Alice Joyce, Gladden James, Aders Randolf, Hedda Hopper, Herbert Evans, George Backus, John P. Wade, L. Rogers Lytton, Edward McGuire.
Howard, disowned by his wealthy father for marrying a waitress, is falsely accused of murdering his best friend and then has a confession beaten out of him. But the waitress comes through and proves her husband's innocence.
Remake of the 1913 Lubin film *The Third Degree*, both versions based on the play of the same name by Charles Klein. It was remade again, by Warner Bros., in 1926.

The Third Degree (Warner Bros., 1926)
d: Michael Curtiz. 8 reels.
Louise Dresser, Dolores Costello, Rockliffe Fellowes, Jason Robards, Kate Price, Tom Santschi, Harry Todd, Mary Louise Miller, David Torrence.
Third film version of the Charles Klein play about a young man wrongly accused of killing his best friend.

The Third Generation (Brentwood Film Corp./Robertson-Cole, 1920)
d: Henry Kolker. 5 reels.
Betty Blythe, Mahlon Hamilton, Jack Pratt, Joseph Swickard, Edward Cecil, Betty Brice, Herbert Jones, Fred Kelsey, Peggy Cartwright.
Alden, a third generation member of a proud industrialist family, is faced with financial disgrace and decides to commit suicide. But providence supplies him with a way out of his difficulties: by impersonating a worker in his own company's mine, he works tirelessly to make the business a success.

The Third Kiss (Famous Players-Lasky/Paramount, 1919)
d: Robert G. Vignola. 5 reels.
Harrison Ford, Vivian Martin, Robert Ellis, Kathleen Kirkham, Edna Mae Cooper, Thomas D. Perse, Jane Keckley.
Missy, an heiress who's determined to give something back to society, does settlement work among the poor. She meets and marries Oliver, who is ignorant of her wealth but loves her anyway.

The Third Woman (Superior Pictures/Robertson-Cole, 1920)
d: Charles Swickard. 5 reels.
Carlyle Blackwell, Louise Lovely, Gloria Hope, Winter Hall, George Hernandez, Walter Long, Frank Lanning, Myrtle Owen.

Luke, a wealthy New Yorker, discovers that his long-deceased mother was an Indian. Stung by taunts of "half-breed!" from his former society friends, Luke goes West to live among his mother's tribe. But his New York girlfriend follows him and convinces him that her love is true, regardless of race distinctions.

13 Washington Square (Universal, 1928)
d: Melville W. Brown. 6 reels.
Jean Hersholt, Alice Joyce, ZaSu Pitts, Helen Foster, Helen Jerome Eddy, Julia Swayne Gordon, Jack McDonald, Jerry Gamble.
A social-climbing woman disapproves of her son's engagement to a grocer's daughter, but has a devil of a time preventing their elopement.

The Thirteenth Chair (Acme Pictures Corp./Pathé, 1919)
d: Leonce Perret. 6 reels.
Yvonne Delva, Creighton Hale, Marie Shotwell, Christine Mayo, Suzanne Colbert, George Deneubourg, Marc McDermott, Walter Law, Fraunie Fraunholz.
In an attempt to solve a murder case, a clairvoyant conducts a séance, and there in the darkened room, the person sitting in the thirteenth chair is himself murdered.

The Thirteenth Commandment (Famous Players-Lasky/Paramount, 1920)
d: Robert G. Vignola. 5 reels.
Ethel Clayton, Charles Meredith, Monte Blue, Anna Q. Nilsson, Irving Cummings, Winter Hall, Lucille Ward, Arthur Maude, Beverly Travers, Lewis Morrison, Jane Wolfe.
Daphne, determined not to depend on anybody but herself, breaks off her engagement and opens her own dress shop.

The Thirteenth Hour (MGM, 1927)
d: Chester Franklin. 6 reels.
Lionel Barrymore, Jacqueline Gadsden, Charles Delaney, Polly Moran, Fred Kelsey.
A prominent criminologist is unmasked as a notorious crook.

The Thirteenth Juror (Universal, 1927)
d: Edward Laemmle. 6 reels.
Anna Q. Nilsson, Francis X. Bushman, Walter Pidgeon, Martha Mattox, Sidney Bracey, Sailor Sharkey, Lloyd Whitlock, George Siegmann, Fred Kelsey.
Complicated thriller about an attorney who refuses to defend his best friend in a murder trial because he desires the friend's wife for himself.

The Thirtieth Piece of Silver (American Film Co., Inc./Pathé, 1920)
d: George L. Cox. 5 reels.
Margarita Fisher, King Baggot, Forrest Stanley, Lillian Leighton.
Tyler Cole believes the rare coin he owns is the thirtieth piece of silver for which Judas betrayed Jesus Christ.

Thirty a Week (Goldwyn, 1918)
d: Harry Beaumont. 5 reels.
Tom Moore, Tallulah Bankhead, Alec B. Francis, Brenda Fowler, Warburton Gamble, Grace Henderson, Ruth Elder.
Barbara, a daughter of wealth, is disowned by her father when she decides to marry a handsome but penniless chauffeur.

Thirty Days (Famous Players-Lasky/Paramount, 1922)
d: James Cruze. 5 reels.
Wallace Reid, Wanda Hawley, Charles Ogle, Cyril Chadwick, Herschel Mayall, Helen Dunbar, Carmen Phillips, Kalla Pasha, Robert Brower.
Comedy about a chap who, to keep a woman's jealous husband from hurting him, has himself sentenced to 30 days in jail.

Thirty Years Later (Micheaux Pictures, 1928)
w, d: Oscar Micheaux. 7 reels.
William Edmonson, A.B. de Comatheire, Mabel Kelly, Ardella Dabney, Gertrude Snelson.
George, a man of mixed race who believes himself to be completely white, feels himself falling in love with a black woman and must confront hostile societal attitudes, including those in his own home.

$30,000 (Robert Brunton Productions/Pathé, 1920)
d: Ernest C. Warde. 5 reels.
J. Warren Kerrigan, Fritzi Brunette, Carl Stockdale, Nancy Chase, Joseph J. Dowling, Arthur Millette, Frank Gereghty, Jack Rollins, Thomas Guise, Gertrude Valentine.
Mystery revolving around a stolen necklace, and the $30,000 in cash that is being used to redeem it.

39 East (Realart Pictures Corp., 1920)
d: John S. Robertson. 5 reels.
Constance Binney, Reginald Denny, Alison Skipworth, Lucia Moore, Blanche Frederici, Edith Gresham, Mildred Arden, Luis Alberni, Albert Carroll, Frank Allworth.
Penelope, a small-town minister's daughter, goes to New York determined to make a success as a stage actress.

This Hero Stuff (William Russell Productions/Pathé, 1919)
d: Henry King. 5 reels.
William Russell, Winifred Westover, J. Barney Sherry, Charles K. French, Mary Thurman, Harvey Clark, J. Farrell MacDonald.
Comedy western about a war hero who returns home to Nevada but can't seem to shake his habit of turning every encounter into an act of heroism.

This is Heaven (Goldwyn/United Artists, 1929)
d: Alfred Santell. 8 reels. (Music, sound effects, part talkie.)
Vilma Banky, James Hall, Fritzi Ridgeway, Lucien Littlefield, Richard Tucker.
There's double deception in this tale about Eva, a poor Hungarian immigrant, who masquerades as an exiled Russian countess. She secretly loves a man she believes to be a chauffeur, but is actually a millionaire's son.

This is the Life (Fox, 1917)
d: Raoul Walsh. 5 reels.
George Walsh, James A. Marcus, Wanda Petit, Ralph Lewis, Jack McDonald, W.H. Ryno, Victor Sarno.
Billy, a movie-struck lad on a mundane mission to South America, meets a beautiful woman on board ship and imagines she is a movie star. When they dock at their destination, the country is in the grips of revolutionary war. But Billy assumes the soldiers are all actors in a film, and his "movie star" charmer is the film's heroine.

This Woman (Warner Brothers, 1924)
d: Phil Rosen. 7 reels.
Irene Rich, Ricardo Cortez, Louise Fazenda, Frank Elliot, Creighton Hale, Marc MacDermott, Helen Dunbar, Clara Bow, Otto Hoffman.
An aspiring singer has to discontinue her voice lessons due to poverty, but an impresario considers whether to come to

the young woman's aid.

Thorns and Orange Blossoms (Preferred Pictures/Al Lichtman Corp., 1922)
d: Louis J. Gasnier. 7 reels.
Estelle Taylor, Kenneth Harlan, Arthur Hull, Edith Roberts, Carl Stockdale, John Cossar, Evelyn Selbie.
On a business trip to Spain, Alan falls in love with a local girl, Rosita. But he's already spoken for at home.

The Thoroughbred (American Film Co./Mutual, 1916)
d: Charles Bartlett. 5 reels.
William Russell, Charlotte Burton, Roy Stewart, Lizette Thorne, Jack Prescott.
Hamilton loves Angela, but she's rich and he isn't. So, he heads West to make his fortune.

The Thoroughbred (New York Motion Picture Corp./Triangle, 1916)
d: Reginald Barker. 5 reels.
Frank Keenan, Margaret Thompson, George Fisher, J.J. Dowling, Walter Perry.
Thomas, a New England minister, is in love with Betty, but there's a problem. Her father races thoroughbred horses for a living, and the minister thinks horse races are the Devil's work.

Those Who Dance (Thomas H. Ince/Associated First National, 1924)
d: Lambert Hillyer. 8 reels.
Blanche Sweet, Bessie Love, Warner Baxter, Matthew Betz, John Sainpolis, Lucille Ricksen, Lydia Knott, Jack Perrin, Frank Campeau, Robert Agnew.
Kane, a man who lost a sister to bootleg booze, helps a girl get her brother out of the liquor smuggling racket.

Those Who Dare (Creative Pictures, 1924)
d: John B. O'Brien. 6 reels.
John Bowers, Marguerite De La Motte, Joseph Dowling, Claire McDowell, Martha Marshall, Edward Burns, Spottiswoode Aitken, Sheldon Lewis, Cesare Gravina.
An old sea captain pilots a ship that is reputed to be haunted.

Those Who Judge (Banner Productions, 1924)
d: Burton King. 6 reels.
Patsy Ruth Miller, Lou Tellegen, Mary Thurman, Flora LeBreton, Edmund Breese, Walter Miller, Coit Albertson, Cornelius Keefe, John Henry.
Angelique, a high society woman, accepts the proposal of a man who believes her to be a widow. In fact, she had merely taken part in a mock wedding ceremony with a British officer who is still alive.

Those Who Pay (Thomas H. Ince, 1917)
d: Raymond B. West. 7 reels.
Bessie Barriscale, Howard Hickman, Dorcas Matthews, Melbourne McDowell.
About to be arrested for shoplifting, Dorothy finds a savior in Graham, a congressman who takes a liking to her. They spend some quality time together and Dorothy falls deeply in love with Graham. But although she becomes pregnant, their love cannot survive, because the congressman is already married.

Those Who Toil (Lubin, 1916)
d: Edgar Lewis. 5 reels.
Nance O'Neil, Victor Sutherland, Herbert Fortier, Tom Tempest, John Sharkey, Fred Chasten, Ray Chamberlain,

Adelaide Hayes.
After her father is killed in an accident at an oil refinery, Jane resolves to investigate working conditions at the plant... and falls in love with the refinery's owner.

Those Without Sin (Lasky Feature Plays/Paramount, 1917)
d: Marshall Neilan. 5 reels.
Blanche Sweet, Tom Forman, C.H. Geldart, Guy Oliver, James Neill, Charles Ogle, George Beranger, Mabel Van Buren, Dot Abril, Edna Wilson, Billy Jacobs, Mayme Kelso.
During the War between the States, a southern belle must fight off the amorous advances of a Yankee officer.

Thou Art the Man (Vitagraph, 1916)
d: S. Rankin Drew. 6 reels.
Virginia Pearson, S. Rankin Drew, Joseph Kilgour, George Cooper, Harold Foshay, Billie Billings, William Davidson, Walter McGrail.
In India, a British government official assigns a clerk to a remote and dangerous post because he covets the clerk's wife.
Drama loosely based on the story of David and Uriah in the Old Testament Book of 2 Samuel.

Thou Art the Man (Famous Players-Lasky/Paramount, 1920)
d: Thomas N. Heffron. 5 reels.
Robert Warwick, Lois Wilson, J.M. Dumont, Clarence Burton, C.H. Geldart, Harry Carter, Jane Wolfe, Dorothy Rosher, Viora Daniel, Richard Wayne, Lorenza Lazzarini, Lillian Leighton, Sylvia Ashton.
Diamond smugglers try to pin their guilt on their innocent courier.

Thou Shalt Not (Fox, 1919)
d: Charles J. Brabin. 6 reels.
Evelyn Nesbit, Ned Burton, Florida Kingsley, Gladden James, Crauford Kent, Eddie Lawrence.
Unforgiving neighbors drive away a woman who has sinned.

Thou Shalt Not Covet (Selig Polyscope, 1916)
d: Colin Campbell. 5 reels.
Tyrone Power, Kathlyn Williams, Guy Oliver, Eugenie Besserer.
When a scientist and his neighbor's wife are shipwrecked together, he finds himself attracted to her.

Thou Shalt Not Steal (Fox, 1917)
d: William Nigh. 5 reels.
Virginia Pearson, Claire Whitney, Eric Mayne, Mathilde Brundage, John Goldsworthy, Robert Elliott, Martin Faust, Lem F. Kennedy, Danny Sullivan, Mrs. Patrick Foy, Dan Mason.
Mary loves Roger, but she is desired by an English nobleman who sweetens his proposal of marriage with a large donation to her father. Incensed when her dad accepts, Mary decides to steal the money from his safe.

Thoughtless Women (Pioneer Film Corp., 1920)
d: Daniel Carson Goodman. 6 reels.
Alma Rubens, Merceita Esmond, Robert Williams, Mathilde Brundage, Gladys Valerie, Lumsden Hare, Mabel Bardine.
Wealthy snobs turn against Annie, a working-class girl who has married into a family of aristocrats.

The Thousand Dollar Husband (Lasky Feature Plays/Paramount, 1916)
d: James Young. 5 reels.

Blanche Sweet, Theodore Roberts, Tom Forman, James Neill, Horace B. Carpenter, Lucille LaVarney, E.L. Delaney, Camille Astor.

Olga, a Swedish girl working as a maid in a boarding house, falls in love with a wealthy college boy. Then, through a double twist of fate, she inherits a fortune and he loses his.

A Thousand to One (J. Parker Read Jr. Productions, 1920)
d: Rowland V. Lee. 6 reels.
Hobart Bosworth, Ethel Grey Terry, Charles West, Landers Stevens, J. Gordon Russell, Fred Kohler.
Though he feels guilty about it, William marries Beatrice for her money. Then, on their honeymoon, he is buried in a train accident and she assumes him dead. Eventually William, who has survived the crash, will return to her a changed man and make her proud of him.

Threads of Destiny (Lubin, 1914)
d: Joseph W. Smiley. 5 reels.
Evelyn Nesbit Thaw, Bernard Siegel, Jack Clifford, Margaret Risser, William Cahill, Joseph W. Smiley, Russell William Thaw, Joseph Standish, Marguerite Marsh.
Ivan, a Russian secret agent, wages a private war against Jews.

Threads of Fate (Columbia/Metro, 1917)
d: Eugene Nowland. 5 reels.
Viola Dana, Augustus Phillips, Richard Tucker, Fred Jones, Helen Strickland, Nellie Grant, Robert Whittier.
After his wife elopes with another man, the despondent Jim leaves their baby girl on a neighbor's doorstep and leaves. The girl is raised by the neighbors and believes them to be her parents. When she is 18 years old, however, her real father re-enters her life, just in time to save his daughter from being seduced by the same scoundrel who stole her mother away.

Three Ages (Metro, 1923)
d: Buster Keaton, Eddie Cline. 6 reels.
Buster Keaton, Margaret Leahy, Wallace Beery, Joe Roberts, Horace Morgan, Lillian Lawrence.
Love is shown in comedic fashion, through the ages— prehistoric, Roman, and modern.

Three Bad Men (Fox, 1926)
d: John Ford. 10 reels.
George O'Brien, Olive Borden, Lou Tellegen, Tom Santschi, J. Farrell MacDonald, Frank Campeau, Priscilla Bonner, Otis Harlan, Phyllis Haver, Georgie Harris, Alec Francis.
Epic western set in the Dakota land rush of the late 1870s. There's a whimsical touch here, when three outlaws (the "three bad men" of the title) befriend a young woman (Miss Borden) who has been robbed and seen her father murdered; and the girl's three protectors then go "husband hunting" for a man who is worthy of her. O'Brien plays their choice.

Three Black Eyes (Triangle, 1919)
d: Charles Horan. 5 reels.
Taylor Holmes, Louise Orth, Clara Moores, Diana Allen, Ida Pardee, Marshall Stedman, Gordon Standing, William Bailey.
In a cabaret, lovesick yachtsman Larry makes a drunken fool of himself in front of the pretty girl he is attracted to. But comes the sober dawn, and Larry redeems himself in the girl's eyes by foiling thieves at her wealthy dad's house.

Three Faces East (Cinema Corp. Of America/Producers Distributing Corp., 1926)
d: Rupert Julian. 7 reels.

Jetta Goudal, Robert Ames, Henry Walthall, Clive Brook, Edythe Chapman, Clarence Burton, Ed Brady.
During World War I, a beautiful British spy masquerades as a German nurse.

The Three Godfathers (Universal, 1916)
d: Edward J. Le Saint. 6 reels.
Harry Carey, Stella Razeto, George Berrill, Frank Lanning, Joe Rickson, Hart Hoxie.
Three outlaws find themselves obliged to care for a newborn baby.

Three Gold Coins (Fox, 1920)
d: Cliff Smith. 5 reels.
Tom Mix, Margaret Loomis, Frank Whitson, Bert Hadley, Dick Rush, Margaret Cullington, Sylvia Jocelyn, Bonnie Hill, Sid Jordan, Walt Robins, Frank Weed.
Out West, a sharpshootin' cowpoke wins the love of a millionaire's daughter.

Three Green Eyes (World Film Corp., 1919)
d: Dell Henderson. 5 reels.
Carlyle Blackwell, Evelyn Greeley, Montagu Love, June Elvidge, Johnny Hines, Jack Drumier, Dorothy Dee, Matilda Brundage, William Black, Yusti Yama, Madge Evans.
Lucille and Alan happily wed... but there's a little matter of Lucille's incriminating love letter to a former suitor, and she means to get it back.

Three Hours (Corinne Griffith Productions/First National, 1927)
d: James Flood. 6 reels.
Corinne Griffith, John Bowers, Hobart Bosworth, Paul Ellis, Anne Schaefer, Mary Louise Miller.
Multiple-hanky weeper about a formerly wealthy woman who loses her child and is then reduced to abject poverty.

Three in Exile (Truart Film Corp., 1925)
d: Fred Windemere. 5 reels.
Louise Lorraine, Art Acord, Tom London.
In the Southwest desert, a man, his dog, and his horse wander about and almost die of thirst. But just as buzzards begin to hover, the trio finds a lady miner who takes them in and feeds them. In gratitude, the man helps her keep her mine going and also fights off a gang of would-be claim jumpers.

Three Jumps Ahead (Fox, 1923)
d: Jack Ford. 5 reels.
Tom Mix, Alma Bennett, Edward Piel, Joe Girard, Virginia True Boardman, Margaret Joslin, Francis Ford, Harry Todd.
Out West, a cowboy captured by outlaws is given a chance at freedom if he brings back a man they want even more. The cowboy agrees, and sets out to do the job. But when he learns that his prey is the father of the girl he loves, all bets are off.

Three Keys (Banner Productions, 1925)
d: Edward J. LeSaint. 6 reels.
Edith Roberts, Jack Mulhall, Gaston Glass, Virginia Lee Corbin, Miss DuPont, Charles Clary, Stuart Holmes, Joseph W. Girard.
In New York, a society girl learns that her fiancé is frequently visited in his apartment by a strange young lady. Suspecting him of infidelity, she abruptly cancels their engagement. Then she learns, to her relief, that the young stranger is actually her sweetheart's ward. But in this convoluted tale by Frederic V.R. Dey, nothing is what it seems. It turns out that the socialite's ex-fiancé actually *is* in

love with his ward. Furthermore, the ward happens to be the socialite's long-lost sister.

Three Live Ghosts (Famous Players-Lasky/Paramount, 1922)
d: George Fitzmaurice. 6 reels.
Anna Q. Nilsson, Norman Kerry, Cyril Chadwick, Edmund Goulding, John Miltern, Claire Greet, Annette Benson, Dorothy Fane, Windham Guise.
Three men—prisoners of war in a German camp during World War I—return home after the armistice, though all three were presumed dead.

Three Men and a Girl (Famous Players-Lasky/Paramount, 1919)
d: Marshall Neilan. 5 reels.
Marguerite Clark, Richard Barthelmess, Percy Marmont, Jerome Patrick, Ida Darling, Charles Craig, Sydney D'Albrook, Betty Bouton, Maggie H. Fisher.
Sylvia, on the rebound from a romance, goes to her late father's country house to relax. Fat chance! The family's realtor has rented the estate to three woman-hating bachelors, and Sylvia's unexpected arrival ruins their vacation plans. That is, until they get to know the lovely newcomer.

Three Miles Out (Associated Exhibitors, 1924)
d: Irwin Willat. 6 reels.
Harrison Ford, Madge Kennedy, Marc McDermott, Ivan Linwo, Walter Lewis, M.W. Rale, Joseph Henderson, Edna Morton, Marie Burke.
Only minutes before her wedding, Molly learns that her intended is a notorious smuggler.

Three Miles Up (Universal, 1927)
d: Bruce Mitchell. 5 reels.
Al Wilson, William Malan, Ethlyne Claire, William Clifford, Frank Rice, Billy "Red" Jones, Joe Bennett, Art Goebel.
Morgan, a World War I flying ace, returns home to friends and family. But his pre-war criminal cohorts refuse to believe Morgan has reformed, and they try to intimidate him back into their gang.

Three Mounted Men (Universal, 1918)
d: Jack Ford. 6 reels.
Harry Carey, Joe Harris, Harry Carter, Neva Gerber, Ruby Lafayette, Charles Hill Mailes.
Cheyenne Harry, serving a sentence in jail, is given an early release after promising the warden he will capture and return a dangerous escaped convict. Harry goes to search for the outlaw, and along the way falls in love with a pretty dance hall girl... not knowing she is the outlaw's sister.

The Three Musketeers (Fairbanks/United Artists, 1921)
d: Fred Niblo. 12 reels.
Douglas Fairbanks, Marguerite De La Motte, Leon Barry, Eugene Pallette, George Siegmann, Adolphe Menjou, Nigel de Brulier, Mary MacLaren, Barbara La Marr, Thomas Holding, Willis Robards, Boyd Irwin, Lon Poff, Walt Whitman, Sydney Franklin, Charles Belcher, Charles Stevens, Leon Bary.
Fairbanks is D'Artagnan, "the best swordsman in France," in this epic adaptation of the famous Alexandre Dumas tale.

The Three Must-Get-Theres (United Artists, 1922)
w, d: Max Linder. 5 reels.
Max Linder, Jobyna Ralston, Jack Richardson, Charles Metzetti, Clarence Wepz, Bull Montana, Frank Cooke, Catharine Rankin.

American-made parody of *The Three Musketeers*, starring (as Dart-In-Again) French comedian Linder, who also wrote, directed, and produced the film.

Three of Many (New York Motion Picture Corp./Triangle, 1916)
d: Reginald Barker. 5 reels.
Clara Williams, Charles Gunn, George Fisher.
Paul and Emil both love Nina, but their romantic pursuits are interrupted by the onset of World War I. Paul and Emil go to war on opposite sides, while Nina becomes an army nurse... and eventually meets both her admirers again.

The Three of Us (B.A. Rolfe Photo Plays, Inc./Alco Film Corp., 1914)
d: John W. Noble. 5 reels.
Mabel Taliaferro, Creighton Hale, Master Stuart, Edwin Carewe, Irving Cummings, Madame Claire, Harry Smith, Mayme Kelso.
In Colorado, a gold miner and his girlfriend embark on a dangerous mountain journey in an attempt to beat a larcenous claim jumper to the registrar's office.

Three Pals (American Film Co./Mutual, 1916)
d: Rea Berger. 5 reels.
C. William Kolb, Max M. Dill, May Cloy.
Two country bumpkins inherit $10,000, but are cheated out of most of it by an unscrupulous attorney. On their way back home, they rescue a pretty girl from thieves and the three of them become fast friends. What the boys don't know is that their new female pal is the daughter of the scheming attorney.

Three Pals (Davis Distributing Division, 1926)
d: Wilbur McGaugh. 5 reels.
Marilyn Mills, Josef Swickard, William H. Turner, Martin Turner, Walter Emerson, James McLaughlin.
Girard, a Southern colonel, is arrested for the crime when his best friend turns up murdered. But Betty, his European-schooled daughter, sets out to prove his innocence and, in the process, falls in love with the dead man's son.

Three Ring Marriage (First National, 1928)
d: Marshall Neilan. 6 reels.
Mary Astor, Lloyd Hughes, Lawford Davidson, Alice White, Yola D'Avril, Harry Earles, Tiny Erales, R.E. Madsen, Rudolph Cameron, George Reed, Anna McGruder, James Neill, Dell Henderson, Richard Skeets Gallagher, Jay Eaton.

Three Sevens (Vitagraph, 1921)
d: Chester Bennett. 5 reels.
Antonio Moreno, Jean Calhoun, Emmett King, Geoffrey Webb, DeWitt Jennings, Starke Patterson, Beatrice Burnham.
The title refers to Convict 777, a prisoner doing time for a crime he didn't commit.

Three Sinners (Paramount, 1928)
d: Rowland V. Lee. 8 reels.
Pola Negri, Warner Baxter, Paul Lukas, Nils Asther, Mary McAllister, Richard Tucker, Phil Strange, Nigel DeBrulier, Robert Fischer, Helene Giere.
In Germany, a beautiful countess who has fallen out of love with her husband, takes a train to Vienna to visit relatives. While on the train, she has an affair with a musician she has just met. Upset and confused, the countess detrains at the next station, and stays there while the train continues on its way. It derails, and all aboard are reported dead, leaving the countess with options: to return to her husband, or drop out of his life completely.

Three Week-Ends (Paramount, 1928)
d: Clarence Badger. 6 reels.
Clara Bow, Neil Hamilton, Harrison Ford, Lucille Powers, Julia Swayne Gordon, Jack Raymond, Edythe Chapman, Guy Oliver, William Holden.
Gladys, a chorus girl with a flirtatious streak, helps her insurance salesman boyfriend overcome a prospect's sales resistance.

Three Weeks (Reliable Feature Film Corp., 1915)
d: Perry N. Vekroff. 5 reels.
H.J. Smith, Madeline Traverse, George Pearce, R.J. Barrett, Joseph Moore, Pauline Seymour, John Webb Dillon, Joseph C. Fay, Arthur Donaldson, Claude Cooper.
In the kingdom of Veseria, the people are distressed that their playboy king, Stefan, has no heir to succeed him. Hearing talk of a possible *coup* to enthrone an outsider, Queen Sonia leaves for Switzerland and coincidentally meets the kingdom's real crown prince, whose father was ousted by Stefan's father years before.

Three Weeks (Goldwyn, 1924)
d: Alan Crosland. 8 reels.
Aileen Pringle, Conrad Nagel, John Sainpolis, H. Reeves Smith, Stuart Holmes, Mitchell Lewis, Robert Cain, Nigel DeBrulier, Claire DeLorez, Dale Fuller, Helen Dunbar, Alan Crosland Jr., Joan Standing, William Haines, George Tustain, Dane Rudhyar.
Dramatization of the Elinor Glyn story *Three Weeks*, about the loves and passions of European royals.

Three Weeks in Paris (Warner Bros., 1926)
d: Roy Del Ruth. 6 reels.
Matt Moore, Dorothy Devore, Willard Louis, Helen Lynch, Gayne Whitman, John Patrick, Frank Bond, Rosa Gore.

A bridegroom is forced to leave his wife on their wedding night, go to Paris, and get into several complicated adventures... but it all turns out to be a dream.

Three Who Paid (Fox, 1923)
d: Colin Campbell. 5 reels.
Dustin Farnum, Fred Kohler, Bessie Love, Frank Campeau, William Conklin, Robert Daly, Robert Agnew.
Out West, a cowpoke sets out to avenge his brother's death.

Three Wise Crooks (Gothic Productions/FBO of America, 1925)
d: F. Harmon Weight. 6 reels.
Evelyn Brent, Fannie Midgley, John Gough, Bruce Gordon, William Humphrey, Carroll Nye, Dodo Newton.
Dolly, a petty thief, and her two cronies turn the tables on a swindling banker.

Three Wise Fools (Goldwyn, 1923)
d: King Vidor. 7 reels.
Claude Gillingwater, Eleanor Boardman, William H. Crane, Alec B. Francis, John Sainpolis, Brinsley Shaw, Fred Esmelton, William Haines, Lucien Littlefield, ZaSu Pitts, Martha Mattox, Fred J. Butler, Charles Hickman, Craig Biddle Jr., Creighton Hale, Raymond Hatton.
Three old bachelors become guardians of the daughter of the woman they once loved.

Three Women (Warner Bros., 1924)
d: Ernst Lubitsch. 8 reels.
Pauline Frederick, May McAvoy, Marie Prevost, Lew Cody, Willard Louis, Pierre Gendron, Mary Carr, Raymond McKee.

Society weeper about a young woman who marries her mother's former lover.

Three Word Brand (Paramount, 1921)
w, d: Lambert Hillyer. 6 reels.
William S. Hart, S.J. Bingham, Jane novak, Gordon Russell, George C. Pearce, Colette Forbes, Ivor McFadden, Herschel Mayall, Leo Willis.
Hart plays three roles in this tale of treachery and romance in the Old West: Twin brothers and their dad.

Three X Gordon (W.W. Hodkinson, 1918)
d: Ernest C. Warde. 5 reels.
J. Warren Kerrigan, Lois Wilson, Charles K. French, Gordon Sackville, John Gilbert, Jay Belasco, Leatrice Joy, Walter Perry, Don Baily, Stanhope Wheatcroft.
H.C.W. Gordon, a dissolute playboy, is disinherited by his father for his shiftless ways. Renaming himself "Three X Gordon," the young man resolves to amend his life, and does so.

Three's a Crowd (Harry Langdon Corp./First National, 1927)
d: Harry Langdon. 6 reels.
Harry Langdon, Gladys McConnell, Cornelius Keefe, Arthur Thalasso, Henry Barrows, Frances Raymond, Agnes Steele, Brooks Benedict, Bobby Young, Julia Brown, Joe Butterworth.
A kindly moving-van worker finds an abandoned mother and her baby in the snow, and takes them in.

The Thrill Chaser (Universal, 1923)
d: Edward Sedgwick. 6 reels.
Hoot Gibson, James Neill, Billie Dove, William E. Lawrence, Bob Reeves, Gino Gerrado, Lloyd Whitlock, Mary Philbin, Norman Kerry, Reginald Denny, Hobart Henley, King Baggot, Edward Sedgwick, Laura LaPlante.
Jenkins, a movie extra and amateur boxer, visits an Arabian kingdom, where he falls for Olala, a desert princess.

The Thrill Hunter (Columbia, 1926)
d: Eugene De Rue. 6 reels.
William Haines, Alma Bennett, Kathryn McGuire, E.J. Ratcliffe, Frankie Darrow.
Mistaken-identity comedy in which a commoner is taken for a king and is very nearly forced to marry the real monarch's princess fiancée.

Through a Glass Window (Realart Pictures/Paramount, 1922)
d: Maurice Campbell. 5 reels.
May McAvoy, Fanny Midgley, Burwell Hamrick, Raymond McKee, Fred Turner, Carrie Clark Ward, Frank Butterworth, Wade Boteler, Russ Powell.
Charming tale of a New York family unit—mother, daughter, son—who struggle to make a happy life for themselves, through good times and bad.

Through Eyes of Men (Radin Pictures, Inc., 1920)
d: Charles A. Taylor. 5 reels.
Frank Mayo, Prudence Lyle, George Gebhardt, Claire McDowell, Ben Alexander, Dell Boone.
Leila, a comely circus performer, is loved by wealthy Franklin—but she has a dark secret that threatens their relationship.

Through Fire to Fortune (Lubin, 1914)
d: Lloyd B. Carleton. 5 reels.
Richard Wangermann, Ormi Hawley, Arthur Matthews,

504

Clay M. Greene, Eleanor Barry, Edward J. Peil, Richard Morris, James Humphrey, Florence McLaughlin, Frankie Man.

Tom, a young coal miner, makes the discovery that there's more than coal in the mine: There's oil!

Through the Back Door (Pickford/United Artists, 1921)
d: Jack Pickford, Alfred E. Green.   6 reels.
Mary Pickford, John Harron, Gertrude Astor, Wilfred Lucas, C. Norman Hammond, Adolphe J. Menjou, Elinor Fair, Helen Raymond, Adolphe Menjou, Peaches Jackson, John Harron, Doreen Turner, George Dromgold.
A young woman who was kidnapped as a child returns to her mother's home as a maid.

Through the Breakers (Gotham Productions/Lumas Film Corp., 1928)
d: Joseph C. Boyle.   6 reels.
Holmes Herbert, Margaret Livingston, Clyde Cook, Natalie Joyce, Frank Hagney.
A lovely socialite whose fiancé is a plantation manager in the South Seas refuses to leave the festive London social scene to join him. Fate, however, brings them together when she embarks on an ocean voyage and is shipwrecked off the coast of his island.

Through the Dark (Cosmopolitan Corp./Goldwyn, 1924)
d: George Hill.   8 reels.
Colleen Moore, Forrest Stanley, Margaret Seddon, Hobart Bosworth, George Cooper, Edward Phillips, Wade Boteler, Tom Bates, Carmelita Geraghty.
Gentleman crook Boston Blackie escapes from San Quentin, only to fall in love with Mary, a recent boarding school graduate.

Through the Toils (World Film Corp., 1919)
d: Hary O. Hoyt.   5 reels.
Montagu Love, Ellen Casity, Gertrude LeBrandt, John Davidson, Thomas Carr, Laura West, Joseph Burke, Lincoln Stedman, Winifred Leighton, Dorothy Walters.
Moffat, an elderly writer looking for inspiration to write a romantic novel, schemes to have two young people fall in love with each other, then makes them break up, so that he can analyze their suffering.

Through the Wall (Vitagraph, 1916)
d: Rollin S. Sturgeon.   6 reels.
George Holt, William Duncan, Nell Shipman, Webster Campbell, Corinne Griffith, Anne Schaeffer, Otto Ledrer, George Kinkel.
A master criminal deceives a wealthy woman and marries her for her money.

Through the Wrong Door (Goldwyn, 1919)
d: Clarence G. Badger.   5 reels.
Madge Kennedy, John Bowers, Herbert Standing, M.B. Manly, Robert Kortman, Kate Lester, Beulah Peyton, Betty Schade.
Humorous happenings, when a young prospector decides to counter a blackmailer's threats by "kidnapping" the blackmailer's daughter—who just happens to be in love with him.

Through Thick and Thin (Camera Pictures/Lumas Film Corp., 1927)
d: Reeves Eason, Jack Nelson.   5 reels.
William Fairbanks, Ethel Shannon, Jack Curtis, George Periolat, Ina Anson, Eddie Chandler, Fred Behrle.
Davis, a Secret Service agent, goes undercover as bouncer in a dance hall to trace down a gang of opium smugglers.

Thrown to the Lions (Universal, 1916)
d: Lucius Henderson.   5 reels.
Mary Fuller, Clifford Gray, Joseph Girard, Augustus Phillips, Finita DeSopia, Clifford Gray, Emil Hick.
Linnie, a cabaret singer, agrees to marry a hoodlum. But he isn't sincere and plans to make it a phony wedding.

Thru the Flames (Phil Goldstone Productions, 1923)
d: Jack Nelson.   5 reels.
Richard Talmadge, Charlotte Pierce, Maine Geary, S.J. Bingham, Taylor Graves, Ruth Langston, Fred Kohler, Edith Yorke, George Sherwood, C.H. Hailes.
Merrill, a fireman who can't stand smoke, finds a way to be useful: He tracks down and captures a criminal gang that has been starting fires.

Thumbs Down (Banner Productions/Sterling Pictures, 1927)
d: Phil Rosen.   5 reels.
Creighton Hale, Lois Boyd, Wyndham Standing, Helen Lee Worthing, Vera Lewis, Scott Seaton.
Helen, a typist, loves a wealthy young man and he loves her. She refuses to marry him, however, because her father is in jail and she wishes to keep that information secret. But love wins in the end, as Helen finally accedes to her sweetheart's proposal and his lawyer discovers that her father was jailed unjustly, and gets him released.

Thunder (MGM, 1929)
d: William Nigh.   9 reels.   (Music score, sound effects.)
Lon Chaney, James Murray, George Duryea, Phyllis Haver, Frances Norris, Wally Albright Jr.
Anderson, a railroad engineer with a grumpy disposition, runs his train with a fanatical devotion to time schedules, often taking unecessary chances by driving through snow drifts and floods.

Thunder Island (Universal, 1921)
d: Norman Dawn.   5 reels.
Edith Roberts, Fred DeSilva, Fred Kohler, Jack O'Brien, Arthur Jasmine.
Isola, a Mexican girl, falls in love with an American sea captain. There's just one hitch: She entered into a marriage of pity with a dying man, but now he seems to have recovered. The report that her husband has survived turns out to be false, however, and Isola sails away to Thunder Island to be with her captain lover.

Thunder Mountain (Fox, 1925)
d: Victor Schertzinger.   8 reels.
Madge Bellamy, Leslie Fenton, Alec B. Francis, Paul Panzer, Arthur Houseman, ZaSu Pitts, Emily Fitzroy, Dan Mason, Otis Harlan, Russell Simpson, Natalie Warfield.
Thunder Mountain, home to the feuding Martin and Givens clans, gets some excitement when Azalea, a circus performer, flees the show and its tyrannical owner, and escapes to the mountain community.

Thunder Riders (Universal, 1928)
d: William Wyler.   5 reels.
Ted Wells, Charlotte Stevens, William A. Steele, Bill Dyer, Leo White, Julia Griffith, Bob Burns, Pee Wee Holmes, Dick L'Estrange.
Betty, an eastern girl, journeys to the Old West to claim the ranch she has inherited.

The Thunderbolt (Katherine MacDonald Pictures/First

National, 1919)
d: Colin Campbell.   5 reels.
Katherine Campbell, Spottiswood Aitken, Thomas Meighan, Forrest Stanley, Ada Gleason, Doc Cannon, Jim Gordon, Antrim Short, Mrs. L.C. Harris, Jim Blackwell.
In Kentucky, a New Yorker marries a southern belle. But soon after, she learns that her new husband plans to keep her childless, a condition she will not accept.

Thunderbolts of Fate   (Edward Warren Productions/Pathé, 1919)
d: Edward Warren.   5 reels.
House Peters, Anna Lehr, Ned Burton, Wildred Lytell, Ben Lewin, Henry Sedley, Corene Uzzell.
When a young man is unjustly convicted of murdering a playboy and sent to death row, his sister goes to the state's governor to plead for a stay of execution. Their meeting is more than simply routine, though, for the sister has been in love with the married governor for a long time, and he with her.

Thunderclap   (Fox, 1921)
d: Richard Stanton.   7 reels.
Mary Carr, J. Barney Sherry, Paul Willis, Violet Mersereau, Carol Chase, John Daly Murphy, Walter McEwen, Maude Hill, Thomas McCann.
A brutal gambler plots to sabotage a horse race in order to win a $40,000 wager. But Thunderclap, the hero's horse, overcomes the obstacles and his owner rides him to victory.

Thundering Dawn   (Universal, 1923)
d: Harry Garson.   7 reels.
Winter Hall, J. Warren Kerrigan, Anna Q. Nillson, Tom Santschi, Charles Clary, Georgia Woodthorpe, Richard Kean, Edward Burns, Winifred Bryson, Anna May Wong.
Standish, a young man feeling the burden of personal loss, goes to the South Seas and falls prey to two formidable seducers: alcohol and a vamp named Lullaby Lou.

The Thundering Herd   (Famous Players-Lasky/Paramount, 1925)
d: William K. Howard.   7 reels.
Jack Holt, Lois Wilson, Noah Beery, Raymond Hatton, Charles Ogle, T.J. McCoy, Lillian Leighton, Eulalie Jensen, Stephen Carr, Maxine Elliott Hicks, Edward J. Brady, Fred Kohler.
Out West, a buffalo hunter falls in love with the stepdaughter of a notorious gang leader.

Thundering Hoofs   (New Era Productions/Anchor Film Distributors, 1922)
d: Francis Ford.   5 reels.
Peggy O'Day, Francis Ford, Florence Murth, Phil Ford, Harry Kelly.
To foil a plot against a prize entry in the Kentucky Derby, a southern girl dons the jockey silks and rides the horse to victory.

Thundering Hoofs   (Monogram/FBO of America, 1924)
d: Albert Rogell.   5 reels.
Fred Thomson, Fred Huntley, Charles Mailes Charles DeRevenna, Ann May, Carrie Clark Ward, William Lowery.
Marshall, an American in love with an aristocratic Mexican girl, must prove himself by entering the bullring—not as a torero, but on horseback.

Thundering Romance   (Action Pictures/Artclass Pictures, 1924)
d: Richard Thorpe.   5 reels.

Buffalo Bill Jr., Jean Arthur, René Picot, Harry Todd, Lew Meehan, J.P. Lockney, George A. Williams, Lafe McKee.
Out West, "Lightning" Bill saves a girl's ranch from foreclosure by taking on the minions of a crooke attorney.

Thundering Through   (Action Pictures/Artclass Pictures, 1925)
d: Fred Bain.   5 reels.
Buddy Roosevelt, Jean Arthur, Charles Colby, Lew Meehan, Frederick Lee, L.J. O'Connor, Lawrence Underwood.
Out West, a rancher falls in love with the daughter of a neighboring rancher, then must put his courtship on hold while he battles a crooked land-grabbing scheme.

Thy Name is Woman   (Metro, 1924)
d: Fred Niblo.   9 reels.
Ramon Novarro, Barbara LaMarr, William V. Mong, Wallace MacDonald, Robert Edeson, Edith Roberts, Claire McDowell.
Ricardo, a Spanish soldier, romances the wife of a notorious smuggler... but it's all in the line of duty.

Tide of Empire   (MGM, 1929)
d: Allan Dwan.   8 reels.
Renee Adoree, George Duryea, George Fawcett, Paul Hurst, Fred Kohler, William Collier Jr., James Bradbury Sr., Harry Gribbon.
Out West, a rancher falls in love with a girl whose brother is under sentence of death for his participation in a failed revolt.

The Tides of Barnegat   (Paramount, 1917)
d: Marshall Neilan.   5 reels.
Blanche Sweet, Harrison Ford, Elliott Dexter, Norma Nichols, Tom Forman, Lillian Leighton, Billy Jacobs, Walter Rogers.
When a sailor dies at sea leaving his girlfriend pregnant, her protective sister shelters her from dishonor by taking her away until the child is born, then claiming it as her own.

The Tides of Fate   (Equitable Motion Pictures Corp./World Film Corp., 1917)
d: Marshall Farnum.   5 reels.
Alexandra Carlisle, Frank Holland, William A. Sheer, Charles Graham, Jane Kent, Walter Ryder.
King, a counterfeiter, skips town when the cops move in, and leaves his innocent bride to take the rap for him.

Tides of Passion   (Vitagraph, 1925)
d: J. Stuart Blackton.   7 reels.
Mae Marsh, Ben Hendricks, Laska Winter, Earl Schenck, Ivor McFadden, Thomas Mills.
In Nova Scotia, an incurable romantic marries a local girl and they set sail for Canada. Aboard ship, however, the new bridegroom flirts with the captain's wife and is thrown overboard into the icy waters. He barely makes it to shore, where he is nursed back to health by an Indian maiden... whom he promptly marries.

The Tie That Binds   (Warner Bros., 1923)
d: Joseph Levering.   7 reels.
Barbara Bedford, Walter Miller, William P. Carlton, Marian Swayne, Effie Shannon, Julia Swayne Gordon.
Familiar tale about a man who confesses to a crime he did not commit, in order to protect a loved one.

The Tiger Lily   (American Film Co./Pathé, 1919)
d: George L. Cox.   5 reels.
Margarita Fisher, Emory Johnson, George Periolat, E. Alyn Warren, J. Barney Sherry, Rosita Marstini, Beatrice Van,

TILLIE'S PUNCTURED ROMANCE (1914). Charlie (Charlie Chaplin) and Mabel (Mabel Normand) get up close and personal behind his hefty new bride's massive back. But the bride will soon hone in on the cheating couple and exact her kind of revenge.

* * * * *

Frank Clark.
The fiery Carmina, a waitress known as "the Tiger Lily," falls in love with David, her boss' landlord.

Tiger Love (Famous Players-Lasky/Paramount, 1924)
d: George Melford. 6 reels.
Estelle Taylor, Antonio Moreno, G. Raymond Nye, Manuel Camero, Egar Norton, David Torrence, Snitz Edwards, Monte Collings.
In Spain, an outlaw falls in love with an aristocratic lady and abducts her on her wedding day.

The Tiger Man (Paramount, 1918)
d: William S. Hart. 5 reels.
William S. Hart, Jane Novak, Robert Lawrence, Milton Ross, J.P. Lockney, Charles K. French.
Desperadoes escape from prison and find a group of immigrants stranded in the desert without water. Hawk, the head outlaw, must decide whether to help the immigrants and thus expose himself to recapture, or leave them and escape into the mountains.

Tiger Rose (Warner Brothers, 1923)
d: Sidney Franklin. 8 reels.
Lenore Ulric, Theodore von Eltz, Forrest Stanley, Joseph Dowling, André de Beranger, Sam De Grasse, Claude Gillingwater.
In Canada, a half-caste girl enchants several males, including a mountie.

Tiger True (Universal, 1921)
d: J.P. McGowan. 5 reels.
Frank Mayo, Fritzi Brunette, Elinor Hancock, Al Kaufman, Walter Long, Charles Brinley, Herbert Bethew, Henry A. Barrows.
Jack, a wealthy big-game hunter, decides to seek adventure in the big city. He finds plenty of it, as newly-appointed bouncer in a popular saloon.

The Tiger Woman (Fox, 1917)
d: J. Gordon Edwards. 5 reels.
Theda Bara, E.F. Rogerman, Glen White, Mary Martin, John Webb Dillon, Louis Dean, Emil De Varney, Herbert Heyes, Edwin Holt, Florence Martin, Kate Blanke, George Clarke, Kittens Reichert.
In a scenario strongly reminiscent of her debut film *A Fool There Was*, Miss Bara plays a heartless woman who betrays her husband and sends him to his death; poisons her lover; blackmails an American playboy; and begins to snare the playboy's brother before she is finally stopped by a dagger-wielding former victim.

The Tiger's Claw (Famous Players-Lasky/Paramount, 1923)
d: Joseph Henabery. 6 reels.
Jack Holt, Eva Novak, George Periolat, Bertram Grassby, Aileen Pringle, Carl Stockdale, Frank Butler, George Field, Evelyn Selbie, Frederick Vroom, Lucien Littlefield, Robert Cain.
In India, an American engineer falls in love with a halfcaste girl who has nursed him back to health after a tiger attack.

The Tiger's Coat (Dial Film Co./W.W. Hodkinson/Pathé, 1920)
d: Roy Clements. 5 reels.
W. Lawson Butt, Tina Modotti, Myrtle Stedman, Myles McCarthy, Frank Weed, Jiquel Lanoe, Nola Luxford, Charles Spere, Helene Sullivan.
Racial prejudice rears its ugly head in this tale about a well-to-do businessman who decides to break off his engagement when he learns that his fiancée is not European, but Mexican.

The Tiger's Cub (Fox, 1920)
d: Charles Giblyn. 6 reels.
Pearl White, Thomas Carrigan, J. Thornton Baston, John Davidson, Frank Evans, John Woodford, Ruby Hoffman, Albert Tavernier.
In Alaska, an adventurer lost in the snow is rescued by a girl known as "Tiger's Cub."

The Tigress (Columbia, 1927)
d: George B. Seitz. 6 reels.
Dorothy Revier, Jack Holt, Howard Truesdell, Frank Leigh, Philippe DeLacy, Frank Nelson.
In Spain, a gypsy girl swears vengeance on the nobleman who killed her father. But in time she learns that the nobleman is innocent of the crime, and even falls in love with him.

Till I Come Back to You (Famous Players-Lasky/Paramount, 1918)
d: Cecil B. DeMille. 6 reels.
Bryant Washburn, Florence Vidor, G. Butler Clonblough, Winter Hall, Georgie Stone, Clarence Geldart, May Giraci, Julia Faye, Lillian Leighton, W.J. Irving, Monte Blue.
During World War I, an American engineer in Belgium falls in love with the wife of a German officer.

Till We Meet Again (Dependable Pictures/Associated Exhibitors, 1922)
d: William Christy Cabanne. 6 reels.
Julia Swayne Gordon, Mae Marsh, J. Barney Sherry, Walter Miller, Norman Kerry, Martha Mansfield, Tammany Young, Danny Hayes, Dick Lee, Cyril Chadwick.
Marion, an escapee from an insane asylum, joins a gang of thieves as their cook. Still seeking vengeance against the man who had her unjustly committed, Marion uses her new connections with the underworld to exact her revenge.

Tillie (Realart Pictures/Paramount Pictures, 1922)
d: Frank Urson. 5 reels.
Mary Miles Minter, Noah Beery, Allan Forrest, Lucien Littlefield, Lillian Leighton, Marie Treboul, Virginia Adair, Robert Anderson, Ashley Cooper.
In Pennsylvania Dutch country, a girl named Tillie learns that she has inherited a small estate, but only on the condition that she become a Mennonite before turning 18.

Tillie the Toiler (Cosmopolitan/MGM, 1927)
d: Hobart Henley. 7 reels.
Marion Davies, Matt Moore, Harry Crocker, George Fawcett, George K. Arthur, Estelle Clark, Claire McDowell, Bert Roach.
Tillie Jones, a stenographer, has eyes for one of the office fellows.
Enjoyable star vehicle based on the popular comic strip.

Tillie Wakes Up (World Film Corp., 1917)
d: Harry Davenport. 5 reels.
Marie Dressler, Johnny Hines. Frank Beamish, Ruby de Remer, Ruth Barrett, Jack Brown.
A man and a woman, both misunderstood by their spouses, get together for a day of relaxation at Coney Island.

Tillie's Night Out—see: Tillie Wakes Up (1917)

Tillie's Punctured Romance (Keystone, 1914)
d: Mack Sennett. 6 reels.

Marie Dressler, Charlie Chaplin, Mabel Normand, Charley Chase, Mack Swain, Charlie Murray, Edgar Kennedy, Chester Conklin, the Keystone Kops.

The first feature-length comedy ever made. Chaplin plays not the Little Tramp, but rather a slimy weasel of a man, a fortune-hunter out to snare a rich wife or, better still, to snare her millions for himself without marriage. No matter. Chaplin is as hilarious as a villain as he would ever be as the hero. Miss Dressler reprises her role from the stage play *Tillie's Nightmare*, playing a love-starved hulk of a woman who naively falls for the scoundrel's deceptions. Miss Normand, the foremost film comedienne of the day, has a key role as the villain's on-again, off-again inamorata.

Tillie's Tomato Surprise (Lubin, 1915)
d: Howell Hansel. 6 reels.
Colin Campbell, Marie Dressler, Eleanor Fairbanks, Sarah McVicker, Clara Lambert, Tom McNaughton.
Tillie and her cousin Percy are aghast when they learn that their wealthy Aunt Sally, who disappeared while riding an aircraft, has willed most of her estate to her pet monkey.

Timber Wolf (Fox, 1925)
d: William S. Van Dyke. 5 reels.
Buck Jones, Elinor Fair, David Dyas, Sam Allen, William Wailing, Jack Craig, Robert Mack.
Standing, a miner also known as the Timber Wolf, battles a gang of claim jumpers.

Time Lock Number 776 (Photo Drama Co., 1915)
d: Hal Reid. 6 reels.
Joe Welch, Dora Dean, Mae Georgina, Hal Reid, Adella Barker, Edward Sullivan, Fred MacKaye, John Starkey, Mae Trado, Jack Murray.
Helen, an aspiring actress, is kidnapped by a gang of counterfeiters who want her gifted father to create phony plates to produce one-hundred-dollar bills.

Time Locks and Diamonds (New York Motion Picture Corp./Triangle, 1917)
d: Walter Edwards. 5 reels.
William Desmond, Gloria Hope, Robert McKim, Rowland Lee, Mildred Harris, George Beranger, Thomas Guise, Milton Ross, Laura Sears, Kate Bruce, Margaret Thompson, Darrell Foss.
Farrel, a reformed thief, agrees to pull one last job to help out a pal.

Time, the Comedian (MGM, 1925)
d: Robert Z. Leonard. 5 reels.
Mae Busch, Lew Cody, Gertrude Olmstead, Creighton Hale.
A singer reveals to her daughter that the man the daughter loves caused the suicide of her father.

Time to Love (Famous Players-Lasky/Paramount, 1927)
d: Frank Tuttle. 5 reels.
Raymond Griffith, William Powell, Vera Voronina, Josef Swichard, Mario Carillo, Pierre De Ramey, Helene Giere, Alfred Sabato.
A man who's unlucky in love tries to commit suicide but fails, and instead he winds up in love again—this time with a beautiful princess. He subsequently fights no fewer than three duels to win her hand, and even feigns death after one duel. In the end, this incurable romantic wins his lady fair.

Times Have Changed (Fox, 1923)
d: James Flood. 5 reels.
William Russell, Mabel Julienne Scott, Charles West, Martha Mattox, Edwin B. Tilton, George Atkinson, Allene Ray, Dick

LaReno, Gus Leonard, Jack Curtis.
Comedy about a chap who is sent to the big city to recover a fancy quilt, then learns that the cops and the crooks are after it too.

Times Square (Gotham Productions/Lumas Film Corp., 1929)
d: Joseph C. Boyle. 6 reels. (Part talkie.)
Alice Day, Arthur Lubin, Emil Chautard, Ann Brady, John Miljan, Arthur Housman, Joseph Swickard, Natalie Joyce, Eddie Kane.
The son of a famous classic musician breaks with family tradition and becomes a songwriter and song plugger in Tin Pan Alley.

The Timid Terror (R-C Pictures/FBO of America, 1926)
d: Del Andrews. 5 reels.
George O'Hara, Edith Yorke, Doris Hill, Rex Lease, George Nichols, Dot Farley.

Trent, a mousy office worker, wants a raise and a promotion but is told by the boss that he's not aggressive enough to handle a higher position. That changes fast, when Trent acquires a taxi cab and takes his boss on a wild ride, demonstrating both his boldness and his tenacity.

Tin Gods (Famous Players-Lasky/Paramount, 1926)
d: Allan Dwan. 9 reels.
Thomas Meighan, Renee Adoree, Aileen Pringle, Hale Hamilton, John Harrington, Joe King, Robert E. O'Connor, Delbert Emory Whitten Jr.
Weepy melodrama about a once-promising engineer whose life is a series of failures.

Tin Hats (MGM, 1926)
d: Edward Sedgwick. 7 reels.
Conrad Nagel, Claire Windsor, George Cooper, Tom O'Brien, Bert Roach, Eileen Sedgwick.
After the armistice that ends World War I, three American doughboys in Europe fall for a trio of frauleins.

Tin Pan Alley (Fox, 1919)
d: Frank Beal. 5 reels.
Elinor Fair, George Hernandez, Albert Ray, Louis Natho, Kate Price, Ardito Mellonino, Frank Weed, Thomas H. Persee.
Tommy, a talented musician and composer, loves June, a cigarette girl. When he writes a song that becomes a big hit, Tommy is swept up in the whirlwind of success and soon forgets June and all his pals. But faithful June waits for him to come back down to earth.

Tinsel (World Film Corp., 1918)
d: Oscar Apfel. 5 reels.
Kitty Gordon, Muriel Ostriche, Frank Mayo, Bradley Barker, Ralph Graves, George DeCarlton, Anthony Merlo, Marie Nau.
Ruth, a simple country girl, is thrilled to learn that her socialite mother, now estranged from Ruth's father, has offered to introduce her daughter into society. But starry-eyed Ruth will learn that not all is gold that glitters, and eventually returns to her simple roots.

The Tip-Off (Universal, 1929)
d: Leigh Jason. 5 reels.
Bill Cody, George Hackathorne, Duane Thompson, L.J. O'Connor, Jack Singleton, Robert Bolder, Monte Montague, Walter Shumway.
Annie, a fortune-teller, sees in her crystal ball that her lover,

a former thief, is about to be betrayed by false friends.

Tipped Off (Harry A. McKenzie/Playgoers Pictures, 1923)
d: Finis Fox. 5 reels.
Arline Pretty, Harold Miller, Tom Santschi, Noah Beery, Stuart Holmes, Zella Gray, Tom O'Brien, Bessie Wong, James Alamo, Jimmie Truax, Si Wilcox, James Wang, Scotty MacGregor.
A stage-struck girl yearns to star in her playwright fiancé's new crime drama, but he won't hear of it. To convince him, she and her siblings arrange a fake robbery to demonstrate her acting ability... but real crooks show up and kidnap her.

The Tired Businessman (Tiffany Productions, 1927)
d: Allen Dale. 6 reels.
Raymond Hitchcock, Dot Farley, Mack Swain, Margaret Quimby, Charles Delaney, Lincoln Plummer, Blanche Mehaffey, Gibson Gowland, James Farley.
Comedy about a pair of paving contractors angling for a valuable city deal.

To a Finish (Fox, 1921)
d: Bernard J. Durning. 5 reels.
Buck Jones, Helen Ferguson, G. Raymond Nye, Norman Selby, Herschel Mayall.
Out West, a corrupt town boss attempts a land grab but is opposed by the son of the rightful owner.

To Have and to Hold (Lasky Feature Plays/Paramount, 1916)
d: George H. Melford. 5 reels.
Mae Murray, Wallace Reid, Tom Forman, Raymond Hatton, James Neill, Lucien Littlefield, Ronald Bradbury, Robert Fleming, Bob Gray, Camille Astor.
Seeking to avoid marriage to a disgusting nobleman, Jocelyn leaves her native England and sets sail for the colonies.

To Have and to Hold (Famous Players-Lasky/Paramount, 1922)
d: George Fitzmaurice. 8 reels.
Betty Compson, Bert Lytell, Theodore Kosloff, W.J. Ferguson, Raymond Hatton, Claire DuBrey, Walter Long, Anne Cornwall, Fred Huntley, Arthur Rankin, Lucien Littlefield.
Remake of Lasky's 1916 feature *To Have and to Hold*, both versions based on the novel of the same name by Mary Johnston.

To Hell With the Kaiser (Screen Classics, Inc./Metro, 1918)
d: George Irving. 7 reels.
Lawrence Grant, Olive Tell, Betty Howe, John Sunderland, Earl Schenck, Mabel Wright, Frank Currier, Carl Dane, Walter P. Lewis, Henry Carvill, Charles Hartley, Emil Hoch.
World War I fantasy-drama, with Germany's Kaiser Wilhelm making a pact with the Devil and eventually replacing the Prince of Darkness in hell.

To Him That Hath — see: The Supreme Sacrifice (1916)

To Him That Hath (World Film Corp., 1918)
d: Oscar Apfel. 6 reels.
Montagu Love, Reginald Carrington, George DeCarlton, George Lessey, Charley Jackson, Gertrude McCoy, Clio Ayres, Marion Barney, Edward Elkas, Dean Raymond, Henry Hebert, Jack Ridgway, Henry West, John Sturgeon.
Remake of the 1916 World Film Corp. Film *The Supreme Sacrifice*, about a struggling writer who takes the blame for a mission director's crime.

To Honor and Obey (Fox, 1917)

d: Otis Turner. 5 reels.
Gladys Brockwell, Bertram Grassby, Charles Clary, Joseph Swickard, Willard Louis, Jewel Carmen.
When an egocentric playboy loses all his money on Wall Street, he persuades his wife to ask her former suitor for help. She does so, and receives a large sum in return for her honor. But her immature husband just goes out and loses it all again.

To Please One Woman (Lois Weber Productions/Paramount, 1920)
w, d: Lois Weber. 7 reels.
Claire Windsor, Edith Kessler, George Hackathorne, Edward Burns, Mona Lisa, Howard Gaye, L.C. Shumway, Gordon Griffith.
Leila, a heartless *femme fatale*, feigns illness to make a play for the local doctor.

To the Death (Metro, 1917)
d: Burton L. King. 5 reels.
Olga Petrova, Mahlon Hamilton, Wyndham Standing, Henry Leone, Evelyn Brent, Violet Reed, Marion Singer, Boris Korlin.
Bianca, a Corsican lace maker, moves to Paris and falls in love with Etienne, leader of a secret society.

To the Highest Bidder (Vitagraph, 1918)
d: Tom Terriss. 5 reels.
Alice Joyce, Percy Standing, Walter McGrail, Edna Murphy, Jules Cowles, Mary Carr, Stephen Carr.
Strapped for funds for herself and her little brother, a young woman auctions herself off as a housewife to the highest bidder.

To the Ladies (Famous Players-Lasky/Paramount, 1923)
d: James Cruze. 6 reels.
Edward Horton, Theodore Roberts, Helen Jerome Eddy, Louise Dresser, Z. Wall Covington, Arthur Hoyt, Jack Gardner.
Comedy about three rivals for an important position with a large firm, all of whom realize that it's the president's wife who makes all the decisions.

To the Last Man (Famous Players-Lasky/Paramount, 1923)
d: Victor Fleming. 7 reels.
Richard Dix, Lois Wilson, Noah Beery, Robert Edeson, Frank Campeau, Fred Huntley, Edward Brady, Eugene Pallette, Leonard Clapham, Guy Oliver, Winifred Greenwood.
Out West, a battle rages between the cattle ranchers and the sheep farmers.

The Toast of Death (New York Motion Picture Corp./Mutual, 1915)
d: Thomas H. Ince. 5 reels.
Louise Glaum, Herschel Mayall, Harry Keenan.
In India, a ballerina marries a Bengalese prince, but she continues her romantic liaisons with a handsome British captain.

Toby's Bow (Goldwyn, 1919)
d: Harry Beaumont. 5 reels.
Tom Moore, Doris Pawn, Macey Harlam, Arthur Housman, Colin Kenny, Augustus Phillips, Catherine Wallace, Violet Schram, Ruby LaFayette, George K. Kuwa, Nick Cogley.
Tom, a published novelist, surreptitiously coaches his landlady Eugenia in writing her manuscript.

Todd of the Times (Robert Brunton Co./Pathé, 1919)
d: Eliot Howe. 5 reels.

Frank Keenan, Buddy Post, Aggie Herring, Herschel Mayall, George Williams, Joe Dowling, Jay Morley, Irene Rich, Arthur Millett, Ruth Langston.

Todd, a city editor on the local paper, is keen to become managing editor, but lacks the drive to go after the job, partly because his domineering wife keeps him perpetually henpecked. Finally Todd gets a break: He learns that a team of crooked stock brokers are actually the brains behind a gambling syndicate in the city, and exposes the whole scheme in a sensational front page story.

Together (Universal, 1918)
d: O.A.C. Lund. 5 reels.
Violet Mersereau, Chester Barnett, Barney Randall, Lindsay J. Hall.
Laura and her long-lost twin, Larry, are reunited when he, now living in desperate property, tries to rob the family home. It's a serendipitous meeting, because now that brother and sister are together again, they can claim inheritance under their father's will.

The Toilers (Tiffany-Stahl Productions, 1928)
d: Reginald Barker. 8 reels.
Douglas Fairbanks Jr., Jobyna Ralston, Harvey Clark, Wade Boteler, Robert Ryan.
Three coal miners buried by an avalanche are rescued when the fiancée of one of the men, following a compelling dream, leads a team to the precise spot where they are trapped.

A Tokyo Siren (Universal, 1920)
d: Norman Dawn. 5 reels.
Tsuru Aoki, Goro Kino, Jack Livingston, Toyo Fujita, Arthur Jasmine, Peggy Pearce, Florence Hart, Frederick Vroom, Dorothy Hipp, Eleanor Hancock, Eugenie Forde.
In Japan, a chivalrous American doctor offers to marry a local girl in name only, and take her to the United States where she can be free.

Tol'able David (First National, 1921)
d: Henry King. 7 reels.
Richard Barthelmess, Gladys Hulette, Ernest Torrence, Warner Richmond, Walter P. Lewis, Ralph Yearsley, Forrest Robinson, Laurence Eddinger, Edmund Gurney, Marion Abbott, Henry Hallam, Patterson Dial.
A young man in a rural town is kept from "growing up" by his overprotective family. However, he must take charge when a brutal gang of thugs moves in and begins destroying the town's peaceful atmosphere.

Told at Twilight (Balboa Amusement Co./Pathé, 1917)
d: Henry King. 5 reels.
Baby Marie Osborne, Daniel Gilfether, Henry King, Beatrice Van, Leon Pardue.
Little Mary Sunshine befriends a crotchety old man who lives next door.

Told in the Hills (Famous Players-Lasky/Paramount, 1919)
d: George Melford. 5 reels.
Robert Warwick, Ann Little, Tom Forman, Wanda Hawley, Charles Ogle, Monte Blue, Margaret Loomis, Eileen Percy, Hart Hoxie, Jack Herbert, Guy Oliver.
Jack, a Kentucky boy, moves to Montana and becomes a prospector and Indian guide. When a tribal chieftain is accidentally killed, Jack is unjustly imprisoned for the crime, but escapes with the help of Rachel, a white woman who's fallen in love with him.

The Toll Gate (Paramount, 1920)

d: Lambert Hillyer. 5 reels.
William S. Hart, Anna Q. Nilsson, Jack Richardson, Joseph Singleton, Richard Headrick.
Black Deering, a notorious outlaw, leads his gang on one last train robbery before going straight—but this time, they're captured by the Army, tipped off by a traitor in the gang. Deering escapes and goes after the traitor on his own.

The Toll of the Sea (Technicolor Motion Picture Corp./Metro, 1922)
d: Chester M. Franklin. 5 reels. (Technicolor.)
Anna May Wong, Kenneth Harlan, Beatrice Bentley, Baby Moran, Etta Lee, Ming Young.
In this updated variant on *Madame Butterfly*, a Chinese girl named Lotus Flower (played wonderfully by the 17-year-old Anna May Wong) rescues an American adventurer shipwrecked on the Chinese coast. They fall in love and, in due course, a child is born to them. But the man returns to America without Lotus Flower and marries his American fiancée.
The Toll of the Sea was the second feature film shot in Technicolor, though the first, *The Gulf Between* (1917), used a more primitive process which required the projection print to be shown through alternating red and green filters. *The Toll of the Sea* contained all the requisite color information on the film itself, though it was still a clumsy process; two strips of exposed film had to be cemented together in precise unison before being run through the projector.

Tom Sawyer (Oliver Morosco Photoplay Co./Paramount, 1917)
d: William D. Taylor. 5 reels.
Jack Pickford, George Hackathorne, Alice Marvin, Edythe Chapman, Robert Gordon, Antrim Short, Clara Horton, Helen Gilmore.
In Hannibal, Missouri, a young mischief maker runs away with his friend Huckleberry Finn and they sail a raft down the Mississippi to a deserted island.

The Tomboy (Fox, 1921)
w, d: Carl Harbaugh. 5 reels.
Eileen Percy, Hal Cooley, Richard Cummings, Paul Kamp, Byron Munson, Harry Dunkinson, James McElhern, Leo Sulky, Grace McClean, Walter Wilkinson, Virginia Stern.
Small-town Minnie, the village hoyden, swears revenge on the bootleggers that got her dad hooked on liquor.

The Tomboy (Chadwick Pictures, 1924)
d: David Kirkland. 6 reels.
Herbert Rawlinson, Dorothy Devore, James Barrows, Lee Moran, Helen Lynch, Lottie Williams, Harry Gribbon, Virginia True Boardman.
A tomboy who runs a small-town boarding house falls hard when a handsome stranger arrives from the city. He's interested in her too, but first he has a job to do: ferreting out liquor smugglers hiding in the town.

Tomorrow's Love (Famous Players-Lasky/Paramount, 1925)
d: Paul Bern. 6 reels.
Agnes Ayres, Pat O'Malley, Raymond Hatton, Jane Winton, Ruby Lafayette, Dale Fuller.
Convoluted romantic comedy in which a wife walks in on her husband while he is dancing with an old girlfriend at her (the girlfriend's) apartment. Though the circumstances are truly innocent, the outraged wife swiftly files for divorce, then takes a trip to Europe while waiting for her final decree. The husband and ex-girlfriend, stunned by all this, decide to

get married when that decree comes in. But the wife, learning of their plans, decides she wants to keep her husband after all, and races back to the U.S. to prevent their marriage.

The Tong Man (Haworth Pictures Corp./Robertson-Cole, 1919)
d: William Worthington. 5 reels.
Sessue Hayakawa, Helen Jerome Eddy, Marc Robbins, Toyo Fujita, Jack Abbe.
In San Francisco's Chinatown, a Tong assassin finds himself unable to carry out his latest assignment because it involves killing the merchant whose daughter he loves.

Tongues of Flame (Universal, 1918)
d: Colin Campbell. 5 reels.
Marie Walcamp, Al Whitman, Alfred Allen, Hugh Sutherland, J.P. Wilde, Lilly Clarke.
In a remoted woodland in California, a preacher's daughter flirts with a half-breed Indian and he imagines he is in love with her.

Tongues of Flame (Famous Players-Lasky/Paramount, 1924)
d: Joseph Henabery. 7 reels.
Thomas Meighan, Bessie Love, Eileen Percy, Berton Churchill, John Miltern, Leslie Stowe, Nick Thompson, Jerry Devine, Kate Mayhew, Cyril Ring.
Out West, a tribe of Indians is swindled out of oil-rich land. Harrington, a white lawyer who has fallen in love with an Indian maiden, leads the fight to reclaim the land for the tribe. It won't be easy.

Tongues of Men (Oliver Morosco Photoplays/Paramount, 1916)
d: Frank Lloyd. 5 reels.
Constance Collier, Forrest Stanley, Herbert Standing, Lamar Johnstone, Lydia Yeamans Titus, Helen Eddy, Elizabeth Burbridge, Charles Marriot, John McKinnon, Howard Davies.
When a small-town minister denounces stage actors in general and one opera diva in particular, the diva resolves to make him fall in love with her.

Tony America (Triangle, 1918)
d: Thomas N. Heffron. 5 reels.
Francis McDonald, Yvonne Paris, Rae Godfrey, Dorothy Giraci, Mrs. Harry Davenport, Harold Holland, Ludwig Lowry, Dick Loreno.
In New York, an Italian fruit peddler loves Rosa. Although they marry and have a child, Rosa still has a flirtatious eye for the other men.

Tony Runs Wild (Fox, 1926)
d: Thomas Buckingham. 6 reels.
Tom Mix, Tony the horse, Jacqueline Logan, Lawford Davidson, Duke Lee, Vivian Oakland, Edward Martindel, Marion Harlan, Raymond Wells, Richard Carter, Lucien Littlefield.
Out West, a beautiful stallion leads a pack of wild horses until he is captured by a cowboy named Tom. Though Tom spends two weeks taming and training the spirited animal—whom he's named "Tony"—at the end he lets him go free. Later, when Tom is ambushed by a gang of roughnecks, Tony and his wild horses come to the rescue.

Too Fat to Fight (Rex Beach Pictures Co./Goldwyn, 1918)
d: Hobart Henley. 6 reels.
Frank McIntyre, Florence Dixon, Henrietta Floyd, Floria de

Martimprey, Harold Entwistle, Jack McLean, Frank Badgley.
When the U.S. enters World War I, chubby Norman tries to enlist but is told he is too fat. Undaunted, he joins a service organization and goes to France, where he serves the troops as a soup carrier.

Too Many Crooks (Vitagraph, 1919)
d: Ralph Ince. 5 reels.
Gladys Leslie, Jean Paige, T.J. McGrane, James Dent, Huntley Gordon, Cecil Chichester, Anders Randolf, George O'Donnell, John P. Wade, James Gaylore.
After attending a play about criminals, wealthy Charlotte grumbles that the script and the actors were unconvincing. To prove her point, she arranges a posh party in her home and invites every real criminal she can find... which leads to several humorous complications.
This film was remade once in the silent era, by Paramount in 1927.

Too Many Crooks (Paramount, 1927)
d: Fred Newmeyer. 6 reels.
Lloyd Hughes, Mildred Davis, George Bancroft, El Brendel, William V. Mong, Betty Francisco, John Sainpolis, Otto Mathiesen, Thomas Ricketts, Cleve Moore, Gayne Whitman, Ruth Cherrington, Pat Hartigan.
Remake of the 1919 Vitagraph comedy *Too Many Crooks*, both versions based on the play of the same name by E.J. Rath.

Too Many Kisses (Famous Players-Lasky/Paramount, 1925)
d: Paul Sloane. 6 reels.
Richard Dix, Frances Howard, Joe Burke, Albert Tavernier, Arthur Ludwig, Alyce Mills, William Powell, Paul Panzer.
Comedy about Gaylord, a playboy whose father disapproves of the young man's many romantic liaisons. To cut him off from contact with the opposite sex, Papa sends him to Spain because he's heard that Basque women never marry outside their race. Papa was misinformed.

Too Many Millions (Famous Players-Lasky/Paramount, 1918)
d: James Cruze. 5 reels.
Wallace Reid, Ora Carew, Tully Marshall, Charles Ogle, Winifred Greenwood, James Neill, Noah Beery, Percy Williams, Richard Wayne.
Comedy about a publisher who learns he has inherited forty million dollars, then has to learn how to be happy with that much money.

Too Much Business (Vitagraph, 1922)
d: Jess Robbins. 7 reels.
Edward Horton, Ethel Grey Terry, Tully Marshall, John Steppling, Carl Gerard, Elsa Lorimer, Helen Gilmore, Mark Fenton, Tom Murray.
Trained in business methods, a chap gets the girl he loves to sign a 30-day option on their love.

Too Much Johnson (Famous Players-Lasky/Paramount, 1919)
d: Donald Crisp. 5 reels.
Bryant Washburn, Lois Wilson, Adele Farrington, C.H. Geldart, Monte Blue, Monte Banks, Elsie Lorimer, Gloria Hope, George Hackathorn, Phil Gastrock.
Comedy of errors involving a husband with a wandering eye who must think fast, to get his marriage back on track after his dalliance with a married woman.

Too Much Money (First National, 1926)

d: John Francis Dillon. 7 reels.

Lewis Stone, Anna Q. Nilsson, Robert Cain, Derek Glynne, Edward Elkas, Ann Brody.

Broadley, a millionaire who feels his wife's love slipping away from him, arranges to "hide" all his money with a business partner and declare bankruptcy. Seemingly reduced to poverty, he and his wife move to a slum and start their life over again. But even as Broadley discovers that his wife's love for him is true, he learns that his business partner's loyalty is decidedly suspect: The scoundrel is planning to steal Broadley's millions for himself.

Too Much Speed (Famous Players-Lasky/Paramount, 1921)

d: Frank Urson. 5 reels.

Wallace Reid, Agnes Ayres, Theodore Roberts, Jack Richardson, Lucien Littlefield, Guy Oliver, Henry Johnson, Jack Herbert.

A professional auto racer and his fiancée try to elope at 100 miles an hour.

Too Much Wife (Realart Pictures/Paramount, 1922)

d: Thomas N. Heffron. 5 reels.

Wanda Hawley, T. Roy Barnes, Arthur Hoyt, Lillian Langdon, Leigh Wyant, Willard Louis, Bertram Johns, John Fox.

Myra, a new bride, smothers her husband with attention when she determines to join him wherever he goes — even on fishing trips with his buddies.

Too Much Youth (Paul Gerson Pictures, 1925)

d: Duke Worne. 5 reels.

Richard Holt, Sylvia Breamer, Eric Mayne, Charles K. French, Walter Leroy, Harris Gordon, Walter Perry, Joseph Belmont.

Kenton, a playboy, resolves not to sleep until he has closed a certain business deal. That's a problem, because the other parties to the transaction purposely delay closing, hoping to force the tiring Kenton into agreeing to their terms.

Too Wise Wives (Famous Players-Lasky/Paramount, 1921)

w, d: Lois Weber. 6 reels.

Louis Calhern, Claire Windsor, Phillips Smalley, Mona Lisa.

Newlyweds David and Marie find their marital bliss imperiled when a former sweeheart tries to entice David back to her.

The Top o' the Morning (Universal, 1922)

d: Edward Laemmle. 5 reels.

Gladys Walton, Harry Myers, Doreen Turner, Florence D. Lee, William Welsh, Don Bailey, Dick Cummings, Margaret Campbell, Ralph McCullough, Ethel Shannon, Harry Carter.

An Irish colleen gets a job in America as governess to a widower's child, and falls in love with her employer.

The Top of the World (Famous Players-Lasky/Paramount, 1925)

d: George Melford. 7 reels.

James Kirkwood, Anna Q. Nilsson, Joseph Kilgour, Mary Mersch, Raymond Hatton, Sheldon Lewis, Charles A. Post, Mabel Van Buren, Frank Jonasson, Lorimer Johnston.

In South Africa, Sylvia falls in love with her sweetheart's cousin. Later, when they are trapped by raging floodwaters, they escape by finding shelter on the highest plateau — the "top of the world" of the title.

Topsy and Eva (United Artists, 1927)

d: Del Lord. 8 reels.

Rosetta Duncan, Vivian Duncan, Gibson Gowland, Noble Johnson, Marjorie Daw, Nils Asther.

The Duncan sisters star as the titular heroines, in a story derived from *Uncle Tom's Cabin*.

The Torch Bearer (American Film Co./Mutual, 1916)

d: Jack Prescott, William Russell. 5 reels.

William Russell, Charlotte Burton, Marie Van Tassell, Harry Keenan, Alan Forrest, Nate Watt, Margaret Nichols.

While a crusading newspaper owner falls in love with an heiress from out West, his sister finds herself attracted to his partner, the district attorney.

Torment (Maurice Tourneur Productions/Associated First National, 1924)

d: Maurice Tourneur. 6 reels.

Owen Moore, Bessie Love, Jean Hersholt, Joseph Kilgour, Maude George, Morgan Wallace, George Cooper.

Following the Russian Revolution, a trio of international crooks trails an exiled count who they believe escaped from Moscow with the crown jewels.

The Torrent (Universal, 1921)

d: Stuart Paton. 5 reels.

Eva Novak, Jack Perrin, Oletta Ottis, L.C. Shumway, Jack Curtis, Harry Carter, Bert Alpino.

During a violent storm, a married woman is washed ashore on an island with a bachelor hydroplaner.

The Torrent (Phil Goldstone Productions/Truart Film Corp., 1924)

d: A.P. Younger. 6 reels.

William Fairbanks, Ora Carew, Frank Elliott, Joseph Kilgour, Gertrude Astor, June Elvidge, Fontaine LaRue, Ashley Cooper, Robert McKim, Charles French.

Aboard a ship on the high seas, a big game hunter and a socialite party too much, wind up drunk, and get married by the captain.

The Torrent (MGM, 1925)

d: Monta Bell. 7 reels.

Greta Garbo, Ricardo Cortez, Gertrude Olmstead, Edward Connelly, Martha Mattox, Lucien Littlefield, Lucy Beaumont, Tully Marshall, Mack Swain, Arthur Edmund Carew.

A Spanish aristocrat loves a poor girl, but his mother prevents their marriage. The girl goes on to become a great success as an opera star and, years later, returns to find her former lover a faded middle-ager.

A Tortured Heart (Fox, 1916)

d: Will S. Davis. 5 reels.

Virginia Pearson, Stuart Holmes, Fuller Mellish, Stephen Grattan, Frances Miller, Joseph Levering, Glenn White, George Larkin, Marian Swayne.

In the antebellum South, an unwed mother leaves her baby girl on the steps of the minister's house, then goes to the river to commit suicide. She is stopped, however, and years later, she finds herself in a position to help her grown daughter through a crisis.

T'Other Dear Charmer (World Film Corp., 1918)

d: William P.S. Earle. 5 reels.

Louise Huff, John Bowers, Charles Dungan, Eugenie Woodward, Jack Raymond, Ida Darling, Florence Billings, Valda Valkyrien, Grace Stevens, Ezra Walck, Herbert Barrington, Patrick Foy.

Improbable but amusing comedy about Tom, a wounded war veteran who falls in love with his landlady and also with his mother's "French maid." The kicker is that the two ladies are one and the same — and she loves Tom, too.

Toton (Triangle, 1919)
d: Frank Borzage. 6 reels.
Olive Thomas, Norman Kerry, Francis McDonald, Jack Perrin.
In Paris, an orphaned girl is raised as a boy and learns to become a pickpocket.

The Tough Guy (Film Booking Offices of America, 1926)
d: David Kirkland. 6 reels.
Fred Thomson, Lola Todd, Robert McKim, William Courtwright, Billy Butts, Leo Willis.
Out West, a cowboy helps the local minister recover money stolen from the collection plate, and wins the heart of the minister's daughter.

The Tower of Jewels (Vitagraph, 1919)
d: Tom Terriss. 5 reels.
Corinne Griffith, Webster Campbell, Henry Stephenson, Maurice Costello, Charles Halton, Estelle Taylor, Edward Elkas, Charles Craig.
Emily, a jewel thief, falls in love and wants to go straight, but her former cronies insist that she pull one last heist with them.

The Tower of Lies (MGM, 1925)
d: Victor Seastrom. 7 reels.
Lon Chaney, Norma Shearer, Ian Keith, William Haines, David Torrence, Claire McDowell.
The daughter of a Swedish farmer saves the family homestead by marrying a man she does not love.

The Town Scandal (Universal, 1923)
d: King Baggot. 5 reels.
Gladys Walton, Edward Hearne, Edward McWade, Charles Hill Mailes, William Welsh, William Franey, Anna Hernandez, Virginia Boardman, Rosa Gore, Nadine Beresford.
Jean, a Broadway chorus girl, visits her small-town sister and discovers that several of her male admirers in the big city are members of the local Purity League.

The Town That Forgot God (Fox, 1922)
d: Harry Millarde. 9 reels.
Bunny Grauer, Warren Krech, Jane Thomas, Harry Benham, Edward Denison, Grace Barton, Raymond Bloomer, Nina Casavant.
A carpenter visits his old home town and finds that David, the son of a woman he once loved, is now friendless and an orphan. They become friends and together escape a violent storm that destroys the town.

Toys of Fate (Screen Classics, Inc./Metro, 1918)
d: George D. Baker. 7 reels.
Mme. Nazimova, Charles Bryant, Irving Cummings, Edward J. Connelly, Dodson Mitchell, Frank Currier, Nila Mac.
Zorah, a gypsy girl, chances to meet the man who seduced her mother many years before, and caused the breakup of their family.

Tracked by the Police (Warner Bros., 1927)
d: Ray Enright. 6 reels.
Rin-Tin-Tin, Jason Robards, Virginia Brown Faire, Tom Santschi, Dave Morris, Theodore Lorch, Ben Walker, Wilfred North.
In the Arizona desert, Rinty saves a young engineer from a rock slide, then rescues his young mistress from a scoundrel bent on seduction.

Tracked in the Snow Country (Warner Bros., 1925)
d: Herman Raymaker. 7 reels.
Rin-Tin-Tin, June Marlowe, David Butler, Mitchell Lewis.
In the Frozen North, a dog is suspected of killing his master. But this is no ordinary dog, this is Rinty — and in no time, he pursues the real killer across the ice and snow and brings him to justice.

Tracked to Earth (Universal, 1922)
d: William Worthington. 5 reels.
Frank Mayo, Virginia Valli, Harold Goodwin, Duke R. Lee, Buck Connors, Arthur Millett, Lon Poff, Percy Challenger.
Out West, an innocent railroad employee is suspected by the sheriff of horse theft.

The Traffic Cop (Thanhouser/Mutual, 1916)
d: Howard M. Mitchell. 5 reels.
Howard M. Mitchell, Gladys Hulette, Ernest Howard, Theodore Von Eltz, Burnett Parker.
With the aid of a pretty girl, traffic cop Casey brings a bank embezzler to justice.

The Traffic Cop (R-C Pictures/FBO of America, 1926)
d: Harry Garson. 5 reels.
Lefty Flynn, Kathleen Myers, James Marcus, Adele Farrington, Ray Ripley, Nigel Barrie, Raymond Turner, Jerry Murphy.
Vacationing at a resort, traffic copy Joe Regan falls for a young socialite. Her mother turns thumbs down on their romance, though, because of Joe's low social standing. That will change after Joe saves the socialite's family from certain death in a mountain traffic accident.

Traffic in Hearts (Columbia, 1924)
d: Scott Dunlap. 6 reels.
Robert Frazer, Mildred Harris, Charles Wellesley, Don Marion, John Herdman, Betty Morrisey.
An architect wants to construct housing for the needy, but his sweetheart's father, a feisty politician, prevents his plan from going through.

Traffic in Souls (Universal, 1913)
d: George Loane Tucker. 6 reels.
Ethel Grandin, Matt Moore, Howard Crampton, Jane Gail, William Turner.
An innocent young woman is lured into a white-slavery brothel, but is rescued by her sister's fiancé.

The Tragedy of Youth (Tiffany-Stahl Productions, 1928)
d: George Archainbaud. 7 reels.
Patsy Ruth Miller, Warner Baxter, William Collier Jr., Claire McDowell, Harvey Clarke, Margaret Quimby, Billie Bennett, Stepin Fetchit.
When newlywed Paula feels neglected by her new husband, she turns her attention to one of her former beaus.

The Trail of '98 (MGM, 1928)
d: Clarence Brown. 10 reels. (Music score, sound effects.)
Dolores Del Rio, Ralph Forbes, Harry Carey, Karl Dane, Tully Marshall, George Cooper, Russell Simpson, Emily Fitzroy, Tenen Holtz, Cesare Gravina, E. Alyn Warren, John Down.
Gold seekers from San Francisco journey to the Klondike to strike it rich.

The Trail of the Axe (Dustin Farnum Productions/American Releasing Corp., 1922)
d: Ernest C. Warde. 5 reels.
Dustin Farnum, Winifred Kingston, George Fisher, Joseph J.

514

Dowling.
A lumber foreman hires his unreliable and alcoholic brother, and soon regrets it.

The Trail of the Cigarette (William Steiner Productions/Arrow Film Corp., 1920)
d: Tom Collins. 5 reels.
Glenn White, Alexander F. Frank, Eugene Acker, Stanley Walpole, David Wall, Ethel Russell, William Fredericks, Vera Grosse, Jack Sharkey.
When a society woman is found murdered, a crushed cigarette is the only clue found at the scene of the crime.

The Trail of the Lonesome Pine (Lasky Feature Plays/Paramount, 1916)
d: Cecil B. DeMille. 5 reels.
Charlotte Walker, Theodore Roberts, Thomas Meighan, Earl Fox, Dick LeStrange, Park Jones.
In the Kentucky mountains, a federal revenue agent tries to locate an illegal still, and winds up falling in love with the moonshiner's daughter.

The Trail of the Lonesome Pine (Famous Players-Lasky/Paramount, 1923)
d: Charles Maigne. 6 reels.
Mary Miles Minter, Antonio Moreno, Ernest Torrence, Edwin J. Brady, Frances Warner, J.S. Stembridge, Cullen Tate.
A big-city engineer goes to the backwoods on a project, and falls in love with one of the local girls.
Remake of sorts of the 1916 Lasky/Paramount production *The Trail of the Lonesome Pine*. Note that in the earlier film, the hero was a revenue agent, while in the 1923 production the hero is an engineer. Both versions were based on the play of the same name by Eugene Walter.

The Trail of the Shadow (Rolfe Photoplays, Inc./Metro, 1917)
d: Edwin Carewe. 5 reels.
Emmy Wehlen, Eugene Strong, Harry S. Northrup, Frank Currier, Fuller Mellish, Kate Blancke, Alice MacChesney, DeJalma West.
Outraged because of Sylvia's refusal of his offer of marriage, an outlaw known as "the Shadow" breaks into her cabin home and tries to force his attentions on her.

The Trail Rider (Fox, 1925)
d: William S. Van Dyke. 5 reels.
Buck Jones, Nancy Deaver, Lucy Fox, Carl Sotckdale, Jack McDonald, George Berrell, Jacques Rollens, Will Walling.
Out West, a drifter is given the job of trail rider for a cattle ranch.

The Trail to Yesterday (Metro, 1918)
d: Edwin Carewe. 5 reels.
Bert Lytell, Anna Q. Nilsson, Harry S. Northrup, Ernest Maupain, John A. Smiley, Danny Hogan.
Out West, a fugitive called "Dakota" offers shelter to a young woman who's caught in a storm. But when he learns that she's the daughter of the man who unjustly accused him and sent him into hiding, Dakota plots his revenge.

Trailin' (Fox, 1921)
d: Lynn F. Reynolds. 5 reels.
Tom Mix, Eva Novak, Bert Sprotte, James Gordon, William Duvall, Sid Jordan, Jay Morley, J. Farrell MacDonald, Carol Holloway, Duke Lee, William Duvall, Harry Dunkinson.
When a young man's adoptive father is killed in a duel with a stranger from Idaho, the youngster swears vengeance and pursues the killer. Only when they confront each other does the truth come out: The stranger is the youngster's real father, and he's been looking for decades for the man who stole his infant son.

Trailin' Back (Trem Carr Productions/Rayart, 1928)
w, d: J.P. McGowan. 5 reels.
Buddy Roosevelt, Betty Baker, Lafe McKee, Leon De La Mothe, Tommy Bay.
A sheriff and his posse search for an outlaw gang, but they are repeatedly frustrated by the gang's last-minute escapes. Finally realizing that a member of his own posse is tipping them off, the sheriff neutralizes the saboteur and captures the gang.

Trail's End (William M. Smith Productions/Merit Film Corp., 1922)
d: Francis Ford. 5 reels.
Franklyn Farnum, Peggy O'Day, George Reehm, Al Hart, Shorty Hamilton, Genevieve Bert.
In a remote western town, a manhunt zeroes in on the missing heir to a fortune.

Tramp, Tramp, Tramp (Harry Langdon Corp./First National, 1926)
d: Harry Edwards. 6 reels.
Harry Langdon, Joan Crawford, Alec B. Francis, Edwards Davis, Carlton Griffin, Brooks Benedict, Tom Murray.
A timid young man enters a cross-country walking contest, partly for the prize money, but also to impress a beautiful girl he has just met.
Langdon's first feature-length film to be released to the public, after a string of outstanding Sennett short comedies. He apparently made one feature film for Mack Sennett Productions in 1925 called *His First Flame*, but its release was delayed until May 1927.

Transcontinental Limited (Chadwick Pictures, 1926)
d: Nat Ross. 7 reels.
Johnnie Walker, Eugenia Gilbert, Alec B. Francis, Edith Yorke, Bruce Gordon, Edward Gillace, George Ovey, Eric Mayne, James Hamel.
A doughboy returns from the war and finds a blackmail plot involving his girlfriend, the daughter of a railroad owner.

Transgression (Vitagraph, 1917)
d: Paul Scardon. 5 reels.
Earle Williams, Billie Billings, Webster Campbell, Edwards Davis, Mary Maurice, Corinne Griffith, Denton Vane, Jack Ellis.
Carline, a conniving woman, allows a suitor to believe he killed his rival... when it was actually she who fired the deadly shot.

The Transgressor (Catholic Art Association, 1918)
d: Joseph Levering. 8 reels.
Marian Swayne, Ben Lyon, Inez Marcel.
A steel mill owner refuses to address serious safety problems in his mill, and nearly pays for his negligence with the loss of his own son.

The Trap (World Film Corp., 1918)
d: George Archainbaud. 5 reels.
Alice Brady, Curtis Cooksey, Crawford Kent, Robert Cummings, Frank Mayo.
Doris, an artist's model, attracts admirers who saw her published picture. Too late, she realizes that Stuart, the artist, is insanely jealous.

The Trap (Universal, 1919)
d: Frank Reicher. 6 reels.
Olive Tell, Jere Austin, Earl Schenck, Joseph Burke, Sidney Mason, Rod LaRocque.
A Yukon schoolteacher travels to New York and marries well, but is threatened with blackmail by a scoundrel who wants to reveal details of her previous marriage.

The Trap (Universal, 1922)
d: Robert T. Thornby. 6 reels.
Lon Chaney, Irene Rich, Alan Hale, Stanely Goethals, Dagmar Godowsky, Spottiswoode Aitken, Herbert Standing, Frank Campeau.
An embittered French-Canadian miner who's been swindled by a con man gets even by framing his enemy for attempted murder. The con artist is eventually released from prison, but now a new irony arises: The miner has taken the con man's son under his wing and has grown to love the boy, and the father's return will almost certainly destroy their relationship.

Travelin' On (William S. Hart Co./Paramount, 1922)
w, d: Lambert Hillyer. 7 reels.
William S. Hart, James Farley, Ethel Grey Terry, Brinsley Shaw, Mary Janes Irving, Robert Kortman, Willis Marks.
Hart plays a mysterious stranger who rides into town and helps a minister and his daughter build their new church before riding away.

The Traveling Salesman (Famous Players/Paramount, 1916)
d: Joseph Kaufman. 5 reels.
Frank McIntyre, Doris Kenyon, Harry Northrup, Russell Bassett, Julia Stuart, Harry Lakemore, James O'Neill Jr.
Blake, a happy-go-lucky traveling salesman, falls for Beth, whose house is due to be sold for unpaid taxes. He travels to the county seat and pays off the taxes just before deadline, but learns that a pair of crooked speculators are interested in Beth's property too, and Blake will have to fight them off.
This comedy was remade in 1921 by Famous Players-Lasky, with Roscoe Arbuckle as the amiable salesman.

The Traveling Salesman (Famous Players-Lasky/Paramount, 1921)
d: Joseph Henabery. 5 reels.
Roscoe "Fatty" Arbuckle, Betty Ross Clark, Frank Holland, Wilton Taylor, Lucille Ward, Jim Blackwell, Richard Wayne, George C. Pearce, Robert Dudley, Gordon Rogers.
Remake of the 1916 Famous Players film *The Traveling Salesman*. Both versions were based on the play of the same name by James Grant Forbes.

Treason (Universal, 1917)
d: Allen Holubar. 5 reels.
Lois Wilson, Dorothy Davenport, Allen Holubar, Joseph Girard, George Pearce, Edward Hearn, Leo Pierson, Burton Law, L.M. Wells.
In the fictitious country of Stratiria, a telegraph operator saves the republic from wartime disaster — twice.

Treason (Mutual, 1918)
d: Burton King. 5 reels.
Edna Goodrich, Howard Hall, Ildred Clair, Clarence Heritage, Stuart Holmes.
While her husband struggles to develop a new formula for the U.S. government, his wife carries on a dalliance with a ladies' man... unaware that the "lothario" is really a German spy, keen on stealing the new formula.

Treasure Island (Fox, 1918)
d: C.M. Franklin, S.A. Franklin. 6 reels.
Francis Carpenter, Eleanor Washington, Virginia Corbin, Violet Radcliffe, Herscel Mayall, Lloyd Perl, Elmo Lincoln, Charles Gorman, Lew Sargent, Buddie Messinger.
In 19th century England, young Jim Hawkins comes by a mysterious treasure map and, with his girlfriend Louise and a contingent of pirates, including the one-legged Long John Silver, sails to the island indicated on the map.

Treasure Island (Maurice Tourneur Productions/Paramount, 1920)
d: Maurice Tourneur. 6 reels.
Lon Chaney, Shirley Mason, Charles Ogle, Sydney Dean, Charles Hill Mailes, Josie Melville, Al Filson, Wilton Taylor, Joseph Singleton, Bull Montana, Harry Holden.
Remake of the 1918 Fox production, both versions based on the novel *Treasure Island* by Robert Louis Stevenson.

Treasure of the Sea (Metro, 1918)
d: Frank Reicher. 5 reels.
Edith Storey, Lew Cody, Lewis Willoughby, Josef Swickard, William DeVaull, Tote DuCrow.
On the Pacific shore, a young woman and the man she thinks she hates discover a wrecked treasure ship. They organize a party of men to uncover the treasure, and in the process the young woman learns that her companion is not the scoundrel she thought him after all.

Treat 'em Rough (Fox, 1919)
d: Lynn Reynolds. 5 reels.
Tom Mix, Jane Novak, Val Paul, Charles LeMoyne, Jack Curtis.
Out West, a daredevil cowpoke clashes with cattle rustlers.

The Trembling Hour (Universal, 1919)
d: George Seigman. 6 reels.
Kenneth Harlan, Helen Jerome Eddy, Henry Barrows, Willis Marks, Clyde Hopkins, Edna Shipman, Gertrude Astor, Anna May Walthall.
Shell-shocked in World War I, a returning veteran is befriended by the district attorney and sent to a western ranch to recuperate. But the vet has a long road to recovery ahead of him.

Trent's Last Case (Fox, 1929)
d: Howard Hawks. 6 reels. (Music score, sound effects.)
Donald Crisp, Raymond Griffith, Raymond Hatton, Marceline Day, Lawrence Gray, Nicholas Soussanin, Anita Garvin, Ed Kennedy.
After the mysterious death of a prominent businessman, the police inspector interrogates five suspects. But it is proved that the victim committed suicide in such a way as to make it look like murder.

Trial Marriage (Columbia, 1929)
d: Erle C. Kenton. 7 reels. (Musical score and sound effects.)
Sally Eilers, Jason Robards, Norman Kerry, Thelma Todd, Charles Clary, Naomi Childers, Rosemary Theby, Gertrude Short.
A wealthy doctor proposes that he and Connie enter into a trial marriage contract, with either able to terminate the arrangement at any time.

A Trick of Fate (B.B. Features/Robertson-Cole/Mutual, 1919)
d: Howard Hickman. 5 reels.
Bessie Barriscale, Alfred Whitman, George Fields, Joe

516

Swickard, Joe Dowling, Frank Whitson.
When a French dancer storms out of the show during an engagement in New York, her manager hires Mary Lee, an American girl and the dancer's exact double, to replace her. Miss Barriscale plays the roles of both the dancer and her lookalike. She previously had played twins in Triangle's *The Snarl* (1917), and would again play a double role in *Life's Twist* (1920).

A Trick of Hearts (Universal, 1928)
d: Reaves Eason. 6 reels.
Hoot Gibson, Georgia Hale, Heine Conklin.
Out West, a woman is elected the town sheriff.

The Triflers (Universal, 1919)
d: W. Christy Cabanne. 5 reels.
Edith Roberts, David Butler, Forrest Stanley, Benny Alexander, Katherine Kirkham, Arthur Shirley, Arthur Hoyt, Lillian Langdon, Frederick Vroom, Nell Craig, Colin Kenny, Magda Lane, Charles Arling, Olita Otis, Helen Broneau.
Janet, a shopgirl, yearns to join the social set. She gets a chance when, at a fashionable resort, she finds herself short of funds and a playboy comes to her aid.

The Triflers (B.P. Schulberg Productions, 1924)
d: Louis Gasnier. 7 reels.
Mae Busch, Elliott Dexter, Frank Mayo, Walter Hiers, Eva Novak, Lloyd Whitlock.
In order to protect herself from fortune-hunting suitors, wealthy Marjorie enters into a marriage of convenience with a man she can trust. The question is, can she trust herself? Because although Marjorie's new husband complies with the terms of their arrangement, she finds herself falling in love with him.

Trifling With Honor (Universal, 1923)
d: Harry A. Pollard. 8 reels.
Fritzi Ridgeway, Rockcliffe Fellowes, Buddy Messinger, Hayden Stevenson, Emmett King, William Welsh, Frederick Stanton, William Robert Daly, Jim Farley, Sidney DeGrey.
A star baseball player refuses to throw a game when would-be blackmailers threaten to expose his prison past.

Trifling Women (Metro, 1922)
d: Rex Ingram. 9 reels.
Barbara LaMarr, Ramon Novarro, Pomeroy Cannon, Edward Connelly, Lewis Stone, Hughie Mack, Gene Pouyet, John George, Jess Weldon.
A novelist tries to instill the value of faithfulness in his flirtatious daughter, but she's no quick learn.

Trilby (Equitable Motion Pictures Corp./World Film Corp., 1915)
d: Maurice Tourneau. 5 reels.
Clara Kimball Young, Wilton Lackaye, Chester Barnesst.
First feature film version of the tale of the mesmerizing Svengali and his Trilby.

Trilby (Richard Walton Tully Productions/Associated First National, 1923)
d: James Young. 8 reels.
Andrée Lafayette, Creighton Hale, Arthur Edmund Carew, Philo McCullough, Wilfred Lucas, Maurice Cannon, Gordon Mullen, Martha Franklin, Gilbert Clayton, Edward Kimball.
Trilby, a Parisian artist's model, falls in love with a student but then meets Svengali, a sinister musician with the power to mesmerize. He hypnotizes her and turns her into a famous concert singer. She enjoys great success on the stage, but when Svengali succumbs to a heart attack she loses her

talent.

Trimmed (Universal, 1922)
d: Harry Pollard. 5 reels.
Hoot Gibson, Patsy Ruth Miller, Alfred Hollingsworth, Fred Kohler, Otto Hoffman, Dick LaReno, R. Hugh Sutherland.
In a western town, the political boss runs a returned war hero for sheriff, thinking he'll be easy to manipulate after the election. But boss man had better think again.

Trimmed in Scarlet (Universal, 1923)
d: Jack Conway. 5 reels.
Kathlyn Williams, Roy Stewart, Lucille Rickson, Robert Agnew, David Torrence, Phillips Smalley, Eve Southern, Bert Sprotte, Grace Carlyle, Gerrard Grassby, Raymond Hatton.
Bitter melodrama about a young socialite who disapproves of her stepmother, then learns that it's her natural mother who has earned her disapproval.

A Trip to Chinatown (Fox, 1926)
d: Robert P. Kerr. 6 reels.
Margaret Livingston, Earle Foxe, J. Farrell MacDonald, Anna May Wong, Harry Woods, Marie Astaire, Gladys McConnell, Charles Farrell, Hazel Howell, Wilson Benge, George Kuwa.
Welland, a wealthy hypochondriac, is given only six months to live by his quack doctors. He decides to travel to that city by the bay, and finds love—and a new lease on life—in San Francisco's Chinatown.

Triple Action (Universal, 1925)
w, d: Tom Gibson. 5 reels.
Pete Morrison, Trilby Clark, Dolores Gardner, Harry von Meter, Lafayette McKee, Harry Belmour, Floyd Ames, Les Bates, Leon Kent, Walter Patterson, Milburn Morante, Fred Burns.
A Texas Ranger parachutes into a ranch where rustlers have corralled a herd of stolen cattle.

The Triple Clue (William Steiner Productions/Arrow Film Corp., 1920)
d: Tom Collins. 5 reels.
Glenn White, Stanley Walpole, Etherl Russell, Clarice Young, Zaidee Burbank, Dave Wall, John B. Cook, Walter Donald, Alexander Frank.
A gumshoe named Tex follows clues to prove a convicted murderer innocent.

Triumph (Universal, 1917)
d: Joseph DeGrasse. 5 reels.
Dorothy Phillips, Lon Chaney, William Stowell, William J. Dyer, Clair DuBrey, Clyde Benson, Helen Wright, Ruth Elder.
Nell, an aspiring actress, attracts the unwanted attentions of the stage manager. He lets her know that, if she wants to be in his play, she will have to reward him with sexual favors.

Triumph (Famous Players-Lasky/Paramount, 1924)
d: Cecil B. DeMille. 8 reels.
Rod LaRocque, Leatrice Joy, Victor Varconi, Charles Ogle, Theodore Kosloff, Robert Edeson, Julia Faye, George Fawcett, Spottiswoode Aitken, ZaSu Pitts, Raymond Hatton, Alma Bennett, Jimmie Adams.
Half brothers vie for their rightful share of their late father's estate.

The Triumph of the Weak (Vitagraph, 1918)
d: Tom Terriss. 5 reels.

Alice Joyce, Walter McGrail, Templar Saxe, Eulalie Jensen, Adele DeGarde, Billy Carr, Bernard Siegel.
When Edith, a destitute widow with a small child, steals to buy food, she is arrested and jailed for theft. After serving her sentence, she snatches her child from the state orphanage and goes on the run... but happiness lies ahead. In a new city, Edith takes a job and finds a man who's willing to forgive her past transgressions and truly love her.

Trixie From Broadway (American Film Co. Inc./Pathé, 1919)
d: R. William Neill. 5 reels.
Margarita Fisher, Emory Johnson, George Periolat, Frank Clark, Olga Grey, J. Farrell MacDonald.
To test his chorus-girl bride's love, a millionaire rancher takes her "home" to a shack.

Trooper 44 (E.I.S. Motion Picture Corp., 1917)
d: Roy Gahris. 5 reels.
George Soule Spencer, June Daye, Walter P. Lewis, W.W. Black, Lynn G. Adams, Roy Sheldon, Roy Gahris, Betty Dodsworth.
Crime drama involving the Pennsylvania Mounted State Police, actually featuring some of the real-life troopers.

Tropic Madness (FBO Pictures, 1928)
d: Robert Vignola. 7 reels.
Leatrice Joy, Lena Malena, George Barraud, Henry Sedley, Albert Valentino, David Durand.
A widow searches frantically for her young son, taken from her by her late husband. Finally giving up hope of finding the boy, she embarks on an ocean cruise to the South Seas—and visits the very island where her son is living with an old trader friend of his dad's.

Tropical Love (Playgoers Pictures/Associated Exhibitors, 1921)
d: Ralph Ince. 5 reels.
Ruth Clifford, Fred Turner, Reginald Denny, Huntley Gordon, Ernest Hilliard, Carl Axzelle, Margaret Fitzroy, Paul Doucet.
After 20 years of searching, an old man finds the daughter he lost during a tropical storm, living in San Juan, Puerto Rico.

Tropical Nights (Tiffany-Stahl Productions, 1928)
d: Elmer Clifton. 6 reels.
Patsy Ruth Miller, Malcolm McGregor, Ray Hallor, Wallace MacDonald, Russell Simpson.
Tale of love, violence and treachery, set on a South Seas island.

Trouble (Jackie Coogan Productions/Associated First National, 1922)
d: Albert Austin. 5 reels.
Jackie Coogan, Wallace Beery, Gloria Hope.
Danny, an orphan boy, struggles to overcome his foster father's indifference.

The Trouble Buster (Pallas Pictures/Paramount, 1917)
d: Frank Reicher. 5 reels.
Vivian Martin, James Neill, Paul Willis, Charles West, Louise Harris, Mary Mersch, Vera Lewis.
Michelna, a poor orphan girl, is befriended by Blackie, a street urchin. He teaches her how to defend herself, how to sculpt in clay, and how to sell newspapers. In time, Michelna cuts her hair short, puts on boys' clothes, and changes her name to Mike.

The Trouble Buster (William Steiner Productions, 1925)
d: Leo Maloney. 5 reels.
Leo Maloney, Josephine Hill, Whitehorse, Evelyn Thatcher, Leonard Clapham, Bud Osborne, Grace Rouch, Barney Furey, Baby Charlotte Johnson, Ray Walters, William Stratton.
Harvey loves Helen and they want to get married, but her mother disapproves.

The Trouble With Wives (Famous Players-Lasky/Paramount, 1925)
d: Malcolm St. Clair. 7 reels.
Florence Vidor, Tom Moore, Esther Ralston, Ford Sterling, Lucy Beaumont, Edward Kennedy, Etta Lee, William Courtright.
The green-eyed monster rears its ugly head when a wife discovers that her husband has been seen visiting the apartment of a lovely Parisienne.

Troublemakers (Fox, 1917)
d: Kenean Buel. 5 reels.
Lillian Concord, Jane Lee, Katherine Lee, Richard Turner, Robert Vivian, William T. Hayes, Stuart Sage, Frances Miller.
Jane and Katy are mischievous sisters who pull boisterous pranks and generally make pests of themselves. But they'll be redeemed in the eyes of their family and friends later, when the girls assist the law in saving an innocent man from the electric chair.

Troubles of a Bride (Fox, 1924)
d: Thomas Buckingham. 5 reels.
Robert Agnew, Mildred June, Alan Hale, Bruce Covington, Dolores Rousse, Charles Conklin, Lew Harvey, Bud Jamieson.
Mildred, engaged to marry Robert, catches him in the act of kissing another girl. To get revenge and throw a scare into her fiancé, she arranges for a stranger to feign a robbery at her house and pretend to kidnap her. All goes well until Mildred realizes that the stranger is a real thief, and he kidnaps her for real. What now?

The Trouper (Universal, 1922)
d: Harry B. Harris. 5 reels.
Gladys Walton, Jack Perrin, Thomas Holding, Kathleen O'Connor, Roscoe Karns, Mary Philbin, Mary True, Tom S. Guise, Florence D. Lee.
The wardrobe lady for a struggling troupe of actors has a crush on the leading man, but in time she'll get over it and find her true love.

Trouping With Ellen (Eastern Productions/Producers Distributing Corp., 1924)
d: T. Hayes Hunter. 7 reels.
Helene Chadwick, Mary Thurman, Gaston Glass, Basil Rathbone, Riley Hatch, Zena Keefe, Kate Blanke, Tyrone Power, John Tansey, Charles McDonald, Ernest Hilliard.
Ellen, a chorus girl in a Boston production, is desired by both the orchestra leader and a wealthy aristocrat.

The Truant Soul (Essanay, 1916)
d: Harry Beaumont. 7 reels.
Henry B. Walthall, Mary Charleson, Patrick Calhoun, Anna Mae Walthall, Mary Parkyn, U.K. Haupt.
When a drug-addicted surgeon makes a costly blunder during an operation, he thoughtlessly blames it on Joan, his nurse. Joan is transferred to a sanitarium to care for lunatics, and goes quietly, without recriminations. Her dedication so moves the surgeon, he resolves to get "clean" and stay that

TRUE HEART SUSIE (1919). Lillian Gish and Robert Harron portray teenagers in love, in the early scenes of this Griffith film. She knows she is in love, but he hasn't a clue–yet.

* * * * *

way, for Joan's sake.

True as Steel (Goldwyn/Metro-Goldwyn Distributing Corp., 1924)
d: Rupert Hughes. 7 reels.
Aileen Pringle, Huntley Gordon, Cleo Madison, Eleanor Boardman, Norman Kerry, William Haines, Louise Fazenda, Louis Payne, William H. Crane, Raymond Hatton, Lucien Littlefield.
After a light dalliance in New York, two business people—a man and a woman—ponder whether to divorce their respective spouses and marry each other.

True Blue (Fox, 1918)
d: Frank Lloyd. 6 reels.
William Farnum, Francis Carpenter, Charles Clary, Katherine Adams, Genevieve Blinn, William Scott, Harry DeVere, Barney Furey, G. Raymond Nye, Marc Robbins, Jack Connelly.
Gilbert, an Englishman who learns he has been proclaimed an earl, suddenly thinks the people nearest to him are his inferiors... including his wife and son.

True Heart Susie (Paramount, 1919)
d: D.W. Griffith. 6 reels.
Lillian Gish, Robert Harron, Wilbur Highby, Loyola O'Connor, George Fawcett, Clarine Seymour, Kate Bruce, Carol Dempster, Raymond Cannon.
A simple country girl loves a neighbor boy and sacrifices much of her own happiness to promote his ambitions to become a minister.
Lillian Gish, as Susie, here delivers the most famous closeup in the silent era. Griffith gave her a giant closeup and let it run for 40 seconds, during which Miss Gish expressed all the passions that Susie is enduring: surprise, resentment, sorrow, puzzlement, supreme heartbreak, and finally bitter resignation. When Miss Gish, at 94, made her final film, *The Whales of August* (1987), her 81-year-old co-star Bette Davis remarked that Gish "invented close-ups."

True Heaven (Fox, 1929)
d: James Tinling. 6 reels.
George O'Brien, Lois Moran, Phillips Smalley, Oscar Apfel, Duke Martin, André Cheron, Donald MacKenzie, Hedwig Reicher, Will Stanton.
During World War I, a British soldier falls in love with a cafe songstress in Belgium. Unfortunately for him, she's an enemy spy.

True Nobility (American Film Co./Mutual, 1916)
d: Donald McDonald. 5 reels.
Charles Newton, Marie Van Tassell, E. Forrest Taylor, Helene Rosson, Eugenie Forde, Harry McCabe, Lizette Thorne, Harry Von Meter.
An old prospector dies and leaves his successful mine to Phil, a young engineer. Soon, however, Phil determines to locate the old man's last known heir.

The Trufflers (Essanay, 1917)
d: Fred E. Wright. 5 reels.
Nell Craig, Sydney Ainsworth, Ernest Maupain, Richard C. Travers, Patrick Calhoun, Harry Dunkinson, John Cossar, Virginia Bowker.
Sue, a small-town girl, yearns to perform on the stage. She gets her chance, but finds that many actors, producers and playwrights are puffed-up hypocrites, and so decides to return home to her true and honest love.

Trumpet Island (Vitagraph, 1920)
d: Tom Terriss. 7 reels.
Marguerite DeLaMotte, Wallace MacDonald, Hallam Cooley, Joseph Swickard, Arthur Hoyt, Marcelle Daly, Percy Challenger.
Eve marries not for love but for money, while her true heart's desire travels to the isolated Trumpet Island to get away from it all. But Eve's honeymoon is cut short when the newlyweds' plane is forced to land in a storm. Where? That's right, Trumpet Island.

The Trunk Mystery (Pathé, 1927)
d: Frank Hall Crane. 5 reels.
Charles Hutchison, Alice Calhoun, Richard Neill, Ben Walker, Ford Sterlng, Otto Lederer, Charles Mack.
A mysterious trunk sold at a police auction suddenly attracts attention from crooks and jewel merchants.

Trust Your Wife (Katherine MacDonald Pictures/Associated First National, 1921)
d: J.A. Barry. 5 reels.
Katherine MacDonald, Dave Winter, Charles Richman, Mary Alden.
A struggling young inventor needs financing to bring his product to market. Holcomb, a contemptible plutocrat, offers to supply the requisite financing if the inventor's lovely wife gives herself to him romantically.

The Truth (Goldwyn, 1920)
d: Lawrence C. Windom. 5 reels.
Madge Kennedy, Tom Carrigan, Helen Green, Kenneth Hill, Frank Doane, Zelda Sears, Horace Haine.
When well-meaning Becky is suspected of amorous feelings for Fred, a married man, his wife and Becky's husband get together to investigate the supposed infidelity.

The Truth About Husbands (Whitman Bennett Productions, 1920)
d: Kenneth Webb. 5 reels.
Anna Lehr, H.E. Herbert, Elizabeth Garrison, May McAvoy, Richard Gordon, Ivo Dawson, Arthur Rankin, Lorraine Frost.
Leslie, a trusting young bride, makes friends with Janet, a private secretary... then discovers that Janet was once engaged to Leslie's husband.

The Truth About Wives (B.B. Productions/American Releasing Corp., 1923)
d: Lawrence Windom. 6 reels.
Betty Blythe, Tyrone Power, William P. Carleton, Ann Luther, Fred C. Jones, John Daly Murphy, Marcia Harris, Nellie Parker Spaulding, Frankie Evans.
Harold marries Helen, but wants to continue romancing his chorus girl mistress.

The Truth About Women (Banner Productions, 1924)
d: Burton King. 6 reels.
Hope Hampton, Lowell Sherman, David Powell, Mary Thurman, Dainty Lee, Louise Carter, Charles Craig, Rosella Ray, Warren Cook, Charles Edwards, Augusta Carey.
An artist decides to leave his wife and child and take up with a worldly vamp.

The Truth Wagon (Masterpiece Film Manufacturing Co., 1914)
d: Max Figman. 5 reels.
Max Figman, Lolita Robertson, H.A. Livingstone, Al W. Wilson.
Ross, a small-time newspaper publisher, wages war against crooked politicians—and watches his circulation skyrocket.

The Truthful Liar (Realart Pictures/Paramount, 1922)
d: Thomas N. Heffron. 6 reels.
Wanda Hawley, Edward Hearn, Charles Stevenson, Casson Ferguson, Lloyd Whitlock, George Siegmann, E.A. Warren, Charles K. French.
Feeling neglected by her husband, Tess goes with a former flame to a gambling hall on the night it is destined to be raided by the police.

The Truthful Sex (Columbia, 1926)
d: Richard Thomas. 6 reels.
Mae Busch, Huntley Gordon, Ian Keith, Leo White, Billy Kent Schaeffer, John Roche, Rosemary Theby, Richard Travers, Joan Meredith.
Sally and Robert, once happily married, become estranged when she accepts the attentions of a lothario.

Truthful Tulliver (Triangle, 1917)
d: William S. Hart. 5 reels.
William S. Hart, Alma Rubens, Nina Byron, Norbert A. Myles, Walter Perry.
Out West, a former frontiersman turns to running a newspaper.

Truxton King (Fox, 1923)
d: Jerome Storm. 6 reels.
John Gilbert, Ruth Clifford, Frank Leigh, Mickey Moore, Otis harlan, Henry Miller Jr., Richard Wayne, Willis Marks, Winifred Bryson, Mark Fenton.
Graustarkian romance about an American who falls in love with a princess.

Try and Get It (Samuel V. Grand/Producers Distributing Corp., 1924)
d: Cullen Tate. 6 reels.
Bryant Washburn, Billie Dove, Edward Horton, Joseph Kilgour, Lionel Belmore, Rose Dione, Hazel Deane, Carl Stockdale.
A young bill collector must collect a debt owed by a contractor with a beautiful daughter and a lot of creditor resistance.

Tumbleweeds (United Artists, 1925)
d: King Baggot, William S. Hart. 7 reels.
William S. Hart, Barbara Bedford, Lucien Littlefield, Gordon Russell, Richard R. Neill, Jack Murphy, Lillian Leighton, Gertrude Claire, T.E. Duncan, James Gordon, Fred Gamble, Turner Savage, Monte Collins, George Marion.
The great Western land rush along the Cherokee strip serves as the basis for this, Hart's last starring film.

Turkish Delight (DeMille Pictures/Pathé, 1927)
d: Paul Sloane. 6 reels.
Julia Faye, Rudolph Schildkraut, Kenneth Thomson, Louis Natheaux, May Robson, Harry Allen, Toby Claude.
In the Arab kingdom of Tamboustan, the sultan dies and seven of his male heirs mysteriously expire. Now the power resides with the sultan's widow, who orders the sole remaining heir, Abdul, to come to the palace to be "inspected" by her. But since Abdul is now a rug dealer living with his niece in the United States, he has different views of the Arab monarchy than the Tamboustanis do.

The Turmoil (Columbia/Metro, 1916)
d: Edgar Jones. 5 reels.
Valli Valli, George LeGuere, Charles Prince, Florida Kingsley, Frank DeVernon, Kate Jepson, Fred Tidmarsh, Robert Stowe Gill, Ilean Hume, Frederic Summer, William Auker.

After his release from a sanitarium, a wealthy young man proposes to a proper young woman, who promptly rejects him on grounds that she would be marrying not for love, but for the young man's money. He respects her decision, but remains determined to win her heart.

The Turmoil (Universal, 1924)
d: Hobart Henley. 7 reels.
Emmet Corrigan, George Hackathorne, Edward Hearn, Theodore von Eltz, Eileen Percy, Pauline Garon, Eleanor Boardman, Winter Hall, Kitty Bradbury, Kenneth Gibson.
Sheridan, a self-made success as a businessman, tries to run the lives of his three sons, with disastrous results.

Turn Back the Hours (Gotham Productions/Lumas Film Corp., 1928)
d: Howard Bretherton. 6 reels.
Myrna Loy, Walter Pidgeon, Sam Hardy, George Stone, Sheldon Lewis, Josef Swickard, Ann Brody, Nanette Villon, Joyzelle Joyner.
A former navy lieutenant valiantly fights off a gang of bandits who are trying to take over the ranch of his sweetheart's father.

The Turn in the Road (Brentwood/Mutual, 1919)
d: King Vidor. 5 reels.
George Nichols, Winter Hall, Helen Jerome Eddy, Pauline Curley, Ben Alexander, Charles Arling.
Paul, the son-in-law of the town minister, has his faith shaken badly when his wife dies in childbirth.

The Turn of a Card (Paralta Plays, Inc./General Film Co., 1918)
d: Oscar Apfel. 7 reels.
J. Warren Kerrigan, Lois Wilson, Eugene Pallette, William Conklin, David M. Hartford, Frank Clark, Clifford Alexander, Eleanor Crowe, Roy Laidlaw, Albert Cody, Wallace Worsley.
Farrell, a high-stakes gambler, wins a large house and property in a card game. He goes to claim it and meets the former owner's daughter, who doesn't know about the bet and mistakes Farrell for her new chauffeur. She's lovely, so Farrell goes along with the deception, and in time wins the lady's hand.

The Turn of the Road (Vitagraph, 1915)
d: Tefft Johnson. 5 reels.
Joseph Kilgour, Naomi Childers, Bobby Connelly, Virginia Pearson, Edwina Robbins, Robert Gaillard, Mabel Kelly.
When Marcia, an irrepressible flirt, vamps her friend's husband, the two decide to elope. But a horrendous auto accident stops them and causes Marcia to become deranged.

The Turn of the Wheel (Goldwyn, 1918)
d: Reginald Barker. 5 reels.
Geraldine Farrar, Herbert Rawlinson, Percy Marmont, Violet Heming, Hassard Short, Maude Turner Gordon, Henry Carvil, Clarence Handysides, Ernest Maupain, Mabel Ballin.
When Rosalie becomes attracted to a handsome gambler at the roulette table, she decides to help him financially and, with the help of Rosalie's money, he wins big. Now the two are in love, but before they can plan for their future, the man is arrested for the murder of his ex-wife. But he's innocent, and in time Rosalie will prove it.

Turn to the Right (Metro, 1922)
d: Rex Ingram. 8 reels.
Alice Terry, Jack Mulhall, Harry Myers, George Cooper, Edward Connelly, Lydia Knott, Betty Allen, Margaret

Loomis, William Bletcher, Eric Mayne, Ray Ripley.
Dramedy about a chap who is unjustly accused by his boss of theft, whereas the real crook is the boss' own son.

The Turning Point (Katherine MacDonald Pictures Corp./First National, 1920)
d: J.A. Barry. 5 reels.
Katherine MacDonald, Leota Lorraine, Nigel Barrie, William Mong, Kenneth Harlan, Edith Yorke, Bartine Burkett, William Clifford, William Colvin, Pat Moore, Walter Hiers.
In New York's social world, a young woman becomes involved in a murder mystery.

Turning the Tables (Paramount, 1919)
d: Elmer Clifton. 5 reels.
Dorothy Gish, Raymond Cannon, Eugenie Besserer, George Fawcett, Kate Toncray, Rhea Haines, Fred Warren, Norman McNeill, Porter Strong.
A lively young woman is so exasperating to her aunt that she has her niece committed to a sanitarium. But once inside, the clever girl switches places with one of the nurses.

'Twas Ever Thus (Bosworth, Inc./Paramount, 1915)
w, d: Elsie Janis. 5 reels.
Elsie Janis, Hobart Bosworth, Owen Moore, Myrtle Stedman, Harry Ham, Helen Wolcott, Joe Ray, Ludloe Goodman, Charles Wainwright.
Love stories through the ages are told with humor: First, in the Stone Age, a caveman courts a prehistoric lovely with—what else?—caveman tactics. Second, during the American Civil War, a Southerner falls for a girl from Boston. Third, in the modern era, a young novelist takes a job as a housemaid to study "real life," and falls for the family's playboy son.

Twelve Miles Out (MGM, 1927)
d: Jack Conway. 5 reels.
John Gilbert, Joan Crawford, Ernest Torrence, Eileen Percy, Dorothy Sebastian, Pauline Duval, Gwen Lee, Edward Earle, Bert Roach, Tim O'Brien.

Rival rum-runners clash at sea, until one of them finds refuge in a woman's seaside home. She threatens to inform the Coast Guard, so he takes her aboard her boat, where more adventures await them.

$20 a Week (Distinctive Pictures/Selznick, 1924)
d: Harmon Weight. 6 reels.
George Arliss, Taylor Holmes, Edith Roberts, Walter Howe, Redfield Clarke, Ronald Colman, Ivan Simpson, Joseph Donohue, William Sellery, George Henry.
Taking a bet that he can't live on only $20 a week, a wealthy man takes a job in a steel mill.

20,000 Leagues Under the Sea (Universal, 1916)
d: Stuart Paton. 8 reels.
Jane Gail, Allen Holubar, Dan Hanlon, Edna Pendleton, William Welsh.
Fantasy-adventure based on the famous Jules Verne story.

23 1/2 Hours Leave (T.H. Ince/Famous Players-Lasky/Paramount, 1919)
d: Henry King. 5 reels.
Douglas MacLean, Doris May, Thomas Guise, Maxfield Stanley, Wade Boteler, Alfred Hollingsorth, Jack Nelson.
Army comedy about a sergeant who falls in love with a general's daughter, on 23 ½ hours leave.

Twilight (DeLuxe Pictures/Film Clearing House, Inc., 1919)
d: J. Searle Dawley. 6 reels.

Doris Kenyon, Frank Mills, Sally Crute, George Lessey, Harry Lee, Edith Warren, William Hartman, Grif Davis, Charles Brooks.
In the North Carolina mountains, an abandoned orphan baby girl is found. Her foster parents name her "Twilight."

Twin Beds (Carter DeHaven Productions/First National, 1920)
d: Lloyd Ingraham. 6 reels.
Carter DeHaven, Flora DeHaven, Helen Raymond, William Desmond, Catherine Lewis, William J. Irving, Lottie Williams, J. Montgomery Carlyle.
A tipsy husband stumbles home late one night and mistakenly enters the wrong apartment, climbs into bed, and is found in the morning by the startled lady of the house, whose own husband is out of town. Fortunately, they have twin beds.

Twin Kiddies (Balboa Amusement Co./Pathé, 1917)
d: Henry King. 5 reels.
Marie Osborne, Henry King, Ruth Lackaye, Daniel Gilfether, R. Henry Grey, Loretta Becker, Edward Jobson, Mignon LeBrun.
Poor little rich girl Fay has everything money can buy, but not the parental affection she desperately wants. Bessie, on the other hand, has a loving family but few possessions. Because the two girls look so much alike, they decide to trade clothes and take each other's place for a few days. Marie Osborne plays both roles.

The Twin Pawns (Acme Pictures Corp./Pathé, 1919)
w, d: Leonce Perret. 5 reels.
Mae Murray, Warner Oland, J.W. Johnston, Henry G. Sell.
Twin girls are separated at birth and grow up in radically different circumstances: One is wealthy, the other is a child of the slums. But fate will bring them together again.
Miss Murray plays a double role as the twins.

The Twin Triangle (Balboa Amusement Co./World Film Corp., 1916)
d: Harry Harvey. 5 reels.
Jackie Saunders, Mollie McConnell, Ruth Lackaye, Edward J. Brady, William Conklin, Robert Grey, Joyce Moore.
Czerta, a gypsy dancer, doesn't know it, but she has a sister who looks just like her... and she's a lady in high society.
Miss Saunders portrays both Czerta and her sister.

Twin Triggers (Action Pictures/Artclass Pictures, 1926)
d: Richard Thorpe. 5 reels.
Buddy Roosevelt, Nita Cavalier, FrederickLee, Laura Lockhart, Lafe McKee, Charles Whitaker, Clyde McClary, Togo Frye, Hank Bell.
Out West, twin brothers clash when one of them tries to smuggle Chinese laborers into the country, while his brother tries to stop him.
Buddy Roosevelt plays both twins, the good and the bad.

The Twinkler (American Film Co./Mutual, 1916)
d: Edward Sloman. 5 reels.
William Russell, Charlotte Burton, Clarence Burton, William Carroll, William Tedmarsh, William Spencer, Robert Klein, Orinel Barney.
In prison, a convict known as "The Twinkler" saves the life of Doc, a prisoner in charge of the facility's power supply. It's an auspicious move, because several months later, "The Twinkler's" girlfriend Rose is unjustly convicted of a capital crime and sentenced to the electric chair... but Doc turns off the power supply at the prison until the arrival of Rose's

TRUE HEART SUSIE (1919). Lillian Gish, as Susie, the girl who has sacrificed all for the man she loves, now learns he plans to marry another. This moment is part of a lengthy close-up in which Susie lays all her emotions bare as she contemplates the trick that fate has played on her.

* * * * *

pardon from the governor.

Twinkletoes (First National, 1926)
d: Charles Brabin. 8 reels.
Colleen Moore, Kenneth Harlan, Tully Marshall, Gladys Brockwell, Lucien Littlefield, Warner Oland, John Philip Kold, Julanne Johnston and William McDonald.
In London's Limehouse district, a street dancer lands a job in a music hall, and becomes a crowd-pleasing favorite.

Twins of Suffering Creek (Fox, 1920)
d: Scott Dunlap. 5 reels.
William Russell, Louise Lovely, E.A. Warren, Bill Ryno, Henry J. Herbert, Joe Ray, Florence Deshon, Malcolm Cripe, Helen Stone.
A saloon owner and a crooked gambler square off in a fight to the death.

Two Arabian Nights (Howard Hughes/United Artists, 1927)
d: Lewis Milestone. 9 reels.
Louis Wolheim, William Boyd, Mary Astor, Michael Vavitch, Ian Keith, DeWitt Jennings, Boris Karloff, Michael Visaroff.
In World War I, two American doughboys are captured by the enemy, then escape to Arabia, where they rescue a damsel in distress.

The Two Brides (Famous Players-Lasky/Paramount, 1919)
d: Edward José. 5 reels.
Lina Cavalieri, Courtenay Foote, Warburton Gamble, Hal Reid, Sherry Tansey, R.E. Milash, Emil Roe.
In Rome, a prince has two brides: His wife Diana and the breathtakingly beautiful statue of Diana sculpted by her father. He has rivals for both as well.

Two Can Play (Encore Pictures/Associated Exhibitors, 1926)
d: Nat Ross. 6 reels.
George Fawcett, Allan Forrest, Clara Bow, Wallace MacDonald, Vola Vale.
A disapproving dad tries to dig up some dirt on his daughter's new sweetheart.

The Two Edged Sword (Vitagraph, 1916)
d: George D. Baker. 5 reels.
Edith Storey, Evart Overton, Josephine Earle, Robert Gaillard, Logan Paul, Marion Henry, Nellie Anderson.
Dorothy, a bored wife, goes on a summer vacation with a friend, and starts up a flirtation with a local farmer.

Two-Fisted Jones (Universal, 1925)
d: Edward Sedgwick. 5 reels.
Jack Hoxie, William Steele, Kathryn McGuire, Harry Todd, Frank Rice, Paul Grimes, William Welsh, Frederick Cole, Byron Douglas, Ed Burns, Art Ortega.
Out West, a cowpoke upsets a sleazy moneylender's plot to take over a family ranch.

A Two-Fisted Sheriff (Ben Wilson Productions/Arrow Pictures, 1925)
d: Ben Wilson, Ward Hayes. 5 reels.
Yakima Canutt, Ruth Stonehouse, Art Walker, Cliff Davidson, Jack Woods, Joe Rickson.
Out West, a two-fisted sheriff falls in love with a girl he's rescued from a runaway team of horses.

Two Flaming Youths (Famous Players-Lasky/Paramount, 1927)
d: John Waters. 6 reels.
W.C. Fields, Chester Conklin, Mary Brian, Jack Luden, George Irving, Cissy Fitzgerald, Jimmy Quinn, Wallace Beery, Raymond Hatton, Rosetta Duncan, Vivian Duncan, Weber and Fields, Moran and Mack.
Gilfoil, owner of a struggling carnival show, is beset by financial problems and also by his apparent resemblance to a wanted criminal. The local sheriff is interested in Gilfoil on both counts.

2 Girls Wanted (Fox, 1927)
d: Alfred E. Green. 7 reels.
Janet Gaynor, Glenn Tryon, Ben Bard, Marie Mosquini, Joseph Cawthorn, Doris Lloyd, Alyce Mills, William Tooker, Pauline Neff, William Blatcher, C.L. Sherwood.
Marianna and Edna answer an ad that reads: "2 Girls Wanted" for the positions of cook and housekeeper. Once on the job, though, the girls discover a plot to swindle the uncle of the wealthy homeowner, and foil the crooks. That done, Marianna and her bachelor boss fall in love.

Two-Gun Betty (Robert Brunton Productions/Pathé, 1918)
d: Robert Brunton. 5 reels.
Bessie Barriscale, L.C. Shumway, Catherine Van Buren, Helen Hawley, Laura Oakley, Albert Cody, Richard Wayne, William Ellingford, C.M. Carlos, George Routh.
Out West, tomboy Betty makes a bet that she can fool the cowboys and impersonate a male ranch hand, with no one being the wiser.

The Two-Gun Man (R-C Pictures/FBO of America, 1926)
d: David Kirkland. 6 reels.
Fred Thomson, Joseph Dowling, Spottiswoode Aitken, Sheldon Lewis, Frank Hagney, Ivor McFadden, Olive Hasbrouck, William Courtwright, Billy Butts, Arthur Millett, Willie Fung.
A returning war hero gets home just in time to redeem his dad's ranch from the greedy moneylenders.

Two Kinds of Love (Universal, 1920)
d: Reaves Eason. 5 reels.
George McDaniel, Ted Brooks, Jimsy May, Reaves Eason Jr., Reaves Eason, Fontaine LaRue, Charles Newton.
Out West, an ex-convict tries to locate the cache of gold he and his late partner had hidden years before. He confides in a small family who nest in his cabin, and together they find the treasure map's missing piece, which will lead them to the gold.

Two Kinds of Women (R-C Pictures, 1922)
d: Colin Campbell. 6 reels.
Pauline Frederick, Tom Santschi, Charles Clary, Dave Winter, Eugene Pallette, Billy Elmer, Jack Curtis, Jim Barley, Sam Appel, Clarissa Selwynne, Otis Harlan, Jean Calhoun.
Judith, an eastern girl, comes West and finds she's inherited a mess. Her father has died and left her his cattle ranch, but a traitorous employee in cahoots with another ranchowner is trying to sabotage Judith's interests.

Two Little Imps (Fox, 1917)
d: Kenean Buel. 5 reels.
Jane Lee, Katherine Lee, Leslie Austen, Edna Hunter, Edwin Holt, Stuart Sage, Sidney D'Albrook, William Harvey.
Jane and Katherine, the "two little imps" of the title, hamper their bachelor uncle's courtship of his neighbor Betty.

Two Lovers (Goldwyn/United Artists, 1928)
d: Fred Niblo. 9 reels.
Ronald Colman, Vilma Banky, Nigel DeBrulier, Noah Beery, Paul Lukas, Virginia Bradford, Helen Jerome Eddy, Eugenie Besserer, Fred Esmelton, Harry Allen, Marcella Daly.

A Flemish patriot dons a mask to fight injustice and woo his lady fair.

Two Men and a Maid (Tiffany-Stahl Productions, 1929)
d: George Archainbaud. 7 reels. (Music, sound effects, part talkie.)
William Collier Jr., Alma Bennett, Eddie Gribbon, George E. Stone, Margaret Quimby.
An Englishman believes his wife to be unfaithful, and joins the French Foreign Legion to try and forget her. There, he will have some romantic adventurous of his own.

Two Men and a Woman (Ivan Film Productions, Inc., 1917)
d: William J. Humphrey. 5 reels.
James Morrison, Guy Coombs, John Reinhard, Christine Mayo, Rubye de Remer, Helen Arnold, Yuka Yamakura.
Donaldson, a bachelor, introduces his young ward to Ethel and they fall in love. But the young man doesn't realize that his guardian is in love with Ethel too.

Two Men of Sandy Bar (Universal, 1916)
d: Lloyd Carleton. 5 reels.
Hobart Bosworth, Charles Hickman, Gretchen Lederer, Emory Johnson, Jack Curtis, Yona Landowska, Frank MacQuarrie, William Mong, A.E. Whiting, Jean Taylor.
Hell hath no fury like.... Out West, when a newly-widowed duchess flirts with a professional gambler and he rejects her, she stacks a deck of his cards so he will be branded as a cheat.

Two Minutes to Go (Charles Ray Productions/Associated First National, 1921)
d: Charles Ray. 6 reels.
Charles Ray, Mary Anderson, Lionel Belmore, Lincoln Stedman, Truman Van Dyke, Gus Leonard, Tom Wilson, Bert Woodruff, François Dumas, Phillip Dunham.
Comedy about Chester, a star football player who is forced to take over a milk route every morning to cover expenses. The extra load of work causes him to cut back on his football practices, and he loses his starting position. But the peppy milkman will bounce back and lead his team to victory in the year-ending Big Game.

Two Moons (Fox, 1920)
d: Edward J. LeSaint. 5 reels.
Buck Jones, Carol Holloway, Gus Saville, Bert Sprotte, Slim Padgett, William Ellingford, Louis Fitzroy, Edward Peil, Edwin Booth Tilton, Eunice Murdock, Eleanor Gawne.
In Wyoming, the never-ending war between the sheep herders and the cattlemen heats up.

The Two Orphans (Fox, 1915)
d: Herbert Brenon. 5 reels.
Theda Bara, Jean Southern, William E. Shay, Herbert Brenon, Gertrude Berkley, Frank Goldsmith, E.L. Fernandez, Sheridan Block, Mrs. Cecil Raleigh.
In Paris, two young women—one of them blind—are forced by disastrous circumstances to beg for food. Unknown to them, one of the girls is the long-lost daughter of a noblewoman.
This film would be remade, as *Orphans of the Storm*, by D.W. Griffith in 1921.

The Two Outlaws (Universal, 1928)
d: Henry MacRae. 5 reels.
Jack Perrin, Kathleen Collins, J.P. McGowan, Cuyler Supplee, Rex the horse.
Rex, leader of a pack of wild horses, gallops to the rescue of a two-legged friend and his sweetheart.

Two Shall be Born (Twin Pictures/Vitagraph, 1924)
d: Whitman Bennett. 6 reels.
Jane Novak, Kenneth Harlan, Sigrid Holmquist, Frank Sheridan, Herman Lieb, Fuller Mellish, Joseph Burke, Blanche Craig, Joseffa DeBok, Catharine Evans, Walter James.
Mayra, a Polish envoy for peace, meets and marries a New York traffic cop. But she must still deliver important documents to the Polish embassy, to foster permanent peace among nations.

Two Sisters (Trem Carr Productions/Rayart Pictures, 1929)
d: Scott Pembroke. 6 reels. (Synchronized music score.)
Viola Dana, Rex Lease, Claire DuBrey, Tom Lingham, Irving Bacon, Tom Curran, Boris Karloff, Adalyn Asbury.
Jean and Jane, twin sisters and shopgirls together, are radically different. One is sweet, honest, and pure... while the other is a cunning thief.
Miss Dana plays both twins.

The Two-Soul Woman (Universal, 1918)
d: Elmer Clifton. 5 reels.
Priscilla Dean, Joseph Girard, Ashton Dearholt, Evelyn Selbie.
Under hypnosis, a young heiress exhibits two different personalities.

Two Weeks (Joseph M. Scheck Productions/First National, 1920)
d: Syndey A. Franklin. 6 reels.
Constance Talmadge, Conway Tearle, Reginald Mason, George Fawcett, Templar Saxe, William Fredericks, Tom Cameron, Mrs. Wensley Thompson, Florence Hope, Gertrude Doyle.
When a broadway showgirl finds that her sponsor is demanding a romantic liaison as the price of her stardom, she escapes and winds up in the home of three confirmed bachelors. Invited to stay with them for two weeks, she so entrances one of the bachelors that he doesn't stay confirmed for long.

Two Weeks Off (First National/Warner Bros., 1929)
d: William Beaudine. 7 reels. (Part talkie.)
Jack Mulhall, Dorothy Mackaill, Gertrude Astor, Jimmy Finlayson, Kate Price, Jed Prouty, Eddie Gribbon, Dixie Gay, Gertrude Messinger.
A plumber masquerades as a film star to impress a salesgirl he's just met.

Two Weeks With Pay (Realart Pictures, 1921)
d: Maurice Campbell. 5 reels.
Bebe Daniels, Jack Mulhall, James Mason, George Periolat, Frances Raymond, Polly Moran, Walter Hiers.
Pansy, a shopgirl who looks a lot like a certain movie star, goes on a two-week vacation at a summer resort, and is quickly mistaken for her illustrious lookalike.
Miss Daniels plays a double role, as the shop girl and her spittin' image movie star.

Two Women (Vitagraph, 1919)
d: Ralph W. Ince. 5 reels.
Anita Stewart, Earle Williams, Julia Swayne Gordon, Harry Northrup.
John, a geologist, finds his wife flirting with his boss and leaves her. In the mountains, he falls in love with a lovely young woman named Enid, and she with him. But now his wife wants him back.

The Typhoon (New York Motion Picture

Corp./Paramount, 1914)
d: Reginald Barker. 5 reels.
Sessue Hayakawa, Gladys Brockwell, Frank Borzage, Henry Katoni, Leona Hutton, Thomas Kurichari, Tsuru Aoki.
Tragic tale of a Japanese diplomat in love with an American chorus girl.

Tyrant Fear (Thomas H. Ince/Paramount, 1918)
d: R. William Neill. 5 reels.
Dorothy Dalton, Thurston Hall, Melbourne MacDowell, William Conklin, Lou Salter, Carmen Phillips.
In the Canadian Northwest, a saloon girl falls in love with the bar's pianist, but their love is put on hold, for she must first deal with her brutish husband.

Tyrant of Red Gulch (FBO Pictures, 1928)
d: Robert DeLacy. 5 reels.
Tom Tyler, Frankie Darro, Josephine Borio, Harry Woods, Serge Temoff, Barney Furey.
Two cowpokes wander into a small mining town ruled by a cruel Russian overseer.

The U. P. Trail (Zane Grey Pictures, Inc./Pathé, 1920)
d: Jack Conway. 7 reels.
Kathlyn Williams, Roy Stewart, Marguerite DeLaMotte, Robert McKim, Joseph J. Dowling, Frederick Starr, Charles B. Murphy, Virginia Caldwell, Walter Perry, George Berrell.

Neale, a railroad engineer helping to build the Union Pacific line (along "the U.P Trail"), falls in love with a girl whose family has been massacred by Indians.

The Unattainable (Universal, 1916)
d: Lloyd Carleton. 5 reels.
Dorothy Davenport, Emory Johnson, Mattie Witting, Richard Morris, Alfred Allen.
Bessie, a theatrical star, leaves her usual Broadway milieu and travels west—and, surprisingly, falls for a shepherd in the high Sierras.

The Unbeliever (Thomas A. Edison, Inc./George Kleine System, 1918)
d: Alan Crosland. 7 reels.
Marguerite Courtot, Raymond McKee, Erich von Stroheim, Kate Lester, Frank de Vernon, Mortimer Martini, Blanche Davenport, Harold Hallacher, Darwin Karr, Earl Schenck, Gertrude Norman, Lew Hart, Thomas Holcomb, J.F. Rorke, Moss Gill, Ross E. Rowell.
Ambitious World War I drama about an atheistic snob who joins the U.S. Marines, sees combat duty in France, and has his outlook on life seriously altered for the better.

The Unborn (Kulee Features, Inc., 1916)
d: Otis B. Thayer. 5 reels.
Gertrude Bondhill, Wharton Jones, Bert Merket, Elinore Jackson, Esther Hough, Edwin Powers, Clark Comstock, Molly Gilmore, Julia Hurley, Lewis Sealy, Charles Hamlin.
Country girl Nancy falls for Richard, a wealthy city boy, but he leaves her and returns to the city to marry his high society girlfriend. Nancy has a baby, but dies soon after and the child is placed in an orphanage. Later, Richard and his wife decide to adopt their paperboy, not realizing the lad is Richard's natural son.

The Unbroken Promise (Sunset Pictures Corp./Triangle, 1919)
d: Frank Powell. 5 reels.
Jane Miller, Sidney Mason, William Human, John Smiley, Dick LeStrange, Robert Taber.

In Texas, a sheep rancher feuds with his cattleman neighbor. The rancher's pacifist daughter tries to smooth things over between the two antagonists—so much so, that she falls in love with the cattleman.

Uncharted Channels (Jesse D. Hampton Productions, 1920)
d: Henry King. 6 reels.
H.B. Warner, Kathryn Adams, Sam DeGrasse, Evelyn Selbie, William Elmer, Percy Challenger, Thomas H. Persse, J.P. Lockney.
Tim, son of a wealthy father who has disinherited him, goes to work in a factory as a plumber. He finds that some of the "workers" are really Bolshevik troublemakers, and proceeds to expose them and rid the factory of them and their poisonous influence.

Uncharted Seas (Metro, 1921)
d: Wesley Ruggles. 6 reels.
Alice Lake, Rudolph Valentino, Carl Gerard, Robert Alden, Charles Mailes, Rhea Haines.
Lucretia, unhappily married to an alcoholic sea captain, boards a ship commanded by a skipper who has loved her from afar, and sails away on an Arctic voyage with him.

The Unchastened Woman (Rialto DeLuxe Productions, 1918)
d: William Humphrey. 7 reels.
Grace Valentine, Mildred Manning, Catherine Tower, Edna Hunter, Frank Mills, Adelaide Barker, Mildred Rankin, Victor Sutherland, Paul Panzer, Mike Donlin, John Hopkins.
Though happily (and wealthily) married, Caroline is an incorrigible flirt.

The Unchastened Woman (Chadwick Pictures, 1925)
d: James Young. 7 reels.
Theda Bara, Wyndham Standing, Dale Fuller, John Miljan, Eileen Percy, Dot Farley, Harry Northrup, Mayme Kelso, Kate Price, Eric Mayne, Frederic Kovert.
A pregnant young wife learns her husband is cheating on her. She takes off for Europe, has her baby, and flirts with several gentlemen. Upon her return to the United States, she makes plans to win her husband back.

Unclaimed Goods (Famous Players-Lasky/Paramount, 1918)
d: Rollin S. Sturgeon. 5 reels.
Harrison Ford, Vivian Martin, Casson Ferguson, George McDaniel, Carmen Phillips, Dick La Reno, George Kunkel, Ann Schaefer.
In this western comedy, the Wells Fargo Express is carrying precious cargo: A C.O.D. package that actually contains Betsy, a live little girl!

Uncle Sam of Freedom Ridge (Harry Levey Productions, 1920)
d: George A. Beranger. 7 reels.
George MacQuarrie, William Corbett, Paul Kelly, Helen Flint, Eugene Keith, Leslie Hunt, Sheridan Tansey, Jack Newton, Nicholas Burnham.
Pro-League of Nations film tracing the story of a Civil War veteran who loses his only son in World War I.

Uncle Tom's Cabin (World Film Corp., 1914)
d: William Robert Daly. 5 reels.
Sam Lucas, Walter Hitchcok, Hattie Delaro, Irving Cummings, Paul Scardon.
Uncle Tom, a faithful slave to the Shelby family, saves Little Eva St. Clair from drowning and is then purchased by her grateful father. Alas, Little Eva dies and her father is killed

during a fight, so Uncle Tom is sold to the vicious Simon Legree.

This was the first feature-length version of the famous Harriet Beecher Stowe novel, after four short interpretations between 1903 and 1910.

Uncle Tom's Cabin (Famous Players-Lasky/Paramount, 1918)
d: J. Searle Dawley. 5 reels.
Marguerite Clark, J.W. Johnston, Florence Carpenter, Frank Losee, Phil Ryley, Harry Lee, Walter Lewis, Augusta Anderson, Ruby Hoffman, Susanne Willis, Thomas Carnahan Jr.
In New Orleans, a warm friendship grows between Little Eva St. Clair and two of her father's slaves, Uncle Tom and Topsy... so much so, that Little Eva asks her father to set them free. But both the girl and her father die before the slaves gain their freedom. As a consequence, Uncle Tom is sold to the brutal Simon Legree.

Uncle Tom's Cabin (Universal, 1927)
d: Harry Pollard. 13 reels. (Music score.)
Virginia Grey, George Siegmann, James Lowe, Margarita Fisher, Mona Ray, Eulalie Jensen, Arthur Edmund Carewe, Aileen Manning, Lucien Littlefield, Adolph Milar, Jack Mower, Vivian Oakland, John Roche.
Harriet Beecher Stowe's famous novel is presented in epic dimensions for its seventh film version.

Unconquered (Lasky Feature Plays/Paramount, 1917)
d: Frank Reicher. 5 reels.
Fannie Ward, Jack Dean, Hobart Bosworth, Tully Marshall, Mabel Van Buren, Jane Wolfe, Billy Jacobs.
A heartless husband forces his wife into a compromising situation with another man, so that he can win a divorce and custody of his son.

Unconquered Woman (Pasha Film Corp./Lee-Bradford Corp., 1922)
d: Marcel Perez. 5 reels.
Rubye DeRemer, Walter Miller, Fred C. Jones, Frankie Mann, Nick Thompson.
To repay money that her wastrel brother has stolen, a young woman offers herself in marriage to the highest bidder.

Under Cover (Famous Players/Paramount, 1916)
d: Robert G. Vignola. 5 reels.
Hazel Dawn, Owen Moore, William Courtleigh Jr., Ethel Fleming, Frank Losee, Ida Darling.
Taylor, an unscrupulous customs official, blackmails Ethel, a young woman, into spying for him on a suspected smuggler. But Ethel's task becomes complicated when she finds herself falling in love with her prey.

Under Crimson Skies (Universal, 1920)
d: Rex Ingram. 6 reels.
Elmo Lincoln, Mabel Ballin, Harry Van Meter, Nancy Caswell, Frank Brownlee, Paul Weigel, Dick La Reno, Noble Johnson.
A ship's captain falls for the wife of one of his passengers.

Under False Colors (Thanhouser/Pathé, 1917)
d: Emile Chautard. 5 reels.
Jeanne Eagels, Frederick Warde, Robert Vaughn, Anne Gregory, Carey Hastings.
Fleeing from revolutionaries, Olga, an exiled Russian countess, makes friends with a young American woman on board ship. When the ship sinks and the young woman is killed, the rescued countess decides to assume her identity.

Under Fire (Clifford S. Elfelt Productions/Davis Distributing Division, 1926)
d: Clifford S. Elfelt. 5 reels.
Bill Patton, Jean Arthur, Cathleen Calhoun, Norbert Myles, William Bertram, Harry Moody.
Brennan, a cavalry lieutenant, is discharged in disgrace when trumped-up evidence suggests he deserted his men during an Indian attack. He wanders into the desert and disappears for a while, then rides furiously back to the cavalry post to warn them of a new Indian uprising.

Under Handicap (Yorke Film Corp./Metro, 1917)
d: Fred J. Balshofer. 8 reels.
Harold Lockwood, W.H. Bainbridge, Anna Little, Lester Cuneo, T.H. Gibson-Gowland, William Clifford, James Youngdeer.
An eastern tenderfoot goes West and signs on to a dam-building project.

Under Northern Lights (Universal, 1920)
d: Jacques Jaccard. 5 reels.
William Buckley, Virginia Brown Faire, Leonard Clapham, Herbert Bethew, Charles Brinley, Ben Corbett, Frank Staples, Oleta Ottis, Kay Harrison.
In the Canadian northwest, a Mountie loves Suzanne, a girl who has adopted a half-breed child. Then the rumors start: Is the baby really Suzanne's?

Under Southern Skies (Universal, 1915)
d: Lucius Henderson. 5 reels.
Mary Fuller, Paul Panzer, Milton Sills, Charles Ogle, Clar Byers, Bert Busby, William Heidoff, John Ridgway, Marie Shotwell, Mary Moore, Harry Blackmore, Nellie Slattery, Margaret Wall, Marie Weirman.
In Civil War days, a Southern belle and her family run afoul of a trouble-making Confederate soldier whose romantic overtures she has rejected.

Under Suspicion (Metro, 1918)
d: Will S. Davis. 5 reels.
Francis X. Bushman, Beverly Bayne, Eva Gordon, Hugh Jeffrey, Frank Montgomery, Sidney D'Albrook, Arthur Housman, Jack Newton, Franklyn Hanna.
Virginia, a newspaper reporter covering a party of swells, is drawn into a mystery surrounding the sudden disappearance of the hostess' diamonds.

Under Suspicion (Universal, 1919)
d: William Dowlan. 5 reels.
Forrest Stanley, Ora Carew, Frank MacQuarrie, Blanche Rose, Charles Clary, Frank Thompson, Burwell Hamrick, Andrew Waldron, Cora Drew.
Mistaken identity animates this crime drama, when a society girl thinks a vacationing millionaire is a burglar, and holds him off with a pistol.

Under the Black Eagle (MGM, 1928)
d: W.S. Van Dyke. 6 reels.
Ralph Forbes, Marceline Day, Flash the dog, Marc MacDermott, Bert Roach, William Fairbanks.
During World War I, a faithful dog comes to his wounded master's rescue.

Under the Greenwood Tree (Famous Players-Lasky/Paramount, 1918)
d: Emile Chautard. 5 reels.
Elsie Ferguson, Eugene O'Brien, Edward Burns, Mildred Havens, John Ardizoni, Robert Milasch, Robert Vivian, Charles Craig, Henry Warwick, James Furey.

An heiress and her secretary journey into the woods to join a gypsy band.

Under the Lash (Famous Players-Lasky/Paramount, 1921)
d: Sam Wood. 6 reels.
Gloria Swanson, Mahlon Hamilton, Russell Simpson, Lillian Leighton, Lincoln Stedman, Thena Jasper, Clarence Ford.
Deborah, the young farm wife of a religious fanatic, is threatened with a beating by her husband for reading *Romeo and Juliet*.

Under the Red Robe (Goldwyn/Cosmopolitan, 1924)
d: Alan Crosland. 10 reels.
Robert Mantell, Alma Rubens, John Charles Thomas, William Powell, Otto Kruger, Sydney Herbert, Genevieve Hamper, Mary MacLaren, Gustaf von Seyffertitz, Paul Panzer, Evelyn Gosnell, Charles Judels, George Nash.
Court intrigue in 17th century France, involving Cardinal Richelieu and his patron, Louis XIII.

Under the Rouge (Encore Pictures/Associated Exhibitors, 1925)
d: Lewis H. Moomaw. 6 reels.
Eileen Percy, Tom Moore, Eddie Phillips, James Mason, Claire DeLorez, William V. Mong, Chester Conklin, Aileen Manning, Stanley Blystone, Peggy Prevost, Frank Clark.
Old war buddies turn to cracking safes for a living.

Under the Tonto Rim (Paramount, 1928)
d: Herman C. Raymaker. 6 reels.
Richard Arlen, Alfred Allen, Mary Brian, Jack Luden, Harry T. Morey, William Franey, Harry Todd, Bruce Gordon, Jack Byron.
Out West, a gold miner searches for his father's poker-playing killer. He finds him when he discovers Sam Spralls doing what the killer was known for: shuffling with one hand.

Under the Top (Famous Players-Lasky/Paramount, 1919)
d: Donald Crisp. 5 reels.
Fred Stone, Ella Hall, Gordon Griffith, Althea Worthley, Lester LeMay, Sylvia Ashton, James Cruze, Guy Oliver, Charles Ogle, Noah Beery, Jane Wolff, Julia N. Stark.
Circus comedy featuring the athletic feats of real-life acrobat Fred Stone.

Under the Yoke (Fox, 1918)
d: J. Gordon Edwards. 5 reels.
Theda Bara, Albert Roscoe, G. Raymond Nye, E.B. Tilton, Carrie Clarke Ward.
In the Philippines, a young Spanish woman is courted by both an evil plantation owner and a dashing American army captain.

Under Two Flags (Fox, 1916)
d: J. Gordon Edwards. 6 reels.
Theda Bara, Herbert Heyes, Stuart Holmes, Stanhope Wheatcroft, Joseph Crehan, Charles Craig, Claire Whitney.
In the Sahara, an Englishman who has joined the French Foreign Legion is unjustly convicted of treason and condemned to die before a firing squad. But at the last possible moment, a Legion "groupie" who loves him takes the bullets meant for him.
This film was remade once in the silent era, by Universal in 1922.

Under Two Flags (Universal, 1922)
d: Tod Browning. 8 reels.
Priscilla Dean, James Kirkwood, Stuart Holmes, John Davidson, Ethel Grey Terry, Robert Mack, Burton Law, Albert Pollet.
French Foreign Legion drama, with a woman sacrificing her life for the man she loves. Second feature film version of the venerable tale by "Ouida" (Marie Louise de la Ramee).

Under Western Skies (Universal, 1926)
d: Edward Sedgwick. 7 reels.
Norman Kerry, Anne Cornwall, Ward Crane, George Fawcett, Kathleen Key, Eddie Gribbon, Harry Todd, Charles K. French, William A. Steele, John S. Peters, Art Artego.
East meets West—in a way—when a New York banker falls for the daughter of an Oregon rancher.

The Undercurrent (Select Pictures Corp./Guy Empey Pictures, 1919)
d: Wilfrid North. 6 reels.
Guy Empey, Florence Evelyn Martin, Vera Boehm, Marguerite Courtot, Betty Blythe, William Dunn, Charles A. Stevenson, Betty Hutchinson, Eugene Strong, Frederick R. Buckley.
Early anti-Communist film, about a returning war veteran who falls in with Russian spies.

The Understanding Heart (MGM, 1926)
d: Jack Conway. 7 reels.
Joan Crawford, Rockcliffe Fellowes, Carmel Myers, Francis X. Bushman Jr., Richard Carle, Jerry Miley, Harvey Clark.
A forest ranger who was forced to kill in self-defense is convicted of murder due to perjured testimony. But he escapes from jail and is protected by the sister of the false witness.

The Understudy (R-C Pictures/FBO of America, 1922)
d: William A. Seiter. 5 reels.
Doris May, Wallace MacDonald, Christine Mayo, Otis Harlan, Arthur Hoyt.
When a wealthy man offers to pay a fortune-hunting stage actress to drop her engagement to his son, she agrees. But instead of showing up herself to pick up the check, she sends her understudy, a girl of such grace and beauty that she soon has both father and son courting her.

The Undertow (American Film Co./Mutual, 1916)
d: Frank Thorne. 5 reels.
Franklin Ritchie, Helene Rosson, Eugenie Forde, Orral Humphrey, Harry Von Meter, George Ahern, Ogden Childe.
Although King, a factory owner, is married, he finds himself strongly attracted to Esther, his foreman's niece.

Underworld (Paramount, 1927)
d: Josef von Sternberg. 8 reels.
George Bancroft, Clive Brook, Evelyn Brent, Larry Semon, Fred Kohler, Helen Lynch, Jerry Mandy, Karl Morse.
An underworld gang leader takes on a clever accomplice who gradually becomes the brains of the outlaw ring. The gang leader lets that pass, but cannot overlook rumors of a romance between his girlfriend and the new accomplice.

Undine (Universal, 1916)
d: Henry Otto. 5 reels.
Ida Schnall, Douglas Gerrard, Edna Mason, Carol Stellson, Caroline Fowler, O.C. Jackson, Josephine Rice, Elijah Zerr, Jack Nelson, Thomas Delmar, Eileen Allen, Grace Astor.
Fantasy about Undine, a water nymph who falls in love with a mortal.

Undressed (Sterling Pictures, 1928)
d: Philip Rosen. 6 reels.

David Torrence, Hedda Hopper, Virginia Brown Faire, Buddy Messenger, Bryant Washburn, Virginia Vance.

An unscrupulous artist paints a portrait of a proper young lady, then alters it to suggest that she posed in the nude.

The Undying Flame (Lasky Feature Plays/Paramount, 1917)
d: Maurice Tourneur. 5 reels.
Olga Petrova, Edwin Mordant, Herbert Evans, Mahlon Hamilton, Warren Cook, Charles W. Martin, Violet Reed.
Drama with mystic overtones, about a princess in ancient Egypt who loves a poor shepherd but is discouraged by her father the king. The two lovers make a death pact to be rejoined in the next life; and to seal the pledge, they break a scarab in two and each keeps a broken half. Centuries later, another pair of mismatched lovers meet and discover that each has a half of a broken scarab.

Uneasy Money (Essanay, 1918)
d: Lawrence C. Windom. 5 reels.
Taylor Holmes, Virginia Valli, Arthur Bates, Charles Gardner, Virginia Bowker, Fred Tiden, Lillian Drew, James F. Fulton, Rod LaRocque.
Comedy about an American millionaire who impulsively wills his entire estate to an Englishman for helping him correct his golf slice. The surprised beneficiary, being an honest man, seeks the millionaire's legal heirs... and finds true love with one of them.

Uneasy Payments (R-C Pictures/FBO of America, 1927)
d: David Kirkland. 5 reels.
Alberta Vaughn, Jack Luden, Gino Corrado, Gene Stone, Victor Potel, Betty Francisco, Amber Norman.
Bee, a country girl, wins a Charleston contest and heads for New York and the big time. But she's got a lot to learn. A cabaret owner offers to install her in a beautifully decorated apartment, and the clueless Bee accepts, thinking it merely a friendly gesture.

Unexpected Places (Metro, 1918)
d: E. Mason Hopper. 5 reels.
Bert Lytell, Rhea Mitchell, Rosemary Theby, Colin Kenny, Louis Morrison, Edythe Chapman, John Burton, Stanton Heck, Jay Dwiggins, Frank Newberry, Martin Best.
During World War I, an ace reporter investigates the mysterious death of a gentleman's gentleman, and discovers that German spies, keen to obtain some secret documents, are the culprits.

The Unfair Sex (Diamant film Co. Of America, 1926)
d: Henri Diamant-Berger. 5 reels.
Hope Hampton, Holbrook Blinn, Nita Naldi, Walter Miller.
Shirley becomes engaged to Billy, her childhood sweetheart. But Calvert, a rival for Shirley's hand, arranges for Billy to meet and fall into the clutches of a vampish chorus girl.

The Unfaithful Wife (Fox, 1915)
d: J. Gordon Edwards. 5 reels.
Robert B. Mantell, Genevieve Hamper, Stuart Holmes, Runa Hodges, Doris Wooldridge, Warner Oland, Lawrence White.
Buried alive by his faithless wife and her lover, an Italian count struggles to free himself, and succeeds. Now seeking revenge, he dons a clever disguise that makes him unrecognizable to his wife, makes the fickle woman fall in love with him... then springs the trap.

The Unfoldment (Producers Pictures/Associated Exhibitors, 1922)
d: George Kern, Murdock MacQuarrie. 6 reels.

Florence Lawrence, Barbara Bedford, Charles French, William Conklin, Albert Prisco, Lydia Knott, Raymond Cannon, Murdock MacQuarrie, Wade Boteler.
A young woman is hired by a newspaper publisher to produce a movie depicting him as a solid citizen and a desirable political candidate.

The Unforseen (Empire All Star Corp./Mutual, 1917)
d: John B. O'Brien. 5 reels.
Olive Tell, David Powell, Lionel Adams, Fuller Mellish, Eileen Dennes, Helen Courtney, Warburton Gamble.
After Margaret's fiancé Henry loses his fortune and commits suicide, she meets a charming blind man and they marry. But when an operation restores his sight, he sees his wife and recognizes her as the woman his friend Henry was engaged to.

The Unguarded Hour (First National, 1925)
d: Lambert Hillyer. 7 reels.
Doris Kenyon, Claude King, Milton Sills, Dolores Cassinelli, Cornelius Keefe, Jed Prouty, Lorna Duveen, Vivia Ogden, Charles Beyer, Tammany Young, J. Moy Bennett.
In Italy for a stay with her father's fiancée, Virginia falls for her nephew, a duke.

Unguarded Women (Famous Players-Lasky/Paramount, 1924)
d: Alan Crosland. 6 reels.
Bebe Daniels, Richard Dix, Mary Astor, Walter McGrail, Frank Losee, Helen Lindroth, Harry Mestayer, Donald Hall, Joe King.
A war hero returns home, but is riddled with guilt over having allowed his buddy to die. Eventually the love of a good woman will help him see things more clearly.

The Unholy Three (MGM, 1925)
d: Tod Browning. 7 reels.
Lon Chaney, Victor McLaglen, Harry Earles, Mae Busch, Matt Moore, Edward Connelly.
A ventriloquist, a midget, and a strong man augment their circus income by picking the customers' pockets... but their larceny doesn't end there. When they try to expand their "business," it leads them to murder and self-destruction.

The Uninvited Guest (Submarine Film Corp./Metro, 1924)
d: Ralph Ince. 7 reels. (Technicolor sequence.)
Maurice B. Flynn, Jean Tolley, Mary MacLaren, William Bailey, Louis Wolheim.
A shipwrecked heiress is found stranded in an island cave.

United States Smith (Gotham Productions/Lumas Film Corp., 1928)
d: Joseph Henabery. 7 reels.
Eddie Gribbon, Lila Lee, Mickey Bennett, Kenneth Harlan, Earle Marsh.
"United States Smith" is really Ugo, a poor Russian orphan boy who's been adopted by a kindly Marine sergeant.

The Unknown (Lasky Feature Plays/Paramount, 1915)
d: George Melford. 5 reels.
Lou Tellegen, Theodore Roberts, Dorothy Davenport, Hal Clements, Tom Forman, Raymond Hatton, Horace B. Carpenter, George Gebhardt.
Richard, a disinherited Briton, joins the Foreign Legion to forget his troubles... but finds more trouble than he's ever known.

The Unknown (Phil Goldstone Productions, 1921)
d: Grover Jones. 5 reels.

Richard Talmadge, Andrée Tourneur, Mark Fenton, J.W. Early.
A young fop leads a consumer rebellion in his other identity, "The Unknown."

The Unknown (MGM, 1927)
d: Tod Browning. 6 reels.
Lon Chaney, Joan Crawford, Norman Kerry, Nick DeRuiz, John George, Frank Lanning.
A sideshow performer goes to horrific lengths to win the heart of a neurotic girl.

The Unknown Cavalier (Charles R. Rogers Productions/First National, 1926)
d: Albert Rogell. 7 reels.
Ken Maynard, Kathleen Collins, David Torrence, T. Roy Barnes, James Mason, Otis Harlan, Joseph Swickard, Bruce Gordon, Fred Burns, Jimsy Boudwin, Pat Harmon.
Out West, a drifter is recruited to try to tame an ornery equine.

The Unknown Love (Perret Productions, Inc./Pathé, 1919)
w, d: Leonce Perret. 6 reels.
Dolores Cassinelli, E.K. Lincoln, Robert Elliott, Bradley Barker.
In a variant on *Cyrano de Bergerac*, a young woman discovers that the overseas soldier she learned to love through his letters is not the man whose photograph first attracted her.

The Unknown Lover (Victory Pictures/Vitagraph, 1925)
d: Victor Hugo Halperin. 7 reels.
Elsie Ferguson, Frank Mayo, Mildred Harris, Peggy Kelly, Leslie Austin.
Seeing that her successful husband is working himself too hard, Elaine surreptitiously changes the bid on one of his contracts. This imposes a financial loss on them, but it also gives the husband some rest from his labors. After a year-long sea voyage, he wins back his health and resolves to be more attentive to his wife and less obsessed about business.

The Unknown Purple (Carlos Productions/Truart Film Corp., 1923)
d: Roland West. 7 reels.
Henry B. Walthall, Alice Lake, Stuart Holmes, Helen Ferguson, Frankie Lee, Ethel Grey Terry, James Morrison, Johnny Arthur, Richard Wayne, Brinsley Shaw, Mike Donlin.
An inventor develops a purple light that makes him invisible.

The Unknown Quantity (Vitagraph, 1919)
d: Thomas R. Mills. 5 reels.
Corinne Griffith, Huntley Gordon, Harry Davenport, Jack Ridgeway, Frederick Buckley, Jack McLean.
After an unscrupulous stock speculator manipulates the market and causes ruination for many, he dies and his son resolves to right some of the wrongs his father caused.

The Unknown Soldier (Renaud Hoffman Productions, 1926)
d: Renaud Hoffman. 8 reels.
Henry B. Walthall, Marguerite De La Motte, Charles Emmett Mack, Claire McDowell, George Cooper, Syd Crossley, Jess Devorska, Willis Marks.
Heavy drama about Fred and Mary, small-town sweethearts, during World War I. Fred goes off to war and encounters Mary in France, entertaining the troops in a variety show. They agree to get married the day before his outfit is to ship out.

Unknown Treasures (Sterling Pictures, 1926)
d: Archie Mayo. 6 reels.
Gladys Hulette, Robert Agnew, John Miljan, Bertram Marburgh, Jed Prouty, Gustav von Seyffertitz.
Mystery drama about a young couple searching for valuable documents in a deserted house.

Unknown 274 (Fox, 1917)
d: Harry Millarde. 5 reels.
June Caprice, Kittens Reichert, Florence Ashbrook, Inez Marcel, Dan Mason, Richard Neill, Tom Burroughs, Jean Armour, William Burns, Alexander Shannon.
"Unknown 274," an orphan girl whose only possession is an old violin, is adopted by a woman seeking to turn a profit by selling her away.

The Unknown Wife (Universal, 1921)
d: William Worthington. 5 reels.
Edith Roberts, Spottiswoode Aitken, Casson Ferguson, Joe Quinn, Joe Neary, Augustus Phillips, Bertram Frank, Mathilde Brundage, Jessie Pratt, Edith Stayart, Hal Wilson.
Grant, a basically decent chap who has served a prison term for petty theft, marries Helen upon his release. Soon, however, the police are questioning him again in connection with a recent robbery.

Unmarried Wives (Gotham Productions/Lumas Film Corp., 1924)
d: James P. Hogan. 6 reels.
Mildred Harris, Gladys Brockwell, Lloyd Whitlock, Bernard Randall, George Cooper, Majel Coleman.
In New York, a married man has a dalliance with Maggie, a stage actress known as Princess Sonya.

The Unnamed Woman (Embassy Pictures/Arrow Pictures, 1925)
d: Harry O. Hoyt. 6 reels.
Katherine MacDonald, Herbert Rawlinson, Wanda Hawley, Leah Baird, John Miljan, Mike Donlin, Grace Gordon, J. Emmett Beck.
Impecunious Doris decides to marry for money—but her new husband is broke, too.

The Unpainted Woman (Universal, 1919)
d: Tod Browning. 6 reels.
Mary MacLaren, David Butler, Thurston Hall, Laura LaVarnie, Fritzie Ridgway, Willard Louis, Carl Stockdale, Lydia Yeamans Titus, Mickey Moore.
Gudrun, a Swedish-American hired girl, marries a wealthy young man, but his snobbish relatives give her the cold shoulder.

The Unpardonable Sin (Shubert Film Corp./World Film Corp., 1916)
d: Barry O'Neil. 5 reels.
Holbrook Blinn, Helen Fulton, Lila Hayward Chester, William a. Norton, Charles D. Mackay, Walter D. Greene.
Norman, a former alcoholic, falls in love with a woman who has a pathological hatred of drinkers.

The Unpardonable Sin (Harry Garson, 1919)
d: Marshall Neilan. 9 reels.
Blanche Sweet, Edwin Stevens, Mary Alden, Matt Moore, Wesley Barry, Wallace Beery, Bull Montana, Bobby Connelly.
During World War I, an American takes his Belgian-born wife to occupied Belgium to search for her mother and sister. But they run afoul of the German commander there, who wishes to abuse the wife just as he has already abused her

sister.

Unprotected (Lasky Feature Plays/Paramount, 1916)
d: James Young. 5 reels.
Blanche Sweet, Theodore Roberts, Ernest Joy, Tom Forman, Walter Long, Mrs. Lewis McCord, Robert Gray, Jane Wolff.
Barbara, a Southern girl convicted of killing her abusive uncle in a fit of rage, is sentenced to hard labor at a privately-owned factory. There, she finds more abuse, in the person of the cruel factory owner, who tries to rape her.

Unseeing Eyes (Cosmopolitan/Goldwyn, 1923)
d: E.H. Griffith. 9 reels.
Lionel Barrymore, Seena Owen, Louis Wolheim, Gustav von Seyffertitz, Walter Miller, Charles Beyer, Helen Lindroth, Jack Johnston, Louis Deer, Frances Red Eagle, Paul Panzer.
In the Canadian Northwest, a young woman engages an aviator to fly her to her brother's mine. The plane is grounded, however, and the two find themselves having to make their way on foot, through the snow, through Indian territory.

Unseen Forces (Mayflower Photoplay Corp./Associated First National, 1920)
d: Sidney A. Franklin. 6 reels.
Sylvia Breamer, Rosemary Theby, Conrad Nagel, Robert Cain, Sam DeGrasse, Edward Martindel, Harry Garrity, James O. Barrows, Aggie Herring, Andrew Arbuckle, Albert Cody.
Miriam, the daughter of a hotel owner, develops psychic powers and uses them to help the hotel guests — in particular Clyde, with whom she's fallen in love.

Unseen Hands (Encore Pictures, 1924)
d: Jacques Jaccard. 6 reels.
Wallace Beery, Joseph J. Dowling, Fontaine LaRue, Jack Rollins, Cleo Madison, Jim Corey, Jamie Gray.
An unscrupulous adventurer weds a wealthy widow, steals her property, and flees to Indian country, where he marries a squaw. But he dies of heart failure upon seeing the avenging spirit of his first wife's ex-husband.

The Unseen Witness (Empire State Film Corp./Arrow Film Corp., 1920)
d: Tom Collins. 5 reels.
Glenn White, William Fredericks, Jan McAlpin, Joseph Striker, Leo Delaney, David Wall, Robert Taber, Joseph Sullivan, Alexander F. Frank.
Tex, a canny private eye, solves a baffling murder case involving a mystery killer who disappeared through a window sixteen stories above the ground.

The Untameable (Universal, 1923)
d: Herbert Blache. 5 reels.
Gladys Walton, Herbert McGregor, John Sainpolis, Etta Lee.
A lady with a split personality is alternately warm and wonderful, and cruelly vampish.

Untamed (Triangle, 1918)
d: Cliff Smith. 5 reels.
Roy Stewart, Ethel Flemkng, May Giraci, H.N. Dudgeon, H.C. Simmons, Graham Pettie, John Lince, Elvira Weil, Eagle Eye.
Out West, two ranchers enter into a partnership... but they really don't trust each other.

The Untamed (Fox, 1920)
d: Emmett J. Flynn. 5 reels.
Tom Mix, Pauline Starke, George Siegmann, P.M.

McCullough, James O. Barrows, Charles K. French, Pat Chrisman, Sid Jordan, J.A. McGuire, Frank M. Clark, Joe Connelly.
Out West, a young rancher is best known for his fierce temper.

Untamed Justice (Biltmore Productions, 1929)
d: Harry Webb. 7 reels.
Gaston Glass, Virginia Browne Faire, David Torrence, Philo McCullough, Alice Lake, Tom London, Sheldon Lewis.
Dog and pony show out West, as a pair of four-footed avengers capture mail bandits.

The Untamed Lady (Famous Players-Lasky/Paramount, 1926)
d: Frank Tuttle. 7 reels.
Gloria Swanson, Lawrence Gray, Joseph Smiley, Charles Graham.
A high society pepperpot sets her cap for a handsome yachtsman, but must overcome her hair-trigger temper before he will accept her affections.

Untamed Youth (R-C Pictures/FBO of America, 1924)
d: Emile Chautard. 5 reels.
Lloyd Hughes, Ralph Lewis, Emily Fitzroy, Joseph Swickard, Joseph J. Dowling, Tom O'Brien, Mickey McBarr, Derelys Perdue.
A pagan gypsy girl saves the life of a seminarian's brother, and that act of courage inspires her to believe in God.

Until They Get Me (Triangle, 1917)
d: Frank Borzage. 5 reels.
Pauline Starke, Jack Curtis, Joe King, Wilbur Higby, Anna Dodge, Walter Perry.
In the Canadian Northwest, a Mountie falls in love with a young woman, not realizing that her protector is the fugitive he has been trailing for years.

Unto Those Who Sin (Selig Polyscope, 1916)
d: William Robert Daly. 5 reels.
Fritzi Brunette, Al W. Filson, Lillian Hayward, Marion Warner, Edward J. Piel, Earle Foxe, George Larkin, William Sheerer, George Hernandez, Louise Sothern, Marie Prevost.
Melodrama about Nadia, a working class girl who yearns for the good life, and resolves to attain it at all costs.

The Unveiling Hand (World Film Corp., 1919)
d: Frank Crane. 5 reels.
Kitty Gordon, Frederick Warde, Irving Cummings, George MacQuarrie, Reginald Carrington, Margaret Seddon, Warren Cook, Anthony Merlo.
Philip, an archeologist in search of ancient Greek ruins, finds a treasure but also loses one: his wife Margaret, who tires of Philip's obsession with relics and finds love with his business manager.

The Unwelcome Mother (Fox, 1916)
d: James Vincent. 5 reels.
Valkyrien, Violet de Biccari, Walter Law, Frank Evans, John Webb Dillon, Warren Cook, Tom Burrough, Lillian Devere, Jane Lee, Katherine Lee.
Elinor, a young woman who was once tricked into a fake marriage with a man who later deserted her, finds true love with a wealthy widower. But his children resent Elinor, and they let her know it.

The Unwelcome Wife (Ivan Film Productions, Inc., 1915)
w, d: Ivan Abramson. 5 reels.
Malvine Lobel, William McNulty, Vivian Prescott, R.G. Don,

Ned Nye, Ordean Stark.
Blanche, a talented but unbalanced actress, is declared insane and institutionalized. After her husband gets an annulment and remarries, years pass and Blanche leaves the sanitarium... but has she recovered sufficiently to accept the presence of a new wife in her home?

An Unwilling Hero (Goldwyn, 1921)
d: Clarence G. Badger. 5 reels.
Will Rogers, Molly Malone, John Bowers, Darrel Foss, Jack Curtis, George Kunkel, Dick Johnson, Larry Fisher, Leo Willis, Nick Cogley, Edward Kimball.
An honest tramp foils the plans of fellow hoboes to rob a grand house on Christmas Eve.

The Unwritten Code (Thomas A. Edison, Inc./World Film Corp., 1919)
d: Bernard J. Durning. 5 reels.
Shirley Mason, Ormi Hawley, Matt Moore, Frank O'Connor, Thomas Tomamoto.
Weepy melodrama about a Japanese girl in love with a white American. They marry, but the strain of being ostracized by both races leads to their separation.

The Unwritten Law (California Motion Picture Corp., 1916)
d: George E. Middleton. 7 reels.
Beatriz Michelena, William Pike, Andrew Robson, Baby Felice Rix, Matt Snyder, Frank Hollins, Clarence Arper, Irene Outtrim, Nina Herbert, Albert Morrison.
Wilson, a successful attorney, decides to run for political office. He loses the election and takes the news so hard that he becomes an alcoholic, winding up in the gutter. His faithful wife sticks with him, though, and in the end Wilson dries out and is reunited with his wife.

The Unwritten Law (Columbia, 1925)
d: Edward J. LeSaint. 7 reels.
Forrest Stanley, Elaine Hammerstein, William V. Mong, Mary Alden, Charles Clary, John Fox Jr., William Carroll.
An employer tricks his secretary into marrying him by telling her that her true love has been killed. But then the deceitful employer himself dies, and his new wife is charged with his murder.

Up and at 'em (R-C Pictures/FBO of America, 1922)
d: William A. Seiter. 5 reels.
Doris May, Hallam Cooley, J. Herbert Frank, Otis Harlan, Clarissa Selwynne, John Gough, Harry Carter.
Comedy about Barbara, a wealthy girl who masquerades as her father's chauffeur and is unwittingly drawn into a major art theft.

Up and Going (Fox, 1922)
d: Lynn Reynolds. 5 reels.
Tom Mix, Eva Novak, Carol Holloway, William Conklin, Sidney Jordan, Cecil Van Auker, Pat Chrisman, Paul Weigel, Helen Field, Marion Feducha.
In Canada, a mountie learns from a strange elderly woman that his childhood sweetheart is being held prisoner. He runs to her aid, fights off her captors after a long chase, and rescues the girl. As a bonus, he learns that the woman who tipped him off is his own mother, who he thought died years before.

Up in Mabel's Room (Producers Distributing Corp., 1926)
d: E. Mason Hopper. 7 reels.
Marie Prevost, Harrison Ford, Phyllis Haver, Harry Myers, Sylvia Breamer, Paul Nicholson, Carl Gerard, Maud Truax, William Orlamond, Arthur Hoyt.

Romantic comedy about Mabel, a young wife who suspects her husband of having an affair and summarily divorces him. Later, she sees him at a party, being pursued by a notorious vamp, and Mabel, her jealousy aroused, determines to win her husband back for herself.

Up in Mary's Attic (Ascher Productions, Inc./Fine Arts Pictures, Inc., 1920)
d: William H. Watson. 5 reels.
Eva Novak, Harry Gribbon, Baby Virginia Stearns, Al Fichlesfield, Clifford Bowes, Edna Gregory, Minnie Ha Ha, Meta Sterling.
Mary's a young heiress who stands to lose her inheritance if she marries without her guardian's approval—and he isn't about to give it. What makes it all so complicated is that Mary has already married, and has given birth to a child, which she keeps hidden in the attic!

Up Romance Road (William Russell Productions, Inc./Mutual, 1918)
d: Henry King. 5 reels.
William Russell, Charlotte Burton, John Burton, Joseph Belmont, Carl Stockdale, Emma Kluge, Claire DuBrey.
World War I comedy about Gregory and Marta, young lovers who decide on a romantic elopement. Gregory hires some men to "kidnap" Marta and take her to him, but by mistake, she lets herself be abducted by a gang of German spies.

Up the Road with Sallie (Select Pictures Corp., 1918)
d: William D. Taylor. 5 reels.
Constance Talmadge, Norman Kerry, Kate Toncray, Thomas D. Persse, Karl Formes.
Sallie, a lively heiress, decides to take her maiden aunt on a trip to seek "adventure."

The Upheaval (Rolfe Photoplays, Inc./Metro, 1916)
d: Charles Horan. 5 reels.
Lionel Barrymore, Marguerite Skirvin, Franklin Hanna, Edgar L. Davenport, John H. Smiley, Paul Lawrence, James Malaidy, Howard Truesdell, George Stevens, Frank Lyons.
Gordon, a noble but misunderstood politician, finally gets legislation passed that endears him to the public... and, not incidentally, to his own wife, who had her doubts about his integrity.

The Uphill Path (Frank A. Keeney Pictures Corp., 1918)
d: James Kirkwood. 5 reels.
Catherine Calvert, Guy Coombs, Dudley Ayers, Frank Beamish, Charles Craig, Russell Simpson, Dorothy Dunn, Winona Bridges, Gene Lenot.
Clarkson, a small-town minister, falls in love with a young woman with a spotted past.

The Upland Rider (First National, 1928)
d: Albert Rogell. 6 reels.
Ken Maynard, Marian Douglas, Lafe McKee, Sidney Jarvis, Robert Walker, David Kirby, Bobby Dunn, Robert Milash.
Out West, a bronco buster wins an important race in spite of attempts at sabotage by his unscrupulous rival.

The Uplifters (Metro, 1919)
d: Herbert Blaché. 5 reels.
May Allison, Pell Trenton, Alfred Hollingsworth, Kathleen Kerrigan, Caroline Rankin, Howard Gaye, Lois Wood.
When Hortense, a stenographer, hears a lecturer who rails against big management and urges the workers to arise, she decides she is a member of the oppressed masses, and quits her job to join the lecturer's cult of "uplifters." But she soon

becomes even more oppressed as a servant to the cultists and their appetite for free love.

The Upper Crust (American Film Co./Mutual, 1917)
d: Rollin S. Sturgeon.   5 reels.
Gail Kane, John Gough, Frank C. Thompson, Douglas MacLean, Edward Peil, Frank Murphy, Eugenie Forde, Joe Holmes.
Molly, housekeeper to the wealthy Mrs. Todd, is mistaken by the neighbors for her employer. The young servant does nothing to correct the impression, and soon finds herself falling for a local millionaire.

Upside Down (Triangle, 1919)
d: Lawrence C. Windom.   5 reels.
Taylor Holmes, Anna Lehr, Ray Applegate, Ruby Hoffman, Harry Lee.
Juliet, a bored wife, consults a fortune teller and is told that her husband is "crushing her freedom of spirit." Mesmerized by the seer's advice, Juliet returns to her startled husband and demands a divorce.

Upstage (MGM, 1926)
d: Monta Bell.   7 reels.
Norma Shearer, Oscar Shaw, Gwen Lee, Dorothy Phillips, Ward Crane.
A Broadway actress gets a swelled head, then finds that to save the show she must humbly stand in as target for a knife-throwing act.

Upstairs (Goldwyn, 1919)
d: Victor L. Schertzinger.   5 reels.
Mabel Normand, Cullen Landis, Hallam Cooley, Edwin Stevens, Robert Olden, Robert Bolder, Buddy Post, Colin Kenny, Beatrice Burnan, Kate Laster.
Elsie, a dishwasher in a fancy hotel, masquerades as a socialite and is pursued by a detective, a chauffeur, and a playboy... all thinking she's someone else.

Upstairs and Down (Selznick/Select, 1919)
d: Charles Giblyn.   5 reels.
Olive Thomas, Rosemary Theby, Mary Charleson, David Butler, Robert Ellis, Andrew Robson, Bertram Grassby, Kathleen Kirkham, Donald MacDonald, Mildred Reardon.
Alice, an incorrigible coquette, flirts with many men, including polo player Terence O'Keefe. But she'll learn that Terence is her sister's man, not Alice's.

The Upstart (Rolfe Photoplays, Inc./Metro, 1916)
d: Edwin Carewe.   5 reels.
George LeGuere, Marguerite Snow, James Lackaye, Frederick Summer, Frederick Sttenham.
A "marriage crusader" tries to save a failing marriage by encouraging the wife to tell her husband she is running off with their chauffeur. The plan works a bit too well, as it plants ideas in the minds of the wife and chauffeur, who *do* try to run away together.

Upstream (Fox, 1927)
d: John Ford.   6 reels.
Nancy Nash, Earle Foxe, Grant Withers, Lydia Yeamans Titus, Raymond Hitchcock, Emile Chautard, Ted McNamara, Sammy Cohen, Judy King, Lillian Worth, Jane Winton.
In London, a wealthy young actor is chosen for a role in *Hamlet* and develops severe egotism.

The Usurper (Vitagraph, 1919)
d: James Young.   5 reels.

Earle Williams, Louise Lovely, Bob Russell, Frank Leigh, Billy Elmer, Jay Morley, Audrey Chapman, Bessie Eyton, Lillian Langdon, Clyde McAtee, Helen Carlisle.
Out West, a formerly misogynistic rancher falls in love with a visiting English girl.

The Vagabond Cub (FBO Productions/RKO, 1929)
d: Louis King.   6 reels.
Buzz Barton, Frank Rice, Sam Nelson, Al Ferguson, Bill Patton, Milburn Morante, Ione Holmes.
Robbins, an old prospector, and Red, his young protégé, confront murder charges, prove them false, and capture the real killer, to boot.

Vagabond Luck (Fox, 1919)
d: Scott Dunlap.   5 reels.
Albert Ray, Elinor Fair, Jack Rollens, John Cossar, William Ryno, George Millum, Al Fremont, Lloyd Bacon, Johnny Ries.
Humorous happenings at the race track. Joy, almost penniless and with no property except for an old horse named "Vagabond," is persuaded to enter the nag in a rich sweepstakes event. The book on Vagabond is that on normal turf, she runs like molasses in January... but on a wet track, the old gal can fly! So Joy and her boyfriend Jimmy—the horse's jockey—pray for rain and, during a torrent, Vagabond is ridden to victory.

The Vagabond Prince (New York Motion Picture Corp./Triangle, 1916)
d: Charles Giblyn.   5 reels.
H.B. Warner, Dorothy Dalton, Roy Laidlaw, Katherine Kirkwood, Charles K. French, J.W. McLaughlin, J. Frank Burke, Agnes Herring.
In San Francisco, a sailor decides to settle down and become an artist. He falls for a Barbary Coast singer after rescuing her from a would-be rapist, and the two contemplate marriage. But what she doesn't know is that this sailor-artist-rescuer is the sole heir to a European throne.

The Vagabond Trail (Fox, 1924)
d: William A. Wellman.   5 reels.
Charles Jones, Marian Nixon, Charles Coleman, L.C. Shumway, Virginia Warwick, Harry Lonsdale, Frank Nelson, George Reed, George Romain.
Out West, a man seeking his long-lost brother teams up with a miner and his daughter.

Valencia (MGM, 1926)
d: Dimitri Buchowetzki.   6 reels.
Mae Murray, Lloyd Hughes, Roy D'Arcy, May Barwyn, Michael Vavitch, Michael Visaroff.
A sailor and the governor are rivals for the hand of a beautiful Spanish dancer.

The Valentine Girl (Famous Players/Paramount, 1917)
d: J. Searle Dawley.   5 reels.
Marguerite Clark, Frank Losee, Richard Barthelemess, Kathryn Adams, Maggie Holloway Fisher, Adolphe Menjou, Edith Campbell Walker.
When her father is convicted for a robbery he did not commit, his tearful daughter Marian runs away and seeks refuge in a church. She is taken in by the clergyman's family and, because she was found on Valentine's Day, she is given the nickname "the Valentine Girl."

The Valiant (Fox, 1929)
d: William K. Howard.   6 reels.
Paul Muni, John Mack Brown, Edith Yorke, Ricahrd Carlyle,

Marguerite Churchill, DeWitt Jennings, Clifford Dempsey, Henry Kolker, Don Terry, George Pearce.

Heavy melodrama about Dyke, a man who kills and then turns himself over to the law, but refuses to give his name. Convicted and sentenced to capital punishment, he goes to his death without letting his mother and sister know he has disgraced the family.

The Valiants of Virginia (Selig Polyscope, 1916)
d: T.N. Heffron. 5 reels.
Kathlyn Williams, Arthur Shirley, Edward J. Piel, Virginia Kraft, Guy Oliver, Fred Carufel, Billy Jacobs, Edith Johnson, Al W. Filson, James Bradbury, Harry Lonsdale, Frank Clark.
In the old South, John Valiant fights a duel with pistols to defend a lady's honor. But although his opponent ends up dead, John insists it wasn't he who pulled the trigger.

The Valley of Decision (American Film/Mutual, 1916)
d: Rea Berger. 5 reels.
Richard Bennett, Adrienne Morrison, Blanche Hanson, George Periolat, Constance Bennett, Joan Bennett, Blanche Bennett, Barbara Bennett.
Arnold, a crusader against child labor, wins election as his state's governor. But the glow of victory hides a dark secret: He wants his own pregnant wife to get an abortion.

The Valley of Doubt (Selznick/Select, 1920)
d: Burton George. 6 reels.
Arline Pretty, Thurston Hall, Anna Lehr, William Davidson, Robert Agnew, John Ardizoni, Jack Costello, T.J. Murray.
In the great northwest, a girl from New York falls for a French Canadian lumberman.

The Valley of Hell (MGM, 1926)
d: Clifford Smith. 5 reels.
Francis McDonald, Edna Murphy, William Steele, Anita Garvin, Joe Bennett.
Out West, a collegian rescues a girl from bandits and locates his long-lost brother.

The Valley of Lost Hope (Lubin, 1915)
d: Romaine Fielding. 5 reels.
Romaine Fielding, Peter Lang, B.K. Roberts, Mildred Gregory, Robin Williamson, Nannie Pearson.
Out West, gold profiteers sell fraudulent claims to unsuspecting miners.

The Valley of Lost Souls (Iroquois Productions/Independent Pictures, 1923)
d: Caryl S. Fleming. 5 reels.
Muriel Kingston, Victor Sutherland, Anne Hamilton, Edward Roseman, Luis Alberni, Stanley Walpole.
In the Canadian Northwest, a mountie tracks a halfbreed killer.

The Valley of Silent Men (Cosmopolitan/Paramount, 1922)
d: Frank Borzage. 7 reels.
Alma Rubens, Lew Cody, Joseph King, Mario Majeroni, George Nash, J.W. Johnston.
In the Canadian Northwest, a man is arrested for murder but is shielded by the woman he loves, in the Valley of Silent Men. Upon investigation, the suspect is cleared of all wrongdoing.

The Valley of the Giants (Famous Players-Lasky/Paramount, 1919)
d: James Cruze. 5 reels.
Wallace Reid, Grace Darmond, William Brunton, Charles

Ogle, Ralph Lewis, Alice Taafe, Kay Laurel, Hart Hoxie, Noah Beery, Guy Oliver, W.H. Brown, Richard Cummings, Virginia Foltz, Ogden Crane.
Bryce, fresh from college, returns home to find that his family is in danger of losing their sprawling land to foreclosure.

The Valley of the Giants (First National, 1927)
d: Charles J. Brabin. 7 reels.
Doris Kenyon, Arthur Stone, Milton Sills, George Fawcett, Paul Hurst, Charles Sellon, Yola D'Avril, Phil Brady.
Remake of the 1919 Famous Players-Lasky film *The Valley of the Giants*, both versions based on the novel of the same name by Peter B. Kyne.

The Valley of the Moon (Bosworth, Inc./W.W. Hodkinson, 1914)
d: Hobart Bosworth. 6 reels.
Myrtle Steadman, Jack Conway, Ernest Garcia, Rhea Haines, Joseph Ray, Hobart Bosworth.
In Sonoma, California, a teamster and his bride settle in a farm they call "The Valley of the Moon."
Based on the novel of the same name by Jack London.

The Valley of Tomorrow (American Film Co./Pathé, 1920)
d: Emmett J. Flynn. 6 reels.
William Russell, Mary Thurman, Frank Brownlee, Pauline Curley, Harvey Clark, Fred M. Malatesta, Frank Clark, Lewis King, Jeffrey Sloan.
Vengeance drives Dabney Morgan to track down the man responsible for his sister's suicide. He'll stick to his grim purpose, even after the man he is seeking saves Morgan from certain death in quicksand.

The Vamp (T.H. Ince/Famous Players-Lasky/Paramount, 1918)
d: Jerome Storm. 5 reels.
Enid Bennett, Charles K. French, Robert McKim, Melbourne MacDowell, Douglas MacLean, John P. Lockney.
Nancy, a wardrobe girl, dons seductive garb and "vamps" her boyfriend into a proposal of marriage.

Vamping Venus (Warner Bros., 1928)
d: Eddie Cline. 7 reels.
Charlie Murray, Louise Fazenda, Russ Powell, Fred O'Beck, Gustav von Seyffertitz, Gus Partos, Thelma Todd.
Cassidy, an Irish-American, dreams he is the King of Ireland in ancient days, annexing Greece along with its lovely goddess Venus.

The Vampire (Popular Plays and Players, Inc./Metro, 1915)
d: Alice Blaché. 5 reels.
Olga Petrova, Vernon Steel, William A. Morse, Wallace Scott, Lawrence Grattan, Albert Howson, Mary Martin.
Jeanne, an American girl, travels to Paris and begins a series of romantic escapades that earns her the nickname of "The Vampire."

The Vanishing American (Famous Players-Lasky/Paramount, 1925)
d: George B. Seitz. 10 reels..
Richard Dix, Lois Wilson, Noah Beery, Malcolm McGregor, Nocki, Shannon Day, Charles Crockett, Bert Woodruff, Guy Oliver, Charles Stevens, Bernard Siegel, Bruce Gordon.
In the Old West, a righteous Navajo secretly loves a white schoolteacher.

The Vanishing Pioneer (Paramount, 1928)
d: John Waters. 6 reels.

Jack Holt, Sally Blane, Fred Kohler, Roscoe Karnes, Tim Holt, William Powell, Guy Oliver, Marcia Manon.

Out West, a pioneer community faces the threat of having their water cut off by corrupt politicians.

Vanity (Popular Plays and Players/Metro, 1916)
d: John B. O'Brien. 5 reels.
Emmy Wehlen, Tom O'Keefe, Edward Martindell, Paul Gordon, W.W. Black, J.W. Hartman, Esther Evans, Norman Kaiser, Tom Cameron, Dixie Marshall, Emile Agoust, Kathleen Townsend.
Phyllis, a fashion model, is used by a vengeful detective to coax a murder confession out of his chief suspect. She tries, but instead of compromising the suspect, she falls in love with him.

Vanity (DeMille Pictures/Producers Distributing Corp., 1927)
d: Donald Crisp. 6 reels.
Leatrice Joy, Charles Ray, Alan Hale, Mayme Kelso, Noble Johnson, Helen Lee Worthing, Louis Payne.
The night before her wedding, a bored socialite accepts an invitation to join a venal yachtsman aboard his ship... and comes to wish she hadn't.

Vanity Fair (Thomas A. Edison, Inc., 1915)
d: Eugene Nowland. 7 reels.
Minnie Maddern Fiske, Helen Fulton, Bigelow Cooper, George A. Wright, Leonie Flugrath, Yale Benner, Richard Tucker, Robert Brower, Frank McGlynn, Helen Strickland.
In early 19th century England, a poor but shrewd young woman maneuvers her way to prosperity through marriage.

Vanity Fair (Goldwyn, 1923)
d: Hugo Ballin. 8 reels.
Harrison Ford, Mabel Ballin, Hobart Bosworth, George Walsh, Earle Foxe, Eleanor Boardman, Willard Louis, Laura LaVarnie, William Humphreys, Robert Mack, Tempe Pigott, James Marcus, Dorcas Matthews, Eugene Acker, Eddie Jones, Rose Gore, Mrs. A. Newton, Laura Pollard, Otto Matiesen.
Social-climbing flirt Becky Sharp succeeds in marrying for money, but continues to "keep her options open."

The Vanity Pool (Universal, 1918)
d: Ida May Park. 6 reels.
Mary MacLaren, Thomas Holding, Franklyn Farnum, Anna Q. Nilsson, Marin Sais, Virginia Chester, Winter Hall, Frank Brownlee, Willis Marks, Mary Talbot.
Harper, married and a candidate for political office, campaigns in the city's tenements and falls for a winsome slum girl.

Vanity's Price (Gothic Pictures/FBO of America, 1924)
d: R. William Neill. 6 reels.
Anna Q. Nilsson, Stuart Holmes, Wyndham Standing, Arthur Rankin, Lucille Rickson, Robert Bolder, Cissy Fitzgerald, Dot Farley, Charles Newton.
Vanna, a successful actress, works hard to form her own theater company.

The Varmint (Oliver Morosco Photoplay Co./Paramount, 1917)
d: William D. Taylor. 5 reels.
Jack Pickford, Louise Huff, Theodore Roberts, Henry Malvern, Ben Suslow, Milton Schumann, Maurice Kessell, Maxfield Stanley, Robert Gordon, Ed Sedgwick, Tom Bates.
A cocky young fellow is sent to school at a private academy, where he engages in schoolboy pranks and falls in love with

his Latin teacher's daughter.

Varsity (Paramount, 1928)
d: Frank Tuttle. 8 reels.
Charles "Buddy" Rogers, Mary Brian, Chester Conklin, Phillips R. Holmes, Robert Ellis, John Westwood.
Pop, a beloved janitor at Princeton University, arranges for Jimmy, an orphan, to be enrolled as an incoming freshman. What Jimmy doesn't know is that Pop is his real father, trying to make up for his neglect of years ago that caused his son to be placed in an orphanage.

The Varsity Girl — see: The Fair Co-Ed

The Veiled Adventure (Select, 1919)
d: Walter Edwards. 5 reels.
Harrison Ford, Constance Talmadge, Stanhope Wheatcroft, Vera Doria, Rosita Marstini, T.D. Crittenden, Eddie Sutherland, Margaret Loomis, Vera Sisson.
Geraldine, a society gadfly, finds a woman's veil in her fiancé's overcoat pocket and suspects the worst.

The Veiled Marriage (Hallmark Pictures Corp., 1920)
d: Keanan Buel. 5 reels.
Anna Lehr, Ralph Kellard, Dorothy Walters, John Charles, Frank J. Murdock, William Carr.
Temporarily blinded in an explosion, a young woman is tricked into marriage with a man she does not know. When she regains her sight, she gazes upon John Browning and falls in love with him, not realizing that they are already husband and wife.

The Velvet Hand (Universal, 1918)
d: Douglas Gerrard. 5 reels.
Eugene Corey, Carmen Phillips, William Conklin, Fritzi Brunette, Fred Turner, Wedgewood Nowell, Nicholas Dunaew.
In Milan, Italy, a famous dancer falls in love with the man she has sworn to destroy.

The Velvet Paw (Paragon Films, Inc./World Film Corp., 1916)
d: Maurice Tourneur. 5 reels.
House Peters, Gail Kane, Ned Burton, Frank Goldsmith, Charles D. Mackay, Charles Edwards, Alex Shannon.
In the shadows of the U.S. Congress, a female lobbyist uses her romantic charms to induce legislators' cooperation.

Vengeance (World Film Corp., 1918)
d: Travers Vale. 6 reels.
Montagu Love, Barbara Castleton, George MacQuarrie, Madge Evans, Jack Drumier, Louise Vale, Lila Chester, Henry Warwick, Irene Blackwell, S.V. Phillips, Charley Jackson.
In India, the son of an Englishman and a Hindu woman swears vengeance on the man who, years earlier, had disgraced his father.

Vengeance is Mine (Centaur Film Co./Mutual, 1916)
d: Robert B. Broadwell. 5 reels.
Crane Wilbur, Carl Von Schiller, Brooklyn Keller, William Jackson, H.C. Demore, Gypsy Abbott, A.B. Ellis, C.A. Foster.
Marion, wife of the governor, is being blackmailed by the man who seduced her, years before.

Vengeance is Mine (Astra Film Corp./Pathé, 1917)
d: Frank Crane. 5 reels.
Irene Castle, Frank Sheridan, Helene Chadwick, Elliott Dexter, Edward Hoyt, Reginald Mason, Ethel Grey Terry, Frank Monroe, Julia Stewart, Fred Teden.

Paula, whose father committed suicide after being ruined financially, swears to wreak vengeance on the man who brokered his downfall. But she is horrified when she learns that the target of her vengeance is the father of the man she loves.

The Vengeance of Durand (Vitagraph, 1919)
d: Tom Terriss. 7 reels.
Alice Joyce, G.V. Seyffertitz, Percy Marmont, William Bechtel, Eugene Strong, Herbert Pattee, Mark Smith.
Durand, a French nobleman, triggers his innocent wife's suicide by accusing her of having an affair with an old friend, Tom. Years later, still consumed with rage and a craving for vengeance against his old friend, Durand persuades his daughter to entice him... with plans to pull out the rug from under their romance once Tom is hooked.
Miss Joyce plays both the suicidal noblewoman and her daughter.

Vengeance of the Deep (A.B. Barringer/American Releasing Corp., 1923)
d: A.B. Barringer. 5 reels.
Ralph Lewis, Virginia Brown Faire, Van Mattimore, Harmon MacGregor, William Anderson, "Smoke" Turner, Maida Vale.
In the South Seas, a diver and a beachcomber find a sunken treasure chest.

The Vengeance of the West —see: Pay Me (1917)

Venus in the East (Famous Players-Lasky/Paramount, 1919)
d: Donald Crisp. 5 reels.
Bryant Washburn, Margery Wilson, Anna Q. Nilsson, Guy Oliver, Clarence Burton, Julia Faye, Helen Dunbar, Arthur Carewe, Henry Barrows, Clarence Geldart, Charles Gerard.
McNair, a wealthy westerner, is so attracted by the newspaper photo of a society woman, he travels to New York to meet his "Venus in the east."

The Venus Model (Goldwyn, 1918)
d: Clarence G. Badger. 5 reels.
Rod LaRocque, Mabel Normand, Alec B. Francis, Edward Elkas, Alfred Hickman, Edward Boulden, Una Trevelyn, Nadia Gary, Albert Hackett.
Braddock, a bathing suit manufacturer, is faced with bankruptcy until a young woman in his employ comes up with a modern style of swimwear.

Venus of the South Seas (Lee-Bradford/Davis Distribution, 1924)
d: James R. Sullivan. 5 reels.
Annette Kellerman, Roland Purdle, Normand French, Robert Ramsey.
A South Seas woman falls in love with a wealthy traveler.

Venus of Venice (Constance Talmadge Productions/First National, 1927)
d: Marshall Neilan. 7 reels.
Constance Talmadge, Antonio Moreno, Julanne Johnston, Edward Martindel, Michael Vavitch, Arthur Thalasso, André Lanoy, Carmelita Geraghty, Mario Carillo, Tom Ricketts, Hedda Hopper.
In Venice, a clever thief named Carlotta finds herself falling for an American artist on vacation.

The Verdict (Phil Goldstone Productions/Truart Film Corp., 1925)
d: Fred Windemere. 7 reels.

Lou Tellegen, Louise Lorraine, William Collier Jr., Gertrude Astor, Joseph Swickard, Paul Weigel, Taylor Holmes, stanton Heck, Elliott Dexter, George Fawcett, Gaston Glass.
Murder mystery about a fashion lothario who is shot to death just as he's starting to put the moves on Carol, wife of the firm's accountant.

The Vermilion Pencil (R-C Pictures, 1922)
d: Norman Dawn. 5 reels.
Sessue Hayakawa, Ann May, Misao Seki, Bessie Love, Sidney Franklin, Thomas Jefferson, Tote DuCrow, Omar Whitehead.
In China, an American-educated engineer falls in love with the daughter of a poor basket weaver. After they are forcibly separated, the engineer finds her and together they plan their escape, aided by the fortuitous eruption of "the Sleeping Dragon," an active volcano.

Very Confidential (Fox, 1927)
d: James Tinling. 6 reels.
Madge Bellamy, Patrick Cunning, Mary Duncan, Joseph Cawthorn, Marjorie Beebe, Isabelle Keith, Carl von Haartmann.
Romantic comedy about a girl who impersonates a famous female athlete to attract the attention of a certain chap, then has to "prove" herself by enduring various grueling athletic sports.

A Very Good Young Man (Famous Players-Lasky/Paramount, 1919)
d: Donald Crisp. 5 reels.
Bryant Washburn, Helene Chadwick, Julia Faye, Sylvia Ashton, Jane Wolfe, Helen Jerome Eddy, Wade Boteler, Anna Q. Nilsson, Noah Beery, Edward Burns, Mayme Kelso.
Hilarious comedy about LeRoy, a young man whose sweetheart will not marry him because he has not "lived" — i.e., he is morally unblemished. To change the lady's mind, LeRoy tries hard to tarnish his reputation: He flirts with a notorious woman, tries to get himself arrested for jewel theft, even tips off the police to come and raid the gambling house he is visiting. But the brazen woman rejects him; the "stolen" jewels turn out not to be stolen after all; and while playing cards in the gambling den, LeRoy breaks the bank and there is nothing left for the police to raid. In the end, he must confront his sweetheart with the sad news that he has no talent for turpitude. She accepts him anyway.

The Very Idea (Taylor Holmes Productions, Inc./Metro, 1920)
d: Lawrence C. Windom. 6 reels.
Taylor Holmes, Virginia Valli, Betty Ross, Jack Levering, Edward Martindale, Jean Robb, Edward Lester, Fay Marbe, George Cooper.
A married couple want desperately to have a baby, and so they contract with their chauffeur and maid to have one for them. The maid does get pregnant; and, now relieved of her anxiety, the lady of the house does too.

Very Truly Yours (Fox, 1922)
d: Harry Beaumont. 5 reels.
Shirley Mason, Allan Forrest, Charles Clary, Otto Hoffman, Harold Miller, Helen Raymond, Hardee Kirkland.
A hotel steno sets her cap for a millionaire, bags her prey, and marries him. But oops! He's not the millionaire—his uncle is.

Via Wireless (Pathé, 1915)
d: George Fitzmaurice. 5 reels.

MARY PICKFORD (1920). The movies' first international superstar was this tiny dynamo from Toronto, known as "Little Mary" to her millions of adoring fans. Miss Pickford began in theater, but once in front of a movie camera she became a master at holding audience attention and using her nimble body to convey specific meaning. She often played young girls, as in 1920's *Pollyanna*, when the 28-year-old Mary played a girl of 14.

* * * * *

Bruce McRae, Gail Kane, Harry Weaver, Brandon Hurst, Paul McAlister.

During a buildup of American war preparedness, a defense contractor turns traitor.

The Vicar of Wakefield (Thanhouser/Pathé, 1917)
d: Ernest Warde. 5 reels.
Frederick Warde, Carey Hastings, Boyd Marshall, Kathryn Adams, Gladys Leslie, William Parke Jr., Tula Bell, Barbara Howard, Thomas A. Curran, Robert Vaughn.
In a modern variant on the Book of Job, a vicar endures the loss of his son, the elopement of his daughter, and prison time for nonpayment of debts.

The Vice of Fools (Vitagraph, 1920)
d: Edward Griffith. 5 reels.
Alice Joyce, Ellen Cassity, Robert Gordon, Raymond Bloomer, William Tooker, Elizabeth Garrison, Agnes Everett.
Marion loves Cameron, but her mother disapproves. On the rebound, Cameron marries a shameless flirt who will bring him only heartbreak.

The Victim (Fox, 1916)
d: Will S. Davis. 5 reels.
Valeska Suratt, Herbert Heyes, Claire Whitney, John Charles, Joseph Cranby, Oscar Nye, Charles Edwards.
Ruth, an innocent woman, is convicted of burglary. Upon her release, she finds love with her doctor, and they marry. But her criminal record will return to haunt her.

The Victim (Catholic Art Association, 1920)
d: Joseph Levering. 6 reels.
Robert T. Haines, Joyce Fair, Inez Marcel, Harry Benham, Armand Cortez.
Father Cosgrove, a Catholic priest, is unjustly convicted of murder and sentenced to die. Only minutes before the priest is to be hanged, a fugitive from justice is struck by lightning and admits he is the real killer. He had confessed his crime to Father Cosgrove, knowing the priest could not repeat any part of his confession.

The Victoria Cross (Lasky Feature Plays/Paramount, 1916)
d: E.J. LeSaint. 5 reels.
Lou Tellegen, Cleo Ridgely, Sessue Hayakawa, Ernest Joy, Mabel Van Buren, Frank Lanning, Harold Skinner.
In British-occupied India, an officer who's in love with his commandant's daughter is awarded the Victoria Cross for bravery in battle.

The Victor (Universal, 1923)
d: Edward Laemmle. 5 reels.
Herbert Rawlinson, Esther Ralston, Otis Harlan, Dorothy Manners, Frank Currier, Eddie Gribbon, Tom McGuire.
An English aristocrat discovers he has a talent for boxing. With encouragement from the poor American girl he loves, he enters the prize ring and vies for the middleweight championship.

Victorine (Majestic/Mutual, 1915)
d: Paul Powell. 5 reels.
Ralph Lewis, Dorothy Gish, Walter Long, Mae Gaston, William Hinckley.
A carnival girl thinks she loves the strong man who uses her as a target for his knife-throwing act.

Victory (Famous Players-Lasky/Paramount, 1919)
d: Maurice Tourneur. 5 reels.
Jack Holt, Seena Owen, Lon Chaney, Wallace Beery, Ben Deely, Laura Winston, Bull Montana, George Nicholls.

Axel, a confirmed loner, lives a life of solitude on a South Sea island. But that doesn't stop him from falling head over heels in love with Alma, a young woman from a neighboring island.

The Victory of Conscience (Lasky Feature Plays/Paramount, 1916)
d: Frank Reicher. 5 reels.
Cleo Ridgely, Lou Tellegen, Elliott Dexter, Thomas Delmar, Laura Woods Cushing, John McKennon.
In France during World War I, a courageous priest inspires a cabaret dancer to become a nun.

The Victory of Virtue (United Photo Plays Co., 1915)
d: Harry McRae Webster. 5 reels.
Gerda Holmes, Wilmuth Merkyl, Bert Howard, J.H. Gilmour, Marie Yould, Rapley Holmes, Arthur Stengard, Cecil Owen.
In a dream, a wealthy young woman imagines herself on a fantasy journey through the Seven Deadly Sins.

The Vigilantes (Bear State Film Co., 1918)
d: Henry Kabierske. 7 reels.
Grant Churchill, Gertrude Kabierske, Joe Ray, William E. Parsons, Joe Ray, William E. Parsons, Kathie Fisher, William Ehfe, Sheldon Johnson, Gale Brooks, Vera Lewis, Robert Cecil.
In 1849 California, New Easterners go for the gold.

The Viking (MGM, 1928)
d: Roy William Neill. 9 reels. (Music, sound effects, Technicolor.)
Donald Crisp, Pauline Starke, LeRoy Mason, Anders Randolf, Richard Alexander, Harry Woods, Albert MacQuarrie, Roy Stewart, Torben Meyer, Claire McDowell, Julia Swayne Gordon.
Pseudo-historical drama about Leif Ericsson and his band of vikings sailing from Norway to the New World, with several battle scenes, an attempted mutiny, and Ericsson's eventual conversion to Christianity.

The Village Blacksmith (Fox, 1922)
d: Jack Ford. 8 reels.
William Walling, Virginia True Boardman, Virginia Valli, Ida McKenzie, David Butler, Gordon Griffith, George Hackathorne, Pat Moore, Tully Marshall, Bessie Love, Lon Poff, Mark Fenton, Eddie Gribbon, Caroline Rankin.
Drama inspired by the Henry Wadsworth Longfellow poem of the same title.

The Village Sleuth (Thomas H. Ince/Paramount, 1920)
d: Jerome Storm. 5 reels.
Charles Ray, Winifred Westover, Dick Rush, Donald MacDonald, George F. Hernandez, Betty Schade, Lew Morrison.
William, a boy straight from the farm, travels to the big city to realize his dream of becoming a famous detective.

The Virgin (Phil Goldstone Productions/Truart Film Corp., 1924)
d: Alvin J. Neitz. 6 reels.
Kenneth Harlan, Dorothy Revier, Sam DeGrasse, Frank Lackteen, Rosa Rosanova, Alice Lake, Walter Hiers, Nell Clarke Keller, Lois Scott, J.P. Lockney.
In Spain, an American falls for a lovely girl with a kind and loving heart.

Virgin Lips (Columbia, 1928)
d: Elmer Clifton. 6 reels.

John Boles, Richard Alexander, Olive Borden, Arline Pretty, Marshall Ruth, Alexander Gill, Erne Veo, Harry Semels, William Tooker.

Blake, an American aviator, crash-lands his plane in a Central American jungle and makes his way to civilization, there finding Norma, an American girl who dances in the local cafe.

The Virgin of Stamboul   (Universal, 1920)
w, d: Tod Browning.   7 reels.
Priscilla Dean, Wallace Beery, Wheeler Oakman, Eugene Forde, E.A. Warren, Edward Burns, Nigel de Brulier, Ethel Ritchie.
A wealthy sheik tries to add a comely virgin to his already thriving harem.

A Virgin Paradise   (Fox, 1921)
d: J. Searle Dawley.   8 reels.
Pearl White, Robert Elliott, J. Thornton Baston, Alan Edwards, Henrietta Floyd, Grace Beaumont, Mary Beth Barnelle, Lynn Pratt, Lewis Seeley, Charles Sutton, Hal Clarendon.
A girl who grew up in the South Seas comes to New York to claim her inheritance.

A Virginia Courtship   (Realart Pictures/Paramount, 1921)
d: Frank O'Connor.   5 reels.
May McAvoy, Alec B. Francis, Jane Keckley, L.M. Wells, Casson Ferguson, Kathlyn Williams, Richard Tucker, Guy Oliver, Verne Winter.
A southern colonel is reunited with his former flame, now a widow, by the colonel's adopted daughter.

The Virginian   (Lasky Feature Plays/Paramount, 1914)
d: Cecil B. DeMille.   5 reels.
Dustin Farnum, J.W. Johnston, Winifred Kingston, Sydney Deane, Billy Elmer, H.B. Carpenter, James Griswold, Tex Driscoll.
Out West, a cowboy known only as The Virginian displays the virtues of hard work, sobriety, and loyalty.

The Virginian   (B.P. Schulberg Productions/Preferred Pictures, 1923)
d: Tom Forman.   8 reels.
Kenneth Harlan, Florence Vidor, Russell Simpson, Pat O'Malley, Raymond Hatton, Milton Ross, Sam Allen, Bert Hadley, Fred Gambold.
A cowboy from Virginia falls in love with a New England schoolmarm

A Virgin's Sacrifice   (Vitagraph, 1922)
d: Webster Campbell.   5 reels.
Corinne Griffith, Curtis Cooksey, David Torrence, Louise Cussing, Nick Thompson, Miss Eagle, George MacQuarrie, Charles Henderson.
In the North Woods, a young woman accepts the generosity of a kind stranger who promises to protect her from unspoken dangers. She fears that the unscrupulous father of her child will blackmail her, or worse, unless she marries him.

Virtue's Revolt   (William Steiner Productions, 1924)
d: James Chapin.   6 reels.
Edith Thornton, Crauford Kent, Betty Morrisey, Charles Cruz, Florence Lee, Edward Phillips, Melbourne MacDowell, Niles Welch.
In New York, a young actress is faced with a choice: remain pure, or compromise her virtue to get a job in show business.

Virtuous Liars   (Whitman Bennett Productions/Vitagraph, 1924)
d: Whitman Bennett.   6 reels.
David Powell, Maurice Costello, Edith Allen, Ralph Kellard, Naomi Childers, Burr McIntosh, Dagmar Godowsky.
Returning to the United States after years in Cuba, a woman's ex-husband finds that she has become wealthy, and threatens her with blackmail.

Virtuous Men   (S-L Pictures/Ralph Ince Film Attractions, 1919)
d: Ralph Ince.   7 reels.
E.K. Lincoln, Grace Darling, Clara Joel, Robert W. Cummings, John P. Wade, William B. Mack, Irving Brooks, Edward Talbot, Danny Hates, Logan Paul, Hugh Jeffrey.
Stokes, a wealthy New Yorker, goes north and becomes a lumberjack. While in the lumber camp, he foils a Bolshevik plot masquerading as a workers' protest, and also falls in love with the camp manager's daughter.

The Virtuous Model   (Albert Capellani Productions, Inc./Pathé, 1919)
d: Albert Capellani.   6 reels.
Dolores Cassinelli, Helen Lowell, May Hopkins, Vincent Serrano, Franklyn Farnum, Paul Doucet, Marie Chambers.
Denise, a poor but virtuous girl from the slums, takes a job as an artist's model.

Virtuous Sinners   (Pioneer Film Corp., 1919)
d: Emmett J. Flynn.   5 reels.
Norman Kerry, Wanda Hawley, Harry Holden, David Kirby, Bert Woodruff, Eunice Woodruff.
Complex drama about a poor girl from New York's Lower East Side who is taken to a mission to recuperate from an illness, and stays to help run the place; and a society thief who robs from the rich to help out the needy souls at the mission.

The Virtuous Thief   (Thomas H. Ince/Famous Players-Lasky, 1919)
d: Fred Niblo.   5 reels.
Enid Bennett, Willis Marks, William Conklin, Dorcas Matthews, Lucille Young, Andrew Robson, Lloyd Hughes.
In Brooklyn, an Alabama-born girl gets work as a stenographer... but her employer has a different kind of "dictation" in mind.

A Virtuous Vamp   (Constance Talmadge Film Co./First National, 1919)
d: David Kirkland.   5 reels.
Constance Talmadge, Harda Daube, Jack Kane, Conway Tearle, Jeanette Horton, Margaret Linden, Wallace McCutcheon, Ned Sparks, William Eville, William Gaunt.
Society comedy about Gwendolyn, a natural-born "vamp" who uses her feminine wiles to get anything she wants from men. Fortunately, she only uses her powers for good.

Virtuous Wives   (Anita Stewart Productions/First National, 1918)
d: George Loane Tucker.   6 reels.
Anita Stewart, Conway Tearle, Hedda Hopper, Edwin Arden, Wiliam Boyd, Virginia Norden, Katharine Lewis, Harold Gwynn, Gwen Williams, Lucille Clayton, Thomas Carr.
While her husband is away on business, Amy flirts with other men.

The Vital Question   (Vitagraph, 1916)
d: S. Rankin Drew.   5 reels.

Virginia Pearson, Charles Kent, George Cooper, Anders Randolf, Leo Delaney, George Lawrence, Denton Vane.
Scarsdale, a candidate for district attorney, is pressured to halt an investigation into financial mischief.

Vive La France!   (Thomas H. Ince/Paramount, 1918)
d: R. William Neill.   5 reels.
Dorothy Dalton, Edmund Lowe, Frederick Starr, Thomas Guise, Bert Woodruff.
During World War I, a French actress returns to her native town to assist in Red Cross work.

Viviette   (Famous Players-Lasky/Paramount, 1918)
d: Walter Edwards.   5 reels.
Harrison Ford, Eugene Pallette, Vivian Martin, Clara Whipple, Kate Toncray, Don Blakemore, Kate Toncray, Clara Whipple.
Viviette, adopted daughter of a wealthy Englishwoman, flirts with both her adoptive mother's sons.

The Vixen   (Fox, 1916)
d: J. Gordon Edwards.   6 reels.
Theda Bara, Mary Martin, A.H. Van Buren, Herbert Heyes, George Clarke, Carl Gerard, George Odell, Jane Lee, Katherine Lee.
In yet another *femme fatale* role for Miss Bara, she plays a vixen who deliberately steals the heart of her sister's fiancé.

The Voice From the Minaret   (Norma Talmadge Productions/Associated First National, 1923)
d: Frank Lloyd.   7 reels.
Norma Talmadge, Eugene O'Brien, Edwin Stevens, Winter Hall, Carl Gerard, Claire DuBrey, Lillian Lawrence, Albert Prisco.
Adrienne, wife of the colonial governor in Bombay, falls in love with a divinity student and is tempted to go away with him.   But a voice from the minaret urges the faithful to keep their vows, and Adrienne takes this as a sign that she should forgo this illicit pleasure.

A Voice in the Dark   (Goldwyn, 1921)
d: Frank Lloyd.   5 reels.
Ramsey Wallace, Irene Rich, Alec Francis, Alan Hale, Ora Carew, William Scott, Richard Tucker, Alice Hollister, Gertrude Norman, James Neill.
When a doctor is shot and killed, the evidence points to his fiancée's sister as the culprit.   Her innocence is proved at trial, however, on the basis of testimony from two witnesses, one of them deaf and the other blind.

The Voice in the Fog   (Lasky Feature Plays/Paramount, 1915)
d: J.P. McGowan.   5 reels.
Donald Brian, Adda Gleason, Frank A. Connor, George Gebhardt, Florence Smythe, Ernest Joy.
Kitty, an American heiress, is robbed of her pendant on a foggy London street.   She can't identify the thief by sight, but remembers the sound of his voice.

The Voice of Conscience   (Metro, 1917)
d: Edwin Carewe.   5 reels.
Francis X. Bushman, Beverly Bayne, Harry S. Northrup, Maggie Breyer, Pauline Dempsey, Walter Broussard, Anthony Byrd.
Potter, a newly paroled prisoner, agrees to visit the home of his cellmate to look in on theman's ailing mother.   He is accepted warmly by the family, and in time falls in love with his cellmate's sister.

The Voice of Destiny   (Diando Film Corp./Pathé, 1918)
d: William Bertram.   5 reels.
Baby Marie Osborne, Jack Connolly, J. Morris Foster, Ellen Cassity, Howard Crampton.
A businessman's dictaphone holds the key to his murder: The killer's voice can be heard on it.

The Voice of Love   (American Film Co./Mutual, 1916)
d: Rea Berger.   5 reels.
Winifred Greenwood, Edward Coxen, George Field, Laura Sears, Harvey Clark, Alfred Ferguson, Howard Crowe, John Singleton, Josephine Phillips, Rena Carlton.
Madame Thebe, an astrologer, becomes involved in a murder mystery... with herself as the chief suspect.

The Voice of the Storm   (FBO Pictures, 1929)
d: Lynn Shores.   7 reels.
Karl Dane, Hugh Allan, Martha Sleeper, Theodore von Eltz, Brandon Hurst, Warner Richmond, Lydia Yeamans Titus.
Powers, an innocent man, is convicted of murder and sentenced to be executed.   But his buddy, a telephone lineman, finds evidence of Powers' innocence and relays it to the governor—even though the lineman has to repair a downed telephone cable in a raging snowstorm to do so, just minutes before the scheduled execution.

The Volcano   (Harry Raver, Inc./Pathé, 1919)
d: George Irving.   6 reels.
Leah Baird, Edward Langford, W.H. Gibson, Jacob Kingsbury, Harry Bartlett, William Fredericks, Elvira Amazar, Becky Bruce, Governor Alfred E. Smith.
In New York's lower East Side, a disgruntled schoolteacher is persuaded to become a Communist.

Volcano   (Famous Players-Lasky/Paramount, 1926)
d: William K. Howard.   6 reels.
Bebe Daniels, Ricardo Cortez, Wallace Beery, Arthur Edmund Carew, Dale Fuller, Eulalie Jensen, Brandon Hurst, Marjorie Gay, Robert Perry, Snitz Edwards, Emily Barrye, Bowditch Turner, Edith Yorke, Mathilde Comont.
Zabette, a convent-bred girl, returns home to the island of Martinique and finds that her father has died.   Destitute, she is forced to auction off her Paris gowns.   The buyer, a handsome Frenchman, takes a romantic interest in Zabette but she rejects him, thinking herself a mulatta.   Mount Pelée erupts and in the turmoil the Frenchman rescues her from disaster; afterwards, he tells her his love knows no color boundaries, and they are married.

The Volga Boatman   (DeMille Pictures, 1926)
d: Cecil B. DeMille.   11 reels.
William Boyd, Elinor Fair, Robert Edeson, Victor Varconi, Julia Faye, Theodore Kosloff, Arthur Rankin, Eugene Pallette.
Romance and intrigue during the Russian revolution.   A rebel falls in love with the princess he has been ordered to execute.

The Volunteer   (World Film Corp., 1917)
d: Harley Knoles.   5 reels.
Madge Evans, Henry Hull, Muriel Ostriche, Victor Kennard, Jack Drumier, Kate Lester, William A. Brady, Kitty Gordon, Ethel Clayton, June Elvidge, Evelyn Greeley.
During World War I, an old Quaker disowns his son for enlisting in the service, as their religion does not allow fighting.   But young Madge Evans (playing herself) gradually wins over the old man, and he not only forgives his son, but welcomes back the daughter he had cast out for

marrying against his will.

The Vortex (Triangle, 1918)
d: Gilbert P. Hamilton. 5 reels.
Mary Warren, Joe King, Eugene Burr, George Hernandez, Myrtle Rishell, Wilbur Higby, R.P. Thompson.
Joan and Albert elope, and register at the hotel as husband and wife while they wait for the minister to arrive. This simple, innocent act unleashes a tempest of accusations and violent emotions, as Joan's honor seems compromised.

Vultures of Society (Essanay, 1916)
d: E.H. Calvert. 5 reels.
Lillian Drew, Marguerite Clayton, Arthur W. Bates, William W. Burns, Charles Stine, Hugh E. Thompson, Edward Arnold, Jack Meredith, Charles Racey, Mae Howard.
Teddy, a vivacious American girl, falls in love with a prince. But before she and the prince can get together, she has to navigate through a maze of complications and false leads.

The Wager (Rolfe Photoplays, Inc./Metro, 1916)
d: George D. Baker. 5 reels.
Emily Stevens, Lyster Chambers, Hugh Jeffrey, Daniel Jarrett, Frank Currier, Harry Mayo, Charles Bowser.
Two jewelers make a bet on whether their most expensive diamonds can be stolen.

Wages for Wives (Fox, 1925)
d: Frank Borzage. 7 reels.
Jacqueline Logan, Creighton Hale, Earle Foxe, ZaSu Pitts, Claude Gillingwater, David Butler, Margaret Seddon, Margaret Livingston, Dan Mason, Tom Ricketts.
Marital comedy about a young woman who assents to her beau's proposal, but only on condition that after marriage he will split his paycheck with her, fifty-fifty.

The Wages of Virtue (Famous Players-Lasky/Paramount, 1924)
d: Allan Dwan. 7 reels.
Gloria Swanson, Ben Lyon, Norman Trevor, Ivan Linow, Armand Cortez, Adrienne D'Ambricourt, Paul Panzer, Joe Moore.
In Algiers, an American legionnaire falls in love with Carmelita, a cafe owner.

The Wagon Master (Universal, 1929)
d: Harry J. Brown. 6 reels. (Part talkie.)
Ken Maynard, Tom Santschi, Edith Roberts, Frederick Dana, Al Ferguson, Jack Hanlon, Billie Dunn, Whitehorse, Frank Rice.
"The Rambler" saves a mining company from making a pact with criminals.

The Wagon Show (First National, 1928)
d: Harry J. Brown. 7 reels.
Ken Maynard, Marian Douglas, Maurice Costello, Fred Malatesta, George Davis, May Boley, Paul Weigel, Henry Roquemore, Sidney Jarvis.
Out West, a cowboy saves a struggling circus when he fills in for its missing stunt rider.

Wagon Tracks (Paramount, 1919)
d: Lambert Hillyer. 5 reels.
William S. Hart, Jane Novak, Robert McKim, Lloyd Bacon, Leo Pierson, Bert Sprotte, Charles Arling.
A wagonmaster swears to avenge his younger brother's death.

The Waif (Aurora Film Plays Corp., 1915)
d: William Roubert. 5 reels.

Matty Roubert, Morgan Philthorpe, Harry Weise, William Heidloff, Jennie Gilbert, Bessie Shaklein.
A penniless street waif lives in a barrel and earns a living by shining shoes. His luck changes when he meets a washed-up actor and gets to share his lodgings, and this leads to his going on a casting call for a new play. The waif gets the role and is such a success, he is signed to appear in the movie version. Now famous, the waif is invited to tea at the home of a wealthy patron of the arts who's still grieving over the kidnapping of her baby boy, years ago. Any bets on how this one ends?

Waifs (Astra Film Corp./Pathé, 1918)
d: Albert Parker. 5 reels.
Gladys Hulette, Creighton Hale, J.H. Gilmour, Walter Hiers.
Marjorie, on the lam from a suitor her father wants her to marry, moves into a boarding house in New York, where she encounters plenty of other pests.

The Waifs (New York Motion Picture Corp./Triangle, 1916)
d: Scott Sidney. 5 reels.
Jane Grey, William Desmond, Robert Kortman, Carol Holloway, J. Frank Burke, Fannie Midgley, Lewis Durham, Truly Shattuck, Harry Keenan.
Arthur, a divinity student, gets drunk on spiked punch and is defrocked by his bishop. Ultimately Arthur will prove he has what it takes to be an effective minister of the Word.

The Waiting Soul (Popular Plays and Players, Inc./Metro, 1917)
d: Burton L. King. 5 reels.
Olga Petrova, Mahlon Hamilton, Mathilde Brundage, Wyndham Standing, Lottie Ford, Anna Laughney, Roy Pilcher, Wilfred DeShields.
Grace, a fallen woman, meets Mr. Right and marries him. But she worries night and day that he will discover her past.

The Wakefield Case (Weber-World/World Film Corp., 1921)
d: George Irving. 6 reels.
Herbert Rawlinson, John P. Wade, J.H. Gilmore, Charles Dalton, Jospeh Burke, Jerry Austin, W.W. Black, H.L. Dewey, Florence Billings.
Transatlantic murder mystery finds a playwright crossing the ocean to find his father's killer.

Waking Up the Town (United Artists, 1925)
d: James Cruze. 6 reels.
Jack Pickford, Norma Shearer, Alec B. Francis, Claire McDowell, Herbert Pryor, Ann May, George Dromgold.
A small-town inventor shakes up the populace with his gadgets and his predictions.

The Walk-Offs (Screen Classics, Inc./Metro, 1920)
d: Herbert Blaché. 6 reels.
May Allison, Emory Johnson, Effie Conley, Darrell Foss, Joseph Kilgour, Richard Morris, Claire DuBrey, Estelle Evans.
When Kathleen overhears her employer's wealthy cousin denouncing "her type" of woman, she determines to make him fall in love with her... and succeeds.

Walking Back (DeMille Pictures/Pathé, 1928)
d: Rupert Julian. 6 reels.
Sue Carol, Richard Walling, Robert Edeson, Ivan Lebedeff, Florence Turner, Jane Keckley, James Bradbury, Arthur Rankin, Billy Sullivan, George Stone.
Thatcher, a jazz-age youth, steals a car to take his girl to the

dance, with disastrous consequences.

The Wall Between (Quality Pictures Corp./Metro, 1916)
d: John W. Noble. 5 reels.
Francis X. Bushman, Beverly Bayne, Edward Brennan, Robert Cummings, Sidney Cushing, Charles Prince, John Davidson, Helen Dunbar, Thomas Brooks, Alice Gordon.
Class-distinction drama about an army sergeant who is criticized for fraternizing with an officer's daughter.

The Wall Flower (Goldwyn, 1922)
w, d: Rupert Hughes. 6 reels.
Colleen Moore, Richard Dix, Gertrude Astor, Laura LaPlante, Tom Gallery, Rush Hughes, Dana Todd, Fanny Stockbridge, Emily Rait.
Tale of a girl who's considered a hopeless wallflower, but dreams about fun and romance all the same. In time, she finds plenty of both.

The Wall Street Mystery (William Steiner Productions/Arrow Film Corp., 1920)
d: Tom Collins. 5 reels.
Glenn White, Jane McAlpine, David Wall, Alexander Frank, Marie Treador, Joseph Striker, Leo Delaney, Augusta Perry, Charles Graham.
Tex, a private detective, solves the baffling murder of a Wall Street broker.

The Wall Street Whiz (Richard Talmadge Productions/FBO of America, 1925)
d: Jack Nelson. 5 reels.
Richard Talmadge, Marceline Day, Lillian Langdon, Carl Miller, Billie Bennet, Dan Mason.
A Wall Street whiz named Dick Butler, fleeing a police raid on a gambling house, jumps into a car owned by Mrs. McCooey and introduces himself as "a Butler." She misunderstands, and soon the financier is employed as a butler in the McCooey home, where he nurtures a romantic interest in Peggy, the McCooey daughter.

The Wallop (Universal, 1921)
d: Jack Ford. 5 reels.
Harry Carey, Mignonne Golden, William Gettinger, Charles LeMoyne, Joe harris, C.E. Anderson, J. Farrell MacDonald, Mark Fenton, Noble Johnson.
Out West, a prospector returns home and finds his girlfriend engaged to another man.

Walloping Wallace (Approved Pictures/Artclass Pictures, 1924)
d: Richard Thorpe. 5 reels.
Buddy Roosevelt, Violet LaPlante, Lew Meehan, N.E. Hendrix, Lillian Gale, Terry Myles, Olin Francis, Dick Bodkins.
Wallace, a ranch foreman, rides to the rescue when his female boss is abducted by a disgruntled former employee.

The Walls of Jericho (Box Office Attraction Co., 1914)
d: Lloyd B. Carleton. 5 reels.
Edmund Breese, Claire Whitney, Stuart Holmes, Edward José.
In England, a titled noblewoman suspects her American husband of murder.

The Wanderer (Famous Players-Lasky/Paramount, 1926)
d: Raoul Walsh. 9 reels.
Greta Nissen, William Collier Jr., Ernest Torrence, Wallace Beery, Tyrone Power, Kathryn Hill, Kathlyn Williams, George Rigas, Holmes Herbert, Snitz Edwards.

Jether, a Jewish shepherd, goes astray and follows a beautiful priestess of the goddess Ishtar.

Wanderer of the Wasteland (Famous Players-Lasky/Paramount, 1924)
d: Irvin Willat. 6 reels. (Technicolor.)
Jack Holt, Noah Beery, George Irving, Kathlyn Williams, Billie Dove, James Mason, Richard R. Neill, James Gordon, William Carroll, Willard Cooley.
Out West, a mining engineer shoots his brother during a quarrel, then flees into the desert. There, he is befriended by a lovely young woman who urges him to return home and face the consequences of his actions — with her at his side.

Wandering Daughters (Sam E. Rork/Associated First National, 1923)
d: James Young. 6 reels.
Marguerite De La Motte, William V. Mong, Mabel Van Buren, Marjorie Daw, Noah Beery, Pat O'Malley, Allan Forrest, Alice Howell.
Bessie, daughter of prim and proper parents, is enticed to join the revels of a bohemian artist and his friends.

Wandering Fires (Arrow Pictures, 1925)
d: Maurice Campbell. 6 reels.
Effie Shannon, George Hackathorne, Constance Bennett, Wallace MacDonald, Henrietta Crosman.
A young married woman is haunted by thoughts of her former lover, reported killed in the war.

Wandering Footsteps (Banner Productions, 1925)
d: Phil Rosen. 6 reels.
Alec B. Francis, Estelle Taylor, Bryant Washburn, Eugenie Besserer, Ethel Wales, Phillips Smalley, Sidney Bracey, Frankie Darro.
A young millionaire befriends an old bum who's tumbled from the upper echelons of society to its bottom rung.

Wandering Girls (Columbia, 1927)
d: Ralph Ince. 6 reels.
Dorothy Revier, Armand Kaliz, Mildred Harris, Robert Agnew, Eugenie Besserer.
A jazz baby falls in with thieves, and winds up being accused of jewel theft.

Wandering Husbands (Regal Pictures/W.W. Hodkinson, 1924)
d: William Beaudine. 7 reels.
James Kirkwood, Lila Lee, Margaret Livingston, Eugene Pallette, Muriel Frances Dana, Turner Savage, George Pearce, George French.
A society wife plots to separate her unfaithful husband from his mistress.

The Waning Sex (MGM, 1926)
d: Robert Z. Leonard. 7 reels.
Norma Shearer, Conrad Nagel, Mary McAllister, George K. Arthur, Martha Mattox.
A female defense attorney wins acquittal for her client, a flirtatious widow, then must do battle with her for the heart of the prosecuting attorney.

Wanted: A Brother (Oakdale Productions/General Film Co., 1918)
d: Robert Ensminger. 5 reels.
Gloria Joy, Mignon LeBrun, H.E. Archer, Daniel Gilfether, Julian Dillon, Edward Jobson, Ruth Lackaye, William Reed.
Bab, a young girl who wants a brother, befriends a neighbor boy.

542

Wanted: A Coward (Banner Productions/Sterling Pictures, 1927)
d: Roy Clements. 6 reels.
Lillian Rich, Robert Frazer, Frank Brownlee, James Gordon, Frank Cooley, Harry S. Northrup, Fred O'Beck, William Bertram.
Rupert, a soldier of fortune, decides that all men are cowards, including himself. Proving it will be the hard part.

Wanted: A Home (Universal, 1916)
d: Lois Weber, Phillips Smalley. 5 reels.
Mary MacLaren, Nannie Wright, Grace Johnson, Jack Mulhall, Charles Marriott, Marian Sigler, Horace "Kewpie" Morgan, Ernest Shields, Dana Ong.
Mina, a homeless girl, impersonates a nurse to get a job.

Wanted: A Husband (Famous Players-Lasky/Paramount, 1919)
d: Lawrence C. Windom. 5 reels.
Billie Burke, James L. Crane, Margaret Linden, Charles Lane, Edward Lester, Bradley Barker, Helen Greene, Gypsy O'Brien, Kid Broad, Mrs. Priestly Morrison, Frank Goldsmith.
Darcy, a lonely and somewhat unkempt young lady, learns that her two roommates have become engaged. So Darcy invents a fiancé of her own, and also gets a makeover from her cousin that transforms her into a fashion plate. Now primed for the mating game, Darcy finds that her fictional fiancé has become the real thing.

Wanted: A Mother (World Film Corp., 1918)
d: Harley Knoles. 5 reels.
Madge Evans, George MacQuarrie, Gerda Holmes, Alec B. Francis, Lionel Belmore, Tom Evans, Rosina Henley, Harry Bartlett.
Grief-stricken after the death of her mother, a young girl is instructed by her father to prepare an ad for a governess. The girl's ad will read: "Wanted, a mother."

Wanted at Headquarters (Universal, 1920)
d: Stuart Paton. 5 reels.
William Marion, Eva Novak, Leonard C. Shumway, Agnes Emerson, Lloyd Sedgwick, Howard Davis, George Chesebro, Frank Clarke.
Kate, the brains of an underworld crime syndicate, falls in love with a detective working to solve one of the heists she's engineered.

Wanted by the Law (Sunset Productions, 1924)
d: Robert N. Bradbury. 5 reels.
J.B. Warner, Frank Rice, Dorothy Woods.
A man assumes the blame for a shooting to save his brother, then heads west.

Wanted For Murder (Harry Rapf Productions/Chatham Pictures Corp., 1918)
d: Frank Crane. 6 reels.
Elaine Hammerstein, Charles Raven, Lillian Hall, Darby Holmes, Burton Green, Irene Franklin, Allen Adams.
During World War I, love blossoms between an American doughboy and a French peasant girl. Together they distribute leaflets bearing a photo of the Kaiser with the inscription: "Wanted for Murder."

The Wanters (Louis B. Mayer Productions/Associated First National, 1923)
d: John M. Stahl. 7 reels.
Marie Prevost, Robert Ellis, Norma Shearer, Gertrude Astor, Huntley Gordon, Lincoln Stedman, Lillian Langdon, Louise

Fazenda, Hank Mann, Lydia Yeamans Titus, Vernon Steele.
Worthington, a millionaire, falls in love with his sister's housemaid and breaks all the "proper" rules of sociey by pursuing her, wooing her, and winning her as his bride.

War and the Woman (Thanhouser/Pathé, 1917)
d: Ernest C. Warde. 5 reels.
Florence LaBadie, Tom Brooke, Wayne Arey, Grace Henderson, Arthur Bower, Ernest C. Warde.
During World War I, a girl falls in love with an army pilot.

War Brides (Herbert Brenon Film Corp./Selznick, 1916)
d: Herbert Brenon. 8 reels.
Alla Nazimova, Charles Hutchinson, Charles Bryant, William Bailey, Richard S. Barthelmess, Nila Mac, Gertrude Berkeley, Alex K. Shannon, Robert Whitworth, Ned Burton.
Gritty anti-war melodrama about a strong-willed woman in a mythical kingdom who refuses to cooperate with her government and its edicts unless the sovereign agrees to end all wars.

The War Bride's Secret (Fox, 1916)
d: Kenean Buel. 6 reels.
Virginia Pearson, Walter Law, Glen White, Stuart Sage, Henry Hallam, Olive Corbett, Robert Vivian, Billy Lynbrook.
Newlywed Jean is still pregnant with her first child when she hears word from the battlefield that her husband has been killed in action. To provide her child with a father, Jean marries an older man who loves and respects her. Then, word comes that her first husband was not killed but merely wounded, and has recuperated.

The War of Wars; or, the Franco-German Invasion (Ramo Film, Inc., 1914)
d: Will S. Davis. 6 reels.
Edith Hallor, Stuart Holmes, Leo A. Kennedy, Miss Mayo, Hugh Jeffrey.
Rare World War I film that paints a marginally sympathetic picture of the German invaders. In occupied France, a German commander rescues a French girl from being raped by the local innkeeper.

War Paint (MGM, 1926)
d: W.S. Van Dyke. 6 reels.
Tim McCoy, Pauline Starke, Charles French, Chief Yowlache, Chief Whitehorse, Karl Dane.
At a western outpost during the 1880s, an American lieutenant forges a friendship with an Indian chief and averts a raid on the garrison.

The Warfare of the Flesh (Edward Warren Productions, 1917)
d: Edward Warren. 7 reels.
Walter Hampden, Marie Shotwell, Harry Benham, Charlotte Ives, Fred Radcliffe, Mary Moore, Theodore Friebus, Mary Elizabeth Forbes.
Allegorical drama pitting good against evil, each represented by a different actor.

Warming Up (Paramount, 1928)
d: Fred Newmeyer. 8 reels. (Music score, sound effects.)
Richard Dix, Jean Arthur, Claude King, Philo McCullough, Billy Kent Schaefer, Roscoe Karns, James Dugan, Mike Donlin, Mike Ready, Chet Thomas, Joe Pirrone, Wally Hood.
A small-town pitcher moves up to the big leagues and falls in love with the team owner's daughter. It's a perilous relationship, though, because the league's home run champ has eyes for her too.

The Warning (Triumph Film Corp./World Film Corp., 1915)
d: Edmund Lawrence. 5 reels.
Henry Kolker, Lily Leslie, Frank Longacre, Christine Mayo, Edna Mayo, Mayme Kelso, Edith Thornton, Cyril Rheinhard, William McKey, Ogden Childe.
Robert, a warmly likeable husband and father, slowly becomes addicted to the bottle. One night he allows himself to be seduced by a "fast" woman, then becomes a thief to satisfy her desires, and is eventually fired from his job and ends up a street derelict. That's when Robert wakes up from his nightmare... and gives thanks for "the warning."

The Warning (Columbia, 1927)
d: George B. Seitz. 6 reels.
Jack Holt, Dorothy Revier.
A female government agent gets mixed up with opium smugglers on the high seas.

The Warning Signal (Ellbee Pictures, 1926)
d: Charles Hunt. 5 reels.
Gladys Hulette, Kent Mead, Lincoln Stedman, Clarence Burton, Martha Mattox, William H. Turner, Joseph Girard.
A young railroad employee finds the warning signal defective just when he needs it to alert two trains on a collision course. Using a radio he himself invented, he is able to contact the engineers and avert disaster.

The Warrens of Virginia (Lasky Feature Plays/Paramount, 1915)
d: Cecil B. DeMille. 5 reels.
James Neill, Mabel Van Buren, Blanche Sweet, P.E. Peters, House Peters, Dick LaReno, Sydney Deane, Raymond Hatton, Milton Brown, Dick LaStrange, Lucien Littlefield, Gerald Ward, Mildred Harris, Mrs. Lewis McCord.
American military heroes, uncle and nephew, find themselves on opposite sides when the Civil War breaks out.

War's Women — see: The Despoiler (1915)

The Wasp (World Film Corp., 1918)
d: Lionel Belmore. 5 reels.
Kitty Gordon, Rockcliffe Fellowes, Charles Gerry, Sadee Burbank, William Calhoun, Edward Roseman, Victor Kennard, Lionel Belmore, Hazel Washburn, Edward Burns.
Grace, a quick-tempered girl nicknamed "The Wasp," is captured by German spies who plan to sabotage her father's war materiels factory.

Wasted Lives (Mission Film Corp./Second National Film Corp., 1923)
d: Clarence Geldert. 5 reels.
Richard Wayne, Catherine Murphy, Winter Hall, Lillian Leighton, Margaret Loomis, Arthur Osborne, Walt Whitman, Philippe DeLacy, Fannie Midgley.
Adams, a devoted husband and doctor, goes off to war, and is reported killed. After a suitable period of mourning, Adams' best friend proposes to the supposed widow; but just before the wedding is to take place, the doctor returns alive and well.

The Wasted Years (Centaur Film Co./Mutual, 1916)
d: Robert B. Broadwell. 5 reels.
Crane Wilbur, Mae Gaston, Jessie Burnett, Thelma Salter, John Oaker, George Harris, Thelma Burns.
Weatherby, a penniless drifter, begs for money and uses it for a theater ticket. To his surprise, the play on stage depicts his own wasted life.

Watch Him Step (Phil Goldstone Productions, 1922)
d: Jack Nelson. 5 reels.
Richard Talmadge, Ethel Shannon, Al Filson, Nellie Peck Saunders, Colin Kenny, Hugh Saxon.
Dick and Dorothy try twice to elope, but are foiled. Third time's the charm.

Watch Your Step (Goldwyn, 1922)
d: William Beaudine. 5 reels.
Cullen Landis, Patsy Ruth Miller, Bert Woodruff, George Pierce, Raymond Cannon, Gus Leonard, Henry Rattenbury, Joel Day, L.J. O'Connor, John Cossar, Lillian Sylvester.
Slocum, a compulsive leadfoot, spends time in jail for speeding. When he gets out, he speeds again, wrecks his car, and knocks down a policeman. But the incident proves to be the catalyst: Once he discovers that the police officer is unhurt, Slocum promises never to speed again.

Watch Your Wife (Universal, 1926)
d: Sven Gade. 7 reels.
Virginia Valli, Nat Carr, Pat O'Malley, Helen Lee Worthing, Albert Conti, Aggie Herring, Nora Hayden.
Domestic comedy about a couple of Type A personalities who quarrel constantly, and finally divorce. The ex-wife finds a new lover, but he's a gigolo interested in her money. The ex-husband hires a young woman to be his platonic companion, but that gets tiresome. In the end, the two exes realize they were meant for each other after all, and decide to remarry.

The Water Hole (Paramount, 1928)
d: F. Richard Jones. 7 reels.
Jack Holt, Nancy Carroll, John Boles, Montague Shaw, Ann Christy, Lydia Yeamans Titus, Jack Perrin, Jack Mower, Paul Ralli, Tex Young, Bob Miles, Greg Whitespear.
Judith, a spoiled eastern girl, vamps Philip, an Arizonan, and gets him to propose, then laughingly rejects him. With her father's permission, Philip "kidnaps" Judith and takes her out west with him. There, in an old Indian pueblo, she is forced to cook and clean for him. Can love be far behind?

Water, Water Everywhere (Goldwyn, 1920)
d: Clarence G. Badger. 5 reels.
Will Rogers, Irene Rich, Roland Lee, Wade Boteler, Marguerite Livingston, Milton Brown, Victor Potel, William Courtwright, Sidney DeGrey, Lillian Langdon, Lydia Yeamans Titus.
The subject of the title is not sea water, but rather soda water, being served by pretty waitresses to try to end alcoholism in their town.

Waterfront (First National, 1928)
d: William A. Seiter. 7 reels.
Dorothy Mackaill, Jack Mulhall, James Bradbury Sr., Knute Erickson, Ben Hendricks Jr., William Norton Bailey, Pat Harmon.
Jack, a seaman, falls in love with the daughter of a fellow skipper and asks her to marry him. At first he is rejected, by both the girl and her father, the latter saying that the bounding main is no place to raise a family. But Jack's intention is not to sail the seven seas forever, but rather to settle down on a farm. That changes things.

The Wax Model (Pallas Pictures/Paramount, 1917)
d: E. Mason Hopper. 5 reels.
Vivian Martin, Thomas Holding, George Fisher, Helen Jerome Eddy, Clarisse Selwyn, Kathryn Vaughn, Pietro Buzzi, Marion Sievers.

544

Julie, a model and the daughter of a man-weary Parisian dancer, tries to defend herself from men by being aloof in their presence. But when a wax image of Julie is displayed in a shop window, one particular man finds her irresistible, and pursues her.

Way Down East (Griffith/United Artists, 1921)
d: D.W. Griffith. 13 reels.
Lillian Gish, Richard Barthelmess, Lowell Sherman, Creighton Hale, Mrs. David Landau, Josephine Bernard, Mrs. Morgan Belmont, Patricia Fruen, Florence Short, Burr McIntosh, Kate Bruce, Porter Strong, George Neville, Edgar Nelson, Mary Hay, Creighton Hale, Emily Fitzroy, Vivia Ogden, Norma Shearer.
A poor country girl is tricked by a scoundrel into a fake marriage. She believes the marriage is real, but once she gets pregnant, her "husband" leaves her.
A popular film, justly famous for the spectacular climactic scene where the girl is rescued from an ice floe by the Barthelmess character.

The Way of a Girl (MGM, 1925)
d: Robert Vignola. 6 reels.
Eleanor Boardman, Matt Moore, Matthew Betz, William Russell, Kate Price.
A reckless jazz baby loves fast, dangerous motor rides... until she winds up as a hostage held by escaped criminals.

The Way of a Maid (Selznick/Select, 1921)
d: William P.S. Earle. 5 reels.
Elaine Hammerstein, Niles Welch, Diana Allen, Charles D. Brown, George Fawcett, Arthur Housman, Helen Lindroth.
A socialite in dire financial straits pretends to be a housemaid.

The Way of a Man With a Maid (Famous Players-Lasky/Paramount, 1918)
d: Donald Crisp. 5 reels.
Bryant Washburn, Wanda Hawley, Fred Goodwins, Clarence H. Geldart, Bessie Eyton, Jay Dwiggins, Billy Elmer, James Neill.
Arthur, a working-class lad who fancies Elsa, a stenographer, finds he must outspend a prosperous broker to win her hand.

The Way of a Woman (Norma Talmadge Film Corp./Select, 1919)
d: Robert Z. Leonard. 5 reels.
Norma Talmadge, Conway Tearle, Gertrude Berkeley, Frank DeVernon, Mae McAvoy, Jobyna Howland, Hassard Short, George LaGuere, William Humphreys, Stuart Holmes.
Nancy, proud daughter of a formerly aristocratic family that has fallen on hard times, tries to marry for money but her new husband dies suddenly and leaves her penniless. Eventually, after being forced to sell her furs and jewelry, Nancy discovers that it is better to marry for love.

The Way of All Flesh (Paramount, 1927)
d: Victor Fleming. 9 reels.
Emil Jannings, Belle Bennett, Phyllis Haver, donald Keith, Fred Kohler, Philippe DeLacey, Mickey McBan, Betsy Ann Lisle, Carmencita Johnson, Gordon Thorpe, Jackie Coombs.
Tragic drama about a devoted family man who is seduced by a vamp and beaten by her gang. Fighting back, he kills the gang leader, then must go into hiding for the rest of his life to avoid prosecution.

The Way of the Strong (Metro, 1919)
d: Edwin Carewe. 5 reels.

Anna Q. Nilsson, Joe King, Harry S. Northrup, Irene Yeager, Arthur Redden, Rita Harlan.
Treachery in the Frozen North, as an Alaskan miner runs off with his partner's wife and son.

The Way of the Strong (Columbia, 1928)
d: Frank Capra. 6 reels.
Mitchell Lewis, Alice Day, Theodore von Eltz, Margaret Livingston, William N. Bailey.
A bootlegger is attracted to a lovely blind girl, but finds she loves another man.

The Way of the Transgressor (Premium Pictures/Independent Pictures, 1923)
d: William J. Craft. 5 reels.
George Larkin, Ruth Stonehouse, Frank Whitson, Al Ferguson, Laura Anson, Carl Silvera, William Vaughn Moody.
Silk, a reformed crook, is framed for a crime he didn't commit and lands in jail. When he gets out, the only "job" he can get is in the gang of the man who framed him. There's a happy ending, though, for after the gang chieftain is stabbed to death, Silk falls in love, goes straight, and gets married, in that order.

The Way of the World (Universal, 1916)
d: Lloyd Carleton. 5 reels.
Hobart Bosworth, Dorothy Davenport, Emory Johnson, Adele Farrington, Jack Curtis, C. Norman Hammond, Gretchen Lederer, Herbert Barrington.
Beatrice, a young woman in love with an up-and-coming politician, books a voyage to Europe. Once on board ship, she meets John, who romances her without revealing that he is already married.

The Way Out (World Film Corp., 1918)
d: George Kelson. 5 reels.
June Elvidge, Carlyle Blackwell, Kate Lester, John Bowers, Muriel Ostriche, Jack Drumier, Marie Pagano.
Alice loves Robert, but her socially ambitious mother withholds her approval, hoping to match Alice with a titled nobleman.

We Americans (Universal, 1928)
d: Edward Sloman. 9 reels.
George Sidney, Patsy Ruth Miller, George Lewis, Eddie Phillips, Beryl Mercer, John Boles, Albert Gran, Michael Visaroff, Kathlyn Williams, Edward Martindel, Josephine Dunn, Daisy Belmore, Rosita Marstini, Andy Devine.
Hugh, a scion of wealth, returns from the war and announces his engagement to Beth, daughter of Russian Jewish immigrants. His parents object strenuously, but drop their objections when they learn that during the war, Beth's brother sacrificed his life to save Hugh.

We Can't Have Everything (Famous Players-Lasky/Paramount, 1918)
d: Cecil B. DeMille. 6 reels.
Kathlyn Williams, Elliott Dexter, Wanda Hawley, Sylvia Breamer, Thurston Hall, Raymond Hatton, Tully Marshall, Theodore Roberts, James Neill, Erest Joy, Billy Elmer, Alvin Wyckoff, Charles Ogle, Sylvia Ashton.
When Jim and his friend Charity go for a drive in the country, a storm forces them to take refuge in an inn for the night. Though the two are innocent of any wrongdoing, Jim's vengeful wife seizes the opportunity to file for divorce.

We Moderns (John McCormick Productions/First National, 1925)

d: John Francis Dillon. 7 reels.
Colleen Moore, Jack Mulhall, Carl Miller, Claude Gillingwater, Clarissa Selwyn, Cleve Morison, Marcelle Corday, Tom McGuire, Blanche Payson, Dorothy Seastrom, Louis Payne.
Mary, a jazz baby addicted to the fast life, scorns the Victorian values of her staid parents, and falls in with a young, devil-may-care crowd. She even fancies one of their number, a worthless humbug who dabbles in poetry. Mary is with the group, partying aboard a zeppelin, when an airplane crashes into the airship, and she almost loses her life. But she is rescued by John, the sensible young man her "staid" parents had picked out for her—and finds love in his arms.

We Should Worry (Fox, 1918)
d: Kenean Buel. 5 reels.
Jane Lee, Katherine Lee, Ruby DeRemer, William Pike, Edward Sturgis, Tammany Young, Henry Clive, Charles Craig, George Humbert, Henry Hallam, Sarah McVicker.
Comedy about Jane and Katherine, a pair of imps who ply their mischief to insure that their aunt will marry the "right" man.

The Weaker Sex (Triangle, 1917)
d: Raymond B. West. 5 reels.
Dorothy Dalton, Louise Glaum, Charles Ray, Robert McKim, Charles K. French, Margaret Thompson, J. Barney Sherry, Nona Thomas, Jack Gilbert.
A district attorney who's married to a lady attorney prefers that she give up her law practice.

The Weaker Vessel (Universal, 1919)
d: Paul Powell. 5 reels.
Mary MacLaren, Anne Schaefer, Johnnie Cooke, Thurston Hall, John Mackay, Ethel Ritchie, Little Zoe Rae, Lena Baskette.
Abby, a waitress in a New York eatery, tries to persuade one of her customers to give up the bottle.

The Weakness of Man (World Film Corp., 1916)
d: Barry O'Neil. 5 reels.
Holbrook Blinn, Eleanor Woodruff, Richard Wangerman, Charles Mackay, Alma Hanlon, Walter D. Greene, Teddy Sampson, John Hines.
Trapped in a marriage to a woman he does not love, David decides to drown himself in the river. Once there, he finds a corpse in the water and impulsively changes clothes and identification with the dead man. Now David starts life anew, in a new region with a new wife.
Bittersweet drama based on the play *The Living Corpse* by Leo Tolstoy.

The Weakness of Strength (Popular Plays and Players, Inc./Metro, 1916)
d: Harry Revier. 5 reels.
Edmund Breese, Clifford Bruce, Ormi Hawley, Evelyn Brent, Florence Moore, Clifford B. Gray.
Daniel, a callous, insensitive shipping executive, cares nothing for those less fortunate than himself. When his employee asks for a raise to help care for his ailing grandmother, Daniel turns him down. The employee embezzles the money anyway, and tells his wife that his request for a raise was granted. Once Daniel discovers the theft, he goes to the employee's home to confront him... and meets the man's pregnant wife, who warmly thanks him for the raise and discloses that in gratitude she plans to name her child after him.

Wealth (Famous Players-Lasky/Paramount, 1921)
d: William D. Taylor. 5 reels.
Ethel Clayton, Herbert Rawlinson, J.M. Dumont, Lawrence Steers, George Periolat, Claire McDowell, Jean Acker, Richard Wayne.
Mary, a young artist, meets playboy Philip aboard a train and they fall in love. His wealthy mother, however, disapproves of the match, having already made plans to marry Philip off to a young woman of her own choosing.

Weary River (First National/Warner Bros., 1929)
d: Frank Lloyd. 8 reels. (Part talkie.)
Richard Barthelmess, Betty Compson, William Holden, Louis Natheaux, George E. Stone, Raymond Turner.
A hoodlum is sent to prison, where he develops a talent for music.

A Weaver of Dreams (Metro, 1918)
d: John H. Collins. 5 reels.
Viola Dana, Clifford Bruce, Mildred Davis, Russell Simpson, Clarissa Selwynne, Vera Lewis.
Judith loves Carter, and they plan to marry and settle down in a home dubbed "The House of Hearts." But there's trouble in Paradise, when an interloper named Margery moves in on the couple's happiness.

Weavers of Life (Edward Warren Productions, 1917)
d: Edward Warren. 5 reels.
Helen Hayes, Howard Hall, Earl Schenck, Gladys Alexandria, Kenneth Hunter, Dorothy Benham, Gilbert Rooney, Isabel West, Edna Hibbard, Beatrice Allen, Harry Hatfield.
Peggy, a shopgirl, finds a masquerade costume and an invitation to a party. On impulse, she dons the costume, shows up at the party, and falls in love.

The Web of Chance (Fox, 1919)
d: Alfred E. Green. 5 reels.
Peggy Hyland, Harry Hamm, E.B. Tilton, William Machin, George Dromgold, Sam Appel.
While on a case with her detective uncle, Dorothy meets Arthur and they fall in love.

The Web of Deceit (Edwin Carewe Productions, Inc./Pathé, 1920)
d: Edwin Carewe. 6 reels.
Dolores Cassinelli, Letty Ford, Hugh Cameron, Mitchell Harris, Franklyn Hanna.
Wanda, a petty criminal, decides to impersonate her sister during a visit to New York. She falls in love with her uncle's protegé and he with her, but her web of deceit begins to unravel when her sister unexpectedly comes to town.

The Web of Desire (World Film Corp., 1917)
d: Emile Chautard. 5 reels.
Ethel Clayton, Rockcliffe Fellowes, Doris Field, Richard Turner, Edward M. Kimball, Madge Evans, William Williams.
Miller, a sudden millionaire through inheritance, becomes deeply involved in business matters and begins to neglect his wife.

Web of Fate (Dallas M. Fitzgerald Productions/Peerless Pictures, 1927)
d: Dallas M. Fitzgerald. 6 reels.
Lillian Rich, Henry Sedley, Eugene Strong, John Cossar, Frances Raymond, Edwin Coxen.
When a theatrical "angel" threatens a stage actress with ruin and is subsequently killed, the girl and her boyfriend are

546

unjustly charged with the crime.

The Web of Life   (Gold Medal Photo Players, 1917)
d: George K. Rolands.   5 reels.
Hilda Nord, James Cruze, George Moss, Redfield Clarke, George Soule Spencer, Billy Quirk, Frank Holland.
Following a shotgun wedding, the groom begins to see other women, thus forcing his distressed wife into the arms of another man.

Wedding Bells   (Constance Talmadge Productions/Associated First National, 1921)
d: Chet Withey.   6 reels.
Constance Talmadge, Harrison Ford, Emily Chichester, Ida Darling, James Harrison, William Roselle, Polly Van, Dallas Welford, Frank Honda.
Newlyweds Rosalie and Reginald have a spat and she goes to Reno for a quick divorce.   Later, however, when she learns that Reggie is planning to marry a young socialite, Rosalie intervenes and tries to win him back for herself.

Wedding Bills   (Paramount, 1927)
d: Erle Kenton.   6 reels.
Raymond Griffith, Anne Sheridan, Hallam Cooley, Iris Stuart, Vivian Oakland, Tom S. Guise, Louis Stern, Edgar Kennedy, John Steppling.
Comedy about Algernon, a perennial best man at weddings, who finally gets himself engaged following a frantic chase after stolen jewels.

The Wedding March   (Paramount, 1928)
d: Erich von Stroheim.   10 reels.
George Fawcett, ZaSu Pitts, Fay Wray, Maude George, Hughie Mack, Mathew Betz, Cesare Gravina, Dale Fuller, Sidney Bracey, Anton Vaverka.
In pre-World War I Vienna, a jaded prince begins a flirtation with Mitzi, a harpist in a wine garden.   His aristocratic mother, however, plans to marry the prince off to the daughter of a wealthy businessman as a means of recouping the family's dissipated fortune.

The Wedding Song   (Cinema Corp. Of America/Producers Distributing Corp., 1925)
d: Alan Hale.   7 reels.
Leatrice Joy, Robert Ames, Charles Gerard, Ruby Lafayette, Rosa Rudami, Jack Curtis, Clarence Burton, Gertrude Claire, Ethel Wales, Gladden James, Casson Ferguson.
Hayes, a Pacific islander, travels to San Francisco to try to dispose of several priceless pearls.   In the city, a con man learns of the pearls and gets his sister to vamp Hayes into marriage.   She does so, and when the trio returns to Hayes' island, the con man tries to seize the cache of pearls for himself.   But now Sis has other plans, for she has fallen in love with her new husband.

Wedlock   (Paralta Plays, Inc./W.W. Hodkinson, 1918)
d: Wallace Worsley.   5 reels.
Louise Glaum, Charles Gunn, Jack Gilbert, Roberta Wilson, W. Lawson Butt, Herschel Mayall, Roy Laidlaw, Joseph J. Dowling, Beverly Randolph, Leatrice Joy, Harry Archer, Ida Lewis, Clifford Alexander, Aggie Herring, Helen Dunbar.
When Granger surprises his wealthy family by marrying Margery, a working-class girl, his snobbish kin object strenuously.   To please them, Granger obtains an annulment and he and Margery sadly go their separate ways.   But in time, he'll want to make himself worthy of her again.

Wee Lady Betty   (Triangle, 1917)
d: Charles Miller.   5 reels.
Bessie Love, Frank Borzage, Charles K. French, Walter Perkins, Walter Whitman, Aggie Herring, Thornton Edwards, Alfred Hollingsorth, J.P. Lockney.
"Wee Lady" Betty and her elderly father occupy an Irish castle, but when they learn that the owner is coming to take possession, they face eviction.   Betty hatches an unusual plan: They will move into the "haunted chamber" and pretend to be ghosts.   But the scheme develops a wee glitch, when Betty falls for the handsome owner.

The Weekend   (American Film Co./Pathé, 1920)
d: George L. Cox.   6 reels.
Milton Sills, Margarita Fischer, Bertram Grassby, Mary Lee Wise, Harvey Clark, Mayme Kelso, Beverly Travers, Harry Lonsdale, Lillian Leighton.
Vera's a fun-loving girl whose wealthy parents want her to marry Spencer... but he's too dull for her, and a fortune-hunter besides.

Weekend Husbands   (Daniel Carson Goodman Corp./Equity Pictures, 1924)
d: E.H. Griffith.   7 reels.
H.J. Herbert, Alma Rubens, Montague Love, Maurice Costello, Sally Cruze, Charles Byer, Paul Panzer, Margaret Dale.
Because his wife expects and demands luxuries, Randall becomes a bootlegger to support her lifestyle.

Welcome Stranger   (Belasco Productions/Producers' Distributors, 1924)
d: James Young.   7 reels.
Lloyd Hughes, Dore Davidson, Florence Vidor, Virginia Brown Faire, Noah Beery, Robert Edeson, William V. Mong, Otis Harlan, Fred J. Butler, Pat Hartigan.
Solomon, a Jew, is prevented from settling in a biased New England town.   But he invests in a power plant that will illuminate the whole town, and becomes one of its honored citizens.

Welcome to Our City   (San Antonio Pictures/Producers Security Corp., 1922)
d: Robert H. Townley.   5 reels.
Maclyn Arbuckle, Bessie Emerick, Fred Dalton, Bessie Wharton, Jack Crosby, Gertrude Robinson, Charles Holleman, Joyce Fair, Gene Baker.
On a visit to New York with his wife, Scott slips out one evening and innocently ends up being jailed with a young lady he tried to help.

We're All Gamblers   (Paramount, 1927)
d: James Cruze.   7 reels.
Thomas Meighan, Marietta Millner, Cullen Landis, Philo McCullough, Gertrude Claire, Gunboat Smith, Spec O'Donnell.
In New York, Sam, an orphan who was raised on the Lower East Side, grows up to be a heavyweight contender, then proprietor of a night club.   Carlotta, a socialite who admires Sam, tries to conceal her affection for him because of the gulf between their social classes.   But when she is implicated in a near-disaster, Sam gallantly comes to her aid and they confess their love for each other.

We're in the Navy Now   (Paramount, 1927)
d: Edward Sutherland.   6 reels.
Wallace Beery, Raymond Hatton, Chester Conklin, Tom Kennedy, Donald Keith, Lorraine Eason, Joseph W. Girard, Max Asher.
Rival boxers find themselves drafted into the Navy together.

WEDDING BILL$ (1927). This publicity still shows Raymond Griffith trying to "rope in" Anne Sheridan (in bridal gown) as her bridesmaids look on in amusement. "Wedding Bill$" is, alas, a "lost" film, but contemporary reviews called it a laugh riot.

* * * * *

548

West is West (Universal, 1920)
d: Val Paul. 5 reels.
Harry Carey, Charles LeMoyne, Joe Harris, Ted Brooks, Ed Lattell, Otto Nelson, Frank Braidwood, Arthur Millett, Adelaide Halleck, Jim O'Neil, Scott McKee, Mignonne, Jack Dill.
Out West, a cowboy takes a job as a mine engineer, but then learns that he's been hired as a strikebreaker.

West of Broadway (Metropolitan Pictures Corp. Of California, 1926)
d: Robert Thornby. 6 reels.
Priscilla Dean, Arnold Gray, Majel Coleman, Walter Long, George Hall, William Austin.
Western comedy about a misogynistic rancher who turns part of his spread into a golf course and hires a New York golf instructor named Freddy. When the instructor arrives from the east, the woman-hating rancher finds that Freddy is a girl—and one who will turn his life upside down.

West of Chicago (Fox, 1922)
d: Scott Dunlap. 5 reels.
Charles Jones, Renee Adoree, Philo McCullough, Sidney D'Albrook, Charles French, Marcella Daly, Kathleen Key.
Out West, a rancher is reported murdered. But his visiting nephew discovers that not only is the old man still alive, the new foreman is the varmint who tried to kill him.

West of Santa Fe (El Dorado Productions/Syndicate Pictures, 1928)
d: J.P. McGowan. 5 reels.
Bob Custer, Peggy Montgomery, Mack V. Wright, J.P. McGowan, Bud Osborne.
A rancher uncovers a plot by crooked cowboys to steal horses from the U.S. cavalry.

West of the Water Tower (Famous Players-Lasky/Paramount, 1924)
d: Rollin Sturgeon. 8 reels.
Glenn Hunter, May McAvoy, Ernest Torrence, George Fawcett, ZaSu Pitts, Charles Abbe, Anne Schaefer, Riley Hatch, Allen Baker, Jack Terry, Edward Elkas, Joseph Burke.
Newlyweds discover that their marriage may have been illegal. Since the wife is now pregnant, bluenose neighbors ostracize the couple, until the missing marriage certificate is uncovered, legal as can be.

West of Zanzibar (MGM, 1928)
d: Tod Browning. 7 reels.
Lon Chaney, Lionel Barrymore, Mary Nolan, Warner Baxter, Jacquelin Gadsden, Roscoe Ward, Kalla Pasha, Curtis Nero.
Bitter because he thinks his wife has been unfaithful to him, a London magician nurtures resentment against their daughter, who he believes is the child of another man.

West Point (MGM, 1927)
d: Edward Sedgwick. 9 reels.
William Haines, Joan Crawford, Ralph Emerson, Neil Neely, William Bakewell, Leon Kellar, Raymond G. Moses.
A West Point cadet has all the talent necessary to excel on the football field, but his selfish ways leave him lacking in school spirit.

The Westbound Limited (Emory Johnson Productions/FBO of America, 1923)
d: Emory Johnson. 7 reels.
Ralph Lewis, Claire McDowell, Ella Hall, Johnny Harron, Taylor Graves, Wedgewood Nowell, David Dirby, Richard Morris, Jane Morgan.
A railroad engineer's quick reflexes save the daughter of the company's president, just before his train would have struck her.

Western Blood (Fox, 1918)
d: Lynn F. Reynolds. 5 reels.
Tom Mix, Victoria Forde, Frank Clark, Barney Furey, Pat Chrisman, Buck Jones.
In California, a visiting Texas rancher gets involved in rounding up German spies as well as wild horses.

Western Courage (Rayart, 1926)
d: Ben Wilson. 5 reels.
Dick Hatton, Elsa Benham, Robert Walker, Ed LaNiece.
A slickster from the city tries to romance a country girl, but a cowboy intervenes.

A Western Demon (Western Feature Productions, 1922)
d: Robert McKenzie. 5 reels.
William Fairbanks, Marilyn Mills, Monte Montague, Murray Miller, Billy Franey.
Rose, a ranch owner out West, meets a friendly cowboy on the train and hires him to investigate a recent spate of cattle rustling. He does more than investigate: He learns that Rose's own foreman is the villain behind the thievery, and later rescues her after the foreman has kidnapped her in a last-ditch effort to escape justice.

Western Feuds (Ashton Dearholt Productions/Arrow Film Corp., 1924)
d: Francis Ford. 5 reels.
Edmund Cobb, Florence Gilbert, Al McCormick, Kathleen Calhoun, William White, Ashton Dearholt, Francis Ford.
Out West, cattlemen and sheep ranchers clash—again.

Western Firebrands (Charles R. Seeling Productions/Aywon, 1921)
d: Charles R. Seeling. 5 reels.
Big Boy Williams, Virginia Adair, J. Conrad Needham, William Horne, Jack Pitcairn, Bert Apling, Helen Yoder.
Man-made forest fires threaten to destroy a lumber company out West.

Western Hearts (Cliff Smith Productions/Associated Photoplays, 1921)
d: Cliff Smith. 5 reels.
Josie Sedgwick, Art Straton, Floyd Taliaferro, Hazel Hart, Edward Moncrief, Bert Wilson.
Treachery and deceit spark this tale of broken hearts among a ranch owner's daughter, a ranch hand, and the cowboy she truly loves.

Western Pluck (Universal, 1926)
d: Travers Vale. 5 reels.
Art Acord, Marceline Day, Ray Ripley, Robert Rose, William Welsh, Helen Cobb, S.E. Jennings, Charles Newton, Helen Cobb.
Out West, Arizona Allen is hired by a rancher to look after his feckless son, Rowdy. After a daring stagecoach robbery in which both men are implicated, Rowdy stands up to his accusers like a man and wins the respect of Allen, his father, and his sister. The latter makes plans to marry Allen.

The Western Rover (Universal, 1927)
d: Albert Rogell. 5 reels.
Art Acord, Ena Gregory, Charles Avery, William Welch.
Estranged from his ranch owner father, a cowpoke becomes a rider in a circus. Later, he returns to ranching as a hand at the spread adjoining his dad's—and discovers that his new

employer is rustling cattle belonging to the cowpoke's father.

The Western Wallop (Universal, 1924)
d: Clifford Smith. 5 reels.
Jack Hoxie, Margaret Landis, Duke R. Lee, James Gordon Russell, Charles Brinley, Fred Burns, Jack Pratt, Herbert Fortier, Joseph W. Girard, William Welsh.
A parolee becomes foreman of a ranch near the Nevada line, but because of the terms of his parole he is forbidden to cross the border. Learning of the foreman's past, an enemy begins rustling cattle and driving them into Nevada. He then kidnaps the ranch owner's daughter and takes her to Nevada as well. That's the last straw—and the parolee-foreman rides to the rescue.

The Western Whirlwind (Universal, 1927)
d: Albert S. Rogell. 5 reels.
Jack Hoxie, Margaret Quimby, Claude Payton, Billy Engle, Edith Yorke, Jack Pratt.
A returning war veteran learns that his father has been killed. He gets the mayor to swear him in as new sheriff, then takes care of business.

Wet Gold (Submarine Film Corp./Goldwyn, 1921)
d: Ralph Ince. 6 reels.
Ralph Ince, Aleen Burr, Alicia Turner, Harry McNaughton, Thomas Megraine, John Butler, Charles McNaughton.
On a treasure hunt in the waters off Havana, a search crew is attacked by pirates.

Wet Paint (Paramount, 1926)
d: Arthur Rosson. 6 reels.
Raymond Griffith, Helene Costello, Bryant Washburn, Natalie Kingston, Henry Kolker.
Comedy of errors follows a wealthy bachelor through a baffling night of chance encounters, mistaken identities, and narrow escapes.

The Wharf Rat (Fine Arts Film Co./Triangle, 1916)
d: Chester Withey. 5 reels.
Mae Marsh, Robert Harron, Spottiswoode Aitken, Josephine Crowell, Pauline Starke, William H. Brown, Jack Brammall.
Polly, unhappy at home, runs away and disguises herself as a boy.

What a Night! (Paramount, 1928)
d: Edward Sutherland. 6 reels.
Bebe Daniels, Neil Hamilton, William Austin, Wheeler Oakman, Charles Sellon, Charles Hill Mailes, Ernie Adams.
Dorothy, a cub reporter, lands a big scoop with the help of Joe, son of the managing editor.

What a Wife Learned (First National, 1923)
d: John Griffith Wray. 7 reels.
Milton Sills, Francelia Billington, John Bowers, Bertram Johns, Ernest Butterworth, John Steppling.
A rancher takes a novelist wife, then suffers envy when he thinks her new literary friend is a threat to their marriage.

What Am I Bid? (Universal, 1919)
d: Robert Z. Leonard. 6 reels.
Mae Murray, Ralph Graves, Willard Louis, Chief Dark Cloud, John Cook, Gertrude Astor, Joseph W. Girard.
Betty, a mountain girl, is sold by her alcoholic father to satisfy his bar bill.

What Do Men Want? (Lois Weber Productions/Wid Gunning, Inc., 1921)
w, d: Lois Weber. 7 reels.

Claire Windsor, J. Frank Glendon, George Hackathorne, Hallam Cooley, Edith Kessler.
Boyd, an inventor, spends more time on his gadgets than with his family.

What Every Girl Should Know (Warner Bros., 1927)
d: Charles F. Reisner. 7 reels.
Patsy Ruth Miller, Ian Keith, Carmelita Geraghty, Carroll Nye, Mickey McBain, Lillian Langdon, Hazel Howell.
A teen-age girl and her younger brother are adopted by a young philanthropist. They run away from his home because of a misunderstanding, and their adoptive father searches for them, but without success. On her own, the girl becomes proficient as a tennis player, and at a tournament the philanthropist finds her and her brother again. The old misunderstandings are cleared up and the philanthropist successfully proposes marriage to his adoptive daughter.

What Every Woman Knows (Famous Players-Lasky/Paramount, 1921)
d: William C. DeMille. 7 reels.
Lois Wilson, Conrad Nagel, Charles Ogle, Fred Huntly, Guy Oliver, Winter Hall, Lillian Tucker, Claire McDowell, Robert Brower.
A railroad porter rises to become a Member of Commons, but his wife is the brains behind his success.

What Every Woman Learns (Thomas H. Ince/Paramount, 1919)
d: Fred Niblo. 5 reels.
Milton Sills, Enid Bennett, Irving Cummings, William Conklin, Lydia Knott, Theodore Roberts.
Amy loves Walter, but marries Gaylord because he's a lot more fun. Too late she discovers she made the wrong choice.

What Every Woman Wants (Jesse D. Hampton Productions/Robertson-Cole, 1919)
d: Jesse D. Hampton. 5 reels.
Wilfred Lucas, Grace Darmond, Forrest Stanley, Percy Challenger, Bertram Grassby, Barbara Tennant, Clare DuBrey, William DeVaull, Mary Warren, Charles French.
After hearing that her boyfriend has been killed in World War I, a young woman consents to marry her employer, although they are a mismatch. Then the boyfriend, who was in a prisoner of war camp, returns home safe and sound.

What Fools Men (First National Pictures, 1925)
d: George Archainbaud. 8 reels.
Lewis Stone, Shirley Mason, Ethel Grey Terry, Barbara Bedford, John Patrick, Hugh Allan, David Torrence, Lewis Dayton, Joyce Compton.
After being divorced from his wife for several years, an industrialist learns that he has a grown daughter.

What Fools Men Are (Pyramid Pictures/American Releasing Corp., 1922)
d: George Terwilliger. 6 reels.
Faire Binney, Lucy Fox, Joseph Striker, Huntley Gordon, Florence Billings, Harry Clay Blaney, Templar Saxe, J. Barney Sherry.
A flirtatious girl marries an admirer, not realizing that his disapproving father will cut him off without a cent.

What Happened at 22 (Frohman Amusement Corp./World Film Corp., 1916)
d: George Irving. 5 reels.
Arthur Ashley, Frances Nelson, Gladden James, Frank Burbeck.

Louise, a governess in a wealthy household, falls in love with her employer's grown son. But she is desired by an extortionist who's trying to rip off her boss.

What Happened to Father (Vitagraph, 1915)
d: C. Jay Williams. 5 reels.
Frank Daniels, Bernice Berner, Adele Kelly, Anna Laughlin, Billy Quirk, William Sloane, John Hollis, William Sellery, Frank Kingsley.
Comedic tale of a flustered father of two daughters who is trying to get his opera produced and his older daughter married at the same time.
This film, based on a short story of the same name by Mary Roberts Rinehart, was remade by Warner Bros. in 1927.

What Happened to Father (Warner Bros., 1927)
d: John Adolfi. 6 reels.
Warner Oland, Flobelle Fairbanks, John Miljan, Hugh Allen, Vera Lewis, William Demarest.
A timid scientist writes musical comedies on the side.
Remake of Vitagraph's 1915 film *What Happened to Father*.

What Happened to Jones (World Film Corp., 1915)
d: Fred Mace. 5 reels.
Fred Mace, Leonia Morgan, William Mandeville, Chester Barnett, Mary Charleson, Marjorie Blossom, Carolyn Rankin, Josie Sadler, Bradley Barker, Joe Daly.
Jones, a traveling salesman, falls for an heiress he meets on a train. At his first stop, though, he barely escapes a police raid and takes refuge in an academy for young ladies.

What Happened to Jones (Famous Players-Lasky/Paramount, 1920)
d: James Cruze. 5 reels.
Bryant Washburn, Margaret Loomis, J. Maurice Foster, Frank Jonasson, Lillian Leighton, Caroline Rankin, Richard Cummings.
Jimmy Jones agrees to transport bootleg hooch for a friend, and just barely escapes arrest.
Remake of the 1915 World Film Corp. film *What Happened to Jones*, both versions based on a play of the same name by George Broadhurst. This tale would be told yet again, in a 1926 Universal film.

What Happened to Jones (Universal, 1926)
d: William A. Seiter. 7 reels.
Reginald Denny, Marian Nixon, Otis Harlan, Melbourne McDowell, Frances Raymond, Emily Fitzroy, ZaSu Pitts, William Austin, Margaret Quimby.

Rapid-fire farce, with an engaged man getting into several complications on the eve of his wedding.
Third film version of the durable *What Happened to Jones*. It was previously filmed in 1915 and 1920.

What Happened to Rosa? (Goldwyn, 1921)
d: Victor L. Schertzinger. 5 reels.
Mabel Normand, Hugh Thompson, Doris Pawn, Tully Marshall, Eugenie Besserer, Buster Trow, Adolphe Menjou.
A bumbling shopgirl believes she is reincarnated from a Spanish noblewoman, and takes it to extremes.

What Love Can Do (Universal, 1916)
d: Jay Hunt. 5 reels.
Adele Farrington, C. Norman Hammond, O.C. Jackson, Kingsley Benedict, Mina Cunard, Mrs. Jay Hunt, H.F. Crane, Harry Mann, Violet Schram, Walter Belasco.
Paige, a widower and a mine owner, falls in love with his employee Lil, and she with him. They have a falling out,

though, when she sides with miners on strike against Paige. Meanwhile, his daughter arrives from New York and she proves to be the soothing balm that unites Paige and Lil and settles the strike to everyone's satisfaction.

What Love Forgives (World Film Corp., 1918)
d: Perry N. Vekroff. 5 reels.
Barbara Castleton, John Hines, John Bowers, Muriel Ostriche, Bobby Connelly, Florence Coventry, Joseph Smiley, Hazel Coates.
David, a New England college boy and fledgling composer, falls for a musical comedy star when she sings one of his own numbers.

What Love Will Do (Fox, 1921)
d: William K. Howard. 5 reels.
Edna Murphy, Johnnie Walker, Glen Cavender, Barbara Tennant, Richard Tucker, Edwin B. Tilton.
Johnny, a lad whose mother deserted him in infancy, grows to teenage and becomes a responsible member of the local church. There, he falls in love with the minister's daughter and coincidentally finds his mother, now repentant and a member of the flock.

What Money Can't Buy (Lasky Feature Plays/Paramount, 1917)
d: Lou Tellegen. 5 reels.
Jack Pickford, Louise Huff, Theodore Roberts, Hobart Bosworth, Raymond Hatton, James Cruze, James Neill, Bliss Chevalier.
Hale, an American financier, bids for the contract to build a transcontinental railway across the European kingdom of Maritizia. Meanwhile, Hale's son meets the Maritizian princess and they fall in love, thus complicating Hale's bargaining position.

What No Man Knows (Harry Garson Productions/Equity Pictures, 1921)
d: Harry Garson. 6 reels.
Clara Kimball Young, Lowell Sherman, Dorothy Wallace, William P. Carleton, Jeanne Carpenter, Dulcie Cooper.
Norma, a young woman who does charity work, still carries a torch for her childhood sweetheart, Craig, now married. She is surprised to find him in the slums, divorced from his wife and disgraced professionally. But Norma still loves him.

What Price Glory (Fox, 1927)
d: Raoul Walsh. 12 reels.
Victor McLaglen, Edmund Lowe, Dolores Del Rio, Phyllis Haver, William V. Mong, Elen Jurado, Leslie Fenton, August Tollaire, Barry Norton, Sammy Cohen, Ted McNamara.
An American army officer and sergeant bicker constantly, but are successful (at least partially) in love and war.

What Shall I Do? (W.W. Hodkinson, 1924)
d: John G. Adolfi. 6 reels.
Dorothy Mackaill, John Harron, Louise Dresser, William V. Mong, Betty Morrissey, Ann May, Ralph McCullough, Joan Standing, Tom O'Brien, Danny Hoy.
A new husband and father suffers an accident that causes him to lose his memory.

What Will People Say? (Popular Plays and Players/Metro, 1916)
d: Alice Blaché. 5 reels.
Olga Petrova, Fritz DeLint, Fraunie Fraunholz, Jean Thomas, Charles Dungan, Zadee Burbank, Marilyn Reid, Elenore Sutter, William Morse, John Dudley.

It's the age-old question: Should a woman marry for love or for money?

What Wives Want (Universal, 1923)
d: Jack Conway. 5 reels.
Ethel Grey Terry, Vernon Steele, Ramsey Wallace, Niles Welsh, Margaret Landis, Lila Leslie, Harry A. Burrows.
A neglected wife starts an affair with a married man.

What Women Love (Sol Lesser/Associated First National, 1920)
d: Nate C. Watt. 6 reels.
Annette Kellerman, Ralph Lewis, Wheeler Oakman, Carl Ullman, Walter Long, Bull Montana.
Miss Kellerman, the Australian swimming champion, stars as a girl who enjoys parading about in revealing bathing costumes.

What Women Want (American Cinema Corp./Pioneer, 1920)
d: George Archainbaud. 5 reels.
Louise Huff, Van Dyke Brooke, Robert Ames, Clara Beyers, Howard Truesdale, Betty Browne.
Francine, a young French woman, is engaged to marry American army officer William Holliday. When she comes to America to be with him, however, she finds he is about to be married to someone else. Francine's love turns to rage at this disclosure—until she discovers that William is simply on an undercover mission for the U.S. Secret Service, and that he has been true to Francine all long.

What Women Will Do (Associated Exhibitors/Pathé, 1921)
d: Edward José. 6 reels.
Anna Q. Nilsson, Earl Metcalfe, Allan Forrest, George Majeroni, Jane Jennings, Riley Hatch.
A young woman masquerades as the daughter-in-law of a dowager whose only son has died.

What Would You Do? (Fox, 1920)
d: Edmund Lawrence. 5 reels.
Madlaine Traverse, George McDaniel, Frank Elliott, Charles K. French, Lenore Lynard, Bud Geary, Edwin Booth Tilton, Cordelia Callahan.
After an American traveler is reported to have died in South America, his wife remarries. But reports of his demise have been greatly exaggerated. Upon returning home, he must decide whether to contact his newly married wife, or keep his silence.

Whatever She Wants (Fox, 1921)
d: C.R. Wallace. 5 reels.
Eileen Percy, Herbert Fortier, Richard Wayne, Otto Hoffman.
Engaged to marry a businessman, Enid impulsively decides to get a job in his office so she can keep an eye on him.

Whatever the Cost (Plaza Pictures/W.W. Hodkinson, 1918)
d: Robert Ensminger. 5 reels.
Ankta King, Bruce Smith, Charles Dudley, Stanley Pembroke, Gordon Sackville, Patrick Calhoun, Corinne Grant.
Out West, a tomboy blossoms forth as a beauty when she takes a job as a saloon dancer.

What's a Wife Worth? (Robertson-Cole Co./R-C Pictures, 1921)
w, d: William Christy Cabanne. 6 reels.
Casson Ferguson, Ruth Renick, Cora Drew, Virginia Caldwell, Alec Francis, Howard Gaye, Lillian Langdon,

Maxfield Stanley, Charles Wyngate, Helen Lynch.
When a young wife has a baby just at the time her husband's ex-wife is having one, the attending physician for both women switches the babies.

What's His Name (Lasky Feature Plays/Paramount, 1914)
d: Cecil B. DeMille. 5 reels.
Max Figman, Lolita Robertson, Fred Montague, Sydney Deane, Dick LaStrange, Merta Carpenter, Theodore Roberts.
Bitten by the showbiz bug, a young wife joins the chorus of a traveling show, leaving her husband and daughter behind.

What's Worth While? (Lois Weber Productions/Paramount, 1921)
w, d: Lois Weber. 6 reels.
Claire Windsor, Arthur Stuart Hull, Mona Lisa, Louis Calhern, Edwin Stevens.
When a sophisticated southern lady meets and falls for a westerner, she loves the man but is repulsed by his rough-hewn ways. To please her, he agrees to go to Europe and take lessons in continental manners for two years. At the end of that time, the two are married. Though the lady continues to love her husband, she soon tires of his artificial sophistication, and is happy at last to surrender to his more natural western manners.

What's Wrong With the Woman? (Goodman Corp./Equity Pictures, 1922)
d: David Carson Goodman. 7 reels.
Wilton Lackaye, Julia Swayne Gordon, Montagu Love, Rod La Rocque, Barbara Castleton, Helen Rowland, Hedda Hopper, Constance Bennett, Huntley Gordon, Paul McAllister.
A young wife discovers the new jazz-age style and insists that her husband get a raise so they can keep up with the times.

What's Your Hurry? (Famous Players-Lasky/Paramount, 1920)
d: Sam Wood. 5 reels.
Wallace Reid, Lois Wilson, Charles Ogle, Clarence Burton, Ernest Butterworth.
Dusty, a race car driver, loves a truck manufacturer's daughter. But her Papa objects.

What's Your Husband Doing? (Thomas H. Ince/Famous Players-Lasky/Paramount, 1920)
d: Lloyd Ingraham. 5 reels.
Douglas MacLean, Doris May, Walter Hiers, William Buckley, Norris Johnson, Alice Elliott, Margaret Livingston, J. P. Lockney.
Humorous happenings, when a suspicious wife hires a pair of bumbling lawyers to shadow her husband and report his comings and goings.

What's Your Reputation Worth? (Vitagraph, 1921)
d: Webster Campbell. 6 reels.
Corinne Griffith, Percy Marmont, Leslie Roycroft, George Howard, Robert Gaillard, Jane Jennings, Louise Prussing.
A secretary agrees to be corespondent in her boss' divorce. Secretly, she wishes she were really the "other woman."

The Wheel (Fox, 1925)
d: Victor Schertzinger. 8 reels.
Claire Adams, Mahlon Hamilton, Harrison Ford, Georgia Harris, Clara Horton, Margaret Livingston, David Torrence, Erin La Bissoniere, J. Russell Powell, Hazel Howell.
The "wheel" of the title is colored in *rouge et noir*, and it leads a young couple to the poorhouse.

Wheel of Chance   (First National, 1928)
d: Alfred Santell.   7 reels.
Richard Barthelmess, Bodil Rosing, Warner Oland, Ann Schaeffer, Lina Basquette, Margaret Livingston, Sidney Franklin, Martha Franklin.
A Russian family emigrates to the United States, where the family's son Nikolai becomes a prominent lawyer and, later, a district attorney. When a young man accused of accidental homicide is brought to trial, the D.A.'s mother instinctively asks Nikolai to go easy on him—resulting in a guilty verdict but only a short jail sentence. After the trial, it is revealed that the young man is Nikolai's brother, thought to have died in infancy.

The Wheel of the Law   (Rolfe Photoplays, Inc./Metro, 1916)
d: George D. Baker.   5 reels.
Emily Stevens, Frank Mills, Raymond McKee, Edwin Holt, Roma Raymond, Harry Davenport, Jerome N. Wilson, Charles Eldridge, Kalman Matus, Thomas McGrath.
Norton, an ambitious lawyer, climbs to the position of district attorney by winning numerous convictions, including some in which he manipulated evidence. But eventually, Norton finds himself having to prosecute his own brother-in-law in a capital case.

When a Girl Loves   (Universal, 1918)
d: Lois Weber, Phillips Smalley.   6 reels.
Mildred Harris, William Stowell, Wharton Jones, Alfred Paget, Willis Marks.
Out West, a notorious outlaw masquerades as a reverend minister... and is surprised to find that he likes the role.

When a Girl Loves   (Halperin Productions/Associated Exhibitors, 1924)
d: Victor Hugo Halperin.   6 reels.
Agnes Ayres, Percy Marmont, Robert McKim, Kathlyn Williams, John George, Mary Alden, George Siegmann, Ynez Seabury, William Orlamond, Rosa Rosanova, Leo White.
Sasha, who fled the Russian revolution and settled in the United States, marries a doctor, but still pines for the sweetheart she lost during the fall of Moscow. Then she meets him, alive and well, and married in America.

When a Man Loves   (Vitagraph, 1919)
d: Chester Bennett.   5 reels.
Earle Williams, Tom Guise, Margaret Loomis, Barbara Tennant, Edward McWade, Margaret McWade, John Elliott, George Hall, Jean Calhoune, William Buckley, Ida Darling.
When an Englishman in Tokyo on a diplomatic mission falls for Yuri, a shopkeeper's daughter, the girl he left behind turns green with envy.

When a Man Loves   (Warner Brothers, 1927)
d: Alan Crosland.   10 reels.
John Barrymore, Dolores Costello, Warner Oland, Sam De Grasse, Holmes Herbert, Stuart Holmes, Bertram Grassby, Tom Santschi, Marcelle Corday, Charles Clary, Templar Saxe, Eugenie Besserer, Rose Dione, Noble Johnson, Tom Wilson.
Picturesque drama based on Prevost's "Manon Lescaut," with Barrymore as a man who escapes from a French prison ship and takes his sweetheart with him.

When a Man Rides Alone   (William Russell Productions/Pathé, 1919)
d: Henry King.   5 reels.
William Russell, Carl Stockdale, Lule Warrenton, Olga Grey, Gordon Russell, Louis Cota, Demetrius Mitsoris.

Sykes, a Texas Ranger, rides into Mexico on the trail of gold-stealing bandidos.

When a Man Sees Red   (Fox, 1917)
d: Frank Lloyd.   5 reels.
William Farnum, Jewel Carmen, G. Raymond Nye, Lulu May Bower, Cora Drew, Marc Robbins, A. Burt Wesner.
Larry, a sailor seeking to avenge his sister's rape, ships out as first mate with Captain Sutton—never realizing that Sutton is the man guilty of violating Larry's sister.
This film was remade once in the silent era, in 1924 by Fox as *The Painted Lady*, which is also the title of the source material, a short story by Larry Evans.

When a Man's a Man   (Principal Pictures/Associated First National, 1924)
d: Edward F. Cline.   7 reels.
John Bowers, Marguerite De La Motte, Robert Frazer, June Marlowe, Forrest Robinson, Elizabeth Rhodes, Fred Stanton, George Hackathorne, Edward Hearne, John Fox Jr.
Helen turns down a marriage proposal from Knight, a wealthy idler, and tells him he needs to become more "manly." He takes her advice seriously, goes west, and becomes a cowboy. These two will meet again.

When a Woman Loves   (Rolfe Photoplays, Inc./Metro, 1915)
d: John W. Noble.   5 reels.
Emmy Wehlen, Arthur Ashley, Carlotta DeFelice, Frank Whitson.
Ruth, a waitress, tries to raise money by betting at the race track, visiting a pool hall (while dressed as a man), and working as a gambling decoy for card sharks.

When a Woman Sins   (Fox, 1918)
d: J. Gordon Edwards.   7 reels.
Theda Bara, Albert Roscoe, Joseph Swickard, Ogden Crane, Alfred W. Fremont, Jack Rollens, Genevieve Blinn.
Michael, a divinity student, falls in love with his father's nurse. But the old man dies, and the nurse, blaming herself, drifts into a life of debauchery.

When Baby Forgot   (Lasalida Film Corp./Pathé, 1917)
d: W. Eugene Moore.   5 reels.
Baby Marie Osborne, Fred Newburg, Margaret Nichols, Lee Hill.
Baby Marie's parents separate due to a misunderstanding, and the devastated girl works herself into a fever, thus uniting her parents in their love for her.

When Bearcat Went Dry   (C.R. Macauley Photoplays, Inc./World Film Corp., 1919)
d: Ollie L. Sellers.   6 reels.
Vangie Valentine, Walt Whitman, Bernard Durning, Winter Hall, Ed Brady, M.K. Wilson, Lon Chaney.
Mountain man "Bearcat" Stacy is a moonshiner, but a missionary's daughter is trying to save him from Demon Rum.

When Broadway Was a Trail   (Shubert Film Corp./World Film Corp., 1914)
d: O.A.C. Lund.   5 reels.
Barbara Tennant, O.A.C. Lund, Edward Roseman, Julia Stuart, Lindsay J. Hall, Mary Navarro, Alec B. Francis, George Cowl.
Historical drama about the love of Henry Minuet for Priscilla Elliott in 17th century New Amsterdam.

When Danger Calls   (Camera Pictures/Lumas Film Corp.,

1927)
d: Charles Hutchison. 5 reels.
William Fairbanks, Eileen Sedgwick, Ethan Laidlaw, Sally Long, Donald MacDonald, Hank Mann.
June, a wealthy welfare worker, buys a building for a settlement house, not realizing it's been condemned by the local fire inspector.

When Dawn Came (Hugh E. Dierker Productions, 1920)
d: Colin Campbell. 7 reels.
L.C. Shumway, James O. Barrows, Colleen Moore, Cathleen Kirkham, William Conklin, Master Isadore Cohen, "Peaches" Jackson.
When a kindly doctor who treats slum patients is persuaded to join a prestigious medical firm and "elevate" his practice, he ends up taking to drugs and alcohol. His benevolent ways will not return until he meets Mary, a blind girl who opens the doctor's eyes and causes his happy return to his charity patients.

When Do We Eat? (Thomas H. Ince/Paramount, 1918)
d: Fred Niblo. 5 reels.
Enid Bennett, Al Ray, Gertrude Claire, Jack Nelson, Robert McKim, Frank Hayes.
Nora, an actress in a touring company of *Uncle Tom's Cabin*, flees the sheriff when he comes to foreclose on the entire cast. After several wild and wooly adventures, Nora settles down with Jimmy Forbes, an undramatic but solidly honest bank clerk.

When Doctors Disagree (Goldwyn, 1919)
d: Victor L. Schertzinger. 5 reels.
Mabel Normand, Walter Hiers, Pomeroy Cannon, George Nichols, Fritzie Ridgeway, Alec B. Francis, William Buckley, James Gordon.
Small-town girl Millie Martin takes a train trip for the first time, and finds adventure, danger, and love with a carpet salesman posing as a doctor.

When Dreams Come True (Trem Carr Productions/Rayart, 1929)
d: Duke Worne. 6 reels.
Helene Costello, Rex Lease, Claire McDowell, Danny Hoy, Ernest Hilliard, Buddy Brown, George Periolat, Emmett King.
Out West, a poor blacksmith falls for wealthy Caroline.

When False Tongues Speak (Fox, 1917)
d: Carl Harbaugh. 5 reels.
Virginia Pearson, Carl Harbaugh, Hardee Kirkland, Claire Whitney, Carl Eckstrom, William E. Meehan.
Mary loves Fred, but it isn't exactly mutual. Although the two wed, Fred continues to see his mistress.

When Fate Decides (Fox, 1919)
d: Harry Millarde. 5 reels.
Madlaine Traverse, William Conklin, Clyde Fillmore, Claire DuBrey, Henry J. Herbert, John Cossar, Genevieve Blinn, Cordelia Callahan.
Vera, a wife whose husband callously carries on with a wealthy woman, is reluctant to file for divorce.

When Husbands Flirt (Columbia, 1925)
d: William Wellman. 6 reels.
Forrest Stanley, Dorothy Revier, Tom Ricketts, Ethel Wales, Maude Wayne, Frank Weed, Erwin Connelly.
The title is deceptive but tantalizing. Actually, this one's about a lawyer who *doesn't* flirt, but whose wife thinks he does.

When It Strikes Home (Charles K. Harris Feature Film Co./World Film Corp., 1915)
d: Perry N. Vekroff. 5 reels.
Edwin August, Grace Washbburn, Muriel Ostriche, William Bailey, Claire Mersereau, George Henry, Harry Knowles, Walter Fenner, Gladys Peck, J. Albert Hall, Charles K. Harris.
Weepy melodrama about Richard, a scion of wealth who impulsively marries Vera, a chorus girl, then has sober regrets in the morning. The marriage is quickly annulled and Richard marries his childhood sweetheart. Since his new wife is unable to have children, they decide to adopt a boy—and sure enough, it's Richard's own son, conceived on his forgotten wedding night with Vera.

When Knighthood Was In Flower
(Cosmopolitan/Paramount, 1922)
d: Robert G. Vignola. 12 reels.
Lyn Harding, Marion Davies, William Norris, Forrest Stanley, Pedro do Cordoba, William Powell, Ernest Glendinning, Arthur Forrest, Johnny Dooley, George Nash.
An aristocratic lady, set to be married to a king, falls for a knight in armor.

When Love Comes (Ray Carroll Productions/FBO of America, 1922)
d: William A. Seiter. 5 reels.
Harrison Ford, Helen Jerome Eddy, Fannie Midgley, Claire DuBrey, Joseph Bell, Gilbert Clayton, Buddy Messinger, Molly Gordon, James Barrows, Fay McKenzie.
A dam engineer whose wife has deserted him and their daughter returns to his home town and, meeting again with his former sweetheart, finds love's flame still simmering.

When Love Grows Cold (R-C Pictures/FBO of America, 1925)
d: Harry O. Hoyt. 7 reels.
Natacha Rambova, Clive Brook, Sam Hardy, Kathryn Hill, John Gough, Kathleen Martyn.
A former stage actress marries an inventor and, using her considerable dramatic skills, persuades the head of a large oil company to give her husband's new invention a chance.

When Love is King (Thomas A. Edison, Inc., 1916)
d: Ben Turbett. 5 reels.
Richard Tucker, Carroll McComas, Bigelow Cooper, Vivian Perry, John Sturgeon, Harold Meltzer, Carlton King, T. Tamamoto, Robert Brower, Charles Sutton, Guido Colucci, Helen Strickland, Lucille Allen, James Harris.
King Felix of Nordland must marry the princess of Trebizond, according to royal tradition. But on a trip to America, the king falls in love with Marcia, a financier's daughter and a commoner. What to do? No problem, says Marcia's dad. He simply buys the entire country of Trebizond, installs his daughter as princess, and... let the wedding march begin!

When Love Was Blind (Thanhouser/Pathé, 1917)
d: Frederick Sullivan. 5 reels.
Florence LaBadie, Thomas Curran, Inda Palmer, Boyd Marshall, Harris Gordon, Gladys Leslie, Ida Darling, Ethyle Cooke.
Burton, a portrait painter, falls in love with a blind girl who also had a gift for art before losing her sight. He arranges for an operation to cure her blindness—and the girl, her sight restored, completes her late father's unfinished masterpiece.

When Men Are Tempted (Vitagraph, 1917)

d: William Wolbert. 5 reels.

Mary Anderson, Alfred Whitman, Otto Lederer, S.E. Jennings.

John and Arthur, though college buddies, fight over the girl they both love.

When Men Desire (Fox, 1919)
d: J. Gordon Edwards. 5 reels.
Theda Bara, Flemming Ward, G. Raymond Nye, Florence Martin, Maude Hill, Edward Elkas.
During World War I, a young woman is desired by both an American aviator and a German army major.

When Odds Are Even (Fox, 1923)
d: James Flood. 5 reels.
William Russell, Dorothy Devore, Lloyd Whitlock, Frank Beal, Allan Cavan.
Rival mine engineers compete for the rights to a rich opal source in the South Seas.

When Rome Ruled (Pathé Frères/Eclectic Film Co., 1914)
d: George Fitzmaurice. 5 reels.
Nelle Craig, Clifford Bruce, Riley Hatch, Walter R. Seymour, Countess de Merstina, A.H. Busby, Charles E. Bunnell.
In ancient Rome, a Christian girl is recruited by a high priest to be a vestal virgin, but she escapes with the aid of the Roman governor's son, who will grow to love her.

When Seconds Count (Duke Worne Productions/Rayart, 1927)
d: Oscar Apfel. 5 reels.
Billy Sullivan, Mildred June, Rose Kimman, Jerome LaGrasse, Marie Messenger, James Aubrey, Earl Wayland Bowman, Joseph Girard.
Billy, a wealthy idler, is sent by his exasperated father to a small town to make good.

When the Clouds Roll By (Fairbanks/United Artists, 1919)
d: Victor Fleming. 6 reels.
Douglas Fairbanks, Kathleen Clifford, Herbert Grimwood, Frank Campeau, Ralph Lewis, Daisy Robinson, Albert MacQuarrie.
A psychiatrist conducts bizarre experiments, using humans as guinea pigs. One of his subjects, Daniel Boone Brown (Fairbanks), endures his experiments and ends up a hero when he rescues his girlfriend from a flood.

When the Desert Calls (Pyramid Pictures/American Releasing Corp., 1922)
d: Ray C. Smallwood. 6 reels.
Violet Heming, Robert Frazer, Sheldon Lewis, Huntley Gordon, J. Barney Sherry, David Wall, Julia Swayne Gordon, Nick Thompson, Tammany Young.
As World War I ends, the British government seeks a mysterious desert sheik to reward him for his bravery. Louise, an army nurse, recognizes the "sheik" as her long-missing husband.

When the Devil Drives (Leah Baird Productions/Associated Exhibitors, 1922)
d: Paul Scardon. 5 reels.
Leah Baird, Arline Pretty, Richard Tucker, Vernon Steel, Katherine Lewis.
Jealousy drives a young woman to wound her lover with a knife when she learns he is planning to marry another woman.

When the Door Opened (Fox, 1925)
d: Reginald Barker. 7 reels.

Jacqueline Logan, Walter McGrail, Margaret Livingston, Robert Cain, Frank Keenan, Roy Laidlaw, Diana Miller, Walter Chung.
A married man unexpectedly walks in on his wife and her lover, and shoots the man. Now a fugitive from justice, he escapes to the Canadian forest and becomes a hermit. But there's a happy ending of sorts, when the fugitive falls in love with a lovely young backwoods woman.

When the Law Rides (FBO Pictures, 1928)
d: Robert DeLacy. 5 reels.
Tom Tyler, Jane Reid, Frankie Darro, Harry O'Connor, Harry Woods, Charles Thurston, Bill Nestel, Barney Furey.
O'Malley, a Secret Service agent, masquerades as a notorious outlaw to infiltrate a gang.

When the Wife's Away (Columbia, 1926)
d: Frank Strayer. 6 reels.
George K. Arthur, Dorothy Revier, Tom Ricketts, Bobby Dunn, Ned Sparks, Lincoln Plummer, Ina Rorke.
Young newlyweds learn that the husband is to inherit a fortune, provided he has "made good." Eager to display affluence, they rent a luxury apartment to entertain his uncle, who's come to check on his nephew's progress.

When We Were Twenty-One (Famous Players/Paramount, 1915)
d: Edwin S. Porter, Hugh Ford. 5 reels.
William Elliott, Charles Waldron, Marie Empress, Helen Lutrell, Winifred Allen, Arthur Hoops, Charles Coleman, George Backus.
Four bachelors comply with a dying friend's request, and adopt his baby boy.

When We Were Twenty-One (Jesse D. Hampton/Pathé, 1920)
d: Henry King. 5 reels.
H.B. Warner, Claire Anderson, James Morrison, Christine Mayo, Claude Payton, Minna Grey.
Remake of the 1915 Paramount film *When We Were Twenty-One*, both versions based on the play of the same name by Henry V. Esmond.

When You and I Were Young (Apollo Pictures, Inc./Art Dramas, Inc., 1917)
d: Alice Guy Blaché. 5 reels.
Alma Hanlon, Louis Thiel, Harry Benham, Florence Short, Robert Mantell Jr., Louis Stearns.
Dorothy, a country girl, meets an artist from the city, and they fall in love.

Where Are My Children? (Universal, 1916)
d: Lois Weber, Phillips Smalley. 5 reels.
Tyrone Power, Helen Riaume, Juan De La Cruz, Marie Walcamp, Cora Drew, Rene Rogers, A.D. Blake, C.Norman Hammond, William J. Hope.
Drama about a man who believes in having large families, married to a woman who refuses to have children.

Where East is East (MGM, 1929)
d: Tod Browning. 7 reels.
Lon Chaney, Estelle Taylor, Lupe Velez, Lloyd Hughes, Louis Stern, Mrs. Wong Wing.
A trapper's wife tries to seduce her daughter's fiancé.

Where is My Father? (Exclusive Features, Inc., 1916)
d: Joseph Adelman. 7 reels.
May Ward, William Sorrell, Ed F. Roseman, Harold J. Jarrett, Agnes Marc, George Henry, Roy Pilcher.

WHERE WAS I? (1925). Reginald Denny, one of the silent film's preeminent light comedians, appears with Marion Nixon, as a man accused of loving two women at once. Of course, he only has eyes for Marion. Or does he?

* * * * *

Fantasy drama about a girl whose deceased father is reincarnated as a powerful black dog. When she is threatened by a scoundrel bent on seducing her, she is rescued by the dog, i.e., her loving Pa!

Where is My Wandering Boy Tonight? (B.F. Zeidman Productions/Equity Pictures, 1922)
d: James P. Hogan, Millard Webb. 7 reels.
Cullen Landis, Carl Stockdale, Virginia True Boardman, Patsy Ruth Miller, Kathleen Key, Ben Beeley, Clarence Badger Jr.
Beecher, a chap who has fallen for a chorus girl and stolen to support her lifestyle, goes to jail for grand larceny. During a jail break, the prisoners capture the warden and are just about to kill him when Beecher steps in and rescues him. This act of bravery secures a pardon for Beecher, who returns home, much wiser, to his mother and small-town sweetheart.

Where is This West? (Universal, 1923)
d: George E. Marshall. 5 reels.
Jack Hoxie, Mary Philbin, Joseph Girard, Bob McKenzie, Sid Jordan, Slim Cole, Bernard Siegel.
A milkman learns he has inherited a half interest in a western ranch.

Where Lights are Low (Hayakawa Feature Play Co./R-C Pictures, 1921)
d: Colin Campbell. 6 reels.
Sessue Hayakawa, Togo Yamamoto, Goro Kino, Gloria Payton, Kiyosho Satow, Misao Seki, Toyo Fujita, Jay Eaton, Harold Holland.
Wong Shih, a Chinese prince, loves a gardener's daughter. Before he can pledge his love, however, his aristocratic father sends him to San Francisco to get a formal education. One day after graduation, he visits a San Francisco slave auction and discoves his beloved is up for sale. Wong Shih bids $5,000 for her, and wins her. Now he must find some way to get the money.

Where Love Is (Thomas A. Edison, Inc./Mutual, 1917)
d: Alan Crosland. 5 reels.
Ann Murdock, Shirley Mason, Mabel Trunnelle, Henry Stanford, Bigelow Cooper, William Wadsworth, Raymond McKee, Helen Strickland, Edith Wright, Jessie Stevens.
Norma is adored by Padgate, a struggling artist, but she's indifferent to him. Instead, she agrees to marry the wealthy young man her mother has picked out for her. But there will be surprises at the wedding ceremony, and just in time Norma will come to realize that Padgate's humble studio is "where love is."

Where Love Leads (Fox, 1916)
d: Frank C. Griffin. 5 reels.
Ormi Hawley, Rockcliffe Fellowes, Royal Byron, Haydn Stevenson, Charles Craig, Herbert Evans, Albert Gran, Maud Hall Macey, Ilean Hume, Dorothy Rogers.
When an Englishwoman sends her two daughters to America for their safety, the girls run afoul of a white slavery ring.

Where Men are Men (Vitagraph, 1921)
d: William Duncan. 5 reels.
William Duncan, Edith Johnson, George Stanley, Tom Wilson, Gertrude Wilson, Harry Lonsdale, George Kunkel, William McCall, Charles Dudley.
Just outside of Death Valley, a prospector meets and falls for a dance hall girl.

Where the North Begins (Warner Brothers, 1923)
d: Chester Franklin. 6 reels.
Rin-Tin-Tin, Claire Adams, Walter McGrail, Pat Hartigan, Myrtle Owen, Charles Stevens, Fred Huntley.
A dog raised in the Wild North by a pack of wolves rescues a fur trapper.

Where the Pavement Ends (Metro, 1923)
d: Rex Ingram. 8 reels.
Edward Connelly, Alice Terry, Ramon Novarro, Harry T. Morey, John George.
In the South Seas, a minister's daughter fights off a drunken trader while trying to join her true love, a young native chief.

Where the West Begins (William Russell Productions/Pathé, 1919)
d: Henry King. 5 reels.
William Russell, Eileen Percy, J. Cullen Landis, Frederick Vroom, Carl Stockdale, Alfred Ferguson.
Depressed and almost suicidal, a young New Yorker goes West to cheer up, and runs into an exciting adventure involving cattle rustlers, bare-knuckle brawls, and the lassoing of a "purty" gal.

Where the Worst Begins (Co-Artists Productions/Truart Film Corp., 1925)
d: John McDermott. 6 reels.
Ruth Roland, Alec B. Francis, Matt Moore, Grace Darmond, Roy Stewart, Derelys Perdue, Theodore Lorch, Ernie Adams, J.P. Lockney, Robert Burns, Floyd Shackelford.
Out West, a city-bred girl tires of the wide open spaces, and seeks a companionate relationship with a New York boy — preferably a rich one.

Where Was I? (Universal, 1925)
d: William A. Seiter. 7 reels.
Reginald Denny, Marion Nixon, Pauline Garon, Tyrone Power Sr., Lee Moran, Otis Harlan, Chester Conklin.
A businessman proposes to his sweetheart and they make wedding plans. Out of the blue, a strange woman turns up and claims to be the man's wife, with convincing proof. Now he has a double dilemma: keeping his "wife" and his fiancée apart, and trying to remember where he really was on his supposed wedding day.

Which Woman? (Universal, 1918)
d: Tod Browning, Harry Pollard. 5 reels.
Ella Hall, Eddie Sutherland, Edward Jobson, Priscilla Dean, Andrew Robson, Harry Carter.
Doris, a runaway bride, dashes from the church and into a parked car, ordering the chauffeur to drive away, quickly. It's all a case of mistaken identity, but the pair in the getaway car fall in love anyway.

While Justice Waits (Fox, 1922)
d: Bernard Dunning. 5 reels.
Dustin Farnum, Irene Rich, Gretchen Hartman, Earl Metcalfe, Junior Delameter, Frankie Lee, Hector Sarno, Peaches Jackson.
A prospector strikes it rich in Alaska, then returns home to find his wife and their infant son gone. They meet again after the prospector spends years searching for his family.

While London Sleeps (Warner Bros., 1926)
d: Howard Bretherton. 6 reels.
Rin-Tin-Tin, Otto Matiesen, De Witt Jennings, Helene Costello.
A sinister killer prowls the streets of London.

While New York Sleeps (Fox, 1920)
d: Charles J. Brabin.   8 reels.
Estelle Taylor, Marc McDermott, William Locke, Harry Southern, Earl Metcalf.
Episodic drama depicting three vignettes of love, passion, and revenge.

While Paris Sleeps (W.W. Hodkinson, 1923)
d: Maurice Tourneur.   6 reels.
Lon Chaney, Mildred Manning, John Gilbert, Hardee Kirkland, Jack McDonald, J. Farrell McDonald.
In Paris, a love-struck sculptor craves his model, but she loves a young American tourist.
This film was produced in 1920 as *The Glory of Love*, but not released until 1923, with a new title.

While Satan Sleeps (Famous Players-Lasky/Paramount, 1922)
d: Joseph Henabery.   7 reels.
Jack Holt, Wade Boteler, Mabel Van Buren, Fritzi Brunette, Will R. Walling, J.P. Lockney, Fred Huntley, Bobby Mack, Sylvia Ashton, Herbert Standing.
Remake of the 1916 Paramount movie *The Parson of Panamint*, both films being on the short story of that name by Peter Bernard Kyne.

While the City Sleeps (MGM, 1928)
d: Jack Conway.   9 reels.
Lon Chaney, Anita Page, Carroll Nye, Wheeler Oakman, Mae Busch, Polly Moran, Lydia Yeamans Titus, William Orlamond, Richard Carle.
Dan, a hard-working city detective, falls in love against his own better judgment—with a girl who's gotten herself involved with gangsters.

While the Devil Laughs (Fox, 1921)
d: George W. Hill.   5 reels.
Louise Lovely, William Scott, G. Raymond Nye, Edwin Booth Tilton, Wilson Hummell, Molly Shafer, Oleta Ottis, Coy Watson Jr., Helen Field.
Mary, a cafe hostess with a touch of larceny (she steals from customers), is persuaded to "go straight" by a young inventor who's taken an interest in her.

Whims of Society (World Film Corp., 1918)
d: Travers Vale.   5 reels.
Ethel Clayton, Frank Beamish, Jack Drumier, Frank Mayo, Katherine Johnson, Zadee Burbank, Pinna Nesbit.
In New England, factories are run as sweat shops, where women work long hours for low pay. One mill owner's son falls in love with Nora, one of the workers, and promises to deliver her from her menial existence. Papa finds out and disowns the boy, but the couple get married anyway.

The Whip (Paragon Films, Inc., 1917)
d: Maurice Tourneur.   8 reels.
Alma Hanlon, June Elvidge, Irving Cummings, Warren Cook, Paul McAllister, Alfred Hemming, Dion Titheradge, Jean Dumar.
A rejected suitor plots to sabotage the vehicle in which his beloved's prize racehorse, nicknamed "The Whip," is being transported to the race track.

The Whip (First National, 1928)
d: Charles J. Brabin.   7 reels.
Dorothy Mackaill, Ralph Forbes, Anna Q. Nilsson, Lowell Sherman, Albert Gran, Marc MacDermott, Lou Payne, Arthur Clayton.
Diana, a wealthy young woman, falls in love with an amnesiac gent who may—or may not—be already married. "The Whip" of the title is the name of Diana's horse, who is entered in a critically important race.

The Whip Woman (First National, 1928)
d: Joseph C. Boyle.   6 reels.
Estelle Taylor, Antonio Moreno, Lowell Sherman, Hedda Hopper, Julanne Johnston, Loretta Young, Jack Ackroyd.
In Hungary, a whip-wielding Hungarian woman rescues a dissolute nobleman from his suicidal tendencies, and they marry.

The Whipping Boss (Monogram, 1924)
d: J.P. McGowan.   6 reels.
Lloyd Hughes, Wade Boteler, Eddie Phillips, J.P. McGowan, Barbara Bedford, Billy Elmer, Andrew Waldron, George Cummings, Lydia Knott, Clarence Geldert.
In the Pacific Northwest, timber men are forced to work under inhumane conditions—one of them being subjected to the whip of a cruel overseer.

The Whirl of Life (Cort Film Corp., 1915)
d: Oliver D. Bailey.   6 reels.
Vernon Castle, Irene Castle, Arthur Stanford, Kate Blanke, William Carleton Sr., Edward Cort.
Vernon and Irene Castle play themselves in this lightweight vehicle, which features the pair performing several dance numbers.

The Whirlpool (Select Pictures Corp., 1918)
d: Alan Crosland.   5 reels.
Alice Brady, H.E. Herbert, J.H. Gilmour, William Davidson, Robert Walker, Warren Cook, W.E. Williams, Louise Lee, Virginia Lee, Mabel Guilford, Wallace Clarke.
Offbeat love story about a young man who runs afoul of the law while trying to impress a young lady. He's convicted but pardoned by the judge, and then the object of his affections marries—that judge!

The Whirlpool of Destiny (Universal, 1916)
d: Otis Turner.   5 reels.
Flora Parker DeHaven, Jack Mulhall, Charles H. Mailes, Edward Hearn, Bertram Grassby, Nanine Wright, Jack Lott, Marjorie Blinn.
Father and son both fall in love with the same young woman.

The Whirlwind of Youth (Paramount, 1927)
d: Rowland V. Lee.   6 reels.
Lois Moran, Vera Voronina, Donald Keith, Alyce Mills, Larry Kent, Gareth Hughes, Charles Lane.
In Paris, two expatriates—an English girl and an American boy—fall in love, but their idylls are interrupted by the onset of World War I.

The Whisper Market (Vitagraph, 1920)
d: George L. Sargent.   5 reels.
Corinne Griffith, George Howard, George MacQuarrie, James O'Neill, Eulalie Jensen, Howard Truesdale, Jacob Kingsbury.
Blackmailers lure a diplomat's wife into a compromising situation, then threaten to use the photographs against her husband.

The Whispered Name (Universal, 1924)
d: King Baggot.   5 reels.
Ruth Clifford, Charles Clary, William E. Lawrence, May Mersch, John Merkyl, Niles Welch, Hayden Stevenson, Buddy Messinger, Herbert Fortier, Joseph North, Emily

Fitzroy, Jane Starr, Carl Stockdale.

Anne, a would-be bride, is saved from a misalliance by the arrival of a wealthy admirer, Van Kreel. Later, however, she learns that Van Kreel's wife is suing him for divorce and naming Anne as corespondent.

Whispering Canyon (Banner Productions, 1926)
d: Tom Forman. 6 reels.
Jane Novak, Robert Ellis, Lee Shumway, Josef Swickard, Eugene Pallette, James Mason, Edward Brady.
In California following World War I, two neighboring ranchers team up to thwart sabotage planned by an unscrupulous timber man.

The Whispering Chorus (Famous Players-Lasky/Artcraft, 1918)
d: Cecil B. DeMille. 7 reels.
Raymond Hatton, Kathlyn Williams, Elliott Dexter, Edythe Chapman, John Burton, Parks Jones, Tully Marshall, Guy Oliver, W.H. Brown, James Neill, Noah Beery, Gustav von Seyffertitz, Walter Lynch, Edna Mae Cooper, Gibson Gowland.
An underpaid bookkeeper decides to embezzle a small sum of money from the company, then panics when he hears of an impending audit.

Whispering Devils (Harry Garson Productions/Equity Pictures Corp., 1920)
d: John M. Voshell. 6 reels.
Conway Tearle, Rosemary Theby, Sam Sothern, Esther Ralston, Warren Millais, Lenore Lynard, Walter Bytell, Hal Wilson.
Faversham, a fire-breathing preacher, condemns a young woman for having had an illegitimate child. But the good reverend discovers his own frailty when he finds himself alone with an attractive parishoner and lets nature, not theology, take its course.

Whispering Smith (Signal Film Corp./Mutual, 1916)
d: J.P. McGowan. 5 reels.
Helen Holmes, Belle Hutchinson, J.P. McGowan, Paul C. Hurst, Leo D. Maloney, F.M. Van Norman, Samuel Appel, Walter Rogers, Thomas G. Lingham.
Railroad detective "Whispering" Smith is hired to solve a series of train robberies.

Whispering Smith (Metropolitan Pictures/Producers Distributing Corp., 1926)
d: George Melford. 7 reels.
H.B. Warner, Lillian Rich, John Bowers, Lilyan Tashman, Eugene Pallette, Richard Neill, James Mason, Warren Rodgers, Nelson McDowell, Robert Edeson.

Remake of the 1916 Signal Film Corp. picture *Whispering Smith*, both versions based on the novel of the same name by Frank Hamilton Spearman.

Whispering Winds (Tiffany-Stahl Productions, 1929)
d: James Flood. 7 reels. (Part talkie.)
Patsy Ruth Miller, Malcolm McGregor, Eve Southern, Eugenie Besserer, James Marcus.
When a New England girl leaves for the big city and a singing career, her forlorn sweetheart marries another local girl. He still carries a torch for the singer, though.

Whispering Wires (Fox, 1926)
d: Albert Ray. 6 reels.
Anita Stewart, Edmund Burns, Charles Clary, Otto Matieson, Mack Swain, Arthur Housman, Charles Conklin,
Frank Campeau, Scott Welsh, Mayme Kelso, Charles Sellon, Cecille Evans.
Mix of mystery and comedy, as two bumbling detectives uncover the machinations of an unbalanced inventor with homocidal tendencies.

Whispers (Selznick Pictures Corp./Select Pictures Corp., 1920)
d: William P.S. Earle. 6 reels.
Elaine Hammerstein, Matt Moore, Phillips Tead, Charles Gerard, Ida Darling, Bernard Randall, Warren Cook, Templar Saxe, Maude Hill, Edgar Hudson, George Stevens.
Darrick, a reporter for a scandal sheet, is assigned to cover the alleged liaisons between a society woman and her married lover... and winds up falling in love with the lady in question.

The Whistle (William S. Hart Productions/Paramount, 1921)
w, d: Lambert Hillyer. 6 reels.
William S. Hart, Myrtle Stedman, Frank Brownlee, Frankie Lee, Will Jim Hatton, Richard Headrick, Robert Kortman.
Tragedy results when a callous mill owner rejects his foreman's recommendation that he make safety repairs to the mill equipment.

White and Unmarried (Famous Players-Lasky/Paramount, 1921)
d: Tom Forman. 5 reels.
Thomas Meighan, Jacqueline Logan, Grace Darmond, Walter Long, Lloyd Whitlock, Fred Vroom, Marian Skinner, Georgie Stone, Jack Herbert.
In Paris, a newly rich reformed burglar meets Dorothea, a young woman he has desired since the day he saw her photograph while robbing her parents' home.

The White Black Sheep (Inspiration Pictures/First National, 1926)
d: Sidney Olcott. 7 reels.
Richard Barthelmess, Patsy Ruth Miller, Constance Howard, Erville Alderson, William H. Tooker, Gino Corrado, Albert Prisco, Sam Appel, G.L. McDonell, Templar Saxe.
A young British officer joins his country's forces in Palestine, and promptly falls in love with Zelie, a Greek dancer.

The White Circle (Paramount, 1920)
d: Maurice Tourneur. 5 reels.
Spottiswoode Aitken, Janice Wilson, Harry S. Northrup, Jack Gilbert, Wesley Barry, Jack McDonald.
In London, a banker foolishly mismanages funds belonging to a criminal syndicate. When the hoodlums come after him, the banker and his daughter flee to the relative safety of an old castle in Scotland.

The White Desert (MGM, 1925)
d: Reginald Barker. 7 reels.
Pat O'Malley, Claire Windsor, Robert Frazer, Frank Currier, William Eugene, Roy Laidlaw, Sojin, Priscilla Bonner, Snitz Edwards, Milton Ross, Matthew Betz.
Railroad engineers prepare to blast a tunnel through a Colorado mountain.

The White Dove (Jesse D. Hampton Productions, 1920)
d: Henry King. 5 reels.
H.B. Warner, James O. Barrows, Clare Adams, Herbert Greenwood, Donald McDonald, Virginia Lee Corbin, Ruth Renick.
Tragically disillusioned, a cuckold severs ties with his family and goes abroad. He soon finds that running away from a

problem is no solution.

White Fang (R-C Pictures/FBO of America, 1925)
d: Lawrence Trimble. 6 reels.
Theodore von Eltz, Ruth Dwyer, Matthew Betz, Walter Perry, Charles Murray, Tom O'Brien, Steve Murphy, John Burch, Margaret McWade.
Molly, daughter of a mine superintendent, marries the owner of White Fang, a man-eating dog, and then discovers that her new husband is robbing her father's mine.

White Flannels (Warner Bros., 1927)
d: Lloyd Bacon. 7 reels.
Louise Dresser, Jason Robards, Virginia Brown Faire, Warner Richmond, George Nichols, Brooks Benedict.
A young man wants to marry his local sweetheart, but his mother insists he get a college education instead.

The White Flower (Famous Players-Lasky/Paramount, 1923)
d: Julia Crawford Ivers. 6 reels.
Betty Compson, Edmund Lowe, Edward Martindel, Arline Pretty, Sylvia Ashton, Arthur Hoyt, Leon Barry, Lily Philips, Reginald Carter, Maui Kaito.
In Hawaii, a halfcaste girl receives a perfect white gardenia from Rutherford, a suitor. David, who was previously rejected by her, becomes insanely jealous and has a local witch doctor place a curse on Rutherford.

White Gold (DeMille Pictures, 1927)
d: William K. Howard. 7 reels.
George Bancroft, Jetta Goudal, Kenneth Thompson, George Nichols, Clyde Cook, Robert Perry.
Heavy drama about a rancher's son who marries a Mexican dancer, and his father's resentment of the girl. The rancher tries to make his son believe his wife is unfaithful, sowing such distrust in their relationship that they quarrel and wind up sleeping in separate rooms. While alone, the wife is visited by a new ranch hand bent on seduction. She shoots and kills him in self-defense, but her hateful father-in-law takes the credit for the killing, saying he caught the pair in an illicit embrace. Which one will the husband believe?

The White Heather (Maurice Tourneur Productions/Paramount, 1919)
d: Maurice Tourneur. 6 reels.
H.E. Herbert, Ben Alexander, Ralph Graves, Mabel Ballin, Jack Gilbert, Spottiswoode Aitken.
The only record of a secret marriage is a certificate in a sunken yacht, "The White Heather." Two men go underwater diving—one to secure the certificate, the other to destroy it.

The White Lie (Paralta Plays, Inc./W.W. Hodkinson, 1918)
d: Howard Hickman. 5 reels.
Bessie Barriscale, Edward Coxen, Charles Gunn, Mary Jane Irving, James Farley, David Kirby, Aggie Herring.
Tangled mystery about a wife who, unable to conceive a child, adopts a baby in her husband's absence and then tells him it is their own.

White Lies (Fox, 1920)
d: Edward J. LeSaint. 5 reels.
Gladys Brockwell, William Scott, Josephine Crowell, Evans Kirk, Violet Schram, Charles K. French, Howard Scott, Lule Warrenton.
A young woman's husband is reported killed in the war, and she then remarries and has a child. But when her first husband returns alive and well, the question arises: Who's the baby's father?

White Man (B.P. Schulberg Productions, 1924)
d: Louis Gasnier. 7 reels.
Kenneth Harlan, Alice Joyce, Walter Long, Clark Gable, Stanton Heck.
Andrea, an impecunious aristocrat, feels compelled to marry for money. She visits the area of South Africa where her fiancé owns a diamond mine and there meets an aviator known among the natives as "White Man" and revered as a god. When she is kidnapped by a rogue thief and is then rescued by the aviator, Andrea comes to realize she's fallen in love with him.

A White Man's Chance (Kerrigan Productions Co./Pathé, 1919)
d: Ernest C. Warde. 5 reels.
J. Warren Kerrigan, Lillian Walker, Joseph J. Dowling, Howard Davies, Andrew Arbuckle, Joseph Hazelton, George Field, Joseph Ray, Richard Loreno.
On undercover assignment to probe a young swain's true character, an attorney himself falls for the lady in the case.

The White Man's Law (Famous Players-Lasky/Paramount, 1918)
d: James Young. 5 reels.
Sessue Hayakawa, Florence Vidor, Jack Holt, Herbert Standing, Mayme Kelso, Forrest Seabury, Joseph Swickard, Ernest Joy, Charles West, Noah Beery, Clarissa Selwynne.
In Africa, a roguish ivory trader seduces a young French woman, then abandons her. But his partner, a British-educated Arab who secretly loves the woman, sets out to avenge her honor.

White Mice (Pinellas Films/Associated Exhibitors, 1926)
d: Edward H. Griffith. 6 reels.
Jacqueline Logan, Ernest Hilliard, Bigelow Cooper, Lucius Henderson, William Powell, Marie Burke, Harlan Knight, Reginald Sheffield, William Wadsworth, Richard Lee.
Forrester, a member of a service organization called the White Mice Club, travels to a Latin American country to rescue a former president being held in captivity.

The White Monkey (Associated Pictures/First National, 1925)
d: Phil Rosen. 7 reels.
Barbara LaMarr, Thomas Holding, Henry Victor, George F. Marion, Colin Campbell, Charles Mack, Flora LeBreton, Tammany Young.
In England, a flirtatious young married woman does nothing to discourage the amorous advances of her husband's best friend.

The White Moth (Maurice Tourneur Productions/Associated First National, 1924)
d: Maurice Tourneur. 7 reels.
Barbara LaMarr, Conway Tearle, Charles DeRoche, Ben Lyon, Edna Murphy, Josie Sedgwick, Kathleen Kirkham, William Orlamond.
In Paris, a young man marries The White Moth, a dancer, and arouses the enmity of her former partner.

White Oak (Paramount, 1921)
d: Lambert Hillyer. 6 reels.
William S. Hart, Vola Vale, Alexander Gaden, Robert Walker, Bert Sprotte, Helen Holly, Standing Bear.
Out West, a gambler known as White Oak searches for the man who betrayed his sister.

560

The White Outlaw (Universal, 1925)
d: Clifford Smith. 5 reels.
Jack Hoxie, Duke R. Lee, Marceline Day, William Welsh, Floyd Shackelford, Charles Brinley.
Lupton, a cowboy accused of horse stealing, proves that it is not he who is releasing the horses from their captivity, but rather a wild horse known as The White Outlaw.

White Pants Willie (B & H Enterprises/First National, 1927)
d: Charles Hines. 7 reels.
Johnny Hines, Leila Hyams, Henry Barrows, Ruth Dwyer, Walter Long, Margaret Seddon, George Kuwa.
Comedy about Willie, a garage mechanic who always dresses in sporty white trousers.

The White Pearl (Famous Players/Paramount, 1915)
d: Edwin S. Porter, Hugh Ford. 5 reels.
Marie Doro, Thomas Holding, Walter Craven, Robert Broderick, Cesare Gravina, Maude Granger, Robert Cain.
Shipwrecked on her way to Japan, a young American woman floats ashore in Yokohama, where she is declared a goddess by the natives because of the Buddhist pearl necklace she wears.

White Pebbles (Action Pictures/Pathé, 1927)
d: Richard Thorpe. 5 reels.
Wally Wales, Olive Hasbrouck, Walter Maly, Tom Bay, Harry Todd, K. Nambu.
Out West, a tenderfoot tries to solve a case involving cattle rustling and the deaths of several ranch hands.

The White Raven (Rolfe Photoplays, Inc./Metro, 1917)
d: George D. Baker. 5 reels.
Ethel Barrymore, William B. Davidson, Walter Hitchcock, George A. Wright, Viola A. Fortescue, Herbert Pattee, Mario Majeroni, Phil Sanford, Etherl Dayton, Ned Finlay.
In Alaska, a saloon singer billed as "The White Raven" offers herself as the prize in a poker game... and nets one thousand dollars in the gamble.

The White Rose (D.W. Griffith, Inc./United Artists, 1923)
d: D.W. Griffith. 12 reels.
Mae Marsh, Ivor Novello, Carol Dempster, Neil Hamilton, Lucille LaVerne, Porter Strong, Jane Thomas, Kate Bruce, Mary Foy.
A simple country girl is seduced by a minister.

The White Rosette (American Film Co./Mutual, 1916)
d: Donald MacDonald. 5 reels.
E. Forrest Taylor, Helen Rosson, Eugenie Forde, Harry Von Meter, William Stowell, Richard LaReno.
Whimsical tale about a white rosette and a mystical love that binds lovers for one thousand years.

The White Scar (Universal, 1915)
d: Hobart Bosworth. 5 reels.
Jane Novak, Anna Lehr, Hobart Bosworth, Norval McGregor, Frank Newburg, Ronald Bradbury, Seymour Zelliff.
In the Great Northwest, a fur trapper falls in love with a young woman engaged to another man.

White Shadows in the South Seas (MGM, 1928)
d: Robert Flaherty, W.S. Van Dyke. 9 reels. (Music score, sound effects, part talkie.)
Monte Blue, Raquel Torres, Robert Anderson.
A doctor with a weakness for the bottle tries to save an island beauty and her tribe from corruption from outsiders.

He partially succeeds, but there's an unexpectedly tragic ending.
Breathtakingly beautiful island scenery won Clyde DeVinna the Academy Award for cinematography.

The White Sheep (Hal Roach Productions/Pathé, 1924)
w, d: Hal Roach. 6 reels.
Glenn Tryon, Blanche Mehaffey, Jack Gavin, Robert Kortman, Leo Willis, Richard Daniels, Chris Lynton, J.J. Clayton, Dick Gilbert.
A small-town mayor with three sons finds himself framed for murder.

White Shoulders (Preferred Pictures/Associated First National, 1922)
d: Tom Forman. 6 reels.
Katherine MacDonald, Lillian Lawrence, Tom Forman, Bryant Washburn, Nigel Barrie, Charles K. French, James O. Barrows, Richard Headrick, Fred Malatesta, Lincoln Stedman, William DeVaull.
A mother tries hard to snare a wealthy husband for her daughter, but the girl does better on her own.

The White Sin (Palmer Photoplay Corp./FBO of America, 1924)
d: William Seiter. 6 reels.
Madge Bellamy, John Bowers, Francelia Billington, Hal Cooley, James Corrigan, Billy Bevan, Norris Johnson, Ethel Wales, Otis Harlan, Myrtle Vane, Arthur Millett, James Gordon.
Hattie Lou, a small-town girl, sails her employer's yacht and falls in love with a young man who sweeps her off her feet. They are married at sea with the captain presiding, but later Hattie Lou comes to suspect the wedding may not be legal and binding.

The White Sister (Essanay, 1915)
d: Fred E. Wright. 6 reels.
Viola Allen, Richard C. Travers, Florence Oberle, Thomas Commerford, Emilie Melville, John Thorn, Sydney Ainsworth, Ernest Maupain, Frank Dayton, John H. Cossar, Camille D'Arcy.
Angela loves Giovanni, a lieutenant who is ordered into combat in Egypt. After word comes that Giovanni died in battle, Angela becomes a nun... but her lover is not dead, only captured by the enemy. Eventually he returns to Angela and asks her to renounce her vows.
This film, based on the novel of the same name by F. Marion Crawford, was remade by Inspiration Pictures in 1923.

The White Sister (Inspiration/Metro, 1923)
d: Henry King. 10 reels.
Lillian Gish, Ronald Colman, Gail Kane, J. Barney Sherry, Charles Lane, Juliette La Violette, Sig Serena, Alfredo Bertone, Ramon Ibanez, Alfredo Martinelli, Carloni Talli, Giovanni Viccola, Giacomo D'Attino, Michele Gualdi, Giuseppe Pavoni.
An Italian girl is engaged to marry a dashing Army officer. However, he is captured by Arabs on an expedition to North Africa, and is presumed dead. His fiancée decides to dedicate her life to his memory, and becomes a nun, unaware that he escaped his captors and has returned to Italy, looking for her.
This production was filmed on location in Italy, and has in one of its climactic scenes an eruption of Mt. Vesuvius.

White Thunder (Ben Wilson Productions/FBO of America, 1925)

d: Ben Wilson. 5 reels.
Yakima Canutt, William H. Turner, Lew Meehan, George Lessey, Nell Brantley, Kingsley Benedict.
Richards, a recent college graduate, returns home to find that his father has been killed by a stranger with the ace of spades tattooed on his arm. To solve the mystery and bring the killer to justice, Richards masquerades as a sissy tenderfoot, hoping to attract trouble... and he succeeds.

The White Tiger (Universal, 1923)
d: Tod Browning. 7 reels.

Priscilla Dean, Wallace Beery, Matt Moore, Raymond Griffith.

A trio of international crooks plays a con game on wealthy victims.

White Youth (Universal, 1920)
d: Norman Dawn. 5 reels.
Edith Roberts, Thomas Jefferson, Alfred Hollingsworth, Arnold Gregg, Hattie Peters, Lucas C. Luke, Sam Konnella, Baldy Delmont, Phyllis Allen, Alida D. Jones, Gertrude Pedlar.
Promised in marriage to an elderly bachelor, a young woman declines the match, and instead falls for a workman laboring on her grandfather's plantation.

Whitewashed Walls (Jesse D. Hampton Productions, 1919)
d: Park Frame. 5 reels.
William Desmond, Fritzi Brunette, Carmen Phillips, Jack Richardson, Arthur Mallete, Frank MacQuarrie, Jay Dwiggins, Jack Cosgrave, Frank Lanning, Walter Perry.
Donovan, an American adventurer in a small Latin American country, runs afoul of the local lawmen.

Whither Thou Goest (Thomas H. Ince, 1917)
d: Raymond West. 5 reels.
Rhea Mitchell, Orrin Johnson, Tom Chatterton, Ida Lewis, Henry Belmar, Phil Thompson, Peggy O'Connell, J. Frank Burke, Lavinia Gre, Ben Hopkins.
After a society youth marries Maizie, a showgirl, they move to Arizona to start a new life together. His status-conscious mother tries to break up the marriage, but when a tearful Maizie tries to cross the Arizona desert, her husband comes after her and reaffirms his love.

Who Am I? (Selznick/Select, 1921)
d: Henry Kolker. 5 reels.
Claire Anderson, Gertrude Astor, Niles Welch, George Periolat, Josef Swickard, Otto Hoffman.
Ruth, a good girl from a small town, is dismayed to learn that she's inherited a gambling hall in New York.

Who Are My Parents? (Fox, 1922)
d: J. Searle Dawley. 9 reels.
Roger Lytton, Peggy Shaw, Florence Billings, Ernest Hilliard, Robert Agnew, Adelaide Prince, Niles Welch, Marie Reichardt, Florence Haas, Jimmie Lapsley.
A southern colonel's daughter marries a man against her father's wishes. Soon, the husband dies in an automobile accident, and the colonel seizes the moment to take away the couple's baby girl, put it into an orphanage, and tell his daughter that her baby died. But that mother, and that little girl, will meet again in the future.

Who Cares? (Select, 1919)
d: Walter Edwards. 5 reels.
Harrison Ford, Donald McDonald, Constance Talmadge, California Truman, Claire Anderson, Gerard Alexander, Beverly Randolph, J. Morris Foster, J.D. Jones, Dorothy Hagger, Tom Bates, Margaret Loomis.
Joan, an impetuous newlywed, adopts a "Who Cares?" attitude and callously ignores her husband.

Who Cares? (Columbia, 1925)
d: David Kirkland. 6 reels.
William Haines, Dorothy Devore, Lloyd Whitlock, Beverly Bayne, Wanda Hawley, Vola Vale, Charlie Murray, Vera Lewis, Ralph Lewis, William Austin, Carrie Clark Ward.
A "social freelancer" tries to horn in on a couple's marriage.

Who Goes There? (Vitagraph, 1917)
d: William P.S. Earle. 5 reels.
Harry T. Morey, Corinne Griffith, Arthur Donaldson, Mary Maurice, Anne Brody, Stanley Dunn.
In Europe during World War I, an American and his friends are captured by the Germans.

Who Is to Blame? (Triangle, 1918)
d: Frank Borzage. 5 reels.
Jack Abbe, Jack Livingston, Maude Wayne, Lillian West, Lillian Langdon.

Though married, Grant falls for the enticements of the vampish Tonia.

Who Killed Walton? (Triangle, 1918)
d: Thomas N. Heffron. 5 reels.
J. Barney Sherry, Mary Mersch, Edwin J. Brady, Dora Rodgers, Frank Bonn.
Mystery surrounding the death of an artist whose body is found in the apartment of a woman who once rejected his romantic advances.

Who Loved Him Best? (Mutual, 1918)
d: Dell Henderson. 5 reels.
Edna Goodrich, Herbert Evans, Miriam Folger, Frank Otto, Charles Martin, Burt Busby, Nadia Cary,Thomas Wallace, Francois DeBarry, Tallulah Bankhead.
Screen queen Doria Dane poses for a statue to be called "American Militant," and falls in love with the sculptor. Her affections, however, are unrequited until the sculptor comes to realize how much Doria has meant to him.

Who Shall Take My Life? (Selig Polyscope, 1917)
d: Colin Campbell. 7 reels.
Thomas Santschi, Fritzi Brunette, Ed Coxen, Bessie Eyton, Harry Lonsdale, Eugenie Besserer, Al W. Filson, Virginia Kirtley.
Anti-capital punishment drama, about an innocent man who is executed by the state just before proof of his innocence comes to light.

Who Was the Other Man? (Universal, 1917)
d: Francis Ford. 5 reels.
Francis Ford, Duke Worne, William T. Horne, Mae Gaston, Beatrice Van.
Espionage and adventure during World War I, involving an American and a German spy who could be his double.
Francis Ford plays the roles of the two lookalikes.

Who Will Marry Me? (Universal, 1919)
d: Paul Powell. 5 reels.
Carmel Myers, Thurston Hall, Betty Schade, William Dyer, Kingsley Benedict, Marian Skinner, Burton Law, Adelaide Elliott.
In New York's "Little Italy" neighborhood, Rosie's parents arrange her marriage, but their daughter isn't having any of it.

The Whole Town's Talking (Universal, 1926)
d: Edward Laemmle. 7 reels.
Edward Everett Horton, Otis Harlan, Virginia Lee Corbin, Dolores Del Rio, Malcolm Waite, Trixie Friganza, Robert Ober, Aileen Manning, Hayden Stevenson.
Comedy about a mild-mannered man who's suddenly the object of excited public attention, due to false rumors that he is the former lover of a famous movie star.

Whom the Gods Destroy (Vitagraph, 1916)
d: William P.S. Earle. 5 reels.
Alice Joyce, Harry T. Morey, Marc MacDermott, Logan Paul, Charles Kent, Thomas R. Mills, Mary Maurice.
Historical drama about Irish rebels who take advantage of England's preoccupation with World War I, and seek to inflict heavy damage on the English forces.

Whom the Gods Would Destroy (C.R. Macauley Photoplays, Inc., 1919)
d: Frank Borzage. 7 reels.
Jack Mulhall, Pauline Starke, Kathryn Adams, Harvey Clarke, Jean Hersholt, Wilton Taylor, Charles French, Millard Wilson, Walter Whitman, Eddie Hearne, Nanine Wright.
World War I drama about a young inventor who saves a Belgian girl from the invading Germans.

Who's Cheating? (Lee-Bradford Corp., 1924)
d: Joseph Levering. 5 reels.
Dorothy Chappell, Ralph Kellard, Zena Keefe, Montague Love, Marie Burke, William H. Tooker, Frank Montgomery, Edward Roseman, Marcia Harris.
Rejected by his fiancée on grounds of cowardice, Fields goes to work in the coal mines to learn to be a man. There, he foils a saboteur's assault on the mines and becomes a hero.

Who's Your Brother? (Curtiss Pictures Corp., 1919)
d: John G. Adolfi. 6 reels.
Edith Taliaferro, Frank Burbeck, Paul Panzer, E. Coit Albertson, Herbert Fortier, Gladden James, Elizabeth Garrison, Elizabeth Kennedy, Edith Stockton.
Morris, a gifted surgeon, is asked to perform life-saving surgery on the boyfriend of the girl Morris himself loves.

Who's Your Friend? (Goodwill Pictures, 1925)
d: Forrest K. Sheldon. 5 reels.
Francis X. Bushman Jr., Jimmy Aubrey, Patricia Palmer, Hal Thompson, Erwin Renard, Laura LaVerne, Hazel Howell, William Moran.
Spirited farce about a young couple who want to get married, but are thwarted at every turn. After several adventures, they wind up saying their "I do's" on a construction loft, high above the city streets and far from their meddling family members.

Who's Your Neighbor? (Master Drama Features, Inc., 1917)
d: S. Rankin Drew. 5 reels.
Christine Mayo, Anders Randolf, Evelyn Brent, Frank Morgan, William Sherwood, Gladys Fairbanks, Franklyn Hanna, Mabel Wright, George Majeroni, Dean Raymond.
Hattie, a prostitute, is forced out of her slum dwelling and turns her seductive attentions to men in the better neighborhoods.

Whose Wife? (American Film Co./Mutual Film Corp., 1917)
d: Rollin S. Sturgeon. 5 reels.
Gail Kane, Elizabeth Taylor, Edward Peil, Harry Von Meter, Ethel Ullman, Frank Rickert, Lucille Younge, Robert Klein, Amelia Widen.
Varden, a licentious playboy, marries one woman but soon tires of her, and proposes to another.

Whoso Findeth a Wife (U.S. Amusement Corp./Art Dramas, Inc., 1916)
d: Frank Crane. 5 reels.
Jean Sothern, William O'Neill, Leo Delaney, Kirk Brown, Ina Brooks, George Henry Trader, J.A. Fury, Eldine Stuart.
After a young woman is "sold" by her parents to a millionaire as his wife, she becomes bitterly determined never to love the husband who has been forced on her. Instead, she falls for a young attorney. Surprisingly, the millionaire sacrifices his own happiness and generously offers to give his wife her freedom. Upon seeing her husband's good will gesture, the young wife realizes her stubborness has blinded her to his good qualities, and they decide to start their married life over again.

Why America Will Win (Fox, 1918)
d: Richard Stanton. 7 reels.
Harris Gordon, Olaf Skavian, Ralph C. Faulkner, W.E. Whittle, Betty Grey, Ernest Maupain, Harry Warwick, John Fox Jr.
Rousingly patriotic study of the life of General John J. Pershing, America's overseas commander during World War I.

Why Announce Your Marriage? (Selznick/Select, 1922)
d: Alan Crosland. 5 reels.
Elaine Hammerstein, Niles Welch, Frank Currier, Arthur Housman, James Harrison, Florence Billings, Marie Burke, Huntley Gordon, Elizabeth Woodmere.
Arline, a successful artist, and Jimmy fall in love and marry, though secretly for fear of damage to her career. But several complications later, the two are forced to admit their union, when an inebriated gent visits their home and discoves the marriage license.

Why Be Good? (First National/Warner Bros., 1929)
d: William A. Seiter. 8 reels. (Synchronized music score.)
Neil Hamilton, Colleen Moore, Edward Martindel, Bodil Rosing, John St. Polis, Louis Natheaux, Lincoln Stedman.
A young man falls for a perky girl who's beneath his social standing, and meets with instant opposition from his wealthy father.

Why Change Your Wife? (Famous Players-Lasky/Paramount, 1920)
d: Cecil B. DeMille. 7 reels.
Gloria Swanson, Bebe Daniels, Thomas Meighan, Theodore Kosloff, Clarence Geldart, Sylvia Ashton, Mayme Kelso, Lucien Littlefield, Edna Mae Cooper, Jane Wolfe.
After ten years of marriage, a couple gets a divorce. The former husband remarries, but now his first wife wants him back.

Why Girls Go Back Home (Warner Bros., 1926)
d: James Flood. 6 reels.
Patsy Ruth Miller, Clive Brook, Jane Winton, Myrna Loy, George O'Hara, Joseph Dowling, Herbert Prior.
A successful actor gets a swelled head and ignores his old girlfriend when she tries her luck on Broadway.

Why Girls Leave Home (Harry Rapf Productions/Warner Bros., 1921)
d: William Nigh. 7 reels.
Anna Q. Nilsson, Maurine Powers, Julia Swayne Gordon, Corinne Barker, Kathryn Perry.

Two girls leave home—one because her father is too strict, the other because her father is too lenient.

Why I Would Not Marry (Fox, 1918)
d: Richard Stanton. 6 reels.
Lucy Fox, Ed Sedgwick, William Davidson.
Adele, a lovely young lady with many suitors, consults a fortune teller to try and sort out the offers of marriage she's received.

Why Men Leave Home (Louis B. Mayer
Productions/Associated First National, 1924)
d: John M. Stahl. 8 reels.
Lewis Stone, Helene Chadwick, Mary Carr, William V. Mong, Alma Bennett, Hedda Hopper, Sidney Bracey, Lila Leslie, E.H. Calvert, Howard Truesdell.
John and Irene marry, but soon drift apart emotionally. John is ensnared by a predatory female and comes home reeking of her perfume, leading Irene to get a divorce. But her grandmother cleverly arranges for the estranged couple to be alone in her house just before a quarantine is declared. After spending some forced "quality time" together, John and Irene come to realize they love each other more than ever.

Why Sailors Go Wrong (Fox, 1928)
d: Henry Lehrman. 6 reels.
Sammy Cohen, Ted McNamara, Sally Phipps, Carl Miller, Nick Stuart, Jules Cowles, Noble Johnson, E.H. Calvert, Jack Pennick.
Zany farce about two cab drivers who get work as deck hands on a millionaire's yacht.

Why Smith Left Home (Famous Players-
Lasky/Paramount, 1919)
d: Donald Crisp. 5 reels.
Bryant Washburn, Lois Wilson, Mayme Kelso, Winter Hall, Walter Hiers, Margaret Loomis, Carrie Clark Ward.
John Smith and his sweetheart Marian elope, but a storm of entanglements postpones their honeymoon night.

Why Trust Your Husband? (Fox, 1921)
d: George E. Marshall. 5 reels.
Eileen Percy, Harry Myers, Ray Ripley, Harry Dunkinson, Milla Davenport, Jane Miller, Hayward Mack, Bess True.
Two husbands sneak out on their wives to attend a masquerade ball. Wouldn't you know, the ladies find out and go to the ball too, in costumes their husbands would never recognize.

Why Women Love (Edwin Carewe Productions/First
National, 1925)
d: Edwin Carewe. 7 reels.
Blanche Sweet, Bert Sprotte, Robert Frazer, Charles Murray, Russell Simpson, Dorothy Sebastion, Alan Roscoe, Fred Warren, Edward Earle.
Molly, the only survivor of a shipwreck, is obliged to look after the orphaned little daughter of her rescuer.

Why Women Remarry (Associated Photoplays, 1923)
d: John Gorman. 5 reels.
Milton Sills, Ethel Terry, William Lowery, Marion Feducha, Jeanne Carpenter, Wilfred Lucas, Clarissa Selwynne, James Barton, Amita Simons, George Hayes, Thomas McGuire, Maine Geary, Carol Holloway, W.B. Clarke, Robert Walker.
A newly-widowed young mother falls for the detective who brings her husband's killer to justice.

Why Women Sin (Wistaria Productions, Inc., 1920)
d: Burton King. 6 reels.
Anne Luther, E.J. Radcliffe, Ivy Ward, Claire Whitney, Charles Gerard, Albert Hart, J.W. Johnston.
The neglected wife of a gubernatorial candidate is duped into helping his opponent create a political scandal.

Why Worry? (Hal Roach/Pathé, 1923)
d: Fred Newmeyer, Sam Taylor. 6 reels.
Harold Lloyd, Jobyna Ralston, Johan Aasen, Leo White, James Mason, Wallace Howe.
A hypochondriac books passage for a South American island country where the climate is reportedly healthful. Unfortunately, when he arrives the natives are involved in a full-scale revolution.
Why Worry? was Lloyd's only attempt at lunatic cinema, a sort of precursor of the films of W.C. Fields and the Marx Brothers.

The Wicked Darling (Universal, 1919)
d: Tod Browning. 6 reels.
Priscilla Dean, Gertrude Astor, Wellington Playter, Lon Chaney, Spottiswoode Aitken, Gertrude Astor, Kalla Pascha.
Mary, a poor girl, becomes a reluctant thief, but determines to mend her ways.

Wickedness Preferred (MGM, 1927)
d: Hobart Henley. 6 reels.
Lew Cody, Aileen Pringle, Mary McAllister, George K. Arthur, Bert Roach.
Though married, Babs falls for Anthony... not realizing that *he's* married, too.

A Wide-Open Town (Selznick/Select, 1922)
d: Ralph Ince. 5 reels.
Conway Tearle, Faire Binney, James Seeley, Harry Tighe, Claude Brooks, Ned Sparks, Danny Hayes, John P. Wade, Alice May, Bobby Connelly, Jerry Devine.
Clifford, proprietor of a gambling hall, rescues the mayor's daughter when she is caught in a raid on his establishment.

Widow by Proxy (Paramount, 1919)
d: Walter Edwards. 5 reels.
Marguerite Clark, Brownie Vernon, Gertrude Norman, Gertrude Claire, Nigel Barrie, Jack Gilbert, A.W. Filson, Rosita Marstini.
After Dolores receives word that her husband Jack has been killed on the battlefields of Europe, she moves in with her girlfriend Gloria. Then Dolores learns that she has inherited a sum of money from Jack's estate, but is too timid to claim the inheritance, so Gloria impersonates her and claims it in her name. Then Gloria falls in love with Jack's brother, who believes she is his widowed sister-in-law. Then Jack shows up, alive and well. Now what?

The Widow's Might (Lasky Feature Plays/Paramount,
1918)
d: William C. DeMille. 5 reels.
Julian Eltinge, Florence Vidor, Gustav von Seyffertitz, Mayme Kelso, James Neill, Larry Steers, George McKenzie, William Elmer.
Tavish, a New Yorker out West, owns a ranch but finds his title threatened by an unscrupulous millionaire. In a comedic escapade, Tavish spies on his foe by impersonating a female, and finds that he has attracted the affections of several men, including the millionaire

Wife Against Wife (Whitman Bennett
Productions/Associated First National, 1921)
d: Whitman Bennett. 6 reels.

Pauline Starke, Percy Marmont, Edward Langford, Emily Fitzroy, Ottola Nesmith.

A sculptor's widow, bitter over the death of her husband, tries to sabotage the marriage of the model who posed for his last masterpiece.

The Wife He Bought (Universal, 1918)
d: Harry Solter. 5 reels.
Carmel Myers, Kenneth Harlan, Howard Crampton, Sydney Deane.

Motivated by revenge, Steele threatens to have his late father's enemy imprisoned unless the man gives his daughter to Steele in marriage. He does so, and the marriage is consummated, but the couple remain unhappy and wary of each other... until one day, they realize they are truly in love.

Wife In Name Only (Pyramid Pictures/Selznick, 1923)
d: George W. Terwilliger. 5 reels.
Mary Thurman, Arthur Housman, Edmund Lowe, William Tucker, Florence Dixon, Edna May Oliver, Tyrone Power.

A spoiled socialite plots revenge against the man who rejected her love.

Wife Number Two (Fox, 1917)
d: William Nigh. 5 reels.
Valeska Suratt, Eric Mayne, Mathilde Brundage, John Goldsworthy, Martin J. Faust, T.J. Lawler, Peter Lang, Dan Mason, William Burton, Dan Sullivan, L.F. Kennedy.

Neglected by her husband, a young wife takes a lover. They arrange to elope, but instead he deserts her, and she commits suicide.

Unmistakably influenced by Flaubert's novel *Madame Bovary*, this film even gives its heroine the same name — Emma — as that used in the novel.

Wife of the Centaur (MGM, 1924)
d: King Vidor. 7 reels.
John Gilbert, Aileen Pringle, Eleanor Boardman, William Haines, Kate Price, Jacquelin Gadsden, Bruce Covington, Philo McCullough, Lincoln Stedman, William Orlamond.

A solid, middle-class wife tries to keep her novelist husband from straying.

A Wife on Trial (Universal, 1917)
d: Ruth Ann Baldwin. 5 reels.
Mignon Anderson, Leo Pierson, L.M. Wells, Julia Jackson, George Pearce.

Inspirational tale about a young woman who marries a paralyzed young man and spends her hours trying to brighten his life.

Wife or Country (Triangle, 1918)
d: E. Mason Hopper. 5 reels.
Harry Mestayer, Gretchen Lederer, Gloria Swanson, Jack Richardson, Charles West.

Barker, an attorney and reformed alcoholic, doesn't know that his wife is a German spy.

Wife Savers (Paramount, 1928)
d: Ralph Cedar. 6 reels.
Sally Blane, Wallace Beery, Raymond Hatton, ZaSu Pitts, Tom Kennedy, Ford Sterling, George Y. Harvey, August Tollaire.

In Switzerland following the Armistice, an American officer falls for Colette, a Swiss girl. When he is ordered to ship out, he gets his buddy to marry Colette and "save" her for him.

The Wife Who Wasn't Wanted (Warner Bros., 1925)

d: James Flood. 7 reels.
Irene Rich, Huntly Gordon, John Harron, Gayne Whitman, June Marlowe, Don Alvarado, Edward Piel.

A district attorney has a double dilemma: He must prosecute his own son for causing a fatal car crash, while his wife — the boy's mother — is making a play for the D.A.'s political rival.

A Wife's Awakening (Robertson-Cole Co./R-C Pictures, 1921)
d: Louis Gasnier. 6 reels.
William P. Carleton, Fritzi Brunette, Sam DeGrasse, Beverly Travers, Edythe Chapman.

A woman who's married to a con artist gets "used" by her husband once too often.

The Wife's Relations (Columbia, 1928)
d: Maurice Marshall. 6 reels.
Gaston Glass, Shirley Mason, Ben Turpin, Armand Kaliz, Flora Finch, Arthur Rankin, Maurice Ryan, James Harrison, Lionel Belmore.

Powers, a struggling inventor, takes a job as caretaker for a wealthy family's estate. Then he meets Patricia, an elevator operator, and they fall in love and get married. Problems arise when it turns out that the wealthy family Powers is working for includes a playboy who's been spurned by Patricia.

A Wife's Romance (Harry Garson Productions/Metro, 1923)
d: Thomas N. Heffron. 6 reels.
Clara Kimball Young, Lewis Dayton, Louise Bates Mortimer, Albert Roscoe, Lillian Adrian, Wedgewood Nowell, Arthur Hull, Robert Cauterio.

In Spain, the wife of an American diplomat falls in love with Ramon, a thief whose portrait she is painting.

A Wife's Sacrifice (Fox, 1916)
d: J. Gordon Edwards. 5 reels.
Robert B. Mantell, Genevieve Blinn, Claire Whitney, Louise Rial, Henry Leone, Genevieve Hamper, Stuart Holmes, Walter Miller, Walter McCullough, Jane Lee.

Society drama about a brother-sister team of crooks who impersonate a deceased pair of siblings in order to inherit a large estate.

A Wife's Story — see: A Mother's Confession (1915)

Wild and Woolly (Artcraft, 1917)
d: John Emerson. 5 reels.
Douglas Fairbanks, Eileen Percy, Walter Bytell, Joseph Singleton, Calvin Carter, Charles Stevens, Sam DeGrasse, Tom Wilson, Forest Seabury, J.W. Jones, Ruth Allen, Ed Burns.

A big-city boy who dreams of being a cowboy gets his chance, when his father sends him out west to investigate a business deal.

Wild Beauty (Universal, 1927)
d: Henry MacRae. 6 reels.
June Marlowe, Hugh Allen, Scott Seaton, Hayes Robinson, William Bailey, J. Gordon Russell, Jack Pratt, Rex the horse, Valerie the horse.

In Europe, an American doughboy saves a filly from shell fire, and then brings the animal home with him. Once home, he learns that his girlfriend's family is in danger of losing their ranch; so to help them, he enters the filly in a high-stakes race.

Wild Bill Hickok (Famous Players-Lasky/Paramount,

1923)
d: Clifford S. Smith. 7 reels.
William S. Hart, Ethel Grey Terry, Kathleen O'Connor, James Farley, Jack Gardner, Carl Gerard, William Dyer, Bert Sprotte, Leo Willis, Naida Carle, Herschel Mayall.
Noted gunfighter Wild Bill Hickok returns to Dodge City after the Civil War, eager for a quiet life. But he is soon recruited by the law to help "clean up" the criminal elements in town.

Wild Blood (Universal, 1929)
d: Henry MacRae. 5 reels.
Jack Perrin, Ethlyn Claire, Theodore Lorch, Nelson McDowell.
Out West, an honest gambler foils a saloon keeper's blackmail plot.

Wild Geese (Tiffany-Stahl, 1927)
d: Phil Stone. 7 reels.
Belle Bennett, Russell Simpson, Eve Southern, Donald Keith, Jason Robards, Anita Stewart, Wesley Barry, Rada Rae, Austin Jewel, Evelyn Selbie, D'Arcy Corrigan, Bert Sprotte.
A Minnesota farmer mercilessly derides his wife because he knows she had an illegitimate child before they were married.

The Wild Girl (Eva Tanguay Film Corp./Selznick/Select, 1917)
d: Howard Estabrook. 5 reels.
Eva Tanguay, Tom Moore, Stuart Holmes, Valerie Bergere, Herbert Evans, Dean Raymond, John Davidson, Norah Cecile.
Gypsies find an abandoned baby girl and raise her as a boy.

The Wild Girl (Truart Film Corp., 1925)
d: William Bletcher. 5 reels.
Louise Lorraine, Art Acord, Andrew Waldron, Rex the dog.
A photographer falls in love with a wild girl who lives in the forest with her pet dog.

The Wild Girl of the Sierras (Fine Arts Film Co./Triangle, 1916)
d: Paul Powell. 5 reels.
Mae Marsh, Wilfred Lucas, Mazie Radford, Olga Grey, Robert Harron, James O'Shea.
In the California Sierra Mountains, a "nature girl" lives among the grizzly bears and rabbits.

The Wild Goose (Cosmopolitan/Paramount, 1921)
d: Albert Capellani. 7 reels.
Mary MacLaren, Holmes E. Herbert, Dorothy Bernard, Joseph Smiley, Norman Kerry, Rita Rogan, Lucia Backus Seger.
An architect's neglected wife falls in love with a handsome stranger.

Wild Honey (DeLuxe Pictures, Inc., 1918)
d: Francis J. Grandon. 6 reels.
Doris Kenyon, Frank Mills, Edgar Jones, John Hopkins, Joseph P. Mack, Howard Kyle, H.J. Hebert, Herbert Standing, Nellie King, Vinnie Burns, Ruth Taylor, Mildred Leary.
"Wild Honey," a dance hall girl, secretly loves the local preacher.

Wild Honey (Universal, 1922)
d: Wesley Ruggles. 7 reels.
Priscilla Dean, Noah Beery, Lloyd Whitlock, Raymond Blathwayt, Percy Challenger, Helen Raymond, Landers Stevens, Robert Ellis, Wallace Beery, Carl Stockdale, Harry DeRoy.
In South Africa, a visiting noblewoman falls in love with a homesteader, then together they save the settlers from an impending flood.

The Wild Horse Stampede (Universal, 1926)
d: Albert S. Rogell. 5 reels.
Jack Hoxie, Fay Wray, William Steele, Marin Sais, Clark Comstock, Jack Pratt, George Kesterson, Bert DeMarc, Monte Montague.
Out West, a rancher tries to corral a herd of wild horses rather than allow a rival to shoot them.

Wild Justice (United Artists, 1925)
d: Chester Franklin. 6 reels.
Peter the Great (the dog), George Sherwood, Frances Teague, Frank Hagney.
In the snow-swept North, a young woman is trapped in a cabin with a cad, but along comes the dashing hero and his faithful dog, and together they save her from a Fate Worse than Death.

Wild Life (Triangle, 1918)
d: Henry Otto. 5 reels.
William Desmond, Josie Sedgwick, Ed Brady, Dot Hagar, Orral Humphreys, Graham Pettie, Eddie Peters, Bill Patton.
Out West, a dance hall girl falls for a gambler.

Wild Oats (George Kleine, 1916)
d: Campbell Gullan. 5 reels.
Malcolm Duncan, Alma Hanlon, William Anker, Herbert Hayes, Frank Belcher, Ruby Hoffman.
When an engineer's son incurs high gambling debts, he conspires to steal his own father's contract and sell it to a competitor.

Wild Oats (Samuel Cummins, 1919)
d: C.J. Williams. 6 reels.
William Jefferson, Emily Marceau, Leslie Hunt, Logan Paul, Caryl Fleming, Gertrude LaBrandt.
U.S. Health Department cautionary film, warning of the dangers of sowing "wild oats" and contracting syphilis.

Wild Oats Lane (Marshall Neilan Productions/Producers Distributing Corp., 1926)
d: Marshall Neilan. 7 reels.
Viola Dana, Robert Agnew, John MacSweeney, Margaret Seddon, George Barnum, Jerry Miley, Scott Welch, Robert Brower, Eddie James, Mitchell Lewis.
A drifter falls in love with an innocent Pennsylvania girl and they plan to get married. However, when she arrives in New York to meet him, he is being held captive by a criminal gang and cannot be there for her. Alone and friendless, the girl turns to prostitution to support herself until she is rescued by a friendly priest who brings her and her sweetheart together again.

The Wild Olive (Oliver Morosco Photoplay Co./Paramount, 1915)
d: Oscar Apfel. 5 reels.
Myrtle Stedman, Forrest Stanley, Mary Ruby, Charles Marriott, Edmund Lowe, Herbert Standing.
Norrie, a college boy, is convicted of murdering his uncle—but it's a frameup. "Wild Olive" is the nickname of the girl who stands by him.

Wild Oranges (Goldwyn, 1924)
d: King Vidor. 7 reels.

Virginia Valli, Frank Mayo, Ford Sterling, Nigel DeBrulier, Charles A. Post.

A yachtsman is lured by the sweet odor of wild oranges to a small island, where he will find his true love.

Wild Orchids (MGM, 1928)
d: Sidney Franklin. 11 reels.
Greta Garbo, Nils Asther, Lewis Stone.
A plantation owner's wife falls for a South Seas prince.

The Wild Party (Universal, 1923)
d: Herbert Blache. 5 reels.
Gladys Walton, Robert Ellis, Freeman Wood, Dorothy Revier, Sidney DeGrey, Lewis Sargent, Esther Ralston, Kate Lester, Joseph W. Girard, Sidney Bracey, William Robert Daly.
After writing a scandalous report on a society party, an editor's secretary is challenged to prove her charges are correct.

Wild Primrose (Vitagraph, 1918)
d: Frederick A. Thomson. 5 reels.
Gladys Leslie, Richard Barthelmess, Eulalie Jensen, Charles Kent, Claude Gillingwater, Ann Warrington, Arthur Lewis, Bigelow Cooper.
Primrose is a Southern mountain girl who was abandoned by her cultured Northern father as an infant. Now that she's grown and has acquired elegant manners, she revisits her father up North and, deeply resentful of him, she poses as a wild, uncouth country girl. Then Primrose meets her father's handsome young ward, and finds incentive to revert to her genteel self.

The Wild Strain (Vitagraph, 1918)
d: William Wolbert. 5 reels.
Nell Shipman, Alfred Whitman, Otto Lederer, Ed Alexander, Ruth Handforth.
A well-bred and proud family finds that their young daughter has a wild, adventurous streak.

Wild Sumac (Triangle, 1917)
d: William V. Mong. 5 reels.
Margery Wilson, Edwin J. Brady, Frank Brownlee, Wilbur Higby, Ray Jackson, Percy Challenger, George Chesebro.
"Wild Sumac" is the charming daughter of a French Canadian fur trapper.

Wild West Romance (Fox, 1928)
d: R. Lee Hough. 5 reels.
Rex Bell, Caryl Lincoln, Neil Neely, Billy Butts, Jack Walters, Fred Parke, Albert Baffert, George Pearce, Ellen Woodston.
Out West, a cowpoke loves the minister's daughter, but his chief rival is a notorious bandit.

The Wild West Show (Universal, 1928)
d: Del Andrews. 6 reels.
Hoot Gibson, Dorothy Gulliver, Allen Forrest, Gale Henry, Monte Montague, Roy Laidlaw, John Hall.
A circus performer foils a robbery of the show's cash box.

Wild Winship's Widow (New York Motion Picture Corp./Triangle,. 1917)
d: Charles Miller. 5 reels.
Dorothy Dalton, Rowland Lee, Joe King, Lillian Hayward, Alice Taafe.
Catherine, a grieving widow, cherishes the memory of her late husband—until she discovers a stack of love letters from a rival for his affections.

Wild, Wild Susan (Famous Players-Lasky/Paramount, 1925)
d: Edward Sutherland. 6 reels.
Bebe Daniels, Rod LaRocque, Henry Stephenson, Jack Kane, Helen Holcombe, Osgood Perkins, Ivan Simpson, Russell G. Medcraft, Warren Cook, Joseph Smiley, Mildred Ryan.
Thrill-loving Susan goes to the big city and takes a job as a private detective.

Wild Women (Universal, 1918)
d: Jack Ford. 5 reels.
Harry Carey, Vester Pegg, Ed Jones, Molly Malone, Martha Mattox, E. Van Beaver, Wilfred Taylor.
Cheyenne Harry and his cowboy pals win several prizes at a rodeo, then celebrate in a Hawaiian-style bar. Overcome by too many Polynesian cocktails, Harry lapses into a deep sleep and dreams he is shipwrecked on an island, where the Hawaiian queen falls in love with him.

Wild Youth (Famous Players-Lasky/Paramount, 1918)
d: George H. Melford. 5 reels.
Louise Huff, Theodore Roberts, Jack Mulhall, James Cruze, Adele Farrington, Charles Ogle.
Unhappily married to a moody man twice her age, Louise falls in love with a young rancher.

The Wildcat (E.D. Horkheimer/Mutual, 1917)
d: Sherwood McDonald. 5 reels.
Jackie Saunders, Daniel Gilfether, Mollie McConnell, Arthur Shirley, Nell Holman.
Hunt loves Beth and wants to marry her, but because he is wealthy her pride will not allow her to admit she loves him.

The Wildcat (Aywon, 1926)
d: Harry L. Fraser. 5 reels.
Gordon Clifford, Charlotte Pierce, Frank Bond, Hooper Phillips, Irwin Renard, Arthur Mille.
A prize-fighter goes to an isolated ranch to concentrate on his training.

Wildcat Jordan (Phil Goldstone Productions, 1922)
d: Al Santell. 5 reels.
Richard Talmadge, Eugenia Gilbert, Harry Van Meter, Jack Waltemeyer.
A rancher is invited to the big city to mix in high society.

The Wildcat of Paris (Universal, 1918)
d: Joseph DeGrasse. 6 reels.
Priscilla Dean, Louis Darclay, Edward Cecil, Lucille Furness.
Colette, a fiery but beautiful Parisienne, leads a band of larcenous Apaches.

The Wilderness Trail (Fox, 1919)
d: Edward J. LeSaint. 5 reels.
Tom Mix, Colleen Moore, Sid Jordan, Frank M. Clark, Lulu Warrenton, Pat Chrisman, Jack Nelson.
When Donald is unjustly accused of being the leader of a gang of thieves who have stolen several valuable furs, he resolves to clear his name by capturing the true criminals.

The Wilderness Woman (Robert Kane Productions/First National, 1926)
d: Howard Higgin. 8 reels.
Aileen Pringle, Lowell Sherman, Chester Conklin, Henry Vibart, Robert Cain, Harriet Sterling, Burr McIntosh.
A pair of con artists prey on a newly wealthy miner and his daughter.

Wildfire (World Film Corp., 1915)
d: Edwin Middleton. 5 reels.
Lillian Russell, Glen White, Leone Morgan, Lionel

Barrymore, William Riley Hatch, William Powers, Stuart R. Morris, Georgie Mack, Walter Kendig, James J. Gorman.
Young lovers learn that the jockey who rides Wildfire, the filly who's favored to win an upcoming race, has been bribed to lose.

Wildfire (Distinctive Pictures/Vitagraph, 1925)
d: T. Hayes Hunter. 7 reels.
Aileen Pringle, Edna Murphy, Holmes Herbert, Edmund Breese, Antrim Short, Tom Blake, Lawford Davidson, Arthur Bryson, Will Archie, Edna Morton, Robert Billoupe.
An unscrupulous racing horse owner tries to "fix" a race by having his own favored filly, Wildfire, lose. His plot backfires, though, and Wildfire wins by a nose.
Remake of World Film Corp.'s 1915 film *Wildfire*, both versions based on the stage play by George V. Hobart and George H. Broadhurst.

Wildness of Youth (Graphic Film Corp., 1922)
d: Ivan Abramson. 8 reels.
Virginia Pearson, Harry T. Morey, Mary Anderson, Joseph Striker, Thurston Hall, Julia Swayne Gordon, Bobby Connelly, Harry Southard, Madeline LaVarre, George J. Williams.
Andrew and Julie, a pair of spoiled rich kids, get mixed up in a murder investigation.

Wilful Youth (Dallas M. Fitzgerald Productions/Peerless Pictures, 1927)
d: Dallas M. Fitzgerald. 6 reels.
Edna Murphy, Kenneth Harlan, Jack Richardson, Walter Perry, James Aubrey, James Florey, Eugenie Forde, Arthur Morrison, Barbara Luddy.
A young lumberjack is suspected of murder, but his fiancée comes to the rescue with evidence that exonerates him.

The Willow Tree (Screen Classic/Metro, 1920)
d: Henry Otto. 6 reels.
Viola Dana, Edward Connelly, Pell Trenton, Harry Dunkinson, Alice Wilson, Frank Tokunago, Togo Yamamato, George Kuwa, Tom Ricketts, Jack Yutaka Abbe.
Whimsical romance drama about an Englishman in Japan, who buys a life-size figure of a mystical princess and finds himself irresistibly drawn to it. When a Japanese beauty pretends to be the statue come to life, the Englishman falls in love with her, and she with him.

Win That Girl (Fox, 1928)
d: David Butler. 6 reels.
David Rollins, Sue Carol, Tom Elliott, Roscoe Karns, Olin Francis, Mack Fluker, Sidney Bracey, Janet MacLeod, Maxine Shelly, Betty Recklaw.
Though he's an underweight runt compared to the other players, Johnny leads the football team to victory over its chief rival, avenging earlier losses suffered by his dad's and grandpa's teams in their college days.

The Winchester Woman (Vitagraph, 1919)
d: Wesley Ruggles. 5 reels.
Alice Joyce, Percy Marmont, Robert Middlemass, Jean Armour, Lucy Fox, Joe Burke.
Mrs. Winchester is accused of killing her husband, but is acquitted at trial. She leaves her home town and settles in Long Island, NY, and changes her name in an effort to start life afresh. But she's soon suspected of murder again.

The Wind (MGM, 1928)
d: Victor Seastrom. 8 reels. (Music, sound effects, part talkie.)

Lillian Gish, Lars Hanson, Montague Love, Dorothy Cummings, Edward Earle, William Orlamonde, Laon Ramon, Carmencita Johnson, Billy Kent Schaefer.
Letty, a wronged woman, shoots her attacker and buries his body outside her cabin in an area of Texas where the harsh wind blows and sandstorms are an almost daily fact of life.

The Winding Stair (Fox, 1925)
d: John Griffith Wray. 6 reels.
Alma Rubens, Edmund Lowe, Warner Oland, Mahlon Hamilton, Emily Fitzroy, Chester Conklin, Frank Leigh.
Ravenal, a legionnaire, discovers that an uprising among the Moroccan natives is really a ruse to distract attention from a massacre elsewhere in the same city.

Winds of Chance (First National, 1925)
d: Frank Lloyd. 10 reels.
Anna Q. Nilsson, Ben Lyon, Viola Dana, Hobart Bosworth, Dorothy Sebastian, Larry Fisher, Fred Kohler, Claude Gillingwater, Charles Crockett, J. Gunnis Davis, Fred Warren, Tom London, Anne M. Wilson, Victor McLaglen, Wade Boteler.
In Alaska during the gold rush, a prospector who is swindled out of his profits winds up working odd jobs for a woman identified as a countess, and falling in love with her.

Winds of the Pampas (Cloninger Productions/Hi-Mark Productions, 1927)
d: Arthur Varney. 6 reels.
Ralph Cloninger, Harry Holden, Vesey O'Davoren, Edwards Davis, Claire McDowell, Anne Drew, Lucille McMurrin, Vincent Padule.
In Argentina, the son of a rancher falls in love with the daughter of Papa's sworn enemy.

Wine (Universal, 1924)
d: Louis Gasnier. 7 reels.
Clara Bow, Forrest Stanley, Huntley Gordon, Myrtle Stedman, Robert Agnew, Walter Long, Arthur Thalasso, Walter Shumway, Grace Carlisle, Leo White.
During Prohibition days, a businessman and his daughter get involved in the bootlegging business.

The Wine Girl (Universal, 1918)
d: Harvey Gates, Stuart Paton. 5 reels.
Carmel Myers, Kenneth Harlan, Rex DeRosselli, E.A. Warren, Katherine Kirkwood.
In Northern California, a vintner and his pretty niece are menaced by a secret society of criminals.

Wine of Youth (MGM, 1924)
d: King Vidor. 7 reels.
Ben Lyon, Eleanor Boardman, William Haines, James Morrison, Johnnie Walker, William Collier Jr., Pauline Garon, Eulalie Jensen, E.J. Ratcliffe, Gertrude Claire, Virginia Lee Corbin, Robert Agnew, Lucille Hutton, Sidney DeGrey.
A girl is loved by two men, but fears marriage because of her parents' marital woes.

Wing Toy (Fox, 1921)
d: Howard M. Mitchell. 5 reels.
Shirley Mason, Raymond McKee, Edward McWade, Harry S. Northrup, Betty Schade, Scott McKee.
At the age of 15, Wing Toy, a Chinese girl, learns that she is pledged to marry Yen Low, a powerful gangster, who plans to divorce his current wife. But she's rescued from that fate when the gangster's wife kills him.

The Winged Horseman (Universal, 1929)

568

d: Arthur Rosson. 6 reels.
Hoot Gibson, Mary Elder, Charles Schaeffer, Allan Forrest, Herbert Prior,.
A motorcycle-riding cowboy halts a stampede, then uses an airplane to chase a kidnapper and rescue the beautiful captive.

The Winged Mystery (Universal, 1917)
d: Joseph DeGrasse.
Franklyn Farnum, Claire DuBrey, Rosemary Theby, Charles Hill Mailes, Sam DeGrasse, T.D. Crittenden, Frederick Montague.
During World War I, twin brothers find themselves on opposite sides—August supports the United States, his brother Louis supports Germany.
Farnum does double duty, portraying both twins.

Wings (Paramount, 1927)
d: William Wellman. 13 reels.
Clara Bow, Charles "Buddy" Rogers, Richard Arlen, Gary Cooper, Jobyna Ralston, El Brendel, Gary Cooper, Arlette Marchal, Gunboat Smith, Richard Tucker, Julia Swayne Gordon, Henry B. Walthall, George Irving, Hedda Hopper, Nigel DeBrulier, Dick Grace, Rod Rogers.
Stirring action film, notable for its photography of air battles, bombing raids, and combat scenes. First movie to win the Academy Award for Best Picture.

Wings of Pride (Jans Pictures, Inc., 1920)
d: B.A. Rolfe. 6 reels.
Olive Tell, John O'Brien, Denton Vane, Ida Pardee, J.D. Walsh, Margaret Seddon, Edwards Davies, Cora DeOrsay, Raye Dean.
Olive Muir, a society girl, behaves in condescending fashion towards a lowly alcoholic and his daughter—until she discovers that the man is her real father.

Wings of the Morning (Fox, 1919)
d: J. Gordon Edwards. 6 reels.
William Farnum, Hershall Mayall, Frank Elliott, G. Raymond Nye, Clarence Burton, Harry DeVere, Louise Lovely, Genevieve Blinn.
To save a lady's reputation, a British officer stationed in Singapore refuses to defend himself against unjust charges of molestation. But in months to come, that officer will perform deeds of heroism that will return him to an honorable position in the service... and win the heart of the woman he loves.

Wings of Youth (Fox, 1925)
d: Emmett Flynn. 6 reels.
Ethel Clayton, Madge Bellamy, Charles Farrell, Freeman Wood, Robert Cain, Katherine Perry, Marion Harlan, George Stewart, Douglas Gerard.
A woman with three flighty daughters tries to bring them to their senses before they ruin their lives.

Winifred, the Shop Girl—see: The Shop Girl (1916)

Winner Take All (Fox, 1924)
d: William S. Van Dyke. 6 reels.
Buck Jones, Peggy Shaw, Edward Hearn, Lilyan Tashman, William Norton Bailey, Ben Deeley, Tom O'Brien.
Out West, a perceived coward enters a winner-take-all boxing match, and wins both the bout and the girl he loves.

Winner Takes All (Universal, 1918)
d: Elmer Clifton. 5 reels.
Monroe Salisbury, Betty Schade, Alfred Allen, Helen Jerome Eddy, Sam DeGrasse, Jack Nelson.
Out West, homesteaders intrude on a cattle baron's peaceful domain.

Winners of the Wilderness (MGM, 1926)
d: W.S. Van Dyke. 7 reels.
Tim McCoy, Joan Crawford, Edward Connelly, Frank Currier, Roy D'Arcy, Louise Lorraine, Edward Hearn, Tom O'Brien, Will R. Walling, Frank Currier, Lionel Belmore.
During the French and Indian wars in colonial days, a young officer rescues a lovely prisoner of war from her captors, and they fall in love.

The Winning Girl (Famous Players-Lasky/Paramount, 1919)
d: Robert G. Vignola. 5 reels.
Shirley Mason, Theodore Roberts, Harold Goodwin, Lincoln Steadman, Clara Horton, Jean Calhoun, Edythe Chapman, Niles Welch, Helen Dunbar, Jose Mellville.
Jemmy, a girl who works at a textile factory, falls in love with an aviator during World War I, but his mother disapproves of their union. That will change.

The Winning Oar (Excellent Pictures, 1927)
d: Bernard McEveety. 6 reels.
George Walsh, Dorothy Hall, William Cain, Arthur Donaldson, Harry Southard, Gladys Frazin.
At a sensational murder trial, the lone juror holding out for acquittal gives an excellent reason: He himself, not the defendant, is the real murderer.

The Winning of Barbara Worth (Goldwyn/United Artists, 1926)
d: Henry King. 9 reels.
Vilma Banky, Ronald Colman, Gary Cooper, Clyde Cook, Erwin Connelly, E.J. Ratcliffe.
A desert romance pits two rivals against each other for the hand of Barbara Worth.

Winning Grandma (Diando Film Co./Pathé, 1918)
d: William Bertram. 5 reels.
Baby Marie Osborne, Morris Foster, Ruth King, William Quinn, Sambo.
An old woman whose wealth has made her avaricious and heartless has her attitude softened by her young granddaughter.

The Winning of Beatrice (Metro, 1918)
d: Harry L. Franklin. 5 reels.
May Allison, Hale Hamilton, Frank Currier, Stephen Grattan, John Davidson, Peggy Parr, Dean Raymond, Frank Joyner, Baby Ivy Ward.
After her father is murdered and her fiancé deserts her, young Beatrice strikes out on her own and becomes a success in the candy manufacturing business.

The Winning of Sally Temple (Lasky Feature Plays/Paramount, 1917)
d: George H. Melford. 5 reels.
Fannie Ward, Jack Dean, Walter Long, Horace B. Carpenter, Billy Elmer, Paul Weigel, Harry J. Smith, Eugene Pallette, Florence Smythe, John McKinnon, Vola Vale.
To protect her from scandal, an actress agrees to impersonate a young woman when her long-absent guardian returns to London. The guardian, a nobleman, is fooled by the masquerade, but the situation becomes complicated when he falls in love with the actress, believing she is his ward.

The Winning Stroke (Fox, 1919)
d: Edward Dillon. 5 reels.
George Walsh, Jane McAlpine, Louis Este, Sidney Marion, Byron Douglas.
Yale students try to get an oarsman to throw the Yale-Harvard race.

Winning the Futurity (Chadwick Pictures, 1926)
d: Scott Dunlap. 6 reels.
Cullen Landis, Clara Horton, Henry Kolker, Pat Harmon, Otis Harlan.
A young mountain man raises his horse to win the Futurity... and it does, in spite of sabotage attempts by his chief rival.

The Winning Wallop (Gotham Productions/Lumas Film Corp., 1926)
d: Charles Hutchinson. 5 reels.
William Fairbanks, Shirley Palmer, Charles K. French, Melvin McDowell, Melbourne MacDowell, Crauford Kent, Jimmy Aubrey, Frank Hagney.
Rex, a champion boxer in his college days, gets a job as trainer in a ladies' gymnasium. His job is threatened when one of the ladies accuses him of flirting, but she's merely jealous because he has *not* flirted with her. All the complications are sorted out and culminate in Rex's victory in a boxing match against a professional champion.

Winning With Wits (Fox, 1922)
d: Howard M. Mitchell. 5 reels.
Barbara Bedford, William Scott, Harry S. Northrup, Edwin B. Tilton, Wilson Hummel.
When her father is convicted of investment fraud, Mary, an actress, goes to his place of business and poses as a wealthy customer. In time, she wrings a confession of guilt from the president of the company, vindicating her father.

A Wise Fool (Famous Players-Lasky/Paramount, 1921)
d: George Melford. 5 reels.
James Kirkwood, Alice Hollister, Ann Forrest, Alan Hale, Fred Huntley, William Boyd, Truly Shattuck, Harry Duffield, John Herdman, Mabel Van Buren.
In Quebec, a neglectful husband and father loses his wife to a stage career and his daughter to marriage against his will.

The Wise Guy (Frank Lloyd Productions/First National, 1926)
d: Frank Lloyd. 8 reels.
Mary Astor, James Kirkwood, Betty Compson, George F. Marion, Mary Carr, George Cooper.
Watson, a charismatic con man, persuades an entire town that he is a minister. He meets his waterloo, however, when Mary, a young and charming member of his "flock," falls in love with him.

Wise Husbands (Pioneer Film Corp., 1921)
d: Frank Reicher. 6 reels.
Gail Kane, J. Herbert Frank, Gladden James, Arthur Donaldson, Lillian Worth.
A playboy falls in love with a Red Cross nurse, and begins to question his own lifestyle.

The Wise Kid (Universal, 1922)
d: Tod Browning. 5 reels.
Gladys Walton, David Butler, Hallam Cooley, Hector Sarno, Henry A. Barrows, C. Norman Hammond.
Rosie, a restaurant cashier, is attracted by the advances of a fashionable customer. But her heart is really with Jimmy, the restaurant's baker.

The Wise Virgin (Peninsula Studios/Producers Distributing Corp., 1924)
d: Lloyd Ingraham. 6 reels.
Patsy Ruth Miller, Edythe Chapman, Lucy Fox, Matt Moore, Leon Bary, Charles A. Stevenson.
Out West, young Billie is attracted to a phony count, but her judicious aunt prefers her to marry her (the aunt's) ranch foreman.

The Wise Wife (DeMille Pictures/Pathé, 1927)
d: E. Mason Hopper. 6 reels.
Phyllis Haver, Tom Moore, Fred Walton, Jacqueline Logan, Joseph Striker, Robert Bolder.
Helen, finding herself neglected by her husband of 10 years, concocts a plan to reawaken his love.

The Wishing Ring (World Film Corp., 1914)
d: Maurice Tourneur. 5 reels.
Vivian Martin, Alec B. Francis, Chester Barnett, Walter Morton, John Hines.
A girl obtains a ring she believes to have magical powers.

The Wishing Ring Man (Vitagraph, 1919)
d: David Smith. 5 reels.
Bessie Love, J. Frank Glendon, Jean Hathaway, Claire DuBrey, Truman Van Dyke, Willis Marks, Alberta Lee, Dorothy Hagan, Colin Kenny.
Joy, a girl who tells her problems to her late aunt's portrait, is overheard one day by a young man who falls in love with her.

The Witch (Fox, 1916)
d: Frank Powell. 5 reels.
Nance O'Neil, Alfred Hickman, Frank Russell, Macey Harlam, Ada Neville, Jane Miller, Sadie Gross, Stuart Holmes, Harry Kendall, Robert Wayne, Jane Janin, Ada Sherin.
In Mexico, a young woman appears to have magical powers, and is branded as a witch.

The Witch Woman (World Film Corp., 1918)
d: Travers Vale. 5 reels.
Ethel Clayton, Frank Myo, John Ardizoni, Jack Drumier, Louise Vale, Robert Tansey.
On a hunting trip, a hypnotist finds a deranged young woman living alone in the mountains.

Witchcraft (Lasky Feature Plays/Paramount, 1916)
d: Frank Reicher. 5 reels.
Fannie Ward, Jack Dean, Paul Weigel, Lillian Leighton.
In old New England, a young woman is thought to possess supernatural powers.

The Witching Hour (Frohman Amusement Corp., 1916)
d: George Irving. 7 reels.
C. Aubrey Smith, Marie Shotwell, Robert Conness, Jack Sherrill, Freeman Barnes, Lewis Sealy, William Eville, Robert Ayerton, Helen Arnold, Etta DeGroff.
By using telepathic powers, a gambler forces a murderer to confess his crime.

The Witching Hour (Famous Players-Lasky/Paramount, 1921)
d: William D. Taylor. 7 reels.
Elliott Dexter, Winter Hall, Ruth Renick, Robert Cain, Edward Sutherland, Mary Alden, Fred Turner, Genevieve Blinn, Charles West, L.M. Wells, Clarence Geldert, Jim Blackwell.
Remake of the 1916 Frohman film *The Witching Hour*, both

based on the play of the same name by Augustus Thomas.

With Hoops of Steel (Paralta Plays, Inc./W.W. Hodkinson, 1918)
d: Eliot Howe. 6 reels.
Henry B. Walthall, Mary Charleson, William DeVaull, Joseph J. Dowling, Howard Crampton, Roy Laidlaw, Jack Standing Jr., Clifford Alexander, Anna Mae Walthall, Paul Hurst.
Out West, a rancher accused of murder discovers that his supposed victim is not dead, but merely hiding from his family.

With Neatness and Dispatch (Metro, 1918)
d: William S. Davis. 5 reels.
Francis X. Bushman, Beverly Bayne, Frank Currier, Walter Miller, Hugh Jeffrey, Sylvia Arnold, Ricca Allen, Adella Barker, John Charles, Arthur Housman, Sidney D'Albrook.
When a young woman asks the New York City Police Commissioner to assign one of his men to work undercover in her aunt's estate, the commissioner's nephew overhears her and, smitten with the lady, volunteers for the task.

With This Ring (B.P. Schulberg Productions, 1925)
d: Fred Windermere. 6 reels.
Alyce Mills, Forrest Stanley, Lou Tellegen, Donald Keith, Dick Sutherland, Martha Mattox, Joan Standing, Eulalie Jensen.
Donald and Cecilie, stranded together on a desert island, conduct their own ceremony and become husband and wife.

Within Our Gates (Micheaux Book and Film Co., 1920)
d: Oscar Micheaux. 7 reels.
Evelyn Preer, William Starks, Mattie Edwards, E.G. Tatum, S.T. Jacks, Grant Edwards, Jack Chenault, Charles D. Lucas, Flo Clements, Jimmie Cook.
In the old South, a sharecropper suspected of murdering his plantation owner is targeted by a lynch mob.

Within the Cup (Paralta Plays, Inc./W.W. Hodkinson, 1918)
d: Raymond B. West. 7 reels.
Bessie Barriscale, George Fisher, Edward Coxen, Aggie Herring.
In Paris, an American woman has a fling with an aristocrat, but he abandons her. Returning home to New York, she draws on her romantic escapades to create lurid romantic novels that bring her wealth, but not contentment.

Within the Law (Vitagraph, 1917)
d: William P.S. Earle. 9 reels.
Alice Joyce, Harry Morey, Adele DeGarde, Anders Randolf, Walter McGrail, Eugene O'Rourke, Billie Billings, Joe Donohue, Bernard Randall, Bernard Seigel, Robert Gaillard.
Mary, a shopgirl unjustly convicted of theft, is sent to jail and swears revenge on the man who framed her. When she is released from prison, she makes a big first step in that direction: She makes her enemy's son fall in love with her.

Within the Law (Joseph M. Schenck Productions/Associated First National, 1923)
d: Frank Lloyd. 8 reels.
Norma Talmadge, Lew Cody, Jack Mulhall, Eileen Percy, Joseph Kilgour, Arthur S. Hull, Helen Ferguson, Lincoln Plummer, Thomas Ricketts, Ward Crane, Catherine Murphy, DeWitt Jennings, Lionel Belmore, Eddie Boland.
Remake of the 1917 Vitagraph film *Within the Law*, both versions based on the play of the same name by Bayard Veiller.

Without Benefit of Clergy (Robert Brunton Productions/Pathé, 1921)
d: James Young. 6 reels.
Virginia Brown Faire, Thomas Holding, Evelyn Selbie, Otto Lederer, Boris Karloff, Nigel DeBrulier, Herbert Prior, Ruth Sinclair, E.G. Miller, Philippe DeLacey.
Tragedy about Holden, a British engineer who falls in love with a girl in Lahore, India, and marries her in a colorful local ceremony. They have a son and are very happy for a time, but a cholera epidemic strikes the area and the woman and her son die.

Without Compromise (Fox, 1922)
d: Emmett J. Flynn. 6 reels.
William Farnum, Lois Wilson, Robert McKim, Tully Marshall, Hardee Kirkland, Otis Harlan, Will Walling, Alma Bennett, Eugene Pallette, Fred Kohler, Jack Dillon.
In the Northwest territory, a sheriff stands his ground against lawless gangs.

Without Fear (Fox, 1922)
d: Kenneth Webb. 5 reels.
Pearl White, Robert Elliott, Charles Mackay, Marie Burke, Robert Agnew, Macey Harlam.
Ruth, a wealthy socialite, is attracted to a man outside her social circle.

Without Honor (Triangle, 1918)
d: E. Mason Hopper. 5 reels.
Margery Wilson, Walt Whitman, Arthur Moon, Darrell Foss, Laura Sears, Anna Dodge, Walter Edwards, A.M. Mallett, Mildred Delfino.
Roy, the son of a hypocritical deacon, deserts his family home and marries a girl in the city and has a child with her. The only problem is, Roy is already married.

Without Limit (S-L Pictures/Metro, 1921)
d: George D. Baker. 7 reels.
Anna Q. Nilsson, Robert Frazer, Frank Currier, Kate Blancke, Charles Lane, Robert Schable, Thomas W. Ross, Nellie Anderson.
A minister's son gets inebriated and then married, in that order.

Without Mercy (Metropolitan Pictures/Producers Distributing Corp., 1925)
d: George Melford. 7 reels.
Dorothy Phillips, Rockliffe Fellowes, Vera Reynolds, Robert Ames, Lionel Belmore, Patricia Palmer, Fred Malatesta, Sidney D'Albrook, Eugene Pallette, Tempe Piggott.
In England, an unscrupulous politician borrows lavishly from a large banking house to finance his campaign for a seat in Parliament. But the woman who heads that bank is the woman he brutally raped and beat in Argentina years before, and she hasn't forgotten. Without mercy and without warning, she calls in the loan and he is ruined.

The Witness for the Defense (Famous Players-Lasky/Paramount, 1919)
d: George Fitzmaurice. 5 reels.
Elsie Ferguson, Vernon Steel, Warner Oland, Wyndham Standing, George Fitzgerlad, J.H. Gilmore, Amelia Summerville, Cora Williams, Blanche Standing, Leslie King, Captain Charles Charles, Henry Warwick.
Stella, an English girl living in India, is accused of murdering her wealthy and alcoholic husband. The chief witness for the defense is a man who happens to be in love with Stella. But there is more, far more, to this mystery than

what appears at trial.

Wits Vs. Wits (Grossman Pictures/Hallmark Pictures Corp., 1920)
d: Harry Grossman. 5 reels.
Marguerite Marsh, Coit Albertson, Charles Middleton, Bernard Randall, Joseph Marba, Leora Spellman, Carolina Lija, George Lessey.
Charles, a bank teller, catches a young woman in the act of picking his pocket. But she's really an undercover detective, working to bring to justice the teller and his felonious business partners.

Wives and Other Wives (American Film Co./Pathé, 1918)
d: Lloyd Ingraham. 5 reels.
Mary Miles Minter, Colin Chase, George Periolat, William Garwood, Margaret Shelby, Virginia Ware, Carl Stockdale, Eugenie Forde, Marie Morledge, John Gough.
Mistaken identity drives this romantic comedy, about two married couples who somehow wind up in seemingly compromising positions with the wrong spouses.

Wives of Men (Pioneer Film Corp., 1918)
d: John M. Stahl. 7 reels.
Florence Reed, Frank Mills, Mathilde Brundage, Edgar Lewis, Charles Jackson, Grace Davison, Bessie Mar English, Robert Lee Keeling.
Lucille, a newlywed, discovers a woman's photograph in her new husband's belongings and assumes the worst.

The Wives of the Prophet (J.A. Fitzgerald Productions/Lee-Bradford Corp., 1926)
d: J.A. Fitzgerald. 7 reels.
Orville Caldwell, Alice Lake, Violet Mersereau, Harlan Knight, Ruth Stonehouse, Warner Richmond, Maurice Costello, Ed Roseman, Mary Thurman.
In the mountains of Virginia, a religious cult prepares each year for the arrival of a prophet by selecting five beautiful young women to be his wives.

The Wizard (Fox, 1927)
d: Richard Rosson. 6 reels.
Edmund Lowe, Leila Hyams, Gustav von Seyffertitz, E.H. Calvert, Barry Norton, Oscar Smith, Perle Marshall, Norman Trevor, George Kotsonaros, Maude Turner Gordon.
A deranged scientist trains an ape to destroy his enemies.

The Wizard of Oz (Chadwick Pictures, 1925)
d: Larry Semon. 7 reels.
Dorothy Dwan, Oliver Hardy, Larry Semon, Bryant Washburn, Virginia Pearson, Charles Murray, Josef Swickard, Mary Carr, G. Howe Black.
On her 18th birthday, a girl has a dream in which she journeys to the magical Kingdom of Oz.

The Wolf (Lubin/General Film Co., 1914)
d: Barry O'Neil. 6 reels.
Bernard Siegel, Ruth Bryan, Soule Spencer, Ferdinand Tidmarsh, Gaston Bell, Joseph Kaufman, Charles Brandt, Edwin Barbour, Richard Wangeman, Mart Heisey.
 Northwest drama about a young man searching in the wilderness for his half-breed half-sister.

The Wolf (Vitagraph, 1919)
 d: James Young. 6 reels.
Earle Williams, Brinsley Shaw, George Nichols, Jane Novak, Robert McKim, Billy Mason.
Remake of the 1914 Lubin film *The Wolf*. Both versions are based on the stage play of the same name, by Eugene Walter.

The Wolf and his Mate (Universal, 1917)
d: Edward le Saint. 5 reels.
Hart Hoxie, Louise Lovely, Betty Schade, George R. Odell, Georgia French, Hector Dion.
In the great Northwest, a trapper known as "The Wolf" marries a young woman to protect her from scandal, but she keeps her distance from him. The uneasy arrangement continues until one day The Wolf proves his love for his wife by foiling her niece's kidnappers.

Wolf Blood (Ryan Brothers Productions/Lee-Bradford Corp., 1925)
d: George Chesebro, George Mitchell. 6 reels.
Marguerite Clayton, George Chesebro, Ray Hanford, Roy Watson, Milburn Morante, Frank Clark.
A man is accidentally injured in the wilds, and his doctor is forced to use wolf blood for his transfusion. Thereafter, unexplained deaths occur and the recovered patient fears he is becoming half beast.

Wolf Fangs (Fox, 1927)
d: Lewis Seiler. 6 reels.
Thunder, the dog, Caryl Lincoln, Charles Morton, Frank Rice, James Gordon.
In the wilds, a dog takes charge of a pack of wolves.

The Wolf Hunters (Ben Wilson Productions/Rayart, 1926)
d: Stuart Paton. 6 reels.
Robert McKim, Virginia Browne Faire, Alan Roscoe, Mildred Harris, David Torrence, Al Ferguson.
In the Canadian Northwest, a mountie is ordered to arrest the girl he loves, on charges of murder.

Wolf Law (Universal, 1922)
d: Stuart Paton. 5 reels.
Frank Mayo, Sylvia Breamer, Tom Guise, Dick Cummings, William Quinn, Nick DeRuiz, Harry Carter, Paul Wismer.
A fugitive from justice joins a gang of roughnecks, but rebels when the gang tries to mistreat an old judge and his daughter.

Wolf Lowry (Triangle, 1917)
d: William S. Hart. 5 reels.
William S. Hart, Margery Wilson, Aaron Edwards, Carl Ullman.
Out West, a rancher falls in love with a young woman searching for her fiancé.

The Wolf Man (Fox, 1924)
d: Edmund Mortimer. 6 reels.
John Gilbert, Norma Shearer, Alma Francis, George Barraud, Eugene Pallette, Edgar Norton, Thomas R. Mills, Max Montisole, Charles Wellesley, Richard Blaydon, Mary Warren.
Stanley's a gentleman while sober but becomes violent when drunk.

The Wolf Woman (New York Motion Picture Corp./Triangle, 1916)
d: Raymond B. West. 5 reels.
Louise Glaum, Howard Hickman, Wyndham Standing, Charles Ray, Gertrude Claire, Marjory Temple.
Following in the footsteps of Theda Bara's "vamp," Miss Glaum essays the role of a heartless woman with great seductive powers. Working her magic spell, she makes adoring men her slaves, quite literally.

Wolfe; or, the Conquest of Quebec (Kalem/General Film Co., 1914)

d: Kenean Buel. 5 reels.
Guy Coombs, Helen Lindroth, Alice Hollister, Jere Austin, Arthur Donaldson, Anna Nilsson, Harold Livingston.
Historical drama about General James Wolfe, who successfully led the British troops in the takeover of Quebec from French forces.

Wolf's Clothing (Warner Bros., 1927)
d: Roy Del Ruth. 8 reels.
Monte Blue, Patsy Ruth Miller, John Miljan, Douglas Gerrard, Lewis Harvey, John Webb Dillon, Lee Moran.
A subway guard is knocked down by a touring automobile and, in his fuzzy mental state, begins to have fantastic dreams.

The Wolf's Fangs (Apfel Productions/Producers Security Corp., 1922)
d: Oscar Apfel. 5 reels.
Wilfred Lytell, Nancy Deaver, Manilla Martans.
In the North Woods, a violent trapper known as "The Wolf" falls in love with the daughter of the local supervisor, but must contend with his more even-tempered rival.

Wolf's Trail (Universal, 1927)
d: Francis Ford. 5 reels.
Edmund Cobb, Dixie Lamont, Edwin Terry, Joe Bennett.
A Texas ranger impersonates a dangerous desperado to align himself with an outlaw he's sworn to bring to justice.

The Wolverine (Spencer Productions/Associated Photoplays, 1921)
d: William Bertram. 5 reels.
Helen Gibson, Jack Connolly, Leo Maloney, Ivor McFadden, Anne Schaefer, Gus Saville.
Out West, a ranch hand is forced to battle cattle rustlers and protect his boss, a lovely 18-year-old named Billie.

Wolves of the Air (Sterling Pictures, 1927)
d: Francis Ford. 6 reels.
Johnnie Walker, Lois Boyd, Maurice Costello, Mildred Harris, Gayne Whitman, William Boyd, Billy Bletcher, Bud Jamieson.
Warne, an aviator and a war hero, returns home and finds he must fly a plane to victory in an air race to win a lucrative contract.

Wolves of the Border (Triangle, 1918)
d: Cliff Smith. 5 reels.
Roy Stewart, Frank MacQuarrie, Jack Curtis, Josie Sedgwick, Louis Durham, Curley Baldwin.
Out West, a rancher is double-crossed by his own foreman.

Wolves of the Border (Phil Goldstone, 1923)
d: Alvin J. Neitz. 5 reels.
Franklyn Farnum, William Dyer, William Lester, Andrew Waldron, Margaret Cullington, Violet Schram.
A cattle rancher battles a gang of rustlers.

Wolves of the City (Universal, 1929)
d: Leigh Jason. 5 reels.
Bill Cody, Sally Blane, Al Ferguson, Monty Montague, Louise Carver, Charles Clary.
Flynn, who works for an art collector and loves the boss' daughter, finds himself having to fight jade thieves and kidnappers.

Wolves of the Night (Fox, 1919)
d: J. Gordon Edwards. 5 reels.
William Farnum, Louise Lovely, lamar Johnston, Charles Clary, Al Fremont, G. Raymond Nye, Carrie Clark Ward,

Irene Rich.
In the Great Northwest, rival miners square off over the love of a woman.

Wolves of the North (Universal, 1921)
d: Norman Dawn. 5 reels.
Herbert Heyes, Percy Challenger, Eva Novak, Starke Patterson, Barbara Tennant, William Eagle Eye, Clyde Tracy, Millie Impolito.
In Alaska, a native youth falls for the daughter of a professor studying Eskimo culture.

Wolves of the Rail (Artcraft Pictures Corp., 1918)
d: William S. Hart. 5 reels.
William S. Hart, Billy Elmer, C. Norman Hammond, Vola Vale, Thomas Kurihara, Melbourne MacDowell, Fanny Midgley.
Hart portrays "Buck," a reformed train robber who saves a large payroll from the clutches of his old gang and falls in love with the station agent's daughter.

Woman (Maurice Tourneur Productions, 1918)
d: Maurice Tourneur. 7 reels.
Florence Billings, Warren Cook, Ethel Hallor, Henry West, Flore Revalles, Paul Clerget, Diana Allen, Escamillo Fernandez, Gloria Goodwin, Chester Barnett, Faire Binney.
Perhaps the first women's rights movie, depicting through allegory a woman's progress through the ages.

The Woman (Lasky Feature Plays/Paramount, 1915)
d: George Melford. 5 reels.
Theodore Roberts, James Neill, Ernest Joy, Raymond Hatton, Mabel Van Buren, Tom Forman, Helen Hill, Lois Meredith.
Two senators, one the father-in-law of the other, scheme to blackmail another senator who is opposing a bill they have introduced, and hire a detective to dig up information. When they discover that their mark spent a night in a hotel with a woman not his wife, the conspirators believe they have the goods on him. But they are stunned to learn that the woman in question is one's own daughter, the other's wife.

A Woman Against the World (Tiffany-Stahl, 1928)
d: George Archainbaud. 6 reels.
Harrison Ford, Georgia Hall, Lee Moran, Harvey Clark, Walter Hiers, Gertrude Olmstead, William Tooker, Ida Darling, Wade Boteler, Charles Clary, Sally Rand, Rosemary Theby, Jim Farley.
Carol, a newspaper reporter, loves a man who's been convicted of killing a chorus girl. Against all odds, she locates evidence to prove him innocent, just minutes before his scheduled execution.

A Woman Alone (World Film Corp., 1917)
d: Harry Davenport. 5 reels.
Alice Brady, Edward T. Langford, Edward M. Kimball, Justine Cutting, J. Clarence Harvey, Arthur Ashley, Walter D. Greene.
Though married, a small-town girl flirts with a wealthy visitor from the big city.

The Woman and the Beast (Graphic Features, 1917)
d: Ernest C. Warde. 5 reels.
Marie Shotwell, Fred Eric, Alphonse Ethier, Kathryn Adams, J.H. Gilmour, Tula Belle.
Lives are imperiled when a lion escapes from the circus.

Woman and the Law (Fox, 1918)
d: Raoul A. Walsh. 7 reels.

Miriam Cooper, Ramsey Wallace, Peggy Hopkins, Jack Connors, George Humbert, Agnes Neilsen, Lewis Dayton, John Laffe, Lillian Satherwaite, Winifred Allen.
An unfaithful husband is divorced by his outraged wife.

The Woman and the Puppet (Goldwyn, 1920)
d: Reginald Barker. 6 reels.
Geraldine Farrar, Lou Tellegen, Dorothy Cumming, Bertram Grassby, Macey Harlam, Cristina Pereda, Amparito Guillot, Milton Ross, Rose Dione.
Don Mateo, a Spanish nobleman, falls in love with Conchita, a carnival dancer.

Woman and Wife (Select Pictures Corp., 1918)
d: Edward José. 5 reels.
Alice Brady, Elliott Dexter, Helen Greene, Helen Lindroth, Victor Benoit, Leonora Morgan.
Jane Eyre takes a position as governess to the daughter of a brooding widower.
This was the second silent feature film to be based on the Charlotte Bronte novel *Jane Eyre*. Other versions, under the novel's original title, were filmed by Whitman Features in 1914 and by Hugo Ballin Productions in 1921.

The Woman Beneath (World Film Corp., 1917)
d: Travers Vale. 5 reels.
Ethel Clayton, Curtis Cooksey, Isabelle Berwin, Frank de Vernon, Crauford Kent, Eugenie Woodward.
When Betty, a young wife, learns that her husband is out to avenge his family against his sister's betrayer, she rushes to the man's apartment to prevent her husband from becoming a murderer. Predictably, Betty is then accused of infidelity herself.

The Woman Between Friends (Vitagraph, 1918)
d: Tom Terriss. 5 reels.
Alice Joyce, Marc MacDermott, Robert Walker, Edith Speare, Katherine Lewis, Mary Maurice, A.B. Conkwright, Bernard Seigel.

In Paris, a young woman unwittingly lets her sweetheart know that his late wife and his best friend were lovers.

The Woman Conquers (Preferred Pictures/Associated First National, 1922)
d: Tom Forman. 5 reels.
Katherine MacDonald, Bryant Washburn, Mitchell Lewis, June Elvidge, Clarissa Selwynne, Boris Karloff, Francis McDonald.
A city-bred eastern girl goes north to the Hudson Bay area and finds herself under attack by a crazed trapper who sets her warehouse afire.

The Woman Disputed (United Artists, 1928)
d: Henry King. 9 reels.
Norma Talmadge, Gilbert Roland, Arnold Kent, Michael Vavitch, Gustave von Seyffertitz, Boris De Fas, Gladys Rockwell, Nicholas Soussanin.
A slum girl who has become a prostitute out of desperation is rescued from her sordid existence by two military officers.

The Woman From Hell (Fox, 1929)
d: A.F. Erickson. 6 reels.
Mary Astor, Robert Armstrong, Dean Jagger, Roy D'Arcy, May Boley, James Bradbury Sr.
In New England, a lighthouse keeper falls for a girl playing the Devil in an amusement park show.

The Woman From Moscow (Paramount, 1928)
d: Ludwig Berger. 7 reels. (Music score, sound effects.)
Pola Negri, Norman Kerry, Otto Matisen, Lawrence Grant, Maude George, Paul Lukas, Bodil Rosing, Mirra Rayo, Martha Franklin, Jack Luden, Tetsu Komai.
In pre-revolutionary Russia, a princess orders a search for the suspected killer of her fiancé. When she finds her man, however, she comes to believe him innocent of the murder, and falls in love with him. Eventually the truth comes out: The man she found did indeed kill the princess' lover, but in self-defense.

The Woman Game (Selznick Pictures/Select Pictures Corp., 1920)
d: William P.S. Earle. 5 reels.
Elaine Hammerstein, Jere Austin, Louis Broughton, Florence Billings, Charles Eldridge, Ida Darling, Blanche Davenport, James Morrison, Charles Duncan.
When Amy, an old-fashioned girl, charms Masters, a wealthy businessman, he thinks it's a match made in heaven. He changes his mind, however, upon hearing that Amy is actually a society flirt. But it's a case of mistaken identity, and when Masters learns that Amy really is the girl he imagined her to be, he quickly returns to her side.

The Woman Gives (Norma Talmadge Film Co./First National, 1920)
d: Roy W. Neill. 6 reels.
Norma Talmadge, John Halliday, Edmund Lowe, Lucille Lee Stewart, John Smiley, Edward Keppler.

Inga, an artists' model, journeys into the opium dens to rescue an artist who has turned to drugs out of depression.

The Woman God Changed (Cosmopolitan Productions/Paramount, 1921)
d: Robert G. Vignola. 7 reels.
Seena Owen, E.K. Lincoln, Henry Sedley, Lillian Walker, H. Cooper Cliffe, Paul Nicholson, Joseph Smiley, Templar Saxe.
Anna, a dancer, shoots and kills her unfaithful lover. She flees to Tahiti, but is followed by a detective bent on her capture. When they meet, however, she charms him and they decide to marry and spend their days together in exile.

The Woman God Forgot (Artcraft Pictures Corp., 1917)
d: Cecil B. DeMille. 5 reels.
Geraldine Farrar, Raymond Hatton, Hobart Bosworth, Wallace Reid, Theodore Kosloff, Walter Long, Charles B. Rogers, Olga Grey, James Neill.
Tecza, daughter of the emperor Montezuma, falls in love with the Spanish soldier being held captive in her father's prison. To save the soldier from certain death, Tecza throws open the city gates and allows the Spanish army to enter and conquer the territory. Just before dying, the emperor condemns his daughter and casts a curse on her. But Tecza finds salvation in the arms of the Spaniard she rescued, and embraces the Christian faith.

The Woman God Sent (Selznick Pictures Corp./Select Pictures Corp., 1920)
d: Larry Trimble. 5 reels.
Zena Keefe, John P. Wade, Barbara Gilroy, Warren Cook, Joe King, William Fredericks, William Gudgeon, Henry Bartley, Louise Powell, William Magner, Thomas O'Donnell.
Social drama about a girl factory worker who helps a senator get a labor reform bill passed.

The Woman Hater (Warner Bros., 1925)
d: James Flood. 7 reels.
Helene Chadwick, Clive Brook, John Harron, Helen Dunbar, Dale Fuller.

A self-professed woman hater has a change of heart, and prevents the marriage of a famous actress so that he can propose to her himself.

The Woman He Loved (J.L. Frothingham/American Releasing Corp., 1922)
d: Edward Sloman. 5 reels.
William V. Mong, Marcia Manon, Eddie Sutherland, Mary Wynn, Charles French, Fred Malatesta, Harvey Clark, Bruce Guerin, Lucille Ward.
Saga of two families of immigrant Jews and the hardships they face in adjusting to life in America.

The Woman He Married (Anita Stewart Productions/Associated First National, 1922)
d: Fred Niblo. 7 reels.
Anita Stewart, Darrel Foss, Donald MacDonald, William Conklin, Shannon Day, Charlotte Pierce, Charles Belcher, Frank Tokawaja.
An artist's model marries a wealthy idler, but because his father disapproves of the match, the new husband is cut off without a cent. Hubby tries his hand at earning a living, but it falls upon the new bride to bring in some income by returning to modeling—exposing her, unjustly, to scandal.

The Woman I Love (FBO Pictures, 1929)
d: George Melford. 7 reels.
Margaret Morris, Robert Frazer, Leota Lorraine, Norman Kerry, Bert Moorehouse.
Tragedy ensues when a young wife is encountered in an apparent dalliance with her neighbor's lover.

The Woman in Black (Biograph/General Film Co., 1914)
d: Lawrence Marston. 4 reels.
Lionel Barrymore, Alan Hale, Mrs. Lawrence Marston, Marie Newton, Millicent Evans, Charles Hill Mailes, Hector V. Sarno, Jack Drumier, Frank Evans.
Zenda, known as "the woman in black," and her daugther Mary concoct an ingenious plan to avenge themselves against Mary's seducer.

The Woman in Chains (Amalgamated Producing Corp., 1923)
d: William P. Burt. 7 reels.
E.K. Lincoln, William H. Tooker, Mrs. Rodolph Valentino, Martha Mansfield, Joseph Striker, Coit Albertson.
A young wife deserts her husband and child to become a cabaret dancer.

The Woman in 47 (Frohman Amusement Corp./World Film Corp., 1916)
d: George Irving. 5 reels.
Alice Brady, William Raymond, John Warwick, George D. Melville, Eric Blind, Lillian Concord, Tom McGrath, Bert Rooney, Jack Sherrill.
Viola and Tony, sweethearts since they lived in their native Italy, find each other again in New York. Planning to marry, they check into a hotel, in room 47. But they are horrified when the man in the next room shoots himself and leaves a suicide note, saying he is Viola's former lover and he did not want to go on living without her.

The Woman in His House (Chaplin-Mayer Pictures Co./First National, 1920)
d: John M. Stahl. 6 reels.
Mildred Harris Chaplin, Ramsey Wallace, Thomas Holding, George Fisher, Gareth Hughes, Richard Hedrick, Winter Hall, Catherine Van Buren, Bob Walker.

Infantile paralysis strikes the young son of a doctor and his wife, and the boy apparently dies. But what seems like death is actually paralysis, and in time, the mother's love and attentions to her son cure the lad.

The Woman in Politics (Thanhouser, /Mutual, 1916)
d: W. Eugene Moore. 5 reels.
Mignon Anderson, Arthur Bauer, Ernest Howard, George Marlo, W. Eugene Moore.
A woman doctor attempts to have a tenement quarantined because of smallpox, but she is rebuffed because the tenement is owned by the mayor.

The Woman in Room 13 (Goldwyn, 1920)
d: Frank Lloyd. 5 reels.
Pauline Frederick, Charles Clary, John Bowers, Robert McKim, Sydney Ainsworth, Charles Arling, Marguerite Snow, Emily Chichester, Kate Lester, Golda Madden, Richard Tucker.
Paul, a newlywed, becomes suspicious of his employer's attentions towards his new wife.

The Woman in the Case (1916)
d: Hugh Ford. 5 reels.
Pauline Frederick, Marie Chambers, Alan Hale, Paul Gordon, George Larkin, Clarence Handysides.
After breaking off his engagement to a woman he has learned is a prostitute, Julian marries Margaret on the rebound. Insanely jealous, his former fiancée frames Julian for a murder he did not commit, and Julian is arrested. Now it's up to his wife, the gentle Margaret, to tart herself up as a lady of the evening and go undercover to learn the prostitute's true motives and exonerate her husband.

The Woman in the Suitcase (Thomas H. Ince/Paramount, 1920)
d: Fred Niblo. 6 reels.
Enid Bennett, William Conklin, Claire McDowell, Dorcas Matthews, Donald McDonald, Roland Lee, Gladys George.
Young Mary finds a strange woman's photo in her father's suitcase, and determines to locate and meet the lady.

The Woman in White (Thanhouser/Pathé, 1917)
d: Ernest C. Warde. 5 reels.
Florence LaBadie, Richard R. Neill, Wayne Arey, Arthur Bower, Gertrude Dallas, J.H. Gilmour, Claude Cooper.
Laura, an heiress, unwisely marries a cad who wants only her money. When he learns that Ann, a mental patient, has escaped from the asylum and died, the cad has Laura committed in Ann's place. Miss LaBadie portrays both Laura and her lookalike, the ill-fated Ann.

The Woman Michael Married (B.B. Features/Mutual, 1919)
d: Henry Kolker. 5 reels.
Bessie Barriscale, Jack Holt, Marcia Manon, Tom Guise, Charles H. West, Bonnie Hill, Cameron Coffey, Mary Jane Irving.
Mira, a girl with the potential to become a successful singer, tricks wealthy Michael into marrying her. But once the honeymoon is over, they quarrel and separate. Three years later, Michael discovers that his wife has become a famous singer, making it on her own.

The Woman Next Door (George Kleine, 1915)
d: Walter Edwin. 5 reels.
Irene Fenwick, Richie Ling, Lawson Butt, Ben L. Taggart, Della Connor, Camille Dalberg, Albert Andruss, John Nicholson, Eddie O'Connor, William Bechtel.

DOUG AND MARY (1922). In the silent era, no one had to ask, "Doug and Mary who?" The athletic Douglas Fairbanks, with his robust swashbucklers and tiny Mary Pickford, with her piquant comedies and dramas, were the most popular couple in pictures. They were, quite simply, the King and Queen of Hollywood–and they wore the mantle gracefully.

* * * * *

576

Jenny, a formerly famous stage actress, lives in seclusion in Connecticut, until her neighbors discover her identity.

The Woman Next Door (Famous Players-Lasky/Paramount, 1919)
d: Robert G. Vignola. 5 reels.
Ethel Clayton, Emory Johnson, Noah Beery, Jane Wolfe, Katherine Griffith, Genevieve Blinn, Josephine Crowell, Clarence Geldart, Mae Hughes, Belle Travers, J.J. Underhill.
Ruth, a neglected wife, decides to teach her husband a lesson by secretly buying the house next door and throwing wild parties as "Miss Victoria."

A Woman of Affairs (MGM, 1928)
d: Clarence Brown. 8 reels. (Music score, sound effects.)
Greta Garbo, John Gilbert, Douglas Fairbanks Jr., Hobart Bosworth, Lewis Stone, Dorothy Sebastian, John Mack Brown.
A socialite unwisely marries a criminal, who dies on their wedding night. Then, in a token of "honor" to him, she orchestrates a series of affairs with men who were victims of her dead husband.

The Woman of Bronze (Samuel Zierler Photoplay Corp./Metro, 1923)
d: King Vidor. 6 reels.
Clara Kimball Young, John Bowers, Kathryn McGuire, Edwin Stevens, Lloyd Whitlock, Edward Kimball.
A sculptor commissioned to create a war memorial titles it "Victory" and falls in love with its model.

A Woman of Impulse (Famous Players-Lasky/Paramount, 1918)
d: Edward José. 5 reels.
Lina Cavalieri, Gertrude Robinson, Raymond Bloomer, Robert Cain, Ida Waterman, Leslie Austen, J. Clarence Handysides, Mathilde Brundage, Corrine Uzzell, Lucien Muratore, Estar Banks.
Leonora, a famed opera singer, marries a Spanish nobleman, but is still desired by her husband's cousin, whom she once rejected.

The Woman of Lies (World Film Corp., 1919)
d: Gilbert Hamilton. 5 reels.
June Elvidge, Earl Metcalfe, Charles Mackay, Gaston Glass, Lillian West, James Laffey, Fanny Cogan, J. Arthur Young, Marion Barney, Horace J. Haines.
Having been blackmailed by an ex-lover, a young woman leaves town but returns three years later, ready to settle accounts.

A Woman of Paris (United Artists, 1923)
w, d: Charles Chaplin. 8 reels.
Edna Purviance, Adolphe Menjou, Carl Miller, Lydia Knott, Charles K. French, Clarence Geldert, Betty Morrissey, Malvina Polo, Karl Gutman, Nellie Bly Baker, Henry Bergman, Harry Northrup, Charles Chaplin (as an extra).
A young Frenchwoman runs away from home and travels to Paris, where she becomes a wealthy man's mistress. Now living in luxury, she imagines she has everything she could hope for—until the boy she loved back home re-enters her life.

A Woman of Pleasure (Jesse D. Hampton Productions/Pathé, 1919)
d: Wallace Worsley. 7 reels.
Blanche Sweet, Wheeler Oakman, Wilfred Lucas, Wesley Barry, Frederick Starr, Milton Ross, Joseph Swickard, Spottiswoode Aitken.

In South Africa, a native revolt endangers the diamond mines owned by Turnbull, an infamous British nobleman. Turnbull travels to the area to witness the turmoil first hand, taking along his reluctant young wife. Once in South Africa, the lady falls in love with her husband's mine superintendent, and he with her.

A Woman of Redemption (World Film Corp., 1918)
d: Travers Vale. 5 reels.
June Elvidge, Charles H. Martin, John Bowers, Alex Shannon, Albert Hart, Marie Pagano.
In a mountain lumber camp, the fire warden's daughter falls in love with Tim, the son of the company's owner.

A Woman of the World (Famous Players-Lasky/Paramount, 1925)
d: Malcolm St. Clair. 7 reels.
Pola Negri, Charles Emmett Mack, Holmes Herbert, Blanche Mehaffey, Chester Conklin, Lucille Ward, Guy Oliver, Dot Farley, May Foster, Dorothea Wolbert.
A countess leaves Europe and settles in a small midwestern town, where her exotic manners stoke the rumor mills.

The Woman on the Index (Goldwyn, 1919)
d: Hobart Henley. 5 reels.
Pauline Frederick, Wyndham Standing, Willard Mack, Ben Hendricks, Jere Austin, Louis Stern, Frank Joyner, Florence Ashbrooke, Florida Kingsley.
Sylvia, an innocent shopgirl who somehow gets involved in a murder plot, is cleared of any complicity, but her name remains on the police index. Years later, a Bolshevik agent discovers her name on the index and threatens to expose her past unless she cooperates with his plans for a workers' revolt.

The Woman on the Jury (Associated First National, 1924)
d: Harry O. Hoyt. 7 reels.
Sylvia Breamer, Jean Hersholt, Frank Mayo, Lew Cody, Bessie Love, Ford Sterling, Stanton Heck, Mary Carr, Hobart Bosworth, Myrtle Stedman, Henry B. Walthall, Roy Stewart.
A woman called to serve as juror in a murder trial is dismayed to discover that the defendant's circumstances closely parallel her own.

The Woman on Trial (Paramount, 1927)
d: Mauritz Stiller. 6 reels.
Pola Negri, Einar Hanson, Arnold Kent, Andre Sarti, Baby Dorothy Brock, Valentina Zimina, Sidney Bracy, Bertram Marburgh, Gayne Whitman.
It was a crime of passion, your honor. A woman on trial for murdering an acquaintance presents as her defense that she was merely a pawn in an elaborate sexual chess match.

The Woman Pays (Columbia/Metro, 1915)
d: Edgar Jones. 5 reels.
Valli Valli, Marie Empress, Edward Brennan, John E. Bowers, Paul Lawrence, Julia Hurley, Mae DeMetz.
A young wife carelessly runs up massive bills and drives her husband into embezzlement.

Woman-Proof (Famous Players-Lasky/Paramount, 1923)
d: Alfred E. Green. 8 reels.
Thomas Meighan, Lila Lee, John Sainpolis, LouiseDresser, Robert Agnew, Mary Astor, Edgar Norton, Charles A. Sellon, George O'Brien, Vera Reynolds, Hardee Krikland.
Comedy about a chap who must marry by a certain date in order to earn his inheritance.

The Woman the Germans Shot (Select Pictures Corp.,

1918)
d: John G. Adolfi. 6 reels.
Julia Arthur, Creighton Hale, Thomas Brooks, George LeGuere, William H. Tooker, J.W. Johnston, Paul Panzer, Joyce Fair, George Majeroni, Sara Alexander, Amy Dennis.
World War I drama about the heroic life and tragic death of Red Cross nurse Edith Cavell.

A Woman There Was (Fox, 1919)
d: J. Gordon Edwards. 5 reels.
Theda Bara, William B. Davidson, Robert Elliot, Claude Payton, John Ardizoni.
In the South Seas, a native girl falls in love with a missionary from New England.

The Woman Thou Gavest Me (Paramount, 1919)
d: Hugh Ford. 6 reels.
Milton Sills, Katherine MacDonald, Jack Holt, Theodore Roberts, Fritzi Brunette, Katherine Griffith.
In Egypt on her honeymoon, a newlywed bride meets Conrad, an explorer.   Considering her new husband neglectful, she makes love to Conrad, who leaves for Antarctica the next morning. But the sinful bride discovers she is pregnant with the explorer's baby, and is soon divorced by her husband and disinherited by her father. But there's a happy ending of sorts, as the long-suffering young woman is reunited with Conrad, and they decide to raise their child together.

The Woman Under Cover (Universal, 1919)
d: George Seigman. 6 reels.
Fritzi Brunette, George McDaniels, Harry Springler, Fontaine LaRue, Edward Cecil, Carl Stockdale, Fred Gamble, Marion Skinner.
Alma, a big-city newspaper reporter, follows a lead in a murder case, hoping for a scoop. But she is alarmed to discover that her own brother is implicated in the affair.

The Woman Under Oath (Tribune Productions, Inc., 1919)
d: John M. Stahl. 6 reels.
Florence Reed, Hugh Thompson, Gareth Hughes, David Powell, Florida Kingsley, Mildred Cheshire, May McAvoy, Harold Entwhistle, Thomas McGuire, Walter McEwen, Edward Brennan, Frank DeCamp, Edward Elkas, Jane Jennings.
Sensational murder mystery centering on the first woman to serve on a jury in New York state. The jury deliberates the case of a young man accused of murdering his employer, an infamous man-about-town. An all-night jury session results only in a deadlock, with all jurors voting for conviction except the woman. With good reason: The woman knows the defendant is not guilty, because she herself killed the playboy for seducing her sister.

Woman, Wake Up! (Florence Vidor Productions/Associated Exhibitors, 1922)
d: Marcus Harrison. 6 reels.
Florence Vidor, Charles Meredith, Louis Calhern.
Monte and Anne fall in love and get married, then discover that they don't march to the same drumbeat.   He's a partygoer, she's a homebody.

The Woman Who Walked Alone (Famous Players-Lasky/Paramount, 1922)
d: George Melford. 6 reels.
Milton Sills, Dorothy Dalton, E.J. Ratcliffe, Wanda Hawley, Mabel Van Buren, Maurice B. Flynn, Frederick Vroom, Mayme Kelso, John Davidson, Harris Gordon, Charles Ogle,

Cecil Holland, John MacKinnon.
In South Africa, an exiled former noblewoman intervenes when she learns that an innocent man who once loved her has been unjustly accused of a crime.

The Woman Who Dared (California Motion Picture Corp., 1916)
d: George E. Middleton. 7 reels.
Beatriz Michelena, Clarence Arper, William Pike, Andrew Robson, Albert Morrison, Leslie Peacocke, John Lord, James Leslie, Frank Hollins, Al McKinnon.
Beatriz, an opera star, is enlisted in a plan to steal a sensitive government document.

The Woman Who Did Not Care (Gotham Productions/Lumas Film Corp., 1927)
d: Phil Rosen. 6 reels.
Lilyan Tashman, Edward Martindel, Arthur Rankin, Philo McCullough, Olive Hasbrouck, Sarah Padden, Guinn Williams.
An embittered man-hater because her father raised her in poverty, Iris seeks to ruin every man she meets.

The Woman Who Gave (Fox, 1918)
d: Kenean Buel. 6 reels.
Evelyn Nesbit, Irving Cummings, Robet Walker, Eugene Ormonde, Dorothy Walters, Russell Thaw.
Colette, an artists' model, marries a Balkan prince but regrets it after experiencing the prince's brutality. Escaping to America, she tries to locate her former patron and ask for his protection.

A Woman Who Sinned (R-C Pictures/FBO of America, 1924)
d: Finis Fox. 7 reels.
Morgan Wallace, Irene Rich, Lucien Littlefield, Mae Busch, Dick Brandon, Rex Lease, Ethel Teare, Cissy Fitzgerald, Hank Mann, Snitz Edwards, Bobby Mack.
Morally compromised by a Wall Street manipulator, a minister's wife leaves home in shame. But she'll return to the fold years later, redeemed by her son, who has followed in his father's footsteps and become a minister.

A Woman Who Understood (Robertson-Cole, 1920)
d: William Parke. 5 reels.
Bessie Barriscale, Forrest Stanley, Dorothy Cumming, Thomas Holding, Stanton Williams, Mary Jane Irving, Gloria Holt, Joe Butterworth.
Madge, a talented sculptor, sacrifices her own career to become a loving wife and mother... then catches her husband in the act of embracing another woman.

The Woman Who Walked Alone (Famous Players-Lasky/Paramount, 1922)
d: George Melford. 6 reels.
Dorothy Dalton, Milton Sills, E.J. Radcliffe, Wanda Hawley, Frederick Vroom, Maym Kelso, John Davidson, Harris Gordon, Charles Ogle, Mabel Van Buren, Maurice B. Flynn.
Iris, trapped in a companionate marriage with a nobleman, is turned out of his house when she is caught trying to retrieve some incriminating letters from a scoundrel.

The Woman Who Was Forgotten (States Cinema Corp., 1930)
d: Richard Thomas. 8 reels.
LeRoy Mason, Belle Bennett, Jack Mower, Gladys McConnell, William Walling, Jack Trent.
A beloved schoolteacher loses her job for protecting a student charged with embezzlement. But in years to come,

the teacher's lifetime of dedication to her students pays off, with a ceremonial banquet and an offer to become a school principal.

Woman Wise (Fox, 1928)
d: Albert Ray. 6 reels.
William Russell, June Collyer, Walter Pidgeon, Theodore Kosloff, Ernie Shields, Raoul Paoli, Duke Kahanamoku, Josephine Borio, Carmen Castillo.
In Persia, the American consul is forced to defend his ne'er-do-well friend from violent locals, who are convinced the chap has insulted a Persian maiden.

Woman, Woman! (Fox, 1919)
d: Kenean Buel. 5 reels.
Evelyn Nesbit, Clifford Bruce, Gareth Hughes, William H. Tooker, William R. Dunn, Frank Goldsmith, Anna Luther, Nora Cecil, Henry Hallam, Florence Flinn.
Alice, a small-town girl, moves to New York and is introduced to the bohemian life style.

Womanhandled (Famous Players-Lasky.Paramount, 1923)
d: Alfred E. Green. 8 reels.
Thomas Meighan, Lila Lee, John Sainpolis, Louise Dresser, Robert Agnew, Mary Astor, Edgar Norton, Charles A. Sellon, George O'Brien, Vera Reynolds, Hardee Kirkland, Martha Mattox, William Gonder, Mike Donlin.
In New York, a playboy loves Molly, but she is unimpressed with his dandified manners and considers him just another of those east coast "womanhandled" fops. He goes out West to learn to become a real man in Molly's eyes. Eventually the ex-playboy takes on real danger and rescues Molly from a cattle stampede, finally erasing the stigma of social class and winning her love.

Womanhood, the Glory of the Nation (Vitagraph, 1917)
d: J. Stuart Blackton, William P.S. Earle. 7 reels.
Alice Joyce, Harry T. Morey, Naomi Childers, Joseph Kilgour, Walter McGrail, Mary Maurice, James Morrison, Peggy Hyland, Templar Saxe, Bobby Connelly, Edward Elkas.
Mary Ward, an American enchantress, receives an offer of marriage from a Ruritanian count. Before she can give him her answer, however, Ruritania launches a surprise invasion of New York, and Mary becomes part of the war effort to drive the invaders back.

Womanpower (Fox, 1926)
d: Harry Beaumont. 7 reels.
Ralph Graves, Kathryn Perry, Margaret Livingston, Ralph Sipperly, William Walling, David Butler, Lou Tellegen, Anders Randolf, Robert Ryan, Frankie Grandetta.
Johnny, a playboy, goes to a prizefighters' training camp to toughen up before asking his coquettish tease of a girlfriend to marry him. He does toughen up, and in the process falls in love with the camp trainer's daughter.

A Woman's Awakening (Fine Arts Film Co./Triangle, 1917)
d: Chester Withey. 5 reels.
Seena Owen, Kate Bruce, A.D. Sears, Spottiswoode Aitken, Charles Gerard, Alma Rueben, Jennie Lee.
Paula, an abused wife, decides to offer her husband money in return for a divorce.

A Woman's Business (Jans Pictures, Inc., 1920)
d: B.A. Rolfe. 5 reels.
Olive Tell, Edmund Lowe, Donald Hall, Lucille Lee Stewart, Warner Richmond, Annette Bade, Stanley Walpole, Jack Davidson.
An avaricious young woman tries marrying for money, but the plan fails when her husband loses his high-paying job.

A Woman's Daring (American Film Co./Mutual, 1916)
d: Edward Sloman. 5 reels.
Winifred Greenwood, George Field, Edward Coxen, Charles Newton, Babe Callis, William Carroll.
Claire, a woman with a past, finally meets and marries a kindly investment banker. But she is terrified when Harding, the man who deceived her and fathered her child, re-enters her life and threatens to reveal details of Claire's past to her new husband.

A Woman's Faith (Universal, 1925)
d: Edward Laemmle. 7 reels.
Alma Rubens, Percy Marmont, Jean Hersholt, ZaSu Pitts, Hughie Mack, André Beranger, Rosa Rosanova.
Shattered by the sight of his fiancée in the arms of another man, Donovan takes to the wilderness and renounces God. But in his sorrow, Donovan will find a young woman who's truly worthy of his love.

A Woman's Fool (Universal, 1918)
d: Jack Ford. 5 reels.
Harry Carey, Betty Schade, Vester Pegg, Ed Jones, Molly Malone, Millard K. Wilson, William A. Carroll, Roy Clark, Sam DeGrasse.
Out West, a lonesome cowboy adopts the abandoned young son of a woman he once loved.

A Woman's Heart (Sterling Pictures, 1926)
d: Phil Rosen. 6 reels.
Enid Bennett, Gayne Whitman, Edward Earle, Mabel Julienne Scott, Lois Boyd, Louis Payne.
Eve, who married for money with her husband's full knowledge and consent, pursues an affair with Ralph, a cad.

The Woman's Law (Arrow Film Corp./Pathé, 1916)
d: Lawrence B. McGill. 5 reels.
Florence Reed, Duncan McRae, Anita d'Este Scott, Jack Curtis, Lora Rogers, John Webb Dillon, William A. Williams, Philip Hahn.
After her husband shoots and kills a man during an argument, Gail Orcutt lets her husband escape, and takes into her life an amnesiac who looks a good deal like her husband. McRae does double duty here, portraying both the felonious husband and his lookalike.

Woman's Man (Screencraft Pictures, Inc., 1920)
d: Warren Gordon. 5 reels.
Romaine Fielding, William Tooker, Velvet Beban, D.W. Reynolds, Emile LaCroix, John Lawlon, Violet Malone, Whitney Drake.
After a gold miner is lost in the desert during a sandstorm, he is presumed dead and his fiancée goes to New York to forget her sorrow. There, she agrees to marry another, not realizing that her sweetheart is still alive.

A Woman's Past (Fox, 1915)
d: Frank Powell. 5 reels.
Nance O'Neil, Alfred Hickman, Clifford Bruce, Carleton Macy.
Falsely accused of killing her husband, a woman faces trial and is defended by a young attorney who grew up in boarding school and doesn't realize his client is his real mother.

Woman's Place (Joseph M. Schenck

Productions/Associated First National, 1921)
d: Victor Fleming. 6 reels.
Constance Talmadge, Kenneth Harlan, Hassard Short, Florence Short, Ina Rorke, Marguerite Linden, Jack Connolly.
Interesting feminist drama, with a woman being nominated to run for mayor and her own fiancé backing an opposition candidate.

A Woman's Power (William A. Brady Picture Plays, Inc./World Film Corp., 1916)
d: Robert W. Thornby. 5 reels.
Mollie King, Charles Mitchell, N.J. Thompson, E.M. Kimball, Douglas MacLean, Simeon Wiltse, Lillian Cook.
During the Spanish-American war, a Kentucky mountain boy who is used to feuding learns that one can love one's enemy.

Woman's Resurrection (Fox, 1915)
d: J. Gordon Edwards. 5 reels.
Betty Nansen, William J. Kelly, Edward José, Bertha Brundage, Arthur Hoops, Stuart Holmes, J.B. Williams, Edgar Davenport, Ann Sutherland, Frances Lorrimore, Cecilia Sydney.
Bitter tale of a Russian peasant woman's unjust sentencing to a Siberian labor camp, and the men who try to come to her aid.

The Woman's Side (Preferred Pictures/Associated First National, 1922)
d: J.A. Barry. 6 reels.
Katherine MacDonald, Edward Burns, Henry Barrows, Dwight Crittenden, Ora Devereaux, Wade Boteler.
Gray, a candidate for governor, faces novel opposition: his wife's divorce attorney.

A Woman's Victory — see: The Evil Eye (1917)

A Woman's Way (World Film Corp., 1916)
d: Barry O'Neil. 5 reels.
Ethel Clayton, Carlyle Blackwell, Alec B. Francis, Pierre LeMay, Ed M. Kimball, Montagu Love, Edith Campbell Walker.
After Marion's society husband tires of her and takes up with another woman, Marion decides to win him back... and does so, in grand style.

A Woman's Way (Columbia, 1928)
d: Edmund Mortimer. 6 reels.
Margaret Livingston, Warner Baxter, Armand Kaliz, Mathilde Comont, Ernie Adams.
A French dancer falls in love with a wealthy American.

A Woman's Woman (United Artists, 1922)
d: Charles Giblyn. 8 reels.
Mary Alden, Holmes Herbert, Louise Lee, Dorothy MacKail, Albert Hackett, J. Barney Sherry, Rod LaRocque, Horace James, Cleo Madison.
A put-upon wife smartens up, starts her own business, then goes into politics.

Women and Gold (Gotham Productions/Lumas Film Corp., 1925)
d: James P. Hogan. 6 reels.
Frank Mayo, Sylvia Breamer, William Davidson, Frankie darrow, Ina Anson, Tote DuCrow, James Olivio, John T. Prince.
Newlyweds enjoying a European vacation find it interrupted by an urgent call that the husband return to work — supervising a gold mine in South America.

Women First (Columbia, 1924)
d: Reeves Eason. 5 reels.
William Fairbanks, Eva Novak, Lydia Knott, Bob Rhodes, Lloyd Whitlock, Andy Waldron, Dan Crimmins, William Dyer, Max Ascher, Merta Sterling, Jack Richardson.
When unscrupulous gamblers try to sabotage her horse and drug the jockey, young Jenny dons racing silks and rides the horse to victory.

Women Love Diamonds (MGM, 1927)
w, d: Edmund Goulding. 7 reels.
Owen Moore, Pauline Starke, Gwen Lee, Lionel Barrymore, Douglas Fairbanks Jr., Cissy Fitzgerald, Pauline Neff, Constance Howard, George Cooper, Dorothy Phillips.
Mavis, a society girl, is attracted to her chauffeur after witnessing the death of his wife.

Women Men Forget (American Cinema Corp., 1920)
d: John M. Stahl. 5 reels.
Mollie King, Edward Langford, Frank Mills, Lucy Fox, Jane Jennings.
Mary's husband Robert has a wandering eye, with a libido to match.

Women Men Love (Bradley Feature Film Co., 1920)
d: Samuel R. Bradley. 6 reels.
William Desmond, Marguerite Marsh, Martha Mansfield, Baby Doris Noldie, Evan Burroughs Fontaine, Denton Vane, Josephine Dempsey, Alice Fleming.
Evelyn loves her husband David, but at times it seems she loves gambling even more.

Women Men Marry (Edward Dillon Productions/Truart Film Corp., 1922)
d: Edward Dillon. 6 reels.
E.K. Lincoln, Florence Dixon, Charles Hammond, Hedda Hopper, Cyril Chadwick, Margaret Seddon, Richard Carlyle, Julia Swayne Gordon, Maude Turner Gordon.
Emmy, raised by a wealthy Englishman as his own child, learns after his death that she is really the daughter of his servants. Regardless of her social status, two gentlemen continue to seek her love.

Women They Talk About (Warner Bros., 1928)
d: Lloyd Bacon. 6 reels. (Part talkie.)
Anders Randolph, Irene Rich, William Collier Jr., Audrey Ferris, Claude Gillingwater, Jack Sanford, John Miljan.
An elected official renews ties with his old sweetheart while her daughter is being romanced by his son.

Women Who Dare (Excellent Pictures, 1928)
d: Burton King. 7 reels.
Helene Chadwick, Charles Delaney, Frank Beal, Jack Richardson, Henry A. Barrows, James Quinn, James Fitzgerald, Grace Elliott, Margaret McWade.
Stella, a nurse in a slum hospital, is deeply moved by the misery she sees around her every day. Unknown to all is the fact that Stella is the daughter of a wealthy family that owns most of the slum property.

Women Who Give (MGM, 1924)
d: Reginald Barker. 8 reels.
Barbara Bedford, Frank Keenan, Renee Adoree, Robert Frazer, Joseph Dowling, Margaret Seddon, Joan Standing, Victor Potel, Eddie Phillips, William Eugene.
In the waters off Cape Cod, a vessel carrying pregnant Emily and her young brother Noah runs into a monstrous storm.

The ship is guided safely to shore by a lighthouse keeper who sets his own house on fire to render enough light for the sailors.

Women's Wares (Tiffany Productions, 1927)
d: Arthur Gregor. 6 reels.
Evelyn Brent, Bert Lytell, Larry Kent, Gertrude Short, Myrtle Stedman, Richard Tucker, Cissy Fitzgerald, Sylvia Ashton, Stanhope Wheatcroft, Gino Corrado, Robert Bolder, James Mack.
Dolly, a New York shopgirl, has an upsetting experience on her first date with Jimmy, the chap she fancies: He lets his amorous impulses overcome his gentlemanliness. Rebounding from that experience, Dolly becomes hardened and decides to become a woman of the world, using men for whatever she can get out of them.

Women's Weapons (Famous Players-Lasky/Paramount, 1918)
d: Robert G. Vignola. 5 reels.
Ethel Clayton, Elliot Dexter, Vera Doria, James Neill, Josephine Crowell, Pat Moore, Dorothy Rosher.
When her husband begins an affair with a free-spirited girl, Anne thinks she knows how to bring hubby back to his senses. She feigns illness and takes to her bed, leaving her rival to do the housework and care for the children. That does it. Inept and impatient with the chores, the mistress storms off, leaving Anne and her repentant husband to work out a reconciliation.

Won in the Clouds (Universal, 1928)
d: Bruce Mitchell. 5 reels.
Al Wilson, Helen Foster, Frank Risco, George French, Joe Bennett, Albert Prisco, Myrtis Crinley, Frank Tomick, Roy Wilson, Evan Unger, Red Sly, Art Goebel.
Spectacular air battles highlight this tale of an aviator trying to save a girl from a ruthless diamond smuggler in the skies over Africa.

The Wonder Man (Robertson-Cole Co., 1920)
d: John G. Adolfi. 7 reels.
Georges Carpentier, Faire Binney, Florence Billings, Downing Clarke, Cecil Owen, Robert Barrat, William Halligan, P.C. Hartigan, John Burkell, William Noell, Gustave Wilson.
Henri, a charming man of mystery, romances a socialite. When Henri is falsely accused of stealing important documents from his sweetheart's father, he offers to clear the matter up by facing his accuser in the boxing ring.

Wonder of Women (MGM, 1929)
d: Clarence Brown. 11 reels. (Part talkie.)
Peggy Wood, Lewis Stone, Leila Hyams, George Fawcett, Harry Myers, Sarah Padden, Blanche Frederici, Wally Albright Jr., Carmencita Johnson, Anita Fremault, Dietrich Haupt, Ullrich Haupt.
A renowned concert pianist falls in love with a widow with three children.

The Wonderful Adventure (Fox, 1915)
d: Frederick Thomson. 5 reels.
William Farnum, Dorothy Green, Mary G. Martin.

Demarest, a wealthy contractor, slides helplessly into drug addiction. In a highly unusual move, he asks a lookalike friend to step into his life and, in effect, become his wife's "husband." Farnum plays a double role, as the addict and his friend.

The Wonderful Chance (Selznick/Select Pictures, 1920)
d: George Archainbaud. 5 reels.
Eugene O'Brien, Tom Blake, Joe Flanagan, Martha Mansfield, Rudolph DeValentino, Warren Cook, Martha Mansfield.
Barlow, a reformed crook, is mistaken for a nobleman whom he closely resembles. Eugene O'Brien does double duty, playing both Barlow and the nobleman.

The Wonderful Thing (Norma Talmadge Productions/Associated First National, 1921)
d: Herbert Brenon. 7 reels.
Norma Talmadge, Harrison Ford, Julia Hart, Howard Truesdale, Robert Agnew, Ethel Fleming, Mabel Bert, Fanny Burke, Walter McEwan, Charles Craig.
The American wife of an honorable but impecunious Englishman tries to reform her younger brother-in-law, who is given to passing bad checks.

A Wonderful Wife (Universal, 1922)
d: Paul Scardon. 5 reels.
Miss DuPont, Vernon Steele, Landers Stevens, Charles Arling, Ethel Ritchie, Harris Gordon, Nick DeRuiz.
Off the coast of Africa, the wife of a British official decides to vamp his superior officer, to try and win her husband a more agreeable post.

The Wood Nymph (Fine Arts Film Co./Triangle, 1916)
d: Paul Powell. 5 reels.
Marie Doro, Frank Campeau, Wilfred Lucas, Charles West, Cora Drew, Fred Graham, Pearl Elsmore.
A "nature girl" is raised in the forest by her mother, and never sees a man until her adulthood. When she finally does see a man, she imagines him to be one of the Greek gods she has heard about.

Wooden Shoes (Triangle, 1917)
d: Raymond B. West. 5 reels.
Bessie Barriscale, Jack Livingston, Joseph J. Dowling, Thomas S. Guise, Howard Hickman, Margaret Thompson, Don Likes, Will H. Bray, J. Frank Burke, Gertrude Claire.
Pampy, a charming Dutch girl, makes a living selling flowers to tourists. But Pampy has a wealthy grandfather living in New York, and when the time comes she travels to America to be with him, arriving just in time to save the old man from being defrauded.

The Wooing of Princess Pat (Vitagraph, 1918)
d: William P.S. Earle. 5 reels.
Gladys Leslie, J. Frank Glendon, Bigelow Cooper, William Dunn, Charles Kent, Carlton King, Templar Saxe, J. Albert Hall.
Tongue-in-cheek fantasy, with Princess Pat of Paxitania being betrothed to King Eric of a neighboring country, Warburg.

Words and Music By--- (Fox, 1919)
d: Scott Dunlap. 5 reels.
Albert Ray, Elinor Fair, Robert Bolder, Eugene Pallette, Edwin Booth Tilton.
Small-town girl Millicent goes to New York and stars in a hit Broadway musical whose authorship is very much in question. Are the lilting melodies the creation of the man who claims them, or are they from the pen of Millicent's small-town boyfriend?

The World Aflame (Frank Keenan Productions, Inc./Pathé, 1919)
d: Ernest C. Warde. 6 reels.

Frank Keenan, Kathleen Kerrigan, Clark Marshall, Janice Wilson, Bert Sprotte, Claire Dubrey, Joseph McManus.
Social drama about the merging of capital and labor, largely as a result of a noble mayor's efforts.

The World Against Him (Paragon Films, Inc./World Film Corp., 1916)
d: Frank Hall Crane. 5 reels.
E.K. Lincoln, June Elvidge, Ruth Findlay, John Sainpolis, Fred Truesdell, Julia Stuart, Nicholas Dunaew, Viola Benton.
Out West, a cowboy fights personal demons when his loving sister dies during an operation and he reacts violently, killing one of the attending physicians.

The World and His Wife (Cosmopolitan Productions/Paramount, 1920)
d: Robert G. Vignola. 6 reels.
Montague Love, Alma Rubens, Gaston Glass, Pedro de Cordoba, Charles Gerard, Mrs. Allan Walker, Byron Russell, Peter Barbier, Leon Gendron, Vincent Macchia, James Savold.
An aging Spanish nobleman loves his young wife and she loves him... but town gossips make their lives miserable by implying that she is carrying on with a young lover.

The World and Its Woman (Goldwyn, 1919)
d: Frank Lloyd. 7 reels.
Geraldine Farrar, Lou Tellegen, May Giraci, Francis Marion, Alec B. Francis, Edward J. Connelly, Naomi Childers, W. Lawson Butt, Arthur Carewe, Rose Dione, Lydia Yeamas Titus.
Marcia, an American opera singer, flees newly Bolshevik Russia with her sweetheart, a Russian prince.

The World and the Woman (Thanhouser/Pathé, 1916)
d: W. Eugene Moore. 5 reels.
Jeanne Eagels, Ethelmary Oakland, Boyd Marshall, Thomas A. Curren, Wayne Arey, Grace DeCarlton, Carey L. Hastings.
A woman of the streets becomes a faith healer.

The World Apart (Oliver Morosco Photoplay Co./Paramount, 1917)
d: William D. Taylor. 5 reels.
Wallace Reid, Myrtle Stedman, John Burton, Eugene Pallette, Florence Carpenter, Henry A. Barrows, Phyllis Daniels.
Out West, a ne'er-do-well scion of wealth disgraces himself by trying to rob the safe at a mining company.

The World at her Feet (Paramount, 1927)
d: Luther Reed. 6 reels.
Florence Vidor, Arnold Kent, Margaret Quimby, Richard Tucker, William Austin, David Torrence.
Richard, neglected husband of a successful attorney, decides that the only way to claim his wife's attention is as a client; therefore, he deliberately drives his car into another car so his wife can take his case. It turns out that the driver of the other car is Alma, who is also being neglected by her mate. Richard and Alma will spend a lot of "quality" time together and arouse suspicions all around, before this farce runs its course.

A World of Folly (Fox, 1920)
d: Frank Beal. 5 reels.
Vivian Rich, Aaron Edwards, Philo McCullough, Daisy Robinson, Augustus Phillips.
Duke, an irresponsible playboy, has his eyes on Helene, a married lady. She has no use for him, but is forced to acknowledge Duke's presence when he saves the lives of her

children in an auto accident.

The World to Live In (Select Pictures Corp., 1919)
d: Charles Maigne. 5 reels.
Alice Brady, Virginia Hammond, Zyllah Shannon, W.P. Carleton Jr., Earl Metcalfe, Robert Schable, Anne Cornwall.
Rita, a gold digger, seeks a wealthy husband, but she settles for love with a young settlement doctor who loves her.

Worldly Goods (Famous Players-Lasky/Paramount, 1926)
d: Paul Bern. 6 reels.
Agnes Ayres, Pat O'Malley, Victor Varconi, Edythe Chapman, Bert Woodruff, Maude George, Cecille Evans, Otto Lederer.
Eleanor falls for a fast-talking salesman with grandiose ideas but little substance. They marry, and it soon becomes apparent that Eleanor must get a job to support them. She plans to file for divorce, but her ne'er-do-well husband then gets a genuinely bright idea and uses borrowed money to buy land on which a major development is planned—thus making money and saving his marriage.

The Worldly Madonna (Harry Garson Productions, 1922)
d: Harry Garson. 6 reels.
Clara Kimball Young, William P. Carleton, Richard Tucker, George Hackathorne, Jean De Limur, William Marion, Milla Davenport.
A convent novice agrees to trade places with her twin sister, a cabaret dancer, to resolve a troubling mystery.

The World's a Stage (Principal Pictures, 1922)
w, d: Colin Campbell. 6 reels.
Dorothy Phillips, Bruce McRae, Kenneth Harlan, Otis Harlan, Jack McDonald.
A screen actress marries a salesman who, daunted by his wife's fame, becomes a hopeless alcoholic.

Worlds Apart (Selznick/Select, 1921)
d: Alan Crosland. 5 reels.
Eugene O'Brien, Olive Tell, William H. Tooker, Florence Billings, Arthur Housman, Louise Prussing, Warren Cook.
Newlyweds Hugh and Elinor greet their houseguests, Lester and Phyllis. When Lester is murdered, accusations are leveled at Hugh, because he once courted Phyllis but lost her to Lester.

The World's Applause (Famous Players-Lasky/Paramount, 1923)
d: William DeMille. 8 reels.
Bebe Daniels, Lewis Stone, Kathlyn Williams, Adolphe Menjou, Brandon Hurst, Bernice Frank, Mayme Kelso, George Kuwa, James Neill.
A famous stage star loves the spotlight a bit too much, it seems.

The World's Champion (Famous Players-Lasky/Paramount, 1922)
d: Philip E. Rosen. 5 reels.
Wallace Reid, Lois Wilson, Lionel Belmore, Henry Miller Jr., Helen Dunbar, Leslie Casey, Stanley J. Sandford, W.J. Ferguson, Guy Oliver.
An expatriate Briton in America becomes middleweight boxing champion, then returns to England to look for the aristocratic lady who once spurned him.

The World's Great Snare (Famous Players/Paramount, 1916)
d: Joseph Kaufman. 5 reels.
Pauline Frederick, Irving Cummings, Ferdinand Tidmarsh,

Frank Evans, Riley Hatch, Buckley Starkey.

Myra, a dance hall girl, falls in love with an American who may be the heir to an English title. She jeopardizes her own safety in order to obtain the necessary entitlement papers from a brute who tries to force himself on her, but at last the would-be nobleman recognizes Myra's sacrifice and elects to remain in America with her.

Wormwood (Fox, 1915)
d: Marshall Farnum. 5 reels.
John Sainpolis, Ethel Kaufman, Charles Arthur, Edgar Davenport, Stephen Grattan, Philip Hahn, Lillian Dilworth, Frank DeVernon, Bertha Brundage, Caroline Harris.
Bitter drama about the corrosive effects of absinthe addiction.

Would You Forgive? (Fox, 1920)
d: Scott Dunlap. 5 reels.
Vivian Rich, Tom Chatterton, Ben Deely, Lilie Leslie, Nancy Caswell.
John and Mary, a married couple, have everything they could want except a child. One day, Mary decides to adopt a baby without telling her husband about it. To everyone's surprise, the baby turns out to be the child of John and his mistress.

Wrath (McClure Pictures, Inc./Triangle, 1917)
d: Theodore Marston. 5 reels.
H.B. Warner, Edith Hallar, Thea Talbot, Shirley Mason, George LeGuere, Charles Wellesley, George Arvine, John Nicholson.
After seventeen years of forced separation, an American woman is reunited with her husband, a Russian prince, just before the Bolshevik Revolution.

Wrath of Love (Fox, 1917)
d: James Vincent. 5 reels.
Virginia Pearson, Louise Bates, Irving Cummings, Nellie Slattery, Frank Glendon, Johnny McCann.
Convinced that her husband is having an affair, Roma begins divorce proceedings. But hubby isn't guilty of infidelity, only of assisting the U.S. Secret Service.

The Wrath of the Gods (New York Motion Picture Corp./Mutual, 1914)
d: Reginald Barker. 6 reels.
Sessue Hayakawa, Tsuru Aoki, Frank Borzage, Thomas Kurikara, Hanoki.
In Japan, a shipwrecked American sailor falls in love with a Japanese maiden, and they marry. But "the wrath of the gods" shows itself when a long-dormant volcano near her village erupts and kills several villagers.

The Wreck (Vitagraph, 1919)
d: Ralph Ince. 5 reels.
Anita Stewart, Harry T. Morey, Gladden James, E.K. Lincoln, Donald Hall, William Dunn.
Carlyle, president of a major railroad, is outraged at the sight of his young wife in the company of one of his male employees, although the meeting is in fact perfectly innocent. In his rage, Carlyle kills the employee, then suffers anguish when his own son is killed in a train wreck.

The Wreck (Columbia, 1927)
d: William J. Craft. 6 reels.
Malcolm McGregor, Shirley Mason, Francis McDonald, James Bradbury Jr., Barbara Tennant, Frances Raymond.
Ann, unjustly convicted as an accomplice to crimes committed by others, is on her way to prison when her train is derailed. In the ensuing commotion, she is mistaken for a prison matron who died in the wreck and is taken to her supposed husband's home, where she charms his mother. The husband, Robert, asks Ann to continue to pose as his wife until his mother's health improves.

The Wreck of the Hesperus (DeMille Pictures/Pathé, 1927)
d: Elmer Clifton. 7 reels.
Sam DeGrasse, Virginia Bradford, Francis Ford, Frank Marion, Alan Hale, Ethel Wales, Josephine Norman, Milton Holmes, James Aldine, Budd Fine.
Drama based loosely on the Henry Wadsworth Longfellow poem of the same name. In New England, the captain of the Hesperus finds a burning ship and from it rescues John, the son of the man who stole the captain's sweetheart from him.

The Wright Idea (C.C. Burr Pictures/First National, 1928)
d: Charles Hines. 7 reels.
Johnny Hines, Louise Lorraine, Edmund Breese, Walter James, Fred Kelsey, Henry Barrows, Henry Hebert, Charles Giblyn, Jack McHugh, J. Barney Sherry, Charles Gerrard.
An inventor named Johnny Wright invents a luminous ink—which comes in handy later, when he and a party of friends are imprisoned on a runaway yacht, and Johnny uses his special ink to write "Help!" on the side of the vessel.

The Writing on the Wall (Vitagraph, 1916)
d: Tefft Johnson. 5 reels.
Joseph Kilgour, Virginia Pearson, Naomi Childers, Charles Wellesley, Bobby Connelly, Robert Gaillard, George Stevens, Josephine Earle, Mabel Kelly.
Lawrence, a tenement owner, lets his buildings deteriorate and, finally, is killed in a tenement fire caused by his own neglect.

The Wrong Door (Universal, 1916)
d: Carter DeHaven. 5 reels.
Carter DeHaven, Flora Parker DeHaven, Ernie Shields, G.A. Williams, Helen Hayward.
Philip, a young businessman, admires a musical comedy star, but doesn't know that she is the daughter of an infamous thief.

The Wrong Mr. Right (Universal, 1927)
d: Scott Sidney. 7 reels.
Jean Hersholt, Enid Bennett, Dorothy Devore, Edgar Kennedy, Walter Hiers, Robert Anderson, Jay Belasco, Mathilde Comont.
Romantic farce about a corset manufacturer named White who finds himself in a sticky love triangle and escapes by swearing that he isn't White, his name is Wright.

The Wrong Woman (Graphic Film Corp., 1920)
d: Ivan Abramson. 5 reels.
Olive Tell, Montagu Love, Jack Crosby, Guy Coombs, Regina Quinn, Ray Allen, Bessie Stinson, Wilfred Lytell.
Foster, a ne'er-do-well, courts and proposes to a young society woman, although he is already married.

The Wrongdoers (Astor Pictures, 1925)
d: Hugh Dierker. 7 reels.
Lionel Barrymore, Anne Cornwall, Henry Hull, Henry Sedley, Blanche Craig, Flora Finch, William Calhoun, Harry Lee, Tammany Young, Tom Brown.
A tender-hearted druggist takes a single mother and her newborn baby girl under his wing.

Wyoming (MGM, 1928)
d: W.S. Van Dyke. 5 reels.

Tim McCoy, Dorothy Sebastian, William Fairbanks, Charles Bell, Chief Big Tree, Blue Washington, Bert Henderson.

Out West, a pioneer's son and an Indian boy are childhood friends. But when they reach adulthood, they find themselves on opposite sides of a deadly clash between the U.S. cavalry and a warlike tribe.

The Wyoming Wildcat (R-C Pictures/FBO of America, 1925)
d: Robert DeLacey. 5 reels.
Tom Tyler, Billie Bennett, Gilbert Clayton, Ethan Laidlaw, Virginia Southern, Alfred Heuston, Thomas Delmar, Frankie Darro.

Out West, a ranch foreman falls for his lady boss, and saves her life when she is attacked by a notorious killer out to steal her property.

The Yankee Clipper (DeMille Pictures/Producers Distributing Corp., 1927)
d: Rupert Julian. 8 reels.
William Boyd, Elinor Fair, Junior Coghlan, John Miljan, Walter Long, Louis Payne, Burr McIntosh, George Ovey, Zack Williams, William Blaisdell, Clarence Burton, Stanton Heck.

Rival ship captains embark on a race from China to Boston Harbor, with the victor to be awarded the valuable tea trade.

The Yankee Consul (Associated Exhibitors, 1924)
d: James W. Horne. 6 reels.
Douglas MacLean, Patsy Ruth Miller, Arthur Stuart, Stanhope Wheatcroft, Eulalie Jensen, George Periolat, Fred Kelsey, Eric Mayne, Leon C. Shumway, Bert Harley.

Comedy about a travel agent who's pressured to impersonate an American consul in Latin America, then gets involved in international intrigue.

Yankee Doodle in Berlin (Mack Sennett Productions, 1916)
d: Richard Jones. 5 reels.
Brothwell, Bowne, Ford Sterling, Mal St. Clair, Bert Roach, Eve Thatcher, Marie Prevost.

The Sennett company mounts a comic spoof of the Kaiser's regime.

The Yankee Girl (Oliver Morosco Photoplay Co./Paramount, 1915)
d: J.J. Clark. 5 reels.
Blanche Ring, Forrest Stanley, Herbert Standing, Howard Davies, Harry Fisher Jr., Robert Dunbar, Joe Ray, Bonita Darling, Lydia Yeamans Titus, Syd de Grey.

Jessie, a lively adventuress, helps her father beat his rivals in a race to buy a South American copper mine.

A Yankee Go-Getter (Berwilla Film Corp./Arrow Film Corp., 1921)
d: Duke Worne. 5 reels.
Neva Gerber, James Morrison, Joseph Girard, Ashton Dearholt.

West, a struggling author, is forced to take a job that involves marriage to his new boss' niece—not realizing that his new employer plans to marry the niece off in order to secure her inheritance for himself.

Yankee Pluck (World Film Corp., 1917)
d: George Archainbaud. 5 reels.
Ethel Clayton, Edward T. Langford, Johnny Hines, Montagu Love, Eric Wayne, Charles Bowser, Isette Monroe.

The spunky daughter of an ex-millionaire learns to move about in social circles and eventually puts her father and

herself back on the fast track.

A Yankee Princess (Vitagraph, 1919)
d: David Smith. 5 reels.
Bessie Love, Robert Gordon, George Pierce, Aggie Herring, J. Carlton Wetherby, Katherine Griffith, Lydia Yeamans Titus, Max Asher.

Patsy, a poor girl who dreams about having wealth and station, realizes her wish when she meets and falls for Larry, an officer who is secretly a member of the Irish nobility.

The Yankee Señor (Fox, 1926)
d: Emmett Flynn. 5 reels.
Tom Mix, Olive Borden, Tom Kennedy, Francis McDonald, Margaret Livingston, Alec B. Francis, Kathryn Hill, Martha Mattox, Raymond Wells.

Don Fernando, a Spanish rancher, seeks the grandson he has never met—and may have found him, when an American adventurer claims to be the missing relative.

Yankee Speed (Sunset Productions/Aywon, 1924)
d: Robert N. Bradbury. 6 reels.
Kenneth McDonald, Jay Hunt, Richard Lewis, Milton Fahrney, John Henry, Viola Yorga, Virginia Ainsworth.

In Arizona, the son of a wealthy oil man goes undercover to help Don Manuel, a neighboring rancher, sort out troubles with his greedy heirs.

The Yankee Way (Fox, 1917)
d: Richard Stanton. 5 reels.
George Walsh, Enid Markey, Joe Dowling, Charles Elder, James O'Shea, Ed Sedgwick, Count Hardenberg, Edward Cecil, Tom Wilson.

Intrepid Dick Mason defends a girl in a Chicago brawl, then learns she is secretly a European princess.

The Yaqui (Universal, 1916)
d: Lloyd B. Carleton. 5 reels.
Hobart Bosworth, Jack Curtis, Golda Caldwell, Charles Hickman, Gretchen Lederer, Alfred Allen, Yona Landowska, Emory Johnson, Louis A. Valderna.

In Mexico, a plantation owner enslaves Yaqui Indians to labor in his fields. They gain their freedom when one of their number leads the Yaquis in a revolt against their captors.

The Years of the Locust (Lasky Feature Plays/Paramount, 1916)
d: George H. Melford. 5 reels.
Fannie Ward, Walter Long, Jack Dean, H.M. Best, Charles Ogle.

Lorraine loves the penniless Dirk, but she marries Aaron for his money.

The Yellow Back (Universal, 1926)
d: Del Andrews. 5 reels.
Fred Humes, Lotus Thompson, Claude Payton, Buck Connors, Willie Fung.

Out West, a ranch hand who's secretly afraid of horses agrees to ride his girlfriend's steed in a prize race.

Yellow Contraband (Pathé, 1928)
d: Leo Maloney. 6 reels.
Leo Maloney, Greta Yoltz, Noble Johnson, Tom London, Joseph Rickson, Robert Burns, Vester Pegg, Walter Patterson, Bill Patton, Bud Osborne, Frank Ellis, Tom Forman.

McMahon, a federal agent who closely resembles a certain notorious gangster, masquerades as his lookalike to foil a heroin smuggling. Actor-director Leo Maloney doubles as both the G-man and his nemesis.

The Yellow Dog (Universal, 1918)
d: Colin Campbell.   6 reels.
Arthur Hoyt, Frank Clark, Clara Horton, Antrim Short, Will Machin, Frank Hayes, Fred Kelsey, Frederick Starr, Ruby Lafayette, Ralph Graves, Lily Clarke.
During World War I, small-town Americans organize to oppose German sympathizers, known as "yellow dogs."

Yellow Fingers (Fox, 1926)
d: Emmett Flynn.   6 reels.
Olive Borden, Ralph Ince, Claire Adams, Edward Piel, Otto Matieson, Nigel DeBrulier, Armand Kaliz, Josephine Crowell, May Foster, John Wallace, Charles Newton.
Saina, a halfcaste girl who has been raised as white, learns she is actually a rajah's granddaughter and an heiress.

The Yellow Lily (First National, 1928)
d: Alexander Korda.   8 reels.
Billie Dove, Clive Brook, Gustav von Seyffertitz, Marc MacDermott, Nicholas Soussanin, Eugenie Besserer, Jane Winton, Charles Puffy.
In Budapest, a roguish archduke forces his attentions on Judith, sister of the local doctor. She shoots and wounds him and is imprisoned for this assault against nobility. But against all odds, the archduke decides he really loves this fiery girl, and sets out to win her heart.

Yellow Men and Gold (Goldwyn, 1922)
d: Irvin V. Willat.   6 reels.
Richard Dix, Helene Chadwick, Henry Barrows, Rosemary Theby, Richard Tucker, Fred Kohler, Henry Hebert, William Moran, Goro Kino, George King, William Carroll, R.T. Frazier.
An author aids a dying man and is given a map supposedly leading to buried treasure.

The Yellow Passport (World Film Corp., 1916)
d: Edwin August.   5 reels.
Clara Kimball Young, Edwin August, John Sainpolis, Alec B. Francis, John Boyle, Edward Kimball, Thomas Charles, Florence Hackett, Silas Feinberg, Robert Cummings.
In Russia, anti-Semites force a Jewish girl to use a yellow passport, marking her as a prostitute.

The Yellow Pawn (Lasky Feature Plays/Paramount, 1916)
d: George H. Melford.   5 reels.
Wallace Reid, Cleo Ridgley, William Conklin, Tom Forman, Irene Aldwin, C.H. Geldart, George Webb.
Kate marries a fiery district attorney instead of her true love, a portrait painter named James. Some years later, the now seriously unbalanced D.A. tries to "set up" his wife in a compromising position with the painter, but she remains faithful... for a while, anyway.

The Yellow Stain (Fox, 1922)
d: Jack Dillon.   5 reels.
John Gilbert, Barbara Bedford, Barbara La Marr, Herschel Mayall, Robert Kortman, William H. Orlamond.
Keith, a young lawyer who's new to town, takes on a case which pits him against a powerful political boss.

The Yellow Streak (Columbia/Metro, 1915)
w, d: William Nigh.   5 reels.
Lionel Barrymore, Irene Howley, Dorothy Gwynn, J.H. Goldsworthy, Niles Welch, R.A. Bresee, William Cowper, William Davidson, Martin J. Faust, John J. Donough.

Two would-be suicides meet at the Brooklyn Bridge, and talk each other out of it.

The Yellow Ticket (Astra Film Corp./Pathé, 1918)
d: William Parke.   5 reels.
Milton Sills, Fannie Ward, Warner Oland, Armand Kaliz, J.H. Gilmour, Helene Chadwick, Leon Barry, Anna Lehr, Dan Mason, Edward Elkas, Richard Thornton.
In Russia, a young Jewish woman is forced to carry a "yellow ticket," which brands her as a prostitute, though she is no such thing.

The Yellow Typhoon (Anita Stewart Productions/Associated First National, 1920)
d: Edward José.   6 reels.
Anita Stewart, Ward Crane, Donald MacDonald, Joseph Kilgour, George Fisher, Edward Brady, Frank Tokunaga.
Berta, a beautiful flirt, leaves her husband and travels to the Far East, where she becomes a courtesan known as "The Yellow Typhoon." Miss Stewart plays two roles here, as Berta and as Hilda, Berta's moral opposite.

The Yellowback (FBO Pictures, 1929)
d: Jerome Storm.   7 reels.
Tom Moore, Irma Harrison, Tom Santschi, William Martin, Lionel Belmore.
In the Canadian Northwest, the sweetheart of a killer helps him escape the mountie who's trying to track him down. But she has a change of heart, falls in love with the mountie, and helps him find and capture the killer.

Yes or No (Norma Talmadge Film Co./First National, 1920)
d: R. Wiliam Neill.   6 reels.
Norma Talmadge, Frederick Burton, Lowell Sherman, Lionel Adams, Rockcliffe Fellowes, Natalie Talmadge, Edward S. Brophy, Dudley Clements, Gladden James.
Tale of two identical ladies with very different backgrounds: wealthy but discontented Margaret and struggling but loyal wife Minnie. Norma Talmadge essays both roles, as Margaret and Minnie.

Yesterday's Wife (Columbia, 1923)
d: Edward J. Le Saint.   6 reels.
Irene Rich, Lewis Dayton, Eileen Percy.
A couple in love are about to be married, but a squabble puts their wedding plans on hold. Then, the man finds a new lady love.

The Yoke of Gold (Universal, 1916)
d: Lloyd Carleton.   5 reels.
Dorothy Davenport, Alfred Allen, Emory Johnson, Richard Morris, Harold Skinner, Gretchen Lederer.
In old California, a misguided young man tries to emulate Lopez, a local thief thought to be glamorous.

The Yokel — see: The Boob

Yolanda (Cosmopolitan/MGM, 1924)
d: Robert G. Vignola.   11 reels.

Marion Davies, Holbrook Blinn, Ralph Graves, Lyn Harding, Leon Errol, Theresa M. Conover, Johnny Dooley, Arthur Donaldson, Martin Faust, Thomas Findley, Mary Kennedy, Gustav von Seyffertitz, Maclyn Arbuckle, Roy Applegate.
A princess, not wishing to be recognized, goes to a public gathering incognito. There she meets a prince who is also traveling anonymously.

The Yosemite Trail (Fox, 1922)
d: Bernard Durning.   5 reels.

Dustin Farnum, Irene Rich, Walter McGrail, Frank Campeau, W.J. Ferguson, Charles French.
Cousins are rivals for the love of the same girl.

You Are Guilty (Mastodon Films, 1923)
d: Edgar Lewis. 5 reels.
James Kirkwood, Doris Kenyon, Robert Edeson, Mary Carr, Russell Griffin, Edmund Breese, Carleton Brickert, William Riley Hatch.
A world traveler returns home and finds that he's been accused of the murder of his half-brother.

You Can't Beat the Law (Trem Carr Productions/Rayart, 1928)
d: Charles J. Hunt. 6 reels.
Lila Lee, Cornelius Keefe, Warner Richmond, Betty Francisco, Charles L. King, Bert Starkey, Frank Clark.
An honest policeman finds himself in a moral dilemma when he falls in love with the sister of the gangster he is pursuing.

You Can't Believe Everything (Triangle, 1918)
d: Jack Conway. 5 reels.
Gloria Swanson, Darrell Foss, Jack Richardson, Edward Peil, George Hernandez, Iris Ashton, James Cope, Claire McDowell, Grover Franke, Kitty Bradbury, Bills Chevalier.
In order to protect the reputation of a young friend, socialite Patria Reynolds refuses to defend herself against false infidelity charges.

You Can't Fool Your Wife (Famous Players-Lasky/Paramount, 1923)
d: George Melford. 6 reels.
Leatrice Joy, Nita Naldi, Lewis Stone, Pauline Garon, Paul McAllister, John Daly Murphy, Julia Swayne Gordon, Tom Carrigan, Dan Pennell, Brownie Roberts, Pete Morris.
A surgeon must operate to save the life of his wife's lover.

You Can't Get Away With It (Fox, 1923)
d: Rowland V. Lee. 6 reels.
Percy Marmont, Malcolm McGregor, Betty Bouton, Barbara Tennant, Grace Morse, Clarissa Selwyn, Charles Cruz.
In New York, a shopgirl falls in love with the store's married owner and they have an affiar. He dies and leaves her a small inheritance, which she uses to search for Mr. Right.

You Never Can Tell (Realart Pictures Corp., 1920)
d: Chester M. Franklin. 5 reels.
Bebe Daniels, Jack Mulhall, Edward Martindel, Helen Dunbar, Harold Goodwin, Neely Edwards, Leo White, Milla Davenport, Graham Pettie, Gertrude Short.
Gold digger Rowena determines to marry a millionaire, but instead falls for a chauffeur. In the final reel, we learn that his "chauffeur" persona is just a pose... and he's really a handsome millionaire who meets all Rowena's criteria.

You Never Know (Vitagraph, 1922)
d: Robert Ensminger. 5 reels.
Earle Williams, Gertrude Astor, George Field, Claire DuBrey, Coy Watson Jr., James Conway, Louis Dumar, Leonard Trainor.
In Latin America, a revolutionary leader is unmasked as a traitor to the people's cause.

You Never Know Women (Famous Players-Lasky/Paramount, 1926)
d: William A. Wellman. 6 reels.
Florence Vidor, Lowell Sherman, Clive Brook, El Brendel, Roy Stewart, Joe Bonomo, Irma Kornelia, Sidney Bracy.

A wealthy stockbroker falls for a dancer in a touring Russian show, but her heart belongs to the show's knife-thrower.

You Never Know Your Luck (Sunset Pictures Corp./World Film Corp., 1919)
d: Frank Powell. 5 reels.
House Peters, Mildred Southwick, Claire Whitney, Bertram Marburgh, Marion Dyer, Frank Nelson, Charles Hammond.
In Canada, a ranch hand is discovered to actually be a wealthy English lord.

You Never Saw Such a Girl (Famous Players-Lasky/Paramount, 1919)
d: Robert G. Vignola. 5 reels.
Harrison Ford, Vivian Martin, Mayme Kelso, Willis Marks, Edna May Cooper, John Burton, Erbert Standing, Gerard Alexander, Claire Anderson, James Farley, J. Morris Foster.
While traveling about the country, selling curios from an old van, a poor young woman discovers that she might be the heiress to a large estate.

You'd Be Surprised (Famous Players-Lasky/Paramount, 1926)
d: Arthur Rosson. 6 reels.
Raymond Griffith, Dorothy Sebastian, Earle Williams, Edward Martindel.
Mystery with comedic overtones, about a district attorney who's murdered by an unknown assailant at his own houseparty.

Young America (Essanay Film Manufacturing Co., 1922)
d: Arthur Berthelet. 5 reels.
Charles Frohman Everett, Madelyn Clare, Howard I. Smith, Wilson Reynolds, Marlow Bowles, William Wadsworth, Leona Ball, Florence Barr, Evelyn Ward, Frances Raymond.
Tender tale about a boy and his dog.

Young April (DeMille Pictures/Producers Distributing Corp., 1926)
d: Donald Crisp. 7 reels.
Joseph Schildkraut, Rudolph Schildkraut, Bessie Love, Bryant Washburn, Clarence Geldert, Alan Brooks, Dot Farley, Carrie Daumery, Baldy Belmont.
In a European kingdom, the crown prince is told he must marry the archduchess Victoria, whom he's never met. Before the wedding, the prince goes to Paris for one last fling. Meanwhile, Victoria is informed that she must marry the prince and decides to go to Paris for—you guessed it— one last fling. Any chance these two will meet and fall in love?

The Young Diana (Cosmopolitan/Paramount, 1922)
d: Albert Capellani, Robert G. Vignola. 7 reels.

Marion Davies, Forrest Stanley, Clara Kimball Young, Gypsy O'Brien, Maclyn Arbuckle, Pedro de Cordoba.
Diana, an impressionable girl, sees her beloved with another woman and believes The Worst. However, the young man returns to her and explains he was merely escorting the lady to her new husband.

Young Ideas (Universal, 1924)
d: Robert F. Hill. 5 reels.
Laura LaPlante, T. Roy Barnes, Lucille Rickson, James O. Barrows, Lydia Yeamans Titus, Jennie Lee, Rolfe Sedan, Buddy Messinger.
Young Octavia is the sole support of her family of leeches, all of whom claim to be too ill to seek employment. When her boss learns of Octavia's plight, he cleverly lures her

away and then has her quarantined, forcing her family members to find work. And while he is at it, he asks for her hand in marriage.

Young Mother Hubbard (Essanay/Perfection Pictures, 1917)
d: Arthur Berthelet. 5 reels.
Little Mary McAllister, William Clifford, Russell McDermott, Bobbie Bolder, Carolyn Irwin, Granville Bates.
Mona, an orphan girl with three young siblings, escapes the clutches of the Welfare Society by making her crusty landlord fall in love with her and give her family a permanent home.

Young Mrs. Winthrop (Famous Players-Lasky/Paramount, 1920)
d: Walter Edwards. 5 reels.
Raymond Hatton, Harrison Ford, Ethel Clayton, Helen Dunbar, Winifred Greenwood, Charles Ogle, Mabel Van Buren, Walter Hiers, Rex Zane, Viora Daniel, Dorothy Rosher.
The Winthrops, Douglas and Constance, find their marriage slowly crumbling. When their only child—a daughter—dies, the parents are driven into grief. But miraculously, it seems, their mutual grief proves to be the tool that will reconcile them and renew their marriage.

The Young Rajah (Famous Players-Lasky, 1922)
d: Philip Rosen. 8 reels.
Rudolph Valentino, Wanda Hawley, Pat Moore, Charles Ogle, Fanny Midgley, Robert Ober, Jack Giddings, Josef Swickard, Bertram Grassby, J. Farrell MacDonald, Edward Jobson, George Periolat, George Field, Maude Wayne, William Boyd, Spottiswoode Aitken.
A young rajah comes to America, where he excels as a student and an athlete, and woos and wins Molly, the prettiest girl in school.

Young Whirlwind (FBO Pictures, 1928)
d: Louis King. 5 reels.
Buzz Barton, Edmund Cobb, Frank Rice, Alma Rayford, Tom Lingham, Eddie Chandler, Bill Patton, Tex Phelps.
Out West, bandits hijack the mail plane, intent on robbery. But they are fought off by the unlikeliest of foes: Young Red Hepner, a small boy with a big slingshot.

The Younger Generation (Columbia, 1929)
d: Frank Capra. 8 reels. (Part talkie.)
Jean Hersholt, Ricard Cortez, Lina Basquette, Rosa Rosanova, Rex Lease, Martha Franklin, Julia Swayne Gordon, Julanne Johnston, Jack Raymond, Syd Crossley, Otto Fries.
A pushcart peddler's family aims to improve their image.

Your Best Friend (Warner Brothers, 1921)
w, d: William Nigh. 7 reels.
Vera Gordon, Doré Davidson, Harry Benham, Stanley Price, Belle Bennett, Beth Mason.
A Jewish mother is spurned by her son's gentile wife.

Your Friend and Mine (S-L Pictures/Metro, 1923)
d: Clarence G. Badger. 6 reels.
Enid Bennett, Huntly Gordon, Willard Mack, Rosemary Theby, J. Herbert Frank, Otto Lederer, Allene Ray.
Patricia, feeling neglected by her husband, decides to get her portrait painted. But the "artist" is a fake, interested only in luring Patricia to his private retreat.

Your Wife and Mine (Excellent Pictures, 1927)

d: Frank O'Connor. 6 reels.
Phyllis Haver, Stuart Holmes, Wallace MacDonald, Barbara Tennant, Katherine Lewis, Blanche Upright, June Lufboro, Jay Emmett.
Marital comedy about a lawyer and his friend and their wives.

You're Fired (Famous Players-Lasky/Paramount, 1919)
d: James Cruze. 5 reels.
Wallace Reid, Wanda Hawley, Henry Woodward, Theodore Roberts, Lillian Mason, Herbert Pryor, Raymond Hatton, William Lesta.
Comedic hi-jinx ensue when a playboy is challenged by his sweetheart's father to hold a job—*any* job—for only one month.

Yours to Command (R-C Pictures/FBO of America, 1927)
d: David Kirkland. 5 reels.
George O'Hara, Shirley Palmer, William Burress, Dot Farley, Jack Luden, William Humphrey.
Duane, a scion of wealth, meets Colleen, a schoolteacher who thinks he's a chauffeur. He's interested in her but wary of scaring her off, so he lets her continue to think he's merely a chauffeur. The scenario changes when Colleen's father strikes it rich, and the family tries to move onto Duane's family's turf.

Youth (World Film Corp., 1917)
d: Romaine Fielding. 5 reels.
Carlyle Blackwell, June Elvidge, Johnny Hines, George Cowl, Muriel Ostriche, Robert Broderick, Victor Kennard, Henrietta Simpson, Henry West.
Bryan, a wealthy idler, is sent by his industrialist father to work on a dam project. There, he meets Jean, a young woman who cures him of his wasteful ways and forces him to earn her love.

Youth and Adventure (Richard Talmadge Productions/FBO of America, 1925)
d: James W. Horne. 6 reels.
Richard Talmadge, Pete Gordon, Joseph Girard, Margaret Landis, Fred Kelsey, Katherine Lewis.
Reggie, a wastrel, inherits a million dollars but squanders most of it on frivolous pursuits. Faced with looming poverty, he hands over the balance of his inheritance to his family lawyer and bets that he can support himself for six months.

Youth For Sale (C.C. Burr Pictures, 1924)
d: William Christy Cabanne. 6 reels.

May Allison, Sigrid Holmquist, Richard Bennett, Charles Emmett Mack, Alice Chapin, Tom Blake, Dorothy Allen, Charles Beyer, Harold Foshay.
Blinded by bootleg hooch, a young woman faces a harrowing choice: Should she remain blind, or marry a wealthy bounder who can finance an operation to restore her sight?

The Youth of Fortune (Universal, 1916)
d: Otis Turner. 5 reels.
Carter DeHaven, Flora Parker DeHaven, Maude George, Harry Carter, Harry Depp, Bertram Grassby.
Young Willie is neglected by his parents, who send him to boarding school. When his grandfather dies and leaves Willie a tidy sum, his parents scramble to regain custody of the lad. But it's too late, for Willie has met and married sweet Mary.

Youth to Youth (Metro, 1922)
d: Emile Chautard. 6 reels.
Billie Dove, Edythe Chapman, Hardee Kirkland, Sylvia Ashton, Jack Gardner, Cullen Landis, Mabel Van Buren, Tom O'Brien, Paul Jeffrey, Carl Gerard, ZaSu Pitts, Lincoln Stedman, Gertrude Short, Noah Beery.
On Broadway, country girl Eve becomes a star but is horrified to hear a completely false rumor that she is the mistress of the show's wealthy backer.

Youthful Folly (Selznick/Select, 1920)
d: Alan Crosland. 5 reels.
Olive Thomas, Crauford Kent, Helen Gill, Hugh Huntley, Charles Craig, Harry Truesdale, Florida Kingsley, Eugenia Woodward, Pauline Dempsey.
In the South, young Nancy is tricked by her married cousin into marrying David, whom her cousin fancies for herself.

Youth's Endearing Charm (American Film Co./Mutual, 1916)
d: William C. Dowlan. 6 reels.
Mary Miles Minter, Wallace MacDonald, Harry VonMeter, Gertrude LeBrandt, Alfred Ferguson, Bessie Banks, Harvey Clark, Margaret Nichols.
Mary, a young orphan, is kept in virtual slavery by a ranch family, until she manages to escape. On her own in the big city, she gets into trouble with the law, but is bailed out by a tipsy young millionaire who takes a shine to the girl.

Yvonne From Paris (American Film Co./Pathé, 1919)
d: Emmett J. Flynn. 5 reels.
Mary Miles Minter, Alan Forrest, Vera Lewis, J. Barney Sherry, Bertram Grassby, Rosemary Theby, E. Alyn Warren, Jack Farrell, Jeanne Robbins, Frank Clark.
Yvonne, an internationally famous Parisian dancer, grows weary of fame and leaves for America. There, she finds love and new fame, and will return to Paris a bigger success than ever.

Zander the Great (Cosmopolitan/MGM, 1925)
d: George Hill. 8 reels.
Marion Davies, Harrison Ford, Emily Fitzroy, Hedda Hopper, Jack Huff, Olin Howlin, Harry Myers, George Siegmann, Hobart Bosworth, Holbrook Blinn.
Fighting to keep her foster mother's young son Alexander—whom she calls Zander—from being sent to a cruel orphan asylum, a young woman takes the boy and sets out to locate the child's missing father.

Zaza (Famous Players/Paramount, 1915)
d: Edwin S. Porter, Hugh Ford. 5 reels.
Pauline Frederick, Julian L'Estrange, Ruth Sinclair, Maude Granger, Blanche Fisher, Helen Sinnott, Mark Smith, Charles Butler, Walter Craven.
Zaza, a brilliant performer in Parisian music halls, falls in love with the handsome Bernard, and they move into an apartment together. For months, Zaza is happy, but then she learns that Bernard is actually married and has a child. Enraged by the deception, she determines to confront him before his wife, but is dissuaded by her meeting with the couple's charming young daughter.
First feature film version of the French play of the same name by Pierre Francois Berton. It was remade once in the silent era, by Famous Players-Lasky in 1923.

Zaza (Famous Players-Lasky/Paramount, 1923)
d: Allan Dwan. 7 reels.
Gloria Swanson, H.B. Warner, Ferdinand Gottschalk, Lucille La Verne, Mary Thurman, Yvonne Hughes, Riley Hatch, Roger Lytton, Ivan Linow.
Zaza, a Parisian music hall performer, loves a diplomat, but she's unaware that he's married. When she learns the truth, Zaza tearfully breaks off the relationship. But there's a happy ending of sorts, when years later the diplomat's wife dies and Zaza and her man are reunited. Remake of the 1915 Paramount film of the same name.

The Zero Hour (World Film Corp., 1918)
d: Travers Vale. 5 reels.
June Elvidge, Frank Mayo, Armand Kaliz, Henry Warwick, Grace Henderson, Clio Ayers, Nora Cecil, Dorothy Walters, Reginald Carrington.
Evelyn, a young boarding school grad, reluctantly agrees to pose as her late twin sister in seances before the sister's grieving fiancé.

Index

595

Corrigan, James, 15, 56, 121, 131, 219, 249, 253, 269, 303, 372, 457, 458, 560

Cortez, Armand, 13, 101, 122, 213, 317, 334, 366, 409, 421, 436, 537, 540

Cortez, Ricardo, 16, 30, 64, 66, 73, 80, 85, 132, 140, 150, 195, 201, 227, 241, 264, 321, 327, 343, 348, 383, 391, 392, 456, 462, 466, 468, 489, 499, 512, 539

Cosen, Edward, 72, 114, 162

Cossar, John H., 10, 27, 44, 76, 92, 100, 126, 127, 150, 164, 176, 181, 195, 196, 209, 214, 228, 251, 284, 289, 298, 305, 312, 324, 344, 354, 366, 367, 385, 390, 409, 427, 496, 498, 500, 519, 532, 543, 545, 553, 560

Costello, Maurice, 68, 70, 93, 101, 112, 163, 187, 188, 235, 253, 267, 269, 290, 296, 302, 306, 307, 333, 347, 420, 439, 471, 480, 491, 513, 538, 540, 546, 571, 572

Coughlan, Rose, 36

Coulson, Roy, 16, 165, 239, 494

Courtot, Marguerite, 36, 98, 99, 111, 126, 149, 249, 259, 340, 374, 416, 492, 525, 527

Courtwright, William, 9, 16, 19, 117, 141, 180, 183, 203, 207, 228, 283, 296, 306, 323, 379, 384, 513, 523, 543

Covert, Fred, 4

Cowl, George, 4, 34, 58, 88, 95, 97, 100, 148, 188, 217, 246, 249, 289, 339, 379, 381, 391, 398, 437, 478, 552, 586

Cowles, Jules, 2, 10, 68, 88, 163, 173, 186, 223, 238, 247, 271, 285, 286, 287, 305, 329, 341, 374, 384, 415, 424, 429, 436, 509, 563

Coxen, Edward, 11, 32, 36, 44, 116, 159, 175, 189, 208, 241, 270, 297, 308, 333, 345, 360, 370, 429, 453, 493, 539, 559, 570, 578

Craft, William J., 14, 38, 146, 175, 206, 234, 385, 496, 544, 582

Craig, Blanche, 1, 36, 84, 91, 111, 163, 219, 290, 294, 298, 327, 382, 418, 524, 582

Craig, Charles, 19, 23, 26, 36, 47, 121, 145, 156, 159, 163, 195, 207, 267, 300, 312, 336, 339, 348, 356, 365, 374, 382, 410, 421, 423, 435, 445, 474, 502, 513, 519, 526, 527, 531, 545, 556, 580, 587

Crampton, Howard, 42, 51, 60, 76, 119, 197, 202, 235, 240, 276, 277, 307, 429, 464, 513, 539, 564, 570

Crane, Frank, 7, 18, 41, 143, 146, 187, 195, 224, 273, 282, 307, 325, 330, 337, 341, 351, 386, 428, 480, 530, 534, 542, 562

Crane, Frank H., 148, 216, 306, 371, 496

Crane, Frank Hall, 18, 519, 581

Craven, Walter, 7, 113, 116, 120, 196, 198, 560, 587

Crawford, Joan, 3, 50, 129, 131, 171, 270, 351, 358, 360, 367, 418, 425, 474, 492, 514, 521, 527, 529, 548, 568

Crisp, Donald, 15, 24, 26, 32, 39, 42, 49, 50, 59, 86, 94, 96, 124, 129, 137, 142, 152, 156, 185, 189, 211, 234, 248, 252, 254, 272, 286, 289, 302, 317, 325, 341, 346, 364, 383, 394, 400, 413, 414, 415, 455, 464, 476, 486, 511, 515, 527, 534, 535, 537, 544, 563, 585

Crolius, Louise, 10

Crosby, Jack, 42, 110, 148, 392, 459, 476, 546, 582

Crosland, Alan, 15, 33, 49, 92, 94, 96, 123, 136, 142, 159, 188, 198, 246, 251, 275, 278, 319, 352, 367, 382, 392, 418, 429, 439, 454, 458, 460, 503, 525, 527, 528, 552, 556, 557, 562, 581, 587

Crossley, Syd, 7, 46, 147, 193, 194, 244, 256, 347, 374, 380, 529, 586

Cruze, James, 8, 10, 17, 31, 32, 66, 72, 77, 84, 85, 97, 99, 120, 123, 130, 131, 136, 140, 152, 163, 175, 176, 177, 194, 205, 220, 222, 227, 246, 252, 271, 272, 286, 288, 309, 313, 316, 319, 322, 334, 339, 343, 352, 354, 355, 383, 405, 416, 421, 454, 461, 468, 495, 499, 509, 511, 527, 533, 540, 546, 550, 566, 586

Cullen, James F., 76, 485

Cullison, Webster, 7, 47, 154, 189, 240

Cumming, Dorothy, 15, 64, 78, 89, 105, 121, 125, 150, 168, 238, 260, 274, 292, 298, 303, 309, 310, 341, 342, 343, 349, 357, 360, 435, 497, 567, 573, 577

Cummings, Charles, 76, 209, 211

Cummings, Dick, 3, 403, 512, 571

Cummings, Irving, 13, 18, 19, 28, 33, 35, 48, 57, 59, 60, 96, 105, 107, 112, 114, 129, 130, 133, 137, 139, 150, 161, 165, 181, 207, 214, 222, 240, 242, 244, 251, 253, 255, 263, 268, 302, 308, 318, 319, 321, 322, 348, 351, 358, 364, 384, 401, 411, 417, 419, 420, 421, 422, 424, 427, 428, 433, 437, 455, 463, 479, 484, 499, 502, 513, 525, 530, 549, 557, 577, 581, 582

Cummings, Robert, 7, 20, 34, 53, 68, 99, 102, 118, 142, 174, 191, 208, 249, 269, 322, 371, 410, 418, 422, 465, 514, 541, 584

Cummins, Miss, 12

Cunard, Grace, 6, 114, 140, 184, 208, 212, 260, 267, 315, 363, 387, 462

Cuneo, Lester, 16, 38, 43, 91, 95, 114, 132, 163, 195, 205, 222, 315, 326, 367, 373, 377, 392, 400, 414, 432, 450, 494, 526

Curley, James, 145, 245

Curley, Pauline, 52, 72, 73, 89, 115, 203, 214, 266, 272, 302, 385, 463, 475, 520, 533

Curran, Thomas A., 11, 69, 207, 244, 334, 537

Currier, Frank, 3, 10, 14, 25, 32, 44, 54, 65, 68, 73, 78, 80, 86, 88, 93, 109, 130, 133, 134, 136, 141, 147, 148, 150, 157, 163, 169, 189, 194, 195, 197, 198, 199, 207, 216, 224, 226, 236, 248, 254, 262, 276, 287, 306, 318, 319, 324, 337, 345, 359, 363, 372, 382, 383, 402, 403, 405, 409, 411, 412, 418, 419, 427, 431, 446, 460, 468, 477, 480, 484, 490, 493, 509, 513, 514, 537, 540, 558, 562, 568, 570

Curry, John, 111, 145

Curtis, Jack, 25, 27, 37, 54, 57, 61, 70, 73, 92, 97, 107, 111, 114, 136, 151, 156, 162, 172, 181, 185, 189, 191, 199, 204, 209, 212, 245, 248, 250, 268, 284, 296, 309, 316, 334, 335, 374, 417, 431, 433, 434, 436, 437, 450, 463, 468, 470, 473, 477, 496, 504, 508, 512, 条515, 523, 524, 530, 531, 544, 546, 572, 578, 583

Custer, Bob, 17, 36, 46, 90, 112, 151, 153, 159, 175, 176, 206, 305, 308, 351, 400, 411, 450, 496, 548

D'Albrook, Sidney, 2, 9, 37, 61, 66, 76, 79, 127, 153, 208, 237, 316, 335, 363, 413, 416, 461, 464, 472, 523, 526, 548, 570

D'Arcy, Roy, 3, 25, 35, 37, 64, 123, 168, 173, 178, 187, 195, 262, 268, 292, 315, 319, 329, 355, 386, 411, 415, 494, 532, 568, 573

D'Auray, Jacques, 8, 85, 335, 478

D'Avril, Yola, 12, 204, 359, 440, 459, 502, 533

D'Elba, H., 8

Dagmarna, Myrda, 145

Dalberg, Camilla, 76, 127, 356

Dalton, Emmett, 36

Daly, Arnold, 4, 166, 240, 337, 384

Daly, William Robert, 3, 18, 93, 101, 106, 218, 411, 428, 516, 525, 530, 566

Dana, Frederick, 15, 123, 284, 540

Dana, Muriel Frances, 148, 447, 488, 541

Dana, Viola, 7, 10, 18, 30, 38, 43, 48, 55, 80, 81, 82, 95, 100, 107, 124, 146, 157, 162, 170, 171, 177, 187, 189, 190, 197, 207, 216, 227, 228, 234, 238, 241, 243, 254, 262, 264, 274, 275, 289, 296, 316, 319, 320, 331, 340, 341, 346, 350, 357, 358, 359, 368, 381, 409, 411, 420, 426, 427, 434, 449, 463, 496, 497, 501, 524, 545, 565, 567

Dane, Karl, 8, 9, 21, 25, 37, 60, 80, 84, 108, 117, 131, 136, 139, 216, 226, 262, 329, 335, 405, 418, 429, 447, 458, 465, 470, 513, 539, 542

Daniels, Bebe, 4, 16, 68, 101, 104, 107, 108, 130, 139, 140, 149, 150, 171, 176, 188, 221, 231, 260, 292, 300, 309, 310, 325, 329,